5374

The
Episcopal
Church
Annual

General Convention Edition
2023

NEW YORK

The Episcopal Church Annual

General Convention Edition

2023

NEW YORK

ISBN 978-1-64065-638-3

THE EPISCOPAL CHURCH ANNUAL

Published by

 Church Publishing
NEW YORK

Church Publishing
19 East 34th Street
New York, NY 10016
Fax (212) 779-3392

© 2023 by Church Publishing

Information and statistics have been compiled from material supplied by the bishops and secretaries of the dioceses, the Executive Office of the General Convention, The Church Pension Fund, the national, provincial, diocesan, and parochial institutions and organizations of The Episcopal Church and the Anglican Consultative Council. This Annual includes information as of January 1, 2023, which is subject to change.

Although extensive effort was made to assure the accuracy and completeness of the information included in this Annual, Church Publishing Incorporated and its affiliates do not guarantee the accuracy of such information and disclaim any liability associated with this Annual. Please write to the Editor, Episcopal Church Annual, 19 East 34th Street, New York, NY 10016 to report any errors and/or omissions.

Any discrepancy between the clerical status of an individual in this Annual and the official records of The Episcopal Church shall be resolved by reference to such official records. All benefits provided to clergy of The Episcopal Church are governed by the terms of the official plan documents and policies.

ISBN-13: 978-1-64065-638-3

Printed in the United States of America

Contents

SERVING THE EPISCOPAL CHURCH THROUGH THE CENTURIES
TIMELINE OF THE EPISCOPAL CHURCH ANNUAL

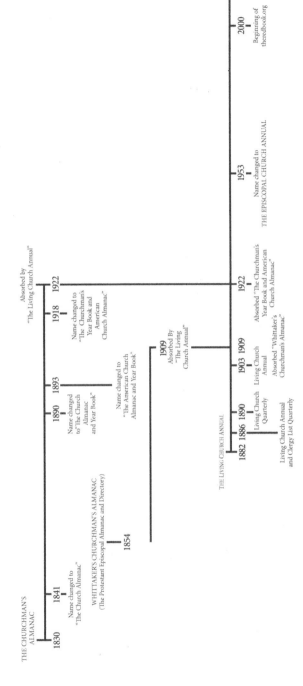

THE CHURCHMAN'S ALMANAC

1830

1841 — Name changed to "The Church Almanac."

WHITTAKER'S CHURCHMAN'S ALMANAC (The Protestant Episcopal Almanac and Directory)

1854

1890 — Name changed to "The Church Almanac and Year Book"

1893 — Name changed to "The American Church Almanac and Year Book"

1918 — Name changed to "The Churchman's Year Book and American Church Almanac."

1922 — Absorbed by "The Living Church Annual"

THE LIVING CHURCH ANNUAL

1882 Living Church Annual and Clergy List Quarterly

1886 **1890** Living Church Quarterly

1903 Living Church Annual

1909 Absorbed "Whittaker's Churchman's Almanac."

1909 — Absorbed By "The Living Church Annual"

1922 — Absorbed "The Churchman's Year Book and American Church Almanac."

1953 — Name changed to THE EPISCOPAL CHURCH ANNUAL

2000 — Beginning of theredbook.org

DIOCESES WITHIN EACH PROVINCE

Province I

Diocese of Connecticut
Diocese of Maine
Diocese of Massachusetts
Diocese of New Hampshire
Diocese of Rhode Island
Diocese of Vermont
Diocese of Western
  Massachusetts

Province II

Diocese of Albany
Diocese of Central New York
Diocese of Cuba
Diocese of Haiti
Diocese of Long Island
Diocese of New Jersey
Diocese of New York
Diocese of Newark
Diocese of Puerto Rico
Diocese of Rochester
Diocese of Virgin Islands
Diocese of Western New York
Convocation of American
  Churches in Europe

Province III

Diocese of Bethlehem
Diocese of Central
  Pennsylvania
Diocese of Delaware
Diocese of Easton
Diocese of Maryland
Diocese of Northwestern
  Pennsylvania
Diocese of Pennsylvania
Diocese of Pittsburgh
Diocese of Southern Virginia
Diocese of Southwestern
  Virginia
Diocese of Virginia
Diocese of Washington
Diocese of West Virginia

Province IV

Diocese of Alabama
Diocese of Atlanta
Diocese of Central Florida

Diocese of Central Gulf
  Coast
Diocese of East Carolina
Diocese of East Tennessee
Diocese of Florida
Diocese of Georgia
Diocese of Kentucky
Diocese of Lexington
Diocese of Louisiana
Diocese of Mississippi
Diocese of North Carolina
The Episcopal Church in
  South Carolina
Diocese of Southeast Florida
Diocese of Southwest Florida
Diocese of Tennessee
Diocese of Upper South
  Carolina
Diocese of West Tennessee
Diocese of Western North
  Carolina

Province V

Diocese of Chicago
Diocese of Eastern Michigan
Diocese of Eau Claire
Diocese of Fond du Lac
Diocese of Indianapolis
Diocese of Michigan
Diocese of Milwaukee
Diocese of Missouri
Diocese of Northern Indiana
Diocese of Northern
  Michigan
Diocese of Ohio
Diocese of Southern Ohio
Diocese of Springfield
Diocese of Western Michigan

Province VI

Diocese of Colorado
Diocese of Iowa
Diocese of Minnesota
Diocese of Montana
Diocese of Nebraska
Diocese of North Dakota
Diocese of South Dakota
Diocese of Wyoming

Province VII

Diocese of Arkansas
Diocese of Dallas
Diocese of Kansas
Diocese of Northwest Texas
Diocese of Oklahoma
Diocese of Rio Grande
Diocese of Texas
Diocese of West Missouri
Diocese of West Texas
Diocese of Western Kansas
Diocese of Western Louisiana

Province VIII

Diocese of Alaska
Diocese of Arizona
Diocese of California
Diocese of Eastern Oregon
Diocese of El Camino Real
Diocese of Hawaii
Diocese of Idaho
Diocese of Los Angeles
Diocese of Navajoland
Diocese of Nevada
Diocese of Northern
  California
Diocese of Olympia
Diocese of Oregon
Diocese of San Diego
Diocese of San Joaquin
Diocese of Spokane
Diocese of Taiwan
Diocese of Utah

Province IX

Diocese of Colombia
Diocese of Dominican
  Republic
Diocese of Ecuador Central
Diocese of Ecuador Litoral
Diocese of Honduras
Diocese of Venezuela

Abbreviations of Dioceses and States

Obvious variants are sometimes used.

A	Albany		NB	Nebraska
AK	Alaska		NC	North Carolina
AL	Alabama		NCA	Northern California
AR	Arkansas		ND	North Dakota
At	Atlanta		NH	New Hampshire
AZ	Arizona		NI	Northern Indiana
BE	Bethlehem		NJ	New Jersey
C	Chicago		Nk	Newark
CA	California		NM	New Mexico (state)
CEcu	Central Ecuador		NMI	Northern Michigan
CF	Central Florida		NT	NW Texas
CGC	Central Gulf Coast		NV	Nevada
CNY	Central New York		NWPA	Northwestern Pennsylvania
CO	Colorado		NY	New York
Colom	Colombia		OH	Ohio
CPA	Central Pennsylvania		OK	Oklahoma
CT	Connecticut		OL	Olympia
Dal	Dallas		OR	Oregon
DC	District of Columbia		PA	Pennsylvania
DE	Delaware		Pgh	Pittsburgh
DomR	Dominican Republic		PR	Puerto Rico
E	Easton		RG	Rio Grande
EauC	Eau Claire		RI	Rhode Island
EC	East Carolina		Roch	Rochester
ECR	El Camino Real		SanD	San Diego
EcuL	Ecuador Litoral		SanJ	San Joaquin
EMI	Eastern Michigan		SC	South Carolina
EO	Eastern Oregon		SD	South Dakota
Er	Erie		SeF	Southeast Florida
ETN	East Tennessee		SO	Southern Ohio
Eur	Europe		Sp	Springfield
FdL	Fond du Lac		Spok	Spokane
FL	Florida		SV	Southern Virginia
GA	Georgia		SwF	Southwest Florida
GU	Guam		SwV	Southwestern Virginia
Hai	Haiti		Tai	Taiwan
HI	Hawaii		TN	Tennessee
Hond	Honduras		TX	Texas
IA	Iowa		USC	Upper South Carolina
ID	Idaho		UT	Utah
IL	Illinois		VA	Virginia
IN	Indiana		VEN	Venezuela
Ind	Indianapolis		VI	Virgin Islands
KS	Kansas		VT	Vermont
KY	Kentucky		W	Washington (dio)
LA	Louisiana		WA	Washington (state)
Lex	Lexington		WI	Wisconsin
LI	Long Island		WKS	Western Kansas
LosA	Los Angeles		WLA	Western Louisiana
MA	Massachusetts		WMI	Western Michigan
MD	Maryland		WMA	Western Massachusetts
ME	Maine		WMO	West Missouri
MI	Michigan		WNC	Western North Carolina
Mil	Milwaukee		WNY	Western New York
MN	Minnesota		WT	West Texas
MO	Missouri		WTN	West Tennessee
MS	Mississippi		WV	West Virginia
MT	Montana		WY	Wyoming
NAM	Navajoland Area Mission			

Abbreviations Used in the Clergy List
That Differ from the Abbreviations of Dioceses and States List

Ala	Alabama	**NI**	Northern Indiana
Alb	Albany	**NMich**	Northern Michigan
Ark	Arkansas	**Nwk**	Newark
CFla	Central Florida	**NwT**	Northwest Texas
Chi	Chicago	**O**	Ohio
Colo	Colorado	**Okla**	Oklahoma
CP	Central Pennsylvania	**Oly**	Olympia
Del	Delaware	**Ore**	Oregon
DR	Dominican Republic	**SeFla**	Southeast Florida
Eas	Easton	**SJ**	San Joaquin
Eau	Eau Claire	**Spr**	Springfield
Fla	Florida	**SVa**	Southern Virginia
Haw	Hawaii	**SwFla**	Southwest Florida
Ida	Idaho	**SwVa**	Southwestern Virginia
Kan	Kansas	**Tenn**	Tennesseeaa
Los	Los Angeles	**Tex**	Texas
Mass	Massachusetts	**WDC**	Washington
Mich	Michigan	**WK**	Western Kansas
Minn	Minnesota	**WMass**	Western Massachusetts
Miss	Mississippi	**WMich**	Western Michigan
Mont	Montana	**WTenn**	West Tennessee
NCal	Northern California	**WTex**	West Texas
Neb	Nebraska	**WVa**	West Virginia
Nev	Nevada	**Wyo**	Wyoming

Acronyms

AandD	Alcohol and Drugs	FODC	Franciscan Order of the Divine Compassion
AIDS	Acquired Immune Deficiency Syndrome (see also HIV)	GTS	General Theological Seminary
BCP	Book of Common Prayer 1979	HIV	Human Immunodeficiency Virus
BSG	Brotherhood of St. Gregory	LAND	Leadership Academy for New Directions
CA	Church Army Community of the Ascension	NCC	National Council of Churches
CDO	Clergy Deployment Office(r)	NECAD	National Episcopal Coalition on Alcohol and Drugs
CDSP	Church Divinity School of the Pacific	OCP	Order of the Community of the Paraclete
CHC	Church Hymnal Corporation	OHC	Order of the Holy Cross
CPF	Church Pension Fund	OSA	Order of St. Augustine
COM	Commission on Ministry		Order of St. Anne
CHS	Community of the Holy Spirit	OSB	Order of St. Benedict
CSJB	Community of St. John the Baptist	OSH	Order of St. Helena
CSM	Community of St. Mary	OSL	Order of St. Luke the Physician
CSSS	Congregation of the Companions of the Holy Savior	RACA	Recovered Alcoholic Clergy Association
DCE	Director/Department of Christian Education	RC	Roman Catholic
EC	Executive Council	SSC	Society of the Holy Cross
ECL	Executive Council Liaison	SSF	Society of St. Francis
ECC	Episcopal Church Center	SSJE	Society of St. John the Evangelist
EDS	Episcopal Divinity School	SSM	Society of St. Margaret
ECW	Episcopal Church Women	SSP	Society of St. Paul
ECS	Episcopal Community Services	USAF	United States Air Force
ESMA	Episcopal Society for Ministry on Aging	USA	United States Army
		USN	United States Navy
ETSW	Episcopal Theological Seminary of the Southwest	WCC	World Council of Churches

Partial List of Abbreviations
NAMES

Adv	Advent	M	Martyr
Alb	Alban	Magd	Magdalene
All SS	All Saints	Mer	Merciful
Amb	Ambrose	Med	Mediator
Ancn	Annunciation	Mem	Memorial
Ang	Angels	Mes	Messiah
Ant(h)	Ant(h)ony	Miss	Mission
Apos	Apostle(s), Apostól	Mt	Mount
Arim	Arimathaea	Mths	Matthias
Ben	Benedict	Mthw	Matthew
Beth	Bethany	O	Our
Ble	Bless, Blessed	Pr	Prince
Cbury	Canterbury	Par	Parish
Chap	Chapel	Raph	Raphael
Chrys	Chrysostom	Rdmn	Redemption, Redemción
Comf	Comforter		
Comm	Communion	Rdmr	Redeemer
Cong	Congregation	Recon	Reconciliation
Crux	Crucifixion	Resr	Resurrection, Resurrección
Cyp	Cyprian		
Dun	Dunstan	S	Saint, San
Edm	Edmund		(in parish name)
Edw	Edward	SS	Saints
Emm	Emmanuel	Sac	Sacrament
Evan	Evangelist	Sav	Savior
Faith	Faithful	Shpd	Shepherd
Fell	Fellowship	Sim	Simon, Simeon
Gab	Gabriel	Seb	Sebastian
Gd	Good	Smtn	Samaritan
Geo	George	St	Saint
Geth	Gethsemane		(in other names)
Gr	Grace	Sta	Santa
H	Holy	Ste	Sainte
Heav	Heavenly		(in other names)
Ign	Ignatius	Thad	Thaddeus
Incsn	Intercession	Theo	Theodore
K	King	Trsfg	Transfiguration, Transfiguracción
Law(u)	Law(u)rence		
Lk	Luke	V	Virgin, Virgen

Other Abbreviations

accom	accommodations	Lit	Liturgy, Liturgics
Admin	Administrative	lm	lay missioner
Amb	Ambassador	lr	lay reader
Angl	Anglican	lt	loc ten
Archdcn	Archdeacon		(locum tenens)
Bdwy	Broadway	lv	lay vicar
Bp	Bishop	Min	Ministry, Minister
c	curate	Miss	Missioner,
cap	capacity		Missionary
cath	cathedral	Mtn	Mountain
chap	chaplain	N	North
ch	church	NT	New Testament
Cn	Canon	NYC	New York City,
Coadj	Coadjutor		New York
Coll	College	Ord	Ordinary
Chanc	Chancellor	OT	Old Testament
Comm	Communion	par	parish
	Committee	Past	Pastoral
	Commission	Pk	Park
	Community	Pkwy	Parkway
Commun	Communication	p-in-c	priest-in-charge
Conf	Conference	prog	program
cont ed	continuing	prov	province, provincial
	education	Pt	part time
Cont	Controller,	Pt	Port, Point
	Comptroller	ptnshp	partnership
convoc	convocation	r	rector
coord	coordinator	res	residence
ctr	center	ret	retirement
dio	diocese, diocesan	retr	retreat
dir	director	Rt	Route
dcn	deacon	sch	school
Dn	Dean	sem	seminary
d-in-c	deacon-in-charge	So	South
E	East	Spg(s)	Spring(s)
ecum	ecumenical	spir	spiritual/spirituality
em	emeritus	spon	sponsor
Episc	Episcopal	sr	sister
fac	facility	Ste	Suite
fam	family	SR	State Rd/Star
grp	group		Route
Hd	Head	svc	service
	(master, mistress)	Theol	Theologian
Hisp	Hispanic	trng	training
Hon	Honorable	Twp	Township
Hse	House	urb	urban
indiv	individual	V	Very
inst	institute	v	vicar
int	interim	W	West
Inter	Interpretation	yr-rnd	year-round
Is	Island	yth	youth
Lib	Library, Librarian		

Provinces of the Episcopal Church
2022–2024 Triennium

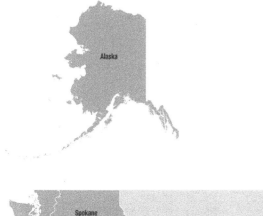

Alaska

Spokane
Olympia
Eastern Oregon
Oregon
Idaho
Northern California
P8
Nevada
Utah
California
San Joaquin
El Camino Real
Los Angeles
San Diego
Arizona
Navajoland Area Mission

Montana
North Dakota
Minnesota
South Dakota
P6
Wyoming
Iowa
Nebraska
Colorado
Western Kansas
Kansas
West Missouri
Oklahoma
Arkansas
The Rio Grande
Northwest Texas
Dallas
P7
Western Louisiana
Texas
West Texas

Additional Province 8 Diocese
Micronesia, Taiwan

Hawaii

Northern Michigan

Eau Claire   Fond Du Lac

Western Michigan   Eastern Michigan

Milwaukee   **P5**

Michigan

Chicago   Northern Indiana   Ohio

Springfield   Indianapolis   Southern Ohio

Missouri

Kentucky   Lexington

West Tenn.   Tennessee   East Tenn.   Western N. Carolina   North Carolina

Upper S. Carolina   East Carolina

Mississippi   Alabama   Atlanta   South Carolina

P4

Central Gulf Coast   Georgia

Louisiana   Florida

Central Florida

Southwest Florida   Southeast Florida

Additional Province 2 Diocese
Convocation of Churches in Europe, Cuba, Haiti, Puerto Rico, and the Virgin Islands

Maine

Vermont   **P1**

P2

Rochester   Central N.Y.   Albany   New Hampshire

Western N.Y.   Western Mass.   Massachusetts

N.W. Penn   Bethlehem   New York   Connecticut   Rhode Island

Newark

Pittsburgh   Central Penn   Penn.   Long Island

New Jersey

Maryland

West Virginia   **P3**   Washington   Delaware

Virginia   Easton

S.W. Virginia   S. Virginia

P9

Colombia, Dominican Republic, Ecuador Central, Ecuador Litoral, Honduras, and Venezuela

11

SUMMARY OF STATISTICS
as of January 2021

	Reported for 2021	Reported for 2020	Net Change	Percent Change
Parishes and Missions....................................	6,294	6,356	-62	-0.98%
Active Baptized Members.............................	1,520,388	1,576,702	-56,314"	-3.57%
Communicants in Good Standing.............	1,083,483	1,217,433	-133,950"	-11.00%
Others Active in Congregation...................	135,868	133,135	2,733"	2.05%
Average Sunday Attendance........................	292,851	458,179	-165,328"	-36.08%
Baptisms...	13,859	7,217	6,642"	92.03%
Confirmations..	9,900	3,513	6,387"	181.81%
Received...	3,086	1,470	1,616"	109.93%
Marriage Services...	4,250	3,594	656	18.25%
Burial Services..	23,127	18,266	4,861"	26.61%
Clergy (incl. non-parochial).......................	18,230	18,257	-27	-0.15%

Notes:

1. These figures, except for clergy, includes only USA Congregational Data from 2021 Parochial Reports. Figures for dioceses outside the USA, see Table of Statistics of the Episcopal Church.

2. Clergy totals include all clergy listed in the clergy list in the Episcopal Church Annual including clergy reported as ordained but not yet entered in the clergy list. Source: The Church Pension Group.

Table of Statistics of the Episcopal Church

From 2021 Parochial Reports. Source: The Office of the General Convention as of October 2022

Province	Diocese	Open Parishes & Missions	Active Baptized Members	Commun. in Good Standing	Others Active in Cong.	Average Worship Attendance	BAPTISMS Children	BAPTISMS Adults	CONFIRMATIONS Children	CONFIRMATIONS Adults	Received	Marriages	Burials
1	Connecticut	156	40,354	27,587	1,665	6,196	404	20	219	51	35	99	699
	Maine	58	9,090	7,250	500	2,268	52	12	4	7	6	22	216
	Massachusetts	162	50,566	34,643	1,671	7,049	393	31	87	72	19	115	828
	New Hampshire	44	11,057	7,000	634	2,096	61	5	19	13	20	22	247
	Rhode Island	52	13,997	8,928	1,936	2,696	122	15	29	37	41	68	268
	Vermont	45	4,743	3,643	195	1,112	23	2	1	6	2	10	94
	Western Massachusetts	50	12,024	7,524	446	2,139	51	6	2	19	23	25	179
	Total	567	141,831	96,575	7,047	23,556	1,106	91	361	205	146	361	2,531
2	Albany	106	10,501	6,923	7235	2,684	68	26	1	4	6	57	273
	Central New York	82	9,776	6,749	560	2,045	66	4	8	23	10	31	221
	Churches in Europe	20	2,374	1,194	203	522	28	3	3	2	11	9	20
	Cuba	44	1,580	1,439	66	621	89	37	0	0	0	0	37
	Haiti	120	97,909	25,331	3,198	10,160	1,375	399	2	2	180	115	247
	Long Island	130	38,482	21,297	1,102	5,764	448	61	72	104	47	113	565
	New Jersey	136	33,769	20,136	2,050	6,469	374	19	218	61	50	100	551
	New York	191	45,112	24,619	3,884	6,945	392	39	147	55	68	136	561
	Newark	96	21,132	15,332	913	3,030	201	13	123	34	18	55	271
	Puerto Rico	51	4,441	3,452	288	1,348	53	7	22	34	82	41	84
	Rochester	51	7,312	5,876	661	1,721	58	12	16	15	17	27	168
	Virgin Islands	13	2,186	1,575	25	711	39	0	8	0	0	6	72
	Western New York	56	7,081	4,176	345	1,544	57	5	0	6	3	32	169
	Total	1,045	277,214	134,647	20,242	42,216	3,195	618	598	306	410	681	3,155
3	Bethlehem	57	8,239	5,903	425	1,605	66	2	9	25	28	21	147
	Central Pennsylvania	62	9,115	7,059	947	2,467	63	12	30	44	45	29	192
	Delaware	33	8,009	5,605	567	1,696	71	9	54	34	25	22	212
	Easton	38	7,233	5,359	456	1,411	79	8	33	17	27	27	166
	Maryland	101	31,968	22,780	2,368	4,181	225	28	75	88	34	53	447
	Northwestern Pennsylvania	32	2,834	2,376	159	823	15	11	1	8	4	12	80
	Pennsylvania	133	35,606	19,225	1,917	5,551	293	16	102	51	37	98	577
	Pittsburgh	34	9,089	7,889	539	1,431	77	6	33	19	55	23	114
	Southern Virginia	101	22,507	16,798	2,102	4,619	144	14	32	108	74	59	359
	Southwestern Virginia	51	9,526	7,174	738	1,911	56	7	7	40	8	26	121
	Virginia	180	65,056	46,646	7,073	11,453	541	50	147	243	126	143	679
	Washington	85	33,265	21,890	3,452	6,150	268	29	76	98	28	83	357
	West Virginia	60	6,405	4,289	202	1,373	28	7	4	14	6	22	92
	Total	967	248,852	172,993	20,945	44,671	1,926	199	603	789	497	618	3,543
4	Alabama	88	30,500	23,292	3,180	5,209	216	26	222	205	33	74	315
	Atlanta	91	45,161	33,258	6,456	6,688	363	32	155	334	155	116	496
	Central Florida	81	23,664	18,846	1,909	6,960	242	22	98	111	75	65	565
	Central Gulf Coast	61	17,474	13,749	1,287	3,092	129	21	62	71	62	67	238
	East Carolina	67	14,852	11,856	1,308	3,476	92	10	29	41	34	45	234

13

Province	Diocese	Open Parishes & Missions	Active Baptized Members	Commun. in Good Standing	Others Active in Cong.	Average Worship Attendance	BAPTISMS Children	BAPTISMS Adults	CONFIRMATIONS Children	CONFIRMATIONS Adults	Received	Marriages	Burials
	East Tennessee	46	13,740	9,865	1,152	2,928	109	16	61	83	86	46	223
	Florida	66	23,075	17,515	1,811	4,902	177	27	94	99	31	59	317
	Georgia	66	12,804	9,588	1,750	2,745	94	6	33	64	35	63	227
	Kentucky	34	6,898	6,026	649	1,555	48	3	38	18	12	23	142
	Lexington	34	6,184	4,964	664	1,231	53	9	16	30	31	20	110
	Louisiana	46	14,686	10,129	1,207	2,437	118	6	38	32	52	61	214
	Mississippi	82	17,648	12,326	1,025	3,471	121	18	68	106	27	61	217
	North Carolina	109	44,695	34,698	6,650	6,003	409	30	229	186	129	105	465
	South Carolina	31	7,254	5,772	885	1,956	76	6	34	12	2	31	89
	Southeast Florida	75	28,336	18,877	1,416	5,618	327	24	25	13	14	73	339
	Southwest Florida	78	25,934	20,711	4,510	6,499	206	36	88	76	42	70	503
	Tennessee	45	15,665	10,830	4,335	3,347	164	21	83	95	25	69	156
	Upper South Carolina	59	21,765	16,487	1,954	4,530	144	18	32	184	38	49	300
	West Tennessee	29	6,736	4,988	1,060	1,375	89	6	45	57	11	25	117
	Western North Carolina	60	13,229	11,215	2,280	3,759	53	10	32	80	68	36	245
	Total	1,248	390,300	294,992	45,488	77,781	3,230	347	1,482	1,897	962	1,158	5,512
5	Chicago	120	28,531	22,362	2,824	5,243	302	28	144	62	89	106	448
	Eastern Michigan	43	4,071	3,312	231	1,080	19	5	0	1	3	20	151
	Eau Claire	19	987	676	148	349	4	0	2	3	4	4	29
	Fond du Lac	32	3,777	2,791	261	936	26	9	9	15	4	8	64
	Indianapolis	48	8,264	6,695	568	2,081	66	14	25	59	54	21	138
	Michigan	74	14,675	10,892	1,393	3,205	101	14	13	44	33	59	345
	Milwaukee	48	6,833	5,839	110	1,929	71	12	21	16	39	26	149
	Missouri	41	9,264	7,821	917	1,915	60	4	30	29	23	31	123
	Northern Indiana	33	3,470	2,731	295	1,031	22	7	5	15	1	18	85
	Northern Michigan	21	1,008	473	74	289	5	1	0	0	5	6	28
	Ohio	82	14,895	10,496	1,117	2,966	89	18	7	30	27	60	288
	Southern Ohio	73	16,688	12,630	2,052	3,787	106	16	37	51	37	52	276
	Springfield	33	3,559	2,379	193	853	27	3	4	15	6	8	71
	Western Michigan	56	6,907	5,805	853	2,046	44	2	1	24	14	35	181
	Total	723	122,929	94,902	11,036	27,710	942	133	298	364	339	454	2,376
6	Colorado	93	21,990	16,761	2,714	4,867	173	23	28	80	47	59	326
	Iowa	58	6,068	4,797	396	1,385	40	5	24	31	12	19	116
	Minnesota	91	16,232	12,181	799	3,137	129	18	48	64	37	35	314
	Montana	32	4,046	3,150	414	815	19	5	10	12	9	8	41
	Nebraska	51	6,843	4,850	172	1,558	60	3	20	2	20	32	120
	North Dakota	18	2,236	1,437	128	416	18	1	6	7	5	5	83
	South Dakota	77	6,507	2,808	194	1,319	147	4	13	15	26	25	285
	Wyoming	44	5,850	4,498	323	1,206	77	12	27	13	20	29	123
	Total	464	69,772	50,482	5,140	14,703	663	71	176	224	176	212	1,408
7	Arkansas	54	13,056	9,251	751	2,460	88	14	43	89	30	51	158
	Dallas	63	29,005	22,629	1,980	5,721	272	27	91	162	65	71	357
	Kansas	44	7,757	6,110	363	1,663	33	5	14	45	21	23	142
	Northwest Texas	28	4,924	2,962	311	1,080	48	2	10	45	11	17	70

Province	Diocese	Open Parishes & Missions	Active Baptized Members	Commun. in Good Standing	Others Active in Cong.	Average Worship Attendance	BAPTISMS Children	BAPTISMS Adults	CONFIRMATIONS Children	CONFIRMATIONS Adults	Received	Marriages	Burials
	Oklahoma	66	14,070	10,934	585	3,215	153	19	77	177	34	27	270
	Rio Grande	48	9,848	7,469	632	1,967	69	12	8	23	18	24	171
	Texas	153	73,617	56,894	6,827	11,888	724	82	420	353	140	149	696
	West Missouri	47	8,807	6,427	1,016	1,879	58	9	12	36	17	33	141
	West Texas	85	19,947	16,072	2,181	4,748	236	29	123	113	47	65	308
	Western Kansas	24	1,267	1,126	54	379	14	4	0	7	8	6	35
	Western Louisiana	42	8,074	4,825	304	2,020	57	2	15	22	28	17	136
	Total	667	193,967	146,356	15,285	38,169	1,785	212	813	1,105	427	492	2,557
8	Alaska	46	5,950	3,944	370	615	55	5	8	0	1	18	139
	Arizona	58	18,472	11,300	2,243	4,182	179	29	23	63	49	46	322
	California	75	21,293	15,513	942	3,800	95	32	37	59	11	27	152
	Eastern Oregon	20	1,770	1,393	456	478	7	1	0	0	5	5	37
	El Camino Real	41	6,600	5,339	337	1,806	30	11	9	15	18	13	111
	Hawaii	35	6,029	4,861	286	1,535	63	21	17	15	27	33	121
	Idaho	27	3,832	2,059	357	807	17	2	4	2	0	13	54
	Los Angeles	128	44,077	23,213	3,901	7,781	195	43	32	76	51	80	383
	Micronesia	2	218	82	0	54	0	0	0	0	0	0	5
	Navajo Missions	10	757	417	84	97	0	0	0	0	0	2	41
	Nevada	29	4,862	4,206	369	1,278	95	5	28	57	17	29	111
	Northern California	65	10,666	8,883	794	2,465	54	18	6	63	42	33	206
	Olympia	90	21,873	15,152	955	3,868	70	13	5	46	48	29	233
	Oregon	70	12,543	9,136	546	2,330	56	13	1	12	19	24	148
	San Diego	42	10,919	8,807	1,743	2,617	102	12	20	36	15	34	188
	San Joaquin	19	1,786	1,645	60	575	10	6	0	12	7	2	27
	Spokane	33	3,861	3,126	187	964	19	3	2	5	5	3	87
	Taiwan	15	1,144	795	95	578	10	21	3	35	69	5	20
	Utah	22	4,282	3,081	547	861	47	3	20	23	5	13	61
	Total	827	180,934	122,952	14,272	36,691	1,104	238	215	519	389	409	2,446
9	Colombia	35	2,552	1,534	507	609	275	90	59	100	143	94	25
	Dominican Republic	65	3,799	2,392	352	1,676	95	54	32	50	44	57	35
	Ecuador, Central	11	708	108	57	51	2	3	0	0	0	1	1
	Ecuador, Litoral	26	7,770	920	283	639	136	25	137	50	19	2	26
	Honduras	110	33,088	28,881	925	2,871	202	48	9	14	15	12	42
	Venezuela	51	4,441	3,452	288	1,348	53	7	22	34	82	41	84
	Total	298	52,358	37,287	2,412	7,194	763	227	259	248	303	207	213
	The Episcopal Church	6,806	1,678,157	1,151,186	141,867	312,691	14,714	2,136	4,805	5,657	3,649	4,592	23,741

Note: These figures are compiled from 2021 Parochial Reports submitted to the Office of the General Convention, 815 Second Avenue, New York, NY 10017-4564.
For further information about the Parochial Report, contact the General Convention office at pr@dfms.org, or phone (212) 716-6159.

Comparative Statistics of the Episcopal Church, U.S.A.

Year Reported	Parishes and Missions	Clergy	Baptized Members	Communicants Domestic	Communicants Overseas	Communicants Total		Church School Pupils*	Day School Staff**	Day School Pupils*	Cand's for Orders	Ordinations Deacons	Ordinations Priests	Baptisms Infant	Baptisms Adult	Baptisms Total	Confirmations (Including Received)	Marriages	Burials	Total Receipts (Gross Receipts)
1850		1,595				89,359	5,039	44,148			175			18,232	2,727	20,959	7,554	2,987	6,226	$ 342,936.49
1855	1,821	1,821				107,560	9,735	82,731			236			18,812	3,618	22,430	10,584	6,777	12,542	727,477.00
1860	2,128	2,156				146,588	15,598	135,925			292	102	83	26,518	5,247	31,765	14,781	7,356	12,989	1,870,914.98
1865	2,322	2,467				154,118	17,538	150,400			220	94	91	24,689	5,297	29,986	15,360	7,487	15,650	2,700,004.08
1870	2,605	2,838				207,762	23,718	213,862			361	102	91			—	21,622	9,261	15,802	4,907,872.57
1875	3,187	3,187				261,003	23,448	235,943			298	110	122			—	22,095	9,690	18,969	6,899,305.94
1880	4,151	3,432		345,433	408	345,841	34,041	299,070			431	136	96	40,557	8,188	48,745	25,903	12,163	22,518	7,013,762.86
1885	4,565	3,787		397,084	108	397,192	36,001	326,203			321	134	108	46,962	11,227	58,189	34,069	14,040	27,893	9,017,155.16
1890	5,330	4,180		504,898	3,394	508,292	40,522	393,795			299			49,777	11,645	61,422	40,911	15,819	30,136	12,754,767.53
1895	6,269	4,610		614,136	5,297	619,433	44,441	418,674			529			48,118	10,418	58,536	44,627	17,242	34,761	13,449,925.95
1900	6,774	5,011		712,997	6,543	719,540	45,901	429,830			506			50,119	12,899	63,018	43,788	19,039	34,138	16,069,580.49
1905	7,480	5,302		817,845	10,548	828,393	47,307	450,212			459			49,981	14,086	64,067	51,341	22,527	37,628	16,296,693.95
1910	7,987	5,543		928,780	17,472	946,252	49,973	456,275			438			53,289	14,537	67,826	55,020	24,044	45,566	18,382,609.85
1915	8,506	5,800		1,040,896	17,908	1,058,804	53,110	483,936			430			50,315	10,025	60,340	61,284	26,231	50,080	20,972,589.78
1920	8,365	5,987		1,075,820	21,075	1,096,895	48,656	417,695			310			54,879	12,181	67,060	60,779	28,485	47,788	24,392,091.64
1925	8,397	6,140		1,164,911	28,410	1,193,321	55,790	498,814			454	177	157	52,200	11,559	63,759	65,064	29,420	50,336	41,746,055.91
1930	8,253	6,304	1,939,453	1,254,227	33,204	1,287,431	58,548	483,413			485	192	193	50,499	12,200	62,699	64,668	30,576	56,163	45,944,896.82
1935	8,098	6,410	2,038,477	1,351,999	37,593	1,389,592	60,952	506,400			426	193	162	56,288	13,130	69,418	67,096	25,639	52,611	30,425,500.75
1940	7,995	6,335	2,171,562	1,449,327	40,057	1,489,384	58,334	492,554			301	152	149	72,377	14,033	86,410	74,318	28,799	53,446	34,618,420.82
1945	7,818	6,449	2,269,962	1,527,762	40,390	1,568,152	46,336	394,456			229	181	209	87,487	16,550	104,037	68,868	31,597	54,650	46,170,035.30
1950	7,784	6,654	2,540,548	1,651,426	37,185	1,688,611	60,151	514,754			486	255	240	98,595	20,388	118,983	85,989	28,695	55,354	73,844,880.41
1955	8,053	7,573	3,013,570	1,781,262	84,653	1,865,915	80,819	696,028			677	415	354	98,312	18,415	116,727	113,443	24,789	53,114	131,354,945.37
1960	7,657	9,079	3,444,265	2,027,671	95,439	2,123,110	105,087	874,550	3,187	44,075	800	424	427	91,695	13,627	105,322	127,861	24,111	57,574	173,013,803.63
1965	7,539	10,309	3,615,643	2,202,607	69,534	2,272,141	105,221	880,912	4,590	58,712	710	442	426			—	128,066	27,728	60,190	223,016,214.03
1970	7,464	11,772	3,475,164	2,238,538	56,017	2,294,555	89,611	711,791	6,088	79,962	510	379	311	74,577	8,359	82,936	102,059	37,836	59,504	299,426,994.00

16

Year Reported	Parishes and Missions	Clergy	Baptized Members	Communicants Domestic	Communicants Overseas	Communicants Total	Others Active in Congregations	Church School Staff*	Church School Pupils*	Day School Staff*	Day School Pupils*	Cand's for Orders	Deacons	Priests	Baptisms Children	Baptisms Adult	Baptisms Total	Confirmations (Including Received)	Marriages	Burials	Total Receipts (Gross Receipts) ‡
1975	7,382	12,035	3,039,136	2,051,914	77,337	2,129,251	—	74,574	559,648	8,897	100,465	702	316	271	63,503	5,965	69,468	77,038	36,535	53,473	411,418,722.00
1980	7,591	13,089	3,037,420	1,933,080	85,790	2,018,870	—	69,459	507,448	—	104,839	425	321	314	64,367	8,611	72,978	64,912	39,862	50,070	648,937,788.00
1985	7,858	14,482	2,972,607	1,881,250	82,375	1,963,625	—	70,383	496,930	—	120,259	563	475	330	65,152	7,142	72,294	59,718	36,073	48,277	1,028,818,309.00
1990	7,354	14,878	2,446,050	1,698,240	—	—	—	72,668	495,537	—	100,589	407	379	296	56,862	7,844	64,706	47,270	31,795	43,568	1,379,782,885.00
1991	7,367	14,879	2,474,625	1,615,505	—	—	—	74,350	336,251	—	95,903	405	380	296	55,869	7,714	63,583	46,068	30,557	43,538	1,433,467,803.00
1992	7,391	15,076	2,491,996	1,614,081	—	—	—	72,153	335,297	—	99,366	407	378	290	53,095	7,071	60,166	46,820	28,844	42,226	1,582,457,015.00
1993	7,403	15,004	2,506,047	1,579,444	—	—	—	75,959	327,157	—	101,752	423	378	290	51,643	8,044	59,687	44,509	28,291	43,010	1,613,697,551.00
1994	7,413	14,645	2,517,520	1,577,951	—	—	142,900	72,988	328,512	13,674	102,145	352	399	317	51,049	6,545	57,594	43,234	27,631	42,259	1,311,990,815.00
1995	7,417	15,138	2,411,841	1,584,760	—	—	150,417	71,773	333,645	—	107,203	372	347	265	50,784	7,250	58,034	43,474	27,324	44,239	1,398,179,032.00
1996	7,395	14,295	2,366,054	1,592,693	—	—	159,199	72,874	325,156	20,416	102,042	329	341	296	49,525	6,688	56,213	42,378	25,931	42,244	1,470,455,496.00
1997	7,379	14,428	2,339,113	1,716,977	—	—	168,595	73,940	319,393	—	103,748	326	332	284	49,545	7,433	56,978	42,486	25,989	41,030	1,577,769,316.00
1998	7,384	14,428	2,318,238	1,763,650	—	—	180,253	75,027	309,713	†	†	326	332	284	48,563	7,191	55,754	41,478	23,974	39,735	1,685,701,827.00
1999	7,368 ◆	16,891 ◆	2,296,936	1,812,434	—	—	196,574	†	275,382	†	†	◊	◊	◊	47,519	7,665	55,184	42,579	23,042	45,587	1,864,447,191.00
2000	7,347	16,783 ◆	2,319,844	1,857,843	—	—	187,927	†	300,010	†	†	◊	◊	◊	46,403	7,231	53,634	44,892	22,341	44,762	2,019,266,027.00
2001	7,344	17,336	2,317,515	1,868,960	—	—	199,446	—	297,635	—	—	—	—	—	45,566	6,969	52,535	42,268	19,354	44,199	1,939,281,740.00
2002	7,305	17,443	2,320,221	1,902,525	—	—	209,416	—	303,061	—	—	—	—	—	44,995	6,299	51,294	40,482	18,798	38,154	1,994,893,155.00
2003	7,220	17,174	2,284,233	1,866,157	—	—	208,094	—	287,998	—	—	—	—	—	43,068	6,248	49,316	39,557	18,260	35,840	2,044,377,792.00
2004	7,200	17,209	2,247,819	1,834,530	—	—	200,917	—	275,087	—	—	—	—	—	41,376	5,754	47,130	36,558	17,149	34,744	2,083,916,019.00
2005	7,155	17,817	2,205,376	1,796,017	—	—	203,390	—	266,080	—	—	—	—	—	38,680	5,620	44,300	36,244	16,190	34,372	2,199,993,228.00
2006	7,095	17,922	2,154,572	1,749,073	71,820	1,820,893	191,460	—	253,304	—	—	—	—	—	36,387	4,501	40,888	32,412	14,805	32,564	2,223,317,477.00
2007	7,055	18,019	2,116,749	1,720,477	75,306	1,795,783	189,671	—	242,557	—	—	—	—	—	34,194	4,020	38,214	23,556	13,438	31,457	2,269,075,042.00
2008	6,964	18,002	2,057,292	1,666,202	68,320	1,734,522	181,367	—	227,619	—	—	—	—	—	32,731	3,816	36,547	23,359	12,816	31,212	2,233,075,961.00
2009	6,895	18,000	2,006,343	1,624,025	69,060	1,693,085	183,674	—	216,693	—	—	—	—	—	30,682	3,978	34,660	22,762	11,647	30,853	2,128,331,169.00
2010	6,794	17,975	1,951,907	1,576,721	75,525	1,652,525	180,360	—	203,774	—	—	—	—	—	28,990	3,746	32,736	22,265	10,990	30,109	2,088,030,689.00
2011	6,736	18,112	1,923,046	1,542,072	70,755	1,612,827	179,256	—	197,754	—	—	—	—	—	28,201	3,939	32,140	20,942	10,950	29,813	2,127,489,576.00
2012	6,667	18,040	1,894,181	1,516,117	71,940	1,588,057	179,000	—	190,606	—	—	—	—	—	27,140	3,836	30,976	20,474	10,366	29,442	2,170,806,058.00
2013	6,622	18,170	1,866,758	1,491,423	57,585	1,549,008	184,035	—	184,859	—	—	—	—	—	25,822	3,675	29,497	20,077	9,933	28,960	2,215,042,224.00
2014	6,553	18,198	1,817,004	1,450,472	53,801	1,504,273	179,638	—	173,682	—	—	—	—	—	24,594	3,530	28,124	19,142	10,337	29,011	2,248,977,732.00
2015	6,510	18,345	1,779,335	1,434,461	60,191	1,494,652	179,353	—	163,301	—	—	—	—	—	24,069	3,305	27,374	17,791	9,149	28,571	2,280,563,637.00
2016	6,473	18,325	1,745,156	1,399,523	87,138	1,486,661	171,526	—	155,614	—	—	—	—	—	22,112	3,160	25,272	17,302	8,343	27,461	2,251,792,484.00

*New category or revised in 1992.
◆ See notes on clergy on page 15

†Statistics on Day Schools and church school staff are no longer maintained.
‡From 1970 on, excludes all non-income items; includes "other parish funds" (not previously reported.)
◊ Not available

A Table of the General Conventions

No.	Opened	Closed	Place of Meeting	Presiding Bishop	Pres. House of Deputies	Preacher
1	Sept. 27	Oct. 7, 1785	Philadelphia.	....	Rev. Wm. White, D.D.	Rev. Wm. Smith, D.D.
2	June 20	June 26, 1786	Philadelphia.	....	Rev. David Griffith.	Rev. Wm. White, D.D.
3	Oct. 10	Oct. 11, 1786	Wilmington, Del.	....	Rev. Samuel Provoost, D.D.	Rev. Samuel Megaw, D.D.
	July 28	Aug. 8, 1789	Philadelphia.	Bp. William White.	Bishop William White.₁	Rev. Wm. Smith, D.D.
	Sept. 29	Oct. 16, 1789	Philadelphia.	Bp. Samuel Seabury.	Rev. Wm. Smith, D.D.	....
4	Sept. 11	Sept.19, 1792	New York.	Bp. Samuel Provoost.	Rev. Wm. Smith, D.D.	Bishop Samuel Seabury.
5	Sept. 8	Sept.18, 1795	Philadelphia.	Bp. William White.	Rev. Wm. Smith, D.D.	Bishop Samuel Provoost.
6	June 11	June 19, 1799	Philadelphia.	Bp. William White.	Rev. Wm. Smith, D.D.	....
7	Sept. 8	Sept.12, 1801	Trenton, N.J.	Bp. William White.	Rev. Abraham Beach, D.D.	Bishop William White.
8	Sept. 11	Sept.18, 1804	New York.	Bp. William White.	Rev. Abraham Beach, D.D.	Bishop Benjamin Moore.
9	May 17	May 26, 1808	Baltimore.	Bp. William White.	Rev. Abraham Beach, D.D.	Bishop William White.
10	May 21	May 24, 1811	New Haven.	Bp. William White.	Rev. Isaac Wilkins.	Bishop William White.
11	May 17	May 24, 1814	Philadelphia.	Bp. William White.	Rev. John Croes, D.D.	Bishop John Henry Hobart.
12	May 20	May 27, 1817	New York.	Bp. William White.	Rev. Isaac Wilkins, D.D.	Bishop Alex. V. Griswold.
					Rev. Wm. H. Wilmer, D.D.	
13	May 16	May 24, 1820	Philadelphia.	Bp. William White.	Rev. Wm. H. Wilmer, D.D.	Bishop Richard C. Moore.
I	Oct. 30	Nov. 3, 1821	Philadelphia.	Bp. William White.	Rev. Wm. H. Wilmer, D.D.	Bishop James Kemp.
14	May 20	May 26, 1823	Philadelphia.	Bp. William White.	Rev. Wm. H. Wilmer, D.D.	Bishop John Cross.
15	Nov. 7	Nov. 15, 1826	Philadelphia.	Bp. William White.	Rev. Wm. H. Wilmer, D.D.	Bishop Nathaniel Bowen.
16	Aug. 12	Aug. 20, 1829	Philadelphia.	Bp. William White.	Rev. Wm. E. Wyatt, D.D.	Bishop Thomas C. Brownell.
17	Oct. 17	Oct. 31, 1832	New York.	Bp. William White.	Rev. Wm. E. Wyatt, D.D.	Bishop Henry U. Onderdonk.
18	Aug. 19	Sept. 1, 1835	Philadelphia.	Bp. Alexander Viets Griswold.	Rev. Wm. E. Wyatt, D.D.	Bishop Wm. Murray Stone.
19	Sept. 5	Sept.17, 1838	Philadelphia.	Bp. Alexander Viets Griswold.	Rev. Wm. E. Wyatt, D.D.	Bishop Wm. Meade.
20	Oct. 6	Oct. 19, 1841	New York.	Bp. Philander Chase.	Rev. Wm. E. Wyatt, D.D.	Bishop Benj. T. Onderdonk.
21	Oct. 2	Oct. 22, 1844	Philadelphia.	Bp. Philander Chase.	Rev. Wm. E. Wyatt, D.D.	Bishop Levi S. Ives.
22	Oct. 6	Oct. 28, 1847	New York.	Bp. Philander Chase.	Rev. Wm. E. Wyatt, D.D.	Bishop John Henry Hopkins.
23	Oct. 2	Oct. 16, 1850	Cincinnati.	Bp. Philander Chase.	Rev. Wm. E. Wyatt, D.D.	Bishop Benj. B. Smith.
24	Oct. 5	Oct. 26, 1853	New York.	Bp. Thomas Church Brownell.	Rev. Wm. Creighton, D.D.	Bishop Charles P. McIlvaine.
25	Oct. 1	Oct. 21, 1856	Philadelphia.	Bp. Thomas Church Brownell.	Rev. Wm. Creighton, D.D.	Bishop Geo. W. Doane.
26	Oct. 5	Oct. 22, 1859	Richmond, Va.	Bp. Thomas Church Brownell.₂	Rev. Wm. Creighton, D.D.	Bishop James H. Otey.
A1	July 3	July 6, 1861₃	Montgomery, Ala.	Bp. Stephen Elliott.	Met as a single house.	None mentioned.
A2	Oct. 16	Oct. 24, 1861₃	Columbia, S.C.	Bp. William Meade.	Met as a single house.	Bishop William Meade.
27	Oct. 1	Oct. 17, 1862	New York.	Bp. Thomas Church Brownell.₄	Rev. James Craik, D.D.	Bishop Sam. A. McCoskry.
A3	Nov. 12	Nov. 22, 1862₅	Augusta, Ga.	Bp. Stephen Elliott.	Rev. Christian Hanckel, D.D.	Bishop Henry C. Lay.
28	Oct. 4	Oct. 24, 1865	Philadelphia.	Bp. John Henry Hopkins.	Rev. James Craik, D.D.	Bishop Fulford of Montreal.
A4	Nov. 8	Nov. 10, 1865₆	Augusta, Ga.	Bp. Stephen Elliott.	Rev. C. C. Pinckney, D.D.	None mentioned.
29	Oct. 7	Oct. 29, 1868	New York.	Bp. Benjamin Bosworth Smith.	Rev. James Craik, D.D.	Bishop Henry W. Lee.
30	Oct. 4	Oct. 26, 1871	Baltimore.	Bp. Benjamin Bosworth Smith.	Rev. James Craik, D.D.	Bishop John Johns.
31	Oct. 7	Nov. 3, 1874	New York.	Bp. Benjamin Bosworth Smith.	Rev. James Craik, D.D.	Bishop Selwyn of Lichfield.
32	Oct. 3	Oct. 25, 1877	Boston.	Bp. Benjamin Bosworth Smith.	Rev. Alex. Burgess, D.D.	Bishop John Williams.
33	Oct. 6	Oct. 27, 1880	New York.	Bp. Benjamin Bosworth Smith.	Rev. E. E. Beardsley, D.D.	Bishop Wm. I. Kip.
34	Oct. 3	Oct. 26, 1883	Philadelphia.	Bp. Benjamin Bosworth Smith.₇	Rev. E. E. Beardsley, D.D.	Bishop Thomas M. Clark.
35	Oct. 6	Oct. 28, 1886	Chicago.	Bp. Alfred Lee.	Rev. Morgan Dix, D.D.	Bishop Gregory T. Bedell.
36	Oct. 2	Oct. 24, 1889	New York.	Bp. John Williams.	Rev. Morgan Dix, D.D.	Bishop Henry B. Whipple.
37	Oct. 5	Oct. 25, 1892	Baltimore.	Bp. John Williams.	Rev. Morgan Dix, D.D.	Bishop Richard H. Wilmer.

18

No.	Dates	Location	Presiding Bishop	Preacher	Chairman/President
40	Oct. 2–Oct. 17, 1901	San Francisco.	Bp. Thomas March Clark.[9]	Rev. J. S. Lindsay, D.D.	Bishop Benj. W. Morris.
41	Oct. 5–Oct. 25, 1904	Boston.	Bp. Daniel Sylvester Tuttle.	Rev. R. H. McKim, D.D.	Bishop Wm. C. Doane.
42	Oct. 2–Oct. 19, 1907	Richmond, Va.	Bp. Daniel Sylvester Tuttle.	Rev. R. H. McKim, D.D.	Bishop Ingram of London.
43	Oct. 5–Oct. 21, 1910	Cincinnati.	Bp. Daniel Sylvester Tuttle.	Rev. R. H. McKim, D.D.	Bp. Wordsworth of Salisbury.
44	Oct. 8–Oct. 25, 1913	New York.	Bp. Daniel Sylvester Tuttle.	Rev. Alex. Mann, D.D.	Bishop William Lawrence.
45	Oct. 11–Oct. 27, 1916	St. Louis.	Bp. Daniel Sylvester Tuttle.	Rev. Alex. Mann, D.D.	Bishop Daniel S. Tuttle.
46	Oct. 8–Oct. 24, 1919	Detroit.	Bp. Daniel Sylvester Tuttle.	Rev. Alex. Mann, D.D.	Bishop Charles H. Brent.
47	Sept. 6–Sept. 23, 1922	Portland, Oreg.	Bp. Daniel Sylvester Tuttle.	Rev. Alex. Mann, D.D.	Bishop Edwin S. Lines.
48	Oct. 7–Oct. 24, 1925	New Orleans, La.	Bp. Ethelbert Talbot.	Rev. Ernest M. Stires, D.D.	Bishop Theo. DuB. Bratton.[10]
49	Oct. 10–Oct. 25, 1928	Washington, D.C.	Bp. John Gardner Murray.	Rev. ZeB. Phillips, D.D.	Bishop Charles P. Anderson.
50	Sept. 16–Sept. 30, 1931	Denver, Colo.	Bp. James DeWolf Perry.	Rev. ZeB. Phillips, D.D.	Bishop Furse of St. Albans.
51	Oct. 10–Oct. 23, 1934	Atlantic City, N.J.	Bp. James DeWolf Perry.	Rev. ZeB. Phillips, D.D.	Bishop James DeWolf Perry.
52	Oct. 6–Oct. 19, 1937	Cincinnati.	Bp. James DeWolf Perry.	Rev. ZeB. Phillips, D.D.	Bishop Edward L. Parsons.
53	Oct. 9–Oct. 19, 1940	Kansas City, Mo.	Bp. Henry St. George Tucker.	Rev. ZeB. Phillips, D.D.	Bishop H. St. George Tucker.
54	Oct. 2–Oct. 11, 1943	Cleveland.	Bp. Henry St. George Tucker.	Rev. Phillips E. Osgood, D.D.	Bishop H. St. George Tucker.
55	Sept. 10–Sept. 20, 1946	Philadelphia.	Bp. Henry St. George Tucker.	Hon. Owen J. Roberts.	Bishop H. St. George Tucker.
56	Sept. 26–Oct. 7, 1949	San Francisco.	Bp. Henry Knox Sherrill.	V.Rev. Claude W. Sprouse, D.D.	Bishop Henry Knox Sherrill.
57	Sept. 8–Sept. 19, 1952	Boston.	Bp. Henry Knox Sherrill.	V.Rev. C. W. Sprouse, D.D.[11]	Bishop Henry Knox Sherrill.
58	Sept. 4–Sept. 15, 1955	Honolulu, T.H.	Bp. Henry Knox Sherrill.	Rev. T. O. Wedel, Ph.D.	Bishop Henry Knox Sherrill.
59	Oct. 5–Oct. 17, 1958	Miami Beach, Fla.	Bp. Henry Knox Sherrill.	Rev. Theodore O. Wedel, Ph.D.	Bishop Henry Knox Sherrill.
60	Sept. 17–Sept. 29, 1961	Detroit, Mich.	Bp. Arthur Lichtenberger.	Rev. Theodore O. Wedel, Ph.D.	Bishop Arthur Lichtenberger.
61	Oct. 11–Oct. 23, 1964	St. Louis, Mo.	Bp. Arthur Lichtenberger.	Clifford P. Morehouse, LL.D.	Bishop Arthur Lichtenberger.[12]
62	Sept. 17–Sept. 27, 1967	Seattle, Wash.	Bp. John Elbridge Hines.	Clifford P. Morehouse, LL.D.	Bishop John Elbridge Hines.
II	Aug. 31–Sept. 5, 1969	South Bend, In.	Bp. John Elbridge Hines.	Clifford P. Morehouse, LL.D.	Bishop John Elbridge Hines.
63	Oct. 11–Oct. 22, 1970	Houston, Tx.	Bp. John Elbridge Hines.	V. Rev. John B. Coburn.	Bishop John Elbridge Hines.
64	Sept. 30–Oct. 11, 1973	Louisville, Ky.	Bp. John Elbridge Hines.	V. Rev. John B. Coburn.	Bishop John Elbridge Hines.
65	Sept. 11–Sept. 22, 1976	Minneapolis, Mn.	Bp. John Maury Allin.	V. Rev. John B. Coburn.	Bishop John Maury Allin.
66	Sept. 6–Sept. 20, 1979	Denver, Co.	Bp. John Maury Allin.	Charles R. Lawrence, Ph.D.	Bishop John Maury Allin.
67	Sept. 5–Sept. 15, 1982	New Orleans, LA	Bp. John Maury Allin.	Charles R. Lawrence, Ph.D.	Bishop John Maury Allin.
68	Sept. 7–Sept. 14, 1985	Anaheim, CA	Bp. John Maury Allin.	Charles R. Lawrence, Ph.D.	Archbishop Robert A. K. Runcie.
69	July 2–July 11, 1988	Detroit, MI	Bp. Edmond Lee Browning.	V. Rev. David B. Collins.	Bishop Edmond Lee Browning.
70	July 11–July 20, 1991	Phoenix, AZ	Bp. Edmond Lee Browning.	V. Rev. David B. Collins.	Bishop Edmond Lee Browning.
71	Aug. 24–Sept. 2, 1994	Indianapolis, IN	Bp. Edmond Lee Browning.	Pamela P. Chinnis.	Pamela P. Chinnis.
72	July 16–July 25, 1997	Philadelphia, PA	Bp. Frank T Griswold.	Pamela P. Chinnis.	Archbishop George Leonard Carey.
73	July 5–July 14, 2000	Denver, CO	Bp. Frank T Griswold.	Pamela P. Chinnis.	Bishop Simon Elija Chiwanga.
74	July 30–Aug 8, 2003	Minneapolis, MN	Bp. Frank T Griswold.	V. Rev. George L. W. Werner.	Archbishop Josiah Idowu-Fearon.
75	June 13–June 21, 2006	Columbus, OH	Bp. Katharine Jefferts Schori.	V. Rev. George L. W. Werner.	Dr. Jenny Te Paa.
76	July 8–July 17, 2009	Anaheim, CA	Bp. Katharine Jefferts Schori.	Bonnie Anderson.	Bishop Katharine Jefferts Schori.
77	July 5–July 12, 2012	Indianapolis, IN	Bp. Katharine Jefferts Schori.	Bonnie Anderson.	Bishop Katharine Jefferts Schori.
78	June 25–July 3, 2015	Salt Lake City, Utah	Bp. Katharine Jefferts Schori.	Rev. Gay Clark Jennings.	Bishop Katharine Jefferts Schori.
79	July 5–July 13, 2018	Austin, Texas	Bp. Michael B. Curry.	Rev. Gay Clark Jennings.	Bishop Katharine Jefferts Schori.
80	July 8–July 11, 2022	Baltimore, Maryland	Bp. Michael B. Curry.	Rev. Gay Clark Jennings.	Bishop Katharine Jefferts Schori.

1) From 1785 through the first session of 1789 the General Convention was a single house and Bishop White was president of the Convention. 2) Absent because of advanced years; Bishop William Meade presided. 3) The First Preliminary meeting of dioceses of the Confederate States was held unofficially. For the Second Preliminary meeting, all dioceses in the Confederate States were officially called by the First Preliminary meeting. In those two meetings there was no official presiding Bishop, but the oldest bishop in point of consecration, who was present, presided. The dioceses involved had not at that time officially withdrawn from The Protestant Episcopal Church in the United States of America, although in practice they had done so. There was no officially appointed Presiding Bishop until the first meeting of the General Council of The Protestant Episcopal Church in the Confederate States of America. 4) Absent because of advanced years; Bishop John Henry Hopkins presided. 5) First General Council of The Protestant Episcopal Church in the Confederate States of America. 6) Second General Council of The Protestant Episcopal Church in the Confederate States of America. 7) Because of Bishop Smith's advanced years, Bishop Alfred Lee presided and signed the minutes. 8) Absent because of illness; Bishop Wm. C. Doane was Chairman of the House of Bishops and signed the minutes. 9) Absent because of illness; Bishop Thomas U. Dudley of Kentucky was Chairman of the House of Bishops and signed the minutes. 10) Read by Bishop T. F. Gailor because of Bishop Bratton's illness. 11) Died during first day's session. 12) Read by Bishop Ned Cole, at the request of Bishop Lichtenberger.

THE CANONICAL STRUCTURE OF THE CHURCH

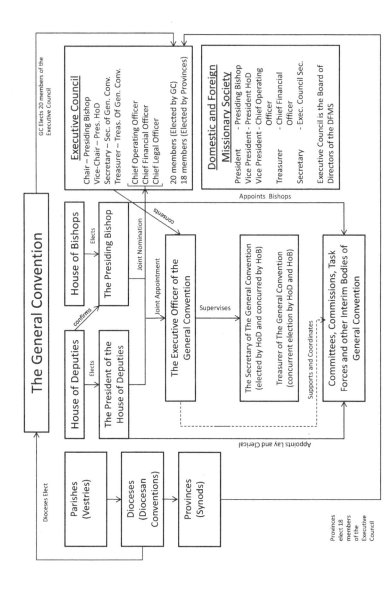

The information listed in this section was generously provided by the Office of the General Convention of The Episcopal Church.

The General Convention of The Episcopal Church
ELECTED OFFICERS OF THE GENERAL CONVENTION

The Most Rev. Michael Bruce Curry, *Presiding Bishop and Primate*; The Rev. Gay Clark Jennings, *President of the House of Deputies*; The Rev. Canon Dr. Michael Barlowe, *Secretary of the General Convention*; Mr. N. Kurt Barnes, *Treasurer*

Most Rev. Michael Curry,
Presiding Bishop and Primate

Rev. Gay Clark Jennings,
President of the House of Deputies

THE EPISCOPAL CHURCH CENTER

815 Second Avenue, New York, NY 10017 (800) 334-7626 Web: www.episcopalchurch.org Staff members may be reached via e-mail using their first initial with their last name (Ex. jdoe@episcopalchurch.org)

EXECUTIVE OFFICE OF THE GENERAL CONVENTION

(800) 334-7626 Fax: (212) 972-9322 Web: www.generalconvention.org

Rev. Canon Dr. Michael Barlowe, *Executive Officer and Secretary of the General Convention;* Rt. Rev. Mary Gray-Reeves, *Vice-President of the House of Bishops*; Rt. Rev. Diane M. Jardine Bruce, *Secretary of the House of Bishops*; The Hon. Byron Rushing, *Vice-President of the House of Deputies*

THE GENERAL CONVENTION

The 81st General Convention will be held June 23–28, 2024, in Louisville, Kentucky.

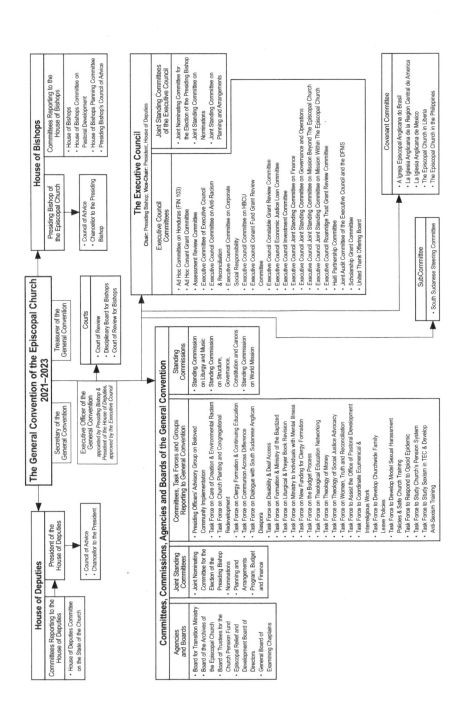

THE HOUSE OF BISHOPS

Chair: **Curry,** Most Rev Michael Bruce; *Vice-Chair*: **Gray-Reeves,** Rt Rev Mary; *Secretary*: **Bruce,** Rt Rev Diane M Jardine

Committees of the House of Bishops

Presiding Bishop's Council of Advice

(*All terms* 2024) **Curry,** Most Rev Michael Bruce (*Chair*); Province III: **Brown,** Rt Rev Kevin ; **Cole,** Rt Rev Brian (IV); **Duncan-Probe,** Rt Rev Dr DeDe (II); **Fisher,** Rt Rev Douglas (I); **Gunter,** Rt Rev Matthew A (V); **León Lorenzo,** Rt Rev Cristobal (IX); **Lucas,** Rt Rev Kimberly (VI); **Owensby,** Rt Rev Jake (VII); **Rehberg,** Ms Gretchen (VIII); *Ex-Officio*: Bruce, Rt Rev Diane Jardin(VIII); Gray-Reeves, Rt Rev Mary (IV); **Ousley** (V)

House of Bishops Committee on Pastoral Development

(*All terms* 2021) **Harris,** Rt Rev Gayle (*Chair*); **Baskerville-Burrows,** Rt Rev Jennifer; **Beauvoir,** Rt Rev Oge; **Daniel,** Rt Rev Clifton; **Goff,** Rt Rev Susan; **Hollerith,** Rt Rev Herman; **Hougland,** Rt Rev Whayne; **Ousley,** Rt Rev Todd; **Owensby,** Rt Rev Jake; **Provenzano,** Rt Rev Lawrence; **Wolfe,** Rt Rev Dean; *SPG Representative*: **Fisher,** Rev Betsy; *Ex Officio*: **Curry,** Most Rev Michael Bruce

THE HOUSE OF DEPUTIES

President: **Jennings,** Rev Gay Clark; *Vice President*: **Rushing,** Hon Byron; *Secretary*: **Barlowe,** Rev Cn Dr Michael; *Chancellor to the President*: **Johnson,** Ms Sally A Johnson, Esq

Committees of the House of Deputies

House of Deputies Committee on the State of the Church

(*All terms* 2024) **Nishibayashi,** Ms Kathryn (*Chair*); **Larson,** Rowan; **Quick-Panwala,** Ms Karma(*Vice-Chairs*); **Brown,** Deputy Nathan (*Secretary*); **Betz Shank,** Rev Erin; **Castellan,** Rev Megan L; **Conley,** Dr Dawn; **Goodhouse,** Rev Angela; **Hardaway,** Lillian; **Hernández Rivas,** Br Luis Enrique; **Kay,** Lauren; **Mendoza,** Rev Milquella; **Ranadive Pooley,** Rev Dr Nina; **Serrano Poveda,** Rev Nelson; **Steele,** Rev Kelly; **Warren,** Ms Evangeline; *Ex Officio*: **Ayala Harris,** Ms Julia; *Representative of the PHoD*: **Millien,** Adia; *Consultant:* **Glass,** Mr Michael

THE COURTS

Disciplinary Board for Bishops

Knudsen, Rt Rev Chilton (*Chair, 2027*); **Alarid,** Hon A Joseph (*2024*); **Bourlakas,** Rt Rev Mark (*2024*); **Brooke-Davidson,** Rt Rev Jennifer (*2024*); **Dean**

Larsen, Cn Julie (*2027*); **Fleener, Jr,** Mr William (*2027*); **Gibbs,** Rt Rev Wendell (*2024*); **Harrison,** Rt Rev Dena (*2024*); **Haynes,** Rt Rev Susan (2027); **Hirschfeld,** Rt Rev A Robert (*2024*); **Hunn,** Rt Rev Michael C B (*2027*; **Jacobs,** Rev Cn Gregory (*2027*); **Knisely,** Rt Rev W Nicholas (2024); **Lloyd,** Rev Mally Ewing (*2024*); **Nichols,** Rt Rev Kevin (2027); **Perrin,** Melissa (*2024*); **Tanabe,** Rev Irene (*2024*); **Wendell,** Rev Chris (*2027*)

Court of Review

(*All terms* 2024) **Burns,** Rev Lisa; **Christian Reynoso,** Sra. Grecia; **Cole,** Dr L Zoe; **Davis,** Rev Rodney; **Glover,** Dr Delbert; **Hazel,** Rev Cn Dorothy d'Rue; **Henes,** Ms Sharon; **Hirshfeld,** Rt Rev A Robert; **Kirby,** Rev Lisa; **Roaf,** Rt Rev Phoebe; **Rodriguez Velez,** Mrs. Brunilda; **Russell,** Ms Laura; **Ryan,** Rt Rev Kathryn; **Schofield-Broadbent,** Rev Carrie; **Wendell,** Rev Chris; **Logue,** Rt Rev Frank (*Bishop Alternate*); **Jacobs,** Rev Cn Gregory (Clergy Alternate); **Dean Larson,** Cn Julie (*Lay Alternate*)

Court of Review for Bishops

Ahrens, Rt Rev Laura (*2024*); **Brewer,** Rt Rev Gregory O (*2027*); **Gunter,** Rt Rev Matthew A. (*2027*); **Lane,** Rt Rev Stephen (*2024*); **Scanlan,** Rt Rev Audrey (*2027*); **White,** Rt Rev Terry (*2024*)

COVENANT COMMITTEE

La Iglesia Anglican de la Region Central de America

(*All terms* 2024) **Gates,** Rt Rev Alan; **Watt,** Ms Linda; *Ex Officio*: **Ayala Harris,** Ms Julia; **Curry,** Most Rev Michael

La Iglesia Anglicana de Mexico

(*All terms* 2024) **Ashby,** Rt Rev Lucinda; **Chavez,** The Rev. David Ulloa; **Compier,** Very Rev Don; **Fisher,** Rt Rev Jeff; **Guerra,** Mr. Jody; *Ex Officio*: **Ayala Harris,** Ms Julia; **Curry,** Most Rev Michael

The Episcopal Church in Liberia

(*All terms* 2024) **Beauvoir,** Rt Rev Oge; **Pham,** Rev Dr J Peter; *Ex Officio*: **Ayala Harris,** Ms Julia; **Curry,** Most Rev Michael

The Episcopal Church in the Philippines

Bruce, Rt Rev Diane Jardine (*2024*); *Ex Officio*: **Ayala Harris,** Ms Julia; **Curry,** Most Rev Michael

EXECUTIVE COUNCIL

(*All terms 2024 unless noted*) **Curry,** Most Rev Michael (*Chair, IV*); **Ayala Harris,** Ms Julia (*Vice-Chair, VII*); **Barlowe,** Rev Cn Dr Michael (*Secretary, VIII*); **Barnes,**

Mr N Kurt; (*Treasurer, II*); VI: **Anderson,** Dr Lisa; **Anderson,** Rev Devon; IX: **Angulo Zamora,** La Rvda Gina (*2027*); II: **Anker,** Mr Kent; **Buchanan,** Cn Annette (*2027*); **Chu,** Mr Thomas (*2027*); VII: **Clare,** Ms Smantha (*2027*); II:**Cooper,** Tivaun (*2027*); II: **Davis-Wilson,** Rev Lillian; III: **Downing,** Rev Patty; VIII: **Eaton,** Rev Cn Cornelia; V: **Eccles,** Very Rev ME; IX: **Echeverry,** Sra Blanca; IV: **Freeman,** Ms Alice; VIII: **Gee,** Mr Timothy (*2027*)**Getz,** Ms Pauline; VI: **Goodhouse,** Rev Angela; VII: **Goodman,** Very Rev Mark; **Graves,** Rev Charles (*2027*); IV: **Haight,** Mr Scott (*2027*); VIII: **Hayashi,** Rt Rev Scott; VI: **Hitt II,** Prof Lawrence (*2027*); IV: **Hodges-Copple,** Rt Rev Anne; **Jackson,** Rev Dr Deborah (*2027*); V: **Johnson,** Rt Rev Deon (*2027*); II: **Kitch,** Rt Rev Cn Anne; IV: **McDaniel,** Mr Joe(*2027*); **McKellar,** Cn Andrea; V: **McKellaston,** Ms Louisa (*2027*); IV: **Merchant,** Rev Cn Dr Wilmot (*2027*);VII: **Montes,** Dr Sandra (*2027*); II: **Morales,** Rt Rev Rafael (*2027*); I: **Perkins,** Ven Aaron; II: **Pollard,** Ms Diane; I: **Ridge,** Ms Betsy (*2027*);II: **Sconiers,** Hon Rose H; V: **Smith,** Ms Diane Audrick (*2027*); III: **Stonesifer Boylan,** Dr Sarah; **Taylor,** Mr Matthew (2027); **Kostel,** Ms Mary (*Chancellor to the PB*); **Taber-Hamilton,** Rev Rachel (*VP HoD*); **Glass,** Mr Michael (*Chancellor HoD);* **Asbil,** Rt Rev Andrew (*Liaison—Anglican Church of Canada*); **Engquist,** Pastor Joanne (*ELCA Liaison*); **Rowe,** Rt Rev Sean (*Parliamentarian*)

EXECUTIVE COUNCIL COMMITTEE OR COMMISSION

Assessment Review Committee

(*All terms 2024*) **Koonce,** Rev Nancy (*Chair*); **Downing,** Rev Patty; **Hunn,** Rt Rev Michael CB; **Lattime**; Rt Rev Mark; **McLoughlin,** Rt Rev José; **Powell Sturm,** Ms Holli; **Rickel,** Rt Rev Gregory; **Simmonds Ballentine,** Cn Rosalie; *Ex Officio*: **Ayala Harris,** Ms Julia; **Curry,** Most Rev Michael; *Treasurer*: **Barnes,** Mr N Kurt

Executive Committee of Executive Council

(*All terms* 2024) **Curry,** Most Rev Michael (*Chair*); **Ayala Harris,** Ms Julia (*Vice-Chair*); **Angulo Zamora,** La Rvda Gina; **Goodman,** Very Rev Mark; **Graves,** Rev Charles; **Hayashi,** Rt Rev Scott; **McKellar,** Cn Andrea; **Pollard,** Ms Diane; **Stonesifer Boylan,** Dr Sarah; *Ex Officio*: **Anker,** Mr Kent; **Barlow,** Rev Cn Dr Michael; **Barnes,** Mr N Kurt

Executive Council Committee on Anti-Racism & Reconciliation

(*All terms 2024*) **McKim,** Mr James (*Chair*); **Bass-Choate,** Rev Yamily; **Brewer-Cotlar,** Ms Deb; **Chiran-Quiñonez,** Rev Jairo, **Harris,** Rt Rev Gayle; **Hayashi,** Rt Rev Scott; **Kershen,** Rev Charles; **McCloud,** Rev Cn Christine; **McLaurin,** Rev Malcolm; **Thompson,** Ms Felicity; *Ex Officio*: **Ayala Harris,** Ms Julia; **Curry,** Most Rev Michael

Executive Council Committee on Corporate Social Responsibility

(*All terms 2024*) **Lawton,** Ms Sarah (*Chair*); **Brown,** Ms Janet; **Burnett,** Rev Richard; **Fisher,** Rt Rev Douglas; **Grieves,** Rev Cn Brian; **Hitt II,** Prof Lawrence; **Pollard,** Ms Diane; **Spalding,** Rev Kirsten; **Taylor,** Rt Rev John Harvey; **Varghese,** Rev Winnie; **Wilcox,** Rev Diana; *Ex Officio*: **Ayala Harris,** Ms Julia; **Curry,** Most Rev Michael

Executive Council Committee on HBCU

(*All terms 2024*) **Shaw,** Very Rev Dr Martini (*Chair*); **Evenbeck,** Dr Scott (*Vice-Chair*); **Alexander,** Dr Martha Bedell; **Callaway,** Rev Cn James; **Cunningham,** Dr Joel; **George,** Dr Anita; **Hagans,** Rev Dr Cn Michele; **Lowe,** Rev Dr Eugene; **Rodman,** Rt Rev Samuel; **Woodliff-Stanley,** Rt Rev Ruth; *Ex Officio*: **Ayala Harris,** Ms Julia; **Curry,** Most Rev Michael

Executive Council Conant Fund Grant Review Committee

(*All terms 2024*) **Kitch,** Rev Anne E (*Chair*); **Butler,** Ms Diane; **Clare,** Ms Samantha; **Grane,** Karen; *Ex Officio*: **Ayala Harris,** Ms Julia; **Curry,** Most Rev Michael; **Barnes,** Mr N Kurt (*Treasurer*); Hercules, Ms Ann (*Staff*)

Executive Council Constable Grant Review Committee

(*All terms 2024*) **Brackett,** Tom; **Clare,** Ms Samantha; **Crosnier de Bellaistre,** Ms Margareth; **Eccles,** Very Rev M E; **James,** Rev Dr Molly; **Ridge,** Ms Betsy; **Taylor,** Rev Jemonde; *Ex Officio*: **Ayala Harris,** Ms Julia; **Curry,** Most Rev Michael

Executive Council Economic Justice Loan Committee

(*All terms 2024*) **Mebane,** Rev Will (*Chair*); **Eccles,** Very Rev M E; **Gee,** Mr Timothy; **Hodges-Copple,** Rt Rev Anne; **McDaniel,** Mr Joe; **Pollard,** Ms Diane; **Rushing,** Mr Byron; **Walter,** Rev Andrew; *Ex Officio*: **Ayala Harris,** Ms Julia; **Curry,** Most Rev Michael

Executive Council Investment Committee

(*All terms 2024*) **Walter,** Rev Andrew (*Chair*); **Akinla,** Mr Dale; **Barnes,** Mr N Kurt; **Brown,** Ms Janet; **Fowler,** Mr Gordon; **Garland,** Charles; **Gee,** Mr Timothy; **McElroy,** Ms Kirsten; **Simon,** Mr James; *Ex Officio*: **Ayala Harris,** Ms Julia; **Curry,** Most Rev Michael

Executive Council Joint Standing Committee on Finance

(*All terms 2024*) **McKellar,** Cn Andrea (*Chair*); **Barnes,** Mr N Kurt (*Treasurer*); **Angulo Zamora,** La Rvda

Gina; **Downing,** Rev Patty; **Eaton,** Rev Cn Cornelia; **Gee,** Mr Timothy; **Haight,** Mr Scott; **Hodges-Copple,** Rt Rev Anne; **Johnson,** Rt Rev Deon; **Kitch,** Rev Cn Anne; **Pollard,** Ms Diane; *Ex Officio*: **Ayala Harris,** Ms Julia; **Curry,** Most Rev Michael

Executive Council Joint Standing Committee on Governance and Operations

(*All terms 2024*) **Hayashi,** Rt Rev Scott (*Chair*); **Getz,** Ms Pauline (*Vice-Chair*); **Anderson,** Dr Liza (*Secretary*); **Anderson,** Rev Devon; **Cooper,** Tivaun; **McKellaston,** Ms Louisa; **Morales,** Rt Rev Rafael; **Perkins** Ven Aaron; **Sconiers,** Hon Rose H; *Ex Officio*: **Ayala Harris,** Ms Julia; **Curry,** Most Rev Michael

Executive Council Joint Standing Committee on Mission Beyond The Episcopal Church

(*All terms 2024*) **Goodman,** Very Rev Mark (*Chair*); **Graves,** Rev Charles (*Vice-Chair*); **Taylor,** Mr Matthew (*Secretary*); **Davis-Wilson,** Rev Lillian; **Freeman,** Ms Alice; **Hitt II,** Prof Lawrence; **Jackson,** Rev Dr Deborah; **Merchant,** Rev Cn Dr Wilmot; **Montes,** Dr Sandra; *Ex Officio*: **Ayala Harris,** Ms Julia; **Curry,** Most Rev Michael

Executive Council Joint Standing Committee on Mission Within The Episcopal Church

(*All terms 2024*) **Stonesifer Boylan,** Dr Sarah (*Chair*); **Buchanan,** Cn Annette; **Chu,** Mr Thomas; **Clare,** Ms Smantha; **Eccles,** Very Rev M E; **Echeverry,** Sra Blanca; **Goodhouse,** Rev Angela; **McDaniel,** Mr Joe; **Ridge,** Ms Betsy; **Smith,** Ms Diane Audrick; *Ex Officio*: **Ayala Harris,** Ms Julia; **Curry,** Most Rev Michael

Executive Council Constable/Roanridge Fund Grant Review Committee

(*All terms 2024*) **Brackett,** Tom; **Clare,** Ms Smantha; **Crosnier de Bellaistre,** Ms Margareth; **Eccles,** Very Rev M E; **James,** Rev Dr Molly; **Ridge,** Ms Betsy; **Taylor,** Rev Jemonde; *Ex Officio*: **Ayala Harris,** Ms Julia; **Curry,** Most Rev Michael

Joint Audit Committee of the Executive Council and the DFMS

(*All terms 2024*) **Judge,** Ms Tess (*Chair*); **Banner,** Rev Shelly; **Bivins, Jr,** Mr. Julian M; **McKellar,** Cn Andrea; **Packard,** Mr Daniel; **Roaf,** Rt Rev Phoebe; *Ex Officio*: **Ayala Harris,** Ms Julia; **Curry,** Most Rev Michael

Scholarship Grant Committee

(*All terms 2024*) **Klusmeyer,** Rt Rev William (*Chair*); **Barnes,** Mr N Kurt; **Crider,** Rev Deon; **Crosnier de Bellaistre,** Ms Margareth; **Grinage.** Ms Penny; **Jackson,** Rev Dr Deborah; **Sondak,** Ms Raphaelle

JOINT STANDING COMMITTEES

Joint Nominating Committee for the Election of the Presiding Bishop

(*All terms 2024*) **Lattime,** Rt Rev Mark; **Nishibayashi,** Cn Dr Steven (Co-Chairs); **Hines,** Ms Deborah (*Secretary);* **Alexander,** Mr Thomas; **Baskerville-Burrows,** Rt Rev Jennifer; **Bucklin,** Rev Cn Lydia K; **Chinguá,** El Rvdo Diego; **Diaz,** Mr Thomas; **Gallardo,** Rev Dr Antonio; **Gonzalez,** Ms Maria; **Hagen,** Rev Maureen-Elizabeth; **Hawk,** Mr Warren; **Jackson,** Rev Dr Deborah; **LeBron,** Mr Eric V; **McLoughlin,** Rev José; **Roaf,** Rt Rev Phoebe; **Scanlan,** Rt Rev Audrey; **Schjonberg,** Rev Mary Francis; **Sconiers,** Hon Rose; **Wang,** Rev Kit; **Barlowe,** Rev Cn Dr (*Secretary GC*)

Joint Standing Committee on Nominations

(*All terms 2024*) **Anderson,** Rev Devon (*Chair*); **Gordon,** Ms Nanci (*Vice-Chair*); **Middleton,** Rev. Tracie (*Secretary*); **Brown,** Rt Rev Kevin; **Cañas,** Ms Wendy; **Collins,** Rev Cn Dr Lynn A; **Rehberg,** Rt Rev Gretchen;　**Scanlan,** Rt Rev Audrey;　**Sweeney-Bender,** Mr Tieran; **Tran,** Mr　Hanh; **Vance,** Mr Eddie; **Ward,** Ms　Delois; *Ex Officio*: **Ayala Harris,** Ms Julia; **Curry,** Most Rev Michael

Joint Standing Committee on Planning and Arrangements

(*All terms* 2024) **Ayala Harris,** Ms Julia; **Barlowe,** Rev Cn Dr Michael; **Barnes,** Mr N Kurt; **Bruce,** Rt Rev Diane Jardine; **Curry,** Most Rev Michael; **Gibbs,** Rt Rev Wendell; **Gray-Reeves,** Rt Rev Mary; **Koonce,** Rev Nancy; **Krislock,** Mr Bryan; **Mellott,** Rev Emily; **Patterson,** Ms Karen; **Real Coultas,** Rev Cn Amy; **Taber-Hamilton,** Rev Rachel; **Wellnitz,** Patricia; **White,** Rt Rev Terry; **Glass,** Mr Michael (*Rep PHoD*); **Bell,** Ms Betsy; **Haizel,** Mr Patrick; **James,** Rev Dr Molly; **Kluysmeyer,** Rt Rev William; **Neiman,** Ms Fiona (*Staff*)

Joint Standing Committee on Finance

(*All terms 2024*) **McKellar,** Cn Andrea (*Chair*); **Barnes,** Mr N Kurt; (*Treasurer*); **Angulo Zamora,** La Rvda Gina; **Downing,** Rev Patty; **Eaton,** Rev Cn Cornelia; **Gee,** Mr Timothy; **Haight,** Mr Scott; **Hodges-Copple,** Rt Rev Anne; **Johnson,** Rt Rev Deon; **Kitch,** Rev Anne E; **Pollard,** Ms Diane; *Ex Officio*: **Ayala Harris,** Ms Julia; **Curry,** Most Rev Michael

STANDING COMMISSIONS

Standing Commission on Liturgy and Music

(*All terms 2024 unless noted*) **Childers,** Cn Mark (*Chair*); **Black,** Rev Cynthia (*Vice-Chair, 2027*); **Baker,** Rev Stannard (*Secretary*); **Boney,** Dr Michael; **Burnett,** Dr Marty (2027); Fennig, Patrick; (2027);

Floberg, Mr Joshua; **Francis,** SSM Kristina; (2027); **Hino**, Rev Cn Robert; **Johnson,** Rt Rev Deon (2027); **Milliken**, Rev Greg (2027); **Montes,** Mr Ellis; **Reddall,** Rt Rev Jennifer; **Rodriguez,** Yuri (2027); **Roque,** Br Angel; **Russell**, Rev Cn Susan (2027); **Santiago,** Sr Jose (2027); **Stevenson,** Rt Rev E Mark (2027); **Whalon**, Rt Rev Pierre; **White**, Rt Rev Terry; **Wright**, Rt Rev Carl (*2024*); *Ex Officio*: **Curry,** Most Rev Michael Bruce; **Moore,** Rev Kathleen (*Rep of the PHoD*);**Anderson,** Dr Liza (*Liaison of Executive Council*); **Alexander,** Rt Rev J Neil (*Custodian of the Book of Common Prayer*)

Standing Commission on Structure, Governance, Constitution, and Canons

(*All terms 2024 unless noted*) **Hayes,** Mr Christopher (*Chair*); **Logue,** Rt Rev Frank (*2027, Vice-Chair*); **Trambley,** Rev Dr Adam (*Secretary*); **Alarid,** Hon A Joseph (*2027*); **Balling,** Rev Cn Valerie; **Baskerville-Burrows,** Rt Rev Jennifer; **Cisluycis,** Ms Jane (2027); **Cohen,** Ms Nancy Mahoney (*2027*); **Edington,** Rt Rev Mark (*2027*); **Figueroa,** Sra Carmen; **Kusumoto,** Mr Ryan; **Little,** Mr Thomas; **Loya,** Rt Rev Craig (*2027*); **Panky,** Rev Dr Steve (*2027*); **Powell,** Mr William; **Randle,** Mr Russell (*2027*); **Rowe,** Rt Rev Sean; **Sammons,** Ms Diane (2027); **Taber-Hamilton,** Rev Rachel (2027); **Tabzon Thompson,** Rev Dr Marisa; *Representative of the Presiding Bishop*: **Mary;** *Ex Officio*: **Ayala Harris,** Ms Julia; **Curry,** Most Rev Michael; **Glass,** Mr Michael (*Rep of the PHoD*); **Perkins,** Ven Aaron (*Liaison of Executive Council*)

Standing Commission on World Mission

(*All terms 2024 unless noted*) **Gardner,** Ms. Martha (*Chair*) **Zacharia,** Rev Dr Manoj Mathew (*Vice-Chair, 2027*); **Tanabe,** Rev Irene (*Secretary*); **Ashby,** Rt Rev Lucinda (*2027*); **Brownridge,** Rev Cn Walter BA; **Carson,** Dr Caroline (*2027*); **Christian Reynoso,** Sra. Grecia; **Conley,** Cn Judith; **Diaz,** Mr Thomas (*2027*); **Elston,** Emily (2027); **Gates,** Rt Rev Alan ; **Hallanan,** Ms Felicity (*2027*); **Keniston,** Ms Emily; **Maggiano,** Rev Grey; **McLoughlin,** Rt Rev José ; **Morales,** Rt Rev Rafael; **Reovan,** Ms. Denise; **Singh,** Rt Rev Prince (*2027*); **Smith,** Ms. Angela; **Wright,** Ms Diane (2027); *Ex Officio*: **Ayala Harris,** Ms Julia; **Curry,** Most Rev Michael; *Liaison of Executive Council*: **Merchant,** Rev Cn Dr Wilmot

TASK FORCES OF GENERAL CONVENTION

Task Force on Care of Creation & Environmental Racism

(*All terms 2024*) **Johnson,** Rev Stephanie (*Chair*); **Link,** Ms Zena (*Vice-Chair*); **Heck,** Dr Delia (*Secretary*); **Bascom,** Rt Rev Cathleen C; **Bennett** Ven Besty; **Berends,** Rev April; **Bleich Weber,** Rev Lynne; **Clifton,** Ver Rev Ellis; **Huber,** Rev Glenna; **Nolan**; Ms Sarah;

Okamoto Bach, Cn Barbie; **Quiñonez,** Bishop Juan Carlos; **Rice,** Rt Rev David; **Richards,** Rt Rev Daniel; **Rickel,** Rt Rev Gregory; **Thompson,** Dr Andrew; **West,** Anna; **Wong,** Mr Warren; *Ex Officio*: **Ayala Harris,** Ms Julia; **Curry,** Most Rev Michael

Task Force to Study Congregational Vitality Indicators[26-C]

(*All terms 2024*) **Doyle,** Rt Rev C Andrew(*Chair*); **Bond,** Ms Kate; **Funston,** Ms Michael; **Griffin,** Stephan; **Hallanan,** Rev Sunny; **Maconaughey,** Rev Debra; **Natta,** Rev Dr Laura; **Phillips Smith,** Ms Karen; **Shepard,** Rev Dr Angela; *Ex Officio*: **Ayala Harris,** Ms Julia; **Curry,** Most Rev Michael

Interim Body to Oversee the Continuing Development of Anti-Harassment Best Practices

(*All terms 2024*) **Russell,** Ms Laura (*Chair*); **Andrews,** Ms Judith; **Brock,** Ven Laurie; **Carmichael,** Rev Cn Anna; **Fry,** Rev Gwen; **Linares,** Rev Ivette; **Sherrod,** Ms Katie; **Shumate,** Rev Gavin; *Ex Officio*: **Ayala Harris,** Ms Julia; **Curry,** Most Rev Michael

Task Force on Clergy Formation & Continuing Education

(*All terms 2024*) **Elfring-Roberts,** Rev Jesse (*Chair*); **Karr-Cornejo,** Dr Katherine (*2027*); **Mandeville,** Jack (*Vice-Chairs*); **Sundberg-Seaman,** Rev Kelly (*Secretary*); **Ahrens,** Rt Rev Laura; **Akiyama,** Rt Rev Dianna (*2027*); **Carmona,** Mr Wilfreddy; **Dail,** Leah; **Denton,** Mr Brian (*2027*); **Doherty,** Ms Sinead; **Gonzales Hernandez,** Rev Yoimel (*2027*); **Harron,** Will (*2027*); **Hurley Hill,** Ms Beverly (*2027*); **Kangrga,** Mr Patrick; **Lytle,** Dr Julie; **Monnot,** Rt Rev Elizabeth (*2027*); **Patridge,** Rev Dr Cn Cameron (*2027*); **Ray,** Rt Rev Rayford (*2027*); **Scharf,** Rt Rev Douglas; **Wallace,** Rev Cn Tanya; *Ex Officio*: **Ayala Harris,** Ms Julia; **Curry,** Most Rev Michael; **Stonesifer Boylan,** Dr Sarah (*Liaison of the Executive Council*); **Kelly,** Rev Shannon (*Staff*)

Task Force on Communion Across Difference

(*All terms 2024*) **Bauerschmidt,** Rt Rev John; **Duncan-Probe,** Rt Rev Dr DeDe (*Co-Chairs*); **Joyce,** Rev Kelli (*Secretary*); **Bartle,** Rev Phyllis; P **England,** Gary; **Faulstich,** Rev Cn Christine; **Hylden,** Rev Cn Jordan; **Michael,** Rev Mark; **Perka,** Karen; **Perry,** Rt Rev Bonnie; **Quezada Mota,** Rt Rev Moises; **Winn,** Mr Randy; *Ex Officio*: **Ayala Harris,** Ms Julia; **Curry,** Most Rev Michael

Task Force on Dialogue with South Sudanese Anglican Diaspora

(*All terms 2024*) **Mathews,** Rev Ranjit (*Chair*); **Scarfe,** Rt Rev Alan (*Vice-Chair*); Blanchard, Mr

Charles; **Field,** Rt Rev Martin; **Kraus,** Ms Jackie; **Paul,** Rev Michael; *Ex Officio:* **Ayala Harris,** Ms Julia; **Curry,** Most Rev Michael

Task Force on Ministry to Individuals with Mental Illness

(*All terms* 2024) **Gortner,** Rev David; (*Chair*); **Beck,** Dr Brandon; **Carlson,** Ms Megan; **Collazo Lugo,** Luis; **Duvall,** Dr Adrienne; **Fox,** Rev Jedediah; **Kincaid,** Jeffrey; **Kingsley,** Myra; **Nichols,** Rt Rev Kevin; **Pallot,** Mrs Tammy; **Phillips,** Rev Dcn Susan; **Simpson,** Rev Matthew; **Stewart,** Rev John; **Wendt,** Ms Liz; ; *Ex Officio:* **Ayala Harris,** Ms Julia; **Curry,** Most Rev Michael

Task Force on Imaging a Church Grounded in Social Justice as Christian Ministry

(*All terms* 2024)**Andrus,** Rt Rev Marc (*Chair*); **Abbott,** Drew; **Danieley,** Rev Dr Victoria; **Felberty-Ruberté;** Dr Victor A; **Frazier,** Ms Caitlan; **Hollis,** Rev Dr Robin; **Lawton,** Ms Sarah; **Leung,** Chris; **Lewis,** Lindsey; **Murray,** Mr Alan; **Rushing,** Mr Byron; **Thompson,** Ms Felicity; **Turnham,** Rev Rena

Task Force to Study Household and Relationship Diversity

(*All terms* 2027 *unless noted*) **Crafton-Tempel,** Connor; **Dunn,** Rev Sarah (*Co-Chairs*); **Cowden,** Rt Rev Matthew; **Dougan,** Mr Bryan; **Ellis,** Mr Fred; **Graves,** Rev Charles; **Haight,** Mr Scott; **Hamilton-Ferguson,** Dr Adam; **Hawthorne,** Ryan; **Knudsen,** Rt Rev Chilton; **Leclaire,** Beckett; **Reddall,** Rt Rev Jennifer; **Shirley,** Dr Melissa; **Thompson,** Ms April; *Ex Officio:* **Ayala Harris,** Ms Julia; **Curry,** Most Rev Michael (2024)

Standing Commission on Ecumenical & Interreligious Work

(*All terms* 2024 *unless noted*) **Franklin,** Rt Rev R William (*Chair*); **Simmons,** Rev David (2027, *Vice Chair*); **Mosher,** Dr Lucinda (2027, *Secretary*); **Anderson,** Dr Liza; **Baer,** Ven Dr Walter (2027); **Booker,** Dr Michael (2027); Ms Kate; **Canela,** El Rvddo Ramon; **Cravens,** Ms Mary Caroline; **Eaton,** Rt Rev Peter; Edington, Rt RevMark (2027); **Fitzpatrick,** Rt Rev Robert (2027); Guidero RevKirsten; **Moore,** Mr Willis HA (2027); **Pigg,** Daniel (2027); Schlesinger, Eugene (2027); Singer, Ellen; Wolf, Erin; Yarbrough, Rev Cn Dr C Denise; *Ex Officio:* **Ayala Harris,** Ms Julia; **Curry,** Most Rev Michael; Jackson, Rev Dr Deborah (*Liaison of the Executive Council*)

Provincial Leadership Council

(*All terms* 2024) **Baer,** Ven Dr Walter ; **Barta,** Rev Heather; **Brown,** Rt Rev Kevin; **Cisluycis,** Ms Jane;

Cochran, Dr Pamela; **Cole,** Rt Rev Brian; **Daniel,** Ms Angela; **De J. Calvo,** El Rvdo Antonis; **Duncan-Probe,** Rt Rev Dr DeDe; **Duque,** Rt Rev Franciso; **Elfring-Roberts,** Ms Rebecca; **Fisher,** Rt Rev Douglas; **Fox,** Ms Neva Rae; **Gregory,** Cn Judith; **Gunter,** Rt Rev Matthew A; **Harron,** Will; **Jones,** Cn Phyllis; **Judge,** Ms Tess; **León Lozano,** Rt Rev Cristobal; **Lucas,** Rt Rev Kimberly; **Mac Auslan,** Ms Rita; **McDonald,** Rev Jim; **Owensby,** Rt Rev Jake; **Petrosh,** Mrs Andrea; **Pierce,** Rev Nathaniel; **Plantz,** Mr Charles; **Rehberg,** Rt Rev Gretchen; **Sramek, Jr.,** Rev Thomas; **Swinski,** Ms Olive; **Weismore,** Ms Betsy; **Williams,** Ms Sandra

Anglican-Roman Catholic Dialogue in the USA

(*All terms* 2024) **Bauerschmidt,** Rt Rev John (*Chair*); **Cover,** Rev Dr Michael; **Joslyn-Siemiatkoski,** Rev Dr Daniel; **Kiess,** Dr John; **McCarron,** Rev Charles; **Yarbrough,** Rev Cn Dr C Denise; *Ex Officio:* **Ayala Harris,** Ms Julia; **Curry,** Most Rev Michael

Lutheran Episcopal Coordinating Committee

(*All terms* 2024) **Sparks,** Rt Rev Douglas (*Chair*); **Goodman,** Very Rev Mark; **Johnson,** Rev Jane; **Karas,** Rev Erik; Lucas, Rev T Stewart; *Ex Officio:* **Ayala Harris,** Ms Julia; **Curry,** Most Rev Michael

Moravian Episcopal Coordinating Committee

(*All terms* 2024) **Tjeltveit,** Rev Maria (*Chair*); **Freeman,** Mrs DeDreana; Grandfield, Rev Dale; **Rodman,** Rt Rev Samuel; **Seward,** Rev Barbara; *Ex Officio:* **Ayala Harris,** Ms Julia; **Curry,** Most Rev Michael

Presbyterian Episcopal Dialogue Committee

(*All terms* 2024) **Johnstone,** Rev Cn Elise B (*Chair*); **Booker,** Dr Michael; **Sutton,** Rt Rev Eugene *Ex Officio:* **Ayala Harris,** Ms Julia; **Curry,** Most Rev Michael

United Methodist Episcopal Committee

(*All terms* 2024) **Good,** Dr Deirdre (*Chair*); **Coleman,** Rev Dr Karen; **Ferguson,** Rev Dr Thomas; **Partee Carlsen,** Rev Cn Mariclair; **Rice,** Rev David; *Ex Officio:* **Ayala Harris,** Ms Julia; **Curry,** Most Rev Michael

White & Dykman Committee

Sammons, Ms Diane (*Chair*); **Geiszler-Ludlum,** Ms Joan (*Vice-Chair*); **Cathcart,** Mr William; **Getz,** Ms Pauline; **Henderson, Jr,** Rt Rev Dorsey; **Hitt II,** Prof Lawrence; **Hutchinson,** Mr Stephen; **Johnson,** Ms Sally A Johnson, Esq; **Little,** Mr Thomas; *Ex-Officio:* **Jennings,** Rev Gay Clark

Board for Transition Ministry

(*All terms* 2027 *unless noted*) **Applegate,** Rev Dr Stephen H (*Chair*); **Ashby,** Rt Rev Lucinda;

Butterworth, Rev Dr Gary *(2024)*; Conrado, Rev Victor H *(2024)*; Gardner, Rt Rev Elizabeth Bonforte *(2024)*; Hunn, Rt Rev Michael CB; Loya, Rt Rev Craig *(2024)*; McVey, Ms Ellen *(2024)*; Montes, Dr Sandra; Rania, Mr Jon; Real Coultas, Rev Cn Amy; Schmidt, Ms Anne *(2024)*; *Ex Officio*: Ayala Harris, Ms Julia; Curry, Most Rev Michael

Episcopal Relief and Development Board of Directors

Lawver, Ms. Teri *(2024, Chair)*; Allen, Ms. Shirley *(2023)*; Baskerville-Burrows, Rt. Rev. Jennifer *(2023)*; Cloos, Ms Putney *(2024)*; Escobar, Mr. Miguel *(2022)*; Faeth, Mr Paul *(2024)*; Hagans, Rev Dr Cn Michelle *(2025)*; Jones, Mr. Kenneth *(2023)*; Longenecker, Ms. Karen *(2023)*; Martin, Mr. David *(2022)*; McCouch, Dr. Robert *(2023)*; Monterroso, Rt Rev Hector (2024); Paulikas, Rev. Steven *(2023)*; Purcell, Rev Christine (2025); Silva, Mr. Matt *(2024)*; van de Weert, Mr John *(2025)*; *Ex Officio*: Barnes, Mr N Kurt; Curry, Most Rev Michael; Radtke, Dr Robert

General Board of Examining Chaplains

(All terms 2027 unless noted) Franklin, Rt Rev William*(Chair)*; Slade, Rev Kara *(2024, Vice-Chair)*; Ahrens, Rt Rev Laura;-Alexander, Dr. Martha Bedell; Bojarski, Beth *(2024)*; Breidenthal, Rt Rev Thomas *(2024)*; Cole, Dr L Zoe; Corbin, Dr Christopher; Duncan-Probe, Rt Rev Dr DeDe *(2024)*; Erdman, Rachel *(2024)*; Hassett, Rev Miranda *(2024)*; Lane, Rev Calvin *(2024)*; Lee, Rhonda; Mendoza, Rev Milquella *(2024)*; Page, Rev Dr Hugh; Robbins, Dr Gregory *(2024)*; Roland Guzman, Dr Carla; Roth, Ms Janet *(2024)*; Story, Rev Mark *(2024)*; Williams, Dr Peter; Wright, Rev Andrew; *Ex Officio*: Ayala Harris, Ms Julia; Curry, Most Rev Michael

DFMS STAFF

Office of the Presiding Bishop

The Presiding Bishop & Primate The Most Rev Michael B Curry *Canon to the Presiding Bishop for Ministry Within the Episcopal Church* The Rt Rev William Michie Klusmeyer *Canon to the Presiding Bishop for Ministry Beyond the Episcopal Church* The Rev Canon Dr Charles K Robertson *Canon to the Presiding Bishop for Evangelism, Reconciliation and Creation* The Rev Canon Stephanie Spellers *Executive Coordinator to the Presiding Bishop* Sharon Jones *Executive Assistant to the Canon for Ministry Within the Episcopal Church* Ednice Baerga *Associate for Evangelism, Reconciliation and Creation Care* Sarah Alphin *Acting Chief Operating Officer,* Jane Cislyucis *Executive Assistant to the COO & Operations Manager* Su Hadden *Chancellor to the Presiding Bishop* Mary E Kostel *Chief Legal Officer* Kent Anker *Deputy General Counsel* Suzanne Baillie *Bishop for the Office of Pastoral Development* The Rt Rev S Todd Ousley *Bishop in*

Charge of the Convocation of American Churches in Europe The Rt Rev Mark D W Edington *Executive Director General Board of Examining Chaplains* Duncan C Ely *Bishop for the Armed Forces and Federal Ministries* TBA *Canon to the Bishop for Armed Forces and Federal Ministries* The Rev Canon Leslie Nuñez Steffensen

Armed Forces & Federal Ministries

Washington National Cathedral
3101 Wisconsin Ave., NW
Washington, DC 20016
Tel: 202-459-9998
www.episcopalchurch.org/armed-forces-and-federal-ministries/

Operations

Acting Chief Operating Officer, Jane Cisluycis *Executive Assistant to the COO & Operations Manager* Su Hadden *Director Human Resources,* TBA *Senior Human Resources Officer* Patricia E Holley *HR Manager for Benefits, Systems & Finance* Michael H Walsh *Director of Information Technology* Darvin D Darling

Office of Communication

Senior Manager for Creative Services & Digital Evangelist Jeremy Tackett *Communications Operations & Language Services Manager* Bernice David *Language Services Coordinator* Cynthia Narvaez *Public Affairs Officer* Amanda Skofstad *Associate Public Affairs Officer* Lisa Webb *Manager, Multimedia Services* Michael F Collins *Web Content & Digital Media Coordinator* Scott Rands *Manager of Digital Sponsorship, Associate Editor & Web Manager, Episcopal News Service* Matthew MacDonald *Senior Graphic Designer* Melissa Walker *Project Manager* Christopher Sikkema *Managing Editor, Episcopal News Service* Lynette Wilson *Editor/Reporter, Episcopal News Service* David Paulsen

Finance

Treasurer and Chief Financial Officer N Kurt Barnes *Assistant to the Treasurer* June A Victor *Director of Investment Management and Banking* Margareth Crosnier de Bellaistre *Controller* JoAnne Brockway *Assistant Controller* Arlissa Dean *Assistant Controller* Tanie Oconer *Payroll Manager* Jacqueline Franco *Finance Support Specialist* Nadyne Duverseau *Travel Loan Supervisor (Episcopal Migration Ministries)* Lisa Gandolfo *Grants and Compliance Officer (Episcopal Migration Ministries)* Florence Etienne

Office of Development Office

Associate Director of Development T.J. Houlihan *Associate Director of Development* Julia Babson Alling

Ministries Beyond the Episcopal Church

Canon to the Presiding Bishop for Ministry Beyond The Episcopal Church The Rev Canon Dr Charles K **Robertson** *Ecumenical and Interreligious Deputy* The Rev. Margaret R **Rose**

Global Partnerships & Mission Personnel

Director The Rev David **Copley** *Mission Personnel Officer* Elizabeth **Boe** *Global Relations & Networking Officer* **Jenny Grant** *Africa Partnership Officer* The Rev Daniel **Karanja** *Asia Pacific Partnership Officer* The Rev Canon Bruce W **Woodcock** *Latin America & the Caribbean Partnership Officer* The Rev Glenda **McQueen** *Middle East Partnership Officer* Archdeacon A Paul **Feheley** *Episcopal Church Representative to the United Nations* Lynnaia **Main**

Office of Government Relations (OGR)

110 Maryland Ave NE Suite 309
Washington DC 20002
Tel: (800) 228 0515 or (202) 547 7300
E-mail: eppn@episcopalchurch.org

Director Rebecca **Blachly** *Policy Advisor* Rushad **Thomas** *Legislative Representative for International Issues* Patricia **Kisare** *Church Relations Manager* Alan **Yarborough** *Policy Advisor* Rushad **Thomas** *Policy Analyst* Lindsey **Warburton**

Episcopal Migration Ministries

Director of Operations Sarah **Shipman** *Senior Manager for Church Relations and Engagement* Allison **Duvall** *Communications Manager* Kendall **Martin** *Senior Program Manager,* Svetlana **Brajdic** *Senior Program Manager,* Claudia **Carrete**

Ministries Within the Episcopal Church

Canon to the Presiding Bishop for Ministry Within the Episcopal Church The Rt Rev William Michie **Klusmeyer**

Department of Faith Formation

Director of Faith Formation & Officer for Young Adult and Campus Ministries The Rev Shannon **Kelly** *Officer for Youth Ministry* Canon Myra **Garnes** *Manager Episcopal Service Corps* Wendy K **Johnson** *Manager for Safe Church and Special Projects* Bronwyn Clark **Skov** *Formation Associate* David **Stickley**

Transition Ministries

Director of Transition Ministries The Rev Meghan F **Froehlich** *Coordinator and Technical Support Specialist* Sabrina **Nealy**

Evangelism, Reconciliation and Creation Ministries

Canon to the Presiding Bishop for Evangelism, Reconciliation and Creation The Rev Canon Stephanie **Spellers**

Ethnic Ministries

Director and Missioner for Latino/Hispanic Ministries The Rev Canon Anthony **Guillén** *Missioner for African Descent Ministries* The Rev Canon Ronald C. **Byrd** *Missioner for Indigenous Ministries* The Rev Dr Bradley S **Hauff** *Missioner for Asiamerica Ministries* TBA *Indigenous Theological Education Coordinator* The Rev Canon Mary Frances **Crist** *Associate for Ethnic Ministries* Angeline **Cabanban**

Church Planting & Redevelopment

Manager of Church Planting & Redevelopment The Rev Tom **Brackett** *Officer for Church Planting Infrastructure* The Rev Katherine Nakamura **Rengers**

Reconciliation, Justice & Creation Care

Director The Rev Melanie **Mullen** *Staff Officer for Evangelism* Jerusalem **Greer** *Staff Officer for Racial Reconciliation* The Rev Isaiah Shaneequa **Brokenleg** *Manager for Racial Justice and Reconciliation* The Rev. Miguel **Bustos**

United Thank Offering

Staff Officer for the United Thank Offering The Rev Canon Heather **Melton** *Administrative Assistant* Isabelle **Watkins**

MISSION COMPANIONS OF THE EPISCOPAL CHURCH

Sending agency key: DFMS - Domestic and Foreign Missionary Society.

Ceylon/Sri Lanka

John Philip Buterbaugh, c/o Mission Personnel, Episcopal Church Center, 815 Second Avenue, New York, NY 10017 – (DFMS)

Costa Rica

Mr. Andrew Lawrence Walker, c/o Mission Personnel, Episcopal Church Center, 815 Second Avenue, New York, NY 10017 – (DFMS)

Dominican Republic

Dr. Thomas Malcolm McGowan, PhD, c/o Mission Personnel, Episcopal Church Center, 815 Second Avenue, New York, NY 10017 – (DFMS)

El Salvador

Mr. Noah Bullock, Diocese of El Salvador, Calle Shafik Handal 5441, Colonia Escalon, San Salvador, El Salvador – (DFMS)

England

Ms. Christi Hosea Cunningham, c/o Mission Personnel, Episcopal Church Center, 815 Second Avenue, New York, NY 10017 – (DFMS)

Mr. Derby Guerrier, c/o Mission Personnel, Episcopal Church Center, 815 Second Avenue, New York, NY 10017 – (DFMS)

Ms. Charlotte Anne Steffensen, c/o Mission Personnel, Episcopal Church Center, 815 Second Avenue, New York, NY 10017 – (DFMS)

France
Mr. Joris Félix Aimé Bürmann, c/o Mission Personnel, Episcopal Church Center, 815 Second Avenue, New York, NY 10017 – (DFMS)

Ms. Madeline Rae Hennig, c/o Mission Personnel, Episcopal Church Center, 815 Second Avenue, New York, NY 10017 – (DFMS)

Ms. Miranda Ruth Wilson, c/o Mission Personnel, Episcopal Church Center, 815 Second Avenue, New York, NY 10017 – (DFMS)

Guatemala
Mr. Gregory Spence Lowden, c/o 53 Ave 9-60 Sector 1 Alamedas de Villaflores, Zona 7, San Miguel Petapa, 01066, Guatemala – (DFMS)

Ms. Sophia Swallow, c/o Mission Personnel, Episcopal Church Center, 815 Second Avenue, New York, NY 10017 – (DFMS)

Honduras
The Rev. Stephen Robinson & Mrs. Rhonda Robinson, c/o Mission Personnel, Episcopal Church Center, 815 Second Avenue, New York, NY 10017 – (DFMS)

Jerusalem
The Rev. Donald Drew Binder - P. O. Box 1248, Jerusalem 91000, Via Israel – (DFMS)

South Africa
Mrs. Jennifer McConnachie, RN, Mariya uMama weThemba Monastery, P.O. Box 6013, Grahamstown, South Africa 6141- (DFMS)

Spain
Ms. Dawn Marie Baity, c/o Anglicana Catedral del Redentor - Calle de la Beneficencia, 18, 28004 Madrid, SPAIN – (DFMS)

Tanzania
Mr. Peter Bak, St. Philip's Theological College, P.O. Box 26, Kongwa, Tanzania – (DFMS)

Ms. Wendy Broadbent, St. Philip's Theological College, P.O. Box 26, Kongwa, Tanzania – (DFMS)

United Arab Emirates
The Rev. James Young, c/o Christ Church Jebel Ali, P.O. Box 7415, Dubai, UAE – (DFMS)

USA
The Rev. John Caleb Collins, c/o Diocese of Arizona, 114 W Roosevelt Street, Phoenix, AZ 85003 – (DFMS)

Mr. Troy Elder, c/o Diocese of San Diego, 2083 Sunset Cliffs Boulevard, San Diego, CA 92107 – (DFMS)

PROVINCIAL CONTACTS

Province I New England
Comprises the dioceses of ME NH VT MA WMA RI CT *Pres* Rt Rev Douglas J Fisher; *VP* Olive Swinski; *Treas* Rita MacAuslan; *Bookkeeper* HarQuin Bookkeeping *Prov Coord* Emily Keniston PO Box 8059 Portland ME 04104 (207) 210-7500 *E-mail:* coordinator@province1. org *Web:* www.Province1 .org; *Reps Exec Council* Alexizendria Link 734 Pleasant Street, Unit 2, Worcester, MA 0160 (617) 447-8039 *Email:* atl029@ mail.harvard. edu; The Rev Aaron C Perkins, 26 Moulton Ln, York, ME 03909-1407 aaron@dunesonthewaterfront.com; *Cultural Competency and Anti-Racism* James McKim *E-mail:* jtmckim@gmail.com; *Campus Min* The Rev Thea Keith-Lucas *E-mail:* theakl@mit.edu; *Deacons* Aaron Perkins aperkins@episcopalmaine.org; *Daughters of the King, Pres* Mariana Bauman (WMA) *E-mail:* marianab@ earthlink.net, marianabauman@doknational.org; ECW *Web:* https://province1episcopalchurchwomen.wordpress.org; ECW Board—Pres Susan Howland (WMA) *E-mail:* howlands@charter.net; *VP* vacant; *Sec* Roberta Stockdale (CT) *E-mail:* rls55@cox.net;*Treas* Phyllis Larson (WMA) *E-mail:* Phyll98617@aol.com; *Prov I Rep to Nat ECW* Margaret (RI) Noel *E-mail:* Margaret_e_noel@ hotmail.com; *National ECW Board Web:* https:// www.ecwnational.org/executive/; *United Thank Offering (UTO) Prov 1 Rep* Jane Jellison (RI) *E-mail:* JaneEJellison@gmail.com; *Church Periodical Club (CPC) Prov 1 Rep* Sally Morelle North (RI) *E-mail:* semorelle@ gmail.com; Members of the Exec Comm at Large: Margaret Sweeney Betsy Ridge Madsen Rev Jennifer Beal

Province II The International Atlantic Province
NY LI A CNY Roch WNY Nk NJ Haiti VI Convoc of Amer Chs in Europe Cuba Puerto Rico. *Web:* www. province2.org. *Pres* Rt Rev Dr. DeDe Duncan-Probe (CNY) (315) 882-0511 *E-mail:* bishop@cnyepiscopal. org; *VP* Archdeacon Walter Baer Office: +33 1 53 23 84 06 *E-mail:* archdeacon@tec-europe.org; *Sec* Rev Jimmie Sue Deppe (R) *Cell:* 586-441-1160 *E-mail:* jsadeppe@gmail.com; *Treas* Cn Phyllis Jones (NJ) (609) 394-5281 x31 *E-mail:* pjones@dioceseseofnj. org; *Prov Coord* Neva Rae Fox (NJ) *E-mail:* nevarae@aol.com; *Chanc* Martha Berrym (CNY) (315) 263-6384 *E-mail:* marthalberry@gmail.com; *Rep to Prov Coun* Rt Rev Carlye Hughes (Nk) (973) 430-9976 *E-mail:* chughes@dioceseofnewark.org; Rev Can Johnnie Ross (R) (859) 285-9361 *E-mail:* smallchurch@episcopaldioceseofrochester.org; Yvonne O'Neal (NY) (347) 776-8010 *E-mail:* yvonne. oneal@gmail.com; *Exec Coun Lay* Thomas K Chu Esq (NY) (212) 882-1128 *E-mail:* thom@tkchulaw. com; *Exec Coun Cler* Rev Dcn Lillian Davis-Wilson (WNY) (716) 553-6200 *E-mail:* ljdwilson1@verizon. net; *Newsletter InProv2* Jan Paxton (NJ) (201) 851-1428 *E-mail:* webeditor@province2.org; *Province II Rep to Exec Coun Comm on Anti-Racism* Rev Yamily Bass-Choate (NY) *Cell:* (914) 826-3349 *E-mail:* ybass-choate@dioceseny.org.

Province III Mid-Atlantic

Comprises the dioceses of BETH CPA DE EASTON MD NWPA PA PGH SVA SWVA VA WASH WV *Pres* Rev Nathaniel W Pierce *E-mail:* nwpierce@verizon.net; *VP* The Rt. Rev. Kevin *E-mail:* bishop@delaware.church; *Sec* Steven Jones *E-mail: swjones836@gmail.com;Treas* Judith Lane Gregory *E-mail:* jgregory@delaware.church; *Coord* Dr Pamela DH Cochran *E-mail:* p3coordinator@gmail.com; *Exec Coun* Matthew Taylor *Email:* matthew.taylor.sjc@gmail.com; Rev Patricia Downing *E-mail:* patricia@trinityparishde.org; *Coun Members* Rev Scott Allen (Beth) *E-mail:* gambaguy@gmail.com; Rev Veronica Chappell (CPA) *E-mail:* vchappell1118@gmail.com; John Michael Sophos (DE) *E-mail:* Jsophos611@comcast.net; Jane Morgan (Easton) *E-mail:* ejanerock@aol.com; Rev Ramelle McCall (MD) *E-mail:* urbanmissioner@episcopalmaryland.org; Rev Geoffrey Wild (NWPA) *E-mail:* gcvicar@gmail.com; Christopher Hart (PA) *E-mail:* chart@lmc.net; Lisa Brown (PGH) *E-mail:* lcbrown15243@gmail.com; Ellyn Crawford (VA) *E-mail:* crawfordellyn@yahoo.com; Russell Bishop (SVA) *E-mail:* rustybishop1974@gmail.com; Jack Barrow (SWVA) *E-mail:* jc.barrow@embarqmail.com; Rev. Gerry Perez (Wash) *E-mail:* gaperez72@gmail.com; Philip Steptoe (WVA) *E-mail:* philtoe@comcast.net; *Altar Guild* Sharon Stewart Nachman (VA) *E-mail:* sharonsnachman@gmail.com; *Chr Form and Yth Min* Joanne Fisher (Easton) *E-mail:* joanne@dioceseofeaston.org and Kate Riley *Email:* kriley@episcopalmaryland.org; *ECW* Nancy Sands (SVA) *E-mail:* beachpeach7@hotmail.com; *Environmental Stew* Steven Jones (DE) *E-mail:* swjones836@gmail.com; *Opioid Task Force* Rev Dina van Klaveren (MD) *E-mail:* dinavk@gmail.comand Karl Colder (VA) *E-mail:* kc.colderalliedllc@consultant.com; *Racial Justice, Reconciliation, and Anti-racism:* Dr Frances Dannenberg (PGH) *E-Mail:* fkdflute1@verizon.net, Rev. Chris McCloud (MD) *E-Mail:* cmccloud@episcopalmaryland.org, and Rev. David Wacaster (WASH) *E-Mail:* raceandjustice@edow.org; *UTO* Mathy Milling Downing (WA) *E-mail:* mathy02@aol.com; *Yth Min* Joanne Fisher (Easton) *E-mail:* joanne@dioceseofeaston.org and Kate Riley *Email:*kriley@episcopalmaryland.org; *Ecumenical Ministries* Rev John P Downey (PA) *Email:* jpdowney@aol.com.

Province IV Southeast

Comprises the dioceses of AL NC EC TECSC CGC GA AT FL LA MS TN WTN ETN KY LEX CF SEF SWF WNC USC *Pres* Kathryn McCormick *E-mail:* kwmccormick@gmail.com; *VP* The Rt Rev Scott A. Benhase, *E-mail:* scottgax@gmail.com; *Treas* Tess Judge *E-mail:* tessjudgeobx@gmail.com; *Sec* Marcellus (Mark) Smith *E-mail:* msmith5864@aol.com; *Reps to Exec Coun: Cler* Rev Steve Pankey, *E-mail:* steve@cecbg.com; *Lay E-mail:* Alice B. Freeman *E-mail* alicebfreeman4@gmail.com; *UTO* Maggie Noland *E-mail* maggienoland@hotmail.com; *ECW Pres* Annie

Jacobs *E-mail: aj34528@aol.com* ; *Altar Guild* Ann McCormick *E-mail* ann.mcc413@gmail.com; *Young Adult & Campus Min* Brian Smith *E-mail:* fb@rugehall.org; *Yth* Cookie Cantwell *E-mail:* cookie@stjames.org; *Envir Min* The Rev Dr Jerry Cappel *E-mail:* jjcappel@hotmail.com; *Companion Dios* Martha B Alexander *E-mail:* marthaebalexander@hotmail.com; *Bishops Chap to the Ret and Surv Spouses* The Rev. Bob and Sandy Cook *E-mail* sandycook8400@icloud.com

Province V Midwest

Comprises the dioceses of OH SO NI Ind C Sp MI WMI NMI EMI FdL Mil EauC MO *Pres* Jane Cisluycis *E-mail:* Jane@Upepiscopal.org; *VP* Matthew Gunter *E-mail:* mgunter@diofdl.org; *Sec* Adrienne Dillon *E-mail:* lemmonsdillon@sbcglobal.net; *Treas* Rebecca Elfring-Robers *E-mail:* rroberts@episcopalchicago.org; *Coord* Heather Barta *E-mail:* provincevcoordinator@gmail.com; *Episcopal Church Exec Coun* ME Eccles *E-mail:* rev.m.e.eccles@gmail.com; Louisa McKellaston *E-mail:* ljhallas@gmail.com; *C:* Laura Jackson *E-mail:* laura.w.jackson@gmail.com; *EC:* Marlene Hogue *E-mail:* mchhogue@gmail.com; *EMI:* Katie Forsyth *E-mail:* kforsyth@eastmich.org; *FdL:* Chris Eggert-Rosenthal *E-mail:* cnor1101@yahoo.com; *Ind:* Lesley MacKellar *E-mail:* lesleymackellar@gmail.com; *MI:* Edie Wakevainen *E-mail:* ewakevainen@gmail.com; *Mil:* Matthew Buterbaugh *E-mail:* rector.stmatts@gmail.com; *MO:* Betty Bowersox *E-mail:* bowersoxb@gmail.com; *NI:* Christopher Hillak *E-mail:* missioner.hillak@ednin.org; *NMI:* Rick Stanitis *E-mail:* chouse@mtu.edu; *OH:* Rachel Harrison *E-mail:* rachel.jagielski@gmail.com; *S:* Jan Goossens *E-mail:* utospil@sbcglobal.net; *SO:* Edward Lasseigne *E-mail:* lasseigne@hotmail.com; *WMI:* Joel Turmo *E-mail:* jturmo@gmail.com; *Young Adult/Campus Ministry* Stacy Alan *E-mail:* stacyalan@brenthouse.org; *Church Periodical Club* Maryfran Crist *E-mail:* maryfrancrist64@gmail.com; *DOK* Celeste Hilliard *E-mail:* hilliacm@gmail.com; *ECCAR* Felicity Thompson *E-mail:* designbyfelicity@comcast.net; *ECW* Kathy Mank *E-mail:* kathymank@gmail.com; *ER&D* Juanita Woods *E-mail:* nitagerman@sbcglobal.net; *Health Min* Maryfran Crist *E-mail:* maryfrancrist64@gmail.com; *JPIC* Cindy Nawrocki *E-mail:* cynrocki@gmail.com; *UTO* Gail Donovan *E-mail:* gadonov@aol.com; *Yth Min* McKenzie Knill *E-mail:* mknill@eastmich.org.

Province VI Land of Mountains Lakes and Plains

Comprises the dioceses of MN IA NE CO MT SD ND WY *Pres*; The Rt Rev Kym Lucas (CO) *E-mail:*bishopkym@episcopalcolorado.org; *VP* Sandy Williams *E-mail:* mtsandylou@gmail.com; *Sec* vacant; *Treas* Mr Charles Plantz *E-mail:* jawa175@aolcom; *Chanc* vacant; *Prov Coord* Ellen Bruckner *E-mail:* ellenwb@mchsi.com; *Lay Reps Clergy Reps*; Rev David Dill (CO); Rev Rick Swenson (MN) *E-mail:* rcswenson@msn.com;

Gretchen Swift (MT) *E-mail:* Gswift84@gmail.com; Julie Gehm (SD) *E-mail:* Julie.Gehm@lifescapesd. com; Rev Steve Godfrey (ND) *E-mail:* sgodfrey@ ndepiscopal.org; Rev Mary Hendricks (NE) *E-mail:* marydh@aya.yale.edu; Jessica Reynolds (WY) *E-mail:* jessica@episcopalwy.org; Ann McLaughlin (IA) *E-mail:* ann.mclaughlin89@yahoo.com *Min High Ed* vacant; *UTO* Elizabeth Campbell *E-mail:* balnamoon@gmail.com; *ECW* Heather Bauer *E-mail:* greenpeacecats121@yahoo.com; *ERD* Barb Hagen *E-mail:* mtbizmgr@qwest.net; *Daughters of the King* Nancy Sevrin *E-mail:* nssfhs@bresnan. net; *Ex Council Reps* Mr Larry Hitt E-mail: Larry@ episcopalcolorado.org; Angela Goodhouse Mauai *Email:* agoodhouse@yahoo.com.

Province VII Southwest

Comprises the diocese of WMO WLA AR TX DAL KS RG NWTX WT OK WKS ECNTX *Pres* The Rt Rev Larry Benfield 5124 Stonewall Rd Little Rock AR 72207 (501) 442-5888 *E-mail:* lbenfield@episcoar. org; *VP* Rev Victoria Heard 8932 Club Creek Circle Dallas TX 75238 (214) 957-3832 *E-mail:* vrtheard@ sbcglobal.net; *Sec* Jo Ann Rachele 2268 North St San Angelo TX 796901 (406) 249-6135 *E-mail:* joannrachele@msn.com; *Treas* Rev Jim McDonald 106 S 5th St Batesville AR 72501 (501) 529-3266 *E-mail:* FatherMcDonald@gmail.com; *Coord* Rev Elizabeth Dabney 14019 Wickersham Ln Houston TX 77077 (832) 462-3228 *E-mail:* elizabethrdowell@ gmail.com; *Members at Large* Rev Scot A McComas 1749 Cimarron St Grapevine TX 76051 (704) 779-6113 *E-mail:* Scot.mccomas@yahoo.com; Lee Spence 160 VZCR 1920 Fruitvale TX 75127 (903) 312-4437 *E-mail:* fiberphys@aol.com; Andrea Marie Rabalais Petrosh 6022 Rosemead Cir Bossier City LA 71111 (318) 426-6564 *E-mail:* mpetrosh@bellsouth.net; *Exec Council* The Very Rev J Mark Goodman 9131 Mabry Ave Albuquerque NM 87109 (505) 328-6157 *E-mail:* goodmankmark@gmail.com; Thomas Alexander 291 Pleasant Valley Dr Little Rock AR 72212 (501) 940-7941 *E-mail:* AlexanderTM@ hendrix.edu; *ECW* JoAnn Rachele PO Box 62711 San Angelo TX 76906 *Cell:* (406) 249-6135 *E-mail:* joannrachele@msn.com; *Commun/Web Page* Susan Hanson; *Prog Coord* Sally Russell 2 Hyde Park Dr Hutchinson KS 67502 (620) 662-8024 *Cell:* (620) 694-9145 *Email:* sallyruss@sbcglobal.net; *Youth* The Rev Karen Schlabach, 10003 W 70th Tr Merriam KS 66203 (913) 708-5927 *E-mail:* KSchlabach@ episcopal-ks.org; *Higher Ed* The Rev Matthew Wise 3908 Faimes Ct College Station TX 77845 (210) 363-9259 *E-mail:* canterburytamu@gmail. com; *Christian Formation* Sabrina Evans 924 N Robinson Oklahoma City OK 73102 (405) 232-4820 *E-mail:* SEvans@epiok.org; *ER&D* The Rev Virginia Holleman 5518 Merrimac Dr Dallas TX 75206 (214) 450-9652 *E-mail:* vfholleman@sbcglobal.net; *Multi-Cultural*; *Restorative Justice/Prison* Dr Ed Davis 2003 Ave P Huntsville TX 77340 (936) 662-3842

E-mail: edsalpc@yahoo.com; *Min to Senior Min:* Janet Nocher 4408 Foxfire Way Ft Worth TX (817) 975-4863 *E-mail:* janet.nocher@sbcglobal.net; Helen Appelberg *Email:* helenappelberg@gmail.com.

Province VIII West and Pacific Rim aka "Province of the Pacific"

Comprises the dioceses of AK AZ CA ECR EO HI ID LosA Navajoland NCA NV OL OR SanD SanJ Spok Tai UT *Pres* The Rt Rev Gretchen Rehberg *Email:* gretchenr@spokanediocese.org; *VP* The Rev Tom Sramek, Jr. *Email:* tomsramekjr@icloud.com; *Treas* Betsy Wiesmore (thru 2022) *Email:* bwiesmore@ gmail.com; *Treas* The Rev Jeff Martinauk (2023 thru 2024) *Email:* jmartinhauk@edsd.org; *Sec* Evita Krislock *Email:* evita@krislock.com; *Chanc* R Miller Adams, Esq *Email:* rma99977@gmail.com; *Reps Exec Coun* Tim Gee *Email:* timgee54@gmail.com; The Rev Cn Cornelia Eaton *Email:* ceaton.ecn@ gmail.com; *Rep ECCAR* The Rev Malcolm McLaurin *Email:* fathermalcolmmclaurin@gmail.com; *FinChr* Nancy Koonce (thru 2022) *Email:* nkoonce@ idahocpa.com; *Comm* Ginny Guzman-Walsh *Email:* ginnygw@icloud.com; *Education & Formation Cluster: Convener* The Rev Maureen Hagen *Email:* maureenhagen@gmail.com; *Sec* Sarah Chesebro *Email:* sarahchesebro@gmail.com; *Altar Guild* Sarah Chesebro *Email:* sarahchesebro@gmail.com; *Healing & Health Min* Susan Wahlstrom *Email:* wahlstrom@ volcano.net; *Stewardship & Planned Giving Min* Ron Hermanson *Email:* ronhermanson@gmail.com and Peter Juvé *Email:* pjuve@aol.com; *Multicultural Cluster: Sec* Melvin Stringer *Email:* mwstrin727@ yahoo.com; *Asian/Pacific Islander Min* The Rev Ruth Casipit Paguio *Email:* ruthcasipit_paguio@yahoo. com; *Black African/Caribbean Min* Stacey Forte-Dupre *Email:* staceydupre@gmail.com and Sherina James *Email:* daringvision@gmail.com; *Indigenous Min* Ronald Braman *Email:* singingflat4you@yahoo. com and The Rev Cn Cathlena Plummer *Email:* ecncplummer@gmail.com; *Latinx:* The Rev. Susana Santibanez Coronado *Email:* sscoronado2013@ gmail.com; *Truth & Reconciliation Cluster: Conv* Alan Murray *Email:* sfalanmurray@gmail.com; *Sec* The Rev Guy Leemhuis *Email:* guyleemhuis@gmail.com; *Peace & Justice* Alan Murray *Email:* sfalanmurray@ gmail.com; *Anti-Sexism & Gender Equity* The Rev. Iain Stanford *Email:* iainstanford@gmail.com; *Care of Creation* Emily Hopkins *Email:* emilyhopkins4@ gmail.com; *Sending & Serving Cluster: Conv* Cn Martha Estes *Email:* marthakestes53@gmail.com; *Brotherhood of St Andrew* Eric Fisher *Email:* eric. on.fisher@gmail.com *CPC* Louise Aloy *Email:* louisealoy63@gmail.com; *Dcns of Prov VIII* The Rev Jon Owens *Email:* owensj2016@fau.edu and The Ven Gen Grewell *Email:* ggrewell21@comcast.net; *ECW* Cn Martha Estes *Email:* marthakestes53@gmail. com; *UTO* Sedona Jacobson *Email:* sedonaj1@gmail. com and Tammy Smecker Hane *Email:* tsmecker@ cox.net

Province IX Caribbean/Latin America/ Northern South America

Comprises the dioceses of Colom DomR CEcu EcuL Hond PR Ven *Pres* The Rt Rev Cristobal Olmedo *E-mail:* padrextobal@hotmail.com; *VP The Rt Rev Francisco Duque E-mail:* obispoduque@hotmail. com; *Canciller* Fausto Chiluisa *E-mail:* fchiluisa@ gmail.com; *Sec Revda Lourde Inapanta E-mail:* lourdes.inapanta@gmail.com; *Treas Carlos Baez E-mail:* cabaezd@gmail.com; *Delegados Clérigos Revdo Richard Acosta E-mail:* richard.ictus@gmail. com y *Rvda Gladys Vasquez E-mail:* gevasquezec@ hotmail.com; *Delegados Laicos: Carlos Alegría E-mail:* aleriacarlos_1995@yahoo.com y *Coromoto Pragredes E-mail:* pragredescjimenez@gmail.com; *Representantes al Consejo Ejecutivo: CLERIGO: Rvda* Gina Angulo Zamora *E-mail:* gina197919@hotmail.com; LAICOS: Blanca Echeverry *E-mail:* blecherry@gmail.com; *ECW Revda Luz María Lambis E-mail* luzlambis@ hotmail.com; *UTO: Carmen Alvarez E-mail:* calvarez. sjes@episcopalhn.org; *Coordinador Provincial:* Revdo Antonis de J Calvo *E-mail:* antonisdej@hotmail.com y coordinador@provincia9.org.

PROGRAM SUPPORT SERVICES

United Thank Offering Board

Staff: UTO Staff Officer The Rev Canon Heather L Melton Episcopal Church Center 815 Second Ave New York NY 10017 (1-800) 334-7626 *E-mail:* hmelton@episcopalchurch.org; *Admin Associate* Isabelle Watkins, iwatkins@episcopalchurch. org; *Province Representatives: Prov I* Rev Rowan Larson; *Prov II* Rev Caroline Carson; *Prov III* Mathy Milling Downing; *Prov IV* Maggie Noland; *Prov V* Gail Donovan; *Prov VI* Karin Elsen; *Prov VII* Daria Condon; *Prov VIII* Sedona Jacobson; *Prov IX* Carmen Alvarez; *Pres* Sherri Dietrich; *VPres* Joyce Landers; *Fin Sec* Kathy Mank; *Young Adult* Erin Sample and Sedona Jacobson; *Appointed Member* Lorraine Candelario.

Episcopal Diocesan Ecumenical and Interreligious Officers (EDEIO)

Pres Rev David Simmons *E-mail:* frsimmons@ gmail.com *Web:* www.edeio.org; *V Pres* Rev Lynne Bleich Weber; *Fin Off* Rev James Biegler *E-mail:* edeioexchequer@comcast.net; *Sec* Richard Mammana; *Prov Coords I* Rev Dr Frederick Moser; *II* Rev Dr Curtis Hart; *III* Rev John Downey; *IV* vacant; *V* Rev David Simmons; *VI* Rev Mary Johnson; *VII* Rev Dr Wayne Carter; *VIII* Rev William Rontani; *IX* vacant; *At large:* Rev Dr Thomas Ferguson.

CHURCHWIDE AGENCIES AND ORGANIZATIONS

Archives of the Episcopal Church, The

107 Denson Drive Austin TX 78752-4148 (512) 472-6816 *Website:* http://episcopalarchives.org *E-mail:* research@episcopalarchives.org. *Exec Dir and Can*

Archivist vacant. Research center for The Episcopal Church, including the Domestic and Foreign Missionary Society, the General Convention, and related churchwide organizations, also individual Episcopalians of note. The Archives collects, preserves, and makes available original source data to Church leaders, members, and the public. Maintains online digital archives, digital repository holdings, and provides consulting services to dioceses and parishes. *Records Administration:* 815 Second Ave New York NY 10017-4594. Administers corporate records. *Rights and Permissions Office:* 107 Denson Drive Austin, TX 78752-4148. Administers rights and permissions for non-current DFMS/ General Convention publications.

The Church Pension Fund

19 East 34th St New York NY 10016 (212) 592-1800 or (800) 223-6602. cpg.org.
The Church Pension Fund (CPF) is a financial services organization that serves The Episcopal Church. CPF and its affiliated companies, collectively the Church Pension Group (CPG), provide retirement, health, life insurance, and related benefits for its clergy and lay employees. For the fiscal year ending March 31, 2022, the benefits paid were $417 million. CPG also serves The Episcopal Church by providing property and casualty insurance as well as book and music publishing, including the official worship materials of The Episcopal Church. Besides CPF, CPG consists of the following companies: Church Life Insurance Corporation (founded 1922), The Episcopal Church Medical Trust (founded 2002), The Church Insurance Company (founded 1929), The Church Insurance Agency Corporation (founded 1930), The Church Insurance Company of Vermont (founded 1999), and Church Publishing Incorporated (founded 1918). The CEO and President of CPF is Mary Kate Wold.

Episcopal Church Building Fund

Established in 1880, the ECBF, an autonomous, self-funding and self-governing agency, provides non-mortgage loans up to $1 million (larger mortgage loans also available) for the purchase, construction, repair, improvement, or refinancing of properties, churches, rectories, schools, and other parochial buildings. Provides consultations on the creative use of church buildings and properties to support a congregations' financial sustainability and increase their connection and relevance to the community. Partners with ecumenical groups to achieve a common mission. Provides guidance on the building planning process. Web resources on accessibility, greening, liturgical design, and full video presentations from national symposiums. *Pres* Dr. Walter Cabe; *Sr VP for Strategic Change* The Rev Ruth Woodliff-Stanley; *Exec Asst and Coord* Linda Van Eckoute PO Box 31039 Chicago IL 60631-3103 *Phone:* (708) 738-9142 *E-mail:* info@ecbf.org *Web:* www.ecbf.org.

Forward Movement
The mission of Forward Movement is inspiring disciples and empowering evangelists. Primary publications include the devotionals *Forward Day by Day* and *Adelante Día a Día* as well as pamphlets, books, and digital resources for study, devotional, pastoral, and congregational development use. Executive Director is the Rev Canon Scott Gunn 412 Sycamore St Cincinnati OH 45202 (513) 721-6659 *E-Mail:* orders@forwardmovement.org *Web:* www.forwardmovement.org.

Institutions and Organizations

EDUCATIONAL
THEOLOGICAL SEMINARIES

Berkeley Divinity School at Yale

Founded in 1854, since 1971 the Berkeley Divinity School has functioned as an affiliate of Yale University. Berkeley has its own dean, board of trustees, and bylaws. Berkeley and Yale Divinity School share a single admissions process, curriculum and faculty, and Yale degrees are granted to all students, with Berkeley diplomas and certificates in Anglican Studies to those undertaking the Berkeley program. Berkeley Center 363 St Ronan St New Haven CT 06511 *Administrative Offices:* 409 Prospect St New Haven CT 06511 (203) 432-9285 *Fax:* (203) 432-9353 *Web:* berkeleydivinity.yale.edu

Dean and Pres, McFaddin Prof of Anglican Studies—V Rev Andrew B McGowan BA BD MA PhD

Assoc Dean and Dir Form—Rev Yejide Peters Pietersen AB MDiv

Dir of Ed Ldrship and Min Prog—Jere Wells BA MA

Bp Percy Goddard Prof of Lit Studies—Rev B Spinks MTh PhD

Prof Hebrew Scriptures—Rev Carolyn Sharp MAR PhD

Noah Porter Prof of Philosophical Theol—John Hare BA PhD

Henry B Wright Prof of Systematic Theol—Miroslav Volf MA DTh

Prof of Asian Theol—Chloe Starr MA DPhil

Lecturer in Art History—Felicity Harley McGowan BA PhD

Frederick Marquand Prof Systematic Theol—Kathryn Tanner MA PhD

Asst Prof of Homiletics—Donyelle McCray BA JD MDiv ThD

Gilbert L Stark Prof of Christian Ethics—Jennifer A Herdt BA MA PhD

Bexley Hall Seabury Western Theological Seminary Federation

www.bexleyseabury.edu

Bexley Seabury Seminary is located in the Hyde Park neighborhood of Chicago, on the campus of Chicago Theological Seminary, and provides a wide range of educational offerings, including the MDiv and DMin, as well as numerous courses through Pathways of Baptismal Living which are available to all who are wanting to deepen their faith, life, and practice. We offer a DMin with specializations in Congregational Development and preaching. The course-based MDiv is primarily undertaken online, with some in-person elements: this allows students to pursue a degree for ordination while not needing to relocate to Chicago, instead remaining rooted in their own context. Bexley Seabury also offers a Diploma in Anglican Studies for students enrolled at non-Episcopal seminaries, or who have previously completed an Mdiv elsewhere but are now pursuing ordination or other leadership opportunities in the Episcopal Church. 1407 E. 60th St. Chicago IL (773) 380-6780 www.bexleyseabury.edu

Pres and Assoc Prof of Preaching—Rev Micah T J Jackson PhD

Academic Dean and Assoc Prof Anglican Theology—Rev Jason A Fout PhD

Asst Prof of NT—Peter Ajer PhD

Asst Prof of OT—Kay Apigo PhD

Director of Distributive and Lifelong Learning Initiatives, Assoc Prof of Educational Leadership—Julie Lytle PhD

Director of Doctor of Ministry Programs, Associate Professor of Pastoral Theology and Leadership—Emlyn Ott DMin

Director of Formation and Contextual Learning; Assistant Professor of the Practice of Ministry—Rev Eileen Shanley Roberts DMin

Affiliate Professor of Church History—Rev Thomas Ferguson PhD

Affiliate Lecturer Sacred Music—M Milner Seifert MM

Affiliate Professor of Pastoral Theology—Rev Lisa Withrow PhD

Church Divinity School of the Pacific

2451 Ridge Rd Berkeley CA 94709 (510) 204-0700 *Fax:* (510) 644-0712 *E-mail:* info@cdsp.edu *Web:* www.cdsp.edu.

Pres and Dean—Rev WM Richardson PhD

Dean Acad Aff—Rev R Meyers PhD

Hodges/Hayes Prof Litur—Rev R Meyers PhD

Assist Prof Theol—S MacDougall PhD

Visiting Prof Ch Hist—Rev W Stafford PhD

Assoc Prof Min Dev—Rev S Singer

Prof ChristianEthics—C Moe-Lobeda PhD

Assist Prof OT—J Gonzalez PhD

DMin Dir—Rev S Singer PhD

Faculty Emer—Rev JL Kater PhD, Rev AG Holder PhD, Rev L Weil PhD, Rev LL Clader PhD

Asst Prof Ch Mus/Dir Chapel Mus—G Emblom MM

Dir Operations and Personal Management—Rev B Rybicki

Dean Stud/Dn of Chapel—Rev LA Hallisey

Dir of Ext Learning / Prof Practical Theo—J Snow PhD

Reg—E Rhee

Dir Recruit—A Hybl

Episcopal Divinity School at Union Theological Seminary in the City of New York (EDS at Union)

3041 Broadway New York NY 10027 (212) 280-1567 *E-mail:* edsinfo@uts.columbia.edu *Web:* utsnyc.edu/eds

In July 2017, the Episcopal Divinity School affiliated with Union Theological Seminary, creating EDS at Union, a place where Episcopal/Anglican faith and scholarship meet to reimagine work of justice. Students who enroll in EDS at Union's Master of Divinity or Master of Sacred Theology program will earn their degree from Union Theological Seminary with a concentration in Episcopal/Anglican studies. EDS was founded in 1974 with the merger of the Episcopal Theological School (ETS) and the Philadelphia Divinity School (PDS).

Dean, Episcopal Divinity School at Union—The Very Rev Dr Kelly Brown Douglas

Executive Director, Anglican Studies—Miguel Escobar

Assoc Prog Dir—The Rev Anna Olson

Assoc Prog Dir—Emilee Walker-Cornetta

Office Manager—Douglas Berger

Communications Manager—Ian Rees

Henry Luce III Prof of Reformation Church History—The Rev Dr Euan K Cameron

Christiane Brooks Johnson Prof of Psychology and Religion—The Rev Dr Pamela Cooper-White

Reinhold Niebuhr Prof of Social Ethics—The Rev Dr Gary Dorrien

Assoc Prof of Theology and World Religions—Dr John J Thatamanil

Adjunct Prof—The Rev Dr Patrick Cheng

Adjunct Prof—The Rev Dr Anderson Jeremiah

Lecturer for Anglican Liturgical History—The Rt Rev Dr William Franklin

Lecturer for Discernment—The Rev Susan Hill

Lecturer for Anglican Liturgy Practicum—The Rt Rev Jeffery D Lee

General Theological Seminary of the Protestant Episcopal Church in the United States

Established by the General Convention, May 27, 1817. Constitution adopted by General Convention, 1822. Incorporated April 5 1822. Adopted in 1999 and reaffirmed in 2015, our Mission Statement reflects the seminary's commitment to education and formation for the whole people of God: Educating and Forming Lay and Ordained leaders for the church in a changing world. 440 West 21 Street New York City, NY 10011-2981 *Phone:* (212) 243-5150 *Fax:* (212) 727-3907 *Web:* www.gts.edu.

Pres and Dean—The Very Rev. Kurt H. Dunkle

Herbert Thompson Professor of Church and Society & Director of The Desmond Tutu Center,

VP and Dean of Academic Affairs and Associate Professor of Sacred Theology
Dr. Michael DeLashmutt

Professor of Ascetical Theology, the Rev. Dr. Clair McPherson

H. Boone Porter Chair and Associate Professor of Liturgics & Director of the Chapel The Rev. Dr. Kevin Moroney

Associate Professor of Biblical Studies—The Rev. Dr. Julie Faith Parker

Lecturer in Practical Theology & Director of Integrative Programs—The Rev. Emily Wachner

Affiliated Professor of Church History—The Rev. Dr. Carla Roland-Guzman

Affiliated Professor of New Testament—Dr. Jee Hei Park

Affiliated Professor of Spiritual Direction and Director of the Center for Christian Spirituality—Dr. Anne Silver

Affiliated Professor of Arts & Pastoral Care—The Rev. Dr. April Stace

Affiliated Professor of Music & the Arts—Dr. Julian Wachner

Interim EVP, Finance, Operations, HR—Amy Ruetten

VP of Advancement—Donna J. Ashley

VP of External Affairs & Special Projects—Joshua A. Bruner

Manager of Keller Library—Patrick Cates

VP of Finance & Controller—Robert Elliot

VP of Operations—Anthony Khani

Director of HR and Financial Aid—Trecia O'Sullivan

Director of Admissions—Logan Nakyanzi Pollard

Director of Preschool and Daycare—Brooke Savitsky

Director of Alumni Relations and Church Partnerships—Jonathan Silver

Director, Doctor of Ministry Program—The Rev. Dr. Hillary Raining

Director, Academic Management andRegistrar—Stacie Waring

Assistant Director, Chapel of the Good Shephard—The Rev. Matthew Jacobson

Associate Dean, Community Life—The Rev. Dr. Rebecca Ehrlich

Manager, Advancement—Anthony Flagiello

Special Proj Manager—Robert Wohner

Special Proj Coordinator—Ekama Eni

Reference Librarian—Melissa Chim

Campus Services—Kadine Madden

Nashotah House

2777 Mission Rd Nashotah WI 53058-9793 (262) 646-6500 *Fax:* (262) 646-6504 *E-mail:* ganderson@nashotah.edu *Web:* www.nashotah.edu

President and Provost / Professor of New Testament—Garwood P. Anderson PhD

Exec VP for Institutional Advancement—Labin Duke, ThM

Senior Director of Operations and Student Services—Rev Jason Terhune, MDiv

St. Benedict Servants of Christ Chair in Ascetical Theology—Hans Boersma PhD

Prof Hist and Syst Theol—Rev Thomas Holtzen PhD

Dir Library and Assoc Prof of Ascetical Theology—David Sherwood, DMin

Assoc Prof Church History—Rev Thomas Buchan III PhD

Prof OT and Hebrew—Rev Travis Bott PhD

Asst Prof of Liturgics and Pastoral Theology —Rev Matthew Olver PhD

Asst Prof of Ethics and Moral Theology—Elisabeth Kincaid PhD

Asst Prof of Church Music and Dir of Chapel Music/ Dir of St Mary's Chapel—Geoffrey Williams, DMA

Instructor in New Testament—Rev Paul Wheatley PhD (ABD) (Cand.)

Research Professor of Monasticism and Ascetical Theology—Rev Greg Peters PhD

Dir of Distributed Education and Affiliate Professor of Theological Aesthetics—Jim Watkins PhD

Dir of Formation and Leadership—Rev Cn Kelly O'Lear DMin

Protestant Episcopal Theological Seminary In Virginia, The

Seminary Post Office 3737 Seminary Rd Alexandria VA 22304 (703) 370-6600 *Fax:* (703) 370-6234 *Web:* www.vts.edu.

Dean and Pres—V Rev Ian Markham PhD

Assoc Dean for Acad Affrs—TF Sedgwick MA PhD

Assoc Dean of Students—A Dyer PhD

Exec Dir Ctr for Ang Comm Studies/Prof Pastoral Theo—Rev JB Hawkins IV MDiv PhD

Dir Field Ed—Rev Allison St Louis MDiv PhD

Doc of Min Prog and Prof of Evan and Cong Ldrshp—Rev David Gortner MA MDiv PhD

Prof NT—Rev LA Lewis MDiv MA MPhil PhD

Prof NT—Rev K Grieb MDiv JD PhD

Prof NT—J Yieh MA MDiv PhD

Prof Ch Hist—Rev RW Prichard MDiv PhD

Asst Prof Ch Hist—Jonathan Gray MA PhD

Prof Theol—Rev K Sonderegger MDiv STM PhD

Asst Prof Hom—Rev R Hooke MAR MA MPhil PhD

Assoc Prof OT—Rev Judy Fentress-Williams MDiv PhD

Prof OT Language and Lit—Stephen L Cook MA MDiv MPhil PhD

Prof of Practical Theol—Rev J Mercer MDiv DMin PhD

Prof of Ch Music—William B Robert MCM DMA

V Pres Admin and Fin—H Zdancewicz MBA

V Pres Inst Advancement—Rev JB Hawkins IV MDiv PhD

Librarian/Prof—M Jarrett-Budde MA MLib DMin

Dir of CMT and Chrs Form and Cong Ldrshp Elizabeth M Kimball MEd PhD

Assoc Prof of Theo and Liturgy—The Rev James W Farwell PhD

The School of Theology, University of the South, Sewanee, Tenn.

335 Tennessee Ave Sewanee TN 37383-0001 *Phone:* (931) 598-1288 *Fax:* (931) 598-1852 *E-mail:* theology @sewanee.edu *Web:* http://theology.sewanee.edu.

Seminary

Dean/ Prof of Liturgy, Charles Todd Quintard Prof of Theol—The V James F Turrell PhD

Assoc Dean of Academic Affairs/Prof of Christian History/Dir ADP program—The Rev Benjamin J King PhD

Assoc Dean for Community Life, Recruitment, and Admission—The Rev Deborah Jackson DMin

Prof of New Testament—The Rev William F Brosend II, PhD

CK Benedict Prof of Old Testament—The Rev Rebecca Abts Wright, PhD

Bishop Frank A. Juhan Prof of Pastoral Theol—The Rev Julia Gatta, PhD

Assoc Prof of Theol—The Rev Robert MacSwain, PhD

Asst Prof of Church Music/Organist/Choir Master for the Chapel of the Apostles—Kenneth Miller, DMA

Asst Prof of Liturgy—The Rev. Hilary Bogert-Winkler, PhD

Theological Librarian—Romulus Stefanut, PhD

Dist Prof of Global Anglicanism—The Rt Rev James Tengatenga PhD

Asst Prof of Theol Ethics and Dir of the Alternative Clergy Training at Sewanee Program—Andrew R H Thompson PhD

Asst Prof in Homiletics—David Stark, ThD

University Prof of Classics and Ancient Christianity—Paul Halloway PhD

Dir of Contextual Education and Lect in Contextual Theol—The Rev Richard Cogill

Instr in Pastoral Spanish and Latino/Hispanic Ministry—The Rev Leigh Preston

Visiting Asst. Professor for Christian Education and Parish Formation —Hilary Ward EdD

Dir of Publications and Media Relations, The School of Theology—Mary Ann Patterson

Assoc Dir for Alumni and Advancement—Bess Turner

Dir of Financial Aid—Connie Patton

Dir for Admission and Recruitment—Walker Adams

The Beecken Center of the School of Theology

Exec Dir of Education for Ministry—Karen Meridith

Asst Dir for Training, Education for Ministry—Elsa Swift Bakkum

Asst Dir of Education for Ministry—Joshua Booher

Seminary of the Southwest (Episcopal Theological Seminary of the Southwest)

501 E 32nd St Austin TX 78705 (512) 472-4133 *Fax:* (512) 472-3098 *E-mail:* info@ssw.edu *Web:* www.ssw.edu.

Dean & Pres and Prof NT—Very Rev Cynthia Briggs Kittredge ThD

Exec VP—Frederick Clement

Acad Dean and Prof Christian Ethics & Moral Theology—Scott Bader-Saye PhD

Director of Beloved Community Initiatives—Rev Valerie Mayo

Prof Theol—Anthony Baker PhD

Dir Library—Alison Poage MLS

Assistant Prof of NT—Jee Hei Park PhD

Dir Loise Henderson Wessendorff Ctr for Chr Min and Voc & Assistant Prof of Counselor Education—Gena St. David PhD

Assistant Prof of Counselor Education—Stephanie Ramirez PhD

Assistant Prof of Counselor Education—Awa Jangha PhD

Associate Prof Lit and Ang Studies—Rev Nathan Jennings PhD

Assistant Prof of Counselor Education—Marlon Johnson PhD

Associate Professor of Leadership and Administration—Steven Tomlinson

Associate Prof OT—Steven Bishop PhD

Dir Hisp Ch Stu—Nancy Frausto PhD

Dir Formational Outreach—Rev Nandra Perry

Assistant Prof of Counselor Education—Maria Spellings PhD

VP Inst Adv—Charley Scarborough

Assistant Prof Pastoral Theology and Dir of Field Ed—Rev Parker Jameson (interim)

Registrar and Dir of Assessment—Madelyn Snodgrass

Dir Information Tech —Erik Morrow

VP Enrollment and Student Services—Rev Hope Benko

VP Commun—Eric Scott

Associate Prof Preaching—Dominique Robinson PhD

BRSG Crump Visiting Prof—Stephen Ray PhD

SCHOOLS OF THEOLOGY

Bloy House, the Episcopal Theological School at Los Angeles

1300 E. Colorado St. Glendale CA 91205 (909) 621-2419 *E-mail:* info@bloyhouse.org *Web:* www. bloyhouse.org. A diocesan theological school offering lay formation programs, clergy continuing education, diaconal ordination preparation, and an Anglican Studies Certificate curriculum.

Pres—Very Rev Gary Hall PhD

Dean—Linda Allport

Prof NT and Greek—James Dunkly PhD

Prof Preaching and Liturgics—Rev Sylvia Sweeney PhD

Prof Ang Studies—Rev Sheryl Kujawa-Holbrook PhD

Prof Theo and Ethics—Michael J McGrath PhD

Prof Church Leadership—Rev Robert Honeychurch DMin

Prof Spiritual Care and Counseling—Rev Karri Backer PhD

Prof of Latinx Spiritualities—Rev Jennifer Hughes PhD

Prof of Hebrew Bible—Rev Mary Toroeiy PhD

George Mercer Jr Memorial School of Theology

65 Fourth St Garden City NY 11530 (516) 248-4800 x140 *Fax:* (516) 248-4883 *E-mail:* merceroffice@ dioceseli.org *Web:* www.mercerschool.org.

Dean of the School – The Very Rev. Dr. Michael T. Sniffen

Director of Academic Programs—Canon Ted Gerbracht PhD

Director of Operations—Diane G Muscarella

Assistant Director of Operations – Aissa Hillebrand

Librarian—Jane Herbst

POST-ORDINATION AND TRAINING INSTITUTIONS

Ecumenical Theological Seminary

DMin MDiv MA in Pas Min and Urban Min Diploma progs. Only ecum Theology sem in SE Mich; accredited by ATS. *Pres* Kenneth E Harris 2930 Woodward Ave Detroit MI 48201. (313) 831-5200. *Fax:* (313) 831-1353. *E-mail:* info@etseminary. edu . *Web:* www.etseminary.edu.

New Directions Ministries Inc

Provides developmental trng prog for laity and clergy in small congs with emphasis on mins of all persons, regional and cluster ministries. Leadership Academy for New Directions (LAND) is available for national, regional, dio levels (urban as well as rural). Ecumenical. *Pres* LaDonna Wind 4434 Buttonbush Glen Dr Louisville KY 40241-4189 (502) 412-0196 *E-mail:* vanzoelen05@gmail.com; *VPres* The Rev John T Harris PO Box 1291 Gridley CA 95948 (530) 846-4257 *E-mail:* +john1@sbcglobal.net; The Rev Warren Frelund 1029 West State St Mason City IA 50401 (641) 423-1138 *E-mail:* wfrelund@q.com.

School of Theology University South

DMin and STM Program 3-week summer session at Sewanee. Write to Advanced Degrees Program 335 Tennessee Ave School of Theology Sewanee TN 37383-0001 (800) 722-1974 *E-mail:* theology@ sewanee.edu *Web:* http://theology.sewanee.edu.

CHURCH COLLEGES AND UNIVERSITIES

Colleges & Universities of the Anglican Communion (CUAC)—Association of Episcopal Colleges (AEC)

815 Second Avenue, New York, NY 10017 (212) 716-6149 *e-Mail:* office@cuac.org *Web:* www.cuac. org. *General Secretary:* Rev Cn James G Callaway, DD, *Prog Assoc:* Mrs Julia DeLashmutt; *Chair:* The Rev Cn Prof Peter Neil, Bishop Grosseteste University, Lincoln, UK; *Treasurer:* Dr Joel Cunningham, Univ of the South (retired) Sewanee, TN, USA; *AEC Pres:* Dr Sean M Decatur PhD; *AEC Sec:* Scott E Evenbeck. The Episcopal colleges are autonomous institutions participating in the overall ministry of the Episcopal Church in areas related to their particular contexts and fields. Included are the ten colleges listed below. The AEC develops programs to support Christian values on and off campus and provides the means for distributing gifts or bequests equitably among some or all members. Colleges & Universities of the Anglican Communion is a worldwide network of Anglican colleges and universities which exists for the mutual flourishing of its members through engaging with each other, their churches, and their society as they seek to enable their students, staff, and faculties to become active and responsive citizens in God's world. Founded in 1962, AEC was instrumental in the 1993 founding of CUAC, a worldwide association of 150 Anglican institutions of higher education on five continents, and continues as the American chapter to serve as its headquarters and staff support. CUAC is a "network" of the Anglican Communion.

Bard College
PO Box 5000 Annandale-on-Hudson NY 125045000 (845) 758-6822. Coed 1860. Liberal arts, sciences, and fine arts offering a four-year BA and a five-year BS/BA degree in economics and finance. MA in curatorial studies, and MS in environmental policy and climate science and policy at the Annandale campus; MFA and MAT at multiple campuses; and MA, MPhil, and PhD in the decorative arts at the Bard Graduate Center in Manhattan. Internationally, Bard confers dual BA degrees at the Faculty of Liberal Arts and Sciences, St Petersburg State University, Russia (Smolny College), and American University of Central Asia in Kyrgyzstan; and dual BA and MAT degrees at Al-Quds University in East Jerusalem. *Pres* Leon Botstein PhD, *Chap* Rev Mary Grace Williams. *E-mail:* admission@bard.edu *Web:* www.bard.edu

Cuttington University
Box 10-0277 1000 Monrovia 10 Liberia West Africa 011-231-886-676-606. 1889. Reopened in fall 1998. Emphasis on trad liberal arts, research, and community partnerships in the context of Christian service. *Pres* Dr Romelle Horton *E-mail:* rhorton@cu.edu.lr, *Chap* Rev James Tamba. Inquiries may also be addressed to CUAC. *E-mail:* vpa@cu.edu.lr *Web:* www.cu.edu.lr.

Hobart and William Smith Colleges
Geneva NY 14456 (315) 789-5500. 1822. Oldest Coll continuously associated with Epis Church in US. William Smith College (for women) and Hobart share faculty, library, and labs. *Pres Emeritus* Mark Gearan, *Chap* Rev Nita Byrd. *E-mail:* admissions@hws.edu *Web:* www.hws.edu.

Kenyon College
Gambier OH 43022 (740) 427-5000. Coed 1824. Fine Arts, Humanities, Natural Sciences, and Social Sciences. Publisher of *Kenyon Review* and *Psychological Record*. New Olin Library. *Pres* Sean M Decatur PhD, *Chap* Rev Dr. Rachel Kessler. *E-mail:* admissions@kenyon.edu *Web:* www.kenyon.edu.

St. Augustine College
1333-1345 W Argyle St Chicago IL 60640-3594 (773) 878-8756. Coed 1980 bilingual: Spanish/English. 3–4-yr technological and vocational prog; fully accredited. Main campus, plus four satellite facilities in areas of high concentration of Hispanic residents. *Pres* Reyes González. *Web:* www.staugustine.edu.

Saint Augustine's University
1315 Oakwood Ave Raleigh NC 27610 (919) 516-4000. Coed 1867. Historically Black. Liberal Arts differential curriculum with an academic focus in STEM, Mass Communication and Journalism, Public Health and Criminal Justice. *Pres* Dr Christine J McPhail, *Chap* Rev Hershey Mallette Stephens. *E-mail:* admissions@st-aug.edu *Web:* www.st-aug.edu.

Sewanee | The University of the South
735 University Ave Sewanee TN 37383 (931) 598-1000. Coed 1857. Coll of Arts and Sciences and School of Theology. Publ *Sewanee Review*, oldest lit-crit quarterly in US and *Sewanee Theological Review*. *Chanc* Rt Rev Robert Skirving, DD, *Vice-Chanc* and *Pres* Dr. Nancy Berner, Acting VC, *Chap* Rev Peter W Gray. *E-mail:* admiss@sewanee.edu *Web:* www.sewanee.edu.

Trinity University of Asia
Address: Cathedral Heights 275 E Rodriguez Sr Ave Quezon City Philippines. +63-2-8702-2882. Co-ed 1963. Episcopal Mission Center complex. Junior high school through graduate school with 4,500 students. Undergraduate courses: Bus Adm, Accountancy, Real Estate Mgt, Hospitality, Tourism, Information Sci, Computer Engg, Educ, Psych, Broadcast, Media Comm, Biology, Nursing, Med Tech, Pharm, Radiologic Tech, Respiratory Therapy. Masters courses: Educ, Nursing, Bus Adm, Management, Pub Adm, Hospital Mgt, Med Tech. Doctorate courses: Educ, Nursing Mgt, Pub Admin. *Pres* Dr Gisela Luna, *Chap* Rev Echanes Cadiogan. *Web:* www.tua.edu.ph

Université Episcopale d'Haiti
14 rue Légitime, Champ de Mars, B.P. Box 2730, Port-au-Prince, Haiti. 509 22 27 7963. Coed 1994. Francophone. Programs in agronomy, education, theology, accounting, management. Affiliated with FSIL Nursing School (Léogâne), Bishop Tharp

Business & Technology Institute (Les Cayes), St. Barnabas Agricultural School (Terrier Rouge), Episcopal Theology Seminary (Port-au-Prince). *Pres* Revd Dr Pierre S Gabaud *E-mail* unephhaiti@hotmail.com *Web* www.uneph.org.

Voorhees University
Voorhees University is a private, diverse, historically black, coeducational, liberal arts, baccalaureate degree-granting institution affiliated with the Episcopal Church located in rural Denmark, South Carolina. This four-year college is organized into three academic departments: Humanities, Education and Social Sciences; Business and Entrepreneurship; Science, Technology, Health, and Human Services; and it offers sixteen majors that are provided on the main campus, the Charleston and Augusta instructional sites, and via online instruction. *Pres* Dr Ronnie Hopkins. For additional information contact the College at 803.780.1234, e-mail Admissions Office at admissions@voorhees.edu, or check the website at www.voorhees.edu.

EPISCOPAL SCHOOLS

National Assoc of Episcopal Schools, Inc. (NAES)
Gov Board Pres: Rev Edmund K Sherrill II, Exton PA. *Office:* 815 Second Ave New York NY 10017. (212) 716-6134, (800) 334-7626 x6134. *Fax:* (212) 286-9366. *E-mail:* info@episcopalschools.org. *Web:* www.episcopalschools.org *Executive Director:* Rev Daniel R Heischman DD *Associate Director:* Ann Mellow *Director of Operations:* Linda A Burnett *Advancement Manager:* Sarah E Tielemans CAE *Communications Manager:* Jonathan F Cooper *Member Services & Events Coordinator:* Heather E Zrubek

The National Association of Episcopal Schools (NAES) is an independent 501(c)(3), voluntary membership organization that supports, serves, and advocates for the vital work and ministry of those who serve nearly 1,200 Episcopal schools, early childhood education programs, and school establishment efforts throughout The Episcopal Church. Chartered in 1965, with historic roots dating to the 1930s, NAES is the only pre-collegiate educational association that is both national in scope and Episcopal in character. The association advances Episcopal education and strengthens Episcopal schools through essential services, resources, conferences, and networking opportunities on Episcopal school identity, leadership, and governance, and on the spiritual and professional development of school leaders.

Church and Church-Related Schools
Episcopal schools and ECE programs vary in size, scope and educational philosophy. They are parish, cathedral, diocesan, seminary, religious order, independent schools; Montessori and military schools; day and boarding schools; co-educational and single-sex schools. Parishes and cathedrals with schools and ECE programs are identified in the

Diocesan Lists with the symbol §. These programs may or may not be NAES members. The following list comprises diocesan, seminary, religious order, and church-related independent schools listed in the NAES database. NAES members, as of January 31, 2019, are identified with the ● symbol. The schools are listed alphabetically by diocese and then by name. The individual listed as contact is in most cases the head of school or director. For a searchable database of current NAES member schools, ECE programs and school establishment efforts, visit www.episcopalschools.org/find-a-school.
●*indicates member of NAES*
Albany *Doane Stuart School* 199 Washington Avenue Rensselaer NY 12144 *Grades:* Comprehensive School (P-12) *Contact:* Cecil Stodghill Jr. *Chaplain(s):* Patricia Hodgkinson
Albany *Hoosac School* P.O. Box 9 Hoosick NY 12089 *Grades:* Secondary School *Contact:* Dean S. Foster
Arizona *Imago Dei Middle School* ● 55 N. Sixth Avenue Tucson AZ 85701 *Grades:* Middle School *Contact:* Cameron Taylor *Chaplain(s):* The Rev. Susan Anderson-Smith
Arkansas *Episcopal Collegiate School* ● 1701 Cantrell Road Little Rock AR 72201 *Grades:* Secondary School *Contact:* James Griffin *Chaplain(s):* The Rev. Sandra Curtis, The Rev. Robert J. Leacock
Atlanta *Saint George's Episcopal School* ● 103 Birch Street Milner GA 30257 *Grades:* Elementary School *Contact:* Blake Monts de Oca *Chaplain(s):* Shelly Melton
Atlanta *St. Benedict's Episcopal School* ● 2160 Cooper Lake Road Smyrna GA 30080 *Grades:* Elementary School *Contact:* The Rev. Brian Sullivan *Chaplain(s):* The Rev. Wendy Porter Cade
Atlanta *The Boyce L. Ansley School* 120 Ralph McGill Blvd. Atlanta GA 30308 *Grades:* Elementary School *Contact:* Dr. Leah Skinner
Bethlehem *Grace Montessori School* ● 814 West Linden Street Allentown PA 18101 *Grades:* Elementary School *Contact:* Radhika Hoshing
California *St. Paul's Episcopal School* ● 116 Montecito Avenue Oakland CA 94610 *Grades:* Elementary School *Contact:* Cheryl Ting
Central Florida *All Saints' Academy* ● 5001 State Road 540 West Winter Haven FL 33880 *Grades:* Comprehensive School (P-12) *Contact:* Elizabeth Hardage *Chaplain(s):* The Rev. Richard H. Gomer Jr.
Central Florida *Holy Trinity Episcopal Academy* ● 5625 Holy Trinity Drive Melbourne FL 32940 *Grades:* Comprehensive School (P-12) *Contact:* Katherine M. Cobb J.D. *Chaplain(s):* Garcia Barnswell-Schmidt, Timothy Rutherford
Central Florida *Saint Edward's School* ● 1895 Saint Edward's Drive Vero Beach FL 32963 *Grades:* Comprehensive School (P-12) *Contact:* Stuart Hirstein *Chaplain(s):* The Rev. John Hammond Barrett
Central Florida *St. Andrew's Episcopal Academy* ● 210 S. Indian River Drive Fort Pierce FL 34950-4337 *Grades:* Elementary School *Contact:* Mandy Doss

Central Florida *Trinity Preparatory School* ● 5700 Trinity Prep Lane Winter Park FL 32792 *Grades:* Secondary School *Contact:* Byron M. Lawson Jr. *Chaplain(s):* The Rev. Russell Wohlever

Central Gulf Coast *Holy Nativity Episcopal School* ● 205 Hamilton Avenue Panama City FL 32401 *Grades:* Elementary School *Contact:* Cynthia Fuller *Chaplain(s):* The Rev. Steven B. Bates

Central Gulf Coast *St. Paul's Episcopal School* ● 161 Dogwood Lane Mobile AL 36608 *Grades:* Comprehensive School (P-12) *Contact:* N. Blair Fisher

Chicago *Rose Hall Montessori Preschool* 1140 Wilmette Avenue Wilmette IL 60091 *Grades:* ECE Program (P-K only) *Contact:* Elizabeth Friedman

Colorado *St. Anne's Episcopal School* ● 2701 S. York Street Denver CO 80210-6098 *Grades:* Elementary School *Contact:* Christopher Cox *Chaplain(s):* The Rev. Alfred Franklin Miller

Colorado *St. Elizabeth's School* ● 1800 N Pontiac St Denver CO 80220 *Grades:* Elementary School *Contact:* Adriana Murphy *Chaplain(s):* The Rev. Paul Garrett

Connecticut *Kent School* ● 1 Macedonia Road Kent CT 06757 *Grades:* Secondary School *Contact:* Michael G. Hirschfeld *Chaplain(s):* The Rev. Kate E. Kelderman, The Rev. John Kennedy, Brian Cheney

Connecticut *Pomfret School* 398 Pomfret St. Pomfret CT 06258 *Grades:* Secondary School *Contact:* J. Timothy Richards *Chaplain(s):* Bobby Fisher

Connecticut *Salisbury School* 251 Canaan Road Salisbury CT 06068 *Grades:* Secondary School *Contact:* William V. Webb *Chaplain(s):* The Rev. Kirk Hall, Sarah Mulrooney

Connecticut *South Kent School* ● 40 Bull's Bridge Road South Kent CT 06785-9747 *Grades:* Secondary School *Contact:* Lawrence Smith *Chaplain(s):* The Rev. Stephen B. Klots

Connecticut *Steward Outdoor School* 253 Bushy Hill Rd. Ivoryton CT 06442 *Grades:* Secondary School *Contact:* Dr. Nancy Nygard Pilon

Connecticut *The Rectory School* 528 Pomfret Pomfret CT 06258 *Grades:* Middle School *Contact:* Frederick W. Williams *Chaplain(s):* Donna Bessette

Connecticut *Wooster School* ● 91 Miry Brook Road Danbury CT 06810 *Grades:* Secondary School *Contact:* Matthew Byrnes

Dallas *Holy Family School* 500 Throckmorton McKinney TX 75069 *Grades:* ECE Program (P-K only) *Contact:* Rachel Pittman

Dallas *Parish Episcopal School* ● 4101 Sigma Road Dallas TX 75244-4439 *Grades:* Elementary School *Contact:* David W. Monaco *Chaplain(s):* The Rev. Alina S. Williams, Rebecca Gingles

Dallas *St. James Day School* ● 5501 N. State Line Texarkana TX 75503-5303 *Grades:* Elementary School *Contact:* Susannah Joyce

Dallas *St. Philip's School & Community Center* 1600 Pennsylvania Avenue Dallas TX 75215 *Grades:* Elementary School *Contact:* Terry J. Flowers Ph.D.

Dallas *The Canterbury Episcopal School* 1708 N.

Westmoreland Road DeSoto TX 75115 *Grades:* Comprehensive School (P-12) *Contact:* Misty Stern *Chaplain(s):* The Rev. Michael G. Wallens

Dallas *The Episcopal School of Dallas* ● 4100 Merrell Road Dallas TX 75229 *Grades:* Comprehensive School (P-12) *Contact:* David L. Baad *Chaplain(s):* The Rev. Nathan L. Bostian, Toni Luc-Tayengo

Delaware *St. Andrew's School* ● 350 Noxontown Road Middletown DE 19709-1605 *Grades:* Secondary School *Contact:* Joy McGrath *Chaplain(s):* The Rev. John F. Hutchinson Jr., The Rev. Elizabeth Preysner

Delaware *St. Anne's Episcopal School* ● 211 Silver Lake Road Middletown DE 19709 *Grades:* Elementary School *Contact:* Barry Davis

Delaware *St. Michael's School and Nursery* 305 E. 7th Street Wilmington DE 19801 *Grades:* ECE Program (P-K only) *Contact:* Johanna Seda

East Tennessee *All Saints' Episcopal School* 3275 Maple Valley Road Morristown TN 37813 *Grades:* Elementary School *Contact:* The Rev. Louis Oats D.Min. *Chaplain(s):* The Rev. J. Mark Holland

East Tennessee *St. Nicholas School* ● 7525 Min-Tom Drive Chattanooga TN 37421-1835 *Grades:* Elementary School *Contact:* Robert McGehee *Chaplain(s):* The Rev. Janice Robbins, Kara Miscio

East Tennessee *St. Peter's Episcopal School* ● 848 Ashland Terrace Chattanooga TN 37415 *Grades:* Elementary School *Contact:* Meredith Ruffner

East Tennessee *The Episcopal School of Knoxville* ● 950 Episcopal School Way Knoxville TN 37932 *Grades:* Elementary School *Contact:* Jack Talmadge Ed.D. *Chaplain(s):* The Rev. Matthew Farr

Ecuador Central *Canterbury School* Box 17-11-6165 Quito Ecuador *Grades:* Comprehensive School (P-12) *Contact:*

Ecuador Central *Escuela Episcopal Chimbacalle* Box 17-11-6165 Quito Ecuador *Grades:* Elementary School *Contact:* Sra. Ana Armijos

El Camino Real *York School* 9501 York Road Monterey CA 93940 *Grades:* Secondary School *Contact:* Doug Key

Episcopal Church in Micronesia *St. John's Episcopal School* ● 911 N. Marine Drive Tamuning GU 96913 *Grades:* Comprehensive School (P-12) *Contact:* Patricia Bennett *Chaplain(s):* The Rev. James R. Moore, The Rev. Bernard Y. Yung

Florida *Episcopal Children's Services, Inc.* 8443 Baymeadows Road #1 Jacksonville FL 32256 *Grades:* ECE Program (P-K only) *Contact:* Connie Stophel

Florida *Episcopal School of Jacksonville* ● 4455 Atlantic Boulevard Jacksonville FL 32207 *Grades:* Secondary School *Contact:* The Rev. Adam S. Greene *Chaplain(s):* The Rev. Teresa R. Seagle, Andy Farmer, The Rev. Christopher Dell

Florida *San Jose Episcopal Day School* ● 7423 San Jose Boulevard Jacksonville FL 32217 *Grades:* Elementary School *Contact:* Dr. Sloane Albright Castleman

Haiti *Holy Trinity School* Box 1309 Port-au-Prince 01309 OU Haiti *Grades:* Comprehensive School (P-12) *Contact:*

Hawaii *Iolani School* ● 563 Kamoku Street Honolulu HI 96826 *Grades:* Comprehensive School (P-12) *Contact:* Timothy R. Cottrell Ph.D. *Chaplain(s):* The Rev. Timothy L. Morehouse, The Rev. Andrew Arakawa, Jenni C. Lallier

Hawaii *Seabury Hall* ● 480 Olinda Road Makawao HI 96768 *Grades:* Secondary School *Contact:* Maureen Madden *Chaplain(s):* The Rev. Christopher P.J. Golding

Hawaii *St. Andrew's Schools* ● 224 Queen Emma Square Honolulu HI 96813 *Grades:* Comprehensive School (P-12) *Contact:* Ruth R. Fletcher Ph.D. *Chaplain(s):* The Rev. Canon Heather L. Patton-Graham

Honduras *El Buen Pastor Episcopal School* 23 Avenida C 21 Calle S.O. Colonia Trejo San Pedro Sula Cortés Honduras *Grades:* Comprehensive School (P-12) *Contact:* Claudia Chicas

Honduras *Holy Family Bilingual School* ● San Pedro Sula Honduras *Grades:* Comprehensive School (P-12) *Contact:* Carlos Duarte *Chaplain(s):* The Rev. Gustavo Galeano

Honduras *Holy Spirit Episcopal School* Tela Atlantida Honduras *Grades:* Comprehensive School (P-12) *Contact:* The Rev. Olga Abelda Barrera

Honduras *Holy Trinity Episcopal School* Avenida Morazan 48 Bario Dantoni La Ceiba Atlantida Honduras *Grades:* Comprehensive School (P-12) *Contact:* Veronica Flowers

Honduras *St. John's Episcopal School* Siguatepeque Comayagua Honduras *Grades:* Comprehensive School (P-12) *Contact:* Sandra Lucia Villatoro

Honduras *St. John's Episcopal School* Bo, El Centro, 6 Calle, 4 Avenida Puerto Cortés 00504 Cortés Honduras *Grades:* Comprehensive School (P-12) *Contact:*

Honduras *St. Mary's Episcopal School* Colonia Florencia Norte 1a Entrada, Boulevard Suyapa Tegucigalpa M.D.C. Honduras *Grades:* Comprehensive School (P-12) *Contact:* Ricardo A. Salinas *Chaplain(s):* The Very Rev. Gerardo A. Alonzo Martinez

Kansas *Bishop Seabury Academy* ● 4120 Clinton Parkway Lawrence KS 66047 *Grades:* Secondary School *Contact:* Donald Schawang Ph.D.

Los Angeles *Campbell Hall (Episcopal)* ● 4533 Laurel Canyon Boulevard Studio. City CA 91607 *Grades:* Comprehensive School (P-12) *Contact:* The Rev. Canon Julian P. Bull *Chaplain(s):* The Rev. Canon Norman S. Hull, The Rev. Joseph Courtney

Los Angeles *Harvard-Westlake School* Upper School Campus 3700 Coldwater Canyon Avenue North Hollywood CA 91604 *Grades:* Secondary School *Contact:* Richard B. Commons

Los Angeles *Saint Mark's School* ● 1050 E. Altadena Drive Altadena CA 91001-2041 *Grades:* Elementary School *Contact:* Jennifer F. Tolbert *Chaplain(s):* The Rev. Elizabeth E. Hooper-Rosebrook

Los Angeles *St. John's Episcopal School* ● 30382 Via Con Dios Rancho Santa Margarita CA 92688-1518 *Grades:* Elementary School *Contact:* Michael D. Pratt Ph.D. *Chaplain(s):* Patti Peebles

Los Angeles *St. Margaret's Episcopal School* ● 31641 La Novia Avenue San Juan Capistrano CA 92675 *Grades:* Comprehensive School (P-12) *Contact:* William N. Moseley *Chaplain(s):* The Rev. Canon Robert D. Edwards, The Rev. Earl Gibson, The Rev. James Livingston, The Rev. KC Robertson, The Rev. Earl Gibson

Los Angeles *St. Mark's Episcopal School* 10354 Downey Avenue Downey CA 90241-2512 *Grades:* ECE Program (P-K only) *Contact:* Glenda Roberts

Los Angeles *The Episcopal School of Los Angeles* ● 6325 Santa Monica Boulevard Los Angeles CA 90038 *Grades:* Secondary School *Contact:* Dr. Kenneth Rodgers *Chaplain(s):* Patrick Hecker, The Rev. Megan Hollaway, The Rev. Alex T. Moreschi

Los Angeles *The Gooden School* ● 192 N. Baldwin Avenue Sierra Madre CA 91024 *Grades:* Elementary School *Contact:* Jo-Anne Woolner *Chaplain(s):* David J Kitch

Louisiana *Episcopal School of Baton Rouge* ● 3200 Woodland Ridge Boulevard Baton Rouge LA 70816 *Grades:* Comprehensive School (P-12) *Contact:* Dr. Carrie Steakley *Chaplain(s):* The Rev. Kirkland W. Knight, Casey Duncan

Louisiana *St. Andrew's Episcopal School* ● 8012 Oak Street New Orleans LA 70118-2708 *Grades:* Elementary School *Contact:* Kathryn Fitzpatrick *Chaplain(s):* Brother Todd van Alstyne

Louisiana *St. George's Episcopal School* ● 923 Napoleon Avenue New Orleans LA 70115 *Grades:* Elementary School *Contact:* Dr. Joseph Kreutziger

Louisiana *St. James Episcopal Day School* ● 445 Convention Street Baton Rouge LA 70802 *Grades:* Elementary School *Contact:* Bridget Henderson *Chaplain(s):* The Rev. John S. Miller, The Rev. Ralph F. Howe Jr.

Louisiana *St. Martin's Episcopal School* ● 225 Green Acres Road Metairie LA 70003-2484 *Grades:* Comprehensive School (P-12) *Contact:* Ford Jones Dieth Jr. *Chaplain(s):* The Rev. Ford Jefferson Millican Jr., The Rev. Deborah W. Scalia, The Rev. Lindsey Ardrey

Louisiana *St. Paul's Episcopal School* ● 6249 Canal Boulevard New Orleans LA 70124-3099 *Grades:* Elementary School *Contact:* Charleen Schwank *Chaplain(s):* The Rev. Gina Brewster Jenkins

Louisiana *Trinity Episcopal School* ● 1315 Jackson Avenue New Orleans LA 70130-5199 *Grades:* Elementary School *Contact:* The Rev. Edgar Garland Taylor *Chaplain(s):* The Rev. Bobby Hadzor

Maryland *Saint James School* ● 17641 College Road Hagerstown MD 21740 *Grades:* Secondary School *Contact:* The Rev. D. Stuart Dunnan D.Phil. *Chaplain(s):* The Rev. Brandt L. Montgomery

Maryland *St. Anne's School of Annapolis* 3112 Arundel-on-the-Bay Road Annapolis MD 21403-4605 *Grades:* Elementary School *Contact:* Andrea Weiss Ph.D.

Maryland *St. Paul's Schools* ● 11232 Falls Road Brooklandville MD 21022 *Grades:* Comprehensive School (P-12) *Contact:* Clark Wight

Maryland *St. Thomas' Preschool* ● 232 St. Thomas' Lane Owings Mills MD 21117 *Grades:* ECE Program (P-K only) *Contact:* Nicole Norris

Maryland *St. Timothy's School* 8400 Greenspring Avenue Stevenson MD 21153 *Grades:* Secondary School *Contact:* Randy S. Stevens

Maryland *The Wilkes School at Grace and St. Peter's* 707 Park Avenue Baltimore MD 21201 *Grades:* Elementary School *Contact:* Sandra G. Shull *Chaplain(s):* The Rev. Frederick S. Thomas

Massachusetts *Brooks School* ● 1160 Great Pond Road North Andover MA 01845-1298 *Grades:* Secondary School *Contact:* John R. Packard *Chaplain(s):* The Rev. James D. Chapman

Massachusetts *Epiphany School* ● 154 Centre Street Dorchester MA 02124 *Grades:* Middle School *Contact:* The Rev. John H. Finley IV

Massachusetts *Epiphany School* ● 154 Centre Street Dorchester MA 02124 *Grades:* Middle School *Contact:* The Rev. John H. Finley IV

Massachusetts *Esperanza Academy* ● 198 Garden Street Lawrence MA 01840 *Grades:* Middle School *Contact:* Jadihel Taveras *Chaplain(s):* The Rev. Jacqueline Clark

Massachusetts *Groton School* ● 282 Farmers Row Groton MA 01450-1848 *Grades:* Secondary School *Contact:* Temba T. Maqubela *Chaplain(s):* The Rev. Allison Read

Massachusetts *St. Mark's School* ● 25 Marlborough Road Southborough MA 01772 *Grades:* Secondary School *Contact:* John Warren *Chaplain(s):* The Rev. Barbara Talcott, The Rev. Katrina H. Solter

Michigan *Little Lambs at Christ Church Cranbrook* ● 470 Church Road Bloomfield Hills MI 48304 *Grades:* ECE Program (P-K only) *Contact:* Kerry Malczewski

Milwaukee *St. John's Northwestern Military Academy* 1101 Genesee Street Delafield WI 53018 *Grades:* Secondary School *Contact:* Paul Edwin Lima Major General, U.S. Army (Reti

Minnesota *Breck School* ● 123 Ottawa Avenue North Minneapolis MN 55422 *Grades:* Comprehensive School (P-12) *Contact:* Dr. Natalia Rico Hernández *Chaplain(s):* Alexis Kent, The Rev. Dr. Dorothy A. White

Minnesota *Shattuck-St. Mary's School* ● 1000 Shumway Avenue Faribault MN 55021 *Grades:* Secondary School *Contact:* Matthew Cavellier *Chaplain(s):* The Rev. Colin S. Maltbie

Mississippi *Coast Episcopal School* ● 5065 Espy Avenue Long Beach MS 39560 *Grades:* Elementary School *Contact:* Jake Winter *Chaplain(s):* The Rev. Clelie McCandless

Mississippi *St. Andrew's Episcopal School* ● 370 Old Agency Road Ridgeland MS 39157 *Grades:* Comprehensive School (P-12) *Contact:* Kevin Lewis *Chaplain(s):* The Rev. Annie Cumberland Elliott, The Rev. Hailey Allin

New Hampshire *Heronfield Academy* 356 Exeter Road Hampton Falls NH 03844 *Grades:* Elementary School *Contact:* John Turner

New Hampshire *Holderness School* ● 33 Chapel Lane Holderness NH 03245 *Grades:* Secondary School *Contact:* John McVeigh *Chaplain(s):* The Rev. Canon Randolph Dales, The Rev. Abby VanderBrug

New Hampshire *St. Paul's School* ● 325 Pleasant Street Concord NH 03301-2591 *Grades:* Secondary School *Contact:* Kathleen Carroll Giles *Chaplain(s):* The Rev. Charles Allen Wynder Jr., The Rev. Charles Allen Wynder Jr., Sam Lovett, The Rev. Walter Joseph Thorne

New Hampshire *The White Mountain School* 371 West Farm Road Bethlehem NH 03574 *Grades:* Secondary School *Contact:* Donald Ball *Chaplain(s):* The Rev. Paul H. Higginson, The Rev. Kathy Boss

New Jersey *Doane Academy* 350 Riverbank Burlington NJ 08016 *Grades:* Comprehensive School (P-12) *Contact:* George B. Sanderson *Chaplain(s):* The Rev. Paul R. Briggs, The Rev. Dr. Michael Giansiracusa Jr.

New York *Eliza Corwin Frost Child Center* ● 17 Sagamore Road Bronxville NY 10708 *Grades:* ECE Program (P-K only) *Contact:* The Rev. Jennifer Brown

New York *Episcopal School for the Performing Arts* One Hudson Street Yonkers NY 10701 *Grades:* *Contact:* Kat Rodriguez

New York *Grace Church School* ● 86 Fourth Avenue New York NY 10003 *Grades:* Comprehensive School (P-12) *Contact:* The Rev. Robert Morgan Pennoyer II *Chaplain(s):* The Rev. Chase Danford, The Rev. Mark W. Hummell

New York *Grace Church School* 254 Hicks Street Brooklyn NY 11201 *Grades:* ECE Program (P-K only) *Contact:* Amy Morgano

New York *St. Hilda's & St. Hugh's School* ● 619 W. 114th Street New York NY 10025 *Grades:* Elementary School *Contact:* Virginia Connor *Chaplain(s):* The Rev. Arden Strasser, Nastia Khlopina

New York *St. Luke's School* ● 487 Hudson Street New York NY 10014 *Grades:* Elementary School *Contact:* W. Barton Baldwin Jr. *Chaplain(s):* The Rev. Andrew Ancona

New York *The Episcopal School in the City of New York* ● 35 E. 69th Street New York NY 10021 *Grades:* ECE Program (P-K only) *Contact:* Susan A. Sheahan

New York *Trinity School* ● 139 W. 91st Street New York NY 10024 *Grades:* Comprehensive School (P-12) *Contact:* John C. Allman *Chaplain(s):* The Rev. Sarah Anne Wood, Cindylisa Muniz, The Rev. Rodney V. Rice

New York *Trinity-Pawling School* ● 700 Route 22 Pawling NY 12564 *Grades:* Secondary School *Contact:* William W. Taylor *Chaplain(s):* The Rev. Daniel D. Lennox

Newark *All Saints Episcopal Day School* ● 707 Washington Street Hoboken NJ 07030 *Grades:* Elementary School *Contact:* Tom Trigg

North Carolina *Canterbury School* ● 5400 Old Lake Jeanette Road Greensboro NC 27455-1322 *Grades:* Elementary School *Contact:* Harrison Stuart *Chaplain(s):* The Rev. Hunter Pearson Silides

North Carolina *Episcopal Day School* ● 340 E. Massachusetts Avenue Southern Pines NC 28387 *Grades:* Elementary School *Contact:* Dr. Amy Jill Connett *Chaplain(s):* Stephen H. Millender II

North Carolina *Palisades Episcopal School* ● 13120 Grand Palisades Parkway Charlotte NC 28278 *Grades:* Elementary School *Contact:* Kerin S. Hughes

North Carolina *Preschool at the Chapel of the Cross* 304 East Franklin Street Chapel Hill NC 27514-3619 *Grades:* ECE Program (P-K only) *Contact:* Laura Gelblum

North Carolina *Saint Mary's School* ● 900 Hillsborough Street Raleigh NC 27603 *Grades:* Secondary School *Contact:* Adam Holden Ed.D. *Chaplain(s):* The Rev. Lauren F. Winner Ph.D., The Rev. Maggie Stoddard

North Carolina *St. David's School* 3400 White Oak Road Raleigh NC 27609 *Grades:* Comprehensive School (P-12) *Contact:* Jonathan Yonan *Chaplain(s):* The Rev. Todd von Helms D.Min.

North Carolina *Trinity Episcopal School* ● 750 E. 9th Street Charlotte NC 28202-3102 *Grades:* Elementary School *Contact:* Imana Legette Sherrill *Chaplain(s):* The Rev. Lindsey Wells Peery, The Rev. Brent Melton, Quantice T. White M.Div.

North Texas *Trinity Episcopal School* ● 3425 Bellaire Drive South Fort Worth TX 76109 *Grades:* ECE Program (P-K only) *Contact:* Melissa Pannell

Northern California *St. Michael's Episcopal Day School* ● 2140 Mission Avenue Carmichael CA 95608 *Grades:* Elementary School *Contact:* Mary Heise

Northwest Texas *All Saints Episcopal School* 3222 103rd Street Lubbock TX 79423 *Grades:* Elementary School *Contact:* Robert Brashear *Chaplain(s):* The Rev. Deacon Paige McKay

Northwest Texas *Trinity School of Midland* 3500 W. Wadley Avenue Midland TX 79707 *Grades:* Comprehensive School (P-12) *Contact:* Shelby Hammer *Chaplain(s):* The Rev. Shannon Weisenfels

Oklahoma *Casady School* ● 9500 N. Pennsylvania Avenue Oklahoma City OK 73120 *Grades:* Comprehensive School (P-12) *Contact:* Nathan L. Sheldon *Chaplain(s):* The Rev. Charles F. Blizzard, The Rev. Canon TimSean Youmans

Oklahoma *Holland Hall School* ● 5666 E. 81st Street Tulsa OK 74137-2099 *Grades:* Comprehensive School (P-12) *Contact:* Jared P. Culley *Chaplain(s):* Christy Utter, The Rev. John A. Thorpe

Oklahoma *Oak Hall Episcopal School* ● 2815 N. Mount Washington Road Ardmore OK 73401 *Grades:* Elementary School *Contact:* Dr. Kenneth R. Willy *Chaplain(s):* The Rev. Michael P. Stephenson

Olympia *Annie Wright Schools* ● 827 N. Tacoma Avenue Tacoma WA 98403 *Grades:* Comprehensive School (P-12) *Contact:* Jake Guadnola *Chaplain(s):* Dymphna Bloodworth

Olympia *Charles Wright Academy* 7723 Chambers Creek Road West Tacoma WA 98467 *Grades:* Comprehensive School (P-12) *Contact:* Susan Rice *Chaplain(s):* Michael Moffitt

Oregon *Oregon Episcopal School* ● 6300 S.W. Nicol Road Portland OR 97223 *Grades:* Comprehensive School (P-12) *Contact:* Mo Copeland *Chaplain(s):* The Rev. Jennifer B. Cleveland, The Rev. Vijendran Sathyaraj, Melissa Robinson

Oregon *St. James Santiago School* 2490 NE Hwy 101 North Lincoln City OR 97367 *Grades:* Elementary School *Contact:* Julie Fiedler

Pennsylvania *St. James School* ● 3217 West Clearfield Street Philadelphia PA 19132 *Grades:* Middle School *Contact:* David J. Kasievich *Chaplain(s):* The Rev. Andrew L. Kellner

Pennsylvania *The Church Farm School* ● 1001 E. Lincoln Highway Exton PA 19341 *Grades:* Secondary School *Contact:* The Rev. Edmund K. Sherrill II

Pennsylvania *The Episcopal Academy* ● 1785 Bishop White Drive Newtown Square PA 19073 *Grades:* Comprehensive School (P-12) *Contact:* Thomas J. Locke Ed.D. *Chaplain(s):* The Rev. Tim Gavin, The Rev. Michael Palmisano

Rhode Island *St. Andrew's School* 63 Federal Road Barrington RI 02806-2407 *Grades:* Secondary School *Contact:* David Tinagero *Chaplain(s):* David Bourk

Rhode Island *St. George's School* ● P.O. Box 1910 Newport RI 02840-0190 *Grades:* Secondary School *Contact:* Alexandra Callen Ed.D. *Chaplain(s):* The Rev. Dr. Jaquelyn Kirby, Virginia Buckles M.Div.

San Diego *The Bishop's School* ● 7607 La Jolla Boulevard La Jolla CA 92037 *Grades:* Secondary School *Contact:* Ron Kim *Chaplain(s):* The Rev. Nicole M. Simopolous-Pigato

South Carolina *Porter-Gaud School* ● 300 Albemarle Road Charleston SC 29407 *Grades:* Comprehensive School (P-12) *Contact:* D. DuBose Egleston Jr. *Chaplain(s):* Henrietta Rivers, David Rowe, Allison Swiger, The Rev. Palmer Kennedy

South Carolina *Trinity-Byrnes Collegiate School* 5001 Hoffmeyer Road Darlington SC 29532 *Grades:* Secondary School *Contact:* Ed Hoffman *Chaplain(s):* The Rev. Charles D. Cooper

Southeast Florida *Good Shepherd Episcopal School* ● 402 Seabrook Road Tequesta FL 33469 *Grades:* Elementary School *Contact:* Heather Vaughn

Southeast Florida *Palmer Trinity School* ● 7900 S.W. 176 Street Palmetto Bay FL 33157 *Grades:* Secondary School *Contact:* Patrick H. F. Roberts *Chaplain(s):* The Rev. Mary Ellen Cassini D.Min.

Southeast Florida *Saint Andrew's School* ● 3900 Jog Road Boca Raton FL 33434-4498 *Grades:* Comprehensive School (P-12) *Contact:* Ethan Shapiro *Chaplain(s):* The Rev. David Taylor, The Rev. Benjamin Anthony

Southeast Florida *Saint Joseph's Episcopal School* ● 3300 S. Seacrest Boulevard Boynton Beach FL 33435-8661 *Grades:* Elementary School *Contact:* Kyle Aubrey

Southeast Florida *St. Stephen's Episcopal Day School* ● 3439 Main Highway Coconut Grove FL 33133 *Grades:* Elementary School *Contact:* Silvia Larrauri *Chaplain(s):* The Rev. Wilifred S. N. Allen-Faiella, The Rev. Jorge Sayago-Gonzalez

Southern Ohio *Bethany School* ● 555 Albion Avenue Glendale OH 45246 *Grades:* Elementary School *Contact:* Holly Moten Fidler *Chaplain(s):* Joseph Snavely

Southern Virginia *Chatham Hall* ● 800 Chatham Hall Circle Chatham VA 24531 *Grades:* Secondary School *Contact:* Rachel Avery Connell *Chaplain(s):* The Rev. Dr. Regina Christianson, The Rev. Becky Crites, Elisabeth S. Barksdale

Southern Virginia *Good Shepherd Episcopal School* 4207 Forest Hill Avenue Richmond VA 23225 *Grades:* Elementary School *Contact:* Ken Seward

Southern Virginia *St. Michael's Episcopal School* ● 10510 Hobby Hill Road Richmond VA 23235 *Grades:* Elementary School *Contact:* Robert E. Gregg III *Chaplain(s):* Christian Hansen

Southern Virginia *Trinity Episcopal School* 3850 Pittaway Drive Richmond VA 23235 *Grades:* Secondary School *Contact:* Robert Short *Chaplain(s):* Brian Griffen

Southwest Florida *Berkeley Preparatory School* ● 4811 Kelly Road Tampa FL 33615-0009 *Grades:* Comprehensive School (P-12) *Contact:* Joseph W. Seivold *Chaplain(s):* The Rev. Carlene Barbeau

Southwest Florida *Saint Paul's School* 1600 St. Paul's Drive Clearwater FL 33764 *Grades:* Elementary School *Contact:* Samantha Campbell

Southwest Florida *Saint Stephen's Episcopal School* ● 315 41st Street West Bradenton FL 34209 *Grades:* Comprehensive School (P-12) *Contact:* Janet S. Pullen Ed.D. *Chaplain(s):* The Rev. Cori Rigney

Southwest Florida *The Canterbury School of Florida* ● 990 62nd Avenue N.E. St. Petersburg FL 33702 *Grades:* Comprehensive School (P-12) *Contact:* Hollis Amley *Chaplain(s):* The Rev. John C. Suhar, David Gould

Southwestern Virginia *Boys Home of Virginia* ● 414 Boys' Home Road Covington VA 24426 *Grades:* Secondary School *Contact:* Chris Doyle *Chaplain(s):* The Rev. Connie Wolfe Gilman, The Rev. Anne Fletcher Grizzle

Southwestern Virginia *Stuart Hall School* ● Middle and Upper School Campus 235 W. Frederick Street Staunton VA 24402 *Grades:* Secondary School *Contact:* Jason Coady *Chaplain(s):* Julie Caran

Southwestern Virginia *Virginia Episcopal School* ● 400 V.E.S. Road Lynchburg VA 24503-1146 *Grades:* Secondary School *Contact:* Garth Q. Ainslie *Chaplain(s):* Chad Hanning, The Rev. Adam White

Tennessee *Episcopal School of Nashville* ● 1310 Ordway Place Nashville TN 37206 *Grades:* Elementary School *Contact:* Dr. James Jordan *Chaplain(s):* The Rev. Melissa Smith, The Rev. Richard Wineland

Tennessee *St. Andrew's-Sewanee School* ● 290 Quintard Road Sewanee TN 37375-3000 *Grades:* Secondary School *Contact:* Karl J. Sjolund *Chaplain(s):* The Rev. Molly Short

Texas *All Saints Episcopal School* ● 2695 South Southwest Loop 323 Tyler TX 75701 *Grades:* Comprehensive School (P-12) *Contact:* Kathy

Wood *Chaplain(s):* The Rev. Tim Kennedy, Jordan Chapman

Texas *All Saints Episcopal School* ● 4108 Delaware Street Beaumont TX 77706 *Grades:* Elementary School *Contact:* Catherine Clark

Texas *Archway Academy* 6221 Main Street Houston TX 77030 *Grades:* Secondary School *Contact:* Sasha Coles

Texas *Episcopal High School* ● 4650 Bissonnet Bellaire TX 77401 *Grades:* Secondary School *Contact:* C. Edward Smith *Chaplain(s):* The Rev. Elizabeth Holden, The Rev. Arthur A. Callaham

Texas *Holy Trinity Episcopal School* ● 11810 Lockwood Houston TX 77044-5392 *Grades:* Comprehensive School (P-12) *Contact:* Troy Roddy Ph.D.

Texas *St. Andrew's Episcopal School* ● 1112 W. 31st Street Austin TX 78705 *Grades:* Comprehensive School (P-12) *Contact:* Melissa Grubb *Chaplain(s):* Ashley Brandon, The Rev. Whitney B. Kirby, The Rev. Nathan S. Speck-Ewer

Texas *St. Stephen's Episcopal School* ● 6500 St. Stephen's Drive Austin TX 78746-1727 *Grades:* Secondary School *Contact:* Christopher L. Gunnin *Chaplain(s):* Morgan Stokes, The Rev. Edward H. Thompson, The Rev. Aimée Eyer-Delevett

Texas *Trinity Episcopal School of Austin* ● 3901 Bee Cave Road Austin TX 78746-6403 *Grades:* Elementary School *Contact:* Jennifer Morgan *Chaplain(s):* Craig L. Cannon, The Rev. Kenneth A. Malcolm, The Rev. Adam Varner

Upper South Carolina *Christ Church Episcopal School* ● 245 Cavalier Drive Greenville SC 29607 *Grades:* Comprehensive School (P-12) *Contact:* David Padilla *Chaplain(s):* Valerie M. Riddle, The Rev. D. Wallace Adams-Riley, John Mark Elliott

Upper South Carolina *Heathwood Hall Episcopal School* ● 3000 South Beltline Boulevard Columbia SC 29201-5199 *Grades:* Comprehensive School (P-12) *Contact:* Christopher P. Hinchey *Chaplain(s):* Raven G. Tarpley, Chaplain Christopher Johnson, The Rev. Jeri Katherine Sipes

Utah *St. Paul's Preschool and Childcare, Inc.* 261 S. 900 East Salt Lake City UT 84102 *Grades:* ECE Program (P-K only) *Contact:* Rhonda Dossett

Vermont *Rock Point School* 1 Rock Point Road Burlington VT 05408 *Grades:* Secondary School *Contact:* CJ Spirito

Virginia *Anna Julia Cooper School* ● 2124 N. 29th Street Richmond VA 23223 *Grades:* Middle School *Contact:* Michael J. Maruca

Virginia *Blue Ridge School* 273 Mayo Drive St. George VA 22935 *Grades:* Secondary School *Contact:* William A. Darrin III *Chaplain(s):* The Rev. David B. McIlhiney Ph.D., Cathy Boyd

Virginia *Christchurch School* ● 49 Seahorse Lane Christchurch VA 23031-9999 *Grades:* Secondary School *Contact:* William Coyle *Chaplain(s):* The Rev. Scott D. Parnell, The Rev. Johan H. Johnson Ph.D.

Virginia *Episcopal High School* ● 1200 N. Quaker Lane Alexandria VA 22302 *Grades:* Secondary

School *Contact:* Charles M. Stillwell *Chaplain(s):* The Rev. Thomas C. Hummel Ph.D., The Rev. Elizabeth Hall Carmody, The Rev. Richmond Ansel Jones

Virginia *St. Anne's-Belfield School* 2132 Ivy Road Charlottesville VA 22903 *Grades:* Comprehensive School (P-12) *Contact:* Dr. Autumn Graves *Chaplain(s):* Robert Clark, Caitlin Thomson

Virginia *St. Catherine's School* ● 6001 Grove Avenue Richmond VA 23226 *Grades:* Comprehensive School (P-12) *Contact:* Cindy Trask *Chaplain(s):* The Rev. Becky McDaniel, Kevin Newell, Miriam Farris

Virginia *St. Christopher's School* ● 711 St. Christopher's Road Richmond VA 23226 *Grades:* Comprehensive School (P-12) *Contact:* Mason Lecky *Chaplain(s):* The Rev. Darren Steadman, Deacon Michael Sweeney

Virginia *St. James' Children's Center* 1205 W. Franklin Street Richmond VA 23220 *Grades:* ECE Program (P-K only) *Contact:* Diahann Whittington

Virginia *St. Margaret's School* ● 444 Water Lane Tappahannock VA 22560 *Grades:* Secondary School *Contact:* Colley Bell

Virginia *St. Stephen's and St. Agnes School* ● 1000 St. Stephen's Road Alexandria VA 22304 *Grades:* Comprehensive School (P-12) *Contact:* Kirsten P. Adams *Chaplain(s):* The Rev. Sean H. Cavanaugh, The Rev. Grace A. Pratt, The Rev. Elizabeth Rees, The Rev. Christopher H. Miller

Virginia *The Butterfly House* Virginia Theological Seminary 3979 Seminary Road Alexandria VA 22304 *Grades:* ECE Program (P-K only) *Contact:* Juanita Sanchez

Washington *Holy Trinity: An Episcopal School* ● 11902 Daisy Lane Glenn Dale MD 20769 *Grades:* Elementary School *Contact:* Michael S. Mullin

Washington *National Cathedral School* ● 3612 Woodley Road NW Washington DC 20016 *Grades:* Comprehensive School (P-12) *Contact:* Elinor M. Scully Ph.D. *Chaplain(s):* The Rev. Eva M. K. Cavaleri, Rachel Mumford, The Rev. Julius Rodriguez

Washington *St. Andrew's Episcopal School* ● 8804 Postoak Road Potomac MD 20854-3553 *Grades:* Secondary School *Contact:* Robert F. Kosasky *Chaplain(s):* The Rev. Sally E. Slater, The Rev. James Isaacs

Washington *The Bishop John T. Walker School for Boys* ● 1801 Mississippi Avenue, SE Washington DC 20020 *Grades:* Elementary School *Contact:* Michael Molina *Chaplain(s):* The Rev. Tim Malone

Washington *Washington Episcopal School* ● 5600 Little Falls Parkway Bethesda MD 20816 *Grades:* Elementary School *Contact:* Daniel Vogelman *Chaplain(s):* The Rev. Kristen Pitts

West Missouri *St. Paul's Episcopal Day School* ● 4041 Main Street Kansas City MO 64111 *Grades:* Elementary School *Contact:* C. Andrew Myler *Chaplain(s):* The Rev. R. Stanley Runnels, The Rev. Steven King, Maria Meli

West Tennessee *Grace-St. Luke's Episcopal School* ● 246 S. Belvedere Boulevard Memphis TN 38104-

3899 *Grades:* Elementary School *Contact:* Andy Surber Ed.D. *Chaplain(s):* The Rev. Broderick Greer, The Rev. Ollie V. Rencher

West Tennessee *St. George's Independent School* ● Collierville Campus 1880 Wolf River Boulevard Collierville TN 38017 *Grades:* Comprehensive School (P-12) *Contact:* Timothy Gibson *Chaplain(s):* The Rev. Jessica Abell, Kim Finch, The Rev. Hester S. Mathes

West Tennessee *St. Mary's Episcopal School* ● 60 Perkins Extended Memphis TN 38117 *Grades:* Comprehensive School (P-12) *Contact:* Albert Throckmorton *Chaplain(s):* Mary Henry Thompson, Rainey Segars, Miranda Cully

West Texas *St. David's Episcopal School* ● 1300 Wiltshire Avenue San Antonio TX 78209-6049 *Grades:* ECE Program (P-K only) *Contact:* Anne Ivy

West Texas *St. James Episcopal School* ● 602 S. Carancahua Corpus Christi TX 78401 *Grades:* Elementary School *Contact:* Galen W. Hoffstadt

West Texas *The Episcopal Day School* ● 34 N. Coria Street Brownsville TX 78520-8310 *Grades:* Elementary School *Contact:* Brian Clyne

West Texas *TMI Episcopal* ● 20955 West Tejas Trail San Antonio TX 78257-9708 *Grades:* Secondary School *Contact:* The Rev. Scott J. Brown *Chaplain(s):* Daniel Forman, The Rev. Dr. Benjamin H. Nelson III

Western Louisiana *Bishop Noland Episcopal Day School* ● 803 North Division Street Lake Charles LA 70601 *Grades:* Elementary School *Contact:* The Rev. Frances C. Kay

Western Louisiana *Episcopal School of Acadiana* ● Cade Campus 1557 Smede Road Broussard LA 70518 *Grades:* Secondary School *Contact:* Paul Baker Ph.D. *Chaplain(s):* Reese Fuller

Western North Carolina *Christ School* ● 500 Christ School Road Arden NC 28704-9914 *Grades:* Secondary School *Contact:* Sean Jenkins Ph.D. *Chaplain(s):* The Rev. John Charles Roberts, Peter Hartwig

CAMP, CONFERENCE, AND RETREAT CENTERS

EPISCOPAL CAMPS AND CONFERENCE CENTERS INC (ECCC)

Organization with advocacy role, providing support and educational opportunities; newsletters; annual conference; consultation services. Membership open to Episcopal Church camps, conference and retreat centers. *Exec Dir* Jess Elfring-Roberts PO Box 180247 Chicago, IL 60618 *Web:* www.episcopalccc.org. *Contact: Dir of Comm & Events* Ashley Graham Wilcox *E-mail:* ashley@episcopalccc.org.

ALABAMA

Camp McDowell 105 DeLong Rd Nauvoo AL 35578 (205) 387-1806 *Fax:* (205) 221-3454 *E-mail:* whitney@campmcdowell.com *Web:* www.campmcdowell.com *Contact: Exec Dir* Whitney Moore. Total Beds: 600.

ARIZONA
Chapel Rock 1131 Country Club Dr Prescott AZ 86303 (928) 445-3499 *Fax:* (928) 445-0370 *E-mail:* info@chapelrock.net *Web:* www.chapelrock.net *Contact: Exec Dir* Kelly Wood. Total Beds: 270.

ARKANSAS
Camp Mitchell 10 Camp Mitchell Rd Morrilton, AR 72110 (501) 727-5451 *Fax:* (501) 727-5761 *E-mail:* director@campmitchell.org *Web:* www.campmitchell. org. Total Beds: 165

ATLANTA
Camp Mikell Honey Creek 299 Episcopal Conference Center Rd Waverly GA 31565 (912) 265-9218 *Fax:* (912) 267-6907 *E-mail:* office@honeycreek.org *Web:* www.honeycreek.org *Contact: Dir* Dade Brantley. Total Beds: 150.

CALIFORNIA
St Columba Church 12835 Sir Francis Drake Blvd (PO Box 430) Inverness CA 04937 (415) 669-1039. 32 person capacity.

St Dorothy's Rest PO Box B Camp Meeker CA 95419 (707) 874-3319 *Fax:* (707) 874-3349 *E-mail:* sdr@monitor.net *Web:* www.stdorothysrest.org *Contact: Interim Dir* Rev Allen Gates *E-mail:* allen@stdorothysrest.org. Total Beds: 120.

The Bishop's Ranch 5297 Westside Rd Healdsburg, CA 95448 (707) 433-2440 *Fax:* (707) 433-3431 *E-mail:* aaron@bishopsranch.org *Web:* www.bishopsranch.org *Contact: Exec Dir* Aaron Wright. Total Beds: 100.

CENTRAL GULF COAST
Beckwith Camp and Retreat Center (Diocese of Central Gulf Coast) 10400 Beckwith Ln Fairhope AL 36532 (251) 928-7844 *Fax:* (251) 928-7811 *E-mail:* Eleanor@BeckwithAL.com *Web:* www.beckwithal.com. Total Beds: 200.

COLORADO
Cathedral Ridge Retreat & Conference Center, 1364 County Road 75, Woodland Park CO 80863, (719) 687-9038. *E-mail:* office@cathedralridge.org. *Contact: Exec Dir* The Rev. Kim Seidman.

CONNECTICUT
Incarnation Center PO Box 577 Ivoryton CT 06442 (860) 767-0848 *Fax:* (860) 767-8432 *E-mail:* info@incarnationcenter.org *Web:* www. incarnationcenter.com *Contact: Dir* Nancy Pilon. Total Beds: 217.

Camp Washington Camp and Retreat Ctr 190 Kenyon Rd Lakeside CT 06758 (860) 567-9623 *Fax:* (860) 567-3037 *E-mail:* camp@campwashington. org *Web:* wwwcampwashington.org *Contact: Dir* Bart Geissinger. Total Beds: 160.

DELAWARE
Camp Arrowhead 913 Wilson Road Wilmington DE 19803 (302) 256-0374 *Fax:* (302) 543-8084 *E-mail:* waltcampa@aol.com *Web:* www.camparrowhead.net *Contact: Exec Dir* Walt Lafontaine. Total Beds: 325.

Memorial House For Contact Information see Camp Arrowhead above. Total Beds: 31.

EASTERN MICHIGAN
Camp Chickagami 111 West Graham Lansing MI 48901 (888) 440-2267 *Fax:* (517) 699-0846 *E-mail:* mbade@eastmich.org *Web:* www.campchickagami. org *Contact:* McKenzie Bade. Total Beds: 130.

EASTON
Camp Wright 400 Camp Wright Ln Stevensville MD 21666 (410) 643-4171 *Fax:* (410) 643-8421 *E-mail:* director@campwright.com *Web:* www. campwright.com *Contact: Exec Dir* Julia Connelly. Total Beds: 185

FLORIDA
Camp Weed and Cerveny Conference Center 11057 Camp Weed Place Live Oak FL 32060 386-364-5250 *Fax:* 386-362-7557 *E-mail:* thomas@campweed.org *Web:* www.campweed.org *Contact: Exec Dir* Thomas Frazer. Total Beds: 278.

Camp Wingmann 3404 Wingmann Rd Avon Park FL 33825 866-526-3380 *E-mail:* wingmann@strato. net *Web:* www.campwingmann.org *Contact:* Rev Deke Miller. Total Beds: 147.

Day Spring Conference Center PO Box 661 Ellenton FL 34222 (941) 776-1018 *Fax:* (941) 776-2678 *E-mail:* execdirctor@dayspringfla.org *Web:* www.dayspringfla.org *Contact: Exec Dir* Carla Odell. Total Beds: 315.

Duncan Conference Center Closed until July 2022.

Canterbury Retreat and Conference Center 1601 Alafaya Trail (SR 434) Oviedo FL 32765 (407) 365-5571 *Fax:* (407) 365-9758 *E-mail:* jim@canterburyretreat.org *Web:* www.canterburyretreat.org *Contact: Exec Dir* Jim Morical. Total Beds: 92.

GEORGIA
Camp Mikell Honey Creek Rt 3 Box 3495 Toccoa GA 30577 (706) 886-7515 *Fax:* (706) 886-7580 *E-mail:* mikell@alltel.net *Web:* www.campmikell. com *Contact: Dir* The Rev Kenneth Struble. Total Beds: 236.

HAWAII
Camp Mokuleia 68-729 Farrington Hwy Waialua HI 96791 (808) 637-6241 *Fax:* (808) 637-5505 *E-mail:* darrell@campmokuleia.org *Web:* www. campmokuleia.com *Contact: Exec Dir* Darrell Whitaker. Total Beds: 212.

IDAHO
Paradise Point Camp PO Box 936 Boise ID 83701 (208) 345-4522 *Fax:* (208) 345-9735 *E-mail:* mbeck@idahodiocese.org *Web:* www.paradisepointcamp.org *Contact: Dir* Marty Beck. Total Beds: 100.

ILLINOIS
Toddhall Retreat and Conference Center 350 Todd Center Dr Columbia IL 62236 (618) 281-8180 *Fax:* (618) 281-8187 *E-mail:* toddhall@htc.net *Web:* www.

toddhallrc.org *Contact: Exec Dir* Mark Mann. Total Beds: 92.

INDIANA
Waycross Episcopal Camp and Conference Center 7363 Bear Creek Rd Morgantown IN 46160 (812) 597-4241 *Fax:* (812) 597-4291 *E-mail:* david@waycross.org *Web:* www.waycrosscenter.org *Contact: Exec Dir* David Ramsey. Total Beds: 226.

Wawasee Episcopal Center 7830 E Vawter Park Rd Syracuse IN 46567 (574) 233-6489 *Fax:* (574) 287-7914 *E-mail:* treasurer@edin.org *Web:* www.ednin.org *Contact: Dir* Sharon Katona. Total Beds: 26.

KENTUCKY
All Saints Episcopal Center 833 Hickory Grove Rd Leitchfield KY 42754 (270) 259-3514 *Fax:* (270) 259-0526 *E-mail:* bill@allsaintscenter.org *Web:* www.allsaintscenter.org *Contact:* Bill Beam. Total Beds: 114.

The Cathedral Domain 800 Highway 1746 Irvine KY 40336-8701 (606) 464-8254 *Fax:* (606) 464-0759 *E-mail:* asigmon@diolex.org *Web:* www.cathedraldomain.org *Contact: Fac Dir* Andy Sigmon. Total Beds: 315.

LOUISIANA
The Solomon Episcopal Conference Center 54296 Highway 445 Loranger LA 70446 (985) 748-6634 *Fax:* (985) 748-2843 *E-mail:* info@solomoncenter.org *Web:* www.solomoncenter.org *Contact: Dir* Tanja Wadsworth Total Beds: 88.

MAINE
Camp Bishopswood 143 State St (Winter) Portland ME 04101 (207) 772-1953 x127 *Fax:* (207) 773-0095 *E-mail:* info@bishopwood.org *Web:* www.bishopwood.org *Contact: Dir* Michael Douglas *E-mail:* mike@bishopswood.org. Total Beds: 100.

MARYLAND
Bishop Clagget Center PO Box 40 Buckeystown MD 21717 (301) 874-5147 *Fax:* (301) 874-0834 *E-mail:* lmryder@claggettcenter.org *Web:* www.bishopclaggett.org *Contact: Exec Dir* Lisa Marie Ryder. Total Beds: 173.

MASSACHUSETTS
Barbara C Harris Camp and Conference Center PO Box 204 Greenfield NH 03047 (603) 547-3400 *Fax:* (603) 547-3038 *E-mail:* info@bchcenter.org *Web:* www.bchcenter.org. Total Beds: 198.

MICHIGAN
Emrich Retreat Center at Parishfield 7380 Teahen Rd Brighton MI (810) 231-1060 *Web:* www.discoveremrich.org. Overnight accommodations for 90 on 26 beatutiful, well kept acres.

MISSISSIPPI
Gray Center 1530 Way Rd Canton 39046 (601) 859-1556 *Fax:* (601) 859-1495 *E-mail:* nisey@graycenter.org *Web:* www.graycenter.com *Contact:* Nisey Ward. Total Beds: 220.

MONTANA
Camp Marshall 41524 Melita Island Rd Polson MT 59860 (406) 849-5718 *E-mail:* campmarshalldirector@diomontana.org *Web:* www.diomontana.com *Contact: Exec Dir.* David Campbell. Total Beds: 150.

NEVADA
Camp Galilee 1776 Highway 50 South PO Box 236 Glenbrook NV 89413 (775) 749-5546 *E-mail:* executivedirector@galileetahoe.org *Web:* www.galileetahoe.org *Contact: Exec Dir* Stuart Campbell. Total Beds: 68.

NEW JERSEY
Crossroads Outdoor Ministries 29 Pleasant Grove Rd Port Murray NJ 07865 (908) 832-7264 *Fax:* (908) 832-6593 *E-mail:* www.crossroadsretreat.com *Web:* www.crossroadsretreat.com *Contact: Dir* Anthony Briggs. Total Beds: 300.

NEW MEXICO
Bishop Stoney Camp and Conferance Center 7855 Old Santa Fe Trail Santa Fe NM 87505 (505) 983-5610 *Fax:* (505) 983-9150 *E-mail:* cjewell@dioceserg.org *Web:* www.campstoney.org *Contact: Exec Dir* Christopher Jewll. Total Beds: 100.

NEW YORK
Camp DeWolfe PO Box 487 Wading River NY 11792 (631) 929-4325 *Fax:* (631) 929-6553 *E-mail:* office@campdewolfe.org *Web:* www.campdewolfe.org *Contact: Dir* Matt Tees. Total Beds: 150.

Christ the King Spiritual Life Center 575 Burton Rd Greenwich NY 12834 (518) 692-9550 *E-mail:* rtodd@ctkcenter.org *Web:* www.Christ-the-King-Center.org *Contact:* Reuben Todd. Total Beds: 160.

NORTH CAROLINA
Kanuga Confererences PO Box 250 Hendersonville NC 28793-0250 (828) 692-9136 *Fax:* (828) 696-3589 *E-mail:* info@kanuga.org *Web:* www.kanuga.org *Contact: Pres* Michael R. Sullivan Total Beds: 750.

Lake Logan Conference Center 154 Suncrest Mill Rd Canton NC 28716 (828) 646-0095 *Fax:* (828) 648-8937 *E-mail:* info@lakelogan.org *Web:* www.lakelogan.org *Contact: Exec Dir* Lauri Sojourner. Total Beds: 196.

Trinity Center PO Box 380 Salter Path NC 28575 (888) 874-6287 *Fax:* (252) 247-3290 *E-mail:* penn@trinityctr.org *Web:* www.trinityctr.com. Total Beds: 180.

Valle Crucis Conference Center PO Box 654 Valle Crucis NC 28691 (828) 963-4453 *Fax:* (828) 963-8806 *E-mail:* vccc@highsouth.com *Web:* www.highsouth.com/vallecrusis *Contact: Exec Dir* Margaret Lumpkin Love. Total Beds: 156.

OHIO
Procter Conference Center 11235 State Rd 38 London OH 43130 (740) 874-3355 *Fax:* (740) 874-3356 *E-mail:* rkimbler@diosohio.org *Web:* www.proctercenter.org *Contact: Exec Dir* Amy Boyd Total Beds: 124.

Sheldon Calvary Camp 4410 Lake Rd Conneaut OH 44030 (440) 593-4381 *Fax:* (440) 593-6250 *E-mail:* executivedirector@calvarycamp.org *Web:* www.calvarycamp.org *Contact:* Dir Tim Green. Total Beds: 250.

Transfiguration Spirituality Center 495 Albion Ave Cincinnati OH 45246 (513) 771-5291 *E-mail:* ctretreats@gmail.com *Contact: Exec Dir* Anne Reed. Total Beds: 50.

OKLAHOMA

St Crispin's Conference Center Rt 2 Box 381 Wewoka OK 74884 (405) 382-1619 *Fax:* (405) 382-1631 *E-mail:* info@stcrispins.org *Web:* www.episcopaloklahoma.org *Contact: Dirs* Joanne & Mike Roberts. Total Beds: 180.

OREGON

Ascension School PO Box 278 Cove OR 97824 (541) 568-4514 *E-mail:* amy@coveascensionschool.com *Web:* www.coveascensionschool.com *Contact: Exec Dir* Amy Jayne. Total Beds: 130.

PITTSBURGH

Sheldon Calvary Camp 4411 Lake Rd Conneaut, OH 44030 (440) 593-4381 *Exec Dir* Tim Green *E-mail:* executivedirector@calvarycamp.org *Web:* www.calvarycamp.org.

RHODE ISLAND

Episcopal Conference Center 872 Reservoir Rd Pascoag RI 02859 (401) 568-4055 *Fax:* (401) 568-7805 *E-mail:* director@eccri.org *Web:* www.eccri.org *Contact: Dir* Rev Meaghan Kelly Brower. Total Beds: 225.

RIO GRANDE

Bishop Stoney Camp and Conference Center 7855 Old Santa Fe Trail Santa Fe NM 87505 (505) 983-5610 *Fax:* (505) 983-9150 *E-mail:* info@campstoney.org *Web:* www.campstoney.org. Total Beds: 100.

SOUTH DAKOTA

Thunderhead Episcopal Center PO Box 890 Lead SD 57754 605-584-2233 (summer) *Fax:* 605-582-2242 *E-mail:* camp.diocese@midconetwork.com *Contact: Missioner for Camp* Rev Lydia Simmons *Email:* lydia@episcopalchurchsd.org. Total Beds: 106.

TENNESSEE

DuBose Conference Center PO Box 339 Monteagle TN 37356 (931) 924-2353 *Fax:* (931) 924-2291 *E-mail:* wendy@duboseconferencecenter.org *Web:* www.duboseconf.org. *Contact: Operations Dir* Wendy Howard. Total Beds: 240.

Grace Point Camp and Retreat Center 300 Chamberlain Cove Rd Kingston TN 37763 (865) 567-1159 *E-mail:* gracepoint@etdiocese.net *Web:* www.etdiocese.net. *Contact: Exec Dir* Rev Brad Jones Total Beds: 46.

St Columba Episcopal Conference Center 4577 Billy Maher Rd Memphis TN 38135 (901) 377-9284 *Fax:* (901) 371-0700 *Web:* www.saintcolumbamemphis.org. *Dir* Brad Thompson. Total Beds: 77.

St Mary's Sewanee PO Box 188 Sewanee TN 37375 (931) 598-5342 *Fax:* (931) 598-5884 *E-mail:* reservations@stmaryssewanee.org *Web:* www.stmaryssewanee.org *Contact: Exec Dir* Rev Andy Anderson. Total Beds: 100.

TEXAS

All Saints Camp and Conference Center 418 Stanton Way Pottsboro TX 75076 (903) 786-3148 *Fax:* (903) 786-7535 *E-mail:* info@allsaintsexoma.org *Web:* www.allsaintsexoma.org *Contact: Operations Dir* Sandi Campbell *E-mail:* sandi@campallsaints.com. Total Beds: 176.

Camp Allen 18800 FM 362 Navasota TX 77868 (936) 825-7175 *Fax:* (936) 825-8495 *E-mail:* frontdesk@campallen.org *Web:* www.campallen.org *Contact: Pres* George Dehan. Total Beds: 600.

Camp Capers PO Box 9 Waring TX 78074 (830) 995-3966 *Fax:* (830) 995-2393 *E-mail:* capers@hctc.net *Web:* www.campcapers.org *Contact:* Rob Watson. Total Beds: 220.

Camp Crucis 2875 Camp Crucis Court Granbury TX 76048 (817) 573-3343 *Fax:* (817) 279-7974 *E-mail:* info@campcrucis.org *Web:* www.campcrucis.org Total Beds: 340.

Mustang Island Conference Center PO Box 130 Port Arkansas TX 78373 (361) 749-1800 *Fax:* (361) 749-1802 *E-mail:* kevin.spaeth@dwtx.org *Web:* www.mustangisland.org *Contact: Oper Mgr* Lynn Corby. *Exec Dir* Kevin Spaeth. Total Beds: 55.

UTAH

Camp Tuttle 80 South 300 East Salt Lake City UT 84110 (801) 322-4131 *Fax:* (801) 322-5096 *E-mail:* kgleeson@episcopal-ut.org *Web:* www.camptuttle.org *Contact: Exec Dir* Karen Gleeson. Total Beds: 165.

VERMONT

Bishop Booth Conference Center 20 Rock Point Circle Burlington VT 05401 (802) 658-6233 *Fax:* (802) 658-8836 *E-mail:* phabersang@diovermont.org *Web:* www.dioceseofvermont.org *Contact: Exec Dir* The Rev. Paul Habersang. Total Beds: 110.

VIRGINIA

Virginia Diocesan Center at Roslyn 8727 River Rd Richmond VA 23229 (804)288-6045 *Fax:* (804) 285-3430 *E-mail:* info@roslyncenter.org *Web:* www.roslyncenter.org *Contact:* Katherine Lawrence. Total Beds: 96.

Shrine Mont 221 Shrine Mont Circle Orkney Springs VA 22845 (540) 856-2141 *Fax:* (540) 856-8520 *E-mail:* shrine@shentel.net *Web:* www.shrinemont.com *Contact: Exec Dir* Kevin Moomaw. Total Beds: 550.

WASHINGTON

Camp Cross 245 E 13th Ave Spokane WA 99202 (509) 624-3191 *Fax:* (509) 747-0049 *E-mail:* campcross@spokanediocese.org *Web:* www.campcross.org. *Contact: Exec Dir* Sara Gunther *E-mail:* SaraG@spokanediocese.org. Total Beds: 110.

Huston Camp and Conference Center PO Box 140 Gold Bar WA 98251 (360) 793-0441 *Fax:* (360)

793-3822 *E-mail:* iiinfo@camphuston.org *Web:* www. huston.org *Contact: Exec Dir* Alida Garcia. Total Beds: 237.

WEST VIRGINIA
Peterkin Camp and Conference Center 286 Clubhouse Rd Romney WV 26757-7521 (304) 822-4519 Fax: (304) 822-7771 *E-mail:* daisymcb1@ hotmail.com *Web:* www.peterkin.org *Contact:* Daisy McBride. Total Beds: 150.

Sandcrest Conference and Retreat Center 143 Sandcrest Dr Wheeling WV 26003 (304) 277-3022 *Fax:* (304) 277-3840 *E-mail:* sdirector@sandcrest.com *Web:* www.sandscrest.com *Contact:* Jessica Thompson. Total Beds: 35.

WESTERN MICHIGAN
Saugatuck Retreat House WMI Diocese PO Box 189 Saugatuck MI 49453 (269) 857-5201. Total 14 rooms. Five bedroom house for overnight and longer retreats run by All Saints Episcopal Church.

WISCONSIN
DeKoven Center 600 21st St Rancine WI 53403 (262) 633-6401 *E-mail:* lbiese@dekovencenter.org *Web:* www.dekovencenter.pair.com *Contact: Exec Dir* Lynn Biese-Carroll. Total Beds: 60.

WYOMING
Wyoming Wilderness Camp 123 S Durbin Casper WY 82601 (307) 265-5200 *Fax:* (307) 577-9939 *E-mail:* stay@tacwyoming.org *Web:* www. wyomingdiocese.org *Contact: Co-directors* Rebecca & Robert Mason. Total Beds: 30.

NATIONAL ALTAR GUILD ASSOCIATION
Formed in 1921. www.nationalaltarguildassociation. org
Pres Marcia Himes *E-mail:* rthimes@wyoming. com; *1VP* David Hawley-Lowry *E-mail:* david8hl@ outlook.com; *2nd VP* The Rev. Laurence G (Larry) Byrne *E-mail:* lgbyrne1129@aol.com; *Sec* Sandy Wilson *E-mail:* slwilson@att.net *Treas* Elizabeth Coffin *E-mail:* eljcoffin22@gmail.com. Meets every 3 years at Gen Conv with program and election of officers. Natl Assn mbrshp is $35/year for individuals; $50/year parish; $100/year for diocese. Member incl quarterly issues of newsletter, *Epistle*.

Provincial Presidents
Province I: Diane Grondin *E-mail:* dmgrondin@ comcast.net
Province II: Barbara Nichols *E-Mail:* tbmee@aol. com
Province III: Sharon Nachman *E-mail:* P3NAGA@ gmail.com
Province IV: Martha Noble Langston *E-mail:* Martha.noble@att.net
Province V: David Hawley-Lowry *E-mail:* david8hl@outlook.com

Province VI: Debbie Mead *E-mail:* altarguild@ holoycomforterchurch.net
Province VII: Rebecca Robertson *E-mail:* Rebecca. robertson@me.com
Province VIII: Sara Chesebro *E-mail:* sarachesebro@ gmail.com

Altar Guild Diocesan Presidents
AL M E Spencer 516 Bennet Dr Alabaster AL 35007 spencermedr@gmail.com
AT Diocesan Altar Guild 2744 Peachtree Rd Atlanta GA 30305
AZ Julia Coleman 2631 S Keene Mesa AZ 85209
CA Jane Phillips 2211 Latham St. #302 Mountain View CA 94040
CFL Kathy Shearer, 1627 Colleen Drive, Belle Isle, FL 32809 wwdassoc@gmail.com
CHICAGO Beth c. Petti c/o Dioc. Of Chicago 65 E Huron St. Chicago IL60611
CT Jean Kelsey 21 Fairview St. Manchester CT 06040
DAL Anna Houston AYhouston@prodigy.net (214) 232-3089
E Barry Passano PO Box 27 Oxford MD 21654
ECR
ETN Joyce Collom 393 Deep Draw Dr Crossville TN 38555
FL Janet Robinson 2150 Spencer Rd Orange Park FL 32073
HI Rosella Newell 229 Queen Emma Sq Honolulu HI 96813
IA Dioc of Iowa 225 37th St. Des Moines IA 50312
LA Carolyn Douglas Box 991 St Francisville LA 70775
LI Jane Ames 21 Melanie Lane Syosset NY 11791 jacamel@juno.com
LOSA Bea Floyd Box 512164 Los Angeles CA 90051-0164 (213) 482-2040
MA Diane Grondin 18 Hilldale Rd. Weymouth MA 02190
ME Vicki Wiederkehr 143 State St Portland ME 04101
MI Novie Duffy PO Box 430357 Pontiac MI 48343
MIL Micki Hoffmn c/o Dioc.of MIL Altar Guild 804 East Juneau Ave Milwaukee WI 53202
MS Ann Mileted 133 Perry St. Gulfport MS eamlstd@yahoo.com
NC Dioc of NC 200 W. Morgan St. Suite 300 Raleigh NC 27601
NE Diocesan Altar Guild 109 18th St Omaha NE 68102 Heather Bauer greenpeacecats121@yahoo. com
NH Sue Ingram PO Box 185 North Hampton NH 03862

NJ NO Diocesan Altar Guild

NK Sr Suzanne Elizabeth CSJB Box 240 Mendham NJ 07945 srse@csjb.org

NT Nancy McReynolds (806) 928-7734

NWPA Mary Blaine Prince 522 W Corydon St Bradford PA 16701

NWTX Paula Howbert 3803 Stanolind Dr Midland TX 79707

NY Molly B. Jones The NY Altar Guild PO Box 881 Millbrook NY 12545

OK Mary Lu Jarvis 3820 S Hiwassee St Choctaw OK 73020

OL Sherry Garman PO Box 12126 Seattle WA 98102

OR Donna Anderson P.O. Box 1576 Roseburg OR 97470

PA Dioc of PA 5421 Germantown Ave Philadelphia PA 19144

PGH Priscilla Castner 165 Summerlawn Dr Sewickley PA 15143

PI Dioc of Pittsburg Shelley Snyder 602 Danbury St. Pittsburg PA 15214

RG Diocesan Altar Guild 4304 Carlisle Blvd NE Albuquerque NM 87107

RI Liz Crawley 275 N Main St. Providence RI 02903

SAND Diocesan Altar Guild 840 Echo Park Ave Los Angeles CA 90026

SANJ Susan Ohanneson 41 Cedarwood Lane Bakersfield CA 93308

SD Vicki Sweet sweetmom@rushmore.com

SOH Craig Foster c/o Altar Guild Dioc. Of SOH 412 Sycamore St. Cincinnati OH 45202

SWF/NORTH Sarah Hill 1906 Carolina Ave NE St Petersburg FL 33703 sarahhill.fl@gmail.com

SWF/SOUTH Sarah Hill 1906 Carolina Ave NE St Petersburg FL 33703 sarahhill.fl@gmail.com

TN Sue Hays 408 N Cameron Ct Hermitage TN 37076

TX Kate Canby 8113 Vailview Cove, Austin, TX 78750

USC Valerie Riley 81 Cannonade Court Irmo SC 29063

VA Sharon Nachman 866 Vine Street Herndon VA 20170 P3NAGA@gmail.com

VT Sarah Maynard 79 Green St St Johnsbury VT 05819

WKS Sally Russell Grace Episcopal Church sallyruss@sbcglobal.net (620) 662-2946

WLA Ginger Norvell 120 Harolyn Park Dr. Lafayette LA 70503

WMA MA Worton 7 Leland Hill Rd South Graft on MA 01560

WMI David Hawley-Lowry 10312 Riley St. Zeeland MI 49464

WMO Grace and Holy Trinity Cathedral (816) 474-8260

WNC Lois Lynn 468 Vision Rd Canton NC 28716

WNY Janice Beam 134 Bridle Path Williamsville NY 14221

WTN Ann McCormick 3071 Dumbarton Rd Memphis TN 38128

WTX Dee Whiteside 234 Five Oaks Dr. San Antonio TX 78209 dwhiteside@satx.rr.com

WVA Holly Mitchell 5119 Brookside Dr Cross Lakes W VA 25313

EPISCOPAL CHURCH WOMEN

Board Officers
Website for national ECW: www.ecwnational. org; *Pres* Karen O Patterson *E-mail:* president@ ecwnational.org; *1st VP* Patricia Wellnitz *E-mail:* firstvp@ecwnational.org; *2nd VP* vacant; *Sec* Samar Fay *E-mail:* secretary@ecwnational.org; *Treas* Jeanne Plecenik *E-mail:* treasurer@ecwnational.org.

Board Members-at-Large
Social Justice Chair vacant

Board Provincial Representatives
I—Margaret Noel *E-mail:* province1@ecwnational. org; *II*—The Rev Jennifer Kenna *E-mail:* province2@ ecwnational.org; *III*—Cindy Mohr *E-mail:* province3@ecwnational.org; *IV*—Mary Beth Welch *E-mail:* province4@ecwnational.org; *V*—Jan Goossens *E-mail:* province5@ecwnational.org; *VI*—Beth Agar *E-mail:* bethagar@live.com; *VII*—Lisa Bortner *E-mail:* province7@ecwnational.org; *VIII*—Madeline Sampson *E-mail:* Madelinesampson15@gmail.com; *IX*—The Rev Consuelo (Connie) Sanchez *E-mail:* province9@ecwnational.org.

Provincial Presidents
I—Susan Howland *E-Mail:* howlands@charter.net; *II*—Carolyn Belvin *E-Mail:* cjb613@hotmail.com *III*—Nancy Polick Sands *E-Mail:* beachpeach7@ hotmail.com; *IV*—Annie Jacobs *E-Mail:* Aj34528@ aol.com *V*—Kathy Mank *E-Mail:* kathymank@ gmail.com; *VI*—Heather Bauer *E-Mail:* greenpeacecats121@yahoo.com; *VII*—The Rev Fran Wheeler *E-Mail:* prov7.ecwpres@gmail.com; *VIII*— Canon Martha K. Estes *E-Mail:* marthakestes53@ gmail.com; *IX*—The Rev Consuelo (Connie) Sanchez *E-Mail:* province9@ecwnational.org

Diocesan Presidents/Contacts: Province I
Connecticut (CT)—Elizabeth Silva *Pres E-mail:* betty.silva@att.net

Maine (ME)—Barbi Tinder *Contact E-mail:* B5tinder@gmail.com

Massachusetts (MA)—Elizabeth Murray *Contact E-mail:* Eg.murray102@gmail.com

New Hampshire (NH)—no contact

Rhode Island (RI)—Linda Guest *Pres E-mail:* lindaeguest@verizon.net

Vermont (VT)—Wendy Grace—Contact *E-mail:* duchs8@gmail.com

Western Massachusetts (WMA)—Susan Howland *Pres E-mail:* howlands@charter.net

Diocesan Presidents/Contacts: Province II
Albany (A)—Mary Young *Contact E-mail:* mar049@yahoo.com

Central New York (CNY)—Jennifer Kenna *Contact E-mail:* province2@ecwnational.org

Cuba—Mayelin A'gueda *Contact E-mail:* mayelin.aj@nauta.cu

Europe (EUR)—no contact

Haiti (Hai)—Bureau Diocesan

Long Island (LI)—Lois Johnson-Rodney *Pres E-mail:* loisjohnsonrodney1@gmail.com

New Jersey (NJ)—Pamela James *Pres E-mail:* jamespej@gmail.com

New York (NY)—Dianne Roberts *Pres E-mail:* drobertslaw@gmail.com

Newark (NK)—no contact

Puerto Rico (PR)—Melva Irizarry *Pres E-mail:* melvacats@yahoo.com

Rochester (ROCH)—no contact

Virgin Islands (VI)—Edith Haynes-Lake *Pres E-mail:* hayneslake@yahoo.com

Western New York (WNY)—no contact

Diocesan Presidents/Contacts: Province III
Bethlehem—Dorothy Shaw *Pres E-mail:* flamingo10@frontier.com

Central Pennsylvania (CPA)—Cindy Mohr *Pres E-mail:* province3@ecwnational.org

Delaware (DE)—Beth Fitzpatrick *Pres E-mail:* gr8art@outlook.com

Easton (E)—vacant

Maryland (MD)—vacant

Northwestern Pennsylvania (NWPA)—vacant

Pennsylvania (PA)—Shirley Smith *Pres E-mail:* granny7sm@gmail.com

Pittsburgh (PGH)—Ann McStay *Pres E-mail:* annmcstay@gmail.com

Southern Virginia (SV)—Laura Manigault *Pres E-mail:* manigault7@gmail.com

Southwestern Virginia (SWV)—vacant

Virginia (VA)—Ericka Masias-Campos *Pres E-mail:* erickamasias@outlook.com

Washington (W)—Elsie E. Kirton *Pres E-mail:* elsiek@aol.com

West Virginia (WV)—Becki Krzywdik *Convener E-mail:* bkrzywdik@msn.com

Diocesan Presidents/Contacts: Province IV
Alabama (AL)—Fran Bramblette *Pres E-mail:* narf96@gmail.com

Atlanta (AT)—Barbara Richards *Pres E-mail:* 2barbie@bellsouth.net

Central Florida (CF)—Christine Allen *Pres E-mail:* ladydr34982@gmail.com

Central Gulf Coast (CGC)—no contact

East Carolina (EC)—Lucia Peel *Pres E-mail:* luciapeel@gmail.com

East Tennessee (ETN)—Mary Lee Baer *Pres E-mail:* volswatcher@comcast.com

Florida (FL)—Dorothy Young Holder *Pres E-mail:* perdor@comcast.net

Georgia (GA)—Christy Jordan *Pres E-mail:* christy@cdrepro.com

Kentucky (KY)—no contact

Lexington (Lex)—Carol Mize *Pres E-mail:* CaroJ11@windstream.net

Louisiana (LA)—Sudee S. Campbell *Pres E-mail:* sudee@bellsouth.com

Mississippi (MS)—Martha E. Morgan *Pres E-mail:* maest55@gmail.com

North Carolina (NC)—Mary E. Hawkins *Pres E-mail:* president@ecw-nc.org

Episcopal Church in South Carolina—Jackie Robe *E-mail:* jrobe18413@aol.com

Southeast Florida (SEF)—Edith Newbold *Pres E-mail:* gladmon7@aol.com

Southwest Florida (SwF)—Michelle Schombs *Pres E-mail:* ml9ma50@verizon.net

Tennessee (TN)—Cathy Links *Pres E-mail:* cathylinrn@gmail.com

Upper South Carolina (USC)—Kathy Siegel *Pres E-mail:* upperscecwpresident@gmail.com

West Tennessee (WTN)—Jean Arehart *Pres E-mail:* jeanarehart@gmail.com

Western North Carolina (WNC)—Mary Ann Ransom *Pres E-mail:* mransom1@bellsouth.net

Diocesan Presidents/Contacts: Province V

Chicago (C)—Jane Schenck *Pres E-mail:* schenckjj@sbcglobal.net

Eastern Michigan (EMI)—Kate Forsyth *Contact E-mail:* kforsyth@eastmich.org

Eau Claire (EAUC)—The Rev Canon Aaron Zook *Contact E-mail:* administrator@dioec.net

Fond du Lac (FDL)—Lisa Baltes *Contact E-mail:* lbaltes@diofdl.org

Indianapolis (IND)—Beverly Ruebeck *Co-Pres E-mail:* beverlyruebeck@gmail.com; Lisa Matucheski *Co-Pres E-mail:* jmatuche@sbcglobal.net

Michigan (MI)—Darlene Williams *Co-Chair E-mail:* darwills1@aol.com; Ged Youngman *Co-Chair E-mail:* amyged@wowway.com

Milwaukee (MIL)—Connie Ott *Pres E-mail:* cott@chorus.net

Missouri (MO)—Sharon Meusch *Pres E-mail:* meuschsharon@gmail.com

Northern Indiana (NI)—The Rt. Rev. Douglas Sparks *Contact E-mail:* bishopsparks@edmin.org

Northern Michigan (NMI)—Teena Maki *Co-Contact E-mail:* makifarm@up.net; Coralie Hambleton Voce *Co-Contact E-mail:* cvhamblet@hotmail.com

Ohio (OH)—Susan Quill *Pres E-mail:* planetquill@roadrunner.com

Southern Ohio (SO)—Kathy Mank *Pres E-mail:* kathymank@gmail.com

Springfield (SP)—Jan Goossens *Pres E-mail:* utospil@sbcglobal.net

Western Michigan (WMI)—Marilee Roth *Contact E-mail:* mjrothfarm@gmail.com

Diocesan Presidents/Contacts: Province VI

Colorado—Samar Fay *Contact E-mail:* samar.fay@gmail.com

Iowa—no contact

Minnesota—LaDonna Boyd *Contact E-mail:* ladonnaboyd@gmail.com

Montana—no contact

Nebraska—Cynthia Dennis *Co-Convener E-mail:* cynden1954@aol.com; Verneda J Kelly *Co-Convener E-mail:* moverneda@gmail.com

North Dakota—no contact

South Dakota—Stephanie Bolman-Altamirano *Pres E-mail:* stephaniebolman@gmail.com

Wyoming—Shirley Wildman *Pres E-mail:* skobielusz@yahoo.com

Diocesan Presidents/Contacts: Province VII

Arkansas—Kaki Roberts *Pres E-mail:* kakir@comcast.net

Dallas— no contact

Kansas—Frances Wheeler *Pres E-mail:* frances.wheeler11@gmail.com

Northwest Texas—Carole Wolf *Pres E-mail:* cwolf3312@sbcglobal.net

Oklahoma—Sherey Sullivan *Pres E-mail:* ssullivan@coxinet.net

Rio Grande—Cindy Davis *Pres E-mail:* cynthiadavisauthor@gmail.com

Texas—no contact

West Missouri—Judy Turner *Pres E-mail:* jannet@cableone.net

West Texas—Linda Hollingsworth *Pres E-mail:* linda1352@hotmail.com

Western Kansas—no contact

Western Louisiana—Shetwan Roberison *Pres E-mail:* sroberison@gmail.com

Diocesan Presidents/Contacts: Province VIII

Alaska—Pearl Chanar *Contact E-mail:* pdchanar@gci.net

Arizona—Winifred Follett *Contact E-mail:* winnieandcj@gmail.com

California—no contact

Eastern Oregon—c/o Episcopal Diocese of Eastern Oregon *E-mail:* diocese@episdioeo.org.

El Camino Real—Charlene McCreight *Pres E-mail:* charlene.mccreight@gmail.com

Hawaii—Louise Aloy *Pres E-mail:* louisealoy63@gmail.com

Idaho—Lisa Brooks *Diocesan Coordinator E-mail:* lbrooks@idahodiocese.org

Los Angeles—Christine Budzowski *Pres E-mail:* Christine@Trinitywebconsulting.com

Micronesia—Archdeacon Irene Egmalis Maliaman *Diocesan Phone:* O: 1-671-649-0690

Navajoland—Margaret Benally *Pres E-Mail:* margaret.benally52@gmail.com

Nevada—Margaret Bouzek *Pres E-mail:* margaret.bouzek@gmail.com

Northern California—Sophie Carrick *Communications Coordinator E-mail:* Sophie@norcalepiscopal.org

Olympia—Daryl Storey *Contact E-mail:* daryl@isomedia.com

Oregon—Charlene McCreight *Pres E-mail:* charlene.mccreight@gmail.com

San Diego—Sandy Bedard *Contact E-mail:* sandybedard@yahoo.com

San Joaquin—The Rev Angela Lerena *Dioc Adm E-mail:* dioadmin@diosanjoaquin.org

Spokane—Evita Krislock *Convener E-mail:* evita@krislock.com

Taiwan—Taiwan Episcopal Church 台灣聖公會 *Contact E-mail:* dioceseoftaiwan@episcopalchurch.org.tw

Utah—Linda Garner *Contact E-mail:* mydietcoke@comcast.net

Diocesan Presidents/Contacts: Province IX
Diocesis en la Nueva Provincia
Diocesis de Colombia—no contact

Diocesis de Ecuador Central—no contact

Diocesis de Ecuador Litoral—Elizabeth Calderón *Pres E-mail:* elicalsa_24@hotmail.com

Diocesis de Honduras—no contact

Diocesis de la Republica Dominicana—Amanda De la Cruz *Pres E-mail:* amandacruzy@gmail.com

Diocesis de Venezuela—Coromoto Jimenez *Pres E-mail:* pragcjimenez04@gmail.com.

CLERGY INCREASE
Church Scholarship Society, The
Aids candidates for Holy Orders who are accountable to Bp of CT. *Pres* Rt Rev Jeffrey William Mello The Episcopal Church in CT 290 Pratt Street Box 52 Meriden CT 06450.

Society for the Increase of the Ministry (SIM)
A national leadership development organization that has, since 1857, identified and funded Postulants and Candidates and other theology students for Holy Orders and other orders of ministry in the Episcopal Church. Inquiries to: Society for the Increase of the Ministry, 815 Second Avenue, Ste. 314, New York, NY 10017, (212) 661-4270. *Exec Dir* Dr. Courtney V. Cowart. *E-mail:* info@simministry.org. *Web:* simministry.org *Facebook:* https://www.facebook.com/SocietyfortheIncreaseoftheMinistry/

SUPPORT SYSTEMS FOR DEACONS
Association for Episcopal Deacons
AED supports the Episcopal diaconate in a variety of ways, such as: offering assistance to diocesan diaconal programs, maintaining a clearinghouse for diaconal ministry and formation best practices, gathering deacons and others involved in diaconal ministry for regular resource-sharing and network-ing, convening affinity groups, and advocating throughout TEC for resources to empower the call to diakonia of all believers. *Website:* www.episcopaldeacons.org. *Contact:* AED's Executive Director and/or President; *E-mail:* director@episcopaldeacons.org or president@episcopaldeacons.org.

Fund for the Diaconate of the Episcopal Church, The
Provides grants for deacons, or persons in formation to become a deacon (and not a priest), who are in financial need. *Pres* The Rev W Keith McCoy *E-mail:* president@fundfordiaconate.org *Web:* www.fundfordiaconate.org. 99 Wall Street #2815 New York, NY 10005 (800) 281-5421

DEVOTIONAL ORGANIZATIONS
Anglican Fellowship of Prayer
International prayer ministry founded in 1958. Our mission: To serve the church by encouraging, facilitating, and promoting the understanding and discipline of prayer in the Anglican Communion. We especially emphasize the value of small group prayer and the parish as a center of prayer. See our website www.afp.org. *Pres* The Rev Dr John R Throop *E-mail:* frjohn@stpetersfalls.org *Web:* www.afp.org.

Brotherhood of St. Andrew
Established in 1883, the Brotherhood of St. Andrew is the official Men's Ministry of the Episcopal Church and Anglican communities. Through their tenants of prayer, study and service their outreach is to men and youth in the church via seven ministries: Scouting, restorative justice (prison reform), veterans affairs, discipleship/mentoring, racial reconciliation, human trafficking and recovery (alcohol, pornography and drugs). Organizational material, newsletters and ministry information is found at www.brothersandrew.net. *Exec Dir* Tom Welch *Office:* 620 South Third Street Louisville KY 40202 *E-mail:* tom.welch@brothersandrew.net *Phone:* 502-450-5640.

Contemplative Outreach, Ltd
An ecumenical spiritual network committed to renewing the contemplative dimension of the Gospel through the practice of Centering Prayer. *Admin* Mary Jane Yates. *E-mail:* office@coutreach.org. *Web:* www.contemplativeoutreach.org.

The Episcopal Community
We are a community of Episcopal women committed to living out our Baptismal Covenant as we nurture and support each other's spiritual journeys. Using the Rule of Benedict as our guide, we develop and follow a personal Rule of Life. While supporting our clergy, our parishes, and The Episcopal Church with our prayers and service, we also provide instruction and mentoring in spiritual disciplines that foster spiritual growth and transformation. *National Pres* Patti Joy Posan *National Office* Box 242, Sewanee TN 37375 *Web:* www.theepiscopalcommunity.org.

Evelyn Underhill Association, Ltd
Established in the US in 1990 to honor the legacy of Anglican spiritual writer Evelyn Underhill, offering an online newsletter and Annual Quiet Day in June at Washington National Cathedral. *Contact:* Kathleen Staudt or Merrill Carrington. *E-mail:* evelynunderhill@gmail.com *Web:* www. evelynunderhill.org.

Fellowship of Contemplative Prayer
Founded in 1949 in England. Members follow a simple Rule stressing daily contemplation of the Word of God and an annual retreat. Clergy and laity. Milo G Coerper 7315 Brookville Rd Chevy Chase MD 20815 (301) 652-8635 *E-mail:* wmcoerp@ verizon.net.

Guild of All Souls
The Guild of All Souls is a prayer guild of people who promise to pray for the sick and departed by name, prayer and an annual Requiem Mass being our only work. Contact: Canon Barry Swain, rector@ resurrectionnyc.org, Website: guildofallsouls.net

Guild of the Living Rosary
Guild of intercessors who use the traditional rosary. The Rev David M Baumann PO Box 303 Salem IL 62881 *E-mail:* guildlivingrosary@gmail.com *Facebook:* facebook.com/guildlivingrosary.

Order of the Thousandfold
Develops Christian spiritual resources by encouraging daily use of The Thousandfold Prayer. Prayer and tracts in 22 languages. *Dir* Rev DA Puckett PO Box 276 Graniteville SC 29829 *E-mail:* dap@gforcecable.com.

Society of King Charles the Martyr (SKCM)
Promotes devotion to King Charles I and his martyrdom in defense of the Catholic faith in the Church of England and encourages commemorations of the anniversary of his martyrdom and other Caroline observances; open to all Christians. *Contact: Pres* The Rev Dr Steven Rice; *E-mail:* membership@ skcm-usa.org *Web:* www.skcm-usa.org.

Society of Mary
A devotional society within the Anglican Communion promoting the honor due the Blessed Virgin Mary. *Sup* The Rev John D Alexander *Sec* Dr Paul Cooper 415 Pennington-Titusville Rd Titusville, NJ 08560-2012 *Membership Adm* Lynne V Walker PO Box 930 Lorton VA 22079 *Web:* www. somamerica.org.

Society of the Companions of the Holy Cross, Potomac River Chapter
Intentional community of women devoted to intercession, thanksgiving, and simplicity and spiritual growth, offering monthly local gatherings and summer conferences and retreats at Adelynrood retreat center. *Local contact* The Rev Sarah Motley Fischer, Associate Companion in Charge *E-mail:* sarahmotleyfischer@gmail.com; *Web:* schccompanions.org.

PRAYER BOOK SOCIETIES

Bible and Common PB Soc of Episc Ch
Society for donation of Bibles, PB's, and Hymnals on request with bishop's endorsement. *Pres* Stephen Storen *Sec* Neva Rae Fox *Mgr* Rev Dr David G Henritzy 247 Broad St Red Bank NJ 07701 (732) 842-2743 *E-mail:* biblesandprayerbooks@gmail.com.

Bishop White PB Society
Donates Prayer Books and Hymnals on Bishop's endorsement. *Sec* Rev Mark J Ainsworth c/o All Hallows Church 262 Bent Rd Wyncote PA 19095 (215) 885-1641 *E-mail:* mainsworth@ allhallowswyncote.org.

Margaret Coffin PB Society
Provides free Prayer Books and Hymnals on request with Bishop's endorsement. Given to parishes, missions, and institutions at home and abroad, unable to purchase them. Rev Marshall W Hunt PO Box 1205 E Harwich MA 02645 (508) 432-2612.

GENERAL ORGANIZATIONS

African American Episcopal Historical Collection (AAEHC)
A joint project of Virginia Theological Seminary and the Historical Society of the Episcopal Church, the AAEHC gathers and preserves letters, journals, records, photographs, minutes, family histories, sermons, personal writing, conference materials, resumes, oral histories, and similar materials from African American individuals, organizations, and others working with African Americans in the Episcopal Church. *Web:* vts.edu/bishop-payne-library/aaehc/ *E-mail:* AskAAEHC@vts.edu.

Alcuin Club
Promotes study of liturgy and worship of the Christian Church by publishing works of scholarship. Members receive two "Liturgical Studies" and a major book *Collection* annually for their dues (US $44 with optional air mail surcharge of US $10)—with occasional disc on other books. For information and membership contact John Collins 5 Saffron St Royston Herts SG8 9TR UK +44 (0) 1763-248676 *E-mail:* alcuinclub@gmail.com *Web:* www.alcuinclub.org.uk.

American Anglican Council
The American Anglican Council is a network of individuals (laity, deacons, priests and bishops), parishes and specialized ministries who affirm biblical authority and Christian orthodoxy within the Anglican Communion and who are working to build up and defend Great Commission Anglican churches in North America and worldwide. *Chairman of the Board* The Rt Rev David C Anderson; *Pres/CEO* The Rev Cn Phil Ashey; *Dir of Human Res* Mary Orr; *Dir of Comm* Robert Lundy; *Admin Asst* Nina Brown-Perry PO Box 2868

Loganville GA 30052 (800) 914-2000 *Fax:* (770) 414-1518 *E-mail:* info@americananglican.org *Web:* www.americananglican.org.

American Bible Society

American Bible Society distributes the Holy Scriptures without doctrinal note or comment. American Bible Society 101 N Independence Mall East, FL 8, Philadelphia, PA 19106-2155 *Web:* www.americanbible.org.

American Friends of the Episcopal Diocese of Jerusalem, The

AFEDJ transforms lives of the vulnerable and displaced in the Middle East through support of the schools, hospitals and centers for children with disabilities that are owned and operated by the Episcopal Diocese of Jerusalem. These institutions are in Palestine, Israel, Jordan, Lebanon and Syria. AFEDJ is an independent, non-political non-profit. Executive Director: John Lent. Email: jlent@afedj.org. Web: www.afedj.org.

Anglican Frontier Missions

Partnering with members of the worldwide Anglican Communion and other Christians who live near or among unreached peoples, the vision of AFM is to plant biblically based, indigenous churches where the church is not, among the 6,000+ unreached people groups still waiting to hear the Gospel. *Dir* The Rev Dr Christopher Royer *E-mail:* info@afm-us.org *Web:* www.anglicanfrontiers.com.

Anglican Musicians, Association of

A nonprofit organization of musicians and clergy serving the Episcopal Church and the larger Anglican tradition that seeks to promote excellence in church music by working with clergy, commissions on liturgy and music, composers, and seminaries, and by endowing the Gerre Hancock Fellowship for organ scholars, hosting an annual conference, and publishing a professional journal. *Pres* Sonya Subbayya Sutton; *Exec Dir* Patrick Fennig; *E-mail:* office@anglicanmusicians.org; *Web:* www.anglicanmusicians.org.

Anglican Society

To promote and maintain Catholic faith and practice in accordance with the principles of the BCP, to explore and affirm Anglican identity and self-understanding. Rev JR Wright 177 9th Ave Apt 2-H NY NY 10011-4977 *E-mail:* wright@gts.edu *Web:* www.anglicansociety.org.

Anglican Women's Empowerment (AWE)

AWE seeks to be an effective and empowered voice for Anglican Women at the United Nations and throughout the Anglican Communion, with particular focus on the UN Commission on the Status of Women committed to worldwide reconciliation, right relationships and shared work for peace and justice through empowerment and education around global issues through the Beijing Platform for Action, the Millennium Development Goals, and working as appropriate for equal representation of women in the Anglican Consultative Council. *Web:* anglicanwomensempowerment.org.

Anglicans for Life

AFL is the only global Anglican/Episcopal ministry that educates, equips, and engages the Church in fulfilling Scripture's mandate to honor, protect, defend and celebrate every human life, through local Life Chapters and published resources for ministry, including adult education curriculums Project Life & Embrace the Journey and youth curriculum Abundant Life: You Were Made for More. *Pres* The Rev Georgette Forney *E-mail:* info@anglicansforlife.org *Web:* www.anglicansforlife.org.

Assembly of Episcopal Healthcare Chaplains

Professional organization of Epis. chaplains and healthcare institutions. Fosters and promotes advocacy, communication and education for chaplaincy. An affiliate of the Joint Commission on the Accreditation of Healthcare Organizations (JCAHO) and the Coalition on Ministry in Specialized Settings (COMISS). For information on ecclesiastical endorsement for AAPC, ACPE or APC call (800) 334-7626 x6068 Rev Margaret Rose. *Pres* Rev S Black *E-mail:* sheryl.black@SIH.net; *Pres-Elect* Rev D Fleenor *E-mail:* dfleenor@gmail.com; *Comm Officer* Rev R Waff Mail: 78 Hillcrest Drive, Weaverville, NC 28787 *E-mail:* RazzW@aol.com *Web:* www.episcopalchaplain.org.

Associated Parishes for Liturgy and Mission (APLM)

Network of Anglicans in North America who promote renewal of liturgy and mission in Episcopal Church and Anglican Church of Canada through education and formation, advocacy, development of resources and cooperation with renewal efforts in other churches. *Mail* 3405 Alman Dr Durham NC 27705 *E-mail:* info@associatedparishes.org *Web:* www.associatedparishes.org.

Bible Reading Fellowship

Produces and distributes daily Bible reading materials and various other resources for church growth. *Pres* Trip Tucker Box 380 Winter Park FL 32790-0380 (407) 628-4330 *E-mail:* brf@biblereading.org *Web:* www.biblereading.org.

Bishops' Executive Secretaries Together—BEST

B+E+S+T empowers our members through networking and education to value our ministry and to support the ministry of our bishops and the wider church. Meets annually. *Pres* Michele King *Email:* michele.king@edfw.org *Web:* www.bestatwork.weebly.com.

Church Periodical Club

Founded in 1888, CPC is dedicated solely to providing free literature and related materials, both religious and secular, through grants requested by member churches and organizations of the Anglican Communion, for people all over the world who need and request them. *Web:* https://churchperiodical.com.

CODE

The Conference of Diocesan Executives was founded in 1963. Membership is open to lay and ordained people who report to Diocesan Bishops while serving on a Bishop's staff. Key is building relationships and sharing experiences. Facilitates collegiality, confidence, and support. Helps members to find healthy solutions to challenges and to build up the body of Christ. Holds annual conference offering best in speakers, seminars and workshops on a wide-ranging variety of topics. Fun is an integral part of CODE Conference experience. *Pres* Jessica Reynolds *E-mail:* jessica@wyomingdiocese.org *VP* Kathy Richey *E-mail:* krichey@diocesewla.org *Treas* Esslie W. Hughes *E-mail:* ehughes@dioceseny.org *Sec* Vanessa Butler *E-mail:* vbutler@dionwwpa.org *Reg* Alexander Graham *E-mail:* acgraham@episcopalhawaii.org *Web:* http://codeepiscopal.org/ *Facebook:* https://www.facebook.com/groups/625497357532880/.

Companions in Mission for Publishing and Communication

Granting agency for miss-related publication projects of the Church. *Pres* Rt Rev Ian T Douglas *E-mail:* CMPC@schrull.us.

Conference of Anglican Religious Orders in the Americas

Association of officially recognized religious orders who live in community under vows; coordinates interest and experience of members, provides opportunities for mutual support, and presents a coherent understanding of religious life to the Church. *Gen Sec* The Rev'd Canon David Brinton OGS *Web:* www.caroa.net.

Cursillo

Cursillo is a movement of the Episcopal Church, under the authority of the Presiding and Diocesan Bishops, whose goal is to bring the world to Christ by empowering adult Christian leaders through the use of a specific method that is taught as part of a three-day weekend. The method, a tool for evangelism, equips and encourages Christians to live out their Baptismal covenant to serve Christ. *E-mail:* admin@episcopalcursilloministry.org *Web:* http://episcopalcursilloministry.org/.

Educational Center, The

A spiritual resource center for seekers, learners and religiouvs educators. Publishers of BibleWorkbench and TeenText; lectionary based studies, discussion guides and sermon preparation. 3200 Park Rd Charlotte NC 28209 (704) 375-1161 *E-mail:* info@educationalcenter.org *Web:* www.educationalcenter.org.

Episcopal Booksellers Association Inc.

Episcopal Booksellers Association Inc. is a non-profit association of and church-owned book and gift stores serving the Episcopal church and general public. *Exec Dir* Kathryn Bissette (888) 589-8020 X101 *E-mail:* director@episcopalbooksellers.org. For listing of nationwide member stores and vendors see www.episcopalbooksellers.org / www.episcopalbooksellers.net.

Episcopal Camps and Conference Centers, Inc

A national network within the Episcopal Church, ECCC links diocesan-related camp and conference center facilities together providing educational services, newsletters and professional support. ECCC sponsors an Annual Conference for executive directors, senior staff and board members. Consultative services focusing on executive search, strategic planning, business plans and board development etc. are also available. For information contact *Director* Bill Slocumb (760) 445-6774 *E-mail:* staff@episcopalccc.org *Web:* www.episcopalccc.org.

Episcopal Church and Visual Arts (ECVA)

Episcopal Church and Visual Arts (ECVA) is a virtual organization that curates visual arts exhibitions online and networks artists and organizations around the country. ECVA assists dioceses and churches in integrating the visual arts into congregational ministry, liturgy, and mission programs. *E-mail:* ecvaexhibitions@ecva.org *Web:* www.ecva.org.

Episcopal Church Foundation (ECF), The

Founded in 1949, The Episcopal Church Foundation is an independent, lay-led and inclusive organization that helps build, vitalize, and transform Episcopal faith communities focusing on formation, finance, and resources. Our purpose is to be a catalyst, agent, and advocate for transformation, renewal, and growth in the Episcopal Church in practical, innovative, and spiritually grounded ways. *Pres* Donald V Romanik *E-mail:* ecf@ecf.org *Web:* www.ecf.org.

Episcopal Communicators

A self-supporting organization of persons with communications responsibilities in the Episcopal Church, whose mission is to foster a community that inspires and supports excellence in church communications. *Chair* Natalee Hill (Class of 2023) *Email:* administrator@episcopalcommunicators.org *Web:* www.episcopalcommunicators.org.

Episcopal Evangelism Society (EES)

Awards grants to Episcopalians in seminaries or local formation programs, for projects of innovative evangelism. *Exec Dir* Day Smith Pritchartt *E-mail:* office@ees1862.org *Web:* www.ees1862.org.

Episcopal Health Ministries

Episcopal Health Ministries (EHM) is a network that promotes health ministry (including parish nursing) in Episcopal congregations and provides health ministry resources to local congs, dioceses and provinces; collaborates with other faith communities, institutions and health orgs; offers education for Episcopal health ministry and parish nursing; and supports those engaged in cong health min. For information see www.EpiscopalHealthMinistries. org 9120 Fredrick Rd Ellicott City MD 21042 *E-mail:* NEHM@episcopalhealthministries.org.

Episcopal Network for Stewardship, The (TENS)

The Episcopal Network for Stewardship is a family of congregations, dioceses, and members who promote, educate, and inspire generosity across The Episcopal Church and the Anglican Church of Canada. Our adaptable, customizable annual pledge campaign has been used by thousands of congregations to help members make their best gifts. In addition to offering the best stewardship campaign resources, TENS hosts webinars, trainings, and conferences to bring faithful people together to learn and share best practices of faith-based fundraising and gathers a robust library of resources to inspire generosity and gratitude. TENS is supported through prayer, diocesan and congregational memberships, and generous financial gifts. *E-mail:* tens@tens.org *Web:* www.tens.org.

Episcopal Parish Network

Episcopal Parish Network is a community of resourced parishes, cathedrals, and other institutions from across the Episcopal Church and around the country. EPN members gather for connection, peer-to-peer learning, and networking throughout the year. Each year EPN hosts the largest annual conference in the Episcopal Church with over 800 lay and clergy leaders. Additionally, EPN convenes regular digital workshops online for lay and clergy leaders on a variety of topics critical to local ministry. Membership in EPN is open to Episcopal parishes, cathedrals, and institutions. *Exec Dir* Joseph R Swimmer, Episcopal Parish Network, 1800 Upshur St NW, Washington, DC 20011; *Phone:* (415) 505-8449 *E-mail:* jswimmer@episcopalparishes.org *Web:* episcopalparishes.org.

Episcopal Peace Fellowship

A national membership organization assisting Episcopalians and others to realize and live out Christ's call for peace, justice and reconciliation; promotes prayer, study, education and action; organizes chapters and action groups around the country, and provides exposure to nonviolence and peacebuilding training. *Exec Dir* Melanie Merkle Atha *Chair* Jackie Lynn *Vice Chair* Christy Close Erskine *E-mail:* epf@epfnational.org *Web:* epfnational.org.

Episcopal Preaching Foundation, Inc

The mission and ministry of the Episcopal Preaching Foundation is to support and enhance preaching in the Episcopal Church. EPF provides educational conferences, seminars and programs, including an annual national conference for seminarians—the Preaching Excellence Program (PEP) and PEP II for clergy 3 to five years into their ministry. Diocesan preaching events are coordinated with Bishops across the US and Canada. *Chair and Founder:* Dr A Gary Shilling (973) 467-0070 *E-mail:* gary@agaryshilling.com; *Phone:* (973) 367-6014 *E-mail:* preachingfoundation@gmail.com *Web:* www.preachingfoundation.org.

Episcopal Public Policy Network (EPPN)

A grassroots network of Episcopalians dedicated to the ministry of public policy advocacy. It is supported by the Office of Government Relations, which represents the policy priorities of the Episcopal Church to the U.S. government in Washington, DC. *Staff contact:* Lindsey Warburton *E-mail:* eppn@episcopalchurch.org *Web:* http://episcopalchurch.org/ogr *Facebook, Twitter, and Instagram:* @TheEPPN.

Episcopal Women's History Project

Organization to raise awareness in the Church of the roles taken by women, highlighting their valuable contributions to the church and society. Funds support research, grants for scholarly work, use of archives, education for church historians, oral history training, and communication encouraging interest in women's history. Publishes quarterly *The Historiographer* with other Episcopal historical organizations. Conferences with speakers and workshops. *Pres* The Rev Dr Jo Ann Barker *E-mail:* joann.barker@gmail.com *Web:* www.ewhp.org.

Evangelical Fellowship in the Anglican Communion (EFAC-USA)

EFAC-USA is a gathering of Evangelicals in the Episcopal and Anglican churches for networking, prayer, Bible study, worship, and mutual encouragement in Gospel ministry, both as lay and ordained ministers of the Gospel. *Contact* The Rev Zac Neubauer *E-mail:* zac@efac-usa.org *Web:* www.efac-usa.org

Faith Alive (Faith Encouragement Ministries)

Faith Alive (Faith Encouragement Ministries) delivers church renewal programs and follow-up tools in line with the church's goals for all churches and missions, regardless of size or denomination of the church. *Contact* Sue Kay *Email:* sueowenkay@gmail.com; *Web:* http://www.faithaliveus.com

Forma

The Network for Christian Formation: We celebrate, equip, support and connect leaders who form followers of Jesus. *Eph. 4:11-16. Exec Dir* Bill Campbell *E-mail:* bill@forma.church *Web:* www.forma.church.

Forward in Faith, North America (FIFNA)

Formerly Episcopal Synod of America. Association of Episcopal and Anglican congregations, chapters, institutions, laity, religious and clergy who embrace the Gospel of Jesus Christ and uphold the Evangelical faith and Catholic order of the Church. Publication: *Forward in Christ.* Membership open to those who subscribe to the FIFNA Declaration of Common Faith and Purpose. *E-mail:* office@fifna.org *Web:* www.fifna.org.

Friends of Canterbury Cathedral in the US (FOCCUS)

A charitable, not-for-profit corporation whose mission is to provide scholarship funds for seminarians from Third World Countries to attend International Study at Canterbury Cathedral; build relationships between Episcopalians and the Cathedral; encourage involvement with Cathedral's mission; strengthen capacity of the Cathedral as retreat center, support the Cathedral's programs, preservation, and restoration. *Chair* The Very Rev Joseph H Britton *V Chairs* Eugene Johnston & Barbara Q Harper 888 17th St NW Ste 608 Washington DC 20006 (202) 822-8994 *Email:* Canterburyus@gmail.com.

Gather the Family Institute for Evangelism and Congregational Development

Provides consultants, training workshops to help congregations and dioceses learn the concepts and skills necessary to develop individualized programs for evangelism and incorporation (assimilation) min. *DMin* Rev GK Sturni PO Box 38447 Germantown TN 38183-0447 (901) 754-7282 *E-mail:* gsturni@gmail.com.

Global Episcopal Mission Network

GEMN gathers, inspires and equips dioceses, congregations, agencies, seminaries, religious orders and individuals to participate in God's global mission. *Exec Dir* Rev Dr Titus Presler *E-mail:* gemn@gemn.org *Web* www.gemn.org.

Guild of St Ives

Association of Episcopal lawyers and judges who live, work or worship in the Diocese of NY; annually observes Law Day with Choral Evensong between Law Day (May 1) and the Feast of St Ives to recognize public service by members of the legal profession on behalf of the community; presents the Servant of Justice Award in recognition of commitment to the legal profession, public service, and mission of the Church. *Phone:* (212) 316-7400

"Happening—A Christian Experience"

A diocesan renewal and evangelism program for and led by High School youth, where participants experience the wonder and love of God as shown through their peers, lay adults and clergy within a sequestered atmosphere full of interactions in both large and small groups. *Exec Dir* Krisan Lamberti

E-mail: happeninginfo@gmail.com *Web:* www.happeningnational.org.

Historical Society of the Episcopal Church

Membership organization for preservation of Episcopal heritage within the Anglican Communion founded in 1910. Fostering research, publishing *Anglican & Episcopal History* since 1932, and *The Historiographer* with other Episcopal historical organizations. *Web:* hsec.us. *Dir of Oper* Matthew P Payne *E-mail:* administration@hsec.us.

Integrity USA

A lesbian, gay, bisexual, and transgender justice ministry in and to the Episcopal Church. There are numerous chapters in 8 provinces. Annual dues start at $25. *Pres* The Rev'd Gwen Fry *E-mail:* info@integrityusa.org *Web:* www.integrityusa.org.

International Order of St Vincent

A fellowship of lay sanctuary ministers of all ages (open to all (men and women, girls and boys) acolytes, lay readers, lectors, lay eucharistic ministers, sacristans, ushers, greeters, vergers, and choristers) serving the One, Holy, Catholic, and Apostolic Church promoting liturgical knowledge, understanding of ritualistic detail and meaning, and encourage intercessory prayer and holy living among our members. Believing that we are also called to serve, we strive to instill reverence, cooperation, responsibility, discipline, mentorship, leadership, humility, quest for excellence, and joy of servanthood by emphasizing a stairway of lay ministry that leads to active adult churchmanship. The OSV is sacramentally centered and encourages living a rule of life (we pray, worship, read, and give). The OSV also publishes a wide range of illustrated liturgical manuals, teaching materials and historical tracts. *Dir Gen* Philip G Dixon, *E-mail:* Director-General@orderstvincent.org *Web:* www.orderstvincent.org.

KEEP (Kiyosato Educational Experiment Project)

American Committee for KEEP (ACK) supports Japanese lay organization since 1950 providing Christian witness of service to others through cross cultural partnerships, international exchange, outreach, and education in the areas of environmental issues, agriculture, youth, and community development. *ACK Pres* Rt Rev Stacy Sauls *E-mail:* ack@ackeep.org.

Living Church Foundation, Inc

Teaching ministry serving the Episcopal Church and Anglican Communion; publisher of *The Living Church* magazine, *Episcopal Musician's Handbook, Covenant* weblog, *The Living Word* preaching resource, and *The Living Church Podcast. Int. Exec Dir* Mark Michael, mmichael@livingchurch.org, *Web:* livingchurch.org.

National Association of Episcopal Christian Communities, The

NAECC is a coalition of Christian Communities recognized under the canons of The Episcopal Church, dedicated to sharing and communicating the fruits of the Gospel—realized in many forms of community—with the church and the world. NAECC also works with communities-in-formation throughout the Church. *Contact*: Secretary, *E-mail*: rafbsg@protonmail.com *Web*: www.naecc.net.

National Episcopal Historians and Archivists

Organization of congregational and diocesan historians and archivists to encourage collection, preservation and organization of church records and sharing of church history; publishes quarterly *The Historiographer* with other Episcopal historical organizations. *Pres pro tem* The Rev Sean Wallace *E-mail* swallace@gts.edu *Web*: episcopalhistorians.org.

North American Committee of St George's College, Jerusalem

St. George's College Jerusalem is an international community for study and pilgrimage in the Holy Land. It is located in the compound of St George's Cathedral, CA interior the seat of the Episcopal Diocese of Jerusalem. The North American Committee links together individuals who have made pilgrimage to Saint George's and works to support the ministry of the College through scholarships, public relations, education and fundraising. *Pres* The Rev James Bimbi *Exec Sec* Nancy Brockway PO Box 12073 (3737 Seminary Rd) Alexandria VA 22304 (404)-386-2924 *E-mail*: nacstgeorges@outlook.com; *Facebook*: www.facebook.com/sgcjerusalem/.

Operation Pass Along

Accepts contributions of new and used books about the church, vestments, clericals and altar fittings and passes them along, without charge, to seminarians, newly ordained priests, and deacons, newly formed parish and mission libraries and others. 805 CR 102 Eureka Springs AR 72632-9705 (800) 572-7929 *E-mail*: OperationPassAlong@anglicandigest.org.

The Order of the Daughters of the King®

An order for lay or ordained women who commit to a lifelong program of prayer, service, and evangelism, dedicated to strengthening the spiritual life of her parish and spreading Christ's Kingdom. *Natl Off*: 101 Weatherstone Dr Ste 870 Woodstock GA 30188-7007 *E-mail*: DOK1885@doknational.org *Web*: www.doknational.org.

OSL

OSL empowers God's people throughout the world with Jesus' healing ministry. *Contact*: Rev Josh Acton *E-mail*: oslnad@osltoday.org *Web*: www.osltoday.org.

Partners for Baptismal Living (PBL)

A partnership dedicated to the ministries of all the baptized in their daily lives. Formed in 2006, PBL's mission within the Episcopal Church, grounded in the Baptismal Covenant, is to recognize, affirm, and empower baptized persons in their Monday through Saturday ministries; to explore common ground and natural alliances with other Episcopal, Anglican, and ecumenical groups; to assist congregations, dioceses, provinces, and seminaries in planning and implementing educational events focused on the calling of all the baptized; and to provide a communications link among partners through our email listserv and blog, www.livinggodsmission.org. PBL is led by a steering committee of laypersons and clergy. Membership is open to all. *Contact*: Pam Tinsley *E-mail*: pbtinsley@icloud.com.

Prayer Book Society of the USA, The

Promotes Anglican doctrine, discipline and worship as expressed in the Common Prayer tradition and Anglican formularies since the first English Prayer Book of 1549, on through the 1928 Book of Common Prayer of the Episcopal Church down to the present day; it advances education in the fullness of what it means to be Episcopalian and Anglican through publications and events, an Annual Conference and Catechetical resources. *Pres* The Revd. Fr. Gavin Dunbar *Web*: www.pbsusa.org and www.anglicanway.org.

Protestant Episcopal Evangelists

Emphasizes inner-city ministries; St Paul's House trains for evangelism. *Exec Dir* Shandra Barahona *Web*: saintpaulshouse.org.

Rock the World Youth Mission Alliance

Engages, equips and empowers young Christians to advance the Kingdom of God. *Exec Dir* The Rev. Whis Hays *E-mail*: info@rocktheworld.org *Web*: www.rocktheworld.org.

SAMS—Society of Anglican Missionaries and Senders

Formerly known as the South American Missionary Society, SAMS is a society of missionaries and senders serving in partnership with the Anglican Church globally. SAMS' purpose is to raise up, send, and support Episcopal and other Anglican missionaries to be witnesses and make disciples for Jesus Christ in fellowship with the Anglican Church globally. *Pres & Dir* Stewart Wicker *E-mail*: info@sams-usa.org *Web*: www.sams-usa.org.

Seedlings Inc

Non-profit corp provides Episcopal curriculum for small churches and other unique educational materials. Sunday School lessons over 4-yr cycle, Every Member Uncanvass, Adult Inquirers, and youth confirmation curricula. *Pres* Rev Betty W Fuller (*E-mail*: seedlings@aol.com *Web*: www.seedlingsinc.com.

Society for Promoting Christian Knowledge (SPCK)

The Society for Promoting Christian Knowledge provides resources for Christian knowledge around the world. Patti Joy Posan, Executive Director. *E-mail:* spck@sewanee.edu *Web:* www.spckusa@sewanee.org

SOMA—Sharing of Ministries Abroad

SOMA USA prepares and sends short-term mission teams across national and cultural boundaries. Teams equip and train leaders to minister in the power of the Holy Spirit who renews individuals, empowers the Church, and transforms society. *Natl Dir* Dr Glen Petta SOMA 2501 Ridgmar Plaza #99 Fort Worth TX 76116 (817) 737-SOMA (7662) *E-mail:* office@somausa.org *Web:* www.somausa.org.

SPEAK

Society for Promoting and Encouraging Arts and Knowledge [of the Church]. *Act Chr Bd* The Rev Charleston David Wilson.

Union of Black Episcopalians

UBE, The Episcopal Church's largest independent advocacy and racial justice membership organization, continues its 200+ years track record of empowering Black leadership to fight racism in and outside The Episcopal Church by advocating for the inclusion of persons of African descent in the life and leadership of the Church at every level and by establishing local chapters that pursue grassroots efforts to achieve racial justice and equality for all people. *Natl Pres* The Very Rev Kim L Coleman *E-mail:* leadership@theube.org *Web:* www.ube.org.

Vergers Guild of the Episcopal Church (VGEC), The

A verger is a layperson who serves the church in a ministry of organization, service, and welcome under the direction of their Rector, Vicar, or Priest in Charge. The Vergers Guild is a source of training, support, fellowship, and mentoring for anybody in the verger ministry as well as those who are interested in starting a ministry in their own church. "The ministry of the vergers is to help to lead the church in bearing witness in the world to the hospitality of God, by helping the church to be a truly hospitable place, by helping us to worship the Lord our God in dignity, in order, in beauty, and in truth in the church so that we can go forth to witness to that God to the world." —The Most Reverend Michael B. Curry. *E-mail:* info@vergers.org *Web:* www.vergers.org.

Vocare International

A Vocare weekend allows young adults to look at God's call and what it means in all areas of life. Primarily in the 19-30 age range, participants share ideas and ways to incorporate Christianity today. *Coord* Liz Williams (404) 202-7284 *E-mail:* lizmaywilliams@gmail.com.

Washington National Cathedral

Washington National Cathedral is a church for national purposes called to embody God's love and to welcome people of all faiths and perspectives. A unique blend of the spiritual and the civic, this Episcopal Cathedral is a voice for generous spirited Christianity and a catalyst for reconciliation and interfaith dialogue to promote respect and understanding. We invite all people to share in our commitment to create a more hopeful and just world. Washington National Cathedral 3101 Wisconsin Ave NW (Massachusetts & Wisconsin Aves NW) Washington DC 20016-5098 (202) 537-6200 *Web:* www.nationalcathedral.org.

GENERAL YOUTH ORGANIZATIONS

Junior Daughters of The Order of the Daughters of the King®

Baptized young women and girls ages 7-21 who make a promise of daily Prayer and Service, which provides a special opportunity for them to grow in their Christian faith and commitment. *Natl Off* 101 Weatherstone Dr #870 Woodstock GA 30188-7003 *E-mail:* DOK1885@doknational.org *Web:* www.doknational.org

GFS/USA—Girls' Friendly Society, USA

International, not-for-profit, faith-based organization affiliated with the Episcopal Church for girls and young women 5-21 with a purpose to provide girls and women with a support system aimed at developing the whole person. *E-mail:* deloresalleyne@aol.com or gfspresident@gmail.com *Facebook:* https://www.facebook.com/gfsusa/info *Web:* www.gfsus.org.

RELIGIOUS ORDERS AND COMMUNITIES

Editor's Note: Beginning with the 2002 Edition of *The Episcopal Church Annual,* only those religious orders and communities officially recognized by the Standing Committee on Religious Communities of the House of Bishops are listed in *The Annual.* For information about applying for official status, please contact The Rt Rev Jeffrey D Lee *Chair,* House of Bishops Committee on Religious Communities.

Traditional Orders

FOR MEN

Brothers of Saint John the Evangelist (OSB)

Contemplative semi-monastic religious community within the Order of S Benedict, clergy and lay, living a life of prayer, personal growth, and service to the Church. Emphasis as a monastic community is on the traditional worship, music and arts of the Church Our Fellowship includes Oblates and Associates, with some residing at the Monastery and others as Externs. *Superior* Br David McClellan EFSJ *Prior & Oblate Director* Br Richard Tussey EFSJ Tanglewood Hill Monastery PO Box 782 Freeland WA 98249 *E-mail:* efsj@whidbey.com

Order of St Benedict, The
Comm of monks in Episcopal Church living Benedictine rule. *Abbot* Rt Rev A Marr OSB S Gregory's
Abbey 56500 Abbey Rd Three Rivers MI 49093-9595
(269) 244-5893 *E-mail:* abbot@saintgregorysthree-
rivers.org *Web:* www.saintgregorysthreerivers.org.

Order of the Holy Cross, The
A Benedictine monastic community for clergy and
laymen. Superior Br Robert James Magliula, OHC.
Holy Cross Monastery Box 99 West Park NY 12493
(845) 384-6660 x3006 Fax: (845) 384-6031. E-mail:
superior@hcmnet.org. Holy Cross Priory 204 High
Park Ave Toronto M6P 2S6 Ontario CANADA
(416) 767-9081. St. Benedict's Priory PostNet
Sandbaai Suite #372 Bag x16 Hermanus South
AFRICA 7200 (011) 27 79 873-0935. Web: www.
holycrossmonastery.com

Society of St Francis
Community of men (lay and ordained) living
under the vows of poverty, chastity, and obedience.
After the example of Francis of Assisi, the brothers
engage in urban ministry, preaching, retreats, prayer
and study. Prov Headquarters, S Damiano Friary
573 Dolores San Francisco CA 94110 Web: www.
ssfamericas.org.

Society of St John the Evangelist
A Monastic Community of brothers, lay and
ordained, who live under a contemporary Rule
of Life and take vows of poverty, celibacy and
obedience. Oldest Anglican religious community
for men, founded by Richard Meux Benson at
Oxford, England in 1866. Arrived in the US in 1870.
Superior Br James Koester SSJE Monastery of St
Mary and St John and the Guesthouse 980 Memorial
Dr Cambridge MA 02138-5717 (617) 876-3037.
Brs E-mail: monastery@ssje.org *Guesthouse E-mail:*
guesthouse@ssje.org *Vocational info:* Br Lucas Hall
E-mail: vocations@ssje.org. Emery House 21 Emery
Ln West Newbury MA 01985 (617) 876-3037 *Web:*
www.ssje.org; www.catchthelife.org

Society of St Paul
Celebrating a life of prayer, personal growth, and
service to others. *Rector* Cn Barnabas Hunt SSP The
Society of St Paul 2567 Second Ave Unit 504 San
Diego CA 92103 (619) 794-2095.

FOR WOMEN
Community of the Holy Spirit
Monastic observance of the Divine Offices, biody-
namic farming, spiritual direction and social justice
ministries underscore the creative charism of the
Community of the Holy Spirit — a community
of life professed sisters, resident companions and
associates. Limited guest facilities. *Leadership:
Community Council.* St Hilda's House 92
Morningside Ave Apt 8B New York NY 10027 212-
666-8249. Bluestone Farm and Living Arts Center at
Melrose Convent 116 Federal Hill Rd Brewster NY

10509 *E-mail:* chssisters@chssisters.org *Web:* www.
chssisters.org.

Community of St Francis, The
Franciscan Sisters living a life in community of
prayer, study, and ministry with special concern for
urban poor and deprived. Associates program and
residential Companions in Franciscan Spirituality
programs available. *Min Prov* Sr Sister Pamela
Clare St Francis House 3743 Cesar Chavez St San
Francisco CA 94110 (415) 824-0288 *E-mail:* csfsfo@
aol.com *Web:* www.communitystfrancis.org.

Community of St John Baptist
A Community of prayer and service, reaching out to
God's people. Retreats, conferences, lay and ordained
ministry, outreach to the needy, spiritual direction
and other ministries. Associate, Oblate, and
Alongsider affiliations for lay and clergy. Mission to
orphans in Cameroon. St Marguerite's Retreat House
open to groups. Convent of St John Baptist Box 240
82 W Main St Mendham NJ 07945 (973) 543-4641
Fax: (973) 543-0327 *E-mail:* superior@csjb.org *Web:*
www.csjb.org.

Community of St Mary (CSM)
Benedictine Community for women with special
dedication to St. Mary expressed through care for the
body, the soul, and the earth - offering retreats, spiritual direction, and private guest accommodations. In
addition to daily worship and special events, we invite
others to connect with the Community as Associates,
Oblates, and through our Organic Prayer Program
internships. *Prioress:* Sr. Hannah, CSM, St Mary's
Convent 1100 St Mary's Ln Sewanee TN 37375-
2614 *Phone:* (931) 598-0046 *Email:* sisterhoodofst-
mary@gmail.com *Web:* communityofstmarysouth.
org *Branch House:* St. Mary's Convent Sagada, Mountain Province, Philippines.

Community of the Teachers of the Children of God, The
Originally founded in 1934 as a traditionally
monastic order for women, now a Community of
both women and men, whose mission is to continue
to support educational organizations to educate
children of all abilities. Consisting of two professed
nuns, who continue to the live the religious life, and
lay members, the Community is dedicated to the
education work of the Episcopal Church and offers
through the *Rule of the Associates* the opportunity
for religious instruction and spiritual development.
Contact: Nannette Akins Associate CTCG 5790
E. 14th Street Tucson, AZ 85711 (520) 591-4178.
E-mail: nannetteak@aol.com.

Community of the Transfiguration
Prayer, worship, hospitality and retreats, educational
and recreational ministry with children. Sup Sr Jean
Gabriel CT Convent of the Transfiguration 495
Albion Ave Cincinnati OH 45246 *E-mail:* inquire@
ctsisters.org *Web:* www.ctsisters.org (513) 771-5291
Fax: (513) 771-0839 Local Ministries: Transfiguration

Spirituality Ctr *Web:*~www.CTRetreats.org. *E-mail:* ctretreats@gmail.com; Bethany Sch: (513) 771-7462 *Web:* www.bethanyschool.org; S Monica's Rec Ctr *E-mail:* mpearl121@gmail.com; Branch Ministry, hospitality and retreats: Tabor Ministry Butler OH 44822 *E-mail:* hilaritas@aol.com. *Feeding ministry:* Food for the Soul *Web:* foodforthesoulct.org.

Episcopal Carmel of Saint Teresa

Semi-enclosed, monastic, contemplative, Carmelite community for women in the tradition of Teresa of Avila and John of the Cross. The community also includes vowed Apostolic Members. Associates are Christian men and women. Life of prayer, silence and solitude lived within community 2525 Pot Spring Rd Unit S 523 Lutherville-Timonium MD 21093 *E-mail:* STIPerk@gmail.com.

Order of Julian of Norwich

Monastic, enclosed, Benedictine contemplative community for women, both lay and clergy, following the spirituality of Dame Julian. Associate and Oblate affiliations for men and women, laity and clergy. Guest accommodations and spiritual direction available. *Guardian* Mthr Hilary OJN Our Lady of the Northwoods Monastery W704 Alft Road White Lake WI 54491-9715 *Phone:* (715) 882-2377 *E-mail:* ojn@orderofjulian.org *Web:* www.orderofjulian.org.

Order of St Anne—Bethany

A religious community for women and a ministry of hospitality and community service within the Bethany Convent and Bethany House of Prayer. Sr Ana Clara OSA *Superior* 25 Hillside Ave Arlington MA 02476 (781) 643-0921 *E-mail:* bethanyconvent@aol.com.

Order of St Anne—Chicago

The Order of St Anne's Chicago is a traditional order of Anglican nuns in the Episcopal Church. Since 1921, we have been an active presence in the heart of the city of Chicago. Currently we are called to parish work at the Episcopal Church of the Ascension, and active ministry to the local community. Sr Judith Marie OSA Superior 1125 N LaSalle Blvd Chicago IL 60610 (312) 642-3638 *E-mail:* stannechicago@hotmail.com.

Order of St Helena

A religious community for lay and ordained women dedicated to prayer, hospitality and service. Living under a vow of monastic poverty, celibate chastity, and obedience to God, we discern new ways to interpret traditional monasticism. *Community Leader* The Rev Sr Miriam Elizabeth, OSH Order of St Helena 414 Savannah Barony Dr North Augusta SC 29841 *E-mail:* sisters@osh.org *Web:* www.osh.org.

Sisterhood of the Holy Nativity

Special dedication to the Incarnation. Religious Order with strong emphasis on life of prayer in community. External ministries are evangelistic in nature and take many forms. Mother House W14164 Plante Dr Ripon WI 54971 (920) 748-5332 *Mother Sup* Sr Abigail *E-mail:* abizac50@hotmail.com *Web:* caroa.net/sites/sisterhoodhn/.

Society of St Margaret

The Society of St Margaret is an Episcopal Religious Order of mission-focused sisters living an ancient tradition with a modern outlook. We were founded in 1855 in East Grinstead, England, by The Rev John Mason Neale. The American House was established in Boston in 1873. Our lives as Sisters are guided by the principle, "Love first, Love midst, Love last." We take vows of poverty, celibate chastity, and obedience; listening for the voice of God in all circumstances. Our mission of hospitality calls us to welcome people to our houses for times of refreshment and renewal. Our mission of service calls us to move out beyond our dwelling places to serve those in need, to go where God leads and to share Christ's light. The central work of the community is worship and prayer, and the Eucharist provides the pattern for our daily lives. As Jesus took bread, blessed, and broke it, so our lives are taken, blessed, broken, and given through our varied ministries. As we work with children, care for the elderly, and do parish work, we seek always to live as Christ's hands and heart in this world. Sr Kristina Frances SSM Superior; St Margaret's Convent PO Box C (50 Harden Hill Rd) Duxbury MA 02331 *Phone:* (781) 934-9477 *E-mail:* sisters@ssmbos.org *Web:* www.ssmbos.org. *Dependencies:* St Margaret's Convent Port-au-Prince HAITI; Sisters of St Margaret, Lower Manhattan NYC.

OTHER CHRISTIAN COMMUNITIES

Anamchara Fellowship

Founded in 2003, Anamchara Fellowship is a dispersed community, open to men and women: single, married and partnered. Dedicated to the Holy Trinity, members use "Celtic Daily Prayer" as part of their daily round of prayer. Members take vows of Simplicity, Fidelity and Obedience and must be approved by their ecclesial authority where they live in order to become part of the Fellowship. Our focus of ministry is pastoral care, catechesis and spiritual direction and we seek to provide these to our parishes and dioceses from which we come. We seek to be guided by our charisms of generosity, hospitality, compassion and love; and the inspiration of the Celtic saints. As a form of the "New Monasticism," Anamchara Fellowship seeks to bridge the gap between the traditional spirit of monastic community and the spirit of the emerging church. For further information view our website: www.anamcharafellowship.org or contact: Brother John Brendan at brjohnbrendan@gmail.com

Anglican Order of Preachers

The Anglican Order of Preachers (also known as the Dominicans) traces its heritage back to Saint

Dominic de Guzman in the thirteen century. The Order is a worldwide, dispersed committed to the proclamation of the Gospel of Jesus Christ, especially through preaching and teaching, as well as other mediums; including, but not limited to scholarship, writing, the arts, and social justice witness. Anglican Dominicans may be celibate or married, lay or ordained, male or female. They take vows of simplicity, purity, and obedience. You can learn more about the Order at http://www.anglicandominicans.com/

Brotherhood of St. Gregory

Open to Anglican men, clergy and lay, without regard to marital status, living under a common Rule and serving the Church on parochial, diocesan and national levels. The brothers live individually, in small groups, or with their families, and support the Community's activities from their secular or church-related employment. Inquiries? Please visit our website: www.gregorians.org.

Community of Celebration

Residential community of men/women, lay/clergy, married/single shares common life under a rule of life and undergirded by Daily Prayer Book Offices, weekly Eucharist.   Members take Benedictine vows of stability, obedience, and conversion of life. Ministry is to be a Christian presence among the poor, to offer hospitality, retreats, sabbaticals, and conferences. Companion relationships welcome. Bill Farra Guardian Box 309 Aliquippa PA 15001 (724) 375-1510. *E-mail:* mail@communityofcelebration.com *Web:* www.communityofcelebration.com.

Community of the Gospel

Founded in 2007, the Community of the Gospel's members express their baptismal vows through daily prayer, reflective study, and service to others. The community is comprised of men and women, single and married, lay and ordained. At the close of 2022 there were twenty-one professed members plus two novices and postulants from across the United States and the Bahamas. An additional group of about 25 "Friends of the CG" accompany and support the community with prayer, finances, and occasional service. They participate in the CG's robust calendar of virtual worship and study events, including prayer vigils around issues of societal concern; Bible study; and exploration of monastic history. The rule of the community is "A Common Rule for Monastics of the Community of the Gospel." The official CG prayer book is the Book of Common Prayer but members are encouraged to draw on resources from diverse faith traditions to nurture their spiritual lives. The CG welcomes like-minded baptized Christians from non-Anglican backgrounds as both members and Friends of the CG. All members and Friends are encouraged to engage deeply in parish and diocesan life. For additional information please visit our website: http://www.communityofthegospel.org/. Inquiries may be sent to the Guardian, Br.

Daniel-Joseph Schroeder, CG, N4028 Morgan Dr Waupaca WI 54981 *E-mail:* brdanjoe@gmail.com *Phone:* (920) 475-8525. he CG Chaplain is the Rev. Canon David Caffrey, of Joshua Tree, California. The CG Bishop Visitor is the Rt. Rev. Megan Traquair of the Diocese of Northern California.

Order of the Ascension

The Order of the Ascension is a dispersed community open to both clergy and laity whose vocations provide opportunities to shape parish life. OA has helped ground and center its members in their daily life and their roles as parish leaders and developers since its founding in 1983. Members take a Promise to seek the presence of Jesus Christ in the people, things, and circumstances of life through stability, obedience and conversion of life. The charism of OA is the development of parish churches grounded in Anglican pastoral and ascetical theology, especially Benedictine spirituality. We also draw on the fields of organization development and organizational psychology in our work, which includes published materials to support parish development. New members engage a multi-year formation process after the first taking of the Promise. For more information, visit http://www.orderoftheascension.org/ or contact the *Presiding Sister* directly: Michelle Heyne, OA *E-mail:* michelleheyne@gmail.com; *Episcopal Visitor:* The Rt. Rev. Barry Howe.

Order of the Community of the Paraclete

Serving since 1971. The Paracletians are men and women, single or married, leading a life of prayer and ministry under a rule and vows. Our work is to bring wholeness to those who need healing in spirit, mind, and body, through the power of the Holy Spirit. Our work is done in three states: AZ, FL, and WA. *Contact:* Min Br Marvin D. Taylor, St Dunstan's Church 722 N 145th St Shoreline WA 98133 *Web:* www.theparacletians.org. *Bishop Visitor:* Bavi Rivera.

Companions of St Luke, OSB

Companions of St Luke OSB is a community founded on the Rule of St Benedict. The Community honors the richness of its tradition, yet knows that each age needs to bring innovation to its history and practice. CSL-OSB is a dispersed community with each member living the Benedictine experience within the context of our parishes and the world. The members of the community live into the Rule of St. Benedict with daily prayer, Lectio Divina, contemplation, study of scripture and the Rule. The Companions of St. Luke, OSB is open to single and partnered persons, lay or ordained. Vocations include Vowed life and Oblation with respective vows and promises made of obedience, *conversatio morum suorum* (fidelity to monastic life), and stability. *E-mail:* csl91.membership@gmail.com *Web:* http://www.csl-osb.org/. *Superior:* Br. David Gerns, OSB. *Bishop Visitor:* The Right Reverend Alan Scarfe.

Congregation of the Companions of the Holy Savior (CCHS)

A community of bishops, priests and deacons, both married and single, both male and female. Founded 1891. Committed to the Sacramental Life of the Episcopal Church and Daily Office in the context of the parish setting. Common Rule; but does not live in community. All attend annual Chapter and retreat. Rule for lay associates, monthly area conferences. *Contact:* Fr Justin A Falciani, CCHS, Father Master, Christ Episcopal Church Box 97, 157 Shore Rd Somers Point NJ 08244 (609) 927-6262. *E-mail:* ccsprector@Verizon.net. *Episcopal Visitor:* The Rt. Rev. William Stokes, Bishop of New Jersey

The Little Sisters of St. Clare, A Franciscan Women's Community

The Little Sisters of St. Clare is a community open to women throughout the Episcopal Church. We guide our lives by the vows of simplicity, fidelity, and purity. Women who seek to live a contemplative life of prayer, study, and service, following St. Clare and St. Francis, are welcome to explore community life with us. We live independently and are single, married, and in committed relationships. As a community, we express our response to God's call in a lifestyle which interprets monastic traditions in a contemporary way. Our beliefs are seen in our actions, in worship, and in our commitment to a common life. We live community life through daily prayer services and monthly formation gatherings online. We serve in a variety of ministries – guiding children and youth; serving the poor, the ill, and the marginalized; nurturing the environment, and healing others. Inquiries Email: lsscmotherguardian@gmail.com or online http://stclarelittlesisters.org. Mother Guardian: Sister Kathryn-Mary Little, LSSC. Bishop Visitor: The Rt. Rev. Diana Akiyama, Bishop of Oregon

Order of the Ascension

The Order of the Ascension is a dispersed community open to both clergy and laity whose vocations provide opportunities to shape parish life. OA has helped ground and center its members in their daily life and their roles as parish leaders and developers since its founding in 1983. Members take a Promise to seek the presence of Jesus Christ in the people, things and circumstances of life through stability, obedience and conversion of life. The charism of OA is the development of parish churches grounded in Anglican pastoral and ascetical theology, especially Benedictine spirituality. We also draw on the fields of organization development and organizational psychology in our work, which includes published materials to support parish development. New members engage a multi-year formation process after the first taking of the Promise. For more information, visit http://www.orderoftheascension. org/ or contact the *Presiding Sister* directly: Michelle Heyne, OA, michelleheyne@gmail.com. *Episcopal Visitor:* The Rt. Rev. Barry Howe.

Order of Saint Anthony the Great

A monastic community of resident and dispersed members, both men and women, who live and pray by a Rule inspired by Saint Anthony of the Desert. Our mission is to help make contemplative spirituality and community accessible to the modern world. *Address:* 5712 St Thomas Dr Lithonia GA 30058 *E-mail:* br.kenneth@gmail.com *Web:* orderofsaintanthony.org.

Rivendell Community, The

Rivendell is a Eucharistic community working and praying to renew and actualize the vision of the Church as a holy priesthood (I Peter 2:5), in and on behalf of the world. Through its Rule, members seek to live Eucharistically, in continual self-offering to God in thanksgiving, intercession and adoration. Among its central interests, the Community seeks to provide lay and ordained leadership for smaller churches and to create and serve houses of prayer and hospitality. Rivendell also supports ministries of spiritual discipleship and social justice in the communities where its members live. Members are women and men, single and married, ordained and lay. The Rivendell Community c/o Noel Schwartz, Interim Guardian, (901)-274-3106, or Martha Colville, Guardian Elect, 210 W First St #115 Mountain View MO 65548 *Phone:* (417) 247-0031 *E-mail:* rivendell-community.inc@gmail.com *Web:* https://rivendell-community.wordpress.com/ *Facebook:* https://www.facebook.com/TheRivendellCommunity

Sisters of Saint Gregory

A religious community of women in the Episcopal Church who have discerned a call to the religious life. Founded in 1987 as a companion order by the Brotherhood of St Gregory, we became autonomous in 1999. We are clergy and lay, without regard to marital status, living dispersed in the world under a common rule as women of prayer and serving the Church on parochial, diocesan, and national levels. The sisters support the community's activities by their secular or church-related employment. All women eighteen years of age and older who are discerning a vocation to the religious life and who are in good standing with the Episcopal or a sister church are welcome to inquire. *Inquiries:* The Rev. Connie Jo McCarroll, SSG, (937) 239-8692, conniejodo@cs.com. Web: www.sistersofsaintgregory.org.

Society of St Anna the Prophet, The (SSAP)

The SSAP is a dispersed vowed community of women, both lay and ordained, called to Godly aging and to ministry with elders and with children. The vows are simplicity, creativity and balance. The SSAP is open to any woman over 50 years old, confirmed in the Episcopal Church, whose vocation to this prophetic life and ministry is discerned. Vows are taken after a minimum of one provisional year and one novice year. Life vows may be taken after five years. The SSAP includes elders living in care, as well as working and retired elders living independently.

Annas are single, married, widowed, and partnered. Founded in the Diocese of Atlanta, the Society is beginning to expand into other areas. Those interested may visit the website at annasisters.org or write the Director of Provisionals and Novices, the Rev. Marilyn Hughes, SSAP, Chapter House 1655 Rainier Falls Drive NE Atlanta GA 30329-4107. *Email:* dpn@annasisters.org.

St. Hildegard's Community

St. Hildegard's Community is a nonresidential, dispersed, beloved community of women and men, single and partnered, with our mother house in Austin, Texas. We began as a local intentional Eucharistic Community in 1996 with commitments to nonviolence and inclusive liturgical language. St. Hildegard's Community Rule of Life (available on amazon.com) describes how Hildegard of Bingen shaped our emerging life in a three-fold pattern of transformation: Contemplation, Action, and intimacy in Community and led to our call as a canonical community embodying a Hildegardian spirituality. We participate in the Spirit's co-creating a lively church in reverent relationship to all of creation, offering hospitality to seekers in a time of flux, including those fed by other spiritual traditions. Professed members take three vows: Open to Christ-Sophia, Cultivate Compassion, and Love the Earth. Chapter members and Companions participate alongside to welcome and create abundance. We sing and dance justice in our weekly Sunday Eucharists and other liturgies as a work-of-the-people (hybrid) and offer online and hybrid classes in our Servant Leadership School. Recent action for social justice has focused on creation care and immigration. Friday Silent Meditation online and silent retreats in Central Texas and online are offered for members

and seekers. *Community Council:* Sr Margo Stolfo, Sr Virginia Marie Rincon+, and Sr Judith Liro+. *Chaplain:* Sr Helena Marie CHS. *Bishop Visitor:* Rt Rev Marc Andrus. See www.facebook.com/ St.Hildegard.Austin and www.hildegard-austin.org for more information. *E-mail:* sthildecommaustin@ gmail.com.

Worker Brothers of the Holy Spirit, The

International Covenant Community for Lay Brothers, Lay Workers and Clergy regardless of marital status. Life commitment to common Rule, Benedictine in orientation but not lived in Community. From a Contemplative model of prayer, meditation, worship, the Eucharist and a focus on the Theology concept of being and the Fruit of the Spirit, come the action of mission and ministry in the local parish, church, and world. For contacts, see Worker Sisters of the Holy Spirit, below *Web:* www.workerbrothers.org.

Worker Sisters of the Holy Spirit, The

International Covenant Community for Lay Sisters, Lay Workers, and Clergy regardless of marital status. Life Commitment to common Rule, Benedictine in orientation but not lived in Community. From a Contemplative model of prayer, meditation, worship, the Eucharist, and a focus on the Theology concept of being and the Fruit of Spirit, come the action of mission and ministry in the local parish, church, and world. *Prioress* Sr LaVerne Peter, WSHS; *American Director* Sr Kathleen Rachel, WSHS *E-mail:* srkathleenrachel@ gmail.com; *Canadian Director* Sr Wendy Samuel, WSHS *E-mail:* srwendysamuel@gmail.com. For more information, visit our website at www.workersisters.org or email Sr. Lucia, WSHS, Coordinator of Admissions at srluciawshs@gmail.com.

PREVIOUS BISHOPS OF THE DIOCESES, DISTRICTS, AND JURISDICTIONS

coadj: coadjutor, const: constituted, dio: diocesan, m: missionary, org: organized, suffr: suffragan

Anking (1910) Daniel T. Huntington 1912-40, Lloyd R Craighill 1940-49. Became Dio of Wan-Gan, H Catholic Church in China 1949.

Asheville Became Dio of WNC 1907.

Boise Became Idaho in 1907.

Central America and Panama Canal Zone (const 1919) Separated into Panama and the Canal Zone, and Central America 1956. See Panama and the Canal Zone.

Central America (const 1956) David E Richards 1957-67. Divided 1967 into 5 districts: CR, ES, Guat, Hond, Nic.

Central Brazil (const 1950) Louis C Melcher 1950-58, Edmund K Sherrill 1959-65. Now part of the Igreja Episcopal do Brasil.

Central Pennsylvania see Bethlehem and Harrisburg.

Central Philippines (const 1901) Chas H Brent 1901-18, Gouveneur F Mosher 1920-40, Robt F Wilner suffr 1936-56, Norman S Binsted 1942-57, Lyman C Ogilby suffr 1953 Bp 1956-67, Ed G Longid suffr 1963-71, CB Manguramas suffr 1969-71, Benito C Cabanban suffr 1957 Bp 1967-78, Manuel C Lumpias coad 1977 Bp 1978-90. Became part of the Province of the Philippines in 1990.

Costa Rica (const 1967) David E Richards 1967-68, Jose Antonio Ramos 1969-76. Became extra-provincial in 1976. Became part of the Province of Central America 1998.

Cuba (const 1901) Albion W Knight 1904-13, Hiram R Hulse 1915-38, Alexander H Blankingship 1939-61, Romualdo Gonzalez 1961-66. Became autonomous dio under metropolitan council in 1966.

Cuernavaca (const 1989) Jose Saucedo 1989-. Became part of the Church of the Province of Mexico 1994.

Dakota Separated into ND and SD in 1883.

Duluth (const 1895) James D Morrison 1897-1922, Granville G Bennett coadj 1920 Bp 1922-23, Benj T Kemerer coadj 1930 Bp 1933-43. Reunited with Minnesota 1944.

Eastern Diocese (org 1810) Alexander V Griswold 1811-43. Incl all of New England except CT. VT separated 1832, NH 1832, RI ME and MA 1843.

Eastern Oklahoma (const 1910) Theodore P Thurston 1911-19. Reunited with Oklahoma 1919.

El Salvador (const w/Bps in charge 1967-1992) Martin Barahona 1992-. Became part of the Province of Central America 1998.

Erie see Northwestern Pennsylvania.

Guatemala (const w/Bps in charge 1967-1981) Armando Guerra 1982-. Became part of the Province of Central America 1998.

Hankow (const 1910) James A Ingle 1902-03, Logan H Roots 1904-37, Alfred A Gilman suffr 1925 Bp 1937-48. Became part of H Catholic Church in China 1948.

Harrisburg (org 1904) James H Darlington 1905-30, Hunter Wyatt-Brown 1931-43, John T Heistand 1943-66, Earl M Honaman suffr 1956-69. *Renamed Central Pennsylvania in 1971.*

Honolulu see Hawaii.

Illinois see Chicago.

Kansas City see West Missouri.

Kearney See Platte.

Kyoto (const 1898) Sidney C Partridge 1900-11, Henry St G Tucker 1912-23, Shirley N Nichols 1926-40. Trans to H Catholic Church in Japan 1941.

Laramie see Platte.

Liberia (const 1851) John Payne 1851-71, John G Auer 1873-74, Chas C Pennick 1877-83, Samuel D Ferguson 1885-1916, Walter H Overs 1919-25, Theophilus M Gardiner suffr 1921-41, Robt E Campbell OHC 1925-36, Leopold Kroll 1936-45, Bravid W Harris 1945-64, Dillard H Brown Jr 1964-69, Geo D Browne 1970-82. Now part of the Province of West Africa.

Marquette see Northern Michigan.

Mexico (est 1879) Sergio Carranza-Gomez 1989. Became part of the Church of the Province of Mexico 1994.

Michigan City see Northern Indiana.

New Mexico and Southwest Texas see Rio Grande.

Nicaragua (const w/Bps in charge 1969-1985) Sturdie Downs 1985-. Became part of the Province of Central America 1998.

Niobrara (1871-83) see South Dakota.

North Central Philippines (const 1989) Artemio M Zabala 1989-90. Became part of the Province of the Philippines in 1990.

67

North Kwanto (org 1893 as No Tokyo, 1938 as No Kwanto) John McKim 1893-1935, Chas S Reifsnyder suff 1924 Bp 1935-41. Became part of the H Catholic Church of Japan.

North Texas Became Dio of Northwest Texas in 1958.

North Tokyo see North Kwanto.

Northern Mexico (const 1973) German Martinez-Marquez 1987-. Became part of the Church of the Province of Mexico 1994.

Northern New Jersey see Newark.

Northern Luzon (const 1986) Richard A Abellon 1986-90. Became part of the Province of the Philippines in 1990.

Northern Philippines (const 1972) Ed G Longid 1972-75, Richard A Abellon 1975-86, Robt LO Longid 1986-90. Became part of the Province of the Philippines in 1990.

Northern Texas see Dallas.

Northwest Diocese Jos C Talbot 1860-65.

Okinawa Edmond L Browning 1968-71. *Transferred to the Nippon Sei Ko Kai 1972.*

Oregon and Washington see Oregon. Washington separated 1880.

Panama (const 1919) James C Morris 1920-30, Harry Beal 1937-44, Reginald H Gooden 1945-72, Lemuel Barnett Shirley 1972-83, Victor Scantlebury suff 1991-94, James H Ottley 1984-95, Clarence Wallace Hayes Dewar 1995-. Became part of the Province of Central America 1998.

Platte, The (const 1889. Name changed to Laramie 1898, Kearney 1908, Western Nebraska 1913) Anson R Graves 1890-1910, Geo A Beecher 1910-43. Reunited with Nebraska 1946.

Puerto Rico (const 1902) James H Van Buren 1902-12, Chas B Colmore 1913-47, Chas F Boynton coadj 1944 Bp 1947-51, A Ervine Swift 1951-65, Francisco Reus-Froylan 1965-79. Became extra-provincial in 1980.

Sacramento see Northern California.

Salina see Western Kansas.

Salt Lake see Utah.

Shanghai Wm J Boone 1844-64, Channing M Williams 1866-74, Samuel IJ Schereschewsky 1877-83, Wm J Boone 1884-91, Fredk R Graves 1893-

1937, John W Nichols suffr 1934-38, Wm P Roberts 1937-49. Became Dio of Kiangsu, H Catholic Church in China 1949.

South Florida (const 1892 as Southern Florida, 1922 as South Florida) Wm C Gray 1892-1913, Cameran Mann m 1913 dio 1922-32, John D Wing coadj 1925 Bp 1932-50, Martin J Bramm suffr 1951-56, Wm F Moses suffr 1956-61 Henry I Louttit suffr 1945 coadj 1948 dio 1951-69, James L Duncan suffr 1961-69, Wm L Hargrave suffr 1961-69. *South Florida divided into Central Fla., Southeast Fla. and Southwest Fla. 1969.*

Southern Brazil (est 1890 rec'd into American Church 1907) Lucien L Kinsolving 1907-28, Wm MM Thomas suffr 1925 Bp 1928-49, Louis C Melcher coadj 1948 Bp 1949-50, Athalicio T Pithan suffr 1940 Bp 1950-55, Egmont M Krischke 1955-65. Now part of Igreja Episcopal do Brasil.

Southern Philippines (const 1972) CB Manguramas 1972-84. Narciso V Ticobay 1986-90. Became part of the Province of the Philippines in 1990.

Southwest Temporary mission jurisdiction 1859-65.

Southwest Texas Included in New Mexico and Southwest Texas since 1895.

Southwestern Brazil Egmont M Krischke 1950-55, Plinio L Simoes 1956-65. Now part of Igreja Episcopal do Brasil.

Southwestern Mexico (const 1989) Claro Huerto-Ramos 1989-. Became part of the Church of the Province of Mexico 1994.

Tohoku (const 1920) Norman S Binsted 1928-41. Transferred to the Holy Catholic Church in Japan 1941.

Washington Territory see Olympia.

Western Colorado (const 1892) Wm M Baker 1894-94, admin by Abiel Leonard 1894-1903, part of Salt Lake 1904-07, recreated 1907, Edward J Knight 1907-08, Benj Brewster 1909-16, Frank H Touret 1917-19. Reunited with Colorado 1919.

Western Mexico (const 1973) Samuel Espinoza 1983-. Became part of the Church of the Province of Mexico 1994.

Western Nebraska see Platte.

Western Texas see West Texas.

Wisconsin see Milwaukee.

Diocesan and Parochial Lists

FOR QUICK REFERENCE, some words have been abbreviated. Please see lists of abbreviations on pages 6–9 and at the beginning of some sections.

ADDRESSES OF THE CLERGY may be found in the alphabetical Clergy List in the last section of the *Annual*.

CHURCH LISTINGS follow this order:

1 *Official postal name of city*
2 *Name of church*
3 *Type of church (capital letter in bold face):*
  P = parish
  M = mission
  PS = preaching station
  CC = college chapel
  SC = summer chapel
  HC = historical church
  NH = nursing home
  CM = campus ministry
  PM = prison ministry
  I = Inactive
  O = Other
4 *Number of communicants in good standing* Actual numbers shown reflect information from the 2008 Parochial Report provided by Congregational Research and the Office of the General Convention, Episcopal Church Center. Information from the 2009 Report will be uploaded to www.theredbook.org in Fall 2010.
5 " § " designates a *Parish Day School.*
6 *St Address*
7 *Zip Code*
8 *Alternate mailing address* if applicable
9 *City* (if applicable) and *church*, if city has more than one, of which the church is a mission, or whose clergy serve the mission.
10 *Members of the Clergy.*
11 *Parish Telephone Number*

EXAMPLES

```
1        2     3  4  5      6
|        |     |  |  |      |
```
Westbury Advent P (726) § 505 Second St
11590 (PO Box 115) JH Krantz (516) 333-0081

```
7        8          10        11
|        |          |         |
```
Church of the Advent is a parish in the city of Westbury, has 726 communicants and a Parish Day School. It is located at 505 Second St with a mailing address of PO Box 115 11590. Its clergy is the Rev J.H. Krantz, and the phone number is (516) 333-0081.

```
1   2   3  4   6      7      9
|   |   |  |   |      |      |
```
Irvington S Paul M (54) 264 E Main St 36544 *S Lk Mobile*

St. Paul's Church is a mission in the city of Irvington, has 54 communicants, and is located at 264 E. Main St., which is also its mailing address. It is either a mission of St. Luke's Church in Mobile, which has more than one church, or is a diocesan mission served by the clergy of St. Luke's.

✠ at beginning of an entry indicates Cathedral or Pro-Cathedral.

PARISH DAY SCHOOLS. Parishes with day schools (above nursery or kindergarten level) are identified by the symbol § . For more information, write directly to the parish or to The National Association of Episcopal Schools, 815 2nd Ave New York NY 10017 (800) 334-7626 x6134 for the *Directory of Episcopal Church Schools.*

To Make Additions or Corrections

Listings for congregations may be updated using CPG's Employee Roster.

Other corrections to diocesan information, information concerning organizations and the governing structures of the Church come from the dioceses, organizations themselves or from The Executive Council.

Please send Clergy List changes to the Recorder of Ordinations, 19 East 34th St, New York, NY 10016.

STATE OF ALABAMA
Dioceses of Alabama and Central Gulf Coast

DIOCESE OF ALABAMA
(PROVINCE IV)
Comprises northern and central counties in the state of Alabama
DIOCESAN OFFICE 521 N 20th St Birmingham AL 35203
TEL (205) 715-2060 FAX (205) 715-2066
E-MAIL diooffice@dioala.org WEB www.dioala.org

Previous Bishops—
Nicholas H Cobbs 1844-61, Richard
H Wilmer 1862-1900, Henry M
Jackson asst 1891-1900, Robt W
Barnwell 1900-02, Chas M Beckwith
1902-28, Wm G McDowell coadj
1922 Bp 1928-38, Chas CJ Carpenter
1938-68, Randolph R Claiborne Jr
suffr 1949-53, Geo M Murray suffr
1953 coadj 1959 Bp 1969-70, Wm
A Dimmick asst 1984, Furman C Stough 1971-88,
Robt O Miller suffr 1986-88 Bp 1988-98, Henry Nutt
Parsley Jr Bp Coad 1996-1998 Bp 1999-2011, Onell
A Soto Asst 1999-01, Mark H Andrus suffr 2002-06,
J McKee Sloan suffr 2008-12 Bp 2013-20

Bishop—Glenda Sharp Curry (2021-)

Assisting Bishop—Brian N. Prior (2022-)

Canon for Mission Support Rev RP Morpeth; *Canon
to the Ordinary* Rev G Evans; *Bookkeeper* J Cook;
Admin Asst to Bp Curry LL Horton; *Dir of Miss
Funding* C Cotten; *Human Res Coord* M Oeder;
Dir of Youth, Campus, and Young Adult Min Kristin
Blackerby; *Miss for Comm* D Donaldson; *Archdcn*
M Holmes; *Miss for Racial Healing and Pilgrimage*
B Mitchell; *Miss for Clergy Transition* Rev K Hudlow

Officers: Sec Rev S Arnold; *Treas* J McCormack; *Asst
Sec-Treas* R Morpeth; *Chanc* A Dowd Esq

Stand Comm—Cler: J Evans K Harper R Webster C
Hartley; *Lay:* A Burress R Norris M Clark J Jolly

Council—Cler: G Curry J Carlson M Waldo R
Lindahl C Ackerman T Joyner B Bridges; *Lay:* J Jolly
L Auman C Ferguson S Young S Griffith R Boylan
G Elliott

PARISHES, MISSIONS, AND CLERGY

Alabaster Epis Church of the Holy Spirit **P** (158)
858 Kent Dairy Road 35007-2027 (Mail to:
858 Kent Dairy Rd 35007-5248) William
Blackerby Elton Wright (205) 621-3418

Albertville Christ Episcopal Church **P** (103) 607
E Main St 35950-2447 (Mail to: PO Box 493
35950-0008) Shari Harrison (256) 878-3243

Alexander City St James Episcopal Church **P**

(285) 347 S Central Ave 35010-2579 (Mail
to: 347 S Central Ave 35010-2579) Robert St
Germain-Iler (256) 234-4752

Alpine Trinity Church **P** (34) 6898 Grist Mill
Road 35014-0095 (Mail to: PO Box 95 35014-
0095) (256) 378-8020

Anniston Grace Episcopal Church **HC** (374) §
1000 Leighton Ave 36207-5702 (Mail to: PO
Box 1791 36202-1791) Walter Lalonde (256)
236-4457

Anniston Ch of St Michael & All Angels **P** (258)
1000 W 18th St 36201-3588 (Mail to: PO Box
1884 36202-1884) (256) 237-4011

Athens St Timothys Episcopal Church **P** (106) §
207 E Washington St 35611-2651 (Mail to: 207
E Washington St 35611-2651) (256) 232-3541

Auburn Holy Trinity Episcopal Church **P** (1006)
§ 100 Church Dr 36830-5903 (Mail to: 100
Church Dr 36830-5903) Robert Blackwell
Michael Harber (334) 887-9506

Auburn St Dunstan Episcopal Church **P** (61)
136 E Magnolia Ave 36830-4722 (Mail to: 136
E Magnolia Ave 36830-4722) Thomas Joyner
Norbert Wilson (334) 887-5657

Bessemer Trinity Episcopal Church **P** (68) 2014
Berkley Ave 35020-4236 (Mail to: PO Box
1563 35021-1563) (205) 966-3938

Birmingham All Saints Episcopal Church **P**
(2008) § 110 W Hawthorne Rd 35209-3999
(Mail to: 110 W Hawthorne Rd 35209-3999)
Bradley Landry John Olson Charles Youngson
(205) 879-8651

Birmingham Birmingham Epis Campus Mnstry
CC 1170 11th Ave S 35205-5236 (Mail to: 1170
11th Ave S 35205-5236) (205) 320-1500

Birmingham Church of the Ascension **P** (475)
§ 1912 Canyon Rd 35216-1753 (Mail to: 1912
Canyon Rd 35216-1799) John Alvey (205)
822-3480

Birmingham Grace Episcopal Church **P** (209)
5712 1st Ave N 35212-1604 (Mail to: 5712 1st
Ave N 35212-1604) (205) 595-4636

Birmingham St Andrews Parish **P** (170) 1024
12th St S 35205-5234 (Mail to: 1024 12th St S
35205-5234) Rebecca Debow (205) 251-7898

Birmingham St Lukes Episcopal Church **P**
(2923) § 3736 Montrose Rd 35213-3832 (Mail

to: 3736 Montrose Rd 35213-3832) Richmond Webster Maurice Goldsmith David Hall (205) 871-3583

Birmingham St Marks Episcopal Church **P** (61) 228 Dennison Ave SW 35211-3803 (Mail to: 228 Dennison Ave SW 35211-3803) Jayne Pool (205) 322-8449

Birmingham St Marys on The Highlands Ch **P** (1946) § 1910 12th Ave S 35205-3804 (Mail to: 1910 12th Ave S 35205-3804) Harry Gardner (205) 933-1140

Birmingham St Stephens Episcopal Church **P** (1786) § 3775 Crosshaven Dr 35223-2832 (Mail to: 3775 Crosshaven Dr 35223-2832) Rebecca Bridges John Burruss Katherine Harper (205) 967-8786

Birmingham St Thomas Episcopal Parish **P** (342) 2870 Acton Rd 35243-2502 (Mail to: 2870 Acton Rd 35243-2502) Josiah Rengers (205) 969-2700

Birmingham The Abbey **P** (50) 131a 41st St S 35222-1930 (Mail to: 131a 41st St S 35222-1930) (205) 703-9538

✠ **Birmingham** Cathedral Church of the Advent **O** (3538) § Attn: Bryan Helm 2017 6th Ave N 35203-2701 (Mail to: C/O Bryan Helm 2017 6th Ave N 35203-2701) Richard Smalley Benjamin Dehart James Gardner Wesley Sharp (205) 251-2324

Boligee Saint Mark's Episcopal Church **P** (5) Rr 1 Box 10 35443-9798 (Mail to: Rr 1 Box 10 35443-9801) (205) 372-4071

Carlowville St Pauls Church Carlowville **P** (10) 310 County Rd 4 36761-3626 (Mail to: PO Box 27 36761-0027) (334) 872-3674

Chelsea St Catherine's Episcopal Church **P** (131) 642 Kings Home Drive 35043 (Mail to: PO Box 577 35043-0577) (205) 6188367

Childersburg St Mary Episcopal Church **P** (37) 5th Ave & 5th St 35044 (Mail to: PO Box 303 35044-0303) (256) 378-8020

Clanton Trinity Episcopal Church **P** (81) 503 Second Avenue South 35045 (Mail to: PO Box 2121 35046-2121) (205) 7553339

Cullman Grace Episcopal Church **P** (320) 305 Arnold St NE 35055-2910 (Mail to: 305 Arnold St NE 35055-2910) (256) 734-6212

Decatur Church of the Good Shepherd **P** (88) 3809 Spring Ave SW 35603-3203 (Mail to: 3809 Spring Ave SW 35603-3203) (256) 351-9955

Decatur St Johns Episcopal Church **P** (645) 202 Gordon Dr SE 35601-2528 (Mail to: 202 Gordon Dr SE 35601-2528) Chase Ackerman (256) 353-9615

Demopolis Trinity Episcopal Church **HC** (149) 401 N Main Ave 36732-2019 (Mail to: PO Box 560 36732-0560) Evan Thayer Paul Andersen (334) 289-3363

Eutaw St Stephens Church **P** (73) 403 Norht Eutaw Ave 35462-0839 (Mail to: PO Box 839 35462-0839) James Vaughn (205) 301-0483

Fairfield Christ Episcopal Church **P** (78) 4912 Richard M Scrushy Pkwy 35064-1456 (Mail to: PO Box 424 35064-0424) (205) 9193240

Faunsdale St Michael/Holy Cross Epis Ch **P** (27) 45 Watkins St 36738-4501 (Mail to: C/O Nancy Terry PO Box 507 36786) (334) 289-3363

Fayette St Michaels Episcopal Church **P** (113) 431 10th St NW 35555-1834 (Mail to: 431 10th St NW 35555-1834) (205) 932-6929

Florence Saint Bartholomew's Epis Ch **P** (89) 1900 Darby Dr 35630-2625 (Mail to: 1900 Darby Dr 35630-2625) Wilbur Eich (256) 764-2000

Florence Trinity Episcopal Church **P** (469) 410 N Pine St 35630-4655 (Mail to: PO Box M 35631-1912) Callie Plunket-Brewton Callie Plunket-Brewton (256) 7646149

Forkland St John in the Prairie Epis Ch **P** (12) A L Issac Rd 36740-4216 (Mail to: PO Box 839 35462-0839) James Vaughn (205) 289-0399

Fort Payne St Philip's Episcopal Church **P** (69) 2813 Godfrey Ave NE 35967-3746 (Mail to: 2813 Godfrey Ave NE 35967-3746) James Elliott (256) 845-1192

Gadsden Church of the Holy Comforter **P** (418) 156 S 9th St 35901-3646 (Mail to: 156 S 9th St 35901-3646) Carl Saxton (256) 547-5361

Gainesville St Alban's Church **P** (4) 290 Chestnut St 35459 (Mail to: C/O Mr William B Stuart PO Box 844 35470-0844) Richard Losch (205) 652-4210

Greensboro St Pauls Episcopal Church **HC** (89) 905 Church St 36744-1520 (Mail to: 905 Church St 36744-1520) (334) 624-8866

Guntersville Church of the Epiphany **P** (267) 1101 Sunset Dr 35976-1003 (Mail to: PO Box 116 35976-0116) Aaron Raulerson (256) 582-4897

Hartselle St Barnabas Episcopal Church **P** (37) 1450 Sparkman St NW 35640-4534 (Mail to: PO Box 614 35640-0614) Elvin Basinger (256) 773-4206

Heflin Church of the Messiah **P** (40) Corner of Lake View & Vaughn 36264 (Mail to: PO Box 596 36264-0596) (256) 463-2928

Hoover St Albans Episcopal Church **P** (140) 429 Cloudland Dr 35226-1100 (Mail to: 429 Cloudland Dr 35226-1100) Margaret Doyle (205) 822-2330

Hoover Church of the Holy Apostles **P** (360) 424 Emery Dr 35244-4548 (Mail to: 424 Emery Dr 35244-4548) Emily Collette Martha Holmes (205) 988-8000

Huntsville Church of the Nativity **P** (1735) 208 Eustis Ave SE 35801-4233 (Mail to: 208 Eustis Ave SE 35801-4293) Thomas Goldsmith Robert Serio (256) 533-2455

Huntsville Holy Cross-St Christopher's **P** (15) 3740 Meridian St N 35811-1116 (Mail to: 3740 Meridian St N 35811-1116) (256) 534-7750

Huntsville St Stephen's Episcopal Church **P** (171) § 8020 Whitesburg Dr SW 35802-3002 (Mail

to: 8020 Whitesburg Dr SW 35802-3002)
Jeffrey Evans (256) 8817223

Huntsville St Thomas Episcopal Church **P**
(953) 12200 Bailey Cove Rd SE 35803-2641
(Mail to: 12200 Bailey Cove Rd SE 35803-
2641) Donavan Cain David Drachlis Virginia
Monroe (256) 880-0247

Indian Springs St Francis of Assisi Church **P**
(139) 3545 Cahaba Valley Rd 35124-3527
(Mail to: 3545 Cahaba Valley Rd 35124-3527)
James Mcadams James Mcadams (205) 988-
4371

Jacksonville St Lukes Church **P** (184) 400
Chinabee Ave SE 36265-2810 (Mail to: Attn:
Penn G Wilson PO Box 55 36265-0055)
Robert Fowler (256) 435-9271

Jasper St Marys Church **P** (140) 801 The Trce W
35504-7454 (Mail to: 801 The Trce W 35504-
7454) (205) 387-7746

Leeds Church of the Epiphany **P** (148) 1338
Montevallo Road 35094-2472 (Mail to: 1338
Montevallo Rd 35094-2472) Monica Carlson
(205) 699-2404

Livingston St James Church **P** (24) C/O T
Raiford Noland 109 Spring 35470 (Mail to:
C/O T Raiford Noland Station Two L U 35470)
(205) 652-7462

Lowndesboro St Pauls Episcopal Church **P** (60) §
164 N Broad St 36752-3002 (Mail to: PO Box
216 36752-0216)

Madison St Matthews Episcopal Church **P** (783)
786 Hughes Rd 35758-8972 (Mail to: PO Box
1187 35758-5187) Chris Hartley (250) 864-0788

Marion St Wilfrids Episcopal Church **P** (60) 104
Clements St 36756-1806 (Mail to: PO Box 43
36756-0043) (334) 683-9628

Mentone St Josephs on the Mountain Ch **P** (97)
21145 Scenic Hwy 35984 (Mail to: PO Box 161
35984-0161) (256) 634-4476

Millbrook St Michael and All Angels Ch **P** (208)
5941 Robinson Sprin 36054 (Mail to: PO Box
586 36054-0012) Mark Waldo (334) 285-3905

Montevallo St Andrews Episcopal Church **P** (52)
925 Plowman St 35115-3809 (Mail to: 925
Plowman St 35115-3809) (205) 665-1667

Montgomery All Saints Episcopal Church **P** (96)
645 Coliseum Blvd 36109-1240 (Mail to: PO
Box 3073 36109-0073) (334) 272-2591

Montgomery Church of the Ascension **P** (762)
§ 315 Clanton Ave 36104-5541 (Mail to: 315
Clanton Ave 36104-5541) Candice Frazer
(334) 263-5529

Montgomery Church of the Holy Comforter **P**
(237) 2911 Woodley Rd 36111-2842 (Mail to:
2911 Woodley Rd 36111-2898) Rosa Lindahl
(334) 281-1337

Montgomery Church of the Good Shepherd **P**
(24) 493 S Jackson St 36104-4749 (Mail to: 493
S Jackson St 36104-4749) (334) 834-9280

Montgomery St Johns Episcopal Church **P**
(1225) 113 Madison Ave 36104-3623 (Mail

to: 113 Madison Ave 36104-3623) Duncan
Johnston Deonna Neal (334) 2621937

Nauvoo Chapel of the Ascension **Chapel** 105
Delong Rd 35578-6550 (Mail to: 105 Delong
Rd 35578-6550) Mark Johnston (205) 387-
1806

Oneonta Calvary Church **P** (34) 1002 Park Ave
35121-0010 (Mail to: PO Box 821 35121-0010)
(205) 274-9444

Opelika Emmanuel Episcopal Church **P** (28) 800
1st AVE 36801-4346 (Mail to: PO Box 2332
36803-2332) (334) 745-2054

Pell City St Simon Peter Church **P** (241) 3702
Mays Bend Rd 35128-7168 (Mail to: PO Box
432 35125-0432) (205) 884-0877

Pike Road Grace Episcopal Church **P** (153) 906
Pike Rd 36064-2242 (Mail to: PO Box 640096
36064-0096) Sarah Halloran (334) 215-1422

Prattville St Marks Episcopal Church **P** (204)
178 E 4th St 36067-3110 (Mail to: 178 E 4th
St 36067-3110) Scott Arnold (334) 365-5289

Rainbow City Church of the Resurrection **P**
(220) 113 Brown Ave 35906-3122 (Mail to: 113
Brown Ave 35906-3122) Richelle Thompson
(256) 442-6862

Roanoke St Barnabas Episcopal Church **P** (26)
809 Rock Mills Rd 36274-5347 (Mail to: Attn:
J Schuessler 266 Guy St 36274-1629) (334)
863-6021

Scottsboro St Lukes Church **P** (128) 402 S Scott
St 35768-1935 (Mail to: 402 S Scott St 35768-
1935) (256) 574-6216

Seale St Matthews in the Pines **P** (36) 38
Longview Ct 36875-3716 (Mail to: PO Box 221
36875-0221) (706) 366-6568

Selma St Pauls Episcopal Church **P** (427) 210
Lauderdale St 36701-4521 (Mail to: PO Box
1306 36702-1306) Amy George (334) 874-
8421

Sheffield Grace Episcopal Church **P** (284) 103
Darby Ave 35660-1505 (Mail to: PO Box 838
35660-0838) Danielle Thompson (256) 383-
2014

Smiths Station St Stephens Episcopal Church
P (64) 45 Lee County Road 567 36877-3285
(Mail to: 45 Lee Road 567 36877-3285) (334)
291-0750

Sylacauga St Andrews Episcopal Church **P** (52)
§ 10 W Walnut St 35150-3312 (Mail to: Atten
Ronald Webster 55 Skyline Dr 35044-1133)
(256) 249-2411

Talladega St Peters Episcopal Church **P** (87) 208
North St E 35160-2110 (Mail to: 208 North St
E PO Box 206 35160-2110) (256) 362-2505

Tallassee Church of the Epiphany **P** (45) 2602
Gilmer Ave 36078-7212 (Mail to: 2602 Gilmer
Ave 36078-7212) David Peeples (334) 252-
8618

Trussville Church of the Holy Cross **P** (195) 90
Parkway Dr 35173-1318 (Mail to: 90 Parkway
Dr 35173-1318) (205) 655-7668

Tuscaloosa Cntbry Chapel and College Ctr **P** (473) 812 5th Ave 35401-1206 (Mail to: 812 5th Ave 35401-1206) William Burnette (205) 345-9590

Tuscaloosa Christ Church **P** (1419) 605 Lurleen B Wallace Blvd N 35401-1712 (Mail to: 605 Lurleen B Wallace Blvd N 35401-1712) Paul Pradat Emily Rowell (205) 758-4252

Tuscaloosa St Matthias Episcopal Church **P** (95) 2310 Skyland Blvd E 35405-4327 (Mail to: 2310 Skyland Blvd E 35405-4327) (205) 553-7282

Tuskegee Institute St Andrews Episcopal Church **P** (72) 701 W Montgomery Rd 36088-1913 (Mail to: PO Box 1213 36087-1213) (334) 727-3210

Uniontown St Michaels/Holy Cross **P** Franklin Street 36786 (Mail to: 515 County Road 54 36738-3310) (334) 289-3363

Wetumpka Trinity Episcopal Church **P** (293) 5371 US Highway 231 36092-3168 (Mail to: 5375 US Highway 231 36092-3168) (334) 567-7534

DIOCESE OF ALASKA
(PROVINCE VIII)
Comprises the State of Alaska
DIOCESAN OFFICE 1205 Denali Way Fairbanks AK 99701-4178
TEL (907) 452-3040 FAX (907) 456-6552
WEB www.episcopalak.org

Previous Bishops— Peter T Rowe 1895-1942, John B Bentley suffr 1931 Bp 1943-48, Wm J Gordon Jr 1948-74, David R Cochran 1974-81, George C Harris 1981-91, Steven Charleston 1991-1996, Mark L McDonald 1997-2008, Rustin Kimsey asst

Bishop—Rt Rev Mark Lattime (1050) (Dio 4 Sept 2010)

Bps Asst M Ward; *Cn for Fin and Adm* S Krull; *Asst Fin and Admin* L Winfrey-Frank; *Treas* M Duggar; *Chanc* E Wohlforth; *V Chanc* S Stanley; *Hunger* vacant; *UTO* vacant; *Safe Church* Rev K Hunt

Stand Comm—Cler: B Glover M Norton L Pifke J Platson; *Lay:* N Burke J Gau D McConachie S Solenberger A Swan Sr

PARISHES, MISSIONS, AND CLERGY

Allakaket St John in the Wilderness Epis **M** (144) General Delivery 99720-9999 (Mail to: General Delivery 99720-9999) (907) 968-2240

Anchorage All Saints Episcopal Church **P** (223) 545 W 8th Ave 99501-3517 (Mail to: PO Box 100686 99510-0686) David Terwilliger David Terwilliger (907) 279-3924

Anchorage Christ Church Episcopal **P** (89) 5101 O'Malley Rd 99507-6850 (Mail to: PO Box 111963 99511-1963) Katherine Hunt Gail Loken (907) 345-7914

Anchorage St Christophers Church **P** (71) 7208 Duben Ave 99504-1321 (Mail to: PO Box 211896 99521-1896) (907) 333-5010

Anchorage St Marys Episcopal Church **P** (757) § 2222 E Tudor Rd 99507-1072 (Mail to: 2222 E Tudor Rd 99507-1300) Michael Burke Dawn

Allen-Herron Dawn Allen-Herron Betty Glover Gayle Nauska Israel Portilla Gomez Robert Thwing (907) 563-3341

Anvik Christ Episcopal Church **M** (88) PO Box 138 99558-0138 (Mail to: PO Box 103 99558-0103) (907) 663-6343

Arctic Vlg Bishop Rowe Chapel **M** (148) General Delivery 99722-9999 (Mail to: General Delivery 99722-9999) (907) 587-5320

Beaver St Matthews Episcopal Church **M** (86) C St 99724 (Mail to: PO Box 24009 99724-0009) (907) 628-6114

Chalkyitsik St Timothys Episcopal Church **M** (77) PO Box 54 99788-0054 (Mail to: PO Box 54 99788-0054) (907) 848-8211

Circle Holy Trinity Episcopal Church **M** (80) No Street Identified 99733 (Mail to: 1205 Denali Way 99701-4137) (907) 457-8823

Cordova St Georges Episcopal Church **P** (78) 100 Lake Ave 99574 (Mail to: PO Box 849 99574-0849) (907) 424-5143

Eagle St Johns Episcopal Church **M** (20) PO Box 17 99738-0017 (Mail to: 1205 Denali Way 99701-4137) (907) 547-2226

Eagle River Holy Spirit Episcopal Church **P** (79) 17545 N Eagle River Loop Rd 99577 (Mail to: PO Box 773223 99577-3223) (907) 694-8201

Fairbanks Chapel of Alaska Saints **Chapel** 1205 Denali Way 99701-4137 (Mail to: 1205 Denali Way 99701-4137) (907) 452-3040

Fairbanks St Matthews Church **P** (1104) § 1029 First Ave 99701 (Mail to: 1030 2nd Ave 99701-4300) John David Charles Davis Shirley Lee Bella Savino Montie Slusher (907) 456-5235

Fort Yukon St Stephens Episcopal Church **M** (219) No Street Address 99740 (Mail to: PO Box 289 99740-0289) Teresa Thomas (907) 662-7556

Fort Yukon St Peters Episcopal Church **M** (25) PO Box KBC 99740 (Mail to: 1205 Denali Way

99701-4137) (907) 662-2383

Grayling St Pauls Episcopal Church **M** (261) General Delivery 99590-9999 (Mail to: General Delivery 99590-9999) (907) 453-5128

Haines St Michael & All Angels **P** (81) 1.5 Mile Haines Hwy 99827-1236 (Mail to: PO Box 1236 99827-1236) Janice Hotze (907) 766-3041

Homer St Augustines Episcopal Church **M** (13) 619 Sterling Hwy 99603 (Mail to: PO Box 4274 99603-4274) (907) 235-1225

Hughes St Pauls Episcopal Church **M** (54) Front St 99745 (Mail to: 1205 Denali Way 99701-4137) (907) 889-2255

Huslia Good Shepherd Mission **M** (130) PO Box 78 99746-0078 (Mail to: PO Box 78 99746-0078) (907) 829-2233

Juneau St Brendans Episcopal Church **P** (77) 4207 Mendenhall Loop Rd 99801-9176 (Mail to: 4207 Mendenhall Loop Rd 99801-9176) Caroline Malseed (907) 789-5152

Juneau Church of the Holy Trinity **P** (164) 415 4th St 99801-1003 (Mail to: 415 4th St 99801-1003) Gordon Blue (907) 586-3532

Kenai St Francis by the Sea Church **P** (20) 110 S Spruce St 99611-7937 (Mail to: 110 S Spruce St 99611-7937) Marian Nickelson (907) 283-6040

Ketchikan Saint John's Church **P** (86) 503 Mission St 99901-6423 (Mail to: PO Box 23003 99901-8003) David Yaw Barbara Massenburg (907) 225-3680

Kivalina Kivalina Epiphany Church **M** (403) General Delivery 99750-9999 (Mail to: General Delivery 99750-9999) Jerry Norton (907) 645-2164

Kodiak St James the Fisherman Church **P** (66) 421 Thorsheim St 99615 (Mail to: PO Box 1668 99615-1668) Wallace Mills (907) 486-5276

Kotzebue St Georges in the Arctic **M** (44) 215 3rd Ave 99752-0269 (Mail to: PO Box 269 99752-0269) Mary Norton (907) 442-2360

Minto St Barnabas Episcopal Church **M** (44) PO Box 58064 99758-0064 (Mail to: PO Box 58041 99758-0041) (907) 798-7414

Nenana Saint Mark's Church **M** (123) Front & Market Sts 99760 (Mail to: PO Box 337 99760-0337) (907) 347-4115

Noatak Episcopal Congregation **PS** (10) General Delivery 99761 (Mail to: General Delivery 99761-9999)

North Pole St Judes Episcopal Church **PS** (29) 3408 Laurance Rd 99705-6705 (Mail to: PO

Box 55458 99705-0458) John Holz (907) 488-9329

Palmer St Bartholomews Episcopal Ch **P** (25) 323 N Alaska St 99645-6233 (Mail to: 323 N Alaska St 99645-6233) James Brisson (907) 745-3526

Petersburg St Andrews Episcopal Church **P** (18) PO Box 1815 99833-1815 (Mail to: PO Box 1815 99833-1815) Dawn Allen-Herron (907) 254-0526

Point Hope St Thomas Episcopal Church **M** (280) Natchiq St 99766 (Mail to: 1205 Denali Way 99701-4137) (907) 368-6200

Point Lay St Albans in the Arctic **M** (59) No Street Identified 99759 (Mail to: 1205 Denali Way 99701-4137) (907) 833-2623

Rampart Episcopal Congregation **PS** (54) General Delivery 99761 (Mail to: General Delivery 99767-9999) (907) 485-2144

Seward St Peters Episcopal Church **P** (12) 239 2nd Ave 99664 (Mail to: PO Box 676 99664-0676) Arthur Thomas (907) 224-3975

Shageluk St Lukes Episcopal Church **M** (124) General Delivery 99665-9999 (Mail to: General Delivery 99665-9999) (907) 473-8292

Sitka St Peters by the Sea **P** (112) 611 Lincoln St 99835-7647 (Mail to: PO Box 1130 99835-1130) Julie Platson (907) 747-3977

Stevens Vlg St Andrews Episcopal Church **M** (43) General Delivery 99774-9999 (Mail to: 1205 Denali Way 99701-4137) (907) 478-7127

Talkeetna Denali Church **M** (1) Talkeetna Spur Rd 99676-0038 (Mail to: PO Box 38 99676-0038) (907) 373-0625

Tanacross St Timothys Episcopal Church **M** (94) General Delivery 99776-9999 (Mail to: General Delivery 99776-9999) (907) 883-5576

Tanana St James Episcopal Church **M** (134) 1 Front St 99777 (Mail to: PO Box 52 99777) (907) 366-7251

Valdez Epiphany Lutheran/Episcopal Ch **HC** (102) 309 Pioneer Dr 99686-0829 (Mail to: PO Box 829 99686) (907) 835-4541

Venetie Church of the Good Shepherd **M** (208) General Delivery 99781-9999 (Mail to General Delivery 99781-9999) (907) 849-8129

Wasilla St David's Epsicopal Church **P** (79) 230 N Wasilla Fishhook Rd 99654-4011 (Mail to: 2301 N Wasilla Fishhook Rd 99654-4011) (907) 373-0625

Wrangell St Philips Episcopal Church **P** (35) 444 Church St 99929 (Mail to: PO Box 409 99929-0409) (907) 874-3047

DIOCESE OF ALBANY
(PROVINCE II)
Comprises 19 counties in Northeast NY
DIOCESAN OFFICE 580 Burton Rd Greenwich NY 12834
TEL (518) 692-3350
E-MAIL Diocese@albanydiocese.org WEB www.albanyepiscopaldiocese.org

Previous Bishops—
Wm C Doane 1869-1913, Richd H Nelson coadj 1904 Bp 1913-29, Geo A Oldham coadj 1922 Bp 1929-49, Fredk L Barry coadj 1945 Bp 1949-60, David E Richards suffr 1951-57, Allen W Brown suffr 1959 Bp 1961-74, Charles B Per sell Jr suffr 1963-76, Wilbur E Hogg 1974-84, David S Ball coadj 1984 Bp 1984-98, Daniel W Herzog coadj 1997-98, Bp 1998-2007, David J Bena suffr 2000-2007; William H Love coadj 2006-07, Bp 2007-21

Bishop—vacant; Standing Committee as Ecclesiastical Authority

Sec Rev S Garno; *Treas* C Curtis; *Asst Treas* S King; *Dir of Admin* Rev M Keegan; *Chanc* Rev W Strickland; *COM* Rev S Troiano; *Deploy* Rev E Papazoglakis; *Acct Mgr* S Denis; *Diaconal Form* Rev T Papazoglakis S Ruetsch

Stand Comm—Cler: Pres T Malionek J DeVaty D Roy B Jones A Garno E Papazoglakis; *Lay:* C Cassidy J Hyde T Mumby J Papa S Ruetsch J Stevens Lauria

Deans: Metro B Jones; *N Adirondack* D Ousley; *S Adirondack* N Goff; *St Lawrence* S Boyce; *U Hudson* T Papazoglakis; *Hudson* T Malionek; *Susquehanna* K Hunter; *W Mohawk* N Longe

PARISHES, MISSIONS, AND CLERGY

✠ **Albany** Cathedral of All Saints **O** (382) § 62 S Swan St 12210-2301 (Mail to: 62 S Swan St 12210-2380) Hugh Wilkes (518) 465-1342

Albany St Andrews Episcopal Church **P** (355) 10 N Main Ave 12203-1403 (Mail to: 10 N Main Ave 12203-1488) Keith Scott (518) 489-4747

Albany St Michaels Episcopal Church **P** (169) 49 Killean Park 12205-4035 (Mail to: 49 Killean Park 12205-4087) Peter Schellhase Peter Schellhase (518) 869-6417

Albany Saint Paul's Episcopal Church **P** (167) 21 Hackett Blvd 12208-3407 (Mail to: 21 Hackett Blvd 12208-3496) Michael Greene Edward Dougherty Nancy Rosenblum (518) 463-2257

Albany St Peters Episcopal Church **P** (435) 107 State St 12207-1622 (Mail to: Mr Richard Bolton 107 State St 12207-1683) Christina Hunter (518) 434-3502

Albany St Francis Mission **P** (55) § 498 Clinton Ave 12206-2705 (Mail to: PO Box 452 12061-0452) (518) 465-1112

Amsterdam St Anns Episcopal Church **P** (224) 37 Division St 12010-4324 (Mail to: 37 Division St 12010-4398) Neal Longe Alan Hart Mary Hart (518) 842-2362

Au Sable Forks St James Episcopal Church **P** (15) 14216 State Rte 9N 12912 (Mail to: C/O Grace E Bushey PO Box 470 12912-0470) David Ousley (518) 647-5312

Ballston Spa Christ Episcopal Church **P** (602) 15 W High St 12020-1912 (Mail to: 15 W High St 12020-1912) Derik Roy Albert Moser William Pearson (518) 885-1031

Bloomville St Pauls Church **P** (27) 464 River St 13739-1173 (Mail to: PO Box 742 13739-0742) (607) 434 5501

Blue Mountain Lake Church of the Transfiguration **SC** (31) 1 Cedar Ln 12812 (Mail to: C/O B Pelton Box 567 Hc 2 13436) (240) 442-2152

Bolton Landing Church of St Sacrement **P** (73) PO Box 1185 4879 Lake Shore Dr 12814-1185 (Mail to: PO Box 1185 12814-1185) (518) 644-9613

Bovina St James Church **P** (18) 55 Lake Delaware Dr 13753 (Mail to: 8 Rothermel Lane Ext 12106-2110) (607) 832-4401

Brant Lake Church of the Good Shepherd **PS** Ny State Route 9 12815 (Mail to: PO Box 119 12815-0119) Michael Webber (518) 494-3314

Brant Lake St Pauls Church **PS** State Rte 8 12815 (Mail to: C/O Nancy Torre PO Box 119 12815-0119) Michael Webber (518) 494-3314

Burnt Hills Calvary Episcopal Church **P** (119) 85 Lake Hill Rd 12027-9597 (Mail to: 85 Lake Hill Rd PO Box 41 12027-9597) Gabriel Morrow (518) 399-7230

Cambridge St Lukes Church **P** (85) 4 St Lukes Pl 12816-1111 (Mail to: 4 St Lukes Pl 12816-1111) (518) 677-2632

Canajoharie The Ch of The Good Shepherd **P** (20) 26 Moyer St 13317-0118 (Mail to: PO Box 118 13317-0118) (518) 673-3440

Canton Grace Episcopal Church **P** (32) 9 E Main St 13617-1416 (Mail to: 9 E Main St 13617-1471) (315) 386-3714

Catskill St Lukes Church **P** (100) 50 William St 12414-1419 (Mail to: PO Box 643 12414-0643) Leander Harding David Sutcliffe Martin Yost (518) 943-4180

Champlain Christ & St John's Parish **P** (73) 8 Butternut St 12919-5121 (Mail to: PO Box 240 12919-0240) Patricia Beauharnois (518) 298-8543

Chatham St Luke Episcopal Church **P** (27) 12 Woodbridge Ave 12037-1314 (Mail to: 12 Woodbridge Ave 12037-1314) (518) 392-2278

Cherry Valley Grace Church **P** (67) 32 Montgomery St 13320-3562 (Mail to: PO Box 382 13320-0382) Thomas Grennen (607) 264-8303

Clifton Park St Georges Episcopal Church **P** (583) 912 Route 146 12065-3702 (Mail to: 912 Route 146 12065-3702) Thomas Papazoglakis Katharine Foster (518) 371-6351

Cobleskill St Christopher's Episcopal Ch **P** (34) 121 St Christopher Pl 12043-5131 (Mail to: PO Box 386 12043-0386) (518) 234-3912

Cohoes St Johns Church **P** (115) § 405 Vliet Blvd 12047-2019 (Mail to: 405 Vliet Blvd 12047-2019) (518) 237-6013

Colton Zion Episcopal Church **P** (75) 91 Main St 13625 (Mail to: C/O Clifton N Duval PO Box 9 13625-0009) (315) 262-3106

Cooperstown Christ Church Episcopal **P** (407) 69 Fair St 13326-1309 (Mail to: 69 Fair St 13326-1309) Nathan Ritter (607) 547-9555

Copake Falls St John in the Wilderness **P** (130) 261 State Route 344 12517-5337 (Mail to: PO Box 180 12517-0180) John Thompson (518) 329-3674

Coxsackie Christ Church **P** (89) 70 Mansion St 12051-1214 (Mail to: PO Box 187 12051-0187) Anne Curtin (518) 731-9883

Delhi St Johns Church **P** (88) 134 1/2 Main St 13753-1213 (Mail to: PO Box 121 13753-0121) Arthur Garno Nancy Truscott (607) 746-3437

Delmar St Stephens Episcopal Church **P** (350) 16 Elsmere Ave 12054-2118 (Mail to: 16 Elsmere Ave 12054-2100) Scott Garno Justine Guernsey (518) 439-3265

Deposit Christ Episcopal Church **P** (83) 14 Monument St 13754-1216 (Mail to: 14 Monument St 13754-1216) Linda Servetas (607) 467-3031

Downsville Saint Mary's Church **P** (43) § 15121 Main St 13755 (Mail to: Attn: Bruce E Dolph 142 Delaware St 13856-1331) (607) 363-2565

Duanesburg Christ Episcopal Church Ch **P** (106) 132 Duanesburg Churches Road 12056 (Mail to: PO Box 92 12056-0092) Deborah Beach Alistair Morrison (518) 895-2383

Elizabethtown Church of the Good Shepherd **P** (102) 10 William St 12932 (Mail to: PO Box 146 12932-0146) (518) 873-2509

Essex St Johns Episcopal Church **P** (116) Church St 12936 (Mail to: PO Box 262 12936-0262) Craig Hacker (518) 963-7775

Franklin St Pauls Episcopal Church **P** (32) Main And Institute Sts 13775 (Mail to: PO Box 72 13775-0072) (607) 829-6404

Gilbertsville Christ Episcopal Church **P** (134) § 36 Marion Ave 13776-1202 (Mail to: PO Box 345 13776-0345) William Lytle (607) 783-2267

Glens Falls Church of the Messiah **P** (317) 296

Glen St 12801-3501 (Mail to: 296 Glen St 12801-3501) Jean Devaty (518) 792-1560

Gouverneur Trinity Episcopal Church **P** (30) § 30 Park St 13642 (Mail to: PO Box 341 13642-0341) Gregory Bailey (315) 287-0755

Greenville Christ Episcopal Church **P** (107) 11226 State Route 32 12083-3600 (Mail to: PO Box 278 12083-0278) (518) 966-5713

Greenwich St Pauls Episcopal Church **P** (46) 145 Main St 12834-1214 (Mail to: PO Box 183 12834-0183) (518) 692-7492

Guilderland St Boniface Episcopal Church **P** (251) 5148 Western Tpke 12084 (Mail to: PO Box 397 12084-0397) Peter Schellhase (518) 355-0134

Hoosick Falls All Saints Church **P** (78) § 4935 Rt. 7 12090 (Mail to: Attn: Ronald W Bovie PO Box 211 12089-0211) Gary Strubel (518) 686-9037

Hoosick Falls Church of the Holy Name **P** (20) § 33 Simmons Rd 12090-5000 (Mail to: 33 Simmons Rd 12090-5000) Susan Troiano (518) 465-3129

Hoosick Falls St Marks Episcopal Church **P** (47) 70 Main St 12090-2004 (Mail to: 70 Main St PO Box 272 12090-2004) (518) 686-4982

Hudson Christ Episcopal Church **P** (150) § 431 Union St 12534-2426 (Mail to: PO Box 411 12534-0411) John Allison (518) 828-1329

Hudson Falls Zion Episcopal Church **P** (63) 224 Main St 12839-1705 (Mail to: 224 Main St 12839-1705) (518) 747-6514

Ilion St Augustines Church **P** (138) 78 2nd St 13357-2118 (Mail to: 78 2nd St 13357-2118) (315) 894-3775

Johnstown St Johns Episcopal Church **P** (424) § 1 N Market St 12095-2139 (Mail to: PO Box 395 12095-0395) Laurie Garramone Alistair Morrison (518) 762-9210

Keene Valley All Souls Church St Huberts **SC** Church St 12943 (Mail to: PO Box 486 12943-0486)

Keeseville St Pauls Church **P** (28) 107 Clinton St 12944-0143 (Mail to: Clinton Street 12944) (518) 563-6836

Kinderhook St Pauls Episcopal Church **P** (53) 10 Silvester St 12106-2013 (Mail to: PO Box 637 12106-0637) Thomas Malionek Jan Volkmann (518) 758-6271

Lake George St James Episcopal Church **P** (67) 172 Ottawa St 12845-1414 (Mail to: Attn: Michele Molldrem-Hotko 172 Ottawa St 12845-1414) Barbara Mitchell (518) 668-2001

Lake Luzerne St Marys Episcopal Church **P** (63) PO Box 211 220 Lake Ave 12846-0211 (Mail to: PO Box 211 12846-0211) Louis Midura Louis Midura (518) 696-3030

Lake Placid St Eustace Church **P** (110) 2450 Main St 12946-3300 (Mail to: 2450 Main St 12946-3300) Kenneth Hitch (518) 523-2564

Lake Pleasant St Hubert of the Lakes Church **P** (10) 2545 State Route 8 12108-4401 (Mail to:

PO Box 119 12815-0119) (518) 494-3314

Latham St Matthews Episcopal Church **P** (111) 129 Old Loudon Rd 12110-4007 (Mail to: 129 Old Loudon Rd 12110-4007) Jacob Evans (518) 785-6029

Little Falls Emmanuel Episcopal Church **P** (152) 588 Albany St 13365-1543 (Mail to: PO Box 592 13365-0592) Jack Whritenour (315) 823-1323

Malone St Marks Episcopal Church **P** (41) § 34 Elm St 12953-1507 (Mail to: PO Box 331 12953-0331) (518) 521-3303

Margaretville St Margarets Church **M** (22) 63 Orchard St 12455 (Mail to: New Academy & Orchard St 12455) (607) 563-9414

Massena St Johns Church **P** (143) 139 Main St 13662-1908 (Mail to: PO Box 15 13662-0015) Sonya Boyce (315) 769-5203

Mechanicville St Lukes Episcopal Church **P** (325) 40 McBride Road 12118-2325 (Mail to: 40 McBride Rd 12118-3512) Michael Todd (518) 664-4834

Morris All Saints Chapel of Zion Ch **Chapel** 1854 State Highway 51 13808 (Mail to: PO Box 156 13808-0156) (607) 263-5783

Morris Zion Church **P** (79) 158 Main Street 13808-0156 (Mail to: PO Box 156 13808-0156) Joseph Norman Joseph Norman (607) 263-5927

Morristown Christ Church **P** (38) Main St 13664 (Mail to: PO Box 1297 13669-6296) Edgar Lacombe (315) 375-4497

N Granville All Saints Chapel **SC** State Route 22 12854 (Mail to: Rt 22 Box 166 12854) (518) 743-1740

New Lebanon Church of Our Saviour **P** (32) 14660 Route 22 12125 (Mail to: PO Box 827 12125-0827) Frank Lockwood (518) 794-8702

Newcomb St Barbaras Church **PS** 65 Sanford Ln 12852-1709 (Mail to: 30 Marcy Ln 12852-2016) Michael Webber (518) 494-3314

North Creek St Christophers Church **PS** Ridge St 12853 (Mail to: PO Box 119 12815-0019) Michael Webber (518) 494-3314

Norwood St Philips Church **P** (51) PO Box 225 13668-0225 (Mail to: PO Box 225 13668-0225) Kathryn Boswell (315) 353-8833

Ogdensburg St Johns Episcopal Church **P** (125) 500 Caroline St 13669-2604 (Mail to: 500 Caroline St PO Box 658 13669-2604) Arthur Garno (315) 393-5470

Old Forge St Peters Church By-the-Lake **SC** 4800 State Route 28 13420-0111 (Mail to: PO Box 111 13331-0111) (315) 360-6879

Oneonta St James Episcopal Church **P** (265) 305 Main St 13820-2520 (Mail to: 305 Main St 13820-2596) Kenneth Hunter Mary Hunter (607) 432-1458

Palenville Gloria Dei Episcopal Church **P** (10) 3393 Route 23a 12463-2318 (Mail to: PO Box 298 12463-0298) John Miller (518) 329-4562

Paul Smiths St Johns in the Wilderness **SC** 350 White Pine Rd 12970 (Mail to: PO Box 23 12945-0023) Allen Cooper (518) 891-6746

Philmont St Marks Episcopal Church **P** (30) Main St Maple Ave 12565 (Mail to: PO Box 628 12565-0628) Mark Mc Darby (518) 672-4062

Plattsburgh Trinity Church **P** (154) 18 Trinity Pl 12901-2933 (Mail to: 18 Trinity Pl 12901-2933) Glen Michaels David Ousley (518) 561-2244

Potsdam Trinity Episcopal Church **P** (233) 8 Maple St 13676-1149 (Mail to: 8 Maple St 13676-1181) Lora Smith (315) 265-5754

Pottersville Adirondack Mission **Cluster** (74) 316 Valentine Pond Rd 12860 (Mail to: PO Box 119 12815-0119) (518) 494-3314

Pottersville Christ Church **P** (14) Nys Route 9 12860 (Mail to: PO Box 119 12815-0119) Michael Webber (518) 494-3314

Rensselaer Church of the Redeemer **P** (40) 1249 3rd St 12144-1821 (Mail to: 1249 3rd St 12144-1821) (518) 326-6722

Rensselaerville Trinity Church Rensselaerville **P** (20) 10 Trinity Ln 12147 (Mail to: PO Box 86 12147-0086) (518) 797-5295

Richfld Spgs St Johns Episcopal Church **P** (36) 98 Main St 13439-2535 (Mail to: PO Box E 13439-1901) (315) 858-1121

Round Lake All Saints Church **P** (85) § Simpson Ave 12151 (Mail to: PO Box 35 12151-0035) Scott Evans (518) 899-5510

Salem St Paul's Church **P** (23) E Broadway 12865 (Mail to: PO Box 484 12865-0484) (518) 854-7294

Saranac Lake St Luke the Beloved Physician **P** (287) 102 Main St 12983 (Mail to: 136 Main St 12983-1734) Andrew Cruz Lillegard Julianna Caguiat (518) 891-3605

Saratoga Spg Bethesda Episcopal Church **P** (302) 41 Washington St 12866-4116 (Mail to: 178 Elm St Ste 5 12866-4086) Paul Evans Marshall Vang (518) 584-5980

Schenectady Christ Church **P** (277) 970 State St 12307-1520 (Mail to: 970 State St Ste 1 12307-1588) Nelson Jones Peter Schofield (518) 374-3064

Schenectady St Andrews Church **P** (172) 50 Sacandaga Rd 12302-1828 (Mail to: 50 Sacandaga Rd 12302-1894) Michael Neufeld (518) 374-8391

Schenectady St George's Episcopal Church **P** (249) 30 N Ferry St 12305-1609 (Mail to: 30 N Ferry St 12305-1697) (518) 374-3163

Schenectady St Pauls Episcopal Church **P** (49) 1911 Fairview Ave 12306-4129 (Mail to: 1911 Fairview Ave 12306-4129) David Culbertson (518) 393-5118

Schenectady St Stephens Church **P** (121) 1229 Baker Ave 12309-5711 (Mail to: 1229 Baker Ave 12309-5711) Patricia Jones (518) 346-6241

Schenevus Church of the Holy Spirit **P** (26) Arch St 12155 (Mail to: PO Box 354 12155-0354) (607) 432-6835

Schroon Lake St Andrews Church **P** St Rte 9 12870 (Mail to: PO Box 334 12870-0334) Michael Webber (518) 494-3314

Schuylerville St Stephens Episcopal Church **P** (55) § 1 Grove St 12871-1403 (Mail to: 1 Grove St 12871-1403) (518) 695-3918

Sidney St Pauls Church **P** (76) 25 River St 13838-1132 (Mail to: 25 River St 13838-1132) (607) 563-3391

Springfld Ctr St Marys Church **P** (50) § 7690 State Highway 80 13468-2018 (Mail to: PO Box 376, 7690 St. Rt. 80 13468) Thomas Grennen (315) 858-4016

Stamford St Peters Church **P** (21) 16155 County Highway 18 12167-1801 (Mail to: 16155 County Highway 18 12167-1801) Arthur Garno (607) 538-9503

Ticonderoga The Episcopal Ch of the Cross **P** (39) § 129 Champlain Ave 12883-1313 (Mail to: 129 Champlain Ave 12883-1313) Richard Roessler (518) 585-4032

Troy St Johns Episcopal Church **P** (156) 146 1st St 12180-4431 (Mail to: Treasurer 146 1st St 12180-4431) Judith Malionek Paul Carney Sandra Tatem (518) 274-5884

Troy St Pauls Church **P** (151) 58 3rd St 12180-3906 (Mail to: PO Box 868 12181) Michael Gorchov (518) 273-7351

Troy Trinity Episcopal Church **P** (100) 545 4th Ave 12182-2616 (Mail to: 585 4th Ave 12182-

2526) Desmond Francis (518) 235-3873

Tupper Lake Church of St Thomas **P** (27) 8 Brentwood Ave 12986-1513 (Mail to: 8 Brentwood Ave 12986-1513) Allen Cooper (518) 359-8786

Twilight Park Memorial Church of All Angels **SC** 69 Balsam Rd 12485 (Mail to: C/O Malcolm Handte 120 Cabrini Blvd Apt 128 10033-3431) (518) 589-5292

Unadilla St Matthews Church **P** (60) § 240 Main St 13849-2245 (Mail to: PO Box 537 13849-0537) (607) 369-3081

Walton Christ Church **P** (61) § 41 Gardiner Pl 13856-1320 (Mail to: 41 Gardiner Pl 13856-1320) (607) 865-4698

Warrensburg Church of the Holy Cross **P** (163) § 3764 Main St 12885-1836 (Mail to: 3764 Main St 12885-1897) Thomas Pettigrew (518) 623-3066

Waterford Grace Church **P** (146) 34 3rd St 12188-2538 (Mail to: 34 3rd St 12188-2538) Katherine Alonge-Coons William Strickland (518) 237-7370

Watervliet Trinity Episcopal Church **P** (126) 1336 1st Ave 12189-3317 (Mail to: 1336 1st Ave 12189-3317) Nicolas Hernandez William Tatem (518) 272-0644

Westford St Timothys Episcopal Church **P** (12) 1776 Co Rte 34 13488 (Mail to: PO Box 74 13488-0074) (607) 369-9214

DIOCESE OF ARIZONA
(PROVINCE VIII)
Comprises the State of Arizona, except for Navajoland,
the Cities of Page and Bullhead City, and Yuma County
DIOCESAN OFFICE 114 W Roosevelt St Phoenix AZ 85003-1406
TEL (602) 254-0976 FAX (602) 495-6603
E-MAIL serrena@azdiocese.org WEB www.azdiocese.org

Previous Bishops—
Ozi W Whitaker (NV and AZ) 1869-74, Wm-F Adams (NMex and AZ) 1875-76, Geo K Dunlap (NMex and AZ) 1880-88, John M Kendrick (NMex and AZ) 1889-1911, Julius W Atwood 1911-25, Walter Mitchell 1926-45, Arthur B Kinsolving II 1959-62, Joseph M Harte 1962-79, Joseph T Heistand coad 1976-79, Bp 1979-92, Wesley Frensdorff Asst 1985-88, Robert R Shahan 1992-2004, Kirk Stevan Smith 2004-19

Bishop—Rt Rev Jennifer Anne Reddall (1113)
(Dio 9 Mar 2019)

Cn to Ord/Trans Min A Braden; *Archdcn* A Bryan; *Cn for Border Min* D Chavez; *Cn for Stew* T Dombek;

Cn for Creation Care P Hyde; *Dir of Finance* L Hansen; *Cn for Native Min* D Royals; *Cn for Youth & Children's Min* J Sundin; *Cn for Hisp & Lat Min* S Santibanez; *Asst to BP* S Fuentes; *Dir of Comm* L Way; *Chanc* D Bivens; *Treas* S Mortenson; *Sec to Conv* P Pauley; *Dn of Cathedral* T Mendez

Stand Comm—Cler: G Brambila M Halle D Hedges R Hollis A Lee S Santibanez; *Lay: Pres* C Kunz C Bro L Derrick S Haas S James M Sinclair

PARISHES, MISSIONS, AND CLERGY

Benson St Raphael In The Vlly Epis Ch **M** (87) 730 S Highway 80 85602-6931 (Mail to: PO Box 1224 85602-1224) (520) 586-4335

Bisbee St Johns Sweet Memorial Church **M** (75) 19 Sowle Ave 85603 (Mail to: C/O Diocese of Arizona 114 W Roosevelt St 85003-1406) (520) 432-7006

Casa Grande St Peters Church **P** (118) 704 E Mcmurray Blvd 85122 (Mail to: 704 E Mcmurray Blvd. 85122) Jeanne Rasmussen (520) 836-7693

Cave Creek Good Shepherd of the Hills **P** (327) 6502 E Cave Creek Rd 85331-8643 (Mail to: 6502 E Cave Creek Rd 85331-8643) Bruce Jackson (480) 488-3283

Chandler Saint Matthew's Church **P** (702) 901 W Erie St 85225-4477 (Mail to: PO Box 1959 85244-1959) Michael Halle David Pettengill Colville Smythe (480) 899-7386

Clarkdale St Thomas of the Valley **M** (65) 889 1st South St 86324 (Mail to: PO Box 1175 86324-1175) (928) 634-8593

Coolidge Saint Michael's Church **M** (91) 800 W Vah Ki Inn Rd 85228-9312 (Mail to: PO Box 547 85128-0010) (520) 723-3845

Douglas St Stephens Episcopal Church **M** (18) 749 E 11th St 85607-2240 (Mail to: 114 W Roosevelt St 85003-1406) (520) 364-7971

Flagstaff Church of the Epiphany **P** (553) 423 N Beaver St 86001-4511 (Mail to: 423 N Beaver St 86001-4511) Katharine Beaumont Bess Driver Alison Lee (928) 774-2911

Glendale St Andrews Church **P** (271) 6300 W Camelback Rd 85301-7305 (Mail to: 6300 W Camelback Rd 85301-7305) Irineo Vasquez Janice Watts (623) 846-8046

Glendale St John the Baptist Church **P** (285) 4102 W Union Hills Dr 85308-1702 (Mail to: 4102 W Union Hills Dr 85308-1702) Timothy Yanni Charles Milhoan (623) 582-5449

Globe St Johns Church **M** (116) 185 E Oak St 85501-2115 (Mail to: PO Box 1051 85502-1051) Byron Mills Byron Mills (928) 425-9300

Green Valley St Francis-in-the-Valley **P** (363) 600 S La Canada Dr 85614-1902 (Mail to: 600 S La Canada Dr 85614-1902) Rebecca Williamson (520) 625-1370

Holbrook St Georges Church **M** (22) 168 W Arizona St 86025-2824 (Mail to: 114 W Roosevelt St 85003-1406) Adrian Tubbs (928) 524-2361

Kingman Trinity Church **M** (70) 425 E Spring St 86402 (Mail to: c/o Diocese of Arizona 114 W Roosevelt St 85003-1406) Benjamin Rodenbeck (928) 754 5658

Lake Havasu City Grace Church **P** (232) 111 Bunker Dr 86403-6856 (Mail to: 111 Bunker Dr 86403-6856) Kim Litsey (928) 8552525

Lakeside Church of Our Saviour **P** (167) 5147 Show Low Lake Rd 85929-5218 (Mail to: 5147 Show Low Lake Rd 85929-5218) Kerry Neuhardt (928) 537-7830

Litchfield Park St Peters Episcopal Church **P** (627) § 400 S Old Litchfield Rd 85340-4721 (Mail to: 400 S Old Litchfield Rd 85340-4721) James Rhodenhiser (623) 935-3279

Mesa Church of the Transfiguration **P** (259) 514 S Mountain Rd 85208-5412 (Mail to: 514 S Mountain Rd 85208-5412) Anne Ellsworth Philip Stowell (480) 986-1145

Mesa St Marks Church **P** (242) 322 N Horne 85203-7933 (Mail to: 322 N Horne 85203-7933) Gerardo Brambila Estrada (480) 964-5820

Morenci SS Philip and James **M** (5) 784 Mountain Ave 85540 (Mail to: C/O Diocese of Arizona 114 W Roosevelt St 85003-1406) (928) 439-4015

Nogales St Andrew's Episcopal Church **P** (193) § 969 W Country Club Dr 85621-3985 (Mail to: 969 W Country Club Dr 85621-3985) Rodger Babnew Derwent Suthers (520) 281-1523

Oro Valley Episcopal Ch of the Apostles **M** (251) 12111 N La Cholla Blvd 85755-9725 (Mail to: PO Box 68435 85737-8435) (520) 544-9660

Paradise Valley Christ Church of the Ascension **P** (656) § 4015 E Lincoln Dr 85253-3946 (Mail to: Attn: Accountant 4015 E Lincoln Dr 85253-3946) Erika Von Haaren (602) 840-8210

Parker St Philips Church **PS** 1209 S Eagle Ave 853445847 (Mail to: PO Box 923 853440923) (928) 770-4589

Payson St Pauls Church **M** (249) 401 E Tyler Pkwy 855413298 (Mail to: 401 E Tyler Pkwy 855413298) Thomas Hawkins (928) 474-3834

Phoenix All Saints Church & Day School **P** (1859) § 6300 N Central Ave 85012-1109 (Mail to: 6300 N Central Ave 85012-1190) James Bade Dan Burner (602) 279-5539

Phoenix Iglesia Episcopal de San Pablo **M** (466) 2801 N 31st St 85008-1126 (Mail to: 114 W Roosevelt St 85003-1406) Guillermo Castillo (602) 255-0602

Phoenix St Lukes at the Mountain Ch **M** (184) 848 E Dobbins Rd 85042 (Mail to: c/o Diocese of Arizona 114 W Roosevelt St 85003-1406) (602) 276-7318

Phoenix St Marys Church **P** (139) 6501 N 39th Ave 85019-1303 (Mail to: 6533 N 39th Ave 85019-1303) Robert Bustrin (602) 354-7540

Phoenix St Stephens Church **P** (158) 2310 N 56th St 85008-2611 (Mail to: 2310 N 56th St 85008-2611) Daniel Tantimonaco Robin Hollis (602) 840-0437

Phoenix Santa Maria Episcopal Church **M** (90) 6501 N 39th Ave 85019-1303 (602) 374-4855

Phoenix St Paul the Apstl Sudan Missn **M** (591) 527 W Pima St 85003-2754 (Mail to: 114 W Roosevelt St 85003-1406) Anderia Lual (602) 253-4094

✠ **Phoenix** Trinity Cathedral **O** (722) 100 W Roosevelt St 85003-1406 (Mail to: 100 W Roosevelt St 85003-1406) Troy Mendez Mark Sutherland (602) 254-7126

Prescott St Lukes Episcopal Church **P** (398) § 2000 Shepard Ln 86301-6143 (Mail to: 2000 Shepherds Ln 86301-6143) Kimball Arnold (928) 778-4499

Safford All Saints Episcopal Church **M** (29) 210 W Main St 85546-2349 (Mail to: 210 W Main

St 85546-2349) (928) 348-9430

Scottsdale Episcopal Ch of the Nativity **P** (432) 22405 N Miller Rd 85255-4939 (Mail to: 22405 N Miller Rd Ste 100 85255-4939) Scot Mccomas Wayne Whitney (480) 307-9216

Scottsdale St Anthony on the Desert **P** (455) 12990 E Shea Blvd 85259-5305 (Mail to: 12990 E Shea Blvd 85259-5305) Holly Herring Susan Cihak Gordon Gilfeather (480) 451-0860

Scottsdale Saint Barnabas On The Desert **P** (1440) 6715 N Mockingbird Ln 85253-4344 (Mail to: 6715 N Mockingbird Ln 85253-4344) James Clark Pamela Bell Robert Berra Sarah Getts (480) 948-5560

Sedona St Andrews Episcopal Church **P** (157) 100 Arroyo Pinon Dr 86336-5004 (Mail to: 100 Arroyo Pinon Dr 86336-5004) Monica Whitaker (928) 282-4457

Sierra Vista St Stephen's Church **P** (82) 2750 E Cardinal Dr 85635 (Mail to: 2750 Cardinal Dr 85635-5447) Allison Cornell (520) 458-4432

Sun City All Saints of the Desert Ch **P** (292) 9502 W Hutton Dr 85351-1462 (Mail to: 9502 W Hutton Dr 85351-1462) (623) 974-8404

Sun City St Christophers Church **P** (252) § 10233 W Peoria Ave 85351-4248 (Mail to: 10233 W Peoria Ave 85351-4248) Sandra Chilese (623) 972-1109

Sun City West Church of the Advent **P** (450) 13150 W Spanish Garden Dr 85375-5052 (Mail to: 13150 W Spanish Garden Dr 85375-5052) Timothy Dombek Janet Gooltz (623) 584-0350

Tempe Church of the Epiphany **P** (628) 2222 S Price Rd 85282-3013 (Mail to: 2222 S Price Rd 85282-3013) Charles Ruffin Lynn Adwell (480) 968-4111

Tempe St Augustines Church **M** (255) 1735 S College Ave 85281-6695 (Mail to: 1735 S College Ave 85281-6695) Chad Sundin Rebecca Williamson Vivian Winter Chaser (480) 967-3295

Tempe St James the Apostle Church **M** (242) 975 E Warner Rd 85284-3232 (Mail to: 975 E Warner Rd 85284-3232) Robin Hollis Robin

Hollis (480) 345-2686

Tombstone St Pauls Church **M** (32) PO Box 1489 85638-1489 (Mail to: PO Box 1489 85638-1489) Heather Rose (520) 553-3290

Tucson Christ the King Church **P** (393) 2800 W Ina Rd 85741-2502 (Mail to: 2800 W Ina Rd 85741-2502) Anita Slovak (520) 297-2551

Tucson The Epis Church of St Matthew **P** (235) 9071 E Old Spanish Trail 85710 (Mail to: PO Box 17116 85731-7116) Richard Wilson Franklyn Bergen Mary Martin (520) 298-9782

Tucson St Mic & All Angels Epis Ch **P** (206) § 602 N Wilmot Rd 85711-2702 (Mail to: 602 N Wilmot Rd 85711-2702) David Hedges Kristin Barberia (520) 886-7292

Tucson Grace St Pauls Epis Church **P** (1294) 2331 E Adams St 85719-4308 (Mail to: 2331 E Adams St 85719-4398) Stephen Keplinger Kathryn Baird Stephen Kelsey Richard Mallory (520) 327-6857

Tucson St Albans Episcopal Church **P** (668) § Sabino Canyon At Old Sabino Canyon Rd 85750 (Mail to: 3738 N Old Sabino Canyon Rd 85750-2102) (520) 296-0791

Tucson St Andrews Church Epis Church **M** (135) § 545 S 5th Ave 85701-2413 (Mail to: PO Box 1165 85702-1165) Deborah Royals (520) 622-8318

Tucson St Philips in the Hills **P** (1826) 4440 N Campbell Ave 85718-6504 (Mail to: PO Box 65840 85728-5840) Robert Hendrickson Clifford Blinman Taylor Devine Peter Helman Thomas Lindell Norma Rogers Rosa Sandwell-Weiss Mary Trainor (520) 299-6421

Wickenburg St Albans Church **P** (112) 357 W Yavapai St 85390-3211 (Mail to: 357 W Yavapai St 85390-3211) (928) 684-2133

Williams St Johns Episcopal-Luth Church **M** (41) 202 W Grant Ave 86046-2535 (Mail to: 114 W Roosevelt St 85003-1406) Cheryl Fox (928) 635-2781

Winslow St Pauls Church **M** (27) 600 Henderson St 86047-2427 (Mail to: PO Box 1018 86047-1018) Adrian Tubbs (928) 289-3851

DIOCESE OF ARKANSAS
(PROVINCE VII)
Comprises the State of Arkansas
DIOCESAN OFFICE 310 W 17th St Little Rock AR 72206
(MAIL: Box 164668 Little Rock AR 72216-4688)
TEL (501) 372-2168 FAX (501) 372-2147
E-MAIL info@episcopalarkansas.org WEB www.episcopalarkansas.org

Previous Bishops—
Leonidas Polk 1838-41, Geo W Freeman 1844-58, Henry C Lay 1859-69, Henry N Pierce m 1870 dio 1871-99, Wm M Brown coadj 1898 Bp 1899-1912, James R Winchester coadj 1911 Bp 1912-31, Edwin W Saphore suffr 1917 Bp 1935-37, Edward T Demby suffr 1918-39, Richard B Mitchell 1938-56, Robt R Brown coadj 1955 Bp 56-70, Christoph Keller Jr coadj 1967 Bp 1970-81, Herbert A Donovan Jr coadj 1980 Bp 1981-93, Larry E Maze dio 1994-2006

Bishop—Rt Rev Larry R Benfield (1011) (Dio 6 Jan 07)

Sec of Conv M Nabors; *Treas and Fin* T Gammill; *Chanc* J Tisdale; *Reg* L Stinnett; *Fin Coord* MJ Hodges; *Deploy* J Alexander; *Cath Affairs* A Dafler Meaux; *Com* M Vano; *Hist* M McNeely; *ECW* K Roberts; *UTO* A Craig; *Yth and YA Coord* R Curtis; *Comm* J Matthews; *Archdcn* S Loudenslager

Stand Comm—Cler: K Alexander *Pres* E Henry-McKeeber S McKinnon; *Lay:* B Greenhill E Matthews R Newell

PARISHES, MISSIONS, AND CLERGY

Batesville St Pauls Episcopal Church **P** (178) 482 E Main St 72501-5628 (Mail to: PO Box 2255 72503-2255) James Mcdonald (870) 793-2203

Bella Vista St Theodores Episcopal Church **P** (246) 1001 Kingsland Rd 72714-5105 (Mail to: 1001 Kingsland Rd 72714-5105) Brandon Hudson Lowell Grisham (479) 855-2715

Benton St Matthews Episcopal Church **M** (65) 1112 Alcoa Rd 72015-3502 (Mail to: 1112 Alcoa Rd 72015-3502) James Bruno (501) 776-4176

Bentonville All Saints Church **M** (574) 2904 NW 3rd St 72712-3426 (Mail to: PO Box 528 72712-0528) Sara Milford (479) 802-0302

Blytheville St Stephens Episcopal Church **M** (23) 1512 Willow St 72315-2361 (Mail to: PO Box 597 72316-0597) (870) 763-8646

Camden St Johns Episcopal Church **M** (14) Corner Of Harrison & Vanburen 71701 (Mail to: PO Box 694 71711-0694) Elizabeth Baumgarten (870) 836-2658

Conway St Peters Episcopal Church **P** (413) 925 Mitchell St 72034-5147 (Mail to: 925 Mitchell St 72034-5147) Gregory Warren (501) 329-8174

Crossett St Marks Episcopal Church **M** (18) 909 Hickory St 71635-3513 (Mail to: 909 Hickory St 71635-3513) Robert Allen Robert Allen (870) 364-2664

Devalls Bluff St Peters Episcopal Church **M** (197) Rr 1 Box 110a 72041-9748 (Mail to: 1002 Highway 86 E 72041-9635) (870) 255-3190

El Dorado St Marys Episcopal Church **P** (198) 512 Champagnolle Rd 71730-4732 (Mail to: 512 Champagnolle Rd 71730-4732) Robert Wetherington (870) 863-7064

Eureka Springs St James Episcopal Church **M** (146) 28 Prospect Ave 72632-3039 (Mail to: 28 Prospect Ave 72632-3039) David Angus (479) 253-8610

Fayetteville St Pauls Episcopal Church **P** (2160) 224 N East Ave 72701-5225 (Mail to: PO Box 1190 72702-1190) Evan Garner Emily Bost Alice Spellman Charles Walling Lora Walsh (479) 442-7373

Foreman Saint Barnabas Church **M** (20) Bell St 2nd Ave 71836 (Mail to: PO Box 9 71836-0009) (870) 542-6880

Forrest City Christ Episcopal Church **M** (44) 1120 Ophelia St 72335-4624 (Mail to: PO Box 1077 72336-1077) Belinda Snyder (870) 633-6118

Forrest City Church of the Good Shepherd **P** (45) 400 Hill Ave 72335-3218 (Mail to: 400 Hill St 72335-3218) Travis Frank (870) 633-3093

Fort Smith St Augustines Episcopal Church **M** (9) 1400 N 9th St 72901-1341 (Mail to: PO Box 8283 72902-8283) (479) 785-1140

Fort Smith St Bartholomews Episcopal Ch **P** (279) 2701 Old Greenwood Rd 72903-3317 (Mail to: 2701 Old Greenwood Rd 72903-3399) Michael Briggs (479) 783-2101

Fort Smith Saint Johns Episcopal Church **P** (624) 215 N 6th St 72901-2105 (Mail to: 214 N 6th St 72901-2106) Michael Lager William Sims (479) 782-9912

Harrison St Johns Episcopal Church **P** (179) § 707 West Central Ave. 72601-4901 (Mail to: 707 W Central Ave 72601-4901) Greg Hoover (870) 741-5638

Heber Springs St Fran in the Pines Epis Ch **M** (60) 20 Woodland Cove Dr 72543-7688 (Mail to: 20 Woodland Cove Dr 72543-7688) Mary Dalby (501) 362-3311

Helena St Johns Episcopal Church **P** (119) 625 Pecan 72342-3201 (Mail to: PO Box 770 72342) (870) 338-8115

Hope St Marks Episcopal Church **M** (17) 301 S Elm St 71801-5219 (Mail to: PO Box 285 71802-0285) (870) 777-3297

Horseshoe Bnd St Stephens Episcopal Church **M** (11) 1005 Third St 72512-3724 (Mail to: 1005 3rd St 72512-3724) (870) 670-5214

Hot Springs St Lukes Episcopal Church **P** (571) § 228 Spring St 71901-4151 (Mail to: PO Box 1117 71902-1117) (501) 623-1653

Hot Springs Village Holy Trinity Episcopal Church **P** (178) 199 Barcelona Rd 71909-3801 (Mail to: 199 Barcelona Rd 71909-3801) Keith Hearnsberger (501) 9220299

Jacksonville St Stephens Episcopal Church **M** (55) 2413 Northeastern Ave 72076-2969 (Mail to: 2413 Northeastern Ave 72076-2969) Bruce Limozaine (501) 982-8701

Jonesboro St Marks Episcopal Church **P** (403) 531 W College Ave 72401-4984 (Mail to: 531 W College Ave 72401-4984) Kevin Gore (870) 932-2124

Lake Village Emmanuel Episcopal Church **M** (32) 422 North Lakeshore Dr 71653 (Mail to: PO Box 389 71653-0389) (870) 265-2230

Little Rock Christ Episcopal Church **P** (441) 509 Scott St 72201-3807 (Mail to: 509 Scott St 72201-3891) Kathryn Alexander Hannah Hooker (501) 375-2342

Little Rock Church of the Good Shepherd **M** (68) 2701 S Elm St 72204-6339 (Mail to: PO Box 164668 72216-4668) Michael Courtney (501) 218-8896

Little Rock St Margarets Episcopal Church **P** (365) § 20900 Chenal Pkwy 72223-9556 (Mail to: 20900 Chenal Pkwy 72223-9556) Mary Vano Michaelene Miller (501) 8211311

Little Rock St Marks Episcopal Church **P** (1447) § 1000 N Mississippi St 72207-5982 (Mail to: 1000 N Mississippi St 72207-5900) Barkley Thompson William Griffin Michael Mccain (501) 225-4203

Little Rock St Michaels Episcopal Church **P** (234) 12415 Cantrell Rd 72223-1727 (Mail to: 12415 Cantrell Rd 72223-1727) Elizabeth Henry-Mckeever (501) 224-1442

✠ **Little Rock** Trinity Episcopal Cathedral **O** (1592) § 310 W 17th St 72206-1461 (Mail to: 310 W 17th St 72206-1461) Amy Meaux (501) 372-0294

Magnolia St James Episcopal Church **M** (34) 901 Highland Cir 71753-2540 (Mail to: PO Box 846 71754-0846) (870) 234-6944

Marianna St Andrews Episcopal Church **P** (29) 49 S Carolina St 72360-2228 (Mail to: PO Box 241 72360-0241) (870) 295-2534

Maumelle St Nicholas Church **M** (80) PO Box 13677 72113-0677 (Mail to: PO Box 13677 72113-0677) Peggy Cromwell (501) 4204840

McGehee St Pauls Episcopal Church **M** (6) 100 N 3rd St 71654-2218 (Mail to: PO Box 246 71654-0246) (870) 222-6519

Mena Christ Episcopal Church **M** (23) 803 Church Ave 71953-3250 (Mail to: 803 Church Ave 71953-3250) (479) 216-2645

Monticello St Marys Episcopal Church **M** (14) 836 N Hyatt St 71655-4036 (Mail to: PO Box 193 71657-0193) Walter Windsor (870) 536-5493

Mountain Home St Andrews Episcopal Church **M** (116) 511 Coley Dr 72653 (Mail to: 511 Coley Dr 72653-2503) (870) 425-3560

N Little Rock Saint Luke's Episcopal Church **P** (304) 4106 John F Kennedy Blvd 72116-8250 (Mail to: C/O Rev.Carey D. Stone 4106 John F Kennedy Blvd 72116-8250) Carey Stone (501) 753-4281

Newport St Pauls Church **P** (122) 301 Hazel St 72112-3825 (Mail to: PO Box 367 72112-0367) (870) 523-2896

Osceola Calvary Episcopal Church **M** (27) 101 N Ash St 72370-2648 (Mail to: PO Box 292 72370-0292) (870) 563-2416

Paragould All Saints Episcopal Church **M** (28) 10th Main Sts 72450 (Mail to: PO Box 212 72451-0212) Evelyn Hornaday (870) 236-2367

Pine Bluff Grace Episcopal Church **P** (45) 4101 S Hazel St 71603-6832 (Mail to: 4101 S Hazel St 71603-6832) (870) 535-3852

Pine Bluff Trinity Episcopal Church **P** (337) 703 W 3rd Ave 71601-4009 (Mail to: PO Box 8069 71611-8069) Jess Reeves (870) 534-3832

Rogers St Andrews Episcopal Church **P** (157) Corner of 9th & Oak Sts 72757 (Mail to: PO Box 339 72757-0339) Craig Gavin (479) 636-4042

Russellville All Saints Episcopal Church **P** (220) 501 S Phoenix Ave 72801-7607 (Mail to: 501 S Phoenix Ave 72801-7607) (479) 968-3622

Searcy Trinity Episcopal Church **P** (59) 200 N Elm St 72143-5271 (Mail to: 200 N Elm St 72143-5271) Mark Harris Thomas Momberg (501) 268-5270

Siloam Springs Grace Episcopal Church **P** (236) 617 N Mt Olive St 72761 (Mail to: PO Box 767 72761-0767) Stanley Mckinnon (479) 524-8782

Springdale St Thomas Episcopal Church **P** (330) 2898 S 48th St 72762-5844 (Mail to: 2898 S 48th St 72762-5844) (479) 751-9184

Stuttgart St Albans Episcopal Church **P** (117) 1201 S Main St 72160-5307 (Mail to: PO Box 726 72160-0726) (870) 673-2848

Van Buren Trinity Episcopal Church **M** (92) 918 N 9th St 72956-2720 (Mail to: PO Box 382 72957-0382) (479) 474-3144

West Memphis Church of the Holy Cross **P** (47) 209 Park Dr 72301-3055 (Mail to: Church Office 209 Park Dr 72301-3055) Andrew Macbeth (870) 735-4517

DIOCESE OF ATLANTA
(PROVINCE IV)
Comprises middle and north GA
DIOCESAN OFFICE 2744 Peachtree Rd Atlanta GA 30305
TEL (404) 601-5320 FAX (404) 601-5330 WATS 800-537-6743
E-MAIL communications@episcopalatlanta.org WEB www.episcopalatlanta.org

Previous Bishops—
Cleland K Nelson 1907-17, Henry J Mikell 1917-42, John M Walker 1942-51, John B Walthour 1952-52, Randolph R Claiborne Jr 1953-72, Milton L Wood suffr 1967-74, Bennett J Sims 1972-83, C Judson Child Jr 1983-88, Frank Kellogg Allan 1989-2000 J Neil Alexander (2001-2012)

Bishop—Rt Rev Robert C Wright (1069) (Dio 13 Oct 12)

Assisting Bishop—Rt Rev Don Wimberly (789) (dio 1984)

Assisting Bishop—Rt Rev Paul Lambert (1031) (dio 2008)

Cn to Ord A Schuster Weltner *Treas* P Farnham; *Chanc* E R Perry; *Chanc* T Christopher; *Sec of Council* Rev R Game; *Min* J Thompson-Quartey; *COM* Rev K Swanson; *Comm* E Davis; *Educ Chair* S Ulrey ; *Stew* T Pallot; *Church Archtr & Constr* L Lowrey; *Mikell Conf Center* K Struble; *Liturg* ; *Annual Council* W Callaway; *Dir ECF* L Hardegree; *Dir Fin* B Schroeder; *Youth Miss* H Tubbs; *Hispanic Miss* Rev Cn I Rodriguez Dismantling Racism C Meeks

Stand Comm—Cler: N Matthis G Crawford Jr L Holder *Lay:* K Sachsenmaier M Cravens T Jenkins

Deans of Convoc—GA Mountains J Hamilton; *Oconee* D Brown; *Chattahoochee Valley* G Burton-Edwards; *Mid-Atlanta* T Black; *Marietta* S Fisher; *N Atlanta* P Templeton; *NE Metro:* R Game; *SW Atlanta* J Jackson; *E Atlanta* C Vaughn; *Middle GA* D Probst; *NW GA* J Herring

PARISHES, MISSIONS, AND CLERGY

Acworth St Teresas Episcopal Church **P** (249) 5725 Fords Rd NW 30101-4674 (Mail to: 5725 Fords Rd NW 30101-4674) (770) 590-9040

Athens Emmanuel Episcopal Church **P** (1269) § 498 Prince Ave 30601-2449 (Mail to: 498 Prince Ave 30601-2467) Samuel Porras (706) 543-1294

Athens St Gregory the Great Epis Ch **P** (317) 3195 Barnett Shoals Rd 30605-4327 (Mail to: Attn: Kendall Kookogey 3195 Barnett Shoals Rd 30605-4327) Thelma Mathis (706) 546-7553

Athens Episcopal Center at UGA **CC** 980 S Lumpkin St 30605-5119 (Mail to: 980 S Lumpkin St 30605-5119) (706) 353-2330

Atlanta Absalom Jones Student Center **CC** C/O The Rev Frank M Ross 634 W Peachtree St SW 30308-1925 (Mail to: C/O The Rev Frank M Ross 634 Peachtree Street SW 30308) (404) 521-1602

Atlanta All Saints Episcopal Church **P** (2695) § 634 W Peachtree St NW 30308-1925 (Mail to: 634 W Peachtree St NW 30308-1981) Simon Mainwaring Andrew Barnett William Clarkson James Donald Judson Mull Nontombi Tutu (404) 881-0835

✠ **Atlanta** Cathedral of St Philip **O** (6667) § 2744 Peachtree Rd NW 30305-2937 (Mail to: 2744 Peachtree Rd NW 30305-2920) Samuel Candler George Maxwell Lauren Holder Julia Mitchener Julia Mitchener Cathy Zappa (404) 365-1000

Atlanta Church of the Epiphany **P** (1038) 2089 Ponce De Leon Ave NE 30307 (Mail to: 2089 Ponce De Leon Ave NE 30307-1345) Amy Dills-Moore (404) 373-8338

Atlanta Church of the Holy Comforter **P** (77) 737 Woodland Ave SE 30316-2454 (Mail to: 737 Woodland Ave SE 30316-2454) Katharine Hilliard-Yntema Bert Smith (404) 627-6510

Atlanta Church of the Incarnation **P** (146) 2407 Cascade Rd SW 30311-3225 (Mail to: 2407 Cascade Rd SW 30311-3286) Lynne Washington (404) 755-6654

Atlanta Emmaus House **P** (116) 993 Hank Aaron Dr SW 30315-1703 (Mail to: Finance Department 2744 Peachtree Rd NW 30305-2937) (404) 525-5948

Atlanta GA Tech/Georgia State Epis Ctr **CC** 2744 Peachtree Rd. NW 30305 (Mail to: 2744 Peachtree Rd NW 30305-2937) (404) 881-0835

Atlanta Holy Innocents Epis Church **P** (1581) § 805 Mount Vernon Hwy 30327-4338 (Mail to: 805 Mount Vernon Rd NW 30327-4396) William Murray Thomas Lucas Ruth Pattison (404) 303-2150

Atlanta Saint Anne's Episcopal Church **P** (841) § 3098 Saint Annes Ln 30327-1638 (Mail to: 3098 Saint Annes Ln NW 30327-1638) Grady Crawford (404) 237-5589

Atlanta St Bartholomews Episcopal Ch **P** (875) 1790 Lavista Rd NE 30329-3604 (Mail to: 1790 Lavista Rd NE 30329-3604) Angela Shepherd Robert Sherrill (404) 634-3336

Atlanta St Bedes Episcopal Church **P** (668) 2601 Henderson Mill Rd NE 30345-2134 (Mail to: 2601 Henderson Mill Rd NE 30345-2199) Steven Vaughn Lynnsay Buehler (770) 938-9797

Atlanta St Dunstan's Episcopal Church **P** (157) 4393 Garmon Rd NW 30327-3831 (Mail to: 4393 Garmon Rd NW 30327-3831) Patricia Templeton Margaret Harney (404) 266-1018

Atlanta St Johns Episcopal Church **P** (98) § 3480 Main St 30337-2064 (Mail to: 3480 Main St 30337-2099) Timothy Black (404) 761-8402

Atlanta St Luke's Episcopal Church **P** (1834) 435 Peachtree St NE 30308 (Mail to: 435 Peachtree St NE 30308) Winnie Varghese Horace Griffin Elizabeth Shows Caffey (404) 873-7600

Atlanta St Martin in the Flds Epis Ch **P** (1281) § 3110 Ashford Dunwoody Rd NE 30319-2751 (Mail to: PO Box 190109 31119-0109) Monica Mainwaring (404) 228-0755

Atlanta St Patricks Episcopal Church **P** (453) 4755 N Peachtree Rd 30338-5812 (Mail to: 4755 N Peachtree Rd 30338-5803) Paul Game (770) 455-6523

Atlanta St Pauls Episcopal Church **P** (684) 294 Peyton Rd SW 30311-2152 (Mail to: 294 Peyton Rd SW 306 Peyton Rd SW 30311-2134) (404) 696-3620

Atlanta Iglesia Epis de Santa Maria **P** (294) 845 Glenway Dr 30344-6703 (Mail to: 845 Glenway Dr 30344-6703) (404) 707-1217

Atlanta Church of Our Saviour **P** (103) § 1068 N Highland Ave NE 30306-3551 (Mail to: 985 Los Angeles Ave NE 30306-3673) Melanie Rowell Carole Maddux (404) 872-4169

Austell Church of the Good Shepherd **P** (286) § 6216 Love St 30168-4714 (Mail to: PO Box 682 30168-1050) (678) 851-2006

Blairsville St Clares Episcopal Church **P** (213) 1272 Ledford Rd 30512-3107 (Mail to: 777 Ledford Rd 30512-3110) Elizabeth Schellingerhoudt (706) 745-0607

Buford St Mary & St Martha of Bethany **P** (585) 4346 Ridge Rd 30519-1853 (Mail to: 4346 Ridge Rd 30519-1853) George Mustard (770) 271-4067

Calhoun St Timothys Episcopal Church **P** (200) PO Box 701 30703-0701 (Mail to: 224 Trammell St 30701-2218) (706) 629-1056

Canton St Clement's Episcopal Church **P** (391) 2795 Ridge Rd 30114-9501 (Mail to: PO Box 4156 30114-0010) James Stutler (770) 345-6722

Carrollton St Margarets Episcopal Church **P** (637) 606 Newnan St 30117-3429 (Mail to: 602 Newnan St 30117-3429) Jeffery Jackson (770) 832-3931

Cartersville Church of the Ascension **P** (265) 205 W Cherokee Ave 30120-3003 (Mail to: 205 W Cherokee Ave 30120-3003) Sandra Brice (770) 382-2626

Cedartown Saint James Church **P** (63) § 302 West Ave 30125-3422 (Mail to: PO Box 85 30125-0085) Paul Anderson (770) 748-2894

Clarkesville Grace Calvary Church **P** (346) 260 E Green St 30523 (Mail to: PO Box 490 30523-0009) (706) 754-2451

Clayton St James Episcopal Church **P** (151) 206 Warwoman Rd 30525-5100 (Mail to: PO Box 69 30525-0002) Anthony Sgro (706) 782-6179

Columbus St Mary Magdalene Episcopal Ch **P** (45) § 4244 Saint Marys Rd 31907-6243 (Mail to: 4244 St Mary Road 31907) (706) 689-2790

Columbus Saint Thomas Episcopal Church **P** (668) § 2100 Hilton Ave 31906-1500 (Mail to: 2100 Hilton Ave 31906-1500) Lydia Burton-Edwards Roxane Gwyn (706) 324-4264

Columbus Trinity Episcopal Church **HC** (623) 1130 First Avenue 31901 (Mail to: 1130 First Avenue 31901) Timothy Graham (706) 322-5569

Conyers St Simons Episcopal Church **P** (197) 1522 Highway 138 NE 30013-1266 (Mail to: PO Box 102 30012-0102) Jane Weston (770) 483-3242

Covington Church of the Good Shepherd **P** (334) 4140 Clark St SW 30014-2713 (Mail to: 4140 Clark St SW 30014-2713) (770) 786-3278

Cumming Church of the Holy Spirit **P** (451) § 724 Pilgrim Mill Rd 30040-2151 (Mail to: Attn: The Rev Brandon Thomas Mozingo PO Box 1010 30028-1010) Brandon Mozingo (770) 8878190

Dahlonega St Elizabeths Episcopal Church **P** (141) 1188 Hamp Mill Rd 30533-4872 (Mail to: 1188 Hamp Mill Rd 30533-4872) John Hamilton Paul Roberts (706) 864-5423

Dalton St Marks Episcopal Church **P** (339) § 901 W Emery St 30720-2330 (Mail to: 901 W Emery St 30720-2330) Richard Tiff (706) 278-8857

Decatur Church of the Holy Cross **P** (327) 2005 S Columbia Pl 30032-5945 (Mail to: 2005 S Columbia Pl 30032-5945) Dennis Patterson (404) 284-1211

Decatur Holy Trinity Parish **P** (456) 515 E Ponce De Leon Ave 30030-1941 (Mail to: 515 E Ponce De Leon Ave 30030-1992) Jimmy Tallant Ellen Purdum Ellen Purdum (404) 377-2622

Decatur St Timothys Episcopal Church **P** (134) 2833 Flat Shoals Rd 30034-1040 (Mail to: 2833 Flat Shoals Rd 30034-1040) Ricardo Bailey (404) 241-7711

Douglasville St Julians Episcopal Church **P** (190) 5400 Stewart Mill Rd 30135-2545 (Mail to: 5400 Stewart Mill Rd 30135-2545) Gregory Gibson (770) 949-9949

Eatonton All Angels Episcopal Church **P** (26) PO Box 4695 31024-4695 (Mail to: PO Box 4695 31024-4695) (478) 718-9189

Elberton St Albans Episcopal Church **P** (23) 109 Brookside Dr 30635-2503 (Mail to: PO Box 733 30635-0733) (706) 376-1489

Fayetteville Church of the Nativity **P** (195) 130 Antioch Rd 30215-5701 (Mail to: 130 Antioch Rd 30215-5701) (770) 460-6390

Fort Valley St Andrews Episcopal Church **P** (42) PO Box 308 31030-0308 (Mail to: 309 Central Ave 31030-3740) (478) 987-8291

Fort Valley St Lukes Episcopal Church **P** (35) PO Box 770 31030-0770 (Mail to: PO Box 770 31030-0770) (706) 975-3264

Gainesville Grace Episcopal Church **P** (894) § 431 Washington St SE 30501-3612 (Mail to: 422 Brenau Ave 30501-3612) Stuart Higginbotham Mary Demmler Michael McCann Cynthia Park (770) 536-0126

Greensboro Episcopal Ch of the Redeemer **P** (134) 303 N Main St 30642-1137 (Mail to: PO Box 93 30642-0093) William Combs (706) 453-7171

Griffin St George's Episcopal Church **P** (334) § 132 N 10th St 30223-2841 (Mail to: 132 N 10th St 30223-2841) Kirk Lafon (770) 227-4453

Hamilton St Nicholas Episcopal Church **P** (82) 69 Mobley Rd 31811 (Mail to: PO Box 752 31811-0752) (706) 628-7272

Hartwell St Andrews Episcopal Church **P** (89) § 579 Fairview Ave 30643-2166 (Mail to: 579 Fairview Ave 30643-2166) Reid Hamilton (706) 376-4986

Jasper Church of the Holy Family **P** (330) § 100 Griffith Rd 30143-4422 (Mail to: 202 Griffith Rd 30143-4422) George Yandell Charles Hackett Byron Tindall (770) 893-4525

Kennesaw Christ Episcopal Church **P** (287) § 1210 Wooten Lake Rd NW 30144-1347 (Mail to: 1210 Wooten Lake Rd NW 30144-1347) Marshall Day (770) 422-9114

Lagrange St Marks Episcopal Church **P** (417) § 207 N Greenwood St 30240-2603 (Mail to: 207 N Greenwood St 30240-2603) (706) 884-8911

Lawrenceville St Edwards Episcopal Church **P** (285) 737 Moon Rd 30045-6109 (Mail to: 737 Moon Rd 30046-6109) Fabio Sotelo (770) 963-6128

Macon Christ Episcopal Church **P** (697) 538 Walnut St 31201-2709 (Mail to: 538 Walnut St 31201-2709) Cynthia Knapp Arthur Villarreal (478) 745-0427

Macon St Francis Episcopal Church **P** (240) § 432 Forest Hill Rd 31210-4824 (Mail to: 432 Forest Hill Rd 31210-4824) Ben Wells Ben Wells (478) 477-4616

Macon St Pauls Episcopal Church **P** (287) 753 College St 31201-1720 (Mail to: 753 College St 31201-1720) Bryan Hinson Pamela Lightsey (478) 743-4623

Madison Church of the Advent **P** (210) 338 Academy St 30650-1545 (Mail to: 338 Academy St 30650-1545) Daniel Brown (706) 342-4787

Marietta Church of the Annunciation **P** (321) 1673 Jamerson Rd 30066-1213 (Mail to: 1673 Jamerson Rd 30066-1213) Paul Mccabe (770) 928-7916

Marietta St Catherines Episcopal Church **P** (1107) § 571 Holt Rd NE 30068-3039 (Mail to: 571 Holt Rd NE 30068-3039) Sarah Fisher (770) 971-2839

Marietta St James Episcopal Church **P** (1430) § 161 Church St NE 30060-1629 (Mail to: 161 Church St NE 30060-1693) Daron Vroon (770) 428-5841

Marietta St Judes Episcopal Church **P** (245) § 220 Windy Hill Rd SW 30060-5547 (Mail to: 220 Windy Hill Rd SW 30060-5547) William Austin (770) 435-0936

Marietta Church of St Peter & St Paul **P** (950) 1795 Johnson Ferry Rd 30062-6400 (Mail to: 1795 Johnson Ferry Rd 30062-6400) Elisa Harres Thomas Pumphrey (770) 977-7473

Mcdonough St Josephs Episcopal Church **P** (318) 1865 Highway 20 W 30253-7316 (Mail to: 1865 Highway 20 E 30252-2264) Ann Barker (770) 957-7517

Milledgeville St Stephens Episcopal Church **P** (291) § 220 S Wayne St 31061-3442 (Mail to: PO Box 309 31059-0309) David Probst (478) 452-2710

Milton Saint Aidan's Episcopal Church **P** (605) § 13560 Cogburn Rd 30004-3648 (Mail to: 13560 Cogburn Rd 30004-3648) Warren Simmons (770) 521-0207

Monroe St Albans Episcopal Church **P** (82) 210 N Broad St 30655-1844 (Mail to: C/O Parish Treasurer PO Box 655 30655-0655) Richard Bardusch Patricia Merchant (855) 398-4597

Montezuma St Marys Episcopal Church **P** (12) 608 Rawls St 31063-1332 (Mail to: 608 Rawls St 31063-1332) (478) 472-8758

Morrow St Augustine of Canterbury **P** (116) 1221 Morrow Rd 30260-1624 (Mail to: PO Box 169 1221 Morrow Rd 30260-0169) (770) 961-9353

Newnan St Pauls Episcopal Church **P** (733) 576 Roscoe Rd 30263-4782 (Mail to: 576 Roscoe Rd 30263-4782) Hazel Glover (770) 253-4264

Norcross Christ Episcopal Church **P** (858) 400 Holcomb Bridge Rd 30071-2040 (Mail to: 400 Holcomb Bridge Rd 30071-2040) Elizabeth Hendrick (770) 447-1166

Oakwood St Gabriels Episcopal Church **P** (111) 2920 Landrum Education Dr 30566-3405 (Mail to: 2920 Landrum Education Dr 30566-3405) (770) 503-7555

Peachtree City St Andrs in the Pines Epis Ch **P** (218) 316 N Peachtree Pkwy 30269-1360 (Mail to: 316 N Peachtree Pkwy 30269-1360) (770) 487-8415

Perry St Christophers at the Xroads **P** (132) 1207 Macon Rd 31069-2612 (Mail to: 1207 Macon Rd 31069-2612) (478) 987-2190

Rome Church of the Transfiguration **P** (46) 304 Coker Dr SW 30165-3416 (Mail to: 304 Coker Dr SW 30165-3416) (706) 234-0197

Rome Saint Peter's Episcopal Church **P** (733) 101 E 4th Ave 30161-3119 (Mail to: 101 E 4th Ave 30161-3119) John Herring David Boyd (706) 2919111

Roswell St Davids Episcopal Church **P** (1976) § 1015 Old Roswell Rd 30076-1607 (Mail to:

1015 Old Roswell Rd 30076-1607) Thomas Slone Michelle Fritch Anne Swiedler (770) 993-6084

Sandy Springs Highpoint Episcopal Community **P** 4945 High Point Rd NE 30342 (Mail to: 4945 High Point Rd 30342-2310) (404) 252-3324

Sautee Nacoochee Epis Ch of the Resurrection **P** (270) § 1755 Duncan Bridge Rd 30571-3611 (Mail to: 1755 Duncan Bridge Rd 30571-3611) Scott Kidd (706) 865-9680

Smyrna St Benedicts Episcopal Church **P** (1378) § 2160 Cooper Lake Rd SE 30080-6328 (Mail to: 2160 Cooper Lake Rd SE 30080-6328) Jenna Strizak (678) 279-4300

Snellville St Matthew's Episcopal Church **P** (566) § 1520 Oak Rd 30078-2230 (Mail to: 1520 Oak Rd 30078-2230) (770) 979-4210

Stone Mountain St Michael And All Angels Ch **P** (258) 6780 James B Rivers Dr 30083-2249 (Mail to: PO Box 1087 30086-1087) Richard Arthur (770) 469-8551

Suwanee St Columbas Episcopal Church **P** (1319) 5400 Laurel Springs Pkwy Ste 1 30024-6056 (Mail to: 939 James Burgess Rd 30024-

1128) Paul Norris (770) 888-4464

Thomaston St Thomas of Cntbry Epis Ch **M** (14) 400 Georgia Ave 30286-3518 (Mail to: 610 Avalon Rd 30286-4002) (706) 646-3364

Toccoa St Matthias Episcopal Church **P** (128) 995 E Tugalo St 30577-1930 (Mail to: 995 E Tugalo St 30577-1938) Scott Harding (706) 886-4413

Trion St Barnabas Episcopal Church **P** (71) 100 Central Ave 30753-1125 (Mail to: PO Box 685 30753-0685) (706) 734-3098

Warner Robins All Saints Episcopal Church **P** (261) 1708 Watson Blvd 31093-3632 (Mail to: 1708 Watson Blvd 31093-3632) Bonnie Underwood Barbara Windom (478) 923-1791

Washington Church of the Mediator **P** (71) PO Box 716 30673 (Mail to: PO Box 716 30673-0716) (706) 678-7226

West Point St Johns Episcopal Church **P** (66) § 501 Avenue C 31833-2037 (Mail to: 502 Avenue C 31833-2026) (706) 645-2156

Winder St Anthonys Episcopal Church **P** (57) 174 Saint Anthonys Dr 30680-1587 (Mail to: 174 Saint Anthonys Dr 30680-1587) (770) 867-5633

AUSTRIA; BELGIUM
See Europe

DIOCESE OF BETHLEHEM
(PROVINCE III)
Comprises 14 counties of Northeastern PA
DIOCESAN OFFICE 333 Wyandotte St Bethlehem PA 18015
TEL (610) 691-5655 FAX (610) 691-1682
E-MAIL office@diobeth.org WEB www.diobeth.org

Previous Bishops— Mark AD Howe 1871-95, Nelson S Rulison coadj 1884 Bp 1895-97, Ethelbert Talbot 1898-1928, Frank W Sterrett coadj 1923 Bp 1928-54, Fred J Warnecke coadj 1953 Bp 1954-71, Lloyd E Gressle coadj 1970 Bp 1971-83, Mark Dyer coadj 1982 Bp 1983-95, Paul V Marshall Bp, 1996-2013, Sean Rowe prov 2014-18

Bishop—Rt Rev Kevin D. Nichols (September 15, 2018)

Northern Cn Miss Rev M Artman; *Southern Cn Miss* Rev B Harrison-Seward; *Cn to Ord for Mission Resources & COO* S Baker; *Sec* Judith Dickerson; *Treas* EH House; *Chanc* L Henry; *Missioner for Fin & Admin* P Lapinski; *Cn for Racial Reconciliation &*

Community Engagement & Asst to the Bp S Milien; *Bookkeeper* C Bakos

Stand Comm—Cler: Pres JD Moyer E Trygar J Bender R Conn; *Lay:* L Holzinger C McMullen L Graham C Dickerson

PARISHES, MISSIONS, AND CLERGY

Allentown Grace Episcopal Church **P** (50) 108 N 5th St 18102-4108 (Mail to: 108 N 5th St 18102-4161) Rodney Conn (610) 435-0782

Allentown St Andrew's Episcopal Church **P** (163) 1901 Pennsylvania Ave 18109-3111 (Mail to: C/O Treasurer 1900 Pennsylvania Ave 18109-3187) Thomas Allen (610) 865-3603

Allentown Church of the Mediator **P** (195) 1620 W Turner St 18102-3637 (Mail to: 1620 W Turner St 18102-3637) Dale Grandfield (610) 434-0155

Ashland Memorial Church of St John **P** 106 N 12th St 17921-1263 (Mail to: C/O North Parish PO Box 82 17921-0082) (570) 874-4532

Athens Trinity Episcopal Church **P** (71) 701 S Main St 18810-1009 (Mail to: 701 S Main St 18810-1009) Benjamin Lentz (570) 888-5715

✠ **Bethlehem** Cathedral Ch of the Nativity **O** (1048) 321 Wyandotte St 18015-1527 (Mail to: 321 Wyandotte St 18015-1592) Jonathan Stratton Barry Harte Maryann Philbrook (610) 865-0727

Bethlehem Trinity Church **P** (304) 44 E Market St 18018-5926 (Mail to: 44 E Market St 18018-5926) Richard Ditterline (610) 8674741

Carbondale St James Church **SC** 2074 State Route 247 18407-7760 (Mail to: PO Box 4 18407-0004) (610) 691-5655

Carbondale Trinity Episcopal Church **P** (121) 58 River St 18407-2306 (Mail to: 58 River St 18407-2306) (570) 282-3620

Dallas Church of the Prince of Peace **P** (182) 420 Main St 18612-1807 (Mail to: 420 Main St 18612-1807) Joseph Rafferty Christine Sutton (570) 675-1723

Dalton The Church of the Epiphany **P** (93) Dalton 25 Church Hl 18414-7739 (Mail to: PO Box 189 18411-0189) (570) 563-1564

Douglassville St Gabriels Episcopal Church **P** (247) § 1188 Ben Franklin Hwy E 19518-1803 (Mail to: PO Box 396 19518-0396) Andrew Vanburen (610) 385-3144

Drifton St James Church **P** (45) Rt. 940, Main St 18221 (Mail to: PO Box 217 18221-0217) (570) 636-3967

Easton Trinity Episcopal Church **P** (550) 234 Spring Garden St 18042-3657 (Mail to: 234 Spring Garden St 18042-3657) (610) 253-0792

Emmaus St Margarets Church **P** (122) 150 Elm St 18049-2622 (Mail to: 150 Elm St 18049-2622) (610) 967-1450

Forest City Christ Church **P** (54) 700 Delaware St 18421-1002 (Mail to: 700 Delaware St 18421-1002) (570) 282-3620

Hamlin St Johns Episcopal Church **P** (181) 564 Easton Turnpike 18427 (Mail to: PO Box 118 18427-0118) (570) 689-9260

Hazleton St Peters Episcopal Church **P** (98) 46 S Laurel St 18201-6311 (Mail to: 46 S Laurel St 18201-6399) (570) 454-6543

Hellertown St Georges Episcopal Church **P** (115) 735 Delaware Ave 18055-1819 (Mail to: 735 Delaware Ave 18055-1899) Harold Mayo (610) 838-9355

Honesdale Christ Church closed **P** (16) 1005 Texas Palmyra Hwy 18431-7672 (Mail to: 333 Wyandotte St 18015-1527) (610) 6915655

Honesdale Grace Episcopal Church **P** (111) 827 Church St 18431-1824 (Mail to: 827 Church St 18431-1824) (570) 253-2760

Jermyn St James-St George Epis Ch **P** (91) 398 Washington Ave 18433-1342 (Mail to: 398 Washington Ave 18433-1342) (570) 876-4896

Jim Thorpe St Marks and St Johns Epis Ch **P** (156) 21 Race St 18229-2003 (Mail to: 21 Race St 18229-2003) (570) 325-2241

Kingston Grace Episcopal Church **P** (159) 30 Butler St 18704 (Mail to: 30 Butler St 18704-4706) Daniel Gross (570) 287-8440

Kutztown St Barnabas Episcopal Church **P** (16) 234 E Main St 19530-1517 (Mail to: PO Box 236 234 E Main St 19530-0236) (484) 6482814

Lebanon St Lukes Church Episcopal **P** (469) 22 S 6th St 17042-5338 (Mail to: 22 S 6th St 17042-5338) David Zwifka (717) 272-8251

Lehighton All Saints Episcopal Church **P** (169) 301 N 2nd St 18235-1418 (Mail to: PO Box 147 18235-0147) (610) 377-2675

Milford Good Shepherd & St Johns Ch **P** (150) 110 W Catherine St 18337-1418 (Mail to: 110 W Catherine St 18337-1418) (570) 296-8123

Montrose St Pauls Church **P** (53) 276 Church St 18801-1271 (Mail to: 276 Church St 18801-1271) (570) 278-2954

Morgantown St Thomas Episcopal Church **P** (75) 6251 Morgantown Rd 19543 (Mail to: PO Box 97 19543-0097) Donald Howells (610) 2869547

Moscow St Marks Episcopal Church **P** (98) 1109 Church St 18444-0678 (Mail to: 1109 Church St PO Box 678 18444-9396) (570) 842-7231

Mount Pocono Trinity Episcopal Church **P** (54) Hcr # Box 1 18344 (Mail to: 137 Trinity Hill Rd 18344-7162) (570) 839-9376

Mountain Top St Martins Church **P** (108) 3085 Church Rd 18707-9035 (Mail to: 3085 Church Rd 18707-9035) Charles Warwick (570) 868-5358

Nanticoke Saint Andrew's Church **P** (46) 12 East Kirmar Avenue 18634-3608 (Mail to: C/O Susan Maza Sr Warden 127 W Union St 18634-2727) Charles Warwick (570) 825-0547

Nazareth St Brigids Church **P** (169) 310 Madison Ave 18064-2613 (Mail to: 310 Madison Ave 18064-2613) John Marcantonio (610) 746-3910

New Milford St Marks Episcopal Church **P** (23) 1148 Main St 18834-2011 (Mail to: 1148 Main St PO Box 406 18834-7434) (570) 465-3896

Palmerton St Johns Episcopal Church **P** (89) 365 Lafayette Ave 18071-1617 (Mail to: 365 Lafayette Ave 18071-1617) (610) 826-2611

Pen Argyl Saint Joseph's Church **P** (14) 1440 Verona Dr 18072-1350 (Mail to: 1440 Verona Dr 18072-1350) (610) 759-0973

Pottsville Trinity Episcopal Church **P** (251) 200 S 2nd St 17901-3520 (Mail to: 200 S 2nd St 17901-3520) Kurt Kovalovich (570) 622-8720

Reading Christ Church **P** (634) 5th & Court St 19603 (Mail to: PO Box 1094 19603-1094) Bryce Wandrey (610) 374-8269

Reading St Albans Episcopal Church **P** (293) § 2848 Saint Albans Dr 19608-1028 (Mail to:

2848 Saint Albans Dr 19608-1028) Michelle Moyer Jeffrey Funk Walter Krieger Nancy Packard (610) 678-7001

Reading St Marys Church **P** (29) 100 W Windsor St 19601-2033 (Mail to: PO Box 13685 19612-3685) (610) 374-7914

Saint Clair Holy Apostles Episcopal Church **P** Nicholas And Hancock Sts 17970 (Mail to: 106 N 12th St 17921-1263) James Smith (570) 429-2771

Sayre Church of the Redeemer **P** (111) 201 S Wilbur Ave 18840-1605 (Mail to: 201 S Wilbur Ave 18840-1605) Melinda Artman (570) 888-2270

Scranton Church of the Good Shepherd **P** (43) 2425 N Washington Ave 18509-1422 (Mail to: 1780 N Washington Ave 18509-1959) Howard Stringfellow (570) 347-1760

Scranton St Lukes Episcopal Church **P** (193) 232 Wyoming Ave 18503-1437 (Mail to: 232 Wyoming Ave 18503-1437) Rebecca Barnes (570) 342-7654

Shuykl Haven St James Episcopal Church **P** (64) 100 Dock St 17972-1208 (Mail to: 100 Dock St 17972-1208) (570) 385-0737

St. Clair North Parish Episcopal Church **P** (172) 307 E. Hancock St. 17970 (Mail to: PO Box 487 17931-0487) Timothy Albright James Smith (570) 429-7107

Stroudsburg Christ Episcopal Church **P** (228) 205 N 7th St 18360-2113 (Mail to: 205 N 7th St 18360-2113) Bruce Gowe (570) 421-7481

Susquehanna Christ Episcopal Church **P** (15) 302 W Main St 18847 (Mail to: PO Box 222 18847-0222) (570) 853-9003

Tamaqua Calvary Episcopal Church **P** (43) 300 W Broad St 18252-1821 (Mail to: C/O Miss Georgine P Feel 309 W Broad St 18252-1820)

(610) 377-0874

Towanda Christ Episcopal Church **P** (155) One Main St 18848-1900 (Mail to: 1 Main St 18848-1900) Joseph Holman (570) 265-5035

Trexlertown St Anne's Episcopal Church **P** (290) 6667 Lower Macungie Rd 18087-0368 (Mail to: PO Box 368 18087-0368) Donald Schaible (610) 3983321

Troy St Pauls Episcopal Church **P** (76) 195 Elmira St 16947-1201 (Mail to: 130 Elmira St 16947-1202) (570) 297-4864

Tunkhannock St Peters Episcopal Church **P** (24) PO Box 459 18657-0459 (Mail to: PO Box 459 18657-0459) (570) 836-2233

West Pittston Trinity Episcopal Church **P** (83) 337 Spring Street 18643-2137 (Mail to: 220 Montgomery Ave 18643-2137) Joseph Rafferty (570) 654-3261

Whitehall St Stephens Episcopal Church **P** (119) § 3900 Mechanicsville Rd 18052-3324 (Mail to: 3900 Mechanicsville Rd 18052-3347) Harold Mayo Harold Mayo (610) 435-3901

Wilkes Barre Holy Cross Episcopal Church **P** (128) 373 N Main St 18702-4409 (Mail to: 373 N Main St 18702-4409) Timothy Alleman (570) 823-2600

✠ **Wilkes Barre** St Stephens Pro-Cathedral **O** (286) 35 S Franklin St 18701-1202 (Mail to: 35 S Franklin St 18701-1299) Timothy Alleman (570) 825-6653

Wilkes Barre St Clement and St Peters Ch **P** (90) 70 Lockhart St 18702-3604 (Mail to: 70 Lockhart St 18702-3604) Charles Warwick (570) 822-8043

Wind Gap St Marys Episcopal Church **P** (32) 340 S Lehigh Ave, 18091-0365 (Mail to: C/O Parish of the Holy Family PO Box 36 18072-0036) (610) 863-8007

STATE OF CALIFORNIA

Dioceses of California (CA), El Camino Real (ECR), Los Angeles (LA), Northern California (NCA), San Diego (SD) and San Joaquin (SanJ).

Alameda—CA	Arroyo Grande—ECR	Bolinas—CA	Chula Vista—SD
Albany—CA	Atascadero—ECR	Bonita—SD	Claremont—LA
Alhambra—LA	Auburn—NCA	Borrego Spgs—SD	Clayton—CA
Alpine—SD	Avery—SanJ	Buena Pk—LA	Cloverdale—NCA
Altadena—LA	Bakersfield—SanJ	Burlingame—CA	Colusa—NCA
Alturas—NCA	Barstow—LA	Calistoga—NCA	Compton—LA
Anaheim—LA	Beaumont—LA	Camarillo—LA	Concord—CA
Anderson—NCA	Belmont—CA	Cambria—ECR	Corning—NCA
Antelope—NCA	Belvedere—CA	Cameron Pk—NCA	Corona—LA
Antioch—CA	Benicia—NCA	Carlsbad—SD	Corona Del Mar—LA
Apple Valley—LA	Ben Lomond—ECR	Carmel—ECR	Coronado—SD
Aptos—ECR	Berkeley—CA	Carmichael—NCA	Corte Madera—CA
Arcadia—LA	Beverly Hills—LA	Castro Valley—CA	Costa Mesa—LA
Arcata—NCA	Big Bear City—LA	Chico—NCA	Covina—LA

Crescent City—NCA
Crockett—CA
Cupertino—ECR
Daly City—CA
Danville—CA
Davis—NCA
Del Mar—SD
Downey—LA
El Cajon—SD
El Centro—SD
El Monte—LA
El Segundo—LA
Encinitas—SD
Encino—LA
Escondido—SD
Eureka—NCA
Fairfield—NCA
Fallbrook—SD
Ferndale—NCA
Fillmore—LA
Folsom—NCA
Ft Bragg—NCA
Fortuna—NCA
Foster City—CA
Fremont—CA
Fullerton—LA
Galt—NCA
Garden Grove—LA
Gardena—LA
Gilroy—ECR
Glendale—LA
Glendora—LA
Granada Hills—LA
Grass Valley—NCA
Gridley—NCA
Gualala—NCA
Hacienda Hgts—LA
Half Moon Bay—CA
Hanford—SanJ
Hawthorne—LA
Healdsburg—NCA
Hemet—SD
Hermosa Bch—LA
Hesperia—LA
Hollister—ECR
Huntington Bch—LA
Huntington Pk—LA
Idyllwild—SD
Indio—SD
Inglewood—LA
Inverness—CA
Irvine—LA
Isla Vista—LA
Jolon—ECR
Kenwood—NCA
Kernville—SanJ
King City—ECR
La Canada—LA
La Crescenta—LA

Lafayette—CA
La Jolla—SD
La Mesa—SD
Lancaster—LA
La Verne—LA
Laguna Bch—LA
Laguna Hills—LA
Laguna Niguel—LA
Lake Elsinore—SD
Lakeport—NCA
Lemon Grove—SD
Lincoln—NCA
Livermore—CA
Lodi—SanJ
Lompoc—LA
Long Bch—LA
Los Altos—CA
Los Angeles—LA
Los Gatos—ECR
Los Olivos—LA
Los Osos—ECR
Madera—SanJ
Malibu—LA
Marina—ECR
Martinez—CA
Marysville—NCA
Menlo Pk—CA
Merced—SanJ
Mill Valley—CA
Modesto—SanJ
Monrovia—LA
Monterey—ECR
Monterey Pk—LA
Monte Rio—NCA
Moreno Valley—LA
Morgan Hill—ECR
Morro Bay—ECR
Mt Shasta—NCA
Mtn View—ECR
Napa—NCA
National City—SD
Needles—LA
Nevada City—NCA
Newport Bch—LA
Norwalk—LA
Novato—CA
Oakland—CA
Oakhurst—SanJ
Oak Park—LA
Ojai—LA
Ontario—LA
Orange—LA
Orinda—CA
Oroville—NCA
Oxnard—LA
Pacific Grove—ECR
Pacific Palisades—LA
Pacifica—CA
Palm Desert—SD

Palm Spgs—SD
Palo Alto—CA & ECR
Palos Verdes Est—LA
Paradise—NCA
Pasadena—LA
Paso Robles—ECR
Pauma Valley—SD
Petaluma—NCA
Pico Rivera—LA
Pinole—CA
Placentia—LA
Placerville—NCA
Pleasant Hill—CA
Pleasanton—CA
Pomona—LA
Portola Valley—CA
Poway—SD
Quincy—NCA
Ramona—SD
Rancho Cordova—
NCA
Rancho Sta Marg—LA
Red Bluff—NCA
Redding—NCA
Redlands—LA
Redondo Bch—LA
Redwood City—CA
Rialto—LA
Richmond—CA
Ridgecrest—SanJ
Rio Vista—NCA
Riverside—LA
Rocklin—NCA
Roseville—NCA
Ross—CA
Sacramento—NCA
St Helena—NCA
Salinas—ECR
San Andreas—SanJ
San Ardo—ECR
San Bernardino—LA
San Bruno—CA
San Carlos—CA
San Clemente—LA
San Diego—SD
San Fernando—LA
San Francisco—CA
San Gabriel—LA
San Jose—ECR
San Juan Capo—LA
San Leandro—CA
San Luis Obispo—ECR
San Marino—LA
San Marcos—SD
San Mateo—CA
San Pedro—LA
San Rafael—CA
Santa Ana—LA
Santa Barbara—LA

Santa Clara—ECR
Santa Clarita—LA
Santa Cruz—ECR
Santa Maria—LA
Santa Monica—LA
Santa Paula—LA
Santa Rosa—NCA
Santee—SD
Saratoga—ECR
Sausalito—CA
Scotts Valley—ECR
Seal Bch—LA
Seaside—ECR
Sebastopol—NCA
Sierra Madre—LA
Simi Valley—LA
Skyforest—LA
Sonoma—NCA
Sonora—SanJ
So Gate—LA
So Pasadena—LA
So San Francisco—CA
Stockton—SanJ
Studio City—LA
Sunnyvale—ECR
Susanville—NCA
Sutter Creek—NCA
Taft—SanJ
Tahoe City—NCA
Temecula—SD
Thousand Oaks—LA
Torrance—LA
Tulare—SanJ
Turlock—SanJ
Tustin—LA
Twentynine Palms—LA
Ukiah—NCA
Upland—LA
Vacaville—NCA
Vallejo—NCA
Van Nuys—LA
Ventura—LA
Visalia—SanJ
Vista—SD
Walnut Creek—CA
Watsonville—ECR
Westwood—NCA
Wheatland—NCA
Whittier—LA
Willits—NCA
Willows—NCA
Wilmington—LA
Winnetka—LA
Woodland Hills—LA
Woodland—NCA
Yuba City—NCA
Yucaipa—LA
Yucca Valley—LA
Yuma—SD

DIOCESE OF CALIFORNIA
The Episcopal Church in the Bay Area
(PROVINCE VIII)
Comprises 5 counties in west-central CA
DIOCESAN OFFICE 1055 Taylor St San Francisco CA 94108
TEL (415) 673-0606 E-MAIL bishopmarc@diocal.org WEB www.diocal.org

Previous Bishops—
Wm I Kip m 1853 dio 1857-93,
Wm F Nichols coadj 1890 Bp 1893-
1924, Edward L Parsons coadj
1919 Bp 1924-40, Karl M Block
coadj 1938 Bp 1941-58, Henry H
Shires suffr 1950-58, James A Pike
coadj 1958 Bp 1958-66, G Richard
Millard suffr 1960-78, C Kilmer
Myers 1966-79, William E Swing
1979-2006

Bishop—Rt Rev Marc Handley Andrus (974)
(Dio 22 Jul 2006)

Chanc C Hayes; *V Chanc* G England; *Can to Ord* D
Low-Skinner (415) 869-7806; *DTM* D Obando (415)
869-7804; *Comm Off* S Martin Taylor (415) 869-
7820; *Faith Form Coord* A Cook (415) 869-7826;
CFO M Racusin; *Camps & Conf* A Wright (707) 433-
2440; *Treas* L Ringlee; *Conv Sec* RE Helmer

Stand Comm—Cler: J Stratford T Bryant M Wilson
C Bolton; *Lay:* G Lintner W Wong R Amos S
McConnell

Exec Coun—Cler: D Erickson K Spalding K Fregoso;
Lay P Fairfield S Lund J Dinwiddie-Moore M
Leeds A Jobe-Sea E Vallecillo Miller B Peguese A
M Vaquero E Woo B Burrell M Buie B Morrow S
Depont-Kalani

PARISHES, MISSIONS, AND CLERGY

Alameda Christ Episcopal Church **P** (509) 1700
Santa Clara Ave 94501-2515 (Mail to: 1700
Santa Clara Ave 94501-2515) Stephen Mchale
Laureen Moyer William Scott (510) 523-7200
Albany St Albans Episcopal Church **P** (95)
1501 Washington Ave 94706-1856 (Mail to:
1501 Washington Ave 94706-1856) Jonathan
Owens Duane Sisson (510) 5251716
Antioch St Annas Episcopal Church **M** (97) 301
E 13th St 94509-1997 (Mail to: 301 E 13th St
94509-1997) Jane Stratford (925) 757-4934
Belmont Good Shepherd Episcopal Church **M**
(41) 1300 Fifth Ave 94002-3831 (Mail to: 1300
Fifth Ave 94002-3831) Michael Barham (650)
593-4844
Belvedere St Stephens Episcopal Church **P** (739)
3 Bayview Ave 94920 (Mail to: PO Box 99
94920-0097) Kyle Seage Robert Gieselmann
Shane Scott-Hamblen (415) 435-4501
Berkeley All Souls Parish **P** (611) § 2220 Cedar
St 94709-1519 (Mail to: 2220 Cedar St 94709-

1586) Philip Brochard Joseph Delgado
Margaret Foote Marguerite Judson Michael
Lemaire Ruth Meyers Paula Nesbitt Margaret
Patterson Daniel Prechtel (510) 848-1755
Berkeley St Clements Episcopal Church **P** (696)
2837 Claremont Blvd 94705-1446 (Mail to:
2837 Claremont Blvd 94705-1446) Bruce
O'Neill (510) 843-2678
Berkeley St Marks Episcopal Church **P** (506)
2300 Bancroft Way 94704-1604 (Mail to: 2300
Bancroft Way 94704-1604) Blake Sawicky
Lizette Larson-Miller (510) 848-5107
Berkeley Good Shepherd Episcopal Church
M (72) 1823 9th St 94710-2102 (Mail to:
1823 9th St 94710-2102) Molly Haws Louis
Countryman Ellen Ekstrom Jay Johnson
Bonnie Ring (510) 549-1433
Bolinas St Aidans Episcopal Church **M** (42) 30
Brighton Ave 94924. (Mail to: PO Box 629
94924-0629) (415) 868-1852
Burlingame St Pauls Episcopal Church **P** (509)
415 El Camino Real 94010-5122 (Mail to: 415
El Camino Real 94010-5197) (650) 348-4811
Castro Valley Holy Cross Episcopal Church **P** (380)
19179 Center St 94546-3616 (Mail to: 19179
Center St 94546-3616) Mark Spaulding Pamela
Cranston Patricia Pearson (510) 889-7233
Clayton St Johns Episcopal Church **M** (131) 5555
Clayton Rd 94517-1013 (Mail to: 5555 Clayton
Rd 94517-1013) John Mcdermott (925) 672-
8855
Concord St Michael and All Angels Epis **M** (124)
2925 Bonifacio St 94519-2511 (Mail to: 2925
Bonifacio St 94519-2511) Stephen Sturgeon
Laina Casillas (925) 685-8859
Corte Madera Holy Innocents Episcopal Ch **P**
(92) 2 Tamalpais Dr 94925 (Mail to: PO Box 5
94976-0005) (415) 924-4393
Crockett St Marks Episcopal Church **P** (30) 800
Pomona St 94525-1400 (Mail to: PO Box 515
94525-0515) (510) 787-2989
Daly City Holy Chld & St Martins Epis Ch **M**
(150) 777 Southgate Ave 94015-3665 (Mail to
777 Southgate Ave 94015-3665) Lynn Bowdish
(650) 991-1560
Danville St Timothys Episcopal Church **P** (705)
§ 1550 Diablo Rd 94526-1952 (Mail to: 1550
Diablo Rd 94526-1952) Todd Bryant Susan
Geissler-O'Neil (925) 837-4993
Foster City St Ambrose Episcopal Church **P**
(164) § 900 Edgewater Blvd 94404-3709 (Mail
to: 900 Edgewater Blvd 94404-3709) Jason
Lucas-Green (650) 574-1369

Fremont St Annes Episcopal Church **P** (49) 2791 Driscoll Rd 94539-4449 (Mail to: 2791 Driscoll Rd 94539-4449) Jeffrey Dodge Robert Partanen (510) 490-0553

Fremont St James Episcopal Church **P** (383) 37051 Cabrillo Dr 94536-5709 (Mail to: PO Box 457 94537-0457) Lori Walton William Hale (510) 797-1492

Half Moon Bay Church of the Holy Family **M** (60) § 1590 Cabrillo Hwy S 94019-2245 (Mail to: 1590 Cabrillo Hwy S 94019-2245) Eric Nefstead

Inverness Saint Columba's Church **P** (77) PO Box 430 94937-0430 (Mail to: PO Box 430 94937-0430) Vincent Pizzuto (415) 669-1039

Lafayette Saint Anselm's Episcopal Church **P** (343) 682 Michael Lane 94549-5399 (Mail to: 682 Michael Lane 94549-5399) Naomi Chamberlain-Harris Kathleen Trapani (925) 284-7420

Livermore St Bartholomews Episcopal Ch **P** (178) 678 Enos Way 94551-5917 (Mail to: 678 Enos Way 94551-5917) Andrew Lobban (925) 447-3289

Los Altos Christ Episcopal Church **P** (325) § 1040 Border Rd 94024-4724 (Mail to: 1040 Border Rd 94024-4724) John Buenz Sheldon Hutchison Julia Nelson (650) 948-2151

Martinez Grace Episcopal Church **P** (257) 130 Muir Station Rd 94553-4420 (Mail to: 130 Muir Station Rd 94553-4420) Deborah White (925) 228-6574

Menlo Park St Bedes Episcopal Church **P** (185) 2650 Sand Hill Rd 94025-7018 (Mail to: 2650 Sand Hill Rd 94025-7018) (650) 854-6555

Menlo Park Holy Trinity Church **P** (929) 330 Ravenswood Ave 94025-3420 (Mail to: 330 Ravenswood Ave 94025-3420) Jude Harmon (650) 326-2083

Mill Valley The Epis Ch of Our Saviour **P** (421) 10 Old Mill St 94941-1813 (Mail to: 10 Old Mill St 94941-1813) Richard Helmer (415) 3881907

Novato St Francis of Assisi Epis Ch **P** (137) § 967 5th St 94945-3105 (Mail to: 967 5th St 94945-3105) Stephanie Tramel (415) 892-1609

Oakland Epis Church of Our Saviour **P** (159) 1011 Harrison St 94607-4426 (Mail to: 1013 Harrison St Ste 202 946074457) Merry Ong (510) 834-6447

Oakland St Augustines Episcopal Church **P** (100) 521 29th St 94609-3512 (Mail to: PO Box 27416 94602-0916) James Dahlin (510) 832-6462

Oakland St Cuthberts Episcopal Church **M** (28) 7932 Mountain Blvd 94605-3708 (Mail to: The Episcopal Diocese of California 1055 Taylor St 94108-2277) (510) 6863146

Oakland St James the Apostle Church **P** (36) 1540 12th Ave 94606-3803 (Mail to: 1540 12th Ave 94606-3803) Maria Munoz (510) 533-2136

Oakland St Johns Episcopal Church **P** (418) 1707 Gouldin Rd 94611-2120 (Mail to: 1707 Gouldin Rd 94611-2120) Scott Denman Fran Toy (510) 339-2200

Oakland St Pauls Episcopal Church **P** (259) § 114 Montecito Ave 94610-4556 (Mail to: 114 Montecito Ave 94610-4599) Mauricio Wilson Carolyn Bolton (510) 834-4314

Orinda St Stephen's Episcopal Church **P** (1085) § 66 Saint Stephens Dr 94563-1949 (Mail to: Attn: Treasurer 66 Saint Stephens Dr 94563-1949) Patrick Collins (925) 254-3770

Pacifica St Edmunds Episcopal Church **M** (43) 1500 Perez Drive 94044 (Mail to: PO Box 688 94044-0688) (650) 359-3364

Palo Alto Saint Mark's Episcopal Church **P** (563) 600 Colorado Ave 94306-2510 (Mail to: 600 Colorado Ave 94306-2599) Matthew Mcdermott Ricardo Avila Nicole Wood (650) 326-3800

Pinole Epis Church of Christ the Lord **M** (85) 592 Tennent Ave 94564-1629 (Mail to: Attn Susan Linnell 592A Tennent Ave 94564-1629) Lois Williams (510) 724-9141

Pleasant Hill Episcopal Church of the Resurrection **P** (341) § 399 Gregory Ln 94523-2837 (Mail to: 399 Gregory Ln 94523-2837) Elizabeth Tichenor (925) 6852288

Pleasanton St Clares Episcopal Church **P** (257) § 3350 Hopyard Rd 94588-5105 (Mail to: 3350 Hopyard Rd 94588-5105) Ronald Culmer Amanda May (925) 462-4802

Portola Valley Christ Episcopal Church **P** (243) 815 Portola Rd 94028-7206 (Mail to: 815 Portola Rd 94028-7206) Elizabeth Phillips Dorothy Jamison David Sheetz (650) 851-0224

Redwood City El Buen Pastor Iglesia Epis **M** (144) 1835 Valota Rd. 94061 (Mail to: 600 Colorado Avenue 90234) (650) 245-7759

Redwood City St Peters Episcopal Church **P** (172) 178 Clinton St 94062-1552 (Mail to: St Peters Episcopal Church 178 Clinton St 94062-1583) (650) 367-0777

Richmond Holy Trinity Episcopal Church **M** (181) 555 37th St 94805-2205 (Mail to: 555 37th St 94805-2205) Jose Torres Bayas Mary Hinse Katherine Salinaro (510) 232-7896

Ross New Skellig Celtic Chrstn Cmty **M** PO Box 217 94957-0217 (Mail to: PO Box 217 94957-0217)

Ross St Johns Episcopal Church **P** (1270) 14 Lagunitas Rd 94957-9661 (Mail to: PO Box 217 94957-0217) Christopher Rankin-Williams Heather Erickson Charlton Fotch Jan West (415) 4561102

S San Fran St Elizabeths Episcopal Church **M** (63) 280 Country Club Dr 94080-5743 (Mail to: Attn: Mrs Ellen Jones 280 Country Club Dr 94080-5743) (650) 583-6678

San Bruno SEA Episcopal Church **M** (63) § 1600 Santa Lucia Ave 94066-4736 (Mail to: C/O

Ellen Jones 1600 Santa Lucia Ave 94066-4798)
David Smith (650) 583-6678

San Carlos Episcopal Ch of the Epiphany **P** (487)
1839 Arroyo Ave 94070-3810 (Mail to: 1839
Arroyo Ave 94070-3899) Annamarie Hoos
Robert Kossler Hailey Mckeefry (650) 591-
0328

San Francisco All Saints Episcopal Church **P**
(117) 1350 Waller St 94117-2986 (Mail to:
1350 Waller St 94117-2986) Daniel Scheid
Thomas Traylor (415) 621-1862

San Francisco Christ Episcopal Ch Sei Ko Kai **M**
(94) 2140 Pierce St 94115-2214 (Mail to: 2140
Pierce St 94115-2214) (415) 921-6395

San Francisco The Advent of Christ the King
P (86) 261 Fell St 94102-5147 (Mail to: 162
Hickory St 94102-5908) Paul Allick Graham
Hill Gregory Martin Roderick Thompson
(415) 431-0454

San Francisco Holy Innocents Episcopal Ch **M**
(281) 455 Fair Oaks St 94110-3618 (Mail to:
455 Fair Oaks St 94110-3618) John Ayers
Kathleen Sylvester (415) 824-5142

San Francisco Episcopal Church of the
Incarnation **P** (56) 1750 29th Ave 94122-4223
(Mail to: 1750 29th Ave 94122-4223) Darren
Miner Franco Kwan (415) 5642324

✠ **San Francisco** Grace Cathedral **O** (2485) §
1100 California St 94108-2206 (Mail to: 1100
California St 94108-2244) Malcolm Young
Michael Barlowe Mary Greene Raymond
Hoche-Mong Gregory Kimura Anna Rossi
(415) 749-6300

San Francisco Iglesia Del Buen Samaritano **M**
1661 15th St 94103-3511 (Mail to: 1661 15th
St 94103-3511) (415) 869-7810

San Francisco Saint Aidan's Church **P** (138) 101
Gold Mine Dr 94131-2538 (Mail to: 101 Gold
Mine Dr 94131-2538) Cameron Partridge
Margaret Dyer-Chamberlain Donald Fox
Mark Henderson David Stickley (415) 285-
9540

San Francisco St Cyprians Episcopal Church **M**
(59) 2097 Turk Blvd 94115-4326 (Mail to: 2097
Turk Blvd 94115-4326) Hannah Cornthwaite
(415) 567-1855

San Francisco St Francis Episcopal Church **P**
(259) 399 San Fernando Way 94127-1913
(Mail to: 399 San Fernando Way 94127-1913)
Clarence Davis George (415) 334-1590

San Francisco St Gregory of Nyssa Epis Ch **P**
(414) 500 De Haro St 94107-2306 (Mail to: 500
De Haro St 94107-2306) Paul Fromberg Paul
Fromberg (415) 255-8100

San Francisco St James Episcopal Church **P** (176)
4620 California St 94118-1225 (Mail to: 4620

California St 94118-1225) John Kirkley Gwen
Buehrens Ronnie Willis (415) 751-1198

San Francisco St Lukes Episcopal Church **P** (176)
1755 Clay St 94109-3612 (Mail to: 1755 Clay St
94109-3682) Jason Cox (415) 673-7327

San Francisco St John the Evangelist Epis Ch
P (97) 1661 Fifteenth Street 94103 (Mail to:
1661 Fifteenth Street 94103-3511) Jacqueline
Cherry Albert Pearson Richard Smith (415)
861-1436

San Francisco Church of St Mary the Virgin **P**
(1090) 2325 Union St 94123-3905 (Mail to:
2325 Union St 94123-3905) David Erickson
Kira Austin-Young Nancy Bryan Mary
Jizmagian Hollinshead Knight (415) 921-3665

San Francisco Trinity Church **M** (80) 1668 Bush
St 94109-5308 (Mail to: 1620 Gough St 94109-
4418) Izabella Sempari (415) 775-1117

San Francisco True Sunshine Episcopal Church
P (178) 1430 Mason St 94133-4222 (Mail to:
1430 Mason St 94133-4222) Merry Ong (415)
956-2160

San Leandro All Saints Episcopal Church **P** (125)
911 Dowling Blvd 94577-2125 (Mail to: 911
Dowling Blvd 94577-2190) Justin Cannon
Pamela Jester Pamela Jester (510) 569-7020

San Mateo Episcopal Church of St Matthew **P**
(878) § 1 S El Camino Real 94401-3800 (Mail
to: 1 S El Camino Real 94401-3800) Eric Hinds
Jay Watan (650) 342-1481

San Mateo Transfiguration Episcopal Ch **P** (362)
3900 Alameda De Las Pulgas 94403-4110
(Mail to: 3900 Alameda De Las Pulgas 94403-
4110) Jennifer Hornbeck (650) 341-8206

San Rafael Episcopal Ch of the Nativity **P** (199)
333 Ellen Dr 94903-1666 (Mail to: 333 Ellen
Dr 94903-1666) Rebecca Morehouse Kirsten
Spalding (415) 479-7023

San Rafael Episcopal Ch of the Redeemer **M** (47)
§ 123 Knight Dr 94901-1427 (Mail to: 123
Knight Dr 94901-1427) (415) 456-0508

San Rafael St Pauls Episcopal Church **P** (284)
1123 Court St 94901-2909 (Mail to: 1123
Court St 94901-2909) Christopher Martin
(415) 456-4842

Sausalito Christ Episcopal Church **P** (188) 70
Santa Rosa Ave 94965-2041 (Mail to: PO Box 5
94966-0005) Sloane Larrimore (415) 332-1539

Walnut Creek St Lukes Episcopal Church **P** (47)
1944 Tice Valley Blvd 94595 (Mail to: PO Box
2088 94595-0088) (925) 937-4820

Walnut Creek St Pauls Episcopal Church **P** (318)
1924 Trinity Ave 94596-4037 (Mail to: 1924
Trinity Ave 94596-4037) Donald Adolphson
Krista Fregoso Laureen Moyer Lynne Sharp
(925) 934-2324

DIOCESE OF CENTRAL FLORIDA
(PROVINCE IV)
Comprises Central Florida
DIOCESAN OFFICE 1017 E Robinson St Orlando FL 32801
Tel (407) 423-3567 FAX (407) 872-0006
WEB www.cfdiocese.org

Previous Bishops —
Wm C Gray 1892-1913, Cameron
Mann m 1913 dio 1922-32, John
D Wing coadj 1925 Bp 1932-50,
Martin J Bram suffr 1951-56, Wm
F Moses suffr 1956-61, Henry I
Louttit suffr 1945 coadj 1948 Bp
1951-69, James L Duncan suffr
1961-69, Wm L Hargrave suffr
1961-69, Wm H Folwell 1970-89, John W Howe
1989-2012

**Bishop—Rt Rev Gregory O Brewer (1063) (Dio
24 March 2012)**

Cn to Ord S Holcombe; *Sec* S Caprani; *Treas* L
Combs 2104 Mallard Cir Winter Park 32789; *Chanc*
C Wooten Jr 236 S Lucerne Ave Orlando 32801-
4490; *COM* O Kimbrough; *Ecum* Rt Rev H Pina-
Lopez (11/03/38–9/23/18)

Stand Comm—Cler: C Rodriguez T Rutherford J
Murbarger J French; *Lay:* H Rodriguez M Myers M
Taffinder

PARISHES, MISSIONS, AND CLERGY
Apopka Church of the Holy Spirit **P** (394) 601
S Highland Ave 32703-5343 (Mail to: 601 S
Highland Ave 32703-5343) Leonard Bartle
Robert Griffith John Pallard Gerald Steidl
(407) 886-1740
Auburndale St Alban's Episcopal Church **P** (82)
202 Pontotoc Plaza 33823-3408 (Mail to: PO
Box 1125 33823-1125) Richard Gomer (863)
967-2130
Avon Park Church of the Redeemer **M** (51) 910
W Martin Road 33825 (Mail to: PO Box 368
33826-0368) (863) 453-5664
Bartow Holy Trinity Episcopal Church **P** (166)
500 W Stuart St 33830-6200 (Mail to: PO Box
197 33831-0197) Rebecca Toalster Patrice
Behnstedt (863) 533-3581
Belleview St Marys Episcopal Church **P** (274)
5750 SE 115th St 34420-4336 (Mail to: PO
Box 2373 34421-2373) Lisa Wimmer (352)
347-6422
Bushnell St Francis of Assisi Church **M** (92) 313
N Grace St 33513-5604 (Mail to: PO Box 566
33513-0030) Karen House (352) 793-3187
Clermont St Matthias Episcopal Church **P** (288)
574 W Montrose St 34711-2261 (Mail to: 528
W Montrose St 34711-2261) James Dorn (352)
3943855
Cocoa St Marks Episcopal Church **P** (272) § 4
Church St 32922-7912 (Mail to: 4 Church St

32922-7999) Nancy Oliver Sara Oxley (321)
636-3781
Cocoa Beach Ch of St David's By The Sea **P** (237)
600 S 4th St 32931-2612 (Mail to: 600 S 4th St
32931-2612) (321) 783-2554
Crystal River St Annes Episcopal Church **P** (381)
9870 W Fort Island Trl 34429-5383 (Mail to:
9870 W Fort Island Trl 34429-5383) Cheryl
Bakker Henry Brown Richard Chandler
Gilbert Larsen (352) 795-2176
Daytona Beach St Marys Episcopal Church **P**
(182) 216 Orange Ave 32114-4312 (Mail to:
216 Orange Ave 32114-4357) Jason Murbarger
(386) 255-3669
Daytona Beach St Timothys Episcopal Church
M (102) C/O Ms Gertrude Sheppard PO Box
10176 32120-0176 (Mail to: C/O Ms Gertrude
Sheppard PO Box 10176 32120-0176) (386)
255-2077
Deland St Barnabas Episcopal Church **P** (505) §
319 W Wisconsin Ave 32720-4132 (Mail to:
319 W Wisconsin Ave 32720-4132) William
Garrison (386) 734-1814
Deland The Ch of the Holy Presence **M** (64)
355 N Kepler Rd 32724-4713 (Mail to: 355 N
Kepler Rd 32724-4713) Carol Mcdonald (386)
734-5228
Dunnellon Church of the Advent **P** (191) 11251
SW Highway 484 34432-6415 (Mail to: 11251
SW Highway 484 34432-6415) (352) 465-7272
Dunnellon Holy Faith Church **P** (94) 19924 W
Blue Cove Dr 34432-5811 (Mail to: 19924 W
Blue Cove Dr 34432-5811) (352) 489-2685
Enterprise All Saints Episcopal Church **P** (296)
155 Clark St 32725-8188 (Mail to: PO Box
4004 32725-0004) Robin Morical Linda
Kromhout Gerald Raschke (386) 668-4108
Eustis Church of St Thomas **P** (228) 317 S Mary St
32726-4201 (Mail to: 317 S Mary St 32726-4201)
Janet Clarke Richard Labud (352) 357-4358
Fort Meade Christ Episcopal Church **M** (7) 1
N Cleveland Ave 33841-3017 (Mail to: 1 N
Cleveland Ave 33841-3017) (863) 368-1465
Fort Pierce Ch of St Simon the Cyrenian **P** (52)
1700 Avenue E 34950-7953 (Mail to: PO Box
1147 34954-1147) (772) 461-2519
Fort Pierce St Andrews Episcopal Church **P** (178)
§ 210 S Indian River Dr 34950-4337 (Mail to:
210 S Indian River Dr 34950-4385) Ellis Brust
(772) 461-5009
Fruitland Pk Holy Trinity Episcopal Church **P**
(191) § 2201 Spring Lake Rd 34731-5256 (Mail
to: 2201 Spring Lake Rd 34731-5256) Samuel
Nsengiyumva Gerald Steidl (352) 787-1500

Haines City St Marks Episcopal Church **P** (107) 102 N 9th St 33844-4314 (Mail to: 102 N 9th St 33844-4314) Angela Ifill (863) 422-1416

Inverness St Margarets Episcopal Church **P** (253) 114 N Osceola Ave 34450-4121 (Mail to: 114 N Osceola Ave 34450-4121) William Brady (352) 726-3153

Kissimmee St Johns Episcopal Church **P** (623) 1709 N John Young Pkwy 34741-3218 (Mail to: 1709 N John Young Pkwy 34741-3200) (407) 847-2009

Lake Mary St Peters Episcopal Church **P** (509) § 700 Rinehart Rd 32746-4875 (Mail to: 700 Rinehart Rd 32746-4875) Jeremy Bergstrom (407) 444-5673

Lake Placid St Francis of Assisi Epis Ch **P** (216) 43 Lake June Rd 33852-8910 (Mail to: 43 Lake June Rd 33852-8910) (863) 465-0051

Lake Wales The Ch of the Good Shepherd **P** (479) 221 S 4th St 33853-3856 (Mail to: 221 4th St S 33853-3856) Timothy Nunez John Motis (863) 676-8578

Lakeland All Saints Episcopal Church **P** (594) 202 S Massachusetts Ave 33801-5012 (Mail to: 209 S Iowa Ave 33801-5018) Larry Hensarling Kathy Hulin (863) 688-4502

Lakeland Christ the King Episcopal Ch **P** (165) 6400 N Socrum Loop Rd 33809-4141 (Mail to: PO Box 1176 33810-1176) (863) 858-1948

Lakeland St Stephens Church **P** (667) 1820 E County Road 540a 33813-3737 (Mail to: 1820 E County Road 540A 33813-3737) David Peoples Robert Moses (863) 646-6115

Lecanto Shepherd of the Hills Epis Ch **P** (424) 2540 W Norvell Bryant Hwy 34461-9422 (Mail to: 2540 W Norvell Bryant Hwy 34461-9422) George Conger Michael Hall Linda Liebert-Hall (352) 527-0052

Leesburg St James Episcopal Church **P** (687) 204 Lee St 34748-4915 (Mail to: 204 Lee St 34748-4915) William Boyer Thomas Trees (352) 787-1981

Longwood Christ Episcopal Church **P** (61) 151 W Church Ave 32750-4105 (Mail to: C/O Heather Kirby 151 W Church Ave 32750-4105) (407) 339-6812

Longwood Church of the Resurrection **P** (504) 251 E Lake Brantley Dr 32779-4808 (Mail to: 251 E Lake Brantley Dr 32779-4808) David Johnson (407) 788-3704

Maitland Church of the Good Shepherd **P** (179) 331 Lake Ave 32751-6331 (Mail to: 331 Lake Ave 32751-6331) (407) 644-5350

Melbourne Christ Episcopal Church **P** (184) 190 Interlachen Rd 32940-1979 (Mail to: 190 Interlachen Rd 32940-1979) Cynthia Brust (321) 259-5810

Melbourne Holy Trinity Episcopal Church **P** (746) 50 W Strawbridge Ave 32901-4438 (Mail to: 1830 S Babcock St 32901-4443) David Newhart Stacey Westphal Stacey Westphal

(321) 723-5272

Melbourne St Johns Episcopal Church **P** (158) 610 Young St 32935-7059 (Mail to: 610 Young St 32935-7059) Eric Turner (321) 254-3365

Melbourne Bch St Sebastians by the Sea **P** (154) 2010 Oak St 32951-2713 (Mail to: 2010 Oak St 32951-2713) Scott Jones (321) 723-3015

Merritt Island St Lukes Episcopal Church **P** (104) 5555 N Tropical Trl 32953-7202 (Mail to: PO Box 541025 32954-1025) (321) 452-5260

Mount Dora St Edward the Confessor **P** (299) 460 N Grandview St 32757-5676 (Mail to: 460 N Grandview St 32757-5676) John Crandall Mark Lafler (352) 383-2832

New Smyrna St Peter the Fisherman Church **P** (274) 4220 Saxon Dr 32169-3923 (Mail to: 4220 Saxon Dr 32169-3923) Peter Tepper (386) 428-7383

New Smyrna Beach Saint Paul's Episcopal Church **P** (368) 1650 Live Oak St 32168-7771 (Mail to: 1650 Live Oak St 32168-7771) Matthew Dallman David Hoag (386) 428-8733

Ocala Grace Episcopal Church **P** (415) 503 SE Broadway St 34471-2250 (Mail to: 510 SE Broadway St Ste 100 34471-2256) Jonathan French Mary Delancey (352) 622-7881

Okahumpka Corpus Christi Epis Church **M** (110) 3430 Country Road 470 34762 (Mail to: PO Box 68 34762-0068) Amanda Bordenkircher (352) 787-8430

Okeechobee Church of Our Saviour **P** (201) 200 NW 3rd St 34972-4125 (Mail to: 200 NW 3rd St 34972-4125) Edward Weiss Kay Mueller Kay Mueller (863) 763-4843

Orange City St Judes Episcopal Church **P** (185) 815 E Graves Ave 32763-5307 (Mail to: 815 E Graves Ave 32763-5307) Phyllis Bartle (386) 775-6200

✠ **Orlando** Cathedral Church of St Luke **O** (1070) Attn: Anne Clarke PO Box 2328 32802-2328 (Mail to: 130 N Magnolia Ave Ste 200 32801-2300) Joshua Bales (407) 849-0680

Orlando Christ the King Episcopal Ch **P** (207) 26 Willow Dr 32807-3220 (Mail to: 26 Willow Dr 32807-3298) Jose Rodriguez-Sanjurjo (407) 277-1151

Orlando Emmanuel Episcopal Church **P** (249) 1603 East Winter Park Rd 32803-2228 (Mail to: 1603 East Winter Park Rd 32803-2296) Robert Lord (407) 894-1641

Orlando Church of the Ascension **P** (683) § 4950 S Apopka Vineland Rd 32819-3104 (Mail to: 4950 S Apopka Vineland Rd 32819-3104) (407) 876-3480

Orlando Holy Family Episcopal Church **P** (573) 1010 N Hiawassee Rd 32818-6711 (Mail to: 1010 N Hiawassee Rd 32818-6711) (407) 293-2236

Orlando Iglesia Epis Jesus de Nazaret **M** (243) 26 Willow Dr 32807-3220 (Mail to: 26 Willow Dr 32807-3220) (407) 222-7995

Orlando Iglesia Epis San Cristobal **M** (167) 7500 Forest City Rd 32810-3710 (Mail to: 7500 Forest City Rd 32810-3710) Carlos Marin (407) 293-5653

Orlando St Mary of the Angels Epis Ch **P** (219) 6316 Matchett Rd 32809-5150 (Mail to: 6316 Matchett Rd 32809-5196) Kevin Bartle Raul Rubiano-Alvarado (407) 855-1930

Orlando St Matthews Episcopal Church **P** (520) 5873 N Dean Rd 32817-3201 (Mail to: 5873 N Dean Rd 32817-3201) (407) 657-9199

Orlando St Michaels Church **P** (647) 2499 N Westmoreland Dr 32804-4934 (Mail to: C/O Tyler Piercy 2499 N Westmoreland Dr 32804-4934) Richard Luoni (407) 843-8448

Orlando St John the Baptist Church **P** (166) 1000 Bethune Dr 32805-3404 (Mail to: 1000 Bethune Dr 32805-3404) (407) 295-1923

Ormond Beach Church of the Holy Child **P** (111) 1225 W Granada Blvd 32174-5914 (Mail to: 1225 W Granada Blvd State Road 40 32174-5914) (386) 672-4470

Ormond Beach St James Episcopal Church **P** (578) 44 S Halifax Dr 32176-6515 (Mail to: 44 S Halifax Dr 32176-6515) Charles Allison Marcia Allison (386) 5621009

Oviedo Church of the Incarnation **M** (130) 1601 Alafaya Trl 32765-9485 (Mail to: 1601 Alafaya Trl 32765-9485) (407) 365-5651

Palm Bay Church of Our Savior **P** (275) 1000 Jersey Ln NE 32905-5519 (Mail to: 1000 Jersey Ln NE 32905-5519) Dee Bright Thomas Williams (321) 723-8032

Palm Bay Epis Ch of the Blessed Rdmr **M** (97) 1225 Degroodt Rd SW 32908-7102 (Mail to: 1225 Degroodt Rd SW 32908-7102) Brian Turner (321) 725-6881

Port Orange Grace Episcopal Church **P** (253) 4110 S Ridgewood Ave 32127-4519 (Mail to: PO Box 290245 32129-0245) Gary Jackson (386) 767-3583

Port St Lucie Church of the Nativity **P** (352) 1151 SW Del Rio Blvd 34953-1520 (Mail to: 1151 SW Del Rio Blvd 34953-1520) Tracy Dugger (772) 343-0401

Port St Lucie Holy Faith Episcopal Church **P** (190) 6990 S Us Highway 1 34952-1416 (Mail to: 6990 S Us Highway 1 34952-1499) (772) 446-9619

Saint Cloud Church of St Luke & St Peter **P** (222) 2745 Canoe Creek Rd 34772-6502 (Mail to: 2745 Canoe Creek Rd 34772-6502) (407) 892-3227

Sanford Holy Cross Episcopal Church **P** (187) 410 S Magnolia Ave 32771-1918 (Mail to: 410 S Magnolia Ave 32771-1918) Ann Kruger Edward Smith (407) 322-4611

Satellite Bch Church of the Holy Apostles **P** (241) 505 Grant Ave 32937-2921 (Mail to: 505 Grant Ave 32937-2921) Todd Schmidtetter Donald Goodheart (321) 777-0024

Sebastian St Elizabeths Episcopal Church **P** (313) 901 Clearmont St 32958-4978 (Mail to: 901 Clearmont St 32958-4978) (772) 589-2770

Sebring Saint Agnes Church **P** (90) 3840 Lakeview Dr 33870-2066 (Mail to: C/O Scott Walker 3840 Lakeview Dr 33870-2066) Scott Walker (863) 385-7649

The Villages St George Episcopal Church **P** (775) 1250 Paige Pl 32159-9315 (Mail to: 1250 Paige Pl 32159-9315) James Taylor Edward Bartle (352) 750-1010

Titusville St Gabriels Episcopal Church **P** (362) PO Box 6584 32782-6584 (Mail to: 414 Pine St 32796-3542) Robert Griffith (321) 267-2545

Vero Beach St Augustine of Canterbury **P** (723) 475 43rd Ave 32968-1836 (Mail to: 475 43rd Ave 32968-1836) John Shields (772) 770-3494

Vero Beach Trinity Episcopal Church **P** (509) 2365 Pine Ave 32960-0528 (Mail to: Attn: Accounts Payable 2365 Pine Ave 32960-0528) Christopher Rodriguez Joshua Gritter (772) 567-1146

Winter Garden Church of the Messiah **P** (391) 241 N Main Street 34787 (Mail to: 241 N Main St 34787-2826) Thomas Rutherford Soner Alexandre Andrew Lazo (407) 656-3218

Winter Haven Holy Cross Church **P** (99) 201 Kipling Ln 33884-2316 (Mail to: 201 Kipling Ln 33884-2316) Woodford Miller (863) 324-4021

Winter Haven St Pauls Church **P** (308) 656 Avenue L NW 33881-4058 (Mail to: 656 Avenue L NW 33881-4030) Paul Head Susan Hansell (863) 294-8888

Winter Park All Saints Episcopal Church **P** (1216) 338 E Lyman Ave 32789-4415 (Mail to: 338 E Lyman Ave 32789-4494) Franck Shelby Elizabeth Tucker (407) 647-3413

Winter Park St Richards Episcopal Church **P** (222) 5151 Lake Howell Rd 32792-1027 (Mail to: 5151 Lake Howell Rd 32792-1095) Alison Harrity Thomas Downs Robert Vanderau (407) 671-4211

DIOCESE OF THE CENTRAL GULF COAST
(PROVINCE IV)
Comprises Southern AL and Northwest FL
DIOCESAN OFFICE 201 N Baylen St Pensacola FL 32502 (MAIL: Box 13330 Pensacola FL 32591-3330)
TEL (850) 434-7337 FAX (850) 434-8577
E-MAIL (staff name)@diocgc.org WEB www.diocgc.org

Previous Bishops—
George Mosley Murray 1971-81, Charles Farmer Duvall DD 1981-2001, Philip Menzie Duncan II 2001-15

Bishop—Rt Rev James Russell Kendrick (Dio July 25 2015)

Dio Admin D Babcock; *Chanc (AL)* K Miller Box 290 Mobile AL 36601; *Chanc (FL)* S Remington Box 13010 Pensacola FL 32591; *Reg & Hist* A Kennington; *Treas* R Snider

Stand Comm—Cler: Pres R Proctor C Hord R Adams W Lowry B Donnell De Freeman; *Lay:* T Moore B Partington C Walters CL Johnson A Gill V Fuller M Crawford R Runderson M Waddell

PARISHES, MISSIONS, AND CLERGY

Alabama

Andalusia St Marys Episcopal Church **P** (184) 1307 E Three Notch St 36420-3403 (Mail to: 1307 E Three Notch St 36420-3403) (334) 222-2487

Atmore St Annas Episcopal Church **M** (133) 100 Lynn Mcghee Dr 36502-5057 (Mail to: 100 Lynn McGhee Dr 36502-5057) (251) 368-8606

Atmore Trinity Episcopal Church **P** (35) 203 S Carney St 36502-2404 (Mail to: 203 S Carney St 36502-2404) (251) 368-5933

Bay Minette Immanuel Episcopal Church **M** (40) 700 Mcmillan Ave 36507-4425 (Mail to: 700 Mcmillan Ave 36507-4425) (251) 937-7900

Bon Secour St Peters Episcopal Church **P** (192) 6270 Bon Secour Hwy 36511 (Mail to: PO Box 29 36511-0029) Bryan Gentry Susan Mckee (251) 949-6254

Brewton St Stephens Episcopal Church **P** (127) 1510 Escambia Ave 36426-1124 (Mail to: PO Box 1261 36427-1261) David Chatel (251) 867-4545

Citronelle St Thomas Episcopal Church **M** (4) 19030 S Center St 36522-2546 (Mail to: PO Box 813 36522-0813) (251) 866-7003

Coden St Marys by the Sea Epis Ch **M** (50) 4875 Highway 188 36523-3703 (Mail to: 4875 Highway 188 36523-3703) Sara Phillips Sara Phillips (251) 873-5602

Daphne St Pauls Episcopal Church **P** (889) § 28788 N Main St 36526-7258 (Mail to: 28788 N Main St 36526-7258) Thack Dyson John Talbert (251) 626-2421

Dauphin Islnd St Francis Episcopal Church **M** (49) 401 Key St 36528 (Mail to: PO Box 407 36528-0407) (251) 861-2300

Dothan Episcopal Ch of the Nativity **P** (577) 205 Holly Ln 36301-1438 (Mail to: 205 Holly Ln 36301-1438) (334) 793-7616

Enterprise Episcopal Ch of the Epiphany **M** (85) § 302 East Grubbs St 36330-2613 (Mail to: 302 E Grubbs St 36330-2613) (334) 347-8210

Eufaula St James Episcopal Church **P** (195) 100 Saint James Pl 36027-1551 (Mail to: 100 Saint James Pl 36027-1551) Neil Kaminski (334) 687-3619

Fairhope St James Episcopal Church **P** (1460) § 860 N Section St 36532-6376 (Mail to: 860 N Section St 36532-6376) Denson Freeman Thomas Sirmon (251) 928-2912

Foley St Pauls Episcopal Church **P** (600) 506 N Pine St 36535-2039 (Mail to: PO Box 1745 36536-1745) Michael Norris (251) 943-2173

Greenville St Thomas Episcopal Church **P** (124) 210 Church St 36037-2606 (Mail to: 210 Church St 36037-2606) (334) 382-8914

Gulf Shores Holy Spirit Episcopal Church **P** (385) 616 W Fort Morgan Rd 36542-4300 (Mail to: PO Box 2346 36547-2346) William Lowry Maurice Goldsmith (251) 968-5988

Jackson St Peters Episcopal Church **M** (17) 100 Hospital Dr 36545-2424 (Mail to: PO Box 146 36545-0146) (251) 246-8092

Lillian Church of the Advent **M** (78) 12099 County Road 99 36549-5128 (Mail to: 12099 County Road 99 36549-5128) Tina Lockett (251) 961-2505

Magnolia Springs St Pauls Episcopal Church **P** (129) 14755 Oak St 36555-6830 (Mail to: PO Box 2 36555-0002) Dennis Day Susan Mckee Susan Mckee (251) 965-7452

Mobile All Saints Episcopal Church **P** (414) 151 S Ann St 36604-2302 (Mail to: 151 S Ann St 36604-2391) James Flowers (251) 438-2492

Mobile Christ Church Cathedral **P** (634) 115 S Conception St 36602-2606 (Mail to: 115 S Conception St 36602-2606) Beverly Gibson Eric Zubler (251) 438-1822

Mobile Church of the Good Shepherd **P** (145) 605 Donald St 36617-3401 (Mail to: 605 Donald St 36617-3401) John George (251) 4529596

Mobile St Andrews Episcopal Church **M** (48) 1854 Staples Rd 36605-4560 (Mail to: 1854 Staples Rd 36605-4560) (251) 479-0336

Mobile St Johns Episcopal Church **P** (82) 1707 Government St 36604-1103 (Mail to: 1707

Government St 36604-1194) John Talbert (251) 479-5474

Mobile St Lukes Episcopal Church **P** (351) § 1050 Azalea Rd 36693-2804 (Mail to: 1050 Azalea Rd 36693-2804) James McElroy Maurice Goldsmith (251) 666-2990

Mobile St Marks For the Deaf **M** (7) 6109 Howells Ferry The Willmer Hall 36618-3147 (Mail to: PO Box 180068 36618-0068) (251) 281-2148

Mobile St Pauls Episcopal Church **P** (2552) § 4051 Old Shell Rd 36608-1337 (Mail to: 4051 Old Shell Rd 36608-1399) John Riggin John Riggin William Burgess (251) 342-8521

Mobile Episcopal Ch of the Redeemer **P** (292) 1100 Cody Rd S 36695-4400 (Mail to: 7125 Hitt Rd 36695-4431) Terry Goff (251) 639-1948

Mobile Trinity Episcopal Church **P** (308) 1900 Dauphin St 36606-1414 (Mail to: 1900 Dauphin St 36606-1414) Mary Jayne Ledgerwood (251) 4732779

Monroeville Saint John's Church **P** (77) 200 Whetstone St 36460-2698 (Mail to: PO Box 853 36461-0853) Kenneth White-Spunner (251) 743-4549

Ozark St Michaels Episcopal Church **M** (30) 427 Camilla Ave 36360-2281 (Mail to: 427 Camilla Ave 36360-2281) (334) 774-2617

Robertsdale St John the Evangelist Epis Ch **M** (102) 22764 Us Highway 90 36567-2805 (Mail to: PO Box 1137 36567-1137) (251) 914-6011

Troy St Mark's Episcopal Church **P** (155) 401 W College St 36081-2108 (Mail to: 401 W College St 36081-2196) Jeffrey Byrd (334) 566-2619

Florida

Apalachicola Trinity Episcopal Church **P** (136) 79 6th St 32329 (Mail to: PO Box 667 32329-0667) (850) 653-9550

Cantonment St Monicas Episcopal Church **P** (119) 699 S Highway 95a 32533-6485 (Mail to: 699 S Highway 95A 32533-6485) Anthony MacWhinnie (850) 937-0001

Chickasaw St Michaels Episcopal Church **M** (60) 300 Grant St 36611-2132 (Mail to: PO Box 11484 36671-0484) (251) 457-6698

Chipley St Matthews Episcopal Church **M** (49) 736 West Blvd 32428-1629 (Mail to: PO Box 345 32428-0345) (850) 638-7837

Crestview Episcopal Ch of the Epiphany **M** (53) PO Box 612 32536-0612 (Mail to: 424 Garden St 32536-1704) (850) 689-1410

Defuniak Spgs St Agathas Episcopal Church **M** (53) 144 Circle Dr 32435-2545 (Mail to: 144 Circle Dr 32435-2545) (850) 892-7254

Destin St Andrew's By-the-Sea Epis Ch **P** (95) 307 Harbor Blvd 32541-2383 (Mail to: PO Box 1658 32540-1658) Jo Popham (850) 650-2737

Ft Walton Bch St Simons on-the-Sound Epis Ch **P** (342) 28 Miracle Strip Pkwy SW 32548-6613

(Mail to: 28 Miracle Strip Pkwy SW 32548-6613) James Knight (850) 244-8621

Gulf Breeze St Francis of Assisi Epis Ch **P** (249) 1 Saint Francis Dr 32561-4825 (Mail to: 1 Saint Francis Dr 32561-4825) (850) 932-2861

Marianna St Lukes Episcopal Church **P** (135) 4362 Lafayette St 32446-2916 (Mail to: 4362 Lafayette St 32446-2916) (850) 482-2431

Milton St Marys Episcopal Church **P** (185) 6841 Oak St 32570-6791 (Mail to: 6849 Oak St 32570-6791) (850) 623-2905

Navarre St Augustine of Canterbury **P** (128) 7810 Navarre Pkwy 32566-7585 (Mail to: PO Box 5425 32566-0425) (850) 939-2261

Niceville St Judes Episcopal Church **P** (306) 200 Partin Dr N 32578-1244 (Mail to: 200 Partin Dr N 32578-1244) Blake Hutson (850) 678-7013

Panama City Holy Nativity Episcopal Church **P** (718) § 222 N Bonita Ave 32401-3853 (Mail to: 1011 E 3rd St 32401-3737) Steven Bates Steven Bates Thomas Weller (850) 747-4000

Panama City St Andrews Episcopal Church **P** (161) 1608 Baker Ct 32401-1900 (Mail to: 1608 Baker Ct 32401-1900) William Adams (850) 763-7636

Panama City St Patricks Episcopal Church **M** (69) 4025 East Fifteenth Street 32404-5862 (Mail to: PO Box 36943 324010061) Julia Phillips (850) 763-7847

Panama City Beach Grace Episcopal Church **P** (135) 9101 Panama City Beach Pkwy 32407-4021 (Mail to: PO Box 9087 32417-9087) Joseph Hagberg (850) 235-4136

Panama City Beach St Thomas by-the-Sea Epis Ch **M** (105) 20408 First Ave 32413-8902 (Mail to: PO Box 7359 32413-0359) (850) 234-2919

Pensacola Christ Episcopal Church **P** (2266) § 18 W Wright St 32501 (Mail to: PO Box 12683 32591-2683) Kathryn Gillett Michael Hoffman James Lord John Phillips (850) 432-5115

Pensacola Holy Cross Episcopal Church **P** (296) 7979 N 9th Ave 32514-6460 (Mail to: 7979 N 9th Ave 32514-6460) Robert Dixon (850) 477-8596

Pensacola Holy Trinity Episcopal Church **P** (138) 850 N Blue Angel Pkwy 32506-6304 (Mail to: 850 N Blue Angel Pkwy 32506-6304) (850) 434-7337

Pensacola St Christophers Episcopal Ch **P** (1211) 3200 N 12th Ave 32503-4007 (Mail to: 3200 N 12th Ave 32503-4007) Susan Sowers Ansley Walker (850) 433-0074

Pensacola St Cyprians Episcopal Church **M** (39) 500 N. Reus St. 32501 (Mail to: PO Box 17165 32522-7165) (850) 438-1958

Pensacola St Johns Episcopal Church **P** (136) 401 Live Oak Ave 32507-3431 (Mail to: 401 Live Oak Ave 32507-3431) (850) 453-9076

Port St Joe St James Episcopal Church **P** (115) 800 22nd St 32456-2298 (Mail to: 800 22nd St 32456-2298) Thomas Dwyer (850) 227-1845

Santa Rosa Beach Christ the King Episcopal Ch **P** (341) 480 N County Highway 393 32459-5362 (Mail to: 480 N County Highway 393 32459-5362) Richard Proctor (850) 267-3332

Wewahitchka St John the Baptist Epis Ch **M** (21) 4060 N Highway 71 PO Box 595 32465-0595 (Mail to: PO Box 595 32465-0595) (850) 639-2280

DIOCESE OF CENTRAL NEW YORK
(PROVINCE II)
Comprises 14 counties in Central NY
DIOCESAN OFFICE 1020 7th North St Ste 200 Liverpool NY 13088
MAILING ADDRESS: PO BOX 3520 Syracuse, NY 13220
Tel (315) 474-6596 FAX (315) 457-2947
E-mail office@cnyepiscopal.org WEB www.cnyepiscopal.org

Previous Bishops—
Frederic D Huntington 1869-1904, Chas T Olm stead coadj 1902 Bp 1904-21, Chas Fiske coadj 1915 Bp 1921-36, Edward H Coley suffr 1924 Bp 1936-42, Malcolm E Peabody coadj 1938 Bp 1942-60, Walter M Higley suffr 1948 coadj 1959 Bp 1960-69, Ned Cole coadj 1964 Bp 1969-83, O'Kelley Whitaker coadj 1981 Bp 1983-92, David B Joslin coadj 1991 Bp 1992-99 David Bowman asst Bp 2000-01 Gladstone B Adams III 2001-16

Bishop — Rt Rev Dr DeDe Duncan-Probe (1097) (Dio 03 Dec 16)

Can to the Ordinary Rev C Schofield-Broadbent; *Can to the Ordinary* Rev T Ferguson; vacant; *Exec Asst* S Alamond; *Conv Sec* K Dengler; *Co-Chanc* J Fellows BS&K, One Lincoln Center, Syracuse, NY 13202 *Co-Chanc* M Berry; *COM* Rev D Handschy; *Cursillo* T Weir; *Ecum Off* vacant; *ER&D* Rev S Banner; *Lit* Rev M Castellan; *Stew* Rev Cn C Schofield-Broadbent; *UTO* vacant; *Yth* vacant; *Safe Church* K Dengler; *Comp Dio* Rev Dcn Dr C Stewart; *Deploy* Rev Cn C Schofield-Broadbent; *Global Miss* Rev Dcn P Kinney

Stand Comm: Cler: JB Benson T Hollowood D-V Mitchell *Lay:* C Adamowsky J Orr, Dr J Chaffee

Dio Bd—Cler: Ch Bp D Duncan-Probe; *Vice Chair* Rev P Frolick; *Treas* S White M Payne-Hardin Rev J Rohde Rev Dr R Drebert; *Lay: Ch* J Fellows *Vice Ch* M Berry J Gendron A Bauder D Kenney

PARISHES, MISSIONS, AND CLERGY
Adams Emmanuel Episcopal Church **P** (72) 40 E Church St 13605 (Mail to: PO Box 29 13605-0029) Jon Lavelle (315) 232-2916
Afton St Anns Church **P** (48) 125 E Main St 13730-2264 (Mail to: PO Box 22 13730-0022) (607) 639-2330
Alexandria Bay Church of St Lawrence **SC** (8) 7 Fuller St 13607 (Mail to: 7 Fuller St 13607-1393) John Andersen

Auburn Epis Ch of Sts Peter and John **P** (269) 169 Genesee St 13021-3534 (Mail to: 169 Genesee St 13021-3403) (315) 252-5721
Aurora United Ministry of Aurora **P** (11) Main St 13026 (Mail to: PO Box 91 13026-0091) (315) 364-8543
Bainbridge St Peters Episcopal Church **P** (174) 1 Church St 13733-1237 (Mail to: 1 Church St 13733-1237) Thomas Margrave (607) 967-3441
Baldwinsville Grace Episcopal Church **P** (206) 110 Oswego St 13027-1129 (Mail to: PO Box 6 13027-0006) Catherine Carpenter (315) 635-3214
Barneveld St Davids Episcopal Church **P** (87) PO Box 344 13304-0344 (Mail to: PO Box 344 13304-0344) Sarah Lewis (315) 896-2595
Berkshire St Johns Episcopal Church **P** (45) 1504 Seventy 6 Rd 13736 (Mail to: C/O The Rev Richard Schaal 877 Mountain Rd 13827-1187) (607) 687-1425
Binghamton Christ Church Episcopal **P** (276) 187 Washington St 13901-2713 (Mail to: 10 Henry St 13901-2789) Katrina Grusell Charles Jones (607) 722-2308
Binghamton St Marks Episcopal Church **P** (295) 728 River Rd 13901-1263 (Mail to: PO Box 458 13745-0458) Dawn-Victoria Mitchell (607) 648-4400
Binghamton Trinity Memorial Church **P** (214) 44 Main St 13905-3108 (Mail to: 44 Main St 13905-3181) Kay Drebert (607) 723-3593
Black River St Johns Episcopal Church **P** (40) 145 W Remington St 13612-3124 (Mail to: PO Box 247 13612-0247) Ninon Hutchinson Wayne Storey (315) 788-3738
Boonville Trinity Episcopal Church **P** (119) Schuyler St 13309-1203 (Mail to: PO Box 151 13309-0151) (315) 942-4726
Brownville St Pauls Episcopal Church **P** (35) 210 Washington St 13615 (Mail to: 314 Clay St 13601-3304) (315) 788-3730
Camden Trinity Episcopal Church **P** (38) 95 Main St 13316-1303 (Mail to: PO Box 102 13316-0102) (315) 245-1987

Camillus St Lukes Episcopal Church **P** (243) 5402 W Genesee St 13031-2138 (Mail to: PO Box 91 13031-0091) Jon White (315) 487-1771

Canastota Trinity Episcopal Church **P** (69) 400 S Peterboro St 13032-1416 (Mail to: PO Box 26 13032-0026) (315) 697-2953

Candor St Marks Episcopal Church **P** (68) 17 Main St 13743-1617 (Mail to: 112 Logue Hill Rd 13743-2043) (607) 659-7479

Cape Vincent St Johns Church **P** (54) 352 S. Market St 13618 (Mail to: PO Box 561 13618-0561) (315) 654-3833

Carthage Grace Episcopal Church **P** (20) 421 State St 13619-1413 (Mail to: 421 State St 13619) (315) 493-0382

Cazenovia St Peters Episcopal Church **P** (176) 10 Mill St 13035-1406 (Mail to: PO Box 419 13035-0419) (315) 655-9063

Chadwicks St Georges Episcopal Church **P** (97) 9389 Elm St PO Box P 13319-3517 (Mail to: 9389 Elm St 13319-3517) Terry Sheldon (315) 737-8124

Chittenango St Pauls Church **P** (166) 204 Genesee St 13037-1705 (Mail to: 204 Genesee St 13037-1705) Charles Grover (315) 687-6304

Clayton Christ Episcopal Church **P** (223) 235 John St 13624-1014 (Mail to: 235 John St 13624-1014) Lisa Busby (315) 686-3703

Clinton St James Episcopal Church **P** (142) 9 Williams St 13323-1705 (Mail to: 9 Williams St 13323-1705) (315) 853-5359

Constableville St Pauls Episcopal Church **P** (13) 27 Church St 13325 (Mail to: PO Box 69 13325-0069) (315) 942-4726

Constantia Trinity Episcopal Church **P** (15) 1492 George Street 13044-0124 (Mail to: PO Box 124 13044-0124) (315) 623-7431

Copenhagen Grace Church **P** (43) 21 Cataract St 13626 (Mail to: Mrs Holly Evans PO Box 6 13626-0006) (315) 688-2867

Cortland Grace and Holy Spirit Church **P** (220) 13 Court St 13045-2603 (Mail to: 13 Court St 13045-2603) Peter Williams (607) 753-3073

East Syracuse Emmanuel Episcopal Church **P** (115) 400 W Yates St 13057-2140 (Mail to: 400 W Yates St 13057-2140) Julie Calhoun-Bryant (315) 463-4310

Elmira Emmanuel Church **P** (51) 380 Pennsylvania Ave 14904-1759 (Mail to: 380 Pennsylvania Ave 14904-1759) Robert Adkins (607) 733-8219

Elmira Grace Episcopal Church **P** (101) 375 W Church St 14901-2620 (Mail to: Attn: Anne H Ferris 375 W Church St 14901-2695) Jennifer Scott-Jones (607) 732-0545

Elmira Trinity Episcopal Church **P** (43) 304 N Main St 14901-2710 (Mail to: 304 N Main St 14901-2778) (607) 732-3241

Endicott St Pauls Episcopal Church **P** (311) 200 Jefferson Ave 13760-5212 (Mail to: 200 Jefferson Ave 13760-5295) John Martinichio (607) 748-8118

Evans Mills St Andrews Church **P** (8) 8520 Leray St 13637-3191 (Mail to: PO Box 233 13637-0233) (315) 350-4844

Fayetteville St Davids Episcopal Church **P** (121) 14 Jamar Dr 13066-1619 (Mail to: PO Box 261 13214-0261) Daniel Handschy Katherine Day (315) 446-2112

Fayetteville Trinity Episcopal Church **P** (298) 106 Chapel St 13066-2004 (Mail to: 106 Chapel St 13066-2052) Renee Tembeckjian (315) 637-9872

Fulton All Saints Episcopal Church **P** (50) 153 S 1st St 13069-1716 (Mail to: PO Box 542 13069-0542) (315) 592-2102

Geneva Grace Church Willowdale **P** (16) 3874 E Lake Rd 14456-9256 (Mail to: C/O Lloyd D Evans PO Box 135 14456-0135) (315) 585-9852

Greene Zion Episcopal Church **P** (351) 10 N Chenango St 13778-1102 (Mail to: PO Box 88 13778-0088) David Hanselman (607) 656-9502

Hamilton St Thomas Episcopal Church **P** (128) 12 1/2 Madison St 13346 (Mail to: 12 1/2 Madison St 13346-1106) Brooks Cato (315) 824-1745

Horseheads St Matthews Episcopal Church **P** (151) 408 S Main St 14845-2409 (Mail to: 408 S Main St 14845-2409) (607) 739-5226

Ithaca Episcopal Church at Cornell **CC** (74) G3 Anabel Taylor Hall Cornell 548 College Ave 14853-4902 (Mail to: Episcopal Church At Cornell University PO Box 7251 14851-7251) Taylor Daynes (607) 351-3784

Ithaca St Johns Episcopal Church **P** (232) 210 N Cayuga St 14850-4333 (Mail to: 210 N Cayuga St 14850-4385) Megan Castellan (607) 273-6532

Johnson City All Saints Episcopal Church **P** (125) 475 Main St 13790-1906 (Mail to: 475 Main St 13790-1999) (607) 797-3354

Jordan Christ Episcopal Church **P** (47) 25 N Main St 13080-9797 (Mail to: PO Box 571 13080-0571) (315) 689-3141

Liverpool St Matthews Episcopal Church **P** (333) 900 Vine St 13088 (Mail to: 900 Vine St 13088) Paul Frolick (315) 457-4633

Lowville Trinity Church **P** (43) § 5411 Trinity Ave 13367-1315 (Mail to: 5411 Trinity Ave 13367-1315) (315) 376-3241

Manlius Christ Church **P** (260) 407 E Seneca St 13104-1910 (Mail to: 407 E Seneca St 13104-1910) (315) 682-5795

Marathon St Johns Chapel **Chapel** (10) West Main St 13803 (Mail to: PO Box 541 13783-0541) Elizabeth Groskoph (607) 637-4952

Marcellus St Johns Episcopal Church **P** (120) 15 Orange St 13108-1215 (Mail to: 15 Orange St 13108-1215) Steven Moore (315) 673-2500

Mexico Grace Episcopal Church **P** (20) 4381 Church St 13114 (Mail to: C/O Ms Janice H

Clark PO Box 539 13114-0539) (315) 297-0254

Moravia St Matthews Church **P** (106) 14 Church St 13118 (Mail to: 14 Church St 13118-2300) (315) 497-1171

✠ **Nedrow** Church of the Good Shepherd **O** Us Rte 11 13120 (Mail to: PO Box 143 13120-0143) (315) 469-0247

New Berlin St Andrews Episcopal Church **P** (98) South Main St 13411 (Mail to: 40 S Main St PO Box 370 13411-3053) William White (607) 847-6361

New Hartford St Stephens Church **P** (149) 25 Oxford Rd 13413-2638 (Mail to: 25 Oxford Rd 13413-2662) (315) 732-7462

Norwich Emmanuel Episcopal Church **P** (176) 37 W Main St 13815-1635 (Mail to: PO Box 203 13815-0203) (607) 334-8801

Oneida St Johns Church **P** (98) 341 Main St 13421-2144 (Mail to: 341 Main St 13421-2144) (315) 363-1940

Oswego Church of the Resurrection **P** (126) 120 W 5th St 13126-2037 (Mail to: C/O Alexander Thompson 120 W 5th St 13126-2037) Anne Wichelns (315) 343-3501

Owego St Pauls Episcopal Church **P** (168) 117 Main St 13827-1587 (Mail to: 117 Main St 13827-1587) Trula Hollywood (607) 687-2830

Oxford St Pauls Church **P** (145) 36 Main St 13830-3439 (Mail to: PO Box 72 13830-0072) David Hanselman (607) 843-7011

Parishville St Pauls Chapel **SC** 310 Montgomery St #200 13429 (Mail to: C/O Saint Stephens Route 12 13429) (315) 733-7575

Pierrepont Manor Zion Church **P** (119) 15639 NY State Rt 193 13674 (Mail to: PO Box 782 13674-0782) John Throop (315) 232-2916

Port Leyden St Marks Episcopal Church **P** (28) 6988 Main St 13433 (Mail to: PO Box 31 13433-0031) (315) 942-4726

Pulaski St James Episcopal Church **P** (30) 24 Lake St 13142-3243 (Mail to: PO Box 433 24 Lake St 13142-0433) Shelly Banner (315) 298-2106

Rome Zion Episcopal Church **P** (109) 140 W Liberty St 13440-5718 (Mail to: 140 W Liberty St 13440-5780) (315) 336-5170

Sackets Hbr Christ Church **M** 207 E Main St 13685-3158 (Mail to: East Main Street 13685) (315) 646-2217

Seneca Falls Trinity Episcopal Church **P** (64) 27 Fall St 13148-1428 (Mail to: PO Box 507 13148-0507) (315) 568-5145

Sherburne Episcopal Ch of the Epiphany **P** (104) 5 Classic St 13460-9797 (Mail to: PO Box 538 13460-0538) Bruce Macduffie (607) 674-4312

Sherrill Gethsemane Episcopal Church **P** (89) 320 Park St 13461-1253 (Mail to: 320 Park St 13461-1253) (315) 363-3244

Skaneateles St James Episcopal Church **P** (655) 96 E Genesee St 13152-1328 (Mail to: 96 E Genesee St 13152-1372) Rebecca Coerper Charles Stewart (315) 685-7600

Slaterville Springs St Thomas Episcopal Church **P** (33) 2720 Slaterville Rd Rte 79 14881 (Mail to: PO Box 51 14817-0051) (607) 227-5118

South New Berlin St Matthews Church **P** (23) State Hwy 8 13843 (Mail to: PO Box 18 13843-0018) (607) 847-6361

Syracuse Church of the Saviour **Chapel** (91) 437 James St 13203-2224 (Mail to: 437 James St 13203-2224) Steven Moore (315) 474-3359

Syracuse Ephphatha Parish for the Deaf **P** (18) 310 Montgomery St Ste 250 13202-2010 (Mail to: 310 Montgomery Street Ste 250 13202) Peter Williams Virginia Nagel (315) 471-3736

Syracuse Grace Church **P** (102) 819 Madison St 13210-1736 (Mail to: 819 Madison St 13210-1793) (315) 478-0901

Syracuse St Albans Episcopal Church **P** (54) 1308 Meadowbrook Dr 13224-1718 (Mail to: 1308 Meadowbrook Dr 13224-1718) Julie Calhoun-Bryant (315) 446-3490

Syracuse St Mark the Evangelist **P** (300) 1612 W Genesee St 13204-1950 (Mail to: 1612 W Genesee St 13204-1950) (315) 488-8511

✠ **Syracuse** St Paul's Syracuse **O** (193) 220 E Fayette St 13202-1904 (Mail to: 310 Montgomery St Ste 1 13202-2096) Philip Major (315) 474-6053

Trumansburg Church of the Epiphany **P** (43) 11 Elm St 14886 (Mail to: PO Box 459 14886-0459) (607) 387-6274

Utica Grace Episcopal Church **P** (453) 193 Genesee St. 13501-2263 (Mail to: 6 Elizabeth St 13501-2263) (315) 733-7575

Waterloo St Pauls Episcopal Church **P** (63) 101 E Williams St 13165-1412 (Mail to: 101 E Williams St 13165-1458) Jeffrey Haugaard (315) 539-3897

Watertown Trinity Episcopal Church **P** (155) 227 Sherman St 13601-3611 (Mail to: 227 Sherman St 13601-3691) Mary Payne-Hardin (315) 788-6290

Waverly Grace Episcopal Church **P** (16) 441 Park Ave 14892-1446 (Mail to: 441 Park Ave 14892-1446) Benjamin Lentz (607) 565-2608

Willard Christ Episcopal Church **P** (24) 1393 Main St 14588 (Mail to: PO Box 275 14588-0275) Arlen Strauss (607) 869-9250

Windsor Zion Episcopal Church **P** (74) § 21 Chapel St 13865-4307 (Mail to: PO Box 85 13865-0085) Geoffrey Doolittle (607) 655-5533

DIOCESE OF CENTRAL PENNSYLVANIA
(PROVINCE III)
Comprises 24 counties in Central Pennsylvania
DIOCESAN OFFICE 101 Pine St Harrisburg PA 17101 (MAIL: Box 11937 Harrisburg PA 17108-1937)
TEL (717) 236-5959 FAX (717) 236-6448
E-MAIL officemailbox@diocesecpa.org WEB www.diocesecpa.org

Previous Bishops—
Central Pennsylvania: Mark AD
Howe 1871-95, Nelson S Rulison
coadj 1884 Bp 1895-97, Ethelbert
Talbot 1898-1928. *Harrisburg:*
James H Darlington 1905-30,
Hunter Wyatt-Brown 1931-43,
John T Heistand 1943-66, Earl M
Honaman suffr 1956-69. *Central Pennsylvania:* Dean
T Stevenson 1966-82, Charlie F McNutt coadj 1980
Bp 1982-95, Michael W Creighton Bp 1995-2006,
Nathan D Baxter Bp 2006-2014, Robert R Gepert
Prov Bp 2014-2015

Bishop—Rt Rev Dr Audrey C Scanlan (1089) (Dio 12 September 2015)

Cn for Fin & Opns C Linder; *Archd for Dcns* Ven J
Miron; *Sec* T Powell Esq; *Treas* T Roche; *Reg* D Ro-
belen; *Chanc* T Schmidt Esq; *V Chanc* M Powell Esq
M McAuliffe Miller Esq; *Dean Stevenson Sch for Min*
Dr S Stonesifer Boylan; *Cn Dioc Events and Comm*
A Guszick; *Cn Mission Dev & Innovation* Rev C
Streeter

Stand Comm—Cler: G Welin K Harrigan E Hillegas
K Barron V Chappell J Mattson; *Lay: Pres* D Dorgan
A Alexander L Gottfried-Letsche K Hettinga N Nor-
ris B Cross D Luo

PARISHES, MISSIONS, AND CLERGY

Altoona St Luke Episcopal Church **P** (129) 806
13th St 16602-2422 (Mail to: 806 13th St
16602-2486) (814) 942-1372

Bedford St James Episcopal Church **P** (55) 309 S.
Richard St 15522-1029 (Mail to: 309 S Richard
St 15522-1744) (814) 623-8822

Bellefonte St John's Episcopal Church **P** (151)
120 W Lamb St 16823-1609 (Mail to: 120
W Lamb St 16823-1609) Carlos De La Torre
Alexander Dyakiw (814) 355-0497

Berwick Christ Episcopal Church **P** (64) 712 E
16th St 18603-2302 (Mail to: 712 E 16th St
18603-2302) (570) 752-6205

Bloomsburg St Pauls Episcopal Church **P** (142)
101 E Main St 17815-1806 (Mail to: PO Box
764 17815-0764) James Jenkins (570) 784-3316

Blue Ridge Summit Calvary Chapel **P** (76) 13646
Summit Avenue 17214-0922 (Mail to: C/O Ch
of the Transfiguration PO Box B 17214-0922)
(717) 794-2229

Blue Ridge Summit Church of the Transfiguration **P** (96) 13646 Summit Ave 17214-9799
(Mail to: Attn: Treasurer PO Box B 17214-
0922) (717) 794-2229

Brookland All Saints Episcopal Church **P** (22)
1568 Fox Hill Rd 16948 (Mail to: PO Box 52
16915-0052) Janis Yskamp (814) 274-8391

Camp Hill Mount Calvary Church **P** (412) 125
N 25th St 17011-3609 (Mail to: 125 N 25th St
17011-3609) Gregory Welin (717) 737-3764

Carlisle Saint John's Episcopal Church **P** (385) §
1 N Hanover St # A 17013-3014 (Mail to: PO
Box 612 17013-0612) Melissa Wilcox Adam
Kradel (717) 243-4220

Chambersburg Trinity Episcopal Church **P** (163)
58 S 2nd St 17201-2208 (Mail to: 58 S 2nd St
17201-2208) Patricia Dickson (717) 264-6351

Columbia Saint Paul's Church **P** (80) 340 Locust
St 17512-1121 (Mail to: PO Box 96 17512-0096)

Coudersport Christ Episcopal Church **P** (76) 601
N Main St 16915-1703 (Mail to: PO Box 52
16915-0052) (814) 274-8391

Danville Christ Memorial Episcopal Ch **P** (134)
120 E Market St 17821-1942 (Mail to: PO Box
363 17821-0363) James Strader-Sasser (570)
275-3903

Danville St James Episcopal Church **P** (16) White
Hall Rd State Route 44 17821 (Mail to: 1261
White Hall Rd 17772-9103) (570) 546-6470

Eagles Mere St Johns Episcopal Church **SC** 50
Jones Ave 17731-0042 (Mail to: Mrs. Caroline
Estey King 260 W. Hartwell Ln 19118) (215)
242-2945

Gettysburg Prince of Peace Memorial Ch **P** (276)
20 W High St 17325-2118 (Mail to: PO Box
3005 17325-0005) Herbert Sprouse (717) 334-
6463

Hanover All Saints Church **P** (177) 890 Mccosh
St 17331-1800 (Mail to: 890 McCosh St 17331-
1800) Carenda Baker (717) 637-5772

✚ **Harrisburg** St Stephens Cathedral **O** (558) §
221 N Front St Ste 101 17101-1407 (Mail to:
221 N Front St 17101-1437) Amy Welin Willis
Nailor (717) 236-4059

Harrisburg St Pauls Episcopal Church **P** (268)
248 Seneca St 17110-1840 (Mail to: 248 Seneca
St 17110-1840) Harry Knisely (717) 233-2175

Harrisburg St Andrews in the Valley Epis **P** (136)
4620 Linglestown Rd 17112 (Mail to: 4620
Linglestown Rd 17112-9521) (717) 657-8583

Harrisburg St Andrews Episcopal Church **P** (23)
1852 Market St 17103-2523 (Mail to: 1854
Market St 17112-9521) Calvin Hoyt (717)
234-8815

Hawk Run Chapel of the Good Shepherd **P** (47)
Leonard J Coval Sr Warden 270 Whitman St
16840-9728 (Mail to: PO Box 23 16840-0023)
Clifford Johnston (814) 345-5576

Hershey All Saints Episcopal Church **P** (471) 310 Elm Ave 17033-1749 (Mail to: 310 Elm Ave 17033-1749) Anjel Scarborough (717) 5332454

Hollidaysburg Church of the Holy Trinity **P** (86) Allegheny & Jones St 16648 (Mail to: 315 Jones St 16648-2007) Jeanne Jacobson (814) 695-7751

Huntingdon Saint John's Episcopal Church **P** (63) 212 Penn St 16652-1444 (Mail to: 212 Penn St 16652-1444) (814) 643-4732

Jersey Shore Trinity Episcopal Church **P** (34) 174 Mount Pleasant Ave 17740-1762 (Mail to: 176 Mount Pleasant Ave 17740-1762) (570) 398-4007

Lancaster St Edward Episcopal Church **P** (424) 2453 Harrisburg Pike 17601-1719 (Mail to: 2453 Harrisburg Pike 17601-1719) Richard Bauer Harold Morrow (717) 898-6276

Lancaster Saint James Episcopal Church **P** (565) 119 N Duke St 17602-2815 (Mail to: 119 N Duke St 17602-2891) David Peck Shayna Watson (717) 397-4858

Lancaster St Johns Episcopal Church **P** (379) 321 W Chestnut St 17603-3509 (Mail to: 321 W Chestnut St 17603-3591) Amanda Knouse Jennifer Trenary (717) 299-1188

Lancaster St Thomas Episcopal Church **P** (261) 301 Saint Thomas Rd 17601-4832 (Mail to: 301 Saint Thomas Rd 17601-4832) Jennifer Mattson (717) 569-3241

Lewisburg St Andrews Episcopal Church **P** (178) 255 S Derr Dr 17837-1722 (Mail to: 255 S Derr Dr 17837-1722) Sarah Weedon (570) 524-2061

Lewistown St Mark's Episcopal Church **P** (91) 21 S Main St 17044-2116 (Mail to: 21 S Main St 17044-2116) (717) 248-8327

Lock Haven Saint Paul's Church **HC** (56) 112 E Main St 17745-1306 (Mail to: PO Box 206 17745-0206) (570) 748-2440

Manheim Hope Episcopal Church **P** (93) 2425 Mountain Rd 17545-8793 (Mail to: 2425 Mountain Rd 17545-8793) (717) 665-6311

Manheim St Pauls Episcopal Church **P** (50) 90 S Charlotte St 17545-1802 (Mail to: 90 S Charlotte St 17545-1802) (717) 665-6584

Mansfield St James Episcopal Church **P** (31) 30 E Wellsboro St 16933-1121 (Mail to: 30 E Wellsboro St 16933-1121) (570) 662-2003

Marietta Saint John's Church **P** (63) 239 E Market St 17547-1533 (Mail to: PO Box 98 17547-0098) (717) 426-3189

Mechanicsburg St Lukes Episcopal Church **P** (198) 8 E Keller St 17055-3826 (Mail to: 8 E Keller St 17055-3826) Robert Schiesler David Ster (717) 766-5182

Milton Christ Episcopal Church **P** (29) 21 Upper Market St 17847-1225 (Mail to: 21 Upper Market St 17847-1225) Robert Van Deusen (570) 742-4153

Montoursville Church of Our Saviour **P** (40) 31 N Loyalsock Ave 17754-1703 (Mail to: 31 N Loyalsock Ave 17754-1703) (570) 368-1860

Montoursville Church of the Good Shepherd **P** (16) 827 Good Shepherd Rd 17754-7532 (Mail to: Mabel B Karschner Rd #1 Box 360 17754) (570) 433-3823

Mount Carmel The Resurrection Mission **M** (16) 120 W 4th St 17851-2003 (Mail to: PO Box 353 17851-0353)

Mount Joy St Lukes Episcopal Church **P** (189) 209 S Market St 17552-3109 (Mail to: 209 S Market St 17552-3109) Eleanor Hart Garner (717) 653-4977

Muncy St James Episcopal Church **P** (49) 215 S Main St 17756-1505 (Mail to: PO Box 95 17756-0095) (570) 546-6470

Narvon Bangor Episcopal Church **P** (77) 2099 Main St 17555-9521 (Mail to: 2099 Main Street 17555-9521) William Murphey (717) 445-0253

Newport Nativity & St Stephs Epis Par **P** (63) 159 S 2nd St 17074-1407 (Mail to: The Church of the Nativity 159 S 2nd St 17074-1407) Rebecca Myers (717) 567-6514

Northumberlnd St Mark Episcopal Church **P** (39) 187 King St 17857-1653 (Mail to: 187 King St 17857-1653) Robert Van Deusen (570) 473-3220

Philipsburg St Pauls Church **P** (198) 406 E Presqueisle St 16866 (Mail to: PO Box 170 16866-0170) (814) 342-3180

Selinsgrove All Saints Episcopal Church **P** (25) 129 N Market St 17870-1905 (Mail to: PO Box 119 17870-0119) (570) 374-8289

Shippensburg St Andrews Episcopal Church **P** (207) 206 E Burd St 17257-1402 (Mail to: 204 E Burd St 17257-1402) Barbara Hutchinson (717) 532-8089

State College St Andrews Church **P** (500) 208 W Foster Ave 16801-4822 (Mail to: 208 W Foster Ave 16801-4822) Jeffry Packard Joseph DeLauter (814) 237-7659

Sunbury St Matthews Episcopal Church **P** (267) 32 N Front St 17801-2140 (Mail to: 32 N Front St 17801-2140) (570) 286-7002

Thompsontown St Stephens Episcopal Church **HC** East Main St 17094 (Mail to: E Main St 17094-9752) (717) 567-6514

Tioga St Andrews Episcopal Church **P** (16) Main St 16946 (Mail to: PO Box 485 16946-0485) (570) 662-7600

Tyrone Trinity Episcopal Church **P** (85) 830 Washington Ave 16686-1345 (Mail to: 830 Washington Ave 16686-1345) Jack Hoffer (814) 684-3100

Waynesboro St Marys Episcopal Church **P** (144) 112 E 2nd St 17268-1603 (Mail to: 112 E 2nd St 17268-1603) Linda Watkins (717) 762-1930

Wellsboro Saint Paul's Church **HC** (202) 29 Charles St 16901-1401 (Mail to: PO Box 701

16901-0701) Edward Erb David Perkins (570) 724-4771

Westfield St Johns Church **P** (26) 205 Elm St 16950-1507 (Mail to: 205 Elm St 16950-1507) (814) 367-2245

Williamsport All Saints Memorial Church **P** (40) 1656 Scott St 17701-4459 (Mail to: 1656 Scott St 17701-4459) (570) 326-0191

Williamsport Christ Episcopal Church **P** (113) 426 Mulberry St 17701-6312 (Mail to: 426 Mulberry St 17701-6375) (570) 322-8157

Williamsport Trinity Episcopal Church **P** (278) 844 W 4th St 17701-5824 (Mail to: 844 W 4th

St 17701-5824) Kenneth Wagner-Pizza (570) 322-0126

York St Andrews Episcopal Church **P** (313) 1502 4th Ave 17403-2623 (Mail to: 1502 4th Ave 17403-2623) Theodore Ambrose (717) 843-3868

York St John The Baptist EpisCh **P** (492) 140 N Beaver St 17403-5324 (Mail to: 140 N Beaver St 17401-5396) Eric Hillegas (717) 848-1862

York Springs Christ Episcopal Church **SC** York Springs Road 17403 (Mail to: C/O Diocese Of Central Pa PO Box 11937 17108) (717) 236-5959

DIOCESE OF CHICAGO
(PROVINCE V)
Comprises Northern and Western Illinois
DIOCESAN OFFICE 65 E Huron St Chicago IL 60611
TEL (312) 751-4200 FAX (312) 787-5872
E-MAIL Bishop@episcopalchicago.org WEB www.episcopalchicago.org

Previous Bishops—
Philander Chase 1835-52, Henry J Whitehouse coadj 1851 Bp 1852-74, Wm E McLaren 1875-1905, Chas P Anderson coadj 1900 Bp 1905-30, Wm E Toll suffr 1911-15, Sheldon M Griswold suffr 1917 Bp 1930-30, Geo C Stewart coadj 1930 Bp 1930-40, Edwin J Randall suffr 1939-47, Wallace E Conkling 1941-53, Chas L Street suffr 1949-63, Gerald F Burrill 1954-71, Quintin E Primo Jr suffr 1972-84, James W Montgomery suffr 1962-65 coadj 1965 Bp 1971-87, William W Wiedrich suffr 1990-97, Frank T Griswold coadj 1985-87 Bp 1987-98, HA Donavan prov 1998-99, William D Persell Bp 1999-2008, Victor A Scantlebury asst 2000-11, John C Buchanan asst Bp 2014-14, C Christopher Epting asst Bp 2012-15, Jeffrey D Lee 2008–20), Chilton R Knudsen asst Bp 2021–22)

Bishop— Rt Rev Paula E Clark (1147) (Dio 17 Sept 2022)

Dir of Min A Mysen; *Treas* K Kampert; *Hist* N Smith; *Chanc* M Peregrine; *Sec Conv* E Saldana; *Dir Operations*; *Dir Networking* C Plummer

Dio Commissions: Anti-Racism: M Briones N Smith

Stand Comm—Cler: D Cody M Briones; *Lay:* A Daniels G Floyd

Deans—Aurora B Linboom; *Chgo-N* K Wagner-Sherer; *Chgo-S* R Cristobal; *Elgin* P Skutch; *Evanston* K Banakis; *Joliet* J Froyen; *Oak Park* J Rumple; *Peoria* M Lee; *Rockford* M Dwyer; *Waukegan* C Makins

PARISHES, MISSIONS, AND CLERGY

Antioch St Ignatius of Antioch Church **P** (92) 500 E Depot St 60002-1564 (Mail to: 500 E Depot St 60002-1564) (847) 395-0652

Arlington Hts Saint Simons Church **P** (250) 717 W Kirchhoff Rd 60005-2339 (Mail to: 717 W Kirchhoff Rd 60005-2339) Jennifer Hulen (847) 259-2930

Aurora Saint David's Episcopal Church **P** (82) 701 N Randall Rd 60506-1923 (Mail to: 701 N Randall Rd 60506-1998) Robert Lambert (630) 896-7229

Aurora Trinity Church **P** (97) 218 E Benton St 60505-4250 (Mail to: 218 E Benton St 60505-4250) Denzil Luckritz (630) 897-7283

Barrington St Marks Episcopal Church **P** (292) 337 Ridge Rd 60010-2331 (Mail to: C/O David A Gibbons 337 Ridge Rd 60010-2331) David Gibbons (847) 381-0596

Barrington St Michaels Episcopal Church **P** (580) § 647 Dundee Ave 60010-4258 (Mail to: 647 Dundee Ave 60010-4299) Jesse Perkins (847) 381-2323

Batavia Calvary Episcopal Church **P** (165) 222 S Batavia Ave 60510-2564 (Mail to: 222 S Batavia Ave 60510-2564) Michael Rasicci (630) 879-3378

Belvidere Church of the Holy Trinity **P** (62) 217 E Hurlbut Ave 61008-3216 (Mail to: 217 E Hurlbut Ave 61008-3216) Randal Wakitsch (815) 544-2635

Berwyn St Mic & All Angels Epis Ch **P** (198) § 6732 W 34th St 60402 (Mail to: 6732 34th St 60402-3412) Jaime Briceno (708) 788-2197

Bloomingdale Church of the Incarnation **M** (43) 261 W Army Trail Rd 60108-1376 (Mail to:

261 W Army Trail Rd 60108-1376) Maurice Strong Louisett Ness (630) 351-3249

Bloomingdale First Asian Church **P** (80) 261 W Army Trail Rd 60108-1376 (Mail to: 261 W Army Trail Rd 60108-1376) (630) 351-3293

Blue Island St Joseph's And St Aidan's Ch **M** (47) Oak St & Greenwood Ave 60406-0275 (Mail to: 2457 Oak St 60406-2032) Rebecca Sperry (708) 389-5933

Bolingbrook Episcopal Ch of St Benedict **P** (128) 909 Lily Cache Ln 60440-3131 (Mail to: 909 Lily Cache Ln 60440-3131) Donna Ialongo (630) 759-5955

Burr Ridge St Helena Episcopal Church **P** (78) 7600 Wolf Rd 60527-8041 (Mail to: 7600 Wolf Rd 60527-8041) (630) 323-4900

Chicago All Saints Episcopal Church **P** (659) 4550`N Hermitage Ave 60640-5304 (Mail to: 4550 N Hermitage Ave 60640-5304) Elizabeth Wille Mary Reid Mary Reid (773) 561-0111

✣ **Chicago** Cathedral of St James **O** (901) 65 E Huron St 60611-2728 (Mail to: C/O Robert Black 65 E Huron St 60611-2728) Steven Balke Christopher Griffin Lisa Hackney (312) 787-7360

Chicago Church of Our Saviour **P** (572) 530 W Fullerton Pkwy 60614-5919 (Mail to: 530 W Fullerton Pkwy 60614-5919) Brian Hastings Jessica Elfring-Roberts Richard Wendel (773) 549-3832

Chicago St Pauls & Redeemer Church **P** (747) 4945 S Dorchester A 60615-2907 (Mail to: 4945 S Dorchester Ave 60615-2907) Catherine Healy Peter Lane Jaime Briceno John Seymour (773) 624-3185

Chicago Church of St Thomas **P** (185) 3801 S Wabash Ave 60653-1520 (Mail to: 3800 S Michigan Ave 60653-1514) Fulton Porter (773) 268-1900

Chicago Church of the Ascension **P** (130) 1133 N La Salle Dr 60610-2601 (Mail to: 1133 N La Salle Dr 60610-2601) Thomas Heard (312) 664-1271

Chicago Church of the Holy Cross **P** (14) 1201 W 111th Pl 60643-4513 (Mail to: PO Box 438507 60643-8507) Tyrone Fowlkes (773) 779-0777

Chicago Church of the Holy Nativity **P** (118) § 9300 S Pleasant Ave 60643-6398 (Mail to: 65 E Huron St 60611-2728) Regina Volpe (773) 4454427

Chicago El Cristo Rey Mission **M** (325) Y814 60646-4217 (Mail to: 5101 W Devon Ave 60646-4217) Alvaro Araica (773) 561-8189

Chicago Church of the Atonement **P** (447) 5749 N Kenmore Ave 60660-4541 (Mail to: 5749 N Kenmore Ave 60660-4541) Ted Durst Scott Elliott Daniel Puchalla Harry Tingley (773) 271-2727

Chicago Grace Episcopal Church **P** (92) 637 S Dearborn St 60605-1839 (Mail to: 637 S Dearborn St Fl 2 60605-1936) Amity Carrubba

Sunny Lopez (312) 922-1426

Chicago Nuestra Senora de las America **M** (45) § 3413 W Medill Ave 60647 (Mail to: 3413 W Medill Ave 60647) (773) 278-1990

Chicago Messiah St Bartholomew Epis Ch **P** (62) 8255 S Dante Ave 60619-4623 (Mail to: 8255 S Dante Ave 60619-4623) Robert Cristobal (773) 721-3232

Chicago St Albans Episcopal Church **P** (130) 6240 N Avondale Ave 60631-2452 (Mail to: 6240 N Avondale Ave 60631-2452) Mary Milano (773) 599-2545

Chicago St Andrews Chaplaincy **PS** (21) 48 N Hoyne Ave 60612-2358 (Mail to: 48 N Hoyne Ave 60612-2358) (312) 226-7205

Chicago Church of St Chrysostoms **P** (1011) § 1424 N Dearborn St 60610-1506 (Mail to: 1424 N Dearborn St 60610-1506) Whayne Hougland Sam Portaro (312) 944-1083

Chicago St Edmunds Episcopal Church **P** (281) 6105 S Michigan Ave 60637-2119 (Mail to: 6105 S Michigan Ave 60637-2119) Alonzo Pruitt (773) 288-0038

Chicago Sts George & Matthias Church **M** (65) 164 E 111th St 60628-4346 (Mail to: 164 E 111th St 60628-4346) Robert Cristobal (773) 468-1148

Chicago St Johns Episcopal Church **P** (277) 3857 N Kostner Ave 60641-2851 (Mail to: C/O Krystyna Gallagher 4650 N Kilbourn Ave 60630-4024) Kara Wagner Sherer (773) 725-9026

Chicago St Margaret of Scotland **M** (83) 2555 E 73rd St 60649-2616 (Mail to: 2555 E 73rd St 60649-2616) (773) 221-5505

Chicago Saint Martin's Church **M** (55) 5710 W Midway Park 60644-1818 (Mail to: 5700 W Midway Park 60644-1818) Christopher Griffin (773) 378-8111

Chicago Church of St Pauls by-the-Lake **P** (453) 7100 N Ashland Blvd 60626-2502 (Mail to: 7100 N Ashland Blvd 60626-2502) John Garland (773) 764-6514

Chicago St Peters Episcopal Church **P** (72) 617 W Belmont Ave 60657-7598 (Mail to: 617 W Belmont Ave 60657-4510) Garth Howe Charlotte Johnson (773) 525-0844

Chicago Santa Teresa de Avila **M** (75) 6201 S Saint Louis Ave 60629-3713 (Mail to: 6201 S Saint Louis Ave 60629-3713) Gary Cox Sandra Castillo (773) 434-9783

Chicago Trinity Church **P** (140) 125 E 26th St 60616-2310 (Mail to: 125 E 26th St 60616-2310) (312) 842-7545

Clarendon Hills Church of the Holy Nativity **P** (224) 275 S Richmond Ave 60514-2711 (Mail to: 275 S Richmond Ave 60514-2711) Bradley Linboom (630) 323-6820

Crystal Lake St Marys Episcopal Church **P** (148) 210 S Mchenry Ave 60014-6009 (Mail to: 210 S Mchenry Ave 60014-6009) Scott Zaucha (815) 459-1009

Deerfield St Gregorys Episcopal Church **P** (243) 815 Wilmot Rd 60015-2723 (Mail to: 815 Wilmot Rd 60015-2723) Anne Jolly Meredith Potter (847) 9451678

Dekalb St Pauls Episcopal Church **P** (91) 900 Normal Rd 60115-1614 (Mail to: 900 Normal Rd 60115-1614) Barbara Wilson Joyce Beaulieu Charles Wilson (815) 756-4888

Des Plaines St Martin's Episcopal Church **HC** (80) 1095 E Thacker St 60016-3361 (Mail to: 1095 E Thacker St 60016-3361) M Eccles (847) 824-2043

Dixon St Lukes Episcopal Church **P** (135) 221 W 3rd St 61021-3015 (Mail to: 221 W 3rd St 61021-3015) (815) 288-2151

Downers Grove St Andrews Episcopal Church **P** (503) 1125 Franklin St 60515-3551 (Mail to: 1125 Franklin St 60515-3599) Gregg Morris Thomas Craighead (630) 968-9188

Dundee St James Episcopal Church **P** (185) 516 Washington St 60118-1245 (Mail to: 516 Washington St 60118-1245) Donald Frye (847) 426-5612

Elgin Church of the Redeemer **P** (733) 40 Center St 60120-5609 (Mail to: 40 Center St 60120-5609) Richard Frontjes Amity Carrubba (847) 742-2428

Elgin Church of St Hugh of Lincoln **P** (160) 36w957 Highland Ave 60123-4875 (Mail to: 36W957 Highland Ave 60123-4875) Marion Phipps (847) 695-7695

Elk Grove Vlg St Nicholas Episcopal Church **M** (170) 1072 Ridge Ave 60007-4642 (Mail to: 1072 Ridge Ave 60007-4642) Manuel Borg (847) 439-2067

Elmhurst Church of Our Saviour **P** (57) 116 E Church St 60126-3404 (Mail to: 116 E Church St 60126-3485) Shireen Baker (630) 530-1434

Evanston St Lukes Episcopal Church **P** (314) 939 Hinman Ave 60202-1801 (Mail to: 939 Hinman Ave 60202-1881) Kathryn Banakis Jeannette Defriest Gloria Hopewell (847) 475-3630

Evanston St Marks Episcopal Church **P** (221) 1509 Ridge Ave 60201-4135 (Mail to: 1509 Ridge Ave 60201-4135) Frances Holliday (847) 864-4806

Evanston St Matthews Episcopal Church **P** (368) 2120 Lincoln St 60201-2282 (Mail to: 2120 Lincoln St 60201-2282) Charles De Kay (847) 869-4850

Evanston St Andrews Episcopal Church **M** (168) 1928 Darrow Ave 60201-3404 (Mail to: 1928 Darrow Ave 60201-3404) Lee Gaede Chukwuemeka Nwachuku (847) 328-4751

Flossmoor Ch of St John the Evangelist **P** (193) 2640 Park Dr 60422-1228 (Mail to: PO Box 25 60422-0025) Jeremy Froyen Jean Hoff Nolan (708) 798-4150

Freeport Grace Episcopal Church **P** (86) 10 S Cherry Ave 61032-5069 (Mail to: 10 S Cherry Ave 61032-5069) Brian Prall (815) 232-4422

Galena Grace Episcopal Church **P** (123) 107 S. Prospect St. 61036-0228 (Mail to: 107 S. Prospect St. 61036-1803) Linda Packard (815) 777-2590

Galesburg Grace Episcopal Church **HC** (18) 60 Public Square 61401 (Mail to: PO Box 218 61402-0218) (309) 255-5916

Geneva St Marks Episcopal Church **P** (987) 320 Franklin St 60134-2639 (Mail to: PO Box 126 60134-0126) Mark Tusken Marcus Johnson Robert Lowe Amy Peeler (630) 232-0133

Glen Ellyn St Barnabas Episcopal Church **P** (152) 22 W 415 Butterfield Rd 60137 (Mail to: 22W415 Butterfield Rd 60137-7164) Carol Kraft Robert Trask (630) 469-1394

Glen Ellyn St Mark's Episcopal Church **P** (2447) 393 North Main Street 60137-5068 (Mail to: 393 N Main St 60137-5098) George Smith Jose Arroyo (630) 858-1020

Glencoe St Elisabeths Episcopal Church **P** (146) 556 Vernon Ave 60022-1647 (Mail to: 556 Vernon Ave 60022-1647) (847) 835-0458

Glenview St Davids Episcopal Church **P** (567) 2410 Glenview Rd 60025-2713 (Mail to: 2410 Glenview Rd 60025-2713) Thomas Atamian Matthew Babcock (847) 724-1341

Grayslake St Andrews Episcopal Church **P** (135) 31 Park Ave 60030-2334 (Mail to: 31 Park Ave 60030-2334) Carlton Kelley (847) 223-2310

Griggsville St James Episcopal Church **M** (20) 409 S Union St 62340 (Mail to: PO Box 463 62340-0463) (573) 221-9111

Gurnee Annunciation of Our Lady **P** (233) 5725 Stearns School Rd 60031-4520 (Mail to: 5725 Stearns School Rd 60031-4520) Jennifer Liem (847) 336-3730

Hanna City Christ Church Limestone **M** 1604 N Christ Church Rd 61536-9011 (Mail to: PO Box 431 61536-0431) (309) 685-8682

Hanover Park Church of St Columba of Iona **P** (26) 1800 W Irving Rd 60103-3253 (Mail to: 1800 Irving Park Rd 60133-3253) (630) 289-1574

Harvey St Clements Episcopal Church **P** (40) 15245 Loomis Ave 60426-3117 (Mail to: PO Box 2307 60426-8307)

Highland Park Trinity Episcopal Church **P** (213) 425 Laurel Ave 60035-2652 (Mail to: 425 Laurel Ave Ste 1 60035-2689) Bryan Cones (847) 432-6653

Hinsdale Grace Episcopal Church **P** (632) 120 E 1st St 60521-4202 (Mail to: 120 E 1st St 60521-4291) Donna Ialongo Donna Ialongo Charles Pierce (630) 323-4900

Joliet St Edward and Christ Epis Ch **P** (190) 206 N Midland Ave 60435-6838 (Mail to: 206 N Midland Ave 60435-6838) Richard Lundgren Richard Lundgren (815) 725-6800

Kankakee St Pauls Episcopal Church **P** (292) St Pauls Episcopal Church 298 S Harrison Ave 60901-4095 (Mail to: 298 S Harrison Ave 60901-4095) (815) 932-6611

Kenilworth The Ch of the Holy Comforter **P** (733) 222 Kenilworth Ave 60043-1243 (Mail to: 222 Kenilworth Ave 60043-1298) Heath Howe (847) 251-6120

Kewanee St Johns Episcopal Church **P** (27) 123 S Chestnut St 61443-2121 (Mail to: PO Box 268 61443-0268) (309) 853-1421

La Grange Emmanuel Episcopal Church **P** (345) 203 S Kensington Ave 60525-2216 (Mail to: 203 S Kensington Ave 60525-2216) David Jackson William Rimkus Katherine Spelman (708) 352-1275

La Salle St Paul Episcopal Church **M** (32) 344 Joliet St 61301-2128 (Mail to: 344 Joliet St 61301-2128) Mark Geisler (815) 220-0238

Lake Forest Church of the Holy Spirit **P** (1425) § 400 E Westminster 60045-2258 (Mail to: 400 E Westminster 60045-2258) Nathaniel Back Jihan Murray-Smith (847) 234-7633

Lake Villa Church of the Holy Family **M** (161) 25291 W Lehmann Blvd 60046-9705 (Mail to: 25291 W Lehmann Blvd 60046-9705) Jose Arroyo (847) 356-7222

Lewistown St James Episcopal Church **M** (69) 420 E. MacArthur Ave. 61542-1250 (Mail to: P.O. Box 63 61542-0063) Barbara Sinclair (309) 543-4248

Libertyville St Lawrence Episcopal Church **P** (419) 125 W Church St 60048-2149 (Mail to: 125 W Church St 60048-2149) (847) 362-2110

Lockport Saint John The Evangelist **M** (130) 324 E 11th St 60441-3421 (Mail to: 324 E 11th St 60441-3421) Roberta Molony (815) 834-1168

Lombard Calvary Episcopal Church **P** (174) 105 W Maple St 60148-2513 (Mail to: 105 W Maple St 60148-2513) James Stanley (630) 620-8899

Macomb Epis Ch of the Good Shepherd **P** (27) 321 1/2 W University Dr 61455-1144 (Mail to: PO Box 294 61455-0294) (309) 421-0142

Mchenry St Paul's Episcopal Church **P** (87) 3717 Main St 60050-5252 (Mail to: 3717 Main St 60050-5252) Eileen Shanley-Roberts (815) 385-0390

Momence Church of the Good Shepherd **M** (57) 123 E 2nd St 60954-1501 (Mail to: 123 E 2nd St 60954-1501) (815) 472-4625

Morris St Thomas Episcopal Church **P** (32) 317 Goold Park Dr 60450-1721 (Mail to: 317 Goold Park Dr 60450-1721) (815) 942-1380

Morrison St Annes Episcopal Church **P** (58) 401 N Cherry St 61270-2606 (Mail to: 401 N Cherry St 61270-2606) James Brzezinski (815) 772-2818

Naperville St Johns Episcopal Church **P** (631) 750 Aurora Ave 60540-6276 (Mail to: 750 Aurora Ave 60540-6276) Thomas Scott (630) 355-0467

New Lenox Grace Episcopal Church **P** (172) 209 N Pine St 60451-1765 (Mail to: 209 N Pine St 60451-1765) Gregory Millikin (815) 485-6596

Northbrook St Giles Episcopal Church **P** (75) 3025 Walters Ave 60062-4370 (Mail to: 3025 Walters Ave 60062-4370) Courtlyn Williams (847) 272-6622

Northfield St James the Less Episcopal Ch **P** (352) 550 Sunset Ridge Rd 60093-1027 (Mail to: 550 Sunset Ridge Rd 60093-1027) (847) 446-8430

Oak Park Grace Church **P** (359) 924 Lake St 60301-1533 (Mail to: Attn: Douglas Van Houten 924 Lake St 60301-1533) John Rumple Jonathan Baumgarten Clayton Thomason (708) 386-8036

Oak Park St Christophers Episcopal Ch **P** (423) 545 S East Ave 60304-1321 (Mail to: 545 S East Ave 60304-1321) Kevin Goodman (708) 386-5613

Oregon St Bride Episcopal Church **M** (47) 1000 W Il Route 64 61061-9350 (Mail to: PO Box 223 61061-0223) (815) 732-7211

Ottawa Christ Episcopal Church **P** (49) C/O Fran Gibson 926 Columbus St 61350-2103 (Mail to Attn: TREASURER 113 E Lafayette St 61350-2114) Mark Geisler (815) 434-0627

Palatine St Philips Episcopal Church **P** (133) 342 E Wood St 60067-5336 (Mail to: 342 E Wood St 60067-5336) (847) 358-0615

Palos Park Church of the Transfiguration **P** (168) § 12219 S 86th Ave 60464-1263 (Mail to 12219 S 86th Ave 60464-1263) Annette Mayer Jason Rayburg-Elliott (708) 448-1200

Park Forest Church of the Holy Family **P** (302) Sauk Trl & Orchard Dr 60466 (Mail to: 102 Marquette St 60466-2016) Elizabeth Lloyd (708) 748-1100

Park Ridge St Marys Episcopal Church **P** (263) 306 S Prospect Ave 60068-4039 (Mail to: 306 S Prospect Ave 60068-4086) Joseph Czolgosz Martha Durham David Grauer Michael Kitt Patrick Skutch (847) 823-4126

Peoria St Paul's Episcopal Church **P** (271) 3601 N North St 61604-1548 (Mail to: 3601 N North St 61604-1548) Jennifer Replogle Jonathan Thomas (309) 688-3436

Pontiac Grace Church **P** (60) 410 E Torrance Ave 61764-2703 (Mail to: 900 S Manlove St 61764-2605) Mark Middleton (815) 842-1743

Prospect Heights One in Christ Episcopal Church **M** (158) 307 W Hintz Rd 60070-1020 (Mail to: 307 W Hintz Rd 60070-1020) Indor Joo (847) 537-0590

River Forest Christ Episcopal Church **P** (50) 515 Franklin Ave 60305-1719 (Mail to: 515 Franklin Ave 60305-1719) (708) 366-7730

Riverside St Pauls Episcopal Church **P** (32) 60 Akenside Rd 60546-1809 (Mail to: 60 Akenside Rd 60546-1809) Luke Wetzel (708) 447-1604

Rock Island All Saints Episcopal Church **M** (105) 3145 31st Ave 61201-5551 (Mail to: PO Box 482 61266-0482) Dustin Fecht (309) 797-2517

Rockford Emmanuel Episcopal Church **P** (237) 412 N Church St 61103-6811 (Mail to: 412 N Church St 61103-6883) Diane Tomlinson Thomas Rosa (815) 964-5514

Rockford St Anskar Episcopal Church **P** (83) 4801 Spring Creek Rd 61114-6321 (Mail to: 4801 Spring Creek Rd 61114-6321) (815) 877-1226

St. Charles St Charles Church Episcopal **P** (332) 994 N 5th Ave 60174-1227 (Mail to: 994 N 5th Ave 60174-1227) Elizabeth Meade Stacy Walker (630) 584-2596

Sterling Grace EpiscopalChurch **P** (121) 707 1st Ave 61081-3622 (Mail to: 707 1st Ave 61081-3622) Margaret Williams (815) 625-0442

Streator Christ Episcopal Church **P** (20) 132 S Vermillion St 61364-2936 (Mail to: 132 S Vermillion St 61364-2936) (815) 672-2479

Sycamore Saint Peter's Episcopal Church **P** (187) 218 Somonauk St 60178-1845 (Mail to: 218 Somonauk St 60178-1845) Georges Jallouf (815) 895-2227

Warsaw St Pauls Episcopal Church **M** (88) 240 S 4th St 62379-1205 (Mail to: 530 S 10th St 62379-1423) Larry Snyder (217) 256-4558

Wauconda Church of the Holy Apostles **M** (59) 26238 N Il Route 59 60084-2332 (Mail to: 26238 N Il Route 59 60084-2399) (847) 5267148

Waukegan Christ Episcopal Church **P** (399) 410 Grand Ave 60085-4227 (Mail to: 410 Grand Ave 60085-4284) Jean Beniste (847) 662-7081

Waukegan Nuestra Senora De Guadalupe **M** (846) 2415 N Butrick St 60087-3048 (Mail to: 2415 N Butrick St 60087-3048) Narciso Diaz (847) 599-3051

Western Sprgs All Saints Episcopal Church **P** (153) 4370 Woodland Ave 60558 (Mail to: 4370 Woodland Ave 60558) Larry Wood-Hull (708) 246-0030

Wheaton Trinity Church **P** (410) 130 N West St 60187-5062 (Mail to: 130 N West St 60187-5097) Kevin Caruso James Lanning (630) 665-1101

Wilmette St Augustines Episcopal Church **P** (346) 1140 Wilmette Ave 60091-2604 (Mail to: 1140 Wilmette Ave 60091-2670) Nadia Stefko Sylvia Nebel (847) 251-6922

Winnetka Christ Church **P** (1246) 784 Sheridan Rd 60093 (Mail to: 470 Maple St 60093-2652) Francis Crittenden (847) 446-2850

Woodstock St Anns Episcopal Church **P** (124) 503 W Jackson St 60098-3143 (Mail to: 503 W Jackson St 60098-3143) Scott Zaucha (815) 338-0950

DIOCESE OF COLOMBIA

(PROVINCIA IX)
Comprende la República de COLOMBIA
OFICINA DIOCESANA Cra 6 No 49-85 Piso 2 Bogotá Colombia
(MAIL: Apartado Aéreo 52964, Bogotá)
TEL 57-1-288-3167
E-MAIL obispoduque@hotmail.com   WEB www.iglesiaepiscopal.org.co

Obispos anteriores-
David B Reed 1964-71 Wm A Franklin 1972-78 Bernardo Merino Botero 1979-2001

Bishop—Rt Rev Francisco José Duque Gómez (1969) (Dio 14 July 2001)

Secretaria de la convención Rvdo Israel Portilla *Tesorero* G Santos; *Registrador* Rvdo Omar Campo (Bogotá); *Presidente* Comité Permanente Rvdo Pastor Elías García Cárdenas (Medellín); *Medios y Comunicaciones* Laura Aristizábal (Medellin); *Con Residencia* Canónica Canciller Rvdo Mauricio Ferro; *Contadora* Sandra Viviana Espitia

PARROQUIAS, MISIONES Y CLERO

Armenia Misión Santo Tomas Apóstol **P** Carrera Dirección Cra 15 No 26-19 +57 (315) 283-6844) Rvdo David Hincapié

Barranquilla: Misión Jesús Sanador, Dirección: Calle 37 C No 6-05, Rvdo Diacono Fabiam Celis +57 (301 2425666)

✠ **Bogotá** Catedral de San Pablo (Dirección: cl. 51 No 6-19 (571) 288-3187) +57 (3102829788) Rvdo Omar Campo

Bogota Mision San Juan Evangelista Dirección Cll 51 6-19, Rvdo Israel Portilla y Rvda. Loida Sardiñas ,+57 (3045825555)+57 (3188449140)

Bogota Parroquia de San Pedro **P** Dirección Calle 22 BIS No 93 A-24 Rvdo Alberto Pinzón +57 (3124984984)

Bogota Mision San Benito de Nursia Rvdo Richard Acosta, Cll 22 No 93 A -24, (3208996564)

Bogotá Parroquia El Divino Salvador Calle 58 Sur 14F78 Este (Dirección : Calle 58 Sur 14F78 Este. Rvdo Bladimir Pedraza +57 (314 5068507) Diacono Jairo Garzón +57 (3208493792)

Bucaramanga Parroquia San Pedro y San Pablo Cra 27 a 51-55 Dirección Cra 27 #51-55) Rvdo Álvaro Javier Prada+57 (312 3233176)

Bucaramanga Misión Santa María Virgen (Dirección Cra 27 No 51-47)Rvdo Álvaro Javier Prada +57 (312 3233176)

Bucaramanga Mison San Esteban, Pueblito Viejo (girón) dirección de correspondencia cra 27 No 51-4 Rvdo Alvaro Javier Prada +57 (312 3233176)

Buenos Aires—Zaragoza Parroquia Nuestra Señora del Carmen **P** (50) (Buenos Aires Palizada Corregimiento: Dirección Cra. 9 No 9A-20) Rvdo José Suarez Elles +57 (313) 526-0209

Cali Parroquia La Trinidad - Cali **P** Calle 7 Oeste No 3-43 AA 52964 (Dirección: Calle 7 Oeste No 3-43) Rvdo Luis López Chicaiza +57 (312 7820463)

Cartagena Parroquia Nuestro Salvador **P** Dirección Pie de popa Camino Arriba 22-109 AA 52964 Rvdo Antonis de Jesús Calvo (310 8146191)

Cartagena Parroquia La Santa Cruz **P** Dirección: 7 de agosto Av. Colombia No 71-15 Rvdo Rvda. Diacona. Luz María Lambis +57 (3114290641)

Cartagena Maria Magdalena Rvdo Diacono Miguel Padilla, Lote 6 Manzana B, Barrio los Santanderes +57 (3046559958)

Cucuta Mision Natividad de Cristo cll 12 No 8-82 Apto 401, Rvdo Martim Hernandez +57 (3158795462)

El Bagre Parroquia la Anunciación **P** Dirección: Carrera 49 # 63 A 74/85/89 Sector Las Delicias Rvdo José Suarez Elles +57 (313) 526-0209

Facatativá Misión Santa Marta de Betania **M**

Dirección Kilometro 4 vía el Rosal: Vereda Noruega Prado Alto Cra 3E 9A-85 INT 2 Casa) Rvdo Javier Aldana +57 (301 6413935)

Ibagué Misión San Juan Bautista **M** (Dirección: Cra. 6 No 16-69-71) Rvdo Julio Salazar +57 (310 8146200)

Malambo Parroquia Nuestra Señora Del Monte Carmelo **P** Dirección: Cra. 3A Sur # 11A-02) Rvdo Gonzalo Rendón +57 (3233320022)

Medellín Mision la Transfiguración Dirección Carrera 80 A 53A-78, Rvdo Sergio Alvarez y Diacono Victor Betancur +57 (311 3336954) +57 (3153123445)

Medellín Parroquia San Lucas **P** Dirección Carrera 80 A 53A-78 Rvdo Pastor Elías García Cárdenas +57 (320 9907669)

Pasto Misión Betania Dirección:Cra. 15 # 20 – 17 Barrio Javeriano, +57 (3164771869)

Pasto Misión Cristo Maestro Dirección:Cra. 15 # 20 – 17 Barrio Javeriano, Rvdo Wilson Davila, Rvdo Hugo Zambrano +57(3166901125) +57 (3113219370)

Soacha Misión del Espíritu Santo **M** Dirección Carrera 5 Este 23-73 Rvdo Ricardo Betancur +57 (316 6664383)

Villavicencio Mision Dios Padre Misericordioso Rvdo Francisco Javier Mejia Cll 85 sur No 40-03, Barrio Cambulos, Manzana I Casa 6 +57 (3182103076)

Villavicencio Parroquia Nuestra Señora de Gracia, Dirección: Cll 1 N No 48-95, Barrio León XIII, +57 (3206777718)

INSTITUCIONES

Centro de Estudios Teológico Pablo Velásquez (CET) Rvdo Rvda Loida Sardiñas CLL 51 No 6-19, (Bogotá) +57 (3045825555)

DIOCESE OF COLORADO

(PROVINCE VI)

Comprises the State of Colorado

DIOCESAN OFFICE 1300 Washington St Denver CO 80203-2008

TEL (303) 837-1173 FAX (303) 837-1311

E-MAIL info@episcopalcolorado.org WEB www.episcopalcolorado.org

THE EPISCOPAL CHURCH IN
COLORADO

Previous Bishops— Geo M Randall (CO and adjacent) 1865-73, John F Spalding m 1873 dio 1887-1902 Chas S Olmstead 1902-18, Irving P Johnson coadj 1917 Bp 1918-38, Fred Ingley coadj 1921 Bp 1938-49, Harold L Bowen coadj 1947 Bp 1949-55, Daniel Corrigan suffr 1958-60, Jos S Minnis coadj 1954 Bp 1955-69, Edwin B Thayer suffr 1960-69 Actg Eccl Auth 1968-69 Bp 1969-73, Wm C Frey coadj 1972 Bp

1973-90, Wm H Wolfrum suffr 1981-91, William J Winterrowd Bp 1991-2004, Robert J O'Neill 2004-19

Bishop — Rt Rev Kimberly Danielle Lucas (1117) (Dio 18 May 2019)

Exec Asst to the Bp N McClung; *Cn for Formation & Pastoral Care* Rev Cn G Foraker; *Cn Transition & Wellness* Rev Cn V Stickler-Glass; *Cn Comm & Evang Cn* M Orr; *Exec Asst to Cns* D Draper; *Miss for Children, Youth, & Cmps Min* E Cervasio; *Event Coord* J Choyce; *Miss for MltiCult Min* Rev Q Cornejo; *Controller* P Greenfield; *Miss for Bptsml*

Lvng T Methe; *Archv* K Ward; *Chanc* L Hitt; *Treas* N Jones; *Dir of Epis Serv Corps* Rev R Crummey; *Colo Episc Found* S Asper.

Stand Comm—Cler: K Bradsen C Greene D Shew W Stanton J Williamson; *Lay: V Pres* D Armstrong D Colville *Treas* N Jones K Schapansky A Shepherd

PARISHES, MISSIONS, AND CLERGY

Arvada The Church of Christ the King **P** (231) § 6490 Carr St 80004-3338 (Mail to: PO Box 6 80001-0006) Austin Leininger (303) 424-5288

Aspen Christ Episcopal Church **P** (242) 536 W North St 81611-1253 (Mail to: C/O Cindy Herndon 536 W North St 81611-1253) William Lupfer (970) 925-3278

Aurora St Martin in the Fields Church **P** (175) PO Box 460906 80046-0906 (Mail to: PO Box 460906 80046-0906) Anna Horen (303) 693-8872

Aurora St Stephens Episcopal Church **P** (236) 1 Del Mar Cir 80011-8225 (Mail to: 1 Del Mar Cir 80011-8225) Kathryn Bradsen (303) 364-3186

Basalt St Peters Episcopal Church **M** (209) 200 Elk Run Dr 81621-9287 (Mail to: 200 Elk Run Dr 81621-9287) E Wendy Huber (970) 927-4235

Battlement Mesa All Saints Episcopal Church **M** (43) 150 Sipprelle Dr 81635-9229 (Mail to: 150 Sipprelle Dr 81635-9229) (970) 285-7908

Boulder St Aidans Episcopal Church **P** (279) 2425 Colorado Ave 80302-6806 (Mail to: 2425 Colorado Ave 80302-6806) Mary Rejouis (303) 443-2503

Boulder St Ambrose Episcopal Church **P** (159) 7520 S Boulder Rd 80303-4640 (Mail to: 7520 S Boulder Rd 80303-4640) Anne Richter Janice Pearson (303) 499-3041

Boulder St Johns Episcopal Church **P** (1468) 1419 Pine St 80304 (Mail to: 1419 Pine St 80302-4895) (303) 442-5246

Boulder Saint Mary Magdalene Church **P** (388) 4775 Cambridge St 80301-4140 (Mail to: PO Box 188 Attn Bookkeeper 80544-0188) Bruce Swinehart (303) 530-1421

Breckenridge St John the Baptist Epis Ch **P** (177) 100 S French St 80424 (Mail to: PO Box 2166 80424-2166) Charles Brumbaugh (970) 453-4264

Brighton St Elizabeths Episcopal Church **M** (56) 76 S 3rd Ave 80601-2008 (Mail to: 76 S 3rd Ave 80601-2008) (303) 659-2648

Broomfield Holy Comforter Epis Church **P** (475) 1700 W 10th Ave 80020 (Mail to: 1700 W 10th Ave 80020-1716) Lyndon Shakespeare (303) 466-2667

Buena Vista Grace Episcopal Church **P** (44) 203 W Main St 81211-9169 (Mail to: PO Box 1559 81211-1559) (719) 395-8868

Canon City Christ Episcopal Church **P** (107) 802 Harrison Ave 81212-3350 (Mail to: 816

Harrison Ave 81212-3350) Mark Meyer (719) 275-2028

Castle Rock Christ's Episcopal Church **P** (470) 615 4th St 80104-2553 (Mail to: C/O Bethany Pedersen 615 4th St 80104-2553) Brian Winter (303) 688-5185

Centennial Good Shepherd Episcopal Church **P** (542) 8545 E Dry Creek Rd 80112-2750 (Mail to: 8545 E Dry Creek Rd 80112-2750) Gary Brower (303) 740-2688

Centennial St Timothys Episcopal Church **P** (469) 1401 E Dry Creek Rd 80122-3087 (Mail to: 1401 E Dry Creek Rd 80122-3087) Kimberly Seidman Lauren Thomas (303) 794-1565

Central City St Pauls Episcopal Church **M** (9) 226 E 1st High St 80427-5001 (Mail to: PO Box 764 80427-0764) (303) 582-0450

Colorado Spg Ch of St Michael the Archangel **P** (564) 7400 Tudor Rd 80919-2615 (Mail to: 7400 Tudor Rd 80919-2615) Matthew Holcombe (719) 598-3244

Colorado Springs Church of Our Saviour **P** (581) 8 4th St 80906-3155 (Mail to: Attn: Desha Thomas 8 4th St 80906-3155) David Dill (719) 6332667

Colorado Springs Grace and St Stephens Epis Ch **P** (736) 601 N Tejon St 80903-1009 (Mail to: 601 N Tejon St 80903-1009) Jeremiah Williamson Martin Pearsall (719) 328-1125

Colorado Springs St Raphael Episcopal Church **P** (131) 802 Leta Dr 80911-1126 (Mail to: 802 Leta Dr 80911-1126) Twyla Zittle (719) 392-3563

Conifer St Laurence Episcopal Church **P** (153) 26812 Barkley Rd 80433-9101 (Mail to: PO Box 361 80433-0361) (303) 838-2457

Cortez St Barnabas of the Valley **P** (136) 110 W North St 81321-3119 (Mail to: 110 W North St 81321-3119) Douglas Bleyle Cynthia Irvin (970) 565-7865

Craig St Marks Ch Grace Eps Luth Min **M** (57) 657 Green St 81625-3029 (Mail to: PO Box 711 81626-3034) Arthur White (970) 824-3470

Creede Saint Augustine's Church **M** (20) 502 S Main 81130 (Mail to: PO Box 803 81130-0803) (719) 658-2394

Crested Butte All Sts of the Mtn Epis Chapel **Chapel** (46) 403 Maroon Ave 81224-9669 (Mail to: PO Box 2733 81224-2733) William Waltz (970) 641-0429

Cripple Creek Saint Andrew's Church **P** (82) 373 Carr St 80813-9613 (Mail to: Attn: Karen Muntzert PO Box 458 80813-0458) (719) 689-2920

Delta St Lukes Episcopal Church **P** (74) 145 W 5th St 81416-1803 (Mail to: Treasurer PO Box 724 81416-0724) (970) 874-9489

Denver Christ Episcopal Church **P** (605) 2950 S University Blvd 80210-6029 (Mail to: 2950 S University Blvd 80210-6029) Terry Mcgugan Joseph Wolyniak (303) 758-3674

Denver Church of St Philip & St James **P** (137) 2797 S Lowell Blvd 80236-2249 (Mail to: 2797 S Lowell Blvd 80236-2249) John Hill (303) 936-3992

Denver Church of the Holy Redeemer **P** (82) 2552 N Williams St 80205-5526 (Mail to: 2552 N Williams St 80205-5526) (303) 831-8963

Denver Church of the Epiphany **P** (256) 100 Colorado Blvd 80206-5533 (Mail to: 100 Colorado Blvd 80206-5533) Stacey Tafoya Gary Stoddard (303) 321-0813

Denver St Peters & St Marys Church **P** (87) 126 W 2nd Ave 80223-1434 (Mail to: 126 W 2nd Ave 80223-1434) Rebecca Crummey Rebecca Crummey (303) 722-8781

Denver Our Merciful Savior Epis Ch **P** (111) 2222 W 32nd Ave 80211-3318 (Mail to: 2222 W 32nd Ave 80211-3318) (303) 477-4555

Denver St Andrews Episcopal Church **P** (297) 2015 Glenarm Pl 80205-3121 (Mail to: 2015 Glenarm Pl 80205-3121) Elizabeth Randall (303) 296-1712

Denver St Barnabas Episcopal Church **P** (156) 1280 Vine St 80206-2912 (Mail to: 1280 Vine St 80206-2912) Jeffrey Nelson (303) 388-6469

Denver St Bede Episcopal Church **P** 2201 S University Blvd 80210 (Mail to: Iliff School of Theology 80210) (303) 744-1287

Denver St Francis Episcopal Chapel **Chapel** (31) 2323 Curtis St 80205-2627 (Mail to: 2323 Curtis St 80205-2627) (303) 244-0766

✠ **Denver** Saint John's Cathedral **O** (1934) 1350 N Washington St 80203-2008 (Mail to: 1350 N Washington St 80203-2008) Richard Lawson Broderick Greer Katie Pearson (303) 831-7115

Denver St Lukes Episcopal Church **P** (461) 1270 Poplar St 80220-3023 (Mail to: PO Box 201296 80220-7296) Amy Lythgoe (303) 355-2331

Denver St Mic & All Angels Epis Ch **P** (405) 1400 S University Blvd 80210-2407 (Mail to: 1400 S University Blvd 80210-2407) Richard Fraser James Johnson (303) 777-5181

Denver St Thomas Episcopal Church **P** (298) 2201 Dexter St 80207-3756 (Mail to: 2201 Dexter St 80207-3756) Terri Hobart Daniel Hopkins Sally Megeath (303) 388-4395

Denver Sudanese Community Church **P** (51) 1350 N Washington St 80203-2008 (Mail to: 1350 N Washington St 80203-2008) (303) 831-7115

Denver Church of the Ascension **P** (351) 600 Gilpin St 80218-3632 (Mail to: 600 N Gilpin St 80218-3632) Louise Blanchard Garrison Horle (303) 388-5978

Durango St Marks Episcopal Church **P** (294) 910 E 3rd Ave 81301-5213 (Mail to: 910 E 3rd Ave 81301-5213) Debra Shew (970) 247-1129

Elizabeth Peace in Christ Church **M** (93) 236 Tabor St 80107 (Mail to: PO Box 2098 80107-2098) (303) 646-6528

Englewood St Gabriel the Archangel Epis **P** (485) 6190 E Quincy Ave 80111-1002 (Mail to:

6190 E Quincy Ave 80111-1002) Christopher Ditzenberger (303) 771-1063

Estes Park Saint Bartholomew's Church **P** (291) 880 Macgregor Ave 80517-9065 (Mail to: PO Box 1559 80517-1559) Seth Richmond (970) 586-4504

Evergreen Church of the Transfiguration **P** (136) 27640 Highway 74 80439-5820 (Mail to: PO Box 1630 80437-1630) (303) 674-4904

Fort Collins St Lukes Episcopal Church **P** (730) 2000 Stover St 80525-1545 (Mail to: 2000 Stover St 80525-1545) Krista Dias (970) 493-7512

Fort Collins Saint Paul's Episcopal Church **P** (144) 301 East Stuart St 80525 (Mail to: 301 East Stuart St 80525) Felicia Smithgraybeal (970) 482-2668

Fort Morgan St Charles the Martyr Epis Ch **P** (68) 505 E 8th Ave 80701-3227 (Mail to: 505 E 8th Ave 80701-3227) (970) 867-6228

Frederick St Brigit Episcopal Church **M** (143) 110 Johnson St 80530-8022 (Mail to: 110 Johnson St 80530-8022) Timothy Backus (720) 208-0280

Georgetown Grace Church **M** (10) 408 Taos St 80444-5103 (Mail to: PO Box 133 80444-0133) (303) 569-2790

Glenwood Spgs St Barnabas Episcopal Church **P** (88) 546 Hyland Park Drive 81601-4276 (Mail to: 546 Hyland Park Dr 81601-4276) (970) 945-6423

Golden Calvary Episcopal Church **P** (916) 1320 Arapahoe St 80401-1815 (Mail to: 1320 Arapahoe St 80401-1815) Scott Campbell Timothy Phenna Bethany Thomas (303) 279-2188

Golden Church of St John Chrysostom **P** (188) 13151 W 28th Ave 80401-1601 (Mail to: 13151 W 28th Ave 80401-1601) Margaret Peel-Shakespeare (303) 279-2760

Granby Cranmer Memorial Chapel **Chapel** 75 High Country Dr 80446-0954 (Mail to: PO Box 954 80446-0954) (970) 887-2742

Granby St John the Baptist Epis Ch **P** (50) 390 Garnet Ave 80446 (Mail to: PO Box 954 80446-0954) Matthew Frey Diane Bielski (970) 887-2742

Grand Jct The Church of the Nativity **P** (117) 2175 Broadway 81503-1086 (Mail to: 2175 Broadway 81507-1086) Lauren Larkin Teri Shecter (970) 245-9606

Grand Jct St Matthew Episcopal Church **P** (523) 3888 27 1/2 Rd 81506-4186 (Mail to: 3888 27 1/2 Rd 81506-4186) Janice Head Stephen Hood (970) 242-3293

Greeley Trinity Episcopal Church **P** (306) 3800 W 20th St 80634-3418 (Mail to: 3800 W 20th St 80634-3418) Lisa Musser (970) 3301877

Gunnison Church of the Good Samaritan **P** (149) 307 W Virginia Ave 81230-3038 (Mail to: PO Box 701 81230-0701) (970) 641-0429

Kremmling Trinity Episcopal Church **M** (18) 805 Central Ave 80459-5128 (Mail to: PO Box 996 80459-0996) Karen Smith (970) 724-3626

La Junta St Andrew Holy Cross Luth Ch **P** (47) 621 Raton Ave 81050-2425 (Mail to: 621 Raton Ave 81050-2449) (719) 383-3504

Lake City St James Episcopal Chapel **M** (60) 5th St & Hwy 149 81235 (Mail to: PO Box 832 81235-0832) (970) 641-0429

Lakewood St Joseph Episcopal Church **P** (146) 11202 W Jewell Ave 80232-6140 (Mail to: 11202 W Jewell Ave 80232-6140) (303) 985-7170

Lakewood St Pauls Episcopal Church **P** (334) 9200 W 10th Ave 80215-4701 (Mail to: 9200 W 10th Ave 80215-4701) Allan Cole (303) 233-4991

Lamar St Pauls Episcopal Church **M** (23) 200 E Parmenter St 81052-3241 (Mail to: 621 Raton 81050) (719) 336-4522

Leadville St George Episcopal Church **M** (61) 200 W 4th St 80461-3632 (Mail to: PO Box 243 80461-0243) (719) 486-3087

Littleton The Epis Parish of St Gregory **P** (420) 6653 W Chatfield Ave 80128-5834 (Mail to: 6653 W Chatfield Ave 80128-5834) Roger Bower (303) 979-5236

Longmont St Stephens Episcopal Church **P** (615) 1303 S Bross Ln 80501-6803 (Mail to: 1303 S Bross Ln 80501-6803) Melissa Adzima Dana Solomon (303) 776-1072

Loveland All Saints Episcopal Church **P** (225) 3448 Taft Ave 80538-2556 (Mail to: 3448 Taft Ave 80538-2596) Cynthia Espeseth (970) 667-0303

Mancos St Pauls Church **M** 479 Bauer Ave 81328-9241 (Mail to: PO Box 226 81328-0226) (970) 533-9104

Manitou Springs Saint Andrew's Church **P** (24) 808 Manitou Ave 80829-1730 (Mail to: 808 Manitou Ave 80829-1730) Frances Mutolo (719) 685-9259

Meeker St James Episcopal Church **P** (107) 368 4th St 81641 (Mail to: PO Box 641 81641-0641) Scott Hollenbeck (970) 878-5823

Monte Vista St Stephen the Martyr **M** (26) 729 3rd Ave 81144-1442 (Mail to: PO Box 489 81144-0489) (303) 921-4440

Monument St Matthias Episcopal Church **P** (170) 18320 Furrow Rd 80132-8790 (Mail to: PO Box 1223 80132-1223) Laura Beck (719) 359-9204

New Castle St Johns Episcopal Church **M** (48) First & Main St 81647 (Mail to: C/O St Johns Church PO Box 82 81647-0082) E Wendy Huber (970) 984-2780

Ouray St Johns Episcopal Church **P** (149) 329 Fifth Ave 81427 (Mail to: PO Box 563 81427-0563) Mark Chambers (970) 325-4655

Pagosa Springs St Patrick Episcopal Church **P** (164) 225 S Pagosa Blvd 81147-8396 (Mail to: 225 S Pagosa Blvd 81147-8396) Wren Blessing (970) 731-5801

Parker St Matthew's Episcopal Church **P** (429) 19580 Pilgrims Pl 80138-7354 (Mail to: 19580 Pilgrims Pl 80138-7354) Karen Smith (303) 841-0121

Pueblo Church of St Peter the Apostle **P** (83) 3939 W Pueblo Blvd 81005-2721 (Mail to: 3939 W Pueblo Blvd 81005-2721) (719) 561-4567

Pueblo Church of the Ascension **P** (347) 420 W 18th St 81003-2625 (Mail to: C/O Janice Parlett 420 W 18th St 81003-2625) (719) 543-4253

Salida Church of the Ascension **P** (95) 349 E St 81201-2631 (Mail to: PO Box 1540 81201-7540) Melissa George (719) 539-4562

Salida Little Shepherd of the Hills **M** PO Box 458 81201 (Mail to: 349 E St 81201-2631) (719) 539-4562

Sedalia St Philip in the Field **P** (137) 397 N Perry Park Rd 80135-8521 (Mail to: 397 N. Perry Road 80135-8521) Janet Fullmer Janet Fullmer (303) 688-5444

Steamboat Sprngs St Pauls Episcopal Church **P** (320) 846 Oak St 80477 (Mail to: PO Box 770722 80477-0722) Margaret Greene (970) 879-0925

Sterling Prince of Peace Episcopal Ch **M** (29) 201 Phelps St 80751-4044 (Mail to: PO Box 164 80751-0164) (970) 522-0539

Thornton Intercession Episcopal Church **P** (187) 3101 E 100th Ave 80229-2687 (Mail to: 3101 E 100th Ave 80229-2687) (303) 451-8085

Vail Church of the Transfiguration **P** (501) 19 Vail Rd 81657 (Mail to: PO Box 1000 81658-1000) Stuart Keith (970) 476-0618

Westcliffe St Lukes Episcopal Mission **M** (64) 201 S 3rd St 81252-9502 (Mail to: PO Box 208 81252-0208) (719) 783-2477

Wheat Ridge Saint James Episcopal Church **P** (95) 8235 W 44th Ave 80033-4426 (Mail to: 8235 W 44th Ave 80033-4426) Rebecca Jones (303) 424-1118

Windsor St Albans Episcopal Church **P** (210) 525 Walnut St 80550-5145 (Mail to: PO Box 697 80550-0697) William Stanton David Tweedale Janice Windsor (970) 686-9658

Woodland Park St David of the Hills Epis Ch **P** (40) 36 Edlowe Rd 80863-8226 (Mail to: 36 Edlowe Rd 80863-8226) (719) 687-9195

THE EPISCOPAL CHURCH IN CONNECTICUT
(PROVINCE I)
Comprises the State of Connecticut
DIOCESAN OFFICE 290 Pratt St Meriden CT 06450
TEL (203) 639-3501 FAX (203) 2035-1008
E-MAIL info@episcopalct.org WEB www.episcopalct.org

Previous Bishops—
Samuel Seabury 1784-96, Abraham Jarvis 1797-1813, Thomas C Brownell 1819-65, John Williams coadj 1851 Bp 1865-99, Chauncey B Brewster coadj 1897 Bp 1899-1928, Edward C Acheson suffr 1915 coadj 1926 Bp 1928-34, Fredk G Budlong coadj 1931 Bp 1934-51, Walter H Gray suffr 1940 coadj 1945 Bp 1951-69, Robert M Hatch suffr 1951-57, John H Esquirol suffr 1958 Bp 1969-71, J Warren Hutchens suffr 1961 Bp 1971-77, Morgan Porteus suffr 1971 coadj 1976 Bp 1977-1981, W Bradford T Hastings suffr 1981-86, Jeffrey W Rowthorn suffr 1987-93, Arthur E Walmsley coad 1979-81 Bp 1981-93, Clarence N Coleridge suffr 1981-93 Bp 1993-99, Andrew D Smith suffr 1996-99 Bp 1999-2010, James E Curry suffr 2000-14, Ian T Douglas Bp 2010-22

Bishop—Rt Rev Jeffrey W Mello (1150) (Dio 15 Oct 2022)

Bishop Suffragan—Rt Rev Laura J Ahrens (1018) (Suffr 30 Jun 2007)

Cn for Miss Adv & Coaching Cn T Hodapp; *Cn for Miss Adv, Racial Justice, & Reconciliation* Cn RK Mathews; *Cn for Mission Fin + Ops* Cn R Rosado; *Bps Exec Sec* A Hollo; *Sec of Dio* Rev S Cosman; *Treas* G Ross; *Chanc* B Babbitt

Stand Comm—Cler: Sec S Jarrett D Burke D Burr J Martinez A Samuel D Stefanovsky; *Lay: Pres* T Hagerth J Aziz S Burke Z Kohl D Welsh P Williams

PARISHES, MISSIONS, AND CLERGY

Ansonia Christ Church Episcopal **P** (136) 56 South Cliff St 06401-1910 (Mail to: 56 S Cliff St 06401-1910) (203) 734-2715

Bantam St Pauls Episcopal Church **P** (93) 802 Bantam Rd 06750-1603 (Mail to: PO Box 449 06750-0449) Brett Figlewski Peter Stebinger (860) 567-8838

Bethany Christ Church Episcopal **P** (151) 526 Amity Rd 06524-3015 (Mail to: 526 Amity Rd 06524-3015) Robert Clements (203) 393-3399

Bethel St Thomas' Episcopal Church **P** (190) 95 Greenwood Ave 06801-2528 (Mail to: 95 Greenwood Ave 06801-2528) Kevin Olds (203) 743-1494

Bethlehem Christ Church Episcopal **P** (36) Main St 06751 (Mail to: PO Box 520 06751-0520) Thomas Peters Thomas Peters (203) 266-7698

Bloomfield Old St Andrews Epis Church **P** (183) 59 Tariffville Rd 06002-1136 (Mail to: 59 Tariffville Rd 06002-1136) Timothy Squier (860) 242-4660

Bloomfield St Stephens Episcopal Church **P** (41) 590 Bloomfield Ave 06002-3044 (Mail to: 590 Bloomfield Ave 06002-3044) Wilborne Austin (860) 242-1152

Bolton St Georges Episcopal Church **P** (54) 1150 BostonTpke 06043-7439 (Mail to: PO Box 158 06040) (860) 643-9203

Branford Trinity Episcopal Church **P** (540) 1109 Main St 06405-3715 (Mail to: 1109 Main St 06405-3770) Thomas Blake (203) 488-2681

Bridgeport Calvary-St George Episcopal Ch **P** (30) 755 Clinton Ave 06604-2302 (Mail to: 755 Clinton Ave 06604-2302) (203) 333-5116

Bridgeport St John's Episcopal Parish **P** (385) 768 Fairfield Ave 06604-3701 (Mail to: 768 Fairfield Ave 06604-3799) Jos Mestre Jean Baptiste Rock (203) 335-2528

Bridgeport St Marks Episcopal Church **P** (292) 401 Newfield Ave 06607-2218 (Mail to: 401 Newfield Ave 06607-2218) (203) 335-5655

Bridgeport St Lukes-St Pauls Episcopal Ch **P** (1299) 594 Kossuth St 06608-2204 (Mail to: PO Box 2156 06608-0156) Jose Martinez (203) 334-8674

Bridgewater St Marks Episcopal Church **P** (38) 5 Main St S 06752-1521 (Mail to: PO Box 143 06752-0143) Daniel Mattila Robert Woodroofe (860) 354-8269

Bristol Good Shepherd Bristol Plnville **M** (145) 851 Stafford Ave 06010-3848 (Mail to: PO Box 2321 06011-2321) Leonard Hullar

Brookfield Saint Paul's Church **P** (460) Attn: Chuck Allen 174 Whisconier Rd 06804-3307 (Mail to: 174 Whisconier Rd 06804-3307) Joseph Shepley William Loring (203) 775-9587

Brooklyn Trinity Episcopal Church **P** (115) 7 Providence Rd 06234-1816 (Mail to: PO Box 276 06234-0276) Gretchen Grimshaw (860) 774-9352

Cheshire St Peters Episcopal Church **P** (1043) § 59 Main St 06410-2405 (Mail to: 59 Main St 06410-2468) Sandra Stayner (203) 272-4041

Clinton Church of the Holy Advent **P** (157) 81 E Main St 06413-2139 (Mail to: PO Box 536 06413-0536) (860) 669-2232

Collinsville Trinity Church Collinsville **P** (247) 55 River Rd 06022 (Mail to: PO Box 374 06022-0374) Linda Spiers (860) 693-8172

Danbury St James Episcopal Church **P** (266) 25 West St 06810-7824 (Mail to: 25 West St

06810-7877) Dustin Trowbridge (203) 748-3561

Darien St Luke's Episcopal Church **P** (2997) § 1864 Post Rd 06820-5802 (Mail to: 1864 Post Rd 06820-5802) Ryan Fleenor Hannah Pommersheim Donald Thompson Susan Wyper (203) 6551456

Derby Immanuel St James Parish **P** (32) 105 Minerva St 06418-1896 (Mail to: 105 Minerva St 06418-1896) George Brower (203) 734-4149

Durham Church of the Epiphany **P** (71) 196 Main St 06422-2106 (Mail to: PO Box 337 06422-0337) Anthony Dinoto (860) 349-9644

East Berlin St Gabriels Church **P** (95) 68 Main St 06023-1130 (Mail to: PO Box 275 06023-0275) Audrey Scanlan (860) 828-3735

East Haddam St Stephens Episcopal Church **P** (417) 29 Main St 06423-1005 (Mail to: PO Box 464 06423-0464) (860) 873-9547

East Hartford All Saints Episcopal Church **P** (45) 444 Hills St 06118-2922 (Mail to: 444 Hills St 06118-2998) Michelle Hansen (860) 568-6175

East Hartford Greater Hartford Regl Mnstry **Cluster** 12 Rector St 06108-2261 (Mail to: 12 Rector St 06108-2261) (860) 528-1474

East Haven Christ and the Epiphany Church **P** (50) 39 Park Pl 06512-2517 (Mail to: 39 Park Pl 06512-2517) (203) 467-2310

East Windsor St Johns Episcopal Church **P** (42) 92 Main St 06088-9651 (Mail to: 92 Main St 06088-9651) (860) 623-3273

Easton Christ Church **P** (243) 59 Church Rd 06612-1411 (Mail to: Attn: Treasurer 59 Church Rd 06612-1411) Allyson Brundige (203) 268-3569

Enfield Holy Trinity Episcopal Church **P** (230) 383 Hazard Ave 06082-4718 (Mail to: 383 Hazard Ave 06082-4718) (860) 749-2722

Essex St John's Episcopal Church **P** (452) 25 Main St 06426-1134 (Mail to: PO Box 422 06426-0422) Kate Wesch (860) 767-8095

Fairfield St Pauls Episcopal Church **P** (561) 661 Old Post Rd 06824-6648 (Mail to: 661 Old Post Rd 06824-6648) Curtis Farr Edrice Viechweg (203) 259-3013

Fairfield St Timothys Church **P** (150) 4670 Congress St 06824-1721 (Mail to: 4670 Congress St 06824-1721) Kevin Olds (203) 255-2740

Fairfield Trinity-St Michaels Church **P** (34) 554 Tunxis Hill Rd 06825-4412 (Mail to: 554 Tunxis Hill Rd 06825-4412) David Norris (203) 368-3225

Farmington St James Episcopal Church **P** (295) 3 Mountain Rd 06032-2339 (Mail to: 3 Mountain Rd 06032-2339) George Roberts (860) 677-1564

Gales Ferry St Davids Episcopal Church **P** (287) 284 Stoddards Wharf Rd 06335-1130 (Mail to: 284 Stoddards Wharf Rd 06335-1130) Jana Branson (860) 464-6516

Glastonbury St James Episcopal Church **P** (310) 2584 Main St 06033-4220 (Mail to: PO Box 206 06033-0206) (860) 633-8333

Greenwich Christ Church Greenwich **P** (1613) § 254 E Putnam Ave 06830-4801 (Mail to: 254 E Putnam Ave 06830-4871) Cheryl Mcfadden Marek Zabriskie (203) 869-6600

Greenwich St Barnabas Episcopal Church **P** (395) 954 Lake Ave 06831-3032 (Mail to: 954 Lake Ave 06831-3099) Margaret Finnerud (203) 661-5526

Guilford Christ Church **P** (486) 11 Park St 06437-2629 (Mail to: PO Box 574 06437-0574) (203) 453-2279

Guilford St Johns Episcopal Church **P** (128) 129 Ledge Hill Rd 06437-1024 (Mail to: 129 Ledge Hill Rd 06437-1024) (203) 457-1094

Hamden Grace And St Peter's Epis Ch **P** (167) 2927 Dixwell Ave 06518-3135 (Mail to: PO Box 5065 06518-0065) Robert Bergner (203) 248-4338

✣ **Hartford** Christ Church Cathedral **O** (204) 45 Church St 06103-1202 (Mail to: 45 Church St 06103-1202) Richard Mansfield Robert Carroon Miguelina Howell Bonnie Matthews (860) 527-7231

Hartford Good Shepherd El Buen Pastor **P** (100) 155 Wyllys St 06106-1957 (Mail to: 155 Wyllys St 06106-1957) Loyda Morales (860) 525-4289

Hartford Grace Episcopal Church **P** (91) 55 New Park Ave 06106-2123 (Mail to: 55 New Park Ave 06106-2123) Rowena Kemp Robert Carroon John Mitman (860) 233-0825

Hartford Saint Martin's Church **M** (207) 290 Cornwall St 06112-1427 (Mail to: 290 Cornwall St 06112-1427) (860) 242-0318

Hartford Saint Monica's Church **P** (224) 3575 Main Street 06120-2326 (Mail to: 3575 Main St 06120-1115) Tracy Johnson Russell (860) 522-7761

Hartford Trinity College Chapel **CC** 300 Summit St 06106 (Mail to: Attn: Marcus Halley 300 Summit St 06106) Marcus Halley (860) 297-2013

Hartford Trinity Episcopal Church **HC** (361) § 120 Sigourney St 06105-2755 (Mail to: 120 Sigourney St 06105-2796) Dorothella Littlepage Norman Macleod (860) 527-8133

Hebron Saint Peter's Episcopal Church **P** (191) 30 Church St 06248-1427 (Mail to: PO Box 513 06248-0513) Ronald Kolanowski (860) 228-3244

Higganum Middlesex Area Cluster Mnstry **P** PO Box 829 06441-0829 (Mail to: PO Box 829 06441-0829) Evelyn Wheeler (860) 345-0058

Higganum St James Episcopal Church **P** (54) 498 Killingworth Rd 06441-4310 (Mail to: PO Box 574 06441-0574) (860) 345-0058

Ivoryton All Saints Episcopal Church **P** (68) 129 Main St 06442-1103 (Mail to: PO Box 576 06442-0576) Brendan Mccormick Brendan Mccormick (860) 767-1698

Kent St Andrews Church **P** (279) 1 N Main St 06757-1512 (Mail to: PO Box 309 06757-0309) Amy Reichman Douglas Worthington (860) 9273486

Killingworth Emmanuel Episcopal Church **P** (44) PO Box 686 06419-0686 (Mail to: 50 Emanuel Church Rd 06419-1019) (860) 663-1800

Lakeville Trinity Church Lime Rock **P** (172) 484 Lime Rock Rd 06039-2404 (Mail to: 484 Lime Rock Rd 06039-2404) Heidi Truax (860) 435-2627

Litchfield St Michaels Church Episcopal **P** (44) 25 South St 06759-4005 (Mail to: PO Box 248 06759-0248) Ian Montgomery (860) 567-9465

Madison St Andrews Church **P** (409) 232 Durham Rd 06443-2451 (Mail to: 232 Durham Rd 06443-2451) Niranjani Molegoda Ronald Steed (203) 245-2584

Manchester St Marys Episcopal Church **P** (201) 41 Park St 06040-5913 (Mail to: 41 Park St 06040-5913) Karen Fedorchak Marjorie Roccoberton (860) 649-4583

Marble Dale St Andrews Episcopal Church **P** (54) 247 New Milford Tpke 06777-0007 (Mail to: PO Box 2007 06777-0007) Daniel Mattila (860) 868-2275

Meriden All Saints Church **P** (44) 201 W Main St 06451-4003 (Mail to: 164 Hanover St 06451-5439) (203) 235-9596

Meriden St Andrews Episcopal Church **P** (444) 20 Catlin St 06450-4204 (Mail to: 20 Catlin St 06450-4294) Mark Byers (203) 237-7451

Middle Haddam Christ Episcopal Church **P** (122) 60 Middle Haddam Rd 06456 (Mail to: PO Box 81 06456-0081) (860) 267-0287

Middlebury St George Episcopal Church **P** (174) Tucker Hill Rd 06762-2517 (Mail to: PO Box 162 06762-0162) Tara Shepley Tara Shepley Andrew Zeman (203) 758-9864

Middletown Holy Trinity Church **P** (263) 381 Main St 06457-3309 (Mail to: 381 Main St 06457-3309) Mary Barnett (860) 347-2591

Milford Saint Andrew's Church **P** (100) 283 Bridgeport Avenue 06460-5431 (Mail to: PO Box 2454 06460-0877) (203) 874-2701

Milford St Peters Church **P** (285) 71 River St 06460-3315 (Mail to: 71 River St 06460-3315) Matthew Lindeman Angela Rowley (203) 874-8562

Monroe St. Peter's Grace Episcopal Church **P** (275) 175 Old Tannery Rd 06468-1932 (Mail to: 175 Old Tannery Rd 06468-1932) (203) 268-4265

Mystic St Marks Episcopal Church **P** (286) 15 Pearl St 06355-2513 (Mail to: 15 Pearl St 06355-2599) Adam Thomas (860) 572-9549

N Branford Zion Episcopal Church **P** (155) 326 Notch Hill Rd 06471-1858 (Mail to: 326 Notch Hill Rd 06471-1858) Lucy Larocca (203) 488-7395

Naugatuck St Michaels Episcopal Parish **P** (326) 210 Church St 06770-4120 (Mail to: 210 Church St 06770-4197) Juliusz Jodko Juliusz Jodko (203) 729-8249

New Britain St Marks Episcopal Church **P** (425) 90 Main St 06051-2509 (Mail to: PO Box 1538 06050-1538) William Eakins Joseph Pace (860) 225-7634

New Canaan St Marks Episcopal Church **P** (1495) § 111 Oenoke Rdg 06840-4105 (Mail to: 111 Oenoke Rdg 06840-4105) Peter Walsh Justin Crisp Justin Crisp Elizabeth Garnsey (203) 9664515

New Haven Christ Episcopal Church **P** (234) 84 Broadway 06511-3412 (Mail to: 84 Broadway 06511-3499) Stephen Holton Louis Mcalister Andrew Osmun Kent Smith (203) 865-6354

New Haven Episcopal Church at Yale **CC** PO Box 201955 06520-1955 (Mail to: PO Box 201955 06520-1955) Alison Donohue (203) 432-5401

New Haven St Johns Church **P** (109) 400 Humphrey St 06511-3711 (Mail to: 400 Humphrey St 06511-3711) (203) 562-1487

New Haven St Lukes Episcopal Church **P** (209) 111 Whalley Ave 06511-3220 (Mail to: 111 Whalley Ave 06511-3293) Paul Jacobson (203) 865-0141

New Haven St Paul - St James Epis Church **P** (78) 57 Olive St 06511-5739 (Mail to: 57 Olive St 06511-5739) Nathan Empsall Stacey Kohl (203) 562-2143

New Haven Church of St Thomas **P** (132) § 830 Whitney Ave 06511-1316 (Mail to: 830 Whitney Ave 06511-1398) Keri Auber Maureen Lederman William Loutrel (203) 777-7623

New Haven Trinity Church on the Green **P** (824) 950 Chapel St Fl 2 06510 (Mail to: 950 Chapel St Fl 2 06510) Luk De Volder Heidi Thorsen (203) 624-3101

New London St James Episcopal Church **P** (326) 76 Federal St 06320-6601 (Mail to: Attn: Treasurer 76 Federal St 06320-6601) Denise Cabana Patricia Hames (860) 443-4989

New Milford Saint John's Church **P** (248) 7 Whittlesey Ave 06776-3023 (Mail to: 7 Whittlesey Ave 06776-3023) Amy Reichman (860) 354-5583

Newington Grace Episcopal Church **P** (153) 124 Maple Hill Ave 06111-2719 (Mail to: 124 Maple Hill Ave 06111-2719) Valerie Miller Robert Stocksdale (860) 666-3331

Newtown Trinity Church Episcopal **P** (225) Attn Ellsworth Stringer 36 Main St 06470-2106 (Mail to: 36 Main St 06470-2181) Andrea Wyatt (203) 426-9070

Niantic St Johns Episcopal Church **P** (603) 406 Main St 06357 (Mail to: PO Box 810 06357-0810) Dianne Warley (860) 739-2324

North Haven St Johns Episcopal Church **P** (226) 3 Trumbull Pl 06473-2522 (Mail to:

Trumbull Pl 06473-2522) (203) 239-0156

Northford St Andrew Episcopal Church **P** (70) Middletown Ave 06472 (Mail to: Middletown Ave PO Box 96 06472-0096) (203) 484-0895

Norwalk Christ Episcopal Church **P** (114) 2 Emerson St 06855-1330 (Mail to: 2 Emerson St 06855-1330) Patricia Coller (203) 866-7442

Norwalk Iglesia Betania Episcopal **P** (83) 1 Union Park 06850-3316 (Mail to: 1 Trinity Pl 06854-2114) Eddie Lopez (203) 853-6767

Norwalk St Paul's on the Green **P** (782) 60 East Ave Ste 1 06851-4891 (Mail to: 60 East Ave 06851-4909) Louise Kalemkerian Daniel Simons (203) 847-2806

Oakville All Saints with Christ Epis Ch **P** (112) 262 Main St 06779-1742 (Mail to: PO Box 33 06779-0033) (860) 274-2352

Old Greenwich St Saviours Church **P** (166) 350 Sound Beach Ave 06870-1930 (Mail to: 350 Sound Beach Ave 06870-1930) Ian Montgomery (203) 637-2262

Old Lyme St Anns Episcopal Church **P** (214) 82 Shore Rd 06371-1726 (Mail to: 82 Shore Rd 06371-1726) Patricia Hames Anita Schell (860) 434-1621

Old Saybrook Grace Episcopal Church **P** (333) 336 Main St 06475-2350 (Mail to: 336 Main St 06475-2350) Charles Hamill (860) 388-0895

Orange Church of the Good Shepherd **P** (163) 680 Racebrook Rd 06477-1931 (Mail to: 680 Racebrook Rd 06477-1931) (203) 795-6577

Oxford Christ Church Quaker Farms **P** (290) 470 Quaker Farms Rd 06478-1307 (Mail to: 470 Quaker Farms Rd 06478-1398) Jillian Morrison (203) 888-4936

Oxford St Peters Episcopal Church **P** (70) 421 Oxford Rd 06478-1692 (Mail to: 421 Oxford Rd 06478-1236) (203) 888-5279

Pine Meadow St Johns Episcopal Church **P** (295) 51 Church St 06061 (Mail to: PO Box 27 06061-0027) (860) 379-3062

Plainfield St Pauls Episcopal Church **P** (120) 27 Babcock Ave 06374-1222 (Mail to: 27 Babcock Ave 06374-1222) (860) 564-3560

Pomfret Christ Church Episcopal **P** (414) 521 Pomfret St 06258 (Mail to: PO Box 21 06258-0021) Virginia Army (860) 315-7780

Portland Trinity Church **P** (133) 345 Main St 06480-1561 (Mail to: 345 Main St 06480-1561) (860) 342-0458

Preston St James Church **P** (179) 95 Route 2a 06365-8538 (Mail to: 95 Rte. 2-A 06365) (860) 889-0150

Redding Christ Church Parish **P** (348) 184 Cross Hwy 06896-2101 (Mail to: PO Box 54 06876-0054) Nicki Kimes (203) 938-2872

Ridgefield St Stephens Church **P** (498) 351 Main St 06877-4601 (Mail to: 353 Main St 06877-4601) Whitney Altopp Leslie Hughs (203) 438-3789

Riverside St Pauls Church **P** (481) § 200 Riverside Ave 06878-2210 (Mail to: 200 Riverside Ave

06878-2206) Stephanie Johnson (203) 637-2447

Rocky Hill St Andrew the Apostle **P** (357) 331 Orchard St 06067-2022 (Mail to: 331 Orchard St 06067-2022) Patrick Bush (860) 529-7622

Roxbury Christ Church **P** (108) 1 Church St 06783-1702 (Mail to: PO Box 4 06783-0004) Stephen Nagy (860) 355-3695

Salisbury St Johns Episcopal Church **P** (196) 12 Main St 06068-1800 (Mail to: PO Box 391 06068-0391) Lance Beizer (860) 435-9290

Seymour Trinity Episcopal Church **P** (129) 91 Church St 06483-2611 (Mail to: 91 Church St 06483-2611) Patricia Leonard-Pasley (203) 888-6596

Sharon Christ Episcopal Church **P** (72) 9 S Main St 06069-1778 (Mail to: PO Box 1778 06069-1778) (860) 364-5260

Shelton Church of the Good Shepherd **P** (100) 182 Coram Ave 06484-3347 (Mail to: 182 Coram Ave 06484-3347) Thomas Mariconda (203) 924-8050

Shelton St Pauls Episcopal Church **P** (263) 25 Church St 06484-5802 (Mail to: 25 Church St 06484-5897) Knute Hansen Amjad Samuel (203) 929-1722

Simsbury St Albans Episcopal Church **P** (76) 197 Bushy Hill Rd 06070-2604 (Mail to: 197 Bushy Hill Rd 06070-2699) Rebekah Hatch (860) 658-0406

South Glastonbury St Lukes Episcopal Church **P** (300) PO Box 155 06073-0155 (Mail to: PO Box 155 06073-0155) Matthew Handi (860) 633-7175

South Windsor St Peters Episcopal Church **P** (141) 99 Sand Hill Rd 06074-2023 (Mail to: 99 Sand Hill Rd 06074-2023) Anne Fraley (860) 644-8548

Southbury Church of the Epiphany **P** (80) 262 Main St N 06488-1808 (Mail to: 262 Main St N 06488-1808) Marston Price (203) 264-8150

Southington St Pauls Episcopal Church **P** (329) 145 Main St 06489-2505 (Mail to: 145 Main St 06489-2590) (860) 628-8486

Southport Trinity Episcopal Church **P** (911) 651 Pequot Ave 06890-1366 (Mail to: PO Box 400 06890-0400) Margaret Hodgkins Catherine Quinn (203) 255-0454

Stafford Springs Grace Church Parish Episcopal **P** (80) 7 Spring St 06076-1504 (Mail to: PO Box 65 06076-0065) (860) 684-2824

Stamford Eglise De L'Epiphanie **M** (44) 628 Main St 06901-2011 (Mail to: C/O St Johns Church 628 Main St 06901-2094) Florencio Ghinaglia Socorro (203) 964-1517

Stamford St Andrews Church **P** (116) 1231 Washington Blvd 06901 (Mail to: 1231 Washington Blvd 06902-2402) Bartlett Gage (203) 325-4359

Stamford St Francis Church **P** (205) 2810 Long Ridge Road 06903-1110 (Mail to: 503 Old

Long Ridge Rd 06903-1110) Mark Lingle Mark Lingle Debra Slade (203) 322-2949

Stamford St Johns Church **P** (988) 628 Main St 06901-2011 (Mail to: 628 Main St 06901-2011) Andrew Kryzak Elizabeth Skaleski (203) 348-2619

Stonington Calvary Church **P** (402) 33 Church St 06378-1344 (Mail to: 27 Church St 06378-1344) Gillian Barr Douglass Lind (860) 535-1181

Storrs St Marks Chapel **P** (121) 42 N Eagleville Rd 06268-1710 (Mail to: 42 N Eagleville Rd 06268-1710) (860) 429-2647

Stratford Christ Episcopal Church **P** (395) 2000 Main St 06615-6340 (Mail to: 2000 Main St 06615-6397) (203) 378-1445

Tariffville Trinity Episcopal Church **P** (430) 11 Church St 06081-9624 (Mail to: C/O Edmond Gaidos 11 Church St 06081-9624) J Taylor Albright Denise Adessa (860) 651-0201

Thomaston St Peters Trinity Church **Chapel** (314) 160 Main St 06787-1720 (Mail to: 160 Main St 06787-1720) Jose Martinez (203) 268-2809

Torrington Trinity Episcopal Church **P** (316) 220 Prospect St 06790-5314 (Mail to: 220 Prospect St 06790-5314) Carrie Combs Amy Reichman (860) 482-6027

Trumbull Christ Episcopal Church Tashua **P** (105) 5170 Madison Ave 06611-1110 (Mail to: 5170 Madison Ave 06611-1110) Jane Jeuland (203) 268-5566

Trumbull Trinity Episcopal Church **P** (204) 1734 Huntington Tpke 06611-5114 (Mail to: 1734 Huntington Tpke 06611-5114) (203) 375-1503

Vernon Rockville St John's Church **P** (290) 523 Hartford Tpke 06066-4900 (Mail to: 523 Hartford Tpke 06066-4900) Marc Eames (860) 872-0517

Wallingford St Pauls Episcopal Church **P** (866) 65 N Main St 06492-3709 (Mail to: 65 N Main St 06492-3795) Debra Dodd (203) 269-5050

Washington St Johns Church **P** (223) 78 Green Hill Rd 06793-1217 (Mail to: PO Box 1278 06793-0278) Susan Mccone (860) 868-2527

Waterbury Christ Church **P** (73) 2030 E Main St 06705-2607 (Mail to: 2030 E Main St 06705-2607) (203) 753-6921

Waterbury St Johns Episcopal Church **P** (252) 16 Church St 06702-2103 (Mail to: 16 Church St 06702-2103) (203) 754-3116

West Hartford St James Church Episcopal **P** (1047) 1018 Farmington Ave 06107-2105 (Mail to: 19 Walden St 06107-1822) Robert

Hooper Alan Murchie (860) 521-9620

West Hartford St Johns Church Episcopal **P** (883) 679 Farmington Ave 06119-1895 (Mail to: 679 Farmington Ave 06119-1895) Hope Eakins Todd Fitzgerald Walter McKenney (860) 523-5201

West Haven Church of the Holy Spirit **P** (170) 28 Church St 06516-4927 (Mail to: 28 Church St 06516-4927) (203) 934-3437

Westbrook St Pauls Episcopal Church **P** (54) 53 S Main St 06498-1902 (Mail to: PO Box 598 06498-0598) (860) 669-7681

Weston Emmanuel Episcopal Church **P** (200) 285 Lyons Plain Rd 06883-2401 (Mail to: 285 Lyons Plain Rd 06883-2441) Katharine Herron-Piazza (203) 227-8565

Westport Christ and Holy Trinity Church **P** (655) § 75 Church Ln 06880-3506 (Mail to: 55 Myrtle Ave 06880-3510) John Betit (203) 2270827

Wethersfield Trinity Episcopal Church **P** (380) 300 Main St 06109-1826 (Mail to: 300 Main St 06109-1892) (860) 529-6825

Willimantic Saint Paul's Episcopal Church **P** (105) 220 Valley St 06226-2332 (Mail to: PO Box 63 06226-) Jaclyn Sheldon (860) 423-8455

Wilton St Matthews Episcopal Church **P** (1253) 36 New Canaan Rd 06897-3310 (Mail to: 36 New Canaan Rd 06897-3310) Marissa Rohrbach (203) 762-7400

Windham St Pauls Church **P** (66) 26 Plains Rd 06280-1324 (Mail to: PO Box 82 06280-0082) (860) 423-9653

Windsor Grace Church Episcopal **P** (232) 311 Broad St 06095-2906 (Mail to: 311 Broad St 06095-2906) Harry Elliott Denise Adessa (860) 688-1232

Winsted St James Episcopal Church **P** (121) 160 Main St 06098-1735 (Mail to: 160 Main St 06098-1735) (860) 379-5657

Wolcott All Saints Episcopal Church **P** (176) 282 Bound Line Rd 06716-2508 (Mail to: PO Box 6015 06716-0015) Susan Davidson (203) 879-2800

Woodbury St Pauls Episcopal Church **P** (200) 249 Main St S 06798-3408 (Mail to: PO Box 5002 06798-5002) Tuesday Rupp David Rhodes (203) 263-3541

Yalesville St John Evangelist Episcopal **P** (40) 360 Church St 06492-2200 (Mail to: 360 Church St 06492-2283) Peter Quinn (203) 269-9526

Yantic Grace Episcopal Church **P** (41) PO Box 126 06389-0126 (Mail to: 4 Chapel Hill Rd 06389-0126) (860) 887-2082

DIOCESE OF CUBA
(PROVINCE II)
Comprises the Island of Cuba
DIOCESAN CENTER Calle 6, No 273, e/11 y 13, Vedado, Plaza Vedado, Cuba 10400
TEL +53 7 8321120 FAX (787) 761-0320
E-MAIL episcopal@enet.cu WEB www.episcopalcuba.org

La Iglesia Episcopal en Cuba

Previous Bishops—
Albion W. Knight 1905–1913, Hiram Richard Hulse 1915–1938, Alexander Hugh Blankingship 1939–1961, Romualdo González Agüeros 1961–1966 (first Cuban citizen bishop, Spain), Iglesia Episcopal de Cuba becomes an extra provincial entity within the Anglican Communion, 1966-2020

Bishop—Rt Rev Griselda Delgado del Carpio (1129) (Dio received 6 March 2020)

PARISHES, MISSIONS, AND CLERGY

Bermeja La Trinidad **P** Independencia 10 (Mail to: Independencia 10)

C Habana C Habana La Santsima Trinidad **P** Calle 11 865e/4 y 6 10400 (Mail to: Calle11 865e/4 y 6 10400)

Cardenas Matanzas San Fco. de Ass **P** Aylln 1074 e/22 y 23 42100 (Mail to: Aylln 1074 e/22 y 23 42100)

Esmeralda Camaguey Buen Pastor **P** Miguel Coyula s/n Nodal y Francisco lvarez 72200 (Mail to: Miguel Coyula s/n Nodal y Francisco lvarez 72200)

Florida Camaguey La Anunciacin **P** Fco Vicente 105 72100 (Mail to: Fco Vicente 105 72100)

Guira de Macurijes Matanzas El Buen Pastor **P** Calle 16 705 (Mail to: Calle 16 705)

La Gloria Camaguey La Santsima Trinidad **P** La Gloria S de Cubita s/n 74190 (Mail to: La Gloria S de Cubita s/n 74190)

Los Arabos Matanzas Cristo Rey **P** Cuatro Esquinas 43300- (Mail to: Cuatro Esquinas 43300-)

Los Arabos Matanzas La Santsima Trinidad **P** Fco Carrillo 45 40200 (Mail to: Fco Carrillo 45 40200)

Luyano C Habana La Resurreccin **P** Municipio 106 10700 (Mail to: Municipio 106 10700)

Manati Las Tunas San Andrs **P** Orlando Canales s/n 77100 (Mail to: Orlando Canales s/n 77100)

Matanzas Matanzas Fieles a Jess **P** S Juan de Dios 27413 40200 (Mail to: S Juan de Dios 27413 40200)

Moron Ciego de Avila La Santsima Trinidad **P** Narciso Lpez 299 67210 (Mail to: Narciso Lpez 299 67210)

S Spiritus S Spiritus San Bernab **P** Calle Martí # 119 60100 (Mail to: Calle Martí # 119 60100)

Santa Cruz Mayabeque La Santa Cruz **P** Calle 13 esquina A 6 32900 (Mail to: Calle 13 esquina A 6 32900)

Tabor-Esmeralda Camaguey La Transfiguracin **P** Ignacio Agramonte 17 74150 (Mail to: Ignacio Agramonte 17 74150)

DIOCESE OF DALLAS
(PROVINCE VII)
Comprises 25 counties in Northeast Texas
DIOCESAN OFFICE 5100 Ross Ave Dallas TX 75206
TEL (214) 826-8310 FAX (214) 826-5968
E-MAIL klanore@edod.org WEB www.edod.org

Previous Bishops—
Alexander C Garrett 1874-1924, Harry T Moore coadj 1917 Bp 1924-46, Chas A Mason coadj 1945 Bp 1946-70, Gerald F Burrill suffr 1950-54, John JM Harte suffr 1954-62, Theodore H McCrea suffr 1962-75, William Paul Barnds suffr 1966-73, A Donald Davies 1970-82, Robert E Terwilliger suffr 1975-86, Donis D Patterson 1983-92, David Bruce MacPherson suffr 1999-02, James Monte Stanton 1993-2014, Paul Emil Lambert suffr 2008-16

Bishop—Rt Rev George Robinson Sumner (1090) (Dio 14 Nov 2015)

Asst Bp M Smith F Lawton; *Cn to the Ord* C Brown; *Treas* G Fox; *Chanc* D Parsons; *Comm* K Durnan; *Sec Conv* R Buchanan; *Dio Serv* SL Mills; *Evang* C Headington; *Budg & Fin* T Young; *Archdcn* R Trei

Stand Comm—Cler: Pres R Corley S Page; *Lay:* T Graves S McCoy

PARISHES, MISSIONS, AND CLERGY

Allen Church of the Savior **P** (48) 110 S Alma Dr 75013-3045 (Mail to: 110 S Alma Dr 75013-3045) (972) 649-4032

Athens Church of St Matthias **P** (113) Attn: Charlene Tucker 205 Willowbrook Dr 75751-3537 (Mail to: Attn: Treasurer 205 Willowbrook Dr 75751-3537) Matthew Frick (903) 675-3210

Atlanta All Saints Episcopal Church **M** (26) 404 N Louise St 75551-2240 (Mail to: PO Box 513 75551-0513) (903) 796-7200

Bonham Church of the Holy Trinity **M** (21) 617 Star St 75418-3630 (Mail to: PO Box 81 75418-0081) (903) 375-3859

Canton St Justin Martyr **PS** (72) 977 W Highway 243 75103-2021 (Mail to: PO Box 87 75103-0087) Marc Dobson (903) 567-4959

Cedar Hill Church of the Good Shepherd **P** (133) 915 Straus Rd 75104-5317 (Mail to: PO Box 429 75106-0429) (972) 291-4528

Coppell Church of the Apostles **P** (559) 322 S Macarthur Blvd 75019-3605 (Mail to: 322 S Macarthur Blvd 75019-3605) Timothy Cherry Leo Loyola (972) 462-0234

Corsicana St Johns Episcopal Church **P** (330) 101 N 14th St 75110-5110 (Mail to: 101 N 14th St 75110-5110) Edward Monk (903) 874-5425

Dallas Christ Episcopal Church **P** (416) 534 West 10th Street 75208-4720 (Mail to: 534 W 10th St 75208-4720) Fabian Villalobos (214) 941-0339

Dallas Epis Church of Our Saviour **M** (34) 1616 N Jim Miller Rd 75217-1320 (Mail to: 1616 N Jim Miller Rd 75217-1320) (214) 391-2824

Dallas Good Samaritan Epis Church **M** (77) 1522 Highland Rd 75218-4420 (Mail to: 1522 Highland Rd 75218-4420) Joel Hatfield (214) 328-3883

Dallas Church of the Good Shepherd **P** (1091) 11122 Midway Rd 75229-4118 (Mail to: 11122 Midway Rd 75229-4199) Michael Mills Thomas Hotchkiss Eric Liles Melody Shobe (214) 351-6468

Dallas Episcopal Ch of the Holy Cross **P** (20) 4052 Herschel Ave 75219-2930 (Mail to: 4052 Herschel Ave 75219-2930) (214) 528-3855

Dallas Church of the Incarnation **P** (4947) 3966 Mckinney Ave 75204-2018 (Mail to: 3966 Mckinney Ave 75204-2099) Christopher Beeley Dorothy Budd Jonathan Jordan James Lee Raleigh Skorburg (214) 5215101

Dallas Episcopal Church of Ascension **P** (297) § 8787 Greenville Ave 75243-7140 (Mail to: 8787 Greenville Ave 75243-7197) Paul Klitzke (214) 340-4196

Dallas Holy Faith **PS** (38) Trinity Episcopal 12727 Hillcrest Rd 75230-2007 (Mail to: C/O Trinity Episcopal 12727 Hillcrest Rd 75230-2007)

Dallas San Francisco de Asis **P** (341) 11540 Ferguson Rd 75228-1825 (Mail to: 11540 Ferguson Rd 75228-1825) Aquilino Lara Juana Lara (972) 279-6501

Dallas St Albans Cntbry House at SMU **CC** 3308 Daniel Ave 75205-1440 (Mail to: 3308 Daniel Ave 75205-1440) (214) 363-2911

Dallas St Andrews Episcopal Church **P** (194) 2783 Valwood Pkwy 75234-3529 (Mail to: 2783 Valwood Pkwy 75234-3529) (972) 247-7702

Dallas St Christophers Episcopal Ch **P** (75) 7900 Lovers Ln 75225-8200 (Mail to: 7900 Lovers Ln 75225-8200) Christopher Steele (214) 363-2792

Dallas St James Episcopal Church **P** (473) 9845 Mccree Rd 75238-3444 (Mail to: 9845 McCree Rd 75238-3444) Jonathan Melton Jacob Nichols (214) 348-1345

Dallas St Johns Episcopal Church **P** (471) 848 Harter Rd 75218-2751 (Mail to: 848 Harter Rd 75218-2792) David Houk Oliver Butler Samuel Cripps Herbert Dewees (214) 321-6451

Dallas Saint Luke's Episcopal Church **P** (204) 5923 Royal Ln 75230-3812 (Mail to: 5923 Royal Ln 75230-3841) Joel Hatfield (214) 368-6304

✠ **Dallas** Cathedral Church of St Matthew **O** (328) 5100 Ross Ave 75206-7709 (Mail to: 5100 Ross Ave 75206-7798) Robert Price Mark Hall Diana Luck Bonnie Slusher (214) 823-8134

Dallas St Michael and All Angels Ch **P** (6101) § 8011 Douglas Ave 75225-6502 (Mail to: C/O Rob Baber 8011 Douglas Ave 75225-6502) Marcia Bhan Nathan Bostian Kenneth Brannon Christopher Girata Andrew Grosso Robert Johnston Mary Lessmann Gregory Pickens (214) 363-5471

Dallas St Augustine of Hippo Epis Ch **P** (187) 1302 W Kiest Blvd 75224-3235 (Mail to: 1302 W Kiest Blvd 75224-3235) Samuel Adams (214) 371-3441

Dallas St Philips Sudanese **P** 8787 Greenville Ave 75243-7140 (Mail to: 8787 Greenville Ave 75243-7140) (877) 829-5500

Dallas St Thomas the Apostle Church **P** (372) 6525 Inwood Rd 75209-5314 (Mail to: 6525 Inwood Rd 75209-5399) Christopher Thomas (214) 352-0410

Dallas The Epis Ch of the Transfig **P** (1179) 14115 Hillcrest Rd 75254-8622 (Mail to: C/O Sophie Lowrance 14115 Hillcrest Rd 75254-8622) Robert Shobe Rebecca Tankersley (972) 233-1898

Denison St Lukes Church **P** (234) 427 W Woodard St 75020 (Mail to: 427 W Woodard St 75020-3138) (903) 465-2630

Denton St Barnabas Episcopal Church **P** (308) 1200 N Elm St 76201-2941 (Mail to: 1200 N Elm St 76201-2941) (940) 382-2748

Denton St Davids Church **P** (337) 623 Ector St 76201-2423 (Mail to: 623 Ector St 76201-2423) (940) 387-2622

Desoto St Anne Episcopal Church **P** (492) 1700 N Westmoreland Rd 75115-2272 (Mail to: 1700 N Westmoreland Rd 75115-2272) David Miller David Miller George Udell (972) 709-0691

Ennis St Thomas Episcopal Church **M** (74) 901 Park St 75119-1607 (Mail to: PO Box 475 75120-0475) (972) 875-2423

Flower Mound Saint Nicholas Church **P** (664) 4800 Wichita Trl 75022-5121 (Mail to: C/O Faith Epley 4800 Wichita Trl 75022-5121) Mark Wright (972) 318-7070

Frisco St Philips Church **P** (2021) § 6400 Stonebrook Pkwy 75034-5711 (Mail to: 6400 Stonebrook Pkwy 75034-5711) Michael Gilton Clayton Elder Clayton Elder (214) 619-5806

Garland Emmanuel Anglican **PS** (114) 2022 Saturn Rd 75041-1640 (Mail to: 2022 Saturn Rd 75041-1640) (972) 840-9044

Garland Holy Trinity Episcopal Church **P** (182) 3217 Guthrie Rd 75043-6121 (Mail to: 3217 Guthrie Rd 75043-6121) Richard Crownover (972) 226-1283

Garland St Barnabas Episcopal Church **P** (716) 1200 N Shiloh Rd 75042-5724 (Mail to: 1200 N Shiloh Rd 75042-5769) Maria Barrios Alyce Schrimsher Alfredo Williams (972) 494-6600

Greenville St Pauls Episcopal Church **P** (168) 8320 Jack Finney Blvd 75402-3004 (Mail to: 8320 Jack Finney Blvd 75402-3004) Nicholas Funk (903) 455-5030

Irving Episcopal Ch of the Redeemer **P** (174) 2700 Warren Cir 75062-9242 (Mail to: 2700 Warren Cir 75062-5799) Victoria Heard (972) 255-4171

Irving St Marks Episcopal Church **P** (146) 516 S O'Connor Rd 75060-4059 (Mail to: 516 S O'Connor Rd 75060-4059) Robert Corley (972) 253-7124

Irving St Marys Episcopal Church **P** (319) 635 N Story Rd 75061-6732 (Mail to: 635 N Story Rd 75061-6728) Luz Elliott Luz Elliott (972) 790-4644

Kaufman Church of Our Merciful Saviour **M** (86) 500 S Jackson St 75142-2330 (Mail to: PO Box 520 75142-0520) (972) 932-4646

Kemp St James on the Lake **P** (98) 10707 County Road 4022 75143-4217 (Mail to: 10707 Cr 4022 75143) (903) 498-8080

Lewisville Church of the Annunciation **P** (403) § 602 N Old Orchard Ln 75077-2869 (Mail to: PO Box 292365 75029-2365) Ames Swartsfager (972) 221-3531

Mc Kinney Church of the Holy Family **M** (211) 406 Lincoln St 75069-4263 (Mail to: PO Box 1039 75070-8147) (972) 542-5799

Mc Kinney St Peters Episcopal Church **P** (621) 400 S College St 75069-5420 (Mail to: 511 Foote St 75069-2707) Katherine Heitmann Janice Honea (972) 562-1166

Mckinney St Andrews Episcopal Church **P** (668) 6400 Mckinney Ranch Pkwy 75070-9601 (Mail to: 6400 Mckinney Ranch Pkwy 75070-9601) Andrew Van Kirk (972) 548-7990

Mineola St Dunstan Episcopal Church **P** (101) 800 N Johnson St 75773-1816 (Mail to: PO Box 81 75773-0081) (903) 569-2478

Mt Pleasant St Marks Episcopal Church **P** (67) 205 E Pecan St 75455-5403 (Mail to: PO Box 1837 75456-1837) (903) 572-3211

Paris Church of the Holy Cross **P** (280) § 322 S Church St 75460-5853 (Mail to: 400 S Church St 75460-5844) Craig Reed (903) 784-6194

Pittsburg St William Laud Epis Church **P** (63) 601 Lafayette St 75686-3057 (Mail to: PO Box 1057 75686-3057) Mary Matthews (903) 856-2675

Plano Iglesia de la Santa Natividad **P** (234) 2200 18th St 75074-4920 (Mail to: 2200 18th St 75074-4920) Noe Mendez

Plano Resurrection Episcopal Church **M** (80) 4500 Quincy Ln 75024-3849 (Mail to: 3609 Steven Dr 75023-3837)

Plano Church of the Holy Nativity **P** (135) C/O Dk Andersen 2200 18th St 75074-4920 (Mail to: 2200 18th St 75074-4920) Samira Page (972) 4244574

Pottsboro St John the Apostle Epis Ch **M** (126) 760 E Fm 120 75076-3097 (Mail to: PO Box 972 75076-0972) Marci Pounders (903) 786-4339

Prosper St Pauls Episcopal Church **M** (461) 420 S Coit Rd 75078-2907 (Mail to: 420 S Coit Rd 75078-2907) (972) 347-9700

Richardson Church of the Epiphany **P** (641) 421 Custer Rd 75080-5628 (Mail to: 421 Custer Rd 75080-5628) Anne Randall Brenda Kroll Anne Randall (972) 690-0095

Rockwall Holy Trinity Episcopal Church **P** (521) 1524 Smirl Dr 75032-7638 (Mail to: Treasurer John Curtis 1524 Smirl Dr 75032-7638) Norman Turbeville Jacob Nichols (972) 771-8242

Sherman St Stephens Episcopal Church **P** (67) 401 S Crockett St 75090-7171 (Mail to: 401 S Crockett St 75090-7171) James Evans (903) 892-6610

Sulphur Spgs St Philips Episcopal Church **P** (59) 1206 College St 75482-3018 (Mail to: PO Box 636 75483-0636) Barbara Kelton

Terrell Church of the Good Shepherd **P** (89) 200 W College St 75160-2625 (Mail to: 200 W College St 75160-2625) Ian Hyde (972) 563-2412

Texarkana St James Episcopal Church **P** (447) § 413 Olive St 75501-5510 (Mail to: 413 Olive St 75501-5510) David Halt (903) 794-9224

Waxahachie Saint Paul's Episcopal Church **M** (535) 624 Ovilla Rd 75167-4801 (Mail to: 624 Ovilla Rd 75167-4801) Terry Reisner (972) 938-2126

Winnsboro St Francis Episcopal Church **M** (30) 103 W Sage St 75494-2541 (Mail to: PO Box 1082 75494-1082) (903) 342-7240

DIOCESE OF DELAWARE
(PROVINCE III)
Comprises State of Delaware
DIOCESAN OFFICE 913 Wilson Road, Wilmington, DE 19803
Tel (302) 256-0374 FAX (302) 543-8084
E-MAIL jgregory@delaware.church WEB www.delaware.church

Previous Bishops— Alfred Lee 1841-87, Leighton Coleman 1888-1907, Fredk J Kinsman 1908-19, Philip Cook 1920-38, Arthur R McKinstry 1939-54, J Brooke Mosley 1955-68, Wm H Mead 1968-74, Wm H Clark 1975-85, Q Primo *Int* 1985-86, C Cabell Tennis 1986-97, Wayne P Wright 1998-2017

Bishop—Rt Rev Kevin S Brown (1107) (Dio 9 December 2017)

Cn to Ord Rev M Kirkpatrick; *Cn Fin and Admin* J Gregory; *Exec Asst to Bp* K Moore; *Chanc* T Willard (302) 645-5470 *E-mail:* tim@fwsslaw.com

Stand Comm—Cler: M Kirkpatrick C Weiss R Bohner B Hinton; *Lay: Pres* T Flanagan J Barrett B Maurer M Wood *Rec Secretary* C Cooper

PARISHES, MISSIONS, AND CLERGY

Bethany Beach St Martha's Episcopal Church **P** (240) PO Box 1478 19930-1478 (Mail to: PO Box 1478 19930-1478) Victoria Pretti (302) 539-7444

Bridgeville St Marys Episcopal Church **P** (48) 114 Delaware Ave 19933-1141 (Mail to: PO Box 21 19933-0021) (302) 337-8981

Camden Wyoming St Pauls Episcopal Church **P** (125) Old North Rd At West St 19934 (Mail to: PO Box 157 19934-0157) (302) 697-7904

Claymont The Church of the Ascension **P** (265) 3717 Philadelphia Pike 19703-3413 (Mail to: 3717 Philadelphia Pike 19703-3413) (302) 798-6683

Delaware City Christ Church Delaware City **P** (57) 222 Third and Clint 19706 (Mail to: Attn: Dan Saunders Treasurer PO Box 523 19706-0523) (302) 834-3328

Delmar All Saints Church Delmar **P** (43) 10th St 19940 (Mail to: PO Box 88 19940-0088) (302) 846-9889

Dover Christ Church Dover **P** (347) S State & Water Sts 19903 (Mail to: PO Box 1374 19903-1374) Charles Weiss Patricia Malcolm Patricia Malcolm (302) 734-5731

Georgetown St Pauls Church Georgetown **P** (85) 122 East Pine Street 19947 (Mail to: C/O Vicki Reinsfelder PO Box 602 19947-0602) (302) 856-2894

Harrington St Stephens Church **P** (56) 190 Raughley Hill Rd 19952-3152 (Mail to: Attn: Judith A Viar 2020 N Tatnall St 19802-4856) (302) 398-8846

Laurel St Philips Episcopal Church **P** (129) 600 S Central Ave 19956-1410 (Mail to: 600 S Central Ave 19956-1410) Howard Backus (302) 875-3644

Lewes St Georges Chapel **SC** Beaver Dam Rd & Chapel Branch 19958 (Mail to: 18 Olive Ave 19971-2806) (302) 227-7202

Lewes St Peters Church Lewes **P** (717) PO Box 464 211 Mulberry St 19958-0464 (Mail to: PO Box 464 19958-0464) Jeffrey Ross Jule Gill Mark Harris (302) 645-8479

Middletown St Andrews School Chapel **Chapel** 350 Noxontown Rd 19709-1621 (Mail to: 350 Noxontown Rd 19709-1605) John Hutchinson (302) 378-9511

Middletown Saint Anne's Episcopal Church **P** (323) 15 E Green St 19709-1497 (Mail to: 15 E Green St 19709-1497) Charles Bohner (302) 3782401

Milford Christ Episcopal Ch Milford **P** (212) 200 N Church Ave 19963-1123 (Mail to: PO Box 191 19963-0191) (302) 422-8466

Millsboro St Marks Church **P** (153) 50 Ellis St 19966-0422 (Mail to: PO Box 422 19966-0422) (302) 934-9464

Milton St John The Baptist **P** (195) 307 Federal St 19968-1606 (Mail to: PO Box 441 19968-0441) (302) 856-6844

New Castle Church of the Nativity **P** (28) 206 Sykes Rd 19720-1814 (Mail to: PO Box 662 19720-0662) (302) 328-3445

New Castle Immanuel Church On The Green **P** (203) 50 Market St 19720-4830 (Mail to: 100 Harmony St 19720-4847) Christopher Keene (302) 3282413

Newark St Nicholas Episcopal Church **P** (98) 10 Old Newark Rd 19713-3944 (Mail to: 10 Old Newark Rd 19713-3944) (302) 368-4655

Newark St Thomas Parish **P** (280) 276 S College Ave 19711-5235 (Mail to: 276 S College Ave 19711-5235) Howell Sasser (302) 368-4644

Newport St James Church Newport **P** (90) 2 S Augustine St 19804-2504 (Mail to: 2 S Augustine St 19804-2504) Sarah Nelson (302) 994-2029

Rehoboth Bch All Saints and St Georges Ch **P** (582) 18 Olive Ave 19971-2806 (Mail to: 18 Olive Ave 19971-2899) Shelley McDade (302) 227-7202

Seaford St Lukes Episcopal Church **P** (36) 202 N North St 19973-2728 (Mail to: 202 N North St 19973-2728) Marianne Ell (302) 6297979

Selbyville St Martins in the Field Church **P** (82) PO Box 697 19975-0697 (Mail to: PO Box 697 19975-0697) (302) 436-8921

Smyrna St Peters Church **P** (116) § 22 N Union St 19977-1147 (Mail to: 22 N Union St 19977-1147) Donna Jean Kiessling (302) 6539691

Wilmington Calvary Church Hillcrest **P** (89) 304 Lore Ave 19809-3134 (Mail to: 304 Lore Ave 19809-3134) (302) 764-2027

Wilmington Christ Ch Christiana Hundred **HC** (1426) § 505 E Buck Rd 19807-2167 (Mail to: PO Box 3510 19807-0510) Ruth Beresford Michael Kurth (302) 655-3379

Wilmington Ch of St Andrews St Matthews **P** (339) 719 N Shipley St 19801-1711 (Mail to: 719 N Shipley St 19801-1727) (302) 6566628

Wilmington Grace Ch Brandywine Hundred **P** (229) 4900 Concord Pike 19803-1412 (Mail to: 4906 Concord Pike 19803-1412) (302) 478-9533

Wilmington Immanuel Church Highlands **P** (203) 2400 W 17th St 19806-1343 (Mail to: 2400 W 17th St Ste A 19806-1346) (302) 658-7326

Wilmington St Barnabas Episcopal Church **P** (600) 2800 Duncan Rd 19808-2306 (Mail to: 2800 Duncan Rd Side 19808-2312) Kenneth Katona (302) 994-6607

Wilmington St Davids Episcopal Church **P** (319) § 2320 Grubb Rd 19810-2702 (Mail to: 2320 Grubb Rd 19810-2798) Bradley Hinton (302) 475-4688

Wilmington St James Epis Ch Mill Creek **HC** (345) 2106 Saint James Church Rd 19808-5225 (Mail to: 2106 Saint James Church Rd 19808-5225) Reuben Rockwell (302) 994-1584

Wilmington Trinity Parish & Old Swedes Ch **P** (824) 1108 N Adams St 19801-1327 (Mail to: 1108 N Adams St 19801-1327) Patricia Downing Charles Cowen (302) 652-8605

DISTRICT OF COLUMBIA

Diocese of Washington

DIOCESE OF THE DOMINICAN REPUBLIC

IGLESIA EPISCOPAL DOMINICANA (PROVINCIA IX)
Comprende la República Dominicana
OFICINA DIOCESANA Calle Santiago No 114 Gazcue, Santo Domingo, REPÚBLICA DOMINICANA
(Correo: Iglesia Episcopal Dominicana DMG [En proceso], 100 Airport Ave Venice Fl 34285 USA)
TELÉFONO (809) 688-6016, (809) 686-7493
CORREO ELECTRÓNICO iglepidom@codetel.net.do / bishopmoisesquezada@gmail.com
WEB www.iglepidom.org

Obispos anteriores— James T. Holly (Haití) a cargo 1897-1911 Charles B. Colmore (Puerto Rico) a cargo 1913- 1922 Harry R. Carson (Haití) a cargo 1923-1948 (dio 1934- 1940) Mis Dist Haití y Dom Rep) Charles Alfred Voegeli (Haití) Bp Coadjutor 1943-1948 Paul A. Kellogg Bp 1960-1972 Telésforo ̣saac Bp 1972-1991 Julio C. Holguín K. Bp 1991-2017

Dbispo Coadjutor—Moisés Quezada (13 Feb 2016-3 Nov 2017)

Dbispo Diocesano—Moisés Quezada (4 Nov 2017)

̤jecutivo del Vicario General Rev Cn: vacante; *Treas* ̄ME Pérez; *Asst fin admin* I De León; *Asst fin admin* ̄enesis Mendez Obispo; *Reg* A Richardson; *Educ of ̤piscopalian Colleges Dept* M Jorge; *Asst Team Coord*

Nederlandn Paulino.; *Sec* K Calzado *Concierge* N Cabrera, B Suero

Archdcns: Central Región S Sanchez; *East Región* J Rosario; *North Región* S Almonte; *South Región* F Encarnación

Consejo Ejecutivo: Cler: M Mota *Sec* B López R Lorenzo Gómez B Diaz D Matos; *Laicos:* A delfa Lara K ugche, Y Diaz

PARROQUIAS, MISIONES Y CLERO

Andrés Boca Chica Iglesia **San José** Calle El Peso No 28 (Mail to Calle El Peso No 28, Andrés Boca Chica) Isaac Emilio Pringle. 849-342-6960.

Azua Iglesia Episcopal **San Jorge** Calle Hernán Cortez No 24, Azua (Mail to Calle Santiago No 114, Gazcue apdo. 764 Santo Domingo) Luis García. 809-404-7470.

Azua Iglesia Episcopal **Espíritu Santo** Calle La Cruz de Ocoa, Las Carreras, Azua (Mail to Hnas. Mirabal No 74, Barrio La Bombita, Azua) Luis García Tel. 809-404-7470.

Azua Iglesia Episcopal **La Reconciliación** Calle Las Carreras No 124, Barrio La Bombita, Azua (Mail to Hnas Mirabal No 74, Barrio La Bombita, Azua) Luis García Tel. 809-404-7470.

Bani Iglesia Episcopal **La Transfiguración** Calle Las Violetas No 2, Urb. Brisas del Canal, Bani (Mail to Calle Las Violetas No 2, Urb. Brisas del Canal, Bani) Juan José Natera Tel. 809-727-0765

Bani Iglesia Episcopal **San Antonio de Padua** Calle Principal No 80, Carretón, Bani (Correo a Calle principal No 80, Carretón, Bani) Juan José Natera Tel. 809-727-0765.

Bani Iglesia Episcopal **San Bernabé** Calle Princiapal Barrio Pizarrete (Mail to Calle Sánchez No 73, Santana D.M. Nizao) Jose M. Abreu Tel. 809-789-9049

Bani Iglesia Episcopal **San Timoteo** Calle Mella No 60, Nizao (Mail to Calle Sánchez No 73, Santana D.M.) Nizao José M. Abreu Tel. 809-789-9049

Bani Iglesia Episcopal **San Matías** Calle Sánchez Vieja No 73, Santana, Nizao (Mail to Calle Sánchez Vieja No 73, Santana, Nizao) Jose M. Abreu Tel. 809-789-9049

Bani Iglesia Episcopal **El Santo Nombre** Calle Altos de los Melones, Catalina, Bani (Mail to Las Violetas No 1, Bani) Juan J Natera Tel. 829-466-8177

Barahona Iglesia Episcopal **Jesús Peregrino** Calle Primera Los Blocks, Batey Central (Correo a Calle Tony Mota Ricart, Esq. Bomba Texaco, Barahona) Jac Marc. Tel. 829-643-2407.

Barahona Iglesia Episcopal **La Redención** Calle Tony Mota Ricart, Esq. Bomba Texaco, Barahona (Correo a Calle Tony Mota Ricart, Esq. Bomba Texaco, Barahona) Jac Marc Tel. 829-643-2407.

Bonao Iglesia Episcopal **San Juan Bautista** Calle Padre Billini No 116, Bonao (Mail to Las Orquídeas No 11, Reside. Mónica VI, Bonao) J Roberts Tel. 809-624-7074

Consuelo, Iglesia Episcopal **San Gabriel** Calle Duarte No 1, Box 70, San Pedro de Macorís (e-mail to Calle Duarte No 1, Box 70, San Pedro de Macorís) Bileisy Díaz Tel. 809-373-9129

Consuelo Misión **La Gran Comisión** Calle Hato Mayor, Batey Doña Lila, Consuelo, San Pedro de Macorís (Mail to Calle Hato Mayor, Batey Doña Lila, Consuelo, San P. Macorís) Bileisy Díaz Tel. 809-373-9129

Dajabon Iglesia Episcopal **Espíritu Consolador** Calle Capotillo No 90, Dajabon (Mail to Calle Capotillo No 90, Dajabon) Jesus Mosquea Tel. 829-879-8996

Gautier Iglesia Episcopal **Santo Tomas** Calle 1era No 7, Gautier (Mail to Calle 1era. No 7, Gautier) Isaac Emilio Pringle. Tel. 809

Guerra Iglesia Episcopal **Divina Providencia** Calle Marcos de Rosario No 39, San Antonio de Guerra (Mail to Calle Marcos del Rosario No 39, San Antonio de Guerra) Alfredo Romero Tel. 829-497-3145

Haina Iglesia Episcopal **San Marcos** Calle Av. Central Rio No 46, Haina (Correo a Central Rio No 46, Haina) Félix Encarnación Tel. 809-764- 1327

Haina Iglesia Episcopal **San Juan Evangelista** Calle Tercera No 25, Barrio Piedra Blanca, Haina (Mail to Calle Tercera No 25, Barrio Piedra Blanca, Haina) Félix Encarnación Tel 809-764- 1327

Hato Mayor Iglesia Episcopal **San Mateo** Batey Jalonga (Correo a: Batey Jalonga, Hato Mayor) Bileisy Díaz Tel. 809-373-9129

Hato Mayor del Rey Iglesia Episcopal **Cristo Libertador** Calle Las Mercedes No 66, Hato Mayor (Mail to Calle Las Mercedes No 66, Hato Mayor) Bileysis Diaz.Tel. 809-373-9129

Jarabacoa Iglesia Episcopal **Monte de la Transfiguración** Calle El Pedregal Abajo Jarabacoa (Mail to Calle Santiago No 114 Gazcue, Santo Domingo) Ramon Canela Tel 809-667-7643

Jimani Iglesia Episcopal **San Pablo Apóstol** Calle Mella, Barrio 50, Jimani (Mail to Calle Mella No 50, Jimani) Divina Matos Tel. 829-364-3982.

Jimani Iglesia Episcopal **San Tito** Boca de Cachón, Jimani (Mail a Calle Mella No 50 Jimani) Daniel Samuel Tel. 809-757-8189

Jimani Iglesia Episcopal **San Ignacio** Calle Segunda Tierra Nueva, Jimani (Mail to Calle Segunda Tierra Nueva, Jimani) Divina Matos Tel. 829-364-3982.

La Caleta, Boca Chica Iglesia Episcopal **De la Gracia** Calle Principal, Barrio Paraíso No 25, La Caleta (Mail to Calle Principal, Barrio Paraíso No 25, La Caleta, Boca Chica) Alfredo Romero.Teléfono 829-497-3145.

La Romana Iglesia Episcopal **Todos los Santos** Calle Dr. Ferry No 75, La Romana (Mail to Calle Dr. Ferry No 75, Apdo. 215, La Romana) Juan Rosario. Tel. 849-352-6649

La Romana Iglesia Episcopal **La Encarnación** Calle Sector Invi, La Romana, (Mail to Calle Sector Invi, La Romana) Juan Rosario Tel. 809 352-6649

La Vega Iglesia Episcopal **Cristo Resucitado** Calle La Riviera No 2, (Mail to: Calle La Riviera No 2, La Vega) Ramon Ant. Garcia Tel. 809-973-6989

Mao, Valverde Iglesia Episcopal **Santa María Llena de Gracia** Calle Constitución No 1, Mao Valverde (Mail to Calle Constitución No 1 Mao) Domingo Rodriguez. Tel. 809-678-7451

Puerto Plata Iglesia Episcopal **Cristo Rey** Calle Sánchez No 21, Esq. José del C. Ariza, Puerto Plata (Mail to Calle Sánchez No 21, Esq. José

correcciones, véase p. 71 del C. Ariza, Puerto Plata) Raul Guaillas Tel. 829-343-2366

Puerto Plata Iglesia Episcopal **San Simón Apóstol** Calle Los Rieles No 1 Barrio San Marcos, Puerto Plata (Mail to Calle Los Rieles No 1, Barrio San Marcos, Puerto Plata) Raul Guaillas Teléfono 829-343-2366

Puerto Plata Iglesia Episcopal **San Francisco de Asís** Calle Las Avispas, Maimón, Puerto Plata (Mail to Las Avispas, Maimón, Puerto Plata) Raúl Guaillas Tel. 829-343-2366

Puerto Plata Iglesia Episcopal **Jesús Mesías** en Imbert, Puerto Plata (Correo a Imbert, Puerto Plata Raúl Guaillas Tel. 829-343-2366

Puerto Plata Iglesia Episcopal **Santa María Virgen** Calle Principal, Barrio Invi-CEA No 36, Monte Llano (Mail to Calle Principal, Barrio Invi-CEA No 36, Monte Llano Ercilia Peralta Tel. 809-545-9280

Puerto Plata Iglesia Episcopal **Divina Gracia** Calle Principal, Mozovi, Puerto Plata (Mail to Calle Principal, Mozovi, Puerto Plata) Pedro Hernández. Tel. 829-720-7724.

Puerto Plata Iglesia Episcopal **San Cornelio** Calle Callejón La Colina, Cabarete, Puerto Plata (Mail to Callejón La Colina, Cabarete, Puerto plata Pedro Hernández Tel. 829-720-7724.

San Cristóbal Iglesia Episcopal **San Bartolomé** Calle Segunda No 3, Barrio Las Flores, San Cristóbal (Mail to Calle Segunda No 3, Barrio Las Flores, San Cristóbal) Carlos Santana Tel. 849- 408-2880

San Cristóbal Iglesia Episcopal **San Miguel** Calle Andrés Bremo, Doña Ana, San Cristóbal (Mail to Calle Andrés Bremo, Doña Ana, San Cristóbal) Carlos Santana Tel. 849-408-2880

✠ **San Francisco de Macorís** Iglesia Episcopal **El Buen Samaritano**, Calle Cesar Agosto Sandino No 8, Barrio San Martin de Porres (Mail to: Calle Cesar Agosto Sandino No 8, Barrio San Martin de Porres, San Fco. De Macorís) Alvaro Yepes.809-268-5423.

San Francisco de Macorís Iglesia Episcopal **Jesús Nazareno** Calle La Cruz No 26, Esq. Ing. Guzmán Abreu, (Mail to: Calle La Cruz No 26, San Francisco de Macorís) Alvaro Yepes. Teléfono 809-268-5423

San Pedro de Macorís Iglesia Episcopal **Santa Cruz,** Calle Salvador Ross, Santa Fe (Correo a: Calle Salvador Ross, Santa Fe, San P. de Macorís) JheraceFleuravil. Tel. 829-215-5657

San Pedro de Macorís Iglesia Episcopal **Santiago Apóstol** Calle Principal, Ingenio Angelina (Mail a: Calle Principal, Ingenio Angelina, San Pedro de Macorís) J Nephtaly Tel. 809-441-0250

San Pedro de Macorís Iglesia Episcopal **El Buen Pastor** Calle Dra. Ana Betances, Barrio Las Flores (Mail to: Calle Dra. Ana Betances, Barrio Las Flores, San P. Macorís) Jonhson Pringle Tel. 829-962-0275.

San Pedro de Macorís Iglesia Episcopal **San Esteban** Calle Sánchez No 9, Miramar, Apdo.128 (Mail to: Calle Sánchez No 9, Miramar Apdo.128, San Pedro de Macorís) Milquella Mendoza Tel. 809-396-5101

San Pedro de Macorís Iglesia Episcopal **San Pedro Apóstol** Los Conucos, Juan Dolio, San P. Macorís (Correo a Los Conucos, Juan Dolio, San Pedro de Macorís) Nimio Hernández Tel. 809-451- 3002.

Santiago Iglesia Episcopal **Cristo Salvador** Calle Proyecto No 52, Mirador del Yaquez, La Yaguita del Pastor (Mail to: Calle Proyecto No 52, Mirador del Yaquez, La Yaguita del Pastor, Santiago) Ercilia Peralta. Tel. 809-545-9280.

Santiago Iglesia Episcopal **San Lucas** Calle Cuba No 128, (Mail a: Calle Cuba No 128, Santiago) Lorenzo Gómez Tel. 829-962-0504

Santiago Iglesia Episcopal **La Anunciación** Calle 6 Esq. Calle 3 No 16, Llanos de Gurabo (Mail to: Calle 6 Esq. Calle 3 No 16 Llanos de Gurabo, Santiago) Ramón Ant. García Tel. 809-973-6989

Santiago Iglesia Episcopal **Jesús Maestro** Tamboril (Correo a: Tamboril Santiago) Nelly Martínez. Teléfono 829-930-6960.

Santo Domingo Catedral Iglesia **Episcopal de la Epifanía** calle Av. Independencia No 253, Gazcue (Mail a: Av. Independencia No 253, Gazcue, Santo Domingo) Sandino Sanchez. Decano Epifania Tel. 809-689-2070

Santo Domingo Iglesia Episcopal **San Andrés** Calle Marcos Ruiz No 26, Villa Juana (Mail to: Calle Marcos Ruiz No 26, Villa Juana Santo Domingo) Estiven Porton. Tel. 829-587-4948.

Santo Domingo Iglesia Episcopal **San Felipe Apóstol Bienvenido Lopez.** Manzana C No 1 Invi Sabana Perdida (Mail. to: Apdo. 764) Diego Sabogal Tel. 829-771-3367

Santo Domingo Iglesia Episcopal **San Pedro y San Pablo** Calle Valera No 60 La Barquita Sabana Perdida (Mail to: Apto 764) Bienvenido Lopez. Fumero Tel. 849-402-6959.

Santo Domingo Este Iglesia Episcopal **Santísima Trinidad** Calle Costa Rica No 21, Ensanche Ozama (Mail to: Calle Costa Rica No 21, Ens. Ozama, Santo Domingo Este) Diego Sabogal. Teléfono 829-771-3367.

Santo Domingo Este Iglesia Episcopal **Sagrada Familia** Calle 4 de Agosto casi Esq. San Vicente de Paul, Los Mina (Mail to: Apdo. 764) Juan Sheen Tel. 809-543-2560

Santo Domingo Este Iglesia Episcopal **Santa Margarita** Calle Orlando Martínez y Alonso Pérez Solares del Almirante (Mail to: Apdo. 764) Cruz Méndez Roberto Castro Tel. 809-530-8289

Santo Domingo Este Iglesia Episcopal **Santa Ana** Calle 1era. Buenaventura, Barrio Mendoza Roberto Castro. Tel. 829-808-5571

DIOCESE OF EAST CAROLINA
(PROVINCE IV)
Comprises eastern North Carolina
DIOCESAN OFFICE 705 Doctors Drive Kinston NC 28501 (MAIL: Box 1336, Kinston, NC 28503)
TEL (252) 522-0885 FAX (252) 523-5272
WEB www.diocese-eastcarolina.org

Previous Bishops—
Alfred A Watson 1884-1905, Robert Strange coadj 1904 Bp 1905-14, Thomas C Darst 1915-45, Thomas H Wright 1945-73, Hunley A Elebash 1973-83, B Sidney Sanders 1979-1997 Clifton Daniel coadj 1996 Bp 1997-2013, Peter James Lee Bp Prov (2013-2014)

Bishop—Rt Rev Robert Stuart Skirving (Dio 8 November 2014)

Stand Comm—Cler: P Stringer J Day P Canady *Lay:* D Trivette J Parrott T Holt

PARISHES, MISSIONS, AND CLERGY

Ahoskie Church of St Thomas **P** (138) PO Box 263 27910-0263 (Mail to: PO Box 263 27910-0263) (252) 332-3263

Bath St Thomas Episcopal Church **P** (128) 101 Craven St 27808-9789 (Mail to: PO Box 257 27808-0257) Copeland Johnston (252) 923-9141

Beaufort St Pauls Episcopal Church **P** (639) 215 Ann St 28516-2103 (Mail to: 215 Ann St 28516-2103) Tambria Lee Ashley Simpson (252) 728-3324

Belhaven St James Episcopal Church **P** (46) 545 E Main St NC 27810-1547 (Mail to: 545 E Main St 27810-1547) (252) 943-6977

Burgaw St Marys Episcopal Church **P** (54) 506 S Mcneil St 28425-5036 (Mail to: PO Box 841 28425-0841) (910) 259-5541

Chocowinity Trinity Episcopal Church **P** (115) 182 NC Highway 33 W 27817 (Mail to: PO Box 332 27817-0332) Stephen Batten (252) 946-9958

Clinton St Pauls Episcopal Church **P** (127) 110 W Main St 28328-4047 (Mail to: 110 W Main St 28328-4047) Eric Grubb (910) 592-3220

Columbia St Andrews Episcopal Church **P** (17) 106 N Road St 27925-8350 (Mail to: PO Box 615 27925-0615) (252) 441-8542

Creswell Christ Episcopal Church **M** (10) 100 S 6th St 27928-8960 (Mail to: Mr. William H. Peal Sixth Street 27928) (252) 482-8581

Creswell Galilee Mission / Lake Phelps **M** (3) 323 Park Rd 27928-9803 (Mail to: Lake Phelps 27928) (252) 441-8542

Currituck St Lukes Episcopal Mission **M** (64) 2864 Caratoke Hwy 27929-9611 Hubert McGee (252) 435-0530

Edenton Saint Paul's Episcopal Church **P** (472) 101 W Gale St 27932-1815 (Mail to: PO Box 548 27932-0548) William Thomas (252) 482-3522

Elizabeth City Christ Episcopal Church **P** (251) 200 S Mcmorrine St 27909-4831 (Mail to: 200 S McMorrine St 27909-4831) Daniel Cenci John Horner Edward Mullins (252) 338-1686

Elizabethtown St Christophers Episcopal Ch **P** (29) 2606 W Broad St 28337-9031 (Mail to: PO Box 1841 28337-1841) (910) 879-2777

Engelhard St Georges Episcopal Church **P** (65) PO Box 101 31655 Hwy 264 27824 (Mail to: PO Box 101 27824-0101) James Lupton (252) 943-6318

Farmville Emmanuel Episcopal Church **P** (27) 3505 S Walnut St 27828-1658 (Mail to: 3505 South Walnut St PO Box 48 27828-1698) (252) 753-3737

Fayetteville Church of the Good Shepherd **P** (15) PO Box 64008 28306-0008 (Mail to: PO Box 64008 28306-0008) (910) 323-1512

Fayetteville Holy Trinity Episcopal Church **P** (674) 1601 Raeford Rd 28305-5031 (Mail to: Attn: Financial Secretary 1601 Raeford Rd 28305-5097) Nancee Cekuta Joseph Running (910) 484-2134

Fayetteville St Johns Episcopal Church **P** (819) 302 Green St 28301-5028 (Mail to: PO Box 722 28302-0722) Robert Alves (910) 483-7405

Fayetteville St Josephs Episcopal Church **P** (51) 509 Ramsey St 28301-4911 (Mail to: PO Box 694 28302-0694) (910) 323-0161

Fayetteville St Pauls in the Pines Epis Ch **P** (144) 1800 Saint Paul Ave 28304-5238 (Mail to: 1800 Saint Paul Ave 28304-5238) (910) 485-7098

Gatesville St Marys Episcopal Church **P** (28) Attn: Edith Bridger PO Box 174 27938-0174 (Mail to: Attn: Edith Bridger PO Box 174 27938-0174) (252) 794-3277

Goldsboro St Andrews Episcopal Church **P** (25) 901 Harris St. 27530-6666 (Mail to: PO Box 1333 27533-1333) (919) 734-0550

Goldsboro St Francis Episcopal Church **P** (99) 503 Forest Hill Drive 27534-1824 (Mail to: PO Box 11406 27532-1406) (919) 735-9845

Goldsboro Saint Stephen's Church **P** (332) 200 North James Street 27530-3631 (Mail to: PO Box 984 27533-0984) (919) 734-4263

Greenville St Pauls Episcopal Church **P** (1056) 401 E 4th St 27858-1916 (Mail to: 401 E 4th St 27858-1916) K Drew Baker Andrew Cannan Skip Walker (252) 752-3482

Greenville St Timothy's Episcopal Church **P** (230) 107 Louis St 27858-8660 (Mail to: 107 Louis St 27858-8660) John Porter-Acee John Robertson (252) 355-2125

Grifton St John Episcopal Church **P** (21) 2016 Price-Cannon Road 28530 (Mail to: PO Box 937 28530-0937) (252) 524-5860

Hampstead Holy Trinity Episcopal Church **P** (80) 107 Deerfield Dr 28443-2135 (Mail to: 107 Deerfield Dr 28443-2135) Ronald Abrams (910) 270-4221

Havelock St Christophers Episcopal Ch **P** (42) 1000 E Main St 28532-2317 (Mail to: PO Box 626 28532-0626) Mary Ogus (252) 447-3912

Hertford Holy Trinity Episcopal Church **P** (134) 207 S Church St 27944-1113 (Mail to: PO Box 125 27944-0125) Robert Beauchamp (910) 270-4221

Holly Ridge St Philips Episcopal Church **P** (43) 661 Tar Landing Rd 28445-7671 (Mail to: PO Box 155 28445-0155) (910) 329-1514

Jacksonville St Annes Episcopal Church **P** (255) § 711 Henderson Dr 28540-4477 (Mail to: 711 Henderson Dr 28540-4477) Cynthia Duffus (910) 347-3774

Kinston St Augustines Episcopal Church **P** (22) 707 E Lenoir Ave 28502 (Mail to: PO Box 2263 28502-2263) (252) 523-4032

Kinston St Marys Episcopal Church **P** (339) 800 Rountree Ave 28501-3655 (Mail to: 800 Rountree Ave 28501-3655) Thomas Warren (252) 523-6146

Leland All Souls Episcopal Church **P** (31) 5087 Blue Banks Loop Rd NE 28451-4009 (Mail to: PO Box 475 28456-0475) Fanny Belanger (910) 655-8935

Lewiston Grace Episcopal Church **P** (14) PO Box 537 27849-0537 (Mail to: PO Box 429 27849-0429) (252) 322-1004

Lumberton Trinity Episcopal Church **P** (372) 1202 N Chestnut St 28358-4713 (Mail to: 1202 N Chestnut St 28358-4713) (910) 739-3717

Morehead City St Andrew's Church **P** (261) 3003 Bridges St 28557-3329 (Mail to: 2005 Arendell St 28557-3999) John Pollock (252) 727-9093

Nags Head Ch of St Andrews by the Sea **P** (292) 4212 S Virginia Dare Trl 27959-9284 (Mail to: PO Box 445 27959-0445) Nathan Finnin Edward Mullins (252) 441-5382

New Bern Christ Episcopal Church **P** (1017) 320 Pollock St 28560-4945 (Mail to: PO Box 1246 28563-1246) Hoyt Canady (252) 633-2109

New Bern St Cyprians Episcopal Church **P** (26) 604 Johnson St 28563 (Mail to: PO Box 809 28563-0809) (252) 633-3816

Newton Grove Iglesia de Sagrada Familia **M** (524) 2989 Easy St 28334-7994 (Mail to: 2989 Easy Street 28334) Marilyn Mitchell (919) 658-1819

Oriental St Thomas Episcopal Church **P** (97) 402 Freemason St 28571-9206 (Mail to: PO Box 461 28571-0461) Bruce Cheney Paul Andersen (252) 249-0256

Plymouth Grace Episcopal Church **P** (46) 107 Madison St 27962-1432 (Mail to: 106 Madison St 27962-1432) Henry Burdick (252) 793-3295

Roper St Lukes & St Annes Epis Ch **P** (26) 206 S Bank St 27970-9181 (Mail to: PO Box 85 27970-0085) (252) 793-3295

Salter Path St Francis by the Sea **P** (201) 920 Salter Path Rd 28512-5938 (Mail to: 920 Salter Path Rd 28512-5938) Leonard Thomas James Sproul (252) 240-2388

Seven Springs Church of the Holy Innocents **P** (90) 6861 Hwy 55 W 28578-9493 (Mail to: 6861 Hwy 55 W 28578-9493) (252) 569-3011

Shallotte St James the Fisherman Church **P** (319) 4941 Main St 28470-4503 (Mail to: PO Box 68 28459-0068) Farrell Graves Jean Miller (910) 754-9313

Southern Shores All Saints Episcopal Church **P** (239) 40 Pintail Trl 27949-3847 (Mail to: 40 Pintail Trl 27949-3847) Cynthia Simpson (252) 261-6674

Southport St Philips Episcopal Church **P** (578) 205 E Moore St 28461-3927 (Mail to: PO Box 10476 28461-0476) Lisa Erdeljon Eric Mills Henrietta Williams (910) 457-5643

Sunbury St Peters Episcopal Church **P** (26) 61 Nc Highway 32 N 27979-9447 (Mail to: PO Box 153 27979-0153) (252) 326-4757

Swansboro St Peters by the Sea Church **P** (225) PO Box 337 28584 (Mail to: PO Box 337 28584-0337) (910) 326-4757

Trenton Grace Episcopal Church **P** (9) PO Box 126 28585-0126 (Mail to: PO Box 126 28585-0126) (252) 448-3241

Washington St Peters Episcopal Church **HC** (571) § 101 N Bonner St 27889-5016 (Mail to: PO Box 985 27889-0985) Christopher Adams (252) 946-8151

Washington Zion Episcopal Church **P** (48) 7322 U.S. Hwy. 264 E 27889-9802 (Mail to: PO Box 1329 27889-1329) Alan Neale (252) 927-9466

Whiteville Grace Episcopal Church **P** (56) 105 S Madison St 28472-4119 (Mail to: 105 S Madison St 28472-4119) (910) 642-4724

Williamston Church of the Advent **P** (98) 124 W Church St 27892-2402 (Mail to: PO Box 463 27892-0463) (252) 792-2244

Wilmington Church of the Good Shepherd **P** (62) 515 Queen St 28401-5243 (Mail to: PO Box 928 28402-0928) (910) 763-6080

Wilmington Church of the Servant **P** (572) 4925 Oriole Dr 28403-1759 (Mail to: Attn: Janet Autry 4925 Oriole Dr 28403-1759) Jody Greenwood (910) 395-0616

Wilmington Holy Cross Episcopal Church **P** (171) 5820 Myrtle Grove Rd 28409-4322 (Mail to: 5820 Myrtle Grove Rd 28409-4322) Lurena Abdy (910) 799-6347

Wilmington St Andrews on-the-Sound Church **P** (857) 101 Arlie Road 28403 (Mail to: 101 Arlie Rd 28403-3701) Richard Elliott (910) 256-3034

Wilmington St James Episcopal Church **P** (1261) 25 S 3rd St 28401-4530 (Mail to: 25 S 3rd St

28401-4595) Claude Craig Cheryl Brainard (910) 763-1628

Wilmington St John Episcopal Church **P** (436) 1219 Forest Hills Dr 28403-2555 (Mail to: 1219 Forest Hills Dr 28403-2555) Eric Moulton (910) 762-5273

Wilmington St Mark Episcopal Church **P** (71) 600 Grace St 28401-4127 (Mail to: 600 Grace

St 28401-4127) Victor Frederiksen (910) 763-3858

Wilmington St Pauls Church **P** (364) 16 N 16th St 28401-4905 (Mail to: 16 N 16th St 28401-4905) Victor Frederiksen Caleb Lee (910) 762-4578

Windsor St Thomas Episcopal Church **P** (126) 302 S Queen St 27983-6728 (Mail to: PO Box 400 27983-0400) (252) 794-3420

DIOCESE OF EAST TENNESSEE
(PROVINCE IV)
Comprises the eastern third of the State of Tennessee
DIOCESAN OFFICE 814 Episcopal School Way Knoxville TN 37932
TEL (865) 966-2110 FAX (865) 966-2535
E-MAIL editor@dioet.org WEB http://dioet.org

Previous Bishops—
Wm E Sanders 1985-91, Robert G Tharp 1992-99; Charles G von Rosenberg 1999-2011; George D Young III 2011-17

Bishop—Rt Rev Brian L Cole (Dio 02 December 2017)

Cn to Ord Rev M Bolt; *Archdcn* Rev J Askew; *Sec* J Humber; *Treas* John Hicks; *Asst Treas* J Anderson; *Chanc* G Arrants Esq; *Comm* A Morehead; *Yth* C Wood; *Cn for Mission & Lay Min* B Hurley Hill; *Dio Admin* M Embler; *Com* Revs D Hill and A Bradley

Stand Comm—Cler: Pres A Berends J Calhoun K Saunders; *Lay:* D Sanders Sr M Everett C Sjoberg

PARISHES, MISSIONS, AND CLERGY

Athens St Pauls Episcopal Church **P** (249) 123 S Jackson St 37303-4710 (Mail to: C/O Kathy Clark PO Box 326 37371-0326) Alice Brown (423) 745-2224

Battle Creek St John the Baptist **P** (39) 12757 Ladds Cove Rd 37380 (Mail to: 335 Tennessee Ave 37383-2001) (931) 598-9546

Bristol St Columbas Episcopal Church **P** (129) 607 Greenfield Pl 37620-6124 (Mail to: 607 Greenfield Pl # 17 37620-6124) (423) 764-2251

Chattanooga Christ Church Episcopal Chattanooga **P** (172) 663 Douglas St 37403-2015 (Mail to: 661 Douglas St 37403-2005) Harry Lawrence (423) 2664263

Chattanooga Grace Episcopal Church **P** (551) 20 Belvoir Ave 37411-4501 (Mail to: 20 Belvoir Ave 37411-4599) April Berends (423) 698-2433

Chattanooga St Martin of Tours Epis Church **P** (580) 7547 E Brainerd Rd 37421-3166 (Mail to: PO Box 21275 37424-0275) (423) 892-9131

Chattanooga Saint Paul's Episcopal Church **P** (1406) 305 W 7th St 37402-1717 (Mail to:

305 W 7th St 37402-1787) Bradford Whitaker (423) 266-8195

Chattanooga St Peter's Episcopal Church **P** (304) 848 Ashland Ter 37415-3538 (Mail to: C/O Parish Administrator 848 Ashland Ter 37415-3538) Fritz Parman (423) 877-2428

Chattanooga St Thaddaeus Episcopal Church **P** (106) 4300 Locksley Ln 37416-2908 (Mail to: PO Box 16305 37416-0305) Robert Hartmans (423) 892-2377

Chattanooga Thankful Memorial Church **P** (143) 1607 W 43rd St 37409-1344 (Mail to: PO Box 2274 37409-0274) Leyla King (423) 821-3135

Cleveland St Lukes Episcopal Church **P** (676) 320 Broad St NW 37311-5038 (Mail to: PO Box 5 37364-0005) Joel Huffstetler (423) 476541

Copperhill St Marks Episcopal Church **P** (60) 124 West Hill Street 37317-0576 (Mail to: PO Box 579 37317-0579) Erik Broeren (423) 496-4681

Crossville St Raphaels Episcopal Church **P** (229) 1038 Sparta Hwy 38572-5746 (Mail to: 1038 Sparta Hwy 38572-5746) Felicity Peck Thomas Schneider (931) 484-2407

Elizabethton St Thomas Church **P** (129) 815 E 2nd St 37643-2324 (Mail to: 815 North Second Street 37644) (423) 543-3081

Ft Oglethorp Episcopal Ch of the Nativity **P** (121) 1201 Cross St 30742-3230 (Mail to: PO Box 2356 30742-2356) Robert Thompson Jason Clark (706) 866-9773

Gatlinburg Trinity Episcopal Church **P** (74) 509 Historic Nature Trail 37738-0055 (Mail to: PO Box 55 37738-0055) Barbara Harper (865) 436-4721

Greeneville St James Episcopal Church **P** (165) 107 W Church St 37745-3803 (Mail to: 107 W Church St 37745-3803) Kenneth Saunders (423) 638-6583

Harriman St Andrews Episcopal Church **P** (79) 190 Circle Dr 37748-7304 (Mail to: 190 Circle Dr 37748-7304) Stephen Jones (865) 882-1272

Hixson St Albans Episcopal Church **P** (121) 7514 Hixson Pike 37343-1721 (Mail to: 7514 Hixson Pike 37343-1721) Robert Hartmans (423) 842-1342

Jefferson City St Barnabas Episcopal Lutheran **P** (27) 807 E Ellis St 37760-2526 (Mail to: 807 E Ellis St 37760-2526) (865) 397-3678985

Johnson City St Johns Episcopal Church **P** (424) 500 N Roan St 37601-4741 (Mail to: 500 N Roan St 37601-4717) Laura Bryant (423) 926-8141

Jonesborough St Mary the Virgin Epis Church **PS** (19) 109 S 2nd Ave 37659-1105 (Mail to: PO Box 273 37659-1105) (423) 753-2350

Kingsport St Christophers Episcopal Ch **P** (74) 584 Lebanon Rd 37663-2908 (Mail to: 584 Lebanon Rd 37663-2908) Jonathan Hermes (423) 239-6751

Kingsport St Pauls Episcopal Church **P** (258) 161 E Ravine Rd 37660-3807 (Mail to: 161 E Ravine Rd 37660-3839) Jonathan Tuttle Christopher Harpster (423) 245-5187

Kingsport St Timothys Episcopal Church **P** (41) 2152 Hawthorne St 37664-3563 (Mail to: PO Box 3248 37664-0248) Richard Shackleford Jonathan Hermes (423) 247-3992

Knoxville Episcopal Ch of the Ascension **P** (1149) 800 S Northshore Dr 37919 (Mail to: 800 S Northshore Dr 37919-7592) William Daniel Christopher Hogin Caroline Vogel (865) 588-0589

Knoxville Church of the Good Samaritan **P** (768) 425 N Cedar Bluff Rd 37923-3600 (Mail to: 425 N Cedar Bluff Rd 37923-3600) Joseph Calhoun (865) 6939591

Knoxville Church of the Good Shepherd **P** (262) 5409 Jacksboro Pike 37918-3330 (Mail to: PO Box 5104 37928-0104) Dorothy Pratt Richard Carter (865) 687-9420

Knoxville St Elizabeths Episcopal Church **P** (317) 110 Sugarwood Dr 37922-4662 (Mail to: 110 Sugarwood Dr 37934-4662) Brett Backus (865) 675-0450

✠ **Knoxville** St Johns Episcopal Cathedral **O** (1201) 413 Cumberland Ave 37902-2302 (Mail to: PO Box 153 37901-0153) John Ross Christopher Hackett Thomas Rasnick (865) 525-7347

Knoxville St Lukes Episcopal Church **P** (31) 600 S Chestnut St 37914-5829 (Mail to: 600 S Chestnut St 37914-5829) Kay Reynolds (865) 522-4244

Knoxville St James Episcopal Church **P** (433) 1101 N Broadway St 37917-6528 (Mail to: 1101 N Broadway St 37917-6592) John Wiggers Kirk Lafon Robert Powell (865) 523-5687

La Follette St Clare Episcopal Church **P** (41) 1720 Jacksboro Pike 37766-3226 (Mail to: 1720 Jacksboro Pike 37766-3226) (423) 566-6707

Lookout Mtn Church of the Good Shepherd **P** (948) § 211 Franklin Rd 37350-1223 (Mail to: 211 Franklin Rd 37350-1223) Robert Childers Janice Robbins (423) 821-1583

Loudon Epis Ch of the Resurrection **P** (137) 917 Pond Rd 37774-6401 (Mail to: 917 Pond Rd 37774-6401) Amy Morehous (865) 986-2390

Maryville St Andrews Church **P** (330) 314 W Broadway Ave 37801-4708 (Mail to: 314 W Broadway Ave 37801-4708) Amy Bradley (865) 983-3512

Morristown All Saints Episcopal Church **P** (493) 601 W Main St 37814-4508 (Mail to: 601 W Main St 37814-4508) (423) 586-6201

Newport Church of the Annunciation **P** (65) 304 Cosby Hwy 37821-2913 (Mail to: PO Box 337 37822-0337) (423) 625-1864

Norris Saint Francis' Church **P** (261) 158 W Norris Rd 37828 (Mail to: Frances Oates PO Box 29 37828-0029) Amanda Lippe Harry Minarik Harry Minarik (865) 494-7167

Oak Ridge St Stephens Episcopal Church **P** (468) 212 N Tulane Ave 37830-6308 (Mail to: 212 N Tulane Ave 37830-6308) Lynn Norman Patricia Reuss (865) 483-8497

Ooltewah St Francis of Assisi Epis Ch **P** (157) 7555 Ooltewah Georgetown Rd 37363-9582 (Mail to: 7555 Ooltewah Georgetown Rd 37363-9582) Martha Tucker-Parsons Joshua Weaver (423) 238-7708

Rugby Christ Church **P** (57) 1332 Rugby Parkway 37733-0025 (Mail to: PO Box 25 37733-0002) (423) 628-5627

S Pittsburg Christ Episcopal Church **P** (113) 302 3rd St 37380-1318 (Mail to: PO Box 347 37380-0347) Kim Hobby (423) 837-7715

Sevierville St Joseph the Carpenter **P** (158) 345 Hardin Ln 37862-4507 (Mail to: 345 Hardin Ln 37862-4507) Paige Buchholz (865) 453-0943

Seymour St Pauls Episcopal Church **PS** (105) 1028 Boyds Creek Hwy 37865-4532 (Mail to: PO Box 907 37865-0907) (865) 577-1255

Signal Mtn St Timothys Episcopal Church **P** (735) 630 Mississippi Ave 37377-2293 (Mail to: 630 Mississippi Ave 37377-2293) Derrick Hill Taylor Dinsmore (423) 886-2281

DIOCESE OF EASTERN MICHIGAN
(PROVINCE V)
Comprises the eastern portion of the lower peninsula of Michigan
DIOCESAN OFFICE 924 N Niagara St Saginaw MI 48602
TEL (989) 752-6020 FAX (989) 752-6120
E-MAIL diocese@eastmich.org WEB www.eastmich.org

Previous Bishops—
Edwin M Leidel Jr 1996-2006; S Todd Ousley 2006-17; Cate Waynick 2017-19 (provisional); Whayne Hougland (provisional) 2019-20; Prince Singh (provisional) 2022

Bps Admin Asst A Krueger; *Financial Mgr* S Philo; *Treas* B Chace; *Chanc* W Fleener; *Cn to Ord* Rev Cn T Little; *Cn for Evangelism* K Forsyth; *Camp Dir and Yth and Young Adult* M Knill; *School Dir* Rev Dr T Little

Stand Comm—Cler: Pres A Kubbe B Ilkka D Davidson; *Lay:* J Lasley N Hargreaves G Geraghty

PARISHES, MISSIONS, AND CLERGY

Alma St John Episcopal Church **P** (23) PO Box 605 48801-0605 (Mail to: PO Box 605 48801-0605) (989) 752-6020

Alpena Trinity Episcopal Church **P** (185) 124 E Washington Ave 49707-2837 (Mail to: 124 E Washington Ave 49707-2869) Daniel Maxwell (989) 752-6020

Atlanta St Marks Episcopal Mission **P** (72) 11847 M 33 N 48638 (Mail to: 11847 M-33 49709) (989) 752-6020

Bad Axe St Pauls Episcopal Church **P** (59) 139 W Huron Ave 48413-1102 (Mail to: 139 W Huron Ave 48413-1102) Thomas Manney (989) 752-6020

Bay City St Albans Episcopal Church **P** (170) 105 S Erie St 48706-4431 (Mail to: 105 S Erie St 48706-4599) Nancy Mayhew Sharon Voelker (989) 752-6020

Bay City Trinity Episcopal Church **P** (205) 815 N Grant St 48708-5006 (Mail to: C/O Patrick Gray 815 N Grant St 48708-5006) Susan Rich (989) 892-5813

Cheboygan St James Church **P** (92) 202 S Huron St 49721-1920 (Mail to: PO Box 253 49721-0253) (989) 752-6020

Corunna St Paul Episcopal Church **P** (32) 111 S Shiawassee St 48817-1357 (Mail to: PO Box 87 48817-0087) (989) 752-6020

Davison St Dunstans Episcopal Church **P** (60) 1523 N Oak Rd 48423-9101 (Mail to: 1523 N Oak Rd 48423-9101) Sue Colavincenzo (810) 875-0541

Dryden St Johns Episcopal Church **P** (39) 4074 S Mill Rd 48428-9233 (Mail to: PO Box 86 48428-0086) Thomas Manney (989) 752-6020

East Tawas Christ Episcopal Church **P** (74) 202 W Westover St 48730-1238 (Mail to: 202 W Westover St 48730-1238) (989) 752-6020

Fenton St Judes Episcopal Church **P** (266) 106 E Elizabeth St 48430-2322 (Mail to: 106 E Elizabeth St 48430-2322) Paul Brunell (810) 629-5681

Flint St Andrews Episcopal Church **P** (163) 1922 Iowa Ave 48506-3539 (Mail to: C/O Patti Gantz 1922 Iowa Ave 48506-3539) Jay Gantz (989) 752-6020

Flint St Pauls Episcopal Church **P** (345) 711 S Saginaw St 48502-1507 (Mail to: 711 S Saginaw St 48502-1589) Donald Davidson Donald Davidson (810) 234-8637

Flushing Trinity Episcopal Church **P** (37) 745 E Main St 48433-2009 (Mail to: 745 E Main St 48433-2009) (989) 752-6020

Gaylord St Andrews Episcopal Church **P** (73) 525 Weiss Rd 49735-1637 (Mail to: PO Box 920 49734-0920) Pamela Lenartowicz (989) 752-6020

Gladwin St Pauls Church **P** (131) 211 E Cedar Ave 48624-2207 (Mail to: 211 E Cedar Ave 48624-2207) Joseph Downs (989) 752-6020

Grand Blanc St Christophers Episcopal Ch **P** (297) 9020 S Saginaw Rd 48439-9576 (Mail to: 9020 S Saginaw Rd 48439-9576) (810) 694-3600

Grayling St Francis Episcopal Church **P** (84) PO Box 501 6441 West M-72 Highway 49738-7787 (Mail to: PO Box 501 49738-0501) (989) 348-5850

Harrisville St Andrews by the Lake **P** (20) PO Box 52 48740-0052 (Mail to: PO Box 52 48740-0052) Joe Jenney (989) 752-6020

Harsens Island St Paul Episcopal Church **P** (72) 208 Orchid Blvd 48028-9556 (Mail to: 2908 S Channel Dr 48028-9577) (989) 752-6020

Hillman Calvary Episcopal Church **P** (52) 330 N State Street 49746-0158 (Mail to: PO Box 158 49746-0158) (989) 752-6020

Indian River Church of the Transfiguration **P** (123) PO Box 460 49749-0460 (Mail to: PO Box 460 49749-0460) (989) 752-6020

Lachine Grace Episcopal Church **P** (40) 13488 Long Rapids Rd 49753-9632 (Mail to: 8528 Long Rapids Rd 49707-9764) John Laycock (989) 752-6020

Lapeer Grace Episcopal Church **P** (80) 735 W Nepessing St 48446-2006 (Mail to: 735 W Nepessing St 48446-2006) Sarah Parks (810) 664-2841

Lexington Trinity Episcopal Church **P** (148) 5646 S Main Street 48450-0315 (Mail to: 5646 Main St 48450-8842) (810) 3598741

Midland Holy Family Episcopal Church **P** (28) 4611 Swede Ave 48642-3861 (Mail to: 4611 Swede Ave 48642-3861) (989) 752-6020

Midland St Johns Episcopal Church **P** (189) 405 N Saginaw Rd 48640-6339 (Mail to: 405 N Saginaw Rd 48640-6339) James Harrison James Harrison James Harrison (989) 631-2260

Mio St Bartholomews Episcopal Ch **P** (37) PO Box 787 48647-0787 (Mail to: PO Box 787 48647-0787) (989) 752-6020

Oscoda Hope-St Johns Parish **P** (30) 223 E. Mill Street 48750-0338 (Mail to: 223 E Mill St 48750-1627) (989) 752-6020

Otter Lake Saint John the Baptist **P** (81) 5811 Forest Ave 48464-9790 (Mail to: C/O Doris Sutton Treasurer 9534 Mcpherson Rd 48746-9481) (989) 752-6020

Owosso Christ Episcopal Church **P** (41) 120 Goodhue St 48867-2320 (Mail to: 120 Goodhue St 48867-2320) Paul Brunell (989) 752-6020

Port Huron Grace Episcopal Church **P** (294) 1213 6th St 48060-5348 (Mail to: 1213 6th St 48060-5348) Linda Crane (810) 985-9539

Rogers City St Lukes Episcopal Church **P** (25) 120 N First St 49779-1602 (Mail to: C/O Ethel Wickersham 278 S 7th St 49779-2017) (989) 752-6020

Roscommon St Elizabeths Episcopal Church **P** (57) 2936 E Higgins Lake Dr 48653-7622 (Mail to: 2936 E Higgins Lake Dr 48653-7622) Charles Curtis Mary Shortt (989) 752-6020

Saginaw St Johns Episcopal Church **P** (263) 123 N Michigan Ave 48602-4235 (Mail to: 123 N Michigan Ave 48602-4235) Curtis Norman (989) 793-9575

Saginaw St Matthews Episcopal Church **P** (65) 1501 N Center Rd 48638-5563 (Mail to: 1501 N Center Rd 48638-5563) (989) 752-6020

Saginaw St Pauls Episcopal Church **P** (161) 720 Tuscola St 48607-1583 (Mail to: 4444 State St Apt F318 48603-4092) Judith Boli (989) 752-6020

Saint Clair Holy Family Episcopal Church **P** (107) 115 N 6th St 48079-4829 (Mail to: 115 N 6th St 48079-4829)

Sand Point St Johns Episcopal Church **P** (24) 8271 Crescent Beach Rd 48755-9648 (Mail to: PO Box 1882 48725-1882) (989) 752-6020

Sandusky St Johns Church **P** (22) 41 N Delaware St 48471-1006 (Mail to: 41 N Delaware St 48471-1006) (989) 752-6020

Standish Grace Episcopal Church **P** (13) PO Box 721 48658-0721 (Mail to: PO Box 721 48658-0721) (989) 752-6020

West Branch Trinity Episcopal Church **P** (50) 100 E Houghton Ave 48661-1124 (Mail to: PO Box 83 48661-0083) Robert Finn (989) 345-0493

DIOCESE OF EASTERN OREGON
(PROVINCE VIII)
Comprises Oregon east of the Cascade Mountains and Klickitat County Washington
DIOCESAN OFFICE 1104 Church St (Box 236) Cove OR 97824
TEL (541) 568-4514
E-MAIL diocese@episdioeo.org WEB www.episdioeo.org

Previous Bishops—
Robert L Paddock 1907-22, Wm P Remington 1922-45, Lane W Barton 1946-68, Wm B Spofford 1967-79, Rustin R Kimsey 1980-2000, Wm O Gregg 2000-2007, Bavi E. Rivera 2009-2016

Bishop—Rt Rev Patrick W. Bell (Dio 2016–)

BP Sec L Boquist; *Sec of Conv* The Rev C Wells; *Treas* P Olson-Lindsey; *Exec Dir Asc Camp* A Jayne; *Dio Coun—Cler:* The Rev RJ Spreier The Rev J Galles *Vacant Lay:* B Mayo B Spell B Palmer A Pursel C Bradshaw D Kosar

Stand Comm—Cler: Pres K Mahon A Hardin A Bonebrake; *Lay:* K Nash E Nesbitt T Rahmsdorff

PARISHES, MISSIONS, AND CLERGY

Baker City St Stephens Episcopal Church **P** (48) 2177 First Street 97814-2606 (Mail to: 2130 Second Street 97814) Aletha Bonebrake (541) 523-4812

Bend All Sts of Cascades Epis Ch **P** (61) 18143 Cottonwood Rd 97707-9317 (Mail to: 18160 Cottonwood Rd #266 97707-9317) (541) 593-5991

Bend Trinity Church **P** (510) C/O Treas Charles W Brisson 469 NW Wall St 97703-2605 (Mail to: 469 NW Wall St 97703-2605) Jedediah Holdorph

Bonanza St Barnabas Episcopal Church **P** (26) 12201 W Langell Valley Rd 97623-9781 (Mail to: C/O Beverly J Yancey 4146 Adelaide Ave Apt 8 97603-3738) Martha Hurlburt (541) 545-1705

Burns St Andrews Episcopal Church **P** (20) 393 E A St 97720-1605 (Mail to: PO Box 627 97720-0627) (541) 573-2632

Canyon City St Thomas Episcopal Church **P** (66) 139 S Washington St 97820-6125 (Mail to: PO Box 164 97820-0164) Daniel Gardner (541) 575-2415

Enterprise St Patricks Episcopal Church **P** (15) 100 NE 3rd St 97828 (Mail to: PO Box 301 97828-0301) Rich Attebury (541) 426-3439

Heppner All Saints Memorial Epis Ch **P** (98) 460 N Gale St 97836 (Mail to: PO Box 246 97836-0246) (541) 676-9970

Hermiston St Johns Episcopal Church **P** (83) 665 E Gladys Ave 97838-1915 (Mail to: 665 E Gladys Ave 97838-1915) Charles Barnes (541) 567-6672

Hood River St Marks Episcopal Church **P** (88) 400 11th Street 97031-1547 (Mail to: 400 11th St 97031-1547) Paul Mahon (541) 386-2077

La Grande St Peters Episcopal Church **P** (38) 1001 O Ave 97850-2424 (Mail to: PO Box 1001 97850-1001) Mary Lujan (541) 963-3623

Lakeview St Lukes Episcopal Church **P** (29) 614 S F St 97630-1751 (Mail to: Attn Barbara Snider 614 S F St 97630-1751) Richard Landrith (541) 947-2360

Madras St Marks Episcopal Church **P** (9) 13 SW F St 97741-1301 (Mail to: Attn: Treasurer PO Box 789 97741-0110) Carol McClelland (541) 546-6250

Milton Frwtr St James Episcopal Church **P** (40) 719 Pierce St 97862-1434 (Mail to: 719 Pierce Street 97862) Ann Marie Hardin (541) 938-7268

Ontario St Matthews Episcopal Church **P** (118) 802 SW 5th St 97914-3417 (Mail to: PO Box 788 97914-0788) Deborah Graham (541) 889-6943

Pendleton Church of the Redeemer **P** (146) 241 SE 2nd St 97801-2222 (Mail to: 241 SE 2nd St 97801-2222) Charlotte Wells (541) 276-3809

Prineville St Andrews Episcopal Church **P** (39) 807 E 1st St 97754-2007 (Mail to: PO Box 299 97754-0299) Raymond Spreier Stephen Uffelman Janet Warner (541) 447-5813

Redmond St Albans Episcopal Church **P** (20) 724 SW 14th St 97756-2619 (Mail to: 724 S.W. 14th St. 97756-2619) Lee Kiefer (541) 548-4212

Sisters Church of the Transfiguration **P** (214) 68825 Brooks Camp Rd 97759 (Mail to: PO Box 130 97759-0130) Joseph Farber (541) 549-7087

The Dalles St Pauls Episcopal Church **P** (191) 1805 Minnesota St 97058-3319 (Mail to: 1805 Minnesota St 97058-3319) Georgia Giacobbe (541) 296-9587

DIOCESE OF EASTON

(PROVINCE III)
Comprises 9 counties on the eastern shore of Maryland
DIOCESAN OFFICE 314 North St Easton MD 21601
TEL: (410) 822-1919 E-MAIL: diocese@dioceseofeaston.org
WEB: www.dioceseofeaston.org

Previous Bishops— Henry C Lay 1869-85, Wm F Adams 1887-1920, Geo W Davenport 1920-38, Wm McClelland 1939-49, Allen J Miller 1949-66, George A Taylor 1967-75, W Moultrie Moore Jr 1975-83, Elliott L Sorge 1983-93, Martin G Townsend 1993-2001, Charles L Longest asst 2002-03, James J Shand 2003-2014, Henry Nutt Parsley Jr. prov 2014-16

Bishop — Rt Rev Santosh K. Marray, DMin, DD

Lay Cn to Ord J J Dragone; *Treas* C Bohn; *Chanc* R Smith; *Sec to Bp* L Anstatt; *Fin Admin* M Timms l; *Dio Youth* J Fisher; *Comm* J Fisher; *Reg* L Anstatt; *Stew* vacant; *Arch* L Collins; *Hist* J Moak; *UTO* E Sturgill; *Deploy* J Dragone; *ER&D* R Gribbon; *COM* C Osberger

Deans—Northern H Sabetti; *Middle* M Delcuze *Southern* D Michaud

Stand Comm—Cler: D Michaud D Dunlap L Webb *Lay:* D Freestate T Mendenhall

PARISHES, MISSIONS, AND CLERGY

Berlin St Pauls Church **P** (142) 3 Church S 21811-1209 (Mail to: PO Box 429 21811-0429) (410) 6414066

Cambridge Christ Ch Great Choptank Paris **P** (444) 601 Church St 21613-1729 (Mail to: 60 Church St 21613-1729) HBW Schroeder HBW Schroeder (410) 228-3161

Cambridge St Johns Chapel **M** (49) 1213 Hudson Rd 21613-3237 (Mail to: 1213 Hudson Rd 21613-3237) Daniel Dunlap Daniel Dunlap (410) 2285056

Centreville St Pauls Parish **P** (297) 301 S Liberty St 21617-1221 (Mail to: PO Box 278 21617

0278) Mary Garner-Friel (410) 758-1553

Chesapeake City Augustine Parish **P** (68) 310 George St 21915-1223 (Mail to: PO Box 487 21915-0487) (410) 885-5375

Chestertown Emmanuel Episcopal Church **P** (310) 101 N Cross St 21620-1527 (Mail to: PO Box 875 21620-0875) Claire Nevin-Field (410) 778-3477

Chestertown Saint Paul's Parish' Kent **P** (109) 7579 Sandy Bottom Rd 21620-4520 (Mail to: 7579 Sandy Bottom Rd 21620-4520) Frank St Amour (410) 7781540

Church Creek Old Trinity Ch-Dorchester Par **P** (46) 1716 Taylors Island Rd 21622 (Mail to: PO Box 157 21622-0157) Daniel Dunlap (410) 2282940

Church Hill St Luke's Parish **P** (125) 403 Main Street 21623-1503 (Mail to: PO Box 38 21623-0038) (410) 5566060

Denton Christ Church **P** (45) 105 Gay St 21629-1019 (Mail to: PO Box 428 21629-0428) Matthew D'Amario (410) 479-0419

Earleville St Stephens Episcopal Church **P** (124) 10 Glebe Rd 21919-2144 (Mail to: 10 Glebe Rd 21919-2144) (410) 2758785

Easton All Faith Chapel **P** (51) 26281 Tunis Mills Rd 21601-5523 (Mail to: 26281 Tunis Mills Rd 21601-5523) (410) 8221464

Easton Christ Church-St Peters Parish **P** (958) § 111 S Harrison St 21601-2907 (Mail to: 111 S Harrison St 21601-2998) William Ortt (410) 8222677

✠ **Easton** Trinity Cathedral Episcopal **O** (207) 314 Goldsborough St 21601-3669 (Mail to: 314 North St 21601-3665) Gregory Powell Sandra Casey-Martus (410) 8221931

Elkton Trinity Episcopal Church **P** (136) 105 N Bridge St 21921-5326 (Mail to: 105 N Bridge St 21921-5326) (410) 398-5350

Hebron St. Paul's Episcopal Center **P** (7) 8700 Memory Gardens Ln 21830 (Mail to: PO Box 28 21830-0028) (443) 6145410

Hurlock St Andrews Episcopal Church **M** (20) 303 S Main St 21643-3511 (Mail to: 303 Main Street 21643-3232) (410) 4630520

Kennedyville Shrewsbury Parish Church **P** (404) 12824 Shrewsbury Church Rd 21645-3400 (Mail to: PO Box 187 21645-0187) Henry Sabetti Stephan Klingelhofer (410) 3485944

Marion St Pauls Episcopal Church **P** (60) St Pauls Church Road 21838 (Mail to: St Pauls Church Road PO Box 245 21838-0245) Michael Lokey (443) 9441651

Massey St Clements **P** (62) 32940 Maryland Line Rd 21650-1703 (Mail to: PO Box 158 32940 Maryland Line Rd 21650-1706) (410) 928-5051

North East St Mary Anne's Epis Church **P** (550) 315 S Main St 21901-3915 (Mail to: 315 S Main St 21901-3915) (410) 287-5522

Ocean City Church of St Pauls By The Sea **P** (127) 302 N Baltimore Ave 21842-3923 (Mail to: 302 N Baltimore Ave 21842-3923) (410) 289-3453

Ocean City The Church of the Holy Spirit **P** (90) 10001 Coastal Hwy 21842-2649 (Mail to: 10001 Coastal Hwy 21842-2649) Joseph Rushton (410) 7231973

Oxford Holy Trinity Church **P** (407) 502 S Morris St 21654-1315 (Mail to: PO Box 387 21654-0387) Kevin Cross Katherine Webb (410) 2265134

Perryville St Marks Episcopal Church **P** (133) 175 Saint Marks Church Rd 21903-2519 (Mail to: PO Box 337 21903-0337) Susan Oldfather (410) 3782592

Pocomoke City St Mary the Virgin Epis Church **P** (88) 18 Third Street 21851-0383 (Mail to: PO Box 383 21851-0383) (410) 9571518

Princess Anne St Andrews Episcopal Church **P** (96) 30513 Washington St 21853-1143 (Mail to: 30513 Washington St 21853-1143) (410) 651-2882

Quantico St Philips Episcopal Church **P** (30) 6457 Quantico Rd 21856 (Mail to: PO Box 92 21856-0092) (443) 5238669

Queenstown St Lukes Chapel **P** C/O Wye Parish 7208 Main St 21658-1628 (Mail to: PO Box 98 21679-0098) (410) 827-8488

Saint Michael Christ Ch St Michaels Parish **P** (517) 301 S Talbot St 21663 (Mail to: Attn Carol A Osborne PO Box S 21663-0570) Steven Mosher (410) 745-9076

Salisbury St Albans Episcopal Church **HC** (123) 302 Saint Albans Dr 21804-5267 (Mail to: PO Box 1511 21802-1511) (410) 742-6595

Salisbury St Peters Church **P** (767) 115 Saint Peters St 21801-4901 (Mail to: 115 Saint Peters St 21801-4901) David Michaud (410) 7425118

Snow Hill All Hallows Episcopal Church **P** (131) 109 W Market St 21863-1047 (Mail to: 109 W Market St 21863-1047) (410) 6322327

Stevensville Christ Ch Parish Kent Island **P** (599) § 830 Romancoke Rd 21666-2790 (Mail to: 830 Romancoke Rd 21666-2790) Mark Delcuze (410) 6435921

Trappe Saint Paul's Church **P** (67) 3936 Main St 21673-1667 (Mail to: PO Box 141 21673-0141) Nathaniel Pierce (410) 4763048

Tyaskin St Mary's - Stepney Parish **P** (11) 21674 Nanticoke Rd 21865-2018 (Mail to: PO Box 76 21865-0076) Dennis Morgan (410) 8732790

Vienna St Pauls Episcopal Church **P** (19) 203 Church St 21869 (Mail to: PO Box 3 21869-0003) Dennis Morgan (410) 376-3376

Worton Christ Episcopal Church **P** (55) 25328 Lambs Meadow Rd 21678-1923 (Mail to: PO Box 161 25328 Lambs Meadow Rd 21678-0161) (410) 7782821

Wye Mills Wye Parish **P** (256) 14114 Old Wye Mills Rd 21679-2002 (Mail to: PO Box 98 21679-0098) (410) 8278484

DIOCESE OF EAU CLAIRE
(PROVINCE V)
Comprises the 26 counties of northwestern Wisconsin
DIOCESAN OFFICE 510 S Farwell St Eau Claire WI 54701
TEL (715) 835-3331
E-MAIL administrator@dioec.net WEB episcopaldioceseofeauclaire.com/

Previous Bishops—
Frank E Wilson 1929-44, Wm W
Horstick 1944-69, Stanley Atkins
1969-80, William C Wantland
1980-99, Keith B Whitmore 1999-
2008, Edwin M Leidel Jr 2008-
2012, William Jay Lambert III
2013-20

Bishop Provisional—Matthew Alan Gunter

Dio Admin Cn A Zook; *Treas* B Weathers; *Chanc* J
Pelish Box 31 Rice Lake WI 54868; *Ecum* Cn A Zook
510 S. Farwell St Eau Claire WI 54701

Stand Comm—Cler: Pres G Usher S Burns B Thomas;
Lay: D Bilderback J Neste C Corbin

PARISHES, MISSIONS, AND CLERGY

Bayfield Epis Ch of Chequamegon Bay **SC** (24)
125 N 3rd St 54814-4872 (Mail to: PO Box 427
54806-0427) (715) 813-0764

Chippewa Falls St Simeons Church **M** (40) 19058
190th St 54729 (Mail to: PO Box 194 54729-
0194) Claudia Hogan Aaron Zook (715) 723-
0050

Chippewa Fls Christ Episcopal Church **P** (60)
624 Bay St 54729-2425 (Mail to: 624 Bay St
54729-2425) Aaron Zook (715) 723-7667

Clear Lake St Barnabas Episcopal Church **M** (9)
365 5th Ave 54005-3738 (Mail to: 944 140th
Ave 54001-2706) Robert Lyga (715) 263-3464

Conrath Holy Trinity Church **M** (19) North 1643
County Hwy G 54731 (Mail to: PO Box 152
54731-0152) (715) 748-2280

✠ **Eau Claire** Christ Church Cathedral **O** (207)
510 S Farwell St 54701-4994 (Mail to: 510
S Farwell St Ste 1 54701-4995) Benjamin
Thomas (715) 835-3734

Hayward Church of the Ascension **M** (119)
10612 California Ave 54843-4604 (Mail to: PO
Box 637 54843-0637) (715) 634-3283

Hudson St Pauls Episcopal Church **P** (187) 502
County Road Uu 54016-7583 (Mail to: 502
County Road Uu 54016-7583) Heather Hill

(715) 386-2348

La Crosse Christ Episcopal Church **P** (207) 111
9th St N 54601-3485 (Mail to: PO Box 2908
54602) Michael Mcelwee Peter Augustine
Kathleen Charles Joanne Glasser Thomas
Winkler (608) 784-0697

Menomonie Grace Episcopal Church **M** (61)
1002 6th St E 54751-2627 (Mail to: Attn: C
Kell E4357 451st Ave 54751-5449) Jacalyn
Broughton (715) 235-7072

New Richmond Church of St Thomas & St John
M (9) 354 N 3rd St 54017-1114 (Mail to:
C/O Lynne RIddle 354 N 3rd St 54017-1114)
Catherine Kuschel (715) 246-6602

Owen St Katherine Episcopal Church **M** (22)
206 E 3rd St 54460-9763 (Mail to: PO Box 148
54460-0148) (715) 229-2643

Phillips Church of Our Saviour **M** (10) Attn:
Kenneth Johnson N11211 Rocky Carrie Rd
54555-7234 (Mail to: Attn: Leonard France
W 7125 Hwy W. 54555) William Radant (715)
339-4281

Rice Lake Grace Episcopal Church **M** (50) 119 W
Humbird St 54868-1642 (Mail to: Mary Ellen
Filken Treas 119-123 W Humbird St 54868-
1642) Harry Kirby (715) 234-4226

Sparta St Johns Episcopal Church **M** (61) 322 N
Water St 54656-1741 (Mail to: 322 N Water St
54656-1741) Peter Augustine (608) 269-4266

Spooner St Albans Episcopal Church **M** (35)
220 Elm St 54801-1328 (Mail to: PO Box 281
54801-0281) (715) 635-4704

Springbrook St Lukes Church **M** (22) N8571
County Hwy 54875-9404 (Mail to: Attn
Lawrence Neste W3399 Highway 63 54875-
9409) (715) 635-4707

Superior St Alban the Martyr Episcopal **M** (53)
1510 New York Ave 54880-2082 (Mail to: 1510
New York Ave 54880-2082) Steven Burns
(715) 392-2536

Tomah St Mary Episcopal Church **M** (51) 1001
Mclean Ave 54660-1941 (Mail to: 1001 Mclean
Ave 54660-1941) Elna McDaniel Mary Rezin
Guy Usher (608) 372-5174

DIOCESES OF ECUADOR
Iglesia Episcopal del Ecuador
(PROVINCE IX)

CENTRAL DIOCESE OF ECUADOR

Previous Bishop—
Adrián Cáceres 1971-90, Wilfrido Ramos-Orench 2006-09; Luis Fernando Ruiz 2009-22

Bishop—Rt Rev Juan Carlos Quiñonez Mera (1144) (Dio 17 May 2022)

Cuenca Iglesia Sagrada Familia **P** (50) No Bartolome de las Casas #534 y Tirso Moliba NO534 (Mail to: Bartolome de las Casas # 534 y Tirso Moliba)
Guaranda Iglesia San Jose **P** Comunidad San Bartolo (Mail to: Comunidad "San Bartolo")
La Hondonada Iglesia Episcopal Resurreccion **P** San Pedro de Echaleche (Mail to: Oficina Central de la Iglesia Episcopal de Ecuador 00017) (593) 245-6948
La Libertad Iglesia de la Santisima Trinidad **P** Avenida 23 entre calle 30-31 (Mail to: Avda 26 y Calle 40 Esquina) Hector Perez Moreira
Pelileo Iglesia Nueva Jerusalem **P** Via La Libertad El Tambo-P. (Mail to: Cascajal de la Libertad)
Pilahuin, Ambato Iglesia San Lucas de Pilahuin **P** Prinicpal San Lucas (Mail to: Oficina

Central Iglesia Episcopal del Ecuador 00017) Raul Herrera Chagna (593) 245-6948
Puyo La Ascencion **P** Manabi y Galapagos (Mail to: Manabi y Galapagos)
✠ **Quito** Catedral de El Senor **O** Av. Real Audiencia #63-47 y Sabanilla (Mail to: Av. Real Audiencia #63-47 y Sabanilla) Juan Salvatierra Serian (2) 534419
Quito Cristo Liberador (Iasa-Refugio) **P** Jose Enriquez 63-55 y Camilo Echanique (Mail to: Jose Enriquez 63-55 y Camilo Echanique) Raul Guaillas Carangui
Quito Iglesia de la Epifania **P** Herman Cortez N58-2 y Vaca De Castro (Mail to: Herman Cortez N58-2 y Vaca De Castro)
Quito Iglesia del Buen Pastor **P** Palemon Morroy S45-75 Y Av. Ecatoriana (Mail to: Palemon Morroy S45-75 y Av. Ecatoriana) Gladys Vasquez-Vera
Quito Iglesia Episcopal Reconciliacion **P** Guayabamba E2-29 y Quilotoa (Mail to: Guayabamba E2-29 y Quilotoa)
Quito Mision Emanuel **P** Avenida Simon Bolivar s/n Guajalo (Mail to: Avenida Simon Bolivar s/n Guagalo)
Santo Domingo de los Tscahila San Pedro del Pupusa-Paraiso **P** Coop 15 de Sep. Calle Julio Jaramillo Pasaje 7 (Mail to: Coop 15 de Sep. Calle Julio Jaramillo Pasaje 7)

LITORAL DIOCESE OF ECUADOR

Previous Bishops—
Adrián D Cáceres 1971-88, Luis Caizapanta 1988-91, M García Montiel 1992-94; Alfredo Morante 1994-2019

Bishop—Rt Rev Cristobal Leon Lozano (Dio 30 March 2019)

Email: padrextobal@hotmail.com celular (593)990230917

Diocesan Office Calle Amarilis Fuentes 603 entre Av JV Trujillo y Calle D Barrio Centenario (Mail: Box 0901-5250) Guayaquil, Ecuador. From the US 011 (593-4) , 2446699 *E-mail* litoralepiscopal@hotmail.com

Treas Rvda G Angulo; *Chanc Abgda* J Contreras Q.; *Sec Conv* D Olvera *Sec Dio* Sra M Zambrano; *Contadora* Ing B Campuzano *Asistente Contable* Ing L Arévalo

Comité Permanente: Pres Rvdo C Villacis Rvda M Loor Rvdo F Orrala *Sec* Sra M Barros Sr W Mejillón Sr. N Neira.

Comité de Ministerio: Rvda G Angulo Rvdo Rvdo C Mora Rvdo F Macías Sra P Vega Sr R Mendoza Sra. C Ortega

Comité de Disciplina: Rvdo G Alava Rvda G Angulo Rvdo C Mora Rvdo F Macias Rvda M Loor Sra. S Carrión

Comité de Nominaciones Y Resoluciones:

Comité de Compañerismo: Rvdmo C León Rvda M Loor Rvda B Juarez Rvda G Angulo Rvdo G Álava Rvdo C Villacís Sra S Carrión.

Comité Desarrollo Diocesano: Presidenta Rvda G Angulo; *Vice Presidente* Rvdo C Villacís; *Secretario* Rvdo F Macías; *Tesorera* M Loor; *Director Ejecutivo* Rvdmo C León L Rvdo C Mora Rvdo F Orrala S Carrión M Zambrano M Juárez

Secretariados: Comuny Relac Públic Rvdo F Macías; *Educ Cristiana* Sr C Villacís; *Mujeres Episcopales* Sra R León; *UTO* Sra J León; *Fondo Desarr Emergente* Sra M Zambrano; *Himnología* Rvda B Juarez y Sra

M Juárez; *Ecumenismo* Rvdo G Alava V; *Justicia y Paz* Rvda M Loor; *Educ Teológica* Rvdo G Alava; *Estadísticas* Rvdo F Orrala *Ministerio Juvenil* Rvda G Angulo

PARISHES, MISSIONS, AND CLERGY

Duran Iglesia de Jesus Obrero de Duran **M** Cooperativa 12 de Noviembre Pedro Vicente Maldonado (Mail to: Box 0901-5250 Guayaquil, Ecuador)

Guayaquil Iglesia de la Resurreccion **P** Shushufindi y Paján Mz. 340 Sl. 07 Pascuales (Mail to: Box 0901-5250 Guayaquil, Ecuador)

Guayaquil Iglesia de la Transfiguracion **M** 33 Ava y Maldonado (Mail to: Box 0901-5250)

Guayaquil Iglesia Espiritu Santo **M** Letamendi entre 38 y 39 (Mail to: Box 090-15250 Guayaquil, Ecuador)

Guayaquil Catedral Cristo Rey Calle D / Bogotá y Amarilís Fuentes (Mail to: Box 09015250 Amarilis Fuentes 603 y Vicente Trujillo Guayaquil, Ecuador)

Guayaquil Iglesia Jesus El Senor **M** Guasmo Sur Cooperativa Battalla de Tarqui , Calle Pública y Pública Mz. 395 Sl. 01 (Mail to: Box 0901 5250 Amarilis Fuente 603 y V. Trujillo)

Guayaquil Iglesia Jesus Obrero **M** Guasmo Norte Coop. Río Guayas Mz. 33 Sol. 64 B (Mail to: Rita Lecumberri y 10 Callejon/ Postal# 09-01-5250 Guayaquil, Ecuador)

Guayaquil Iglesia San Pedro **M** 18 y la N Plan Piloto (Mail to: Box 09015250)

Guayaquil Iglesia Santa Maria **M** Sauces 3 Mz 1406 Sl. 018 Calle peatonal (Mail to: Box 0901 5250 Guayaquil, Ecuador)

Guayaquil Iglesia Todos los Santos **M** 25 y la "Q" (Mail to: 0901-5250 Guayaquil, Ecuador)

Guayaquil Iglesia Virgen Maria **M** Calle 23 Y Tercer Callejon P Mz. 195 Sol. 26 (Mail to: Box 09015250 Amarilis Fuentes 603 y Vicente Trujillo)

Guayaquil Iglesia Santísima Trinidad Calle Sedalana y la 11 ava (Mail to: Box 09015250 Guayaquil, Ecuador)

Guayaquil Mision de Jesus **M** Mapasinguie (Coop la Esperanza) Mz. 234 Sol. 1 (Mail to: 09-01-5250 Amarilis Fuentes 603 y Vicente Trujillo Guayaquil, Ecuador)

Guayaquil San Mateo **M** Callejon "O" Entre 23 y 24 Mz. 01341 Sol 11 (Mail to: Box 0901-5250 Guayaquil, Ecuador)

Manta San Esteban-Manabi **M** Sector 10 de Agosto Cdla. Eloy Alfaro Mz. 216 Av, 221 Calle 321 B. (Mail to: Box 0901 5250)

Manta San Jose Obrero-Manabi **M** Ciudadela 15 de Abril, Sl. 4 Mz. 136 Parroquia E Alfaro (Mail to: Box. 0901-5250)

Manta San Pablo **M** (50) § Calle 19 #208 y Ave 10 Barrio Cordova (Mail to: Box 0901-5250 Guayaquil, Ecuador)

MonteCristi Iglesia Santiago el Apostolo **M** Parroquia La Pila Calle Pública y Pública (Mail to: Box 0901-5250 Guayaquil, Ecuador)

Santa Elena Iglesia Virgen Maria Salanguillo **M** Comuna de Salanguillo, Parroquia Colonche, Cantón Santa Elena (Mail to: Apdo Box 0901-5250 Guayaquil, Ecuador)

Santa Elena Iglesia Santísima Trinidad Cantón La Libertad, Cdla. San Vicente Avda. 32 entre calles 30 y 31 Sl. 2 Mz. 11 (Mail to P.O. Box 0901-5250 Guayaquil, Ecuador)

Ventanas Iglesia San Eduardo **M** Recinto San Eduardo Canton Ventanas Vía Panamericana (Mail to: Amarilis Fuentes 603 y Jose V. Trujillo 0901-5250 Guayaquil, Ecuador)

Ventanas Iglesia San Gerardo **M** Recinto San Gerardo, Canton Ventanas Vía Panamericana (Mail to: Amarilis Fuentes 603 y Jose Vicente Trujillo Box 0901-5250 Guayaquil, Ecuador)

Ventanas La Gracia de Dios **M** Sixto Escalona y Pablo Palacios, Parroquia 10 de Noviembre, Ventanas (Mail to: Amarilis Fuertes 603 y Jose V. Trujillo Box 0901-5250 Guayaquil, Ecuador)

Quevedo Iglesia San Pablo Calle Otto Arosemena entre las calles E y F Sl. 63-64 Mz. 6, San Camilo—Quevedo (Mail to: 0901-5250 Guayaquil, Ecuador)

Babahoyo Iglesia Belén Recinto Pueblo Nuevo, Parroquia Febres Cordero (Mail To: Box 09015250 Guayaquil, Ecuador)

INSTITUCIONES

Escuela de Educación Básica Ann Stevens, Box. 0901-5250 San Eduardo, Ventanas

Campamento Episcopal "Adrián Cáseres" Playas Km. 14 ½ Vía Data Posorja, Playas Box 0901-5250 Guayaquil

Centro de Estudios Teologicos San Patricio

IMEL Instituto para el Ministerio Episcopal Laico

CLÉRIGOS ACTIVOS

Rvdmo Cristobal León Lozano Amarilis Fuentes 603 y José Vicente Trujillo, Barrio Centenario (Mail to: P.O. Box 0901 5250 Guayaquil, Ecuador)

Rvdo P. Gerónimo Álava Calle Sedalana y la 11 ava.—Cisne 2 (Mail to: P.O. Box 0901-5250 Guayaquil, Ecuador)

Rvda P. Gina Angulo Rcto. San Eduardo, Prov. Los Ríos (Mail to: P.O. Box 0901-5250 Guayaquil, Ecuador)

Rvdo P. Jairo Chirán Guasmo Sur Cooperativa Battalla de Tarqui, Calle Pública y Pública Mz. 395 Sl. 01 (Mail to: P.O. Box 09015250 Guayaquil, Ecuador)

Rvdo P. Betty Juárez Villamar Mapasingue Este. Coop La Esperanza Mz 233 Sl 7 (Mail to: P.O. Box 0901–5250 Guayaquil, Ecuador)

Rvdo P. Carlos Mora Calle Otto Arosemena entre la D y la F, Quevedo (Mail to: P.O. Box 0901-

5250 Guayaquil, Ecuador)
Rvdo Franklín Macías Coop 12 de Noviembre Mz A solar 3 Cantón Duran (Mail to: P.O. Box 0901-5250 Guayaquil, Ecuador)
Rvdo Francisco Orrala Callejón "O" entre la 20 y 21 ava-Sector P.Piloto (Mail to: P.O. Box 0901-5250 Guayaquil, Ecuador)
Rvdo Carlos Villacís. Cdla. San Vicente Av. 32 entre calles 30 y 31 La Libertad, Península (Mail to: P.O. 0901-5250 Guayaquil, Ecuador)
Rvda Goldí Santana Mera Vera Cruz, Mexico. Ave. Laguna Real 605 entre Laberinto y Manglares Fraccionamiento Laguna Real. Veracruz Ver. C.P.91790

Clérigos Jubilados
Rvda Diác. Mérida León F. Cdla. Alborada (Mail to: P.O. Box 09015250 Guayaquil, Ecuador)
Rvda. P. Marina Loor Calle 22 ava y 4 Callejón P. (Mail to: P.O. Box 0901-5250 Guayaquil, Ecuador)
Rvdo P. Hugo Mendoza Cdla. 15 de Abril, Manta (Mail to: P.O. Box 09015250 Guayaquil, Ecuador)
Rvdo P. Héctor Pérez Coop. Ríos Guayas, Guasmo Norte (Mail to: P.O. Box 09015250 Guayaquil, Ecuador) Fallecido

DIOCESE OF EL CAMINO REAL
(PROVINCE VIII)
Comprises 5 counties in central coastal CA except St Mark's Palo Alto and Christ Church Los Altos
DIOCESAN OFFICE 154 Central Ave Salinas, CA 93901 (MAIL: Box 689 Salinas CA 93902)
TEL (831) 394-4465 FAX (831) 394-7133
E-MAIL mbpowell@realepiscopal.org   WEB www.realepiscopal.org

Previous Bishops—
Wm I Kip m 1853 dio 1857-93, Wm F Nichols coadj 1890 Bp 1893-1924, Edward L Parsons coadj 1919 Bp 1924-40, Karl M Block coadj 1933 Bp 1941-58, Henry H Shires suffr 1950-58, James A Pike 1958-66, G Richard Millard suffr 1960-76, C Kilmer Myers 1966-79, William E Swing coadj 1979 Bp 1980 (California), C Shannon Mallory 1980-90, R Shimpfky 1990-2004; S Romero asst 2004-7; M Gray-Reeves 2007-20

Bishop—Rt Rev Lucinda B. Ashby (11 Jan 2020)

Conv Sec J Diehl; *Treas* J Shreve; *Dio Admin* Rev B Nordwick; *Admin Asst* MB Powell; *Chanc* S Kottmeier; *Archdcn* None *Cong Growth & Dev* J Reyes

Board of Trustees—Cler: A Leininger J Wild S Symington J Wild M Blessing; *Lay:* E Fisher D Mora MJ Kelly L Gonzalez S Byrd

Stand Comm—Cler: Pres K Doar C Hall M Juarez; *Lay:* E Frost J Melvin S Pearson M Cameron

PARISHES, MISSIONS, AND CLERGY
Aptos Epis Ch of St John the Baptist **P** (135) 125 Canterbury Dr 95003-4367 (Mail to: 125 Canterbury Dr 95003-4367) Tracy Wells Miller Eliza Linley (831) 708-2278
Arroyo Grande St Barnabas Episcopal Church **P** (299) 301 Trinity Ave 93420-3384 (Mail to: 301 Trinity Ave 93420-3384) Robert Keim (805) 489-2990

Atascadero St Lukes Episcopal Church **P** (75) 5318 Palma Ave 93422-3338 (Mail to: 5318 Palma Ave 93422-3338) (805) 466-0379
Ben Lomond St Andrew Episcopal Church **P** (74) 101 Riverside Ave 95005-9509 (Mail to: PO Box 293 95005-0293) (831) 336-5994
Cambria St Paul Episcopal Church **P** (57) 2700 Eton Rd 93428-4106 (Mail to: 2700 Eton Rd 93428-4106) (805) 927-3239
Carmel All Saints Episcopal Church **P** (164) 100 Lincoln St 93923 (Mail to: PO Box 1296 93921-1296) Amber Sturgess (831) 624-3883
Carmel St Dunstan's Episcopal Church **P** (332) § 28005 Robinson Canyon Rd 93923-8572 (Mail to: 28005 Robinson Canyon Rd 93923-8572) Laurel Coote Marcia Lockwood (831) 624-6646
Cupertino St Jude the Apostle Episcopal **P** (491) 20920 Mcclellan Rd 95014-2967 (Mail to: 20920 McClellan Rd 95014-2967) (408) 252-4166
Gilroy St Stephen Episcopal Church **P** (147) 651 Broadway 95020-4304 (Mail to: 651 Broadway 95020-4398) Ernest Boyer (408) 842-4415
Hollister St Lukes Episcopal Church **P** (141) 720 Monterey St 95023-3826 (Mail to: 720 Monterey St 95023-3826) Kenneth Wratten (831) 637-7570
Jolon St Lukes Church Episcopal **M** (56) Jolon Rd & Mission Rd 93928 (Mail to: PO Box 233 93928-0233) Robert Seifert (831) 227-1202
King City St Mark Church **M** (65) 301 Bassett St 93930-2901 (Mail to: 301 Bassett St 93930-2901) (831) 385-5119
Los Gatos St Luke Episcopal Church **P** (177) 20 University Ave 95030-6009 (Mail to: 20

University Ave 95030-6099) Ricardo Avila Richard Emerson (408) 354-2195

Los Osos St Benedict Episcopal Church **P** (112) 2220 Snowy Egret Ln 93402 (Mail to: PO Box 6877 93412-6877) Caroline Hall Donna Ross Carlton Turner (805) 528-0654

Marina Epiphany LutheranEpiscopal Ch **P** 425 Carmel Ave 93933-3305 (Mail to: 425 Carmel Ave 93933-3305) Jon Perez Patricia Catalano (831) 384-6323

Monterey St James Episcopal Church **P** (43) 381 High St 93940-2161 (Mail to: 381 High St 93940-2199) (831) 375-8476

Monterey St John Episcopal Chapel **P** (165) 1490 Mark Thomas Dr 93940-4919 (Mail to: 1490 Mark Thomas Dr 93940-4919) (831) 375-4463

Morgan Hill St John the Divine Epis Church **P** (196) 17740 Peak Ave 95037-4121 (Mail to: 17740 Peak Ave 95037-4121) (408) 779-9510

Morro Bay St Peters by the Sea Epis Ch **P** (95) 545 Shasta Ave 93442-2541 (Mail to: 545 Shasta Ave 93442-2541) Sidney Symington (805) 772-2368

Mountain View St Timothy's Episcopal Church **P** (277) 2094 Grant Rd 94040-3802 (Mail to: 2094 Grant Rd 94040-3899) Nicholas Roosevelt (650) 967-4724

Pacific Grove Church of St Marys by the Sea **P** (476) 146 12th St 93950-2749 (Mail to: 146 12th St 93950-2760) Kristine Johnson Wendy Howe Scott Taylor (831) 373-4441

Palo Alto All Saints Episcopal Church **P** (219) 555 Waverley St 94301-1721 (Mail to: 555 Waverley St 94301-1721) Craig Vance (650) 322-4528

Paso Robles St James Episcopal Church **P** (147) 1335 Oak Street 93446-2262 (Mail to: 514 14th St 93446-2262) Barbara Miller Jacqueline Sebro (805) 238-0819

Salinas Church of the Good Shepherd **P** (209) 301 Corral De Tierra Rd 93908-8917 (Mail to: 301 Corral De Tierra Rd 93908-8917) Linda Mcconnell Cynthia Montague (831) 484-2153

Salinas St Georges Episcopal Church **P** (56) 98 Kip Dr 93906-2909 (Mail to: 98 Kip Dr 93906-2909) (831) 449-6709

Salinas St Paul's/San Pablo Epis Ch **P** (287) 1071 Pajaro St 93901-3001 (Mail to: 1071 Pajaro St 93901-3099) Alejandra Trillos Arnold Hedlund (831) 424-7331

San Ardo St Matthews Church **M** (7) Jolon St & Railroad St 93450 (Mail to: C/O Janyce E Lacoume PO Box 114 93450-0114) (805) 740-2024

San Jose Episcopal Church in Almaden **P** (174) 6581 Camden Ave 95120-1908 (Mail to: 6581 Camden Ave 95120-1908) (408) 268-0243

San Jose Good Samaritan Episcopal Church **P** (75) 15040 Union Ave 95124-5135 (Mail to: 15040 Union Ave 95124-5199) (408) 377-0158

San Jose Holy Family Episcopal Church **P** (199) 5038 Hyland Ave 95127-2212 (Mail to: 5038 Hyland Ave 95127-2212) Ruth Paguio

San Jose St Francis Episcopal Church **P** (475) 1205 Pine Ave 95125-3459 (Mail to: 1205 Pine Ave 95125-3400) Mary London Hughes Stephenie Cooper John Palmer (408) 292-7090

San Jose St Stephens in the Field Epis **P** (114) 7269 Santa Teresa Blvd 95139-1352 (Mail to: 7269 Santa Teresa Blvd 95139-1352) Karen Cuffie (408) 629-1836

✠ **San Jose** Trinity Episcopal Cathedral **O** (772) 81 N 2nd St 95113-1205 (Mail to: 81 N 2nd St 95113-1205) David Bird Lee Barford Lee Barford Lance Beizer Jerry Drino Julia McCray-Goldsmith (408) 293-7953

Santa Clara St Mark Episcopal Church **P** (87) 1957 Pruneridge Ave 95050-6515 (Mail to: 1957 Pruneridge Ave 95050-6515) Karin White (408) 296-8383

Santa Cruz Calvary Episcopal Church **P** (386) 532 Center St 95060-4313 (Mail to: 532 Center St 95060-4313) Robert Keim Ann-Lining Smith (831) 423-8787

Saratoga Saint Andrew's Church **P** (2030) § 13601 Saratoga Ave 95070-5055 (Mail to: PO Box 2789 95070-0789) Kathleen Crowe Janet Wild (408) 867-3493

Scotts Valley St Philip the Apostle **M** (205) 5271 Scotts Valley Dr 95066-3514 (Mail to: 5271 Scotts Valley Dr 95066-3577) Katherine Doar (831) 438-4360

✠ **Seaside** La Iglesia De San Pablo **P** (239) 1092 Noche Buena St 93955-6221 (Mail to: 1092 Noche Buena St 93955-6221) Rachel Bennett Jose Juarez

Sn Luis Obispo St Stephens Episcopal Church **P** (142) 1344 Nipomo St 93401-3935 (Mail to: 1344 Nipomo St 93401-3987) Karen Siegfriedt Anne Wall (805) 543-7212

Sunnyvale St Thomas Episcopal Church **P** (170) 231 Sunset Ave 94086-5969 (Mail to: 231 Sunset Ave 94086-5938) Sheldon Hutchison Michael Ridgway Sally Wong (408) 736-4155

Watsonville All Saints Episcopal Church **P** (363) 437 Rogers Ave 95076-3320 (Mail to: 437 Rogers Ave 95076-3398) (831) 724-5338

CONVOCATION OF EPISCOPAL CHURCHES IN EUROPE
(PROVINCE II)
Under the Jurisdiction of the Presiding Bishop
Convocation Office American Cathedral of the Holy Trinity
23 Ave George F-75008 Paris
TEL +33 1 53 23 84 06
E-MAIL office@tec-europe.org WEB www.tec-europe.org

Previous Bishops in Charge— EL Browning 1971-74, AE Swift 1974-77, R Millard 1979-80, JM Krumm 1980-83, RB Appleyard 1983-86, AD Davies 1986-88, MP Bigliardi 1988-91, JM Krumm int 1992, MP Bigliardi int 1992-93, JM Rowthorn 1994-2001, Pierre W Whalon Bp in Charge 2001-19

Bishop—The Rt Rev Mark David Wheeler Edington (Dio 6 Apr 2019)

Archdeacon: Ven Dr WJ Baer; *Convocation Adm:* S Plé: *Digital Min:* M Rios

Convocation Officers: Treas D Le Moullac (France); *Sec Rev* R Cole Dcn (Geneva); *COMB Chair Rev Dr* A Gray (Munich); *Chris Ed Chair* J Day-Strehlow (Munich); *Ecumenical Rep Rev* C Easthill (Wiesbaden); *Mission Com Chair* L Litman (Rome)

Council of Advice: Cler: Rev R Easterling Rev S Hallanan Rev JD Chavanne Rev D Morrow; *Lay* P Mahoney W Greenburg D Groby L Stuckenbruck; *Ex-Off* Rt Rev M Edington D Le Moullac Ven W Baer S Plé Rev Dn R Cole H Mbele-Mbong

Youth Commission Chair S Hinkley (Paris)

PARISHES, MISSIONS, AND CLERGY

Austria

Muhlbach Am Hochkonig Ecumenical Chp of Holy Fmly **Chapel** Mandlwandstrasse 437 05505 (Mail to: Mandlwandstrasse 437) (239) 331-5641

Belgium

Braine-l'Alleud All Saints Episcopal Church **P** (130) Chaussée de Charleroi #2 1420 (Mail to: Chaussée de Charleroi #2 1420) Sunny Hallanan (322) 384-7780
Charleroi Christ Church **M** Boulevard Audent, 20, Sunny Hallanan
Mons Saint-Esprit **M** Sunny Hallanan
Namur Mission Station **M** Sunny Hallanan

France

Montpellier Grace Church **P** (8) Rue Leon Blum c/o Eglise Don Bosco 34000 (Mail to: 10 rue Moilere)

✠ **Paris** Cathedral of the Holy Trinity **O** (715) § 23, Avenue George V (Mail to: 23 Avenue George V 75008) Timothy Safford Nathaniel Katz (1) 4-723-9530
Royat Christ Church Clermont **M** (52) 1 Bis avenue Jeanne Heitz 63130 (Mail to: 1 Bis avenue Jeanne Heitz 63130)

Georgia (Republic of)

Tbilisi St. Nino's Episcopal Mission **M** Kedia street #6 Tbilisi, +995 555 33 25 31

Germany

Augsburg St Boniface **P** (56) Evangelisch-Lutherische Auferstehungskirche Garmischer Straße 2a 86163 (Mail to: C/O Dagmar Hamberger Am Anger 5 85256) Lutz Ackermann (498) 964-8185
Frankfurt am Main, Germany Church of Christ the King **P** (218) Sebastian-Rinz Strasse 22 60323 (Mail to: Christ The King Parish Sebastian-Rinz-Str 22 60323) 69550184
Karlsruhe, St. Columban's **M** Röntgenstraße 1, 76133 Karlsruhe Robert Vukovic
Munich Church of the Ascension **P** (241) Seybothstrasse 4 81545 (Mail to: Seyboth Strasse 4 Munich, Germany 81545 00000) Daniel Morrow (498) 964-8185
Nuremberg St James, the Less **P** (36) St. Jakob Kirche Jakobsplatz 1 90402 (Mail to: c/o Sonja March Schillerstrasse 17 90409) Scott Moore 964-8185
Weimar St Michael's Church of Thuringia **M** William-Shakespeare-Straße 13 99423 Weimar, Scott Moore +49 176 22387296
Wiesbaden St Augustine of Canterbury **P** (244) Frankfurter Strasse 3 (Mail to: Frankfurter Strasse 3 C/O 65 Parish Treasurer 65189) Christopher Easthill 611306674

Italy

Florence St James Episcopal Church **P** (150) Via Bernardo Rucellai 9 50123 (Mail to: C/O Mr Sandro Sanavio Via Bernardo Rucellai 9 50123) Richard Easterling 294417
Rome Church of the Resurrection **M** (25) In care of St Pauls Via Napoli 58 00184 (Mail to: c/o St Pauls Church Via Napoli 58) (392) 258-6513
Rome St Pauls within the Walls **P** (265) Via Napoli 58 00184 (Mail to: Via Napoli 58 00184) Austin Rios Francisco Alberca Merino (06) 488 3339

Santa Maria a Ferrano Santa Maria Chapel, Santa Maria a Ferrano Retreat Center (Mail to: Via de' Renai 19, 50060 Pelago (Fi)) Thomas Muller +39 055 0456 959

Switzerland

Geneva 1201 Emmanuel Episcopal Church **P** (290) 3 Rue de Monthoux (Mail to: C/O Convocation Of American Churches 3 Rue De Monthoux 1201) Michael Rusk

STATE OF FLORIDA
Dioceses of Central Florida (CF), Central Gulf Coast (CGC), Florida (FL), Southeast Florida (SeF), and Southwest Florida (SwF)

Apalachicola—CGC
Apopka—CF
Arcadia—SwF
Auburndale—CF
Avon Pk—CF
Bartow—CF
Belleview—CF
Big Pine Key—SeF
Biscayne Park—SeF
Boca Grande—SwF
Boca Raton—SeF
Bonita Spgs—SwF
Boynton Bch—SeF
Bradenton—SwF
Brooksville—SwF
Bushnell—CF
Cantonment—CGC
Cape Coral—SwF
Carrabelle—FL
Cedar Key—FL
Chickasaw—CGC
Chiefland—FL
Chipley—CGC
Clearwater—SwF
Clermont—CF
Clewiston—SeF
Cocoa—CF
Cocoa Bch—CF
Coral Gables—SeF
Crescent City—FL
Crestview—CGC
Crystal River—CF
Dade City—SwF
Daytona Bch—CF
Deerfield Bch—SeF
Defuniak Spgs—CGC
Deland—CF
Delray Bch—SeF
Destin—CGC
Dunedin—SwF
Dunnellon—CF
E Palatka—FL
Englewood—SwF
Enterprise—CF
Eustis—CF
Fernandina Bch—FL
Ft Lauderdale—SeF

Ft Meade—CF
Ft Myers—SwF
Ft Pierce—CF
Ft Walton Bch—CGC
Fruitland Pk—CF
Gainesville—FL
Green Cove Spgs—FL
Gulf Breeze—CGC
Haines City—CF
Hallandale Beach—SeF
Hawthorne—FL
High Spgs—FL
Hilliard—FL
Hobe Sound—SeF
Hollywood—SeF
Holmes Bch—SwF
Homestead—SeF
Hudson—SwF
Indian Rocks Bch—SwF
Interlachen—FL
Inverness—CF
Islamorada—SeF
Jacksonville—FL
Jacksonville Bch—FL
Jensen Bch—SeF
Key Biscayne—SeF
Key West—SeF
Kissimmee—CF
LaBelle—SwF
Lake City—FL
Lake Mary—CF
Lake Placid—CF
Lake Wales—CF
Lake Worth—SeF
Lakeland—CF
Largo—SwF
Lecanto—CF
Leesburg—CF
Lehigh Acres—SwF
Live Oak—FL
Longboat Key—SwF
Longwood—CF
Madison—FL
Maitland—CF
Marathon—SeF
Marco Is—SwF

Marianna—CGC
Mayo—FL
Melbourne—CF
Melbourne Bch—CF
Melrose—FL
Merritt Is—CF
Miami—SeF
Miami Bch—SeF
Miami Lakes—SeF
Micanopy—FL
Milton—CGC
Monticello—FL
Mt Dora—CF
Naples—SwF
Navarre—CGC
Newberry—FL
New Pt Richey—SwF
New Smyrna—CF
Niceville—CGC
N Ft Myers—SwF
N Miami Bch—SeF
N Port—SwF
Ocala—CF
Okahumpka—CF
Okeechobee—CF
Opa Locka—SeF
Orange City—CF
Orange Pk—FL
Orlando—CF
Ormond Bch—CF
Osprey—SwF
Oviedo—CF
Palatka—FL
Palm Bay—CF
Palm Bch—SeF
Palm Bch Gdn—SeF
Palm City—SeF
Palm Coast—FL
Palm Hbr—SwF
Palmetto—SwF
Panama City—CGC
Panama City Bch—CGC
Pensacola—CGC
Perry—FL
Pinellas Pk—SwF
Plant City—SwF

Pompano Bch—SeF
Ponte Vedra—FL
Ponte Vedra Bch—FL
Pt Charlotte—SwF
Pt Orange—CF
Pt St Joe—CGC
Pt St Lucie—CF
Punta Gorda—SwF
Quincy—FL
Riviera Beach—SeF
Safety Hbr—SwF
St Augustine—FL
St Cloud—CF
St James City—SwF
St Johns—FL
St Petersburg—SwF
Sanford—CF
Sanibel—SwF
Santa Rosa Bch—CGC
Sarasota—SwF
Satellite Bch—CF
Sebastian—CF
Sebring—CF
Seminole—SwF
Spring Hill—SwF
Starke—FL
Stuart—SeF
Sun City Ctr—SwF
Tallahassee—FL
Tampa—SwF
Tarpon Spgs—SwF
Temple Terrace—SwF
Tequesta—SeF
The Villages—CF
Titusville—CF
Valrico—SwF
Venice—SwF
Vero Bch—CF
Welaka—FL
W Palm Bch—SeF
Wesley Chapel—SwF
Wewahitchka—CGC
Williston—FL
Winter Garden—CF
Winter Haven—CF
Winter Pk—CF
Zephyrhills—SwF

DIOCESE OF FLORIDA
(PROVINCE IV)
Comprises the northern part of the State of Florida
DIOCESAN OFFICE 325 N Market St Jacksonville FL 32202
TEL (904) 356-1328 FAX (904) 355-1934
E-MAIL sengemann@diocesefl.org WEB www.diocesefl.org

Previous Bishops—
Francis H Rutledge 1851-66, John F Young 1867-85, Edwin G Weed 1886-24, Frank A Juhan 1924-56, Ed Hamilton West 1956-74, Frank S Cerveny coadj 1974-75 Bp 1975-92, Stephen H Jecko 1994-2004

Bishop—Rt Rev Samuel J Howard (992) (Dio 1 Nov 03)

Cn to Ord & DDO A Defoor; *Reg Cns: First Coast East* BW Ammons; *First Coast West* T Murray; *River* R Goolsby; *Santa Fe* A Powel; *Apalachee* S Pessah; *Sec* S Minton; *Treas* D Lester; *Dn* K Moorehead; *Comp* K Hartwig N Castiov; *Bp Exec Asst* V Haskew; *Chanc* Hon F Isaac; *Ecum & Outrch* Rev Cn RV Lee III; *Camp & Conf Ctr* R Winton-

Stand Comm—Cler: Pres J Gibbes T Seagle *Lay:* A Crofton E Hill R Williams

PARISHES, MISSIONS, AND CLERGY

Carrabelle Church of the Ascension **M** (42) 110 NE 1st St 32322-2172 (Mail to: PO Box 546 32322-0546) (850) 545-2578

Cedar Key Christ Episcopal Church **M** (48) Corner of Hwy 24 & 5th Street 32625-5154 (Mail to: PO Box 210 32625-0210) Robert Davis (352) 543-6407

Chiefland St Alban Episcopal Church **M** (68) 7550 NW 149th Pl 32626 (Mail to: PO Box 997 32644-0997) (352) 493-2770

Crescent City Church of the Holy Comforter **M** (44) 223 N Summit St 32112-2301 (Mail to: 223 N Summit St 32112-2301) Timothy Thomas (386) 698-1983

East Palatka St Paul Episcopal Church **P** (44) 124 Commercial Ave 32131-4363 (Mail to: PO Box 6 32145-0006) Joe Dunagan (904) 692-1967

Fernandina Bch St Peter's Episcopal Church **P** (893) 801 Atlantic Ave 32034-3628 (Mail to: 801 Atlantic Ave 32034-3628) Joseph Woodfin (904) 261-4293

Gainesville Chapel of the Incarnation **CC** (60) 1522 W University Ave 32603-1812 (Mail to: 325 N Market St 32202-2732) Adam Young (352) 372-8506

Gainesville Holy Trinity Episcopal Church **P** (1247) 100 NE 1st St 32601-5379 (Mail to: 100 NE 1st St 32601-5379) John Montgomery (352) 372-4721

Gainesville St Michael Episcopal Church **P** (51) 4315 NW 23rd Ave 32606-6542 (Mail to: 4315

NW 23rd Ave 32606-6587) (352) 376-8184

Green Cv Spg St Mary Episcopal Church **P** (221) 400 Saint Johns Ave 32043-3051 (Mail to: PO Box 1346 32043-1346) (904) 284-5434

Hawthorne Church of the Holy Communion **M** (31) 21810 SE 69th Ave 32640-3959 (Mail to: PO Box 655 32640-0655) (352) 481-3600

High Springs St Bartholomews Episcopal Ch **M** (126) 105 NW 2nd St 32643-0004 (Mail to: PO Box 906 32655-0906) (386) 454-9812

Hilliard Bethany Episcopal Church **M** (24) 15860 County Road 108 PO Box 1005 32046-6711 (Mail to: PO Box 1005 32046-1005) William Smith (904) 845-2304

Interlachen St Andrew's Episcopal Church **M** (118) 111 S. Francis St 32148-7305 (Mail to: PO Box 41 107 S Frances Street 32148) (386) 684-4506

Jacksonville All Saints Episcopal Church **P** (441) 4171 Hendricks Ave 32207-6323 (Mail to: 4171 Hendricks Ave 32207-6398) Elizabeth Greenman (904) 737-8488

Jacksonville Church of Our Saviour **P** (1364) 12236 Mandarin Rd 32223-1813 (Mail to: 12236 Mandarin Rd 32223-1877) Joseph Gibbes (904) 268-9457

Jacksonville The Ch of the Good Shepherd **P** (252) 1100 Stockton St 32204 (Mail to: 1100 Stockton St 32204) Brent Owens (904) 387-5691

Jacksonville Resurrection Episcopal Church **P** (67) 12355 Fort Caroline Rd 32225-1708 (Mail to: 12355 Fort Caroline Rd 32225-1708) (904) 641-8177

Jacksonville St Andrew's Episcopal Church **P** (203) 7801 Lone Star Rd 32211-6001 (Mail to: 7801 Lone Star Rd 32211-6095) Lisa Meirow (904) 725-6566

Jacksonville St Catherine Episcopal Church **P** (202) 4758 Shelby Ave 32210-1716 (Mail to: 4758 Shelby Ave 32210-1716) (904) 387-2061

Jacksonville St Elizabeths Episcopal Church **P** (70) 1735 Leonid Rd 32218-4727 (Mail to: 1735 Leonid Rd 32218-4727) (904) 751-2626

Jacksonville St Gabriel Episcopal Church **M** (68) 5235 Moncrief Rd W 32209-1042 (Mail to: PO Box 12252 32209-0252) (904) 765-0964

Jacksonville Saint George Episcopal Church **P** (124) 10560 Fort George Rd 32226-2442 (Mail to: 10560 Fort George Rd 32226-2442) Jonathan Baugh (904) 251-9272

✠ **Jacksonville** St John Episcopal Cathedral **O** (1437) 256 E Church St 32202-3132 (Mail to: 256 E Church St 32202-3186) Kate Moorehead

Jean Dodd Saundra Kidd Saundra Kidd (904) 356-5507

Jacksonville St Lukes Episcopal Church **P** (238) 2961 University Boulevard N 32211-3398 (Mail to: 2961 University Blvd N 32211-3398) (904) 744-2133

Jacksonville St Mark Episcopal Church **P** (1580) § 4129 Oxford Ave 32210-4425 (Mail to: 4129 Oxford Ave 32210-4404) Thomas Murray (904) 388-2681

Jacksonville St Marys Episcopal Church **M** (296) PO Box 3243 32206-0243 (Mail to: 1924 N Laura St 32206-3633) Marie Tjoflat (904) 354-5075

Jacksonville St Pauls Episcopal Church **P** (89) 5616 Atlantic Blvd 32207-2204 (Mail to: 5616 Atlantic Blvd 32207-2204) (904) 725-1150

Jacksonville St Peters Episcopal Church **P** (898) 5043 Timuquana Rd 32210-7440 (Mail to: 5042 Timuquana Rd 32210-7475) (904) 778-1434

Jacksonville St Philips Episcopal Church **P** (216) 321 Union St W 32202-4020 (Mail to: 321 Union St W 32202-4020) (904) 354-1053

Jacksonville San Jose Episcopal Church **HC** (450) § 7423 San Jose Blvd 32217-3429 (Mail to: 7423 San Jose Blvd Ste A 32217-3498) Stephen Britt Sara Rich (904) 733-1811

Jacksonville The Church of the Redeemer **P** (254) 7500 Southside Blvd 32256-7095 (Mail to: 7500 Southside Blvd 32256-7095) Benjamin Ammons (904) 642-4575

Jaxville Bch St Pauls by the Sea Episcopal **P** (549) 465 11th Ave N 32250-4722 (Mail to: 465 11th Ave N 32250-4722) Connie Loch (904) 249-4091

Lake City St James Episcopal Church **P** (216) 2423 SW Bascom Norris Dr 32025-4912 (Mail to: 2423 SW Bascom Norris Dr 32025-4912) (386) 752-2218

Live Oak St Luke's Episcopal Church **P** (317) 1391 SW 11th Street 32064 (Mail to: PO Box 1238 32064-1238) Phyllis Doty (386) 362-1837

Madison St Mary Episcopal Church **M** (103) 104 N Horry Ave 32340 (Mail to: PO Box 611 32341-0611) (850) 973-8338

Mayo St Matthew Episcopal Church **M** (5) PO Box 1570 32066-1570 (Mail to: PO Box 1570 32066-1570) (386) 294-1839

Melrose Trinity Episcopal Church **P** (172) 204 State Road 26 32666-3901 (Mail to: PO Box 361 32666-0361) Anthony Powell (352) 475-2177

Micanopy Church of the Mediator **M** (51) PO Box 184 32667-4108 (Mail to: PO Box 184 32667-0184) (352) 466-3364

Monticello Christ Church Episcopal **P** (115) 425 N Cherry St 32344-2001 (Mail to: 425 N Cherry St 32344-2001) Stephen Pessah (850) 997-4116

Newberry St Joseph Episcopal Church **P** (144) 16921 W Newberry Rd 32669-2811 (Mail to: 16921 W Newberry Rd 32669-2811) Michael Snider (352) 472-2951

Orange Park Grace Episcopal Church **P** (343) § 151 Kingsley Ave 32073-5640 (Mail to: 245 Kingsley Ave 32073-5695) Aaron Smith Aaron Smith (904) 264-9981

Palatka St Mark's Episcopal Church **P** (114) 211 Main Street 32177-3508 (Mail to: PO Box 370 32178-0370) (386) 328-1474

Palatka St Marys Episcopal Church **M** (15) Mrs Edith Alexander 809 Saint Johns Ave 32177-4647 (Mail to: 312 N 2nd St 32177-3508) (386) 328-6394

Palm Coast St Thomas Epis Ch of Flagle **P** (441) 5400 Belle Terre Pkwy 32137-8824 (Mail to: 5400 Belle Terre Pkwy 32137-8824) Robert Goolsby Horace Johnson Alfred Stefanik (386) 446-2300

Perry St James Episcopal Church **P** (67) 1100 W Green St 32347-3107 (Mail to: 1100 W Green St 32347-3107) (850) 584-7636

Ponte Vedra St Francis in the Field **P** (722) 895 Palm Valley Rd 32081-4315 (Mail to: 895 Palm Valley Rd 32081-4315) Justin Yawn (904) 615-2130

Ponte Vedra Beach Christ Episcopal Church **M** (5376) § 400 San Juan Dr 32082-2836 (Mail to: PO Box 1558 32004-1558) Tom Reeder Keith Oglesby Andreis Diaz Dorta Tom Reeder Amy Slater (904) 285-6127

Quincy St Paul Episcopal Church **P** (61) 10 W King St 32351-1702 (Mail to: 10 W King St 32351-1702) (850) 627-6257

Saint Johns St Patricks Episcopal Church **P** (264) 1221 State Road 13 32259-3184 (Mail to: 1221 State Road 13 32259-3184) John Palarine (904) 287-2807

St Augustine St Cyprian Episcopal Church **M** (181) 37 Lovett St 32084-4858 (Mail to: 37 Lovett St 32084-4858) (904) 829-8828

St Augustine Trinity Episcopal Parish **P** (1215) 215 Saint George St 32084-4410 (Mail to: 215 Saint George St 32084-4410) Matthew Marino Curtis Benham Kenneth Herzog (904) 824-2876

Starke St Mark Episcopal Church **P** (85) 212 N Church St 32091-3414 (Mail to: PO Box 487 32091-0487) (904) 964-6126

Tallahassee Episcopal Church of the Advent **P** (213) § 815 Piedmont Dr 32312-2422 (Mail to: 815 Piedmont Dr 32312-2400) Bret Hays (850) 386-5109

Tallahassee Episcopal University Center **Chapel** (49) 655 W Jefferson St 32304-8013 (Mail to: 325 N Market St 32202-2732) James Hill (850) 296-7843

Tallahassee Grace Mission Church **M** (184) 303 W Brevard St 32301-1117 (Mail to: PO Box 10472 32302-2472) Jeanie Beyer (850) 224-3817

Tallahassee Church of the Holy Comforter **P** (541) § 2015 Fleischmann Rd 32308 (Mail to:

2015 Fleischmann Rd 32308-0561) Elizabeth Pessah (850) 877-2712

Tallahassee St John's Episcopal Church **P** (1574) 211 N Monroe St 32301-7619 (Mail to: 211 N Monroe St 32301-7691) Thomas Lacy (850) 222-2636

Tallahassee St Mic & All Angels Epis Ch **P** (140) 1405 Melvin St 32301-4232 (Mail to: 1405

Melvin St 32301-4232) Hugh Chapman (850) 681-0844

Welaka Emmanuel Episcopal Church **M** (11) PO Box 302 672 Third Ave 32193-0302 (Mail to: PO Box 302 32193-0302) (386) 698-1983

Williston St Barnabas Episcopal Church **M** (26) PO Box 615 32696-2050 (Mail to: PO Box 615 32696-0615) (352) 528-2593

EPISCOPAL DIOCESE OF FOND DU LAC

(PROVINCE V)
The northeast and northcentral part of Wisconsin
DIOCESAN OFFICE 1051 N Lynndale Dr Ste 1B
Appleton WI 54914-3094
TEL (920) 830-8866
E-MAIL diofdl@diofdl.org WEB diofdl.org

Previous Bishops—
John HH Brown 1875-88, Chas C Grafton 1889-1912, Reginald H Weller coadj 1900 Bp 1912-33, Harwood Sturtevant coadj 1929 Bp 1933-56, William H Brady coadj 1953 Bp 1956-80, William L Stevens 1980-94; Russell E Jacobus 1994-2013

Bishop—Rt Rev Matthew A Gunter (1081) (Dio 26 Apr 2014)

Sec Rev J Biegler; *Admin* MP Payne; *Treas* J Limberger; *Reg* MP Payne; *Chanc* G Stillings; *Cursillo* J Barnes; *Trans Min* Rev M Albright; *Dcn Cncl* Ven M Whitford; *Dcn Schl* Rev G Kanestrom; *Sisterhood of the Hly Nat* Sr Abigail; *UTO* C Dobrzynski; *Yth Min* E Wolf; ; *Com Min* Rev M Burkert-Brist; *CPC* K Powers; *EfM* Rev R Patience; *Trustees* Rev J Biegler; *Sum Cmp* E Wolf; *Const & Cns* M Payne; *Fin Rvw Tm* EA Peterson; *Archivist* MP Payne; *Historiographer* MP Payne; *Chaps Ret Clergy* Rev J & K Peterson; *Intake Ofcr* Rev J Hendrix; *Deaneries Chairs: Lake Winnebago* Rev R Osborne; *Green Bay* Rev G Kanestrom; *Wisconsin River* Rev M Albright; *Mosaic Task Force* M Mims & Rev C Wilkerson; *Companion Diocese* R Alexander; *Faithful Innovations* C Cowling; *Clergy Spouse Council* L Gunter

Stand Comm—Cler: Pres Rev J Hendrix W Bulson P Coey J Throop; *Lay:* S Gilbert EA Peterson C Sampson M Mims

PARISHES, MISSIONS, AND CLERGY

Algoma St. Agnes Episcopal Church **M** (19) 806 4th St 54201-1348 (Mail to: 806 4th St 54201-1348) Robert Hoppe (920) 4872015

Amherst St. Olaf's Episcopal Church **M** (28) 277 N Main St 54406-9101 (Mail to: PO Box 204 54406-0204) (715) 8242577

Antigo St. Ambrose Episcopal Church **M** (11) 800 6th Ave 54409-1856 (Mail to: PO Box 134 54409-0134) (715) 6235532

Appleton All Saints Episcopal Church **P** (218) 100 N Drew St 54911-5421 (Mail to: 100 N Drew St 54911-5421) (920) 7343656

De Pere St. Anne's Episcopal Church **P** (218) 347 Libal St 54115-3460 (Mail to: 347 Libal St 54115-3460) Tyler Richards Mary Adams (920) 3369571

Eagle River St. Francis Episcopal Church **M** (14) 120 Silver Lake Rd 54521-8017 (Mail to: PO Box 1625 54521-1625) (715) 4804237

Elkhart Lake All Saints Episcopal Chapel **SC** N7902 County Rd P 53020 (Mail to: C/O Grace Episcopal Church 630 Ontario Ave 53081-4029) Karl Schaffenburg (920) 4529659

Fish Creek Atonement Episcopal Chapel **SC** 9415 Cottage Row 54212 (Mail to: PO Box 241 54212-0241) (920) 8682700

✠ **Fond du Lac** Cathedral Church of St. Paul **O** (172) 51 W Division St 54935-4028 (Mail to: 51 W Division St 54935-4028) Cecil Perkins Christopher Arnold Michael Hackbarth Ezgi Perkins (920) 9213363

Gardner Precious Blood Episcopal Church **M** (11) County Rd C And County Rd N 54204 (Mail to: c o Janice Englebert 9834 County Rd N 54204-9779) Robert Hoppe (920) 4872015

Manitowoc St. James Episcopal Church **P** (98) 434 N 8th St 54220-4010 (Mail to: 434 N 8th St 54220-4010) (920) 6848256

Marinette St. Paul's Episcopal Church **P** (93) 917 Church St 54143-2408 (Mail to: 917 Church St 54143-2408) Glenn Kanestrom (715) 7353719

Menasha St. Thomas Episcopal Church **P** (853) 226 Washington St 54952-3353 (Mail to: 226 Washington St 54952-3396) Ralph Osborne Aran Walter (920) 7255601

Merrill Ascension Episcopal Church **M** (54) 218 Pier St 54452-2449 (Mail to: 218 Pier St 54452-2449) Linda Schmidt (715) 5390857

Minocqua St. Matthias Episcopal Church **P** (178) 403 E Chicago Ave 54548-9300 (Mail to: PO Box 936 54548-0936) (715) 3566758

Mosinee St. James Episcopal Church **M** (46) 409 2nd St 54455-1420 (Mail to: PO Box 24 54455-0024) (715) 5738830

New London St. John's Episcopal Church **M** (57) 1513 Pinewood Ln 54961-2449 (Mail to: 1513 Pinewood Ln 54961-2449) Portia Corbin (920) 2505752

Oneida Holy Apostles Episcopal Church **M** (281) 2937 Freedom Rd 54155-8926 (Mail to: 2937 Freedom Rd 54155-8926) Rodger Patience Deborah Heckel (920) 8692565

Oshkosh Trinity Episcopal Church **P** (147) 203 Algoma Blvd 54901-4739 (Mail to: 311 Division St 54901-4884) Nancy Behm Christopher Corbin (920) 2312420

Plymouth St. Paul's Episcopal Church **M** (95) 312 E Main St 53073-1817 (Mail to: PO Box 192 53073-0192) Michele Whitford (920) 8924894

Rhinelander St. Augustine's Episcopal Church **P** (80) 39 S Pelham St 54501-3458 (Mail to: PO Box 771 54501-0771) Meredyth Albright (715) 3623184

Ripon St. Peter's Episcopal Church **P** (52) 217 Houston St 54971-1566 (Mail to: 217 Houston St 54971-1566) Ezgi Perkins (920) 7482422

Shawano St. John's Episcopal Church **M** (27) 141 S Smalley St 54166-2347 (Mail to: 141 S Smalley St 54166-2347) (715) 5263686

Sheboygan Grace Episcopal Church **P** (178) 1011 N 7th St 53081-4019 (Mail to: 1011 N 7th St 53081-4019) William Bulson Nicole Beeck Michael Burg (920) 4529659

Sheboygan Falls St. Peter's Episcopal Church **P** (102) 104 Elm St 53085-1592 (Mail to: Attn: Financial Admin 104 Elm St 53085-1592) (920) 4676639

Sister Bay St. Luke's Episcopal Church **P** (101) 2336 Canterbury Ln 54234 (Mail to: PO Box 559 54234-0559) (920) 8549600

Stevens Point Intercession Episcopal Church **P** (126) 900 Brilowski Rd 54482-8461 (Mail to: Beloved Community 900 Brilowski Rd 54482-8461) Jane Johnson (715) 3413233

Sturgeon Bay Christ the King Episcopal Church **M** (54) 512 Michigan St 54235-2220 (Mail to: PO Box 828 54235-0828) (920) 7433286

Sturgeon Bay Holy Nativity Episcopal Church **M** 3434 County Road Cc 54235-8611 (Mail to: PO Box 828 54235-0828) George Hillman (920) 7433286

Suamico St Barnabas Episcopal Church **M** (52) 2809 Flintville Rd 54313-7917 (Mail to: PO Box 225 54173-0225) Brien Beck (920) 434-2247

Waupaca St. Mark's Episcopal Church **P** (110) 415 S Main St 54981-1746 (Mail to: PO Box 561 54981-0561) (715) 2585125

Waupun Holy Trinity Episcopal Church **M** (43) 315 E Jefferson St 53963-2032 (Mail to: PO Box 488 53963-0488) (920) 3245700

Wausau St. John's Episcopal Church **P** (177) 330 Mcclellan St 54403-4841 (Mail to: 330 Mcclellan St 54403-4841) Barbara Sajna (715) 8456947

Wautoma St. Mary's Episcopal Chapel **SC** N2616 Bughs Lake Rd 54982-7130 (Mail to: 217 Houston St 54971-1566) (920) 7482422

Wisconsin Rapids St. John's Episcopal Church **P** (52) 320 Oak St 54494-4363 (Mail to: 320 Oak St 54494-4363) David Klutterman (715) 4232332

FRANCE

See Europe

STATE OF GEORGIA

Dioceses of Atlanta and Georgia

DIOCESE OF GEORGIA
(PROVINCE IV)
Comprises South Georgia
DIOCESAN OFFICE 18 E 34th St Savannah GA 31401
TEL (912) 236-4279 FAX (912) 236-2007
E-MAIL mlyons@gaepiscopal.org WEB www.gaepiscopal.org

Previous Bishops— Stephen Elliott 1841-66, John W Beckwith 1868-90, Cleland K Nelson 1892-1907, Frederick F Reese 1908-36, Middleton S Barnwell 1936-54, Albert R Stuart 1954-71, Paul Reeves 1972-85, Harry W Shipps 1985-94, Henry I Louttit 1995-2010, Scott Benhase 2010-20

Bishop—Rt Rev Frank Logue (1130) (Dio 31 May 2020)

Cn to Ord Rev L Lasch; *Chanc* Rev J Elliott 3016 N Patterson St Valdosta 31402; *Min Com* Rev L Byrd 1802 Abercorn St Savannah GA 31401; *Cong Dev* Dio Ofc Rev Cn L Lasch; *Comm Off & Reg Dio Ofc* L Williams; *Const & Can* B Cheatham 2 Sandy Point Savannah 31404; *ECW* C Jordan 7604 Arcola Rd Brooklet GA 30415; *Hist* Bishop F Logue; *Treas* B Robinson 366 E 56 St Savannah GA 31405 ; *Yth Progs* Rev Cn J Varner *E-mail:* jvarner@gaepiscopal.org *Web:* youth.georgiaepiscopal.org *Addiction Rec Dio Off* Rev RK Kelly; *Anti-Racism Dio Off* Dcn Y Owens; *Conf Ctr* B Rowell; *Cursillo* Rev K Brinson; *ER&D* Rev C Todd

Deans: Albany Rev R Nelson 408 South Lee St Americus GA 31709; *Augusta* Rev B Alford 2321 Lumpkin Rd Augusta 30906; *Central* Rev D Vaughn PO Box 30475 Vidalia GA 30475; *Savannah* W Willoughby III 1802 Abercorn St Savannah GA 31401 *Southeastern* Rev T Purdy 6329 Frederica Rd St Simons Island GA 31522; *Southwestern* Rev L Dellenbarger 516 East Broughton St Bainbridge GA 39817-4040

Stand Comm—Cler: Pres D Ronn A Crumpton T Clarkson RK Kelly W Willoughby; *Lay:* B Kitterman M Stevenson S Jennings C Wooten

PARISHES, MISSIONS, AND CLERGY

Albany St Patricks Episcopal Church **P** (248) 4800 Old Dawson Rd 31721-9151 (Mail to: 4800 Old Dawson Rd 31721-9151) Timothy Burger Kedron Nicholson (229) 432-7964

Albany St Pauls Episcopal Church **P** (307) 212 N Jefferson St 31701-2523 (Mail to: 212 N Jefferson St 31701-4892) Galen Mirate (229) 436-0196

Albany St John & St Marks Epis Church **P** (86) 2425 Cherry Laurel Ln 31705-4507 (Mail to: 2425 Cherry Laurel Ln 31705-4507) Ridenour Lamb (229) 436-5268

Americus Calvary Episcopal Church **P** (181) 408 Lee St 31709-3918 (Mail to: 408 S Lee St 31709-3918) Dianne Hall Johnny Lane (229) 924-3908

Augusta Christ Church **P** (29) 1904 Greene St 30904-3906 (Mail to: PO Box 2965 30914-2965) (706) 736-5165

Augusta Our Savior Episcopal Church **P** (174) 4227 Columbia Rd 30907-1466 (Mail to: 4227 Columbia Rd 30907-1466) Alvin Crumpton Saundra Turner (706) 863-1718

Augusta St Albans Episcopal Church **P** (156) 2321 Lumpkin Rd 30906-3014 (Mail to: 2321 Lumpkin Rd 30906-3014) Rosalyn Panton (706) 798-1482

Augusta St Augustine Cntbry Epis Ch **P** (263) 3321 Wheeler Rd 30909-3104 (Mail to: 3321 Wheeler Rd 30909-3199) Terri Degenhardt Elizabeth Forbes Kurt Miller John Warner (706) 738-6676

Augusta St Marys Church **M** (58) 1114 12th St 30901-2706 (Mail to: PO Box 2303 30903-2303) (706) 722-6061

Augusta St Pauls Church **P** (794) 605 Reynolds St 30901-1431 (Mail to: 605 Reynolds St 30901-1431) Eric Biddy William Dolen (706) 724-2485

Augusta Church of the Good Shepherd **P** (1525) 2230 Walton Way 30904-4302 (Mail to: 2230 Walton Way 30904-4302) Ted Clarkson Talmadge Bowden Sonia Sullivan-Clifton (706) 738-3386

Bainbridge St Johns Episcopal Church **P** (47) 516 E Broughton St 39817-4040 (Mail to: 516 E Broughton St 39817-4040) (229) 246-3554

Baxley St Thomas Aquinas Church **M** (15) 5686 Golden Isle W 31513-7937 (Mail to: PO Box 1283 31515-1283) Phillip Runge (912) 705-0287

Blakely Holy Trinity Episcopal Church **M** (8) PO Box 186 39823-0186 (Mail to: PO Box 186 39823-0186) (229) 723-3971

Brunswick Good Shepherd Church **M** (22) 1601 Macon Ave 31520-6653 (Mail to: 1601 Macon Ave 31520-6653) John Butin (912) 265-2663

Brunswick St Athanasius Episcopal Church **P** (162) C/O Mr Charles L Scott PO Box 977 31521-0977 (Mail to: C/O Mr Charles L Scott PO Box 977 31521-0977) (912) 342-8461

Brunswick St Marks Church **P** (460) § 900 Gloucester Street 31520 (Mail to: PO Box 1155 31521-1155) Alan Akridge Gary Jackson (912) 265-0600

Cochran Trinity Episcopal Church **M** (80) Corner of 5th & Cherry St 31014 (Mail to: PO Box 294 31014-0294) Joy Fisher George Porter Eschol Wiggins (478) 934-2771

Cordele Christ Episcopal Church **M** (158) 408 S 1st St 31015-1573 (Mail to: PO Box 264 31010-0264) (229) 273-2439

Darien St Andrews Episcopal Church **P** (217) PO Box D929 31305-0930 (Mail to: PO Box D929 31305-0930) (912) 437-4562

Darien St Cyprian Episcopal Church **M** (70) C/O Drawer Box 929 Fort King George Dr 31305 (Mail to: C/O Drawer Box 929 31305) Ted Clarkson (912) 437-4562

Dawson Church of the Holy Spirit **M** (7) 1170 Georgia Ave SE 39842-2112 (Mail to: Attn: Ann O Duskin 398 7th Ave NE 39842-1504) (229) 995-4729

Douglas St Andrew's Episcopal Church **P** (35) 204 Coffee Ave S 31533-0006 (Mail to: 204 Coffee Ave S 31533-0006) (912) 384-1712

Dublin Christ Church **P** (75) PO Box 417 31040-0417 (Mail to: PO Box 417 31040-0417) (478) 272-3003

Fitzgerald St Matthews Episcopal Church **M** (16) 212 W Pine St 31750-5800 (Mail to: PO Box 1153 212 W Pine St 31750-1153) Frank Christian Frank Christian (229) 423-5268

Hawkinsville St Lukes Episcopal Church **P** (91) Dooley At Broad Sts 31036 (Mail to: PO Box 273 31036-0273) Craig Dolack (478) 892-9373

Hephzibah Church of the Atonement **M** (53) 2616 Tobacco Rd 30815-7015 (Mail to: PO Box 5785 30916-5785) Lawrence Jesion (706) 796-3545

Hinesville St Philips Episcopal Church **P** (89) 302 E General Stewart Way 31313-2640 (Mail to: 302 E General Stewart Way 31313-2640) (912) 876-2744

Jekyll Island St Rich of Chichester Epis Msn **M** (14) PO Box 13007 31527-0007 (Mail to: PO Box 13007 31527-0007) Jesse Yarborough (912) 230-6341

Jesup St Pauls Episcopal Church **M** (297) PO Box 1291 31598-1291 (Mail to: PO Box 1291 31598-1291) Nathan Wilson (912) 427-3900

Kingsland King of Peace **P** (232) 6230 Laurel Island Pkwy 31548-6056 (Mail to: 6230 Laurel Island Pkwy 31548-6056) Aaron Brewer Doris Johnson (912) 510-8958

Louisville Epis Ch of St Mary Magdalene **M** (26) 321 W 7th St 30434-1307 (Mail to: PO Box 2 30434-0002) (478) 685-7019

Martinez Holy Comforter Church **M** (238) 473 Furys Ferry Rd 30907-8221 (Mail to: 473 Furys Ferry Rd 30907-8221) Lynn Prather (706) 210-1133

Moultrie St Margaret of Scotland Church **M** (41) 1499 S Main St 31768-5811 (Mail to: 112 1st Ave NE PO Box 925 31768-3902) (229) 616-1116

Pooler St Patricks Church **M** (86) PO Box 576 31322-0576 (Mail to: PO Box 576 31322-0576) (912) 748-6016

Quitman St James Episcopal Church **M** (68) 306 N Court St 31643-2036 (Mail to: PO Box 864

31643-0864) James Elliott James Elliott (229) 263-5053

Richmond Hill St Elizabeths Episcopal Church **P** (236) 16491 Ga Highway 144 31324-5367 (Mail to: 16491 GA Highway 144 31324-5367) Dwayne Varas (912) 727-2650

Rincon St Lukes Episcopal Church **M** (162) 155 Goshen Rd 31326-5546 (Mail to: 155 Goshen Rd 31326-5546) David Rose (912) 826-3332

Saint Marys Christ Episcopal Church **P** (95) 305 Wheeler St 31558-8431 (Mail to: 305 Wheeler St 31558-8431) (912) 882-5308

Sandersville Grace Episcopal Church M (30) PO Box 771 114 2nd Ave W 31082-0771 (Mail to: PO Box 771 31082-0771) (478) 552-5295

Savannah Christ Church Episcopal **P** (531) 28 Bull Street 31401 (Mail to: 18 Abercorn St 31401-2712) Michael White Patricia Davis Samantha Mckean Helen White Helen White (912) 236-2500

Savannah St Bartholomews Church **HC** C/O Dio Of Georgia 611 E Bay St 31401-1238 (Mail to: C/O Dio Of Georgia 611 E Bay St 31401-1238) William Willoughby (912) 232-0274

Savannah St Francis of Islands Epis Ch **P** (149) 590 Walthour Rd 31410-2610 (Mail to: 590 Walthour Rd 31410-2610) Ian Lasch (912) 897-5725

Savannah St Georges Episcopal Church **P** (92) 15 Willow Rd 31419-2627 (Mail to: PO Box 61297 31420-1297) David Lemburg (912) 925-6517

Savannah St Johns Episcopal Church **P** (736) 1 W Macon St 31401-4307 (Mail to: 1 W Macon St 31401-4399) Gavin Dunbar (912) 232-1251

Savannah Saint Matthews Church **P** (265) § 1401 Martin L King Jr Blvd 31415-7201 (Mail to: 1401 Martin L King Jr Blvd 31415-7201) Guillermo Arboleda Ella Roundtree (912) 234-4440

Savannah St Mic All Angels Epis Ch **P** (203) 3101 Waters Ave 31404-6259 (Mail to: 3101 Waters Ave 31404-6259) Roger Kelly (912) 3547230

Savannah St Peters Episcopal Church **P** (449) 3 Westridge Rd 31411-2951 (Mail to: 3 Westridge Rd 31411-2951) Kelly Steele William Lea David Wantland (912) 598-7242

Savannah St Thomas Episcopal Church **P** (383) 2 Saint Thomas Ave 31406-7533 (Mail to: 2 Saint Thomas Ave 31406-7533) William Collins Melanie Lemburg (912) 355-3110

✣ **Savannah** Colgte Ch of St Paul the Apstl **O** (356) 1802 Abercorn St 31401-8122 (Mail to: 1802 Abercorn St 31401-8122) William Willoughby Lauren Flowers William Willoughby James Carter Susan Gahagan Leonel Polanco De La Cruz (912) 232-0274

St Simons Is Christ Church Frederica **P** (938) 6329 Frederica Rd 31522-5812 (Mail to: 6329 Frederica Rd 31522-5812) Thomas Purdy Jan Saltzgaber James Wethern Ashton Williston (912) 638-8683

St Simons Is Church of the Holy Nativity **M** (97) 615 Mallory St 31522-4018 (Mail to: 615 Mallery St 31522-4018) Thomas Townsend (912) 638-3733

Statesboro Trinity Episcopal Church **P** (135) 4401 Country Club Rd 30458-9188 (Mail to: PO Box 2005 30459-2005) Charles Todd (912) 489-4208

Swainsboro Church of the Good Shepherd **M** (43) 621 W Main St 30401-3108 (Mail to: PO Box 74 30401-0074) (478) 237-7122

Thomasville All Saints Episcopal Church **P** (359) 443 S Hansell St 31792-5512 (Mail to: PO Box 2626 31799-2626) Paul Hancock George Brown (229) 228-9242

Thomasville Church of the Good Shepherd **M** (22) 515 N Oak St 31792-5046 (Mail to: PO Box 3136 31799-3136) (229) 403-7515

Thomasville St Thomas Episcopal Church **P** (302) § 216 Remington Ave 31792-5521 (Mail to: 216 Remington Ave 31792-5521) Judith Keith Charles Marsh (229) 226-5145

Thomson Holy Cross Episcopal Church **M** (24) 515 Fluker St 30824-3018 (Mail to: PO Box 211 30824-0211) Erwin Veale (706) 595-4342

Tifton St Annes Episcopal Church **P** (528) 2411 Central Ave N 31794-2855 (Mail to: C/O Emily Guerry PO Box 889 31793-0889)

Leeann Culbreath (229) 386-5989

Tybee Island All Saints Episcopal Church **M** (98) 804 Jones Ave 31328-8735 (Mail to: PO Box 727 31328-0727) (912) 786-5845

Valdosta Christ Episcopal Church **P** (631) 1521 N Patterson St 31602-3848 (Mail to: 1521 N Patterson St 31602-3848) (229) 242-5115

Valdosta Christ the King Episcopal Ch **P** (295) 101 E Central Ave Fl 3 31601-5500 (Mail to: PO Box 5531 31603-5531) (229) 247-6859

Valdosta St Barnabas Episcopal Church **M** (106) 3565 Bemiss Rd 31605-6074 (Mail to: 3565 Bemiss RD 31605-6074) Susan Gage (229) 242-5332

Vidalia Church of the Annunciation **P** (119) 1512 Meadows Ln 30474-4425 (Mail to: PO Box 1311 30475-1311) Denise Vaughn (912) 537-3776

Waycross Grace Episcopal Church **P** (176) 401 Pendleton St 31501-3645 (Mail to: 401 Pendleton St 31501-3645) (912) 283-8582

Waynesboro St Michaels Episcopal Church **P** (136) 515 S Liberty St 30830-1508 (Mail to: PO Box 50 30830-0050) Lawrence Jesion (706) 554-3465

Woodbine St Marks Episcopal Church **M** (16) 209 Bedell Ave 31569 (Mail to: PO Box 626 31569-0626) (912) 576-5005

GERMANY

See Europe

DIOCESE OF HAITI

EGLISE EPISCOPALE D'HAITI
(PROVINCE II)
Comprises the Republic of Haiti
DIOCESAN OFFICE BP 1309 Port-au-Prince HAITI
Tel 011 (509) 257-8116 FAX 011 (509) 257-3412
E-mail epihaiti@yahoo.com WEB www.egliseepiscopaledhaiti.org

Previous Bishops— James Theodore Holly (106A) 1874-1911, Harry R Carson (327) 1923-43, Spence Burton SSJE (417) suffr 1939-42, C Alfred Voegeli (441) 1943-71, Luc Anatole Jacques Garnier (660) 1971-94, Jean-Zaché Duracin (881) (1994-2019)

Bishop Suffragan—Rt RevOgé Beauvoir (1064) 2012)

Executive secretary RP F Cole WBHS; *Acct*; J-M J Gilles; *Dir Off of Dev; Chair of Stand Comm* RevF Desire; *Sec* M-E Duracin; *Hist* Rev Y François; *Chr*

Ed Off Rev F Casseus; *Prep of Dio Synods* G Orelien; *Comm to Examine* Rev M Jean Rev R Auguste; *COM* Rev N Bernier Rev F Valdema E Xavier

Standing Committee—Cler RP F Desiré RP M St Louis RP S Saint Louis; *Lay* J Plantin M Desjardins R Louis Charles

PARISHES, MISSIONS, AND CLERGY

Ambouchure St Joseph, **M** Rev Milor Medela

Anse-A-Galets St Francois D'Assise **M** (100) Bas Bureau #20 (Mail to: PO Box 1309), Rev Mardoche Vil

Arcahaie Christ-Roi (Leger) **M** (100) Leger (Mail to: Leger), Rev Max Accime

Arcahaie St Jean L'Evangeliste, **P** Jean Dumas (Mail to: Jean Dumas) Rev Max Accime

Aux Parques Dumale St Thomas, Rev Pierre Reginal Valliere

Arcahaie St Thomas, **P** Rev Max Accime

Bahot St Barthelemy, **M** Rev Michelet Jacob

Bainet Ascension, **P** Rev Jean Jean Junior

Bainet St Cyprien, **M** Labiche (Mail to: Labiche) Rev Jean Jean Junior

Bainet St Luc, **SC** La Bresilienne (Mail to: La Bresilienne) Rev Jean Jean Junior

Bainet St Matthieu, **SC** Begin-Laurent Rev Jean Jean Junior

Bayonnais Saint Mathieu, **M** Rev Wallin Descamps

Beaudin Jn Pierre St Paul, **S** Rev Michelet Jacob

Begin St Mathieu, **S** Rev Michelet Jacob

Belair Port-au-Prince, S La Redemption Ven. Kerwin Delicat

Bel-Air, Saint Innocents, Rév Gracia Kesner

Belladère, Transfiguration, Rev Jean Jacques Deravil

Bellevue Les Saints Innocents, **S** Rev Jean Jean Junior

Bernaco Annonciation, Rév Gracia Kesner

Beraud Ascension, Rev Abiade Lozama

Bero St Pierre, **S** Rev Michelet Jacob

Bigonet Bonne Nouvelle, **M** Rev Yves Semé

Bire St Marc, **S** Rev Yves Semé

Blanchard Ascension, Rév Gracia Kesner

Boc Banique ND de l'annonciation, Rev Père Noé Bernier

Bois Blanc Saint Marc, S Rev Wilfrid Plantin

Bois Brule St Jacques, Rev Mardoche Vil

Bois Joly, Christ-Roi, Rév Gracia Kesner

Bois Neuf Notre Dame, **S** Rev Michelet Jacob

Bondeau Bon Samaritain,Rev Bertold Phanor

Bonbon Sainte Madeleine, Rev Jean Daniel Fils

Bongnotte Christ Roi, **S** Rev Pierre Reginald Valliere

Boucan carre St Timothe, Rev Jean Saint Vil Renaud

Boromain St innocents, Rev Jean Alphonse Jean Philippe

Bras de gauche Bon samaritain, S Rev Jean Jean Junior

Buteau St Etienne, **P** Rev Milor Medela

Cabaret St Francois D'Assise, **S** Rev Samuel Louis Charles

Cabestor, St Marc, Rév Gracia Kesner

Cajouc-Franc Saint Mathias, Rév Gracia Kesner

Campan St Barthelemy, **M** Rev Pierre Reginald Valliere

Camp Perrin Saint Mathias, Rev Père Rosannas Toussaint

Cange Bon Sauveur, **M** (400) Plateau Central Rte #3, Rév Gracia Kesner

Cange Hopital, Rév Gracia Kesner

Cap-Haitien Notre Dame, Molas Rev Wisnel Desjardins

Cap-Haitien St Esprit, Rev Wisnel Desjardins

Cavanack St Andre, **S** Rev Michelet Jacob

Cavaillon St Esprit, Rev Pierre Auguste

Caracol Saint Paul, Rev Gracia Kesner

Carrefour Ascension, **P** Rev Roldano Auguste

Carrefour Feuille St John The Evangelist, **S** Rev Fritz Desire

Carrefour Sainte Croix, **M** (100) Taifer Rev Roldano Auguste

Casse, St Barthelemy, Rév Gracia Kesner

Cayes St Jn Baptiste, **M** Savanette Rev Rogenor Joseph

Cayes St Sauveur, **P** Rev Pierre Auguste

Cayes Ste Croix, **M** Ravine-a-L'Anse Rev Pierre Auguste

Cayes Bishop Tharp Institute, **DI** Rev Abiade Lozama

Cazale St Andre, **M** (700) Route Port Salut, Rev Samuel Louis Charles

Chanlsome Transfiguration, **M** Rev Wilky Avril

Chapoteau Saint Mathieu, Rév Gracia Kesner

Château St Thimothee, Rév Gracia Kesner

Cerca Saint Marc, Rev Jean Alphonse Jean Philippe

Cerca la source St Marc, Rev Père Schneider Couloute

Chemins a boeuf St Esprit, **S** Rev Jean Jean Junior

Cherident St Mathias, **P** Rev Michelet Jacob

Chermaitre St Paul, **M** Rev Jonas Laborde

Civol Christ Roi, Rev Jean Alphonse Jean Philippe

College St Martin of Tour, DI Rev Jean Jeanno Joseph

Collin St Philippe & St Jacques, **S** Rev Yves Semé

Corail Christ-Roi, **S** Rev St Louis Michelin

Corps La transfiguration, **S** Rev Yves Seme

Corosse St Philippe St Jacques, Rev Jean Jacques Deravil

Cote de fer Bon Berger, **S** Rev Jean Jean Junior

Croix–des-Bouquets St Simeon, Rev Yonel Pierre

Crochu St Alban, Rev Yonel Pierre

Darbonne Annonciation, **P** Rev St Louis Michelin

David St Jacques, **S** Rev Michelet Jacob

Deslande St Mathias, Rev Jean Fruito Michaud

Delices St Mathias, **M** Rev Samuel Louis Charles

Delmas St Martin de Tours, Rev Jean Jeanno Joseph

Denard St Jacques, **S** Rev Jean Jean Junior

Diocese of Haiti partnership program, **DI** Rev Ajax Kesner

Diamond, Epiphanie, Rev Jean Alphonse Jean Philippe

Dubreuil St Barthelemy, Rev Rosanas Louis Toussaint

Dumal aux Parques St Thomas, **M** Rev Pierre Reginald Valliere

Duny St Simon & St Jude, Rev Mondesir Peti Frere

Dupera Porte Etroite, **S** Rev Jean Jean Junior

Dutete Saint Thomas, **S** Rev Jean Jean Junior
Epin St Jn Baptiste, Rév Gracia Kesner
Embourchure St Joseph, **P** Rev Milor Medela
Fiervil St Michel, **M** Rev Jonas Laborde
Flande St Andre, Rev Jean Jacques Deravil
Francoise St Barnabas, **S** Rev St Louis Michelin
Fond Grand St Paul, **S** Rev Pierre Reginald Valliere
Fond Parisien St Sacrement, Rev Michel Guerrier
Gaillard Chateau St Timothee, **M** Rev St Louis Michelin
Gascogne St Paul, Rev Jean Alphonse Jean Philippe
Gazou Saint Croix, **S** Rev Jean Jean Junior
Gandou Epiphanie, **S** Rev Jean Jean Junior
Gateau Tom St Patrick, **S** Rev Milor Medela
Gde Colline St Barthelemy, **M** Nan Mangot Rev Michelet Jacob
Gorman Transfiguration, Rev Michel Guerrier
Gonaives (Gros-Morne) Bon Samaritain, **P** Rev Jonas Laborde
Gonaives La Resurrection, **M** Rev Pere Wallin Descamps
Gonaives-Treille St Barnabas, **M** (200) Treille Rev Jonas Laborde
Gonaive Saint Basile le Grand, **P** Rev Wallin Descamps
Gonaives St Mathieu, **SC** Bayonnais Rev Wallin Descamps
Gracette St Matthias, Rev Frederick Menelas
Grande Colline St Mathias, Rev Michelet Jacob
Grand Colline Transfiguration, **S** Rev Max Accime
Grand Goave Danot bon Berger, **S** Rev Yves Seme
Grand Goave St Matthias, **M** Cherident—Rev Michelet Jacob
Grand Savane Christ the King, **S** Rev Willy Banna
Grand Riviere du Nord, S St Mathias, Rev Wisnel Desjardins
Gressier Saint Phillipe et Saint Jacques, Rev Mackenzy Jean
Gros Mornes Gonaive La Resurrection, Rev Colbert Estil
Gros Morne St Pierre, **M** Rev St Louis Michelin
Gros Mangles St Esprit, Rev Mardoche Vil
Hinche St Andre, **P** Rev Père Noé
Hicaque Saint Croix, Rev Gracia Kesner
Holy Trinity Cathedral Holy Trinity Fondamental and Secondary School, Rev Ricot Geffrard
Il de La Tortue St Aidan, **SC** Montry Rev André Wildaine
Jasmin St Joseph D'Arimathea, **M** Rev Yves Semé
Jacmel Christ Roi, Rev Jonas Beauvoir
Jacmel Duvillon Transfiguration, **S** Rev Jonas Beauvoir
Jacmel Lavano St Thomas, **S** Rev Jonas Beauvoir
Jacmel Marigot, St Esprit, **S** Rev Jonas Beauvoir
Jacmel Monchil, Christ-Roi, **P** Rev Jonas Beauvoir
Jean Dumas St Jean l'Evangelique, **M** Rev Max Accime

Jeanjean St Jean Baptiste, **M** Rev Pierre Reginald Valliere
Jeannette St Marc, Rev Moise Dorceus
Jeremie Sainte Croix, Rev Daniel Fils
Jacmel Mission St Joseph Embouchure, **SC** Embouchure, Rev Milor Medela
L'Acul Bon Samarithain, Rev Estil Colbert
Labegue Sts Innocents, Rev Père Noé
Lacorbe St Patrick, Rev Laguerre Jackson
Labiche Saint Cyprien, **M** Rev Jean Jean Junior
La Colline St Agnes, **S** Rev St Louis Michelin
La Chappelle St Michel, Rev Jean Alphonse Jean Philippe
La Bresilienne St Luc, **M** Rev Jean Jean Junior
La Feuillade la Toussaint, **S** Rev Jean Jean Junior
La Gonave (Bois Brule) St Jacques, **P** Bois Brule Anse-A-Galets, Rev Jean Madoché Vil
La Gonave Saint Jacques, **M** Rev Jean Madoché Vil
La Gonave Sainte Croix, **M** Rev Jean Madoché Vil
La Gonave St Innocents, **M** Anse-a-Galets, Rev Jean Madoché Vil
Lahoye Saint Jacques, Rev Jean Jacques Deravil,
La Ville de Jacmel St Barnabee, **S** Rev Jonas Beauvoir
La Tortue St Aidan, **P** Rev Wildaine André
Lascahobas Ascension, **M** (200) Pouly Rev Jean Jacques Deravil
Lascahobas St Andre, **M** (200) Flande Rev Jean Jacques Deravil
Lascahobas St Esprit, **P** Rev Jean Jacques Deravil
Lasile St Luc, **M** Rev Milor Medela
Latoumelle Ste Marguerite, **M** Rev Pierre Reginald Valliere
Larevoie Saint Thimothee, **S** Rev Jean Jean Junior
Leba Bonne Nouvelle, **S** Rev Michelet Jacob
Leger Christ-Roi, **M** Rev Max Accime
Leogane Bonne Nouvelle, **M** (300) Bigonet, Rev Yves Semé
Leogane Epiphanie l'Acul, **P** Rev Carmel Chery
Leogane Mission Saint Pierre, **M** Rev Jean Michelin Saint Louis
Leogane Mission St Andre, **M** (200) Citronnier Mithon, Rev Jean Michelin Saint Louis
Leogane Mission St Luc, **M** (100) L'Azile Citronier, Rev Medela Milor
Leogane Mission St Michel, **M** (300) Petit Orangers, Rev Jean Michelin Saint Louis
Leogane Mission St Timothee, **M** (300) Chateau Gaillard, Rev Jean Michelin Saint Louis
Leogane Paroisse Annonciation, **M** (400) Darbonne, Rev Jean Michelin Saint Louis
Leogane Ste Croix, **P** Rev Yves Semé
Leogane St Barthelemy, **M** (100) Campan , Rev Pierre Reginald Valliere
Leogane St Étienne, **P** Rev Milor Medela
Leogane St Jean Baptiste Jean Jean, Rev Pierre Reginald Valliere
Leogane St Jean L'Evangeliste, **M** Rev Pierre Reginald Valliere

Leogane St Joseph D'Arimathee, **SC** Jasmin Morne a Chandelle ,Rev Pierre Reginald Valliere

Leogane St Matthieu, **P** Rev Pierre Reginald Valliere

Leogane St Nicolas, **M** Rue Nicolas Rev Jean Makendy

Leogane Ste Marguerite, **M** (200) Latournelle Rev Pierre Reginal Valliere

Leprete Incarnation, Rev Frederick Menelas

Les Bayes St Jacques, Rev Jean Alphonse Jean Philippe

Lilavois St Marc, Rev Lionel Pierre

Limonade St Etienne, **P** Rev St Louis Samuel

Lotore St Barnabas, Rev Mardoche Vil

Loranette Epiphanie, Rev Père Noé

Lorcorbre Saint Patrick, Terviné Denise

Lhomond St Marc, Rev Frederick Menelas

M. Thomonde St Paul, Rév Denise Tervine Desire

Macabe St Andre, Rev Menelas Frederick

Machecana St Etienne, Rev Jean Alphonse Jean Philippe

Maissade St Barthelmy, Rev Père Noé

Maniche St Augustin **M** (200) Maniche, Rev Petit Homme Pierre

Mathieu St Mathieu, **P** Rev Pierre Reginald Valliere

Mercery St Luc, **M** Rev Seme Yves

Mersan Saint Thomas, Rev Pere Rosannas Toussaint

Meyer St Marguerite, **S** Rev Michelet Jacob

Miragoane St Marc, **M** Jeannette Paillant, Rev Père Moise Dorceus

Mirebalais St Jacques, **M** Rev Jean Alphonse Jean Philippe

Mirebalais St Luc, **M** (200) Pouille Rev Jean Alphonse Jean Philippe

Mirebalais St Pierre, Rev Jean Alphonse Jean Philippe

Mirebalais St Matthias, **M** (400) Deslandes, Rev Jean Fruito Michaud

Mirebalais St Paul **M** (100) Gascogne, Rev Jean Alphonse Jean Phillipe

Mirebalais St Pierre Episcopal Church, **P** Rev Jean Alphonse Jean Philippe

Mithon St Andre, **M** Rev St Louis Michelin

Moge Saint Jacques, Rév Gracia Kesner

Moise Christ-Roi, **S** Rev Joseph Rogenor

Molas Notre Dame, **M** Rev Andre Wildaine

Mombin Crochu St Benoit, Rev Celestin Gousse

Montrouis St Paul, **P** Rev Vetinel Jean Marc

Moreau St Jean Baptiste, **S** Rev Jonas Beauvoir

Morin Epiphanie, **S** Rev Michelet Jacob

Morin St Jean Baptiste, **S** Rev Roldano Auguste

Nordette St Patrick, Rev Jean Alphonse Jean Philippe

Morne Michel Saint Jean, Rév Gracia Kesner

Nan Mango St Barthelemy, Rev Mardoche Vil

Nicolas Saint Nicolas, **S** Rev Seme Yves

Nouvelle Cite Sainte Croix, Rev Mardoche Vil

Orangers St Michel, **M** Rev St Louis Michelin

Palissa St Philippe et St Jacques, Rév Gracia Kesner

Parcasse Confession de st Pierre, Rev Père Noé

Petionvile St Jacques Le Juste, **P** Rev Ricot Geffrard

Petion ville Cathedral Holy Trinity Holy Trinity Music school, **DI** Rev David Cesar

Petit Boucan St Jacques, **S** Rev Pierre Reginald Valliere

Petite Cotelette St Innocents, Rev Mardoche Vil

Petit Harpon St Jean Evangeliste, **M** Rev Willy Banna

Petit Trou de Nippes St Paul, Rev Desire Luc

Petite Rivière St Hilaire de Poltier, Rev Frederick Menelas

Petite Rivière de l'Artibonite Transfiguration, Rev Jean Fruito Michaud

Petite Riviere de l'Artibonite Saint Luc, Rev Jean Fruito Michaud

Petite Rivière de Nippes Saint Jacques Lindor, Rev Bertold Phanor

Pilard St Joseph D'Arimathe, **S** Rev Michelet Jacob

Palto St Thomas, Rev Jean Alphonse Jean Philippe

Platon Balai Sts Simon & Jude, Rev Mardoche Vil

Petite Riviere St Philippe et St Jacques, **S** Rev Jean Jean Junior

Plaine Mapou St Jean Baptiste, **M**, Rev Mardoche Vil

Pouille St Luc, Rev Jean Alphonse Jean Philippe

Pouly Ascension, Rev Jean Jacques Deravil

Port-au-Prince Annonciation Our Lady, **P** Rev Frantz Cole

Port-au-Prince Holy Trinity Cathedral, Rev Kerwin Delicat

Port-Au-Prince Paroisse Epiphanie, **P** Rev Fritz Desiré

Croix Des Bouquets St Alban **M** Rev Yonel Pierre

Port-Au-Prince St Marc, **P** Lilavois, Rev Yonel Pierre

Port-au-Prince St Martin de Tours, **P** Rev Jean Jeannot Joseph

Thomazeau St Michel & Tous, Les Anges Rev Irnel Duveaux

Croix des Bouquets St Simeon, **P** Père Yonel Pierre

Port-au-Prince Collège Saint Pierre, **DI** Rev Fritz Desire

Port-au-Prince Séminaire de Theologie, **DI** Rev Simpson Gabeaud

Port-de-Paix Sts Innocents, **P** Rev Wilky Avril

Ravine à l'Anse Sainte Croix, Rev Pierre Auguste

Roche Mulatre Saint Thomas, RévGracia Kesner

Rosette St Jacques, **M** Rev Fanfan Luckner

Salmadère St Etienne, Rev Père Noé

Saint Vincent School For Handicaped Children, Rev Inel Duveaux

Saurel Incarnation, **S** Rev Joseph Rogenor

Savanette-Plateau Central Mission St Philippe & St Jacques, **M** (200) Corosse, Rev Deravil Jean Jacques

Savanette-Sud St Jean Baptiste, Rev Rogenor Joseph
Sept, S St Thomas la Mer, Rev Père Noé
Siline Christ Roi, Rev Petit Homme Pierre
Taifer Ste Croix, **M** Rev Roldano Auguste
Terre-Casse St Jacques, Rev Père Noé Bernier
Terrier Rouge Christ Roi, **P** Rev Esperance Jabnel
Terrier Rouge St Barnabas, Rev Esperance Jabnel
Ticotelette Saints Innocents, Rev Jean Madoché Vil
Tierra Muscady Transfiguration, Rev D. Laguerre Jackson
Thomonde St Mathias, Rev Terviné Denise
Thomonde St Patrick, **M** (200) Locorbe, Rev Laguerre Jackson
Thomassique St Luc, Rev Fiefe Guirlene
Thor Ascension, **P** Rev Roldano Auguste
Torbeck Incarnation, **M** (100) Route Platon (Rev Louis Toussaint Rosanas)
Torbeck St Barthelemy, **M** Route Ducis Dubreuil, Rev Louis Toussaint Rosanas

Torbeck St Hilaire, **M** Route de Saint Jean, Rev Louis Toussaint Rosanas
Torbeck St Paul, Rev Menelas Frederick
Trade School St Esprit, **L** St Louis Samuel
Trade school Holy Trinity, **DI** Ven. Kerwin Delicat
Treille St Barnabas, Rev Jonas Laborde
Trou du Nord Saint Luc, **M** Rev Père Jean Nesly Ais
Trou-Jacques Sts Philippe & Jacques, Rev Mardoche Vil
Trouin St Marc, **P** Rev Petit Frere Mondesir
Trouin St Simeon et St Jude, **M** Platon Balai Duny, Rev Petit Frere Mondesir
Triano St André, Rev Jean Alphonse Jean
Tomazeau St Michel, Rev Inel Duveaux
Thor Ascension, Rev Roldano Auguste
Venant Saint Nom de Jesus, **S** Rev Jean Jean Junior
Vieux Cayes St Luc, Rév Gracia Kesner
4e Ave Bolosse Notre Dame, Rev Frantz Cole

DIOCESE OF HAWAII
(PROVINCE VIII)
DIOCESAN OFFICE 229 Queen Emma Sq Honolulu HI 96813
Tel (808) 536-7776 FAX (808) 538-7194
E-mail desposito@episcopalhawaii.org WEB www.episcopalhawaii.org

Previous Bishops—
Eng Bps: Thomas N Staley 1862-70, Alfred Willis 1872-1902. US Bps: Henry B Restarick 1902-20, John D La Mothe 1921-28, S Harrington Littell 1930-42, Chas P Gilson suffr 1961-67, Harry S Kennedy 1944-69, E Lani Hanchett 1967-75, Edmond L Browning 1976-85, Donald P Hart 1986-94, Richard SO Chang 1997-2007

Bishop—Rt Rev Robert L Fitzpatrick (1015) (Dio 10 Mar 2007)

Chanc W Yoshigai; *Treas* R Kusumoto; *Conv Sec* A Pasalo; *Reg* R Costa; *Hist* S Ching; *Cn to the Bishop* A Graham; *Ops Mgr* R Costa; *Controller* D Casey; *Exec Asst to Bishop* D Esposito; *Admin Asst* S Liu

Stand Comm—Cler: E Berman G King J Tomoso R Woo *Lay:* W Bonnet J Decker D Adams F Kramer

PARISHES, MISSIONS, AND CLERGY

Island of Hawaii

Hilo Church of the Holy Apostles **P** (198) 1407 Kapiolani St 96720 (Mail to: 1407 Kapiolani St 96720-4026) Katlin Mccallister (808) 935-5545

Kamuela Saint James Episcopal Church **P** (289) 65-1237 Kawaihae Rd 96743 (Mail to: Attn: Jaisy Jardine PO Box 278 96743-0278) David Stout Linda Lundgren (808) 885-4923
Kapaau St Augustines Episcopal Church **M** (140) 54-3801 Akoni Pule Hwy 96755 (Mail to: PO Box 220 96755-0220) Jennifer Masada Heather Mueller (808) 889-5390
Ocean View St Jude Episcopal Mission **M** (61) Paradise Circle Hov 96737 (Mail to: Star Rt Box 6026 96737) (808) 939-7000

Island of Kauai

Eleele Episcopal Church on West Kauai **M** (107) 322 A Mehana Rd 96705 (Mail to: PO Box 247 96705-0247) Maurice Goldsmith Kerry Holder-Joffrion (808) 335-5533
Kapaa All Saints Episcopal Church **P** (297) § 1065 Kuhio Hwy 96746 (Mail to: PO Box 248 96746-0248) David Jackson (808) 822-4267
Kilauea Christ Memorial Church **M** (56) 2509 Kolo Rd 96754-5576 (Mail to: PO Box 293 96754-0293) (808) 482-4824
Lihue St Michael & All Angels Church **P** (290) 4364 Hardy St 96766-1263 (Mail to: 4364 Hardy St 96766-1263) Andrew Mcmullen (808) 245-3796

Island of Maui

Kihei Trinity By-the-Sea Episcopal Church **P** (110) 100 Kulanihakoi St 96753-7300 (Mail to: 100 Kulanihakoi St 96753-7300) John Tomoso (808) 8790161

Kula St Johns Episcopal Church **P** (330) 8992 Kula Hwy 96790-7420 (Mail to: 8992 Kula Hwy 96790-7420) Andrew Walmisley George Wong (808) 878-1485

Lahaina Holy Innocents' Episcopal Ch **P** (106) 561 Front St 96761-1116 (Mail to: 561 Front St 96761-1116) (808) 661-4202

Wailuku Church of the Good Shepherd **P** (364) 2140 Main St 96793-1637 (Mail to: 2140 Main St 96793-1695) Linda Decker Robert Hino (808) 244-4656

Island of Molokai

Hoolehua Grace Episcopal Church **M** (46) 2210 Farrington Ave 96729 (Mail to: PO Box 157 96729-0157) (808) 567-6420

Island of Oahu

Aiea St Timothy's Episcopal Church **M** (159) 98-939 Moanalua Rd 96701-5012 (Mail to: Attn: Treasurer 98-939 Moanalua Rd 96701-5012) Karen Swanson (808) 488-5747

Honolulu Church of the Epiphany **P** (138) 1041 10th Ave 96816-2210 (Mail to: 1041 10th Ave 96816-2210) Christopher Bridges (808) 734-5706

Honolulu Church of the Holy Nativity **P** (123) § 5286 Kalanianaole Hwy 96821-1826 (Mail to: 5286 Kalanianaole Hwy 96821-1883) Elizabeth Berman Elizabeth Berman Jennifer Latham (808) 373-2131

Honolulu Good Samaritan Episcopal Church **M** (78) 1801 10th Ave 96816-2907 (Mail to: 1801 10th Ave 96816-2907) Malcolm Hee (808) 7355944

Honolulu Parish of St Clement **P** (309) § 1515 Wilder Ave 96822-4614 (Mail to: 1515 Wilder Ave 96822-4699) (808) 955-7745

✠ **Honolulu** Cathedral Church of St Andrew **O** (516) 229 Queen Emma Sq 96813-2334 (Mail to: 229 Queen Emma Sq 96813-2334) Heather Patton-Graham Steven Costa (808) 524-2822

Honolulu St Elizabeths Episcopal Church **P** (335) 720 N King St 96817-4511 (Mail to: 720 N King St 96817-4511) David Gierlach Imelda Padasdao (808) 845-2112

Honolulu St Luke Episcopal Church **M** (33) 45 N Judd St 96817-1760 (Mail to: 45 N Judd St 96817-1792) Raymond Woo (808) 533-3481

Honolulu St Mark Episcopal Parish **HC** (148) § 539 Kapahulu Ave 96815-3855 (Mail to: 539 Kapahulu Ave 96815-3855) Paul Lillie (808) 732-2333

Honolulu St Mary's Episcopal Ch **P** (64) 2062 S King St 96826-2219 (Mail to: 2062 S King St 96826-2219) Charles Browning (808) 949-4655

Honolulu St Paul Episcopal Church **M** (584) 229 Queen Emma Sq 96813-2334 (Mail to: 229 Queen Emma Sq 96813-2334) Randolph Albano Randolph Albano Peter Wu (808) 538-3275

Honolulu St Peters Episcopal Church **P** (305) 1317 Queen Emma St 96813-2301 (Mail to: 1317 Queen Emma St 96813-2394) (808) 533-1943

Honolulu St Albans Chapel Iolani School **M** 563 Kamoku St 96826-5245 (Mail to: Michelle Sugihara 563 Kamoku St 96826-5245) Timothy Morehouse (808) 943-2333

Kahuku Holy Cross **M** (8) 56-356 Kamehameha Hwy 96731-2213 (Mail to: PO Box 51 96731-0051) (808) 293-7330

Kailua Emmanuel Episcopal Church **M** (60) 780 Keolu Dr 96734-3508 (Mail to: 780 Keolu Dr 96734-3508) (808) 262-4548

Kailua St Christophers Church **P** (175) 93 N Kainalu Dr 96734-2331 (Mail to: 93 N Kainalu Dr 96734-2331) Giovan King (808) 262-8176

Kaneohe Calvary Episcopal Church **M** (133) 45-435 Aumoku St 96744 (Mail to: 45-435 Aumoku St 96744-2037) (808) 247-2733

Kaneohe St John's By-the-Sea Epis Ch **M** (98) 47-074 Lihikai Dr 96744-4762 (Mail to: 47-074 Lihikai Dr 96744-4762) Paul Lucas (808) 239-7198

Kapolei Halau Wa'a Episcopal **M** 91-1122 Kamaaha Loop 96707 (Mail to: C/O Diocesan Support Center 229 Queen Emma Sq 96813-2334) Mark Haworth

Kealakekua Christ Church Episcopal **P** (121) 81-1004 Konawaena School Rd 96750-8188 (Mail to: PO Box 545 96750-0545) Dwight Brown (808) 323-3429

Wahiawa St Stephen's Episcopal Church **P** (98) 1679 California Ave 96786-2511 (Mail to: 1679 California Ave 96786-2511) Baldo Patterson (808) 621-8662

Waianae St John the Baptist Epis Ch **M** (134) 87-227 St Johns Rd 96792-3259 (Mail to: 87-227 Saint Johns Rd 96792-3259) Helen Harper Marilyn Watts Mark Haworth (808) 696-5772

Waimanalo St Matthew Episcopal Church **M** (41) 41-054 Ehukai St 96795-0070 (Mail to: 41-054 Ehukai St PO Box 70 96795-1603) CS Honey Becker Ernesto Pasalo (808) 259-8664

DIOCESE OF HONDURAS
IGLESIA EPISCOPAL DE HONDURAS
(PROVINCE IX)
(Comprises the Republic of Honduras)
DIOCESAN OFFICE Colonia Trejo 23 Ave 21 Calle (MAIL: Apdo 586) San Pedro Sula Cortés 21105
TEL: 011 (504) 556-6155   FAX 011 (504) 556-6467
International Mail: IMC-SAP Dept 215 PO Box 523900 Miami FL 33152-3900
E-MAIL: honduras@anglicano.hn   WEB: www.avanzamedia.net/anglicano/

Previous Bishops—
Bishops in Charge: David E Richards
1968, Wm C Frey 1968-72, Albert E
Swift 1973, Anselmo Carral 1973-
78; Diocesan Bishops: Hugo L Pina
1978-83, Leopold Frade 1984-2000
James H Ottley int 2000-01

Bishop — Rt Rev Lloyd Emmanuel Allen (971)
(Dio 20 Oct 2001)

Cn to Ord Rev Cn A Brooks; *Oficina Pastoral* V Rev
Oscar López; *Dn Atlántida e Islas de la Bahía* V Rev
Rosa Angélica Gámez-Cordona; *Dn Tegucigalpa* M
Consuelo Cartegena de Arevalo; *Dn Comayagua* V
Rev H Madrid-Paz; *Dn Copán* V Rev JA Mejia; *Dn
El Paraíso* V Rev Dagobert Chacón-Rodríguez; *Dn
Omoa y Puerto Cortéz* V Rev F Midence; *Dn San
Pedro Sula* V Rev O López; *Dn St Bárbara* V Rev
José Luis Mendoza-Barahona-y-Rodríguez; *Treas* C
Antunez; *Sec* Rev J Francisco Lone; *ECW* R de Allen;
Com Min Rev A Brooks; *Social Min* JJ Calerón;
Comm & Pub Rel Cn E Monzón; *Finances* Dr G
Frazier; *Global Rel* C de Brooks; *Theology Ed* V Rev
Pascual Torres; *Faith* V Rev H Madrid-Paz; *Chris Ed*
Lic Elizabeth P de Torres; *Exam Chap* RA Gómez-
Cordona; *Stew* Rev F Midence-Valdés; *Bd Gov El
Hogar Proj* Rev H Madrid; *Cursillo* LP Consuelo
de Brenes; *Const and Can* V Rev P Torres; *Ecum* V
Rev P Torres; *Yth* Prof W Barret; *Reg* V Madisson de
Molina; *Chanc* V Rev P Torres; *Health* EM Galindo
MD Jose Arnaldo Mejia

Stand Comm–Cler: Pres Maria Consuelo Cartagena
de Arevalo Juan José Diaz Jose Alejandro Chirinos;
Lay Claudia Castro Wendy Avila Nativi Jethy
Yolanda Portillo Pedro Herrera

To call Honduras from the US, dial (011) 504, then
the number.

PARISHES, MISSIONS, AND CLERGY

Agua Caliente Misión Episcopal San Antonio **PS**
(198) San Antonio (Mail to: San Antonio)
Atima Iglesia Jesus Nazareno **M** (495) § Barrio de
Jesus (Mail to: Apdo. 586) (504) 556-6155
Cabanas San Francisco De Asis **M** (112) § San
Francisco de Asis (Mail to: San Francisco de
Asis)
Carrizalito Misión Epis San Juan Bautista **SC**
(623) Calle Central San Juan Bautista (Mail to:
San Juan Bautista)
Cedral Misión Episcopal San José **SC** (602)

Mision San Jose La Union (Mail to: La Union,
Cedral)
Chinda Mision Santa Maria Magdalena **SC** (413)
§ El Retiro (Mail to: Apartado Postal #586)
Choloma Iglesia Episcopal Cristo Rey **M** (457) §
Col. Exitos de Anach No 2 (Mail to: Apartado
586)
Comayaguela MDC Iglesia Epis Cristo Redentor
P (282) § Col America (Mail to: Lomas
Miraflores Sur Bloque D 4318) Luis Brenes
Vargas Aida Sanchez Navarro (504) 236-7116
Concepcion del Norte Iglesia Episcopal Santa
Ana **M** (430) § Apdo 24 Sta Barbara (Mail to:
Apdo 24 Sta Barbara)
Concepcion del Norte Iglesia Episcopal San
Mateo **M** (23) § El Cerron (Aldea) (Mail to:
Apartado No 586)
Concepcion del Norte Proteccion Santa Lucia **M**
(600) § Proteccion (Aldea) (Mail to: Apartado
No 586) Hector Madrid
Concepcion del Norte Vstacn de Bendita Virgen
Maria **M** (722) § Barrio Nuevo (Mail to:
Apartado No 586)
Copan Iglesia Epis Espiritu Santo **P** (127) § Santa
Rita (Mail to: Escuela Iglesia Espritu Santo PO
Box 071) Olga Barrera Flores
Copan Misión Epis El Buen Pastor **PS** (83) §
Las Juntas El Paraiso (Mail to: Las Juntas El
Paraiso)
Copan Misión Episcopal San Mateo **PS** (78) § San
Jose Miramar (Mail to: San Jose Miramar)
Copan Ruinas Misión Episcopal San Jorge **SC**
(156) § Agua Caliente (Mail to: Agua Caliente)
Copan Ruinas Misión San Juan Evangelista **SC**
(613) Sesemil II Principal (Mail to: Sesemil
Segundo CO)
Copan Ruinas Mssn Epis Santa María Virgen **PS**
(87) § Santa María Virgen 000000 (Mail to:
Santa María Virgen 000000)
Corralitos Mssn Epis San Miguel Arcangel **PS**
(575) § San Miguel Arcangel (Mail to: San
Miguel Arcangel)
Danli Iglesia Episcopal Cristo Rey **M** (411) §
Barrio El Carmelo (Mail to: El Carmelo)
Danli Iglesia Episcopal Manos de Dios **P**
(581) Colonia Nueva Esperanza (Mail to:
Iglesia Episc Manos de Dios Colonia Nueva
Esperanza) Victor Velasquez Martinez (504)
763-4096
Dona Ana Iglesia Episcopal San Miguel **M** (45) §
Andres Bremo (Mail to: Andres Bremo) (809)
420-1867

El **Cordoncillo** Iglesia Episcopal San Marcos **SC** (367) El Cordoncillo (Mail to: El Cordoncillo)

El **Paraiso** Misión Epis la Resurrección **PS** (640) Barrio San Jose (Mail to: Barrio San Jose)

El **Progreso** San Patricio **M** (362) § Barrio San Jose #1, 4 Ave 9 calle N.E. SPS 586 (Mail to: Barrio San Jose #1, 4 ave. 9 calle N.E. SPS 586)

El **Quebracho** Mision Episcopal San Nicolas **SC** (498) § El Quebracho (Mail to: El Quebracho)

El **Tigre** Misión Episcopal San Ignacio **PS** (331) § San Ignacio (Mail to: San Ignacio)

Guaimaca Mssn Epis la Transfiguración **PS** (441) § Barrio Arriba (Mail to: Barrio Arriba)

La **Ceiba** Igles Epis Santisima Trinidad **M** (344) § Avenida Morazan # 1175 28 (Mail to: Avenida Morazan # 1175 28) Nery Varela Zuniga Ethelridge Brooks (504) 440-2772

La **Laguna** Misión Episcopal San Felipe **SC** (27) San Felipe La Laguna (Mail to: San Felipe La Laguna)

Nueva Arcadia Cristo Salvador **M** (425) § Chalmeca (Mail to: Apartado Postal # 586)

Nueva Esperanza Misión Episcopal Santa Cruz **SC** (108) § Mision Santa Cruz (Mail to: Mision Santa Cruz)

Omoa Conversion de San Pablo **M** (168) § Principal, Frente al Centro Comunal (Mail to: Principal, Frente al Centro Comunal)

Omoa Iglesia Episcopal San Agustin **M** (180) § Aldea Barba Cheles (Mail to: Barba Cheles)

Omoa Iglesia Epis San Fernando Rey **M** (300) § Principal, Frente al Castillo (Mail to: Bo. San Martin 12 Calle 6/7 Ave Puerto C) 658-9062

Omoa Iglesia Episcopal San Marcos **M** (230) § Principal (Mail to: Principal)

Omoa Igle Epis Snta Mgrita Escocia **M** (38) § Principal Chachahuala (Mail to: Principal, Chachahuala)

Omoa Nativd de la Bndta Virg Maria **M** (96) § Real Asia Guatemala Centsica N-O 35 (Mail to: San Pedro Sula 35)

Omoa Igles Epis San Franco de Asis **SC** (44) § Principal Muchilena 586 (Mail to: Apartado Postal # 35)

Oropoli Misión Epis la Anunciación **PS** (26) Melaisipio Oropoli (Mail to: La Anunciacion)

Petoa Iglesia Episcopal San Joaquin **M** (462) § San Joaquin (Mail to: Apartado 586)

Petoa Iglesia Epis San Pedro Apostol **P** (146) Calle Real Principal (Mail to: Apartado Postal 1106)

Petoa La Resurrección **M** (39) § Plan del Portillo (Aldea) (Mail to: Apartado No 586)

Pozo Azul el Rosario Santo Tomas Apostol **M** (350) § Principal (Mail to: Apartado Postal # 30)

Proteccion Misión Episcopal en Nuevas Delicias **PS** (90) Nuevas Delicias (Mail to: Nuevas Delicias)

Proteccion Misión Epis en Nuevo Porvenir **PS** (94) Pueblo Nuevo (Mail to: Pueblo Nuevo)

Proteccion Santo Tomás Cranmer **SC** (456) § Comunidad Los Mayas (Mail to: Apartado 856)

Pueblo Viejo Misión Episcopal San Esteban **PS** (384) § Pueblo Viejo (Mail to: Pueblo Viejo)

Puerto Cortes Iglesia Epis San Juan Bautista **M** (658) § 6 Calle 4 Ave Barrio El Centro (Mail to: Bo El Centro 6 Calle 4 Ave) Pascual Torres Fuentes (504) 665-0200

Puerto Cortes Jesús El Salvador **M** (514) 15 Calle, 4ta Avenida, La Curva Barrio Buenos Aires (Mail to: 15 Calle 4ta Avenida La Curva Barrio Buenos Aires) 665-5859

Puerto Cortes Nstra Snra de los Desamparados **PS** (53) Autopista Region el Chile (Mail to: Colonia Episcopal)

Rio Negro Misión Episcopal Pentecostés **PS** (225) § Mision Pentecostes (Mail to: Mision Pentecostes)

Roatan Iglesia Epis San Pedro del Mar **P** (52) Brick Bay (Mail to: Apartado Postal 193) (504) 445-3891

✠ **San Pedro Sula** Catedral Epis El Buen Pastor **O** (732) § 21 Calle 23 Ave C SO Colonia Trejo Colonia Trejo (Mail to: Apartado 586) Hector Ortega Caballero (504) 556-7140

San Pedro Sula Iglesia Epis Cristo Redentor **M** (468) § Vado Ancho (Mail to: Vado Ancho DCPN 06-52)

San Pedro Sula Iglesia Episcopal Fe y Alegria **M** (545) § Calle Principal, Colonia Episcopal El Ocotillo (Mail to: 23 Ave C 21 Calle Trejo)

San Pedro Sula Iglesia Episcopal San Andres **M** (767) § 12 Calle, 10-11 Ave, SE Barrio Cabañas (Mail to: Apartado 586) Oscar Lopez (504) 554-2292

San Pedro Sula Igl Eps San Jose de la Montana **M** (585) § Calle Principal (Mail to: Col. Nueva Primavera)

San Pedro Sula Iglesia Episcopal San Lucas **M** (99) § Delicias del Norte (Mail to: Col Trejo 23 Ave C Calle 21 Apartado 586) Oscar Lopez

San Pedro Sula Iglesia Epis San Pablo Apostol **M** (224) § 3 y 4 Calle, 2nd Ave Col Satelite II Etapa 586 (Mail to: Iglesia Episcopal Hondurena 586) Roberto Martinez Amengual (504) 559-3055

San Pedro Sula Misión Epis la Divina Gracia **M** (332) § Colonia Stibys (Mail to: Apartado 586) Jaqueline Rapalo De Ruiz

Santa Ana Iglesia Episcopal San Isidro **M** (536) § El Cruce 11001 (Mail to: Iglesia Episcopal San Isidro Apdo. Postal 15023)

Santa Barbara Iglesia Epis Santa Barbara **M** (325) § Calle Principal, Barrio Llano del Conejo 22101 (Mail to: Calle Principal, Barrio Llano del Conejo 22101) (504) 643-2754

Santa Rita Misión Epis San Juan Apóstol **M** (74) § Londres (Mail to: Mision San Juan Apostol) Jose Lone

Santa Rita Misn Epis Santiago Ápóstol **PS** (93) § La Castellana (Mail to: La Castellana)

Siguatepeque Igl Epis San Bartolome Apostol **M** (1145) § Calle Principal la Esperanza (Mail to: Apartado Postal 30 21105) Jose Lone Hector Madrid

Siguatepeque Mision Epis San Matias Apostol **M** (520) § Aldea La Laguna (Mail to: La Laguna Siguatepeque) Hector Madrid

Siguatepeque Iglesia Epis Santiago Apostol **M** (562) § Barrio Zaragoza 2 cuadras al este de la gasolinera uno (Mail to: Barrio Zaragoza) Hector Madrid

Siguatepeque San Juan Apostol **P** (1062) 3 Ave 5 Calle S.O. Bo. San Juan ave. Gabriela Nunez 504 (Mail to: Apartado Postal 30) (504) 773-5660

Soroguara Iglesia Episcopal San Isidro **M** (155) § Santa Cruz Arriba 4063 (Mail to: Col. Florencia Norte 1era Entrada 1era calle 4063)

Talanga Misión Episcopal San Felipe **M** (389) § Calle Agua Blanca Bo Sabanetilla (Mail to: Residencial San Miguel Agua Blanca)

Tegucigalpa Igles Santa Maria de los Angeles **P** (2031) § 1era Entrada, Col. Florencia Norte 1100 (Mail to: Iglesia Episcopal Santa Maria Apartado Postal 15023 11101) Gerardo Alonzo Martinez (504) 232-0353

Tegucigalpa Misión Episcopal Emmanuel **PS** § Las Moritas, Aldea Yaguacire Germania Carreterra al Sur (Mail to: Germania Carreterra al Sur Las Moritas)

Tegucigalpa Mision Epis Nuevea Esperanza **PS** (20) § Col Nueva Esperanza Amarateca (Mail to: Catedral Santa Maria de los Angeles)

Tegucigalpa Igle San Pedro Cerca del Rio **M** (644) § Km 9. Carretera a Salida Talanga El Guanabano (Mail to: Km 9. Carretera a Talanga)

Tegucigalpa, A.M.D.C. Misión Episcopal San Esteban **SC** (56) § El Mulular, Quiscamote, A.M.D.C. (Mail to: Catedral Santa Maria de los Angeles)

Tegucigalpa, A.M.D.C. Misión Episcopal San Simón **PS** (74) El Jocomico, Nueva Aldea Santa Cruz Arriba (Mail to: Catderal Santa Maria de los Angeles)

Tegucigalpa, M.D.C Iglesia San Juan Evangelista **P** (536) § Terminal de buses, Mano derecha 4063 (Mail to: Apartado Postal #4063)

Tegucigalpa, M.D.C. Iglesia Epis La Anunciacion **M** (64) § Rincon de Dolores A.M.D.C. (Mail to: Catedral "Santa Maria de los Angeles" Aptdo. 15023)

Tegucigalpa, M.D.C. Misión Episcopal Mesías **PS** (177) Caserio Laguna del Pedregal (Mail to: Col Florencia N 1era entrada 1era calle Blvd Suyapa)

Tegucigalpa, M.D.C. St Mary of the Angels Epis Ch **M** (6) 1st St. Col. Florencia N. y Blvd. Suyapa (Mail to: 1st St. Col. Florencia N. y Blvd. Suyapa)

Trinidad Iglesia La Trinidad **P** (689) § Las Americas (Mail to: Apartado Postal 586)

Trinidad San Miguel Arcángel **M** (87) § Real Principal (Matazanales) (Mail to: Apartado Postal # 586)

Villa De San Francisco Natividad Nstro Snr Jesucristo **M** (14) § La Natividad de Nuestra Sr Jesucristo (Mail to: Bo Nuevo Progreso)

Villanueva Iglesia Episl de la Epifania **M** (695) § Barrio El Centro (Mail to: Apartado Postal No 586) Jose Pena-Regalado

Villanueva Santiago de Jerusalén **M** (451) § Santa Ana de Chasnigua (Mail to: Apartado Postal No 586)

Yuscaran Iglesia Episcopal San Antonio **M** (673) § Aldea Los Lainez (Mail to: Apdo 56 Danli Lainez)

Yuscaran Iglesia Episcopal San Jose **M** (340) § Aldea Corral Quemado (Mail to: Aldea Corral Quemado)

Yuscaran Igles Epis San Miguel Arcangel **P** (703) Aldea Ojo de Agua (Mail to: Oficina del Deanato de El Paraiso)

Yuscaran Misión Episcopal La Ascensión **PS** (46) Aldea Agua Viva (Mail to: Aldea Agua Viva)

Yuscaran Misión Epis la Presentación **SC** (186) Barrio San Juan (Mail to: Barrio San Juan)

Yuscaran Misión Episcopal la Santa Cruz **PS** (136) Aldea Chaguite Oriente (Mail to: Aldea Chaguite Oriente)

Yuscaran Mssn Epis la Transfiguración **PS** (121) Aldea Las Crucitas (Mail to: Aldea Las Crucitas)

Yuscaran Snta María Virgen de Mercedes **M** (59) § Aldea Rancho del Obispo (Mail to: Aldea Rancho del Obispo)

STATE OF IDAHO
Dioceses of Idaho and Spokane

DIOCESE OF IDAHO
(PROVINCE VIII)
Comprises Idaho South of the Salmon River
DIOCESAN OFFICE 1858 W Judith Ln Boise ID 83705
TEL (208) 345-4440 FAX (208) 345-9735
E-MAIL sledwich@idahodiocese.org WEB www.episcopalidaho.org

Previous Bishops—
Daniel S Tuttle 1867-87, Ethelbert Talbot 1887-1898, James B Funsten 1899-1918, Herman Page 1919, Frank H Touret 1919-24, Herbert HH Fox 1925-26, Middleton S Barnwell 1926-35, Fredk B Bartlett 1935-41, Frank A Rhea 1942-57, Norman L Foote 1957-72, Hanford L King Jr 1972-81, David B Birney IV 1982-89, John S Thornton 1990-98, Harry B Bainbridge III 1998-2008, Brian Thom 2008-22

Bishop—Rt Rev Jos Tharakan (1146) (Dio 25 June 2022)

Canon to the Ord E Van Hise; *Treas* B Rudin; *Archdcn* E O'Shea; *Cn for Public Relations* M Dembi; *Dio Coord* A O'Connor; *Chair of Comm on Min* L Speir; *Chap to Ret Clergy* J Attonen; *Camp Exec Dir* M Beck; *Camp Dir* M Kittridge; *Asst Camp Dir* C Martin

Stand Comm— Cler: J Farnes J Herndon R Schoeck; *Lay:* K Kissell R Ash J Ashton

PARISHES, MISSIONS, AND CLERGY

Alta St Francis of Tetons Epis Ch **P** (146) 20 Alta School Rd 83414-4518 (Mail to: 20 Alta School Rd 83414-4518) (307) 3538100

American Fls St Johns Episcopal Church **P** (5) 328 Roosevelt St 83211-1219 (Mail to: Ms Nancy Ross 257 Polk St 83211-1421) (208) 226-2646

Arco Church of the Epiphany **M** (12) 448 Yvonne St 83213-8760 (Mail to: PO Box 672 83213-0672) (208) 220-9785

Blackfoot St Pauls Episcopal Church **P** (39) 72 N Shilling Ave 83221-2846 (Mail to: 72 N Shilling Ave 83221-2846) (208) 785-4474

Boise All Saints Episcopal Church **P** (348) 704 S Latah St 83705-1547 (Mail to: 704 S Latah St 83705-1547) Joseph Farnes (208) 344-2537

✠ **Boise** St Michaels Epis Cathedral **O** (1499) 518 N 8th St 83702-5515 (Mail to: 518 N 8th St 83702-5515) Sean Wall James Brooks Rick Harvey Margaret Kurtz Mary Weiner (208) 342-5601

Boise St Stephens Episcopal Church **P** (364) 2206 N Cole Rd 83704-7313 (Mail to: 2206 N Cole Rd 83704-7313) Scott Ellsworth Debra Greenleaf James Mahoney Eileen O'Shea Jeffrey Shankles (208) 375-3862

Buhl Holy Trinity Episcopal Church **P** (37) 229 9th Ave N 83316-1216 (Mail to: PO Box 26 83316-0026) Marilyn Butler (208) 543-8496

Caldwell St Davids Episcopal Church **P** (53) Arlington Ave & East Pine 83605 (Mail to 1800 Arlington Ave 83605-5254) Wallace Lonergan (208) 459-9261

Emmett St Mary's Episcopal Church **P** (78) 219 F 1st St 83617-2903 (Mail to: PO Box 215 83617 0215) Gretchen Downer Gretchen Downe: (208) 365-2309

Fort Hall Church of the Good Shepherd **P** (85 PO Box 608 83203 (Mail to: PO Box 60: 83203-0608) Daniel Buchin Daniel Buchin (208) 223-7053

Glenns Ferry Grace Episcopal Church **P** (20) 10: E Cleveland Ave 83623-2400 (Mail to: PO Box 786 83623-0786) (208) 366-7425

Gooding Trinity Episcopal Church **P** 125 7th Ave W 83330-1227 (Mail to: 125 7th Ave W 83330 1227) (208) 934-4779

Hailey Emmanuel Episcopal Church **P** (90) 101 2nd Ave 83333-8604 (Mail to: C/O Nancy Gur ney PO Box 576 83333-0550) (208) 788-3547

Idaho Falls St Lukes Episcopal Church **P** (206 270 N Placer Ave 83402-4021 (Mail to: 270 N Placer Ave 83402-4021) (208) 522-8465

Jerome Calvary Episcopal Church **P** (18) 201 Adams St 83338-2600 (Mail to: 201 S Adams S 83338-2600) Richard Goetsch Barbara Ware (208) 324-8480

Mccall St Andrews Episcopal Church **P** (102 Forest And Gamble 83638 (Mail to: PO Bo 1045 83638-1045) (208) 634-2796

Meridian Church of the Holy Nativity **P** (198) 102 W 8th St 83642-2003 (Mail to: 828 W Cherry L: 83642-1619) Paula Egbert (208) 888-4342

Mountain Home St James Episcopal Church **P** (51) 315 N 3rd E 83647-2736 (Mail to: PO Bo 761 83647-0761) Paul Walsh (208) 587-3516

Nampa Grace Episcopal Church **P** (145) 91 4th St S 83651-4104 (Mail to: 411 10th Ave 83651-4137) Karen Hunter (208) 466-0782

Placerville Emmanuel Epis Ch Placerville **P** (15) 123 S Main St 83666-4065 (Mail to: 301 Granite St 83666-4022) (208) 392-9701

Pocatello Trinity Episcopal Church **P** (153) 248 N Arthur Ave 83204-3104 (Mail to: PO Box 1214 83204-1214) Diane Paulson Donald Paulson Donald Paulson (208) 233-2640

Rupert St Matthews Episcopal Church **P** (65) 6th & I St 83350 (Mail to: PO Box 324 83350-0324) Randy Fagg Tammy Jones Barbara Ward (208) 436-4904

Salmon Church of the Redeemer **P** (91) 204 Courthouse Dr 83467-3943 (Mail to: 204 Courthouse Dr 83467-3943) Joseph Marek Robert Perry (208) 756-3720

Shoshone Christ Episcopal Church **P** (15) 106 W B St 83352-5365 (Mail to: Attn: Kenneth Crothers PO Box 548 83352-0548) Kenneth Crothers (208) 886-2617

Sun Valley St Thomas Episcopal Church **P** (428) 201 Sun Valley Rd 83353 (Mail to: PO Box 1070 83353-1070) Michael Kendall Kathleen Bean (208) 726-5349

Twin Falls The Episcopal Church of the Ascension **P** (189) 371 Eastland Dr N 83301-4417 (Mail to: 371 Eastland Dr N 83301-4417) Shawn Carty (208) 733-1248

Weiser St Lukes Episcopal Church **P** (40) 106 E Liberty St 83672-2259 (Mail to: 101 E Liberty St 83672-2258) Deborah Graham (208) 549-1552

STATE OF ILLINOIS
Dioceses of Chicago (C) and Springfield (Sp)

Albion—Sp
Alton—Sp
Antioch—C
Arlington Hts—C
Aurora—C
Barrington—C
Batavia—C
Belleville—Sp
Belvidere—C
Berwyn—C
Bloomingdale—C
Bloomington—Sp
Blue Is—C
Bolingbrook—C
Burr Ridge—C
Cairo—Sp
Carbondale—Sp
Carlinville—Sp
Centralia—Sp
Champaign—Sp
Chesterfield—Sp
Chicago—C
Clarendon Hills—C
Crystal Lake—C
Danville—Sp
Decatur—Sp
Deerfield—C
DeKalb—C
Des Plaines—C
Dixon—C

Downers Grove—C
Dundee—C
Edwardsville—Sp
Elgin—C
Elk Grove Village—C
Elmhurst—C
Evanston—C
Flossmoor—C
Freeport—C
Galena—C
Galesburg—C
Geneva—C
Glen Carbon—Sp
Glen Ellyn—C
Glencoe—C
Glenview—C
Granite City—Sp
Grayslake—C
Griggsville—C
Gurnee—C
Hanna City—C
Hanover Pk—C
Harrisburg—Sp
Harvey—C
Havana—Sp
Highland Pk—C
Hinsdale—C
Jacksonville—Sp
Joliet—C
Kankakee—C

Kenilworth—C
Kewanee—C
La Grange—C
Lake Forest—C
Lake Villa—C
LaSalle—C
Lewistown—C
Libertyville—C
Lincoln—Sp
Lockport—C
Lombard—C
Macomb—C
Marion—Sp
Mattoon—Sp
McHenry—C
Momence—C
Morris—C
Morrison—C
Morton—Sp
Mt Carmel—Sp
Mt Vernon—Sp
Naperville—C
New Lenox—C
Normal—Sp
Northbrook—C
Northfield—C
Oak Pk—C
O'Fallon—Sp
Oregon—C
Ottawa—C

Palatine—C
Palos Pk—C
Pk Forest—C
Pk Ridge—C
Pekin—Sp
Peoria—C
Pontiac—C
Prospect Heights—C
Rantoul—Sp
River Forest—C
Riverside—C
Robinson—Sp
Rockford—C
Rock Island—C
Salem—Sp
Springfield—Sp
St Charles—C
Sterling—C
Streator—C
Sycamore—C
Warsaw—C
Wauconda—C
Waukegan—C
W Frankfort—Sp
Western Springs—C
Wheaton—C
Wilmette—C
Winnetka—C
Woodstock—C

STATE OF INDIANA

Dioceses of Indianaoplis and Northern Indiana

DIOCESE OF INDIANAPOLIS
(PROVINCE V)
Comprises central and southern Indiana
DIOCESAN OFFICE 125 Monument Circle Indianapolis IN 46204
TEL (317) 926-5454
TOLL FREE (800) 669-5786 FAX (317) 926-5456.
E-MAIL brinkworth@indydio.org WEB www.indydio.org

Previous Bishops—
Jackson Kemper (MO and IN) 1835-49, Geo Upfold 1849-72, Jos C Talbot coadj 1865 Bp 1872-83, David B Knickerbocker 1883-94, John H White 1895-99, Jos M Francis 1899-1939, Richard A Kirchhoffer coadj 1939 Bp 1939-59, John P Craine coadj 1957 Bp 1959-77, Edward W Jones coadj 1977 Bp 1977-97, Catherine M Waynick coadj 1997 Bp 1997-2017

Bishop — Rt Rev Jennifer Baskerville-Burrows (1100) (Dio 29 April 2017)

Cn to Ord for Admin & Evan Cn B O'Sullivan-Hale; *Cn to Ord for Cong Dev & Ldrshp* Rev Cn K White; *Treas* L Cornell 402 S Rogers St Bloomington IN 47403; *Chanc* G Plews 1346 N Delaware Indianapolis IN 46202; *Sec* S Sullivan; *Coord Yth Min* vacant; *Hist* B Roberts; *Bps Exec Sec* J Brinkworth; *Admin Sec* K Christopher

Stand Comm—Cler: Chair K Sullivan M Seddon M Slenski; *Lay:* G Eastman M McGraw J Ridder

PARISHES, MISSIONS, AND CLERGY

Anderson Trinity Episcopal Church **P** (90) 1030 Delaware St 46016 (Mail to: 1030 Delaware St 46016) William Smalley (765) 644-2566

Beanblossom St Davids Episcopal Church **P** (88) 11 State Road 45 46160 (Mail to: PO Box 1798 47448-1798) Catherine Wilson (812) 988-1038

Bedford St Johns Episcopal Church **P** (108) 1219 14th St 47421-3228 (Mail to: 1219 14th St 47421-3228) Kelsey Hutto (812) 275-6620

Bloomington Epis Cmps Mnstry at IU Blmgton **CM** (15) 719 E 7th St 47408 (Mail to: PO Box 127 47402-0127) (812) 361-7971

Bloomington Trinity Episcopal Church **P** (649) 111 S. Grant Street 47408 (Mail to: Attn: Lori Miller 111 S Grant St 47408-4031) Matthew Seddon Connie Peppler (812) 336-4466

Brownsburg Good Samaritan Epis Church **P** (176) 725 S Green St 46112-1612 (Mail to: 1100 W 42nd St 46208-3346) (317) 926-5454

Cannelton St Lukes Episcopal Church **P** (19) 101 S 3rd St 47520-1504 (Mail to: PO Box 7 47520-0007) (812) 988-1038

Carmel St Christophers Episcopal Ch **P** (623) 1402 W Main St 46032-1442 (Mail to: C/O Cindy Short 1402 W Main St 46032-1442) Cara Spaccarelli Cara Spaccarelli Chana Tetzlaff (317) 846-8716

Columbus Saint Paul's Church **P** (148) 2651 California St 47201-3650 (Mail to: 2651 California St 47201-3650) Aelred Dean (812) 372-7869

Crawfordsvlle St Johns Episcopal Church **P** (111) 212 S Green St 47933-2508 (Mail to: PO Box 445 47933-0445) Christian Baron (765) 362-2331

Danville St Augustine Episcopal Church **P** (298) 600 N Washington St 46122-1246 (Mail to: PO BOX 141 46122) William Barfield (317) 745-2741

Elwood St Stephens Episcopal Church **P** (10) 11706 N State Road 37 46036-8318 (Mail to: PO Box 291 46036-0291) (765) 552-5356

Evansville St Pauls Episcopal Church **P** (213) 301 SE 1st St 47713-1003 (Mail to: 301 SE 1st St 47713-1003) (812) 422-9009

Fishers Holy Family Episcopal Church **M** (276) 11445 Fishers Point Blvd 46038-2997 (Mail to: 11445 Fishers Point Blvd 46038-2997) Bruce Gray (317) 842-4133

Franklin St Thomas Episcopal Church **P** (121) 600 Paul Hand Blvd 46131-6922 (Mail to: 600 Paul Hand Blvd 46131-6922) Whitney Smith Karen Sullivan (317) 535-8985

Greencastle St Andrew's Episcopal Church **P** (122) 520 E Seminary St 46135-1745 (Mail to: 520 E Seminary St 46135-1745) Jennifer Oldstone-Moore (765) 653-3921

Indianapolis All Saints Episcopal Church **P** (206) 1559 Central Ave 46202-2606 (Mail to: 1559 Central Ave 46202-2698) Andrea Arsene Daniel Billman (317) 635-2538

✠ **Indianapolis** Christ Church Cathedral **O** (641) 125 Monument Cir 46204-2921 (Mail to: 125 Monument Cir 46204-2921) William Lesesne Gregory Baker Jodi Baron Hipolito Fernandez-Reina Thomas Kryder-Reid Fatima Yakubu-Madus (317) 636-4577

Indianapolis Church of the Nativity **P** (164) 7300 Lantern Rd 46256-2118 (Mail to: 7300 Lantern Rd 46256-2118) Catherine Wilson (317) 915-1020

Indianapolis St Alban's Episcopal Church **P** (53) 4601 N Emerson Ave 46226-2218 (Mail to: 4601 N Emerson Ave 46226-2218) Debra Dehler Walter Sherman Jean Smith (317) 546-8037

Indianapolis St Johns Episcopal Church **P** (144) 5625 W 30th St 46224-3013 (Mail to: 5625 W 30th St 46224-3013) (317) 293-0372

Indianapolis Saint Matthew's Church **P** (115) 8320 E 10th St 46219-5331 (Mail to: 8320 E 10th St 46219-5399) Frank Impicciche (317) 898-7807

Indianapolis St Paul's Episcopal Church **HC** (1070) 6050 N Meridian St 46208-1549 (Mail to: 6050 N Meridian St 462081549) John Denson Jeffrey Bower Patrick Burke Barbara Kempf (317) 253-1277

Indianapolis St Philips Episcopal Church **P** (72) 720 Dr Martin L King Jr St 46202-3116 (Mail to: 720 Dr Martin L King Jr St 46202-3116) Michelle Roos Jean Smith Karen Sullivan (317) 636-1133

Indianapolis St Timothys Episcopal Church **P** (201) 2601 East Thompson Road 46227-4496 (Mail to: 2601 E Thompson Rd 46227-4496) Rebecca Nickel (317) 784-6925

Indianapolis Trinity Episcopal Church **P** (796) 3243 N Meridian St 46208-4645 (Mail to: 3243 N Meridian St 46208-4645) Julia Whitworth Karen King Adam Pierce (317) 926-1346

Jeffersonvlle St Pauls Episcopal Church **P** (67) 321 E Market St 47130-3309 (Mail to: 321 E Market St 47130-3309) (812) 282-1108

Lafayette St Johns Episcopal Church **P** (388) 600 Ferry St 47901-1142 (Mail to: 600 Ferry St 47901-1142) Bradley Pace (765) 742-4079

Lawrenceburg Trinity Episcopal Church **P** (49) 101 W. Center St. 47025-1942 (Mail to: PO Box 3883 Center And Lake Streets 47025-3883) Jason Haddox (812) 537-2619

Lebanon St Peters Episcopal Church **M** (51) 950 E Washington St 46052-1901 (Mail to: 950 E Washington St 46052-1901) Christopher Beasley (765) 482-2322

Madison Christ Episcopal Church **P** (70) 506 Mulberry St 47250-3440 (Mail to: C/O Linda Wenning 506 Mulberry St 47250-3440) Mary Slenski (812) 265-2158

Martinsville St Marys Episcopal Church **M** (32) 1109 E Morgan St 46151-1746 (Mail to: 1109 E Morgan St 46151-1746) Todd Kissam (765) 342-1682

Mount Vernon St Johns Episcopal Church **P** (56) 602 Mulberry Street 47620 (Mail to: PO Box 503 47620-0503) Allen Rutherford (812) 838-5445

Muncie Grace Episcopal Church **P** (105) 300 S Madison St 47305-2464 (Mail to: PO Box 1732 47308-1732) Paul Jacobson (765) 289-7931

New Albany St Pauls Episcopal Church **P** (238) 1015 E Main St 47150-5842 (Mail to: 1015 E Main St 47150-5842) Gordon Anderson (812) 944-0413

New Castle St James Episcopal Church **P** (42) 2020 Bundy Ave 47362-2920 (Mail to: 2020 Bundy Ave 47362-2920) (765) 529-5309

New Harmony St Stephens Episcopal Church **P** (33) 318 Main St 47631 (Mail to: PO Box 173 47631-0173) Elizabeth Macke (812) 682-4604

Noblesville St Michaels Episcopal Church **P** (174) 444 S Harbour Dr 46062-9107 (Mail to: 444 S Harbour Dr 46062-9109) Tyler Tetzlaff (317) 773-6157

Plainfield St Marks Episcopal Church **P** (200) 710 E Buchanan St 46168-1514 (Mail to: 710 E Buchanan St 46168-1514) Kirsteen Wilkinson (317) 839-6730

Richmond St Pauls Episcopal Church **P** (44) 800 N A St 47374-3120 (Mail to: 800 N A St 47374-3120) Barbara Fisher (765) 962-6988

Rockport Peace Episcopal Church **M** (34) 223 Cnty. Rd. 350 W. 47635 (Mail to: PO Box 127 47635-0127) (812) 6495500

Shelbyville St Lukes Church **P** (30) 1201 N Riley Hwy 46176-9432 (Mail to: 1201 N Riley Hwy 46176-9432) (317) 392-1379

Terre Haute St Stephens Episcopal Church **P** (150) 215 N 7th St 47807-3103 (Mail to: 215 N 7th St 47807-3193) Andrew Downs (812) 232-5165

Vincennes St James Episcopal Church **HC** (46) 610 Perry St 47591-2130 (Mail to: 610 Perry St 47591-2130) Mary Becker (812) 882-9640

W Lafayette Church of the Good Shepherd **P** (121) 610 Meridian St 47906-2656 (Mail to: 610 Meridian St 47906-2656) (765) 743-1347

Washington St Johns Episcopal Church **P** (34) 509 E Walnut St 47501-2766 (Mail to: 805 W Main St 47501-2514) Dennis Latta (812) 726-5333

West Terre Haute Saint George Episcopal Church **M** (54) 1337 N Smith Pl 47885-9644 (Mail to: Att Rick Baldomero 2382 W Highland Ave 47885-9254) (812) 242-4893

Zionsville St Fran in the Fields Epis Ch **P** (393) 1525 Mulberry St 46077-1146 (Mail to: 1525 Mulberry St 46077-1146) C Davies Reed (317) 873-4377

DIOCESE OF IOWA
(PROVINCE VI)
Comprises the State of Iowa
DIOCESAN OFFICE 225 37th St Des Moines IA 50312-4305
TEL (515) 277-6165 FAX (515) 277-0273
E-MAIL diocese@iowaepiscopal.org WEB http://www.iowaepiscopal.org

Previous Bishops—
Henry W Lee 1854-74, Wm S Perry
1876-98, Theodore N Morrison
1899-1929, Harry S Longley suffr
1912 coadj 1917 Bp 1929-44, Elwood
L Haines 1944-49, Gordon V Smith
1950-71, Walter C Righter 1972-88,
C Christopher Epting 1988-2001,
Alan Scarfe 2003-21

Bishop—Rt Rev Betsey Monnot (Dio 18 Dec 2021)

Sec/Conv Rev KS Milligan; *Cn to the Ord* Rev Cn M Wagner; *Archdcn* Ven J Crossett; *Fin Ofc* A Wagner; *Exec Asst to Bp* J Allaway; *Chanc* W Graham; *Hist* W Chase; *Treas* W Smith; *Intake Officer* Rev K Leaman; *Ecum Off* Rev J McCarthy; *ER&D* Rev H Scherff; *Global Miss* Rev M Rockwell; *Prison Min* Rev A Moats Williams; *UTO* Rev D Eddy & D Eddy; *Children & Yth* A Mellies; *Editor/Comm/Young Adult* T Ruhland Petty; *Coord for Convention, EfM, Small Ch Min* J Doherty; *Dio Asst* E Adams; *Fin Asst* T Austin; *Altar Guild* S Murphy; *Trans Off* Rev Cn M Wagner; *Int Dir Beloved Community Initiative* Rev N Boerner; *Span Speaking Miss* Rev S Hughes Empke

Stand Comm—Cler: E Popplewell S Benitz N Bowler; *Lay:* K Brooke E Gillott J Cornfortht

PARISHES, MISSIONS, AND CLERGY

Algona Church of St Thomas **M** (62) 213 E Call St 50511-2453 (Mail to: PO Box 611 50511-0611) (515) 295-2113

Ames Iowa State Univ Chaplaincy **CC** 2338 Lincoln Way 50014-7113 (Mail to: 2338 Lincoln Way 50014) (515) 292-6655

Ames St Johns by the Campus **P** (326) 2338 Lincoln Way 50014-7113 (Mail to: 2338 Lincoln Way 50014-7113) Thomas Early (515) 292-6655

Anamosa St Marks Episcopal Church **M** (12) 107 W 1st St 52205-1831 (Mail to: 201 S Garnavillo St 52205-1939) (319) 462-2933

Ankeny St Annes by the Fields **P** (94) 2110 W 1st St 50023-2487 (Mail to: 2110 W 1st St 50023-2487) Vincent Bete (515) 964-5152

Bettendorf St Peters Episcopal Church **P** (84) 2400 Middle Rd 52722-3250 (Mail to: 2400 Middle Rd 52722-3250) Elaine Caldbeck (563) 355-4640

Boone Grace Episcopal Church **M** (15) 707 8th St 50036-2727 (Mail to: 707 8th St 50036-2727) (515) 432-7586

Burlington Christ Episcopal Church **P** (76) Attn: Treasurer 623 N 5th St 52601-5029 (Mail to: 623 N 5th St 52601-5029) Carl Mann (319) 752-1381

Carroll Trinity Episcopal Church **M** (12) 127 W 9th St 51401-2305 (Mail to: 1700 Pike Ave 51401-1627) Diana Wright (712) 792-2836

Cedar Falls St Luke's Episcopal Church **P** (224) 2410 Melrose Dr 50613-5234 (Mail to: 2410 Melrose Dr 50613-5234) Elizabeth Popplewell Liane Nichols Ruth Ratliff (319) 277-8520

Cedar Rapids Christ Episcopal Church **P** (608) 220 40th St NE 52402-5616 (Mail to: 220 40th St NE 52402-5616) Mark Eccles Brian Gross Melody Rockwell (319) 363-2029

Cedar Rapids Grace Episcopal Church **P** (88) 525 A Ave NE 52401-1015 (Mail to: 525 A Ave NE 52401-1015) John Greve (319) 362-1929

Chariton St Andrews Episcopal Church **M** (42) 1112 N 7th St 50049-1208 (Mail to: PO Box 838 50049-0838) (641) 774-4911

Charles City Grace Episcopal Church **M** (12) 902 5th Ave 50616-3006 (Mail to: 902 5th Ave 50616-3006) (641) 228-4519

Clermont Church of the Saviour **M** (22) 610 - 702 Mill St 52135 (Mail to: 225 37th St 50312-4305) (515) 2776165

Clinton Christ Episcopal Church **P** (99) 2100 N 2nd St 52732-2418 (Mail to: 2100 N 2nd St PO Box 3052 52732-2418) (563) 242-5740

Coralville New Song Episcopal Church **P** (159) 912 20th Ave 52241-1404 (Mail to: 912 20th Ave 52241-1404) Jane Stewart (319) 351-3577

Council Blfs St Pauls Episcopal Church **P** (83) 22 Dillman Dr 51503-1641 (Mail to: 22 Dillman Dr 51503-1692) (712) 323-7188

Davenport St Albans Episcopal Church **P** (176) 3510 W Central Park Ave 52804-2753 (Mail to: 3510 W Central Park Ave 52804-2753) (563) 386-4087

✠ **Davenport** Trinity Cathedral **O** (607) 121 W 12th St 52803-5227 (Mail to: 121 W 12th St 52803-5227) (563) 323-9989

Decorah Grace Episcopal Church **M** (40) 506 W Broadway St 52101-1704 (Mail to: PO Box 4 52101-0004) (563) 382-4246

Denison Trinity Church **M** (15) 14 S. 16th St. 51442 (Mail to: C/O Carol Block 801 1st Ave S 51442-2603) (712) 263-6907

Des Moines St Andrews Episcopal Church **P** (289) 5720 Urbandale Ave 50310-1250 (Mail to: 5720 Urbandale Ave 50310-1295) Eric Rucker (515) 2552101

Des Moines St Lukes Episcopal Church **P** (347) 3424 Forest Ave 50311-2615 (Mail to: 3424 Forest Ave 50311-2615) Martha Kester (515) 277-0875

Des Moines St Marks Episcopal Church **P** (27) 3120 E 24th St 50317-3609 (Mail to: 3120 E 24th St 50317-3609) Sheryl Hughes-Empke Kathleen Travis (515) 266-1304

✠ **Des Moines** Cathedral Church of St Paul **O** (351) 815 High St 50309-2714 (Mail to: 815 High St 50309-2733) Michael Barlowe Nicola Bowler (515) 288-7297

Des Moines Trinity Cush **P** 5720 Urbandale Ave 50310-1250 (Mail to: 5720 Urbandale Ave 50310-1250) (515) 554-8312

Dubuque St Johns Episcopal Church **P** (170) 1410 Main St 52001-4740 (Mail to: 1458 Locust St 52001-4714) Kevin Goodrich (563) 556-0252

Durant St Pauls Episcopal Church **P** (39) 206 6th St 52747-9742 (Mail to: PO Box 865 52747-0865) Alice Haugen (563) 785-6228

Emmetsburg Trinity Church **M** (20) 2219 Main St 50536-2446 (Mail to: PO Box 332 50536-0332) Elizabeth Preston (712) 852-3809

Fort Dodge St Marks Episcopal Church **P** (68) 1007 1st Ave S 50501-4801 (Mail to: 1007 1st Ave S 50501-4801) Kristine Leaman (515) 576-2019

Fort Madison St Lukes Episcopal Church **P** (56) 605 Avenue E 52627-4805 (Mail to: 605 Avenue E 52627-4805) Lyle Brown Lyle Brown (319) 372-6409

Glenwood St Johns Episcopal Church **M** (10) 111 N Vine St 51534-1516 (Mail to: PO Box 109 51534-0109) (712) 527-2971

Grinnell St Pauls Episcopal Church **P** (108) 1026 State St 50112 (Mail to: 1026 State St 50112) Wendy Abrahamson (515) 236-6254

Harlan St Pauls Episcopal Church **M** (9) 712 Farnam St 51537-1637 (Mail to: PO Box 526 51537-0526) (712) 755-2793

Independence St James Episcopal Church **M** (21) 202 2nd Ave NE 50644-1905 (Mail to: PO Box 264 202 2nd Ave 50644-0264) Sean Burke Sue Ann Raymond (319) 334-4297

Indianola All Saints Episcopal Church **M** (10) 119 N Buxton St 50125-2412 (Mail to: 4901 Westbrooke Pl 50266-5487) (319) 2906306

Iowa City Trinity Episcopal Church **P** (564) 320 E College St 52240-1628 (Mail to: 320 E College St 52240-1628) Lauren Lyon Judith Crossett Lori Erickson Marcus Haack Elizabeth Koffron-Eisen William Moorhead Catherine Quehl-Engel (319) 337-3333

Iowa City University of Iowa Chaplaincy **CC** 26 E Market St 52245-1742 (Mail to: 26 E Market St 52245-1742) Jan Horn (319) 337-3333

Iowa Falls St Matthews-by-the-Bridge **M** (19) 507 Railroad St 50126-2240 (Mail to: PO Box 206 50126-0206) (641) 648-6779

Keokuk St Johns Episcopal Church **P** (91) 208 N 4th St 52632-5602 (Mail to: 208 N 4th St 52632-5602) (319) 524-4672

Le Mars St Georges Episcopal Church **M** (5) 400 1st Ave SE 51031-2045 (Mail to: 401 1st Ave SE 51031-2044) (712) 546-4604

Maquoketa St Marks Episcopal Church **M** (41) 208 W Maple St 52060-2929 (Mail to: 208 W Maple Street 52060-2929) (563) 652-4970

Marshalltown St Pauls Episcopal Church **P** (66) 201 E Church St 50158-2944 (Mail to: 201 E Church St 50158-2944) Kay Beach (641) 753-6317

Mason City St Johns Episcopal Church **P** (122) 120 1st St NE 50401-3302 (Mail to: 120 1st St NE 50401-3302) Stephen Benitz (641) 424-1300

Mt Pleasant St Michaels Episcopal Church **P** (37) 202 E Washington St 52641-1933 (Mail to: PO Box 624 52641-0624) (319) 385-2633

Muscatine Trinity Episcopal Church **P** (108) 211 Walnut St 52761-4130 (Mail to: 211 Walnut St 52761-4130) Martha Lang (563) 263-2177

Newton St Stephens Episcopal Church **P** (101) 223 E 4th St N 50208-3214 (Mail to: 223 E 4th St N 50208-3214) Karen Crawford Merle Smith (641) 792-6971

Orange City Church of the Savior **M** (39) 415 Third St NW 51041-1313 (Mail to: 530 Arizona Ave SW 51041-1935) (712) 737-3930

Oskaloosa St James Episcopal Church **P** (50) 207 S 3rd St 52577-3137 (Mail to: PO Box 545 52577-0545) Terence Kleven (641) 673-4218

Ottumwa Trinity Episcopal Church **M** (36) 204 E 5th St 52501-2626 (Mail to: 204 E 5th St 52501-2626) Kevin Emge (641) 682-5624

Perry St Martins Episcopal Church **P** (70) & 10th Iowa Sts 50220 (Mail to: PO Box 486 50220-0486) (515) 465-3468

Shenandoah St Johns Episcopal Church **M** (16) 401 Church St 51601-1987 (Mail to: PO Box 105 51601-0105) (712) 246-4790

Sioux City Calvary Episcopal Church **M** (32) 1308 S Cleveland St 51106-1942 (Mail to: 1308 S Cleveland St 51106-1942) (712) 276-3561

Sioux City St Thomas Episcopal Church **P** (79) 406 12th St 51105-1305 (Mail to: PO Box 5394 51102-5394) Stacey Gerhart (712) 258-0141

Sioux City St Pauls Indian Mission **M** (110) 524 Center St 51103-3648 (Mail to: PO Box 895 51102-0895) (712) 255-5162

Spirit Lake St Alban's Episcopal Church **P** (100) 2011 23rd & Zenith 51360 (Mail to: PO Box 85 51360-0085) (712) 336-1117

Storm Lake All Saints Episcopal Church **P** (37) 121 W Marina Rd 50588-7473 (Mail to: 121 W Marina Rd 50588-7473) Stacey Gerhart (712) 732-1314

W Des Moines St Timothys Episcopal Church **P** (659) 1020 24th St 50266-2107 (Mail to: 1020 24th St 50266-2107) Kyle Carswell (515) 225-2020

Waterloo Trinity Episcopal Parish **P** (153) 4535 Kimball Ave 50701-9087 (Mail to: 4535 Kimball Ave 50701-9087) Cathi Bencken Peter Fones (319) 232-4714

Waverly St Andrews Episcopal Church **M** (13)

717 W Bremer Ave 50677-2926 (Mail to: PO Box 176 50677-0176) (319) 352-1489

Webster City Church of the Good Shepherd **M** (39) 1100 Mary Ln 50595-2746 (Mail to: PO Box 108 50595-0108) (515) 576-2019

ITALY

See Europe

STATE OF KANSAS

Dioceses of Kansas and Western Kansas

DIOCESE OF KANSAS

(PROVINCE VII)
Comprises eastern Kansas
DIOCESAN OFFICE 835 SW Polk Topeka KS 66612-1688
TEL (785) 235-9255 FAX (785) 235-2449
E-MAIL mfunston@episcopal-ks.org WEB www.episcopal-ks.org

Previous Bishops—
Thomas H Vail 1864-89, Elisha S Thomas coadj 1887 Bp 1889-95, Frank R Millspaugh 1895-1916, James Wise coadj 1916 Bp 1916-39, Goodrich R Fenner coadj 1937 Bp 1939-59, Edward C Turner coadj 1956 Bp 1959-81, Richard F Grein 1981-88, William E Smalley Bp 1989-2003
Dean E Wolfe coadj 2003 Bp 2004-2017

Bishop—The Rt Rev Cathleen Bascom (1112) (2019-)

Cn to Ord & Deploy Off AP Funston; *Bp Assist* M Funston; *Comp* J Currie; *Digital Comm* Yth *and Campus Miss* K Schlabach; *Sec Conv* K Baker-Lampe; *Comm and Yng Adlt* C Senuta; *Chanc* LF Taylor 7450 W 130th Street Ste 140

Overland Park KS 66213; *V Chanc* J Bullock 529 Ohio St Lawrence KS 66044; *V Chanc* K Harper 833 N Waco Wichita KS 67203; *Treas* B Geary 12061 S Troost St Olathe KS 66061; *Hist* J Beck

Stand Comm—Cler: J Cummins G Doll H Hoch M McDonald A O'Connor D Rice C Rohleder *Lay:* E Fitz-Gibbon L Hannan D Littrell M Morrow T Ryther J Smittle D Waddell-Gilbert

PARISHES, MISSIONS, AND CLERGY

Abilene St Johns Episcopal Church **P** (34) 519 N Buckeye Ave 67410-2531 (Mail to: PO Box 461 67410-0461) (785) 263-3592

Arkansas City Trinity Episcopal Church **P** (80) 224 N A St 67005-2204 (Mail to: PO Box 544 67005-0544) (620) 442-1720

Atchison Trinity Episcopal Church **P** (97) 300 S 5th St 66002-2809 (Mail to: 300 S 5th St 66002-2809) Jon Hullinger (913) 3673171

Blue Rapids St Marks Church **P** (32) 601 Lincoln St 66411-1545 (Mail to: C/O Joe Warders 400 E 4th St 66411-1545) (785) 363-7542

Chanute Grace Episcopal Church **P** (36) 209 S Lincoln Ave 66720-2463 (Mail to: 209 S Lincoln Ave 66720-2463) Joyce Holmes (620) 431-1210

Clay Center St Pauls Episcopal Church **P** (87) 1010 6th St 67432-2506 (Mail to: PO Box 625 67432-0625) (785) 632-3200

Coffeyville St Paul's Episcopal Church **P** (77) 613 Elm St 67337-4935 (Mail to: 613 Elm St 67337-4935) (620) 251-4890

Derby St Andrews Episcopal Church **P** (103) 1062 E Chet Smith Ave 67037-2354 (Mail to: PO Box 8 67037-0008) Michael Loyd (316) 788-2595

Edwardsville St Martin in the Fields Church **P** (60) 1501 Edwardsville Dr 66111-1127 (Mail to: PO Box 13012 66113-0012) (913) 422-5879

El Dorado Trinity Episcopal Church **P** (75) PO Box 507 67042-0507 (Mail to: PO Box 507 67042-0507) Jimmy Jackson (316) 321-6606

Emporia St Andrew's Episcopal Church **P** (97) 828 Commercial St 66801-2915 (Mail to: 828 Commercial St 66801-2915) Marc Mcdonald (620) 342-1537

Galena St Marys Episcopal Church **P** (24) 415 S Washington St 66739-1733 (Mail to: 415 S Washington St 66739-1733) Gary Kennedy (620) 783-5075

Holton Church of St Thomas **P** (5) 512 Wisconsin Ave 66436-1645 (Mail to: 512 Wisconsin Ave 66436) (785) 979-8411

Independence Church of the Epiphany **P** (95) 400 E Maple St 67301-3822 (Mail to: PO Box 655 67301-0655) Gerald Eytcheson (620) 331-4794

Iola St Timothys Episcopal Church **P** (44) 202 S Walnut St 66749-3245 (Mail to: 202 S Walnut St 66749-3245) David Kent (620) 365-7306

Junction City Church of the Covenant **P** (90) 314 N Adams St 66441-3071 (Mail to: PO Box 366 66441-0366) (785) 238-2897

Kansas City St Pauls Episcopal Church **P** (116) 1300 N 18th St 66102-2733 (Mail to: 1300 N 18th St 66102-2798) Dixie Junk Gail Reynolds (913) 321-3535

Lawrence St Margarets Episcopal Church **P** (313) 5700 W 6th St 66049-4829 (Mail to: 5700 W 6th St 66049-4829) (785) 865-5777

Lawrence Trinity Episcopal Church **P** (551) 1011 Vermont St 660442921 (Mail to: 1027 Vermont Stt 660442921) Robert Baldwin (785) 843-6166

Leavenworth St Pauls Episcopal Church **P** (170) 209 N 7th St 66048-1930 (Mail to: PO Box 233 66048-0233) Machrina Blasdell Randall Lipscomb (913) 682-1033

Manhattan St Pauls Episcopal Church **P** (103) 601 Poyntz Ave 66502-6006 (Mail to: 601 Poyntz Ave 66502-6006) Robert Pearce (785) 776-9427

Marysville St Pauls Episcopal Church **P** (25) 306 N 17th St 66508-1405 (Mail to: 1103 Elm St 66508-1935) (785) 562-5182

Mission St Michael and All Angels Ch **P** (973) 6630 Nall Ave 66202-4325 (Mail to: 6630 Nall Ave 66202-4399) Samuel Cox Monte Giddings James Robertson Donald Williams (913) 236-8600

Neodesha Church of the Ascension **P** (38) 702 Osage St 66757-1466 (Mail to: 702 Osage St 66757-1466) Gerald Eytcheson (620) 331-4794

Newton St Matthews Episcopal Church **P** (92) 2001 Windsor Dr 67114-1250 (Mail to: PO Box 342 67114-0342) (316) 283-3310

Olathe St Aidans Episcopal Church **P** (111) 14301 S Blackbob Rd 66062-2537 (Mail to: 14301 S Blackbob Rd 66062-2537) Thomas Baker (913) 764-3050

Ottawa Grace Episcopal Church **P** (28) PO Box 601 66067-0601 (Mail to: 315 W 5th St 66067-2842) (785) 242-5390

Overland Park Ch of St Thomas the Apostle **P** (1054) 12251 Antioch Rd 66213-1517 (Mail to: 12251 Antioch Rd 66213-1517) Gar Demo Kelly Demo (913) 451-0512

Parsons St Johns Episcopal Church **P** (100) 1801 Corning 67357-4265 (Mail to: PO Box 753 67357-0753) Sharon Billman (620) 421-3775

Pittsburg St Peters Episcopal Church **P** (103) 306 W Euclid St 66762-5106 (Mail to: 306 W Euclid St 66762-5106) (620) 231-3790

Sedan Church of the Epiphany **P** (32) 309 W Elm St 67361-1216 (Mail to: PO Box 367 67361-0367) (620) 725-3701

Shawnee St Lukes Episcopal Church **P** (178) 5325 Nieman Rd 66203-1939 (Mail to: 5325 Nieman Rd 66203-1939) Jonathan Brice (913) 631-8597

Stilwell St Francis of Assisi Epis Ch **P** (54) 17890 Metcalf Ave 66085-9326 (Mail to: PO Box 118 66085-0118) Kevin Schmidt (913) 897-2588

✠ **Topeka** Grace Cathedral **O** (759) 701 SW 8th Ave 66603-3219 (Mail to: 701 SW 8th Ave 66603-3219) Torey Lightcap Donald Chubb (785) 235-3457

Topeka St Davids Episcopal Church **P** (519) 3916 SW 17th St 66604-2438 (Mail to: 3916 SW 17th St 66604-2497) (785) 272-5144

Wamego St Lukes Episcopal Church **P** (79) 700 Lincoln St 66547-1638 (Mail to: PO Box 109 66547-0109) Catherine Rohleder (785) 456-9310

Wellington St Judes Episcopal Church **P** (11) 1323 N Jefferson Ave 67152-4356 (Mail to: PO Box 222 67152-0222) Catherine Shield (620) 326-6406

Wichita Good Shepherd Episcopal Church **P** (421) 8021 W 21st St N 67205-1743 (Mail to: 8021 W 21st St N 67205-1743) Andrew O'Connor Robert Hirst Michael Loyd (316) 721-8096

Wichita St Bartholomews Episcopal Ch **P** (21) 2799 S Meridian Ave 67217-1461 (Mail to: 2799 S Meridian Ave 67217-1461) Walter Miescher (316) 941-4744

Wichita Saint James Church **P** (1070) 3750 E Douglas Ave 67208-3708 (Mail to: C/O Bookkeeper 3750 E Douglas Ave 67208-3784) Dawn Frankfurt Carthur Criss (316) 683-5686

Wichita St Johns Episcopal Church **P** (120) 402 N Topeka Ave 67202-2414 (Mail to: 402 N Topeka St 67202-2414) (316) 262-0897

Wichita St Stephens Episcopal Church **P** (180) 7404 Killarney Pl 67206-1627 (Mail to: 7404 E Killarney Pl 67206-1699) Laurie Lewis Barbara Gibson (316) 634-2513

Winfield Grace Episcopal Church **P** (192) 715 Millington St 67156-2838 (Mail to: PO Box 490 67156-0490) (620) 221-4252

Yates Center Calvary Episcopal Church **P** (39) 200 S Grove St 66783 (Mail to: PO Box 214 66783-0214) (620) 625-2358

STATE OF KENTUCKY
Dioceses of Kentucky and Lexington

DIOCESE OF KENTUCKY
(PROVINCE IV)
Comprises western Kentucky
DIOCESAN OFFICE 425 S 2nd St Ste 200 Louisville KY 40202
TEL (502) 584-7148 FAX (502) 587-8123
WEB www.episcopalky.org

Previous Bishops—
Benj B Smith 1832-84, Geo D
Cummins asst 1866-74, Thomas U
Dudley coadj 1875 Bp 1884-1904,
Chas E Woodcock 1905-35, Chas
Clingman 1936-54, CG Marmion
1954-74, DB Reed coadj 1972 Bp
1974-94, Edwin F Gulick Jr Bp
1994-2010

Bishop—Terry Allen White (1051) (Dio 25
Sept 2010)

Cn to Ord Rev AR Coultas *Chanc* W Robinson Beard
400 W Market St Ste 1800 Louisville; *Sec of Dio* KS
Wilkinson; *Treas* D Brooks; *Bp's Staff: All Saints Epis
Center Compt* B Meyer; *Comm* Brian Kinnaman;
Yth K Badgett; *Transition* M Linder; *Ecum* Rev A
Coultas; *Ch Form* Rev K Doyle; *Fin & Stew* D Brooks
4010 Fox Meadow Way Prospect KY 40059; *Evang
& Cong Dev* B Blodgett 57 Ironwood Dr Murray
KY 42071; *COM* Rev P Connell 720 Ford Ave
Owensboro 42301; *Cn for Cong Vitality* Rev J Lewis

Stand Comm—Cler: Pres A Vouga J Trimble E
Markham; *Lay:* C Stone J Donahue

PARISHES, MISSIONS, AND CLERGY

Bardstown Episcopal Ch of the Ascension **P**
(104) 211 N 3rd St 40004-1527 (Mail to: 211 N
3rd St 40004-1527) (502) 348-4317

Bowling Green Christ Episcopal Church **P** (664)
1215 State St 42101-2650 (Mail to: 1215 State
St 42101-2650) Steven Pankey Rebecca Kello
(270) 843-6563

Brandenburg Holy Trinity Church **M** (85) 319
Oaklawn Rd 40108-1033 (Mail to: PO Box 645
40108-0645) (270) 422-3721

Campbellsvlle St Thomas Church **M** (43) 116
S Columbia Ave 42718-1339 (Mail to: 116 S
Columbia Ave 42718-1339) (270) 789-1601

Elizabethtown Christ Episcopal Church **P** (87)
206 W Poplar St 42701-1537 (Mail to: PO Box
1054 42702-1054) (270) 765-5606

Fulton Trinity Church **M** (38) 1104 Vine St
42041-1758 (Mail to: 1100 Vine Street 40065)
(270) 472-1870

Gilbertsville St Peters of the Lakes Epis Ch **M**
(49) 47 Black River Rd 42044-9053 (Mail to:

PO Box 183 42044-0183) Meghan Ryan (270)
362-8301

Harrods Creek St Fran in the Fields Epis Ch **P**
(1295) 6710 Wolf Pen Branch Rd 40027 (Mail
to: PO Box 225 40027-0225) Clinton Wilson
Walter Langley (502) 228-1176

Henderson St Pauls Episcopal Church **P** (206) 5
S Green St 42420-3536 (Mail to: 5 S Green St
42420-3536) (270) 826-2937

Hickman St Paul Episcopal Church **M** (6) 611
Church St 42050 (Mail to: 511 E Moulton St
42050) Barbara Burgess Ellen Ekevag (270)
236-3619

Hopkinsville Grace Episcopal Church **P** (166)
216 E 6th St 42240-3433 (Mail to: 216 E 6th
St 42240-3433) Stephen Spicer (270) 885-8752

Louisville Calvary Church **P** (216) 821 S 4th St
40203-2115 (Mail to: 821 S 4th St 40203-2191
Lee Shafer (502) 587-6011

✠ **Louisville** Christ Church Cathedral **O** (244)
421 S 2nd St 40202-1417 (Mail to: 421 S 2nd St
40202-1475) Matthew Bradley (502) 587-135-

Louisville Church of Our Merciful Saviour **P** (38)
473 S 11th St 40203-1875 (Mail to: 473 S 11th
St 40203-1875) Harold Price (502) 587-6129

Louisville Church of the Advent **P** (316) 901
Baxter Ave 40204-2046 (Mail to: 901 Baxter
Ave 40204-2046) Timothy Mitchell John
Fritschner John Fritschner Drusilla Kemp
(502) 451-6066

Louisville Messiah Trinity Episcopal Ch **P** (109)
8701 Shepherdsville Rd 40219-5037 (Mail to
8701 Shepherdsville Rd 40219-5037) John
Allen (502) 969-1422

Louisville Resurrection Episcopal Church **M**
(157) 4100 Southern Pkwy 40214-1648 (Mail
to: 4100 Southern Pkwy 40214-1648) Ev
Markham (502) 368-1146

Louisville St Andrews Episcopal Church **P** (415)
2233 Woodbourne Ave 40205-2105 (Mail to
2233 Woodbourne Ave 40205-2195) (502)
452-9581

Louisville St Clement Episcopal Church **M** (25)
4112 Wimpole Rd 40218-2369 (Mail to: 609 W
Main St 40202-2951) (502) 491-6085

Louisville St George Episcopal Church **M** (32)
PO Box 3652 40201-3652 (Mail to: PO Box
3652 40201-3652) (502) 776-2030

Louisville St Lukes Chapel **Chapel** (32) C/O Joy Moll 1201 Lyndon Ln 40222-4319 (Mail to: C/O Chris Ward 7504 Westport Rd 40222-4108) John Allen Mary Cherry Lisa Tolliver (502) 736-7800

Louisville St Lukes Episcopal Church **P** (376) 1206 Maple Ln 40223-2406 (Mail to: PO Box 23336 40223-0336) Mark Feather (502) 245-8827

Louisville St Marks Episcopal Church **P** (405) 2822 Frankfort Ave 40206-2640 (Mail to: 2822 Frankfort Ave 40206-2692) (502) 895-2429

Louisville St Matthew Episcopal Church **P** (683) 330 N Hubbards Ln 40207-2253 (Mail to: 330 N Hubbards Ln Frnt 40207-2394) Benjamin Hart Helen Jones Kelly Kirby Harvey Roberts (502) 895-3485

Louisville St Pauls Episcopal Church **P** (179) 4700 Lowe Rd 40220-1532 (Mail to: 4700 Lowe Rd 40220-1532) Andrew Shirota (502) 491-7417

Louisville St Peter Episcopal Church **P** (177) 8110 Saint Andrews Church Rd 40258-3832 (Mail to: 8110 Saint Andrews Church Rd 40258-3832) John Hines (502) 937-3613

Louisville St Thomas Episcopal Church **P** (181) § 9616 Westport Rd 40241-2224 (Mail to: 9616 Westport Rd 40241-2224) (502) 425-3727

Madisonville St Marys Episcopal Church **P** (214) 163 N Main St 42431-1952 (Mail to: PO Box 768 42431-0016) John Heidel (270) 821-3674

Murray Saint John's Church **P** (128) 1620 Main St 42071-2275 (Mail to: 1620 Main St 42071-2275) Zebulun Treloar Rosemarie Bogal-Allbritten (270) 753-6908

Owensboro Trinity Church Episcopal **P** (408) 720 Ford Ave 42301-4632 (Mail to: 720 Ford Ave 42301-4632) David Carletta (270) 684-5326

Paducah Grace Episcopal Church **P** (298) 820 Broadway St 42001-6808 (Mail to: 820 Broadway St 42001-6887) Richard Paxton Charles Uhlik (270) 443-1363

Pewee Valley St James Episcopal Church **P** (161) § 401 Lagrange Rd 40056 (Mail to: PO Box 433 40056-0433) (502) 241-8136

Russellville Trinity Episcopal Church **M** (59) PO Box 162 42276-0162 (Mail to: PO Box 162 42276-0162) Geoffrey Butcher (270) 726-3481

Shelbyville St James Episcopal Church **P** (129) 230 Main St 40065-1024 (Mail to: PO Box 166 40066-0166) (502) 633-2718

DIOCESE OF LEXINGTON
(PROVINCE IV)
Comprises eastern Kentucky
DIOCESAN OFFICE 203 E Fourth St
(MAIL: Box 610 Lexington KY 40588-0610) Lexington KY 40508-1515
TEL (859) 252-6527 FAX (859) 231-9077
E-MAIL diocese@diolex.org WEB www.diolex.org

Previous Bishops—
Lewis W Burton 1896- 1928, Henry PA Abbott 1929-45, Wm R Moody 1945-71, Addison Hosea coadj 1970 Bp 1971-85, Don A Wimberly coadj 1984 Bp 1985-99, Rogers S Harris asst 1999-2000, Stacy F Sauls Bp 2000-2011, Chilton R Knudsen asst 2011-2012, W Douglas Hahn Bp 2012-17, Bruce Caldwell Bp prov (2016-18), Mark Van Koevering Bp prov (2018-19)

Bishop—Mark Van Koevering (2019-)

Dn of Lex C Wade; *Miss for Operation and Fin* K Luchtefeld; *Chanc* MT Yeiser; *Cn to Ord* A Cortright; J Kimbrough; *Comm* C Buterbaugh; *Hist* D Wilkins; *Admin Asst* M Yankey; *Depts and Comms: Yth* C Sigmon

Stand Comm—Cler: Pres J Trimble A Dean G Harrison: *Lay:* T Pope D Sevigny E Pitts

PARISHES, MISSIONS, AND CLERGY

Ashland Calvary Episcopal Church **P** (110) 1337 Winchester Ave 41101-7553 (Mail to: PO Box 109 41105-0109) (606) 325-2328

Beattyville St Thomas Episcopal Church **M** (6) 1 Madison St 41311 (Mail to: PO Box 626 41311-0626) (606) 464-9714

Corbin St Johns Episcopal Church **P** (61) 701 Engineer St 40701-1037 (Mail to: PO Box 1512 40702-1512) Jennifer Woodruff Jennifer Woodruff (606) 5281659

Covington Trinity Episcopal Church **P** (432) 16 E 4th St 41011-1510 (Mail to: 16 E 4th St 41011-1510) Peter D'Angio (859) 431-1786

Cynthiana Advent Church **P** (38) 122 N Walnut St 41031-1224 (Mail to: PO Box 308 41031-0308) (859) 234-4163

Danville Trinity Episcopal Church **P** (208) 320 W Main St 40422-1814 (Mail to: 320 W Main St 40422-1814) Joseph Chambers (859) 236-3374

Flemingsburg Chp of St Fran of Flemingsburg **M** (24) 444 Fountain Ave 41041-1032 (Mail to: 444 Fountain Ave 41041-1032) Mary Kilbourn-Huey (606) 845-4001

Florence Grace Episcopal Church **HC** (60) 7111 Price Pike 41042-1665 (Mail to: 7111 Price Pike 41042-1665) Sherilyn Pearce (859) 371-5951

Fort Thomas St Andrews Episcopal Church **P** (635) 3 Chalfonte Pl 41075-1927 (Mail to: PO Box 75027 41075-0027) John Pennington Jeffrey Queen Jeffrey Queen (859) 441-1092

Frankfort Episcopal Ch of the Ascension **P** (303) 311 Washington St 40601-1823 (Mail to: 311 Washington St 40601-1823) Peter Doddema Rebecca Saager (502) 2230557

Georgetown Church of the Holy Trinity **P** (171) PO Box 1433 209 S Broadway St 40324-6433 (Mail to: PO Box 1433 40324-1340) Karen Booth (502) 863-0505

Harlan Christ Episcopal Church **P** (31) 119 E Central St 40831-2348 (Mail to: PO Box 858 40831-0858) (606) 573-4210

Harrodsburg St Philips Episcopal Church **HC** (112) 118 W Poplar St 40330-1641 (Mail to: 118 W Poplar St 40330-1641) (859) 734-3569

Hazard St Marks Episcopal Church **M** (21) 317 Walnut St 41701-1853 (Mail to: 317 Walnut St 41701-1853) (606) 273-7826

Irvine St Timothys Church **M** (8) 170 St. Timothy's Rd. 40336 (Mail to: PO Box 656 40336-0656) Bryant Kibler (606) 726-0607

✣ **Lexington** Christ Church Cathedral **O** (1009) 166 Market St 40507-1139 (Mail to: 166 Market St 40507-1139) Carol Wade (859) 254-4497

Lexington Church of the Good Shepherd **P** (819) § 533 E Main St 40508-2341 (Mail to: C/O Scott Heersche DOF 533 E Main St 40508-2341) G Hendree Harrison Christian Brady Jon Hall (859) 2521744

Lexington Ch St Michael The Archangel **P** (611) § 2025 Bellefonte Dr 40503-2601 (Mail to: 2025 Bellefonte Dr 40503-2601) Laurie Brock William Neat (859) 277-7511

Lexington St Andrews Episcopal Church **P** (37) 401 N Upper St 40508-1450 (Mail to: 401 N Upper St 40508-1450) Michael Henderson Marcia Hunter (859) 254-8325

Lexington St Augustine Episcopal Chapel **CM** 472 Rose St 40508-3342 (Mail to: 472 Rose St 40508-3342) (859) 2543726

Lexington St Huberts Episcopal Church **P** (89) 7559 Grimes Mill Rd 40515-9600 (Mail to: PO Box 21987 40522-1987) Duane Smith Charles Ellestad Duane Smith (859) 527-6440

Lexington St Raphael Episcopal Church **P** (284) 1891 Parkers Mill Rd 40504-2041 (Mail to: 1891 Parkers Mill Rd 40504-2041) Helen Van Koevering (859) 255-4987

Lexington St Marthas Episcopal Church **P** (56) 1870 Armstrong Mill RD 40517 (Mail to: 1870 Armstrong Mill RD 40517) (859) 271-7641

Maysville Episcopal Ch of the Nativity **P** (31) 31 E 3rd St 41056-1149 (Mail to: PO Box 3 41056-0003) Roxanne Ruggles (606) 564-5850

Middlesboro St Marys Episcopal Church **P** (46) 131 Edgewood Rd 40965-2840 (Mail to: PO Box 744 40965-0744) (606) 248-6450

Morehead St Albans Church **M** (42) 145 E 5th St 40351-1205 (Mail to: 145 E 5th St 40351-1205) Keila Thomas (606) 784-6427

Mt Sterling Church of the Ascension **P** (60) 48 W High St 40353-0653 (Mail to: PO Box 653 40353-0653) (859) 498-3730

Newport St Pauls Episcopal Church **P** (166) 7 Court Pl 41071-1005 (Mail to: 7 Court Pl 41071-1098) Stephen Young Thomas Runge (859) 581-7640

Nicholasville Epis Ch of the Resurrection **P** (161) 3220 Lexington Rd 40356-9798 (Mail to: 3220 Lexington Rd 40356-9798) (859) 885-6391

Paris St Peters Episcopal Church **P** (104) 311 High St 40361-2002 (Mail to: PO Box 27 40362-0027) Keila Thomas (859) 987-2760

Prestonsburg St James Episcopal Church **P** (16) 562 University Dr 41653-1800 (Mail to: 562 University Dr 41653-1800) (606) 886-8046

Richmond Episcopal Church of Our Saviour **M** (81) 2323 Lexington Rd 40475-9135 (Mail to: 2323 Lexington Rd 40475-9135) Carol Ruthven (859) 6231226

Somerset St Patricks Episcopal Church **P** (88) 206 West Columbia Street 42501-1674 (Mail to: PO Box 633 42502-0633) Christina Brannock (606) 678-4262

Versailles St Johns Episcopal Church **P** (297) 210 N Main St 40383-1206 (Mail to: 210 N Main St 40383-1206) (859) 873-3481

Winchester Emmanuel Episcopal Church **P** (64) 2410 Lexington Rd 40391-9522 (Mail to: 2410 Lexington Rd 40391-9522) James Trimble (859) 744-4889

DIOCESE OF LONG ISLAND
(PROVINCE II)
Comprises the 4 counties of Brooklyn, Queens, Nassau, and Suffolk
DIOCESAN HOUSE 36 Cathedral Ave Garden City NY 11530
TEL (516) 248-4800 FAX (516) 877-1349
E-MAIL communication@dioceseli.org WEB www.dioceselongisland.org

Previous Bishops—
Abram N Littlejohn 1868-1901, Fredk Burgess 1901-25, Ernest M Stires 1925-42, John I Larned suffr 1929-47, Frank W Creighton suffr 1933-37, James P DeWolfe 1942-66, Jonathan G Sherman suffr 1949-65 Bp 1966-77, Richd B Martin suffr 1967-74, Chas W MacLean suffr 1962-75, C Shannon Mallory asst bp 1979-80, Henry B Hucles III suffr 1981-88, Robert C Witcher coadj 1975 Bp 1977-91, Rodney R Michel suffr 1997-2007, Orris G Walker Jr coadj 1991-2009, Rt Rev James H Ottley Asst Bp 2007-09

Bishop—Rt Rev Lawrence C Provenzano (1037)
(Dio 14 Nov 09)

Chanc R Fardella; *Dir of Yth Min* M Garnes; *Sec* Rev KDM Davis-Lawson; *Treas* P Griffith; *Hist Reg* C Egleston

Stand Comm–Cler: Pres S Foster EC Nesmith D Sibley L Womack; *Lay:* M Thorstenn R Murphy A McPartland V Hinkson

PARISHES, MISSIONS, AND CLERGY

Amagansett St Thomas Episcopal Chapel **SC** Rt 27 & Indian Wells Hwy 11930 (Mail to: PO Box 103 11930-0103) (313) 242-7356

Amityville St Marys Episcopal Church **P** (409) 175 Broadway 11701-2703 (Mail to: C/O Kevin C Fowler 175 Broadway 11701-2703) (631) 264-0004

Astoria Church of the Redeemer **P** (742) 30-14 Crescent St 11102 (Mail to: 3014 Crescent St 11102-3249) Juan Quevedo-Bosch Thomas Carey (718) 278-8093

Astoria St George's Episcopal Church **P** (66) 14-02 27th Ave 11102 (Mail to: 1420 27th Ave 11102-3873) (718) 721-5154

Babylon Christ Episcopal Church **P** (245) 12 Prospect St 11702-3407 (Mail to: 12 Prospect St 11702-3407) Elizabeth Nesmith (631) 661-5757

Baldwin All Saints' Episcopal Church **P** (477) 2375 Harrison Ave 11510-3214 (Mail to: 2375 Harrison Ave 11510-3214) Maxine Barnett (516) 223-3731

Bay Shore St Peters by the Sea Epis Ch **P** (419) § 500 S Country Rd 11706-8295 (Mail to: 500 S Country Rd 11706-8295) Doyle Dietz Allen Johncy Itty (631) 665-0051

Bayside All Saints Church **P** (264) 21435 40th Ave 11361-2145 (Mail to: 21435 40th Ave 11361-2151) Laurence Byrne (718) 229-5631

Bellmore St Matthias Episcopal Church **M** (8) 2856 Jerusalem Ave 11710 (Mail to: PO Box 573 11710-0573) (516) 783-0558

Bellport Christ Episcopal Church **P** (146) 64 S Country Rd 11713-2519 (Mail to: 64 S Country Rd 11713-2519) Terrence Buckley (631) 286-0299

Brentwood Christ Church **M** (61) 155 3rd Ave 11717-5322 (Mail to: 155 3rd Ave 11717-5322) (631) 273-9504

Bridgehampton St Anns Episcopal Church **P** (220) 2463 Main St 11932 (Mail to: PO Box 961 11932-0961) James Erwin (631) 537-1527

Brookhaven St James Episcopal Church **M** (70) 260 Beaver Dam Rd 11719-9756 (Mail to: 260 Beaver Dam Rd 11719-9756) Hickman Alexandre (631) 286-0726

Brooklyn All Saints Church **P** (334) 286-88 7th Ave 11215-3601 (Mail to: 286-88 Seventh Ave 11215-3601) Steven Paulikas Spencer Cantrell Jennifer VanCooten-Webster (718) 768-1156

Brooklyn Bushwick Abbey **P** 22 Wyckoff Ave 11237-2635 (Mail to: 22 Wyckoff Ave 11237-2635)

Brooklyn Christ Church Cobble Hill **P** (35) Attn: Mr Alan Mc Dougal 326 Clinton St 11231-3702 (Mail to: Attn: Mr Alan Mcdougal 326 Clinton St 11231-3702) Mark Genszler

Brooklyn Christ Church Bay Ridge **P** (108) 7301 Ridge Blvd 11209-2113 (Mail to: C/O Theresa DeStasio 7301 Ridge Blvd 11209-2113) Lawrence De Lion (718) 745-3698

Brooklyn Ch of Calvary and St Cyprian **P** (236) 966 Bushwick Ave 11221-3740 (Mail to: 966 Bushwick Ave 11221-3740) Charles Holdbrooke (718) 453-3764

Brooklyn Church of St Thomas **P** (623) 1405 Bushwick Ave 11207-1408 (Mail to: 1405 Bushwick Ave 11207-1408) Sully Guillaume-Sam (718) 452-2332

Brooklyn St Stephen & St Martin Church **P** (264) 809 Jefferson Ave 11221-3504 (Mail to: 789 Jefferson Ave 11221) Richard Pike (718) 453-0651

Brooklyn Church of the Ascension **P** (163) 127 Kent St 11222 (Mail to: 127 Kent St 11222-2103) David Fleenor John Merz (718) 383-5402

Brooklyn Church of the Holy Apostles **P** (125) 612 Greenwood Ave 11218-1302 (Mail to: Attn: Treasurer 612 Greenwood Ave 11218-

1302) Kimberlee Auletta Sarah Kooperkamp (718) 871-1615

Brooklyn Church of the Holy Spirit **M** (143) 81-17 Bay Pkwy 11214 (Mail to: 8117 Bay Pkwy 11214-2513) (718) 837-0412

Brooklyn Church of the Nativity **M** (186) 121 Amersfort Pl 11210-2321 (Mail to: 1099 Ocean Ave 11230-1905) (718) 859-8654

Brooklyn Emmanuel Episcopal Church **P** (142) 2635 E 23rd St 11235 (Mail to: 2635 E 23rd St 11235-2825) (718) 934-0189

Brooklyn Grace Church **P** (1131) § 254 Hicks St 11201-4028 (Mail to: 254 Hicks St 11201-4097) Allen Robinson Leandra Lambert Erika Meyer (718) 624-1850

Brooklyn Iglesia de la Santa Cruz **M** (46) 172 Saint Nicholas Ave 11237 (Mail to: 172 Saint Nicholas Ave 11237) (917) 507-7088

Brooklyn Saint Alban's Church **P** (1737) 9408 Farragut Rd 11236-2028 (Mail to: 9408 Farragut Rd 11236-2028) (718) 342-5215

Brooklyn St Andrew Episcopal Church **P** (494) 4917 4th Ave 11220-1819 (Mail to: 4917 4th Ave 11220-1819) Francisco Rodriguez-Padron (718) 439-6056

Brooklyn St Ann and the Holy Trinity Ch **P** (155) 157 Montague St 11201-3587 (Mail to: 157 Montague St 11201-3587) John Denaro Elise Hanley (718) 875-6960

Brooklyn St Augustines Episcopal Church **P** (1198) 4301 Ave D 11203 (Mail to: 4301 Avenue D 11203-5723) Lawrence Womack Joseph Diele Anthony Jones Howard Williams (718) 629-0930

Brooklyn St Barnabas Episcopal Church **P** (507) 417 Elton St 11208 (Mail to: 417 Elton St 11208-2129) Sylvester Taylor (718) 277-5407

Brooklyn St Bartholomews Church **P** (97) 1227 Pacific St 11216 (Mail to: C/O Nancy Signore 36 Cathedral Ave 11530-4435) Pierre Damus (718) 467-8750

Brooklyn St Gabriels Episcopal Church **P** (902) 331 Hawthorne St 11225-5909 (Mail to: 331 Hawthorne St 11225-5909) Donovan Leys (718) 774-5248

Brooklyn St Georges Episcopal Church **P** (261) 800 Marcy Ave 11216-1513 (Mail to: 800 Marcy Ave 11216-1513) Landon Moore Jason Moskal (718) 789-6036

Brooklyn St Johns Park Slope **P** (211) 139 Saint Johns Pl 11217-3401 (Mail to: 139 Saint Johns Pl 11217-3401) Stephen Setzer Sean Wallace (718) 783-3928

Brooklyn Church of St Mark **P** (3620) 1417 Union St 11213 (Mail to: 1417 Union St 11213-4337) Kino Vitet Kino Vitet (718) 756-6607

Brooklyn St Marys Episcopal Church **P** (100) 230 Classon Ave 11205-1441 (Mail to: 230 Classon Ave 11205-1441) Gerald Keucher (718) 638-2090

Brooklyn St Pauls Episcopal Church **P** (250) 199 Carroll St 11231-4203 (Mail to: 199

Carroll St 11231-4203) William Ogburn (718) 625-4126

Brooklyn St Pauls Church in the Village **P** (369) 157 St Pauls Pl 11226-2708 (Mail to: 157 Saint Pauls Pl 11226-2708) Sheldon Hamblin (718) 282-2100

Brooklyn St Philip's Episcopal Church **P** (75) 1072 80th St 11228 (Mail to: 1072 80th St 11228-2620) (718) 745-2505

Brooklyn St Philips Episcopal Church **P** (501) 334 Macdonough St 11233-1013 (Mail to: C/O Susan Ransom 265 Decatur St 11233-1704) (718) 778-8700

Brooklyn Church of St Luke & St Matthew **P** (217) 520 Clinton Ave 11238-2211 (Mail to: 520 Clinton Ave 11238-2211) Andrew Durbidge Edwin Chase (718) 638-0686

Brooklyn Church The Epiphany & St Simon **P** (165) 2910 Avenue M 11210 (Mail to: 2910 Avenue M 11210-4699) Allen George (718) 258-1166

Cambria Heights St Davids Episcopal Church **P** (606) 117-35 235th St 11411 (Mail to: 117-35 235th St 11411-1821) Karen Davis-Lawson (718) 528-2095

Carle Place St Marys Episcopal Church **P** (55) 252 Rushmore Ave 11514-1431 (Mail to: PO Box 201 11514-0201) (516) 333-2290

Central Islip Church of the Messiah **M** (72) 53 Carleton Ave 11722-3018 (Mail to: PO Box 161 11722-0161) (631) 234-5161

Cold Spring Harbor St John's Church **P** (1137) 1675 Route 25a 11724-1513 (Mail to: PO Box 266 11724-0266) Gideon Pollach (516) 692-6368

Ctr Moriches Church of St John the Baptist **P** (170) 33 Railroad Ave 11934 (Mail to: PO Box 602 11934-0602) (631) 878-0022

Deer Park St Patricks Episcopal Church **P** (116) 305 Carlls Path 11729-5415 (Mail to: 305 Carlls Path 11729-5415) (631) 242-7530

Douglaston Zion Episcopal Church **P** (273) 243-01 Northern Blvd 11363 (Mail to: 243-01 Northern Blvd 11363) Lindsay Lunnum Carl Adair (718) 225-0466

East Elmhurst Epis ch of Grace and Rsurctn **P** (423) 10017 32nd Ave 11369-2501 (Mail to: 10017 32nd Ave 11369-2501) Gilberto Hinds (718) 899-5227

East Hampton St Lukes Episcopal Church **P** (638) 18 James Ln 11937 (Mail to: 18 James Ln 11937-2796) (631) 329-0990

East Hampton St Peter Epis Summer Chapel **SC** 463 Old Stone Hwy 11937 (Mail to: 18 James Ln 11937-2710) (631) 329-0990

East Setauket Caroline Church of Brookhaven **P** (745) 1 Dyke Rd 11733-3052 (Mail to: 1 Dyke Rd 11733-3014) J Cooper Conway (631) 941-4245

Elmhurst St James Episcopal Church **P** (67) 8407 Broadway 11373-5727 (Mail to: 8407

Broadway 11373-5727) Paul Lai Winfred Vergara (718) 592-2555

Far Rockaway St Joseph Episcopal Chapel **SC** 327 Beach 19th St 11691-4423 (Mail to: 327 Beach 19th St 11691-4423) Cecily Broderick y Guerra Barbara Jean Maxwell (718) 869-7320

Farmingdale St Thomas Episcopal Church **P** (43) 298 Conklin St 11735-2609 (Mail to: 298 Conklin St 11735-2609) (516) 752-9254

Fishers Island St Johns Episcopal Church **SC** Oriental Ave 06390 (Mail to: PO Box 475 06390-0475) Michael Spencer (631) 788-7497

Floral Park St Elisabeths Episcopal Church **P** (53) 6 Harvard St 11001-2822 (Mail to: 6 Harvard St 11001-2822) T Abigail Murphy (516) 354-6867

Floral Park St Thomas Episcopal Church **P** (103) 6 Commonwealth Blvd 11001-4141 (Mail to: 6 Commonwealth Blvd 11001-4141) Brian Barry (516) 354-6866

Flushing St Georges Episcopal Church **P** (1130) 13532 38th Ave 11354-4417 (Mail to: 13532 38th Ave 11354-4483) Paul Xie Paul Xie (718) 359-1171

Flushing St John's Episcopal Church **P** (182) 149-49 Sanford Ave 11355-1038 (Mail to: 14949 Sanford Ave 11355-1092) (718) 961-1333

Forest Hills St Lukes Episcopal Church **P** (239) 85 Greenway S 11375 (Mail to: 85 Greenway S 11375-5942) Cecily Broderick Y Guerra William Doubleday (718) 268-6021

Freeport Church of the Transfiguration **P** (312) Pine St S Long Beach Ave 11520 (Mail to: 69 South Long Beach Ave 11520) Raymond Wilson (516) 379-1230

✠ **Garden City** Cathedral of the Incarnation **O** (1224) 50 Cathedral Ave 11530-4435 (Mail to: 36 Cathedral Ave 11530-4435) Michael Sniffen Edmund Alleyne Katherine Salisbury (516) 746-2955

Garden City Christ Episcopal Church **P** (99) 33 Jefferson St 11530-3929 (Mail to: 33 Jefferson St 11530-3929) (516) 775-2626

Garden City Good Shepherd Episcopal Chapel **CC** 65 4th St 11530-4313 (Mail to: 65 4th St 11530-4313) John Mcginty (516) 248-4800

Glen Cove St Paul's Episcopal Church **P** (113) 28 Highland Rd 11542-2630 (Mail to: 28 Highland Rd 11542-2698) Shawn Williams (516) 676-0015

Great Neck All Saints Episcopal Church **P** (210) 855 Middle Neck Rd 11024-1441 (Mail to: 855 Middle Neck Rd 11024-1441) Joseph Pae (516) 482-5392

Great River Emmanuel Episcopal Church **HC** (106) 320 Great River Rd 11739-0571 (Mail to: 320 Great River Rd 11739-3010) Ellis Tommaseo (631) 581-3964

Greenport Church of the Holy Trinity **P** (96) 768 Main St 11944-1446 (Mail to: PO Box 502 11944-0502) (631) 477-0855

Hampton Bays Church of St Marys **P** (438) 165 Ponquogue Ave 11946-3069 (Mail to: 165 Ponquogue Ave 11946-3069) Philip Hubbard (631) 7280776

Hempstead St Georges Episcopal Church **P** (174) 319 Front St 11550-4024 (Mail to: 319 Front St 11550-4083) Imlijungla Sojwal (516) 483-2771

Hewlett Trinity St Johns Epis Church **P** (680) 1142 Broadway 11557 (Mail to: 1142 Broadway 11557-2302) John Ballard (516) 374-1415

Hicksville Holy Trinity Episcopal Church **P** (337) 130 Jerusalem Ave 11801-4918 (Mail to: 130 Jerusalem Ave 11801-4934) (516) 931-1920

Hollis St Gabriels Episcopal Church **P** (322) 196-10 Woodhull Ave 11423 (Mail to: 19610 Woodhull Ave 11423-2984) Ryan Boyce Charles Nelson (718) 465-2876

Huntington St Johns Episcopal Church **P** (446) 12 Prospect St 11743-3375 (Mail to: 12 Prospect St 11743-3375) Duncan Burns John Morrison (631) 427-1752

Islip St Marks Episcopal Church **P** (484) 754 Montauk Hwy 11751-3696 (Mail to: 754 Montauk Hwy 11751-3696) Maurice Beckham (631) 581-4950

Jackson Heights St Marks Church **P** (256) 33-50 82nd Street 11372-1499 (Mail to: 3350 82nd St 11372-1499) Pedro Cuevas Feliz Jason Moskal Jason Moskal (718) 639-8893

Jamaica Church of St James the Less **P** (676) 107-66 Merrick Blvd 11433 (Mail to: Attn: Glenn Stewart 10766 Merrick Blvd 11433-2417) Dennison Richards (718) 262-0535

Jamaica Grace Episcopal Church **P** (339) 15524 90th Ave 11432-3825 (Mail to: C/O Deena Alleyne 15524 90th Ave 11432-3825) (718) 291-4901

Jamaica St Stephens Episcopal Church **P** (186) 89-26 168th St 11432-4334 (Mail to: 8926 168th St 11432-4334) Frederick Walker (718) 523-1917

Kew Gardens Church of the Resurrection **P** (160) 8509 118th St 11415-2907 (Mail to: 8509 118th St 11415-2907) (718) 847-2649

Lindenhurst St Boniface Episcopal Church **P** (181) 100 46th St 11757-2050 (Mail to: 100 46th St Unit 2 11757-2050) Diane Deblasio (631) 957-2666

Locust Valley St John's Ch of Lattingtown **P** (562) 325 Lattingtown Rd 11560-1022 (Mail to: 325 Lattingtown Rd 11560-1022) Mark Fitzhugh Catherine Wieczorek (516) 671-3226

Long Beach St James of Jerusalem Epis Ch **P** (133) 220 W Penn St 11561-3933 (Mail to: 220 W Penn St 11561-3933) (516) 432-1080

Long Island City All Saints' Episcopal Church **P** (55) 4312 46th St 11104-2002 (Mail to: 43-12 46th St 11104-2002) (718) 784-8031

Lynbrook St John the Evangelist Epis Ch **P** (155) 49 Blake Ave 11563-2505 (Mail to: 49 Blake Ave 11563-2505) (516) 792-6050

Manhasset Christ Episcopal Church **P** (182) 1351 Northern Blvd 11030-3007 (Mail to: 1351 Northern Blvd 11030-3007) Stephen Tamke (516) 627-2184

Massapequa Grace Episcopal Church **P** (377) § 23 Cedar Shore Dr 11758 (Mail to: 23 Cedar Shore Dr 11758-7318) Walter Hillebrand (516) 798-1122

Mastic Beach Saint Andrew's Church **M** (49) 250 Main St 11951-3623 (Mail to: PO Box 488 11951-0488) (631) 281-9133

Mattituck Church of the Redeemer **P** (133) 13225 Sound Ave 11952 (Mail to: PO Box 906 13225 Sound Ave 11952-0912) Edward Blatz Roger Joslin (631) 298-4277

Medford St Marks Episcopal Church **P** (25) 208 Jamaica Ave 11763-3290 (Mail to: PO Box 527 11763-0527) (631) 475-7406

New Hyde Park St Philip and St James Church **M** (31) 432 Lakeville Rd 11042-1121 (Mail to: 432 Lakeville Rd 11042-1121) (516) 354-0458

North Bellmore St Francis Episcopal Church **P** (70) 1692 Bellmore Ave 11710-5530 (Mail to: 1692 Bellmore Ave 11710-5530)

Northport Trinity Episcopal Church **P** (209) 130 Main St 11768-1723 (Mail to: 130 Main St Ste 1 11768-1784) (631) 261-7670

Oakdale St Johns Episcopal Church **M** (11) 1 Berard Blvd 11769-1701 (Mail to: One Berard Blvd 11769) (631) 589-0213

Oyster Bay Christ Episcopal Church **P** (452) 55 East Main St 11771-2400 (Mail to: 55 E Main St 11771-2493) Michael Piret (516) 922-6377

Patchogue St Pauls Episcopal Church **P** (111) 31 Rider Ave 11772-3915 (Mail to: 31 Rider Ave 11772-3999) Guilherme De Azevedo (631) 475-3078

Plainview St Margarets Church **P** (187) 1000 Washington Ave 11803-1831 (Mail to: 1000 Washington Ave 11803-1831) Christina Van Liew (516) 692-5268

Prt Jefferson Christ Episcopal Church **P** (154) 127 Barnum Ave 11777-1621 (Mail to: 127 Barnum Ave 11777-1621) Anthony Di Lorenzo (631) 473-0273

Prt Washington St Stephens Episcopal Church **P** (420) 9 Carlton Ave 11050-3105 (Mail to: 9 Carlton Ave 11050-3105) Lauren Mcleavey (516) 767-0363

Queens Vlg St Josephs Episcopal Church **P** (912) 9910 217th Ln 11429-1214 (Mail to: 9910 217th Ln 11429-1214) Kassinda Ellis (718) 465-4193

Quogue Church of the Atonement **SC** 17 Quogue St 11959 (Mail to: PO Box 928 11959-0928) (631) 653-6798

Riverhead Grace Episcopal Church **P** (178) 573 Roanoke Ave 11901-2760 (Mail to: 573 Roanoke Ave 11901-2760) (631) 727-3900

Rockville Ct The Church of the Ascension **P** (353) 71 N Village Ave 11570-4605 (Mail to: 71 N Village Ave 11570-4605) Kevin Morris (516) 766-0693

Ronkonkoma St Marys Episcopal Church **P** (280) 315 Lake Shore Rd 11779-3180 (Mail to: 315 Lake Shore Rd 11779-3147) John Shirley (631) 588-1888

Roosevelt St Pauls Episcopal Church **M** (130) 25 W Centennial Ave 11575-2028 (Mail to: PO Box 514 11575-0514) (516) 546-2754

Rosedale St Peters Episcopal Church **P** (277) 13728 244th St 11422-1828 (Mail to: 13728 244th St 11422-1828) Steve Foster (718) 528-1356

Roslyn Trinity Episcopal Church **P** (46) 1579 Northern Blvd 11576-1103 (Mail to: 1579 Northern Blvd Unit A 11576-1137) George Sherrill (516) 621-7925

Sag Harbor Christ Episcopal Church **P** (100) 5 Hampton St 11963-4242 (Mail to: PO Box 570 11963-0012) James Erwin (631) 725-0128

Saint Albans St Alban the Martyr Church **P** (253) 11642 Farmers Blvd 11412-3026 (Mail to: 11642 Farmers Blvd 11412-3026) Keith Voets (718) 528-1891

Saint James St James Episcopal Church **P** (407) 490 Route 25a 11780-1953 (Mail to: 490 Route 25a 11780-1953) Ian Wetmore (631) 584-5560

Saltaire St Andrews-by-the-Sea **SC** (35) 113 Broadway 11706 (Mail to: Attn Peter M R Kendall 300 W End Ave # 8b 10023-8156) (631) 583-8382

Sayville Saint Ann's Church **HC** (505) 262 Middle Rd 11782-3242 (Mail to: 262 Middle Rd 11782-3242) Jeffrey Stevenson (631) 589-6522

Sea Cliff St Lukes Episcopal Church **P** (211) 253 Glen Avenue 11579-1544 (Mail to: 253 Glen Ave 11579-1544) Jesse Lebus (516) 676-4222

Seaford St Michael & All Angels **P** (10) 2197 Jackson Ave 11783-2607 (Mail to: 2197 Jackson Ave 11783-2607) (516) 785-3762

Selden St Cuthberts Episcopal Church **P** (63) 18 Magnolia Pl 11784-2902 (Mail to: PO Box 1367 11784-0995) (631) 475-4555

Shelter Island St Marys Church **P** (135) 26 St Marys Rd 11964 (Mail to: PO Box 1660 11964-1660) Charles Mccarron (631) 749-0770

Shoreham St Anselms Episcopal Church **P** (372) § 4 Woodville Rd 11786-1329 (Mail to: PO Box 606 11786-0606) (631) 744-7730

Smithtown St Thomas of Canterbury Church **P** (249) 29 Brookside Drive 11787-3495 (Mail to: 90 Edgewater Ave 11787-3467) Judith Carrick John Purchal (631) 265-4520

South Ozone Park Saint John's Church **P** (171) 13304 109th Ave 11420-1703 (Mail to: 13304 109th Ave 11420-1703) Frederick Opare-Addo Frederick Opare-Addo (718) 529-0366

Southampton St Johns Episcopal Church **P** (329) 100 S Main St 11968-4804 (Mail to: PO Box 5068 11969-5068) William Edwards (631) 283-0549

Sprngfld Gdn St Johns Episcopal Church **P** (97) 13767 Belknap St 11413-2619 (Mail to: 13767 Belknap St 11413-2619) (718) 525-1444

Stony Brook All Souls Episcopal Church **M** (85) 61 Main Street 11790-1816 (Mail to: 10 Mill Pond Rd 11790-1816) Thomas Reese (631) 751-0034

Valley Stream Holy Trinity Episcopal Church **P** (88) 87 7th St 11581-1214 (Mail to: 87 7th St 11581-1290) (516) 825-2903

Wading River St Lukes Chapel **SC** 408 N Side Rd 11792 (Mail to: 1 N Side Rd 11792-1112) Matthew Tees (631) 929-4325

Wantagh Church of St Jude **P** (509) 3606 Lufberry Ave 11793-3031 (Mail to: 3606 Lufberry Ave 11793-3031) Jimmie Sue Deppe (516) 221-2505

Westbury Church of the Advent **P** (348) 555 Advent St 11590-1309 (Mail to: 555 Advent St 11590-1309) T Abigail Murphy (516) 333-0081

Westhampton Beach St Marks Episcopal Church **P** (257) § 40 Main St 11978-2673 (Mail to: PO Box 887 11978-0887) Christopher Jubinski (631) 288-2111

Whitestone Grace Episcopal Church **P** (126) 14-15 Clintonville Street 11357 (Mail to: 1415 Clintonville St 11357-1825) Karen Sherrill (718) 767-6305

Williston Pk Resurrection **P** (40) 147 Campbell Ave 11596-1606 (Mail to: 147 Campbell Ave 11596-1606) Anandsekar Manuel (516) 746-5527

Woodhaven All Saints Episcopal Church **P** (253) 85-45 96th Street 11421 (Mail to: 8545 96th St 11421-1727) Norman Whitmire (718) 849-2352

Woodside St Paul Episcopal Church **M** (38) 39-04 61st St 11377 (Mail to: PO Box 23 11377) (718) 672-8565

Yaphank St Andrew Episcopal Church **P** (155) 244 E Main St 11980-9656 (Mail to: PO Box 249 11980-0249) Gerardo Romo-Garcia (631) 924-5083

DIOCESE OF LOS ANGELES
(PROVINCE VIII)
Comprises southern California, except San Diego
DIO OFC 840 Echo Pk Ave Los Angeles CA 90026
TEL (213) 482-2040 FAX (213) 482-5304
E-MAIL communications@ladiocese.org WEB www.ladiocese.org
The Bishop of the Protestant Episcopal Church in the Diocese of Los Angeles, a Corporation Sole

Previous Bishops—
Jos H Johnson 1896-1928, W Bertrand Stevens coadj 1920 Bp 1928-47, Robt B Gooden suffr 1930-47, F Eric Bloy 1948-73, Donald J Campbell suffr 1949-59, Ivol I Curtis suffr 1960-64, C Rusack suffr 1964-73 Bp 1974-86, Oliver B Garver suffr 1985-90, Frederick Houk Borsch 1988-2002, Chester L Talton suffr 1991-2010, Mary D Glasspool suffr 2010-15, J on Bruno 2002-17, Diane J. Bruce suffr 2010-21

Bishop—Rt Rev John Harvey Taylor (1101) Dio 8 Jul 2017)

Sec Conv Cn S Nishibayashi; *Treas* Cn A Tomat; Canon to the Ordinary, *Chief of Staff* Cn M McCarthy; *CFO* S Stanton; *Chanc* Cn R Zevnik; *Cn Form/Deploy* Rev T Quijada-Discavage; *COM* Rev . Crow & C Johnson; *Sch* Rev R Newman; *Missions Cong Cn* C Bangao; *Parish Cong* Cn A Urquidi

tand Comm—Cler: Pres G Leemhuis A Gallardo D ustin L Mackenzie; *Lay:* R Hayden-Smith D Askren Cn J Wylie R Verma

PARISHES, MISSIONS, AND CLERGY

Alhambra Holy Trinity St Benedict Ch **P** (262) 412 N Garfield Ave 91801-2438 (Mail to: 412 N Garfield Ave 91801-2498) Brent Quines (626) 282-9118

Altadena St Marks Episcopal Church **P** (677) § 1014 E Altadena Dr 91001-2041 (Mail to: 1014 E Altadena Dr 91001-2041) Carri Grindon Elizabeth Hooper Joseph Lane Sylvia Sweeney (626) 798-6747

Anaheim St Michaels Episcopal Church **M** (2475) 311 W South St 92805-4517 (Mail to: 311 W South St 92805-4598) Juan Jimenez (714) 535-4654

Apple Valley St Timothy's Episcopal Church **P** (230) 15757 St Timothy Rd 92307-2554 (Mail to: 15757 St Timothy Rd 92307-2590) John Limo (760) 242-2405

Arcadia Church of the Transfiguration **P** (192) 1881 S 1st Ave 91006-4618 (Mail to: 1881 S 1st Ave 91006-4618) (626) 445-3340

Barstow St Paul's Episcopal Church **M** (37) 512 E Williams St 92311-2941 (Mail to: PO Box 726 92312-0726) (760) 256-2822

Beaumont St Stephens Episcopal Church **M** (141) 225 E 8th St 92223-5903 (Mail to: 225 E 8th St 92223-5903) William Dunn (951) 845-1358

Beverly Hills All Saints Episcopal Parish **P** (1702) 504 N Camden Dr 90210-3299 (Mail to: 504 N Camden Dr 90210-3299) Janet Broderick Andrea Mcmillin Andrea Mcmillin Michael Sahdev (310) 275-0123

Big Bear City St Columbas Episcopal Church **M** (137) 42324 North Shore Dr 92314 (Mail to: PO Box 1681 92315-1681) (909) 866-7239

Buena Park St Joseph Episcopal Church **P** (101) 8300 Valley View St 90620-2738 (Mail to: 8300 Valley View St 90620-2738) Matthew Parker Lucinda Voien (714) 828-8950

Camarillo St Columbas Church **P** (232) 1251 Las Posas Rd 93010-3001 (Mail to: 1251 Las Posas Rd 93010-3001) Mark Asman (805) 482-8831

Claremont St Ambrose Episcopal Church **P** (192) 830 W Bonita Ave 91711-4113 (Mail to: 830 W Bonita Ave 91711-4113) Jessica Smith (909) 626-7170

Compton St Timothys Episcopal Church **P** (135) § 312 S Oleander Ave 90220 (Mail to: 312 S Oleander Ave 90220-3118) Anthony Miller (310) 638-6319

Corona St John's Church **P** (292) 526 Magnolia Ave 92879-3113 (Mail to: PO Box 152 92878-0152) Patricia Stansfield (951) 737-1363

Corona Del Mar St. Michael and All Angels Episcopal Church **P** (100) 3233 Pacific View Dr 92625-1109 (Mail to: 3233 Pacific View Dr 92625-1109) Shane Scott-Hamblen (949) 644-0463

Costa Mesa St John The Divine Church **P** (90) 183 E Bay St 92627-2145 (Mail to: 183 E Bay St 92627-2145) George Okusi (949) 548-2237

Covina Holy Trinity Episcopal Church **P** (230) § 100 Third Ave 91723 (Mail to: 100 N Third Ave 91723-0595) Steven De Muth (626) 967-3939

Downey St Marks Episcopal Church **P** (56) § 10354 Downey Ave 90241-2512 (Mail to: 10354 Downey Ave 90241-2597) (562) 862-3268

El Monte Immanuel Episcopal Church **M** (162) 4366 Santa Anita Ave 91731-1606 (Mail to: 4366 Santa Anita Ave 91731-1606) Hector Limatu (626) 448-1908

El Segundo St Michael the Archangel Par **P** (113) § 361 Richmond St 90245-3729 (Mail to: 361 Richmond St 90245-3729) (310) 322-2589

Encino St Nicholas Episcopal Church **P** (428) 17114 Ventura Blvd 91316-4003 (Mail to: 17114 Ventura Blvd 91316-4003) Michael Cooper (818) 788-4486

Fillmore Trinity Episcopal Church **P** (91) 600 Saratoga St 93015-1444 (Mail to: PO Box 306 93016-0306) Lawrence Brown (805) 524-1910

Fullerton Emmanuel Episcopal Church **P** (135) § 1145 W Valencia Mesa Dr 92833-2218 (Mail to: 1145 W Valencia Mesa Dr 92833-2218) Susan Cardone (714) 8798070

Fullerton St Andrews Episcopal Church **P** (161) § 1231 E Chapman Ave 92831-3908 (Mail to:

1231 E Chapman Ave 92831-3987) (714) 870-4350

Garden Grove St Anselm of Cntbry Epis Ch **P** (226) 13091 Galway St 92844-1633 (Mail to: 13091 Galway St 92844-1698) Thomas Lee Hector Limatu (714) 537-0604

Gardena Church of the Holy Communion **M** (63) 1160 W 141st St 90247-2220 (Mail to: 1160 W 141st St 90247-2220) (310) 324-1441

Glendale Iglesia de la Magdalena **M** (196) 1011 S Verdugo Rd 91205-3831 (Mail to: 1011 S Verdugo Rd 91205-3831) Roberto Martinez-Morales (818) 243-8670

Glendale St Marks Episcopal Church **P** (556) § 1020 N Brand Blvd 91202-2907 (Mail to: 1020 N Brand Blvd 91202-2983) Mark Weitzel Susie Kenny James Prendergast James Prendergast (818) 240-3853

Glendora Grace Episcopal Church **P** (296) 555 E Mountain View Ave 91741-2764 (Mail to: 555 E Mountain View Ave 91741-2764) Susan Scranton (626) 335-3171

Granada Hills St Andrew & Charles Episcopal **P** (218) 16651 Rinaldi St 91344-3632 (Mail to 16651 Rinaldi St 91344-3698) Gregory Fros (818) 366-7542

Hacienda Hgts St Thomas Episcopal Church **M** (113) 15694 Tetley St 91745-4543 (Mail to 15694 Tetley St 91745-4543) Hsin Fen Chang (626) 330-7649

Hawthorne St Georges Episcopal Church **M** (48 4679 W El Segundo Blvd 90250-4349 (Mail to PO Box C 90251-0165) (310) 324-1617

Hermosa Beach St Cross Episcopal Church **P** (905) 1818 Monterey Blvd 90254-2906 (Mai to: 1818 Monterey Blvd 90254-2906) Rache Nyback Patrice Angelo Stephen Smith (310 376-8989

Hesperia St Hilarys Episcopal Church **M** (103 11305 Hesperia Rd 92345-2170 (Mail to 11305 Hesperia Rd 92345-2170) Jonathan S (760) 244-6444

Huntington Beach St Wilfrid of York Epi Church **P** (661) 18631 Chapel Ln 92646 1831 (Mail to: 18631 Chapel Ln 92646-1831 Nathan Biornstad William Wells (714) 962 7512

Huntington Park St Clement's Church **M** (207 6909 Rugby Ave 90255-4721 (Mail to: 84 Echo Park Ave 90026-4209) Santos Flore (323) 587-1277

Inglewood Ch of the Holy Faith Parish **P** (160 260 N Locust St 90301-1204 (Mail to: 260 N Locust St 90301-1298) Kathryn Derose Gu Leemhuis (310) 674-7700

Irvine St Andrew Episcopal Church **M** (237 § 4400 Barranca Pkwy 92604-4739 (Ma to: 4400 Barranca Pkwy 92604-4739) Pete Browning (949) 559-4699

Isla Vista St Michaels University Epis Ch **M** (106 6586 Picasso Rd 93117-4651 (Mail to: 658

Picasso Rd 93117-4651) Scott Claassen Toni Stuart (805) 968-2712

La Canada Saint George's Parish **P** (129) § 808 Foothill Blvd 91011-3336 (Mail to: 808 Foothill Blvd 91011-3336) Amy Pringle (818) 790-3323

La Crescenta St Luke's of the Mountains Ch **M** (186) 2563 Foothill Blvd 91214-3508 (Mail to: 2563 Foothill Blvd 91214-3596) Guy Leemhuis (818) 248-3639

La Verne St John's Episcopal Church **M** (187) 4745 Wheeler Ave 91750-1960 (Mail to: 4745 Wheeler Ave 91750-1960) Jana Milhon-Martin Robert Van Buren Robert Van Buren (909) 596-1321

Laguna Beach St Marys Church Episcopal **P** (152) 428 Park Ave 92651-2337 (Mail to: 428 Park Ave 92651-2337) Lester Mackenzie (949) 494-3542

Laguna Hills St Georges Episcopal Church **M** (179) 23802 Ave De La Carlota 92653-3117 (Mail to: 23802 Avenida De La Carlota 92653-3148) Patricia McCaughan (949) 837-4530

Laguna Niguel Faith Episcopal Church **M** (110) 27802 El Lazo 92677-3915 (Mail to: 27802 El Lazo 92677-3915) Emily Bell Dawn Vukich (949) 448-8114

Lancaster St Pauls Episcopal Church **P** (290) 502 W Avenue K 93534 (Mail to: PO Box 8836 93539) (661) 945-6704

Lompoc Saint Mary's Parish **P** (410) 2800 Harris Grade Rd 93436-2211 (Mail to: C/O Dina Brown 2800 Harris Grade Rd 93436-2211) James Sprague (805) 7334400

Long Beach St Thomas of Canterbury Church **M** (96) 5306 E Arbor Rd 90808-1109 (Mail to: 5306 E Arbor Rd 90808-1109) Sharon Sheffield (562) 425-4457

Long Beach St Gregorys Episcopal Church **P** (433) 6201 E Willow St 90815-2247 (Mail to: 6201 E Willow St 90815-2296) Michael Fincher (562) 420-1311

Long Beach St Lukes Episcopal Church **P** (571) 525 E 7th St 90813-4559 (Mail to: PO Box 20038 90801-3038) Steven Alder Holway Farrar Antonio Gallardo Jane Gould Beryl Nyre-Thomas (562) 436-4047

Los Angeles All Saints Episcopal Church **P** (109) 5619 Monte Vista St 90042-3425 (Mail to: 5619 Monte Vista St 90042-3425) (323) 255-6806

Los Angeles Christ the Good Shepherd Ch **P** (122) 3303 W Vernon Ave 90008-5229 (Mail to: 3303 W Vernon Ave 90008-5295) (323) 295-4139

Los Angeles Church of the Epiphany **M** (269) 2808 Altura St 90031-2305 (Mail to: 2808 Altura St 90031-2399) (323) 227-9931

Los Angeles Episcopal Church of the Advent **P** (202) 4976 W Adams Blvd 90016-2852 (Mail to: 2614 S Longwood Ave 90016-2811) Vanessa Mackenzie (323) 731-8831

Los Angeles Holy Nativity Church **P** (139) 6700 W 83rd St 90045-2730 (Mail to: 6700 W 83rd St 90045-2730) Michael Foley (310) 670-4777

Los Angeles St Albans Episcopal Church **P** (115) 580 Hilgard Ave 90024-3234 (Mail to: 580 Hilgard Ave 90024-3297) (310) 208-6516

Los Angeles St Bedes Episcopal Church **P** (159) 3590 Grand View Blvd 90066-1904 (Mail to: 3590 Grand View Blvd 90066-1904) Ryan Newman (310) 391-5522

Los Angeles Saint James Parish **P** (585) § 3903 Wilshire Blvd. 99010-3301 (Mail to: 3903 Wilshire Blvd 90010-3301) Katherine Cress Jonathan Feuss John Kim (213) 388-3417

Los Angeles St Marys Episcopal Church **P** (433) 961 S Mariposa Ave 90006-1413 (Mail to: 961 S Mariposa Ave 90006-1413) Joy Magala (213) 387-1334

Los Angeles St Philips Ch Igles de Felipe **P** (103) 801 E 28th St 90011-5506 (Mail to: Attn: Ms Ann Young 2800 Stanford Ave 90011-2018) (323) 232-3494

Los Angeles St Thomas the Apostle Hollywood **P** (606) 7501 Hollywood Blvd 90046-2813 (Mail to: 7501 Hollywood Blvd 90046-2813) Ian Davies Ian Davies Walter Johnson Mark Stuart (323) 876-2102

✠ **Los Angeles** St Athanasius **O** (245) 840 Echo Park Ave 90026-4209 (Mail to: 840 Echo Park Ave 90026-4209) (213) 482-2040

✠ **Los Angeles** St John's Cathedral **O** (439) 514 W Adams Blvd 90007-2616 (Mail to: 514 W Adams Blvd 90007-2616) (213) 747-6285

Los Angeles St Mary in Palms **P** (172) 3647 Watseka Ave 90034-3914 (Mail to: 3647 Watseka Ave 90034-3914) (310) 558-4124

Los Angeles St Stephen's Episcopal Church **P** (235) 6128 Yucca St 90028-5214 (Mail to: 6128 Yucca St 90028-5214) Jaime Edwards-Acton (323) 469-3993

Los Angeles Trinity Episcopal Church **P** (215) 650 N Berendo St 90004-2104 (Mail to: 4274 Melrose Ave. 90029) Nancy Frausto (323) 660-1110

Los Olivos St Mark's-In-The-Valley Epis **P** (525) § 2905 Nojoqui 93441 (Mail to: PO Box 39 93441-0039) Randall Day (805) 688-4454

Malibu St Aidans Episcopal Church **P** (151) 28211 Pacific Coast Hwy 90265-3911 (Mail to: 28211 Pacific Coast Hwy 90265-3999) Joyce Stickney (310) 457-7966

Monrovia St Lukes Episcopal Church **P** (59) 122 S California Ave 91016-2948 (Mail to: 122 S California Ave 91016-2948) Brian O'Rourke Neil Tadken (626) 357-7071

Monterey Park St Gabriels Episcopal Church **P** (163) 133 E Graves Ave 91755-3915 (Mail to: 133 E Graves Ave 91755-3915) (626) 571-2714

Moreno Valley Grace Episcopal Church **M** (61) 11349 Perris Blvd 92557-5657 (Mail to: 19091 Seaton Ave 92570-8722) Barbara Barnum Bonnie Brandon (951) 9246760

Needles St John the Evangelist Church **M** (38) 2020 J St 92363-2622 (Mail to: PO Box 817 92363-0817) (760) 326-6673

Newport Beach St James Episcopal Church **M** (224) 3209 Via Lido 92663-3973 (Mail to: 3209 Via Lido 92663-3973) Cynthia Voorhees (949) 675-0210

Norwalk St Francis Episcopal Church **M** (65) 12700 Paddison Ave 90650-3059 (Mail to: 12700 Paddison Ave 90650-3059) Joy Magala (562) 863-9212

Oak Park Episcopal Ch of the Epiphany **M** (706) § 5450 Churchwood Dr 91377-4797 (Mail to: 5450 Churchwood Dr 91377-4797) (818) 991-4797

Ojai St Andrews Episcopal Church **P** (184) 409 Topa Topa Dr 93023-3233 (Mail to: 409 Topa Topa Dr 93023-3233) Mikel Morrison (805) 646-1885

Ontario Christ Church Parish **P** (96) 1127 N San Antonio Ave 91762-1803 (Mail to: 1127 N San Antonio Ave 91762-1899) Walter Donaldson Gian Luigi Gugliermetto (909) 983-1859

Orange Trinity Episcopal Church **P** (676) 2400 N Canal St 92865-3614 (Mail to: 2400 N Canal St 92865-3614) (714) 637-1390

Oxnard All Saints Episcopal Church **P** (142) 144 S C St 93030-5615 (Mail to: 144 S C St 93030-5693) Melissa Campbell-Langdell (805) 483-2347

Pacific Plsds St Matthew's Episcopal Church **P** (1549) § Attn: Craig Ehlers 1031 Bienveneda Ave 90272-2314 (Mail to: C/O Chief Financial Officer 1031 Bienveneda Ave 90272-2314) Gregory Brown Bruce Freeman Christine Purcell William Wallace (310) 454-1358

Palos Verdes Estates St Francis Episcopal Church **P** (592) PO Box 772 2200 Via Rosa 90274-0772 (Mail to: PO Box 772 90274-0772) Jerry Sather (310) 375-4617

Pasadena All Saints Episcopal Church **P** (7209) 132 N Euclid Ave 91101-1722 (Mail to: 132 N Euclid Ave 132 N Euclid Ave 91101-1796) Michael Kinman Alfredo Feregrino Sally Howard Sally Howard Susan Russell (626) 5832742

Pasadena Church of the Angels **P** (200) 1100 Avenue 64 91105-2712 (Mail to: 1100 Avenue 64 91105-2712) Robert Gaestel (323) 255-3878

Pasadena St Barnabas Episcopal Church **P** (87) 1062 N Fair Oaks Ave 91103-3011 (Mail to: PO Box 93096 91109-3096) Jamesetta Glosson Hammons Victoria Zahn (626) 798-2996

Pico Rivera St Bartholomews Episcopal Ch **M** (378) 7540 Passons Blvd 90660-4233 (Mail to: Episcopal Diocese of La 840 Echo Park Ave 90026-4209) Juan Barragan (562) 949-5228

Placentia Blessed Sacrament Church **P** (117) § 1314 N Angelina Dr 92870-3442 (Mail to: 1314 N Angelina Dr 92870-3442) (714) 528-2995

Pomona St Pauls Episcopal Church **P** (199) 242 E Alvarado St 91767-4634 (Mail to: 242 E Alvarado St 91767-4698) Thomas Hallahan (909) 622-2015

Rancho Santa Margarita St Johns Chrysostom Church **M** (825) § 30382 Via Con Dios 92688-1518 (Mail to: 30382 Via Con Dios 92688-1518) Paul Potter (949) 888-4595

Redlands Trinity Church **P** (943) § 419 S 4th St 92373-5952 (Mail to: 419 S 4th St 92373-5952) (909) 793-2014

Redondo Beach Christ Episcopal Church **P** (152) 408 S Broadway 90277-3717 (Mail to: 408 S Broadway 90277-3717) Julie Beals Bonnie McNaughton (310) 540-1722

Rialto St Peter's Episcopal Church **P** (79) 777 N Acacia Ave 92376-5246 (Mail to: 777 N Acacia Ave 92376-5246) David Smith (909) 875-5689

Riverside All Saints Episcopal Church **P** (432) 3847 Terracina Dr 92506-0149 (Mail to: 3847 Terracina Dr 92506-0149) Kelli Kurtz (951) 683-8466

Riverside St Georges Episcopal Church **P** (96) 950 Spruce St 92507-2503 (Mail to: 950 Spruce St 92507-2503) Karri Backer Guy Leemhuis (951) 686-9936

San Clemente St Clements by the Sea **P** (495) 202 Avenida Aragon 92672-5015 (Mail to: 202 Avenida Aragon 92672-5098) Patrick Crerar William Wells (949) 492-3401

San Fernando St Simons Episcopal Church **P** (155) 623 N Hagar St 91340-2005 (Mail to: 623 N Hagar St 91340-2005) (818) 361-3317

San Gabriel Church of Our Saviour **P** (589) § 535 W Roses Rd 91775-2205 (Mail to: 535 W Roses Rd 91775-2205) Jeffrey Thornberg William Doulos Timothy Hartley Huiliang Ni (626) 282-5147

San Juan Capo St Margaret of Scotland Church **P** (761) § 31641 La Novia Ave 92675-2752 (Mail to: C/O Kim Ashby 31641 La Novia Ave 92675-2752) Robert Edwards Earl Gibson James Livingston Linda Wirt (949) 661-0110

San Marino St Edmunds Episcopal Church **P** (412) § 1175 S San Gabriel Blvd 91108-2226 (Mail to: PO Box 80038 91118-8038) Jenifer Chatfield (626) 793-9167

San Pedro St Peters Episcopal Church **P** (176) 1648 W 9th St 90732-3404 (Mail to: 1648 W 9th St 90732-3404) Jeanette Repp Ruth Eller (310) 831-2361

Santa Ana Church of the Messiah **P** (908) 614 N Bush St 92701-4157 (Mail to: 614 N Bush St 92701-4157) Abel Lopez James Lee Katharine MacKenzie (714) 543-9389

Santa Barbara Ch of All Saints-by-the-Sea **P** (916) § 83 Eucalyptus Ln 93108-2901 (Mail to: 83 Eucalyptus Ln 93108-2901) Glen Mitchel (805) 969-4771

Santa Barbara Christ the King Episcopal Ch **P** (115) 5073 Hollister Ave 93111-2637 (Mail to:

PO Box 6188 93160-6188) Israel Anchan (805) 964-9966

Santa Barbara Trinity Episcopal Church **P** (762) 1500 State St 93101-2514 (Mail to: 1500 State St 93101-2514) Elizabeth Molitors Sarah Thomas (805) 965-7419

Santa Clarita St Stephen's Episcopal Church **P** (366) § 24901 Orchard Village Rd 91355-3074 (Mail to: 24901 Orchard Village Rd 91355-3074) Christopher Montella (661) 259-7307

Santa Maria St Peter Episcopal Church **P** (108) 402 S Lincoln St 93454 (Mail to: PO Box 1868 93456-1868) Hi-Jae Kang (805) 922-3575

Santa Monica St Augustines by the Sea **P** (265) 1227 4th St 90401-1303 (Mail to: 1227 4th St 90401-1390) Nathan Rugh Katherine Cadigan (310) 395-0977

Santa Paula St Pauls Episcopal Church **P** (61) 117 N 7th St 93060-2615 (Mail to: 117 N 7th St 93060-2615) Cynthia Jew (805) 5253811

Seal Beach St Theodore of Canterbury Ch **M** (20) 1240 Oakmont Rd Ste 52b 90740-3650 (Mail to: Leisure World 1240 Oakmont Rd Ste 52B 90740-3650) (562) 430-8619

Sierra Madre Church of the Ascension **P** (405) 25 E Laurel Ave 91024-1915 (Mail to: 25 E Laurel Ave 91024-1915) Michael Bamberger Jennifer Beal Edward Sniecienski (626) 355-1133

Simi Valley Church of St Francis of Assisi **M** (407) 280 Royal Ave 93065 (Mail to: PO Box 940516 93094-0516) Sarah Kitch (805) 526-5141

Skyforest St Richards Episcopal Church **M** (59) 28708 Hwy 18 92385 (Mail to: PO Box 1317 92352-1317) (909) 337-3889

Sn Bernrdno St Johns Episcopal Church **M** (44) 1407 N Arrowhead Ave 92405-4813 (Mail to: 1407 N Arrowhead Ave 92405-4813) (909) 889-1195

South Gate St Margaret's Episcopal Church **P** (460) 4704 Tweedy Blvd 90280-5208 (Mail to: 4704 Tweedy Blvd 90280-5208) Eduardo Bresciani (323) 569-9901

South Pasadena St James Episcopal Church **P** (638) § 1325 Monterey Rd 91030-3228 (Mail to: 1325 Monterey Rd 91030-3291) Michelle Baker-Wright (626) 799-9194

Studio City St Michael All Angels **P** (310) 3646 Coldwater Canyon Ave 91604-4062 (Mail to: 3646 Coldwater Canyon Ave 91604-4099) Daniel Justin (818) 7639193

Thousand Oaks St Patricks Church **P** (293) § 1 Church Rd 91362-1809 (Mail to: 1 Church Rd 91362-1809) George Daisa (805) 495-6441

Torrance St Andrews Church **P** (40) 1432 Engracia Ave 90501-3201 (Mail to: 1432 Engracia Ave 90501-3201) (310) 328-3781

Tustin St Pauls Episcopal Church **P** (344) § 1221 Wass St 92780-2855 (Mail to: 1221 Wass St 92780-2855) Valerie Hart Kathleen Sylvester (714) 544-3141

Twentynine Palms St Martin in-the-Fields Church **M** (31) 72348 Larrea Ave 92277-2181 (Mail to: 72348 Larrea Ave 92277-2181) (760) 367-7133

Upland St Marks Episcopal Church **P** (289) § 330 E 16th St 91784-2050 (Mail to: 330 E 16th St 91784-2050) Keith Yamamoto Sally Monastiere (909) 920-5565

Van Nuys St Marks Episcopal Church **P** (200) 14646 Sherman Way 91405-5860 (Mail to: 14646 Sherman Way Ste A 91405-2297) Robin Kassabian (818) 785-4251

Ventura St Paul's Episcopal Church **P** (449) 3290 Loma Vista Rd 93003-3002 (Mail to: 3290 Loma Vista Rd 93003-3002) Susan Bek Raymond Steever Richard Swanson (805) 6435033

Whittier St Matthias Episcopal Church **P** (286) 7056 Washington Ave 90602-1415 (Mail to: 7056 Washington Ave 90602-1496) James Lander (562) 698-9741

Wilmington St Johns & Holy Child Epis Ch **M** (384) 1537 N Neptune Ave 90744-2003 (Mail to: PO Box 1716 90748-1716) (310) 835-7870

Winnetka St Martin in-the-Fields Church **M** (142) 7136 Winnetka Ave 91306-3647 (Mail to: 7136 Winnetka Ave 91306-3647) Christopher Eade Gabriel Ferrer Christopher Montella (818) 348-1419

Woodland Hls Church of the Prince of Peace **P** (924) 5700 Rudnick Ave 91367-6238 (Mail to: 5700 Rudnick Ave 91367-6299) Rand Reasoner Onesmus Tayebwa Onesmus Tayebwa (818) 346-6968

Yucaipa St Alban's Episcopal Church **M** (45) 12692 5th St 92399-2571 (Mail to: PO Box 695 92399-0695) Cecelia Schroeder (909) 797-3266

Yucca Valley St Joseph of Arimathea Mission **M** (18) 56312 Onaga Trl 92284-3636 (Mail to: 56312 Onaga Trl 92284-3636) (760) 365-7133

STATE OF LOUISIANA
Dioceses of Louisiana and Western Louisiana

DIOCESE OF LOUISIANA
(PROVINCE IV)
Comprises all parishes east of the Atchafalaya River and including all of St Mary's Parish
DIOCESAN OFFICE 1623 Seventh St New Orleans LA 70115
TEL (504) 895-6634 FAX (504) 895-6637 WEB www.edola.org

Previous Bishops—
Leonidas Polk 1841-64, Jos PB
Wilmer 1866-78, John N Galleher
1880-91, Davis Sessums coadj
1891 Bp 1891-1929, James C
Morris 1930-39, John L Jackson
1940-48, Girault M Jones 1949-
69, Iveson B Noland suffr 1952-61
coadj 1961 Bp 1969-75, R Heber
Gooden asst 1972-75 acting 1975-76, James B Brown
1976-98, Charles Edward Jenkins III Bp 1998-2010,
Morris K Thompson Jr 2010-22

**Bishop—Rt Rev Shannon R Duckworth (1151)
(Dio November 19 2022)**

Cn to Ord Rev Cn M MacIntire *Sec/Reg* M Wade;
Treas A Brackett; *Chanc* CJ Geary 201 St Charles
New Orleans LA 70170-5100; *Hist* K Mackey; *Com*
Rev J Angerer

Stand Comm—Cler: Pres B Hadzor D Harmon S
Roberts S Fox; *Lay:* J Johnson E Mitchell A Martinez
B Soileau

PARISHES, MISSIONS, AND CLERGY

Amite Epis Church of the Incarnation **M** (20) 111
E Olive St 70422-2539 (Mail to: PO Box 722
70422-0722) (985) 748-9706

Angola Transfig at Angola State Pris **M** Angola
State Prison 70712 (Mail to: 3112 Green Acres
Rd 70003-1820) (225) 387-0396

Baton Rouge St Albans Episcopal Chapel **Chapel**
(348) Dalrymple Highland Lsu 70808 (Mail
to: 5261 Highland Rd Pmb 376 70808-6547)
Andrew Rollins (225) 343-2070

Baton Rouge St Augustines Episcopal Church **M**
(42) 12954 Joor Rd 70837 (Mail to: PO Box
78123 70837-8123) (225) 261-4344

Baton Rouge St James Episcopal Church **P**
(1560) § 205 N 4th St 70801-1403 (Mail to:
PO Box 126 70821-0126) Christopher Duncan
Andrew Harmon Paul White (225) 387-5141

Baton Rouge Saint Luke's Church **P** (1560) §
8833 Goodwood Blvd 70806-7919 (Mail to:
8833 Goodwood Blvd 70806-7995) Charles
Owen (225) 926-5343

Baton Rouge St Margaret's Episcopal Church **P**
(243) 12663 Perkins Rd 70810-1909 (Mail to:

12663 Perkins Rd 70810-1909) Tommy Dillon
(225) 766-8314

Baton Rouge St Michael & All Angels **M** (71)
1666 77th Ave 70807-5405 (Mail to: 1620
77th Ave 70807-5496) Stewart Cage (225)
357-8852

Baton Rouge Trinity Episcopal Church **HC** (781)
§ 3552 Morning Glory Ave 70808-2865 (Mail
to: 3552 Morning Glory Ave 70808-2865)
Peter Wong Peter Wong (225) 387-0396

Bogalusa St Matthews Church **P** (51) 208
Georgia Ave 70427-3824 (Mail to: 208 Georgia
Ave 70427-3824) (985) 732-4328

Clinton St Andrews Episcopal Church **M** (96)
1 St Andrew St 70722 (Mail to: PO Box 8259
70722-1259) Walter Windsor (225) 683-5498

Covington Christ Episcopal Church **P** (1148) §
120 S New Hampshire St 70433-3500 (Mail to:
129 N New Hampshire St 70433-3235) David
Donald Winston Rice Winston Rice Philip
Wild (985) 8923177

Denham Spgs St Francis Church **P** (178) 726
Maple St 70726-3026 (Mail to: 726 Maple St
70726-3026) Margaret Sullivan (225) 665-
2707

Franklin St Marys Episcopal Church **P** (52) 805
1st St 70538-5415 (Mail to: PO Box 95 70538-
0095) Stephen Crawford (337) 828-0918

Hammond Grace Memorial EpisChurch **P** (509)
100 W Church St 70401-3205 (Mail to: PO
Box 1086 70404-1086) (985) 345-2764

Harvey St Marks Episcopal Church **P** (145) 3245
Manhattan Blvd 70058-5112 (Mail to: 3245
Manhattan Blvd 70058-5112) (504) 366-0123

Houma St Matthew Episcopal Church **P** (349)
239 Barrow St 70360-4403 (Mail to: 243
Barrow St 70360-4403) (985) 872-5057

Innis Saint Stephen's Church **P** (203) 9795
Highway 418 70747 (Mail to: PO Box 1020
70747-1020) (225) 492-2234

Kenner St Johns Episcopal Church **M** (56) 2109
17th St 70062-6351 (Mail to: 2109 17th St
70062-6351) Charmaine Kathmann (504)
469-4535

La Place St Timothys Episcopal Church **M** (41)
§ 1101 Belle Alliance Dr 70068-3201 (Mail
to: 1101 Belle Alliance Dr 70068-3201) (985)
652-2121

Luling St Andrews Episcopal Church **M** Audbon & Early St 70070 (Mail to: PO Box 621 70070-0621) (985) 758-1607

Mandeville St Michael's Episcopal Church **M** (167) § 4499 Sharp Rd 70471-8919 (Mail to: 4499 Sharp Rd 70471-8919) Robert Beazley Robert Beazley (985) 626-5781

Metairie St Augustines Episcopal Church **P** (854) 3412 Haring Rd 70006-3902 (Mail to: 3412 Haring Rd 70006-3902) Julia Rusling Michael Hackett (504) 8874801

Metairie St Martin's Episcopal Church **P** (330) 2216 Metairie Rd 70001-4205 (Mail to: 2216 Metairie Rd 70001-4200) Frederick Devall Ford Millican (504) 835-7357

Morgan City Trinity Episcopal Church **P** (67) PO Box 1776 70381-1776 (Mail to: PO Box 1776 302 Greenwood 70381-1776) (985) 384-7629

Morganza St Marys Episcopal Church **M** (22) 331 W Tircuit St 70759 (Mail to: PO Box 173 70759-0173) (225) 694-3609

Napoleonville Christ Episcopal Church **PS** 4829 Highway 1 70390-2002 (Mail to: PO Box 27 70390-0027) (985) 369-2106

New Orleans All Saints' Episcopal Church **P** (249) 100 Rex Dr 70123-3531 (Mail to: 100 Rex Dr 70123-3531) John Angerer (504) 737-2421

New Orleans Chapel of the Holy Comforter **CC** (40) 2220 Lakeshore Dr 70122-3502 (Mail to: 2220 Lakeshore Dr 70122-3502) John Craft (504) 282-4593

✠ **New Orleans** Christ Church Cathedral **O** (768) 2919 Saint Charles Ave 70115-4421 (Mail to: 2919 Saint Charles Ave 70115-4498) David Duplantier Steven Roberts (504) 895-6602

New Orleans Chapel of the Holy Spirit **CC** (33) 1100 Broadway St 70118-5243 (Mail to: 1100 Broadway St 70118-5243) Watson Lamb (504) 866-7438

New Orleans Mt Olivet Episcopal Church **P** (109) 530 Pelican Ave 70114-1051 (Mail to: 530 Pelican St 70114-1051) (504) 366-4650

New Orleans St Andrew Episcopal Church **P** (484) § 1116 Short St 70118-2712 (Mail to: 1031 S Carrollton Ave 70118-1145) James Morrison (504) 866-0123

New Orleans St Annas Episcopal Church **P** (251) 1313 Esplanade Ave 70116-1836 (Mail to: 1313 Esplanade Ave 70116-1894) William Terry (504) 947-2121

New Orleans St George's Episcopal Church **P** (234) § 4600 Saint Charles Ave 70115-4834 (Mail to: 4600 Saint Charles Ave 70115-4897) Stephanie Fox (504) 899-2811

New Orleans St Lukes Episcopal Church **P** (102) 1222 N Dorgenois St 70119-3445 (Mail to: 1222 N Dorgenois St 70119-3445) Donald Muth (504) 821-0529

New Orleans St Pauls Episcopal Church **P** (471) § 6249 Canal Blvd 70124-3099 (Mail to: 6249 Canal Blvd 70124-3099) Robert Courtney Elizabeth Embler-Beazley (504) 488-3749

New Orleans St Philips Episcopal Church **P** (341) 3643 Aurora Dr 70131-5507 (Mail to: 3643 Aurora Dr 70131-5507) Stephen Craft (504) 394-2408

New Orleans The Church of the Annunciation **P** (138) 4505 S Claiborne Ave 70125-5007 (Mail to: 4505 S Claiborne Ave 70125-5007) David Casey (504) 8958697

New Orleans Trinity Episcopal Church **P** (2518) § 1329 Jackson Ave 70130-5131 (Mail to: C/O Gabriella Frank 1329 Jackson Ave 70130-5198) Andrew Thayer Robert Price-Hadzor Edgar Taylor (504) 522-0276

New Roads St Pauls Holy Trinity **P** (58) 607 E Main St 70760-3641 (Mail to: PO Box 386 70760-0386) (225) 638-8433

Plaquemine Church of the Holy Communion **P** (135) 58040 Court St 70764-2704 (Mail to: PO Box 474 70765-0474) John Miller (225) 687-2611

Ponchatoula All Saints Episcopal Church **M** (43) 250 W Hickory St 70454 (Mail to: 250 W Hickory St 70454) Katherine Mclean (985) 386-8126

Rosedale Church of the Nativity **M** (40) 302 Laurel St 70772 (Mail to: C/O Shirley Best PO Box 195 70772-0195) (225) 241-2556

Slidell Christ Episcopal Church **P** (165) 1534 7th St 70458-2847 (Mail to: 1534 7th St 70458-2897) Harry Jenkins Harry Jenkins (985) 643-4531

St Francisvlle Grace Church Of West Feliciana **P** (354) 11621 Ferdinand St 70775-4339 (Mail to: Attn: Margaret E Kendrick PO Box 28 70775-0028) Craig Dalferes (225) 635-4065

Theriot St Andrews Episcopal Church **M** (306) 3027 Bayou Dularge Rd 70397-9743 (Mail to: 3027 Bayou Dularge Rd 70397-9743) (985) 872-2508

Thibodaux St Johns Episcopal Church **P** (109) 718 Jackson St 70301-2732 (Mail to: 718 Jackson St 70301-2732) Holly Burris (985) 447-2910

Zachary St Patricks Episcopal Church **P** (356) § 1322 Church St 70791-2743 (Mail to: 1322 Church St 70791-2743) Charles Krutz (225) 6544091

DIOCESE OF MAINE
(PROVINCE I)
Comprises the State of Maine
DIOCESAN OFFICE PO Box 4036 (143 State St) Portland ME 04101-3799
TEL (207) 772-1953
E-MAIL info@episcopalmaine.org WEB www.episcopalmaine.org

Previous Bishops—
Geo Burgess 1847-66, Henry A Neely 1867-99, Robt Codman 1900-15, Benj Brewster 1916-40, Oliver L Loring 1941-68, Fredk B Wolf 1968-86, Edward C Chalfant coadj 1984-86 Bp 1986-1996, Chilton R Knudsen 1998-2008, Stephen T Lane 2008-19

Bishop — Rt Rev Thomas James Brown (Dio 23 June 2019)

Cn to the Ordinary M Ambler; *Cn Fin & Stew* T Reimer; *Cn for Admin, Reg & Arch* B Martin; *Faith Form Dir* E Keniston; *Camp Dir* M Douglass; *Chanc* G Gayer 16 Mare's Hollow Ln Cape Elizabeth ME 04107

Stand Comm—Cler: Pres K Mansir S Gavit A McAlhany *Lay:* M Spahr P Ryan L Lindsay

PARISHES, MISSIONS, AND CLERGY

Auburn St Michaels Episcopal Church **P** (98) 78 Pleasant St 04210-5940 (Mail to: 78 Pleasant St 04210-5940) George Sheats (207) 782-1346

Augusta St Marks Church **P** (69) 9 Summer St 04330-5128 (Mail to: 9 Summer St 04330-5128) (207) 622-2424

Bailey Island All Sts by the Sea Summer Chap **SC** Washington Ave 04003 (Mail to: 20 Cedar Beach Rd C/O Dana R Baggett 04003-2521) (207) 772-1953

Bangor St Johns Episcopal Church **P** (206) 225 French St 04401-5012 (Mail to: 234 French St 04401-5013) (207) 947-0156

Bar Harbor St Saviours Church **P** (122) 41 Mount Desert St 04609-1753 (Mail to: 41 Mount Desert St 04609-1753) Holly Hoffmann (207) 288-4215

Bath Grace Episcopal Church **P** (426) 1100 Washington St 04530-2762 (Mail to: 1100 Washington St 04530-2762) Pamela Mott (207) 443-3792

Belfast Saint Margaret's Church **P** (164) 95 Court St 04915-6135 (Mail to: 95 Court St 04915-6135) Barbara Briggs (207) 338-2412

Biddeford Christ Church **P** 18 1/2 Crescent St 04005-2520 (Mail to: 35 SOUTH ST 040052520) (207) 283-1783

Biddeford Pool St Martins in Field Summer Chp **SC** St Martins Ln 04006 (Mail to: Martins Lane 04006) Daniel Meck (207) 772-1953

Blue Hill St Francis by the Sea **P** (397) 330 Hinckley Ridge Rd 04614-5816 (Mail to: PO Box 76 04614-0076) Stephen Hayward (207) 374-5200

Brewer St Patricks Episcopal Church **P** (85) 21 Holyoke St 04412-1905 (Mail to: 21 Holyoke St 04412-1905) (207) 989-1308

Bridgton St Peters Episcopal Church **P** (111) 42 Sweden Rd 04009-3528 (Mail to: PO Box 134 04009-0134) (207) 647-8549

Brownville St Johns Episcopal Church **M** (29) 26 Henderson St 04414-3735 (Mail to: PO Box 751 04414-0751) (207) 943-5168

Brunswick St Pauls Church Episcopal **P** (603) 27 Pleasant St 04011-2222 (Mail to: PO Box 195 04011-0195) Carolyn Eklund Kathryn Holicky (207) 725-5342

Calais St Annes Church **P** (86) 29 Church St 04619-1636 (Mail to: 29 Church St 04619-1669) Sara Gavit Sara Gavit (207) 454-8016

Camden Christ Church Dark Harbor **SC** Attn S Russell Schatz Fletcher 87 Elm St Ste 215 04843-1959 (Mail to: PO Box 147 04848-0147) (207) 734-8207

Camden Church of St Thomas **P** (262) 33 Chestnut St 04843-2209 (Mail to: PO Box 631 33 Chestnut Street 04843-0631) Lisa Fry (207) 236-3680

Cape Elizabeth St Alban Episcopal Church **P** (1261) 885 Shore Rd 04107-1540 (Mail to: 885 Shore Rd 04107-1540) Joshua Hill George Cooper (207) 799-4014

Castine Trinity Episcopal Church **P** (89) Perkins and Tarrant 04421 (Mail to: PO Box 433 04421-0433) Emily Stribling (207) 326-4180

Damariscotta St Cuthbert Summer Chapel **SC** C/O Jane Kennedy Hc 61 Box 124 04543 (Mail to: C/O Jane Kennedy Hc 61 Box 124 04543) (207) 371-2517

Deer Isle St Brendan's Episcopal Church **P** (21) PO Box 305 04627-0305 (Mail to: PO Box 305 04627-0305) (207) 348-6240

Dovr Foxcroft St Augustines Episcopal Church **M** (51) PO Box 504 04426-0504 (Mail to: PO Box 504 04426-0504) Douglas Beck (207) 564-7075

East Boothbay St Columbas Episcopal Church **P** (170) 32 Emery Ln 04538-1965 (Mail to: 32 Emery Ln 04538-1965) Maria Hoecker Susan Kraus (207) 633-6313

Eastport Christ Episcopal Church **P** (41) PO Box 12 04631-0012 (Mail to: PO Box 12 04631-0012) (207) 853-4598

Ellsworth St Dunstans Episcopal Church **P** (123) 134 State Stree 04605-1832 (Mail to: PO Box 711 04605-0711) Carolyn Rosen (207) 667-5495

Falmouth St Mary the Virgin Epis Church **P** (653) 43 Foreside Rd 04105-1708 (Mail to: 43 Foreside Rd 04105-1708) Nathan Ferrell Jack Haney (207) 781-3366

Farmington St Lukes Church **P** (74) High And School Sts 04938 (Mail to: PO Box 249 04938-0249) John Balicki (207) 645-2639

Ft Fairfield St Pauls Episcopal Church **P** (64) 170 Main St 04742-1220 (Mail to: PO Box 389 04742-0389) (207) 492-4211

Gardiner Christ Church Episcopal **P** (173) 2 Dresden Ave 04345-2633 (Mail to: 2 Dresden Ave 04345-2633) Kerry Mansir (207) 582-3354

Hallowell St Matthews Episcopal Church **P** (171) 20 Union St 04347-1369 (Mail to: 20 Union St 04347-1369) (207) 623-3041

Harborside Our Lady of Evrgrns Summer Chp **SC** 44 Emerson Point Rd 04642-3330 (Mail to: PO Box 94 04642)

Houlton Church of the Good Shepherd **P** (114) 116 Main St 04730-2113 (Mail to: PO Box 1672 04730-5672) Jessie Drysdale (207) 532-2927

Hulls Cove Church of Our Father **P** (85) State Hwy #3 3 04644 (Mail to: PO Box 186 04644-0186) Holly Hoffmann (207) 288-4849

Jefferson St Giles Episcopal Church **P** (55) 72 Gardiner Rd 04348-3973 (Mail to: PO Box 34 04348-0034) Dana Stivers (207) 549-3158

Kennebunk St Davids Episcopal Church **P** (299) 138 York St 04043-7108 (Mail to: 138 York St 04043-7108) Andrew White (207) 985-3073

Kennebunk Beach Trinity Summer Chapel **SC** 3 Woodland Ave 04043 (Mail to: C/O Norman Kellett PO Box 1130 04043) (207) 967-3056

Kennebunkport St Anns Episcopal Church **SC** 1 Ocean Ave 04046-6003 (Mail to: PO Box 44 04046-0044) Peter Cheney (207) 967-8043

Lewiston Trinity Episcopal Church **P** (28) 247 Bates St 04240-7331 (Mail to: PO Box 2324 04241-2324) (207) 312-9410

Limestone Church of the Advent **M** (7) 37 Church St 04750 (Mail to: 650 Main St Ste A 04736-4422) (207) 492-4211

Lisbon Falls St Matthews Episcopal Church **P** (65) 496 Lisbon St 04250 (Mail to: PO Box 879 04250-0879) David Matson David Matson (207) 353-8453

Machias St Aidans Episcopal Church **M** (33) 36 Hill St 04654-1309 (Mail to: PO Box 271 04654-0271) (207) 255-4995

Millinocket St Andrews Episcopal Church **P** (78) 40 Highland Ave 04462-1413 (Mail to: 40 Highland Ave 04462-1413) Robert Landry (207) 723-5893

Newcastle Saint Andrew's Church **P** (268) PO Box 234 04553-3401 (Mail to: PO Box 234 04553-0234) Suzannah Rohman (207) 563-3533

North Haven North Haven Summer Services **SC** Church St 04853 (Mail to: PO Box 318 04853)

Northeast Harbor Parish of St Mary & St Jude **P** (224) PO Box 105 04662-0105 (Mail to: PO Box 105 04662-0105) Stephen Muncie (207) 276-5588

Norway Christ Episcopal Church **P** (112) 35 Paris St 04268-5630 (Mail to: 35 Paris St 04268-5630) Nancy Moore (207) 743-6782

Old Town St James Episcopal Church **P** (44) 149 Center St 04468-1502 (Mail to: PO Box 183 04468-0183) M Jane White-Hassler (207) 827-5013

Orrs Island All Saints Summer Chapel **SC** 9 Cooper Ln 04066-2112 (Mail to: 9 Cooper Ln 04066) (207) 833-7745

Palmyra St Martins Episcopal Church **M** (55) 900 Main St 04965-3408 (Mail to: PO Box 107 04965-0107) Leslie Nesin (207) 938-3385

Peaks Island Holy Trinty Epis Summer Chapel **SC** 69 Knickerbocker Ln 04108-1562 (Mail to: Robin Walden 60 Centennial St 04108-1102) (207) 766-3376

✠ **Portland** Cathedral Church of Saint Luke **O** (699) 143 State St 04101-3701 (Mail to: PO Box 4141 04101-0341) Benjamin Shambaugh Suzanne Roberts (207) 772-5434

Portland St Peters Church **P** (127) 10 Alton St 04103-4906 (Mail to: 10 Alton St 04103-4906) Mary Ann Hoy Thomas Mousin (207) 775-1179

Portland Trinity Episcopal Church **P** (458) 580 Forest Ave 04101-1509 (Mail to: 580 Forest Ave 04101-1509) James Swarr (207) 772-7421

Presque Isle St Johns Episcopal Church **P** (37) 52 2nd St 04769-2636 (Mail to: PO Box 8 04769-0008) Judith Burleigh Stephen Summerson (207) 764-4298

Rangeley Church of the Good Shepherd **P** (67) 2614 Main St 04970-4114 (Mail to: PO Box 156 04970-0156) (207) 864-3381

Rockland Saint Peter's Church **P** (342) White St 04841 (Mail to: 11 White St 04841-2982) Lael Sorensen (207) 594-8191

Rumford Saint Barnabas Church **P** (22) 71 Rumford Ave 04276-1973 (Mail to: PO Box 591 04276-0591) Timothy Parsons (207) 364-2193

Saco Trinity Episcopal Church **P** (207) 403 Main St 04072-1522 (Mail to: 403 Main St 04072-1522) Linda Cappers (207) 284-4852

Sanford St Georges Episcopal Church **P** (177) 1 Emerson St 04073-3903 (Mail to: 3 Emerson St 04073-3903) (207) 324-8119

Scarborough St Nicholas Episcopal Church **M** (89) 350 US Route 1 04074-8307 (Mail to: 350 US Route 1 04074-8307) Ted Gaiser (207) 883-9437

Skowhegan All Saints Episcopal Church **M** (25) 169 Malbons Mills Rd 04976-4122 (Mail to: PO Box 412 04976-0412) (207) 474-2629

Sorrento Ch of the Rdmr Summer Chapel **SC** 62 Bayview Ave 04677 (Mail to: PO Box 123 04677-0123) (207) 422-3955

Southport All Sts by the Sea Summer Chap **SC** PO Box 377 04576-0377 (Mail to: PO Box 377 04576-0377) (207) 633-7301

Southwest Hbr Sts Andrew & John Episcopal Ch **P** (110) 315 Main St 04679-4403 (Mail to: PO Box 767 04679-0767) Holly Hoffmann (207) 244-3229

Thomaston Epis Church of St John Baptist **P** (198) 200 Main St 04861-3800 (Mail to: 200 Main St 04861-3800) Peter Jenks (207) 354-8734

Waterville St Marks Church **P** (238) 60 Eustis Pkwy 04901-4932 (Mail to: 60 Eustis Pkwy 04901-4932) (207) 872-7869

Windham St Anns Episcopal Church **P** (392) 40 Windham Center Rd. 04062 (Mail to: PO Box 911 04062-0911) Timothy Higgins (207) 892-8447

Winn St Thomas Episcopal Church **M** (39) 14 Main Street 04495 (Mail to: PO Box 106 04495-0106) (207) 736-2010

Winter Harbor St Christopher Summer Chapel **SC** 9 Clubhouse Rd 04693 (Mail to: C/O Margaret F Bennett 6 Holly Villa Drive 33436) Thomas Van Culin Ralph Warren (207) 963-5554

Winthrop St Andrews Episcopal Church **M** (53) 219 Winthrop Center Rd. 04364 (Mail to: PO Box 66 04364) (207) 395-2015

Wiscasset St Philips Episcopal Church **P** (57) 12 Hodge St 04578-4021 (Mail to: 12 Hodge St 04578-4021) (207) 882-7184

Yarmouth St Bartholomews Episcopal Ch **P** (533) 396 Gilman Rd 04096-5731 (Mail to: 396 Gilman Rd 04096-5731) (207) 846-9244

York St George's Episcopal Church **P** (352) 407 York St 03909-1060 (Mail to: PO Box 364 407 York St 03911-0364) Ryan Mails Aaron Perkins (207) 363-7376

York Harbor Trinity Church **SC** 546 York Street 03911 (Mail to: 546 York St 03911) (207) 363-5095

STATE OF MARYLAND
Dioceses of Easton (E), Maryland (MD), and Washington (W)

Abingdon—MD	Damascus—W	Kennedyville—E	Pikesville—MD
Accokeek—W	Darlington—MD	Kensington—W	Pocomoke City—E
Annapolis—MD	Denton—E	Kingsville—MD	Pt of Rocks—MD
Aquasco—W	Earleville—E	La Plata—W	Poolesville—W
Avenue—W	Easton—E	Laurel—W	Pt Republic—MD
Baltimore—MD	Edgewater—MD	Leonardtown—W	Potomac—W
Bel Air—MD	Elkridge—MD	Linthicum Hts—MD	Prince Frederick—MD
Beltsville—W	Elkton—E	Lonaconing—MD	Princess Anne—E
Berlin—E	Ellicott City—MD	Long Green—MD	Quantico—E
Bethesda—W	Essex—MD	Lothian—MD	Queenstown—E
Boonsboro—MD	Forest Hill—MD	Lusby—MD	Reisterstown—MD
Braddock Hts—MD	Forrestville—W	Lutherville Timon—	Ridge—W
Brandywine—W	Ft Washington—W	MD	Rockville—W
Brookeville—W	Frederick—MD	Marion—E	St Marys City—W
Brownsville—MD	Frostburg—MD	Massey—E	St Michael—E
Brunswick—MD	Gaithersburg—W	Mayo—MD	Salisbury—E
California—W	Germantown—W	Monkton—MD	Severna Pk—MD
Cambridge—E	Glen Burnie—MD	Mt Airy—MD	Sharpsburg—MD
Centreville—E	Glencoe—MD	Mt Rainier—W	Silver Spg—W
Chaptico—W	Glenwood—MD	Mt Savage—MD	Smithsburg—MD
Charlotte Hall—W	Glenn Dale—W	Nanjemoy—W	Snow Hill—E
Chesapeake City—E	Gwynn Oak—MD	New Carrolton—W	Stevensville—E
Chestertown—E	Hagerstown—MD	New Market—MD	Street—MD
Chevy Chase—W	Halethorpe—MD	Newburg—W	Sunderland—MD
Church Creek—E	Hampstead—MD	North East—E	Sykesville—MD
Church Hill—E	Hancock—MD	Oakland—MD	Temple Hills—W
Churchville—MD	Havre de Grace—MD	Ocean City—E	Thurmont—MD
Clear Spg—MD	Hebron—E	Odenton—MD	Timonium—MD
Clinton—W	Highland—MD	Olney—W	Towson—MD
Cockeysville—MD	Hughesville—W	Owings Mills—MD	Tracys Landing—MD
College Pk—W	Hurlock—E	Oxford—E	Trappe—E
Columbia—MD	Hyattsville—W	Parkton—MD	Tyaskin—E
Crownsville—MD	Indian Head—W	Pasadena—MD	Upper Marlboro—W
Cumberland—MD	Joppatowne—MD	Perryville—E	Vienna—E

Waldorf—W   W River—MD   Westminster—MD   Wye Mills—E
Washington—W   Westernport—MD   Worton—E

DIOCESE OF MARYLAND
(PROVINCE III)
Comprises western shore of Maryland excluding Charles,
Montgomery, Prince George's & St Mary's Counties
DIOCESAN OFFICE 4 East University Pkwy Baltimore MD 21218
TEL (410) 467-1399, (800) 443-1399 FAX (410) 554-6387
E-MAIL communications@episcopalmaryland.org WEB www.episcopalmaryland.org

Previous Bishops—
Thomas J Claggett 1792-1816,
James Kemp suffr 1814 Bp
1816-27, Wm M Stone 1830-38,
Wm R Whittingham 1840-79,
Wm Pinkney coadj 1870 Bp
1879-83, Wm Paret 1885-1911,
John G Murray coadj 1909 Bp
1911-29, Edward T Helfenstein
coadj 1926 Bp 1929-44, Noble
C Powell coadj 1941 Bp 1944-63, Harry L Doll
suffr 1955 coadj 1958 Bp 1963-71, William J Cox
suffr 1972-80, David K Leighton Sr coadj 1968 Bp
1972-85, Barry Valentine asst 1986-88, A Theodore
Eastman coadj 1982 Bp 1986-94, Charles L Longest
suffr 1989-97, Robert W Ihloff Bp 1995-2007, John L
Rabb Bp-in-Charge 2007-08 Suffr 1998-2010, Joe G
Burnett asst 2011-2013, Heather E Cook suffr 2014-
15, Chilton R. Knudsen asst 2015-18

**Bishop—Rt Rev Eugene Taylor Sutton (1030)
(Dio 28 June 2008)**

**Assisting Bishop—Rt Rev Robert W Ihloff
(909)**

Staff: Interim Cn to the Ord Rev MC Sulerud; *Cn for
Mission* Rev CL McCloud; *Interim Cn for Cong Vit* K
Lindh-Payne; *Cn for Admin & Transitions Ministry*
Rev SW Wright; *Cn for Youth Ministry* K Riley; *Cn
for Latino Min* Rev RM Santana; *Cn for Comms*
CS Graves; *Cn for Pastoral Services* Rev MJ White;
Archivist MO Klein

Officers: Cn for Finance JE Kamrath; *Treas* J Lindsey;
Chanc N Baroody c/o Baroody & O'Toole 201 N
Charles St Suite 2102 Baltimore MD 21201; *Sec of
Convention* Rev MJ White

Stand Comm—Cler: KA Shahinian TK Smith *VP*
MR Hanisian AM Richards; *Lay: Pres* K-AF Lynne
JA Henderson K McAllister V Willard

Archdeacons: Ven RA Elder Ven FH Bailey

PARISHES, MISSIONS, AND CLERGY

Abingdon St Marys Episcopal Church **P** (262) 1
Saint Marys Church Rd 21009-1565 (Mail to:

1 Saint Marys Church Rd 21009-1569) (410)
569-0180

Annapolis St Annes Episcopal Parish **P** (1642)
199 Duke Of Gloucester St 21401-2520 (Mail
to: 199 Duke Of Gloucester St 21401-2520)
Manoj Zacharia Olivia Hilton Meredith Olsen
Katharine Shahinian M Dion Thompson (410)
2679333

Annapolis St Lukes Church **P** (103) 1101 Bay
Ridge Ave 21403-2901 (Mail to: 1101 Bay
Ridge Ave 21403-2901) David Showers (410)
268-5419

Annapolis St Margarets Episcopal Church **P** (1298)
§ 1601 Pleasant Plains Rd 21401-5928 (Mail to:
1601 Pleasant Plains Rd 21409-5928) Peter Mayer Patti Sachs Patti Sachs (410) 974-0200

Annapolis St Philips Episcopal Church **P** (215)
730 Bestgate Rd 21401-2137 (Mail to: 730
Bestgate Rd 21401-2137) Randy Callender
(410) 266-9755

✠ **Baltimore** Cathedral of the Incarnation **O**
(679) 4 E University Pkwy 21218-2437 (Mail
to: 4 E University Pkwy 21218-2490) Robert
Boulter Charles Cloughen (410) 467-3750

Baltimore Nativity and Holy Comforter **P** (109)
419 Cedarcroft Rd 21212-2523 (Mail to: 419
Cedarcroft Rd 21212-2599) Kathleen Schotto
(410) 433-4811

Baltimore St Katherine of Alexandria **P** (85)
2001 Division St 21217-3323 (Mail to: 2001
Division St 21217-3323) (410) 523-2207

Baltimore Church of St Mary the Virgin **P** (70)
3121 Walbrook Ave 21216-3031 (Mail to: 3121
Walbrook Ave 21216-3031) Charles Mercer
(410) 383-1575

Baltimore Ch of the Advent -Federal Hill **P** (177)
1301 S Charles St 21230-4218 (Mail to: 1301
S Charles St 21230-4218) Tobias Haller (410)
539-7804

Baltimore Church of the Guardian Angel **P** (40)
2629 Huntingdon Ave 21211-3111 (Mail to:
2629 Huntingdon Ave 21211-3111) (443) 879-
9453

Baltimore Church of the Holy Nativity **M** (53)
4238 Pimlico Rd 21215-6961 (Mail to: 4238
Pimlico Rd 21215-6961) (410) 542-9554

Baltimore Church of the Holy Trinity **P** (176) 2300 W Lafayette Ave 21216-4816 (Mail to: 2300 W Lafayette Ave 21216-4898) Benita Keene-Johnson (410) 945-0002

Baltimore Church of the Messiah **P** (83) 5801 Harford Rd 21214-1848 (Mail to: 5801 Harford Rd 21214-1848) Monique Ellison (410) 426-0709

Baltimore Church of the Redemption **P** (65) 1401 Towson St 21230-5301 (Mail to: 1401 Towson St 21230-5301) Mary Davisson (410) 539-8270

Baltimore Church of the Resurrection **M** (128) 2900 E Fayette St 21224-1316 (Mail to: 2900 E Fayette St 21224-1316) Lewis Bradford Rosa Santana-Honrado (443) 631-0115

Baltimore Emmanuel Episcopal Church **P** (341) 811 Cathedral St 21201-5201 (Mail to: 811 Cathedral St 21201-5201) Anne Marie Richards (410) 685-1130

Baltimore Christ the King Episcopal Ch **P** (129) 1930 Brookdale Rd 21244-1704 (Mail to: 1930 Brookdale Rd 21244-1704) Mary Eliot Robert Frederick (410) 944-6683

Baltimore Grace & St Peters Church **P** (413) 707 Park Ave 21201-4703 (Mail to: 707 Park Ave 21201-4799) Christopher Pyles (410) 539-1395

Baltimore Memorial Episcopal Church **P** (302) 1407 Bolton St 21217-4202 (Mail to: 1407 Bolton St 21217-4202) Natalie Conway Grey Maggiano (410) 669-0220

Baltimore St Bartholomews Episcopal Ch **P** (336) 4711 Edmondson Ave 21229-2404 (Mail to: 4711 Edmondson Ave 21229-1440) Virginia Boyd Neva Brown Maria Fedock Thelma Smullen (410) 945-7263

Baltimore Saint David's Church **P** (758) § 4700 Roland Ave 21210-2320 (Mail to: Attn: Christine Naylor 4700 Roland Ave 21210-2320) William McPherson (410) 4670476

Baltimore St James Episcopal Church **P** (441) 829 N Arlington Ave 21217-2534 (Mail to: 1020 W Lafayette Ave 21217-2555) Carole Douglas Richard Meadows Melvin Truiett (410) 523-4588

Baltimore St Johns Church **P** (75) 3001 Old York Rd 21218-3544 (Mail to: 3009 Greenmount Ave 21218-3599) (410) 467-4793

Baltimore St Johns Episcopal Church **P** (35) 2209 W Rogers Ave Apt 211 21209-4453 (Mail to: Attn: Assistant Treasurer 1702 South Rd 21209-4504) (410) 367-7287

Baltimore St Matthias Episcopal Church **P** (55) 6400 Belair Rd 21206-1840 (Mail to: 6400 Belair Rd 21206-1899) (410) 426-1002

Baltimore Ch of St Michael & All Angels **P** (147) 2013 Saint Paul St 21218-5929 (Mail to: 2013 Saint Paul St 21218-5998) Richard Meadows Richard Meadows (410) 685-3128

Baltimore Saint Paul's Parish **P** (502) 233 Charles St 21225-2846 (Mail to: 309 Cathedral St 21201-4410) Mary Stanley Mark Stanley (443) 6829587

Baltimore Church of the Redeemer **P** (1544) § 5603 N Charles St 21210-2006 (Mail to: 5603 N Charles St 21210-2097) David Ware Freda Brown Rebecca Ogus Maria Cristina Paglinauan Caroline Stewart (410) 435-7333

Bel Air Emmanuel Episcopal Church **P** (416) Main St & Broadway 21014 (Mail to: PO Box 628 21014-0628) Mark Gatza William Smith (410) 838-7699

Boonsboro St Marks Episcopal Church **P** (495) 18313 Lappans Rd 21713-1918 (Mail to: 18313 Lappans Rd 21713-1918) (301) 582-0417

Braddock Heights Church of the Transfiguration **P** (151) 6909 Maryland Ave 21714 (Mail to: PO Box 87 21714-0087) (301) 371-7505

Brownsville Saint Luke's Church **M** (29) 2150 Boteler Rd 21715-2008 (Mail to: 2150 Boteler Rd 21758-1002) Edie Holton (301) 432-4209

Brunswick Grace Episcopal Church **P** (116) 114 E A St 21716-1406 (Mail to: 114 E A St 21716-1406) Edie Holton (301) 834-8540

Churchville Holy Trinity Church **P** (133) 2929 Level Rd 21028-1820 (Mail to: PO Box 25 21028-0025) Joseph Zollickoffer Gail Landers (410) 914-5531

Clear Spring St Andrew's Episcopal Church **M** (136) 22 Cumberland St 21722 (Mail to: PO Box 189 21722-0189) Steven Mccarty (301) 842-2433

Cockeysville Sherwood Episcopal Church **P** (101) 5 Sherwood Rd 21030-2346 (Mail to: 5 Sherwood Rd Ste A 21030-2354) Nancy Hennessey (410) 666-2180

Columbia Christ Episcopal Church **P** (1083) 6800 Oakland Mills Rd 21045-4706 (Mail to: 6800 Oakland Mills Rd 21045-4706) Emmanuel Mercer (410) 381-9365

Crownsville St Stephens - Severn Parish **P** (370) § 1112 Saint Stephens Church Rd 21032-1908 (Mail to: 1110 Saint Stephens Church Rd 21032-1908) Victor Hailey (410) 721-2881

Cumberland Emmanuel Episcopal Church **P** (668) 16 Washington St 21502-2924 (Mail to: 16 Washington St 21502-2976) John Reardon (301) 777-3364

Darlington Grace Memorial Church **P** (100) 1022 Main St 21034-1434 (Mail to: C/O Cole Nelson PO Box 35 21034-0035) Lynn Hade (410) 836-3587

Edgewater The Vestry of All Hallows Par **P** (204) 3600 Solomons Island Rd 21037-3620 (Mail to: 3600 Solomons Island Rd 21037-3620) Jeffrey Hual (410) 798-0808

Elkridge Grace Episcopal Church **P** (665) 6725 Montgomery Rd 21075-5723 (Mail to: 6725 Montgomery Rd 21075-5723) Travis Smith Miriam Mathews (410) 796-3270

Elkridge Trinity Episcopal Church **P** (195) 7474 Washington Blvd 21075-6330 (Mail to: 7474

Washington Blvd 21075-6330) Frank Bailey Anne Wright (410) 220-3628

Ellicott City St Johns Episcopal Church **P** (2276) § 9120 Frederick Rd 21042-3912 (Mail to: 9120 Frederick Rd 21042-3978) Ann Ritonia Stephen Hagerty Wanhong Lee (410) 461-7793

Ellicott City St Peters Church **P** (75) § 3695 Rogers Ave 21043-4125 (Mail to: 3695 Rogers Ave 21043-4175) (410) 465-2273

Essex Holy Trinity Episcopal Church **P** (168) C/O The Reverend Eric Zile 1131 Mace Ave 21221-3316 (Mail to: C/O The Reverend Eric Zile 1131 Mace Ave 21221-3316) Cynthia Christopher (410) 687-5531

Forest Hill Christ Episcopal Church **P** (77) 2100 Rock Spring Rd 21050-2632 (Mail to: PO Box 215 21050-0215) Kirk Kubicek (410) 838-6606

Frederick All Saints Church **P** (1263) 108 W Church St 21701-5411 (Mail to: 106 W Church St 21701-5411) Joseph Pagano Amy Richter (301) 663-5625

Frostburg St Johns Episcopal Church **P** (35) 52 S Broadway 21532-1710 (Mail to: PO Box 229 21532-0229) Karen Crosby (301) 689-6634

Glen Burnie St Albans Episcopal Parish **P** (185) 105 1st Ave 21060-7627 (Mail to: 105 1st Ave SW 21061-3453) Pamela Conrad (410) 766-1455

Glencoe Immanuel Episcopal Church **P** (198) 1509 Glencoe Rd 21152-9439 (Mail to: 1509 Glencoe Rd 21152-9349) Megan Stewart-Sicking

Glenwood St Andrews Episcopal Church **P** (681) Rte 97 At Union Chapel Rd 21738 (Mail to: PO Box 52 21738-0052) Dina Van Klaveren Charles Shaffer (410) 489-4035

Gwynn Oak St Mary Episcopal Church **P** (62) 5610 Dogwood Rd 21207-5906 (Mail to: 5610 Dogwood Rd 21207-5985) (410) 944-4236

Hagerstown St Johns Episcopal Church **P** (317) 101 S Prospect St 21740-5409 (Mail to: 101 S Prospect St 21740-5495) Gary Young (301) 733-2560

Halethorpe The Ch of the Holy Apostles **P** (124) 4922 Leeds Ave 21227-2412 (Mail to: 4922 Leeds Ave 21227-2412) Diane Fadely (410) 242-5477

Hampstead St Georges Episcopal Church **P** (393) 2434 Cape Horn Rd 21074-1123 (Mail to: PO Box 255 21074-0255) Mario Conliffe Anthony Warner (410) 374-9748

Hancock St Thomas Church **P** (833) 2 E High St 21750-1216 (Mail to: 2 E High St 21750-1216) Kirk DeVore (301) 6786569

Havre De Grace St Johns Episcopal Church **P** (103) 114 N Union Ave 21078-3008 (Mail to: 114 N Union Ave 21078-3008) (410) 939-2107

Highland St Marks Episcopal Church **P** (459) 12700 Hall Shop Rd 20777-9544 (Mail to: 12700 Hall Shop Rd 20777-9544) (301) 854-2304

Joppatowne Copley Parish **P** (111) 700 Anchor Dr 21085-0222 (Mail to: PO Box 222 21085-0222) (410) 679-8700

Kingsville St Johns Episcopal Church **P** (86) 11901 Belair Rd 21087-1155 (Mail to: PO Box 187 21087-0187) Elizabeth Anne Sipos (410) 592-8570

Linthicum Hts St Christopher Epis Church **P** (44) 116 Marydel Rd 21090-2130 (Mail to: 116 Marydel Rd 21090-2130) (410) 859-5633

Lonaconing St Peters Episcopal Church **M** (69) 6 Saint Peters Place 21562 (Mail to: 6 Saint Peters Pl 21539-1135) Garrett Carskadon (301) 463-6144

Long Green Trinity Episcopal Church **P** (185) § 12400 Manor Rd 21092 (Mail to: PO Box 4001 12400 Manor Rd 21057-1001) Jessica Sexton (410) 592-6224

Lothian St James Parish **P** (359) 5757 Solomons Island Rd 20711-9707 (Mail to: 5757 Solomons Island Rd 20711-9792) John Verdon (410) 867-2838

Lusby Middleham and St Peters Parish **P** (259) 10210 H G Trueman Rd 20657 (Mail to: PO Box 277 20657-0277) Nathan Beall (410) 326-4948

Luthvle Timon The Ch of the Holy Comforter **P** (350) 130 W Seminary Ave 21093-5523 (Mail to: 130 W Seminary Ave 21093-5599) Christopher Tang Joanne Tetrault (410) 252-2711

Mayo St Andrew the Fisherman **P** (129) Central Ave & Carrs Wharf Rd 21106 (Mail to: PO Box 175 21106-0175) Rock Schuler (410) 798-1533

Monkton St James Episcopal Church **P** (1464) § 3100 Monkton Rd 21111-2113 (Mail to: 3100 Monkton Rd 21111-2199) Joseph Cochran Joseph Cochran Matthew Rogers (410) 771-4466

Mount Airy St James' Episcopal Church **P** (345) 1307 N Main St 21771-7499 (Mail to: 1307 N Main St 21771-7499) Kristin Krantz (301) 829-0325

Mount Airy St Pauls Episcopal Church **P** (34) 16457 Old Frederick Rd 21771-3331 (Mail to: 16457 Old Frederick Rd 21771-3331) (410) 489-4411

Mount Savage St Georges Episcopal Church **P** (23) 12811 Saint Georges Ln NW 21545-1001 (Mail to: 12811 Saint Georges Ln NW 21545-1001) (301) 264-3524

New Market Grace Episcopal Church **P** (119) 4 E Main St 21774 (Mail to: PO Box 17 21774-0017) Sharon Watts (301) 865-3270

Oakland Garrett County Episcopal Ch **P** 5234 Maryland Hwy 21550-4807 (Mail to: 5234 Maryland Highway 21550)

Oakland Our Fathers House **SC** 109 C St 21550-3507 (Mail to: PO Box 414 21550-4414) William Lee (301) 334-1197

Oakland St Johns Church **M** (144) 5234 Maryland Hwy 21550-4807 (Mail to: PO Box 414 21550-4414) (301) 334-2510

Oakland St Matthews Church **P** (209) 126 E Liberty St 21550-1202 (Mail to: PO Box 303 21550-0303) Anne Byrne William Lee (301) 334-2510

Odenton Epiphany Episcopal Church **P** (887) PO Box 110 21113-0110 (Mail to: PO Box 110 21113-0110) Julian Eibin (410) 336-8383

Owings Mills St Thomas Episcopal Church **P** (1028) 232 Saint Thomas Ln 21117-3806 (Mail to: 232 Saint Thomas Ln 21117-3800) Thomas Murphy (410) 363-1043

Parkton St James Episcopal Church **P** (87) 19200 York Rd 21120-9207 (Mail to: PO Box 420 21120-0420) William Alford (410) 357-4473

Pasadena St Andrews Episcopal Church **P** (246) 7859 Tick Neck Rd 21122-2264 (Mail to: 7859 Tick Neck Rd 21122-2264) Jason Poling (410) 255-1070

Pikesville Church Of St Marks On The Hill **P** (105) 1620 Reisterstown Rd 21208-2902 (Mail to: 1620 Reisterstown Rd 21208-2900) Julia Fritts (410) 486-3016

Port Republic Christ Church **P** (155) 3100 Broomes Island Rd 20676-2101 (Mail to: 3100 Broomes Island Rd 20676-2101) Christopher Garcia (410) 586-0565

Prnc Frederck St Pauls Episcopal Church **P** (201) 25 Church St 20678-4116 (Mail to: 25 Church St 20678-4116) Richard Humm (410) 535-2897

Pt of Rocks St Pauls Episcopal Church **P** (38) 1914 Ballenger Creek Rd 21777 (Mail to: PO Box 216 21777-0216) (301) 874-2995

Reisterstown St. John's Church' Western Run Parish **P** (457) 3738 Butler Rd 21136-3830 (Mail to: 3738 Butler Rd 21136-3830) John Stonesifer (410) 4294690

Severna Park St Martins in-the-Fld Epis Ch **P** (906) § 375 Benfield Rd 21146-2794 (Mail to: 375 Benfield Rd 21146-2794) Nathan Erdman Matthew Hanisian (410) 647-6248

Sharpsburg St Pauls Episcopal Church **P** (87) 209 W Main St 21782-1743 (Mail to: PO Box 364 21782-0364) Connor Newlun (301) 432-7098

Smithsburg St Anns Episcopal Church **P** (54) 9 N Maple Ave 21783-9702 (Mail to: PO Box 177

21783-0177) Sandra Kline-Mortimer (301) 824-3033

Street Church of the Ascension **P** (47) 3460 Mill Green Rd 21154-1724 (Mail to: C/O Mr Gregory Buckler 3460 Mill Green Rd 21154-1724) (410) 836-3587

Street Holy Cross Episcopal Church **M** (141) 4603 Rocks Rd 21154-1210 (Mail to: PO Box 103 21154-0103) (410) 452-5502

Sunderland All Saints Parish **P** (164) 100 Lower Marlboro Rd 20689 (Mail to: PO Box 40 20689-0040) (410) 257-6306

Sykesville St Barnabas Episcopal Church **P** (78) 13135 Forsythe Rd 21784-5818 (Mail to: PO Box 1426 21784-1426) Timothy Grayson (410) 489-2800

Thurmont Catoctin Parish Harriet Chapel **P** (122) 12625 Catoctin Furnace Rd 21788-3008 (Mail to: 12625 Catoctin Furnace Rd 21788-3008) Barbara Sears (301) 271-4554

Timonium St Francis Episcopal Parish **P** (353) 2216 Pot Spring Rd 21093-2724 (Mail to: 2216 Pot Spring Rd 21093-2797) Kristofer Lindh-Payne Kristofer Lindh-Payne Amy Myers (410) 252-4465

Towson Church of the Good Shepherd **P** (537) § 1401 Carrollton Ave 21204-6518 (Mail to: 1401 Carrollton Ave 21204-6518) Arianne Rice (410) 823-0122

Towson Trinity Episcopal Church **P** (447) § 120 Allegheny Ave 21204-4019 (Mail to: 120 Allegheny Ave 21204-4095) Henrietta Wiley (410) 823-3588

Tracys Landing St Marks Chapel **Chapel** 361 Deale Rd 20779-9713 (Mail to: C/O St James 5757 Solomons Island Rd 20711-9707) (410) 867-2838

West River Christ Episcopal Church **P** (203) 220 Owensville Rd 20778-9704 (Mail to: 220 Owensville Rd 20778-9704) Richard Laribee (410) 867-0346

Westernport St James Episcopal Church **P** (65) 32 Main St 21539 (Mail to: PO Box 279 21562-0279) Garrett Carskadon John Martin (301) 359-6001

Westminster Church of the Ascension **P** (236) 23 N Court St 21157-5109 (Mail to: 23 N Court St 21157-5352) (410) 848-3251

STATE OF MASSACHUSETTS

Dioceses of Massachusetts and Western Massachusetts

DIOCESE OF MASSACHUSETTS

(PROVINCE I)
Comprises Eastern Massachusetts
DIOCESAN OFFICE 138 Tremont St Boston MA 02111-1318
TEL (617) 482-5800
E-MAIL info@diomass.org   WEB www.diomass.org

Previous Bishops—
Edward Bass 1797-1803, Samuel Parker 1804-04, Alexander V Griswold (Eastern Dio) 1811-43, Manton Eastburn coadj 1842 Bp 1843-72, Benj H Paddock 1873-91, Phillips Brooks 1891-93, Wm Lawrence 1893-1927, Charles L Slattery coadj 1922 Bp 1927-30, Saml G Babcock suffr 1913-38, Henry K Sherrill 1930-47, Raymond A Heron suffr 1938-54, Norman B Nash coadj 1947 Bp 1947-56, Frederic C Lawrence suffr 1956-68, Anson P Stokes Jr coadj 1954 Bp 1956-70, John M Burgess suffr 1962-69 coadj 1969 Bp 1970-75, Morris F Arnold suffr 1972-82, John B Coburn 1976-86, David E Johnson coadj 1985 Bp 1986-1995, Barbara C Harris suffr 1989-2002, Roy F Cederholm Jr suffr 2001-11, M Thomas Shaw III SSJE 1995-2014

Bishop—Rt Rev Alan M. Gates (1082) (Dio 13 Sep 2014)

Bishop Suffragan—Rt Rev Gayle Elizabeth Harris (981) (Suffr 18 Jan 2003)

Chanc E Notis-McConarty; *Sec* R Wildman; *Asst Sec* C Smith; *Treas* T Ts'o; *Reg-Hist* L Smith; *Dean* A McCreath; *Cn to Ord* W Parnell; *Bps Exec Asst* L Simons; *Suffr Bps Exec Asst* D Ames; *Exec Dir Epis City Miss* A Chambliss

Stand Comm—Cler: K Coleman D Dice K Elledge T Soughers ; *Lay: Pres* L Gant D Dilday G Knowles S Owayda

PARISHES, MISSIONS, AND CLERGY

Acton Church of the Good Shepherd **P** (311) 164 Newtown Rd 01720-3114 (Mail to: 164 Newtown Rd 01720-3114) Eleanor Terry Ruthann Savage-King (978) 263-5782

Amesbury St James Episcopal Church **P** (207) 120 Main St 01913-2809 (Mail to: PO Box 25 01913-0001) John Satula (978) 388-0030

Andover Parish of Christ Church **P** (922) 25 Central St 01810-3737 (Mail to: 25 Central St 01810-3780) Michael Hodges (978) 475-0529

Arlington Church of Our Saviour **P** (99) 21 Marathon St 02474-6940 (Mail to: 21 Marathon St 02474-6940) Malia Crawford Patricia De Beer (781) 648-5962

Arlington St Johns Church **P** (116) 74 Pleasant St 02476-6516 (Mail to: 74 Pleasant St 02476-6516) Diane Wong (781) 648-4819

Attleboro All Saints Episcopal Church **P** (52) 121 N Main St 02703-2221 (Mail to: 121 N Main St 02703-2221) Meghan Sweeney Ronald Tibbetts (508) 222-2233

Ayer St Andrews Episcopal Church **P** (182) 7 Faulkner St 01432-1611 (Mail to: PO Box 298 01432-0298) (978) 772-2615

Barnstable St Marys Episcopal Church **P** (627) 3055 Main St 02630-1132 (Mail to: PO Box 395 02630-0395) Scott Bellows (508) 362-3977

Bedford St Pauls Episcopal Church **P** (444) 100 Pine Hill Rd 01730-1641 (Mail to: 100 Pine Hill Rd 01730-1698) Christopher Wendell Diane Keith-Lucas (781) 275-8262

Belmont All Saints Episcopal Church **P** (152) 17 Clark St 02478-2448 (Mail to: 17 Clark St 02478-2448) Cheryl Minor Paul Minor (617) 484-2228

Beverly St John's Church **P** (1537) 705 Hale St 01915-2118 (Mail to: PO Box 5610 01915-0522) Kathryn Elledge (978) 927-0229

Beverly St Peters Episcopal Church **P** (280) 4 Ocean St 01915-5220 (Mail to: 4 Ocean St 01915-5299) Sarah Conner Brett Johnson (978) 922-3438

Boston Emmanuel Episcopal Church **P** (367) 15 Newbury St 02116-3105 (Mail to: 15 Newbury St 02116-3185) Pamela Werntz Frederick Stecker (617) 536-3355

Boston Grace Federated Church **M** (2) 760 Saratoga St 02128-1513 (Mail to: 760 Saratoga St 02128-1513) (617) 569-5358

Boston Old North Christ Church **P** (290) 193 Salem St 02113-1123 (Mail to: 193 Salem St 02113-1123) Matthew Cadwell Holly Hartman (617) 523-6676

Boston St Augustine and St Martin **P** (92) 29 Lenox St 02118-3201 (Mail to: 31 Lenox St 02118-3201) (617) 442-6395

Boston St Cyprians Episcopal Church **P** (223) 1073 Tremont St 02120-2163 (Mail to: 1073 Tremont St 02120-2163) Julian Fredie (617) 427-6175

Boston St Mary Episcopal Church **P** (137) 14 Cushing Ave 02125-2009 (Mail to: 14 Cushing Ave 02125-2009) John Finley (617) 282-3181

Boston St Stephen Episcopal Church **M** (246) 419 Shawmut Ave 02118-3822 (Mail to: 419 Shawmut Ave 02118-3825) Amy Whitcomb Slemmer (617) 262-9070

✣ **Boston** Cathedral Church of St Paul **O** 138 Tremont St 02111-1318 (Mail to: C/O Human Resources 138 Tremont St 02111-1318) Amy Mccreath Jennifer Mccracken Tamra Tucker (617) 482-5800

Boston The Church of the Advent **P** (492) 30 Brimmer St 02108-1002 (Mail to: 30 Brimmer St 02108-1098) Douglas Anderson Thomas Adams Jay James Daphne Noyes David Thompson (617) 523-2377

Boston Parish of All Saints **P** (365) 209 Ashmont St 02124-3803 (Mail to: 209 Ashmont St 02124-3898) Michael Godderz (617) 436-6370

Boston Trinity Church Episcopal **P** (2805) 206 Clarendon St 02116-3722 (Mail to: 206 Clarendon St 02116-3722) Morgan Allen Michael Battle Karen Coleman Paige Fisher Kathleen Lonergan Abigail Moon (617) 536-0944

Braintree Emmanuel Episcopal Church **P** (212) 519 Washington St 02184-4655 (Mail to: 519 Washington St 02184-4655) Thomas Mulvey (781) 843-0170

Bridgewater Trinity Episcopal Church **P** (221) 91 Main Street 02324-1406 (Mail to: 91 Main St 02324-1406) (508) 697-4311

Brookline All Saints Parish **P** (431) 1773 Beacon St 02445-4214 (Mail to: 1773 Beacon St 02445-4299) Richard Burden

Brookline Boston Univ Episcopal Chapel **CC** 40 Prescott St 024464038 (Mail to: 40 Prescott St 024464038) (617) 277-5523

Brookline Church of Our Saviour **P** (141) 25 Monmouth St 02446-5604 (Mail to: 25 Monmouth St 02446-5604) Joel Ives (617) 277-7334

Brookline St Pauls Episcopal Church **P** (539) 15 Saint Paul St 02446-6501 (Mail to: 15 Saint Paul St 02446-6501) Elise Feyerherm Paul Kolbet (617) 566-4953

Burlington St Marks Episcopal Church **P** (117) C/O Sherley Estrella 10 Saint Marks Rd 01803-3622 (Mail to: C/O Sherley Estrella 10 Saint Marks Rd 01803-3622) John De Beer Daniel Bell (781) 272-1586

Buzzards Bay Ch of St Peters on the Canal **P** (381) PO Box 265 02532-0265 (Mail to: PO Box 265 02532-0265) Robert Sherwood (508) 759-5641

Cambridge Christ Church **P** (567) 0 Garden St 02138-3631 (Mail to: 0 Garden St 02138-3656) Katherine Ekrem Rowan Larson Patricia Zifcak (617) 876-0200

Cambridge Epis Chaplaincy at Harvard **CC** 2 Garden St 02138-3631 (Mail to: 2 Garden St 02138-3631) Rita Powell

Cambridge Episcopal Chapel at MIT **CC** 77 Massachusetts Ave 02139-4307 (Mail to: MIT W11 77 Massachusetts Ave 02139-4307) (617) 253-2983

Cambridge Saint Bartholomew's Church **P** (171) 239 Harvard St 02139-2640 (Mail to: 239 Harvard St 02139-2640) Patricia Zifcak (617) 354-8582

Cambridge St James Episcopal Church **P** (799) 1991 Massachusetts Ave 02140-1306 (Mail to: 1991 Massachusetts Ave 02140-1342) Robert Massie Matthew Stewart (617) 547-4070

Cambridge St Johns Memorial Chapel **CC** 99 Brattle St 02138-3402 (Mail to: 99 Brattle St 02138-3402) (617) 868-3450

Cambridge St Peters Episcopal Church **P** (141) 838 Massachusetts Ave 02139-3004 (Mail to: Attn: Pat Drake 15 Sellers St 02139-3005) (617) 547-7788

Canton Trinity Church Episcopal **P** (49) 1 Blue Hill River Rd 02021-1001 (Mail to: 1 Blue Hill River Rd 02021-1001) Rachel Wildman (781) 828-1810

Charlestown St John's Episcopal Church **P** (116) 27 Devens St 02129-3735 (Mail to: 27 Devens St 02129-3735) Gregory Johnston Lyn Brakeman (617) 242-1272

Chatham St Christophers Church **P** (863) 625 Main St 02633-2233 (Mail to: Attn: Treasurer 625 Main St 02633-2233) Brian Mcgurk John Martiner (508) 945-2832

Chelmsford All Saints Church **P** (556) 10 Billerica Rd 01824-3011 (Mail to: 10 Billerica Rd 01824-3097) Sean Maloney (978) 256-5673

Chelsea St Lukes-San Lucas Epis Church **M** (193) 201 Washington Ave 02150-3914 (Mail to: 201 Washington Ave 02150-3914) Edgar Gutierrez-Duarte (617) 884-4278

Chestnut Hill Boston College Campus Ministry **CC** Episcopal Chaplain-McElroy 105 379 Hammond St 02467-1224 (Mail to: C/O Church of the Redeemer 02467-1224) James Hairston James Weiss (617) 285-6577

Chestnut Hill Church of the Redeemer **P** (779) 379 Hammond St 02467-1224 (Mail to: 379 Hammond St 02467-1224) Michael Dangelo Nancy Gossling (617) 566-7679

Cohasset St Stephens Episcopal Church **P** (805) 16 Highland Ave 02025-1819 (Mail to: 16 Highland Ave 02025-1819) Margaret Arnold (781) 383-1083

Concord Trinity Episcopal Church **P** (1397) 81 Elm St 01742-2252 (Mail to: 81 Elm St 01742-2252) Christopher Whiteman (978) 369-3715

Danvers All Saints Church North Shore **P** (290) 46 Cherry St 01923-2820 (Mail to: 46 Cherry St 01923-2820) Marya Decarlen (978) 774-1150

Dartmouth St Peter's Episcopal Church **P** (89) 351 Elm St 02748-3407 (Mail to: 351 Elm St

02748-3407) Scott Ciosek Scott Ciosek (508) 997-0903
Dedham Church of the Good Shepherd **P** (58) 62 Cedar St 02026-3237 (Mail to: 62 Cedar St 02026-3237) Chitral De Mel (781) 326-3052
Dedham St Pauls Church Episcopal **P** (482) 59 Court St 02026-4301 (Mail to: 59 Court St 02026-4301) Melanie Mccarley (781) 326-4553
Dorchester St Marks Episcopal Church **P** (97) 73 Columbia Rd 02121-3347 (Mail to: 73 Columbia Rd 02121-3347) (617) 436-4319
Dover St Dunstans Episcopal Church **P** (223) 18 Springdale Ave 02030-2353 (Mail to: Attn: Richard Crispin PO Box 515 02030-0515) Sean Leonard (508) 7850879
Duxbury Ch Of St John The Evangelist **P** (664) 410 Washington St 02332-4552 (Mail to: 410 Washington St PO Box 2893 02331-2893) Daniel Dice (781) 934-8911
Edgartown St Andrews Episcopal Church **P** (150) PO Box 1287 02539-1287 (Mail to: PO Box 1287 02539-1287) Vincent Seadale (508) 627-5330
Everett Grace Episcopal Church **P** (168) 67 Norwood St 02149-2722 (Mail to: PO Box 490285 02149-0004) James Hairston (617) 387-7526
Fall River Church of the Holy Spirit **P** (111) 160 Rock St 02720-3233 (Mail to: 160 Rock St 02720-3283) James Medley Jeremi Colvin (508) 672-5571
Fall River St Luke's Episcopal Church **P** (80) 315 Warren St 02721-3919 (Mail to: 315 Warren St 02721-3919) James Hornsby (508) 678-5118
Falmouth St Barnabas Memorial Church **P** (430) 91 Main St 02540-2652 (Mail to: PO Box 203 02541-0203) Willie Mebane (508) 548-3863
Foxborough St Marks Episcopal Church **P** (257) 116 South St 02035-1760 (Mail to: 116 South St 02035-1760) Lauren Lukason (508) 543-8191
Framingham Framingham State Colg Prot Min **CC** 100 State St 01701-9101 (Mail to: 63a Highland St 02119-1536) (508) 626-4610
Framingham St Andrews Episcopal Church **P** (577) 3 Maple St 01702 (Mail to: 3 Maple St 01702) (508) 875-5095
Franklin St Johns Episcopal Church **P** (145) 237 Pleasant St 02038-3620 (Mail to: PO Box 287 02038-0287) Kathleen McAdams Margaret Geller Deborah Woodward (508) 528-2387
Gloucester St Johns Episcopal Church **P** (423) 48 Middle St 01930-5716 (Mail to: 48 Middle St 01930-5795) M Lise Hildebrandt (978) 2831708
Groton St Johns Chapel **Chapel** 282 Farmers Row 01450-1848 (Mail to: Groton School 06340) (978) 448-7257
Groveland St James Episcopal Church **P** (186) 119 Washington St 01834-1535 (Mail to: C/O

Mrs Elaine Hatch 119 Washington St 01834-1535) (978) 373-1270
Hanover St Andrews Church **P** (564) 17 Church St 02339-2315 (Mail to: 17 Church St 02339-2315) (781) 826-2062
Harwich Port Christ Church Episcopal **P** (150) 671 Route 28 02646-1913 (Mail to: 671 Route 28 02646-1913) Donna Foughty (508) 432-1787
Haverhill Trinity Episcopal Church **P** (138) 26 White St 01830-5702 (Mail to: 26 White St 01830-5702) Jacqueline Clark (978) 372-4244
Hingham Par of St John the Evangelist **P** (1646) 172 Main St 02043-1911 (Mail to: 172 Main St 02043-1999) Sarah Mato (781) 749-1535
Holbrook St Johns Episcopal Church **P** (75) 322 S Franklin St 02343-1430 (Mail to: 322 S Franklin St 02343-1430) (781) 767-4656
Holliston St Michaels Church **P** (281) 1162 Highland St 01746-1602 (Mail to: 1162 Highland St 01746-1602) Kathryn Bast (508) 429-4248
Hopkinton St Pauls Church Episcopal **P** (35) 61 Wood St 01748 (Mail to: PO Box 165 01748-0165) Michael Billingsley (508) 435-4536
Hudson St Lukes Episcopal Church **P** (83) 5 Washington St 01749-2409 (Mail to: 5 Washington St 01749-2409) T James Kodera (978) 562-2701
Hyannis Port St Andrew by the Sea **SC** Irving Ave 02647 (Mail to: PO Box 386 02647-0386)
Hyde Park Parish of Christ Church **P** (114) PO Box 366202 02136-0022 (Mail to: PO Box 366202 02136-0022) (617) 361-2457
Hyde Park Iglesia de San Juan **M** (42) PO Box 366202 02136-0022 (Mail to: PO Box 366202 02136-0022) (617) 361-3081
Ipswich Ascension Memorial Church **P** (416) 31 County St 01938-2224 (Mail to: PO Box 547 01938-0547) Bradford Clark (978) 356-2560
Jamaica Plain St Johns Episcopal Church **P** (230) 1 Roanoke Ave 02130-2828 (Mail to: PO Box 300230 02130-0031) Cecil Cole (617) 524-2999
Lawrence Grace Episcopal Church **P** (196) 35 Jackson St 01840-1626 (Mail to: 29 Jackson St 01840-1627) Joel Almono Roque Ennis Duffis Fox (978) 682-6003
Lexington Church of Our Redeemer **P** (405) 6 Meriam St 02420-5309 (Mail to: C/O Frank A Kern 6 Meriam St 02420-5309) Emily Garcia Virginia Solaqua (781) 862-6408
Lincoln St Annes Church **P** (515) 147 Concord Rd 01773-4108 (Mail to: PO Box 6 01773-0006) Joseph Kimmel Christopher Yates David Holroyd (781) 259-8834
Lowell Saint Anne's Church **P** (282) 10 Kirk St 01852-1005 (Mail to: 8 Kirk St 01852-1086) Jeremi Colvin Sarah Lewis (978) 452-2150
Lowell St Johns Episcopal Church **P** (76) 82 Luce St 01852-3034 (Mail to: 260 Gorham St 01852-3345) (978) 453-5423

Lynn St Stephen's Memorial Church **P** (299) 74 Sagamore St 01902-3436 (Mail to: 74 S Common St 01902-4594) Gregory Perez (781) 599-4220

Lynnfield St Pauls Episcopal Church **P** (383) 127 Summer St 01940-1827 (Mail to: 127 Summer St 01940-1827) Robert Bacon (781) 334-4594

Malden St Pauls Church **P** (117) 26 Washington St 02148-4903 (Mail to: 26 Washington St 02148-8299) (781) 324-9544

Manchester Emmanuel Chapel **SC** PO Box 705 01944-0705 (Mail to: PO Box 705 01944-0705) Luther Zeigler (978) 526-0085

Marblehead St Michaels Church Episcopal **P** (269) 26 Pleasant St 01945-3432 (Mail to: 26 Pleasant St 01945-3432) (781) 631-0657

Marblehead Wyman Memorial Ch of St Andrew **P** (397) 135 Lafayette St 01945-0805 (Mail to: 135 Lafayette St 01945-1113) Charles Elledge (781) 631-4951

Marion St Gabriels Episcopal Church **P** (527) 124 Front St 02738-1634 (Mail to: PO Box 545 02738-0010) Eric Fialho Catherine Harper (508) 748-1507

Marshfield Trinity Episcopal Church **P** (157) 229 Highland St 02050-6202 (Mail to: PO Box 388 02051-0388) (781) 834-8575

Mattapan Church of the Holy Spirit **P** (405) 525 River St 02126-3013 (Mail to: 525 River St 02126-3096) Zenetta Armstrong Harry Jean-Jacques H Mark Smith (617) 2980577

Mattapan St John St James Church **P** (91) 891 Cummins Hwy 02126-2039 (Mail to: 31 Lenox St 02118-3201) Rospignac Ambroise (617) 445-8843

Mattapoisett St Phil of Bethsaida Sumr Chpl **SC** 34 Water St 02739 (Mail to: 40 Water St 02109-3604) (508) 758-1346

Medfield Church of the Advent **P** (244) 28 Pleasant St 02052-2613 (Mail to: 28 Pleasant St 02052-2613) Lynn Campbell (508) 359-6303

Medford Grace Episcopal Church **P** (472) 160 High St 02155-3818 (Mail to: 160 High St 02155-3818) Carol Morehead (781) 396-7215

Medford Tufts University Epis Chapel **CC** 520 Boston Ave 02155-5500 (Mail to: Tufts University 02155) (781) 628-5000

Medway Christ Church **P** (167) 14 School St 02053-1306 (Mail to: 14 School St 02053-1306) (508) 533-7171

Melrose Trinity Episcopal Church **P** (156) 131 W Emerson St 02176-3136 (Mail to: 131 W Emerson St 02176-3136) David Prentice (781) 665-3890

Methuen St Andrews Church **P** (237) 90 Broadway 01844-3838 (Mail to: 90 Broadway 01844-3838) Eleanor Prior (978) 689-0463

Middleboro Church of Our Saviour **P** (163) 120 Centre St 02346-2233 (Mail to: PO Box 89 02346-0089) David Milam (508) 947-1900

Milton Epis Church of Our Saviour **P** (64) 453 Adams St 02186-4359 (Mail to: 453 Adams St 02186-4359) Rachael Pettengill-Rasure (617) 698-4757

Milton Saint Michael's Church **P** (719) 112 Randolph Ave 02186-3401 (Mail to: 112 Randolph Ave 02186-3401) Hall Kirkham Jennifer Grumhaus (617) 698-1813

N Attleboro Grace Church **P** (113) 104 N Washington St 02760-1633 (Mail to: 104 N Washington St 02760-1633) Austin Almon Kathleen McAdams (508) 695-5471

Nantucket St Pauls Episcopal Church **P** (495) 20 Fair St 02554-3705 (Mail to: 20 Fair Street 02554) Max Wolf (508) 228-0916

Natick St Pauls Episcopal Church **P** (507) 39 E Central St 01760-4612 (Mail to: 39 E Central St 01760) Rebecca Gettel (508) 655-5880

Needham Hgts Christ Episcopal **P** (601) 1132 Highland Ave 02494-1131 (Mail to: 1132 Highland Ave 02494-1131) Nicholas Morris-Kliment (781) 444-1469

New Bedford Grace Church **P** (651) 133 School St 02740-5928 (Mail to: 133 School St 02740-5928) Melissa Howell (508) 993-0547

New Bedford St Andrews Church **P** (329) 169 Belleville Rd 02745-5220 (Mail to: 169 Belleville Rd 02745-5220) Isabel Geller (508) 992-9274

New Bedford St Martin's Episcopal Church **P** (127) 136 Rivet St 02744-1814 (Mail to: 136 Rivet St 02744) (508) 994-8972

Newburyport St Pauls Episcopal Church **P** (409) 166 High St 01950-3948 (Mail to: 166 High St 01950-3948) Jarred Mercer Margaret Ingall (978) 465-5351

Newton Grace Episcopal Church **P** (248) 76 Eldredge St 02458-2017 (Mail to: 76 Eldredge St 02458-2098) David Killian Rowan Larson Regina Walton (617) 244-3221

Newton Center Trinity Par of Newton Centre **P** (58) 1097 Centre St 02459-1536 (Mail to: 11 Homer S 02459-1510) Todd Miller (617) 527-2790

Newton Highlands St Pauls Episcopal Church **P** (191) 1135 Walnut St 02161 (Mail to: 1135 Walnut St 02461-1242) (617) 527-6642

Newton Lower Falls St Marys Episcopal Church **P** (247) 258 Concord St 02462-1315 (Mail to: 258 Concord St 02462-1315) Ann Bonner Stewart (617) 527-4769

Newtonville St Johns Episcopal Church **P** (112) 297 Lowell Ave 02460-1826 (Mail to: 297 Lowell Ave 02460-1826) (617) 964-2591

North Andover Brooks School Chapel **Chapel** 1160 Great Pond Rd 01845-1298 (Mail to: 1160 Great Pond Rd 01845-1298) Rober Flanagan (508) 686-6101

North Andover St Pauls Episcopal Church **P** (218) 390 Main St 01845-3952 (Mail to: 390 Main St 01845-3952) Frederick Emrich (978) 683-0671

North Billerica St Annes Episcopal Church **P** (189) 14 Treble Cove Rd 01862-2117 (Mail to

PO Box 134 01862-0134) Jennifer Beal (978) 663-4073

North Dartmouth Univ of Mass - Darmouth Chapel **CC** 285 Old Westport Rd 02747-2300 (Mail to: Old Westport Rd 02747) (508) 999-8875

North Easton Bristol Trinity Epis Church **P** (88) 143 Lincoln St 02356-1709 (Mail to: 143 Lincoln St 02356-1709)

Norwood Grace Episcopal Church **P** (191) 150 Chapel St 02062-3130 (Mail to: 150 Chapel St 02062-3130) Robert Brockmann (781) 762-0959

Oak Bluffs Trinity Episcopal Church **SC** 5 Ocean Ave 02557 (Mail to: PO Box 2147 02557-2147) (508) 693-3780

Orleans The Church of the Holy Spirit **P** (394) 204 Monument Rd 02653-3512 (Mail to: 204 Monument Rd 02653-3512) Joseph Robinson Patrick Ward (508) 255-0433

Osterville St Peters Church Episcopal **P** (249) 421 Wianno Ave 02655-1918 (Mail to: 421 Wianno Ave 02655-1918) Elizabeth Grundy (508) 428-3561

Plymouth Christ Church Parish **P** (766) 149 Court St 02360-4003 (Mail to: 149 Court St 02360-4003) (508) 746-4959

Provincetown Ch Of St Mary of the Harbor **P** (155) 517 Commercial St 02657-2412 (Mail to: 517 Commercial St 02657-2412) (508) 487-2622

Quincy Christ's Church Quincy **P** (150) 12 Quincy Ave 02169-6712 (Mail to: 12 Quincy Ave 02169-6712) Clifford Brown (617) 773-0310

Quincy St Chrysostom's Episcopal Ch **P** (160) 1 Linden St 02170-1809 (Mail to: 1 Linden St 02170-1809) Christopher Capaldo (617) 472-0737

Randolph Trinity Church **P** (191) 120 North Main St 02368 (Mail to: Attn: Mildred Mukasa 120 N Main St 02368-4629) Philip Kuhn (781) 963-2366

Reading Church of the Good Shepherd **P** (462) 95 Woburn St 01867-2907 (Mail to: 95 Woburn St 01867-2907) Brian Raiche (781) 944-1572

Rockland Trinity Episcopal Church **P** (99) 3 Goddard Ave 02370-2325 (Mail to: 3 Goddard Ave 02370-2325) Sarah Brockmann (781) 871-0096

Rockport St Marys Episcopal Church **P** (290) 24 Broadway 01966-1537 (Mail to: PO Box 299 01966-0399) Karin Wade (978) 546-3421

S Hamilton Christ Church **P** (320) 149 Asbury St 01982-1813 (Mail to: 149 Asbury St 01982-1813) Patrick Gray (978) 468-4461

S Weymouth Church of the Holy Nativity **P** (613) 8 Nevin Rd 02190-1611 (Mail to: 8 Nevin Rd 02190-1611) Laurie Rofinot (781) 335-2030

S Yarmouth St Davids Church **P** (289) 205 Old Main St 02664-4529 (Mail to: 205 Old Main

St 02664-4529) Andrea Taylor (508) 394-4222

Salem Grace Episcopal Church **P** (568) 385 Essex St 01970-3260 (Mail to: 385 Essex St 01970-3292) Deborah Phillips (978) 744-2796

Salem St Peters Episcopal Church **P** (367) 24 Saint Peter St 01970-3820 (Mail to: 24 Saint Peter St 01970-3820) Nathan Ives Nathan Ives (978) 745-2291

Sandwich St. John's Episcopal Church **P** (557) 159 Main St 02563-2283 (Mail to: 159 Main St 02563-2283) (508) 888-2828

Saugus St Johns Episcopal Church **P** (247) 265 Central St 01906-2142 (Mail to: 8 Prospect St 01906-2155) John Beach (781) 233-1242

Scituate Saint Luke's Episcopal Church **P** (499) 465 First Parish Rd 02066-3334 (Mail to: 465 First Parish Rd 02066-3334) Natasha Stewart (781) 545-9482

Sharon St Johns Church **P** (17) 23 High St 02067-1417 (Mail to: 23 High St 02067-1417) (781) 784-3400

Shirley Trinity Chapel **P** (114) 188 Center Rd 01464-2115 (Mail to: PO Box 1488 01464) Marsha Hoecker Suzanne Wade (978) 425-9041

Somerset Church of Our Saviour **P** (297) 2112 County St 02726-5501 (Mail to: 2112 County St 02726-5501) Virgilio Fortuna Tara Soughers (508) 678-9663

Somerville St James Episcopal Church **P** (21) PO Box 440185 02144-0002 (Mail to: PO Box 440185 02144-0002) Kevin Sparrow (617) 666-1063

South Dartmouth St Aidan's Chapel **SC** 188 Smith Neck Rd 02748-1310 (Mail to: PO Box P183 02748-0310) (508) 996-2008

Southborough St Marks Church **P** (586) 27 Main St 01772-1508 (Mail to: 27 Main St 01772-1508) Philip Labelle Christine Whittaker-Navez (508) 481-1917

Southborough St Marks Chapel **Chapel** 25 Marlboro Rd 01772-1207 (Mail to: St Marks School 25 Marlboro Rd 01772-1299) (508) 786-6000

Stoughton Trinity Episcopal Church **P** (143) PO Box 513 02072-0513 (Mail to: 414 Sumner St 02072-3470) Rachel Wildman (781) 344-4592

Sudbury St Elizabeths Episcopal Church **P** (347) 1 Morse Rd 01776-1746 (Mail to: 1 Morse Rd 01776-1746) Andrew Suitter (978) 443-6035

Swampscott The Church of the Holy Name **P** (115) 60 Monument Ave 01907-1968 (Mail to: 40 Hardy Rd 01907-1981) Mark Templeman (781) 595-1674

Swansea Christ Episcopal Church **P** (296) 57 Main St 02777-4624 (Mail to: 57 Main St 02777-4624) (508) 678-0923

Taunton Episcopal Church of St Thomas **P** (172) 111 High St 02780-3901 (Mail to: Attn: Ritch Price PO Box 149 02780-0149) Joseph Mumita (508) 824-9595

Topsfield Trinity Church **P** (574) 124 River Rd 01983-2111 (Mail to: PO Box 308 01983-0408) Jennifer Vath (978) 887-5570

Vineyard Haven Grace Episcopal Church **P** (144) 36 Woodlawn Ave 02568 (Mail to: PO Box 1197 02568-0903) Stephen Harding Gloria Wong (508) 693-0332

Waban Church of the Good Shepherd **P** (233) 1671 Beacon St 02468-1401 (Mail to: 1671 Beacon St 02468-1401) James Weldon (617) 244-4028

Wakefield Emmanuel Episcopal Church **P** (195) 5 Bryant St 01880-5008 (Mail to: 5 Bryant St 01880-5008) (781) 245-1374

Walpole Epiphany Church **P** (200) 62 Front St 02081-2810 (Mail to: 62 Front St 02081-2810) Christian Beukman Rebecca Black (508) 668-2353

Waltham Christ Church **P** (381) 750 Main St 02451-0603 (Mail to: 750 Main St Ste 1 02451-0697) Kapya Kaoma (781) 891-6012

Wareham Church of the Good Shepherd **P** (281) 74 High St 02571-2014 (Mail to: PO Box 719 74 High St 02571-0719) Daniel Bernier (508) 295-2840

Watertown Church of the Good Shepherd **P** (196) 9 Russell Ave 02472-3452 (Mail to: 9 Russell Ave 02472-3452) Andrew Goldhor (617) 924-9420

Wellesley St Andrews Episcopal Church **P** (1782) 79 Denton Rd 02482-6404 (Mail to: 79 Denton Rd 02482-6400) Adrian Robbins-Cole Karen Budney Sarah Robbins-Cole Margaret Schwarzer (781) 235-7310

Wellfleet Chpl of St James the Fisherman **SC** 2317 State Hwy Rte 6 02667 (Mail to: PO Box 1334 02667-1334) (508) 349-2188

West Newbury All Saints Episcopal Church **P** (34) 895 Main St 01985-1302 (Mail to: 25 Storey Ave # 228 01950-1869) John Satula

(978) 462-4244

West Roxbury Parish of Emmanuel Church **P** (56) 21 Stratford St 02132-2008 (Mail to: 21 Stratford St 02132-2020) (617) 323-1440

Westford Saint Mark's Church **P** (124) 75 Cold Spring Rd 01886-2410 (Mail to: 75 Cold Spring Rd 01886-2410) Suzanne Wade (978) 692-7849

Weston St Peters Church Episcopal **P** (608) 320 Boston Post Rd 02493-1540 (Mail to: 320 Boston Post Rd 02493-1540) George Stevens (781) 891-3200

Westwood St Johns Episcopal Church **P** (233) 95 Deerfield Ave 02090-1612 (Mail to: 95 Deerfield Ave 02090-1612) Vincent Bousquet (781) 329-2442

Whitman All Saints Parish **P** (129) 44 Park Ave 02382-1419 (Mail to: 44 Park Ave 02382-1419) Michele Matott (781) 447-6106

Wilmington St Elizabeths Episcopal Church **P** (174) 4 Forest St 01887-2811 (Mail to: C/O Pat Fregeau PO Box 294 01887-0294) Christopher Fike (978) 657-8178

Winchester Parish of the Epiphany **P** (892) 70 Church St 01890-2523 (Mail to: 70 Church St 01890-2523) Nicholas Myers (781) 729-1922

Winthrop St Johns Episcopal Church **P** (130) 222 Bowdoin St 02152-3123 (Mail to: 222 Bowdoin St 02152-3123) Walter Connelly (617) 846-2363

Woburn Trinity Episcopal Church **P** (35) 535 Main St 01801-2991 (Mail to: 535 Main St 01801-2991) (781) 935-0219

Woods Hole Church of the Messiah Epis Ch **P** (297) 13 Church St 02543-1007 (Mail to: 16 Church St 02543-1006) Storm Swain (508) 548-2145

Wrentham Trinity Episcopal Church **P** (185) 47 East St 02093-1369 (Mail to: PO Box 55 02093-0055) Lauren Lukason (508) 384-3958

STATE OF MICHIGAN

Dioceses of Eastern Michigan (EMI), Michigan (MI), Northern Michigan (NMI),
and Western Michigan (WMI)

Adrian—M
Albion—WMI
Allegan—WMI
Allen Pk—MI
Alma—EMI
Alpena—EMI
Ann Arbor—MI
Atlanta—EMI
Bad Axe—EMI
Battle Creek—WMI
Bay City—EMI
Beaver Is—WMI
Belmont—WMI
Benton Hbr—WMI
Beulah—WMI
Big Rapids—WMI
Birmingham—MI
Bloomfield Hills—MI
Bloomfield Township—MI
Boyne City—WMI
Brighton—MI
Brooklyn—MI
Cadillac—WMI
Charlevoix—WMI
Charlotte—WMI
Cheboygan—EMI
Chelsea—MI
Clarkston—MI
Clinton—MI
Coldwater—WMI
Corunna—EMI
Crystal Falls—NMI
Davison—EMI
Dearborn—MI
DeTour Vil—NMI
Detroit—MI
Dewitt—MI
Dexter—MI
Dowagiac—WMI
Dryden—EMI
Eagle Harbor—NMI
E Lansing—MI

E Tawas—EMI
Ecorse—MI
Elk Rapids—WMI
Escanaba—NMI
Farmington—MI
Fenton—EMI
Ferndale—MI
Flint—EMI
Flushing—EMI
Fremont—WMI
Gaylord—EMI
Gladstone—NMI
Gladwin—EMI
Grand Blanc—EMI
Grand Haven—WMI
Grand Ledge—WMI
Grand Rapids—WMI
Grayling—EMI
Greenville—WMI
Grosse Ile—MI
Grosse Pte—MI
Grosse Pte Farms—MI
Hamburg—MI
Harbert—WMI
Harbor Spgs—WMI
Harrisville—EMI
Harsens Is—EMI
Hastings—WMI
Hillman—EMI
Hillsdale—MI
Holland—WMI
Houghton—NMI
Howell—MI
Indian River—EMI
Inkster—MI
Ionia—MI
Iron Mtn—NMI
Iron River—NMI
Ironwood—NMI
Ishpeming—NMI
Jackson—MI
Kalamazoo—WMI
Kentwood—WMI

Lachine—EMI
Lake Orion—MI
Lansing—MI and WMI
Lapeer—EMI
Larium—NMI
Leland—WMI
Lexington—EMI
Lincoln Pk—MI
Livonia—MI
Ludington—WMI
Mackinac Is—NMI
Madison Hts—MI
Manistee—WMI
Manistique—NMI
Marquette—NMI
Marshall—WMI
Menominee—NMI
Michigan Ctr—MI
Midland—EMI
Milford—MI
Mio—EMI
Monroe—MI
Montague—WMI
Mt Clemens—MI
Mt Pleasant—WMI
Munising—NMI
Muskegon—WMI
Negaunee—NMI
Newaygo—WMI
Newberry—NMI
Niles—WMI
Northport—WMI
Norton Shores—WMI
Novi—MI
Onekama—WMI
Oscoda—EMI
Otter Lake—EMI
Owosso—EMI
Paw Paw—WMI
Pentwater—WMI
Petoskey—WMI
Plainwell—WMI
Pleasant Lake—MI

Plymouth—MI
Pte Aux Pins—NMI
Pontiac—MI
Pt Huron—EMI
Portage—WMI
Richland—WMI
Rochester—MI
Rogers City—EMI
Romeo—MI
Roscommon—EMI
Royal Oak—MI
Saginaw—EMI
St Clair—EMI
St Clair Shores—MI
St Joseph—WMI
Saline—MI
Sand Pt—EMI
Sandusky—EMI
Saugatuck—WMI
Sault Ste Marie—NMI
Shelbyville—WMI
Southfield—MI
Southgate—MI
S Haven—WMI
Standish—EMI
Sturgis—WMI
Three Rivers—WMI
Traverse City—WMI
Trenton—MI
Troy—MI
Utica—MI
Van Buren Twp—MI
Waterford—MI
W Bloomfield—MI
W Branch—EMI
Westland—MI
Williamston—MI
Wyandotte—MI
Wyoming—WMI
Ypsilanti—MI

DIOCESE OF MICHIGAN
(PROVINCE V)
Comprises the southeastern and southcentral portion of Michigan's lower peninsula
DIOCESAN OFFICE 4800 Woodward Ave Detroit MI 48201
TEL (313) 832-4400 TOLL FREE (866) 545-6424 FAX (313) 831-0259
E-MAIL Info@edomi.org WEB www.edomi.org

Previous Bishops—
Samuel A McCoskry 1836-78, Samuel S Harris 1879-88, Thomas F Davies 1889-1905, Chas D Williams 1906-23, Herman Page 1923-39, Frank W Creighton coadj 1937 Bp 1940-48, Donald B Aldrich coadj 1945-46, Russell S Hubbard suffr 1948-54, Archie H Crowley suffr 1954-72, Richard S Emrich suffr 1946-48 coadj 1948 Bp 1948-73, Robt L DeWitt suffr 1960-64, C Kilmer Myers suffr 1964-66, WJ Gordon Jr asst 1976-86, H Coleman McGehee Jr coadj 1971 Bp 1973-89, H Irving Mayson suffr 1976-92, R Stewart Wood Jr coadj 1989-90 Bp 1990-2000, Wendell N Gibbs Jr coadj 1999-2000 Bp 2000-19

Bishop—Rt Rev Dr Bonnie A. Perry (Dio 8 February 2020)

Cn for Cong Life E Ekevag; *Cn to Ord* JA Hardy; *Cn for Fin* M Miliotto; *Accountant* K Chapman; *Ex Asst to Bishop* S. Mason; *Dir of Admin* C Ramirez; *Assoc for Comm* A Trupiano; *Miss for Spirituality and Race* V Dunbar; *Miss for Young People's Min* C Piggins; *Assoc for Transitions/Local Form* S Shaefer; *Chanc* S Ott; *Asst Chanc* M Norris

Stand Comm—Cler: R Byrd A Estes A Martin R Alltop *chair; Lay:* H Santiz G Swan J Messimer J Powell

PARISHES, MISSIONS, AND CLERGY

Adrian Christ Episcopal Church **P** (25) 720 Riverside Ave 49221-1445 (Mail to: 720 Riverside Ave 49221-1445) (517) 263-1162

Allen Park St Lukes Episcopal Church **P** (44) 15603 Wick Rd 48101-1532 (Mail to: 15603 Wick Rd 48101-1532) William Hale (313) 381-6345

Ann Arbor Church of the Incarnation **M** (149) 3257 Lohr Rd 48108-9515 (Mail to: 3257 Lohr Rd 48108-9515) Joseph Summers Joseph Summers (734) 769-7900

Ann Arbor St Aidans Episcopal Church **P** (33) 1679 Broadway St 48105-1811 (Mail to: 1679 Broadway St 48105-1811) (734) 663-5503

Ann Arbor St Andrews Episcopal Church **HC** (1015) 306 N Division St 48104-1441 (Mail to: 306 N Division St 48104-1497) Walter Labatt Everette Rollins (734) 663-0518

Ann Arbor St Clare of Assisi Epis Church **P** (273) 2309 Packard St 48104-6321 (Mail to: 2309 Packard St 48104-6321) Anne Clarke (734) 6622449

Birmingham St James Episcopal Church **P** (532) 355 W Maple Rd 48009-3347 (Mail to: 355 W Maple Rd 48009-3348) Christine Fentress-Gannon Robert Hart Joshua Hoover (248) 644-0820

Bloomfield Hills Christ Church Cranbrook **P** (1698) 470 Church Rd 48304-3400 (Mail to: 470 Church Rd 48304-3400) William Danaher (248) 644-5210

Bloomfield Township Nativity Episcopal Church **P** (23) 21220 W 14 Mile Rd 48301-4000 (Mail to: Attn: Treasurer 21220 W 14 Mile Rd 48301-4000) Robert Alltop William Bales (248) 646-4100

Brighton St Pauls Episcopal Church **P** (422) 200 W Saint Paul St 48116-1202 (Mail to: 200 W Saint Paul St 48116-1202) Jeanne Hansknecht Jenny Housner-Ritter (810) 229-2821

Brooklyn All Saints Episcopal Church **P** (55) 151 N Main St 49230-8979 (Mail to: PO Box 367 49230-0367) (517) 592-2244

Brooklyn St Michael and All Angels **P** (35) 11646 Old Monroe Pike 49230-8706 (Mail to: PO Box 287 49265-0287) Winifred Cook Cynthia Corner Mark Hastings Diana Walworth (517) 467-7855

Chelsea St Barnabas Episcopal Church **M** (42) 20500 W Old US Highway 12 48118-1309 (Mail to: 20500 W Old US Highway 12 48118-1309) David Glaser Ernest Stech (734) 475-8818

Clarkston Church of the Resurrection **P** (49) 6490 Clarkston Rd 48346-1500 (Mail to: 6490 Clarkston Rd 48346-1500) (248) 625-2325

Clinton St Johns Episcopal Church **M** (257) 122 E Church St 49236-9762 (Mail to: 122 E Church St PO Box 518 49236-9762) (517) 456-4828

Dearborn Christ Episcopal Church **P** (161) 120 N Military St 48124-1035 (Mail to: 120 N Military St 48124-1035) Terri Pilarski (313) 565-8450

Detroit All Saints Episcopal Church **P** (72) 3837 West Seven Mile Road 48221-2218 (Mail to: 3837 W 7 Mile Rd 48221-2218) (313) 341-5320

✠ **Detroit** Cathedral Church of St Paul **O** (407) 4800 Woodward Ave 48201-1310 (Mail to: 4800 Woodward Ave 48201-1399) S Scott Hunter Anthony Estes (313) 831-5000

Detroit Christ Episcopal Church **P** (448) 960 E Jefferson Ave 48207 (Mail to: Attn: Randy Gilchrist 960 E Jefferson Ave 48207) Emily Guffey (313) 259-6688

Detroit Church of the Messiah **P** (372) 231 E Grand Blvd 48207-3739 (Mail to: 231 E Grand Blvd 48207-3788) (313) 567-1158

Detroit Grace Episcopal Church **P** (37) 1926 Virginia Park St 48206-2422 (Mail to: 1926 Virginia Park St 48206-2422) (313) 895-6442

Detroit St Cyprians Episcopal Church **P** (22) 6114 28th St 48210-1400 (Mail to: 6114 28th St 48210-1400) (313) 896-7515

Detroit St Johns Episcopal Church **P** (231) 2326 Woodward Ave 48201-3431 (Mail to: 50 E Fisher Fwy 48201-3405) Steven Kelly (313) 962-7358

Detroit St Matthews & St Josephs Ch **P** (143) 8850 Woodward Ave 48202-2137 (Mail to: 8850 Woodward Ave 48202-2137) (313) 871-4750

Detroit St Peters Episcopal Church **P** (20) 1950 Trumbull St 48216-1529 (Mail to: 1950 Trumbull St 48216-1529) (313) 757-2985

Detroit Trinity Episcopal Church **P** (15) 1519 Martin Luther King Jr Bl 48208-2867 (Mail to: 1519 Martin Luther King Jr Bl 48208) Robert Smith (313) 964-3113

Dewitt Christ United St Annes **M** (26) 1000 W Webb Rd 48820-8396 (Mail to: 1000 W Webb Rd 48820-8396) (517) 669-9308

Dexter St James Episcopal Church **P** (84) 3279 Broad St 48130-1016 (Mail to: 3279 Broad St 48130-1016) Jenny Housner-Ritter Carol Mader (734) 426-8247

East Lansing All Saints Episcopal Church **P** (415) 800 Abbott Rd 48823-3103 (Mail to: 800 Abbot Rd 48823-3103) Katherine Carlson (517) 351-7160

East Lansing Cntbry at Michigan State Univ **CC** 800 Abbot Rd 48823-3103 (Mail to: C/O All Saints 800 Abbot Rd 48823-3194) Donna McNiel (517) 351-1885

Ecorse Church of the Resurrection **M** (26) 27085 W Outer Dr 48229-1282 (Mail to: 27085 W Outer Dr 48229-1282) (313) 382-1781

Farmington Trinity Episcopal Church **P** (198) 26880 La Muera St 48334-4614 (Mail to: 26880 La Muera St 48334-4614) Julia Huttar Bailey (248) 474-2860

Ferndale St Lukes Episcopal Church **P** (141) 540 W Lewiston Ave 48220-1204 (Mail to: 540 W Lewiston Ave 48220-1204) Clare Hickman (248) 677-1804

Grosse Ile St James Episcopal Church **P** (396) 25150 E River RD 48138-1789 (Mail to: 25150 E River RD 48138-1789) Philip Dinwiddie (734) 676-1727

Grosse Pointe Saint Michael's Church **P** (486) 20475 Sunningdale Park 48236-1637 (Mail to: 20475 Sunningdale Park Attn: Michael Rothgery 48236-1637) Michael Bradley (313) 884-4820

Grosse Pointe Farms Christ Church Grosse Pointe **P** (1447) 61 Grosse Pointe Blvd 48236-

3712 (Mail to: 61 Grosse Pointe Blvd 48236-3712) Thomas Van Culin Paul Spann (313) 885-4841

Hamburg St Stephens Episcopal Church **P** (78) 10585 Hamburg Rd 48139-1214 (Mail to: PO Box 436 48139-0436) James Pashturro (810) 231-3220

Hillsdale St Peters Episcopal Church **P** (27) 3 N Broad St 49242-1601 (Mail to: 3 N Broad St 49242-1601) (517) 437-2833

Howell St Johns Episcopal Church **P** (77) 504 Prospect St 48843-1440 (Mail to: 504 Prospect St 48843-1440) James Pashturro (517) 546-3660

Inkster St Clements Episcopal Church **P** (60) 4300 Harrison St 48141-2963 (Mail to: Attn: The Treasurer 4300 Harrison St 48141-2963) (734) 728-0790

Jackson St Pauls Episcopal Church **P** (372) 309 S Jackson St 49201-2214 (Mail to: Attn: Diane Billingsley 309 S Jackson St 49201-2214) (517) 787-3370

Lake Orion St Marys-in-the-Hills Epis Ch **P** (133) 2512 Joslyn Ct 48360-1938 (Mail to: Attn: Treasurer 2512 Joslyn Ct 48360-1938) (248) 391-0663

Lansing St Michael Episcopal Church **P** (86) 6500 Amwood Dr 48911-5955 (Mail to: 6500 Amwood Dr 48911-5955) Roger Walker (517) 882-9733

Lansing St Paul's Episcopal Church **P** (405) 218 W Ottawa St 48933-1309 (Mail to: 218 W Ottawa St 48933-1374) Karen Lewis Karen Lewis (517) 482-9454

Lincoln Park St Mics & All Angels Epis Ch **P** (219) 1325 Champaign Rd 48146-3302 (Mail to: 1325 Champaign Rd 48146-3302) (313) 382-5525

Livonia St Andrews Episcopal Church **P** (112) 16360 Hubbard St 48154-6100 (Mail to: 16360 Hubbard St 48154-6100) Daniel Lawson (734) 421-8451

Madison Hts St Patrick's Episcopal Church **P** (67) 1434 E 13 Mile Rd 48071-1515 (Mail to: 1434 E 13 Mile Rd 48071-1515) Linda Ferguson Paul Leclair Judith Marinco Vincent Marinco (248) 585-9591

Michigan Ctr St Aidans Episcopal Church **P** (29) 361 E Grove Ave 49254-1511 (Mail to: 361 E Grove Ave 49254-1511) (517) 764-2950

Milford St George's Episcopal Church **P** (122) 801 E Commerce St 48381-1727 (Mail to: 801 E Commerce St 48381-1727) Susan Williams (248) 684-0495

Monroe Trinity Episcopal Church **P** (59) 11 W 3rd St 48161-6536 (Mail to: 11 W 3rd St 48161-2340) (734) 242-3113

Mount Clemens Grace Episcopal Church **P** (151) 115 S Main St 48043-2379 (Mail to: Attn: Treasurer 115 S Main St 48043-2379) Steven Domienik (586) 465-4573

Novi Church of the Holy Cross **P** (118) 46200 W 10 Mile Rd 48374-3004 (Mail to: 40700 W 10 Mile Rd 48375-3510) Ian Twiss (248) 427-1175

Pleasant Lake Christ Church **P** (97) 9900 N Meridian Rd 49272-9630 (Mail to: 9900 N Meridian Rd 49272-9630) (517) 769-2333

Plymouth St Johns Episcopal Church **P** (314) 574 S Sheldon Rd 48170-1565 (Mail to: 574 S Sheldon Rd 48170-1565) (734) 453-0190

Pontiac All Saints Episcopal Church **P** (143) 171 W Pike St 48341-1750 (Mail to: PO Box 430357 48343-0357) Christopher Johnson (248) 334-4571

Rochester St Philips Episcopal Church **P** (187) 100 Romeo St. 48307-1557 (Mail to: 100 Romeo Rd 48307-1557) Eric Williams (248) 651-6188

Romeo St Pauls Episcopal Church **P** (64) 11100 W St Clair St 48065 (Mail to: PO Box 148 48065-0148) (586) 752-3212

Royal Oak St Johns Episcopal Church **P** (510) 26998 Woodward Ave 48067-0923 (Mail to: 26998 Woodward Ave 48067-0923) Gerardo Aponte-Safe Timothy Spannaus Marjorie Taylor (248) 546-1255

Saline Holy Faith Episcopal Church **M** (113) 6299 Saline Ann Arbor Rd 48176-8805 (Mail to: 6299 Saline Ann Arbor Rd 48176-8805) Donald Dersnah Andrea Martin (734) 429-2991

Southfield St Davids Episcopal Church **P** (612) 16200 W 12 Mile Rd 48076-2959 (Mail to: 16200 W 12 Mile Rd 48076-7357) Christopher Yaw (248) 557-5430

Southfield Episcopal Ch of the Redeemer **P** (76) 18140 Cornell Rd 48075-4146 (Mail to: 18140 Cornell Rd 48075-4146) (248) 569-4418

Southgate Grace Episcopal Church **P** (81) 15650 Reeck Rd 48195-3237 (Mail to: 15650 Reeck Rd 48195-3237) Lynda Carter (734) 285-0380

St Clair Shrs Trinity Episcopal Church **P** (66) 30205 Jefferson Ave 48082-1787 (Mail to: 30205 Jefferson Ave 48082-1787) (586) 294-0740

Trenton St Thomas Episcopal Church **M** (109) 2441 Nichols St 48183-2419 (Mail to: 2441 Nichols St 48183-2419) Maryjane Peck (734) 676-3122

Troy St Stephen's Episcopal Church **P** (295) 5500 N Adams Rd 48098-2399 (Mail to: 5500 N Adams Rd 48098-2399) Brian Alberti (248) 6418080

Utica St Lukes Episcopal Church **P** (35) 7700 22 Mile Rd 48317-2312 (Mail to: 7700 22 Mile Rd 48317-2312) (586) 731-1221

Van Buren Twp Trinity Episcopal Church **P** (162) § 11575 Belleville Rd 48111-2401 (Mail to: 11575 Belleville Rd 48111-2401) Alice Sawyer (734) 699-3361

Waterford St Andrews Episcopal Church **P** (188) 5301 Hatchery Rd 48329-3440 (Mail to: 5301 Hatchery Rd 48329-3440) (248) 673-7635

West Bloomfield Spirit of Grace **P** (166) 2399 Figa Ave 48324-1808 (Mail to: 2399 Figa Ave 48324-1808) Stephen Bancroft (248) 338-3505

Westland St Johns Episcopal Church **P** (82) 555 S Wayne Rd 48186-4301 (Mail to: 555 S Wayne Rd 48186-4301) (734) 721-5023

Williamston Saint Katherine's Church **P** (113) 4650 Meridian Rd 48895-9317 (Mail to: 4650 Meridian Rd # Rt 48895-9317) (517) 349-4120

Wyandotte St Stephens Episcopal Church **P** (211) 2803 1st St 48192-5113 (Mail to: 2803 1st St 48192-5113) Andrea Morrow (734) 284-8777

Ypsilanti St Lukes Episcopal Church **P** (279) 120 North Huron St. 48197-2610 (Mail to: 120 N Huron St 48197-2610) Elizabeth Scriven (734) 483-4253

EPISCOPAL CHURCH IN MICRONESIA

Under the jurisdiction of the Presiding Bishop
BISHOP'S OFFICE The Episcopal Church in Hawaii 229 Queen Emma Square Honolulu HI 96813
TEL (808) 536-7776 FAX (808) 538-7194 WEB www.episcopalhawaii.org; episcopalmicronesia.org/guam/
LOCAL ADMINISTRATIVE OFFICES 911 N Marine Dr Tamuning GU 96913-4302
TEL (671) 649-0690 FAX (671) 649-0690

Previous Bishops—
HS Kennedy 1957-69, L Hanchett 1969, EL Browning
1969-71, L Hanchett 1971-75, EL Browning 1975-78,
CL Burgreen 1978-86, JF Ashby 1986-87, DP Hart
1987-94, CL Keyser 1994-99, GE Packard 1999-2009

Bishop-in-charge—Rt Rev RL Fitzpatrick (1015)

Archdcn Ven Irene Egmalis Maliaman

MISSIONS AND CLERGY

Saipan St Pauls Episcopal Church **M** (42) Gualo
Rai Middle Rd 96950 (Mail: PO Box 506610
Saipan MP 96950-4339) (670) 233-6081
Tamuning Epis Ch of St John the Divine **M** (60)
§ 911 N Marine Corps Dr 96913-4302 (Mail:
911 N Marine Corps Dr Tamuning GU 96913-
4302) Dcn Lisa Pang Irene Maliaman (671)
646-1708

DIOCESE OF MILWAUKEE

(PROVINCE V)
Comprises Southern Wisconsin
DIOCESAN OFFICE 804 E Juneau Ave Milwaukee WI 53202-2798
TEL (414) 272-3028 FAX (866) 499-1973
E-MAIL info@diomil.org WEB www.diomil.org

Previous Bishops—
Jackson Kemper 1854-70, Wm
E Armitage coadj 1866 Bp 1870-
73, Edward R Welles 1874-88,
Cyrus F Knight 1889-91, Isaac
L Nicholson 1891-1906, Wm
W Webb 1906-33, Benj FP
Ivins coadj 1925 Bp 1933-53,
Donald HV Hallock coadj 1952
Bp 1953-73, Charles T Gaskell
coadj 1973 Bp 1974-85, Roger
White coadj 1984 Bp 1984-03, Steven A Miller Bp
2003-20, Jeffrey Lee Bp Prov 2021

Financial Controller C Senn; *CN for Min* Rev S
Leannah; *Treas* M Weber; *Chanc* M Ehrmann; *Vice
Chanc* E Orelup; *Hist* Dr R Miller

Stand Comm—Cler: Pres J Troutman-Miller T
Garner D Mowers M Skoglund; *Lay:* G Bell M White
Sec M Done J Watter

PARISHES, MISSIONS, AND CLERGY

Baraboo Trinity Episcopal Church **P** (117) 111
6th St 53913-2157 (Mail to: 111 6th St 53913-
2177) David Mowers (608) 356-3620
Beaver Dam St Marks Episcopal Church **P** (69)
700 E Mill St 53916-2435 (Mail to: PO Box 126
53916-0126) Michael Tess (920) 885-3536
Beloit St Pauls Episcopal Church **P** (87) 212 W
Grand Ave 53511-6109 (Mail to: 212 W Grand
Ave 53511-6193) Gregg Schneider (608) 362-
4312

Burlington Church of St John the Divine **P** (86)
216 E Chandler Blvd 53105-1901 (Mail to:
216 E Chandler Blvd 53105-1901) Matthew
Buterbaugh (262) 763-7482
Delafield St John Chrysostom Church **P** (87)
1111 Genesee St 53018-1411 (Mail to: PO Box
180082 53018-0082) (262) 646-2727
Delavan Christ Church **P** (80) 503 E Walworth
Ave 53115-1209 (Mail to: PO Box 528 53115-
0528) Pedro Lara William Pelnar Marlyne
Seymour (262) 728-5292
Dousman Saint Mary's Episcopal Church **P** (179)
36014 Sunset Dr 53118 (Mail to: PO Box 126
53118-0126) Philippa Lindwright Charles
Zellermayer (262) 965-3924
Elkhorn St Johns in the Wilderness **P** (36) 13 S
Church St 53121-1707 (Mail to: 13 S Church
St 53121-1707) (262) 723-4229
Fort Atkinson St Peters Episcopal Church **P**
(80) 302 Merchants Ave 53538-2248 (Mail
to: 302 Merchants Ave 53538-2248) Melinda
Valentine Davis (920) 563-3889
Greendale St Thomas Of Canterbury Church **P**
(162) 7255 W Grange Ave 53129-1132 (Mail
to: PO Box 342 53129-0342) Melesa Skoglund
Margaret Kiss (414) 421-0130
Hartford St Aidans Episcopal Church **SC** (170)
670 E Monroe Ave 53027-2574 (Mail to: Attn:
Treasurer 670 E Monroe Ave 53027-2574)
Esther Kramer (262) 673-7273
Hartland St Anskar's Episcopal Church **P** (78)
N48w31340 State Road 83 53029-8500 (Mail

to: N48w31340 State Road 83 53029-8500) Thomas Buchan (262) 367-2439

Janesville Trinity Episcopal Church **P** (319) 419 E Court St 53545-4009 (Mail to: 409 E Court St 53545-4009) Kathleen Lutes (608) 754-3402

Kenosha Saint Matthew's Church **P** (224) 5900 7th Ave 53140-4133 (Mail to: 5900 7th Ave 53140-4162) (262) 605-5526

Lake Geneva Church of the Holy Communion **P** (97) § 320 Broad St 53147-1812 (Mail to: 320 Broad St 53147-1812) Elizabeth Meade (262) 248-3522

Madison Grace Episcopal Church **P** (450) 116 W Washington Ave 53703-2740 (Mail to: Attn: Financial Administrator 116 W Washington Ave Ste 1 53703-2740) Dale Grieser Margaret Irwin John Maher Carol Smith (608) 255-5147

Madison St Andrews Episcopal Church **P** (389) 1833 Regent St 53726-4119 (Mail to: 1833 Regent St 53726-4198) Andrew Jones (608) 233-3249

Madison St Dunstans Episcopal Church **P** (283) 6205 University Ave 53562 (Mail to: 6205 University Ave 53705-1056) Miranda Hassett (608) 238-2781

Madison St Lukes Church **P** (119) 4011 Major Ave 53716-1133 (Mail to: 4011 Major Ave 53716-1133) Donald Fleischman (608) 222-6921

Menomonee Falls St Francis Episcopal Church **P** (76) N84 W16525 Menomonee Ave. 53051 (Mail to: PO Box 194 53052-0194) Stephen Capitelli (262) 251-7420

Mequon St Boniface Episcopal Church **P** (384) 3906 W Mequon Rd 53092-2728 (Mail to: 3906 W Mequon Rd 53092-2799) Terrance Garner (262) 242-2994

✠ **Milwaukee** All Saints Cathedral **O** (231) 818 E Juneau Ave 53202-2714 (Mail to: 818 E Juneau Ave 53202-2714) Kevin Carroll Theodore Parks (414) 271-7719

Milwaukee Christ Church Episcopal **P** (571) 5655 N Lake Dr 53217-4849 (Mail to: 5655 N Lake Dr 53217-4849) Thomas Binder Oswald Bwechwa Seth Dietrich (414) 964-3368

Milwaukee St Christophers Church **P** (342) 7845 N River Rd 53217-3025 (Mail to: 7845 N River Rd 53217-3025) Geoffrey Ward (414) 352-0380

Milwaukee St Lukes Episcopal Church **P** (130) 3200 S Herman St 53207-2852 (Mail to: 3200 S Herman St 53207-2899) Jason Lavann (414) 744-3736

Milwaukee St Marks Episcopal Church **P** (221) 2618 N Hackett Ave 53211-3832 (Mail to: 2618 N Hackett Ave 53211-3832) Ian Burch (414) 962-0500

Milwaukee St Pauls Church **P** (219) 914 E Knapp St 53202-2825 (Mail to: 914 E Knapp St 53202-2898) Lane Hensley Sheila Scott (414) 276-6277

Milwaukee St Peters Episcopal Church **P** (109) 7929 W Lincoln Ave 53219-1752 (Mail to: 7929 W Lincoln Ave 53219-1752) Karen Buker Theodore Parks (414) 543-6040

Milwaukee Trinity Church **P** (442) 1717 Church St 53213-2105 (Mail to: 1717 Church St 53213-2199) Gary Manning Kevin Stewart (414) 453-4540

Mineral Point Trinity Church **P** (31) 409 High St 53565-1220 (Mail to: 403 High St 53565-1220) John Hector (608) 987-3019

Monroe St Andrews Episcopal Church **P** (13) 2810 6th St 53566-1901 (Mail to: 2810 6th St 53566-1901) (608) 328-8265

North Lake St Peters Episcopal Church **P** (37) W314n7412 Hwy 83 53064 (Mail to: PO Box 267 53064-0267) (262) 966-7312

Oconomowoc St Pauls Episcopal Church **P** (49) N982 County Road P 53066-9517 (Mail to N982 County Road P 53066-9517) Thomas Holtzen (920) 355-1006

Oconomowoc Zion Episcopal Church **P** (100) 135 Rockwell St 53066-2854 (Mail to: 135 Rockwell St 53066-2896) Scott Seefeldt (262) 567-7507

Pewaukee St Bartholomews Episcopal Ch **P** (132) N27W24000 Paul Ct 53072-6239 (Mail to N27W24000 Paul Ct 53072-6239) Joel Prather (262) 691-0836

Platteville Trinity Episcopal Church **P** (23) 250 Market St 53818-2543 (Mail to: 250 Market S 53818-2543) (608) 348-6402

Port Washington St Simon the Fisherman Epi Ch **SC** (62) 3448 Green Bay Rd 53074-9765 (Mail to: PO Box 34 53074-0034) Julian Hill (262) 284-0510

Portage St John the Baptist Epis Ch **P** (26) 211 W Pleasant St 53901-1744 (Mail to: 201 W Pleasant St 53901-1744) (608) 742-6054

Prairie Du Chien Church of the Holy Trinity **P** (16) 220 S Michigan St 53821-1713 (Mail to: PO Box 365 53821-0365) Carson Culver (608) 326-6085

Racine St Lukes Episcopal Church **P** (125) 61 Main St 53403-1210 (Mail to: 614 Main S 53403-1210) (262) 634-5025

Racine St Michaels Episcopal Church **P** (294) 4701 Erie St 53402-2513 (Mail to: 4701 Erie St 53402-2513) Lars Skoglund (262) 639-2502

Richland Ctr St Barnabas Episcopal Church **P** (70) 297 N Main St 53581-2240 (Mail to: PO Box 487 53581-0487) (608) 649-6003

S Milwaukee St Marks Church **P** (97) 1314 Rawson Ave 53172-1939 (Mail to: 1314 Rawson Ave 53172-1939) (414) 762-1772

Sun Prairie Church of the Good Shepherd (59) 3416 Swansee Ridge 53590 (Mail to: 341 Swansee Rdg 53590-9495) Donald Fleischman (608) 837-3308

Sussex St Albans Episcopal Church **P** (89) W23 N5924 Maple Ave 53089 (Mail to: PO Box 20 53089-0202) Stephen Capitelli (262) 246-443

Watertown St Pauls Episcopal Church **P** (70) 413 S 2nd St 53094-4420 (Mail to: 413 S 2nd St 53094-4420) Monica Burkert-Brist William Dunlop (920) 261-1150

Waukesha St Matthias Episcopal Church **P** (414) 111 E Main St 53186 (Mail to: Attn: Sandra Krueger PO Box 824 53187-0824) David Simmons Richard Fox (262) 547-4838

West Bend St James Episcopal Church **P** (150) 148 S 8th Ave 53095-3207 (Mail to: 148 S 8th Ave 53095-3207) Benjamin Hankinson (262) 334-4242

Wisconsin Dells Holy Cross Episcopal Church **P** (62) 322 Unity Dr 53965-9761 (Mail to: 322 Unity Dr 53965-9761) Michael Caldwell Kenneth Foster (608) 254-8623

DIOCESE OF MINNESOTA
(PROVINCE VI)
Comprises the State of Minnesota
DIOCESAN OFFICE 1101 W Broadway, Minneapolis MN 55411
TEL (612) 871-5311; In MN (800) 596-3839
E-MAIL info@episcopalmn.org WEB www.episcopalmn.org

Previous Bishops— Henry B Whipple 1859-1901, Mahlon N Gilbert coadj 1886 1900, Samuel C Edsall 1901-17, Frank A Mc Elwain suffr 1912 Bp 1917-43, Benj T Kemerer suffr 1944-48, Stephen E Keeler coadj 1931 Bp 1944-56, Hamilton H Kellogg coadj 1952 Bp 1956-70, Philip F McNairy suffr 1958 coadj 1968 Bp 1971-78, Robert M Anderson 1978 93, Sanford ZK Hampton suffr 1989-95, James L Jelinek 1993-2010, Brian N Prior 2010-20

Bishop—Rt Rev Craig William Loya (1132) (Dio 6 June 2020)

Miss for Min Cn K Olson; *Miss for Comm Engagement* R Babbitt; *Miss for Indian Work and Multicultural Min* Rev Cn R Two Bulls; *Miss for Children, Yth, and Camp* S Barnett; *Miss for Form* Rev S Daughtry; *Miss for Admin* E Chelgren; *Miss for Comm* K Schuster; *Miss for Fin* J Gamberg; *Miss for the Bp* J Ricardo; *Miss for Networking* S Stevenson

Stand Comm—Cler: D Anderson A Arthur B Pogue S Hustad R Scarpace D Brown; *Lay:* J New-Landrum R Simons A Roy L Bathke S Grove C Commers

PARISHES, MISSIONS, AND CLERGY

Aitkin St Johns Church **M** (10) 222 1st St SE 56431-1706 (Mail to: 417 1st Ave SW 56431-1818) (218) 927-6040

Albert Lea Christ Church **P** (52) 204 W Fountain St 56007-2406 (Mail to: 204 W Fountain St 56007-2446) Henry Doyle (507) 373-3188

Alexandria Emmanuel Episcopal Church **P** (40) PO Box 231 56308-0231 (Mail to: PO Box 231 56308-0231) Thomas Sinning (320) 763-3201

Annandale St Marks Church **SC** 10536 108th St NW 55302-2912 (Mail to: 10536 108th St NW 55302-2912) (320) 230-6337

Anoka Trinity Episcopal Church **P** (313) 1415 6th Ave 55303-5250 (Mail to: 1415 6th Ave 55303-5250) Phillip Boelter (763) 421-1196

Austin Christ Episcopal Church **P** (108) 301 3rd Ave NW 55912-3023 (Mail to: 301 3rd Ave NW 55912-3023) John Sullivan (507) 433-3782

Bagley St Philips Church **M** (186) 16101 290th St 56621-4980 (Mail to: C/O Rev Lisa White Smith PO Box 8 56566-0008) (218) 358-0723

Bemidji St Bartholomews Episcopal Ch **M** (45) 1800 Irvine Ave NW 56601-2552 (Mail to: 1800 Irvine Ave NW 56601-2552) (218) 444-6831

Brainerd St Pauls Church **P** (63) 408 N 7th St 56401-3019 (Mail to: 408 N 7th St 56401-3019) (218) 829-3834

Burnsville Episcopal Ch of the Nativity **P** (394) 15601 Maple Island Rd 55306-5541 (Mail to: 15601 Maple Island Rd 55306-5541) Dana Strande (952) 435-8687

Cannon Falls Church of the Redeemer **P** (17) 123 3rd St N 55009-2012 (Mail to: PO Box 122 55009) (507) 263-3469

Cass Lake St Peters Church **M** (62) 301 Cedar Ave NW 56633 (Mail to: PO Box 222 56633-0222) (218) 536-0834

Chatfield St Matthew Episcopal Church **P** (19) 100 Fillmore St SE 55923-1219 (Mail to: 114 Valley St SE 55923-1429) Alice Applequist (507) 867-3707

Detroit Lakes St Lukes Episcopal Church **P** (101) 1400 Corbett Rd 56501-4508 (Mail to: C/O Treasurer PO Box 868 56502-0868) (218) 847-5858

Duluth St Andrews by the Lake **M** (124) 2802 Minnesota Ave 55802-2526 (Mail to: 2802 Minnesota Ave 55802-2526) (218) 727-1262

Duluth St Pauls Episcopal Church **P** (536) 1710 E Superior St 55812-2045 (Mail to: 1710 E Superior St 55812-2045) Margaret Nancarrow Patricia Benson (218) 724-3535

Edina St Albans Episcopal Church **P** (369) 6716 Gleason Rd 55439-1130 (Mail to: 6716

Gleason Rd 55439-1130) John Peters (952) 941-3065

Elk River Holy Trinity Episcopal Church **P** (111) 1326 4th St 55330-1809 (Mail to: PO Box 65 1326 4th Street NW 55330-0065) (763) 441-5482

Ely St Mary's Church **M** (34) 715 S. Central Avenue 55731-0513 (Mail to: PO Box 513 55731-0513) (218) 365-4914

Excelsior Trinity Episcopal Church **P** (491) 221 Center St 55331-1817 (Mail to: 322 2nd St 55331-1893) Devon Anderson (952) 474-5263

Fairmont St Martins Episcopal Church **P** (43) 102 N Park St 56031-2822 (Mail to: 102 N Park St 56031-2822) Marilla Whitney (507) 238-2686

✠ **Faribault** Cathd of Our Merciful Saviour **O** (129) PO Box 816 515 2nd Ave NW 55021-0816 (Mail to: PO Box 816 55021-0816) James Zotalis (507) 334-7732

Farmington Church of the Advent **P** (23) 412 Oak St 55024-1326 (Mail to: 412 Oak St 55024-1326) (651) 460-6636

Fergus Falls St James Episcopal Church **P** (78) 321 S Lakeside Dr 56537-2219 (Mail to: 321 S Lakeside Dr 56537-2219) (218) 736-6736

Frontenac Christ Episcopal Church **M** (52) 29036 Westervelt Ave Way 55026-0058 (Mail to: PO Box 58 55026-0058) (651) 345-5986

Grand Marais Spirit of the Wilderness **M** (95) 121 Maple Hill Dr 55604 (Mail to: PO Box 1115 55604-1115) Mary Ashcroft Carolyn Schmidt (218) 387-1536

Grand Rapids Christ Episcopal Church **P** (87) 520 N Pokegama Ave 55744-2646 (Mail to: 520 N Pokegama Ave 55744-2646) (218) 326-6279

Hastings St Lukes Episcopal Church **P** (109) 615 Vermillion St 55033-1939 (Mail to: PO Box 155 55033-0155) Elizabeth Herman Robert Langenfeld Darcy Valentine Franklin Van De Steeg (651) 437-9855

Hastings St Mary's Afton-Basswood Grove **P** (58) § 8435 Saint Croix Trl S 55033-9495 (Mail to: PO Box 362 55001-0362) Scott Monson (651) 338-5364

Hermantown Trinity Episcopal Church **M** (55) 4903 Maple Grove Rd 55811-1446 (Mail to: 4903 Maple Grove Rd 55811-1446) Cheryl Harder David Hill (218) 729-7957

Hibbing St James Episcopal Church **P** (33) 2028 7th Ave E 55746-1706 (Mail to: 2028 7th Ave E 55746-1706) Sally Maxwell (218) 263-5764

Intl Falls Holy Trinity Episcopal Church **P** (83) 820 4th St 56649-2213 (Mail to: PO Box 170 56649-0170) (218) 283-8606

Kasson St Peter's Episcopal Church **P** (70) 101 1st St NE 55944-1419 (Mail to: PO Box 205 55944-0205) (507) 634-6081

Lake City St Marks Episcopal Church **P** (50) 110 S Oak St 55041-1629 (Mail to: 112 S Oak St 55041-1629) (651) 345-2674

Litchfield Trinity Episcopal Church **P** (17) 3 E 4th St 55355-2121 (Mail to: 3 E 4th St 55355-2121) (320) 693-6035

Mankato St Johns Episcopal Church **P** (52) Warren & Broad St 56002 (Mail to: PO Box 1119 56002-1119) Cynthia Brickson (507) 388-1969

Marshall St James Episcopal Church **P** (44) 101 N 5th St 56258-1303 (Mail to: 101 N 5th St 56258-1303) Marilyn Leach (507) 532-6632

Minneapolis All Sts Epis Indian Mission **M** (170) 3044 Longfellow Ave 55407-1811 (Mail to: 3044 Longfellow Ave 55407-1811) James Shoulak (612) 722-2342

✠ **Minneapolis** Cathedral Church of St Mark **O** (691) 519 Oak Grove St 55403-3230 (Mail to: 519 Oak Grove St 55403-3270) Paul Lebens Englund Siri Hustad Timothy Kingsley Neptali Rodriguez Espinel (612) 870-7800

Minneapolis Church of the Epiphany **P** (307) 4900 Nathan Ln N 55442-3156 (Mail to: 4900 Nathan Ln N 55442-3156) Alissa Smith (763) 5593144

Minneapolis Gethsemane Church **M** (30) 905 Fourth Avenue South 55404-1093 (Mail to: 905 4th Ave S 55404-1020) (612) 332-5407

Minneapolis Holy Trinity - St Anskars Ch **P** (47) 1808 Riverside Ave 55454-1022 (Mail to: 1219 University Ave SE # 309 55414-2038) (612) 331-1544

Minneapolis St Andrews Episcopal Church **P** (187) 1832 James Ave N 55411-3164 (Mail to: PO Box 11745 55411-0745) (612) 529-1320

Minneapolis St James on the Parkway **P** (76) 3225 E Minnehaha Pkwy 55417-1431 (Mail to: 3225 E Minnehaha Pkwy 55417-1431) (612) 724-3425

Minneapolis St John the Baptist Epis Ch **P** (566) 4201 Sheridan Ave S 55410-1618 (Mail to: 4201 Sheridan Ave S 55410-1618) Lisa Wiens Heinsohn (612) 922-0396

Minneapolis Saint Luke's Church **P** (386) 4557 Colfax Ave S 55419-4736 (Mail to: 4557 Colfax Ave S 55419-4736) Susan Daughtry (612) 824-2697

Minneapolis St Nicholas Episcopal Church **P** (134) 7227 Penn Ave S 55423-2820 (Mail to: Treasurer 7227 Penn Ave S 55423-2899) Julie Luna (612) 869-7551

Minneapolis St Pauls Episcopal Church **P** (150) 1917 Logan Ave S 55403-2856 (Mail to: 1917 Logan Ave S Ste 1 55403-2899) Ramona Scarpace (612) 377-1273

Minneapolis St Stephen the Martyr Church **P** (908) 4439 W 50th St 55424-1327 (Mail to: 4439 W 50th St 55424-1399) Thomas Cook (952) 920-0595

Minneapolis St George's Episcopal Church **P** (238) 5224 Minnetonka Blvd 55416-2104 (Mail to: 5224 Minnetonka Blvd 55416-2104) Thomas Gehlsen Diane Mcgowan (952) 926-1646

Minnetonka The Epis Parish of St David **P** (293) 13000 Saint Davids Rd 55305-4119 (Mail to: 13000 Saint Davids Rd 55305-4119) Katherine Lewis Leonard Freeman Lindsay Freeman Katherine Lewis (952) 935-3336

Moose Lake St Andrews Episcopal Church **M** (13) 114 Elm Ave 55767-0840 (Mail to: PO Box P 55767) (218) 485-4945

Morton Bishop Whipple Mission **M** (313) 38378 Reservation Highway 101 56270-1272 (Mail to: PO Box 369 56270-0369) David Sams (507) 697-6433

Naytahwaush Samuel Memorial Church **M** (98) 36 Church Street 56566 (Mail to: PO Box 8 56566-0008) (218) 935-2192

Northfield All Saints Episcopal Church **P** (146) 419 Washington St 55057-2028 (Mail to: PO Box 663 550570663) Cody Maynus (507) 645-7417

Owatonna St Pauls Episcopal Church **P** (280) 222 S Cedar Ave 55060-2915 (Mail to: 220 S Cedar Ave 55060-2915) Steven Judd Michael Tippett (507) 451-5319

Park Rapids Trinity Church **M** (43) 212 Court Avenue 56470-0262 (Mail to: PO Box 262 56470-0262) (218) 732-4393

Ponsford Breck Memorial Mission **M** (62) PO Box 141 56575-0141 (Mail to: PO Box 8 56566-0008) (218) 255-1535

Red Lake St John in the Wilderness **M** (25) 15341 St Marys Mission Rd 56671 (Mail to: PO Box 54 56671-0054) (218) 679-4330

Red Wing Christ Episcopal Church **P** (236) 321 West Ave 55066-2250 (Mail to: 321 West Ave 55066-2250) Barbara Von Haaren (651) 388-0411

Redby St Antipas Episcopal Church **M** (46) 19050 State Highway 1 56670 (Mail to: PO Box 273 56670-0273) (218) 679-3900

Rochester Calvary Episcopal Church **P** (590) 111 3rd Ave SW 55902-3150 (Mail to: 111 3rd Ave SW 55902-3198) Virginia Royalty (507) 282-9429

Rochester St Lukes Episcopal Church **P** (241) 1884 22nd St NW 55901-0618 (Mail to: 1884 22nd St NW 55901-0618) Justin Chapman (507) 288-2469

Rushford Emmanuel Episcopal Church **P** (70) 217 W Jessie St 55971-9103 (Mail to: PO Box 443 55971-0443) (507) 864-2164

Saint Cloud St Johns Episcopal Church **P** (140) 1111 Cooper Ave S 56301-4829 (Mail to: 1111 Cooper Ave S 56301-4829) Priscilla Gray (320) 251-8524

Saint Paul Christ Church Episcopal Parish **P** (487) 7305 Afton Rd 55125-1501 (Mail to: 7305 Afton Rd 55125-1501) Anna Doherty (651) 735-8790

Saint Paul Church of the Holy Apostles **M** (1013) 2200 Minnehaha Ave 55119-3932 (Mail to: 2200 Minnehaha Ave E 55119-3999) Cher Lor (651) 735-3016

Saint Paul Church of the Epiphany **P** (16) Attn: Kenneth Johnson Treasurer 1636 Van Buren Ave 55104-1818 (Mail to: Attn: Kenneth Johnson Treasurer 1636 Van Buren Ave 55104-1818) (612) 645-4466

Saint Paul Holy Trinity Episcopal Church **P** (103) 1636 Van Buren Ave 55104-1818 (Mail to: 1636 Van Buren Ave 55104-1818) Lawrence Bussey (651) 228-0930

Saint Paul La Mision El Santo Nino Jesus **M** (190) 463 Maria Ave 55106-4428 (Mail to: 463 Maria Ave 55106-4428) Neptali Rodriguez Espinel (651) 295-7481

Saint Paul Messiah Episcopal Church **P** (385) 1631 Ford Pkwy 55116-2130 (Mail to: 1631 Ford Pkwy 55116-2130) Christina Boehm Carlson David Langille (651) 698-2590

Saint Paul St Annes Episcopal Church **P** (213) 2035 Charlton Rd 55118-4704 (Mail to: 2035 Charlton Rd 55118-4704) Jennifer McNally (651) 455-9449

Saint Paul St Christophers Episcopal Ch **P** (284) 2300 Hamline Ave N 55113-4200 (Mail to: C/O Ruth Thillen 2300 Hamline Ave N 55113-4200) Randy Johnson Janet Macnally (651) 633-4589

Saint Paul St Clements Episcopal Church **P** (489) 901 Portland Ave 55104-7032 (Mail to: 901 Portland Ave 55104-7032) Joy Caires (651) 228-1164

Saint Paul St John in the Wilderness Epis **P** (607) 2175 1st St 55110-3462 (Mail to: 2175 1st St 55110-3488) Arthur Hancock (651) 429-5351

Saint Paul St John the Evangelist Epis Ch **P** (443) 60 Kent St 55102-2232 (Mail to: 60 Kent St 55102-2232) Jered Weber-Johnson Craig Lemming (651) 228-1172

Saint Paul St Mary Episcopal Church **P** (381) 1895 Laurel Ave 55104-5938 (Mail to: 1895 Laurel Ave 55104-5998) (651) 646-6175

Saint Paul St Matthews Episcopal Church **P** (382) 2136 Carter Ave 55108-1708 (Mail to: 2136 Carter Ave 55108-1708) Dwight Zscheile (651) 645-3058

Saint Paul Sts Martha & Mary Church **M** (81) 4180 Lexington Ave S 55123-1534 (Mail to: 4180 Lexington Ave S 55123-1534) Bruce Henne Alfred Hopwood (651) 681-0219

Saint Peter Church of the Holy Communion **HC** (103) 118 North Minnesota Ave 56082-2412 (Mail to: PO Box 176 56082-0176) (507) 934-2542

Sauk Centre Church of the Good Samaritan **P** (18) 529 Main St S 56378-1510 (Mail to: PO Box 205 56378-0205) (320) 352-6882

Stillwater Ascension Episcopal Church **P** (604) 214 3rd St N 55082-4806 (Mail to: 215 4th St N 55082-4806) George Mcdonnell (651) 439-2609

Virginia Sts John & Paul Episcopal Ch **P** 231 3rd St S 55792-2619 (Mail to: PO Box 376 55792-0376) (218) 741-1379

Wabasha Grace Memorial Church **P** (119) 936 Gambia Ave 55981-1011 (Mail to: 205 3rd St E 55981-1401) (651) 565-4827

Wadena St Helens Episcopal Church **M** (34) 22 Dayton Ave SW 56482-1450 (Mail to: PO Box 311 56482-0311) (218) 583-2206

Walker Saint Johns Episcopal Church **M** (59) PO Box 1192 8819 Onigum Rd NW 56484-1192 (Mail to: PO Box 1192 56484-2673) (218) 547-2570

Warroad St Peters Church **M** (27) PO Box 117 56763-0875 (Mail to: PO Box 875 56763-0875) (218) 386-4334

Waterville St Andrews Episcopal Church **P** (27) 210 Lake St W 56096-1320 (Mail to: 208 Lake St W 56096-1320) (507) 720-5251

Wayzata St Edward the Confessor Epis Ch **P** (102) 865 Ferndale Road N 55391-1011 (Mail to: 865 Ferndale Rd N 55391-1011) Aron Kramer (952) 473-2262

Wayzata Ch of St Martins by the Lake **P** (435) 2801 Westwood Rd S 55391-9787 (Mail to: PO Box 38 55361-0038) Jeffrey Hupf (952) 4718429

Welch Church of the Messiah **M** (96) 1760 Chakya St 55089-9416 (Mail to: 21449 County 18 Blvd 55089-6402) Martin Balfe (612) 388-7531

White Earth Saint Columba **M** (102) 26094 370th Street 56591-0388 (Mail to: PO Box 388 56591-0388) (218) 935-0259

Windom Church of the Good Shepherd **P** (18) 453 10th St 56101-1407 (Mail to: PO Box 69 56101-0069) (507) 831-1797

Winona St Pauls Episcopal Church **P** (84) 265 Lafayette St 55987-3535 (Mail to: 265 Lafayette St 55987-3535) Jonathan Spinillo Grzywa (507) 452-5355

DIOCESE OF MISSISSIPPI
(PROVINCE IV)
Comprises the State of Mississippi
DIOCESAN OFFICE 118 N Congress St PO Box 23107 Jackson 39225-3107
TEL (601) 948-5954 FAX (601) 354-3401
E-MAIL info@dioms.org WEB www.dioms.org

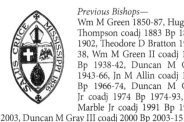

Previous Bishops—
Wm M Green 1850-87, Hugh M Thompson coadj 1883 Bp 1887-1902, Theodore D Bratton 1903-38, Wm M Green II coadj 1919 Bp 1938-42, Duncan M Gray 1943-66, Jn M Allin coadj 1961 Bp 1966-74, Duncan M Gray Jr coadj 1974 Bp 1974-93, AC Marble Jr coadj 1991 Bp 1993-2003, Duncan M Gray III coadj 2000 Bp 2003-15

Bishop—Rt Rev Brian R. Seage (1085) (Dio 8 Feb 2015)

Cn to Ord Rev P Stephens; *Sec* Rev B Ponder; *Treas* M Calcote; *Cn Adm & Fin* Rev B Ponder; *Reg* P Jones; *Chanc* G Tate; *V Chanc* R Ireland and C Ketner; *Chm Fin* B Howard; *Ecum* Rev Dr. J Switzer; *Yth Adv* W Robinson

Stand Comm—Cler: C Duncan J Deaton J Burnett B Robertson; *Lay:* M Baria A Gwin T Bowie Goodman J Woodrick

PARISHES, MISSIONS, AND CLERGY

Aberdeen St Johns Episcopal Church **M** (121) 402 W Commerce St 39730-2523 (Mail to: PO Box 54 39730-0054) (662) 369-4854

Batesville St Stephens Episcopal Church **P** 113 Panola Ave 38606-2121 (Mail to: C/O Rev S Walley - St Peters 113 S 9th St 38655-3916) (662) 526-5166

Bay Saint Louis Christ Church **P** (160) 912 S Beach Blvd 39520-4105 (Mail to: 912 S Beach Blvd 39520-4105) Tucker Dawson (228) 467-7757

Belzoni Mission of St Thomas **M** (18) 210 Castleman St 39038-3924 (Mail to: PO Box 401 39038-0401) (662) 746-5082

Biloxi Church of the Redeemer **P** (341) 1904 Popps Ferry Rd 39532-2125 (Mail to: 1904 Popps Ferry Rd 39532-2125) Christopher Robinson (228) 594-2100

Bolton St Mary Episcopal Church **P** (8) 209 E Madison St 39041 (Mail to: 900 First North St 39183-2616) (601) 209-8044

Brandon St Lukes Church **P** (148) 104 N College St 39042-3180 (Mail to: PO Box 1899 39043-1899) Gates Elliott (601) 825-5839

Brandon St Peters by the Lake **P** (257) 1954 Spillway Rd 39047-6064 (Mail to: PO Box 5026 39047-5026) Carol Mead Roy Wilson (601) 992-2691

Brookhaven Church of the Redeemer **P** (210) 230 W Monticello St 39601-3204 (Mail to: PO Box 804 39602-0804) William Mclarty (601) 833-7399

Canton Grace Episcopal Church **P** (136) 161 E Peace St 39046-4519 (Mail to: PO Box 252 161 E Peace St 39046-0252) Elizabeth Foose (601) 859-2680

Carrollton Mission of Grace **M** (23) Washington St 38917 (Mail to: Washington 38917) (601) 445-8432

Clarksdale St Georges Episcopal Church **P** (181) 106 Sharkey Ave 38614-4402 (Mail to: 106 Sharkey Ave 38614-4402) Charles Deaton (662) 627-7875

Cleveland Calvary Episcopal Church **P** (163) 409 S Court St 38732 (Mail to: 107 S Victoria Ave 38732-3231) Julia Moore (662) 843-5964

Clinton Epis Church of the Creator **P** (107) 1445 Clinton Raymond Rd 39056-5443 (Mail to: 1445 Clinton Raymond Rd 39056-5443) (601) 924-2261

Collins St Elizabeths Mission **M** (18) 1200 S 4th St 39428 (Mail to: PO Box 652 39428-0652) (601) 765-6809

Columbia St Stephens Episcopal Church **M** (77) 1300 Church St 39429-3128 (Mail to: PO Box 761 39429-0761) (601) 736-5496

Columbus St Pauls Episcopal Church **P** (350) § 318 College St 39701-5701 (Mail to: 318 College St 39701-5701) Jason Shelby (662) 328-6673

Columbus Epis Ch of the Good Shepherd **M** (120) 321 Forrest Blvd 39702-5313 (Mail to: PO Box 2023 39704-2023) (662) 327-1953

Como Holy Innocents Epis Church **M** (69) 311 N Main St 38619-7305 (Mail to: PO Box 391 38619-0391) (662) 526-5166

Corinth St Pauls Episcopal Church **P** (80) 250 Highway 2 NE 38834-6906 (Mail to: PO Box 1225 38835-1225) Michael Shipman (662) 286-2922

Crystal Springs Mission of Holy Trinity **M** (16) 204 W Railroad Ave S 39059-2772 (Mail to: PO Box 812 39059-0812) (601) 892-5142

Diamondhead St Thomas Episcopal Church **P** (223) 5303 Diamondhead Cir 39525-3203 (Mail to: 5303 Diamondhead Cir 39525-3203) (228) 255-9213

Enterprise Mission of St Mary **M** (17) 106 Saint John St 39330-8909 (Mail to: St John St PO Box 177 39330-0177) (601) 656-2938

Gautier St Pierre Episcopal Church **P** (132) 4412 Gautier Vancleave Rd 39553-4807 (Mail to: PO Box 145 39553-0145) John Switzer John Switzer (228) 497-9819

Greenville Church of the Redeemer **M** (18) 632 W Ohea St 38701-3663 (Mail to: PO Box 494 38702-0494) (601) 332-8658

Greenville St James Episcopal Church **P** (195) 1026 S Washington Ave 38701-6307 (Mail to: 1026 S Washington Ave 38701-6307) Brandt Dick (662) 334-4582

Greenwood Church of the Nativity **P** (275) 400 Howard St 38930-4338 (Mail to: PO Box 1006 38935-1006) Donald Chancellor (662) 453-7786

Grenada All Saints Episcopal Church **P** (160) 469 S Main St 38901-3816 (Mail to: PO Box 345 38902-0345) Abram Jones (662) 2268234

Gulfport St Marks Episcopal Church **P** (704) 11322 West Taylor Road 39503 (Mail to: 11322 W Taylor Rd 39503-4097) Stephen Kidd Clelie Mccandless (258) 8967597

Gulfport St Peters by the Sea **P** (599) 1909 15th St 39501-2117 (Mail to: 1909 15th St 39501-2117) Patrick Sanders (228) 863-2611

Hattiesburg Episcopal Ch of the Ascension **P** (248) 3600 Arlington Loop 39402-1618 (Mail to: 3600 Arlington Loop 39402-1618) Susan Bear (601) 264-6773

Hattiesburg Trinity Episcopal Church **P** (282) § 509 W Pine St 39401-3833 (Mail to: PO Box 1483 39403-1483) Carrie Duncan (601) 544-5551

Hollandale St Pauls Episcopal Church **M** (18) PO Box 596 38748-0596 (Mail to: C/O The Rev R E Sanders PO Box 267 38756-0267) (662) 822-4863

Holly Springs Christ Episcopal Church **P** (81) 100 N Randolph St 38635-2411 (Mail to: PO Box 596 38635-0596) (662) 252-2435

Indianola St Stephens Episcopal Church **P** (103) PO Box 1004 38751-1004 (Mail to: PO Box 1004 38751-1004) Jennifer Deaton (662) 887-4365

Inverness All Saints Episcopal Church **M** (15) US Hwy 49 W 38753 (Mail to: PO Box 9 387530009) (662) 265-5775

Jackson All Saints Episcopal Church **P** (63) 147 Daniel Lake Blvd 39212-4942 (Mail to: 147 Daniel Lake Blvd 39212-4942) William Ndishabandi (601) 372-5185

Jackson St Alexis Episcopal Church **M** (136) 650 E South St 39201-5307 (Mail to: PO Box 783 39205-0783) (601) 944-0415

✠ **Jackson** St Andrews Episcopal Cathedral **O** (1160) 305 E Capitol St 39201-3414 (Mail to: Business Admin PO Box 1366 39215-1366) Anne Maxwell Katie Bradshaw (601) 354-1535

Jackson St Christophers Church **M** (58) 643 Beasley Rd 39206-3827 (Mail to: 643 Beasley Rd 39206-2826) (601) 366-6768

Jackson St James Episcopal Church **P** (2184) 3921 Oakridge Dr 39216-3412 (Mail to: 3921 Oakridge Dr 39216-3412) Elizabeth Wheatley-Jones Gates Elliott (601) 982-4880

Jackson St Marks Episcopal Church **P** (67) 903 Dr Robert Smith Sr Pkwy 39203-3036 (Mail to: PO Box 3191 39207-3191) Charles Ashford Robert Spencer (601) 353-0246

Jackson St Philips Episcopal Church **P** (601) 5400 Old Canton Rd 39211-4254 (Mail to: 5400 Old Canton Rd 39211-4277) (601) 956-5788

Kosciusko St Matthews Church **P** (44) 317 St Matthew Street 39090-3455 (Mail to: PO Box 1455 39090-1455) (662) 289-5326

Laurel St Johns Episcopal Church **P** (293) 541 N 5th Ave 39440-3410 (Mail to: PO Box 1766 39441-1766) Jeffrey Reich (601) 428-7252

Leland St Johns Episcopal Church **M** (53) 405 California Ave 38756-3305 (Mail to: PO Box 267 38756-0267) (662) 686-4260

Lexington St Mary Episcopal Church **M** (15) 402 Hillside St 39095 (Mail to: PO Box 63 39095-0063) (662) 834-2973

Long Beach Lighthouse - St Nicholas **PS** (22) 310 N Cleveland Ave 39560-4739 (Mail to: 310 N Cleveland Ave 39560-4739) (601) 3851818

Long Beach St Patricks Episcopal Church **P** (65) 310 N Cleveland Ave 39560-4739 (Mail to: 310 N Cleveland Ave 39560-4739) Jane Bearden (228) 863-7882

Madison The Chapel of the Cross **P** (909) 674 Mannsdale Rd 39110-7991 (Mail to: 674 Mannsdale Rd 39110-7991) Benjamin Robertson William Compton (601) 856-2593

Mccomb Parish of the Mediator Rdmr **P** (104) 215 N Broadway 39648-3905 (Mail to: 217 N Broadway St 39648-3905) Victor Mcinnis (601) 684-5682

Meridian St Pauls Episcopal Church **P** (239) 1116 23rd Ave 39301-4017 (Mail to: 1116 23rd Ave 39301-4091) Andrew McGehee (601) 693-2502

Meridian Church of the Mediator **P** (244) 3825 35th Ave 39305-3617 (Mail to: PO Box 3400 39303-3400) Joshua Messick Morris Thompson (601) 483-3959

Michigan City Mission of Calvary **M** (12) 43 Fort St 38647-8554 (Mail to: Route 1 38647) (662) 401-3089

Natchez Christ Episcopal Church **P** (16) RR 2 Box 296 39120-9608 (Mail to: Rt 2 Box 296 39120) (601) 445-8432

Natchez Trinity Episcopal Church **P** (396) PO Box 1323 39121-1323 (Mail to: 305 S Commerce St 39120-3503) Kenneth Ritter (601) 445-8432

Newton Trinity Episcopal Church **M** (2) PO Box 418 39345-0418 (Mail to: PO Box 418 39345-0418)

Ocean Springs St Johns Episcopal Church **P** (591) 705 Rayburn Ave 39564-3762 (Mail to: 705 Rayburn Ave 39564-3762) Charles Hawkins Robert Lenoir John Switzer (228) 875-4454

Okolona St Bernard **P** (12) 400 W Main St 38860-1305 (Mail to: PO Box 150 38860-0150) (662) 447-2752

Olive Branch Holy Cross Episcopal Church **M** (68) 8230 Highway 178 38654-1116 (Mail to: 8230 Highway 178 38654-1116) (662) 895-5029

Oxford St Peters Episcopal Church **P** (754) 113 S 9th St 38655-3916 (Mail to: 113 S 9th St 38655-3916) Joseph Burnett Penny Sisson Jennifer Southall (662) 234-1269

Pascagoula St Johns Episcopal Church **P** (485) 3507 Pine St 39567-3117 (Mail to: 3507 Pine St 39567-3100) Thomas Fanning (228) 762-1705

Pass Christian Trinity Episcopal Church **P** (262) 125 Church Ave 39571-4302 (Mail to: 125 Church Ave 39571-4302) Kyle Bennett Richard Devenport (228) 452-4563

Philadelphia Mssn of St Francis of Assisi **M** (42) 10701 Saint Francis Dr 39350-2170 (Mail to: Attn: Rae Gordon Sr Warden 10701 Saint Francis Dr 39350-2170) Betty Melton (601) 656-2938

Picayune St Pauls Episcopal Church **P** (49) 1421 Goodyear Blvd 39466-3152 (Mail to: 1421 Goodyear Blvd 39466-3152) Arthur Johnson (601) 798-2802

Port Gibson St James Episcopal Church **M** (25) 305 Jackson St 39150-2327 (Mail to: Mrs Rochelle Abraham 1073 Rattlesnake Rdg 39150-2543) (601) 437-4244

Raymond St Marks Church **M** (36) 201 Main St 39154-9712 (Mail to: PO Box 113 39154-0113) Janet Ott (601) 826-2128

Ridgeland St Columbs Episcopal Church **P** (532) 550 Sunnybrook Rd 39157-1810 (Mail to: 550 Sunnybrook Rd 39157-1810) Calvin Meaders (601) 853-0205

Rolling Fork Chapel of the Cross **P** (70) 35 Mclaurin Ave 39159-2906 (Mail to: C/O William Moore PO Box 336 39054-0336) Frederick Proctor Robert Weatherly (662) 873-2226

Rosedale Mission of Grace **M** (17) Main St 38769 (Mail to: Main St 38769) Sylvia Czarnetzky

Southaven St Timothy Episcopal Church **P** (461) 8245 Getwell Rd 38672-6420 (Mail to: PO Box 325 38671-0004) Robert Calhoun (662) 393-3100

Starkville Church of the Resurrection **P** (390) 105 N Montgomery St 39759-2903 (Mail to: 105 N Montgomery St 39759-2903) Walton Jones George Rambow (662) 323-3483

Sumner Episcopal Church of the Advent **P** (73) 224 Monroe St 38957 (Mail to: PO Box 366 38957-0366) (662) 375-8848

Terry Mission of the Good Shepherd **M** (46) 109 E Claiborne St 39170-7805 (Mail to: PO Box 325 39170-0325) (601) 878-5612

Tunica Episcopal Ch of the Epiphany **P** (77) 1045 Shady Ln 38676-9499 (Mail to: PO Box 224 38676-0224) (662) 363-2393

Tupelo All Saints' Episcopal Church **P** (412) 608 W Jefferson St 38804-3736 (Mail to: 608 W Jefferson St 38804-3736) Phillip Parker (662) 842-4386

Vicksburg Christ Episcopal Church **P** (208) 1115 Main St 39183-2527 (Mail to: 1115 Main St 39183-2527) Samuel Godfrey (601) 638-5899

Vicksburg Church of the Holy Trinity **HC** (230) 900 South St 39180-3256 (Mail to: 900 South St 39180-3256) Elizabeth Hunter (601) 636-0542

Vicksburg St Albans Episcopal Church **P** (123) 5930 Warriors Trl 39180-0878 (Mail to: 5930 Warriors Trl 39180-0878) Josie Williams (601) 6366687

Vicksburg St Marys Episcopal Church **M** (34) 900 First North St 39183-2616 (Mail to: 900 First North St 39183-2699) Denny Allman (601) 636-4811

Water Valley Mission of the Nativity **M** (3) Main St 38965 (Mail to: C/O Glen Evans 749 Highway 7 S 38655-8244)

West Point Church of the Incarnation **P** (123) 103 W Broad St 39773-2801 (Mail to: PO Box 316 39773-0316) Patricia Cantrell (662) 494-1378

Woodville St Pauls Episcopal Church **P** (127) 259 S Church St 39669 (Mail to: PO Box 207 39669-0207) Walter Windsor Mary Anne Heine (601) 888-6704

Yazoo City Trinity Church **P** (47) 323 N Main St 39194-4262 (Mail to: PO Box 145 39194-0145) George Woodliff (662) 746-5082

DIOCESE OF MISSOURI
(PROVINCE V)
Comprises eastern Missouri
DIOCESAN OFFICE 1210 Locust St Louis MO 63103
TEL (314) 231-1220 FAX (314) 231-3373
E-MAIL info@diocesemo.org WEB www.diocesemo.org

Previous Bishops— Jackson Kemper 1835-44, Cicero S Hawks 1844-68, Chas F Robertson 1868-86, Daniel S Tuttle 1886-1932, Fredk F Johnson coadj 1912 Bp 1923-32, Wm Scarlett coadj 1930 Bp 1932-52, Arthur Lichtenberger coadj 1951 Bp 1952-59, George L Cadigan 1959-75, WA Jones Jr 1975-93 Hays H Rockwell 1993-2002, George Wayne Smith 2002-20

Bishop—Rt Rev Deon K. Johnson (Dio June 13, 2020)

Cn to Ord Rev D Westfall; *Exec Dir Fin/Admin* D Brattin; *Chanc* HR Burroughs 211 N Broadway St Louis MO 63102; *Treas* A Ludwig; *Sec of Conv* B Bowersox; *Comm* J Greenbaum

Stand Comm—Pres C Whitson; *Cler:* S Lawler K Adams-Shepherd S Goodlow E Hillquist-Davis C Hines DK Johnson S Weaver; *Lay:* A Brewen S Ferguson P O'Brien T Korte R Walz; *Chanc* H Burroughs; *Staff* D Westfall D Brattin

Diocesan Council—Chair DK Johnson; *Vice-Chair* TBD; *Cler:* Rev N Emmel Gunn J Huber Rev H Leip M Nchimbi C Wesley; *Lay:* A. Binggeli A Bleyer A Breeher L Cornelius J Smith W Haggerty S Kekec L Kramer R Lowe J Martin C Nield K Quinlisk M Reier J Smith A Webb E Yount; *Chanc* H Burroughs; *Treas* A Ludwig; *Staff:* D Westfall D Brattin

Diocesan Committees and Commissions—Commission on Min: Chair The Rev A Dieterle; *Companion Diocese Committee:* Chair Dcn D Goldfeder; *Daughters of the King:* Pres M Steiling; *Dismantling Racism Commission:* Chair Rev S Goodlow; *Bishop's Deputy for Gun Violence Prevention* The Rev M Haggerty; *Jubilee Officer* Dcn B Click; *Task Force for the Hungry:* Chair J Mayfield; *Creation Care Min* The Rev K McGrane; *Hispanic/Latinx Min* The Rev V Mulvey Sherer; *Indigenous Min* The Rev L Scoopmire; *LGBTQIA+ Min* B O'Conner; *Rural Min* The Rev. A Joseph; *Public Advocacy* The Rev T Mithen Danieley

PARISHES, MISSIONS, AND CLERGY

Ballwin Faith Christian Ch of India **M** 444 Bright Field Trl 63021-7460 (Mail to: 444 Bright Field Trl 63021-7460) Seelam Raj Clive Samson (314) 737-7796

Cape Girardeau Christ Episcopal Church **P** (110) 101 N Fountain St 63701-7338 (Mail to: 38 N Fountain St 637017338) Annette Joseph (573) 335-2997

Columbia Calvary Episcopal Church **P** (813) 123 S 9th St 65201-4815 (Mail to: 123 S 9th St 65201-4815) Ann Dieterle Joshua Huber Elizabeth Simpson Elizabeth Simpson (573) 4493194

De Soto Trinity Episcopal Church **M** (34) PO Box 9 63020-0009 (Mail to: PO Box 9 63020-0009) (636) 586-2542

Ellisville St Martins Episcopal Church **P** (315) 15764 Clayton Rd 63011-2330 (Mail to: 15764 Clayton Rd 63011-2330) Leslie Scoopmire Leslie Scoopmire (636) 227-1484

Eolia St John's Church Prairieville **P** (9) Hwy H 63344 (Mail to: 515 N Main Cross St 63334-1416) (573) 754-6423

Eureka St Francis' Episcopal Church **M** (120) § 602 Rockwood Arbor Dr 63025-1023 (Mail to: 602 Rockwood Arbor Dr 63025-1023) Laura Anzilotti (636) 938-3733

Farmington All Saints Episcopal Church **M** (68) 1151 W. Columbia 63640 (Mail to: 1151 W. Columbia St 63640) Richard Wiskus (573) 756-3225

Florissant St Barnabas Episcopal Church **P** (69) 2900 Saint Catherine St 63033-3628 (Mail to: 2900 Saint Catherine St 63033-3628) Pamela Stuerke (314) 837-7113

Fulton St Albans Episcopal Church **M** (42) 6 W 9th & Nichols St 65251 (Mail to: PO Box 6065 65251-6065) (573) 291-9886

Hannibal Trinity Church **P** (106) 213 N 4th St 63401-3508 (Mail to: 213 N 4th St Attn Treasurer Robert H Gilstrap 63401-3508) Maria Evans Michael Kyle (573) 221-0298

Ironton St Pauls Episcopal Church **M** (20) 106 N Knob St 63650-1219 (Mail to: PO Box 62 63650-0062) (573) 546-2397

Jefferson City Grace Episcopal Church **P** (359) 217 Adams St 65101-3203 (Mail to: 217 Adams St 65101-3298) Paula Hartsfield William Nesbit (573) 635-4405

Kirksville Trinity Episcopal Church **M** (81) PO Box 652 63501-0652 (Mail to: PO Box 652 63501-0652) Carrol Davenport Amy Fallon (660) 665-6155

Kirkwood St Thomas Church for the Deaf **M** (14) C/O Grace Episcopal Church 514 E Argonne Dr 63122-4526 (Mail to: c/o Grace Episcopal Church 514 E Argonne Dr 63122-4526) (314) 560-6731

Lake Saint Louis Church of the Transfiguration **P** (100) 1860 Lake Saint Louis Blvd 63367-1318 (Mail to: 1860 Lake Saint Louis Blvd 63367-1318) Lu-Anne Conner (636) 561-8951

Louisiana Calvary Church **P** (29) 706 Georgia St 63353-1612 (Mail to: PO Box 528 63353-0528) (573) 754-6423

Manchester St Lukes Episcopal Church **P** (75) 1101 Sulphur Spring Rd 63021-7419 (Mail to: 444 Brightfield Trl 63021-7460) Charles Mahan (636) 227-1227

Mexico St Matthews Episcopal Church **P** (24) 1100 S Grove St 65265-2292 (Mail to: 1100 Grove St 65265-2292) (573) 581-1498

Poplar Bluff Church of the Holy Cross **P** (49) 420 N Main St 63901-5108 (Mail to: 420 N Main St 63901-5108) (573) 785-1098

Portland St Marks Episcopal Church **M** (58) 8645 Co. Road 466 65067 (Mail to: PO Box 148 65067-0148) (573) 291-9886

Rolla Christ Episcopal Church **P** (152) 1000 N Main St 65401-2865 (Mail to: PO Box 845 65402-0845) Mary Korte (573) 364-1499

Saint Charles Trinity Episcopal Church **P** (324) 318 S Duchesne Dr 63301-1655 (Mail to: 318 S Duchesne Dr 63301-1655) Tamsen Whistler (314) 949-0160

Saint James Trinity Episcopal Church **M** (51) 120 E Scioto St 65559-1718 (Mail to: PO Box 126 65559-0126) (573) 265-7667

✠ **Saint Louis** Christ Church Cathedral **O** (582) 1210 Locust St 63103-2322 (Mail to: 1210 Locust St 63103-2322) Kathleen Adams-Shepherd Robert Franken (314) 231-3454

Saint Louis Church of the Advent **P** (135) 9373 Garber Rd 63126-2849 (Mail to: 9373 Garber Rd 63126-2849) Emily Davis (314) 843-0123

Saint Louis Church of the Good Shepherd **P** (77) 1166 S Mason Rd 63131-1039 (Mail to: 1166 S Mason Rd 63131-1039) (314) 576-5502

Saint Louis Church of the Holy Communion **P** (351) 7401 Delmar Blvd 63130-4035 (Mail to: 7401 Delmar Blvd 63130-4093) Michael Angell Julie Graham (314) 721-7401

Saint Louis Emmanuel Episcopal Church **P** (791) 9 S Bompart Ave 63119-3225 (Mail to: 9 S Bompart Ave 63119-3282) Seelam Raj Valori Sherer (314) 961-2393

Saint Louis Epis Ch of All Saints & Ascen **P** (188) 4520 Lucas And Hunt Rd 63121-2737 (Mail to: 4520 Lucas And Hunt Rd 63121-2737) Renee Fenner

Saint Louis Grace Church **HC** (505) 514 E Argonne Dr 63122-4526 (Mail to: C/O Grace Bonham 514 E Argonne Dr 63122-4526) Mary Haggerty (314) 821-1806

Saint Louis St Johns Church **P** (305) 3664 Arsenal St 63116-4801 (Mail to: 3672-B Arsenal St 63116) (314) 772-3970

Saint Louis St Marks Episcopal Church **P** (169) 4714 Clifton Ave 63109-2701 (Mail to: 4714 Clifton Ave 63109-2701) Mark Kozielec Jerre Birdsong (314) 832-3588

Saint Louis St Michael And St George **P** (1543) PO Box 11887 63105-0687 (Mail to: PO Box 11887 63105-0687) Andrew Archie Stewart Clem (314) 721-1502

Saint Louis St Pauls Episcopal Church **P** (89) 6518 Michigan Ave 63111-2803 (Mail to: 6518 Michigan Avenue 63111-2803) Rebecca Ragland (314) 352-0370

Saint Louis St Peters Episcopal Church **P** (1220) 110 N Warson Rd 63124-1327 (Mail to: 110 N Warson Rd 63124-1327) David Hodges (314) 9932306

Saint Louis St Stephens Episcopal Church **P** (293) 33 N Clay Ave 63135-2418 (Mail to: 3 N Clay Ave 63135-2484) (314) 521-0138

Saint Louis St Timothy's Episcopal Church **P** (370) 808 N Mason Rd 63141-6306 (Mail to: 808 N Mason Rd 63141-6306) Meghan Ryan (341) 4345906

Saint Louis Trinity Church **HC** (238) 600 N Euclid Ave 63108-1606 (Mail to: 600 N Euclid Ave 63108-1606) Barbara Click Harry Leip Beverly Van Horne (314) 361-4655

Sikeston St Pauls Episcopal Church **P** (46) 101 N Main St 63801-5044 (Mail to: PO Box 424 63801) (573) 471-2680

Ste Genevieve St Vincents-in-the-Vineyard **M** (17) 24345 State Route WW 63670-9022 (Mail to: 23 The Villages at Chaumette 24345 State Route Ww 63670-9022) (314) 397-3050

Sullivan St John and St James Church **M** (15) 463 N Church St 63080-1505 (Mail to: 463 N Church St 63080-1505) (573) 468-3753

DIOCESE OF MONTANA
(PROVINCE VI)
Comprises the State of Montana
DIOCESAN OFFICE 515 N Park Ave Helena MT 59601 (MAIL: PO Box 2020 Helena MT 59624)
TEL (800) 247-1391 FAX (406) 442-2238
E-MAIL admin@diomontana.com WEB https://diomontana.com/

Previous Bishops—
Daniel S Tuttle 1866-1880, Leigh R Brewer m 1880 dio 1904-16, Wm F Faber coadj 1914 Bp 1916-34, Herbert HH Fox suffr 1920 coadj 1925 Bp 1934-39, Henry H Daniels coadj 1939 Bp 1939-57, Chandler W Sterling coadj 1956 Bp 1957-68, Jackson E Gilliam 1968-85, Charles I Jones, 1986-2001, Charles L Keyser Bp asst 2001-2003, C Franklin Brookhart 2003-18

Bishop—Rt Rev E. Martha Stebbins (dio 7 December 2019)

Cn to Ord & Deploy Off Rev Canon M Dunfee *Dio Adm* B Hagen; *Sec* L Catlin *Treas* M Dvarishkis; *Chanc* B Foster

Stand Comm—Cler: D Gleaves M St Clair T Kelley Bergmann; *Lay: Pres* S Williams D Martin **L Solorzano Work**

PARISHES, MISSIONS, AND CLERGY

Anaconda St Marks Episcopal Church **P** (25) 600 Main St 59711 (Mail to: PO Box 1021 59703) Theresa Kelley (405) 563-3625

Big Sky All Saints in Big Sky **P** (95) Meadow Village Big 59716 (Mail to: PO Box 161026 59716-1026) (406) 995-7988

Big Timber St Marks Episcopal Church **P** (73) 203 W 4th Ave 59011 (Mail to: PO Box 626 59011-0626) (406) 932-5712

Bigfork St Patricks Episcopal Church **P** (101) 105 S Crane Mountain Rd 59911 (Mail to: PO Box 431 59911-0431) (406) 849-5465

Billings Saint Luke's Church **P** (258) 119 N 33rd St 59101-2018 (Mail to: 119 N 33rd St 59101-2018) Melinda St Clair (406) 252-7186

Billings St Stephens Church **P** (271) 1241 Crawford Dr 59102-2442 (Mail to: 1241 Crawford Dr 59102-2442) Stephen Day Gerald Jasmer (406) 259-5017

Bozeman St James Episcopal Church **P** (604) 5 West Olive St 59715-4624 (Mail to: 5 W Olive St 59715-4624) John Honeychurch David Smith Sylvia Sweeney (406) 586-9093

Butte St John's Episcopal Church **P** (60) 15 N Idaho St 59701-9229 (Mail to: PO Box 613 59703-0613) (406) 723-4017

Columbia Falls All Saints Episcopal Church **P** (218) 2048 Conn Road 59912 (Mail to: PO Box 1923 59937-1923) Charles Knuth (406) 862-2863

Deer Lodge St James-Pintler Cluster **P** (32) 307 Cottonwood Ave 59722-1040 (Mail to: 657 Prairie Ln 59722-2365) (406) 563-3625

Dillon St James Episcopal Church **P** (67) 203 E Glendale St 59725-2707 (Mail to: PO Box 1374 59725-1374) (406) 683-2735

Emigrant St Johns Episcopal Church **P** (115) 8 Story Rd 59027 (Mail to: PO Box 176 59027-0176) (406) 222-0222

Ennis Trinity Episcopal Church **P** (86) 93 Jeffers Rd 59729-9026 (Mail to: PO Box 336 59729-0336) Jaime Leonard (406) 600-1128

Eureka St Michael & All Angels Church **P** (49) PO Box 342 59917-0342 (Mail to: PO Box 342 59917-0342) (406) 297-7233

Forsyth Church of the Ascension **M** (13) 380 15th Ave N 59327 (Mail to: PO Box 876 59327-0876) (406) 234-5188

Fort Benton St Paul Episcopal Church **P** (11) 1112 14th St 59442 (Mail to: PO Box 217 59442-0217) (406) 265-2638

Great Falls Church of the Incarnation **P** (120) 600 3rd Ave N 59401-2426 (Mail to: PO Box 3046 59403-3046) (406) 453-4167

Hamilton St Pauls Episcopal Church **P** (107) 600 S 3rd St 59840-2730 (Mail to: C/O Carol Shipman 130 S 6th St E 59801-4222) Gretchen Strohmaier (406) 360-2661

✠ **Helena** St Peters Cathedral **O** (504) 511 N Park Ave 59601-2703 (Mail to: PO Box 819 59624-0819) Scott Anderson Raymond Brown John Moran (406) 442-5175

Kalispell Christ Church Episcopal **P** (114) 215 3rd Ave E 59901-4531 (Mail to: 215 3rd Ave E 59901-4531) (406) 257-6182

Lewistown St James Episcopal Church **P** (117) 502 W Montana St 59457-2631 (Mail to: PO Box 744 59457-0744) Jean Collins (406) 538-5151

Livingston St Andrews Episcopal Church **P** (165) 310 W Lewis St 59047-3015 (Mail to: PO Box 835 59047-0835) (406) 222-0222

Manhattan Gethsemane Episcopal Church **P** (22) 305 5th Ave 59741 (Mail to: PO Box 84 59741-0085) (406) 5869093

Miles City Emmanuel Episcopal Church **M** (15) 208 North 11th 59301 (Mail to: PO Box 1526 59301-1526) (406) 234-5188

Missoula Church of the Holy Spirit **P** (828) 130 S 6th St E 59801-4222 (Mail to: 130 S 6th St E 59801-4222) Dorcie Dvarishkis Dorcie Dvarishkis Terri Grotzinger Gretchen Strohmaier Gretchen Strohmaier (406) 542-2167

Philipsburg St Andrews Episcopal Church **P** (17) 101 E Kearney St 59858 (Mail to: PO Box 601 59858-0601) (406) 563-3625

Polson St Andrews Episcopal Church **P** (103) 110 6th Ave E 59860-2728 (Mail to: 110 6th Ave E 59860-2728) (406) 883-5524

Red Lodge Calvary Episcopal Church **M** (97) PO Box 348 59068-0348 (Mail to: PO Box 348 59068-0368) Aimee Altizer (406) 425-0388

Sheridan Christ Episcopal Church **P** (48) 304 S Main St 59749 (Mail to: Attn: Jennifer Boucher

PO Box 152 59749-0152) (406) 842-7539

Stevensville St Stephens Episcopal Church **M** (12) 203 Main St 59870-2112 (Mail to: Attn: Donald Artley PO Box 35 59870-0035) (406) 777-0028

Troy Holy Trinity Episcopal Church **P** (6) PO Box 892 59935-0892 (Mail to: 218 Missoula Ave 59935-7504)

Virginia City St Paul Episcopal Church **P** (21) 102 E Idaho St 59755-7757 (Mail to: PO Box 206 59755-0206) (406) 600-1128

NAVAJOLAND AREA MISSION
(PROVINCE VIII)
Comprises portions of Navajo Reservation in Arizona, New Mexico, and Utah
OFFICE: 1257 Mission Ave Farmington NM 87499-0720 (MAIL: Box 720 Farmington NM 87499-0720)
TEL (505) 327-7549
E-MAIL ceaton.ecn@gmail.com WEB www.ecofnavajoland.org

Previous Bishops— Frederick W Putnam 1979-83, Wesley Frensdorff int 1983-88, Wm F Wolfrum int 1988-90, Wm C Wantland int 1990-2005 Steven T Plummer 1990-2005, Rustin R Kimsey 2005-06, Mark L MacDonald 2006-2009.

Bishop—Rt Rev David E Bailey (1049) (Dio 7 Aug 2010)

Admin MM Putnam Box 720 Farmington NM 87499; *Sec* C Eaton Box 720 Farmington NM 87499

Dio Coun—Cler: C Eaton L Sampson CA Plummer P Henson M Sells J Hubbard; *Lay:* A Fowler M Brown R Dick L Bekise L Henderson M Benally

Standing Committee—Cler: Pres C Eaton L Sampson; *Lay:* M Brown A Fowler M Benally

PARISHES, MISSIONS, AND CLERGY

Bluff St Christophers Church **M** (60) 3315 East Old Mission Rd 1.7 Mile Utah Route 162 84512 (Mail to: PO Box 28 84512-0028) (435) 672-9940

Farmington All Saints Church **M** (105) 1271 Mission Ave 87401 (Mail to: PO Box 720 87499-0720) (505) 327-7549

Farmington St Luke in the Desert **M** (43) PO Box 720 87499-0720 (Mail to: PO Box 720 87499-0720) (505) 327-7549

Fort Defiance Church of the Good Shepherd **M** (175) 618 Kit Carson Drive 86504 (Mail to: Epis Church In Navajoland PO Box 720 87499-0720) (928) 729-2322

Fort Defiance Saint Mark's, Coalmine **M** (80) Coalmine 86504 (Mail to: PO Box 720 87499-0720) (928) 729-2322

Many Farms St Joseph Church **M** (11) Indian Route 59 86538 (Mail to: PO Box 618 86504-0618) (928) 729-2322

Montezuma Creek Saint John The Baptizer **M** (64) Mile 129 Route 162 3599 W Hwy 162 84534 (Mail to: PO Box 720 87499-0720) (435) 444-0484

Oljato St Mary of the Moonlight **M** (39) Rte 6420 - Oljato Wash Road 84536 (Mail to: PO Box 28 84512-0028) (435) 727-0200

Upper Fruitland St Michaels Episcopal Church **M** (83) Highway N36 87416 (Mail to: PO Box 720 87499-0720) (505) 327-7549

DIOCESE OF NEBRASKA
(PROVINCE VI)
Comprises the State of Nebraska
DIOCESAN OFFICE 109 N 18th St Omaha NE 68102
TEL (402) 341-5373 FAX (402) 341-8683
WEB www.episcopal-ne.org

Previous Bishops—
Robt H Clarkson 1865-84, George Worthington 1885-1908, Arthur L Williams coadj 1899 Bp 1908-19, Ernest V Shayler 1919-38, Howard R Brinker 1940-62, Russell T Rauscher coadj 1961 Bp 1962-72, Robert P Varley coadj 1971 Bp 1972-75, Jas D Warner 1976-89, James E Krotz, 1990-03, Joe Goodwin-Burnett 2003-2011

Bishop—Rt Rev J Scott Barker (Dio 8 Oct 2011)

Archdcn B Bennett; *Cn to Ord* Rev Cn E Easton; *Chanc* D Bradford III; *Sec Reg* Rev Cn E Easton; *Treas* J Pirruccello; *Dio Admin* L Baskin; *Dir of Fin* B Byrne

Stand Comm—Cler: Pres Susanna DesMarais Rev B Bennett Rev T Anderson Rev C Loya; *Lay:* N Cloudt D Kennell C Schrader J Wisniewski

Comm on Min—Cler: Rev S King Rev K Watson Rev J Long Rev S Swinnea Rev J Wood; *Lay: Chair* M Schaefer D Hendricks G Clarke J Jordan J Stribley

PARISHES, MISSIONS, AND CLERGY

Alliance St Matthews Episcopal Church **P** (103) 312 W 16th St 69301-2205 (Mail to: PO Box 430 69301-0430) John Adam Cheryl Harris (308) 762-1965

Arapahoe St Pauls Episcopal Church **P** (32) 909 4th St 68922-2776 (Mail to: PO Box 583 68922-0583) (308) 962-7271

Bassett St Marys Episcopal Church **M** (28) 212 Clark St 68714-5503 (Mail to: PO Box 361 68714-0361) Randall Goeke (402) 684-3943

Beatrice Christ Episcopal Church **P** (147) 524 N 5th St 68310-2903 (Mail to: 524 N 5th St 68310-2903) (402) 223-5515

Bellevue Church of the Holy Spirit **P** (245) 1305 Thomas Dr 68005-2973 (Mail to: 1305 Thomas Dr 68005-2973) Thomas Jones (402) 291-7732

Blair St Marys Episcopal Church **P** (117) 1743 Grant St 68008-1916 (Mail to: 1734 Grant St 68008-1917) Kimberly Culp (402) 426-2057

Broken Bow St Johns Episcopal Church **P** (51) 602 N 10th Ave 68822-1222 (Mail to: 610 N 10th Ave 68822-1222) Mary Gockley (308) 872-5900

Central City Christ Church **P** (14) 1414 15th St 68826-1416 (Mail to: 1414 15th St 68826-1416) (308) 946-2640

Chadron Grace Episcopal Church **P** (48) 450 Bordeaux St 69337-2607 (Mail to: 450 Bordeaux St 69337-2607) (308) 432-2229

Columbus Grace Episcopal Church **P** (44) 2053 23rd Ave 68601-3329 (Mail to: PO Box 306 68602-0306) Jan With (402) 564-0116

Cozad St Christophers Church **P** (13) 1520 Avenue B 69130-1645 (Mail to: 1520 Avenue B 69130-1645) (308) 784-2056

Creighton St Marks Church **P** (9) 901 Garfield St 68729-2949 (Mail to: PO Box 653 68729-0653) (402) 358-3295

Crete Trinity Memorial Chruch **P** (11) 14th & Juniper Sts 68333 (Mail to: 660 Franklin Dr 68333-2513) (402) 826-3390

De Witt St Augustines Episcopal Church **P** (30) 108 N Quince 68341-5001 (Mail to: PO Box 201 68341-0201) (402) 683-4110

Elkhorn St Augustine of Canterbury **P** (332) 285 S 208th St 68022-1811 (Mail to: 285 S 208th St 68022-1811) Benedict Varnum Patricia Sheldon (402) 289-4058

Falls City St Thomas Episcopal Church **P** (23) 1602 Harlan St 68355-2655 (Mail to: PO Box 117 68355-0117) (402) 245-2868

Fremont St James Episcopal Church **P** (95) 301 E 5th St 68025-5025 (Mail to: PO Box 2421 68026-2421) (402) 721-3327

Gordon St Marks Episcopal Church **P** (11) Attn: Amy Moore 116 Lariat St 69343-1143 (Mail to: Attn: Amy Moore 924 N Elm St 69343-1135) (308) 282-1303

Grand Island St Stephens Episcopal Church **P** (115) 422 W 2nd St 68801-5936 (Mail to: 422 W 2nd St 68801-5936) (308) 382-4961

Harrisburg Good Shepherd of Plains **P** (18) Maryland Avenue 69345-0025 (Mail to: PO Box 25 69345-0025) (308) 436-4465

Harvard Saint John's Mission **P** (10) 410 North Harvard 68944 (Mail to: 422 N Burlington Ave 68901-5059) (402) 462-4126

✠ **Hastings** St Marks Pro Cathedral **O** (253) 422 N Burlington Ave 68901-5059 (Mail to: 422 N Burlington Ave 68901-5059) Kathleen Hargis (402) 462-4126

Holdrege St Elizabeths Church **P** (31) 512 Tilden St 68949-2245 (Mail to: PO Box 864 68949-0864) (308) 995-4528

Hyannis Calvary Church Hyannis **M** (21) 302 E Highway 2 69350 (Mail to: Attn: Kleo Dredla PO Box 80 69350-0080) Robert Mcclure (308) 458-2336

Kearney St Lukes Church **P** (200) 2304 Second Ave 68847-5317 (Mail to: PO Box 2285 68848-2285) Stephanie Swinnea (308) 236-5821

Kimball St Hilda Church **P** (24) 601 S. Chesnut 69145-1423 (Mail to: 509 Adams St 69145-1709) (308) 235-4588

Lexington St Peters in the Valley Church **P** (7) 903 E 13th St 68850-1741 (Mail to: 905 E 13th St 68850-1741) Kay Knudson (308) 324-6199

Lincoln Church of the Holy Trinity **P** (313) 6001 A St 68510-5006 (Mail to: 6001 A St 68510-5098) Clay Lein Daniel Coffman John Long (402) 488-7139

Lincoln St David of Wales Epis Church **P** (156) 8800 Holdrege St 68505-9417 (Mail to: 8800 Holdrege St 68505-9417) David Stock (402) 489-2772

Lincoln St Marks on the Campus Church **P** (266) 1309 R St 68508-1219 (Mail to: 1309 R St 68508-1219) Sidnie Crawford (402) 474-1979

Lincoln St Matthews Church **P** (426) 2325 S 24th St 68502-4005 (Mail to: 2325 S 24th St 68502-4099) Stephen Lahey (402) 435-2226

McCook St Albans Episcopal Church **P** (115) 509 W 1st St 69001-3102 (Mail to: 509 W 1st St 69001-3102) (308) 345-4844

Mitchell Holy Apostles Church **P** (81) 1730 18th St 69357-1138 (Mail to: 1730 18th St 69357-1138) (308) 623-1969

Mullen St Josephs Church **P** (23) 402 Northwest 1st St 69152 (Mail to: Attn: Evelyn Elliott PO Box 453 69152-0453) (308) 546-2262

Nebraska City Grace Episcopal Church **P** (3) 1416 1st Corso 68410-2238 (Mail to: 1416 1st Corso 68410-2238) Richard Swenson (402) 335-2331

Nebraska City St Mary Episcopal Church **P** (30) 116 S 9th St 68410-2403 (Mail to: Attn: Jaymi Victor 1729 S 70th Rd 68410-6568) Mavis Hall (402) 873-6517

Norfolk Trinity Episcopal Church **P** (152) 111 S 9th St 68701-5166 (Mail to: 111 S 9th St 68701-5166) Sylvia Landers (402) 371-3080

North Platte Church of Our Savior **P** (77) 203 W 4th St 69101-3916 (Mail to: 203 W 4th St 69101-3916) (308) 532-0515

Ogallala St Pauls Episcopal Church **P** (19) 318 E A St 69153-2609 (Mail to: 318 E A St 69153-2609) (308) 203-1141

Omaha All Saints Episcopal Church **P** (803) 9302 Blondo St 68134-6036 (Mail to: 9302 Blondo St 68134-6099) Marisa Thompson Stephanie Ulrich (402) 393-8612

Omaha Church of the Resurrection **P** (259) 3004 Belvedere Blvd 68111-1232 (Mail to: 3004 Belvedere Blvd 68111-1232) Mary Forsythe Juanita Johnson (402) 455-7015

Omaha St Andrews Episcopal Church **P** (773) 925 S 84th St 68114-5207 (Mail to: 925 S 84th St 68114-5207) Keith Winton (402) 391-1950

Omaha St Martin of Tours Church **P** (36) 2312 J St 68107-1815 (Mail to: 2324 J St 681071815) Kim Roberts Ralph Agar (402) 733-8815

✠ **Omaha** Trinity Cathedral **O** (566) 113 N 18th St 68102-4903 (Mail to: 113 N 18th St 68102-4969) Vanessa Clark (402) 342-7010

Oshkosh St Georges Church **P** (3) 421 West 5th Street 69154 (Mail to: PO Box 436 69154) (308) 778-7177

Papillion St Marthas Episcopal Church **P** (345) 801 Magnolia Ave 68046-6264 (Mail to: 780 Pinnacle Dr 68046-6268) Emily Schnabl Ralph Agar (402) 331-1564

Plattsmouth St Lukes Church **P** (76) 302 Ave A 68048 (Mail to: 3rd Street & Avenue A, Box 446 68048) Phillip Chapman (402) 296-4718

Rushville St Marys Church **M** (23) 6919 State Highway 87 69360 (Mail to: PO Box 71 69360-0071) William Graham (308) 327-2506

Scottsbluff St Francis Episcopal Church **P** (290) 14 E 20th St 69361 (Mail to: PO Box 1201 69363) Erin Rath Karen Anderson Robert Manasek Robert Manasek (308) 632-4626

Seward St Andrews Church **P** (68) 1014 N 6th St 68434-1243 (Mail to: 1014 N 6th St 68434-1243) Pamela Williams (402) 643-3829

Sidney Christ Episcopal Church **P** (10) 1205 10th Ave 69162-2045 (Mail to: Attn: Zac Peterson PO Box 141 69162-0141) Charles Cook (308) 254-2166

Valentine St Johns Episcopal Church **P** (14) 372 N Main St 69201-1842 (Mail to: PO Box 261 69201-0261) (402) 376-1723

DIOCESE OF NEVADA
(PROVINCE VIII)
Comprises the State of Nevada and 1 church in Arizona
DIOCESAN OFFICE 9480 S Eastern Ave Ste 236 Las Vegas NV 89123-8037
TEL (702) 737-9190 FAX (702) 737-6488
E-MAIL office@episcopalnevada.org WEB www.episcopalnevada.org

Previous Bishops—
Ozi W Whitaker (NV and AZ) 1869-86, Henry D Robinson 1908-24, Geo C Hunting 1914-24, Thomas Jenkins 1929-42, Wm F Lewis 1942-59, Wm G Wright 1960-72, Wesley Frensdorff 1972-85, Stewart C Zabriskie 1986-99, Katharine Jefferts Schori 2001-06, Dan T Edwards 2008-18, James E Waggoner Jr Asst Bp (2019-2021)

Bishop – Rt Rev Elizabeth Bonforte Gardner (1142)

Conv Sec E Tattersall; *Treas* E McGarry; *Finan Off* vacant *Chanc* R Caffertata; *Cn to Ord* vacant

Stand Comm—Cler: Pres J Paull *Chap:* vacant; *Treas* vacant; *Lay:* P Avery P Turner A Flint T Cain M Stringer *Clergy* K Rackley C Schuller J McClatchy J Paul T Snyder

Dio Staff—Admin and Comm Off: S Sims; *Fin Off:* vacant; *Cn to Ordinary & Chief of Staff* vacant

PARISHES, MISSIONS, AND CLERGY

Austin St George Episcopal Church **P** (6) 156 Main St 89310-0181 (Mail to: PO Box 181 89310-0181) (775) 964-1477

Boulder City St Christophers Episcopal Ch **P** (86) 812 Arizona St 89005-2604 (Mail to: C/O Nancy MacFarlane 812 Arizona St 89005-2604) (702) 293-4275

Bullhead City Church of the Holy Spirit **P** (53) 580 Hancock Rd 86442-4902 (Mail to: 580 Hancock Rd 86442-4902) (928) 763-1881

Carson City St Nicholas Mission **M** 1721 Snyder Ave 89701-7812 (Mail to: PO Box 7000 89702-7000) (775) 882-9203

Carson City St Peters Episcopal Church **P** (240) 314 S Division St 89703-4172 (Mail to: 305 N Minnesota St 89703-4172) Jeffrey Paul (775) 882-1534

Elko St Pauls Episcopal Church **P** (95) 777 Sage St 89801-3318 (Mail to: 777 Sage St 89801-3318) Karen Albrethsen David Grube Julie Vice (775) 738-3264

Ely St Bartholomews Church **P** (54) 209 7th St 89301-1583 (Mail to: PO Box 151585 89315-1207) Richard Sims (775) 289-6208

Fallon Holy Trinity Episcopal Church **P** (67) 507 Churchill St 89406-3902 (Mail to: 507 Churchill St 89406-3902) Patrick Leclaire (775) 423-3551

Glenbrook St Johns in the Wilderness Ch **P** (101) 1776 Us Highway 50 89413 (Mail to: 1776 US Highway 50 89413-9714) Eric Heidecker Peter Skewes-Cox (775) 588-6793

Henderson St Timothys Episcopal Church **P** (169) 43 W Pacific Ave 89015-7351 (Mail to: 43 W Pacific Ave 89015-7351) John Jordan Christopher Schuller (702) 565-8033

Incline Vlg St Patrick's Episcopal Church **P** (251) 341 Village Blvd 89451-8237 (Mail to: 341 Village Blvd 89451-8237) Sarah Dunn (775) 831-1418

Las Vegas All Saints Episcopal Church **P** (317) 4201 W Washington Ave 89107-2005 (Mail to: 4201 W Washington Ave 89107-2005) Nicholas Neubauer Rafael Pereira Alvarez (702) 878-2373

Las Vegas Christ Episcopal Church **P** (570) 2000 S Maryland Pkwy 89104-3200 (Mail to: 2000 S Maryland Pkwy # 1 89104-3200) Jorge Hernandez (702) 7357655

Las Vegas Epiphany Episcopal Church **P** (168) 10450 Gilespie St 89183-4112 (Mail to: 10450 Gilespie St 89183-4112) Richard O' Brien (702) 427-9588

Las Vegas Grace in the Desert EpisCh **P** (659) 2004 Spring Gate Ln 89134-6246 (Mail to: 2004 Spring Gate Ln 89134-6246) John Agbaje Mary Bredlau Sherman Frederick Clelia Garrity James Hobart Barbara Lewis Nicholas Neubauer Barbara Preas James Wallis (702) 838-7444

Las Vegas St Lukes Episcopal Church **P** (200) 832 N Eastern Ave 89101-2345 (Mail to: 820 H Street 89106) (702) 642-4459

Las Vegas St Matthews Episcopal Church **P** (176) 4709 S Nellis Blvd 89121-3113 (Mail to: C/O Johnson Watts 6540 Bourbon Way 89107-3331) Christie Leavitt Lionel Starkes (702) 451-2483

Las Vegas St Thomas Episcopal Church **P** (13) 5383 E Owens Ave 89110-1624 (Mail to: C/O Ms Marge Tucker Treasurer 111 N Lamb Blvd 279 89110) Timothy Swonger (702) 452-1199

Lovelock Grace - St Francis Epis Church **P** (14) 801 Cornell Ave 89419 (Mail to: C/O Charles M Harris PO Box 1043 89419-1043) (775) 273-7720

Minden Coventry Cross Episcopal Ch **P** (24) 1631 Esmeralda Ave 89423-4202 (Mail to: Treasurer PO Box 518 89423-0518) Elizabeth Ann Tattersall Elizabeth Ann Tattersall (775) 782-4161

Nixon St Mary the Virgin Epis Church **P** (63) 240 Church St 89424 (Mail to: PO Box 217 89424) (775) 574-0280

Pahrump St Martins in the Desert **P** (66) 631 W Irene St 89060-3929 (Mail to: PO Box 1385 89041-1385) Johnny Mcclatchy Julie Platson (775) 537-1115

Pioche Christ Episcopal Church **P** (18) Cedar St 89043 (Mail to: PO Box 126 89043-0126) (775) 962-5835

Reno St Catherine of Siena **M** (113) 110 Bishop Manogue Dr 89511-4809 (Mail to: PO Box 17831 89511-1033) Eric Heidecker (775) 851-4168

Reno Trinity Episcopal Church **P** (933) 200 Island

Ave 89505-2246 (Mail to: PO Box 2246 89505-2246) Patricia Pumphrey (775) 329-4279

Sparks St Pauls Episcopal Church **P** (322) 1135 12th St 89431-3607 (Mail to: PO Box 737 89432-0737) Kirk Woodliff William Arnold (775) 358-4474

Tonopah St Marks Episcopal Church **P** (5) 210 University St 89043 (Mail to: PO Box 447 89049-0447) (775) 482-5546

Virginia City Old St Pauls Episcopal Church **P** (19) F & Taylor St 89440 (Mail to: PO Box 13 89440-0013) (775) 847-9700

Wadsworth St Michael & All Angels Church **P** (53) 445 Reservation Rd 89442 (Mail to: PO Box 310 89442-0310) (775) 835-6440

DIOCESE OF NEW HAMPSHIRE
(PROVINCE I)
Comprises the State of New Hampshire
DIOCESAN OFFICE 63 Green St Concord NH 03301
TEL (603) 224-1914 FAX (603) 225-7884
E-MAIL info@nhepiscopal.org WEB www.nhepiscopal.org

Previous Bishops—
Alexander V Griswold 1811-43, Carlton Chase 1844-70, Wm W Niles 1870-1914, Edward M Parker coadj 1906 Bp 1914-25, John T Dallas 1926-48, Chas F Hall 1948-73, Philip A Smith 1973-86, Douglas E Theuner 1986-2004, V Gene Robinson 2004-13

Bishop—Rt Rev A Robert Hirschfeld (1067) (Dio 5 Jan 2013)

CFO B Ambrogi; *Sec* K Kennerson; *Treas* C Porter; *Dir of Fin & Benefits* L Tennet; *Chanc* RA Wells Jr; *Exec Asst to Bp* S Gay; *Dean of Clergy* L Howlett; *Cn to Ord* T Pickering; *Comm and Prog Admin* K Traynor

Stand Comm—Cler: K Atkinson Z Harmon; T Gocha *Lay: Pres* M Porter J Stevens B Chapell

PARISHES, MISSIONS, AND CLERGY

Berlin St Barnabas Church **P** (46) 1 Main St 03570-2414 (Mail to: C/O Christine Lindsey PO Box 545 03570-0545) (603) 752-3504

Bretton Woods Church of the Transfiguration **SC** Rt 302 03860-0382 (Mail to: C/O Christ Church PO Box 382 03860-0382) Susan Buchanan (603) 356-2062

Canterbury Kairos Earth Church of the Woods **M** (55) 92 Foster Rd 03224-2517 (Mail to: PO Box 698 03302-0698) Stephen Blackmer (603) 7315013

Claremont Trinity Episcopal Church **P** (85) 120 Broad St 03743-3621 (Mail to: PO Box 172

03743-0172) (603) 542-2103

Claremont Union-St. Luke's Episcopal Ch **P** (32) 133 Old Church Rd 03743-4519 (Mail to: PO Box 902 03743-0902) (603) 542-7209

Colebrook St Stephens Episcopal Mission **M** (14) 16 Parsons St 03576 (Mail to: 1935 US Route 3 03576-6520) Marlyn Neary (603) 237-8229

Concord Chapel of St Peter and Paul **CC** (50) 325 Pleasant St 03301 (Mail to: 325 Pleasant St 03301) (603) 229-4659

Concord Grace Episcopal Church **M** (98) 30 Eastman St 03301-5409 (Mail to: 30 Eastman St 03301-5409) Katherine Siberine (603) 224-2252

Concord St Pauls Church **P** (827) 21 Centre St 03301-6301 (Mail to: 21 Centre St 03301-6301) Kate Atkinson Denis Brunelle Charles Leclerc Peggy Schnack (603) 224-2523

Contoocook St Andrews Episcopal Church **P** (473) 354 Main St 03229-2627 (Mail to: 354 Main St 03229-2627) Reed Loy John Mccausland (603) 746-3415

Derry Church of the Transfiguration **P** (153) 1 Hood Rd 03038-2046 (Mail to: 1 Hood Rd 03038-2046) Raymond Bonin (603) 432-2120

Dover Church of St Thomas **P** (272) 5 Hale St 03820-3712 (Mail to: 5 Hale St 03820-3773) Suzanne Poulin (603) 742-3155

Dublin Emmanuel Church **SC** Dublin Rd 03444 (Mail to: PO Box 499 03444-0499) (603) 563-8029

Dunbarton Ch of St John the Evangelist **M** (29) 270 Stark Hwy N 03046-4714 (Mail to: 270 Stark Hwy N 03046-4714) (603) 774-3678

Durham St Georges Episcopal Church **P** (200) 1 Park Ct 03824-2407 (Mail to: 1 Park Ct 03824-

2400) (603) 868-2785

Exeter Christ Church Episcopal **P** (1160) 43 Pine St 03833-2720 (Mail to: C/O Lucia Savage 43 Pine St 03833-2720) Mark Pendleton Charles Nichols Melissa Remington (603) 772-3332

Goffstown St Matthews Episcopal Church **P** (643) 7 N Mast St 03045-1709 (Mail to: 7 N Mast St 03045-1709) Jason Wells (603) 497-2003

Hampstead St Christophers Episcopal Ch **M** (374) 187 East Rd 03841-5302 (Mail to: C/O Brenda Getchell 187 East Rd 03841-5340) Zachary Harmon (603) 329-4674

Hampton Trinity Episcopal Church **M** (130) 200 High St 03842-2286 (Mail to: 200 High St 03842-2286) Kit M David Nathan Wang (603) 926-5688

Hanover St Thomas Episcopal Church **P** (746) 9 W Wheelock St 03755-1710 (Mail to: 9 W Wheelock St 03755-1710) Guy Collins (603) 643-4155

Holderness Chapel of Holy Cross **M** (195) Holderness School 33 Chapel Ln 03245-5007 (Mail to: Holderness School PO Box 1879 03264-1879) (603) 536-1257

Keene Parish of St James Church **P** (326) 44 West St 03431-3371 (Mail to: 44 West St 03431-3371) Geoffrey Smith Elsa Worth (603) 352-1019

Laconia St James Episcopal Church **P** (92) 2238 Parade Rd 03246-1520 (Mail to: 2238 Parade Rd 03246-1520) Janet Lombardo William Gannon Janet Lombardo (603) 524-5800

Lancaster St Pauls Church **P** (97) 113 Main St 03584-3028 (Mail to: 113 Main St 03584-3028) Weldon Brooks (603) 788-4654

Lisbon Church of the Epiphany **M** (10) 90 School St 03585-6514 (Mail to: 90 School St 03585-6514) (603) 838-8961

Littleton All Saints Episcopal Church **P** (165) 35 School St 03561-4820 (Mail to: 35 School St 03561-4820) Curtis Metzger Paul Higginson (603) 444-3414

Londonderry St Peters Episcopal Church **P** (292) 3 Peabody Row 03053-3302 (Mail to: 3 Peabody Row 03053-6609) Colin Chapman (603) 437-8222

Lost Nation St Timothys Chapel **SC** Lost Nation Road 03584 (Mail to: C/O St Pauls Church 113 Main St 03584) (603) 788-4654

Manchester Grace Episcopal Church **P** (346) Attn: Treasurer Richard Feren 106 Lowell St 03101-1625 (Mail to: Attn: Treasurer Gail Austin 106 Lowell St 03101-1625) Marjorie Gerbracht William Knight Jane Van Zandt Wesley Wasdyke (603) 622-9813

Manchester St Andrews Episcopal Church **P** (38) 102 Main St 03102-4028 (Mail to: 102 Main St Ste 1 03102-4079) Sarah Rockwell (603) 622-8632

Marlborough St Francis Chapel **SC** Stone Pond 03444 (Mail to: PO Box 368 03455-0368) Anne Webb Richard Webb (603) 876-4407

Meredith Trinity Episcopal Church **P** (100) 93 Route 25 East 03253-0635 (Mail to: PO Box 635 03253-0635) Amanda Sampey (603) 279-6689

Merrimack Faith Episcopal Church **M** (87) 590 Daniel Webster Hwy 03054-3429 (Mail to: PO Box 422 03054-0422) (603) 424-6806

Milford Church of Our Saviour **P** (181) 10 Amherst St 03055-4009 (Mail to: PO Box 237 03055-0237) (603) 673-3309

Nashua Church of the Good Shepherd **P** (1085) 214 Main St 03060-2939 (Mail to: Laurie Ascani PO Box 412 03061-0412) Nancy Meyer (603) 882-5352

New London St Andrews Church **P** (450) 15 Gould Rd 03257-5533 (Mail to: PO Box 294 03257-0294) John Macleod John Macleod (603) 526-6344

North Conway Christ Episcopal Church **P** (118) 16 Pine St 03860-5210 (Mail to: PO Box 382 03860-0382) (603) 356-2062

North Woodstock Church of the Messiah **M** (83) School St 03262 (Mail to: PO Box 267 03262-0267) Teresa Gocha (603) 745-3148

Peterborough All Saints Church **P** (359) 51 Concord St 03458-1510 (Mail to: C/O Treasurer 51-53 Concord St 03458-1510) Jennifer Walters Louise Howlett (603) 924-3202

Pittsfield St Stephens Episcopal Church **P** (73) 50 main st 03263 (Mail to: C/O Curtis Metzger PO Box 435 03263-0435) Stephen Blackmer Stephen Blackmer Stephen Ekerberg (603) 435-7908

Portsmouth Christ Church **M** (82) 1035 Lafayette Rd 03801-5468 (Mail to: Attn: Treasurer 1035 Lafayette Rd 03801-7416) (603) 436-8842

Portsmouth St John's Episcopal Church **P** (1047) 100 Chapel St 03801-3808 (Mail to: C/O Finance Administration 100 Chapel St 03801-3808) Robert Stevens Anne Williamson (603) 436-8283

Rye Beach St Andrews by the Sea **SC** Church Rd 03871 (Mail to: PO Box 555 03871-0555) (207) 964-8432

Salem St Davids Episcopal Church **P** (71) 231 Main St 03079-3186 (Mail to: Attn: Treasurer 231 Main St 03079-3186) Carolyn Stevenson (603) 893-0342

Sanbornville Church of St John the Baptist **P** (104) 118 High St 03872-4367 (Mail to: Attn: Treasurer PO Box 249 03872-0249) (603) 522-3329

Sugar Hill St Matthews Summer Chapel **SC** Rte 117 03585 (Mail to: 71 Sunset Hill Rd 03586-4235) (603) 823-5667

Sunapee St James Episcopal Church **SC** 378 Lake Avenue 03782-0178 (Mail to: C/O Mr. A.H. Hardt PO Box 178 03782) (603) 526-9070

Tamworth Church of St Andrew in Valley **P** (70) 678 Whittier Road 03886-0436 (Mail to: PO Box 436 03886-0436) (603) 323-8515

Walpole St Johns Episcopal Church **P** (56) Westminister and Elm Sts 03608 (Mail to: PO Box 179 03608-0179) (603) 756-4533

Weare Church of the Holy Cross **M** (31) 118 Center Rd 03281-4605 (Mail to: PO Box 161 03281-0161) David Ferner (603) 529-1042

Whitefield Church of the Transfiguration **SC** 277 Water St 03598 (Mail to: C/O Mr Christopher

Smith Water Street 03598) Gordon Owen (603) 837-2098

Wolfeboro All Saints Episcopal Church **P** (340) 359 S Main St 03894-4413 (Mail to: PO Box 359 03894-0359) (603) 569-3453

Woodsville St Lukes Episcopal Church **M** (71) 3 Church St 03785-1259 (Mail to: PO Box 167 03785-0167) (603) 747-2670

STATE OF NEW JERSEY

See Dioceses of Newark and New Jersey

DIOCESE OF NEW JERSEY

(PROVINCE II)

Comprises 14 counties in central and southern New Jersey

DIOCESAN OFFICE 808 W State St Trenton NJ 08618-5326

TEL (609) 394-5281 FAX (609) 394-9546 BISHOP'S FAX (609) 394-8015

E-MAIL diocese@dioceseofnj.org WEB www.dioceseofnj.org

Previous Bishops— John Croes 1815-32, Geo W Doane 1832-59, Wm H Odenheimer 1859-74, John Scarborough 1875-1914, Paul Matthews 1915-37, Albion W Knight coadj 1923-35, Ralph E Urban suffr 1932-35, Wallace J Gardner 1937-54, Alfred L Banyard suffr 1945-55 Bp 1955-73, Albert W Van Duzer suffr 1966-72 Bp 1973-82, VK Pettit suffr 1983-91, GPM Belshaw suffr 1975-82 coadj 1982 Bp 1983-94, Joe Morris Doss Bp 1995-2001, David B Joslin asst 2000-03, Sylvestre D Romero 2008-10, George E Councell, DD 2003-2013

Bishop—Rt Rev William H. Stokes, D.D. (Dio 2 Nov 2013)

Cn to Ord Rev Cn J Izzo; *Trans Off* Rev Cn J Izzo; *COO* Cn P Jones; *Sec of Conv* Cn P Ambos; *Treas* J Gloster; *Chanc* Cn P Ambos; *Esq; COP Co-Chairs:* Rev S Connor P Jackson; *Dir of Comm* S Welch; *Com Chair* C White; *Cong Dev* Cn R Droste

Stand Comm—Cler: *Pres* EW Zelley J Hollis L Hoffman A Moore; *Lay:* B Bach P Wolfgang S Espenshade D Freidel

PARISHES, MISSIONS, AND CLERGY

Allenhurst Ch of St Andrews by the Sea **SC** (12) 150 Norwood Ave S 07711-1218 (Mail to: PO BOX 245 07712-0245) (508) 740-2115

Asbury Park St Augustine Episcopal Church **P** (137) Atlantic And Prospect Aves 07712 (Mail to: PO Box 245 07712-0245) Eddie Lillard William Ndishabandi (732) 774-3069

Asbury Park Trinity Church **P** (332) 503 Asbury Ave 07712-6104 (Mail to: 503 Asbury Ave 07712-6189) Nicholas Danford (732) 775-5084

Atlantic City St Augustines Church **P** (132) 170 Arctic Ave PO Box1657 08401-4304 (Mail to: PO Box 1657 08404-1657) (609) 345-0718

Avalon St Johns by the Sea **SC** 25th & Avalon Ave 08202 (Mail to: C/O Frederick A Bluefield 62 Pancoast Road 08202) (609) 996-7715

Avon By Sea St Johns Episcopal Church **SC** 10 Woodland Ave 07717-1341 (Mail to: 11 Woodland Ave box 375 07717-1341) (732) 988-9577

Barnegat Light St Peters at the Light Church **M** (107) 607 Central Ave 08006 (Mail to: 70 Central Ave 08006) Donald Turner Lee Power (609) 494-2398

Basking Ridge St Marks Church **P** (389) 140 Finley Ave 07920-1428 (Mail to: 140 S Finley Av 07920-1428) Richard Morley (908) 766-9058

Bay Head All Saints Church **P** (394) 500 Lak Ave 08742-5366 (Mail to: 500 Lake Ave 08742 0053) Kathryn King (732) 892-7478

Beach Haven Holy Innocents Church **P** (232) Marine St 08008-1635 (Mail to: 410 S Atlanti Ave 08008-1699) Charles Arlin Judith Kror Gretchen Zimmerman (609) 4927571

Bellmawr Church of the Holy Spirit **M** (64) 2 E. Browning Rd 08031 (Mail to: 300 Smith L 08078-1346) (856) 931-0990

Berlin Church of the Good Shepherd **P** (130) 10 W Broad St 08009-1438 (Mail to: 108 W Broa St 08009-1438) Frances Clark (856) 767-016

Bernardsville St John on the Mountain **P** (20 379 Mount Harmony Rd 07924-1414 (Mail t

379 Mount Harmony Rd 07924-1414) (908) 766-2282

Bernardsville St Bernards Episcopal Church **P** (187) 88 Claremont Rd 07924-2210 (Mail to: 88 Claremont Rd 07924-2210) Elizabeth Sciaino (908) 766-0602

Beverly St Stephens Episcopal Church **P** (148) 158 Warren St 08010-1342 (Mail to: 158 Warren St 08010-1342) Frederick Pray Anne Wrede (609) 387-0169

Blackwood St John Episcopal Church **P** (380) 1720 Old Black Horse Pike 08012-5218 (Mail to: 1720 Old Black Horse Pike 08012-5218) Richard Wrede (856) 227-1051

Bordentown Christ Church **P** (206) 124 Prince St 08505-1318 (Mail to: 130 Prince St 08505-1318) James Tucker (609) 298-2348

Bound Brook St Pauls Episcopal Church **P** (98) 214 Church St 08805-1934 (Mail to: 214 Church St 08805-1934) Kristen Foley (732) 356-0247

Bradley Beach St James Episcopal Church **P** (260) 605 4th Ave 07720-1250 (Mail to: PO Box 1 07720-0001) Paul Chalakani James Yarsiah (732) 775-5414

Brick St Raphael the Archangel **P** (94) 1520 Route 88 08724-2320 (Mail to: 1520 Route 88 08724-2320) Maria Sanzo Nancy Hite Speck (732) 458-5743

Bridgewater St Martins Episcopal Church **P** (243) § 1350 Washington Valley Rd 08807-1418 (Mail to: 1350 Washington Valley Rd 08807-1418) Robert Laws (908) 526-1353

Burlington St Marys Episcopal Church **P** (251) 145 W Broad St 08016-1341 (Mail to: 145 W Broad St 08016-1341) John Haynes (609) 386-0902

Camden Ch of St Andrew the Apostle **M** (504) 3050 River Rd 08105-4134 (Mail to: PO Box 1333 08105-0333) Pedro Guzman (856) 365-0111

Camden St Augustine Episcopal Church **P** (64) Broadway & Royden St 08101 (Mail to: PO Box 1925 Broadway Royden Street 08101-1925) (856) 365-3243

Camden St Pauls Episcopal Church **P** (202) 422 Market St 08102-1526 (Mail to: PO Box 1551 08101-1551) Zachary Smith (856) 365-5880

Camden St Wilfreds Church **M** (11) 83 N Dudley St 08105-2425 (Mail to: 3012 Westfield Ave 08105-2411) (856) 365-4924

Cape May Church of the Advent **P** (336) Washington & Franklin Sts 08204 (Mail to: PO Box 261 08204-0261) Henry Leonard Daniel Hall (609) 884-3065

Cape May Point St Peters by the Sea **SC** 102 Lake Dr 08212-0261 (Mail to: 603 Arctic Ave 08204-1819) (609) 898-4318

Cherry Hill St Bartholomews Episcopal Ch **P** (279) 1989 Marlton Pike E 08003-1830 (Mail to: 1989 Marlton Pike E 08003-1830) Lynn Johnson Colleen Spaeth (856) 424-2229

Clarksboro St Peter's Episcopal Church **P** (62) 304 Kings Hwy 08020-1404 (Mail to: 304 Kings Hwy 08020-1404) Martha Bradley (856) 423-4116

Clementon St Mary Episcopal Church **M** (93) 33 Berlin Rd 08021-4501 (Mail to: PO Box 219 08021-0222) Douglas Reans (856) 435-2009

Collingswood Holy Trinity Church **P** (195) 839 Haddon Ave 08108-1941 (Mail to: 839 Haddon Ave 08108-1993) (856) 858-0491

Cranbury St Davids Episcopal Church **P** (440) 90 S Main St 08512-3144 (Mail to: 90 S Main St 08512-3144) Amy Cornell Henry Bristol Donald Caron (609) 655-4731

Cranford Trinity Church **P** (338) 205 North Avenue East 07016-2040 (Mail to: North Avenue At Forest Avenue 07016) Andrew Kruger (908) 276-4047

Dunellen St Francis Episcopal Church **P** (170) 400 New Market Rd 08812-1505 (Mail to: 400 New Market Rd 08812-1505) Margaret Forsythe Francis Hubbard (732) 968-6781

Eatontown St James Memorial Episcopal Ch **P** (127) 69 Broad St # O 07724-1528 (Mail to: PO Box 207 07724-0207) Agostino Rivolta (732) 542-0818

Edison Saint James Church **HC** (73) 2136 Woodbridge Ave 08817-4421 (Mail to: PO Box 1286 08818-1286) (732) 985-2023

Elizabeth St Elizabeths Church **P** (218) 305 N Broad St 07208-3704 (Mail to: PO Box 510 07207-0510) Andy Moore Theodore Moore (908) 289-0681

Elizabeth St Johns Episcopal Church **P** (447) 61 Broad St 07201-2205 (Mail to: PO Box 278 07207-0278) Jorge Liriano Martinez (908) 352-2220

Elizabeth San Jose Episcopal Church **M** (432) 38 W End Pl 07202-1724 (Mail to: 38 W End Pl 07202-1724) Toribio Rodriguez-Santos (908) 289-7070

Flemington Calvary Episcopal Church **P** (318) 44 Broad St 08822-1404 (Mail to: 44 Broad St 08822-1404) John Hain Ann Holt (908) 782-7227

Florence Sts Stephen & Barnabas Epis Ch **M** (87) Second & Spring Sts 08518 (Mail to: PO Box 365 08518-0365) Ryan Paetzold Fernando Paiva (609) 499-0998

Freehold St Peters Episcopal Church **P** (346) 33 Throckmorton St 07728-1946 (Mail to: 33 Throckmorton St 07728-1946) Dirk Reinken (732) 431-8383

Galloway St Marks and All Saints Church **P** (179) 429 S Pitney Rd 08205-9780 (Mail to: 429 S Pitney Rd 08205-9780) Terrence O'Connor Richard Wisniewski (609) 652-6222

Gladstone St Lukes Episcopal Church **P** (696) 182 Main St 07934-2063 (Mail to: PO Box 605 07934-0605) Kent Walley Karen Lewis (908) 234-0002

Glassboro St Thomas Episcopal Church **P** (188) 212 N Main St 08028-1919 (Mail to: Dr Harold Lucius 212 N Main St 08028-1919) Todd Foster Louis De Sheplo (856) 881-9144

Gloucester City Church of the Ascension **P** (102) 110 S Sussex St 08030-1942 (Mail to: 110 S Sussex St 08030-1942) (856) 456-4394

Haddon Heights St Marys Episcopal Church **P** (71) 70 White Horse Pike 08035 (Mail to: 501 Green St 08035-1987) (856) 547-3240

Haddonfield Grace Episcopal Church **P** (931) 19 Kings Hwy E 08033-2001 (Mail to: 19 Kings Hwy E 08033-2097) Kimberly Reinholz (856) 429-0007

Keansburg St Marks Episcopal Church **M** (57) 247 Carr Ave 07734-1452 (Mail to: 247 Carr Ave 07734-1452) (732) 787-1075

Keyport St Mary the Virgin **M** (17) 10 E Front St 07735-1525 (Mail to: PO Box 2 07735-0002) Walter Leigh (732) 264-5288

Lakewood All Saints Church **P** (282) 213 Madison Ave 08701-3316 (Mail to: 213 Madison Ave 08701-3316) (732) 367-0933

Lambertville St Andrews Episcopal Church **P** (235) 50 York St 08530-2024 (Mail to: 50 York St 08530-2024) (609) 397-2425

Laurel Springs Holy Family **M** 233 Fairmount Ave 08021-2115 (Mail to: 233 Fairmount Ave 08021-2115) Naomi Cressman Carmen Viola (856) 784-8666

Lebanon Church of the Holy Spirit **P** (330) 3 Haytown Rd 08833-4009 (Mail to: 3 Haytown Rd 08833-4009) Philip Carr-Jones Johnine Byrer Dorothea Hospador (908) 236-6301

Linden Epis Ch of St John the Baptist **P** (47) 2018 Dewitt Ter 07036-3700 (Mail to: 2018 Dewitt Ter 07036-3700) Terry Blackburn Peter Defranco (908) 925-1535

Little Silver St John's Episcopal Church **P** (232) 325 Little Silver Point Rd 07739-1757 (Mail to: 325 Little Silver Point Rd 07739-1757) (732) 741-7826

Long Branch St James Church **P** (209) 300 Broadway 07740-6930 (Mail to: 300 Broadway 07740-6930) William Noble Robert Sullivan (732) 222-1411

Longport Church of the Redeemer **SC** 108 S 20th Ave 08403-1135 (Mail to: Attn Mr Philip S Demig 1013 W 9th Ave Ste 9e 19406-1208) (609) 822-7222

Lumberton St Martin in the Fields **P** (124) 489 Main St 08048-1101 (Mail to: 489 Main St 08048-1101) Margaret Smyth (609) 261-4882

Magnolia Christ Church **M** (74) 413 W Evesham Ave 08049-1726 (Mail to: PO Box 67 08049-0067) (856) 783-4281

Maple Shade St Johns Episcopal Church **M** (79) 41 E Linwood Avenue 08052-2535 (Mail to: 41 E Linwood Ave 08052-2535) John Powell (856) 779-0389

Matawan Trinity Episcopal Church **P** (194) 18 Ryers Ln 07747 (Mail to: 18 Ryers Ln 07747)

(732) 591-9210

Medford St Peters Episcopal Church **P** (496) 1 Hartford Rd 08055-9051 (Mail to: 1 Hartford Rd 08055-9051) Valerie Balling Helen Orlando (609) 654-2963

Merchantville Grace Episcopal Church **P** (281) 7 E Maple Ave 08109-5005 (Mail to: 7 E Maple Ave 08109-5096) Robert Fitzpatrick (856) 665-4117

Metuchen St Lukes Episcopal Church **P** (233) 17 Oak Ave 08840-1529 (Mail to: 17 Oak Ave 08840-1529) Edmund Zelley (732) 548-4308

Middletown Christ Church **P** (236) 90 Kings Hwy 07748-2025 (Mail to: 90 Kings Hwy 07748-2025) Frances Bickerton Michael Way (732) 671-2524

Millville Christ Episcopal Church **M** (15) 225 Sassafras Street 08332-3353 (Mail to: PO Box 357 08332-0357) Donald Richey (856) 825-1163

Millville Church of the Resurrection **P** (150) 1209 West Main Street 08332 (Mail to: PO Box 1525 08332-8525) Ellen Rutherford (856) 451-3233

Mnchstr Twp St Elisabeths Chpl by-the-Sea **SC** 2 Stonybrook Ct 08759-2032 (Mail to: 31 Ocean Bay Blvd 08735-1922) (732) 830-0450

Monmouth Jct St Barnabas Episcopal Church **HC** (174) 142 Sand Hills Rd 08852-3103 (Mail to: 142 Sand Hills Rd 08852-3103) (732) 297-4607

Moorestown Trinity Church Episcopal **P** (553) § 207 W Main St 08057-2325 (Mail to: 207 W Main St 08057-2381) Emily Mellott Angela Cipolla John Salmon (856) 235-0811

Mount Holly St Andrews Church Episcopal **P** (474) 121 High St 08060-1401 (Mail to: 121 High St 08060-1401) Andrew Hanyzewski (609) 267-0225

Mullica Hill Saint Stephen's Church **M** (105) 51 N Main St 08062-9414 (Mail to: 51 N Main St 08062-9414) Sharon Patterson Sharon Patterson (856) 478-6931

Navesink All Saints Memorial Church **P** (233) 202 Navesink Ave 07752-0326 (Mail to: PO Box 326 07752-0326) Deborah Cook Rosemarie Broderick (732) 291-0214

New Brunswick Christ Church **P** (445) 5 Paterson St 08901-1204 (Mail to: 5 Paterson St 08901-1204) Joanna Hollis Peter Cornell (732) 545-6262

New Brunswick St Albans Episcopal Church **M** (101) 148 Lee Ave 08901-2919 (Mail to: 148 Lee Ave 08901-2919) Sharon Sutton (732) 247-0808

New Brunswick Ch of St John the Evangelist **P** (91) 189 George St 08901-1319 (Mail to: 189 George St 08901-1399) (732) 545-5619

New Brunswick Epis Cmps Ministr at Rutgers **CC** 5 Mine St 08901-1111 (Mail to: 5 Mine St 08901-1111) (732) 932-1278

New Providence St Andrews Episcopal Church **P** (293) 419 South St 07974-2131 (Mail to: 419 South St 07974-2194) Daniel Gunn Daniel Gunn (908) 464-4875

Ocean City Holy Trinity Episcopal Church **P** (140) 2998 Bay Ave 08226-2361 (Mail to: 2998 Bay Ave 08226-2361) Stephen Connor Elizabeth Ohlson (609) 399-1019

Palmyra Christ Church **M** (26) 638 Parry Ave 08065-2502 (Mail to: 638 Parry Ave 08065-2599) Ryan Paetzold (856) 829-1764

Paulsboro St James Episcopal Church **M** (22) 190 E Jefferson St 08066 (Mail to: 349 Lincoln Ave 08066-1132) (856) 845-4878

Pemberton Grace Episcopal Church **P** (139) 43 Elizabeth St 08068-1215 (Mail to: 43 Elizabeth St 08068-1215) Kyle Cuperwich (609) 894-8001

Pennington St Matthews Episcopal Church **P** (550) 300 S Main St 08534-2804 (Mail to: Attn: Bruce Weise 300 S Main St 08534-2804) Ophelia Laughlin John Merz (609) 737-0985

Penns Grove Church of Our Merciful Saviour **P** (125) 110 E Maple Ave 08069-2066 (Mail to: 110 E Maple Ave 08069-2097) (856) 299-6038

Pennsville St Georges Church **P** (64) 305 N Broadway 08070-1216 (Mail to: 305 N Broadway 08070-3010) William Boatwright Sally Maurer (856) 678-7979

Perth Amboy St Peters Episcopal Church **P** (263) 183 Rector St 08861-4739 (Mail to: 183 Rector St 08861-4739) Kathleen Dejohn (732) 826-1594

Pitman Church of the Good Shepherd **P** (537) 315 Highland Ter 08071-1550 (Mail to: 315 Highland Ter 08071-1550) Andrew Reinholz (856) 589-8209

Pittstown St Thomas Episcopal Church **P** (319) 98 Sky Manor Rd 08867-4032 (Mail to: PO Box 348 08867-0348) Debra Clarke (908) 996-4091

Plainfield Grace Episcopal Church **P** (55) 600 Cleveland Ave 07060-1727 (Mail to: 600 Cleveland Ave 07060-1727) Theodore Moore (908) 756-1520

Plainfield Church of the Holy Cross **P** (126) 40 Mercer Ave 07060-4630 (Mail to: Att Office Admin C Hall 40 Mercer Ave 07060-4630) Kwabena Owusu-Afriyie Stephanie Shockley (908) 756-2438

Plainfield St Marks Episcopal Church **P** (458) 1430 Park Ave 07060-2911 (Mail to: 1430 Park Ave 07060-2911) Angelo Wildgoose (908) 754-9483

Pleasantville St Marys Episcopal Church **M** (88) 118 W Bayview Ave 08232-3106 (Mail to: 118 W Bayview Ave 08232-3106) James Wilson (609) 646-1604

Princeton All Saints Church **P** (563) 16 All Saints Rd 08540-3634 (Mail to: 16 All Saints Rd 08540-3634) John Frederick Jane Hague Karl Morrison (609) 921-2420

Princeton Episcopal Church at Princeton **Chapel** (75) C/O Diocese of New Jersey 808 State Rd 08540-1416 (Mail to: 53 University Pl 08540-5100) (609) 252-9469

Princeton Trinity Episcopal Church **P** (1394) 33 Mercer St 08540-6807 (Mail to: 33 Mercer St 08540-6893) Paul Jeanes Joanne Epply-Schmidt Kara Slade (609) 924-2277

Pt Pleas Bch Church Of St Mary's By The Sea **P** (323) 804 Bay Ave 08742-3006 (Mail to: 804 Bay Ave 08742-3006) Debra Brewin-Wilson (732) 892-9254

Rahway Church of the Good Shepherd **P** (168) 749 Seminary Ave 07065-3413 (Mail to: 749 Seminary Ave 07065-3413) (732) 388-3460

Red Bank St Thomas Episcopal Church **P** (137) 26 East Sunset Ave 07701-1408 (Mail to: PO Box 502 07701-0502) Eddie Lillard (732) 747-1039

Red Bank Trinity Episcopal Church **P** (208) 65 W Front St 07701-1621 (Mail to: Attn: Treasurer 65 W Front St 07701-1621) John Lock (732) 741-4581

Riverside Saint Stephen's Church **P** (79) 324 Bridgeboro St 08075-3205 (Mail to: 158 WARREN ST 08010-1342) Sharon Sutton (856) 461-1037

Riverton Christ Church **P** (477) 500 4th St 08077-1214 (Mail to: 500 4th St 08077-1214) (856) 829-1634

Rocky Hill Trinity Episcopal Church **M** (33) 1 Crescent Ave 08553 (Mail to: PO Box 265 08553-0265) (609) 921-8971

Rumson St Georges- by- the- River **P** (1154) Waterman Ave 07760 (Mail to: 7 Lincoln Ave 07760-2051) Jeffrey Roy James Jones (732) 842-0596

Salem St Johns Church **HC** (116) 76 Market St 08079-1911 (Mail to: 76 Market St 08079-1911) Charles Messer (856) 935-1798

Scotch Plains All Saints Episcopal Church **P** (415) 559 Park Ave 07076-1705 (Mail to: 559 Park Ave 07076-1777) Susanna Cates (908) 322-8047

Sea Girt Ch of St Uriel the Archangel **P** (394) § 219 Philadelphia Blvd 08750-2718 (Mail to: 219 Philadelphia Blvd 08750-2718) (732) 449-6173

Sewaren St Johns Church **M** (155) 7 Woodbridge Ave 07077-1423 (Mail to: 17 Woodbridge Ave 07077-1423) Martin Oguike (732) 634-2397

Shrewsbury Christ Episcopal Church **P** (303) 380 Sycamore Ave 07702-4513 (Mail to: 380 Sycamore Ave 07702-4513) Lisa Mitchell Victoria Cuff (732) 741-2220

Somers Point Christ Church Episcopal **P** (250) 157 Shore Rd 08244-2752 (Mail to: PO Box 97 08244-0097) Justin Falciani (609) 927-6262

Somerville St Johns Episcopal Church **P** (753) 158 W High St 08876-1818 (Mail to: 158 W High St 08876-1881) Ronald Pollock William Mccoy (908) 722-1250

South Amboy Christ Church **P** (131) 220 Main Street 08879-1304 (Mail to: 257 4th St 08879-1304) Ann Urinoski (732) 721-6262

South River Holy Trinity Episcopal Church **P** (186) § 90 Leonardine Ave 08882-2507 (Mail to: C/O Treasurer 90 Leonardine Ave 08882-2507) Gregory Bezilla (732) 254-1734

Spotswood St Peters Episcopal Church **P** (514) 505 Main St 08884-1734 (Mail to: Attn: Finance Chair 505 Main St 08884-1734) Marshall Shelly (732) 251-2449

Spring Lake Holy Trinity Episcopal Church **SC** 301 Monmouth Ave 07762-1128 (Mail to: PO Box 317 07762-0317) Peter Stimpson (734) 477-4363

Stone Harbor St Marys Episcopal Church **P** (145) 9425 3rd Ave 08247-1926 (Mail to: 9425 3rd Ave 08247-1926) Peter Stube (609) 368-5922

Summit St Simons by the Sea Church **SC** C/O Mr Sandy White 206 Oak Ridge Ave 07901-3237 (Mail to: Attn Jennifer Buck PO Box 532 08738-0532) (860) 236-5321

Swedesboro Trinity Epis Old Swedes Church **M** (82) 1208 Kings Hwy 08085-0031 (Mail to: PO Box 31 08085-0031) Gregory Wilson (856) 467-1227

Toms River Christ Episcopal Church **P** (649) 415 Washington St 08753-6742 (Mail to: 415 Washington St 08753-6742) Lisa Hoffman Jose Cantos Delgado Jose Cantos Delgado Theodore Foley Emily Holman Lewis McCrum (732) 349-5506

Trenton Christ Church-Cristo Rey **M** (1313) 331 Hamilton Ave 08609-2716 (Mail to: 331 Hamilton Ave 08609-2716) Ramon Liz Lopez (609) 394-8926

Trenton Grace St Pauls Church **P** (218) 3715 E State St Ext 08619-2447 (Mail to: 3715 E State Street Ext 08619-2447) (609) 586-6004

Trenton Holy Apostles Episcopal Church **P** (315) 1040 Yardville-Allentown Rd 08620 (Mail to: 1040 Yardville Allentown Rd 08620-9711) Arthur Powell Denise Cavaliere (609) 208-0228

Trenton St Luke's Episcopal Church **P** (149) 1620 Prospect St 08638-3031 (Mail to: 1620 Prospect St 08638-3031) Alexandra Van Kuiken (609) 882-7614

Trenton St Michaels Episcopal Church **M** (38) 140 N Warren St 08608-1308 (Mail to: 140 N Warren St 08608-1308) (609) 392-8086

Trenton St Peters IGBO Church **M** (141) 1300 Brunswick Ave 08638-3316 (Mail to: 1300 Brunswick Ave 08638-3316) (609) 599-2880

✠ **Trenton** Trinity Cathedral **O** (493) 801 W State St 08618-5325 (Mail to: C/O William Harmer 801 W State St 08618-5325) Rene

John Peter Bridge Christopher Cox Carol Gilbert (609) 392-3805

Tuckerton Church of the Holy Spirit **M** (169) 220 E. Main 08087-2627 (Mail to: PO Box 174 08087-0174) (609) 296-9618

Union St Luke & All Saints Epis Ch **P** (44) 398 Chestnut St 07083-9413 (Mail to: 398 Chestnut St 07083-9413) James Kollin (908) 688-7253

Villas St Barnabas by the Bay Church **M** (108) 13 W Bates Ave 08251-2502 (Mail to: 13 W Bates Ave 08251-2502) Susan Cushinotto (609) 886-5960

Vincentown Trinity Episcopal Church **M** (40) 18 Mill St 08088-8824 (Mail to: 18 Mill St 08088-8824) Robert Haller (609) 859-2299

Wall Township St Michaels Episcopal Church **P** (114) 2015 Allenwood Rd 07719-4633 (Mail to: 2015 Allenwood Rd 07719-4633) James Yarsiah (732) 681-1863

Waretown St Stephens Episcopal Church **P** (377) 367 Route 9 08758-1702 (Mail to: 367 Route 9 08758-1702) Jon Graves Lisa Graves (609) 698-8561

Wenonah Holy Trinity Episcopal Church **P** (416) 11 N Monroe Ave 08090-1735 (Mail to: 11 N Monroe Ave 08090-1735) Benjamin Maddison (856) 468-0295

Westfield St Pauls Episcopal Church **P** (1537) § 414 E Broad St 07090-2124 (Mail to: 414 E Broad St 07090-2124) E Michael Morgan (908) 232-8506

Whiting St Stephens Episcopal Church **P** (280) 180 Route 539 08759-1248 (Mail to: 180 Route 539 08759-1248) Paul Van Sant (732) 350-2121

Wildwood St Simeons by the Sea Church **P** (78) 2502 Central Ave 08260-5235 (Mail to: 2502 Central Ave 08260-5235) (609) 522-8389

Williamstown St Marks at the Crossing Ch **M** (60) 131 W Malaga Rd 08094-3852 (Mail to: 131 W Malaga Rd 08094-3852) (856) 629-8762

Willingboro Church of Christ the King **M** (275) C/O Clint Jackson 40 Charleston Rd 08046-2066 (Mail to: 40 Charleston Rd 08046-2066) (609) 877-2987

Woodbridge Trinity Episcopal Church **P** (379) 650 Rahway Ave 07095-3530 (Mail to: 650 Rahway Ave 07095-3530) Fernando Paiva (732) 634-7422

Woodbury Christ Episcopal Church **P** (866) 62 Delaware St 08096-5912 (Mail to: 62 Delaware St 08096-5989) John Alexander (856) 845-0190

Woodstown Saint Luke's Church **M** (59) 37 E Grant St 08098-1401 (Mail to: 37 E Grant St PO Box 197 08098-1401) (856) 769-0760

STATE OF NEW MEXICO
Diocese of Rio Grande (RG)

STATE OF NEW YORK
Dioceses of Albany (A), Central New York (CNY), Long Island (LI), New York (NY), Rochester (Roch),
and Western New York (WNY)

Adams—CNY
Addison—Roch
Afton—CNY
Albany—A
Albion—WNY
Alden—WNY
Alexandria Bay—CNY
Amagansett—LI
Amenia—NY
Amityville—LI
Amsterdam—A
Angelica—Roch
Angola—WNY
Arden—NY
Ardsley—NY
Armonk—NY
Astoria—LI
Attica—WNY
Auburn—CNY
Aurora—CNY
Au Sable Forks—A
Avon—Roch
Babylon—LI
Bainbridge—CNY
Baldwin—LI
Baldwinsville—CNY
Ballston Spa—A
Barneveld—CNY
Batavia—WNY
Bath—Roch
Bay Shore—LI
Bayside—LI
Beacon—NY
Bedford—NY
Bellmore—LI
Bellport—LI
Berkshire—CNY
Binghamton—CNY
Black River—CNY
Boonville—CNY
Bloomville—A
Blue Mountain
Lake—A
Bolton Landing—A
Bovina—A
Branchport—Roch
Brant Lake—A
Brentwood—LI
Brewster—NY

Briarcliff—NY
Bridgehampton—LI
Brockport—Roch
Bronx—NY
Bronxville—NY
Brookhaven—LI
Brooklyn—LI
Brownville—CNY
Buffalo—WNY
Burnt Hills—A
Burt—WNY
Caledonia—Roch
Callicoon—NY
Cambria Hts—LI
Cambridge—A
Camden—CNY
Camillus—CNY
Canajoharie—A
Canandaigua—Roch
Canaseraga—Roch
Canastota—CNY
Candor—CNY
Canton—A
Cape Vincent—CNY
Carle Pl—LI
Carthage—CNY
Catskill—A
Cazenovia—CNY
Ctr Mariches—LI
Central Islip—LI
Chadwicks—CNY
Champlain—A
Chappaqua—NY
Chatham—A
Chautauqua—WNY
Chelsea—NY
Cherry Valley—A
Chester—NY
Chittenango—CNY
Clayton—CNY
Clifton Park—A
Clifton Spgs—Roch
Clinton—CNY
Cobleskill—A
Cohoes—A
Cold Spg—NY
Cold Spg Hbr—LI
Colton—A
Constableville—CNY

Constantia—CNY
Cooperstown—A
Copake Falls—A
Copenhagen—CNY
Corning—Roch
Cornwall—NY
Cortland—CNY
Coxsackie—A
Croton on Hudson—
NY
Cuba—Roch
Dansville—Roch
Deer Pk—LI
Delhi—A
Delmar—A
Deposit—A
Dobbs Ferry—NY
Douglaston—LI
Dover Plains—NY
Downsville—A
Duanesburg—A
Dunkirk—WNY
Eastchester—NY
E Aurora—WNY
E Elmhurst—LI
E Hampton—LI
E Setauket—LI
E Syracuse—CNY
Elizabethtown—A
Ellenville—NY
Ellicottville—WNY
Elmhurst—LI
Elmira—CNY
Endicott—CNY
Essex—A
Evans Mills—CNY
Fairport—Roch
Far Rockaway—LI
Farmingdale—LI
Fayetteville—CNY
Fishers Is—LI
Fishkill—NY
Floral Pk—LI
Flushing—LI
Forest Hills—LI
Ft Montgomery—NY
Franklin—A
Franklinville—WNY
Fredonia—WNY

Freeport—LI
Fulton—CNY
Garden City—LI
Garnerville—NY
Garrison—NY
Gates—Roch
Geneseo—Roch
Geneva—Roch & CNY
Gilbertsville—A
Glen Cove—LI
Glens Falls—A
Goshen—NY
Gouverneur—A
Gowanda—WNY
Grand Is—WNY
Granite Spgs—NY
Great Neck—LI
Great River—LI
Greene—CNY
Greenport—LI
Greenville—A
Greenwich—A
Greenwood Lake—NY
Guilderland—A
Hamburg—WNY
Hamilton—CNY
Hammondsport—Roch
Hampton Bays—LI
Harrison—NY
Hartsdale—NY
Hastings on Hudson—
NY
Hempstead—LI
Henrietta—Roch
Hewlett—LI
Hicksville—LI
Highland Falls—NY
Hilton—Roch
Holley—WNY
Hollis—LI
Honeoye Falls—Roch
Hoosick Falls—A
Hopewell Jct—NY
Hornell—Roch
Horseheads—CNY
Hudson—A
Hudson Falls—A
Huntington—LI
Hyde Park—NY

Ilion—A
Irving—WNY
Irvington—NY
Islip—LI
Ithaca—CNY
Jackson Hts—LI
Jamaica—LI
Jamestown—WNY
Johnson City—CNY
Johnstown—A
Jordan—CNY
Katonah—NY
Keene Valley—A
Keesville—A
Kenmore—WNY
Keuka Park—Roch
Kew Gardens—LI
Kinderhook—A
Kingston—NY
Lake George—A
Lake Luzerne—A
Lake Placid—A
Lake Pleasant—A
Lancaster—WNY
Larchmont—NY
Latham—NY
LeRoy—WNY
Lewiston—WNY
Lindenhurst—LI
Little Falls—A
Liverpool—CNY
Lockport—WNY
Locust Valley—LI
Long Bch—LI
Long Is City—LI
Lowville—CNY
Lynbrook—LI
Lyons—Roch
Mahopac—NY
Malone—A
Mamaroneck—NY
Manhasset—LI
Manlius—CNY
Marathon—CNY
Marcellus—CNY
Margaretville—A
Marlboro—NY
Massapeque—LI
Massena—A
Mastic Bch—LI
Mattituck—LI
Mayville—WNY
Mechanicville—A
Medford—LI
Medina—WNY
Mexico—CNY
Middletown—NY
Millbrook—NY
Mohegan Lake—NY
Monroe—NY
Montgomery—NY

Monticello—NY
Montrose—NY
Moravia—CNY
Morris—A
Morristown—A
Mt Kisco—NY
Mt Vernon—NY
Nedrow—CNY
Newark—Roch
New Berlin—CNY
New City—NY
New Hamburg—NY
New Hartford—CNY
New Hyde Park—LI
New Lebanon—A
New Paltz—NY
New Rochelle—NY
New Windsor—NY
New York—NY
Newburgh—NY
Newcomb—A
Niagara Falls—WNY
N Belmore—LI
N Creek—A
N Granville—A
N Salem—NY
N Tonawanda—WNY
Northport—LI
Norwich—CNY
Norwood—A
Nyack—NY
Oakdale—LI
Odessa—Roch
Ogdensburg—A
Old Forge—A
Olean—WNY
Oneida—CNY
Oneonta—A
Orchard Pk—WNY
Ossining—NY
Oswego—CNY
Oxford—CNY
Oyster Bay—LI
Palenville—A
Palmyra—Roch
Parishville—CNY
Patchogue—LI
Patterson—NY
Paul Smiths—A
Pawling—NY
Pearl River—NY
Peekskill—NY
Pelham—NY
Penfield—Roch
Penn Yan—Roch
Perry—WNY
Philmont—A
Pierrepont Manor—
  CNY
Pine Plains—NY
Pittsford—Roch

Plainview—LI
Plattsburgh—A
Pleasant Valley—NY
Pleasantville—NY
Pt Chester—NY
Pt Jefferson—LI
Pt Jervis—NY
Pt Leyden—CNY
Pt Washington—LI
Potsdam—A
Pottersville—A
Poughkeepsie—NY
Pulaski—CNY
Queens Village—LI
Quogue—LI
Randolph—WNY
Red Hook—NY
Rensselaer—A
Rensselaerville—A
Rhinebeck—NY
Richfield Spgs—A
Riverhead—LI
Rochester—Roch
Rockville Ctr—LI
Rome—CNY
Ronkonkoma—LI
Roosevelt—LI
Roosevelt Is—NY
Rosedale—LI
Roslyn—LI
Round Lake—A
Rye—NY
Sackets Hbr—CNY
Sag Hbr—LI
St Albans—LI
St James—LI
Salamanca—WNY
Salem—A
Saltaire—LI
Saranac Lake—A
Saratoga Spgs—A
Saugerties—NY
Savona—Roch
Sayville—LI
Scarsdale—NY
Schenectady—A
Schenevus—A
Schroon Lake—A
Schuylerville—A
Scottsville—Roch
Sea Cliff—LI
Seaford—LI
Selden—LI
Seneca Falls—CNY
Shelter Is—LI
Sherburne—CNY
Sherrill—CNY
Shoreham—LI
Sidney—A
Silver Creek—WNY
Skaneateles—CNY

Slaterville Springs—
  CNY
Smithtown—LI
Sodus—Roch
Sodus Point—Roch
Somers—NY
So Fallsburgh—NY
Southampton—LI
So New Berlin—CNY
S Ozone Park—LI
So Salem—NY
Sparkill—NY
Spring Valley—NY
Springfield Ctr—A
Springfield Gdns—LI
Springville—WNY
Staatsburg—NY
Stafford—WNY
Stamford—A
Staten Is—NY
Stone Ridge—NY
Stony Brook—LI
Stony Pt—NY
Suffern—NY
Syracuse—CNY
Tarrytown—NY
Ticonderoga—A
Tivoli—NY
Tomkins Cove—NY
Tonawanda—WNY
Troy—A
Trumansburg—CNY
Tupper Lake—A
Tuxedo Park—NY
Twilight Park—A
Unadilla—A
Utica—CNY
Valley Cottage—NY
Valley Stream—LI
Wading River—LI
Walden—NY
Walton—A
Wantagh—LI
Wappingers Falls—NY
Warrensburg—A
Warsaw—WNY
Warwick—NY
Washingtonville—NY
Waterford—A
Waterloo—CNY
Watertown—CNY
Watervliet—A
Watkins Glen—Roch
Waverly—CNY
Webster—Roch
Wellsville—Roch
W Park—NY
Westbury—LI
Westfield—WNY
Westford—A
Westhampton Bch—LI

White Plains—NY   Williston Pk—LI   Woodside—LI   Youngstown—WNY
Whitestone—LI   Wilson—WNY   Woodstock—NY
Willard—CNY   Windsor—CNY   Yaphank—LI
Williamsville—WNY   Woodhaven—LI   Yonkers—NY

DIOCESE OF NEW YORK
(PROVINCE II)
Comprises 10 counties in southern New York
DIOCESAN OFFICE 1047 Amsterdam Ave New York NY 10025
TEL (212) 316-7400 FAX (212) 316-7405
E-MAIL info@diioceseny.org WEB www.dioceseny.org

Previous Bishops—
Samuel Provoost 1787-1815, Benj
Moore asst 1801 Bp 1815-16,
John H Hobart asst 1811 Bp 1816-
30, Benj T Onderdonk 1830-61,
Jonathan M Wainwright provis
1852-54, Horatio Potter provis
1854 Bp 1861-87, Henry C Potter asst 1883 Bp 1887-1908, David
H Greer coadj 1904 Bp 1908-19, Chas S Burch suffr
1911 Bp 1919-20, Wm T Manning 1921-46, Arthur
S Lloyd suffr 1921-36, Herbert Shipman suffr 1921-
30, Chas K Gilbert suffr 1930 Bp 1947-50, Chas F
Boynton suffr 1951-69, Horace WB Donegan suffr
1947-50, coadj 1950 Bp 1950-72, Harold L Wright
suffr 1974-78, James S Wetmore suffr 1960-87, Paul
Moore Jr coadj 1969 Bp 1972-89, Walter D Dennis suffr 1979-1998, Richard F Grein coadj 1989 Bp
1989-2001, Mark S Sisk coadj 1998-2001 Bp 2001-
2013, Catherine S Roskam suffr 1996-2012

**Bishop—Rt Rev Andrew ML Dietsche (Dio 2
Feb 2013)**

Bishop Suffragan—Rt Rev Allen K Shin

Bishop Assistant—Rt Rev Mary D Glasspool

Chanc A Yurke; *V-Chanc* J Harbeson; *Treas* Sr F
Margaret CHS; *Sec of Conv & Reg* KG Flexer; *Senior
Asst Sec of Conv* S Saavedra; *Cn to Ord* Rev Cn JD
Perris; *Hist* W Kempton *Cn Min* Rev Cn C Simmons;
Cn Trans Min Rev Cn L Smith; *Cn Pastor* Rev Cn KJ
Person; *Cn for Cong Vit & Form* Rev Cn V Conrado;
Liaison for Global Miss Rev Y Bass-Choate; *Religious
Life Adviser & Epis Campus Chap for Harlem,
Uptown and the Bronx* Rev R Kuratko

Stand Comm—Cler: S Owen JA Zahl J Kotuby ML
Foulke; *Lay:* C Burns M Hendricks S Auchincloss
V O'Neal

PARISHES, MISSIONS, AND CLERGY
  Amenia St Thomas Church **P** (31) 40 Leedsville Rd
  12501-5836 (Mail to: 40 Leedsville Rd 12501-
  5836) Gene Stack Lois Szost (845) 373-9161

Arden St Johns Church **P** (41) 26 Homestead Dr
  10910-0051 (Mail to: General Delivery 10910-
  9999) (845) 351-4696
Ardsley St Barnabas Church **P** (79) 2 Revolution-
  ary Rd 10502 (Mail to: 2 Revolutionary Rd
  10502-1512) (914) 693-3366
Armonk St Stephens Church **P** (275) 50 Bedford
  Rd 10504-1830 (Mail to: 50 Bedford Rd 10504-
  1814) Garrett Mettler (914) 273-3812
Beacon St Andrew & St Luke Epis Ch **P** (102) 850
  Wolcott Ave 12508-4081 (Mail to: 15 South
  Ave 12508-3114) John Williams
Bedford St Matthews Church **P** (1220) 382
  Cantitoe St 10507 (Mail to: PO Box 293 10506-
  0293) Andrew Courtright John Zahl (914)
  234-9636
Brewster St Andrews Church **P** (94) 26 Prospect
  St 10509-1216 (Mail to: 26 Prospect St 10509-
  1216) (845) 279-4325
Briarcliff All Saints Church **P** (195) 201
  Scarborough Rd 10510-2043 (Mail to: 201
  Scarborough Rd 10510-2043) Kevin Veitinger
  Ann Douglas (914) 941-6955
Bronx Christ Church Riverdale **P** (400) 5030
  Henry Hudson Pkwy 10471-3297 (Mail to:
  5030 Henry Hudson Pkwy 10471-3297) Emily
  Lukanich (718) 543-1011
Bronx Church of the Atonement **P** (61) 1344-44
  Beach Ave 10472-1909 (Mail to: 1344 Beach
  Ave 10472-1909) (718) 828-6078
Bronx Church of the Good Shepherd **P** (286)
  4401 Matilda Ave 10470-1502 (Mail to: 4401
  Matilda Ave 10470-1502) Calvin Mcintyre
  (718) 324-2347
Bronx Church of the Holy Nativity **P** (91) 3061
  Bainbridge Ave 10467-3904 (Mail to: 3061
  Bainbridge Ave 10467-3999) (718) 652-0443
Bronx Church of the Mediator **P** (103) 260 W
  231st St 10463-3904 (Mail to: 260 W 231st St
  10463-3904) (718) 548-0944
Bronx Grace Church **P** (40) 104 City Island
  Ave 10464-1660 (Mail to: 116 City Island
  Ave 10464-0131) John Covington (718) 885-
  1080

Bronx Grace Church (West Farms) **P** (110) 1909 Vyse Ave 10460-4343 (Mail to: 1909 Vyse Ave 10460-4343) (718) 542-1946

Bronx Haitian Congreg of Good Smrtn **P** (123) 1858 Hunt Ave 10462-3623 (Mail to: 1858 Hunt Ave 10462-3623) (718) 881-3779

Bronx Iglesia de San Juan Bautista **M** (45) 948 E 156th St 10455-1998 (Mail to: 948 E 156th St 10455-1914) Maria Servellon (718) 893-0376

Bronx St Andrews Episcopal Church **P** (371) 781 Castle Hill Ave 10473-1330 (Mail to: Attn: Linda Philip 781 Castle Hill Ave 10473-1396) Allen George (718) 863-2244

Bronx St Anns Church **P** (508) 295 St Ann Ave 10454 (Mail to: 295 Saint Anns Ave 10454-2597) Martha Overall (718) 585-5632

Bronx St Davids Church **P** (152) 384 E 160th St # 200 10451-4404 (Mail to: PO Box 200 10451-0200) (718) 665-2747

Bronx St Edmunds Church **P** (95) 1905 Morris Ave 10453-5903 (Mail to: 1905 Morris Ave 10453-5903) Benjamin Nnaji (718) 299-7567

Bronx St James Church, Fordham **P** (199) 2500 Jerome Ave 10468-4300 (Mail to: 2500 Jerome Ave 10468-4300) William Cusano (718) 367-0655

Bronx Saint Joseph's Church **P** (186) 155 Dreiser Loop 10475-2703 (Mail to: Attn: Glynis Bruce 155 Dreiser Loop 10475-2703) Simeon Johnson (718) 320-0844

Bronx Saint Luke's Episcopal Church **P** (989) Attn: Mr Bookal 777 E 222nd St 10467-5105 (Mail to: Attn: Janet William 777 E 222nd St 10467-5105) Pierre-Andre Duvert (718) 8823060

Bronx St Margarets Church (Longwood) **P** (133) 940 E 156th St 10455-1914 (Mail to: 940 E 156th St 10455-1998) Theodora Brooks (718) 589-4430

Bronx St Marthas Church **P** (28) 1858 Hunt Ave 10462-3623 (Mail to: 1858 Hunt Ave 10462-3623) Eliza Davies-Aryeequaye (718) 792-3681

Bronx St Pauls Church **P** (52) 489 Saint Pauls Pl 10456-1935 (Mail to: PO Box 507 10456-0520) Horton Scott (347) 269-7604

Bronx St Peters Church **P** (191) 2500 Westchester Ave 10461-3543 (Mail to: 2500 Westchester Ave 10461-4588) Joade Dauer-Cardasis (718) 931-9270

Bronx St Simeons Church **P** (105) 1858 Hunt Ave 10462-3623 (Mail to: C/O St Marthas Church PO Box 950A 10451) (718) 824-9188

Bronx St Stephens Church (Woodlawn) **P** (69) 439 E 238th St 10470-1701 (Mail to: 439 E 238th St 10470-1701) (718) 324-5427

Bronx Trinity Church of Morrisania **P** (78) 698 East 166th Street 10456-5699 (Mail to: 698 E 166th St 10456-5699) Howard Blunt (718) 542-1309

Bronxville Christ Church **P** (686) § Att: Katherine Gojkovich 17 Sagamore Rd 10708-1502 (Mail to: Att: Jocelyn Angelone 17 Sagamore Rd 10708-1599) Kurt Gerhard Jennifer Brown (914) 337-3544

Callicoon St James Church **P** (15) Route 17b 12723 (Mail to: PO Box 296 12723-0296) Elizabeth Groskoph Ralph Groskoph (845) 887-4742

Chappaqua Church of St Mary the Virgin **P** (278) 191 South Greeley Avenue 10514 (Mail to: PO Box 380 10514-0380) (914) 238-8751

Chelsea St Marks Ch, Chelsea on Hudson **P** (9) 9 Liberty St 12512 (Mail to: PO Box 252 12512-0252) (845) 838-1886

Chester St Pauls Church **P** (94) 101 Main St 10918-1328 (Mail to: 101 Main St 10918-1328) (845) 469-2616

Cold Spring St Marys Ch in the Highlands **P** (102) 1 Chestnut St 10516-2516 (Mail to: PO Box 351 10516-0351) Steven Schunk (845) 265-2539

Cornwall St John's Church **P** (118) 66 Clinton St 12518-1558 (Mail to: PO Box 783 12518-0783) Suzanne Toro David McDonald (845) 534-5475

Croton Hdsn St Augustines Episcopal Church **P** (277) 6 Old Post Rd N 10520-2016 (Mail to: 6 Old Post Rd N 10520-2016) Jennifer Owen Sharon Manning-Lew (914) 271-3501

Dobbs Ferry Zion Episcopal Church **P** (80) 55 Cedar St 10522-1711 (Mail to: 55 Cedar S 10522-1711) Mary Grambsch (914) 693-9320

Dover Plains Mision Ep Santiago Apostol **P** (30) 12 Reimer Ave 12522-5136 (Mail to: PO Box 336 12522-0336) (203) 605-0090

Eastchester St Lukes Church **P** (21) 100 Stewart Ave 10709-5799 (Mail to: 98 Stewart Ave 10709-5799) Charles Pridemore (914) 961-3856

Ellenville St Johns Memorial Church **P** (124) 46 Market St 12428-2132 (Mail to: PO Box 26 12428) (845) 647-7084

Fishkill Trinity Church **P** (94) 1200 Main S 12524-1849 (Mail to: PO Box 484 12524-0484) (845) 896-9884

Fort Montgomery Saint Mark's Church **M** 9 S Marks Pl 10922 (Mail to: PO Box 116 10928 0116) (845) 446-2197

Garnerville Trinity Church **P** (117) 28 Chapel St 10923 (Mail to: 28 Chapel St 10923-1209 (845) 947-1090

Garrison St Philips in the Highlands **P** (376) 1101 Route 9d 10524-3638 (Mail to: PO Box 15 10524-0158) Amanda Eiman (845) 424-3571

Goshen St James Church **P** (472) 1 Saint James F 10924-2013 (Mail to: 1 Saint James Pl 10924 2013) Michael Lunden Thomas Liotta (845 294-6225

Granite Spgs Church of the Good Shepherd (139) 39 Granite Springs Rd 10527-1108 (Ma to: 39 Granite Springs Rd 10527-1108) Harr Roark (914) 248-5631

Greenwood Lake Church of the Good Shepherd **P** (19) 62 Windermere Ave 10925-0011 (Mail to: PO Box 11 10925-0011) (845) 477-2191

Harrison All Saints Church **P** (80) 300 Harrison Ave 10528-3328 (Mail to: 300 Harrison Ave 10528-3360) (914) 835-4716

Hartsdale St Andrews Episcopal Church **P** (44) 101 N Central Ave 10530-1912 (Mail to: 101 N Central Ave 10530-1912) (914) 946-7931

Hastings Hdsn Grace Episcopal Church **P** (208) 78 Main St 10706-1602 (Mail to: 78 Main St 10706-1602) Lauren Kuratko (914) 478-1779

Highland Falls Holy Innocents **P** (210) 401 Main St 10928-0116 (Mail to: PO Box116 10928-0116) Judith Ferguson (845) 446-2197

Hopewell Junction Church of the Resurrection **P** (85) 182 Route 376 12533-6083 (Mail to: 182 Route 376 12533-6083) Janice Kotuby (845) 226-5727

Hyde Park Saint James Church **P** (177) 4526 Albany Post Rd 12538-1564 (Mail to: 4526 Albany Post Rd 12538-1564) David Bender Gail Ganter-Toback Meredith Sanderson (845) 229-2820

Irvington St Barnabas Church **P** (313) 15 N Broadway 10533-1802 (Mail to: 15 N Broadway 10533-1898) Gareth Evans (914) 591-8194

Katonah St Luke's Episcopal Church **P** (85) 68 Bedford Rd 10536-2117 (Mail to: PO Box 602 10536-0602) Patrick Ward (914) 232-5220

Kingston Church of the Holy Cross **P** (146) 30 Pine Grove Ave 12401-5408 (Mail to: 30 Pine Grove Ave 12401-5408) Frank Alagna Maria Servellon (845) 331-6796

Kingston St Johns Episcopal Church **P** (164) 207 Albany Ave 12401-2511 (Mail to: 207 Albany Ave 12401-2511) Susan Bonsteel Michelle Meech (845) 331-2252

Larchmont St Johns Church **P** (495) 4 Fountain Sq 10538-4106 (Mail to: 4 Fountain Sq 10538-4199) Lisa Mason (914) 834-2981

Mahopac Church of the Holy Communion **P** (108) 1055 Route 6 10541-3402 (Mail to: 1055 Route 6 10541-3402) David Morris David Morris (845) 628-6144

Mamaroneck St Thomas Church **P** (236) 168 W Boston Post Rd 10543-3605 (Mail to: 168 W Boston Post Rd 10543-3605) Tami Burks (914) 698-0300

Marlboro Christ Church **P** (84) 222 Old Post Rd 12542-6534 (Mail to: PO Box 27 12542-0027) (845) 220-7478

Middletown Grace Church **P** (400) 58 North St 10940-5011 (Mail to: 12 Depot St 10940-5707) Victor Sarrazin (845) 343-6101

Millbrook Grace Church **P** (246) 3328 Franklin Ave 12545-5969 (Mail to: PO Box 366 12545-0366) Matthew Calkins Alison Quin (845) 677-3064

Millbrook St Peters Church Lithgow **P** (300) 692 Deep Hollow Rd 12545-1502 (Mail to: PO Box 1502 12545-1502) Jacob Dell (845) 677-9286

Mohegan Lake St Marys Church **P** (149) 1836 E Main St 10547-1226 (Mail to: 1836 E Main St 10547-1226) Ronnie Stout-Kopp (914) 528-3972

Monroe Grace Episcopal Church **P** (70) 1 Forest Ave 10950-2809 (Mail to: 1 Forest Ave 10950-2809) (845) 782-8535

Montgomery St Francis of Assisi **P** (28) 74 Wallkill Ave 12549 (Mail to: PO Box 708 12586-0708) (845) 457-7545

Monticello St Johns Episcopal Church **P** (70) 15 St John St 12701-2118 (Mail to: 14 Saint John St 12701-2118) (845) 807-3050

Montrose Church of the Divine Love **P** (127) 80 Sunset Rd 10548 (Mail to: 80 Sunset Rd 10548-1334) Jean Quatorze (484) 737-1080

Mount Kisco St Marks Church **P** (181) 85 E Main St 10549 (Mail to: 85 E Main St 10549-2313) William Doubleday Kyle Martindale (914) 666-8058

Mount Vernon Sts John Paul & Clement **P** (66) 126 S 9th Ave 10550-3019 (Mail to: 126 S 9th Ave 10550-3019) (914) 668-0551

Mount Vernon Church of the Ascension **P** (201) 104 Park Ave 10550-1410 (Mail to: 104 Park Ave 10550-1410) George Taylor (914) 668-4851

New City St Johns Church **P** (260) 365 Strawtown Rd 10956-6632 (Mail to: Attn: Margaret Gillespie 365 Strawtown Rd 10956-6632) Shawn Duncan Victoria Duncan (845) 634-3601

New Hamburg St Nicholas on the Hudson **M** (293) 37 Point St 12590-5529 (Mail to: 37 Point St 12590-5529) Leigh Hall (845) 297-2010

New Paltz St Andrews Episcopal Church **P** (153) 163 Main St 12561-1116 (Mail to: 163 Main St 12561-1116) (845) 255-5098

New Rochelle Ch of St Simon the Cyrenian **P** (96) 135 Remington Pl 10801 (Mail to: 135 Remington Pl 10801-3925) Evette Austin Paulette Remppel (914) 632-5911

New Rochelle St Johns Church Wilmot **P** (108) 11 Wilmot Rd 10804-1514 (Mail to: 11 Wilmot Rd 10804-1514) Jennie Talley William Cusano Jennie Talley (914) 636-0047

New Rochelle Trinity St Pauls Episcopal **P** (175) 311 Huguenot St 10801-7208 (Mail to: 311 Huguenot St 10801-7208) Hollis Galgano Hyacinth Lee (914) 632-5368

New Windsor St Thomas Episcopal Church **P** (103) 47 Old Route 9w 12553-5480 (Mail to: PO Box 4221 12553-0221) (845) 562-4712

New York All Angels Church **P** (350) 251 W 80th St 10024-5743 (Mail to: 251 W 80th St 10024-5798) Walter Kerbel (212) 362-9300

New York All Saints Church **P** (225) 230 E 60th St 10065 (Mail to: 230 E 60th St 10022-1402) Andrew Mullins (212) 758-0447

New York All Souls Church **P** (62) 88 Saint Nicholas Ave 10026-2926 (Mail to: 88 Saint Nicholas Ave 10026-2926) (212) 663-2351

New York Calvary & St George Church **P** (980) § 61 Gramercy Park N Fl 2 10010-5406 (Mail to: 61 Gramercy Park N Fl 2 10010-5406) Janet Broderick Molly Layton Jacob Smith (646) 723-4178

✠ **New York** Cathd of St John the Divine **O** § 1047 Amsterdam Ave 10025-1747 (Mail to: ClO William Wagner 1047 Amsterdam Ave 10025-1747) Kenton Curtis Kenton Curtis Steven Lee Patrick Malloy (212) 316-7401

New York Christ & St Stephens Church **P** (679) 120 W 69th St 10023-5194 (Mail to: 120 W 69th St Ste 1 10023-5194) Bert Breiner Jay Gordon James Hagen Kathryn Person (212) 787-2755

New York Church Of St Mary The Virgin **P** (366) 145 W 46th St 10036-8591 (Mail to: 145 W 46th St 10036-8591) Matthew Jacobson James Pace Peter Powell Rebecca Weiner Tompkins Sammy Wood (212) 869-5830

New York Church of the Ascension **P** (207) 12 W 11th St 10011-8602 (Mail to: 12 W 11th St 10011-8695) Edwin Chinery Lisa Krakowsky Lisa Krakowsky Elizabeth Maxwell (212) 254-8620

New York Church of the Crucifixion **P** (145) 459 W 149th St 10031-2704 (Mail to: 459 W 149th St 10031-2704) (212) 281-0900

New York Church of the Good Shepherd **P** (88) 240 E 31st St 10016 (Mail to: 236 E 31st St 100166303) Mary Grambsch (212) 689-1595

New York Church of the Heavenly Rest **P** (1866) 1085 Fifth Avenue 10128-0114 (Mail to: 1085 Fifth Avenue 10128-0144) Euan Cameron Matthew Heyd Cynthia Stravers Philippa Turner Anne Witchger (212) 289-3400

New York Church of the Holy Apostles **P** (177) 296 9th Ave 10001-5703 (Mail to: C/O Michael Ottley 296 9th Ave 10001-5703) Anna Pearson Susan Hill Robert Jacobs (212) 807-6799

New York Church of the Holy Trinity **P** (723) 316 E 88th St 10128-4909 (Mail to: 316 E 88th St 10128-4999) John Beddingfield Paul Feuerstein (212) 289-4100

New York Church of the Incarnation **P** (503) 209 Madison Ave 10016-3814 (Mail to: 209 Madison Ave 10016-3814) Adrian Dannhauser Nathaniel Lee (212) 689-6350

New York Church of the Intercession **P** (210) 550 W 155th St 10032 (Mail to: 550 W 155th St 10032-7899) (212) 283-6200

New York Church of the Resurrection **P** (150) § 119 E 74th St 10021 (Mail to: 119 E 74th St 10021-3299) Barry Swain Earl Michael Allen Horace Hitchcock (212) 879-4320

New York Church of the Transfiguration **P** (193) 1 E 29th St 10016-7405 (Mail to: 1 E 29th St 10016-7405) John Van Dooren (212) 684-6770

New York Congregation of St Saviour **P** (207) 1047 Amsterdam Ave 10025-1747 (Mail to: Attn: Aaron W Koch 1047 Amsterdam Ave

10025-1747) (212) 316-7483

New York Episcopal Church of Our Savior **P** (64) 48 Henry St 10002-6901 (Mail to: 48 Henry St 10002-6901) (212) 233-2899

New York Eglise Du St Esprit **P** (167) 109-111 E 60th St 10022-1113 (Mail to: 111 E 60th St 10022-1113) Nigel Massey (212) 838-5680

New York Grace Church In New York **P** (1028) 802 Broadway 10003-4804 (Mail to: 802 Broadway 10003-4831) James Waring Julia Offinger (212) 2542000

New York Holy Trinity Church - Inwood **P** (16) 20 Cumming St 10034-4804 (Mail to: 20 Cumming St 10034-4804) Rebecca Barnes (212) 567-1177

New York Church of the Holyrood **P** (211) 715 W 179th St 10033 (Mail to: 715 W 179th St 10033-6020) Eugene Bourquin James Hagen (212) 923-3770

New York St Ambrose Church **P** (64) 9 W 130th St 10037 (Mail to: C/O Reuben Best 9 W 130th St 10037-3638) Wayne Dodson (212) 283-2175

New York St Andrews Church **P** (144) 2067 5th Ave 10035-1219 (Mail to: 2067 5th Ave 10035-1297) Terry Jackson Edward Johnston (212) 534-0896

New York St Ann's Church For the Deaf **M** (22) 209 E 16th St 10003-3702 (Mail to: 209 E 16th St 10003-3702) William Krengel (347) 458-9571

New York St Augustines Church **P** (61) 290 Henry St 10002 (Mail to: 333 Madison St 10002-5706) Nathanael Saint-Pierre (212) 673-5300

New York St Clements Church **P** (28) 423 W 46th St 10036-3510 (Mail to: 423 W 46th St 10036-3592) (212) 246-7277

New York St James Church **P** (1540) 865 Madison Ave 10021-4103 (Mail to: 865 Madison Ave 10021-4195) Brenda Husson John Sidebotham John Sidebotham Eva Suarez Zachary Thompson (212) 774-4240

New York St Johns in Village Church **P** (72) 224 Waverly Pl 10014-2405 (Mail to: 224 Waverly Pl 10014-2405) Graeme Napier Denise Lavetty (212) 243-6192

New York St Johns Korean American Ch **P** 1047 Amsterdam Ave 10025-1747 (Mail to: 84 Ehrhardt Rd 10965-1930) (212) 316-7432

New York St Lukes Church **P** (53) 435 W 141st St 10031-6401 (Mail to: 435 W 141st St 10031-6401) (212) 926-2713

New York St Marks Church in the Bowery **P** (104) 131 E 10th St 10003-7504 (Mail to: 131 E 10th St 10003-7590) Winnie Varghese Nathaniel Lee (212) 674-6377

New York St Martins Church **P** (36) 230 Lenox Avenue 10027-6340 (Mail to: 230 Malcolm X Blvd 10027-6396) Johan Johnson (212) 534-4531

New York St Michaels Church **P** (701) 225 W 99th St 10025-5014 (Mail to: 225 W 99th St 10025-5014) Katharine Flexer Julie Hoplamazian Richard Limato (212) 222-2700

New York St Peters Church **P** (89) 346 W 20th St 10011-3302 (Mail to: 346 W 20th St 10011-3398) Christine Lee (212) 929-2390

New York St Philip's Church **P** (197) 204 W 134 St 10030 (Mail to: 204 W 134th St 10030-3098) Terence Lee Chloe Breyer Fitzroy Edwards (212) 862-4940

New York Saint Thomas Church **P** (2815) § 1 W 53rd St 10019-5496 (Mail to: 1 W 53rd St 10019-5496) Anne Mallonee David McNeeley Matthew Moretz Nathan Ritter Mark Schultz Carl Turner (212) 757-7013

New York St Marys Ch Manhattanville **P** (146) 521 W 126th St 10027-2496 (Mail to: 521 W 126th St 10027-2496) Mary Foulke Jacqueline Sanchez-Shabazz (212) 864-4013

New York St Bartholomews Church **P** (2210) § 325 Park Ave 51st Street 10022-6814 (Mail to: 325 Park Ave 51st Street 10022-6814) Dean Wolfe Peter Thompson Clayton Crawley Andrew Mullins Zachary Nyein Meredith Ward (212) 378-0222

New York Church of St Edward the Martyr **P** (79) 14 E 109th St 10029-3402 (Mail to: 14 E 109th St 10029-3402) Matthew Buccheri (212) 369-1140

New York The Ch of St Igns of Antioch **P** (259) 552 W End Ave 10024-2707 (Mail to: 552 W End Ave 10024-2796) Andrew Blume Paul Kahn Paul Kahn (212) 580-3326

New York Ch of Saint Luke in the Fields **P** (885) 487 Hudson St 10014-2851 (Mail to: 487 Hudson St 10014-6397) Caroline Stacey Andrew Ancona Milton Gatch Bo Reynolds (212) 924-0562

New York Ch of St Matthew & St Timothy **P** (343) 26 W 84th St 10024-4702 (Mail to: 26 W 84th St 10024-4702) Carla Roland George Diaz (212) 362-6750

New York The Church of the Epiphany **P** (294) 1393 York Ave 10021-3407 (Mail to: 351 E 74th St 10021-3701) R Anne Auchincloss Roy Cole Jennifer Reddall Horace Whyte Joseph Zorawick (212) 7372720

New York Trinity Parish **P** (970) § 76 Trinity Pl 10006-1818 (Mail to: 76 Trinity Pl 10006-1818) Phillip Jackson Michael Bird Elizabeth Blunt Mark Bozzuti-Jones Clayton Crawley Yein Kim Cece Loua Kristin Miles (212) 602-0800

Newburgh Church of the Good Shepherd **P** (10) 271 Broadway 12550-5452 (Mail to: PO Box 2865 12550-0119) (845) 562-8545

Newburgh Iglesia Del Buen Pastor **M** (167) 270 Broadway & Mill St 12550 (Mail to: PO Box 2865 12550-0119) (845) 562-8545

Newburgh St Georges Episcopal Church **P** (118) 105 Grand St 12550 (Mail to: 105 Grand St

12550-4613) Mavourneen Hubbard (845) 561-5355

North Salem St James Church **P** (148) 296 Titicus Road 10560 (Mail to: PO Box 459 10560-0459) Kenneth Citarella (914) 669-5563

Nyack Grace Church **P** (896) 130 1st Ave 10960-2633 (Mail to: 130 1st Ave 10960-2633) Dustin Trowbridge Anne Ross (845) 358-1297

Ossining Grace Episcopal Church **P** 7 S Highland Ave 10562 (Mail to: PO Box 108 10562) Dorothee Caulfield (914) 523-8464

Patterson Christ Church **P** (24) 590 Route 11 12563-0569 (Mail to: PO Box 569 12563-0569) (845) 878-8027

Pawling Holy Trinity Church **P** (184) 22 Coulter Ave 12564-1109 (Mail to: 22 Coulter Ave 12564-1109) Ann Conti (845) 855-5276

Pearl River St Stephens Church **P** (335) 84 Ehrhardt Rd 10965-1930 (Mail to: 84 Ehrhardt Rd 10965-1930) (845) 735-8588

Peekskill St Peters Episcopal Church **P** (152) 137 N Division St 10566 (Mail to: 137 N Division St 10566-2788) Cheryl Parris (914) 737-6312

Pelham Parish of Christ the Redeemer **P** (662) 1415 Pelhamdale Ave 10803-3312 (Mail to: 1415 Pelhamdale Ave 10803-3312) Matthew Mead Chisara Alimole John Zacker (914) 738-5516

Pine Plains Church of the Regeneration **P** (27) 18 Pine St 12567-5209 (Mail to: PO Box 321 12567-0321) (518) 398-5628

Pleasant Valley St Pauls Episcopal Church **P** (122) 808 Traver Rd 12569-7653 (Mail to: PO Box 1449 12569-1449) (845) 6352854

Pleasantville Saint John's Church **P** (169) 8 Sunnyside Ave 10570-3125 (Mail to: C/O Treasurer Ken Foley 8 Sunnyside Ave 10570-3125) (914) 769-0053

Port Chester St Peters Church **P** (305) Westchester Ave at Pearl St 10573 (Mail to: 19 Smith St 10573-4505) Mario Martinez (914) 939-1244

Port Jervis Grace Church **P** (152) 84 Seward Ave 12771 (Mail to: 84 Seward Ave 12771-2006) (845) 856-3026

Poughkeepsie Christ Church **P** (333) 20 Carroll St 12601-4314 (Mail to: 20 Carroll St 12601-4396) Arnulfo Arambulo Susan Fortunato (845) 452-8220

Poughkeepsie Igle de la Virgen de Guadalupe **M** (100) 20 Carroll St 12601 (Mail to: 20 Carroll St 12601-4314) (845) 452-8225

Poughkeepsie St Pauls Church **P** (199) 161 Mansion St 12601-2524 (Mail to: 161 Mansion St 12601-2524) (845) 452-8440

Red Hook Christ Church of Red Hook **P** (81) 7423 S Broadway 12571-1747 (Mail to: 7423 S Broadway 12571-1747) Linda Duval (845) 758-1591

Red Hook St John the Evangelist **P** (179) 1114 River Rd 12571-2938 (Mail to: 1114 River Rd 12571-2938) (845) 758-6433

222 *Diocese of New York* [For Corrections, see p. 69]

Rhinebeck Church of the Messiah **P** (631) 6436 Montgomery St 12572-1359 (Mail to: PO Box 248 12572-0248) Richard Mckeon Gwyneth Murphy (845) 876-3533

Roosevelt Island Good Shepherd Ch Roosevelt Isl **M** (75) 543 Main St 10044 (Mail to: PO Box 361 10044-0207) (917) 843-3338

Rye Christ's Church **P** (1397) 2 Rectory St 10580-3818 (Mail to: C/O Finance Office 2 Rectory St 10580-3818) Catherine Lawrence Katherine Malin Mary Mccarthy (914) 9671749

Saugerties Trinity Church **P** (41) 32 Church St 12477-1809 (Mail to: 32 Church St 12477-1809) (845) 246-6312

Scarsdale Church of St James the Less **P** (571) 10 Church Ln 10583-4216 (Mail to: 10 Church Ln 10583-4216) Astrid Storm (914) 723-6100

Somers Saint Luke's Church **P** (230) 331 Rte 100 10589-3204 (Mail to: Attn: Kay 331 Route 100 10589-3204) Michael Watson (914) 277-3122

South Fallsburg St Andrews Church **M** (13) 5277 State Route 42 12779-5726 (Mail to: PO Box 55 12788-0055) (845) 436-7539

South Salem St Johns Church **P** (122) 82 Spring St 10590-1417 (Mail to: PO Box 394 10590-0394) (914) 763-8273

Sparkill Christ Church **P** (60) New St 10976-1203 (Mail to: PO Box 177 10976-0177) Karen Lynn Depue Stephen Holton (646) 373-6013

Spring Valley St Pauls Church **P** (167) 26 S Madison Ave 10977-5512 (Mail to: 26 S Madison Ave 10977-5512) (845) 356-1857

Staatsburg St Margarets Church **P** (70) 68 Old Post Rd 12580 (Mail to: PO Box 395 12580-0395) Charles Ford (845) 889-4181

Staten Island All Saints Church **P** (109) 2329 Victory Blvd 10314-6621 (Mail to: 2329 Victory Blvd 10314-6689) (718) 698-1338

Staten Island Christ Church New Brighton **P** (271) 76 Franklin Ave 10301-1239 (Mail to: 76 Franklin Ave 10301-1239) Trevor Babb (718) 727-6100

Staten Island Church of the Ascension **P** (129) 1 Kingsley Ave 10314-2420 (Mail to: 1 Kingsley Ave 10314-2420) (718) 442-4187

Staten Island St Albans Episcopal Church **P** (172) 76 Saint Albans Pl 10312-5131 (Mail to: 76 Saint Albans Pl 10312-5199) John Morgan (718) 984-7756

Staten Island Church of St Andrew **P** (290) 40 Old Mill Rd 10306-1122 (Mail to: 40 Old Mill Rd 10306-1197) Aaron Hudson Frederick Fausak (718) 351-0900

Staten Island St Johns Church **P** (195) 1333 Bay St 10305 (Mail to: 1333 Bay St 10305-3199) Geraldine Swanson Henry Tuell (718) 447-1605

Staten Island St Mary's Church Castleton **P** (95) 347 Davis Ave 10310-1557 (Mail to: 347 Davis Ave 10310-1557) Sylvester Ekunwe (718) 442-1527

Staten Island St Pauls Church **P** (67) C/O Gwendloyn Simmons 77 Bard Ave 10310-1605 (Mail to: C/O Richard Mingoia 225 St Pauls Ave 10304-2246) (718) 273-9572

Staten Island St Simons Church **P** (63) 1055 Richmond Rd 10304-2401 (Mail to: 1055 Richmond Rd 10304-2401) (718) 987-5252

Stone Ridge Christ the King Church **P** (192) 3021 St Rt 213 E 12484-5101 (Mail to: 3021 State Route 213 E 12484-5101) Marcella Gillis Robin Beveridge Judith Borzumato (845) 687-9414

Stony Point St Johns in the Wilderness **M** (75) 119 St John's Rd 10980-3624 (Mail to: 16 Johnsontown Road 10980) (845) 578-6036

Suffern Christ Church of Ramapo **P** (190) 65 Washington Ave 10901-5619 (Mail to: 65 Washington Ave 10901-5619) Dale Cranston (845) 357-1615

Tarrytown Christ Church **P** (239) 43 S Broadway 10591-4012 (Mail to: 43 S Broadway 10591-4095) William Baker Dorothee Caulfield Dorothee Caulfield (914) 631-2074

Tivoli St Pauls Church **P** (36) 39 Woods Rd 12583-5433 (Mail to: PO Box 68 12583-0068) (845) 757-3131

Tomkins Cove Church of St John the Divine **P** (68) 170 Mott Farm Rd 10986-1411 (Mail to: PO Box 92 10986-0092) (845) 786-5203

Tuxedo Park St Marys Church **P** (298) 10 Fox Hill Rd 10987-4224 (Mail to: PO Box 637 Fox Hill Road 10987-0637) Richard Datos-Robyn (845) 351-5122

Valley Cottage All Saints Episcopal Church **P** (40) 182 Ridge Rd 10989-2351 (Mail to: 182 Ridge Rd 10989-2351) (845) 268-9542

Walden Saint Andrew's Church **P** (60) 15 Walnut St 12586-1709 (Mail to: Attn: Jody Gridley PO Box 708 12586-0708) Nicole Hanley Charles Kramer (845) 778-5310

Wappingers Falls Zion Church **P** (626) 12 Saterlee Pl 12590-2600 (Mail to: 12 Saterlee Pl 12590-2600) (845) 297-9797

Warwick Christ Church **P** (701) 50 South St 10990-1638 (Mail to: 50 South St 10990-1638) Amber Carswell (845) 986-3440

Washingtonville St Annes Church **P** (107) 179 E Main St 10992 (Mail to: 179 E Main St 10992-1723) (845) 496-3961

West Park Ch of Ascension & Holy Trinity **P** (37) 1585 Rte 9W 12493 (Mail to: PO Box 1512 12528-8512) Jennifer Barrows William Owen (845) 384-6723

White Plains Grace Church **P** (691) 33 Church St 10601 (Mail to: 33 Church St 10601-1995) Buddelov Adolfo Moronta (914) 949-2874

White Plains St Bartholomews Church **P** (91) 82 Prospect St 10606-3421 (Mail to: 82 Prospect St 10606-3499) Este Gardner (914) 949-5577

White Plains St Francis & St Marthas Church **P** (52) 575 Tarrytown Rd 10607 (Mail to: 133

Augustine Rd 10603-2039) Audrey Bailey (914) 946-8846

White Plains St Joseph of Arimathea Church **P** (71) 2172 Saw Mill River Rd 10607 (Mail to: 2172 Saw Mill River Rd 10607-2205) (914) 592-7163

Woodstock St Gregorys Episcopal Church **P** (95) 2578 Rte 212 12498 (Mail to: PO Box 66 12498-0066) Matthew Wright Matthew Wright (845) 679-6394

Yonkers Church of the Holy Cross **P** (56) 81 Locust Hill Ave 10701 (Mail to: 81 Locust Hill Ave 10701-2801) (914) 965-4070

Yonkers St Johns Church Gettys Sq **P** (112) 1 Hudson St 10701 (Mail to: 1 Hudson St 10701-

3599) Yesupatham Duraikannu (914) 963-3033

Yonkers St Johns Church of Tuckahoe **P** (236) 100 Underhill St 10710-3615 (Mail to: 100 Underhill St 10710-3615) Stephen Trever (914) 779-7024

Yonkers St Marks Church **P** (27) 1373 Nepperhan Ave 10703-1011 (Mail to: 1373 Nepperhan Ave 10703-1011) (914) 965-3455

Yonkers Saint Paul's Church **P** (18) 636 Palisade Ave 10703-2122 (Mail to: 636 Palisade Ave 10703-2122) (914) 965-4967

Yonkers San Andres Church **P** (80) 22 Post St 10705 (Mail to: 22 Post St 10705-2241) (914) 963-9523

DIOCESE OF NEWARK
(PROVINCE II)
Comprises Northern New Jersey
DIOCESAN OFFICE 31 Mulberry St Newark NJ 07102
TEL (973) 430-9900 FAX (973) 622-3503
E-MAIL jking@dioceseofnewark.org WEB www.dioceseofnewark.org

Previous Bishops—
Wm H Odenheimer 1874-79, Thomas A Starkey 1880-1903, Edwin S Lines 1903-27, Wilson R Stearly suffr 1915 coadj 1917 Bp 1927-35, Benj M Washburn coadj 1932 Bp 1935-58, Theodore R Ludlow suffr 1936-53, Donald MacAdie suffr 1958-63, Leland Stark coadj 1953 Bp 1958-73, George E Rath suffr 1964 coadj 1970 Bp 1974-78, John S Spong coadj 1976 Bp 1979-2000, Jack M McKelvey suffr 1991-99, John P Croneberger coadj 1998 Bp 2000-2007, Mark M Beckwith Bp 2007-18

Bishop—The Rt Rev Carlye J. Hughes (1109) (Dio 22 Sep 2018)

Bp Exec Asst K Lark; *Dio Admin Off* JA King; *Cn to Ord* Rev AR Wright; *Asst* R Johnson; *CFO* S Reckford; *Chanc* DE Sammons

Stand Comm—Cler: Pres E Ellis-Thomas D Brewin-Wilson N Darville R Griner; *Lay:* N Boccino B Milano M Simon N Horsky

PARISHES, MISSIONS, AND CLERGY

Allendale Trinity Epis Ch of Bergen Cnty **P** (119) 55 George St 07401-1426 (Mail to: 55 George St 07401-1426) Raul Ausa (201) 327-3012

Bayonne Calvary Episcopal Church **P** (35) 956 Avenue C 07002-3022 (Mail to: C/O Sr Warden 956 Avenue C 07002-3022) (201) 339-3112

Bayonne Trinity Church **P** (159) 141 Broadway 07002-2459 (Mail to: 141 Broadway 07002-2459) (201) 858-4460

Belvidere Epis Ch of St Luke and St Mary **P** (85) 408 3rd St 07823-1834 (Mail to: 408 3rd St 07823-1834) (908) 818-9661

Bergenfield All Saints Episcopal Korean Ch **M** (35) 12 W Central Ave 07621-1302 (Mail to: 12 W Central Ave 07621-1302) Hogil Won (201) 244-1004

Boonton St Johns Episcopal Church **P** (242) 226 Cornelia St 07005-1712 (Mail to: 226 Cornelia St 07005-1712) (973) 334-3655

Budd Lake Christ Episcopal Church **P** (60) 369 Sand Shore Rd 07828-2215 (Mail to: 369 Sand Shore Rd 07828-2215) (973) 347-1866

Chatham St Pauls Episcopal Church **P** (428) 200 Main St 07928-2406 (Mail to: 200 Main St 07928-2467) Ellen Kohn-Perry (973) 635-8085

Chester Church of the Messiah **P** (183) 50 State Route 24 07930-2410 (Mail to: 50 State Route 24 07930-2410) (908) 879-7208

Cliffside Pk Trinity Church **P** (54) 555 Palisade Ave 07010-3035 (Mail to: 555 Palisade Ave 07010-3035) (201) 943-1034

Clifton St Peters Episcopal Church **P** (63) 380 Clifton Ave 07011-2643 (Mail to: 380 Clifton Ave 07011-2643) (973) 546-5020

Denville The Church of the Saviour **P** (309) 155 Morris Ave 07834-1736 (Mail to: 155 Morris Ave 07834-1736) James Petroccione (973) 627-3304

Dover St Johns Episcopal Church **P** (109) 11 S Bergen St 07801-4634 (Mail to: 11 S Bergen St 07801-4634) John Habecker Rodrigo Perez-Vega (973) 366-2772

East Orange St Agnes & St Pauls Church **P** (141) 206 Renshaw Ave 07017-3313 (Mail to: 206

Renshaw Ave 07017-3313) Esar Budhu (973) 678-6716

Englewood St Pauls Episcopal Church **P** (407) 113 Engle St 07631-2508 (Mail to: 113 Engle St 07631-2508) William Allport (201) 568-3276

Essex Fells St Peters Episcopal Church **P** (560) 271 Roseland Ave 07021-1313 (Mail to: PO Box 96 07021-0096) Nathaniel Darville (973) 226-6500

Fair Lawn Church of the Atonement **P** (54) 1-36 30th St 07410-3946 (Mail to: 1-36 30th St 07410-3946) Kevin Coffey (201) 797-0760

Fort Lee Church of the Good Shepherd **P** (87) 1576 Palisade Ave 07024-6929 (Mail to: 1576 Palisade Ave 07024-6993) (201) 461-7260

Glen Ridge Christ Episcopal Church **P** (297) § 74 Park Ave 07028-2309 (Mail to: 74 Park Ave 07028-2309) Diana Wilcox Robert Solon (973) 743-5911

Glen Rock All Saints Episcopal Church **P** (311) 40 Central Ave 07452-1837 (Mail to: 40 Central Ave 07452-1837) Mark Collins (201) 444-6874

Hackensack Christ Episcopal Church **P** (226) 251 State St 07601-5512 (Mail to: PO Box 1097 07602-1097) (201) 342-2365

Hackensack Church of St Anthony Padua **P** (723) 72 Lodi St 07601-5350 (Mail to: 72 Lodi St 07601-5363) Brian Laffler (201) 489-3286

Hackensack St Cyprians Church **M** (25) 269 1st St 07601-3434 (Mail to: 269 1st St 07601-3434) (201) 342-5560

Hackettstown St James Episcopal Church **P** (129) 214 Washington St 07840-2146 (Mail to: 214 Washington St 07840-2146) Wayne Sherrer (908) 852-3968

Harrington Park St Andrews Episcopal Church **P** (110) Lynn St And La Roche Ave 07640 (Mail to: 31 Lynn Street 07640-0161) Elizabeth Wigg-Maxwell (201) 768-0819

Harrison Christ Church **M** (58) 100 Frank E Rodgers Blvd N 07029-1402 (Mail to: 100 Frank E Rodgers Blvd N 07029-1402) (973) 483-1260

Hasbrouck Hts Church of St John the Divine **M** (50) 229 Terrace Ave 07604-1917 (Mail to: 229 Terrace Ave 07604-1917) (201) 288-0002

Haworth St Lukes Episcopal Church **P** (65) 43 Massachusetts Ave 07641-1950 (Mail to: 43 Massachusetts Ave 07641-1950) (201) 384-0706

Hawthorne St Clements Episcopal Church **P** (179) 271 Lafayette Ave 07506-1921 (Mail to: 271 Lafayette Ave 07506-1921) Erik Soldwedel (973) 427-8118

Hillsdale Holy Trinity Episcopal Church **P** (121) 326 Hillsdale Ave 07642-2209 (Mail to: 326 Hillsdale Ave 07642-2209) (201) 664-2428

Ho Ho Kus St Bartholomews Episcopal Ch **P** (185) 70 Sheridan Ave 07423-1541 (Mail to: 70 Sheridan Ave 07423-1541) Cathleen Studwell

(201) 444-5025

Hoboken All Saints Episcopal Parish **P** (351) § 701 Washington St 07030-5001 (Mail to: 701 Washington St 07030-5001) Elaine Thomas John Morgan (201) 792-3563

Jersey City Church of the Incarnation **P** 68 Storms Ave 07306-3316 (Mail to: 68 Storms Ave 07306-3316) (201) 434-4810

Jersey City Grace Van Vorst Church **P** (421) 39 Erie St 07302-2821 (Mail to: 39 Erie St 07302-2821) Laurie Wurm (201) 659-2211

Jersey City St Paul's Episcopal Church **P** (243) 38 Duncan Ave 07304-2102 (Mail to: Attn: Susan M Den Herder 38 Duncan Ave 07304-2102) (201) 433-4922

Kinnelon St Davids Episcopal Church **P** (100) 91 Kinnelon Rd 07405-2335 (Mail to: Mrs Arther 91 Kinnelon Rd 07405-2335) Jon Richardson (973) 838-6696

Leonia All Saints Episcopal Church **P** (92) 150 Park Ave 07605-2012 (Mail to: 150 Park Ave 07605-2091) (201) 947-1233

Little Falls St Agnes Episcopal Church **P** (83) 65 Union Ave 07424-1321 (Mail to: 65 Union Ave 07424-1397) Young Yoon (973) 256-5020

Livingston St Peter's Episcopal Church **P** (113) 94 E Mount Pleasant Ave 07039-3004 (Mail to: 94 E Mount Pleasant Ave 07039-3094) (973) 992-1932

Lyndhurst St Thomas Episcopal Church **P** (37) PO Box 207 300 Forest Ave 07071-0207 (Mail to: 300 Forest Ave 07071-2330) (201) 438-5668

Madison Grace Church **P** (850) 4 Madison Ave 07940-1433 (Mail to: 4 Madison Ave 07940-1433) Susan Ironside Asa Coulson (973) 377-0106

Maplewood St Georges Episcopal Church **P** (437) 550 Ridgewood Rd 07040-2135 (Mail to: 550 Ridgewood Rd 07040-2198) Robert Mansfield (973) 762-1319

Maywood St Martins Episcopal Church **P** (48) 29 Parkway 07607-1558 (Mail to: 670 Oak Ave 07607) Ruben Jurado (201) 843-5360

Mendham St Marks Church **P** (132) 9 E Main St 07945-1501 (Mail to: 9 E Main St 07945-1501) Lorna Erixson (973) 543-4471

Millburn St Stephens Church **P** (243) 119 Main St 07041-1115 (Mail to: 119 Main St 07041-1115) Paula Toland (973) 376-0688

Millington All Saints Church **P** (229) 15 Basking Ridge Rd 07946-1407 (Mail to: 15 Basking Ridge Rd 07946-1407) Victoria Mcgrath Victoria Mcgrath (908) 647-0067

Montclair St James Episcopal Church **P** (626) § 581 Valley Rd 07043-1826 (Mail to: 581 Valley Rd 07043-1826) David Casto Charlotte Hall Audrey Hasselbrook (973) 744-0270

Montclair St Johns Episcopal Church **P** (323) 55 Montclair Ave 07042-4109 (Mail to: 55 Montclair Ave 07042-4109) Candace Sandfort (973) 746-2474

Montclair Saint Luke's Episcopal Church **P** (677) 73 S Fullerton Ave 07042-2618 (Mail to: 73 S Fullerton Ave Ste A 07042-2685) John Mennell (973) 7446220

Montvale Saint Paul's Church **P** (379) 4 Woodland Rd 07645-2134 (Mail to: 4 Woodland Rd 07645-2134) (201) 391-3181

Morris Plains Saint Paul's Episcopal Church **P** (161) 29 Hillview Ave 07950-2114 (Mail to: 29 Hillview Ave 07950-2114) (973) 285-0884

Morristown Church of the Redeemer **P** (324) 36 South St 07960-4136 (Mail to: 36 South St 07960-7260) Cynthia Black (973) 539-0703

Morristown St Peters Episcopal Church **P** (1271) 121 South Street 07960 (Mail to: 70 Maple Ave 07960-5293) Anne Thatcher Elizabeth Ivell (973) 538-0555

Mountain Lks St Peters Episcopal Church **P** (392) 215 Boulevard 07046-1209 (Mail to: 215 Boulevard 07046-1209) Michael Muller (973) 334-4429

Mt Arlington St Peters Episcopal Church **P** (35) 50 Edgemere Ave 07856-1164 (Mail to: PO Box 403 50 Edgemere Ave 07856-0403) Elizabeth Myers (973) 398-1890

Newark Grace Episcopal Church **P** (191) 950 Broad St 07102-2614 (Mail to: 950 Broad St 07102-2684) James Bates Marjorie Lindstrom (973) 623-1733

Newark House of Prayer Episcopal Ch **M** (68) 407 Broad St 07104-3310 (Mail to: 407 Broad St 07104-3310) Kathleen Ballard Wade Renn (973) 483-8202

Newark St Andrews Episcopal Church **M** (104) 933 S 17th St 07108-1136 (Mail to: 933 S 17th St 07108-1136) (973) 375-3012

Newark Trinity St Philips Cathedral **O** (62) 2 Park Pl 07102 (Mail to: 2 Park Pl 07102) (973) 622-3505

Newton Christ Church **P** (614) 62 Main St 07860-2024 (Mail to: 62 Main St 07860-2024) (973) 383-2245

Norwood Church of the Holy Communion **P** (81) 66 Summit St 07648-1841 (Mail to: 66 Summit St 07648-1841) (201) 768-0634

Nutley Grace Episcopal Church **P** (559) 200 Highfield Ln 07110-2448 (Mail to: 200 Highfield Ln 07110-2499) Pamela Bakal Nancy Read (973) 235-1177

Oak Ridge St Gabriels Episcopal Church **M** (25) 153 Milton Rd 07438-9598 (Mail to: C/O Dorothy Skelton 153 Milton Rd 07438-9598) (973) 697-5688

Oakland St Albans Episcopal Church **P** (156) 1 Church Ln 07436-4036 (Mail to: 1 Church Ln 07436-4036) (201) 337-4909

Oradell The Church of the Annunciation **P** (85) 343 Kinderkamack Rd 07649-2123 (Mail to: 343 Kinderkamack Rd 07649-2151) (201) 262-7222

Orange Ch of the Epiphany & Christ Ch **P** (246) 105 Main St 07050-4026 Lorraine Harris

Paramus Saint Matthew's Church **M** (98) 167 Spring Valley Rd 07652-5333 (Mail to: 167 Spring Valley Rd Ste 1 07652-5396) (201) 262-5286

Parsippany St Gregorys Episcopal Church **M** (83) 480 S Beverwyck Rd 07054-3328 (Mail to: 480 S Beverwyck Rd 07054-3328) Aaron Oliver (973) 887-5879

Passaic St Johns Episcopal Church **P** (135) 215 Lafayette Ave 07055-4711 (Mail to: 215 Lafayette Ave 07055-4711) (973) 779-0966

Paterson St Pauls Episcopal Church **P** (430) 422 Broadway 07501 (Mail to: 422 Broadway 07501) Beth Glover Erik Soldwedel (973) 278-7900

Phillipsburg St Luke Episcopal Church **P** (222) 500 Hillcrest Blvd 08865-1407 (Mail to: 500 Hillcrest Blvd 08865-1499) Anne Kitch (908) 859-1479

Pompton Lake Christ Episcopal Church **P** (523) 400 Ramapo Ave 07442-1825 (Mail to: 400 Ramapo Ave 07442-1825) Stephen Rozzelle (973) 835-2207

Ramsey St Johns Memorial Episcopal Ch **P** (262) 301 E Main St 07446 (Mail to: Attn: Ellen Joyce 301 E Main St 07446) William Cruse (201) 327-0703

Ridgefield St James Episcopal Church **P** (242) 514 Abbott Ave 07657-2413 (Mail to: 514 Abbott Ave 07657-2413) (201) 945-0079

Ridgewood Christ Episcopal Church **P** (386) 105 Cottage Pl 07450-3213 (Mail to: 105 Cottage Pl 07450-3217) Thomas Mathews (201) 652-2350

Ridgewood St Elizabeths Church **P** (722) 169 Fairmount Rd 07450-1422 (Mail to: 169 Fairmount Rd 07450-1422) David Olivo (201) 444-2299

Ringwood Church of the Good Shepherd **M** (66) 80 Margaret King Ave 07456-1703 (Mail to: PO Box 727 07456-0727) (973) 962-9510

Rutherford Grace Episcopal Church **P** (170) 128 W Passaic Ave 07070-1935 (Mail to: 128 W Passaic Ave 07070-1935) (201) 438-8623

Secaucus Church of Our Saviour **M** (55) 191 Flanagan Way 07094-3435 (Mail to: 191 Flanagan Way 07094-3435) Barbara Lewis (201) 863-1449

Short Hills Christ Episcopal Church **P** (584) 66 Highland Ave 07078-2829 (Mail to: 66 Highland Ave 07078-2829) A Bowie Snodgrass (973) 3792898

South Orange St Andrew and Holy Commun Ch **P** (645) 160 W South Orange Ave 07079-1731 (Mail to: 160 W South Orange Ave 07079-1731) Anne Bolles-Beaven Rosemarie Hassan (973) 763-2355

Sparta St Marys Episcopal Church **P** (175) 85 Conestoga Trl 07871-2537 (Mail to: 85 Conestoga Trl 07871-2537) (973) 729-3136

Succasunna St. Dunstan's Church **P** (89) 179 S Hillside Ave 07876-1197 (Mail to: 179 S Hillside Ave 07876-1197) (973) 927-1485

Summit Calvary Church **P** (918) 31 Woodland Ave 07901-2157 (Mail to: C/O Pamela Kuhn 31 Woodland Ave 07901-2157) (908) 277-1814

Sussex Church of the Good Shepherd **M** (131) 200 State Rt 23 07461-3100 (Mail to: 200 State Rt 23 07461-3100) Elizabeth Ostuni (973) 875-0919

Teaneck Christ Church **M** (111) 480 Warwick Ave 07666-2926 (Mail to: 480 Warwick Ave 07666-2926) Michelle White (201) 833-4502

Teaneck St Marks Episcopal Church **P** (520) 118 Chadwick Rd 07666-4204 (Mail to: C/O Anne Beemsterboer 118 Chadwick Rd 07666-4204) Joan Conley (201) 836-7275

Tenafly Church of the Atonement **P** (212) 97 Highwood Ave 07670-1834 (Mail to: 97 Highwood Ave 07670-1834) Lynne Weber (201) 568-1763

Towaco Good Shepherd Episcopal Church **P** (96) 9 Two Bridges Rd 07082-1318 (Mail to: 9 Two Bridges Rd 07082-1318) (973) 334-2882

Union City Grace Episcopal Church **P** (99) 3901 Park Ave 07087-6127 (Mail to: 3901 Park Ave 07087-6127) Arthur Fouts (201) 863-6334

Verona The Church of the Holy Spirit **P** (152) 36 Gould St 07044-1928 (Mail to: 36 Gould St 07044-1928) Gerard Racioppi (973) 239-2850

Washington St Peters Church **P** (170) 127 Broad St 07882-1801 (Mail to: 127 Broad St 07882-1801) (908) 689-1019

Wayne St Michaels Episcopal Church **P** (108) 1219 Ratzer Rd 07470-2310 (Mail to: 1219 Ratzer Rd 07470-2310) (973) 694-1026

West Orange Church of the Holy Innocents **P** (77) 681 Prospect Ave 07052-3212 (Mail to: 681 Prospect Ave 07052-3212) (973) 731-0259

West Orange Church of the Holy Trinity **M** (40) 315 Main St 07052-5630 (Mail to: 315 Main St 07052-5624) Miguel Hernandez (973) 325-0369

Westwood Grace Episcopal Church **P** (63) 9 Harrington Ave 07675-1801 (Mail to: 9 Harrington Ave 07675-1899) Anthony Puca (201) 664-0407

Wood Ridge Church of St Paul and Resurrection **P** (94) 483 Center St 07075-2311 (Mail to: 483 Center St 07075-2311) Jacob Nanthicattu Charles Nelson (201) 438-8333

STATE OF NORTH CAROLINA
Dioceses of East Carolina (EC), North Carolina (NC), and Western North Carolina (WNC)

Advance—NC
Ahoskie—EC
Albemarle—NC
Ansonville—NC
Asheboro—NC
Asheville—WNC
Bat Cave—WNC
Bath—EC
Battleboro—NC
Beaufort—EC
Belhaven—EC
Bessemer City—WNC
Black Mtn—WNC
Blowing Rock—WNC
Boone—WNC
Brevard—WNC
Burgaw—EC
Burlington—NC
Burnsville—WNC
Canton—WNC
Cary—NC
Cashiers—WNC
Chapel Hill—NC
Charlotte—NC
Chocowinity—EC
Clayton—NC
Clemmons—NC
Cleveland—NC
Clinton—EC
Columbia—EC

Concord—NC
Cooleemee—NC
Creswell—EC
Cullowhee—WNC
Currituck—EC
Davidson—NC
Denver—WNC
Durham—NC
Eden—NC
Edenton—EC
Edneyville—WNC
Elizabeth City—EC
Elizabethtown—EC
Elkin—NC
Engelhard—EC
Erwin—NC
Farmville—EC
Fayetteville—EC
Flat Rock—WNC
Fletcher—WNC
Franklin—WNC
Fuquay Varina—NC
Garner—NC
Gastonia—WNC
Gatesville—EC
Glendale Spgs—WNC
Goldsboro—EC
Greensboro—NC
Greenville—EC
Grifton—EC

Hamlet—NC
Hampstead—EC
Havelock—EC
Haw River—NC
Hayesville—WNC
Henderson—NC
Hendersonville—WNC
Hertford—EC
Hickory—WNC
High Pt—NC
Highlands—WNC
Hillsborough—NC
Holly Ridge—EC
Huntersville—NC
Jackson—NC
Jacksonville—EC
Kernersville—NC
Kinston—EC
Laurinburg—NC
Leland—EC
Lenoir—WNC
Lewiston—EC
Lexington—NC
Lincolnton—WNC
Linville—WNC
Little Switzerland—WNC
Littleton—NC
Louisburg—NC
Lumberton—EC

Marion—WNC
Mars Hill—WNC
Matthews—NC
Mayodan—NC
Mills River—WNC
Monroe—NC
Mooresville—NC
Morehead City—EC
Morganton—WNC
Mt Airy—NC
Murphy—WNC
Nags Head—EC
New Bern—EC
Newland—WNC
Newton—WNC
Newton Grove—EC
Oriental—EC
Oxford—NC
Pittsboro—NC
Plymouth—EC
Raleigh—NC
Reidsville—NC
Ridgeway—NC
Roanoke Rapids—NC
Robbinsville—WNC
Rockingham—NC
Rocky Mt—NC
Roper—EC
Roxboro—NC
Rutherfordton—WNC

Salisbury—NC
Salter Path—EC
Saluda—WNC
Sanford—NC
Scotland Neck—NC
Seven Lakes—NC
Seven Sprs—EC
Shallotte—EC
Shelby—WNC
Smithfield—NC

Southern Pines—NC
Southern Shores—EC
Southport—EC
Sparta—WNC
Speed—NC
Spruce Pine—WNC
Statesville—NC
Sunbury—EC
Swansboro—EC
Sylva—WNC

Tarboro—NC
Trenton—EC
Tryon—WNC
Valle Crucis—WNC
Wadesboro—NC
Wake Forest—NC
Walnut Cove—NC
Warrenton—NC
Washington—EC
Waxhaw—NC

Waynesville—WNC
Weldon—NC
Whiteville—EC
Wilkesboro—WNC
Williamston—EC
Wilmington—EC
Wilson—NC
Windsor—EC
Winston-Salem—NC

DIOCESE OF NORTH CAROLINA
(PROVINCE IV)
Comprises central North Carolina
DIOCESAN OFFICE 200 W Morgan St Ste 300 Raleigh NC 27601-1338
Tel (919) 834-7474 FAX (919) 834-7546
Tel (336) 273 5770 FAX (336) 273 9253
E-Mail communications@episdionc.org WEB www.episdionc.org

Previous Bishops—
John S Ravenscroft 1823-30, Levi S Ives 1831-53, Thomas Atkinson 1853-81, Theodore B Lyman coadj 1873 Bp 1881-93, Jos B Cheshire coadj 1893 Bp 1893-1932, Henry B Delany suffr 1918-28, Edwin A Penickcoadj 1922 Bp 1932-59, Richard H Baker coadj 1950 Bp 1959-65, W Moultrie Moore Jr suffr 1967-75, Thomas A Fraser coadj 1960 Bp 1965-83, Frank H Vest Jr suffr 1985-89, Robt W Estill coadj 1980 Bp 1983-94, Huntington Williams Jr suffr 1990-96, Robert C Johnson Jr 1994-2000, J Gary Gloster suffr 1996-2004; Michael B Curry (955) (2000-15), Anne E Hodges-Copple suffr 2013-2022

Bishop Diocesan—The Rt Rev Samuel S Rodman III (1102) (Dio 15 July 2017)

Assistant Bishop—The Rt Rev Jennifer Brooke-Davison (1104) (Dio 18 Nov 2022)

Cn to Bishop and Trans and Pastoral Mins C Massey; *Reg Cn* E Graham *(Northwest)*; *Reg Cn* S French *(East)*; *Reg Dcn* B McKee-Hugar; *Exec Asst to Bishops* E Dawkins P Sarazen; *CFO* M Gillespie; *Fin Coord* E Sweeney; *Comm Dir* C McTaggart; *Comm Coord* S Walter; *Lead Yth Miss* L Aycock; *Asst Yth Miss* L Dail; *Child Fam Miss* A Campbell; *Black Min Miss* K Walker; *Archdcn* J Lamb; *Sec* C Till; *Treas* G Small; *Chanc* M Brinkley; *Hist* B Graebner; *Archiv* L Hoke; *Ecum & Interfaith Off* J Beimdiek

Stand Comm—Cler: N Cox K Edrington P Haynes G Jones D Umphlett; *Lay:* M Clarke S Florimonte A Freeman M Wellman

Diocesan Council—Cler: J Bernacki V Colbert L Nye J Pahl M Saxon V Wilder; *Lay:* D Bland P Harvey C

Long R Mitchell S Owens J Price A Ragland D Tamer A Van Noppen

Deans of Convoc—Rocky Mt S Browne; *Raleigh* R Thomas; *Durham* G Lamazares; *Sandhills* B Heyvaert; *Greensboro* G Silides; *Winston-Salem* V Wilder; *Charlotte* A Stephenson; *Lay Wardens of Convoc—Rocky Mt* C Putney; *Raleigh* M Harvey; *Durham* M Gardner-Woods; *Sandhills* L Holden; *Greensboro* S Mercier; *Winston-Salem* B Morphis; *Charlotte* A Badgett

PARISHES, MISSIONS, AND CLERGY

Advance Church of the Ascension **M** (88) 183 Fork Bixby Rd 27006-7217 (Mail to: 183 Fork Bixby Rd 27006-7217) Gus Chrysson (336) 998-0857

Albemarle Christ Episcopal Church **P** (148) 428 Pee Dee Ave 28001-4934 (Mail to: PO Box 657 28002-0657) (704) 982-1428

Ansonville All Souls Episcopal Church **M** (3) 52 Highway 52 N 28007-9798 (Mail to: C/O Jennie Thomas 211 Camden Rd 28170-2629) (704) 694-3223

Asheboro Epis Ch of the Good Shepherd **P** (250) 505 Mountain Rd 27205-4219 (Mail to: 505 Mountain Rd 27205-4219) Joe Mitchell (336) 625-5234

Battleboro St Johns Episcopal Church **M** (14) 211 E. Main Street 27809 (Mail to: PO Box 577 27809-0577) (252) 446-8852

Burlington Holy Comforter Episcopal Church **P** (370) § 320 East Davis Street 27215 (Mail to: PO Box 1336 27216-1336) George Silides (336) 227-4251

Cary St Pauls Episcopal Church **P** (907) § 221 Union St 27511-3763 (Mail to: C/O Church Administrator 221 Union St 27511-3763)

George Adamik Javier Almendarez Bautista Alice Grant (919) 467-1477

Chapel Hill The Chapel of the Cross **P** (1947) § 304 E Franklin St 27514-3619 (Mail to: 304 E Franklin St 27514-3624) Elizabeth Melchionna Mary Young (919) 9292193

Chapel Hill Church of the Holy Family **P** (732) 200 Hayes Rd 27517-5633 (Mail to: 200 Hayes Rd 27517-5633) Clarke French Sarah Ball-Damberg Jason Eslicker (919) 942-3108

Chapel Hill Church of the Advocate **M** (155) 8410 Merin Road 27516 (Mail to: 8410 Merin Rd 27516-9231) Marion Sprott-Goldson (919) 933-3221

Charlotte Chapel of Christ the King **M** (32) 425 E 17th St 28206-3407 (Mail to: 425 E 17th St 28206-3407) Reginald Payne-Wiens (704) 334-3097

Charlotte Christ Episcopal Church **P** (5440) 1412 Providence Rd 28207-2543 (Mail to: 1412 Providence Rd 28207-2543) Henry Edens James Case Connor Gwin Joan Kilian Robert Pruitt Elizabeth Saunders Elizabeth Saunders (704) 333-0378

Charlotte Church of the Holy Comforter **P** (664) § 2701 Park Rd 28209-1311 (Mail to: 2701 Park Rd 28209-1357) Gregory Brown James Vaughn (704) 332-4171

Charlotte St Johns Episcopal Church **P** (1612) 1623 Carmel Rd 28226-5015 (Mail to: 1623 Carmel Rd 28226-5097) Peter Floyd Richard Clark Bradford Smith Michael Thompson (704) 366-3034

Charlotte St Martins Episcopal Church **P** (692) 1510 E 7th St 28204-2410 (Mail to: 1510 E 7th St 28204-2410) Joshua Bowron Rebecca Schunior (704) 376-8441

Charlotte Ch of St Michael & All Angels **M** (102) 750 East 9th Street 28202-3102 (Mail to: PO Box 11318 28220-1318) (704) 399-3151

Charlotte St Peters Episcopal Church **P** (919) 115 W 7th St 28202-2127 (Mail to: 115 W 7th St Ste 300 28202-0401) (704) 332-7746

Clayton Grace Episcopal Mission **M** (47) 111 Lee Ct 27520-7927 (Mail to: PO Box 752 27528-0752) Teresa Daily (919) 553-2810

Clemmons St Clement's Episcopal Church **P** (233) 3600 Harper Rd 27012-8681 (Mail to: PO Box 1547 27012-1547) Jamie Edwards (336) 766-4323

Cleveland Christ Episcopal Church **P** (96) 3430 Old Us Highway 27013-9733 (Mail to: PO Box 37 27013-0037) Sarah Blaies-Diamond (704) 278-4652

Concord All Saints Episcopal Church **P** (472) 525 Lake Concord Rd NE 28025-2925 (Mail to: 525 Lake Concord Rd NE 28025-2925) Nancy Cox (704) 782-2024

Cooleemee Church of the Good Shepherd **P** (11) 141 Church St 27014 (Mail to: PO Box 1047 27014-1047) (336) 284-4359

Davidson St Albans Episcopal Church **P** (598) § 301 Caldwell Lane 28036 (Mail to: 301 Caldwell Lane 28036-0970) Carmen Germino Kevin Lloyd (704) 892-0173

Durham Epis Center Duke University **Chapel** 505 Alexander Ave 27705-4707 (Mail to: 505 Alexander Ave 27705-4707) (919) 286-0624

Durham Iglesia El Buen Pastor **M** (503) 1852 Liberty St 27703-2271 (Mail to: 1852 Liberty St 27703-2271) (919) 6823301

Durham St Josephs Episcopal Church **M** (44) 1902 W Main St 27705-4838 (Mail to: 1902 W Main St 27705-4838) Lauren Winner (919) 286-1064

Durham St Lukes Church **P** (313) 1737 Hillandale Rd 27705-3045 (Mail to: 1737 Hillandale Rd 27705-3045) James Craven (919) 286-2273

Durham St Philips Episcopal Church **P** (1524) 403 E Main St 27701-3719 (Mail to: 403 E Main St 27701-3719) Maryann Younger Jill Bullard Gabriel Lamazares (919) 682-5708

Durham St Stephens Church **P** (605) 82 Kimberly Dr 27707-5446 (Mail to: 82 Kimberly Dr 27707-5446) Sanford Key Gail Davis William Shows (919) 493-5451

Durham Church of St Titus **P** (183) 400 Moline St 27707-2348 (Mail to: 400 Moline St 27707-2348) Alicia Alexis (919) 682-5504

Eden Church of the Epiphany **P** (146) 538 Henry St 27288-6103 (Mail to: 538 Henry St 27288-6103) Linda Nye (336) 623-9410

Eden St Lukes Episcopal Church **P** (94) 604 Morgan Rd 27288-2526 (Mail to: 604 Morgan Rd 27288-2526) Wheigar Bright (336) 627-4668

Elkin Galloway Memorial Chapel **M** (42) 310 W Main St 28621-3314 (Mail to: PO Box 747 28621-0747) Jonathan Pucik (336) 526-2172

Erwin St Stephens Episcopal Church **P** (122) 201 Denim Dr 28339 (Mail to: 209 Denim Dr 28339-2125) Raymond Hanna (910) 897-5291

Fuquay Varina Trinity Episcopal Church **P** (133) 1128 S Main St 27526-9700 (Mail to: 1128 S Main St 27526-9700) Robert Henderson (919) 552-1056

Garner St Christopher's Epis Church **M** (68) 1101 Vandora Springs Rd 27529-3746 (Mail to: PO Box 505 27529-0505) (919) 772-7125

Greensboro All Saints Church **P** (152) 4211 Wayne Rd 27407-7314 (Mail to: 4211 Wayne Rd 27407-7314) Paula Rachal (336) 299-0705

Greensboro Church of the Holy Spirit **M** (55) 3910 Yanceyville St 27405-3350 (Mail to: 3910 Yanceyville St 27405-3350) Audra Abt (336) 621-7321

Greensboro Church of the Redeemer **P** (157) 901 E Friendly Ave 27401-3103 (Mail to: 901 E Friendly Ave 27401-3103) (336) 275-0033

Greensboro Holy Trinity Episcopal Church **P** (2553) § 607 N Greene St 27401-2023 (Mail to: 607 N Greene St 27401-2023) David Umphlett Sarah Carver (336) 272-6149

Greensboro St Andrews Episcopal Church **P** (377) 2105 W Market St 27403-1718 (Mail to: Attn: Kimberly Rathburn 2105 W Market St 27403-1799) Virginia Inman Robert Hamilton Virginia Inman (336) 275-1651

Greensboro St Barnabas Episcopal Church **M** (238) 1300 Jefferson Rd 27410-3529 (Mail to: 1300 Jefferson Rd 27410-3529) Randall Keeney (336) 294-1282

Greensboro St Francis Episcopal Church **P** (660) § 3506 Lawndale Dr 27408-2804 (Mail to: C/O Linda Allgood 3506 Lawndale Dr 27408-2804) Matthew Addington Milton Williams (336) 288-4721

Greensboro St Marys House **Chapel** (27) 930 Walker Ave 27403-2530 (Mail to: 930 Walker Ave 27403-2530) (336) 334-5219

Hamlet All Saints Episcopal Church **M** (84) 217 Henderson St 28345-3311 (Mail to: PO Box 687 28345-0687) (910) 582-0861

Haw River Saint Andrew's Church **M** (82) PO Box 1088 27258 (Mail to: PO Box 1088 Route 70 27258-1088) (336) 578-3623

Henderson St James Church **M** 3415 Cameron Dr 27536-3820 (Mail to: PO Box 245 27544-0245) (252) 257-3542

Henderson St Johns Episcopal Church **M** (28) N Church & Main Sts 27536 (Mail to: PO Box 974 27536-0974) (252) 492-0082

Henderson Church of the Holy Innocents **P** (347) 210 S Chestnut St 27536-4223 (Mail to: 210 S Chestnut St 27536-4223) (252) 492-0904

High Point St Christophers Episcopal Ch **P** (120) Corner Of Eastchester & High 27262 (Mail to: 303 Eastchester Dr 27262-7628) Niel Lentz (336) 869-5311

High Point St Marys Episcopal Church **P** (779) 108 W Farriss Ave 27262-3008 (Mail to: 108 W Farriss Ave 27262-3099) Robert Travis Foster Mays (336) 886-4756

Hillsborough St Matthews Parish Church **P** (345) 210 St Marys Rd 27278-2518 (Mail to: PO Box 628 27278-0628) Robert Fruehwirth Lisa Frost-Phillips Jean Vail (919) 732-9308

Huntersville St Marks Episcopal Church **P** (354) 8600 Mount Holly Hntrsvlle Rd 28078-8475 (Mail to: 8600 Mount Holly Hntrsvlle Rd 28078-8475) John Edwards (704) 399-5193

Jackson The Church of the Saviour **M** (54) Calhoun & Church Sts 27845 (Mail to: C/O Dana Boone PO Box 613 27845-0613) (919) 534-0911

Kernersville St Matthews Episcopal Church **M** (72) 1110 Salisbury St 27284-3302 (Mail to: PO Box 1173 27285-1173) (336) 996-4422

Laurinburg St Davids Episcopal Church **Cluster** (52) Covington Azure 28353 (Mail to: C/O Donald Nisben PO Box 334 28353-0334) (919) 276-1757

Lexington Grace Episcopal Church **P** (272) 419 S Main St 27292-3234 (Mail to: 419 S Main St

27292-3234) Edward Kelaher (336) 249-7211

Littleton St Alban Episcopal Church **M** (25) 300 Mosby Avenue 27850-0955 (Mail to: PO Box 955 27850-0955) (252) 586-4700

Louisburg St Matthias Episcopal Church **M** (15) Attn Miss Mary L Hill Treas 102 Harris St 27549-2722 (Mail to: Attn Miss Mary L Hill Treas 102 Harris St 27549) (919) 853-2278

Louisburg St Pauls Episcopal Church **M** (87) 301 North Church Street 27549-2417 (Mail to: PO Box 247 27549-0247) Amy Huacani (919) 496-4180

Matthews Thompson Child & Family Focus **P** 6800 Saint Peters Ln 28105 (Mail to: 6800 Saint Peters Ln 28105-8458) (704) 536-0375

Mayodan Church of the Messiah **M** (55) 114 S 2nd Ave 27027-2712 (Mail to: 114 S 2nd Ave 27027-2712) (336) 548-2801

Monroe St Pauls Episcopal Church **P** (212) 116 S Church St 28112-5605 (Mail to: PO Box 293 28111-0293) (704) 289-8434

Mooresville St James Episcopal Church **M** (53) 851 Shinnville Rd 28115-7111 (Mail to: 851 Shinnville Rd 28115-7111) (704) 664-7115

Mooresville St Patrick's Episcopal Church **P** (393) § 164 Fairview Rd 28117-9512 (Mail to: PO Box 295 28123-0295) Gregory McIntyre (704) 663-5659

Mount Airy Trinity Episcopal Church **P** (114) 472 N Main St # 1043 27030-3814 (Mail to: PO Box 1043 27030-1043) Sarah Morris (336) 786-6067

Oxford St Cyprians Episcopal Church **M** (62) 408 Granville St 27565-3673 (Mail to: 408 Granville St 27565-3673) Scott Benhase (919) 693-1351

Oxford St Stephens Episcopal Church **P** (219) 140 College St 27565-2947 (Mail to: 140 College St 27565-2956) Vincent Kopp (919) 693-9740

Pittsboro St Bartholomews Episcopal Ch **P** (77) 204 W Salisbury St 27312-9483 (Mail to: Attn Bookkeeper 204 W Salisbury St 27312-9483) (919) 542-5679

Raleigh Christ Episcopal Church **P** (3039) § 120 E Edenton St 27601-1014 (Mail to: 120 E Edenton St 27601-1014) James Adams Mary Davila David Frazelle Daniel Reeves (919) 8346259

Raleigh Church of the Good Shepherd **P** (800) 121 Hillsborough St 27603-1762 (Mail to: 121 Hillsborough St 27603-1762) Imogen Rhodenhiser Imogen Rhodenhiser Miriam Saxon (919) 831-2000

Raleigh Church of the Nativity **P** (550) 8849 Ray Rd 27613-1232 (Mail to: 8849 Ray Rd 27613-1232) Stephanie Allen Nancy Allison (919) 846-8338

Raleigh NC State Campus Ministry **P** 2208 Hope St 27607-7334 (Mail to: 2208 Hope St 27607-7334) (919) 834-2428

Raleigh St Ambrose Episcopal Church **P** (398) 813 Darby St 27610-4017 (Mail to: 813 Darby St 27610-4017) Robert Taylor (919) 833-8055

Raleigh St Augustines Chapel **P** 1315 Oakwood Ave 27610-2247 (Mail to: 1315 Oakwood Ave 27610-2247) (919) 516-4000

Raleigh St Marks Episcopal Church **P** (256) 1725 N New Hope Rd 27604-8304 (Mail to: 1725 N New Hope Rd 27604-8304) (919) 231-6767

Raleigh St Marys School Chapel **School** 900 Hillsborough St 27603-1610 (Mail to: 900 Hillsborough St 27603-1689) Margaret Leidheiser-Stoddard (919) 424-4122

Raleigh St Michaels Episcopal Church **P** (2118) § 1520 Canterbury Rd 27608-1106 (Mail to: C/O Susan Little 1520 Canterbury Rd 27608-1106) Samuel Jones James Pahl Holly Gloff David Nichols (919) 782-0731

Raleigh St Timothys Church **P** (275) 4523 Six Forks Rd 27609-5709 (Mail to: 4523 Six Forks Rd 27609-5709) Allen Waller (919) 787-7590

Reidsville St Thomas Episcopal Church **P** (109) § 315 Lindsey St 27320-3649 (Mail to: PO Box 72 27323-0072) (336) 349-3511

Ridgeway Chapel of the Good Shepherd **M** (9) 1202 Ridgeway-Warrenton Road 27570-0070 (Mail to: PO Box 70 27570-0070) (252) 456-2412

Roanoke Rapids All Saints Episcopal Church **P** (128) 635 Hamilton St 27870-2703 (Mail to: 635 Hamilton St 27870-2703) Joseph Browne Joseph Browne (252) 537-3610

Roanoke Rapids St Mark Episcopal Church **P** (14) PO Box 234 27870-0234 (Mail to: C/O Senior Warden PO Box 234 27870) (252) 537-8835

Rockingham Church of the Messiah **P** (15) 202 N Lawrence St 28379-3668 (Mail to: PO Box 1313 28380-1313) (910) 895-4739

Rocky Mount Church of the Good Shepherd **P** (470) 231 N Church St 27804-5404 (Mail to: 231 N Church St 27804-5404) Louise Anderson Susan Michelfelder (252) 442-1134

Rocky Mount St Andrews Episcopal Church **P** (355) 301 S Circle Dr 27804-3613 (Mail to: 301 S Circle Dr 27804-3613) George Greer (252) 443-2070

Roxboro St Marks Episcopal Church **M** (25) 422 N Main St 27573-5037 (Mail to: PO Box 1071 27573-1071) (336) 597-2171

Salisbury St Lukes Episcopal Church **P** (621) 131 W Council St 28144-4320 (Mail to: 131 W Council St 28144-4320) Robert Black Bonnie Duckworth (704) 633-3221

Salisbury Saint Matthew Church **M** (28) 4401 Statesville Blvd 28147-7463 (Mail to: 4401 Statesville Blvd 28147-7463) Edwin Cox (704) 636-0821

Salisbury St Pauls Church **M** (32) 930 S Main St 28144-6453 (Mail to: PO Box 1852 28145-1852) (704) 637-9404

Sanford St Thomas Episcopal Church **P** (226) 312 N Steele St 27330-3922 (Mail to: 312 N Steele St 27330-3922) Bruce Heyvaert Barbara Cooke (919) 774-8644

Scotland Neck Trinity Episcopal Church **P** (34) 1305 Main St 27874-1346 (Mail to: PO Box 372 27874-0372) John Fulton (252) 826-4616

Seven Lakes St Mary Magdalene Episcopal Ch **M** (68) 1143 7 Lks N 27376-9757 (Mail to: PO Box 456 27376-0456) (910) 6733838

Smithfield St Paul's Episcopal Church **P** (215) 218 S 2nd St 27577-4532 (Mail to: 218 S 2nd St 27577-4532) Katherine Byrd (919) 934-2675

Smithfield San Jose Mission **M** (35) 218 South Second St 27577 (Mail to: 218 S 2nd St 27577-4532) (910) 989-9742

Southern Pines Emmanuel Parish Episcopal Ch **P** (612) 340 S Ridge St 28387-6036 (Mail to: 340 S Ridge St 28387-6036) Patricia Grace (910) 692-3171

Speed St Marys Episcopal Church **M** (25) 169 Kilquick Rd 27886 (Mail to: 1264 Rogister Rd 27886-4366) (252) 903-3555

Statesville Trinity Episcopal Church **P** (302) 801 Henkel Rd 28677-3215 (Mail to: 801 Henkel Rd PO Box 1103 28677-3215) Robert Mullis (704) 872-6314

Tarboro Calvary Episcopal Church **P** (293) § 411 E Church St 27886-4403 (Mail to: PO Box 1245 27886-1245) Deborah Shaffer (252) 823-8192

Tarboro St Luke Episcopal Church **M** (10) PO Box 64 27886-0064 (Mail to: PO Box 64 27886-0064) (252) 641-5853

Tarboro St Michael Episcopal Church **M** (109) 3204 Western Blvd 27886-1828 (Mail to: PO Box 331 27886-0331) (252) 823-4926

Wadesboro Calvary Episcopal Church **P** (153) 223 E Morgan St 28170-2222 (Mail to: PO Box 942 28170-0942) (704) 694-3223

Wake Forest St Johns Episcopal Church **P** (876) § 830 Durham Rd 27587-8792 (Mail to: 834 Durham Rd 27587-8792) Sarah Phelps Stephen Mazingo (919) 556-3656

Walnut Cove Christ Church **P** (53) 412 Summit Ave. 27052-0476 (Mail to: PO Box 476 27052-0476) (336) 591 7727

Warrenton Emmanuel Episcopal Church **M** (52) 133 N Main St 27589-1921 (Mail to: PO Box 704 27589-0704) (252) 257-2557

Waxhaw St Margarets Episcopal Church **P** (1031) 8515 Rea Rd 28173-6801 (Mail to: 8515 Rea Rd 28173-6801) Todd Dill (704) 243-3523

Weldon Grace Episcopal Church **P** (26) Washington Ave 5th St 27890 (Mail to: PO Box 308 27890-0308) (252) 536-4312

Wilson La Iglesia de la Guadalupana **M** (1338) 106 Reid St SE 27893-6230 (Mail to: PO Box 4032 27893-0032) Jose Pinell Mendieta (252) 206-9996

Wilson St Marks Episcopal Church **M** (66) C/O Louie Tabron 2404 Nash St N 27896-1309 (Mail to: C/O Louie Tabron 2404 E Nash Street 27893) Jose Pinell Mendieta (252) 291-6076

Wilson St Timothys Church **P** (417) 202 N Goldsboro Street 27893 (Mail to: PO Box 1527 27894-1527) Paul Castelli James Reed Robert Thomas (252) 291-8220

Winston Salem St Annes Episcopal Church **P** (244) 2690 Fairlawn Dr 27106-3802 (Mail to: Attn: Treasurer PO Box 11437 27116-1437) Virginia Wilder (336) 768-0174

Winston Salem St Pauls Episcopal Church **P** (2152) 520 Summit St 27101-1115 (Mail to: 520 Summit St 27101-1195) Sara Ardrey-

Graves David Kinser Nancy Vaders Lauren Villemuer-Drenth (336) 723-4391

Winston Salem St Stephen Episcopal Church **P** (76) 810 Highland Ave 27101-4209 (Mail to: 810 Highland Ave 27101-4209) Hector Sintim (336) 724-2614

Winston Salem St Timothys Episcopal Church **P** (1132) 2575 Parkway Dr 27103-3522 (Mail to: 2575 Parkway Dr 27103-3522) Steven Rice (336) 765-0294

DIOCESE OF NORTH DAKOTA
(PROVINCE VI)
Comprises the State of North Dakota and Clay County, Minnesota
DIOCESAN OFFICE 3600 South 25th St Fargo ND 58104-6861
TEL (701) 235-6688 WEB http://www.ndepiscopal.org/

Previous Bishops—
Wm D Walker 1883-96, Samuel C Edsall 1899-1901, Cameron Mann 1901-13, John P Tyler 1914-31, Fredk B Bartlett 1931-35, Douglass H Atwill 1937-51, Richard R Emery 1951-64, George T Masuda 1965-79, Harold A Hopkins Jr 1980-88 Andrew H Fairfield 1989-2003, Michael G Smith 2004-2019

Bishop Provisional—Thomas C. Ely (2021-)

Conv Sec T Enockson; *Treas* C Peterson; *Chanc* L Wilking; *Dio Min* S Godfrey; *Dio Admin* J Thielke; *Indian Work* A Goodhouse-Mauai; *Fin* C Peterson; *ER&D* A Stomberg; *Evang Off* vacant; *UTO* V Strobel M Massad; *NW Coord* K Becker

Stand Comm—Cler: Pres M Strobel T Overbo H Weidman; *Lay:* R Fox J Thoms J Baird

PARISHES, MISSIONS, AND CLERGY

Bismarck St George's Episcopal Church **P** (201) 601 N 4th St 58501-3685 (Mail to: PO Box 1241 58502-1241) Hal Weidman (701) 223-1942

Cannon Ball St James Episcopal Church **P** (122) General Delivery 58528 (Mail to: PO Box 612 58528) Neil Two Bears (701) 854-7325

Cartwright St Michael & All Angels Church **P** (21) 14 Route 1 Box Box 58838 (Mail to: General Delivery 58838-9999) (701) 572-9278

Devils Lake Episcopal Church of the Advent **P** (34) 501 6th St NE 58301-2523 (Mail to: PO Box 703 58301-0703) (701) 662-3726

Dickinson St Johns Episcopal Church **P** (50) 822 5th Ave W 58601-3832 (Mail to: PO Box 48 58602-0048) (701) 225-5026

Dunseith St Sylvans Church **P** (84) 1025 61st Ave NW 58329 (Mail to: PO Box 10337 58106-

0337) (701) 891-2911

✠ **Fargo** Gethsemane Cathedral **O** (302) 3600 25th St S 58104-6861 (Mail to: 3600 25th St S 58104-6861) Mark Strobel Terry Overbo Charlotte Robbins Crystal Towers Glenn Williams (701) 232-3394

Fargo St Stephens Episcopal Church **P** (245) 120 21st Ave N 58102-2015 (Mail to: 120 21st Ave N 58102-2015) Jamie Parsley (701) 2322076

Fort Totten St Thomas Church **P** (143) PO Box 43 58335-9999 (Mail to: PO Box 10337 58106-0337) (701) 766-4630

Fort Yates St Lukes Church **P** (304) 501 S River Rd 58538 (Mail to: PO Box 612 58538-0612) Lindsey Dwarf Sloane Floberg Virginia Luger Neil Two Bears (701) 854-2323

Garrison St Pauls Church **P** (86) 1025 61st Ave NW 58540-9384 (Mail to: PO Box 10337 58106-0337)

Grand Forks St Pauls Episcopal Church **P** (187) 319 S 5th St 58201-4607 (Mail to: 319 S 5th St 58201-4607) Harvey Henderson Harvey Henderson James Shannon (701) 775-7955

Jamestown Grace Episcopal Church **P** (167) 405 2nd Ave NE 58401-3308 (Mail to: 405 2nd Ave NE 58401-3308) Robert Hoekstra (701) 252-4499

Minot All Saints' Episcopal Church **P** (60) 301 Main St S 58701-3917 (Mail to: 301 Main St S 58701-3917) (701) 839-1037

Moorhead St John the Divine Epis Church **P** (290) 120 8th St S 56560-2809 (Mail to: PO Box 641 56561-0641) (218) 233-0423

Oakes St Mary & St Mark Epis Church **M** (15) 211 N 6th St 58474-1218 (Mail to: 9034 111th Avenue SE 58474-9105) (701) 742-2213

Selfridge Church of the Cross **P** (30) 25 N Main St 58568-6801 (Mail to: PO Box 73 58568-0073) John Floberg (701) 891-2911

Valley City All Saints Episcopal Church **P** (14) 516 Central Ave N 58072-2544 (Mail to: PO Box 366 58072-0366) (701) 845-0819

Walhalla St Peters Church **P** 508 Delano Ave 58282 (Mail to: 12707-109th St NE 58282-9460) Elsie Magnus

Williston St Peters Episcopal Church **P** (100) 111 East 14th Street 58802-1181 (Mail to: PO Box 1181 58802-1181) (701) 572-9278

DIOCESE OF NORTHERN CALIFORNIA
(PROVINCE VIII)
Comprises the northern third of the State of California
DIOCESAN OFFICE 350 University Avenue, Suite 280, Sacramento CA 95825
TEL (916) 442-6918 FAX (916) 442-6927
E-MAIL info@norcalepiscopal.org WEB www.norcalepiscopal.org

Previous Bishops—
John HD Wingfield 1874-98; William H Moreland m 1899 Bp 1910-33; Archie WN Porter coadj 1933 Bp 1933-57; Edward McNair suffr 1967-73; Clarence R Haden coadj 1957 Bp 1958-78; John L Thompson III 1978-91; Jerry A Lamb coadj 1991 Bp 1992-2006; Barry L Beisner coad 2006 Bp 2006

Bishop—Rt Rev Megan McClure Traquair (1121) (Dio Jun 2019)

Sec Conv Rev M Warren; *Canon to Ord* Rev Cn J Wakelee; *Board of Trustees Pres* Rt Rev M. Traquair; *Board of Trustees VP* M Harrison-Smith; *Sec* Rev Dr P Dolan *Treas* J Nykamp; *Chanc* B Jewell; *Dir of Ops* K Braak; *Comm on Min* Rev K Sefton L Maxwell; *Cong Dev* Rev Cn J Wakelee; *Epis Comm Serv* Rev Cn. B Clark; *Health Min* S Wahlstrom; *Companion Diocese* Rev D Green; *Sust Dev Goals; ERD* C Maloney; *Chap to Ret Clergy* Rev Cn L Walker

Stand Comm—Cler: Sec S Hubbell *P* S Kellerman VP T McDonald M Woodward; *Lay:* M McMillen L Parks S Takagi D Wallace

PARISHES, MISSIONS, AND CLERGY

Alturas St Michaels Episcopal Church **M** (23) 310 W North St 96101-3957 (Mail to: 310 W North St 96101-3957) David Cohen (530) 233-2251

Anderson St. Michael's Episcopal Church **P** (58) 3001 Rupert Rd 96007-3746 (Mail to: PO Box 144 96007-0144) (530) 365-4344

Antelope St Andrew's Episcopal Church **M** (64) 7850 Watt Ave 95843-2001 (Mail to: 7850 Watt Ave 95843-2001) Peter Rodgers (916) 332-1476

Arcata St Albans Episcopal Church **P** (215) 1675 Chester Ave 95521-6827 (Mail to: 1675 Chester Ave 95521-6827) Sara Potter Nancy Streufert (707) 822-4102

Auburn St Lukes Church **P** (155) 124 Orange St 95603-5233 (Mail to: 124 Orange St 95603-5233) Brian Rebholtz (530) 885-2316

Benicia St Pauls Episcopal Church **P** (271) 120 East J Street 94510-3235 (Mail to: 120 E J St 94510-3298) Anne Mertz Mary Goshert Arthur Holder (707) 745-0307

Calistoga St Lukes Episcopal Church **M** (50) 1504 Myrtle St 94515-1633 (Mail to: PO Box 381 94515-0381) William Mcilmoyl (707) 942-6007

Cameron Park Faith Episcopal Church **P** (398) 2200 Country Club Dr 95682-7703 (Mail to: PO Box 966 95682-0966) Thomas Gartin (530) 676-5348

Carmichael St Georges Church **P** (74) 5600 Winding Way 95608-1213 (Mail to: 5600 Winding Way 95608-1213) Raymond Hess Raymond Hess Christine Leigh-Taylor Christine Leigh-Taylor Robert Olsen William Rontani Julie Vice (916) 487-5600

Carmichael St Michaels Episcopal Church **P** (795) § 2140 Mission Ave 95608-5635 (Mail to: 2140 Mission Ave 95608-5699) Mary Claugus Rodney Davis Wesley Whitten (916) 488-3550

Chico St John the Evangelist Church **P** (345) 2341 Floral Ave 95926-7311 (Mail to: 2341 Floral Ave 95926-7311) Lewis Powell William Stomski Ann Sullivan (530) 894-1971

Cloverdale Church of the Good Shepherd **M** (59) 122 N Main St 95425-3346 (Mail to: PO Box 337 95425-0337) Robert Scott Jane Snibbe (707) 891-6015

Colusa St Stephens Episcopal Church **P** (31) 642 5th St 95932-2611 (Mail to: PO Box 1044 95932-1044) John Vafis (530) 458-2470

Corning St Andrew Episcopal Church **M** (33) 820 Marin St 96021-3230 (Mail to: PO Box 276 96021-0276) (530) 824-2321

Crescent City St Pauls Episcopal Church **M** (47) 220 E Macken Ave 95531-2745 (Mail to: 220 E Macken Ave 95531-2745) (707) 464-2708

Davis Church of St Martin **P** (558) 640 Hawthorne Ln 95616-3463 (Mail to: 640 Hawthorne Ln 95616-3463) Anne Beatty Pamela Dolan Margaret Grayden Ernest Lewis (530) 756-0444

Eureka Christ Episcopal Church **P** (167) 625 15th St 95501-2328 (Mail to: PO Box 861

95502-0861) Daniel London Pamela Gossard Kathleen McCloghrie David Shewmaker (707) 442-1797

Fairfield Grace Episcopal Church **P** (346) 1405 Kentucky St 94533-4715 (Mail to: 1405 Kentucky St 94533-4715) Karen Freeman Perry Polk (707) 425-4481

Ferndale St Mary Episcopal Church **M** (7) 400 Shaw Ave 95536 (Mail to: PO Box 366 95536-0366) (707) 786-9843

Folsom Trinity Episcopal Church **P** (557) 803 Figueroa St 95630-2404 (Mail to: 801 Figueroa St 95630-2404) Jason Bruce Michael Kerrick Anne Smith Anne Smith Elizabeth Vincent (916) 985-2495

Fort Bragg St Michael & All Angels Parish **P** (85) 201 Fir St 95437-3110 (Mail to: PO Box 124 95437-0124) Tansy Chapman Randy Knutson (707) 964-1900

Fortuna St Francis Episcopal Church **M** (47) 568 16th St 95540-2415 (Mail to: 568 16th St 95540-2415) Gerarlyn Cunningham Kathleen McCloghrie (707) 725-4686

Galt St Lukes Episcopal Church **M** (53) 200 Third St 95632 (Mail to: PO Box 897 95632-0897) Barbara Nixon (209) 745-2784

Grass Valley Emmanuel Episcopal Church **P** (361) 235 S Church St 95945-6703 (Mail to: 235 S Church St 95945-6793) Alan Kellermann Gary Brown (530) 273-7876

Gridley St Timothys Episcopal Church **M** (54) 410 Jackson St 95948-2513 (Mail to: PO Box 176 95948-0176) (530) 846-4147

Gualala Shepherd by the Sea MIssion **M** (63) 39141 Church St 95445-8306 (Mail to: PO Box 691 95445-0691) (707) 785-3682

Healdsburg St Pauls Episcopal Church **P** (262) 209 Matheson St 95448-4109 (Mail to: 209 Matheson St 95448-4109) Sally Hubbell (707) 433-2107

Kenwood St Patricks Episcopal Church **P** (132) 9000 Sonoma Hwy 95452-9028 (Mail to: PO Box 247 95452-0247) Edward Howell Karen King Leslie King (707) 833-4228

Lakeport St Johns Episcopal Church **P** (33) 1190 N Forbes St 95453-3824 (Mail to: 1190 N Forbes St 95453-3824) (707) 263-4785

Lincoln St James Episcopal Church **P** (196) 479 L St 95648-1633 (Mail to: 490 K St 95648-1627) (916) 645-1739

Marysville St Johns Episcopal Church **P** (67) 800 D St 95901-5321 (Mail to: 800 D St 95901-5321) (530) 742-8829

Monte Rio St Andrews in the Redwoods **M** 20329 Highway 116 95462-9747 (Mail to: PO Box 721 95462-0721) (707) 865-0834

Mount Shasta St Barnabas **M** (49) 701 Lassen Ln 96067-9711 (Mail to: 701 Lassen Ln 96067-9711) Lawrence Holben (530) 926-5326

Napa St Marys Episcopal Church **P** (323) 1917 Third St 94558 (Mail to: 1917 3rd St 94559-2312)

Robin Denney John Morris (707) 255-0991

Nevada City Holy Trinity Episcopal Church **P** (279) 201 Nevada St 95959-2605 (Mail to: 201 Nevada St 95959-2605) Bradley Helmuth (530) 265-8836

Oroville St Pauls Episcopal Church **P** (25) 1430 Pine St 95965-4836 (Mail to: 1430 Pine St 95965-4836) David Englund Susan Fay William Rontani (530) 533-5035

Paradise Church of St Nicholas **P** (174) 5872 Oliver Rd 95969-3835 (Mail to: 5872 Oliver Rd 95969-3835) Susan Fay (530) 877-7006

Petaluma St Johns Episcopal Church **P** (156) 40 5th St 94952-3042 (Mail to: 40 5th St 94952-3042) Daniel Green (707) 762-8872

Placerville Epis Church of Our Saviour **P** (220) 2979 Coloma St 95667-4440 (Mail to: PO Box 447 95667-0447) Debra Warwick-Sabino (530) 622-2441

Quincy Christ the King Episcopal Ch **M** (79) 545 Lawrence St 95971-9432 (Mail to: 545 Lawrence St 95971-9432) Matthew Warren (530) 283-0254

Rancho Cordova St Clements Episcopal Church **P** (127) 2376 Zinfandel Dr 95670-4953 (Mail to: 2376 Zinfandel Dr 95670-4953) Zachary Neubauer (916) 635-5282

Red Bluff Saint Peter's Episcopal Church **P** (81) 510 Jefferson St 96080-3408 (Mail to: 510 Jefferson St 96080-3408) (530) 5275205

Redding All Saints Episcopal Church **P** (244) 2150 Benton Dr 96003-2151 (Mail to: 2150 Benton Dr 96003-2151) (530) 243-1000

Rio Vista St Brigid of Kildare **P** (6) 218 California Street 94571-1923 (Mail to: PO Box 580 94571-0580) (707) 374-2667

Rocklin St Augustine of Canterbury **P** (290) 1800 Wildcat Blvd. 95765 (Mail to: 1800 Wildcat Blvd 95765-5471) (916) 435-9552

Roseville St Johns Episcopal Church **P** (427) 2351 Pleasant Grove Blvd 95747-8918 (Mail to: C/O The Rev Cliff Haggenjos 2351 Pleasant Grove Blvd 95747-8918) Clifford Haggenjos Babette Haggenjos (916) 786-6911

Sacramento All Saints Episcopal Church **P** (207) 2076 Sutterville Rd 95822-1320 (Mail to: 2076 Sutterville Rd 95822-1384) Merritt Greenwood Virginia Mcneely (916) 455-0643

Sacramento St Matthews Episcopal Church **P** (30) 2300 Edison Ave 95821-1714 (Mail to: 2300 Edison Ave 95821-1796) Anne Arthur Babette Haggenjos Cynthia Long Rik Rasmussen (916) 927-0115

Sacramento St Pauls Episcopal Church **P** (146) 1430 J St 95814-2918 (Mail to: PO Box 160914 95816) Michael Backlund Anne McKeever Rik Rasmussen Rik Rasmussen Anne Slakey (916) 446-2620

Sacramento St Marys Church **P** (105) 9085 Calvine Rd 95829-9451 (Mail to: 9085 Calvine Rd 95829-9451) (916) 689-1099

✠ **Sacramento** Trinity Episcopal Cathedral **O** (1334) 2620 Capitol Ave 95816-5905 (Mail to: 2620 Capitol Ave 95816-5991) Matthew Woodward Leah Hallisey William Adams Megan Anderson Anne Arthur Kathryn Hopner Anne McKeever Mary Morrison Peter Rodgers Claudia Weber (916) 446-2513

Saint Helena Grace Episcopal Church **P** (510) 1314 Spring St 94574-2050 (Mail to: 1314 Spring St 94574-2050) Amy Denney-Zuniga (707) 9634157

Santa Rosa The Church of the Incarnation **P** (448) 550 Mendocino Ave 95401-5213 (Mail to: 550 Mendocino Ave 95401-5213) Stephen Shaver James Knutsen Margaret Moore (707) 579-2604

Sebastopol St Stephens Episcopal Church **P** (194) 500 Robinson Rd 95472-4110 (Mail to: 500 Robinson Rd 95472-4110) Christy Laborda Harris (707) 823-3281

Sonoma Trinity Episcopal Church **P** (176) 275 East Spain Street 95476-5732 (Mail to: 275 E Spain St 95476-5732) James Thomas (707) 938-4846

Susanville Good Shepherd Episcopal Church **M** (21) 1155 North St 96130-4051 (Mail to: 1155 North St 96130-4051) David Cohen (530) 257-6002

Sutter Creek Trinity Episcopal Church **P** (99) 430 Highway 49 95685-4144 (Mail to: 430 State Highway 49 95685-4144) (209) 267-0255

Tahoe City St Nicholas Episcopal Church **M** (54) 855 W Lake Blvd Hwy 89 96145 (Mail to: PO Box 855 96145-0855) (530) 583-4713

Ukiah Holy Trinity Episcopal Church **P** (62) 640 South Orchard Avenue 95482-5012 (Mail to: Barbara Webster 640 S Orchard Ave 95482-5012) (707) 462-8042

Vacaville Epiphany Episcopal Church **P** (322) 300 West St 95688-4516 (Mail to: 300 West St 95688-4516) Beatryce Clark Stacey Grossman (707) 448-2275

Vallejo Ascension Episcopal Church **P** (168) 2420 Tuolumne St 94589-2345 (Mail to: 2420 Tuolumne St 94589-2345) Bayani Rico Richard Von Grabow (707) 644-5505

Westwood Holy Spirit Mission **M** (9) 462-520 Forest Path 96137-9403 (Mail to: 462-520 Forest Path 96137-9403) Matthew Warren (530) 375-0994

Wheatland Grace Episcopal Church **M** (25) 610 3rd St 95692-9459 (Mail to: 610 3rd St 95692-9459) Richard Laughman (530) 483-7050

Willits St Fran in the Redwoods Mssn **M** (46) 1 N Main Street 95490 (Mail to: 66 E Commercial St 95490-3102) Betsy Bruneau Donnalee Hart (707) 272-0177

Willows Holy Trinity Episcopal Church **P** (26) 556 East Sycamore Street 95988-3250 (Mail to: Mrs R W Danley PO Box 339 95988-0339) (530) 934-3778

Woodland St Lukes Episcopal Church **P** (125) 515 Second Street 95695-4029 (Mail to: 515 2nd S 95695-4029) Alex Leach (530) 662-7152

Yuba City St James of Jerusalem Mission **M** (35 556 N George Washington Blvd 95993 (Mail to: 556 N George Washington Blvd 95993 8995) Richard Laughman (530) 673-1790

DIOCESE OF NORTHERN INDIANA
(PROVINCE V)
Comprises Northern Indiana
DIOCESAN OFFICE 117 N Lafayette Blvd South Bend IN 46601
TEL (574) 233-6489
E-MAIL info@ednin.org WEB www.ednin.org

Previous Bishops— John H White 1895-1925, Campbell Gray 1925-44, Reginald Mallett 1944-63, Walter Conrad Klein 1963-72, William CR Sheridan 1972-87, Francis C Gray 1987-98, Edward S Little II 2000-2016

Bishop—Rt Rev Dr Douglas E Sparks (Dio 25 Jun 16)

Miss for Admin and Governance Rev Cn M Walker; *Miss for Formation and Trans* Rev Cn TL Bays; *Miss for Fin* Cn C Bianchini & Cn S Katona; *Miss for Dcns* Rev Cn A Wietstock; *Miss for Communication and Operations* Cn CA Hillak

Officers: Sec E Doye; *Treas* J Walker; *Chanc* J Rigdo PO Box 585 North Webster IN 46555 (574) 268-822

Stand Comm: Cler: N Warne P Hooper TJ Freeman *Lay:* D Stacy R Powers P Kincaid

Depts: COM Marie Gambetta

PARISHES, MISSIONS, AND CLERGY

Angola Church of the Holy Family **P** (90) 909 A Darling St 46703-1857 (Mail to: 909 S Darlin St 46703-1857) Thomas Adamson (260) 665 5067

Berne St George Episcopal Church **M** (27) 119 Hendricks St 46711-2391 (Mail to: 119 Hendricks St 46711-2391) (260) 589-3315

Bristol Saint John of the Cross **P** (101) 601 E Vistula St 46507-8904 (Mail to: PO Box 433 46507-0433) (574) 848-7114

Chesterton St Francis Episcopal Church **P** (92) 237 E 1200 N 46304-9360 (Mail to: PO Box 621 46304-0621) (219) 926-3497

Crown Point St Christophers Episcopal Ch **P** (46) 12718 Marshall St 46307-8386 (Mail to: 12718 Marshall St 46307-8386) (219) 663-0559

Culver St Elizabeths Episcopal Church **M** (20) 820 Academy Rd 46511-1106 (Mail to: 515 State St 46511-1131) (574) 339-0235

Elkhart St David Episcopal Church **P** (51) 26824 County Road 4 46514-5851 (Mail to: 26824 County Road 4 46514-5851) (574) 264-4039

Elkhart Ch of St John the Evangelist **P** (219) 226 W Lexington Ave 46516-3128 (Mail to: PO Box 1155 46515) (574) 295-1725

Fort Wayne Grace Episcopal Church **P** (74) 10010 Aurora Pl 46804-8500 (Mail to: 10010 Aurora Pl 46804-8500) (260) 432-9221

Fort Wayne St Alban Episcopal Church **P** (116) 7308 Saint Joe Rd 46835-1581 (Mail to: 7308 Saint Joe Rd 46835-1596) Michael Roeske (260) 485-8022

Fort Wayne Trinity Episcopal Church **P** (447) 611 W Berry St 46802-2105 (Mail to: 611 W Berry St 46802-2192) TJ Freeman Paul Greve Phillip Hooper Gordon Samra (260) 423-1693

Gary St Augustine Episcopal Church **P** (123) 2425 W 19th Ave 46404-2749 (Mail to: PO Box 4156 46404-4156) (219) 944-8383

Gary St Barnabas in the Dunes **P** (28) PO Box 2608 46403-0608 (Mail to: 1125 N Pike St 46403-1380) Michael Dwyer (219) 938-2834

Goshen St James Episcopal Church **P** (46) 105 S 6th St 46528-3303 (Mail to: 105 S 6th St 46528-3398) (574) 533-4984

Griffith St Timothy Episcopal Church **P** (60) 1115 N Cline Ave 46319-1563 (Mail to: 1115 N Cline Ave 46319-1563) (219) 838-8379

Hobart St Stephen Episcopal Church **P** (45) 1360 State St 46342-6056 (Mail to: PO Box 647 46342-0647) John Blakslee (219) 696-4819

Howe St Mark's Episcopal Church **P** (15) 5755 N State Road 9 46746-9228 (Mail to: PO Box 336 46746-0336) (260) 497-9718

Huntington Church of Christ the King **P** (68) § 1224 N Jefferson St 46750-1848 (Mail to: 1224 N Jefferson St 46750-1848) (260) 356-3570

Kokomo St Andrew Episcopal Church **HC** (177) 602 W Superior Street 46901-5299 (Mail to: 602 W Superior St 46901-5299) Richard Lightsey (765) 457-2075

Laporte St Pauls Episcopal Church **P** (83) 708 Harrison St 46350-3418 (Mail to: 708 Harrison St 46350-3418) Michelle Walker (219) 362-2784

Logansport Trinity Episcopal Church **P** (73) 319 7th St 46947-3128 (Mail to: 319 7th St 46947-3128) Clark Miller (574) 753-2733

Marion Gethsemane Episcopal Church **P** (175) 111 E 9th St 46953-1968 (Mail to: 803 S Washington St 46953-1968) (765) 664-4638

Michigan City Trinity Episcopal Church **P** (101) 600 Franklin St 46360-3412 (Mail to: 600 Franklin St 46360-3412) Robert Rhodes (219) 874-4355

Mishawaka St Paul Episcopal Church **P** (176) 616 Lincolnway E 46544-2210 (Mail to: 616 Lincolnway E 46544-2210) (574) 255-9090

Munster St Paul Episcopal Church **P** (75) 1101 Park Dr 46321-2544 (Mail to: 1101 Park Dr 46321-2544) (219) 838-3803

Plymouth St Thomas Church Episcopal **HC** (153) N. Center Street at Adams 46563-1728 (Mail to: 400 N Center St 46563-1728) Bernadette Hartsough Bernadette Hartsough (574) 936-2735

South Bend Church of the Holy Trinity **P** (34) 915 N Olive St 46628-2521 (Mail to: PO Box 3679 46619-0679) Terri Bays (574) 234-9582

South Bend St Mich & All Angels Epis Ch **P** (191) 53720 Ironwood Rd 46635-1532 (Mail to: 53720 Ironwood Rd 46635-1532) Mark Van Wassenhove Cynthia Van Parys (574) 243-0632

✠ **South Bend** Cathedral of St James **O** (238) 117 N Lafayette Blvd 46601-1507 (Mail to: 117 N Lafayette Blvd 46601-1587) Brian Grantz Janice Miller (574) 232-4837

Syracuse All Saints Episcopal Church **M** (50) 7812 E Vawter Park Rd 46567-9515 (Mail to: 7830 E Vawter Park Rd 46567-9515) (574) 457-2178

Valparaiso St Andrew's Episcopal Church **P** (192) 505 Bullseye Lake Rd. 46383-4813 (Mail to: 505 Bullseye Lake Rd 46383-1951) (219) 462-4946

Warsaw St Anne Episcopal Church **P** (193) 424 W Market St 46580-2831 (Mail to: 424 W Market St 46580-2831) Ryan Fischer (574) 267-6266

DIOCESE OF NORTHERN MICHIGAN
(PROVINCE V)
Comprises the northernmost part of the State in the Upper Peninsula of Michigan
DIOCESAN OFFICE 131 E Ridge St Marquette MI 49855
TEL (906) 228-7160 FAX (906) 228-7171
E-MAIL diocese@upepiscopal.org WEB www.upepiscopal.org

Previous Bishops—
Gershom M Williams 1896-1919, Robt L Harris coadj 1918 Bp 1919-29, Hayward S Ablewhite 1930-39, Herman Page prov 1940-42, Herman R Page 1942-64, George R Selway 1964-71, Sam J Wylie 1972-74, Wm A Dimmick 1975-82, Thomas K Ray 1982-99, James A Kelsey 1999-2007,

Bishop—Rayford J Ray (April 1, 2011)

Treas R Graybill; *Chanc* J Spray; *Standing Comm Pres* W Davis; *Missioners:* D Carlisle M Franson S Harries V Mannisto B Pickens S Ray; *COM* V Mannisto; *Trans* LK Bucklin; *Cn to Ord* J Cisluycis; *Cn for Disc & Vit* LK Bucklin; *Dir Diversity, Equity & Inclusion* L Tadgerson

PARISHES, MISSIONS, AND CLERGY

Crystal Falls St Marks Church **P** (30) 809 Crystal Ave 49920-1104 (Mail to: C/O T R Harrison Treasurer 127 Iron St 49920-1124) Christine Mello-Maki Carolyn Orchard Margaret Padilla (906) 875-3921

De Tour Village St Stephens Episcopal Church **P** (21) 124 S Ontario St 49725 (Mail to: PO Box 413 49725-0413) (906) 297-3207

Eagle Harbor St Peters by the Sea **SC** (6) 435 Front Street 49950 (Mail to: PO Box 265 49950-0265) (906) 289-4567

Escanaba St Stephens Episcopal Church **P** (268) 500 Ogden Ave 49829-3930 (Mail to: 510 Ogden Ave 49829-3930) (906) 786-7970

Gladstone Trinity Episcopal Church **P** (139) 901 Dakota Ave 49837-1616 (Mail to: PO Box 428 49837-0428) Dale Jamison Maria Maniaci Suzanne Ray (906) 428-4116

Houghton Trinity Episcopal Church **P** (39) 205 E Montezuma Ave 49931-2110 (Mail to: 205 E Montezuma Ave 49931-2110) (906) 482-2010

Iron Mountain Church of the Holy Trinity **P** (24) 221 W B St 49801-3336 (Mail to: PO Box 805 49801-0805) Candice Lauk Norris Satterly (906) 774-3722

Iron River St Johns Church **P** (14) 527 N 2nd Ave 49935-1446 (Mail to: 527 N 2nd Ave 49935-

1446) (906) 265-9013

Ironwood Church of the Transfiguration **P** (15) 336 E Aurora St 49938-2114 (Mail to: 334 E Aurora St 49938-2114) Geri Sola John Kangas (906) 932-4395

Ishpeming Grace Episcopal Church **P** (45) 1st Canda Sts 49849 (Mail to: PO Box 601 49849-0601) (906) 485-1623

Larium Christ Episcopal Church **P** (17) 57031 Fifth St 49913 (Mail to: 3906 5th St 49913-1809) Laura Eaton (906) 337-5242

Mackinac Island Trinity Episcopal Church **P** (31) 1623 Fort St 49757 (Mail to: PO Box 472 49757-0472) (906) 847-3798

Manistique St Albans Church **P** (32) 301 Range St 49854-1562 (Mail to: PO Box 302 49854-0302) (906) 286-2881

Marquette Holy Innocents Episcopal Ch **P** (21) 131 E Ridge St 49855-4208 (Mail to: PO Box 333 49833-0333) (906) 942-7178

Marquette St Pauls Episcopal Church **P** (301) 201 E Ridge St 49855-4210 (Mail to: 201 E Ridge St 49855-4210) Marcia Franz Coralie Hambleton (906) 226-2912

Menominee Grace Episcopal Church **P** (60) 922 10th Ave 49858-3033 (Mail to: 922 10th Ave 49858-3033) Mary Miron Bonnie Turner (906) 863-2385

Munising St Johns Church **P** (15) 121 W Onota Street 49862-1119 (Mail to: 121 W Onota St 49862-1119) Virginia Mannisto Marion Luckey Kimberly Moote (906) 387-2468

Negaunee St Johns Episcopal Church **P** (30) 101 W Main St 49866-1607 (Mail to: PO Box 29 49866-0029) John Lenten James Martindale Kevin Thew Forrester (906) 475-4012

Newberry All Saints Church **P** (11) 314 W Truman St 49868-1227 (Mail to: 314 W Truman St 49868-1227) (906) 293-3180

Pointe Aux Pins Church of the Tranfiguration **SC** (7) Island Rd 49775 (Mail to: PO Box 850 49775-0850) (231) 634-7323

Sault Sainte Marie St James Episcopal Church **P** (71) 533 Bingham Ave 49783-2141 (Mail to: 533 Bingham Ave 49783-2199) Dawn Aldrich Robert Aldrich Susan Harries Diane Horst Lawrence Rice (906) 632-2451

DIOCESE OF NORTHWEST TEXAS
(PROVINCE VII)
Comprises 80 counties of Texas
DIOCESAN OFFICE The Hulsey Episcopal Center 1802 Broadway Lubbock TX 79401-3016
TEL (806) 763-1370
E-MAIL ejones@nwtdiocese.org WEB www.nwtdiocese.org

Previous Bishops—
Edward A Temple 1910-24, Eugene C Seaman 1925-45, George H Quarterman 1946-72, Willis R Henton 1972-80, Sam B Hulsey 1980-1997, Charles Wallis Ohl Jr 1997-2008

Bishop—J Scott Mayer (1035) (Dio 21 Mar 09)

Cn to Ord JM Ehmer; *Dio Adm* E Jones; *Fin Mgr* A Mora; *Treas* F Deaderick; *Asst* C Holley; *Reg* E Jones; *Chanc* T Choate; *COM* JM Ehmer

Stand Comm—Cler. Pres J Haney V R Hennagin R Lopez; *Lay:* B Easton A House D Copeland

PARISHES, MISSIONS, AND CLERGY

Abilene Ch of the Hvnly Rest Abilene **P** (1190) 602 Meander St 79602-1027 (Mail to: 602 Meander St 79602-1099) David Romanik Karen Boyd Douglas Thomas Amanda Watson Amanda Watson (325) 677-2091

Abilene Saint Mark's Episcopal Church **P** (45) 341 Pine St 79601-5913 (Mail to: PO Box 3313 79604-3313) Mary Glover Mary Glover James Smart Peggy Valentine (325) 261-1612

Albany Trinity Episcopal Church **P** (4) 140 N Ave B 76430 (Mail to: PO Box 818 76430-0818) (325) 513-7983

Amarillo St Andrews Episcopal Church **P** (1176) 1601 S Georgia St 79102-2315 (Mail to: 1601 S Georgia St 79102-2315) Nina Jo Craig Jared Houze Diedre Ballou Dave Blakley Erin Jones Erin Jones Mildred Rugger Christopher Wrampelmeier (806) 376-6316

Amarillo St Peters Episcopal Church **P** (40) 4714 NW 4th Ave 79106-5220 (Mail to: 4714 NW 4th Ave 79106-5220) Beverly Couzzourt (806) 353-9594

Big Spring St Mary the Virgin Epis Church **P** (50) 1001 Goliad St 79720-2848 (Mail to: PO Box 2949 79721-2949) Christian Rabone Connetta Fowler John Marshall (432) 267-8201

Borger St Peters Church **P** (15) 620 Hemlock St 79007-4554 (Mail to: PO Box 138 79008-0138) (806) 274-2944

Clarendon St John the Baptist Mission **M** (37) 301 South Park 79226 (Mail to: Attn: Kade L Matthews PO Box 1078 79226-1078) (806) 874-2511

Coleman St Marks Episcopal Church **M** (68) 601 S Neches St 76834-4026 (Mail to: PO Box 838 76834-0838) (325) 625-4995

Colorado City All Saints Episcopal Church **M** (25) 304 Locust St 79512-6428 (Mail to: PO Box 336 79512-0336) (325) 728-2243

Levelland St Lukes Episcopal Church **I** (13) 1103 West State Road 300 79336 (Mail to: 1103 West State Road 79336) (804) 894-8097

Lubbock Canterbury Eps Cmp Min TX Tech **CC** 2407 16th St 79401-4434 (Mail to: 2407 16th St 79401-4434) (806) 765-0037

Lubbock St Christophers Episcopal Ch **P** (265) 2807 42nd St 79413-3223 (Mail to: 2807 42nd St 79413-3223) (806) 7998208

Lubbock St Pauls On The Plains Epis Ch **P** (791) 1510 Ave X 79401 (Mail to: 1510 Avenue X 79401-4423) James Haney Becky Orem (806) 762-2893

Lubbock St Stephens Episcopal Church **P** (327) 1101 Slide Rd 79416-5419 (Mail to: 1101 Slide Rd 79416-5419) Paige Mckay (806) 799-3439

Midland Church of the Holy Trinity **P** (241) 1412 W Illinois Ave 79701-6537 (Mail to: 1412 W Illinois Ave 79701-6593) Robert Hennagin (432) 683-4207

Midland St Nicholas Episcopal Church **P** (138) 4000 W Loop 250 N 79707-3419 (Mail to: 4000 W Loop 250 N 79707-3419) Amy Haynie Thomas Burns (432) 694-8856

Odessa St Barnabas Episcopal Church **P** (102) 4141 Tanglewood Ln 79762-7224 (Mail to: PO Box 14225 79768-4225) Ricardo Lopez

Odessa St Johns Episcopal Church **P** (31) 401 N County Road West 79763 (Mail to: PO Box 3346 401 N County Road W 79760-3346) Ricardo Lopez Ricardo Lopez (432) 333-6022

Odessa San Miguel Arcangel Epis Ch **M** (448) 907 Adams Ave 79761-4111 (Mail to: 907 Adams Ave 79761-4111) Ricardo Lopez (432) 332-2074

Pampa St Matthews Episcopal Church **P** (113) 727 W Browning Ave 79065-6204 (Mail to: 727 W Browning Ave 79065-6204) Mark Lang (806) 665-0701

Plainview St Marks Episcopal Church **M** (13) 710 Joliet St 79072-7716 (Mail to: 710 Joliet St 79072-7716) (806) 296-7185

San Angelo Emmanuel Episcopal Church **P** (394) 3 S Randolph St 76903-5828 (Mail to: 3 S Randolph St 76903-5828) Matthew Rowe (325) 653-2446

San Angelo Church of the Good Shepherd **P** (59) 720 S Abe Street 76903 (Mail to: 720 S Abe St 76903-6734) (325) 659-3800

Shamrock St Michaels All Angels Ch **P** (6) 304 S Madden St 79079-2518 (Mail to: 304 S Madden St 79079-2518) (806) 256-5181

Sweetwater St Stephens Episcopal Church **M** (41) 502 Locust St 79556-3250 (Mail to: 502 Locust St 79556-3250) (325) 235-8408

Vernon Grace Episcopal Church **M** (15) 3207 Indian St 76384-5923 (Mail to: PO Box 1404 76385-1404) (940) 552-7008

DIOCESE OF NORTHWESTERN PENNSYLVANIA
(PROVINCE III)
Comprises 13 counties in Northwest PA
DIOCESAN OFFICE 145 W 6th St Erie PA 16501
TEL (814) 456-4203 FAX (814) 454-8703
WEB www.episcopalpartnership.org

Previous Bishops— Rogers Israel 1911-21, John C Ward 1921-43, Edward P Wroth 1943-46, Harold E Sawyer 1946-51, Wm Crittenden 1952-1973, Donald J Davis coadj 1973 Bp 1974-91 Robt D Rowley Jr coadj 1989-1991 Bp 1991-2007

Bishop—Rt Rev Sean Rowe (1019) (Dio 8 Sep 07)

Archdcn GG Winslow; *Treas* R Armstrong; *Chanc* J Steadman; *Sec* A Trambley

Deans: SW Rev A Trambley *NE* Rev S Fussell *NW* Rev M Norton *SE* Rev B Ellis

Stand Comm—Cler Pres S Fussell M Ishman S Clerkin B Ellis *Lay:* D Billioni C Dressler C Dinger J Croskey

PARISHES, MISSIONS, AND CLERGY

Bradford Church of the Ascension **P** (172) 26 Chautauqua Pl 16701-1915 (Mail to: PO Box 337 16701-0337) Stacey Fussell Gail Winslow (814) 368-8915

Brookville Church of the Holy Trinity **M** (38) 62 Pickering St 15825-1246 (Mail to: 62 Pickering St 15825-1246) Timothy Kroh (814) 849-7235

Clearfield St Andrews Church **M** (23) 102 E Cherry St 16830-2350 (Mail to: 102 E Cherry St 16830-2350) (814) 849-7235

Corry Emmanuel Episcopal Church **P** (63) 327 N Center St 16407-1628 (Mail to: 327 N Center St 16407-1676) Mary Norton (814) 665-7535

Dubois Church of Our Saviour **P** (55) 400 Liberty Blvd 15801-2408 (Mail to: PO Box 503 15801-0503) Timothy Kroh (814) 371-8810

Edinboro St Augustine of Canterbury Ch **M** (82) 427 W Plum St 16412-2145 (Mail to: PO Box 479 16412-0479) (814) 734-4116

Emporium Emmanuel Episcopal Church **P** (75) 144 E 4th St 15834-1445 (Mail to: PO Box 88 15834-0088) Matthew Ryan (814) 486-0711

✠ **Erie** Cathedral of St Paul **O** (275) 134 W 7th St 16501-1004 (Mail to: 134 W 7th St 16501-1004) Melinda Hall (814) 452-3779

Erie St Marks Episcopal Church **P** (324) 4701 Old French Rd 16509-3631 (Mail to: 4701 Old French Rd 16509-3699) Sarah Brock (814) 868-9704

Erie St Marys Episcopal Church **M** (41) 662 Silliman Ave 16511-2057 (Mail to: 662 Silliman Ave 16511-2057) (814) 899-0118

Fairview St Stephens Church **P** (182) 1070 Dutch Rd 16415-1627 (Mail to: 1070 Dutch Rd 16415-1627) (814) 474-5490

Foxburg Memorial Church of Our Father **M** (34) 110-136 Church Rd R 16036 (Mail to: PO Box 332 16036-0332) (724) 659-4541

Franklin St Johns Episcopal Church **P** (227) 1145 Buffalo St 16323-1254 (Mail to: PO Box 550 16323-0550) Shawn Clerkin (814) 432-5161

Greenville St Clements Episcopal Church **P** (46) 103 Clinton St 16125-2051 (Mail to: 103 Clinton St 16125-2051) (724) 588-6440

Grove City Church of the Epiphany **M** (32) 870 Liberty St Ext 16127-6438 (Mail to: Rd 3 PO Box 287 16127) (724) 458-6720

Hermitage Church of the Redeemer **P** 5130 E State St 16148-9447 (Mail to: 5130 E State St 16148-9489) (724) 347-4602

Houtzdale Church of the Holy Trinity **M** (46) 222 Brisbin St 16651-1301 (Mail to: 222 Brisbin St 16651) William Ellis (814) 378-8543

Kane St Johns Episcopal Church **P** (16) 427 Chase St 16735-1320 (Mail to: 427 Chase St 16735-1320) (814) 837-6351

Lake City Grace Episcopal Church **M** (37) 10121 Hall Avenue 16423 (Mail to: 10121 Hall Ave 16423-1220) Donald Baxter (814) 774-8288

Meadville Christ Episcopal Church **P** (102) 870 Diamond Park 16335-2606 (Mail to: 870 Diamond Park 16335-2606) Rebecca Lash (814) 724-7389

New Castle Trinity Episcopal Church **P** (107) 212 N Mill St 16101-3612 (Mail to: 212 N Mill St 16101-3612) (724) 654-8761

North East Holy Cross Episcopal Church **M** (40) 51 W Main St 16428-1103 (Mail to: 51 W Main St 16428-1103) (814) 725-2910

Oil City Christ Church **P** (39) 16 Central Ave 16301-2734 (Mail to: 16 Central Ave 16301-2734) Mark Elliston (814) 677-3023

Osceola Mills St Laurence Episcopal Church **M** (35) 501 Lingle St 16666-1121 (Mail to: R.R. Box 569 16666) (814) 342-2379

Port Allegan St Joseph Church **M** (46) 116 E Arnold Ave 16743-1247 (Mail to: PO Box 117 16743) Joann Piatko (814) 558-5876

Ridgway Grace Episcopal Church **P** (52) 216 Center St 15853-1203 (Mail to: PO Box 404 15853-0404) Timothy Dyer Bonnie Skellen (814) 776-6132

Saint Marys St Agnes Episcopal Church **P** (21) 209 N Saint Marys St 15857-1237 (Mail to: 209 N Saint Marys St 15857-1271) Timothy Dyer (814) 781-1909

Sharon St Johns Episcopal Church **P** (500) 226 W State St 16146-1341 (Mail to: 226 W State St 16146-1395) Adam Trambley Randall Beck (724) 347-4501

Smethport Saint Luke's Episcopal Church **P** (48) 600 W Main & Church 16749 (Mail to: PO Box 1475 16749-1146) (814) 887-5841

Titusville St James Memorial Church **P** (106) 112 E Main St 16354-1849 (Mail to: 112 E Main St 16354-1849) (814) 827-3590

Warren Trinity Memorial Church **P** (134) 444 Pennsylvania Ave W 16365-2238 (Mail to: 444 Pennsylvania Ave W 16365-2238) Matthew Scott (814) 723-9360

Waterford St Peters Church **M** (35) 100 E 3rd St 16441-9766 (Mail to: PO Box 804 16441-0804) (814) 796-9011

Youngsville St Francis of Assisi Epis Ch **P** (44) 343 E Main St 16371-1125 (Mail to: 343 E Main St 16371-1177) (814) 563-7586

STATE OF OHIO

Dioceses of Ohio and Southern Ohio

DIOCESE OF OHIO

(PROVINCE V)
Comprises the northern portion of Ohio
DIOCESAN OFFICE Trinity Commons 2230 Euclid Ave Cleveland OH 44115-2499
TEL (216) 771-4815 FAX (216) 623-0735
WEB www.dohio.org

Previous Bishops— Philander Chase 1819-31, Chas P McIlvaine 1832-73, Gregory T Bedell coadj 1859 Bp 1873-89, Wm A Leonard 1889-30, Frank De Moulin coadj 1914-24, Warren L Rogers coadj 1925 Bp 1930-38, Beverley D Tucker coadj 1938 Bp 1938 -52, Nelson M Burroughs coadj 1949 Bp 1952-68, John H Burt coadj 1967 Bp 1968-1984, William Davidson asst 1980-86, James R Moodey coadj 1983 Bp 1984-93, Arthur Benjamin Williams Jr Bp Suffr 1986-2002, J Clark Grew II Bp 1994-2004

Bishop—Rt Rev Mark Hollingsworth Jr (997) (Dio 17 Apr 04)

Assisting Bishop—Rt Rev William D Persell (999)

Assisting Bishop—Rt Rev Arthur B Williams Jr (812)

Cn to Ord WA Powel III; *Sec* D Arrington; *Treas* PT Austin; *Chanc* WA Powel III; *Archiv* B Wilbert;

Cn for Cong B Purdom; *Cn for Min* P Grant; *Cn for Chr Frm* A Sutterisch; *Cn for Mission* M D'Anieri; *CFO* S Leishman; *Comm* J Rocha; *Bp Admin Asst* E Cole

Stand Comm—Cler: D Bennett J Hardy Dorsey A Martin B Wilbert; *Lay:* H Marsh D McCallops P O'Halloran D Audrick Smith

PARISHES, MISSIONS, AND CLERGY

Akron Church of Our Saviour **P** (242) 471 Crosby St 44302-1518 (Mail to: 471 Crosby St 44302-1500) Debra Bennett (330) 535-9174

Akron St Andrews Church **P** (25) 765 Thayer St 44315-0001 (Mail to: 765 Thayer St 44310-3099) (330) 253-6447

Akron St Pauls Church **P** (1683) 1361 W Market St 44313-7123 (Mail to: C/O Gail Wild 1361 W Market St 44313-7123) Mark Pruitt Polly Glanville Susan Tiffany (330) 836-9327

Akron St Philips Church **P** (64) 1130 Mercer Ave 44320-3646 (Mail to: 1130 Mercer Ave 44320-3646) Clark West (330) 535-7295

Alliance Trinity Church **P** (85) 1200 S Union Ave 44601-4021 (Mail to: 1200 S Union Ave 44601-4021) (330) 821-8498

Ashland St Matthews Church **P** (90) 1515 Mifflin Ave 44805-3648 (Mail to: 1515 Mifflin Ave 44805-3648) Alice Kay Ashby (419) 281-1420

Ashtabula St Peters Church **P** (142) 4901 Main Ave 44004-7018 (Mail to: PO Box 357 44005-0357) C David Evans Peter Nielsen (440) 992-8100

Barberton St Andrews Episcopal Church **P** (136) 267 5th St NW 44203-2103 (Mail to: 583 W Hopocan Ave 44203-2256) Michael Petrochuk (330) 753-9026

Bellevue St Pauls Church **P** (27) 285 W Main St 44811-1333 (Mail to: PO Box 372 44811-0372) John Reinheimer (419) 483-4628

Berea Church of St Thomas **P** (302) 50 E Bagley Rd 44017-2009 (Mail to: 50 E Bagley Rd 44017-2009) (440) 234-5241

Boardman St James Church **P** (90) 7640 Glenwood Ave 44512-5897 (Mail to: 7640 Glenwood Ave 44512-5897) Maureen Major John Wigle (330) 758-2727

Bowling Green St Johns Church **P** (12) 1505 E Wooster St 43402-3392 (Mail to: 1505 E Wooster St 43402-3392) (419) 353-0881

Brecksville St Matthews Church **P** (167) 9549 Highland Dr 44141-2729 (Mail to: 9549 Highland Dr 44141-2799) Stephanie Pace (440) 526-9865

Brunswick St Patricks Church **P** (34) 3611 Center Rd 44212-0397 (Mail to: PO Box 397 44212-0397) Brian Pavlac (330) 220-2777

Canton St Marks Church **P** (341) 515 48th St NW 44709-1369 (Mail to: 515 48th St NW 44709-1369) Ronald Johnson (330) 449-2662

Canton St Pauls Church **P** (212) 425 Cleveland Ave SW 44702-1625 (Mail to: 425 Cleveland Ave SW PO Box 21333 44702-1625) Robin Woodberry (330) 455-0286

Chagrin Fall St Martin's Episcopal Church **P** (315) 6295 Chagrin River Rd 44022-3544 (Mail to: 6295 Chagrin River Rd 44022-3599) John Cerrato (440) 247-7406

Chardon St Lukes Church **P** (83) 11519 Wilson Mills Rd 44024-9406 (Mail to: PO Box 244 11519 Wilson Mills Rd 44024-0244) Christopher Mccann (440) 285-4641

Cleveland All Saints Church **P** (183) 8911 W Ridgewood Dr 44130-4122 (Mail to: 8911 W Ridgewood Dr 44130-4100) (440) 888-4055

Cleveland St Albans Church **P** (31) 2555 Euclid Heights Blvd 44106-2709 (Mail to: 2555 Euclid Heights Blvd 44106-2799) (216) 932-8080

Cleveland St Andrews Church **P** (129) 2171 E 49th St 44103-4401 (Mail to: 2171 E 49th St 44103-4401) Sharon Williams (216) 391-2632

Cleveland St Bartholomew's Episcopal Ch **P** (115) 435 Som Center Rd 44143-1519 (Mail to: 435 Som Center Rd 44143-1519) Stephen Secaur (440) 449-2290

Cleveland St Johns Church **P** 2600 Church Ave 44113-2908 (Mail to: PO Box 309 44107-0309) (216) 781-5546

Cleveland St Pauls Episcopal Church **P** (1318) 2747 Fairmount Blvd 44106-3606 (Mail to: 2747 Fairmount Blvd 44106-3696) Brandon Ashcraft Jessie Gutgsell Jeanne Leinbach (216) 932-5815

Cleveland St Lukes Episcopal Church **P** (65) 1349 W 78th St 44102-1915 (Mail to: 1349 W 78th St 44102-1915) (216) 631-2841

✠ **Cleveland** Trinity Cathedral **O** (774) 2230 Euclid Ave 44115-2405 (Mail to: 2230 Euclid Ave 44115-2405) Bernard Owens Adrienne Koch Nancy Rich (216) 771-3630

Coshocton Trinity Episcopal Church **P** (78) 705 Main St 43812-1616 (Mail to: 705 Main St 43812-1616) (740) 622-0860

Cuyahoga Fls St Johns Episcopal Church **P** (161) 2220 2nd St 44221-2502 (Mail to: 2220 2nd St 44221-2502) (330) 928-2139

Defiance Grace Church **P** (43) 308 W 2nd St 43512-2131 (Mail to: 308 Second Street 43512) (419) 782-0766

E Liverpool St Stephens Church **P** (114) 220 W 4th St 43920-4510 (Mail to: 220 W 4th St 43920-4510) (330) 385-3828

Elyria St Andrews Church **P** (320) 300 3rd St 44035-5618 (Mail to: 300 3rd St 44035-5693) Martha June Dorsey (440) 322-2126

Euclid Church of the Epiphany **P** (292) 21000 Lakeshore Blvd 44123-1800 (Mail to: 21000 Lake Shore Blvd 44123-1800) Rosalind Hughes (216) 731-1316

Findlay Trinity Episcopal Church **P** (166) 128 W Hardin St 45840-3104 (Mail to: C/O Todd Russell 128 W Hardin St 45840-3104) John Drymon (419) 422-3214

Fremont St Pauls Church **P** (155) 206 N Park Ave 43420-2430 (Mail to: 206 N Park Ave 43420-2430) Matthew Wahlgren (419) 332-3032

Gambier Harcourt Parish **P** (115) Church of the Holy Spirit 102 College Park Dr 43022-5020 (Mail to: PO Box 377 43022-0377) Rachel Kessler (740) 427-2187

Gates Mills St Christophers by the Riv Ch **P** (146) 7601 Old Mill Rd 44040 (Mail to: PO Box 519 44040) Ann Kidder (440) 423-4451

Geneva Christ Church **P** (76) 66 South Eagle St 44041-1547 (Mail to: 66 S Eagle St 44041-1547) (440) 466-3706

Hudson Christ Church Episcopal **P** (375) 21 Aurora St 44236-2902 (Mail to: Attn: Kathy Garber 21 Aurora St 44236-2902) Charlotte Collins Reed (330) 650-4359

Huron Christ Episcopal Church **P** (80) 120 Ohio St 44839-1537 (Mail to: 120 Ohio St 44839-1537) Michael Floyd (419) 433-4701

Kent Christ Episcopal Church **P** (167) 118 S Mantua St 44240-3437 (Mail to: 118 S Mantua St 44240-3437) Mary Staley (330) 673-4604

Lakewood Church of the Ascension **P** (164) 13216 Detroit Ave 44107-2842 (Mail to: 13216 Detroit Ave 44107-2894) Vincent Black (216) 521-8727

Lakewood St Peters Episcopal Church **P** (585) 18001 Detroit Ave 44107-3417 (Mail to: 18001 Detroit Ave 44107-3491) Brian Wilbert (216) 226-1772

Lisbon Holy Trinity Church **P** (41) 310 E Lincoln Way 44432-1420 (Mail to: PO Box 323 44432-0323) (330) 424-5442

Lorain Church of the Redeemer **P** (139) 647 Reid Ave 44052-1737 (Mail to: PO Box 521 44052-0521) Alexander Barton (440) 244-3134

Lyndhurst Church of the Good Shepherd **P** (65) 23599 Cedar Rd 44122-1065 (Mail to: 23599 Cedar Rd 44122-1065) Stephen Ashby Anne Pillot (216) 382-7770

Macedonia St Timothys Church **P** (233) 8667 Shepard Rd 44056-2010 (Mail to: PO Box 560204 44056-0204) Albert Jennings Anne Pillot (330) 467-1103

Mansfield Grace Church **P** (324) 41 Bowman St 44903-1650 (Mail to: 41 Bowman St 44903-1650) Joe Ashby Daniel Orr (419) 524-2661

Massillon St Timothys Church **P** (248) 226 3rd St SE 44646-6702 (Mail to: 226 3rd St SE 44646-6702) George Baum (330) 833-3183

Maumee St Pauls Church **P** (490) § 310 Elizabeth St 43537-3322 (Mail to: 310 Elizabeth St 43537-3322) John Board (419) 893-3381

Medina St Pauls Church **P** (509) 317 E Liberty St 44256-2108 (Mail to: 317 E Liberty St 44256-2108) Kelly Aughenbaugh (330) 725-4131

Mentor St Andrews Church **P** (261) 7989 Little Mountain Rd 44060-7802 (Mail to: 7989 Little Mountain Rd 44060-7802) Lisa O'Rear (440) 255-8842

Mentor St Huberts Church **P** (243) 8870 Baldwin Rd 44060-7835 (Mail to: 8870 Baldwin Rd 44060-7835) Daniel Schoonmaker John Hayden (440) 256-1280

Mount Vernon St Paul's Episcopal Church **HC** (72) 100 E High St 43050-3402 (Mail to: 100 E High St 43050-3402) Karl Stevens (740) 392-8601

Napoleon St Johns Church **P** (26) 1400 Glenwood Ave 43545-9032 (Mail to: PO Box 227 43545-0227) (419) 592-8466

New Phila Trinity Church **P** (59) 122 3rd St NW 44663-3719 (Mail to: 122 3rd St NW 44663-3719) (330) 339-6439

Niles St Lukes Church **P** (124) 348 Robbins Ave 44446-2408 (Mail to: 348 Robbins Ave 44446-2489) (330) 652-2952

Norwalk St Pauls Church **P** (52) 87 W Main St 44857-1439 (Mail to: 87 W Main St 44857-1439) (419) 668-1937

Oberlin Christ Church **P** (96) 162 S Main St 44074-1629 (Mail to: 162 S Main St 44074-1629) (440) 775-2501

Oregon St Pauls Church **P** (123) 798 S Coy Rd 43616-3008 (Mail to: 798 S Coy Rd 43616-3008) (419) 691-9400

Painesville St James Church **P** (171) 131 N State St 44077-3939 (Mail to: 131 N State St 44077-3991) (440) 354-3526

Perrysburg St Timothy's Epis Church, Inc. **P** (268) 871 E Boundary St 43551-2451 (Mail to: 871 E Boundary St 43551-2451) Sarah Shofstall (419) 874-5704

Port Clinton Church of St Thomas **P** (51) 214 E 2nd St 43452-1117 (Mail to: 214 E 2nd St 43452-1117)

Put In Bay St Pauls Church **P** (43) 623 Catawba Ave 43456-6539 (Mail to: PO Box 248 43456-0248) Robert Solon (419) 285-5981

Ravenna Grace Church **P** (151) 250 Cedar Ave 44266-2740 (Mail to: 250 Cedar Ave 44266-2740) Carol Evans William Snyder James Wichman (330) 296-3443

Salem Church of Our Saviour **P** (53) 870 E State St 44460-2224 (Mail to: PO Box 120 44460-0120) Jerome Colegrove (330) 332-5701

Sandusky Grace Church **P** (254) 315 Wayne St 44870-2619 (Mail to: 315 Wayne St 44870-2658) Seth Wymer (419) 625-6919

Shaker Heights Christ Church **P** (363) 3445 Warrensville Center Rd 44122-5206 (Mail to: 3445 Warrensville Center Rd 44122-5206) James Greer (216) 991-3432

Shelby St Marks Episcopal Church **P** (72) 31 N Gamble St 44875-1201 (Mail to: 31 N Gamble St 44875-1201) (419) 347-7701

Sidney St Mark's Episcopal Church **P** (21) 231 N Miami Ave 45365-2707 (Mail to: 231 N Miami Ave 45365-2707) Stephanie Brugger (937) 492-8584

Steubenville St Pauls Church **P** (54) 415 Adams St 43952-2809 (Mail to: 415 Adams St 43952-2809) (740) 282-5366

Steubenville St Stephens Episcopal Church **P** (102) 284 Lovers Ln 43953-3401 (Mail to: 284 Lovers Ln 43953-3401) (740) 264-5005

Tiffin Old Trinity Church **P** (74) 125 E Market St 44883-3903 (Mail to: 125 E Market St 44883-3903) Aaron Gerlach (419) 447-0728

Toledo All Saints Episcopal Church **P** (112) 563 Pinewood Ave 43604-8009 (Mail to: 563 Pinewood Ave 43604-8009) (419) 246-2461

Toledo St Andrew's Episcopal Church **P** (192) 2770 W. Central Ave 43606-3462 (Mail to: 2770 W Central Ave 43606-3462) Bridget Coffey (419) 473-1367

Toledo St Matthews Church **P** (165) 5240 Talmadge Rd 43623-2138 (Mail to: 5240 Talmadge Rd 43623-2138) Christopher Coughlin (419) 473-1187

Toledo St Michaels in the Hills Ch **P** (241) 4718 Brittany Rd 43615-2314 (Mail to: 4718 Brittany Rd 43615-2314) (419) 531-1616

Toledo Trinity Church **P** (241) 316 Adams St 43604-1557 (Mail to: 316 Adams St 43604-1557) Lisa Tucker-Gray (419) 243-1231

Uniontown New Life Episcopal Church **P** (77) 13118 Church Ave NW 44685-8452 (Mail to: 13118 Church Ave NW 44685-8452) (330) 699-3554

Wadsworth St Marks Episcopal Church **P** (44) 146 College St 44281-1852 (Mail to: 146 College St 44281-1852) Allan Belton (330) 336-0212

Warren Christ Episcopal Church **P** (209) 2627 Atlantic St NE 44483-4423 (Mail to: 2627 Atlantic St NE 44483-4498) (330) 372-4998

Westlake Church of the Advent **P** (134) 3760 Dover Center Rd 44145-5433 (Mail to: 3760 Dover Center Rd 44145-5433) (440) 871-6685

Willoughby Grace Church **P** (114) 36200 Ridge Rd 44094-4161 (Mail to: 36200 Ridge Rd 44094-4194) Rose Anne Lonsway (440) 942-1015

Wooster Saint James Episcopal Church **P** (133) 122 E. North St. 44691 (Mail to: 122 E North St 44691-4350) Evan Fischer (330) 262-4476

Youngstown St Johns Church Episcopal **P** (370) 323 Wick Ave 44503-1003 (Mail to: 323 Wick Ave 44503-1095) Gayle Catinella (330) 743-3175

DIOCESE OF OKLAHOMA
(PROVINCE VII)
Comprises the State of Oklahoma
DIOCESAN OFFICE 924 N Robinson Oklahoma City 73102
TEL (405) 232-4820 FAX (405) 232-4912
WEB www.epiok.org

Previous Bishops— Theology P Thurston 1919-27, Thomas Casady m 1927 dio 1937-53, WR Chilton Powell 1953-77, Frederick W Putnam suffr 1963-79, Gerald N McAllister 1977-89, William J Cox asst 1980-88, Robert Manning Moody 1988-2007, Edward Joseph Konieczny 2007-20

Bishop—Rt Rev Poulson Connell Reed Jr. (1131) (Dio 30 May 2020)

Staff: Cn for Cong Vit S Carlsen; *Cn for Fin & Admin/CFO* W Buchanan; *Bp Exec Asst* L Graft; *Executive Asst to Cn to the Ord* J Rodriguez; *Prison Miss* N Brock; *Dir of Faith Form and Discipleship* K Carney Bond; *Payroll & Benefits* M Smith; *Dir of Comm* S LeMasters; *Arch* P Bell; *OU Chaplain* B Woods; *OSU Chaplain* J Huston; *Staff Acct* C Roberts; *Staff Acct* C Floyd; *Acct Mgr* Y Griffin; *Children and Yth Coord and Summer Camp Dir* T Phares; *Dean of Iona School of Formation* S Orwig; *Dean of School of Spiritual Direction* S Joplin; *Dio Military Miss* D Plummer; *Dio Music Miss* J Ripka

Officers: Conv Sec L Graft; *Chanc* W Cathcart 2807 Classen Blvd OK; *Vice Chanc* G Derrick, T Williams; *Treas* H Baer

Stand Comm—Cler: T Baer S Jenkins T Dahlman; *Lay: Pres* M Moon S Urbach W Young

PARISHES, MISSIONS, AND CLERGY

Ada St Lukes Episcopal Church **P** (137) 110 E 17th St 74820-7802 (Mail to: PO Box 890 74821-0890) Tammy Wooliver (580) 332-6429

Altus St Pauls Episcopal Church **P** (64) 721 N Thomas St 73521-2871 (Mail to: 721 N Thomas St 73521-2800) Carol Mollison Michael Trachman (580) 482-2102

Antlers St James Episcopal **M** (41) 700 N High St 74523-2245 (Mail to: 700 N High St 74523-2245) (580) 298-5123

Ardmore St Philips Episcopal Church **P** (314) 516 Mclish St 73401-4710 (Mail to: 516 Mclish St 73401-4742) Michael Stephenson Joyce Spurgin (580) 226-2191

Bartlesville St Lukes Episcopal Church **P** (296) 210 E 9th St 74003-4905 (Mail to: 210 E 9th St 74003-4961) Nicholas Phares (918) 336-1212

Broken Arrow St Patricks Episcopal Church **P** (445) 4250 W Houston St 74012-4538 (Mail to: 4250 W Houston St 74012-4538) Shelb Scott (918) 294-9444

Chickasha St Lukes Episcopal Church **M** (97) 124 S 6th St 73018-3420 (Mail to: 124 S 6th St 73018-3420) (405) 224-1296

Claremore St Pauls Episcopal Church **P** (139) 1310 N Sioux Ave 74017-4416 (Mail to: 1310 N Sioux Ave 74017-4416) (918) 341-0168

Clinton St Pauls Episcopal Church **M** (22) 321 7th St 73601-3903 (Mail to: 321 S 7th St 73601-3903) Lynn Borrego (580) 323-2160

Coalgate St Peters Episcopal Church **M** (15) 10 W Hanover Ave 74538-1839 (Mail to: PO Box 165 74538-0165) (580) 927-3310

Duncan All Saints' Episcopal Church **P** (130) 809 W Cedar Ave 73533-4135 (Mail to: 809 W Cedar Ave 73533-4135) David Galletly Gar Templeton (580) 255-6165

Durant St Johns Episcopal Church **P** (141) 51 W Beech St 74701-4335 (Mail to: PO Box 116 74702-1168) James Blagg (580) 924-1332

Edmond St Marys Episcopal Church **P** (749) 3100 N Broadway 73034-3730 (Mail to: 3100 N Broadway 73034-3730) Mark Story William Hesse (405) 341-3855

El Reno Christ Memorial Episcopal Ch **M** (34) 500 S Bickford Ave 73036-3844 (Mail to: 500 S Barker Ave 73036-3801) (405) 262-1710

Enid St Matthews Church **P** (175) 518 W Randolph Ave 73701-3828 (Mail to: 518 W Randolph Ave 73701-3897) John Toles (580) 237-4737

Eufaula Trinity Episcopal Church **M** (96) S 3rd & High Sts 74432 (Mail to: PO Box 759 74432-0759) Therese Starr (918) 689-2369

Grove St Andrews Episcopal Church **P** (160) 555 E 3rd St 74344-7139 (Mail to: 555 E 3rd St 74344-7139) Philip Lawrence Melissa Harris Philip Lawrence (918) 786-4113

Guthrie Trinity Church **P** (116) 310 E Noble Ave 73044-3311 (Mail to: 310 E Noble Ave 73044-3311) (405) 282-0982

Guymon St Stephens Episcopal Church **M** (12) 1803 N Lelia St 73942-2832 (Mail to: PO Box 1952 73942-1952) (580) 338-8747

Holdenville St Pauls Episcopal Church **M** (9) 8th and Oak Sts 74848 (Mail to: PO Box 69 74848-0069) Cyntha Gilks (405) 379-5879

Hugo St Mark's Episcopal Church **P** (13) 803 S 3rd St 74743-6809 (Mail to: 803 South 3rd 74743) (580) 326-9197

Idabel St Luke the Beloved Physician **M** (34) 211 SE Ave N 74745-5728 (Mail to: 211 SE Ave N 74745) (580) 286-3672

Lawton St Andrews Episcopal Church **P** (152) 1313 SW D Ave 73501-4252 (Mail to: PO Box 1256 73502-1256) Stephanie Jenkins Katherine Dutcher (580) 355-9543

Mcalester All Saints Episcopal Church **P** (117) 325 E Washington Ave 74501-4757 (Mail to: PO Box 534 74502-0534) Janie Koch (918) 423-1915

Miami All Saints Episcopal Church **P** (113) 225 B St NW 74354-5806 (Mail to: 225 B St NW 74354-5806) (918) 542-3662

Midwest City St Christophers Church **P** (201) 800 S Midwest Blvd 73110-4730 (Mail to: PO Box 10722 73140-1722) Dale Plummer (405) 732-4802

Muskogee Grace Episcopal Church **HC** (254) Attn: Mary Emily Basolo 218 N 6th St 74401-6209 (Mail to: 218 N 6th St 74401-6209) David Cole Thomas Harrington (918) 687-5416

Norman St Anselm Canterbury Assn **Chapel** 800 Elm Ave 73069-8837 (Mail to: 800 Elm Ave 73069-8837) Kay Greenshields (405) 360-6453

Norman St Johns Episcopal Church **P** (885) 325 W Duffy St 73069-5827 (Mail to: PO Box 2088 73070-2088) James Detrich (405) 321-3020

Norman St Michaels Episcopal Church **P** (221) 1601 W Imhoff Rd 73072-7408 (Mail to: PO Box 720326 73070-4242) Joseph Farber (405) 321-8951

Oklahoma City All Souls Episcopal Church **P** (1616) 6400 N Pennsylvania Ave 73116-5626 (Mail to: 6400 N Pennsylvania Ave 73116-5694) Andrew Johnson Graham Marsh (405) 842-1461

Oklahoma City Church of the Redeemer **P** (91) 2100 N Martin Luther King Ave 73111-2402 (Mail to: PO Box 11272 73136-0272) (405) 427-2106

Oklahoma City Epis Ch of the Resurrection **P** (182) 13112 N Rockwell Ave Attn: Administrator 73142-2717 (Mail to: Attn Administrator 13112 N Rockwell Ave 73142-2700) Sean Ekberg Beth Bell Dion Crider (405) 721-2929

Oklahoma City St Augustine of Canterbury **M** (364) 14700 N May Ave 73134-5009 (Mail to: 14700 N May Ave 73134-5008) Joseph Alsay Anthony Moon Anthony Moon Robert Trammell (405) 751-7874

Oklahoma City St Davids Episcopal Church **M** (70) 3333 No Meridian Ave 73112 (Mail to: 3333 N Meridian Ave 73112-3198) Beth Bell (405) 942-1740

Oklahoma City St James Episcopal Church **M** (110) 8400 S Pennsylvania Ave 73159-5205 (Mail to: 8400 S Pennsylvania Ave 73159-5205) Robert Trammell Nathan Carr Jeffrey Huston (405) 6823405

Oklahoma City St Johns Episcopal Church **P** (260) 5401 N Brookline Av 73112-3514 (Mail to: 5401 N Brookline Ave 73112-3598) Nathan Carr Lisa Chronister Dana Orwig (405) 943-8548

✠ **Oklahoma City** St Pauls Cathedral **O** (1125) 127 NW 7th St 73102-6004 (Mail to: 127 NW 7th St 73102-6004) Katherine Churchwell (405) 2353436

Oklahoma City Santa Maria Virgen **M** (958) 5500 S Western Ave. 73109 (Mail to: 5500 S Western Ave 73109-4511) (405) 631-6747

Okmulgee Church of the Redeemer **M** (44) 213 N Seminole Ave 74447-7334 (Mail to: PO Box 1012 74447-1012) (918) 756-2384

Owasso Church of the Holy Cross **M** (65) 9309 N 129th East Ave 74055-5314 (Mail to: 9309 N 129th East Ave 74055-5314) Bryan Beard (918) 271-1075

Pauls Valley St Timothys Church **M** (21) 1820 S Walnut St 73075-6902 (Mail to: PO Box 485 73075-0485) (405) 238-2133

Pawhuska St Thomas Episcopal Church **M** (43) 817 Leahy Ave 74056-3219 (Mail to: PO Box 1476 74056-1476) (918) 287-3513

Pawnee Church of the Ascension **M** (11) Seventh And Ash Sts 74058 (Mail to: PO Box 26 74058-0026) (918) 762-2771

Perry St Mark Episcopal Church **M** (14) 701 N 7th St 73077-4227 (Mail to: PO Box 507 73077-0507) William Powell Stephen Miller (580) 336-9720

Ponca City Grace Episcopal Church **P** (233) 109 N 13th St 74601-7314 (Mail to: 109 N 13th St 74601-7314) Caleb Roberts Steven Mallory (580) 765-7609

Poteau St Barnabas Episcopal Church **M** 506 College Ave 74953-3114 (Mail to: RR 3 Box 100 74953-9803) (918) 647-9092

Pryor St Martin of Tours Epis Church **M** (75) 612 SE 1st St 74361-4614 (Mail to: PO Box 1153 74362-1153) (918) 825-1115

Sand Springs St Matthews Episcopal Church **M** (79) 601 N Lake Dr 74063-8716 (Mail to: 601 N Lake Dr 74063-8716) (918) 245-7552

Sapulpa Church of the Good Shepherd **P** (100) 1420 E Dewey Ave 74066 (Mail to: PO Box 335 74067-0335) Nancy Brown Robert Fallis (918) 224-5144

Seminole St Marks Episcopal Church **M** (21) 800 N Highland St 74868 (Mail to: PO Box 1304 74818-1304) Lynn Borrego William Bales (405) 382-2192

Shawnee Emmanuel Episcopal Church **P** (452) 501 N Broadway Ave 74801-6926 (Mail to: PO Box 1905 74802-1905) Thomas Dahlman John Belzer (405) 273-1374

Stillwater St Andrews Church **P** (404) 516 W 3rd Ave 74074-3001 (Mail to: PO Box 938 74076-0938) Jeromy Matkin Jeffrey Huston (405) 3723357

Stillwater St Augustine Canterbury Ctr **CM** 519 W University Ave 74074-3033 (Mail to: 519 W University Ave 74074-3033) (405) 624-0141

Tahlequah St Basils Episcopal Church **M** (73) 814 N Vinita Ave 74464-2235 (Mail to: 814 N Vinita Ave 74464-2235) Larry Rogers (918) 456-3649

Tulsa Christ Episcopal Church **M** (475) 10901 S Yale Ave 74137-7211 (Mail to: 10901 S Yale Ave 74137-7211) Everett Lees Justin Boyd Judith Gann (918) 2997510

Tulsa St Adrian of Canterbury **CM** 1115 S Florence Ave 74104-4104 (Mail to: 1115 S Florence Ave 74104-4104) (918) 631-2993

Tulsa Saint Aidan's Episcopal Church **M** (29) 4045 N Martin L King Jr Blvd 74106-6452 (Mail to: PO Box 480874 74148-0874) William Eller (918) 425-7882

Tulsa St Dunstans Episcopal Church **P** (515) 5635 E 71st St 74136-6538 (Mail to: 5635 E 71st St 74136-6538) Alan Barrow Mary Hill (918) 492-7140

Tulsa St Johns Episcopal Church **P** (1091) 4200 S Atlanta Pl 74105-4331 (Mail to: 4200 S Atlanta Pl 74105-4300) David Bumsted (918) 742-7381

Tulsa St Lukes Episcopal Church **P** (123) 4818 E 9th St 74112-4240 (Mail to: 4818 E 9th St 74112-4240) John Rule (918) 834-4800

Tulsa St Peters Episcopal Church **P** (58) 9100 E 21st St 74129-1421 (Mail to: 9100 E 21st St 74129-1421) Mary Lord (918) 627-2713

Tulsa Trinity Episcopal Church of Tulsa Inc **P** (1050) 501 S Cincinnati Ave 74103-4801 (Mail to: 501 S Cincinnati Ave 74103-4800) Warren Domenick Cheryl Harder (918) 5824128

Vinita Saint John's Episcopal Church **M** (59) 522 W Canadian Ave 74301-3612 (Mail to: PO Box 165 74301-0165) (918) 256-3766

Wagoner St James Church **M** (36) 303 E Church St 74467-5209 (Mail to: 303 E Church St 74467-5209) Edmund James (918) 485-5681

Watonga Whirlwind Msn of the Holy Fmly **M** (72) 1000 E Russworm Dr 73772 (Mail to: PO Box 26 73772-0026) James Kee-Rees (580) 623-5585

Westport St Bedes Episcopal Church **M** (59) 1 2 Miles North Hwy 64 74020 (Mail to: RR 3 Box 4A 74020-9502) Penni Chambers (918) 743-2686

Woodward St Johns Episcopal Church **M** (59) 917 Texas St 73801-3125 (Mail to: 917 Texas St 73801-3125) (580) 256-7713

Yukon Grace Church - Episcopal **P** (272) 600 N Mustang Rd 73099 (Mail to: 600 N Mustang Rd 73099) Timothy Baer (405) 3547277

DIOCESE OF OLYMPIA
(PROVINCE VIII)
Comprises western Washington
DIOCESAN OFFICE 1551 10th Ave E Seattle WA 98102
TEL (206) 325-4200
E-MAIL info@ecww.org WEB ecww.org

Previous Bishops—
John A Paddock 1880-94, Wm M Barker 1894-1901, Frederic W Keator 1902-24, S Arthur Huston 1925-47, Stephen F Bayne Jr 1947-60, Wm F Lewis 1960-64, Ivol I Curtis 1964-76, Robt H Cochrane 1976-89, Sanford ZK Hampton asst 1996-2004, Vincent W Warner 1990-2007, Bavi Edna Rivera Suff 2004-10

Bishop—Rt Rev Gregory H Rickel (1021) (Dio 15 Sep 2007)

Assisting Bishop—Rt Rev Brian Prioer

Assisting Bishop—Most Rev Melissa Skelton

Cn to Ord Rev A Davison; *Cn for Governance & Human Resources* D Moore; *Cn for Faith Formation* V Reinke; *Cn for Cong Dev* Rev A Newton; *Dir of Fin* C Thorne; *Commun Dir* J Hornbeck; *Dir Resource Ctr* S Tait; *Ex Asst* A Caballero; *Dio Property Mgr* Rev D Tierney; *Iona School Dean* G La Torra; *Int Strategist* K Allman; *Veterans Min Missioner* Rev B Wright; *Refugee Resettl* G Hope; *Mission to Seafarers Exec Dir* Rev C Chapman; *Huston Ctr Dir* B Tubbs; *SA Hse Mgr* D Oberg

Officers—Treas J Beckwith; *Sec* Rev M Steedman Sanborn; *Chanc* J Andrews; *V Chanc* B Krislock; *Hist* Br C Griffin; *Archive* D Wells

Stand Comm—Cler: C Crippen S Danzey J Daugherty C Robinson *Lay:* C Connor C Loudenback *Pres* V Day T Nakatani L Sylvester

PARISHES, MISSIONS, AND CLERGY

Aberdeen St Andrews Episcopal Church **P** (230) 400 E 1st St 98520-4116 (Mail to: 400 E 1st St 98520-4116) Sarah Monroe (360) 533-2511

Allyn St Hugh of Lincoln Epis Church **M** (73) 280 E Wheelwright St S 98524 (Mail to: PO Box 156 98524-0156) Sylvia Haase Christie Logan Jennifer Pratt (360) 275-8450

Anacortes Christ Episcopal Church **M** (115) 1216 7th St 98221-1809 (Mail to: 1216 7th St 98221-1809) Eric Johnson Brian Lennstrom (360) 293-5790

Auburn St Matthews Episcopal Church **P** (84) 123 L St NE 98002-4434 (Mail to: 123 L St NE 98002-4434) Patricia Trytten (253) 833-0890

Bainbridge Island Grace Episcopal Church **M** (857) 8595 NE Day Rd E 98110-1395 (Mail to: C/O Trustee For Human Resource 8595 NE Day Rd E 98110-1395) Mary Anderson (206)

842-9997

Bainbridge Island St Barnabas Episcopal Church **P** (398) 1187 Wyatt Way NW 98110-2722 (Mail to: 1187 Wyatt Way NW 98110-2722) Martha Haig Daniel Fowler Nancy Tiederman (206) 842-5601

Battle Ground Church of the Holy Spirit **M** (35) 2400 NW 9th Ave 98604-1117 (Mail to: PO Box 1117 98604-1117) (360) 687-3301

Bellevue All Saints Church **M** (20) 1307 120th Ave NE 98005-2124 (Mail to: 1307 120th Ave NE 98005-2124) (425) 646-1136

Bellevue Church of the Holy Apostles **M** (74) 15220 Main St 98007-5228 (Mail to: Attn: Mr Torres Hui 15220 Main St 98007-5228) (425) 351-1423

Bellevue Church of the Resurrection **P** (48) 15220 Main St 98007-5228 (Mail to: 15220 Main St 98007-5228) (425) 746-0322

Bellevue St Margarets Episcopal Church **P** (933) 4228 Factoria Blvd SE 98006-1929 (Mail to: 4228 Factoria Blvd SE 98006-1929) Beverly Tasy (425) 7466650

Bellingham St Paul's Episcopal Church **P** (625) 2117 Walnut St 98225-2836 (Mail to: 2117 Walnut St 98225-2836) Jonathan Weldon Charles Whitmore (360) 733-2890

Blaine Christ Episcopal Church **M** (70) 382 Boblett St 98230-4003 (Mail to: 382 Boblett St 98230-4003) (360) 332-4113

Bremerton St Pauls Episcopal Church **P** (223) 700 Callahan Dr 98310-3304 (Mail to: 700 Callahan Dr 98310-3304) Kathleen Kingslight Susan Stroup (360) 377-0106

Castle Rock St Matthew Church **M** (35) 412 Pioneer Ave NE 98611-9234 (Mail to: PO Box 1467 98611-1467) Elizabeth Cochran Linda Santman Suzanne Streiff (360) 274-9393

Cathlamet Saint James Episcopal Church **M** (30) 1134 Columbia St 98612-9535 (Mail to: 1134 Columbia St 98612-9535) Irene Martin Joann Prestegard Rachael Wolford (360) 795-8612

Chehalis St Timothy Episcopal Church **P** (116) 1826 SW Snively Ave 98532-4022 (Mail to: PO Box 277 98532-0277) Katherine Flores (360) 748-8232

Darrington Church of the Transfiguration **M** (18) 836 Commercial Ave 98241-7743 (Mail to: PO Box 55 98241-0055) Janet Loyd (360) 436-1552

Eastsound Emmanuel Episcopal Church **P** (216) 242 Main St 98245-5510 (Mail to: PO Box 8 98245-0008) Jose Gandara-Perea Hugh Grant Kathleen Kinney (360) 376-2352

Edmonds St Albans Episcopal Church **P** (132) 21405 82nd Pl W 98026-7434 (Mail to: 21405 82nd Pl W 98026-7434) Gregory Peters (425) 778-0371

Edmonds St Hilda-St Patrick Church **M** (157) 15224 52nd Ave W 98026-4304 (Mail to: 15224 52nd Ave W 98026-4304) Joseph Peters-Mathews (425) 743-4655

Elma St Lukes Episcopal Church **M** (7) 626 E Young St 98541-9357 (Mail to: C/O Mr Steve Brown 103 Heritage Dr 98541-9339) John Nemes (360) 482-3231

Everett Trinity Episcopal Church **P** (371) 2301 Hoyt Ave 98201-2898 (Mail to: 2301 Hoyt Ave 98201-2898) Rachel Taber-Hamilton (425) 252-4129

Federal Way Church of the Good Shepherd **P** (136) 345 S 312th St 98003-4031 (Mail to: PO Box 3108 98063-3108) Joshua Hosler (253) 839-6100

Forks St Swithin **M** Prince Of Peace Lutheran Ch 98331 (Mail to: 660 G St 98331-9183) (360) 457-4862

Freeland St Augstns in-the-Woods Epis **P** (133) 5217 Honeymoon Bay Rd 98249-9712 (Mail to: PO Box 11 98249-0011) Malcolm Davis (360) 331-4887

Friday Harbor St Davids Episcopal Church **P** (85) 780 Park St 98250-9609 (Mail to: PO Box 2714 98250-2714) Cristi Chapman Margaret Lewis-Headden (360) 378-5360

Gig Harbor St Johns Episcopal Church **P** (366) 7701 Skansie Ave 98335-8330 (Mail to: 7701 Skansie Ave 98335-8330) Marilyn Behrens Robert Mayor Eric Stelle (253) 8583777

Hoodsport St Germain Episcopal Church **M** (32) 600 N Lake Cushman Rd 98548-9781 (Mail to: PO Box 222 98548-0222) Peter Van Zanten (360) 866-9870

Issaquah St Michael and All Angels Ch **P** (303) 325 SE Darst St 98027-4326 (Mail to: 325 SE Darst St 98027-4326) Katherine Sedwick R Richard Marchand (425) 392-3215

Kenmore Church of the Redeemer **P** (111) 6211 NE 182nd St 98028-9419 (Mail to: PO Box 82677 98028-0677) Jedediah Fox Jill Zimmerschied (425) 486-3777

Kent St Columba's Episcopal Church **M** (137) 26715 Military Rd S 98032-7011 (Mail to: 31811 Pacific Hwy S Ste B342 98003-5646) Meghan Mullarkey (253) 8549912

Kent St James Episcopal Church **P** (765) 24447 94th Ave S 98030-4746 (Mail to: 24447 94th Ave S 98030-4746) Ruth Anne Garcia (253) 852-4450

Kirkland St Johns Episcopal Church **P** (218) § 105 State St S 98033-6610 (Mail to: 127 State St S 98033-6687) Michael Ryan (425) 827-3077

Lacey St Benedicts Episcopal Church **M** (269) 910 Bowker St SE 98503-1212 (Mail to: PO Box 3811 98509-3811) Eldwin Lovelady (360) 456-2240

Lakewood St Joseph & St John Church **P** (66) 11111 Old Military Rd SW 98498 (Mail to: PO Box 88550 98388-0550) Zula Johnston (253) 584-6143

Lakewood St Marys Episcopal Church **P** (234) 10630 Gravelly Lake Dr SW 98499-1328 (Mail to: Attn: Rosemary Doupe 10630 Gravelly Lake Dr SW 98499-1328) James Evans Andrew Cooley Eldwin Lovelady Marian Stinson (253) 588-6621

Longview St Stephens Episcopal Church **P** (187) 1428 22nd Ave 98632-2828 (Mail to: 1428 22nd Ave 98632-2828) Kathleen Patton Nicholas Mather (360) 423-5600

Lopez Island Grace Church **P** (90) 70 Sunset Ln 98261-5518 (Mail to: PO Box 324 98261-0324) (360) 468-3477

Maple Valley St Georges Episcopal Church **M** (247) § 24219 Witte Rd SE 98038-6827 (Mail to: PO Box 510 98038-0510) Bonnie Malone (425) 432-5481

Marysville St Philip Episcopal Church **P** (61) 4312 84th St NE 98270-3447 (Mail to: 4312 84th St NE 98270-3447) Dawn Foisie (360) 659-1727

Medina St Thomas Episcopal Church **P** (1230) § 8398 NE 12th St 98039-3100 (Mail to: PO Box 124 98039-0124) Elizabeth Costello (425) 454-9541

Mercer Island Emmanuel Episcopal Church **P** (272) 4400 86th Ave SE 98040-4146 (Mail to: 4400 86th Ave SE 98040-4146) Elizabeth Riley Brian Gregory Jonathan Myers (206) 232-1572

Montesano St Marks Episcopal Church **M** (25) 124 N Sylvia St 98563-3717 (Mail to: C/O Joyce Avery 124 N Sylvia St 98563-3717) Joyce Avery F Lorraine Dierick (360) 249-3281

Mount Vernon St Pauls Episcopal Church **P** (115) 415 S 18th St 98273 (Mail to: 415 S 18th Street 98274-4658) Paul Moore (360) 424-1822

Oak Harbor St Stephens Episcopal Church **P** (70) 555 SE Regatta Dr 98277-3981 (Mail to: PO Box 2754 98277-6754) Paul Price Richard Scott (360) 279-0715

Olympia St John's Episcopal Church **P** (592) 114 20th Ave SE 98501-2923 (Mail to: PO Box 977 98507-0977) Albin Fogelquist Robert Laird (360) 352-8527

Olympia St Christophers Community **M** (175) 7902 Steamboat Island Rd NW 98502-9389 (Mail to: 7902 Steamboat Island Rd NW 98502-9389) James Thibodeaux (360) 866-2111

Port Angeles Saint Andrews Episcopal Church **P** (223) 510 E Park Ave 98362-6938 (Mail to: 510 E Park Ave 98362-6938) Laura Murray (360) 457-4862

Port Orchard St Bede Episcopal Church **M** (116) 1578 SE Lider Rd 98367-7516 (Mail to: PO Box 845 98366-0845) (360) 876-1182

Port Townsend St Pauls Episcopal Church **P** (294) 1020 Jefferson St 98368-6618 (Mail to: PO Box 753 98368-0753) Dianne Andrews (360) 385-0770

Poulsbo Faith Episcopal Church **M** (88) 20295 Little Valley Rd NE 98370-6514 (Mail to: PO Box 1362 98370-0136) Raymond Sheldon (360) 471-7522

Puyallup Christ Episcopal Church **P** (146) 210 5th St SW 98371-5383 (Mail to: 210 5th St SW 98371-5383) Robert Mayor (253) 848-2323

Redmond Church of the Holy Cross **P** (421) 11526 162nd Ave NE 98052-2645 (Mail to: 11526 162nd Ave NE 98052-2645) Carlos Caguiat Malcolm Mclaurin Jane Rohrer (425) 885-5822

Renton St Luke Episcopal Church **P** (278) 99 Wells Ave S 98057-2153 (Mail to: C/O Kate Martin 99 Wells Ave S 98057-2153) Kevin Pearson Sara Carlson Susan Dean (425) 255-3323

Rockport St Martin-St Francis **M** 55223 Conrad Rd 98283-9740 (Mail to: 55223 Conrad Rd 98283-9740) (425) 876-4628

Sammamish Good Samaritan Epis Church **P** (267) 1757 244th Ave NE 98074-3323 (Mail to: 1757 244th Ave NE 98074-3323) (425) 868-2123

Seattle Christ Church **P** (199) 4548 Brooklyn Ave NE 98105-4537 (Mail to: 4548 Brooklyn Ave NE 98105-4537) Shelly Fayette (206) 633-1611

Seattle Church of the Apostles **M** 4272 Fremont Ave N 98103-7279 (Mail to: 4272 Fremont Ave N 98103-7279) (206) 851-8962

Seattle Church of the Ascension **P** (187) 2330 Viewmont Way W 98199-3939 (Mail to: 2330 Viewmont Way W 98199-3939) Heather Wenrick Mary Shehane (206) 283-3967

Seattle Epiphany Parish of Seattle **P** (1002) 1805 38th Ave 98122-3447 (Mail to: 1805 38th Ave 98122-3447) Doyt Conn (206) 324-2573

Seattle St Andrews Episcopal Church **P** (832) 111 NE 80th St 98115-4033 (Mail to: 111 NE 80th St 98115-4033) Danae Ashley Rachel Endicott Kay Kessel-Hanna Rebecca Kirkpatrick Rebecca Kirkpatrick (206) 523-7476

Seattle St Clement of Rome Epis Church **P** (77) 1501 32nd Ave S 98144-3917 (Mail to: 1501 32nd Ave S 98144-3917) Kevin Smith Thomas Bigelow Robert Gallagher (206) 324-3072

Seattle St Elizabeths Episcopal Church **P** (144) 1005 SW 152nd St 98166-1845 (Mail to: PO Box 66579 98166-0579) John Forman (206) 243-6844

Seattle Church of St John the Baptist **P** (417) 3050 California Ave SW 98116-3302 (Mail to: 3050 California Ave SW 98116-3302) Elise Johnstone (206) 937-4545

Seattle St Lukes Episcopal Church **P** (161) 5710 22nd Ave NW 98107-3144 (Mail to: 5710 22nd Ave NW 98107-3144) Britt Olson (206) 784-3119

✠ **Seattle** St Marks Episcopal Cathedral **O** (3027) 1245 10th Ave E 98102-4323 (Mail to: 1245 10th Ave E 98102-4323) Steven Thomason Jennifer Daugherty Jennifer Daugherty Earl Grout Eliacin Rosario-Cruz Linzi Stahlecker (206) 323-0300

Seattle St Pauls Episcopal Church **P** (330) 15 Roy St 98109-4019 (Mail to: PO Box 9070 98109-0070) Stephen Crippen Kerry Kirking Charles Ridge Jay Rozendaal (206) 282-0786

Seattle St Stephens Episcopal Church **P** (228) 4805 NE 45th St 98105-3803 (Mail to: 4805 NE 45th St 98105-3897) Karen Robertson (206) 522-7144

Seattle St Peter's Episcopal Parish **P** (162) 1610 S King St 98144-2115 (Mail to: 1610 S King St 98144-2115) Edmund Harris (206) 323-5250

Seattle Trinity Church Episcopal **P** (460) 609 8th Ave 98104-1921 (Mail to: 609 8th Ave 98104-1997) Robert Davidson Malcolm Davis Elisabeth Fitzgibbons (206) 624-5337

Seaview St Peters Episcopal Church **M** (17) 5000 N Pl 98644-2124 (Mail to: PO Box 268 98644-0268) (360) 642-3115

Sedro Woolley St James Church **P** (45) 1013 Polte Rd 98284-9478 (Mail to: 1013 Polte Rd 98284-9478) (360) 424-1822

Sequim St Lukes Episcopal Church **P** (238) 525 N 5th Ave 98382-3079 (Mail to: PO Box 896 98382-4314) Clayola Gitane (360) 683-4862

Shelton Church of St David of Wales **P** (115) 324 W Cedar St 98584-3443 (Mail to: PO Box 339 98584-0339) (360) 426-8472

Shoreline St David Emmanuel Episcopal Ch **M** (48) 18842 Meridian Ave N 98133-4232 (Mail to: PO Box 77322 98177-0322) Gerald Hanna (206) 362-2565

Shoreline St Dunstans Church **P** (305) 722 N 145th St 98133-6502 (Mail to: 722 N 145th St 98133-6502) David Marshall Catharine Reid (206) 363-4319

Silverdale St Antony of Egypt Epis Church **P** (163) § 10239 Old Frontier Rd NW 98383-8895 (Mail to: PO Box 2822 98383-2822) Craig Vocelka Craig Vocelka (360) 698-0555

Snohomish St John's Episcopal Church **P** (243) 913 2nd St 98290-2918 (Mail to: 913 2nd St 98290-2918) (360) 568-4622

Snoqualmie St Clare of Assisi Epis Church **M** (92) 8650 Railroad Pl SE 98065-5181 (Mail to: PO Box 369 98065-0369) Patricia Baker (425) 831-6175

Stanwood St Aidans Episcopal Church **M** (198) 1318 State Highway 532 98282-8836 (Mail to: PO Box 145 98292-0145) Stephen Foisie (360) 629-3969

Tacoma All Saints' Episcopal Church **M** (43) 205 E 96th St 98445-2003 (Mail to: 205 E 96th St 98445-2003) (253) 537-2970

Tacoma Christ Church **P** (299) 310 N K St 98403-1617 (Mail to: 310 N K St 98403-1696) Robert

Carver Samuel Torvend William Tudor (253) 383-1569

Tacoma Holy Family of Jesus Episcopal Church **M** (14) 1427 E 40th St 98404 (Mail to: Attn: Sue Bernstein PO Box 112376 98411) (253) 471-9838

Tacoma St Andrews Episcopal Church **P** (224) 7410 S 12th St 98465-1500 (Mail to: 7410 S 12th St 98465-1500) Thomas Ortung Edward Sterling (253) 564-4402

Tacoma St Lukes Episcopal Church **P** (479) § 3615 N Gove St 98407-4815 (Mail to: 3615 N Gove St 98407-4899) Marlene Jacobs (253) 759-3534

Tacoma Saint Matthew Church **P** (173) 6800 East Side Dr NE 98422-1116 (Mail to: 6800 East Side Dr NE 98422-1116) Kendall Haynes (253) 927-9808

Tahuya St Nicholas Episcopal Church **M** (25) 15000 NE North Shore Rd 98588 (Mail to: PO Box 101 98588-0101) Robert Williams (360) 275-7141

Vancouver All Saints Episcopal Church **M** (120) 2206 NW 99th St 98665-6253 (Mail to: PO Box 65825 98665-0028) (360) 573-8106

Vancouver Church of the Good Shepherd **P** (601) § 805 SE Ellsworth Rd 98664-5120 (Mail to: 805 SE Ellsworth Rd 98664-5120) William Warne (360) 892-7770

Vancouver St Lukes Church **P** (473) 426 E Fourth Plain Blvd 98663-3085 (Mail to: 426 E Fourth Plain Blvd Ste 11 98663-3085) Jesus Reyes (360) 696-0181

Vashon Church of the Holy Spirit **P** (88) 15420 Vashon Hwy SW 98070-3841 (Mail to: PO Box 508 98070-0508) Evan Clendenin (206) 567-4488

Washougal St Anne Episcopal Church **M** (138) 2350 Main St 98671-4115 (Mail to: PO Box 62 98671-0062) Ann Calhoun (360) 835-5301

STATE OF OREGON

Dioceses of Oregon and Eastern Oregon

DIOCESE OF OREGON

(PROVINCE VIII)
Comprises Oregon west of the Cascade Mountains
DIOCESAN OFFICE 11800 S Military Ln Portland OR 97219-8436
TEL (503) 636-5613 FAX (503) 636-5616
E-MAIL info@diocese-oregon.org WEB www.diocese-oregon.org

Previous Bishops— Thomas F Scott 1854-67, Benj W Morris m 1868 (OR and WA) 1880 (OR) dio 1889-1906, Chas Scadding 1906-14, Walter T Sumner 1915-35, Benj D Dagwell 1936-58, James WF Carman 1958-74, Hal R Gross suffr 1965-79, Matthew P Bigliardi 1974-85, Robert L Ladehoff coadj 1985 Bp 1986-2003, Johncy Itty 2003-8, Michael Hanley 2010-21

Bishop—Rt Rev Diana D Akiyama (Dio 30 Jan 2021)

Thriving Cong C Craun; *Treas* K Gordon; *Ex Asst* T Esguerra; *Chanc Emily Karr*

Fin C Buresch; *Lifelong Learning* D Moyer; *Comm* A Gannett; *Prog/Budg* A Fraizer; *COM* D Moyer; *Archivist* M Bagwell

Deans: Metro-East Rev M McDowell; *Columbia* Rev S McCauley; *Sunset* Rev B Mallon; *Willamette* Rev C Hertlein; *Central* Rev J Jones; *South* Rev E Flemister; *S Coast* Rev P Hale

Stand Comm—Cler: Pres A Valadez P Hale G Shumate G Rainey; *Lay:* T Phipps D Metheny M Colwell J Weber

PARISHES, MISSIONS, AND CLERGY

Albany St Albans Episcopal Church **M** (140) 1730 Hill St SE 97322-4246 (Mail to: PO Box 1556 97321-0465) Robert Morrison (541) 967-7051

Ashland Trinity Episcopal Church **P** (346) 44 N 2nd St 97520-1927 (Mail to: 44 N 2nd St 97520-1927) Bert Anderson Anne Bartlett Meredith Pech (541) 201-3418

Astoria Grace Episcopal Church **P** (92) 1545 Franklin Ave 97103-3717 (Mail to: 1545 Franklin Ave 97103-3717) Carren Sheldon Patricia Morris-Rader (503) 325-4691

Bandon Church of St John by the Sea **M** (37) 795 Franklin Avenue 97411-0246 (Mail to: PO Box

246 97411-0246) Beth Hoffmann Douglas Hale (541) 347-2152

Beaverton St Bartholomew's Church **P** (512) 11265 SW Cabot St 97005-2295 (Mail to: 11265 SW Cabot St 97005-2219) Jeffrey Littlefield Mikel Mcclain (503) 644-3468

Brookings St Timothy Episcopal Church **M** (120) 401 Fir St 97415-9222 (Mail to: PO Box 1237 97415-0115) James Lindley (541) 469-3314

Cave Junction Church of St Matthias **M** (4) 25904 97523-0805 (Mail to: PO Box 805 97523-0805) (541) 592-2006

Coos Bay Emmanuel Episcopal Church **P** (186) 370 Market Ave 97420-2229 (Mail to: PO Box 1028 97420-0226) Patricia Hale (541) 269-5829

Coquille St James Episcopal Church **M** (40) 210 E 3rd St 97423-1871 (Mail to: Attn: Treasurer 210 E 3rd St 97423-1871) Cathy Clark (541) 396-2322

Corvallis St Anselm of Cntbry Epis Ch **CC** 2615 NW Arnold Way 97330-5308 (Mail to: 2615 NW Arnold Way 97330-5308) Douglas Hale (541) 752-3734

Corvallis Church of the Good Samaritan **P** (679) § 333 NW 35th St 97330-4908 (Mail to: 333 NW 35th St 97330-4956) (541) 757-6647

Cottage Grove St Andrews Episcopal Church **M** (28) 1301 W Main St 97424-1802 (Mail to: 1301 W Main St 97424-1802) (541) 767-9050

Dallas Church of St Thomas **M** (52) 1486 SW Levens St 97338-3225 (Mail to: 1486 SW Levens St 97338-3225) (503) 623-8522

Drain St Davids Episcopal Church **M** (5) 239 East B Ave 97436 (Mail to: C/O Jane B Stewart PO Box 97 97435-0097) (541) 972-7085

Eugene Church of the Resurrection **P** (279) 3925 Hilyard St 97405-3957 (Mail to: 3925 Hilyard St 97405-3957) Kenneth Dorsch Nancy Gallagher Thomas Rambo Maron Van (541) 686-8462

Eugene St Marys Episcopal Church **P** (661) 1300 Pearl St 97401-3539 (Mail to: 1300 Pearl St 97401-3539) Robert Powell Nancy Crawford Thomas English Nancy Muhlheim Ann Rose (541) 343-9253

Eugene St Matthews Episcopal Church **P** (130) 4110 River Rd 97404-1235 (Mail to: 4110 River Rd 97404-1235) (541) 689-4010

Eugene St Thomas Episcopal Church **P** (163) 1465 Coburg Rd 97401-5006 (Mail to: 1465 Coburg Rd Ste 2 9740l-5006) (541) 343-5241

Florence St Andrews Episcopal Church **M** (73) 2135 19th St 97439-9730 (Mail to: PO Box 15 97439-0001) (541) 997-6600

Forest Grove St Bede Episcopal Church **M** (154) 1609 Elm St 97116-2503 (Mail to: 1609 Elm St 97116-2503) Marlene Mutchler (503) 357-5300

Gardiner St Mary Episcopal Church **M** (20) North 2nd & High Sts 97441 (Mail to: PO Box 208 97441-0208) (541) 271-0413

Gold Beach St Matthews Episcopal Church **M** (27) 94261 Moore St 97444 (Mail to: PO Box 651 97444-0651) George Walter (541) 247-7878

Grants Pass St Lukes Episcopal Church **P** (115) 244 NW 'D' St 97526-2042 (Mail to: 224 NW D St 97526-2042) Ernestein Flemister Joan Bristol (541) 476-2493

Gresham St Lukes Episcopal Church **P** (135) 120 SW Towle Ave 97080-6750 (Mail to: 120 SW Towle Ave 97080-6750) (503) 665-9442

Hillsboro All Saints Parish of Hillsboro **P** (102) 372 NE Lincoln St 97124-3146 (Mail to: 372 NE Lincoln St 97124-3196) Thomas Sramek David Brownmiller (503) 648-2514

Hillsboro Todos Los Santos **P** (175) 372 NE Lincoln St 97124-3146 (Mail to: 372 NE Lincoln St 97124-3146) (503) 640-9425

Lake Oswego Christ Episcopal Church **P** (665) § 1060 Chandler Rd 97034-2874 (Mail to: C/O Charles Mansfield PO Box 447 97034-0048) Carolynne Fairweather (503) 636-5618

Lebanon St Martins Episcopal Church **P** (47) 257 E Milton St 97355-3493 (Mail to: 1461 Grove St 97355-3428) (541) 451-1159

Lincoln City St James Episcopal Parish **P** (42) 2490 NE Highway 101 97367-4148 (Mail to: PO Box 789 97367-0789) Kristina Burbank (541) 994-2426

McMinnville St Barnabas Episcopal Church **P** (157) 822 W Second St 97128 (Mail to: PO Box 539 97128-0539) Elizabeth Mcwhorter (503) 472-5831

Medford St Marks Episcopal Parish **P** (206) 140 N Oakdale Ave 97501-2629 (Mail to: 140 N Oakdale Ave 97501-2629) Jedediah Holdorph Jane Maynard Betty Pinnock (541) 7733111

Milwaukie Ch of St John the Evangelist **P** (359) 2036 SE Jefferson St 97222-7660 (Mail to: 2036 SE Jefferson St 97222-7660) Jeanne Kaliszewski Stephen Denny Richard Simpson (503) 653-5880

Monmouth St Hildas Episcopal Church **M** (27) 245 Main St W 97361-2024 (Mail to: 245 Main St W 97361-2024) Pauline Morrison Ronald Wynn (503) 838-6087

Nehalem St Catherine Episcopal Church **M** (51) 36335 Highway 101 N 97131-9732 (Mail to: PO Box 251 97130) (503) 368-7890

Newberg St Michael/San Miguel **M** (219) 110 S Everest Rd 97132-2113 (Mail to: PO Box 358 97132-0358) Wilson Ferreira Sandoval Juan Guerra-Diaz (503) 538-3080

Newport St Stephens Episcopal **P** (70) 331 SW 9th St 97365-4637 (Mail to: PO Box 1014 97365-0076) George Goold Janis Goold (541) 265-5251

Oregon City St Pauls Episcopal Church **P** (228) 822 Washington St 97045-1945 (Mail to: 822 Washington St 97045-1945) Shawn Dickerson

Port Orford St Christophers Church **M** (17) 9th & Washington Sts 97465 (Mail to: PO Box 214

97465-0214) Norman Goldman (541) 347-1504

Portland All Saints Episcopal Church **P** (221) 4033 SE Woodstock Blvd 97202-7661 (Mail to: 4033 SE Woodstock Blvd 97202-7661) Andria Skornik (503) 777-3829

Portland Ascension Parish **P** (87) 1823 SW Spring St 97201-2345 (Mail to: 1823 SW Spring St 97201-2345) Robert Ladehoff Jeremy Lucas (503) 227-7806

Portland Parish of St John the Baptist **P** (513) 6300 SW Nicol Rd 97223-7566 (Mail to: 6300 SW Nicol Rd 97223-7566) Robert Bryant Marianne Allison Julia Jensen Colin Williams (503) 245-3777

Portland Grace Memorial Church **P** (435) 1535 NE 17th Ave 97232-1417 (Mail to: 1535 NE 17th Ave 97232-1417) Martin Elfert Daniel Carlson Darrah Clark (503) 287-0418

Portland St Aidan's Episcopal Church **P** (83) 17405 NE Glisan St 97230-6414 (Mail to: 17405 NE Glisan St 97230-6414) Sandra Ragan (503) 252-6128

Portland St Andrew Episcopal Church **M** (67) 7600 N Hereford Ave 97203-3432 (Mail to: 7600 N Hereford Ave 97203-3498) Jennifer Creswell (503) 285-0631

Portland St Barnabas Episcopal Church **P** (151) 2201 SW Vermont St 97219-1935 (Mail to: 2201 SW Vermont St 97219-1935) Bonnie Stewart (503) 246-1949

Portland St Davids Episcopal Church **P** (137) 2800 SE Harrison St 97214-5650 (Mail to: 2800 SE Harrison St 97214-5699) John Nesbitt P Joshua Griffin James Joiner Kerlin Richter (503) 232-8461

Portland St Gabriel the Archangel Epis **M** (467) 17435 NW West Union Rd 97229-2190 (Mail to: AttnRevCraig Mac Coll 17435 NW West Union Road 97229) Thomas Lang Roger Reynolds (503) 645-0744

Portland St James Episcopal Church **P** (137) 11511 SW Bull Mountain Rd 97224-2716 (Mail to: 11511 SW Bull Mountain Rd 97224-2716) Beth Mallon (503) 639-3002

Portland St Michael & All Angels Church **P** (828) 1704 NE 43rd Ave 97213-1402 (Mail to: 1704 NE 43rd Ave 97213-1402) Samuel Borbon Sallie Bowman David Perry (503) 284-7141

Portland Saints Peter and Paul **P** (177) 247 SE 82nd Ave 97216-1005 (Mail to: PO Box 16127 97292-0127) Sara Fischer Tracy LeBlanc (503) 254-8168

Portland St Philip the Deacon Epis Ch **P** (62) 120 NE Knott St 97212-3010 (Mail to: 120 NE Knott St 97212-3010) Maria Mcdowell (503) 281-5802

Portland St Stephens Episcopal Parish **P** (100) 1432 SW 13th Ave 97201-3356 (Mail to: 1432 SW 13th Ave 97201-3390) Dale Carr Maureen Hagen (503) 223-6424

✠ **Portland** Trinity Episcopal Cathedral **O** (1487) 147 NW 19th Ave 97209-1901 (Mail to: 147 NW 19th Ave 97209-1901) Joseph Dubay Valerie Ivey Nathanael Lerud Shana Mccauley John Scott Scannell Maureen Tighe Patrick Tomter (503) 2229811

Riddle Church of the Ascension **M** (7) 135 D St 97469-8640 (Mail to: PO Box 460 97469-0460) (541) 874-2936

Roseburg St Georges Episcopal Church **P** (82) 1024 SE Cass Ave 97470-4912 (Mail to: 1024 SE Cass Ave 97470-4984) (541) 673-4048

Saint Helens Christ Episcopal Church **M** (72) 35350 E Division Rd 97051-3202 (Mail to: PO Box 478 97051-0478) (503) 397-1033

Salem St Pauls Episcopal Church **P** (625) 1444 Liberty St SE 97302-4344 (Mail to: 1444 Liberty St SE 97302-4384) Anne Emry (503) 362-3661

Salem St Timothys Episcopal Church **P** (169) 3295 Ladd Ave NE 97301-1750 (Mail to: PO Box 7416 97303-0089) Brandon Filbert Anthony Petrotta Donald Wilson (503) 363-0601

Salem Epis Ch of the Prnc Of Peace **M** (88) PC Box 5757 1525 Glen Creek Rd NW 97304-0757 (Mail to: PO Box 5757 97304) Steven Ellis Anne Moore (503) 585-1479

Seaside Calvary Parish **P** (154) 503 N Holladay Dr 97138-6923 (Mail to: 503 N Holladay Dr 97138-6923) David Sweeney (503) 738-5773

Shady Cove St Martins Church **M** (59) 95 Cleveland St 97539-9730 (Mail to: C/O Diocese of Oregon 11800 S Military Ln 97219 8436) Laura Sheridan-Campbell (541) 878-2166

Silverton St Edwards Episcopal Church **M** (134 211 W Center St 97381-1905 (Mail to: PO Box 344 97381-0344) (503) 873-6188

Springfield Church of St John the Divine **P** (55 2537 Game Farm Rd 97477-7577 (Mail to: PC Box 1537 97477-0166) (541) 746-3322

St Portland Holy Cross Episcopal Church **M** (125) 17405 NE Glison St 17405 (Mail to: PC Box 669 97009-0669) Roberto Maldonado Mercado (503) 663-4223

Stayton Christ the King on the Santiam **M** (9) 55 W Regis St 97383-1164 (Mail to: PO Box 40 97383-0403) Thomas Moehl (503) 394-4113

Sutherlin Church of the Holy Spirit **M** (26) 120 Umatilla St 97479-9548 (Mail to: PO Box 139 97479-1398) (541) 459-4697

Tillamook St Albans Episcopal Parish **P** (179 2102 6th St 97141-3900 (Mail to: PO Box 28 97141-0285) Alison Lufkin (503) 842-6192

Toledo St Johns Episcopal Church **M** (15) 110 N. Alder St 97391-1520 (Mail to: 110 NE Alder S 97391-1520) (541) 336-3161

Waldport Saint Luke's Church **M** (79) 135 Highway 101 S 97394 (Mail to: PO Box 42 97394-0422) (541) 563-4812

Wilsonville St Francis of Assisi Episcopal **P** (591) 8818 SW Miley Rd 97070 (Mail to: PO Box 445 97070-0445) Brendan Barnicle Kenneth Russell (503) 678-5422

Woodburn St Marys Episcopal Church **M** (50) 1560 W Hayes St 97071-4314 (Mail to: PO Box 362 97071-0362) Agustin Valadez-Jaime (503) 982-6262

STATE OF PENNSYLVANIA
Dioceses of Bethlehem (Be), Central Pennsylvania (CPA), Northwestern Pennsylvania (NWPA), Pennsylvania (PA), and Pittsburgh (Pgh)

Abington—PA
Allentown—Be
Altoona—CPA
Ambler—PA
Ardmore—PA
Ashland—Be
Athens—Be
Bala Cynwyd—PA
Bedford—CPA
Bellefonte—CPA
Berwick—CPA
Bethlehem—Be
Blairsville—Pgh
Bloomsburg—CPA
Blue Bell—PA
Blue Ridge Summit—CPA
Boothwyn—PA
Brackenridge—Pgh
Bradford—NWPA
Bridgeport—PA
Brighton Heights—Pgh
Bristol—PA
Brookland—CPA
Brookville—NWPA
Bryn Mawr—PA
Buckingham—PA
Camp Hill—CPA
Canonsburg—Pgh
Carbondale—Be
Carlisle—CPA
Carnegie—Pgh
Chambersburg—CPA
Chester—PA
Clearfield—NWPA
Clifton Hts—PA
Coatesville—PA
Collegeville—PA
Columbia—CPA
Conshohocken—PA
Corry—NWPA
Coudersport—CPA
Dalton—Be
Dallas—Be
Danville—CPA
Donora—Pgh
Downingtown—PA
Douglassville—Be

Doylestown—PA
Drexel Hill—PA
Drifton—Be
Dubois—NWPA
Eagles Mere—CPA
Easton—Be
Edinboro—NWPA
Elkins Pk—PA
Emmaus—Be
Emporium—NWPA
Erie—NWPA
Essington—PA
Exton—PA
Fairview—NWPA
Forest City—Be
Ft Washington—PA
Foxburg—NWPA
Franklin—NWPA
Gap—PA
Gettysburg—CPA
Gladwyne—PA
Glen Mills—PA
Glenmoore—PA
Glenside—PA
Greensburg—Pgh
Greenville—NWPA
Grove City—NWPA
Hamlin—Be
Hanover—CPA
Harleysville—PA
Harrisburg—CPA
Hatboro—PA
Hawk Run—CPA
Hazleton—Be
Hellertown—Be
Hermitage—NWPA
Hershey—CPA
Hilltown—PA
Hollidaysburg—CPA
Homestead—Pgh
Honesdale—Be
Honey Brook—PA
Houtzdale—NWPA
Hulmeville—PA
Huntingdon—CPA
Huntingdon Valley—PA
Indiana—Pgh

Jeannette—Pgh
Jenkintown—PA
Jermyn—Be
Jersey Shore—CPA
Jim Thorpe—Be
Johnstown—Pgh
Kane—NWPA
Kennett Sq—PA
King of Prussia—PA
Kingston—Be
Kittanning—Pgh
Kutztown—Be
Lafayette Hill—PA
Lake City—NWPA
Lancaster—CPA
Langhorne—PA
Lansdowne—PA
Lebanon—Be
Lehighton—Be
Levittown—PA
Lewisburg—CPA
Lewistown—CPA
Ligonier—Pgh
Lock Haven—CPA
Lower Gwynedd—PA
Malvern—PA
Manheim—CPA
Mansfield—CPA
Maple Glen—PA
Marietta—CPA
McKeesport—Pgh
Meadville—NWPA
Mechanicsburg—CPA
Media—PA
Milford—Be
Milton—CPA
Monogehela—Pgh
Montoursville—CPA
Montrose—Be
Morgantown—Be
Moscow—Be
Mountaintop—Be
Mt Carmel—CPA
Mt Joy—CPA
Mt Pocono—Be
Muncy—CPA
Nanticoke—Be
Narvon—CPA

Nazareth—Be
New Castle—NWPA
New Hope—PA
New Milford—Be
Newport—CPA
Newtown—PA
Newtown Sq—PA
Norristown—PA
North East—NWPA
North Versailles—Pgh
Northern Cambria—Pgh
Northumberland—CPA
Norwood—PA
Oakmont—Pgh
Oaks—PA
Oil City—NWPA
Oreland—PA
Osceola Mills—NWPA
Oxford—PA
Palmerton—Be
Paoli—PA
Parkesburg—PA
Pen Argyl—Be
Peters Township—Pgh
Philadelphia—PA
Philipsburg—CPA
Phoenixville—PA
Pittsburgh—Pgh
Pt Alleghany—NWPA
Pottstown—PA
Pottsville—Be
Prospect Pk—PA
Quakertown—PA
Reading—Be
Ridgway—NWPA
Ridley Pk—PA
Rockledge—PA
Royersford—PA
St Clair—Be
St Marys—NWPA
Sayre—Be
Schuylkill Haven—Be
Scottdale—Pgh
Scranton—Pe
Selinsgrove—CPA
Sewickley—Pgh
Sharon—NWPA

Shippensburg—CPA	Tamaqua—Be	Warren—NWPA	Williamsport—CPA
Smethport—NWPA	Thompsontown—CPA	Waterford—NWPA	Wind Gap—Be
Solebury—PA	Tioga—CPA	Wayne—PA	Wrightstown—PA
Somerset—Pgh	Titusville—NWPA	Waynesboro—CPA	Wyncote—PA
Southampton—PA	Towanda—Be	Wayne Township—Pgh	Wynnewood—PA
Springfield—PA	Trexlertown—Be	Wellsboro—CPA	Yardley—PA
State College—CPA	Troy—Be	W Chester—PA	York—CPA
Stroudsburg—Be	Tunkhannock—Be	W Pittston—Be	York Springs—CPA
Sunbury—CPA	Tyrone—CPA	Westfield—CPA	Youngsville—NWPA
Susquehanna—Be	Valley Forge—PA	Whitehall—Be	
Swarthmore—PA	Villanova—PA	Wilkes-Barre—Be	

DIOCESE OF PENNSYLVANIA
(PROVINCE III)
Comprises Bucks, Chester, Delaware, Montgomery, and Philadelphia Counties
DIOCESAN OFFICE Diocesan House 23 East Airy Street, Norristown, PA 19401
Tel (215) 627-6434 FAX (267) 900-2928
E-MAIL mail@diopa.org WEB www.diopa.org

Previous Bishops—
Wm White 1787-1836, Henry U Onderdonk coadj 1827 Bp 1836-44, Alonzo Potter 1845-65, Samuel Bowman suffr 1858-61, Wm B Stevens coadj 1862 Bp 1865-87, Ozi W Whitaker coadj 1886 Bp 1887-1911, Alexander Mackay-Smith coadj 1902 Bp 1911, Philip McRhinelander coadj 1911 Bp 1911-23, Thomas J Garland suffr 1911 Bp 1924-31, Francis M Taitt coadj 1929 Bp 1931-43, Wm P Remington suffr 1945-51, Oliver J Hart coadj 1942 Bp 1943-63, J Gillespie Armstrong suffr 1949 coadj 1960 Bp1963-64, Robert L DeWitt coadj 1964 Bp 1964-73, Lyman C Ogilby coadj 1973 Bp 1974-87, Allen L Bartlett Jr coadj 1986 Bp 1987-98, Franklin D Turner suffr 1988-2000, Charles E. Bennison Jr coadj 1997-98 Bp 1998-2012, Clifton Daniel Bp prov 2013-2016

Bishop—Daniel G.P. Gutiérrez (955) (2016)

Chanc M Kohart; *Treas* J Pope; *Bp's Staff: Asst for Op* C Fisher *Exec Asst* M Hain; *Cn for Fin* D Horner; *Cn for Trans Min* A Benoit Joseph; *Property Manager* S McCauley; *Cn Growth and Support* B Ivey; *Cn Growth and Support* K Berlenbach; *Cn for Miss* T Smyth; *Cn for Comm* J Tucker; *Cn to Ord* S Wamsley; *Sr Acct Spec* N Clothier; *Sr Acct* K Sherman; *Conv Sec* H Njenga

Deans: Brandywine K Dellaria; *Bucks* M Ruk; *Delaware* E Thompson; *Merion* vacant; *Montgomery* W Smith; *Pennypack* S Murangi; *Schuylkill* M Shaw; *Southwark* S Mullen; *Valley Forge* S Kirabi; *Wissahickon* B McCrickard

Stand Comm—Cler: Pres J LaRoche-Wikel; *Lay: Sec* C Johnstone; D Parker P Smith R Francis A Kellner M Ruk H Greer

PARISHES, MISSIONS, AND CLERGY

Abington St Annes Episcopal Church **P** (493) 2119 Welsh Rd 19001-1013 (Mail to: 2119 Old Welsh Rd 19001-1013) (215) 659-1674

Ambler Trinity Episcopal Church **P** (462) 708 S Bethlehem Pike 19002-5809 (Mail to: 708 S Bethlehem Pike 19002-5899) Emmanuel Williamson (215) 646-0416

Ardmore Nevil Memorial Ch of St George **P** (242) 1 W Ardmore Ave 19003-1017 (Mail to: 1 W Ardmore Ave # C 19003-1017) Joel Daniels (610) 642-3500

Ardmore Saint Mary's Episcopal Church **P** (246) 36 Ardmore Ave 19003-1334 (Mail to: 36 Ardmore Ave 19003-1334) Sean Lanigan Joseph Schaller (610) 649-1486

Bala Cynwyd St. Asaph's **P** (341) § 27 Conshohocken State Rd 19004-2400 (Mail to: 27 Conshohocken State Rd 19004-2496) Andrew Kellner (610) 664-0966

Bala Cynwyd St Johns Episcopal Church **P** (104) 404 Levering Mill Rd 19004-2703 (Mail to: 404 Levering Mill Rd 19004-2700) Frank Wallner (610) 664-4517

Blue Bell St Dunstans Episcopal Church **P** (51) 750 Skippack Pike 19422-1712 (Mail to: 750 Skippack Pike 19422-1712) (215) 643-0522

Boothwyn Trinity Church **P** (207) 700 Meetinghouse Rd 19061-3503 (Mail to: 700 Meetinghouse Rd 19061-3503) Paul Gitimu (610) 213-9587

Bridgeport Christ Episcopal Church **P** (26) 740 Schuylkill River Rd 19405-1761 (Mail to: 740 River Rd 19405-1761) Theodore Henderson (610) 272-6036

Bristol St James Church Episcopal **P** (100) 225 Walnut St 19007-4940 (Mail to: 225 Walnut St 19007-4940) (215) 788-2228

Bryn Mawr Church of the Redeemer **P** (2278) 230 Pennswood Rd 19010 (Mail to: 230 Pennswood Rd 19010-3616) Peter Vanderveen Joann Jones (610) 525-2486

Bryn Mawr The Ch of the Good Shepherd **P** (30) 1116 E Lancaster Ave 19010-2615 (Mail to: 1116 E Lancaster Ave 19010-2693) (610) 525-7070

Buckingham Trinity Episcopal Church **P** (354) 2631 Durham Rd 18912 (Mail to: PO Box 387 18912-0387) Nancy Dilliplane (215) 794-7921

Chester St Mary Episcopal Church **M** (92) 703 Edwards St 19013 (Mail to: PO Box 595 19016-0595) Deirdre Whitfield (610) 874-8565

Chester St Pauls Episcopal Church **P** (70) 301 E 9th St 19013-6020 (Mail to: 301 E 9th St 19013-6088) (610) 872-5711

Clifton Hgts St Stephen's Episcopal Church **P** (76) 119 W Baltimore Ave 19018-1405 (Mail to: 199 W Baltimore Ave 19018-1494) (610) 622-3636

Coatesville The Church of the Trinity **P** (118) 323 E Lincoln Hwy 19320-3409 (Mail to: 323 E Lincoln Hwy 19320-3409) Sherry Deets (610) 384-4771

Collegeville St James Church Collegeville **P** (597) 3768 Germantown Pike 19426-3151 (Mail to: 3768 Germantown Pike 19426-3151) William Sowards (610) 489-7564

Conshohocken Calvary Episcopal Church **P** (120) 325 Fayette St 19428-0546 (Mail to: PO Box 546 19428-0546) Thomas McClellan (610) 825-5959

Downingtown St James Episcopal Church **P** (305) 409 E Lancaster Ave 19335-2722 (Mail to: 409 E Lancaster Ave 19335-2722) (610) 269-1774

Doylestown St Pauls Episcopal Church **P** (507) 84 E Oakland Ave 18901-4647 (Mail to: 84 E Oakland Ave 18901-4647) Daniel Moore (215) 348-5511

Drexel Hill Incrntn Holy Sacrament Epis **P** (288) 3000 Garrett Rd 19026-2217 (Mail to: 3000 Garrett Rd 19026-2217) Diane Faison Benjamin Wallis (610) 259-5148

Drexel Hill Holy Comforter **P** (247) 1000 Burmont Rd 19026-4533 (Mail to: 1000 Burmont Rd 19026-4533) Christopher Decatur (610) 789-6754

Elkins Park St Paul's Episcopal Church **P** (226) 7809 Old York Rd 19027-2508 (Mail to: 7809 Old York Rd 19027-2593) (215) 635-4185

Essington St. John the Evangelist **P** (82) 16 W 3rd St 19029-1200 (Mail to: 16 W 3rd St 19029-1200) Denise Leo (215) 687-1204

Exton St Pauls Episcopal Church **P** (550) 901 E Lincoln Hwy 19341-2806 (Mail to: 1105 E Lincoln Hwy 19341-2824) (610) 363-2363

Fort Washington St Thomas Church Whitemarsh **P** (1425) § 7020 Camp Hill Rd 19034-2202 (Mail to: 7020 Camp Hill Rd 19034-2202) Emily Richards Lorna Williams (215) 233-3970

Gap St Johns Episcopal Church **P** (89) 1520 W Kings Hwy 17527-9009 (Mail to: 1520 W Kings Hwy 17527-9009) John Obenchain (717) 442-4302

Gladwyne Saint Christopher's Church **P** (687) § 226 Righters Mill Rd 19035-1533 (Mail to: 226 Righters Mill Rd 19035-1597) Hillary Raining (610) 642-8920

Glen Mills St Johns Episcopal Church **P** (616) 576 Concord Rd 19342-1402 (Mail to: 576 Concord Rd 19342-1402) Jill Laroche Wilson (610) 459-2994

Glenmoore St Andrews Episcopal Church **P** (364) 7 Saint Andrews Ln 19343-9559 (Mail to: 7 Saint Andrews Ln 19343-9559) (610) 458-5277

Glenside St Peters Episcopal Church **P** (413) 654 N Easton Rd 19038-4310 (Mail to: 654 N Easton Rd 19038-4391) (215) 887-1765

Harleysville The Church of the Holy Spirit **P** (634) 2871 Barndt Rd 19438-1150 (Mail to: PO Box 575 19438-0575) Kathryn Andonian (215) 234-8020

Hatboro Church of the Advent **P** (216) 12 Byberry Rd 19040-3405 (Mail to: 12 Byberry Rd 19040-3405) Nazareno Javier (215) 675-5737

Hilltown Good Shepherd Epis Church **P** (97) 1634 Hilltown Pike 18927-9701 (Mail to: PO Box 132 18927-0132) George Master (215) 822-3930

Honey Brook St Marks Church **P** (91) 1040 Chestnut Tree Rd 19344-9645 (Mail to: 1040 Chestnut Tree Rd 19344-9645) (610) 942-2365

Hulmeville Grace Episcopal Church **P** (99) 313 Main St 19047-5801 (Mail to: 313 Main St 19047-5801) (215) 757-6025

Huntingdon Valley St John's Episcopal Church **P** (69) 1309 Old Welsh Rd 19006-5899 (Mail to: 1309 Old Welsh Rd 19006-5899) Eric Bond Eric Bond (215) 947-3212

Jenkintown Church of Our Saviour **P** (44) Old York & Homestead Rds 19046 (Mail to: Homestead & Old York Roads 19046) Eric Bond (215) 887-0500

Kennett Square Church of the Advent **P** (704) 401 N Union St 19348-2427 (Mail to: 401 N Union St 19348-2427) Timothy Johnson (610) 4444624

King of Prussia Grace Ch and the Incarnation **P** (66) C/O John Loftus 966 Trinity Lane 19406 (Mail to: Treasurer 2645 E Venango St 19134-5529) (610) 828-1500

King of Prussia Trinity Church Gulph Mills **P** (89) 966 Trinity Ln 19406-3636 (Mail to: Attn: J Smith 966 Trinity Ln 19406-3636) Deborah Payson (610) 828-1500

Lafayette Hill St. Jude and the Nativity **P** (56) 203 Germantown Pike 19444-1323 (Mail to: 203 Germantown Pike 19444-1323) (610) 941-6666

Langhorne St James Episcopal Church **P** (256) 330 S Bellevue Ave 19047-2808 (Mail to: 330 S Bellevue Ave 19047-2808) Sean Slack (215) 7573766

Lansdowne St Michaels Episcopal Church **P** (84) 813 Longacre Blvd 19050-3319 (Mail to: 813 Longacre Blvd 19050-3319) Jordan Casson (610) 2597871

Levittown All Saints Church **P** (34) 9 Old Locust Ave 19054-1107 (Mail to: 9 Old Locust Ave 19054-1107) (215) 2955196

Levittown St Paul Church **P** (65) 89 Pinewood Dr 19054-3609 (Mail to: 89 Pinewood Dr 19054-3609) (215) 946-8559

Lower Gwynedd Church of the Messiah **P** (638) 1001 Dekalb Pike 19002-1941 (Mail to: 1001 Dekalb Pike 19002-1941) Keith Marsh Maryjo Melberger (215) 699-9204

Malvern St Peters Ch in the Great Vly **P** (511) 2475 Saint Peters Rd 19355-8791 (Mail to: 2475 Saint Peters Rd 19355-8791) Abigail Nestlehutt (610) 644-7967

Malvern St Francis-in-the Field **P** (443) 689 Sugartown Rd 19355-3305 (Mail to: 689 Sugartown Rd 19355-3305) Kevin Dellaria Diane Faison (610) 647-0130

Maple Glen St. Matthew's Church **P** (579) § 919 Tennis Ave 19002-2312 (Mail to: 919 Tennis Ave 19002-2312) Rodney Roehner (215) 646-4092

Media Christ Episcopal Church **P** (368) 311 S Orange St 19063-3111 (Mail to: 311 S Orange St 19063-3190) Ernest Galaz (610) 566-7525

New Hope St Philips Episcopal Church **P** (132) 10 Chapel Rd 18938-1006 (Mail to: 10 Chapel Rd 18938-1006) Michael Ruk (267) 897-3050

Newtown St Lukes Church, Newtown **P** (383) 100 E Washington Ave 18940-1980 (Mail to: 100 E Washington Ave 18940-1980) (215) 968-2781

Newtown Square Saint Alban's Church **P** (163) 3625 Chapel Rd 19073-3602 (Mail to: 3625 Chapel Rd 19073-3698) Matthew Dayton-Welch (610) 356-0459

Norristown All Saints Episcopal Church **P** (174) 535 Haws Ave 19401-4542 (Mail to: 535 Haws Ave 19401-4542) Sandra Etemad Geoffrey West (610) 279-3990

Norristown St Augustine of Hippo Church **P** (139) 1208 Green St 19401-3402 (Mail to: 1208 Green St 19401-3402) (610) 279-8890

Norristown St Johns Episcopal Church **M** 23 E Airy St 19401-4815 (Mail to: 23 E Airy St 19401-4815) Christopher Schwenk (610) 2724092

Norwood St Stephen Church **P** (99) 128 Chester Pike 19074-1702 (Mail to: 128 Chester Pike 19074-1702) (610) 4610490

Oaks St Pauls Episcopal Church **P** (82) 126 Black Rock Rd 19456 (Mail to: PO Box 404 19456) (610) 650-9336

Oreland St Philip in the Fields **P** (118) Lorraine Ave & Oreland Mill Rd 19075 (Mail to: 317 Oreland Mill Rd 19075-2256) (215) 233-0409

Oxford St Christophers Episcopal Ch **P** (279) 116 Lancaster Pike 19363-1171 (Mail to: 116 Lancaster Pike 19363-1171) Mary Mertz (610) 932-8134

Paoli Church of the Good Samaritan **P** (1085) § 212 W Lancaster Ave 19301-1723 (Mail to: 212 W Lancaster Ave 19301-1758) Phillip Ellsworth (610) 644-4040

Parkesburg Church of the Ascension **P** (118) 406 W 2nd Ave 19365-1402 (Mail to: PO Box 193 19365-0193) (610) 857-9176

Philadelphia All Saints Church Torresdale **P** (294) 9601 Frankford Ave 19114-2813 (Mail to: 9601 Frankford Ave 19114-2895) James Walton (215) 637-8787

Philadelphia All Saints Church (Rhawnhurst) **P** (73) 7939 Frontenac St 19111 (Mail to: 1811 Loney St 19111-2911) (215) 342-6310

Philadelphia Calvary-St Augustine Church **P** (112) 814 N 41st St 19104-4813 (Mail to: 814 N 41st St 19104-4813) Isaac Miller (215) 222-2070

✠ **Philadelphia** Cathedral Ch of Our Saviour **O** (255) 13-19 S 38th St 19104-3843 (Mail to: 3717 Chestnut St Ste 200 19104-3164) Judith Sullivan Phillip Bennett Tyrone Fowlkes Pamela Nesbit (215) 386-0234

Philadelphia Igles de Christo y San Ambrsio **M** (2403) 3552 N 6th St 19140-4506 (Mail to: 6th and Venango Sts 19140) (215) 226-1444

Philadelphia Christ Church & St Michaels Ch **P** (72) 29 W Tulpehocken St 19144-2607 (Mail to: 29 W Tulpehocken St 19144-2607) (215) 844-7274

Philadelphia Christ Church **P** (536) 20 N American St 19106-4509 (Mail to: 20 N American St 19106-4592) Carol Anthony Susan Richardson (215) 922-1695

Philadelphia St Andrew & St Monica Church **M** (184) 3600 Baring St 19104-2333 (Mail to: 3600 Baring St 19104-2333) (215) 222-7606

Philadelphia Ch of St Luke & the Epiphany **P** (225) 330 S 13th St 19107-5916 (Mail to: 330 S 13th St 19107-5916) Joseph Wallace-Williams (215) 732-1918

Philadelphia St Martin in the Fields **P** (897) 8000 Saint Martins Ln 19118-4101 (Mail to: 8000 Saint Martins Ln 19118-4101) James Littrell (215) 2477466

Philadelphia Church of the Annunciation **P** (98) 324 Carpenter Ln 19119-3003 (Mail to: 324 Carpenter Ln 19119-3003) (215) 844-3059

Philadelphia Memorial Ch of the Good Shphd **P** (81) 3820 the Oak Road 19129-1030 (Mail to: 3820 the Oak Rd 19129-1030) (215) 844-0580

Philadelphia Emmanuel Resurrection **P** (101) 8201 Frankford Ave 19136-2735 (Mail to: 8201 Frankford Ave 19136-2735) Samuel Murangi (215) 624-8520

Philadelphia Church of the Advocate **P** (76) 1801 W Diamond St 19121-1519 (Mail to: 1801 W Diamond St 19121-1519) (215) 978-8000

Philadelphia Gloria Dei Episcopal Church **P** (169) 916 S Swanson St 19147-4332 (Mail to: 916 S Swanson St 19147-4396) (215) 389-1513

Philadelphia Grace Epiphany Church **P** (84) 224 E Gowen Ave 19119-1020 (Mail to: 224 E Gowen Ave 19119-1020) (215) 248-2950

Philadelphia Holy Apostles And Mediator **P** (250) Spruce & 51st Sts 19139 (Mail to: 260 S 51st St 19139) (215) 472-3000

Philadelphia Holy Innocents St Pauls Church **P** (89) 7001 Torresdale Ave 19135-1914 (Mail to: 7001 Torresdale Ave 19135-1914) Brian Rallison (215) 624-1144

Philadelphia House of Prayer **P** (97) 1747 Church Ln 19141-1309 (Mail to: 1747 Church Ln 19141-1309) (215) 549-7650

Philadelphia Memorial Church of St Luke **P** (134) 1946 Welsh Rd 19115-4654 (Mail to: 1946 Welsh Rd 19115-4712) (215) 969-3645

Philadelphia St Albans Church Roxborough **P** (176) 6769 Ridge Ave 19128-2444 (Mail to: 6769 Ridge Ave 19128-2444) Paul Adler (215) 482-2627

Philadelphia St Andrews in the Field Church **P** (41) 500 Somerton Ave 19116-2027 (Mail to: 500 Somerton Ave 19116-2027) (215) 673-5938

Philadelphia St Clements Church **P** (129) 2013 Appletree St 19103-1409 (Mail to: 2013 Appletree St 19103-1409) Richard Alton Justin Lanier (215) 563-1876

Philadelphia St Davids Episcopal Church **P** (41) 156 Dupont St 19127 (Mail to: PO Box 29102 19127-0102) Frank Wallner (215) 482-2345

Philadelphia St Dismas Episcopal Mission **M** (20) 3717 Chestnut St 19104 (Mail to: PO Box 244 19426-0244) George Master (215) 985-5751

Philadelphia St Gabriels Episcopal Church **M** (143) 101 E Roosevelt Blvd 19120-4243 (Mail to: 101 E Roosevelt Blvd 19120-4243) Joseph Schaller (215) 329-3807

Philadelphia St George & St Barnabas **P** (98) 520 S 61st St 19143-2234 (Mail to: 520 S 61st St 19143-2234) James Wynn (215) 747-2605

Philadelphia St James Kingsessing Epis Ch **P** (221) 6838 Woodland Ave 19142-1822 (Mail to: 6838 Woodland Ave 19142-1822) (215) 727-5265

Philadelphia St Lukes Church Germantown **P** (437) 5421 Germantown Ave 19144-2223 (Mail to: 5421 Germantown Ave 19144-2223) David Morris (215) 844-8544

Philadelphia St Mark's Episcopal Church **P** (486) 1625 Locust St 19103-6304 (Mail to: 1625 Locust St 19103-6388) Sean Mullen Nicholas Phelps (215) 735-1416

Philadelphia St Marks Church Frankford **P** (155) 4442 Frankford Ave 19124-3659 (Mail to: 4442 Frankford Ave 19124-3659) (215) 535-0635

Philadelphia St Marys Church Cathedral Road **P** (205) 630 E Cathedral Rd 19128-1935 (Mail to: 630 E Cathedral Rd 19128-1935) Peter Carey (215) 482-6300

Philadelphia St Marys Ch Hamilton Village **P** (225) 3916 Locust Walk 19104-6152 (Mail to: 3916 Locust Walk 19104-6152) (215) 386-3916

Philadelphia St Marys Episcopal Church **P** (38) 1831 Bainbridge St 19146-1429 (Mail to: 1831 Bainbridge St 19146-1429) (215) 985-0360

Philadelphia St Pauls Church Chestnut Hill **P** (245) 22 E Chestnut Hill Ave 19118-2715 (Mail to: 22 E Chestnut Hill Ave 19118-2764) Eric Hungerford Josiah Daniels (215) 242-2055

Philadelphia St Peter's Church **P** (444) 313 Pine St 19106-4212 (Mail to: 313 Pine St. 19106-4299) Sarah Hedgis (215) 925-5968

Philadelphia St Simon the Cyrenian Church **P** (31) 22nd and Reed Sts 19146 (Mail to: 1401 S 22nd St 19146-4530) (215) 468-1926

Philadelphia St Stephens Church **HC** (21) 19 S 10th St 19107-4224 (Mail to: PO Box 417 19105-0417) (215) 9223807

Philadelphia St Timothy Episcopal Church **HC** (292) 5720 Ridge Ave 19128-1734 (Mail to: 5720 Ridge Ave 19128-1734) Bonnie Mccrickard (215) 483-1529

Philadelphia The Afrcn Epis Ch of St Thomas **P** (1128) 6361 Lancaster Ave 19151-2622 (Mail to: 6361 Lancaster Ave 19151-2622) Martini Shaw (215) 473-3065

Philadelphia The Church of the Holy Trinity **HC** (457) 1904 Walnut St 19103-5733 (Mail to: 1904 Walnut St 19103-5796) John Gardner Rachel Wenner Gardner (215) 567-1267

Philadelphia Church of St John the Free **M** (120) 3089 Emerald St 19134-0498 (Mail to: 3554 N 6th St 19140-4506) (215) 226-1444

Philadelphia Trinity Church, Oxford **P** (151) 601 Longshore Ave 19111 (Mail to: 601 Longshore Ave 19111-4330) (215) 745-1258

Philadelphia Trinity Memorial Church **P** (110) 2212 Spruce St 19103-6503 (Mail to: 2212 Spruce St 19103-6503) (215) 732-2515

Phoenixville St Peters Episcopal Church **P** (398) 121 Church St 19460-3438 (Mail to: 121 Church St 19460-3438) Samuel Ndungu Joseph Dietz (610) 933-2195

Pottstown Christ Episcopal Church **P** (279) 316 E High St 19464-5538 (Mail to: 316 E High St PO Box 252 19464-5538) Joshua Caler (610) 323-2895

Prospect Park St James Church Episcopal **P** (117) 11th & Lincoln Aves 19076 (Mail to: 732 11th Ave 19076-1313) (610) 461-6698

Quakertown Emmanuel Episcopal Church **P** (34) 560 S Main St 18951-1570 (Mail to: 560 S Main St 18951-1570) (215) 536-3040

Ridley Park Christ Church Episcopal **P** (312) 104 Nevin St 19078-2108 (Mail to: 104 Nevin St 19078-2195) Jane Gober Dennis Bingham (610) 521-1626

Rockledge Memorial Ch of the Holy Nativity **P** (364) 205 Huntingdon Pike 19046-4444 (Mail to: C/O Heather Sherman 205 Huntingdon Pike 19046-4444) John Daniels (215) 663-9903

Royersford Church of the Epiphany **P** (107) 209 S 3rd Ave 19468-2551 (Mail to: 209 S 3rd Ave 19468-2551) (610) 948-9655

Solebury Trinity Episcopal Church **P** (548) § 6587 Upper York Rd 18963 (Mail to: PO Box 377 18963-0377) Emory Byrum Virginia Sheay (215) 297-5135

Southampton Church of the Redemption **P** (142) 1101 2nd Street Pike 18966-3956 (Mail to: 1101 2nd Street Pike 18966-3956) (215) 357-0303

Springfield Church of the Redeemer **P** (354) 145 W Springfield Rd 19064-1414 (Mail to: 145 W Springfield Rd 19064-1414) (610) 544-8113

Swarthmore Trinity Church **P** (210) 301 N Chester Rd 19081-1496 (Mail to: 301 N Chester Rd 19081-1496) Edward Thompson (610) 544-2297

Valley Forge Washington Memorial Chapel **P** (241) RR 23 19481-0098 (Mail to: PO Box 98 19481-0098) Tommy Thompson (610) 7830120

Villanova Christ Church **P** (254) 536 Conestoga Rd 19085-1131 (Mail to: 536 Conestoga Rd 19085-1131) Veronika Travis (610) 688-1110

Wayne St David Episcopal Church **P** (3135) § 763 Valley Forge Rd 19087-4724 (Mail to: 763 Valley Forge Rd 19087-4794) William Allen

Elizabeth Colton H Kenneth Mccaslin Thomas Szczerba (610) 688-7947

Wayne St Martins Church **P** (235) 400 King of Prussia Rd 19087-2342 (Mail to: 400 King of Prussia Rd 19087-2342) (610) 688-4830

Wayne St Marys Episcopal Church **P** (398) 104 Louella Ave 19087-4121 (Mail to: 104 Louella Ave 19087-4195) Joseph Smith (610) 688-1313

West Chester The Church of the Holy Trinity **P** (415) 212 S High St 19382-3404 (Mail to: 212 S High St 19382-3499) Paul Hunt (610) 696-4640

Wrightstown Church of the Holy Nativity **M** (44) 749 Durham Rd 18940-9679 (Mail to: 749 Durham Rd 18940-9679) (215) 598-3405

Wyncote All Hallows Church **P** (100) 262 Bent Road 19095 (Mail to: 262 Bent Rd 19095-1503) (215) 885-1641

Wynnewood All Saints Episcopal Church **P** (149) Montgomery Ave & Gypsy Ln 19096 (Mail to: 1325 Montgomery Ave 19096-1037) (610) 642-4098

Wynnewood Church of the Holy Apostles **P** (225) 1020 Remington Rd 19096-2326 (Mail to: 1020 Remington Rd 19096-2394) James Stambaugh (610) 642-6617

Yardley Church of the Incarnation **P** (122) 1505 Makefield Rd 19067-3149 (Mail to: 1505 Makefield Rd 19067-3149) (215) 295-2259

Yardley St. Andrews Church **P** (257) 47 W Afton Ave 19067-1444 (Mail to: 47 W Afton Ave 19067-1444) Hilary Greer (215) 493-2636

DIOCESE OF PITTSBURGH
(PROVINCE III)
Comprises the southwestern portion of Pennsylvania
DIOCESAN OFFICE 325 Oliver Avenue, Suite 300, Pittsburgh, PA 15222
TEL (412) 721-0853
E-MAIL office@episcopalpgh.org   WEB www.episcopalpgh.org

Previous Bishops— John B Kerfoot 1866-81, Cortlandt Whitehead 1881-1922, Alexander Mann 1923-43, Austin Pardue 1944-68, William S Thomas suffr 1954-70, Robert B Appleyard 1968-82, Alden M Hathaway 1983-97, Robert Duncan 1997-2008, Kenneth L Price 2009-2012, Dorsey McConnell 2012-21

Bishop—Rt Rev Ketlen A. Solak (1138) (Dio 14 Nov 2021)

Treas & Dir of Admin E Zevkovich; *Cn to the Ord* Rev K Karashin; *Cn for Evangelism & Faith Formation* Rev N Hall; *Cn for Beloved Community Initiative*

Rev E McIntosh; *Program Coord for Beloved Community Initiative* S Alam-Denlinger; *Coord for Episcopal/Anglican House of Study* Rev C Brall; *Exec Asst & Comm Specialist* A Muhl; *Fin Admin* M Rihn; *Admin Specialist* J A McLaughlin-Klemencic; *Dir of Ext Relations* R Creehan; *Chanc* A Roman, Reed Smith LLP 225 Fifth Ave Pittsburgh PA 15222 (412) 288-3131; *Pres Brd of Trustees* Sh Stagnitta; *Child Min Team Coord* J Yoon; *Univ Chaplain* Rev D Isadore; *Comm on Min Chr* Rev J Smith; *Comm on Race and Reconciliation Chr* Rev N Chalfant-Walker; *Emergency Prep Coord* T Austin; *Epis Ch Women Pres* A McStay; *Social Justice Comm* M Novy

Stand Comm—Cler: A Rogers N Raman M McIntyre N Threadgill; *Lay:* L Brown St Stagnitta K Baird F Atwood

PARISHES, MISSIONS, AND CLERGY

Blairsville St Peters Episcopal Church **P** (16) 36 W Campbell St 15717-1312 (Mail to: 36 W Campbell St 15717-1312) (724) 459-8804

Brackenridge St Barnabas Episcopal Church **P** (129) 989 Morgan St 15014-1164 (Mail to: 989 Morgan St 15014-1164) Francis Yesko (724) 224-9280

Brighton Heights All Saints Episcopal Church **P** (57) 3577 McClure Ave 15212-2147 (Mail to: 3577 McClure Ave 15212-2147) Bruce Robison (412) 766-8112

Canonsburg St Thomas Episcopal Church **P** (68) 139 N Jefferson Ave 15317-1307 (Mail to: 139 N Jefferson Ave 15317-1307) Catherine Brall (724) 745-2013

Carnegie Church of the Atonement **P** (40) 618 Washington Ave 15106-2837 (Mail to: 618 Washington Ave 15106-2837) (412) 279-1944

Carnegie Old St Luke's Church **P** 330 Old Washington Pike 15106-3730 (Mail to: PO Box 9089 15224-0089)

Donora St Johns Episcopal Church **P** (33) 998 Thompson Ave 15033-2146 (Mail to: 998 Thompson Ave 15033-2146) (724) 969-6427

Greensburg Christ Episcopal Church **P** 132 Sherwood Drive 15601 (Mail to: 122 N Maple Ave 15601-2580) (724) 216-4717

Homestead St Matthews Episcopal Church **P** (64) 336 E 10th Ave 15120-1613 (Mail to: 336 E 10th Ave 15120-1613) (412) 461-5291

Indiana Christ Episcopal Church **P** (84) 902 Philadelphia St 15701-3912 (Mail to: 902 Philadelphia St 15701-3912) William Geiger (724) 465-6129

Jeannette Church of the Advent **P** (63) 51 S 1st St 15644-2102 (Mail to: 51 S 1st St 15644-2102) Martin Wright (724) 523-9390

Johnstown St Marks Episcopal Church **P** (138) 335 Locust St 15901-1606 (Mail to: 335 Locust St 15901-1606) (814) 535-6797

Kittanning St Pauls Episcopal Church **P** (110) 112 N Water St 16201-1516 (Mail to: 112 N Water St 16201-1516) (724) 543-5402

Ligonier St Michaels of the Valley **P** (256) 2535 Route 381 15658 (Mail to: PO Box 336 15658-0336) (724) 238-9411

Mckeesport St Stephens Episcopal Church **P** (68) 220 8th St 15132-2744 (Mail to: 220 8th St 15132-2744) Moni Mcintyre (412) 664-9379

Monongahela St Pauls Episcopal Church **P** (47) § 130 W. Main Street 15063-2332 (Mail to: 130 W Main St 15063-2332) (724) 258-7792

North Versailles All Souls Church **P** (15) 215 Canterbury Ln 15137-2111 (Mail to: 215 Canterbury Ln 15137-2198) (412) 823-1440

Northern Cambria St Thomas Episcopal Church **P** (18) § 1201 Chestnut Ave 15714-1469 (Mail to: Attn: Marlene Rihn 325 Oliver Ave Ste 300 15222-2403) Annis Rogers Annis Rogers (814) 659-9805

Oakmont St Thomas Memorial Church **P** (716) 378 Delaware Ave 15139-1618 (Mail to: 378 Delaware Ave 15139-1618) Jeffrey Murph Daniel Isadore (412) 828-9680

Peters Township St Davids Episcopal Church **P** (337) 905 E McMurray Rd 15367-1094 (Mail to: 905 E McMurray Rd 15367-1094) Kristian Opat Kristian Opat (724) 941-4060

Pittsburgh Calvary Episcopal Church **P** (1645) 315 Shady Ave 15206-4388 (Mail to: 315 Shady Ave 15206-4388) Jonathon Jensen Neil Raman Cameron Soulis (412) 661-0120

Pittsburgh Christ Episcopal Church **P** (1387) 5910 Babcock Blvd 15237-2548 (Mail to: 5910 Babcock Blvd 15237-2588) James Shoucair Jean McIlvain Lorena Ringle (412) 364-2442

Pittsburgh Church of the Good Shepherd **P** (43) 124 Johnston Ave 15207-1739 (Mail to: 5200 Gertrude St. 15207-0054) (412) 421-8497

Pittsburgh Church of the Holy Cross **P** (128) 7507 Kelly St 15208-1914 (Mail to: 7507 Kelly St 15208-1914) (412) 242-3209

Pittsburgh Church of the Nativity **P** (134) 33 Alice St 15205-2801 (Mail to: 33 Alice St 15205-2801) Shawn Malarkey (412) 921-4103

Pittsburgh Emmanuel Episcopal Church **P** (206) 957 W North Ave 15233-1693 (Mail to: 957 W North Ave 15233-1693) Don Youse (412) 231-0454

Pittsburgh St James Episcopal Church **P** (55) 11524 Frankstown Rd 15235-3199 (Mail to: 325 Oliver Ave Ste 300 15222-2403) Eric Mcintosh (412) 721-0853

Pittsburgh St Pauls Episcopal Church **P** (1521) 1066 Washington Rd 15228-2061 (Mail to: 1066 Washington Rd 15228-2024) Noah Evans Jean Chess (412) 531-7153

Pittsburgh St Peters Episcopal Church **P** (406) 4048 Brownsville Rd 15227-3499 (Mail to: 4048 Brownsville Rd 15227-3499) (412) 884-5225

Pittsburgh St Stephens Episcopal Church **P** (133) 600 Pitt St 15221-3136 (Mail to: 600 Pitt St 15221-3136) Charles Esposito (412) 243-6100

Pittsburgh St Andrews Episcopal Church **P** (417) 5801 Hampton St 15206-1615 (Mail to: 5801 Hampton St 15206-1615) Christopher Cole (412) 661-1245

Pittsburgh Church of the Redeemer **P** (127) 5700 Forbes Ave 15217-1526 (Mail to: 5700 Forbes Ave 15217-1526) Natalie Hall (412) 422-7100

✠ **Pittsburgh** Trinity Cathedral **O** (94) 325 Oliver Avenue 15222-2403 (Mail to: 325 Oliver Ave 15222-2467) (412) 232-6404

Scottdale St Bartholomew Trinity Church **P** (25) 149 Walnut Ave 15683-1936 (Mail to: 149 Walnut Ave. 15683-1936) (724) 887-5110

Sewickley St Brendan's Episcopal Church **P** (418) 2365 Mcaleer Rd 15143-8762 (Mail to: 2365 McAleer Rd 15143-8762) Robin Jarrell (412) 364-5974

Somerset St Francis in the Flds Epis Ch **P** (45) 2081 Husband Rd 15501-7253 (Mail to: 2081 Husband Rd 15501-7253) (814) 445-7149

Wayne Township St Michaels Episcopal Church **P** (10) 274 St Michaels Rd 16222 (Mail to: PO Box 218 16249-0544) (724) 664-7522

DIOCESE OF PUERTO RICÒ
PROVINCE II
Comprises the Island of Puerto Rico
DIOCESAN CENTER 1409 Ave Ponce de León, 4to Piso San Juan PR 00907-4025
(MAIL: 1409 Ave. Ponce de León, 4to Piso San Juan PR 00907-4025)
TEL (787) 761-9800
E-MAIL iep@episcopalpr.org WEB www.episcopalpr.org

Previous Bishops—
WW Jackson (Antigua) in charge 1860-1895, James H Van Buren 1902-1912, Charles B Colmore 1913-1947, Charles F Boynton 1948-1950, Albert E Swift 1951-1964, Francisco Reus Froylan 1964-1986, David Andres Alvarez Velazquez 1986-2013, Wilfrido Ramos Orench 2013-2017 (Provisional Bishop)

Bishop—The Rt Rev Rafael L. Morales Maldonado – July 22, 2017

Archdcns: Northeastern Rev A Méndez; *North I* Rev F Guzmán; *North II* Rev A Rivera; *Southern* Rev J Restrepo; *Southwest* Rev J Franco; *Southeastern* Rev C Vélez; *Mountains* Rev E Vélez; *Archdeacon* D Guzmán

Staff Off.: Canon to the Ordinary Very Rev M Santos; *Bishop Chaplain and Asst* A Rivera; *Bp Exec Asst* Y Torres; *Social Pastoral, Spirituality and Ecumenism* Can A Dávila; *Evangelism, Pastoral and Formation* Can G Garcés; *Comm* J Delgado; *Admin* Y Salinas; *Human Resourses* B Alameda

Sec of Conv Mrs C Pérez; *Treas* Rev N Lopez; *Chanc* Lic F Nieves; *Chaplains of Cler* Rev M Santos, Rev J Velazquez; *Aff Extra diocesan* Rev A Rivera; *Church Development* Rev L Gómez; *Christian Ed* Can A Alvarez and D A Lugo; *Hist* Rev I Buxeda; *Yth Min* A Rivera

Dean of the Cathedral: Very Rev Dr M Rodríguez

Dean of the Seminary: Very Rev Dr G Garcés

Stand Comm—Cler: D Guzmán, J Muñoz, C Vélez, F Rivera; *Lay:* I Torres, L Heylegier, A Rodríguez, S Restrepo

PARISHES, MISSIONS, AND CLERGY

Aibonito Espiritu Santo la Tea **M** (14) Bo. Caonillas Sector La Tea Carr. 726, Km 4.2 00705 (Mail to: PO Box 00705-0127) (787) 313-7015

Aibonito Mision San Judas Tadeo **M** (153) Barrio Pasto Carr. 717 Km. 0.9 Sector La Playita

00705 (Mail to: PO Box 612 00705-0612) (787) 735-2299

Añasco San Jose de Arimatea **P** (53) Carr. 109 Km 2.4 00610 (Mail to: PO Box 239 00610-0239) (787) 645-3971

Arecibo Mision San Pablo **M** (255) Carr. 653 Avenida Universidad Barrio Villa Los Santos 00613 (Mail to: Apartado 1051 00613) (787) 878-2084

Bayamon Parroquia San Pedro y Pablo **P** (79) IC33 Ave Lomas Verdes 00956 (Mail to: IC33 Ave. Lomas Verdes 00956) (787) 785-6472

Bayamon Mision San Bernabe **M** (37) Carr 167 Km 147 Bo Buena Vista 00956 (Mail to: RR 5 Box 8100 Bo Buena Vista 00956) (787) 730 8265

Bayamon San Timoteo **P** (26) 49-13 Calle 36 Esq North Main Urb Sierra Bayamon 00961 (Mail to: 49-13 Calle 36 Esq North Main Urb Sierra Bayamon 00961)

Cabo Rojo Nuestra Senora de Walsingham **M** (46) Carr. 103 Residencia #3 Bario Bajura Sector Coqui 00623 (Mail to: PO Box 127 00623) (787) 685-6766

Caguas Mision Cristo Rey **M** (60) Call Mayagüez, Esquina Ponce Urb Villa de Carmen 00725 (Mail to: PO Box 6271 00726 Juan Garcia De Jesus (787) 746-2543

Carolina Mision El Adviento **M** (33) Urb Vill Fontana Calle Via 19 Qr 16 00985 (Mail to Condominio La Rada Ashford 1020 Apt. 2 Condado 00907) (787) 724-9217

Carolina Mision Santo Tomas Apostol **M** (54) B Martin Gonzalez Carr 860 Km 1.1 00987 (Mail to: PO Box 757 00986-0757) (787) 276-1283

Coamo Nueva Msn San Simon de Cirineo **M** (40) Bo Las Flores #47 A Paseo Los Tulipane 00769 (Mail to: Urb. Valle de Andalucia 314 Calle Almeria 00728) (787) 387-0889

Dorado Mision Emmanuel **M** (60) Bo Maguay Sector Maysonet II Carr 694 00646 (Mail to HC 46 Box 5667 00646) (787) 466-8970

Ensenada Mision Santa Cecilia **M** (80) Cal Brandon #1 00647 (Mail to: PO Box 44 00647-0445) (787) 821-1201

Fajardo Mision El Buen Pastor **M** (66) 399 Ave General Valero 00738-3990 (Mail to: 399 Ave General Valero 00738) (939) 400-1278

Guayama Mision San Pedro **M** (18) Hospital Epis S Lucas Guayama Ave Pedro Albizu Campos 00785 (Mail to: Hospital Epis San Luca Guayama Ave Pedro Albizu Campos 00784) (787) 989-2369

Guaynabo Mision San Esteban El Martir **M** (54) Urb. San Ramón Calle Nogal Final 00970 (Mail to: Urb Santiago Iglesias 1308 Ave Paz Granela Pmb 160 00921-4183) (787) 367-1128

Hato Rey Parroquia la Encarnacion **P** (196) Calle Juan Davila Esq Juan BR Urb Roosevelt 00918 (Mail to: GPO Box 361067 00936-1067) (787) 459-8374

Humacao Mision San Gabriel Arcangel **M** (173) Ave. Los Sauces Lote B 00792 (Mail to: Villa Humacao A-2 00791) (787) 645-3971

Lares Mision la Santa Cruz **M** (158) Carr 135 Km 64.4 Poblado de Castañer 00631 (Mail to: PO Box 1012 00631-1012) Tomas Pixcar-Pol (787) 439-7111

Lares Mision San Bartolome **M** (37) Carr. 128 Km 37.9 Bo Bartolo 00631 (Mail to: PO Box 1005 00631-1005) (787) 553-0401

Lares Mision San Matias **M** (39) Carr 111 Km 24 Ave Los Patriotas 00669 (Mail to: PO Box 499 00669) (787) 800-3960

Levittown Mision Santa Maria Magdalena **M** (218) Ave Boulevard Esq Paseo Conde 00949 (Mail to: PO Box 580497 00950) (787) 604-3135

Loiza Msn San Felipe y Santiago Apsl **M** (106) Carr 187 Km 5.8 Mediania Alta 00772 (Mail to: HC - 01 Buzon 5460 00772-9726) (787) 536-1700

Manati Parroquia la Resurreccion **P** (204) Bo. Cantera Carr 2 Km 47 00674 (Mail to: 88 Bo Cantera 00674-4805) (787) 368-1625

Maricao Mision la Epifania **M** (30) Barrio Indiera Alta Sector 30 Km 128 Carr 428 00606 (Mail to: HC-01 Box 4766 00606) (787) 553-0401

Maricao Mision La Transfiguracion **M** (80) Carr. 365, Int 105 Sector Indiera Baja 00606 (Mail to: PO Box 551 00606-0551) (787) 838-2629

Mayaguez Parroquia San Andres **P** (211) 156 Calle Santiago R Palmer 00680 (Mail to: PO Box 4297 00681-4297) (787) 832-1116

Morovis Parroquia Ayudada La Ascencion **P** (123) Carr 633 Km 3.9 Bo Barahona 00674 (Mail to: HC-02 Box 5830 00687) (787) 862-4206

Penuelas Sn Mateo Apostol y Evangelista **M** (251) Km 2.3 Sector La Gelpa Bo Quebrada Ceiba 00624 (Mail to: HC - 01 Buzon 8219 00624) (787) 969-0164

Ponce Mision San Lucas Evangelista **M** (179) Torre Medica Hosp Epis S Lucas 909 Ave Tito Castro 00716-4728 (Mail to: 2703 Paseo De La Reina 00717) (787) 996-4504

Ponce Parroquia Ayudada La Recon **P** (116) Bo. Quebrada Limon Carr. 502, Km 4.5 00728

(Mail to: Parcelas Pastillo Canas 818 Calle Jesus T Pineiro 00728-3601) (787) 612-0381

Ponce Mision Principe de Paz **M** (18) 469 Calle 13 Urb Brisas Del Caribe El Tuque 00728 (Mail to: PO Box 271 Brisas Del Caribe 00728-5312) (787) 514-5994

Ponce Mision San Marcos Evangelista **M** (100) Carr 123 Km 10 Hm 5 Bo Magueyes 00731 (Mail to: PO Box 8453 00732-8453) (787) 848-4681

Ponce Mision San Miguel Arcangel **M** (54) Calle Lolita Tizol #49 00731 (Mail to: HC - 01 Box 10100 00624) (787) 470-5894

Ponce Par Ayudada Santa Maria Virgen **M** (124) Bo. Clausells Calle Central #15 00780 (Mail to: PO Box 10010 00732-0010) (787) 454-9161

Ponce Parroquia Santisima Trinidad **P** (124) Calle Marina Esq Abolicion 00732 (Mail to: Apartado 335693 00732) (787) 841-6719

Ponce Parroquia Santo Nombre de Jesus **P** (194) Parcelas Pastillos Canas 806 Calle Jesus T Pineiro 00728-3601 (Mail to: Parcelas Pastillo Canas 806 Calle Jesus T Pineiro 00728-3601) (787) 844-3955

Rio Piedras Mision San Francisco de Asis **M** (42) Urb El Comandante 876 Calle Manuel Guerra 00924-2534 (Mail to: Urb El Comandante 876 Calle Manuel Guerra 00924-2534) (787) 762-0835

Rio Piedras Parroquia San Jose **P** (133) Carr 842 Km 2.4 Caimito 00926 (Mail to: RR 6 Box 9615 00926) (787) 720-5834

Sabana Grande Mision Santa Ana **M** (59) Urb El Arrendado 97 Calle A 00637-2155 (Mail to: PO Box 445 00647) (787) 821-1201

✤ **Santurce** Catedral San Juan Bautista **O** (84) Ave Ponce de León Esq. Calle Canals Pda. 20 00908 (Mail to: PO Box 9262 00908-9262) (787) 721-2395

✤ **Santurce** Cathedral St John the Baptist **O** (95) 1401 Ponce de Leon Ave Esquina Calle Canals Parada 20 00907 (Mail to: Box 9262 Santurce 00708) (787) 722-3254

Trujillo Alto Parroquia la Sagrada Familia **P** (80) Carr 848 Km 1.1 Bo Saint Just 00978 (Mail to: PO Box 360145 00936-0145) (787) 616-9174

Trujillo Alto Parroquia Ayudada Santa Hilda **P** (120) Carr 848 Bo Saint Just 00978 (Mail to: Apartado 902 00978) (787) 755-7675

Vieques Mision Todos los Santos **M** (104) Calle Plinion Peterson 557 765 (Mail to: PO Box 308 00765-0308) (787) 741-2668

Yauco Msn la Anunciacion a la Virgen **M** (44) Bo Rancheras Carr 371 Km 122 00698 (Mail to: 1925 Calle Afrodita Urb Alta Vista 00716-2945) (787) 856-6256

Yauco Msn San Juan Apostol y Evnglst **M** (25) Calle Marcial Santana, #73 Parcelas Viejas,Barinas 00698 (Mail to: HC 03 Box 15683 00698) (787) 460-1001

Yauco Mision San Rafael Arcangel **M** (59) Calle Barbosa #21 00698 (Mail to: PO Box 1967 00698-1967) (787) 460-1001

DIOCESE OF RHODE ISLAND
(PROVINCE I)
Comprises the State of Rhode Island
DIOCESAN OFFICE 275 N Main St Providence 02903-1298
TEL (401) 274-4500 FAX (401) 331-9430
E-MAIL diocese@episcopalri.org   WEB www.episcopalri.org

Previous Bishops—
Samuel Seabury 1790-96, Edward Bass 1798-1803, Alexander V Griswold 1811-43, John PK Henshaw 1843-52, Thomas M Clark 1854-1903, Wm M McVickar coadj 1898 Bp 1903-10, James D Perry 1911-46, Granville G Bennett suffr 1939 Bp 1946-54, John S Higgins coadj 1953 Bp 1955-72, Frederick H Belden coadj 1971 Bp 1972-79, George N Hunt 1980-94, Geralyn Wolf 1996-2012

Bishop—The Rt Rev W Nicholas Knisely SOSc (1071) (Dio 17 Nov 2012)

Bps Exec Asst: K Knudson-Groh; *Epis Char* B Fornal; *Sec Conv Rev* B Besier; *Treas* V Escalera 275 N Main Providence 02903; *Cn to Ord* D Cleaver-Bartholomew; *CFO* E Biddles

Stand Comm—Cler: E Habecker K Beelsey J Kirby *Pres* S Wrathall; *Lay:* O Forbes R Silliman D Monroe W Willis

PARISHES, MISSIONS, AND CLERGY

Barrington St Johns Episcopal Church **P** (785) 191 County Rd 02806-4501 (Mail to: 191 County Rd 02806-4501) Patrick Greene (401) 245-4065

Barrington Sts Matthew & Mark Epis Church **P** (194) 3 Chapel Rd 02806-1807 (Mail to: 5 Chapel Rd 02806-1861) (401) 245-3690

Block Island St Anns by the Sea **M** (19) 25 Spring St 02807-7794 (Mail to: PO Box 622 02807-0622) Eletha Buote-Greig (401) 4662911

Bristol St Michaels Church **P** (207) 399 Hope St 02809-1803 (Mail to: 399 Hope St # 414 02809-1803) Michael Horvath Michael Horvath Paul Twelves (401) 253-7717

Central Falls St George & San Jorge **P** (795) 12 Clinton St 02863-2906 (Mail to: 12 Clinton St 02863-2906) (401) 722-9449

Charlestown Church of the Holy Spirit **M** (79) 4150 Old Post Rd 02813-2551 (Mail to: PO Box 241 02813-0241) (401) 364-6368

Coventry St Francis Episcopal Church **M** (258) 132 Peckham Ln 02816-5125 (Mail to: PO Box 142 02816-0003) Sean Manchester (401) 397-7757

Cranston Church of the Ascension **P** (315) 390 Pontiac Ave 02910-3322 (Mail to: 390 Pontiac Ave 02910-3322) Sarah Saxe (401) 461-5811

Cranston Church of the Transfiguration **P** (924) § 1665 Broad St 02905-2727 (Mail to: 1665 Broad St 02905-2727) (401) 461-3142

Cranston St Davids on the Hill Epis Ch **P** (258) 200 Meshanticut Valley Pkwy 02920-3917 (Mail to: 200 Meshanticut Valley Pkwy 02920-3997) (401) 942-4368

Cranston Trinity Episcopal Church **P** (473) 139 Ocean Ave 02905-3628 (Mail to: 139 Ocean Ave 02905-3628) (401) 941-4324

Cumberland Emmanuel Episcopal Church **P** (496) § 120 Nate Whipple Hwy 02864-1410 (Mail to: 120 Nate Whipple Hwy 02864-1410) Joan Testin Noel Bailey (401) 658-1506

E Greenwich Saint Luke's Episcopal Church **P** (1058) 99 Peirce St 02818-3814 (Mail to: 99 Peirce St 02818-3814) John Higginbotham Timothy Rich (401) 884-4116

East Providence St Marys Episcopal Church **M** (22) 81 Warren Ave 02914-5165 (Mail to: 81 Warren Ave 02914-5165) Peter Michaelson Michele Matott (401) 434-7456

Greenville St Thomas Episcopal Church **P** (432) 1 Smith Avenue 02828 (Mail to: PO Box 505 02828-0505) Susan Carpenter Donald Parker Dante Tavolaro (401) 949-0261

Hope Valley St Elizabeths Church **M** (155) 63 Canonchet Rd 02832-2401 (Mail to: Attn: Robert Olsen PO Box 48 02832-0048) Edward Beaudreau Richard Schweinsburg (401) 539-7346

Jamestown St Matthews Parish **P** (438) § 87 Narragansett Ave 02835-1149 (Mail to: PO Box 317 02835-0317) Christa Moore-Levesque (401) 423-1762

Kingston St Augustines Church **P** (111) 35 Lower College Rd 02881-1307 (Mail to: 15 Lower College Rd 02881-1307) Elizabeth Sherman (401) 783-2153

Lincoln Christ Church in Lonsdale **P** (188) 1643 Lonsdale Ave 02865-1707 (Mail to: 1643 Lonsdale Ave 02865-1707) (401) 725-1920

Little Compton St Andrew's by-the-Sea **P** (207) § 182 Willow Ave 02837-1535 (Mail to: PO Box 491 02837-0491) (401) 635-2452

Middletown St Columbas Chapel **P** (308) § 55 Vaucluse Ave 02842-5742 (Mail to: 55 Vaucluse Ave 02842-5742) Anne Bolles-Beaven Everett Greene (401) 847-5571

Middletown Church of the Holy Cross **M** (60) 1439 West Main Rd 02842-7315 (Mail to: PO Box 4121 02842-0121) (401) 846-7076

N Kingstown St Pauls Wickford **P** (2026) 55 Main St 02852-5017 (Mail to: 55 Main St 02852-5017) Mark Reece (401) 294-4357

N Providence St James Episcopal Church **M** (71) § 474 Fruit Hill Ave 02911-2636 (Mail to: 474

Fruit Hill Ave 02911-2636) John Reardon (401) 353-2079

Narragansett St Peters-by-the-Sea Church **P** (375) § 72 Central St 02882-3647 (Mail to: 72 Central St 02882-3647) Craig Swan (401) 783-4623

Newport Emmanuel Church **P** (215) § 42 Dearborn St 02840-3408 (Mail to: 42 Dearborn St 02840-3408) Della Wells (401) 847-0675

Newport St Johns Church **P** (131) 61 Poplar St 02840-2434 (Mail to: 61 Poplar St 02840-2434) (401) 848-2561

Newport Trinity Church **P** (600) 1 Queen Anne Sq 02840-6855 (Mail to: 1 Queen Anne Sq 02840-6855) Timothy Watt Christine Cassels (401) 846-0660

North Scituate Trinity Church **P** (568) 249 Danielson Pike 02857-1906 (Mail to: 249 Danielson Pike 02857-1906) Johanna Marcure (401) 647-2322

Pawtucket Church of the Good Shepherd **P** (130) 490 Broadway 02860-1340 (Mail to: 490 Broadway 02860-1340) Dennis Bucco (401) 723-0408

Pawtucket St Lukes Episcopal Church **P** (251) 670 Weeden St 02860-1649 (Mail to: 670 Weeden St 02860-1649) Dennis Bucco Joyce Thorne (401) 723-9216

Pawtucket St Pauls Church **P** (252) 50 Park Pl 02860-4010 (Mail to: 50 Park Pl 02860-4010) (401) 728-4300

Portsmouth St Marys Episcopal Church **P** (436) 324 East Main Rd. 02871-2113 (Mail to: 324 E Main Rd 02871-2113) Jennifer Pedrick (401) 846-9700

Portsmouth St Pauls Episcopal Church **P** (40) 2679 E Main Rd 02871-2613 (Mail to: 2679 E Main Rd 02871-2613) (401) 683-1164

Providence All Saints Memorial Church **P** (139) 674 Westminster St 02903-4066 (Mail to: 674 Westminster St 02903-4066) Julianne Hanavan Maryalice Sullivan (401) 751-1747

Providence Cathedral of St John **P** 271 N Main St 02903-1237 (Mail to: 271 N Main St 02903-1237) (401) 274-4500

Providence Church of the Redeemer **P** (101) 655 Hope St 02906-2652 (Mail to: 655 Hope St 02906-2652) Patrick Campbell (401) 331-0678

Providence Grace Episcopal Church **P** (473) 175 Mathewson St 02903-3410 (Mail to: 300

Westminster St 02903-3303) Jonathan Huyck (401) 331-3225

Providence St Martins Episcopal Church **P** (528) § 50 Orchard Ave 02906-5418 (Mail to: 50 Orchard Ave 02906-5418) Mark Sutherland Lawrence Bradner Linda Griggs (401) 751-2141

Providence St Peters & St Andrews Epis **P** (72) 25 Pomona Ave 02908-5255 (Mail to: 25 Pomona Ave 02908-5244) (401) 272-9649

Providence St Stephens Church **P** (75) § 114 George St 02906-1189 (Mail to: 114 George St 02906-1189) Benjamin Straley Leroy Close (401) 4216702

Rumford Church of the Epiphany **P** (214) 1336 Pawtucket Ave 02916-1412 (Mail to: 1336 Pawtucket Ave 02916-1412) Jennifer Zogg Dorothy Brightman (401) 434-5012

Saunderstown Chapel of St John the Divine **P** (186) 10 Church Way 02874-3807 (Mail to: PO Box 541 02874-0541) (401) 295-0193

Tiverton Church of the Holy Trinity **P** (375) 1956 Main Rd 02878-4637 (Mail to: 1956 Main Rd 02878-4698) John Higginbotham (401) 624-4759

Wakefield Church of the Ascension **P** (144) 370 Main St 02879-7407 (Mail to: 370 Main St 02879-7407) (401) 783-2911

Warwick All Saints Church in Pontiac **P** (70) 111 Greenwich Ave 02886-1279 (Mail to: 111 Greenwich Ave 02886-1279) (401) 739-1238

Warwick St Barnabas Episcopal Church **P** (210) 3257 Post Rd 02886-7145 (Mail to: 3257 Post Rd 02886-7196) Scott Lee (401) 737-4141

Warwick St Marks Church **P** (341) 111 W Shore Rd 02889-1145 (Mail to: 111 W Shore Rd 02889-1145) Susan Wrathall (401) 737-3127

Westerly Christ Church **P** (587) 7 Elm St 02891-2125 (Mail to: Attn: Treasurer 7 Elm St 02891-2198) Kuruvilla Chandy Sandra Haines-Murdocco David Joslin Richard Morgan (401) 596-0197

Wood River Jct St Thomas Episcopal Church **M** (68) 322 Church St 02894-1119 (Mail to: PO Box 33 02894-0033) Bettine Besier Bettine Besier (401) 364-3113

Woonsocket St James Church **P** (261) § 24 Hamlet Ave 02895-4408 (Mail to: 24 Hamlet Ave 02895-4427) Peter Tierney (401) 762-2222

DIOCESE OF THE RIO GRANDE
(PROVINCE VII)
Comprises New Mexico and Far West Texas
DIOCESAN OFFICE 318 Silver Avenue SW Albuquerque NM 87102
TEL (505) 881-0636 FAX (505) 883-9048
E-MAIL office@dioceserg.org WEB www.dioceserg.org

Previous Bishops—
John M Kendrick 1889 (NM and AZ) 1892-1911, Frederick B Howden 1914-40, James M Stoney M 1942 dio 1952-56, Charles James Kinsolving III 1956-72, Richard M Trelease Jr 1972-87 Terence Kelshaw 1989-2005, Jeffrey N Steenson 2005-07, Michael L. Vono 2010-18

Bishop—Rt Rev Michael B. Hunn (1110) (Dio 3 November 2018)

Treas Rev JP Arrossa; *Chanc for NM* K Aubrey; *Chanc for TX* C Pine; *Archivist* CE Davies; *Reg* M Jewell; *ECW* C Davis; *Recov Min* J Cline; *Inv Bd* Rev JP Arrossa; *Cn to Ord* Rev Cn WL Curtis; *Archdcn* P Soukup; *Cn Theol* Very Rev Cn S Ruthven; *Trans Off* Rev Cn WL Curtis; *Bishop's Ridge: Stoney Camp and Rec Ctr* C Jewell; *Yth Min* A Roque; *Border Min* Rev M Wallens; *Comm* Rev Cn WL Curtis; *School for Min* Very Rev Cn S Ruthven; *Disciplinary Board* P Lamb; *COMB* Rev S Miller-Mutia

Stand Comm—Cler: J Hosea K Kopren K McNellis; *Lay:* D Butler K Daly P Siefert *Pres* K Kopren

Regional Deans: NE Very Rev TBA; *NW* Very Rev A Lenzo; *SE* Very Rev TBA; *SW* Very Rev J Tober

PARISHES, MISSIONS, AND CLERGY

Alamogordo St Johns Episcopal Church **P** (113) § 1114 Indiana Ave 88310-6720 (Mail to: 1114 Indiana Ave 88310-6720) Michael Drinkwater (575) 437-3891

Albuquerque Hope in the Desert Epis Church **P** (118) 8700 Alameda Blvd NE 87122-3789 (Mail to: 8700 Alameda Blvd NE 87122-3789) Daniel Tuton Ruth Morgan (505) 830-0572

Albuquerque Our Lady in the Valley Epis Ch **M** (18) 2805 Don Felipe Rd 87105-6748 (Mail to: PO Box 4126 87196-4126) (505) 873-2011

Albuquerque St Chads Episcopal Church **P** (365) 7171 Tennyson St NE 87122-1081 (Mail to: 7171 Tennyson St NE 87122-1081) Jeremiah Griffin (505) 856-9200

✣ **Albuquerque** Cathedral Church of St John **O** (2220) 318 Silver Ave SW 87102-3328 (Mail to: PO Box 1246 87103-1246) Kristina Maulden Spencer Brown (505) 247-1581

Albuquerque St Marks Episcopal Church **P** (291) § 431 Richmond Pl NE 87106-2150 (Mail to: 431 Richmond Pl NE 87106-2150) Christopher Mclaren David Martin Sylvia Miller-Mutia (505) 262-2484

Albuquerque St Marys Episcopal Church **P** (330) 1500 Chelwood Park Blvd NE 87112-4620 (Mail to: 1500 Chelwood Park Blvd NE 87112-4620) (505) 293-1911

Albuquerque St Michael & All Angels Church **P** (1082) § 601 Montano Rd NW 87107-5226 (Mail to: 601 Montano Rd NW 87107-5226) Mary Allison-Hatch Jean Arrossa Hermon Lowery (505) 345-8147

Albuquerque St Thomas of Canterbury Church **P** (82) 425 University Blvd NE 87106-4556 (Mail to: 425 University Blvd NE 87106-4556) (505) 247-2515

Alpine St James Church **M** (3) 510 N 6th St # 877 79830-3510 (Mail to: 510 N 6th St # 877 79830-3510) (432) 837-7313

Anthony St Luke's Episcopal Church **P** (239) 7050 McNutt Rd 88021-9221 (Mail to: 7050 McNutt Rd 88021-9221) Daniel Cave (575) 874-3972

Artesia St Pauls Church **P** (19) 807 S 10th St 88210-2388 (Mail to: PO Box 1308 88211-1308) Maurice Geldert (575) 746-3380

Belen St Philips Episcopal Church **M** (81) PO Box 955 87002-0955 (Mail to: 113 La Luna Place 87002-1096) (505) 864-7954

Carlsbad Grace Episcopal Church **P** (136) 508 W Fox St 88220-5721 (Mail to: PO Box PP 88221-7529) Rodney Hurst (575) 885-6200

Chama St Jeromes Church **M** (31) 331 North Pine 87520 (Mail to: PO Box 399 87575-0399) (575) 753-1503

Cloudcroft Church of the Ascension **SC** (13) 60 Chipmunk Ave 88317 (Mail to: PO Box 263 88317-0263) (575) 404-1590

Clovis Curry St James Episcopal Church **P** (84) 1117 N Main St 88102-0249 (Mail to: PO Box 249 88102-0249) Alan Brockmeier (575) 763-4638

Deming St Lukes Episcopal Church **M** (46) 419 W. Spruce Street 88030-3640 (Mail to: PO Box 1258 88031-1258) (575) 546-8088

Edgewood Church of the Holy Cross **P** (120) 367 State Road 344 87015-1090 (Mail to: PO Box 1090 87015-1090) Kristin Kopren Michael Coburn (505) 281-7722

El Paso All Saints Episcopal Church **P** (114) 3500 Mcrae Blvd 79925-2807 (Mail to: 3500 Mcrae Blvd 79925-2897) Philip Dougharty (915) 598-0721

El Paso Holy Spirit Episcopal Church **P** (51) 10500 Kenworthy St 79924-1738 (Mail to: 10500 Kenworthy St 79924-1738) (915) 821-1362

El Paso St Albans Episcopal Church **P** (107) 1810 Elm St 79930-3110 (Mail to: 1810 Elm St 79930-3110) (915) 565-2727

El Paso Saint Christopher's Epis Ch **P** (74) 300 Riverside Dr 79915-4527 (Mail to: 300 Riverside Dr 79915-4527) (915) 859-9329

El Paso St Francis on the Hill Epis Ch **M** (127) § 6280 Los Robles Dr 79912-1958 (Mail to: 6280 Los Robles Dr 79912-1958) Kristin Kopren (915) 581-9500

Espanola St Stephens Episcopal Church **M** (24) 703 Bond St 87532-2729 (Mail to: PO Box 1303 87532-1303) Constance Delzell (505) 753-3010

Farmington St Johns Episcopal Church **P** (363) 312 N Orchard Ave 87401-6227 (Mail to: 312 N Orchard Ave 87401-6227) Guy Mackey (505) 325-5832

Fort Stockton St Stephens Episcopal Church **M** (17) 401 East Second St 76054-2941 (Mail to: PO Box 330 79735-0330) (432) 336-3180

Gallup Church of the Holy Spirit **M** (74) 1334 Country Club Dr 87301-5665 (Mail to: 1334 S Country Club Dr 87301-5665) Lynn Perkins Roger Perkins (505) 863-4695

Glencoe St Anne Chapel **HC** Highway 70 88324 (Mail to: 121 Mescalero Trl 88345-6090) (575) 257-2356

Hillsboro Christ Episcopal Church **M** (3) Eleanora St 88042 (Mail to: PO Box 91 88042) (575) 895-5644

Hobbs St Christophers Church **M** (52) 207 E Permian Dr 88240-4434 (Mail to: 207 E Permian Dr 88240-4434) (575) 393-3237

Las Cruces St Andrews Episcopal Church **P** (574) Canon Scott A Ruthven 518 N Alameda Blvd 88005-2540 (Mail to: PO Box 266 88004-0266) Jonathan Hanneman (575) 526-6333

Las Cruces St James Episcopal Church **P** (160) 102 Saint James 88005-3713 (Mail to: PO Box 2427 88047-2427) John Tober Francis Williams (575) 526-2389

Las Vegas St Pauls Peace Church **M** (40) 810 8th St 87701-4242 (Mail to: PO Box 2576 87701-2576) William Mckay Thomas Woodward (505) 425-8479

Los Alamos Trinity on the Hill Epis Ch **P** (230) 3900 Trinity Dr 87544-1871 (Mail to: 3900 Trinity Dr 87544-1871) (505) 662-5107

Los Lunas St Matthews Episcopal Church **M** (133) 400 Huning Ranch Loop W 87031-4325 (Mail to: 400 Huning Ranch Loop W 87031-4325) Robert Mundy (505) 865-6548

Marfa St Paul's Church **M** (75) 101 E Washington 79843-0175 (Mail to: PO Box 175 79843-0175) (830) 660-2971

Milan All Saints Episcopal Church **M** (37) 600 Hwy 605 87021 (Mail to: PO Box 157 87020-0157) Patricia Eustis (505) 285-5074

Portales Trinity Episcopal Church **M** (10) § 1116 W 3rd St 88130-6618 (Mail to: 1116 W 3rd St 88130-6618) Larry Mote (575) 356-6860

Raton Holy Trinity Episcopal Church **HC** (60) 240 Rio Grande Ave 87740-3945 (Mail to: PO Box 1016 87740-1016) Timothy Sexton (575) 445-9884

Rio Rancho St Francis Episcopal Church **P** (321) 2903 Cabezon Blvd SE 87124-1741 (Mail to: 2903 Cabezon Blvd SE 87124-1741) Alexander Lenzo (505) 896-1999

Roswell St Andrews Church **P** (205) § 505 N Pennsylvania Ave 88201-4736 (Mail to: PO Box 1495 88202-1495) Dale Plummer (575) 622-1353

Ruidoso Epis Church in Lincoln County **P** (194) 121 Mescalero Trl 88345-6090 (Mail to: 121 Mescalero Trl 88345-6090) Laurie Benavides (575) 257-2356

Santa Fe Church of the Holy Faith **P** (818) 311 E Palace Ave 87501-2221 (Mail to: 311 E Palace Ave 87501-2221) Robin Dodge James Gordon Madelynn Johnston (505) 9824447

Santa Fe Epis Church of the Holy Family **M** (48) 10A Bisbee Ct 87508-4865 (Mail to: 10A Bisbee Ct 87508-4865) Corinne Hodges Elisabeth Noland (505) 424-0095

Santa Fe St Bedes Episcopal Church **P** (313) 550 W San Mateo Rd 87505-4028 (Mail to: 550 W San Mateo Rd 87505-4028) Lucas Grubbs Robert Davenport Edward Fellhauer Sheila Fellhauer George Kunkle Peter Vazquez-Schmitt (505) 982-1133

Silver City Church of the Good Shepherd **P** (190) 615 N Texas St 88061-5422 (Mail to: PO Box 2795 88062-2795) Thomas Bates Francoise Gelineau (575) 538-2015

Socorro Church of the Epiphany **M** (80) 908 Leroy Pl 87801-4744 (Mail to: PO Box 692 87801-0692) Steve Stephens Morrill Peabody (575) 835-1818

Taos St James Episcopal Church **P** (265) 214 Camino De Santiago 87571-4306 (Mail to: 208 Camino De Santiago 87571-4306) Fred Brown Dana Cline (575) 758-2790

Terlingua Santa Inez Episcopal Church **M** (4) Terlingua Ghost Town & Ivey Rd 79852 (Mail to: PO Box 88 79830) (432) 371-4399

Truth Consq St Pauls Episcopal Church **M** (52) 407 N Cedar St 87901-2335 (Mail to: PO Box 949 87901-0949) (575) 894-9596

Tucumcari St Michaels Episcopal Church **M** (42) 2602 S 2nd St 88401-4221 (Mail to: 2602 S 2nd St 88401-4221) (575) 461-4222

DIOCESE OF ROCHESTER
(PROVINCE II)
Comprises 8 western New York counties
DIOCESAN OFFICE 3825 E Henrietta Rd, Ste 100, Henrietta, NY 14467
TEL (585) 473-2977
E-MAIL communications@episcopaldioceseofrochester.org
WEB www.episcopalrochester.org

Previous Bishops—
David L Ferris 1931-38, Bartel H
Reinheimer coadj 1936 Bp 1938-
49, Dudley S Stark 1950-62, Geo W
Barrett 1963-69, Robert R Spears Jr
1970-84, William G Burrill 1984-
99, Jack M McKelvey 1999-2008

Bishop—Rt Rev Prince Gren-
ville Singh (1029) (Dio 31 May 2008)

Cn to Ord J Ross; *Cn for Stew & Fin CFO* T Rubiano;
Operations & Benefits K Estey; *Exec to the Bishop* C
McConnell; *Audit* C Shoemaker; *Comm* S Richards;
Accounting K Woodward; *Sec to Conv* Rev A
Stridiron; *Treas* T Butwid; *Asst Treas* B Owen; *Chanc*
PR Fileri; *Asst Chanc* CT Wright, FP Greene; *Reg* C
McConnell

Stand Comm— *Cler:* R Hamlin L Burkardt C Miller
R Picken; *Lay: Pres* S Peters J DaBall-Lavoie C Mok
S Woodhouse

PARISHES, MISSIONS, AND CLERGY

Addison Church of the Redeemer **P** (66) 1
Wombaugh Sq 14801-1032 (Mail to: 1
Wombaugh Sq 14801-1032) (607) 359-2300
Angelica St Pauls Church **P** (10) 1 Park Cir 14709
(Mail to: PO Box 472 14709) (585) 466-3546
Avon Zion Church **P** (61) 10 Park Pl 14414-1055
(Mail to: 10 Park Pl 14414-1055) Virginia
Mazzarella (585) 226-3722
Bath St Thomas Church **P** (101) 122 Liberty St
14810-1509 (Mail to: 122 Liberty St 14810-
1509) (607) 776-4503
Branchport St Lukes Church **P** (55) § 121 West
Lake Rd 14418-9754 (Mail to: 187 W Lake Rd
14418-9768) Philip Kasey Philip Kasey (315)
595-6162
Brockport Saint Luke's Church **P** (177) 14 State St
14420-1922 (Mail to: 14 State St 14420-1922)
(585) 637-6650
Caledonia St Andrews Episcopal Church **M** (46)
175 North St 14423-1036 (Mail to: C/O Laurie
Mcmeremy 175 North St 14423-1036) (585)
538-2112
Canandaigua St Johns Church **P** (266) 183 N
Main St 14424-1226 (Mail to: 183 N Main St
14424-1226) David Hefling (585) 394-4818
Canaseraga Trinity Church **P** (3) 20 N. Church
St 14822 (Mail to: PO Box 202 14822-0202)
Bruce Torrey (607) 545-6211

Clifton Springs Saint John's Church **P** (80) 32
E Main St 14432-1233 (Mail to: PO Box 622
14432-0622) Donald Schranz (315) 462-6611
Corning Christ Episcopal Church **P** (213) 33 East
First St 14830-2620 (Mail to: 33 E 1st St 14830-
2699) Troy Preston (607) 9375449
Cuba Christ Church **P** (21) 19 South St 14727-
1411 (Mail to: PO Box 112 14727-0112) (585)
268-7622
Dansville St Peters Memorial **P** (32) 25 Clara
Barton Street 14437 (Mail to: PO Box 127
14437-0127) John Thompson (585) 335-5434
Fairport Saint Luke's Church **P** (177) 77 Country
Corner Ln 14450-3034 (Mail to: PO BOX 146
14450-0146) Kenneth Pepin (585) 598-3037
Gates The Church of the Epiphany **P** (190) 3285
Buffalo Rd 14624-2413 (Mail to: 3285 Buffalo
Rd 14624-2483) (585) 247-4190
Geneseo St Michael's Episcopal Church **P** (265)
23 Main St 14454-1213 (Mail to: 23 Main St
14454-1213) Michael Laver (585) 243-1220
Geneva St Johns Chapel **Chapel** South Main St
14456 (Mail to: 300 Pulteney St 14456-3304)
(315) 781-3671
Geneva St Peters Memorial **P** (388) 151 Genesee
St 14456-2320 (Mail to: PO Box 147 14456-
0147) James Adams (315) 789-4910
Geneva Trinity Church **P** (55) 78 Castle St 14456-
2621 (Mail to: PO Box 287 14456-0287) (315)
7162284
Hammondsport St James Church **P** (98) 38 Lake
St 14840 (Mail to: PO Box 249 14840-0249)
Craig Hacker (607) 569-2647
Henrietta St Peter's **P** (83) 3825 E Henrietta Rd
14467-9147 (Mail to: 3825 E Henrietta Rd
14467-9147) (585) 334-1110
Hilton St Georges Church **P** (116) 635 Wilder Rd
14468-9701 (Mail to: 635 Wilder Rd 14468-
9701) (585) 392-4099
Honeoye Falls St Johns Episcopal Church **P** (96)
11 Episcopal Ave 14472-1001 (Mail to: 11
Episcopal Ave 14472-1001) (585) 624-4074
Hornell Christ Episcopal Church **P** (100) Main
And Center St 14843 (Mail to: PO Box 336
14843-0336) (607) 324-3620
Keuka Park Garrett Chapel **O** C/O John Barden
213 West Main St 14478 (Mail to: Skyline Dr
14478) (315) 536-3955
Lyons Grace Episcopal Church **P** 7 Phelps St
14489-1420 (Mail to: 9 Phelps St 14489-1509)
Richard Witt (315) 946-9687

Newark St Marks Church **P** (69) 400 S Main St 14513-1723 (Mail to: 400 S Main St Ste 3 14513-1795) (315) 331-3610

Odessa Saint John's Church **O** (45) 4938 County Route 14 14869-9729 (Mail to: Interchurch Office 112 Sixth Street 14891) (607) 535-2321

Palmyra Zion Episcopal Church **P** (144) 120 E Main St 14522-1018 (Mail to: 120 E Main St 14522-1018) Keisha Stokes (315) 597-9236

Penfield Church of the Incarnation **P** (249) 1957 Five Mile Line Rd 14526-1000 (Mail to: 1957 Five Mile Line Rd 14526-1000) Mitchell Bojarski Miriam Owens (585) 586-7860

Penn Yan St Marks Episcopal Church **P** (91) 179 Main St 14527-1202 (Mail to: PO Box 424 14527-0424) Ryan Salamony (315) 536-3955

Pittsford Christ Church **P** (1185) 36 S Main St 14534-1939 (Mail to: 36 S Main St 14534-1999) Ronald Young Ronald Young (585) 586-1226

Rochester Christ Church **P** (134) 141 East Ave 14604-2521 (Mail to: 141 East Ave 14604-2597) Ruth Ferguson (585) 454-3878

Rochester Church of the Ascension **P** (158) 2 Riverside St 14613-1222 (Mail to: 2 Riverside St 14613-1222) Abidhananthar John (585) 458-5423

Rochester St Luke & St Simon Cyrene Epis **P** (101) 17 S Fitzhugh St 14614-1401 (Mail to: PO Box 14577 14614-0577) Keith Patterson (585) 546-7730

Rochester St Marks St Johns Church **P** (114) 1245 Culver Rd 14609-5340 (Mail to: 1245 Culver Rd 14609-5340) Cynthia Rasmussen Michael Finn (585) 654-9229

Rochester St Pauls Church **P** (775) § 41 Westminster Rd 14607-2223 (Mail to: 25 Westminster Rd 14607-2223) Robert Picken Jay Burkardt (585) 271-2240

Rochester St Stephens Episcopal Church **P** (58) 350 Chili Ave 14611-2555 (Mail to: 350 Chili Ave 14611-2555) Gloria Fish (585) 328-0856

Rochester St Thomas Episcopal Church **P** (643) 2000 Highland Ave 14618-1125 (Mail to: 2000 Highland Ave 14618-1125) Leslie Burkardt (585) 442-3544

Rochester South Wedge Mission **M** (50) 125 Caroline St 14620-2127 (585) 746-0348

Rochester Chapel of the Good Shepherd **Chapel** 505 Mount Hope Ave 14620-2251 (Mail to: 505 Mount Hope Ave 14620-2251) (585) 546-8400

Rochester Trinity Episcopal Church **P** (200) § 3450 Ridge Rd W 14626 (Mail to: Attn: Administrative Asst 3450 W Ridge Rd 14626-3432) Deborah Duguid-May Deborah Duguid-May (585) 225-7848

Savona Church of the Good Shepherd **HC** (47) § 31 Church St 14879-9658 (Mail to: PO Box 466 14879-9658) (607) 569-2647

Scottsville Grace Episcopal Church **P** (112) 9 Browns Ave 14546-1345 (Mail to: PO Box 158 14546-0158) Johnnie Ross (585) 889-2028

Sodus St Johns Episcopal Church **P** (46) 54 W Main St 14551-1134 (Mail to: 54 W Main St 14551-1134) Mary Brody (315) 483-4235

Sodus Point Christ Church **SC** 8350 Bay St 14555-9533 (Mail to: 935 East Ave 14607-2570) (315) 331-8251

Watkins Glen Saint James' Church **HC** (64) 597 S Decatur St 14891-1610 (Mail to: 112 6th St 14891-1359) (607) 535-2321

Webster Church of the Good Shepherd **P** (445) 1130 Webster Rd 14580-9320 (Mail to: 1130 Webster Rd 14580-9321) Lance Robbins (585) 872-2281

Webster St Andrews by the Lake **SC** 1206 Lake Rd 14580-9708 (Mail to: 935 East Ave 14607-2216) (716) 872-2281

Wellsville St John Episcopal Church **P** (33) 12 E Genesee St 14895-1032 (Mail to: 12 E Genesee St 14895-1032) (585) 593-5592

DIOCESE OF SAN DIEGO
(PROVINCE VIII)
Comprises San Diego, Imperial and part of Riverside Counties, CA and Yuma County, AZ
DIOCESAN OFFICE 2083 Sunset Cliffs Blvd, San Diego CA 92107
TEL (619) 291-5947
E-MAIL emcdougal@edsd.org WEB www.edsd.org

Previous Bishops—
Robert M Wolterstorff 1974-82, C
Brinkley Morton 1982-92, Gethin
B Hughes 1992-2005, James R.
Mathes 2005-17

Bishop—The Rt Rev Dr Susan Brown Snook (Dio June 2019)

Assisting Bishops—Rt Rev John B Chane, Rt Rev Sanford Z Hampton, Rt Rev James R Mathes

Cn to Ord G Lynch; *Ecum Off* R Dinovo; *Sec* G Lynch; *Treas* J Martinhauk; *Reg* A Terry; *Archivist/ Historiographer* J Will; *Chanc* D Bagley

Standing Comm—Cler: Pres C Mathewson P Bridges P Carmona J Schenone; *Lay:* D Peralta J Brown J Jow P Carson

PARISHES, MISSIONS, AND CLERGY

Alpine Church of Christ the King **P** (64) 1460 Midway Dr 91901-3714 (Mail to: 1460 Midway Dr 91901-3714) (619) 445-3419

Bonita Epis Ch of the Good Shepherd **P** (115) 3990 Bonita Rd 91902-1260 (Mail to: 3990 Bonita Rd 91902-1260) George Calvert (619) 479-8391

Borrego Spgs St Barnabas Episcopal Church **P** (111) 2680 Country Club Rd 92004 (Mail to: PO Box 691 92004-0691) (760) 767-4038

Carlsbad Holy Cross Episcopal Church **M** (78) 2510 Gateway Rd 92009-1727 (Mail to: 2647 Gateway Rd Ste 105 290 92009-1757) (760) 930-1270

Carlsbad Ch of St Michaels-by-the-Sea **P** (337) 2775 Carlsbad Blvd 92008-2210 (Mail to: 2775 Carlsbad Blvd 92008-2210) Doran Stambaugh Doran Stambaugh (760) 729-8901

Chula Vista St Johns Epis Ch **P** (212) § 760 First Ave 91910-6012 (Mail to: 760 1st Ave 91910-6012) Roger Haenke (619) 422-4141

Coronado Christ Episcopal Church **P** (581) § 1114 Ninth St 92118 (Mail to: 1114 9th St 92118-2602) Regan Schutz (619) 435-4561

Del Mar St Peters Episcopal Church **P** (960) 334 14th St 92014-2519 (Mail to: PO Box 336 92014-0336) Paige Blair-Hubert Gary Gruberth (858) 755-1616

El Cajon St Albans Episcopal Church **P** (243) 490 Farragut Cir 92020-5203 (Mail to: 490 Farragut Cir 92020-5203) David Madsen (619) 444-8212

El Centro Sts Peter & Paul Episcopal Ch **P** (37) 500 S 5th St 92243-3333 (Mail to: PO Box 3446 92244-3446) (760) 352-6531

Encinitas St Andrew-the-Apostle Church **P** (699) 890 Balour Dr 92024-3943 (Mail to: 890 Balour Dr 92024-3943) Brenda Sol (760) 753-3017

Escondido Trinity Episcopal Church **P** (273) 845 Chestnut St 92025-5257 (Mail to: 845 Chestnut St 92025-5257) Carolyn Richardson (760) 743-1629

Fallbrook St Johns Episcopal Church **P** (103) § 434 Iowa St 92028-2109 (Mail to: 434 Iowa St 92028-2109) Leland Jones (760) 728-2908

Hemet The Ch of the Good Shepherd **P** (133) § 308 E Acacia Ave 92543-4228 (Mail to: 308 E Acacia Ave 92543-4228) Susan Latimer (951) 929-1152

Idyllwild St Hugh of Lincoln Epis Church **M** (92) § 25525 Tahquitz Rd 92549 (Mail to: PO Box 506 92549-0506) (951) 659-4471

Indio St Johns Episcopal Church **P** (104) 45319 Deglet Noor St 92201-4315 (Mail to: 45319 Deglet Noor St 92201-4315) Brian Johnson (760) 347-3265

La Jolla St James by-the-Sea Epis Ch **P** (1062) 743 Prospect St 92037-4229 (Mail to: 743 Prospect St 92037-4290) Darlyn Dinovo Mark Hargreaves Steven Strane (858) 459-3421

La Mesa Saint Andrew's Church **P** (163) 4816 Glen St 91941-5498 (Mail to: 4816 Glen S 91941-5498) Robert Blessing (619) 460-7272

Lake Elsinore St Andrews by the Lake Epis Ch **M** (69) 111 S. Kellogg St 92530-3538 (Mail to 111 S. Kellogg Street 92530) Kenneth Simon (951) 674-4087

Lemon Grove Ch of St Philip the Apostle **P** (452) § 2660 Hardy Dr 91945-2936 (Mail to: 2660 Hardy Dr 91945-2936) Carlos Garcia-Tuira (619) 466-8055

National City St Matthews Episcopal Church **P** (267) § 521 E 8th St 91950-2343 (Mail to: 521 E 8th St 91950-2398) Roberto Maldonado Mercado (619) 474-8916

Palm Desert St Margarets Episcopal Church **P** (505) § 47535 Highway 74 92260-5946 (Mail to: 47-535 Highway 74 92260-5946) Andrew Butler Kathleen Dale Patricia Horkey Clark Trafton Richard Wilmington (760) 346-2697

Palm Springs St Paul in the Desert **P** (373) § 125 W El Alameda 92262-5662 (Mail to: 125 W El Alameda 92262-5662) (760) 320-7488

Pauma Valley St Francis Episcopal Church **P** (123) § 16608 State Highway 76 92061 (Mail to: PO Box 1220 92061-1220) (760) 742-1738

Poway St Bartholomews Episcopal Ch **P** (1789) § 16275 Pomerado Rd 92064-1826 (Mail to: 16275 Pomerado Rd 92064-1826) William Doggett William Zettinger (858) 487-2159

Ramona St Marys in the Valley Church **M** (84) § 1010 12th St 92065-2848 (Mail to: PO Box 491 92065-0491) Hannah Wilder (760) 789-0890

San Diego All Saints Church **P** (187) § 625 Pennsylvania Ave 92103-4321 (Mail to: 625 Pennsylvania Ave 92103-4393) Victor Krulak Anthony Noble (619) 298-7729

San Diego All Souls' Episcopal Church **P** (377) 1475 Catalina Blvd 92107-3763 (Mail to: Attn: Finance Office 1475 Catalina Blvd 92107-3798) William Garrison (619) 223-6394

✠ **San Diego** Cathedral Church of St Paul **O** (749) 2728 6th Ave 92103-6301 (Mail to: 2728 6th Ave 92103-6301) Penelope Bridges Richard Hogue Brooks Mason (619) 298-7261

San Diego Good Samaritan Epis Church **P** (354) § 4321 Eastgate Mall 92121-2102 (Mail to: 4321 Eastgate Mall 92121-2102) Janine Schenone (858) 458-1501

San Diego St Andrews by the Sea Church **P** (210) § 1050 Thomas Ave 92109-4161 (Mail to: 1050 Thomas Ave 92109-4194) Mary Coulson (858) 273-3022

San Diego St Davids Episcopal Church **P** (176) § 5050 Milton St 92110-1250 (Mail to: 5050 Milton St 92110-1299) Susan Astarita (619) 276-4567

San Diego St Dunstans Episcopal Church **P** (475) 6556 Park Ridge Blvd 92120-3236 (Mail to: 6556 Park Ridge Blvd 92120-3297) Henry Mann (619) 460-6442

San Diego St Lukes Episcopal Church **P** (360) 3725 30th St 92104-3607 (Mail to: 3725 30th St 92104-3697) Colin Mathewson Laurel Mathewson (619) 298-2130

San Diego St Marks Episcopal Church **P** (132) § 4227 Fairmount Ave 92105-1243 (Mail to: PO Box 5788 92165-5788) Richard Lee Hannah Wilder (619) 283-6242

San Diego St Timothy's Episcopal Church **P** (162) § 10125 Azuaga St 92129-4000 (Mail to: 10125 Azuaga St 92129-4000) Judith Allison Edward Busch (858) 538-1267

San Marcos Grace Episcopal Church **M** (137) § 1020 Rose Ranch Rd 92069-1161 (Mail to: 1020 Rose Ranch Rd 92069-1161) William Lieber (760) 744-7667

Santee St Columbas Episcopal Church **M** (18) § 9720 Cuyamaca St 92071-2626 (Mail to: 9720 Cuyamaca St 92071-2626) (619) 857-6749

Temecula St Thomas of Cntbry Epis Ch **M** (267) § 44651 Avenida De Missiones 92592-3098 (Mail to: 44651 Avenida De Missiones 92592-3098) Carole Horton-Howe (951) 302-4566

Vista All Saints Episcopal Church **P** (47) § 651 Eucalyptus Ave 92084-6241 (Mail to: 651 Eucalyptus Ave 92084-6298) Kirby Smith (760) 726-4280

Yuma St Pauls Episcopal Church **P** (238) 1550 S 14th Ave 85364-4414 (Mail to: 1550 S 14th Ave 85364-4498) Robert Lewis (928) 782-5155

DIOCESE OF SAN JOAQUIN
(PROVINCE VIII)
Comprises the central third of California
DIOCESAN OFFICE 4147 E Dakota Ave Fresno CA 93726
TEL (209) 576-0104
E-MAIL dioadmin@diosanjoaquin.org   WEB www.diosanjoaquin.org

Previous Bishops— Louis C Sanford 1911-42, Sumner FD Walters 1944-68, Victor M Rivera 1968-88, John-David Schofield 1989-2008, Jerry A Lamb 2008-11, Chester L Talton (2011-14)

Bishop—Rt Rev. David C. Rice (2014)

Cn to Ord Rev Dr AR Carmichael; *Chanc* MO Glass 1101 Fifth Avenue Suite 100 San Rafael CA 94901; *Treas* C Peck; *Dio Admin* N Pardo; *Comm* N Pardo

Stand Comm—Cler: Pres S Ward C Woodall S Colley-Toothaker; *Lay: Sec* L Toia J Brock J Partridge L Masztal

Dio Coun—Cler: Sec M Muncey T March C Kline; *Lay:* S Carlson J Fennacy C List S Van Mater J Dunlap S Gilmer

Comm on Min: Chair Rev L Rodriguez N Fitzgerald W Patterson Rev C Kline Rev G Masztal M Crider B Shoemaker Dcn L Jacoby Rev B Woods

PARISHES, MISSIONS, AND CLERGY

Avery St Clare of Assisi **M** (25) 4351 Highway 4 95224 (Mail to: PO Box 278 95224-0278) Michael Backlund (209) 795-5970

Bakersfield St Paul's Episcopal Church **P** (146) 2216 17th St 93301-3605 (Mail to: 2216 17th St 93301-3605) Vernon Hill Luis Rodriguez (661) 869-1630

Hanford Church of the Saviour Parish **P** (63) 519 N Douty St 93230-3910 (Mail to: 519 N Douty St 93230-3910) (559) 584-7706

Kernville St Sherrian Episcopal Church **M** (16) Meets At 251 Big Blue Road 93238 (Mail to: 50 Tobias St 93238) Robert Woods (760) 376-2455

Lodi Church of St John The Baptist **P** (333) 1055 S Lower Sacramento Rd 95242 (Mail to: 1055 S Lower Sacramento Rd 95242-9339) (209) 369-3381

Madera Holy Trinity Episcopal Church **M** (23) 500 Sunset Ave 93637-3012 (Mail to: PO Box 517 93639-0517) (559) 975-9037

Merced Church of the Resurrection **M** (11) 1455 E Yosemite Ave 95340-9322 (Mail to: 1455 E Yosemite Ave 95340-9322) (209) 761-8180

Modesto St Pauls Episcopal Church **P** (295) § 1528 Oakdale Rd 95355-3306 (Mail to: Attn: Allison 1528 Oakdale Rd 95355-3306) (209) 522-3267

Oakhurst St Raphael Episcopal Church **M** (23) PO Box 13 93644 (Mail to: PO Box 13 93644-0013) (559) 683-4023

Ridgecrest St Michaels Episcopal Church **P** (30) 200 Drummond Ave 93555-3119 (Mail to: 200 Drummond Ave 93555-3119) Jorge Pallares Arellano (760) 446-5816

San Andreas St Matthew's Church **P** (56) 414 Oak Street 95249-9612 (Mail to: PO Box 520 95249-0520) (209) 754-3878

Sonora St James Episcopal Church **P** (81) 42 Snell St 95370-5600 (Mail to: 42 Snell St 95370-5600) (209) 532-1580

Stockton Church of St Anne **P** (170) 1020 W Lincoln Rd 95207-2516 (Mail to: 1020 W Lincoln Rd 95207-2516) Lynette Morlan Justo Andres Rebecca Blair Carolyn Woodall (209) 473-2313

Taft St Andrews Mission **M** (7) 703 5th St 93268-2407 (Mail to: 703 5th St 93268-2407) Heather Mueller (661) 765-2378

Tulare St Johns Episcopal Church **P** (49) § 1701 E Prosperity Ave 93274-2345 (Mail to: 1701 E Prosperity Ave 93274-2345) (559) 631-3663

Turlock St Francis Episcopal Church **M** (73) 915 East Main Street 95380 (Mail to: 915 E Main St 95380-3404) Kathryn Galicia (209) 324-1677

Visalia St Pauls Episcopal Church **P** (78) 120 N Hall St 93291-5833 (Mail to: 120 N Hall St 93291-5833) Suzanne Ward (559) 6278265

STATE OF SOUTH CAROLINA

Dioceses of Upper South Carolina and The Episcopal Church in South Carolina

---

DIOCESE OF SOUTH CAROLINA

(PROVINCE IV)
Comprising churches in Southern and Eastern South Carolina
DIOCESAN OFFICE: 98 Wentworth St Charleston SC 29401 (MAIL: Box 20485 Charleston SC 29413)
TEL: (843) 259-2016　E-MAIL: info@episcopalchurchsc.org
WEB: www.episcopalchurchsc.org

Previous Bishops—
Gladstone B Adams prov 2016-19

Bishop—The Rt Rev Ruth M Woodliff-Stanley (1137) (Dio 2 Oct 2021)

Chancellor T S Tisdale; *Comm* M Hamilton; *Min Dev* A McKellar; *Cn to Ord* P Linder

*Stand Comm: Cler—*J Richardson T Wilson R Donehue J Olbrych B Watson A Shoemaker; *Lay—*A Davidow T Skardon M Dianish C Wingard G Decosta T Miller

Diocesan Council—Cler: W Keith F Thompson D Trogdon C Jenkins P Farhner L Rezac; *Lay:* G King J Bullock E Phillips J Chewning C Sparks J Rutter

Trustees—Lay: B Beak B Mann D Billings *Cler:* D McPhail M Brinkmann

Comm on Ministry—Cler: C Davis-Shoemaker W Keith R Lindsey C Walpole D Sanderson; *Lay:* C Hayes A Webb JH Lewis

PARISHES, MISSIONS, AND CLERGY

Allendale Church of Holy Communion **M** (23) 401 Main St N 29810-3717 (Mail to: PO Box 202 29810-0202) (803) 812-9912

Charleston Calvary Episcopal Church **P** (170) 106 Line St 29403-5305 (Mail to: 106 Line St 29403-5305) Ann Broomell (843) 723-3878

Charleston Church of the Holy Communion **P** (554) 218 Ashley Ave 29403-5245 (Mail to: 218

Ashley Ave 29403-5245) Jeffrey Richardson Michael Smith (843) 722-2024

Charleston The Ch of the Good Shepherd **P** 1393 Miles Dr 29407-5163 (Mail to: 1393 Miles Dr 29407-5163) (843) 571-2993

Charleston Grace Church Cathedral **P** (3251) § 98 Wentworth St 29401-1424 (Mail to: 98 Wentworth St 29401-1473) Jonathan Wright Robertson Donehue Lynwood Magee (843) 723-4575

Charleston Holy Trinity Episcopal Church **M** 95 Folly Road Blvd 29407-7532 (Mail to: 95 Folly Road Blvd 29407-7532) (843) 556-2560

Charleston St James Episcopal Church **M** 1872 Camp Rd 29412-3540 (Mail to: 1872 Camp Rd 29412-3540) (843) 795-1623

Charleston St Marks Episcopal Church **P** (95) 18 Thomas St 29403-6839 (Mail to: 16 Thomas St 29403-6024) Fred Thompson Fred Thompson (843) 722-0267

Charleston St. Stephen's Episcopal Church **P** (318) 67 Anson St 29401-1529 (Mail to: 67 Anson St 29401-1529) Adam Shoemaker Courtney Davis-Shoemaker Laura Rezac Gregory Smith Gregory Smith (843) 723-8818

Charleston St Francis Episcopal Church **M** (64) Stuhrs Chapel 3360 Glenn Mcconnell Pkwy 29414-5759 (Mail to: 2245 Ashley Crossing Dr Unit C Pmb 174 29414-5704) James Shaffer Gregory Smith (843) 442-2692

Cheraw St Davids Church **M** 420 Market St 29520-2637 (Mail to: PO Box 926 29520-0926) (843) 537-3832

Conway St Anne's Episcopal Church **P** (130) Lackey Chapel 105 University Dr 29526-8832 (Mail to: PO Box 752 29528-0752) (843) 246-1247

Denmark Christ Episcopal Church **M** (23) 5266 Carolina Hwy 29042-1684 (Mail to: PO Box 237 29042-0237) (803) 793-4837

Denmark St Phil Epi Ch Voorhees Colg **M** (20) 386 Porter Dr 29042 (Mail to: Attn: Accounts Payable PO Box 678 29042-0678) (803) 780-1264

Edisto Island Episcopal Church on Edisto **P** (80) 1650 Hwy 174 29438 (Mail to: PO Box 239 29438-0239) Robert Blackwell William Coyne (843) 869-3568

Estill Church of the Heavenly Rest **M** (7) 152 Corley Rd 29918-0152 (Mail to: PO Box 1190 29918-1190) (843) 524-1644

Florence St Catherine's Episcopal Ch **M** (65) 3123 W Palmetto St 29501-5937 (Mail to: C/O Earl Phillips 4205 Byrnes Blvd 29506-8335) Eunice Dunlap (843) 259-2016

Hampton All Saints Episcopal Church **M** (18) § 511 Jackson Ave E 29924-3605 (Mail to: Attn: Mr Wes Shore 511 Jackson Ave E 29924-3605) (803) 943-2300

Hartsville St Bartholomews Episcopal Ch **M** 103 Campus Dr 29550-3874 (Mail to: 103 Campus

Dr 29550-3874) (843) 332-8765

Hilton Head Island All Saints Episcopal Church **P** (350) § 3001 Meeting St 29926-1673 (Mail to: 3001 Meeting St 29926-1673) Denise Trogdon Pamela Fahrner Pamela Fahrner George Moyser (843) 6818333

Johns Island St Johns Episcopal Church **P** 3673 Maybank Hwy 29455-4825 (Mail to: St Johns Episcopal Church 3673 Maybank Hwy 29455-4825) (843) 559-9560

Kingstree St Albans Church **M** (16) 305 Hampton Ave 29556-3417 (Mail to: PO Box 866 29556-0866) (843) 355-7575

Mc Clellanville St James Santee **M** (127) 144 Oak St 29458-9746 (Mail to: PO Box 123 29458-0123) (843) 887-4386

Mount Pleasant The East Cooper Epis Church **M** (32) 1494 Mathis Ferry Rd 29464-9727 (Mail to: PO Box 511 29465-0511) Laura Cantrell (883) 873-1941

Mt Pleasant Christ Episcopal Church **M** § 2304 N Highway 17 29466-9172 (Mail to: 2304 N Highway 17 29466-9172) (843) 884-9090

Myrtle Beach Epis Church of the Messiah **M** (62) 4221 N Kings Hwy 29577-2722 (Mail to: PO Box 70367 29572-0025) Randolph Ferebee (843) 999-0888

N Charleston St Thomas Episcopal Church **P** (275) 1150 E Montague Ave 29405-4719 (Mail to: 1150 E Montague Ave 29405-4719) Matthew Mccormick Charles Jett (843) 747-0479

N Myrtle Bch St Stephens Episcopal Church **P** (247) 801 11th Ave N 29582-2644 (Mail to: 801 11th Ave N 29582-2644) Wilmot Merchant (843) 249-1169

Pawleys Island Holy Cross Faith Mem Epis Ch **P** (582) 88 Baskervill Dr 29585-6191 (Mail to: PO Box 990 29585-0990) William Keith Lee Ragsdale (843) 237-3459

Pinewood St Augustines Episcopal Church **M** (25) 5450 Milford Plantation Rd 29125 (Mail to: Attn: Mr John Spann PO Box 247 29168-0247) (803) 259-2016

Port Royal St Mark's Episcopal Church **P** (393) 1110 Paris Ave Ste A 29935-2322 (Mail to: PO Box 761 29935-0761) Clairoy Tripp (843) 379-1020

Ridgeland The Episcopal Church in Okatie **M** (61) Ste 1 2 231 Hazzard Creek Vlg 29936-8285 (Mail to: 4467 Spring Is 29909-4756) (843) 259-2016

Saint Stephen St Stephens Episcopal Church **M** (44) 245 Mendel St 29479 (Mail to: PO Box 517 29479-0517) (843) 567-3419

St Matthews St Matthews Episcopal Church **M** Off Hwy 601 Fort Motte Rd 29135 (Mail to: PO Box 447 29135-0447) (803) 874-1333

Summerville Epis Ch of the Good Shepherd **M** (126) 119b W Luke Ave 29483-6423 (Mail to: 119b W Luke Ave 29483-6423) Marshall Sanderson (843) 225-7590

Summerville St Georges Episcopal Church **P** (537) 9110 Dorchester Rd 29485-8647 (Mail to: 9110 Dorchester Rd 29485-8647) Hugh Wallace (843) 873-0772

Summerville Church of the Epiphany **M** (55) 212 Central Ave 29483-6004 (Mail to: 807 W 2nd North St 29483-3829) Robert Switz (843) 851-3467

Sumter Church of the Good Shepherd **M** (22) 401 Dingle St 29150-5155 (Mail to: PO Box 1701 29151-1701) (803) 773-8341

DIOCESE OF SOUTH DAKOTA
(PROVINCE VI)
Comprises South Dakota, 2 churches in Nebraska, and 1 church in Minnesota
DIOCESAN OFFICE 408 N Jefferson Ave Pierre SD 57501-2626
TEL (605) 494-2020 FAX (605) 494-2025
E-MAIL office@episcopalchurchsd.org WEB www.episcopalchurchsd.org

Previous Bishops—
Wm H Hare 1873-1909, Fred F Johnson asst 1905 Bp 1910-11, Geo Biller Jr 1912-15, Hugh L Burleson 1916-31, Wm P Remington suffr 1918-22, W Blair Roberts suffr 1922 Bp 1931-53, Conrad H Gesner coadj 1945-54 Bp 1954-69, Lyman C Ogilby coadj 1967-70, Harold S Jones suffr 1970-75, Walter H Jones 1970-83, Craig B Anderson 1984-92, Creighton L Robertson Bp 1994-2009, John T Tarrant 2009-19

Bishop—Rt Rev Dr Jonathan H Folts (Dio 2 Nov 2019)

Admin M Fratzke; *Archdcn* P Sneve; *Treas* E Walker; *Chan* S Sanford 200 E 10th St Ste 200 Sioux Falls SD 57104; *Cn for Mission* vacant; *Cn to Ord* L Stanley; *Cn for Fin and Property* M Honan; *Thunderhead Episcopal Center* L Simmons

Stand Comm—Cler: Pres K Fonder *Sec* M Garwood JD Barnes P White Horse-Carda *Lay:* R Minor R Bowen S Crane C Cloud Eagle

Dio Counc: S Altamirano D Hanson R Thompson Jr W Simpson A Henninger B Klein W Hawk T TwoBulls D Stands

Departments: COM: C O'Hara; *Theol Edu:* vacant; *Chm Niobrara Council:* R Zephier

PARISHES, MISSIONS, AND CLERGY

Aberdeen St Marks Episcopal Church **P** (66) 1410 N Kline St 57401-2103 (Mail to: 1410 N Kline St 57401-2103) (605) 225-0474

Batesland St Michaels Episcopal Church **M** (141) Hwy 18 57716 (Mail to: 408 N Jefferson Ave 57501-2626) (605) 494-2020

Bear Creek St James Church **M** 5 Miles North of Hwy 212 57636 (Mail to: PO Box 80 57625-0080) (605) 494-2020

Belle Fourche St James Episcopal Church **P** (49) 806 6th Ave 57717-1707 (Mail to: PO Box 414 57717-0414) (605) 892-2446

Blackfoot Church of the Ascension **M** Blackfoot 57601 (Mail to: PO Box 80 57625-0080) (605) 200-0899

Brookings St Pauls Episcopal Church **P** (114) 725 5th St 57006-2102 (Mail to: 726 6th St 57006-2108) (605) 692-2617

Browns Valley St Johns Church **M** (73) Browns Valley 56219 (Mail to: 716 7th Ave W 57262-1248) (605) 494-2020

Bullhead St John the Baptist **PS** (12) Bullhead Rd 57621 (Mail to: PO Box 80 57273-0080) (605) 404-2020

Chamberlain Christ Episcopal Church **M** (30) 207 S Main St 57325-1420 (Mail to: PO Box 221 57325-0221) (605) 234-6327

Cherry Creek St Andrews Station **M** Cherry Creek 57623 (Mail to: PO Box 80 57625-0080) (605) 494-2020

Deadwood St Johns Episcopal Church **P** (70) 401 Williams St 57732-1113 (Mail to: PO Box 130 57732-0130) (605) 920-8818

Dupree St Philips Church **M** Main St & Hwy 212 57623 (Mail to: PO Box 80 57625-0080) (605) 200-0899

Eagle Butte Cheyenne River Epis Mission **Cluster** Eagle Butte 57625 (Mail to: PO Box 812 57625-0812) (605) 964-7283

Eagle Butte St John the Evangelist **M** (100) North Main St 57625-0080 (Mail to: PO Box 80 57625-0080) (605) 494-2020

Firesteel Church of the Holy Spirit **M** (99) State Rte 20 57633 (Mail to: PO Box 80 57658-0080) (605) 494-2020

Flandreau St Mary & Our Blessed Redeemer **M** (48) 223 E 2nd Ave 57028-1224 (Mail to: 408 N Jefferson Ave 57501-2626) (605) 494-2020

Fort George Holy Name Church **M** (25) Iron Nation St 57548 (Mail to: C/O The Rev Craig West 209 S Main St 57325-1420) (605) 730-0626

Fort Pierre St Peters Episcopal Church **M** (37) 713 S 1st St 57532-2074 (Mail to: PO Box 391 57532-0391) (605) 670-7195

Fort Thompson Christ Episcopal Church **M** (89) Ft Thompson 57339 (Mail to: 405 N Madison

Ave 57501-2630) (605) 494-2020

Herrick All Saints Episcopal Church **M** (22) 352 Avenue 57538 (Mail to: 105 E 12th Street 57533) (605) 494-2020

Hot Springs St Lukes Episcopal Church **M** (54) Hammond Ave & Minnekah 57747 (Mail to: PO Box 716 57747-0716) (605) 494-2020

Huron Grace Episcopal Church **P** (54) 1617 McClellan Dr 57350-1361 (Mail to: PO Box 1361 57350-1361) Jean Mornard (605) 352-3096

Ideal Church of the Holy Spirit **M** (91) Rural Tripp Co Gravel Rd 57541 (Mail to: 105 E 12th St 57533-1140) (605) 494-2020

Iron Lightning St Lukes Church **SC** Iron Lightning 57623 (Mail to: PO Box 80 57625-0080) (605) 200-0899

Kyle Church of the Mediator **M** (445) Kyle Village Rd 57752 (Mail to: 408 N Jefferson Ave 57501-2626) (605) 494-2020

Lake Andes Saint Philip the Deacon Church **M** (18) 29273 383rd Ave 57356 (Mail to: 126 Park St NE 57380) (605) 494-2020

Lead Christ Episcopal Church **P** (65) 631 W Main St 57754-1532 (Mail to: PO Box 675 57754-0675) (605) 584-3607

Little Eagle St Pauls Episcopal Church **M** (46) Little Eagle 57639 (Mail to: PO Box 80 57658-0080) (605) 494-2020

Little Oak Creek Church of the Good Shepherd **M** (86) Little Oak Creek 57639 (Mail to: PO Box 80 57658-0080) (605) 494-2020

Lower Brule Holy Comforter Episcopal Ch **M** (457) 412 Spotted Tail Lane 57548 (Mail to: 405 N Madison Ave 57501-2630) (605) 494-2020

Lower Brule Messiah Episcopal Church **P** (33) Iron Nation 57548 (Mail to: PO Box 227 57548-0227)

Madison Grace Episcopal Church **M** (17) 306 NW 3rd St 57042-2115 (Mail to: 804 Best Point Dr 57042-9001) (605) 256-2325

Martin St Katharines Episcopal Church **M** (201) 4th Avenue & School Street 57551-0207 (Mail to: PO Box 207 57551-0207) (605) 685-6173

McLaughlin St Peters Episcopal Church **M** (101) 307 3rd Ave W 57642 (Mail to: PO Box 80 57273-0080) (605) 404-2020

Milbank Christ Episcopal Church **M** (43) 203 N 4th St 57252 (Mail to: 10108th Ave NE 57201) (605) 494-2020

Mission St Philip and St James Station **M** (37) PO Box 256 57579 (Mail to: PO Box 256 575550256) (605) 828-3892

Mission Rosebud Episcopal Mission **Cluster** Bishop Hare Rd 57555 (Mail to: PO Box 257 57570-0257) (605) 828-3892

Mission Trinity Episcopal Church **M** (265) 180 Main Street 57601 (Mail to: PO Box 188 57555-0188) (605) 494-2020

Mitchell St Marys Episcopal Church **P** (78) 214 W 3rd Ave 57301-2547 (Mail to: PO Box 866 57301-0866) (605) 996-3025

Mobridge St James Episcopal Church **P** (34) 802 N Main St 57601-2134 (Mail to: PO Box 80 57273-0080) (605) 494-2020

Niobrara Church of the Blessed Redeemer **M** (40) 535 Ave Howe Creek 68760 (Mail to: 126 N Park St NE 57380-9407) (605) 494-2020

Norris Tiwahe ed wacekiyapi **M** S Main St 57560 (Mail to: PO Box 188 57555-0188) (605) 494-2020

Oglala St Johns Episcopal Church **M** Pine Ridge Mission 57764 (Mail to: PO Box 207 57551-0207) (650) 867-1502

Okreek Calvary Episcopal Church **M** (28) Highway 18 57563 (Mail to: 105 E. 12th Street 57533) (605) 494-2020

On The Tree St Thomas Station **PS** Green Grass-Whitehorse Rd Rural Dewey County 57265 (Mail to: PO Box 80 57625-0080) (605) 200-0899

Parmelee Holy Innocents Episcopal Ch **M** (186) 7 1st St 57566 (Mail to: PO Box 80 57555-0080) (605) 494-2020

Peever St Marys, Old Agency Episcopal Church **M** (94) 12889 Whipple Rd 57257-7628 (Mail to: 716 7th Ave W 57262-1248) (605) 494-2020

Pierre Trinity Episcopal Church **P** (155) 408 N Jefferson Ave 57501-2626 (Mail to: 408 N Jefferson Ave 57501-2626) Mercy Hobbs Judith Flagstad (605) 224-5237

Pine Ridge Church of the Advent **PS** (102) Calico 57770 (Mail to: 408 N Jefferson Ave 57501-2626) (605) 494-2020

Pine Ridge Holy Cross Episcopal Church **M** (92) Highway 407 57770 (Mail to: 408 N Jefferson Ave 57501-2626) (605) 494-2020

Pine Ridge Pine Ridge Episcopal Mission **Cluster** Pine Ridge Reservation 57770 (Mail to: Box J 57770) (605) 685-6173

Porcupine St Julias Episcopal Church **PS** (53) 92 Main St 57772 (Mail to: 408 N Jefferson Ave 57501-2626) (605) 494-2020

Promise St Marys Episcopal Church **M** Whitehorse-Promise Rd 57625 (Mail to: PO Box 80 57625-0080) (605) 200-0899

Pukwana St John the Baptist Epis Ch **M** (62) Crow Creek Reservation 57370 (Mail to: 405 N Madison Ave 57501) (605) 494-2020

Rapid City Emmanuel Episcopal Parish **P** (300) 717 Quincy St 57701-3631 (Mail to: 717 Quincy St 57701-3631) John Barnes (605) 342-0909

Rapid City St Andrew's Episcopal Church **P** (132) 910 Soo San Dr 57702-8115 (Mail to: 910 Soo San Dr 57702-8115) Martha Garwood (605) 343-4210

Rapid City St Matthews Episcopal Church **M** (465) 620 N Haines Ave 57701 (Mail to: PO Box 1606 57709-1606) (605) 342-6199

Red Scaffold St Stephens Station **SC** Red Scaffold 57626 (Mail to: PO Box 80 57625-0080) (605) 200-0899

Red Shirt Table Christ Episcopal Church **SC** (221) RR 57701 (Mail to: PO Box 168 57744-0168) (605) 255-4914

Reliance St Albans Episcopal Church **P** (25) 23792 340th Ave 57569-5622 (Mail to: 405 N Madison Ave 57501-2630) (605) 494-2020

Rosebud Church of Jesus **M** (140) Rosebud Mission 57570 (Mail to: C/O Frank Gangone PO Box 897 57555-0897) (605) 828-3892

Santee Ch of Our Most Merciful Savior **M** (214) 65 Santee Rt. 22 68760 (Mail to: 126 N Park St NE 57380-9407) (605) 494-2020

✤ **Sioux Falls** Calvary Cathedral **O** (880) 500 S Main Ave 57104-6814 (Mail to: 500 S Main Ave 57104-6814) Ward Simpson (605) 336-3486

Sioux Falls Church of the Good Shepherd **P** (101) 2707 W 33rd St 57105-4302 (Mail to: 2707 W 33rd St 57105-4302) Christina O'Hara (605) 332-1474

Sioux Falls Church of the Holy Apostles **M** (188) 1415 S Bahnson Ave 57103-3443 (Mail to: 408 N Jefferson Ave 57501-2626) (605) 494-2020

Sisseton Gethsemane Episcopal Church **M** (36) Sisseton 57262 (Mail to: 7 5th Ave E 57262-2014) (605) 494-2020

Soldier Creek Grace Station **PS** (43) Soldier Creek Rd 57570 (Mail to: Bishop Hare Rd 57566) (605) 494-2020

Spearfish Church of All Angels **P** (183) 1044 N 5th St 57783-2009 (Mail to: 1044 N 5th St 57783-2009) John Riley (605) 642-4349

Sturgis St Thomas Episcopal Church **P** (30) 1222 Junction Ave 57785-1937 (Mail to: 1222 Junction Ave 57785-1937) (605) 347-5683

Thunder Butte St Peters Church **M** Thunder Butte Rd 57623 (Mail to: PO Box 80 57625-0456) (605) 964-6180

Vermillion St Pauls Episcopal Church **M** (64) 10 Linden Ave 57069-3203 (Mail to: 10 Linden Ave 57069-3203) (605) 659-5997

Wagner Church of the Holy Spirit **M** (90) 613 S Main St 57380 (Mail to: PO Box 686 57380-0686) (605) 494-2020

Wakpala St Elizabeths Episcopal Church **M** (137) Standing Rock Mission 57658 (Mail to: PO Box 80 57658-0080) (605) 494-2020

Wanblee Gethsemane Episcopal Church **M** (36) 6th Main St 57577 (Mail to: 408 N Jefferson Ave 57501-2626) (605) 494-2020

Watertown Trinity Episcopal Church **P** (43) 202 E Kemp 57201-3642 (Mail to: 612 3rd St NE 57201) (605) 280-4927

Waubay St James Episcopal Church **M** (84) Enemy Swim Lake 57273 (Mail to: 716 7th Ave W 57262-1248) (605) 494-2020

Webster St Marys Episcopal Church **M** (8) 8th Main 57274 (Mail to: 716 7th Ave W 57262-1248) (605) 494-2020

White Horse Emmanuel Episcopal Church **M** White Horse 57661 (Mail to: PO Box 80 57625-0080) (605) 200-0899

Yankton Christ Episcopal Church **P** (145) 513 Douglas Ave 57078-4030 (Mail to: Attn: Richard Unruh 513 Douglas Ave 57078-4030) Michael Newago (605) 665-2456

DIOCESE OF SOUTHEAST FLORIDA
(PROVINCE IV)
Comprises 7 counties in SE Florida
DIOCESAN OFFICE 525 NE 15th St Miami FL 33132
TEL (305) 373-0881 FAX (305) 375-8054
E-MAIL info@diosef.org WEB www.diosef.org

Previous Bishops— James L Duncan suffr 1961-69 Bp 1970-80, Calvin O Schofield Jr Bp 1980-2000, John Said suffr 1995-2002, James Ottley Asst Bp 2002-2006, Leopold Frade 2000-2016, Peter Eaton coadj 2015-16

Bishop—Rt Rev Peter Eaton 1087 (2016)

Cn to Ord Rev Cn L Affer; *Cn Miss for Cong Vita and Tran* Rev Cn J Roberson; *Archdcn for Imm and Soc Just Ven* JF Bazin; *Cn Miss for Hispanic Min* Rev Cn E Lopez; *Archdcn for Cong of African Descent* Ven H Hurley; *Sec* K Neely; *Treas* Cn T Huston; *Chanc* C Johnson ESQ; *Vice Chanc* B Reid; K Grantham; *COO*

C Valdes; *Ex Dir Episc Charities* R Clinton; *ComM co-chairs* Rev L Hague Rev S Groff Ven H Hurley

Deans: N Palm Beach Very Rev A Holder; *South Palm Beach* Very Rev C Olson; *Broward* Very Rev L Davis; *North Dade* Very Rev R Knowles; *South Dade* Very Rev T Fleck; *Keys* Very Rev D Mote; *Trinity Cathedral* vacant

Stand Comm—Cler: Pres W Wright C Titcomb R Fox; *Lay:* A Carty M Smyser P Delvaille

PARISHES, MISSIONS, AND CLERGY

Big Pine Key St Francis in the Keys Church **M** (30) 1600 Key Deer Blvd 33043 (Mail to: PO Box 430645 33043-0645) Christopher Todd Christopher Todd (305) 872-2547

Biscayne Park Santa CruzResurrection Epis Ch P (297) 11173 Griffing Blvd 33161 (Mail to: 11173 Griffing Blvd 33161-7249) Jose Ortez (305) 893-8523

Boca Raton Chapel Of Saint Andrew M (213) 2707 NW 37th St 33434-4497 (Mail to: 3900 Jog Rd, Building 13 33434) Winnie Bolle Faye Somers (561) 210-2700

Boca Raton St Gregorys Episcopal Church P (1101) § 100 NE Mizner Blvd 33432-4008 (Mail to: PO Box 1503 33429-1503) Andrew Sherman (561) 395-8285

Boynton Beach St Cuthberts Episcopal Church M (39) Attn: Mrs Barbara Smith 417 NW 7th Ave 33435-3754 (Mail to: Attn: Mrs Barbara Smith 417 NW 7th Ave 33435-3754) (561) 732-7422

Boynton Beach St Josephs Episcopal Church P (935) § 3300a S Seacrest Blvd 33435-8661 (Mail to: 3300a S Seacrest Blvd 33435-8661) Martin Zlatic Gwendolyn Pinzino (561) 732-3060

Clewiston St Martins Episcopal Church M (95) 207 N W C Owen Ave 33440-3030 (Mail to: 207 N W C Owens Ave 33440-3030) (863) 983-7960

Coral Gables Chapel of the Venerable Bede CC (77) 1150 Stanford Dr 33146-2002 (Mail to: 1150 Stanford Dr 33146-2002) Frank Corbishley (305) 284-2333

Coral Gables St Philips Episcopal Church P (479) 1121 Andalusia Ave 33134-5509 (Mail to: 1121 Andalusia Ave 33134-5509) Mary Conroy (305) 444-6176

Coral Springs Ch of St Magdalene St Martin P (521) § 1400 Riverside Dr 33071-6070 (Mail to: PO Box 771145 33077-1145) Ronald Davis Lorna Goodison (954) 753-1400

Deerfield Beach St Marys Episcopal Church M (126) 417 S Dixie Hwy 33441-4627 (Mail to: 417 S Dixie Hwy 33441-4627) (954) 428-3040

Delray Beach St Matthews Episcopal Church M (99) 404 SW 3rd St 33444-2402 (Mail to: 404 SW 3rd St 33444-2402) Mercedes Busto (561) 272-4143

Delray Beach St Pauls Church P (905) § 188 S Swinton Ave 33444-3656 (Mail to: 188 S Swinton Ave 33444-3698) Paul Kane Bernard Pecaro (561) 276-4541

Fort Lauderdale St Ambrose Episcopal Church M (54) 2250 SW 31st Ave 33312-4398 (Mail to: 2250 SW 31st Ave 33312-4398) Andrew Hudson Rosa Lindahl (954) 584-3372

Fort Lauderdale St Mark the Evangelist Church P (755) 1750 E Oakland Park Blvd 33334-5239 (Mail to: 1750 E Oakland Park Blvd 33334-5299) Grant Wiseman (954) 3340126

Ft Lauderdale All Saints Episcopal Church P (526) 333 Tarpon Dr 33301-2337 (Mail to: 333 Tarpon Dr 33301-2337) Carl Beasley Leslie Hague (954) 467-6496

Ft Lauderdale St Christophers Episcopal Ch M (122) 318 NW 6th Ave 33311-9154 (Mail to: PO Box 228 33302-0228) (954) 306-6148

Ft Lauderdale Episcopal Ch of the Atonement P (515) § 4401 W Oakland Park Blvd 33313-1826 (Mail to: 4401 W Oakland Park Blvd 33313-1826) (954) 731-6100

Ft Lauderdale St Benedicts Episcopal Church P (1294) 7801 NW 5th St 33324-1911 (Mail to: 7801 NW 5th St 33324-1999) Albert Cutie (954) 473-6578

Hallandale Beach St. Anne's Episcopal Church M (35) 705 NW 1st Avenue 33020 (Mail to: PO Box 695 33004-0695) (301) 253-2130

Hallandale Beach St Anne's Episcopal Church M (196) 705 NW 1st Ave 33009-2301 (Mail to: 705 NW 1st Ave 33009-2301) (954) 454-2811

Hobe Sound Christ Memorial Chapel SC 52 S Beach Rd 33455-2225 (Mail to: PO Box 582 33475-0582) Heidi Kinner (772) 546-8329

Hollywood Holy Sacrament Epis Church P (351) § 2801 N University Dr 33024-2547 (Mail to: 2801 N University Dr 33024-2547) William Eaton (954) 432-8686

Hollywood St James in the Hills Church P (154) 3329 Wilson St 33021-4836 (Mail to: 3329 Wilson St 33021-4836) (954) 987-2203

Hollywood St Johns Episcopal Church P (71) § 1704 Buchanan St 33020-4030 (Mail to: 1704 Buchanan St 33020-4030) Harry Walton (954) 921-3721

Homestead St Johns Episcopal Church M (536) § 145 NE 10th St 33030-4633 (Mail to: 145 NE 10th St 33030-4698) (305) 247-5343

Islamorada St James the Fisherman P (256) § 87500 Overseas High 33036 (Mail to: PO Box 509 33036-0509) (305) 852-2161

Jensen Beach All Saints Episcopal Church P (469) 2303 NE Seaview Dr 34957-5533 (Mail to: 2303 NE Seaview Dr 34957) Anthony Holder Alan Gellert (772) 334-0610

Key Biscayne St Christopher's By-the-Sea Church P (171) § 95 Harbor Dr 33149-1411 (Mail to: 95 Harbor Dr 33149-1411) Miguel Baguer Amanda Brady (305) 361-5080

Key West St Pauls Episcopal Church P (387) 401 Duval St 33040-6550 (Mail to: 401 Duval St 33040-6550) Donna Mote (305) 296-5142

Key West St Peters Episcopal Church M (69) 807 Center St 33040-7435 (Mail to: 800 Center St 33040-7435) (305) 296-2346

Lake Worth St Johns Episcopal Church M (25) 810 Washington Ave 33460-5555 (Mail to: 1524 Douglas St 33460-5510) (561) 547-4480

Lake Worth Holy Redeemer Episcopal Church M (112) 3730 Kirk Rd 33461-3431 (Mail to: 3730 Kirk Rd 33461-3431) (561) 965-8632

Lake Worth St Andrews Episcopal Church P (424) 100 N Palmway 33460-3515 (Mail to: 100 N Palmway 33460-3515) Corinna Olson (561) 582-6609

Marathon St Columba Episcopal Church **P** (130) § 451 52nd Street Gulf 33050-2614 (Mail to: PO Box 500426 451 52nd Street Gulf 33050-0426) Debra Andrew-Maconaughey (305) 7436412

Miami All Angels Episcopal Church **M** (107) § 1801 Ludlam Dr 33166-3165 (Mail to: 1801 Ludlam Dr 33166-3165) Ann Kathleen Goraczko Kimberly Knight (305) 885-1780

Miami Christ Church **P** (368) § 3481 Hibiscus St 33133-5717 (Mail to: 3481 Hibiscus St 33133-5717) Jonathan Archer Vivian Hopkins (305) 442-8542

Miami Episcopal Ch of the Ascension **P** (326) § 11201 SW 160th St 33157-2701 (Mail to: 11201 SW 160th St 33157-2701) (305) 238-5151

Miami Holy Comforter Epis Church **P** (697) § 150 SW 13th Ave 33135-2412 (Mail to: 150 SW 13th Ave 33135-2491) Sixto Garcia (305) 643-2711

Miami Epis Church of the Incarnation **P** (322) 1835 NW 54th St 33142-3065 (Mail to: PO Box 420050 33242-0050) Roberta Knowles (305) 633-2446

Miami Church of the Holy Family **P** (426) 18501 NW 7th Ave 33169-4441 (Mail to: 18501 NW 7th Ave 33169-4441) Horace Ward (305) 652-6797

Miami Igles Epis de Todos Los Santos **P** (128) 1023 SW 27th Ave 33135-4614 (Mail to: 1023 SW 27th Ave 33135-4614) Alejandro Hernandez (305) 642-2951

Miami Igles Epis Santisima Trinidad **P** (106) 6744 N Miami Ave 33150-4030 (Mail to: 6744 N Miami Ave Suite 201 33150-4030) Marivel Milien (305) 758-8546

Miami Historic St Agnes Episcopal Ch **P** (469) 1750 NW 3rd Ave 33136-1610 (Mail to: PO Box 12943 33101-2943) Doris Ingraham Denrick Rolle (305) 573-5330

Miami St Andrews Episcopal Church **P** (543) 14260 Old Cutler Rd 33158-1347 (Mail to: 14260 Old Cutler Rd 33158-1347) Spencer Potter George Ronkowitz (305) 238-2161

Miami St Faith Episcopal Church **P** (141) 10600 Caribbean Blvd 33189-1361 (Mail to: 10600 Caribbean Blvd 33189-1361) (305) 235-3621

Miami St Luke the Physician **M** (351) 12355 SW 104th St 33186-3602 (Mail to: 12355 SW 104th St 33186-3602) (305) 279-4265

Miami Ch of St Matthew the Apostle **P** (79) § 7410 Sunset Dr 33143-4130 (Mail to: 7410 Sunset Dr 33143-4130) (305) 665-7333

Miami St Simons Episcopal Church **M** (55) 10950 SW 34th St 33165-3542 (Mail to: 10950 SW 34th St 33165-3542) Carlos Sandoval (305) 221-4753

Miami St Stephens Episcopal Church **P** (538) § 2750 Mcfarlane Rd 33133-6026 (Mail to: 2750 McFarlane Rd 33133-6026) Wilifred Allen-Faiella Jo-Ann Murphy Jo-Ann Murphy (305) 448-2601

Miami St Thomas Episcopal Church **P** (1048) § 5690 SW 88th St 33156-2199 (Mail to: 5690 SW 88th St 33156-2199) Timothy Fleck Harold Walker (305) 661-3436

Miami St Paul et Les Martyrs D'Haiti **M** (204) 6744 N Miami Ave 33150-4030 (Mail to: 6744 N Miami Ave 33150-4000) Marivel Milien Smith Milien (305) 758-8546

✠ **Miami** Trinity Cathedral **O** (1102) 464 NE 16th St 33132-1222 (Mail to: 464 NE 16th St 33132-1222) Richard Benedict Sixto Garcia Elaine Jessup (305) 374-3372

Miami Beach All Souls' Episcopal Church **P** (121) § 4025 Pine Tree Dr 33140-3601 (Mail to: 4025 Pine Tree Dr 33140-3677) Timothy Carr (305) 520-5410

Miami Lakes Church of the Epiphany **M** (81) § 15650 Miami Lakeway N 33014-5517 (Mail to: 15650 Miami Lakeway N 33014-5517) (305) 558-3961

N Miami Beach St Bernard deClairvaux Epis Ch **P** (949) § 16711 W Dixie Hwy 33160-3714 (Mail to: 16711 W Dixie Hwy 33160-3714) Gregory Mansfield (305) 945-1461

Opa Locka Church of the Transfiguration **M** (159) 15260 NW 19th Ave 33054-2960 (Mail to: PO Box 272 33054) Terrence Taylor (305) 681-1660

Opa Locka St Kevins Episcopal Church **M** (125) 3280 NW 135th St 33054-4812 (Mail to: PO Box 540668 33054-0668) Simeon Newbold Simeon Newbold (305) 688-8517

Palm Beach Epis Ch of Bethesda-by-the-Sea **P** (1608) 141 S County Rd 33480 (Mail to: 141 S County Rd 33480-1057) Timothy Schenck Susan Beebe Elizabeth Geitz Elizabeth Geitz Cecily Titcomb (561) 655-4554

Palm Beach Garden Saint Mark's Church **P** (1576) § 3395 Burns Rd 33410-4322 (Mail to: Attn: Treasurer Accounting Dept 3395 Burns Rd 33410-4322) James Cook Sanford Groff Jean Wright (561) 622-0956

Palm City Church of the Advent **P** (224) 448 SW Citrus Blvd 34990 (Mail to: 4484 SW Citrus Blvd 34990-8760) (772) 283-6221

Pompano Beach St Nicholas Episcopal Church **P** (104) 1111 E Sample Rd 33064-5113 (Mail to: 1111 E Sample Rd 33064-5113) Mark Jones (954) 942-5887

Pompano Beach St Philips Episcopal Church **M** (37) 465 NW 15th St 33060-5416 (Mail to: 465 NW 15th St 33060-5416) (954) 785-2437

Riviera Beach St Georges Episcopal Church **P** (16) 21 W 22nd St 33404-5509 (Mail to: PO Box 10584 33419-0584) (561) 844-7713

Stuart St Lukes Episcopal Church **P** (450) 515 SE Railway Ave 34997-3305 (Mail to: PO Box 117 34992-0117) Paul Hartt (772) 286-5455

Stuart St Marys Episcopal Church **P** (1628) 623 South East Ocean Blvd 34994-2329 (Mail to: 623 SE Ocean Blvd 34994-2376) Christia Anderson Patricia Mcgregor (772) 287-3244

Stuart St Monicas Episcopal Church **M** (64) PO Box 1798 34995-1798 (Mail to: PO Box 1798 33494) (772) 221-0552

Tequesta Church of the Good Shepherd **P** (1476) § 400 Seabrook Rd 33469-2685 (Mail to: 400 Seabrook Rd 33469-2685) (561) 746-4674

West Palm Bch Grace Episcopal Church **P** (647) 3600 N Australian Ave 33407-4513 (Mail to: 3600 N Australian Ave 33407-4599) Winston Wright (561) 845-6060

West Palm Bch Holy Spirit Episcopal Church **P** (247) § 1003 Allendale Rd 33405-1347 (Mail to: 1003 Allendale Rd 33405-1347) (561) 833-7605

West Palm Bch Holy Trinity Episcopal Church **P** (552) § 211 Trinity Pl 33401-6119 (Mail to: 211 Trinity Pl 33401-6119) Rutger-Jan Heijmen Donald Griffin Rutger-Jan Heijmen (561) 655-8650

West Palm Bch St Christophers Episcopal Ch **M** (225) § 1063 N Haverhill Rd 33417-5844 (Mail to: PO Box 222068 33422-2068) (561) 683-8167

West Palm Bch St David in the Pines Epis Ch **P** (363) § 465 W Forest Hill Blvd 33414-4705 (Mail to: 465 W Forest Hill Blvd 33414-4705) William Thomas (561) 793-1976

West Palm Beach Saint Patricks Church **P** (356) § 418 North Sapodilla Avenue 33401-4138 (Mail to: 418 N Sapodilla Ave 33401-4138) (561) 833-1903

DIOCESE OF SOUTHERN OHIO
(PROVINCE V)
Comprises 40 counties of Southern Ohio
DIOCESAN OFFICE 412 Sycamore St Cincinnati OH 45202-4179
TEL (513) 421-0311; (800) 582-1712
WEB www.diosohio.org

Previous Bishops— Thomas A Jaggar 1875-1904, Boyd Vincent coadj 1889 Bp 1904-29, Theodore I Reese coadj 1913 Bp 1929-31, Henry W Hobson coadj 1930 Bp 1931-59, Roger W Blanchard coadj 1958 Bp 1959-70, John M Krumm 1971-80, WG Black coadj 1979 Bp 1980-91, Herbert Thompson Jr coadj 1988 Bp 1992-05, Kenneth Price Jr suffr 1994-2012, Thomas E Breidenthal 2007-20, Kenneth Price Jr asst Bp 2020-21

Bishop Provisional—The Rt. Rev. Wayne Smith

Cn to Ord Rev Cn J Johanssen;; *CFO* C Perme ; *Pres of Trustees* J Boss; *Sec to Conv* J Murray; *Chanc* JJ Dehner 3300 Great American Tower 301 E Fourth St Cincinnati 45202; *Hist* Rev AW Wilson; *Treas* R Krantz

Stand Comm—Cler: E Cook S Gunn D Kendall-Sperry; *Lay:* J Allsop B Fiest E Barker

PARISHES, MISSIONS, AND CLERGY

Amelia Church of the Good Samaritan **M** (30) 25 Amelia-Olive Branch Rd 45102-0889 (Mail to: PO Box 889 45102-0889) (513) 753-4115

Athens Church of the Good Shepherd **P** (170) § 64 University Ter 45701-2913 (Mail to: 64 University Ter 45701-2982) Deborah Woolsey (740) 593-6877

Cambridge St Johns Episcopal Church **M** (25) 1025 Steubenville Ave 43725-2401 (Mail to: PO Box 1044 43725-6044) Robert Howell (740) 432-7508

Chillicothe St Pauls Episcopal Church **P** (92) 33 E Main St 45601-2504 (Mail to: 33 E Main St 45601-2595) Paul Daggett (740) 772-4105

Cincinnati All Saints Episcopal Church **P** (124) 6301 Parkman Pl 45213-1123 (Mail to: 6301 Parkman Pl 45213-1123) Meredith Day (513) 531-6333

Cincinnati Calvary Episcopal Church **P** (323) 3766 Clifton Ave 45220-1238 (Mail to: 3766 Clifton Ave Ste B 45220-1255) Allison English Gary Givler Olivia Hamilton Olivia Hamilton (513) 861-4437

Cincinnati Holy Chd Chapel-Childrens Hosp **PS** 3333 Burnet Ave # 5022 45229-3026 (Mail to: 3333 Burnet Ave MLC 5022 45229) (513) 636-4200

✠ **Cincinnati** Christ Church Cathedral **O** (809) 318 E 4th St 45202-4202 (Mail to: C/O Judy Hering 318 E 4th St 45202-4202) Owen Thompson Brian Blayer Paul Williams (513) 621-1817

Cincinnati Church of Our Saviour **P** (95) 65 E Hollister St 45219-1703 (Mail to: 65 E Hollister St 45219-1796) (513) 241-1870

Cincinnati Church of the Advent **HC** (40) 2366 Kemper Lane 45206-2686 (Mail to: 2366 Kemper Ln 45206-2686) (513) 961-2100

Cincinnati Grace Episcopal Church **M** (54) 5501 Hamilton Ave 45224-3111 (Mail to: 5501 Hamilton Ave 45224-3301) (513) 541-2415

Cincinnati Holy Trinity Episcopal Church **M** (17) 7190 Euclid Ave 45243-2544 (Mail to: 7190 Euclid Ave 45243-2544) (513) 984-8400

Cincinnati Indian Hill Church **P** (247) 6000 Drake Rd 45243-3308 (Mail to: 6000 Drake Rd 45243-3395) Simon Barnes (513) 561-6805

Cincinnati St Andrews Episcopal Church **P** (236) 1809 Rutland Ave 45207-1219 (Mail to: 1809 Rutland Ave 45207-1219) Anne Reed (513) 531-4337

Cincinnati St Barnabas Church **P** (533) 10345 Montgomery Rd 45242-5113 (Mail to: 10345 Montgomery Rd 45242-5113) Elizabeth Gerdsen (513) 984-8401

Cincinnati St James Episcopal Church **P** (160) 3207 Montana Ave 45211-6609 (Mail to: 3207 Montana Ave 45211-6697) Mary Carson (513) 661-1154

Cincinnati St Simon of Cyrene Episcopal **P** (190) 810 Matthews Dr 45215-1837 (Mail to: 810 Matthews Dr 45215-1837) Theorphlis Borden Colenthia Hunter (513) 771-4828

Cincinnati St Timothys Episcopal Church **P** (813) § 8101 Beechmont Ave 45255-3190 (Mail to: 8101 Beechmont Ave 45255-3196) Roger Greene (513) 474-4445

Cincinnati Ascension and Holy Trinity **P** (479) § 334 Burns Ave 45215-4320 (Mail to: 334 Burns Ave 45215) Eric Miller (513) 821-5341

Cincinnati The Church of the Redeemer **P** (1446) 2944 Erie Ave 45208-2404 (Mail to: 2944 Erie Ave 45208-2404) Philip Devaul Melanie Slane (513) 321-6700

Circleville St Philips Episcopal Church **HC** (124) 129 W Mound St 43113-1623 (Mail to: PO Box 484 43113-0484) David Getreu Rowena Macgregor Michael Ralph (740) 474-4525

Columbus St Edwards Church Whitehall **M** (43) 214 Fairway Blvd 43213-2012 (Mail to: 214 Fairway Blvd 43213-2012) Fredric Shirley (614) 861-1777

Columbus St Albans Epis Ch of Bexley **P** (353) 333 S Drexel Ave 43209-2139 (Mail to: 333 S Drexel Ave 43209-2139) James Rodgers Harry Harper John Jupin Meribah Mansfield (614) 253-8549

Columbus St James Episcopal Church **P** (121) § 3400 Calumet St 43214-4106 (Mail to: 3400 Calumet St 43214-4106) Phillip Harris Elise Feyerherm Alan Smith (614) 262-2360

Columbus St Johns Episcopal Church **M** (243) 1003 W Town St 43222-1438 (Mail to: 1003 W Town St 43222-1438) Meribah Mansfield (614) 221-9328

Columbus Saint Mark's Episcopal Church **P** (785) 2151 Dorset Rd 43221-3103 (Mail to: 2151 Dorset Rd 43221-3194) Vicki Zust (614) 486-9452

Columbus St Philip Episcopal Church **P** (148) 166 Woodland Ave 43203-1774 (Mail to: 166 Woodland Ave 43203-1774) Karl Ruttan Brenda Taylor (614) 253-2771

Columbus St Stephen's Epis Ch & Univ **P** (150) 30 W Woodruff Ave 43210-1118 (Mail to: 30

W Woodruff Ave 43210-1118) Karl Stevens Pamela Elwell (614) 294-3749

Columbus Trinity Episcopal Church **P** (257) 125 E Broad St 43215-3605 (Mail to: 125 E Broad St 43215-3605) Stephen Applegate Brian Shaffer (614) 221-5351

Dayton Christ Episcopal Church **P** (371) 20 W 1st St 45402-1269 (Mail to: 20 W First St 45402) Peter Homeyer (937) 815-0236

Dayton St Georges Episcopal Church **P** (583) 5520 Far Hills Ave 45429-2204 (Mail to: 5520 Far Hills Ave 45429-2232) Benjamin Phillips David Cottrill Lewis Lane (937) 434-1781

Dayton St Margarets Episcopal Church **P** (205) 3010 Mccall St 45417-2034 (Mail to: 5301 Free Pike 45426-2441) Benjamin Speare-Hardy Jeanette Manning (937) 837-7741

Dayton St Marks Episcopal Church **P** (100) 456 Woodman Dr 45431-2099 (Mail to: 456 Woodman Dr 45431-2099) George Snyder (937) 256-1082

Dayton St Pauls Church Episcopal **P** (379) 33 W Dixon Ave 45419-3431 (Mail to: 33 W Dixon Ave 45419-3431) Daniel Mcclain (937) 293-1154

Delaware St Peters Episcopal Church **P** (205) 45 W Winter St 43015-1934 (Mail to: 45 W Winter St 43015-1934) David Kendall-Sperry (740) 369-3175

Dublin St Patricks Episcopal Church **P** (978) 7121 Muirfield Dr 43017-2863 (Mail to: 7121 Muirfield Dr 43017-2863) Jason Emerson Robert Rideout (614) 766-2664

Fairborn St Christophers Church **P** (104) 1501 N Broad St 45324-5575 (Mail to: PO Box 1026 45324-1026) John Paddock (937) 878-5614

Gallipolis St Peters Episcopal Church **P** (66) 541 2nd Ave 45631-1250 (Mail to: 541 2nd Ave 45631-1250) (740) 446-2483

Glendale Christ Church - Glendale **P** (507) 965 Forest Ave 45246-4405 (Mail to: 965 Forest Ave 45246-4499) David Pfaff Scott Gunn Lori O'Riley Anne Reed (513) 771-1544

Granville St Luke Episcopal Church **P** (385) 107 Broadway E 43023-1303 (Mail to: PO Box 82 43023-0082) Elizabeth Hoster (740) 587-0167

Greenville St Pauls Episcopal Church **P** (60) 201 S Broadway St 45331-1978 (Mail to: 201 South Broadway & Water 45331) David Brower Richard Larsen (937) 548-5575

Hamilton Trinity Church **P** (174) § 115 N 6th St 45011-3541 (Mail to: PO Box 851 45012-0851) Suzanne Levesconte (513) 896-6755

Hillsboro St Marys Episcopal Church **P** (50) § 234 N High St 45133-1129 (Mail to: 234 N High St 45133-1129) (937) 393-2043

Ironton Christ Church **M** (87) 501 Park Ave 45638-1546 (Mail to: PO Box 555 45638-0555) (740) 532-3528

Lancaster St Johns Episcopal Church **P** (291) 134 N Broad St 43130-3701 (Mail to: 134 N Broad St 43130-3701) (740) 653-3052

Lebanon St Patricks Church **P** (213) 232 E Main St 45036-2230 (Mail to: 232 E Main St 45036-2230) Cortney Dale (513) 932-7691

Logan St Pauls Episcopal Church **P** (29) 375 E Main St 43138-1307 (Mail to: PO Box 736 43138-0736) (740) 385-1005

London Christ Chapel **SC** 11235 State Route 38 SE 43140-9716 (Mail to: 11235 State Route 38 SE 43140-9716)

London Trinity Episcopal Church **P** (56) Corner of 4th and Main St 43140-0468 (Mail to: PO Box 468 43140-0468) Frank Edmands George Glazier (740) 852-9298

Marietta St Lukes Episcopal Church **P** (69) § 320 2nd St 45750-2919 (Mail to: 320 2nd St 45750-2919) William Field Dale Sheppard (740) 373-5132

Mc Arthur Trinity Church **M** (6) 202 W High St 45651-1009 (Mail to: 202 W High St 45651-1009) (740) 596-5562

Mechanicsburg Church of Our Saviour **M** (63) § 56 S Main St 43044-1111 (Mail to: 230 Scioto St 43078-2128) (937) 653-3497

Middletown Church of the Ascension **P** (160) § 2709 Mcgee Ave 45044-4836 (Mail to: 2709 Mcgee Ave 45044-4899) Thomas Fehr (513) 424-1254

Nelsonville Church of the Epiphany **M** (32) 193 Jefferson St 45764-1207 (Mail to: 193 Jefferson St 45764-1207) (740) 753-3434

New Albany All Saints Episcopal Church **P** (627) 5101 Johnstown Rd PO Box 421 43054-8964 (Mail to: PO Box 421 43054-0421) Jason Prati (614) 855-8267

Newark Trinity Episcopal Church **P** (82) 76 E Main St 43055-5604 (Mail to: 76 E Main St 43055-5672) (740) 345-5643

Oxford Holy Trinity Episcopal Church **P** (196) 25 E Walnut St 45056-1892 (Mail to: 25 E Walnut St 45056-1892) Julie Fisher (513) 5237559

Pickerington Saint Andrew's Church **P** (221) 8630 Refugee Rd 43147-9509 (Mail to: 8630 Refugee Rd 43147-9509) Seth Wymer (614) 626-2720

Piqua St James Episcopal Church **P** (64) 200 W High St 45356-2218 (Mail to: 200 W High St 45356-2218) (937) 773-1241

Pomeroy Grace Episcopal Church **M** (38) 326 E Main St 45769-1023 (Mail to: 326 E Main St 45769-1023) (740) 992-3968

Portsmouth All Saints' Episcopal Church **P** (145) 610 4th St 45662-3921 (Mail to: 610 4th St 45662-3921) Richard Schisler (740) 353-7919

Springboro St Francis Episcopal Church **P** (84) 225 N Main St 45066-9255 (Mail to: 225 N Main St 45066-9255) (937) 748-2592

Springfield Christ Epis Ch Of Springfield **P** (382) 409 E High St 45505-1007 (Mail to: 409 E High St 45505-1007) (937) 323-8651

Terrace Park St Thomas Episcopal Church **P** (1559) § 100 Miami Ave 45174-1175 (Mail to: 100 Miami Ave 45174-1175) Darren Elin Daniel Grossoehme Noel Julnes-Dehner (513) 831-2052

Troy Trinity Episcopal Church **P** (126) § 60 S Dorset Rd 45373-5616 (Mail to: 60 S Dorset Rd 45373-5616) Joan Smoke (937) 335-7747

Urbana Church of the Epiphany **M** (46) § 230 Scioto St 43078-2128 (Mail to: 230 Scioto St 43078-2128) (937) 653-3497

Waynesville St Marys Episcopal Church **M** (18) 107 S 3rd St 45068-9011 (Mail to: PO Box 653 45068-0653) Pamela Gaylor (513) 897-2435

West Chester St Anne Episcopal Church **P** (524) § 6461 Tylersville Rd 45069-1435 (Mail to: 6461 Tylersville Rd 45069-1435) (513) 779-1139

Westerville St Matthews Episcopal Church **M** (129) § 30 E College Ave 43081-1601 (Mail to: 30 E College Ave 43081-1601) Joseph Kovitch (614) 882-2706

Worthington St Johns Episcopal Church **P** (473) 700 High St 43085-4137 (Mail to: 700 High St 43085-4152) Gianetta Hayes-Martin Alice Herman Denise Mueller Denise Mueller (614) 846-5180

Wshngtn Ct Hs All Saints Lutheran Epis Ch **M** (100) 733 State Route 41 SW 43160-8797 (Mail to: 733 State Route 41 SW 43160-8797) Warren Huestis (740) 335-2129

Xenia Christ Episcopal Church **P** (89) 63 E Church St 45385-3001 (Mail to: 68 E Church St 45385-3002) (937) 372-1594

Zanesville St James Episcopal Church **P** (163) 155 N 6th St 43701-3603 (Mail to: PO Box 1445 43702-1445) Robert Willmann (740) 453-9459

DIOCESE OF SOUTHERN VIRGINIA
(PROVINCE III)
Comprises 26 southern VA counties
DIOCESAN OFFICE 11832 Rock Landing Drive Ste 100 Newport News VA 23606
TEL (757) 423-8287 In VA only (800) 582-8292 FAX (757) 595-0783
E-MAIL 600@diosova.org WEB www.diosova.org

Previous Bishops— Alfred M Randolph 1892-1918, Beverley D Tucker coadj 1906 Bp 1918-30, Arthur C Thomson suffr 1917 coadj 1919 Bp 1930-37, Wm A Brown 1938-50, Geo P Gunn coadj 1948 Bp 1950-71, David S Rose suffr 1958 coadj 1964 Bp 1971-1978, C Charles Vaché coadj 1976 Bp 1978-91, O'Kelley Whitaker Asst 1992-97 Frank H Vest Jr coadj 1989 Bp 1991-98 Donald P Hart asst 1998-2001, Carol Joy WT Gallagher suffr 2002-5, David C Bane coadj 1997 Bp 1998-2006, John C Buchanan Bp Int 2006-9, Herman Hollerith IV Bp 2009-18, James B Magness diocesan pro tempore 2019-20

Bishop—Susan B Haynes (Diocesan 1 Feb 2020)

Sec Rev S Grimm; *Chanc* A Bibeau; *Cn to the Ordinary* R Hoffman; *Treas* J Fogarty

Stand Comm—Cler: Pres A Rohrs S Vincent-Alexander G Stokes; *Lay:* R Bishop R Parker Kathy Wootton *Deans: 1st or Eastern Shore* V Rev R Coniglio; *2nd or Virginia Beach* V Rev A Buchanan; *3rd or Norfolk* V Rev S Tabb; *4th* V Rev K Emerson; *5th or Jamestown* V Rev Dr R Ramsey *6th or Petersburg* V E Butler-Gee; *7th or South Richmond* V Rev Dr J Godsey; *8th or Farmville* V Rev N Meck; *9th or Danville* V Rev Dr S Grimm

PARISHES, MISSIONS, AND CLERGY

Accomac St James Episcopal Church **P** (33) 23309 Back St 23301-1742 (Mail to: PO Box 540 23301-0540) (757) 787-4892

Amelia Ct Hse Christ Church **P** (80) 16401 Court St 23002-4870 (Mail to: PO Box 468 23002-0468) Michael Stone (804) 561-2441

Appomattox St Anne Episcopal Church **P** (56) 311 Oakleigh Ave 24522 (Mail to: PO Box 387 24522-0387) (434) 352-8296

Baskerville St Andrew Episcopal Church **M** (8) 4118 Baskerville Rd 23915-2045 (Mail to: PO Box 124 23915-0124) (434) 447-4914

Blackstone St Lukes Episcopal Church **P** (66) Corner of S Main & Church 23824 (Mail to: PO Box 36 23824-0036) William Muller (434) 298-7650

Bloxom Emmanuel Episcopal Church **M** (21) Route # Box 1 23308 (Mail to: 637 Williams Rd 24562-4115) (434) 969-4814

Bon Air St Michael Episcopal Church **P** (227) § 2040 McRae Rd 23235 (Mail to: 2040 McRae Rd 23235) Jeunee Godsey (804) 272-0992

Bracey St Mark Episcopal Church **M** (20) 3906 Highway Nine O Three 23919-9997 (Mail to: James A Mckeathern PO Box 227 23919-0227) (434) 689-2219

Cape Charles Emmanuel Episcopal Church **M** (32) 601 Tazewell Ave 23310-0601 (Mail to: PO Box 601 23310-0601) Robert Coniglio (757) 678-7802

Cartersville St James Episcopal Church **P** (54) C/O Mr John R Martin 35 Boone Trl 23027-9630 (Mail to: C/O Mr John R Martin 35 Boone Trl 23027-9630) (804) 375-3019

Chase City St John Episcopal Church **P** (33) 338 E 4th St 23924-1226 (Mail to: 338 E 4th St 23924-1226) (434) 372-3318

Chatham St Marys Chapel **Chapel** 800 Chatham Hall Cir 24531-3084 (Mail to: 800 Chatham Hall Cir 24531-3084) (757) 489-9096

Chatham Emmanuel Episcopal Church **P** (47) 66 North Main Street 24531-0026 (Mail to: PO Box 26 24531-0026) Rebecca Crites (434) 432-0316

Chesapeake St Bride Episcopal Church **P** (47) 621 Sparrow Rd 23325-2504 (Mail to: 621 Sparrow Rd 23325-2504) (757) 420-7033

Chesapeake St Thomas Episcopal Church **P** (628) 233 Mann Dr 23322-5215 (Mail to: 233 Mann Dr 23322-5215) Mark Mckone-Sweet (757) 547-4662

Chesapeake Church of the Messiah **M** 816 Kempsville Rd 23320-5002 (Mail to: 816 Kempsville Rd 23320-5002) (757) 436-2545

Chester Saint John's Church **P** (350) 12201 Richmond St 23831-4440 (Mail to: PO Box 3886 23831-8471) (804) 748-2182

Chesterfield St Matthew Episcopal Church **P** (113) 9300 Shawonodasee Rd 23832-6330 (Mail to: PO Box 2187 23832-9111) (804) 790-1211

Claremont Ritchie Memorial Episcopal Ch **P** 115 Virginian 23899 (Mail to: PO Box 27 23899-0027) (804) 866-8629

Clarksville St Timothy Episcopal Church **P** (86) 111 6th St 23927-9285 (Mail to: 111 6th St 23927-9285) Timothy Fulop (434) 374-8611

Colonial Heights St Michael Episcopal Church **P** (125) § 501 Old Town Dr 23834-1734 (Mail to: 501 Old Town Dr 23834-1734) John Boucher (804) 526-1790

Courtland St Luke Episcopal Church **M** (40) 22430 Main St 23837-1027 (Mail to: PO Box 156 23837-0156) (757) 653-2442

Danville Christ Episcopal Church **P** (76) 9 Ridgecrest Dr 24540-0115 (Mail to: PO Box

10355 24543-5006) Timothy Fulop (434) 836-2060

Danville Church of the Epiphany **P** (150) 781 Main St 24541-1803 (Mail to: 115 Jefferson Ave 24541-1921) Jon Anderson (434) 792-4321

Disputanta Brandon Episcopal Church **P** (36) 18706 James River Dr 23842-9045 (Mail to: 18706 James River Dr 23842-9045) Macon Walton (757) 866-8977

Eastville Christ Church **P** (78) 16304 Courthouse Rd 23347 (Mail to: PO Box 367 23347-0367) Robert Johnson Janet Wheelock

Farmville Johns Memorial Epis Church **P** (272) 400 High St 23901-1812 (Mail to: 400 High St 23901-1812) Nancy Meck (434) 392-5695

Franklin Emmanuel Episcopal Church **P** (71) 400 N High St 23851-1420 (Mail to: PO Box 146 23851-0146) Jean Mackay Vinson (757) 562-4542

Freeman St Thomas Episcopal Church **M** (41) § 6271 Belfield Rd 23856-2413 (Mail to: PO Box 71 23856-0071) (434) 336-1132

Gretna St Johns Episcopal Church **M** (7) 1357 Hickeys Rd 24557-4689 (Mail to: 1357 Hickeys Rd 24557-4689) (434) 656-1735

Halifax Christ Episcopal Church **M** (13) 545 N Main St 24558 (Mail to: 545 N Main St 24558) (434) 476-4421

Halifax Emmanuel Episcopal Church **M** 3120 Mountain Rd 24558-2228 (Mail to: PO Box 905 24558-0905) (434) 476-6696

Halifax St John Episcopal Church **P** (167) § 197 Mountain Rd 24558-2010 (Mail to: PO Box 905 24558-0905) Timothy Jones (434) 476-6696

Hampton Emmanuel Episcopal Church **P** (187) 179 E Mercury Blvd 23669-2461 (Mail to: 179 E Mercury Blvd 23669-2461) Rhonda Wheeler (757) 723-8144

Hampton St Cyprian Episcopal Church **P** (120) 1242 W Queen St 23669-3843 (Mail to: PO Box 65 23669-0065) (757) 723-8253

Hampton St John Church **P** (408) 100 W Queens Way 23669-4014 (Mail to: 100 W Queens Way 23669-4014) Mark Riley Samantha Vincent-Alexander (757) 722-2567

Hampton St Mark Episcopal Church **P** (125) 100 W Queens Way 23669-4014 (Mail to: 100 W Queens Way 23669-4014) (757) 826-3515

Hopewell St John Episcopal Church **P** (168) 505 Cedar Ln 23860-1517 (Mail to: 505 Cedar Ln 23860-1517) William Taylor (804) 458-8142

Java St Paul Episcopal Church **M** (10) 13953 Halifax Rd 24565 (Mail to: PO Box 43 24565-0043) (804) 432-3776

Kenbridge Church of St Paul & St Andrew **P** (128) 512 S Broad St 23944-2012 (Mail to: PO Box 248 23944-0248) (434) 676-3448

Lawrenceville St Andrew Episcopal Church **P** (39) 400 Windsor Ave 23868-1202 (Mail to:

PO Box 26 23868-0026) (434) 848-3939

Lawrenceville Saint Paul's Memorial Chapel **CC** (51) § 115 James Solomon Russell Dr 23868-1299 (Mail to: PO Box 268 23868-1200) (434) 848-2544

Machipongo Hungars Parish **P** (188) 10107 Bayside Rd 23405-1816 (Mail to: PO Box 367 23347-0367) Janet Wheelock (757) 678-7837

Mc Kenney Church of the Good Shepherd **P** (65) 7800 Lew Jones 23872 (Mail to: PO Box 357 23872-0357) (804) 478-4280

Midlothian Episcopal Ch of the Redeemer **P** (807) 2341 Winterfield Rd 23113-4157 (Mail to: 2341 Winterfield Rd 23113-4157) Augusta Martien (804) 3798899

Midlothian Manakin Episcopal Church **P** (487) 985 Huguenot Trl 23113-9224 (Mail to: 985 Huguenot Trl 23113-9224) Virginia Distanislao Rebecca Dean Judith Lee (804) 794-6401

Midlothian St Matthias Episcopal Church **P** (433) 11300 W Huguenot Rd 23113-1121 (Mail to: PO Box 73537 23235-8042) Brenda Smiley-Lykins (804) 272-8588

Newport News St Andrew Episcopal Church **P** (499) § 45 Main St 23601-4011 (Mail to: 45 Main St 23601-4088) Anne Kirchmier Marcus Vance (757) 595-0371

Newport News St Augustine Episcopal Church **P** (129) 2515 Marshall Ave 23607-4605 (Mail to: 2515 Marshall Ave 23607-4605) (757) 245-4613

Newport News St George Episcopal Church **P** (57) § 15446 Warwick Blvd 23608-1506 (Mail to: 15446 Warwick Blvd 23608-1506) (757) 877-0088

Newport News St Paul Episcopal Church **P** (76) 221 34th St 23607-2903 (Mail to: 221 34th St 23607-2903) (757) 247-5086

Newport News St Stephen Episcopal Church **P** (247) 372 Hiden Blvd 23606-2934 (Mail to: 372 Hiden Blvd 23606-2934) Kyle Mackey (757) 595-5521

Norfolk Christ & St Lukes Epis Church **P** (1508) § 560 W Olney Rd 23507-2135 (Mail to: PO Box 11499 23517-0499) Noah Van Niel Jess Stribling (757) 627-5665

Norfolk Episcopal Ch of the Ascension **P** (191) § 405 Talbot Hall Rd 23505-4309 (Mail to: 405 Talbot Hall Rd 23505-4309) Stewart Tabb (757) 423-6715

Norfolk Episcopal Ch of the Epiphany **P** (101) 1530 Lafayette Blvd 23509-1112 (Mail to: 1530 Lafayette Blvd 23509-1112) Julia Ashby (757) 622-7672

Norfolk Church of the Good Shepherd **P** (541) 7400 Hampton Blvd 23505-1775 (Mail to: Attn: Accounting Dept 7400 Hampton Blvd 23505-1780) Jacqueline Soltys (757) 423-3230

Norfolk Grace Episcopal Church **P** (867) 1400 E Brambleton Ave 23504-4394 (Mail to: PO Box 1003 23501-1003) Harold Cobb (757) 625-2868

Norfolk St Andrew Episcopal Church **P** (525) 1009 W Princess Anne Rd 23507-1219 (Mail to: 1009 W Princess Anne Rd 23507-1219) Marguerite Alley (757) 622-5530

Norfolk St Paul Episcopal Church **P** (434) 201 Saint Pauls Blvd 23510-2701 (Mail to: C/O Judy Best 201 Saint Pauls Blvd 23510-2701) (757) 627-4353

Norfolk St Peter's Episcopal Church **P** (227) § 224 S Military Hwy 23502-5231 (Mail to: 224 S Military Hwy 23502-5231) (757) 466-9392

Norfolk St Stephen's Episcopal Church **P** (64) 1445 Norview Ave 23513-1552 (Mail to: 1445 Norview Ave 23513-1552) Gwynneth Mudd Carlotta Cochran (757) 855-2788

Norfolk Episcopal Church of the Advent **P** (113) 9620 Sherwood Pl 23503-1723 (Mail to: 9629 Norfolk Ave 23503-1701) (757) 587-0125

North Chesterfield St Barnabas Episcopal Church **P** (104) 5155 Iron Bridge Rd 23234-4703 (Mail to: 5155 Iron Bridge Rd 23234-4703) (804) 275-1648

North Chesterfield St David Episcopal Church **P** (324) § 1801 Camborne Rd 23236-2126 (Mail to: 1801 Camborne Rd 23236-2126) Elizabeth Felicetti (804) 276-4348

North Prince George Merchants Hope Epis Church **M** (66) 11500 Merchants Hope Rd 23860-8933 (Mail to: 11500 Merchant Hope Rd 23860-8933) Charles Moore (804) 458-1356

Onancock Holy Trinity Episcopal Church **P** (120) 66 Market St 23417-4224 (Mail to: PO Box 338 23417-0338) Edward Hunt (757) 787-4430

Petersburg Christ & Grace Epis Church **P** (318) 1545 S Sycamore St 23805-1314 (Mail to: 1545 S Sycamore St 23805-1314) Mary Thorpe (804) 733-7202

Petersburg St John Episcopal Church **P** (66) 842 W Washington St 23804-1187 (Mail to: 842 W Washington St 23803-3060) (804) 732-8107

Petersburg St Paul's Episcopal Church **P** (350) 110 N Union St 23803 (Mail to: PO Box 564 23804-0564) (804) 733-3415

Petersburg St Stephen Episcopal Church **P** (124) 228 Halifax St 23803-6312 (Mail to: 228 Halifax St 23803-6312) (804) 733-6228

Portsmouth Saint Christopher's Epis Ch **P** (113) 3300 Cedar Ln 23703-4104 (Mail to: 3300 Cedar Ln 23703-4104) Eileen Walsh (757) 484-5155

Portsmouth St James Episcopal Church **M** (93) 928 Effingham St 23704-3438 (Mail to: 928 Effingham St 23704-3438) (757) 399-7707

Portsmouth St John Episcopal Church **P** (396) 424 Washington St 23704-2435 (Mail to: 424 Washington St 23704-2435) J Derek Harbin (757) 399-4967

Portsmouth Trinity Episcopal Church **P** (101) 500 Court St 23704-3606 (Mail to: 500 Court St 23704-3606) Grant Stokes Connie Gilman (757) 393-0431

Powhatan St Luke Episcopal Church **P** (258) 2245 Huguenot Trl 23139-4403 (Mail to: 2245 Huguenot Trl 23139-4403) Raymond Custer (804) 794-6953

Pungoteague St George's Episcopal Church **P** (69) 30241 Bobtown Rd 23422 (Mail to: PO Box 172 23422-0172) (757) 787-4892

Richmond Church of the Good Shepherd **P** (222) 4206 Springhill Ave 23225-3345 (Mail to: 4206 Springhill Ave 23225-3345) William Miller (804) 233-2278

Smithfield Christ Episcopal Church **P** (134) 111 S Church St 23430-1332 (Mail to: 111 S Church St 23430-1332) (757) 357-2826

South Boston Trinity Episcopal Church **P** (98) § 520 Yancey St 24592-3322 (Mail to: 520 Yancey St 24592-3323) Timothy Fulop (434) 572-4513

South Hill All Saints Episcopal Church **P** (79) 203 Franklin St 23970-2009 (Mail to: PO Box 58 23970-0058) Terrence Walker (434) 955-2271

South Hill Trinity Episcopal Church **P** (38) 926 Thomason Ln 23970 (Mail to: Attn: Treasurer PO Box 903 23970-0903) (434) 447-6533

Suffolk Glebe Episcopal Church **P** (132) § 4400 Nansemond Pkwy 23435-2136 (Mail to: PO Box 5042 23435-0042) Ross Keener (757) 538-8842

Suffolk St John Episcopal Church **P** (35) 828 Kings Hwy 23432-1112 (Mail to: C/O Susan Kirkpatrick 828 Kings Hwy 23432-1112) Leslie Ferguson (757) 255-4168

Suffolk St Mark Episcopal Church **P** (22) 142 Tynes St 23434-4625 (Mail to: 142 Tynes St 23434-4625) (757) 934-0830

Suffolk St Paul Episcopal Church **P** (271) 213 North Main Street 23434-4420 (Mail to: 213 N Main St 23434-4420) Keith Emerson (757) 539-2478

Surry St Paul Episcopal Church **M** (69) 11891 Rolfe Hwy 23883-2738 (Mail to: PO Box 298 23883-0298) (757) 569-6280

Temperanceville Emmanuel Episcopal Church **M** (56) 26405 Horsey Rd 23442 (Mail to: PO Box 186 23416-0186) (757) 824-5043

Toano Hickory Neck Episcopal Church **P** (565) 8300 Richmond Rd 23168-9206 (Mail to: 8300 Richmond Rd 23168-9206) Jennifer Andrews-Weckerly (757) 566-0276

Victoria St Luke Episcopal Church **M** (2) C/O Charlie W Allen 601 Mecklenburg Ave 23974-4721 (Mail to: C/O Cathy Johnson PO Box 437 23974-0437) (434) 676-3432

Virginia Bch Church of the Holy Apostles **P** (84) 1598 Lynnhaven Pkwy 23453-2008 (Mail to: 1593 Lynnhaven Pkwy 23453-2008) Alan Mead (757) 427-0963

Virginia Bch Galilee Episcopal Church **P** (974) § 3928 Pacific Ave 23451-2636 (Mail to: 3928 Pacific Ave 23451-2636) Andrew Buchanan Benjamin Randall (757) 428-3573

Virginia Bch Good Samaritan Episcopal Ch **P** (54) 848 Baker Rd 23462-1035 (Mail to: 848 Baker Rd 23462-1035) Ann Truitt (757) 497-0729

Virginia Bch Old Donation Episcopal Church **P** (871) § 4449 N Witchduck Rd 23455-6151 (Mail to: 4449 N Witchduck Rd 23455-6151) Robert Randall Elisabeth Rhoton (757) 497-0563

Virginia Bch St Aidan's Episcopal Church **P** (428) 3201 Edinburgh Dr 23452-5803 (Mail to: 3201 Edinburgh Dr 23452-5803) Julia Messer-Croteau (757) 340-6459

Virginia Bch St Francis Episcopal Church **P** (243) 509 S Rosemont Rd 23452-4131 (Mail to: 509 S Rosemont Rd 23452-4131) Conor Alexander (757) 340-6884

Virginia Beach St Simons by the Sea **M** (63) 308 Sandbridge Rd 23456-4522 (Mail to: 308 Sandbridge Rd 23456-4522) Dale Hirst (757) 426-5427

Virginia Beach All Saints' Episcopal Church **P** (515) § 1969 Woodside Ln 23454-1031 (Mail to: 1969 Woodside Ln 23454-1031) Ashley Urquidi (757) 481-0577

Virginia Beach Eastern Shore Chapel **P** (992) 2020 Laskin Rd 23454-4208 (Mail to: 2020 Laskin Rd 23454-4208) (757) 428-6763

Virginia Beach Emmanuel Episcopal Church **P** (428) § 5181 Singleton Way 23462-4241 (Mail to: 5181 Singleton Way 23462-4241) Mary Lacy (757) 499-1271

Warfield St James Episcopal Church **M** (22) 275 Waqua Creek Rd 23889-2048 (Mail to: C/O Mrs Lena G Pierson PO Box 248 23868-0248) (434) 949-7720

Waverly Christ Episcopal Church **M** (19) 203 E Main St 23890-3240 (Mail to: PO Box 928 23890-0928) (804) 834-2393

Williamsburg Bruton Parish Church **HC** (2071) 331 E Duke of Gloucester St 23185-4251 (Mail to: PO Box 3520 23187-3520) Christopher Epperson Charles Bauer Lauren Mcdonald (757) 229-2891

Williamsburg St Martins Episcopal Church **P** (752) 1333 Jamestown Rd 23185-3335 (Mail to: 1333 Jamestown Rd 23185-3335) Elizabeth Green (757) 229-1111

Yorktown Christ the King Church **P** (227) 4109 Big Bethel Rd 23693-3821 (Mail to: 4109 Big Bethel Rd 23693-3821) Thomas Haynes (757) 8657227

Yorktown Grace Episcopal Church **P** (693) § 111 Church St 23690-4002 (Mail to: PO Box 123 23690-0123) Seldon Walker (757) 8983261

DIOCESE OF SOUTHWEST FLORIDA
(PROVINCE IV)
Comprises 12 counties of SW Florida
DIOCESAN OFFICE 8005 25th St E Parrish FL 34219
TEL (941) 556-0315 FAX (941) 556-0321
E-MAIL wmartucci@episcopalswfl.org WEB www.episcopalswfl.org

Previous Bishops–
Francis H Rutledge 1851–1866, John F Young 1867-1885, Edwin G Weed 1886-1924, Wm C Gray 1892-1914, Cameron Mann 1914-1932, John D Wing coadj 1925 Bp 1932-1950, Martin J Bramm suffr 1951-1956, Wm F Moses suffr 1956-1961, Henry I Louttit suffr 1945 coadj 1948 Bp 1951-1969, James L Duncan suffr 1961-1969, Wm L Hargrave suffr 1961-1969 Bp 1970-1975, E Paul Haynes 1975-1988, Rogers S Harris 1989-1997, Telesforo A Issac assist 1991-1996, John B Lipscomb 1997-2007

Bishop—Rt Rev Dabney T Smith (1014) (Dio 5 Sep 07)

Assisting Bishops—Rt Rev J Michael Garrison and Rt Rev Barry R Howe

Chanc TL Tripp Jr; *Cn for Fin & Admin*/CFO AM Vickers; Archdeacon Ven Dr KM Moore; *COM*

Chair Rev A Andujar; *Cn for Stew & Pastoral Care* Rev CN Gray; *Cn for Mis & Min* Rev RH Norman; *Dir Yth Min & Prog* MR Bowers; *Mis for Church Extension* Rev AM Hymes; *Dir Comm* L Nickel; *Dir Cong Supp* ; *Ex Dir DaySpring* CJ Odell

Deans: Clearwater V Rev R Bonoan; *Ft Myers* V Rev R Buchanan; *St Petersburg* V Rev R Whitley; *Manasota* V Rev W Farrell; *Tampa* V Rev B O'Carroll; *Naples* V Rev EC Gleason; *Venice* V Rev M Robertshaw

Stand Comm–Cler: Pres CB McCook RR Whitley AC Cannon M Robertshaw JC Teets; *Lay: VP* RU Stoll JH Corn J Smith D Hollier

PARISHES, MISSIONS, AND CLERGY

Arcadia Church of St Edmund the Martyr **M** (79) 327 W Hickory St 34266-3905 (Mail to: 327 W Hickory St 34266-3905) James Mcconnell Robert Vaughn James Williamson (941) 740-5817

Boca Grande St Andrews Church **P** (334) 390 Gilchrist Ave 33921-1011 (Mail to: PO Box

272 33921-0272) Michelle Robertshaw (941) 9642257

Bonita Springs Saint Mary's Episcopal Church **P** (362) § 9801 Bonita Beach Rd 34135-4628 (Mail to: PO Box 1923 34135-1923) David Faupel Ryan Wright Gail Tomei (239) 992-4343

Bradenton Christ Church **P** (471) 4030 Manatee Ave W 34205-1717 (Mail to: 4030 Manatee Ave W 34205-1789) Gretchen Platt Richard Visconti (941) 747-3709

Bradenton St George's Episcopal Church **P** (194) 912 63rd Ave W 34207-4849 (Mail to: 912 63rd Ave W 34207-4800) (941) 755-3606

Bradenton St Mary Magdalene **P** (362) 11315 Palmbrush Trail 34202-2938 (Mail to: 11315 Palmbrush Trl 34202-2938) James Hedman (941) 751-5048

Brooksville St John Episcopal Church **P** (152) § 200 S Brooksville Ave 34601-3311 (Mail to: 200 S Brooksville Ave 34601-3311) Kenneth Taber (352) 796-9112

Cape Coral Church of the Epiphany **P** (128) 2507 Del Prado Blvd South 33904-5768 (Mail to: 2507 Del Prado Blvd S 33904-5768) Aubrey Cort Edward Gibbons Priscilla Gray Susan Henderson (239) 574-3200

Clearwater Epis Church of the Ascension **P** (861) 701 Orange Ave 33756-5232 (Mail to: 701 Orange Ave 33756-5232) James Sorvillo William Burkett Leo Crawford William Shiflet (727) 447-3469

Clearwater Epis Ch of Good Samaritan **M** (96) 2165 NE Coachman Rd 33765-2616 (Mail to: 2165 NE Coachman Rd 33765-2616) Sandra Jamieson Jamie Samilio (727) 461-1717

Clearwater Holy Trinity Episcopal Church **P** (208) § 3240 N McMullen Booth Rd 33761-2009 (Mail to: 3200 N McMullen Booth Road 33761-2009) Daniel Lemley (727) 796-5514

Clearwater St Johns Episcopal Church **P** (204) § 1676 South Belcher Rd 33764-6517 (Mail to: 1676 S Belcher Rd 33764-6517) Andrew Gerns (727) 531-6020

Dade City St Marys Episcopal Church **P** (219) Attn: Sandra Sartain 37637 Magnolia Ave 33523-3744 (Mail to: C/O Sandra Sartain PO Box 452 33526-0452) James Teets (352) 567-3888

Dunedin Church of the Good Shepherd **P** (231) 639 Edgewater Dr 34698-6916 (Mail to: 639 Edgewater Dr 34698-6916) Whitney Burton Cynthia Roehl (727) 733-4125

Englewood St Davids Episcopal Church **P** (175) 401 South Broadway 34223-3802 (Mail to: 401 S Broadway 34223-3802) Vincent Scotto Micki-Ann Thomas (941) 474-3140

Fort Myers Iona-Hope Episcopal Church **P** (177) 9650 Gladiolus Dr 33908-7616 (Mail to: 9650 Gladiolus Dr 33908-7616) Herman Buchanan John Gamble Margaret Harker (239) 454-4778

Fort Myers Lamb Of God Episcopal Church **P** (206) § 19691 Cypress View Dr 33967-6217 (Mail to: 19691 Cypress View Dr 33967-6217) (239) 267-3525

Fort Myers St Hilarys Episcopal Church **P** (430) § 5011 McGregor Blvd 33901-8840 (Mail to: 5011 McGregor Blvd 33901-8840) Alberry Cannon (239) 936-1000

Fort Myers St Lukes Episcopal Church **P** (756) § 2635 Cleveland Ave 33901-5803 (Mail to: 2635 Cleveland Ave 33901-5803) Richard Grady Alan Kelmereit Michael Rowe (239) 334-2479

Fort Myers Beach St Raphaels Church **M** (60) 5601 Williams Dr 33931-4031 (Mail to: 5601 Williams Dr 33931-4097) John Adler Jean Hite (239) 463-6057

Holmes Beach Episcopal Ch of Annunciation **P** (135) 4408 Gulf Dr 34217-1829 (Mail to: 4408 Gulf Dr 34217-1829) Matthew Grunfeld Bruce Gillies Kathlyn Gilpin (941) 7781638

Hudson St Martin's Episcopal Church **P** (104) § 15801 US 19 34667-3602 (Mail to: PO Box 7199 34674-7199) Ronald Kowalski (727) 863-8560

Indian Rk Bc Calvary Episcopal Church **P** (320) 1615 1st St 33785-2809 (Mail to: 1615 1st St 33785-2809) Charles Roberts (727) 595-2374

Labelle Church of the Good Shepherd **M** (39) 1098 Collingswood Pkwy 33935-2306 (Mail to: 1098 Collingswood Pkwy 33935-2306) (863) 675-0385

Largo Resurrection Episcopal Church **M** (93) 10888 126th Ave 33778-2710 (Mail to: 10888 126th Ave 33778-2710) (727) 586-6968

Lehigh Acres St Anselms Church **M** (107) 2201 E 6th Street 33936-4376 (Mail to: 2201 E 6th S 33936-4399) (239) 369-1916

Longboat Key All Angels by the Sea **P** (224) 563 Bay Isles Rd 34228-3142 (Mail to: Attn Sandy L Wood 563 Bay Isles Rd 34228-3142) Frederick Emrich Margaret Gat Davie Marshall (941) 383-8161

Marco Island St Mark's Episcopal Church **P** (628) 1101 N Collier Blvd 34145-2507 (Mail to: PO Box 339 34146-0339) Jessica Babcock Kathryn Schillreff (239) 394-7242

Naples St Johns Episcopal Church **P** (560) 500 Park Shore Dr 34103-3537 (Mail to: 500 Park Shore Dr 34103-3537) Joseph Maiocco (239) 261-2355

Naples St Monica Episcopal Church **P** (593) 707 Immokalee Rd 34119-8845 (Mail to: 707 Immokalee Rd 34119-8845) (239) 591-4550

Naples St Pauls Episcopal Church **P** (240) 3901 Davis Blvd 34104-5010 (Mail to: 3901 Davis Blvd 34104-5010) Thomas Thoeni Wende Meyer (239) 643-0197

Naples Trinity by the Cove **P** (1574) 553 Galleon Dr 34102-7639 (Mail to: 553 Galleon D 34102-7639) Edward Gleason Nichola Caccese Stephen Zimmerman (239) 262-658

New Prt Rchy St Stephens Episcopal Church **P** (183) 5326 Charles St 34652-3906 (Mail to: 5326 Charles St 34652-3906) Walcott Hunter (727) 849-4330

North Fort Myers All Souls Episcopal Church **P** (80) 14640 N Cleveland Ave 33903-3806 (Mail to: 14640 N Cleveland Ave 33903-3806) Sandra Johnson Walter Mycoff Nancy Smith (239) 997-7685

North Port St Nathaniel Episcopal Church **P** (215) 4200 S Biscayne Dr 34287-1626 (Mail to: 4200 S Biscayne Dr 34287-1626) Andrea Hayden Margaret Koor Margaret Koor (941) 426-2520

Osprey Church of the Holy Spirit **P** (94) § 129 S Tamiami Trl 34229-9211 (Mail to: 129 S Tamiami Trl 34229-9211) (941) 966-1924

Palm Harbor St Alfreds Episcopal Church **P** (457) 1601 Curlew Rd 34683-6515 (Mail to: 1601 Curlew Rd 34683-6515) Peter Lane (727) 7851601

Palmetto St Marys Episcopal Church **P** (239) 1010 24th Ave W 34221-3540 (Mail to: 1010 24th Ave W 34221-3540) William De la Torre Glen Graczyk (941) 722-5292

Pinellas Park St Giles Episcopal Church **P** (368) 8271 52nd St N 33781-1518 (Mail to: 8271 52nd St N 33781-1558) Douglas Remer (727) 544-6856

Plant City St. Peter's Episcopal Church **P** (554) 302 N Carey St 33563-4316 (Mail to: 302 Carey St 33563-4316) Alissa Anderson (813) 752-5061

Pt Charlotte Saint James Episcopal Church **P** (445) 1365 Viscaya Dr 33952-2519 (Mail to: 1365 Viscaya Dr 33952-2519) Cesar Olivero Cesar Olivero (941) 627-4000

Punta Gorda Church of the Good Shepherd **P** (238) § 401 W Henry St 33950-5905 (Mail to: 401 W Henry St 33950-5905) Roy Tuff (941) 639-2757

Safety Harbor Church of the Holy Spirit **P** (185) 601 Phillippe Pkwy 34695-3148 (Mail to: 601 Phillippe Pkwy 34695-3148) Raynald Bonoan (727) 725-4726

Sanibel Ch of St Mic & All Angls Ep Ch **P** (413) 2304 Periwinkle Way 33957-3209 (Mail to: 2304 Periwinkle Way 33957-3209) William Van Oss Alan Kelmereit Anne Kimball Douglass Lind (239) 472-2173

Sarasota Church of the Nativity **P** (499) 5900 N Lockwood Ridge Rd 34243-2523 (Mail to: 5900 N Lockwood Ridge Rd 34243-2523) Michael Durning Rosalind Hall (941) 355-3262

Sarasota Church of the Redeemer **P** (2424) 222 S Palm Ave 34236-6727 (Mail to: 222 S Palm Ave 34236-6799) Charleston Wilson Mario Castro Arthur Cheney Michael Hurst Ralph Strohm Charleston Wilson (941) 955-4263

Sarasota Saint Boniface Church **P** (549) § 5615 Midnight Pass Rd 34242-1721 (Mail to: 5615

Midnight Pass Rd 34242-1721) Wayne Farrell Elisa Hansen Ralph Mcgimpsey Nikki Seger (941) 349-5616

Sarasota St Margaret of Scotland Church **P** (197) 8700 State Road 72 34241-9578 (Mail to: 8700 State Road 72 34241-9578) Carla Mccook Lisa Parker (941) 925-2525

Sarasota St Wilfred Episcopal Church **P** (236) 3773 Wilkinson Rd 34233-3607 (Mail to: 3773 Wilkinson Rd 34233-3608) (941) 924-7436

Seminole St Anne of Grace Church **M** (377) 6650 113th St 33772-6214 (Mail to: 6650 113th St 33772-6214) Robert Crow (727) 392-4483

Spring Hill St Andrews Episcopal Church **P** (355) 2301 Deltona Blvd 34606 (Mail to: PO Box 5026 34611-5026) Lance Wallace Elaine Cole Frederick Scharf (352) 683-2010

St James City St Johns Episcopal Church **M** (64) 7771 Stringfellow Rd 33956-2805 (Mail to: 7771 Stringfellow Rd 33956-2805) Aubrey Cort Susan Henderson (239) 283-1820

St Petersburg St Albans Episcopal Church **P** (171) 330 85th Ave 33706-1525 (Mail to: 330 85th Ave 33706-1546) Muriel Debussy (727) 360-8406

St Petersburg St Augustine's Episc Church **P** (62) § 2920 26th Ave South 33712-3328 (Mail to: 2920 26th Ave S 33712-3328) Mack Bauknight Josie Rose (727) 867-6774

St Petersburg St Bartholomews Episcopal Ch **P** (100) § 3747 34th St South 33711-3836 (Mail to: 3747 34th St S 33711-3836) Ethan Cole Lucien Watkins (727) 867-7015

St Petersburg St Matthews Church **M** (64) 738 Pinellas Point Dr S 33705-6255 (Mail to: 738 Pinellas Point Dr S 33705-6255) Harry Parsell (727) 866-2187

St Petersburg St Thomas Episcopal Church **P** (1108) 1200 Snell Isle Blvd NE 33704-3036 (Mail to: 1200 Snell Isle Blvd NE 33704-3036) Ryan Whitley Martha Goodwill (727) 896-9641

St Petersburg St Vincents Episcopal Church **P** (273) § 5441 Ninth Ave N 33710-6546 (Mail to: 5441 9th Ave N 33710-6599) Richard Earle Richard Earle Chester Trow (727) 321-5086

St. Petersburg St Peters Episcopal Cathedral **O** (1011) 140 4th St N 33701-3807 (Mail to: PO Box 1581 33731-1581) Earl Beshears Ronald Brokaw Peter Fleming Stephen Morris Thomas Williams (727) 822-4173

St. Petersburg St Bede Episcopal Church **P** (155) 2500 16th St N 33704-3132 (Mail to: 2500 16th St N 33704-3132) Marcus Crim (727) 823-7649

Sun City Center St John the Divine Epis Church **P** (408) 1015 Del Webb East 33573 (Mail to: 1015 E Del Webb Blvd 33573-6673) Kevin Warner Leewin Miller (813) 633-3970

Tampa Grace Episcopal Church **P** (343) 15102 Amberly Dr 33647-1618 (Mail to:

15102 Amberly Dr 33647-1618) Benjamin Twinamaani (813) 971-8484

Tampa St Andrews Episcopal Church **P** (870) 509 E Twiggs St 33602-3916 (Mail to: 509 E Twiggs St 33602-3934) John Reese (813) 221-2035

Tampa St Chads Episcopal Church **M** (44) 5609 N Albany Ave 33603-1005 (Mail to: 5609 N Albany Ave 33603-1005) (813) 872-7545

Tampa St Clement's Church **P** (238) 706 W 113th Ave 33612-5605 (Mail to: 706 W 113th Ave 33612-5605) Andrew Heyes (813) 932-6204

Tampa St Francis Episcopal Church **M** (285) 912 E Sligh Ave 33604-5636 (Mail to: PO Box 9332 33674-9332) Livan Echazabal (813) 238-1098

Tampa St James House of Prayer **P** (152) § 2708 N Central Ave 33602-1602 (Mail to: 2708 N Central Ave 33602-1699) Lynn Grinnell (813) 223-6090

Tampa St Mark's Epis Church Of Tampa **P** (502) 13312 Cain Rd 33625-4004 (Mail to: 13312 Cain Rd 33625-4004) Robert Douglas (813) 962-3089

Tampa St Marys Episcopal Church **P** (252) § 4311 W San Miguel St 33629-5623 (Mail to: 4311 W San Miguel St 33629-5691) Mario Milian Douglas Remer (813) 251-1660

Tampa St Johns Episcopal Church **P** (1273) 906 S Orleans Ave 33606-2941 (Mail to: 906 S Orleans Ave 33606-2941) Christian Wood Donald Goodheart Dale Van Wormer (813) 259-1570

Tarpon Spgs All Saints Episcopal Church **P** (233) 1700 Keystone Rd 34688-4928 (Mail to: PO Box 2584 34688-2584) Janet Tunnell Janet Tunnell (727) 937-3881

Temple Terrace St Catherine of Alexandria Ch **P** (323) 502 Druid Hills Rd 33617-3853 (Mail to: 502 Druid Hills Rd 33617-3853) James Reho (813) 988-6483

Valrico Church Of the Holy Innocents **P** (506) 604 N Valrico Rd 33594 (Mail to: 604 N Valrico Rd 33594-6874) Bryan O'Carroll Stephen Rudacille (813) 689-3130

Venice St Marks Episcopal Church **P** (676) § 513 Nassau St S 34285-2816 (Mail to: 513 Nassau St S 34285-2816) Michael Rau Oliver Backhaus Leonard Brusso Lisa Hamilton John Lawrence Judith Roberts Joyce Treppa John Warfel (941) 4887714

Venice Epis Ch of the Good Shepherd **P** (390) 1115 Center Rd 34292-3812 (Mail to: 1115 Center Rd 34292-3812) Joseph Hudson Michael Kitt Robert Miller (941) 497-7286

Wesley Chapel St Paul's Episcopal Church **M** (40) 3836 Flatiron Loop Ste 101 33544-7823 (Mail to: 3836 Flatiron Loop Unit 101 33544-7823) Adrienne Hymes (813) 803-7489

Zephyrhills St Elizabeths Episcopal Church **P** (105) § 5855 16th St 33542-3761 (Mail to: 5855 16th St 33542-3761) Dewey Brown Hugh Wilkes (813) 782-1202

DIOCESE OF SOUTHWESTERN VIRGINIA
(PROVINCE III)
Comprises 32 Southwestern VA counties
DIOCESAN OFFICE 1002 1st St. SW Roanoke VA 24016 (MAIL: Box 2279 Roanoke VA 24009-2279)
TEL (540) 342-6797, (800) 346-7982 FAX (540) 343-9114
E-MAIL mfurlow@dioswva.org WEB www.dioswva.org

Previous Bishops—
Robt C Jett 1920-38, Henry D Phillips 1938-54, Wm H Marmion 1954-79, A Heath Light 1979-96, F Neff Powell 1996-2013

Bishop—Rt Rev Mark Allen Bourlakas (1077) (Dio 20 Jul 2013)

COO Cn Mark Furlow; *Treas* A Heron 4525 Farmwood Dr Roanoke VA 24018; *Chanc* M Loftis PO Box 14125 Roanoke VA 24038; *Reg* K Hester PO Box 2279 Roanoke VA 24009; *Hist* Rev S West PO Box 164 Blacksburg VA 24063; *Ecum* Rev SR Stanley 1826 Mount Vernon Road SW Roanoke VA 24015

Stand Comm—Cler: Pres C Roussell T Vie G Goldmsith; *Lay:* S Duerson B Garrison D Williams

PARISHES, MISSIONS, AND CLERGY

Abingdon Church of St Thomas **P** (178) Attn: Elizabeth K Hurley 124 E Main St 24210-2808 (Mail to: Attn: Treasurer 124 E Main St 24210-2808) Boyd Evans (276) 628-3606

Altavista St Peters Episcopal Church **P** (41) 1010 Broad St 24517-1806 (Mail to: PO Box 207 24517-0207) (434) 369-5291

Amherst Ascension Episcopal Church **P** (33) 253 S Main St 24521-2636 (Mail to: PO Box 810 24521-0810) (434) 946-5498

Amherst Saint Mark's Church **P** (55) 670 Patrick Henry Hwy 24521-3982 (Mail to: PO Box 36 24533-0036) David Perkins (434) 946-1121

Amherst St Pauls Episcopal Mission **M** (143) 2009 Kenmore Road 24521-3239 (Mail to: PO Box 2279 24009-2279) (434) 946-2531

Arrington Trinity Episcopal Church **P** (67) 475 Oak Ridge Rd 22922-2610 (Mail to: 475 Oak

Ridge Rd 22922-2610) Donna Steckline (434) 263-5721

Bedford St Johns Episcopal Church **P** (182) 314 N Bridge St 24523-1928 (Mail to: 314 N Bridge St 24523-1928) Francis Brown (540) 586-9582

Bedford St Thomas Episcopal Church **M** (24) 9575 Big ISland Highway 24523 (Mail to: C/O Edward Marshall PO Box 695 24523-0695) (540) 586-4768

Big Stone Gap Christ Episcopal Church **P** (50) PO Box 778 106 Clinton Ave 24219-0778 (Mail to: PO Box 778 24219-0778) Robert Moore (276) 523-0401

Blacksburg Christ Episcopal Church **P** (585) 120 Church St NE 24060-3923 (Mail to: PO Box 164 24063-0164) Scott West (540) 5522411

Blue Grass Epis Ch of the Good Shepherd **P** (40) 3678 Blue Grass Valley Rd 24413-0007 (Mail to: PO Box 7 24413-0007) Robert Gilman (540) 474-2175

Bristol Emmanuel Episcopal Church **P** (286) 760 Cumberland St 24201-4124 (Mail to: PO Box 1376 24203-1376) Thomas Day (276) 669-9488

Buchanan Trinity Episcopal Church **P** (22) 19460 Main St 24066-2701 (Mail to: PO Box 459 24066-0459) (540) 254-1574

Buena Vista Christ Episcopal Church **P** (43) 2246 Walnut Ave 24416-2702 (Mail to: 2246 Walnut Ave 24416-2702) (540) 261-3929

Callaway St Peters Episcopal Church **P** (110) 65 Rock Ridge Rd 24067-5701 (Mail to: 65 Rock Ridge Rd 24067-5701) John Heck John Heck (540) 483-5370

Christiansbrg St Thomas Episcopal Church **P** (172) 103 E Main St 24073-3032 (Mail to: 103 E Main St 24073-3032) Phyllis Spiegel Mark Frazier (540) 382-4365

Clifton Forge St Andrews Episcopal Church **P** 516 Mccormick Blvd 24422-1137 (Mail to: 516 McCormick Blvd 24422-1137) (540) 863-3041

Covington All Saints Chapel **Chapel** 414 Boys Home Rd 24426-5539 (Mail to: 414 Boys Home Rd 24426-5539) Connie Gilman (540) 965-7700

Covington Emmanuel Episcopal Church **P** (44) 138 N Maple Ave 24426-1545 (Mail to: PO Box 709 24426-0709) Lebaron Taylor Ann Doyle (540) 965-5626

Fincastle St Marks Episcopal Church **P** (120) 111 S Roanoke St 24090 (Mail to: PO Box 277 24090-0277) George Logan (540) 473-2370

Forest St Stephens Episcopal Church **P** (104) 1695 Perrowville Rd 24551-2258 (Mail to: 1695 Perrowville Rd 24551-2258) Matthew Rhodes (434) 525-5511

Galax Church of the Good Shepherd **P** (36) 9441 Grayson Parkway 24333 (Mail to: PO Box 1266 24333-1266) (276) 236-4957

Glasgow Saint John's Episcopal Church **M** (15) 1002 Blue Ridge Rd 24555-2160 (Mail to:

C/O Elaine S Massie PO Box 507 24555-0507) (540) 258-2959

Hot Springs St Lukes Episcopal Church **P** (79) Rte 220 24445 (Mail to: Attn: Treasurer PO Box 779 24445-0779) Jerry Heidel (540) 839-2279

Lexington Grace Episcopal Church **P** (339) 123 W Washington St 24450-2122 (Mail to: 123 W Washington St 24450-2122) Ellis Bowerfind (540) 463-4981

Lynchburg Grace Memorial Epis Church **P** (219) 1021 New Hampshire Ave 24502-1216 (Mail to: 1021 New Hampshire Ave 24502-1216) Alan Cowart (434) 846-3156

Lynchburg St Johns Episcopal Church **P** (935) § 200 Boston Ave 24503-0123 (Mail to: PO Box 3123 24503-0123) Christopher Roussell (434) 528-1138

Lynchburg St Pauls Episcopal Church **P** (612) 7th & Clay St 24504 (Mail to: 605 Clay St 24504-2460) William Bumgarner Nina Salmon Todd Vie (434) 845-7301

Lynchburg Trinity Episcopal Church **P** (99) 104 Walnut Hollow Rd 24503-4778 (Mail to: PO Box 3278 24503-0278) (434) 384-2257

Marion Christ Episcopal Church **P** (101) 401 W Main St 24354-2417 (Mail to: 401 W Main St 24354-2417) Emily Edmondson (276) 783-8050

Martinsville Christ Episcopal Church **P** (213) 321 E. Church Street 24112-2981 (Mail to: 311 E Church St 24112-2981) John Adams (276) 632-2896

Martinsville St Pauls Episcopal Church **M** 904 Fayette St 24112-3432 (Mail to: 904 West Fayette 24112) Gene Anderson (276) 790-2612

Massies Mill Grace Episcopal Church **P** (72) 1934 Crabtree Falls Hwy 22967-2008 (Mail to: PO Box 762 22958-0762) (434) 277-8926

Moneta Trinity Ecumenical Parish **P** (103) 40 Lakemount Dr 24121-1915 (Mail to: 40 Lakemount Dr 24121-1915) (540) 721-4330

Monroe St Lukes Episcopal Church **M** (5) 3788 Buffalo Springs Tpke 24574-3104 (Mail to: C/O Mr Thomas C Wallace Iv PO Box 688 24572-0688) (434) 845-3446

Norton All Saints Episcopal Church **P** (35) Virginia Ave & 11th St 24273 (Mail to: PO Box 227 24273-0227) (276) 679-3185

Pearisburg Christ Episcopal Church **P** (48) 529 Wenonah Ave. 24134 (Mail to: PO Box 360 24134-0360) (540) 921-3033

Pocahontas Christ Episcopal Church **M** (10) Water St 24635-0322 (Mail to: PO Box 322 24635-0322) (276) 322-0487

Pulaski Christ Episcopal Church **P** (74) 144 N Washington Ave 24301-0975 (Mail to: PO Box 975 24301-0975) (540) 980-2413

Radford Grace Episcopal Church **P** (154) 210 4th St 24141-1523 (Mail to: 210 4th St 24141-1523) Sarah Morris (540) 639-3494

Richlands Trinity Episcopal Church **P** (10) 107 Hill Creek Rd 24641-2032 (Mail to: 107 Hill Creek Rd 24641-2032) (276) 963-9600

Roanoke Christ Episcopal Church **P** (358) 1101 Franklin Rd SW 24016-4309 (Mail to: 1101 Franklin Rd SW 24016-4397) Alexander Macphail (540) 343-0159

Roanoke St Elizabeths Episcopal Church **P** (80) 2339 Grandin Rd SW 24015-3916 (Mail to: PO Box 4706 24015-0706) Karin Macphail (540) 774-5183

Roanoke St James Episcopal Church **P** (190) 4515 Delray St NW 24012-2209 (Mail to: 4515 Delray St NW 24012-2209) Susan Bentley William Eanes (540) 366-4157

Roanoke St John Episcopal Church **P** (1892) 1 Mountain Ave SW 24016-5109 (Mail to: PO Box 257 24002-0257) Eric Long (540) 343-9341

Rocky Mount Trinity Episcopal Church **P** (85) 15 East Church Street 24151 (Mail to: PO Box 527 24151) David Taylor (540) 483-5038

Saint Paul St Marks Episcopal Church **P** (22) Broad And Fifth Ave 24283 (Mail to: PO Box 1138 24283-1138) (276) 679-3185

Salem St Pauls Episcopal Church **P** (492) § 42 E Main St 24153-3807 (Mail to: 42 E Main St 24153-3807) David Dixon James Hubbard (540) 389-9307

Saltville St Pauls Episcopal Church **M** (14) 370 E Main St 24370-2808 (Mail to: Attn: Helen W Barbrow PO Box 235 24370-0235) (276) 791-3175

Staunton Good Shepherd Folly Mills **M** (53) 809 Lee Jackson Hwy 24401-5510 (Mail to: 809 Lee Jackson Hwy 24401-5510) (540) 377-9449

Staunton Emmanuel Episcopal Church **P** (231) 300 W Frederick St 24401-3328 (Mail to: 300 W Frederick St 24401-3328) (540) 886-8172

Staunton Trinity Episcopal Church **P** (451) 214 W Beverley St 24401-4205 (Mail to: PO Box 208 24402-0208) William Heine (540) 886-9132

Tazewell Stras Memorial Epis Church **P** (33) 211 Central Ave 24651-6235 (Mail to: PO Box 563 24651-0563) (540) 988-2889

Waynesboro St Johns Episcopal Church **P** (342) 473 S Wayne Ave 22980-4739 (Mail to: PO Box 945 22980-0693) Benjamin Badgett (540) 942-4136

Wytheville St John's Episcopal Church **P** (218) § 275 E Main St 24382-2323 (Mail to: 275 E Main St 24382-2323) Paul Hicks (276) 228-2562

DIOCESE OF SPOKANE
(PROVINCE VIII)
Comprises Eastern Washington and North Idaho
DIOCESAN OFFICE 245 E 13th Ave Spokane WA 99202-1114
TEL (509) 624-3191 FAX (509) 747-0049
E-MAIL malloryd@spokanediocese.org WEB www.spokanediocese.org

Previous Bishops—
Lemuel H Wells 1892-1913, Herman Page 1915-23, Edward M Cross 1924-54, Russell S Hubbard m 1954 dio 1964-67, John R Wyatt 1967-78, Leigh A Wallace Jr 1979-90, Frank J Terry coadj 1990-91 Bp 91-99, James E Waggoner Jr 2000-17

Bishop — Gretchen M Rehberg (1099) (Dio 18 Mar 2017)

Cn to Ord Rev Cn S Cleveley; *Trans Min* Rev Cn S Cleveley; *Cn For Discipleship* A Farley; *Cn for Youth and Families* S Gunter; *Arch for Congregational Development* C McCall; *Sec Conv* Rev K Lamphere; *Treas* S Nitz; *Chanc* S Miller of J Scott Miller 115 N Washington St Ste 201 Jockey Club Bldg Spokane WA 99201-0657; *Arch* K Lamphere; *Arch dcn* Rev T Nitz; *Trustee Bd Chair Foundation* Rev D Walker; *Fin Off* L Boss; *B Exec Asst and Reg* M Davis; *COM Co-Chairs* Very Rev H VanDeventer and K Karr-Cornejo

Stand Comm Rev J Schmoetzer

PARISHES, MISSIONS, AND CLERGY

Bonners Ferr St Marys Church **Chapel** (13) 6633 Buchanan St 83805-8616 (Mail to: 6633 Buchanan St 83805-8616) (208) 267-3202

Cashmere St James Episcopal Church **M** (68) 222 Cottage Ave 98815-1004 (Mail to: PO Box 351 98815-0351) Carol Forhan (509) 782-1590

Chelan St Andrews Episcopal Church **P** (54) 120 East Wooden Ave 98816 (Mail to: PO Box 1226 98816-1226) Linda Mayer (509) 682-2851

Cheney St Pauls Episcopal Church **M** (23) 625 C St 99004-1747 (Mail to: 625 C St 99004-1747) (509) 235-6150

Coeur D Alene St Lukes Episcopal Church **P** (320) 501 E Wallace Ave 83814-2955 (Mail to: 501 E Wallace Ave 83814-2955) David Gortner (208) 664-5533

Dayton Grace Episcopal Church **M** (17) 301 S 3rd St 99328-1332 (Mail to: 301 S 3rd St 99328-1332) (509) 382-4795

Dover Holy Spirit Episcopal Church **M** (53) 55 Rocky Point Road 83825 (Mail to: 217 Cedar St PMB 336 83864-1410) David Walker Marjorie Stanley (208) 263-7078

Ellensburg Grace Episcopal Church **P** (74) 1201 N B Street 98926-2578 (Mail to: PO Box 644 98926-1918) (509) 962-2951

Ephrata St John the Baptist Epis Ch **M** (35) 701 1st Ave NW 98823-1504 (Mail to: PO Box 295 98823-0295) Anthony Green (509) 754-4949

Grangeville Holy Trinity Episcopal Church **M** (24) 311 S Hall St 83530-2011 (Mail to: 311 S Hall St 83530-2011) Chris Hagenbuch (208) 451-0645

Kennewick St Paul's Episcopal Mission **P** (342) 1609 W 10th Ave 99336-5200 (Mail to: PO Box 6857 99336-0529) Richard Matters Marilynn Yule (509) 582-8635

Lewiston Church of the Nativity **P** (104) 731 8th St 83501-2626 (Mail to: 731 8th St 83501-2626) Katherine Kelly (208) 743-9121

Moscow St Marks Episcopal Church **P** (124) 111 S Jefferson St 83843-2859 (Mail to: 111 S Jefferson St 83843-2859) (208) 882-2022

Moses Lake St Martins Episcopal Church **P** (76) 416 E Nelson Rd 98837-2383 (Mail to: 416 E Nelson Rd 98837-2383) Brent Tilson Gayle Gaither (509) 765-3369

Omak St Annes Episcopal Church **M** (67) 639 W Ridge Dr 98841-3251 (Mail to: PO Box 3251 98841-3251) (509) 826-5815

Oroville Trinity Episcopal Church **M** (109) 604 Central Ave 98844-9222 (Mail to: PO Box 1270 98844-1270) (509) 476-2230

Pomeroy St Peters Church **P** (46) 710 High St 99347-5007 (Mail to: PO Box 490 99347-0490) (509) 843-1871

Prosser St Matthews Episcopal Church **M** (70) 317 7th St 99350-1180 (Mail to: PO Box 828 99350-0828) (509) 830-6318

Pullman Saint James **P** (219) § 1410 NE Stadium Way 99163-3841 (Mail to: 1410 NE Stadium Way 99163-4619) Dianne Lowe Theodore Nitz Wilhelmina Sarai-Clark Linda Young (509) 332-1742

Republic Episcopal Ch of the Redeemer **M** (4) 3 Klondike Rd 99166-9701 (Mail to: PO Box 342 99166-0342) (509) 775-3096

Richland All Saints' Episcopal Church **P** (410) 1322 Kimball Ave 99354-3206 (Mail to: 1322

Kimball Ave 99354-3206) Jane Schmoetzer Shanna Hawks (509) 9431169

South Cle Elum Church of the Resurrection **M** (89) Kelly Clift PO Box 23 98943-0023 (Mail to: PO Box 701 98941-0701) (509) 649-2283

✠ **Spokane** Cathd of St John the Evnglst **O** (433) 127 E 12th Ave 99202-1199 (Mail to: C/O Rosie Banta 127 E 12th Ave 99202-1199) Heather Vandeventer (509) 8384277

Spokane St Andrews Episcopal Church **P** (74) 2404 N Howard St 99205-3215 (Mail to: 2404 N Howard St 99205-3215) (509) 325-5252

Spokane Saint David's Church **P** (348) 7315 N Wall St 99208-6102 (Mail to: PO Box 18917 99228-0917) (509) 466-3100

Spokane St Stephens Episcopal Church **P** (221) 5720 S Perry St 99223-6349 (Mail to: 5720 S Perry St 99223-6349) William Osborne Elaine Pitzer (509) 448-2255

Spokane West Central Episcopal Mission **M** (15) 1832 W Dean Ave 99201-1829 (Mail to: 1832 W Dean Ave 99201-1829) Jonathan Myers (206) 554-1544

Spokane Valley Church of the Resurrection **P** (158) 15319 E 8th Ave 99037-8828 (Mail to: PO Box 14771 99214-0771) James Andrews (509) 926-6450

Sunnyside Holy Trinity Episcopal Church **P** (35) 327 E Edison Ave 98944-1435 (Mail to: 327 E Edison Ave 98944-1435) Peter Kalunian (509) 837-4727

Walla Walla Saint Paul's Church **P** (190) 323 Catherine St 99362-3021 (Mail to: 323 Catherine St 99362-3082) David Sibley Ernest Campbell (509) 529-1083

Wenatchee St Luke's Episcopal Church **P** (106) § 428 King St 98801-2846 (Mail to: PO Box 1642 98807-1642) Frances Twiggs (509) 662-5635

Yakima St Michaels Episcopal Church **P** (22) 5 S Naches Ave 98901-2726 (Mail to: 5 S Naches Ave 98901-2726) David Hacker (509) 453-4881

Yakima St Timothys Episcopal Church **P** (202) 4105 Richey Rd 98908-2662 (Mail to: 4105 Richey Rd 98908-2662) Colby Roberts (509) 966-7370

DIOCESE OF SPRINGFIELD
(PROVINCE V)
Comprises 60 counties of central and southern Illinois
DIOCESAN CENTER 821 S Second St Springfield IL 62704
TEL (217) 525-1876 FAX (217) 525-1877
E-MAIL Diocese@episcopalspringfield.org WEB www.episcopalspringfield.org

Previous Bishops—
Geo F Seymour 1878-1906, Chas R Hale coadj 1892-1900, Edward W Osborne coadj 1904 Bp 1906-16, Granville H Sherwood 1917-23, John C White 1924-47, Richard T Loring 1947-48, Chas A Clough 1948-61, Albert A Chambers 1962-72, Albert W Hillestad 1972-81, Donald M Hultstrand 1982-91, Peter H Beckwith 1992-2010, Daniel H Martins 2011-21

Bishop—The Rt Rev Brian K Burgess (1145) (Dio 21 May 2022)

Cn to Ord The Rev Can ME Evans; *V Pres* The Rev SW Denney; *Sec* The Rev GT Leighton; *Asst Sec* Rev RE Armidon; *Treas* G Smith; *Chanc* KJ Babb; *Trustee* D Monty; *COM* The Very Rev AS Hook; *Exec Asst to the Bishop* E McCrary; *Depts—Fin* C Rice; *Audit* E Burbage; *Mission* The Rev M Clark and D Shuler

Stand Comm—Cler: Pres SW Denney JK Muriuki AS Hook ZD Brooks; *Lay:* G Smith R Winn A Cornelius R Laws

Deans—Darrow MW Ohlemeier; *Eastern* GW Howard III; *Hale* SL Black; *Northern* JD Richmond; *Northeastern* RI Lewis; *Northwestern* ZD Brooks

PARISHES, MISSIONS, AND CLERGY

Albion St Johns Episcopal Church **M** (13) 20 E Cherry St 62806-1302 (Mail to: PO Box 747 62864-0015) George Howard (618) 2426594

Alton St Pauls and Trinity Chapel **P** (343) § 10 E 3rd St 62002-6201 (Mail to: 10 E 3rd St 62002-6201) Cynthia Sever (618) 4659149

Alton Trinity Chapel **SC** 1901 State St 62002-3370 (Mail to: 10 E 3rd St 62002-6201) (618) 4659149

Belleville St Georges Episcopal Church **P** (341) § 105 E D St 62220-1205 (Mail to: 105 E D St 62220-1295) Mark Ohlemeier (618) 2336320

Bloomington St Matthews Episcopal Church **P** (274) § 1920 E Oakland Ave 61701-5755 (Mail to: 1920 E Oakland Ave 61701-5798) Gregory Leighton (309) 6624646

Cairo Church of the Redeemer **M** (48) 606 Washington Ave 62914-2229 (Mail to: C/O Diocese of Springfield 821 S 2nd St 62704-2601) James Muriuki (618) 3063607

Carbondale St Andrews Episcopal Church **P** (126) 402 W Mill St 62901-2728 (Mail to: 402 W Mill St 62901-2728) Dale Coleman (618) 5294316

Carlinville St Pauls Episcopal Church **P** (45) § 415 S Broad St 62626-2111 (Mail to: 415 S Broad St 62626-2111) William Aikin (217) 8546431

Centralia St Johns Episcopal Church **M** (24) 700 E Broadway 62801-3261 (Mail to: PO Box 1512 62801-9122) Sylvia Howard Gene Tucker (618) 5323767

Champaign Chapel of St John The Divine **P** (253) 1011 S Wright St 61820-6249 (Mail to: 1011 S Wright St 61820-6249) Sean Ferrell (217) 3441924

Champaign Emmanuel Memorial Episcopal Ch **P** (395) 102 N State St 61820-3908 (Mail to: 208 W University Ave 61820-3997) (217) 3529827

Chesterfield St Peters Episcopal Church **M** 110 East Lincoln Ave 62630 (Mail to: C/O St Pauls Church 415 S Broad St 62626-2111) (217) 854-6431

Danville Church of the Holy Trinity **P** (65) § 308 N Vermilion St 61832-4770 (Mail to: 308 N Vermilion St 61832-4770) (217) 442-3498

Decatur St Johns Episcopal Church **P** (170) § 130 W Eldorado St 62522-2111 (Mail to: 130 W Eldorado St 62522-2111) (217) 428-4461

Edwardsville St Andrews Episcopal Church **P** (112) 406 Hillsboro Ave 62025-1730 (Mail to: 406 Hillsboro Ave 62025-1730) (618) 656-1929

Glen Carbon St Thomas Episcopal Church **M** (38) § 182 Summit Ave 62034-1446 (Mail to: 182 Summit Ave 62034-1446) (618) 288-5620

Granite City St Bartholomews Episcopal Ch **M** (15) § 2167 Grand Ave 62040-4724 (Mail to: 2165 Grand Ave 62040-4724) (618) 876-9097

Harrisburg St Stephen's Church **M** (37) § 101 E Church St 629461704 (Mail to: 101 E Church St 629461704) Timothy Goodman (618) 252-8239

Havana St Barnabas Episcopal Church **M** (33) § 420 N Plum St 62644-1129 (Mail to: 420 N Plum St 62644-1129) (309) 5432430

Jacksonville Trinity Episcopal Church **P** (83) § 359 W State St 62650-2007 (Mail to: 359 W State St 62650-2007) Zachary Brooks Thomas Langford (217) 245-5901

Lincoln Church of St John the Baptist **SC** PO Box 386 62656-0386 (Mail to: PO Box 386 62656-0386) James Cravens (217) 732-7609

Lincoln Trinity Episcopal Church **P** (62) 402 Pekin St 62656-2033 (Mail to: PO Box 386 62656-0386) Christopher Simpson (217) 732-7609

Marion St James Episcopal Church **Chapel** § 301 E Thorn St 62959-3159 (Mail to: 301 E Thorn St 62959-3159) (618) 993-2074

Mattoon Trinity Episcopal Church **M** (45) PO Box 302 61938-0302 (Mail to: PO Box 302 61938-0302) Anne Flynn (217) 234-4514

Morton All Saints Episcopal Church **M** (33) § 201 W Chicago St 61550-1909 (Mail to: 329 S Plum Ave 61550-1856) Laurie Kellington (309) 266-9894

Mount Carmel St John the Baptist Epis Ch **P** (49) § 600 N Mulberry St 62863-2045 (Mail to: PO Box 674 62863-0674) (618) 262-7382

Mount Vernon Trinity Episcopal Church **P** (70) 1100 Harrison St 62864-3814 (Mail to: 1100 Harrison St 62864-3814) (618) 242-3434

Normal Christ The King Episcopal Ch **P** (63) 1210 S Fell Ave 61761-3641 (Mail to: 1210 S Fell Ave 61761-3641) John Richmond (309) 454-4903

O Fallon St Michaels Episcopal Church **M** (119) 111 Ofallon Troy Rd 62269-6703 (Mail to: 111 Ofallon Troy Rd 62269-6703) Gregory Wilde (618) 632-6168

Pekin St Pauls Church Episcopal **P** (48) § 349 Buena Vista Ave 61554-4288 (Mail to: 343 Buena Vista Ave 61554-4227) Jonathan

Butcher Laurie Kellington (309) 346-2615

Rantoul St Christopher Epis Church **M** (26) § 1501 E Grove Ave 61866-2735 (Mail to: 1501 E Grove Ave 61866-2735) Steven Thorp (217) 892-2476

Robinson St Marys Episcopal Church **M** (14) § 8996 E 1050th Ave 62454-4822 (Mail to: PO Box 442 62454-0442) (618) 544-8974

Salem St Thomas Episcopal Church **M** (13) § PO Box 622 512 W Main St 62881-0622 (Mail to: PO Box 622 62881-0622) (618) 548-3560

Springfield Christ Episcopal Church **P** (124) 611 E Jackson St 62701-1815 (Mail to: 611 E Jackson St 62701-1898) Gregory Tournoux (217) 523-1871

Springfield St Lukes Episcopal Church **M** (108) 3813 Bergamot Dr 62712-5813 (Mail to: 1218 South Grand Ave E 62703-2621) Shawn Denney (217) 528-5915

✠ **Springfield** Cathedral Church of St Paul **O** (445) § 815 So 2nd St 62704 (Mail to: 815 S 2nd St 62704-2696) Martha Bradley Andrew Hook Gerald Raschke (217) 544-5135

W Frankfort St Marks Episcopal Church **M** (32) § 212 N Ida St 62896-2311 (Mail to: PO Box 97 62896-0097) Sheryl Black (618) 937-4976

SWITZERLAND

See Europe

DIOCESE OF TAIWAN

(PROVINCE VIII)
Comprises Taiwan and neighboring islands
DIOCESAN OFFICE 7 Ln 105 Hangchow S Rd Sec 1 Taipei Taiwan 10060 ROC
TEL 886-2-2341-1265 FAX 886-2-2396-2014
E-MAIL dioceseoftaiwan@episcopalchurch.org.tw WEB https://episcopalchurch.org.tw/

Previous Bishops—
Harry S Kennedy 1954-60, Chas P Gilson suffr 1961-64, James CL Wong 1965-70, James TM Pong 1971-79, PY Cheung 1980-87 John Chien 1988-2001, David Jung-Hsin Lai (2000-2020)

Bishop—Rt Rev Lennon YR Chang (Dio 22 Feb 2020)

Sec Conv CN Yang *Treas* May SC Hsy *Chanc* HHP Ma

Stand Comm—Cler: LF Lin LL Chang CC Lee WB Tzeng JC Lee CC Cheng *Lay:* BS Hu YC Chiu CH Chang Jude Chu Gung Chern HW Chuang *Honorable Chairperson* HHP Ma

PARISHES, MISSIONS, AND CLERGY

✠ **Taipei** St John Cathedral **O** 280 Fu-Hsing S Rd Sec 2 TAIWAN 10663 (Mail to: 280 Fu-Hsing S Rd Sec 2 Taipei TAIWAN 10663) Philip Lin, Anthony Liang

Keelung Holy Trinity **P** 163 Tung-Ming Road TAIWAN 20141 (Mail to: 163 Tung-Ming Road Keelung TAIWAN 20105) Justin Lin

Keelung St Stephen **M** 1F No 9 Aly 6 Ln 168 Zhonghe Rd Zhongshan Dist TAIWAN 20347 (Mail to: 1F No 9 Aly 6 Ln 168 Zhonghe Rd Zhongshan Dist Keelung TAIWAN 20347) Julia Lin

Taipei Good Shepherd **P** 509 Chung-Cheng Rd Shihlin Dist TAIWAN 11168 (Mail to:

509 Chung-Cheng Rd Shihlin Dist Taipei TAIWAN 11168) Keith Lee

New Taipei City Advent **P** 499 Sec 4 Tam King Rd Tamsui TAIWAN 25135 (Mail to: 499 Sec 4 Tam King Rd Tamsui New Taipei City TAIWAN 25135) Lennon Chang, Irving Wu

Taoyuan City Christ **M** No 33, Chongyi 3rd St., Pingzhen Dist., Taoyuan City, TAIWAN 32453, (Mail to: No 33, Chongyi 3rd St., Pingzhen Dist., Taoyuan City, TAIWAN 32453) Deledda Tsai

Taichung St James **P** No 23 Wu-Chuan West Road Sec 1 TAIWAN 40348 (Mail to: No 23 Wu-Chuan West Road Sec 1 Taichung TAIWAN 40348) Lily Chang

Taichung Leading Star **M** No 8 Ln 530 Guangxing Rd Taiping Dist TAIWAN 41148 (Mail to: No 8 Ln 530 Guangxing Rd Taiping Dist Taichung AIWAN 41148) Lily Chang

Chiayi St Peters **M** 8 Hsing Chung St TAIWAN 60047 (Mail to: 8 Hsing Chung St Chiayi TAIWAN 60047) Simon Tsou

Chiayi County Goubei Mission **PS** No 70-1 . Goubei Village Dalin Township TAIWAN 62245 (Mail to: No 70-1 Goubei Village Dalin Township Chiayi County TAIWAN 62245) Simon Tsou

Tainan Grace **M** No 4 Ln 550 Chongde Rd East Dist TAIWAN 70171 (Mail to: No 24 Ln 550 Chongde Rd East Dist Tainan TAIWAN 70171) Philip Ho

Kaohsiung St Andrew **PS** No 11 Sec 2 Jiading Rd Qieding Dist TAIWAN 85241 (Mail to: No 11 Sec 2 Jiading Rd Qieding Dist Kaohsiung TAIWAN 85241) Philip Ho

Kangshan All Saints **P** No5 Jieshou Rd Gangshan Dist TAIWAN 82044 (Mail to: No 5 Jieshou Rd Gangshan Dist Kaohsiung TAIWAN 82044) Leo Tzeng

Kaohsiung St Paul **M** 200 Tzu Chiang 1 Rd San Min Dist TAIWAN 80749 (Mail to: 200 Tzu Chiang 1 Rd San Min Dist Kaohsiung TAIWAN 80749) Chen-Chang Cheng

Kaohsiung St Timothy **P** 3F # 262 Chung-Hsiao 1 Rd Hsin-Hsing Dist TAIWAN 80055 (Mail to: 3F # 262 Chung-Hsiao 1 Rd Hsin-Hsing Dist Kaohsiung TAIWAN 80055) Richard Lee

Pingtung St Mark **M** 120-11 Chung Hsiao Rd TAIWAN 90063 (Mail to: 120-11 Chung Hsiao Rd Pingtung Taiwan 90063) Joseph Ho

Hualien St Luke **M** No 1-6 Ming Hsin St TAIWAN 97050 (Mail to: 1-6 Ming Hsin St Hualien TAIWAN 97050) Joseph Wu

STATE OF TENNESSEE
Dioceses of East Tennessee (ETN), Tennessee (TN), and West Tennessee (WTN)

Antioch—TN	Dickson—TN	La Grange—WTN	Pulaski—TN
Athens—ETN	Dyersburg—WTN	Lebanon—TN	Ripley—TN
Atoka—WTN	Elizabethton—ETN	Lookout Mtn—ETN	Rugby—ETN
Battle Creek—ETN	Fayetteville—TN	Loudon—ETN	Saint Andrews—TN
Bolivar—WTN	Franklin—TN	Madison—TN	Sevierville—ETN
Brentwood—TN	Ft Ogelthorpe—ETN	Manchester—TN	Sewanee—TN
Bristol—ETN	Gallatin—TN	Maryville—ETN	Seymour—ETN
Brownsville—WTN	Gatlinburg—ETN	Mason—WTN	Shelbyville—TN
Chattanooga—ETN	Germantown—WTN	McMinnville—TN	Sherwood—TN
Clarksville—TN	Greeneville—ETN	Memphis—WTN	Signal Mtn—ETN
Cleveland—ETN	Harriman—ETN	Millington—WTN	Smyrna—TN
Collierville—WTN	Hendersonville—TN	Monteagle—TN	Somerville—WTN
Columbia—TN	Hixson—ETN	Morristown—ETN	So Pittsburg—ETN
Cookeville—TN	Humboldt—WTN	Murfreesboro—TN	Spring Hill—TN
Copperhill—ETN	Jackson—WTN	Nashville—TN	Springfield—TN
Covington—WTN	Jefferson City—ETN	Newport—ETN	Tracy City—TN
Cowan—TN	Johnson City—ETN	New Johnsonville—TN	Tullahoma—TN
Crossville—ETN	Jonesborough—ETN	Norris—ETN	Union City—WTN
Cumberland Furnace—	Kingsport—ETN	Oak Ridge—ETN	Winchester—TN
TN	Knoxville—ETN	Ooltewah—ETN	
Decherd—TN	LaFollette—ETN	Paris—WTN	

DIOCESE OF TENNESSEE
(PROVINCE IV)
Comprises the middle section of the State of Tennessee
DIOCESAN OFFICE 3700 Woodmont Blvd Nashville TN 37215
TEL (615) 251-3322 FAX (615) 251-8010
E-MAIL info@edtn.org WEB http://edtn.org/

Previous Bishops— James H Otey 1834-63, Chas T Quintard 1865-98, Thomas F Gailor coadj 1893 Bp 1898-1935, Troy Beatty coadj 1919-22, James HM Maxon coadj 1922 Bp 1935-47, Edmund P Dandridge coadj 1938 Bp 1947-53, Theodore N Barth coadj 1948 Bp 1953-61, John Vander Horst suffr 1955-1961 coadj 1961 Bp 1961-1977, William E Sanders coadj 1962 Bp 1977-1984, W Fred Gates Jr suffr 1966-1982, Geo L Reynolds 1985-91, Bertram N Herlong 1993-2006

Bishop—Rt Rev John C Bauerschmidt (1013) (Dio 27 Jan 2007)

Cn to Ord Rev Cn J Howard; Cn to Ord; Treas WA Stringer; Chanc J Weatherly; V Chanc W Longmire; Asst Treas J Ramsey; COM Chair E Arning; *AF* S Abington; *Exec Asst* S Beld

Stand Comm—Cler: W Dennler J Davis L Smith; *Lay:* S Huggins B Gittens E LeBlanc

PARISHES, MISSIONS, AND CLERGY

Antioch St Marks Episcopal Church **P** (136) 3100 Murfreesboro Pike 37013-2202 (Mail to: PO Box 741 37011-0741) Battle Beasley (615) 361-4100

Brentwood Church of the Good Shepherd **P** (1091) § 1420 Wilson Pike 37027-7701 (Mail to: 1420 Wilson Pike 37027-7701) Natalie Van Kirk Frederick Schmidt (615) 661-0890

Clarksville Grace Chapel **M** (24) 1950 Rossview Rd 37043-1516 (Mail to: C/O Julia Meadows Treasurer 3270 Port Royal Rd 37010-9018) (931) 3582111

Clarksville Trinity Episcopal Church **P** (473) § 317 Franklin St 37040-3421 (Mail to: 317 Franklin St 37040-3421) (931) 645-2458

Columbia St Peters Episcopal Church **P** (565) 311 W 7th St 38401-3132 (Mail to: 311 W 7th St 38401-3132) Christopher Bowhay (931) 388-3331

Cookeville St Michael Episcopal Church **P** (314) 640 N Washington Ave 38501-2659 (Mail to: 640 N Washington Ave 38501-2659) Antoinette Azar (931) 526-4654

Cowan St Agnes Mission **M** (49) England At Cherry 37318 (Mail to: PO Box 356 37318) (931) 636-6313

Cumberland Furnace Calvary Episcopal Church **M** (10) 1086 Old Highway 48 N 37051-5000 (Mail to: 1086 Old Highway 48 N 37051-5000) (615) 566-5247

Decherd Christ Episcopal Church **M** (17) 9616 Old Alto Hwy 37324 (Mail to: Leona Hawk 311 Kelly Dr 37324-3803) (931) 967-0898

Dickson St James Episcopal Church **M** (48) § 205 Church St 37055-1303 (Mail to: 205 Church St 37055-1303) David Yancey David Yancey (615) 446-8916

Fayetteville St Mary Magdalene Episcopal Ch **P** (78) § 106 Washington St E 37334-2544 (Mail to: PO Box 150 37334-0150) Patrick Soule (931) 433-2911

Franklin St Pauls Episcopal Church **P** (819) § 510 W Main St 37064-2722 (Mail to: 510 W Main St 37064-2722) William Mccown Monna Mayhall (615) 790-0527

Franklin Church of the Resurrection **P** (259) § 1216 Sneed Rd W 37069-6927 (Mail to: 1216 Sneed Rd W 37069-6927) Stephen Jones (615) 3779144

Gallatin Church of Our Saviour **P** (107) 704 Hartsville Pike 37066-2525 (Mail to: PO Box 307 37066-0307) Jacob Bottom (615) 452-7146

Hendersonvlle St Joseph of Arimathea Epis Ch **P** (171) 103 Country Club Dr 37075-4024 (Mail to: 103 Country Club Dr 37075-4024) Robert Osborne (615) 824-2910

Lebanon Episcopal Ch of the Epiphany **P** (61) § 1500 Hickory Ridge Rd 37087-5702 (Mail to: 1500 Hickory Ridge Rd 37087-5702) Cynthia Seifert (615) 444-7336

Madison St James the Less **P** (117) 411 W Due West Ave 37115-4403 (Mail to: PO Box 1419 37116-1419) John Smith (615) 8654496

Manchester St Bedes Episcopal Church **P** (67) § 93 Saint Bedes Dr 37355-5900 (Mail to: PO Box 305 37349-0305) (931) 728-4463

Mcminnville St Matthews Episcopal Church **M** (138) 105 Edgewood Ave 37110-1565 (Mail to: 105 Edgewood Ave 37110-1565) (931) 473-8233

Monteagle Church of the Holy Comforter **M** (5) 1st Ave & Fairmont 37356 (Mail to: PO Box 541 37366-0541) (931) 967-0898

Murfreesboro Church of the Holy Cross **M** (80) 1140 Cason Ln 37128-7660 (Mail to: 1140 Cason Ln 37128-7660) (615) 867-7116

Murfreesboro Saint Paul's Episcopal Church **P** (1022) 116 N Academy St 37130-3717 (Mail to: 116 N Academy St 37130-3717) Kristine Blaess Michael Whitnah (615) 893-3780

✛ **Nashville** Christ Church Cathedral **O** (2118) 900 Broadway 37203-3807 (Mail to: 900

Broadway 37203-3854) Timothy Kimbrough Anna Russell Friedman Hassell Hurst Timothy Kimbrough Matthew Lewis Melissa Smith Richard Wineland (615) 255-7729

Nashville Church of the Advent **P** (618) 5501 Franklin Pike 37220-2115 (Mail to: 5501 Franklin Pike 37220-2115) James McVey (615) 373-5630

Nashville Church of the Holy Trinity **P** (92) 615 6th Ave S 37203-4613 (Mail to: 615 6th Ave S 37203-4613) William Dennler Rebecca Weiner Tompkins (615) 256-6359

Nashville Church of the Holy Spirit **P** (90) 222 Franklin Limestone Rd 37217-3004 (Mail to: 5325 Nolensville Pike 37211-6415) (615) 333-9979

Nashville St Anns Episcopal Church **P** (135) 419 Woodland St 37206-4207 (Mail to: 419 Woodland St 37206-4207) (615) 254-3534

Nashville St Anselms Episcopal Chapel **M** (59) 2008 Meharry Blvd 37208-2916 (Mail to: 2008 Meharry Blvd 37208-2916) Richard Britton (615) 329-9640

Nashville Saint Augustine's Chapel **CC** (669) 200 24th Ave S 37235 (Mail to: PO Box 6330-B 37235-0001) Ian Cron Francisco Garcia Rebecca Stevens-Hummon Rebecca Stevens-Hummon Richard Wineland (615) 322-4783

Nashville St Bartholomews Episcopal Ch **P** (1143) § 4800 Belmont Park Terrace 37215-4422 (Mail to: 4800 Belmont Park Ter 37215-4422) Serena Sides Harold Wilson (615) 377-4750

Nashville Saint David's Episcopal Church **P** (374) § 6501 Pennywell Dr 37205-3005 (Mail to: 6501 Pennywell Dr 37205-3005) Carolyn Coleman (615) 352-0293

Nashville Saint George's Church **P** (3914) § 4715 Harding Pike 37205-2809 (Mail to: 4715 Harding Pike 37205-2896) John Gilliam Colin Ambrose Colin Ambrose David Barr Christopher Jones Margery Kennelly (615) 3852150

Nashville Saint Philip's Church **P** (380) 85 Fairway Dr 37214-2148 (Mail to: 85 Fairway Dr 37214-2148) Caroline Osborne (615) 883-4595

New Johnsonville St Andrews Episcopal Church **M** (22) 539 Hillcrest Dr 37134-9668 (Mail to: PO Box 522 37134-0522) (931) 535-2314

Pulaski Church of the Messiah **P** (117) § 114 N 3rd St 38478-3203 (Mail to: 114 N 3rd St 38478-3203) (931) 363-1454

Saint Andrews St Andrews-Sewanee **SC** 290 Quintard Rd 37375-3000 (Mail to: 290 Quintard Rd 37375-3000) (931) 598-5651

Sewanee Parish of St Mark and St Paul **P** (442) 216 University Ave 37375-2202 (Mail to: Box 267 37375-0267) Robert Lamborn (931) 598-5926

Sewanee St James Episcopal Church **P** (38) 898 Midway Rd 37375-2701 (Mail to: PO Box 336 37375-0336) (931) 598-0153

Shelbyville Church of the Redeemer **P** (51) 203 E Lane St 37160-3429 (Mail to: PO Box 274 37162-0274) Michael Blaess (931) 619-5493

Sherwood Church of the Epiphany **M** (90) 62 Mountain Ave E 37376 (Mail to: 62 Mountain Ave W 37376-2000) (931) 967-0898

Smyrna All Saints Episcopal Church **M** (310) 1401 Lee Victory Pkwy 37167-6299 (Mail to: 1401 Lee Victory Pkwy 37167-6299) (615) 223-7157

Spring Hill Grace Episcopal Church **M** (92) 5291 Main St 37174-2495 (Mail to: 5291 Main St 37174-2449) Joseph Davis (931) 486-3223

Springfield St Lukes Church **M** (40) 103 7th Ave W 37172-2826 (Mail to: 103 7th Ave W 37172-2826) Hassell Hurst (615) 382-7505

Tracy City Christ Episcopal Church **M** (145) PO Box 457 37387-0457 (Mail to: PO Box 457 37387-0457) (931) 967-0898

Tullahoma St Barnabas Episcopal Church **P** (292) 110 E Lincoln St 37388-3631 (Mail to: 110 E Lincoln St 37388-3632) Michael Murphy (931) 455-3170

Winchester Trinity Episcopal Church **P** (22) § 213 1st Ave NW 37398-1645 (Mail to: 213 1st Ave NW 37398-1645) William Barton (931) 967-0898

STATE OF TEXAS

Dioceses of Dallas (Dal), Northwest Texas (NT), Rio Grande (RG), Texas (TX), and West Texas (WT)

Abilene—NT	Alvin—TX	Athens—Dal	Beaumont—TX
Albany—NT	Amarillo—NT	Atlanta—Dal	Beeville—WT
Alamogordo—RG	Angleton—TX	Austin—TX	Belen—RG
Albuquerque—RG	Anthony—RG	Bandera—WT	Bellville—TX
Alice—WT	Aransas Pass—WT	Bastrop—TX	Big Spg—NT
Allen—Dal & WT	Arlington—TX	Bay City—TX	Blanco—WT
Alpine—RG	Artesia—RG	Baytown—TX	Boerne—WT

Bonham—Dal
Borger—NT
Bracketville—WT
Brady—WT
Brenham—TX
Brownsville—WT
Bryan—TX
Buda—WT
Burnet—TX
Calvert—TX
Cameron—TX
Canton—Dal
Canyon Lake—WT
Carlsbad—RG
Carrizo Spgs—WT
Carthage—TX
Cedar Hill—Dal
Cedar Pk—TX
Center—TX
Chama—RG
Clarendon—NT
Cloudcroft—RG
Clovis Curry—RG
Coleman—NT
College Sta—TX
Colorado City—NT
Columbus—TX
Comfort—WT
Conroe—TX
Coppell—Dal
Copperas Cove—TX
Corpus Christi—WT
Corsicana—Dal
Cotulla—WT
Crockett—TX
Cuero—WT
Cypress—TX
Cypress Mill—WT
Dallas—Dal
Decatur—TX
Del Rio—WT
Deming—RG
Denison—Dal
Denton—Dal
De Soto—Dal
Devine—WT
Dickinson—TX
Dripping Spgs—WT
Eagle Lake—TX
Eagle Pass—WT
Edgewood—RG
Edinburg—WT
Edna—WT
El Paso—RG
Ennis—Dal
Espanola—RG
Farmington—RG
Fort Stockton—RG

Flower Mound—Dal
Ft McKavett—WT
Ft Worth—TX
Fredericksburg—WT
Freeport—TX
Friendswood—TX
Frisco—Dal
Gallup—RG
Galveston—TX
Garland—Dal
Georgetown—TX
George West—WT
Glencoe—RG
Goliad—WT
Gonzales—WT
Granbury—TX
Greenville—Dal
Hallettsville—WT
Hamilton—TX
Harlingen—WT
Hearne—TX
Hebbronville—WT
Hempstead—TX
Henderson—TX
Hillsboro—RG & TX
Hitchcock—TX
Hobbs—RG
Houston—TX
Humble—TX
Huntsville—TX
Hurst—RG & TX
Irving—Dal
Jacksonville—TX
Jasper—TX
Jefferson—TX
Junction—WT
Katy—TX
Kaufman—Dal
Keller—TX
Kemp—Dal
Kenedy—WT
Kerrville—WT
Kilgore—TX
Killeen—TX
Kingsville—WT
Kingwood—TX
Lago Vista—TX
La Grange—TX
La Marque—TX
La Porte—TX
Lake Jackson—TX
Lampasas—TX
Laredo—WT
Las Cruces—RG
Las Vegas—RG
League City—TX
Levelland—NT
Lewisville—Dal

Liberty—TX
Lindale—TX
Livingston—TX
Llano—WT
Lockhart—WT
Longview—TX
Los Alamos—RG
Los Lunas—RG
Lubbock—NT
Lufkin—TX
Luling—WT
Madisonville—TX
Manor—TX
Marble Falls—TX
Marfa—RG
Marlin—TX
Marshall—TX
Matagorda—TX
McAllen—WT
McKinney—Dal
Menard—WT
Mexia—TX
Midland—NT
Milan—RG
Mineola—Dal
Mission—WT
Missouri City—TX
Montell—WT
Mt Pleasant—Dal
Nacogdoches—TX
Navasota—TX
New Braunfels—WT
Odessa—NT
Orange—TX
Palacios—TX
Palestine—TX
Pampa—NT
Paris—Dal
Pasadena—TX
Pearland—TX
Pflugerville—TX
Pharr—WT
Pittsburg—Dal
Plainview—NT
Plano—Dal
Pleasanton—WT
Portales—RG
Pt Aransas—WT
Pt Isabel—WT
Pt Lavaca—WT
Portland—WT
Pt Neches—TX
Pottsboro—Dal
Prairie View—TX
Prosper—Dal
Raton—RG
Refugio—WT
Richardson—Dal

Richmond—TX
Rio Rancho—RG
Rockdale—TX
Rockport—WT
Rockwall—Dal
Roswell—RG
Round Rock—TX
Ruidoso—RG
Salado—TX
San Antonio—WT
San Angelo—NT
San Augustine—TX
San Benito—WT
San Marcos—WT
San Saba—WT
Santa Fe—RG
Sealy—TX
Seguin—WT
Shamrock—NT
Sherman—Dal
Silsbee—TX
Silver City—RG
Socorro—RG
Sonora—WT
Spring—TX
Stafford—TX
Stephenville—TX
Sugar Land—TX
Sulphur Spgs—Dal
Sweetwater—NT
Taos—RG
Taylor—TX
Temple—TX
Terlingua—RG
Terrell—Dal
Texarkana—Dal
Texas City—TX
The Woodlands—TX
Tomball—TX
Truth Consq—RG
Tucumcari—RG
Tyler—TX
Universal City—WT
Uvalde—WT
Vernon—NT
Victoria—WT
Waco—TX
Waxahachie—Dal
Weslaco—WT
W Columbia—TX
Wharton—TX
Wichita Falls—TX
Wimberley—WT
Windcrest—WT
Winnie—TX
Winnsboro—Dal
Woodville—TX

DIOCESE OF TEXAS
(PROVINCE VII)
Comprises 57 counties of southeast and central Texas
DIOCESAN OFFICE 1225 Texas Ave Houston TX 77002-3504
TEL (713) 520-6444, (800) 318-4452 FAX (713) 520-5723
E-MAIL Individual e-mail addresses may be found on the diocesan website WEB www.epicenter.org

Previous Bishops—
Alexander Gregg 1859-93, Geo H Kinsolving coadj 1892 Bp 1893-1928, Clinton S Quin coadj 1918 Bp 1928-55, F Percy Goddard suffr 1955-72, James P Clements suffr 1956-60, Scott Field Bailey suffr 1964-75, John E Hines coadj 1945 Bp 1955-64, James M Richardson 1965-80, Roger H Cilley suffr 1976-85, Gordon T Charlton suffr 1982-89, Maurice M Benitez 1980-95, William E Sterling suffr 1989-99 James B Brown asst Bp 2000-2003, Claude E Payne Bp 1995-2003, Leopoldo J Alard suffr 1995-2003, Rayford B High Jr suffr 2003-2011, Don A Wimberly Bp 2003-09, Dena A Harrison suffr 2006-19, Jeff W Fisher suffr 2012-19

Bishop—Rt Rev C Andrew Doyle (1033) (Dio 7 June 09)

Bishop Suffragan—Rt Rev Kathryn McCrossen Ryan (1118) (1 June 2019)

Bishop Assistant—Rt Rev Hector F Monterroso (7 June 2019)

Cn to Ord Rev Cn KM Ryan; *Sec* Rev Cn JA Logan Jr; *Treas and CFO* L Mitchell; *Chanc* DT Harvin; *Chief of Staff* Rev Cn C Faulstich; *Cn for Wellness & Care* Rev Cn L Hines; *Trans Off* Rev B Rider; *Dir Fdns* D Fisher; *Chr Form* J Martin-Currie; *Yth* S Townes; *Missional Communities* J Evans; *Comm* LK Eaglin; *Camps* G Dehan; *Mission Amp* Rev Cn J Saylors; *Archdcn* R Oechsel; *Intercultural Dev* D Trevino

Deans: Austin B Pearson; *Central* D Hay; *Northeast* M Tollett; *Northwest* J Jones; *San Jacinto* G Sevick; *Southeast* K Giblin; *Southwest* T Smith; *West Harris* J Condon; *East Harris* V Thomas; *Galveston* J Liberatore

Stand Comm—Cler: Sec M Tollett J Pevehouse G Razim; *Lay: Pres* D Bollinger M Quintanilla E Ziegler

PARISHES, MISSIONS, AND CLERGY
Alvin Grace Episcopal Church **P** (163) 200 W Lang St 77511-2396 (Mail to: 112 W Lang St 77511-2300) Suzanne Smith Carol Mills Joseph Mills (281) 331-5657
Angleton Church of the Holy Comforter **P** (249) § 234 South Arcola 77515 (Mail to: PO Box 786 77516-0786) Travis Smith (979) 849-1269
Arlington St Alban Episcopal Church **P** (205) 316 W Main St 76010-7114 (Mail to: 316 W Main St 76010-7114) Kevin Johnson (817) 264-3083
Austin All Saints Episcopal Church **P** (1537) § 209 W 27th St 78705-1043 (Mail to: 209 W

27th St 78705-1043) Genevieve Razim Robert Chambers Kendrah Mcdonald (512) 4763589
Austin Church of the Resurrection **P** (365) 2200 Justin Ln 78757-2417 (Mail to: 2200 Justin Ln 78757-2417) William Tweedie (512) 459-0027
Austin Episcopal Church of the Cross **P** (114) PO Box 340821 78734-0014 (Mail to: PO Box 340821 78734-0014) Paul Johnson
Austin Iglesia San Francisco de Asis **M** (1220) 7000 Woodhue Dr 78745-5454 (Mail to: 7000 Woodhue Dr 78745-5454) Albert Pearson (512) 439-0721
Austin St Albans Episcopal Church **P** (488) 11819 S I H 35 78747-1804 (Mail to: PO Box 368 78652-0368) (512) 282-5631
Austin St Christophers Episcopal Ch **P** (200) 8724 Travis Hills Dr 78735-8171 (Mail to: 8724 Travis Hills Dr 78735-8171) Kenneth Malcolm Sharon Williams (512) 288-0128
Austin St Davids Episcopal Church **P** (1934) § 301 E 8th St 78701-3203 (Mail to: 301 E 8th St 78701-3280) William Treadwell Angela Cortinas Chad Mccall (512) 610-3500
Austin St. George's Episcopal Church **P** (130) 4301 N Interstate 35 78722-1103 (Mail to: 4301 N Interstate 35 78722-1103) Matthew Boulter (512) 4542523
Austin St James' Episcopal Church **P** (746) 1941 Webberville Rd 78721-1679 (Mail to: 1941 Webberville Rd 78721-1679) Erin Hensley Albert Rodriguez Robert Vickery (512) 926-6339
Austin St Johns Episcopal Church **P** (216) 11201 Parkfield Dr 78758-4264 (Mail to: PO Box 81493 78708-1493) Victoria Mason (512) 836-3974
Austin St Lukes on the Lake Epis Ch **P** (772) 5600 Ranch Road 620 N 78732-1823 (Mail to: 5600 Ranch Road 620 N 78732-1823) James Cook Ann Mclemore (512) 266-2455
Austin St Marks Episcopal Church **P** (820) 2128 Barton Hills Dr 78704-4651 (Mail to: 2128 Barton Hills Dr 78704-4651) Zachary Koons Nathan Jennings (512) 444-1449
Austin St Matthews Episcopal Church **P** (1295) § 8134 Mesa Dr 78759-8615 (Mail to: 8134 Mesa Dr 78759-8678) Catherine Wright Andrew Benko Marcia Bhan Jerry Chapman (512) 345-8314
Austin St Michaels Episcopal Church **P** (571) 6317 Bee Caves Rd 78746-5148 (Mail to: 1500 N Capital of Texas Hwy 78746-3320) John Newton Hope Benko Joshua Kulak Nancy Ricketts Sharon Williams (512) 327-1474

Austin Soco Episcopal Community **M** (24) 1502 Eva St 78704-3011 (Mail to: 1502 Eva St 78704-3011) Paul Skeith

Austin The Ch of the Good Shepherd **P** (3670) 3201 Windsor Dr 78703-2239 (Mail to: PO Box 5176 78763-5176) Channing Smith Holmes Adams Brin Bon Terence Gleeson Paige Hanks Whitney Kirby Cynthia Kittredge Laurence Wainwright-Maks (512) 476-3523

Bastrop Calvary Episcopal Church **P** (422) § 603 Spring St 78602-3226 (Mail to: PO Box 721 78602-0721) Matthew Stone Kenneth Kesselus (512) 303-7515

Bay City St Marks Episcopal Church **P** (209) 2200 Avenue E 77414-5009 (Mail to: 2200 Avenue E 77414-5009) John Myers (979) 245-2557

Baytown Trinity Episcopal Church **P** (448) 5010 N Main St 77521-9606 (Mail to: 5010 N Main St 77521-9606) Meredith Crigler Lajunta Rios Lajunta Rios (281) 421-0090

Beaumont St Mark's Episcopal Church **P** (653) 680 Calder St 77701-2303 (Mail to: 680 Calder St 77701-2398) James Pevehouse (409) 832-3405

Beaumont St Stephens Episcopal Church **P** (494) 4090 Delaware St 77706-7801 (Mail to: 4090 Delaware St 77706-7801) (409) 892-4227

Bellville St Marys Episcopal Church **P** (117) 24 N Masonic St 77418-1444 (Mail to: 24 N Masonic St 77418-1444) (979) 865-2330

Brenham St Peters Episcopal Church **P** (208) 2310 Airline Dr 77833-5509 (Mail to: 2310 Airline Dr 77833-5509) Stephen Whaley (979) 836-7248

Bryan Saint Andrew's Episcopal Church **P** (300) 217 W 26th St 77803-3215 (Mail to: PO Box 405 77806-0405) Daryl Hay David Hoster (979) 8225176

Burnet Epis Church of the Epiphany **P** (135) 601 N Wood St 78611-0002 (Mail to: PO Box 2 78611-0002) (512) 756-2334

Calvert Church of the Epiphany **M** (14) 700 E Gregg St 77837-7801 (Mail to: PO Box 129 77837) (512) 217-6314

Cameron All Saints Episcopal Church **M** (39) 200 N Travis Ave 76520-3312 (Mail to: PO Box 510 76520) Durwood Bagby (254) 697-2167

Carthage St Johns Episcopal Church **M** (44) Attn: Maudie Leach 904 N Daniels St 75633-1126 (Mail to: Attn: Maudie Leach 904 N Daniels St 75633-1126) Jennene Laurinec (903) 693-5566

Cedar Park Christ Episcopal Church **P** (331) 3520 W Whitestone Blvd 78613 (Mail to: 3520 W Whitestone Blvd 78613-7973) Richard Pelkey (512) 267-2428

Center St Johns Episcopal Church **M** (16) 1063 Southview Cir 75935-4544 (Mail to: PO Box 1026 75935-1026) Jane Barker (936) 598-4101

College Station St Francis Episcopal Church **P** (78) 1101 Rock Prairie Rd 77845-8344 (Mail to: 1101 Rock Prairie Rd 77845-8344) Lacy Largent (979) 696-1491

College Station St Thomas Episcopal Church **P** (588) § 906 George Bush Dr 77840-3056 (Mail to: 906 George Bush Dr 77840-3056) (979) 696-1726

Columbus Saint John's Episcopal Church **P** (42) 913 Travis St 78934-2436 (Mail to: PO Box 746 78934-0746) (979) 732-2590

Conroe St James The Apostle Epis Ch **P** (802) 1803 Highland Hollow Dr 77304-4092 (Mail to: C/O Financial Secretary PO Box 559 77305-0559) Jerald Hyche (936) 756-8831

Copperas Cove St Martins Episcopal Church **M** (89) 1602 S Fm 116 76522-4204 (Mail to: 1602 S Fm 116 76522-4204) (254) 547-0331

Crockett All Saints Episcopal Church **M** (17) 1301 E Houston Ave 75835-1749 (Mail to: PO Box 103 75835-0103) John Chase (936) 544-8914

Cypress St Aidans Episcopal Church **M** (502) 13131 Fry Rd 77433-3339 (Mail to: 13131 Fry Rd 77433-3339) Leslie Carpenter Warren Miedke (281) 373-3203

Cypress St Marys Episcopal Church **P** (480) 15415 N Eldridge Pkwy 77429-2005 (Mail to: PO Box 1542 77410-1542) (281) 370-8000

Decatur Epis Ch of the Resurrection **M** (35) 905 S Church St 76234-2211 (Mail to: 905 S Church St 76234-2211) Anthony Hiatt

Dickinson Holy Trinity Episcopal Church **P** (316) 4613 Highway 3 77539-6852 (Mail to: 4613 Highway 3 77539-6852) (281) 337-1833

Eagle Lake Christ Church **P** (76) PO Box 577 77434-0577 (Mail to: PO Box 577 77434-0577) Ray Wilson (979) 234-3437

Fort Worth All Saints Episcopal Church **P** (1317) § 9700 Saints Cir 76108-5985 (Mail to: PO Box 100609 76185-0609) Christopher Jambor Lynne Waltman (817) 732-1424

Fort Worth St Christopher's Epis Church **P** (301) § 5709 Wedgwood Dr 76133-2540 (Mail to: PO Box 34971 76162-4971) (817) 926-8277

Fort Worth St Luke-in-the-Meadow Epis Ch **P** (96) 3021 E Rosedale St 76105-2331 (Mail to: PO Box 8695 76124-0695) Karen Calafat (817) 534-4925

Fort Worth Trinity Episcopal Church **P** (1071) § 3401 Bellaire Dr S 76109-2133 (Mail to: 3401 Bellaire Dr S 76109-2133) Robert Pace (817) 926-4631

Freeport St Pauls Episcopal Church **P** (79) 1307 W 5th St 77541-5311 (Mail to: 1307 W 5th St 77541-5311) Robert Dohle (979) 233-3673

Friendswood Church of the Good Shepherd **P** (690) § 1207 Winding Way Dr 77546-4808 (Mail to: 1207 W Winding Way Dr 77546-4808) Justin Briggle (281) 482-7630

Galveston Grace Episcopal Church **P** (246) 1115 36th St 77550-4113 (Mail to: 1115 36th St 77550-4113) (409) 762-9676

Galveston St Augustine of Hippo Church **M** (88) § 1410 Jack Johnson Blvd 77550-3953 (Mail to:

1410 Jack Johnson Blvd 77550-3953) Michael Brady Chester Makowski (409) 763-4254

Galveston Trinity Episcopal Church **P** (609) 2216 Ball St 77550-2224 (Mail to: 2216 Ball St 77550-2224) James Abbott (409) 765-6317

Galveston William Temple Episl Ctr **Chapel** 427 Market St 77550-2703 (Mail to: Attn: Mr Tim R Mack Treas 427 Market St 77550-2703) (409) 539-2077

Georgetown Grace Episcopal Church **P** (677) 1314 E University Ave 78626-6115 (Mail to: 1314 E University Ave 78626-6115) Albert Pearson Mary Ann Huston (512) 863-2068

Granbury Church of the Good Shepherd **P** (164) 4530 Acton Hwy 76049-2907 (Mail to: 4530 Acton Hwy 76049-2907) (817) 326-6074

Hamilton Saint Mary's Church **M** (16) 1101 S Rice St 76531-9600 (Mail to: PO Box 562 76531-0562) (254) 386-4412

Hearne St Philips Episcopal Church **M** (30) 408 Cedar St 77859-2545 (Mail to: Ina F Boyle PO Box 952 77859) (979) 279-3234

Hempstead St Bartholomews Church **P** (38) 811 14th St 77445-5146 (Mail to: PO Box 961 77445-0961) (979) 826-2525

Henderson St Matthews Episcopal Church **P** (64) 214 College Ave 75654-4131 (Mail to: 214 College Ave 75654-4131) Patsy Barham (903) 657-3154

Hillsboro Saint Mary's Church **M** (11) 301 S Waco Street 76645 (Mail to: C/O David Skelton MD 109 Corsicana St 76645-2133) (254) 582-2255

Hitchcock All Saints Episcopal Church **M** (31) 10416 Highway 6 77563-4580 (Mail to: 10416 Highway 6 77563-4580) Mark Marmon (409) 925-2544

✣ **Houston** Christ Church Cathedral **O** (3970) § 1117 Texas St 77002-3113 (Mail to: C/O J David Simpson 1117 Texas St 77002-3113) Simon Bautista Gary Jones Gary Jones Kathleen Pfister Kathleen Pfister Stephen-Phillip Varnell Rebecca Zartman (713) 590-3308

Houston Christ the King Episcopal Ch **M** (235) 15325 Bellaire Blvd 77083-3110 (Mail to: 15325 Bellaire Blvd 77083-3110) Wendy Wilkinson (281) 933-6800

Houston Church of the Ascension **P** (376) 2525 Seagler Rd 77042-3119 (Mail to: 2525 Seagler Rd 77042-3119) Mark Mcdonald (713) 781-1330

Houston Church of the Epiphany **P** (732) § 9600 S Gessner Dr 77071-1002 (Mail to: 9600 S Gessner Rd 77071-1099) Patrick Hall (713) 774-9619

Houston Church of the Redeemer **M** (28) § 5700 Lawndale St 77023-3842 (Mail to: PO Box 9564 77261-9564) Lacy Largent (713) 928-3221

Houston Emmanuel Episcopal Church **P** (676) § 3785 Barker Cypress Rd 77084-3930 (Mail to: 3785 Barker Cypress Rd 77084-3930) Patrick Ousley Bradley Sullivan (281) 493-3161

Houston Grace Episcopal Church **M** (117) 4040 W Bellfort Ave 77025-5307 (Mail to: 4040 W Bellfort St 77025-5307) Randall Painter (713) 666-1408

Houston Church of the Holy Spirit **P** (689) § 12535 Perthshire Rd 77024-4106 (Mail to: 12535 Perthshire Rd 77024-4186) Joshua Condon (713) 468-7796

Houston Hope Episcopal Church **P** (66) 1613 W 43rd St 77018-1849 (Mail to: 1613 W 43rd St 77018-1849) Lyn Briggs (713) 681-6422

Houston Santa Maria Virgen Epis Church **M** (958) § 9600 Huntington Place Dr 77099-2316 (Mail to: 9600 Huntington Place Dr 77099-2316) Uriel Osnaya-Jimenez (281) 879-6000

Houston Iglesia Episcopal San Mateo **P** (629) 6635 Alder Dr 77081-5201 (Mail to: 6635 Alder Dr 77081-5201) Janssen Gutierrez (713) 664-7792

Houston Lord of the Streets Epis Ch **M** (22) 3401 Fannin St. 77004-3806 (Mail to: 3401 Fannin St 77004-3806) (713) 526-0311

Houston Palmer Memorial Episcopal Ch **P** (1671) 6221 Main St 77030-1506 (Mail to: 6221 Main St 77030-1506) Ryan Hawthorne Katharine Wallingford Neil Willard (713) 529-6196

Houston St Albans Episcopal Church **M** (103) 420 Woodard St 77009-1824 (Mail to: 420 Woodard St 77009-1824) (713) 692-3080

Houston St Christophers Episcopal Ch **P** (159) 1656 Blalock Rd 77080-7396 (Mail to: 1656 Blalock Rd 77080-7396) Richard Houser (713) 465-6015

Houston St Cuthbert Episcopal Church **P** (1194) § 17020 West Rd 77095-7758 (Mail to: 17020 West Rd 77095-5578) Malcolm Ellis Margaret Williams (281) 463-7330

✣ **Houston** St Dunstans Episcopal Church **O** (1141) 14301 Stuebner Airline Rd 77069-3529 (Mail to: 14301 Stuebner Airline Rd 77069-3529) Roman Roldan (713) 855-0310

Houston St Francis Episcopal Church **P** (1455) 345 Piney Point Rd 77024-6505 (Mail to: 345 Piney Point Rd 77024-6505) Stuart Bates David Price Robert Wismer (713) 952-5812

Houston St James Episcopal Church **P** (503) § 3129 Southmore Blvd 77004-6298 (Mail to: 3129 Southmore Blvd 77004-6298) Elizabeth Divine Victor Thomas (713) 526-9571

Houston St John the Divine Epis Church **P** (4501) § 2450 River Oaks Blvd 77019-5826 (Mail to: 2450 River Oaks Blvd 77019-5826) Robert Spruill Reagan Cocke Neal Mcgowan Louise Samuelson Louise Samuelson (713) 622-3600

Houston St Luke the Evangelist Church **P** (160) 3530 Wheeler St 77004-5527 (Mail to: 3530 Wheeler St 77004-5527) Francene Young (713) 748-5974

Houston St Marks Episcopal Church **P** (924) § 3816 Bellaire Blvd 77025-1209 (Mail to: 3816

Bellaire Blvd 77025-1296) Patrick Miller David Goldberg (713) 664-3466

Houston St Martin's Episcopal Church **P** (9590) § 717 Sage Rd 77056-2111 (Mail to: 717 Sage Rd 77056-2111) Russell Levenson John Sundara Robert Arning Martin Bastian Sharron Cox James Cunningham Alexander Graham Susannah Mcbay Lisa Neilson (713) 985-3802

Houston St Pauls Episcopal Church **P** (615) § 7843 Park Place Blvd 77087-4639 (Mail to: 7843 Park Place Blvd 77087-4698) (713) 645-5031

Houston St Stephen's Episcopal Church **P** (298) § 1805 W Alabama St 77098-2601 (Mail to: Attn: Finance Office 1805 W Alabama St 77098-2601) Lisa Hunt (713) 528-6665

Houston Saint Thomas Church **P** (330) § 4900 Jackwood St 77096-1505 (Mail to: 4900 Jackwood St 77096-1599) David Browder Geoffrey Simpson (713) 666-3111

Houston St Thomas the Apostle Epis Ch **P** (597) § 18300 Upper Bay Rd 77058-4110 (Mail to: 18300 Upper Bay Rd 77058-4110) Michael Stone James Mcgill (281) 333-2384

Houston St Andrews Episcopal Church **P** (459) § 1819 Heights Blvd 77008-4025 (Mail to: 1819 Heights Blvd 77008-4025) James Grace Clint Brown (713) 8615596

Houston Trinity Episcopal Church **P** (781) 1015 Holman St 77004-3810 (Mail to: 1015 Holman St 77004-3899) Hannah Atkins Luz Montes (713) 528-4100

Humble Christ the King (Atascocita) **P** (203) 19330 Pinehurst Trail Dr 77346-2224 (Mail to: 19330 Pinehurst Trail Dr 77346-2224) David Nelson (281) 852-1990

Huntsville St Stephens Episcopal Church **P** (325) 5019 Sam Houston Ave 77340-6653 (Mail to: PO Box 388 77342-0388) William Rider (936) 295-7226

Hurst St Stephen Episcopal Church **P** (85) 463 W Harwood Rd 76054-2941 (Mail to: 463 W Harwood Rd 76054-2941) Allison Liles (915) 479-4669

Jacksonville Trinity Episcopal Church **M** (59) 1000 S Jackson St 75766-3016 (Mail to: PO Box 472 75766-0472) (903) 586-4336

Jasper Trinity Episcopal Church **P** (14) § 800 N Main St 75951-3018 (Mail to: PO Box 1598 75951-0016) (409) 384-3719

Jefferson Christ Episcopal Church **M** (41) 703 S Main St 75657-2227 (Mail to: 703 S Main St 75657-2227) (903) 665-2693

Katy Holy Apostles Epis Church-Katy **P** (420) 1225 W Grand Pkwy S 77494-8283 (Mail to: 1225 W Grand Pkwy S 77494-8283) Alexander Large Desmond Goonesekera (281) 3923310

Katy St. Paul's Epis Church-Katy **P** (365) 5373 Franz Rd 77493-1732 (Mail to: 5373 Franz Rd 77493-1732) Mark Wilkinson (281) 391-2785

Keller St Martin in-the-Fields Church **P** (282) § 223 S Pearson Ln 76248-5348 (Mail to: PO Box

1149 76244-1149) Alan Bentrup (817) 431-2396

Kilgore St Pauls Episcopal Church **P** (40) § 314 N Henderson Blvd 75662-2712 (Mail to: 314 N Henderson Blvd 75662-2712) (903) 984-3929

Killeen St Christophers Episcopal Ch **P** (456) 2800 Trimmier Rd 76542-6003 (Mail to: 2800 Trimmier Rd 76542-6003) (254) 634-7474

Kingwood Church of the Good Shepherd **P** (758) 2929 Woodland Hills Dr 77339-1406 (Mail to: 2929 Woodland Hills Dr 77339-1406) William Richter Linda Geldreich (281) 358-3154

La Grange St James Episcopal Church **P** (183) 156 N Monroe St 78945-2651 (Mail to: PO Box 507 78945-0507) Rchristopher Heying (979) 968-3910

La Marque St Michaels Episcopal Church **HC** (89) § 1601 Lake Rd 77568-5242 (Mail to: 1601 Lake Rd 77568-5242) Robert Moore (409) 935-3559

La Porte St Johns Episcopal Church **P** (252) 815 S Broadway St 77571-5323 (Mail to: 815 S Broadway St 77571-5323) Nan Doerr Stacy Stringer (281) 471-0383

Lago Vista St Peters Episcopal Church **P** (51) 3305 Pinnacle Cv 78645-6567 (Mail to: 3305 Pinnacle Cv 78645-6567) (512) 267-2744

Lake Jackson St Timothys Episcopal Church **P** (209) 200 Oyster Creek Dr 77566-4402 (Mail to: 200 Oyster Creek Dr 77566-4402) Robin Reeves-Kautz (979) 297-6003

Lampasas St Marys Episcopal Church **P** (184) 501 S Chestnut St 76550-3225 (Mail to: PO Box 29 76550-0001) William Fowler Mildred Williams (512) 556-5433

League City St Christopher Epis Church **P** (570) 2508 St Christopher Ave 77573-4258 (Mail to: 2508 St Christopher Ave 77573-4258) Brian Cannaday Viktoria Gotting (281) 332-5553

Liberty St Stephens Episcopal Church **P** (142) 2041 Trinity St 77575-4831 (Mail to: PO Box 10357 77575-7857) Glennda Hardin (936) 336-3762

Lindale St Lukes Episcopal Church **M** (72) 16292 FM 849 75771 (Mail to: PO Box 1766 75771-1766) John Carr Kenneth Martin (903) 882-8118

Livingston St Lukes Episcopal Church **P** (85) 832 W Jones St 77351-2721 (Mail to: 836 W Jones St 77351-2721) Leonard Hullar (936) 327-8467

Longview St Mic & All Angels Epis Ch **P** (104) 909 Reel Rd 75604-2528 (Mail to: 909 Reel Rd 75604-2528) Tracey Carroll (903) 759-2051

Longview Trinity Episcopal Church **P** (350) § 906 Padon St 75601-6734 (Mail to: 906 Padon St 75601-6797) Roland Carroll Vivian Orndorff (903) 753-3366

Lufkin St Cyprians Episcopal Church **P** (549) § 919 S John Redditt Dr 75904 (Mail to: 919 S John Redditt Dr 75904-4326) David Faulkner (936) 639-1253

Madisonville Holy Innocents Episcopal Ch **M** (21) 600 N McIver St 77864-3270 (Mail to: Attn Treasurer PO Box 1344 77864-1344) (936) 348-2034

Manor St Mary Magdalene Episcopal Ch **M** (127) 12800 Lexington St 78653-3333 (Mail to: PO Box 33 78653) Alex Montes (512) 423-8897

Marble Falls Trinity Episcopal Church **P** (228) § 909 Avenue D 78654-5217 (Mail to: 909 Avenue D 78654-5217) David Sugeno Claire Field (830) 693-2822

Marlin St Johns Episcopal Church **P** (55) 514 Carter St 76661-2326 (Mail to: 514 Carter St 76661-2326) Judy Filer (254) 803-3800

Marshall St Pauls Church **P** (8) Fm Rd 134 75670 (Mail to: 4512 Fern Ave 71105-3116) (903) 407-0117

Marshall Trinity Episcopal Church **P** (422) 106 N Grove St 75670-3237 (Mail to: 106 N Grove St 75670-3237) Sean Duncan (903) 938-4246

Matagorda Christ Episcopal Church **M** (65) § 206 Cypress St 77457 (Mail to: PO Box 673 77457-0673) (979) 863-7239

Mexia Christ Episcopal Church **M** (54) 505 E Commerce St 76667-2862 (Mail to: 505 E Commerce St 76667-2862) (254) 562-5918

Missouri City St Catherine of Sienna Epis Ch **M** (445) 4747 Sienna Pkwy 77459-6052 (Mail to: 4747 Sienna Pkwy 77459-6052) Andrew Ellison (281) 778-2046

Nacogdoches Christ Church **P** (404) 1430 N Mound St. 75961-4052 (Mail to: 1320 N Mound St 75961-4029) Karl Griswold-Kuhn (936) 564-0421

Navasota St Pauls Episcopal Church **P** (84) 414 E Mcalpine St 77868-3645 (Mail to: 414 E McAlpine St 77868-3645) (936) 825-7726

Orange St Pauls Episcopal Church **P** (148) 1401 W Park Ave 77630 (Mail to: 1401 W Park Ave 77630-4950) Petroula Ruehlen (409) 883-2969

Palacios St Johns Episcopal Church **M** (55) 3rd & Main Sts 77465 (Mail to: PO Box 895 77465-0895) William Bullard (361) 972-2744

Palestine St Philips Episcopal Church **P** (221) 106 E Crawford St 75801-2805 (Mail to: 106 E Crawford St 75801-2805) (903) 729-4214

Pasadena St Peters Episcopal Church **M** (457) 705 Williams St 77506-3639 (Mail to: 705 Williams St 77506-3694) Pedro Lopez (713) 473-8090

Pearland St Andrews Episcopal Church **P** (896) 2535 Broadway St 77581-4901 (Mail to: 2535 Broadway St 77581-4901) Michael Gemignani (281) 485-3843

Pflugerville St Paul's Episcopal Church **M** (71) § 507 E Pflugerville Loop 78660-1904 (Mail to: PO Box 28 78691-0028) Kelly Koonce (512) 990-1350

Port Neches Holy Trinity Episcopal Church **P** (220) § 2425 Nall St 77651-4703 (Mail to: 2425 Nall St 77651-4703) (409) 722-6238

Prairie View St Francis of Assisi Epis Ch **P** (21) § PO Box 246 77446-0246 (Mail to: PO Box 246 77446-0246) (936) 857-3272

Richmond Calvary Episcopal Church **P** (464) § 806 Thompson Rd 77469-3334 (Mail to: 806 Thompson Rd 77469-3334) Ralph Morgan (281) 342-2147

Richmond Saint Mark's Episcopal Church **P** (206) § 7615 FM 762 77469 (Mail to: 7615 Fm 762 Rd 77469-9505) (281) 545-1661

Rockdale St Thomas Episcopal Church **M** (25) 302 E Davilla Ave 76567-2986 (Mail to: PO Box 997 76567-0997) (512) 446-5932

Round Rock St Richards Episcopal Church **P** (555) 1420 E Palm Valley Blvd 78664-4549 (Mail to: 1420 E Palm Valley Blvd 78664-4549) Christopher Nations Kelly Jennings (512) 255-5436

Round Rock St Julian of Norwich Episl Ch **M** (352) 7700 Cat Hollow Dr Ste 204 78681-5799 (Mail to: 7700 Cat Hollow Dr Ste 204 78681-5799) Miles Brandon (512) 284-7983

Salado St Joseph's Episcopal Church **M** (133) 881 North Main Street 76571-0797 (Mail to: PO Box 797 76571-0797) Robert Bliss (254) 947-3160

San Augustine Christ Episcopal Church **M** (51) 201 N Ayish St 75972-2105 (Mail to: PO Box 85 75972-0085) (936) 275-6993

Sealy St James Episcopal Church **M** (69) 311 6th St 77474-2719 (Mail to: PO Box 1477 77474-1477) Eric LeBrocq (979) 885-2359

Silsbee St Johns Episcopal Church **P** (111) 1305 Roosevelt Dr 77656-3309 (Mail to: 1305 Roosevelt Dr 77656-3309) (409) 385-4371

Spring Holy Comforter Epis Church **P** (488) 2322 Spring Cypress Rd 77388-4717 (Mail to 2129 Fm 2920 Rd Ste 190-165 77388-3671 John Soard (281) 288-8169

Stafford All Saints Episcopal Church **P** (244 § 605 Dulles Ave 77477-5222 (Mail to: 605 Dulles Ave 77477-5222) (281) 499-9602

Stephenville Saint Luke's Episcopal Church **P** (112) 595 N Mcilhaney St 76401-5625 (Mail to: PO Box 2506 76401-0041) Bradley Dyche (254) 968-6949

Sugar Land Holy Cross Episcopal Church **P** (203) 5653 W River Park Dr 77479-7900 (Mail to: 5653 W River Park Dr 77479-7900) Scot Thompson (281) 633-2000

Taylor St James Episcopal Church **M** (50) 61 Davis St 76574-2729 (Mail to: C/O Treasure PO Box 268 76574-0268) Terry Pierce (512 352-2330

Temple Christ Episcopal Church **P** (576) § 30 N Main St 76501-3210 (Mail to: 300 N Mai St 76501-3210) Keith Pozzuto Rebecca Spark James Wilburn James Wilburn (254) 773-165

Temple St Francis Episcopal Church **P** (176) 5001 Hickory Rd 76502-3012 (Mail to: 500 Hickory Rd 76502-3099) Tamara Clothie David Krause (254) 773-4255

Texas City St. George's Episcopal Church **P** (188) § 510 13th Ave N 77590-6250 (Mail to: 510 13th Ave N 77590-6250) (409) 945-2583

The Woodlands Trinity Episcopal Church **P** (1690) § 3901 S Panther Creek Dr. 77381-2736 (Mail to: 3901 S Panther Creek Dr 77381-2736) Gerald Sevick Frank Samuelson (281) 367-8113

Tomball Church of the Good Shepherd **P** (248) 715 Carrell St 77375-4899 (Mail to: 715 Carrell St 77375-4899) Cecil Mcgavern (281) 351-1609

Tyler Christ Episcopal Church **P** (1678) § 118 S Bois D Arc Ave 75702-7101 (Mail to: 118 S Bois D Arc Ave 75702-7199) David Luckenbach (903) 597-9854

Tyler St Francis Episcopal Church **P** (159) 3232 Jan Ave 75701-9115 (Mail to: 3232 Jan Ave 75701-9115) Mitchell Tollett (903) 5938459

Tyler St John's Episcopal Church **M** (26) 514 W Vance St 75702-3251 (Mail to: 514 W Vance St 75702-3251) (903) 597-5923

Waco Epis Church of the Holy Spirit **P** (130) 1624 Wooded Acres Dr 76710-2852 (Mail to: 1624 Wooded Acres Dr 76710-2852) Jason Ingalls (254) 772-1982

Waco St. Alban's Episcopal Church **P** (738) 305 N 30th St 76710-7225 (Mail to: 2900 W. Waco Drive 76610) Aaron Zimmerman Andrew Armond Neal Mcgowan Alberto Melis Alberto Melis Kara Wischmeyer Kara Wischmeyer (254) 752-1773

Waco St Pauls Episcopal Church **P** (1161) § 515 Columbus Ave 76701-1347 (Mail to: 601 Columbus Ave 76701-1347) Samantha Smith (254) 753-4501

West Columbia St Marys Episcopal Church **P** (74) 16th & Clay Sts 77486 (Mail to: PO Box 786 77486-0786) (979) 345-3456

Wharton St Thomas Church **P** (112) 207 Bob O Link Lane 77488-3205 (Mail to: PO Box 586 77488-0586) Michael Paul (979) 532-1723

Wichita Falls The Epis Ch of Wichita Falls **M** (41) 1437 Southwest Pkwy 76302-5114 (Mail to: PO Box 9321 76308-9321) (940) 692-3982

Winnie Trinity Episcopal Church **M** (75) 1324 Highway 124, 77665-0630 (Mail to: C/O Travis Pair PO Box 630 77665-0630) (409) 267-6582

Woodville St Pauls Episcopal Church **M** (24) Hwy 190 W 75979 (Mail to: PO Box 546 75979-0546) (409) 283-3710

DIOCESE OF UPPER SOUTH CAROLINA
(PROVINCE IV)
Comprises Northwestern South Carolina
DIOCESAN OFFICE 1115 Marion St Columbia SC 29201
TEL (803) 771-7800 FAX (803) 799-5119
E-MAIL diocese@edusc.org WEB www.edusc.org

Previous Bishops— Kirkman G Finlay 1922-38; John J Gravatt 1939-53; C Alfred Cole 1953-63; John A Pinckney 1963-72; George M Alexander 1973-79; Rogers S Harris suffr 1985-89; Wm A Beckham 1979-94; Wm F Carr asst 1991-94; Dorsey F Henderson Jr 1995-2009

Bishop—Rt Rev W Andrew Waldo (1046) (Dio 22 May 2010)

Chanc K Shealy; *Asst Chanc* JP Lee; *Sec ; Asst to BP* T Forman; *Cn for Vis & Min Dev* Rev DM Hazel; *Aging Min* Rev D Thompson; *Pres ECW* K Siegle; *Cursillo* J Jendron; *DOK* D Dunlap; *ER&D* M Jennings-Todd; *Com* M Langford Kennedy; *Treas* B Sandberg; *Sec to Conv* N Grimball

Stand Comm—Cler: S Cate C Darnell M Balfour-Dunlap G Eichelberger S Franklin P Griffin J Hardaway P Wall; *Lay:* F Boineau E Cashwell S Clawson R Gilliam S Johnson R Kenner M Langford J Ray J Rippy J Webb F Wideman

PARISHES, MISSIONS, AND CLERGY

Abbeville Trinity Episcopal Church **M** (27) 200 Church St 29620-2456 (Mail to: PO Box 911 29620-0911) (864) 366-5186

Aiken St Augustine of Canterbury **M** (138) 1630 Silver Bluff Rd 29803-9200 (Mail to: 1630 Silver Bluff Rd 29803-9200) Dale Klitzke (803) 641-1913

Aiken St Thaddeus Episcopal Church **P** (514) § 125 Pendleton St SW 29801-3861 (Mail to: 125 Pendleton St SW 29801-3861) Joseph Whitehurst (803) 648-5497

Anderson Grace Episcopal Church **P** (429) § 711 S Mcduffie St 29624-2334 (Mail to: 711 S McDuffie St 29624-2334) John Hardaway (864) 225-8011

Anderson St George Episcopal Church **P** (40) 2206 N Highway 81 29621-2548 (Mail to: 2206 E Greenville St 29621) Susan Hardaway (864) 224-1104

Batesburg St Pauls Episcopal Church **PS** 116 S Perry St 29006-2244 (Mail to: 116 S Perry St 29006-2244) Teddy Higgins (803) 532-0950

Beech Island All Saints Episcopal Church **M** (11) 305 Williston Rd 29842-8407 (Mail to: 137 Summerwood Way 29803-7702) (803) 302-9900

Boiling Springs St Margarets Episcopal Church **P** (267) 4180 Highway 9 29316-8580 (Mail to: PO Box 160024 29316-0002) (864) 578-3238

Camden Grace Episcopal Church **P** (358) 1315 Lyttleton St 29020-3617 (Mail to: 1315 Lyttleton St 29020-3600) Michael Bullock Henry Wall (803) 432-7621

Cayce All Saints' Episcopal Church **P** (161) 1001 12th St 29033-3302 (Mail to: 1001 12th St 29033-3302) Patricia Sexton (803) 796-5735

Chapin St Francis of Assisi **P** (587) 735 Old Lexington Hwy 29036-7980 (Mail to: PO Box 265 29036-0265) (803) 345-1550

Chester Saint Mark's Church **M** (13) 132 Center St 29706-1703 (Mail to: PO Box 41 29706-0041) (803) 581-3273

Clemson Holy Trinity Episcopal Parish **P** (365) § 193 Old Greenville Hwy 29631-1335 (Mail to: 193 Old Greenville Hwy 29631-1335) Suzanne Cate (864) 654-5071

Clinton All Saints Episcopal Church **P** (92) § 505 Calvert Ave 29325-2620 (Mail to: 505 Calvert Ave 29325-2620) Charles Davis (864) 833-1388

Columbia Church of the Cross **M** (62) PO Box 9561 7244 Patterson Rd 29290-0561 (Mail to: PO Box 9561 29290-0561) (803) 776-1864

Columbia Church of the Good Shepherd **P** (376) 1512 Blanding St 29201-2907 (Mail to: 1512 Blanding St 29201-2907) James Lyon (803) 779-2960

Columbia St Davids Episcopal Church **P** (388) 605 Polo Rd 29223-2905 (Mail to: 605 Polo Rd 29223-2905) William Brock (803) 736-0866

Columbia St Johns Episcopal Church **P** (956) 2827 Wheat St 29205-2515 (Mail to: 2827 Wheat St 29205-2515) Nicholas Beasley (803) 799-4767

Columbia St Lukes Episcopal Church **P** (262) 1300 Pine St 29204-1846 (Mail to: 1300 Pine St 29204-1846) Charles Ashford (803) 254-2327

Columbia St Martins-in-the-Fields **P** (729) § 5220 Clemson Ave 29206-3011 (Mail to: 5220 Clemson Ave 29206-3011) Mitchell Smith Caitlyn Keith (803) 7870392

Columbia St Marys Episcopal Church **P** (224) § 170 Saint Andrews Rd 29210-4107 (Mail to: PO Box 1487 29063-1487) Anna Brawley (803) 798-2776

Columbia St Michael and All Angels **P** (191) § 6408 Bridgewood Rd 29206-2126 (Mail to: 6408 Bridgewood Rd 29206-2198) Charles Smith (803) 782-8080

Columbia St Timothys Episcopal Church **P** (116) 900 Calhoun St 29201-2308 (Mail to: 900 Calhoun St 29201-2308) Alice Mills (803) 7651519

✠ **Columbia** Trinity Episcopal Cathedral **O** (4010) § 1100 Sumter St 29201-3717 (Mail to: 1100 Sumter St 29201-3717) Dane Boston Charles Davis James Hartley James Hartley (803) 771-7300

Easley St Michaels Episcopal Church **P** (217) 1200 Powdersville Rd 29642-2422 (Mail to: 1200 Powdersville Rd 29642-2422) (864) 859-6296

Eastover St Thomas Church **M** (63) 115 Yelton Rd 29044-9770 (Mail to: PO Box 614 29044-0614) (803) 479-4101

Fort Mill Saint Paul's Episcopal Church **P** (254) 501 Pine St 29715-1750 (Mail to: PO Box 753 29716-0753) Sarah Franklin (803) 547-5968

Gaffney Epis Church of the Incarnation **P** (81) 308 College Dr 29340-3007 (Mail to: 308 College Dr 29340-3007) Jeannette Gettys (864) 489-6183

Graniteville St Pauls Episcopal Church **P** (54) 111 Hard St 29829 (Mail to: PO Box 276 29829-0276) Douglas Puckett (803) 663-9457

Great Falls St Peters Episcopal Church **M** (22) 30 Hampton St 29055-1636 (Mail to: PO Box 521 29055-0521) (803) 482-6755

Greenville Christ Episcopal Church **P** (3719) § 10 N Church St 29601-2809 (Mail to: 10 N Church St 29601-2864) Harrison Mcleod Linda Bunch Scott Fleischer Kellie Wilson (864) 271-8773

Greenville Church of the Redeemer **P** (249) 120 Mauldin Rd 29605-1257 (Mail to: 120 Mauldin Rd 29605-1257) Catherine Tatem (864) 2774562

Greenville St Andrews Episcopal Church **P** (222) 1002 S Main St 29601-3335 (Mail to: 1002 S Main St 29601-3335) John Eichelberger (864) 235-5884

Greenville St Francis Episcopal Church **P** (165) 301 Piney Mountain Rd. 29609 (Mail to: 506 Edwards Rd 29615-1247) (864) 268-2845

Greenville St James Episcopal Church **P** (705) § 301 Piney Mountain Rd 29609-3035 (Mail to: Attn: Accounts Payable 301 Piney Mountain Rd 29609-3035) Lathrop Mosley John Nieman (864) 244-6358

Greenville St Peters Episcopal Church **P** (713) § 910 Hudson Rd 29615-3430 (Mail to: PO Box 25817 29616-0817) Stephen Bolle Marie Cope (864) 268-7280

Greenville St Philip's Episcopal Church **M** (45) 31 Allendale Ln 29607-2208 (Mail to: PO Box 17521 29606-8521) (864) 271-1382

Greenwood Church of the Resurrection **P** (488) 700 Main St W 29646-3211 (Mail to: PO Box 3283 29648-3283) Mary Dunlap Timothy Ervolina (864) 223-5426

Greer Church of the Good Shepherd **P** (146) 200 Cannon St 29651-3705 (Mail to: PO Box 1408 29652-1408) Leslie Horvath (864) 877-2330

Hopkins St Johns Episcopal Church **P** (187) 1151 Elm Savannah Rd 29061-8938 (Mail to: 1151 Elm Savannah Rd 29061-8938) (803) 776-9292

Irmo Church of St Simon and St Jude **P** (344) 1110 Kinley Rd 29063-9633 (Mail to: 1110 Kinley Rd 29063-9633) Jill Williams (803) 732-0153

Jenkinsville St Barnabas Episcopal Church **M** (71) 1056 St Barnabas Rd 29065-9400 (Mail to: PO Box 18 29065-0018) (803) 635-4995

Lancaster Christ Episcopal Church **P** (116) 534 Plantation Rd 29720 (Mail to: PO Box 488 29721-0488) Philip Emanuel (803) 286-5224

Laurens Church of the Epiphany **P** (82) 225 W Main St 29360-2940 (Mail to: 225 W Main St 29360-2940) Kelly Ayer (864) 984-7000

Lexington St Albans Episcopal Church **P** (183) 403 Park Rd 29072-9060 (Mail to: PO Box 882 29071-0882) Thomas Dimarco (803) 359-2444

Newberry St Lukes Episcopal Church **M** (44) 1605 Main St 29108-3456 (Mail to: 1605 Main St 29108-3456) Slaven Manning (803) 276-8513

North Augusta St Bartholomews Episcopal Ch **P** (578) 471 W Martintown Rd 29841-3105 (Mail to: 471 W Martintown Rd 29841-3105) Joseph Shippen (803) 279-4622

Pauline Calvary Episcopal Church **M** (27) C/O Claude Finney 305 Quinn Rd 29374-2834 (Mail to: C/O Claude Finney 305 Quinn Rd 29374-2834) (864) 582-3952

Ridgeway St Stephens Episcopal Church **M** (66) 335 Longtown Rd 29130-6814 (Mail to: PO Box 26 29130-0026) Mark Werner (803) 337-2905

Rock Hill Church of Our Saviour **P** (562) § 144 Caldwell St 29730-4534 (Mail to: 144 Caldwell St 29730-4534) Jane Wilson (803) 327-1131

Seneca Church of the Ascension **P** (32) 214 Northampton Road 29672-2221 (Mail to: 214 Northampton Rd 29672-2221) (864) 882-2006

Simpsonville Holy Cross Episcopal Church **P** (834) § 205 E College St 29681-2616 (Mail to: PO Box 187 29681-0187) Micah Del Priore (864) 967-7470

Spartanburg Episcopal Church of the Advent **P** (1239) § 141 Advent St 29302-1904 (Mail to: 141 Advent St 29302-1904) Jonathan Morris Pauline Griffin (864) 585-2268

Spartanburg Epis Church of the Epiphany **M** (25) 121 W Park Dr 29306-5010 (Mail to: PO Box 726 29304-0726) (864) 583-0405

Spartanburg St Christophers Church Epis **M** (180) 400 Dupre Dr 29307-2976 (Mail to: 400 Dupre Dr 29307-2976) Leslie Horvath (864) 585-2858

Spartanburg St Matthews Episcopal Church **P** (540) 101 Saint Matthews Ln 29301-1378 (Mail to: 101 Saint Matthews Ln 29301-1378) Robert Brown (864) 576-0424

Trenton Episcopal Church of the Ridge **M** (120) 212 Church Street 29847-0206 (Mail to: PO Box 206 29847-0206) (803) 275-3934

Union Church of the Nativity **M** (46) 320 S Church St 29379-2307 (Mail to: PO Box 456 293790456) (864) 427-8610

Winnsboro St Johns Episcopal Church **P** (78) 301 W Liberty St 29180-1423 (Mail to: 301 W Liberty St 29180-1423) (803) 635-4398

York Church of the Good Shepherd **P** (177) 108 E Liberty St 29745-1549 (Mail to: PO Box 437 29745-0437) Amanda Robertson Paul Greeley (803) 684-4021

DIOCESE OF UTAH
(PROVINCE VIII)

Comprises the State of Utah, excluding Navajoland and including Page, AZ

DIOCESAN OFFICE 75 South 200 East Salt Lake City UT 84111-2147

TEL (801) 322-4131 FAX (801) 322-5096

E-MAIL mdaly@episcopal-ut.org WEB www.episcopal-ut.org

Previous Bishops— Daniel S Tuttle 1867-86, Abiel Leonard 1888-1903, Franklin S Spalding 1904-14, Paul Jones 1914-18, Arthur W Moulton 1920-46, Stephen C Clark 1946-50, Richard S Watson 1951-71, E Otis Charles 1971-86, George E Bates 1986-97, Carolyn T Irish coadj 1996-97 Bp 1997-2010, Scott B Hayashi 2010-22.

Bishop—Rt Rev Phyllis A Spiegel (1148) (Dio 17 September 2022)

Bp Exec Asst M Daly; *Comm* C Wirth; *Chanc* S Hutchinson; *Treas* D Lingo; *Conv Sec* D Sakrison; *Fin Off* W Potts; *Cn to the Ordinary & Exec Off* vacant; *Latino Missioner* P Ramos

Stand Comm—Cler: Rev M Carney; *Lay:* K Cook

Diocesan Council—Cler: Pres Rt Rev P Spiegel; *VP* Rev Cn P Ramos DD

Comm on Min: Cler: Chair Rev K Wiesner

PARISHES, MISSIONS, AND CLERGY
Brigham City St Michaels Episcopal Church **M** (47) 589 S 200 E 84302-2903 (Mail to: 80 S 300 E 84111-1607) (801) 391-2185

Cedar City St Judes Episcopal Church **M** (61) 70 N 200 W 84720-2570 (Mail to: 70 N 200 W 84720-2570) (435) 586-3623

Centerville Church of the Resurrection **P** (105) 1131 S Main St 84014-2217 (Mail to: 92 E Pages Lane 84014-2216) (801) 295-1360

Clearfield St Peters Episcopal Church **P** (62) 1204 E 1450 S 84015-1643 (Mail to: 80 S 300 E 84111-1607) (801) 825-0177

Ivins Spirit of the Desert **M** (31) 873 Coyote Gulch Ct Ste D 84738-6708 (Mail to: 873 Coyote Gulch Ct Ste D 84738-6708) (435) 592-0034

Logan St Johns Episcopal Church **P** (144) 85 E 100 N 84321-4624 (Mail to: 85 E 100 N 84321-4624) (435) 752-0331

Midvale St James Episcopal Church **P** (447) 7486 S Union Park Ave 84047-4164 (Mail to: 6905 South 1300 East PO Box 203 84121) Christopher Szarke John Dillon (801) 5661311

Moab Mision de San Francisco **P** (157) 250 Kane Creek Blvd 84532-2538 (Mail to: PO Box 596 84532-0596) (435) 259-3113

Moab St Francis Episcopal Church **P** (161) 250 Kane Creek Blvd 84532-2950 (Mail to: PO Box 96 84532-0096) (435) 259-5831

Ogden Church of the Good Shepherd **P** (220) 2374 Grant Ave 84401-1408 (Mail to: 2374 Grant Ave 84401-1408) Patricia Sanchez (801) 392-8168

Page St Davids Episcopal Church **M** (26) 421 S Lake Powell Blvd 86040-0856 (Mail to: PO Box 125 86040-0125) (928) 645-4965

Park City St Lukes Church **P** (294) 4595 N. Silver Springs Dr. 84098 (Mail to: PO Box 981208 84098-1208) (435) 649-4900

Price Ascension St Matthew's Epis Ch **M** (126) 522 Homestead Blvd 84501-2261 (Mail to: PO

Box 881 84501-0881) (435) 637-0106

Provo Saint Mary's Church **P** (65) 50 W 200 N 84601-2806 (Mail to: 50 W 200 N 84601-2806) Craig Klein Timothy Yanni (801) 373-3090

Randlett Church of the Holy Spirit **M** (128) 4250 South 10000 E 84063 (Mail to: PO Box 630016 84063) (435) 545-2400

Salt Lake City All Saints Episcopal Church **P** (478) 1710 Foothill Dr 84108-3052 (Mail to: 1710 S Foothill Dr 84108-3052) Tracy Browning Garang Atem Antoinette Catron Miner (801) 581-0380

✠ **Salt Lake City** Cathedral Church of Saint Mark **O** (560) 231 E 100 S 84111-1604 (Mail to: 231 E 100 S 84111-1604) Tyler Doherty Tyler Doherty Elizabeth Hunter Michael Milligan (801) 322-3400

Salt Lake City St Pauls Episcopal Church **P** (709) 261 S 900 E 84102-2308 (Mail to: C/O Selma Afridi 261 S 900 E 84102-2308) Kurt Wiesner Christine Contestable (801) 322-5869

St George Grace Episcopal Church **P** (108) 1072 E 900 S 84790-4099 (Mail to: 1072 E 900 S 84790-4099) (435) 628-1181

Vernal St Pauls Episcopal Church **P** (30) 226 W Main St 84078-2506 (Mail to: 226 W Main St 84078-2506) (435) 781-1806

West Valley City Iglesia Episcopal San Esteban **P** (220) 4615 S 3200 W 84119-5943 (Mail to: 4615 S 3200 W 84119-5943) (801) 968-2731

West Valley City St Stephens Episcopal Church **P** (157) 4615 S 3200 W 84119-5943 (Mail to: 4615 S 3200 W 84119-5943) (801) 968-2731

Whiterocks St Elizabeths Episcopal Church **P** (62) 11700 N 3900 E 84085 (Mail to: 80 S 300 E 84111-1607) (435) 353-4279

DIOCESE OF VENEZUELA
IGLESIA ANGLICANA/EPISCOPAL EN VENEZUELA
(PROVINCE IX)

DIOCESAN OFFICE Centro Diocesano, Ave Caroni No 100, Colinas de Bello Monte Caracas
(Mail: 49-143 Colinas de Bello Monte Caracas 1042-a Venezuela)
TEL: (58) 212-7513046 or (58) 212-7530723 FAX (58) 212-7513180
E-MAIL: obispoguerrero@iglesianglicanavzla.org WEB www.iglesianglicanavzla.org

Previous Bishops—
Guy Marshall 1967-76, Hyden Jones 1976-1986, Onell Soto 1987-1995

Bishop—Rt Rev Orlando JT Guerrero (1004)

Dio Admin: Sr Marco A Ramos C; *Treas:* Sr José Francisco; *Chris Ed:* Lic Adrían E Cárdenas T

PARISHES, MISSIONS, AND CLERGY

Barquisimeto Misión San Judas Tadeo **M** Av. Florencio Jimenez - KM14 Via Quibor (Mail

to: Ave Florencio Jimenez Manzana Caja No L-95)

Caraballeda Misión Anglicana San Mateo **M** Vista al Mar (Mail to: Centro Diocesano) (212) 615-4440

Caracas Capilla de la Reconciliacion **P** Ave Caroni #100, Colinas Bello Monte (Mail to: Ave Caroni #100, Colinas Bello Monte) (212) 753-0723

Caripe Misión de la Sagrada Familia **M** El Potrero de Teresen (Mail to: Calle El Cementerio Arriba No 27- Teresen) 2925551022

Caripe Misión de San Miguel Arcangel **M** Sector Alto de las Brisas (Mail to: Sector Alto de las Brisas) (281) 808-0882

Caripe 6224 Misión Bendita Virgen Maria **M** Sector La Sabana (Mail to: Sector La Sabana) 2925551022

El Callao, 8017 Misión de San Agustin de Cantorbery **M** Via Santa Elena de Uairen Km 72 (Mail to: Calle Orinoco #3) 2887621206

El Callao, 8056 Iglesia de la Resurreccion **M** Calle Heres Con Bolivar #14 (Mail to: Calle Heres # 14) 2887621206

Puerto La Cruz, 6023 Iglesia de la Santisima Trinidad **M** Valdez No 46 Tierra Adentro (Mail to: Valdez No 102 Tierra Adentro)

San Felix, 8050 Iglesia de la Santisima Cruz **M** Tumutu, Urb Bella Vista (Mail to: Calle Bakairies, Detras Semaforo El Roble) (414) 894-9254

San Flaviano Misión de San Flaviano **M** Carretera Nacional via la Gran Sabana (Mail to: Calle Orinoco #3) 2887621206

Steenrijk, Curacao Iglesia de Todos los Santos **P** Heelsumstraat #18 (Mail to: Heelsumstraat #18)

INSTITUTIONS

ISTESAC Insituto Superior de Teología San Agustine de Cantórbery *E-mail* istesac@iglesianglicanavzla.org; *Web* www.iglesiangli-canavzla.org/ISTESAC.htm

DIOCESE OF VERMONT
(PROVINCE I)
Comprises the State of Vermont
DIOCESAN OFFICE 5 Rock Pt Rd Burlington VT 05408-2735
TEL (802) 863-3431 FAX (802) 860-1562
E-MAIL adminasst@diovermont.org WEB http://diovermont.org/

Previous Bishops—
John H Hopkins 1832-68, Wm HA Bissell 1868-93, Arthur AC Hall 1894-1929, Wm F Weeks coadj 1913-14, Geo Y Bliss coadj 1915-24, Samuel B Booth coadj 1925 Bp 1929-35, Vedder Van Dyck 1936-60, Harvey D Butterfield 1961-74, Robert S Kerr 1974-86, Daniel L Swenson coadj 1986 Bp 1987-93, Mary Adelia R McLeod Bp 1993-2001, Thomas Clark Ely Bp 2001-19

Bishop—Rt. Rev. Shannon MacVean-Brown (Dio 28 Sept 2019)

Cn to Ord for Transition Min Rev A Watersong; *Cn to Ord for Cultural Transformation* Rev W Brownridge; *Cn Miss for Cong Vit* Rev S Ohlidal; *Archdcn* C Cooke; *Archdcn* S Baker; *Fin-Property Adm* R Sagui; *Rock Point Exec Dir* Rev P Habersang; *Bishop's Asst* K Torrisi; *Bookeeper and Data Support* K Robinson *Treas* P Horn; *Chanc* T Little; *V Chanc* W Meub; *COM COD Chair* Rev T Presler; *Earth Stew Convener* W Grace; *Oversight & Audit Comm* Very Rev G Getlein; *UTO Coord* W Grace

Stand Comm—Cler: J Anderson *Pres* L Ransom S Baker S Ginolfi; *Lay:* S Ginn T Ingalls *Sec* T Rees M Thompson

PARISHES, MISSIONS, AND CLERGY

Alburg St Lukes Episcopal Mission **M** (8) 33 N Main St 05440-9726 (Mail to: Attn: Senior Warden PO Box 113 05440-0113) (802) 863-8036

Arlington St James Episcopal Church **P** (87) 46 Church St 05250-4457 (Mail to: PO Box 25 05250-0025) (802) 375-9952

Barre Church of the Good Shepherd **P** (94) 39 Washington St 05641-4236 (Mail to: PO Box 726 05641-0726) William Kooperkamp (802) 476-3929

Bellows Falls Immanuel Episcopal Church **HC** (27) 20 Church St 05101-1515 (Mail to: PO Box 64 05101-0064) Steven Fuller Steven Fuller Charles Mansfield (802) 463-3100

Bennington St Peters Episcopal Church **P** (301) 200 Pleasant St 05201-2526 (Mail to: 200 Pleasant St 05201-2526) (802) 442-2911

Bethel Christ Episcopal Church **P** (29) 5 Main St 05032-9002 (Mail to: PO Box 383 05032-0383) (802) 234-5680

Brandon St Thomas and Grace Church **P** (45) 19 Conant Sq 05733-1011 (Mail to: 19 Conant Sq 05733-1011) (802) 247-6759

Brattleboro St Michaels Episcopal Church **P** (316) 16 Bradley Ave 05301-3429 (Mail to: 16 Bradley Ave 05301-3429) Mary Lindquist Jean Jersey Jean Smith (802) 254-6048

✠ **Burlington** Cathedral Church of St Paul **O** (382) 2 Cherry St 05401-7304 (Mail to: 2 Cherry St 05401-7304) Greta Getlein Joseph Baker Joseph Baker (802) 864-0471

Canaan St Paul-Border Parish **P** (2) 55 Power House Rd 05903 (Mail to: 55 Power House Rd 05903) Robert Lee (802) 266-8269

Chester St Lukes Episcopal Church **P** (142) 313 Main St 05143-9864 (Mail to: PO Box 8 05143-0008) (802) 875-6000

Colchester St Andrew's Episcopal Church **P** (101) 1063 Prim Rd 05446 (Mail to: PO Box 78 05446-0078) Robert Leopold (802) 658-0533

Enosburg Fls St Matthews Episcopal Church **P** (47) C/O Michael Burfoot Md 1650 Water Tower Rd 05450-5422 (Mail to: PO Box 276 05450-0276) Jane Presler (802) 933-6127

Essex Jct St James Episcopal Church **P** (128) 4 St James Pl 05452-3223 (Mail to: 4 St James Pl 05452-3223) Kim Hardy G David Ganter (802) 878-4014

Fair Haven St Luke's Episcopal Mission **M** (24) 146 N Main St 05743-1152 (Mail to: PO Box 293 05743-0293) Melanie Combs (802) 558-2670

Fairlee St Martins Episcopal Church **P** (70) 1 Lake Morey Rd 05045-9595 (Mail to: PO Box 158 05045-0158) (802) 333-9725

Hardwick Church of St John the Baptist **P** (76) PO Box 424 05843-0424 (Mail to: PO Box 424 05843-0424) John Perry (802) 472-5979

Island Pond Christ Ch Episcopal Mission **M** (22) 5 Walnut Ave 05846 (Mail to: PO Box 341 05846-0341) (802) 723-6381

Killington Church of Our Saviour **M** (20) 316 Mission Farm Rd 05751-9451 (Mail to: PO Box 272 05751-0272) Lisa Ransom (802) 422-9064

Lyndonville St Peter Episcopal Mission **M** (40) 51 Elm St 05851-9255 (Mail to: PO Box 41 05851-0041) (802) 626-5705

Manchestr Ctr Zion Church **P** (400) 5167 Main St 05255-9772 (Mail to: PO Box 717 05255-0717) David Fredrickson (802) 362-1987

Middlebury St Stephens Episcopal Church **P** (383) 3 Main St 05753-1450 (Mail to: 3 Main St 05753-1450) Paul Olsson Lucy Pellegrini (802) 388-7200

Montpelier Christ Episcopal Church **P** (213) 64 State St 05602-2933 (Mail to: 64 State St 05602-2933) Kevin Sparrow (802) 223-3631

Newport St Marks Episcopal Church **HC** (179) 44 2nd St 05855-2178 (Mail to: PO Box 125 05855-0125) Christine Moseley Robert Wilson Robert Wilson (802) 334-7365

Northfield St Marys Episcopal Church **P** (31) 203 S. Main St. 05663-5670 (Mail to: 203 S Main St 05663-5670) (802) 485-8221

Norwich St Barnabas Episcopal Church **P** (68) 262 Main St 05055 (Mail to: PO Box 306 05055-0306) Jennie Anderson Todd Mckee (802) 649-1923

Proctorsville Gethsemane Church **P** (43) Depot St 05153 (Mail to: PO Box 217 05153-0217) (802) 226-7967

Randolph St Johns Episcopal Church **P** (62) 15 Summer St 05060-1162 (Mail to: PO Box 278 05060-0278) (802) 728-9910

Rutland Trinity Episcopal Church **P** (443) 85 West St 05701-3452 (Mail to: 85 West St 05701-3452) Sarah Ginolfi (802) 775-1004

S Burlington All Saints Episcopal Church **P** (242) 1250 Spear St 05403-7407 (Mail to: 1250 Spear St 05403-7407) David Hamilton Daniel MacDonald Margaret Mathauer Margaret Mathauer (802) 862-9750

Saint Albans St Lukes Church **P** (86) 8 Bishop St 05478-1639 (Mail to: 8 Bishop St 05478-1639) James Ballard (802) 524-6212

Shelburne Trinity Episcopal Church **P** (399) 5171 Shelburne Rd 05482-6509 (Mail to: 5171 Shelburne Rd 05482-6509) Frederick Moser (802) 985-2269

Sheldon Grace Church **M** (11) Beth Crane Senior Warden 215 Pleasant St 05483-9696 (Mail to: 215 Pleasant St 05483-9696) (802) 899-1188

Springfield St Marks Church **P** (21) 33 Fairground Rd 05156-2112 (Mail to: 33 Fairground Rd 05156-2112) (802) 885-2723

St Johnsbury St Andrews Episcopal Church **P** (15) 1265 Main St 05819-2697 (Mail to: Diane Simons Bookkeeper 1129 Main St 05819-2601) (802) 748-2121

Stowe St Johns in the Mountains **P** (111) 1994 Mountain Road 05672-1175 (Mail to: PO Box 1175 05672-1175) Richard Swanson Zarina O'Hagin Zarina O'Hagin (802) 253-7578

Swanton Holy Trinity Episcopal Church **P** (157) 38 Grand Ave 05488-0273 (Mail to: 38 Grand Ave 05488-1427) John Spainhour (802) 868-7185

Underhill Calvary Episcopal Church **P** (31) 372 Vermont Route 15 05489-0057 (Mail to: PO Box 57 05489-0057) (802) 899-2326

Vergennes St Paul's Episcopal Church **P** (99) 6 Park St 05491-1129 (Mail to: PO Box 196 05491-0196) (802) 877-3322

Waitsfield St Dunstans Episcopal Mission **M** (9) § 6307 Main Street 05673 (Mail to: PO Box 1133 05673-1133) Laurian Seeber (802) 479-7920

Wells St Pauls Episcopal Church **M** (53) 587 E Wells Rd 05774-3847 (Mail to: PO Box 726 05774-0726) William Davidson (518) 499-1850

White Riv Jct St Pauls Episcopal Church **P** (165) 749 Hartford Ave 05001-8037 (Mail to: 749 Hartford Ave 05001-1693) Scott Neal (802) 295-5415

Wilmington St Mary in the Mountain Epis **P** (46) 13 E Main St 05363-9645 (Mail to: PO Box 1366 05363-1366) (802) 464-9341

Windsor St Pauls Episcopal Church **P** (12) 27 State St 05089-1201 (Mail to: PO Box 725 05089-0725) (802) 674-6576

Woodstock St James Episcopal Church **P** (146) 2 St. James Place 05091-1214 (Mail to: 2 St. James Place 050911214) (802) 457-1727

DIOCESE OF THE VIRGIN ISLANDS
(PROVINCE II)
Comprises the American and British Virgin Islands
DIOCESAN OFFICE #13 Commandant Gade Charlotte Amalie St Thomas
US Virgin Islands 00801
(MAIL: PO Box 7488 St Thomas VI 00801)
TEL (340) 776-1797 FAX (340) 777-8485

Previous Bishops—
Cedric E Mills 1963-72, Edward M Turner 1972-86, Richard B Martin int 1985-87, E Don Taylor 1987-94, Telesforo A Isaac int (1996-May 1997) Theodore A Daniels 1997-2003 Telesforo Issac 2004-05 E Ambrose Gumbs 2005-21

Treas J Williams; *Hist* B Hodge-Smith; *Chanc* Atty R Simmonds-Ballentine; *Conv Sec* C Callwood; *Fin Comm Chr* R Javois; *COM Chr* Rev E Georges

Stand Comm—Cler: Cn L S Rymer *Pres* Cn JC Clarke
Lay: M Hennessey C Jeremiah-Ambrose A Wells

PARISHES, MISSIONS, AND CLERGY

Christiansted St Croix St John's Episcopal Church **P** (151) 27 King St 00820 (Mail to: PO Box 486 00821-0486) (340) 778-8221 Rev Gregory Gibson

Christiansted St Croix St Peter's Episcopal Church **P** (185) Castle Coakley 38-40 00820 (Mail to: PO Box 7974 00823-7974) Rev Alric Francis (340) 778-6471

Cruz Bay St John St Ursula Church **M** (33) 295 Contant 00831 (Mail to: PO Box 199 00831-0199) (340) 777-6306 Cn Lionel Rymer

Frederiksted St Croix Iglesia San Francisco Episcopal **M** (19) 20 Estate Diamond 00840 (Mail to: PO Box 1796 00851-1796) (340) 776-1797 Dcn Aida Nieves

Frederiksted St Croix St Paul's Episcopal Church **P** (103) 25-26-27 Prince St 00841-0745 (Mail

to: PO Box 745 00841-0745) (340) 772-0818

Kingshill St Croix Episcopal Church of the Holy Cross **P** (35) Estate Upper Love 00850 (Mail to: RR 1 Box 8005 00850-9860) (340) 778-3272 Rev Amonteen Doward

SCB St Paul's Episcopal Church **M** (85) (Mail to: PO Box 3066 Tortola VG1110) (284) 494-4732 Rev Sandra Walters Malone

St Thomas Cathedral Church of All Saints **P** (227) § PO Box 1148 Charlotte Amalie Street 00804 (340) 774-0217

St Thomas Church of the Holy Spirit **M** (36) (Mail to: PO Box 301827 00803-1827) (340) 776-1797

St Thomas Nazareth by the Sea M 6501 Red Hook Ste 201 St Thomas VI 00802 (44) (340) 776-1797

St Thomas St Andrew's Episcopal Church **P** (450) 31-33 Frist Ave Sugar Estate 00802 (Mail to: PO Box 7386 008010386) (340) 774-1223 Rev Lenroy Cabey

St Thomas St Luke's Episcopal Church **P** (49) Smith Bay #10A & 115A 00801 (Mail to: PO Box 7335 00801-0335) (340) 775-3100 Rev Stedwart Lee

Tortola St George the Martyr Church **P** (229) 170 Main St Road Town VG1110 (Mail to: PO Box 28 Road Town VG1110) (284) 3894 Rev Dr Ian Rock Rev E Georges

Tortola Rev Esther Georges (non-serving)

Virgin Gorda VG 1150 St Mary the Virgin Church (40) **P** Church Hill Road The Valley VG 1150 (Mail to: PO Box 65 The Valley VG 1150) (284) 495-5769

STATE OF VIRGINIA
Dioceses of Southern Virginia (SV), Southwestern Virginia (SwV), and Virginia (VA)

Abingdon—SwV
Accomac—SV
Aldie—VA
Alexandria—VA
Altavista—SwV
Amelia Court House—SV
Amherst—SwV
Annandale—VA

Appomattox—SV
Arlington—VA
Arrington—SwV
Ashburn—VA
Ashland—VA
Aylett—VA
Baskerville—SV
Batesville—VA
Bedford—SwV

Berryville—VA
Big Stone Gap—SwV
Blacksburg—SwV
Blackstone—SV
Bloxom—SV
Blue Grass—SwV
Bon Air—SV
Bluemont—VA
Boonesville—VA

Bowling Green—VA
Bracey—SV
Brandy Sta—VA
Bremo Bluff—VA
Bristol—SwV
Buchanan—SwV
Buena Vista—SwV
Burke—VA
Callaway—SwV

Cape Charles—SV	Glen Allen—VA	Mathews—VA	Rocky Mt—SwV
Cartersville—SV	Gloucester—VA	McKenney—SV	St Paul—SwV
Casanova—VA	Goochland—VA	McLean—VA	Salem—SwV
Catlett—VA	Gordonsville—VA	Mechanicsville—VA	Saltville—SwV
Centreville—VA	Great Falls—VA	Middleburg—VA	Scottsville—VA
Charles City—VA	Greenwood—VA	Midlothian—SV	Shenandoah—VA
Charlottesville—VA	Gretna—SV	Millers Tavern—VA	Smithfield—SV
Chase City—SV	Grottoes—VA	Millwood—VA	S Boston—SV
Chatham—SV	Hague—VA	Mineral—VA	S Hill—SV
Chesapeake—SV	Halifax—SV	Moneta—SwV	Spotsylvania—VA
Chester—SV	Hampton—SV	Monroe—SwV	Springfield—VA
Chesterfield—SV	Hanover—VA	Montpelier—VA	Stafford—VA
Christchurch—VA	Harrisonburg—VA	Montross—VA	Stanardsville—VA
Christiansburg—SwV	Haymarket—VA	Mt Jackson—VA	Stanley—VA
Claremont—SV	Heathsville—VA	Mt Vernon—VA	Staunton—SwV
Clarksville—SV	Henrico—VA	New Kent—VA	Sterling—VA
Clifton Forge—SwV	Herndon—VA	Newport News—SV	Suffolk—SV
Colonial Bch—VA	Hopewell—SV	Norfolk—SV	Surry—SV
Colonial Hts—SV	Hot Spgs—SwV	Norton—SwV	Tappahannock—VA
Columbia—VA	Ivy—VA	N Chesterfield—SV	Tazewell—SwV
Courtland—SV	Java—SV	N Prince George—SV	Temperanceville—SV
Covington—SwV	Kenbridge—SV	Oak Grove—VA	The Plains—VA
Culpeper—VA	Keswick—VA	Oak Hill—VA	Toano—SV
Danville—SV	Kilmarnock—VA	Onancock—SV	Upperville—VA
Delaplane—VA	King and Queen	Orange—VA	Victoria—SV
Disputanta—SV	Cthse—VA	Orkney Spgs—VA	Vienna—VA
Doswell—VA	King George—VA	Pearisburg—SwV	Virginia Bch—SV
Dunn Loring—VA	Lancaster—VA	Petersburg—SV	Warfield—SV
Earlysville—VA	Lawrenceville—SV	Pocahontas—SwV	Warrenton—VA
Eastville—SV	Leesburg—VA	Pt Royal—VA	Warsaw—VA
Elkton—VA	Lexington—SwV	Portsmouth—SV	Washington—VA
Fairfax—VA	Loretto—VA	Powhatan—SV	Waverly—SV
Fairfax Sta—VA	Lorton—VA	Pulaski—SwV	Waynesboro—SwV
Falls Church—VA	Louisa—VA	Pungoteague—SV	West Pt—VA
Farmville—SV	Luray—VA	Purcellville—VA	White Marsh—VA
Farnham—VA	Lynchburg—SwV	Radford—SwV	White Post—VA
Fincastle—SwV	Machipongo—SV	Rapidan—VA	Wicomico Church—VA
Forest—SwV	Madison—VA	Reedville—VA	Williamsburg—SV
Franklin—SV	Manakin Sabot—VA	Remington—VA	Winchester—VA
Fredericksburg—VA	Manassas—VA	Reston—VA	Woodbridge—VA
Freeman—SV	Marion—SwV	Richlands—SwV	Woodstock—SV
Front Royal—VA	Markham—VA	Richmond—VA & SV	Wytheville—SwV
Galax—SwV	Martinsville—SwV	Rixeyville—VA	Yorktown—SV
Glasgow—SwV	Massies Mill—SwV	Roanoke—SwV	

DIOCESE OF VIRGINIA
(PROVINCE III)
Comprises 38 northern and northwestern VA counties
DIOCESAN OFFICE 110 W Franklin St Richmond VA 23220
TEL (804) 643-8451, 1-800-DIOCESE
E-MAIL bishopsoffice@thediocese.net

NORTHERN VA OFFICE 115 E Fairfax St Falls Church VA 22046
TEL (703) 241-0441
WEB www.thediocese.net

Previous Bishops—
James Madison 1790-1812, Richard C Moore 1814-41, Wm Meade coadj 1829 Bp 1842-62, John Johns coadj 1842 Bp 1862-76, Francis M Whittle coadj 1868 Bp 1876-1902, Alfred M Randolph coadj 1883-1892, John B Newton coadj 1894-97, Robt A Gibson coadj 1897 Bp 1902-19, Arthur S Lloyd coadj 1909-10, Wm C Brown coadj 1914 Bp 1919-27, Henry StG Tucker coadj 1926 Bp 1927-44, Wiley R Mason suffr 1942-50, Fredk D Goodwin coadj 1930 Bp 1944-60, Robt F Gibson Jr suffr 1949-54 coadj 1954 Bp 1960-74, Samuel B Chilton suffr 1960-69, Phil A Smith suffr 1970-73, John A Baden suffr 1973-79, Robt B Hall coadj 1966 Bp 1974-85, David H Lewis Jr suffr 1980-87, Robt P Atkinson asst 1989-93, FC Matthews suffr 1993-99, Francis C Gray ret asst 1999-2006, Peter James Lee coadj 1984 Bp 1985-2009, David C Jones suffr 1995-2012, Edwin F Gulick Jr ret asst 2011-17, Shannon S Johnston coadj 2007 Bp 2009-18, Robert Ihloff ret asst 2018-19, Jennifer Brooke-Davidson asst 2019-22, G. Porter Taylor ret asst 2020-22, Susan E. Goff suffr 2012-22 and eccl auth 2018-22

Bishop Diocesan—Rt Rev E Mark Stevenson (1152)

Chanc JP Causey Jr Esq; *Pres Exec Bd* Rt Rev EM Stevenson; *Dio Sec* M Eastham; *Treas* T Smith; *Cn to Ord* Rev d'Rue Hazel; *Dep Off* Rev Shirley Smith-Graham; *Stew* S Higgins; *Comm Off* N Chafin

Stand Comm—Cler: L Lockey *Sec* C Love Mendoza C Ramey S Rodriguez K Wickersham N York-Simmons; *Lay:* J Atkinson *Pres* T Baker T Beatty T Gilpin H Penrod M Woody

Deans of Regions: PH Buisson K Dougherty C Dupree B Franklin F Gardner-Smith R Gordon S Hartzell J Ivatts E Keeler K Murray R Razzino L Ronaldi S Schlossberg M Smith K Tomlin

PARISHES, MISSIONS, AND CLERGY

Aldie Church of Our Redeemer **M** (244) § PO Box 217 20105-0217 (Mail to: PO Box 217 20105-0217) (703) 327-4060

Alexandria All Saints Sharon Chapel **P** (197) 3421 Franconia Rd 22310-2320 (Mail to: PO Box 3074 22302-0074) Valerie Hayes (703) 9604808

Alexandria Christ Church **P** (1541) § 118 N Washington St 22314-3023 (Mail to: 118 N Washington St 22314-3078) Diane Murphy Noelle York-Simmons (703) 549-1450

Alexandria Church of the Resurrection **P** (123) 2800 Hope Way 22311-2220 (Mail to: 2800 Hope Way 22311-2220) Jo Belser Theresa Lewallen (703) 9980888

Alexandria Church of the Spirit **P** (72) § C/O Olivet Episcopal Church 6107 Franconia Rd 22310-2542 (Mail to: C/O Olivet Episcopal Church 6107 Franconia Rd 22310-2542) (703) 971-5242

Alexandria Emmanuel Church **P** (728) § 1608 Russell Rd 22301-1926 (Mail to: 1608 Russell Rd 22301-1998) Charles Mccoart Joan Peacock (703) 683-0798

Alexandria Grace Episcopal Church **P** (1008) § 3601 Russell Rd 22305-1731 (Mail to: 3601 Russell Rd 22305-1799) Anne Turner (703) 549-1980

Alexandria La Iglesia de San Marcos **M** (152) 6744 S Kings Hwy 22306-1318 (Mail to: The Diocese of Virginia 110 W Franklin St 23220-5010) (804) 643-8451

Alexandria Immanuel Church on the Hill **P** (1048) 3606 Seminary Rd 22304-5200 (Mail to: 3606 Seminary Rd 22304-5200) Joseph Alexander Patricia Alexander (703) 370-6555

Alexandria Meade Memorial Church **P** (113) § 322 N Alfred St 22314-2423 (Mail to: 322 N Alfred St 22314-2423) Collins Asonye (703) 549-1334

Alexandria Olivet Church **P** (91) § 6107 Franconia Rd 22310-2508 (Mail to: 6107 Franconia Rd 22310-2508) Robert Tedesco (703) 971-4733

Alexandria St Aidans Church **P** (288) 8531 Riverside Rd 22308-2206 (Mail to: 8531 Riverside Rd 22308-2200) Laura Cochran (703) 360-4220

Alexandria St Luke's Church **P** (354) § 8009 Fort Hunt Rd 22308-1207 (Mail to: 8009 Fort Hunt Rd 22308-1293) Nicholas Hull (703) 765-4342

Alexandria Saint Mark's Church **P** (250) § 6744 S Kings Hwy 22306-1318 (Mail to: 6744 S Kings Hwy 22306-1318) (703) 765-3949

Alexandria Saint Paul's Episcopal Church **P** (3254) § 228 S Pitt Steet 22314 (Mail to: 228 S Pitt St 22314-3797) Oran Warder Rosemary

Beales Anne Monahan Jennifer Ovenstone (703) 549-3312

Alexandria Church of St Clement **P** (211) § 1701 N Quaker Ln 22302-2339 (Mail to: 1701 N Quaker Ln 22302-2339) Cynthia Park Robin Razzino (703) 998-6166

Annandale St Albans Church **P** (572) 6800 Columbia Pike 22003-3431 (Mail to: 6800 Columbia Pike 22003-3431) Jeffrey Shankles (703) 256-2966

Annandale St Barnabas' Church **P** (207) 4801 Ravensworth Rd 22003-5551 (Mail to: 4801 Ravensworth Rd 22003-5551) John Shellito (703) 941-2922

Arlington La Iglesia de Cristo Rey **M** (179) 415 S Lexington St 22204-1226 (Mail to: 415 S Lexington St 22204-1226) (703) 524-4716

Arlington St Andrews Church **P** (253) 4000 Lorcom Ln 22207-3937 (Mail to: 4000 Lorcom Ln 22207-3937) Dorota Wright-Pruski Alfred Moss (703) 522-1600

Arlington St Georges Church **P** (555) § 915 N Oakland St 22203-1916 (Mail to: 915 N Oakland St 22203-1916) Shearon Williams (703) 525-8286

Arlington St Johns Episcopal Church **P** (47) 415 S Lexington St 22204-1226 (Mail to: 415 S Lexington St 22204-1226) Julie Bryant (703) 671-6834

Arlington Saint Mary's Episcopal Church **P** (1645) 2609 N Glebe Rd 22207-3501 (Mail to: 2609 N Glebe Rd 22207-3501) Andrew Merrow Sara Palmer (703) 527-6800

Arlington St Michael's Episcopal Church **P** (235) 1132 N Ivanhoe St 22205-2445 (Mail to: 1132 N Ivanhoe St 22205-2499) Elizabeth Franklin (703) 2412474

Arlington St Peters Episcopal Church **P** (1082) 4250 N Glebe Rd 22207-4508 (Mail to: 4250 N Glebe Rd 22207-4500) Jenifer Gamber (703) 536-6606

Arlington San Jose Church **M** (124) 911 N Oakland St 22203-1916 (Mail to: 911 N Oakland St 22203-1916) (703) 524-4716

Arlington Trinity Church **P** (231) 2217 Columbia Pike 22204-4405 (Mail to: 2217 Columbia Pike 22204-4497) Kim Coleman Elliott Waters (703) 920-7077

Ashburn Saint David's Church **P** (487) § 43600 Russell Branch Pkwy 20147-2903 (Mail to: C/O Lisa Gager 43600 Russell Branch Pkwy 20147-2903) Susan Pinkerton (703) 729-0570

Ashland Church of St James the Less **P** (388) 125 Beverly Rd 23005-1821 (Mail to: 125 Beverly Rd 23005-1821) Jeffrey Higgins (804) 798-6336

Aylett St Davids Church **M** (51) 11291 W River Rd 23009-3000 (Mail to: PO Box 125 23009-0125) (804) 737-6685

Batesville Holy Cross Episcopal Church **P** (71) 2523 Craigs Store Road 22924 (Mail to: PO Box 12 22924-0012) Ryan Lesh (434) 361-9651

Berryville Grace Episcopal Church **P** (164) 110 N Church St 22611-1109 (Mail to: PO Box 678 22611-0678) Justin Ivatts (540) 955-1610

Berryville St Marys Church **M** (16) N Buckmarsh St 22611 (Mail to: PO Box 252 22611-0252) (540) 955-1610

Bluemont Church of the Good Shepherd **M** (23) 27 Good Shepherd Rd 20135-4725 (Mail to: PO Box 324 20135-0324) Ralph Bayfield (540) 554-8351

Boonesville Good Shepherd-of-the-Hills **M** (18) Intersection of SR601 & SR810 22940 (Mail to: PO Box 31 22940-0031) (434) 973-7688

Bowling Green St Asaphs Church **P** (115) 130 S Main St 22427-9424 (Mail to: PO Box 1178 22427-1178) (804) 633-5660

Brandy Station Christ Church **P** (68) 14586 Alanthus Rd 22714-0025 (Mail to: PO Box 25 22714-0025) (434) 286-3914

Bremo Bluff Grace Episcopal Church **M** (55) 754 Bremo Bluff Rd 23022-2104 (Mail to: PO Box 95 23022-0095) Thomas Hendrickson (804) 266-1410

Burke Church of the Good Shepherd **P** (591) 9350 Braddock Rd 22015-1521 (Mail to: 9350 Braddock Rd 22015-1521) Christine Mendoza (703) 323-5400

Burke St Andrews Church **P** (807) § 6509 Sydenstricker Rd 22015-4210 (Mail to: 6509 Sydenstricker Rd 22015-4210) William Packard (703) 455-2500

Casanova Grace Church Emmanuel Parish **P** (38) 5108 Weston Rd 20139 (Mail to: PO Box 18 20139-0018) (540) 788-4419

Catlett St Stephens Church **P** (157) 8695 Old Dumfries Road 20119-1922 (Mail to: 8695 Old Dumfries Rd 20119-1943) Peter Gustin (540) 788-4252

Centreville Saint John's Church **P** (113) § 5649 Mount Gilead Rd 20120-1906 (Mail to: 5649 Mount Gilead Rd 20120-1906) Steven Busch Philene Ware Dunn (703) 803-7500

Charles City Westover Parish Church **P** (170) 6401 John Tyler Mem High 23030 (Mail to: 6401 John Tyler Memorial Hwy 23030-3310) Eleanor Mcdaniel (804) 829-2488

Charlottesville Mcilhany Parish **M** (30) 960 Monacan Trail Rd 22903-7704 (Mail to: 960 Monacan Trail Rd 22903-7704) (434) 293-3455

Charlottesville Saint Luke's, Simeon **M** (101) 1333 Thomas Jefferson Pkwy 22902-7518 (Mail to: PO Box 694 22902-0694) (434) 970-5020

Charlottesville St Paul's Ivy Church **P** (835) 851 Owensville Road 22901-9594 (Mail to: PO Box 37 22945-0037) Justin Mcintosh Sara Kotval Richard Lord (434) 979-6354

Charlottesville Trinity Episcopal Church **P** (166) 1118 Preston Ave 22903-2002 (Mail to: 1118 Preston Ave 22903-2002) Bertram Bailey (434) 293-3157

Charlottesvlle Christ Episcopal Church **P** (2028) 120 W High St 22902 (Mail to: 100 W Jefferson St 22902-5023) Paul Walker Marilu Thomas (434) 977-1227

Charlottesvlle Church of Our Saviour **P** (554) 1165 Rio Rd E 22901-1810 (Mail to: 1165 E Rio Rd 22901-1810) David Stoddart Kathleen Sturges Kathleen Sturges (434) 973-6512

Charlottesvlle St Pauls Memorial Church **P** (649) 1701 University Ave 22903-2619 (Mail to: 1701 University Ave 22903-2619) William Peyton Heather Warren Mark Wastler (434) 295-2156

Christchurch Christ Church Parish **P** (113) 56 Christchurch Labe Rt 33 638 23031 (Mail to: PO Box 476 23149-0476) Stuart Wood (804) 758-2006

Colonial Beach St Mary's Church **P** (131) 203 Dennison St 22443-2311 (Mail to: 203 Dennison St 22443-2311) Nicholas Szobota Thomas Hughes (804) 224-7186

Columbia St Johns Church **M** (25) 43 Washington St 23038 (Mail to: PO Box 853 23038-0853) Richard Singleton (434) 842-3715

Culpeper St Stephens Episcopal Church **P** (363) 115 N East St 22701-3021 (Mail to: 115 N East St 22701-3021) Emmetri Beane Emmetri Beane (540) 825-8786

Delaplane Emmanuel Episcopal Church **P** (194) 9668 Maidstone Rd 20144-2211 (Mail to: 9668 Maidstone Rd 20144-2211) Pierre-Henry Buisson (540) 364-2772

Doswell The Fork Church **P** (179) 12566 Old Ridge Rd 23047-1710 (Mail to: 12566 Old Ridge Rd 23047-1710) Kenneth Forti (804) 227-3413

Dunn Loring Church of the Holy Cross **P** (321) 2455 Gallows Road 22027-1225 (Mail to: 2455 Gallows Rd 22027-1225) Kelly Moughty (703) 698-6991

Earlysville Buck Mountain Church **P** (279) 4133 Earlysville Rd 22936-2504 (Mail to: PO Box 183 22936-0183) Constance Clark (434) 973-2054

Elkton St Stephen & the Good Shepherd **P** (40) 7078 Rocky Bar Rd 22827-3503 (Mail to: 211 Spring Lane 22840) Laura Minnich-Lockey Stuart Wood (540) 249-4121

Fairfax Holy Cross Korean Epis Church **M** (41) 10520 Main St 22030-3380 (Mail to: 10520 Main St 22030-3380) (703) 563-6333

Fairfax Station St Peters in the Woods **M** (320) 5911 Fairview Woods Dr 22039-1427 (Mail to: 5911 Fairview Woods Dr 22039-1427) Susan Hartzell (703) 503-9210

Falls Church La Iglesia de Santa Maria **M** (476) 7000 Arlington Blvd 22042-1827 (Mail to: 7000 Arlington Blvd 22042-1827) Roberto Orihuela (703) 533-9220

Falls Church St Patricks Episcopal Church **M** (108) § 3241 Brush Dr 22042-2569 (Mail to: 3241 Brush Dr 22042-2569) Julie Bryant Tinh Huynh (703) 532-5656

Falls Church St Pauls Episcopal Church **P** (69) § 3439 Payne St 22041-2019 (Mail to: 3439 Payne St 22041-2019) (703) 820-2625

Falls Church The Falls Church Episcopal **P** (803) 115 E Fairfax St 22046-2903 (Mail to: 115 E Fairfax St 22046-2903) Walter Salmon Steven Busch (703) 241-0003

Farnham North Farnham Parish Church **P** (32) 231 N Farnham Church Rd 22460 (Mail to: PO Box 343 22460-0343) (804) 333-4333

Fredericksbrg Church of the Messiah **M** (106) 5875 Plank Rd 22407-6229 (Mail to: 12201 Spotswood Furnace Ln 22407-2265) Kyle Tomlin (540) 786-3100

Fredericksbrg Trinity Church **P** (621) 825 College Ave 22401-5469 (Mail to: 825 College Ave 22401-5469) Cynthia Mckenna (540) 373-2996

Fredericksbrg St Georges Episcopal Church **P** (776) § 905 Princess Anne St 22401-5821 (Mail to: PO Box 7127 22404-7127) Joseph Hensley Rosemary Beales William Dickinson (540) 373-4133

Front Royal Calvary Church **P** (304) 132 N Royal Avenue 22630-2603 (Mail to: 11 West 2nd Street 22630) Valerie Hayes (540) 635-2763

Glen Allen Christ Church **P** (1283) § 5000 Pouncey Tract Rd 5000 Pouncey Tract Rd 23059-5301 (Mail to: 5000 Pouncey Tract Rd 5000 Pouncey Tract Rd 23059-5301) Charles Goldsborough (804) 3640394

Gloucester Ware Episcopal Church **P** (235) 7825 John Clayton Memorial Hwy 23061-5108 (Mail to: PO Box 616 23061-0616) Scott Parnell (804) 693-3821

Goochland Grace Church **P** (261) 2955 River Rd W 23063-3230 (Mail to: PO Box 698 23063-0698) Emily Dunevant (804) 556-3051

Gordonsville Christ Church **P** (79) 310 N High Street 22942 (Mail to: PO Box 588 22942-0588) Mary Wells (540) 832-3209

Great Falls St Francis Church **P** (297) 9220 Georgetown Pike 22066-2726 (Mail to: 9220 Georgetown Pike 22066-2726) David Lucey (703) 759-2082

Greenwood Emmanuel Episcopal Church **P** (389) 7500 Rockfish Gap Tpke 22943-1802 (Mail to: 7599 Rockfish Gap Tpke 22943-1802) John Thomas (540) 456-6334

Grottoes Grace Memorial Church **P** (55) C/O Sally Jensen 1203 Randall Rd Apt A6 24441-2435 (Mail to: 7120 Ore Bank Rd 24471-2206) Stuart Wood (540) 249-4121

Hague Cople Parish **P** (141) 72 Coles Point Rd 22469 (Mail to: PO Box 249 22488-0249) (804) 472-2593

Hanover Calvary Episcopal Church **P** (99) 13312 Courthouse Road 23069-0307 (Mail to: PO Box 307 23069-0307) (804) 537-5061

Hanover St Paul's Episcopal Church **P** (225) 8050 St Paul's Church Rd 23069 (Mail to: PO Box 441 23069-0441) Rachel Rickenbaker Benson Shelton (804) 537-5516

Harrisonburg Emmanuel Church **P** (223) 660 S Main St 22801-5819 (Mail to: 660 S Main St 22801-5819) Edward Bachschmid Joseph Butler (540) 434-2357

Haymarket St Pauls Church **P** (177) St Pauls Episcopal Church 6750 Fayette St 20169-2913 (Mail to: 6750 Fayette St 20169-2913) Sean Rousseau (703) 753-2443

Heathsville St Stephens Episcopal Church **P** (65) 6807 Northumberland Hwy 22473-3334 (Mail to: PO Box 40 22473-0040) Pilar Parnell (804) 724-4238

Henrico Varina Church **P** (226) 2385 Mill Rd 23231-7019 (Mail to: 2385 Mill Rd 23231-7019) Whitney Edwards (804) 795-5340

Herndon St Timothys Church **P** (628) § 432 Van Buren St 20170-5104 (Mail to: 432 Van Buren St 20170-5199) Charles Cowherd (703) 437-3790

Ivy St John the Baptist Church **M** (36) § State Route 637 22945 (Mail to: Attn: Treasurer PO Box 351 22945-0351) Anthony Andres Kathleen Sturges (434) 295-0744

Keswick Grace Church **P** (245) 5607 Gordonsville Rd 22947-1906 (Mail to: PO Box 43 22947-0043) Gary Smith (434) 293-3549

Kilmarnock Grace Church **P** (573) 303 S Main St 22482-9595 (Mail to: PO Box 1059 22482-1059) Kim Glenn R Jeffrey Patnaude (804) 435-1285

King and Queen Courthouse Immanuel Church **M** (7) 190 Allens Cir 23085 (Mail to: General Delivary 23085) (804) 785-6461

King George Emmanuel Church **P** (10) 17062 James Madison Pkwy 22485-2613 (Mail to: PO Box 134 22485-0134) (540) 775-3635

King George Hanvr With Brnswk Par St John **P** (50) 9403 Kings Hwy 22485-3425 (Mail to: PO Box 134 22485-0134) Richard Fichter (540) 775-3635

King George Saint Paul's, Owens **P** (160) 5486 Saint Pauls Rd 22485-5436 (Mail to: 5486 Saint Pauls Rd 22485-5436) Leonard Gandiya (540) 663-3085

Lancaster St Marys Whitechapel **P** (69) 5940 White Chapel Rd 22503-3029 (Mail to: 5940 White Chapel Rd 22503-3029) Megan Limburg (804) 462-5908

Lancaster Trinity Episcopal Church **P** (72) § 8484 Mary Ball Rd, Lancaster 22503 (Mail to: C/O Craig H Giese PO Box 1546 22503) (804) 462-0610

Leesburg Christ Church Lucketts **M** (61) 14861 Newvalley Church Rd 20176-6031 (Mail to: 14861 Newvalley Church Rd 20176-6031) (703) 771-2196

Leesburg St Gabriels Episcopal Church **M** (170) 14 Cornwall St NW 20176-2801 (Mail to: 8

Cornwall St NW 20176-2801) Daniel Velez-Rivera (703) 779-3616

Leesburg St James Church **P** (729) § 14 Cornwall St NW 20176-2801 (Mail to: 14 Cornwall St NW 20176-2801) Chad Martin (703) 777-1124

Loretto Vauters Church **P** (83) 3661 Tidewater Trl 22438 (Mail to: PO Box 154 22438-0154) (804) 443-4788

Lorton Pohick Church **P** (623) § 9301 Richmond Hwy 22079-1519 (Mail to: 9301 Richmond Hwy 22079-1519) Lynn Ronaldi Celal Kamran (703) 339-6572

Louisa St James Church **P** (169) 102 Ellisville Dr 23093-6550 (Mail to: PO Box 1216 23093-1216) Rodney Caulkins (540) 967-1665

Luray Christ Church **P** (81) § PO Box 231 22835-0231 (Mail to: 16 Amiss Ave 22835-1310) Catherine Tibbetts (540) 743-5734

Madison Piedmont Bromfield Parish **P** (119) 214 Church St 22727-3013 (Mail to: PO Box 305 22727-0305) Anne West Brad Jackson (540) 948-6787

Manakin Sabot St Francis Episcopal Church **P** (53) 1484 Hockett Rd 23103-2603 (Mail to: PO Box 303 23103-0303) John Maher (804) 784-6116

Manassas Trinity Church **P** (1159) 9325 West St 20110-5128 (Mail to: 9325 West St 20110-5197) Vinnie Lainson John Talk (703) 368-4231

Markham Episcopal Ch of Leeds Parish **P** (325) 4332 Leeds Manor Rd 22643-1906 (Mail to: 4332 Leeds Manor Rd 22643-1906) Denise Guinta (540) 364-2849

Mathews Kingston Parish **P** (209) 370 Main Street 23109-0471 (Mail to: PO Box 471 23109-0471) Gary Barker (804) 725-2175

Mc Lean St Dunstans Church **P** (400) § 1830 Kirby Rd 22101-5323 (Mail to: 1830 Kirby Rd 22101-5399) Stephen Shepherd Anna Scherer (703) 356-7533

Mclean St Johns Episcopal Church **P** (1201) § 6715 Georgetown Pike 22101 (Mail to: PO Box 457 22101) Joshua Walters Stuart Kenworthy Andrew Moore (703) 356-4902

Mclean St Thomas Church **P** (352) § 8991 Brook Rd 22102-1510 (Mail to: 8991 Brook Rd 22102-1599) Fran Gardner-Smith (703) 442-0330

Mclean St Francis Korean Church **M** (30) 1830 Kirby Rd 22101-5323 (Mail to: 1830 Kirby Rd 22101-5323) (804) 2210153

Mechanicsville All Souls Episcopal Church **M** (202) 9077 Atlee Rd 23116-2501 (Mail to: 9077 Atlee Rd 23116-2501) (804) 229-4998

Mechanicsvlle Church of the Creator **P** (173) 7159 Mechanicsville Tpke 23111-3663 (Mail to: 7159 Mechanicsville Tpke 23111-3663) William Burk (804) 746-8765

Mechanicsvlle Immanuel Church **P** (290) 3263 Old Church Rd. 23111 (Mail to: 3263 Old

Church Rd 23111-6224) Robin Teasley (804) 779-3454

Middleburg Emmanuel Church **P** (161) 105 E Washington St 20117 (Mail to: C/O Norris Beavers PO Box 306 20118-0306) Eugene LeCouteur (540) 687-6297

Millers Tavern Grace Church **P** (14) 604 Howerton Road 23115 (Mail to: PO Box 126 23115-0126) (804) 843-3587

Millers Tavern St Paul's Episcopal Church **P** (182) 360 Highway 23115 (Mail to: PO Box 278 23115-0278) Johan Johnson Theodore Mcconnell (804) 443-2341

Millwood Cunningham Chapel Parish **P** (159) 809 Bishop Meade Road 22646-0153 (Mail to: PO Box 153 22646-0153) (540) 837-1112

Mineral Church of the Incarnation **M** (66) Rt 552 Lee St 23117 (Mail to: PO Box 307 23117-0307) (540) 894-0136

Montpelier Church of Our Saviour **M** (159) 17102 Mountain Rd 23192-2550 (Mail to: PO Box 11 23192-0011) Emily Krudys (804) 883-5943

Montross St James Church **P** (104) 15870 Kings Hwy 22520 (Mail to: PO Box 177 22520-0177) Alan Hooker (804) 493-8285

Montross St Pauls Church Nomini Grove **P** (40) 21983 Kings Hwy 22520-2912 (Mail to: Attn: Treasurer 1819 Neenah Rd 22520-3115) (804) 493-8994

Mount Jackson St Andrews Church **P** (51) 5890 Main St 22842-9406 (Mail to: PO Box 117 22842-0117) Kathleen Murray (540) 477-3335

Mount Vernon St James' Episcopal Church **P** (112) 5614 Old Mills Rd 22309 (Mail to: 5614 Old Mill Rd 22309-3300) Charles Brock (703) 780-3081

New Kent St Peters Parish Church **P** (329) 8400 St Peters Ln 23124-2718 (Mail to: 8400 St Peters Ln 23124-2718) (804) 932-4846

Oak Grove St Peters **P** (125) 2961 Kings Hwy 22443-5310 (Mail to: Attn: Alice Payne PO Box 757 22520-0757) Rodney Gordon Linda Murphy (804) 224-0163

Oak Hill Epiphany Episcopal Church **P** (235) 3301 Hidden Meadow Dr 20171-4068 (Mail to: 3301 Hidden Meadow Dr 20171-4068) Dina Widlake Susannah Harding (703) 466-5200

Orange St Thomas Episcopal Church **P** (148) 119 Caroline St 22960-1532 (Mail to: 119 Caroline St 22960-1532) Linda Hutton (540) 672-3761

✠ **Orkney Springs** Cathd Shrine of the Transfig **O** (5) 221 Shrine Mont Cir 22845 (Mail to: 221 Shrine Mont Cir 22845) (540) 856-2141

Port Royal St Peters Church **P** (62) 823 Water St 22535-2171 (Mail to: PO Box 399 22535-0399) Catherine Hicks (804) 742-5908

Purcellville St Peters Church **P** (263) 37018 Glendale St 20132-3422 (Mail to: PO Box 546 20134-0546) Thomas Simmons (540) 338-7307

Rapidan Emmanuel Church **P** (57) 28279 Rapidan Rd 22733-2431 (Mail to: PO Box 81 22733-0081) (540) 672-1395

Reedville St Marys Church **P** (83) 3020 Fleeton Rd 22539-4221 (Mail to: PO Box 278 22539-0278) Johanna Pierce (804) 453-6712

Remington St Lukes Church **P** (48) 400 N Church St 22734-9708 (Mail to: PO Box 267 22734-0267) Nancy Betz (540) 439-3733

Reston St Anne's Church **P** (1025) 1700 Wainwright Dr 20190-5500 (Mail to: 1700 Wainwright Dr 20190-5500) Jessica Holthus Harold Johnson (703) 437-6530

Richmond All Saints Episcopal Church **P** (738) § 8787 River Rd 23229-8303 (Mail to: 8787 River Rd 23229-8303) Penny Nash (804) 2887811

Richmond Christ Ascension Church **P** (61) § 1704 W Laburnum Ave 23227-4312 (Mail to: 1704 W Laburnum Ave 23227-4312) (804) 264-9474

Richmond Church of the Holy Comforter **P** (233) 4819 Monument Ave 23230-3615 (Mail to: 4819 Monument Ave 23230-3615) Hilary Smith Joseph Klenzmann (804) 355-3251

Richmond Emmanuel Church at Brook Hill **P** (326) § 1214 Wilmer Ave 23227-2405 (Mail to: 1214 Wilmer Ave 23227-2405) (804) 266-2431

Richmond Epiphany Church **P** (355) 8000 Hermitage Rd 23228-3704 (Mail to: 8000 Hermitage Road 23228) (804) 266-2503

Richmond Grace and Holy Trinity Church **P** (540) 8 N Laurel St 23220-4700 (Mail to: 8 N Laurel St 23220-4797) Duane Nettles (804) 359-5628

Richmond St Andrews Church **P** (227) 240 S Laurel St 23220 (Mail to: 236 S Laurel St 23220-6229) Barbara Ambrose (804) 648-7980

Richmond St Bartholomews Episcopal Ch **P** (167) § 10627 Patterson Ave 23238-4701 (Mail to: PO Box 29626 23242-0626) John Cadaret (804) 740-2101

Richmond St Johns Church **P** (265) 2401 E Broad St 23223-7128 (Mail to: 2319 E Broad St 23223-7126) Sandra Levy Amelie Wilmer Anne Lane Witt (804) 649-7938

Richmond St Marks Church **P** (410) 520 N Boulevard 23220-3309 (Mail to: 520 N Boulevard 23220-3309) Judith Davis (804) 358-4771

Richmond St Martins Episcopal Church **M** (309) 9000 Saint Martin Ln 23294-4448 (Mail to: 9000 St Martins Ln 23294-4448) Lee Hutchson (804) 270-6786

Richmond St Mary's Episcopal Church **P** (1334) § Attn: Carl Hayslett 12291 River Rd 23238-6112 (Mail to: 12291 River Rd 23238-6112) David May Eleanor Wellford (804) 784-5678

Richmond St Matthews Episcopal Church **P** (471) § 1101 Forest Ave 23229-5845 (Mail to: 1101 Forest Ave 23229-5800) Stephen Schlossberg (804) 288-1911

Richmond St Pauls Church **P** (573) 815 E Grace St 23219-3409 (Mail to: 815 E Grace St 23219-3409) Charles Dupree Mary Crichton Susan Rainey Dankel (804) 643-3589

Richmond St Peters Episcopal Church **M** (93) 1719 N 22nd St 23223-4431 (Mail to: 1719 N 22nd St 23223-4431) Karla Hunt (804) 643-2686

Richmond St Philips Church **P** (311) 2900 Hanes Ave 23222-3607 (Mail to: 2900 Hanes Ave 23222-3607) Marlene Forrest (804) 3211266

Richmond St Stephens Church **P** (4769) § 6000 Grove Ave 23226-2601 (Mail to: 6000 Grove Ave 23226-2601) John Rohrs William Stanley (804) 288-2867

Richmond St Thomas Church **P** (358) 3602 Hawthorne Ave 23222-1824 (Mail to: 3602 Hawthorne Ave 23222-1824) Herbert Jones (804) 321-9548

Richmond St James Church **P** (2932) § 1205 W Franklin St 23220-3711 (Mail to: 1205 W Franklin St 23220-3793) John Mccard Amelia Arthur John Wigner (804) 355-1779

Rixeyville Little Fork Episcopal Church **P** (82) 16471 Oak Shade Rd 22737-2927 (Mail to: PO Box 367 22737-0367) Stacy Williams-Duncan (540) 937-4306

Scottsville St Annes Parish **P** (180) § 410 Harrison St 24590 (Mail to: PO Box 337 24590-0337) (434) 286-3437

Shenandoah St Pauls Church **P** (14) 3075 Comertown Rd 22849-4047 (Mail to: 1012 Wahmona Ave 22849-1023) (540) 962-7112

Spotsylvania Christ Church **P** (227) 8951 Courthouse Rd 22553-2517 (Mail to: 8951 Courthouse Rd 22553-2517) Daniel Johnson (540) 582-5033

Springfield St Christopher's Church **P** (563) 6320 Hanover Ave 22150-4099 (Mail to: 6320 Hanover Ave 22150-4099) Carey Connors (703) 451-1088

Stafford Aquia Church **P** (1136) 2938 Jefferson Davis Hwy 22554-1730 (Mail to: PO Box 275 22555-0275) John Morris James Rickenbaker (540) 659-4007

Stanardsville Grace Church **M** (75) 97 Main St 22973 (Mail to: 112 Main St PO Box 112 22973-2970) Anne West Grace Cangialosi (434) 985-7716

Stanley St Georges Church **M** (14) The Diocese Of Virginia 3380 Pine Grove Rd 22851-5411 (Mail to: The Diocese of Virginia 110 W Franklin St 23220-5010) Stuart Smith (540) 778-3462

Sterling St Matthews Church **P** (940) § 201 E Frederick Dr 20164-2387 (Mail to: 201 E Frederick Dr 20164-2387) Carl Merola (703) 430-2121

Tappahannock St Johns Episcopal Church **P** (115) 216 Duke St 22560-2200 (Mail to: PO Box 336 22560-0336) Candine Johnson Robert Friend (804) 649-7938

The Plains Grace Church **P** (365) § 6507 Main St 20198 (Mail to: PO Box 32 20198-0032) Edward Mathews (540) 253-5177

Upperville Trinity Church **P** (459) 9108 John S Mosby Hwy 20184-1776 (Mail to: PO Box 127 20185-0127) Jonathan Adams (540) 592-3343

Vienna Church of the Holy Comforter **P** (2174) § 543 Beulah Rd NE 22180-3510 (Mail to: 543 Beulah Rd NE 22180-3599) Jon Strand Ann Gillespie (703) 938-6521

Warrenton St Andrews Church **M** (65) Attn Mr Ordie L Frazier 75 Frazier Rd 20186-2704 (Mail to: 75 Frazier Rd 20186-2704) (540) 675-3616

Warrenton St James Church **P** (646) § 73 Culpeper St 20186-3321 (Mail to: 73 Culpeper St 20186-3321) Benjamin Maas (540) 347-4342

Warsaw St Johns Church **P** (40) 5987 Richmond Rd 22572-1093 (Mail to: C/O Anne Douglas PO Box 1093 22572-1093) (804) 333-4333

Washington Trinity Church **P** (228) 379 Gay St 22747-1978 (Mail to: PO Box 299 22747-0299) Elizabeth Keeler (540) 675-3716

West Point St Johns Episcopal Church **P** (95) § C/O H V Perry 916 Main St 23181-9548 (Mail to: PO Box 629 23181-0629) Theresa Brion (804) 843-4594

West Point St Pauls Church **P** (40) 532 15th St 23181-0767 (Mail to: PO Box 767 23181-0767) (804) 843-3587

White Marsh Abingdon Church **P** (317) 4645 Geo Washington Mem Hwy 23183 (Mail to: PO Box 82 23183-0082) Sven Vanbaars Jennifer Kimball (804) 693-3035

White Post Meade Memorial Church **M** (36) 192 White Post Road 22663-0007 (Mail to: PO Box 7 22663-0007) (540) 837-2354

Wicomico Church Wicomico Parish Church **P** (261) § 5195 Jessie B Dupont Mem Hwy 22579 (Mail to: PO Box 70 22579-0070) (804) 580-6445

Winchester Christ Episcopal Church **P** (681) § 114 W Boscawen St 22601-4116 (Mail to: 114 W Boscawen St 22601-4116) Webster Gibson Martin Geiger (540) 662-5843

Winchester St Pauls on the Hill Church **P** (213) 1527 Senseny Rd 22602-6423 (Mail to: PO Box 1442 22604-7942) (540) 667-8110

Woodbridge St Margaret's Episcopal Church **P** (151) 5290 Saratoga Ln 22193-3455 (Mail to: 5290 Saratoga Ln 22193-3455) (703) 590-3990

Woodstock Emmanuel Church **P** (94) 122 E Court St 22664-1727 (Mail to: 122 E Court St 22664-1727) Kathleen Murray (540) 459-2720

STATE OF WASHINGTON
Dioceses of Olympia and Spokane

DIOCESE OF WASHINGTON
(PROVINCE III)
Comprises DC and 4 counties of Maryland
DIOCESAN OFFICE Episcopal Church House Mt S Alban Washington DC 20016-5094
TEL (202) 537-6555 FAX (202) 364-6605
WEB www.edow.org

Previous Bishops—
Henry Y Satterlee 1896-1908, Alfred Harding 1909-23, James E Freeman 1923-43, Angus Dun 1944-62, William F Creighton coadj 1959 Bp 1962-77, Paul Moore Jr suffr 1964-70, John T Walker suffr 1971-76 coadj 1976 Bp 1977-89, Ronald H Haines suffr 1986-90 Bp 1990-2000, Jane H Dixon suffr 1992-2002; John Bryson Chane 2002-11

Bishop—Rt Rev Mariann Edgar Budde (1061) (Dio 12 Nov 2011)

Cn to Ord & COO Rev Cn A Walter; *Chanc* J Van de Weert; *Treas* J Nicholas; *Hist* S Stonesifer; *Sec* K Roachford; *Cn for Lead Dev & Cong Care* Rev Dr R Phillips; *Archddcn* Rev S Seely; *Dean for the Dio Latino Deacons' School* Rev Y González Hernández; *Miss for Latino/Hispanic Min & Dio Initiatives* M Reyes; *Cn for Congregational Vitality* Rev. Dr. A Jeffery; *Miss for Faith Form & Dev't* Rev A Akes-Cardwell; *Miss for Equity & Justice* R Logan

Stand Comm—Cler: S McJilton M Jenkins M Heffner M Kane; *Lay:* K Pierson E Gilmore J Little A Vanterpool

PARISHES, MISSIONS, AND CLERGY

Accokeek Christ Ch, St John's Parish **P** (133) 600 Farmington Rd W 20607-9732 (Mail to: 600 Farmington Rd W 20607-9732) (301) 292-5633

Aquasco St Mary **Chapel** 13500 Baden Westwood Rd 20608 (Mail to: C/O St Pauls Church 20613) Mary McCarty (301) 579-2643

Avenue All Saints Church **P** (14) 22598 Oakley Rd 20609 (Mail to: PO Box 307 20609-0307) (301) 769-4288

Beltsville St Johns Church **P** (264) 11040 Baltimore Ave 20705-2118 (Mail to: PO Box 14 20704-0014) Joseph Constant Anne Nicholson (301) 937-9242

Bethesda St Dunstans Episcopal Church **P** (202) 5450 Massachusetts Ave 20816-1653 (Mail to: 5450 Massachusetts Ave 20816-1653) Patricia Alexander (301) 229-2960

Bethesda St Lukes Church Trinity Parish **P** (390) 6030 Grosvenor Ln 20814-1852 (Mail to: 6030 Grosvenor Ln 20814-1852) Jessica Hitchcock Owen Thompson (301) 530-1800

Bethesda Church of the Redeemer **P** (309) 6201 Dunrobbin Dr 20816-1044 (Mail to: 6201 Dunrobbin Dr 20816-1044) David Schlafer (301) 229-3770

Brandywine St Pauls Parish **P** (75) 13500 Baden Westwood Rd 20613-8419 (Mail to: 13500 Baden Westwood Rd 20613-8419) Christian Lehrer (301) 579-2643

Brandywine St Philips Church **P** (109) 13801 Baden Westwood Rd 20613-8426 (Mail to: 13801 Baden Westwood Rd 20613-8426) Christopher Wilkins (301) 888-1536

Brookeville St Lukes Church **P** (97) PO Box 131 20833-0131 (Mail to: PO Box 131 20833-0131) Victoria Clayton (301) 570-3834

California St Andrews Church **P** (357) 44078 St Andrews Church Rd 20619 (Mail to: 44078 Saint Andrews Church Rd 20619-2100) (301) 862-2247

Chaptico Christ Church **P** (194) 25390 Maddox Rd 20621 (Mail to: 37497 Zach Fowler Road PO Box 8 20621) Peter Ackerman (301) 884-3451

Charlotte Hall All Faith Episcopal Church **P** (134) 38885 New Market Turner Rd 20659 (Mail to: PO Box 24 20622-0024) (301) 884-3773

Chevy Chase All Saints Church Chevy Chase Parish **P** (1905) § 3 Chevy Chase Cir 20815-3408 (Mail to: Attn: Lois McDonald 3 Chevy Chase Cir 20815-3408) William Buracker Matthew Kozlowski (301) 6542488

Chevy Chase St Johns Church **P** (985) 6701 Wisconsin Ave 20815-5351 (Mail to: 6701 Wisconsin Ave 20815-5399) Sari Ateek Anne Derse Sarah Reynolds (301) 654-7767

Clinton Christ Church **P** (124) 8710 Old Branch Ave 20735-2522 (Mail to: 8710 Old Branch Ave 20735-2522) (301) 868-1330

College Park St Andrews Episcopal Church **P** (480) 4510 College Ave 20740-3302 (Mail to: 4512 College Ave 20740-3302) Linda Calkins (301) 864-8881

College Park University of Maryland Mission **CC** University of Maryland 2116 Memorial Chapel 20742 (Mail to: 2116 Memorial Chapel 20740) (301) 405-8453

Damascus St Anne's Church **P** (298) 25100 Ridge Rd 20872-1832 (Mail to: 25100 Ridge Rd 20872-1832) Jonathan Musser (301) 253-2130

Forestville Church of the Epiphany **P** (173) 3111 Ritchie Rd 20747-4434 (Mail to: 3111 Ritchie Rd 20747-4434) Prince Decker (202) 726-2080

Ft Washington St Johns Broad Creek **P** (167) § 9801 Livingston Rd 20744-4925 (Mail to: 9801 Livingston Rd 20744-4925) (301) 248-4290

Gaithersburg Church of the Ascension **P** (877) 205 S Summit Ave 20877-2315 (Mail to: Attn: Linett Keene 205 S Summit Ave 20877-2399) Kimberly Becker Javier Garcia-Ocampo (301) 948-0122

Gaithersburg St Barnabas Church of the Deaf **M** (35) C/O Church of the Ascension 205 S Summit Ave 20877-2399 (Mail to: C/O Church of the Ascension 205 S Summit Ave 20877-2399) (301) 907-2955

Gaithersburg St Bartholomews Church **P** (168) 21615 Laytonsville Rd 20882-1627 (Mail to: Attention William Fitts PO Box 5005 20882-0005) Victoria Clayton Margaret Pollock (301) 3557189

Germantown St Nicholas Episcopal Church **P** (310) 15575 Germantown Road 20874-3012 (Mail to: 15575 Germantown Rd 20874-3012) Elizabeth O'Callaghan (240) 631-2800

Glenn Dale St Georges Ch Glenn Dale Par **P** (300) 7010 Glenn Dale Rd 20769 (Mail to: PO Box 188 20769-0188) Constance Reinhardt (301) 262-3285

Hughesville Old Fields Chapel **Chapel** 15837 Prince Frederick Rd 20637-2926 (Mail to: PO Box 178 20637-0178) (301) 934-1424

Hughesville Trinity Parish **P** (40) PO Box 178 20637-0178 (Mail to: PO Box 178 20637-0178) (301) 934-1424

Hyattsville St Matthews Episcopal Church **P** (1191) § 5901 36th Ave 20782-2925 (Mail to: 5901 36th Ave 20782-2925) Vidal Rivas Elena Thompson (301) 559-8686

Hyattsville St Michael and All Angels Ch **P** (123) 8501 New Hampshire Ave 20783-2411 (Mail to: 8501 New Hampshire Ave 20783-2411) (301) 434-4646

Indian Head St James' Church **P** (147) 7 Potomac Ave 20640-1714 (Mail to: 7 Potomac Ave 20640-1798) Denise Cabana (301) 743-2366

Kensington Christ Church Parish **P** (514) 4001 Franklin St 20895-3827 (Mail to: 4001 Franklin St 20895-3827) Emily Guthrie (301) 9424673

La Plata Christ Church **P** (165) 112 E Charles Street 20646-0760 (Mail to: PO Box 760 20646-0760) Katherine Heichler Eric Shoemaker (301) 392-1051

Laurel St Philips Church **P** (476) 522 Main St 20707-4118 (Mail to: 522 Main St 20707-4118) Robert Bunker (301) 776-5151

Leonardtown Resurrection Parish **P** (256) 44965 Blake Creek Rd 20650 (Mail to: PO Box 30 20692-0030) Gregory Syler (301) 9940585

Mount Rainier St Johns Episcopal Church **P** (246) 4104 34th St 20712-1948 (Mail to: 4112 34th St 20712-1948) (301) 927-1156

Nanjemoy Christ Church (Durham Parish) **P** (180) 8700 Ironsides Rd 20662-3430 (Mail to: 8685 Ironsides Rd 20662-3430) Catharine Gibson (301) 743-7099

New Carrollton Saint Christopher's Church **P** (330) 8001 Annapolis Rd 20784-3009 (Mail to: 8001 Annapolis Rd 20784-3009) Melana Nelson-Amaker (301) 577-1281

Newburg Chrst Ch Wayside WM & Mary Par **P** (79) 13050 Rock Point Rd 20664-2503 (Mail to: PO Box 177 20664-0177) (301) 259-4327

Olney St Johns Church **P** (631) § 3427 Olney Laytonsville Rd 20832-1743 (Mail to: PO Box 187 20830-0187) Henry Mcqueen Janice Hicks Shivaun Wilkinson Shivaun Wilkinson (301) 774-6999

Poolesville St Peters Parish **P** (396) 20100 Fisher Ave 20837-2080 (Mail to: PO Box 387 20837-0387) Emily Lloyd (301) 349-2073

Potomac St Francis Church **P** (1021) § 10033 River Rd 20854-4902 (Mail to: 10033 River Rd 20854-4975) Mark Michael (301) 365-2055

Potomac St James Church **P** (323) § 11815 Seven Locks Rd 20854-3340 (Mail to: 11815 Seven Locks Rd 20854-3340) Meredith Heffner James Isaacs (301) 762-8040

Ridge St Marys Chapel **Chapel** 12960 Point Lookout Road 20680 (Mail to: PO Box 207 20686-0207) (301) 862-4597

Rockville Christ Church, Rockville **P** (633) § 107 S Washington St 20850-2319 (Mail to: 109 S Washington St 20850-2319) (301) 762-2191

Silver Spring Our Saviour Hillandale **P** (744) 1700 Powder Mill Rd 20903-1514 (Mail to: 1700 Powder Mill Rd 20903-1500) Jose Valle Jose Valle (301) 439-5900

Silver Spring Church of the Ascension **P** (836) 632 Sligo Ave 20910-4764 (Mail to: 634 Silver Spring Ave 20910-4657) Joan Beilstein (301) 587-3272

Silver Spring Church of the Transfiguration **P** (346) 13925 New Hampshire Ave 20904-6218 (Mail to: 13925 New Hampshire Ave 20904-6218) Stephen Marcoux (301) 384-6264

Silver Spring Good Shepherd Episcopal Church **P** (246) § 818 University Blvd W 20901-103 (Mail to: 818 University Blvd W 20901-1095) Anna Olson (301) 593-3282

Silver Spring Grace Episcopal Church **P** (1003) § 1607 Grace Church Rd 20910-1509 (Mail to: Attn: Gib Baily 1607 Grace Church Rd 20910-1563) Sarah Odderstol Anna Broadbent Evelyn (301) 585-3515

Silver Spring St Marks Church Fairland **P** (233) 12621 Old Columbia Pike 20904-1614 (Mail to: 12621 Old Columbia Pike 20904-1614) Christopher Wilkins (301) 622-5860

Silver Spring St Mary Magdalene Church **P** (342) 3820 Aspen Hill Rd 20906-2904 (Mail to: 3820 Aspen Hill Rd 20906-2904) (301) 871-7660

St Marys City St Marys Parish **HC** (374) PO Box 145 20686-0145 (Mail to: PO Box 207 20686-0207) Jeanie Martinez-Jantz (301) 862-4597

Temple Hills St Barnabas Episcopal Church **P** (111) 5203 St Barnabas Rd 20748-5837 (Mail to: 5203 Saint Barnabas Rd 20748-5837) Shell Kimble (301) 894-9100

Uppr Marlboro St Thomas Parish **P** (137) 14300 Saint Thomas Church Rd 20772-8222 (Mail to: 14300 Saint Thomas Church Rd 20772-8222) Peter Antoci (301) 627-8469

Uppr Marlboro Chapel of the Incarnation **Chapel** 14300 Thomas Church 20772 (Mail to: 14300 Saint Thomas Church Rd 20772-8222) (301) 627-8469

Uppr Marlboro St Barnabas Church **P** (234) § 14111 Oak Grove Rd 20774-8424 (Mail to: PO Box 5168 20775-1168) Phillip Cato Robyn Franklin-Vaughn

Uppr Marlboro Trinity Episcopal Church **P** (318) 14515 Church St 20772-3039 (Mail to: PO Box 187 20773-0187) (301) 627-2636

Waldorf St Pauls Episcopal Church **P** (338) Piney Church Rd St Pauls Dr 20604 (Mail to: 4535 Piney Church Rd 20604-0272) Maria Kane (301) 645-5000

Washington All Souls Memorial Church **P** (199) 2300 Cathedral Ave NW 20008-1505 (Mail to: 2300 Cathedral Ave NW 20008-1505) Julianne Buenting Elizabeth Orens (202) 232-4244

Washington Calvary Church **P** (296) 509 I St NE 20002-4345 (Mail to: 820 6th St NE 20002-4326) Peter Jarrett-Schell (202) 546-8011

✣ **Washington** Washington National Cathedral **O** (1320) Attn: Debbie L Marr HR DEPT 3101 Wisconsin Ave NW 20016-5015 (Mail to: Attn: Debbie L Marr HR Dept 3101 Wisconsin Ave NW 20016-5015) Randolph Hollerith Lisa Barrowclough Eva Maria Cavaleri Leslie Chadwick Jeannette Cope Dana Corsello Rosemarie Duncan Melissa Hollerith Brooks Hundley Patrick Keyser (202) 537-2348

Washington Christ Ch Washington Parish **P** (458) 620 G St SE 20003-2722 (Mail to: C/O Washington Parish 620 G St SE 20003-2722) John Kellogg (202) 547-9300

Washington Christ Church Georgetown **P** (1452) 3116 O St NW 20007-3116 (Mail to: 3116 O St NW 20007-3198) Timothy Cole Nathan Huddleston (202) 333-6677

Washington Church of Our Saviour **P** (95) 1616 Irving St NE 20018-3826 (Mail to: 1616 Irving St NE 20018-3826) (202) 635-7804

Washington Ch Of St Stephen & The Incrntn **P**

(233) 1525 Newton St NW 20010-3103 (Mail to: 1525 Newton St NW 20010-3199) Frank Dunn Rondesia Jarrett-Schell Linda Kaufman (202) 232-0900

Washington Ch of the Ascension & St Agnes **P** (182) 1217 Massachusetts Ave NW 20005-5301 (Mail to: 1217 Massachusetts Ave NW 20005-5396) Mary McCue Dominique Peridans (202) 347-8161

Washington Church of the Atonement **P** (236) 5073 E Capitol St SE 20019-5327 (Mail to: 5073 E Capitol St SE 20019-5327) Ricardo Sheppard (202) 582-4200

Washington Church of the Holy Comforter **P** (102) 701 Oglethorpe St NW 20011-2021 (Mail to: 701 Oglethorpe St NW 20011-2021) (202) 726-1862

Washington Church of the Holy Communion **P** (54) 3640 Martin L King Jr Ave SE 20032-1546 (Mail to: 3640 Martin L King Jr Ave SE 20032-1546) (202) 562-8153

Washington Howard University Epis Mission **CC** 2225 Georgia Ave 20059-1014 (Mail to: Howard University MS 59017 20059-0001) (202) 806-5747

Washington Grace Church **P** (349) 1041 Wisconsin Ave NW 20007-3635 (Mail to: 1041 Wisconsin Ave NW 20007-3635) David Wacaster (202) 333-7100

Washington Holy Trinity Episcopal Church **P** § C/O Church House Mount St Alban 20016 (Mail to: 13106 Annapolis Rd 20720-3829) (301) 262-5353

Washington Parish of St Monica & St James **P** (159) 222 8th St NE 20002-6106 (Mail to: 222 8th St NE 20002-6188) John Coleman William Stafford-Whittaker (202) 546-1746

Washington St Albans Episcopal Parish **P** (942) 3001 Wisconsin Ave NW 20016-5095 (Mail to: Attn: Doug Dykstra 3001 Wisconsin Ave NW Bldg 1 20016-5069) Yoimel Gonzalez Hernandez Emily Griffin James Quigley (202) 363-8286

Washington St Augustine's Episcopal Ch **P** (139) 555 Water St SW 20024 (Mail to: 555 Water St SW 20024) Leonard Lipscomb (202) 554-3222

Washington St Columba's Episcopal Church **P** (2789) § 4201 Albemarle St NW Unit 402 20016-2009 (Mail to: 4201 Albemarle St NW 20016-2098) Ledlie Laughlin Joshua Daniel Susan Flanders (202) 363-4119

Washington St Davids Episcopal Church **P** (484) 5150 Macomb St NW 20016-2612 (Mail to: 5150 Macomb St NW 20016-2699) Kristen Hawley Sarah Miller (202) 966-2093

Washington St Georges Church **P** (258) 160 U St NW 20001-1606 (Mail to: C/O James O Williams 160 U St NW 20001-1606) Marilyn Jenkins (202) 387-6421

Washington St Johns Church **P** (545) Georgetown Parish 3240 O St NW 20007-2842 (Mail to:

3240 O St NW 20007-2880) Virginia Gerbasi Sarah Duggin (202) 338-1796

Washington St Johns Church **P** (1900) 1525 H St NW 20005-1005 (Mail to: 1525 H St NW 20005-1098) Robert Fisher Sarah Cardwell (202) 347-8766

Washington St Lukes Church **P** (259) 1514 15th St NW 20036 (Mail to: 1514 15th St NW 20005-1922) Kim Baker (202) 667-4394

Washington St Margarets Church **P** (220) 1820 Connecticut Ave NW 20009-5732 (Mail to: 1830 Connecticut Ave NW 20009-5706) Richard Weinberg Diana Gustafson (202) 232-2995

Washington St Marks Church **P** (716) 301 A St SE 20003-3812 (Mail to: Attn: Patricia Braley or M Morgan 301 A St SE 20003-3812) Marcella Gillis Michele Morgan Thomas Sinclair (202) 543-0053

Washington St Marys Church **P** (96) 728 23rd St NW 20037-2501 (Mail to: 728 23rd St NW 20037-2598) (202) 333-3985

Washington St Patricks Church **P** (410) § 4700 Whitehaven Pkwy NW 20007-1554 (Mail to: 4700 Whitehaven Pkwy NW 20007-1586) Edward Thornley (202) 342-2800

Washington St Pauls Parish **P** (765) 2430 K St NW 20037-1703 (Mail to: 2430 K St NW 20037-1703) James Jelinek Lloyd Lewis John Pham Richard Wall (202) 337-2020

Washington St Pauls Rock Creek Parish **P** (197) 201 Allison St NW 20011-7305 (Mail to: 201 Allison St NW 20011-7305) Douglas Greenaway Robert Trache (202) 7262080

Washington St Philip the Evangelist Epis **P** (102) § 2001 14th St SE 20020-4817 (Mail to: 2001 14th St SE 20020-4817) (202) 678-4300

Washington St Thomas Parish **P** (153) 1777 Church St NW 20036-1301 (Mail to: 1517 18th St NW 20036-1305) Lisa Ahuja Linda Kaufman (202) 332-0607

Washington St Timothys Church **P** (330) § 3601 Alabama Ave SE 20020-2425 (Mail to: 3601 Alabama Ave SE 20020-2425) (202) 582-7740

Washington The Church of the Epiphany **P** (260) 1317 G St NW 20005-3102 (Mail to: 1317 G St NW 20005-3165) Glenna Huber (202) 347-2635

Washington Trinity Church **P** (363) 7005 Piney Branch Rd NW 20012-2417 (Mail to: 7005 Piney Branch Rd NW 20012-2417) John Harmon (202) 726-7036

DIOCESE OF WEST MISSOURI
(PROVINCE VII)
Comprises counties of the western half of Missouri
DIOCESAN OFFICE 420 W 14th St Kansas City MO 64105
TEL (816) 471-6161
E-MAIL info@diowestmo.org WEB www.diowestmo.org

Previous Bishops—
Edward R Atwill 1890-1911, Sidney C Partridge 1911-30, Robert N Spencer 1930-49, Robt R Spears Jr suffr 1967-70, Edward R Welles 1950-72, Arthur A Vogel 1973-89, John C Buchanan coadj 1989 Bp 1989-99 Barry R Howe 1998-2011 Martin S Field 2011-21

Bishop Provisional—Diane M Jardine Bruce (1 December 21)

Sec C Hamilton *Comm Dir* G Allman; *Treas* T Kokjer; *Chanc* M Galus

Stand Comm—Cler: T Estes L Ehren A Kyle *Pres* J Spicer; *Lay:* J Chesman A Connors M Patterson E Rhodes

Deans: C Jackson R James I Petty

Chairs: COM R Maynard; *Hist* C Jackson; *ECW* J Turner; *Christian Form* K Snodgrass

PARISHES, MISSIONS, AND CLERGY

Belton St Mary Magdalene **P** (130) 16808 S Holmes Road 64012 (Mail to: 16808 S State Route D 64012-9661) (816) 331-2222

Blue Springs Church of the Resurrection **P** (131) 1433 NW R D Mize Rd 64015-3666 (Mail to: 1433 NW R D Mize Rd 64015-3666) (816) 228-4220

Bolivar St Albans Episcopal Church **M** (76) 201 South Killingsworth 65613 (Mail to: PO Box 844 65613-0844) Catherine Cox Brenda Sickler (417) 777-2233

Boonville Christ Episcopal Church **M** (22) 524 4th St 65233-1552 (Mail to: 524 4th St 65233-1552) Martha Byer Kimberly Taube (660) 882-6444

Branson Shepherd of the Hills Church **P** (47) 107 Walnut Ln 65616-2220 (Mail to: 107 Walnut Ln 65616-2220) (417) 334-3968

Camdenton St George Episcopal Church **Chapel** (64) § 423 North Business Route 5 65020-9591 (Mail to: PO Box 1043 65020-1043) Lauretta Hughes (573) 346-4686

Carthage Grace Church **P** (837) 820 Howard St 64836-2318 (Mail to: PO Box 596 64836-0596) (417) 358-4631

Cassville St Thomas a Becket Epis Ch **M** (17) 13628 State Highway AA 65625-8529 (Mail to: PO Box 613 65625-0613) (417) 846-2155

Chillicothe Grace Episcopal Church **P** (20) 421 Elm St 64601-2610 (Mail to: 421 Elm St 64601-2610) (660) 646-4288

Clinton St Pauls Episcopal Church **M** (18) 181 E Highway 7 64735-9504 (Mail to: PO Box 453 64735-0453) (660) 885-8008

Excelsior Springs St Luke Episcopal Church **M** (60) 404 Regents Street 64024-2649 (Mail to: PO Box 551 64024-0551) (816) 476-2932

Fairfax St Oswalds in the Field Church **M** (12) 30996 X Ave 64446 (Mail to: Route 1 Box 123 64487) (660) 442-5897

Fayette St Marys Episcopal Church **M** (20) 104 W Davis St 65248-1453 (Mail to: PO Box 57 65248-0057) (660) 248-3219

Harrisonville St Peters Episcopal Church **P** (117) 400 W Wall St 64701-2251 (Mail to: PO Box 425 64701-0425) John Richardson (816) 884-4025

Independence Saint Michael's Episcopal Ch **P** (51) 4000 S Lees Summit Rd 64055-4005 (Mail to: 4000 S Lees Summit Rd 64055-4005) (816) 373-5333

Independence Trinity Episcopal Church **P** (119) 409 N Liberty St 64050-2701 (Mail to: PO Box 58 64051-0058) Karen Mann Karen Mann (816) 254-3644

Joplin St Philips Episcopal Church **P** (246) 706 Byers Ave 64801-4304 (Mail to: 706 Byers Ave 64801-4304) (417) 623-6893

Kansas City Church of the Good Shepherd **P** (301) 4947 NE Chouteau Drive 64119 (Mail to: 4947 NE Chouteau Dr 64119-4815) Galen Snodgrass (816) 452-0745

Kansas City Church of the Redeemer **P** (376) 7110 N State Route 9 64152-2930 (Mail to: 7110 N State Route 9 64152-2930) Ralph Behen Ralph Behen (816) 741-1136

✠ **Kansas City** Grace Holy Trinity Cathedral **O** (545) 415 W 13th St 64105-1350 (Mail to: 415 W 13th St 64105-1350) Andrew Keyse (816) 474-8260

Kansas City St Andrews Episcopal Church **P** (1553) 6401 Wornall Ter 64113-1755 (Mail to: 6401 Wornall Ter 64113-1789) John Spicer (816) 523-1602

Kansas City St Augustines Church **P** (63) 2732 Benton Blvd 64128-1130 (Mail to: 2732 Benton Blvd 64128-1130) Charles Marks (816) 921-8534

Kansas City Saint Mary's Episcopal Church **P** (166) 1307 Holmes St 64106-2845 (Mail to: 1307 Holmes St 64106-2845) Charles Everson Charles Everson (816) 842-0975

Kansas City St Matthews Episcopal Church **P** (82) 9349 E 65th St 64133-4907 (Mail to: 9349

E 65th St 64133-4907) William Hurst (816) 353-4592

Kansas City St Pauls Church **P** (670) § 11 E 40th St 64111-4909 (Mail to: 11 E 40th St 64111-4909) Steven King Jonathan Callison (816) 931-2850

Kansas City St Luke's Chapel **Chapel** 4401 Wornall Rd 64111-3220 (Mail to: MT PO1606927B CP PO1490888B PO Box 5870 64171-0870) Mark Jeske Susan Roberts Ronald Verhaeghe (816) 932-2180

Kansas City St. Peter & All Saints Epis Ch **P** (231) § 100 E Red Bridge Rd 64114-5412 (Mail to: 100 E Red Bridge Rd 64114-5499) Jonathan Frazier (816) 942-1066

Kimberling City St Marks Episcopal Church **M** (42) 3 Northwoods Blvd 65686 (Mail to: PO Box 153 65686-0153) (417) 739-2460

Lebanon Trinity Episcopal Church **M** (87) PO Box 1615 65536-1615 (Mail to: PO Box 1615 65536-1615) Jerry Miller (417) 532-3433

Lees Summit St Annes Church **P** (167) § 1815 NE Independence Ave 64086-5415 (Mail to: 1815 NE Independence Ave 64086-5415) Margaret Rhodes (816) 524-5552

Lees Summit St Pauls Episcopal Church **P** (186) 416 Grand St 64063 (Mail to: PO Box 372 64063-0372) Timothy Coppinger Nancy Nevins (816) 524-3651

Lexington Christ Episcopal Church **P** (68) 13th And Franklin St 64067 (Mail to: PO Box 307 64067-0307) (660) 259-3605

Liberty Grace Episcopal Church **P** (175) 520 S State Route 2 64068-1915 (Mail to: 520 S State Route 291 64068-1915) Robin James (816) 781-6262

Monett St Stephens Episcopal Church **M** (12) 601 E Benton St 65708-1770 (Mail to: PO Box 126 65708-0126) (417) 235-3330

Mountain Grove Church of the Transfiguration **M** (25) 215 N Wall St 65711-1766 (Mail to: PO Box 160 65689-0160) Bradford Ellsworth Linda Milholen (417) 926-5217

Neosho St Johns Church **M** (22) 305 W Spring St 64850-1762 (Mail to: 305 W Spring St 64850-1762) (417) 451-3644

Nevada All Saints Episcopal Church **P** (151) 425 E Cherry St 64772-3418 (Mail to: PO Box 456 64772-0456) (417) 667-2607

Noel St Nicholas Episcopal Church **M** (115) § 101 Sulphur St 64854 (Mail to: PO Box 248 64854-0248) (417) 475-3852

Overland Park St Luke's South Chapel **Chapel** 12300 Metcalf Ave 66213-1324 (Mail to: Spiritual Wellness Dept 12300 Metcalf Ave 66213-1324) (816) 932-2190

Ozark St Matthews Episcopal Church **P** (35) PO Box 704 1932 E Hwy 14 65721-0704 (Mail to: 203A E Brick St 65721-8906) (417) 581-1350

Saint Joseph Christ Episcopal Church **P** (117) 207 N 7th St 64501-1905 (Mail to: 207 N 7th St 64501-1975) (816) 279-6351

Savannah St Marys Episcopal Church **M** (16) 401 W Chestnut St 64485-1439 (Mail to: 401 W Chestnut St 64485-1439) (816) 387-6862

Sedalia Calvary Episcopal Church **P** (82) 713 S Ohio Ave 65301-4415 (Mail to: 713 S Ohio Ave 65301-4415) Anne Kyle (660) 826-4873

Springfield Christ Episcopal Church **P** (1182) 601 E Walnut St 65806-2419 (Mail to: 601 E Walnut St 65806-2491) Ronald Keel (417) 866-5133

Springfield St James Episcopal Church **P** (129) 2645 E Southern Hill Blvd 65804-3433 (Mail to: 2645 E Southern Hills Blvd 65804-3433) Suzanne Lynch (417) 881-3073

Springfield St Johns Episcopal Church **P** (161) § 515 E Division St 65803-2815 (Mail to: 515 E Division St 65803-2815) David Kendrick (417) 869-6351

Trenton St Philips Church **M** (11) 205 E 9th St 64683-2202 (Mail to: PO Box 46 64683-0046) (660) 684-6825

Warrensburg Christ Episcopal Church **P** (148) 136 E Gay St 64093-1810 (Mail to: PO Box 3 64093-0003) Ronald Verhaeghe (660) 429-1130

West Plains All Saints Church **P** (55) 107 S Curry St 65775-3943 (Mail to: PO Box 1012 65775-1012) (417) 256-2215

DIOCESE OF WEST TENNESSEE
(PROVINCE IV)
Comprises twenty counties lying west of the Tennessee River including all of Hardin County
DIOCESAN OFFICE 692 Poplar Ave Memphis TN 38105
TEL (901) 526-0023 FAX (901) 526-1555
E-MAIL diocese@episwtn.org WEB www.edwtn.org

Previous Bishops—
Alex D Dickson 1983-94, James M Coleman 1994-2001, Don E Johnson 2001-19 (967)

Bishop—Rt Rev Phoebe A Roaf (1116) (Dio 4 May 19)

Cn to Ord SA Alexander; *Cn for Fin and Admin* A Kelly; *Sec* S Smith; *Treas* M McLean; *Chanc* MA Cobb Jr; *V Chanc* M Marshall; *V Chanc* S Haight; *Hist* F Washburn; *Reg* M Jones

Stand Comm—Cler: C Senyoni H Mathes S Cowan; *Lay:* P Evans S Claybon R McLain J Chapman

Bishop & Council—Cler: R Fletcher G Meade M Cully J Abell S Webb; *Lay:* E Noel S Smith A Duncan S Kenny

PARISHES, MISSIONS, AND CLERGY

Atoka Ravenscroft Chapel **M** (32) C/O Shelly Nichols 33 Sarah Cv 38004-4904 (Mail to: C/O Brenda F Scott PO Box 251 38011-0251) (901) 837-1312

Bolivar St James Episcopal Church **M** (59) PO Box 85 38008-0085 (Mail to: PO Box 85 38008-0085) (731) 658-4439

Brownsville Christ Episcopal Church **HC** (16) 140 N Washington Ave 38012-2519 (Mail to: 140 N Washington Ave 38012-2519) (901) 772-9156

Collierville Church of the Holy Apostles **P** (512) 1380 Wolf River Blvd 38017-8687 (Mail to: 1380 Wolf River Blvd 38017-8687) Lisa Mcindoo Gerri Endicott (901) 937-3830

Collierville Saint Andrew's Epis Church **P** (311) 106 Walnut St 38017-2672 (Mail to: PO Box 626 38027-0626) Jeffery Marx Christian Senyoni (901) 853-0425

Covington St Matthew Episcopal Church **HC** (38) 303 S Munford St 38019-2555 (Mail to: 303 S Munford St 38019-2555) (901) 476-6577

Dyersburg St Mary's Episcopal Church **P** (94) 108 N King Ave 38024-4610 (Mail to: 108 N King Ave 38024-4610) Gary Meade (731) 285-3522

Germantown St George Episcopal Church **P** (568) § 2425 S Germantown Rd 38138-5946 (Mail to: 2425 S Germantown Rd 38138-5946) Dorothy Wells (901) 7547282

Humboldt St Thomas the Apostle **M** (38) 6 Esquire Lewis Rd 38343-6426 (Mail to: PO Box 442 38343-0442) Bill Burks (901) 784-2872

Jackson St Lukes Episcopal Church **HC** (232) 309 E Baltimore St 38301-6304 (Mail to: 309 E Baltimore St 38301-6304) Timothy True (731) 424-0556

La Grange Immanuel Episcopal Church **HC** (48) PO Box 21 38046-0021 (Mail to: PO Box 21 38046-0021) (901) 754-7282

Mason St Paul Episcopal Church **M** (38) 2406 Highway 59 38049-7522 (Mail to: C/O John Cochran PO Box 158 38049-0158) (901) 294-2641

Mason Trinity Episcopal Church **M** (10) 260 N Main St 38049 (Mail to: 206 North Main Street 38049) (901) 594-5012

Memphis All Saints Episcopal Church **M** (32) 1508 S White Station Rd 38117-6826 (Mail to: 1508 S White Station Rd 38117-6899) (901) 685-7333

Memphis Calvary Episcopal Church **HC** (785) 102 N 2nd St 38103-2203 (Mail to: 102 N 2nd St 38103-2287) Katherine Bush Lewis McKee Paul Mclain James Walters (901) 525-6602

Memphis Church of the Holy Communion **P** (1155) 4645 Walnut Grove Rd 38117-2537 (Mail to: 4645 Walnut Grove Rd 38117-2537) Alexander Webb Jonathan Chesney (901) 7676987

Memphis Emmanuel Episcopal Church **M** (102) 4150 Boeingshire Dr 38116-6007 (Mail to: 4150 Boeingshire Dr 38116-6007) (901) 346-7434

Memphis Grace - St Lukes Church **P** (1046) § 1720 Peabody Ave 38104-6124 (Mail to: 1720 Peabody Ave 38104-6100) Ollie Rencher Jesse Abell Anne Carriere Laura Gettys (901) 272-7425

Memphis Holy Trinity Episcopal Church **M** (29) 3749 Kimball Ave 38111-6420 (Mail to: PO Box 111163 38111-1163) (901) 743-6421

Memphis St Johns Episcopal Church **P** (721) 3245 Central Ave 38111-4409 (Mail to: 3245 Central Ave 38111-4409) James Biedenharn (901) 323-8597

Memphis St Joseph Episcopal Church **M** (24) 604 Saint Paul Ave 38126-2865 (Mail to: C/O Diocese of W Tennessee 2029 Woodchase Cv 38016-5082)

✠ **Memphis** St Mary's Episcopal Cathedral **O** (735) 692 Poplar Ave 38105-4512 (Mail to: 692 Poplar Ave 38105-4512) (901) 527-3361

Memphis St Philip Episcopal Church **P** (226) 9380 Davies Plantation Rd 38133-4250 (Mail to: 9380 Davies Plantation Rd 38133-4250) Terry Street (901) 388-9830

Memphis Church of the Good Shepherd **M** (49) 1971 Jackson Ave 38107-4614 (Mail to: 1971 Jackson Ave 38107-4614) (901) 725-9768

Millington St Annes Church **M** (134) 4063 Sykes Rd 38053-7930 (Mail to: 4063 Sykes Rd 38053-7930) (901) 872-0303

Paris Grace Episcopal Church **M** (59) 103 S Poplar St 38242-4103 (Mail to: PO Box 447 38242-0447) (731) 642-1721

Ripley Immanuel Episcopal Church **M** (55) Ro Winslow 153 Highland St 38063-1815 (Mail to: PO Box 513 38063-0513) (731) 635-5593

Somerville St Thomas Episcopal Church **M** (41) Attn: Rev William Fry 203 W Market St 38068-1593 (Mail to: Attn Rev William Fry 10 North Highland 38068) (901) 465-7112

Union City St James Episcopal Church **P** (79) 422 E Church St 38261-3906 (Mail to: PO Box 838 38281-0838) William Mcmillen (731) 885-9575

DIOCESE OF WEST TEXAS

(PROVINCE VII)
Comprises 60 West Texas counties
DIOCESAN OFFICE 111 Torcido Dr San Antonio TX 78209 (MAIL: Box 6885)
TEL (210) 824-5387 (888) 824-5387 FAX (210) 824-2164
E-MAIL general.mail@dwtx.org WEB www.dwtx.org

Previous Bishops—
Robt WB Elliott miss 1874-87, James S Johnston miss 1888-1904 dio 1905-16, Wm T Capers 1916-43, Everett H Jones 1943-69, R Earl Dicus suffr 1955-75, Harold C Gosnell coadj 1968 dio 1969-77, Scott Field Bailey 1976-87, Stanley F Hauser suffr 1979-87, John H MacNaughton coadj 1986, dio 1987-95 Earl N McArthur suffr 1988-93, James Folts coadj 1994-96, dio 1996-2006, Robert B Hibbs 1996-2003; Gary R Lillibridge (coadj 2004; Dio 2006-17), Jennifer Brooke-Davidson suffr 2017-19

Bishop—Rt Rev David M Reed (1005) (suff 2006-14; coadj 2014-17; Dio June 2017)

Assistant Bishop—Rt Rev Rayford B High Jr (988) (Jan 2021)

Lay Cn C Mowen; *Sec* Rev DG Read; *Treas* T Burkhart; *Reg* L Saunders; *Chanc* K Kimble 11 Tanglewood St Uvalde TX 78801-6502; *Asst Chanc* J Norman; *Comm* L McGrew A Thompson; *Stew* vacant; *Camp& Conf* R Watson; *Cong Dev* M Besson; *Hisp Off* F Saldivar; *Hist* T Lee; *Deploy Off* M Besson

Stand Comm—Cler: Pres B Nelson M Wise S Brown; *Lay:* R Mosty N Beauchamp E Manning

Deans: Central D Read; *Eastern* S Carson; *North Eastern* S Shortess; *Northern* B Stephenson; *Southern* J Wickham; *Valley* C Nalven; *Western* M Marsh

PARISHES, MISSIONS, AND CLERGY

Alice The Epis Church of the Advent **P** (25) 200 N Wright 78332 (Mail to: PO Box 1937 78333-1937) Thomas Turner (361) 664-7881

Aransas Pass The Epis Church of Our Saviour **M** (20) 822 S McCampbell St 78336-2316 (Mail to: 822 S McCampbell St 78336-2316) (361) 727-9101

Bandera St Christophers Church **P** (224) 395 State Highway 173 N 78003 (Mail to: PO Box

314 78003-0314) Robert Harris (830) 796-4387

Beeville St Philip's Episcopal Church **P** (91) § 311 E Corpus Christi St 78102-4813 (Mail to: 311 E Corpus Christi St 78102-4813) Andrew Green (361) 358-2730

Blanco St Michaels & All Angels Epis **M** (80) 218 Pittsburg St 78606-5768 (Mail to: PO Box 684 78606-0684) (830) 833-4816

Boerne St Helena's Epis Ch and Sch **P** (713) § 410 N Main St 78006 (Mail to: PO Box 1765 78006-6765) David Read (830) 249-3228

Brackettville St Andrews Episcopal Church **M** (24) 300 E Henderson St 78832 (Mail to: PO Box 927 78832) (830) 563-3666

Brady St Pauls Episcopal Church **P** (29) 1111 S Blackburn 76825 (Mail to: PO Box 1148 76825-1148) (325) 597-1330

Brownsville Church of the Advent **P** (330) § 104 W Elizabeth St 78520-5547 (Mail to: 104 W Elizabeth St 78520-5594) Laurie McKim Laurie McKim (956) 542-4123

Brownsville St Pauls Episcopal Church **M** (40) 16th And Taft St 78521-3132 (Mail to: PO Box 4191 78523-4191) (956) 542-3869

Buda St Elizabeths Episcopal Church **M** (230) 723 Ranch Road 967 78610-9297 (Mail to: PO Box 292 78610-0292) Michael Woods (512) 295-3674

Canyon Lake St Francis by the Lake **P** (310) 121 Spring Mountain Drive 78133 (Mail to: PO Box 2031 78133-0023) David Chalk Nancy Springer (830) 9643820

Carrizo Springs Holy Trinity Episcopal Church **M** (19) 1807 Pena St 78834-3515 (Mail to: Attn: Treasurer PO Box 919 78834-6919) Nicholas Mayer (830) 876-9729

Comfort St Boniface Episcopal Church **Chapel** (78) § 116 US 87 78013 (Mail to: PO Box 676 78013-0676) (830) 995-3897

Corpus Christi All Saints Episcopal Church **P** (307) 3026 S Staples St 78404-3610 (Mail to: 3026 S Staples St 78404-3691) Jonathan Wickham (361) 855-6294

Corpus Christi Church of the Good Shepherd **P** (1132) § 700 S Upper Broadway 78401-3521 (Mail to: 700 S Upper Broadway St 78401-3521) Milton Black William Campbell Philip May (361) 882-1735

Corpus Christi St Andrews Episcopal Church **M** (28) 13026 Leopard St 78410-4515 (Mail to: 13026 Leopard St 78410-4515) (361) 241-9240

Corpus Christi St Bartholomews Episcopal Ch **P** (339) § 622 Airline Rd 78412 (Mail to: 622 Airline Rd 78412-3156) (361) 991-2954

Corpus Christi St Marks Episcopal Church **P** (233) 2727 Airline Rd 78414-3306 (Mail to: 2727 Airline Rd 78414-3306) Douglas Wasinger (361) 994-0285

Cotulla St Timothys Church **M** (18) 305 North Choctaw Ave 78014 (Mail to: PO Box 738 78014-0738) (830) 879-2239

Cuero Grace Episcopal Church **P** (75) 102 E Live Oak St 77954 (Mail to: 102 E Live Oak St 77954-2957) Aloysius Thaddeus (361) 275-3423

Cypress Mill St Lukes Episcopal Church **M** (106) 263 Spur 962 78663-8486 (Mail to: 263 Spur 962 78663-8486) Tommy Bye (830) 825-8001

Del Rio St James Episcopal Church **P** (112) § 206 W Greenwood St 78841-1129 (Mail to: PO Box 1129 78841-1129) (830) 775-7292

Devine St Matthias **M** (28) 901 N. Teel Dr. 78016-1701 (Mail to: PO Box B 78016-0684) (210) 385-7668

Dripping Spgs The Church of the Holy Spirit **P** (255) § 301 Hays Country Acres Rd 78620-4282 (Mail to: 301 Hays Country Acres Rd 78620-4282) Evan Hierholzer (512) 858-4924

Eagle Pass Church of the Redeemer **P** (82) § 648 Madison St 78852 (Mail to: 648 Madison St 78852-4246) (830) 773-5122

Edinburg St Matthews Episcopal Church **P** (143) § 2620 Crestview Dr 78539-6296 (Mail to: C/O Rev Charles Mahan 2620 Crestview Dr 78539-6219) (956) 383-4202

Edna Trinity Episcopal Church **P** (31) 102 W Church St 77957 (Mail to: PO Box 305 77957-0305) (361) 782-2204

Fort McKavett St James Episcopal Church **M** (32) 3232 Runge Ranch Rd 76841-2020 (Mail to: 2685 County RD 76935)

Fredericksburg St Barnabas Episcopal Church **P** (635) 601 W Creek St 78624 (Mail to: 601 W Creek St 78624-3117) Richard Elwood Jeffrey Hammond G Thomas Luck (830) 997-5762

George West Church of the Good Shepherd **Chapel** (42) 809 N San Antonio St 78022 (Mail to: PO Box 1582 78022-1582) John Rayls George Keeble (361) 449-2737

Goliad St Stephens Episcopal Church **M** (5) 152 N Chilton Ave 77963-3906 (Mail to: PO Box 739 77963-0739) (361) 645-2234

Gonzales Epis Church of the Messiah **P** (57) 721 Saint Louis St 78629-4154 (Mail to: PO Box 139 78629-0139) (830) 672-3407

Hallettsville St James Episcopal Church **M** (12) 1103 E 4th St 77964-3219 (Mail to: 1103 E 4th St 77964-3219) (361) 798-4119

Harlingen St Albans Episcopal Church **P** (806) § 1417 E Austin Ave 78550 (Mail to: 1417 E Austin Ave 78550-8855) John Inserra (956) 428-2305

Hebbronville St James Episcopal Church **M** (48) 112 W North 78361 (Mail to: PO Box 68 78361-0068) Ernest Buchanan (361) 527-3433

Junction Trinity Episcopal Church **M** (57) 1119 Main 76849 (Mail to: Attn: Pat Thomson Treasurer PO Box 3 76849-0003) (325) 446-4416

Kenedy St Matthews Episcopal Church **M** (23) 309 S 5th 78119 (Mail to: 315 S 5th St 78119-2607) (830) 583-2589

Kerrville St Peters Episcopal Church **P** (666) § 956 Main St 78028-3549 (Mail to: 320 Saint Peter St 78028-4650) Bertrand Baetz (830) 2578162

Kingsville Episcopal Ch of the Epiphany **P** (151) 206 N 3rd St 78363-4409 (Mail to: PO Box 1476 78364-1476) Janet Dantone (361) 595-5535

Laredo Christ Episcopal Church **P** (207) 2320 Lane St 78043-2711 (Mail to: 2320 Lane St 78043-2711) Paul Frey (956) 723-5714

Llano Grace Episcopal Church **P** (48) 1200 Oatman St 78643-2730 (Mail to: 1200 Oatman St 78643-2730) (325) 247-5276

Lockhart Emmanuel Episcopal Church **P** (138) 118 N Church St 78644 (Mail to: 118 N Church St 78644-2102) (512) 398-3342

Luling Church of the Annunciation **P** (113) 301 S Walnut Ave 78648-2925 (Mail to: PO Box 106 78648-0106) James Kee-Rees (830) 875-5155

McAllen St Johns Episcopal Church **P** (342) § 2500 N. 10th St. 78501-4008 (Mail to: 2500 N 10th St 78501-4090) William Clark (956) 687-6191

Menard Calvary Episcopal Church **M** (16) 201 Callan St 76859 (Mail to: PO Box 863 76859-0863) (325) 396-2696

Mission St Peter & St Paul Church **M** (183) 2310 N Stewart Rd 78574 (Mail to: 2310 N Stewart Rd 78574-8842) Michael Scolare (956) 585-5005

Montell Church of the Ascension **M** (35) 27851 N Hwy 55 78802-0808 (Mail to: PO Box 808 78802-0808) (830) 597-4284

New Braunfels St Johns Episcopal Church **P** (345) 312 S Guenther Ave 78130-5639 (Mail to: 312 S Guenther Ave 78130-5639) Ripp Hardaway (830) 625-2532

Pharr Trinity Episcopal Church **P** (108) 210 W Caffery Ave 78577-4713 (Mail to: PO Box 692 78577-1613) Richard Speer (956) 787-1243

Pleasanton All Saints Episcopal Church **M** (29) 1435 W Oaklawn Rd 78064 (Mail to: PO Box 732 78064-0732) (830) 277-2222

Port Aransas Trinity by the Sea **P** (166) § 431 Trojan St. 78373 (Mail to: PO Box 346 78373-0346) John Derkits Douglas Schwert (361) 749-6449

Port Isabel St Andrews by the Sea **HC** (50) 1022 N Yturria St 78578 (Mail to: PO Box 1168 78578-1168) Claudia Nalven (956) 943-1962

Port Lavaca Grace Episcopal Church **P** (33) 213 E Austin St 77979 (Mail to: PO Box 172 77979-0172) Robert Dewolfe (361) 552-2805

Portland St Christophers by the Sea **P** (39) 720 7th St 78374 (Mail to: PO Box 386 78374-0386) (361) 643-3514

Refugio Church of the Ascension **M** (5) 602 E Plasuela St 78377-3241 (Mail to: PO Box 903 78377-0903) (361) 526-4262

Rockport Saint Peter's Episcopal Church **P** (347) 555 Enterprise Blvd 78382 (Mail to: PO Box

1807 78381-1807) James Friedel (361) 729-2649

San Antonio Christ Episcopal Church **P** (1197) 510 Belknap Pl 78212-3400 (Mail to: 510 Belknap Pl 78212-3493) William Gahan Eric Fenton Scott Kitayama Justin Lindstrom (210) 736-3132

San Antonio Church of Reconciliation **P** (449) 8900 Starcrest Dr 78217-4741 (Mail to: 8900 Starcrest Dr 78217-4741) Joshua Woods (210) 655-2731

San Antonio Church of the Holy Spirit **P** (310) § 11093 Bandera Road 78250-6814 (Mail to: 11093 Bandera Rd 78250-6806) Jason Roberts John Padgett (210) 314-6729

San Antonio Grace Episcopal Church **M** (165) All Saints Chapel at TMI 20955 W Tejas Trl 78257-1603 (Mail to: 6275 Camp Bullis Road 78257) Jacob George (210) 462-6901

San Antonio St Andrews Episcopal Church **P** (280) 6110 NW Loop 410 78238-3305 (Mail to: 6110 NW Loop 410 78238-3399) David Archibald David Archibald (210) 684-0845

San Antonio St Davids Episcopal Church **P** (666) § 1300 Wiltshire Ave 78209-6049 (Mail to: 1300 Wiltshire Ave 78209-6049) Brian Tarver (210) 824-2481

San Antonio St George Episcopal Church **P** (834) § 6904 West Ave 78213-1820 (Mail to: 6904 West Ave 78213-1893) Ramiro Lopez (210) 342-4261

San Antonio St Lukes Episcopal Church **P** (990) § Angie Hudgins 11 Saint Lukes Ln 78209-4445 (Mail to: Attn: Angie Hudgins 11 Saint Lukes Ln 78209-4445) Irving Cutter Reagan Gonzalez (210) 828-6425

San Antonio St Margarets Episcopal Church **M** (131) § 5310 Stahl Rd 78247-1522 (Mail to: 5310 Stahl Rd 78247-1500) (210) 657-3328

San Antonio St Marks Episcopal Church **P** (1423) 315 E Pecan St 78205-1819 (Mail to: 315 E Pecan St 78205-1819) Elizabeth Knowlton Ann Fraser Christopher Wise (210) 226-2426

San Antonio Saint Paul's Episcopal Church **P** (264) § 1018 E Grayson St 78208-1224 (Mail to: 1018 E Grayson St 78208-1299) Robert Carabin Martha Vasquez Joseph Webb (210) 226-0345

San Antonio St Philips Episcopal Church **P** (84) 1310 Pecan Valley Dr 78210-3416 (Mail to: 1310 Pecan Valley Dr 78210-3416) (210) 333-6256

San Antonio St Stephens Episcopal Church **P** (21) 3726 S New Braunfels Ave 78223 (Mail to: 3726 S New Braunfels Ave 78223-1706) (210) 534-5400

San Antonio St Thomas Epis Church & School **P** (982) § 1416 N Loop 1604 E 78232-1427 (Mail to: 1416 N Loop 1604 E 78232-1400) Michael Michie (210) 494-3507

San Antonio Sante Fe Episcopal Church **M** (249) 1108 Brunswick Blvd 78211-1502 (Mail to: 1108 Brunswick Blvd 78211-1502) John Wauters Donald Wilkinson (210) 923-0822

San Antonio St Francis Episcopal Church **Chapel** (187) 4242 Bluemel Rd 78240-1063 (Mail to: PO Box 690670 78269) Carrie Guerra (210) 696-0834

San Benito All Saints Episcopal Church **P** (39) 499 N Reagan 78586 (Mail to: PO Box 1948 78586-0041) (956) 399-1795

San Marcos St Marks Episcopal Church **P** (594) § 3039 Ranch Road 12 78666-2488 (Mail to: 3039 Ranch Road 12 78666-2488) Christian Hawley (512) 353-1979

San Saba St Lukes Episcopal Church **P** (26) 601 W Dry St 76877-5611 (Mail to: 601 W Dry St 76877-5611) William Grusendorf (325) 372-4731

Seguin St Andrew's Episcopal Church **P** (343) 201 E Nolte 78155 (Mail to: 201 E Nolte St 78155-6123) Stephen Shortess (830) 372-4330

Sonora St Johns Episcopal Church **P** (106) 404 E Poplar St 76950 (Mail to: PO Box 1100 76950-1100) (325) 387-2955

Universal City St Matthews Episcopal Church **P** (114) 810 Kitty Hawk Rd 78148-3822 (Mail to:

PO Box 2337 78148-1337) Timothy Vellom (210) 658-5956

Uvalde St Philips Episcopal Church **P** (246) § 343 N Getty St 78801-4690 (Mail to: 343 N Getty St 78801-4690) Michael Marsh (830) 278-5223

Victoria St Francis Episcopal Church **P** (121) 3002 Miori Ln 77901-3618 (Mail to: 3002 Miori Ln 77901-3618) Stephen Carson (361) 575-0441

Victoria Trinity Episcopal Church **P** (352) § 1501 N Glass St 77901 (Mail to: 1501 N Glass St 77901-5130) Michael Koehler (361) 573-3228

Weslaco Grace Episcopal Church **P** (214) 701 S Missouri 78596 (Mail to: 701 S Missouri Ave 78596-6941) (956) 968-7014

Wimberley St Stephen's Episcopal Church **P** (776) § 6000 Fm 3237 78676-5832 (Mail to: 6000 FM 3237 Unit A 78676-6386) Kevin Schubert (512) 847-9956

Windcrest Church of the Resurrection **P** (361) § 5909 Walzem Rd 78218-2197 (Mail to: 5909 Walzem Rd 78218-2197) Christopher Cole (210) 655-5484

DIOCESE OF WEST VIRGINIA
(PROVINCE III)
Comprises State of West Virginia
DIOCESAN OFFICE 1608 Virginia St E Charleston WV 25311-2114
(MAIL: PO Box 5400 Charleston WV 25361-0400)
TEL (304) 344-3597; Toll-free (866) 549-8346 FAX (304) 343-3295
E-MAIL thannah@wvdiocese.org WEB www.wvdiocese.org

Previous Bishops—
Geo W Peterkin 1878-1916, Wm L Gravatt coadj 1899 Bp 1916-39, Robt EL Strider coadj 1923 Bp 1939-55, WC Campbell coadj 1950 Bp 1955-76, Robt P Atkinson coadj 1973 Bp 1976-88, W Franklin Carr suffr 1985-90, John H Smith 1989-99, Michie Klusmeyer 2001-22

Bishop—Right Rev Matthew Davis Cowden (1143) (Dio 14 Oct 2022)

Canon to the Ordinary—Rev Chadwick Slater

Treas TC Farnsworth 111 McCulloch Dr Wheeling WV 26003; *Chanc* K Klein; VChanc L Javins; *VChanc* J Canfield;; Controller A Combs; *COM* K Javins;; *Publications* L Comins; *Dio Admin* T Hannah

Stand Comm—Cler: G Pennington J Trumble S Claytor K Webster; *Lay:* P Steptoe M Jaennson D Lumsden C Andrus

PARISHES, MISSIONS, AND CLERGY

Ansted Church of the Redeemer **M** (25) 102 Taylor St 25812 (Mail to: PO Box 625 25812-0625) 1304 658-5857

Beckley St Stephens Episcopal Church **P** (158) § 200 Virginia St 25801-5243 (Mail to: 200 Virginia St 25801-5299) Susan Claytor (304) 253-9672

Berkeley Spg St Marks Episcopal Church **P** (92) 180 S Washington St 25411-1646 (Mail to: 180 S Washington St 25411-1646) (304) 258-2440

Bluefield Christ Episcopal Church **P** (207) 200 Duhring St 24701-2910 (Mail to: 200 Duhring St 24701-2910) (304) 327-6861

Buckhannon Church of the Transfiguration **M** (45) 65 S Kanawha St 26201-2636 (Mail to: 65 S Kanawha St 26201-2636) (304) 472-4418

Bunker Hill Christ Episcopal Church **HC** Runnymeade Rd 25413 (Mail to: Runnymeade Road 25413) (304) 344-3597

Charles Town St Philips Episcopal Church **M** (31) 411 S Lawrence St 25414-1645 (Mail to: PO Box 368 25414-0368) Elwyn Mackov (304) 725-4236

Charles Town Zion Episcopal Church **P** (402) 301 East Congress Street 25414 (Mail to: 221 E Washington St 25414-1073) James Lawrence (304) 725-5312

Charleston Chapel of the Resurrection **Chapel** 1608 Virginia St E 25311-2114 (Mail to: 1608 Virginia St E 25311-2114) (304) 344-3597

Charleston St Johns Episcopal Church **P** (235) 1105 Quarrier St 25301-2410 (Mail to: 1105 Quarrier St 25301-2410) (304) 346-0359

Charleston St Matthews Episcopal Church **P** (555) 36 Norwood Rd 25314-1327 (Mail to: 36 Norwood Rd 25314-1399) Alan Webster (304) 343-3837

Charleston St Christopher Episcopal Ch **P** (182) 821 Edgewood Dr 25302-2811 (Mail to: 821 Edgewood Dr 25302-2811) (304) 342-3272

Chester St Matthews Episcopal Church **M** 4th And Indiana Ave 26034 (Mail to: 336 Indiana Ave Rear 26034-1148) (304) 387-2206

Clarksburg Christ Episcopal Church **P** (67) 123 S 6th St 26302 (Mail to: PO Box 1492 26302-1492) (304) 622-3694

Colliers Olde St John Episcopal Church **M** (51) 2308 Eldersville Rd 26035 (Mail to: PO Box 347 26035) (304) 527-4746

Elkins Grace Episcopal Church **P** (80) 212 John St 26241-3823 (Mail to: Attn: E W Carter Treasurer 212 John St 26241-3823) Frederick Bird (304) 636-4251

Fairmont Christ Church **P** (112) 824 Fairmont Avenue 26554-5138 (Mail to: 824 Fairmont Ave 26554-5190) (304) 366-3471

Glenville St Mark Episcopal Church **M** (7) 607 Main St 26351 (Mail to: 607 W Main St 26351-1057) Teresa Wayman (304) 462-7455

Grafton St Matthias Episcopal Church **M** (7) 330 W Francis St 26354-1720 (Mail to: PO Box 27 26354-0027) Frederick Bird (304) 265-3112

Hansford Church of the Good Shepherd **P** (86) 1203 Center St 25103 (Mail to: C/O Donald L Smith Treasurer PO Box 41 25103-0041) (304) 595-6224

Harpers Ferry St Johns Episcopal Church **M** (24) 898 W Washington St 25425-6910 (Mail to: PO Box 999 25425-0999) (304) 579-5586

Hedgesville Mt Zion Episcopal Church **M** (100) PO Box 2246 1 Zion Street 25427 (Mail to: PO Box 2246 25427-2246) David Shoda (304) 702-7111

Hinton Ascension Episcopal Church **M** (25) 222 5th Ave 25951-2210 (Mail to: 222 5th Ave 25951-2210) (304) 627-1232

Huntington St John Episcopal Church **P** (404) 3000 Washington Blvd 25705-1633 (Mail to: 3000 Washington Blvd 25705-1633) (304) 525-9105

Huntington St Peters Episcopal Church **P** (125) 2248 Adams Ave 25704-1424 (Mail to: 435 23rd St W 25704-1349) (304) 429-2241

Huntington Trinity Episcopal Church **P** (273) 520 11th St 25701-2211 (Mail to: 520 11th St

25701-2292) James Morgan (304) 529-6084

Hurricane Ch St Timothys in the Valley **P** (226) 3434 Teays Valley Rd 25526-9279 (Mail to: PO Box 424 25526-0424) Cheryl Winter (304) 5629325

Kearneysville Grace Episcopal Church **M** (41) East & Church St 25430 (Mail to: Attn: William W Grantham 159 East St 25430-5691) (304) 725-7073

Kearneysville St Bartholomews Church **M** (18) PO Box 896 25430 (Mail to: C/O Judith Schroder PO Box 684 25414-0684) (304) 725-1707

Keyser Emmanuel Episcopal Church **P** (48) 303 S Mineral St 26726-2641 (Mail to: 303 S Mineral St 26726-2641) Martin Townsend (304) 788-4475

Kingwood St Michaels Episcopal Church **M** (23) 107 Mcdonald St 26537-1017 (Mail to: Attn: Richard V Wolfe PO Box 543 26537-0543) (304) 329-3207

Lewisburg St James Episcopal Church **P** (145) 218 Church St 24901-1330 (Mail to: 468 Church Street 24901-1330) (304) 645-2588

Logan Holy Trinity Church **P** (10) 604 Stratton St 25601-4029 (Mail to: 604 Stratton St 25601) (304) 752-6900

Marlinton St Johns Church **M** 415 9th St 24954-1236 (Mail to: 717 8th Ave 24954-1214) (304) 704-2014

Martinsburg Trinity Episcopal Church **P** (144) 200 West King Street 25401-3212 (Mail to: 200 W King St 25401-3212) (304) 263-0994

Morgantown St Thomas a Becket Episcopal **P** (221) 75 Old Cheat Rd 26508-4103 (Mail to: 75 Old Cheat Rd 26508-4103) (304) 296-0270

Morgantown Trinity Episcopal Church **P** (81) 247 Willey St 26505-5522 (Mail to: 247 Willey St 26505-5522) E Michael Morgan (304) 292-7364

Moundsville Trinity Church **P** (95) 1 Oak Ave 26041-1107 (Mail to: PO Box P 26041-0966) (304) 845-5982

N Martinsvlle St Anns Episcopal Church **P** (46) 453 Maple Ave 26155-7000 (Mail to: PO Box 161 26155-0161) Richard Heller (304) 455-5143

Oak Hill St Andrews Episcopal Church **P** (67) 345 Kelley Ave 25901-2916 (Mail to: 345 Kelly Ave 25901-2916) (304) 469-3223

Parkersburg Memorial Ch of the Good Shphd **P** (589) 903 Charles St 26101-4825 (Mail to: 903 Charles St 26101-4825) Marjorie Bevans (304) 428-1525

Parkersburg Trinity Episcopal Church **P** (218) 430 Juliana St 26101-5335 (Mail to: 430 Juliana St 26101-5335) (304) 422-3362

Point Pleasant Christ Church **P** (91) C/O Jack Sturgeon 804 Main St 25550-1229 (Mail to: C/O Jack Sturgeon PO Box 819 25550) Katharine Foster Raymond Hage (304) 675-3120

Princeton Church of the Heavenly Rest **M** (41) 1207 Mercer St 24740-3031 (Mail to: 1207 Mercer St 24740-3031) (304) 425-9345

Ravenswood Grace Episcopal Church **M** (35) 405 Walnut St 26164-1649 (Mail to: 405 Walnut St 26164-1649) Marie Mulford (304) 273-0980

Ripley St Johns Episcopal Church **M** (30) 702 Main St W 25271-1110 (Mail to: PO Box 558 25271-0558) Katharine Foster (304) 372-9183

Romney St Stephens Church **M** (36) 316 E Main St 26757-1822 (Mail to: 332 E Main St Apt A 26757-1845) (304) 822-5054

Ronceverte Church of the Incarnation **M** (23) 707 W Main St 24970-1754 (Mail to: PO Box 276 24970-0276) (304) 536-3320

Saint Albans St Marks Episcopal Church **P** (172) 405 B St 25177-2716 (Mail to: PO Box 204 25177-0204) (304) 722-4284

Salem Prince of Peace Episcopal Ch **M** (35) 53 Sacred Heart Ln 26426-8647 (Mail to: PO Box 215 26426-0215) Pamela Shier (304) 906-7540

Shepherdstown Trinity Church **P** (452) 200 W German St 25443 (Mail to: PO Box 308 25443-0308) George Schramm Frank Coe (304) 876-6990

Sistersville St Pauls Episcopal Church **P** (12) 313 N Wells St 26175-1437 (Mail to: PO Box 79 26175-0079) (304) 652-1801

Snowshoe Chapel on the Mount **Chapel** (14) 10 Snowshoe Dr 26209-1700 (Mail to: 354 Locust Glen Dr 26291-9028) (304) 572-3333

St Marys Grace Episcopal Church **P** (23) 317 Riverside Dr 26170-1030 (Mail to: 317 Riverside Dr 26170-1030) Richard Heller (304) 684-7976

Summersville St Martins in the Fields **M** (6) § 221 Mckees Creek Rd 26651-1601 (Mail to: 221 Mckees Creek Rd 26651-1601) (304) 872-5594

Union All Saints Church **M** (29) 1 Greenhill Rd 24983 (Mail to: PO Box 401 24983-0401) (304) 772-3120

Weirton St Thomas Episcopal Church **P** (39) 300 Three Springs Dr 26062-4922 (Mail to: PO Box 2232 Three Springs Dr 26062) (304) 723-4120

Welch St Lukes Episcopal Church **M** PO Box 204 24801-2414 (Mail to: 71 Riverside Dr 24801-2544) (304) 436-2641

Wellsburg Christ Episcopal Church **P** (54) 1014 Main St 26070-1632 (Mail to: 1014 Main St 26070-1632) (304) 737-1866

Weston St Pauls Church **P** (95) 206 E 2nd St 26452-1927 (Mail to: 206 E 2nd St 26452-1927) John Valentine (304) 269-5266

Wheeling St Lukes Episcopal Church **M** (55) 200 S Penn St 26003-2028 (Mail to: 200 S Penn St 26003-2028) (304) 232-2395

Wheeling St Matthews Church **P** (333) PO Box 508 26003-0064 (Mail to: PO Box 508 26003-0064) Joshua Saxe (304) 233-0133

Wheeling Lawrencefield Parish Church **P** (128) Table Rock Ln 44 Kirkside Dr 26003 (Mail to: PO Box 4063 26003-0414) Nancy Woodworth-Hill (304) 277-2353

Wht Sphr Spgs St Thomas Episcopal Church **P** (124) 205 W Main St 24986-2411 (Mail to: PO Box 148 24986-0148) (304) 536-3320

Williamson St Pauls Episcopal Church **M** (33) 411 Prichard St 25661-3140 (Mail to: 415 Prichard St 25661-3140) (304) 235-4056

Williamstown Christ Memorial Episcopal Ch **M** (13) 409 Columbia Ave 26187-1122 (Mail to: 409 Columbia Ave 26187-1122) Richard Heller (304) 375-6506

DIOCESE OF WESTERN KANSAS
(PROVINCE VII)
Comprises Western Kansas
DIOCESAN OFFICE 1 North Main Ste 418 Hutchinson KS 67504
TEL (620) 669-0006
WEB http://www.diowks.org

Previous Bishops—
Sheldon M Griswold 1903-17, John C Sage 1918-19, Robt H Mize 1921-38, Shirley H Nichols 1943-55, Arnold M Lewis 1956-64, Wm Davidson mb 1966-71, Bp 1971-80, John F Ashby 1981-95, Vernon E Strickland 1995-2002, James M Adams Jr 2002-10, Michael Milliken 2011-18

Current Bishop- The Rt. Rev. Mark A. Cowell (Dio 1 Dec 2018)

Dio Admin T Cottrell; *Chanc* M Kliewer 2751 Arrowhead Road, Amarillo TX 79124 *Treas* M Hixson; *Bus & Fin* M Wamsley; *COM* Rev M Milliken; *Sec Dio Conv* T Cottrell *Dispatch of Business for Dio Conv* C Peterson; *ECW* vacant; *UTO Chair* H Von Fange; *Yth* vacant; *Cn to Ord* Rev Cn J Jones 1113 Pinehurst Hays KS 67601 (785) 623-1736

Stand Comm—Cler: Pres K Lemon   D Martin S Schneider; *Lay:* N Pyle P Smith J Higgins

PARISHES, MISSIONS, AND CLERGY

Bavaria St Onesimus Chapel **Chapel** St Francis Academy 5097 W Cloud St 67401-9743 (Mail to: 5097 W Cloud St 67401-9743) (913) 825-0563

Colby Ascension-on-the-Prairie Epis **P** (27) 1170 Wheat Ridge Rd 67701-3530 (Mail to: PO Box 842 67701-0842) Donald Martin (785) 462-7198

Dodge City St Cornelius Episcopal Church **P** (116) 200 W Spruce St 67801-4425 (Mail to: PO Box 1414 67801-1414) Jose Bernal (620) 227-6975

Garden City St Thomas Episcopal Church **M** (48) 710-712 N Main St 67846-5433 (Mail to: PO Box 2410 67846-8410) (620) 276-3173

Goodland St Pauls Episcopal Church **M** (35) 121 W 13th St 67735-2926 (Mail to: PO Box 452 67735-0452) Donald Martin (785) 890-2115

Great Bend St Johns Episcopal Church **M** (39) 2701 17th St 67530-2303 (Mail to: 2701 17th St 67530-2303) Basil Price (620) 792-4288

Hays St Andrews Episcopal Church **M** (21) 2422 Hyacinth Ave 67601 (Mail to: Attn: Mrs Gwen Johnson PO Box 247 67601-0247) (785) 625-6476

Hays St Michaels Episcopal Church **P** (42) 2900 Canal Blvd 67601-1704 (Mail to: 2900 Canal Blvd PO Box 1352 67601-1704) (758) 628-8442

Hutchinson Grace Episcopal Church **P** (420) § 2 Hyde Park Dr 67502-2824 (Mail to: 2 Hyde Park Dr 67502-2824) James Blakley Larry Carver Larry Steadman William Waln (620) 662-8024

Kingman Christ Episcopal Church **M** (16) 332 N Spruce St 67068-1651 (Mail to: PO Box 323 67068-0323) (620) 532-2488

Kinsley Holy Nativity Episcopal Church **M** (13) 714 E 8th St 67547-1326 (Mail to: PO Box 233 67547-0233) (620) 659-2539

Lakin Epis Church of the Upper Room **M** (22) 406 W Kingman Ave 67860-9463 (Mail to: PO Box 634 67860-0634) (620) 355-6077

Larned Sts Mary and Martha of Bethany **M** (35) PO Box 333 67550-0333 (Mail to: PO Box 333 67550-0333) Kevin Schmidt (620) 285-6503

Liberal St Andrews Church **M** (44) 521 N Sherman Ave 67901-3205 (Mail to: PO Box 250 67905-0250) (620) 624-3944

Lyons Saint Mark's Church **M** (16) 524 East Ave S 67554-3804 (Mail to: 524 East Ave S 67554-3804) Kevin Schmidt (620) 257-5955

Mcpherson St Annes Episcopal Church **M** (63) 105 W Sutherland St 67460-4719 (Mail to: 105 W Sutherland St # 577 67460-4719) (866) 363-8850

Medicine Ldg St Marks Episcopal Church **M** (5) 208 N Walnut St 67104-1319 (Mail to: 1109 Goodview St 67104-1040) Karen Lemon (620) 866-5131

Norton Trinity Episcopal Church **M** (18) § 319 N. State St. 67654 (Mail to: 319 N State St 67654-1811) (785) 877-2589

Pratt All Saints Episcopal Church **M** (41) 218 N Main St 67124-1739 (Mail to: C/O Warden Gary Skaggs 542 Terrace Dr 67124-1354) Karen Lemon (620) 672-2308

Russell Springs St Francis Episcopal Church **M** (19) 525 Hilts Ave 67764 (Mail to: Hilts Street 67764) Donald Martin (785) 751-4278

Salina Armstrong Memorial Chapel **CC** 110 E Otis Ave 67402 (Mail to: PO Box 827 67402-0827) (785) 823-7231

✠ **Salina** Christ Cathedral Church **O** (223) § 138 S 8th St 67401-2808 (Mail to: 138 S 8th St 67401-2808) Shay Craig Bruce Le Barron Basil Price Robert Seaton (785) 825-0974

Salina St Francis of Assisi Chapel **Chapel** 509 E Elm St 67401-2348 (Mail to: PO Box 1340 67402-1340) (800) 423-1342

Scott City St Lukes Episcopal Church **M** (31) 303 Epperson Dr 67871-1841 (Mail to: Attn: Harriet Jones 303 Epperson Dr 67871-1841) Donald Martin (620) 872-3666

Ulysses St Johns Episcopal Church **M** (10) 104 S Maxwell St 67880-2327 (Mail to: 104 S Maxwell St 67880-2327) Floyd Daharsh (620) 356-3690

DIOCESE OF WESTERN LOUISIANA
(PROVINCE VII)
Comprises Thirty-Two Civil Parishes and Eleven Missions in Western Louisiana
DIOCESAN OFFICE 335 Main St Pineville LA 71360 (MAIL: Box 4330 Pineville LA 71361)
TEL (318) 442-1304 FAX (318) 442-8712
E-MAIL bishopjake@diocesewla.org WEB www.epiwla.org

Previous Bishops—
Willis R Henton 1980-90, Robert J Hargrove 1990-2002, D Bruce MacPherson 2002-12

Bishop—Rt Rev Jacob W Owensby (21 July 2012)

Sec K Hayward; *Chanc* K McInnis 1080 Avery St Shreveport 71106; *Treas* W Harp 1310 Plantation Dr Alexandria 71301; *Reg* H Davis; *Ecum* Rev WE Carter

Standing Comm—Cler: *Pres* D Stodghill A Perry R Snow; *Lay:* S Broussard S Hamm L Smith

Deans: Acadiana M McLain; *Alexandria* R Snow; *Lake Charles* S Donald; *Monroe* D Stodghill; *Shreveport* T Nsugbuga

PARISHES, MISSIONS, AND CLERGY

Abbeville St Pauls Episcopal Church **P** (43) 101 E Vermilion St 70510 (Mail to: PO Box 1101 70511-1101) Madge Mclain (337) 893-3195

Alexandria St Timothy's Episcopal Church **P** (131) 2627 Horseshoe Dr 71301-2664 (Mail to: 2627 Horseshoe Dr 71301-2664) Walter Friese George Snow (318) 487-0875

Alexandria St James Epis Ch and Schl **P** (280) § 1620 Murray Street 71301-6882 (Mail to: 1620 Murray St 71301-6882) John Bedingfield John Parham (318) 445-9845

Bastrop Christ Episcopal Church **P** (77) 204 S Locust St 71220-4554 (Mail to: 206 S Locust St 71220-4554) (318) 281-5276

Bossier City St Georges Episcopal Church **P** (241) 1959 Airline Dr 71112-2407 (Mail to: 1959 Airline Dr 71112-2407) Teresa Deokaran (318) 746-2571

Bunkie Calvary Church **P** (52) 401 S Lexington Ave 71322-1842 (Mail to: PO Box 679 71322-0679) (318) 445-7651

Cheneyville Trinity Episcopal Church **M** (19) PO Box 223 71325-0223 (Mail to: PO Box 223 71325-0223) Andre Bordelon Joseph Bordelon (318) 473-9811

Deridder Trinity Episcopal Church **P** (40) C/O Marjorie H Adams PO Box 661 70634-0661 (Mail to: C/O Marjorie H Adams PO Box 661 70634) (337) 463-6322

Grambling St Lukes Chapel **M** (9) 1991 S Main & Adams St 71245 (Mail to: PO Box 365 71245-0365) (318) 247-6669

Jennings St Lukes Mission Episcopal Ch **M** (40) PO Box 461 70546-0461 (Mail to: PO Box 461 70546-0461) Johnny Clark (337) 824-4397

Lafayette Episcopal Ch of The Ascension **P** (754) § 1030 Johnston St 70501-7810 (Mail to: C/O Frank Limouze 1030 Johnston St 70501-7810) Jordan Hylden Emily Hylden (337) 232-2732

Lafayette St Barnabas Episcopal Church **HC** (536) § 400 Camellia Blvd 70503-4316 (Mail to: 400 Camellia Blvd 70503-4316) Michael Bordelon Michael Bordelon (337) 984-3848

Lake Charles Church of the Good Shepherd **P** (374) § 715 Kirkman St 70601-4350 (Mail to: C/O Ann Lindsay 715 Kirkman St 70601-4350) Mitzi George Frances Kay Frances Kay James Lueckenhoff (337) 433-5244

Lake Charles St Andrews Episcopal Church **M** (59) 1532 Sam Houston Jones Pkwy 70611 (Mail to: 1532 Sam Houston Jones Pkwy 70611-5457) (337) 855-1344

Lake Charles St Mich & All Angels Epis Ch **P** (293) 123 W Sale Rd 70605-2821 (Mail to: 123 W Sale Rd 70605-2821) Andrew Christiansen (337) 477-1881

Lecompte Holy Comforter Episcopal Ch **M** (63) 1708 Hardy St 71346 (Mail to: 3215 Madonna Dr 71301-4816) Andre Bordelon Joseph Bordelon (318) 776-5287

Leesville Leonidas Polk Memo Epis Mssn **M** (13) PO Box 1546 71496-1546 (Mail to: PO Box 1546 71496-1546) (337) 239-3083

Lk Providence Grace Episcopal Church **M** (34) PO Box 566 71254-0566 (Mail to: PO Box 566 71254-0566) William Echols (318) 559-1620

Mansfield Christ Memorial Episcopal Ch **P** (120) 401 Washington Ave 71052-3103 (Mail to: 401 Washington Ave 71052-3103) (318) 872-1144

Mer Rouge St Andrews Episcopal Church **P** (61) 201 Davenport Ave 71261 (Mail to: PO Box 65 71261-0065) Dawnell Stodghill (318) 647-3683

Minden St Johns Episcopal Church **P** (197) § 1107 Broadway St 71055-3314 (Mail to: 1107 Broadway St 71055-3314) (318) 377-1259

Monroe Grace Episcopal Church **P** (670) § 405 Glenmar Ave 71201-5307 (Mail to: 405 Glenmar Ave 71201-5307) Donald Smith (318) 387-6646

Monroe St Albans Episcopal Church **P** (198) 2816 Deborah Dr 71201-1942 (Mail to: 2816 Deborah Dr 71201-1942) Thomas Stodghill (318) 323-3139

Monroe St Thomas Episcopal Church **P** (67) 3706 Bon Aire Dr 71203-3009 (Mail to: 3706 Bon Aire Dr 71203-3009) (318) 343-4089

Natchitoches Trinity Episcopal Church **P** (142) § 533 Second Street 71457-4619 (Mail to: 148

Touline St 71457-4639) Mary Wolfenbarger (318) 352-3113

New Iberia Episcopal Ch of the Epiphany **P** (239) 303 W Main St 70560-3642 (Mail to: 303 W Main St 70560-3642) Anne Etheredge (337) 369-9966

Oak Ridge Church of the Redeemer **M** (7) 206 N Oak St 71264-9385 (Mail to: PO Box 238 71264-0238) (318) 647-3683

Opelousas Church of the Epiphany **P** (149) 1103 S Union St 70570-5952 (Mail to: 1103 S Union St 70570-5952) Laurent De Prins (337) 942-3336

Pineville Mount Olivet Chapel **HC** 335 Main St 71360-6929 (Mail to: PO Box 2031 71309) Jacob Owensby (318) 442-1304

Pineville St Michael's Episcopal Church **P** (251) 500 Edgewood Dr 71360-4525 (Mail to: 500 Edgewood Dr 71360-4525) (318) 640-0030

Rayville St Davids Episcopal Church **P** (76) 834 Louisa St 71269-2633 (Mail to: PO Box 276 71269-0276) (318) 728-2367

Ruston Church of the Redeemer **P** (133) 504 Tech Dr 71270-4938 (Mail to: 504 Tech Dr 71270-4938) (318) 255-3925

Shreveport Church of the Holy Cross **P** (108) 875 Cotton St 71101-3462 (Mail to: PO Box 1627 71165-1627) James Boyte Donald Heacock (318) 222-3325

Shreveport St James Episcopal Church **P** (152) 2050 Bert Kouns Loop 71118-3315 (Mail to: 2050 Bert Kouns Loop 71118-3315) Morgan Macintire (318) 686-1261

✠ **Shreveport** St Marks Episcopal Cathedral **O** (1774) § 908 Rutherford St 71104-4246 (Mail to: 908 Rutherford St 71104-4297) William Bryant Wayne Carter Alston Johnson Thomas Nsubuga Rowena White (318) 221-3360

Shreveport St Matthias Episcopal Church **P** (101) 3301 St Matthias Dr 71119-5600 (Mail to: 3301 Saint Matthias Dr 71119-5600) (318) 635-5354

Shreveport St Pauls Episcopal Church **P** (487) § 275 Southfield Rd 71105-3608 (Mail to: 275 Southfield Rd 71105-3608) Michael Cannon (318) 865-8469

St Joseph Christ Episcopal Church **P** (15) 120 Hancock St 71366 (Mail to: PO Box 256 71366-0256) Gregg Riley (318) 766-3518

Sulphur Church of the Holy Trinity **P** (123) C/O Mrs Heather Reddoch 1700 Maplewood Dr 70663-6002 (Mail to: C/O Mrs Heather Reddoch 1700 Maplewood Dr 70663-6002) (337) 625-4288

Tallulah Trinity Episcopal Church **P** (50) PO Box 208 71284-0208 (Mail to: PO Box 208 71284-0208) William Echols (318) 362-9728

West Monroe St Patricks Episcopal Church **P** (87) 1712 Wellerman Rd 71291 (Mail to: 1712 Wellerman Rd 71291-7429) (318) 396-1341

Winnfield St Pauls Episcopal Church **M** (13) 206 Pecan St 71483-3363 (Mail to: PO Box 206 71483-0206) Richard Taylor (318) 628-6971

Winnsboro St Columbas Episcopal Church **M** (11) 201 N Franklin St 71295-2245 (Mail to: PO Box 83 71378-0083) (318) 435-6269

DIOCESE OF WESTERN MASSACHUSETTS
(PROVINCE I)
Comprises the central and western half of the state of Massachusetts
DIOCESAN OFFICE 37 Chestnut St Springfield MA 01103
TEL (413) 737-4786, 737-4787, (800) 332-8513 FAX (413) 746-9873
E-MAIL diocese@diocesewma.org WEB www.diocesewma.org

Previous Bishops— Alexander H Vinton 1902-11, Thomas F Davies 1911-36, William A Lawrence 1937-57, Robert M Hatch 1957-70, Alexander D Stewart 1970-84, Andrew F Wissemann 1984-92, Robert S Denig 1993-95, Gordon P Scruton 1996-2012

Bishop—Rt Rev Douglas John Fisher (1073) (Dio 1 Dec 2012)

Sec of Conv Rev Wm Murray; *Cns to Ord* Rev Dr R Simpson Rev P Mott; *Cn for Mission Resources* S Abdow; *Exec Asst to Bp Dio* J Senecal; *Treas* W Gass; *Asst Treas* S Abdow; *Chanc* D Allison 69 S Pleasant

St Suite 201 Amherst MA 01002; *Exec Dir Trustees* N Kalber

Stand Comm—Cler: Chair N Webb Stroud C Jones C Munz S Smith; *Lay:* L Cheek P Kite N Lowry C Loy

PARISHES, MISSIONS, AND CLERGY

Amherst Grace Episcopal Church **P** (713) 14 Boltwood Ave 01002-2301 (Mail to: 14 Boltwood Ave 01002-2301) (413) 256-6754

Ashfield St Johns Episcopal Church **M** (135) Main & South St 01330-9602 (Mail to: PO Box 253 01330-0253) Victoria Ix (413) 628-4402

Athol St Johns Episcopal Church **P** (86) 15 Park Ave 01331-2515 (Mail to: 15 Park Ave 01331-2500) J Eliot Moss (978) 249-9553

Auburn Church of St Thomas **P** (68) 35 School St 01501-2917 (Mail to: 35 School St 01501-2917) (508) 832-2598

Chicopee Trinity Church **P** (43) 27 Streiber Dr 01020-3055 (Mail to: 27 Streiber Dr 01020-3055) (413) 533-7872

Clinton Church of the Good Shepherd **P** (264) 209 Union St 01510-2903 (Mail to: 209 Union St 01510-2903) Ann Scannell (978) 365-5169

E Longmeadow Saint Mark's Episcopal Church **P** (362) 1 Porter Rd 01028-1348 (Mail to: 1 Porter Rd 01028-1348) Maria Kano (413) 525-6341

Easthampton Saint Philip's Church **P** (81) 128 Main St 01027-2023 (Mail to: 128 Main St 01027-2023) Jill Rierdan (413) 527-0862

Feeding Hills St Davids Episcopal Church **P** (242) 699 Springfield St 01030-2134 (Mail to: 699 Springfield St 01030-2134) Benjamin Hill (413) 786-6133

Fitchburg Christ Church **P** (517) 569 Main St 01420-8012 (Mail to: 569 Main St 01420-8057) Bennett Jones Carolyn Jones (978) 342-0007

Gardner St Pauls Episcopal Church **P** (134) 79 Cross St 01440-2214 (Mail to: 79 Cross St 01440-2214) (978) 632-0925

Great Barrington Grace Ch in Sthrn Berkshires **P** (138) 67 State Road 01230 (Mail to: 352 Main St 01230-1814) Ray Wilson (413) 644-0022

Greenfield Epis Ch of St James & Andrew **P** (325) 8 Church St 01301-2901 (Mail to: 8 Church St 01301-2901) Heather Blais (413) 773-3925

Holden St Francis Episcopal Church **P** (512) 70 Highland St 01520-2594 (Mail to: 70 Highland St 01520-2594) (508) 829-3344

Holyoke St Pauls Episcopal Church **P** (228) 485 Appleton St 01040-3255 (Mail to: 485 Appleton St 01040-3295) (413) 532-5060

Lanesborough St Lukes Episcopal Church **M** (52) 20 S Main St 01237-9656 (Mail to: 20 S Main St # 593 01237-9656) Noreen Suriner (413) 443-0165

Lenox St Helenas Chapel **M** (74) 245 New Lenox Rd 01240-2242 (Mail to: 221 New Lenox Rd 01240-2223) Jennifer Gregg (413) 637-1483

Lenox Trinity Parish **P** (180) 88 Walker St 01240-2725 (Mail to: Attn: Eugenie Fawcett 88 Walker St 01240-2797) (413) 637-0073

Leominster St Marks Episcopal Church **P** (625) 60 West St 01453-5653 (Mail to: 60 West St 01453-5653) (978) 537-3560

Longmeadow St Andrews Episcopal Church **P** (656) 335 Longmeadow St 01106-1367 (Mail to: 335 Longmeadow St 01106-1367) Charlotte Laforest Benjamin Hill (413) 567-5901

Milford Trinity Episcopal Church **HC** (525) 17 Congress St 01757-4152 (Mail to: Dio of Western Massachusetts 37 Chestnut St 01103-1705) (508) 473-8464

Millville Saint John's Church **M** (159) 49 Central St 01529-1714 (Mail to: PO Box 395 01529-0395) (508) 883-4480

North Adams All Sts Ch of the Berkshires **P** (190) 59 Summer St 01247-4009 (Mail to: PO Box 374 01247-0374) James Duncan (413) 663-5389

North Brookfield Christ Memorial Church **P** (76) 133 N Main St 01535-1413 (Mail to: 65 E Huron St 60611-2728) Jane Beebe (508) 867 2789

Northampton St Johns Episcopal Church **P** (419) 48 Elm St 01060-2903 (Mail to: 48 Elm St 01060-2932) Michael Ramsey-Musolf (413) 584-1757

Northborough Church of the Nativity **P** (315) 45 Howard St 01532-1441 (Mail to: 45 Howard St 01532-1441) (508) 393-3146

Oxford Good Shepherd Church **P** (130) 270 Main St 01540-2359 (Mail to: 268 Main St 01540-2359) (508) 987-1004

Pittsfield St Stephens Episcopal Church **P** (602) 67 East St 01201-5313 (Mail to: 67 East St 01201-5383) Nina Pooley William Loutrel (413) 448-8276

Rochdale Christ Episcopal Church **P** (119) 1089 Stafford St 01542-1003 (Mail to: PO Box 142 01542-0142) (508) 892-8460

Sheffield Christ Epis Trnty Lutheran Ch **P** (45) 180 S Main St 01257 (Mail to: PO Box 127 01257-0127) William Karas (413) 229-8811

Shrewsbury Trinity Episcopal Church **P** (190) 440 Main St 01545-2208 (Mail to: 440 Main St 01545-2208) (508) 842-6040

South Hadley All Saints Church **P** (238) 7 Woodbridge St 01075-1117 (Mail to: 7 Woodbridge St 01075-1117) (413) 532-8917

Southbridge Holy Trinity Episcopal Church **P** (74) 446 Hamilton St 01550-1859 (Mail to: 446 Hamilton St 01550-1859) (508) 765-9559

Southwick Southwick Community Epis Ch **M** (141) PO Box 1069 01077-1069 (Mail to: PO Box 1069 01077-1069) (413) 569-9650

✠ **Springfield** Christ Church Cathedral **O** (581) 35 Chestnut St 01103-1705 (Mail to: 37 Chestnut St 01103-1786) (413) 736-2742

Springfield St Peters Church **P** (184) 45 Buckingham St 01109-3926 (Mail to: 45 Buckingham St 01109-3926) Michael Devine (413) 736-8567

Stockbridge St Pauls Episcopal Church **P** (181) 29 Main St 01262 (Mail to: PO Box 784 01262-0784) Jane Tillman (413) 298-4913

Sutton Holy Spirit Episcopal Church **P** (601) 3 Pleasant St 01590-3890 (Mail to: 3 Pleasant St 01590-3890) Julie Carson (508) 865-6448

W Springfield Church of the Good Shepherd **P** (18) 214 Elm St 01089-2709 (Mail to: PO Box 483 01090-0483) (413) 734-1976

Ware Trinity Episcopal Church **P** (79) PO Box 447 01082-0447 (Mail to: PO Box 447 01082-0447) (413) 967-6100

Webster The Ch of the Reconciliation **P** (100) 5 N Main St 01570-2229 (Mail to: 5 N Main St 01570-2229) Janice Ford (508) 943-8714

Westborough Saint Stephen's Church P (236) 3 John St 01581-2510 (Mail to: 3 John St 01581-2510) (508) 366-4134

Westfield Church of the Atonement P (312) 36 Court St 01085-3667 (Mail to: 36 Court St 01085-3667) Sandra Albom (413) 562-5461

Whitinsville Trinity Episcopal Church P (232) 33 Linwood Ave 01588-2309 (Mail to: 29 Linwood Ave 01588-2309) (508) 234-5303

Wilbraham Church of the Epiphany P (207) 10 Highland Ave 01095-1932 (Mail to: 20 Highland Ave 01095-1932) (413) 596-6080

Williamstown St Johns Church P (427) 35 Park St 01267-2114 (Mail to: 35 Park St 01267-2114) Nathaniel Anderson Valerie Bailey Fischer (413) 458-8144

Worcester All Saints Episcopal Church P (803) 10 Irving St 01609-3210 (Mail to: 10 Irving St 01609-3229) (508) 752-3766

Worcester St Lukes Episcopal Church P (278) 921 Pleasant St 01602-1908 (Mail to: c/o Dio of W Massachusetts 37 Chestnut St 01103) (508) 756-1990

Worcester St Marks Episcopal Church P (56) 0 Freeland St 01603-2603 (Mail to: 0 Freeland St 01603-2603) William Hobbs (508) 791-6027

Worcester St Matthews Church P (297) 695 Southbridge St 01610-2914 (Mail to: 695 Southbridge St 01610-2914) (508) 755-4433

Worcester St Michaels on the Heights P (210) 340 Burncoat St 01606-3101 (Mail to: 340 Burncoat St 01606-3101) (508) 853-9400

DIOCESE OF WESTERN MICHIGAN
(PROVINCE V)
Comprises the western half of the Lower Peninsula
DIOCESAN OFFICE Diocese of Western Michigan
1815 Hall St SE, Ste 200, Grand Rapids, MI 49506
TEL (616) 319-2006 Bishop's Office (616) 319-2006 x1
E-MAIL office@edwm.org WEB www.edwm.org

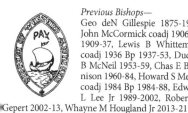

Previous Bishops—
Geo deN Gillespie 1875-1909, John McCormick coadj 1906 Bp 1909-37, Lewis B Whittemore coadj 1936 Bp 1937-53, Dudley B McNeil 1953-59, Chas E Bennison 1960-84, Howard S Meeks coadj 1984 Bp 1984-88, Edward L Lee Jr 1989-2002, Robert R Gepert 2002-13, Whayne M Hougland Jr 2013-21

Bishop Provisional—Rt Rev Prince G. Singh (1 Feb 2021)

Sec Conv Rev Joel Turmo; *Chanc* WJ Fleener Jr; *Admin Staff, Bp Admin Asst* C Cameron-Heldt; *Cn Missioner* V Ambrose; *Cn Missioner* A Hallmark; *Cn Missioner* A James; *Cn for Evang and Networking* K Forsyth; *Dir of Children, Yth, and Young Adult Form* M Knill

Stand Comm: Cler: R Warren; *Lay:* C Redwine M Bartlett F Gilbert M Bosscher A Schnaare F Skidmore E Stoffan

Council: Cler: J Cramer J Perra J Turmo; *Lay:* L Atwater J Buchanan A Hager R Kaminski M Neddo N Love-Parish M Porter l Raisanen S Reed P Vinge

Extended Staff: Arch Dcn B Drew; *Dcn for International Mission* B Drew

Comm on Ministry—Cler: Co-Chair L Marx *Co-Chair* M Wood D Meyers J Enlow J Johnson; *Lay:* S Lund-Coyle M Pridgeon N Foster P Redinger C Searles

PARISHES, MISSIONS, AND CLERGY

Albion St James Church P (53) 119 W Erie St 49224-1756 (Mail to: 119 W Erie St 49224-1756) (517) 629-8710

Allegan Church of the Good Shepherd P (54) 101 N Walnut St 49010-1249 (Mail to: 101 N Walnut St 49010-1249) (269) 673-2254

Battle Creek Church of the Resurrection P (27) 2589 Capital Ave SW 49015-4160 (Mail to: 2589 Capital Ave SW 49015-4160) (269) 965-2840

Battle Creek Church of St Thomas P (362) 16 Van Buren St E 49017-3916 (Mail to: 16 Van Buren St E 49017-3916) Brian Coleman (269) 9652244

Beaver Island St James Episcopal Mission M 26055 Pine St 49782 (Mail to: PO Box 281 49782-0281) (231) 448-2241

Belmont Holy Spirit Episcopal Church P (87) 1200 Post Dr NE 49306-9723 (Mail to: 1200 Post Dr NE 49306-9723) David Meyers Daniel Buchin (616) 784-1111

Benton Harbor St Augustine's Church P (91) 1753 Union St 49022-6261 (Mail to: 1753 Union Ave 49022-6298) (269) 925-2670

Beulah St Philips Church P (104) 785 Beulah Hwy 49617-9297 (Mail to: 785 Beulah Hwy 49617-9297) (231) 882-4506

Big Rapids St Andrews Episcopal Church P (39) § 323 S State St 49307-1760 (Mail to: 323 S State St 49307-1760) Gary Hamp (231) 796-5473

Boyne City Church of the Nativity P (22) 209 E Main St 49712-1306 (Mail to: PO Box 228 49712-0228) (231) 582-5045

Cadillac St Marys Church **P** (51) 815 Lincoln St 49601-2033 (Mail to: 815 Lincoln St 49601-2033) (231) 775-9641

Charlevoix Christ Church **P** (128) PO Box 385 49720-0385 (Mail to: PO Box 385 49720-0385) (231) 547-6322

Charlotte St Johns Episcopal Church **P** (30) 201 W Shepherd St 48813-1868 (Mail to: 201 W Shepherd St 48813-1868) Wendy Brown (517) 543-4430

Coldwater St Marks Church **P** (268) § 27 E Chicago St 49036-1605 (Mail to: 27 E Chicago St 49036-1605) Frederick Schark (517) 278-5752

Dowagiac St Pauls Episcopal Church **P** (40) 306 Courtland St 49047-1198 (Mail to: 306 Courtland St 49047-1198) (269) 782-7033

Elk Rapids St Pauls Episcopal Church **P** (95) § 403 Traverse St 49629-9721 (Mail to: 403 Traverse St 49629-9721) (231) 264-8871

Fremont St Johns Episcopal Church **P** (16) 124 S Sullivan Ave 49412-1546 (Mail to: PO Box 277 49412-0277) (231) 924-3280

Grand Haven St Johns Episcopal Church **P** (273) 524 Washington Ave 49417-1455 (Mail to: 524 Washington Ave 49417-1455) Jared Cramer (616) 8426260

Grand Ledge Trinity Church **P** (118) 201 E Jefferson St 48837-0116 (Mail to: PO Box 116 48837-0116) (517) 627-6287

Grand Rapids Grace Church **P** (202) 1815 Hall St SE 49506-4005 (Mail to: 1815 Hall St SE 49506-4099) Anne Schnaare (616) 241-4631

Grand Rapids St Andrews Church **P** (508) 1025 3 Mile Rd NE 49505-3419 (Mail to: 1025 3 Mile Rd NE 49505-3419) Molly Bosscher (616) 361-7887

Grand Rapids St Marks Episcopal Church **P** (475) 134 Division Ave N 49503-3103 (Mail to: 134 Division Ave N 49503-3173) Christian Brocato Susan York (616) 456-1684

Grand Rapids St Philips Church **P** (65) 558 Henry Ave SE 49503-5547 (Mail to: 558 Henry Ave SE 49503-5547) Zachariah Char (616) 451-9865

Grand Rapids Sudanese Grace Episcopal Church **M** (159) 1550 Oswego St NW 49504-4963 (Mail to: 1550 Oswego St NW 49504-4963) Zachariah Char Abraham Anei (616) 724-4052

Greenville St Paul the Apostle Epis Ch **P** (65) 305 S Clay St 48838-1917 (Mail to: 305 S Clay St 48838-1917) (616) 754-3163

Harbert Church of the Mediator **P** (131) 14280 Red Arrow Hwy 49115 (Mail to: PO Box 223 49115-0223) Darlene Kuhn (269) 469-1441

Harbor Spgs St Johns Chapel **SC** Third & Traverse 49740 (Mail to: PO Box 52 49740-0052) Phillip Ellsworth (231) 526-3914

Hastings Emmanuel Church **P** (130) 315 W Center St 49058-1615 (Mail to: 315 W Center St 49058-1615) William Ericson (269) 945-3014

Holland Grace Church **P** (659) 555 Michigan Ave 49423-4748 (Mail to: 555 Michigan Ave 49423-4794) Jennifer Adams (616) 3967459

Ionia St John the Apostle Epis Ch **P** (30) 107 W Washington St 48846-1623 (Mail to: PO Box 307 48846-0307) (616) 527-2290

Kalamazoo St Lukes Church **P** (417) § 247 W Lovell St 49007-5207 (Mail to: 247 W Lovell St 49007-5276) Randall Warren (269) 345-8553

Kalamazoo St Martin of Tours Epis Church **P** (143) 2010 Nichols Rd 49004-3200 (Mail to: 2010 Nichols Rd 49004-3200) Mary Perrin (269) 381-3188

Kentwood Church of the Holy Cross **P** (104) 4252 Breton Rd SE 49512-3858 (Mail to: 4252 Breton Rd SE 49512-3858) Michael Wernick (616) 949-7034

Lansing St Davids Church **P** (214) 1519 Elmwood Rd 48917-1543 (Mail to: 1519 Elmwood Rd 48917-1543) Andrew Downs Carol Spangenberg (517) 323-2272

Leland St Peters Chapel **SC** 203 Cedar St 49654-5015 (Mail to: C/O Shep Burr 525 10th Ave S 34102-7194) (231) 271-3081

Ludington Grace Epis Church Of Ludington **P** (33) 301 N James St 49431-1723 (Mail to: 301 N James St 49431-1723) Domingo Shriver (231) 843-9366

Manistee Holy Trinity Episcopal Church **P** (83) 410 2nd St 49660-1534 (Mail to: PO Box 577 49660-0577) (231) 723-2078

Marshall Trinity Episcopal Church **P** (128) 101 E Mansion St 49068-1117 (Mail to: 101 E Mansion St 49068-1186) (269) 781-7881

Montague St Peters by the Lake Epis **P** (125) 8435 Old Channel Trl 49437-1360 (Mail to: 8435 Old Channel Trl 49437-1360) David Meyers (231) 893-2425

Mt Pleasant St Johns Church Episcopal **P** (123) 206 W Maple St 48858-3103 (Mail to: 206 W Maple St 48858-3103) Nancy Fulton (989) 773-7448

Muskegon St Pauls Episcopal Church **P** (147) 1006 3rd St 49440-1206 (Mail to: 1006 3rd St 49440-1206) (231) 722-2112

Newaygo St Marks Church **P** (95) 30 Justice S 49337-8519 (Mail to: PO Box 211 49337-0211) Bobbi Heyboer (231) 652-7284

Niles Trinity Episcopal Church **P** (54) § 9 S 4th St 49120-2708 (Mail to: 9 S 4th St 49120-2708) (269) 683-6060

Northport St Christophers Church **P** (26) § 70 N Warren St 49670 (Mail to: PO Box 98 49670-0098) (231) 386-5037

Norton Shores St Gregorys Episcopal Church **P** (132) 1200 Seminole Rd 49441-4375 (Mail to: 1200 Seminole Rd 49441-4375) Lily Mar. (231) 780-2955

Onekama St Johns by the Lake Chapel **SC** 466 Highway 22 49675-9748 (Mail to: Chuc. Andrews 1131 Conlon Ave SE 49506-3566 (231) 935-1898

Paw Paw St Marks Episcopal Church **P** (67) § 412 Cedar St 49079-1113 (Mail to: PO Box 307 49079-0307) (269) 657-3762

Pentwater St James Church **P** (26) 82 S Wythe St 49449-7526 (Mail to: PO Box 412 49449-0412) (231) 869-7351

Petoskey Emmanuel Episcopal Church of Petoskey Michigan **P** (227) 1020 E Mitchell St 49770-2636 (Mail to: Attn: Office Manager 1020 E Mitchell St 49770-2636) Kay Houck (231) 3472350

Plainwell St Stephens Episcopal Church **P** (20) 309 Union St 49080-1248 (Mail to: 309 Union St 49080-1248) (269) 685-8230

Portage St Barnabas Episcopal Church **P** (35) 929 E Centre Ave 49002-5571 (Mail to: 929 E Centre Ave 49002-5571) Michael Wood (269) 327-7878

Richland St Timothys Church **P** (78) 9800 E BC Ave 49083-9577 (Mail to: 9800 E BC Ave 49083-9577) Joel Turmo (269) 629-9436

Saugatuck All Saints Church **P** (177) 252 Grand St 49453-9627 (Mail to: PO Box 189 49453-0189) Jay Johnson (269) 857-5201

Shelbyville St Francis Episcopal Church **P** (20) 11850 9 Mile Rd 49344-9441 (Mail to: 11850 9 Mile Rd 49344-9441) (269) 664-4345

South Haven Church of the Epiphany **P** (122) 410 Erie St 49090-1324 (Mail to: 410 Erie St 49090-1324) (269) 637-2521

St Joseph St Pauls Episcopal Church **P** (67) § 914 Lane Dr 49085-2053 (Mail to: 914 Lane Dr 49085-2053) (269) 983-4761

Sturgis St John Episcopal Church **P** (94) 110 S Clay St 49091-1711 (Mail to: 110 S Clay St 49091-1711) James Lively (269) 651-5811

Three Rivers Trinity Episcopal Church **P** (83) 321 N Main St 49093-1422 (Mail to: 321 N Main St 49093-1422) (269) 273-3795

Traverse City Grace Episcopal Church **P** (387) 341 Washington St 49684-2547 (Mail to: 341 Washington St 49684-2547) James Perra Derek Quinn (231) 947-2330

Wyoming Holy Trinity Episcopal Church **P** (140) 5333 Clyde Park Ave SW 49509-9527 (Mail to: 5333 Clyde Park Ave SW 49509-9527) Bradley Allard (616) 538-0900

DIOCESE OF WESTERN NEW YORK
(PROVINCE II)
Comprises 7 Western New York counties
DIOCESAN OFFICE 1064 Brighton Rd Tonawanda NY 14150
TEL (716) 881-0660 FAX (716) 881-1724
WEB www.episcopalpartnership.org

Previous Bishops—
Wm H Delancey 1839-65, Arthur C Coxe coadj 1865 Bp 1865-96, Wm D Walker 1897-1917, Chas H Brent 1918-29, David L Ferris suffr 1920-24 coadj 1924 Bp 1929-31, Cameron J Davis coadj 1930 Bp 1931-47, Lauriston L Scaife 1948-70, Harold B Robinson coadj 1968 Bp 1970-1987, David C Bowman coadj 1986 Bp 1987-98, J Michael Garrison 1999-2011, R William Franklin 2011-2019

Bishop—Rt Rev Sean Rowe (1019) (Provisional 3 Apr 2019)

Sec H Gondree; *Treas* W Palmer; *Chanc* C Fisher; *Trustees* R Sconiers R Rowe M Lincoln K Gengo R Matson P LaLonde; *Ex Sec* H Gondree; *Archdcn* D Leiker

Standing Comm—Cler: H Harper K Rossi N Evancho L Fodor; *Lay: Pres* J Isaac D Clarke-Merriweather S Cobb Deck L Mazuchowski

Deans: Central Erie M Hadaway; *Cattaraugus & Chautauqua* L Fodor; *Eastern Erie* R Harvey; *Genesee Region* C O'Connor; *Northern Region* R Rowe; *Southern Erie* A Tillman

PARISHES, MISSIONS, AND CLERGY

Albion Christ Episcopal Church **P** (42) § 26 S Main St 14411-1401 (Mail to: 26 S Main St 14411-1401) (585) 589-5314

Alden St Aidans Church **M** (34) 13021 Main St 14004-1225 (Mail to: 13021 Main St 14004-1225) (716) 937-6922

Angola St Pauls Episcopal Church **P** (90) 930 Lake St 14006-9200 (Mail to: PO Box 344 14006-0344) (716) 549-0063

Attica St Luke's Episcopal Church **P** (22) 30 Favor St 14011-1257 (Mail to: PO Box 178 14011) (585) 591-0301

Batavia St James Church **P** (151) 405 E Main St 14020-2496 (Mail to: 405 E Main St 14020-2496) Steven Metcalfe (585) 343-6802

Buffalo St Andrews Church **P** (43) 3107 Main St 14214-1305 (Mail to: 3107 Main St 14214-1305) (716) 834-9337

Buffalo St Davids Episcopal Church **P** (84) 3951 Seneca St 14224-3412 (Mail to: 3951 Seneca St 14224-3412) Claudia Scheda (716) 674-4670

Buffalo St Johns Grace Church **P** (74) 51 Colonial Cir 14222-1399 (Mail to: 51 Colonial Cir 14222-1399) (716) 885-1112

Buffalo St Judes Episcopal Church **P** (184) 124 Macamley St 14220-1242 (Mail to: 124 Macamley St 14220-1242) (716) 824-4322

Buffalo St Marks & All Saints Epis Ch **P** (41) 311 Ontario St 14207-1548 (Mail to: 311 Ontario St 14207-1548) (716) 875-8374

Buffalo St Matthews Church **P** (51) 1182 Seneca St 14210-1545 (Mail to: 1182 Seneca St 14210-1545) (716) 822-4830

Buffalo St Michael & All Angels Church **P** (59) 81 Burke Dr 14215-1305 (Mail to: 81 Burke Dr 14215-1305) Jason Miller (716) 836-0220

Buffalo St Patricks Episcopal Church **P** (77) 1395 George Urban Blvd 14225-3807 (Mail to: 1395 George Urban Blvd 14225-3807) Bonnie Morris (716) 684-4206

✛ **Buffalo** Saint Paul's Cathedral **O** (248) 4 Cathedral Park 14202-4002 (Mail to: 4 Cathedral Park 14202-4002) Twila Smith Michael Hadaway (716) 855-0900

Buffalo St Pauls Episcopal Church **P** (481) 4275 Harris Hill Rd 14221-7437 (Mail to: 4275 Harris Hill Rd 14221-7437) (716) 632-8221

Buffalo St Peters Episcopal Church **P** (127) 205 Longmeadow Rd 14226-2905 (Mail to: Rev Daniel Pinti 205 Longmeadow Rd 14226-2905) Daniel Pinti (716) 832-9764

Buffalo St Philips Episcopal Church **P** (138) 18 Sussex Street 14215 (Mail to: 15 Fernhill Ave 14215-3032) Lillian Davis-Wilson Stephen Lane (716) 833-0444

Buffalo St Simons Episcopal Church **P** (60) 200 Cazenovia St 14210-2451 (Mail to: 200 Cazenovia St 14210-2499) Ralph Strohm Linda Malia (716) 822-1901

Buffalo The Ch of the Good Shepherd **P** (74) § 96 Jewett Pkwy 14214-2451 (Mail to: 96 Jewett Pkwy 14214-2451) Michael Hadaway Elizabeth Hadaway Leann Mcconchie (716) 833-1151

Buffalo Trinity Episcopal Church **P** (402) 371 Delaware Ave 14202-1601 (Mail to: 371 Delaware Ave Ste 1 14202-1699) Matthew Lincoln (716) 852-8314

Burt St Andrews Episcopal Church **P** (146) 2239 W Creek Rd 14028-9724 (Mail to: PO Box 133 14028-0133) Randi Rowe (716) 778-7633

Chautauqua Chapel of the Good Shepherd **SC** Clark Ave 14722 (Mail to: PO Box 81 14722-0081) (716) 753-2172

Dunkirk Church of St John the Baptist **P** (65) 16 W 4th St 14048-2056 (Mail to: PO Box 14 14048-0014) (716) 366-1979

East Aurora St Matthias Episcopal Church **P** (275) 374 Main St 14052-1715 (Mail to: 374 Main St 14052-1715) Ann Tillman Ann Tillman (716) 652-0377

Ellicottville St Johns Episcopal Church **P** (5) Washington & Jefferson Sts 14731 (Mail to: PO Box 137 14731-0137) Michael Lonto (716) 945-1820

Franklinville St Barnabas Episcopal Church **M** (12) PO Box 105 14737-0105 (Mail to: PO Box 105 14737-0105) (716) 676-3468

Fredonia Trinity Episcopal Church **P** (110) 11 Day St 14063-1813 (Mail to: PO Box 467 11 Day St 14063-0467) James Clement (716) 679-7901

Gowanda St Marys Episcopal Church **P** (34) 75 Center St 14070-1106 (Mail to: PO Box 166 14070-0166) W David Noves (716) 532-4352

Grand Island Ch of St Martin in the Fields **P** (207) § 2587 Baseline Rd 14072-1656 (Mail to: 2587 Baseline Rd 14072-1656) Nicholas Evancho (716) 773-3335

Hamburg Trinity Episcopal Church **P** (318) § 261 E Main St 14075-5345 (Mail to: 261 E Main St 14075-5345) Shannon Collis (716) 649-4320

Holley St Pauls Episcopal Church **P** (30) 2 Jackson St 14470-1106 (Mail to: 2 Jackson St 14470-1106) John Boyer (585) 638-5142

Irving Church of the Good Shepherd **M** (108) 12114 Route 438 Ext 14081-9661 (Mail to: PO Box 179 14081-0179) (716) 934-3328

Jamestown St Lukes Episcopal Church **P** (482) 410 N Main St 14701-5008 (Mail to: 410 N Main St 14701-5008) Lucas Fodor Cathleen Smith (716) 483-6405

Kenmore Church of the Advent **P** (318) § 54 Delaware Rd 14217-2402 (Mail to: 54 Delaware Rd 14217-2402) Bonnie Morris Penelope Foster (716) 876-6504

Lancaster Trinity Church **P** (70) 5448 Broadway 14086-2124 (Mail to: 5448 Broadway St 14086-2124) Ann Markle (716) 683-1111

Le Roy St Marks Episcopal Church **P** (189) § 1 E Main St 14482-1209 (Mail to: 1 E Main Street 14482-1209) (585) 768-7200

Lewiston St Pauls Episcopal Church **P** (46) § 400 Ridge St 14092-1206 (Mail to: PO Box 354 14092-0354) Neil Johnson Barbara Price Barbara Price Randi Rowe (716) 754-4591

Lockport Christ Church **P** (229) 7145 Fieldcrest Dr 14094-1613 (Mail to: 7145 Fieldcrest Dr 14094-1613) Jeffery Edmister (716) 433-9229

Lockport Grace Episcopal Church **P** (65) 100 Genesee St 14094-4318 (Mail to: 100 Genesee St 14094-4395) (716) 433-2878

Mayville St Pauls Episcopal Church **P** (129) 99 S Erie St 14757-1120 (Mail to: 99 S Erie St 14757-1120) Patricia Guinn Claudia Scheda (716) 753-2172

Medina St Johns Church **P** (42) 200 E Center St 14103-1623 (Mail to: 200 E Center St 14103-1623) Nancy Guenther (585) 798-0920

Niagara Falls Niagara Falls Epis Urb Mnstry **P** (70) 140 Rainbow Blvd 14303-1214 (Mail to: 140 Rainbow Blvd 14303-1214) (716) 282-1717

Niagara Falls St Stephen's Episcopal Church **P** (56) 616 Cayuga Drive 14304-3499 (Mail to: 616 Cayuga Dr 14304-3499) (716) 283-2774

North Tonawanda St Mark Episcopal Church **P** (344) 61 Payne Ave 14120-6012 (Mail to: 61 Payne Ave 14120-6012) Elizabeth Hadaway Michael Hadaway (716) 692-3735

Olean St Stephens Church **P** (96) 109 S Barry St 14760-3626 (Mail to: Attn: Treasurer PO Box 446 14760-0446) Kim Rossi (716) 372-5628

Orchard Park St Marks Episcopal Church **P** (670) 6595 E Quaker St 14127-2501 (Mail to: 6595 E Quaker St 14127-2585) John Marshall Leland Rose (716) 662-4418

Perry Holy Apostle Episcopal Church **P** (40) 88 Main St S 14530-1524 (Mail to: 88 Main St S 14530-1524) (585) 237-5883

Randolph Grace Episcopal Church **P** (90) 21 N Washington St 14772-1207 (Mail to: 21 Washington Street 14772) Michelle Boomgaard Lucas Fodor (716) 358-6124

Salamanca St Marys Episcopal Church **P** (82) 99 Wildwood Ave 14779-1523 (Mail to: 99 Wildwood Ave 14779-1523) (716) 945-1820

Silver Creek St Albans Episcopal Church **P** (51) 4 Lake Ave 14136-1012 (Mail to: PO Box 214 14136-0214) (716) 934-2174

Springville St Pauls Episcopal Church **M** (109) § 591 E Main St 14141-1437 (Mail to: 591 E Main St 14141-1437) Gerald Hilfiker (716) 592-2153

Stafford St Pauls Episcopal Church **P** (23) § 6188 Main Rd 14143-9546 (Mail to: 6188 Main Rd 14143-9546) (585) 356-0769

Tonawanda St Anthony of Padua Chapel **Chapel** 1064 Brighton Rd 14150-8204 (Mail to: 1064 Brighton Rd 14150-8204) (716) 881-0660

Warsaw Trinity Church **P** (26) 62 W Buffalo St 14569-1209 (Mail to: PO Box 396 14569-0396) Sarah Anuszkiewicz (585) 786-5285

Westfield St Peters Episcopal Church **P** (68) § 12 Elm St 14787-1402 (Mail to: 12 Elm St 14787-1402) (716) 326-2064

Williamsville Calvary Episcopal Church **P** (495) 20 Milton St 14221-6704 (Mail to: 20 Milton St 14221-6704) Robert Harvey (716) 633-7800

Wilson St Johns Episcopal Church **P** (59) 431 Lake St 14172-9798 (Mail to: C/O A Malangelo PO Box 28 14172-0028) (716) 751-6109

Youngstown St Johns Episcopal Church **P** (68) 110 Chestnut St 14174-1002 (Mail to: PO Box 366 14174-0366) Barbara Price (716) 745-3369

DIOCESE OF WESTERN NORTH CAROLINA
(PROVINCE IV)
Comprises the 28 westernmost counties of North Carolina
DIOCESAN OFFICE 900-B Centre Park Dr Asheville NC 28805
TEL (828) 225-6656
E-MAIL bishopjose@diocesewnc.org WEB www.diocesewnc.org

Previous Bishops—
Junius M Horner 1898-1933, Robt E Gribbin 1934-47, Matt G Henry 1948-75, Wm G Weinhauer coadj 1973 Bp 1975-89, Robert H Johnson 1990-2004, Granville Porter Taylor 2004-2016

Bishop — Rt Rev José McLoughlin (1096) (Dio 1 Oct 2016)

Cn to Ord Rev Cn A Anderson; *Treas* J Parsons; *Chanc* GS Hilderbran 301 College St, Ste 110 Asheville NC 28801; *CFO* C Tannenbaum; *Latino Missioner* Rev O Rozo; *Yth & Young Adult Min* E Lewis; *Archdcn* Ven B Gilbert

Stand Comm—Cler: Chair M Jolly J Stepp A Hege S Buchanan; *Lay:* C Longoria W Hasskamp J Dunbar J Schronce

Deans: Asheville Rev Dn K Neal; *Foothills* Rev T Árnason; *Hendersonville* Rev J Clarkson; *Mountain* Rev A Hege; *Piedmont* Rev C Kramer; *Western* Rev J Stepp

PARISHES, MISSIONS, AND CLERGY

Asheville St Matthias Episcopal Church **P** (73) 1 Dundee Street 28802-7375 (Mail to: PO Box 7375 28802-7375) David Sailer (828) 285-0033

Asheville Church of the Advocate **P** (20) 60 Church St 28801-3622 (Mail to: 60 Church St 28801-3622) (828) 243-3932

Asheville Church of the Redeemer **P** (130) 1201 Riverside Dr 28804-3019 (Mail to: 1201 Riverside Dr 28804-3019) (828) 253-3588

Asheville Grace Church **P** (257) 871 Merrimon Ave 28804-2404 (Mail to: 871 Merrimon Ave 28804-2492) Mildred Morrow Wendy Cade Robert Reese (828) 254-1086

Asheville St Johns Episcopal Church **P** (112) 290 Old Haw Creek Rd 28805-1436 (Mail to: 290 Old Haw Creek Rd 28805-1436) (828) 298-3553

Asheville Saint Luke's Episcopal Church **P** (120) 219 Chunns Cove Rd 28805-1210 (Mail to: 219 Chunns Cove Rd 28805-1210) Patricia Mouer (828) 254-2133

Asheville St Marys Church **P** (183) 337 Charlotte Street 28801-1437 (Mail to: 337 Charlotte St 28801-1437) Richard Rowe Stephen Weissman (828) 254-5836

Asheville St Georges Episcopal Church **P** (37) 1 School Rd 28806-1633 (Mail to: 1 School Rd 28806-1633) Carol Jablonski (828) 258-0211

✠ **Asheville** Cathedral of All Souls **O** (934) § 9 Swan St 28803-2674 (Mail to: 9 Swan St 28803-2674) Sarah Hurlbert Brian Cole Rosa Harden Nancy Mccarthy (828) 274-2681

Asheville Trinity Episcopal Church **P** (1097) 60 Church St 28801-3622 (Mail to: 60 Church St 28801-3690) Robert White (828) 253-9361

Bat Cave Church of the Transfiguration **P** (112) 106 Saylor Lane 28710 (Mail to: PO Box 130 28710-0130) (828) 625-9244

Bessemer City St Andrews Episcopal Church **P** (41) 1303 N 12th St 28016-6739 (Mail to: PO Box 611 28016-0611) (704) 629-3021

Black Mtn Saint James Church **P** (376) 424 W State St 28711-3345 (Mail to: Attn: Andrea Blankinship PO Box 1087 28711-1087) Judith Whelchel (828) 669-2754

Blowing Rock St Mary of the Hills Church **P** (291) § 140 Chestnut Cir 28605-9214 (Mail to: PO Box 14 28605-0014) James Gloster (828) 295-7323

Boone St Lukes Episcopal Church **P** (388) 170 Councill St 28607-3727 (Mail to: 170 Councill St 28607-3727) Cynthia Banks (828) 264-8943

Brevard St Philip's Episcopal Church **P** (613) 317 E Main St 28712-3834 (Mail to: 256 E Main St 28712-3724) Elizabeth Roles William Livingston (828) 884-3666

Burnsville St Thomas Episcopal Church **P** (102) PO Box 591 28714-0591 (Mail to: PO Box 591 28714-0591) Alicia Turner (828) 682-0037

Canton St Andrews Church **P** (262) 99 Academy St 28716-4445 (Mail to: PO Box 947 28716-0947) Karen Barfield Todd Donatelli (828) 648-7550

Cashiers Church of the Good Shepherd **P** (569) 1448 Highway 107 S 28717 (Mail to: PO Box 32 28717-0032) Alison Schultz Robert Wood (828) 743-2359

Cullowhee St Davids Episcopal Church **P** (70) PO Box 152 28723 (Mail to: PO Box 152 28723-0152) (828) 293-9496

Denver Ep Ch of St Peters by the Lake **P** (503) 8433 Fairfield Rd 28037-9130 (Mail to: 8433 Fairfield Forest Rd 28037-9166) Ronald Taylor Judith Cole (704) 483-3460

Edneyville St Pauls Episcopal Church **P** (53) 1659 St Pauls Rd 28727 (Mail to: PO Box 70 28727-0070) Harriet Shands Kevin Todd Kevin Todd (828) 685-3644

Flat Rock Ch Of St John In The Wildrness **P** (453) 1895 Greenville Hwy 28731-9646 (Mail to: PO Box 185 28731-0185) Joshua Stephens Joyce Beschta William Mccleery Harry Viola (828) 693-9783

Fletcher Calvary Episcopal Church **P** (425) PO Box 187 Hwy 25 28732-0187 (Mail to: PO Box 187 28732-0187) (828) 684-6266

Franklin All Saints Episcopal Church **P** (82) 216 Roller Mill Rd 28734-9089 (Mail to: 84 Church Street 28734-2946) Jonathan Stepp

Franklin St John's Episcopal Church **P** (77) 542 St John's Church Rd 28734-8201 (Mail to: 542 Saint Johns Church Rd 28734-8201) (828) 524-6370

Gastonia All Saints Episcopal Church **P** (185) 1201 S New Hope Rd 28054-5833 (Mail to: 1201 S New Hope Rd 28054-5833) Lynn Orville (704) 864-7201

Gastonia St Marks Episcopal Church **P** (603) 258 W Franklin Blvd 28052-4108 (Mail to: 258 W Franklin Blvd 28052-4108) Shawn Griffith (704) 864-4531

Glendale Springs Parish of Holy Communion **P** (102) 120 Glendale School Rd 28629 (Mail to: PO Box 177 28629-0177) Shirley Long (336) 982-3076

Hayesville Church of the Good Shepherd **P** (232) 495 Herbert Hills Dr 28904-4716 (Mail to: PO Box 677 28904-0677) William Breedlove (828) 389-3397

Hendersonvlle La Capilla de Santa Maria **P** (205) PO Box 296 28793-0296 (Mail to: C/O Mrs Margaret Dowsett Rt 9 Box 313 28792) (828) 697-5292

Hendersonvlle St James Episcopal Church **P** (482) 766 N Main St 28792-5078 (Mail to: 766 N Main St 28792-3612) Timothy Jones Christiana Olsen Kevin Todd (828) 693-7458

Hickory Church of the Ascension **P** (392) 726 1st Ave NW 28601-6062 (Mail to: 726 1st Ave NW 28601-6062) Karla Woggon Jared Grant (828) 328-5393

Hickory St Albans Episcopal Church **P** (746) 130 39th Ave Pl NW 28601-8029 (Mail to: 130 39th Avenue Pl NW 28601-8029) Tryggvi Arnason (828) 324-1351

Highlands Church of the Incarnation **P** (341) 520 Main St 28741 (Mail to: PO Box 729 28741-0729) Kellan Day (828) 5262968

Lenoir St James Episcopal Church **P** (160) 806 College Ave SW 28645-5426 (Mail to: 806 College Ave SW 28645-5426) Susan Buchanan (828) 754-3712

Lincolnton Our Saviour Episcopal Church **P** (27) PO Box 203 28092 (Mail to: PO Box 203 28093-0203) (704) 732-3585

Lincolnton St Lukes Church **P** (147) § 325 N Cedar St 28092-2802 (Mail to: 315 N Cedar St 28092-2802) Elizabeth Tester (704) 732-9179

Linville All Saints Episcopal Chapel **SC** Carolina Ave 28646 (Mail to: C/O Edgar A Terrell Jr 2820 Rothwood Drive 28646) (828) 733-4311

Little Switzerland Church of the Resurrection **SC** PO Box 217 160 High Ridge Rd 28749-0217 (Mail to: PO Box 217 160 High Ridge Rd 28749-0217) Robert Hansel (828) 765-1808

Marion St Johns Episcopal Church **P** (74) 311 S Main St 28752-4526 (Mail to: PO Box 968 28752-0968) Erin Kirby (828) 652-4144

Mars Hill Epis Church of the Holy Spirit **P** (195) 433 Bone Camp Rd 28753 (Mail to: C/O Treasurer PO Box 956 28754-0956) David Mcnair Robert Magnus (828) 689-2517

Mills River Church of the Holy Family **P** (87) 419 Turnpike Rd 28729 (Mail to: 419 Turnpike Rd 28759-9548) Tracey Kelly (828) 891-9375

Morganton Grace Episcopal Church **P** (184) 303 S King St 28655-3536 (Mail to: 303 S King St 28655-3536) Marshall Jolly (828) 437-1133

Morganton St Pauls Episcopal Church **P** (62) 4656 E Shores Dr 28655-8278 (Mail to: 4656 E Shores Dr 28655-8278) Jeffrey Mackey Harry Rains (704) 584-0955

Morganton St Marys & St Stephens Epis Ch **P** (146) 140 Saint Marys Church Rd 28655-9096 (Mail to: 140 Saint Marys Church Rd 28655-9096) (828) 448-8490

Murphy Church of the Messiah **P** (107) 76 Peachtree St 28906-2940 (Mail to: Attn: Ann Taaffe PO Box 67 28906-0067) (828) 837-2021

Newland Church of the Savior **P** (20) 2118 Elk Park Hwy 28657-8827 (Mail to: 2118 Elk Park Hwy 28657-8827) David Booher (828) 733-2513

Newton Episcopal Ch of the Epiphany **P** (38) 750 W 13th St 28658-3826 (Mail to: PO Box 270 28658-0270) (828) 464-1876

Robbinsville Grace Mountainside Luth Epi Ch **P** (20) 129 S. Main St. 28771-9802 (Mail to: Route 2 Box 7 28771) (828) 479-1184

Rutherdforton St Gabriels Episcopal Church **P** (26) PO Box 2121 28139 (Mail to: C/O Debbie Johnson 311 Mt View Street 28043) Bobby Lynch (828) 980-1466

Rutherfordton St Francis Episcopal Church **P** (105) § 395 N Main Street 28139-2415 (Mail to: 395 N Main St 28139-2505) (828) 287-3888

Saluda Church of the Transfiguration **P** (141) 72 Church St 28773-9716 (Mail to: PO Box 275 28773-0275) Walter Broadfoot (828) 749-9740

Shelby Church of the Redeemer **P** (193) 502 W Sumter St 28150-4329 (Mail to: 502 W Sumter St 28150-4329) Caroline Kramer (704) 487-5404

Sparta Christ Episcopal Church **P** (96) 2543 Us Hwy 21 S 28675 (Mail to: PO Box 1866 28675-1866) (336) 372-7983

Spruce Pine Trinity Episcopal Church **P** (169) 15 Hemlock Ave 28777-2981 (Mail to: 15 Hemlock Ave 28777-2981) Richard Biega (828) 520-1151

Sylva St Johns Episcopal Church **P** (101) 18 Jackson St 28779-3034 (Mail to: PO Box 175 28779-0175) Erin Johnson (828) 586-8358

Tryon Church of the Good Shepherd **P** (73) § 814 Markham Rd 28782-2819 (Mail to: PO Box 186 27925-0186) (828) 859-9961

Tryon Church of the Holy Cross **P** (275) 150 Melrose Ave 28782-3327 (Mail to: PO Box 279 28782-0279) Robert Ard Mary Turner (828) 859-9741

Valle Crucis Church of the Holy Cross **P** (402) § 122 Skiles Way 28604 (Mail to: PO Box 645 28691-0645) Robert Mccaslin (828) 963-4609

Waynesville Grace Church in the Mountains **P** (297) § 394 N Haywood St 28786-5718 (Mail to: 394 N Haywood St 28786-5718) Joslyn Schaefer (828) 456-6029

Wilkesboro St Pauls Episcopal Church **P** (328) 200 W Cowles St 28697-2410 (Mail to: PO Box 95 28697-0095) Stephanie Parker (336) 667-4231

STATE OF WISCONSIN
Dioceses of Eau Claire (EauC), Fond du Lac (FdL), and Milwaukee (Mil)

Algoma—FdL	Elkhart Lake—FdL	Menasha—FdL	Phillips—EauC
Amherst—FdL	Elkhorn—Mil	Menomonee Falls—Mil	Platteville—Mil
Antigo—FdL	Fish Creek—FdL	Menomonie—EauC	Plymouth—FdL
Appleton—FdL	Fond du Lac—FdL	Mequon—Mil	Pt Washington—Mil
Baraboo—Mil	Ft Atkinson—Mil	Merrill—FdL	Portage—Mil
Bayfield—EauC	Gardner—FdL	Milwaukee—Mil	Prairie du Chien—Mil
Beaver Dam—Mil	Greendale—Mil	Mineral Pt—Mil	Racine—Mil
Beloit—Mil	Hartford—Mil	Minocqua—FdL	Rhinelander—FdL
Burlington—Mil	Hartland—Mil	Monroe—Mil	Rice Lake—EauC
Chippewa Falls—EauC	Hayward—EauC	Mosinee—FdL	Richland Ctr—Mil
Clear Lake—EauC	Hudson—EauC	New London—FdL	Ripon—FdL
Conrath—EauC	Janesville—Mil	New Richmond—EauC	Shawano—FdL
Delafield—Mil	Kenosha—Mil	North Lake—Mil	Sheboygan—FdL
Delavan—Mil	La Crosse—EauC	Oconomowoc—Mil	Sheboygan Falls—FdL
De Pere—FdL	Lake Geneva—Mil	Oneida—FdL	Sister Bay—FdL
Dousman—Mil	Madison—Mil	Oshkosh—FdL	So Milwaukee—Mil
Eagle River—FdL	Manitowoc—FdL	Owen—EauC	Sparta—EauC
Eau Claire—EauC	Marinette—FdL	Pewaukee—Mil	Spooner—EauC

Springbrook—EauC
Stevens Pt—FdL
Sturgeon Bay—FdL
Suamico—FdL
Sun Prairie—Mil

Superior—EauC
Sussex—Mil
Tomah—EauC
Watertown—Mil
Waukesha—Mil

Waupaca—FdL
Waupun—FdL
Wausau—FdL
Wautoma—FdL
W Bend—Mil

Wis Dells—Mil
Wis Rapids—FdL

DIOCESE OF WYOMING
(PROVINCE VI)
Comprises the State of Wyoming
DIOCESAN OFFICE 123 S Durbin Casper WY 82601
TEL (307) 265-5200 FAX (307) 577-9939
E-MAIL jessica@episcopalwy.org WEB www.episcopalwy.org

Previous Bishops—
Ethelbert Talbot 1887-98, Nathaniel S Thomas 1909-27, Elmer N Schmuck 1929-36, Winifred H Ziegler 1936-49, James W Hunter 1949-69, David R Thornberry 1969-77, Bob G Jones 1977-96, Bruce Caldwell 1997-2010, John S Smylie 2010-21

Bishop—Rt Rev Paul-Gordon Chandler (Dio 13 February 2021)

Deploy J Reynolds *Sec/Treas* W Tanner; *Chanc* B Lance; *Comm* G Osburn; *Admin* J Reynolds; *Ed* L Gilbert; *Rec* J Reynolds

Stand Comm—Cler: Pres M Nickles P Bright L Anderson ; *Lay:* V Miller L McElwain MB Evers

COM—Cler: W Seeley D McElwain C Clarke R Veit K Walker; *Lay: Sec* J Reynolds L Turnell M Tepper C Lev

Diocesan Council: *Cler:* M Evers, A Mayes W Seeley L Modesitt; *Lay:* K McAtee S Donahue M Appel J Sullivan P Larson J Angst S Wildman B Knox

PARISHES, MISSIONS, AND CLERGY

Atlantic City St Andrews Episcopal Church **M** (22) 50 E Forbes St 82520-8812 (Mail to: 123 S Durbin St 82601-2511) (307) 332-4327

Basin St Andrews Episcopal Church **P** (72) 401 S 8th St 82410-9550 (Mail to: PO Box 407 82410-0407) Jean McLean (307) 568-2072

Big Piney St John the Baptist Church **M** (47) 340 Smith Ave 83113 (Mail to: PO Box 205 83113-0205) Jami Anderson (307) 276-3805

Bondurant St Hubert the Hunter **SC** Us 191 189 82922 (Mail to: 104 S 4th St 82070-3102) (307) 733-4166

Buffalo St Lukes Episcopal Church **P** (115) 178 S Main St 82834-0909 (Mail to: PO Box 909 82834-0909) Camie Dewey (307) 684-7529

Casper St Marks Church **P** (297) § 701 S Wolcott St 82601-3159 (Mail to: 701 S Wolcott St 82601-3159) James Shumard (307) 234-0831

Casper St Stephens Church **P** (57) 4700 S Poplar St 82601-6257 (Mail to: 4700 S Poplar St 82601-6257) Katherine Flores Judy Likwartz Wendy Owens (307) 265-4105

Cheyenne St Christophers Church **P** (97) 2602 Deming Blvd 82001-5708 (Mail to: 2602 Deming Blvd 82001-5708) (307) 632-4488

Cheyenne St Marks Episcopal Church **P** (260) § 1908 Central Ave 82001-3743 (Mail to: 1908 Central Ave 82001-3743) Richard Veit David Mcelwain James Stewart (307) 634-7709

Cody Christ Church **P** (549) § 825 Simpson Ave 82414-4140 (Mail to: PO Box 1718 82414-1718) Mary Caucutt David Fox Douglas Sunderland (307) 587-3849

Cokeville St Bartholomews Church **M** (6) 220 Pine St 83114 (Mail to: PO Box 365 83114-0365) (307) 279-3519

Dixon St Pauls Episcopal Church **M** (114) PO Box 68 82323-0068 (Mail to: PO Box 68 82323-0068) (307) 383-7645

Douglas Christ Episcopal Church **P** (112) 411 E Center St 82633-2438 (Mail to: PO Box 1419 82633-1419) (307) 358-5609

Dubois St Thomas Episcopal Church **P** (81) 5 S 1st St 82513 (Mail to: PO Box 735 82513-0735) Lyndie Duff (307) 455-2313

Encampment St James Church **M** (10) 812 Mccaffrey 82325 (Mail to: PO Box 685 82325-0685) (307) 710-5464

Evanston St Pauls Episcopal Church **P** (117) § 10th And Sage Sts 82930 (Mail to: PO Box 316 82931-0316) Constance Clark Suzanne Mac Ewen George Snow (307) 444-2601

Fort Washakie Shoshone Mission **M** (80) 189 Trout Creek Rd 82514 (Mail to: PO Box 175 82514-0175) Carl Means (307) 332-7925

Gillette Holy Trinity Episcopal Church **P** (110) 5101 Tanner Dr 82718-7849 (Mail to: 5101 Tanner Dr 82718-4332) Anetta Davenport (307) 682-4296

Glendo St John the Baptist Church **M** (14) § Attn Mrs John H Hughes PO Box 412 82213-0008 (Mail to: PO Box 412 82213-0412) (307) 331-8405

Glenrock Christ Episcopal Church **M** (90) § 415 W Cedar St 82637-0849 (Mail to: PO Box 298 82637-0298) Leigh Earle (307) 436-8804

Green River St Johns Episcopal Church **P** (65) 350 Mansface St 82935-4904 (Mail to: PO Box 400 82935-0321) (307) 875-3419

Hartville Our Saviour Church **M** (10) 9 Lincoln St 82215 (Mail to: PO Box 64 82215-0064) Rex Martin William Walker (307) 836-2321

Jackson Chapel of the Transfiguration **SC** 170 N Glenwood 83001 (Mail to: PO Box 1690 83001-1690) (307) 733-2603

Jackson St Johns Episcopal Church **P** (1046) § 170 N Glenwood St 83001-8761 (Mail to: PO Box 1690 83001-1690) James Bartz Mary Erickson William Helms Brian Nystrom (307) 733-2603

Kaycee All Souls Episcopal Church **M** (34) 414 Sullivan St 82639 (Mail to: PO Box 12 82639-0012) (307) 738-2416

Kemmerer St James Episcopal Church **M** (67) 506 Cedar Ave 83101-3015 (Mail to: 506 Cedar Ave 83101-3015) Walt Seeley (307) 877-3652

Kinnear Holy Nativity Church **M** (17) 10925 US Hwy 26 82516-0160 (Mail to: PO Box 160 82516-0160) Sally Bub

Lander Our Father's House **M** (207) 3 Saint Michael Cir 82520-9373 (Mail to: PO Box 8610 82520-8060) Patricia Bergie (307) 332-2660

Lander Trinity Episcopal Church **P** (64) 806 S 3rd St 82520-3712 (Mail to: 860 S 3rd St 82520-3712) Terry Robeson Walt Seeley (307) 332-5977

✠ **Laramie** St Matthews Epis Cathedral **O** (298) 104 S 4th St 82070 (Mail to: 104 S 4th St 82070-3102) Jami Anderson Candice Corrigan Paul Mottl Richard Naumann (307) 742-6608

Lusk St Georges Episcopal Church **P** (71) 120 W 5th St 82225-5048 (Mail to: PO Box 38 82225-0038) (307) 334-2870

Medicine Bow St Lukes Church **M** (15) 220 Pine Street 82329 (Mail to: PO Box 23 82329-0085) (307) 745-8472

Meeteetse St Andrews Episcopal Church **M** (49) 1116 Park Ave 82433 (Mail to: PO Box 88 82433-0088) (307) 868-2534

Newcastle Christ Episcopal Church **M** (26) 310 S Summit Ave 82701-0519 (Mail to: PO Box 519 82701-0519) (307) 746-9684

Pinedale St Andrews in the Pines **P** (271) 524 West Pine St 82941 (Mail to: PO Box 847 82941-0847) Melinda Bobo Raleigh Denison (307) 367-2674

Powell St Johns Episcopal Church **M** (97) 308 Mountain View St 82435-2231 (Mail to: PO Box 846 82435-0846) Megan Nickles (307) 754-4000

Rawlins St Thomas Episcopal Church **P** (22) 6th And Pine Sts 82301 (Mail to: PO Box 608 82301-0608) Karen Buckingham (307) 324-5447

Riverton St James Episcopal Church **P** (102) § 519 E Park Ave 82501-3652 (Mail to: 519 E Park Ave 82501-3652) (307) 856-2369

Rock Springs Church of the Holy Communion **P** (160) 205 2nd St 82901 (Mail to: PO Box 567 82902-0567) (307) 362-3002

Saratoga St Barnabas Episcopal Church **M** (25) 204 W Main Ave 82331-5171 (Mail to: PO Box 250 82331-0250) Margaret Hotchkiss Margaret Hotchkiss (307) 326-8514

Sheridan St Peters Episcopal Church **P** (707) One S Tschirgi St 82801 (Mail to: 1 S Tschirgi St 82801-4229) Joel Dingman John Meyer (307) 674-7655

Sundance Good Shepherd Episcopal Church **M** (40) 120 N 6th St 82729-5044 (Mail to: Attn: Norma Lambert Treas PO Box 246 82729-0246) Katherine Moore (307) 283-1863

Thermopolis Holy Trinity Episcopal Church **P** (88) § 642 Arapahoe St 82443-2712 (Mail to: PO Box 950 82443-0950) Anetta Davenport (307) 864-3629

Torrington All Saints Episcopal Church **P** (133) 2601 Main St 82240-1925 (Mail to: 2601 Main St 82240-1925) Ellen Carleton (307) 532-5495

Wheatland All Saints Episcopal Church **P** (160) § 605 11th Street 82201-2805 (Mail to: PO Box 997 82201-0997) Lori Modesitt Jill Zimmerschied (307) 322-9067

Worland St Albans Episcopal Church **P** (79) § 1126 US Highway 16 82401-3011 (Mail to: PO Box 84 82401-0084) David Mcelwain (307) 347-4704

Wright St Francis On The Prairie Church **M** (33) 357 Willow Creek Dr 82732-5097 (Mail to: PO Box 161 82732-0161) Sally Boyd (307) 464-0028

The Succession of American Bishops

See end of list for lettered entries.

		Consecrators			Born	Date Consecrated	Died
1	SEABURY SAMUEL	AAA	AAB	AAC	1729	1784	1796
2	WHITE WILLIAM	AAD	AAE	AAF	1748	1787	1836
3	PROVOOST SAMUEL	AAD	AAE	AAF	1742	1787	1815
4	MADISON JAMES	AAG	AAD	AAH	1749	1790	1812
5	CLAGGETT THOMAS JOHN	3	1	2	1743	1792	1816
6	SMITH ROBERT	2	3	4	1732	1795	1801
7	BASS EDWARD	2	3	5	1726	1797	1803
8	JARVIS ABRAHAM	2	3	7	1739	1797	1813
9	MOORE BENJAMIN	2	5	8	1748	1801	1816
10	PARKER SAMUEL	2	5	8	1744	1804	1804
11	HOBART JOHN HENRY	2	3	8	1775	1811	1830
12	GRISWOLD ALEXANDER V	2	3	8	1766	1811	1843
13	DEHON THEODORE	2	8	11	1776	1812	1817
14	MOORE RICHARD C	2	11	12	1762	1814	1841
15	KEMP JAMES	2	11	14	1764	1814	1827
16	CROES JOHN	2	11	15	1762	1815	1832
17	BOWEN NATHANIEL	2	11	15	1779	1818	1839
18	CHASE PHILANDER	2	11	15	1775	1819	1852
19	BROWNELL THOMAS C	2	11	12	1779	1819	1865
20	RAVENSCROFT JOHN S	2	12	15	1772	1823	1830
21	ONDERDONK HENRY U	2	11	15	1789	1827	1858
22	MEADE WILLIAM	2	11	12	1789	1829	1862
23	STONE WILLIAM MURRAY	2	14	21	1779	1830	1838
24	ONDERDONK BENJAMIN T	2	19	21	1791	1830	1861
25	IVES LEVI SILLIMAN	2	21	24	1797	1831	1867
26	HOPKINS JOHN HENRY	2	12	17	1792	1832	1868
27	SMITH BENJAMIN B	2	19	21	1794	1832	1884
28	MCILVAINE CHARLES P	2	12	22	1799	1832	1873
29	DOANE GEORGE W	2	24	25	1799	1832	1859
30	OTEY JAMES HERVEY	2	21	24	1800	1834	1863
31	KEMPER JACKSON	2	14	18	1789	1835	1870
32	MCCOSKRY SAMUEL ALLEN	21	29	31	1804	1836	1886
33	POLK LEONIDAS	22	27	28	1806	1838	1864
34	DELANCEY WILLIAM H	12	21	24	1797	1839	1865
35	GADSDEN CHRISTOPHER E	12	29	32	1785	1840	1852
36	WHITTINGHAM WILLIAM R	12	14	24	1805	1840	1879
37	ELLIOT STEPHEN	22	25	35	1806	1841	1866
38	LEE ALFRED	12	14	18	1807	1841	1887
39	JOHNS JOHN	12	22	25	1796	1842	1876
40	EASTBURN MANTON	12	19	24	1801	1842	1872
41	HENSHAW JOHN P K	19	24	26	1792	1843	1852
42	CHASE CARLTON	18	19	24	1794	1844	1870
43	COBBS NICHOLAS HAMNER	18	22	28	1795	1844	1861
44	HAWKS CICERO STEPHENS	18	31	32	1812	1844	1868
45	BOONE WILLIAM JONES	18	29	30	1811	1844	1864
46	FREEMAN GEORGE W	18	31	33	1789	1844	1858
47	SOUTHGATE HORATIO	18	36	37	1812	1844	1894
48	POTTER ALONZO	18	19	29	1800	1845	1865
49	BURGESS GEORGE	18	19	40	1809	1847	1866
50	UPFOLD GEORGE	27	28	31	1796	1849	1872
51	GREEN WILLIAM MERCER	30	33	43	1798	1850	1887
52	PAYNE JOHN	22	38	39	1815	1851	1874
53	RUTLEDGE FRANCIS H	35	37	43	1799	1851	1866
54	WILLIAMS JOHN	19	26	34	1817	1851	1899
55	WHITEHOUSE HENRY JOHN	19	38	40	1803	1851	1874
56	WAINWRIGHT JONATHAN M	19	29	31	1792	1852	1854
57	DAVIS THOMAS F	19	26	27	1804	1853	1871
58	ATKINSON THOMAS	19	28	29	1807	1853	1881
59	KIP WILLIAM INGRAHAM	31	38	45	1811	1853	1893
60	SCOTT THOMAS FIELDING	37	43	57	1807	1854	1867
61	LEE HENRY WASHINGTON	26	32	34	1815	1854	1874
62	POTTER HORATIO	19	26	29	1802	1854	1887
63	CLARK THOMAS MARCH	19	26	29	1812	1854	1903
64	BOWMAN SAMUEL	31	34	38	1800	1858	1861
65	GREGG ALEXANDER	26	27	30	1819	1859	1893
66	ODENHEIMER WILLIAM H	22	32	39	1817	1859	1879

		Consecrators			Born	Cons.	Died
67	BEDELL GREGORY T	22	28	39	1817	1859	1892
68	WHIPPLE HENRY B	31	34	43	1822	1859	1901
69	LAY HENRY C	22	28	33	1823	1859	1885
70	TALBOT JOSEPH C	31	27	44	1816	1860	1883
71	STEVENS WILLIAM B	26	38	48	1815	1862	1887
72	WILMER RICHARD H	22	37	39	1816	1862	1900
73	VAIL THOMAS H	31	55	61	1812	1864	1889
74	COXE ARTHUR CLEVELAND	26	49	58	1818	1865	1896
75	QUINTARD CHARLES T	26	49	58	1824	1865	1898
76	CLARKSON ROBERT H	26	31	32	1826	1865	1884
77	RANDALL GEORGE M	26	27	40	1810	1865	1873
78	KERFOOT JOHN B	26	28	36	1816	1866	1881
79	WILLIAMS CHANNING M	26	38	39	1829	1866	1910
80	WILMER JOSEPH P B	26	51	72	1812	1866	1878
81	CUMMINS GEORGE D	26	27	61	1822	1866	1876
82	ARMITAGE WILLIAM E	31	32	61	1830	1866	1873
83	NEELY HENRY A	26	54	62	1830	1867	1899
84	TUTTLE DANIEL S	26	62	66	1837	1867	1923
85	YOUNG JOHN F	26	52	65	1820	1867	1885
86	BECKWITH JOHN W	51	58	72	1831	1868	1890
87	WHITTLE FRANCIS M	39	38	67	1823	1868	1902
88	BISSELL WILLIAM H A	32	54	62	1814	1868	1893
89	ROBERTSON CHARLES F	27	32	39	1835	1868	1886
90	MORRIS BENJAMIN W	38	66	73	1819	1868	1906
91	LITTLEJOHN ABRAM N	62	39	66	1824	1869	1901
92	DOANE WILLIAM C	62	66	83	1832	1869	1913
93	HUNTINGTON FREDERIC D	27	40	62	1819	1869	1904
94	WHITAKER OZI W	28	38	40	1830	1869	1911
95	PIERCE HENRY N	51	55	72	1820	1870	1899
96	NILES WILLIAM W	27	54	83	1832	1870	1914
97	PINKNEY WILLIAM	27	39	58	1810	1870	1883
98	HOWE WILLIAM B W	27	36	57	1823	1871	1894
99	HOWE MARK A DE W	27	28	38	1809	1871	1895
100	HARE WILLIAM H	27	38	54	1838	1873	1909
101	AUER JOHN GOTTLIEB	27	38	52	1832	1873	1874
102	PADDOCK BENJAMIN H	27	38	54	1828	1873	1891
103	LYMAN THEODORE B	36	58	69	1815	1873	1893
104	SPALDING JOHN F	32	67	70	1828	1873	1902
105	WELLES EDWARD R	27	54	58	1830	1874	1888
106	ELLIOTT ROBERT W B	65	72	75	1840	1874	1887
A	HOLLY JAMES THEODORE	27	38	62	1829	1874	1911
107	WINGFIELD JOHN H D	39	58	69	1833	1874	1898
108	GARRETT ALEXANDER C	76	84	100	1832	1874	1924
109	ADAMS WILLIAM F	51	80	86	1833	1875	1920
110	DUDLEY THOMAS U	27	39	71	1837	1875	1904
111	SCARBOROUGH JOHN	62	71	78	1831	1875	1914
112	GILLESPIE GEORGE D	32	70	88	1819	1875	1909
113	JAGGAR THOMAS A	27	38	62	1839	1875	1912
114	MC LAREN WILLIAM E	32	67	68	1831	1875	1905
115	BROWN JOHN H H	62	88	92	1831	1875	1888
116	PERRY WILLIAM S	71	74	78	1832	1876	1898
117	PENICK CHARLES C	58	87	97	1843	1877	1914
118	SCHERESCHEWSKY SAMUEL	27	62	67	1831	1877	1906
119	BURGESS ALEXANDER	27	54	63	1819	1878	1901
120	PETERKIN GEORGE W	67	78	87	1841	1878	1916
121	SEYMOUR GEORGE F	62	66	69	1829	1878	1906
B	RILEY HENRY CHAUNCEY	38	67	71		1879	1904
122	HARRIS SAMUEL S	72	70	76	1841	1879	1888
123	STARKEY THOMAS A	63	73	91	1818	1880	1903
124	GALLEHER JOHN N	51	71	89	1839	1880	1891
125	DUNLOP GEORGE K	68	89	102	1830	1880	1888
126	BREWER LEGH R	93	84	88	1839	1880	1916
127	PADDOCK JOHN A	27	38	62	1825	1880	1894
128	WHITEHEAD CORTLANDT	71	67	99	1842	1882	1922
129	THOMPSON HUGH M	51	72	122	1830	1883	1902
130	KNICKERBACKER DAVID B	74	89	103	1833	1883	1894
131	POTTER HENRY C	27	54	63	1835	1883	1908
132	RANDOLPH ALFRED M	38	98	110	1836	1883	1918
133	WALKER WILLIAM D	63	74	76	1839	1883	1917
134	WATSON ALFRED A	51	83	98	1818	1884	1905
135	BOONE WILLIAM J	79	AAK	AAL	1846	1884	1891

		Consecrators			Born	Cons.	Died
136	RULISON NELSON S	38	99	114	1842	1884	1897
137	PARET WILLIAM	38	71	99	1826	1885	1911
138	WORTHINGTON GEORGE	74	100	114	1840	1885	1908
139	FERGUSON SAMUEL DAVID	38	71	91	1842	1885	1916
140	WEED EDWIN GARDNER	75	98	106	1847	1886	1924
141	GILBERT MAHLON NORRIS	38	67	68	1848	1886	1900
142	THOMAS ELISHA SMITH	68	73	84	1834	1887	1895
143	TALBOT ETHELBERT	68	73	84	1848	1887	1928
144	JOHNSTON JAMES S	72	110	122	1843	1888	1924
145	LEONARD ABIEL	73	75	84	1848	1888	1903
146	COLEMAN LEIGHTON	99	94	109	1837	1888	1907
147	KENDRICK JOHN MILLS	84	110	130	1836	1889	1911
148	VINCENT BOYD	104	110	117	1845	1889	1935
149	KNIGHT CYRUS F	114	116	119	1831	1889	1891
150	GRAFTON CHARLES C	114	119	121	1832	1889	1912
151	LEONARD WILLIAM A	54	68	92	1848	1889	1930
152	DAVIES THOMAS F	54	68	84	1831	1889	1905
153	GRAVES ANSON ROGERS	84	100	119	1842	1890	1931
154	NICHOLS WILLIAM FORD	54	75	83	1849	1890	1924
155	ATWILL EDWARD ROBERT	84	114	121	1840	1890	1911
156	JACKSON HENRY M	72	98	120	1848	1891	1900
157	SESSUMS DAVIS	75	84	108	1858	1891	1929
158	BROOKS PHILLIPS	54	63	68	1835	1891	1893
159	NICHOLSON ISAAC LEA	114	94	109	1844	1891	1906
160	NELSON CLELAND K	75	98	103	1852	1892	1917
161	HALE CHARLES REUBEN	116	121	133	1837	1892	1900
162	KINSOLVING GEORGE H	72	75	94	1849	1892	1928
163	WELLS LEMUEL HENRY	54	83	90	1841	1892	1936
164	GRAY WILLIAM CRANE	75	110	140	1835	1892	1919
165	BROOKE FRANCIS KEY	84	95	104	1852	1893	1918
166	BARKER WILLIAM MORRIS	90	104	114	1854	1893	1901
167	MCKIM JOHN	91	103	110	1852	1893	1936
168	GRAVES FREDERICK R	91	103	110	1858	1893	1940
169	CAPERS ELLISON	103	134	140	1837	1893	1908
170	GAILOR THOMAS FRANK	75	110	116	1856	1893	1935
171	LAWRENCE WILLIAM	54	63	83	1850	1893	1941
172	CHESHIRE JOSEPH B	103	134	169	1850	1893	1932
173	HALL ARTHUR CRAWSHAY	83	96	146	1847	1894	1930
174	NEWTON JOHN B	87	110	120	1839	1894	1897
175	WHITE JOHN HAZEN	84	114	128	1849	1895	1925
176	MILLSPAUGH FRANK R	68	84	104	1848	1895	1916
177	ROWE PETER TRIMBLE	92	94	123	1856	1895	1942
178	BURTON LEWIS WILLIAM	110	120	132	1852	1896	1940
179	JOHNSON JOSEPH H	152	138	143	1847	1896	1928
180	SATTERLEE HENRY YATES	74	93	110	1843	1896	1908
181	WILLIAMS GERSHOM MOTT	84	75	114	1857	1896	1923
182	MORRISON JAMES DOW	92	93	111	1844	1897	1934
183	BREWSTER CHAUNCEY B	91	92	94	1848	1897	1941
184	GIBSON ROBERT A	87	117	120	1846	1897	1919
185	MC VICKAR WILLIAM N	92	94	113	1843	1898	1910
186	BROWN WILLIAM M	114	121	128	1855	1898	1937
187	HORNER JUNIUS MOORE	172	134	169	1859	1898	1933
C	KINSOLVING LUCIEN LEE	110	92	111	1862	1899	1929
188	MORELAND WILLIAM HALL	154	145	147	1861	1899	1946
189	EDSALL SAMUEL COOK	114	121	133	1860	1899	1917
190	MORRISON THEODORE N	114	121	133	1850	1899	1929
191	FUNSTEN JAMES BOWEN	84	94	117	1856	1899	1918
192	FRANCIS JOSEPH M	114	121	152	1862	1899	1939
193	WILLIAMS ARTHUR L	138	104	153	1853	1899	1919
194	GRAVATT WILLIAM L	87	117	120	1858	1899	1942
195	PARTRIDGE SIDNEY C	167	118	168	1857	1900	1930
196	CODMAN ROBERT	96	92	93	1859	1900	1915
197	ANDERSON CHARLES P	114	112	121	1863	1900	1930
198	BARNWELL ROBERT W	129	140	144	1849	1900	1902
199	WELLER REGINALD H	150	114	159	1857	1900	1935
200	TAYLOR FREDERICK W	121	150	159	1853	1901	1903
201	MANN CAMERON	84	143	155	1851	1901	1932
202	BRENT CHARLES H	92	131	171	1862	1901	1929
203	KEATOR FREDERIC W	114	100	159	1855	1902	1924
204	BURGESS FREDERICK	131	92	111	1853	1902	1925
205	INGLE JAMES A	168	167	195	1867	1902	1903

		Consecrators			Born	Cons.	Died
206	VINTON ALEXANDER H	152	93	173	1852	1902	1911
207	OLMSTED CHARLES S	84	144	145	1853	1902	1918
208	MACKAY SMITH A	92	111	128	1850	1902	1911
209	VAN BUREN JAMES H	120	171	173	1850	1902	1917
210	RESTARICK HENRY B	154	113	147	1854	1902	1933
211	OLMSTED CHARLES T	93	96	131	1842	1902	1924
212	BECKWITH CHARLES M	110	108	157	1851	1902	1928
213	GRISWOLD SHELDON M	92	121	133	1861	1903	1930
214	BRATTON THEODORE D	110	140	144	1862	1903	1944
215	LINES EDWIN S	84	92	111	1845	1903	1927
216	FAWCETT EDWARD	84	121	150	1865	1904	1935
217	GREER DAVID H	131	92	94	1844	1904	1919
218	NELSON RICHARD H	92	94	133	1859	1904	1931
219	OSBORNE EDWARD W	121	131	150	1845	1904	1926
220	STRANGE ROBERT	169	132	172	1857	1904	1914
221	ROOTS LOGAN H	168	167	171	1870	1904	1945
222	SPALDING FRANKLIN S	84	94	111	1865	1904	1914
223	AVES HENRY D	108	144	157	1853	1904	1936
224	KNIGHT ALBION W	84	140	157	1859	1904	1936
225	WOODCOCK CHARLES E	84	121	138	1854	1905	1940
226	DARLINGTON JAMES H	94	121	128	1856	1905	1930
227	JOHNSON FREDERIC F	84	94	113	1866	1905	1943
228	WILLIAMS CHARLES D	84	113	148	1860	1906	1923
229	PARKER EDWARD M	96	171	173	1855	1906	1925
230	MC CORMICK JOHN N	84	112	160	1863	1906	1939
231	WEBB WILLIAM W	159	150	175	1857	1906	1933
232	SCADDING CHARLES	84	121	128	1861	1906	1914
233	TUCKER BEVERLEY D	132	120	172	1846	1906	1930
234	GUERRY WILLIAM A	84	140	170	1861	1907	1928
235	PADDOCK ROBERT L	84	131	180	1869	1907	1939
236	KNIGHT EDWARD J	111	143	208	1864	1907	1908
237	ROBINSON HENRY D	84	150	189	1859	1908	1913
238	REESE FREDERICK F	160	140	170	1854	1908	1936
239	KINSMAN FREDERICK J	84	94	96	1868	1908	1944
240	HARDING ALFRED	84	109	111	1852	1909	1923
241	THOMAS NATHANIEL S	84	94	111	1867	1909	1937
242	BREWSTER BENJAMIN	84	154	183	1860	1909	1941
243	MURRAY JOHN G	137	109	132	1857	1909	1929
244	LLOYD ARTHUR S	84	120	132	1857	1909	1936
245	BEECHER GEORGE A	84	108	153	1868	1910	1951
246	TEMPLE EDWARD A	84	108	144	1867	1910	1924
247	PERRY JAMES D	84	126	171	1871	1911	1947
248	ATWOOD JULIUS W	171	173	183	1857	1911	1945
249	THURSTON THEODORE P	84	126	165	1867	1911	1941
250	SANFORD LOUIS C	154	179	188	1867	1911	1948
251	BURCH CHARLES S	217	92	111	1855	1911	1920
252	ISRAEL ROGERS	128	143	148	1854	1911	1921
253	WINCHESTER JAMES R	84	140	162	1852	1911	1941
254	DAVIES THOMAS F	84	171	183	1872	1911	1936
255	RHINELANDER PHILIP M	84	128	171	1869	1911	1939
256	GARLAND THOMAS J	84	111	128	1866	1911	1931
257	TOLL WILLIAM E	84	151	175	1843	1911	1915
258	TUCKER HENRY ST G	167	AAM	AAN	1874	1912	1959
259	HUNTINGTON DANIEL T	168	221	AAO	1868	1912	1950
260	BILLER GEORGE JR	84	126	165	1874	1912	1915
261	LONGLEY HARRY S	84	190	193	1868	1912	1944
262	MC ELWAIN FRANK A	84	189	193	1875	1912	1957
263	WEEKS WILLIAM F	173	218	229	1859	1913	1914
264	REESE THEODORE I	148	151	171	1873	1913	1931
265	BABCOCK SAMUEL G	171	196	202	1851	1913	1942
266	COLMORE CHARLES B	84	140	170	1879	1913	1950
267	TYLER JOHN P	84	120	132	1862	1914	1931
268	DU MOULIN FRANK	151	128	148	1870	1914	1947
269	HOWDEN FREDERICK S	84	143	148	1869	1914	1940
270	CAPERS WILLIAM T	84	140	144	1867	1914	1943
271	BROWN WILLIAM C	84	132	184	1861	1914	1927
272	FABER WILLIAM F	84	126	151	1860	1914	1934
273	HUNTING GEORGE C	84	154	179	1871	1914	1924
274	JONES PAUL	84	154	179	1880	1914	1941
275	DARST THOMAS C	84	172	187	1875	1915	1948
276	SUMNER WALTER T	197	151	175	1873	1915	1935

		Consecrators			Born	Cons.	Died
277	HULSE HIRAM RICHARD	217	151	163	1868	1915	1938
278	MATTHEWS PAUL	148	151	192	1866	1915	1954
279	PAGE HERMAN	84	163	171	1866	1915	1942
280	BLISS GEORGE YEMENS	173	196	229	1864	1915	1924
281	FISKE CHARLES	84	199	211	1868	1915	1942
282	STEARLY WILSON REIFF	215	128	143	1869	1915	1941
283	ACHESON EDWARD C	183	171	215	1858	1915	1934
284	WISE JAMES	84	162	177	1875	1916	1939
285	BURLESON HUGH LATIMER	84	171	189	1865	1916	1933
286	JOHNSON IRVING PEAKE	84	189	193	1866	1917	1947
287	TOURET FRANK HALE	84	270	272	1875	1917	1945
288	SHERWOOD GRANVILLE H	84	190	193	1878	1917	1923
289	SAPHORE EDWIN W	84	162	195	1854	1917	1944
290	THOMSON ARTHUR C	84	132	172	1871	1917	1946
291	MOORE HARRY TUNIS	84	108	162	1874	1917	1955
292	MIKELL HENRY JUDAH	170	140	164	1873	1917	1942
293	REMINGTON WILLIAM P	84	228	249	1879	1918	1963
294	SAGE JOHN CHARLES	84	190	193	1866	1918	1919
295	HARRIS ROBERT LE ROY	84	151	175	1874	1918	1948
296	DEMBY EDWARD THOMAS	84	170	195	1869	1918	1957
297	QUIN CLINTON SIMON	84	223	225	1883	1918	1956
298	DELANY HENRY B	172	233	275	1858	1918	1928
299	GREEN WILLIAM M	84	157	170	1876	1919	1942
300	SHAYLER ERNEST V	203	163	272	1868	1919	1947
301	BEATTY TROY	84	170	253	1866	1919	1922
302	PARSONS EDWARD L	154	179	188	1868	1919	1960
303	OVERS WALTER H	84	226	252	1870	1919	1934
304	MORRIS JAMES C	84	170	224	1870	1920	1944
305	MOSHER GOUVERNEUR F	168	259	258	1871	1920	1941
306	JETT ROBERT C	84	233	194	1865	1920	1950
307	MOULTON ARTHUR W	84	171	173	1873	1920	1962
308	DAVENPORT GEORGE W	84	233	151	1870	1920	1956
309	STEVENS WILLIAM B	179	154	167	1884	1920	1947
310	FERRIS DAVID L	202	128	173	1864	1920	1947
311	COOK PHILIP	84	143	201	1875	1920	1938
312	FOX HERBERT H H	84	184	262	1871	1920	1943
313	BENNETT GRANVILLE G	84	151	192	1882	1920	1975
314	MIZE ROBERT HERBERT	84	213	245	1870	1921	1956
315	FINLAY KIRKMAN GEORGE	234	172	238	1877	1921	1938
316	MANNING WILLIAM T	84	148	171	1866	1921	1949
317	INGLEY FRED	84	286	128	1878	1921	1951
318	GARDINER THEOPHILUS M	84	170	244	1870	1921	1941
319	LA MOTHE JOHN D	84	243	233	1868	1921	1928
320	WARD JOHN C	84	128	148	1873	1921	1949
321	SHIPMAN HERBERT	84	316	215	1869	1921	1930
322	PENICK EDWIN A	172	234	275	1887	1922	1959
323	MAXON JAMES M	170	216	225	1875	1922	1948
324	MC DOWELL WILLIAM G	170	210	233	1882	1922	1938
325	OLDHAM GEORGE A	218	151	316	1877	1922	1963
326	SLATTERY CHARLES L	171	233	265	1867	1922	1930
327	ROBERTS WILLIAM BLAIR	84	285	286	1881	1922	1964
328	CARSON HARRY R	84	170	316	1869	1923	1948
329	MANN ALEXANDER	201	171	215	1860	1923	1948
330	FREEMAN JAMES E	170	171	243	1866	1923	1943
331	STRIDER ROBERT E L	194	271	329	1887	1923	1969
332	STERRETT FRANK W	143	226	194	1885	1923	1976
D	FERRANDO MANUEL	170	316	244	1866	1923	1934
333	REIFSNIDER CHARLES S	167	179	151	1875	1924	1958
334	CROSS EDWARD MAKIN	262	261	330	1880	1924	1965
335	WHITE JOHN CHANLER	143	216	197	1867	1924	1956
336	COLEY EDWARD H	143	244	310	1861	1924	1949
337	JUHAN FRANK A	143	253	315	1887	1924	1967
338	SEAMAN EUGENE CECIL	170	162	270	1881	1925	1950
339	BOOTH SAMUEL B	173	229	247	1883	1925	1935
340	GILMAN ALFRED A	168	259	221	1878	1925	1966
341	ROGERS WARREN L	151	279	148	1877	1925	1938
342	GRAY CAMPBELL	199	216	231	1879	1925	1944
343	IVINS BENJAMIN F P	231	199	213	1884	1925	1962
344	HUSTON SIMEON A	162	270	309	1876	1925	1963
345	WING JOHN D	201	238	170	1882	1925	1960
346	STIRES ERNEST M	143	243	316	1866	1925	1951

		Consecrators			Born	Cons.	Died
347	CAMPBELL ROBERT E	143	170	303	1884	1925	1977
348	THOMAS WILLIAM M M	143	172	C	1878	1925	1951
349	BARNWELL MIDDLETON S	143	170	212	1882	1925	1957
350	MITCHELL WALTER	243	278	248	1876	1926	1971
351	CREIGHTON FRANK W	243	218	256	1879	1926	1948
352	NICHOLS SHIRLEY HALL	167	333	AAN	1884	1926	1964
353	DALLAS JOHN T	243	173	171	1880	1926	1961
354	HELFENSTEIN EDWARD T	243	194	233	1865	1926	1947
355	CASADY THOMAS	243	190	245	1881	1927	1958
356	THOMAS ALBERT S	243	172	214	1873	1928	1967
357	BINSTED NORMAN S	243	167	258	1890	1928	1961
358	JENKINS THOMAS	243	177	250	1871	1929	1955
359	LARNED JOHN I B	243	177	250	1883	1929	1955
360	WILSON FRANK E	243	170	197	1885	1929	1944
361	ABBOTT HENRY P A	243	178	225	1881	1929	1945
362	TAITT FRANCIS M	256	226	241	1862	1929	1943
363	STURTEVANT HARWOOD	199	213	231	1888	1929	1977
364	SCHMUCK ELMER N	197	238	241	1882	1929	1936
365	DAVIS CAMERON J	310	281	285	1873	1930	1952
366	LITTELL SAMUEL H	285	167	210	1873	1930	1967
367	ABLEWHITE HAYWARD S	285	230	279	1887	1930	1964
368	HOBSON HENRY W	148	151	194	1891	1930	1983
369	SCARLETT WILLIAM	148	227	248	1883	1930	1973
370	GOODEN ROBERT B	309	188	250	1874	1930	1976
371	STEWART GEORGE C	247	213	225	1879	1930	1940
372	SHERRILL HENRY KNOX	247	171	221	1890	1930	1980
373	GOODWIN FREDERICK D	258	194	244	1888	1930	1968
374	GILBERT CHARLES K	247	224	244	1878	1930	1958
375	SPENCER ROBERT N	270	216	227	1877	1930	1961
376	KEMERER BENJAMIN T	269	230	262	1874	1930	1960
377	WYATT BROWN HUNTER	247	310	320	1884	1931	1952
378	KEELER STEPHEN E	269	230	262	1887	1931	1956
379	BENTLEY JOHN B	247	170	177	1896	1931	1989
380	SALINAS Y VELASCO E	247	170	244	1886	1931	1968
381	BUDLONG FREDERICK G	247	183	242	1881	1931	1953
382	BARTLETT FREDERICK B	285	250	317	1882	1931	1941
383	WASHBURN BENJAMIN M	247	224	244	1887	1932	1966
384	URBAN RALPH E	247	224	278	1875	1932	1935
385	PORTER ARCHIE W N	188	250	302	1885	1933	1963
386	GRIBBIN ROBERT E	247	322	275	1887	1934	1976
387	NICHOLS JOHN WILLIAMS	AAI	168	340	1878	1934	1940
388	LUDLOW THEODORE R	247	282	311	1883	1936	1961
389	DAGWELL BENJAMIN D	278	177	250	1890	1936	1963
390	KROLL LEOPOLD	247	244	316	1874	1936	1946
391	VAN DYCK VEDDER	247	353	372	1889	1936	1960
392	REINHEIMER BARTEL H	247	281	310	1889	1936	1949
393	CLINGMAN CHARLES	247	178	225	1883	1936	1971
394	WHITTEMORE LEWIS B	247	230	342	1885	1936	1965
395	GARDNER WALLACE J	278	188	311	1883	1936	1954
396	ESSEX WILLIAM L	247	192	261	1886	1936	1959
397	ZIEGLER WINFRED H	371	177	245	1885	1936	1972
398	LAWRENCE WILLIAM A	171	247	242	1889	1937	1968
399	BEAL HARRY	309	250	370	1885	1937	1944
400	ATWILL DOUGLASS H	378	261	262	1881	1937	1960
401	FENNER GOODRICH R	284	270	286	1891	1937	1966
402	ROBERTS WILLIAM P	AAI	168	AAJ	1888	1937	1971
403	WILNER ROBERT F	305	333	AAK	1889	1938	1960
404	HERON RAYMOND A	258	171	242	1886	1938	1960
405	BROWN WILLIAM A	258	275	306	1878	1938	1965
406	CARPENTER CHARLES C J	258	214	270	1899	1938	1969
407	DANDRIDGE EDMUND P	258	214	266	1881	1938	1961
408	PHILLIPS HENRY D	258	275	292	1882	1938	1955
409	TUCKER BEVERLEY D	258	194	275	1882	1938	1969
410	PEABODY MALCOLM E	258	248	307	1888	1938	1974
411	BLOCK KARL M	302	309	358	1886	1938	1958
412	MITCHELL RICHARD B	350	214	289	1887	1938	1961
413	KIRCHHOFFER RICHARD A	258	342	349	1890	1939	1977
414	MC KINSTRY ARTHUR R	258	309	320	1894	1939	1991
415	BLANKINGSHIP A H	258	266	328	1894	1939	1975
416	BURTON SPENCE	258	247	286	1881	1939	1966
417	GRAVATT JOHN J	258	194	275	1881	1939	1965

	Consecrators			Born	Cons.	Died
418	MC CLELLAND WILLIAM	258	268	308	1883	1939	1949
419	DANIELS HENRY HEAN	312	307	344	1885	1939	1958
420	RANDALL EDWIN J	258	177	262	1869	1939	1962
421	BRINKER HOWARD R	258	245	300	1893	1940	1965
422	PITHAN ATHALICIO T	348	380	415	1898	1940	1966
423	JACKSON JOHN L	258	275	292	1884	1940	1948
424	GRAY WALTER H	258	247	381	1898	1940	1973
425	CRAIGHILL LLOYD R	402	AAI	AAL	1886	1940	1971
426	CONKLING WALLACE E	258	347	395	1896	1941	1979
427	LORING OLIVER L	258	247	391	1904	1941	1979
428	POWELL NOBLE C	258	354	330	1891	1941	1968
429	STONEY JAMES M	258	406	412	1888	1942	1965
430	RHEA FRANK A	307	334	358	1887	1942	1963
431	DE WOLFE JAMES P	258	316	346	1895	1942	1966
432	LEWIS WILLIAM F	258	307	358	1902	1942	1964
433	MASON WILEY R	258	306	373	1879	1942	1967
434	WALKER JOHN M	258	337	412	1888	1942	1951
435	HART OLIVER J	258	330	362	1892	1942	1977
436	PAGE HERMAN R	258	351	394	1892	1942	1977
437	GRAY DUNCAN M	258	214	412	1898	1943	1966
438	HEISTAND JOHN T	258	332	435	1895	1943	1979
439	WROTH EDWARD P	258	329	331	1889	1943	1946
440	JONES EVERETT H	258	401	414	1902	1943	1995
441	VOEGELI CHARLES A	258	325	383	1904	1943	1984
442	BOYNTON CHARLES F	266	343	395	1906	1944	1999
443	WALTERS SUMNER F D	258	250	309	1898	1944	1979
444	KENNEDY HARRY S	258	317	350	1901	1944	1986
445	PARDUE AUSTIN	258	365	421	1899	1944	1981
446	DUN ANGUS	258	372	368	1892	1944	1971
447	CARRUTHERS THOMAS N	258	323	356	1900	1944	1960
448	HAINES ELWOOD L	258	406	423	1893	1944	1949
449	HORSTICK WILLIAM W	258	363	420	1902	1944	1973
450	MALLETT JAMES R	343	363	395	1893	1944	1965
451	HARRIS BRAVID W	258	405	322	1896	1945	1965
452	GESNER CONRAD H	258	327	378	1901	1945	1993
453	ALDRICH DONALD B	258	251	374	1892	1945	1961
454	GOODEN REGINALD H	258	370	415	1910	1945	2003
455	LOUTTIT HENRY I	345	350	416	1903	1945	1984
456	KINSOLVING II ARTHUR	258	350	409	1894	1945	1964
457	BARRY FREDERICK L	258	325	346	1897	1945	1960
458	MASON CHARLES A	258	291	426	1904	1945	1970
459	BANYARD ALFRED L	258	383	395	1908	1945	1992
460	WRIGHT THOMAS H	258	275	428	1904	1945	1997
461	HINES JOHN E	258	297	411	1910	1945	1997
462	MOODY WILLIAM R	258	393	368	1900	1945	1986
463	EMRICH RICHARD S M	258	262	351	1910	1946	1997
464	SAWYER HAROLD E	258	320	410	1890	1946	1969
465	BARTON Ln W	258	368	378	1899	1946	1997
466	QUARTERMAN GEORGE H	258	355	401	1906	1946	2002
467	CLARK STEPHEN C	258	307	309	1892	1946	1950
468	NASH NORMAN B	372	353	398	1888	1947	1963
469	BAYNE JR STEPHEN F	372	344	424	1908	1947	1974
470	BOWEN HAROLD L	372	317	426	1886	1947	1967
471	LORING JR RICHARD T	372	335	426	1900	1947	1948
472	DONEGAN HORACE W B	372	374	468	1900	1947	1991
473	GUNN GEORGE P	372	306	405	1903	1948	1973
474	HALL CHARLES F	372	353	468	1908	1948	1992
475	MELCHER LOUIS C	372	407	417	1898	1948	1965
476	HUNTER JAMES W	372	397	440	1904	1948	1987
477	BLOY FRANCIS E I	258	302	370	1904	1948	1993
478	SCAIFE LAURISTON L	372	365	420	1907	1948	1970
479	GORDON JR WILLIAM J	372	322	379	1918	1948	1994
480	HUBBARD RUSSELL S	343	335	445	1902	1948	1972
481	CLOUGH CHARLES A	343	335	427	1903	1948	1961
482	BARTH THEODORE N	372	323	407	1898	1948	1961
483	HENRY MATTHEW G	258	408	447	1910	1948	1975
484	WEST EDWARD H	372	337	349	1906	1948	1977
485	HIGLEY WALTER M	372	336	410	1899	1948	1969
486	SHERMAN JONATHAN G	372	394	431	1907	1949	1989
487	CAMPBELL DONALD J	372	302	477	1903	1949	1973
488	JONES GIRAULT M	372	337	417	1904	1949	1998

		Consecrators			Born	Cons.	Died
489	CLAIBORNE RANDOLPH R	258	406	428	1906	1949	1986
490	GIBSON JR ROBERT F	258	373	433	1906	1949	1990
491	ARMSTRONG JOSEPH G	372	293	435	1901	1949	1964
492	St CHARLES L	372	343	426	1891	1949	1968
493	MILLER ALLEN J	428	446	464	1901	1949	1991
494	BURROUGHS NELSON M	258	368	408	1899	1949	1998
495	KRISCHKE EGMONT M	475	379	422	1909	1950	1972
496	STARK DUDLEY S	372	368	378	1894	1950	1971
497	WELLES EDWARD R	372	375	428	1907	1950	1991
498	SMITH GORDON V	372	327	394	1906	1950	1997
499	CAMPBELL WILBURN C	258	331	373	1910	1950	1997
500	BURRILL G FRANCIS	258	291	432	1906	1950	2001
501	SHIRES HENRY H	372	370	411	1886	1950	1961
502	BAKER RICHARD H	372	322	428	1897	1951	1981
503	LICHTENBERGER A C	372	340	369	1900	1951	1968
504	HATCH ROBERT M	372	381	424	1910	1951	2009
505	WATSON RICHARD S	372	307	430	1902	1951	1987
506	SWIFT A ERVINE	372	379	442	1913	1951	2003
507	EMERY RICHARD R	372	378	424	1910	1951	1964
508	RICHARDS DAVID E	372	347	451	1921	1951	2018
509	BRAM MARTIN J	455	458	416	1897	1951	1956
510	POWELL CHILTON	372	355	421	1911	1951	1994
511	WALTHOUR JOHN B	372	322	435	1904	1952	1952
512	HALLOCK DONALD H V	343	426	363	1908	1952	1996
513	KELLOGG HAMILTON H	372	297	378	1899	1952	1977
514	CRITTENDEN WILLIAM	372	368	409	1908	1952	2003
515	NOLAND IVESON B	488	412	437	1916	1952	1975
516	OGILBY LYMAN C	357	403	424	1922	1953	1990
517	HIGGINS JOHN S	372	313	378	1904	1953	1992
518	WARNECKE FREDERICK J	372	332	383	1906	1953	1977
519	BRADY WILLIAM H	363	481	343	1912	1953	1996
520	STARK LELAND	372	378	383	1907	1953	1986
521	MURRAY GEORGE M	406	393	498	1919	1953	2006
522	MC NEIL DUDLEY B	372	394	470	1908	1953	1977
523	THOMAS WILLIAM S	445	435	478	1901	1953	1986
524	COLE CLARENCE ALFRED	322	417	447	1909	1953	1963
525	KINSOLVING III C J	429	401	456	1904	1953	1984
526	MOSLEY J BROOKE	372	368	414	1915	1953	1988
527	MARMION CHARLES G	372	393	458	1905	1954	2000
528	MARMION WILLIAM H	372	408	414	1907	1954	2002
529	HARTE JOSEPH M	500	297	510	1914	1954	1999
530	MINNIS JOSEPH S	470	421	449	1904	1954	1977
531	CROWLEY ARCHIE H	372	436	468	1907	1954	1996
532	STUART ALBERT R	372	347	488	1906	1954	1973
533	STOKES JR ANSON P	372	368	468	1905	1954	1986
534	VANDERHORST JOHN	372	407	482	1912	1955	1980
535	DOLL HARRY L	372	373	428	1903	1955	1984
536	DICUS RICHARD E	440	350	412	1910	1955	1996
537	GODDARD FREDERICK P	297	440	461	1903	1955	1983
538	BROWN ROBERT R	412	414	373	1910	1955	1994
539	LEWIS ARNOLD M	372	337	484	1904	1956	1994
540	CARMAN JAMES W F	372	389	293	1903	1956	1979
541	HONAMAN EARL M	372	438	435	1904	1956	1982
542	SIMOES PLINIO L	475	379	495	1915	1956	1994
543	TURNER EDWARD C	401	470	421	1915	1956	1997
544	CLEMENTS JAMES P	372	297	461	1911	1956	1977
545	MOSES WILLIAM F	372	455	345	1898	1956	1961
546	STERLING CHANDLER W	419	421	530	1911	1956	1984
547	LAWRENCE FREDERIC C	372	398	533	1899	1956	1989
548	FOOTE NORMAN L	372	430	449	1915	1957	1974
549	CRAINE JOHN P	413	411	368	1911	1957	1977
550	HADEN CLARENCE R	372	385	497	1910	1957	2000
551	SAUCEDO JOSE G	372	380	440	1924	1958	
552	MC NAIRY PHILIP F	372	368	513	1911	1958	1989
553	ESQUIROL JOHN HENRY	372	424	504	1900	1958	1970
554	CORRIGAN DANIEL	372	530	449	1900	1958	1994
555	PIKE JAMES ALBERT	372	302	472	1913	1958	1969
556	ROSE DAVID S	372	473	405	1913	1958	1997
557	LICKFIELD FRANCIS W	500	396	519	1908	1958	1997
558	MACADIE DONALD	383	520	503	1899	1958	1963
559	BLANCHARD ROGER W	372	368	484	1909	1958	1998

		Consecrators			Born	Cons.	Died
560	SHERRILL EDMUND K	372	495	542	1925	1959	2015
561	BROWN ALLEN W	503	457	410	1908	1959	1990
562	CABANBAN BENITO C	516	444	587	1911	1959	1990
563	CADIGAN GEORGE L	503	496	538	1910	1959	2005
564	CREIGHTON WILLIAM F	503	446	480	1909	1959	1987
565	MILLARD G RICHARD	503	432	443	1914	1960	2018
566	WRIGHT WILLIAM G	503	432	443	1904	1960	1973
567	BENNISON SR CHARLES E	503	394	470	1917	1960	2004
568	KELLOGG PAUL A	503	441	506	1910	1960	1999
569	WETMORE JAMES STUART	503	472	478	1915	1960	1999
570	CURTIS IVOL I	503	370	477	1908	1960	1994
571	CHILTON SAMUEL B	503	373	490	1900	1960	1984
572	FRASER JR THOMAS A	503	373	502	1915	1960	1989
573	DE WITT ROBERT L	503	446	468	1916	1960	2003
574	THAYER EDWIN B	530	470	498	1905	1960	1989
575	TEMPLE GRAY	503	424	427	1914	1961	1999
576	BUTTERFIELD HARVEY D	503	424	427	1908	1961	1998
577	RAUSCHER RUSSELL T	503	421	510	1908	1961	1989
578	GILSON CHARLES P	503	444	402	1899	1961	1980
579	GONZALEZ AGUEROS R	503	415	379	1906	1961	1966
580	BROWN JR DILLARD H	503	446	564	1912	1961	1969
581	ALLIN JOHN M	503	488	437	1921	1961	1998
582	HUTCHENS JOSEPH W	424	427	553	1913	1961	1979
583	DUNCAN JAMES L	503	455	534	1913	1961	2000
584	HARGRAVE WILLIAM L	503	455	424	1903	1961	1975
585	MAC LEAN CHARLES W	431	472	486	1903	1962	1985
586	SANDERS WILLIAM E	503	534	532	1919	1962	2021
587	MONTGOMERY JAMES WINCHESTER	503	500	492	1921	1962	2019
588	CHAMBERS ALBERT A	503	472	450	1906	1962	1993
589	MCCREA THEODORE H	503	458	500	1908	1962	1986
590	BURGESS JOHN MELVILLE	503	526	446	1909	1962	2003
591	LONGID EDWARD G	503	516	533	1908	1963	1993
592	PERSELL JR CHARLES B	503	561	478	1909	1963	1988
593	MILLS CEDRIC EARL	428	379	506	1903	1963	1992
594	BARRETT GEORGE W	472	496	554	1908	1963	2000
595	PUTNAM JR FREDERICK W	538	510	543	1917	1963	2007
596	KLEIN WALTER C	450	500	549	1904	1963	1980
597	PINCKNEY JOHN A	483	356	417	1905	1963	1972
598	MOORE JR PAUL	503	549	564	1919	1964	2003
599	ROMERO LEONARDO	503	551	506	1930	1964	1986
600	SAUCEDO MELCHOR	503	551	506	1920	1964	
601	RATH GEORGE E	503	472	520	1913	1964	1995
602	COLE JR NED	503	410	485	1917	1964	2000
603	REED DAVID B	503	454	529	1927	1964	
604	BAILEY SCOTT FIELD	461	466	537	1916	1964	2005
605	MYERS C KILMER	549	463	531	1914	1964	1981
606	RUSACK ROBERT C	477	370	570	1926	1964	1986
607	SELWAY GEORGE R	549	529	436	1905	1964	1989
608	REUS FROYLAN F	503	506	442	1919	1964	2008
609	WONG JAMES CHANG L	AAK	AAO	AAP		1960	1970
610	MASUDA GEORGE T	452	476	546	1913	1965	1995
611	RICHARDSON J MILTON	461	604	537	1913	1965	1980
612	GROSS HAL R	461	540	550	1914	1965	2002
613	DAVIDSON WILLIAM	461	466	610	1919	1966	2006
614	VAN DUZER ALBERT W	461	459	486	1917	1966	1999
615	GATES JR WILLIAM F	461	534	586	1912	1966	1987
616	BARNDS WILLIAM PAUL	461	458	589	1904	1966	1973
617	STEVENSON DEAN T	461	438	518	1915	1966	1994
618	HALL ROBERT BRUCE	461	490	500	1921	1966	1985
619	TAYLOR GEORGE A	461	493	414	1903	1966	1978
620	MARTIN RICHARD B	461	486	478	1913	1967	2012
621	BURT JOHN HARRIS	461	494	409	1918	1967	2009
622	MOORE JR WILLIAM M	532	572	502	1916	1967	1998
623	WYATT JOHN R	461	529	605	1913	1967	2004
624	SPEARS JR ROBERT R	461	472	497	1918	1967	2008
625	WOOD JR MILTON L	461	406	489	1922	1967	2015
626	KELLER CHRISTOPH JR	461	581	538	1916	1967	1995
627	FREY WILLIAM C	461	508	608	1930	1967	2020
628	MCNAIR EDWARD	461	477	550	1913	1967	1986
629	HANCHETT EDWIN LANI	461	444	540	1919	1967	1975
630	BROWNING EDMOND LEE	461	AAQ	444	1929	1968	2016

		Consecrators			Born	Cons.	Died
631	APPLEYARD ROBERT B	461	445	523	1917	1968	1999
632	ROBINSON HAROLD B	461	478	AAR	1922	1968	1994
633	GOSNELL HAROLD C	461	440	494	1908	1968	1999
634	GILLIAM JACKSON EARL	461	521	546	1920	1968	2000
635	RIVERA VICTOR MANUEL	461	443	570	1916	1968	2005
636	ELEBASH HUNLEY AGEE	461	460	484	1923	1968	1993
637	WOLF FREDERICK BARTO	461	424	517	1922	1968	1998
638	MEAD WILLIAM HENRY	461	414	526	1921	1968	1974
639	LEIGHTON DAVID K SR	461	535	523	1922	1968	2013
640	HAYNSWORTH GEORGE E	608	508	510	1925	1969	2012
641	RAMOS JOSE ANTONIO	461	608	508	1937	1969	
642	MANGURAMAS C B	562	591	630	1933	1969	
643	SPOFFORD WILLIAM B J	461	548	465	1921	1969	2013
644	THORNBERRY DAVID R	461	368	476	1911	1969	1995
645	ATKINS STANLEY H	449	512	519	1912	1969	1996
646	REEVES GEORGE PAUL	532	455	Nassau	1918	1969	2010
647	SMITH PHILIP A	461	490	618	1920	1970	2010
648	FOLWELL WILLIAM H	455	583	646	1924	1970	2022
649	HOSEA ADDISON	462	527	488	1914	1970	1986
650	DAVIES A DONALD	461	577	581	1920	1970	
651	JONES WALTER H	498	452	610	1925	1970	2003
652	BROWNE GEORGE D	461	520	441	1933	1970	1993
653	STEWART ALEXANDER D	461	590	504	1926	1970	1999
654	GRESSLE LLOYD EDGAR	461	526	518	1918	1970	1999
655	PONG JAMES T M	461	AAK	AAJ	1911	1971	1988
656	HOBGOOD CLARENCE E	461	539	572	1914	1971	2008
657	CACERES V ADRIAN D	461	627	600	1922	1971	2006
658	STOUGH FURMAN C	461	521	581	1928	1971	2004
659	KRUMM JOHN MC GILL	461	474	559	1913	1971	1995
660	GARNIER LUC A J	461	527	620	1928	1971	1999
661	VARLEY ROBERT P	461	577	619	1921	1971	2000
662	VOGEL ARTHUR ANTON	461	497	512	1924	1971	2012
663	HENTON WILLIS RYAN	461	466	599	1925	1971	2006
664	WALKER JOHN THOMAS	461	564	590	1925	1971	1989
665	CHARLES EDGAR OTIS	461	505	582	1926	1971	2013
666	BELDEN FREDERICK H	461	517	561	1909	1971	1979
667	MCGEHEE HARRY C JR	461	490	463	1923	1971	2013
668	PORTEUS MORGAN	461	582	424	1917	1971	2019
669	TRELEASE JR RICHARD M	461	526	621	1921	1971	2005
670	JONES HAROLD STEPHEN	461	452	651	1909	1972	2002
671	RIGHTER WALTER C	461	474	498	1923	1972	2011
672	ARNOLD MORRIS F	461	590	659	1915	1972	1992
673	FRANKLIN WILLIAM A	603	514	454	1916	1972	1998
674	HILLESTAD ALBERT W	461	588	637	1924	1972	2007
675	SHIRLEY LEMUEL B	454	603	584	1916	1972	1999
676	SIMS BENNETT J	461	489	613	1920	1972	2006
677	FRENSDORFF WESLEY	461	505	566	1926	1972	1988
678	ISAAC TELESFORO A	461	568	441	1929	1972	
679	WYLIE SAMUEL J	461	472	659	1918	1972	1974
680	TURNER EDWARD MASON	461	593	506	1918	1972	1996
681	KING HANFORD L JR	461	548	651	1921	1972	1986
682	SHERIDAN WILLIAM CR	461	587	AAQ	1917	1972	2005
683	PRIMO QUINTIN E JR	461	587	463	1913	1972	1998
684	COX WILLIAM JACKSON	461	639	535	1921	1972	
685	ALEXANDER GEORGE M	461	521	583	1914	1973	1983
686	CARRAL-SOLAR ANSELMO	600	675	514	1925	1973	2002
687	ATKINSON ROBERT P	461	499	586	1927	1973	2012
688	BADEN JOHN ALFRED	490	618	556	1913	1973	1983
689	GASKELL CHARLES T	461	512	645	1919	1973	2000
690	WEINHAUER WILLIAM G	461	636	572	1924	1973	2007
691	PARSONS DONALD JAMES	461	587	512	1922	1973	2016
692	DAVIS DONALD JAMES	461	514	549	1929	1973	2007
693	BIGLIARDI MATTHEW P	540	612	570	1920	1974	1996
694	WRIGHT HAROLD LOUIS	598	590	472	1929	1974	1978
695	HOGG WILBUR EMORY JR	461	561	637	1918	1974	1986
696	KERR ROBERT SHAW	461	576	624	1917	1974	1988
697	WOLTERSTORFF ROBERT M	461	477	552	1914	1974	2007
698	GRAY DUNCAN M JR	461	581	515	1926	1974	2016
699	CERVENY FRANK S	461	543	484	1933	1974	
700	COCHRAN DAVID REA	581	479	610	1915	1974	2001
701	HAYNES EMERSON PAUL	581	584	455	1918	1974	1988

		Consecrators		Born	Cons.	Died
702	BELSHAW GEORGE PHELPS MELLICK	581	614	444	1928	1975	2020
703	WITCHER ROBERT CAMPBELL	581	486	515	1926	1975	2021
704	JONES WILLIAM AUGUSTUS JR	581	563	614	1927	1975	2020
705	CLARK WILLIAM HAWLEY	581	590	613	1919	1975	1997
706	DIMMICK WILLIAM ARTHUR	581	534	582	1919	1975	1984
707	ABELLON RICHARD ABELARDO	562	591	614	1924	1975	
708	TERWILLIGER ROBERT ELWIN	581	560	699	1917	1975	1991
709	COCHRANE ROBERT HUME	581	570	677	1924	1976	2010
710	CILLEY ROGER HOWARD	581	611	537	1918	1976	1986
711	BROWN JAMES BARROW	581	488	454	1932	1976	
712	VACHE CLAUDE CHARLES	581	556	564	1926	1976	2009
713	SPONG JOHN SHELBY	581	601	618	1931	1976	2021
714	HEISTAND JOSEPH THOMAS	581	438	618	1924	1976	2008
715	COBURN JOHN BOWEN	581	590	472	1914	1976	2009
716	MAYSON HENRY IRVING	581	667	683	1925	1976	1995
717	WARNER JAMES DANIEL	581	519	543	1924	1976	2009
718	McALLISTER GERALD NICHOLAS	581	613	633	1923	1977	2014
719	JONES EDWARD WITKER	581	549	617	1929	1977	2007
720	LUMPIAS MANUEL CAPUYAN	562	707	655	1930	1977	
721	JONES BOBBY GORDON	581	644	479	1932	1977	
722	ANDERSON ROBERT MARSHALL	581	552	665	1933	1978	2011
723	CHILD CHARLES JUDSON	581	676	489	1923	1978	2004
724	BURGREEN CHARLES LEE	581	539	633	1924	1978	2006
725	PINA HUGO LUIS	581	675	648	1938	1978	2018
726	THOMPSON JOHN LESTER	581	550	635	1926	1978	2004
727	WALLACE LEIGH ALLEN	581	623	634	1927	1979	2010
728	SCHOFIELD CALVIN ONDERDONK	581	583	455	1933	1979	
729	LIGHT ARTHUR HEATH	581	528	516	1929	1979	
730	MERINO BERNARDO	581	675	657	1930	1979	2021
731	HAUSER STANLEY FILLMORE	581	604	670	1922	1979	1989
732	SWING WILLIAM EDWIN	581	605	664	1936	1979	
733	BECKHAM WILLIAM ARTHUR	581	685	586	1927	1979	2005
734	DENNIS WALTER DECOSTER	598	472	569	1932	1979	2003
735	SANDERS BRICE SIDNEY	581	460	636	1930	1979	1997
736	WALMSLEY ARTHUR EDWARD	581	668	637	1928	1979	2017
737	BLACK WILLIAM GRANT	581	368	659	1920	1979	2013
738	CHEUNG PUI-YEUNG	581	655	642	1919	1980	1987
739	LEWIS DAVID H JR	581	618	490	1918	1980	2002
740	HOPKINS HAROLD A JR	581	610	637	1930	1980	2019
741	ESTILL ROBERT W	581	572	650	1927	1980	2019
742	MARTINEZ-RESENDEZ ROBERTO	581	551	600	1938	1980	
743	HUERTA-RAMOS CLARO	581	551	600	1929	1980	
744	HUNT GEORGE N III	581	732	517	1931	1980	2022
745	KIMSEY RUSTIN R	581	465	643	1935	1980	2015
746	STEVENS WILLIAM L	581	519	689	1932	1980	1997
747	BENITEZ MAURICE M	581	461	604	1928	1980	2014
748	DONOVAN HERBERT A JR	581	626	538	1931	1980	
749	ALLISON C FITZSIMONS	581	575	685	1927	1980	
750	WANTLAND WILLIAM C	581	645	718	1934	1980	
751	MALLORY C SHANNON				1936	1972	2018
752	McNUTT CHARLIE FULLER JR	581	617	687	1931	1980	
753	HULSEY SAM BYRON	581	466	663	1932	1980	2020
754	WOLFRUM WILLIAM H	581	627	574	1926	1981	2007
755	DUVALL CHARLES F	581	521	733	1935	1981	2020
756	WHITAKER O'KELLEY	581	602	648	1926	1981	2015
757	ASHBY JOHN F	581	718	750	1929	1981	2001
758	GREIN RICHARD F	581	543	552	1932	1981	
759	HARRIS GEORGE C	581	700	651	1925	1981	2000
760	HUCLES HENRY B III	581	703	486	1923	1981	1989
761	HATHAWAY ALDEN M	581	631	618	1933	1981	
762	ESPINOZA-VENEGAS SAMUEL	581	600	551	1942	1981	2013
763	COLERIDGE CLARENCE L	581	736	AAA	1930	1981	
764	HASTINGS W BRADFORD	581	736	AAA	1919	1981	1992
765	GUERRA-SORIA ARMANDO R	675	686	678	1949	1982	
766	HULTSTRAND DONALD M	581	689	719	1927	1982	2018
767	EASTMAN ALBERT THEODORE	581	639	535	1928	1982	2018
768	BIRNEY DAVID B IV	581	654	681	1929	1982	2004
769	RAY THOMAS K	581	567	706	1934	1982	2018
770	CHARLTON GORDON T JR	581	747	650	1923	1982	2020
771	MORTON CHARLES B	581	697	658	1926	1982	1994
772	DYER JM MARK	581	654	590	1930	1982	2014

		Consecrators			Born	Cons.	Died
773	DICKSON ALEX D JR	581	698	586	1926	1983	2021
774	MOODEY JAMES R	581	621	494	1932	1983	2005
775	SORGE ELLIOTT L				1929	1971	2011
776	PATTERSON DONIS D	581	604	724	1930	1983	2006
777	LONGID ROBERT LEE OMENGAN	707	591	720	1935	1983	1996
778	SHIPPS HARRY WOOLSTON	581	646	773	1926	1984	2016
779	OTTLEY JAMES HAMILTON	581	730	599	1936	1984	
780	FRADE LEOPOLD	581	711	765	1943	1984	
781	PETTIT VINCENT KING	581	702	734	1924	1984	2006
782	BALL DAVID STANDISH	581	508	695	1926	1984	2017
783	WISSEMANN ANDREW FREDERICK	581	782	504	1928	1984	2014
784	BURRILL WILLIAM GEORGE	581	500	550	1934	1984	
785	LEE PETER JAMES	581	741	618	1938	1984	2022
786	ANDERSON CRAIG BARRY	581	452	634	1942	1984	
787	WHITE ROGER JOHN	581	766	587	1941	1984	2012
788	CHALFANT EDWARD COLE	581	559	659	1937	1984	
789	WIMBERLY DON ADGER	581	749	699	1937	1984	
790	MEEKS HOWARD SAMUEL	581	567	776	1932	1984	2016
791	POPE CLARENCE CULLAM JR	581	645	711	1929	1985	
792	GARCIA-MONTEIL MARTINIANO	581	650	762	1933	1985	
793	DOWNS-HIGGS STURDIE WYMAN	599	787	678	1947	1985	
794	GRISWOLD FRANK TRACY III	581	500	587	1937	1985	
795	HARRIS ROGERS SANDERS	581	733	773	1930	1985	2017
796	VEST FRANK HARRIS JR	581	741	572	1936	1985	2008
797	GARVER OLIVER BAILEY JR	581	745	746	1925	1985	1996
798	CARR WILLIAM FRANKLIN	581	687	499	1938	1985	2022
799	REYNOLDS GEORGE LAZENBY JR	581	722	773	1927	1985	1991
800	JOHNSON DAVID ELLIOT	581	538	500	1933	1985	1995
801	LADEHOFF ROBERT LOUIS	581	693	755	1932	1985	
802	MacNAUGHTON JOHN HERBERT	630	604	731	1929	1986	2022
803	JONES CHARLES IRVING	630	634	603	1943	1986	
804	BARTLETT ALLEN LYMAN JR	630	516	603	1929	1986	
805	THEUNER DOUGLAS EDWIN	630	647	736	1938	1986	2013
806	SWENSON DANIEL LEE	630	722	696	1928	1986	2014
807	TICOBAY NARCISCO VALENTIN	692	707	777	1932	1986	2014
808	MILLER ROBERT ORAN	630	698	608	1935	1986	2009
809	ZABRISKIE STEWART CLARK	677	740	771	1936	1986	1999
A810	VALENTINE BARRY						
811	BOWMAN DAVID CHARLES	630	494	621	1932	1986	2015
812	WILLIAMS ARTHUR BENJAMIN JR	630	774	621	1935	1986	
813	BATES GEORGE EDMOND	677	745	643	1933	1986	1999
814	HAINES RONALD HAYWARD	630	664	690	1934	1986	2008
815	GRAY FRANCIS CAMPBELL	630	648	719	1940	1986	
816	TENNIS CALVIN CABELL	729	804	712	1932	1986	
817	HART DONALD PURPLE	630	479	647	1937	1986	
818	ALLAN FRANK KELLOGG	723	586	676	1935	1987	2019
819	TAYLOR EGBERT DON	630	632	680	1937	1987	2014
820	MARTINEZ-MARQUEZ GERMAN	802	779	551	1933	1987	
821	ROWTHORN JEFFERY WILLIAM	630	657	736	1934	1987	
822	McARTHUR EARL NICHOLAS	630	802	718	1925	1988	2016
823	MacBURNEY EDWARD HARDING	630	746	813	1927	1988	
824	MOODY ROBERT MANNING	630	718	785	1939	1988	
825	CHIEN JOHN CHIH-TSUNG	630	817		1923	1988	2013
826	WALKER ORRIS GEORGE	630	812	703	1942	1988	2015
827	CAISAPANTA LUIS	779	692	657	1932	1988	1991
828	BORSCH FREDERICK HOUK	630	702	664	1935	1988	2017
829	THOMPSON HERBERT	630	737	620	1933	1988	2006
830	EPTING C CHRISTOPHER	630	648	671	1946	1988	
831	TURNER FRANKLIN D	630	804	664	1933	1988	2013
832	SCHOFIELD DAVID MERCER	630	635	732	1938	1988	2013
833	WOOD RAYMOND STEWART	664	667	659	1934	1988	
834	HARRIS BARBARA CLEMENTINE	630	800	804	1930	1989	2020
835	BUCHANAN JOHN CLARK	630	755	622	1933	1989	2020
836	KELSHAW TERENCE	630	761	747	1936	1989	
837	JOHNSON ROBERT HODGES	630	690	723	1934	1989	
838	HAMPTON SANFORD ZANGWILL KAYE	630	722	834	1935	1989	
839	HOWE JOHN W	630	761	627	1942	1989	
840	ROWLEY ROBERT D	630	692	772	1941	1989	2010
841	SMITH JOHN H	630	690	774	1939	1989	2012
842	HARGROVE ROBERT JEFFERSON	630	663	711	1937	1989	2005
843	WARNER VINCENT WAYDELL JR	709	637	800	1940	1989	

		Consecrators			Born	Cons.	Died
844	CARRANZA-GOMEZ SERGIO	678	826	675	1941	1989	
845	STERLING WILLIAM E	630	747	686	1927	1989	2005
846	KROTZ JAMES E	630	717	830	1948	1989	
847	LEE EDWARD L JR	719	769	516	1934	1989	
848	LONGEST CHARLES L	630	639	767	1933	1989	
849	ZABALA ARTEMIO MASLENG	707	777	807		1989	
850	FAIRFIELD ANDREW H	630	610	740	1943	1989	
851	SMALLEY WILLIAM E	630	758	767	1940	1989	
852	SALMON EDWARD L JR	630	749	640	1934	1990	2016
853	PLUMMER STEVEN T	630	670	595	1944	1990	2005
854	KEYSER CHARLES L	630	699	785	1930	1990	2022
855	WILLIAMS HUNTINGTON JR	630	741	676	1925	1990	2013
856	LARREA-MORENO JOSE N	630	779	780	1949	1990	
857	THORNTON JOHN STUART	658	745	801	1932	1990	
858	SHIMPFKY RICHARD LESTER	630	834	713	1940	1990	2011
859	TERRY FRANK JEFFREY	630	516	623	1939	1990	1999
860	WINTERROWD WILLIAM JERRY	630	627	754	1938	1991	
861	TALTON CHESTER LOVELLE	630	722	826	1941	1991	
862	WIEDRICH WILLIAM W	719	587	794	1931	1991	2014
863	ROCKWELL HAYS HAMILTON	630	758	704	1936	1991	
864	SCANTLEBURY VICTOR A	630	779	675	1945	1991	2020
865	CHARLESTON STEVEN	630	853	750	1949	1991	
866	MCKELVEY JACK MARSTON	756	713	831	1941	1991	
867	THARP ROBERT G	630	648	586	1928	1991	2003
868	LAMB JERRY A	630	726	801	1940	1991	
869	MARBLE ALFRED CLARK JR	581	698	735	1936	1991	2017
870	HOLGUIN-KHOURY JULIO CESAR	856	779	678	1948	1991	
871	JOSLIN DAVID BRUCE	630	631	830	1936	1991	
872	BECKWITH PETER HESS	630	829	794	1939	1991	2019
873	BARAHONA-PASCASIO MARTIN DE JESUS	630	779	856	1943	1992	
874	HUGHES GETHIN BENWIL	630	828	842	1942	1992	
875	SHAHAN ROBERT R	630	529	714	1939	1992	2020
876	DIXON JANE HOLMES	630	814	834	1937	1992	2012
877	TOWNSEND MARTIN GOUGH	630	775	772	1943	1992	
878	DENIG ROBERT S	630	847	783	1946	1993	1995
879	STANTON JAMES M	630	828	832	1946	1993	
880	IKER JACK L	630	791	659	1949	1993	
881	DURACIN JEAN Z	630	660	867	1947	1993	
882	HERLONG BERTRAM N	630	785	752	1934	1993	2011
883	MATTHEWS FRANK CLAY	630	785	687	1947	1993	
884	PAYNE CLAUDE E	630	461	581	1932	1993	
885	JELINEK JAMES L	630	722	838	1942	1993	
886	DOSS JOE MORRIS	630	732	780	1943	1993	
887	MCLEOD MARY ADELIA R	630	808	834	1938	1993	2022
888	COLEMAN JAMES MALONE	630	711	773	1929	1993	2020
889	FOLTS JAMES EDWARD	630	802	604	1940	1994	
890	GREW JOSEPH CLARK	630	812	794	1939	1994	
891	GULICK EDWIN FUNSTEN JR	630	796	883	1948	1994	
892	JECKO STEPHEN HAYS	630	699	661	1940	1994	2007
893	JOHNSON ROBERT CARROLL JR	630	741	855	1938	1994	2014
894	JACOBUS RUSSELL EDWARD	630	746	787	1944	1994	
895	MAZE LARRY EARL	630	698	748	1943	1994	
896	ROBERTSON CREIGHTON LELAND	630	786	670	1944	1994	2014
897	ACKERMAN KEITH LYNN	630	691	823	1946	1994	
898	SHAW MARVIL THOMAS III SSJE	630	800	834	1945	1994	2014
899	ESPAÑA ALFREDO TERENCIO MORANTE	D A	906	856	1947	1994	
900	PRICE KENNETH LESTER	630	829	841	1943	1994	
901	LOUTITT HENRY IRVING JR	630	778	675	1938	1995	2020
902	HENDERSON DORSEY FELIX JR	630	583	746	1939	1995	
903	SAID JOHN LEWIS	630	728	583	1932	1995	2019
904	STRICKLAND VERNON EDWARD	630	721	830	1938	1995	
905	HAYES CLARENCE WALLACE	630	454	730	1928	1995	
A906	SOTO ONELL ASISELO	779	648	730	1932	1987	2015
907	JONES DAVID COLIN	630	785	687	1943	1995	
908	ALARD LEOPOLDO J	630	884	845	1941	1995	2003
909	IHLOFF ROBERT W	630	763	834	1941	1995	
910	CREIGHTON MICHAEL W	630	752	843	1940	1995	
911	HIBBS ROBERT B	630	889	802	1932	1996	2017
912	ROSKAM CATHERINE A	630	834	758	1943	1996	
913	WOLF GERALYN	630	794	744	1947	1996	
914	LIPSCOMB JOHN B	630	888	795	1950	1996	

		Consecrators			Born	Cons.	Died
915	SKILTON WILLIAM J	630	852	575	1940	1996	
916	DUNCAN ROBERT WILLIAM	630	761	785	1948	1996	
917	SMITH ANDREW DONNAN	630	763	736	1944	1996	
918	IRISH CAROLYN TANNER	630	813	665	1940	1996	2021
919	MARSHALL PAUL VICTOR	840	772	654	1947	1996	
920	GLOSTER JAMES GARY	630	893	741	1936	1996	
921	LEIDEL JR EDWIN MAX	630	833	719	1938	1996	2022
922	DANIEL III CLIFTON	630	735	712	1947	1996	
923	PARSLEY JR HENRY NUTT	630	808	785	1948	1996	
924	SCRUTON GORDON PAUL	630	653	783	1947	1996	
925	POWELL FRANK NEFF	630	729	796	1947	1996	
926	CHANG RICHARD SUI ON	630	744	745	1941	1997	2017
927	BENNISON JR CHARLES ELLSWORTH	630	804	831	1943	1997	
928	MICHEL RODNEY RAE	630	826	703	1943	1997	
929	WAYNICK CATHERINE MAPLES	812	719	667	1948	1997	
930	OHL JR CHARLES WALLIS	752	753	860	1943	1997	
931	DANIELS THEODORE ATHELBERT	734	819	675	1944	1997	
932	BANE JR DAVID CONNER	829	796	687	1942	1997	
933	MACDONALD MARK LAWRENCE	630	853	750	1954	1997	
934	CALDWELL BRUCE EDWARD	846	721	850	1947	1997	
935	HERZOG DANIEL	630	782	924	1941	1997	
936	JENKINS CHARLES EDWARD III	794	711	852	1951	1998	2021
937	HOWE BARRY ROBERT	794	835	795	1942	1998	
938	KNUDSEN CHILTON ABBIE RICHARDSON	794	637	913	1946	1998	
939	SISK MARK SEAN	794	758	734	1942	1998	
940	BAINBRIDGE HARRY BROWN	812	867	857	1939	1998	2010
941	WRIGHT WAYNE PARKER	840	936	887	1951	1998	
942	RABB JOHN LESLIE	840	909	767	1944	1998	
943	CRONEBERGER JOHN PALMER	812	713	866	1938	1998	
944	VONROSENBERG CHARLES GLENN	867	586	733	1947	1999	
945	PERSELL WILLIAM D	794	812	890	1943	1999	
946	WHITMORE KEITH BERNARD	794	750	904	1945	1999	
947	GARRISON J MICHAEL	794	811	809	1945	1999	
948	KELSEY JAMES ARTHUR	794	769	847	1952	1999	2007
949	MACPHERSON DAVID BRUCE	851	879	828	1940	1999	2017
950	GIBBS WENDELL NATHANIEL	812	587	834	1954	2000	
951	PACKARD GEORGE ELDEN	794	854	758	1944	2000	
952	LITTLE EDWARD STUART	812	815	832	1947	2000	
953	BRUNO JOSEPH JON	858	828	861	1946	2000	2021
954	BENA DAVID JOHN	794	935	782	1943	2000	
955	CURRY MICHAEL BRUCE	837	920	834	1953	2000	
956	GRAY III DUNCAN MONTGOMERY	794	869	698	1949	2000	
957	GREGG WILLIAM OTIS	630	745	801	1951	2000	
958	SAULS STACY FRED	837	789	891	1955	2000	
959	CURRY JAMES E.	805	917	763	1948	2000	
960	RAMOS-ORENCH WILFRIDO	805	917	763	1940	2000	
961	WAGGONER JAMES EDWARD	868	687	900	1947	2000	
962	LAI DAVID JUNG-HSIN	926	825		1948	2000	
963	SCHORI KATHARINE JEFFERTS	868	801	918	1954	2001	
964	CEDARHOLM ROY FREDERICK JR	805	898	834	1944	2001	
965	ELY THOMAS CLARK	805	887	806	1951	2001	
966	DUNCAN PHILIP MENZIE II	794	755	937	1944	2001	
967	JOHNSON DON EDWARD	794	888	586	1949	2001	
968	ALEXANDER JOHN NEIL	794	818	723	1954	2001	
969	DUQUE FRANCISCO JOSÉ	794	730	856	1950	2001	
970	KLUSMEYER WILLIAM MICHIE	794	945	687	1955	2001	
971	ALLEN LLOYD EMMANUEL	779	780		1956	2001	
972	ADAMS GLADSTONE BAILEY III	866	671	891	1952	2001	
973	WHALON PIERRE WELTÉ	794	821	839	1952	2001	
974	ANDRUS MARK HANDLEY	794	923	785	1956	2002	
975	SMITH GEORGE WAYNE	890	863	830	1955	2002	
976	ADAMS JAMES MARSHALL JR	851	904	894	1948	2002	
977	GALLAGHER CAROL JOY WT	840	932	834	1955	2002	
978	GEPERT ROBERT R	812	847	772	1948	2002	
979	CHANE JOHN BRYSON	794	876	814	1944	2002	
980A	SCRIVEN HENRY WM	AAD			1951	1995	
981	HARRIS GAYLE ELIZABETH	812	898	834	1951	2003	
982	SHAND JAMES JOSEPH	909	877	775	1946	2003	
983	SCARFE ALAN	885	830	981	1950	2003	
984A	ALVAREZ DAVID ANDRES	779	772	608	1941	1987	
985	BURNETT JOE GOODWIN	885	717	846	1948	2003	

		Consecrators			Born	Cons.	Died
986	ITTY JOHNCY	794	630	801	1963	2003	
987	BROOKHART C FRANKLIN	794	970	854	1948	2003	
988	HIGH RAYFORD BAINES JR	949	789	884	1941	2003	
989	O'NEILL ROBERT JOHN	885	860	898	1955	2003	
990	COUNCELL GEORGE EDWARD	794	783	945	1949	2003	2018
991	MILLER STEVEN ANDREW	950	787	662	1957	2003	
992	HOWARD SAMUEL JOHNSON	936	892	699	1951	2003	
993	ROBINSON V GENE	794	630	767	1947	2003	
994	WOLFE DEAN ELLIOTT	949	851	758	1956	2003	
995	LILLIBRIDGE GARY	794	889	911	1956	2004	
996	HOLLINGSWORTH MARK JR	950	890	898	1954	2004	
997	SMITH KIRK STEVAN	794	875	953	1951	2004	
998	SMITH MICHAEL GENE	794	850	740	1955	2004	
999	TAYLOR GRANVILLE PORTER	893	968	818	1950	2004	
1000	STEENSON JEFFREY NEIL	794	836	791	1952	2005	
1001	RIVERA BAVI EDNA	940	843	732	1946	2005	
1002	MATHES JAMES ROBERT	926	874	995	1959	2005	
1003	GUMBS EDWARD AMBROSE	812	678	826	1949	2005	
1004A	GUERRERO ORLANDO JESUS	AAS	870	AAT		2005	
1005	REED DAVID MITCHELL	949	995	889	1957	2006	
1006	OUSLEY STEVEN TODD	950	921	948	1961	2006	
1007	LOVE WILLIAM H	794	935	954	1957	2006	
1008	BEISNER BARRY L	940	963	868	1951	2006	
1009	HARRISON DENA A	949	789	988	1947	2006	
1010	BAXTER NATHAN D	794	910	979	1948	2006	
1011	BENFIELD LARRY R	963	748	895	1955	2007	
1012	BECKWITH MARK M	963	722	943	1951	2007	
1013	BAUERSCHMIDT JOHN C	922	882	711	1959	2007	
1014	SMITH DABNEY T	922	914	648	1953	2007	
1015	FITZPATRICK ROBERT L	963	926	962	1958	2007	
1016	BREIDENTHAL THOMAS E	963	900	737	1951	2007	
1017	JOHNSTON SHANNON S	963	785	907	1958	2007	
1018	AHRENS LAURA J	963	959	912	1962	2007	
1019	ROWE SEAN W	963	840	772	1975	2007	
1020	KONIECZNY EDWARD J	963	952	824	1954	2007	
1021	RICKEL GREGORY	926	843	1001	1963	2007	
1022	GRAY-REEVES MARY	963	1027	728	1962	2007	
1023	EDWARDS DAN	963	968	868	1950	2008	
1024	SLOAN JOHN MCKEE	963	923	808	1955	2008	
1025	LAWRENCE MARK	922	870	897	1950	2008	
1026	LEE JEFFREY	963	950	938	1957	2008	
1027A	ROMERO SYLVESTRE	AAU			1943	1994	
1028	LN STEPHEN	963	866	938	1949	2008	
1029	SINGH PRINCE	963	866	1012	1962	2008	
1030	SUTTON EUGENE	963	979	1010	1954	2008	
1031	LAMBERT PAUL	949	879	998	1950	2008	
1032	THOM BRIAN	963	940	868	1955	2008	
1033	DOYLE CHARLES A	963	789	1009	1966	2008	
1034	HOLLERITH HERMAN	963	785	925	1955	2009	
1035	MAYER J SCOTT	963	753	930	1955	2009	
1036	RUIZ LUIS F	963	969	960	1956	2009	
1037	PROVENZANO LAWRENCE	963	924	990	1955	2009	
1038	TARRANT JOHN J	963	896	786	1952	2009	2020
1039	BENHASE SCOTT A	963	901	1030	1957	2010	
1040	PRIOR BRIAN N	963	885	961	1959	2010	
1041	HANLEY MICHAEL J	963	1021	1001	1954	2010	
1042	DOUGLAS IAN T	963	955	952	1958	2010	
1043	THOMPSON MORRIS K	963	958	956	1955	2010	
1044	BRUCE DIANE	963	953	1037	1956	2010	
1045	GLASSPOOL MARY D	963	953	997	1954	2010	
1046	WALDO ANDRE W	963	881	923	1953	2010	
1047	MAGNESS JAMES B	963	891	951	1947	2010	
1048	SMYLIE JOHN S	963	1040	955	1952	2010	
1049	BAILEY DAVID E	963	918	745	1940	2010	
1050	LATTIME MARK A	963	1029	866	1966	2010	
1051	WHITE TERRY ALLEN	963	891	937	1959	2010	
1052	VONO MICHAEL LOUIS	963	906	973	1949	2010	
1053	HAYASHI SCOTT B	963	918	1008	1953	2010	
1054	MILLIKEN MICHAEL P	963	994	1011	1947	2011	
1055	FIELD MARTIN S	963	937	994	1956	2011	
1056	MARTINS DANIEL H	963	952	894	1951	2011	

		Consecrators			Born	Cons.	Died
1057	FRANKLIN RALPH WILLIAM	963	939	973	1947	2011	
1058	RAY RAYFORD JEFFREY	963	1006	950	1956	2011	
1059	YOUNG GEORGE DIBRELL III	963	1013	967	1955	2011	
1060	BARKER JOSEPH SCOTT	963	985	939	1964	2011	
1061	BUDDE MARIANN EDGAR	963	1040	1012	1959	2011	
1062	DIETSCHE ANDREW ML	963	939	990	1953	2012	
1063	BREWER GREGORY O	922	839	1007	1951	2012	
1064	BEAUVOIR OGÉ	963	881	939	1956	2012	
1065	OWENSBY JACOB W	963	949	975	1957	2012	
1066	GOFF SUSAN E	963	1017	891	1953	2012	
1067	HIRSCHFELD ALFRED ROBERT	963	993	924	1961	2012	
1068	FISHER JEFF W	963	1033	1009	1964	2012	
1069	WRIGHT ROBERT C	963	968	955	1964	2012	
1070	MCCONNELL DORSEY WM	963	900	898	1953	2012	
1071	KNISELY W NICHOLAS JR	963	996	1028	1960	2012	
1072	MARRAY SANTOSH KUMAR					2005	
1073	FISHER DOUGLAS J	963	924	939	1954	2012	
1074	HAHN WILLIAM DOUGLAS	963	968	1051	1952	2012	
1075	LAMBERT WILLIAM JAY III	963	894	1063	1948	2013	
1076	HODGES-COPPLE ANNIE ELLIOTT	963	955	1039	1957	2013	
1077	BOURLAKAS MARK ALLEN	963	955	968	1963	2013	
1078	HOUGLAND WHAYNE MILLER JR	963	955	958	1962	2013	
1079	STOKES WILLIAM HALLOCK	963	990	780	1957	2013	
1080	RICE DAVID	963			1961	2014	
1081	GUNTER MATTHEW ALAN	963	1026	991	1957	2014	
1082	SHIN ALLEN KUNHO	963	1062	1037	1956	2014	
1083	COOK HEATHER ELIZABETH	963	1030	982		2014	
1084	GATES ALAN MCINTOSH	1028	898	990	1958	2014	
1085	SEAGE BRIAN RICHARD	963	956	953	1963	2014	
1086	SKIRVING ROBERT	963	1006	870	1960	2014	
1087	EATON PETER DAVID	963	780	989	1958	2015	
1088	KENDRICK JAMES RUSSELL	963	966	1033	1960	2015	
1089	SCANLAN AUDREY CADY	963	1042	1018	1958	2015	
1090	SUMNER GEORGE ROBINSON	955	1031	1013	1955	2015	
1091	MOTA MOISES QUEZADA	955	870	678	1956	2016	
1092a	VAN KOEVERING MARK				1957	2016	
1093	BELL PATRICK WILLIAM	955	1001	961	1952	2016	
1094	SPARKS DOUGLAS EVERETT	955	952	1040	1956	2016	
1095	GUTIERREZ DANIEL GEORGE POLYCARP	955	922	1052	1964	2016	
1096	MCLOUGHLIN JOSÉ ANTONIO	955	999	1020	1969	2016	
1097	DUNCAN-PROBE DEDE	955	1017	834	1962	2016	
1098	WRIGHT CARL WALTER	955	1047	1030	1959	2017	
1099	REHBERG GRETCHEN MARY	955	961	1016	1964	2017	
1100	BASKERVILLE-BURROWS JENNIFER	955	929	1094	1966	2017	
1101	TAYLOR JOHN HARVEY	955	953	1044	1954	2017	
1102	RODMAN SAMUEL SEWELL	955	1084	1076	1959	2017	
1103	MORALES MALDONADO RAFAEL LUIS	955	960	984	1963	2017	
1104	DAVIDSON JENNIFER BROOKE	955	1005	1018	1960	2017	
1105a	MONTERROSO GONZALEZ HECTOR FIDEL					2017	
1106	COLE BRIAN LEE	955	950	1077	1967	2017	
1107	BROWN KEVIN SCOTT	955	967	941	1968	2017	
1108	NICHOLS KEVIN DONNELLY	955	1019	1067	1962	2018	
1109	HUGHES CARLYE JEAN	955	1097	1035	1958	2018	
1110	HUNN MICHAEL BUERKEL	955	1052	1022	1970	2018	
1111	COWELL MARK ANDREW	955	1054	1055	1965	2018	
1112	BASCOM CATHLEEN CHITTENDEN	955	974	983	1962	2019	
1113	REDDALL JENNIFER ANNE	955	996	1099	1975	2019	
1114	LOZANO CRISTOBAL LEON	955				2019	
1115	EDINGTON MARK DAVID WHEELER	955	1084	973	1961	2019	
1116	ROAF PHOEBE ALISON	955	1100	938	1964	2019	
1117	LUCAS KIMBERLY DANIELLE	955	989	1100	1970	2019	
1118	RYAN KATHRYN MCCROSSEN	955	1033	1035	1964	2019	
1119	SNOOK SUSAN BROWN	963	1020	1022	1962	2019	
1120	BROWN THOMAS JAMES	955	1060	1100	1970	2019	
1121	MCCLURE TRAQUAIR MEGAN	955	1096	1022	1962	2019	
1122	MACVEAN-BROWN SHANNON	955	1100	981	1967	2019	
1123	FOLTS JONATHAN HUNTER	955	1005	1042	1968	2019	
1124	STEBBINS MARTHA ELIZABETH	955	1102	1048	1960	2019	
1125	ASHBY LUCINDA BETH	955	1022	1032	1959	2020	
1126	HAYNES SUSAN BUNTON	955	1119	1054	1959	2020	
1127	PERRY BONNIE ANNE	955	1026	1061	1962	2020	

1128	CHANG LENNON YUAN-RUNG	955	962	1015		2020
1129	DEL CARPIO GRISELDA	955				2020
1130	LOGUE FRANK SULLIVAN	1039	1069	1019	1963	2020
1131	REED JR. POULSON CONNELL	1011	1020	1087	1970	2020
1132	LOYA CRAIG WILLIAM	1040	1060	934	1977	2020
1133	JOHNSON DEON	975	1127	1116	1977	2020
1134	CURRY GLENDA SHARP	1039	1024	1116	1953	2020
1135	AKIYAMA DIANA D	1099	1015	1041	1958	2021
1136	CHANDLER PAUL-GORDON	963	1117	1040	1964	2021
1137	WOODLIFF-STANLEY RUTH M	955	1117	1019	1962	2021
1138	SOLAK KETLEN ADRIEN	955	1107	1109	1961	2021
1139	MONNOT ELIZABETH LOCKWOOD HAWLEY	955	1125	983	1967	2021
1140	LAWTON FRASER					2022
1141	RICHARDS DANIEL PAUL	955	1113	1137	1975	2022
1142	GARDINER ELIZABETH BONFORTE	955	1087	1099	1965	2022
1143	COWDEN MATTHEW DAVIS	955	970	1094	1969	2022
1144	MERA JUAN CARLOS QUINONEZ	955	971	1103		2022
1145	BURGESS BRYAN KENDALL	955	1063	1013	1960	2022
1146	THARAKAN JOS	955	1032	1044	1964	2022
1147	CLARK PAULA	955	1100	1133	1962	2022
1148	SPIEGEL PHYLLIS	963	1053	1146	1966	2022
1149	SCHARF DOUGLAS FREDERICK	955	1014	1129	1979	2022
1150	MELLO JEFFREY WILLIAM	955	1120	981	1968	2022
1151	DUCKWORTH SHANNON ROGERS	955	1043	1110	1974	2022
1152	STEVENSON EDWARD MARK	955	1066	1019	1964	2022

Codes for other Anglican and Old Catholic Consecrators

AAA Aberdeen	AAE York	AAI North China	AAM Rangoon	AAQ Rowinski (PNC)
AAB Ross	AAF Bath and Wells	AAJ Singapore	AAN Kyushu	AAR Zielinski (PNC)
AAC Skinner	AAG London	AAK Hong Kong	AAO Borneo	AAS Costa Rica
AAD Canterbury	AAH Rochester	AAL Honan	AAP Korea	AAT Colombia
				AAU Belize

Key to Single-Letter Entries
These entries refer to Bishops consecrated for foreign lands which subsequently became missionary jurisdictions of this church: A Haiti; B Mexico; C Brazil; D Puerto Rico.

Key to "A" + Number
These entries refer to Bishops consecrated outside the American episcopate, later transferred in as Assistant Bishops under Canon III.12.(b)(2) or a Bishop whose diocese has joined The Episcopal Church under Article V of the Constitution.

A Table of Presiding Bishops*

1. WILLIAM WHITE (2) (Bishop of Pennsylvania), from July 28, 1789, to October 3, 1789.

2. SAMUEL SEABURY (1) (Bishop of Connecticut), from October 5, 1789 to September 8, 1792.

3. SAMUEL PROVOOST (3) (Bishop of New York), from September 13, 1792, to September 8, 1795.

4. WILLIAM WHITE (2) (Bishop of Pennsylvania), from September 8, 1795, to July 17, 1836.

5. ALEXANDER VIETS GRISWOLD (12) (Bishop of the Eastern Diocese), from July 17, 1836, to February 15, 1843.

6. PHILANDER CHASE (18) (Bishop of Illinois), from February 15, 1843, to September 20, 1852.

7. THOMAS CHURCH BROWNELL (19) (Bishop of Connecticut), from September 20, 1852, to January 13, 1865.

8. JOHN HENRY HOPKINS (26) (Bishop of Vermont), from January 13, 1865, to January 9, 1868.

9. BENJAMIN BOSWORTH SMITH (27) (Bishop of Kentucky), from January 9, 1868, to May 31, 1884.

10. ALFRED LEE (38) (Bishop of Delaware), from May 31, 1884, to April 12, 1887.

11. JOHN WILLIAMS (54) (Bishop of Connecticut), from April 12, 1887, to February 7, 1899.

12. THOMAS MARCH CLARK (63) (Bishop of Rhode Island), from February 7, 1899, to September 7, 1903.

13. DANIEL SYLVESTER TUTTLE (84) (Bishop of Missouri), from September 7, 1903, to April 17, 1923.

14. ALEXANDER CHARLES GARRETT (108) (Bishop of Dallas), from April 17, 1923, to February 18, 1924.

15. ETHELBERT TALBOT (143) (Bishop of Bethlehem), from February 18, 1924, to January 1, 1926.

ELECTIVE

16. JOHN GARDNER MURRAY (243) (Bishop of Maryland), from January 1, 1926, to October 3, 1929 (died in office).

17. CHARLES PALMERSTON ANDERSON (197) (Bishop of Chicago), from November 13, 1929, to January 30, 1930 (died in office).

18. JAMES DEWOLF PERRY (247) (Bishop of Rhode Island), from March 26, 1930, to serve until General Convention of 1931. Reelected September 25, 1931, at General Convention held in Denver, Colo., for a term of six years to end December 31, 1937.

19. HENRY ST. GEORGE TUCKER (258) (Bishop of Virginia, resigned** in 1944), from January 1, 1938, to December 31, 1946.

20. HENRY KNOX SHERRILL (372) (Bishop of Massachusetts, resigned June 1, 1947), from January 1, 1947, to November 14, 1958.

21. ARTHUR LICHTENBERGER (503) (Bishop of Missouri, resigned in 1959), from November 15, 1958. Resigned for ill health, October, 1964.

22. JOHN ELBRIDGE HINES (461) (Bishop of Texas, resigned December 31, 1964), from January 1, 1965 to May 31, 1974.

23. JOHN MAURY ALLIN (581) (Bishop of Mississippi, resigned 1974), from June 1, 1974 to December 31, 1985.

24. EDMOND LEE BROWNING (630) (Bishop of Hawaii, resigned 1986) from January 1, 1986 to December 31, 1997.

25. FRANK TRACY GRISWOLD III (794) (Bishop of Chicago, resigned 1998) from January 1, 1998 to October 31, 2006.

26. KATHARINE JEFFERTS SCHORI (963) (Bishop of Nevada, resigned October 31, 2006) from November 1, 2006, to October 31, 2015.

27. MICHAEL BRUCE CURRY (955) (Bishop of North Carolina, resigned October 31, 2015), from November 1, 2015.

*NOTE—The title *Presiding Bishop* was not used in the Journals of General Convention until 1795. This table is based on the premise that the Bishop who was President of General Convention or of the House of Bishops before 1795 was *de facto* Presiding Bishop.

The General Convention of 1789 during its first session (July 28-August 8), and for the first five days (September 29-October 3) of its second session (September 29-October 16), consisted of one House only. Bishop White was *President of the General Convention* throughout its first session and for the first five days of its second session, and as such signed the minutes of the first session.

When, on October 5, 1789, a separate House of Bishops was first organized, Bishop Seabury became President of the House of Bishops in accordance with the rule of seniority, based on the date of consecration to the episcopate.

On September 13, 1792, Bishop Provoost became President of the House of Bishops by the adoption of the rule that the office should "be held in rotation, beginning from the North."

In 1795, under the above rule, Bishop White automatically became President of the House of Bishops, and for the first time the title *Presiding Bishop* appears in the signing of the minutes of that

House. In 1799, "the Bishop whose turn it would have been to preside" not being present, "Bishop White was requested to preside." In 1801 the rule of rotation was suspended. On September 12, 1804, the rule of seniority was again adopted and continued in effect for 115 years.

The General Convention of 1919 provided for the election of the Presiding Bishop by the Convention. The first such election took place at the General Convention of 1925.

**NOTE—The Presiding Bishop is currently elected by and from the House of Bishops and confirmed by the House of Deputies. The Presiding Bishop resigns from being a Diocesan within six months of taking office and retires after nine years (or at age seventy). The term begins on the first day of November following the election. (See Canon I.2 for further detail.)

RECENTLY CONSECRATED BISHOPS

DANIEL PAUL RICHARDS

On September 25, 2021, The Rt. Rev. Daniel Paul Richards was elected to serve as the ninth bishop of The Episcopal Diocese of Upper South Carolina.

Daniel was born in Cleveland, Mississippi, and grew up in Mississippi and Tennessee before moving with his family to Phoenix, Arizona, in high school. He graduated *summa cum laude* from Grand Canyon University in 1994, with a Bachelor of Arts in Creative Arts in Worship: Speech and Performance. He was ordained a Southern Baptist minister by the First Baptist Church of Buckeye, Arizona, on February 2, 1996.

Daniel's faith journey led him to leave the Southern Baptist tradition shortly after his ordination, and he found a home in The Episcopal Church. In 1997, Daniel was confirmed in The Episcopal Church and was hired by The Episcopal Diocese of Arizona as the Youth and Young Adult Coordinator for the diocese. He attended the Church Divinity School of the Pacific in Berkeley, California, and graduated with a Master in Divinity (MDiv) in 2003. He was ordained to the Sacred Order of Deacons on May 25, 2003, and to the Sacred Order of Priests on December 3, by Bishop Robert Reed Shahan (Arizona).

Daniel first served as a Curate at Saint Michael and All Angels in Tucson before serving as a Curate at the Church of the Holy Spirit in Phoenix for four years. During this time, he also served on the Commission on Ministry for the Diocese of Arizona and as spiritual director for the annual high school program at Chapel Rock Camp and Conference Center.

Daniel accepted a call to serve as Rector of Grace Episcopal Church in Traverse City, Michigan, in 2009, which has a long-standing commitment to hands-on ministry to the homeless and underserved. In 2010, Daniel was appointed Dean of the Grand Traverse Deanery and served as Dean until 2015, the same year he ended his tenure as Rector at Grace Episcopal Church. While in the Diocese of Western Michigan, he also served on the bishop nominating committee for the ninth bishop of Western Michigan and local interdenominational and inter-religious boards.

In 2015, Daniel returned to Arizona to serve as Rector of Christ Church of the Ascension Episcopal Church and School in Paradise Valley. Shortly thereafter, he was elected Dean of the East Phoenix Deanery and

served as President of the Board of Chapel Rock Camp and Conference Center in Prescott. While Rector of Christ Church of the Ascension, Daniel also served as a volunteer chaplain for the Phoenix Fire Department from 2018 to 2021, a ministry that has left a deep impression on him.

Daniel is an experienced minister of the gospel, a gifted preacher, and a thoughtful leader in the Church. His spiritual life is marked by a deep love for and commitment to the Benedictine tradition, especially its discipline of deep prayer, challenging study, and hard work. In the midst of the constant demands and the weight of ministry, Daniel finds peace and draws spiritual strength from time in the wilderness.

Daniel is married to Amy Rose Richards of West Bloomfield, Michigan, and they have three children: Rachel Richards, Jolie Richards, and Henri Richards. They reside in Columbia, South Carolina.

ELIZABETH BONFORTE GARDINER

Although Elizabeth was born in the same hospital as her mother and grandmother in Pueblo, Colorado, her family moved to San Diego, and she graduated from Torrey Pines High School. Since going to school on the beach is always a good idea, Elizabeth earned a Bachelor of Arts in Political Science with an emphasis in Public Policy from the University of California Santa Barbara.

After college, Elizabeth moved to Washington, DC, to "save the world." She participated in all aspects of politics before taking a hiatus to work at Nordstrom, Inc., where she was the buyer for women's career clothing. She went back into politics, eventually settling on the campaign side, and founded a successful consulting firm, The Townsend Group, with two other women. Her rector at St. John's Lafayette Square, however, had other plans and encouraged Elizabeth to consider ordained ministry. "While saving the world is admirable, perhaps you should first consider saving souls," he told her. Unfortunately, Virginia Theological Seminary was not on the beach, but Elizabeth graduated anyway with a Master of Divinity, cum laude.

Elizabeth is the 11th Bishop of Nevada elected October 8, 2021, and consecrated and ordained on

March 5, 2022. The Diocese of Nevada has offices in Las Vegas and Reno to support a camp on Lake Tahoe, two preaching stations, and thirty churches scattered throughout the state, including one in Bullhead City, Arizona.

Elizabeth previously served in the dioceses of Virginia and Washington, DC, focusing on church growth, leadership, and young adults. She helped start a 20s & 30s ministry at St. John's Lafayette Square, where she met her husband, Chris. They have been married for twenty-two years and have two daughters. Annie, a graduate of Columbia Chicago, is a filmmaker and currently working for NBC on the television show *Chicago PD*. Carolyn attends the University of the South in Sewanee, Tennessee, and is a bio-chemistry major. The whole family is excited for skiing and snowboarding in the beautiful Sierra mountains.

MATTHEW D. COWDEN

The Rt. Rev. Matthew D. Cowden is the VIII Bishop of West Virginia. He was consecrated as Bishop Coadjutor on March 12, 2022, and Bishop Diocesan on October 14, 2022.

With family roots in West Virginia, Bishop Cowden was born and reared in northern Virginia. After an early career as a college theater professor, he received his Master of Divinity degree at Virginia Theological Seminary in 2006 and served parishes in the Dioceses of Virginia and Northern Indiana. As a Trainer in Congregational Development ministries, Bishop Cowden has led rural and suburban congregations in developing a shared vision for implementing new ministry.

He is married to Melissa Cowden, his best friend and partner in ministry. Melissa is an early childhood teacher with a master's degree in multicultural education. They have three young adult children: Meghan, a nurse; Nicholas, a ballet dancer; and Joshua, a computer science major. Bishop Cowden loves hiking, running, making memorable meals, folklore, and storytelling.

BRIAN KENDALL BURGESS

A native of Southwest Florida, The Right Reverend Brian K. Burgess grew up attending Episcopal day schools and public schools while singing in an Anglican choir of men and boys. He attended Ball State University in Muncie, Indiana, as a Music Edu-

cation major (B.S.) where he studied Applied Percussion and served as Drum Major of the Ball State *Pride of Mid-America* Marching Band.

Bishop Burgess began his career as band and choral director at Rockville High School in the Wabash Valley area of Indiana. From there, he taught within the Lee County, Florida, school district where his senior high band programs were consistently recognized with superior ratings by the State Bandmasters Association.

He served as a fully certified law enforcement officer for the Lee County Port Authority Police Department prior to being hired by the nationally recognized Lee County Division of Emergency Management as their Training Coordinator and then Operations Coordinator. Bishop Burgess is licensed by the Federal Communications Commission (FCC) as a General Class amateur radio operator, call sign KD4UTL. In the immediate aftermath of Hurricane Andrew in 1992, he was dispatched to Florida City on the southeast coast of Florida as part of the Lee County Department of Public Safety's Response and Recovery Team.

Bishop Burgess attended seminary at The University of the South in Sewanee, Tennessee (MDiv., *cum laude*). After being invited into and completing the required canonical process, Bishop Burgess was ordained deacon and priest by The Right Reverend John Bailey Lipscomb of Southwest Florida. As priest, he has served parishes within the Episcopal dioceses of Southwest Florida, Louisiana, and New Jersey. Throughout these tenures, he served on diocesan council, standing committee, ecumenical and inter-faith relations committee, the Episcopal Community Services board, clerical compensation committee, and fifteen (nonconsecutive) years as dean of a three-country deanery of parishes and missions. In addition, he was elected by the Associated Alumni of The University of the South to represent their interests as a Clerical Trustee on the University Board of Trustees.

On December 11, 2021, while in his seventeenth year as rector of Christ Church Woodbury, New Jersey, Bishop Burgess was elected the XII Diocesan of Springfield on the second ballot. He was ordained and consecrated a bishop and seated within the Cathedral Church of St. Paul the Apostle in Springfield, Illinois, on May 21, 2022, by the Most Reverend Michael B. Curry, Presiding Bishop of the Episcopal Church USA, The Right Reverend Gregory O. Brewer of Central Florida, and The Right Reverend Dr. John C. Bauerschmidt of Tennessee. Other co-consecrators included The Right Reverend

Dr. J. Neil Alexander of Atlanta (retired), The Right Reverend William H. Stokes of New Jersey, and The Right Reverend Daniel H. Martins of Springfield (retired).

Bishop Burgess is married to his college sweetheart, Denise Lee (née Swing), and together, they have two grown children, Robert Kendall and Catherine Marian.

JOS THARAKAN

Fr. Jos Tharakan, Rector at St. James Episcopal Church, Springfield, Missouri, was born and brought up in a traditional and devout Roman Catholic Eastern Rite home in Kerala, India. His parents and four siblings grew up in a poor but religiously diverse and rich place, among Hindus and Muslims. After completing high school at the age of 15, he joined the Religious Order of Friars Minor Capuchins, First Order Franciscans. He was ordained on December 30, 1994, and served in the North Indian Missions of the Capuchins. While in Delhi, he served as priest and chaplain to the Missionaries of Charity of St. Mother Teresa and was blessed to know her. Besides being the Assistant Director of the Media House Publication Center, he was an itinerant preacher, music composer, spiritual director, theology professor, and interim high school principal for St. Paul's and Holy Angels in Uttar Pradesh, India.

At the invitation of Bishop Andrew J. McDonald, Fr. Jos came to the Catholic Diocese of Little Rock, and he served as associate priest at the Immaculate Conception Church in Fort Smith and St. Leo's in Hartford, Arkansas. Receiving a 'call within a call,' he came out of the Roman church on the day of Pentecost in 2001 and moved into a small town of 98 people in Chester, Arkansas. There he lived a simple life and worked on a cow farm, caring for 900 cows. After completing eight units of Clinical Pastoral Education in San Antonio and Pine Bluff from 2001 to 2003, he returned to Chester. He then started a successful business providing internet access to poor and rural communities. In 2006, Fr. Jos was accepted into the Episcopal Church and served Christ Church, a small mission in Mena, and All Saints' in Russellville, Arkansas.

During these years, he presented popular teleconferences on Pastoral Care and Complementary Healing through the University of Texas, and taught the same in hospitals and the CASA in Scottsdale, Arizona. In 2004 he received a certificate of recognition for his innovative Healing Ministry presentation for chaplains at the International Conference of the National Association of the Catholic Chaplains in Kansas City, Missouri. His workshops also were approved for continuing education credits through the Association of Clinical Pastoral Education and the National Association of Massage Therapists and Bodyworks. In 2015, five years before the projected date, he achieved his CREDO BHAG (Big Hairy Audacious Goal) when he founded the House of Blessings Foundation, a nonprofit renewal center for clergy and laity to grow spiritually. Being technology savvy, Fr. Jos designed several websites and church apps, and he currently publishes an online newspaper called the *Episcopal Daily* (www.episcopaldaily.net). Fr. Jos also is a nationally commissioned Centering Prayer Facilitator and member of Spiritual Directors International. He now serves as the Dean of the Southern Deanery of the Diocese of West Missouri, besides being the rector at St. James.

Fr. Jos married Kimby, a preschool teacher and an excellent children's minister. Combined, they have six children and three grandchildren. They also have a dog named Mia and a cat named Bunny FuFu. Together they serve a beautiful growing congregation in Springfield and are proud and humbled to be loved and cared for by the community of St. James.

PAULA E. CLARK

The Rt. Rev. Canon Paula E. Clark was elected on December 12, 2020, and ordained and consecrated on September 17, 2022, as the thirteenth bishop of the Episcopal Diocese of Chicago. She leads more than 30,000 Episcopalians in 122 congregations across northern and west central Illinois, and is the first Black person and the first woman to hold the position.

Clark, who previously served as canon to the ordinary and chief of staff in the Episcopal Diocese of Washington, was chosen unanimously on the fourth ballot in an election conducted on Zoom from a slate originally composed of four candidates. She received 229 clergy votes and 284 lay votes.

Clark was baptized into the Episcopal Church at age ten by Bishop John Walker, the first Black dean of Washington National Cathedral and first Black bishop of the Diocese of Washington. She received her undergraduate education at Brown University and earned a Master of Public Policy degree from the University of California, Berkeley.

Before entering the seminary, Clark served as public information officer for the Office of the Mayor and the District of Columbia's Board of Parole for nine years and spent five years as director of human resources and administration for an engineering and consulting firm in the District.

In 2004, she received a Master of Divinity degree from the Virginia Theological Seminary in Alexandria, Virginia, and served at St. Patrick's Episcopal Church in Washington, DC, and St. John's Episcopal Church in Beltsville, Maryland, before joining the staff of Bishop Mariann Edgar Budde. Her work for the diocese focused initially on clergy development and multicultural and justice issues.

PHYLLIS SPIEGEL

The Rt. Rev. Phyllis Spiegel was consecrated as the 12th Bishop of Utah on September 17, 2022. She is passionate about The Episcopal Church's work of deepening discipleship through daily practices of faith, believing that deepening our daily walk with God profoundly changes the way we walk in the world. Bishop Spiegel has a commitment to finding sustainable solutions for providing stability and dignity for the unhoused and those with mental illness.

Bishop Spiegel was ordained a priest in 2004. She served as a Priest-in-Charge to St. Thomas in Christiansburg, Virginia, from 2006 to 2015. In 2015, she was called as rector to St. Anne in West Chester, Ohio.

The Bishop graduated from Virginia Theological Seminary in 2004. Her undergraduate work was at Emory & Henry where she received a Bachelor of Arts degree in Business Management, French, and International Studies. After graduation, she interned with Southern Empowerment Project (SEP) and spent her time learning grassroots organizing in Appalachia. She then taught Business and Commerce at a secondary school in Kenya for nine months. Upon returning to the U.S., she answered the call to the priesthood.

She has a daughter, who lives in England with her husband. The Bishop's hiking partner is a 90-pound Dutch Shepherd mix named Samson, who loves his morning hike with her.

DOUGLAS FREDERICK SCHARF

The Rt. Rev. Douglas Frederick Scharf was elected bishop coadjutor of the Diocese of Southwest Florida on April 2, 2022. He was ordained and consecrated as a bishop on September 24, 2022, in Sarasota, Florida. He was seated as the sixth bishop of the diocese on December 10, 2022, at the Cathedral Church of St. Peter in St. Petersburg.

Prior to his 2022 election, Bishop Scharf was the Rector of Good Shepherd Episcopal Church and School in Tequesta, Florida, since January 2017. A thriving congregation, Good Shepherd includes more than 500 active members and a vibrant, fully accredited early childhood program and elemen-

tary school of 140 students. He served as rector of Holy Innocents' Episcopal Church (October 2007–2016) in Valrico, Florida. He also served as associate rector of Church of the Holy Spirit (June 2004–October 2007) in Osprey, Florida.

Bishop Scharf earned a B.A. in English from Florida Gulf Coast University (2002); an M.Div. from Virginia Theological Seminary (2004); and a D.Min. from Emory University, Candler School of Theology (2018), with a concentration in Biblical Interpretation and Proclamation.

In addition to parish ministry, Bishop Scharf has served in various leadership roles within his diocesan communities and the wider Episcopal Church, including Standing Committee President, Convocation Dean, and two-time Deputy to General Convention.

Born in 1979, Bishop Scharf was raised in the Diocese of Southwest Florida, the son of the Rev. Frederick Scharf and Carol Scharf. He and his wife Shannon are the parents of three children: Clayton, Parker, and Grady. His hobbies include music (he plays piano), reading, hiking, kayaking, and spending time in the beauty of God's creation.

JEFFREY WILLIAM MELLO

The Rt. Rev. Jeffrey W. Mello is the 16th Bishop Diocesan of the Episcopal Church in Connecticut. Elected in May 2022, he was ordained bishop in October 2022. As Bishop Diocesan, Bishop Jeff oversees and is responsible for the spiritual and temporal needs of the Episcopal Church in Connecticut; together, we participate in God's mission.

The *Book of Common Prayer* says that "a bishop in God's Holy Church is called to be one with the apostles in proclaiming Christ's resurrection and interpreting the Gospel. . . . The bishop is called to guard the faith, unity, and discipline of the Church; to celebrate and provide for the administration of the sacraments of the New Covenant; to ordain priests and deacons and to join in ordaining bishops; and to be in all things a faithful pastor and wholesome example for the entire flock of Christ."

For fun, Bishop Jeff enjoys running, attending live theater, hiking with his dog, and especially coffee ice cream.

SHANNON ROGERS DUCKWORTH

The Rev. Canon Shannon Rogers Duckworth was elected XII Bishop of the Episcopal Diocese of Louisiana during a special convention on May 14, 2022, at Christ Church Cathedral, New Orleans. She was elected on the first ballot after attaining a majority of both clergy and lay votes. She is the first woman to be elected bishop in the Episcopal Diocese of Louisiana.

A native of Mississippi, Bishop-elect Duckworth, received her BA in English and History in 1997 from Millsaps College. She was ordained a priest in 2001 after receiving her M.Div. from The General Theological Seminary.

Since 2013, Bishop-elect Duckworth has served as canon to the ordinary of the Episcopal Diocese of Louisiana. Prior to this position, she served as curate at St. John's Episcopal Church, Ocean Springs, Mississippi (May 2001–May 2002); vicar at St. Mary's Episcopal Church, Lexington, Mississippi (July 2002–July 2005); chaplain at St. Andrew's Episcopal School, Jackson, Mississippi (July 2005–September 2007); and associate rector of St. James' Episcopal Church, Jackson, Mississippi (September 2007–October 2013).

Bishop-elect Duckworth has held several diocesan and wider church leadership positions. These include Province IV Transition Officers (2013–present); Client Council, Church Pension Group (2018–present); St. Martin's Episcopal School, Metairie, Louisiana, Board member (2020–present); Transition in Progress Co-Facilitator, Diocese of Louisiana; Chair, General Convention Deputation, Diocese of Louisiana (2020); Co-Chair, Young Adult Discernment Committee, Diocese of Mississippi; Commission on Ministry member; Diocesan Liturgical Coordinator, Episcopal Diocese of Mississippi; and Transition Committee member for the tenth bishop of Mississippi 2012–13.

She is married to James Duckworth and has two sons, Nicholas and Tucker.

E. MARK STEVENSON

The Rt. Rev'd E. Mark Stevenson is the 14th Bishop of the Episcopal Diocese of Virginia. He was elected on June 4, 2022, at St. Stephen's and St. Agnes School, Alexandria, and was ordained and consecrated on December 3, 2022, at The Saint Paul's Baptist Church in Richmond. More than thirty-five bishops from around the United States, England, Tanzania, and Ghana joined in the laying on of hands along with Presiding Bishop Michael Bruce Curry, Chief Consecrator.

Bishop Stevenson centers his ministry—and that of the Diocese of Virginia—on the teaching and love of Jesus. Central to that is an emphasis on truth telling and reckoning as we address issues of systemic racism; life-giving formation as followers of Jesus; and transparency and accountability as we interact with each other as the family of God.

Prior to his ministry in the Diocese of Virginia, Bishop Stevenson served as Canon to the Presiding Bishop for Ministry Within The Episcopal Church. In this role he was the principal liaison between Presiding Bishop Michael Curry and the House of Bishops, the various dioceses, and many of the governing bodies of The Episcopal Church. Before being called to that role in September 2018, he was the Director of Episcopal Migration Ministries leading a dedicated team in executing a national program of refugee resettlement. Previously, he served as Domestic Poverty Missioner for The Episcopal Church.

Bishop Stevenson served as Canon to the Ordinary in the Diocese of Louisiana from August 2005 until September 2013. Following hurricane Katrina, he worked closely with local, regional, national, and international leaders and groups to put into place the processes for effective relief and other ministry. He was the rector in two parishes: the Church of the Annunciation in New Orleans, and the Church of the Good Shepherd in Maitland, Florida. His time a both churches focused on developing ministries with youth and revitalizing ministries of stewardship, Christian education, and community outreach.

Bishop Stevenson and his wife of twenty-seven years, Joy, reside in Richmond with their border collie Franklin.

The Anglican Communion

Introduction
The Anglican Communion comprises 40 self-governing *Member Churches* or *Provinces* that share several things in common including doctrine, ways of worshipping, mission, and a focus of unity in the Archbishop of Canterbury. Formal mechanisms for meeting include the Lambeth Conference, the Anglican Consultative Council, and the Primates' Meeting, together with the Archbishop, known as the *Instruments of Communion*.

Most Communion life, however, is found in the relationships between Anglicans at all levels of church life and work around the globe; dioceses linked with dioceses, parishes with parishes, people with people, all working to further God's mission. There are tens of millions of people on six continents who call themselves Anglican (or Episcopalian), in more than 165 countries. These Christian brothers and sisters share prayer, resources, support and knowledge across geographical and cultural boundaries.

As with any family, the Anglican Communion's members have a range of differing opinions. The Anglican Christian tradition has long valued its diversity, and has never been afraid to tackle publicly the hard questions of life and faith.

History
IIn continuity with the ancient Celtic and Saxon churches of the British Isles, and Britain's place within Catholic Europe, Anglicanism found its distinctive identity in the 16th and 17th centuries. At the Reformation national Churches emerged in England, Ireland and Scotland. With the American Revolution an autonomous Episcopal Church was founded in the United States and later Anglican or Episcopal Churches were founded across the globe as a result of the missionary movements of the 18th and 19th centuries. Many of these Churches became autonomous Provinces in the course of the 19th and 20th centuries. In South Asia, the United Churches formed between Anglican and Protestant denominations, joined the Anglican Communion, as did Churches elsewhere such as the Spanish Episcopal Reformed Church and the Lusitanian Church of Portugal.

Official structures
It was in 1867 that Lambeth Palace hosted the first conference for Anglican bishops from around the world. From 1948 each Archbishop of Canterbury has called a *Lambeth Conference* every ten years. The last, in 2008, saw more than 800 bishops from around the world invited to Canterbury. The Conference has no authority of itself: rather it is a chance for bishops to meet and explore aspects of Anglican Communion life and ministry. The next Lambeth Conference takes place in July and August 2020.

Bishops attending the 1968 Lambeth Conference called for a body representative of all sections of the churches—laity, clergy and bishops—to co-ordinate aspects of international Anglican ecumenical and mission work. The resulting body was the *Anglican Consultative Council*. This council comprising elected and appointed members from around the globe meets approximately every three years.

Since 1979 the Archbishop of Canterbury has also regularly invited the chief bishops of the Provinces (known as *Primates*) to join him in a meeting for consultation, prayer and reflection on theological, social and international matters. These *Primates' Meetings* take place approximately every two years.

These Instruments of Communion are served by a secretariat with staff based at the Anglican Communion Office in London, England, and New York.

(See below for more information on the Anglican Communion Office)

Beliefs
There can be many differences between individual Anglican churches, but all uphold and proclaim the Catholic and Apostolic faith, proclaimed in the Scriptures, interpreted in the light of tradition and reason. Anglicans hold these things in common:

- The Holy Bible, comprising the Old and New Testament, as a basis of our faith;

- The Nicene and Apostles' Creeds as the basic statements of Christian belief;

- Recognition of the Sacraments of Baptism and Holy Communion; and

- The Historic Episcopate—ours is a Christian tradition with bishops.

This *quadrilateral*, drawn up in the 19th Century, is one of the definitions of Anglican faith and ministry. Another is a style of worship which has its roots in the Book of Common Prayer and the Services of Ordination (the Ordinal). Anglicans also celebrate the Eucharist (also known as the Holy Communion, the Lord's Supper or the Mass), the Sacrament of Baptism and other rites including Confirmation, Reconciliation, Marriage, Anointing of the Sick, and Ordination.

Anglicanism rests on the three pillars of Scripture, Tradition and Reason as it seeks to chart 'a middle way' among the other Christian traditions.

Mission
Following the teachings of Jesus Christ, Anglicans are committed to proclaiming the good news of the Gospel to all creation as expressed in the Marks of Mission:

- To proclaim the Good News of the Kingdom;

- To teach, baptise and nurture new believers;

- To respond to human need by loving service;

- To seek to transform unjust structures of society, to challenge violence of every kind and to pursue peace and reconciliation

- To strive to safeguard the integrity of creation and sustain and renew the life of the earth.

These Marks are to be expressed in all areas of a Christian's life: their words and their actions. Therefore, members of the Anglican Communion around the world are involved with a range of life-changing activities that include evangelism and church growth; providing food, shelter and clothing to those in need; speaking out with and for the oppressed; and setting up schools, hospitals, clinics and universities.

PROVINCES

The Anglican Church in Aotearoa, New Zealand & Polynesia
The Anglican Church of Australia
The Church of Bangladesh
Igreja Episcopal Anglicana do Brasil
The Anglican Church of Burundi
The Anglican Church of Canada
The Church of the Province of Central Africa
Iglesia Anglicana de la Region Central de America
Iglesia Anglicana de Chile
Province de L'Eglise Anglicane Du Congo
The Church of England
Hong Kong Sheng Kung Hui
The Church of the Province of the Indian Ocean
The Church of Ireland
The Nippon Sei Ko Kai
(The Anglican Communion in Japan)
The Episcopal Church in Jerusalem & the Middle East
The Anglican Church of Kenya
The Anglican Church of Korea
The Church of the Province of Melansia
La Iglesia Anglicana de Mexico
The Church of the Province of Myanmar (Burma)
The Church of Nigeria (Anglican Communion)
The Church of North India (United)
The Church of Pakistan (United)
The Anglican Church of Papua New Guinea
The Episcopal Church in the Philippines
Eglise Anglicane du Rwanda
The Scottish Episcopal Church
Church of the Province of South East Asia

The Church of South India (United)
The Anglican Church of Southern Africa
The Anglican Church of South America
Province of the Episcopal Church of South Sudan
Province of the Episcopal Church of Sudan
The Anglican Church of Tanzania
The Church of the Province of Uganda
The Episcopal Church *(Includes 100 dioceses in the United States, and 12 additional dioceses or jurisdictions in 15 nations)*
The Church in Wales
The Church of the Province of West Africa
The Church in the Province of the West Indies

Extra-Provincial Churches and other dioceses
The Church of Ceylon
(Extra-Provincial to Canterbury)
Bermuda (Extra-Provincial to Canterbury)
The Lusitanian Church
(Extra-Provincial to Canterbury)
The Reformed Episcopal Church of Spain
(Extra-Provincial to Canterbury)
Falkland Islands (Extra-Provincial to Canterbury)

Churches in Communion
The Mar Thoma Syrian Church of Malabar
The Old Catholic Churches of the Union of Utrecht
The Philippine Independent Church
(Iglesia Filipina Independiente - IFI)
NB: Anglicans/Episcopalians in certain parts of the Communion are in full communion with some Lutheran Churches.

THE ANGLICAN COMMUNION OFFICE

Sec Gen for Ang Com Archbishop Dr Josiah Idowu-Fearon; *Dir for Unity Faith and Order* Revd Dr Will Adams; *Executive Dir for Anglican Alliance* Revd Rachel Carnegie; *Dir for Com* Gavin Drake; *Dir for Finance and Resources* Michaela Southworth; *Dir for Mission* Rev John Kafwanka; *Dir for Gender Justice* Mandy Marshall; *Rep to UN institutions in Geneva* Jack Palmer-White-Anglican Communion; *Wdn of the Gst Hse* Stefan Tkaczek; *Chief Operating Officer:* David White

Anglican Communion Office: St Andrew's House, 16 Tavistock Crescent, London, W11 1AP
Tel: +44 (0)207 313 3900   *Fax:* +44 (0)207 313 3999
E-mail: aco@anglicancommunion.org
Web: www.anglicancommunion.org   ACNS: www.anglicannews.org
Lambeth Conference: www.lambethconference.org

The permanent secretariat (the Anglican Communion Office) serves the Anglican Communion and is responsible for facilitating all meetings of the conciliar Instruments of Communion as well as the commissions, working groups and networks of the Communion. Anglican Communion Office staff from countries including Colombia, Nigeria, the United States, and Zambia also maintain the Anglican Communion website where visitors can find the official prayer cycle (daily prayer intentions for the dioceses of the Communion) and vast amounts of official information and documentation about the Anglican Communion's Instruments and its ministries. The very latest news from around the Anglican world is available via the Anglican Communion News Service (ACNS) website. Most of the funding for the work of the office comes from the Inter-Anglican budget supported by all Member Churches according to their means.

The Anglican Episcopate

THE ANGLICAN CHURCH IN AOTEAROA, NEW ZEALAND AND POLYNESIA

General Secretary The Revd Michael M Hughes PO BOX 87188 Meadowbank Auckland 1742 NEW ZEALAND *Tel:* + 64 (0)9 521 4439 *Email:* gensecm@anglicanchurch.org.nz *Web:* www.anglican.org.nz

Aotearoa Vacant Aotearoa is the overall See for all the Maori diocese in NZ PO Box 568 Gisborne 4040 NEW ZEALAND *Tel:* + 64 (0)6 867 8856

Auckland The Rt Revd Ross Bay Bishop of Auckland PO Box 37 242 Parnell Auckland 1151 NEW ZEALAND *Tel:* + 64 (0)9 302 7201 *Email:* bishop.office@auckanglican.org.nz

Auckland The Rt Revd James White Assistant bishop of Auckland PO Box 37 242 Parnell Auckland 1151 NEW ZEALAND *Tel:* + 64 (09) 302 7288 *Web:* www.auckanglican.org.nz

Christchurch The Rt Revd Victoria Matthews Bishop of Christchurch PO Box 4438 Christchurch 8140 NEW ZEALAND *Tel:* + 64 (0)3 379 5950 *Fax:* + 64 (0)3 372 3357 *Email:* bishopspa@anglicanlife.org.nz *Web:* www.anglicanlife.org.nz

Dunedin The Rt Revd Steven Benford Bishop of Dunedin 1A Howden Street Green Island Dunedin 9052 NEW ZEALAND *Tel:* + 64 (0)3 488 0820 *Fax:* + 64 (0)3 488 2038 *Email:* bishop.steven@calledsouth.org.nz *Web:* www.calledsouth.org.nz

Nelson The Rt Revd Victor Richard Ellena Bishop of Nelson PO Box 100 Nelson 7040 NEW ZEALAND *Tel:* + 64 (0)3 548 3124 *Fax:* + 64 (0)3 548 2125 *Email:* bprichard@nelsonanglican.org.nz *Web:* www.nelsonanglican.org.nz

Polynesia The Most Revd Winston Halapua Bishop of Polynesia and Primate and Archbishop of the Anglican Church in Aotearoa, New Zealand and Polynesia Box 35 Suva Fiji *Tel:* + 679 3 304 716 *Fax:* + 679 3 302 553 *Email:* archbishop@dioceseofpolynesia.org *Web:* www.dioceseofpolynesia.org

Polynesia The Rt Revd Apimeleki Nadoki Qiliho Bishop of Vanua Levu and Taveuni, Fiji PO Box 117 Lautoka FIJI *Tel:* + 679 666 0124 *Email:* qiliho@gmail.com *Web:* www.dioceseofpolynesia.org

Polynesia The Rt Revd Gabriel Sharma Bishop of Viti Levu West, Fiji PO Box 117 Lautoka FIJI *Email:* gabsharma@yahoo.com *Web:* www.dioceseofpolynesia.org

Polynesia The Rt Revd Afa Vaka Bishop in Tonga Box 35 Suva FIJI *Email:* afavaka@yahoo.co.nz

Te Pihopatanga o Manawa o Te Wheke The Rt Revd Ngarahu Katene Pihopa ki Te Manawa o Te Wheke (Bp Central North Island Region) PO Box 146 Rotorua 3040 NEW ZEALAND *Tel:* + 64 (0)7 348 4043 *Email:* ngarahukatene@ihug.co.nz

Te Pihopatanga o Tai Tokerau The Rt Revd Te Kitohi Wiremu Pikaahu Pihopa ki Te Tai Tokerau (Bp, Northern Region) PO Box 25 Paihia Bay of Islands 247 NEW ZEALAND *Tel:* + 64 (0)9 402 6788 *Fax:* + 64 (0)9 402 6663 *Email:* tkwp@tokerau.ang.org.nz

Te Pihopatanga o Tairawhiti The Rt Revd Don Tamihere Bishop of Te Hui Amorangi ki Te Tairawhiti PO Box 568 Gisborne 4040 NEW ZEALAND *Tel:* + 64 (0)6 867 8856 *Fax:* + 64 (0)6 867 8859 *Email:* bishop@tairawhiti.org.nz

Te Pihopatanga o Upoko o Te Ika The Rt Revd Muru Walters Pihopa ki Te Upoko o Te Ika (Bp, Wellington / Taranaki Region) 14 Amesbury Drive Churton Park Wellington 6037 NEW ZEALAND *Tel:* + 64 (0)4 478 3549 *Email:* muru.walters@xtra.co.nz

Te Pihopatanga o Upoko o Te Waipounamu The Rt Revd Richard R Wallace Pihopa ki Te Waipounamu (Bp, South Island) PO Box 10 086 Christchurch 8145 NEW ZEALAND *Tel:* + 64 (0)3 389 1683 *Fax:* + 64 (0)3 389 0912

Waiapu The Rt Revd Andrew Hedge Bishop of Waiapu PO Box 227 Napier 4140 NEW ZEALAND *Tel:* + 64 (0)6 835 8230 *Fax:* + 64 (0)6 835 0680 *Web:* www.waiapu.anglican.org.nz

Waikato & Taranaki The Most Revd Philip Richardson Bishop of Taranaki and Senior Bishop of New Zealand Dioceses and Primate and Archbishop of the Anglican Church in Aotearoa, New Zealand and Polynesia PO Box 547 566 Mangorei Road New Plymouth 4340 NEW ZEALAND *Tel:* + 64 (0)6 759 1178 *Fax:* + 64 (0)6 759 1180 *Email:* bishop@taranakianglican.org.nz

Waikato & Taranaki The Rt Revd Helen-Ann Hartley Bishop of Waikato PO Box 21 Hamilton 3240 NEW ZEALAND *Tel:* + 64 (0)7 857 0020 *Email:* bishopspa@waikatoanglican.org.nz *Web:* www.waikatotaranakianglican.org.nz/

Wellington The Rt Revd Justin Duckworth Bishop of Wellington PO Box 12-046 Wellington 6144 NEW ZEALAND *Tel:* + 64 04 472 1057 *Fax:* + 64 04 499 1360 *Email:* reception@wn.ang.org.nz *Web:* wn.anglican.org.nz

Wellington The Rt Revd Eleanor Sanderson Assistant Bishop of Wellington PO Box 12-046 Wellington 6144 NEW ZEALAND *Tel:* + 64 04 472 1057 *Email:* reception@wn.ang.org.nz *Web:* wn.anglican.org.nz

THE ANGLICAN CHURCH OF AUSTRALIA

General Secretary Ms Anne Hywood General Synod Office Suite 4 Level 5 189 Kent Street Sydney 2000 AUSTRALIA *Tel:* + 61 (0)2 8267 2701 *Fax:* + 61

(0)2 8267 2727 *Email:* generalsecretary@anglican.org.au

Finance and Administration Manager Ms Marianne Yacoel General Synod Office Suite 4 Level 5 189 Kent Street Sydney 2000 AUSTRALIA *Tel:* + 61 2 8267 2700 *Fax:* + 61 2 8267 2727 *Web:* www.anglican.org.au

Adelaide-South Australia The Rt Revd Geoffrey Martyn Smith Archbishop elect of Adelaide 18 King William Road North Adelaide 5006 AUSTRALIA *Tel:* + 61 (0)8 8305 9350 *Email:* office@adelaideanglicans.com

Adelaide-South Australia The Rt Revd Christopher McLeod Assistant Bishop of Adelaide & National Aboriginal Bishop 18 King William Road North Adelaide 5006 AUSTRALIA *Tel:* + 61 (0)8 305 9350 *Web:* www.adelaide.anglican.com.au

Adelaide-South Australia The Rt Revd Tim J Harris Bishop for Mission and Evangelism 18 King William Road North Adelaide 5006 AUSTRALIA *Tel:* + 61 8 8305 9352 *Email:* tharris@adelaide.anglican.com.au

Armidale-New South Wales The Rt Revd Richard Lewers Bishop of Armidale Anglican Diocesan Registry PO Box 198 Armidale 2350 AUSTRALIA *Tel:* + 61 (02) 6772 4491 *Fax:* + 61 (02) 6772 9261 *Email:* bishop@armidaleanglicandiocese.com *Web:* www.armidaleanglicandiocese.com

Ballarat-Victoria The Rt Revd Garry Weatherill Bishop of Ballarat PO Box 89 Ballarat 3352 AUSTRALIA *Tel:* + 61 (0)35 331 1183 *Fax:* + 61 (0)35 333 2982 *Email:* bishop@ballaratanglican.org.au *Web:* www.ballaratanglican.org.au

Bathurst-New South Wales The Rt Revd Ian Palmer Bishop of Bathurst PO Box 23 Bathurst 2795 AUSTRALIA *Tel:* + 61 (0)26 331 1722 *Fax:* + 61 (0)26 332 2772 *Web:* www.bathurst.anglican.org

Bendigo-Victoria The Rt Revd Andrew William Curnow Bishop of Bendigo PO Box 2 Post office Bendigo 3552 AUSTRALIA *Tel:* + 61 (0)35 443 4711 *Fax:* + 61 (0)35 441 2173 *Email:* bishop@bendigoanglican.org.au *Web:* www.bendigoanglican.org.au/

Brisbane-Queesland The Most Revd Phillip John Aspinall Archbishop of Brisbane PO Box 421 Brisbane 4001 AUSTRALIA *Tel:* + 61 (0)7 3835 2218 *Fax:* + 61 (0)7 3832 5030 *Email:* ajoseph@anglicanbrisbane.org.au *Web:* www.brisbane.anglican.org

Brisbane-Queensland The Rt Revd Ian Keese Lambert Aglican Bishop to the Australian Defence Force PO Box 421 Brisbane 4001 AUSTRALIA

Brisbane-Queensland The Rt Revd Cameron Venables Bishop of Brisbane - Western Region PO Box 2600 Toowoomba 4350 AUSTRALIA *Tel:* + 61 (0)7 4639 1875 *Fax:* + 61 (0)7 4632 6882

Brisbane The Rt Revd Alison Taylor Bishop of Brisbane - Southern Region PO Box 5384 Gold Coast Mail Centre 9726 Queensland AUSTRALIA

Brisbane-Queensland The Rt Revd Jonathan Holland Bishop of Brisbane - Northern Region GPO Box 421 Brisbane 4001 AUSTRALIA *Tel:* + 61 (0)7 3835 2213 *Fax:* + 61 (0)7 3832 5030 *Email:* jholland@anglicanbrisbane.org.au

Bunbury-Western Australia The Rt Revd Alan Ewing Bishop of Bunbury Bishopscourt PO Box 15 Bunbury 6231 AUSTRALIA *Tel:* + 61 9721 2100 *Email:* office@bunbury.org.au *Web:* www.bunbury.org.au

Canberra & Goulburn-ACT The Rt Revd Stuart Robinson Bishop of Canberra & Goulburn Jamieson House 43 Constitution Avenue Reid 2612 AUSTRALIA

Canberra & Goulburn-ACT The Rt Revd Trevor W Edwards Assistant Bishop of Canberra & Goulburn 28 McBryde Crescent Wanniassa 2903 AUSTRALIA *Tel:* + 61 (0)2 6231 7347 *Fax:* + 61 (0)2 6231 7500 *Email:* trevor@stmattswanniassa.org.au

Canberra & Goulburn-ACT Vacant Regional Bishop in Wagga Wagga Jamieson House 43 Constitution Avenue Reid 2612 AUSTRALIA

Gippsland-Victoria The Rt Revd Kay Goldsworthy Bishop of Gippsland PO Box 928 Sale 3850 AUSTRALIA *Tel:* + 61 (0)35 144 2044 *Fax:* + 61 (0)35 144 7183 *Email:* bishopkay@gippsanglican.org.au *Web:* www.gippsanglican.org.au

Grafton-New South Wales The Rt Revd Sarah Macneil Bishop of Grafton Bishopsholme PO Box 4 Grafton 2460 AUSTRALIA *Tel:* + 61 (0)2 6642 4122 *Fax:* + 61 (0)2 6643 1814 *Email:* bishop@graftondiocese.org.au *Web:* www.graftondiocese.org.au

Melbourne-Victoria The Most Revd Philip Leslie Freier Archbishop of Melbourne & Primate of Australia The Anglican Centre 209 Flinders Lane Melbourne 3000 AUSTRALIA *Tel:* + 61 (0)3 9653 4204 *Email:* archbishopsoffice@melbourneanglican.org.au *Web:* www.melbourne.anglican.com.au/

Melbourne-Victoria The Rt Revd Genieve Blackwell Bishop of Melbourne - Marmingatha Episcopate The Anglican Centre 209 Flinders Lane Melbourne 3000 AUSTRALIA *Tel:* + 61 (0)3 9653 4220

Melbourne-Victoria The Rt Revd Philip J Huggins Bishop of Melbourne - Oodthenong Episcopate The Anglican Centre 209 Flinders Lane Melbourne 3000 AUSTRALIA *Tel:* + 61 (0)3 9653 4220 *Fax:* + 61 (0)3 9653 4266 *Email:* phuggins@melbourne.anglican.com.au

Melbourne-Victoria The Rt Revd Paul White Bishop of Melbourne - Jumbunna Episcopate The Anglican Centre 209 Flinders Lane Melbourne 3000 AUSTRALIA *Tel:* + 61 3 9653 4220 *Fax:* + 61 3 9650 2184 *Email:* paulwhite49@iinet.net.au

Newcastle (AUS)-New South Wales The Rt Revd Greg E Thompson Bishop of Newcastle The Bishop's Registry PO Box 817 Newcastle 2300 AUSTRALIA *Tel:* + 61 (0)2 4926 3733 *Fax:* + 61 (0)2 4926 1968 *Web:* www.newcastleanglican.org.au

Newcastle (AUS)-NEW SOUTH WALES The Rt Revd Peter Stuart Assistant Bishop of Newcastle The Diocesan Office PO Box 817 Newcastle 2300 AUSTRALIA *Tel:* + 61 (02) 4926 3733 *Email:* bishoppeter@newcastleanglican.org.au *Web:* www. newcastleanglican.org.au

North Queensland-Queensland The Rt Revd William J Ray Bishop of North Queensland PO Box 1244 Townsville 4810 AUSTRALIA *Tel:* + 61 (0)7 4771 4175 *Fax:* + 61 (0)7 4721 1756 *Email:* bishop@ anglicannq.org *Web:* www.anglicannq.com

North West Australia-Western Australia The Rt Revd Gary Nelson Bishop of North West AUSTRALIA PO Box 2783 Geraldton 6531 AUSTRALIA *Tel:* + 61 (0)8 9921 7277 *Fax:* + 61 (0)8 9964 2220 *Email:* bishop@anglicandnwa.org *Web:* www.anglicandnwa.org

Northern Territory, The- NT The Rt Revd Greg Anderson Bishop of the Northern Territory GPO Box 2950 Darwin 801 AUSTRALIA *Tel:* + 61 (0)8 8941 7440 *Fax:* + 61 (0)8 8941 7446 *Email:* ntdiocese@ internode.on.net *Web:* www.anglicanchurchnt.org.au

Perth-Western Australia The Most Revd Roger A Herft Archbishop of Perth GPO Box W2067 Perth 6846 AUSTRALIA *Tel:* + 61 (0)8 9425 7201 *Fax:* + 61 (0)8 9325 6741 *Email:* archbishop@perth.anglican. org *Web:* www.perth.anglican.org/

Perth-Western Australia The Rt Revd Tom Wilmot Assistant Bishop of Perth, Eastern and Rural Region GPO Box W2067 Perth 6846 AUSTRALIA *Tel:* + 61 08 9325 7455 *Fax:* + 61 08 9325 6741 *Email:* twilmot@perth.anglican.org

Perth-Western Australia The Rt Revd Jeremy James Assistant Bishop of Perth Goldfields-Country Region GPO Box W2067 Perth 6846 AUSTRALIA *Tel:* + 61 (0)8 9430 7224 *Fax:* + 61 (0)8 9336 3374

Perth-Western Australia The Rt Revd Kate Wilmot Assistant Bishop of Perth GPO Box W2067 Perth 5846 AUSTRALIA *Tel:* + 1 (0)8 9425 7201 *Web:* www.perth.anglican.org

Riverina-New South Wales The Rt Revd Rob Gillion Bishop of Riverina PO Box 10 58 Arthur Street Narrandera 2700 AUSTRALIA *Tel:* + 61 (0)2 6959 1648 *Fax:* + 61 (0)2 6959 2903 *Email:* bishoprob@ anglicanriverina.com *Web:* www.riverina.anglican.org

Rockhampton-Queensland The Rt Revd David Robinson Bishop of Rockhampton PO Box 6158 Central Queensland Mail Centre Rockhampton 4702 AUSTRALIA *Tel:* + 61 (0)7 4927 3188 *Fax:* + 1 (0)7 4922 4562 *Email:* bishop@anglicanrock.org. au *Web:* www.anglicanrock.org.au

Sydney-New South Wales The Most Revd Glenn N Davies Archbishop of Sydney PO Box 190 Q.V.B Post Office Sydney 1230 AUSTRALIA *Tel:* + 61 2 9265 1527 *Fax:* + 61 2 9265 1543 *Email:* gdavies@ sydney.anglican.asn.au *Web:* www.sydneyanglicans. net

Sydney-New South Wales The Rt Revd Robert C Forsyth Assistant Bishop of Sydney - South PO Box Q190 QVB Post Office Sydney 1230 AUSTRALIA *Tel:* + 61 (0)292 651 523 *Fax:* + 61 (0)292 651 543 *Email:* robforsyth@sydney.anglican.asn.au *Web:* www.anglicanmediasydney.asn.au/

Sydney-New South Wales The Rt Revd Ivan Y Lee Assistant Bishop of Sydney - West PO Box Q190 QVB Post Office 1230 AUSTRALIA *Tel:* + 61 (0)296 353 186 *Fax:* + 61 (0)296 333 636 *Email:* office@ westernsydney.anglican.asn.au

Sydney-New South Wales The Rt Revd Al Stewart Assistant Bishop of Sydney - Wollongong 74 Church Street PO Box A287 Wollongong 2500 AUSTRALIA *Tel:* + 61 (0)2 4225 2800 *Fax:* + 61 (0)2 4228 4296 *Email:* office@wollongong.anglican.asn.au *Web:* www.anglicanmediasydney.asn.au

Sydney-New South Wales The Rt Revd Peter J Tasker Assistant Bishop of Sydney - Liverpool PO Box Q190 QVB Post Office Sydney 1230 AUSTRALIA *Tel:* + 61 2 9265 1572 *Fax:* + 61 2 9265 1543 *Email:* ptasker@ sydney.anglican.asn.au

Sydney-New South Wales The Rt Revd Chris Edwards Assistant Bishop of Sydney - North PO Box Q190 QVB Post Office Sydney 1230 AUSTRALIA *Tel:* + 61 2 9265 1527 *Fax:* + 61 2 9265 1543 *Web:* www.sydneyanglicans.net

Tasmania-Tasmania The Rt Revd Richard Condie Bishop of Tasmania GPO 748H Hobart 7001 AUSTRALIA *Tel:* + 61 (0)3 6220 2020 *Email:* bishop@anglicantas.org.au *Web:* www.anglicantas. org.au

Tasmania-Tasmania The Rt Revd Christopher R J Jones Assistant Bishop of Tasmania GPO Box 1620 Hobart 7001 AUSTRALIA *Tel:* + 61 (0)3 6231 9602 *Fax:* + 61 (0)3 6231 9589 *Email:* c.jones@anglicare-tas.org.au *Web:* www.anglicare-tas.org.au

Tasmania-Tasmania The Rt Revd Ross J Nicholson Assistant Bishop of Tasmania 157 St John Street Launceston 7250 AUSTRALIA *Tel:* + 61 (0)3 6331 4896 *Fax:* + 61 (0)3 6334 1719 *Email:* rnicholson@ stjohns.net.au

The Murray-South Australia The Rt Revd John Frank Ford Bishop of The Murray PO Box 269 Murray Bridge 5253 AUSTRALIA *Tel:* + 61 (0)8 8532 2270 *Fax:* + 61 (0)8 8532 5760 *Email:* registry@ murray.anglican.org *Web:* www.murray.anglican.org

Wangaratta-Victoria The Rt Revd John Parkes Bishop of Wangaratta Bishop's Lodge PO Box 457 Wangaratta 3677 AUSTRALIA *Tel:* + 61 (0)3 5721

3643 *Email:* bishop@wangaratta.anglican.org *Web:* www.wangaratta-anglican.org.au

Willochra-South Australia The Rt Revd John Stead Bishop of Willochra PO Box 96 Gladstone 5497 AUSTRALIA *Tel:* + 61 (0)8 8662 2249 *Fax:* + 61 (0)8 8662 2027 *Email:* bishop@diowillochra.org.au *Web:* www.willochra.anglican.org

THE CHURCH OF BANGLADESH

Provincial Secretary Dr James Tejosh Das 54/1 Barobagh Mirpur-2 Dhaka 1216 Bangladesh *Email:* tejoshd@gmail.com

Hon Treasurer Mr Lawrence Mondol 54/1 Barobagh Mirpur-2 Dhaka 1216 Bangladesh *Email:* lorance_mondol@yahoo.com

Barisal The Rt Revd Shourabh Pholia Bishop of Barisal Awaiting Details

Dhaka The Most Revd Paul Shishir Sarker Moderator, Church of Bangladesh & Bishop of Dhaka 54/1 Barobagh Mirpur-2 Dhaka 1216 Bangladesh *Tel:* + 880 2 805 3729 *Email:* pssarker19@gmail.com

Kushtia The Rt Revd Samuel Sunil Mankhin Bishop of Kushtia St Thomas Church 391 New Eskaton Road Moghbazar Dhaka 1000 Bangladesh *Tel:* + 880 2 711 6546 *Fax:* + 880 2 712 1632

IGREJA EPISCOPAL ANGLICANA DO BRASIL

Provincial Secretary The Revd Arthur P Cavalcante Praça Olavo Bilac nº 63-Campos Elseos São Paulo SP 01201-050 BRAZIL *Email:* arthurieab@gmail.com

Provincial Treasurer Mrs Silvia Fernandes Campos Elíseos São Paulo SP 01201-050 BRAZIL *Tel:* + 55 (0)11 3667 8161 *Fax:* + 55 (0)11 3667 8161 *Email:* sec.geral@ieab.org.br

Amazon The Rt Revd Saulo Mauricio de Barros Bishop of the Amazon Avenida Serzedelo Corrêa 514 Batista Campos Belem PA 66033-265 BRAZIL *Tel:* + 55 (0)91 3241 9720 *Email:* saulomauricio@gmail.com *Web:* www.daa.ieab.org.br/

Brasilia The Rt Revd Maurício Jose Araujo De Andrade Bishop of Brasilia Gabinete Episcopal - Catedral Anglicana EQS 309/310 sala 1 - Asa Sul Brazilia DF 70362-400 BRAZIL *Tel:* + 55 (0)61 3443 4305 *Fax:* + 55 (0)61 3443 4337 *Email:* mandrade@ieab.org.br *Web:* www.dab.ieab.org.br

Curitiba The Rt Revd Naudal Alves Gomes Bishop of Curitiba Av. Sete de Setembro 3927 sl. 8 Centro Curitiba PR 80250-210 BRAZIL *Tel:* + 55 (0)41 3079 9992 *Fax:* + 55 (0)41 3079 9992 *Email:* naudal@yahoo.com.br *Web:* www.dac.ieab.org.br

Missionary District of Oeste-Brasil Vacant The Most Revd Francisco de Assis da Silva is currently Bishop in Charge Av. Rio Branco 880 Santa Maria RS 97010-422 BRAZIL *Tel:* + 55 (0)55 3221 4328 *Fax:*

+ 55 (0)55 8131 0709 *Email:* xicosilva@gmail.com *Web:* www.dmo.ieab.org.br/

Pelotas The Rt Revd Renato Da Cruz Raatz Bishop of Pelotas Rua Goncalves Chaves, 665 Pelotas RS 96015-560 BRAZIL *Tel:* + 55 (0)53 3202 8618 *Email:* rcaatz@ieab.org.br *Web:* www.dapsul.com.br/

Recife The Rt Revd João Cancio Peixoto Bishop of Recife Av. Boa Viagem 5130 apto 701 Recife PE 51.030-000 BRAZIL *Tel:* + 55 (0)81 33410791 *Fax:* + 55 (0)81 88330791 *Email:* joao.peixoto01@uol.com.br *Web:* www.dar.ieab.org.br

Rio de Janeiro The Rt Revd Filadelfo Oliviera Neto Bishop of Rio de Janeiro Rua Haddock Lobo 258 Rio de Janeiro RJ 20260-142 BRAZIL *Tel:* + 55 (0)21 2220 2148 *Fax:* + 55 (0)21 2252 9686 *Email:* oliveira.ieab@gmail.com *Web:* www.anglicanarj.org

Sao Paulo The Rt Revd Flavio Augusto Borges Irala Bishop of São Paulo Rua Borges Lagoa 172 Vila Clementino Sao Paulo SP 04038-030 BRAZIL *Tel:* + 55 (0)11 5549 9086 *Email:* flavioirala@ieab.org.br

South Western Brazil The Most Revd Francisco De Assis Da Silva Primate of Brazil & Bishop of South-Western Brazil Av. Rio Branco 880 Santa Maria RS 97010-422 BRAZIL *Tel:* + 55 55 3221 4328 *Fax:* + 55 55 3221 4328 *Email:* xicoasilva@gmail.com *Web:* www.ieab.org.br

Southern Brazil The Rt Revd Humberto Maiztegue Bishop of Southern Brazil Av Eng Ludolfo Boehl 278 Teresópolis Porto Alegre RS 91720-150 BRAZIL *Tel:* + 55 (0)51 3318 6199 *Fax:* + 55 (0)51 3318 6199 *Email:* humbertox@uol.com.br *Web:* www.dm.ieab.org.br

THE ANGLICAN CHURCH OF BURUNDI

Provincial Secretary The Revd Félibien Ndintore BP 2098 Bujumbura Burundi *Tel:* + 257 22 22 9129

Provincial Treasurer Mrs Christine Niyonkuru BP 2098 Bujumbura Burundi

Buhiga The Rt Revd Evariste Nijimbere Bishop of Buhiga Awaiting Details

Bujumbura The Rt Revd Eraste Bigirimana Bishop of Bujumbura BP 1300 Bujumbura Burundi *Tel:* - 257 22 249 104 *Fax:* + 257 22 227 496 *Email:* eraste@bethesdaburundi.org

Buye The Rt Revd Sixbert Macumi Bishop of Buye Eglise Episcopale du Burundi BP 94 Ngozi Burundi *Tel:* + 257 22 302 210 *Fax:* + 257 22 302 317 *Email:* buyedioc@yahoo.fr

Gitega The Rt Revd John W Nduwayo Bishop c Gitega BP 23 Gitega Burundi *Tel:* + 257 22 402 24 *Fax:* + 257 22 402 247 *Email:* eab.diogitega@gmail.com

Gitega The Rt Revd Aimé Joseph Kimararung Coadjutor Bishop of Gitega BP 23 Gitega Burundi *Tel:* + 257 22 402 247

Makamba The Most Revd Martin B Nyaboho Archbishop of Burundi & Bishop of Makamba BP 96 Makamba Burundi *Tel:* + 257 22 508 080 *Fax:* + 257 22 229 129 *Email:* mgrmartinyaboho@gmail.com

Matana The Rt Revd Seth Ndayirukiye Bishop of Matana DS 30 Bujumbura Burundi *Tel:* + 257 79923832 *Email:* canonseth@gmail.com *Web:* www. anglicanburundi.org

Muyinga The Rt Revd Paisible Ndacayisaba Bishop of Muyinga BP 55 Muyinga Burundi *Tel:* + 257 22 306 019 *Fax:* + 257 22 306 157 *Email:* ndacp@yahoo. com *Web:* www.anglicanchurchmuyinga.moonfruit. com

Rumonge The Rt Revd Pedaculi Birakengana Bishop of Rumonge Awaiting Details *Tel:* + 257 79 970 926 *Email:* birakepeda@yahoo.fr

Rutana The Rt Revd Pontien Ribakare Bishop of Rutana Awaiting Details

THE ANGLICAN CHURCH OF CANADA

The Most Revd Frederick J Hiltz Primate of the Anglican Church of Canada 80 Hayden Street Toronto ON M4Y 3G2 CANADA *Tel:* + 1 416 924 9199 *Fax:* + 1 416 924 0211 *Email:* primate@ national.anglican.ca *Web:* www.anglican.ca/

General Secretary of the General Synod The Ven Michael Thompson 80 Hayden Street Toronto ON M4Y 3G2 CANADA *Tel:* + 1 416 924 9199 *Fax:* + 1 416 924 0211 *Email:* mthompson@national. anglican.ca

General Treasurer of the General Synod Ms Hanna Goschy 80 Hayden Street Toronto ON M4Y 3G2 CANADA *Tel:* + 1 416 924 9199 *Email:* hgoschy@ national.anglican.ca

Algoma-Ontario The Rt Revd Anne Germond Bishop of Algoma PO Box 1168 619 Wellington Street East Sault Ste. Marie ON P6A 5N7 CANADA *Tel:* + 1 705 256 5061 *Fax:* + 1 705 673 4979 *Email:* bishop@dioceseofalgoma.com *Web:* www. dioceseofalgoma.com

Anglican Parishes of the Central Interior (formerly Cariboo)-British Columbia The Rt Revd Barbara Jean Andrews Bishop of Anglican Parishes of the Central Interior 360 Nicola Street Kamloops BC V2C 2P5 CANADA *Tel:* + 1 778 471 5573 *Fax:* + 1 778 471 5586 *Email:* apcibishop@shaw.ca *Web:* www.territoryofthepeople.ca

Athabasca-Alberta The Rt Revd Fraser W Lawton Bishop of Athabasca Box 6868 Peace River AB T8S 1S6 CANADA *Tel:* + 1 780 624 2767 *Fax:* + 1 780 624 2365 *Email:* bpath@telusplanet.net *Web:* www. dioath.ca

Brandon-MB The Rt Revd William Cliff Bishop of Brandon 403 13th Street Brandon MB R7A 4P9

CANADA *Tel:* + 1 204 727 2380 *Fax:* + 1 204 724 4135 *Email:* bishop@brandon.anglican.ca *Web:* www.dioceseofbrandon.org

British Columbia-British Columbia The Rt Revd Logan McMenamie Bishop of British Columbia 900 Vancouver Street Victoria BC V8V 3V7 CANADA *Tel:* + 1 250 386 7781 *Fax:* + 1 250 386 4013 *Email:* bishop@bc.anglican.ca *Web:* www.bc.anglican.ca

Caledonia-British Columbia The Revd David TJ Lehmann Bishop elect of Caledonia #201 - 4716 Lazelle Avenue Terrace BC V8G 1T2 CANADA *Tel:* + 1 250 635 6016 *Fax:* + 1 250 635 6026 *Email:* caledonia@telus.net *Web:* www.caledoniaanglican.ca

Calgary-Alberta The Most Revd Gregory Kerr-Wilson Metropolitan of Rupert's Land & Archbishop of Calgary 180 1209 - 59th Avenue SE Calgary AB T2H 2P6 CANADA *Tel:* + 1 403 243 3673 *Fax:* + 1 403 243 2182 *Email:* info@calgary.anglican.ca *Web:* www.calgary.anglican.ca

Central Newfoundland-Canada The Rt Revd John Watton Bishop of Central Newfoundland 34 Fraser Road Gander NL A1V 2E8 CANADA *Tel:* + 1 709 256 2372 *Fax:* + 1 709 256 2396 *Email:* centraldiocese@ bellaliant.com *Web:* www.centraldiocese.ca

Eastern Newfoundland & Labrador-Canada The Rt Revd Geoffrey Peddle Bishop of Eastern Newfoundland & Labrador 16 King's Bridge Road St John's NL A1C 3K4 CANADA *Tel:* + 1 709 576 6697 *Fax:* + 1 709 576 7122 *Email:* geoffpeddle48@gmail. com *Web:* www.anglicanenl.net

Edmonton-Alberta The Rt Revd Jane Alexander Bishop of Edmonton 10035-103 Street Edmonton AB T5J 0X5 CANADA *Tel:* + 1 780 439 7344 *Fax:* + 1 780 439 6549 *Email:* bishop@edmonton.anglican.ca *Web:* www.edmonton.anglican.org

Fredericton-Canada The Rt Revd David Edwards Bishop of Fredericton 115 Church Street Fredericton NB E3B 4C8 CANADA *Tel:* + 1 506 459 1801 *Fax:* + 1 506 460 0520 *Email:* bishop@anglican.nb.ca *Web:* www.fredericton.anglican.org

Huron-Ontario The Rt Revd Linda Nicholls Bishop of Huron 190 Queen's Avenue London ON N6A 6H7 CANADA *Tel:* + 1 519 434 6893 *Fax:* + 1 519 673 4151 *Email:* lnicholls@huron.anglican.ca

Huron-Ontario The Rt Revd Terrance Arthur Dance Suffragan Bishop of Huron 190 Queens Avenue London ON N6A 6H7 CANADA *Tel:* + 1 519 434 6893 *Fax:* + 1 519 673 1451 *Email:* bishops@ huron.anglican.ca *Web:* www.diohuron.org

Keewatin-Ontario The Rt Revd David Norman Ashdown Bishop of Keewatin 915 Ottawa Street PO Box 567 Keewatin ON P0X 1C0 CANADA *Tel:* + 1 807 547 3353 *Fax:* + 1 807 547 3356 *Email:* keewatinbishop@shaw.ca *Web:* www. dioceseofkeewatin.ca/

Kootenay-British Columbia The Most Revd John Elswood Privett Metropolitan of BC and Yukon and Archbishop of Kootenay #201 - 380 Leathead Road Kelowna BC V1X 2H8 CANADA *Tel:* + 1 250 762 3306 *Fax:* + 1 250 762 4150 *Email:* diocese_of_kootenay@telus.net *Web:* www.kootenay.anglican.ca/

Mishamikoweesh-Ontario The Rt Revd Lydia Mamakwa Bishop of Indigenous Spiritual Ministry of Mishamikoweesh PO Box 65 Kingfisher Lake ON P0V 1Z0 CANADA *Tel:* + 1 807 532 2085 *Fax:* + 1 807 532 2344 *Email:* lydiam@kingfisherlake.ca

Montreal-Canada The Rt Revd Mary Irwin-Gibson Bishop of Montreal 1444 Union Avenue Montreal QCH3A 2B8 CANADA *Tel:* + 1 514 843 6577 *Fax:* + 1 514 843 3221 *Email:* bishops.office@montreal.anglican.ca *Web:* www.montreal.anglican.ca

Moosonee-Ontario The Rt Revd Thomas A Corston Bishop of Moosonee 113 Third St PO Box 735 Cochrane ON P0L 1C0 CANADA *Tel:* + 1 705 360 1129 *Fax:* + 1 705 360 1120 *Email:* bishop@moosoneeanglican.ca *Web:* www.moosonee.anglican.org

National Indigenous Bishop-Ontario The Rt Revd Mark Lawrence MacDonald National Indigenous Anglican Bishop 80 Hayden Street Toronto ON M4Y 3G2 CANADA *Tel:* + 1 416 924 9199 *Fax:* + 1 416 968 7983 *Email:* mmacdonald@national.anglican.ca *Web:* www.anglican.ca

New Westminster-British Columbia The Rt Revd Melissa M Skelton Bishop of New Westminster 1410 Nanton Avenue Vancouver BC V6H 2E2 CANADA *Tel:* + 1 604 684 6306 *Fax:* + 1 604 684 7017 *Email:* bishop@vancouver.anglican.ca *Web:* www.vancouver.anglican.ca

Niagara-Ontario The Rt Revd Michael Allan Bird Bishop of Niagara Cathedral Place 252 James Street North Hamilton ON L8R 2L3 CANADA *Tel:* + 1 905 527 1316 *Fax:* + 1 905 527 1281 *Email:* bishop@niagara.anglican.ca *Web:* www.niagara.anglican.ca

Nova Scotia & Prince Edward Island-Canada The Most Revd Ronald Wayne Cutler Metropolitan of the Ecclesiastical Province of Canada & Bishop of Nova Scotia & Prince Edward Island 1340 Cathedral Lane Halifax NS B3H 2Z1 CANADA *Tel:* + 1 902 420 0717 *Fax:* + 1 902 425 0717 *Email:* rcutler@nspeidiocese.ca *Web:* www.nspeidiocese.ca

Ontario-Ontario The Rt Revd Michael D Oulton Bishop of Ontario 90 Johnson Street Kingston ON K7L 1X7 CANADA *Tel:* + 1 613 544 4774 *Fax:* + 1 613 547 3745 *Email:* moulton@ontario.ca *Web:* www.ontario.anglican.ca

Ottawa-Ontario The Rt Revd John Holland Chapman Bishop of Ottawa 71 Bronson Avenue Ottawa ON K1R 6G6 CANADA *Tel:* + 1 613 232 7124 *Fax:* + 1 613 232 7088 *Email:* bishopsoffice@ottawa.anglican.ca *Web:* www.ottawa.anglican.ca

Ottawa-Ontario The Rt Revd Nigel Shaw Anglican Bishop Ordinary to the Canadian Armed Forces N.D.H.Q. (CFSU Ottawa – Uplands) 101 Colonel By Drive Ottawa ON K1A 0K2 CANADA *Email:* Nigel.Shaw@gc.forces.ca

Qu'Appelle-Rupert's Land The Rt Revd Robert Hardwick Bishop of Qu'Appelle 1501 College Avenue Regina SK S4P 1B8 CANADA *Tel:* + 1 306 522 1608 *Fax:* + 1 306 352 6808 *Email:* bishop.rob@sasktel.net *Web:* www.quappelle.anglican.ca/

Quebec-Canada The Rt Revd Bruce Myers Bishop of Quebec 31 rue des Jardins Quebec QC G1R 4L6 CANADA *Tel:* + 1 418 692 3858 *Email:* bishopqc@quebec.anglican.ca *Web:* www.quebec.anglican.org

Rupert's Land-Rupert's Land The Rt Revd Donald David Phillips Bishop of Rupert's Land 935 Nesbitt Bay Winnipeg MB R3T 1W6 CANADA *Tel:* + 1 204 992 4200 *Fax:* + 1 204 992 4219 *Email:* dphillips@rupertsland.anglican.ca *Web:* www.rupertsland.ca/

Saskatchewan-Rupert's Land The Rt Revd Michael William Hawkins Bishop of Saskatchewan 1308 Fifth Avenue East Prince Albert SK S6V 2H7 CANADA *Tel:* + 1 306 763 2455 *Fax:* + 1 306 764 5172 *Email:* synod@sasktel.net *Web:* www.saskatchewan.anglican.org

Saskatchewan-Rupert's Land The Rt Revd Adam Halkett Suffragan Bishop of Saskatchewan-Indigenous Ministry 1308 Fifth Avenue East Prince Albert SK S6V 2H7 CANADA *Tel:* + 1 306 763 2455 *Fax:* + 1 306 764 5172 *Web:* www.saskatchewan.anglican.org

Saskatoon-Rupert's Land The Rt Revd David M Irving Bishop of Saskatoon PO Box 1965 1403 9th Avenue North Saskatoon SK S7K 3S5 CANADA *Tel:* + 1 306 244 5651 *Fax:* + 1 306 933 4606 *Email:* bishopdavid@sasktel.net *Web:* www.saskatoon.anglican.org

The Arctic-Rupert's Land The Rt Revd David Parsons Bishop of the Diocese of the Arctic Box 190 Yellowknife NT X1A 2N2 CANADA *Tel:* + 1 867-873-5432 *Email:* arctic@arcticnet.org *Web:* www.arcticnet.org

The Arctic-Rupert's Land The Rt Revd Darren McCartney Suffragan Bishop of the Diocese of the Arctic PO Box 57 Iqaluit NU X0A 0H0 CANADA *Tel:* + 1 867-979-5595 *Email:* darren@arcticnet.org

Toronto-Ontario The Most Revd Colin Robert Johnson Metropolitan of Ontario and Archbishop of Toronto 135 Adelaide St East Toronto ON M5C 1L8 CANADA *Tel:* + 1 416 363 6021 *Fax:* + 1 416 363 7678 *Email:* cjohnson@toronto.anglican.ca *Web:* www.toronto.anglican.ca

Toronto-Ontario The Rt Revd Riscylla Shaw Suffragan Bishop of Toronto - Trent-Durham Area Suite 207 965 Dundas St. West Whitby ON L1P 1G8 CANADA *Tel:* + 1 905 668 1558 *Fax:* + 1 905 668 8216 *Email:* rshaw@toronto.anglican.ca *Web:* www. trentdurhamanglicans.ca

Toronto-Ontario The Rt Revd Peter Fenty Suffragan Bishop of Toronto - York - Simcoe 2174 King Road Unit 2 King City ON L7B 1L5 CANADA *Tel:* + 1 905 833 8327 *Fax:* + 1 905 833 8329 *Email:* ysimcoe@ toronto.anglican.ca

Toronto-Ontario The Rt Revd Jenny Andison Suffragan Bishop of Toronto - York-Credit Valley 135 Adelaide St East Toronto ON M5C 1L8 CANADA *Tel:* + 1 416 363 6021 *Fax:* + 1 416 363 7678 *Email:* jandison@toronto.anglican.ca

Toronto-Ontario The Rt Revd Kevin Robertson Suffragan Bishop of Toronto - York - Scarborough 135 Adelaide St East Toronto ON M5C 1L8 CANADA *Tel:* + 1 416 363 6021 *Email:* krobertson@ toronto.anglican.ca

Western Newfoundland-Canada The Rt Revd Percy David Coffin Bishop of Western Newfoundland 25 Main Street Corner Brookl NF A2H 1C2 CANADA *Tel:* + 1 709 639 8712 *Email:* dsown@nf.aibn.com *Web:* www.westernnewfoundland.anglican.org/

Yukon-Yukon The Rt Revd Larry David Robertson Bishop of Yukon Box 31136 Whitehorse YK Y1A 5P7 CANADA *Tel:* + 1 867 667 7746 *Fax:* + 1 867 667 6125 *Email:* synodoffice@klondiker.com *Web:* www.yukon.anglican.org

THE CHURCH OF THE PROVINCE OF CENTRAL AFRICA

Acting Provincial Secretary **Eastern Zambia** The Rt Revd William Mchombo Bishop of Eastern Zambia & PO Box 510154 Chipata ZAMBIA *Tel:* + 260 216 221 294 *Email:* dioeastzm@zamnet.zm

Provincial Treasurer Mr Evans Mwewa CPCA PO Box 22317 Kitwe ZAMBIA *Tel:* + 260 267 351 081 *Fax:* + 260 267 351 668

Botswana The Rt Revd Metlhayotlhe Rawlings Belemi Bishop of Botswana PO Box 769 Gaaborone BOTSWANA *Tel:* + 267 (0)3 953 779 *Fax:* + 267 (0)3 913 015 *Email:* angli_diocese@info.bw *Web:* www. diobot.org

Central Zambia The Rt Revd Derek Gary Kamukwamba Bishop of Central Zambia PO Box 70172 Ndola ZAMBIA *Tel:* + 260 (0)2 612 431 *Fax:* + 260 (0)2 615 954 *Email:* adcznla@zamnet.zm

Central Zimbabwe The Rt Revd Ishmael Mukuwanda Bishop of Central Zimbabwe PO Box 25 Gweru ZIMBABWE *Tel:* + 263 (0)5 421 030 *Fax:* + 263 (0)5 421 097 *Email:* diocent@telconet.co.zw

Harare The Rt Revd Chad Nicholas Gandiya Bishop of Harare Diocese of Harare CPCA 2nd Floor Paget House 87 Kwame Nkurumah Avenue Harare ZIMBABWE *Tel:* + 263 4 702 253 *Fax:* + 263 4 300 419 *Web:* www.hreanglicancpca.org.zw

Lake Malawi The Rt Revd Francis Kaulanda Bishop of Lake Malawi PO Box 30349 Lilongwe 3 MALAWI *Tel:* + 265 1 797 858 *Fax:* + 265 1 797 548

Luapula The Rt Revd Robert Mumbi Bishop of Luapula PO Box 710 210 Mansa ZAMBIA *Tel:* + 260 (0)2 821 680 *Email:* diopula@zamtel.zm

Lusaka The Rt Revd David Njovu Bishop of Lusaka Bishop's Lodge PO Box 30183 Lusaka ZAMBIA *Tel:* + 260 (0)1 264 515 *Fax:* + 260 (0)1 262 379

Manicaland The Rt Revd Erick Ruwona Bishop of Manicaland 113 Herbert Chitepo Street Mutare ZIMBABWE *Tel:* + 263 20 68418 *Email:* ruwonaerick@gmail.com

Masvingo The Rt Revd Godfrey Tawonezwi Bishop of Masvingo PO Box 1421 Masvingo ZIMBABWE *Tel:* + 263 39 362 536 *Email:* bishopgodfreytawonezvi@ gmail.com *Web:* www.masvingo.anglican.org/

Matabeleland The Rt Revd Cleophas Lunga Bishop of Matabeleland PO Box 2422 Bulawayo ZIMBABWE *Tel:* + 263 09 613 70 *Fax:* + 263 09 683 53 *Email:* clunga@aol.com

Northern Malawi The Rt Revd Fanuel Emmanuel Magangani Bishop of Northern Malawi PO Box 120 Mzuzu MALAWI *Tel:* + 265 (0) 1312 858 *Email:* anglicandnm@gmail.com *Web:* www. nmalawianglican.org

Northern Zambia The Most Revd Albert Chama Archbishop of Central Africa & Bishop of Northern Zambia PO Box 20798 Kitwe ZAMBIA *Tel:* + 260 2 223 264 *Fax:* + 260 2 224 778 *Email:* chama_albert@ yahoo.ca

Southern Malawi The Rt Revd Alinafe Kalemba Bishop of Southern Malawi PO Box 30220 Chichiri Blantyre 3 MALAWI *Tel:* + 265 1 841 218 *Fax:* + 265 1 841 235 *Email:* dean@sdnp.org.mw

Upper Shire The Rt Revd Brighton Vitta Malasa Bishop of Upper Shire Bishop's House Private Bag 1 Chilema Zomba MALAWI *Email:* malasab@ yahoo.co.uk *Web:* www.malawipartnership.co.uk/ uppershire/

IGLESIA ANGLICANA DE LA REGION CENTRAL DE AMERICA

Provincial Treasurer Mr Harold Charles Apartado R Balboa REPUBLIC OF PANAMA *Tel:* + 507 262 2052 *Email:* iarcahch@sinfo.net

Costa Rica The Rt Revd Hector Monterroso Gonzalez Bishop of Costa Rica & Provincial Secretary Apartado 2773-1000 San José COSTA

RICA *Tel:* + 506 22250209 *Fax:* + 506 22538331 *Email:* iarca@me.com

El Salvador The Rt Revd Juan David Alvarado Melgar Bishop of El Salvador 47 Avenida Sur 723 Col Flor Blanca Apt Postal (01) San Salvador 274 EL SALVADOR *Tel:* + 503 2 223 2252 *Email:* anglican. es@gmail.com

Guatemala The Most Revd Armando R Guerra Soria Bishop of Guatemala Apartado 58a Avenida La Castellana 40-06 Guatemala City Zona 8 GUATEMALA *Tel:* + 502 (0)2 472 0852 *Fax:* + 502 (0)2 472 0764 *Email:* agepiscopal@yahoo.com

Guatemala The Revd Silvestre Romero Bishop Coadjutor elect of Guatemala Apartado 58a Avenida La Castellana 40-06 Guatemala City Zona 8 Guatemala *Tel:* + 502 (0)2 472 0852 *Email:* agepiscopal@yahoo.com

Nicaragua The Most Revd Sturdie Downs Primate of IARCA & Bishop of Nicaragua Apartado 1207 Managua NICARAGUA *Tel:* + 505 22225174 *Fax:* + 505 22545248 *Email:* secretaria_diocesana@hotmail. com

Panama The Rt Revd Julio Murray Bishop of Panama Box R Balboa REPUBLIC OF PANAMA *Tel:* + 507 212 0062 *Email:* bpmurray@hotmail.com

PROVINCE DE L'EGLISE ANGLICANE DU CONGO

Provincial Secretary The Ven Anthonio Kibwela The Province of the Anglican Church of Congo 11 AV Basalakala Commune de Kalamu Kinshasa DR CONGO *Tel:* + 243 995412138 *Email:* anthoniokibwela@gmail.com

Provincial Treasurer Mr Alain Batondela PO Box 16482 Kinshasa 1 DR CONGO

Aru The Rt Revd Georges Titre Ande Bishop of Aru PO Box 226 Arua UGANDA *Tel:* + 243 8 1039 3071 *Email:* revdande@yahoo.co.uk

Boga The Rt Revd Mugenyi William Bahemuka Bishop of Boga Awaiting Details *Email:* mugenywiliam@yahoo.com

Bukavu The Rt Revd Sylvestre Bahati Bishop of Bukavu Evache Anglican Av. Pagni No2 Q/ Nyalukemba, C/ Ibanda Bukavu DR CONGO *Email:* bahati_bali@yahoo.fr

Kamango The Rt Revd Sabiti Tibafa Daniel Bishop of Kamango c/o The Congo Church Liaison Office PO Box 25586 Kampala UGANDA *Tel:* + 243 99 779 1013 *Email:* revsabiti@yahoo.fr

Kasai The Rt Revd Marcel Kapinga Bishop of Kasai No 05, Avenue Makenga District Bonzola Common Dibindi Mbuji-Mayi Kasai Oriental DR CONGO *Tel:* + 243 8160 61423 *Email:* anglicanekasai2@ gmail.com

Katanga The Rt Revd Bertin Subi Bishop of Katanga C/O U.M.M PO Box 22037 Kitwe ZAMBIA *Tel:* + 342 97 047 173 *Email:* peacbertinsubi@yahoo.fr *Web:* www.katanga.anglican.org

Kindu The Most Revd Zacharie Masimango Katanda Archbishop of the Congo & Bishop of Kindu Av. Penemisenga No 4, C/ Kasuku Kindu Maniema RWANDA *Email:* angkindu@yahoo.fr

Kinshasa The Rt Revd Achille Mutshindu Bishop of Kinshasa PO Box 16482 Kinshasa 1 DR CONGO

Kisangani The Rt Revd Lambert F Botolome Bishop of Kisangani Bowane Street, No 10 Quartier des Musiciens C/ Makiso BP 861 Kisangani DR CONGO

Nord Kivu The Rt Revd Muhindo Isesomo Bishop of Nord Kivu CAZ Butembo PO Box 506 Bwera-Kasese UGANDA *Fax:* + 871 166 1121

Nord Kivu The Rt Revd Enoch WM Kayeeye Assistant Bishop of Nord Kivu C/O PO Box 506 Bwera/Kasese UGANDA *Tel:* + 243 09 9414 8579 *Email:* bpkayeeye@hotmail.com

THE CHURCH OF ENGLAND

Provincial Secretary Mr William Nye Church House Great Smith Street London SW1P 3NZ UK *Tel:* + 44 (0)207 898 1360 *Fax:* + 44 (0)207 898 1369 *Email:* william.nye@churchofengland.org

Bath & Wells-Canterbury The Rt Revd Peter Hancock Bishop of Bath & Wells The Palace Wells Somerset BA5 2PD ENGLAND *Tel:* + 44 (0)1749 672 341 *Fax:* + 44 (0)1749 679 355 *Email:* bishop@ bathwells.anglican.org *Web:* www.bathwells. anglican.org

Bath & Wells- Canterbury The Rt Revd Ruth Worsley Suffragan Bishop of Taunton The Palace Wells Somerset BA5 2PD ENGLAND *Tel:* + 44 (0)1749 672 341 *Fax:* + 44 (0)1749 679 355 *Email:* bishop.taunton@bathwells.anglican.org *Web:* www. bathandwells.org.uk

Birmingham-Canterbury The Rt Revd David Andrew Urquhart Bishop of Birmingham Birmingham Diocese Office 1 Colmore Row Birmingham B3 2BJ ENGLAND *Tel:* + 44 (0)121 427 1163 *Fax:* + 44 (0)121 426 1322 *Email:* bishop@ birmingham.anglican.org *Web:* www.birmingham. anglican.org

Birmingham-Canterbury The Rt Revd Anne Elizabeth Hollinghurst Suffragan Bishop of Birmingham - Aston Birmingham Diocese Office 1 Colmore Row Birmingham B3 2BJ ENGLAND *Tel:* + 44 (0)121 426 0400 *Fax:* + 44 (0)121 428 1114 *Email:* bishopofaston@birmingham.anglican.org *Web:* www.birmingham.anglican.org

Blackburn-York The Rt Revd Julian Tudor Henderson Bishop of Blackburn Bishop's House Ribchester Road Clayton-le-Dale Blackburn BB1

9EF ENGLAND *Tel:* + 44 (0)1254 248 234 *Fax:* + 44 (0)1254 246 668 *Email:* bishop@bishopofblackburn.org.uk *Web:* www.blackburn.anglican.org

Blackburn-York The Rt Revd Philip North Suffragan Bishop of Blackburn - Burnley Church House Cathedral close Blackburn BB1 5AA ENGLAND *Tel:* + 44 01254 503087 *Email:* bishop.burnley@blackburn.anglican.org

Blackburn-York The Rt Revd Geoffrey Seagrave Pearson Suffragan Bishop Lancaster The Vicarage Whinney Brow Lane Shireshead, Forton Preston PR3 0AE ENGLAND *Tel:* + 44 (0)1524 799 900 *Fax:* + 44 (0)1524 799 901 *Email:* bishop.lancaster@ukonline.co.uk

Bristol-Canterbury The Rt Revd Michael Arthur Hill Bishop of Bristol 58a High Street Winterbourne Bristol BS36 1JQ ENGLAND *Tel:* + 44 (0)1454 777 728 *Fax:* + 44 (0)1454 777 814 *Email:* bishop@bristoldiocese.org *Web:* www.bristol.anglican.org

Bristol-Canterbury The Rt Revd Lee Stephen Rayfield Bishop of Swindon Mark House Field Rise Swindon SN1 4HP England *Tel:* + 44 (0)1793 538 654 *Fax:* + 44 (0)1793 525 181 *Email:* bishop.swindon@bristoldiocese.org

Canterbury-Canterbury The Most Revd and Rt Hon Justin Welby Archbishop of Canterbury Lambeth Palace London SE1 7JU United Kingdom *Tel:* + 44 (0)20 7898 1238 *Fax:* + 44 (0)20 7261 9836 *Email:* pa.archbishop@lambethpalace.org.uk *Web:* www.archbishopofcanterbury.org/

Canterbury-Canterbury The Rt Revd Roderick Charles Howell H Thomas Suffragan Bishop of Maidstone Bishop's House Pett Lane Charing Ashford TN27 0DL ENGLAND *Tel:* + 44 (0)1233 712 950 *Fax:* + 44 (0)1233 713 543 *Email:* bishop@bishmaid.org *Web:* www.bishopofmaidstone.org

Canterbury-Canterbury The Rt Revd Trevor Willmott Bishop in Canterbury and Bishop of Dover The Old Palace The Precincts Canterbury CT1 2EE ENGLAND *Tel:* + 44 (0)1227 459 382 *Fax:* + 44 (0)1227 784 985 *Email:* bishop@bishcant.org

Canterbury-Canterbury The Rt Revd Norman N Banks Suffragan Bishop of Richborough Parkside House Abbey Mill Lane St Albans AL3 4HE ENGLAND *Tel:* + 44 (0)1727 836 358 *Email:* bishop@richborough.org.uk

Canterbury-Canterbury The Rt Revd Jonathan Goodall Suffragan Bishop of Ebbsfleet Hill House The Mount Caversham Reading RG4 7RE UK *Tel:* + 44 (0)1865 288 030 *Email:* bishop@ebbsfleet.org.uk

Carlisle-York The Rt Revd James Scobie WS Newcome Bishop of Carlisle Bishop's House Ambleside Road Keswick CA12 4DD ENGLAND *Tel:* + 44 (0)1768 773 430 *Email:* bishop.carlisle@carlislediocese.org.uk *Web:* www.carlislediocese.org.uk

Carlisle-York The Rt Revd Robert Freeman Suffragan Bishop of Penrith Holm Croft 13 Castle Road Kendal LA9 7AU ENGLAND *Tel:* + 44 (0)1539 727 836 *Email:* bishop.penrith@carlislediocese.org.uk

Chelmsford-Canterbury The Rt Revd Stephen Geoffrey Cottrell Bishop of Chelmsford Bishopscourt Main Road Margretting Ingatestone Essex CM4 0HD ENGLAND *Tel:* + 44 (0)1277 352 001 *Fax:* + 44 (0)1277 355 374 *Email:* bishopscourt@chelmsford.anglican.org *Web:* www.chelmsford.anglican.org

Chelmsford-Canterbury The Rt Revd Peter Hill Bishop of Barking Barking Lodge 35A Verulam Avenue Walthamstow London E17 8ES ENGLAND *Tel:* + 44 (0)20 8509 7377 *Fax:* + 44 (0)20 8514 6049 *Email:* b.barking@chelmsford.anglican.org

Chelmsford-Canterbury The Rt Revd Anthony Brett Morris Bishop of Colchester 1 Fitzwalter Road Colchester CO3 3SS ENGLAND *Tel:* + 44 (0)1206 576 648 *Fax:* + 44 (0)1206 763 868 *Email:* b.colchester@chelmsford.anglican.org *Web:* www.chelmsford.anglican.org

Chelmsford-Canterbury Vacant Bishop elect of Bradwell Bishop's House Orsett Road Hordon-on-the-Hill Stanford-le-Hope SS17 8NS ENGLAND *Tel:* + 44 (0)1375 673 806 *Fax:* + 44 (0)1375 674 222 *Email:* b.bradwell@chelmsford.anglican.org

Chester-York The Rt Revd Peter Robert Forster Bishop of Chester Bishop's House Abbey Square Chester CH1 2JD ENGLAND *Tel:* + 44 (0)1244 350 864 *Fax:* + 44 (0)1244 314 187 *Email:* bpchester@chester.anglican.org *Web:* www.chester.anglican.org/

Chester-York The Rt Revd Keith Sinclair Bishop of Birkenhead Bishops Lodge 67 Bidston Road Prenton Wirral CH43 6TR ENGLAND *Tel:* + 44 (0)151 652 2741 *Fax:* + 44 (0)151 651 2330 *Email:* bpbirkenhead@chester.anglican.org

Chester-York The Rt Revd Libby Lane Suffragan Bishop of Chester - Stockport Bishop's Lodge Back Lane Dunham Town Altrincham WA14 4SG ENGLAND *Tel:* + 44 (0)161 928 5611 *Fax:* + 44 (0)161 929 0692 *Email:* bpstockport@chester.anglican.org

Chichester-Canterbury The Rt Revd Martin C Warner Bishop of Chichester The Palace Canon Lane Chichester West Sussex PO19 1PY ENGLAND *Tel:* + 44 (0)1243 782 161 *Fax:* + 44 (0)1243 531 332 *Email:* bishop@chichester.anglian.org *Web:* www.chichester.anglican.org

Chichester-Canterbury The Rt Revd Mark Sowerby Suffragan Bishop of Horsham Bishop's House 21 Guildford Road Horsham Sussex RH12 1LU ENGLAND *Tel:* + 44 (0)1403 211 139 *Fax:* + 44 (0)1403 217 349 *Email:* bishop.horsham@chichester.anglican.org

Chichester-Canterbury The Revd Richard Charles Jackson Suffragan Bishop of Lewes The Palace

Canon Lane Chichester West Sussex PO19 1PY ENGLAND

Coventry-Canterbury The Rt Revd Christopher J Cocksworth Bishop of Coventry Bishop's House 23 Davenport Road Coventry CV5 6PW ENGLAND *Tel:* + 44 (0)2476 672 244 *Fax:* + 44 (0)24 76 713 271 *Email:* bishop@bishop-coventry.org *Web:* www.dioceseofcoventry.org

Coventry-Canterbury The Rt Revd John RA Stroyan Suffragan Bishop of Warwick Warwick House School Hill Offchurch Leamington Spa CV33 9AL UK *Tel:* + 44 (0)1926 427465 *Email:* Bishop.Warwick@covcofe.org

Derby-Canterbury The Rt Revd Alastair Redfern Bishop of Derby The Bishop's House 6 King Street Duffield Belper DE56 4EU ENGLAND *Tel:* + 44 (0)1332 840 132 *Fax:* + 44 (0)1332 842 743 *Email:* pa@bishopofderby.org *Web:* www.derby.anglican.org/

Derby-Canterbury The Rt Revd Janet Elizabeth McFarlane Suffragan Bishop of Derby - Repton Repton House Lea Matlock Derby DE4 5JP ENGLAND *Tel:* + 44 (0)1629 534 644 *Fax:* + 44 (0)1629 534 003 *Email:* bishop@repton.free-online.co.uk

Diocese in Europe The Rt Revd Robert Innes Bishop of Gibraltar in Europe 47 rue Capitaine Crespel - boite 49 Brussels 1050 Belgium *Tel:* + 32 2 213 7480 *Email:* robert.innes@churchofengland.org *Web:* www.europe.anglican.org

Diocese in Europe The Rt Revd David Hamid Suffragan Bishop of the Diocese in Europe 14 Tufton Street Westminster London SW1P 3QZ ENGLAND *Tel:* + 44 (0)20 7898 1160 *Fax:* + 44 (0)20 7898 1166 *Email:* david.hamid@churchofengland.org

Durham-York The Rt Revd Paul R Butler Bishop elect of Durham Auckland Castle Bishop Auckland Durham DL14 7NR ENGLAND *Tel:* + 44 (0)1388 602 576 *Fax:* + 44 (0)1388 605 264 *Email:* bishop.of.durham@durham.anglican.org *Web:* www.durham.anglican.org

Durham-York The Rt Revd Mark Watts Bryant Suffragan Bishop of Jarrow Bishop's House Ivy Lane Low Fell Gateshead NE9 6QD ENGLAND *Tel:* + 44 (0)191 491 0917 *Fax:* + 44 (0)191 491 5116 *Email:* bishop.of.jarrow@durham.anglican.org *Web:* www.durham.anglican.org

Ely-Canterbury The Rt Revd Stephen David Conway Bishop of Ely The Bishop's House Ely Cambs CB7 4DW ENGLAND *Tel:* + 44 (0)1353 662 749 *Fax:* + 44 (0)1353 669 477 *Email:* bishop@ely.anglican.org *Web:* www.ely.anglican.org

Ely-Canterbury The Rt Revd David Thomson Suffragan Bishop of Huntingdon 14 Lynn Road Ely CB6 1DA ENGLAND *Tel:* + 44 (0)1353 662 137 *Fax:* + 44 (0)1353 662 137 *Email:* bishop.huntingdon@ely.anglican.org

Exeter-Canterbury The Rt Revd Robert Atwell Bishop of Exeter The Palace Exeter EX1 1HY ENGLAND *Tel:* + 44 (0)1392 272 362 *Fax:* + 44 (0)1392 430 923 *Email:* sarah.johnson@exeter.anglican.org *Web:* www.exeter.anglican.org

Exeter-Canterbury The Rt Revd Sarah Mullally Suffragan Bishop of Crediton 32 The Avenue Tiverton Devon EX16 4HW ENGLAND *Tel:* + 44 (0)1884 250 002 *Fax:* + 44 (0)1884 257 454 *Email:* Sarah.mullally@exeter.anglican.org

Exeter-Canterbury The Rt Revd Nick McKinnel Suffragan Bishop of Plymouth 31 Riverside Walk Tamerton Foliot Plymouth PL5 4AQ ENGLAND *Tel:* + 44 (0)1752 769 836 *Fax:* + 44 (0)1752 769 818 *Email:* bishop.of.plymouth@exeter.anglican.org

Gloucester-Canterbury The Rt Revd Rachel Treweek Bishop of Gloucester Church House 2 College Green Gloucester GL1 2LR ENGLAND *Tel:* + 44 (0)1452 835 512 *Email:* bgloucester@glosdioc.org.uk *Web:* www.gloucester.anglican.org

Gloucester-Canterbury The Rt Revd Robert Wilfrid WS Springett Suffragan Bishop of Gloucester-Tewkesbury Bishop's House Church Road Staverton Gloucester GL51 0TW ENGLAND *Tel:* + 44 (0)1242 680 188 *Email:* btewkesbury@glosdioc.org.uk *Web:* www.gloucester.anglican.org

Guildford-Canterbury The Rt Revd Andrew John Watson Bishop of Guildford Willow Grange Woking Road Guildford Surrey GU4 7QS ENGLAND *Tel:* + 44 01483 590 500 *Fax:* + 44 01483 590 501 *Email:* bishop.guildford@cofeguildford.org.uk *Web:* www.cofeguildford.org.uk

Guildford-Canterbury The Rt Revd Jo Bailey Wells Suffragan Bishop of Guildford-Dorking Dayspring 13 Pilgrim's Way Guildford GU4 8AD ENGLAND *Tel:* + 44 01483 570829 *Email:* muriel.mulvany@cofeguildford.org.uk

Hereford-Canterbury The Rt Revd Richard MC Frith Bishop of Hereford Bishop's House The Palace Hereford HR4 9BN ENGLAND *Tel:* + 44 (0)1432 373 300 *Email:* diooffice@hereford.anglican.org

Hereford-Canterbury The Rt Revd Alistair James Magowan Suffragan Bishop of Ludlow Bishops' House Corvedale Road Cavern Arms Shropshire SY7 9BT ENGLAND *Tel:* + 44 (0)1588 673 571 *Fax:* + 44 (0)1588 673 571 *Email:* bishopalistair@btinternet.com

Leeds-York The Rt Revd Nicholas Baines Bishop of Leeds St Mary's Street Leeds West Yorkshire LS9 7DP ENGLAND *Tel:* + 44 01274 545414 *Fax:* + 44 01274 544831 *Email:* bishop.nick@leeds.anglican.org *Web:* www.leeds.anglican.org

Leeds-York The Rt Revd Anthony W Robinson Area Bishop of Wakefield 181A Manygates Lane Sandal Wakefield WF2 7DR ENGLAND *Tel:* + 44 (0)1924 250 781 *Fax:* + 44 (0)1924 240 490 *Email:* bishop.tony@leeds.anglican.org

Leeds-York The Rt Revd James H Bell Area Bishop of Ripon Thistledown Exelby Bedale DL8 2HD ENGLAND *Tel:* + 44 (0)1677 423 525 *Fax:* + 44 (0)1677 427 515 *Email:* bishop.james@leeds.anglican.org

Leeds-York The Rt Revd Paul Slater Area Bishop of Richmond St Mary's Street Leeds West Yorkshire LS9 7DP ENGLAND *Tel:* + 44 (0)113 284 4304 *Email:* bishop.paul@leeds.anglican.org

Leeds-York The Rt Revd Jonathan Gibbs Area Bishop of Huddersfield Stone Royd 9 Valley Head Huddersfield HD2 2DH ENGLAND *Tel:* + 44 (0)1484 471801 *Email:* bishop.jonathan@leeds.anglican.org

Leeds-York The Rt Revd Toby Howarth Area Bishop of Bradford 47 Kirkgate Shipley BD18 3EH ENGLAND *Email:* bishop.toby@leeds.anglican.org

Leicester-Canterbury The Rt Revd Martyn James Snow Bishop of Leicester Bishop's Lodge 10 Springfield Road Leicester LE2 3BD ENGLAND *Tel:* + 44 (0)116 270 8985 *Email:* leicester@leccofe.org *Web:* www.leicester.anglican.org

Leicester-Canterbury The Revd Canon Guli Francis-Dehqani Bishop elect of Loughborough Bishop's Lodge 10 Springfield Road Leicester LE2 3BD ENGLAND *Web:* www.leicester.anglican.org

Leicester-Canterbury The Rt Revd Christopher John Boyle Assistant Bishop in the Diocese of Leicester Church House St Martin's East Leicester LE1 5FX ENGLAND *Tel:* + 44 (0) 116 248 7411 *Email:* bishop.boyle@leccofe.org

Lichfield-Canterbury The Rt Revd Michael Ipgrave Bishop of Lichfield The Bishop's House 22 The Close Lichfield WS13 7LG ENGLAND *Tel:* + 44 (0)1543 306 000 *Fax:* + 44 (0)1543 306 009 *Email:* bishop.lichfield@lichfield.anglican.org *Web:* www.lichfield.anglican.org

Lichfield-Canterbury The Rt Revd Mark James Rylands Bishop of Shrewsbury Athlone House 68 London Road Shrewsbury SYZ 6PG ENGLAND *Tel:* + 44 (0)1743 235 867 *Fax:* + 44 (0)1743 243 296 *Email:* bishop.shrewsbury@lichfield.anglican.org *Web:* www.lichfield.anglican.org

Lichfield-Canterbury The Rt Revd Geoffrey Peter Annas Suffragan Bishop of Stafford Ash Garth 6 Broughton Crescent Barlaston Stoke on Trent ST12 9DD ENGLAND *Tel:* + 44 01782 373 308 *Fax:* + 44 01782 373 705 *Email:* bishop.stafford@lichfield.anglican.org

Lichfield-Canterbury The Rt Revd Clive Gregory Bishop of Wolverhampton 61 Richmond Road Merridale Wolverhampton WV3 9JH ENGLAND *Tel:* + 44 (0)1902 824 503 *Fax:* + 44 (0)1902 824 504 *Email:* bishop.wolverhampton@lichfield.anglican.org

Lincoln-Canterbury The Rt Revd Christopher Lowson Bishop of Lincoln The Old Palace Minster Yard Lincoln LN2 1PU ENGLAND *Tel:* + 44 (0)1522 504 090 *Fax:* + 44 (0)1522 511 095 *Email:* bishop.lincoln@lincoln.anglican.org *Web:* www.lincoln.anglican.org

Lincoln-Canterbury The Rt Revd David Eric Court Suffragan Bishop of Grimsby Bishop's House Church Lane Irby Upon Humber Grimsby DN37 7JR ENGLAND *Tel:* + 44 (0)1472 371 715 *Fax:* + 44 (0)1472 371 716 *Email:* bishop.grimsby@lincoln.anglican.org

Lincoln-Canterbury The Rt Revd Nicholas Alan Chamberlain Suffragan Bishop of Grantham Saxonwell Vicarage Church Street Long Bennington Newark NG23 5ES ENGLAND *Tel:* + 44 (0)1400 283 344 *Fax:* + 44 (0)1400 283 321 *Email:* bishop.grantham@lincoln.anglican.org

Liverpool-York The Rt Revd Paul Bayes Bishop of Liverpool Bishop's Lodge Woolton Park Liverpool L25 6DT ENGLAND *Tel:* + 44 (0)151 421 0831 *Fax:* + 44 (0)151 428 3055 *Email:* Bishopslodge@liverpool.anglican.org *Web:* www.liverpool.anglican.org

Liverpool-York The Rt Revd Richard Finn Blackburn Suffragan Bishop of Warrington St James House 20 St James Road Liverpool L1 7BY ENGLAND *Tel:* + 44 (0)151 705 2140 *Fax:* + 44 (0)151 709 2885 *Email:* bishopofwarrington@liverpool.anglican.org

London-Canterbury The Rt Revd & Rt Hon Richard John Carew Chartres Bishop of London The Old Deanery Dean's Court London EC4V 5AA ENGLAND *Tel:* + 44 (0)20 7248 6233 *Fax:* + 44 (0)20 7248 9721 *Email:* bishop@londin.clara.co.uk *Web:* www.london.anglican.org

London-Canterbury The Rt Revd Adrian Newman Suffragan Bishop of London - Stepney 63 Coborn Road Bow London Kent E3 2DB ENGLAND *Tel:* + 44 (0)1634 843 366 *Fax:* + 44 (0)1634 401 410 *Email:* bishop.stepney@london.anglican.org

London-Canterbury The Rt Revd Peter Allan Broadbent Bishop of Willesden 173 Willesden Lane London NW6 7YN ENGLAND *Tel:* + 44 (0)20 8451 0189 *Fax:* + 44 (0)20 8451 4606 *Email:* bishopwillesden.pa@btinternet.com

London-Canterbury The Rt Revd Graham Tomlin Suffragan Bishop of London - Kensington Dial House Riverside Twickenham Middlesex TW1 3DT ENGLAND *Tel:* + 44 (0)208 8892 7781 *Fax:* + 44 (0)208 8891 3969 *Email:* bishop.kensington@london.anglican.org

London-Canterbury The Rt Revd Robert Wickham Suffragan Bishop of London - Edmonton 27 Thurlow Road Hampstead London NW3 5PP ENGLAND *Tel:* + 44 (0)20 7435 5890 *Fax:* + 44 (0)20 7435 6049 *Email:* bishop.edmonton@london.anglican.org

London-Canterbury The Rt Revd Ric Thorpe Suffragan Bishop of London - Islington Bishop of Islington's Office St Edmund the King Lombard Street London EC3V 9EA ENGLAND *Tel:* + 44 020 3837 5275 *Email:* bishop.islington@london.anglican. org

London-Canterbury The Rt Revd Jonathan Mark Richard Baker Suffragan Bishop of Fulham The Old Deanery Dean's Court London EC4V 5AA ENGLAND *Tel:* + 44 (0)20 7932 1130 *Email:* bishop. fulham@london.anglican.org

Manchester-York The Rt Revd David S Walker Bishop of Manchester Bishopscourt Bury New Road Salford Manchester M7 4LE ENGLAND *Tel:* + 44 (0)161 792 2096 *Fax:* + 44 (0)161 792 6826 *Email:* bishop@bishopscourt.manchester.anglican.org *Web:* www.manchester.anglican.org

Manchester-York The Rt Revd Mark Davies Suffragan Bishop of Middleton The Hollies Manchester Road Rochdale OL11 3QY ENGLAND *Tel:* + 44 (0)1706 358 550 *Fax:* + 44 (0)1706 354 851 *Email:* bishopmark@manchester.anglican.org

Manchester-York The Rt Revd Mark David Ashcroft Suffragan Bishop of Bolton Bishop's Lodge Walkden Road Worsley Manchester M28 2WH ENGLAND *Tel:* + 44 (0)161 790 8289 *Fax:* + 44 (0)161 703 9157 *Email:* bishopofbolton@manchester.anglican.org *Web:* www.manchester.anglican.org

Newcastle-York The Rt Revd Christine Hardman Bishop of Newcastle Bishop's House 29 Moor Road South Gosforth Newcastle upon Tyne NE3 1PA ENGLAND *Tel:* + 44 (0)191 285 2220 *Fax:* + 44 (0)191 284 6933 *Email:* bishop@newcastle.anglican. org *Web:* www.newcastle.anglican.org

Newcastle-York The Rt Revd Mark Tanner Suffragan Bishop of Berwick Bishop's House 29 Moor Road South Gosforth Newcastle upon Tyne NE3 1PA ENGLAND*Email:* bishopofberwick@newcastle. anglican.org

Norwich-Canterbury The Rt Revd Graham James Bishop of Norwich Bishop's House Norwich Norfolk NR3 1SB ENGLAND *Tel:* + 44 (0)1603 629 001 *Fax:* + 44 (0)1603 761 613 *Email:* bishop@norwich. anglican.org *Web:* www.norwich.anglican.org

Norwich-Canterbury The Rt Revd Jonathan Meyrick Suffragan Bishop of Lynn The Old Vicarage Castle Acre King's Lynn Norfolk PE32 2AA ENGLAND *Tel:* + 44 (0)1760 755 553 *Fax:* + 44 (0)1760 755 085 *Email:* bishop.lynn@norwich. anglican.org

Norwich-Canterbury The Rt Revd Alan Peter Winton Suffragan Bishop of Thetford The Red House 53 Norwich Street Stoke Holy Cross Norwich Norfolk NR14 8AB ENGLAND *Tel:* + 44 (0)1508 491 014 *Fax:* + 44 (0)1508 492 105 *Email:* bishop. thetford@norwich.anglican.org

Oxford-Canterbury The Rt Revd Steven Croft Bishop of Oxford Diocesan Church House North Hinksey Oxford OX2 0NB ENGLAND *Tel:* + 44 (0)1865 208 222 *Fax:* + 44 (0)1865 790 470 *Email:* bishopoxon@dch.oxford.anglican.org *Web:* www. oxford.anglican.org

Oxford-Canterbury The Rt Revd Alan Thomas Lawrence Wilson Suffragan Bishop of Buckingham Sheridan Grimms Hill Great Missenden Bucks HP16 9BD ENGLAND *Tel:* + 44 (0)1494 862 173 *Fax:* + 44 (0)1494 890 508 *Email:* bishopbucks@ oxford.anglican.org

Oxford-Canterbury The Rt Revd Colin William Fletcher Suffragan Bishop of Dorchester Arran House Sandy Lane Yarnton Kidlington OX5 1PB ENGLAND *Tel:* + 44 (0)1865 208 218 *Fax:* + 44 (0)1865 379 890 *Email:* bishopdorchester@oxford. anglican.org

Oxford-Canterbury The Rt Revd Andrew Proud Suffragan Bishop of Reading Bishop's House Tidmarsh Lane Reading Berks RG8 8HA ENGLAND *Tel:* + 44 (0)118 984 1216 *Fax:* + 44 (0)118 984 1218 *Email:* bishopreading@oxford.anglican.org

Peterborough-Canterbury The Rt Revd Donald Spargo Allister Bishop of Peterborough Bishop's Lodging The Palace Peterborough Cambs PE1 1YA ENGLAND *Tel:* + 44 (0)1733 562 492 *Fax:* + 44 (0)1733 890 077 *Email:* bishop@peterborough-diocese.org.uk *Web:* www.peterborough-diocese. org.uk

Peterborough-Canterbury The Rt Revd John F Holbrook Suffragan Bishop of Brixworth Orchard Acre 11 North Street Mears Ashby Northampton NN6 0DW ENGLAND *Tel:* + 44 (0)1733 562 492 *Email:* bishop.brixworth@peterborough-diocese. org.uk

Portsmouth-Canterbury The Rt Revd Christopher RJ Foster Bishop of Portsmouth Bishopsgrove 26 Osborn Road Fareham Hants PO16 7DC ENGLAND *Tel:* + 44 (0)1329 280 247 *Fax:* + 44 (0)1329 231 538 *Email:* bishports@portsmouth. anglican.org *Web:* www.portsmouth.anglican.org/

Rochester-Canterbury The Rt Revd James F Langstaff Bishop of Rochester Bishopscourt 24 St Margaret's Street Rochester K entME1 1T ENGLAND *Tel:* + 44 (0)1634 842 721 *Fax:* + 44 (0)1634 831 136 *Email:* bishop.rochester@rochester. anglican.org *Web:* www.rochester.anglican.org/

Rochester-Canterbury Vacant Suffragan bishop elect of Rochester - Tonbridge Bishop's Lodge 48 S Botolph's Road Sevenoaks TN13 3AG ENGLAND *Tel:* + 44 (0)1732 456 070 *Fax:* + 44 (0)1732 741 44 *Email:* bishop.tonbridge@rochester.anglican.org

Salisbury-Canterbury The Rt Revd Nicholas Holtam Bishop of Salisbury South Canonry 71 The Close Salisbury Wiltshire SP1 2ER ENGLAND *Tel:*

44 (0)1722 334 031 *Fax:* + 44 (0)1722 413 112 *Email:* bishop.salisbury@salisbury.anglican.org *Web:* www. salisbury.anglican.org

Salisbury-Canterbury The Rt Revd Karen Gorham Suffragan Bishop of Sherborne The Sherborne Area Office St Nicholas' Church Centre 30 Wareham Road Corfe Mullen Dorset BH21 3LE ENGLAND *Tel:* + 44 (0)1202 691 418 *Email:* gsherborne@salisbury. anglican.org *Web:* www.salisbury.anglican.org

Salisbury-Canterbury The Rt Revd Edward Condry Suffragan Bishop of Ramsbury Diocesan Office Church House Crane Street Salisbury Wilts SP1 2QB ENGLAND *Tel:* + 44 (0)1722 438 662 *Fax:* + 44 (0)1380 848 247 *Email:* ramsbury.office@salisbury. anglican.org

Sheffield-York The Rt Revd Pete Wilcox Bishop of Sheffield Bishopscroft Snaithing Lane Sheffield S10 3LG ENGLAND *Tel:* + 44 (0)114 230 2170 *Email:* bishop@sheffield.anglican.org *Web:* www.sheffield. anglican.org

Sheffield-York The Rt Revd Peter Burrows Suffragan Bishop of Doncaster Doncaster House Church Lane Fishlake Doncaster DN7 5JW ENGLAND *Tel:* + 44 (0)1302 846 610 *Fax:* + 44 (0)1709 730 230 *Email:* bishoppeter@bishopofdoncaster.org.uk

Sodor & Man-York The Rt Revd Peter Eagles Bishop elect of Sodor & Man Thie yn Aspick 4 The Falls Tromode Road Douglas IM4 4PZ Isle of Man *Tel:* + 44 (0)1624 622 108 *Fax:* + 44 (0)1624 672 890 *Email:* bishop@sodorandman.im *Web:* www.sodorandman. im

Southwark-Canterbury The Rt Revd Christopher T Chessun Bishop of Southwark Trinity House 4 Chapel Court Borough High Street London SE1 1HW ENGLAND *Tel:* + 44 (0)207 939 9241 *Email:* bishop.christopher@southwark.anglican.org   *Web:* www.southwark.anglican.org

Southwark-Canterbury The Rt Revd Richard I Cheetham Suffragan Bishop of Kingston 620 Kingston Road Raynes Park London SW20 8DN ENGLAND *Tel:* + 44 (0)20 8545 2440 *Fax:* + 44 (0)20 8545 2441 *Email:* bishop.richard@southwark. anglican.org

Southwark-Canterbury The Rt Revd Johnathan Clark Suffragan Bishop of Croydon St Matthew's House 100 George Street Croydon Surrey CR0 1PE ENGLAND *Tel:* + 44 (0)208 256 9630 *Fax:* + 44 (0)208 256 9631 *Email:* bishop.jonathan@ southwark.anglican.org

Southwark-Canterbury The Rt Revd Karowei Dorgu Suffragan Bishop of Woolwich Trinity House 4 Chapel Court Borough High Street London SE1 1HW ENGLAND *Tel:* + 44 (0)207 939 9405 *Fax:* + 44 (0)207 939 9467 *Email:* bishop@southwark. anglican.org *Web:* www.southwark.anglican.org

Southwell & Nottingham-York The Rt Revd Paul Gavin Williams Bishop elect of Southwell & Nottingham Bishop's Manor Southwell Notts NG25 0JR ENGLAND *Tel:* + 44 (0)1636 812 112 *Fax:* + 44 (0)1636 815 401 *Email:* bishop@southwell.anglican. org *Web:* www.southwell.anglican.org

Southwell & Nottingham-York The Rt Revd Anthony Porter Suffragan Bishop of Southwell - Sherwood Dunham House 8 Westgate Southwell Notts NG25 0JL ENGLAND *Tel:* + 44 (0)1636 819 133 *Fax:* + 44 (0)1636 819 085 *Email:* bishopsherwood@ southwell.anglican.org

St Albans-Canterbury The Rt Revd Alan GC Smith Bishop of St Albans Abbey Gate House 4 Abbey Mill Lane St Albans Herts AL3 4HD ENGLAND *Tel:* + 44 (01727 853 305 *Fax:* + 44 (01727 846 715 *Email:* bishop@stalbans.anglican.org *Web:* www.stalbans. anglican.org/

St Albans-Canterbury The Rt Revd Richard Atkinson Bishop of Bedford Bishop's Lodge Bedford Road Cardington MK44 3SS ENGLAND *Tel:* + 44 (0)1234 831 432 *Fax:* + 44 (0)1234 831 484 *Email:* bishopbedford@stalbans.anglican.org

St Albans-Canterbury The Rt Revd Michael Beasley Suffragan Bishop of Hertford Bishopswood 3 Stobarts Close Knebworth Herts SG3 6ND ENGLAND *Tel:* + 44 (0)1438 817 260 *Email:* bishophertford@stalbans. anglican.org

St Edmundsbury & Ipswich-Canterbury The Rt Revd Martin Seeley Bishop of St Edmundsbury & Ipswich The Bishop's House 4 Park Road Ipswich Suffolk IP1 3ST ENGLAND *Tel:* + 44 01473 252829 *Fax:* + 44 01473 232552 *Email:* bishops.office@ cofesuffolk.org *Web:* www.stedmundsbury.anglican. org

St Edmundsbury & Ipswich-Canterbury The Rt Revd Michael Harrison Suffragan Bishop of Dunwich The Bishop's House 4 Park Road Ipswich Suffolk IP1 3ST ENGLAND *Tel:* + 44 (0)1473 222 276 *Email:* bishop.mike@cofesuffolk.org

Truro-Canterbury The Revd Christopher David Goldsmith Suffragan Bishop of St Germans 32 Falmouth Road Truro Cornwall TR1 2HX ENGLAND *Tel:* + 44 (0)1872 273 190 *Fax:* + 44 (0)1872 277 883 *Email:* bishop@stgermans.truro. anglican.org

Winchester-Canterbury The Rt Revd Tim Dakin Bishop of Winchester Wolvesey Winchester Hampshire SO23 9ND ENGLAND *Tel:* + 44 (0)1962 854 050 *Fax:* + 44 (0)1962 897 088 *Email:* joyce.cockell@winchester.anglican.org *Web:* www. winchester.anglican.org

Winchester-Canterbury The Rt Revd David Grant Williams Suffragan Bishop of Basingstoke Bishop's Lodge Colden Lane Old Alresford Hampshire SO24

9DY ENGLAND *Tel:* + 44 (0)1962 737 330 *Email:* lindsey.demaudave@winchester.anglican.org

Winchester-Canterbury The Rt Revd Jonathan H Frost Suffragan Bishop of Southampton Bishop's House St Mary's Church Close Wessex Lane Southampton Hants SO18 2ST ENGLAND *Tel:* + 44 (0)23 8067 2684 *Email:* bishop.jonathan@ winchester.anglican.org

Worcester-Canterbury The Rt Revd John G Inge Bishop of Worcester The Bishop's Office The Old Palace Deans Way Worcester Worcs WR1 2JE ENGLAND *Tel:* + 44 (0)1905 731 599 *Fax:* + 44 (0)1299 250 027 *Email:* generalinfo@cofe-worcester. org.uk

Worcester-Canterbury The Rt Revd Graham B Usher Suffragan Bishop of Dudley Bishop's House 60 Bishop's Walk Cradley Heath Warley West Midlands B64 7RH ENGLAND *Tel:* + 44 (0)121 550 3407 *Fax:* + 44 (0)121 550 7340 *Email:* bishop.dudley@cofe-worcester.org.uk

York-York The Most Revd & Rt Hon Dr John TM Sentamu Archbishop of York Bishopthorpe Palace Bishopthorpe York North Yorks YO23 2GE ENGLAND *Tel:* + 44 (0)1904 707 021 *Fax:* + 44 (0)1904 709 204 *Email:* alison.cundiff@ archbishopofyork.org *Web:* www.dioceseofyork.org. uk/

York-York The Rt Revd Glyn Webster Suffragan Bishop of Beverley Holy Trinity Rectory Micklegate York YO1 6LE ENGLAND *Tel:* + 44 (0)113 265 4280 *Fax:* + 44 (0)113 265 4281 *Email:* bishopofbeverley@ yorkdiocese.org

York-York The Rt Revd Paul John Ferguson Bishop of Whitby 21 Thornton Rd Middlesbrough TS8 9DS ENGLAND *Tel:* + 44 (0)1642 593273 *Fax:* + 44 (0)1642 710 685 *Email:* bishopofwhitby@ yorkdiocese.org

York-York The Rt Revd John Bromilow Thomson Bishop of Selby Bishop's House Barton-le-Street Malton YO17 6PL ENGLAND *Tel:* + 44 (0)1653 627 191 *Fax:* + 44 (0)1653 627 193 *Email:* bishselby@ clara.net

York-York The Rt Revd Alison White Suffragan Bishop of Hull Hullen House Woodfield Lane Hessle HU13 0ES ENGLAND *Tel:* + 44 (0)1482 649 019 *Fax:* + 44 (0)1482 647 449 *Email:* bishopofhull@ yorkdiocese.org

HONG KONG SHENG KUNG HUI

Provincial Secretary The Revd Peter D Koon 16/F Tung Wai Commercial Building 109-111 Gloucester Road Wan Chai Hong Kong PEOPLE'S REPUBLIC OF CHINA *Tel:* + 852 25 265 355 *Fax:* + 852 25 212 199 *Email:* peter.koon@hkskh.org

Hong Kong Island The Most Revd Paul Kwong Archbishop of Hong Kong Sheng Kung Hui & Bishop of Hong Kong Island 71 Bonham Road Shek Tong Tsui Hong Kong PEOPLE'S REPUBLIC OF CHINA *Tel:* + 852 2526 5366 *Fax:* + 852 2523 3344 *Email:* paul.kwong@hkskh.org *Web:* dhk.hkskh.org

Western Kowloon The Rt Revd Andrew Chan Bishop of Western Kowloon 11 Pak Po Street Mongkok Kowloon Hong Kong PEOPLE'S REPUBLIC OF CHINA *Tel:* + 852 27 830 811 *Fax:* + 852 27 830 799 *Email:* dwk@hkskh.org *Web:* dwk.hkskh.org

THE CHURCH OF THE PROVINCE OF THE INDIAN OCEAN

Provincial Secretary The Revd Canon Samitiana J Razafindralambo Jhonson Diocesan Church House 37th St Paul Road Vacoas MAURITIUS *Tel:* + 230 686 5158 *Fax:* + *Email:* psec.acio@gmail.com

Provincial Treasurer Mr Philip Tse Rai Wai 21 Dr, J. Riviere St Port Louis REPUBLIC OF MAURITIUS *Tel:* + 230 465 1235 *Fax:* + *Email:* pptrw@intnet.mu

Antananarivo The Rt Revd Samoela Jaona Ranarivelo Bishop of Antananarivo Evêché Anglican Lot VK57 ter Ambohimanoro 101 Antananarivo MADAGASCAR *Tel:* + 261 (0)20 222 0827 *Fax:* + 261 (0)2 226 1331 *Email:* eemdanta@yahoo.com

Antananarivo The Rt Revd Todd Andrew McGregor Bishop of Tulear and Assistant Bishop of Antananarivo Evêché Anglican Lot VK57 ter Ambohimanoro 101 Antananarivo MADAGASCAR*Email:* revmctodd@yahoo.com

Antsiranana The Rt Revd Theophile Botomazava Bishop of Antsiranana Evêché Anglican BP 278 4 Rue Grandidier Antsiranana 201 MADAGASCAR *Tel:* + 261 (0)20 822 2776

Fianarantsoa The Rt Revd Gilbert Rateloson Rakotondravelo Bishop of Fianarantsoa Eveque du Diocese Fianarantsoa BP 1418 Fianarantsoa 301 MADAGASCAR *Tel:* + 261 20 755 1583 *Email:* eemdiofianara@yahoo.fr

Mahajanga The Rt Revd Jean Claude Andrianjafimanana Bishop of Mahajanga Eveche Anglican 401 Mahajanga B.P 570 Mahajanga 501 MADAGASCAR *Email:* andrianjajc@yahoo.fr

Mauritius The Rt Revd Ian Gerald James Ernest Bishop of Mauritius Bishops House Nallatamby Road Phoenix MAURITIUS *Tel:* + 230 686 5158 *Fax:* + 230 697 1096 *Email:* dioang@intnet.mu

Seychelles The Most Revd James Richard Wong Yin Song Archbishop, Province of Indian Ocean & Bishop of the Seychelles PO Box 44 Victoria Mahe SEYCHELLES *Tel:* + 248 321 977 *Fax:* + 248 323 879 *Email:* angdio@seychelles.net

Toamasina The Rt Revd Jean Paul Solo Bishop of Toamasina Evêché Anglican Lot VK57 ter Ambohimanoro Antananarivo 101 MADAGASCAR *Tel:* + 261 20 533 1663 *Fax:* + 261 20 533 1689 *Email:* eemdtoam@wanadoo.mg

Toliara The Rt Revd Todd McGregor Bishop of Toliara Awaiting Details *Email:* Bishopmctodd@yahoo.com

THE CHURCH OF IRELAND

Provincial Secretary Mr David Ritchie Church of Ireland House Church Avenue Rathmines Dublin 6 REPUBLIC OF IRELAND *Tel:* + 353 (0)1 497 8422 *Fax:* + 353 (0)1 497 8792 *Email:* chiefofficer@rcbdub.org

Armagh-Dublin The Most Revd Richard Lionel Clarke Archbishop of Armagh and Primate of All Ireland and Metropolitan Church House 46 Abbey Street Armagh BT61 7DZ NORTHERN IRELAND *Tel:* + 44 (0)28 375 27144 *Fax:* + 44 (0)28 375 1059 *Email:* archbishop@armagh.anglican.org *Web:* www.armagh.anglican.org/

Cashel & Ossory-Dublin The Rt Revd Michael Andrew James J Burrows Bishop of Cashel, Ferns & Ossory Bishop's House Troysgate Kilkenny REPUBLIC OF IRELAND *Tel:* + 353 (0)56 778 6633 *Fax:* + 353 (0)56 775 1813 *Email:* cashelossorybishop@eircom.net *Web:* www.cashel.anglican.org/

Clogher-Armagh The Rt Revd John McDowell Bishop of Clogher The See House 152A Ballagh Road Fivemiletown Co Tyrone BT75 0QP NORTHERN IRELAND *Tel:* + 44 (0)28 6634 7879 *Fax:* + 44 (0)28 8952 2475 *Email:* bishop@clogher.anglican.org *Web:* www.clogher.anglican.org

Connor-Armagh The Rt Revd Alan Francis Abernethy Bishop of Connor Bishop's House 1 Marlborough Gate Marlborough Park Malone, Belfast BT9 6GB NORTHERN IRELAND *Tel:* + 44 (0)28 902 33188 *Fax:* + 44 (0)28 902 37802 *Email:* bishop@connor.anglican.org *Web:* www.connor.anglican.org/

Cork, Cloyne & Ross-Dublin The Rt Revd William Paul Colton Bishop of Cork, Cloyne & Ross The Palace Bishop Street Cork REPUBLIC OF IRELAND *Tel:* + 353 (0)21 5005 080 *Fax:* + 353 (0)21 4320 960 *Email:* bishop@ccrd.ie *Web:* www.cork.anglican.org

Derry & Raphoe-Armagh The Rt Revd Kenneth Raymond Good Bishop of Derry & Raphoe The See House 112 Culmore Road Londonderry BT48 8JF NORTHERN IRELAND *Tel:* + 44 (0)28 7135 1206 *Fax:* + 44 (0)28 7135 2554 *Email:* bishop@derry.anglican.org *Web:* www.derry.anglican.org

Down & Dromore-Armagh The Rt Revd Harold Creeth Miller Bishop of Down & Dromore The See House 32 Knockdene Park South Belfast BT5 7AB

NORTHERN IRELAND *Tel:* + 44 (0)28 9082 8850 *Fax:* + 44 (0)28 902 31902 *Email:* bishop@down.anglican.org *Web:* www.down.anglican.org

Dublin & Glendalough-Dublin The Most Revd Michael Geoffrey St Aubyn Jackson Archbishop of Dublin & Glendalough The See House 17 Temple Road Dartry Dublin 6 REPUBLIC OF IRELAND *Tel:* + 353 (0)1 497 6981 *Fax:* + 353 (0)1 497 6355 *Email:* archbishop@dublin.anglican.org *Web:* www.dublin.anglican.org

Kilmore, Elphin & Ardagh-Armagh The Rt Revd Ferran Glenfield Bishop of Kilmore, Elphin & Ardagh The Rectory Cootehill Co Cavan IRELAND *Tel:* + 353 49 555 9954 *Email:* bishop@kilmore.anglican.org *Web:* www.kilmore.anglican.org

Limerick & Killaloe-Dublin The Rt Revd Kenneth Kearon Bishop of Limerick & Killaloe Rien Roe Adare Co Limerick REPUBLIC OF IRELAND *Tel:* + 353 (0)61 396 244 *Fax:* + 353 (0)66 451 100 *Email:* bishop@limerick.anglican.org *Web:* www.limerick.anglican.org

Meath & Kildare-Dublin The Rt Revd Patricia Louise Storey Bishop of Meath & Kildare Bishop's House Mayglare Maynooth Co Kildare REPUBLIC OF IRELAND *Tel:* + 353 (0)1 629 2163 *Fax:* + 353 (0)1 628 9354 *Email:* bishop@meath.anglican.org *Web:* www.meath.anglican.org/

Tuam, Killala & Achonry-Armagh The Rt Revd Patrick William Rooke Bishop of Tuam, Killala & Achonry Bishop's House 2 Summerfield Cahergowan Claregalway Co Galway IRELAND *Tel:* + 353 (0)91 799 359 *Email:* bishop@tuam.anglican.org *Web:* www.tuam.anglican.org

THE NIPPON SEI KO KAI (THE ANGLICAN COMMUNION IN JAPAN)

General Secretary The Revd Jesse Shin-Ichi Yahagi 65-3 Yarai Cho Shinjuku-Ku Tokyo 162-0805 JAPAN *Tel:* + 81 (0)3 5228 3171 *Fax:* + 81 (0)3 5228 3175 *Email:* general-sec.po@nskk.org

Provincial Treasurer Mr Shigeo Ozaki Provincial Office 65-3 Yarai-cho Shinjuku-ku Tokyo 162-0805 JAPAN *Tel:* + 81 (0)3 5228 3171 *Fax:* + 81 (0)3 5228 3175

Chubu The Rt Revd Peter Ichiro Shibusawa Bishop of Chubu 2-28-1 Meigetsu-cho Showa-ku Nagoya-shi Aichi-ken 466-0034 JAPAN *Tel:* + 81 (0)52 858 1007 *Fax:* + 81 (0)52 858 1008 *Email:* bishop.chubu@nskk.org

Hokkaido The Most Revd Nathaniel Makoto Uematsu Primate of The Nippon Sei Ko Kai & Bishop of Hokkaido Kita 15 Jo Nishi 5-1-12 Kita-Ku Sapporo 001-0015 JAPAN *Tel:* + 81 (0)11 717 8181 *Fax:* + 81 (0)11 736 8377 *Email:* fwjh6169@mb.infoweb.ne.jp *Web:* www.nskk.org/hokkaido

Kita Kanto The Rt Revd Zerubbabel Katsuichi Hirota Bishop of Kita Kanto 2-172 Sakuragi-cho

Omiya-ku Saitama-shi Saitama-ken 330-0854 JAPAN *Tel:* + 81 (0)48 642 2680 *Fax:* + 81 (0)48 648 0358 *Email:* horotaz@nifty.com

Kobe The Rt Revd Andrew Yatuka Nakamura Bishop of Kobe 5-11-1 Shimo Yamate Dori Chuo-ku Kobe City Hyogo 650 0011 JAPAN *Tel:* + 81 (0)78 351 5469 *Fax:* + 81 (0)78 382 1095 *Email:* nakamurayutaka6@msn.com *Web:* www.kobe.anglican.org

Kyoto The Rt Revd Stephen Takashi Kochi Bishop of Kyoto 380 Okakuen-cho, Shimotachiuri-agaru Karasumadori Kamikyo-ku Kyoto-shi Kyoto-hu 602-8011 JAPAN *Tel:* + 81 (0)75 431 7204 *Fax:* + 81 (0)75 441 4238 *Email:* aset@kje.biglobe.ne.jp *Web:* www.nskk.org/kyoto

Kyushu The Rt Revd Luke Ken-ichi Muto Bishop of Kyushu 2-9-22 Kusagae Chuo-ku Fukuoka-shi Fukuoka-ken 810 -0045 JAPAN *Tel:* + 81 (0)92 771 2050 *Fax:* + 81 (0)92 771 9857 *Web:* www.kyushu.anglican.org

Okinawa The Rt Revd David Eisho Uehara Bishop of Okinawa 3-3-5 Aza Meada Urasoe-shi Okinawa-ken 901-2102 JAPAN *Tel:* + 81 (0)98 942 1101 *Fax:* + 81 (0)98 942 1102 *Email:* rtrev.david-uehara@anglican-okinawa.jp

Osaka The Rt Revd Andrew Haruhisa Iso Bishop of Osaka 2-1-8 Matsuzaki-cho Abeno-ku Osaka-shi Osaka-fu 545-0053 JAPAN *Tel:* + 81 (0)6 6621 6530 *Fax:* + 81 (0)6 6621 9148 *Email:* iso.osaka@nskk.org *Web:* www.nskk.org/osaka/

Tohoku The Rt Revd John Hiromichi Kato Bishop of Tohoku 2-13-15 Kokubun-cho Aoba-ku Sendai-shi Miyagi-ken 980-0803 JAPAN *Tel:* + 81 (0)22 223 2349 *Fax:* + 81 (0)22 223 2387 *Email:* bishop.tohoku@nskk.org *Web:* www.tohoku.anglican.org

Tokyo The Rt Revd Andrew Yoshimichi Ohata Bishop of Tokyo 3-6-18 Shiba Koen Minato-ku Tokyo Tokyo-to 105-0011 JAPAN *Tel:* + 81 (0)3 3433 0987 *Fax:* + 81 (0)3 3433 8678 *Email:* bishop.tko@nskk.org *Web:* www.tokyo.anglican.org

Yokohama The Rt Revd Laurence Yutaka Minabe Bishop of Yokohama 14-57 Mitsuzawa Shimo-cho Kanagawa-ku Yokohama-shi Kanagawa-ken 221-0852 JAPAN *Tel:* + 81 (0)45 321 4988 *Fax:* + 81 (0)45 321 4978 *Email:* laurence.yokohama@anglican.jp *Web:* www.anglican.jp/yokohama/

THE EPISCOPAL CHURCH IN JERUSALEM AND THE MIDDLE EAST

Provincial Secretary Ms Georgia K Katsantonis 2 Grigori Afxentiou Nicosia PO Box 22075 1515 CYPRUS *Email:* georgia@spidernet.com.cy

Provincial Treasurer The Ven Canon William Schwartz PO Box 3210 Doha QATAR *Tel:* + 974 4416 5726 *Email:* archdeacon.bill@cypgulf.org

Cyprus and the Gulf The Rt Revd Michael Augustine Owen A O Lewis Bishop of Cyprus and

the Gulf Bishop's Office PO Box 22075 CY 1517 Nicosia CYPRUS *Tel:* + 357 (0)22 332 206 *Fax:* + 357 (0)22 672 241 *Email:* bishop@spidernet.com.cy *Web:* www.cypgulf.org/

Egypt The Rt Revd Mouneer Hanna Anis Bishop in Egypt with North Africa and the Horn of Africa Diocesan Office PO Box 87 Zamalek Distribution 11211 Cairo EGYPT *Tel:* + 20 (0)2 738 0821/3/9 *Fax:* + 20 (0)2 735 894 *Email:* bishopmouneer@gmail.com *Web:* www.dioceseofegypt.org/

Egypt The Rt Revd Grant Lemarquand Area Bishop for the Horn of Africa Gambella Anglican Centre Gambella Town Gambella ETHIOPIA *Tel:* + 20 (0)2 738 0821/3/9 *Fax:* + 20 (0)2 735 894 *Email:* bishopgrant777@gmail.com

Egypt The Rt Revd Samy Fawzy Area Bishop for North Africa Diocesan Office PO Box 87 Zamalek Distribution 11211 Cairo EGYPT *Tel:* + 20 (0)2 738 0821/3/9

Iran Vacant Bishop elect of Iran St Thomas Center Raiwind Road PO Box 688 Lahore Punjab 54000 PAKISTAN *Tel:* + 92 (0)42 542 0452

Jerusalem The Most Revd Suheil S Dawani Archbishop, Jerusalem & the Middle East & Archbishop in Jerusalem St George's Cathedral Close Nablus Road Box 19122 Jerusalem 91191 ISRAEL *Tel:* + 972 (0)2 627 1670 *Fax:* + 972 (0)2 627 3847 *Email:* bishop@j-diocese.org *Web:* www.j-diocese.org

THE ANGLICAN CHURCH OF KENYA

Provincial Secretary The Revd Canon Rosemary Mbogo Bishops Road Off Ngong Road PO Box 40502 - 00100 Nairobi KENYA *Tel:* + 254 20 271 4752/3/4 *Fax:* + 254 20 2718442 *Email:* ackpsoffice@ackenya.org

Provincial Treasurer Mr William Ogara PO Box 40502 Bishop's Gardens Bishop's Road Nairobi KENYA *Tel:* + 254 (0)20 2333 324/5 *Fax:* + 254 (0)20 2728 139

Provincial Accountant Mr John Muhoho PO Box 40502 Bishop's Gardens Bishop's Road Nairobi KENYA *Tel:* + 254 (0)20 2714 755 *Fax:* + 254 (0)20 2718 442

All Saints Cathedral Diocese The Most Revd Jackson Ole Sapit Primate and Archbishop of All Kenya PO Box 678 Kericho 20200 KENYA *Tel:* + 254 (0)20 2714 752/3/5 *Fax:* + 254 (0)20 2718 442 *Email:* archoffice@ackenya.org

All Saints Cathedral Diocese The Rt Revd Cleti Ogeto Suffragan Bishop - All Saints Cathedral Diocese PO Box 40502 Nairobi 100 KENYA

All Saints Cathedral Diocese The Rt Revd David Mutisya Suffragan Bishop of All Saints Cathedral Diocese - Garissa Missionary Area All Saints Cathedral PO Box 60 Garissa 70100 KENYA

Bondo The Rt Revd Johannes O Angela Bishop of the Diocese of Bondo PO Box 240 Bondo 40601 KENYA *Tel:* + 254 (0)335 20415 *Email:* ackbondo@swiftkenya.com

Bungoma The Revd George Mechumo Bishop elect of Bungoma PO Box 2392 Bungoma 50200 KENYA *Tel:* + 254 (0)337 30 481 *Fax:* + 254 (0)337 30 481 *Email:* ackbungoma@swiftkenya.com

Butere The Rt Revd Timothy Wambunya Bishop of Butere PO Box 54 Butere 50101 KENYA *Tel:* + 254 056 620 412 *Fax:* + 254 056 620 038 *Email:* ackbutere@swiftkenya.com

Eldoret The Rt Revd Christopher Ruto Bishop of Eldoret PO Box 3404 Eldoret 30100 KENYA*Email:* ackeldoret@africaonline.co.ke

Embu The Rt Revd David Muriithi Ireri Bishop of Embu PO Box 189 Embu 60100 KENYA *Tel:* + 254 068 30614 *Email:* ack-embu@swiftkenya.com

Kajiado The Rt Revd Gadiel Katanga Lenini Bishop of Kajiado PO Box 203-01100 Kajiado 1100 KENYA *Tel:* + 254 (0)45 21105 *Email:* ackajiado@swiftkenya.com

Kapsabet The Rt Revd Paul Korir Bishop of Kapsabet Awaiting Details

Katakwa The Rt Revd John OKude Omuse Bishop of Katakwa PO Box 68 Amagoro 50244 KENYA *Tel:* + 254 (0)337 54 079 *Fax:* + 254 (0)337 54 017 *Email:* ackatakwa@swiftkenya.com

Kericho The Rt Revd Ernest Kiprotich Bishop of Kericho PO Box 678 Kericho 20200 KENYA *Tel:* + 254 (0)52 20112

Kirinyaga The Rt Revd Joseph Kibuchua Bishop of Kirinyaga PO Box 95 Kutus 10304 KENYA *Tel:* + 254 (0)163 44 221 *Fax:* + 254 (0)163 44 020 *Email:* ackirinyaga@swiftkenya.com

Kitale The Rt Revd Stephen Kewasis Bishop of Kitale PO Box 4176 Kitale KENYA *Tel:* + 254 054 31631 *Email:* ack.ktl@gmail.com

Kitui The Rt Revd Josephat V Mule Bishop of Kitui PO Box 1054 Kitui 90200 KENYA *Tel:* + 254 (0)141 226 82 *Fax:* + 254 (0)141 221 19 *Email:* ackitui@swiftkenya.com

Machakos The Rt Revd Joseph Mutungi Bishop of Machakos PO Box 282 Machakos 90100 KENYA *Tel:* + 254 044 21379 *Fax:* + 254 044 20178 *Email:* ackmachakos@gmail.com

Makueni The Rt Revd Joseph M Kanuku Bishop of Makueni PO Box 282 Machakos KENYA *Tel:* + 254 044 21379 *Fax:* + 254 044 20178 *Email:* ackmachakos@swiftkenya.com

Malindi The Rt Revd Lawrence K Dena Bishop of Malindi Ukumbusho House Nkrumah Road PO Box 80072 Mombasa KENYA *Web:* www.ackenya.org

Marsabit The Rt Revd Robert Martin Bishop of Marsabit PO Box 51 Marsabit 6500 KENYA *Email:* ackbishopmarsabit@gmail.com

Maseno North The Rt Revd Simon M Oketch Bishop of Maseno North PO Box 416 Kakemega 50100 KENYA *Tel:* + 254 56 2/3 *Email:* ackmnorth@jambo.co.ke

Maseno South The Rt Revd Francis Abiero Bishop of Maseno South PO Box 114 Kisumu 40100 KENYA *Tel:* + 254 (0)35 45 147 *Fax:* + 254 (0)35 21 009 *Email:* ackmsouth@swiftkenya.com

Maseno West The Rt Revd Joseph J Wasonga Bishop of Maseno West PO Box 793 Siaya 40600 KENYA *Email:* wbishopjoseph@yahoo.com

Mbeere The Rt Revd Moses Masamba Nthukah Bishop of Mbeere PO Box 122 Siakago 60104 KENYA *Tel:* + 254 721423840 *Email:* bishopmbeere@gmail.com *Web:* http://www.ackenya.org/dioceses/mbeere.html

Meru The Rt Revd Charles N Mwendwa Bishop of Meru PO Box 427 Meru 60200 KENYA *Tel:* + 254 16 430 719 *Email:* ackmeru@swiftkenya.com

Mombasa The Rt Revd Julius R M Katio Kalu Bishop of Mombasa Ukumbusho House Mkrumah Road PO Box 80072 Mombasa 80100 KENYA *Tel:* + 254 (0)11 311 105 *Fax:* + 254 (0)11 227 837 *Email:* ackmombasa@swiftmombasa.com

Mount Kenya Central The Rt Revd Isaac M Ng'ang'a Bishop of Mount Kenya Central PO Box 1040 Muranga 10200 KENYA *Tel:* + 254 (0)60 30559 *Fax:* + 254 (0)60 30148 *Email:* ackmkcentral@wananchi.com

Mount Kenya Central The Rt Revd Allen M Waithaka Suffragan Bishop of Mount Kenya Central PO Box 1040 Muranga 10200 KENYA *Tel:* + 254 156 305 59

Mount Kenya South The Rt Revd Timothy Ranji Bishop of Mount Kenya South PO Box 886 Kiambu 900 KENYA *Tel:* + 254 (0)154 22 997 *Fax:* + 254 (0)154 22 408 *Email:* ackmtksouth@swiftkenya.com

Mount Kenya South The Rt Revd Charles Muturi Suffragan Bishop Mt Kenya South Mount Kenya South Diocese PO Box 886 Kiambu 900 KENYA *Email:* ackmtkenyasouth@swiftkenya.com

Mount Kenya West The Rt Revd Joseph M Kagunda Bishop of Mount Kenya West PO Box 229 Nyeri 10100 KENYA *Tel:* + 254 (0)171 302 14 *Fax:* + 254 (0)171 2954 *Email:* ackmtkwest@wananchi.com

Mumias The Rt Revd Beneah Okumu Salala Bishop of Mumias PO Box 213 Mumias 50102 KENYA *Fax:* + 254 333 41232 *Email:* ackmumias@swiftkenya.com *Web:* www.ackmumiasdiocese.org

Muranga South The Rt Revd Julius Karanu Wa Gicheru Bishop of Muranga South Awaiting Details

Nairobi The Rt Revd Joel Waweru Mwangi Bishop of Nairobi PO Box 72846 Nairobi 200 KENYA *Tel:* + 254 020 4440524 *Fax:* + 254 2 226259

Nakuru The Rt Revd Joseph Muchai Bishop of Nakuru PO Box 56 Moi Road Nakuru 20100 KENYA *Tel:* + 254 (0)37 212 155 *Fax:* + 254 (0)37 44 379

Nakuru The Rt Revd Musa Kamuren Suffragan Bishop of Nakuru - Baringo Area PO Box 56 Moi Road Nakuru 20100 KENYA *Tel:* + 254 (0)37 212 155

Nambale The Rt Revd Robert Magina Barasa Bishop of Nambale PO Box 4 Nambale 50409 KENYA *Tel:* + 254 (0)336 24040 *Fax:* + 254 (0)336 24071 *Email:* acknambale@swiftkenya.com

Nyahururu The Rt Revd Stephen Kabora Bishop of Nyahururu PO Box 926 Nyahururu 20300 KENYA *Tel:* + 254 365 32179 *Email:* nyahu_dc@africaonline.co.ke

Nyahururu The Rt Revd Jacob Lesuuda Suffragan Bishop of Maralal Area PO Box 42 Maralal KENYA *Email:* jlesuuda@yahoo.com

Southern Nyanza The Rt Revd James Ochiel Bishop of Southern Nyanza PO Box 65 Homa Bay 40300 KENYA *Tel:* + 254 0385 221 27 *Fax:* + 254 0385 220 56 *Email:* acksnyanza@swiftkenya.com

Taita-Taveta The Rt Revd Samson Mwaluda Bishop of Taita Taveta ACK Taita-taveta Diocese PO Box 75 Voi 80300 KENYA *Tel:* + 254 (0)147 30 096 *Fax:* + 254 (0)147 30 364 *Email:* acktaita@swiftmombasa.com

Taita-Taveta The Rt Revd Liverson Mng'onda Coadjutor Bishop of Taita-Taveta ACK Taita-taveta Diocese PO Box 75 Voi 80300 KENYA

Thika The Rt Revd Julius Njuguna Wanyoike Bishop of Thika PO Box 214 Thika 1000 KENYA *Tel:* + 254 (0)151 217 35 *Fax:* + 254 (0)151 315 44

THE ANGLICAN CHURCH OF KOREA
General Secretary The Revd Stephen Si-Kyung Yoo 16, Sejong-daero 19-gil Jung-gu Seoul 100-120 KOREA *Tel:* + 82 (0)2 738 8952 *Fax:* + 82 (0)2 737 4210 *Email:* 08skyoo@naver.com *Web:* www.skh.or.kr

Busan The Most Revd Onesimus Dongsin Park Primate of the Anglican Church of Korea & Bishop of Busan Bishop's Office 18 Daecheng-dong 2Ga Jung-Ku Busan 600-092 KOREA *Tel:* + 82 (0)51 463 5742 *Fax:* + 82 (0)51 463 5957 *Email:* primate.ack@gmail.com *Web:* skhpusan.onmam.com/

Daejeon The Revd Moses Nak Jun Yoo Bishop elect of Daejeon Bishop's Office 87-6 Sunhwa 2-dong Jung-gu Daejeon 301-823 KOREA *Tel:* + 82 (0)42 256 9988 *Fax:* + 82 (0)42 255 8918 *Email:* tdio@unitel.co.kr *Web:* www.djdio.or.kr

Seoul The Rt Revd Peter Lee Bishop of Seoul Bishop's Office 16 Sejong-daero 19-gil Jung-gu Seoul 100-120 KOREA *Tel:* + 82 (0)2 735 6157 *Fax:* + 82 (0)2 723 2640 *Web:* www.skhseoul.or.kr

THE CHURCH OF THE PROVINCE OF MELANESIA
Tel: +

Provincial Secretary Dr Abraham Hauriasi Anglican Church of Melanesia PO Box 19 Honiara SOLOMON ISLANDS *Tel:* + 677 20407

Provincial Accountant Mr Jimmy Maeigoa PO Box 19 Dogura MBP PAPUA NEW GUNIEA *Tel:* + 677 21 892 *Fax:* + 677 23 301

Banks & Torres The Rt Revd Alfred Patterson Worek Bishop of Banks & Torres C/O PO Box 19 Sola Vanualava Torba Province VANUTU *Tel:* + 678 38520 *Fax:* + 678 38520 *Email:* worek_p@comphq.org.sb

Central Melanesia The Most Revd George Takeli Archbishop of the Anglican Church of Melanesia and Bishop of Central Melanesia Church of Melanesia PO Box 19 Honiara SOLOMON iSLANDS *Tel:* + 677 242 10 *Email:* g.takeli@comphq.org.sb

Central Solomons The Rt Revd Ben Seka Bishop of Central Solomons PO Box 52 Tulagia CIP SOLOMON ISLANDS *Tel:* + 677 32 042 *Email:* d.bindon@xtra.co.nz

Guadalcanal The Rt Revd Nathan Tome Bishop of Guadalcanal Awaiting Details *Tel:* + 677 23337 *Email:* ntome4080@gmail.com

Hanuato'o The Rt Revd Alfred Karibongi Bishop of Hanuato'o C/O Post Office Kirakira Makira/Ulawa Province SOLOMON ISLANDS

Malaita The Rt Revd Samuel Sahu Bishop of Malaita Bishops House PO Box 7 Auki Malaita Province SOLOMON ISLANDS *Tel:* + 611 45 121 071 *Fax:* + 677 21 098

Malaita The Revd Rickson George Maomaoru Assistant Bishop elect of Malaita Bishops House PO Box 7 Auki Malaita Province SOLOMON ISLANDS

Temotu The Rt Revd Leonard Dawea Bishop of Temotu PO Box 50 Lata Santa Cruz Temotu Province SOLOMON ISLANDS *Tel:* + 677 530 80 *Fax:* + 677 530 92 *Email:* bjdawea@gmail.com

Vanuatu The Rt Revd James M Ligo Bishop of Vanuatu Bishop's House PO Box 238 Luganville Santo VANUATU *Tel:* + 678 370 65 *Fax:* + 678 363 31 *Email:* comdov@vanuatu.com.vu

Ysabel The Revd Ellison Quity Bishop elect of Ysabel Bishop's House PO Box 6 Buala Jejevo Ysabel Province SOLOMON ISLANDS *Tel:* + 677 350 34 *Fax:* + 677 350 71 *Email:* ellison.jejevo@gmail.com

LA IGLESIA ANGLICANA DE MEXICO

Provincial Secretary The Revd Canon Alfonso Walls Acatlán 102 Oriente Col. Mitras Centro Monterrey Nuevo Leon 64460 MEXICO *Tel:* + 52 81 8333 0992 *Fax:* + 52 81 8348 7362 *Email:* awalls@anglicanmx. org

Ms Laura Gracia Provincial Treasurer Acatlán 102 Ote Mitras Centro Monterrey NL 64460 MEXICO *Tel:* + 52 (0)81 8333 0992 *Email:* lgracia@anglicanmx.org

Cuernavaca The Rt Revd Enrique Treviño Cruz Bishop of Cuernavaca Minerva #1 Fracc. Delicias Cuernavaca Morelos 62330 MEXICO *Tel:* + 52 777 315 2870 *Email:* diocesisdecuernavaca@hotmail. com

Mexico The Rt Revd Carlos Touche-Porter Bishop of Mexico San Jeronimo #117 Col. San Angel Delegacion Alvaro Obregón MEXICO City DF 1000 MEXICO *Tel:* + 52 (0)33 5616 2205 *Email:* diocesisdemexico@gmail.com

Northern Mexico The Most Revd Francisco Moreno Presiding Bishop of La Iglesia Anglicana de Mexico & Bishop of Northern Mexico Acatlán 102 Oriente Col. Mitras Centro Monterrey Nuevo Leon 64460 MEXICO *Tel:* + 52 81 8333 0992 *Fax:* + 52 81 8348 7362 *Email:* primado@anglicanmx.org

Southeastern Mexico The Rt Revd Benito Juarez-Martinez Bishop of Southeastern Mexico Av Las Americas #73 Col. Aguacatal Xalapa Veracruz 91130 MEXICO *Tel:* + 52 (0)228 814 6951 *Email:* obispobenito.49@gmail.com

Western Mexico The Rt Revd Lino Rodriguez-Amaro Bishop of Western Mexico Torres Quintero # 15 Col. Seattle Zapopan Jalisco 45150 MEXICO *Tel:* + 52 333 560 4727 *Fax:* + 52 333 560 4726 *Email:* obispolino@hotmail.com *Web:* www.iamoccidente. org.mx

THE CHURCH OF THE PROVINCE OF MYANMAR (BURMA)

General Secretary The Revd Paul Myint Htet Htin Ya No 140 Pyidaungsu Yeiktha Street PO Box 11191 Yangon MYANMAR *Tel:* + 95 1 395 279 *Email:* myinthtet@gmail.com

Provincial Treasurer Ms Helen Myint Htwe Yee 140 Pyidaungsu-Yeiktha Road Dagon PO Yangon MYANMAR *Tel:* + 95 (0)1 395 279 *Email:* cpm.140@nptmail.com.mm

Hpa-an The Rt Revd Saw Stylo Bishop of Hpa-an Bishop Kone: Ward 4 Hpa-an Kayin State MYANMAR *Tel:* + 95 58 216 96

Mandalay The Rt Revd David Nyi Nyi Naing Bishop of Mandalay Diocesan Office 22 Pinya Road Mandalay MYANMAR *Tel:* + 95 (0)2 341 10 *Email:* davidnaing@gmail.com

Mytikyina The Rt Revd John Zau Li Bishop of Mytikyina 147 Thankin Net Pe Road Thinda Quarters Mytikyina Kachin State MYANMAR *Tel:* + 95 (0)74 231 04 *Email:* john.zauli@gmail.com

Mytikyina The Rt Revd Vacant Assistant Bishop elect of Mytikyina Diocesan Office 147 Thakin Net Pe Road Thida Quarter Mytikyina Kachin State MYANMAR *Tel:* + 95 074 25428

Sittwe The Rt Revd James Min Dein Bishop of Sittwe May Yu Stree Sittwe Rakhine State MYANMAR *Tel:* + 95 43 536 22 *Email:* mindein3@gmail.com

Toungoo The Rt Revd Saw Wilme Bishop of Toungoo Diocesan Office Nat-shin-Naung Street Ward 20 Toungoo Myanmar *Tel:* + 95 54 231 59 *Email:* bishop.wilme@gmail.com

Yangon The Most Revd Stephen Than Myint Oo Archbishop of Myanmar and Bishop of Yangon No 140 Pyidaungsu Yeiktha Street PO Box 11191 Yangon MYANMAR *Tel:* + 95 (0)1 395 279 *Fax:* + 95 (0)1 395 314 *Email:* stephenthan777@gmail.com

Yangon The Rt Revd Samuel Htang Oak Assistant Bishop of Yangon No 44 Bishop Home Pyay Road Yangon MYANMAR *Tel:* + 95 1 372 300 *Email:* sthangoak40@gmail.com

THE CHURCH OF NIGERIA (ANGLICAN COMMUNION)

Provincial Secretary Vacant Episcopal House 24 Doula Street PO Box 212 ADCP Abuja NIGERIA *Tel:* + 234 9 5236950 *Email:* communicator1@anglican-nig.org

Provincial Treasurer Chief O Adekunle PO Box 78 Lagos NIGERIA *Tel:* + 234 (0)1 263 3581

The Rt Revd Michael Olurohunbi Episcopal House 24 Douala Street Wuse District, Zone 5 PO Box 212 ADCP, Garki, Abuja NIGERIA *Tel:* + 234 (0)9 523 6950 *Email:* mikefarohunbi08@gmail.com

Aba-Province of the Niger Delta The Most Revd Ugochukwu U Ezuoke Archbishop of the Province of Niger Delta & Bishop of Aba Bishopscourt 70-72 St Michael's Road PO Box 212 Aba NIGERIA *Tel:* + 234 (0)82 227 666 *Email:* aba@anglican-nig.org

Aba Ngwa North-Province of Niger Delta The Rt Revd Nathan C Kanu Bishop of Aba Ngwa North Bishopscourt - All Saints Cathedral Abayi-Umuocham No 161-165 Owerri Road PO Box 43 Aba Abia State NIGERIA *Email:* odinathnfe@sbcglobal.net

Abakaliki-Province of Enugu The Rt Revd Monday C Nkwoagu Bishop of Abakaliki All Saints Cathedral PO Box 112 Abakaliki Ebonyi State NIGERIA *Tel:* + 234 (0)43 20 762 *Email:* abakaliki@anglican-nig.org

Abuja-Province of Abuja The Most Revd Nicholas Okoh Metropolitan & Primate of all Nigeria &

Bishop of Abuja Episcopal House 24 Douala Street Wuse District, Zone 5, PO Box 212 Abuja ADCP Garki NIGERIA *Tel:* + 234 (0)56 280 682 *Email:* nickorogodo@yahoo.com

Afikpo-Province of Enugu The Rt Revd Paul Uduogu Bishop of Afikpo Bishop's House PO Box 699 Afikpo Ebonyi State NIGERIA *Email:* udogupaul@yahoo.com

Aguata-Province of Niger The Most Revd Christian O Efobi Archbishop of the Province of the Niger & Bishop of Aguata Bishopscourt PO Box 1128 Ekwulobia Anambra State Rivers State NIGERIA *Tel:* + 234 (0)803 750 1077 *Email:* christianefobi@yahoo.com

Ahoada-Province of Niger Delta The Rt Revd Clement Ekpeye Bishop of Ahoada Bishopscourt PO Box 4 Ahoada Rivers State NIGERIA *Tel:* + 234 (0)806 357 6242 *Email:* ahoada@anglican-nig.org

Ajayi Crowther-Province of Ibadan The Rt Revd Olugbenga Oduntan Bishop of Ajayi Crowther Bishopscourt PO Box 430 Iseyin Oyo State NIGERIA *Tel:* + 234 (0)803 719 8182 *Email:* ajayicrowtherdiocese@yahoo.com

Akoko-Province of Ondo The Rt Revd Gabriel Akinbiyi Bishop of Akoko Bishopscourt PO Box 572 Ikare-Akoko Ondo State NIGERIA *Tel:* + 234 (0)31 801 011 *Email:* bishopgabrielakinbiyi@yahoo.com

Akoko Edo-Province of Bendel The Rt Revd Jolly Oyekpen Bishop of Akoko Edo Bishopscourt PO Box 10 Igarra Edo State NIGERIA *Tel:* + 234 (0)803 470 5941 *Email:* venjollye@yahoo.com

Akure-Province of Ondo The Rt Revd Simeon O Borokini Bishop of Akure Bishopscourt PO Box 1622 Akure Ondo state NIGERIA *Tel:* + 234 (0)34 241 572 *Fax:* + 234 (0)34 241 572

Amichi-Province of Niger The Rt Revd Ephraim Ikeakor Bishop of Amichi Bishopscourt PO Box 13 Amichi Anambra State NIGERIA *Tel:* + 234 (0)803 317 0916 *Email:* eoikeakor@yahoo.com

Arochukwu/Ohafia-Province of Aba The Rt Revd Johnson Onuoha Bishop of Arochukwu/Ohafia Bishopscourt PO Box 193 Arochukwu Abia State NIGERIA *Tel:* + 234 (0)802 538 6407 *Email:* aroohafia@anglican-nig.org

Asaba-Province of Bendel The Rt Revd Justus N Mogekwu Bishop of Asaba Bishopscourt PO Box 216 Asaba Delta State NIGERIA *Tel:* + 234 (0)802 819 2980 *Email:* justusmogekwu@yahoo.com

Awgu/Aninri-Province of Niger The Rt Revd Emmaunuel Ugwu Bishop of Awgu/Aniniri Bishopscourt PO Box 305 Agwu Enungu State NIGERIA *Tel:* + 234 (0)803 334 9360 *Email:* afamnonye@yahoo.com

Awka-Province of Niger The Rt Revd Alexander C Ibezim Bishop of Awka Bishopscourt PO Box 130 Awka Anambra State NIGERIA *Tel:* + 234 (0)48 550 058 *Email:* chioma1560@aol.com

Awori-Province of Lagos The Rt Revd J Akin Atere Bishop of Awori Bishopscourt PO Box 10 Ota Ogun State NIGERIA *Tel:* + 234 (0)803 553 7284 *Email:* dioceseofawori@yahoo.com

Badagry-Province of Lagos The Rt Revd Joseph B Adeyemi Bishop of Badagry Bishopscourt PO Box 7 Badagry Lagos State NIGERIA *Email:* badagry@anglican-nig.org

Bari-Province of Kaduna The Rt Revd Idris A Zubairu Bishop of Bari Bishopscourt Gidan Mato Bari Kano State NIGERIA *Tel:* + 234 (0)808 559 7183

Bauchi-Province of Jos The Rt Revd Musa Tula Bishop of Bauchi Bishop's House 2 Hospital Road PO Box 2450 Bauchi NIGERIA *Tel:* + 234 (0)77 543 460 *Email:* bauchi@anglican-nig.org

Benin-Province of Bendel The Rt Revd Peter J Imasuen Bishop of Benin Bishopscourt PO Box 82 Benin City Edo State NIGERIA *Tel:* + 234 30799560 *Email:* Beninanglican@yahoo.com

Bida-Province of Abuja The Rt Revd Jonah G E Kolo Bishop of the Missionary Diocese of Bida Bishop's House St John's Mission Compound PO Box 14 Bida NIGERIA *Tel:* + 234 (0)66 461 694

Bukuru-Province of Jos The Rt Revd Jwan Zhumbes Bishop of Bukuru Bishopscourt Citrus Estate PO Box 605 Sabon Bariki Plateau State NIGERIA

Calabar-Province of Niger Delta The Rt Revd Tunde Adeleye Bishop of Calabar Bishopscourt PO Box 74 Calabar Cross Rivers State NIGERIA *Tel:* + 234 (0)87 232 812 *Fax:* + 234 (0)88 220 835 *Email:* calabar@anglican-nig.org

Damaturu-Province of Jos The Rt Revd Abiodur Ogunyemi Bishop of Damaturu PO Box 312 Damaturu Yobe State NIGERIA *Tel:* + 234 (0)74 522 142 *Email:* damaturu@anglican-nig.org

Diocese on the Coast formerly (Ikale-Ilaje) Province of Ondo The Rt Revd Joshua E Ogunele Bishop of the Diocese on the Coast Bishopscourt Ikoya Road PMB 3 Ilutitun-Osooro Ondo State NIGERIA *Tel:* + 234 (0)803 467 1879 *Email:* joshuaonthecoast@yahoo.ca

Doko-Province of Lokoja The Rt Revd Uriah Kolo Bishop of Doko PO Box 1513 Bida Niger State NIGERIA *Tel:* + 234 (0)803 590 6327 *Email:* uriahkolo@gmail.com

Dutse-Province of Kaduna The Rt Revd Yesufu Lumu Bishop of Dutse PO Box 67 Yadi Dutse Jigawa State NIGERIA *Tel:* + 234 (0)64 721 379 *Email:* dutse@anglican-nig.org

Egba-Province of Lagos The Rt Revd Emmanuel O Adekunle Bishop of Egba Bishopscourt Cathedral of St Peter PO Box 46 Ile-oluji Ondo State NIGERIA

Egba West-Province of Lagos The Rt Revd Samuel O Ajani Bishop of Egba-West Bishopscourt Oke-Ata Housing Estate PO Box 6204 Sapon Abeokuta NIGERIA *Tel:* + 234 (0)80 5518 4822 *Email:* samuelajani@yahoo.com

Egbu-Province of Owerri The Rt Revd Geoffrey E Okoroafor Bishop of Egbu PO Box 1967 Owerri Imo State NIGERIA *Tel:* + 234 (0)83 231 797 *Email:* egbu@anglican-nig.org

Eha-Amufu-Province of Enugu The Rt Revd Daniel Olinya Bishop of Eha - Amufu St Andrews Cathedral Bishopscourt PO Box 85 Eha-Amufu Enugu State NIGERIA *Tel:* + 234 (0)803 089 2131 *Email:* dankol@yahoo.com

Ekiti-Province of Ondo The Most Revd Samuel Abe Archbishop of the Province of Ondo & Bishop of Ekiti Bishopscourt PO Box 12 Okesa Street Ado-Ekiti Ekiti State NIGERIA *Tel:* + 234 (0)30 250 305 *Email:* adedayoekiti@yahoo.com

Ekiti Kwara-Province of Ibadan The Rt Revd Andrew O Ajayi Bishop of Ekiti Kwara Awaiting Details *Tel:* + 234 (0)803 470 3522 *Email:* andajayi@yahoo.com

Ekiti Oke-Province of Ondo The Rt Revd Isaac Olubowale Bishop of Ekiti - Oke PMB 207 Usi-Ekiti Ekiti State NIGERIA *Email:* ekitioke@anglican-nig.org

Ekiti West-Province of Ondo The Rt Revd Samuel Oke Bishop of the Diocese of Ekiti West Bishop's Residence 6 Ifaki Street PO Box 477 Ijero-Ekiti NIGERIA *Tel:* + 234 (0)30 850 314

Enugu-Province of Niger The Rt Revd Emmanuel C Chukwuma Bishop of Enugu Bishop's House PO Box 418 Enugu NIGERIA *Tel:* + 234 (0)42 435 804 *Fax:* + 234 (0)42 259 808 *Email:* enugu@anglican-nig.org

Enugu North-Province of Niger Delta The Rt Revd Sosthenes Eze Bishop of Enugu North Bishopscourt St Marys Cathedral Ngwo-Enugu NIGERIA *Tel:* + 234 (0)803 870 9362 *Email:* bishopsieze@yahoo.com

Esan-Province of Bendel The Most Revd Friday J Imaekhai Archbishop of Bendel Province & Bishop of Esan Bishopscourt Ojoelen PO Box 921 Ekpoma Edo State NIGERIA *Tel:* + 234 (0)55 981 079 *Email:* bishopimaekhai@yahoo.com

Etche-Province of Niger Delta The Rt Revd Precious Nwala Bishop of Etche Bishopscourt PO Box 89 Okehi Etche Rivers State NIGERIA

Etsako-Province of Bendel The Rt Revd Jacob Bada Bishop of Etsako Bishopscourt PO Box 11 Jattu Auchi Edo State NIGERIA

Evo-Province of Niger Delta The Rt Revd Innocent Ordu Bishop of Evo Bishopscourt PO Box 3576 Port Harcourt Rivers State NIGERIA *Tel:* + 234 (0)803 715 2706 *Email:* innocent-ordu@yahoo.com

Gboko-Province of Abuja The Rt Revd Emmanuel Nyitsse Bishop of Gboko Awaiting Details

Gombe-Province of Jos The Rt Revd Henry Ndukuba Bishop of Gombe Cathedral Church of St Peter PO Box 39 Gombe NIGERIA *Tel:* + 234 (0)72 221 212 *Fax:* + 234 (0)72 221 141 *Email:* gombe@anglican-nig.org

Gusau-Province of Kaduna The Rt Revd John Garba Bishop of Gusau PO Box 64 Gusau Zamfara State NIGERIA *Tel:* + 234 (0)63 204 747 *Email:* gusau@anglican.skannet.com

Gwagwalada-Province of Abuja The Rt Revd Moses Tabwaye Bishop of Gwagwalada Diocesan Headquarters Secretariat Road PO Box .287 Gwagwalada Abuja NIGERIA *Tel:* + 234 (0)9 882 2083 *Email:* anggwag@skannet.com.ng

Ibadan-Province of Ibadan The Most Revd Joseph Akinfenwa Archbishop of Province of Ibadan & Bishop of Ibadan PO Box 3075 Mapo Ibadan NIGERIA *Tel:* + 234 (0)2 810 1400 *Fax:* + 234 (0)2 810 1413 *Email:* ibadan@anglican.skannet.com.ng

Ibadan North-Province of Ibadan The Rt Revd Segun Okubadejo Bishop of Ibadan North Bishopscourt Moyede PO Box 182 Dugbe Ibadan NIGERIA *Tel:* + 234 (0)2 810 7482 *Email:* angibn@skannet.com

Ibadan South-Province of Ibadan The Rt Revd Jacob Ajetunmobi Bishop of Ibadan South Bishopscourt PO Box 166 St David's Compound Kudeti Ibadan NIGERIA *Tel:* + 234 (0)2 231 9141 *Fax:* + 234 (0)2 231 9141 *Email:* jacajet@skannet.com.ng

Idah-Province of Abuja The Rt Revd Joseph Musa Bishop of Idah Bishopscourt PO Box 25 Idah Kogi State NIGERIA *Email:* idah@anglican-nig.org

Ideato-Province of Owerri The Rt Revd Caleb A Maduoma Bishop of Ideato Bishopscourt PO Box 2 Ndizuogu Imo State NIGERIA*Email:* bpomacal@hotmail.com

Idoani-Province of Ondo The Rt Revd Ezekiel B Dahunsi Bishop of Idoani Bishopscourt PO Box 100 Idoani Ondo State NIGERIA *Tel:* + 234 (0)803 384 4029 *Email:* bolaezek@yahoo.com *Web:* www.dioceseofidoani.org

Ife-Province of Ibadan The Rt Revd Oluwole Odubogun Bishop of Ife Bishopscourt PO Box 312 Ife Osun State NIGERIA *Tel:* + 234 (0)36 230 046 *Email:* rantiodubogun@yahoo.com

Ife East-Province of Ibadan The Rt Revd Oluseyi Oyelade Bishop of Ife East Bishop's House PMB

505 Modakeke-Ife Osun State NIGERIA *Tel:* + 234 (0)802 332 4962 *Email:* seyioyelade@yahoo.com

Ifo-Province of Lagos The Rt Revd Nathaniel Oladejo Ogundipe Bishop of Ifo Bishopscourt Trinity House KM1 Ibogun Road Ifo Ogun State NIGERIA *Tel:* + 234 (0)802 778 4377 *Email:* dioceseofifo@gmail.com

Igbomina-Province of Kwara The Ven Emmanuel Adekola Bishop elect of Igbomina Bishopscourt PO Box 102 Oro Kwara State NIGERIA *Tel:* + 234 (0)803 669 1940

Igbomina-West-Province of Kwara The Rt Revd James O Akinola Bishop of Igbomina West Bishop's House PO Box 32 Oke Osin Kwara State NIGERIA *Tel:* + 234 (0)803 392 3720 *Email:* olaotimuyiwa@yahoo.com *Web:* www.dioceseofigbominawest.org/igbomina/

Ijebu-Province of Lagoa The Rt Revd Ezekiel Awosoga Bishop of Ijebu Bishopscourt Ejirin Road PO Box 112 Ijebu-Ode NIGERIA

Ijeb-North-Province of Lagos The Rt Revd Solomon Kuponu Bishop of Ijebu - North Bishopscourt Oke-Sopen Ijebu-Igbo NIGERIA *Tel:* + 234 (0)803 741 9372 *Web:* www.ijebunorthdiocese.org

Ijesa North East-Province of Ibadan The Rt Revd Joseph A Olusola Bishop of Ijesa North East PO Box 40 Ipetu Ijesa Osun State NIGERIA *Tel:* + 234 (0)803 942 8275 *Email:* bpjafsola@gmail.com *Web:* www.ijesanortheastdiocese.org

Ijesha North-Province of Ibadan The Rt Revd Isaac Oluyamo Bishop of Ijesha North Bishopscourt PO Box 4 Ijebu-Jesa Osun State NIGERIA *Tel:* + 234 (0)802 344 0333

Ijumu-Province of Lokoja The Rt Revd Ezekiel Ikupolati Bishop of Ijumu Bishopscourt PO Box 90 Iyara-Ijumi Kogi State NIGERIA *Tel:* + 234 (0)807 500 8780 *Email:* efikupolati@yahoo.com

Ikara-Province of Kaduna The Rt Revd Yusuf I Janfalan Bishop of Ikara Bishopscourt PO Box 23 Ikara Kaduna State NIGERIA *Tel:* + 234 (0)803 679 3865 *Email:* ikara@anglican-nig.org

Ikeduru-Province of Owerri The Rt Revd Emmanuel C Maduwike Bishop of Ikeduru Bishop's House PO Box 56 Atta Imo State NIGERIA *Tel:* + 234 (0)803 704 4686 *Email:* emmamaduwike@yahoo.com

Ikka-Province of Bendel The Rt Revd Peter Onekpe Bishop of Ikka St John's Cathedral PO Box 5 Agbor Delta State NIGERIA *Tel:* + 234 (0)55 250 14

Ikwerre-Province of Niger Delta The Rt Revd Blessing Enyindah Bishop of Ikwerre Bishopscourt St Peter's Cathedral PO Box 14229 Port Harcourt Rivers State NIGERIA *Tel:* + 234 (0)802 321 2824 *Email:* blessingenyindah@yahoo.com

Ikwo-Province of Enugu The Rt Revd Kenneth C Ifemene Bishop of Ikwo Bishops Residence PO Box 998 Agubia Ikwo Abakaliki Ebonyi State NIGERIA *Tel:* + 234 (0)805 853 4849 *Email:* bishopikwoanglican@yahoo.com

Ikwuano-Province of Aba The Rt Revd Chigozirim Onyegbule Bishop of Ikwuano Bishopscourt St Phillip's Cathedral PO Box 5 Ahaba-Oloko Abia State NIGERIA *Tel:* + 234 (0)803 085 9319 *Email:* ikwuano@anglican-nig.org

Ilaje-Province of Ondo The Rt Revd Fredrick I Olugbemi Bishop of Iiaje Bishopscourt PO Box 147 Igbokoda Ondo State NIGERIA *Tel:* + 234 (0)806 624 8662 *Email:* forogbemi@yahoo.com

Ile-Oluji-Province of Ondo The Rt Revd Samson O Adekunle Bishop of Ile - Oluji Bishopscourt Cathedral of St PEter PO Box 46 Ile-Oluji Ondo State NIGERIA *Tel:* + 234 (0)803 454 1236 *Email:* adekunlesamson86@yahoo.co.uk

Ilesa-Province of Ibadan The Rt Revd Olubayu Sowale Bishop of Ilesa Diocesan Headquarters Muroko Road PO Box 237 Ilesa Osun State NIGERIA *Tel:* + 234 (0)36 460 138 *Email:* ilesha@anglican-nig.org

Ilesa South West-Province of Ibadan The Rt Revd Samuel Egbebunmi Bishop of Ilesa South West Bishopscourt Cathedral of the Holy Trinity Imo Ilesa Osun State NIGERIA *Tel:* + 234 (0)803 307 1876 *Email:* segbebunmi@yahoo.com

Irele-Eseodo-Province of Ondo The Rt Revd Felix O Akinbuluma Bishop of Irele - Eseodo Bishopscourt Sabomi Road Ode Irele Ondo State NIGERIA *Tel:* + 234 (0)805 671 2653 *Email:* felixgoke@yahoo.com

Isiala-Ngwa-Province of Aba The Rt Revd Owen N N Azubuike Bishop of Isiala-Ngwa Bishopscourt St Georges Cathedral Compound PNB 2033 Mbawsi Abia State NIGERIA *Tel:* + 234 (0)805 467 0528 *Email:* bpowenazubuike@yahoo.com

Isial-Ngwa South-Province of Aba The Rt Revd Isaac Nwaobia Bishop of Isiala-Ngwa South St Peter's Cathedral Compound PO Box 15 Owerrinta Abia State NIGERIA *Tel:* + 234 (0)803 711 9317 *Email:* isialangwasouth@anglican-nig.org

Isikwuato-Province of Aba The Rt Revd Manasses Chijiokem Okere Bishop of Isikwuato Bishopscourt PO Box 350 Ovim Abia State NIGERIA *Tel:* + 234 (0)803 386 221 *Email:* isiukwuato@anglican-nig.org

Jalingo-Province of Jos The Rt Revd Timothy Yahaya Bishop of Jalingo PO Box 4 Magami Jalingo Tabara State NIGERIA *Tel:* + 234 806 594 4694 *Email:* timothyyahaya@yahoo.com

Jebba-Province of Kwara The Rt Revd Timothy S Adewole Bishop of Jebba Bishopscourt PO Box 2 Jebba Kwara State NIGERIA *Tel:* + 234 (0)803 572 5298 *Email:* bishopadewole@yahoo.com

Jos-Province of Jos The Most Revd Benjamin A Kwashi Archbishop of the Province of Jos & Bishop of Jos Bishopscourt PO Box 6283 Jos Plateau State NIGERIA *Email:* benkwashi@gmail.com

Kabba-Province of Lokoja The Rt Revd Steven K Akobe Bishop of Kabba Bishopscourt Obara Way PO Box 62 Kabba Kogi State NIGERIA *Tel:* + 234 (0)58 300 633 *Fax:* + 234 (0)803 471 4759

Kaduna-Province of Kaduna Vacant Bishop elect of Kaduna PO Box 72 Kaduna NIGERIA *Tel:* + 234 (0)62 240 085 *Fax:* + 234 (0)62 244 408

Kafanchan-Province of Abuja The Rt Revd Marcus Dogo Bishop of Kafanchan Bishopscourt PO Box 29 Kafanchan Kaduna State NIGERIA *Tel:* + 234 (0)61 20 634 *Web:* www.anglicankafanchan.blogspot.co.uk

Kano-Province of Kaduna The Rt Revd Zakka L Nyam Bishop of Kano Bishopscourt PO Box 362 Kano Kano State NIGERIA *Tel:* + 234 (0)64 647 816 *Fax:* + 234 (0)64 647 816 *Email:* kano@anglican. skannet.com.ng

Katsina-Province of Kaduna The Rt Revd Jonathan S Bamaiyi Bishop of Katsina Bishop's Lodge PO Box 904 Katsina Katsina State NIGERIA

Kebbi-Province of Kaduna The Most Revd Edmund E Akanya Archbishop of the Province of Kaduna & Bishop of Kebbi Bishops Residence PO Box 701 Birnin Kebbi Kebbi State NIGERIA *Tel:* + 234 (0)68 321 179 *Fax:* + 234 (0)803 586 1060 *Email:* eekanya@ yahoo.com

Kontagora-Province of Lokoja The Rt Revd Jonah Ibrahim Bishop of Kontagora Bishop's House GPA PO Box 1 Kontagora Niger State NIGERIA *Tel:* + 234 (0)803 625 2032 *Email:* jonahibrahim@yahoo.co.uk

Kubwa-Province of Abuja The Rt Revd Duke Akamisoko Bishop of Kubwa Bishop's House PO Box 67 Kubwa Abuja FCT NIGERIA *Tel:* + 234 (0)803 451 9437 *Email:* dukesoko@yahoo.com

Kutigi-Province of Lokoja The Rt Revd Jeremiah N N Kolo Bishop of Kutigi Bishop's House St John's Mission Compound PO Box 14 Bida NIGERIA *Tel:* + 234 (0)803 625 2032 *Email:* bishopkolo@yahoo.com

Kwara-Province of Kwara The Most Revd Olusegun S Adeyemi Archbishop of Province of Kwara & Bishop of Kwara Bishopscourt Fate Road PO Box 1884 Ilorin Kwara State NIGERIA *Tel:* + 234 (0)31 220 879 *Fax:* + 234 (0)803 325 8068 *Email:* bishopolusegun@yahoo.com

Kwoi-Province of Abuja The Rt Revd Paul S Zamani Bishop of Kwoi Bishop's Residence Cathedral Compound Samban Gida PO Box 173 Kwoi Kaduna State NIGERIA *Tel:* + 234 (0)80 651 8160 *Email:* paulzamani@yahoo.com

Lafia-Province of Abuja The Rt Revd Miller K Maza Bishop of the Missionary Diocese of Lafia PO Box 560 Lafia Nasarawa State NIGERIA *Tel:* + 234 (0)803 973 5973 *Email:* anglicandioceseoflafia@yahoo.com

Lagos-Province of Lagos The Most Revd Ephraim Ademowo Archbishop of the Province of Lagos & Bishop of Lagos 29 Marina PO Box 13 Lagos NIGERIA *Tel:* + 234 (0)1 263 6026 *Fax:* + 234 (0)803 403 1358 *Email:* adebolaademowo@dioceseoflagos.org

Lagos Mainland-Province of Lagos The Rt Revd Adebayo Akinde Bishop of Lagos Mainland Bishops House PO Box 849 Ebute Lagos State NIGERIA *Tel:* + 234 (0)703 390 5522 *Email:* adakinde@gmail.com *Web:* www.lagosmainlanddiocese.org

Lagos West-Province of Lagos The Rt Revd James Odedeji Bishop of Lagos West Vining House 3rd Floor Archbishop Vining Memorial Cathedral Oba Akinjobi Road GRA Ikeja NIGERIA *Tel:* + 234 (0)1 493 7333 *Fax:* + 234 (0)1 493 7337 *Email:* dioceseoflagoswest@yahoo.com

Langtang-Province of Jos The Rt Revd Stanley D Fube Bishop of Langtang No 87 Solomon Lar Road PO Box 38 Langtang Plateau State NIGERIA *Tel:* + 234 (0)803 605 8767 *Email:* stanleyfube@gmail.com

Lokoja-Province of Lokoja The Most Revd Emmanuel Sokowamju Egbunu Archbishop of the Province of Lokoja & Bishop of Lokoja Bishopscourt PO Box 11 bethany Lokoja Koji State NIGERIA *Tel:* + 234 (0)58 220 588 *Fax:* + 234 (0)803 592 5698 *Email:* emmanuelegbunu@yahoo.co.uk *Web:* www. anglican-lokojadiocese.org

Maiduguri-Province of Jos The Ven Emmanuel Morris Bishop elect of Maiduguri Bishopscourt PO Box 1693 Maiduguri Borno State NIGERIA *Tel:* + 234 (0)76 234 010 *Email:* bishope-45@yahoo.com

Makurdi-Province of Abuja The Rt Revd Nathan Nyitar Inyom Bishop of Makurdi Bishopscourt PO Box 1 Makurdi Benue State NIGERIA *Tel:* + 234 (0)44 533 349 *Fax:* + 234 (0)803 614 5319 *Email:* makurdi@anglican.skannet.com.ng

Mbaise-Province of Owerri The Rt Revd Chamberlain Chinedu Ogunedo Bishop of Mbaise Bishopscourt PO Box 10 Ife Imo State NIGERIA *Tel:* + 234 (0)803 336 9836 *Email:* ogunedochi@yahoo. com

Mbamili-Province of Niger The Rt Revd Henry S Okeke Bishop of Mbamili Bishopscourt PO Box 2653 Onitsha Anambra State NIGERIA *Tel:* + 234 (0)803 644 9780 *Email:* bishopokeke@yahoo.com

Minna-Province of Lokoja The Rt Revd Daniel Abu Yisa Bishop of Minna Bishopscourt Dutsen Kura PO Box 2469 Minna NIGERIA *Tel:* + 234 (0)803 588 6552 *Email:* danyisa2007@yahoo.com

Ndokwa-Province of Bendel The Rt Revd David Obiosa Bishop of Ndokwa Bishopscourt 151 Old Sapele Road Obiaruka Delta State NIGERIA *Tel:* + 234 (0)803 776 9464 *Email:* dfao1963@yahoo.com

New Busa-Province of Kwara The Rt Revd Israel Amoo Bishop of New Busa Bishoscourt PO Box 208 New Busa Niger State NIGERIA *Tel:* + 234 (0)803 677 3839 *Email:* bishopamoo@yahoo.com

Ngbo-Province of Enugu The Rt Revd Christian Ebisike Bishop of Ngbo Bishop's House PO Box 93 Abakaliki Ebonyi State NIGERIA *Tel:* + 234 (0)806 979 4899 *Email:* vendchris@yahoo.com

Niger Delta North-Province of Niger Delta The Most Revd Ignatius C/O Kattey Archbishop of Niger Delta Province & Bishop of Niger Delta North PO Box 53 Diobu Port Harcourt Rivers State NIGERIA *Tel:* + 234 (0)803 309 4331 *Email:* bishopicokattey@yahoo.com

Niger Delta West-Province of Niger Delta The Rt Revd Emmanuel Oko-Jaja Bishop of Niger Delta West PO Box 10 Yenagoa Bayelsa NIGERIA *Tel:* + 234 (0)803 870 2099 *Email:* nigerdelta-west@anglican-nig.org

Niger Delta, The-Province of the Niger Delta The Rt Revd Ralph Ebirien Bishop of the Niger Delta Bishopscourt PO Box 115 Port Harcourt Rivers State NIGERIA *Tel:* + 234 (0)708 427 9095 *Email:* revpalph_ebirien@yahoo.com

Niger West-Province of Niger The Rt Revd Johnson Ekwe Bishop of Niger West Bishop's House Anambra Anambra State NIGERIA *Tel:* + 234 (0)803 384 3339

Nike-Province of Enugu The Rt Revd Evans Jonathan Ibeagha Bishop of Nike Bishopscourt Trans-Ekulu PO Box 2416 Enugu Enugu State NIGERIA *Tel:* + 234 (0)803 324 1387 *Email:* pnibeagha@yahoo.com

Nnewi-Province of Niger The Rt Revd Godwin Izundu Nmezinwa Okpala Bishop of Nnewi Bishopscourt (opp Total filling station) PO Box 2630 Uruagu-Nnewi Anambra State NIGERIA *Tel:* + 234 (0)803 348 5714 *Fax:* + 234 (0)46 462 676 *Email:* okpalagodwin@yahoo.co.uk

Northern Izon-Province of Niger Delta The Rt Revd Fred Nyanabo Bishop of Northern Izon Bishopscourt PO Box 705 Yenagoa Bayelsa State NIGERIA *Tel:* + 234 (0)803 316 0938 *Email:* fred_nyanabo@yahoo.co.uk

Nsukka-Province of Enugu The Rt Revd Aloysius Agbo Bishop of Nsukka Bishopscourt St Cyprian's Compound PO Box 516 Nsukka Enugu State NIGERIA *Tel:* + 234 (0)803 932 7840 *Email:* nsukka@anglican-nig.org

Offa-Province of Kwara The Rt Revd Akintunde Popoola Bishop of Offa Bishop's House 78-80 Ibrahim Road PO Box 21 Offa Kwara State NIGERIA *Tel:* + 234 (0)805 925 0011 *Email:* tpopoola@anglican-nig.org

Ogbaru-Province of Niger The Rt Revd Samuel Ezeofor Bishop of Ogbaru Bishopscourt PO Box 46 Atani Anambra State NIGERIA *Web:* www.ogbaruanglicandiocese.org

Ogbia-Province of Niger Delta The Rt Revd James Oruwori Bishop of Ogbia Bishop's House No 10 Queens Street Ogbia Town Bayelsa State NIGERIA *Tel:* + 234 (0)803 73 4746 *Email:* jaoruwori@yahoo.com

Ogbomoso-Province of Ibadan The Rt Revd Matthew Osunade Bishop of Ogbomoso Bishopscourt St David's Anglican Cathedral PO Box 1909 Ogbomoso Osun State NIGERIA *Tel:* + 234 (0)805 593 6164 *Email:* maaosunade@yahoo.com

Ogoni-Province of Niger Delta The Rt Revd Solomon Gberegbara Bishop of Ogoni Bishopscourt PO Box 73 Bori Rivers State NIGERIA *Tel:* + 234 (0)803 339 2545 *Email:* ogoni@anglican-nig.org

Ogori-Magongo-Province of Lokoja The Rt Revd Festus Davies Bishop of Ogori-Magongo Bishop's House St Peter's Cathedral Ogori Kogi State NIGERIA *Tel:* + 234 (0)803 451 0378 *Email:* fessyoladiran@yahoo.com

Ohaji/Egbema-Province of Owerri The Rt Revd Chidi Collins Oparaojiaku Bishop of Ohaji/Egbema Bishop's House PO Box 8026 New Owerri Imo State NIGERIA *Tel:* + 234 (0)803 312 1063 *Email:* chidioparachiaku@yahoo.com

Oji River-Province of Enugu The Most Revd Amos Amankechinelo Madu Archbishop of the Province of Enugu & Bishop of Oji River St Paul's Cathedral Church PO Box 123 Oji River Enuga NIGERIA *Tel:* + 234 (0)803 670 4888 *Email:* amosmadu@yahoo.com

Okene-Province of Lokoja The Ven Emmanuel Onsachi Bishop elect of Okene Bishopscourt PO Box 43 Okene Kogi State NIGERIA *Tel:* + 234 (0)803 700 0016 *Email:* okenediocese@yahoo.com

Oke-Ogun-Province of Ibadan The Rt Revd Solomon Amusan Bishop of Oke-Ogun Bishopscourt PO Box 30 Saki Oyo State NIGERIA *Tel:* + 234 (0)802 323 3365 *Email:* solomonamusan@yahoo.com

Oke-Osun-Province of Ibadan The Rt Revd Abraham Akinlalu Bishop of Oke-Osun Bishopscourt PO Box 251 Gbongan Osun State NIGERIA *Tel:* + 234 (0)803 771 7194 *Email:* abrahamakinlalu@yahoo.com *Web:* www.okeosunanglicandiocese.org

Okigwe-Province of Owerri The Rt Revd Edward Osuegbu Bishop of Okigwe Bishopscourt PO Box 156 Okigwe Imo State NIGERIA *Tel:* + 234 (0)803 724 6374 *Email:* edchuc@justice.com

Okigwe North-Province of Owerri The Rt Revd Godson Udochukwu Ukanwa Bishop of Okigwe North Bishopscourt PO Box 127 Anara Imo State NIGERIA *Tel:* + 234 (0)803 672 4314 *Email:* venukanwa@yahoo.com

Okigwe South-Province of Owerri The Rt Revd David Onuoha Bishop of Okigwe South Bishopscourt PO Box 235 Nsu Imo State NIGERIA *Email:* okisouth@yahoo.com

Okrika-Province of Niger Delta The Rt Revd Tubokosemie Atere Bishop of Okrika Bishopscourt PO Box 11 Okrika Rivers State NIGERIA *Tel:* + 234 (0)803 312 5226 *Email:* dioceseofokrika@yahoo.com

Oleh-Province of Bendel The Rt Revd John Usiwoma Aruakpor Bishop of Oleh Bishopscourt PO Box 8 Oleh Delta State NIGERIA *Tel:* + 234 (0)53 701 062 *Fax:* + 234 (0)802 307 4008 *Email:* angoleh2000@yahoo.com

Omu-Aran-Province of Kwara The Rt Revd Philip Adeyemo Bishop of Omu-Aran Bishop's House PO Box 224 Omu-Aran Kwara State NIGERIA *Tel:* + 234 (0)806 592 4891 *Email:* rtrevadeyemo@yahoo.com

On the Lake-Province of Owerri The Rt Revd Chijioke Oti Bishop of on the Lake Bishopscourt PO Box 36 Oguta Imo State NIGERIA *Tel:* + 234 (0)802 788 8738 *Email:* chijiokeoti72@yahoo.com

On the Niger-Province of Niger The Rt Revd Owen Chidozie Nwokolo Bishop of On the Niger Bishopscourt Ozala Road Onitsha Anambra State NIGERIA *Tel:* + 234 (0)803 726 0548 *Email:* owenelsie@yahoo.com

Ondo-Province of Ondo The Rt Revd George Lasebikan Bishop of Ondo Bishopscourt PO Box 265 Ife Road Ondo Ondo State NIGERIA *Tel:* + 234 (0)34 610 718 *Fax:* + 234 (0)803 472 1813 *Email:* ondoanglican@yahoo.co.uk

Ondo-Province of Ondo The Rt Revd Christopher Tayo Omotunde Suffragan Bishop of Ondo Bishopscourt PO Box 265 Ife Road Ondo Ondo State NIGERIA *Tel:* + 234 (0)802 919 1866 *Email:* chrisomotunde@yahoo.com

Orlu-Province of Owerri The Most Revd Bennett C I Okoro Archbishop of Province of Owerri & Bishop of Orlu Bishopscourt PO Box 260 Nkwerre Imo State NIGERIA *Tel:* + 234 (0)82 440 538 *Fax:* + 234 (0)803 671 1271 *Email:* anglicannaorlu@yahoo.com

Oru-Province of Owerri The Rt Revd Geoffrey Chukwunenye Bishop of Oru PO Box 191 Mgbidi Imo State NIGERIA *Tel:* + 234 (0)803 308 1270 *Email:* geoinlagos@yahoo.com

Osun-Province of Ibadan The Rt Revd James Afolabi Popoola Bishop of Osun Bishopscourt PO Box 285 Osogbo Osun State NIGERIA *Tel:* + 234 (0)35 240 325 *Fax:* + 234 (0)803 356 1628 *Email:* folapool@yahoo.com

Osun North East-Province of Ibadan The Rt Revd Humphery Olumakaiye Bishop of Osun North East Bishopscourt PO Box 32 Otan Ayegbaju Osun State NIGERIA *Tel:* + 234 (0)803 388 2678

Email: bamisebi2002@yahoo.co.uk *Web:* www.osunnortheastdiocese.org

Otukpo-Province of Abuja The Rt Revd David Bello Bishop of Otukpo Bishopscourt PO Box 360 Otukpo Benue State NIGERIA *Tel:* + 234 (0)803 309 1778 *Email:* bishopdkbello@yahoo.com

Owerri-Imo State The Rt Revd Cyril Chukwunonyerem Okorocha Bishop of Owerri Bishop's Bourne PMB 1063 Owerri NIGERIA *Tel:* + 234 (0)83 230 784 *Fax:* + 234 (0)803 338 9344 *Email:* owerri_anglican@yahoo.com

Owo-Province of Ondo The Rt Revd Stephen Ayodeji Fagbemi Bishop of Owo Bishopscourt PO Box 472 Owo Ondo State NIGERIA *Tel:* + 234 (0)51 241 463 *Fax:* + 234 (0)803 475 4291

Oyo-Province of Ibadan The Rt Revd Williams Oluwarotimi Aladekugbe Bishop of Oyo PO Box 23 Oyo Oyo State NIGERIA *Tel:* + 234 (0)38 240 225 *Fax:* + 234 (0)803 857 2120 *Email:* oyo@anglican-nig.org

Pankshin-Province of Jos The Rt Revd Olumuyiwa Ajayi Bishop of Pankshin Diocesan Secretariat PO Box 196 Pankshin Plateau State NIGERIA *Tel:* + 234 (0)803 344 7318 *Email:* olumijayi@yahoo.com

Remo-Province of Lagos The Rt Revd Michael Fape Bishop of Remo Bishopscourt PO Box 522 Sagama Ogun State NIGERIA *Tel:* + 234 (0)37 640 598 *Fax:* + 234 (0)803 726 7949 *Email:* remo@anglican-nig.org

Sabongidda-Ora-Province of Bendel Vacant Bishop elect of Sabongidda-Ora Bishopscourt PO Box 13 Sabongidda-Ora - Edo State NIGERIA *Tel:* + 234 (0)57 54 132

Sapele-Province of Bendel The Rt Revd Blessing A Erifeta Bishop of Sapele Bishopscourt PO Box 52 Sapele Delta State NIGERIA *Tel:* + 234 (0)803 662 4282 *Email:* dioceseofsapele@yahoo.com

Sokoto-Province of Kaduna The Rt Revd Augustin Omole Bishop of Sokoto Bishop's Lodge 68 Shuni Road PO Box 3489 Sokoto Sokoto State NIGERIA *Tel:* + 234 (0)60 234 639 *Fax:* + 234 (0)803 542 3765 *Email:* akin_sok@yahoo.com *Web:* www.dosac.org

Udi-Province of Enugu The Rt Revd Chjioke Augustine Aneke Bishop of Udi Bishopscourt PO Box 30 Udi Enugu State NIGERIA *Tel:* + 234 (0)806 908 9690 *Email:* bpchijiokeudi@yahoo.com

Ughelli-Province of Bendel The Rt Revd Cyril Odutemu Bishop of Ughelli Bishopscourt PO Box 760 Ughelli Delta State NIGERIA *Tel:* + 234 (0)53 600 403 *Fax:* + 234 (0)803 530 7114 *Email:* ughellianglican@yahoo.com

Ukwa-Province of Aba The Rt Revd Samuel Kelechi Eze Bishop of Ukwa PO Box 20468 Aba Abia State NIGERIA *Tel:* + 234 (0)803 789 2431 *Email:* kelerem53878@yahoo.com

Umuahia-Province of Aba The Most Revd Ikechi Nwachukwu Nwosu Archbishop of Province of Aba & Bishop of Umuahia St Stephen's Cathedral Church Compound PO Box 96 Umuahia Abia State NIGERIA *Tel:* + 234 (0)88 221 037 *Fax:* + 234 (0)803 549 9066

Uyo-Province of Niger Delta The Rt Revd Prince Asukwo Antai Bishop of Uyo Bishopscourt PO Box 70 Uyo Akwa Ibom State NIGERIA *Tel:* + 234 (0)802 916 2305 *Email:* uyo@anglican-nig.com

Warri-Province of Bendel The Rt Revd Christian Esezi Ideh Bishop of Warri Bishopscourt 17 Mabiaku Road PO Box 4571 Warri Delta State NIGERIA *Tel:* + 234 (0)53 255 857 *Fax:* + 234 (0)805 102 2680 *Email:* angdioceseofwarri@yahoo.com

Western Izon-Province of Bendel The Rt Revd Edafe B Emamezi Bishop of Western Izon Bishopscourt PO Box 5 Patani Delta State NIGERIA *Tel:* + 234 (0)822 05 6228 *Email:* anglizon@yahoo.co.uk

Wusasa-Province of Kaduna The Rt Revd Ali Buba Lamido Bishop of Wusasa PO Box 28 Wusasa Zaria Kaduna State NIGERIA *Tel:* + 234 (0)69 334 594 *Fax:* + 234 (0)803 727 2504 *Email:* lamido2sl@aol.co.uk

Yewa (form. Egbado)-Province of Lagos The Rt Revd Michael Adebayo Oluwarohunbi Bishop of Yewa Bishopscourt PO Box 484 Ilaro Ogun State NIGERIA *Tel:* + 234 (0)39 440 695

Yola-Province of Jos The Rt Revd Markus A Ibrahm Bishop of Yola PO Box 601 Yola Adamawa State Adamawa State NIGERIA *Tel:* + 234 (0)75 624 303 *Fax:* + 234 (0)803 045 7576 *Email:* marcusibrahim2002@yahoo.com

Zaki-Biam-Province of Abuja The Rt Revd Benjamin A Vager Bishop of Zaki-Biam Bishopscourt PO Box 600 Yam Market Road Zaki-biam Benue State NIGERIA *Tel:* + 234 (0)803 676 0018 *Email:* rubavia@yahoo.com

Zaria-Province of Kaduna The Rt Revd Cornelius Salifu Bello Bishop of Zaria Bishopscourt PO Box 507 Zaria Kaduna State NIGERIA *Tel:* + 234 (0)802 708 9555 *Email:* cssbello@hotmail.com

Zonkwa-Province of Abuja The Rt Revd Jacob W Kwashi Bishop of Zonkwa Bishop's Residence PO Box 26 Zonkwa 802002 Kaduna State NIGERIA *Tel:* + 234 (0)803 331 0252 *Email:* zonkwa@anglican-nig.org

THE CHURCH OF NORTH INDIA

Provincial Secretary Mr Alwan Masih CNI Synod Post Box 311 16 Pandit Pant Marg New Delhi 110 001 INDIA *Tel:* + 91 11 2373 1079 *Fax:* + 91 11 2371 6901 *Email:* alwanmasih@cnisynod.org *Web:* www. cnisynod.org

Provincial Treasurer Mr Prem Masih CNI Synod Post Box 311 16 Pandit Pant Marg New Delhi 110 001 INDIA *Tel:* + 91 11 4321 4000 *Fax:* + 91 11 4321 4006 *Email:* ucnita1@gmail.com

Agra The Rt Revd Prem Prakash Habil Bishop of Agra Bishop's House 4/116-B Church Road Civil Lines Agra Uttarr Pradesh 282 002 INDIA *Tel:* + 91 (0)562 285 4845 *Fax:* + 91 (0)562 252 0074 *Email:* doacni@gmail.com

Amritsar The Rt Revd Pradeep K Samantaroy Bishop of Amritsar 26 R B Prakash Chand Road Opp Police Ground Amritsar Punjab 143 001 INDIA *Tel:* + 91 (0)183 256 2010 *Fax:* + 91 (0)183 222 2910 *Email:* bishoppradeep@gmail.com *Web:* www. amritsardiocese.org/

Andaman & Car Nicobar Islands The Rt Revd Christopher Paul Bishop of Andaman & Car Nicobar Islands Cathedral Church Compound Car Nicobar MUS 744 301 ANDAMAN & NICOBAR ISLANDS *Tel:* + 91 (0)319 223 1362 *Fax:* + 91 (0)319 223 1362 *Email:* cniportblair@yahoo.co.in

Barrackpore The Rt Revd Brojen Malakar Bishop of Barrackpore Bishop's Lodge 86 Middle Road Barrackpore Kolkata West Bengal 700 120 INDIA *Tel:* + 91 (0)332 593 1852 *Fax:* + 91 (0)332 593 1852 *Email:* malakar.brojen@rediffmail.com *Web:* www. barrackporediocesecni.org

Bhopal The Rt Revd Robert Ali Bishop of Bhopal Bishop's House 57 Residency Area Behind Narmada Water Tank Indore Madhya Pradesh 452 001 INDIA *Tel:* + 91 (0)731 271 0551 *Fax:* + 91 (0)731 405 5452 *Email:* bhopal_diocese@yahoo.com

Calcutta The Rt Revd Ashok Biswas Bishop of Kolkatta Bishop's House 51 Chowringhee Road Kolkatta West Bengal 700 071 INDIA *Tel:* + 91 (0)336 534 7770 *Fax:* + 91 (0)332 282 6340 *Email:* ashoke.biswas@vsnl.net

Chandigarh The Rt Revd Younas Massey Bishop of Chandigarh Bishop's House CNI Mission Compound Brown Road Ludhiana Punjab 141 008 INDIA *Tel:* + 91 (0)161 222 5706 *Fax:* + 91 (0)161 222 5706 *Email:* massey.younas@yahoo.in

Chhattisgarh The Rt Revd Purna Sagar Nag Bishop of Chhattisgarh Opp. Rajbhavan Gate No 1 Civil Lines Raipur Chhattisgarh 492 001 INDIA *Tel:* + 91 (0)771 221 0015 *Email:* doccni@reiffmail.com

Chotanagpur The Rt Revd B Baskey Bishop of Chotanagpur Bishop's Lodge PO Box 1 Old Hazari Bagh Road Ranchi Jharkhand 834 001 INDIA *Tel:* + 91 651 235 1181 *Fax:* + 91 651 235 1184 *Email:* rch_cndta@sancharnet.in

Cuttack The Rt Revd Surendra Kumar Nanda Bishop of Cuttack Bishop's House Mission Road Cuttack Orissa 753 001 INDIA *Tel:* + 91 6712300102 *Email:* doccni@gmail.com

Delhi Vacant Bishop elect of Delhi 1 Church Lane Off North Avenue New Delhi Delhi 110 001 INDIA *Tel:* + 91 (0)112 371 7471 *Fax:* + 91 (0)112 335 8006

Durgapur The Rt Revd Probal K Dutta Deputy Moderator of CNI & Bishop of Durgapur St Michael's Church Compound Alderin Path Bidhan Nagar Durgapur West Bengal 713 212 INDIA *Tel:* + 91 (0)343 253 4552 *Email:* probaldutta@ymail.com

Eastern Himalayas Vacant Bishop elect of Eastern Himalayas Bishop's House 1B K Gongba Road Darjeeling West Bengal 734 001 INDIA *Tel:* + 91 (0)354 225 8183 *Email:* easternhimalaya2004@yahoo.co.in

Gujarat The Rt Revd Silvans S Christian Bishop of Gujarat Bishop's House I.P Mission Compound Ellis Bridge Ahmedabad Gujarat State380 006 INDIA *Tel:* + 91 (0)792 656 1950 *Fax:* + 91 (0)792 656 1950 *Email:* gujdio@yahoo.co.in

Jabalpur The Most Revd Dr Prem Chand P C Singh Moderator of CNI & Bishop of Jabalpur Bishop's House 2131 Napier Town Jabalpur Madhya Pradesh 482 001 INDIA *Tel:* + 91 (0)761 262 2109 *Fax:* + 91 (0)761 262 2109 *Email:* bishoppcsingh@yahoo.co.in

Kolhapur The Rt Revd Bathuel R Tiwade Bishop of Kolhapur Bishop's House EP School Compound Nagala Park Kolhapur Maharashatra 416 003 INDIA *Tel:* + 91 (0)231 265 4832 *Fax:* + 91 (0)231 265 4832 *Email:* kdcdbss@yahoo.com

Lucknow The Rt Revd Peter Baldev Bishop of Lucknow Bishop's House 25/11 Mahatma Gandhi Marg Allahabad Uttar Pradesh 211 001 INDIA *Tel:* + 91 (0)532 242 7053

Marathwada The Rt Revd Madhukar Kasab Bishop of Marathwada Bungalow 28/A Mission Compound Cantt Aurangabad Maharashtra 431 002 INDIA *Tel:* + 91 (0)240 237 3136 *Email:* revmukasab@yahoo.co.in

Mumbai (Form. Bombay) The Rt Revd Prakash D Patole Bishop of Mumbai Bishop's House 19 Hazarimal Somani Marg Mumbai Maharashtra 400 001 INDIA *Tel:* + 91 (0)222 206 0248 *Fax:* + 91 222 206 0248 *Email:* cnibombaydiocese@yahoo.com

Nagpur The Rt Revd Paul B K Dupare Bishop of Nagpur Bishop's House Cathedral House, Opp Indian Coffee House Sadar Nagpur Maharashtra 440 001 INDIA *Tel:* + 91 (0)712 255 3351 *Fax:* + 91 (0)712 255 3351 *Email:* nagpurdiocese@rediffmail.com

Nasik The Rt Revd Pradip Kamble Bishop of Nasik Bishop's House 1 Outram Road Tarakpur Ahmednagar Maharashtra 414 003 INDIA *Tel:* + 91 (0)241 241 1806 *Fax:* + 91 (0)241 242 2314 *Email:* bishopofnasik@rediffmail.com

North East India The Rt Revd Michael Herenz Bishop of North East India Bishop's Kuti Shillong Meghalaya 1 793 001 INDIA *Tel:* + 91 (0)364 222 4155 *Fax:* + 91 (0)364 250 1178

Patna The Rt Revd Philip P Marandih Bishop of Patna Bishop's House Christ Church Compound

Bhagalpur Bihar 812 001 INDIA *Tel:* + 91 (0)641 240 0033 *Email:* cnipatna@rediffmail.com

Phulbani The Rt Revd Bijay K Nayak Bishop of Phulbani Bishop's House, Mission Compound Gudripori G. Udayagiri Phulbani Kandhmal 762 100 INDIA *Tel:* + 91 (0)684 726 0569 *Email:* bpnayakbijaykumar@gmail.com *Web:* www.cniphulbanidiocese.org

Pune The Rt Revd Andrew B K Rathod Bishop of Pune 1A Stavley Road General Bhagat Marg Pune Maharashtra 411 001 INDIA *Tel:* + 91 (0)202 633 4374 *Email:* punediocese@yahoo.co.in

Rajasthan The Rt Revd Darbara Singh Bishop of Rajasthan 2/10 Civil Lines Opp. Bus Stand Jaipur Road Ajmer Rajasthan 305 001 INDIA *Tel:* + 91 (0)145 242 0633 *Fax:* + 91 (0)145 262 1627

Sambalpur The Rt Revd Pinuel Dip Bishop of Sambalpur Bishop's House Mission Compound Bolangir Orissa 767 001 INDIA *Tel:* + 91 (0)665 223 0625 *Email:* pinuel_dip@rediffmail.com

THE CHURCH OF PAKISTAN (UNITED)

General Secretary Mr Anthony Lamuel Bishopsbourne Cathedral Close The Mall Lahore 54000 PAKISTAN

Provincial Treasurer Mr Irshad Nawab 113 Quasim Road PO Box 204 Multan Cantt PAKISTAN *Email:* treasurersynod.cop@gmail.com

Faisalabad The Rt Revd John Samuel Bishop of Faisalabad and Deputy Moderator of the Church of Pakistan Bishop's House PO Box 27 Mission road Gojra Dist Toba Tek Sing PAKISTAN *Tel:* + 92 (0)46 351 4689 *Email:* jsamuel51@hotmail.com

Hyderabad The Rt Revd Kaleem John Bishop of Hyderabad 27 - Liaqat Road Civil Lines Hyderabad 71000 PAKISTAN *Email:* kaleemjohn@aol.com

Karachi The Rt Revd Sadiq Daniel Bishop of Karachi Trinity Close Abdullah Haroon Road Karachi 4 PAKISTAN *Tel:* + 92 021 356556913 *Email:* sadiqdaniel@hotmail.com

Lahore The Rt Revd Irfan Jamil Bishop of Lahore Bishopsbourne Cathedral Close The Mall Lahore 54000 PAKISTAN *Tel:* + 92 (0)42 3723 3560 *Fax:* + 92 (0)42 3712 0766 *Email:* 9thbishopoflahore@gmail.com *Web:* www.dol.com.pk

Multan The Rt Revd Leo Roderick Paul Bishop of Multan 113 Quasim Road PO Box 204 Multan Cantt PAKISTAN *Tel:* + 92 (0)61 458 3694 *Email:* bishop_mdcop@live.com

Peshawar The Most Revd Humphrey S Peters Bishop of Peshawar & Moderator of the Church of Pakistan St Johns Cathedral 1 Sir Syed Road Peshawar 25000 PAKISTAN *Tel:* + 92 (0)91 527 6519 *Email:* bishopdop@hotmail.com

Raiwind The Rt Revd Azad Marshall Bishop of Raiwind 17 Warris Road Lahore 54000 PAKISTAN *Tel:* + 92 (0)42 3758 8950 *Email:* bishop@saintthomascenter.org

Sialkot The Rt Revd Alwin John Samuel Bishop of Sialkot Lal Kothi Bara Pathar Christian Town Sialkot 2 PAKISTAN *Tel:* + 92 052 4264828 *Email:* alwinsialkot@gmail.com

THE ANGLICAN CHURCH OF PAPUA NEW GUINEA

The Most Revd Allan Migi Archbishop of Papua New Guinea PO Box 673 Lae 411 Morobe Province PAPUA NEW GUINEA *Tel:* +*Email:* archbishopmigi95@gmail.com

Provincial Secretary Mr Dennis Kabekabe PO Box 673 Lae 411 Morobe Province PAPUA NEW GUINEA *Tel:* + 675 4724262 *Email:* dpk07jan@gmail.com

Aipo Rongo The Rt Revd Nathan Ingen Bishop of Aipo Rongo PO Box 893 Mount Hagen Western Highlands Province PAPUA NEW GUINEA *Tel:* + 675 54 211 31 *Fax:* + 675 54 211 81 *Email:* bishopnathan2@gmail.com

Dogura The Rt Revd Tennyson Bogar Bishop of Dogura PO Box 19 Dogura MBP PAPUA NEW GUINEA *Tel:* + 675 641 1530

New Guinea Islands, The Vacant Bishop elect of The New Guinea Islands Bishop's House PO Box 806 Kimbe NGIP PAPUA NEW GUINEA *Tel:* + 675 9 835 120 *Fax:* + 675 9 835 120

Popondota The Rt Revd Lindsley Ihove Bishop of Popondota Diocese of Popondota PO Box 26 Popondetta Oro Province PAPUA NEW GUINEA *Tel:* + 675 329 7194 *Fax:* + 675 329 7476 *Email:* bplndsleyihove@gmail.com

Port Moresby The Rt Revd Denny Bray Guka Bishop of Port Morsby PO Box 6491 Boroko NCD PAPUA NEW GUINEA*Email:* dennyguka@gmail.com

THE EPISCOPAL CHURCH IN THE PHILIPPINES

Provincial Secretary Mr Floyd Lalwet PO Box 10321 Broadway Centrum Quezon City 1112 PHILIPPINES *Fax:* + 63 (0)2 721 1923 *Email:* flaw997@gmail.com

Provincial Treasurer Mrs Bridget Lacdao Provincial Office PO Box 10321 Broadway Centrum 1112 Quezon City PHILIPPINES *Tel:* + 63 (0)2 722 8510 *Fax:* + 63 (0)2 721 1923

Central Philippines The Rt Revd Dixie Copanut Taclobao Central Philippines 281 E Rodriguez Sr Avenue 1102 Quezon City PHILIPPINES *Tel:* + 63 (0)2 412 8561 *Fax:* + 63 (0)2 721 1923 *Email:* central@i-next.net

Davao The Rt Revd Jonathan Labasan Casimina Bishop of Davao Km. 3 McArthur Highway Matina Davao City PHILIPPINES *Tel:* + 63 82 299 1511 *Fax:* + 63 82 296 9629 *Email:* episcopaldioceseofdavao@yahoo.com *Web:* www.eddphilippines.com

North Central Philippines The Most Revd Joel Atiwag Pachao Prime Bishop of the Philippines & Bishop of North Central Philippines 358 Magsaysay Avenue Baguio City 2600 PHILIPPINES *Tel:* + 63 27228481 *Fax:* + 63 (0)74 442 2432 *Email:* bpjoelpachao@yahoo.com

Northern Luzon Vacant Bishop elect of Northern Luzon Bulanao Tabuk Kalinga-Apayao 3800 PHILIPPINES

Northern Philippines- Mt Province The Rt Revd Brent W Alawas Bishop of Northern Philippines Diocesan Office Bontoc 2616 PHILIPPINES *Tel:* + 63 (0)74 602 1026 *Fax:* + 63 (0)74 462 4099 *Email:* ednpvic@hotmail.com

Northern Philippines The Rt Revd Miguel P Yamoyam Suffragan Bishop of the Northern Philippines PO Box 10321 Broadway Centrum Quezon City 1112 PHILIPPINES *Tel:* + 63 (0)2 722 8481/8460 *Fax:* + 63 (0)2 721 1923 *Email:* ecpnational@yahoo.co.ph

Santiago-Isabela The Rt Revd Alexander A Wandag Bishop of Santiago Episcopal Diocese of Santiago Maharlika Highway 3311 Divisoria Santiago City 3311 PHILIPPINES *Tel:* + 63 (0)78 682 3756 *Fax:* + 63 (0)78 682 1256 *Email:* alexwandageds@yahoo.com

Southern Philippines The Rt Revd Danilo Labacanacruz Bustamante Bishop of Southern Philippines 186 Sinsuat Avenue Cotabato City 9600 PHILIPPINES *Tel:* + 63 (0)64 421 2960 *Fax:* + 63 (0)64 421 1703 *Email:* edsp_ecp@yahoo.com *Web:* www.edspphilippines.com

L'EGLISE EPISCOPAL AU RWANDA

Provincial Secretary The Revd Francis Karemera PO Box 2487 Kigali RWANDA *Email:* frkaremera@yahoo.co.uk

Butare The Rt Revd Nathan K Gasatura Bishop o Butare BP 255 Butare RWANDA *Tel:* + 250 30 71 *Fax:* + 250 30 504 *Email:* nathan.gasatura@gmail.com

Byumba The Rt Revd Emmanuel Ngendahaye Bishop of Byumba BP 17 Byumba RWANDA *Tel:* - 250 64 242 *Fax:* + 250 64 242 *Email:* engendahayo@ymail.com

Cyangugu The Rt Revd Nathan Amooti Ruseng Bishop of Cyangugu PO Box 52 Cyangugu RWAND *Tel:* + 250 788 409 061 *Email:* nathanamooti@gmai com

Gahini The Rt Revd Alexis Bilindabagabo Bishop o Gahini BP 22 Gahini RWANDA *Tel:* + 250 67 42 *Fax:* + 250 77 831 *Email:* abilindabagabo@gmail.com

Gasabo The Most Revd Onesphore Rwaje Archbishop of L'Eglise Episcopal au Rwanda and Bishop of Gasabo PO Box 2487 Kigali RWANDA *Fax:* + 250 64 242 *Email:* onesphorerwaje@yahoo. fr

Kibungo The Rt Revd Emmanuel Ntazinda Bishop of Kibungo BP 719 Kibungo RWANDA *Tel:* + 250 566 194

Kigali The Rt Revd Louis Muvunyi Bishop of Kigali PO Box 61 Kigali RWANDA *Tel:* + 250 576 340 *Fax:* + 250 573 213 *Email:* louismuvunyi@hotmail.com

Kigeme The Rt Revd Augustin Mvunabandi Bishop of Kigeme BP 67 Gikongoro RWANDA *Tel:* + 250 535 086 *Email:* dkigemeear@yahoo.fr

Kivu The Rt Revd Augustin Ahimana Bishop of Kivu PO Box 166 Gisenyi RWANDA *Tel:* + 250 78 830 5119 *Email:* aamurekezi@gmail.com

Shyira The Rt Revd Laurent Mbanda Bishop of Shyira EER - Shyira PO Box 52 Ruhengeri RWANDA *Tel:* + 250 466 02 *Fax:* + 250 546 449 *Email:* mbandalaurent@yahoo.com

Shyira The Rt Revd Samuel Mugisha Mugiraneza Coadjutor Bishop of Shyira EER - Shyira PO Box 52 Ruhengeri RWANDA *Tel:* + 250 466 02

Shyogwe The Rt Revd Jered Kalimba Bishop of Shyogwe BP 27 Gitarama RWANDA *Tel:* + 250 62 372 *Fax:* + 250 62 460 *Email:* kalimbaj60@yahoo.fr

THE SCOTTISH EPISCOPAL CHURCH

Secretary General Mr John Stuart 21 Grosvenor Crescent Edinburgh EH12 5EE SCOTLAND *Tel:* + 44 (0)131 225 6357 *Fax:* + 44 (0)131 346 7247 *Email:* secgen@scotland.anglican.org

Provincial Treasurer Mr Malcolm G Bett 21 Grosvenor Crescent Edinburgh EH12 5EE SCOTLAND *Tel:* + 44 (0)131 225 6357 *Fax:* + 44 (0)131 346 7247

Aberdeen & Orkney The Rt Revd Robert Gillies Bishop of Aberdeen & Orkney Diocesan Office St Clement's Church House Mastrick Drive Aberdeen AB16 6UF SCOTLAND *Tel:* + 44 (0) 1224 662 247 *Fax:* + 44 (0)1224 662 168 *Email:* bishop@aberdeen. anglican.org *Web:* www.aberdeen.anglican.org

Argyll & The Isles-Argyll The Rt Revd Kevin Pearson Bishop of Argyll & The Isles St Moluag's Diocesan Centre Croft Avenue Oban PA34 5JJ SCOTLAND *Tel:* + 44 (0)1631 570 870 *Fax:* + 44 (0)1631 570 411 *Email:* bishop@argyll.anglican.org *Web:* www.argyllandtheisles.org.uk

Brechin The Rt Revd Nigel Peyton Bishop of Brechin The Brechin Diocesan Office 38 Langlands Street Dundee DD4 6SZ SCOTLAND *Tel:* + 44 (0)1382 562 24 *Email:* office@brechin.anglican.org *Web:* www.thedioceseofbrechin.org

Edinburgh The Rt Revd John Armes Bishop of Edinburgh Diocesan Centre 21A Grosvenor Crescent Edinburgh EH12 5EL SCOTLAND *Tel:* + 44 (0)131 538 7044 *Fax:* + 44 (0)131 538 7088 *Email:* bishop@edinburgh.anglican.org *Web:* www.edinburgh.anglican.org

Glasgow & Galloway The Rt Revd Gregor Duncan Bishop of Glasgow & Galloway Bishop's Office Diocesan Centre 5 St Vincent Place Glasgow G1 2DH SCOTLAND *Tel:* + 44 (0)141 221 6911 *Fax:* + 44 (0)141 221 7014 *Email:* bishop@glasgow.anglican. org *Web:* www.glasgow.anglican.org

Moray, Ross & Caithness The Most Revd Mark Strange Primus of the Scottish Episcopal Church & Bishop of Moray, Ross & Caithness Diocesan Office 9-11 Kenneth Street Inverness IV3 5NR SCOTLAND *Tel:* + 44 (0)1463 237503 *Fax:* + *Email:* bishop@moray. anglican.org *Web:* www.moray.anglican.org

St Andrews Dunkeld & Dunblane Vacant Bishop of St Andrews, Dunkeld & Dunblane Diocesan Office 28A Balhousie Street Perth PH1 5HJ SCOTLAND *Tel:* + 44 01738 580426 *Email:* bishopsec@standrews. anglican.org

CHURCH OF THE PROVINCE OF SOUTHEAST ASIA

Provincial Secretary The Revd Kenneth Thien Su Yin PO Box 10811 88809 Kota Kinabalu Sabah 88809 MALAYSIA *Email:* kenneththien@gmail.com

Provincial Treasurer Mr Keith Chua 35 Ford Avenue Singapore 268714 SINGAPORE *Tel:* + 65 (0)2 6235 3344 *Fax:* + 65 (0)2 6736 1201 *Email:* keithchu@ singnet.com.sg

Kuching The Rt Revd Danald Jute Bishop of Kuching Bishop's House PO Box 347 Kuching Sarawak 93704 MALAYSIA *Tel:* + 60 (0)82 240 187 *Fax:* + 60 (0)82 426 488 *Email:* bpofkuching@gmail.com *Web:* www. diocesekuching.org

Kuching The Rt Revd Solomon Cheong Sung Voon Assistant Bishop of Kuching Bishop's House PO Box 347 Kuching Sarawak 93704 MALAYSIA *Tel:* + 60 (0)82 429 755

Sabah The Rt Revd Melter Jiki Tais Bishop of Sabah PO Box 10811 88809 Kota Kinabalu Sabah 88809 MALAYSIA *Tel:* + 60 (0)89 521 448 *Fax:* + 60 (0)89 521 448 *Email:* uskupmjtais@gmail.com

Sabah The Rt Revd John Yeo Assistant Bishop of Sabah 201 Jalan Dunlop Tawau sabah 91000 MALAYSIA *Tel:* + 60 (0)89 772 212 *Fax:* + 60 (0)89 761 451 *Email:* ad.johnyeo@gmail.com

Singapore The Rt Revd Rennis Ponniah Bishop of Singapore St Andrew's Village 1 Francis Thomas Drive #01-01 Singapore 359340 SINGAPORE *Tel:* + 65 6288 7585 *Fax:* + 65 6288 5574 *Email:* bpoffice@ anglican.org.sg

West Malaysia The Most Revd Ng Moon Hing Archbishop of South East Asia & Bishop of West Malaysia 16 Jalan Pudu Kuala Lumpur 50200 MALAYSIA *Tel:* + 60 (0)32 031 3213 *Fax:* + 60 (0)32 031 2728 *Email:* canonmoon@gmail.com

West Malaysia The Rt Revd Charles K Samuel Assistant Bishop of West Malaysia St George's Church 1 Lebuh Farquhar Georgetown Pulau Pinang 10200 MALAYSIA *Tel:* + 60 (0)16 922 1618 *Email:* vencan.cs@gmail.com

West Malaysia The Rt Revd Jayson Selvaraj Assistant Bishop of West Malaysia Christ Church Melaka 48 Jalan Gereja Melaka 75000 West MALAYSIA *Tel:* + 60 06 2848 804 *Email:* jasondaphne101@gmail.com

CHURCH OF SOUTH INDIA

General Secretary CSI The Revd D R Sadananda CSI Centre, No 5 Whites Road Royapettah Chennai 6000 014 INDIA *Tel:* + 91 044 2852 1566 *Email:* synodcsi@gmail.com

Provincial Treasurer Advocate C. Robert Bruce 5 Whites Road Royapettah Chennai 600014 INDIA *Tel:* + 91 044 2852 1566 *Email:* treasurercsi@eth.net

Cochin The Rt Revd Baker Ninan Fenn Bishop of Cochin CSI Diocesan Office P.B. No 104 Shoranur Palakkad Kerala 679 121 INDIA *Tel:* + 91 (0)466 222 4454 *Fax:* + 91 (0)466 222 2545 *Email:* revbnfenn@gmail.com

Coimbatore The Rt Revd Timothy Ravinder Bishop of Coimbatore Bishop's House 256 Race Course Road Coimbatore TN 1 641018 INDIA *Tel:* + 91 (0)422 221 3605 *Fax:* + 91 (0)422 221 3369 *Email:* csi.bpcbe@gmail.com

Dornakal The Rt Revd Vadapalli Prasada Rao Deputy Moderator of CSI & Bishop of Dornakal Bishop's House Epiphany Cathedral Compound SC Railway Dornakal Andhra Pradesh 506 381 INDIA *Tel:* + 91 (0) 8719 227 535 *Fax:* + 91 (0) 8719 227 376 *Email:* dkbpoff@hotmail.com

East Kerala The Rt Revd Kayalakkakathu George Daniel Bishop of East Kerala CSI Bishop's House Melukavumattom - Kerala 686 652 INDIA *Tel:* + 91 (0)4822 219 044 *Email:* bishopkgdaniel@rediffmail.com

Jaffna The Rt Revd Daniel Selvaratnam Thiagarajah Bishop of Jaffna Bishop's House Vaddukoddai SRI LANKA *Tel:* + 94 (0)60 221 2424 *Email:* dsthiagarajah@yahoo.com

Kanyakumari The Rt Revd Gnanasigamony Devakadasham Bishop of Kanyakumari 71-A Dennis Street Nagercoil Tamil Nadu629 001 INDIA *Tel:* + 91 (0)4652 231 539 *Fax:* + 91 (0)4652 226 560 *Email:* csikkd@bsnl.com

Karimnagar The Rt Revd Reuben Mark Bishop of Karimnagar 2-8-95 CV Raman Road PO Box 40 Makarampura Karimnagar Andhra Pradesh 505 001 INDIA *Tel:* + 91 878 226 2971 *Fax:* + 91 878 226 2972

Karnataka Central The Rt Revd Prasana Kumar Samuel Bishop of Karnataka Central Diocesan Office 20 Third Cross CSI Compound Bangalore Karnataka 560 027 INDIA *Tel:* + 91 (0)80 2222 3766 *Email:* admin@csikcd.org

Karnataka North The Rt Revd Ravikumar J. Niranjan Bishop of Karnataka North Bishop's House All Saints Church Compound Dharwad - Karnataka 580 008 INDIA *Tel:* + 91 (0)836 244 7733 *Email:* haradoni.rn@gmail.com

Karnataka South The Rt Revd Mohan Manoraj Bishop of Karnataka South Bishop's House Balmatta Mangalore 575 002 INDIA *Tel:* + 91 (0)824 2432 657 *Fax:* + 91 (0)824 2432 363 *Email:* csikcd2014@gmail.com

Kollam-Kottarakkara Vacant Bishop elect of Kollam - Kottarakkara CSI Kollam - Kottarakkara Diocesan Office N. H. 208 Chinnakkada Kollam-Kerala 691001 INDIA *Email:* revbhanusamuel@gmail.com

Krishna-Godavari The Rt Revd Govada Dyvasirvadam Bishop of Krishna-Godavari St Andrew's Cathedral Compound Main Road Machilipatnam - Andhra Pradesh 521 002 Krishna-Godaviri District INDIA *Tel:* + 91 (0)8672 220 623 *Fax:* + 91 (0)8672 220 771 *Email:* bishopkrishna@yahoo.com

Madhya Kerala The Most Revd Thomas Kanjirappally Oommen Moderator of CSI & Bishop of Madhya Kerala CSI Bishop's House Cathedral Road Kottayam Kerala State 686 001 INDIA *Tel:* + 91 (0)481 2566 536 *Fax:* + 91 (0)481 2566 531 *Email:* csimkdbishopsoffice@gmail.com

Madras The Rt Revd George Stephen Jeyaraj Bishop of Madras Diocesan Office PB No 4914 226 Cathedral Road Chennai Tamil Nadu 600 086 INDIA *Tel:* + 91 (0)44 2811 3933 *Fax:* + 91 (0)44 2811 0608 *Web:* www.csimadrasdiocese.org

Madurai-Ramnad The Rt Revd Marialouis Joseph Bishop of Madurai-Ramnad #5 Bhulabai Road Chockikulam Madurai District Tamil Nadu 625 002 INDIA *Tel:* + 91 (0)452 256 3196 *Fax:* + 91 (0)452 256 0864 *Email:* bishop@csidmr.net

Malabar The Rt Revd Royce Manoj Victor Bishop of Malabar CSI Diocesan Office Bank Road Calicut Kerala 673001 INDIA *Tel:* + 91 495 2721748 *Email:* csimalabardiocese@gmail.com

Medak Vacant Bishop elect of Medak 10-3-65, Church House Golden Jubilee Bhavan Old Lancer Lane Secunderabad Andhra Pradesh 500 025 INDIA *Tel:* + 91 (0)40 2783 3151 *Fax:* + 91 (0)40 2782 0843 *Email:* medakdiocese@yahoo.com

Nandyal The Rt Revd Eggoni Pushpalalitha Bishop of Nandyal Bishop's House Nandyal RS Kurnool District Andhra Pradesh 518 502 INDIA *Tel:* + 91 (0)8514 222 477 *Fax:* + 91 (0)8514 242 255

Rayalaseema The Rt Revd B D Prasada Rao Bishop of Rayalaseema CSI Compound Kadapa Andhra Pradesh 516 001 INDIA *Tel:* + 91 (0) 8562 325320 *Fax:* + 91 (0) 8562 275200 *Email:* lbd_prasad@yahoo.com

South Kerala The Rt Revd Dharmaraj Rasalam Bishop of South Kerala Bishop's House LMS Compound Trivandrum Kerala State 695 033 INDIA *Tel:* + 91 (0)471 231 5490 *Fax:* + 91 (0)471 231 6439

Thoothukudi-Nazareth The Rt Revd Samuel Devasahayam Ebenezer E Clement Bishop of Thoothukudi - Nazareth Diocesan Road Caldwell Hr. Sec. School Campus Beach Road Thoothukudi Tamil Nadu 628 001 INDIA *Tel:* + 91 (0) 461 2329 408 *Fax:* + 91 (0)461 2328 408 *Email:* csitnd@bsnl.in

Tirunelveli The Rt Revd Jayaraj J Christdoss Bishop of Tirunelveli Bishopstowe PO Box 118 Palayamkottai Tirunelveli Tamil Nadu 627 002 INDIA *Tel:* + 91 (0)462 2578 744 *Fax:* + 91 (0)462 2574 525

Trichy-Tanjore The Rt Revd Gnanamuthu Paul Vasanthakumar Bishop of Trichy-Tanjore CSI Diocesan Office Allithurai Road Pathur Tiruchirappalli Tamil Nadu 620 017 INDIA *Tel:* + 91 (0)431 771 254 *Email:* csittd@tr.net.in

Vellore The Rt Revd A Rajavelu Bishop of Vellore 3/1 Anna Salai Vellore Tamil Nadu 632 001 INDIA *Tel:* + 91 (0)416 2232 160 *Fax:* + 91 (0)416 2223 835 *Email:* csi.vlrdiocese@gmail.com

THE CHURCH OF THE PROVINCE OF SOUTHERN AFRICA

Provincial Executive Officer The Ven Horace Arenz 20 Bishopscourt Drive Bishopscourt Claremont Western Cape 7708 SOUTH AFRICA *Tel:* + 27 (0)21 763 1325 *Fax:* + 27 (0)21 797 1329 *Email:* peo@anglicanchurchsa.org.za

Provincial Treasurer and Diocesan Secretary of Cape Town Mr Rob S Rogerson PO Box 53014 Kenilworth 7745 SOUTH AFRICA *Tel:* + 27 (0)21 797 8324 *Fax:* + 27 (0)21 683 4603 *Email:* rogerson@cpsa-province.org.za

Angola (Missionary Diocese) The Rt Revd Andre Soares Bishop of Angola Off Caixa Postal No 10341 Luanda ANGOLA *Tel:* + 244 946463780 *Email:* anglicangola@yahoo.com

Cape Town The Most Revd Thabo C Makgoba Archbishop of Capetown and Primate of Southern Africa 20 Bishopscourt Drive Bishopscourt Claremont Cape Town Western Cape 7708 SOUTH AFRICA *Tel:* + 27 021 763 1320 *Fax:* + 27 021 761

4193 *Email:* archpa@anglicanchurchsa.org.za *Web:* www.anglicanchurchsa.org/

Cape Town The Rt Revd Garth Q Counsell Bishop of Table Bay PO Box 1932 Cape Town 8000 SOUTH AFRICA *Tel:* + 27 (0)21 469 3774 *Fax:* + 27 (0)21 469 3774 *Email:* bishop.suffragan@ctdiocese.org.za

Christ the King The Rt Revd Peter J Lee Bishop of Christ the King Diocese of Christ the King PO Box 1653 Rosettenville Gauteng 2130 SOUTH AFRICA *Tel:* + 27 (0)11 435 0097 *Fax:* + 27 (0)11 435 2868 *Email:* bishop@ctkdiocese.co.za *Web:* www.christthekingdiocese-anglican.org

Diocese of the Free State (formerly Bloemfontein) The Rt Revd Dintoe Letloenyane Bishop of Diocese of the Free State PO Box 411 Bloemfontein 9300 SOUTH AFRICA *Tel:* + 27 (0)51 447 6053 *Fax:* + 27 (0)51 447 5874 *Email:* bishopdintoe@dsc.co.za *Web:* www.dsc.co.za

False Bay The Rt Revd Margaret Brenda Vertue Bishop of False Bay PO Box 2804 Somerset West 7129 SOUTH AFRICA *Tel:* + 27 (0)21 852 5243 *Fax:* + 27 (0)21 852 9430 *Email:* bishopm@falsebaydiocese.org.za *Web:* www.falsebaydiocese.org.za

George The Rt Revd Brian Marajh Bishop of George PO Box 227 George Cape Province 6530 SOUTH AFRICA *Tel:* + 27 (0)44 873 5680 *Fax:* + 27 (0)44 873 5680 *Email:* bishopbrian@georgediocese.org.za

Grahamstown The Rt Revd Ebenezer StM Ntlali Bishop of Grahamstown Bishopsbourne PO Box 181 Grahamstown Eastern Cape 6140 SOUTH AFRICA *Tel:* + 27 (0)46 636 1996 *Fax:* + 27 (0)46 622 5231 *Email:* bpgtn@intekom.co.za

Highveld The Rt Revd David H Bannerman Bishop of the Highveld PO Box 17642 Benoni West Gauteng 1503 SOUTH AFRICA *Tel:* + 27 (0)11 422 2231/2 *Fax:* + 27 (0)11 420 1336 *Email:* diohveld@iafrica.com *Web:* www.diocesehighveld.org.za

Johannesburg The Rt Revd Stephen Mosimanegape Moreo Bishop of Johannesburg Diocesan Office PO Box 157 Westhoven Gauteng 2142 SOUTH AFRICA *Tel:* + 27 (0)11 375 2700 *Fax:* + 27 (0)11 477 1337 *Email:* steve.moreo@anglicanjoburg.org.za

Kimberley & Kuruman The Rt Revd Oswald P P Swartz Bishop of Kimberley and Kuruman PO Box 45 Kimberley 8300 SOUTH AFRICA *Tel:* + 27 (0)53 833 2433 *Fax:* + 27 (0)53 831 2730 *Email:* oppswartz@onetel.com

Lebombo The Rt Revd Carlos Simao Matsinhe Bishop of Lebombo Caixa Postale 120 Maputo MOZAMBIQUE *Tel:* + 258 860 278 712 *Email:* carlosmatsinhe@rocketmail.com

Lesotho The Rt Revd Adam Mallane A Taaso Bishop of Lesotho PO Box 87 Maseru 100 LOSOTO *Tel:* + 266 (0)22 3311 974 *Fax:* + 266 (0)22 310 161 *Email:* dioceselesotho@ecoweb.co.ls

Matlosane (formerly Klerksdorp) The Rt Revd Stephen M Diseko Bishop of Matlosane PO Box 11417 Klerksdorp 2570 SOUTH AFRICA *Tel:* + 27 (0)18 464 2260 *Fax:* + 27 (0)18 462 4939 *Email:* diocesematlosane@telkomsa.net

Mbhashe The Rt Revd Elliot S Williams Bishop of Mbhashe PO Box 1184 Butterworth 4960 SOUTH AFRICA *Tel:* + 27 (0)47 491 8127 *Fax:* + 27 (0)47 491 9218 *Email:* dioceseofmbhashe@telkomsa.net

Mpumalanga The Rt Revd Daniel M Kgomosotho Bishop of Mpumalanga PO Box 4327 White River 1240 SOUTH AFRICA *Tel:* + 27 (0)13 751 1960 *Fax:* + 27 (0)13 751 3638 *Email:* bishopdan@telkomsa.net

Mthatha (formerly St John's) The Rt Revd Sitembele T Mzamane Bishop of Mthatha PO Box 25 Umtata Transkei 5100 SOUTH AFRICA *Tel:* + 27 (0)47 532 4450 *Fax:* + 27 (0)47 532 4191 *Email:* anglicbspmthatha@intekom.co.za *Web:* www.mthatha.anglican.org

Namibia The Rt Revd Natanael Nakwatumba Bishop of Namibia PO Box 57 Windhoek 9000 NAMIBIA *Tel:* + 264 (0)61 238 920 *Fax:* + 264 (0)61 225 903 *Email:* bishop@anglicanchurchnamibia.com

Namibia The Rt Revd Petrus Hilukiluah Suffragan Bishop of Namibia PO Box 65 Windhoek NAMIBIA *Tel:* + 264 (0)61 236 009 *Fax:* + 264 (0)61 225 903 *Email:* bpertus@iafrica.com.na

Natal The Rt Revd Dino Gabriel Bishop of Natal PO Box 47439 Greyville Durban 4023 SOUTH AFRICA *Tel:* + 27 (0)31 308 9302 *Fax:* + 27 (0)31 308 9316 *Email:* bishop@dionatal.org.za *Web:* www.anglican-kzn.org.za

Natal The Rt Revd Hummingfield C Ndwandwe Suffragan Bishop of the South Episcopal Area PO Box 889 Pietermaritzburg 3200 SOUTH AFRICA *Tel:* + 27 (0)33 394 1560 *Fax:* + 27 (0)33 394 8785 *Email:* bishopndwandwe@dionatal.org.za

Natal The Rt Revd Tsietse Edward Seleoane Suffragan Bishop of the North West Episcopal Area PO Box 463 Ladysmith 3370 SOUTH AFRICA *Tel:* + 27 (0)36 631 4650 *Fax:* + 27 (0)36 637 4949 *Email:* seleoanet@vodamail.co.za

Niassa The Revd Vicente Msossa Bishop elect of Niassa Diocese of Niassa CP 264 Lichinga Niassa MOZAMBIQUE *Tel:* + 258 2712 0735 *Email:* bishop.niassa@gmail.com

Niassa The Rt Revd Manuel Ernesto Suffragan Bishop of Niassa Diocese of Niassa CP 264 Lichinga Niassa MOZAMBIQUE *Tel:* + 258 27 121 377 *Email:* mernesto.diocese.niassa@gmail.com

Port Elizabeth The Rt Revd Nceba B Nopece Bishop of Port Elizabeth PO Box 7109 Newton Park 6055 SOUTH AFRICA *Tel:* + 27 (0)41 365 1387 *Fax:* + 27 (0)41 365 2049 *Email:* pebishop@iafrica.com *Web:* www.anglicandiocesepe.org.za

Pretoria The Rt Revd Allan John Kannemeyer Bishop of Pretoria PO Box 1032 Pretoria 1 SOUTH AFRICA *Tel:* + 27 (0)12 430 2345 *Fax:* + 12 (0)12 430 2224 *Email:* ptabish@dioceseofpretoria.org *Web:* www.pretoriadiocese.org.za

Saldanha Bay The Rt Revd Raphael B V Hess Bishop of Saldanha Bay PO Box 420 Malmesbury Cape Province 7299 SOUTH AFRICA *Tel:* + 27 (0)22 487 3885 *Fax:* + 27 (0)22 487 3187 *Email:* bishop@dioceseofsaldanhabay.org.za

St Helena The Rt Revd Richard D Fenwick Bishop of St Helena Bishopsholme PO Box 62 St Helena Island South Atlantic *Tel:* + 290 4471 *Fax:* + 290 4728 *Email:* bishop@helanta.sh *Web:* www.sthelena.anglican.org

St Mark the Evangelist The Rt Revd Martin A Breytenbach Bishop of St Mark the Evangelist PO Box 643 Polokwane 700 SOUTH AFRICA *Tel:* + 27 (0)15 297 3297 *Fax:* + 27 (0)15 297 0408 *Email:* martin@stmark.org.za *Web:*

Swaziland The Rt Revd Ellinah Ntfombi Wamukoya Bishop of Swaziland PO Box 118 Mbabane SWAZILAND *Tel:* + 268 4 04 3624 *Fax:* + 268 404 6759 *Email:* bishopen@swazilanddiocese.org.sz *Web:*

Ukhahlamba The Rt Revd Mazwi E Tisani Bishop of Ukhahlamba PO Box 1673 Queenstown Eastern Cape 116 SOUTH AFRICA *Tel:* + 27 (0)45 838 3261 *Fax:* + 27 (0)45 838 2874 *Email:* bishopmazwi@mweb.co.za

Umzimvubu The Rt Revd Mlibo M Ngewu Bishop of Umzimvubu PO Box 644 Kokstad 4700 SOUTH AFRICA *Tel:* + 27 (0)39 727 4117 *Fax:* + 27 (0)39 727 4117 *Email:* mzimvubu@futurenet.co.za *Web:*

Zululand The Rt Revd Monument Makhanya Bishop of Zululand PO Box 147 Eshowe Zululand 3815 SOUTH AFRICA *Tel:* + 27 (0)35 474 2047 *Fax:* + 27 (0)35 474 2047 *Email:* bishopzld@nctactive.co.za

IGLESIA ANGLICANA DEL CONO SUR DE AMERICA

Provincial Secretary Mrs Cristina Daly Awaiting Details *Email:* cristindaly@gmail.com

Provincial Treasurer The Revd Walter Toro Awaiting Details *Email:* wabricii@gmail.com

Argentina The Most Revd Gregory James Venables Presiding Bishop of the Anglican Church of South America & Bishop of Argentina 25 de Mayo 282 Capital Federal Buenos Aires 1001 ARGENTINA *Tel:* + 54 11 4342 4618 *Fax:* + 54 11 4784 1277 *Email:* bpgreg@fibertel.com.ar *Web:* www.anglicana.org.ar

Bolivia The Rt Revd Raphael Samuel Bishop of Bolivia Inglesia Anglicana Episcopal de Bolivia Casilla 848 Cochabamba BOLIVIA *Tel:* + 591 4440 1168 *Email:* raphaelsamuel@gmail.com

Chile The Rt Revd Hector Zavala Muñoz Bishop of Chile Casilla 50675 Correo Central Santiago CHILE *Tel:* + 56 (0)2 638 3009 *Fax:* + 56 (0)2 639 4581 *Email:* tzavala@iach.cl *Web:* www.iach.cl

Chile The Rt Revd Abelino Manuel Apeleo Suffragan Bishop of Chile Pasaje Viña Poniente 4593 Puente Alto Santiago CHILE *Tel:* + 56 (0)2 638 3009 *Email:* aapeleo@gmail.com *Web:* www.iach.cl

Northern Argentina The Rt Revd Nicholas James Quested Drayson Bishop of Northern Argentina Iglesia Anglicana Casilla 187 Salta 4400 ARGENTINA *Tel:* + 54 387 431 1718 *Fax:* + 54 371 142 0100 *Email:* nicobispo@gmail.com

Northern Argentina The Rt Revd Cristiano Rojas Suffragan Bishop of Northern Argentina Iglesia Anglicana Casilla 187 Salta 4400 ARGENTINA

Northern Argentina The Rt Revd Mateo Alto Suffragan Bishop of Northern Argentina Iglesia Anglicana Casilla 187 Salta 4400 ARGENTINA

Northern Argentina The Rt Revd Urbano Duarte Suffragan Bishop of Northern Argentina Iglesia Anglicana Casilla 187 Salta 4400 ARGENTINA

Paraguay The Rt Revd Peter John Henry Bartlett Bishop of Paraguay Iglesia Anglicana Paraguya Casilla de Correo 1124 Asuncion Paraguay PARAGUAY *Tel:* + 595 (0)21 200 933 *Fax:* + 595 (0)21 214 328 *Email:* peterparaguay@gmail.com

Paraguay The Rt Revd Andrés Rodríguez Erben Assistant Bishop of Paraguay España # 1357 (casi Gral. Santos) Asuncion 1124 PARAGUAY *Tel:* + 59 5331 242 533

Peru The Rt Revd Jorge Luis Aguilar Bishop of Peru Calle Doña María 141 Los Rosales Surco Lima 33 PERU *Tel:* + 51 (0)1 449 0600 *Email:* cocosac59@ hotmail.com

Peru The Rt Revd Eulogio Alejandro Mesco Suffragan bishop of Peru Residencial Monte Bello D4 Cerro Colorado Arequipa PERU *Tel:* + 51 054 9943 51781 *Email:* alejandromesco@hotmail.com

Peru The Rt Revd Juan Carlos Revilla Suffragan Bishop of Peru Calle Doña María 141 Los Rosales Surco Lima 33 PERU *Tel:* + 51 (0)1 449 0600 *Email:* jucareli1208@hotmail.es

Uruguay The Rt Revd Michael Pollesel Bishop of Uruguay Reconquista # 522 Montevideo 11000 URUGUAY *Tel:* + 598 (0)2 915 9627 *Fax:* + 598 (0)2 916 2519 *Email:* iglesiaau@gmail.com *Web:* www. anglicanchurch.uy

Uruguay The Rt Revd Gilberto Obdulio Porcal Martínez Suffragan Bishop of Uruguay Reconquista # 522 Montevideo 11000 URUGUAY *Tel:* + 598 (0)2 915 9627 *Fax:* + 598 (0)4 732 8237 *Email:* gilbertoporcal@hotmail.com

THE EPISCOPAL CHURCH OF SOUTH SUDAN

Acting Provincial Secretary Mr John Augustino Lumori PO Box 110 Juba SOUTH SUDAN *Email:* provincialsecretary@sudan.anglican.org

Provincial Treasurer Mr Evans Sokiri PO Box 110 Juba SOUTH SUDAN *Email:* ecsprovince@hotmail. com

Akot-Bahr El Ghazal The Rt Revd Isaac Dhieu Ater Bishop of Akot PO Box 110 Juba SOUTH SUDAN *Email:* bishop@akot.anglican.org *Web:* www.akot. anglican.org

Attooch-Upper NIle The Rt Revd Moses Anur Bishop of Attooch Awaiting Details *Tel:* + 211 91489017 *Email:* athoochdiocese@gmail.com

Aweil-Bahr El Ghazal The Rt Revd Abraham Yel Nhial Bishop of Aweil e/o ECS PO Box 110 Northern Bah el Ghazal SOUTH SUDAN *Tel:* + 211 (0)955 621 584 *Email:* bishop@aweil.anglican.org *Web:* www. aweil.anglican.org

Aweil-Bahr El Ghazal The Rt Revd Michael Deng Assistant Bishop of Aweil - Abyei Area Awaiting Details *Tel:* + 211 (0)9257 73333 *Email:* mbol55@ hotmail.com

Awerial -Bahr El Ghazal The Rt Revd David Akau Kuol Bishop of Awerial Awaiting Details *Tel:* + 211 (0)955 526 396 *Email:* bpkuol2@gmail.com

Bor-Upper Nile The Rt Revd Ruben Akurdid Ngong Bishop of Bor C/O ECS PO Box 110 Juba SOUTH SUDAN *Tel:* + 211 (0)926 572 471 *Web:* www.bor. anglican.org

Cueibet-Bahr El Ghazal The Rt Revd Elijah Matueny Awet Bishop of Cueibet C/O ECS PO Box 110 Juba SOUTH SUDAN *Tel:* + 211 (0)926 572 471 *Email:* bishop@cueibet.anglican.org *Web:* www. cueibet.anglican.org

Duk-Upper Nile The Rt Revd Daniel Deng Abot Bishop of Duk Awaiting Details *Email:* danieldengabot@gmail.com

Duk-Upper Nile The Rt Revd Thomas Tut Assistant Bishop of Duk - Ayod Area Awaiting Details*Email:* tutgany@gmail.com

Ezo-Minye The Rt Revd John Kereboro Zawo Bishop of Ezo C/O ECS PO Box 110 Juba SOUTH SUDAN *Tel:* + 211 (0)818 593 217 *Web:* www.ezo. anglican.org

Ibba-Minye The Rt Revd Wilson Elisa Kamani Bishop of Ibba C/O ECS PO Box 110 Juba SOUTH SUDAN *Email:* bishopkamani@gmail.com *Web:* www.ibba.anglican.org

Juba-Loryco The Most Revd Daniel Deng Bul Yak Archbishop of the Province of the Episcopal Church of South Sudan & Bishop of Juba Province of the Episcopal Church of South Sudan PO Box 110 Juba

SOUTH SUDAN *Email:* archbishopdeng@gmail. com *Web:* www.juba.anglican.org

Juba-Loryco The Rt Revd Fraser Yugu Elias Assistant Bishop of Juba Episcopal Church of Sudan PO Box 110 Juba SOUTH SUDAN *Email:* bishopyugu@gmail.com

Kajo Keji-Loryco The Rt Revd Emmanuel Murye Bishop of Kajo Keji C/O ECS PO Box 110 Juba SOUTH SUDAN *Email:* bishop@kajokeji.anglican. org *Web:* www.kajokeji.anglican.org

Kongor-Upper Nile The Rt Revd Gabriel Thuch Agoth Deng Bishop of Kongor St Peter's Cathedral Panyagor SOUTH SUDAN *Tel:* + 211 955225139 *Email:* ecsdkongor@gmail.com

Lainya-Loryco The Rt Revd Eliaba Lako Obed Bishop of Lainya C/O ECS PO Box 110 Juba SOUTH SUDAN *Email:* eliabalakoobed@gmail.com

Lomega-Loryco The Rt Revd Paul Yugusuk Bishop of Lomega Awaiting Details *Email:* lomegarea@yahoo.com

Lui-Central The Rt Revd Stephen Dokolo Ismail Bishop of Lui C/O ECS PO Box 110 Juba SOUTH SUDAN *Email:* stephen.dokolo@gmail.com *Web:* www.lui.anglican.org

Malakal-Upper Nile The Rt Revd Hilary Garang Deng Bishop of Malakal PO Box 114 Malakal SOUTH SUDAN *Email:* bishop@malakal.anglican. org *Web:* www.malakal.anglican.org

Malakal-Upper Nile The Rt Revd Peter Gatbel Kunen Assistant Bishop of Malakal - Nasir Area PO Box 114 Malakal SOUTH SUDAN *Email:* pgkunen2014@gmail.com

Malakal-Upper Nile The Rt Revd John Gettek Assistant Bishop of Malakal - Bentiu Area PO Box 114 Malakal SOUTH SUDAN *Tel:* + 211 (0)955 039476 *Email:* jgattek@yahoo.com

Malakal-Upper Nile The Rt Revd David Kiir Mayath Assistant Bishop of Malakal - Pariang Area PO Box 114 Malakal SOUTH SUDAN

Malek-Upper Nile The Rt Revd Peter Joh Mayom Bishop of Malek C/O PO Box 110 Diocese of Malek SOUTH SUDAN *Email:* malekdiocese@gmail.com

Maridi-Minye The Rt Revd Justin Badi Arama Bishop of Maridi C/O ECS Office PO Box 7576 Kampala UGANDA *Tel:* + 256 77 3304 965 *Email:* bishop@maridi.anglican.org *Web:* www.maridi. anglican.org

Mundri-Central The Rt Revd Bismark Monday Avokaya Bishop of Mundri PO Box 127 Juba SUDAN *Tel:* + 88 216 2197 4812 *Email:* bishop@mundri.anglican.org *Web:* www.mundri.anglican. org

Nzara-Minye The Rt Revd Samuel Enosa Peni Bishop of Nzara c/o ECS PO Box 110, WES/Yambio SOUTH SUDAN *Email:* samuelpeni@yahoo.com *Web:* www.nzara.anglican.org

Olo-Minye The Rt Revd Tandema O Andrew Bishop of Olo Awaiting Details *Email:* bishopolo65@gmail. com

Pacong-Bahr El Ghazal The Rt Revd Joseph Maker Atot Bishop of Pacong C/O CMS PO Box 40360 Nairobi KENYA *Email:* ecs.pacongdiocese@yahoo. com *Web:* www.pacong.anglican.org

Rejaf-Loryco The Rt Revd Enock Tombe Bishop of Rejaf PO Box 110 Juba SOUTH SUDAN *Tel:* + 249 811 20040 *Fax:* + 249 183 20065 *Web:* www.rejaf. anglican.org

Renk-Upper Nile The Rt Revd Joseph Garang Atem Bishop of Renk c/o ECS PO Box 110 S Upper Nile State SOUTH SUDAN *Email:* josephatem@gmail. com *Web:* www.renk.anglican.org

Rokon-Loryco The Rt Revd Francis Loyo Mori Bishop of Rokon c/o ECS PO Box 110CES-Juba SOUTH SUDAN *Tel:* + 211 928 122 065 *Email:* bployo@yahoo.co.uk *Web:* www.rokon.anglican.org

Rumbek-Bahr El Ghazal The Rt Revd Alapayo Manyang Kuctiel Bishop of Rumbek c/o ECS PO Box 110Lake State SOUTH SUDAN *Email:* kuctiel@yahoo.com *Web:* www.rumbek.anglican.org

Terekeka-Loryco The Rt Revd Paul Modi Bishop of Terekeka PO Box 110 Juba SOUTH SUDAN*Email:* modipaul5@gmail.com *Web:* www.terekeka. anglican.org

Torit-Loryco The Rt Revd Bernard Oringa Balmoi Diocesan Bishop of Torit Awaiting Details *Email:* bishop@torit.anglican.org *Web:* www.torit.anglican.org

Torit-Loryco The Rt Revd Isaac Deu Chon Assistant Bishop of Torit - Kapoeta Area Awaiting Details

Torit-Loryco The Rt Revd Martin Abuni Assistant Bishop of Torit - Magwi Area Awaiting Details

Twik East-Upper Nile The Rt Revd Ezekiel Diing Bishop of Twik East Awaiting Details *Tel:* + 211 (0)955 682118 *Email:* malangajang@gmail.com

Wau-Bahr El Ghazal The Rt Revd Moses Deng Bol Bishop of Wau c/o ECS PO Box 110 Western Bahr El Ghazal SOUTH SUDAN*Email:* mosesdengbol@gmail.com *Web:* www.wau.anglican.org

Wondurba-Loryco The Rt Revd Matthew Taban Peter Bishop of Wondurba Awaiting Details *Email:* bp.matthewpeter@gmail.com

Yambio-Minye The Rt Revd Peter Munde Yacoub Bishop of Yambio c/o ECS PO Box 110 WES/Yambio SOUTH SUDAN *Email:* mundepeter@gmail.com *Web:* www.yambio.anglican.org

Yei-Loryco The Rt Revd Hilary Luate Adeba Bishop of Yei c/o ECS PO Box 110 CES-Juba SOUTH SUDAN *Email:* hill_shepherd@yahoo.com *Web:* www.yei.anglican.org

Yirol-Bahr El Ghazal The Rt Revd David Akau Bishop of Yirol C/O ECS PO Box 110 Lakes State SOUTH SUDAN *Email:* ecsyiroldiocese@yahoo.com *Web:* www.yirol.anglican.org

Yirol-Bahr El Ghazal The Rt Revd Isaac Nyaryiel Aleth Assistant Bishop of Yirol - Aluakluak Area C/O ECS PO Box 110 Lakes State SOUTH SUDAN *Tel:* + 211 (0)923 045451 *Email:* aluakluakarea@gmail.com

Yirol-Bahr El Ghazal The Rt Revd Paul Tokmach Lual Assistant Bishop of Yirol - Nyang Area C/O ECS PO Box 110 Lakes State SOUTH SUDAN *Tel:* + 211 (0)955 990351 *Email:* nyangarea@gmail.com

THE EPISCOPAL CHURCH OF SUDAN

Provincial Secretary The Revd Musa Abujam Awaiting Details *Email:* msabujam@gmail.com

El-Obeid The Rt Revd Ismail Gabriel Abudigin Bishop of El-Obeid PO Box 211 El Obeid SUDAN *Web:* www.elobeid.anglican.org

Kadugli & Nuba Mountains The Rt Revd Andudu Adam Elnail Bishop of Kadugli and Nuba Mountains PO Box 35 Kadugli SUDAN *Tel:* + 249 63 182 2898 *Fax:* + 249 63 182 2898 *Email:* bpkadugli@gmail.com *Web:* www.kadugli.anglican.org

Kadugli & Nuba Mountains The Rt Revd Hassan J Osman Assistant Bishop of Kadugli & Nuba Mountains PO Box 35 Kadugli SUDAN *Email:* Hassan.ojamis@gmail.com *Web:* kadugli.anglican.org

Khartoum The Most Revd Ezekiel Kumir Kondo Archbishop of the Province of Sudan & Bishop of Khartoum PO Box 65 Omdurman SUDAN *Email:* bishop@khartoum.anglican.org *Web:* www.khartoum.anglican.org

Port Sudan The Rt Revd Abdu Elnur Kodi Bishop of Port Sudan PO Box 278 Red Sea State SUDAN *Tel:* + 249 31 212 24 *Email:* bunukaa@live.com *Web:* www.portsudan.anglican.org

Wad Medani The Rt Revd Saman Farajalla Mahdi Bishop of Wad Medani Awaiting Details*Email:* bishop@wadmedani.anglican.org *Web:* www.wadmedani.anglican.org

THE ANGLICAN CHURCH OF TANZANIA

Provincial Secretary The Revd Canon Capt. Johnson Chinyong'ole PO Box 899 Dodoma TANZANIA *Tel:* + 255 (0) 26 232 4574 *Fax:* + 255 (0) 26 232 4565 *Email:* chinyongole@gmail.com *Web:* www.anglican.or.tz

Central Tanganyika The Rt Revd Dickson Chilongani Bishop elect of Central Tanganyika Makay House PO Box 15 Dodoma TANZANIA *Tel:*

+ 255 (0)26 232 4518 *Email:* chilongani@anglican.or.tz *Web:* www.d-c-t.org

Dar-es-Salaam The Rt Revd Valentino Mokiwa Bishop of Dar-es-Salaam St Mark's Theological College PO Box 25016 Dar es Salaam TANZANIA *Fax:* + 255 (0)22 286 5840 *Email:* mokiwa_valentine@hotmail.com *Web:* www.diodar.org

Kagera The Rt Revd Aaron Kijanjali Bishop of Kagera PO Box 18 Ngara TANZANIA *Tel:* + 255 (0)28 222 3624 *Fax:* + 255 (0)28 222 2518 *Email:* dkagera@gmail.com *Web:* www.kageradiocese.info

Kibondo The Rt Revd Awaiting Details Bishop of Kibondo PO Box 15 Kibondo Kigoma TANZANIA

Kiteto The Rt Revd Isaiah Chambala Bishop of Kiteto PO Box 74 Kibaya Kiteto TANZANIA *Email:* bishopiofkiteto@yahoo.com

Kondoa The Rt Revd Given Gaula Bishop of Kondoa PO Box 7 Kondoa TANZANIA *Tel:* + 255 687424428 *Fax:* + 255 762080083 *Email:* gmguala@gmail.com

Lake Rukwa The Rt Revd Mathayo Kasagara Bishop of Lake Rukwa PO Box 19 Mpanda TANZANIA *Email:* kasagarajr@gmail.com

Lweru The Rt Revd Jackton Yeremiah Lugumira Bishop of Lweru PO Box 12 Muleba TANZANIA *Tel:* + 255 (0)28 222 2796 *Email:* act@bukobaonline.com

Mara The Rt Revd George Okoth Bishop of Mara PO Box 131 Musoma TANZANIA *Tel:* + 255 (0)28 262 2376 *Email:* frokoth@yahoo.com

Masasi The Rt Revd James Almasi Bishop of Masasi Private Bag PO Masasi Mtwara Region TANZANIA *Tel:* + 255 (0)23 251 0016 *Fax:* + 255 (0)23 251 0351 *Email:* Bishopjamesalmasi@yahoo.com

Morogoro The Rt Revd Godfrey Sehaba Bishop of Morogoro PO Box 320 Morogoro TANZANIA *Tel:* + 255 (0)23 260 3356 *Fax:* + 255 (0)23 260 4602 *Email:* bishopgsehaba@yahoo.com

Mount Kilimanjaro The Rt Revd Stanley Elilekia Hotay Bishop of Mount Kilimanjaro PO Box 1057 Arush TANZANIA *Tel:* + 255 (0)27 254 8396 *Fax:* + 255 (0)27 254 4187 *Email:* hotaystanley@gmail.com *Web:* www.mountkilimanjaro.anglican.org

Mpwapwa The Most Revd Jacob Erasto Chimeledya Archbishop of Tanzania & Bishop of Mpwapwa PO Box 2 Mpwapwa TANZANIA *Tel:* + 255 (0)26 232 0117 *Fax:* + 255 (0)26 232 0063 *Email:* jacobchimeledya@hotmail.com *Web:*

Newala The Rt Revd Oscar Mnung'a Bishop of Newala PO Box 92 Newala TANZANIA *Email:* oscarnewala.diocese@yahoo.com

Rift Valley The Rt Revd John Daudi Lupaa Bishop of the Rift Valley PO Box 16 Manyoni TANZANIA *Tel:* + 255 (0)26 254 0013 *Fax:* + 255 (0)26 250 3014 *Email:* jlupaa@yahoo.com *Web:* www.dioceseofriftvalley.weebly.com

Rorya The Rt Revd John Adiema Bishop of Rorya PO Box 38 Musoma TANZANIA *Tel:* + 255 (0)752 893957

Ruaha The Rt Revd Joseph D Mgomi Bishop of Ruaha PO Box 1028 Iringa TANZANIA *Email:* sanbalatchisewo@yahoo.com

Ruvuma The Rt Revd Maternus Kapinga Bishop of Ruvuma Bishop's Office PO Box 1357 Songea TANZANIA *Tel:* + 255 (0)25 260 0090 *Fax:* + 255 (0)25 260 2987 *Email:* matemask@gmail.com

Shinyanga The Rt Revd Charles Kija Ngusa Bishop of Shinyanga C/O PO Box 421 Shinyanga TANZANIA *Tel:* + 255 (0)28 276 3584 *Email:* ckngusa@yahoo.com

South West Tanganyika The Rt Revd Matthew Mhagama Bishop of South West Tanganyika Bishop's House PO Box 32 Njombe TANZANIA *Tel:* + 255 (0)26 278 2010 *Fax:* + 255 (0)26 278 2403

Southern Highlands The Rt Revd John Mwela Bishop of Southern Highlands PO Box 198 Mbeya TANZANIA *Tel:* + 255 (0)25 250 0216 *Email:* mwelajohn@yahoo.co.uk

Tabora The Rt Revd Elias S Chakupewa Bishop of Tabora Diocese of Tabora PO Box 1408 Tabora TANZANIA *Tel:* + 255 (0)26 260 4124 *Fax:* + 255 (0)26 260 4899 *Email:* chakupewalucy@yahoo.com *Web:* www.anglicantabora.wordpress.com

Tanga The Rt Revd Maimbo Mndolwa Bishop of Tanga PO Box 35 Korogwe Tanga TANZANIA *Tel:* + 255 (0)27 264 0631 *Fax:* + 255 (0)27 264 0631

Tarime The Rt Revd R Mwita Akiri Bishop of Tarime PO Box 410 Tarime TANZANIA *Tel:* + 255 (0)28 269 0153 *Fax:* + 255 (0)28 269 0153 *Email:* bishop.tarime@gmail.com *Web:* www.anglicantarime.org/

Victoria Nyanza The Rt Revd Boniface Kwangu Bishop of Victoria Nyanza PO Box 278 Mwanza TANZANIA *Tel:* + 255 (0)75 439 6020 *Fax:* + 255 (0)28 250 0676 *Email:* bandmkwangu@yahoo.co.uk

Western Tanganyika The Rt Revd Sadock Makaya Bishop of Western Tanganyika PO Box 13 Kasulu TANZANIA *Tel:* + 255 (0)26 260 4124 *Fax:* + 255 (0)26 260 4899

Zanzibar The Rt Revd Michael Hafidh Bishop of Zanzibar PO Box 5 Mkunazini Zanzibar TANZANIA *Tel:* + 255 (0)24 223 5348 *Fax:* + 255 (0)24 223 6772 *Email:* secactznz@zalink.com

THE CHURCH OF THE PROVINCE OF UGANDA

Provincial Secretary The Revd Canon Amos Magezi Wills Road Namirembe PO Box 14123 Kampala UGANDA *Tel:* + 256 414 272 757 *Email:* pschurchofuganda@gmail.com

Provincial Treasurer Mr Richard M Obura Box 14123 Kampala UGANDA *Tel:* + 256 (0)41 270 218 *Fax:* + 256 (0)41 251 925 *Email:* richardobura@gmail.com

Ankole The Rt Revd Sheldon F Mwesigwa Bishop of Ankole PO Box 14 Mbarara UGANDA *Tel:* + 256 787 084 301 *Email:* ruharo@utlonline.co.ug *Web:* www.ankolediocese.org

Bukedi The Rt Revd Samuel Egesa Bishop of Bukedi PO Box 170 Tororo UGANDA *Tel:* + 256 772 542 164 *Email:* bukedidiocese@yahoo.com

Bunyoro-Kitara The Rt Revd Samuel Kahuma Bishop of Bunyoro-Kitara PO Box 20 Hoima UGANDA *Tel:* + 256 772 55 83 83 *Email:* can.kahuma@gmail.com

Busoga The Rt Revd Paul Moses Samson Naimanhye Bishop of Busoga PO Box 1658 Jinja UGANDA *Tel:* + 256 0752 598 955 *Fax:* + 256 (0)43 20 547 *Email:* busogadiocese@gmail.com

Central Buganda The Rt Revd Michael Lubowa Bishop of Central Buganda PO Box 1200 Kanoni-Gomba Mpigi UGANDA *Tel:* + 256 772 475 640 *Fax:* + 256 772 242 742 *Email:* michaelluwalira@yahoo.com *Web:* www.centralbuganda.com

Central Busoga The Rt Revd Patrick Wakula Bishop of Central Busoga Awaiting Details *Tel:* + 256 782 510 482

East Ruwenzori The Rt Revd Edward Bamucwanira Bishop of East Ruwenzori PO Box 1439 Kamwenge UGANDA *Tel:* + 256 772 906 236 *Email:* edward_bamu@yahoo.com

Kampala The Most Revd Stanley Ntagali Archbishop of Uganda & and Bishop of Kampala Box 335 Kampala UGANDA *Tel:* + 256 (0)41 270 218 / 9 *Fax:* + 256 (0)41 251 925 *Email:* abpcou@gmail.com

Kampala The Rt Revd Hannington Mutebi Assistant Bishop of Kampala Box 335 Kampala UGANDA *Tel:* + 256 (0)414 342 601 *Email:* mutebihanning@gmail.com

Karamoja The Rt Revd Joseph Abura Bishop o Karamoja PO Box 44 Moroto UGANDA *Tel:* + 256 782 658 502 *Email:* loukomoru@gmail.com

Kigezi The Rt Revd George Bagamuhunda Bishop o Kigezi PO Box 3 Kabale UGANDA *Tel:* + 256 772 450 019 *Email:* bishopkigezi@infocom.co.ug

Kinkiizi The Rt Revd Dan J Zoreka Bishop c Kinkizi PO Box 77 Kanungu UGANDA *Tel:* + 256 782 316 238 *Email:* zoekadan@gmail.com *Web:* www.kinkiizidiocese.com

Kitgum Vacant Bishop elect of Kitgum PO Box 18 Kitgum UGANDA *Tel:* + 256 772 959 924

Kumi The Rt Revd Thomas E Irigei Bishop of Kumi PO Box 18 Kumi UGANDA *Tel:* + 256 772 659 46

Fax: + 256 (0)45 613 25 *Email:* kumimothersunion@ yahoo.com

Lango The Revd Canon Alfred Olwa Bishop elect of Lango PO Box 6 Lira UGANDA *Tel:* + 256 772 614 000 *Email:* bishoplango@yahoo.com

Luwero The Rt Revd Eridard Kironde Nsubuga Bishop of Luwero PO Box 125 Luwero UGANDA *Tel:* + 256 772 349 669 *Email:* eridard.nsubuga@gmail.com

Madi & West Nile The Rt Revd Charles Collins Andaku Bishop of Madi & West Nile PO Box 370 Arua UGANDA *Tel:* + 256 772 382 324 *Email:* andakucollins@gmail.com

Masindi-Kitara The Rt Revd George Kasangaki Bishop of Masindi-Kitara PO Box 515 Masindi UGANDA *Tel:* + 256 772 624 461 *Email:* georgewakasa@gmail.com

Mbale The Rt Revd Patrick M Gidudu Bishop of Mbale Bishop's House PO Box 473 Mbale UGANDA *Tel:* + 256 782 625 619 *Email:* mbalediocese7@ rocketmail.com

Mityana The Rt Revd Stephen Kaziimba Bishop of Mityana PO Box 102 Mityana UGANDA *Tel:* + 256 772 512 175 *Email:* skaziimba@yahoo.com

Muhabura The Rt Revd Cranmer Mugisha Bishop of Muhabura PO Box 22 Kisoro UGANDA *Tel:* + 256 712 195 891 *Email:* cranhopmu@yahoo.co.uk

Mukono The Rt Revd William K Ssebaggala Bishop of Mukono PO Box 39 Mukono UGANDA *Tel:* + 256 772 603 348 *Email:* jamesebagala@yahoo.co.uk *Web:* www.mukonodiocese.or.ug

Namirembe The Rt Revd Wilberforce Kityo Luwalira Bishop of Namirembe PO Box 14297 Kampala UGANDA *Tel:* + 256 712 942 161 *Email:* omulabirizi@gmail.com *Web:* www.namirembe-diocese.org

Nebbi The Rt Revd Alphonse Watho-kudi Bishop of Nebbi PO Box 27 Nebbi UGANDA *Tel:* + 256 772 650 032 *Email:* bpalphonse@ekk.org

North Ankole The Rt Revd Stephen Namanya Bishop of North Ankole PO Box 1 Rushere-Kiruhura UGANDA *Tel:* + 256 772 622 116 *Email:* Nadsrushere@yahoo.com

North Karamoja The Rt Revd James Nasak Bishop of North Karamoja PO Box 26 Kotido UGANDA *Tel:* + 256 772 660 228 *Email:* jn.nasak@yahoo.com

North Kigezi The Rt Revd Benon Magezi Bishop of North Kigezi PO Box 23 Kinyasano-Rukungiri UGANDA *Tel:* + 256 782 561 217 *Email:* northkigezi@infocom.co.ug

North Mbale The Rt Revd Samuel Gidudu Bishop of North Mbale PO Box 2357 Mbale UGANDA *Tel:* +

256 782 853 094 *Email:* northmbalediocese@yahoo. com

Northern Uganda The Rt Revd Johnson Gakumba Bishop of Northern Uganda PO Box 232 Gulu UGANDA *Tel:* + 256 772 601 421 *Email:* dnu@ utlonline.co.ug *Web:* dioceseofnorthernuganda. blogspot.co.uk

Ruwenzori The Rt Revd Reuben Kisembo Bishop of Ruwenzori PO Box 37 Fort Portal UGANDA *Tel:* + 256 (0)45 51 072 *Email:* dioruwenzori@yahoo.com *Web:* www.ruwenzoridiocese.com

Sebei The Rt Revd Paul Kiptoo Masaba Bishop of Sebei PO Box 23 Kapchorwa UGANDA *Tel:* + 256 772 312 502 *Email:* revpkmasaba@yahoo.com

Soroti The Rt Revd George Erwau Bishop of Soroti Soroti Diocese PO Box 107 Soroti UGANDA *Tel:* + 256 772 653 607 *Email:* georgeerwau@yahoo.com *Web:* www.soroti.anglican.org

South Ankole The Rt Revd Nathan Ahimbisibwe Bishop of South Ankole PO Box 39 Ntungamo UGANDA *Tel:* + 256 772 660 636 *Email:* revnathan2000@yahoo.com

South Rwenzori The Rt Revd Jackson Nzerebende Bishop of South Rwenzori PO Box 142 Kasese UGANDA *Tel:* + 256 772 713 736 *Email:* srdiocese@ gmail.com *Web:* www.southrd.org

West Ankole The Rt Revd Johnson Twinomujuni Bishop of West Ankole PO Box 140 Bushenyi UGANDA *Tel:* + 256 752 377 192 *Email:* wad@ westankolediocese.org

West Buganda The Rt Revd Henry Katumba-Tamale Bishop of West Buganda PO Box 242 Masaka UGANDA *Tel:* + 256 772 770 828 *Email:* hkatumbatamale@gmail.com

West Lango The Rt Revd Alfred Acur Okodi Bishop of West Lango Awaiting Details *Tel:* + 256 772 523 153 *Email:* revalfredac@yahoo.co.uk

THE CHURCH IN WALES

Provincial Secretary Canon Simon Lloyd 2 Callaghan Square Cardiff CF10 5BT WALES *Tel:* + 44 (0)2920 348 200 *Email:* simonlloyd@churchinwales.org.uk *Web:* www.churchinwales.org.uk

Bangor The Rt Revd Andrew T G John Bishop of Bangor Ty'r Esgob Upper Garth Road Bangor Gwynedd LL57 2SS WALES *Tel:* + 44 (0)1248 362 895 *Fax:* + 44 (0)1248 372 454 *Email:* bishop. bangor@churchinwales.org.uk *Web:* bangor. churchinwales.org.uk

Llandaff The Rt Revd June Osborne Bishop of Llandaff Llys Esgob The Cathedral Green Llandaff Cardiff CF5 2YE WALES *Tel:* + 44 (0)292 056 2400 *Fax:* + 44 (0)292

057 7129 *Email:* bishop.llandaff@churchinwales.org.uk *Web:* llandaff.churchinwales.org.uk

Monmouth The Rt Revd Richard R Pain Bishop of Monmouth Bishopstow 91 Stow Hill Newport Gwent NP20 4EA WALES *Tel:* + 44 (0)1633 263 510 *Fax:* + 44 (0)1633 259 946 *Email:* bishop.monmouth@churchinwales.org.uk *Web:* monmouth.churchinwales.org.uk

St Asaph The Rt Revd Gregory K Cameron Bishop of St Asaph Esgobty St Asaph Denbighshire LL17 0TW WALES *Tel:* + 44 (0)1745 583 503 *Fax:* + 44 (0)1745 584 301 *Email:* Bishop.stasaph@churchinwales.org.uk *Web:* stasaph.churchinwales.org.uk

St Davids The Rt Revd Joanna Penberthy Bishop of St Davids Llys Esgob Abergwili Carmarthen SA31 2JG WALES *Tel:* + 44 (0)1267 236 597 *Fax:* + 44 (0)1267 243 403 *Email:* bishop.stdavids@churchinwales.org.uk *Web:* stdavids.churchinwales.org.uk

Swansea & Brecon The Most Revd John E Davies Archbishop of Wales & Bishop of Swansea & Brecon Bishop's House Ely Tower Castle Square Brecon Powys LD3 9DJ WALES *Tel:* + 44 (0)1874 622 008 *Fax:* + 44 (0)1874 610 927 *Email:* archbishop@churchinwales.org.uk *Web:* swanseaandbrecon.churchinwales.org.uk

THE CHURCH IN THE PROVINCE OF WEST AFRICA

Provincial Secretary The Revd Canon Anthony M K Eiwuley PO Box KN 2023 Kaneshie Accra GHANA *Email:* morkeiwuley@gmail.com

Provincial Treasurer The Revd Canon Andrew Torgbor P. O. Box GP8 Accra GHANA *Tel:* + 233 208 237 424 *Email:* ayorkor33@yahoo.com

Accra-Ghana The Rt Revd Daniel Sylvanus Mensah Torto Bishop of Accra Bishopscourt PO Box 8 Accra 233 GHANA *Tel:* + 233 302 662 292 *Fax:* + 233 277 496 479 *Email:* dantorto@yahoo.com *Web:* http://www.accraanglican.org/

Asante-Mampong-Ghana The Rt Revd Cyril K Ben-Smith Bishop of Asante-Mampong PO Box 220 Mampong Ashanti GHANA*Email:* bishop.mampong@yahoo.co.uk *Web:* www.mampong.anglican.org

Bo (Sierra Leone)-West Africa The Rt Revd Emmanuel J S Tucker Bishop of Bo PO Box 21 Bo Southern Province SIERRA LEONE *Tel:* + 232 766 778 62 *Fax:* + 232 (0)32 605 *Email:* ejstucker@gmail.com

Cameroon-West Africa The Rt Revd Dibo T B Elango Bishop of Cameroon BP 15705 Akwa Douala CAMEROON *Tel:* + 237 7 555 8276 *Email:* revdibo2@yahoo.com

Cape Coast-Ghana The Rt Revd Victor R Atta-Baffoe Bishop of Cape Coast Bishopscourt PO Box A233 Adiadel Estates Cape Coast GHANA *Tel:* + 233 20 650 2319 *Email:* victorattabaffoe@yahoo.com

Dunkwa-on-Offin-Ghana The Rt Revd Edmund K Dawson Ahmoah Bishop of Dunkwa-on-Offin PO Box DW42 Dukwa-on-Offin GHANA *Tel:* + 233 244 464 764 *Email:* papacy11@yahoo.co.uk

Freetown (Sierra Leone)-West Africa The Rt Revd Thomas Arnold Ikunika Wilson Bishop of Freetown (Sierra Leone) Bishopscourt PO Box 537 105 Fourah Bay Road Freetown SIERRA LEONE *Tel:* + 232 (0)22 251 307 *Email:* vicnold2003@gmail.com

Gambia-West Africa The Rt Revd James Allen Yaw Odico Bishop of the Gambia Bishopscourt PO Box 51 Banjul THE GAMBIA *Tel:* + 220 4227084 *Email:* jayawodico@gmail.com

Guinea-West Africa The Rt Revd Jacques Boston Bishop of Guinea BP 1187 Conakry GUINEA *Tel:* + 224 632 204 660 *Email:* dioceseanglicanguinee@yahoo.fr

Ho-Ghana The Rt Revd Matthias K Mededues-Badohu Bishop of Ho Bishopslodge PO Box MA300 Ho Volta Region GHANA *Tel:* + 233 20 816 2246 *Email:* matthiaskwab@gmail.com

Koforidua-Ghana The Rt Revd Francis F B Quashie Bishop of Koforidua PO Box 980 Koforidua GHANA *Tel:* + 233 26 681 9414 *Email:* fbquashie@yahoo.com

Kumasi-Ghana The Most Revd Daniel Y Sarfo Primate & Metropolitan, CPWA; Archbishop of the Internal province of Ghana and Bishop of Kumasi Bishop's House PO Box 144 Kumasi GHANA *Tel:* + 233 32 204 7717 *Email:* anglicandioceseofkumasi@yahoo.com *Web:* www.anglicandioceseofkumasi.com

Liberia-West Africa The Most Revd Jonathan Bau-Bau Bonaparte Hart Archbishop for the internal province of West Africa and Bishop of Liberia PO Box 10-0277 1000 Monrovia 10 LIBERIA West Africa *Tel:* + 231 88 651 6343 *Email:* bishopecl12@yahoo.com

Sekondi-Ghana The Rt Revd Alexander K Asmah Bishop of Sekondi PO Box 85 Sekondi GHANA *Tel:* + 233 208 378 295 *Email:* alexasmah@yahoo.com

Sunyani-Ghana The Rt Revd Festus Yeboah-Asuamah Bishop of Sunyani PO Box 23 Sunyani GHANA *Tel:* + 233 208 124 378 *Email:* fyasuamah@yahoo.com

Tamale-Ghana The Rt Revd Jacob K Ayeebo Bishop of Tamale PO Box 110 Tamale NR GHANA *Tel:* + 233 24 341 9864 *Email:* ayeebojacob@gmail.com

Wiawso-Ghana The Rt Revd Abraham K Ackah Bishop of Wiawso PO Box 4 Sefwi Wiawso GHANA

Tel: + 233 20 816 1826 *Email:* bishopackah@yahoo.
com

THE CHURCH IN THE PROVINCE OF THE WEST INDIES

Provincial Secretary Mrs Elenor I Lawrence Bamford House Society Hill St John BB2008 BARBADOS *Tel:* + 1 246 423 0842 *Fax:* + 1 246 423 0855 *Email:* cpwi@ caribsurf.com

Barbados The Most Revd & The Hon John W D Holder Archbishop of West Indies & Bishop of Barbados Mandeville House Henry's Lane Collymore Rock St Michael BARBADOS *Tel:* + 1 246 426 2761 *Fax:* + 1 246 426 0871 *Email:* jwdh@ outlook.com *Web:* www.barbados.anglican.org

Belize The Rt Revd Philip S Wright Bishop of Belize Diocesan Office 2 Rectory Lane PO Box 535 Belize City BELIZE *Tel:* + 11 501 227 3029 *Fax:* + 11 501 227 6898 *Email:* bzediocese@btl.net *Web:* anglicandioceseofbelize.com

Diocese of The Bahamas and The Turks and Caicos Islands The Rt Revd Laish Z Boyd Bishop of The Bahamas and The Turks and Caicos Islands Addington House Sands Road PO Box N-7107 New Providence Nassau BAHAMAS *Tel:* + 1 (0)242 322 3015/6/ *Fax:* + 1 (0)242 322 7943 *Email:* bishop@bahamasanglican. org *Web:* www.bahamasanglicans.org

Guyana The Rt Revd Charles Davidson Bishop of Guyana Diocesan Office 49 Barrack Street PO Box 10949 Georgetown GUYANA *Tel:* + 592 226 4183 *Fax:* + 592 226 6091 *Email:* dioceseofguyana@gmail. com

Jamaica & The Cayman Islands The Rt Revd Howard K A Gregory Bishop of Jamaica & The Cayman Islands Church House 2 Caledonia Avenue Kingston JAMAICA *Tel:* + 1 876 920 2712 *Email:* hkagregory@ hotmail.com *Web:* www.anglicandioceseja.org

Jamaica & The Cayman Islands The Rt Revd Robert M Thompson Suffragan Bishop of Kingston 3 Duke Street Kingston JAMAICA *Tel:* + 1 876 924 9044 *Fax:* + 1 876 948 5362 *Email:* bishop.kingston@ anglicandiocese.com

Jamaica & The Cayman Islands Vacant Suffragan Bishop elect of Mandeville 8 Morningside Drive PO Box 346 Montego Bay JAMAICA *Tel:* + 1 876 625 6817 *Fax:* + 1 876 625 6819

Jamaica & The Cayman Islands The Rt Revd Leon Paul Golding Suffragan Bishop of Montego Bay 8 Clieveden Avenue Kingston 6 JAMAICA *Tel:* + 876 920 2712

North Eastern Caribbean & Aruba The Rt Revd Leroy E Brooks Bishop of North Eastern Caribbean & Aruba Bishop's Lodge Redcliffe Street PO Box 23 St John's ANTIGUA *Tel:* + 1 268 462 0151 *Fax:* + 1 268 462 2090 *Email:* brookx@anguillanet.com

Trinidad & Tobago The Rt Revd Claude Berkley Bishop of Trinidad & Tobago Diocesian Office 21 Maraval Road Port of Spain TRINIDAD *Email:* claberk@yahoo.com

Windward Islands The Rt Revd Calvert L Friday Bishop of the Windward Islands Diocesan Pastoral Centre Montrose PO Box 502 Kingstown ST VINCENT *Tel:* + 1 784 456 1895 *Fax:* + 1 784 456 2591 *Email:* diocesewi@vincysurf.com

THE CHURCH OF CEYLON

Mrs Ramola Sivasunderam Secretary to General Assembly C/O The Polytechnic Galle Road Colombo 600 Sri Lanka *Tel:* + 94 1 1258 6603 *Fax:* + 94 (0) 777 35 23 73

Colombo The Rt Revd Dhiloraj Ranjit Canagasabey Bishop of Colombo Bishop's Office 368/3A Bauddhaloka Mawatha Colombo - 07 Sri Lanka *Fax:* + 94 (0)11 268 4811 *Email:* anglican@sltnet.lk

Kurunagala Vacant Bishop elect of Kurunagala Bishop's House 31 Kandy Road Kurunagala 60000 Sri Lanka *Tel:* + 94 (0)37 222 2191 *Email:* bishopkg@ sltnet.lk

IGLESIA EPISCOPAL DE CUBA

Provincial Secretary Mr Francisco De Arazoza Calle 6 No 273 Vedado Plaza de la revolucion Ciudad de la Habana CUBA *Tel:* + 53 7 832 1120 *Fax:* + 53 7 834 3293 *Email:* episcopal@enet.cu

Cuba The Rt Revd Griselda Delgado Del Carpio Bishop of Cuba Calle 6 No 273 Vedado Plaza Cuidad de la Habana 10400 CUBA *Tel:* + 53 (0)7 833 5760 *Email:* griselda@enet.cu

Cuba The Rt Revd Ulises A Prendes Suffragan Bishop of Cuba Calle Escario No 459 entre 3 Y 4 Santiago de Cuba 90100 CUBA *Tel:* + 53 (0)22 627 815 *Email:* bpulises@enet.cu

BERMUDA (EXTRA-PROVINCIAL TO CANTERBURY)

Provincial Treasurer HM CX Mr Campbell McBeath PO Box HM769 Hamilton BERMUDA *Tel:* + 1 441 292 6987 *Fax:* + 1 441 292 5421 *Email:* diocese@ anglican.bm *Web:* www.anglican.bm

Bermuda The Rt Revd Nicholas Dill Bishop of Bermuda Diocesan Office PO Box HM769 Hamilton HM CX BERMUDA *Tel:* + 1 441 292 6987 *Fax:* + 1 441 292 5421 *Email:* bishop@anglican.bm *Web:* www.anglican.bm

THE LUSITANIAN CHURCH (EXTRA-PROVINCIAL TO CANTERBURY)

Provincial Treasurer The Revd Sérgio Filipe Pinho Alves Diocesan Centre of Lusitanian Church Rua Afonso de Albuquerque, No 86 4430-003 Vila Nova de Gaia PORTUGAL *Tel:* + 351 22 375 4018 *Fax:* + 351 22 375 2016 *Email:* sergioalves@igreja-lusitana. org *Web:* www.igreja-lusitana.org

Lusitanian Church The Rt Revd José Jorge De Pina Cabral Bishop of the Lusitanian Church Diocesan Centre of Lusitanian Church Rua Afonso de Albuquerque, No 86 4430-003 Vila Nova de Gaia PORTUGAL *Tel:* + 351 (0)22 375 4018 *Fax:* + 351 (0)22 375 2016 *Email:* bispopinacabral@igreja-lusitana.org *Web:* www.igreja-lusitana.org

THE REFORMED CHURCH OF SPAIN

Senor Jose Antonio Rodriguez Provincial Treasurer Calle Beneficencia 18 Madrid 28004 SPAIN *Tel:* + 34 91 445 25 60 *Email:* secretario@anglicanos.org *Web:* www.anglicanos.org

The Reformed Episcopal Church of Spain The Rt Revd Carlos López-Lozano Bishop of Spanish Reformed Episcopal Church Calle Beneficencia 18 Madrid 28004 SPAIN *Tel:* + 34 (0)91 445 2560 *Fax:* + 34 (0)91 594 4572 *Email:* eclesiae@arrakis.es

PARISH OF THE FALKLAND ISLANDS

Falkland Islands (Parish of) The Rt Revd Timothy M Thornton Bishop to the Forces and Bishop to the Falkland Islands Lambeth Palace London SE1 7JU United Kingdom *Email:* tim.thornton@lambethpalace.org.uk

CHURCHES IN FULL COMMUNION
WITH THE EPISCOPAL CHURCH

The Episcopal Church seeks the full, visible unity of Christ's Church in one Eucharistic fellowship. The Episcopal Church notes in Called to Common Mission that in full communion, "churches become interdependent while remaining autonomous. Diversity is preserved, but this diversity is not static. Neither church seeks to remake the other in its own image, but each is open to the gifts of the other as it seeks to be faithful to Christ and his mission."

The Office of Ecumenical and Interreligious Relations promotes relationships between the Episcopal Church and other Christian communities and supports interreligious relationships globally and locally.

The Presiding Bishop is the Ecumenical Officer of the Episcopal Church. The Rev. Margaret Rose is the Deputy to the Presiding Bishop for Ecumenical and Interreligious Relations. Email: mrose@episcopalchurch. org. Mr. Richard Mammana is Associate for Ecumenical and Interreligious Relations. Email: rmammana@ episcopalchurch.org.

EVANGELICAL LUTHERAN CHURCH IN AMERICA

In 2001, the Episcopal Church and the Evangelical Lutheran Church in America (ELCA) entered into a relationship of full communion, *Called to Common Mission*, culminating thirty years of dialogue. The two churches have committed themselves to joint mission and witness, including mutual participation in consecrations and installations of bishops and the exchangeability of clergy between the two churches. The Lutheran Episcopal Coordinating Committee meets regularly to support this relationship, and maintains a directory of documentation and other resources at lutheran-episcopal.org.

THE MORAVIAN CHURCH
(Northern and Southern Provinces)

Following centuries of friendly relations between the two traditions, the Episcopal Church and the Moravian Church in America's Northern and Southern Provinces established an official dialogue in 1997. In 2003, the two churches entered into an agreement on interim Eucharistic sharing. In 2009, the General Convention approved *Finding Our Delight in the Lord*, a proposal for full communion between the two churches. The Moravian provinces approved the same agreement in 2010. The ELCA is also in full communion with these Moravian provinces. The Moravian Episcopal Coordinating Committee supports this relationship, and provides background material at moravian-episcopal.org.

CHURCHES BEYOND BORDERS

Churches Beyond Borders is a full communion body of Anglicans and Lutherans in North America consisting of The Episcopal Church (domestic dioceses and provinces), the Anglican Church of Canada, the Evangelical Lutheran Church in America (domestic synods); and the Evangelical Lutheran Church in Canada. Working collaboratively, Churches Beyond Borders offers devotions, resources, workshops and statements on such issues as the Doctrine of Discovery, climate change, racial reconciliation, gender justice, missional leadership,

and other matters of common gospel urgency. It builds on the 2001 Waterloo Declaration and the 1999-2000 Called to Common Mission an expression of full communion among Anglicans and Lutherans in North America. The 2022 General Convention formalized these full communion relationships through a Memorandum of Mutual Recognition.

THE OLD CATHOLIC CHURCHES OF THE UNION OF UTRECHT

The Old Catholic Churches of the Union of Utrecht are our oldest and longest termed Full Communion partners. (In 1934, the Episcopal Church entered full communion with the Old Catholic Churches in communion with the See of Utrecht during the ratification of the Bonn Agreement of 1931, which stipulated that:

- Each Communion recognizes the catholicity of the other and maintains its own.
- Each Communion agrees to admit members of the other communion to participate in the sacraments.
- Intercommunion does not require from either communion the acceptance of all doctrinal opinion, sacramental devotion, or liturgical practice characteristic of the other, but implies that each believes the other to hold all the essentials of the Christian faith.

Mutual ministry, primarily through the Convocation of Episcopal Churches in Europe, is being accomplished by our cooperation and shared ministries.

The Presiding Bishop has designated a permanent representative to the annual Old Catholic Bishops' Conference in order to assure continued communication, mutual ministry and understanding.

PHILIPPINE INDEPENDENT CHURCH

In 1961, the Philippine Independent Church, also known as the Iglesia Filipina Independiente (IFI), and the Episcopal Church agreed to "establish a concordat of full communion." A Concordat Panel supports this relationship, and members of the IFI often attend the General Convention of the Episcopal Church as observers. The Episcopal Church assists the IFI in its efforts to minister to members in the United States.

MAR THOMA SYRIAN CHURCH OF MALABAR

Following an agreement acknowledged by the General Convention in 1976, the Episcopal Church is in full communion with the Mar Thoma Syrian Church of Malabar, based in southern India. When requested by the Metropolitan of the Mar Thoma Church, bishops of dioceses of the Episcopal Church shall exercise episcopal oversight of clergy and laity of the Mar Thoma Church within their jurisdictions. Members of the Mar Thoma Church in the jurisdiction of an Episcopal diocese shall be treated as members of the Episcopal Church, with the understanding that they also remain members of the Mar Thoma Church.

THE CHURCH OF SWEDEN

The General Convention adopted a resolution in 2015 accepting a report identifying the grounds for full communion and ongoing shared mission in the following areas: practical work in parishes; areas of tripartite interest with common partners; issues of common concern in the strategy and programmatic work of the World Council of Churches; and specific questions which the two churches prioritize, such as climate change, peace, gender justice, etc. General Convention 2018's Resolution D085 requested that the Presiding Bishop prepare "a memorandum of understanding setting forth the terms and procedures of the full communion between The Episcopal Church and the Church of Sweden." A memorandum of understanding was acknowledged at the 2022 General Convention, establishing a contact group for the relationship, which will be ratified at a future date.

Ecumenical Relations

The Episcopal Church maintains ecumenical relations through dialogues with other Christian traditions; coordinating committees or concordat panels supporting existing full communion relationships; membership in the World Council of Churches and the National Council of Churches as well as other national and international conciliar or ecumenical bodies; and diocesan and local ecumenical efforts conducted through the network of Episcopal Diocesan Ecumenical and Interreligious Officers (EDEIO)..

ECUMENICAL DIALOGUES

The Episcopal Church is engaged in formal bilateral talks with the following churches. These dialogues have been established by act of General Convention and are provided with oversight by the Office of Ecumenical and Interreligious Relations (EIR) in conjunction with clergy and laity appointed by the EIR and the Office of General Convention.

United Methodist-Episcopal Dialogue

The United Methodist-Episcopal dialogue was established by act of the 2000 General Convention and began meeting in 2002. The 2006 General Convention approved interim Eucharistic sharing with the United Methodist Church. Episcopal parishes are now authorized to hold joint celebrations of the Eucharist with United Methodist churches under the guidelines established by General Convention. The Episcopal Church participated with the United Methodist Church as part of the Consultation on Church Union. The ecumenical work of the United Methodist Church is carried out by the Council of Bishops Office of Christian Unity and Interreligious Relationships. The committee's proposal for full communion is under discussion. The dialogue's resources are available online at umc-tec.org.

Presbyterian-Episcopal Dialogue

The Presbyterian Church (U.S.A.) was formed in 1983 through the merger of the United Presbyterian Church and the Presbyterian Church in the United States. The Episcopal Church participated in dialogue with the Presbyterian Church (U.S.A.) within the context of the earlier Consultation on Church Union. A bilateral dialogue was established in 2000 and began meeting in 2002. General Convention in 2009 approved an agreement with the Presbyterian Church (U.S.A.). While this relationship is not full communion or Eucharistic sharing, the agreement encourages cooperation and joint ministry. General Convention 2018 also authorized a further round of ongoing dialogue.

Anglican-Roman Catholic Dialogue

The Episcopal Church has been in dialogue with the Roman Catholic Church for more than 40 years through the Anglican-Roman Catholic Dialogue in the USA (ARC-USA), and on the international level through the Anglican Communion Office in the Anglican-Roman Catholic International Consultations (ARCIC). In a common declaration signed in 2006 by Rowan Williams, then Archbishop of Canterbury, and Pope Benedict XVI, the two leaders renewed the historic commitment to the goal of "full visible communion in the truth of Christ." ARC-USA continues its discussions through its current round of dialogue on the topic of reconciliation. A roster, directory of documentation, and other resources are available at arcusa.church.

OTHER ECUMENICAL RELATIONS
Evangelical Lutheran Church in Bavaria
Beginning in 2015, members of the Episcopal Church and the Evangelical Lutheran Church in Bavaria (Evangelisch-Lutherische Kirche in Bayern/ELKB) have conducted conversations about areas of shared mission and ministry, particularly in Europe. Observers from the Anglican Communion Office; the Inter-Anglican Standing Commission for Unity, Faith and Order; the Lutheran World Federation; the Convocation of Episcopal Churches in Europe; and the United Evangelical Lutheran Church of Germany have joined in these ongoing conversations. General Convention 2018's Resolution C059 commended "the process of exploring deeper relations and the dialogue toward full communion between The Episcopal Church and the ELKB." In 2022, the General Convention commended "Sharing the Gifts of Communion" (the Augsburg Agreement) for study throughout the church.

The Polish National Catholic Church
The Episcopal Church was in a relationship of full communion with the Polish National Catholic Church (PNCC) on the basis of the Bonn Agreement and a supplemental concordat of intercommunion by the 1946 General Convention. In 1978, the PNCC terminated this full communion agreement after the ordination of women in the Episcopal Church. The Episcopal Church did not take a similar action. In 2003, the PNCC ceased to be in communion with the Archbishop of Utrecht and is no longer a member of the Old Catholic Churches of the Union of Utrecht. The PNCC is a member of the World Council of Churches.

Episcopal Diocesan Ecumenical and Interreligious Officers
EDEIO is the national network of individuals designated by their diocesan bishops with special responsibility for encouraging the visible unity of Christ's Church and collegial relationships with members of other religions. It maintains a website (edeio.org) with a wide variety of resources, including the Ecumenical Handbook. EDEIO is also a sponsor of the annual National Workshop on Christian Unity (nwcu.org), a gathering of ecumenical officers from several denominations for education, formation, mutual encouragement, and worship. Each province of the Episcopal Church has an EDEIO-elected coordinator supporting regional ecumenical and interreligious work.

WORLD COUNCIL OF CHURCHES
The World Council of Churches (WCC) is a fellowship of churches which confess the Lord Jesus Christ as God and Savior according to the Scriptures and therefore seeks to fulfill together their common calling to the glory of the one God: Father, Son, and Holy Spirit. The WCC is constituted by member churches to serve the ecumenical movement. It incorporates the work of the world movements for Faith and Order and Life and Work, the International Missionary Council, and the World Council of Christian Education. The primary purpose of the fellowship of churches in the WCC is to call one another to visible unity in one faith and in one Eucharistic fellowship, expressed in worship and common life in Christ, through witness and service to the world. The WCC has more than 350 member churches. Almost every province of the Anglican Communion is included, together with most independent Orthodox churches and Protestant traditions. The Roman Catholic Church has sent official observers to all main WCC meetings since 1960. In the United States, most churches that belong to the National Council of Churches belong to the WCC.

NATIONAL COUNCIL OF CHURCHES OF CHRIST IN THE USA
The National Council of Churches (NCC) is a major expression in the U.S. of the movement toward Christian unity. The NCC's 38 member communions, including Protestant, Orthodox, and Anglican church bodies, work together on a wide range of activities that further Christian unity, that promote peace and justice, and that serve people throughout the world. The council was formed in 1950 by the action of representatives of the member churches and by the merger of 12 previously existing ecumenical agencies, each of which had a different program focus. Episcopalians participate annually in the NCC's Christian Unity Gathering and convening tables on Christian education, Faith and Order, and interreligious relations.

CHRISTIAN CHURCHES TOGETHER IN THE USA
In 2006, 34 churches and national Christian organizations officially formed the broadest fellowship of Christian churches and organizations in the U.S. Those participating as founding members represent the Episcopal Church, Orthodox, Roman Catholic, Evangelical, Pentecostal, and Charismatic churches, among others. Christian Churches Together (CCT) provides a context in which churches can develop relationships, share common work, make public witness, and pray together. Its website is christianchurchestogether.org.

CHURCHES UNITING IN CHRIST
After 40 years of study and prayer through the Consultation on Church Union (COCU), nine

churches—the African Methodist Episcopal Church, the African Methodist Episcopal Zion Church, the Christian Church (Disciples of Christ), the Christian Methodist Episcopal Church, the Episcopal Church, International Council of Community Churches, the Presbyterian Church (U.S.A.), the United Church of Christ, and the United Methodist Church—in 2002 agreed to start living their unity in Christ more fully through a relationship called Churches Uniting in Christ (CUIC). In 2006, the Moravian Church (Northern Province) became a full member. Each church maintains its own identity and decision-making structures, but each also pledges to draw closer in sacred things and common mission, especially the mission to combat racism. Recent work has focused on issues of racial justice among our churches. On Pentecost of 2017, a joint celebration in Dallas acknowledged and deepened this work while proclaiming the recognition of ministries among our member denominations. At the 2019 Assembly in Montgomery, CUIC called on to rethink its goals and purposes, identifying these foci for future work:

- to continue and expand the work of the Young Adult Task Force to include a component to equip additional young adults as ecumenical leaders

- to work with other organizations who promote grassroots activity to combat racism

- to envision a new structure for CUIC that will provide additional opportunities for bilateral and multilateral agreements among the member denominations. This work will be directed by the Coordinating Council, which includes three members from each member denomination.

CONSULTATION ON COMMON TEXTS

The Episcopal Church is a member of the Consultation on Common Texts, an ecumenical group of liturgical scholars and denominational representatives from the United States and Canada who produce liturgical materials and a three-year lectionary for common use by Christian churches worldwide. Through the CCT, the Episcopal Church is also represented in the international corollary body, the English Language Liturgical Consultation. Its website is www.commontexts.org.

INTERRELIGIOUS RELATIONS

The Episcopal Church's primary participation in interreligious dialogue focuses principally on:

- Ecumenical efforts with other Christians through the Interfaith Relations Commission of the National Council of Churches of Christ (NCC). The 1999 Assembly of the NCC unanimously approved a policy statement giving a theological rationale for participating

in interreligious dialogue; in 2019 the NCC issued a Policy Statement entitled "Interreligious Relations with a Focus on Peace;"

- International efforts through the Anglican Communion Office, including the Anglican Inter Faith Commission launched in 2017;

- Particular initiatives taken by the Presiding Bishop as primate of the church;

- Task force initiatives and programs created by Episcopal Church institutions, such as Episcopal Relief and Development;

- Diocesan, congregational, and individual efforts in peacemaking and interreligious dialogue and with the support of EDEIO;

- Participation in the interreligious organizations listed below, among others.

In 2003, the General Convention officially located oversight of the church's interreligious work with the Standing Commission on Ecumenical Relations, which was renamed the Standing Commission on Ecumenical and Interreligious Relations (SCEIR). During the 2006-2009 triennium, the Interreligious Relations Subcommittee of the SCEIR worked to develop a more substantive statement to clarify the theological and historical rationale for the Episcopal Church's interreligious engagement, and in 2009 a resolution was adopted by General Convention—and reaffirmed in 2012—establishing a canonical teaching on interreligious relations known as "Toward Our Mutual Flourishing." The SCEIR was reestablished by the 2022 General Convention. Updated guidelines for interreligious Muslim, and Jewish relations were circulated by the 2022 convention: https://www.edeio.org/about-interreligious-relations.html.

RELIGIONS FOR PEACE USA

The Episcopal Church actively participates in Religions for Peace USA (RfPUSA). Religions for Peace USA works to contribute to the well-being of civil society and to advance peace-building effort and reconciliation in the U.S. and internationally Religions for Peace USA is part of a network of Religions for Peace with nearly 100 affiliate globally. The Presiding Bishop is a member of the organization's Council of Presidents, and representatives from the Episcopal Church are members of its Executive Council. This organization website is at www.rfpusa.org.

THE ANTI-DEFAMATION LEAGUE

The Anti-Defamation League (ADL) was founded in 1913 "to stop the defamation of the Jewish people and to secure justice and fair treatment to all." is a major civil rights and human relations agency fighting anti-Semitism and all forms of bigotry. defends democratic ideals and protects civil rights for all. The Episcopal Church partners with the ADL in advocacy.

THE AMERICAN JEWISH COMMITTEE

The American Jewish Committee (AJC) is an international advocacy organization, founded in 1906 to protect the human rights of Jewish persons throughout the world. The AJC sends an observer to the General Convention of the Episcopal Church, and consults with the Episcopal Church's Office of Government Relations on matters of common interest and concern. The AJC's website is at www.ajc.org.

THE ISLAMIC CIRCLE OF NORTH AMERICA

Established in 1968, the Islamic Circle of North America (ICNA) is an umbrella organization focusing on development, education, outreach and social services. The Episcopal Church participates in conversation with ICNA through the National Council of Churches Muslim-Christian Dialogue. ICNA is online at www.icna.org.

THE ISLAMIC SOCIETY OF NORTH AMERICA

The goal of the Islamic Society of North America (ISNA), founded in 1982, is "to be an exemplary and unifying Islamic organization in North America that contributes to the betterment of the Muslim community and society at large." The Episcopal Church participates in conversation with ISNA through the National Council of Churches Muslim-Christian Dialogue, and has sent an observer to the General Convention of the Episcopal Church. The Episcopal Church also partners with ISNA in special events and educational initiatives. ISNA is online at www.isna.net.

SHOULDER TO SHOULDER

Shoulder to Shoulder (shouldertoshouldercampaign.org) is an interfaith organization dedicated to ending anti-Muslim sentiment by strengthening the voice of freedom and peace. Founded in November 2010 by over 20 national religious groups, Shoulder to Shoulder works not only on a national level, but offers strategies and support to local and regional efforts to address anti-Muslim sentiment and seeks

to spread the word abroad. Episcopalians serve on the steering committee of Shoulder to Shoulder and engage in advocacy work as well as the development of congregational resources.

BREAD FOR THE WORLD

Bread for the World (www.bread.org) provides nonpartisan policy analysis on hunger and strategies to end it. The Episcopal Church works with Bread for the World in its poverty and hunger initiatives. The Circle of Protection, of which the Episcopal Church is a member, is an alliance of Christian leaders working to monitor policy, legislation, and programs addressing the needs of the most vulnerable in society.

CHURCHES FOR MIDDLE EAST PEACE

Churches for Middle East Peace (CMEP) is a coalition of 27 national Church denominations and organizations in Catholic, Orthodox and Protestant traditions. Each of these denominations and organizations is represented on the CMEP Board of Directors, which sets CMEP's mission, positions and policy. Decisions are made by consensus of this group. The Episcopal Church is on the Executive Committee and the board of this organization. CMEP works to encourage U.S. policies that actively promote a just, lasting, and comprehensive resolution of the Israeli-Palestinian conflict, ensuring security, human rights and religious freedom for all the people of the region. The Episcopal Church primarily works through CMEP on Middle East-related policy advocacy. CMEP is online at cmep.org.

CHRISTIANS AGAINST CHRISTIAN NATIONALISM

The Episcopal Church is an endorser of the Christians Against Christian Nationalism campaign organized in 2019 by the Baptist Joint Committee for Religious Liberty. The Presiding Bishop's statement that "the violence, intimidation and distortion of scripture associated with 'Christian nationalism' does not reflect the person and teachings of Jesus Christ" can also be endorsed by individuals through the initiative's website at christiansagainstchristiannationalism.org.

Clergy List of The Episcopal Church

Any changes to this list should be addressed to the Recorder of Ordinations, Church Pension Group, 19 East 34th Street, New York, NY 10016.

The symbol ✠ indicates bishop.

CLERGY LIST

The names, addresses, and canonical residences in the Clergy List section are supplied by The Recorder of Ordinations and reflect changes reported by **31 December 2022**. Any request for a change in the Clergy List should be addressed to The Recorder of Ordinations, CHURCH PENSION GROUP, 19 East 34th Street, New York, NY 10016.

NECROLOGY
1/22-12/22

Bishops

CARR, William Franklin	8/7/22
FOLWELL, William Hopkins	2/7/22
HUNT III, George Nelson	10/23/22
KEYSER, Charles Lovett	7/31/22
LEE, Peter	7/2/22
LEIDEL JR, Ed	6/5/22
MACNAUGHTON, John Herbert	2/28/22
MCLEOD, Mary Adelia Rosamond	10/12/22

Priests and Deacons

ADAM, Betty	6/30/22
ADAMS, David Robert	5/18/22
ADAMS, Frank George	10/13/22
ALLEMEIER, James Elmer	7/6/22
ALLMAN, M K	12/27/22
ANDERSEN, Steven C	7/1/22
ANDERSON, Elizabeth May	12/21/22
ANDERSON, James Desmond	2/4/22
ANDERSON, William C	9/4/22
ANGLE, Nancy Scott	12/12/22
ANTHONY, Robert Williams	8/26/22
APPELBERG, Helen Marie Waller	4/21/22
APPLEYARD JR, Robert Bracewell	7/3/22
ARENTS, Gina	2/24/22
ARMER, MaryCay	12/24/22
ARNOLD, Robyn Elizabeth	7/5/22
ATKINSON JR, Joel Walter	11/7/22
AUSTIN, William Paul	1/17/22
AYERS, Phillip Wallace	5/25/22
BAKELY, Catherine Mae	8/11/22
BAKER, Robert	8/14/22
BARDOS, Gordon	2/3/22
BARTON, Charles Denis Hampden	6/26/22
BEACHY, William Nicholas	7/22/22
BECKER, Robert Andrew	5/3/22
BELLAIS, William	2/5/22
BENZ, Charles Frederick	10/15/22
BLOTTNER, William Eugene	4/16/22
BOATRIGHT-SPENCER, Angela	11/4/22
BOESSER, Mark Alan	10/13/22
BONADIE, Leroy Rowland	11/17/22
BOND, Jeremy	4/8/22
BOWERSOX, Ned Ford	7/31/22
BOWYER, Charles Lester	5/5/22

BRAMLETT, Bob	11/13/22
BRENTNALL, Burden	1/26/22
BRIDGES, Melva Gayle	6/11/22
BRILL, Steven G	5/5/22
BRISON, William Stanly	10/27/22
BROCKMAN, John Martin	8/25/22
BROUGHTON, William	9/22/22
BROWN, Ian Frederick	1/14/22
BUCK, Elizabeth Salmon	3/30/22
BUHRER, Richard Albert	10/5/22
BURCHILL, George Stuart	12/12/22
BURDETT, Audrey Brown	9/3/22
BUTLER, Barbara Thayer	3/11/22
BUTLER, Robert Mitchell	1/23/22
BUTTS, Stephen	9/4/22
CALDWELL, Edward F	5/22/22
CALDWELL, Steve	8/18/22
CALLAGHAN, Carol L	8/19/22
CANNON JR, Alberry Charles	10/27/22
CANNON, David Lawrence	3/22/22
CAREY, Peter R	12/3/22
CARLSON, Robert Warren	2/22/22
CARROLL, James Earle	1/16/22
CARSON, Boyd Rodney	11/5/22
CARTER, James Lee	2/25/22
CARTIER, Fred Claire	10/21/22
CASSELL JR, Mike	9/28/22
CHATTIN, Mark Haney	8/27/22
CHRISMAN JR, John Aubrey	6/23/22
CHRISTIANSEN, Anthony	6/19/22
CLAY, Thomas Davies	9/10/22
CLEMMONS, Geraldine Dobbs	4/26/22
COFFEY, E Allen	6/9/22
COIL, Doug	4/24/22
COLES, Constance C	8/10/22
COLLINS, Diana Garvin	5/31/22
COLLINS, Stanley Penrose	3/1/22
COOK, Carol	11/17/22
COOLIDGE, Ted	4/5/22
CORKERN, Matthew Thomas Locy	4/24/22
COX, Mildred Louise	5/14/22
CRAPSEY II, Marc	6/8/22
CREWDSON, Robert	7/27/22
CROCKER JR, John Alexander Frazer	7/10/22
CRUZ, Hector	9/18/22
DALMASSO, Judith Connie	2/3/22
DALTON JR, James Albert	7/28/22
DANIEL, Wilfred	12/28/22
DAUPHIN, Joanne Coyle	1/18/22
DEAN, Gordon Joy	8/17/22
DE FONTAINE-STRATTON, James	7/9/22

DEMING, Robert	7/11/22
DICKEY, Robert William	6/29/22
DICKS, Paul Richard	2/7/22
DUDLEY, Michael Devere	6/25/22
DURANT, Jack Davis	1/2/22
EDWARDS, Lloyd	2/21/22
EKLO, Thomas	11/17/22
EMERSON, James Carson	12/18/22
EMERY-GINN, Margaret Elizabeth	9/24/22
ENGLE, Cynthia L	7/2/22
ERICKSON JR, Joseph Austin	12/28/22
EVANS, John Frederick	11/30/22
EVERETT, Sherman Bradley	7/2/22
EXNER, William Edward	4/24/22
FAIRMAN, Henry Francis	4/29/22
FALCONE, John Francis	12/5/22
FENN, Richard Lewis	5/25/22
FENTON, David Henry	7/8/22
FENWICK, Robert Donald	4/28/22
FERNANDEZ-LIRANZO, Hipolito Secundino	11/14/22
FINCH JR, Floyd William	3/2/22
FINEANGANOFO, Sosaia Ala	1/6/22
FINKENSTAEDT JR, Harry Seymour	4/19/22
FISHER, Davis Lee	7/16/22
FITCH, William Babcock	11/1/22
FLYNN, Michael T	4/30/22
FORBES, David Reineman	4/26/22
FRANK, Beth	1/21/22
FREEMAN JR, Monroe	7/15/22
FREEMAN, Reed H	10/26/22
FRENSLEY, James Monroe	8/25/22
FREW, Randolph Lloyd	12/27/22
FRIEDRICH JR, Robert E	1/18/22
FRITTS, John Clinton	2/5/22
FULTON JR, Charles Britton	12/12/22
GADDY, Anna Lee	8/2/22
GERVAIS JR, Sidney Joseph	3/5/22
GIBSON, John Noel Keith	2/5/22
GILMER, Lyonel Wayman	9/23/22
GLAUDE, Ron	3/22/22
GOLDBLOOM, Ruth Alice	1/8/22
GRABHER, Jerald	10/12/22
GRAHAM, Pamela Louise	5/29/22
GRAY, Bruce	3/17/22
GRAY, Peter Hanson	6/3/22
GRECO, John Anthony	4/16/22
GREEN, David Edward	12/25/22
GREENE, Ed	3/12/22
GREENFIELD, Peter Alan	1/16/22
GRIFFIN, Calvin Russell	2/17/22
GROSS, Robert A	11/10/22
GRUBBS, Michael Conway	12/19/22
GUERNSEY, Jacqueline Louise	10/16/22
GWIN JR, Lawrence Prestidge	7/4/22
HAAS, Michael James	4/20/22
HABERKORN, Violet Marie	3/22/22
HAGUE, Sally	6/6/22
HALL, Allen Keith	12/24/22
HALL, Donald	3/15/22
HALL, Lisbeth Jordan	1/4/22
HAMILTON, David Hendry	8/23/22
HAMLYN, Robert Cornelius	12/3/22
HANCHEY, Howard	5/17/22
HANNA, William James	12/24/22
HARGIS, Jim	10/11/22
HARKINS, James Robert	5/27/22
HARRIS, Robert Charles	1/27/22
HARRIS, William Henry	2/5/22
HARRISON, Merritt Raymond	2/24/22
HASSERIES, Robert Alan	3/11/22
HAWES III, Charles M	7/18/22
HAYDEN, John Carleton	6/29/22
HAYS-SMITH, Melissa Beth	9/16/22
HAYWARD, Dennis Earl	8/31/22
HAZELETT, William Howard	12/6/22
HENKING, Patricia Ellen	8/18/22
HERRING, Dianne Lerae	6/2/22
HILL, Jerry Echols	1/30/22
HODGKINS, Nelson	8/15/22
HOFFACKER, Michael Paul Niblett	10/8/22
HOFFMANN, Beth	12/22/22
HOGAN, Faye	6/5/22
HOLLEY, Richard Hedge	8/9/22
HOLT, Timmothy	4/30/22
HOOVER, John	2/7/22
HOUSER, Lucy Anne Latham	1/16/22
HOWARD, Norman	9/16/22
HUBERT, Lawrence William	5/13/22
HUMMEL, Gini	2/1/22
HUNKINS, Claire	8/15/22
HUNT, Donald Aldrich	1/26/22
HUNTER, Kay Smith	9/14/22
HUNTER JR, Victor Edward	1/5/22
HUSBAND, John Frederick	6/30/22
HUTTON, Linda Arzelia	10/14/22
INNES, Neil Fraser	3/22/22
JACKSON, Jared Judd	3/28/22
JACKSON, Thomas Lee	1/8/22
JAMES, Robert Arthur	12/18/22
JAMES, William Evans	3/27/22
JASPER SR, John Weaver	4/7/22
JEFFERY, David Luce	5/17/22
JEWSON, Alfred Joseph	11/6/22
JOHNSON, Frances Kay	11/26/22
JOHNSON, Ira Joseph	8/20/22
JONES, Frederick Lamar	9/11/22
JONES, Peter Hoyt	11/13/22
JONES, Teresa Crawford	12/15/22
KARDALEFF, Patricia Payne	7/17/22
KARNEY JR, George James	7/7/22
KEESTER, John Carl	5/23/22
KELLETT, James William	1/20/22
KEMPSTER, Jane	3/12/22
KEMPSTER, Patricia Sue	5/5/22
KENNEY, Christine Swarts	5/14/22
KILLINGSTAD, Mary Louise	9/3/22
KIMMEY, Jimmye Elizabeth	2/3/22
KING, Robert A	7/31/22
KIRKMAN, John Raymond	7/7/22
KITAGAWA, Chisato	1/14/22
KLINE, John William	11/18/22
KNIGHT II, Steve	10/1/22
KOVIC, Fenton Hubert	1/18/22
KRAMER, Frederick Ferdinand	3/29/22
KUNZ JR, Andy	11/27/22
LANGI, Viliami	1/6/22
LARSEN, Erik	6/9/22
LEDYARD, Christopher Martin	3/24/22
LEE, Darry Kyong Ho	11/7/22
LEE, Shiane Marlena	12/30/22
LEHMANN, Richard B	7/11/22
LEWIS, Ken	1/20/22
LEWIS, Maurine Ann	2/13/22
LILLPOPP, Donald R	9/23/22
LINDSEY, Kenneth Lewis	4/28/22

LINK, Mike	12/19/22
LLOYD, James Edward	1/28/22
LLOYD III, Samuel Thames	8/31/22
LOUIS, Richard Mortimer	11/11/22
LOVE, Leon Lewis	1/31/22
LOW, Melvin Leslie	4/19/22
LOWE, Lori	4/25/22
LUCAS, Alison C	2/3/22
LUCKEY III, Thomas Hannan	12/20/22
LUSIGNAN, Louise Jennet	9/28/22
MACINTOSH, Neil Keith	10/26/22
MACNEICE, Alan Donor	5/20/22
MAGERS, James Hugh	11/3/22
MANGUM, Frank Burnett	6/26/22
MANNING, Ronald Francis	1/29/22
MAPPLEBECKPALMER, Richard Warwick	12/7/22
MARANVILLE, Joyce Margaret	8/18/22
MARQUAND, Betty Harlina	2/9/22
MARR, Jon Aidan	5/19/22
MARSH, Karl Edwin	12/3/22
MARSHALL, Carol Phillips	4/11/22
MARSHALL, Richard G	6/10/22
MARTIN, Terry L	6/5/22
MATLACK, David Russell	4/19/22
MAXWELL, William F	11/11/22
MCCABE III, Charles Peyton	11/2/22
MCCALL, Richard David	12/30/22
MCCALLUM, Bruce Allan	2/2/22
MCCLOSKEY JR, Robert Johnson	11/3/22
MCCLOUD, Linda	12/11/22
MCDOWELL, Harold Clayton	5/22/22
MCDOWELL, Lynn	5/16/22
MCGEE-STREET, Eleanor Lee	2/21/22
MCKEAN, Deborah Adams	4/23/22
MCLEOD, James Wallace	3/26/22
MCMANIS, Dennis Ray	4/26/22
MERRILL, George Richard	4/17/22
METZ, susanna	4/30/22
MILLER, Alden Scott	2/23/22
MINTURN, Sterling Majors	10/31/22
MONICA, Ted	6/5/22
MONTANARI, Albert Ubaldo	4/26/22
MONZON-MOLINA, Eduardo	8/20/22
MOORE, Kathleen Mary	2/18/22
MORGAN, Barbara Jean	5/30/22
MORGAN, Ed	12/13/22
MORGAN, Elaine Ludlum	9/27/22
MORRIS, Clayton L	10/24/22
MORRIS, Jim	4/24/22
MUSHORN, Richard C	8/6/22
MUSSATTI, David James	8/26/22
NARVAEZ, Alfonso Anthony	3/30/22
NATOLI, Anne Marie	5/9/22
NEAL, James Frederick	12/28/22
NEILSON, John Robert	5/4/22
NEUHAUS, Ted	3/14/22
NICHOLSON, Aleathia Dolores	10/20/22
NIEHAUS, Tom	12/29/22
NIESE JR, Alfred Moring	8/15/22
NORGREN, William Andrew	2/24/22
NYGREN, Adam	9/9/22
O'BRIEN, Charles Harold	1/25/22
ODA-BURNS, John Macdonald	1/1/22
OLSEN, David Logie	9/22/22
O'STEEN, Joe	6/7/22
PAIN, Mary Reed	5/13/22
PANASEVICH, Eleanor Jones	7/13/22
PARTRIDGE, Edmund Bruce	4/23/22
PAUL, Kenneth Wayne	10/9/22
PAULIS, Marion Helen	2/7/22
PEABODY, William Nelson	10/19/22
PEREZ JR, Juan Francisco	9/5/22
PETERSON, Ralph	6/7/22
PETLEY, Dale Alfred	6/24/22
PETTERSON, Ted Ross	11/8/22
PEVERLEY, Stephen Richard	10/25/22
PFAB, Martin William	8/24/22
PHELPS, Cecil Richard	6/17/22
PHILIPS, J Kevin	1/21/22
PICKUP JR, Ezra Alden	1/1/22
PINDER, Nelson Wardell	7/10/22
PITT JR, Louis Wetherbee	3/24/22
PLATT, Nancy	9/14/22
PLATT, Thomas Walter	2/14/22
POLK, Thomas Robb	9/24/22
POLLEY, Bonnie Bonnabel	8/5/22
PONG, Tak Yue	11/18/22
PORTER, Gerry	7/5/22
PORTERFIELD, David	8/14/22
PORTEUS, Bev	8/8/22
POTTER-NORMAN, Ricardo T	2/3/22
POWELL, David Richardson	12/11/22
POWELL JR, Festus Hilliard	11/13/22
PRITTS, Clarence Edward	10/29/22
PULLIAM, James Millard	8/28/22
PUMMILL, Joseph Howard	12/26/22
PUMPHREY, Margaret K	10/15/22
QUINN, Eugene Frederick	11/27/22
RADKE, Pamela Kay	11/3/22
RAMSDEN, Charlie	2/7/22
RANKIN II, William Wright	7/22/22
REARDIN, Lois Arline	2/25/22
REEVES, Frank	12/28/22
REINECKE, Rod	12/27/22
RETTGER, John Hubbard	2/13/22
RHODES, Diane Lynn	9/14/22
RIEBE, Norman W	5/17/22
ROBBINS, Anne Wilson	3/23/22
ROBILLARD, Roger Manuel	3/5/22
RODGERS, Robert Christopher	12/23/22
ROEGER JR, William Donald	6/16/22
ROLLINSON, John	2/21/22
ROOS, Carl	4/3/22
ROSS, Robert Layne	4/7/22
SALLEY JR, George Bull	8/10/22
SAMMONS, Margaret Holt	8/3/22
SCHACHT, Lawrence Arthur	11/25/22
SCHROETER, George Hieronymus	4/28/22
SCHWAB, Wayne Wayne	5/19/22
SCOTT, Nolie Edward	11/2/22
SEARS, Gwen W	8/12/22
SEAY, Donald Robert	5/31/22
SEIBERT, Thomas E	8/8/22
SELL, Jim	9/30/22
SERACUSE, Linda	11/12/22
SERPA-ORDONEZ, Pedro Abel	11/1/22
SHOBERG, Warren E	12/20/22
SHOULDERS, David	7/16/22
SINGLETON, Lester Brian	6/25/22
SIVRET, David Otis	11/23/22
SIX, George	12/27/22
SLACK, James Cooper Simmons	3/26/22
SMITH, Bardwell Leith	11/28/22
SMITH, Charles L	5/19/22
SMITH, Edwin Ball	8/4/22
SMITH, Harold Vaughn	11/2/22

SMITH, Myrl Elden	4/30/22
SMITH, Perry Michael	7/20/22
SMITH, Philip Kingsley	12/27/22
SMITH, Ralph	12/24/22
SPAID, William John	3/20/22
SPARKS-LUNDELIUS, Heulette C	5/7/22
SPEARS, Melanie Lea	5/10/22
SPEIR, Susan	5/15/22
SPENCER, Bob	1/25/22
SPRUHAN, John Halsey	2/5/22
STANTON JR, Barclay Reynolds	2/7/22
STEELE, Nancy J	4/5/22
STELK, Lincoln Frank	6/6/22
STERLING, Franklin Mills	12/11/22
STIEFEL, Jennifer H	6/9/22
STIEPER, John Richard	10/25/22
STIVERS, Donald Austin	6/28/22
ST JOHNS, Ernest Keys	10/26/22
STOCKARD, Matthew	3/13/22
STONE, Sandra Elizabeth	2/4/22
STRIMER, Peter	10/18/22
STUART, Charles Moore	9/28/22
SULLIVAN, Herbert Patrick	6/6/22
SURUDA, Teresa Ann	10/4/22
SYMONDS, John W	6/19/22
SZYMANSKI, Walter	10/19/22
THIGPEN III, Mac	9/20/22
THOMPSON, Robert Gaston	1/12/22
TIFFANY, Roger Lyman	7/15/22
TIPTON, Harry Steadman	9/10/22
TROEGER, Thomas Henry	4/3/22
TRUMBORE, Frederick Rhue	1/23/22
TUOHY, James Fidelis	4/8/22
TUTTLE, Peggy Elaine Wills	4/3/22
TWO BULLS, Robert G	2/5/22
TWO HAWK, Webster Aaron	10/21/22
VANDERSLICE, Thomas Arthur	4/24/22
VAN SCOYOC, Gardner Warren	8/9/22
VERRETTE, Sallie Cheavens	1/6/22
VIE, Diane	6/15/22
VINCE, Gail Lynne	1/28/22
WARD JR, Herbert Arthur	5/31/22
WARD IV, Samuel Mortimer	7/28/22
WARRINGTON, James Malcolm	8/17/22
WEAVER, Roger Warren	9/22/22
WEBSTER, Edwin Crowe	6/28/22
WEDDLE, Karl G	8/3/22
WEIL, Louis	3/9/22
WEST JR, Irvin D	3/29/22
WESTERHOFF III, John Henry	2/25/22
WHELAN, Edgar Joseph	11/13/22
WHELAN, Peter H	10/1/22
WHISENHUNT, Bill	1/28/22
WHITE, Warner Clock	4/16/22
WHITEFORD, Cecily S	4/22/22
WILDER III, Tracy	1/6/22
WILKINS, Palmer Oliver	3/22/22
WILLIAMS, Gary Wayne	2/20/22
WILLIAMS, Priscilla Mudge	6/14/22
WILSON, Linda Latham	8/24/22
WILSON, Steven Clark	2/14/22
WILSON, Thomas Stuart	2/28/22
WING III, Arthur K	8/1/22
WINGERT JR, John Alton	11/26/22
WINTERS JR, Charles Layfaette	5/17/22
WISSINK, Charles Jay	1/21/22
WOGGON, Harry	11/26/22
WORLEY, James Paul	7/6/22

WRIGHT, Jeannene F	9/11/22
WRIGHT, John Robert	1/12/22
YAO, Ting Chang	7/9/22
YUROSKO, Steven	6/15/22
ZIMMERMAN, Jervis Sharp	2/27/22

CLERGY RECEIVED FROM CHURCHES IN FULL COMMUNION 1/22-12/22

BECK, Douglas A (Angl Ch of Can)	4/1/22
CONNOLLY, Catherine Hannah Victoria (Ch Of Engl)	5/11/22
GALLES, Jonathan Wesley (Angl Ch of Can)	2/9/22
HALL, Natalie (Evang Luth Ch in Amer)	10/4/22
HILL III, James Allen (Iglesia Anglicana del Cono Sur de Amer)	4/13/22
JOSEPH, Yves-Eugene (Angl Ch of Can)	4/14/22
KERR, Donald G (Ch in the Prov Of The W Indies)	2/1/22
KIM, Kyrie (Angl Ch Of Korea)	7/15/22
NJOKU, Benjamin (Ch Of Nigeria)	5/22/22
OWUOR, Shadrack (Angl Ch Of Kenya)	10/29/22
SAMUEL, Joshua (Ch of So India)	8/24/22
SMITH-FIRESTONE, Tammy (Iglesia Anglicana del Cono Sur de Amer)	3/8/22
STEPHEN, Christopher (Angl Ch Of Pakistan)	4/28/22
WALL, Dawna D (Angl Ch of Can)	3/31/22
WALLACE, Charles F (Angl Ch of Can)	7/19/22

CLERGY RECEIVED FROM CHURCHES IN HISTORIC SUCCESSION 1/22-12/22

ANDERSON, Jack D (RC)	10/30/22
COOK, Millard S (RC)	8/20/22
GARNETT, Andrew M (RC)	4/23/22
GONZALEZ, Emilio (RC)	1/31/22
KELLEY, Patrick (The Orth Ch in Amer)	10/2/22
LATOUR, Charles H (RC)	6/15/22
LOPEZ BOLANOS, Eddy E (RC)	6/30/22
MORRIS, Stephen Michael (The Orth Ch in Amer)	5/15/22
PLEKON, Michael P (Gk Orth)	3/27/22
REEVES, Thomas Daniel (Angl Ch in No Amer)	7/14/22
WHARFF GALVIS, Arian Hernando (RC)	2/19/22

RESTORATIONS 1/22-12/22

ANDERSON SCHUTZ, Ann Johnston (ND)	5/5/22
KRAMER, Beaman K (SwVa)	6/14/22
SILVA-GONZALEZ, Alvaro (PR)	9/4/22

SUSPENSIONS
1/22-12/22

OECHSEL JR, Russell Harold (Tex)   10/27/22

DEPOSITIONS
1/22-12/22

BATES, Percy Quin (La)   7/29/22
LEATHERMAN, Daniel Lee   10/21/22
  (The Episcopal Church in Haw)
MARSHALL, Robert K (SVa)   11/2/22
SHOEMAKE, Daniel O (At)   2/21/22
WATTS, Timothy Joe (At)   2/21/22

REMOVALS
1/22-12/22

ADAMS-RILEY, Gena D (Fla)   10/26/22

AGIM, Emeka (Tex)   3/24/22
ALLISON, Christopher FitzSimons (SC)   10/31/22
BATARSEH, Peter B (Tenn)   4/4/22
CLEMENTS, Michael Stuart (Okla)   5/6/22
COMPTON, David O (SwVa)   6/16/22
CORDOBA, Guillermo (Fla)   10/26/22
DALY, Richard R (Dal)   10/26/22
DEPRIEST, Sandra Moss (Miss)   12/7/22
DICKINSON, Garrin William (Dal)   2/8/22
GRAY, Marie Therese (FdL)   7/18/22
HATHAWAY, Alden Moinet (SC)   10/31/22
HYBL, Andrew David (Cal)   5/17/22
KANNENBERG, James Gordon (Ia)   12/2/22
KAVAL, Lura (Va)   2/23/22
LOEWEN-SAMUELS, Joshua (Fla)   8/24/22
LOVELESS, Phillip Lyman (SanD)   8/23/22
MACMILLAN, Cameron P (CFla)   8/18/22
SHEVLIN, James Charles (CFla)   2/17/22
SPICER, John Tildsley (Fla)   9/21/22
THEODORE, Margaret Bessie (Alb)   5/16/22
VANDERMARK, Roy James (Alb)   12/5/22
WHITE, Kevin Gerard (WMo)   3/22/22

CLERGY:
BISHOPS, PRIESTS, AND DEACONS

The names, addresses, and canonical residences in the Clergy List, as well as the preceding lists (Necrology, Receptions, Transfers, Restorations, Suspensions, Depositions, Removals), are supplied by The Recorder of Ordinations and reflect changes reported by 31 December 2022. Any request for a change in the Clergy List should be addressed to The Recorder of Ordinations, CHURCH PENSION GROUP, 19 East 34th Street, New York, NY 10016.

A

AALAN, Joshua Canon (Pa) 2013 Appletree St, Philadelphia, PA 19103
AARON, Stephen Craig (Wyo) 618 Saunders Cir, Evanston, WY 82930
AARON LUDWIG, Stephanie (Wyo)
ABBOTT, Gail Eoline (Mil)
ABBOTT SR, Gary Louis (Ga) 2028 Maggie Dr, Macon, GA 31204
ABBOTT, Grant H (Minn) 2163 Carter Ave, Saint Paul, MN 55108
ABBOTT, James Michael (Tex) 1723 Mechanic St, Galveston, TX 77550
ABBOTT, Samuel Bassett (Alb) 1 Church St, Cooperstown, NY 13326
ABBOTT, Sefton Frank James (WNC) 27 Hildebrand St, Asheville, NC 28801
ABDELNOUR, Mark Anthony (USC) St Simon St Jude Epis Ch, 1110 Kinley Rd, Irmo, SC 29063
ABDY, Anne (EC) 2106 Sapling Ct, Wilmington, NC 28411
ABELL, Jesse (WTenn) 1720 Peabody Ave, Memphis, TN 38104
ABELL, Jessica Tankersley (WTenn)
ABER, Jack Albert (Chi) 522 Portsmouth Cir, Doylestown, PA 18901

ABERNATHEY, James Milton (Tex) 1903 E Bayshore Dr, Palacios, TX 77465
ABERNATHY, Paul (WA) 1050 Willis Rd, Spartanburg, SC 29301
ABERNATHY JR, W Harry (NY) 50 Bedford Rd, Armonk, NY 10504
ABERNETHY-DEPPE, David Edward (Cal) 19938 Josh Pl, Castro Valley, CA 94546
ABERNETHY-DEPPE, Jonathan (Cal) 2322 Oakcrest Dr, Palm Springs, CA 92264
ABEYARATNE, Keshini Anoma (Mass) 4 Greenough Cir, Brookline, MA 02445
ABIDARI, Mehrdad (Cal) Cathedral School for Boys, 1275 Sacramento St, San Francisco, CA 94108
ABRAHAM, Billie (Miss) P.O. Box 921, Vicksburg, MS 39181
ABRAHAM, Hebert (Hai)
ABRAHAM, John Laurence (Az) 9138 N Palm Brook Dr, Tucson, AZ 85743
ABRAHAMSON, Wendy (Ia) St Pauls Episcopal Church, 1026 State St, Grinnell, IA 50112
ABRAMS, Mary Elizabeth (Ky) 4100 Southern Pkwy, Louisville, KY 40214

ABRAMS, Ronald (EC) 3309 Upton Ct, Wilmington, NC 28409
ABREU ABREU, Jose Martin Altagracia (DomRep)
ABSHIER, Patsy Ann (Kan) Po Box 1175, Wichita, KS 67201
ABSHIRE, Lupton P (Colo) St. Gregory's Episcopal Church, 6653 W. Chatfield Avenue, Littleton, CO 80128
ABSTEIN II, WIlliam Robert (Tenn) 9210 Sawyer Brown Rd, Nashville, TN 37221
ABT, Audra (NC) 2105 W Market St, Greensboro, NC 27403
ABUCHAR CURY, Rafael (Colom)
ACCIME, Max (Hai) C O Lynx Air, PO Box 407139, Fort Lauderdale, FL 33340
ACEVEDO, Miriam (NH) 92 Nashua Rd, Pelham, NH 03076
ACEVEDO, Sheila Devine (SeFla) St. Andrew's Episcopal Church, 100 N Palmway, Lake Worth, FL 33460
ACKAAH, Vincent Abisi (NY) PO Box 950a, Bronx, NY 10451
ACKER, Patricia Small (CFla) PO Bo 290245, Pt Orange, FL 32129
ACKERMAN, Chase Dumont (Ala) 202 Gordon Dr SE, Decatur, AL 3560

ACKERMAN, Patricia Elizabeth (NY) 86 Piermont Ave, Nyack, NY 10960

ACKERMAN, Peter (Episcopal SJ) PO Box 70, 37501 Zach Fowler Rd, Chaptico, MD 20621

ACKERMAN, Thomas Dieden (Mil) 4875 Easy St, Unit # 12, Hartland, WI 53029

ACKERMANN, Frauke (Eur)

ACKERMANN, John Frederick (Oly)

ACKERMANN, Lutz (Eur) Garmischer Str 2A, Augsburg, 86163, Germany

ACKERSON, Charles Garrett (LI) PO Box 113, Mastic Beach, NY 11951

ACKLAND III, Lauren (Nwk) 321 N Wyoming Ave Apt 1b, South Orange, NJ 07079

ACKLEY, Susan M (NH) 28 River St, Ashland, NH 03217

ACOSTA PORTA, Yordanis (Cu)

ACOSTA RODRIGUEZ, Richard (Colom)

ACOSTA-ZAPATA, Pedro Jose (Mil)

ADAIR, Carl C (LI)

ADAIR, Maryly S (The Episcopal NCal)

ADAM, Barbara Ann (Kan) 10500 W 140th Ter, Overland Park, KS 66221

ADAM, John Todd (Neb) 2621 County Road 59, Alliance, NE 69301

ADAMIK, George F (NC) 221 Union St, Cary, NC 27511

ADAMO, Michele (RI)

ADAMS, Chris (EC) 231 Amberleigh Dr Apt 102, Wilmington, NC 28411

ADAMS JR, David Morrison (Spr)

ADAMS, Deanna Sue (U) 603 W 2350 S, Perry, UT 84302

ADAMS, Debra Jeanne (Ida)

ADAMS, Eloise Ellen (Ct) 495 Laurel Hill Rd Apt 4B, Norwich, CT 06360

ADAMS JR, Enoch (Ak)

ADAMS III, Gladstone Bailey (CNY) The TEC Ch in S Ca, PO Box 20485, Charleston, SC 29413

ADAMS JR, H Stanford (Tex) Good Shepherd, 3201 Windsor Rd, Austin, TX 78703

ADAMS, Helen Kandl (CFla) 103 Shady Branch Trl, Ormond Beach, FL 32174

ADAMS, James Harold (Roch) 517 Castle St, Geneva, NY 14456

ADAMS JR, James Marshall (FdL) 428 W Cobblestone Loop, Hernando, FL 34442

ADAMS, Jennifer Lin (WMich) 536 College Ave, Holland, MI 49423

ADAMS JR, Jesse Roland (La) 6306 Prytania St, New Orleans, LA 70118

ADAMS, Jim (NC) 120 E Edenton St, Raleigh, NC 27601

ADAMS, John (SwVa) 422 W 2nd St, Grand Island, NE 68801

ADAMS, John Stockton (ECR) 24745 Summit Field Road, Carmel, CA 93923

ADAMS, Jonathan Vaughn (Va) 9108 John S Mosby Hwy, Upperville, VA 20184

ADAMS, Lesley (Roch) 6200 Mount Rd, Trumansburg, NY 14886

ADAMS, Margaret Louise (Tenn) 411 Annex Ave Apt F1, Nashville, TN 37209

ADAMS, Mary Lynn (FdL)

ADAMS, Patricia Wessels (Ak) 3506 Cherokee Dr S, Salem, OR 97302

ADAMS, Samuel Bowman (Dal) 4715 Harding Pike, Nashville, TN 37205

ADAMS JR, Thomas Edwin (Mass) PO Box 522, Falmouth, MA 02541

ADAMS, Timothy Boyd (Miss) 5155 Wayneland Dr Apt B, Jackson, MS 39211

ADAMS, William C (Ky)

ADAMS, William J (The Episcopal NCal) 95 Malaga Ct, Ukiah, CA 95482

ADAMS, William Rian (CGC) 6329 Frederica Rd, St Simons Island, GA 31522

ADAMS, William Seth (Oly) 2707 Silver Crest Ct, Langley, WA 98260

ADAMS-HARRIS, Anne Jane (Wyo) Po Box 4086, Santa Barbara, CA 93140

ADAMS-MASSMANN, Jennifer Helen (Eur)

ADAMSON, Tom (NI) 909 S Darling St, Angola, IN 46703

ADAMS-RILEY, Wallace (USC) 33 Bromes Way, Greenville, SC 29607

ADAMS-SHEPHERD, Kathleen E (Mo) Christ Church Cathedral, 1210 Locust St, Saint Louis, MO 63103

ADAMS-THOMPSON, Larry (Tex)

ADDIEGO, Jeffrey Clark (Nev) 1429 Bronco Rd, Boulder City, NV 89005

ADDINGTON, Matt (NC) 309 Robert Keever Rd, Stanley, NC 28164

ADDISON, Orlando J (CFla) 6990 S US Highway 1, Port St Lucie, FL 34952

ADE, Daniel Gerard George (Los) 252 Vineyard Rd, Huntington, NY 11743

ADEBONOJO, Mary Bunton (Pa) 50 Bagdad Rd, Durham, NH 03824

ADELIA, Laura A (Az) 100 W Roosevelt St, Phoenix, AZ 85003

ADER, Thomas Edmund (At) 3596 Liberty Ln, Marietta, GA 30062

ADERS, Magdalena Mary (NJ) 18 Ryers Ln, Matawan, NJ 07747

ADESSA, Denise Mcgovern (Ct) 311 Broad St, Windsor, CT 06095

ADINOLFI, Debora (At) 9180 E Sunset Point Rd, Tucson, AZ 85749

ADINOLFI JR, Jerry (Kan) 131 Country Estates Rd, Greenville, NY 12083

ADKINS JR, Robert Frederick (CNY) 956 Graylea Cir, Elmira, NY 14905

ADLER, John Stuart (SwFla) 1406 S Larkwood Sq, Fort Myers, FL 33919

ADLER, Paul (Pa) 6769 Ridge Ave, Philadelphia, PA 19128

ADOLPHSON, Donald Richard (Cal) 552 Old Orchard Dr, Danville, CA 94526

ADORNO ANDINO, Hector Luis (PR) Ch TEC PR, PO Box 902, Saint Just, PR 00978

ADWELL, Lynn (Minn) 334 E Fremont Dr, Tempe, AZ 85282

ADZIMA, Melissa (Colo) 307 Western Sky Cir, Longmont, CO 80501

AFANADOR-KAFURI, Hernan (Ala) 176 Ridgewood Dr., Remlap, AL 35133

AFFER, Licia (SeFla) 3098 Saint Annes Ln NW, Atlanta, GA 30327

AGAR JR, Ralph Wesley (Neb) 2315 Georgetown Pl, Bellevue, NE 68123

AGBAJE, John (SO) 1 Paddle Ct, Portsmouth, VA 23703

AGBO, Godwin (Ct) 61 Grove St, Putnam, CT 06260

AGGELER, Harold Griffith (Ida)

AGNER, Georgia Ellen (Eau) 17823 57th Ave, Chippewa Falls, WI 54729

AGNEW, Christopher Mack (Va) 12433 Richards Ride, King George, VA 22485

AGNEW JR, ML (WLa) 1903 Royal Oak Dr, Tyler, TX 75703

AGUILAR, Lisa (Neb)

AGUILAR, Norman (Hond)

AGUILAR FAJARDO, Ana Roselia (Hond)

AHLENIUS, Robert Orson (Dal) 2541 Pinebluff Drive, Dallas, TX 75228

AHLVIN, Judith L (ECR) 18325 Crystal Dr, Morgan Hill, CA 95037

AHN, Matthew Y (Los) 10555 Bel Air Dr, Cherry Valley, CA 92223

AHN, Paul C (Chi) 5801 N Pulaski Rd #348, Chicago, IL 60646

✠ **AHRENS**, Laura (Ct) 2 Cannondale Dr, Danbury, CT 06810

AHUJA, Lisa S (WA) 833 W Wisconsin Ave, Milwaukee, WI 53233

AIDNIK, Aileen Marie (The Episcopal NCal) 988 Collier Dr, San Leandro, CA 94577

AIKEN JR, Charles Duval (Va) 4210 Hanover Ave, Richmond, VA 23221

AIKIN, William Carter (Spr)

AIN, Judith Pattison (ECR) 286 Thompson Rd Rear, Watsonville, CA 95076

AINSLEY, Matthew Brian (CFla)

AINSWORTH, Mark J (Pa) 262 Bent Road, Wyncote, PA 19095

AIS, Jean (Hai) Eglesi Episcopal DHaiti, Boite Postale 1309, Port-au-Prince, Haiti

AJAX, Kesner (Hai) C/O Agape Flights Acc. #2519, 100 Airport Avenue, Venice, FL 34285

AKAMATSU, Mary Catherine (Ala) St Matthew's Episcopal Church, 786 Hughes Rd, Madison, AL 35758

AKER, Edwina (Mont) 32413 Skidoo Ln, Polson, MT 59860

AKES, Amanda Ann (WA) Grace Church, 1607 Grace Church Rd, Silver Spring, MD 20910

AKIN, Mary Anne ANNE (Ala) 8546 Sawyer Brown Rd, Nashville, TN 37221

AKINKUGBE, Felix Olagboye (Tex) 2995 Celian Dr, Grand Prairie, TX 75052

✠ **AKIYAMA**, Diana D (Ore) PO Box 44915, Kamuela, HI 96743

AKRIDGE, Alan M (Ga) 108 Worthing Rd, St Simons Island, GA 31522

ALAGNA, Frank J (NY) Po Box 1, Rhinecliff, NY 12574

ALAN, Stacy (Chi) 5540 S Woodlawn Ave, Chicago, IL 60637

ALAVA VILLAREAL, Geronimo (Litoral Diocese Of Ecuador) Casilla 0901-5250, Guayaquil, Ecuador

ALBANO, Randy (The Episcopal Church in Haw) St Pauls Episcopal Church, 229 Queen Emma Sq, Honolulu, HI 96813

ALBARRAN, Rodolfo A (Ve)

ALBERCA MERINO, Francisco Venito (Eur) Via Napoli 58, Roma Italy, 00184, Italy

ALBERGATE, Scott P (Pa) 249 N Belfield Ave, Havertown, PA 19083

ALBERS, Barbara Ann (RG) 8540 S Southpoint Rd, Empire, MI 49630

ALBERT II, Edwin Edward (SO) 1924 Timberidge Dr., Loveland, OH 45140

ALBERT, Hilario (NY) 535 King St, Port Chester, NY 10573

ALBERT III, Jules Gilmore (La) 6249 Canal Blvd, New Orleans, LA 70124

ALBERTI, Brian Christopher (Fla)

ALBINGER JR, Bill (The Episcopal Church in Haw)

ALBINSON, Thomas R (Mo)

ALBOM, Sandra Janet (NH) 51 Concord St, Peterborough, NH 03458

ALBRETHSEN, Karen Anne (Nev) 777 Sage St, Elko, NV 89801

ALBRIGHT, J Taylor Taylor (Ct) 525 Suffield St, Agawam, MA 01001

ALBRIGHT, Meredyth L (FdL)

ALBRIGHT, Timothy Scott (Be) 383 N Hunter Hwy, Drums, PA 18222

ALDANA ROJAS, Javier (Colom)

ALDAY, Kristen Nowell (CFla) 1017 E Robinson St, Orlando, FL 32801

ALDER, Steve (Los) 2215 Molino Ave Apt A, Signal Hill, CA 90755

ALDRICH, Dawn Marie (NMich) 1310 Ashmun St, Sault Sainte Marie, MI 49783

ALDRICH JR, Kenneth Davis (NJ) 400 4th St, Huntingdon, PA 16652

ALDRICH, Robert Paul (NMich)

ALEJANDRO, Yesenia (Pa)

ALEXANDER, Brantley (Ind)

ALEXANDER, Conor Matthew (SVa)

ALEXANDER, Gerald G (Fla) 4311 Ortega Forest Dr, Jacksonville, FL 32210

✠ **ALEXANDER**, J Neil (At) 3100 Kramer Ln Apt 216, Austin, TX 78758

ALEXANDER JR, J Randolph (Va) 3606 Seminary Rd, Alexandria, VA 22304

ALEXANDER, Jane Biggs (WLa) 2015 E Northside Dr, Jackson, MS 39211

ALEXANDER, Jason (Ark) The⁻ Episcopal Diocese of Arkansas, PO Box 164668, Little Rock, AR 72216

ALEXANDER, John David (RI) 974 Pine St, Seekonk, MA 02771

ALEXANDER, Kathryn Bellm (Ark) CHRIST CHURCH, 509 Scott St, Little Rock, AR 72201

ALEXANDER, Patricia Phaneuf (WA) 3600 Seminary Rd, Alexandria, VA 22304

ALEXANDER, Sharon (WTenn) 692 Poplar Ave, Memphis, TN 38105

ALEXANDER, Stephen Gray (Lex) 5300 Hamilton Ave Apt 906, Cincinnati, OH 45224

ALEXANDER, William David (Okla)

ALEXANDRE, Hickman (LI) 260 Beaver Dam Rd, Brookhaven, NY 11719

ALEXANDRE, Soner (CFla)

ALEXIS, Alicia (NC) PO Box 20427, Greensboro, NC 27420

ALEXIS, Judith (Ct) 7 Allen Oneill Dr # B, Darien, CT 06820

ALFORD JR, Ben (Ala) 680 Calder St, Beaumont, TX 77701

ALFORD, Billy J (Ga) 3520 Woodlake Rd, Hephzibah, GA 30815

ALFORD, Joseph Stanley Trowbridge (Kan) 2618 W 24th Terrace, Lawrence, KS 66047

ALFORD, William T (CPa) 302 S Liberty St, Centreville, MD 21617

ALFORD-HARKEY, April L (Ct)

ALGERNON, Marcel (SwFla) 1700 NW 27th St, Cape Coral, FL 33993

ALICEA SOTO, Leida Iris (PR)

ALIER, John (Dal)

ALIMOLE, Chisara Rose (NY) 1415 Pelhamdale Ave, Pelham, NY 10803

ALLAGREE, The Rev Harry R (The Episcopal NCal) 361 Lincoln Avenue, Cotati, CA 94931

ALLAIN, Thomas A (Miss) 615 18th St S, Birmingham, AL 35233

ALLARD, Bradley Richard (WMich) 1145 N Hampton Dr NE, Grand Rapids, MI 49505

ALLEE, Roger G (SeFla) 2212 S Cypress Bend Dr Apt 107, Pompano Beach, FL 33069

ALLEMAN, Timothy Lee (Be) 20b Buckingham St, Luzerne, PA 18709

ALLEN, Abraham Claude (Mass) 17 Winthrop St, Marlborough, MA 01752

ALLEN, Charles William (Ind) 4118 Byram Ave, Indianapolis, IN 46208

ALLEN, David Edward (Mass) PO Box 1052, Barnstable, MA 02630

ALLEN, Donald Frederick (Ct) 34 Ashlar Vlg, Wallingford, CT 06492

ALLEN, Earl Michael (Nwk) 55 George St, Allendale, NJ 07401

ALLEN II, George Curwood (SO) 988 Duxbury Ct, Cincinnati, OH 45255

ALLEN, Jennifer Marie (Kan)

ALLEN JR, John (Ky) 1512 Valley Brook Rd, Louisville, KY 40222

ALLEN, John Shepley (NH) 229 Shore Dr, Laconia, NH 03246

ALLEN, John Tait (Mil) 515 Oak St., South Milwaukee, WI 53172

ALLEN, Joyce Corbin (NC) 300 Finsbury St Apt 204, Durham, NC 27703

ALLEN, Lainie Acridge (Ore)

ALLEN, Larry J (WMo) 3212 S Jeffrey Cir, Independence, MO 64055

✠ **ALLEN**, Lloyd Emmanuel (Hond) Diocese of Honduras, PO Box 523900, Miami, FL 33152

ALLEN, Mark (The Episcopal NCal) 5872 Oliver Rd, Paradise, CA 95969

ALLEN, Mary (Del) 12395 SE Main St, Portland, OR 97233

ALLEN, Megan A (O)

ALLEN, Morgan S (Mass) 3201 Windsor Rd, Austin, TX 78703

ALLEN, Robert Edward (Ark) 109 N Fork Dr, Sherwood, AR 72120

ALLEN, Roger D (At) 175 Wright St SW, Marietta, GA 30064

ALLEN, Russell Harvey (Ct) 28 Seaward Ln, Harwich, MA 02645

ALLEN, Stephanie Perry (NC) Church of the Nativity, 8849 Ray Rd, Raleigh, NC 27613

ALLEN, T Scott (Be) 713 Cherokee St, Bethlehem, PA 18015

ALLEN, W Frank (Pa) 763 Valley Forge Rd, Wayne, PA 19087

ALLEN-FAIELLA, Willie (SeFla) 16745 SW 74th Ave, Miami, FL 33157

ALLEN-HERRON, Dawn (Ak) 3886 S Tongass Hwy, Ketchikan, AK 99901

ALLEY, Ann Leonard (Spr) 913 W Washington St, Champaign, IL 61821

ALLEY, Charles Dickson (Va) 1101 Forest Ave, Richmond, VA 23229

ALLEY, Marguerite Cole (SVa) 1917 Indian Run Rd, Virginia Beach, VA 23454

ALLEYNE, Edmund Torrence (LI) 972 E 93rd St, Brooklyn, NY 11236

ALLICK, Paul Delain (Cal) 162 Hickory St, San Francisco, CA 94102

ALLIN, Hailey Wile (Miss) PO Box 1366, Jackson, MS 39215

ALLING JR, Roger (Ct) 125 N 28th St, Camp Hill, PA 17011

ALLISON II, Charles Roy (CFla) 453 Palm Ave, Ormond Beach, FL 32174

ALLISON, John Leroy (Me) PO Box 186, Hulls Cove, ME 04644

ALLISON, Judith (SanD)

ALLISON, Marcia A (CFla) 453 Palm Ave, Ormond Beach, FL 32174

ALLISON, Marianne Stirling (Ore) 3012 Club House Ct, West Linn, OR 97068

ALLISON, Nancy Jean (NC) 3110 Belvin Dr, Raleigh, NC 27609

ALLISON-HATCH, Mary Susan (RG) 1625 Escalante Ave SW, Albuquerque, NM 87104

ALLMAN, Denny Paul (Miss) 8008 Bluebonnet Blvd Apt 13-2, Baton Rouge, LA 70810

ALLMAN, Susan (U) 1016 E H Cedar Highland Dr, Cedar City, UT 84720

ALLPORT II, Bill (Nwk) 113 Engle St, Englewood, NJ 07631

ALLRED, Jennifer Allison (Minn) 901 Portland Ave, Saint Paul, MN 55104

ALLTOP, Bob (Mich) Cathedral Church of St Paul, 4800 Woodward Ave, Detroit, MI 48201

ALMENDAREZ BAUTISTA, Javier E (NC)

ALMODIEL JR, Arsolin Diones (Nev) Dioces of Nevada, 9480 S Eastern Ave, Las Vegas, NV 89123

ALMON JR, Austin Albert (RI) 116 Daggett Ave, Pawtucket, RI 02861

ALMONO ROQUE, Joel (Mass) 1524 Summit Ave, Saint Paul, MN 55105

ALMONTE, Salvador (DomRep) Calle Santiago #114 Gazcue, Santo Domingo, Dominican Republic

ALMOS, Richard Wayne (La) 996 Marina Dr, Slidell, LA 70458

ALMQUIST, Curtis Gustav (Mass) St John the Evangelist, 980 Memorial Dr, Cambridge, MA 02138

ALONGE-COONS, Katherine Grace (Alb) Grace Church, 34 3rd St, Waterford, NY 12188

ALONSO COLOMAR, Rodhin (Cu)

ALONSO MARINA, Jesus Daniel (EcuC) Ava Y Maldonado, Guayaquil, Ecuador

ALONZO, Mary Parsons (Roch) 541 Linden St, Rochester, NY 14620

ALONZO MARTINEZ, Gerardo (Hond)

ALSAY, Joseph Caldwell (Okla) 14700 N May Ave, Oklahoma City, OK 73134

AL-SHATTI, Patrice (Az)

ALTENBACH, Julie Kay (CFla)

ALTIZER, Aimee Marie (U) PO Box 1081, Red Lodge, MT 59068

ALTIZER, Caryl Jean (WTenn) 1830 S 336th St Apt C-202, Federal Way, WA 98003

ALTON, Frank (Los) 840 Echo Park Ave, Los Angeles, CA 90026

ALTON, Richard (Pa) St. Clement's Church, 2013 Appletree Street, Philadelphia, PA 19103

ALTOPP, Whitney F (Ct) 355 Main St, Ridgefield, CT 06877

ALVARADO FIGUEROA, Luis A (PR)

ALVARADO-PALADA, Carlos (Hond)

ALVAREZ, Jose Antonio (Episcopal SJ)

ALVAREZ, Miguel (WNC) 5383 E Owens Ave, Las Vegas, NV 89110

ALVAREZ-ADORNO, Aida (PR)

✠ **ALVAREZ-VELAZQUEZ**, David Andres (PR) 4735 Ave Isla Verde, Villas del Mar Oeste Apt 3-E, Carolina, PR 00979

ALVAREZ VELEZ, Sergio Leon (Colom) Cra 6 #49-85, Bogota, Colombia

ALVES, David Alan (The Episcopal NCal) 13840 Tulsa Ct, Magalia, CA 95954

ALVES, Robert (EC) St Johns Episcopal Church, 302 Green St, Fayetteville, NC 28301

ALVEY JR, John Thomas (Ala) 110 W Hawthorne Rd, Birmingham, AL 35209

ALWINE, David W (Tex) 527 Shem Butler Ct, Charleston, SC 29414

AMADIO, Carol M (FdL) PO Box 51, Washington Island, WI 54246

AMANOR-BOADU, Yvonne (Kan)

AMAYA MARTINEZ, Ana Victoria (Hond)

AMBELANG, John (Eau) 506 Fairway Dr, Sheboygan, WI 53081

AMBLER JR, Michael (Me) 912 Middle St, Bath, ME 04530

AMBROISE, Rospignac (Mass) Box 1309, Port-Au-Prince, Haiti

AMBROSE, Barbara (Va) 236 S Laurel St, Richmond, VA 23220

AMBROSE, Colin Moore (Tenn) 116 N. Academy St., Murfreesboro, TN 37130

AMBROSE, Theodore (CPa) 2609 N Glebe Rd # P, Arlington, VA 22207

AMBROSE, Val Twomey (WMich) 6308 Greenway Dr SE, Grand Rapids, MI 49546

AMBURGEY, Cristina Goubaud (Oly) 3213 17th Street Pl Se, Puyallup, WA 98374

AMEND, Russell Jay (WNY) 25 Caspian Ct, Amherst, NY 14228

AMERMAN, Lucy SL (Pa) PO Box 57, Buckingham, PA 18912

AMES, David A (RI) 200 Exchange St Unit 517, Providence, RI 02903

AMES, Richard Kenneth (SeFla) 4917 Ravenswood Dr Apt 1709, San Antonio, TX 78227

AMMONS JR, B Wiley (Fla) 7500 Southside Blvd, Jacksonville, FL 32256

AMPAH, Rosina A (NY) 3042 Eagle Dr, Augusta, GA 30906

AMPARO TAPIA, Milton (DomRep) Juan Luis Franco Bido #21, Santo Domingo, Dominican Republic

AMSDEN, Helen Prince (Neb) 9459 Jones Cir, Omaha, NE 68114

AMUZIE, Charles (WA) 3601 Alabama Ave SE, Washington, DC 20020

ANAYA, Chan (NAM) 1115 Main St, Vicksburg, MS 39183

ANCHAN, Israel D (Los) 298 S. Harrison Ave., Kankakee, IL 60901

ANCONA, Andrew Joseph (NC)

ANDERS, Florence Kay (RG) 8 Well Tank Rd, Santa Fe, NM 87508

ANDERSEN, John Day (CNY) 2702 W Old State Road 34, Lizton, IN 46149

ANDERSEN, Judith Ann (NMich) 500 Ogden Ave, Escanaba, MI 49829

ANDERSEN, Paul (Va) 905 Runaway Bay, Trent Woods, NC 28562

ANDERSEN, Raynor Wade (Ct) 199 Eastgate Dr, Cheshire, CT 06410

ANDERSEN, Richard Belden (Nwk) 275 E Franklin Tpke, Ho Ho Kus, NJ 07423

ANDERSON, Alicia F (WTenn)

ANDERSON, Alissa Goudswaard (SwFla) 802 Broadway, New York, NY 10003

ANDERSON, Angela Mary (Nev) 2908 Laverton Dr, Las Vegas, NV 89134

ANDERSON, Augusta (WNC) 2 Cedarcliff Rd, Asheville, NC 28803

ANDERSON, Becky (RI) 719 Hope St Apt 1, Bristol, RI 02809

ANDERSON JR, Bert A (Los) 612 Chestnut St, Ashland, OR 97520

ANDERSON, Betsy (Los) 315 Lorraine Blvd, Los Angeles, CA 90020

ANDERSON, Bettina Galer (Colo) 822 Fox Hollow Ln, Golden, CO 80401

ANDERSON, Bill (At) 2510 Two Oaks Dr, Charleston, SC 29414

ANDERSON, Carmen Marie (Kan) 375 Lake Shore Drive, Alma, KS 66401

ANDERSON, Carol (NY) 115 E 87th St Apt 16b, New York, NY 10128

ANDERSON, Christian S (SeFla) St Marys Episcopal Church, 623 Se Ocean Blvd, Stuart, FL 34994

ANDERSON JR, Claude Newell (At) 1884 Rugby Ave, College Park, GA 30337

✠ **ANDERSON**, Craig (SD) PO Box 1316, Ranchos De Taos, NM 87557

ANDERSON, David (Pa) Saint Luke's Parish, 1864 Post Rd, Darien, CT 06820

ANDERSON, Devon (Minn) 4644 Upton Ave S, Minneapolis, MN 55410

ANDERSON, Douglas Evan (Mass) 413 Olive St, Texarkana, TX 75501

ANDERSON, Douglas Reid (Mont) 408 Westview Dr, Missoula, MT 59803

ANDERSON JR, E Bernard (Md) 3800 Rodman St NW Apt 304 Apt 304, Washington, DC 20016

ANDERSON, Eldon Wayne (Episcopal SJ) P O Box 146, 18232 Smoke St, Jamestown, CA 95327

ANDERSON III, Elenor Lucius 'Andy' (Ala) 1008 Broadmont Ter, Falls Church, VA 22046

ANDERSON, Eric A (WMo) 2001 Windsor Dr, Newton, KS 67114

ANDERSON, Gene (SwVa) 5631 Warwood Dr, Roanoke, VA 24018

ANDERSON, Gordon James (Ind) 2522 E Elm St, New Albany, IN 47150

ANDERSON, Hannah (NH) 54 Dunklee St, Concord, NH 03301

ANDERSON, Howard (Los) PO Box 37, Pacific Palisades, CA 90272

ANDERSON, Jack D (Del)

ANDERSON, James Arthur (Mil) 10041 Beckford St, Pickerington, OH 43147

ANDERSON, James Russell (WA) 3111 Ritchie Rd, Forestville, MD 20747

ANDERSON, Jami (Wyo) PO Box 847, Pinedale, WY 82941

ANDERSON, Jennie (Vt) PO Box 265, Norwich, VT 05055

ANDERSON, Jerry (Los) PO Box 271, Herrin, IL 62948

ANDERSON, Joan Wilkinson (ECR) 425 Carmel Ave, Marina, CA 93933

ANDERSON, John Peter (ND)

ANDERSON, Jon (SVa) 663 Douglas St, Chattanooga, TN 37403

ANDERSON, Judith Kay Finney (Mont) 408 Westview Dr, Missoula, MT 59803

ANDERSON, Juliana Collins (Mass) 620 Old Creamery Rd, Williston, VT 05495

ANDERSON, Karen Elizabeth (At)

ANDERSON, Karen Sue (Neb) 1517 Broadway Ste 104, Scottsbluff, NE 69361

ANDERSON III, Lennel Vincent (Eau) 2081 Husband Rd, Somerset, PA 15501

ANDERSON, Linda Lee (Wyo)

ANDERSON, Louise Thomas (NC) 901 N Main St, Tarboro, NC 27886

ANDERSON, Marilyn Lea (Ct) 180 Cross Hwy, Redding, CT 06896

ANDERSON, Mark S (Fla)

ANDERSON, Martha (SanD) P. O. Box 334, Del Mar, CA 92014

ANDERSON, Mary Kathleen (Minn)

ANDERSON, Mary Petty (Oly) 10450 NE Yaquina Ave, Bainbridge Island, WA 98110

ANDERSON, Mary Sterrett (O) 7250 Harris Farm Road, Chagin Falls, OH 44023

ANDERSON, Megan Elizabeth (The Episcopal NCal) 10697 Biscay Way, Rancho Cordova, CA 95670

ANDERSON, Michael Eddie (Chi) 1225 Asbury Ave, Evanston, IL 60202

ANDERSON, Nathaniel (WMass) 35 Park St, Williamstown, MA 01267

ANDERSON, Otto Suen (SO) 409 E High St, Springfield, OH 45505

ANDERSON III, Paul Kemper (At) PO Box 85, 302 West Ave, Cedartown, GA 30125

ANDERSON, Philip Alden (O) 7250 Harris Farm Dr, Chagrin Falls, OH 44023

ANDERSON, Polly Chambers (WLa) 4037 Highway 15, Calhoun, LA 71225

ANDERSON JR, Ralph W (WMass) 114 Lake St, Shrewsbury, MA 01545

ANDERSON, Richard John (NY) 2635 2nd Ave Apt 203, San Diego, CA 92103

ANDERSON, Robert Jay (WVa) 1006 Frostwood St, Huntsville, TX 77340

ANDERSON, Robert Melville (CFla) 350 Lake Talmadge Rd., Deland, FL 32724

ANDERSON, Rosemarie (ECR) 355 Redwood Dr, Boulder Creek, CA 95006

ANDERSON, Scott Crawford (Mont) St Peters Cathedral, PO Box 819, Helena, MT 59624

ANDERSON, Scott Keith (CFla)

ANDERSON JR, Theodore Lester (NJ) 127 West Liebig Ave, Egg Harbor City, NJ 08215

ANDERSON, Tim (Neb) P.O. Box 64, Ashland, NE 68003

ANDERSON, Tony (Neb)

ANDERSON, Tracy Lynn (EO)

ANDERSON, Vicky Lyn (WMo)

ANDERSON III, William Marcellus (NY)

ANDERSON SCHUTZ, Ann Johnston (ND) 2405 W Country Club Dr S, Fargo, ND 58103

ANDERSON-SMITH, Susan (Az) Third Floor, 232 E 11th St, New York, NY 10003

ANDOH, Samuel (Pa) 1121 Serrill Ave, Yeadon, PA 19050

ANDONIAN, Kathryn Ann (Pa) 942 Masters Way, Harleysville, PA 19438

ANDRE, Wildaine (Hai)

ANDRES, Justo Rambac (Episcopal SJ) 115 E Miner Ave, Stockton, CA 95202

ANDRES, Michael James (NH) 239 South Rd, Deerfield, NH 03037

ANDRES, Tony (Ind) 795 Elk Mountain Rd, Afton, VA 22920

ANDREW, Carol (Ga) 3042 Eagle Dr, Augusta, GA 30906

ANDREW SR, Robert Nelson (O) 3800 W 33rd St, Cleveland, OH 44109

ANDREW-MACONAUGHEY, Debra Elaine (SeFla) 111 W Indies Dr, Ramrod Key, FL 33042

ANDREWS, Alfred John (Neb) PO Box 141, Sidney, NE 69162

ANDREWS III, Andy (Miss) 1086 Avondale St, Jackson, MS 39216

ANDREWS, Arthur Edward (Ore) 350 SE 48th Ave, Portland, OR 97215

ANDREWS, Carl Machin (Colo) The Diocese of Colorado, 1300 Washington Street, Denver, CO 80203

ANDREWS JR, David Tallmadge (Del) 732 Nottingham Rd, Wilmington, DE 19805

ANDREWS, David Thomas (WA) 500 Merton Woods Way, Millersville, MD 21108

ANDREWS, Dianne (Oly) 1613 California Ave SW Apt 301, Seattle, WA 98116

ANDREWS II, George Edward (SeFla) 20 Vine St, Marion, MA 02738

ANDREWS III, Jake (Spok)

ANDREWS, John (Colo) 5968 S Zenobia Ct, Littleton, CO 80123

ANDREWS, John Anthony (NY) PO Box 547, Lima, NY 14485

ANDREWS, Lyde Coley (Ga) St Philips Episcopal Church, 302 E General Stewart Way, Hinesville, GA 31313

ANDREWS, Pati Mary (Va) 8217 Roxborough Loop, Gainesville, VA 20155

ANDREWS, Shirley May (Mass) 2 Palmer St, Barrington, RI 02806

ANDREWS-WECKERLY, Jennifer N (SVa) 8300 Richmond Rd, Toano, VA 23168

ANDRUS, Archie Leslie (HB) 2701 Bellefontaine St, Houston, TX 77025

✠ **ANDRUS**, Marc (Cal) Tec Dio Of Ca, 1055 Taylor St, San Francisco, VA 20118

ANDUJAR, Alexander (SwFla)

ANEI, Abraham Muong (WMich)

ANGELICA, David M (Mass) 1218 Heatherwood, Yarmouth Port, MA 02675

ANGELL, Debra Lanning (Colo) 13866 W 2nd Ave, Golden, CO 80401

ANGELL, Mike (Mo) 7401 Delmar Blvd, Saint Louis, MO 63130

ANGELO, Jean Marie (NY)

ANGELO, Patrice Lonnette (Los) 1818 Monterey Blvd, Hermosa Beach, CA 90254

ANGERER JR, John David (La) 112 Hazel Dr, River Ridge, LA 70123

ANGLIN, Dante' (Spr)

ANGULO ZAMORA, Gina (Litoral Diocese Of Ecuador)

ANGUS, David E (Ark) Grace Cathedral, 415 W 13th St, Kansas City, MO 64105

ANGUS SR, Joslyn Lloyd (Ga) 88 Oakwood Dr, Hardeeville, SC 29927

ANSCHUTZ, Mark Semmes (Mass) 162 Pleasant Street, South Yarmouth, MA 02664

ANSCHUTZ, Maryetta Madeleine (Los) 111 Louisiana Circle, Sewanee, TN 37375

ANTHONY, Benjamin J (SeFla)

ANTHONY, Carol (Pa) 4961 Buttonbush Dr, Durham, NC 27712

ANTHONY, Catherine (Va)

ANTHONY, Joan (Oly) 1549 Mw 57th St, Seattle, WA 98107

ANTHONY JR, Joseph Daniel (At) 389 Dorsey Cir Sw, Lilburn, GA 30047

ANTHONY, Lloyd Lincoln (LI) 115 Willow Ln, Valley Stream, NY 11580

ANTHONY-CHARLES, Ana Graciela (Ve)

ANTOCI, Peter M (WA) 3117 Perry St, Mount Rainier, MD 20712

ANTOLINI, Holly Lyman (Mass) 11 Quincy St, Arlington, MA 02476

ANTRIM, Nancy Mae (RG)

ANTTONEN, Jennifer Parker (Ida) 288 E Kite Dr, Eagle, ID 83616

ANUSZKIEWICZ, Sarah Elisabeth (WNY) St Paul's Episcopal Church, 4275 Harris Hill Rd, Williamsville, NY 14221

ANZILOTTI, Laurie Niemann (Mo) 816 S Hanley Rd Apt 15a Unit 15a, Saint Louis, MO 63105
APARICIO, Paul Douglas (FdL)
APOLDO, Deborah D (USC)
APONTE-SAFE, Gerardo Joel (Mich)
APPLEGATE, Stephen Holmes (SO) 117 S Plum St, Granville, OH 43023
APPLEQUIST, Alice Mae (Minn) 17221 Highway 30 Se, Chatfield, MN 55923
APPLETON, Mary Ellen (CFla) 200 Saint Andrews Blvd, 1406, Winter Park, FL 32792
APPLEYARD, Dan (Mo) 9 S Bompart Ave, Webster Groves, MO 63119
APPLEYARD, Jonathan Briggs (Me) 26 Montsweag Rd, Woolwich, ME 04579
APPLING, Elizabeth Faragher (Oly) St Pauls Episcopal Church, PO Box 753, Port Townsend, WA 98368
APPOLLONI, Sharyn L (Nev) 1965 Golden Gate Dr, Reno, NV 89511
ARACK, Mara (The Episcopal NCal) St Francis Episcopal Church, 568 16th St, Fortuna, CA 95540
ARAICA, Alvaro (Chi) 4609 Main St, Skokie, IL 60076
ARAKAWA, Andrew (The Episcopal Church in Haw)
ARAMBULO, Arnulfo (NY) 231 City View Ter, Kingston, NY 12401
ARAQUE GALVIS, Alirio (PR) Ch Tec Pr, PO Box 902, Saint Just, PR 00978
ARBOGAST, Stephen Daniel Kirkpatrick (WA) St Marks School of Texas, 10600 Preston Rd, Dallas, TX 75230
ARBOLEDA, Guillermo Alejandro (Ga)
ARBUCKLE, Jacquelyn Fenelon (Vt) 54 Morse Pl, Burlington, VT 05401
ARCENEAUX, George (Mil)
ARCHER, Carolyn (Ct)
ARCHER, John Richard (Cal) 80 Harmon St, Hamden, CT 06517
ARCHER, Jonathan Gurth Adam (SeFla) 3481 Hibiscus St, Miami, FL 33133
ARCHER, Nell B (LI) 199 Carroll St, Brooklyn, NY 11231
ARCHIBALD, David Jost (Del) 32216 Bixler Rd, Selbyville, DE 19975
ARCHIBALD, David Roberts (WTex) 6110 NW Loop 410, San Antonio, TX 78238
ARCHIE, Andrew John (Mo) 6345 Wydown Blvd, Saint Louis, MO 63105
ARCINIEGA, Roberto (Ore) 2065 SE 44th Ave Apt 248, Hillsboro, OR 97123
ARD JR, Robert (WNC) 6518 Michigan Ave, St. Louis, MO 63111
ARD, Roger Hoyt (At) 104 Sequoia Dr SE, Rome, GA 30161
ARDREY, Lindsey R (La)

ARDREY-GRAVES, Sara (NC) St Paul Episc Church, 520 Summit St, Winston Salem, NC 27101
ARELLANO, Donna (Oly)
ARENAS TORO, William Henry (Colom)
ARGUE, Douglas (SO) 22 Glencoe Rd, Columbus, OH 43214
ARIAS, Javier Enrique (NC)
ARLEDGE JR, Thomas Lafayette (At) 909 Massee Ln, Perry, GA 31069
ARLIN, Charles (Nwk) 1078B Long Beach Blvd, Long Beach Twp., NJ 08008
ARMENTROUT, Katharine Jacobs (At) 202 Griffith Rd, Jasper, GA 30143
ARMER, Susan Charlee (Az) 10064 E Durham Rd, Dewey, AZ 86327
ARMIDON, Hannah (Spr) Oaks Of Rtns Tec Min, 2331 15th St, Troy, NY 12180
ARMIDON, Robert Edward (Spr) 417 E Washington St, Riverton, IL 62561
ARMINGTON, Shawn Aaron (NJ) 118 Jefferson Rd, Princeton, NJ 08540
ARMOND, Andrew D (Tex)
ARMSTRONG, Barbara Keegan (NC) 509 Sleepy Valley Rd, Apex, NC 27523
ARMSTRONG, Elizabeth (The Episcopal NCal) 1008 Linier Ct, Roseville, CA 95678
ARMSTRONG, Geoffrey Macgregor (NY) 10 Lanes End, Mervin Village, NH 03850
ARMSTRONG, Michael N (Fla) 12581 Mandarin Road, Jacksonville, FL 32223
ARMSTRONG, Phyllis (SO) 2841 Urwiler Ave, Cincinnati, OH 45211
ARMSTRONG, Richard Sweet (Mass) 35 Old Fields Way, Castine, ME 04421
ARMSTRONG, Susan J (The Episcopal NCal) 1765 Virginia Way, Arcata, CA 95521
ARMSTRONG, William H (WVa) 320 Old Bluefield Rd, Princeton, WV 24740
ARMSTRONG, Zenetta (Mass) 58 Crawford St Apt 2, Dorchester, MA 02121
ARMY, Virginia (Ct) 5 Winslow Rd, PO Box 268, Little Compton, RI 02837
ARNASON, Tryggvi Gudmundur (WNC) 130 39th Avenue Pl NW, Hickory, NC 28601
ARNEY, Carol Mary (The Episcopal Church in Haw) 2542 Date St Apt 402, Honolulu, HI 96826
ARNHART, James Rhyne (Tenn) 1710 Riverview Dr, Murfreesboro, TN 37129
ARNING, Robert W (Tenn) 411 W Due West Ave, Madison, TN 37115
ARNOLD, Beth Kelly (Los) 5863 Caradco Rd, Winston Salem, NC 27106
ARNOLD, Christopher John (FdL) St Andrew's, 828 Commercial Street, Emporia, KS 66801

ARNOLD, Donna J (Alb) 4 Pine Ledge Ter, Gansevoort, NY 12831
ARNOLD, Duane Wade-Hampton (NY) 5815 Lawrence Dr., Indianapolis, IN 46226
ARNOLD, Kimball Clark (Az) 3150 Spence Springs Rd, Prescott, AZ 86305
ARNOLD, Margaret L (Mass) 149 High St Apt 1, Wareham, MA 02571
ARNOLD, Robert D (WNY) 29 University Park, Fredonia, NY 14063
ARNOLD, Scott A (Ala) 1204 Valridge N, Prattville, AL 36066
ARNOLD, Susan Louise (ECR) Cdsp, Morro Bay, CA 93442
ARNOLD, William Bruce (SwFla) 114 Fairway Ct, Greenwood, SC 29649
ARNOLD JR, William Stevenson Maclaren (Nev) 1855 Baring Blvd Apt 301, Sparks, NV 89434
ARNOLD-BOYD, Annette (Oly) 12420 SW Tremont St, Portland, OR 97225
ARPEE, Stephen Trowbridge (WA) 7416 Spring Village Dr Apt 112, Springfield, VA 22150
ARRINGTON, Sandra Clark (Roch) 20 Trumbull Ln, Pittsford, NY 14534
ARROSSA, Jean Pierre (RG)
ARROYO, Jose Del Carmen (Chi) 25291 W Lehmann Blvd, Lake Villa, IL 60046
ARROYO, Margarita E (WTex) 7528 Crimson Shade St, Austin, TX 78744
ARROYO-SANCHEZ, Jose (PR)
ARRUNATEGUI, Herbert (CFla) 3468 Capland Ave, Clermont, FL 34711
ARSENE, Andrea Thornton (Ind)
ARSENIE, Linda Sue (Az)
ARTHUR, Amelia Ruth (Va) 3918 Hanover Ave, Richmond, VA 23221
ARTHUR, Anne Tilley (The Episcopal NCal) 2620 Capitol Ave, Sacramento, CA 95816
ARTHUR, Richard Winston (At) 6780 James B Rivers Dr, Stone Mountain, GA 30083
ARTMAN, Melinda May (Be) 638 Stevenson St, Sayre, PA 18840
ARTRESS, Lauren (Cal) 309 Coleridge St, San Francisco, CA 94110
ASEL, John Kenneth (WTex) 225 Yorktown Blvd, Kerrville, TX 78028
ASGILL, Edmondson Omotayo (CFla) 381 N Lincoln St, Daytona Beach, FL 32114
ASH JR, Evan Arnold (Kan) 1114 E Northview St, Olathe, KS 66061
ASH, Linda D (EMich) 111 S Shiawassee St, Corunna, MI 48817
ASH, Patricia Bryan (Los)
ASHBY, Alice Kay Neel (O) 344 Shepard Rd, Mansfield, OH 44907
ASHBY, Joe (O) 402 Channel Rd, N Muskegon, MI 49445
ASHBY, Julia Sizemore (SVa) 4205 Cheswick Ln, Virginia Beach, VA 23455
✠ ASHBY, Lucinda Beth (ECR) 1858 W Judith Ln, Boise, ID 83705

ASHBY, Stephen Neel (O) 7000 Fullerton Ave, Cleveland, OH 44105

ASHCRAFT, Brandon Cole (O)

ASHCROFT, Ernie (Minn) 4015 Sunnyside Rd, Edina, MN 55424

ASHCROFT, Mary Ellen (Minn) PO Box 1093, Grand Marais, MN 55604

ASHER, Charles William (Los)

ASHFORD, Raphiell (USC) 643 Beasley Rd, Jackson, MS 39206

ASHLEY, Danae (Oly) 111 NE 80th St, Seattle, WA 98115

ASHMORE, Christopher Lee (Spr) 17 Forest Park W, Jacksonville, IL 62650

ASHMORE JR, Robert Michael (WNC) PO Box 956, Mars Hill, NC 28754

ASIS, Debra (Az) 12111 N La Cholla Blvd, Oro Valley, AZ 85755

ASKEW, Jerry Wayne (ETenn) 600 S Chestnut St, Knoxville, TN 37914

ASKEW, Patricia Tanzer (Wyo)

ASKEW, Stephen (Wyo) 203 Heathcote Rd, Hendersonvlle, NC 28791

ASMAN, Mark Elliott (Los) 1500 State St, Santa Barbara, CA 93101

ASONYE, Collins (Va)

ASSON, Marla Lynn (Nev) Holy Cross/ St Christopher, 3740 Meridian St N, Huntsville, AL 35811

ASTARITA, Susan Gallagher (WA) PO Box 816, Del Mar, CA 92014

ASTLEFORD, Elise Linder (Oly) 2515 NE 80th St, Vancouver, WA 98665

ASTON, Geraldine Patricia (Ala) 544 S Forest Dr, Homewood, AL 35209

ATAMIAN, Thomas Michael (Chi) 272 Presidential Ln, Elgin, IL 60123

ATCHLEY, Joyce Eileen (EO)

ATCITTY, Janice Nacke (Ida) Po Box 388, Fort Hall, ID 83203

ATEEK, Sari N (WA) 6701 Wisconsin Ave, Chevy Chase, MD 20815

ATELON, Marie P (NY)

ATEM, Garang Gabriel (U) 1710 S Foothill Dr, Salt Lake City, UT 84108

ATHEY JR, Ken (Del) PO Box 88, 10719 Grove St, Delmar, DE 19940

ATKINS, Elisabeth L (Neb)

ATKINS, Hannah (Tex) Trinity Episcopal Church, 1015 Holman St, Houston, TX 77004

ATKINS JR, Henry (NJ) 3210 Louisiana St Apt 1413, Houston, TX 77006

ATKINS, James Jackson (RG)

ATKINS, Janet (USC)

ATKINS, John Merritt (SO) 5800 Cantella Ct, Dayton, OH 45429

ATKINSON, Andrew James (EC) 321 Pettigrew Dr, Wilmington, NC 28412

ATKINSON, Kate Bigwood (NH)

ATKINSON, Mark W (Fla) 7801 Lone Star Rd, Jacksonville, FL 32211

ATTEBURY, Rich Earl (EO) Po Box 123, Lostine, OR 97857

ATWOOD, Mary Hill (Los) 546 Bradford Ct, Claremont, CA 91711

AUBERT, Keri T (Ct) 830 Whitney Ave, New Haven, CT 06511

AUBREY, Norman Edward (WMass) 5 College View Hts, South Hadley, MA 01075

AUCHINCLOSS, R Anne (NY) 250 W 94th St # 4F, New York, NY 10025

AUCHINCLOSS, Susan Carpenter (NY) 2342 Glasco Tpke, Woodstock, NY 12498

AUELUA, Royston Toto'A Stene (The Episcopal NCal) 6963 Riata Dr, Redding, CA 96002

AUER, Dorothy Kogler (NJ) 320 Glenburney Dr Apt 106, Fayetteville, NC 28303

AUER, Nancy Ann (NMich)

AUGHENBAUGH, Kelly Anne (O) 18001 Detroit Ave, Lakewood, OH 44107

AUGUSTE, Pierre (Hai)

AUGUSTE, Roldano (Hai)

AUGUSTIN, Dale Lee (Nev) 422 Red Canvas Pl, Las Vegas, NV 89144

AUGUSTINE, Anne Logan (Va)

AUGUSTINE, Peter John (Eau) 111 9th St N, La Crosse, WI 54601

AULENBACH JR, Bil (The Episcopal Church in Haw) The Groves 59, 5200 Irvine Blvd, Irvine, CA 92620

AULETTA, Kimberlee (NY)

AULT, Jessica (WA)

AURAND, Benjamin Kyte (Tex) 2421 Gate 11 Rd, Two Harbors, MN 55616

AUSA, Raul Ernesto (Nwk)

AUSTIN, Dorothy Ann (Nwk) Harvard Yard, Cambridge, MA 02138

AUSTIN, Evette Eliene (Alb) 9 E Main St, Canton, NY 13617

AUSTIN, Henry Whipple (Neb) 4509 Anderson Cir, Papillion, NE 68133

AUSTIN, Jean E (Vt) 545 Shore Road, Digby, NS B0V 1A0, Canada

AUSTIN, Margaret (Colo) 2526 Gates Cir Apt 2611, Baton Rouge, LA 70809

AUSTIN, Victor Lee (Dal) 3966 Mckinney Ave, Dallas, TX 75204

AUSTIN, Wilborne Adolphus (Ct) 18 Richard Rd, East Hartford, CT 06108

AUSTIN, William Bouldin (CFla) 3508 Lakeshore Dr SW, Smyrna, GA 30082

AUSTIN-YOUNG, Kira (Tenn) 650 Masonic Ave Apt 4, San Francisco, CA 94117

AVCIN, Janet Elaine (CPa) 228 Charles St, Harrisburg, PA 17102

AVENI JR, James Vincent (NwT) Po Box 1064, Clarendon, TX 79226

AVERY, Daniel Thomas (SVa) 15231 ROYAL CREST DR #306, Haymarket, VA 20169

AVERY, Gail (NH) Seafarer's Friend, 77 Broadway, Chelsea, MA 02150

AVERY, Joyce Marie (Oly) 1022 Monte Elma Rd, Elma, WA 98541

AVERY, Steven Walter (Ore) PO Box 2617, Florence, OR 97439

AVILA, Ricardo (ECR) 20 University Ave, Los Gatos, CA 95030

AVILA-NATIVI, Rigoberto (NY) PO Box 3786, Poughkeepsie, NY 12603

AVRIL, Wilky (Hai)

AWAN, Abraham Kuol (Chi) 7100 N Ashland Blvd, Chicago, IL 60626

AXBERG, Keith (Mont) Trinity Church Jeffers, PO Box 336, Ennis, MT 59729

AYALA TORRES, Carlos Anibal (EcuC) Bogota S/N Jose Vicente T, Guayaquil, Ecuador

AYBAR-MARTE, Pantaleon (PR)

AYER, Kelly Lane (Roch) 10 Park Pl, Avon, NY 14414

AYERBE, Reynaldo (SwFla) 4012 Penhurst Park, Sarasota, FL 34235

AYERS, Barbara (Alb)

AYERS, Gregory Garrett (USC)

AYERS, John Cameron (Cal) 13601 Saratoga Ave, Saratoga, CA 95070

AYERS, Margaret (WLa) St James Episcopal Church, PO Box 494, Port Gibson, MS 39150

AYERS, Mary L (Spok) 7315 N Wall St, Spokane, WA 99208

AYERS, Robert Curtis (CNY) 6010 E. Lake Rd., Cazenovia, NY 13035

AYERS, Russell C (Mass) 3737 Seminary Rd, Alexandria, VA 22304

AYRES, Steve (Mass) 104 Ridge Rd, PO Box 1340, Basalt, CO 81621

AZAR, Antoinette Joann (Tenn) 316 Stone Creek Dr, Cookeville, TN 38501

AZARIAH, Khushnud (Los) 6563 East Ave, Etiwanda, CA 91739

B

BAAR, David Josef (The Episcopal Church in Haw)

BABB, Trevor (NY) 76 Franklin Ave, Staten Island, NY 10301

BABCOCK, Jessica H (SwFla) St Marks Episcopal Church, 1101 N Collier Blvd, Marco Island, FL 34145

BABCOCK, Linda Mae (WMo) Saint Anne'S Church, Lebanon, MO 65536

BABCOCK, Lori Hale (Md) 1700 South Rd, Baltimore, MD 21209

BABCOCK, Margaret (Wyo) 336 E Desert Tree Dr, Tucson, AZ 85704

BABCOCK, Mary Kathleen (Kan) 400 E. Maple St, Independence, KS 67301

BABCOCK, Matthew Ray (Chi) 1105 Shermer Rd, Glenview, IL 60025

BABCOCK, Ted (Pgh) The TEC Dio of Pittsburgh, 325 Oliver Ave, Pittsburgh, PA 15222

BABENKO-LONGHI, Julie P (Chi) 1850 Landre Ct, Burlington, WI 53105

BABIN, Kyle James (Pa)

BABLER, Emmett John (Minn) 9411 E Parkside Dr, Sun Lakes, AZ 85248

BABNEW JR, Rodger Allan (Az) 969 W Country Club Dr, Nogales, AZ 85621

BABSON, Katharine E (Me) 149 Pennellville Rd, Brunswick, ME 04011

BACAS, Nina Liggett (Va)

BACHMANN, Douglas P (Cal) 419 Orchard View Ave, Martinez, CA 94553

BACHSCHMID, Edward Karl (RG) 9024 N Congress St, New Market, VA 22844

BACIGALUPO, Joseph Andrew (ECR) 1343 Wylie Way, San Jose, CA 95130

BACK, George H (Chi) 160 E Laurel Ave Apt E 110, Lake Forest, IL 60045

BACK, Luke (Chi) 400 E Westminster, Lake Forest, IL 60045

BACK BECKER, Heather E (Minn) 2367 Glen Eagle Dr, Louisville, KY 40222

BACKER, Karri Anne (Los) 1030 North Towne Avenue, Claremont, CA 91711

BACKHAUS, Oliver Keith (SwFla) St Marks Episcopal Church, 513 Nassau St S, Venice, FL 34285

BACKLUND, Michael Anders (Episcopal SJ) 10449 Oak Valley Rd, Angels Camp, CA 95222

BACKSTRAND, Brian E (Mil) 804 E Juneau Ave, Milwaukee, WI 53202

BACKUS, Brett Paul (ETenn) 2605 Smoky Hill Ln, Knoxville, TN 37932

BACKUS, Howard G (NC) 600 S Central Ave, Laurel, DE 19956

BACKUS, Timothy Warren (Colo) PO Box 12683, Pensacola, FL 32591

BACON JR, James Edwin (Ala) 3239 Heathrow Downs, Hoover, AL 35226

BACON JR, Robert (Mass) 51 Ledgelawn Ave, Lexington, MA 02420

BADDERS JR, John D (WTex) 1632 Santa Fe Trail Dr, San Antonio, TX 78232

BADE, James Robert (Az) 6300 N Central Ave, Phoenix, AZ 85012

BADER-SAYE, Demery Letisha (Be) 334 Knapp Rd, Clarks Summit, PA 18411

BADGETT, Benjamin R (SwVa)

BAER, Kirsten Herndon (Okla) 13316 SW 3rd St, Yukon, OK 73099

BAER, Timothy Christopher (Okla) 13316 SW 3rd St, Yukon, OK 73099

BAER, Walter Jacob (Eur) Convocation in EU, 23 avenue George V, Paris, AS 75008, France

BAETZ III, Bertrand O (WTex) 320 Saint Peter St, Kerrville, TX 78028

BAGAY, Martin (At) all saints episcopal church, 1708 Watson Blvd, Warner Robins, GA 31093

BAGBY, John Blythe (Ala) 3516 Country Club Road, Birmingham,, AL 35213

BAGBY, Ray (Tex) 2515 Richards Dr, Waco, TX 76710

BAGGETT, Heather Kathleen (Va) 401 N 4th St, Bismarck, ND 58501

BAGIONI, Elizabeth A (WA) 2304 George St Apt 3 Unit 3, Grand Island, NE 68803

BAGLEY, Robert Chambers (Mil) 701 Erie St, Racine, WI 53402

BAGUER II, Miguel A (SeFla) 300 Sunrise Dr Apt 1b, Key Biscayne, FL 33149

BAGUYOS, Avelino (Kan) PO Box 40222, Overland Park, KS 66204

BAGWELL, Rob (Mass) 401 E 60th St, Savannah, GA 31405

BAHLOW, Harry (ETenn) 4026 Starview Ln, Evans, GA 30809

BAILEY, Abbott (Va)

BAILEY, Anne Cox (Cal) 750 Adella Ave, Coronado, CA 92118

BAILEY, Audrey Veronica (NY) 777 E 222nd St, Bronx, NY 10467

BAILEY, BErtram Cass (Va) 1118 Preston Ave, Charlottesville, VA 22903

BAILEY, Charles James (Lex)

BAILEY, Charles Leroy (Alb) 15 Richards Ave, Oneonta, NY 13820

BAILEY, David Bruce (SO) 9097 Cascara Dr, West Chester, OH 45069

✠ **BAILEY**, David Earle (NAM) PO Box 720, Farmington, NM 87499

BAILEY III, Douglass Moxley (NC)

BAILEY, Frank Hudson (Md) 7474 Washington Blvd, Elkridge, MD 21075

BAILEY, Gregory Bruce (Alb) Trinity Episcopal Church, 30 Park St, Gouverneur, NY 13642

BAILEY, Jefferson Moore (Az) PO Box 492, Tucson, AZ 85702

BAILEY, Lydia Collins (O) 21000 Lake Shore Blvd, Euclid, OH 44123

BAILEY, Max (Colo) 1902 Lochmore Dr, Longmont, CO 80504

BAILEY, Noel (RI) Emmanuel Church, 120 Nate Whipple Hwy, Cumberland, RI 02864

BAILEY, Paul Milton (La) PO Box 1086, Hammond, LA 70404

BAILEY, Pauline Rose (Alb) 15 Richards Ave, Oneonta, NY 13820

BAILEY, Ricardo Z (At) 2744 Peachtree Rd NW, Atlanta, GA 30305

BAILEY, Sarah E (WVa) 401 S Washington St, Berkeley Springs, WV 25411

BAILEY FISCHER, Valerie (WMass) 735 Pine Cobble Rd, Williamstown, MA 01267

BAILLARGEON JR, Henri Albert (SVa) 11106 N 51st St, Tampa, FL 33617

BAIN, Robert Walker (WMass) 1673 Huasna Dr, San Luis Obispo, CA 93405

BAIRD, Carolyn Alice (Cal) 1026 Springhouse Dr, Ambler, PA 19002

BAIRD, Gary Clifton (Ark) 617 Tahlequah, POB 6827, Siloam Springs, AR 72761

BAIRD, Joseph Paul (Pgh) St. Peter's Episcopal Church, 36 W Campbell St, Blairsville, PA 15717

BAIRD, Kathryn Jo Anne (Az) 4442 E Bermuda St, Tucson, AZ 85712

BAKAL, Pamela (Nwk) 200 Highfield Ln, Nutley, NJ 07110

BAKER, Andrea (The Episcopal NCal) 2620 Capitol Ave, Sacramento, CA 95816

BAKER, Brian (The Episcopal NCal) 46 078 Emepela Pl, Apt B203, Kaneohe, HI 96744

BAKER, Brock (Alb) PO Box 1374, Lake Placid, NY 12946

BAKER, Carenda Diane (CPa) 206 E Burd St, Shippensburg, PA 17257

BAKER JR, Charles Mulford (Ct) PO Box 296, Gales Ferry, CT 06335

BAKER, Clarence (Ark) 692 Poplar Ave, Memphis, TN 38105

BAKER, Danielle (Nwk)

BAKER, Douglas Macintyre (NJ)

BAKER, Gregory James (Ind) 726 Weghorst St, Indianapolis, IN 46203

BAKER, Jeff (O) 160 Keagler Dr, Steubenville, OH 43953

BAKER, John (Va) 8531 Riverside Rd, Alexandria, VA 22308

BAKER JR, John Thurlow (Cal) 2055 Northshore Rd, Bellingham, WA 98226

BAKER, Joseph Scott (SVa) St. Stephen's Episcopal Church, 372 Hiden Blvd., Newport News, VA 23606

BAKER, Joseph Stannard (Vt) 2 Cherry St., Burlington, VT 05401

BAKER, Josephine Louise Redenius (Pa) Po Box 429, Wayne, PA 19087

BAKER, K Drew (Me) 2411 Shiraz Lane, Charleston, SC 29414

BAKER, Kim Turner (WA) 2420 14th St NW Apt 524, Washington, DC 20009

BAKER, Louise (Mont) 52120 Lake Mary Ronan Rd, Proctor, MT 59929

BAKER, Marjorie Freeouf (Ct)

BAKER, Mark James (At) 126 Wild Horse Cove Cir, Cleveland, GA 30528

BAKER, Milledge Leonard (CGC) 699 S Highway 95a, Cantonment, FL 32533

BAKER, Patricia Lucile (Oly) PO Box 369, Snoqualmie, WA 98065

BAKER, Paul Edgar (Alb) 4 St Lukes Pl, Cambridge, NY 12816

BAKER, Rhonda (Va) PO Box 2066, Crystal Lake, IL 60039

BAKER, Richard Henry (Mo) 3139 Barrett Station Rd, Saint Louis, MO 63122

BAKER, Shireen R (Chi) 116 E Church St, Elmhurst, IL 60126

BAKER, Thomas Joseph (Kan)

BAKER, Ursula Paula (Az)

BAKER, William (NY) 1 Kingsley Ave, Staten Island, NY 10314

BAKER-BORJESON, Susan C (Alb) PO Box 340, 10 Mansion St Apt 3, Coxsackie, NY 12051

BAKER-FONES, Ryan Jacob (Ore)

BAKER-WRIGHT, Michelle (Los) 1325 Monterey Rd, South Pasadena, CA 91030

BAKEWELL JR, Rev Grant McNeill (The Episcopal NCal) 2300 Edison Ave, Sacramento, CA 95821

BAKKER, Cheryl Anne (CFla) 7416 W Seven Rivers Dr, Crystal River, FL 34429

BAKKER, Gregory Kendall (Episcopal SJ) 41 Station Road, Sholing, Southampton, SO19 8FN, Great Britain (UK)

BAKKER, Joseph Harold (Fla) 211 N Monroe St, Tallahassee, FL 32301

BAKKUM, Carleton B (SVa) 107 Lafayette Rd, Yorktown, VA 23690

BALABANIS, Achilles (Spok)

BALDERSON, Scott (NC) 304 E Franklin St, Chapel Hill, NC 27514

BALDRIDGE SR, Kempton Dunn (Eur) 605 Woodland Dr, Paducah, KY 42001

BALDWIN, Frederick (NJ) 3401 38th St NW Apt 122, Apt TWR 122, Washington, DC 20016

BALDWIN, Gary (CGC) 188 Grindstone Creek Dr, Clarkesville, GA 30523

BALDWIN, Gayle R (Wyo) ????, Greybull, WY 82426

BALDWIN, Jerome M (SO) 9477 N Maura Ln., Brown Deer, WI 53223

BALDWIN, John (SVa) 5181 Singleton Way, Virginia Beach, VA 23462

BALDWIN, Judith Anne (Nwk) 119 Main St, Millburn, NJ 07041

BALDWIN, Marilyn E (Minn) 12336 Eagle Cir NW, Coon Rapids, MN 55448

BALDWIN, Rob (Kan) 1011 Vermont St, Lawrence, KS 66044

BALDWIN, Victoria Evelyn (Ct) 27 Babcock Ave, Plainfield, CT 06374

BALDWIN-MCGINNIS, Carissa E. (Tex) 1220 Omar St, Houston, TX 77008

BALE, Harvey Edgar (WA)

BALES, Janice Stebing (RG) 3112 La Mancha Pl Nw, Albuquerque, NM 87104

BALES, Joshua Morris (CFla) 130 N Magnolia Ave, Orlando, FL 32801

BALES, William Oliver (SO) 29405 Blosser Rd, Logan, OH 43138

BALFE, Martin Kevin (Minn) 315 State St W, Cannon Falls, MN 55009

BALICKI, John (Me) 104 Echo Rd, Brunswick, ME 04011

BALIIRA, Nelson Kuule (CPa)

BALKE JR, Steven M (Chi) B, 1829 N Cleveland Ave, Chicago, IL 60614

BALL, Edwin (CFla) 3740 Pinebrook Cir, Bradenton, FL 34209

BALL, John Arthur (WA) 46455 Hyatt Ct, Drayden, MD 20630

BALLANTINE, Lucia (NY) 402 Route 22, North Salem, NY 10560

BALLARD, Chris Christopher (LI) St Lukes St Matts Tec Ch, 520 Clinton Ave, Brooklyn, NY 11238

BALLARD, James David (Vt) 139 Sanderson Rd, Milton, VT 05468

BALLARD JR, Joseph (Tenn) 17525 Shady Elm Ave, Baton Rouge, LA 70816

BALLARD, Kathleen Miller (Nwk)

BALLARD, Michael Eugene Lewis (CGC)

BALL-DAMBERG, Sarah (NC) 915 Monmouth Ave, Durham, NC 27701

BALLENGER, Barbara (Pa)

BALLENTINE, Jabriel Simmonds (CFla) 1000 Bethune Dr, Orlando, FL 32805

BALLERT JR, Irving Frank (Alb) 25 Sharon St, Sidney, NY 13838

BALLEW, Thelma Johnanna (NH) 1 Park Ct, Durham, NH 03824

BALLING, Valerie L (NJ) 4 Christopher Mill Rd, Medford, NJ 08055

BALLINGER, Carolyn Tucker (WK)

BALLINGER, Catherine Ann (WA)

BALLINGER, Kathryn Elisabeth (Oly) 9210 Ne 123rd St, Kirkland, WA 98034

BALLOU, Diedre Schuler (NwT) 6304 Roadrunner Ct, Amarillo, TX 79119

BALMER, Randall (Ct) 720 Pattrell Road, Norwich, VT 05055

BALMER, William John (NJ) 380 Sycamore Ave, Shrewsbury, NJ 07702

BALTZ, Ann Marie Halpin (Ida) 8947 Springhurst Dr, Boise, ID 83704

BALTZ, Frank (At) 369 Merrydale Dr SW, Marietta, GA 30064

BAMBERGER, Michael Andrew (Los) 241 Ramona Ave, Sierra Madre, CA 91024

BAMBRICK, Barbara Nichols (SeFla) 1802 Pine St, Perry, IA 50220

BANACH, Karla (Alb)

BANAKIS, Kathryn Loretta (Chi) 939 Hinman Ave, Evanston, IL 60202

BANCROFT, John Galloway (At) 1865 Highway 20 W, Mcdonough, GA 30253

BANCROFT, Stephen (Mich) 27310 Wellington Rd, Franklin, MI 48025

BANDY, Talmage Gwaltney (NC) 22 Bogie Dr, Whispering Pines, NC 28327

☩ **BANE JR**, David Conner (SVa) 163 Pelican Pointe Dr, Elizabeth City, NC 27909

BANKOWSKI, Thomas (CFla)

BANKS, Cynthia Kay Rauh (WNC) 272 Maple Ridge Dr, Boone, NC 28607

BANKS JR, Ralph Alton (SeFla) 940 Eucalyptus Rd, North Palm Beach, FL 33408

BANKS, Richard Allan (La) 1444 Cabrini Ct, New Orleans, LA 70122

BANKSTON, Van (Be) 69 Northport Ave, Belfast, ME 04915

BANNA, Willy (Hai)

BANNER, Shelly Ann (CNY) 41 Highmore Dr, Oswego, NY 13126

BANSE JR, Robert (Va) 221 Orr Rd, Pittsburgh, PA 15241

BAPTISTE-WILLIAMS, Barbara Jeanne (SeFla) 6041 SW 63rd Ct, Miami, FL 33143

BARBARE, Mikel J (Fla) 7801 Lone Star Rd, Jacksonville, FL 32211

BARBARITO, Melanie Repko (Nwk) 3981 River Pointe Pl Apt 1f, High Point, NC 27265

BARBER, Barbara Jean (Kan) 5518 Sw 17th Ter, Topeka, KS 66604

BARBER, Elaine Elizabeth Rybak Clyborne (Minn) 4830 Acorn Ridge Rd, Minnetonka, MN 55345

BARBER, Grant Woodward (Mass) 318 Franklin St, Whitman, MA 02382

BARBER, Grethe Ann (Oly) 690 N Shepherd Rd, Washougal, WA 98671

BARBER, James Frederick (Tex) 3217 Chaparral Ln, Fort Worth, TX 76109

BARBER, Mary Ellen (NY)

BARBERIA, Kristin Neily (Los) 5254 N Fairway Heights Dr, Tucson, AZ 85749

BARBOUR, Grady Frederic Waddell (Ala) 565 12th Ct, Pleasant Grove, AL 35127

BARBUTO, Judith Steele (U) 11146 S Heather Grove Ln, South Jordan, UT 84095

BARDEN III, Albert A (Ct) 254 Father Rasle Rd, Norridgewock, ME 04957

BARDSLEY, Nancy Louise (Ida) 1154 Camps Canyon Rd, Troy, ID 83871

BARDUSCH, Richard Evans (At) 1581 Flat Rock Rd, Covington, GA 30014

BAREBO, Charles Vincent (Be) 333 Wyandotte St, Bethlehem, PA 18015

BARFIELD, Bill (Ind) PO Box 141, Danville, IN 46122

BARFIELD, David S (Ala) 4908 Masters Rd, Pell City, AL 35128

BARFIELD, DeOla Edwina (Ct) 744 Lakeside Dr, Bridgeport, CT 06606

BARFIELD, Karen (WNC) 65 Belmont Ave, Asheville, NC 28806

BARFORD, Lee Alton (ECR) 561 Keystone Ave #434, Reno, NV 89503

BARGER, Rebecca Sue (Mo)

BARGETZI, David (O) 1417 Larchmont Ave, Lakewood, OH 44107

BARGIEL, Mary Victoria (Ind) 3243 N Meridian St, Indianapolis, IN 46208

BARHAM, Michael (Cal) 2480 Virginia St Apt 2, Berkeley, CA 94709

BARHAM, Patsy Griffin (Tex) St Matthew's Episcopal Church, 214 College Ave, Henderson, TX 75654

BARKER, Ann (At) 6231 Kilmer Ct, Falls Church, VA 22044

BARKER, Christie Dalton (NC) 981 Valiant Dr., Statesville, NC 28677

BARKER, Christopher Haskins (Pgh) 1062 Old Orchard Dr, Gibsonia, PA 15044

BARKER, Gary Joseph (Va) 87 Edwards Ct, Dutton, VA 23050

BARKER, Herbert James (SanD) 11727 Mesa Verde Dr, Valley Center, CA 92082

BARKER, Jane Daugherty (Tex)

BARKER, Jo Ann D (Del) 100 Rattlesnake Spring Ln, Sewanee, TN 37375

Clergy List

BARKER, Lynn (Miss) 29 Melody Ln, Purvis, MS 39475

BARKER, Patrick Morgan (Ark) 1521 Mcarthur Dr, Jacksonville, AR 72076

BARKER, Paul R (Pgh)

✠ **BARKER**, Scott (Neb) 109 N 18th St, Omaha, NE 68102

BARLEY, Linda Elizabeth (SwFla) 10922 106th Ave, Largo, FL 33778

BARLING, Kenli (Wyo)

BARLOWE, Michael (Cal) 815 Second Avenue, New York, NY 10017

BARNARD, Nancy Alexandra Sandra (ECR) 1267 Black Sage Cir, Nipomo, CA 93444

BARNES, Chuck (EO) Po Box 317, Hermiston, OR 97838

BARNES, Jeffry Parker (SD) 21285 Highway 20 Apt 127, Bend, OR 97701

BARNES, John David (SD) 717 Quincy St, Rapid City, SD 57701

BARNES, Rebecca A (Be) 801 Wheeler Ave, Scranton, PA 18510

BARNES, Simon (Pgh) 8050 Buckingham Rd, Cincinnati, OH 45243

BARNES, Susan Johnston (Minn) St John The Baptist Episc Ch, 4201 Sheridan Ave S, Minneapolis, MN 55410

BARNETT, Andrew K (WA) Washington National Cathedral, 3101 Wisconsin Ave NW, Washington, DC 20016

BARNETT, Becca Fleming (Cal) 435 Euclid Ave Apt 1, San Francisco, CA 94118

BARNETT, Edwin Wilson (Tex) 1232 S Timberline Dr, Benbrook, TX 76126

BARNETT, Jamelia Cooper (Los)

BARNETT, Mary Russell (Ct)

BARNETT, Maxine Maria Veronica (LI) Church of Saint Jude, 3606 Lufberry Ave, Wantagh, NY 11793

BARNETT, Thomas C (EC) 6454 Pleasant Hill Rd SE, Gnadenhutten, OH 44629

BARNEY, David Marshall (Mass) 310 Hayward Mill Rd, Concord, MA 01742

BARNEY, Roger Alexander (ECR) 19040 Portos Dr, Saratoga, CA 95070

BARNHILL JR, James W (Fla) 5043 Timuquana Rd, Jacksonville, FL 32210

BARNICLE, Brendan John (Ore) PO Box 445, Wilsonville, OR 97070

BARNS, G Stewart Stewart (Mass) PO Box 381164, Cambridge, MA 02238

BARNSWELL-SCHMIDT, Garcia C (CFla)

BARNUM, Barbara Coxe (Los) 11359 Perris Blvd, Moreno Valley, CA 92557

BARNUM, Elena (NY) 112 Bentwood Dr, Stamford, CT 06903

BARON, Christian John (Ind) 555 Michigan Ave, Holland, MI 49423

BARON, Jodi Lynn (Ind) 8948 River Ridge Dr, Brownsburg, IN 46112

BAROODY, Roger Anis (NY) 218 Luke Mountain Rd, Covington, VA 24426

BARR, David Lee (Fla) 8227 Bateau Rd S, Jacksonville, FL 32216

BARR, David Mason (Tenn)

BARR, Donna Faulconer (Lex) 2140 Woodmont Dr, Lexington, KY 40502

BARR, Gillian Rachel (Ct) 31 Church St, Stonington, CT 06378

BARR, Jane Wallace (Va) 209 Macarthur Rd, Alexandria, VA 22305

BARR, Norma Margaret (Chi)

BARRAGAN, Juan (Los) 9046 Gallatin Rd., Pico Rivera, CA 90660

BARRAZA, Rene (Los) St Athanasius And St Pauls, 840 Echo Park Ave, Los Angeles, CA 90026

BARRE, James Lyman (Vt) 1009 Robert E. Lee Drive, Wilmington, NC 28412

BARRERA FLORES, Olga I (Hond) IMS SAP Dept 215, PO BOX 523900, Miami, FL 33152-3900, Honduras

BARRETT, Constance Yvonne (Mil) 3560 N Summit Ave, Shorewood, WI 53211

BARRETT, Jo (Mass) Trinity Church, 124 River Rd, Topsfield, MA 01983

BARRETT, John Hammond (CFla) 3527 Vancouver Dr, Dallas, TX 75229

BARRETT, John Richard (Tex) St Martin's Episcopal Church, 1602 S Fm 116, Copperas Cove, TX 76522

BARRETT, Joshua Patrick (Roch)

BARRETT, Patricia Callan (Mass)

BARRETT, Rilla (Oly) 670 Rainbow Dr, Sedro Woolley, WA 98284

BARRETT, Sr Helena (Nwk)

BARRETT, Timothy Lewis (Nwk) 10 Crestmont Rd, Montclair, NJ 07042

BARRIE, David Paul (NY) 2109 Broadway # 1241, New York, NY 10023

BARRINGTON, Dominic M J (Chi) 65 E Huron St, Chicago, IL 60611

BARRINGTON JR, Tom (Mass) 27 6th Ave, North Chelmsford, MA 01863

BARRIOS, Luis (NY)

BARRIOS, Maria Trevino (Dal) 534 W 10th St, Dallas, TX 75208

BARRON JR, Alex (USC) 168 Club Cir, Pawleys Island, SC 29585

BARRON, Carol (SeFla) 3954 SE Fairway E, Stuart, FL 34997

BARRON, Kevin Wayne (CPa)

BARRON, Scott William (Chi) 1148 N Douglas Ave, Arlington Heights, IL 60004

BARRON, Thomas Lemuel (Ga) PO Box 211106, Augusta, GA 30917

BARROW, Alan Lester (Okla) 5635 E. 71st St., Tulsa, OK 74136

BARROW, Suzanne (Ky)

BARROWCLOUGH, Lisa Shirley (WA) St Marks Tec Ch Sch, 3395 Burns Road, Palm Beach Gardens, FL 33410

BARROWS, Dustin Kyle (WTex)

BARROWS, Jennifer Eve (NY) 1585 Route 9 West, West Park, NY 12493

BARRY, Brian Clark (LI) 54 Brooklyn Ave, Valley Stream, NY 11581

BARRY, Eugenia Clare Mackenzie (WNC) 11 Lone Pine Rd, Asheville, NC 28803

BARTA, Heather Marie (EMich) 156 Guanonocque St, Auburn Hills, MI 48326

BARTELS, Judith Tallman (Oly) none----moved from there, lacey, WA 98117

BARTH, Barbara L (Me) 42 Tailwind Ct Apt 78 D, Auburn, ME 04210

BARTHELEMY, Paul Berge (Ore) 18160 Cottonwood Rd Pmb 789, Sunriver, OR 97707

BARTHLE, Donna (CPa)

BARTHOLOMEW, Adam (NY) 802 Broadway, New York, NY 10003

BARTHOLOMEW, Linda (Spok) Church Of The Resurrection, 15319 E 8th Ave, Spokane Valley, WA 99037

BARTHOLOMEW, Tara Anne (Az) 6715 N Mockingbird Ln, Paradise Valley, AZ 85253

BARTKUS, Carolyn Jennifer (Alb)

BARTLE, Edward Bartholomew (CFla) 330 Hickory Ave, Orange City, FL 32763

BARTLE, John Dixon (Alb) PO Box E, Richfield Springs, NY 13439

BARTLE, Kevin B (CFla) 700 Rinehart Rd, Lake Mary, FL 32746

BARTLE, Leonard William (CFla) 3520 Curtis Dr, Apopka, FL 32703

BARTLE, Phyllis (CFla) 4 Sweetgum Dr Apt A, Orange City, FL 32763

✠ **BARTLETT JR**, Allen Lyman (Pa) 600 E Cathedral Rd Apt L 209, Apt L-209, Philadelphia, PA 19128

BARTLETT, Anne Kristin (Ore) 204 W. Clearpine Dr., Sisters, OR 97759

BARTLETT, Laurie Lee (Alb) Calvary Church, PO Box 41, Burnt Hills, NY 12027

BARTLETT, Lois Sherburne (Be) 2716 Tennyson Ave, Sinking Spring, PA 19608

BARTLETT, Stephen Ives (WMich) 8975 Shawbacoung Trail, Shelby, MI 49455

BARTLETT, Thomas Albert (NJ) 25 Monmouth St, Brookline, MA 02446

BARTOLOMEO, Michael Edward (LI) 124 Balaton Ave, Lake Ronkonkoma, NY 11779

BARTON, Alexander Doyle (O) PO Box 521, Lorain, OH 44052

BARTON, Anne (Spok) 5205 Sycamore Dr, Yakima, WA 98901

BARTON III, Bill (Ga) Trinity Episcopal Church, 213 1st Ave NW, Winchester, TN 37398

BARTON, Charlie (Md) 105 Somerset Ave, Cambridge, MD 21613

BARTON JR, John Clib (Ark) 1024 Stanford Dr Ne, Albuquerque, NM 87106

BARTZ, James Perkins (Wyo) St John's Church, 170 N Glenwood St, Jackson, WY 83001

BARWICK III, Frederick Ernest (NC) 5941 Leasburg Rd., Roxboro, NC 27574

BARWICK, Mark (Eur) avenue du Preau 16, Brussels, 01040, Belgium

✠ **BASCOM**, Cathleen (Kan) Cathedral Church of St. Paul, 815 High Street, Des Moines, IA 50309

BASCOM, Joshua L (Va)

BASDEN, Michael (SwFla) 495 Galleon Dr, Naples, FL 34102

BASEL, Christian P (SC)

BASINGER JR, Elvin David (Ala) 21526 Silver Oaks Circle, Athens, AL 35613

✠ **BASKERVILLE-BURROWS**, Jennifer (Ind)

BASKIN, Cynthia Oppen (WA) 10924 Citreon Ct, N Potomac, MD 20878

BASS, Francis Arthur (ETenn)

BASS, Phillip Michael (NC)

BASS-CHOATE, Yamily (NY) 4 Gateway Rd Apt 1d, Yonkers, NY 10703

BASSUENER, Barbara A. (Colo) 20 3rd St, Pocomoke City, MD 21851

BAST, Kathryn A (SwVa) 131 W Emerson St, Melrose, MA 02176

BAST, Robert Lee (Eas) 201 Crosstown Dr Apt 3013, Peachtree City, GA 30269

BASTIAN, Martin James (Tex) 5714 Jackwood St, Houston, TX 77096

BATEMAN, David (CPa) 3312 Brisban St, Harrisburg, PA 17111

BATES, Allen Layfield (Ark) 1902 W Magnolia St, Rogers, AR 72758

BATES, J Barrington (Nwk) 4600 N Lake Shore Drive, Harbor Springs, MI 49740

BATES, James Brent (Nwk) 950 Broad St, Newark, NJ 07102

BATES, Robert Seaton (Chi) 4243 Ahlstrand Dr, Rockford, IL 61101

BATES, Steven Byron (CGC) 7115 Thomas Dr Unit 1402, Panama City Beach, FL 32408

BATES, Stuart Alan (Tex) 345 Piney Point Rd, Houston, TX 77024

BATES, Thomas Justin (RG)

BATES, Toppie (CNY) 5623 Mack Rd, Skaneateles, NY 13152

BATIZ MEJIA, Jos David (Hond) IMS SAP Dept 215, PO BOX 523900, Miami, FL 33152-3900, Honduras

BATSON, Lloyd Samuel (Nwk) 160 W South Orange Ave, South Orange, NJ 07079

BATSON, Sara Chapman (Pa) 6102 Treyburn Point Dr, Durham, NC 27712

BATSON III, Stephen Radford (NY) 3721 Wares Ferry Rd Apt 500, Montgomery, AL 36109

BATTEN, Stephen John (EC) PO Box 332, Chocowinity, NC 27817

BATTEN-KALANTZIS, Kendall (Chi)

BATTERMAN, Stephanie (Me) 3 Fairview Ln, Bath, ME 04530

BATTLE, Michael Jesse (NC) 1611 East Millbrook Rd, Raleigh, NC 27609

BATTON JR, Robert Nolton (RG) 4304 Carlisle Blvd NE, Albuquerque, NM 87107

BAUER, Charles (SVa)

BAUER, Charles David (Eau)

BAUER, Kathryn Ann (WMo) Po Box 996, Kremmling, CO 80459

BAUER, Richard C (CPa) 1608 Russell Rd, Alexandria, VA 22301

BAUER, Ronald Coleman (Los) 27292 Via Callejon Apt B, San Juan Capistrano, CA 92675

BAUER, Thomas William (Md) 3148 Gracefield Rd Apt C1412, Silver Spring, MD 20904

✠ **BAUERSCHMIDT**, John (Tenn) 50 Vantage Way Ste 107, Nashville, TN 37228

BAUGH, Jonathan Earle (Fla) Saint Margarets, 8515 Rea Rd, Waxhaw, NC 28173

BAUGHMAN, David Lee (Chi) 804 James Court, Wheaton, IL 60189

BAUKNIGHT JR, Mack Miller (SwFla) 2440 26th Ave S, Saint Petersburg, FL 33712

BAUM, George R (O) 13415 Ardoon Ave, Cleveland, OH 44120

BAUM, Nancy Louise (Mich) 411 Walnut St # 3371, Green Cove Springs, FL 32043

BAUMAN, Dwayne Ray (Ark) 176 State Road YY, Tunas, MO 65764

BAUMAN, Ward J (Minn) 1111 Upton Ave N, Minneapolis, MN 55411

BAUMGARTEN, Betsy (Ark) 14294 John Lee Road, Biloxi, MS 39532

BAUMGARTEN, Jonathan David (Chi) 41 E. 8th St. Apt. 2001, Chicago, IL 60605

BAUMGARTEN, William (Mont) 845 2nd Ave E, Kalispell, MT 59901

BAUSCHARD, Michael Robert Thomas (NwPa) 5 Cottage Pl, Warren, PA 16365

BAUTISTA, Gina (CPa) 2712 Crestwyck Circl, Mount Joy, PA 17552

BAUTISTA, Simon (Tex) Christ Church Cathedral, 1117 Texas St, Houston, TX 77002

BAVARO, Carolyn Margaret (Chi) PO Box 648, Wood Dale, IL 60191

BAXLEY, Todd Lee (NwT) 1601 S Georgia St, Amarillo, TX 79102

BAXTER, Antonio Jermaine (WA)

BAXTER, Barbara W (WNY) 16 N Phetteplace St, Falconer, NY 14733

BAXTER JR, Donald Leslie (NwPa) 300 Hilltop Rd, Erie, PA 16509

BAXTER, Jane Ann (CNY) 151 Hawkins Rd, Ferrisburgh, VT 05456

BAXTER, Lisette Dyer (Vt) 112 Lakewood Pkwy, Burlington, VT 05408

BAXTER, Nancy Julia (At) 1223 Clifton Rd NE, Atlanta, GA 30307

✠ **BAXTER**, Nathan Dwight (CPa) 115 N Duke St, Lancaster, PA 17602

BAXTER, Rae Lee (Mich) 430 Nicolet St, Walled Lake, MI 48390

BAYANG, Martin Eugenio (RG) 1406 S Cliff Dr, Gallup, NM 87301

BAYFIELD, Ralph Wesley (Va) 300 Westminster Canterbury Dr Apt 405, Winchester, VA 22603

BAYLES, Joseph Austin (Kan) 1341 N River Blvd, Wichita, KS 67203

BAYLES, Richard Allen (Oly) Po Box 1115, South Bend, WA 98586

BAYNES, Leopold Cornelius (LI) Grace Church, 3434 98th St, Corona, NY 11368

BAYONNE, Zacher (CFla)

BAYS, Terri (NI) 117 N Lafayette Blvd, South Bend, IN 46601

BAZIN, Jean Jacques Emmanuel Fritz (SeFla) 525 NE 15 Street, Miami, FL 33132

BEACH, Deborah Elizabeth (Alb) 132 Duanesburg - Churches Road, Duanesburg, NY 12056

BEACH, Diana (Nwk) 88 Main St, Thomaston, ME 04861

BEACH II, John Tappan (Mass) 39 Route De Malagnou, Geneva, 01208, Switzerland

BEACH, Joseph Lawrence (ETenn) 4768 Edens View Rd, Kingsport, TN 37664

BEACH, Kay Joan (Ia) 201 E Church St, Marshalltown, IA 50158

BEACHAM III, Albert Burton (U) 1420 N 3000 W, Vernal, UT 84078

BEADLE, David L (Dal)

BEAL, Jennifer D (Mass) 1745 Wedgewood Cmn, Concord, MA 01742

BEAL, Stephen Thomas (The Episcopal NCal) 2301 Polk St Apt 3, San Francisco, CA 94109

BEALE, Mary I (NH) 45 Derryfield Ct, Manchester, NH 03104

BEALES, Rosemary Elizabeth (Va) St Aidans Episcopal Church, 8531 Riverside Rd, Alexandria, VA 22308

BEALL, Nathan Andrew (Md) 1110 El Dorado Dr, Lusby, MD 20657

BEALS, Julie (Los) 4499 Via Marisol Apt 334, Los Angeles, CA 90042

BEAM, Barbara (WMo) 6336 SE Hamilton Rd, Lathrop, MO 64465

BEAM, Marcia Mckay (SeFla) 805 SW 6th Ave, Delray Beach, FL 33444

BEAN, Kathleen Tedrow (Ida) PO Box 2249, Hailey, ID 83333

BEAN, Kevin D (WMass) All Saints Church, 10 Irving St., Worcester, MA 01609

BEAN, Rebecca Anne (EC) PO Box 1333, Goldsboro, NC 27533

BEANE, Emmetri Monica (Va) PO Box 367, Rixeyville, VA 22737

BEAR, Susan (Miss) 3600 Arlington Loop, Hattiesburg, MS 39402

BEARD, Bryan Benjamin (Okla) 9309 N 129th East Ave, Owasso, OK 74055

BEARDEN, Jane Bostick (Miss) 77 Westchester Dr, Haverhill, MA 01830

BEASLEY, Battle (Tenn) 1613 Fatherland St, Nashville, TN 37206

BEASLEY, Carl (Eas) 720 NE 4th Ave Apt 506, Fort Lauderdale, FL 33304

BEASLEY, Christopher Ryan (Ind) 9540 N County Road 1025 E, Brownsburg, IN 46112

BEASLEY, Helen Roberts (SwVa) PO Box 1266, Galax, VA 24333

BEASLEY, Nicholas Madden (USC) St Johns, 2827 Wheat St, Columbia, SC 29205

BEASLEY, Robert L (ETenn) 121 E. Harper Avenue, Maryville, TN 37804

BEASLEY JR, Thomas Edward (Fla) 6003 Brookridge Rd, Jacksonville, FL 32210

BEATON-OAKLEY, Michael (Oly)

BEATTIE, Casandra Marie (Nev)

BEATTIE, Richard Edward (Ct) 438 Old Tavern Rd, Orange, CT 06477

BEATTY, Anne M (The Episcopal NCal) 1515 Shasta Dr Apt 1335, Davis, CA 95616

BEATTY, Steve (Va) 10267 Lakeridge Square Ct Apt B, Ashland, VA 23005

BEATY, Maureen Kay (Colo) St Mary Magdalene, 4775 Cambridge St, Boulder, CO 80301

BEAUCHAMP, Robert William (EC) PO Box 227, Norton, VA 24273

BEAUDREAU JR, Edward Gil (RI) 63 Canonchet Rd, Hope Valley, RI 02832

BEAUHARNOIS, Patricia Ann (Alb) 18 Butternut St, Champlain, NY 12919

BEAULIEU, Cynthia Rae (Me) 650 Main St, Caribou, ME 04736

BEAULIEU, Delores Joyce (Minn) Rr 2 Box 246, Bagley, MN 56621

BEAULIEU, Joyce (Chi) 745 Honey Creek Ln, Lomax, IL 61454

BEAUMONT, Katharine Jenetta (Az)

BEAUVOIR, Jonas (Hai) Eglesi Episcopal DHaiti, Boite Postale 1309, Port-au-Prince, Haiti

✠ **BEAUVOIR**, Oge (Hai) 76 Avenue Christophe, Port-Au-Prince, Haiti

BEAVEN, John Clinton (Me) 22 Willow Grove Rd, Brunswick, ME 04011

BEAVER, Kathryn Elizabeth (WA)

BEAZLEY, Robert William (La) 4499 Sharp Rd, Mandeville, LA 70471

BEBBER, Donald (Az)

BEBBER, Gerald King (Chi) 1821 Mcgougan Rd, Fayetteville, NC 28303

BECHERER, Carl John (Minn)

BECHTEL, Brian Matthew (O)

BECHTOLD, Bryant Coffin (Tex) 3290 Lackland Rd, Fort Worth, TX 76116

BECK, Brien Patrick (FdL) 347 Libal St, De Pere, WI 54115

BECK, Douglas A (Me) 16 Mckinley St, Bangor, ME 04401

BECK, Jonathon Paul (Alb)

BECK, Judith Taw (Pa) 3300 W Penn St, Philadelphia, PA 19129

BECK, Laura E (Colo)

BECK, Randy (NwPa) St Johns Episcopal Church, 226 W State St, Sharon, PA 16146

BECK, Sue Ann (Los) St. John The Divine, 183 E. Bay St., Costa Mesa, CA 92627

BECK-EI, Katherine (Mich)

BECKER, CS Honey (The Episcopal Church in Haw) PO Box 819, Kailua, HI 96734

BECKER, Kim (ND) PO Box 177, Glendale Springs, NC 28629

BECKER, Mary Clovis (Kan)

BECKER, Mary Elizabeth (Ind) 2076 E County Rd 375 S, Winslow, IN 47598

BECKER, Nora A (WVa)

BECKER, Stephen (NC) 3613 Alamosa Dr, High Point, NC 27265

BECKETT, Kimberly Youngblood (Ala) 113 Brown Ave, Rainbow City, AL 35906

BECKETT JR, Norman James (Los) 3157 E Avenue, #B-4, Lancaster, LA 93535, Costa Rica

BECKHAM JR, M Edwin (At) 16 Saint Marks Ln, Islip, NY 11751

BECKLES, William Anthony (NY) Po Box 1067, Mount Vernon, NY 10551

✠ **BECKWITH**, Mark M (Nwk) Episcopal Diocese of Newark, 312 Mulberry St, Newark, NJ 07102

BEDARD, Caren Marie (Minn) 408 N 7th St, Brainerd, MN 56401

BEDDINGFIELD, John Floyd (NY) wwwjfbeddingfieldcom, 316 E 88th St, New York, NY 10128

BEDELL, Bryan Douglas (Roch) 28 Village Trl, Honeoye Falls, NY 14472

BEDFORD, Michael John (Mich) 25831 Lexington Dr Unit 1, South Lyon, MI 48178

BEDINGFIELD, John Davis (WLa) 1620 Murray St, Alexandria, LA 71301

BEE, Robert D (Neb) 13850 W 91st Ter Apt 312d, Lenexa, KS 66215

BEEBE, Christine Fair (Minn) 395 N Main St, Rutherfordton, NC 28139

BEEBE SR, Fred H (Fla) 124 Peninsular Dr, Crescent City, FL 32112

BEEBE, James Russell (Nev) 205 Mackinaw Ave, Akron, OH 44333

BEEBE, Jane Alice (WMass)

BEEBE SR, Jeffrey (SeFla) 151 S County Rd, Palm Beach, FL 33480

BEEBE, Susan Rafter (SeFla) 151 S County Rd, Palm Beach, FL 33480

BEEBE-BOVE, Polly (Vt) 3 Cathedral Sq Apt 2g, Burlington, VT 05401

BEECHAM, Troy (Ia) 815 High St, Des Moines, IA 50309

BEECK, Nicole Misoni (FdL) 4609 Ashley Ln, Sheboygan, WI 53083

BEELEY, Christopher Alfred (Dal) 6811 Aberdeen Ave, Dallas, TX 75230

BEEN, Tyler Joe (Dal)

BEER, David Frank (Tex) 6810 Thistle Hill Way, Austin, TX 78754

BEERS, William Rogers (Chi) 120 1st St, Lodi, WI 53555

BEERY, Bill (NY) 905 Osprey Ct, New Bern, NC 28560

BEERY, Susan Beem (U) 228 S Pitt St, Alexandria, VA 22314

BEESLEY, Kevin D (RI)

BEHEN, Ralph Joseph (WMo)

BEHM, Nancy Anne (FdL) 1703 Doemel St, Oshkosh, WI 54901

BEHNKE, Cathleen Ann (Mich) 4800 Woodward Ave, Detroit, MI 48201

BEHNSTEDT, Patrice Faith (CFla) 500 W Floral Ave, Bartow, FL 33830

BEHRENS, Marilyn Jean (Oly) 7417 Hill Ave Apt 2, Gig Harbor, WA 98335

BEIKIRCH, Paula Marie (CFla) 4915 Deter Rd, Lakeland, FL 33813

BEILSTEIN, Joan Elizabeth (WA) 400 Hinsdale Ct, Silver Spring, MD 20901

BEIMDIEK, Jill (NC) St Stephens Episcopal Church, 200 N James St, Goldsboro, NC 27530

BEIMES, Phyllis Mahilani (The Episcopal Church in Haw) St Matthew's Episcopal Church, Po Box 70, Waimanalo, HI 96795

✠ **BEISNER**, Barry (The Episcopal NCal) Dio Of Northern CA, 350 University Ave Ste 280, Sacramento, CA 95825

BEITZEL, Wallace Dickens (U) 9475 Brookside Ave, Ben Lomond, CA 95005

BEIZER, Lance Kurt (ECR) P.O. Box 1047, 9 Blackberry Way, Canaan, CT 06018

BEK, Susan (Los) 3290 Loma Vista Rd, Ventura, CA 93003

BELA, Robert (Mass) 475 Breeding Loop, Breeding, KY 42015

BELANGER, Fanny Sohet (Va) 3602 Calabash Ct, Wilmington, NC 28405

BELCHER, Nancy Spencer (Mo) PO Box 6065, Fulton, MO 65251

BELCHER, Sandra Alves (Ct) 165 Grassy Hill Rd, Woodbury, CT 06798

BELHU, Cheryl Antoinette (WNC)

BELKNAP, Charles (Los) 1386 Beddis Road, Salt Spring Island, BC V8K2C, Canada

BELKNAP, Sarah (Los) 2066 Empress Ave, South Pasadena, CA 91030

BELL, Beth Ann (Okla) 13112 N Rockwell Ave, Oklahoma City, OK 73142

BELL, Daniel Peter (Mass) Tufts U Protestant Chaplaincy, 3 Thegreen, Medford, MA 02155

BELL, Emily Susan Richardson (Los) 190 Avenida Aragon, San Clemente, CA 92672

BELL, Gerald Michael (Miss) 602 Riverview Dr, Florence, AL 35630

BELL JR, Hugh Oliver (Tex) 960 Starkey Rd Unit 6201, Largo, FL 33771

BELL, Jocelyn (ETenn) 105 Morningside Dr, Soddy Daisy, TN 37379

BELL, Mary Cynthia (Mass) 22 Hathaway Pond Circle, Rochester, MA 02770
BELL, Michael S (Los) PIH Health Spiritual Care Dept, 12401 Washington Blvd, Whittier, CA 90602
BELL, Mike (WMich) 406 2nd St, Manistee, MI 49660
BELL, Pamela Corbin (Az) 7525 E Gainey Ranch Rd # U 181, Scottsdale, AZ 85258
✠ **BELL**, Pat (EO) 501 E Wallace Ave, Coeur D Alene, ID 83814
BELL JR, William R (Md) 2901 Boston St Apt 601, Baltimore, MD 21224
BELLAIMEY, John Edward (Minn) 4233 Linden Hills Blvd, Minneapolis, MN 55410
BELLISS, Richard (Los) 25454 Via Heraldo, Santa Clarita, CA 91355
BELLNER, Elisabeth Ann (Md)
BELLOWS, Carol Hartley (WMass) 33 Fernald Street, Wilton, ME 04294
BELLOWS, Richard S (WMass) 21 Briarcliff Dr, Westfield, MA 01085
BELLOWS, Scott P (Md) St Marys Episcopal Church, PO Box 395, Barnstable, MA 02630
BELL-WOLSKI, Dedra Ann (Ga) 32464 Willow Parke Circle, Fernandina Beach, FL 32034
BELMONT JR, Jack (NJ) 300 S Main St, Pennington, NJ 08534
BELMONTES, Mervyn Lancelot (LI) 812 Nebraska Ave, Bay Shore, NY 11706
BELMORE, Constance (Nev) 4626 Grand Dr Unit 2, Las Vegas, NV 89169
BELNAP, Ronald Victor (U) 8952 S Golden Field Way, Sandy, UT 84094
BELSER, Jo J (Va) 2800 Hope Way, Alexandria, VA 22311
BELSHAW, Richard W (NH) 18 Highland St, Ashland, NH 03217
BELSKY, Emil Eugene (U) 2714 Sierra Vista Rd, Grand Junction, CO 81503
BELT, Michel (Ct) 141 Kings Rd, Madison, NJ 07940
BELTON, Allan Edgar (O) 3490 E Prescott Cir, Cuyahoga Falls, OH 44223
BELTON, Colin Charles (Alb) 18 Trinity Pl., Plattsburgh, NY 12901
BELTON, Randy Samuel (Wyo) St Andrews In The Pines, PO Box 847, Pinedale, WY 82941
BELZER, John Alfred (Okla) 13 Lake Ln, Shawnee, OK 74804
BENAVIDES, Laurie Pauline (RG) 112 Goldenrod Ln, Alto, NM 88312
BENBROOK, Jim (WLa) 125 Woodstone Dr, Ruston, LA 71270
BENCKEN, Cathi Head (Ia) 26 Hampshire Rd, Madison, CT 06443
BENCKEN, Charles F (WNY) 26 Hampshire Road, Madison, CT 06443
BENDALL, Douglas (Nwk) 26 Howard Ct, Newark, NJ 07103

BENDER, David Randa (NY) 104 Fairview Avenue, Poughkeepsie, NY 12601
BENDER, Jane (Be) 557 W 3rd St Apt K, Bethlehem, PA 18015
BENDER, John Charles (Tenn) Our Saviour Episcopal Church, 704 Hartsville Pike, Gallatin, TN 37066
BENDER, William (Ala) 402 S Scott St, Scottsboro, AL 35768
BENDER-BRECK, Barbara (Cal) 3226 Adeline St, Oakland, CA 94608
BENEDICT, Richard Alan Davis (NJ) 1625 SE 10th Ave Apt 602, Fort Lauderdale, FL 33316
BENES, Sandra S (Mich) 122 White Lake Dr, Brooklyn, MI 49230
BENESH, Jimi Brown (The Episcopal NCal) 334 D St, Redwood City, CA 94063
✠ **BENFIELD**, Larry (Ark) Episcopal Diocese Of Arkansas, 310 W 17th St, Little Rock, AR 72206
BENHAM, Curt (Fla)
BENHAM, David D (Ark) 2701 Old Greenwood Rd, Fort Smith, AR 72903
✠ **BENHASE**, Scott Anson (Ga) 18 E 34th St, Savannah, GA 31401
BENISTE, Jean C (Chi) 2430 K St NW, Washington, DC 20037
BENITEZ, Wilfredo (Ct) St George's Church, 13532 38th Ave, Flushing, NY 11354
BENITZ, Stephen M (Ia) 120 1st St NE, Mason City, IA 50401
BENJAMIN, Judy (Cal) 1400 Loma Drive, Ojai, CA 93023
BENKO, Andrew Grayson (Tex) 908 Rutherford St, Shreveport, LA 71104
BENKO, Hope (Tex) 501 E 32nd St, Austin, TX 78705
BENNER, Stephen T (Ind) 1206 Nicki Dr, Bloomington, IL 61704
BENNET, Richard Wilson (FdL) 7220 Newell Road, Hazelhurst, WI 54531
BENNETT III, Arthur Lasure (WVa) 16 Ashwood Dr, Vienna, WV 26105
BENNETT JR, Bertram George (NY) 384 E 160th St, Bronx, NY 10451
BENNETT, Betsy Blake (Neb) 325 W. 11th St., Hastings, NE 68901
BENNETT, Christine Aikens (Me) 30 Turtle Cove Rd, Raymond, ME 04071
BENNETT, Dale Koch (WMich) 110 Quail St, Battle Creek, MI 49037
BENNETT, Debra Q (O) 1933 Kingsley Ave, Akron, OH 44313
BENNETT, Denise C (Va)
BENNETT, Denise Harper (Roch) 2882 Country Road 13, Clifton Springs, NY 14432
BENNETT, Ernest L (CFla) 42 Indianhead Dr, Ormond Beach, FL 32174
BENNETT JR, Franklin Pierce (EMich) 1051 Virginia Ave, Marysville, MI 48040
BENNETT, Gail Louise (NJ) 803 Prospect Ave, Spring Lake, NJ 07762

BENNETT, Gerald L (SwFla) 5134 Wedge Ct E, Bradenton, FL 34203
BENNETT, JoAnne (Ore) PO Box 1791, Roseburg, OR 97470
BENNETT, Kyle Vernon (Miss) St. Mark's Episcopal Church, 1101 N. Collier Blvd, Marco Island, FL 34145
BENNETT, Lisa Carol (Oly)
BENNETT, Marionette Elvena (SC) 15625 E Atlantic Cir, Aurora, CO 80013
BENNETT, Martha Kimsey (SwVa)
BENNETT, Pattiann (Mont) 324 Terning Dr W, Eureka, MT 59917
BENNETT, Paul (Md)
BENNETT, Phillip (Pa) 2001 Hamilton St Apt 303, Philadelphia, PA 19130
BENNETT, Rachel Marybelle (ECR) 201 Glenwood Cir Apt 19e, Monterey, CA 93940
BENNETT, Robert Avon (Mass) PO Box 380367, Cambridge, MA 02238
BENNETT, Susan P (Ind) 610 Perry St, Vincennes, IN 47591
BENNETT, Thaddeus A (Vt) 1165 Shelburne Falls Rd, Conway, MA 01341
BENNETT, Virginia Lee (Spr) 1404 Gettysburg Lndg, Saint Charles, MO 63303
BENNETT, Vivian Rose Kerr (Pa) 934 Overfield RD, Meshoppen, PA 18630
BENNETT, William (Tex) 3711 Hidden Holw, Austin, TX 78731
BENNETT JR, William Doub (NC) Po Box 28024, Raleigh, NC 27611
✠ **BENNISON JR**, Charles Ellsworth (Pa) 279 S 4th St, Philadelphia, PA 19106
BENO, Brian Martin (SwFla) 17 Yorkshire Dr, Fond Du Lac, WI 54935
BENOIT JOSEPH, Arlette Dierdre (Pa) 294 Peyton Rd SW, Atlanta, GA 30311
BENSHOFF, Bruce L (Mass) 11 Meadowlark Dr, Middleboro, MA 02346
BENSKIN, Joanna (Ind)
BENSON, Brad Bradley (CNY) 110 Robie St, Bath, NY 14810
BENSON, E Heather (CNY) 60 Elm St, Ilion, NY 13357
BENSON, George Andrew (Neb) 8800 Holdrege St, Lincoln, NE 68505
BENSON, Patricia B (Minn) PO Box 5888, Collegeville, MN 56321
BENSON, Virginia (Los) 1432 Engracia Ave, Torrance, CA 90501
BENTER JR, Harry William (SwFla) 1010 American Eagle Blvd Apt 348, Apt 348, Sun City Center, FL 33573
BENTLEY JR, John R (Tex) 15410 Misty Forest Ct, Houston, TX 77068
BENTLEY, Stephen Richard (Episcopal SJ) 316 N El Dorado St, Stockton, CA 95202
BENTLEY, Susan Bliss Emmons (SwVa) 4515 Delray St NW, Roanoke, VA 24012

BENTRUP, Alan Dale (Tex) 223 S Pearson Ln, Keller, TX 76248

BENVENUTI, Anne Cecilia (Chi) 4945 S Dorchester Ave, Chicago, IL 60615

BERARD, Jeffrey Jerome (Mil) 1622 Quincy Ave, Racine, WI 53405

BERCOVICI, Hillary R (NY) 20 Kettle Close, Westerly, RI 02891

BERDAHL, Peder (Ind) 5 Oak Brook Club Dr Apr P2s, Oak Brook, IL 60523

BERENDS, April (ETenn) St Marks Episcopal Church, 2618 N Hackett Ave, Milwaukee, WI 53211

BERESFORD, David Charles (Pa) 507 E Buck Rd, Wilmington, DE 19807

BERESFORD, Ruth (Del) 507 E Buck Rd, PO Box 3510, Wilmington, DE 19807

BERG, Dustin (The Episcopal Church in Haw) 770b Wilfred Rd, Hudson, WI 54016

BERG, James Christopher (Mich) 642 Woodcreek Dr, Waterford, MI 48327

BERGE JR, William Clark (Oly) PO Box 399, Mount Sinai, NY 11766

BERGEN, Franklyn Joseph (Az) 4076 N Hidden Cove Pl, Tucson, AZ 85749

BERGER, Fred (Ia) 25111 Valley Drive, Pleasant Valley, IA 52767

BERGER, Martha (Mil) 1616 Martha Washington Dr, Wauwatosa, WI 53213

BERGH JR, Palmer A (Ida) 180 kings court, mountain home, ID 83647

BERGHUIS, Michael Robert (WMich)

BERGIE, Patricia Ann (Wyo) Po Box 903, Fort Washakie, WY 82514

BERGMANN, William (WMass) 85 E Main St, Ayer, MA 01432

BERGMANS, Susan Estelle (Cal) 1320 Addison St Apt C130, Berkeley, CA 94702

BERGNER, Mario J (Spr) 149 Asbury St, South Hamilton, MA 01982

BERGNER, Robert A (Ct) 200 Seabury Dr, Bloomfield, CT 06002

BERGSTROM, Fiona Mabel (NC) 11 Fleet St, Umina Beach NSW, NC 02257, Australia

BERGSTROM, Jeremy W (CFla) 700 Rinehart Rd, Lake Mary, FL 32746

BERITELA, Gerry (CNY) 360 S Collingwood Ave, Syracuse, NY 13206

BERK, Dennis (Be) 27 Grace Ave, Schuylkill Haven, PA 17972

BERKHOUSE, Casey Stephen (WTex) 343 N Getty St, Uvalde, TX 78801

BERKLEY, John Clayton Ashton (NI) 26824 County Road 4, Elkhart, IN 46514

BERKOWE, Kathleen (NY) 16 Truesdale Dr, Croton On Hudson, NY 10520

BERKTOLD, Brenda Clare (Ore) 170 Brookside Dr, Eugene, OR 97405

BERKTOLD, Ted (Ore) 170 Brookside Dr, Eugene, OR 97405

BERLENBACH, Betty Lorraine (Vt) 1961 Plains Rd., Perkinsville, VT 05151

BERLENBACH, Kirk Thomas (Pa) 6429 Sherwood Rd, Philadelphia, PA 19151

BERLIN II, George Albert (Colo) 3155 Kendall St, Wheat Ridge, CO 80214

BERLIN, Sarah Aline (Colo) 3155 Kendall St, Wheat Ridge, CO 80214

BERMAN, Elizabeth Sievert (The Episcopal Church in Haw) 144 Nenue St, Honolulu, HI 96821

BERNACCHI, Jacqueline A (Minn) 1730 Clifton Pl Ste 201, Minneapolis, MN 55403

BERNACKI, James (NC) 2479 Willow Pond Ln SE, Concord, NC 28025

BERNAL, Jose Juan (WK) 635 N Story Rd, Irving, TX 75061

BERNARD, Michael Allen (NwT) 305 Old Colony Ct, North Newton, KS 67117

BERNARDEZ JR, Teogenes Kalaw (Nev) 832 N Eastern Ave, Las Vegas, NV 89101

BERNARDI, Frank Alan (Episcopal SJ) 1815 S Teddy St, Visalia, CA 93277

BERNHARD, Margaret (Ore) 1180 NW Country Ct, Corvallis, OR 97330

BERNIER, Daniel L (Mass) PO Box 719, Wareham, MA 02571

BERNIER, Noe (Hai)

BERNTHAL, Gail Elizabeth (Episcopal SJ) 519 N Douty St, Hanford, CA 93230

BERRA, Robert M (Az) St Augustines Tec Ch, 1735 S College Ave, Tempe, AZ 85281

BERRY, Beverly (Pa) 212 W Lancaster Ave, Paoli, PA 19301

BERRY JR, Charles (WTex) 1100 Grand Blvd Apt 223, Boerne, TX 78006

BERRY, John Emerson (NMich)

BERRY, Mary (Miss)

BERRY, William T (Lex)

BERRYMAN II, Jerome Woods (Colo) 5455 Landmark PL Unit 807, Greenwood Village, CO 80111

BERSIN, Ruth (Ct) 4 Holmes Rd, Boxford, MA 01921

BERTOLOZZI, Michael Alan (Nev) 3625 Marlborough Ave, Las Vegas, NV 89110

BERTRAND, Michael Elmore (WTex) 2310 N Stewart Rd, Mission, TX 78574

BESCHTA, Gerald Thomas (WNC) 175 Mimosa Way, Hendersonville, NC 28739

BESCHTA, Joyce Marie (WNC) 65 Mimosa Way, Hendersonville, NC 28739

BESENBRUCH, Peter Ray (The Episcopal Church in Haw) 1679 California Ave, Wahiawa, HI 96786

BESHEARS, Earl (SwFla) 331 56th Ave S, St Petersburg, FL 33705

BESHEER, Kimbrough Allan (Oly) 600 1st Ave Ste 632, Seattle, WA 98104

BESIER, Bettine Elisabeth (RI) 30 Scotch Cap Rd, Quaker Hill, CT 06375

BESS JR, Walter (Cal) 118 Tamalpais Rd, Fairfax, CA 94930

BESSLER, Jeffrey L (Ind)

BESSON JR, Michael Wallace (WTex) 9610 Roarks Psge, Missouri City, TX 77459

BEST, Stephen W (Oly) 10670 NE Manor Ln, Bainbridge Island, WA 98110

BETANCES, Gregoria Cedano De (At) 6216 Love St, Austell, GA 30168

BETANCES, Ramon Antonio (At) 925 Whitlock Ave SW Apt 1308, Marietta, GA 30064

BETANCUR ORTIZ, Ricardo Antonio (Colom) c o Diocese of Colombia, Cra 6 No 49-85 Piso 2, Bogota BDC, Colombia

BETE, Vincent Songaben (Ia) 204 E. 5th St., Ottumwa, IA 52501

BETENBAUGH, Helen R (CGC)

BETHANCOURT JR, A Robert (Los) 1145 W Valencia Mesa Dr, Fullerton, CA 92833

BETHEA, Mary (Los) 31641 La Novia Ave, San Juan Capistrano, CA 92675

BETHELL, John Christian (USC) Holy Trinity, 193 Old Greenville Hwy, Clemson, SC 29631

BETHELL, Talbot James (Tex) 290 Fall Creek Dr, Tillamook, OR 97141

BETIT, John D (Ct) 5 Pleasant St, Sutton, MA 01590

BETSINGER, Vicki Lynn (Oly) 280 E Wheelright St, Allyn, WA 98524

BETTINGER, Robert L (Cal) 3940 Park Blvd Apt 911, San Diego, CA 92103

BETTS, Ian Randolph (NY) 5069 Route 108, Millerton, NB E1V 5B7, Canada

BETZ, David Emanuel (NwPa)

BETZ, Nancy (CNY) 412 Hugunin St, Clayton, NY 13624

BETZ SHANK, Erin L (NwPa)

BEUKMAN, Christian Arnold (Mass) 12 Quincy Ave, Quincy, MA 02169

BEVANS, Bruce (WVa) PO Box P, Moundsville, WV 26041

BEVANS, Marjorie (WVa) 903 Charles St, Parkersburg, WV 26101

BEVENS, Myrna Eloise (Colo) 46 N Albion St, Colorado Springs, CO 80911

BEVERIDGE, Robin Lorraine (NY)

BEYER, Jeanie Tillotson (Fla) 2872 N. Hannon Hill Dr., Tallahassee, FL 32309

BEZILLA, Gregory (NJ) 134 Mercer St, Princeton, NJ 08540

BEZY, Bernard Anthony (Lex) 1407 Gemstone Blvd, Hanahan, SC 29410

BHAN, Marcia Chanta (Mass) 10301 Burnet Rd Apt 2408, Austin, TX 78758

BIBENS, Robert Lee (Okla) 4642 E 57th Pl, Tulsa, OK 74135

BICE, Michael Kenneth (Chi) 1244 N Astor St, Chicago, IL 60610

BICKERTON, Frances Catherine Baur (NJ) 164 Buttonwood Dr, Fair Haven, NJ 07704

BICKFORD, Wayne Elva (HB) 8212 Kelsey Whiteface Rd, Cotton, MN 55724

BICKING, David (WVa) 813 Bowling Green Rd, Front Royal, VA 22630

BIDDLE III, Craig (Va) 364 Friar Trl, Annapolis, MD 21401

BIDDY, Eric (Ga) 545 S East Ave, Oak Park, IL 60304

BIDWELL, Mary Almy (NH) 1145 Jerusalem Rd, Bristol, VT 05443

BIDWELL-WAITE, Davidson (Cal) 3641 20th St., San Francisco, CA 94110

BIEDENHARN III, Jay (WTenn) 10 N Church St, Greenville, SC 29601

BIEGA, Richard (WNC) 426 English Rd, Spruce Pine, NC 28777

BIEGLER, James Cameron (FdL) 211 E Carrington Ln, Appleton, WI 54913

BIELSKI, Diane Irene (Colo) P O Box 1558, Fraser, CO 80442

BIEVER, Robert Ray (Oly) 3310 N Bennett St, Tacoma, WA 98407

BIFFLE, Robin (Spok) 1400 Le Grande Cannon Blvd, Helena, MT 59601

BIGELOW, Thomas Seymour (Oly) Box 20489, Seattle, WA 98102

BIGGADIKE, Maylin Teresa (Nwk) 398 Shelbourne Ter, Ridgewood, NJ 07450

BIGGERS, Jackson Cunningham (Miss) 10100 Hillview Dr Apt 537, Pensacola, FL 32514

BIGGS, Carolyn (CFla) 6071 Sabal Hammock Cir, Port Orange, FL 32128

BIGGS, John (WMo) 2632 S Wallis Smith Blvd, Springfield, MO 65804

BIGLEY, Mark Charles (WTex) Church of the Annunciation, PO Box 106, Luling, TX 78648

BILBY, Gary Eugene (NwT) 1501 S Grinnell St, Perryton, TX 79070

BILLER, Larry Ray (NI) 9064 E Koher Rd S, Syracuse, IN 46567

BILLHARDT, Andrea (Chi)

BILLINGS, Leopoldo Samuel (Ve)

BILLINGSLEA, Wendy Ward (Fla) 400 San Juan Dr, Ponte Vedra Beach, FL 32082

BILLINGSLEY, Michael (Mass) Saint Paul's Episcopal Church, 61 Wood St., Hopkinton, MA 01748

BILLINGTON, James Hadley (Los) 1 S El Camino Real, San Mateo, CA 94401

BILLMAN, Daniel Robert (Ind) 8165 Gwinnett Pl, Indianapolis, IN 46250

BILLMAN, Sharon Lynn (Kan) 1738 24000 Rd, Parsons, KS 67357

BILLOW JR, William Pierce (WA) PO Box 242, Barboursville, VA 22923

BILOW, Alexandra Lynn (Colo)

BIMBI, Jim (Del) 4828 Hogan Dr, Wilmington, DE 19808

BINDER, Donald Drew (Va) 9301 Richmond Hwy, Lorton, VA 22079

BINDER, Thomas Francis (Mil)

BINGHAM, Dennis J (Pa)

BINGHAM, Elizabeth Jane (Mich)

BINGHAM, John Pratt (The Episcopal NCal) 17538 Caminito Balata, San Diego, CA 92128

BINGHAM, Sally Grover (Cal) 7 Laurel St, San Francisco, CA 94118

BIORNSTAD, Nathan A (Los) 122 S California Ave, Monrovia, CA 91016

BIPPUS JR, William Lloyd (Ky) 917 Church St, Marinette, WI 54143

BIRCHER, Victor Malcolm (Miss) 102 Edie St, Columbia, MS 39429

BIRD, David John (ECR) 770 Shetland Ct, San Jose, CA 95127

BIRD, Edith (Mo) 1325 Margaret St, Cape Girardeau, MO 63701

BIRD IV, Edward (Ed) T. (Ind) 2897 South Walnut Street Pike, Bloomington, IL 47401

BIRD, Frederick L (WVa) 1009 S Henry Ave, Elkins, WV 26241

BIRD JR, John Edwin (NJ) 304 S Girard St, Woodbury, NJ 08096

BIRD, Julie Childs (SC)

BIRD, Michael Andrew (NY) 40 Broad St Rm 4c, New York, NY 10004

BIRD, Patricia (Del) 30851 Crepe Myrtle Dr Unit 60, Millsboro, DE 19966

BIRD, Robert Dale (Mich) 824 W Maple Ave, Adrian, MI 49221

BIRD, Robert Vincent (Los) 2701 Blue Fox Dr, Ontario, CA 91761

BIRD, Virginia Lee (SD) PO Box 9412, Rapid City, SD 57709

BIRDSEY, Bruce (EC) 2206 Rosewood Ave, Richmond, VA 23220

BIRDSONG, Jerre Eugene (Mo) 4714 Clifton Ave, Saint Louis, MO 63109

BIRKBY, Charles H (CNY) 1505 Pershing Pl Apt A, Rolla, MO 65401

BIRKENHEAD, Harold George (Mass) 8 Nevin Rd, South Weymouth, MA 02190

BIRNBAUM, Rachelle (Va) 942a Heritage Vlg, Southbury, CT 06488

BIRNEY, Edith Hazard (Me) 11 Perkins St, Topsham, ME 04086

BIRNEY III, James Gillespie (Me) 1110 North Rd, North Yarmouth, ME 04097

BIRTCH, John Edward Mckay (SwFla) 1001 Carpenters Way Apt H108, Lakeland, FL 33809

BISHOP, Chris (Pa)

BISHOP, Edwin (Ore) 1900 Lauderdale Dr Apt D115, Henrico, VA 23238

BISHOP, Genevieve R (NJ)

BISHOP, Kathleen Gayle (NJ) St Mary's by-the-sea, 804 Bay Ave, Point Pleasant Beach, NJ 08742

BISHOP-HENCHMAN, Ethan John (WA)

BISSELL-THOMPSON, Geraldine Vina (Alb) 225 Back West Creek Rd, Newark Valley, NY 13811

BITTNER, Merrill (Me) 118 Lone Pine Rd, Newry, ME 04261

BJORNBERG JR, Philip John (SVa) 1 Mill Rd, East Haddam, CT 06423

BLACK, Cynthia (Nwk) 36 South St, Morristown, NJ 07960

BLACK, Katharine C (Mass) 13 Louisburg Sq, Boston, MA 02108

BLACK JR, Milton England (WTex) 149 Cordula St, Corpus Christi, TX 78411

BLACK, Rebecca Lynn (Mass) 6 Daniels St, Millis, MA 02054

BLACK JR, Robert William (NC) 131 W Council St, Salisbury, NC 28144

BLACK, Sherry Leonard (Spr) 12806 Mallard Dr., Whittington, IL 62897

BLACK, Timothy H (At) 1001 Euclid Ave NE, Atlanta, GA 30307

BLACK, Vicki Kay (Me) 73 Bristol Rd, Damariscotta, ME 04543

BLACK, Vincent (O) 2230 Euclid Ave, Cleveland, OH 44115

BLACKBURN, Elliot Hillman (Spr) 603 South Grant, Mason City, IA 50401

BLACKBURN, Gerald Jackson (EC) 4531 Regent Dr, Wilmington, NC 28412

BLACKBURN, John Louis (WTex)

BLACKBURN, Terry Gene (NJ) 35-50 85th Street 5J, Jackson Heights, NY 11372

BLACKERBY JR, William (Ala) 4307 Clairmont Ave S, Birmingham, AL 35222

BLACKHAM, Todd Patten (Los) 1325 Monterey Rd, South Pasadena, CA 91030

BLACKLOCK, Martha Grace (NJ) POBox 2973, Silver City, NM 88062

BLACKMER, Stephen D (NH) Kairos Earth, 107 Hackleboro Rd, Canterbury, NH 03224

BLACKMON, Andrew Thomas (La) 120 S New Hampshire St, Covington, LA 70433

BLACKWELL, Norma Lee (WA) 10754 Main St Apt 202, Fairfax, VA 22030

BLACKWELL, Robert Hunter (Ala) 1016 Broadway Ave SW, Cullman, AL 35055

BLACKWOOD, Deb (NC) 14103 Wilford Ct, Charlotte, NC 28277

BLADON, Doyle Gene (Az) 310 W Union Ave, Monticello, AR 71655

BLAESS, Kristine (Tenn) 1002 Glastonbury Way, Murfreesboro, TN 37129

BLAESS, Michael (Tenn)

BLAGG, James Raymond (Okla) 117 Sandpiper Cir, Durant, OK 74701

BLAIES-DIAMOND, Sarah (NC) PO Box 37, Cleveland, NC 27013

Clergy List

BLAINE, Carol McGown (Tex) 307 Palm Dr, Marlin, TX 76661

BLAINE, Patti (Roch) 3825 E Henrietta Rd Ste 100, Henrietta, NY 14467

BLAINE-WALLACE, Bill (Me) 161 Wood Street, Lewiston, ME 04240

BLAIR, Rebecca H (Episcopal SJ) 1020 W Lincoln Rd, Stockton, CA 95207

BLAIR JR, Thom Williamson (Va) Po Box 1059, Kilmarnock, VA 22482

BLAIR-HUBERT, Paige (SanD) PO Box 336, Del Mar, CA 92014

BLAIR-LOY, Mary Frances (SanD) North Augusta, SC 29841

BLAIS, Heather Jeanette (WMass) 73 Federal St, Wiscasset, ME 04578

BLAKE, Sandy (Colo)

BLAKE, Susan Lynn (CFla) 460 N Grandview St, Mount Dora, FL 32757

BLAKE, Thomas William (Nev) 49 Elizabeth St, Branford, CT 06405

BLAKEMORE, Andrew Thomas (At)

BLAKLEY, Dave Edward (NwT)

BLAKLEY, J Ted (WK) 1101 Prairie St, Hutchinson, KS 67501

BLAKLEY, Raymond Leonard (WTenn) 761 Spaulding Dr, Roseville, CA 95678

BLAKSLEE, John Charles (NI) 15606 W 103rd Ln, Dyer, IN 46311

BLANCH, Paul F (The Episcopal NCal) 2150 Benton Dr, Redding, CA 96003

BLANCHARD, Louise Browner (Colo) 600 N Gilpin St, Denver, CO 80218

BLANCHARD, Louise Sharon (Colo) 6774 Tabor St, Arvada, CO 80004

BLANCHARD, Margaret (WVa)

BLANCHARD, Sudie Mixter (Me) St. George's Episcopal Church, PO Box 364, York Harbor, ME 03911

BLANCHETT SR, David Harvey (The Episcopal Church in Haw) 1100 Pullman Dr, Wasilla, AK 99654

BLANCO, Patricia Dugan (Los) 3455 Mountain Ave, San Bernardino, CA 92404

BLANCO-MONTERROSO, Leonel (Okla) 5500 S Western Ave., Oklahoma City, OK 73109

BLAND, John Dilkes (Minn) 1431 Cherry Hill Rd, Mendota Heights, MN 55118

BLAND, Leslie Rasmussen (NC)

BLAND SR, Thomas James (NC) 4608 Pine Cove Rd, Greensboro, NC 27410

BLASCO, Natalie (SeFla) 1801 Ludlam Dr, Miami Springs, FL 33166

BLASDELL, Machrina Loris (Cal) 504 Cottonwood Dr., Lansing, KS 6043

BLATZ, Edward Nils (LI) 79 Zophar Mills Rd, Wading River, NY 11792

BLAUSER, Dennis Alan (NwPa) 215 Permod Rd, Hermitage, PA 16148

BLAUVELT II, Charles (NH) 32 Church St, Saugerties, NY 12477

BLAUVELT, Jeremy David (USC) 125 Church Ave, Pass Christian, MS 39571

BLAVIER JR, Donald Charles (WTex) 404 Salisbury Ln, Victoria, TX 77904

BLAYER, Brian David (Ct) 15117 14th Rd, Whitestone, NY 11357

BLAYLOCK, Joy Harrell (CGC) 6121 Rawson Ln, Pensacola, FL 32503

BLAZEK, Laura Sue (Okla) 1601 W Imhoff Rd, Norman, OK 73072

BLEDSOE, Alwen Grace (Colo)

BLEDSOE, Faith (SC) Order of Saint Helena, 414 Savannah Barony Dr, North Augusta, SC 29841

BLEDSOE, Sharon Calloway (SVa) 116 Victorian Lane, Jupiter, FL 33458

BLEND, Jennifer Davis (Colo) 4775 Cambridge St, Boulder, CO 80301

BLESSING, Bob (SanD) 12539 Sundance Ave, San Diego, CA 92129

BLESSING, Kamila Abrahamova (Pgh) 6211 Wrightsville Ave # U 147, Wilmington, NC 28403

BLESSING, Pastor Mary (ECR) 5271 Scotts Valley Dr, Scotts Valley, CA 95066

BLESSING, Wren Tyler (Oly) St Patricks Episcopal Church, 225 S Pagosa Blvd, Pagosa Springs, CO 81147

BLEVINS, Isaac (ETenn)

BLEYLE, Douglas Karl (Colo) 318 Silver Ave Sw, Albuquerque, NM 87102

BLIND, Carlisle (Me)

BLINDHEIM, Mark (Oly)

BLINMAN, Clifford (Ore) 2092 E Bighorn Mountain Dr, Oro Valley, AZ 85755

BLISS, Bryan B (Minn)

BLISS, John Derek Clegg (Cal) 4 Edgewater Hillside, Westport, CT 06880

BLISS, Robert Francis (Tex) 881 North Main Street, PO Box 797, Salado, TX 76571

BLOOM, Barry Moffett (Mass) 3030 Union St, Oakland, CA 94608

BLOOM, Lauren Marie (Md)

BLOOMER, Nancy Hester (NY) 4 Grant St, Essex Junction, VT 05452

BLOSS, Matthew Robert (WTex)

BLOSSOM JR, John Dickson (Chi) 125 Sw Jefferson Ave, Peoria, IL 61602

BLUBAUGH, Susan Jo (NI) 1305 S 2nd St, Lafayette, IN 47905

BLUE, Eddie Michael (Md) 7 Park Ave Apt 1, Westminster, MD 21157

BLUE, Gordon K (Ak) 2902 Sawmill Creek Rd, Sitka, AK 99835

BLUE, Susan (WA) 270 El Diente Dr., Durango, CO 81301

BLUE COAT TRAVERSIE, Iva (SD)

BLUME, Andrew C (NY) 160 W 95th St Apt 8b, New York, NY 10025

BLUMENSTOCK, Robert (The Episcopal NCal) 732 Shoreside Dr, Sacramento, CA 95831

BLUNDELL, Gayle Ann (ECR) 2100 Emmons Rd, Cambria, CA 93428

BLUNT, Elizabeth E (NY) Christ Church of the Ascension, 4015 E Lincoln Dr, Paradise Valley, AZ 85253

BLUNT JR, Howard Elton (LI) 125 Eastern Parkway #5D, Brooklyn, NY 11238

BOARD, John Curtis (Mont) 2704 Gold Rush Ave, Helena, MT 59601

BOARD III, Paul (O) 313 E Wayne St, Maumee, OH 43537

BOASE, David John (Spr) 4902 Blu Fountain Dr, Godfrey, IL 62035

BOATWRIGHT, William (NJ) 1901 N Dupont Hwy, New Castle, DE 19720

BOBBITT, Kathleen Morrisette (SVa) 1005 Windsor Rd, Virginia Beach, VA 23451

BOBO, Melinda (Wyo) PO Box 1177, Dubois, WY 82513

BOCCINO, Kenneth Robert (Nwk) 550 Ridgewood Rd, Maplewood, NJ 07040

BOCK, Susan Kay (Mich) 529 E Kirby St, Detroit, MI 48202

BODIE, Park (NY) 235 W 56th St Apt 11m, New York, NY 10019

BOEGER, Daniel Edward (The Episcopal NCal)

BOEGER, Mary Rose Steen (The Episcopal NCal)

BOEHM CARLSON, Christina Mae (Minn)

BOELTER, Phillip R (Minn) Gethsemane Episcopal Church, 905 4th Ave S, Minneapolis, MN 55404

BOELTER, Sally (Cal) 41485 S I-94 Service Drive, Belleville, MI 48111

BOERNER, Nora BC (Ia)

BOESCHENSTEIN, Kathryn C (Colo)

BOEVE, Phillip Dale (Spr) 303 Merchants Ave, Fort Atkinson, WI 53538

BOGAL-ALLBRITTEN, Rose (Ky) 1504 Kirkwood Dr, Murray, KY 42071

BOGAN III, Leslie Eugene (CGC) 1336 Greenvista Ln, Gulf Breeze, FL 32563

BOGEL, Marianne (Oly) 11844 Bandera Rd # 148, Helotes, TX 78023

BOGERT-WINKLER, Hilary Megan (WMass) 14 Boltwood Ave, Amherst, MA 01002

BOGGS, Timothy A (Me) 12 Oakhurst Road, Cape Elizabeth, ME 04107

BOGHETICH, Barbara (Hond) IMC-SAP 564, PO Box 523900, Miami, FL 33152

BOHANSKI, Jeffrey John (Tex)

BOHLER JR, Lewis Penrose (Los) PO Box 16216, Augusta, GA 30919

BOHNER, Charles Russell (Del) 6 Sands Ct, Middletown, DE 19709

BOIVIN, Barbara Ann (Nev)

BOJARSKI, Mitchell T (Roch) 116 S. Columbia St., Campbellsville, KY 42718

BOLAND, Geoffrey Allan (CFla) 1861 Peninsular Dr, Haines City, FL 33844

BOLDINE, Charles Stanley (RG) 6009 Costa Brava Ave NW, Albuquerque, NM 87114

BOLI, Judith Davis (EMich) 4444 State St Apt F-318, Saginaw, MI 48603

BOLLE, Stephen (NY) 1 Chipping Ct, Greenville, SC 29607

BOLLE, Winnie Mckenzie Hoilette (SeFla) 6055 Verde Trl S Apt H316, Boca Raton, FL 33433

BOLLES-BEAVEN, Anne (RI) 32 Yale St, Maplewood, NJ 07040

BOLLINGER II, David Glenn (CNY) 206 John St, Binghamton, NY 13905

BOLLINGER, Matthew D (NJ) 514 W Adams Blvd, Los Angeles, CA 90007

BOLT, Michelle Warriner (ETenn) 413 Cumberland Ave, Knoxville, TN 37902

BOLTON, Carolyn Marie (Cal) 1125 Brush St, Oakland, CA 94607

BOLTON, John (At) 16245 Birmingham Hwy, Milton, GA 30004

BOLTON, Virginia Cassady (CFla)

BOMAN, Ruth Kay (Okla) 424 E St Nw, Miami, OK 74354

BOMAN, Samuel Ratliff (Neb) 1111 S 70th St Apt 211, Apt. 211, Lincoln, NE 68510

BON, Brin Carol (Tex) 1500 N Capital Of Texas Hwy, Austin, TX 78746

BOND, Barbara Lynn (O) 455 Santa Clara St Nw, Canton, OH 44709

BOND, Eric (Pa) 2122 Washington Ln, Huntingdon Valley, PA 19006

BOND, Leonard Wayne (Oly) 5810 Fleming St Unit 66, Everett, WA 98203

BOND, Michael David (Chi) PO Box 438, Cedar Lake, IN 46303

BOND, Michele (Eas) 19524 Meadowbrook Dr, Hagerstown, MD 21742

BONDURANT, Stephen Bryce (SO) 785 Ludlow Ave, Cincinnati, OH 45220

BONE, Patrick Joseph (ETenn) Po Box 129, Church Hill, TN 37642

BONEBRAKE, Aletha Green (EO) 2347 Campbell St, Baker City, OR 97814

BONELL, John Winston (NH) 332 Us Route 202, Rindge, NH 03461

BONIN, Raymond Thomas (NH) 1 Hood Rd, Derry, NH 03038

BONNER, Bruce (Tex) 17119 Horseshoe Bnd, Waller, TX 77484

BONNER, George Llewellyn (LI) 783 E 35th St, Brooklyn, NY 11210

BONNER III, John Hare (ETenn) Holy Trinity Episcopal Church, 207 S Church St, Hertford, NC 27944

BONNER, Michele Christiane (Tex)

BONNER-STEWART, Ann (Mass) 258 Concord St # 258, 258, Newton, MA 02462

BONNEVILLE, Jerome (Spok)

BONNEY, Isaac Kojo Nyame (WA) Saint Marks Church, 12621 Old Columbia Pike, Silver Spring, MD 20904

BONNYMAN, Anne Berry (Mass) 101 Mill Rd, Wilmington, DE 19806

BONOAN, Raynald Sales (SwFla) 18612 Chemille Dr, Lutz, FL 33558

BONSEY, Steven (Mass) 138 Tremont St, Boston, MA 02111

BONSEY, WIlliam Edwin (The Episcopal Church in Haw) 401 Santa Clara Ave Apt 309, Oakland, CA 94610

BONSTEEL, Susan Layh (NY) 94 Clifton Ave, Kingston, NY 12401

BONWITT, Martha (WA) 14303 Old Marlboro Pike, Upper Marlboro, MD 20772

BOODT, Mary Ione (Ind) 100 Oakview Dr, Mooresville, IN 46158

BOOHER, David Lewis (SVa) 724 West H St., Elizabethton, TN 37643

BOOK, Robert TM (At) 170 Trinity Ave SW, Atlanta, GA 30303

BOOKER JR, James Howard (Az) 700 E Georgia Ave, Deland, FL 32724

BOOKSTEIN, Nancey Johnson (Colo) 110 Johnson St, St Brigit Episcopal Church, Frederick, CO 80530

BOOMGAARD, Michelle (WVa)

BOONE, Arthur Robinson (Vt) 1616 Harmon St, Berkeley, CA 94703

BOONE, Connie Louise (EO) 42893 Pocahontas Rd, Baker City, OR 97814

BOONE JR, Robert Augustus (WNC) 266 Merrimon Avenuer, Asheville, NC 28801

BOOTH, Errol Kent (WA) 2811 Deep Landing Rd, Huntingtown, MD 20639

BOOTH, James Alexander (ECR) 48 Miramonte Rd, Carmel Valley, CA 93924

BOOTH, Karen (Lex) 7423 San Jose Blvd, Jacksonville, FL 32217

BOOTH, Stephen P (WMass)

BOOZER, Alcena Elaine Caldwell (Ore) 5256 NE 48th Ave, Portland, OR 97218

BORBON, Samuel (Ore) 1704 NE 43rd Ave, Portland, OR 97213

BORDA, Julian M (Dal)

BORDADOR, Noel Estrella (NY)

BORDELON, Andre (WLa) 1285 Lake Dr., Woodworth, LA 71485

BORDELON, Joseph Ardell (WLa) 5704 Monroe Hwy, Ball, LA 71405

BORDELON, Michael Joseph (WLa) 554, East Middlebury, VT 05740

BORDEN, Robert Bruce (Vt) PO Box 554, East Middlebury, VT 05740

BORDEN, Theorphlis Marzetta (SO) St Simon Of Cyrene, 810 Matthews Dr, Cincinnati, OH 45215

BORDENKIRCHER, Amanda (CFla) 942 Cobbler Ct, Longwood, FL 32750

BORDNER, Ken (Roch) 3471 Cerrillos Rd Trlr 78, Santa Fe, NM 87507

BORG, Manuel (Chi) 1072 Ridge Ave, Elk Grove Village, IL 60007

BORG, Marianne (Ore) 1133 Nw 11th Ave Apt 403, Portland, OR 97209

BORGEN, Linda Suzanne (CGC)

BORGES ALVAREZ, Maria Cristina (SanD) 521 E 8th St, National City, CA 91950

BORGESON, Josephine (The Episcopal NCal) 458 Occidental Cir, Santa Rosa, CA 95401

BORGMAN, Dean Wylie (Mass) 5 Heritage Dr, Rockport, MA 01966

BORNT, Lisa Ashley (Md)

BORREGO, John Edward (Okla) 422 E Noble Ave, Guthrie, OK 73044

BORREGO, Lynn Griffith (Okla) 422 E Noble Ave, Guthrie, OK 73044

BORSCH, Kathleen Ann (Ore)

BORZUMATO, Judith Alice (NY) 500 State Rte 299 Apt 24C, Highland, NY 12528

BOSLER, Sarah Mather (Be) 1188 Ben Franklin Hwy E, Douglassville, PA 19518

BOSQUE, Monica (Fla)

BOSS, Bruce William (Ind) 133 Belvedere Dr, Georgetown, KY 40324

BOSS, Katherine Danielle (NH)

BOSSCHER, Molly Boscher (WMich) 251 E Lake Brantley Dr, Longwood, FL 32779

BOST, Emily Catherine (Ark) 217 N East Ave, Fayetteville, AR 72701

BOSTIAN, Nathan Louis (WTex) 20955 W Tejas Trl, San Antonio, TX 78257

BOSTOCK, Jasmine Hanakaulani (The Episcopal Church in Haw) 1020 Green St Apt 204, Honolulu, HI 96822

BOSTON, Dane Ethan (USC) 1100 Sumter St, Columbia, SC 29201

BOSTON, James Terrell (Ore) 518 NE Dean Dr, Grants Pass, OR 97526

BOSWELL JR, Frederick Philip (Colo) 9200 W 10th Ave, Lakewood, CO 80215

BOSWELL, Kathryn Mary (Alb) 21 Cherry St, Potsdam, NY 13676

BOTH, M Blair (EC) 305 S 5th Ave, Wilmington, NC 28401

BOTTOM, Jacob A (Tenn) Saint David's Episcopal Church, 623 Ector St, Denton, TX 76201

BOTTONE, Doreen Ann (Ct) 68 Main St, Berlin, CT 06037

BOUCHER, Edward Charles (RI) 341 Seaview Ave, Swansea, MA 02777

BOUCHER, John (SVa) 600 Farnham Ct, North Chesterfield, VA 23236

BOULTER, Matthew Rutherford (Tex) 118 S Bois Darc, Tyler, TX 77702

BOULTER, Richard Ottmuller (Mich) 11575 Belleville Rd, Belleville, MI 48111

BOULTER, Robert J (Md) Cathedral of the Incarnation, 4 E University Pkwy, Baltimore, MD 21218

BOURGEAULT, Cynthia Warren (Colo) 8 Pacific St, Rockland, ME 04841

BOURHILL, John William (NY) 26 Huron Rd, Yonkers, NY 10710

Clergy List

BOURLAKAS, Mark (SwVa) 4556 Royal Oak Dr SW, Roanoke, VA 24018

BOURNE, Amanda (Va)

BOURNE, Nathaniel Francis (NH)

BOURNE-RAISWELL, Margaret Lafayette (ECR) 20025 Glen Brae Dr, Saratoga, CA 95070

BOURQUE, Mary Elizabeth (Me) 20 Union St., Hallowell, ME 04347

BOURQUIN, Eugene Alphonse (NY) 296 9th Ave, New York, NY 10001

BOUSFIELD, Nigel J (Mil) 1432 Foxfire Ct, Waupaca, WI 54981

BOUSQUET, Michael (Mass) 1671 Beacon St, Waban, MA 02468

BOUVEL, William (Chi)

BOWDEN, George Edward (Mo) 624 Saffron Ct, Myrtle Beach, SC 29579

BOWDEN JR, Talmadge Arton (Ga) 3409 Wheeler Rd, Augusta, GA 30909

BOWDISH, Lynn (Cal) 172 Northgate Ave, Daly City, CA 94015

BOWEN, Anthony DeLisle (LI) 180 Kane St, Brooklyn, NY 11231

BOWEN, Carol Staley (Cal) 2019 Monroe Ave, Belmont, CA 94002

BOWEN, Elizabeth Anne (Mo) Trinity Episcopal Church, 318 S Duchesne Dr, Saint Charles, MO 63301

BOWEN, George Harry (Nwk) 308 River Oaks Dr, Rutherford, NJ 07070

BOWEN, Kristin Elaine (Mich)

BOWEN, Paul Roger (Tex) 324 Sherwood Ave, Staunton, VA 24401

BOWEN, Pauline Mason (WNY) 138 Castle Hill Rd, East Aurora, NY 14052

BOWEN, Peter Scott (Me) 20 Sky Harbor Dr, Biddeford, ME 04005

BOWEN, Shirley (Me) 20 Sky Harbor Dr, Biddeford, ME 04005

BOWER, Alice W (Oly) 2400 NW 9th Ave, Battle Ground, WA 98604

BOWER, Bruce E (WMo) 6401 Wornall Ter, Kansas City, MO 64113

BOWER, Jeffrey L (Ind) 4160 Broadway St, Indianapolis, IN 46205

BOWER, John Allen (SO) 418 Sugar Maple Ln, Springdale, OH 45246

BOWER, Richard Allen (CNY) 681 N Hill Cross Rd, Ludlow, VT 05149

BOWER, Roger Andrew (Colo) Unit 3223, 10200 Park Meadows Dr, Littleton, CO 80124

BOWERFIND, Ellis Tucker (SwVa) 8727 Bluedale St, Alexandria, VA 22308

BOWERS, David Douglas (SwFla) 513 Nassau St S, Venice, FL 34285

BOWERS, John Edward (SO) 1276 Coonpath Rd Nw, Lancaster, OH 43130

BOWERS, Marvin Nelson (The Episcopal NCal) 202 Tucker St, Healdsburg, CA 95448

BOWERS, Terry L (Colo) 1900 Etton Dr, Fort Collins, CO 80526

BOWERS, Thomas Dix (NY) 304 Lord Granville Dr, Morehead City, NC 28557

BOWERSOX, Sally (Colo) 620 S Alton Way Apt 4d, Denver, CO 80247

BOWES, Bruce (NY) 254 Bloomer Rd, Lagrangeville, NY 12540

BOWHAY, Christopher Andrew (Tenn) St Peters Episcopal Church, 311 W 7th St, Columbia, TN 38401

BOWLER, Nicola (Ia) 3700 SW 37th St, Des Moines, IA 50321

BOWLIN, Howard Bruce (ETenn) 348 Deer Run Dr, Maryville, TN 37803

BOWMAN, Lani Louise (The Episcopal Church in Haw)

BOWMAN, Sallie (Ore) Department Of Spiritual Care, 1015 NW 22nd Ave, Portland, OR 97210

BOWMAN, Susan B (Alb) 790 Route 9w Apt 104, Glenmont, NY 12077

BOWRON, Josh (At) 1623 Carmel Rd, Charlotte, NC 28226

BOYCE, Ryan Antonio (LI) 1709 Arctic Ave, Atlantic City, NJ 08401

BOYCE, Sonya Anna (Alb)

BOYD, Catherine Tyndall (SVa) 19 Lothrop St, North Easton, MA 02356

BOYD, David (Tex) 19 Lothrop St, North Easton, MA 02356

BOYD III, David Emory (At) 101 E 4th Ave, Rome, GA 30161

BOYD, Jeffrey Howard (Mass) 57 Bethany Woods Rd, Bethany, CT 06524

BOYD, Jim (WTenn) 135 Ross M Lynn Dr, Memphis, TN 38111

BOYD, Justin Andrew (Okla) 5666 E 81st St, Tulsa, OK 74137

BOYD, Karen Pisarz (NwT) 602 Meander St, Abilene, TX 79602

BOYD, Larry (Neb) 176 Dome Peak Ter, Dripping Springs, TX 78620

BOYD, Linda Koerber (Md)

BOYD, Sally Ann (Wyo) 436 Sundance Circle, Wright, WY 82732

BOYD, Samuel L (Tex) Po Box 1884, Chandler, TX 75758

BOYD, Sandra Hughes (Colo) 8251 E Phillips Pl, Englewood, CO 80112

BOYD, Virginia Ann (Md) 370 River Rd, Cambridge, VT 05444

BOYD, William Marvin (Fla) 338 River Rd, Carrabelle, FL 32322

BOYD-ELLIS, Sue (WNY) 1439 Schoellkopf Rd, Lake View, NY 14085

BOYDEN-EDMONDS, Marjorie Jennifer (LI) 10017 32nd Ave, East Elmhurst, NY 11369

BOYER JR, Ernest L (ECR) PO Box 360832, Milpitas, CA 95036

BOYER, Geoffrey Thomas (Mich) 2600 Milscott Dr Apt 1335, Decatur, GA 30033

BOYER, John Paul (WNY) 3885 Teachers Ln Apt 8, Orchard Park, NY 14127

BOYER, Marcia M (Vt) Po Box 494, Woodstock, VT 05091

BOYER, William James (CFla) 126 E Palmetto Ave, Howey in the Hills, FL 34737

BOYLAN JR, Russell Brooks (Va)

BOYLE, Patton Lindsay (Spok) 1342 Bartlett Ave, Wenatchee, WA 98801

BOYLE, Peter (Nwk) 185 Newman St, Metuchen, NJ 08840

BOYLES, David Joseph (Fla) St Mary's Episcopal Church, PO Box 611, Madison, FL 32341

BOYLES, William R (Ala)

BOYNTON, Caroline Cochran (NY)

BOYTE, James Garrett Asa (WLa) 3847 Maryland Ave, Shreveport, LA 71106

BOZARTH, Alla Rene (Minn) 43222 SE Tapp Rd, Sandy, OR 97055

BOZZUTI-JONES, Mark Francisco (NY) 74 Trinity Pl, New York, NY 10006

BRACK, Margaret S (Eas)

BRACKETT, Tom (WNC) 11 Waverly Ct, Asheville, NC 28805

BRACKETT KNIGHT, Donna Marie (Tex)

BRADA, Netha Nadine (Ia) 345 Lincoln Ave, Iowa Falls, IA 50126

BRADBURY, John Saferian (Ind)

BRADBURY, Stephanie Chase (Mass) 95 Tyler Park, Lowell, MA 01851

BRADBURY, William J (Mass) 95 Tyler Park, Lowell, MA 01851

BRADEN, Anita (Az) 11527 N Luckenbach St, Surprise, AZ 85388

BRADEN, Lawrence Frank (Ark)

BRADFORD, Kathleen Diane Ross (Cal) 1713 Daisy Way, Antioch, CA 94509

BRADFORD, Larry (Colo) 4131 E 26th Ave, Denver, CO 80207

BRADFORD, Lewis Gabriel (Md) 2900 E Fayette St, Baltimore, MD 21224

BRADLEY, Amy Smith (ETenn)

BRADLEY, Carolyn Ann (NJ) 503 Asbury Ave, Asbury Park, NJ 07712

BRADLEY, Gary J (Los) PO Box 3748, Lake Arrowhead, CA 92352

BRADLEY, James (Ct) 95 Cornwall Ave, Cheshire, CT 06410

BRADLEY, Jeremy Charles (Tex)

BRADLEY, Martha Jean (Spr) 3621 Troon DR, Springfield, IL 62712

BRADLEY, Martha Mantelle (NJ) 318 Elton Ln, Galloway, NJ 08205

BRADLEY, Matthew Bryant (Ky) Christ Church Cathedral, 421 S 2nd St, Louisville, KY 40202

BRADLEY, Michael Lee (Mich) 1780 Allard Ave, Grosse Pointe Woods, MI 48236

BRADLEY, Patrick John (WNY) 505 Riverdale Ave, Lewiston, NY 14092

BRADLEY, Peg (Los) PO Box 3748, Lake Arrowhead, CA 92352

BRADLEY, Raymond Earle (Ind) 7235 East Glen Ct., Mooresville, IN 46158

BRADNER, Lawrence Hitchcock (RI) 500 Angell St Apt 504, Providence, RI 02906

BRADSEN, Kate (Colo)

BRADSHAW, Katie Ann (Miss)

BRADSHAW, Mark D (Los) PO Box 93096, Pasadena, CA 91109

BRADSHAW, Michael Ray (NC) St Pauls Episcopal Church, 520 Summit St, Winston Salem, NC 27101

BRADSHAW, Paul Frederick (NI) University of Notre Dame, 1 Suffolk Street, London, SW1Y 4HG, Great Britain (UK)

BRADSTREET, Charissa Joy (Oly)

BRADTMILLER, Katharine (Minn)

BRADY, Amanda B Mandy (At) 1501 Ridge Ave, Evanston, IL 60201

BRADY, Christian Mark (Lex) 94 Penmoken Park, Lexington, KY 40503

BRADY, Michael (Tex) 1921 Harbour Cove Dr, Seabrook, TX 77586

BRADY, Susan Jane (Colo) 3250 Lee Hill Dr, Boulder, CO 80302

BRADY II, William Donald (CFla) 7135 W Sunripe Loop, Crystal River, FL 34428

BRADY-CLOSE, Jane (NJ)

BRAINARD, Cheryl Elaine (EC) 25 S 3rd St, Wilmington, NC 28401

BRAINARD, Mary-Lloyd (Ct) 3A Gold St, Stonington, CT 06378

BRAINE, Beverly Barfield (Md) 1314 Second Avenue, Tybee Island, GA 31328

BRAKE, Mary Wood (Va)

BRAKEMAN, Lyn G (Mass) 203 Pemberton St Unit #, Cambridge, MA 02140

BRALL, Cathy (Pgh) 321 Parkside Ave, Pittsburgh, PA 15228

BRAMBILA ESTRADA, Gerardo Brambila (Az) 483 W. 80Th. Avenue, Denver, CO 80221

BRAMBLE, Peter Wilkin Duke (LI) 1417 Union St, Brooklyn, NY 11213

BRAMBLE, Sandra Russline (WA)

BRAMLETT, Bruce (ECR) 6028 El Dorado Ave, El Cerrito, CA 94530

BRANCH, Caroline E (At) 2089 Ponce De Leon Ave NE, Atlanta, GA 30307

BRANCHE, Ronald Clifford (Episcopal VI) PO Box 28, Main Street, Tortola, British Virgin Islands

BRANDENBURG, Nancy Lee Hamman (SO) Saint Johns Church, Worthington, OH 43085

BRANDON, Bonnie (Los) 1874 W Nutwood Pl, Anaheim, CA 92804

BRANDON, Karen Dale (RG) 226 Jupiter Dr, White Sands Missile Range, NM 88002

BRANDON II, Miles (Tex) 1501 W 30th St, Austin, TX 78703

BRANDT JR, George (NY) 16 Park Ave Apt 9c, New York, NY 10016

BRANDT, Robert G (LI) 414 SW Horseshoe Bay, Port Saint Lucie, FL 34986

BRANNOCK, Chris (Lex) PO Box 27, Paris, KY 40362

BRANNOCK-WANTER JR, Henry Paul (Vt) 257 Us Route 5, Hartland, VT 05048

BRANNON, Kenneth Hoffman (Dal) St Thomas Episcopal Church, PO Box 1070, Sun Valley, ID 83353

BRANNON, Lecia Elaine (Tex)

BRANNON, Stephen Nave (The Episcopal NCal) 19275 Robinson Rd, Sonoma, CA 95476

BRANSCOMBE, Mike (SwFla) 1010 Charles St, Clearwater, FL 33755

BRANSON, Jana Mauck (Ct) 124 Orange St, Auburn, CA 95603

BRANSON, John Hood (Ct) 827 Fearrington Post, Pittsboro, NC 27312

BRANSTETTER, Kent A (SanD) St Dunstans Episcopal Church, 6556 Park Ridge Blvd, San Diego, CA 92120

BRANT, George Henry (Nwk) 601 Park St Apt 11d, Bordentown, NJ 08505

BRANTINGHAM, Nancy Marie (Minn) 3185 County Road 6, Long Lake, MN 55356

BRATHWAITE, Christopher Ethelbert (CFla) 102 N 9th St, Haines City, FL 33844

BRAUN, Eric (Mich)

BRAUN, Kristin Leigh (Tex)

BRAUZA, Ellen Lederer (WNY) 4210 Gunnville Rd, Clarence, NY 14031

BRAWLEY, Anna P (USC) St Marys Episcopal Church, PO Box 1487, Irmo, SC 29063

BRAWLEY, Joan Biddles Kirby (CFla) 631 W Lake Elbert Dr NE, Winter Haven, FL 33881

BRAXTON JR, Louis (Nwk) 480 Warwick Ave, Teaneck, NJ 07666

BRAY, Doris S (Be) 443 Franklin Ave, Palmerton, PA 18071

BRDLIK, Christopher (Nwk) 914 Ridge Rd, Newton, NJ 07860

BREAKEY, Pamela Jean (WMich) 54581 California Rd, Dowagiac, MI 49047

BRECHT, Laura (SanD) 600 Brennan St, Erie, CO 80516

BRECKENRIDGE, Allen (Az) 2721 N Dos Hombres Rd, Tucson, AZ 85715

BRECKENRIDGE, Elaine (Episcopal SJ) 2927 Sweetwood Dr, Lodi, CA 95242

BRECKENRIDGE, Ella (WLa) 1825 Albert Street, Alexandria, LA 71301

BRECKINRIDGE IV, Lex (Oly) 8398 NE 12th St, Medina, WA 98039

BREDLAU, Mary Theresa (Nev) 8520 W Hammer Ln, Las Vegas, NV 89149

BREEDLOVE, William L (WNC) Church Of The Good Shepherd, PO Box 677, Hayesville, NC 28904

BREESE, Mary Schrom (WMo) 606 Woodcrest Dr, Saint Joseph, MO 64506

BREESE, Sidney Samuel (WMo) 2533 Francis St, Saint Joseph, MO 64501

BREEZE, Jacob P (Tex)

BREHE, Steve (Mont) 912 Stuart St., Helena, MT 59601

✠ **BREIDENTHAL**, Thomas Edward (SO) Diocese Of Southern Ohio, 412 Sycamore St, Cincinnati, OH 45202

BREINER, Bert Fredrick (NY) 401 W 24th St, New York, NY 10011

BREITBARTH, Tammy Marie (NwT)

BRENEMEN, Betty Jo (CGC) 18 West Wright Street Street, Pensacola, FL 32501

BRENES CHAVARRIA, Jose Vinicio (PR)

BRENES VARGAS, Luis Gustavo (Hond) Ch TEC Custo Redentor, AP 15029 Col Kennedy, Tegucigalpa, 11101, Honduras

BRENMARK-FRENCH, Regina Kay (Chi) 2105 Cumberland St, Rockford, IL 61103

BRENNAN, Gerry L (Oly)

BRENNEIS, Michael Joseph (Va) 2309 N Kentucky St, Arlington, VA 22205

BRENNEN, Scott O (SwFla)

BRENNOM, Kesha Mai (Los) 4366 Santa Anita Ave., El Monte, CA 91731

BRENTLEY, David J (SO) 804 Clearfield Ln, Cincinnati, OH 45240

BRENY, Judith Mary (WNY) 745 Ashland Ave, Buffalo, NY 14222

BRESCIANI, Eduardo Roberto (Los) 9037 Park St, Bellflower, CA 90706

BRESNAHAN, Paul B (Mass) 17 King St Unit 1, Lynn, MA 01902

BRETSCHER, Robert George (SwFla) 240 Hancock Ln, Athens, GA 30605

BRETTMANN, William Sims (EC) 557 Fearrington Post, Pittsboro, NC 27312

BREUER, David R (ECR) 20 University Ave, Los Gatos, CA 95030

BREWER, Aaron Keith (Ga) 239 Laurel Landing Blvd, Kingsland, GA 31548

BREWER, Anne (NY) 1275 Summer St, Stamford, CT 06905

✠ **BREWER**, Gregory Orrin (CFla) 1017 E Robinson St, Orlando, FL 32801

BREWER, Johnny Lyvon (CGC) 7810 Navarre Pkwy, Navarre, FL 32566

BREWER JR, Luther Gordon (ETenn) 1417 Warpath Dr Ste B, Kingsport, TN 37664

BREWER III, Richard Frederick (LI) Prestwick Farm, 2260 County Route 12, Whitehall, NY 12887

BREWER, Rick (Okla) 5174 E 29th St, Tulsa, OK 74114

BREWIN-WILSON, Debbie (NJ) 622 Forman Ave, Point Pleasant Beach, NJ 08742

BREWSTER, John Pierce (At) 1064 Can Tex Dr, Sewanee, TN 37375

BREWSTER JR, William (O) 7 Bond Rd, Kittery Point, ME 03905

BREWSTER-JENKINS, Regina (La) 6249 Canal Blvd, New Orleans, LA 70124

BREYER, Chloe Anne (NY) 1800 Adam Clayton Powell Jr Blvd Apt 7b, New York, NY 10026

BREYFOGLE, Elizabeth (Dal) 511 Foote St., McKinney, TX 75069
BREZNAU, Nancy Ann (EMich) PO Box 1882, Caseville, MI 48725
BRICE, Jonathan Andrew William (Kan) St Lukes Episcopal Church, 5325 Nieman Rd, Shawnee, KS 66203
BRICE, Theresa (At) 302 West Ave, Cedartown, GA 30125
BRICENO, Jaime A (Chi)
BRICKSON, Cynthia Jean (Minn) 905 4th Ave S, Minneapolis, MN 55404
BRIDEWELL, Laurie Bridewell (Ark)
BRIDGE, Melvin Alden (Tex) 2102 Lakeforest Dr, Weatherford, TX 76087
BRIDGE, Michael James (WK)
BRIDGE, Peter (NJ) 1509 Esther Ln, Yardley, PA 19067
BRIDGEMOHAN, Areeta D (Va)
BRIDGERS, Anne (SanD) 187 Greenville Ave Unit 104 Apt 104, Arden, NC 28704
BRIDGES, Christopher Mark (The Episcopal Church in Haw) 5286 Kalanianaole Hwy, Honolulu, HI 96821
BRIDGES, Dr David L (Okla)
BRIDGES, Nancy Kilbourn (Okla) 408 Ridge Rd, Edmond, OK 73034
BRIDGES, Penelope Maud (SanD) 6935 Camino Pacheco, San Diego, CA 92111
BRIDGES, Rebecca Bridges (Ala) Saint Stephens Episcopal Church, 3775 Crosshaven Dr, Vestavia, AL 35223
BRIDGFORD, Richard Oliver (SVa) 707 Steiner Way, Norfolk, VA 23502
BRIGGLE, Justin David (Tex) 262 Clearwood Dr, League City, TX 77573
BRIGGS, Barbara (Me) 51 Northport Ave, Belfast, ME 04915
BRIGGS, Lindsey (Minn)
BRIGGS, Lyn (Tex) 661 Redondo Ave, Salt Lake City, UT 84105
BRIGGS, Michael (Ark) PO Box 954, Granby, CO 80446
BRIGGS II, Paul R (Ct) 306 S Main St, Pennington, NJ 08534
BRIGHT, Barbara Pamela (WNC) Tec Ch Of The Redeemer, 502 W Sumter St, Shelby, NC 28150
BRIGHT, Carl Connell (CGC) 198 Beardsley Ct, Muscle Shoals, AL 35661
BRIGHT SR, Dee (CFla) 4hiking Trl, Melbourne, FL 32904
BRIGHT, John Adams (Cal) 812 SW Saint Clair Ave Apt 1, Portland, OR 97205
BRIGHT, Pamela (Wyo)
BRIGHT, Patrick Edmund (Okla) 11901 Maple Hollow Ct, Oklahoma City, OK 73120
BRIGHT, Wheigar J (NC) PO Box 858, Yanceyville, NC 27379
BRIGHTMAN, Dorothy Louise (RI) 17 N Country Club Dr, Warwick, RI 02888
BRIGHTMAN, Mikel Fisher (WTex)

BRIMM, Martha Carol (NC) 7 Surrey Lane, Durham, NC 27707
BRINKMAN, Charles Reed (Pa) 219 Hanover Rd, Phoenixville, PA 19460
BRINKMANN, Mark (SC) All Saints Episcopal Church, 3001 Meeting St, Hilton Head Island, SC 29926
BRINKMOELLER, Leonard Joseph (WMich) 312 Maple St, Paw Paw, MI 49079
BRINSON, Katherine Herrington (Ga) 4227 Columbia Rd, Martinez Branch, GA 30907
BRION, Theresa Markley (Va) 415 10th St, West Point, VA 23181
BRIONES, Miguel Angel (Chi) 5101 W Devon Ave, Chicago, IL 60646
BRISBANE, Paul Owen (Colo) 513 N Union City Rd, Coldwater, MI 49036
BRISLIN, Andrew S (Ala)
BRISSON JR, James L (Ak) 868 Satinwood Ct, Fayetteville, NC 28312
BRISTOL II, Henry Platt (NJ) St David's Church, 90 S Main St, Cranbury, NJ 08512
BRISTOL, Joan Esther (Ore) 2529 Bel Abbes Ave, Medford, OR 97504
BRITCHER, Sharon Ann (CFla) 1010 Pennsylvania Avenue, Fort Pierce, FL 34950
BRITNELL, Offie Wayne (Ak) 18609 S. Lowrie Loop, Eagle River, AK 99577
BRITO, Napoleon Ramon (DomRep) Box 764, Santo Domingo, Dominican Republic
BRITO PEGUERO, Antonio P (At) 1015 Old Roswell Rd, Roswell, GA 30076
BRITT, Diane (LI) St Anns Church, 257 Middle Rd, Sayville, NY 11782
BRITT, Larry (WNC) 236 Camelot Dr, Morganton, NC 28655
BRITT, Marc Lawrence (WA) 2 Amy Ct, Pittsfield, MA 01201
BRITT, Sarah Eugenia Swiss (At) 253 Lake Somerset Dr Nw, Marietta, GA 30064
BRITT, Stephen (Fla) San Jose Episcopal, 7423 San Jose Blvd, Jacksonville, FL 32217
BRITTON, John Clay (Chi) 680 Madrona Ave S, Salem, OR 97302
BRITTON, Joseph Harp (RG) St Michael All Angels Ch, 601 Montano Rd NW, Albuquerque, NM 87107
BRITTON SR, Judith Ann (NMich) 365 Kirkpatrick Ln, Gwinn, MI 49841
BRITTON JR, Richard (Tenn) 509 Laurel Park Dr, Nashville, TN 37205
BROAD, Thomas M (WNY) 3036 Moon Rd, Jamestown, NY 14701
BROADBENT-EVELYN, Anna (WA)
BROADFOOT III, Walter Walter (WNC) 146 Episcopal Church Dr, Saluda, NC 28773
BROADHEAD, Alan John (ND) 107 Heartwood Drive, Lansdale, PA 19446
BROADLEY, Rodger (Pa) 250 S 17th St Apt 400, Apt 400, Philadelphia, PA 19103

BROCATO, Christian (WMich) St Peters Episcopal Church, 838 Massachusetts Ave, Cambridge, MA 02139
BROCHARD, Philip Thomas (Cal) 1118 Santa Fe Ave, Albany, CA 94706
BROCK, Charles F (Va) St James Episcopal Church, Alexandria, VA 22309
BROCK, Laurie M (Lex) 2025 Bellefonte Dr, Lexington, KY 40503
BROCK, Sarah Kathleen (NwPa) 613 Japan St, Erie, PA 16502
BROCK, Scott (USC) 230 Pinecrest Dr Apt 25, Fayetteville, NC 28305
BROCKENBROUGH, Sarah (Va) PO Box 3520, Williamsburg, VA 23187
BROCKMAN, Bennett Albert (Ct) 362 Lake St, Vernon, CT 06066
BROCKMANN, Robert (Mass) 78 Mann Hill Rd, Scituate, MA 02066
BROCKMANN, Sarah (Mass) 78 Mann Hill Road, Scituate, MA 02066
BROCKMEIER, Alan Lee (RG) 8516 N Prince St, Clovis, NM 88101
BROCKMEIER, Suzanne Carroll (RG) St James Episcopal Church, PO Box 249, Clovis, NM 88102
BRODERICK, Janet (Los) 268 2nd St, Jersey City, NJ 07302
BRODERICK, Rosemarie (NJ) P.O. Box 326, Navesink, NJ 07752
BRODERICK Y GUERRA, Cecily (LI) 80 N Centre Ave Apt 133, Rockville Centre, NY 11570
BRODIE, Robert (SwVa) 1612 Valhalla Ct, Salem, VA 24153
BRODY, Mary Ann (Roch) 190 Penarrow Rd, Rochester, NY 14618
BROEREN, Erik Stephanus Simon (ETenn)
BROGAN, Betty Jean (Mich) 17665 E Kirkwood Dr, Clinton Township, MI 48038
BROGAN, Margaret C (Cal) 1432 Eastshore Ave, Alameda, CA 94501
BROKAW, Ronald Gene (CFla) 1106 Dorchester St, Orlando, FL 32803
BROKENLEG, Isaiah Shaneequa (SD) 2701 E Tranquility Pl, Sioux Falls, SD 57108
BROME, Henderson LeVere (Mass) 1201 Davenport Ave, Canton, MA 02021
BROMILEY, Hugh (CFla) 1250 Paige Pl, The Villages, FL 32159
BRONDSTED, Linda J (Eur) 1880 Taylor Ave, Winter Park, FL 32789
BRONOS, Sarah L (CFla) 7718 White Ash Street, Orlando, FL 32819
BROOK, Robert Charles (Mich) 6112 W Longview Dr, East Lansing, MI 48823
✠ BROOKE-DAVIDSON, Jennifer (WTex) 1005 Hadley Meadows Dr, Raleigh, NC 27603
✠ BROOKHART JR, Frank (Mont) PO Box 2020, Helena, MT 59624
BROOKMAN, Cathleen Anne (Chi) 29 W 410 Emerald Green Dr, Warrenville, IL 60555

BROOKS, Albert (Hond) Aptd 28, La Ceiba Atlantida, 31101, Honduras

BROOKS, Ashton Jacinto (DomRep) Cath Ch of the Epiphany, P O BOX 764, Santo Domingo, Dominican Republic

BROOKS, Donald Edgar (WTenn) 1436 Forest Drive, Union City, TN 38261

BROOKS, Dub (Tex) 1917 Revere St, Houston, TX 77019

BROOKS, James Buckingham (Ida) Po Box 36, Letha, ID 83636

BROOKS, Rebecca Rae (Ky)

BROOKS, Reverend Kimberly Brooks (CPa) 248 Seneca St, Harrisburg, PA 17110

BROOKS, Richard Smith (WK) 1333 Crescent Ln, Concordia, KS 66901

BROOKS JR, Robert Brudon (NY) 4 Quail Ridge Rd, Hyde Park, NY 12538

BROOKS, Teddy (NY) 750 Kelly St, Bronx, NY 10455

BROOKS, Weldon Timothy (NH) 113 Main St, Lancaster, NH 03584

BROOKS, Zachary D (Spr) 359 W State St, Jacksonville, IL 62650

BROOME JR, William Bridges (Chi) 504 E Earle St, Landrum, SC 29356

BROOMELL, Ann Johnson (Ct) 1745 Blalock St, Mount Pleasant, SC 29466

BROSEND II, William Frank (Ky) 335 Tennessee Ave, Sewanee, TN 37383

BROTHERTON, E Ann (Tex) 203 Austin Sq Apt 230, Houston, TX 77077

BROUCHT, Mary Louise (CPa) 126 N. Water St., Lancaster, PA 17603

BROUGHTON, Jacalyn Irene (Eau) E4357 451st Ave, Menomonie, WI 54751

BROWDER, David O'Neal (Tex) St Dunstan's Episcopal Church, 14301 Stuebner Airline Rd, Houston, TX 77069

BROWDER III, James Wilbur (SVa) Po Box 133, Courtland, VA 23837

BROWER, David (WMich) 7895 Adams St, Zeeland, MI 49464

BROWER, Gary (Colo) 2050 E Evans Ave Ste 29, Denver, CO 80208

BROWER, George C (Ct) 503a Heritage Vlg, Southbury, CT 06488

BROWER, Katherine Moore (WMich) 335 Bridge St NW Apt 2301, Grand Rapids, MI 49504

BROWER, Meaghan M (RI) Tec Dio Of Ri, 275 N Main St, Providence, RI 02903

BROWER, Sally (NC) 164 Fairview Rd, Mooresville, NC 28117

BROWN, Aston George (Tex)

BROWN, Barton (NJ)

BROWN, Becky (Colo) 6820 W 84th Cir Unit 26, Arvada, CO 80003

BROWN, Bernard Owen (Chi) 5417 S Blackstone Ave, Chicago, IL 60615

BROWN JR, Bill (Ida) 5605 N Lynwood Pl, Boise, ID 83706

BROWN, Christopher Aubrey (Dal) 3200 Mckinney Ave Apt 432, Dallas, TX 75204

BROWN, Claire (ETenn) 123 S Jackson St, Athens, TN 37303

BROWN, Cliff (Mass) 351 Pearl St # 1, Cambridge, MA 02139

BROWN, Clint Edward (Tex) 1812 Stanford St Apt 1, Houston, TX 77006

BROWN, Craig Howard (WK) 3710 Summer Ln, Hays, KS 67601

BROWN, Daniel Aaron (NC) 652 Forest Glen Cir, Murfreesboro, TN 37128

BROWN, Daniel Barnes (At) Po Box 490, Clarkesville, GA 30523

BROWN, David Colin (At)

BROWN, David Crane (NY) 125 Prospect Ave Apt 9g, Hackensack, NJ 07601

BROWN, David Wooster (Ct) 729 W Beach Rd, Charlestown, RI 02813

BROWN, Debbie (Minn) 1297 Wilderness Curv, Eagan, MN 55123

BROWN, Deborah (Ore) Diocese of Oregon, 11800 SW Military Ln, Portland, OR 97219

BROWN, Deborah Bennett (SwFla)

BROWN, Dennis Roy Alfred (CGC) 306 Grant St, Chickasaw, AL 36611

BROWN JR, Dewey E (SwFla) 9508 Front Nine Ln, Dade City, FL 33525

BROWN, Don (La) 224 Pecan Ave, New Roads, LA 70760

BROWN, Donald Gary (Cal) 12705 SE River Rd Apt 508a, Portland, OR 97222

BROWN, Donn H (At) 217 Booth St Apt 119, Gaithersburg, MD 20878

BROWN, Donna Hvistendahl (WA) 1318 Charlottesville Blvd, Knoxville, TN 37922

BROWN, Dorothy (At) 1197 Skyline Dr, Toccoa, GA 30577

BROWN, Dwight (The Episcopal Church in Haw) 489 Ridge Rd, Moscow, ID 83843

BROWN, Eleanor Beverly (CFla)

BROWN, Elly Sparks (WA) 5006-B Barbour Dr, Alexandria, VA 22304

BROWN, Enrique (WA) 5248 Colorado Ave Nw, Washington, DC 20011

BROWN JR, F Wilson (SwVa) 715 Sunset Dr, Bedford, VA 24523

BROWN, Fred McKelder (RG) 208 Camino Del Santiago, 375 Upper Ranchitos Rd, Taos, NM 87571

BROWN, Freda Marie (Md) St Vincents Episcopal House, 2817 Alfreda Houston Place, Galveston, TX 77550

BROWN, Frederick Ransom (Vt) 346 Gladys Avenue, Long Beach, CA 90814

BROWN, Gary N (The Episcopal NCal)

BROWN, Gaye (NC) 308 W Main St, Elkin, NC 28621

BROWN III, George W (Dal) 409 Prospect St, New Haven, CT 06511

BROWN, Greg (NC) 2701 Park Rd, Charlotte, NC 28209

BROWN, Greg (Los) The Church of the Epiphany, 5450 Churchwood Drive, Oak Park, CA 91377

BROWN III, Henry William (CFla) Po Box 1420, Homosassa Springs, FL 34447

BROWN JR, H (Horace) Frederick (WTex) 309 S Someday Dr, Boerne, TX 78006

BROWN III, Hugh Eldridge (NJ) 16 All Saints Rd, Princeton, NJ 08540

✠ **BROWN**, James Barrow (La) 2136 Octavia St, New Orleans, LA 70115

BROWN, James Louis (O) 1533 N 85th Ct, Kansas City, KS 66112

BROWN, Jan Michelle (SVa)

BROWN, Janet Easson (CPa) 140 N Beaver St, York, PA 17401

BROWN, Janet Kelly (Vt) Po Box 351, Jericho, VT 05465

BROWN, Jennifer (NY) 1558 Unionport Rd Apt 7c, Bronx, NY 10462

BROWN, Jennifer Clarke (NC) 1005 Norris Street, Raleigh, NC 27604

BROWN JR, John Ashmore (USC) 9 Sweet Branch Ct, Columbia, SC 29212

BROWN, John Clive (Ore) 431-A Red Blanket Rd, Prospect, OR 97536

BROWN, John Daniel (Dal) 7610 Rockingham Rd, Prospect, KY 40059

BROWN, John Thompson (Ala) 400 University Park Dr Apt 381, Homewood, AL 35209

BROWN, Keith B (Episcopal SJ) 1776 S Homsy Ave, Fresno, CA 93727

BROWN, Ken (WA) 1318 Charlottesville Blvd, Knoxville, TN 37922

BROWN, Kevin Clayton (Del)

✠ **BROWN**, Kevin S (Del) 2106 N Grant Ave, Wilmington, DE 19806

BROWN, Kirk (WNC) 500 Christ School Rd, Arden, NC 28704

BROWN, Lawrence Mitchell (Los) 44550 Denmore Ave, Lancaster, CA 93535

BROWN, Lila Byrd (Fla) 2358 Riverside Ave. #704, Jacksonville, FL 32204

BROWN, Linda Josephine (Colo) 1700 W 10th Ave, Broomfield, CO 80020

BROWN, Lydia Huttar (Minn) 10 Buffalo Rd, North Oaks, MN 55127

BROWN, Lyle L (Ia) 605 Avenue E, Fort Madison, IA 52627

BROWN, Marilynn (Ore) 332338 109Th Pl SE Apt 102, Auburn, WA 98092

BROWN, Marion Mackey (SwFla) 208 Ne Monroe Cir N Apt 103-C, Saint Petersburg, FL 33702

BROWN, Mark M (NY) 1331 BAY ST, #411, STATEN ISLAND, NY 10305

BROWN, Mary Kay (Va) 228 S Pitt St, Alexandria, VA 22314

BROWN, Nancy (Okla) 3914 E. 37th Street, Tulsa, OK 74135
BROWN, Nancy (Los) 2095 Stoneman St, Simi Valley, CA 93065
BROWN, Neva Wilkins (Md)
BROWN, Peter (Minn)
BROWN, Ray (EC) 205 Bedell Pl, Fayetteville, NC 28314
BROWN, Raymond Dutson (Mont) 6162 Lazy Man Gulch, Helena, MT 59601
BROWN, Reed Haller (Vt) 49 Brewer Pkwy, South Burlington, VT 05403
BROWN, Rob (USC) 531 Old Iron Works Rd, Spartanburg, SC 29302
BROWN, Robert Charles (Ark) 501 S Phoenix Ave, Russellville, AR 72801
BROWN, Robert Henry (Pa) 117 Pine Lake Dr, Whispering Pines, NC 28327
BROWN, Robert Labannah (Neb) 9302 Blondo St, Omaha, NE 68134
BROWN, Rodney K (Eas) 32659 Seaview Loop, Millsboro, DE 19966
BROWN, Rosa Maria (Az) 50 N Illinois St, Indianapolis, IN 46204
BROWN, Royce Walter (Wyo) Central Wyoming Hospice, 319 S Wilson St, Casper, WY 82601
BROWN, Sally Sims (Colo) 85 Rampart Way Uniit 510, Denver, CO 80230
BROWN, Scott Jeffrey (WTex) 1417 E Austin Ave, Harlingen, TX 78550
BROWN, Sharman Jones (Mont)
BROWN, Spencer Wade (RG) 2004 Hubbard St SE, Albuquerque, NM 87123
✠ **BROWN**, Thomas James (Me) 70 Church St, Winchester, MA 01890
BROWN, Tricia Lynn (Ore)
BROWN, Virginia Wood (Colo) 706 E. 3rd Avenue, Durango, CO 81301
BROWN JR, Walter R (Ark) 12415 Cantrell Rd, Little Rock, AR 72223
BROWN, Wendy Jo (WMich) 409 W Randolph St, Lansing, MI 48906
BROWN, William Garland (Lex) 311 Washington St, Frankfort, KY 40601
BROWN III, Wm Hill (Va) 5103 Harlan Cir, Richmond, VA 23226
BROWN DOUGLAS, Kelly Delaine (WA) 12519 Hawks Nest Ln, Germantown, MD 20876
BROWNE, Bliss Williams (Chi) 7743 SE Loblolly Bay Dr, Hobe Sound, FL 33455
BROWNE, Frances Louise (NC) 303 Eastchester Dr, High Point, NC 27262
BROWNE, Gayle (SO) 212 Tulane Ave, Oak Ridge, TN 37830
BROWNE, Marigold Sandreen (Episcopal VI)
BROWNE III, Sonny (NC) 117 River Rd N, Roanoke Rapids, NC 27870
BROWNE, Sr Thea Joy (Ky) 2907 Sunset Ave, Bakersfield, CA 93304
BROWNING JR, Bob (Nwk) Grace Church, 128 W Passaic Ave, Rutherford, NJ 07070

BROWNING II, Charles Alex (The Episcopal Church in Haw) 2707 NW 37th Street, Boca Raton, FL 33434
BROWNING, Peter (Los) 2 Hidalgo, Irvine, CA 92620
BROWNING JR, Robert Guy Shipton (SwFla) 7038 West Brandywine Circle, Fort Myers, FL 33919
BROWNING, Trace (U) All Saints Episcopal Church, 1710 S Foothill Dr, Salt Lake City, UT 84108
BROWNLEE, Annette Geoffrian (Colo) 410 W 18th St, Pueblo, CO 81003
BROWNMILLER, David Clark (Ore) 16379 NW Charlais St, Beaverton, OR 97006
BROWN-NOLAN, Virginia (WA) 12613 Meadowood Dr, Silver Spring, MD 20904
BROWNRIDGE, Walter Bruce Augustine (Vt) The Episcopal Diocese of Vermont, 5 Rock Point Rd, Burlington, VT 05048
BROYLES, Elizabeth Ruth (NY) 37 Chipmunk Hollow Rd, Kerhonkson, NY 12446
BRUBAKER GARRISON, Tasha Vache (Ore) 418 Stonewood Dr, Eugene, OR 97405
BRUCE, David Allison (Mass) Brighams Cove Road, Box 243 HCR 63, West Bath, ME 04530
✠ **BRUCE**, Diane Jardine (Los) 5 W Trenton, Irvine, CA 92620
BRUCE, Jane (NC) 750 Weaver Dairy Rd Apt 1225, Chapel Hill, NC 27514
BRUCE, Todd (The Episcopal NCal)
BRUCE, Tracy Ann (Md) 3738 Butler Rd, Reisterstown, MD 21136
BRUCKART, Robert Monroe (CFla) 2327 Saint Andrews Cir, Melbourne, FL 32901
BRUGGER, Stephanie Black (SO) 335 Lincoln Ave, Troy, OH 45373
BRUMBAUGH, Charlie (Colo) PO Box 2166, Breckenridge, CO 80424
BRUNDIGE, Allyson Paige (Nwk) 333 Christian St, Wallingford, CT 06492
BRUNEAU, Betsy (The Episcopal NCal) 66 E. Commercial St., Willits, CA 95490
BRUNELL, Paul Thomas (EMich)
BRUNELLE, Denis Charles (LI) 160 Brunelle Ave, Manchester, NH 03103
BRUNETT, Harry (Md) 9855 S Iris Ct, Littleton, CO 80127
BRUNNER, Arthur Fischer (Pa) 100 Halcyon Dr Apt F202, Media, PA 19063
BRUNO, James Ernest (Ark)
BRUNO, Jean Monique (DomRep) Box 1309, Port-Au-Prince, Haiti
BRUNO, Suzanne Lee (CFla) 9528 Spurwig Ct, Charlotte, NC 28278
BRUNS, Thomas Charles (Mo) 222 Montwood, Seguin, TX 78155
BRUNSON, Catherine E (NJ) 124 Harrow Dr, Somerset, NJ 08873
BRUNSON, Christine (Tex)

BRUSCO, Kathleen Kyle (Minn) 112 Crestridge Dr, Burnsville, MN 55337
BRUSSO, Leonard George (SeFla) 1225 Knollcrest Ct, Venice, FL 34285
BRUST, Cynthia Patrick (CFla)
BRUST, Ellis English (CFla) 463 Peregrine Dr, Indialantic, FL 32903
BRUTTELL, Susan (SeFla) 706 Glenwood Ln, Plantation, FL 33317
BRUTTELL, Tom (SeFla) 706 Glenwood Ln, Plantation, FL 33317
BRUTUS, Joseph Mathieu (Hai) Box 1309, Port-Au-Prince, Haiti
BRYAN, Amelia S (Az)
BRYAN, Elizabeth (SD) 1521 Forest Dr, Rapid City, SD 57701
BRYAN, Joan C (Fla) PO Box 1584, Ponte Vedra Beach, FL 32004
BRYAN, Jonathan (Va) 7815 Midday Ln, Alexandria, VA 22306
BRYAN, Michael John Christopher (Tenn) The Sch of Theology, U of the South, 335 Tennessee Ave, Sewanee, TN 37398
BRYAN, Nancy Henry (Cal) 2111 Hyde St # 404, San Francisco, CA 94109
BRYAN, Peggy (ECR) 1359 Arroyo Seco Dr, Campbell, CA 95008
BRYAN, Walter Lee (WNC) PO Box 1356, Columbus, NC 28722
BRYANT, Bronson Howell (Miss) 5408 Vinings Lake Vw SW, Mableton, GA 30126
BRYANT, Julie Diane (Los) St Pauls Episcopal Church, 502 W Avenue K, Lancaster, CA 93534
BRYANT, Katherine Seavey (Va) 17 Union St NW, Leesburg, VA 20176
BRYANT, Laura Annette (ETenn) 2456 Tanglewood Rd, Decatur, GA 30033
BRYANT, Peter F (Roch) 4160 Back River Rd, Scio, NY 14880
BRYANT, Richard Gordon (Md) 678 Dave Ct, Covington, KY 41015
BRYANT, Robert (Ore) 6300 SW Nicol Rd, Portland, OR 97223
BRYANT, Todd (Cal) 5826 Doliver Dr, Houston, TX 77057
BRYANT, William Reid (WLa) 715 Lewisville Rd, Minden, LA 71055
BRYANT, William S (WNC)
BRYCE, Christopher David Francis (USC) 819 Angela Ln, Cross, SC 29436
BRYSON, Nancy Gretchen (CFla)
BRZEZINSKI, James (Chi) 405 N Cherry St, Morrison, IL 61270
BUB, Sally (Wyo) 30 Diversion Dam Rd, Kinnear, WY 82516
BUCCHERI, Matthew Paul (NY) 14 E 109th St, New York, NY 10029
BUCCO, Dennis M (RI) 58 Arrowhead Ln, West Greenwich, RI 02817
BUCHAN III, Thomas Nicholson (CFla) 1716 River Lakes Rd N, Oconomowoc, WI 53066

BUCHANAN, Andrew Douglas (SVa) 3928 Pacific Ave, Virginia Beach, VA 23451

BUCHANAN, Ernest Ray (WTex) PO Box 68, Hebbronville, TX 78361

BUCHANAN, Furman Lee (SC) 2815 Dearmin Dr, Mt Pleasant, SC 29466

BUCHANAN, H Ray (SwFla) 9650 Gladiolus Dr, Fort Myers, FL 33908

BUCHANAN, Margaret Grace (WNC) 827 Montreat Rd, Black Mountain, NC 28711

BUCHANAN, Susan Jill (WNC) 806 College Ave Sw, Lenoir, NC 28645

BUCHHOLZ, Paige (ETenn) 1211 Oakdale Trl, Knoxville, TN 37914

BUCHIN, Daniel Arthur (Mich) 2655 Grand Castle Blvd SW Apt T0613, Grandville, MI 49418

BUCK, David E (NC) 616 Watson Street, Davidson, NC 28036

BUCK, Leonard Frank (HB)

BUCK, Martha (ECR) 651 Sinex Ave Apt L115, Pacific Grove, CA 93950

BUCK, Robert Allen (Colo) 3070 Indiana St, Golden, CO 80401

BUCK-GLENN, Judith (Pa) 1031 N Lawrence St, Philadelphia, PA 19123

BUCKINGHAM, Carole Sylmay (Wyo) PO Box 12, Kaycee, WY 82639

BUCKINGHAM, Karen Burnquist (Wyo) 608 6th St, Rawlins, WY 82301

BUCKLEY, Rev Mx AJ (Ore) 7403 SE Harold St, Portland, OR 97206

BUCKLEY, Terrence Patrick (LI) 64 S Country Rd, Bellport, NY 11713

BUCKLIN, Lydia K (NMich) 225 37th St, Des Moines, IA 50312

BUCKO, Adam (LI)

BUCKWALTER, Georgine (Ky) 2511 Cottonwood Dr, Louisville, KY 40242

BUDD, Dorothy Reid (Dal) 3707 Crescent Ave, Dallas, TX 75205

BUDD, Richard Wade (SVa) 120 Cypress Crk, Williamsburg, VA 23188

✠ **BUDDE**, Mariann (WA) Diocese Of Washington, Mount St Alban, Washington, DC 20016

BUDEZ, Jorge Horacio (WNY)

BUDHU, Esar (Nwk) 206 Renshaw Ave, East Orange, NJ 07017

BUDNEY, Karen Vickers (CNY) 18 Cross St., Dover, MA 02030

BUECHELE, Thomas John (The Episcopal Church in Haw) 15-2686 Hinalea St, Pahoa, HI 96778

BUECHNER, Deborah Ann (CFla) 1078 Coastal Cir, Ocoee, FL 34761

BUECHNER, Frederick Alvin (Ga) Po Box 2626, Thomasville, GA 31799

BUEHLER, Lynnsay Anne (At) 147 Shadowmoor Dr, Decatur, GA 30030

BUEHRENS, Gwen Langdoc (Mass) 1333 Gough St. Apt 1-D, San Francisco, CA 94109

BUELOW, Peggy Butterbaugh (SVa) 23397 Owen Farm Rd, Carrollton, VA 23314

BUENO BUENO, Francisco Javier (Colom) Kra 80 #53a-78, Medellin, Colombia

BUENTING, Julianne (Chi) 3857 N Kostner Ave, Chicago, IL 60641

BUENZ JR, John Frederick (ECR) 22115 Dean Ct, Cupertino, CA 95014

BUFFONE, Gregory James (Tex) 3 Westridge Rd, Savannah, GA 31411

BUICE, Samuel Walton (At) 3 Westridge Rd, Savannah, GA 31411

BUICE, William Ramsey (Hond) 10100 Hillview Dr #4A, Pensacola, FL 32514

BUIE, Delinda Stephens (Ky) 2341 Strathmoor Blvd, Louisville, KY 40205

BUISSON, Pierre-Henry Paul (Va) 808 Red Bud Ln, Front Royal, VA 22630

BUKER, Karen Elaine (Mil) 3380 S Jeffers Dr, New Berlin, WI 53146

BULL, Julian (Los) 5049 Gloria Ave, Encino, CA 91436

BULL, Terry Wayne (WNY) 633 Harrison Ave, Buffalo, NY 14223

BULLARD, Carol Ann (Neb) 1603 17th St, Mitchell, NE 69357

BULLARD, Jill Staton (NC) 403 E Main St, Durham, NC 27701

BULLARD, Lynn Huston (Ala) 8020 Whitesburg Dr S, Huntsville, AL 35802

BULLARD, William Thomas (Tex)

BULLER, Reverend Deacon Alberta Brown (The Episcopal Church in Haw) 15-2660 Pahoa Village Rd Ste 203-404, Pahoa, HI 96778

BULLION, Jim (Ga) 512 Flamingo Ln., Albany, GA 31707

BULLITT-JONAS, Margaret (WMass) 109 Olander Dr, Northampton, MA 01060

BULLOCK, Ashley (EC)

BULLOCK, Debra K (Chi) St Marks Episcopal Church, 1509 Ridge Ave, Evanston, IL 60201

BULLOCK, Jeff (Los) 3474 NW Bryce Canyon Ln, Bend, OR 97703

BULLOCK, John Thomas (Kan)

BULLOCK, Kenneth R (Pa) 213 Stable Rd, Carrboro, NC 27510

BULLOCK, Michael (WMass) 1040 Brentwood Dr, Columbia, SC 29206

BULSON, William Lawrence (FdL) 13000 Saint Davids Rd, Minnetonka, MN 55305

BUMGARNER, William Ray (SwVa) 605 Clay St, Lynchburg, VA 24504

BUMP, Anne (Mich) 1708 Jamestown Place, Pittsburgh, PA 15235

BUMSTED, David S (Okla) Church Of The Redeemer, 222 S Palm Ave, Sarasota, FL 34236

BUNCH, Linda Lauren (USC) 33 Station Ct Apt 205, Greenville, SC 29601

BUNDER, Peter J (Ind) 610 Meridian St, West Lafayette, IN 47906

BUNKE, Jeff L (O) 223 W Harrison St, Maumee, OH 43537

BUNKER, Oliver Franklin (Kan) Grace Episcopal Church, 209 S Lincoln Ave, Chanute, KS 66720

BUNKER, Robert Monroe (WA) 522 Main St, Laurel, MD 20707

BUNSY, Martin (Episcopal SJ) 1327 N Del Mar Ave, Fresno, CA 93728

BUNTING, Drew Andrew (ETenn) 290 Quintard Rd # 19, Sewanee, TN 37375

BUNTING SR, Norman Richard (Eas) St Paul's Episcopal Church, 3 Church St, Berlin, MD 21811

BUOTE-GREIG, Eletha (Mass) PO Box 192, North Scituate, RI 02857

BUQUOR, Anthony Francis (SD) 1357 Old Marlboro Rd, Concord, MA 01742

BURACKER II, William Joseph (CFla)

BURBANK, Kristina Dawn (Ore)

BURCH, Ian C (Mil) 1424 N Dearborn St, Chicago, IL 60610

BURCH, Suzanne (ETenn) 4111 Albemarle Ave, Chattanooga, TN 37411

BURCHARD, Russell Church (SwVa) 51 Mayapple Gln, Dawsonville, GA 30534

BURDEKIN, Edwina Amelia (Colo) 4566 Winewood Village Dr, Colorado Springs, CO 80917

BURDEN, Richard James (Mass) 1789 Beacon St Unit 1, Brookline, MA 02445

BURDESHAW, Charles Abbott (Tenn) 139 Brighton Close, Nashville, TN 37205

BURDICK III, Henry C (Ct) 152 Wharf Landing Dr Unit A, Edenton, NC 27932

BURETTE, Stephanie (Eur)

BURG, Michael (FdL) 2515 Lakeshore Dr, Sheboygan, WI 53081

BURGDORF, David (Los) 36270 Avenida de Las Montanas, Cathedral City, CA 92234

BURGER, Charles Sherman (Ida) 9640 W. Sleepy Hollow Ln, Garden Valley, ID 83714

BURGER, Douglas Clyde (RI) 214 Oakley Rd, Woonsocket, RI 02895

BURGER, Robert Franz (Wyo) Po Box 579, Estes Park, CO 80517

BURGER, Tim (Ga) 11 Berkeley Pl, Glen Rock, NJ 07452

✠ **BURGESS**, Brian (Spr) 450 Hickory, Petersburg, IL 62675

BURGESS, Candis (NC) PO Box 1547, Clemmons, NC 27012

BURGESS, Judy (RG) 134 Hillcrest Loop, Capitan, NM 88316

BURGESS, Vicki (Tenn) 4016 Brush Hill Rd, Nashville, TN 37216

BURGESS, Walter F (Eas) 105 Gay St, Denton, MD 21629

BURGESS, William (CGC)

BURGOS, Joe A (Tex) 305 Sunset Drive, North Manchester, IN 46962

BURHANS III, Rick (CFla)

Clergy List

BURHOE, Alden Read (Mass) 54 Grant Ave, Somerset, MA 02726

BURK, John H (Episcopal SJ) 599 Colton St, Monterey, CA 93940

BURK, William H (Va) 7159 Mechanicsville Tpke, Mechanicsville, VA 23111

BURKARDT, Jay P (Roch) St Paul Episcopal Church, 25 Westminster Rd, Rochester, NY 14607

BURKARDT, Leslie S (Roch) 2000 Highland Ave, Rochester, NY 14618

BURKE, Anne B (RI) 66 Elm St Apt 1, Westerly, RI 02891

BURKE, Celine (WMich) 1033 NW Stannium Rd, Bend, OR 97701

BURKE, Cyril Casper (Ct) 26 Hoskins Rd, Bloomfield, CT 06002

BURKE, Darryl Clifford (Ct)

BURKE, Geneva Frances (Mich) 21514 Deguindre, #202, Warren, MI 48091

BURKE, Gregory (Neb)

BURKE, Michael (Ak) 3221 Amber Bay Loop, Anchorage, AK 99515

BURKE, Norman Charles (Az) 9552 West Wild Turkey Lane, Strawberry, AZ 85544

BURKE, Patrick Timothy (Ind) 11524 Long Sotton Cir, Fishers, IN 46037

BURKE, Richard Early (Mass) 3279 Flamingo Blvd, Hernando Beach, FL 34607

BURKE, Robert Thomas (NwPa) Grace Episcopal Church, 10121 Hall Ave, Lake City, PA 16423

BURKE, Sean Dennis (Ia) 201 Hollihan St, Decorah, IA 52101

BURKERT-BRIST, Monica Anne (FdL) 315 E Jefferson St, Waupun, WI 53963

BURKETT, William Vernard (SwFla) 2902 Weset San Rafael Street, Tampa, FL 33629

BURKHART, John Delmas (Lex) 701 E Engineer St, Corbin, KY 40701

BURKS, Bill (WTenn) 98 Jim Dedmon Rd., Dyer, TN 38330

BURKS, Tami Louise (NY)

BURLEIGH, Judith Cushing (Me) PO Box 8, Presque Isle, ME 04769

BURLESON, Saul Lars (RG) Unit 00341 Box 41, FPO, AE 09564

BURLEY, Aloysius Englebert John Timothy (Minn) 615 W Tanglewood Dr, Arlington Heights, IL 60004

BURLEY III, Clarence Augustus (ECR) 651 Broadway, Gilroy, CA 95020

BURLINGTON, Robert Craig (RI) 1070 Homewood Blvd Apt 306, Delray Beach, FL 33445

BURMAN, David F (ETenn)

BURMEISTER, Melissa Lynne (Mil) 1556 E. Colonial Oaks Dr., Monticello, IN 47960

BURNARD, Karen Kartsimas (SO) 264 Gemstone Sq W, Westerville, OH 43081

BURNER, Dan E (Az)

✠ **BURNETT**, Joe Goodwin (Neb) PO Box 506, Rapid City, SD 57709

BURNETT, Joseph or Jody Goodwin (Miss) St Peters Episcopal Church, 113 S 9th St, Oxford, MS 38655

BURNETT, Nancy Jo (SanD)

BURNETT, Richard Alvin (SO) 125 E Broad St, Columbus, OH 43215

BURNETTE, Marc (Ala) 1930 Fairfax Dr, Florence, AL 35630

BURNHAM, Karen Lee (Colo) 2029 Pine St, Pueblo, CO 81004

BURNHAM, Susan E (WTex)

BURNS, ANn Lyn (Colo) PO Box 635, La Veta, CO 81055

BURNS, Deborah Stansbrough (Kan) 3021 Steven Dr, Lawrence, KS 66049

BURNS, Duncan Adam (LI) 209 Albany Ave, Kingston, NY 12401

BURNS, Jacquelyn Mae (SO) St John's Episcopal Church, 700 High St, Worthington, OH 43085

BURNS, James Lee (NY) 1936 Eastlake Ave E # 312, Seattle, WA 98102

BURNS, Jason A (WMass)

BURNS, Jerome (SO) 1316 Villa Paloma Blvd, Little Elm, TX 75068

BURNS, Leonetta Faye (Me) 52 Dondero Rd, Chelsea, ME 04330

BURNS, Lisa (Tex) Calvary Episcopal Church, PO Box 721, Bastrop, TX 78602

BURNS, Steven Thomas (Eau)

BURNS, Thomas Dale (NwT) 3402 W Ohio Ave, Midland, TX 79703

BURNS LAGRECA, Allison Marie (NJ)

BURR II, Donald Field (Ct)

BURR, John Terry (Roch) 594 Stearns Rd, Churchville, NY 14428

BURR, Whitney Haight (Mass) 175 Shane Dr, Chatham, MA 02633

✠ **BURRILL**, William George (Az) 7550 N. 16th Street #5204, Phoenix, AZ 85020

BURRIS, Holly (La) 407 Saint Bernard St, Thibodaux, LA 70301

BURRIS, Richard R (Okla) 900 Schulze Dr, Norman, OK 73071

BURROUGHS, Joseph Parker (Md) 7236 Gaither Rd, Sykesville, MD 21784

BURROWS, Judith Anne (WNY) 106 Hickory Hill Rd Apt A, Buffalo, NY 14221

BURROWS, Paul Anthony (Cal) 474 48th Ave Apt 23a, Long Island City, NY 11109

BURRUSS, John (Ala) 3775 Crosshaven Dr, Birmingham, AL 35223

BURT, William R (Ct) 813 Marla Dr, Point Pleasant Boro, NJ 08742

BURTON, Anthony John (Dal) 3966 Mckinney Ave, Dallas, TX 75204

BURTON, Bob (Az) 9502 W Hutton Dr, Sun City, AZ 85351

BURTON, Cassandra Yvonne (WA)

BURTON, Christine Hazel (RI) PO Box 48, Hope Valley, RI 02832

BURTON, Jack C (SO) Norton Orchard Rd, PO Box 5195, Edgartown, MA 02539

BURTON, James M (SC) 126 Taylor Cir, Goose Creek, SC 29445

BURTON, John (Ct)

BURTON, John (Ark) 807 COUNTY ROAD 102, EUREKA SPRINGS, AR 72632

BURTON, John Peter (Chi) 4839 W Howard, Skokie, IL 60076

BURTON, Laurel Arthur (Mil)

BURTON, Whitney A (SwFla)

BURTON-EDWARDS, Grace (At) St Thomas Episcopal Church, 2100 Hilton Ave, Columbus, GA 31906

BURTS, Ann (NC) 8804 Broadmore Ct, Raleigh, NC 27613

BUSBY, Lisa Jo (CNY) 412 Hugunin St, Clayton, NY 13624

BUSCH, Edward Leonard (SanD) 11650 Calle Paracho, San Diego, CA 92128

BUSCH, Glenn Edward (NC) 3024 Cardinal Pl, Lynchburg, VA 24503

BUSCH, Richard Alan (Los) 4125 36th St S, Arlington, VA 22206

BUSCH, Steven (Va) 9111 Hunting Pines Pl, Fairfax, VA 22032

BUSER, Carolyn Elizabeth (Md) Carolyn Buser, 601 Pennsylvania Ave NW Apt 1108, Washington, DC 20004

BUSH, Emilie Chaudron (Colo) St. Paul's, PO Box 726, Barstow, CA 92312

BUSH, Katherine (WTenn) 718 Charles Place, Memphis, TN 38112

BUSH, Lydia (Fla)

BUSH, Patrick (Ct) 327 Orchard St, Rocky Hill, CT 06067

BUSH, Samuel Prescott (Va)

BUSHEE, Grant Sartori (Cal) 1225 Rosefield Way, Menlo Park, CA 94025

BUSHEY JR, Howard (La) 8833 Goodwood Blvd, Baton Rouge, LA 70806

BUSHNELL, Peter Emerson (Ct) Holy Trinity Church, 383 Hazard Ave, Enfield, CT 06082

BUSHONG JR, Edward Stuart (SVa) 2806 E Marshall St, Richmond, VA 23223

BUSSE, Mary Ruth (Fla) 3580 Pine St, Jacksonville, FL 32205

BUSSEY, Gregory (RG)

BUSSEY, Lawrence (Minn)

BUSTARD-BURNSIDE, Carol (Md) 1106 Woodheights Ave, Baltimore, MD 21211

BUSTO, Mercedes (SeFla)

BUSTOS, Miguel (Cal)

BUSTRIN, Robert C (Az) 118 Lafayette Ave, Brooklyn, NY 11217

BUTCHER, Geoffrey (Ky) 310 N Pearl St, Natchez, MS 39120

BUTCHER, Gerald Alfred (Okla) 1720 W Carolina Ave, Chickasha, OK 73018

BUTCHER, Jonathan Mark (Spr) 111 Bess St, Washington, IL 61571

BUTCHER, Julie Ann (CFla)

BUTCHER, Kenneth Pf (Colo) 3306 Morris Ave, Pueblo, CO 81008

BUTCHER, William (Minn)

BUTERBAUGH, Matthew L (Mil) St Matthews Church, 5900 7th Ave, Kenosha, WI 53140

BUTIN, John Murray (Ga) 303 Cannon Ct, St Simons Island, GA 31522

BUTLER III, Andrew Garland (SanD) 59 Montclair Ave, Montclair, NJ 07042

BUTLER, Charles Roger (CNY) 28205 Nc 73 Hwy, Albemarle, NC 28001

BUTLER, Clarence Elliot (Mass) 19 Russell Ave., Watertown, MA 02472

BUTLER, David Floyd (Kan) PO Box 65, Independence, KS 67301

BUTLER, Joseph Gilbert (WTenn) 2044 Elm Tree Ct, Charlottesville, VA 22911

BUTLER, Joseph Green (O) 471 Crosby St, Akron, OH 44302

BUTLER, Julett Noreene (NY)

BUTLER, Marilyn M (Ida) 4251 N 1800 E, Buhl, ID 83316

BUTLER, Mark Hilliard (LI) 225 Arbutus Ln, Hendersonville, NC 28739

BUTLER, Oliver Martin (Dal) 8011 Douglas Ave, Dallas, TX 75225

BUTLER, Pauline Felton (CFla) 815 E Graves Ave, Orange City, FL 32763

BUTLER, Susan J (ETenn) 20 Belvoir Ave, Chattanooga, TN 37411

BUTLER, Tony Eugene (Cal) PO Box 4380, Sparks, NV 89432

BUTLER-GEE, Eve (SVa) Martins Bron Tec Ch, 18706 James River Dr, Disputanta, VA 23842

BUTTERWORTH, Gary Wayne (WNC) 510 Sabine Dr, Laurel Park, NC 28739

BUTWILL, Norman M (Cal)

BUXEDA-DIAZ, Ivan Rene (PR)

BUXO, David Carlysle (Mich) 3601 W 13 Mile Rd, Royal Oak, MI 48073

BUXTON-SMITH, Sarah Wallace (WNY) 100 Beard Ave, Buffalo, NY 14214

BUZZARD, Henry Lewis (NY) 71 Wayne Ave, White Plains, NY 10606

BUZZINI W, Walter (WTex)

BWECHWA, Oswald (Mil) 3400 E Debbie Drive, Oak Creek, WI 53154

BYE, Mike (SC) PO Box 942, Wadesboro, NC 28170

BYE, Tommy Frank (Tex) 1201 Overhill St, Bedford, TX 76022

BYER, Martha Russell (WMo) 3907 Ivanhoe Blvd, Columbia, MO 65203

BYERS, Mark (Ct) 38 Grove St, Thomaston, CT 06787

BYERS, Sara Shovar (Ga) PO Box 925, Moultrie, GA 31776

BYERS, William (WMass) 35 Nedwied Rd, Tolland, CT 06084

BYRD, Bear (CGC) 403 W College St, Troy, AL 36081

BYRD, Frederick Colclough (USC) 1115 Marion St, Columbia, SC 29201

BYRD, Katherine H (NC) 166 Market St, Lexington, KY 40507

BYRD, Nita Charlene Johnson (Roch) St Paul Episcopal Church, 221 Union St, Cary, NC 27511

BYRD SR, Ronald Charles (Mich) 634 Canoga Ln, Haslett, MI 48840

BYRER, Johnine Vaughn (Pa) 6 Juniper Dr, Whitehouse Station, NJ 08889

BYRNE, Anne SC (Md) 126 E. Liberty St., Oakland, MD 21550

BYRNE, Larry (LI) 21433 40th Ave, Bayside, NY 11361

BYRUM, Emory Etheridge (Nwk) Trinity Episcopal Church, 6587 Upper York Rd. PO Box 377, Solebury, PA 18963

BYRUM, Philip Robert (NC) 1207 Cambridge Rd NW, Wilson, NC 27896

BYRUM, Rick Edward (Los) 28648 Greenwood Pl, Castaic, CA 91384

C

CABALLERO, Daniel (Mil) 4305 Rolla Ln, Madison, WI 53711

CABALLERO-ELIZALDE, Gilberto Tadeo (Cu)

CABANA, Denise (Ct) 2584 Main St, Glastonbury, CT 06033

CABES, Corrie M (NwT)

CABEY, Lenroy Kirtley (Episcopal VI)

CABRERA AMADOR, Fredy (Hond) IMS SAP Dept 215, PO Box 523900, Miami, FL 22152-3900, Honduras

CABRERO-OLIVER, Juan (LI) 443 Maren St, West Hempstead, NY 11552

CABUSH, Carrie Grace (Nwk)

CABUSH, David Walter (Nwk) 2 Pond Hill Rd # 7960, Morristown, NJ 07960

CACCESE, Nicholas Michael (SwFla) 553 Galleon Dr, Naples, FL 34102

CACOPERDO, Peter Anthony (RG) 103 Taos Ct, PO Box 1747, Elephant Butte, NM 87935

CADARET, John Michael (Va) 8411 Freestone Ave, Richmond, VA 23229

CADDELL, Bryn S (WTex)

CADDELL, Christopher Len (WTex) C Of Holy Spirit, 301 Hays Country Acres Rd, Dripping Springs, TX 78620

CADE, Wendy P (At) 1323 N Dupont St, Wilmington, DE 19806

CADENA, Enrique (Az) 2801 N 31st Street, Phoenix, AZ 85008

CADIGAN, Charles Richard (Mo) 1625 Masters Drive, DeSoto, TX 75115

CADIGAN, Katie (Los) St. Augustine by-the-Sea, 1227 4th St, Santa Monica, CA 90401

CADWELL, Matthew P (Mass) 94 Newbury Ave Apt 309, Quincy, MA 02171

CADY, Donald Holmes (Va) Grace Episcopal Church, PO Box 43, Keswick, VA 22947

CAFFERATA, Gail (The Episcopal NCal) 4794 Hillsboro Cir, Santa Rosa, CA 95405

CAFFREY, David (Los) PO Box 514, Joshua Tree, CA 92252

CAGE JR, Stewart B (La) 8932 Fox Run Ave, Baton Rouge, LA 70808

CAGGIANO, Diane Ruth (Ct) 11 Overvale Rd, Wolcott, CT 06716

CAGGIANO, Joyce (Mass) 27 Curtis Rd, Milton, MA 02186

CAGUIAT, Carlos J (Mich) 10901 176th Cir NE Apt 2421, Redmond, WA 98052

CAGUIAT, Julianna (Oly) 20 Oakwood Road, Saranac Lake, NY 12983

CAHALL, Michael Sheldon (WA) 22879 Kimberly Ct, Lexington Park, MD 20653

CAHILL, Elizabeth Ann (EO)

CAHILL, Pat (ETenn) 317 Windy Hollow Dr, Chattanooga, TN 37421

CAHOON, Vernon John (NC) 428 Pee Dee Ave, Albemarle, NC 28001

CAIMANO, Catherine Anne (NC) 13804 Hill St, Huntersville, NC 28078

CAIN, Donavan (Ala) All Saints Episcopal Church, 4171 Hendricks Ave, Jacksonville, FL 32207

CAIN JR, Everett Harrison (Tex) 7705 Merrybrook Circle, Austin, TX 78731

CAIN, George Robert (SwFla) Box 1033, 6 Hickory Rd, Wolfeboro, NH 03894

CAIRES, Joy Marielouise (Minn) 12671 Woodside Dr, Chesterland, OH 44026

CAIRNS, John Carter (Alb) 316 Valentine Pond Rd, Pottersville, NY 12860

CALAFAT, KAREN A (Tex) 1145 Fairweather Dr, Fort Worth, TX 76120

CALANDRIELLO, Andrew Michael (NJ)

CALCOTE, ALan Dean (Tex) 5615 Duff St, Beaumont, TX 77706

CALDBECK, Elaine S (Ia) 2400 Middle Rd, Bettendorf, IA 52722

CALDWELL, Brenda Ann (Wyo) 1167 Hidalgo Dr, Laramie, WY 82072

✠ **CALDWELL**, Bruce (Wyo) 104 S 4th St, Laramie, WY 82070

CALDWELL, George M (Va) 501 Slaters Ln Apt 521, Alexandria, VA 22314

CALDWELL, James Hardy (Chi) 1307nW Logan St, Freeport, IL 61032

CALDWELL, Kevin Lee (Ala) 905 E Mcmurray Rd, Venetia, PA 15367

CALDWELL, Margaret Caldwell (ETenn) 1264 Duane Rd, Chattanooga, TN 37405

CALDWELL, Michael (Mil) C O Holy Cross Episcopal Church Wisonsin Dells, 322 Unity Dr, Wisconsin Dells, WI 53965

CALDWELL, Wallace Franklin (Mo) 1115 Woodleigh Ct, Harrisonburg, VA 22802

CALER, Joshua M (Pa) 900 Broadway, Nashville, TN 37203

CALEY BOWERS, Elizabeth Ann Ann (Fla) 9252 San Jose Blvd. Apt. 3703, Jacksonville, FL 32257

CALHOUN, Annie (Los) St Annes Church, 2350 Main St, Washougal, WA 98671

CALHOUN, Dolores Moore (CPa) Po Box 32, Jersey Mills, PA 17739

CALHOUN, Joseph 'Cal' William (ETenn) 9420 States View Dr, Knoxville, TN 37922

CALHOUN, Nancy Ellen (Del) 31 Dresner Cir, Boothwyn, PA 19061

CALHOUN, Robert Clay (Miss)

CALHOUN, Royce (WTex) 103 Bluff Vista, Boerne, TX 78006

CALHOUN-BRYANT, Julie (CNY) 104 Single Dr, North Syracuse, NY 13212

CALKINS, Linda (WA) 10617 Eastwood Ave, Silver Spring, MD 20901

CALKINS, Matthew H(amilton)) (NY) PO Box 366, Millbrook, NY 12545

CALLAGHAN, Alice Dale (Los) 307 E 7th St, Los Angeles, CA 90014

CALLAHAM, Arthur A (Tex) 4428 Basswood Ln, Bellaire, TX 77401

CALLAHAN, Gary Edward (ETenn) PO Box 21275, Chattanooga, TN 37424

CALLARD, Tom Adams (WMass) 35 Chestnut St, Springfield, MA 01103

CALLAWAY, James Gaines (NY) 549 W 123rd St Apt 13a, New York, NY 10027

CALLAWAY, Richard H (At) 6513 Blue Creek Ct, Douglasville, GA 30135

CALLEN, Bryan (NwT)

CALLENDER, Francis Charles (Episcopal SJ) 1060 Cottage Ave, Manteca, CA 95336

CALLENDER, Randy (Md) Saint Philip's Church, 730 Bestgate Rd, Annapolis, MD 21401

CALLISON, Donald Walter (The Episcopal NCal)

CALLISON, Jonathan David (WMo) 11 E 40th St, Kansas City, MO 64111

CALVERT, George (SanD) 3990 Bonita Rd, Bonita, CA 91902

CALVO PEREZ, Antonis (Colom) C165 No. 36 A-30, Bogota, Colombia

CAMERON, David Albert (SD) 2417 Holiday Ln, Rapid City, SD 57702

CAMERON, Euan Kerr (NY)

CAMERON, Jackie (Chi) 513 W Aldine Ave Apt 2h, Chicago, IL 60657

CAMERON, Krista (Roch) 3345 Edgemere Dr, Rochester, NY 14612

CAMERON, Meigan Cameron (Chi) 4140 N Lavergne Ave, Chicago, IL 60641

CAMERO SANABRIA, Elizabeth (Colom)

CAMPBELL, Anne (U) 3438 161st Pl SE Apt 51, Bellevue, WA 98008

CAMPBELL, Benjamin Pfohl (Va) 1310 Whitby Rd, Richmond, VA 23227

CAMPBELL, Boneta R (Oly)

CAMPBELL, Bruce Alan (Mich) 649 Merrimac Rd, Canton, MI 48188

CAMPBELL, Catherine (Va) 3420 Flint Hill Pl, Woodbridge, VA 22192

CAMPBELL, Dana LOu (Ct) 58 Greenwood St, East Hartford, CT 06118

CAMPBELL, David Noah (WTenn)

CAMPBELL, Dennis Gail (Ark) 1938 Petit Jean Mountain Rd, Morrilton, AR 72110

CAMPBELL, Ernest Francis (Spok) 825 Wauna Vista Dr, Walla Walla, WA 99362

CAMPBELL, Ernestina Rodriguez (The Episcopal NCal) 1617 32nd Ave, Sacramento, CA 95822

CAMPBELL, Fr Ken (WMass) 5 Peace Lane, Box 306, South Orleans, MA 02653

CAMPBELL III, George Latimer (NJ) 257 4th St, South Amboy, NJ 08879

CAMPBELL, James Donald (La) 525 N Laurel St, Amite, LA 70422

CAMPBELL, Janet Bragg (Oly) 9022 SW 51st Ave, Portland, OR 97219

CAMPBELL, Jean C (RG) 7250 Pajarito Rd NE, Rio Rancho, NM 87144

CAMPBELL, John Mark (Tex)

CAMPBELL, Karen (LI) PO Box 570, Hampton East Union Street, Sag Harbor, NY 11963

CAMPBELL, Katherine C (WLa)

CAMPBELL, Kathryn Sue (Ia) 106 3rd Ave, Charles City, IA 50616

CAMPBELL, Lynn Marie (Mass) 53 South St, Medfield, MA 02052

CAMPBELL, Maurice Bernard (Episcopal SJ) 1151 Park View Ct, Sheridan, WY 82801

CAMPBELL, Patrick Alan (RI) The Church Of The Redeemer, 655 Hope St, Providence, RI 02906

CAMPBELL, Peter Nelson (Chi) 519 Franklin Ave, River Forest, IL 60305

CAMPBELL II, Ralph (LI) 9825 Georgetown St, Louisville, OH 44641

CAMPBELL, Scott (Colo) PO Box 1961, Monument, CO 80132

CAMPBELL, Solomon Sebastian (SeFla) P.O. Box 50222, Nassau, Bahamas

CAMPBELL, Thomas Wellman (Minn) 234 W Kansas St, Spearfish, SD 57783

CAMPBELL, William Thomas (WTex) Church of the Good Shepherd, 700 S Upper Broadway St, Corpus Christi, TX 78401

CAMPBELL-LANGDELL, Alene (Los) 144 S C St, Oxnard, CA 93030

CAMPBELL-LANGDELL, Melissa (Los) 144 S C St, Oxnard, CA 93030

CAMPBELL-PEARSON, Constance (Mont)

CAMPO, JoAnne Crocitto (NY) 48 Spring St S, South Salem, NY 10590

CAMPO, Joseph John (NY)

CAMPO CAMAYO, Omar Julio (Colom)

CAMPOS, Cynthia Lou (SanD)

CANADY III, Paul (EC) Christ Church, PO Box 1246, New Bern, NC 28563

CANAN, Dave (Pa) 36791 Crooked Hammock Way Unit 2206, Lewes, DE 19958

CANAVAN, Mary Ann (RI)

CANDLER, Samuel Glenn (At) 2744 Peachtree Rd Nw, Atlanta, GA 30305

CANELA CANELA, Ramon (DomRep) Ms Digna Valdez, Box 764, Dominican Republic, Dominican Republic

CANGIALOSI, Grace Louise (Va) 2209 E Grace St, Richmond, VA 23223

CANHAM, Liz (WNC) 51 Laurel Ln, Black Mountain, NC 28711

CANNADAY, Brian W (Tex) 410 N Main St, Boerne, TX 78006

CANNADY, Jessie Edmonia (Colo)

CANNAN, Andrew (EC) St Lukes Episc Church, 435 Peachtree St NE, Atlanta, GA 30308

CANNELL, John Edward (WTex) 11107 Wurzbach Rd Ste 401, San Antonio, TX 78230

CANNING, Michael Jacob Brinton (Ida) 2333 W Duck Alley Rd, Eagle, ID 83616

CANNON III, Charles (SwFla) 87500 Overseas Highway, Islamorada, FL 33036

CANNON, Charles Wilcken (The Episcopal Church in Haw) 290 Shady Glen Ave, Point Roberts, WA 98281

CANNON, Justin R (Cal) 911 Dowling Blvd, San Leandro, CA 94577

CANNON, Michael D (WLa) 210 S Indian River Dr, Fort Pierce, FL 34950

CANO, George Luciano (Episcopal SJ) 3605 Shady Valley Ct, Modesto, CA 95355

CANTELLA, Frances French (Los) 30015 Buchanan Way, Castaic, CA 91384

CANTER, Matthew A (SanD) PO Box 127, Carlsbad, CA 92018

CANTOS DELGADO, Jose (NJ)

CANTRELL, Darla (Nev) PO Box 181, Austin, NV 89310

CANTRELL, Laura (Ga) Christ Church, 1521 N Patterson St, Valdosta, GA 31602

CANTRELL, Patricia Martin (Miss) PO Box 316, West Point, MS 39773

CANTRELL, Spencer Daniel (ETenn) 286-88 7th Ave, Brooklyn, NY 11215

CANTRELL, Teresa M (Ark)

CAPALDO, Christopher James (Mass) 801 Atlantic Ave, Fernandina Beach, FL 32034

CAPELLARO, John (Los) 15021 Ventura Blvd # 1114, Sherman Oaks, CA 91403

CAPITELLI, Stephen Richard (Mil) St John in the Wilderness, 13 S Church St, Elkhorn, WI 53121

CAPPEL, Jerry (Ky) 344 Reed Ln, Simpsonville, KY 40067

CAPPER, Steve (Tex) 6700 County Road 1229, Godley, TX 76044

CAPPERS, Linda Frances (Me) 30 Hemlock Dr, Saco, ME 04072

CAPPS, Benjamin (Pa)

CAPWELL, Kim (Del) 2400 W 17th St, Wilmington, DE 19806

CARABIN, Robert Jerome (WTex) 203 Panama Ave, San Antonio, TX 78210

CARBERRY, Timothy Oliver (SO) 49 Dipper Cove Rd, Orrs Island, ME 04066

CARDEN, Larry Edward (Tenn) University Of The South, Spo, Sewanee, TN 37375

CARDONA CIERO, Leandro (Cu)

CARDONE, Susan Holliday (Los) 6125 Carlos Ave, Los Angeles, CA 90028

CARDOZA, Edward Miguel (Mass) 181 Grove St, Peterborough, NH 03458

CARDWELL, Emily Marie (Lex) 210 N Main St, Versailles, KY 40383

CARDWELL, Sarah Layne (WA)

CAREY, Brenton Henderson (SanD) 232 Cushing Rd, Newmarket, NH 03857

CAREY, Pamela Hann (Cal) 525 29th St, Oakland, CA 94609

CAREY, Peter (Pa) 1390 Jolly Rd, Blue Bell, PA 19422

CAREY, Tom (Los) 880 N Alameda St Apt 304, Los Angeles, CA 90012

CARL, Elizabeth (WA) 1414 Montague St NW, Washington, DC 20011

CARLETON, Ellen Diane (Wyo) 519 E Park Ave, Riverton, WY 82501

CARLETTA, David (Ky) Trinity Episcopal Church, 720 Ford Ave, Owensboro, KY 42301

CARLIN, Christine (EC) 810 Fisher St Apt 4, Morehead City, NC 28557

CARLIN II, William B (Okla) 3508 Robert Dr, Duncan, OK 73533

CARLING, Paul Joseph (Ct) Saint Pauls Episcopal Church, 661 Old Post Rd, Fairfield, CT 06824

CARLISLE, Cathleen Ann (Tex)

CARLISLE, Christopher Arthur Elliott (WMass) 758 N Pleasant St, Amherst, MA 01002

CARLISLE, Corky (Lex) 85 Mikell Ln, Sewanee, TN 37375

CARLISLE, David (NMich)

CARLISTO SR, John Bradley (Ala) 6558 Spring St, Trussville, AL 35173

CARLSEN, Gail (Az) 3756 E Marble Peak Pl, Tucson, AZ 85718

CARLSEN, Steve (Okla) 444 N Central Ave Apt 211, #211, Oklahoma City, OK 73104

CARLSON, Carol Emma (NwPa) Po Box 328, Mount Jewett, PA 16740

CARLSON, Constance (Oly) St Andrew's Episc Church, 111 NE 80th St, Seattle, WA 98115

CARLSON, Daniel Stephen (SO) 1633 NE Halsey St, Portland, OR 97232

CARLSON, David (Alb)

CARLSON, David John (Mich) 28217 Edward Ave, Madison Heights, MI 48071

CARLSON, David Lee (NY) 84 Seward Ave, Port Jervis, NY 12771

CARLSON, Geraldine Beatrice (WMich) 1287 La Chaumiere Drive # 5, Petoskey, MI 46770

CARLSON, Jeremy Lloyd (Ala)

CARLSON, Kelly B (Mo) 580 1st St Apt 16, Lake Oswego, OR 97034

CARLSON, Kit (Mich) 907 Southlawn Ave, East Lansing, MI 48823

CARLSON, Michael Shane (Oly)

CARLSON, Monica (Ala) 2310 Skyland Blvd E, Tuscaloosa, AL 35405

CARLSON, Philip Lawrence (Az) 7147 N 78th St, Scottsdale, AZ 85258

CARLSON, Reed (Mass)

CARLSON, Robert Bryant (Ore) 15242 Sw Millikan Way Apt 517, Beaverton, OR 97006

CARLSON, Sally (Oly) 17320 97th Pl Sw Apt 603, Vashon, WA 98070

CARLTON-JONES, Anne Helen (SwFla) 15608 Fiddlesticks Blvd, Fort Myers, FL 33912

CARLYON, Robert David (Be) PO Box 262, Orwigsburg, PA 17961

CARMAN, Charles Churchill (RG) 94 Winterhaven Dr, Nellysford, VA 22958

CARMICHAEL, Alisa Roberts (WMo) 502 Druid Hills Rd, Temple Terrace, FL 33617

CARMICHAEL, Anna R (Episcopal SJ) 1528 Oakdale Rd, Modesto, CA 95355

CARMIENCKE JR, Bayard Collier (LI) 1145 Walnut Ave, Bohemia, NY 11716

CARMODY, Alison (Ala) 1708 Wickingham Cv, Vestavia, AL 35243

CARMODY, Betsy Carmody (WA) 1200 N Quaker Ln, Alexandria, VA 22302

CARMONA, Paul B (SanD) -, San Diego, CA 92115

CARMONA-ROMERO, Miguel A (Dal)

CARNAHAN, Allison Jan (CPa) 125 E Main St, Bloomsburg, PA 17815

CARNAHAN, Patricia King (Pgh) 4201 Saltsburg Rd, Murrysville, PA 15668

CARNES, Valerie Folts (Mil) 4507 Dayton Blvd, Chattanooga, TN 37415

CARNEY, Georgia Martyn (Roch) 350 Chili Ave, Rochester, NY 14611

CARNEY, Michael (U) PO Box 55, Whiterocks, UT 84085

CARNEY, Paul Martin (Alb) 146 1st St, Troy, NY 12180

CARNEY, Paulette Louise (WNY) 131 Lincoln Blvd, Kenmore, NY 14217

CARNEY, Susan Roberta (NJ) 9924 Pointe Aux Chenes Road, Ocean Springs, MS 39564

CARON, Don (NJ) 116 Forte Dr NW, Milledgeville, GA 31061

CARON II, Joseph A (Alb) 271 Stevenson Rd, Greenwich, NY 12834

CARPENTER, Allen Douglas (Alb) 62 S. Swan St., Albany, NY 12210

CARPENTER, Catherine E (CNY) PO Box 6, Baldwinsville, NY 13027

CARPENTER, Charlie (Ind) 91 Smiths Rd, Mitchell, IN 47446

CARPENTER, Doug (Ala) 3037 Overton Rd, Birmingham, AL 35223

CARPENTER, Elizabeth Kincaid (Tenn) 216 University Ave, Sewanee, TN 37375

CARPENTER, Francis Newton (Chi) 337 Ridge Rd, Barrington Hills, IL 60010

CARPENTER, Gene (EC) 1603 E Walnut St, Goldsboro, NC 27530

CARPENTER, George Harrison (Oly) Po Box 343, Medina, WA 98039

CARPENTER, John Paul (Pa) 3937 Netherfield Rd, Philadelphia, PA 19129

CARPENTER, Judith Perry (Mass) 192 N. Main Street, Rockland, ME 04841

CARPENTER, Laura Michelle (Md)

CARPENTER, Leslie Scott (Tex) 6050 N Meridian St, Indianapolis, IN 46208

CARPENTER II, Marion George (NI) Saint Annes, 424 W Market St, Warsaw, IN 46580

CARPENTER, Nicholas (Los) 15757 Saint Timothy Rd, Apple Valley, CA 92307

CARPENTER, Stacey (Del)

CARPENTER, Stephen (The Episcopal NCal) 1020 Westview Dr, Napa, CA 94558

CARPENTER, Susan (RI) 10 Justin St, Bristol, RI 02809

CARPENTER, William E (Pgh)

CARPINELLI, Kenneth Scott (NJ) 1 Hartford Rd, Medford, NJ 08055

CARR, Clifford Bradley (Be) 526 11th Avenue, Bethlehem, PA 18018

CARR, Dale R (Ore) 1205 SW 19th Ave., Portland, OR 97205

CARR, John Joseph (WNY) 56 Mckinley Ave, Kenmore, NY 14217

CARR, John Philip (Tex)

CARR, Michael (SanD) 651 Eucalyptus Ave, Vista, CA 92084

CARR, Michael Leo (Mich) 9132 Pine Valley Dr, Grand Blanc, MI 48439

CARR, Nathan Daniel (Okla) 6400 N Pennsylvania Ave, Nichols Hills, OK 73116

CARR, Timothy Patrick (SeFla) 3133 Connecticut Ave NW Apt 1016, Washington, DC 20008

CARR, Virginia Rose (WNY) 12 Elm St, Westfield, NY 14787

✠ **CARRANZA-GOMEZ**, Sergio (Los) PO Box 512164, Los Angeles, CA 90051

CARREKER, Michael Lyons (Ga) 1 West Macon Street, Savannah, GA 31401

CARRICK, Judith Trautman (LI) 4 Kenny St, Hauppauge, NY 11788

CARRIERE, Anne Stone (WTenn) 31 Stonecrest Ct, Mountain Home, AR 72653

CARR-JONES, Philip (NJ) 3 Haytown Rd, Lebanon, NJ 08833

CARROCCINO, Michael Jonathan (Oly) 541 W Morondo Ave, Ajo, AZ 85321

CARROLL III, Bill William (Tex) 924 N Robinson Ave, Oklahoma City, OK 73102

CARROLL, Charles Moisan (Me) PO Box 195, Brunswick, ME 04011

CARROLL, Christian (Nwk) 173 Oakland Rd, Maplewood, NJ 07040

CARROLL, Diana (Md) 2 Horseshoe Way, Market Rasen Lincolnshire, LN83F, Great Britain (UK)

CARROLL, Diane Phyllis (Va) 218 Claymor Oaks Est, Dunnsville, VA 22454

CARROLL, Kevin Charles (Mil) 3309 N Knoll Ter, Wauwatosa, WI 53222

CARROLL, Michael Edward (Ct) 16 Church St, Waterbury, CT 06702

CARROLL, Steven (NJ) 5120 E Hampton Ave Apt 1128, Mesa, AZ 85206

CARROLL, Tracey F (Tex) 335 Tennessee Ave, Sewanee, TN 37383

CARROLL, Vincent John (SwVa) 2518 2nd St, Richlands, VA 24641

CARROLL, William Wesley (Fla) 465 11th Ave N, Jacksonville, FL 32250

CARROON, Robert Girard (Ct) 24 Park Pl Apt 8f, Hartford, CT 06106

CARR RIVERA, Liselotte (LI)

CARRUBBA, Amity (Chi) 2258 W Cullerton St Apt 2, Chicago, IL 60608

CARSKADON, Garrett Harvey (Md) 32 Main St, Westernport, MD 21562

CARSON, Caroline P (NJ)

CARSON, Julie (Mass) 500 Brook St, Framingham, MA 01701

CARSON, Mary Claypoole (SO) 3207 Montana Ave, Cincinnati, OH 45211

CARSON, Rebecca Jayne (CGC) 1707 Government St, Mobile, AL 36604

CARSON, Stephen Wilson (WTex) 3002 Miori Ln, Victoria, TX 77901

CARSWELL, Amber B (NY) 102 N 2nd St, Memphis, TN 38103

CARSWELL, Kyle Reed (Ia) 3853 Woodland Ave Apt 5, West Des Moines, IA 50266

CARTAGENA MEJIA DE AREVALO, Maria (Hond) San Angel B-26, C4202, Tegucigalpa, Honduras

CARTER, Bente (Cal) 60 Pinehurst Way, San Francisco, CA 94127

CARTER, Charles Robert (Eau) 1001 McLean Ave, Tomah, WI 54660

CARTER, Cynthia A (CGC) 2005 Boxwood Ave, Andalusia, AL 36421

CARTER, David Morgan (Ct) 90 Salem Rd, Lyme, CT 06371

CARTER, Davis Blake (WTex) Po Box 707, Aberdeen, MS 39730

CARTER JR, Frederick Leroy (U) 472 Gordon Cir, Tooele, UT 84074

CARTER, Grayson Leigh (RG) 1602 Palmcroft Dr Sw, Phoenix, AZ 85007

CARTER, Halcott Richardson (USC) 4708 Seahurst Ave, Everett, WA 98203

CARTER, James Currie Mackechnie (Va) 3510 Hastings Dr, Richmond, VA 23235

CARTER JR, James Robert (Ga) 601 Washington Ave, Savannah, GA 31405

CARTER, John Franklin (Ct) John Carter, 19 Willow Dr, Lakeville, CT 06039

CARTER, L Susan (Mich) 1102 Portage Path, East Lansing, MI 48823

CARTER, Lynda Anne (Mich) 2803 1st St, Wyandotte, MI 48192

CARTER III, Philander Lothrop (WMich) 1296 Siena Way, Boulder, CO 80301

CARTER JR, Richard Blair (ETenn) PO Box 5104, Knoxville, TN 37928

CARTER, Robert Douglas (SwFla) Berkeley Preparatory School, 4811 Kelly Rd, Tampa, FL 33615

CARTER, Thomas Brooke (Md) 2860 Hill Top Dr, Salisbury, NC 28147

CARTER, Wayne (WLa) 396 Country Club Cir, Minden, LA 71055

CARTER-EDMANDS, Lynn (SO) 4667 Wenham Park, Columbus, OH 43230

CARTWRIGHT, Gary Earle (SwFla) 2202 Wildwood Hollow Dr, Valrico, FL 33596

CARTWRIGHT, Thomas Lisson (Ore) 1720 Ten Oaks Ln, Woodburn, OR 97071

CARTY, Shawn (Nwk) PO Box 139, Greenbank, WA 98253

CARUSO, Cynthia Woodham (WMich) 1215 W 22nd 1/2 St, Austin, TX 78705

CARUSO, Frank (Mass) 112 Spring St, Hopkinton, MA 01748

CARUSO, Kevin (Chi) 647 Dundee Ave, Barrington, IL 60010

CARUTHERS, Mary C (Ark) 509 Scott St, Little Rock, AR 72201

CARVER, Barbara Schenkel (Spok) 1904 Browning Way, Sandpoint, ID 83864

CARVER, JP (Spok) 1904 Browning Way, Sandpoint, ID 83864

CARVER, Larry A (WK) 18 E 28th Ave, Hutchinson, KS 67502

CARVER, Lynne (Ia) St Peters Episcopal Church, 2400 Middle Rd, Bettendorf, IA 52722

CARVER, Robert Cody (Oly) 1701 N Juniper St, Tacoma, WA 98406

CARVER, Sarah Frances (NC) 5500 Rambling Rd, Greensboro, NC 27409

CASE, Jaime Jay (Oly) 6535 Littlerock Rd SW, Tumwater, WA 98512

CASE, James J (NC) H Innocents Tec Ch, 805 Mount Vernon Hwy, Atlanta, GA 30327

CASE, Margaret Timothy (RG)

CASE, Michael Allen (Ida) 704 S Latah St, Boise, ID 83705

CASEY, David P (La) 2518 Belmont Terrace Apt 3D, Fredericksburg, VA 22401

CASEY, Dayle Alan (Colo) 2059 Glenhill Rd, Colorado Springs, CO 80906

CASEY-MARTUS, Sandra (WTex) St. Stephen's Episcopal Church, Wimberley, TX 78676

CASHELL, Douglas Hanson (NwT)

CASHMAN, Patricia (Pa) 2 Riverside St, Rochester, NY 14613

CASIANO BOFFIL, Ruth (PR)

CASILLAS, Laina Wood (Cal) 4942 Thunderhead Ct, El Sobrante, CA 94803

CASKEY, Charles C (Chi) 24410 Reserve Ct Apt 103, Bonita Springs, FL 34134

CASON JR, Charles Edward (FdL) 1080 N Westfield St Apt 213, Oshkosh, WI 54902

CASPARIAN, Peter (LI) 705 Snyder Hill Dr, San Marcos, TX 78666

CASSELL, Jonnie Lee (Mo) 12025 Willow Ln Apt 916, Overland Park, KS 66213

CASSELS, Christine Helen (RI) 1 Queen Anne Sq, Newport, RI 02840

CASSEUS, Frantz (Hai) 7835 Jean Vincent, Montreal, QC H1E 3C4, Canada

CASSINI, Mary Ellen Dakin (SeFla) 19740 Cutler Ct, Miami, FL 33189

CASSON, Jordan Francis Martin (Pa) 813 Longacre Blvd, Yeadon, PA 19050

CASTELLAN, Megan (CNY) 11 E 40th St, Kansas City, MO 64111

CASTELLANOS FLORES, Marcos Antonio (DomRep)

CASTELLI, Paul Henry (NC)

CASTELLO, Kenneth August (Mil)

CASTELLON, Paul Frank (NJ) 7403 Dress Blue Cir, Mechanicsville, VA 23116

CASTILLO, Antonio J (Ve)

CASTILLO, Guillermo Antonio (Ark) 3777 E Mcdowell Rd # Apt1165, Phoenix, AZ 85008

CASTILLO, Sandra Ann (Chi) 322 N Water St, Sparta, WI 54656

CASTLES, Charles William (Ga) 1552 Pangborn Station Dr, Decatur, GA 30033

CASTO, David Cameron (Pgh) 9 Cliff Rd Apt B2, Woodland Park, NJ 07424

CASTRO, Jose Roberto (DomRep)

CASTRO, Mario (SwFla) Church of the Redeemer, 222 S Palm Ave, Sarasota, FL 34236

CASTRO, Reinel (WLa) 29655 Circle R Greens Dr, Escondido, CA 92026

CASURELLA, Rae Ann (SO)

CATALANO, Patricia (ECR) 300 C Street NE, Washington, DC 20002

CATANIA, Libby (Mass) Saint Marys Episcopal Church, 3055 Main St, Barnstable, MA 02630

CATCHINGS, Robert Mitchell (WA)

CATE, Rex Vasa (Ga) 615 Mallery St, St Simons Is, GA 31522

CATE, Suzanne (USC) Holy Trinity Parish, 193 Old Greenville Hwy, Clemson, SC 29631

CATES, Susanna (NJ) 602 Meander St, Abilene, TX 79602

CATIGANO, Stacey Dawn (CPa)

CATINELLA, Gayle (O) 16507 S Red Rock Dr, Strongsville, OH 44136

CATIR JR, Norman Joseph (Tex) 31 John St, Providence, RI 02906

CATO, Brooks (CNY) Saint Thomas', 12 1/2 Madison St, Hamilton, NY 13346

CATO, Phillip (WA) 8617 Hidden Hill Ln, Potomac, MD 20854

CATO, Vanessa Gisela (U) 2374 Grant Ave, Ogden, UT 84401

CATON, Lisa Elfers (NJ) 23 E Welling Ave, Pennington, NJ 08534

CATRON MINER, Antoinette (U) 1710 S Foothill Dr, Salt Lake City, UT 84108

CAUCUTT, Mary (Wyo) 820 River View Dr, Cody, WY 82414

CAUDLE, Stephen (WLa) 7714 Albany Ave Apt B, Lubbock, TX 79424

CAULFIELD, Dorothee Renee (NY) 7 Sleator Dr, Ossining, NY 10562

CAULKINS, Rodney Leroy (SVa) 267 Jefferson Dr, Palmyra, VA 22963

CAUSTON, Michele Lynn (Be) 205 N 7th St, Stroudsburg, PA 18360

CAVAGNARO, Deborah Daggett (NwPa) St Luke's Church, 600 W Main St, Smethport, PA 16749

CAVALCANTE, Jose Ivanildo (Los) 48 Old Post Rd, Mount Sinai, NY 11766

CAVALERI, Eva (WA) 3612 Woodley Rd NW, Washington, DC 20016

CAVALIERE, Denise B (NJ) 15 Papermill Rd, Cherry Hill, NJ 08003

CAVANAUGH, Jean Marie (Me)

CAVANAUGH, Sean Harris (Va) 1795 Johnson Ferry Rd, Marietta, GA 30062

CAVANAUGH, William Jeffrey (Dal) 38 Fair St, Guilford, CT 06437

CAVANNA, Robert Charles (Minn) 6910 43rd Ave Se, Saint Cloud, MN 56304

CAVE, Daniel Eugene (RG) 7052 McNutt Rd, La Union, NM 88021

CAVE, Jeffrey Paull (At)

CAVIN, Barbara (EMich) Saint Pauls Episcopal Church, 711 S Saginaw St, Flint, MI 48502

CAWTHORNE, John Harry (Md) 1597 Amberlea Dr. S, Dunedin, FL 34698

CAZDEN, Jan (Cal) 2901 Verona Ct, Arlington, TX 76012

CECCHINI, Bruce Cox (NJ)

CEDERBERG, Todd (SeFla) 623 SE Ocean Blvd, Stuart, FL 34994

✠ **CEDERHOLM JR**, Bud (Mass) 499 Webster St, Needham, MA 02494

CEKUTA, Nancee A (EC) 471 W Martintown Rd, North Augusta, SC 29841

CELESTIN, Jois Goursse (Hai)

CELIS, Edgar Fabiam (Colom)

CEMBALISTY INNES, Susan Eve (Be) 108 Fern Way, Clarks Summit, PA 18411

CENCI, Daniel M (EC) 110 W Main St, Clinton, NC 28328

CENDESE, William Ivan (U) 520 E 9th Ave, Salt Lake City, UT 84103

CERRATO III, John A (O) 2813 Market Bridge Ln Unit 101, Raleigh, NC 27608

CERTAIN, Robert (WTex) 3776 Loch Highland Pkwy NE, Roswell, GA 30075

✠ **CERVENY**, Frank Stanley (Fla) 3711 Ortega Blvd, Jacksonville, FL 32210

CESARETTI, Charles Antony (NJ) Po Box 408, New Milford, PA 18834

CEYNAR, Marlene Hruby (Minn) 1811 Southbrook Ln, Wadena, MN 56482

CHABOT, Bruce Guy (Tex) 5919 Wild Horse Run, College Station, TX 77845

CHACE, Brian David (EMich) Trinity Episcopal Church, PO Box 83, West Branch, MI 48661

CHACE, Elizabeth Marian Maxwell (EMich) PO Box 109, Frederic, MI 49733

CHACON, Frank Joe (The Episcopal NCal)

CHACON-RODRIGUEZ, Dagoberto (Hond)

CHADWICK, Leslie (WA) 11290 Spyglass Cove Ln, Reston, VA 20191

CHADWICK, Thora Louise Libbey (Vt) 267 Hildred Dr, Burlington, VT 05401

CHAFFEE, Barb (EC) 5301 Creedmoor Rd Apt 306, Raleigh, NC 27612

CHALAKANI, Paul Scott (NJ) 7 Lincoln Ave, Rumson, NJ 07760

CHALARON, Janice Belle Melbourne (USC) 144 Caldwell St, Rock Hill, SC 29730

✠ **CHALFANT**, Edward Cole (Me) PO Box 2056, Ponte Vedra Beach, FL 32004

CHALFANT-WALKER, Nancy Oliver (Pgh) 33 Thorn St, Sewickley, PA 15143

CHALK, David Paul (WTex) 651 Pecan St, Canyon Lake, TX 78133

CHALK, Michael Dulaney (WTex) 155 El Rancho Way, San Antonio, TX 78209

CHALKER, Gae M (The Episcopal Church in Haw) 9817 Villa Ridge Dr, Las Vegas, NV 89134

CHALMERS, Glenn (NY) 296 9th Ave, New York, NY 10001

CHAMBERLAIN, Carol Moore (Pa) 22 Pin Oak Rd, Newport News, VA 23601

CHAMBERLAIN, David Morrow (EC) 136 Fairway Oaks Dr, Perry, GA 31069

CHAMBERLAIN, Eve Yorke (NJ) 325 Little Silver Point Rd, Little Silver, NJ 07739

CHAMBERLAIN-HARRIS, Naomi Redman (Cal) 4467 Crestwood Cir, Concord, CA 94521

CHAMBERS, Joseph Michael Cortright (Lex) 3906 Tropical Ln, Columbia, MO 65202

CHAMBERS, Mark Ellis (Colo) PO Box 1167, Ouray, CO 81427

CHAMBERS, Penni Howell (RG) 10 Sundance Cir, Santa Fe, NM 87506

CHAMBERS, Rex (Colo) PO Box 237, Windsor, CO 80550

CHAMBERS, Richard Graeff Mark (CFla) 91 Church St, Seymour, CT 06483

CHAMBERS, Robert Karl (NY)

CHAMBLISS, Arrington (Mass) 7 Eldridge Rd, Jamaica Plain, MA 02130

CHAMORRO, Hector Manuel (SwFla)

CHAMPION, Peter (Cal) 703 Mariposa Ave, Rodeo, CA 94572

CHAMPION, Susan Manley (Cal) 315 Welch St, Silverton, OR 97381

CHAMPION-GARTHE, Mo Vinck (Mont) 2101 W Broadway Ste 103-190, Columbia, MO 65203

CHAMPLIN, Charles (Minn)

CHAMPLIN, Jeffrey (Ark) 2701 Old Greenwood Rd, Fort Smith, AR 72903

CHAN, Charles Yang-Ling Ping-Fai (Colo) Po Box 662, Mukwonago, WI 53149

CHAN, Henry Albert (LI) 1212 Foulk Rd Apt 4c, Wilmington, DE 19803

CHANCE, Robin (Wyo) 6516 Weaver Rd, Cheyenne, WY 82009

CHANCELLOR JR, Donald Wood (Miss) PO Box 391, Como, MS 38619

CHANDLER, Belinda (Chi) 3025 Walters Ave, Northbrook, IL 60062

CHANDLER, Gail Stearns (Me) St Davids Episcopal Church, 138 York St, Kennebunk, ME 04043

CHANDLER, John Herrick (Los) 2286 Vasanta Way, Los Angeles, CA 90068

CHANDLER, Nan Elizabeth (EC) 301 Bretonshire Rd, Wilmington, NC 28405

✠ **CHANDLER**, Paul-Gordon (Wyo)

CHANDLER JR, Richard Anthony (CFla) Saint Annes Church, 9870 W

Fort Island Trl, Crystal River, FL
34429
CHANDLER, Susan (Mass) 195
Patmos Rd, Sawyers Island, Rowley,
MA 01969
CHANDY, Sunil Kulangana (RI) 1115
New Pear St, Vineland, NJ 08360
✠ **CHANE**, John Bryson (WA) 5309
Pendleton St, San Diego, CA 92109
CHANEY JR, Michael Jackson (Ga)
1802 Abercorn St, Savannah, GA
31401
CHANG, Hsin Fen (Los) 15694 Tetley
St, Hacienda Heights, CA 91745
✠ **CHANG**, Lennon Yuan-Rung (Tai)
Wen-Hua 3rd Road, 4th Place #75, Pei-
Tan, Taiwan
CHANG, Lily (Tai) 280 Fu-Hsing
South Road, Sec 2, Taipei, Taiwan
CHANGO, Georgianna (NwPa) Rr 6
Box 324, Punxsutawney, PA 15767
CHANNON, Ethel M (Dal) 2304
County Ave, Texarkana, AR 71854
CHAPARRO MUNOZ, Benny (PR)
CHAPMAN JR, Chuck (Ark) 1721
Monzingo, Magnolia, AR 71753
CHAPMAN, Colin (NH) Christ
Church, 2 Rectory St, Rye, NY 10580
CHAPMAN, Cristi Elizabeth (Oly)
3434 39th Ave W, Seattle, WA 98199
CHAPMAN, George Memory (Mass)
41 Garth Rd, West Roxbury, MA
02132
CHAPMAN, Hugh William (Fla) 13
Bb Misgunsi, St. Thomas, VI 802
CHAPMAN, James Dreger (Mass) 201
Washington Ave, Chelsea, MA 02150
CHAPMAN, Jennifer Marie (NMich)
CHAPMAN, Jerry Wayne (Dal) 11201
Pickfair Dr, Austin, TX 78750
CHAPMAN, Justin P (Minn) 2021
13th Ave NW, Rochester, MN 55901
CHAPMAN, Michael (Alb) 22 Bergen
St, Brentwood, NY 11717
CHAPMAN, Phillip (Neb) 322 S 15th
St, Plattsmouth, NE 68048
CHAPMAN, Rebecca Ann (CFla)
CHAPMAN, Tansy (Mass) PO Box
832, Mendocino, CA 95460
CHAPPELL, Annette M (Md)
CHAPPELL, Katherine Cantelou
(ETenn)
CHAPPELL, Veronica Donohue
(CPa) 1118 State Route 973 E, Cogan
Station, PA 17728
CHAPPELLE, Laurinda (Nev) 1230
Riverberry Dr, Reno, NV 89509
CHAR, Zachariah Jok (WMich) 4232
Alpinehorn Dr Nw, Comstock Pk, MI
49321
CHARD, Art (WVa) 1206 Maple Ln,
Anchorage, KY 40223
CHARLES, D Maurice (Chi)
Rockefeller Memorial Chapel, 5850 S
Woodlawn Avenue, Chicago, IL 60637
CHARLES, Kathleen J (Eau) 2816
Mesa Grande Pl, La Crosse, WI 54601
CHARLES, Leonel (SeFla) Box 1309,
Port-Au-Prince, Haiti

CHARLES, Randolph (WA) 11178
Kilkenny Rd, Marshall, VA 20115
CHARLES, Winston (NC) 114 E
Drewry Ln, Raleigh, NC 27609
✠ **CHARLESTON**, Steven (Okla) 2702
Silvertree Dr, Oklahoma City, OK
73120
CHARTERS IV, Everett Wallace
(Ore)
CHASE, Alexis M (At) PO Box 286,
Decatur, GA 30031
CHASE, Benjamin O (Vt) 95
Worcester Village Rd, Worcester, VT
05682
CHASE, Christopher (Cal) 10885
Caminito Cuesta, San Diego, CA
92131
CHASE IV, Edwin Theodore Ted (LI)
432 Lakeville Rd, New Hyde Park, NY
11042
CHASE JR, John Garvey (Tex) P.O.
Box 103, Crockett, TX 75835
CHASE, Katharine Barnhardt (SwVa)
PO Box 810, Amherst, VA 24521
CHASE, Peter Gray Otis (Mass) 258
Concord St, Newton, MA 02462
CHASE JR, Ran (Mass) PO Box 924,
Barnstable, MA 02630
CHASSE, Katherine (Az)
CHASSE, Richard P (Nwk) 176
Palisade Ave, Jersey City, NJ 07306
CHASTAIN, Gordon Lee (Ind) 1769
Dunaway Ct, Indianapolis, IN 46228
CHATEL, David R (CGC)
CHATFIELD, Jane Sheldon (Me) 11
White St, Rockland, ME 04841
CHATFIELD, Jenifer (Los)
CHATHAM, Charles Erwin (Az) 500 S
Jackson St, Wickenburg, AZ 85390
CHAVANNE, Jean Dummond (Eur) 23
Avenue George V, Paris, 75008, France
CHAVEZ, Chloe Ann Tischler (RG)
CHAVEZ, David Ulloa (Az)
CHAVEZ, Juan Rafael (Hond)
CHAVEZ, Karen Sue (Los) 3160
Graceland Way, Corona, CA 92882
CHAVEZ FRANCO, Juan Eloy
(Litoral Diocese Of Ecuador) Amarilis
Fuente 603, Ave Vicente Trujillo y la
D, Apartado Postal 09015250,
Guayaquil, Ecuador
CHEE, David T (Los) 700 Devils Drop
Ct, El Sobrante, CA 94803
CHEESMAN JR, Benbow Palmer
(Mil) 2501 S 60th St, Milwaukee, WI
53219
CHEFFEY, Anne Davis (WMo) 3
Northwoods Dr, Kimberling City, MO
65686
CHEN, Charles Chin-Ti (Tai) 23 Wu-
Chuan West Road, 403, Taichung,
Taiwan
CHEN, Luke Hh (Tai) No 67 Lane 314
Ming Shen Rd, Shin Hua County,
Tainan Hsien, 71246, Taiwan
CHENEY III, Arthur Milton (WMass)
38 Barnes Ln, West Greenwich, RI
02817
CHENEY, Barbara T (Ct) 90 Rogers
Rd, Hamden, CT 06517

CHENEY SR, Bruce David (EC) 497
Church St, Oriental, NC 28571
CHENEY, Dexter (Ct) 90 Rogers Rd,
Hamden, CT 06517
CHENEY, Michael Robert (Mass) 117
Forest St, Malden, MA 02148
CHENEY, Peter Gunn (Az) 5090 N
Via Gelsomino, Tucson, AZ 85750
CHENG, Chen Chang (Tai) 499, Sec 4
Tam King Rd, New Taipei City
Taiwan, 25135, Taiwan
CHENG, Ching-Shan (Tai) 40 Ta
Tung Rd, Wu Feng, Taichung County,
852, Taiwan
CHENG, Patrick S (NY) 19 E 34th St,
New York, NY 10016
CHERBONNEAU, Allen Robert (Ala)
4367 East River Road, Box 282,
Mentone, AL 35984
CHERISME, Charles M. (Hai) 472
Beech St, Roslindale, MA 02131
CHERRY, Charles Shuler (Minn) 734
7th St S, Breckenridge, MN 56520
CHERRY, Jacqueline Ann (Cal) 1076
De Haro St, San Francisco, CA 94107
CHERRY, Mary Jane (Ky) Tec Ch
Home, 7504 Westport Rd, Louisville,
KY 40222
CHERRY, Timothy B (Dal) 56 Cedar
Ln, Osterville, MA 02655
CHERY, Jean Fils (Hai)
CHERY, Marie Carmel (Hai)
CHESHIRE, Grady Patterson (WNC)
1131 S Edgemont Ave, Gastonia, NC
28054
CHESNEY, Jonathan C (WTenn)
4577billy Maher Rd, Bartlett, TN
38135
CHESS, Jean D (Pgh) 1500 Cochran
Rd Apt 901, Pittsburgh, PA 15243
CHESTERMAN JR, Thomas Charles
(DomRep) 2418 Hidden Valley Dr,
Santa Rosa, CA 95404
CHEVES, Henry Middleton (SC) 635
Foredeck Lane, Edisto Island, SC
29438
CHILDERS, Robert T J (ETenn)
Church Of The Good Shepherd, 211
Franklin Rd, Lookout Mountain, TN
37350
CHILDRESS JR, John (Ark) 7404
Fleming Island Dr, Fleming Island, FL
32003
CHILES, Bob (USC) The Reverend
Robert L Chiles, 103 Underwood Dr,
Hendersonville, NC 28739
CHILESE, Sandra Lee (Az)
CHILLINGTON, Joseph Henry (Ind)
46 Lakeview Dr, Terre Haute, IN
47803
CHILTON, Bruce (NY) Bard College,
Annandale-on-Hudson, NY 12504
CHILTON, Mary Habel (Alb) 3 Woods
Edge Ln, West Sand Lake, NY 12196
CHILTON, William Parish (Eas) 214
Wye Ave, Easton, MD 21601
CHIN, Mary Louise (Me) Po Box
650397, Fresh Meadows, NY 11365
CHINERY, Edwin Thomas (NY) 12 W
11th St, New York, NY 10011
CHINGUA, Diego A (EcuC)

CHIPPS, Kathleen Dawn (Va) 3604 Secret Grove Ct, Dumfries, VA 22025

CHIRAN QUINONEZ, Jairo Ernesto (Litoral Diocese Of Ecuador) Santiago Apostol, Parroquia La Pila Calle Mexico, La Pila, 593, Ecuador

CHIRINOS-HERNANDEZ, Jose A (Hond)

CHISHAM, Anne Beardsley (SanD) 47568 Hawley Boulevard, San Diego, CA 92116

CHISHOLM, Alan Laird (NY) 13801 York Rd Apt F6, Cockeysville, MD 21030

CHITTENDEN, Nils Philip (NY) St Stephens Church, 50 Bedford Rd, Armonk, NY 10504

CHO, Francis Soonhwan (NJ) 16 Rodak Cir, Edison, NJ 08817

CHOI, Sang (Va)

CHOI, Stephen Young Sai (NY) 5 77th St # 7047, North Bergen, NJ 07047

⚜ **CHOI**, William Chul-Hi (Los) 8105 232nd St Se, Woodinville, WA 98072

CHOI, Young Kwon Kwon (Va) 1830 Kirby Rd, Mclean, VA 22101

CHOLLET, Mariclea (U) 944 W Bloomsbury Cv, Salt Lake City, UT 84123

CHOQUETTE, Michael (Chi)

CHORNYAK, Christopher John (Me) 3 Spring House Ln, Ellsworth, ME 04605

CHOU, Yun-Kuang (Tai) St. Mark, 120-11 Chung Hsiao Road, Ping Tung, 900, Taiwan

CHOYCE, George (ETenn) 27 Cool Springs Rd, Signal Mountain, TN 37377

CHRISMAN, Robert (Oly) 1214 184th Pl, Long Beach, WA 98631

CHRISNER, Marlen Ronald (At) 6517 SW 85th St, Ocala, FL 34476

CHRISTENSEN, Alan (Oly)

CHRISTENSEN, Bonniejean Mcguire (ND) 4001 Beneva Rd Apt 334, Sarasota, FL 34233

CHRISTENSEN, Hope Alice Jee (WA)

CHRISTIAN, Carol Jean (SO) 5701 Makati Cir Apt E, San Jose, CA 95123

CHRISTIAN, Charles Ellis (Ind) 3627 E Crystal Valley Dr, Vincennes, IN 47591

CHRISTIAN, David Victor (U) 8282 Macon Rd, Cordova, TN 38018

CHRISTIAN, Earl Rix (SVa) 25 Tripp Ter, Hampton, VA 23666

CHRISTIAN JR, Frank Stanaland (Ga) 212 W Pine St, Fitzgerald, GA 31750

CHRISTIANSEN, Andrew Lee (WLa) 908 Rutherford St, Shreveport, LA 71104

CHRISTIANSON, Regina (Vt) PO Box 57, Underhill, VT 05489

CHRISTIANSSEN, Paul Jerome (The Episcopal NCal) 1016 W. Arrow Hwy, Apt. C, Upland, CA 91786

CHRISTOFFERSEN, Timothy Robert (Cal) 611 Foxwood Way, Walnut Creek, CA 94595

CHRISTOPHER JR, Chuck (EO) 19529 Sugar Mill Loop, Bend, OR 97702

CHRISTOPHER, Cynthia Ann (Md) Holy Trinity Episcopal Church, 1131 Mace Ave, Essex, MD 21221

CHRISTOPHER, Edward Barse (CPa)

CHRISTOPHER, John S (Az) 440 Red Rock Rd, Durango, CO 81301

CHRISTOPHER, Mary (Ia) 2110 Summit St, Sioux City, IA 51104

CHRISTOPHER, Melanie (Colo) 371 Upham St, Lakewood, CO 80226

CHRISTOPHERSEN, Lynn (Okla) 4604 E 54th St Apt 203, Tulsa, OK 74135

CHRISTOPHERSON, Paul Conrad (Minn) Wildlife Run, New Vernon, NJ 07976

CHRISTY, Christine Lavon (Az)

CHRISTY, Stephen James (Wyo)

CHRONISTER, Lisa Marie (Okla)

CHRYSSON, Gus P (NC) 320 Hanover Arms Ct, Winston Salem, NC 27104

CHRYSTAL, Susan (Nwk) 33 Woodstone Cir, Short Hills, NJ 07078

CHUBB JR, Donald Allen (Kan) 1011 SW Cambridge Ave, Topeka, KS 66604

CHUBOFF, Esther Lois (Ct) 83 E Main St, Clinton, CT 06413

CHUMBLEY, Ken (WMo) 601 E Walnut St, Springfield, MO 65806

CHUN, Franklin (The Episcopal Church in Haw) 1163 Lunaanela St, Kailua, HI 96734

CHURCH JR, John L (SwVa)

CHURCH, Susan (Ore) Po Box 605, John Day, OR 97845

CHURCH, Susan Jean (NMich) Christ Church, 3906 5th St, Calumet, MI 49913

CHURCHILL, Gregg Hardison (Los) Po Box 1082, Lompoc, CA 93438

CHURCHMAN, Nina Wood (Colo) 3224 S Eudora St, Denver, CO 80222

CHURCHWELL, Katherine C (Okla) PO Box 1581, St Petersburg, FL 33731

CIANNELLA, J oseph Domenic Kennith (Mass) 13 Park Dr, West Springfield, MA 01089

CICCARELLI, Sharon Lynn (Mass) 13 Turner Ter, Newton, MA 02460

CICERO, Rose (Chi)

CICORA, Julie Anne (Roch) 556 Forest Lawn Rd, Webster, NY 14580

CIESEL, Barbara Bitney (SD) 126 N Park St Ne, Wagner, SD 57380

CIESEL, Conrad Henry (SD) Po Box 216, Lake City, SD 57247

CIHAK, Susan Elizabeth (Az) 12990 E Shea Blvd, Scottsdale, AZ 85259

CIMIJOTTI, Jerry Anthony (SD) 2822 S Division St, Spokane, WA 99203

CINTRON, Julio A (PR)

CIOSEK, Scott Andrew (Mass) 351 Elm St, South Dartmouth, MA 02748

CIPOLLA, Angela Marie (NJ) 24 Perilli Dr, Hamilton, NJ 08610

CIPRIAN VIZCAINO, Luis (PR)

CIRIELLO, Mary Anne (Ct) 3768 Anslow Drive, Leland, NC 28451

CIRILLO, Jim (Va) PO Box 847, Buckingham, PA 18912

CIRVES, Judith Melanie (Mil) 510 Ludington Ave, Madison, WI 53704

CISNEROS, Hilario (Nev) 2657 Chimney Rock Rd, Hendersonville, NC 28792

CISNEROS, Omar (Okla)

CITARELLA, Kenneth Christopher (NY) PO Box 459, North Salem, NY 10560

CIVALE, Lawrence J (Mass)

CIVALIER, Rick (NJ) 161 Lakebridge Dr, Deptford, NJ 08096

CLAASSEN, Scott Allen (Los) 714 Mission Park Dr, Santa Barbara, CA 93105

CLADER, Linda (The Episcopal NCal) 5555 Montgomery Dr Apt N201, Santa Rosa, CA 95409

CLAMP, Adrienne Joann (WA)

CLANCE, Bennett Bolton (Fla)

CLAPP JR, Schuyler Lamb (EMich) 2830 Arborview Dr Apt 2, Traverse City, MI 49685

CLARAGE, Thelma Lou (NMich)

CLARK, Beatryce Arlene (The Episcopal NCal) 581 Ridgewood Dr, Vacaville, CA 95688

CLARK, Brad (Mass) PO Box 547, 31 County St, Ipswich, MA 01938

CLARK, Carol Ruth (NMich) 10401 V.05 Rd, Rapid River, MI 49878

CLARK, Carole Sue (Okla) Hc 67 Box 82, Indianola, OK 74442

CLARK, Cathy A (Ore) 1545 N Dean St, Coquille, OR 97423

CLARK, Cheryl L (Ark) 5113 Dorset Mews, Williamsburg, VA 23188

CLARK, Cindy Lou (Tex) 501 E Gregg St, Calvert, TX 77837

CLARK, Constance Lee (Va) PO Box 183, Earlysville, VA 22936

CLARK, Corbet (Oly) 11520 SW Timberline Dr, Beaverton, OR 97008

CLARK, David Norman (Md) 12265 Boyd Rd, Clear Spring, MD 21722

CLARK, Diana Doyle (Nwk) 44 Clark St, Chatham, NJ 07928

CLARK, Diane Catherine Fitzgerald (WA) 13 Eleanor Avenue, Saint Albans, Hertfordshire, AL35TA, Great Britain (UK)

CLARK, Donald Lewis (WNC)

CLARK, Douglas Burns (NY) 116 Prospect Park W # 2r, Brooklyn, NY 11215

CLARK, Frances M (NJ) 201 Penbryn Rd, Berlin, NJ 08009

CLARK, Frank H (Az) 7810 W Columbine Dr, Peoria, AZ 85381

Clergy List

CLARK, Jacqueline (Mass) St Elizabeths Tec Ch, 1 Morse Rd, Sudbury, MA 01776

CLARK II, James Boyd (Az) 6715 N Mockingbird Ln, Paradise Valley, AZ 85253

CLARK, Jane (Chi) 1608 W Plymouth Dr, Arlington Heights, IL 60004

CLARK, Jason (ETenn)

CLARK, John E (CFla) 414 Pine St, Titusville, FL 32796

CLARK, John Leland (SO) 1712 - 8888 Riverside Dr E, Windsor, ON N8S 1H2, Canada

CLARK SR, John Warren (WLa) 321 Horseshoe Dr, Crowley, LA 70526

CLARK, Joseph Madison (WA) 402 Grove Ave, PO Box 1098, Washington Grove, MD 20880

CLARK, Judith Freeman (Mass) 10 Ida Rd, Worcester, MA 01604

CLARK, Katherine Hampton (Los) 3969 Bucklin Pl, Thousand Oaks, CA 91360

CLARK, Martha (WA) 600 M St SW, Washington, DC 20024

CLARK, Michael Thomas (Spr)

CLARK, Paula E (Chi) 1534 W Highland Ave, Chicago, IL 60660

CLARK, Philip C (Minn) 128 Canterbury Cir, Le Sueur, MN 56058

CLARK, Ralph (EC) 801 Bobby Jones Drive, Fayetteville, NC 28312

CLARK JR, Richard Johnston (NC) 4624 Crooked Oak Ln, Charlotte, NC 28226

CLARK, Richard Neece (WMich) 900 Pivot Rock Rd, Eureka Springs, AR 72632

CLARK, Richard Tilton (Mass) 16 Timothy St, Fairhaven, MA 02719

CLARK, Robbin (Cal) 36 Larkhay Road, Hucclecote Gloucester, AE GL3 3NS, Great Britain (UK)

CLARK, Susan Mccarter (EMich) W180n7890 Town Hall Rd, D315, Menomonee Falls, WI 53051

CLARK, Taylor Brooks (EO) 991 Normandy Ave S, Salem, OR 97302

CLARK, Vanessa E B (Neb) 113 N 18th St, Omaha, NE 68102

CLARK, William Roderick (WTex) 1417 E Austin Ave, Harlingen, TX 78550

CLARK, William Whittier (NH) Po Box 56, Medusa, NY 12120

CLARKE, Anne Elizabeth (Mich) 350 University Ave Ste 280, Sacramento, CA 95825

CLARKE, Barbara Jean (Me) 11 Daisey Ln, Brewer, ME 04412

CLARKE, Charles Ray (Wyo) 796 Garner Dr, Lander, WY 82520

CLARKE JR, Daniel L (SC) 1110 Northbridge Dr, 160 Carolina Dr, Charleston, SC 29407

CLARKE, Debra M (NJ) 187 Aster Ct, Whitehouse Station, NJ 08889

CLARKE, James Munro (Alb) Po Box 05, Downsville, NY 13755

CLARKE, Janet Vollert (SeFla) 33406 Fairway Rd, Leesburg, FL 34788

CLARKE, John David Blackmore (NY) 790 11th Ave Apt 29a, New York, NY 10019

CLARKE, John Robert (Mass) 2 Ridgewood Rd, Malden, MA 02148

CLARKE, Julian Maurice (Episcopal VI) 123 Circle Dr, Saint Simons Island, GA 31522

CLARKE, Kenneth Gregory (SO) 3090 Montego Ln. Apt. 1, Maineville, OH 45039

CLARKE, Richard Kent (WMass) 162 Laurelwood Dr, Hopedale, MA 01747

CLARKE, Robert B (Chi) 524 Sheridan Sq Apt 3, Evanston, IL 60202

CLARKE, Sheelagh (Nwk) 119 Main St, Millburn, NJ 07041

CLARKE, Thomas George (Los) PO Box 5830, Palm Springs, CA 92263

CLARK-KING, Ellen Jane (Cal) 1100 California St, San Francisco, CA 94108

CLARK-KING, Jeremy (Cal)

CLARKSON, Frederick C (EC) 4401 Statesville Blvd, Salisbury, NC 28147

CLARKSON, J (WNC)

CLARKSON, Julie Cuthbertson (NC) 1420 Sterling Rd, Charlotte, NC 28209

CLARKSON JR, Ted H (Tex)

CLARKSON, Ted Hamby (Ga) PO Box 929, Darien, GA 31305

CLARKSON IV, William (WA) 1424 W Paces Ferry Rd Nw, Atlanta, GA 30327

CLASSEN, Ashley Molesworth (Dal) 635 N Story Rd, Irving, TX 75061

CLAUGUS, Mary Case (The Episcopal NCal) 1240 Mission Ave., Sacramento, CA 95608

CLAUSEN, Kathryn (SO) 3623 Sellers Drive, Millersport, OH 43046

CLAUSEN, Ruth Lucille (Mich) 100 N. College Row Apt. 165, Brevard, NC 28712

CLAVIER, Anthony Forbes Moreton (Spr) 193 Summit Ave, Glen Carbon, IL 62034

CLAVIJO, Joseph Maria (La) 4600 Saint Charles Ave, New Orleans, LA 70115

CLAWSON, Donald Richard (SeFla) 1605 Paseo Del Lago Ln, Vero Beach, FL 32967

CLAWSON, Jeffrey David (Los) 2626 Ivan Hill Ter, Los Angeles, CA 90039

CLAXTON, Constance Colvin (Minn) 312 Church St, Audubon, IA 50025

CLAYTON JR, Paul Bauchman (NY) 4 Townsend Farm Rd, Lagrangeville, NY 12540

CLAYTON, Sharon Hoffman Chant (NY) 4 Townsend Farm Rd, Lagrangeville, NY 12540

CLAYTON, Vikki (WA) 17100 Conoy Rd, Barnesville, MD 20838

CLAYTOR, Susan Quarles (WVa) 310 Elm Ave, Hershey, PA 17033

CLAYVILLE, Stephanie B (Eas)

CLEARY, Brian Poul (SwFla)

CLEAVER-BARTHOLOMEW, Dena (RI) 74 Benefit St, Providence, RI 02904

CLEAVES JR, George Lucius (WMo) 9020 S Saginaw Rd, Grand Blanc, MI 48439

CLECKLER, Michael Howard (Ala) 1513 Edinburgh Way, Birmingham, AL 35243

CLEGHORN, Charlotte Dudley (WNC) 37 Cherry St, Arden, NC 28704

CLEGHORN, Maxine Janetta (NY) 4401 Matilda Ave, Bronx, NY 10470

CLELAND, Carol Elaine (Cal) 1550 Portola Ave, Palo Alto, CA 94306

CLEM, Stewart Douglas (Okla) 3022 Clearview Dr, Saint Louis, MO 63121

CLEMENT, Betty Cannon (Dal) 4120 Jasmine St, Paris, TX 75462

CLEMENT, James Marshall (WNY) Trinity Episcopal Church, 11 Day St, Fredonia, NY 14063

CLEMENT, Thomas M A (Md)

CLEMENTS, CHarles Christopher (USC) 1523 Delmar St, West Columbia, SC 29169

CLEMENTS, Elaine Gant (La) St Andrew's Episcopal Church, 1101 S Carrollton Ave, New Orleans, LA 70118

CLEMENTS, Mercedes McDaniel (Ark)

CLEMENTS, Robert (Ct) PO Box 426, Waterford, CT 06385

CLEMONS, Roland (NJ) 132 S Adelaide Ave Apt 1b, Highland Park, NJ 08904

CLENDENIN, Evan Graham (Oly) 621 Ensley Ln SE, Tumwater, WA 98501

CLENDINEN JR, James H (Ga) 2621 Cotuit Ln, Tallahassee, FL 32309

CLERKIN, Shawn J (NwPa) 662 Silliman Ave, Erie, PA 16510

CLEVELAND, Jenny (Oly) 125 SW Eckman St, Mcminnville, OR 97128

CLEVELEY, Susan Lynn (Spok) 1005 E B St, Moscow, ID 83843

CLEVENGER, Mark R (U) PO Box 606, Shoreham, NY 11786

CLICK, Barbara G (Mo) 600 N Euclid Ave, Saint Louis, MO 63108

CLIFF, Wendy D (Cal) 1632 NW Riverscape St, Portland, OR 97209

CLIFFORD III, George Minott (The Episcopal Church in Haw)

CLIFT, Joe Walter (Ga) 343 Gander Rd, Dawson, GA 39842

CLIFTON JR, Ellis Edward (Episcopal VI) St. Clement'S Episcopal Church, 4300 Harrison Road, Inkster, MI 48141

CLIFTON, Steve (Ga) 3137 Denham Ct, Orlando, FL 32825

CLINE, Jill (RG) 26558 E Us Highway 64, Taos, NM 87571

CLINEHENS JR, Hal (The Episcopal NCal) 714 Lassen Ln, Mount Shasta, CA 96067

C37

CLINGENPEEL, Ronald Harvey (La) 1906 Cedarwood Ave, Gretna, LA 70056
CLODFELTER, Jon (Pa) 4442 Frankford Ave, Philadelphia, PA 19124
CLOSE, David Wyman (Ore) 7990 Headlands Way, Clinton, WA 98236
CLOSE, Leroy Gregorius (RI) 316 W Main Rd, Little Compton, RI 02837
CLOSE, Patrick (NJ)
CLOSE ERSKINE, Christine Elaine (Ore) 60960 Creekstone Loop, Bend, OR 97702
CLOTHIER, David Michael (CGC)
CLOTHIER, Tamara Ann (Tex) 5001 Hickory Rd, Temple, TX 76502
CLOUGHEN JR, Charles (Md) 1 Southerly Ct Apt 606, Towson, MD 21286
CLOWERS, Grantland Hugh (Kan) 2007 Miller Dr, Lawrence, KS 66046
CLUETT JR, Rick (Be) 119 W. Johnston St., Allentown, PA 18103
COATS, Bleakley Irving (Ida)
COATS, Christopher Vincent (CGC) Wharf Marina Slip #38, Orange Beach, AL 36561
COATS, John R (Cal) 15814 Champion Forest Dr, Spring, TX 77379
COATS, William Russell (Nwk) 19 Elmwood Ave., Ho Ho Kus, NJ 07423
COBB, Christina Rich Rich (Mo) 1212 Ringo St, Mexico, MO 65265
COBB, David (Chi) 34 Running Knob Hollow Rd, Sewanee, TN 37375
COBB JR, Harold James (SVa) 1931 Paddock Rd, Norfolk, VA 23518
COBB, Julia Kramer (NwT) St Barnabas Episcopal Church, 4141 Tanglewood Ln, Odessa, TX 79762
COBB, Matthew M (Minn) 1367 Willow St Apt 500, Minneapolis, MN 55403
COBB-ANDERSON, Vienna (Va) 1138 West Ave, Richmond, VA 23220
COBDEN JR, Edward Alexander Morrison (Mich) PO Box 295, South Egremont, MA 01258
COBDEN III, Edward Alexander Morrison (NY) 374 Sarles St, Bedford Corners, NY 10549
COBIELLAS TOLEDO, Yohanes (Cu)
COBLE JR, John Reifsnyder (Be) 1929 Pelham Rd, Bethlehem, PA 18018
COBLE, Robert Henry (Pa) 36 Crescent Cir, Harleysville, PA 19438
COBURN, Ann Struthers (Mass) PO Box 1988, Berkeley, CA 94709
COBURN, Michael (RI) 55 Linden Road, Barrington, RI 02806
COBURN, Michael Stanton (RG) 4131 Marla Dr. NE, Albuquerque, NM 87109
COCHRAN, Elizabeth Jane (Oly) St Matthew's Episcopal Church, 412 Pioneer Ave, Castle Rock, WA 98611
COCHRAN, Joseph M (Md)

COCHRAN, Laura (Va) 46590 Drysdale Ter Unit 101, UNIT 101, Sterling, VA 20165
COCHRAN, Lottie (SVa) 713 Seagrass Reach, Chesapeake, VA 23320
COCKBILL, Douglas J (Chi) 3310 Coventry Ct, Joliet, IL 60431
COCKE, Reagan Winter (Tex) 2450 River Oaks Blvd, Houston, TX 77019
COCKRELL, Ernest (ECR) 1538 Koch Ln, San Jose, CA 95125
COCKRELL, John Grafton (SC) 275 Warden Ave, Bluefield, WV 24701
COCKRELL, Richard (USC) 8700 N La Cholla Blvd Apt 2137, Anderson, SC 29625
CODE, David (NJ) 729 Partridge Ln, State College, PA 16803
CODY, Daphne (Chi) 400 Park Ave Apt B, Highland Park, IL 60035
COE III, Frank S (WVa) 74 Rhodes Court, Harpers Ferry, WV 25425
COE, Wayland Newton (Tex) 5934 Rutherglenn Dr, Houston, TX 77096
COENEN, Susan Ann (FdL)
COERPER, Becky (CNY) 98 E Genesee St, Skaneateles, NY 13152
COEY, Paul S (FdL)
COFFEY, Bridget (O) 1808 Berkshire Pl, Toledo, OH 43613
COFFEY, Gary Keith (WNC) 23 Forest Knoll Dr, Weaverville, NC 28787
COFFEY, Janet Paris (Chi) 7736 Weaver Ave, Saint Louis, MO 63143
COFFEY JR, Jon (Fla) 4903 Robert D Gordon Rd, Jacksonville, FL 32210
COFFEY, Kevin PJ (Nwk) 17-14 Radburn Rd, Fair Lawn, NJ 07410
COFFIN, Peter R (NH) 35 Woodbury St, Keene, NH 03431
COFFMAN, Daniel Brian (Neb) Holy Trinity Episcopal Church, 6001 A St, Lincoln, NE 68510
COFFMAN, Mary Ann (Okla) 3333 N Meridian Ave, Oklahoma City, OK 73112
COGAN, Timothy Bernard (NJ) 38 The Blvd/RFD659, Edgartown, MA 02539
COGAR, Carolyn Christine (SO) 541 2nd Ave, Gallipolis, OH 45631
COGGI, Lynne Marie Madeleine (NY) 3206 Cripple Creek St Apt 39b, San Antonio, TX 78209
COGGIN, Bruce W (Tex) 3700 Ellsmere Ct, Fort Worth, TX 76103
COGILL, Richard (Minn) 175 Magnolia Ave, Sewanee, TN 37375
COGSDALE, Mike (WNC) 845 Cherokee Place, Lenoir, NC 28645
COHEE, William Patrick (Az) 114 W Roosevelt St, Phoenix, AZ 85003
COHEN, David Michael (The Episcopal NCal) 310 W North St, Alturas, CA 96101
COHEN, Georgia S (NJ) Po Box 5, Blawenburg, NJ 08504

COIL, John Albert (WMo) 7917 Lamar Ave, Prairie Village, KS 66208
COKE, Paul Tyler (Tex) 9426 Peabody Ct, Boca Raton, FL 33496
COLANGELO, Preston Hart (Ala) 1663 Bradford Ln, Bessemer, AL 35022
COLAVINCENZO, Sue (EMich) St Dunstan's Episcopal Church, 1523 N Oak Rd, Davison, MI 48423
COLBERT, Paul A (The Episcopal NCal) 642 Mayflower Rd, Claremont, CA 91711
COLBERT, Valerie Davis (NC)
COLBURN, Suzanne (Mass) PO Box 185, Boothbay Harbor, ME 04538
COLBURN, Therese Jean (Colo)
COLBY, Richard Everett (Me) 3702 Haven Pines Dr, Kingwood, TX 77345
COLE, Allan Hunter (Colo) 9200 W 10th Ave, Lakewood, CO 80215
COLE, Anson Dean (O) 565 S Cleveland Massillon Rd, Akron, OH 44333
COLE, Anthony Richard (Eur) 3 Rue de Monthoux, Geneva, 1201, Switzerland
✠ **COLE**, Brian (ETenn) Church of the Good Shepherd, 533 E Main St, Lexington, KY 40508
COLE JR, C Alfred (CFla) 125 Larkwood Dr, Sanford, FL 32771
COLE, Chris (Okla)
COLE, Christopher A (Pgh) H Innocents Tec Ch, Pittsburgh, PA 30327
COLE, Christopher Owen (WTex) 5909 Walzem Rd, San Antonio, TX 78218
COLE, Elaine Agnes (SwFla) 330 Forest Wood Ct, Spring Hill, FL 34609
COLE, Enid Omodele (WA)
COLE, Ethan J (SwFla) 5083 Thompson Rd, Clarence, NY 14031
COLE, Frantz (Hai) Box 1309, Port-Au-Prince, Haiti
COLE JR, Howard Milton (Pa)
COLE, Judith Hampton Poteet (WNC) 8015 Island View Ct, Denver, NC 28037
COLE, Lisa Jeanne (The Episcopal NCal) 275 E Spain St, Sonoma, CA 95476
COLE, Mary Catherine (Be)
COLE, Patrice Clark (Az)
COLE JR, Ray (WTex) 3614 Hunters Dove, San Antonio, TX 78230
COLE, Roy A (NY) 1385 York Ave Apt 29f, 29F, New York, NY 10021
COLE, Suzanne (Me) 16 Belmont Dr, Jay, ME 04239
COLE JR, Ted (Mass) 31 Manion Rd, Hyde Park, MA 02136
COLE, Timothy Alexander Robertson (WA) Christ Church, 3116 O St NW, Washington, DC 20007
COLEGROVE, Jerome Higgins (O) 475 Laurel Dr, Kent, OH 44240
COLEMAN, Barbara Alicia (Eas)

COLEMAN, Bernice (LI) 10206 Farmers Blvd, Hollis, NY 11423
COLEMAN, Betty Ellen Gibson (SO) 4325 Skylark Dr, Englewood, OH 45322
COLEMAN, Brian Ray (WMich) 406 Second Street, Manistee, MI 49660
COLEMAN, Carolyn (Tenn) Saint Davids Episcopal Church, 6501 Pennywell Dr, Nashville, TN 37205
COLEMAN JR, Dale D (Spr) 105 E. D St., Belleville, IL 62220
COLEMAN, Dennis E (Pa) 121 Church St, Phoenixville, PA 19460
COLEMAN, Edwin Cabaniss (Tenn) 4715 Harding Pike, Nashville, TN 37205
COLEMAN JR, Fred George (NY) 2048 Lorena Ave, Akron, OH 44313
COLEMAN, John Charles (CGC) 2 Chateau Place, Dothan, AL 36303
COLEMAN, Karen (Mass) 59 Fayerweather St # 2138, Cambridge, MA 02138
COLEMAN, Kim (Va) 912 S Veitch St, Arlington, VA 22204
COLEMAN, M Joan (Spr) 9 Teakwood Dr, Belleville, IL 62221
COLERIDGE, Clarence Nicholas (Ct) 29 Indian Rd, Trumbull, CT 06611
COLES, Suzanne M (LI)
COLLAMORE JR, Harry Bacon (Ct) 899 Turtle Ct, Naples, FL 34108
COLLEGE, Philip (SO) 5691 Great Hall Ct, Columbus, OH 43231
COLLER, Patricia Marie (Ct) Church Pension Group, 19 E 34th St, New York, NY 10016
COLLETTE, Emily C (Ala)
COLLEY, Ashley Taylor (NwT)
COLLEY-TOOTHAKER, Sam Scott (Episcopal SJ) 437 Hawthorne Dr, Danville, VA 24541
COLLIER, Catherine (Ala) 605 Lurleen B Wallace Blvd N, Tuscaloosa, AL 35401
COLLIER, Daniel R (NH) 155 Salem Rd, Billerica, MA 01821
COLLIER JR, John Winston (CFla)
COLLIER, Mary Anne (NwT) 1605 W Pecan Ave, Midland, TX 79705
COLLIN, Winifred Nohmer (Roch) 2696 Clover St, Pittsford, NY 14534
COLLINS, Charles Blake (WTex) 431 Richmond Pl NE, Albuquerque, NM 87106
COLLINS, David (SeFla) 365 La Villa Dr., Miami Springs, FL 33166
COLLINS, Emily Selden (NMich) 1628 W Town Line Rd, Pickford, MI 49774
COLLINS, Gerald (Pa) 4700 City Ave Apt 11310, Philadelphia, PA 19131
COLLINS, Guy JAmes DOuglas (NH) 9 W Wheelock St, Hanover, NH 03755
COLLINS, James Edward (ECR) 615 Santa Paula Dr, Salinas, CA 93901
COLLINS, Jean Griffin (Mont) 1000 Fountain Terrace Dr Unit 402, Lewistown, MT 59457

COLLINS, John Caleb (Az)
COLLINS III, John Milton (SanD) 701 Kettner Blvd Unit 94, San Diego, CA 92101
COLLINS, John Robert (EO) PO Box 130, Sisters, OR 97759
COLLINS, Loretta (Eas) 21 S Main St, Lewistown, PA 17044
COLLINS, Lynn (LI) 10 Kimmer Ct, Fredericksburg, VA 22406
COLLINS, Mac (SanD) 3847 Balsamina Dr, Bonita, CA 91902
COLLINS, Mark Robin (Nwk) 11, Glen Rock, NJ 07452
COLLINS, Patrick (Eas) 66 Saint Stephens Dr, Orinda, CA 94563
COLLINS, Paul Michael (Oly) PO Box 1204, Summerland, CA 93067
COLLINS, William Gerard (Ga) 209 Maple St, Saint Simons Island, GA 31522
COLLINS-BOHRER, Padraic Michael (Roch) 111 East Ave Apt 330, Rochester, NY 14604
COLLINS REED, Charlotte Collins (O) 409 E High St, Springfield, OH 45505
COLLINSWORTH, Beverly (NI)
COLLIS, Shannon J (WNY) 11305 Hesperia Rd., Hesperia, CA 92345
COLMENAREZ, Gustavo Adolfo (Ve) Iglesia Episcopal de Venezuela, Colinas de Bello Monte, Centro Diocesano Av. CaronÂ No. 100, Caracas, 1042A, Venezuela
COLMORE III, Charles Blayney (SanD) PO Box 516, Jacksonville, VT 05342
COLON, Cristobal (NY)
COLON TORRES, Lydia (PR) PO Box 902, Saint Just, PR 00978
COLTON, Elizabeth Wentworth (Pa) 966 Trinity Ln, King Of Prussia, PA 19406
COLVILL, Lea Nadine (Mont)
COLVIN, Jeremi Ann (Mass) 160 Rock St, Fall River, MA 02720
COLVIN, Sarah M (Oly) 3737 Seminary Rd, Alexandria, VA 22304
COLWELL, Charles Richard (NY) 172 Ivy St, Oyster Bay, NY 11771
COLWELL II, Kirby (O) 4449 Lander Rd, Chagrin Falls, OH 44022
COMBS, Carrie Anne (Ct) 153 Sharon Ave, Torrington, CT 06790
COMBS, Jaqueline Suzanne (WNC)
COMBS, Leslie David (NY) 123 Franklin St., Concord, NH 03301
COMBS, Melanie J (Vt) 21 Whitlock Rd, Castleton, VT 05735
COMBS, Nikolaus M (Ct)
COMBS, William (At) 2920 Landrum Education Dr, Oakwood, GA 30566
COMEAU, Molly Stata (Vt) 400 Wake Robin Dr Apt 304, Shelburne, VT 05482
COMEAUX, Andrew Anthony (WLa) 3728 Sabine Pass Dr, Bossier City, LA 71111

COMER JR, Fletcher (Ala) 898 Running Brook Dr, Prattville, AL 36066
COMER, Judith Walton (Ala) 2813 Godfrey Ave NE, Fort Payne, AL 35967
COMER, Kathleen Susan (La) 4105 Division St, Metairie, LA 70002
COMER, Skip (WMich) 1231 Fran Dr, Frankfort, MI 49635
COMERFORD, Marilee (Mass)
COMFORT, Alexander Freeman (WNC) 105 Sunny Ln, Mars Hill, NC 28754
COMMINS, Gary (Los) 954 Avenue C, Bayonne, NJ 07002
COMPIER, Don Hendrik (WMo) 701 SW 8th Ave, Topeka, KS 66603
COMPTON, William Hewlett (Miss) 674 Mannsdale Rd, Madison, MS 39110
CONANT, Louise Ritchey (Mass) 24 Bowdoin St, Cambridge, MA 02138
CONDELLO II, Frank Michael (The Episcopal Church in Haw)
CONDON, Joshua T (Tex) Holy Spirit Episcopal Church, 12535 Perthshire Rd, Houston, TX 77024
CONDON, Sarah Taylor (Tex)
CONES, Bryan Matthew (Chi) 1140 Wilmette Ave, Wilmette, IL 60091
CONGDON, William Hopper (Ct)
CONGER, George (CFla) 3155 N Sandpiper Dunes Pt, Lecanto, FL 34461
CONGER, George Mallett (NY) 9 Angel Rd, New Paltz, NY 12561
CONGER, John Peyton (Cal)
CONGLETON, Melissa Ann (Mich)
CONIGLIO, Robert Freeman (SVa) 21313 Metompkin View Lane, Parksley, VA 23421
CONKLIN, Andrea Caruso (Tex) 1819 Heights Blvd, Houston, TX 77008
CONKLIN, Caroline Elizabeth (Mont) 13231 15th Ave N.E., Seattle, WA 98125
CONKLIN, Daniel G (Oly) Neue Jakob Str 1, Berlin, 10179, Germany
CONKLING JR, Allan (WTex) PO Box 314, Bandera, TX 78003
CONKLING, Kelly S (WTex) 10642 Newcroft Pl, Helotes, TX 78023
CONLEY, Joan Frances (Nwk) 169 Fairmount Rd, Ridgewood, NJ 07450
CONLEY, Kristina Mellor (Me) 17 Littlefield Dr, Kennebunk, ME 04043
CONLEY, Patricia Ann (Chi) 1993 Yasgur Dr, Woodstock, IL 60098
CONLIFFE, Mario Romain Marvin (Md) PO Box 255, 2434 Cape Horn Rd, Hampstead, MD 21074
CONN JR, Doyt Ladean (Oly) 1805 38th Ave, Seattle, WA 98122
CONN, John Hardeman (Mass) 4 Alton Court, Brookline, MA 02446
CONN, Rodney Carl (Be) 108 N. 5th St., Allentown, PA 18102

CONNELL, George Patterson (Ky) 11 Saint Lukes Ln, San Antonio, TX 78209

CONNELL, John Baade (The Episcopal Church in Haw) 95-1050 Makaikai St Apt 17m, Mililani, HI 96789

CONNELL, Susan (Okla) 57200 E Hwy 125, Unit 3431, Monkey Island, OK 74331

CONNELLY III, Albert Pinckney (CFla) 16 Hawks Lndg, Weaverville, NC 28787

CONNELLY, Charles Evans (SwFla) 2401 Bayshore Blvd Unit 505, Tampa, FL 33629

CONNELLY, Constance R (NC) 1950 S Wendover Rd, Charlotte, NC 28211

CONNELLY, John Vaillancourt (FdL) 3500 Lacey Rd, Suite 700, Downers Grove, IL 60515

CONNELLY JR, Walter (Mass) 231 Bowdoin St, Winthrop, MA 02151

CONNER, Georgene Gigi D (SwFla) 958 Felicity St, New Orleans, LA 70130

CONNER, John W (Pa)

CONNER, Lu-Anne (Mo) Church Of The Transfiguration, 1860 Lake Saint Louis Blvd, Lake St Louis, MO 63367

CONNER, Marty H (Az) 19801 N Concho Cir, Sun City, AZ 85373

CONNER, Sarah (Mass) 4 Ernest Rd Apt 3, Arlington, MA 02474

CONNERS, John H (EC) 14703 Dorset Dr, Noblesville, IN 46062

CONNERY, Vincent George (SVa)

CONNOLLY, Catherine Hannah Victoria (NC)

CONNOLLY, Emma French (WTenn) 480 S. Greer St., Memphis, TN 38111

CONNOR, Alice Elizabeth (SO) 5751 Marmion Ln, Cincinnati, OH 45212

CONNOR, The Rev Stephen J (NJ) 15 Sunnyside Ct, Ocean City, NJ 08226

CONNORS, Carey D (Va) 905 Princess Anne St, Fredericksburg, VA 22401

CONRAD JR, James Wallace (Az) 2540 Ontario Dr, Las Vegas, NV 89128

CONRAD, John (Los) All Saints Episcopal Church, 3847 Terracina Dr, Riverside, CA 92506

CONRAD JR, Larry Brown (NC)

CONRAD, Matthew MacMillan (ECR) 7620 Cristobal Ave, Atascadero, CA 93422

CONRAD, Pamela Gales (Md) 105 1st Ave SW, Glen Burnie, MD 21061

CONRADO VARELA, Victor H (Chi)

CONRADS, Alexandra (Los)

CONRADS, Nancy Alice (Chi) 4801 Spring Creek Rd, Rockford, IL 61114

CONRADT, James Robert (FdL) W1693 Echo Valley Rd, Kaukauna, WI 54130

CONROE, Jon Wallace (RG)

CONROY, Mary Elizabeth (SeFla) 1121 Andalusia Ave, St Philips Episcopal Church and School, Coral Gables, FL 33134

CONSIDINE, H James (NwPa) 11733 SW 17th Ct, Miramar, FL 33025

CONSTANT, Donna Rittenhouse (Pa) 167 Hermit Hollow Lane, Middleburg, PA 17842

CONSTANT, Joseph (WA) 701 Oglethorpe St NW, Washington, DC 20011

CONTESTABLE, Christine Marie (U) 673 Wall St, Salt Lake City, UT 84103

CONTI, Ann (NY) 22 Coulter Ave, Pawling, NY 12564

CONWAY, Cooper (NY) 1514 Palisade Ave, Union City, NJ 07087

CONWAY, Marta Therese-Pea (RG)

CONWAY, Natalie (Md)

CONWAY, Thomas Bradley (NJ) 22wickapecko Drive, Interlaken, NJ 07712

CONYERS, Kacei (Cal)

COOK, Ashley Michele (Tex) 919 S John Redditt Dr, Lufkin, TX 75904

COOK, Bill E (Tex) 11245 Shoreline Dr., Apt 308, Tyler, TX 75703

COOK, Charles James (Tex) PO Box 2247, Austin, TX 78768

COOK, Charles Robert (Neb) 2666 El Rancho Rd, Sidney, NE 69162

COOK, Debbie (NJ) 202 Navesink Ave, Atlantic Highlands, NJ 07716

COOK, Ellen Piel (SO) 2768 Turpin Oaks Ct, Cincinnati, OH 45244

COOK, Harvey Gerald (Lex) 20129 N Painted Sky Dr, Surprise, AZ 85374

COOK, James Bonham (Okla) 10407 Button Quail Dr, Austin, TX 78758

COOK, Jim (SeFla) 3395 Burns Road, Palm Beach Gardens, FL 33410

COOK JR, Joe (Mass) 28 Highland Ave, Roxbury, MA 02119

COOK, Johnny Walter (CGC) 206 Fig Ave, Fairhope, AL 36532

COOK, Kay Kellam (U) 2425 Colorado Ave, Boulder, CO 80302

COOK, Laura Lynn (CFla)

COOK, Millard S (Be)

COOK, Nancy Bell (Ark) 1112 Alcoa Rd, Benton, AR 72015

COOK, Patricia Ann (NAM) PO Box 85, Bluff, UT 84512

COOK, Paul Raymond (WMo) 4 Burton Rd, Kingston, KT25TE, Great Britain (UK)

COOK, Peter John Arthur (WLa) 4100 Bayou Rd, Lake Charles, LA 70605

COOK JR, Robert (NC) 8400 Goose Landing Ct, Browns Summit, NC 27214

COOK, Ryan Arthur (CFla)

COOK, Thomas R (Minn) 4439 W 50th St, Edina, MN 55424

COOK, Winifred Rose (Mich) PO Box 287, Onsted, MI 49265

COOKE, Barbara Jane (NC) 5205 Ainsworth Dr, Greensboro, NC 27410

COOKE, Catherine Cornelia Hutton (Vt) 500 South Union, Burlington, VT 05401

COOKE, Douglas Tasker (Ct) 19 Ridgebrook Dr, West Hartford, CT 06107

COOKE, Hilary (Ind)

COOKE, Hugh Mabee (Episcopal SJ) 67 W Noble St, Stockton, CA 95204

COOKE JR, James Coffield (EC) 10004 Netherton dr., Las Vegas, NV 89134

COOKE, James Daniel (Ct) 23 Parsonage Road, HIgganum, CT 06441

COOKE, Philip Ralph (ECR) 401 S 1st St Unit 202, Minneapolis, MN 55401

COOK-QUARRY, Cassandra (Minn)

COOL, Opal Mary (Neb) 3525 N. 167Th Cir. Apt. 206, Omaha, NE 68116

COOLEY, Andrew A (Colo) 3415 N 30th St, Tacoma, WA 98407

COOLIDGE, Robert T (Cal) PO Box 282, Westmount, QC H3Z 2T2, Canada

COOLIDGE, William Mccabe (NC) 118 Cumberland Ave, Asheville, NC 28801

COOLING, David (USC) 280 Holcombe Way, Lambertville, NJ 08530

COOMBER, Matthew JM (ND)

COON JR, Bob (CFla) 3236 Shamrock E, Tallahassee, FL 32309

COON, David Paul (The Episcopal Church in Haw) PO Box 690, Kamuela, HI 96743

COON, Nancy (WTex) 200 Crossroads Dr, Dripping Springs, TX 78620

COOPER JR, ALlen William (Alb) 60 Church St Apt 6h, Saranac Lake, NY 12983

COOPER, Brandon P (Pgh)

COOPER, Cricket S (WMass) PO Box 1104, Quechee, VT 05059

COOPER, Deborah Silas (Ark)

COOPER IV, Francis Marion (CGC) PO Box 1677, Santa Rosa Beach, FL 32459

COOPER, Gale Hodkinson (NC) 1636 Hqtr Plantation Dr, Charleston, SC 29455

COOPER, George L (Me) 980 Sawyer St, South Portland, ME 04106

COOPER, James Herbert (Fla) 1314 Ponte Vedra Blvd, Ponte Vedra Beach, FL 32082

COOPER, Joseph Wiley (EC) 4925 Oriole Dr, Wilmington, NC 28403

COOPER, Michael Francis (Los) 23206 La Granja Dr, Valencia, CA 91354

COOPER, Michael Scott (CPa) 181 S 2nd St, Hughesville, PA 17737

COOPER, Miles Oliver (CFla) 423 Forest Ridge Dr, Aiken, SC 29803

COOPER, Milton Norbert (SeFla) 11201 Sw 160th St, Miami, FL 33157

COOPER, Richard Randolph (Tex) 4805 E Columbary Dr, Rosenberg, TX 77471

COOPER, Robert Norman (WLa) 108 Blue Ridge, Site 41, Comfort, TX 78013

COOPER, Stephenie Rose (ECR) 1205 Pine Ave, San Jose, CA 95125
COOPER-WHITE, Pamela (NY) Union Theological Seminary, 3041 Broadway, New York, NY 10027
COOTE, Laurel (ECR) 28005 Robinson Canyon Rd, Carmel, CA 93923
COOTER, Eric Shane (Okla) 10702 Rio Mar Cir, Estero, FL 33928
COPE, Gerald D (Ga)
COPE, Jan Naylor (WA) Washington National Cathedral, 3101 Wisconsin Avenue, NW, Washington, DC 20016
COPE, Marie S (USC) 910 Hudson Rd, Greenville, SC 29615
COPELAND, Richard (Dal) 1141 N Loop 1604 E, Suite 105-614, San Antonio, TX 78232
COPELAND, Wanda Ruth (CNY) St Matthews Episcopal Church, 408 S Main St, Horseheads, NY 14845
COPENHAVER, Robert Thomas (SwVa) 50 Draper Pl, Daleville, VA 24083
COPLAND, Edward Mark (SwFla) 5301 Popoli Way, Sarasota, FL 34238
COPLEY, David (NY) 10 W Elizabeth St, Tarrytown, NY 10591
COPLEY, Susan Kay (NY) 10 W Elizabeth St, Tarrytown, NY 10591
COPP, Ann (Md) 444 Garrison Forest Rd, Owings Mills, MD 21117
COPPERSMITH, Curtis Joseph (Mass)
COPPINGER, Tim (WMo) 107 W Perimeter Dr, San Antonio, TX 78227
CORBETT, Ian (NAM) Po Box 28, Bluff, UT 84512
CORBETT-WELCH, Kathy (WA) 793 E Lighton Trl, Fayetteville, AR 72701
CORBIN, Christopher Wesley (FdL) 1215 Liberty St, Oshkosh, WI 54901
CORBIN, Peter Reed (Fla)
CORBIN, Portia (FdL) 500 S Main Ave, Sioux Falls, SD 57104
CORBISHLEY, Frank J (SeFla) 921 Sorolla, Coral Gables, FL 33134
CORDINGLEY, Saundra Lee (Roch) 23 Seneca Road, Rochester, NY 14622
CORDOBA MENESES, Nolberto (Colom)
CORIOLAN, Simpson (Hai) Box 1309, Port-Au-Prince, Haiti
CORKLIN, Stanley Earl (Vt) 744 Parker Rd, West Glover, VT 05875
CORL, James Alexander (CNY) 2435 Fleming Scipio T L Rd, Auburn, NY 13021
CORLEY, Robert M (Dal) 10837 Colbert Way, Dallas, TX 75218
CORNEJO, Quirino H. (Colo) 193 Bristlecone St, Brighton, CO 80601
CORNELL, Allison Lee (Az) 2252 Cherry Hills Dr, Sierra Vista, AZ 85635
CORNELL, Amy S (NJ)

CORNELL, Charles Walton (The Episcopal NCal) 813 Mormon St, Folsom, CA 95630
CORNELL, Peter Stuart (Del) 5 Paterson St, New Brunswick, NJ 08901
CORNER, Cynthia Ruth (Mich) PO Box 287, Onsted, MI 49265
CORNILS, Calvin Stanley (The Episcopal NCal)
CORNMAN, Jane Elizabeth (Me) Po Box 105, Northeast Harbor, ME 04662
CORNNER, Robert Wyman (Los) 8170 Manitoba St Unit 1, Unit #1, Playa Del Rey, CA 90293
CORNTHWAITE, Hannah Elyse (Cal)
CORNWELL, Marilyn (Oly) 9010 SE 47th St, Mercer Island, WA 98040
CORREA AMARILES, Maria Ofelia (Colom) Parroquia San Lucas, Cr 80 No 53A-78, Medellin, Antioguia, Colombia
CORREA GALVEZ, Jose William (Colom) Carrera 6 No 49-85, Piso 2, Bogota, Colombia
CORREIRA, Susan (Mass)
CORRELL, Ruth E (Va) 15639 John Diskin Cir, Woodbridge, VA 22191
CORRIGAN, Candice Lyn (Oly) 506 21st St SW, Austin, MN 55912
CORRIGAN, Michael (Mass) Northfield Mount Hermon School, 1 Lamplighter Way #4702, Mt. Hermon, MA 01354
CORRIGAN, Michael Edward (Los) 1500 State St, Santa Barbara, CA 93101
CORRY, Lisa Marie (Ark)
CORSELLO, Dana Colley (WA) 1755 Clay St, San Francisco, CA 94109
CORT, Aubrey Ebenezer (SwFla) 2507 Del Prado Blvd S, Cape Coral, FL 33904
CORTINAS, Angela Maria (Tex) 9821 Evening Canopy Dr, Manor, TX 78653
CORTRIGHT, Amy Ethel Marie Chambers (Lex) Episcopal Diocese of Lexington, PO Box 610, Lexington, KY 40588
COSBY, Arlinda (Cal) 36458 Shelley Ct, Newark, CA 94560
COSCA-WARFIELD, Sara Nichole (Ore)
COSMAN, Sandra Lee (Ct) 220 Prospect St, Torrington, CT 06790
COSSLETT, Ashley (WNC) 1885 Long Branch Rd, Marshall, NC 28753
COSTA, Steven James (The Episcopal Church in Haw) St Timothy's Episcopal Church, 98-939 Moanalua Rd, Aiea, HI 96701
COSTAS, Catherine Stephenson (Cal) 905 W Middlefield Rd Apt 946, Mountain View, CA 94043
COSTAS, J Kathryn (Ind) 238 Margaret Ridge Rd, Boone, NC 28607
COSTELLO, Elizabeth R (Oly) 1252 NE 89th St, Seattle, WA 98115
COSTIN, Richard Banks (Fla) 1601 Alafaya Trl, Oviedo, FL 32765
COTTER, Barry Lynn (SO) 308 Heard St, Mckinney, TX 75069

COTTING, Jean (SO)
COTTRELL, Jan M (Lex) 1445 Copperfield Ct, Lexington, KY 40514
COTTRILL, Dave (SO) 3724 Mengel Dr, Kettering, OH 45429
COUCH, Michelle A (Oly) 105 State St., Kirkland, WA 98033
COUDRIET, Alan P (NwPa) 10 Woodside Ave, Oil City, PA 16301
COUFAL, M(ary) Lorraine (Neb) 3819 Green Arbor Way #812, Indianapolis, IN 46220
COUGHLIN, Christopher Anthony (O) 7640 Glenwood Ave, Boardman, OH 44512
COULOUTE, Schneyder (Hai)
COULSON, Asa David (CPa) 4 Madison Ave, Madison, NJ 07940
COULSON, Mary Lynn (SanD) 16275 Pomerado Rd, Poway, CA 92064
COULTAS, Amy (Ky) 612 Myrte St, Louisville, KY 40208
COULTER, Clayton Roy (Ore) 7430 Sw Pineridge Ct, Portland, OR 97225
COULTER, Elizabeth (Ia) 3148 Dubuque St NE, Iowa City, IA 52240
COULTER, Linda M (CFla)
COULTER, Sherry Lynn (At) 681 Holt Rd Ne, Marietta, GA 30068
COUNSELMAN, Robert Lee (NJ) 119 S Hondo St, P O Box 1478, Sabinal, TX 78881
COUNTRYMAN, LOuis William (Cal) 5805 Keith Ave, Oakland, CA 94618
COUPER, David Courtland (Mil) 5282 County Road K, Blue Mounds, WI 53517
COUPLAND, Geoffrey D (Va) 5110 Park Ave., Richmond, VA 23226
COURTNEY, Joseph Bradley (Los) 4533 Laurel Canyon Blvd, Studio City, CA 91607
COURTNEY, Larry Edward (Ky) 5 S Green St, Henderson, KY 42420
COURTNEY, Michael David (Ark) 235 Caroline Acres Road, Hot Springs, AR 71913
COURTNEY, Peter (At) 339 Reeds Lndg, Springfield, MA 01109
COURTNEY II, Robert Wickliff (La) 15 Drifter Ln, New Orleans, LA 70124
COURTRIGHT, Alice Hodgkins (NH)
COURTRIGHT, Andrew Michael (NY) 40 Jefferson Ln, Bedford, NY 10506
COUVILLION, Brian Neff (Chi) 4370 Woodland Ave, Western Springs, IL 60558
COUZZOURT, Beverly Schmidt (NwT) 2106 7th Avenue, 2106 7th Anvenue, Canyon, TX 79015
COVENTRY, Donald Edgar (Spr) 246 Southmoreland Pl, Decatur, IL 62521
COVENTRY, Jon (O)
COVER, Michael Benjamin (Dal) 616 Lincolnway E., Mishawaka, IN 46544
COVERSTON, Harry Scott (ECR) 630 Roberta Ave, Orlando, FL 32803

COVERT, Edward Martin (SwVa) Po Box 126, Fort Defiance, VA 24437

COVINGTON, John E (NY) 410 W 24th St Apt 8k Apt 8k, New York, NY 10011

COWAN, Sarah Bliss (WTenn)

COWARDIN, Eustis Barber (ND) 510 E Lake County Rd, Jamestown, ND 58401

COWART, Alan B (SwVa) 1021 New Hampshire Ave, Lynchburg, VA 24502

COWART, Valerie (Mass)

✠ **COWDEN**, Matthew D (WVa) 16341 Parkwood Ct, Granger, IN 46530

COWELL, Curtis Lyle (Kan) 2601 SW College Ave, Topeka, KS 66611

✠ **COWELL**, Mark Andrew (WK) 501 W 5th St, Larned, KS 67550

COWEN, Charles Lane (Del) 2009 Shallcross Ave, Wilmington, DE 19806

COWGILL, Allison Mackenzie (SwVa)

COWGILL, Benjamin (SwVa)

COWHERD, Charles Robison (Va) 2609 Claxton Dr, Herndon, VA 20171

COWPER, Judy (Ct) 54 Dora Dr, Middletown, CT 06457

COWPERTHWAITE, Robert W (Fla) 6535 Jean Dr, Raleigh, NC 27612

COX, Amy Eleanor (WMo) Stfrancis In The Pines, 17890 Metcalf Ave, Overland Park, KS 66085

COX, Amy Gabrielle (Los)

COX, Anne Elizabeth (Mich) 8 Ridge Rd, Tenants Harbor, ME 04860

COX IV, Brian (Los) 871 Serenidad Pl, Goleta, CA 93117

COX, Catherine Rodman (WK)

COX, Catherine Susanna (WMo) 365 E 372nd Rd, Dunnegan, MO 65640

COX, Celeste O'Hern (Del) 568 Willowwood Dr, Smyrna, DE 19977

COX, Christopher Edward (NJ) 801 W State St, Trenton, NJ 08618

COX, David (Kan) 1455 E 37th St, Sedalia, MO 65301

COX, Diane (WNY)

COX, Edwin Manuel (NC) 4510 Highberry Rd, Greensboro, NC 27410

COX, Frances Fosbroke (Md) 4510 Highberry Rd, Greensboro, NC 27410

COX, Gary (Chi)

COX, Jason (Cal) 1330 Chestnut St, San Francisco, CA 94123

COX, Nancy L J (NC) 525 Lake Concord Rd NE, Concord, NC 28025

COX, R David (SwVa) 107 Lee Ave., Lexington, VA 24450

COX, The Rev Sharron L (Tex) 201 E Clay St, West Columbia, TX 77486

COX ONEY, Erin Kathleen (Az)

COYNE, William (SC) 1615 Ellsworth St, Mount Pleasant, SC 29466

COZZOLI, John David (Md) 17524 Lincolnshire Rd, Hagerstown, MD 21740

CRAFT, Bernadine Louise (Wyo) Po Box 567, Rock Springs, WY 82902

CRAFT, Carolyn Martin (SVa) 1702 Briery Rd, Farmville, VA 23901

CRAFT, John Harvey (La) 4505 S Claiborne Ave, New Orleans, LA 70125

CRAFT, Stephen Frank (La) 3101 Plymouth Pl, New Orleans, LA 70131

CRAFTON, Barbara Cawthorne (NY) 99 New St Apt 309, Metuchen, NJ 08840

CRAIG, Carrie (EC) 825 Peninsula Dr Apt 321, Apt 321, Davidson, NC 28036

CRAIG SR, Claude Phillep (EC) 400 Avinger Ln, Apt 246, Davidson, NC 28036

CRAIG JR, Claude Phillip (EC) 6300 SW Nicol Rd, Portland, OR 97223

CRAIG JR, Harry Walter (Kan) 5041 Sw Fairlawn Rd, Topeka, KS 66610

CRAIG, Idalia S (NJ) 85 Stone Rd, Mcdonough, GA 30253

CRAIG III, James (WMass) 11 Cotton St, Leominster, MA 01453

CRAIG, Jo Roberts (NwT) 2401 Parker St, Amarillo, TX 79109

CRAIG III, Richard Edwin (Mil) 517 Issa Cir, El Paso, TX 79932

CRAIG, Shay (WK)

CRAIGHEAD, Thomas Gray (Chi) St Andrew's Church, 1125 Franklin St, Downers Grove, IL 60515

CRAIGHEAD JR, Tom Thomas (Oly) 28203 137th Ave SW, Vashon, WA 98070

CRAIG-JONES, Christopher (SanD)

CRAIN II, Lee Bryan (LI) 518 Brooklyn Blvd, Brightwaters, NY 11718

CRAIN, William Henry (WMo) 9208 Wenonga Rd, Leawood, KS 66206

CRAM JR, Norman Lee (The Episcopal NCal) PO Box 224, Vineburg, CA 95487

CRAMER, Alan Barry (Ind)

CRAMER, Jared C (WMich) 524 Washington Ave, Grand Haven, MI 49417

CRAMER, Roger Weldon (Mass) 16 Aubin Street, Amesbury, MA 01913

CRAMPTON, Susan Harris (WMass) 16595 Warren Ct Apt 305, Chagrin Falls, OH 44023

CRANDALL, John Davin (Mass) 404 Juniper Way, Tavares, FL 32778

CRANE, Linda Sue (EMich) 1213 6th St, Port Huron, MI 48060

CRANE, Rebecca Mai (Mass) 13 Trinity St., Danvers, MA 01923

CRANSTON, Dale L (NY) 21 Stone Fence Rd, Mahwah, NJ 07430

CRANSTON, Pamela Lee (Cal) 207 Taurus Ave, Oakland, CA 94611

CRARY, Kathleen (Cal) 733 Baywood Rd, Alameda, CA 94502

CRAUN, Chris (Ore) 3236 NE Alberta St., Portland, OR 97211

CRAVEN III, James Braxton (NC) 17 Marchmont Ct, Durham, NC 27705

CRAVEN, Sam (Tex) 6221 Main St, Houston, TX 77030

CRAVENS, James Owen (Spr) 4 Canterbury Ln, Lincoln, IL 62656

CRAVER III, Marshall P (CGC) 613 Highland Woods Dr E, Mobile, AL 36608

CRAWFORD, Alicia Leu Lydon (Chi) 550 N Green Bay Rd, Lake Forest, IL 60045

CRAWFORD II, Gerald Gene (Ark)

CRAWFORD JR, Grady J (At) 1011 Nottingham Ln NE, Atlanta, GA 30319

CRAWFORD, Hayden G (SeFla) 701 45th Ave S, Saint Petersburg, FL 33705

CRAWFORD, Karen Graham (Ia) 223 E 4th St N, Newton, IA 50208

CRAWFORD JR, Kelly (Los) 450 NW Ivy Ave, Dallas, OR 97338

CRAWFORD, Lee (Vt) PO Box 67, Plymouth, VT 05056

CRAWFORD, Leo (SwFla) 2694 Grove Park Rd, Palm Harbor, FL 34583

CRAWFORD, Malia (Mass) 21 Marathon St., Arlington, MA 02474

CRAWFORD, Mark (Tex) PO Box 20269, Houston, TX 77225

CRAWFORD, Nancy (Ore) 1595 E 31st Ave, Eugene, OR 97405

CRAWFORD, Sidnie White (Be)

CRAWFORD, Stephen Howard (La) 3552 Morning Glory Ave, Baton Rouge, LA 70808

CRAWFORD, Susan Kaye (Miss) 1026 S Washington Ave, Greenville, MS 38701

CRAWLEY, Clayton D (NY) 20 Pine St Apt 2106, New York, NY 10005

CREAN, Charleen (Los) 931 E. Walnut St. #114, Pasadena, CA 91106

CREAN JR, Very Rev Canon Dr John E (Los) 49475 Marne Ct, La Quinta, CA 92253

CREASY, James Arthur (Ala) 3228 Lee Road 56, Auburn, AL 36832

CRECCA, Kimberly Diane (Az)

CREED, Christopher Duflon (ECR) 501 Portola Rd Apt 8185, Portola Valley, CA 94028

CREELMAN JR, Benjamin Lambert (SwFla)

✠ **CREIGHTON**, Michael Whittington (CPa) 2716 Gingerview Ln, Annapolis, MD 21401

CREIGHTON, Susan (Oly) 15 Huckleberry Ct, Bellingham, WA 98229

CRELLIN, Timothy Edward (WMass) 25 Boylston St, Jamaica Plain, MA 02130

CRERAR, Patrick (Los) 202 Avenida Aragon, San Clemente, CA 92672

CRESPO, Willy (SanD) 10125 Azuaga St, San Diego, CA 92129

CRESS, Katherine E (Los) 3903 Wilshire Blvd, Los Angeles, CA 90010

CRESSMAN, Lisa Kraske (Minn) 3 Blue Iron Dr, Missouri City, TX 77459

CRESSMAN, Louise A (NJ) 25 Lakeshore Dr, Hammonton, NJ 08037

CRESSMAN, Naomi May (NJ) 305 Main St, Riverton, NJ 08077

Clergy List

CRESWELL, Jennifer (Ore) 4411 NE Beech St, Portland, OR 97213
CRETEN, Claude Daniel (NMich) E4929 State Highway M35, Escanaba, MI 49829
CREWS, Norman Dale (Md) 201 Porter Dr, Annapolis, MD 21401
CREWS, Warren Earl (Mo) 25 Country Club Ter, Saint Louis, MO 63122
CREWS, William Eugene (Colo) 4042 Xerxes Ave. S., Minneapolis, MN 55410
CRICHLOW, Neville Joseph (CFla) 381 N Lincoln St, Daytona Beach, FL 32114
CRICHTON, Mary Gwynn (Va) 815 Egrace St, Richmond, VA 23225
CRIDER, Dion Gregory (Okla)
CRIGLER, Meredith Holt (Tex) 4507 Crescent Lake Cir, Baytown, TX 77521
CRIM, Marcus Jacob (Cal) 385 Eddy St Apt 613, San Francisco, CA 94102
CRIMI, Lynne B (Alb) 7 Sweet Rd, Stillwater, NY 12170
CRIPPEN, Stephen Daniel (Oly) 1922 12th Ave W, Seattle, WA 98119
CRIPPS, David Richard (Roch) 139 Lake Bluff Rd, Rochester, NY 14622
CRIPPS, Samuel Cassidy Roth (Dal)
CRIPS, Paul (Wyo)
CRISE, Rebecca Ann (WMich) Saint Mark's Episcopal Church, PO Box 307, Paw Paw, MI 49079
CRISP, Justin E (Ct) 111 Oenoke Rdg, New Canaan, CT 06840
CRISS, Carthur Paul (Kan) 4138 E 24th St N, Wichita, KS 67220
CRIST, John (Chi) PO Box, 131 Fifth St, Mc Nabb, IL 61335
CRIST, Mary Frances (Los) St Michaels Episcopal Church, 4070 Jackson St, Riverside, CA 92503
CRIST JR, William Harold (Los) 2091 Business Center Dr Ste 130, Irvine, CA 92612
CRISTE-TROUTMAN, Bob (Be) 137 Trinity Hill Rd., Mt. Pocono, PA 18344
CRISTOBAL, Robert S (Chi) 1000 West Rt 64, Oregon, IL 61061
CRITCHFIELD, Margot (Mass) 3 Boardwalk Rd, Sandwich, MA 02563
CRITCHLOW II, Fitzgerald St Clair Jerry (Tex) 3700 Kingwood Dr Apt 1806, Kingwood, TX 77339
CRITELLI, Robert J (NJ) 13 King Arthurs Ct, Sicklerville, NJ 08081
CRITES, Becky (SVa) Emmanuel Episcopal Church, PO Box 26, Chatham, VA 24531
CRITES, Karry D (Nev) 1035 Munley Dr, Reno, NV 89503
CRITTENDEN, Francis Thomas Glasgow (SwVa) 208 N Market St, Staunton, VA 24401
CRITTENDEN, Joan Marie (WA)
CRITTENDEN, William S (WNY) Po Box 93, Chautauqua, NY 14722

CROCKER, Edna Irene (Fla) 10560 Fort George Rd, Jacksonville, FL 32226
CROCKER, Ronald Conrad (Va) 3 Hamilton Ct, Uxbridge, MA 01569
CROCKETT, Daniel L (SVa) PO Box 102, Conyers, GA 30012
CROCKETT, Jennie L (SO) 2700 Kenview Rd S, Columbus, OH 43209
CROCKETT, Larry Joe (Minn) 4525 Alicia Dr, Inver Grove Heights, MN 55077
CROES, John Rodney (NJ) 20 Claremont Ave, South River, NJ 08882
CROFTS, Marisa D (Dal)
CROMEY, Edwin Harry (NY) St. Luke's Church, 850 Wolcott Ave. Box 507, Beacon, NY 12508
CROMEY, Robert Warren (Cal) 3839 - 20th, San Francisco, CA 94114
CROMMELIN-DELL, Sally Huntress (SVa) 500 Court St., Portsmouth, VA 23704
CROMPTON, Jennifer Jen Anna (ECR) 11353 Los Osos Valley Rd Apt C, Apt C, San Luis Obispo, CA 93405
CROMWELL, Peggy Lynn (Ark)
CRON, Ian Morgan (Ct) 226 5th Ave S, Franklin, TN 37064
✠ CRONEBERGER, John Palmer (Be) 1079 Old Bernville Rd, Reading, PA 19605
CRONIN, Audrey Ann (WMass)
CRONIN, Micah Connor (NJ)
CROPPER, Andrew C (Eas)
CROSBY, Benjamin David (Mass)
CROSBY, David (Va) Immanuel Church-on-the-Hill, 3606 Seminary Rd, Alexandria, VA 22304
CROSBY, Karen Ann (Md) 52 S Broadway, Frostburg, MD 21532
CROSIER, Allen Duane (Spok)
CROSKEY, Christine Lucille (CFla) Holy Apostles Episcopal Church, 505 Grant Ave, Satellite Beach, FL 32937
CROSS, Carol (SwVa)
CROSS II, Eugenia Sealy (NC) 1032 Wessyngton Rd, Winston Salem, NC 27104
CROSS, Kevin (Eas) PO Box 387, Oxford, MD 21654
CROSS, Myrick Tyler (SO) 52 Pleasant St, Freedom, ME 04941
CROSS, Samuel Otis (WTenn) 330 Fletcher Hollow Rd, Collierville, TN 38017
CROSSETT, Judith Hale Wallace (Ia) 320 E College St, Iowa City, IA 52240
CROSSLEY, Pamela S (SC)
CROSSNOE, Marshall E (Mo) 217 Adams St, Jefferson City, MO 65101
CROSSWAITE, John (CNY) PO Box 961, 182 Vincent Street, Cape Vincent, NY 13618
CROTHERS, Kenneth Delbert (Ida) Po Box 374, Shoshone, ID 83352
CROUCH, Billy Gene (NY) 3604 Balcones Dr, Austin, TX 78731
CROW, Lyn (Los) 1145 W Valencia Mesa Dr, Fullerton, CA 92833

CROW, Robert B (SwFla) St Andrews TEC Ch, PO Box 1658, Destin, FL 32540
CROWE, Amy Beth (The Episcopal Church in Haw)
CROWE, Kathleen A (ECR) The Rev Kathleen Crowe, 4271 N 1st St Spc 74, San Jose, CA 95134
CROWELL, Larry A (SO)
CROWELL, Paul (Az) 2800 Huntsman Ct, Jamestown, NC 27282
CROWLEY, Daniel Fenwick (Mass) 76 Olde Towne Lane, West Chatham, MA 02669
CROWNOVER, Richard Matthew (Dal)
CROWSON, Steven Franklin (LI) 360 Fountain St Apt 10, New Haven, CT 06515
CROZIER, Richard Lee (USC) 125 Pendleton St Sw, Aiken, SC 29801
CRUIKSHANK, Charles Clark (CPa) 208 W Foster Ave, State College, PA 16801
CRUMB, Lawrence Nelson (Ore) 1674 Washington St, Eugene, OR 97401
CRUMBAUGH III, Frank (NJ) 410 S Atlantic Ave, Beach Haven, NJ 08008
CRUMLEY, Carole (WA) 3039 Beech St Nw, Washington, DC 20015
CRUMMEY, Rebecca (Colo) 967 Marion St Apt 7, Denver, CO 80218
CRUMP, Carl Calvin (ETenn) St Martins St Stephens, 15801 Us Highway 19, Hudson, FL 34667
CRUMPTON IV, Alvin Briggs (Ga) 4227 Columbia Rd, Martinez, GA 30907
CRUPI, Hilary (FdL) Our Lady Of The Northwoods, W 704 Alft Rd, White Lake, WI 54491
CRUSE, William C (Nwk) PO Box 389, Jackson, NH 03846
CRUSOE, Lewis D (EMich)
CRUZ-DIAZ, Nora (At) 5148 Victor Trail, Norcross, GA 30071
CRUZ LILLEGARD, Andrew R (Alb)
CRYSLER JR, Fred (Ct) PO Box 9324, Louisville, KY 40209
CUBILLAS, Angelito Conde (Az) 2135 19th St, Florence, OR 97439
CUBINE, James W (WTenn) 7910 Gayle Ln, Memphis, TN 38138
CUDD, Anne Grover (Ida) 3024 Sw 98th Way, Gainesville, FL 32608
CUEVAS FELIZ, Pedro G (RG) 7004 31st Ave Fl 2, East Elmhurst, NY 11370
CUFF, Stephen James (SO) 451 N Galloway St, Xenia, OH 45385
CUFF, Victoria Slater Smith (NJ) 45 2nd St, Keyport, NJ 07735
CUFFIE, Karen Ann (ECR) 2094 Grant Rd, Mountain View, CA 94040
CULBERTSON, David Paul (Alb) 210 S Washington St, Muncy, PA 17756
CULBERTSON, Thomas Leon (Md) 6 Yearling Way, Lutherville, MD 21093

CULBREATH, Leeann D (Ga) 2411 Madison Dr, Tifton, GA 31793
CULBREATH, Lola Annette (Nev)
CULLEN, Kathleen Mary (NH) St Andrews Episcopal Church, 102 N Main St, Manchester, NH 03102
CULLEN, Peter (LI) 199 Carroll St, Brooklyn, NY 11231
CULLINANE, Kathleen Jean (The Episcopal Church in Haw) 15422 Nantucket St, Westminster, CA 92683
CULLIPHER III, James Robert (USC) 800 Stillpoint Way, Balsam Grove, NC 28708
CULLY, Miranda (WTenn) 3245 Central Ave, Memphis, TN 38111
CULMER, Ron (Cal) 3350 Hopyard Rd, Pleasanton, CA 94588
CULP, Kimberly H (Neb)
CULP JR, Robert S (Roch) 19 Arbor Ct, Fairport, NY 14450
CULPEPPER, Judith (Ind) 6736 Prince Regent Ct, Indianapolis, IN 46250
CULPEPPER, Polk (Ind) 1301 Summit Ave, Washington, NC 27889
CULTON, Douglas (Del) 1212 E Holly St, Goldsboro, NC 27530
CULVER, Carson Kies (Mil) 590 N Church St, Richland Center, WI 53581
CULVER, Esme Jo R (Ore) Grace Memorial Church, 1535 NE 17th Ave, Portland, OR 97232
CUMBIE II, Walter Kenneth (CGC) 172 Hannon Ave, Mobile, AL 36604
CUMMER, Edwin West (SwFla)
CUMMINGS, Carolsue J (NJ) 322 So Second St, Surf City, NJ 08008
CUMMINGS, Patricia L (Cal) 110 Wood Rd Apt C-104, Los Gatos, CA 95030
CUMMINGS, Sally Ann (Minn) 520 N Pokegama Ave, Grand Rapids, MN 55744
CUMMINGS, Sudduth (NC) 3990 Meandering Ln, Tallahassee, FL 32308
CUMMINS, James Michael (Kan)
CUMMINS, Thomas W (Ore) 11100 Sw Riverwood Rd, Portland, OR 97219
CUNDIFF IV, Joseph Lawrence (LI)
CUNIFF, Wanda Wood (Tex) Christ Episcopal Church, 1320 Mound St., Nacogdoches, TX 75961
CUNNINGHAM, Arthur Leland (Mil) 1320 Mill Rd, Delafield, WI 53018
CUNNINGHAM, Chris (Mich) 400 High St, Farmville, VA 23901
CUNNINGHAM, Gerarlyn E (The Episcopal NCal) 1780 Greenfield Pl, Fortuna, CA 95540
CUNNINGHAM, James Earl (Tex) 2227 Woodland Springs Dr, Houston, TX 77077
CUNNINGHAM, Lynn Edward (Wyo) 3403 Ordway St Nw, Washington, DC 20016
CUNNINGHAM, Margaret Taylor (Los) 1122 Wabash St, Pasadena, CA 91103

CUNNINGHAM, Michael Ray (Los) St Marys Episcopal Church, 2800 Harris Grade Rd, Lompoc, CA 93436
CUNNINGHAM, Philip John (Mil) 2500 N. 10th St., McAllen, TX 78501
CUNNINGHAM, Trish (Cal) 1668 Bush St, San Francisco, CA 94109
CUNNINGHAM, William Wallace (Ala)
CUPERWICH, Kyle Andrew (NJ) 485 Main St, Lumberton, NJ 08048
CUPP, Jean Carol (EO) 1239 Nw Ingram Ave, Pendleton, OR 97801
CURL, James Fair (WNC) 461 Crowfields Dr., Asheville, NC 28803
CURNS, Mary S (WMass) All Saints Episcopal Church, PO Box 374, North Adams, MA 01247
CURRIE, Ryan Daniel (SC)
CURRY, Dorothy Reed (Cal) 4351 Ridgeway Dr, San Diego, CA 92116
CURRY, Gene E (Mich) 2735 Manchester Rd, Ann Arbor, MI 48104
✠ **CURRY**, Glenda (Ala) 4304 Bonwood Dr, Vestavia, AL 35243
✠ **CURRY**, James (Ct) 18 Nash St Apt 2, New Haven, CT 06511
✠ **CURRY**, Michael B (NC) 200 W Morgan St Ste 300, Raleigh, NC 27601
CURTIN, Anne (Alb) Healing A Womans Soul Inc, 68 Sswan St, Albany, NY 12210
CURTIN JR, Ernest Albert (Pa) St Lukes Episcopal Church, 100 E Washington Ave, Newtown, PA 18940
CURTIS, Chuck (EMich) 3260 E Midland Rd, Bay City, MI 48706
CURTIS, David (Va)
CURTIS, Frederick L (Alb) 262 Main St N, Southbury, CT 06488
CURTIS, Kenton (NY) 200 Bennett Ave Apt 3g, New York, NY 10040
CURTIS, Lynne Marsh Piret (Alb) 912 Route 146, Clifton Park, NY 12065
CURTIS, Mary Page (NC) 212 Edinboro Dr, Southern Pines, NC 28387
CURTIS, Pattie (WNC) St Johns Episcopal Church, PO Box 175, Sylva, NC 28779
CURTIS, Sandra King (Roch) 10 Shether St # 272, Hammondsport, NY 14840
CURTIS, Sandra O (Ark) Episcopal Collegiate School, 1701 Cantrell Rd, Little Rock, AR 72201
CURTIS, Susan Bradbury (Me) 8 Pine Ln, Cumberland Foreside, ME 04110
CURTIS, Ted (RG) 637 S Dearborn St Fl 1, Chicago, IL 60605
CURTIS III, William L (RG) 2407 Cascade Rd Sw, Atlanta, GA 30311
CURTIS JR, William Shepley (Nev) 1654 County Rd, Minden, NV 89423
CURTIS, Yvonne Marie (WNY) PO Box 14, Dunkirk, NY 14048
CURTISS, Geoff (Nwk) 202 3RD AVE, Bradley Beach, NJ 07720
CUSANO, William Alan (NY) 2500 Jerome Ave, Bronx, NY 10468

CUSHING, Nan Chenault Marshall (NC) 69 Crystal Oaks Ct, Durham, NC 27707
CUSHINOTTO, Susan Elizabeth (NJ) 9425 3rd Ave, Stone Harbor, NJ 08247
CUSHMAN, Mary Toohey (NY) PO Box 211, Chebeague Island, ME 04017
CUSHMAN, Thomas Spaulding (NY) PO Box 211, Chebeague Island, ME 04017
CUSIC, Georgeanne Hill (FdL) 1510 N Broadway Ave, Marshfield, WI 54449
CUSTER, Dale (SVa) 14404 Roberts Mill Ct, Midlothian, VA 23113
CUTAIAR, Michael Louis (NMich)
CUTIE, Albert R (SeFla) 11173 Griffing Blvd, Miami, FL 33161
CUTLER, Cliff (Pa) 18 E Chestnut Hill Ave, Philadelphia, PA 19118
CUTLER, Howard Taylor (HB) 1124 Westhampton Glen Dr, Richmond, VA 23238
CUTOLO, Mark Anthony (WNY) 351 E 74th St, New York, NY 10021
CUTSHALL, Jason Edward (Minn) 2801 Westwood Rd, Minnetonka Beach, MN 55391
CUTTER IV, Irv (WTex) 11 Saint Lukes Ln, San Antonio, TX 78209
CYR, Gary A (CNY) 3 J St, Bangor, ME 04401
CYR, Mark Bernard (Eas) 25 Addy Road, P.O. Box 191, Bethany Beach, DE 19930
CZARNETZKY, Sylvia Yale (Miss) 148 French Br, Madison, MS 39110
CZARNIECKI, Lynn (Pa) 30 Gildersleeve Pl, Watchung, NJ 07069
CZOLGOSZ, Joseph Tamborini (NI) 707 S Chester Ave, Park Ridge, IL 60068

D

DABNEY, Elizabeth Ruth (Tex) PO Box 746, Columbus, TX 78934
DAGG, Kay (Kan) 1427 SW Macvicar Ave, Topeka, KS 66604
DAGGETT, Paul (SO) 115 N 6th St, Hamilton, OH 45011
DAHARSH, Floyd Arthur (Okla) 112 W 9th St, Hugoton, KS 67951
DAHL, Joan Elizabeth (Spok) 8991 State Route 24, Moxee, WA 98936
DAHLIN, Jim (Cal) 525 29th St, Oakland, CA 94609
DAHLMAN, Thomas A (Okla) 1321 N Broadway Ave, Shawnee, OK 74801
DAIGLE, Deborah Heft (Tex) 15357 Ben Wiggins Rd, Conroe, TX 77303
DAIL, Jonathan G (Tex)
DAILEY, Beulah Huffman (Dal) 2929 Hickory St, Dallas, TX 75226
DAILEY, Douglas G (At) 3603 Tradition Dr, Gainesville, GA 30506
DAILY JR, Charles W (FdL) N 6945 Ash Road, Shawano, WI 54166
DAILY, Teresa Wooten (Ark) 925 Mitchell St, Conway, AR 72034

Clergy List

DAISA IV, George (Los) 1 Church Rd, Thousand Oaks, CA 91362
DAKAN, Karen Nugent (SwFla) 14 Sandy Hook Rd N, Sarasota, FL 34242
D'ALCARAVELA, Joao Antonio Alpalhao (Mass) Palmoinho, Serra do Louro, Palmela, 2950-305, Portugal
DALE, Anne (SVa)
DALE, Cortney H (EC)
DALE, Kathleen Askew (Los) Stmargarets Tec Ch, 47535 Highway 74, Palm Desert, CA 92260
DALES, Randolph Kent (NH) PO Box 1363, Wolfeboro, NH 03894
DALEY, Joy (Dal) 13355 Pandora Cir, Dallas, TX 75238
DALFERES, Craig (La) 11637 Ferdinand St # 864, Saint Francisville, LA 70775
DALGLISH, William Anthony (Tenn) 1911 Hampton Dr, Lebanon, TN 37087
DALLMAN, Matthew Christian (CFla)
DALLY, John A (Chi) 2650 N Lakeview Ave Apt 2501, Chicago, IL 60614
DALMASSO, Gary Lee (Chi) 215 29th Ave, East Moline, IL 61244
DALRYMPLE, Sharon Gladwin (ECR) 5147 Show Low Lake Rd, Lakeside, AZ 85929
DALTON, Harlon L (Ct) 329 Greene St Unit 9, New Haven, CT 06511
DALTON, Joyce Foley (Ark) St Stephens Episcopal Church, 2413 Northeastern Ave, Jacksonville, AR 72076
DALY, Joseph Erin (WLa) 1030 Johnston St, Lafayette, LA 70501
DALY III, Raymond Ernest (Fla) 160 Sea Island Dr, Ponte Vedra Beach, FL 32082
DALZON, Wilfrid (Hai)
D'AMARIO, Matthew Justin (Eas) 302 North Baltimore Avenue, Ocean City, MD 21842
DAMON, Robert Edward (CFla) 3329 Wilson St, Hollywood, FL 33021
DAMROSCH, Tom (WMass) PO Box 512, Stockbridge, MA 01262
DAMUS, Pierre Gasner (LI) 1227 Pacific St, Brooklyn, NY 11216
DANAHER JR, William Joseph (Mich) 470 Church Rd, Bloomfield Hills, MI 48304
DANDRIDGE, Robert Floyd (WLa) 702 Elm St, Minden, LA 71055
DANFORD, Nicholas Chase (NJ) 4 Fountain Sq, Larchmont, NY 10538
DANFORTH, John Claggett (Mo) 911 Cirrill Farms Rd, Saint Louis, MO 63124
DANGELO, Michael B (Mass) 10600 Preston Rd, Dallas, TX 75230
D'ANGIO, Peter David (Lex) 16 E 4th St, Covington, KY 41011
DANIEL III, Clifton (NY) 1047 Amsterdam Ave, New York, NY 10025

DANIEL, Joshua Timothy Kenyon (WA) 531 W College Ave, Jonesboro, AR 72401
DANIEL JR, William Otis (ETenn) 23 Main St, Geneseo, NY 14454
DANIELEY, Teresa K M (Mo) 3887 Wyoming St, Saint Louis, MO 63116
DANIELLI, Helena Mary Corinne (Tex)
DANIELS, Garron (Mo)
DANIELS, Janet (NJ) St Mary's by the Sea, 804 Bay Ave, Point Pleasant, NJ 08742
DANIELS, Joel C. (Pa) 1 W. 53rd St., New York, NY 10019
DANIELS, John D (WA) 1001 E Lincoln Hwy, Exton, PA 19341
DANIELS, Josiah Mark (NC) 22 E Chestnut Hill Ave, Philadelphia, PA 19118
DANIELS, Paul Anthony (NC)
✠ **DANIELS**, Theodore Athelbert (Episcopal VI) 3208 Prairie Clover Path, Austin, TX 78732
DANIEL-TURK, Patricia (Fla) 15 East Manor, Beaufort, SC 29906
D'ANIERI, Margaret C (O) 18369 State Route 18, Wellington, OH 44090
DANITSCHEK, Thomas K (Colo) 6930 E 4th Ave, Denver, CO 80220
DANKEL, Rainey (Va) 1500 Westbrook Ct Apt 1136, Richmond, VA 23227
DANNALS, James Clark (SC) 2 W Manor, Beaufort, SC 29906
DANNALS, Robert S (Dal) 8011 Douglas At Colgate, Dallas, TX 75225
DANNHAUSER, Adrian (NY) St James' Church, 865 Madison Ave, New York, NY 10021
DANSDILL, Dorothy Newton (NMich) 501 N Ravine St, Sault Sainte Marie, MI 49783
DANSON, Michelle Anne (Colo) 7776 Country Creek Dr, Longmont, CO 80503
DANTONE, Jan (WTex)
DANZEY, Charles (Oly) 6009 W Parker Rd Ste 149-425, Plano, TX 75093
DARBY, Steven Lanier (Ga) 114 W Mockingbird Ln, Statesboro, GA 30461
DARDEN, John Webster (Dal) 1852 E Mulberry, PPrescott Valley, AZ 89314
DARISME, Joseph Wilkie (Hai) Boite Postale 1309, Port-Au-Prince, Haiti
DARKO, Daniel Dodoo (WA) 1510 Erskine St, Takoma Park, MD 20912
DARLING, Elizabeth Ann (WNC) 1045 Jamestown Rd, Williamsburg, VA 23185
DARLING, Laura (Cal) 13785 Old Morro Rd, Atascadero, CA 93422
DARLING, Mary (Roch) 2704 Darnby Dr, Oakland, CA 94611
DARLINGTON, Diane Lillie (NMich) 301 N 1st St, Ishpeming, MI 49849
DARRESS, Gary (Colo)

DARVES-BORNOZ, Derek (NY) Church Pension Group, 19 E 34th St, New York, NY 10016
DARVILLE, Nathaniel Kirk Michael (Nwk) 906 Pike Rd, Pike Road, AL 36064
DASS, Stephen (CFla) 1108 SE 9th Ave, Ocala, FL 34471
DATOS-ROBYN, Richard James (NY) St Marys-in-Tuxedo, PO Box 637, Tuxedo Park, NY 10987
DATSKO, Paula Suzanne (Az) 3783 N Forgeus Ave, Tucson, AZ 85716
DAUER-CARDASIS, Joade (NY) 227 E 87th St Apt 1B, New York, NY 10128
DAUGHERTY, Jennifer King (Oly) 1245 10th Ave E, Seattle, WA 98102
DAUGHTRY, Susan (Minn) 1325 Nottoway Ave, Apt. A, Richmond, VA 23227
DAUNT, Francis Thomas (La) 815 E Guenther St, San Antonio, TX 78210
DAUTEL, Terrence Pickands (O) Po Box 62, Gates Mills, OH 44040
DAVENPORT, Anetta Lynn (Wyo) Holy Trinity Episcopal Church, PO Box 950, Thermopolis, WY 82443
DAVENPORT, Carrol Kimsey (Mo) 17 Broadview, Kirksville, MO 63501
DAVENPORT, Dave (SVa) 6051 River Road Pt, Norfolk, VA 23505
DAVENPORT, Elizabeth Jayne Louise (Chi)
DAVENPORT, Karen Geddes (CFla) 3840 Lakeview Dr, Sebring, FL 33870
DAVENPORT, Marcia EM (SwFla) 1606 Chickasaw Rd, Arnold, MD 21012
DAVENPORT JR, Richard (NH) PO Box 85, Colebrook, NH 03576
DAVENPORT, Robert (SVa) 1509 N Shore Rd, Norfolk, VA 23505
DAVENPORT III, Stephen Rintoul (WA) 4700 Whitehaven Pkwy NW, Washington, DC 20007
DAVID, Charles Wayne Laskin (Mass) 6390 Sagewood Way, Delray Beach, FL 33484
DAVID, Christopher (LI) PO Box 110, 482 County Route 30, Salem, NY 12865
DAVID, Jacob Thandasseril (Nwk) 1 Paddock Court, Dayton, NJ 08810
DAVID, John Spencer (WMich) 157 Lost Creek Lane, Kalispell, MT 59901
DAVID, Ronald (Los) 1225 Wilshire Blvd, Los Angeles, CA 90017
DAVIDSON, Charles Alexander (Pa) 814 N 41st St, Philadelphia, PA 19104
DAVIDSON, Don (EMich) 5333 Clyde Park Ave SW, Wyoming, MI 49509
DAVIDSON, Jon Paul (Nev) PO Box 8822, Incline Village, NV 89452
DAVIDSON, Mark Alan (NC) 3205 S Main St, Winston Salem, NC 27127
DAVIDSON, Patricia Foote (Ct) 118 Bill Hill Rd, Lyme, CT 06371
DAVIDSON, Robert Michael (Pa) 22 E Chestnut Hill Ave, Philadelphia, PA 19118

DAVIDSON, Robert Paul (Colo) 29 Lakeview Rd, Winchester, MA 01890

DAVIDSON, Susan (Ct) 808 Hunters Creek Dr, Melbourne, FL 32904

DAVIDSON, William A (Vt) Prestwick Farm, 2260 County Route 12, Whitehall, NY 12887

DAVIDSON-METHOT, David G (Los) 2945 Bell Rd Pmb 325, Auburn, CA 95603

DAVIES, Ian (Los) 7501 Hollywood Blvd, Los Angeles, CA 90046

DAVIES-ARYEEQUAYE, Eliza Ayorkor (NY) 23 Water Grant St Apt 9e, Yonkers, NY 10701

DAVILA, Mary Fisher (NC) 117 Rivana Terr SW, Leesburg, VA 20175

DAVILA, Willie Rodriguez (SeFla) 525 Pasadena Pl, Corpus Christi, TX 78411

DAVILA COLON, Angel Michael (PR)

DAVILA FIGUEROA, Wilson Jaime (Colom) c/o Diocese of Colombia, Cra 6 No. 49-85 Piso 2, Bogota, BDC, Colombia

DAVINICH, George Lawrence (Mich) 945 Palmer St, Plymouth, MI 48170

DAVIOU, Albert G (At) 432 Noelle Ln, Dahlonega, GA 30533

DAVIS JR, Albin P (Los) 209 S. Detroit St., Los Angeles, CA 90036

DAVIS, Alice Downing (Va) 1357 Botetourt Gdns, Norfolk, VA 23517

DAVIS, Angus Kenneth (Pa) PO Box 329, Kimberton, PA 19442

DAVIS, Bancroft Gherardi (Pa) 419 Chandlee Dr, Berwyn, PA 19312

DAVIS, Calvin Lee (SwFla) 725 Nokomis Ave S, Venice, FL 34285

DAVIS, Catherine Ward (EC) St James Parish, 25 S 3rd St, Wilmington, NC 28401

DAVIS, Charles Lee (Ak) ST MATTHEW'S EPISCOPAL CHURCH, 1030 2ND AVE, FAIRBANKS, AK 99701

DAVIS SR, Charles Meyer (USC) 232 Elstow Rd, Irmo, SC 29206

DAVIS JR, Charles Meyer (USC) 3709 Greenbriar Dr, Columbia, SC 29206

DAVIS, Charlotte Murray (NC) 3120 Sunnybrook Dr, Charlotte, NC 28210

DAVIS, Clifford Bruce (Kan) 1070 W Antelope Creek Way, Tucson, AZ 85737

DAVIS, David Joseph (EC) 208 Country Club Dr, Shallotte, NC 28470

DAVIS, Donald Henry Kortright (WA) 11414 Woodson Ave, Kensington, MD 20895

DAVIS, Elizabeth Hill (Okla)

DAVIS, Emily Hillquist (Mo) 9441 Engel Lane, Saint Louis, MO 63132

DAVIS, Fletcher (WMass) 4490 Smugglers Cove Rd, Freeland, WA 98249

DAVIS, Gae K (EC)

DAVIS, Gail E (Kan) 1228 Auburn Village Dr, Durham, NC 27713

DAVIS, Gale Davis (Mass) 25 Central St, Andover, MA 01810

DAVIS, Gena Lynn (Tex) 5010 N Main St, Baytown, TX 77521

DAVIS, James Frazier (ETenn)

DAVIS, James Lloyd (Ia) 6617 Romford Ct, Johnston, IA 50131

DAVIS, Jane Lowe (EC) PO Box 7386, St Thomas, VI 00801

DAVIS, Jean Marie (Ia)

DAVIS, John Bartley (ND) 7940 45r Street Southeast, Jamestown, ND 58401

DAVIS, John William (Be) Church of the Good Shepherd, 1780 N Washington Ave, Scranton, PA 18509

DAVIS JR, Johnnie (USC) PO Box 2959, West Columbia, SC 29171

DAVIS, Jon (Fla) 1412 Palomino Way, Oviedo, FL 32765

DAVIS, Joseph Norman (Tenn) 1205 Cornerstone Ct, Nashville, TN 37221

DAVIS, Joy Ruth (Ga) St Patrick's Episcopal Church, 4800 Old Dawson Rd, Albany, GA 31721

DAVIS, Judith Anne (Mass) 671 Route 28, Harwich Port, MA 02646

DAVIS, Judy (Va) 236 S Laurel St, Richmond, VA 23220

DAVIS, Keith A (WTex)

DAVIS, Margaret Callender (CFla) 2445 Plum Creek Dr, Roaming Shores, OH 44084

DAVIS, Mary (Okla) c o Rita Kuda, 232 Bridge St Apt 434, Burlington, WI 53105

DAVIS, Mary Elizabeth (Nwk) 200 Main St, Chatham, NJ 07928

DAVIS, Maryan Elizabeth (NH)

DAVIS, Matthew Steven (Episcopal SJ) 1710 Verde St, Bakersfield, CA 93304

DAVIS, Michael (WTex) 8401 Kearsarge Dr, Austin, TX 78745

DAVIS, Milbrew (WTex) 338 Hub Ave, San Antonio, TX 78220

DAVIS, Orion Woods (Nwk) 2 Pasadena St, Canton, NC 28716

DAVIS, Patricia Rhoads (Ga) 215 Grimball Point Rd, Savannah, GA 31406

DAVIS, Philip Arthur (SwFla) 1603 52nd St W, Bradenton, FL 34209

DAVIS, Rodney (The Episcopal NCal) 2140 Mission Ave., Carmichael, CA 95608

DAVIS, Ronald Lee (SeFla) Saint Anne's Church, 25100 Ridge Rd, Damascus, MD 20872

DAVIS, Roy Jefferson (Tex)

DAVIS, Steven Jay (Wyo)

DAVIS, Vicki (WMo) 4551 PA Ave U 1523, Kansas City, MO 64111

DAVIS, West Richard (Oly) 790 Smugglers Cove Rd, Friday Harbor, WA 98250

DAVIS III, Zabron A Chip (Miss) 70 Pine Cv, Senatobia, MS 38668

DAVIS-HELLER, Lisa Ann (WVa)

DAVIS-LAWSON, Karen Dm (LI) 1420 27th Ave, Astoria, NY 11102

DAVISON, Arienne Siu Ling (Oly) 2151 4th St, Bremerton, WA 98312

DAVIS-SHOEMAKER, Courtney (SC) 54 Society St, Charleston, SC 29401

DAVISSON, Mary Thomsen (Md) 2363 Hamiltowne Cir, Baltimore, MD 21237

DAVIS-WILSON, Lillian Juanita (WNY) St Philip's Episc Church, 15 Fernhill Ave, Buffalo, NY 14215

DAVY, Brian Kendall (At) 589 Martins Grove Rd, Dahlonega, GA 30533

DAW JR, Carl Pickens (Ct) 171 Highland Ave, Watertown, MA 02472

DAWKINS, Adam L (Mass)

DAWSON, Adrien P (Md) 4412 Eastway, Baltimore, MD 21218

DAWSON, Barbara Louise (Cal) 399 Gregory Ln, Pleasant Hill, CA 94523

DAWSON, Cynthia Louise (Me)

DAWSON, Eric Emmanuel (Episcopal VI) 19-5 Hope, Saint Thomas, VI 00801

DAWSON, George (WTex) 4426 Dolphin Pl, Corpus Christi, TX 78411

DAWSON, Margaret G (La) 320 Sena Dr, Metairie, LA 70005

DAWSON, Mark Douglas (Los) 514 W Adams Blvd, Los Angeles, CA 90007

DAWSON JR, Marshall Allen (Lex) 1375 Weisenberger Mill Rd, Midway, KY 40347

DAWSON, Paul Sweeting (Md) 145 Main St Apt A1, Vineyard Haven, MA 02568

DAWSON JR, Tucker Edward (La) 321 State St, Bay Saint Louis, MS 39520

DAWSON, Walter (Mich) 18017 Grand Lake Blvd, Presque Isle, MI 49777

DAY, Christine Jane (CNY) 35 Second St, Johnson City, NY 13790

DAY, Dennis Lee (CGC) PO Box 2066, Fairhope, AL 36533

DAY, Ginny (Be) 1006 Eisenhower Way, Tobyhanna, PA 18466

DAY, James Meredith (Eur)

DAY, Jeremiah (EC) 109 Skipper Circle, Oriental, NC 28571

DAY, John Edward (The Episcopal NCal) 9843 Derby Way, Elk Grove, CA 95757

DAY, Kate Lufkin (CNY) 106 Ardsley Dr, Syracuse, NY 13214

DAY, Kellan (WNC)

DAY, Margaret Ann (Me) 777 Stillwater Ave Lot 63, Old Town, ME 04468

DAY, Marshall Benjamin (At) 1210 Wooten Lake Rd NW, Kennesaw, GA 30144

DAY, Meredith Jane (SO) 1747 Peabody Ave # R, Memphis, TN 38104

DAY, Michael Henry (SwFla) 1070 54th St N, Saint Petersburg, FL 33710

DAY, Randall Carl Kidder (Los) 2901 Nojoqui Avenue, P.O. Box 39, Los Olivos, CA 93441

DAY, Stephen (Mont) 1241 Crawford Dr, Billings, MT 59102

DAY, Tom (Tex) 221 Edgewood Rd, Bristol, TN 37620

DAYNES, Taylor Darlington (CNY) 25 Westminster Rd, Rochester, NY 14607

DAYTON, Douglas Kennedy (NwPa) 3600 Mcconnell Rd, Hermitage, PA 16148

DAYTON, Michelle Suzanne (SD) Lindenhurst, NY 11757

DAYTON-WELCH, Matthew H (Pa) 3625 Chapel Rd, Newtown Square, PA 19073

DEACON, Jonathan (NJ) 12 Bryan Dr, Voorhees, NJ 08043

DEADERICK, Dianna LaMance (USC) 1300 Pine St, Columbia, SC 29204

DEAKLE, David Wayne (La) 4350 SE Brooklyn St, Portland, OR 97206

DEAL, Karen Kay (Kan)

DEAN, Aelred B (Lex) 200 Jackson St Apt 308, Columbus, IN 47201

DEAN, Bobby Wayne (CGC) PO Box 1677, Santa Rosa Beach, FL 32459

DEAN JR, Edward Carroll (RI) St Davids Episcopal Church, 200 Meshanticut Valley Pkwy, Cranston, RI 02920

DEAN, Jay Judson (Me) 33 Baker St, Dover, NH 03820

DEAN, Rebecca Anderson (SVa) 985 Huguenot Trl, Midlothian, VA 23113

DEAN, Steve (Los) 25211 Via Tanara, Santa Clarita, CA 91355

DEAN, Susan Chanda (Oly) 3714 90th Ave SE, Mercer Island, WA 98040

DE ANAYA, Nilda Lucca (PR) 2100 Washington Ave Apt 2c, Silver Spring, MD 20910

DEANE JR, William Boyd (Pa) 812 Lombard St, Philadelphia, PA 19147

DEAR, Tyrrel (CFla) PO Box 668, New Smyrna, FL 32170

DEARING, Jed J (SO)

DEARING, Trevor (Oly) 4 Rock House Gardens, Radcliffe Road, Stamford, PE9 1AS, Great Britain (UK)

DEARMAN, David (Tex) 6 Broad St, Galveston, TX 77554

DEARMAN JR, William Benjamin (NY) 7 Oakridge Pkwy, Peekskill, NY 10566

DEASY, James Scott (Az) Epiphany Episcopal Church, 423 N Beaver St, Flagstaff, AZ 86001

DEATON JR, Charles Milton (Miss) 1616 52nd Ct, Meridian, MS 39305

DEATON, Jennifer Deaton (Miss) PO Box 23107, Jackson, MS 39225

DEATS, Cathy (NC) 6625 Battleford Dr, Raleigh, NC 27613

DEAVOURS, Cipher A (NJ) 112 Union St, Montclair, NJ 07042

DE AZEVEDO, Guilherme B (LI) 7486 S Union Park Ave, Midvale, UT 84047

DE BEER, John Michael (Mass) 2905 Wynnewood Dr, Greensboro, NC 27408

DE BEER, Patricia Jean (Mass) 2905 Wynnewood Dr, Greensboro, NC 27408

DEBENHAM JR, Warren Warren (Cal) 143 Arlington Ave, Berkeley, CA 94707

DEBLASIO, Diane L (LI) 100 46th St, Lindenhurst, NY 11757

DEBOW, Rebecca (Ala) 3519 W Lakeside Dr, Birmingham, AL 35243

DEBUSSY, Muriel S (NJ) 825 Summerset Dr, Hockessin, DE 19707

DEBUYS III, John Forrester (Ala) 2501 Country Club Cir, Birmingham, AL 35223

DECAMPS, Walin (Hai)

DECARLEN, Marya Louise (Mass) Same, Boxford, MA 01921

DECARVALHO, Maria Elena (RI) 18 Vassar Ave, Providence, RI 02906

DECATUR, Christopher M (NJ)

DE CHAMBEAU, Franck Alsid (Ct) 163 Belgo Rd, PO Box 391, Lakeville, CT 06039

DECKER, Dallas (The Episcopal Church in Haw) 18218 Paradise Mountain Rd Spc 88, Valley Center, CA 92082

DECKER, Georgia Ann (WK) 509 16th Ter, Hutchinson, KS 67501

DECKER, Linda McCullough (The Episcopal Church in Haw) 307 S Alu Rd, Wailuku, HI 96793

DECKER, Margaret Sharp (SanD) 1651 S Juniper St Unit 26, Escondido, CA 92025

DECKER, Prince A (WA) 3918 Wendy Ln, Silver Spring, MD 20906

DECOSS, Donald Albion (Cal) 26 Overlake Ct, Oakland, CA 94611

DEDDE, Joseph Colin (WNY) 233 Brantwood Rd, Amherst, NY 14226

DEDEAUX JR, James Terrell (Miss) 5303 Diamondhead Cir, Diamondhead, MS 39525

DEDMON JR, Robert Aaron (Chi) 1804 Sycamore Circle, Manchester, TN 37355

DEERY, Laurel Pierson (Mass) 44 School St, Manchester, MA 01944

DEETHS, Margaret Edith (Cal) 576 Cedarberry Ln, San Rafael, CA 94903

DEETS, Sherry (Pa) 2717 Shelburne Road, Downingtown, PA 19335

DEETZ, Susan Maureen (Minn) 4210 Robinson St, Duluth, MN 55804

DEFOOR II, Allison (Fla) 325 N Market St, Jacksonville, FL 32202

DEFOREST, Bill (Tex) 47 Witherbee Pl, The Woodlands, TX 77375

DEFOREST, Nancy (Tex) 47 Witherbee Pl, The Woodlands, TX 77375

DEFRANCO JR, Peter (NJ) 230 Melrose Ter, Linden, NJ 07036

DEFRIEST, Jeannette (Chi) 400 Main St Apt 5a, Evanston, IL 60202

DEGAVRE, Susan Williams (Va) 7120 S. Wenatchee Way Unit C, Aurora, CO 80016

DEGENHARDT, Terri Walker (Ga) St Michael's Episcopal Church, 515 S Liberty St, Waynesboro, GA 30830

DEGOOYER, Bruce Underwood (The Episcopal Church in Haw)

DE GRAVELLES, Charlie (La) 3651 Broussard St, Baton Rouge, LA 70808

DEGWECK, Stephen William (Ala) 1336 Round Hill Rd, Vestavia Hills, AL 35216

DEHART, Benjamin (Ala) 2844 Fairway Dr Apt 191a, Birmingham, AL 35213

DEHART, Elsa Arp (Ak) St James the Fisherman, PO Box 1668, Kodiak, AK 99615

DEHART, Steven Darrell (Mont)

DEHETRE, Donna (Chi) 31 Edgehill Rd, New Haven, CT 06511

DEHLER, Debra Rae (Ind) St Albans Episcopal Church, 4601 N Emerson Ave, Indianapolis, IN 46226

DEJARDIN, Wisnel (Hai)

DE JESUS-JIMENEZ, Justo (PR) Par Sto Nombre de Jesus, 806 Calle Jesus T Pineiro, Ponce, PR 00728

DE JESUS LAGARES, Jose Joaquin (DomRep)

DEJOHN, Kathleen Ann Gillespie (NJ) 138 Rector St, Perth Amboy, NJ 08861

DE KAY, Charlie (Chi) 901 Forest Ave Apt 1e, Evanston, IL 60202

DEKKER, ROBERT P (Chi) 15145 Smarty Jones Dr, Noblesville, IN 46060

DE LA CRUZ, Luis Manuel (CFla) 1709 N John Young Pkwy, Kissimmee, FL 34741

DELAFIELD, Audrey Sawtelle (Me) 32 Ship Channel Rd, South Portland, ME 04106

DELAMATER, Joanie (Minn) 6287 Crackleberry Trl, Woodbury, MN 55129

DELANCEY, Mary Louise (CFla) 510 SE Broadway St, Ocala, FL 34471

DE LANEROLLE, Nihal Chandra (Ct) 500 Prospect St Apt 2-F, New Haven, CT 06511

DELANEY, Conrad Todd (SanD)

DELANEY, Mary Joan (Az) 5611E Alta Vista St, Tucson, AZ 85712

DELANEY, Mary Timothea Kathleen (EMich) 1038 W Center St, Alma, MI 40001

DELANEY, Michael F (LI) 191 Kensington Road, Garden City, NY 11530

DELANEY, Ryan Ray (Alb) W304s10624, Sandy Beach Rd, Mukwonago, WI 53149

DE LA PAZ COT, Aurelio Bernabe (Cu)

DE LA PAZ COT, Marianela (Cu)

DELA ROSA MUNOZ, Jorge Alberto (Okla)

DELASHMUTT, Michael W. (Mil)

DE LA TORRE, Carlos Enrique (CPa)

DE LA TORRE, William Jhon (SwFla) 8271 52nd St N, Pinellas Park, FL 33781

DELAURA, Gilbert Frank (Alb) Church of the Messiah, 296 Glen St, Glens Falls, NY 12801

DELAUTER, Joseph Halvor (CPa) 598 Longbarn Rd, State College, PA 16803

DE LA VARS, Gordon (Md) 115 S Erie St, Mayville, NY 14757

DEL BENE, Ronald Norman (Ala) 2841 Floyd Bradford Rd, Trussville, AL 35173

DEL CASTILLO, Gloria (Cal) 622 Lois Lane, El Sobrante, CA 94803

DELCUZE, Mark Stewart (Eas) 623 Cloverfields Dr, Stevensville, MD 21666

DELEERY, Seth Mabry (Tex) 9002 Clithea Cv, Austin, TX 78759

DE LEEUW, Gawain (NY) 20 Cumming St, New York, NY 10034

DELEUSE, Betsey W (Me) 27 Arlington St. Unit 1, Portland, ME 04101

DELFS, Carin Bridgit (SO) 4500 twp Rd 21, Marengo, OH 43334

DELGADO, Annemarie (Wyo)

DELGADO, Joseph Anthony (Cal) 2220 Cedar St, Berkeley, CA 94709

✠ **DELGADO DEL CARPIO**, Maria Griselda (Cu)

DELGADO-MARKSMAN, Adams Felipe (Ve)

DELGADO OROZCO, Armando Alfonso (Cu)

DELGADO-VERA, Ramiro Mario (WTex) 697 W White Ave, Raymondville, TX 78580

DELICAT, Joseph Kerwin (Hai)

DELINGER, Ian M (ECR)

DE LION, Lawrence Raymond (LI) 15 Greenwich Rd, Smithtown, NY 11787

DELK, Michael (SVa) 205 Castle Ln, Williamsburg, VA 23185

DELL, Christopher G (Fla)

DELL, Jacob William (NY) PO Box 1064, Millbrook, NY 12545

DELL, Mary Lynn (La) 2741 Sherbrooke Road, Shaker Heights, OH 44122

DELLARIA, Kevin (Pa) Saint Francis-In-The-Fields, 689 Sugartown Rd, Malvern, PA 19355

DELLENBARGER, Leslie Ann (Ga)

DEL PRIORE, Dorian (USC) 120 Meadowbrook Dr, Mauldin, SC 29662

DEL VALLE-ORTIZ, Efrain Edgardo (PR) 557 Calle Plinio Peterson, Vieques, PR 00765

DEL VALLE-TIRADO, Jose A (PR)

DELZELL, Constance Kay Clawson (Colo) 3 Calle de Montanas, Santa Fe, NM 87507

DEMAREST, Richard Alan (Ida) 518 N Eighth Street, Boise, ID 83702

DEMARSICO, Jonnette Marie (CFla)

DEMBI, Megan E (Ida) 6030 Grosvenor Ln, Bethesda, MD 20814

DE MEL, Chitral S (Mass)

DEMING, Nancy James (Pa) 1912 Harbour Links Cir, Longboat Key, FL 34228

DE MIRANDA, Mario Eugenio (SeFla) 15650 Miami Lakeway N, Miami Lakes, FL 33014

DEMLER, Maureen Ann (Alb) 912 Route 146, Clifton Park, NY 12065

DEMMLER, Mary Reynolds Hemmer (At) 995 E Tugalo St, Toccoa, GA 30577

DEMO, Gar R (Kan) 8144 Rosehill Rd, Lenexa, KS 66215

DEMO, Kelly Marie (Kan) 8144 Rosehill Rd, Lenexa, KS 66215

DE MONTMOLLIN, Dee Ann Ann (SwFla) 394 N Main St, Rutherfordton, NC 28139

DEMPESY-SIMS, Catherine Biggs (WNY) St Pauls Cathedral, 128 Pearl St, Buffalo, NY 14202

DEMPZ, Julia A (Mich) 61 Grosse Pointe Blvd, Grosse Pointe Farms, MI 48236

DEMURA, Christie (Oly) 10042 Main St Apt 410, Bellevue, WA 98004

DE MUTH, Steven H (Los) Holy Trinity Parish, PO Box 4195, Covina, CA 91723

DENARO, John (LI) 157 Montague St, Brooklyn, NY 11201

DENAUW, Elizabeth Anne (NH)

DENDTLER, Robert Blanchard (At) 4409 Links Blvd, Jefferson, GA 30549

DENEAU, Elizabeth Ann (NMich) 500 Ogden Ave, Escanaba, MI 49829

DENEKE, Bill (At) 515 E Ponce de Leon Ave, Decatur, GA 30031

DENG DENG, William (Oly) 4759 Shattuck Pl S Unit B101, Renton, WA 98055

DENHAM, John (WA) 767 N Cambridge Way, Claremont, CA 91711

DENISON, Charles Wayne (Wyo) 2502 Overland Rd, Laramie, WY 82070

DENISON JR, Raleigh Edmond (Dal) 1504 S Ash St, Georgetown, TX 78626

DENMAN, Scott (Cal) 7917 Outlook Ave, Oakland, CA 94605

DENNEY, Robin (The Episcopal NCal)

DENNEY, Shawn W (Spr) 3813 Bergamot Dr, Springfield, IL 62712

DENNEY, Shelley Booth (ECR) 424 Montecito Ave, Monterey, CA 93940

DENNEY-ZUNIGA, Amy (The Episcopal NCal)

DENNIS, Alan Godfrey (NY) 45 Orchard Ln, Torrington, CT 06790

DENNIS, Fredrick Hogarth (Alb) 455 Park Ave, Saranac Lake, NY 12983

DENNIS, Loretta Anne (Roch) 240 S 4th St, Philadelphia, PA 19106

DENNIS, William J (WLa) 501 Springfield Ave, Eutaw, AL 35462

DENNISON JR, Bryant Whitman (Mich) PO Box 3974, Ann Arbor, MI 48106

DENNLER, William David (Tenn) 615 6th Ave S, Nashville, TN 37203

DENNY, Stephen Michael (Ore) 10143 Se 49th Ave, Milwaukie, OR 97222

DENSON JR, John (Ind) 5 Granite St, Exeter, NH 03833

DENTON, Edna Marguerite (SO) 1021 Crede Way, Waynesville, OH 45068

DENTON, Jean Margaret (Ind) 607 Alden Rd, Claremont, CA 91711

DENTON, Maria Anna (Colo) 7068 Kiowa Rd, Larkspur, CO 80118

DEOKARAN, Teresa J (WLa) 209 S Walnut St, Medicine Lodge, KS 67104

DEPHOUSE, John R (Los) 1325 Monterey Rd, South Pasadena, CA 91030

DEPPE, Jimmie Sue (LI) 1400 Poulson St, Wantagh, NY 11793

DEPPE, Thomas W (SVa) 2020 Laskin Rd, Virginia Beach, VA 23454

DEPPEN, G(ehret) David (NJ) 35 Queens Way, Wellfleet, MA 02667

DE PRINS, Laurent Fabrice (WLa) 903 James Paul Ave, Opelousas, LA 70570

DEPUE, Karen Lynn Joanna (NY) 7 Heather Ln, Orangeburg, NY 10962

DE PUY KERSHAW, Susan Lynn (NH) PO Box 485, Walpole, NH 03608

DERAVIL, Jean-Jacques (Hai) Diquini 63b #8, Carrefour, Haiti

DERBY, William (NY) 14 E 109th St, New York, NY 10029

DERBYSHIRE, John Edward (CNY) 229 Twin Hills Dr, Syracuse, NY 13207

DERKITS III, J James (WTex) Trinity By The Sea Tec Ch, PO Box 346, Port Aransas, TX 78373

DEROSE, Kathryn Pitkin (Los) 2621 6th St Apt 5, Santa Monica, CA 90405

DERRICK, John Burton (Ga) 1512 Meadows Ln, Vidalia, GA 30474

DERSE, Anne Elizabeth (WA) 6701 Wisconsin Ave, Chevy Chase, MD 20815

DERSNAH, Donald L (Mich) 4354 Weber Rd, Saline, MI 48176

DE RUFF, Elizabeth Anslow (Cal) PO Box 1137, Ross, CA 94957

DESALVO, David (Del) 350 Noxontown Rd, Middletown, DE 19709

DESCHAINE, Thomas Charles (Me) Po Box 467, Augusta, ME 04332

DESHAIES, Robert Joseph (SeFla)

DE SHEPLO, Louis John (NJ) 551 Saint Kitts Dr, Williamstown, NJ 08094

DE SILVA, Dinushka M (Ct)

DE SILVA, Sumi (Az) 9533 E. Kokopelli Circle, Tucson, AZ 85748

DESIR, Jean (DomRep) Iglesia Episcopal Dominicana, Apartado 764, Santo Domingo, Dominican Republic
DESIRE, Fritz (Hai)
DESIRE, Luc (Hai)
DESMARAIS, Susanna (Neb) 4545 S 58th St, Lincoln, NE 68516
DESMITH, David John (Nwk) 90 Kiel Ave, Kinnelon, NJ 07405
DESROSIERS JR, Norman (CFla) St Sebastian By The Sea, 2010 Oak St, Melbourne Beach, FL 32951
DESUEZA, Edmond (NY) 271 Broadway, Newburgh, NY 12550
DESUEZA-SAVINON, Edmond (PR) Urb. Fairview, D11 Calle 10, San Juan, PR 00926
DETRICH, James Paul (Okla) 239 Brandon Cir, Washington, OK 73093
DETTWILLER II, George Frederick (Tenn) 108 Savoy Cir., Nashville, TN 37205
DEVALL IV, Frederick D (La) St Martins Episcopal Church, 2216 Metairie Rd, Metairie, LA 70001
DEVATY, Jean M (Alb) 508 4th Ave, Beaver Falls, PA 15010
DEVAUL, Philip (SO) 3019 Springer Ave, Cincinnati, OH 45208
DEVEAU, Peter (WMo) 5916 Oak St, Kansas City, MO 64113
DEVENPORT, Richard Lindsey (Miss) 7096 ROLLING GREEN DR, PASS CHRISTIAN, MS 39571
DEVENS, Philip (RI) 111 Greenwich Ave # 2886, Warwick, RI 02886
DEVINE, Mike (WMass) 47 Ruskin St, Springfield, MA 01108
DEVINE, Taylor Poindexter (Az)
DEVINE, Whitney Alford Jones (Oly) 4420 137th Ave NE, Bellevue, WA 98005
DE VOLDER, Luk Jozef (Ct) 950 Chapel St Fl 2, New Haven, CT 06510
DEVORE, Christopher Scott (Tex)
DEVORE, Kirk Eugene (Md) 2 E High St, Hancock, MD 21750
DEWEES, Herbert Reed (Dal) 9511 Meadowknoll Dr, Dallas, TX 75243
DE WETTER, Robert Emerson (Colo) PO Box 5310, Snowmass Village, CO 81615
DEWEY, Camie Marie (Wyo) 1910 Newport, Casper, WY 82609
DEWEY, Edward Robinson (SC) 598 E Hobcaw Dr, Mount Pleasant, SC 29464
DEWEY, Joseph Denton (CFla)
DEWITT, Edward Leonard (NMich) 90 Croix St Apt 2, Negaunee, MI 49866
DEWITT, Phyllis M (NMich) 301 N 1st St, Ishpeming, MI 49849
DEWITT, William Henry (NMich) 301 N 1st St, Ishpeming, MI 49849
DEWLEN, Janet Marie (Colo) 2500 22nd Drive, Longmont, CO 80503
DEWOLFE, Robert F (WTex) 3412 Pebblebrook Dr, Tyler, TX 75707
DEWRELL, Heath Daniel (NJ)

DEXTER, Beverly (SanD) 325 Kempton St Apt 400, Spring Valley, CA 91977
DEYO, Bonnie (Wyo)
DEYOUNG, Lily A (Mass) 1118 Jaffrey Rd, Marlborough, NH 03455
DEZHBOD, Esmail Shahrokh (Ct) 294 Main St S, Woodbury, CT 06798
DEZHBOD, Melina (Ct)
DHARMARAJ, Brainerd Solomon (Los)
DIAS, Krista K (Colo) Church Of Our Saviour, 8 4th St, Colorado Springs, CO 80906
DIAZ, George (NY) 257 Clinton St Apt 19n, New York, NY 10002
DIAZ, Gladys (NY) Po Box 617, Bronx, NY 10473
DIAZ, Jose (Pa) 3554 N 6th St, Philadelphia, PA 19140
DIAZ, Joseph Herbert (SwFla) 3396 Deerfield Ln, Clearwater, FL 33761
DIAZ, Juan Jose (Hond)
DIAZ, Maytee De La Torre (CFla)
DIAZ, Narciso (Chi) 400 E Westminster, Lake Forest, IL 60045
DIAZ DORTA, Andreis (Fla) Christ Episcopal Church, 400 San Juan Dr, Ponte Vedra Beach, FL 32082
DIAZ ESTEVEZ, Manuel Jesus (DomRep)
DIAZ SORIANO, Bileisy Anajai (DomRep)
DIBENEDETTO, Aileen Elizabeth (WMass) 36 Chevy Chase Rd, Worcester, MA 01606
DICARLO, Michael Joseph (Los) 1400 W. 13th St. Spc 139, Upland, CA 91786
DICE, Daniel (Mass) St John the Evangelist, PO Box 2893, Duxbury, MA 02331
DICK, Brandt (Miss) 1026 S Washing Ave, Greenville, MS 38701
DICKERSON, Russell Sturges (NwT)
DICKERSON, Shawn E (Ore) 822 Washington St, Oregon City, OR 97045
DICKEY, Michael Patrick (CGC)
DICKHAUT, Walter R (Me)
DICKINSON, Albert Hugh (Pa) NW Apt A-205, 2510 Lake Michigan Dr NW, Grand Rapids, MI 49504
DICKINSON, Will (Va) 606 Amelia St Apt 404, Fredericksburg, VA 22401
DICKSON JR, Elton Robert (Mass) 6102 Buckhorn Rd, Greensboro, NC 27410
DICKSON, Patricia (Va) 3883 Connecticut Ave Nw, 715, Washington, DC 20008
DIEBEL, Mark H (Alb) 3207 Shadewood Ter, Owensboro, KY 42303
DIEGUE, Joseph (Hai) Box 1309, Port-Au-Prince, Haiti
DIEHL, Jane Cornell (EMich) 3201 Gratiot Ave, Port Huron, MI 48060
DIELE, Joseph (LI) 4301 Avenue D, Brooklyn, NY 11203

DIENER-SCHLITT, Sarah Ruth (NMich)
DIERICK, F Lorraine (Oly) 102 Glenn Ln, Montesano, WA 98563
DIETER, David (Mich) 847 Grand Marais St, Grosse Pointe Park, MI 48230
DIETERLE, Ann (Mo) 200 W Cowles St, Wilkesboro, NC 28697
DIETRICH, Seth (Mil) 4234 N Larkin St, Milwaukee, WI 53211
✠ **DIETSCHE**, Andy (NY) 1047 Amsterdam Ave, New York, NY 10025
DIETZ, Joseph Bland (Pa) 2619 N Charlotte St, Pottstown, PA 19464
DIETZ ALLEN, Doyle (LI) 3 Grace Ln, Lindenhurst, NY 11757
DIEUDONN, Vinsot (Hai)
DIEZ MOREIRA, Juan Carlos (Cu)
DILEO, John (Fla) 1505 NW 91st Ter, Gainesville, FL 32606
DILG, Arthur Charles (Pgh) 1371 Washington St, Indiana, PA 15701
DILL, David (Colo) Church of the Good Shepherd, 3809 Spring Ave SW, Decatur, AL 35603
DILL, Todd R (NC) 8515 Rea Rd, Waxhaw, NC 28173
DILLER, Sallie Winch (NMich) 733n E Gulliver Lake Rd, Gulliver, MI 49840
DILLIPLANE, Nancy Burton (Pa) PO Box 245, 2645 Durham Rd, Buckingham, PA 18912
DILLON, John Lawrence (U) 8738 Oakwood Park Cir, Sandy, UT 84094
DILLON, Karla Lewis (Okla)
DILLON II, Tommy J (La) 601 Spain St, Baton Rouge, LA 70802
DILLS, Robert Scott (Oly) 919 - 21st Avenue East, Seattle, WA 98112
DILLS-MOORE, Amy Sarah (At) 3110 Ashford Dunwoody Rd NE, Brookhaven, GA 30319
DI LORENZO, Anthony (LI) 40 Warren Ave, Lake Ronkonkoma, NY 11779
DIMARCO, Tom (USC) PO Box 206, Trenton, SC 29847
DIMMICK, Kenneth Ray (Tex) Lorenzstaffel 8, Stuttgart, 70182, Germany
DINGES, John Albert (Mil) Box 27671, West Allis, WI 53227
DINGLEY, Alison M (The Episcopal Church in Haw) 1255 Nuuanu Ave., #E1513, Honolulu, HI 96817
DINGMAN, Joel (Wyo) 419 Circle Dr, Gillette, WY 82716
DINKINS, David Duane (RG) 1400 Decatur Ave, Bremerton, WA 98337
DINOTO, Anthony Charles (Ct) PO Box 810, Niantic, CT 06357
DINOVO, Darlyn Rebecca (SanD) St John Tec Ch, 2036 SE Jefferson St, Milwaukie, OR 97222
DINSMORE, Taylor Whitehead (ETenn) 9125 Candlewood Dr, Knoxville, TN 37923

DINSMORE, Virginia Carol (Nwk) 681 Prospect Ave, West Orange, NJ 07052

DINWIDDIE, Philip Matthew (Mich) 25150 East River, Grosse Ile, MI 48138

DI PANFILO, Laura (Pgh)

DIRBAS, Joseph James (SanD) 1475 Catalina Blvd, San Diego, CA 92107

DIRBAS, Terry Shields (SanD) 1114 9th St, Coronado, CA 92118

DISBROW, Jimme Lynn (Okla) 1737 Churchill Way, Oklahoma City, OK 73120

DISCHINGER III, George Lane (Mich)

DISHAROON, Susan Clay (Miss) 3030 Highway 547, Port Gibson, MS 39150

DISTANISLAO, Virginia Gates (SVa) 512 S Broad St, Kenbridge, VA 23944

DITEWIG, Luke (Mass)

DITTERLINE, Richard Charles (Pa) 1350 Spring Valley Rd, Bethlehem, PA 18015

DITZENBERGER, Christopher Steven (Colo) 6190 E. Quincy Avenue, Englewood, CO 80111

DIVINE, Elizabeth Baird (Tex) 1616 Fountain View Dr Apt 203, Houston, TX 77057

DIVIS, Mary Lou (Be) 408 E Main St, Nanticoke, PA 18634

DIXON III, David Lloyd (SwVa) 42 E Main St, Salem, VA 24153

DIXON, Elizabeth Lovette (WA)

DIXON JR, John Henry (RG) Av. C. Leon de Nicaragua 1, Esc. 3, 1-B, Alicante, 03015, Spain

DIXON, Mary Lenn (Tex) 1101 Rock Prairie Rd, College Station, TX 77845

DIXON, Rob (CGC) Saint Stephen's Church, 1510 Escambia Ave, Brewton, AL 36426

DIXON, Valerie Wilde (Ct) 23 Bayview Ave, Niantic, CT 06357

DIXON WALTON JR, Richard (WNC) 11 Flycatcher Way Unit 301, Arden, NC 28704

DMYTRIW, Carey-Lea Anne (Wyo) 506 Cedar Ave, Kemmerer, WY 83101

DOAR, Katherine (ECR) 1225 Pine Ave, San Jose, CA 95125

DOBBIN, Robert A (Cal) 24 Van Gordon Pl, Danville, CA 94526

DOBBINS, Burford C (WTex) 1501 N Glass St, Victoria, TX 77901

DOBBINS, Timothy (Pa) 292 Militia Dr, Radnor, PA 19087

DOBBINS JR, William David (RI) 205 Lindley Ave, North Kingstown, RI 02852

DOBSON, Marc (Dal) 6021 Shady Valley Ct, Garland, TX 75043

DOBYNS, Nancy (Ind) 1021 SW 15th St, Richmond, IN 47374

DOBYNS, Richard (Ind) 1021 SW 15th St, Richmond, IN 47374

DOD, David Stockton (ECR) 8294 Carmelita Ave, Atascadero, CA 93422

DODD, Debra Dee Anne (Ct) 37 Bailey Dr, North Branford, CT 06471

DODD, Jean Carrison (Fla) 1860 Edgewood Ave S, Jacksonville, FL 32205

DODDEMA, Peter (Lex) 118 W Poplar St, Harrodsburg, KY 40330

DODGE, Jeffrey Alan (Cal) 39600 Fremont Blvd Apt 10, Fremont, CA 94538

DODGE, Robin Dennis (RG) Church Of The Holy Faith, 311 E Palace Ave, Santa Fe, NM 87501

DODSON, Wayne J (NY) 9 W 130th St, New York, NY 10037

DOERR, Nan (Tex) 901 S Johnson St, Alvin, TX 77511

DOGARU, Vickie A (Oly) 22405 Ne 182nd Ave, Battle Ground, WA 98604

DOGGETT, William Jordan (WA) 66 Via del Pienza, Rancho Mirage, CA 92270

DOHERTY, Anna Clay (Minn) 3308 North View Ln, Woodbury, MN 55125

DOHERTY, Jerry (Minn) 201 Bayberry Avenue Ct, Stillwater, MN 55082

DOHERTY, John S (Ia) Cathedral Church Of St Paul, 815 HIGH ST, Des Moines, IA 50309

DOHERTY, Maureen (RG) 417 Olive St, Cedar Falls, IA 50613

DOHERTY, Noel (Okla) 6910 E 62nd St S, Tulsa, OK 74133

DOHERTY, Tyler Britton (U) 231 E 100 S, Salt Lake City, UT 84111

DOHLE, Robert Joseph (Tex) St Paul's Episcopal Church, 1307 W 5th St, Freeport, TX 77541

DOHONEY, Ed (WTex) 14906 Grayoak Frst, San Antonio, TX 78248

DOLACK, Craig A (Ga) Saint Michael And All Angels, 3101 Waters Ave, Savannah, GA 31404

DOLAN, Mary Ellen (Eur) 110 W Catherine St, Milford, PA 18337

DOLAN, Pamela (The Episcopal NCal) 9 S Bompart Ave, Saint Louis, MO 63119

DOLAN-HENDERSON, Susan Mary (Tex) 3104 Harris Park Ave, Austin, TX 78705

DOLEN, William Kennedy (Ga) 605 Reynolds St, Augusta, GA 30901

DOLL, Gregory Allen (Kan)

DOLLAHITE, Damian DeWitt Gene (Dal) 226 Oakhaven Dr, Grand Prairie, TX 75050

DOLLHAUSEN, Matthew Mark (CGC) 6849 Oak St, Milton, FL 32570

DOLNIKOWSKI, Edie (Mass) The TEC Dio Of MA, 138 Tremont St, Boston, MA 02111

DOLPH, Scott (Ore) 4233 SE Ash St, Portland, OR 97215

DOLS, Timothy Walters (Va) 5705 Oak Bluff Ln, Wilmington, NC 28409

DOMBEK, Timothy (Az) 11242 N 50th Ave, Glendale, AZ 85304

DOMENICK, Julia J (Colo)

DOMENICK JR, W Lee (Okla) Trinity Episcopal Church, 501 S Cincinnati Ave, Tulsa, OK 74103

DOMIENIK, Steve (Mich) St. John's Episcopal Church, 555 S Wayne Rd, Westland, MI 48186

DOMINGUEZ REYEZ, Jesus David (Hond)

DONAHOE, Melanie (Cal) Church of the Epiphany, 1839 Arroyo Ave, San Carlos, CA 94070

DONALD, David Seth (La) 715 Kirkman St, Lake Charles, LA 70601

DONALD, James (WA) 1 Peachtree Battle Ave NW, Atlanta, GA 30305

DONALDSON, Audley (LI) 1345 President St, Brooklyn, NY 11213

DONALDSON, Walker Alexander (Los) 7631 Klusman Ave, Rancho Cucamonga, CA 91730

DONATELLI, Todd (WNC) Cathedral of All Souls, 9 Swan St, Asheville, NC 28803

DONATHAN, William Larry (WA) 105 15th Street SE, Washington, DC 20003

DONCASTER, Diana (The Episcopal NCal) 495 Albion Ave, Cincinnati, OH 45246

DONDERO, Christina Downs (At) 460 Franklin St, Athens, GA 30606

DONECKER, Paul (CPa) 351 Bull Run Crossing, Lewisburg, PA 17837

DONEHUE, The Rev Cn Robertson Carr (SC) 1530 Clark Sound Cir, Charleston, SC 29412

DONELSON JR, Frank Taylor (WTenn) 475 N Highland St Apt 7e, Memphis, TN 38122

DONNELL, Robert Mark (CGC)

DONNELLY, Frances Ellen (Nwk) 852 Bullet Hill Rd, Southbury, CT 06488

DONNELLY, Jeffrey Joseph (Cal)

DONNELLY, John Allen (Ct) 470 Quaker Farms Road, Oxford, CT 06478

DONOHUE, Alison (Ct)

DONOHUE, Mary Jane (Mass) 51 Ryder Ave, Melrose, MA 02176

DONOHUE-ADAMS, Amy (Oly) 11703 Oakwood Dr, Austin, TX 78753

✠ **DONOVAN JR**, Herbert Alcorn (NY) 3085 Mill Vista Rd Unit 2322, Highlands Ranch, CO 80129

DONOVAN, Mary (Kan)

DONOVAN, Nancy Lu (SD) 9412 Saint Joseph St, Silver City, SD 57702

DOOLEY, Martha M (NJ) 4735 Cedar Ave, Philadelphia, PA 19143

DOOLITTLE, Geoffrey D (CNY) 7 1 2 Monell St Apt 1, Greene, NY 13778

DOPP, Cynthia Hill (WA) 301 A St SE, Washington, DC 20003

DOR, Wilson (Hai)

DORAN, Judith Ann (Chi) 1350 N Western Ave Apt 111, Lake Forest, IL 60045

DORAN, Michelle Stuart (Md) All Saints, PO Box 40, Sunderland, MD 20689

DORCEUS, Jean Moiise (Hai)

DORN, Christy (WMo) 13134 Lamar Ave, Overland Park, KS 66209
DORN III, James M (CFla) 528 W Montrose St, Clermont, FL 34711
DORNEMANN, Deanna Maxine (EC) 60 Bethlehem Pike Rm 1401, Philadelphia, PA 19118
DORNER, Mary Anne (SwFla) 27127 Fordham Dr, Wesley Chapel, FL 33544
DORNHECKER, Douglas Boyd (Oly) 114 20th Ave SE, Olympia, WA 98501
DOROW, Robert M (NI) 1007 Moore Rd, Michigan City, IN 46360
DORR, Kathleen (Ct) 39 Whalers Pt, East Haven, CT 06512
DORRIEN, Gary John (NY) Union Theological Seminary, 3041 Broadway, New York, NY 10027
DORSCH, Ken (Ore) 15625 NW Norwich St, Beaverton, OR 97006
DORSEY, Jennifer Hull (Alb)
DORSEY, June Hardy (O) 352 West College Street, Oberlin, OH 44074
DORSEY, Laura Miller (Eas) 28333 Mount Vernon Rd, Princess Anne, MD 21853
DORVIL, Renès (Hai)
DORWICK, Keith (Oly)
DOSHER, Amanda Harbert (CGC)
DOSHER, Joy (EC)
✠ **DOSS**, Joe (NJ) 15 Front St, Mandeville, LA 70448
DOSTAL FELL, Margaret Ann (Minn) 1765 Upper 55th St E, Inver Grove Heights, MN 55077
DOSTER, Daniel Harris (Ga) 724 Victoria Cir, Dublin, GA 31021
DOTY, DAvid Michael (ETenn) 143 Caledonia Rd, Landrum, SC 29356
DOTY, Phyllis Marie (Fla) P.O. Box 4366, Dowling Park, FL 32064
DOUBLEDAY, William Alan (NY) 31 Croton Ave, Mount Kisco, NY 10549
DOUGHARTY, Phil (WNY) 427 Loma Hermosa Dr NW, Albuquerque, NM 87105
DOUGHERTY JR, Edward Archer (SeFla) 10 Eighth St., Biddeford Pool, ME 04006
DOUGHERTY, Janet Hayes (Minn) 5844 Deer Trail Cir, Woodbury, MN 55129
DOUGHERTY, Katherine G (Va)
DOUGLAS, Ann Leslie (NY) 201 Scarborough Rd, Briarcliff Manor, NY 10510
DOUGLAS, Carole Robinson (Md) 7521 Rockridge Rd, Pikesville, MD 21208
✠ **DOUGLAS**, Ian Theodore (Ct) TEC Dio Of Connecticut, 290 Pratt St Ste 52, Meriden, CT 06450
DOUGLAS, Jeff (EC) 907 Colony Ave N, Ahoskie, NC 27910
DOUGLAS, Michael John (Az) 400 S Old Litchfield Rd, Litchfield Park, AZ 85340
DOUGLAS, Robert Charles (SwFla)
DOUGLAS, Roger Owen (Az) 47280 Amir Dr, Palm Desert, CA 92260

DOUGLASS, David George (NI) 6085 N 190 W, Howe, IN 46746
DOULOS, William Lane (Los) 535 W Roses Rd, San Gabriel, CA 91775
DOWARD, Amonteen Ravenden (Episcopal VI) PO Box 486, Christiansted, VI 00821
DOWDESWELL, Eugenia Hedden (WNC) Po Box 132, Flat Rock, NC 28731
DOWDLE, Catherine Ellen (SanD) 726 Second Ave, Chula Vista, CA 91910
DOWER, Ron (NJ) 3500 Penny Ln, Zanesville, OH 43701
DOWER, Sandra Nichols (WNY)
DOWLING, Shelley (Ia)
DOWLING-SENDOR, Elizabeth (NC) 6 Davie Cir, Chapel Hill, NC 27514
DOWNER, Gretchen Marie (Ida) 1419 Butte View Cir, Emmett, ID 83617
DOWNEY, John (NwPa) 220 W 41st St, Erie, PA 16508
DOWNIE, Elizabeth Morris (EMich) 668 Elder Ln, Winnetka, IL 60093
DOWNING, George (WNC) 824 Aumond Pl E, Augusta, GA 30909
DOWNING, John Wesley (Mil) c o Patricia Haley, 18130 Kamkoff Ave, Eagle River, AK 99577
DOWNING, Patricia S (Del) 1108 N Adams St, Wilmington, DE 19801
DOWNS, Alice Lacey (NJ) 14 Winding Ln, Southwest Harbor, ME 04679
DOWNS, Andrew D (Ind) Saint Stephen's Church, 215 N 7th St, Terre Haute, IN 47807
DOWNS, Donna (Ct) 64 Philip Dr, Shelton, CT 06484
DOWNS JR, Joseph Thomas (EMich) 3225 N Branch Dr, Beaverton, MI 48612
DOWNS, Lee Daniel (Mil) N77w17700 Lake Park Dr Apt 311, Menomonee Falls, WI 53051
DOWNS, Thomas Alexander (CFla) 390 Lake Lenelle Dr, Chuluota, FL 32766
DOYLE, Ann K (Ky) Calvary Episcopal Church, 821 S 4th St, Louisville, KY 40203
✠ **DOYLE**, C Andrew (Tex) 1225 Texas St, Houston, TX 77002
DOYLE, Henry (Minn) 1000 Shumway Ave, Faribault, MN 55021
DOYLE, Margaret E (Ala) 429 Cloudland Dr, Hoover, AL 35226
DOYLE, Seamus (Ark) 1802 W Cambridge Dr, Harrison, AR 72601
DRACHLIS, David Bernard (Ala) 188 Ridgewood Cir, Union Grove, AL 35175
DRAESEL JR, Herbert Gustav (NY) 215 W 84th St Apt 515, New York, NY 10024
DRAKE, Deborah Rucki (Nwk) 380 Clifton Ave, Clifton, NJ 07011
DRAKE, Elliott Theodore (CFla)

DRAKE, Jo-Ann Jane (RI) 104 Lafayette St, Pawtucket, RI 02860
DRAKE, Lesley-Ann (At) 2160 Cooper Lake Rd SE, Smyrna, GA 30080
DRAKE, Kay Marie (CNY) 227 W Walnut Dr, Sturgeon Bay, WI 54235
DRAKE, Leslie Sargent (USC) 1630 Silver Bluff Rd, Aiken, SC 29803
DRAPER, John G (Los)
DRAPER, Rick (Ind) 11974 State Highway M26, Eagle Harbor, MI 49950
DRAWDY, Marcella J (SwFla)
DRAZDOWSKI, Tar (Ga) 408 S 1st St, Cordele, GA 31015
DREBERT, Kay Marie (CNY) 227 W Walnut Dr, Sturgeon Bay, WI 54235
DREBERT, Rebecca Ellen (CNY) St Peters Episcopal Church, 1 Church St, Bainbridge, NY 13733
DREDDEN III, George E (Nwk)
DREISBACH, Christopher (Md) 1040 Deer Ridge Dr Apt 504, Baltimore, MD 21210
DRENNEN, Zachary Polk (WVa) 1102 Juliana St Apt B, Parkersburg, WV 26101
DRESBACH, Michael (ECR) 490 Vivienne Dr, Watsonville, CA 95076
DRESSEL, Marilyn Kaye (EMich) 3725 Woodside Dr, Traverse City, MI 49684
DRESSER, Deborah Metcalf (NY) 105 Grand St, Newburgh, NY 12550
DREWRY, John Colin (EC) 2513 Confederate Dr, Wilmington, NC 28403
DRINKWATER, Michael (RG) PO Box 1246, Albuquerque, NM 87103
DRINO, Jerry (ECR) 14801 Whipple Ct, San Jose, CA 95127
DRISCOLL, Jeanine (RG) PO Box 1071, Roxboro, NC 27573
DRISKILL, Lorinda Elizabeth (Tex) Trinity Episcopal Church, PO Box 777, Anahuac, TX 77514
DRIVER, Bess D (Az) 2137 W. University Ave., Flagstaff, AZ 86001
DROSOS, William (Va)
DROSTE, Rob (NJ) 911 Dowling Blvd, San Leandro, CA 94577
DRUBE, Bruce James (Ala) 1219 Quail Run Dr Sw, Jacksonville, AL 36265
DRUCE, Glenn Edward (NJ) 202 Broadway, Westville, NJ 08093
DRUMM, Elizabeth Prentice (Kan)
DRURY, Susan R (Kan) 7311 Legler Road, Shawnee, KS 66217
DRYMON, John A (O) Trinity Church, 128 W Hardin St, Findlay, OH 45840
DRYNAN, Thomas Steele (Ore) 6431 Ganon St Se, Salem, OR 97317
DRYSDALE, Jessie Cookson (Me) 136 Butterfield Landing Rd., Weston, ME 04424
DRYSDALE-SCHRUTH, Sherry (Minn) Grace Mem TEC Ch, PO Box 27, Wabasha, MN 55981
DUBAY, Joe (Ore) 1805 Nw 34th Ave, Portland, OR 97210

DUBAY, Noreen (WA) 1510 Oakview Dr, Silver Spring, MD 20903

DUBOIS, Charles (NJ) 33509 Anns Choice Way, Warminster, PA 18974

DUBOSE, Georgia (WVa) Po Box 999, Harpers Ferry, WV 25425

DUBOVENKO, Sandra Raye (NMich)

DUCKWORTH, Bonnie (NC)

DUCKWORTH, Penelope Tulleys (Cal) St Jude the Apostle Episcopal Church, 20920 Mcclellan Rd, Cupertino, CA 95014

✠ **DUCKWORTH**, Shannon (La) 5335 Suffolk Dr, Jackson, MS 39211

DUDDING II, Burton Arthur (Nev) 7000 Mae Anne Ave Apt 1521, Reno, NV 89523

DUDLEY JR, Thomas Lee (USC) 134 E Boscawen St, Winchester, VA 22601

DUERR, Robert Edward (Mass) 15 Millbrook Rd, Beverly, MA 01915

DUFF, Eric T (The Episcopal NCal) 524 Old Wagon Rd, Trinidad, CA 95570

DUFF, Lyndie (Wyo) 1117 West Ramshorn Boulevard, Box 844, Dubois, WY 82513

DUFFEY, Ben Rosebro (SVa) 1401 N High St., Apt. 102, Franklin, VA 23851

DUFFEY, Bill (Pa) 3300 Darby Rd, Cottage 304, Haverford, PA 19041

DUFFIELD, Barbara (WTex)

DUFFIELD, Sue (U) St Eliizabeth Episcopal Church, PO Box 100, Whiterocks, UT 84085

DUFFIS FOX, Ennis (Mass) Bello Horizonte S-1-4, Manuagua, Nicaragua

DUFFTY, Bryan (ECR) 3020 Daurine Ct, Gilroy, CA 95020

DUFFUS, Cynthia Slaughter (EC) 711 Henderson Dr, Jacksonville, NC 28540

DUFFY, Christopher Gregory (NJ) 338 Ewingville Rd., Trenton, NJ 08628

DUFFY, Glenn Alan (Del) 63 Battersea Rd., Berlin, MD 21811

DUFORD, Donald John (Mich) 16889 Club Drive, Southgate, MI 48195

DUFOUR, Matthew John (Ak) PO Box 773223, Eagle River, AK 99577

DUGAN II, Haynes Webster (Okla) 305 Camino Norte, Altus, OK 73521

DUGAN, Jeffrey Scott (Ct) 102 Seabury Dr, Bloomfield, CT 06002

DUGAN, Raymond Paul (Az) 534 W Wilshire Dr, Phoenix, AZ 85003

DUGARD, Debra Harris (WTenn) Emmanuel Episcopal Church, 4150 Boeingshire Dr, Memphis, TN 38116

DUGGAN, Joe F (Cal) 351 W James St # 4, Lancaster, PA 17603

DUGGAR, Marilyn (Ak) St Marks Episcopal Church, PO Box 469, Nenana, AK 99760

DUGGER, Rita Jacqueline Carney (WNY) 24 Linwood Ave, Buffalo, NY 14209

DUGGER, Tracy Michelle (CFla) 241 N Main St, Winter Garden, FL 34787

DUGGIN, Sarah Helene (WA) 3240 O St NW, Washington, DC 20007

DUGGINS, Amy E (NC)

DUGUID-MAY, Deborah Lee (Roch) 3450 W Ridge Rd, Rochester, NY 14626

DUGUID-MAY, Melanie Ann (Roch)

DUH, Michael (Tai) 952 Sec 2 Chading Road Chading, Kaohsiung Hsien 85202, Taiwan, China

DUKE, Brandon (At) 1850 N Akin Dr NE, Atlanta, GA 30345

DUKE, Ceci (At) 597 Haralson Dr SW, Lilburn, GA 30047

DUKES, John (At) 626 Mississippi Ave, Signal Mountain, TN 37377

DUKES, Lynne (WMich) 115 3rd St S Apt 913, Jacksonville Beach, FL 32250

DULFER, John Guidi (NY) 110 W 15th St Apt 1, New York, NY 10011

DULGAR, Sandra Lee (Nev) P.O. Box 3522, Tonopah, NV 89049

DULL, Stanley Lynn (Pa) 2215 Palm Tree Dr, Punta Gorda, FL 33950

DUMKE, Barbara (Colo) 11684 Eldorado St Nw, Coon Rapids, MN 55433

DUMKE, Edward John (Cal) 805 Barneson Ave, San Mateo, CA 94402

DUNAGAN, Joe (Fla) 914 Chippewa Dr, Bristol, VA 24201

DUNBAR, Donald Machell (Mass) 160 Longmeadow Rd, Fairfield, CT 06824

DUNBAR, Gavin Gunning (Ga) 1 W Macon St, Savannah, GA 31401

DUNBAR, Julia Brown (WMass) 20 Whitney Ave, Cambridge, MA 02139

DUNBAR, Pamela (Dal) 9221 Flickering Shadow Dr, Dallas, TX 75243

DUNBAR, Robert Barron (USC) PO Box 36155, Rock Hill, SC 29732

DUNBAR, Timothy Andrew (Colo)

DUNBAR, Veronica (Mich) 4800 Woodward Ave, Detroit, MI 48201

DUNCAN, Carol (Pa) 503 W Springer St, Philadelphia, PA 19119

DUNCAN, Carrie Barnes (Miss) PO Box 267, Leland, MS 38756

DUNCAN, Christopher R (La) PO Box 5176, Austin, TX 78763

DUNCAN, David (Los) 6700 Woodland Hills Rd, Rushville, IL 62681

DUNCAN, Hugh C (Ida) 5120 W Overland Rd PMB-276, Boise, ID 83705

DUNCAN, James Bruce (Los) 45 Chestnut St Unit A, North Adams, MA 01247

DUNCAN, John L (The Episcopal NCal) B 207, 925 Freedom Blvd, Watsonville, CA 95076

✠ **DUNCAN II**, Philip (CGC) 7208 Mitra Dr, Austin, TX 78739

DUNCAN, Rosemarie Logan (WA) 1329 Hamilton St NW, Washington, DC 20011

DUNCAN, Sean David (Tex) 10488 State Highway 154, Marshall, TX 75670

DUNCAN, Shawn P (NY) 27 W 55th St Apt 52, New York, NY 10019

DUNCAN, Victoria D (NY) 27 W 55th St Apt 52, New York, NY 10019

DUNCAN-O'NEAL III, William McKinley (Ark) 9669 Wedd St, Overland Park, KS 66212

✠ **DUNCAN-PROBE**, DeDe (CNY) 2 Audubon Dr, Cazenovia, NY 13035

DUNEVANT, Emily Hope (Va) 2955 River Rd W, Goochland, VA 23063

DUNFEE, Mikayla S (Mont)

DUNHAM, Rick (WTex) 4137 Harry St, Corpus Christi, TX 78411

DUNKLE, Kurt H (Fla) 1038 River Rd, Orange Park, FL 32073

DUNKS, Andrew Andrew (Va) Saint Bartholomew's Church, 10627 Patterson Ave, Richmond, VA 23238

DUNLAP, Daniel K (Eas) 715 Carrell St., Tomball, TX 77375

DUNLAP, Eunice Rosalie (SC) 1016 Cheraw Dr, Florence, SC 29501

DUNLAP, Garland Edward (Va) 537 Chattooga Place Dr, Wilmington, NC 28412

DUNLAP, Mary Balfour (USC) Emmanuel Episcopal Church, 340 S Ridge St, Southern Pines, NC 28387

DUNLOP, William Henry (Mil) 413 S 2nd St, Watertown, WI 53094

DUNN JR, Carlton Willard (NJ) St Andrew's Church, 121 High St, Mount Holly, NJ 08060

DUNN, Douglas Robert (Colo) 12925 E Colorado Ave, Aurora, CO 80012

DUNN, Frank (WA) St Stephen The Inct Par, 1525 Newton St NW, Washington, DC 20010

DUNN, George Mervyn (Ga) 8 Woodbridge Crescent, Kanata, ON K2M 2N6, Canada

DUNN, Prentiss Carroll (La) 422 W Hickory Ave, Bastrop, LA 71220

DUNN, Robert Ellis (Oly) PO Box 1377, Granite Falls, WA 98252

DUNN, Sarah Amelia (Nev) 930 Tahoe Blvd Ste 802-1290, Incline Village, NV 89451

DUNN, Sharon Kay Estey (Nev) 3500 San Mateo Ave, Reno, NV 89509

DUNN, William (Los) 1803 Highland Hollow Dr # 559, Conroe, TX 77304

DUNNAM, Thomas Mark (Eur) Via Bernardo Rucellai 9, Firenze, 50123, Italy

DUNNAN, Donald Stuart (Md) Saint James School, Saint James, MD 21781

DUNNAVANT, Charles Randall (Tenn) 817 Stonebrook Blvd, Nolensville, TN 37135

DUNNING, Jane Romeyn (WMass) 44 Main St, Shelburne Falls, MA 01370

DUNNING, William (Md) 1612 Trebor Ct, Lutherville, MD 21093

DUNNINGTON, Michael Gerard (Mo) 1620 Forestview Ridge Ln, Ballwin, MO 63021

DUNST, Earl Walter (Mil) 8121 N Seneca Rd, Milwaukee, WI 53217

Clergy List

DUPLANTIER, David Allard (La) 225 Girod St Apt 203, New Orleans, LA 70130

DUPRE, Stacey F (Los)

DUPREE, Charlie (Va) 111 S Grant St, Bloomington, IN 47408

DUPREE, Hugh Douglas (Fla) 325 N Market St, Jacksonville, FL 32202

DUPREY, David Luke (Wyo) 1 S Tschirgi St, Sheridan, WY 82801

DUQUE-GOMEZ, Francisco (Colom) Calle 122-A 1211, Bogota, Colombia

DURACIN, Zache (Hai) P.O.BOX 295, Port-Au-Prince, Haiti

DURAIKANNU, Yesu (NY) StJames Church, 1 Saint James Pl, Goshen, NY 10924

DURAND, Sally Elaine (Az) 7813 N. Via De La Luna, Scottsdale, AZ 85258

DURANY, Helen Marie (Ore)

D'URBANO, Faith Jeanne (Be) 340 W Orange St, Lancaster, PA 17603

DURBIDGE, Andrew John (LI) 519 Vanderbilt Ave, Brooklyn, NY 11238

DURE, Lucy Ann (Pa) 46 Montrose Ave, Verona, NJ 07044

DURHAM, Martha Hemenway (Az) St Marys Episcopal Church, 306 S Prospect Ave, Park Ridge, IL 60068

DURNING, Michael (SwFla) 12002 Summer Meadow Dr, Bradenton, FL 34202

DURREN, Paula Ellen (WMich) 19 S Jameson St, New Buffalo, MI 49117

DURST, Ted (Chi) 4900 N Marine Dr Apt 411, Chicago, IL 60640

DUTCHER, Katherine Grant (Okla) St Andrew's Episcopal Church, PO Box 1256, Lawton, OK 73502

DUTTON-GILLETT, Matthew Richard (Cal) 472 Ravenswood Ave, Menlo Park, CA 94025

DUVAL, Linda Marie (NY) 16 Boulder Ave, Kingston, NY 12401

DUVALL, Mary Duvall (Ia) 2001 S 40th Ct, West Des Moines, IA 50265

DUVEAUX, Irnel (Hai) Box 1309, Port-Au-Prince, Haiti

DUVERT, Pierre-Andre (NY) 777 E 222nd St, Bronx, NY 10467

DVARISHKIS, Dorcie (Mont) Church Of The Holy Spirit, 130 S 6th St E, Missoula, MT 59801

DWARF, Lindsey Craig (ND) PO Box 45, Cannon Ball, ND 58528

DWYER, John F (Cal) 2300 Hamline Ave N, Roseville, MN 55113

DWYER, Michael W (Chi) 1101 Park Dr, Munster, IN 46321

DWYER, Patricia Marie (Be)

DWYER, Tommy (CGC) 800 22nd St, Port St Joe, FL 32456

DYAKIW, Alexander Raymond (CPa) t John's Episc Ch, 120 W Lamb St, Bellefonte, PA 16823

DYCHE, Bradley (Tex) 6 Old Post Rd N, Croton On Hudson, NY 10520

DYER, Alex (Colo) 51 Crown St, New Haven, CT 06510

DYER II, Maurice (Pa)

DYER, Susan Jeinine (Wyo) PO Box 399, Saratoga, WY 82331

DYER, Timothy D (NwPa) 444 Pennsylvania Ave W, Warren, PA 16365

DYER-CHAMBERLAIN, Margaret Elizabeth (Cal)

DYKE, Nicolas Roger David (Tex) 3815 Echo Mountain Dr, Humble, TX 77345

DYKES, Deborah White (Miss) 3524 Old Canton Rd, Jackson, MS 39216

DYKSTRA, Danny Jon (Ky) 9616 Westport Rd, Louisville, KY 40241

DYNER, Marthe (NH) Po Box 347, Charlestown, NH 03603

DYSON, Elizabeth Wheatley (Mass) 451 Birchbark Dr, Hanson, MA 02341

DYSON, Martha Lynn (Vt) 123 Caroline St, Burlington, VT 05401

DYSON, Thack Harris (CGC) 28788 N Main St, Daphne, AL 36526

DZUGAN, Joseph Mark (NC)

E

EADE, Christopher K (Los) 1031 Bienveneda Ave, Pacific Palisades, CA 90272

EADES, Susan (Mont) 1603 Casino Creek Dr, Lewistown, MT 59457

EAGER, Donald Bates (SO) 2102 Scenic Dr Ne, Lancaster, OH 43130

EAGLEBULL, Harold L (SD) Po Box 1149, Cass Lake, MN 56633

EAKINS, Bill (Ct) 25 Scarborough St, Hartford, CT 06105

EAKINS, Hope Howlett (Ct) 605 Park Ave Apt 14c, New York, NY 10065

EAMES, Marc (Ct) The Church of the Advent, 523 Hartford Tpke, Vernon, CT 06066

EANES II, William Raymond (SwVa) St James Episcopal Church, 4515 Delray St NW, Roanoke, VA 24012

EARL, John Keith (WNC) 1650 5th St Nw, Hickory, NC 28601

EARL, Nicholas Edward (Tex)

EARLE, Charles Douglas (WTex) 7302 Robin Rest Dr, San Antonio, TX 78209

EARLE, Leigh Christensen (Wyo) 1745 Westridge Cir, Casper, WY 82604

EARLE, Mary Colbert (WTex) 7302 Robin Rest Dr, San Antonio, TX 78209

EARLE, Patty Ann Trapp (NC) Po Box 1103, Statesville, NC 28687

EARLE III, Richard Tilghman (SwFla) 555 13th Avenue NE, Saint Petersburg, FL 33701

EARLS, John G (USC)

EARLY, Nancy Davis (WA) 402 Montrose Ave, Catonsville, MD 21228

EARLY, Thomas M (Ia)

EASLEY, Barbara Ann (Ia) 605 Avenue H, Fort Madison, IA 52627

EASLEY, Julia Kathleen (Ia) 26 E Market St, Iowa City, IA 52245

EASTER, James Dennis (WMo)

EASTER, Mary Kathleen (WMo) 973 Evergreen Ave, Hollister, MO 65672

EASTERDAY, Pamela Kay (CFla) 2130 Spring Creek Cir NE, Palm Bay, FL 32905

EASTERDAY, Stephen Wayne (CFla) 2130 Spring Creek Cir NE, Palm Bay, FL 32905

EASTERLING JR, Richard Brooks (Eur) via Bernardo Rucellai 9, Firenze, 50123, Italy

EASTERLING SR, William Ramsay (WLa) 504 Tech Dr, Ruston, LA 71270

EASTES, Suzanne Hardey (Mo) 312 Clayton Crossing Dr., #108, Ellisville, MO 63011

EASTHILL, Christopher Mark (Eur) Schuetzenstrasse 2, Wiesbaden, 65195 DE, Germany

EASTMAN, Susan Grove (NC) 4604 Brodog Ter, Hurdle Mills, NC 27541

EASTON, Elizabeth Lavender (Neb) 9302 Blondo St, Omaha, NE 68134

EASTON, Stanley Evan (Ala) 1104 Church Avenue Northeast, Jacksonville, AL 36265

EASTWOOD, Jack (Cal) 30 Ogden Ave, San Francisco, CA 94110

EATON, Carol Ann (EC) St Francis By the Sea Church, 920 Salter Path Rd, Salter Path, NC 28512

EATON, Cornelia Kay (NAM) PO Box 720, Farmington, NM 87499

EATON, Karen A (Oly) PO Box 753, Port Townsend, WA 98368

EATON, Laura Mary (NMich)

✠ **EATON**, Peter David (SeFla) 525 NE 15th St, Miami, FL 33132

EATON, Robert G (Spr) 1571 E Glenwood Ave, Tulare, CA 93274

EATON, William (SeFla) C O Passavant Retirement Community, 300 W Beaver St 118 Mountain Laurel, Zelienople, PA 16063

EAVES, Lindon John (Va) 10835 Old Prescott Rd, Richmond, VA 23238

EAVES, Sue (Va) 3207 Hawthorne Ave, Richmond, VA 23222

EBEL, Ann Teresa (PR)

EBENS, Richard Frank (Mass) 4-C Autumn Dr, Hudson, MA 01749

EBERHARDT, Karen Anne (Nwk) 18 Ute Ave., Lake Hiawatha, NJ 07034

EBERHARDT, Timothy Charles (Vt) 2460 Braintree Hill Rd, Braintree, VT 05060

EBERLE, Bill (Va) P.O. Box 367, Rixeyville, VA 22737

EBERLY, George Douglas (NJ) 500 19th St, Ocean City, NJ 08226

EBERLY, Laura (Cal)

EBERT, Bernhard (Colo) 802 Raton Ave, La Junta, CO 81050

ECCLES, Mark Eldon (Ia) 1619 21st St Nw, Cedar Rapids, IA 52405

ECCLES, M.E. (Chi) 311 N. Westgate Rd., Mount Prospect, IL 60056

ECHAZABAL, Livan (SwFla) 6709 N Nebraska Ave, Tampa, FL 33604

ECHOLS, Mary W (SwFla) 917 11th St N, Naples, FL 34102
ECHOLS, Stephen Gregory (RG)
ECHOLS, William Joseph (WLa) 104 Ingram St, Lake Providence, LA 71254
ECKART JR, Richard Joseph (Roch) 38 Dale Rd, Rochester, NY 14625
ECKEL, Malcolm David (Mass) 11 Griggs Ter., Brookline, MA 02446
ECKIAN, Deirdre (WA) 200 Saint Andrews Blvd Apt 1707, Winter Park, FL 32792
EDDY, Diane Lynn (Ia) 1458 Locust St, Dubuque, IA 52001
EDDY, Elizabeth (NJ) 913 Fassler Ave, Pacifica, CA 94044
EDDY, William Welles (Mass) PO Box 3615, Waquoit, MA 02536
EDELMAN, Walter Lucian (SanD) 17427 Gibraltar Ct, San Diego, CA 92128
EDEN, Holly (CNY) 120 W 5th St, Oswego, NY 13126
EDEN, Jonathan T (Mass) 865 Madison Ave, New York, NY 10021
EDENS III, Chip (NC) 1412 Providence Rd, Charlotte, NC 28207
✠ **EDINGTON**, Mark David Wheeler (Eur) PO Box 455, Hardwick, MA 01037
EDLEMAN JR, Samuel Warren (Md) 1257 Weller Way, Westminster, MD 21158
EDMAN, David (Tex)
EDMAN, Elizabeth Marie (Nwk) 690 Fort Washington Ave., New York, NY 10040
EDMANDS II, Frank A (SO) 55 S Vernon Ln, Fort Thomas, KY 41075
EDMISTER, Jeffery Ray (WNY) Christ Episcopal Church, 7145 Fieldcrest Dr, Lockport, NY 14094
EDMONDS, Curtis M (Nev) Po Box 70342, Las Vegas, NV 89170
EDMONDS, John B (NY) 15 Wabun Rd, Blue Hill, ME 04614
EDMONDSON, Emily F (SwVa)
EDMONSON, Hal (Mass)
EDMUNDS, Robert Douglas (Mass) PO Box 9000, Edgartown, MA 02539
EDRINGTON, Kristin Nicole (NC)
EDSON, Heidi L (Vt) 6795 W 19th Pl Apt 304, Lakewood, CO 80214
EDSON, Robert Bruce (Mass) 4 Home Meadows Ln, Hingham, MA 02043
EDWARD, Gadi M (ND) 120 8th St S, Moorhead, MN 56560
EDWARDS, Bonnie (RG) 4908 Corrales Rd Ste B, Corrales, NM 87048
EDWARDS, Carl Nickel (Kan)
EDWARDS, Carl Norris (Md) 201 Box Turtle Trl, Chapel Hill, NC 27516
✠ **EDWARDS**, Dan Thomas (Colo) 9480 S Eastern Ave Ste 236, Las Vegas, NV 89123
EDWARDS, Doug (Los) 4255 Harbour Island Ln, Oxnard, CA 93035
EDWARDS, Fitzroy Foster (NY) 72 Carnegie Ave, Elmont, NY 11003

EDWARDS, Halbert D (Okla) 1728 NW 42nd St, Oklahoma City, OK 73118
EDWARDS, James Dennison (LI) 4 S Aspen Pl, Lewisburg, PA 17837
EDWARDS, James Paul (Nev) 1400 Ebbetts Dr, Reno, NV 89503
EDWARDS, Jamie L (NC) 1902 N Holden Rd, Greensboro, NC 27408
EDWARDS, John Garry (NC) 1122 Thoroughbred Dr, Iron Station, NC 28080
EDWARDS, Kathleen Louise (Minn)
EDWARDS, Laura MacFarland (WA) 13118 Collingwood Ter, Silver Spring, MD 20904
EDWARDS, Lydia Alice (NJ) 81 Hillside Ave, Metuchen, NJ 08840
EDWARDS, Paul David (Los) 734 W Maplewood Ave, Fullerton, CA 92832
EDWARDS, Rebecca (Cal) 4321 Eastgate Mall, San Diego, CA 92121
EDWARDS, Robert Daniel (Los) 31641 La Novia Ave, San Juan Capistrano, CA 92675
EDWARDS, Terry Ann (SVa) 2515 Marshall Ave, Newport News, VA 23607
EDWARDS JR, Theodore Whitfield (SwFla) 114 John Pott Dr, Williamsburg, VA 23188
EDWARDS III, Tilden Hampton (WA) 9615 Page Ave, Bethesda, MD 20814
EDWARDS, Whitney (Va) St Jame's Episcopal, 1205 W Franklin St, Richmond, VA 23220
EDWARDS, William Glover (WNC) 38 Wildwood Ave, Asheville, NC 28804
EDWARDS, William Patrick (LI) St Johns Episc Ch, PO Box 5069, Southampton, NY 11969
EDWARDS-ACTON, Jaime Kendall (Los) 727 Olympic Ave, Costa Mesa, CA 92626
EFFINGER, Richard W (SeFla) 141 S County Rd, Palm Beach, FL 33480
EGBERT, David (Okla) 2817 Natchez Trl, Edmond, OK 73012
EGBERT, Paula Sue (Ida) 5780 Millwright Ave, Boise, ID 83714
EGERSTROM, Marisa (WMass) PO Box 9359, North Amherst, MA 01059
EGERTON, Karen (CFla) 1404 Chapman Cir, Winter Park, FL 32789
EHLING, Paul (Minn)
EHMER, Joseph Michael (NwT) Diocese of Northwest Texas, 1802 Broadway, Lubbock, TX 79401
EHREN, Lawrence Glenn (WMo)
EHRICH, Thomas Lindley (NC) 505 W 54th St Apt 812, New York, NY 10019
EIBIN, Julian Raymond (Md) 406 Elizabeth St, Harrisburg, PA 17109
EIBNER, Susan (NH) 97 Halls Mill Rd, Newfields, NH 03856
EICH III, Wilbur Fuster (Ala) 1600 Darby Dr, Florence, AL 35630
EICHELBERGER JR, J Gary (USC) 1002 S Main St, Greenville, SC 29601

EICHENLAUB, Patricia (Mich) 2745 Lake Pine Path Apt 219, Saint Joseph, MI 49085
EICHLER, Stephen (ETenn) 1151 Gudger Rd, Sewanee, TN 37375
EICHNER, James F (Oly)
EICK, John David (WMo) 8030 Ward Pkwy, Kansas City, MO 64114
EICK, Mary Herron (Ore) 11511 Sw Bull Mountain Rd, Tigard, OR 97224
EIDAM JR, John Mahlon (SVa) 224 S Military Hwy, Norfolk, VA 23502
EIMAN, Amanda (NY) St Philips Church in the Highlands, PO Box 158, Garrison, NY 10524
EINERSON, Dean Alfred (FdL) 29 S Pelham St, Rhinelander, WI 54501
EISENSTADT-EANS, Elizabeth Anne (Pa) 50 Fleming Dr, Glenmoore, PA 19343
EKBERG, Sean A (Okla) 210 E 9th St, Bartlesville, OK 74003
EKERBERG, Stephen Matthew (NH)
EKEVAG, Ellen Poole (Mich) 209 N Pine St, New Lenox, IL 60451
EKIZIAN, Hagop J (NY) 137 N Division St, Peekskill, NY 10566
EKLUND, Carolyn (Me) Episcopal Church St Paul, PO Box 195, Brunswick, ME 04011
EKLUND, Virginia Jane Rouleau (Lex) 130 Winterhawk Rd, Danville, KY 40422
EKREM, Katherine Boyle (Mass) 12 White Pine Ln, Lexington, MA 02421
EKSTROM, Ellen Louise (Cal) 1017 Virginia Street, Berkeley, CA 94710
EKUNWE, Sylvester Osa (NH)
ELAM III, Walter L (CGC) 153 Orange Ave, Fairhope, AL 36532
ELBERFELD, Katherine Ann Fockele (At) 123 Church St NE # 150, Marietta, GA 30060
ELBERFELD, Richard (NwPa) 3105 Springland Terrace, Erie, PA 16506
ELCOCK, Frank Ulric (LI) 257 Leaf Ave, Central Islip, NY 11722
ELDER, Clayton L (Dal) 311 E Corpus Christi St, Beeville, TX 78102
ELDER, Paul Robert (Los) 580 Hilgard Ave, Los Angeles, CA 90024
ELDER, Robert Macrum (Va) 218 2nd St, Huntingdon, PA 16652
ELDER, Ruth Annette (Md) 4238 Pimlico Rd, Baltimore, MD 21215
ELDER-HOLIFIELD, Donna Ellen Carter (ECR) 64 San Pedro St, Salinas, CA 93901
ELD MAFFEO, Amy Joanne (Mich)
ELDREDGE, Martha Josephine (WA) 19167 Poplar Hill Ln, Valley Lee, MD 20692
ELDRIDGE, Barbara Adelle (CFla) 2143 Kings Cross St, Titusville, FL 32796
ELDRIDGE, Buel (EMich)
ELDRIDGE JR, Robert William (USC) Hq Forscom, 1777 Hardee Ave Sw, Atlanta, GA 30310

ELEK, Hentzi (Colo) 3625 Chapel Rd, Newtown Square, PA 19073
ELEY, Gary (Vt) 33 Adams Ct, Burlington, VT 05401
ELFERT, Martin (Ore) 127 E 12th Ave, Spokane, WA 99202
ELFRING-ROBERTS, Jess (Chi) Church of our Saviour, 530 W Fullerton Pkwy, Chicago, IL 60614
ELFVIN, Robert Roger (Ia) 8 Poinciana Lane, Palm Coast, FL 32164
ELIN, Darren (SO) 100 Miami Ave, Terrace Park, OH 45174
ELIOT, Mary (Md) 1930 Brookdale Rd, Baltimore, MD 21244
ELKINS-WILLIAMS, Stephen (NC) 100 Black Oak Pl, Chapel Hill, NC 27517
ELL, Marianne Sorge (Del) 8190 Beechley Rd, Wittman, MD 21676
ELLEDGE II, Clyde (Mass) 54 Robert Rd, Marblehead, MA 01945
ELLEDGE, Kate (Mass) 54 Robert Rd, Marblehead, MA 01945
ELLER, Ruth (U) 700 S Silver Ridge St Spc 85, Ridgecrest, CA 93555
ELLER III, William Everett (Okla) 3767 E 82nd St, Tulsa, OK 74137
ELLERY, Celia (NwT) 2661 Yale Ave, San Angelo, TX 76904
ELLESTAD, Charles (Lex) 837 Isaac Shelby Cir E, Frankfort, KY 40601
ELLEY, Eric M (WMass) PO Box 528, Somersville, CT 06072
ELLGREN SHEPLEY, Neysa (Ore) 11800 S Military Ln, Portland, OR 97219
ELLINGBOE, Shirley Kay (RG) 5794 Ndcbu, Taos, NM 87571
ELLINGTON, Meta Louise Turkelson (NC) 521 Marlowe Rd, Raleigh, NC 27609
ELLIOTT, Annie (Miss) 370 Old Agency Rd, Ridgeland, MS 39157
ELLIOTT, Barb (Minn) St Paul's Episcopal Church, 1710 E Superior St, Duluth, MN 55812
ELLIOTT, Beverley Florence (At) 5458 E Mountain St, Stone Mountain, GA 30083
ELLIOTT, Bianca Lynn (Kan)
ELLIOTT III, David Augustus (Miss) 205 Autumn Ridge Dr, Jackson, MS 39211
ELLIOTT, Diane Lynn (Minn)
ELLIOTT, Gates Safford (Miss) 4130 Crestview Dr, 118 N Congress St, Jackson, MS 39201
ELLIOTT III, Harry Arnold (Ct) 104 Seabury Dr, Bloomfield, CT 06002
ELLIOTT, James Lawrence (Ga) PO Box 864, Quitman, GA 31643
ELLIOTT JR, Jim (Ala) 2714 Hilltop Cir, Gadsden, AL 35904
ELLIOTT, Jim (The Episcopal NCal) 1407 N Anderson St, Tacoma, WA 98406
ELLIOTT, Lawrence (Va)

ELLIOTT, Luz Adriana (Dal) St Anne Episcopal Church, 1700 N Westmoreland Rd, Desoto, TX 75115
ELLIOTT, Paul Alexander (At) 5458 E Mountain St, Stone Mountain, GA 30083
ELLIOTT, Paul C (Ala) 2762 Hanover Cir S, Birmingham, AL 35205
ELLIOTT III, Richard G (EC) 2322 Metts Ave, Wilmington, NC 28403
ELLIOTT, Rodger Neil (RG) 1262 Birch Pond Trail, White Bear Lake, MN 55110
ELLIOTT, Scott Fuller (Chi) 2222 W Belmont Ave Unit 205, # 205, Chicago, IL 60618
ELLIS, Jane Fielding (Ala) 556 Mohave Cir, Huntington, CT 06484
ELLIS, Kassinda Rosalind Tabia (LI)
ELLIS, Malcolm (Md) 232 Saint Thomas Ln, Owings Mills, MD 21117
ELLIS, Michael Elwin (Fla) 6126 Cherry Lake Dr N, Jacksonville, FL 32258
ELLIS, Nana Kwasi (Md) All Saints Episcopal Church, Po Box 279, Reisterstown, MD 21136
ELLIS, Richard Alvin (Ct) 15 Piper Rd Apt J313, Scarborough, ME 04074
ELLIS, Russell Ray (Vt) 328 Shore Rd, Burlington, VT 05408
ELLIS, Steven MacDonald (ECR) 1408 Beaumont St NW, Salem, OR 97304
ELLIS, Walter L (Tex) 2419 Lansing Cir, Pearland, TX 77584
ELLIS, William Joseph (NwPa) 222 Brisbin St, Houtzdale, PA 16651
ELLISON, Andrew Duncan (Tex) 4321 Us Highway 80 W, Marshall, TX 75670
ELLISON, Monique (Md) 6060 Charles Edward Terrace, Columbia, MD 21045
ELLISTON, Mark Sanford (NwPa) 16 Central Ave, Oil City, PA 16301
ELLSWORTH, Anne (Az) 6300 N Central Ave, Phoenix, AZ 85012
ELLSWORTH, Bradford Edwin (WMo) Po Box 160, Cabool, MO 65689
ELLSWORTH, Eleanor (SanD) 2205 Caminito Del Barco, Del Mar, CA 92014
ELLSWORTH, Phillip (Cal) 7 Sierra Ct, Belvedere Tiburon, CA 94920
ELLSWORTH, Scott Anthony (Ida) 2887 Snowflake Dr, Boise, ID 83706
ELMIGER-JONES, Mary Kathleen (Cal) St Timothy's Church, 1550 Diablo Rd, Danville, CA 94526
ELPHEE, David T (SwVa)
ELSBERRY, Terry (NY) PO Box 293, Bedford, NY 10506
ELSE, Dave (Pgh) 272 Caryl Dr, Pittsburgh, PA 15236
ELSENSOHN, David Dirk (Ak) PO Box 406, Seaview, WA 98644
ELSER, Claire (Colo)
ELVIN, Peter Thurston (WMass) 35 Park St, Williamstown, MA 01267

ELWELL, Pamela (SO) 321 East Kanawha Ave, Columbus, OH 43214
ELWOOD, Frederick Campbell (Mich) 1334 Riverside Dr, Buhl, ID 83316
ELWOOD, Richard Hugh (Tex) 308 E San Antonio St, Fredericksburg, TX 78624
ELY, Elizabeth Wickenberg (NC) 1223 Midvale Ave, Charleston, SC 29412
ELY, James Everett (Tex) 1700 Golden Ave, Bay City, TX 77414
✠ **ELY**, Thomas C (Vt) 34 Blueberry Cir, Newfane, VT 05345
EMANUEL, Philip Grantham (SC) PO Box 990, Pawleys Island, SC 29585
EMBLER-BEAZLEY, Liz (La) 6249 Canal Blvd, New Orleans, LA 70124
EMENHEISER, Ed (WMich) 174 Wakulat Ln, Traverse City, MI 49686
EMERSON, Angela Angela (Vt) Gates Briggs Blgd Ste 315, White River Junction, VT 05001
EMERSON, Jason (SO) 2511 Hixson St, Powell, OH 43065
EMERSON, Keith (SVa) St Pauls Church, 213 N Main St, Suffolk, VA 23434
EMERSON, Mary Beth (Mass) 305 Mayflower Street, Duxbury, MA 02332
EMERSON, Richard Clark (ECR) 1412 Maysun Ct, Campbell, CA 95008
EMERY, Dana Karen (Minn) 1400 Corbett Rd, Detroit Lakes, MN 56501
EMGE, Kevin Ray (Ia)
EMMERT, John Howard (CPa) 648 Laurel View Dr., Manheim, PA 17545
EMPSALL, Glenda Mascarella (Spok) 501 E Wallace Ave, Coeur D Alene, ID 83814
EMPSALL, Nathan Santway (Spok)
EMRICH III, Frederick Ernest (WMass) PO Box 318, 7 Smith St, North Haven, ME 04853
EMRICH III, Richard Stanley Merrill (Chi) 1804 Hacienda Dr, Stevensville, MI 49127
EMRY, Anne (Ore) 1444 Liberty St SE, Salem, OR 97302
ENCARNACION-CARABALLO, Felix Antonio (DomRep) C/Santiago 114, Santo Iomingo, Dominican Republic
ENCINOSA, Christina (SeFla) 68 Paxford Ln, Boynton Beach, FL 33426
ENDER, Sinclair Conrad Paul (Ia) Building 241 Chaplains Office, Portsmouth Naval Shipyard, Portsmouth, NH 03804
ENDICOTT, Gerri LaVerne (WTenn) PO Box 318, Somerville, TN 38068
ENDICOTT, Rachel (Oly) 15114 SE 48th Dr, Bellevue, WA 98006
ENELOW, James (WMich)
ENGDAHL JR, Frederick Robert (Mich) 6490 Clarkston Rd., Clarkston, MI 48346
ENGELHARDT, Hanns Christian Joachim (Eur) Stephanienstrasse, 72, Karlsruhe, 76133, Germany
ENGELHORN, Paula Elaine (Chi)

ENGELS, Allen Robert (Colo) 3081 Evanston Ave, Grand Junction, CO 81504

ENGELS, Jimichael (Mass) 1190 Adams St Apt 213, Dorchester Center, MA 02124

ENGFER, Michael (Nev) 957 Buffalo River Ave, Henderson, NV 89002

ENGLAND, Edward Gary (ETenn) 408 Oak Ave, South Pittsburg, TN 37380

ENGLAND, Gary William (Cal) 7404 Arrowwood Rd, Louisville, KY 40222

ENGLAND, Loy David (WTex) Po Box 1025, Pflugerville, TX 78691

ENGLAND, Margaret Jefferson (Az) 11058 Portobelo Dr, San Diego, CA 92124

ENGLAND, Nicholas B (SO) 134 N Broad St, Lancaster, OH 43130

ENGLAND JR, Nick Arnold (WVa) 411 Prichard St, Williamson, WV 25661

ENGLE SR, Mark Christoph (NMich) 22975 Pine Lake Rd, Battle Creek, MI 49014

ENGLEBY, Matt (NY) 379 Mount Harmony Rd, Bernardsville, NJ 07924

ENGLERT, Martha Ann (Mil) 3109 Churchill Dr, Madison, WI 53713

ENGLISH, Allison Rainey (SO) 3766 Clifton Ave, Cincinnati, OH 45220

ENGLISH, Ann Cantwell (Spok) Rr 1 Box 241-B, Touchet, WA 99360

ENGLISH, Linda (WK) 114 W Roosevelt St, Phoenix, AZ 85003

ENGLISH, Rev Carrie (Fla) 11601 Longwood Key Dr W, Jacksonville, FL 32218

ENGLISH, Thomas Ronald (Ore) 2530 Fairmount Blvd, Eugene, OR 97403

ENGLISH, William H (Roch) 248 Commons Ln, Foster City, CA 94404

ENGLUND, David (The Episcopal NCal) 1624 10th St, Oroville, CA 95965

ENGLUND, Henry C (NJ) 90 Dillon Way, Washington Crossing, PA 18977

ENGSTROM, Marilyn (Wyo) 1714 Mitchell St, Laramie, WY 82072

ENGWALL, Douglas Brian (Ct) Trinity Episcopal Church, 55 River Rd, Collinsville, CT 06019

ENNIS, Kathleen Knox (SwFla) 6180 Golden Oaks Ln, Naples, FL 34119

ENSOR, Amelia Jeanne (Oly) 8235 36th Ave Ne, Seattle, WA 98115

EOYANG JR, Thomas (Pa) 6622 Germantown Ave Apt 3a, Philadelphia, PA 19119

EPES, Gail E (Va) 1200 N Quaker Ln, Alexandria, VA 22302

EPPERSON, Christopher Larry (SVa) PO Box 3520, Williamsburg, VA 23187

EPPLY-SCHMIDT, Joanne (NJ) 26 Nelson Ridge Rd, Princeton, NJ 08540

✠ **EPTING**, Chris Christopher (Ia) 86 Broadmoor Ln, Iowa City, IA 52245

ERB, Ed (Be) 827 Church St., Honesdale, PA 18431

ERDELJON, Lisa Michele (EC) 4157 Cambridge Cove Cir SE Unit 3, Southport, NC 28461

ERDMAN, Dan (Mich) 1 Swanage Dr, Bella Vista, AR 72715

ERDMAN, Nathan (Md) 637 Whittier Pkwy, Severna Park, MD 21146

ERICKSON, David L (Cal) 1818 Monterey Blvd, Hermosa Beach, CA 90254

ERICKSON, Frederick David (Los) 10700 Keswick St, Garrett Park, MD 20896

ERICKSON, Gregory Charles (WNC) 1359 Lamb Mountain Rd, Hendersonville, NC 28792

ERICKSON, Heather B (Los) St Margaret's Episcopal Church, 31641 La Novia Ave, San Juan Capistrano, CA 92675

ERICKSON, Ken (Mich) 310 Star Bend Rd, Yuba City, CA 95991

ERICKSON, Lori Jean (Ia)

ERICKSON, Mary (At) 4 Jones St, Cartersville, GA 30120

ERICKSON, Mary Cobb (Wyo) PO Box 1690, Jackson, WY 83001

ERICKSON, Richard Paul (Alb) 901 Ridge View Circle, Castleton-On-Hudson, NY 12033

ERICKSON, Scott (Cal) 420 Eureka St, San Francisco, CA 94114

ERICKSON, Susan Joan (Az)

ERICKSON, Winifred Jean (NMich) 1506 Us #2 Highway West, Crystal Falls, MI 49920

ERICSON, Bill (Mich) Po Box 267, Dewitt, MI 48820

ERIXSON, Lorna (Nwk) 7 E Main St, Mendham, NJ 07945

ERKMAN, Charles Philip (Fla)

ERNST, Katie N (Minn)

ERQUIAGA, Trudel Nada (Nev) 1128 Green Valley Drive, Fallon, NV 89406

ERSKINE, Jack Arthur (EO) 69787 Pine Ridge Rd, Sisters, OR 97759

ERVOLINA, Timothy Mark (WNC) 120 Ridgewood Cir, Greenwood, SC 29649

ERWIN, Ginny (Los) 2157 Birdie Dr, Banning, CA 92220

ERWIN JR, Jim (LI) 5 Second St, Warwick, NY 10990

ESBENSHADE, Burnell True (Mo) 1116 E Linden Ave, Saint Louis, MO 63117

ESCALERA, Jose Refugio (Okla) 8400 S Pennsylvania Ave, Oklahoma City, OK 73159

ESCOTT, Raymond Philip (WNC) 12 Misti Leigh Ln, Waynesville, NC 28786

ESKAMIRE-JACKSON, Joyce (La) 1313 Esplanade Ave, New Orleans, LA 70116

ESKITE, Rachel Christine (Va)

ESLICKER, Jason Thornton (Tex) 2003 Wa Wa Ave, Durham, NC 27707

ESONU, Clinton (WA) 2031 Powhatan Rd, Hyattsville, MD 20782

ESPERANCE, Jabnel (Hai)

ESPESETH, Cynthia A (Colo) 464 Wagon Bend Rd, Berthoud, CO 80513

ESPINOSA-AREVALO, Carlos (EcuC) Apartado Postal 10-04-21, Atuntaqui-Imbabura, Ecuador

ESPOSITO, Catherine Patricia (NJ) 14 Edgemere Dr, Matawan, NJ 07747

ESPOSITO, Charles Paul (Pgh) 315 Shady Ave, Pittsburgh, PA 15206

ESPOSITO, Keith Callahan (NC)

ESSING, Rachael (WMass)

ESTES, Anthony Carlos (Mich)

ESTES, Diane (La)

ESTES, James Gray (SanD) 1427 Rimrock Dr, Escondido, CA 92027

ESTES, Robert Theodore (WMo) 425 East Cherry St, Nevada, MO 64772

ESTES, William Thomas (Tex) Grace Church, 405 Glenmar Ave, Monroe, LA 71201

ESTEY, Lawrence Mitchell (Me) 53 Mcauley Way Unit 302, Portland, ME 04103

ESTIL, Colbert (Hai) Eglesi Episcopal DHaiti, Boite Postale 1309, Port-au-Prince, Haiti

ESTIL, Wilson (NY)

ESTRADA, Carolyn Sullivan (Los) 2516 E Willow St Unit 108, Signal Hill, CA 90755

ESTRADA, Richard Roger (Los) 2808 Altura St, Los Angeles, CA 90031

ESWEIN, Nancy G (Cal) 5040 E Timrod St, Tucson, AZ 85711

ETEMAD, Sandra L (Pa) 535 Haws Ave, Norristown, PA 19401

ETHELSTON, Sally A (WA)

ETHEREDGE, Annie (WLa) 905 Dafney Dr, Lafayette, LA 70503

ETIENNE, Balde (Hai)

ETTENHOFER, Karen Ruth (NMich) 500 Ogden Ave, Escanaba, MI 49829

EUSTACE, Warren Paul (ECR) 1604 E. Nectarine Ave., Lompoc, CA 93436

EUSTIS, Patricia Anne (ND) 1323 N 38th St, Apt A, Seattle, WA 98103

EVANCHO, Nicholas James (WNY) 3116 O St NW, Washington, DC 20007

EVANGREENE, Gaelyn Lei (WNC)

EVANS, Aaron (WMich) 1115 W Summit Ave, Muskegon, MI 49441

EVANS, Amber (Cal) 1357 Natoma St, San Francisco, CA 94103

EVANS III, Boyd Mccutchen (SwVa) Church of St Thomas, 124 E Main St, Abingdon, VA 24210

EVANS, Carol (O) 246 Cedar Ave, Ravenna, OH 44266

EVANS, Caryllou Deedee (Kan) St. James Episcopal Church, 3750 E. Douglas, Wichita, KS 67208

EVANS, Courtenay B (Va)

EVANS II, David (NwPa) 506 Young Rd, Erie, PA 16509

EVANS, David Hugh (Mich) 1926 Morris St, Sarasota, FL 34239

EVANS, Dolores Elaine (Be) 184 Meadow Lane, Conestoga, PA 17516

EVANS, Gareth C (NY) 148 Newtown Rd, Acton, MA 01720

EVANS, Gary T (NMich) 1000 Bluff View Dr Apt 112, Houghton, MI 49931

EVANS, Geoffrey Parker (Ala) 1727 Post Oak Ct., Auburn, AL 36830

EVANS, Gregory Myles (Ala)

EVANS, Haydn Barry (Pa) 214 New St Apt 4n, Philadelphia, PA 19106

EVANS, Holly Sue (CNY) PO Box 319, Copenhagen, NY 13626

EVANS, Jacob Joseph (Alb) 5 Simpson Ave, Round Lake, NY 12151

EVANS, James Eston (Pa) 1013 Balfour Cir, Phoenixville, PA 19460

EVANS, James W (Oly) 8648 Onyx Dr SW Unit D, Lakewood, WA 98498

EVANS, Jeffrey Keith (Ala) St Stephens Episcopal Church, 8020 Whitesburg Dr SW, Huntsville, AL 35802

EVANS, John Miles (Md) PO Box 1272, PO Box 1272, Portsmouth, NH 03802

EVANS, Jonathan W (SwFla)

EVANS, Karen Patricia (At) 3750 Peachtree Rd NE Apt 276, Atlanta, GA 30319

EVANS, Katharine (Mass) 18 Lafayette Rd, Ipswich, MA 01938

EVANS, Len (U) 259 S Byron Ct, Wichita, KS 67209

EVANS, Maria Louise (Mo) 12776 Suncrest Way, Greentop, MO 63546

EVANS, Mark E (Spr) 402 Pekin St., P.O. Box 386, Lincoln, IL 62656

EVANS, Noah H (Pgh) 240 Woodhaven Dr, Pittsburgh, PA 15228

EVANS, Paul Fredric (Cal) 23 Seward St Apt C2, Saratoga Springs, NY 12866

EVANS, Paul M (Va)

EVANS, Scott Charles (Alb) 15 W High St, Ballston Spa, NY 12020

EVANS, Theodore H (WMass) 235 Walker St. Apt. 236, Lenox, MA 01240

EVELYN, Shawn (WA)

EVENBECK, Katherine L (The Episcopal NCal)

EVENSON, Bruce (SC) 34 Krier Ln, Mt Pleasant, SC 29464

EVERETT, Isaac J (Mass) 77 Wachusett St, Boston, MA 02130

EVERHARD, Darby (NC) 520 Summit St, Winston Salem, NC 27101

EVERS, Michael (Wyo)

EVERSLEY, Walter Vl (Md) 214 Lambeth Rd, Baltimore, MD 21218

EVERSMAN, Karen Lynn (O) 2041 W Reserve Cir, Avon, OH 44011

EVERSON, Charles (WMo) 1307 Holmes St, Kansas City, MO 64106

EVERSON, Jacquelyn (NMich) 711 11th Ave, Menominee, MI 49858

EWART, Craig Kimball (NY)

EWING, Elizabeth (CNY) 233 Marlboro Rd, Ardmore, PA 19003

EWING, Judith (SC) 203 Magnolia Bluff Dr, Columbia, SC 29229

EWING, Ward Burleson (ETenn) P O Box 6, 213 Baker Cemetery Road, Ten Mile, TN 37880

EXLEY, Christopher Wright (Pa)

EXLEY, Lori Tucker (Pa)

EXPOSITO IRARRAGORRI, Carlos Eduardo (SanD)

EYER-DELEVETT, Aimee (Los) All Saints By The Sea, 83 Eucalyptus Ln, Santa Barbara, CA 93108

EYTCHESON, Gerald Leonard (Kan) 2400 Gary Ave, Independence, KS 67301

EZELL II, Jim (ECR) 105 Dogwood Trl, Elizabeth City, NC 27909

F

FAASS, Peter (O) 3566 Avalon Rd, Shaker Heights, OH 44120

FABIAN, Rick (Cal) 2525 Lyon St, San Francisco, CA 94123

FABRE, Julie Kilbride (U) 38105 Redwood Road #2191, West Valley City, UT 84119

FACCIO, David Franceschi (PR)

FACKLER, Phillip Joseph Augustine (Pa) 6130 Mccallum St, Philadelphia, PA 19144

FACTOR, Beverly A (Los) 2620 Catherine Rd, Altadena, CA 91001

FADELY, Diane Camille (Md) Trinity Episcopal Church, 120 Allegheny Ave, Towson, MD 21204

FAETH, Margaret Ann (Va) 4529 Peacock Ave, Alexandria, VA 22304

FAGEOL, Suzanne Antoinette (Oly) Po Box 303, Langley, WA 98260

FAGG, Randy Jay (Ida) PO Box 324, Rupert, ID 83350

FAHRNER, Pamela Henry (SC) All Saints Episcopal Church, 3001 Meeting St, Hilton Head Island, SC 29909

FAIN, Beth Ann Jernigan (Tex) 10515 Laneview Dr, Houston, TX 77070

FAIR, Verna M (Chi) 1134 Highpointe Dr, Dekalb, IL 60115

FAIRBANKS, Barbara Jean (Minn) 3044 Longfellow Ave, Minneapolis, MN 55407

FAIRFIELD, Roger Louis (EO) 69793 Pine Glen Rd, Sisters, OR 97759

FAIRLESS, Caroline (NH) 8 Whispering Pines Rd, Wilmont, NH 03287

FAIRLEY, Pamela Sue (SO) 6400 Mckinney Ranch Pkwy, Mckinney, TX 75070

FAIRWEATHER, Carolynne Marie (Ore) 4061 Hayes St. #28, Newberg, OR 97132

FAISON, Dee Doheny (Pa) 405 Warren Rd, West Chester, PA 19382

FAISON, Diane Elizabeth (Pa) 657 11th Ave, Prospect Park, PA 19076

FAIT JR, Harold Charles (Minn)

FALCIANI, Justin Anthony (NJ) 16 W Wilmont Ave, Somers Point, NJ 08244

FALCONER, Allan (Miss) 11593 Avondale Dr, Fairfax, VA 22030

FALES, Stephen Abbott (Ind) 1402 W Main St, Carmel, IN 46032

FALLIS, Robert Keith (Okla) 4500 W 168th St N, Skiatook, OK 74070

FALLON, Amy (Mo) Grace Place Campus Ministry, 401 Normal Rd, Dekalb, IL 60115

FALLOWFIELD, Bill (Md) 2622 N Calvert St, Baltimore, MD 21218

FALLS, Michael Lee (Tex) 5831 Secrest Dr, Austin, TX 78759

FAMULARE JR, Joseph Anthony (Alb) 119 Southern Ave, Little Falls, NY 13365

FAN, Peter Sheung-Mau (The Episcopal Church in Haw) St Elizabeth Episcopal Church, 720 N King St, Honolulu, HI 96817

FANFAN, Luckner (Hai)

FANGUY, Mabel Matheny (Pgh) 1114 1st St, Canonsburg, PA 15317

FANNING, Thomas H (Miss) 24 Greystone Dr, Madison, MS 39110

FARABEE, Allen W (WNY) 31837 Larkenheath Dr, Wesley Chapel, FL 33543

FARAMELLI, Norman Joseph (Mass) 29 Harris St, Waltham, MA 02452

FARBER, Joseph W (EO) 31934 Sparrow Rd, Norman, OK 73072

FARGO, David Rolland (La) 17 Hastings Ct, Asheville, NC 28803

FARGO, Valerie (EMich) 2805 Georgetown Dr, Midland, MI 48642

FARIA III, Manuel P (Mass) 4 Ocean St, Beverly, MA 01915

FARINA, Gaspar Miran (Mil) 154 Club Wildwood, Hudson, FL 33568

FARKAS, Hazel Daphne Martin (SVa) 111 Montrose, Williamsburg, VA 23188

FARLEY, Arlen Thomas (Spok)

FARLEY, Nancy Stone (Lex) 151 Vine St, Sadieville, KY 40370

FARMER, Eyleen Hamner (WTenn) 102 N 2nd St, Memphis, TN 38103

FARMER, Jennie Marietta (EMich) 453 S 26th St, Saginaw, MI 48601

FARNES, Joseph E (Ida) 704 S Latah St, Boise, ID 83705

FARONE, Martha Jeanete (WNY) 7145 Fieldcrest Dr, Lockport, NY 14094

FARQUHAR-MAYES, Alice Fay (Ida) 1560 E Lenz Ln, Boise, ID 83712

FARQUHAR-MAYES, Thomas (Ida) 1115 W Clarinda Dr, Meridian, ID 83642

FARR, Beau Anthony (At)

FARR, Curtis Andrew (Ct) St James Church, 19 Walden St, West Hartford, CT 06107

FARR, Elizabeth (ETenn)

FARR, Matthew R (ETenn)

FARR, Meghan J (Eau) St Luke's Episcopal Church, PO Box 605, Gladstone, NJ 07934

FARRAND, Gregory C (NC)

FARRAR, Charles Thomas (Me) 2390 Rfd 201, Gardiner, ME 04345

FARRAR III, Dean (Los) 4091 E La Cara St, Long Beach, CA 90815
FARRELL, Mary Beth (Minn)
FARRELL JR, Reid Dwyer (Vt) PO Box 273, Swanton, VT 05488
FARRELL, Wayne (SwFla) 1700 Keystone Rd, Tarpon Springs, FL 34688
FARRINGTON, Kristen Johanna (Md) 11232 Falls Rd, Timonium, MD 21093
FARSTAD, Joan Elizabeth (RG) 2410 Melrose Dr, Cedar Falls, IA 50613
FARWELL JR, James William (At) Virginia Theological Seminary, 3737 Seminary Rd, Alexandria, VA 22304
FASEL, William Jay (WMo) 824 W 62nd St, Kansas City, MO 64113
FAT YERO, Gil (Cu)
FAUCETTE, Louis H (At) 2998 Kodiak Ct, Marietta, GA 30062
FAULKNER, David M (Tex) St Cyprians Church, 919 S John Redditt Dr, Lufkin, TX 75904
FAULKNER, Tom (NY) 131 E 66th St Apt 10b, New York, NY 10065
FAULSTICH, Christine (Tex) 9600 S Gessner Rd, Houston, TX 77071
FAULSTICH, Matthew (SeFla) 1704 Buchanan St, Hollywood, FL 33020
FAUPEL, David William (SwFla) 7447 Emilia Ln, Naples, FL 34114
FAUSAK, Frederick Emil (NY) 41 Alter Ave, Staten Island, NY 10304
FAVAZZA, Gregory Emanuel (CFla)
FAY, Michael (Colo) 8010 W Us Highway 50, Salida, CO 81201
FAY, Susan D (The Episcopal NCal) 2508 Tom Polk Ave, Chico, CA 95973
FAYA AMARO, Barbaro Roberto (Cu)
FAYETTE, Shelly Lynn (Oly) 4548 Brooklyn Ave NE, Seattle, WA 98105
FEAGIN JR, Jerre Willis (WNY) 3751 N Franklin Ave, Loveland, CO 80538
FEATHER, Mark (Va) 15036 Tradition Dr, Louisville, KY 40245
FECHT, Dustin Michael (Chi) St Johns Episcopal Church, 405 N Saginaw Rd, Midland, MI 48640
FEDEWA, Mike (WMich) 1025 3 Mile Rd Ne, Grand Rapids, MI 49505
FEDOCK, Maria Michele (Md) 2115 Southland Rd, Baltimore, MD 21207
FEDORCHAK, Karen Christina Russell (Ct) 48 S Hawthorne St, Manchester, CT 06040
FEELY, Mary Josephine (Minn) 8055 Morgan Ave N, Stillwater, MN 55082
FEES, Nancy Fardelius (Wyo)
FEHR, Thomas James (SO) Com Of The Transfiguration, 495 Albion Ave, Cincinnati, OH 45246
FEHR, Wayne L (Mil) 8220 Harwood Ave Apt 334, Wauwatosa, WI 53213
FEIDER, Paul A (FdL) 1511 Cedarhurst Dr, New London, WI 54961
FEINS, Amy Matthews (SwFla)
FELICETTI, Elizabeth (SVa) 1217 Yarbrough Way, Virginia Beach, VA 23455

FELLHAUER, Edward William (Miss) 9b Deans Ct, Santa Fe, NM 87508
FELLHAUER, Sheila Rose (Miss) 9b Deans Ct, Santa Fe, NM 87508
FELLOWS, Richard Greer (SwFla) 15801 Country Lake Dr, Tampa, FL 33624
FELLOWS, Robert Hayden (Okla) 5820 W Garden Pointe Dr, Stillwater, OK 74074
FELS, Charles Wentworth Baker (ETenn)
FELSOVANYI, Andrea (The Episcopal NCal) 4 Bishop Ln, Menlo Park, CA 94025
FELTMAN-MAHAN SR, Peter Joseph (WMass)
FELTNER, Allan L (EMich) 1210 S Fell Ave, Normal, IL 61761
FELTY, Rose Ann (Alb) 960 Toledo Dr, Brownsville, TX 78526
FENG, Katherine Ying (Los)
FENLON, Mathew Charles (Tex) 2450 River Oaks Blvd, Houston, TX 77019
FENN, Richard Kimball (Pa) 43 Hibben Rd, Princeton, NJ 08540
FENNER, Renee Lynette (Mo)
FENTON, Douglas (NY) 1410 Nanton St, Vancouver, BC V6H 2E2, Canada
FENTON, Eric Denis (WTex) 14207 Bold Ruler St, San Antonio, TX 78248
FENTON, Fred (Los) 1670 Interlachen Rd Apt 43g, Seal Beach, CA 90740
FENTON, Graham (Minn) 4720 Zenith Ave S, Minneapolis, MN 55410
FENTRESS-GANNON, Christine (Mich) 19100 Chelton Dr, Beverly Hills, MI 48025
FEREBEE, Randy (WNC) 201 E Howard St Apt 3a, Tryon, NC 28782
FEREGRINO, Alfredo (Los)
FERGUESON, John Frederick (Oly) 14449 90th Ct Ne, Bothell, WA 98011
FERGUSON, Anthony David Norman (Fla) 5128 Falling Water Rd, Nolensville, TN 37135
FERGUSON, Dina McMullin (Los) St. Michael the Archangel, El Segundo, CA 90245
FERGUSON, Dru (NwT) 510 Newell Ave, Dallas, TX 75223
FERGUSON, Judy (NY) 391 Main St, Highland Falls, NY 10928
FERGUSON, Katherine (Va)
FERGUSON, Les (SVa) 5537 Greenefield Dr S, Portsmouth, VA 23703
FERGUSON, Linda Jean (Mich) 1434 E 13 Mile Rd, Madison Heights, MI 48071
FERGUSON, Ronald L (Chi)
FERGUSON, Ruth (Roch) 377 Rector Pl Apt 95, New York, NY 10280
FERGUSON, Stephen Keith (Tex) 20171 Chasewood Park Drive, Houston, TX 77070
FERGUSON, Thomas A (Mich)
FERGUSON, Tom (CNY) 583 Sheridan Ave, Columbus, OH 43209

FERLO, Roger (NY) 1700 E 56th St Apt 2601, Chicago, IL 60637
FERNANDEZ, Jose Pascual (NY) 107 Se Superior Way, Stuart, FL 34997
FERNANDEZ, Jose R (Ala)
FERNANDEZ, Jureck Zamudio (Cal) 3900 Alameda de Las Pulgas, San Mateo, CA 94403
FERNANDEZ, Linda (Md) 30 Tiffany St, Englewood, FL 34223
FERNANDEZ-POLA, Rosali (PR)
FERNANDEZ-REINA, Hipolito (Ind)
FERNANDEZ TRIANA, Frank Miguel (Cu)
FERNER, Dave (NH) 180 Red Coat Ln, Stoddard, NH 03464
FERNÉLUS, Jean Samuel (Hai)
FERREE, Angela (Mo)
FERREIRA SANDOVAL, Wilson (Ore) 1217 NE 155th Ave, Portland, OR 97230
FERRELL, Nathan Wilson (Me) 41 Foreside Road, Falmouth, ME 04105
FERRELL, Sean Daniel (Spr) 2203 Fletcher St, Urbana, IL 61801
FERRER, Gabriel V (Los) All Saints Parish, 504 N Camden Dr, Beverly Hills, CA 90210
FERRIANI, Nancy Ann (Ind) 5010 Washington Blvd, Indianapolis, IN 46205
FERRITO, Michael Louis (ECR) 1391 Market St, Santa Clara, CA 95050
FERRO, Mauricio (Colom) Carrera 16 #94-A-30, Bogota, Colombia
FESSLER, Robert H (Mil) 2275 De Carlin Dr, Brookfield, WI 53045
FETTERMAN, James Harry (WLa) 1755 NE 46th St, Oakland Park, FL 33334
FETZ, Robert D (SO) 30 Warren Ter, Longmeadow, MA 01106
FEUERSTEIN, John Mark (Pgh) 1066 Washington Rd, Mt Lebanon, PA 15228
FEUERSTEIN, Paul (NY) 431 E 118th St, New York, NY 10035
FEUS, William Frederick (USC) St. Mark's Church, 132 Center Street, Chester, SC 29706
FEUSS, Jon (Los) 255 W 5th St Apt 1113, San Pedro, CA 90731
FEYERHERM, Elise Anne (Mass) 3400 Calumet St, Columbus, OH 43214
FEYRER, David (Ct) 70 S Dogwood Trl, Southern Shores, NC 27949
FHUERE, Brenda Lee (Colo) 520 Jaylee St Unit A, Clifton, CO 81520
FIALHO, Eric Edward (Mass)
FICHTER JR, Richard E (Va) 10360 Rectory Ln, King George, VA 22485
FICKS III, Robert Leslie (Ct) PO Box 1283, Houlton, ME 04730
FIDDLER, Andrew (Ct) 215 Highland St, New Haven, CT 06511
FIDLER, Brian Ernest (SanD) The Bishop's School, 7607 La Jolla Blvd, La Jolla, CA 92037
FIEFIE, Guilene (Hai)

FIELD, Claire Cowden (NwT) 1601 S Georgia St, Amarillo, TX 79102

✠ **FIELD**, Martin Scott (WMo) 919 Pleasant St, Worcester, MA 01602

FIELD, Norman Grover (NwPa) 747 E 41st St, Erie, PA 16504

FIELD, Rachel E (Vt)

FIELD, Robert Durning (WNC) 256 E. Main St., Brevard, NC 28712

FIELD, William Overstreet (Del) 1611 Spring Dr Apt 5b, Louisville, KY 40205

FIELDSTON, Heidi A (Mass) 24 Court St, Dedham, MA 02026

FIFE, Richard (SwVa) 2515 Wycliffe Ave SW, Roanoke, VA 24014

FIGGE, Diane (RG) 3900 Trinity Dr, Los Alamos, NM 87544

FIGLEWISKI, Brett Michael (Ct) 770 E Main St, Waterbury, CT 06702

FIKE, Christopher John (Mass) 24 Oakland St, Medford, MA 02155

FIKES, Gerald David (Tex) PO Box 100014, Arlington, VA 22210

FILBERT, Brandon Lee (Ore) 2090 High St SE, Salem, OR 97302

FILER, Judy Kathleen (Tex) St John's Episcopal Church, 514 Carter St, Marlin, TX 76661

FILL, Michael (Be) 151 Prospect Ave Apt 16d, Hackensack, NJ 07601

FILLER, John Arthur (U) 514 Americas Way # 4603, Box Elder, SD 57719

FILS, Jean Daniel (Hai)

FINAN, Alice Jeanne (Vt) 24 Highbridge Xing Apt 1406, Asheville, NC 28803

FINCH, Barbara Jo (Ore) 11865 SW Tualatin Rd Apt 45, Tualatin, OR 97062

FINCH, Robin Lee (Ida) All Saints' Episcopal Church, 704 S Latah St, Boise, ID 83705

FINCHER, Michael (Los) 1242 E 4th St Unit 8, Long Beach, CA 90802

FINLEY IV, John Huston (Mass) 717 Atlantic Ave Apt 3b, Boston, MA 02111

FINLEY, Rosamond Stelle (Los) 212 W Franklin St, Tucson, AZ 85701

FINN, Anne Marie (NwT) 2630 S 11th St, Abilene, TX 79605

FINN, Emilie Aurora (Az) 13150 W Spanish Garden Dr, Sun City West, AZ 85375

FINN, Laurie Ann (Az)

FINN, Michael John (Roch) 1245 Culver Rd, Rochester, NY 14609

FINN, Patrick Shawn (WMich) 1006 3rd Street, Muskegon, MI 49440

FINN, Robert Patrick (EMich) PO Box 83, West Branch, MI 48661

FINNEGAN, Lynn Marie (RG)

FINNERUD, Margaret A (Ct) 29 Cary Rd, Riverside, CT 06878

FINNIN, Nathan McBride (EC) 4212 S Virginia Dare Trl, Nags Head, NC 27959

FIRESTINE, Susan Lee (WNY)

FIRTH, Harry Warren (WMo) 4024 W 100th Ter, Overland Park, KS 66207

FISCHBECK, Lisa (NC) 8410 Merin Rd, Chapel Hill, NC 27516

FISCHER, Alison (Episcopal SJ)

FISCHER III, Charles L (Pgh) Pittsburgh Theological Seminary, 616 N. Highland Ave., Pittsburgh, PA 15206

FISCHER, Evan (O) 127 W North St, Wooster, OH 44691

FISCHER, Ryan David (NI) PO Box 1373, Warsaw, IN 46581

FISCHER, Sara (Ore) 2800 SE Harrison Street, Portland, OR 97214

FISCHER, Sarah Motley (WA) Grace Episcopal Church, 1041 Wisconsin Ave NW, Washington, DC 20007

FISCHER-DAVIES, Clare (RI) 50 Orchard Ave, Providence, RI 02906

FISH, Cameron Hoover (CNY) 6 Canberra Ct, Mystic, CT 06355

FISH, Charles Tad Cramer (Ct) PO Box 335, Antrim, NH 03440

FISH, Gloria Hoyer (Roch) 46 Azalea Rd, Rochester, NY 14620

FISH, Sonnie Eriksen (Ct) PO Box 335, Antrim, NH 03440

FISHBECK, Nadine B (Tenn)

FISHBURNE, Donald Allston (SC) 57 Sweet Water Ct, Pawleys Island, SC 29585

FISHER, Barbara Anne (Ind)

FISHER, David (Chi) 1012 Churchill Dr, Naperville, IL 60563

✠ **FISHER**, Doug (WMass) 37 Chestnut St, Springfield, MA 01103

FISHER, Elizabeth B (WMass) PO Box 974, Millbrook, NY 12545

FISHER, Ernest Wilkin (SwFla) 550 1st Ave S Apt 514, #514, Saint Petersburg, FL 33701

FISHER, James Alfred (NJ) 15 Maple Street, South Seaville, NJ 08246

✠ **FISHER**, Jeff (Tex) 2695 S Southwest Loop 323, Tyler, TX 75701

FISHER, Jerry William (NC) 5450 Trinity Landing Way Apt 346, Wilmington, NC 28409

FISHER, Jill Carmen (ETenn) 1175 Pineville Rd Apt 85, Chattanooga, TN 37405

FISHER, John Coale (SC) 8244 Crooked Creek Ln, Edisto Island, SC 29438

FISHER, Joy (Ga) 147 SouthSecond Street, Cochran, GA 31014

FISHER, Julie Blake (SO) 410 W Chestnut St, Oxford, OH 45056

FISHER, Margaret (Spok) 522 W Park Pl, Spokane, WA 99205

FISHER, Mary Carlton (The Episcopal NCal) 72 Mill Creek Dr, Willits, CA 95490

FISHER, Paige Ford (Mass) 206 Clarendon St, Boston, MA 02116

FISHER, Richard Lingham (WNC) 175 Vinal St, Rockport, ME 04856

FISHER, Robert William (WA)

FISHER, Ronald Spencer (Md) 24 Evergreen Trail, Severna Park, MD 21146

FISHER JR, Russell Ellsworth (Tex) Po Box 192, Santa Anna, TX 76878

FISHER, Sarah (At) 4755 N Peachtree Rd, Atlanta, GA 30338

FISHER, Scott Owen (Ak) PO Box 10153, Fairbanks, AK 99710

FISHER, William A (Ct) 200 Elk Run Dr, Basalt, CO 81621

FISHER-STEWART, Gayle Antoinette (WA) 820 6th St NE, Washington, DC 20002

FISHWICK, Jeffrey Palmer (Va) 1260 River Chase Ln, Charlottesville, VA 22901

FISKE, Thomas W (U) 123 Linden Ave, Fairmont, MN 56031

FITTZ, Joan Ellen (Ct)

FITZGERALD, Joseph Michael (Az) 2288 W Silverbell Tree Dr, Tucson, AZ 85745

FITZGERALD, Todd (Ct) St Stephens School, 6528 Saint Stephens Dr, Austin, TX 78746

FITZGIBBONS, Michael John (Spok) 8505 W Hood Ave, Kennewick, WA 99336

FITZGIBBONS, Sabeth S (Oly) 1706 NW 60th St, Seattle, WA 98107

FITZHUGH, Bobbe Kay (Wyo) PO Box 1419, Douglas, WY 82633

FITZHUGH, Mark Lee (LI) 325 Lattingtown Rd, Locust Valley, NY 11560

FITZPATRICK, Michael Carl (Mich) 24699 Grand River Ave, Detroit, MI 48219

FITZPATRICK, Robert (NJ) Grace Episcopal Church, 7 E Maple Ave, Merchantville, NJ 08109

✠ **FITZPATRICK**, Robert LeRoy (The Episcopal Church in Haw) Episcopal Diocese Of Hawaii, 229 Queen Emma Sq, Honolulu, HI 96813

FITZSIMMONS, Daniel (Be) 16 Allenberry Dr, Wilkes Barre, PA 18706

FITZSIMMONS, James (Az) 1741 North Camino Rebecca, Nogales, AZ 85621

FLAGSTAD, Judith Marie (SD) 101 W Prospect Ave Apt 3, Pierre, SD 57501

FLAHERTY, Jane (SVa) 614 E 7th St, Alton, IL 62002

FLAHERTY, Jessica Barbara (Mass)

FLAHERTY, Philip John (Mass) 44 Park Ave, Whitman, MA 02382

FLAK, Maureen (NC)

FLAMINIO, Robert Joseph (NMich)

FLANAGAN, Carol Cole (WA) St Barnabas Episcopal Church, 4801 Ravensworth Rd, Annandale, VA 22003

FLANAGAN, Jakki Renee (Ct)

FLANAGAN, Michael P (USC) 104 Brockman Dr, Mauldin, SC 29662

FLANAGAN, Robert D (NY) PO Box 267, Bridgewater, CT 06752

FLANDERS, Alden Beaman (Mass) 145 Weyland Cir, North Andover, MA 01845

FLANDERS JR, James W (WA) 3714 Harrison St Nw, Washington, DC 20015

FLANDERS, Susan (WA) Susan Flanders, 3714 Harrison St NW, Washington, DC 20015

FLECK, Timothy R (SeFla) 5401 Banyan Dr, Coral Gables, FL 33156

FLEENER SR, William Joseph (WMich) 297 W Clay Ave Apt 214, Muskegon, MI 49440

FLEENOR, David (LI) 4310 48th Ave Apt 2f, Woodside, NY 11377

FLEENOR, Ryan (Ct) 27 Rings End Rd, Darien, CT 06820

FLEETWOOD, Zachary William Maddrey (Eur) 4418 Slate River Mill Rd, Dillwyn, VA 23936

FLEISCHER, Marie M (NC) 118 Leonard Ave, Newton, NC 28658

FLEISCHER, Scott (USC) 2827 Wheat St, Columbia, SC 29205

FLEISCHMAN, Donald M (Mil) 297 N Main St, Richland Center, WI 53581

FLEMING, Carol (SwFla) 70865 Wayne St, Union, MI 49130

FLEMING, Christie Shelburne (WLa) PO Box 52, Bastrop, LA 71221

FLEMING, Joan (NJ) 183 Hartley Ave., Princeton, NJ 08540

FLEMING, Linda Lee (Wyo) St Paul's Episcopal Church, PO Box 68, Dixon, WY 82323

FLEMING JR, Peter Wallace (SwFla) 1 Beach Dr SE Apt 2214, Saint Petersburg, FL 33701

FLEMING JR, Raymond Edgar (Los) 484 Cliff Dr Apt 10, Laguna Beach, CA 92651

FLEMISTER, Ernestein (Ore) 212 W Idlewild Ave, Tampa, FL 33604

FLEMMING, Leslie (SO) 1 Kent Dr, Athens, OH 45701

FLENTJE, Gregory Laurence (WMich) 4210 Honey Creek Ave Ne, Ada, MI 49301

FLES, Jacob C (Me) 2 Dresden Ave, Gardiner, ME 04345

FLETCHER, Margaret Ann Laurie (Vt) St Peters Episcopal Church, 300 Pleasant St, Bennington, VT 05201

FLETCHER JR, Richard James (WTenn) 108 N King Ave, Dyersburg, TN 38024

FLETCHER, Wayne Alexander (WLa) 500 Edgewood Dr, Pineville, LA 71360

FLETT, Carol Ann (WA) 34002 Darlington St, Lewes, DE 19958

FLEXER, Katharine Grace (NY) 225 W 99th St, New York, NY 10025

FLICK, Robert Terry (Tex) 1410 Cambridge Dr, Friendswood, TX 77546

FLINN, Erin Leigh Lapham (Ct)

FLINT, Grace A (LI)

FLINTOM, Jack Glenn (Md) 2030 Marshall Ln, Hayes, VA 23072

FLOBERG, John (ND) PO Box 612, Fort Yates, ND 58538

FLOBERG, Sloane (ND) 820 West Central Ave, Bismarck, ND 58501

FLOCKEN, Robin (CNY) 1721 Stanley Rd, Cazenovia, NY 13035

FLOOD, Dr Charles TA (Pa) 7 E Knight Ave, Collingswood, NJ 08108

FLOOD, James Andrew (CFla)

FLORES, Katherine Doris (Wyo) 4700 S Poplar St, Casper, WY 82601

FLORES, Santos (Los) Maravillas 606, Col Guillen, Piedras Negras, Colombia

FLORY, Phyllis Brannon (WK) 1551 Briargate Dr, Salina, KS 67401

FLOWERS JR, James Byrd (CGC)

FLOWERS JR, James Edgar (WLa) 946 Ockley Dr, Shreveport, LA 71106

FLOWERS, Lauren F (Ga) 3 Ridge Rd, Savannah, GA 31405

FLOWERS, Mary Miller (WA)

FLOYD, Donna (Tenn)

FLOYD, Michael Hinnant (DomRep) 5505 Stuart Cir Unit B, Austin, TX 78721

FLOYD, Michael Stephen (O) 120 Ohio St, Huron, OH 44839

FLOYD, Peter M (NC) 7408 Tudor Rd, Colorado Springs, CO 80919

FLOYD, Peter Winslow (Ct) 18 Hidden Lake Rd, Higganum, CT 06441

FLOYD, Theresa Ann (Ore) 4177 Nw Thatcher Rd, Forest Grove, OR 97116

FLY, David Kerrigan (Mo) 4400 Lindell Blvd Apt 11n, Saint Louis, MO 63108

FLYNN, Anne Regina (Kan) 21 Copperfield Ln, Charleston, IL 61920

FLYNN, Peggy Rishel (Kan)

FLYNN, Timothy (Mich)

FODOR, Luke (WNY) 410 N Main St, Jamestown, NY 14701

FOERSTER III, Frederick Henry (CNY) 183 Capn Crosby Rd, Centerville, MA 02632

FOGELQUIST, Albin Hilding (Spok) 1307 Regents Blvd Apt D, Fircrest, WA 98466

FOISIE, Dawn Ann Campbell (Oly) 5757 Solomons Island Rd, Lothian, MD 20711

FOISIE, Stephen D (Oly) 228 Wall St, Camano Island, WA 98282

FOLEY, Kristen Claire (NJ) 375 Brook Ave, North Plainfield, NJ 07062

FOLEY, Michael (Los) 5700 Forbes Ave, Pittsburgh, PA 15217

FOLEY, Theodore Archer (NJ) Christ Church, 415 Washington St, Toms River, NJ 08753

✠ **FOLTS**, James Edward (WTex) PO Box 6885, San Antonio, TX 78209

✠ **FOLTS**, Jonathan H (SD) Episcopal Diocese Of South Dakota, 408 N Jefferson Ave, Pierre, SD 57501

FOLTS, Kimberly S (SD) 40 Main St, Essex, CT 06426

FOLTZ, Marvin Lee (Mo) 600 S Dearborn St Apt 301, Apt 301, Chicago, IL 60605

FONCREE, Rose Mary Ivas (Miss) 4526 Meadow Hill Road, Jackson, MS 39206

FONDER SR, Kim Michael (SD) Holy Comforter/Messiah, PO Box 242, Lower Brule, SD 57548

FONES, Peter Alden (Ore) 1405 Ashworth Drive, Cedar Falls, IA 50613

FONT SANCHEZ, William (Okla)

FOOSE, Elizabeth Boutwell (Miss) 6697 Bee Lake Rd, Tchula, MS 39169

FOOTE, Beth Lind (Cal) 705 Grand St, Alameda, CA 94501

FOOTE, Margaret Lloyd Foster (Cal) 255 Best Ave, San Leandro, CA 94577

FOOTE, Roger (SO) 7 E Interwood Pl, Cincinnati, OH 45220

FOOTE, Stephen Williams (Me) 574 Turner Rd, Bremen, ME 04551

FORAKER, Greg (Colo) The Episcopal Church in Colorado, 1300 N Washington St, Denver, CO 80203

FORAKER-THOMPSON, Jane (Nev) P.O. Box 2665, Gardnerville, NV 89410

FORBES, Elizabeth Faye (Ga) 3321 Wheeler Rd, Augusta, GA 30909

FORBES, Mark S (Ala) 156 Lavender Bloom Loop, Mooresville, NC 28115

FORBES, Michael Philip (Minn) 402 31st St Ne Apt 224, Rochester, MN 55906

FORD, Berkley (SVa) 140 Mariners Way, Moyock, NC 27958

FORD, Charles Allan (NY) 205 Stone Rd, West Hurley, NY 12491

FORD, Cheri Lynn (NMich) Rr 2 Box 939-A, Newberry, MI 49868

FORD, Denis B (Colo) 3231 Olive St., Jacksonville, FL 32207

FORD, Janice Celeste (WMass)

FORD, Joann (Colo) 3231 Olive St, Jacksonville, FL 32207

FORD, John Mark (Ala) 90 Gibson Rd, Asheville, NC 28804

FORD, Larry (Oly) PO Box 3276, Bellevue, WA 98009

FORD, Linda Alexander (Tex) 3807 Tanglewood Dr, Bryan, TX 77802

FORD, Richard Barlow (Cal) 2165 West Dry Creek Road, Healdsburg, CA 95448

FORD, Steven E (NMich) Rr 2 Box 939-A, Newberry, MI 49868

FOREMAN JR, Harold Vandon (Ala) 3013 Boundary Oaks Dr SE, Owens Cross Roads, AL 35763

FORESMAN, R Scott (Ia) Po Box 306, Bishop, CA 93515

FORHAN, Carol Lynn (Spok) 9327 E Leavenworth Rd, Leavenworth, WA 98826

FORINASH JR, Joseph Lynn (Colo) PO Box 1026, Eagle, CO 81631

FORMAN, John P (Oly) 1005 S.W. 152nd Street, Burien, WA 98166

FORNALIK, Barbara Horn (Roch) 1130 Webster Rd, Webster, NY 14580

FORNARO, Frank (Mass) 11 Alaska Ave, Bedford, MA 01730

FORNEA, Stanley Wayne (EC) 2111 Jefferson Davis Hwy, Apt 603S, Arlington, VA 22202

FORNEY, John C (Los) 316 W Green St., Claremont, CA 91711

FORREST, Elizabeth Louise (Mass) 41 Hall Ave, Watertown, MA 02472

FORREST, Marlene Eudora (Va) 1309 N 31st St, Richmond, VA 23223

FORREST, William (FdL) 56500 Abbey Rd, Three Rivers, MI 49093

FORREST, William Clifford (Az) 24922 S Lakewood Dr, Sun Lakes, AZ 85248

FORRESTER, Shelley (Okla) St Andrews Church, PO Box 1256, Lawton, OK 73502

FORSHAW, Lee (Ct) 2000 Main St, Stratford, CT 06615

FORSHEY, Susan Lynn (Ia)

FORSYTHE, Margaret Ann Kroy (NJ) 687 Donald Dr S, Bridgewater, NJ 08807

FORSYTHE, Mary Louise (Neb) 420 Shorewood Ln, Waterloo, NE 68069

FORTE, Jeanne (The Episcopal NCal) 700 Wellfleet Dr, Vallejo, CA 94591

FORTI, Nicholas (Va) 1700 University Ave, Charlottesville, VA 22903

FORTNER, Jason (Ind)

FORTNER, Marian Dulaney (Miss) 301 S 21st Ave, Hattiesburg, MS 39401

FORTUNA, Lisa (Cal) Christ Church Iglesia San Juan, 1220 River St, Hyde Park, MA 02136

FORTUNA, Virgilio (Mass) 2112 County St, Somerset, MA 02726

FORTUNATO, Susan (NY) 82 Ehrhardt Rd, Pearl River, NY 10965

FOSS, Charlie (USC) 1646 SW Spence Ave, Troutdale, OR 97060

FOSTER III, Andrew (NY) 790 Plymouth Rd, Claremont, CA 91711

FOSTER, Craig A (SO) 508 Thistle Dr, Delaware, OH 43015

FOSTER, Katharine K (SO) 7919 N Coolville Ridge Rd, Athens, OH 45701

FOSTER JR, Kenneth Earl (Mil) 418 Valley Dr, Wisconsin Dells, WI 53965

FOSTER, Margaret Reidpath (WNY) 088 Delaware Ave Apt 5a, Buffalo, NY 14209

FOSTER, Pamela Lamotte (Mass) 19 Warren Point Rd, Wareham, MA 02571

FOSTER, Penelope Hope (WNY) 54 Delaware Rd, Kenmore, NY 14217

FOSTER, Randal Arthur (NC) 105 Pettingill Pl, Southern Pines, NC 28387

FOSTER, Simon (LI) 808 Driggs Ave Apt 5B, Brooklyn, NY 11211

FOSTER, Steve Leslie (LI) 13728 144th St, Rosedale, NY 11422

FOSTER, Todd E (NJ)

FOSTER, Willis Renard (SVa) 6303 Ashcrest Ct, Suffolk, VA 23435

FOTCH JR, Charlton Harvey (Cal) 681 S Eliseo Dr, Greenbrae, CA 94904

FOTINOS, Dennis George (Tex) 248 Birchbark Dr., Mills River, NC 28759

FOUGHTY, Donna (Mass) 10 Samuels Path, Harwich, MA 02645

FOUKE, Scherry Vickery (ETenn) 1601 Forest Dr, Morristown, TN 37814

FOULKE, Mary (NY) 521 W 126th St, New York, NY 10027

FOUNTAIN, Timothy L (SD) 2707 W. 33rd St, Sioux Falls, SD 57105

FOUT, Jason A (SO) 161 S Cassady Ave, Bexley, OH 43209

FOUTS, Guy (WA) 603 Ramapo Ave, Pompton Lakes, NJ 07442

FOWLE, Elizabeth Heller (WMass) 15 Old Hancock Rd, Hancock, NH 03449

FOWLER, Anne Carroll (Mass) 39 Prospect Street, Portland, ME 04103

FOWLER, Connetta Bertrand (NwT) 430 Dallas St, Big Spring, TX 79720

FOWLER, Daniel Lewis (Oly) 4335 NE Rhodes End Rd, Bainbridge Island, WA 98110

FOWLER III, Robert (Ala) St Margaret's Episcopal Church, 606 Newnan St, Carrollton, GA 30117

FOWLER, Stanley Gordon (Oly) 111 NE 80th St, Seattle, WA 98115

FOWLER IV, William Young (Tex) PO Box 292, Buda, TX 78610

FOWLKES, Tyrone (NC) 530 W Fullerton Pkwy, Chicago, IL 60614

FOX, Brian Francis (WTex)

FOX, Carol Rogers (NY) 312 West 22nd Street, New York, NY 10011

FOX, Cheryl Lynn (Az) 5000 E Palomino Ln Unit 27, Flagstaff, AZ 86004

FOX, David Coblentz (Okla) 2455 Sulpher Creek St, Cody, WY 82414

FOX, Don (Cal) 185 Baltimore Way, San Francisco, CA 94112

FOX III, Frederick Carl (Nwk) 441 Lockhart Mountain Rd # U 4, Lake George, NY 12845

FOX, Jedediah Wynn (Oly) 19649 15th Ave NE, Shoreline, WA 98155

FOX, Loren Charles (CFla) Tang-Lin, Minden Road, 248816, Singapore

FOX, Matthew Timothy (Cal) 287 17th St Ste 400, Oakland, CA 94612

FOX, R. Steven (U) 6230 Hyderabad Pl., Dulles, VA 20189

FOX, Richard George (Mil) S 24 W 26835 Apache Pass, Waukesha, WI 53188

FOX, Ronald Napoleon (SeFla) 3464 Oak Ave, Miami, FL 33133

FOX, Stephanie Donaldson (La) New Orleans, 1500 Cadiz St, New Orleans, LA 70115

FOX, Susann (Pa) 76 S Forge Manor Dr, Phoenixville, PA 19460

FOX SR, Wesley D (ND) Hc 2 Box 176, Garrison, ND 58540

FOXWORTH, George Marion (The Episcopal NCal) 4338 Walali Way, Fair Oaks, CA 95628

FOXX, Nelson (Mass) 397 Putnam Ave., Cambridge, MA 02139

✠ **FRADE**, Leo (SeFla) 525 NE 15th St, Miami, FL 33132

FRAIOLI, Karen Ann (Mass) 20 Rhodes Ave, Sharon, MA 02067

FRALEY, Anne (Ct) 109 Sand Hill Rd, South Windsor, CT 06074

FRALEY, Patricia (Mich)

FRANCE JR, Andrew Menaris (CPa) 651 Harding Ave, Williamsport, PA 17701

FRANCIS SR, Alric H (Episcopal VI) PO Box 7974, Christiansted, VI 00823

FRANCIS, Desmond (Alb) 2011 Trotter Ln, Bloomington, IL 61704

FRANCIS, James Woodcock (Mich) 1404 Joliet Pl, Detroit, MI 48207

FRANCIS, John Robert (Be) PO Box 1094, 435 Court St, Reading, PA 19603

FRANCIS, Mary Jane Jane (Oly) 725 9th Ave Apt 2109, Seattle, WA 98104

FRANCKS, Robert (NY) 360 W 21st St, New York, NY 10011

FRANCO ESTEVEZ, Juan Bautista (PR) Ch Tec Pr, PO Box 902, Saint Just, PR 00978

FRANCOIS, Yvan (Hai) Box 1309, Port-Au-Prince, Haiti

FRANK, Anna (Ak) 1578 Bridgewater Dr, Fairbanks, AK 99709

FRANK, Richard Lloyd (U) 13640 N 21st Ave, Phoenix, AZ 85029

FRANK, Travis (Ark) 400 Hill St, Forrest City, AR 72335

FRANK JR, William George (Va) 11 Wakefield Dr Apt 2004, Asheville, NC 28803

FRANKEN, Robert Anton (Colo) 101 E Main St Unit 204, PO Box 2073, Frisco, CO 80443

FRANKFURT, Dawn M (Kan) 3750 E Douglas Ave, Wichita, KS 67208

FRANK-HAND, Kathleen (Chi)

FRANKLIN, Ann (Mass) 143 Gillespie Circle, Brevard, NC 28712

FRANKLIN, Beth (Va) 301 E 8th St, Austin, TX 78701

FRANKLIN III, James (NC) Young Adult Ministry, PO Box 7204, Winston Salem, NC 27109

✠ **FRANKLIN**, Ralph William (WNY) 1064 Brighton Road, Tonawanda, NY 14150

FRANKLIN, Sally (USC) 7128 Caggy Ln, Fort Mill, SC 29707

FRANKLIN-VAUGHN, Robyn (WA) 319 Bryant St NE, Washington, DC 20002

FRANKS, Laurence Edward Alexander (FdL) 299 Corey St, Boston, MA 02132

FRANSON, Marna (NMich)

FRANTZ-DALE, Heidi Hallett (NH) 247 Pound Road, Madison, NH 03849

FRANZ, Marcia Wheatley (NMich)

FRASER, Ann (WTex) St Pauls Episcopal Church, PO Box 1225, Corinth, MS 38835

FRASER, Richard Trent (Colo) 1400 S University Blvd, Denver, CO 80210

FRASER, Thomas A (Chi) 60 Akenside Rd, Riverside, IL 60546

FRASER-MORRIS, Peter Zvarych (Va)

FRAUSTO, Nancy Aide (Los) 12800 Harrisglenn Dr Apt 227, Austin, TX 78753

FRAZELLE, David (NC) 304 E Franklin St, Chapel Hill, NC 27514

FRAZER, Candice Burk (Ala) St Johns Episcopal Church, 113 Madison Ave, Montgomery, AL 36104

FRAZIER, Brittany Bjurstrom (Los)

FRAZIER, John (EC) 5324 Bluewater Pl, Fayetteville, NC 28311

FRAZIER, Jonathan E (WMo) 422 W 111th Ter, Kansas City, MO 64114

FRAZIER, Mark William (SwVa) 6030 Catawba Creek Road, Troutville, VA 24175

FRAZIER, Raymond Malcom (SwFla) 8017 Fountain Ave, Tampa, FL 33615

FREARSON, Andrew Richard (At) 3136 Lynnray Dr, Doraville, GA 30340

FREDERIC, Eliot Garrison (Eas) 51 Columbine Ave N, Hampton Bays, NY 11946

FREDERICK, Jessica L (WNY)

FREDERICK, John Bassett Moore (Ct) 32 Chestnut St, Princeton, NJ 08542

FREDERICK, Robert John (Md) 1930 Brookdale Rd, Baltimore, MD 21244

FREDERICK, Sherman Richardson (Nev) 2724 Brienza Way, Las Vegas, NV 89117

FREDERICK, Warren (WMass) 19 Rydal St, Worcester, MA 01602

FREDERIKSEN III, Victor (EC) PO Box 7672, Wilmington, NC 28406

FREDHOLM, Everett Leonard (Tex) 201 Nicholas Dr, Asheville, NC 28806

FREDIE JR, Julian Von Kessel (Mass)

FREDRICK, Lawrence Edward (EO) 1220 Tasman Dr Spc 1k, Sunnyvale, CA 94089

FREDRICKSON, David A (Vt) 149 Court Street, Plymouth, MA 02360

FREDRICKSON, Mark Alan (Neb)

FREE JR, Horace D (NY) PO Box 125, Johns Island, SC 29457

FREEBERN, Douglas Wayne (Okla) 210 E 9th St, Bartlesville, OK 74003

FREEMAN, Ashley B (CGC)

FREEMAN, Bruce A (Los) 2944 Erie Ave, Cincinnati, OH 45208

FREEMAN JR, De (CGC) St James Church, 860 N Section St, Fairhope, AL 36532

FREEMAN, Diana G (Dal) 6400 Stonebrook Pkwy, Frisco, TX 75034

FREEMAN, John (WTenn)

FREEMAN, Karen Lynn (The Episcopal NCal) 1405 Kentucky St, Fairfield, CA 94533

FREEMAN, Leonard Wilbur (Minn) 190 Cygnet Pl, Long Lake, MN 55356

FREEMAN, Lindsay Hardin (Minn) 190 Cygnet Pl, Long Lake, MN 55356

FREEMAN JR, Norman (Los) St Georges Church And Academy, 23802 Avenida de la Carlota, Laguna Hills, CA 92653

FREEMAN, Sarah (Colo) 726 W Elati Cir, Littleton, CO 80120

FREEMAN, Sollace Mitchell (At) 5194 Glenstone Ct, Gainesville, GA 30504

FREEMAN, TJ (NI) 611 W Berry St, Fort Wayne, IN 46802

FREES, Mooydeen Claire (SO) 3826 Portrush Way, Amelia, OH 45102

FREGEAU, Stephen Alfred (Mass) 3798 NW Adriatic Ln, Jensen Beach, FL 34957

FREGOSO, Krista (Cal) 345 Pimlico, Walnut Creek, CA 94597

FREIRE-SOLORZANO, Luis Hernan (EcuC) Barrio El Tambo, Sector Bomba De Aqua, Pelileo, 24, Ecuador

FRENCH, Alan C (NJ) 237 Summer Winds Cir, Aiken, SC 29803

FRENCH, Clarke (NC) 814 Churchill Dr, Chapel Hill, NC 27517

FRENCH, Dick (Oly) 23500 Cristo Rey Dr Unit 520G, Cupertino, CA 95014

FRENCH, Jonathan D (CFla) 2304 SE 12th St, Ocala, FL 34471

FRENCH, Peter (NJ) 53 University Pl., Princeton, NJ 08540

FRENCH, Sally (NC) 200 W Morgan St Ste 300, Suite 300, Raleigh, NC 27601

FRENS, Mary Jean (WMich) 934 Clubview Dr, Fremont, MI 49412

FREY, Louane Florence Virgilio (NC) 801 Footbridge Pl, Cary, NC 27519

FREY, Matthew V (Colo) PO Box 1593, Granby, CO 80446

FREY, Paul Anthony (WTex) 139 Kentucky St, Laredo, TX 78041

FRIAS, Miguel (Chi) 941 W Lawrence Ave, Chicago, IL 60640

FRIBOURGH, Cindy (Ark) 11123 Bainbridge Dr, Little Rock, AR 72212

FRICK, Matthew M (Dal) 718 S Prairieville St, Athens, TX 75751

FRIDAY, Rawlin (Wyo)

FRIDAY, Roxanne L (Wyo)

FRIEDEL, James (WTex) 11905 E Maple Dr, Claremore, OK 74019

FRIEDMAN, Anna Russell (Ala) PO Box 27, Minter, AL 36761

FRIEDMAN, Maurice Lane (WTex) 7958 Schaefer Crst, Breinigsville, PA 18031

FRIEDRICH, James Louis (Los) 4685 Taylor Ave Ne, Bainbridge Island, WA 98110

FRIEND, Robert Douglas (Va) 4011 College Valley Ct, Richmond, VA 23233

FRIESE JR, Walter Edward (WLa) 107 Shady Ave, Pineville, LA 71360

FRINK, James Phillip (RI) 3a Grouse Trl, Smithfield, RI 02917

FRISCH, Floyd Charles (ECR) 2 N Santa Cruz Ave, Los Gatos, CA 95030

FRITCH, Charles Oscar (CFla) 324 S Lost Lake Ln, Casselberry, FL 32707

FRITCH, Michelle (At) 10900 Wittenridge Dr Unit 16, Alpharetta, GA 30022

FRITSCH, Andrew John (WMo) 3702 Poplar Dr, Joplin, MO 64804

FRITSCH, Peter (Ore) 6310 W Ford Ave, Las Vegas, NV 89139

FRITSCHE, Janet Yvonne (NMich) 122 Hunter Rd, Iron River, MI 49935

FRITSCHNER, Annie (WNC) 110 Country Ridge Rd, Hendersonville, NC 28739

FRITSCHNER, John (Ky) Church of the Advent, 901 Baxter Ave, Louisville, KY 40204

FRITTS, Julia Anne (Md) 702 Brookwood Rd, Baltimore, MD 21229

FRITZ, Janice Vary (CPa) 109 Hope Dr, Boiling Springs, PA 17007

FRITZ, Susan C (WA) 372 Buckeye Circle, La Plata, MD 20646

FRIZZELL, Judith Ann (Dal) 5200 Fairway Circle, Granbury, TX 76049

FRNKA, Virginia H (WTex) 314 W Gayle St, Edna, TX 77957

FROEHLICH, Burt H (SeFla) 406-B Coopers Cove Rd, St Augustine, FL 32095

FROEHLICH, Meghan F (O) Presiding Bishops Staff, 815 2nd Ave, New York, NY 10017

FROILAND, Paul Vincent (Minn) 12525 Porcupine Ct, Eden Prairie, MN 55344

FROLICK, Betty Roberson (NI) 3360 Riverside Ct, Canton, MI 48188

FROLICK, Paul (CNY) St Matthews Episcopal Chruch, 900 Vine St, Liverpool, NY 13088

FROMBERG, Paul D (Cal) 500 De Haro Street, San Francisco, CA 94107

FRONTJES, Rich (Chi) 910 Normal Rd, DeKalb, IL 60115

FROST, Edward David James (NH)

FROST, Gregory Hayden (Los) 18354 Superior St, Northridge, CA 91325

FROST, Jeffrey Louis (Cal) Saint Timothy's Church, 1550 Diablo Rd, Danville, CA 94526

FROST-PHILLIPS, Lisa (NC) 128 Creekview Cir, Carrboro, NC 27510

FROTHINGHAM, Christen Struthers (Mass) 6 Sunset Ave, North Reading, MA 01864

FROYEN, Jeremy C (Chi) St John the Evangelist, 2640 Park Dr, Flossmoor, IL 60422

FRUEHWIRTH, Robert Alan (NC) 66 Ella Road, Norwich, NR1 4BS, Great Britain (UK)

FRY, Gwenneth Jeri (Ark) 1200 Washington Rd, Waldoboro, ME 0457

FRY, Lisa (Me) 1000 N Mississippi St, Little Rock, AR 72207

FRY III, William Nall (WTenn) 10 N Highland St, Memphis, TN 38111

FRYE, Don Jay (Chi) 2843 Gypsum Cir, Naperville, IL 60564

FRYE, Linda Lou (Eau) 21836 Gladestone Ave, Tomah, WI 54660

FULFORD, David Edward (NwPa)

FULGHUM, Peter Clopper (Md) 13007 Still Meadow Rd, Smithsburg, MD 21783

FULGONI, Dina Loreen (Los) PO Box 1681, Big Bear Lake, CA 92315

FULK, Michael Thomas (WTex) 909 S Darling St, Angola, IN 46703

FULKS, William B (Pa) 112 Elite Hts, Hurricane, WV 25526

FULLER, Betty WL Works (WTex) 823 S Water St Apt 3g, Corpus Christi, TX 78401

FULLER, Edward Beaty (At) 3826 Courtyard Drive, Atlanta, GA 30339

FULLER JR, Frank (WLa)

FULLER III, Frank E (Tex) 823 S Water St Apt 3g, Corpus Christi, TX 78401

FULLER, Glen C (WNY)

FULLER, Jan (SwVa) 2247 Saddle Club Rd, Burlington, NC 27215

FULLER, Lynnette (NJ) 10085 State Road 156, Patriot, IN 47038

FULLER SR, Steven George (Vt) 10 South St # 5101, Bellows Falls, VT 05101

FULLER, Walter Harry (LI) 1692 Bellmore Ave, North Bellmore, NY 11710

FULLMER, Janet (Colo) 1700 Esther Way, The Dalles, OR 97058

FULOP, Timothy Earl (SVa)

FULTON, Bill (Oly) 32 NE Tracy Hill Way, Bremerton, WA 98311

FULTON III, Charles Newell (NY) 815 2nd Ave, New York, NY 10017

FULTON, Jennifer (NI)

FULTON, John Gary (EC) 307 North Main St, Farmville, NC 27828

FULTON, Nancy Casey (WMich) 807 South University, Mt Pleasant, MI 48858

FULTON, Norman Hamilton (NY) Macaulay Road, Rd #2, Katonah, NY 10536

FULTON, Sharline Alahverde (Pa) 1207 Foulkeways, Gwynedd, PA 19436

FUNK, Jeffrey Lawrence (Be) 46 S Laurel St, Hazleton, PA 18201

FUNK, Kathyleen Allen (Nev) PO Box 1385, Pahrump, NV 89041

FUNK, Nicholas (Dal) 8320 Jack Finney Blvd, Greenville, TX 75402

FUNKHOUSER, David Franklin (Pa) 456 66th St, Oakland, CA 94609

FUNSTON, Charles Eric (O) St Pauls Episcopal Church, 317 E Liberty St, Medina, OH 44256

FUNSTON, Patrick Patrick K (Kan) 3133 SW Canterbury Lane, Topeka, KS 66604

FURLONG, Angela (Md)

FURLOW, Mark D (SwVa)

FURNISS III, Robert Hosmer (Minn) 2132 Cameron Dr, Woodbury, MN 55125

FURRER, Tom (Ct) 5 Trout Dr, Granby, CT 06035

FUSSELL, Stacey Marie (NwPa) 138 Clarence St, Bradford, PA 16701

G

GABAUD, Pierre Simpson (SeFla) St Paul Et Les Martyrs Dhaiti, 6744 N Miami Ave, Miami, FL 33150

GABB, James Neil (Neb) 114 S 122nd St, Omaha, NE 68154

GABBARD, Justin E (Lex)

GABEL, Mark Francis (Fla) 5139 Marbella Isle Dr, Orlando, FL 32837

GABLE, David Lee (Nwk) 101 Bickford Ext, Avon, CT 06001

GABLE, Stephen Louis (Ind) 1045 E Sassafras Cir, 1129 Linden Dr, Bloomington, IN 47408

GABRIEL, Dani (Cal)

GADDIS, Mona Elaine (WNY) 4275 Harris Hill Rd, Williamsville, NY 14221

GADSDEN, Carol D (NY) 168 W Boston Post Rd, Mamaroneck, NY 10543

GAEDE, Lee A (Chi) 342 Custer Ave. Apt. 2, Evanston, IL 60202

GAEDE, Sarah (Ala) 830 Willingham Rd, Florence, AL 35630

GAESTEL, Bob (Los) 1100 Avenue 64, Pasadena, CA 91105

GAFFORD, Donna Elizabeth Goodman (Ala) 38 Longview Ct, Seale, AL 36875

GAFFORD, Happy Lawton (CFla) 1330 Arthur St, Orlando, FL 32804

GAFNEY, Wilda Clydette (Pa) 7301 Germantown Ave, Philadelphia, PA 19119

GAGE, Bartlett Wright (Ct) 26 Edmond St, Darien, CT 06820

GAGE, Susan Chase (Ga) 1407 St Meridian St, Tallahassee, FL 32301

GAHAGAN, Susan Elisabeth (Ga) 1802 Abercorn St, Savannah, GA 31401

GAHAN III, WIlliam Patrick (WTex) Christ Episcopal Church, 510 Belknap Pl, San Antonio, TX 78212

GAHLER, Robert Edward (NY) 67 Woodmere Rd, Stamford, CT 06905

GAILLARD, Ann (Ore)

GAINES, Elizabeth Juliet (The Episcopal NCal)

GAINES, Mary Moore Thompson (Cal) 128 Beaumont Ave, San Francisco, CA 94118

GAISER, Ted J (Me) 641 Allen Ave, Portland, ME 04103

GAITHER, Gayle Lee (Spok) 416 E Nelson Rd, Moses Lake, WA 98837

GAJDEL, Lydia (Chi)

GALAGAN, Christine Kay (Wyo) PO Box 1718, Cody, WY 82414

GALANO, Frederick (NJ)

GALANTE, Anahi T (NY) 30 Newport Pkwy Apt 304, Jersey City, NJ 07310

GALANTOWICZ, Deena McHenry (Fla) 49 Ocean Ct, Saint Augustine, FL 32080

GALAS, Veronica (Nev) 1767 Carson River Road, Carson City, NV 89701

GALAZ, Ernest M (Az) 969 W Country Club Dr, Nogales, AZ 85621

GALBREATH, Janet Louise (CFla) 01236 Miller Blvd, Fruitland Park, FL 34731

GALEANO FRANCO, Gustavo Adolfo (SeFla)

GALEY, Hilary (NMich)

GALEY, Patrick (NMich)

GALGANO, Hollis H (NY) 311 Huguenot St, New Rochelle, NY 10801

GALGANOWICZ, Henry (Pa) 1115 Country Berry Ct, Middletown, DE 19709

GALICIA, Kathie (Episcopal SJ) 3308 Swallow Dr, Modesto, CA 95356

GALINDO-PAZ, Elvia Maria (Hond)

GALIPEAU, Steven Arthur (Los) 8805 Azul Drive, West Hills, CA 91304

✠ **GALLAGHER**, Carol Joy (NY) 40 Charlotte St, Haverhill, MA 01830

GALLAGHER, Daniel P (NY) 29 Halcyon Rd, Millbrook, NY 12545

GALLAGHER, Gerald J (NY) 1001 Leesburg Dr, Leland, NC 28451

GALLAGHER, John Merrill (Cal) 212 Riviera Cir, Larkspur, CA 94939

GALLAGHER, Mary Ellen Turner (Ida) 13118 W Picadilly St, Boise, ID 83713

GALLAGHER, Nancy Elizabeth (Ore) 1800 Lakewood Ct, Spc 58, Eugene, OR 97402

GALLAGHER, Patricia Marie-Portley (Ct) 9134 Town Walk Dr, Hamden, CT 06518

GALLAGHER, Robert A (Me) 4752 41st Ave SW Apt 405, Seattle, WA 98116

GALLAGHER, Robert Joseph (Mich) 78 Nason St, Maynard, MA 01754

GALLARDO, Antonio J (Los) 132 N Euclid Ave, Pasadena, CA 91101

GALLEHER, Stephen C (Nwk) 7855 Boulevard East, 21d Apt 22k, North Bergen, NJ 07047

GALLES, Jonathan Wesley (EO)

GALLETLY, David P (Okla) 1412 W Illinois Ave, Midland, TX 79701

GALLIGAN, Joe (Wyo) PO Box 950, Thermopolis, WY 82443

GALLOWAY, David Alan (At) 845 Edgewater Dr, Atlanta, GA 30328

GALLOWAY, Denise Althea (LI) 35 Cathedral Ave, Garden City, NY 11530

GALLOWAY, Richard Kent (NC) 120 Mauldin Rd, Greenville, SC 29605

GALLOWAY, Sarah (Tex) 7002 Rusty Fig Dr, Austin, TX 78750

GALLUP, Deacon Dale J (Az)

GALUSZKA, Lorenzo M (Dal)
GALVIN, Kathleen M (Minn) 2242 Downing Ave, Shakopee, MN 55379
GALVIN, Mike Joseph (Ind) 9621 Claymount Ln, Fishers, IN 46037
GAMBER, Jenifer Chestora (WA) 3738 N Woodrow St, Arlington, VA 22207
GAMBLE, Deborah E (SO) 5020 Dovetail Lane, Cincinnati, OH 45223
GAMBLE, John Robert (SwFla) 1005 Sleepy Hollow Rd, Venice, FL 34285
GAMBLING, Paul (SanD) 5079 E 30th Pl, Yuma, AZ 85365
GAMBRILL, James Howard (Nwk) PO Box 1929, York Beach, ME 03910
GAME, Dick (At) Trinity Episcopal Church, 1130 First Ave, Columbus, GA 31901
GAMEZ-CARDONA, Rosa Angelica (Hond)
GAMMONS JR, Edward Babson (NJ) 7 Oak St, Warren, RI 02885
GANDARA-PEREA, Jose Roberto (Oly) PO Box 8, Eastsound, WA 98245
GANDELL, Dahn Dorann Dean (Roch) 21 Warwick Dr, Fairport, NY 14450
GANDIYA, Leonard F (Va) 5486 Saint Pauls Rd, King George, VA 22485
GANN, Judith Fara Walsman (Okla) 6335 S 72nd East Ave, Tulsa, OK 74133
GANNON, Kathleen (SeFla) 2014 Alta Meadows Ln Apt 302, Delray Beach, FL 33444
GANNON, William Sawyer (Nwk) 11 French Dr, Bedford, NH 03110
GANTER, G David (Vt) 12 Beechwood Lane, Jericho, VT 05465
GANTER-TOBACK, Gail Sage (NY) 32 Center St, New Paltz, NY 12561
GANTZ, Jay John (EMich) 10095 E Coldwater Rd, Davison, MI 48423
GARAFALO, Robert Christopher (Los) 19988 Promenade Cir, Riverside, CA 92508
GARBARINO, Harold William (Mass) 2038 Laurel Park Hwy, Laurel Park, NC 28739
GARCEAU, John Earle (Alb) 2050 N San Clemente Rd, Palm Springs, CA 92262
GARCES TORRES, Gilberto Goen (PR) Ch Tec Pr, PO Box 902, Saint Just, PR 00978
GARCIA, Carlos Alberto (EcuC)
GARCIA, Christine Joyce (Va) 1704 W Laburnum Ave, Richmond, VA 23227
GARCIA, Christopher (Md) 3090 Broomes Island Rd, The Rectory at Christ Church, Port Republic, MD 20676
GARCIA, David Allen (PR) 165 Hoyt St, Brooklyn, NY 11217
GARCIA, Emily J (Mass) 379 Hammond St, Chestnut Hill, MA 02467

GARCIA JR, Francisco J (Los) St Augustines Chapel, PO Box 6330-B, Nashville, TN 37235
GARCIA, Hope Jufiar (ECR) Po Box 3994, Salinas, CA 93912
GARCIA, Michael George (Az)
GARCIA, Ruth Anne (Oly) Grace Episcopal Church, 116 City Island Avenue, Bronx, NY 10464
GARCIA, Sixto Rafael (SeFla) 150 SW 13th Ave, Miami, FL 33135
GARCIA, Teodosio R (HB)
GARCIA-APONTE, Jorge (PR)
GARCIA CARDENAS, Pastor Elias (Colom)
GARCIA CORREA, Luis Alberto (DomRep)
GARCIA DE JESUS, Juan (PR)
GARCIA DE LOS SANTOS, Tony (DomRep) Guarionex #19, Ensanche Quisqueya, La Romana, Dominican Republic
GARCIA-JUAREZ, Jose L (Los)
GARCIA-OCAMPO, Xabo (WA) Av San Jeronimo 117, Col San Angel, Alvaro Obregon, CMX 01000, Mexico
GARCIA-PEREZ, Jose Rafael (PR)
GARCIA-TUIRAN, Carlos (SanD) 2660 Hardy Drive, Lemon Grove, CA 91945
GARD, Mary Anne (EO) 147 NW 19th Ave, Portland, OR 97209
GARDE, Mary Ann (LI) 573 Roanoke Ave, Riverhead, NY 11901
GARDNER, Anne (Mass) 718 E 8th St, Boston, MA 02127
GARDNER, Bruce Norman (Eau) 221 Twin Oak Dr, Altoona, WI 54720
GARDNER, Calvin George (SVa) 1405 Bruton Ln, Virginia Beach, VA 23451
GARDNER, Carol Hartsfield (WTenn) 215 Windsor Terrace Dr, Nashville, TN 37221
GARDNER, Daniel Wayne (EO) 571 Yakima St S, Vale, OR 97918
GARDNER, Edward Morgan (WNC) 1045 Jamestown Road, Williamsburg, VA 23185
✠ **GARDNER**, Elizabeth (Va) St Johns Church, 6715 Georgetown Pike, Mclean, VA 22101
GARDNER, Este (NY) 1105 High Ct, Berkeley, CA 94708
GARDNER, E Ugene Clifton (Dal) 6505 Brook Lake Dr., Dallas, TX 75248
GARDNER, Harry Huey (Ala) 1910 12th Ave S, Birmingham, AL 35205
GARDNER III, James Wynn (Ala) 61 Gramercy Park N Apt 201, New York, NY 10010
GARDNER, Joan (ECR) 1970 Cerra Vista Dr, Hollister, CA 95023
GARDNER, John (Pa) Ascension Holy Trinity, 420 W 18th St, Pueblo, CO 81003
GARDNER, Mark William (Los) 1031 Lanza Ct, San Marcos, CA 92078

GARDNER, Randal B (Cal) PO Box 2375, 2416 Pine Ridge Dr, Gearhart, OR 97138
GARDNER-SMITH, Fran (Va) 1588 Moorings Dr Apt 2c, Reston, VA 20190
GARFIELD, Elizabeth Ann (Colo) St Luke's Episcopal Church, 1270 Poplar St, Denver, CO 80220
GARFIELD, Elizabeth C (CFla)
GARFIELD, Liston (Ala) 2060 Mohican Dr, Auburn, AL 36879
GARGIULO, Mariano (Nwk) 384 Hilltop Ave # 7605, Leonia, NJ 07605
GARLAND III, John G (Chi) 251 E Lake Brantley Dr, Longwood, FL 32779
GARMA, Joann Marie (La) 1014 Marigny Ave, Mandeville, LA 70448
GARMAN, Cynthia (Mich) 426 Cottonwood Ln, Saline, MI 48176
GARNER, Evan D (Ark) 2319 N Covington Park Blvd, Fayetteville, AR 72703
GARNER, Jeffery Ray (CGC)
GARNER, Terry (Mil) 10328 N Stanford Dr, Mequon, WI 53097
GARNER-FRIEL, Mary P (Eas) 302 S Liberty St, Centreville, MD 21617
GARNETT, Andrew M (LI)
GARNIER, Maryellen (The Episcopal NCal) 1800 Wildcat Blvd, Rocklin, CA 95765
GARNO, Arthur S (Alb) 13 High St, Delhi, NY 13753
GARNO, Scott (Alb) Po Box 537, Unadilla, NY 13849
GARNSEY, Elizabeth H (NY) St Marks Episcopal Church, 1 Hampton Ln, New Canaan, CT 06840
GARRAMONE, Laurie Marie (Alb) 28 S. Market Street, Johnstown, NY 12095
GARRATT, Steve (Oly) 19247 40th Pl NE, Lake Forest Park, WA 98155
GARREN, Ben (Az)
GARRENTON, Linwood Wilson (Roch) 599 E 7th St Apt 6e, Brooklyn, NY 11218
GARRETT, David (ETenn) 515 5th St, Newport, TN 37821
GARRETT, George Kenneth (Mass) 12 Academy Ave, Fairhaven, MA 02719
GARRETT, Jane Nuckols (Vt) 206 Fairway Vlg, Leeds, MA 01053
GARRETT, Mary Ann (La) PO Box 126, Baton Rouge, LA 70821
GARRETT, Paul (Colo) 2530 Leyden St, Denver, CO 80207
✠ **GARRISON**, Michael (WNY) 207 Pineneedle Dr, Bradenton, FL 34210
GARRISON, Thomas Martin (Minn)
GARRISON, William (Los) 7056 Washington Ave, Whittier, CA 90602
GARRISON, William Brian (CFla) 212 Brevity Ln, DeLand, FL 32724
GARRITY, Clelia Pinza (CGC) 3081 Margarita Ave, Pahrump, NV 89048

GARTIN, Tom (The Episcopal NCal) Faith Episcopal Church, PO Box 966, Shingle Springs, CA 95682
GARTON, Mary Pamela (CFla) 190 Interlachen Rd, Melbourne, FL 32940
GARWOOD, Carolyn Sue (Kan)
GARWOOD, Martha Jayne (SD) 4640 Sturgis Rd Lot 49, Rapid City, SD 57702
GARZA JR, Frederico Eloy (Va) 3306 Fendall Ave, Richmond, VA 23222
GARZA LOPEZ, Carlos (Hond) Santa Maria Virgen, Bamo San Pedrito, Copan Ruinas, Copan, Honduras
GARZA SALVADOR, Sergio Danilo (Hond) San Juan Bautista, Carrizalito Copan Ruinas, Copan Ruinas, Copan, Honduras
GARZON RESTREPO, Jairo Alfonso (Colom)
GASKILL JR, John Joseph (EC) 174 Windy Point Rd, Beaufort, NC 28516
GASKIN, Hershell (Cu)
GASSOUMIS, Athena Marie (RG)
GASTON, Katherine Elizabeth (Neb) 7625 Lafayette Ave, Omaha, NE 68114
GASTON III, Paul Lee (O) 2389 Brunswick Lane, Hudson, OH 44236
GASTON, Ruth (Chi)
GAT, Maggie (Nwk) 4230 Cascade Falls Dr, Sarasota, FL 34243
GATCH JR, Milton Mccormick (NY) 575 W End Ave Apt 7c, New York, NY 10024
GATELEY, Gail (Dal) 15264 SW Peachtree Dr, Tigard, OR 97224
GATES, Alan (Cal)
GATES, Alan (Mass) TEC Dio of MA, 138 Tremont St, Boston, MA 02111
GATES, Mary May (Ct) 16 Church St, Waterbury, CT 06702
GATES JR, Robert J (Okla)
GATLIN, Lonny J (O)
GATTA, Julia Milan (Ct) 243 Tennessee Ave, Sewanee, TN 37375
GATTIS, Larry R (Chi) 20326 Harding Ave, Olympia Fields, IL 60461
GATZA, Mark Francis (Md) 703 Peppard Dr, Bel Air, MD 21014
GAUMER, Susan (La) 7820 Jeannette St., New Orleans, LA 70118
GAUVIN, Joseph Henri Armand (NJ) 25 Southwood Drive, St CatharineS, ON L2M 4M5, Canada
GAVENTA, Sarah Kinney (Va)
GAVIN, Craig Edmonds (Ark) 196 Dawn Dr, Centerton, AR 72719
GAVIN, Timothy (Pa) The Episcopal Academy, 1785 Bishop White Dr, Newtown Square, PA 19073
GAVIT, Sara (Me) 2222 E Tudor Rd, Anchorage, AK 99507
GAY, Jean Ricot (SeFla) 465 NE 100th St, Miami Shores, FL 33138
GAY, Karen (La) Tec Ch Of The H Communion, PO Box 474, Plaquemine, LA 70765
GAY, Robert George (SVa) 100 W Queens Way, Hampton, VA 23669

GAYLE JR, William Gedge (La) 227 Helios Ave, Metairie, LA 70005
GAYLOR, Pamela Elaine (SO) 3149 Indian Ripple Rd, Dayton, OH 45440
GDULA, Peter Mark (CPa) St Luke's Episcopal Church, 8 E Keller St, Mechanicsburg, PA 17055
GEARS, Wallace E (Minn) 3240 Jersey Ave S, Minneapolis, MN 55426
GEDDES, Robert Douglas (Va) 269 Johnson Point Rd, Hallieford, VA 23068
GEDRICK III, John Paul (Ind) 700 Route 22, Pawling, NY 12564
GEER, Francis Hartley (NY) PO Box 158, Garrison, NY 10524
GEERDES, Patricia Seney (WVa) 900 Hillsborough St, Raleigh, NC 27603
GEFFRARD, Ricot (Hai)
GEHLSEN, Tom (Minn) 1232 Lakemoor Dr., Woodbury, MN 55129
GEHRIG, Stephen James (Oly) 1828 Field Pl NE, Renton, WA 98059
GEIB, Lanny Roland (Tex) 5087 Galileo Dr, Colorado Springs, CO 80917
GEIGER SR, Clifford T (Me) 369 Pond St Unit 307, Ashland, MA 01721
GEIGER, Martin Richard (Va) 1542 Senseny Rd, Winchester, VA 22602
GEIGER, William Linwood (Pgh)
GEISLER, Jay (Pgh) 408 Howard St, East Pittsburgh, PA 15112
GEISLER, Mark (Chi) 113 E Lafayette St, Ottawa, IL 61350
GEISLER, William Fredric (Cal) PO Box 2624, San Anselmo, CA 94979
GEISSLER-O'NEIL, Susan (Cal) 3350 Hopyard Rd, Pleasanton, CA 94588
GEITZ, Elizabeth Rankin (NJ) 431 Twin Lakes Rd, Shohola, PA 18458
GELDERT, Maurice William (RG) 121 Mescalero Tr, Ruidoso, NM 88345
GELDREICH, L Celeste (Tex) 315 W Drew St, Houston, TX 77006
GELFER, Miriam C (Mass) 689 Willow St, South Yarmouth, MA 02664
GELIEBTER, Phillip Lincoln (Pa) 4442 Frankford Ave, Phila, PA 19124
GELINEAU, Francoise (Mich) PO Box 351, Roscommon, MI 48653
GELLER, Isabel Roberts (Mass) 27 Caswell St, New Bedford, MA 02745
GELLER, Maggie (Mass) 160 Farm St, Millis, MA 02054
GELLERT, Alan Cranston (SeFla) 2303 NE Seaview Dr, Jensen Beach, FL 34957
GEMIGNANI, Michael (Tex) 1816 Dublin Dr, League City, TX 77573
GEMINDER, Randolph Jon (LI) 175 Broadway, Amityville, NY 11701
GENATO, Ann-Marie (The Episcopal NCal)
GENEREUX, Patrick Edward (Ia) 385 SE Telby Ln, Waukee, IA 50263

GENNETT JR, Paul (Del) 2415 Westwind Dr, Ames, IA 50010
GENNUSO JR, George (WLa) 500 Edgewood Dr, Pineville, LA 71360
GENSZLER, Mark (LI)
GENTLE, Judith Marie (Pgh) 315 Turnpike St, North Andover, MA 01845
GENTRY, Bryan Massey (CGC) 624 Camden Rdg, Birmingham, AL 35226
GENTRY, Keith Alan (SVa) 1107 Rockbasket Ln, Chester, VA 23836
GENTY, Marc Daniel (Colo) St Luke's Episcopal Church, 2000 Stover St, Fort Collins, CO 80525
GEORGE, Allen Winnie Sie (NY) 781 Castle Hill Ave, Bronx, NY 10473
GEORGE, Amy Martin (Ala) Grace - Saint Luke's Church, 1720 Peabody Ave, Memphis, TN 38104
GEORGE, Clarence Davis Dominic (NY) 797 Corbett Ave Apt 3, San Francisco, CA 94131
GEORGE, Eldred (Chi)
GEORGE, Erminie A (Episcopal VI) PO Box 1148, Charlotte Amalie, VI 00804
GEORGE, Jamie (WTex)
GEORGE JR, Jay Charles (WTex) 7714 Moss Brook Dr, San Antonio, TX 78255
GEORGE, Joanna Elizabeth (Dal) St Philip's Episcopal Church, 6400 Stonebrook Pkwy, Frisco, TX 75034
GEORGE, Johannes (Tex) 15325 Bellaire Boulevard, Houston, TX 77083
GEORGE, John C (CGC)
GEORGE, Juan (Del) Trinity Episcopal Church, 1108 N Adams St, Wilmington, DE 19801
GEORGE, Melissa Roberts (Colo) PO Box 984, Salida, CO 81201
GEORGE, Mitzi (WLa) 1020 Sutherland Rd, Lake Charles, LA 70611
GEORGE, Reverend Cathy Hagstrom George (Mass) 409 Prospect St, New Haven, CT 06511
GEORGE, Susanne T (Cal) 60 Brunswick Park, Melrose, MA 02176
GEORGE GUISER, Asha Mary (Pa)
GEORGE-HACKER, Nina (Alb)
GEORGES, Esther Mathilda (Episcopal VI)
GEORGI, Geoffrey Mack (NJ) Po Box 13, Rougemont, NC 27572
✠ **GEPERT**, Robert R (WMich) Tec Dio Of Central Pa, 101 Pine St, Harrisburg, PA 17101
GERBASI, Virginia Kaye (WA) St Johns Church Georgetown, 3240 O St NW, Washington, DC 20007
GERBER, Mary Kate (Dal)
GERBRACHT, Madge (NH) 106 Lowell St, Manchester, NH 03101
GERDING, Susan Ann (Tex) 836 W. Jones St., Livingston, TX 77351
GERDSEN, Elizabeth Jane (SO) 1219 Amherst Pl, Dayton, OH 45406

GERHARD, Ernest J (Neb) 14214 Briggs Cir, Omaha, NE 68144

GERHARD, Kurt (NY) 7 Library Ln, Bronxville, NY 10708

GERHARDT, Michael Joseph (NJ) 171 Larch Ave, Bogota, NJ 07603

GERHART, Stacey P (Ia) 1308 S Cleveland St, Sioux City, IA 51106

GERLACH, Aaron R (O) 125 E Market St, Tiffin, OH 44883

GERMINO, Carmen (NC) 123 Williams Rd, Davidson, NC 28036

GERNS, Andrew Timothy (SwFla) 4986 Pointe Cir, Oldsmar, FL 34677

GEROLD, Donna (Ala) 103 Windhaven Rd, Homewood, AL 35209

GERTH JR, Stephen (NY) 832 Tanbark Dr Apt 206, Naples, FL 34108

GESSNER, Barbara (Be)

GESTON, Alejandro Sumadin (The Episcopal Church in Haw) 91-1746 Bond St, Ewa Beach, HI 96706

GETCHELL, Philip Armour (ECR) 6524 Hercus Ct, San Jose, CA 95119

GETLEIN, Greta (Vt) Saint Pauls Church, 50 Park Pl, Pawtucket, RI 02860

GETREU, David Edward (SO) 316 Northridge Rd, Circleville, OH 43113

GETTEL, Rebecca Elizabeth Binns (Mass) 39 E Central St, Natick, MA 01760

GETTS, Sarah Jane (Az)

GETTYS, Jeannette Cooper (USC) 308 College Dr, Gaffney, SC 29340

GETTYS, Laura (WTenn) 692 Poplar Ave, Memphis, TN 38105

GETZ, Peter (Dal) 808 Oak Hollow Ln, Rockwall, TX 75087

GHEEN, Stephen Harris (Minn)

GHINAGLIA SOCORRO, Florencio Armando (Ct) PO Box 2321, Bristol, CT 06011

GIACOBBE, Georgia Bates (EO) 3564 E. Second St. #26, The Dalles, OR 97058

GIACOMA, Claudia Louder (U) 7362 Tall Oaks Dr, Park City, UT 84098

GIANNINI, Robert Edward (Ind) 55 Monument Cir Ste 600, Indianapolis, IN 46204

GIANSIRACUSA JR, Michael (Pa) 300 N Essex Ave Apt 105a, Narberth, PA 19072

GIARDINA, Denise Diana (WVa)

GIBBES, Joseph A (Fla) 12236 Mandarin Rd, Jacksonville, FL 32223

GIBBONS, David Austen (Chi) 339 Ridge Rd, Barrington, IL 60010

GIBBONS, Edward Francis Patrick (SwFla) St Hilarys Episcopal Church, 5011 Mcgregor Blvd, Fort Myers, FL 33901

GIBBS, Charles Philip (Cal) 9900 Kensington Pkwy, Kensington, MD 20895

GIBBS, Dennis (ECR) 840 Echo Park Ave, Los Angeles, CA 90026

GIBBS, Lee Wayland (O) 2413 Weymouth Dr, Springfield, VA 22151

✠ **GIBBS JR**, Wendell Nathaniel (Mich) 6505 Nature Nook Dr, Lewis Center, OH 43035

GIBLIN, Keith Fredrick (Tex) 1401 W Park Ave, Orange, TX 77630

GIBSON, Alan (Mich) St Andrew Episcopal Church, 306 N Division St, Ann Arbor, MI 48104

GIBSON, Barbara Jean (Kan) 400 Sutton Dr, Newton, KS 67114

GIBSON, Beverly Findley (CGC) 24 Blacklawn St, Mobile, AL 36604

GIBSON, Catharine (WA)

GIBSON, Catherine S (ETenn) 7782 Pine Island Way, West Palm Beach, FL 33411

GIBSON, David Warren (Dal)

GIBSON, Earl Dodridge (Az) 31641 La Novia Ave, San Juan Capistrano, CA 92675

GIBSON, Emily Stearns (Me) 732 Nottingham Rd, Wilmington, DE 19805

GIBSON, Gregory H (Episcopal VI) St Johns Episcopal Church, PO Box 486, Christiansted, VI 00821

GIBSON, John (NC) 1520 Canterbury Rd, Raleigh, NC 27608

GIBSON, Justin Thomas (NwT)

GIBSON II, Nathaniel John (Md)

GIBSON III, Owen S (HB) 2926 Maple Springs Blvd, Dallas, TX 75235

GIBSON, Robert Burrows (At) 20 Lucky Ln, Blairsville, GA 30512

GIBSON, Tom (CFla) 570 Capri Rd, Cocoa Beach, FL 32931

GIBSON, Webster S (Va) 111 Stonebrook Rd, Winchester, VA 22602

GIDDINGS, Monte Carl (Kan) 26755 W 103rd St, Olathe, KS 66061

GIERLACH, David Joseph (The Episcopal Church in Haw) 231 Miloiki Pl, Honolulu, HI 96825

GIESELMANN, Rob (Ida) 211 N 2nd Ave, Hailey, ID 83333

GIFFORD-COLE, Irene Margarete (Minn) 225 Hoylake Rd W, Qualicum Beach, BC V9K 1K5, Canada

GILBERT, Brenda Marie (WNC) 8433 Fairfield Forest Rd, Denver, NC 28037

GILBERT, Carol Beverly (Az) 34 Mystic Way, Burlington, NJ 08016

GILBERT, Lara (Wyo)

GILBERT, Marilynn D (Ct) 28 Windemere Pl, Grosse Pointe Farms, MI 48236

GILBERT, Paul (LI) 1760 Parc Vue Ave, Mount Pleasant, SC 29464

GILBERT, Trimble (Ak) General Delivery, Arctic Village, AK 99722

GILBERTSON, Gary (WMo) 12301 West 125th Terr, Overland Park, KS 66213

GILCHRIST, James Edwin (Neb) 124 1st Ave Se, Ronan, MT 59864

GILCHRIST, James F (Colo) 1616 Fernstone Dr NW, Acworth, GA 30101

GILCHRIST, John Richard (Ct) Po Box 361, Winter Harbor, ME 04693

GILES, James D (CFla)

GILES, Richard Stephen (Pa) 105 Lansdowne Ct, Lansdowne, PA 19050

GILES, Walter Crews (Tex) 1649 Park Ln, Alvarado, TX 76009

GILES, Walter Edward (CNY) 12914 US Route 11, Adams Center, NY 13606

GILFEATHER, Gordon Grant (Az) 12990 E Shea Blvd, Scottsdale, AZ 85259

GILHOUSEN, Dennis Ray (Kan) 6501 Maple Dr, Mission, KS 66202

GIL JIMENEZ, Ramon Antonio (DomRep)

GILKES, Overton Weldon (Ct) 262 Shelton Ave, New Haven, CT 06511

GILKEY JR, Sam (CFla) 3670 Northgate Dr., Apt 1, Kissimmee, FL 34746

GILKS, Cyntha Ann (Okla) 903 E Main St, Holdenville, OK 74848

GILL JR, Charles (Eur) 3451 South Washington Ave., Titusville, FL 32780

GILL, Cynthia Elizabeth (SeFla) 2750 Mcfarlane Rd, Miami, FL 33133

GILL, Jeffrey (Oly) Trinity Parish, Vashon, WA 98070

GILL JR, John Nicholas (SO) 3429 Live Oak Place, Columbus, OH 43221

GILL, Jule Carlyle (WA) 431 Park Ave, Lewes, DE 19958

GILL, Nancy Michelle (Okla)

GILL, Robert Clarence (CPa) 139 N Findlay St, York, PA 17402

GILLESPIE, Ann (Va) Christ Church, 118 N Washington St, Alexandria, VA 22314

GILLESPIE, Devin Scott (Az)

GILLETT, Elizabeth (CNY) 1213 River Rd, Hamilton, NY 13346

GILLETT, Kathryn Sarah (CGC) 18 W Wright St, Pensacola, FL 32501

GILLETT, Richard Walker (Oly) 719 N 67th St, Seattle, WA 98103

GILLETTE, Martha Carol (Chi) 154 Timber Ridge Ln, Lake Barrington, IL 60010

GILLIAM, John Malone (Tenn) 1217 Davidson Rd, Nashville, TN 37205

GILLIES, Bruce Nelson (WNY) 1082 Brookwood Dr, Derby, NY 14047

GILLIES, Clara (WNY) 18 N Pearl St, Buffalo, NY 14202

GILLIS, Marcella R (NY) 55 Myrtle Ave, Westport, CT 06880

GILLISS, Columba (Md) 3200 Baker Cir Unit I209, Adamstown, MD 21710

GILLMAN, Elizabeth Walters (Ia)

GILLOOLY, Bryan Charles (O) 19636 Scottsdale Blvd, Cleveland, OH 44122

GILMAN, Bob (SwVa) 16918 Paynes Creek Dr, Cypress, TX 77433

GILMAN, Connie (SVa) 306 Boys Home Rd, Covington, VA 24426

GILMAN, James Earl (Oly) 719 Opie St, Staunton, VA 24401

GILMORE, Elizabeth Lameyer (Me) 24 Fairmount St, Portland, ME 04103

GILMORE, William Kennedy (SwFla)

GILPIN, John Mitchell (Ct) St John's Episcopal Church, 7 Whittlesey Ave, New Milford, CT 06776

GILPIN, Kathlyn Castiglion (SwFla)

GIL RESTREPO, Silvio (Colom) Carrera 6 No 49-85, Piso 2, Bogota, Colombia

GILSDORF, John Walter (EO) 1971 Sw Quinney Ave, Pendleton, OR 97801

GILSON, Anne Elizabeth (WA) 5 Fernwood Cir, Harwich, MA 02645

GILSON, Christine (Kan) PO Box 883, El Dorado, KS 67042

GILTON, Michael (Dal)

GINN JR, Robert Jay (WMass) Oratory Of Saint Francis, Box 300, Templeton, MA 01468

GINNEVER, Richard Arthur (Md) 595 Grant Dr, Gettysburg, PA 17325

GINOLFI, Priscilla Grant (CPa) 156 Warren Way, Lancaster, PA 17601

GINOLFI, Sarah C (Vt) 85 West St, Rutland, VT 05701

GINSON, Isaias Gonzales (Tex) 1805 W.Alabama st., Houston, TX 77098

GIOVANGELO, Steven Michael (Ind) 337 N Kenyon St, Indianapolis, IN 46219

GIRALDO OROZCO, Edgar (PR) 1409 Av Juan Ponce de Len, San Juan, PR 00909

GIRARD, Jacques Andre (Nwk) 8 Shore Rd, Staten Island, NY 10307

GIRARDEAU, Charles Michael (At) 1446 Edinburgh Dr, Tucker, GA 30084

GIRARDEAU, Doug (Eas) 211 E Isabella St, Salisbury, MD 21801

GIRARDIN, Barbara Jeanine (Colo) 2604 S Troy Ct, Aurora, CO 80014

GIRATA, Christopher D (Dal) St Michael All Angels Church, 8011 Douglas Ave, Dallas, TX 75225

GIROUX, Mark Alan (CNY) 355 Hyde St, Whitney Point, NY 13862

GIRVIN, Calvin Shields (NwT) 4541 County Road 127, Colorado City, TX 79512

GITANE, ClayOla (SanD) 476 Sycamore St, Sequim, WA 98382

GITAU, John N (Mass)

GITAU, Samson Njuguna (Ark) 243 N Mcneil St, Memphis, TN 38112

GITIMU, Paul Wainaina (Pa) 1747 Church Ln, Philadelphia, PA 19141

GIVEN, Mark E (Ct) 1113 Abrams Rd # 4-121, Richardson, TX 75081

GIVLER, Gary Bruce (SO) 6215 Kenwood Rd, Madeira, OH 45243

GLANCEY, Bryan Eaton (Eas) 1205 Frederick Ave, Salisbury, MD 21801

GLANDON, Clyde Calvin (Okla) 4223 E 84th St, Tulsa, OK 74137

GLANVILLE, Polly Ann (O) 1945 26th Street, Cuyahoga Falls, OH 44223

GLASER, David Charles (The Episcopal Church in Haw) 20500 W OLD US HIGHWAY 12, Chelsea, MI 48118

GLASER, Geoffrey Scott (ECR) 9868 N Niobrara Way, Tucson, AZ 85742

GLASS, Rosalee Tyree (Me)

GLASS, Vanessa (Colo) The Episcopal Church in Colorado, 1300 N Washington St, Denver, CO 80203

GLASSER, Joanne Kathleen (Eau) 111 9th St N, La Crosse, WI 54601

✠ GLASSPOOL, Mary Douglas (NY) Episcopal Diocese of New York, 1047 Amsterdam Ave, New York, NY 10025

GLAZIER JR, George H (SO) 10 E Weber Rd Apt 305, Columbus, OH 43202

GLEASON, Dorothy Jean (Episcopal SJ) Po Box 399, Ambridge, PA 15003

GLEASON, Edward Campbell (SwFla) 553 Galleon Dr, Naples, FL 34102

GLEASON, Patricia Ellen (Tex) 1534 Milam St, Columbus, TX 78934

GLEAVES, Donna Jeanne (Mont) PO Box 819, 5112 N Park Ave, Helena, MT 59624

GLEAVES, Glen Lee (Mont) 1226 Wildflower Trl, Livingston, MT 59047

GLEESON, Terry Patrick (ECR) 700 Zennia St, Austin, TX 78751

GLENDENNING, Audrey Geraldine (SeFla) 3322 Meridian Way N Apt A, Palm Beach Gardens, FL 33410

GLENDINNING, David Cross (Me) 221 Shelburne Rd, Burlington, VT 05401

GLENN, Kimberly Baker (SwVa) PO Box 1059, 303 S Main St, Kilmarnock, VA 22482

GLENN, Michael Eugene (Okla) 106 E Crawford St, Palestine, TX 75801

GLENN, Patricia Foster (Mo) 19424 Highway 54, Louisiana, MO 63353

GLENNIE, Jannel (Mich) 294 Willoughby Rd, Mason, MI 48854

GLICK, Phillip Randall (EC) 63 Beech Glen Dr, Black Mountain, NC 28711

GLIDDEN, Charles Aelred (FdL) 56500 Abbey Rd, Three Rivers, MI 49093

GLIDDEN, Richard Mark (Chi) 49 Larbert Rd # 6490, Southport, CT 06890

GLOFF, Holly (NC) 1520 Canterbury Rd, Raleigh, NC 27608

GLOSSON HAMMONS, Jamesetta (Los) 1508 W 145th St, Compton, CA 90220

✠ GLOSTER, James Gary (NC) 2236 Fernbank Dr, Charlotte, NC 28226

GLOVER, Beth Faulk (Nwk) 29 Village Gate Way, Nyack, NY 10960

GLOVER, Betty Marie (Ak) 1200 I St Unit 705, Anchorage, AK 99501

GLOVER, Hazel (At) 606 Newnan St, Carrollton, GA 30117

GLOVER, Marsha Bacon (NY) 122 Grandview Ave, White Plains, NY 10605

GLOVER, Mary Elizabeth (NwT) 891 Davis Dr, Abilene, TX 79605

GOBER, Jane A (Pa) 323 Catherine St, Walla Walla, WA 99362

GOBER, Wallace Gene (Mass) 17 Leroy St, Attleboro, MA 02703

GOCHA, Teresa Payne (NH) 477 Main St, Plymouth, NH 03264

GOCKERMAN, Janet Pierce (WMich) 134 Division Ave N, Grand Rapids, MI 49503

GOCKLEY, Mary Jane (Neb) PO Box 353, Broken Bow, NE 68822

GODBOLD, Richard Rives (Ind) 829 Wiltshire Dr, Evansville, IN 47715

GODDEN, Edward Eastman (Del) 610 Lindsey Rd, Wilmington, DE 19809

GODDERZ, Michael John (Mass) 209 Ashmont Street, Boston, MA 02124

GODFREY, Sam (Miss) 1115 Main St, Vicksburg, MS 39183

GODFREY, Steven R (ND) 3102 Hackberry St, Bismarck, ND 58503

GODFREY, William Calvin (LI) 102 Thompson Blvd, Greenport, NY 11944

GODLEY, Robert James (NY) 4440 E Lady Banks Ln, Murrells Inlet, SC 29565

GODSEY, Jeunee (SVa) 8706 Quaker Ln, North Chesterfield, VA 23235

GODWIN, Jerry D (Oly) 5001 California Ave SW #611, Seattle, WA 98136

GODWIN, Shea (Va)

GOEHRING, Dorothy (Mass)

GOEKE, Randall Fred (Neb) 87993 482nd Ave, Atkinson, NE 68713

GOERTZ, Linda Ruth (Ore)

GOETSCH, Richard William (Ida) 213 E Avenue D, Jerome, ID 83338

GOFF, Nancy L (Alb) Adirondack Mission, PO Box 119, Brant Lake, NY 12815

✠ GOFF, Susan (Va) 110 W Franklin St, Richmond, VA 23220

GOFF, Terry Lynn (CGC) 7125 Hitt Rd, Mobile, AL 36695

GOFORTH, Lisa (Az) 1310 N Sioux Ave, Claremore, OK 74017

GOFORTH, Thomas Robert (Chi) 1126 W Wolfram St, Chicago, IL 60657

GOGLIA, Bette Mack (CFla) 9203 Glascow Dr, Fredericksburg, VA 22408

GOING, Virginia Lee (NC) 400 S Boylan Ave, Raleigh, NC 27603

GOKEY, Mary Jordheim (ND) 1742 9th St S, Fargo, ND 58103

GOLDBERG, David Michael (Tex) 705 Williams St, Pasadena, TX 77506

GOLDBERG, Mike William (CFla) 460 38th Sq Sw, Vero Beach, FL 32968

GOLDBERG, Rebecca Lee (Cal) 777 Southgate Ave, Daly City, CA 94015

GOLDEN JR, John Anthony (Pgh) 5 Devon Ave, Lawrenceville, NJ 08648

GOLDEN, Peter (LI) 2115 Albemarle Ter, Brooklyn, NY 11226

GOLDFARB, Ronald Allen (WTenn) 8853 Mission Hills Dr Apt 104, Memphis, TN 38125

GOLDFEDER, Deborah Baker (Mo) 4520 Lucas and Hunt Rd, Saint Louis, MO 63121

GOLDHOR, Andrew (Mass) 6 Meriam St, Lexington, MA 02420

GOLDING, Christopher Pj (The Episcopal Church in Haw) 1266 Oakley Dr, Baton Rouge, LA 70806

GOLDMAN, Norman Clifford (Ore) 94416 Langlois Mountain Rd, Langlois, OR 97450

GOLDMAN, Paul D'Wayne (Ala)

GOLDONE, Jeffrey (Mo)

GOLDSBOROUGH, Neal Neal (Va) PO Box 12683, Pensacola, FL 32591

GOLDSMITH, Gail Austin (SwVa)

GOLDSMITH, Maurice Rusty (Tex) Saint Luke's Episcopal Church, 3736 Montrose Rd., Birmingham, AL 35213

GOLDSMITH SR, Michael (Ala) 904 Wellman Ave NE, Huntsville, AL 35801

GOLDSMITH III, Robert (Eas) 314 North St, Easton, MD 21601

GOLDSTEIN, Margaret Barry (Mo)

GOLENSKI, John Donald (Cal) 1360 Montgomery St Apt 1, San Francisco, CA 94133

GOLLIHER, Jeff (NY) 150 W End Ave Apt 30m, New York, NY 10023

GOLUB, Elizabeth Kress (Nwk) 18 Wittig Ter # 7470, Wayne, NJ 07470

GOMAN, Jon Gifford (Ore) 2615 Nw Arnold Way, Corvallis, OR 97330

GOMER JR, Richard Henry (CFla) 6400 N Socrum Loop Rd, Lakeland, FL 33809

GOMES, Elizabeth (Kan) 912 N Amidon Ave, Wichita, KS 67203

GOMEZ, Ed (Tex) 2404 Marcus Abrams Blvd, Austin, TX 78748

GOMEZ, Lisa (Wyo)

GOMEZ, Luis Enrique (NY) 26 W 84th St, New York, NY 10024

GOMEZ ALMONTE, Lorenzo (DomRep) Calle Las Mercedes #66, Bigalindo, Hato Mayor Del Rey, DR

GOMEZ MOLINA, Lydia Esther (PR)

GONZALES, Pat Marie (Okla) PO Box 26, Watonga, OK 73772

GONZALES JR, Ricardo (Los) 859 Jessica Pl, Nipomo, CA 93444

GONZALEZ, Alfredo Pedro (USC) 1115 Marion St, Columbia, SC 29201

GONZALEZ, Emilio (CFla)

GONZALEZ, Isabel Tapia (U) 4024 S Redhawk Rd, West Valley City, UT 84119

GONZALEZ, Reagan Len (WTex) 11 Saint Lukes Ln, San Antonio, TX 78209

GONZALEZ, Richard (CFla)

GONZALEZ AQUDELO, Luis Mariano (Colom) Carrera 84 North 50 A-112, Ap 301, Medellin, Antioquia, Colombia

GONZALEZ DEL SOLAR, Mario Sebastian (Va) 800 Brantley Rd, Richmond, VA 23235

GONZALEZ-FIGUEROA, Efrain (PR)

GONZALEZ GARAVITO, Jose Pio (PR) PO Box 902, Saint Just, PR 00978

GONZALEZ HERNANDEZ, Yoimel (WA) 1525 Newton St NW, Washington, DC 20010

GONZALEZ-MESA, Gustavo (Ore) 700 Se 7th St, Gresham, OR 97080

GONZALEZ SANTOS, Rosa Ari (PR)

GOOCH, Gary (Kan) 236 Jumping Laurel St, San Marcos, TX 78666

GOOD, Elizabeth (Mass) 17 Church St, Hanover, MA 02339

GOODALE-MIKOSZ, Desiree Ann (Chi) 20913 W Snowberry Ln, Plainfield, IL 60544-416

GOODALL, Sally (O)

GOODFELLOW, Willa Marie (EO) 1745 5th St Apt 8, Coralville, IA 52241

GOODHEART, Donald P (NC) 1303 Hwy A1A #201, Satellite Beach, FL 32937

GOODHOUSE-MAUAI, Angela (ND)

GOODING, Ludwick E (Pa) 5910 Cobbs Creek Pkwy, Philadelphia, PA 19143

GOODISON, Lorna Fay (SeFla) 1400 Riverside Dr, Coral Springs, FL 33071

GOODKIND, Caroline Cox (USC) 45 Crooked Island Cir, Murrells Inlet, SC 29576

GOODLETT, Cal Calvin (Fla)

GOODLOW, Suzzane D (Mo)

GOODMAN, Kevin M (Chi) 6033 N Sheridan Rd Apt 29g, Chicago, IL 60660

GOODMAN, Mark (RG) P.O. Box 1246, Albuquerque, NM 87103

GOODMAN, Timothy Allen (Spr) 9267 HERRIN RD, JOHNSTON CITY, IL 62951

GOODNESS, DONALD (NY) 4800 Fillmore Ave Apt 651, Alexandria, VA 22311

GOODPANKRATZ, Gretchen (WK) Po Box 851, Liberal, KS 67905

GOODPASTER, David Thomas (Tenn)

GOODPASTURE, Terrance Martin (Episcopal SJ) 2315 Merriment Ct, Turlock, CA 95380

GOODRICH, Kevin P (Ia) St John Episc Ch, 1458 Locust St, Dubuque, IA 52001

GOODRIDGE, Rob (CFla) 2669 W Brookfield Way, Vero Beach, FL 32966

GOODWILL, Martha E (SwFla) 8005 25th St E, Parrish, FL 34219

GOODWIN, Joan Carolyn (Az) 413 N San Francisco St, Flagstaff, AZ 86001

GOODWIN, Laura (WMass) St Andrews Church, 53 N Main St, North Grafton, MA 01536

GOODWIN, Marilyn Marie (Minn) 27309 County Road 4, Naytahwaush, MN 56566

GOODWIN, Sarabeth (WA) 382 S Hills Dr, Shepherdstown, WV 25443

GOOLD, George Charles (Ore) St Stephen's Church, SW Ninth & Hurbert Sts, Newport, OR 97365

GOOLD, Janis Leigh (Ore) 16530 Nottingham Dr, Gladstone, OR 97027

GOOLSBY, Robert Patrick (Fla) 5400 Belle Terre Pkwy, Palm Coast, FL 32137

GOOLTZ, Janet R (Az) 12607 W Westgate Dr, Sun City West, AZ 85375

GOONESEKERA, Desmond Joel Peter (Tex) 2806 Belham Creek Dr, Katy, TX 77494

GOORAHOO, Ephraim Basant (LI) 111-16 116th St, South Ozone Park, NY 11420

GORACZKO, Ann Kathleen (SeFla) 1801 Ludlam Drive, Miami Springs, FL 33166

GORANSON, Paul Werner (WMass) 130 Sachem Ave, Worcester, MA 01606

GORCHOV, Michael Ivan (Alb) 58 3rd St, Troy, NY 12180

GORDAY, Peter J (WNC) 34 Lullwater Pl NE, Atlanta, GA 30307

GORDON, Andrew (At)

GORDON, Billie Mae (Mass) 290 Kingstown Way Unit 395, Duxbury, MA 02332

GORDON, Constance Leigh (U) 789 White Pine Dr, Tooele, UT 84074

GORDON, David Walter (Cal) 130 Avenida Barbera, Sonoma, CA 95476

GORDON JR, Harrington Manly (RI) 108 Columbia Ave, Warwick, RI 02888

GORDON, James Donald (RG) 3223 Calle de Molina, Santa Fe, NM 87507

GORDON, Jay (NY) 382 Central Park W Apt 17p, New York, NY 10025

GORDON, Katherine (SanD)

GORDON, Rodney E (Va) 701 S Providence Rd, North Chesterfield, VA 23236

GORDON, Walt (Minn) 834 Marshall Ave, Saint Paul, MN 55104

GORDON, Walter Bernard (WTenn) PO Box 622, Grand Junction, TN 38039

GORDON-BARNES, Janice E (Md) 3117 Raven Croft Ter, The Villages, FL 32163

GORE, Gina Lee (NY) 18631 Chapel Ln, Huntington Beach, CA 92646

GORE, Kevin Wesley (Ark) 510 Shadow Ln, Jonesboro, AR 72401

GORES, Ariail Fischer (Dal) 4229 Tomberra Way, Dallas, TX 75220

GORMAN, James Michael (Chi) 5388 W Harvey Rd, Oregon, IL 61061

GORMAN, W Kenneth (NJ) 684 Sunrise Dr, Avalon, NJ 08202

GORMLEY, Shane P (Chi)

GORTNER, David T (Spok) 3737 Seminary Road, Alexandria, VA 22304

GORTON, James Fredrick (Okla)

GOSHERT, Mary Linda (The Episcopal NCal) 882 Oxford Way, Benicia, CA 94510

GOSHGARIAN, Martin John (Mass) 85 Glenwood Rd, Somerville, MA 02145

GOSHORN, Alice Elizabeth Gill (Ind) 4921 E State Road 252, Franklin, IN 46131

GOSS, Frank (NJ) PO Box 1, Bradley Beach, NJ 07720

GOSS III, James Paul (Cal) 792 Penny Royal Ln, San Rafael, CA 94903

GOSSARD, Pamela Ann (The Episcopal NCal)

GOSSETT JR, Earl Fowler (Ala) 1811 Cedar Crest Rd, Birmingham, AL 35214

GOSSLING, Nancy (Mass) 25 Chapman Dr, Glastonbury, CT 06033

GOTAUTAS, Patricia Marie (USC)

GOTKO, Raymond Morgan (At) PO Box 713, Sewanee, TN 37375

GOTT, Amanda Katherine (Neb)

GOTTARDI-LITTELL, Laura (Chi) Church Of Our Saviour, Chicago, IL 60614

GOTTING, Viktoria Johanna Petra (Tex) Saint Johns Church, 815 S Broadway St, La Porte, TX 77571

GOUGH, Karen (WNY) 315 Oakbrook Dr, Williamsville, NY 14221

GOULD, Glenn Hamilton (USC) 30 Moise Dr, Sumter, SC 29150

GOULD, Jane (Los) 19 Nahant Pl, Lynn, MA 01902

GOULD, Jennie Ruth (NH) 19 Maplewood St, Watertown, MA 02472

GOULD, Katherine E (Tex)

GOULD, Mary Dolores (Oly) Po Box 1193, Maple Valley, WA 98038

GOWDY-JAEHNIG, Christine Annette (Ia) 506 W Broadway St, Decorah, IA 52101

GOWE, Bruce E (Be) 398 Greentree Dr # M107, East Stroudsburg, PA 18301

GOWETT, Randall James (Episcopal SJ) 1224 E Sample Ave, Fresno, CA 93710

GOWING, Michael LeVern (Mich) 2696 Indian Trl, Pinckney, MI 48169

GOWLAND, James David (NJ) 11 N Monroe Ave, Wenonah, NJ 08090

GOWTY, Richard Newton (Tex) 21 Mclean Street, Brighton, 4017, Australia

GRAB, Virginia (NY) 74 Montgomery St, Tivoli, NY 12583

GRABINSKI, Kenneth Lee (Oly) 5240 46th Ave Sw, Seattle, WA 98136

GRABNER, John David (Spok) 165 SW Spruce St, Apt 1, Pullman, WA 99163

GRABNER-HEGG, Linnae Marie (Minn) 1619 31st Ave S, Fargo, ND 58103

GRACE JR, Harry Tyler (NC) 36 Parkside Ct, Buffalo, NY 14214

GRACE SR, James McKay Lykes (Tex) 4221 Riley St, Houston, TX 77005

GRACE, Patricia M (NC) 2208 Landings Way, Raleigh, NC 27615

GRACEN, Sharon Kay (Ct) 1109 Main St, Branford, CT 06405

GRACIA, Kesner (Hai)

GRACZYK, Glen Gerard (SwFla) St Marys Episcopal Church, 1010 24th Ave W, Palmetto, FL 34221

GRADY, Ann (EMich) 815 N. Grant St, Bay City, MI 48708

GRADY, Jennifer (CFla)

GRADY, Richard C (SwFla) 6985 Edgewater Cir, Fort Myers, FL 33919

GRAEBNER, Brooks (NC) Po Box 628, Hillsborough, NC 27278

GRAFF, Donald T (Pa) 1434 Alcott St, Philadelphia, PA 19149

GRAFF, Stephen John (SeFla) St Gregory's Episcopal Church, 100 NE Mizner Blvd, Boca Raton, FL 33432

GRAHAM III, Alexander D (Tex) 2783 Valwood Pkwy, Farmers Branch, TX 75234

GRAHAM III, Bob (Alb) 153 Billings Ave, Ottawa, ON K1H 5K8, Canada

GRAHAM, Carolyn Jane (Kan) 1107 W 27th Ter, Lawrence, KS 66046

GRAHAM, Deborah Marie Therese (Ida) 1867 W Belmont St, Boise, ID 83706

GRAHAM III, Earnest Newt (NC) 828 Kings Hwy, Suffolk, VA 23432

GRAHAM, Elizabeth Folk (Miss)

GRAHAM, John (WA) 1041 Wisconsin Ave NW, Washington, DC 20007

GRAHAM, John Kirkland (Tex) 6231 Ella Lee Ln, Houston, TX 77057

GRAHAM, Julie Ann (Mo) 2605 Louisiana Ave, Saint Louis, MO 63118

GRAHAM IV, Sandy (The Episcopal Church in Haw) 563 Kamoku St, Honolulu, HI 96826

GRAHAM, Suzanne H (NY) 279 Piermont Ave, Nyack, NY 10960

GRAHAM, Tim (At) 1130 First Ave, Columbus, GA 31901

GRAHAM, Wells Newell (CGC) 771 Simon Park Cir, Lawrenceville, GA 30045

GRAHAM JR, William James (Neb) 607 Toluca Ave, Alliance, NE 69301

GRAMBSCH, Mary Frances (My) 55 Cedar St, Dobbs Ferry, NY 10522

GRAMLEY, Thomas S (Roch) 13 Prospect Ave, Canisteo, NY 14823

GRANDFIELD, Dale Terence (Be) 417 Linden St, Bethlehem, PA 18018

GRANGER JR, Charles Irving (Okla) 305 E Douglas Dr, Midwest City, OK 73110

GRANT, Alice Graham (NC) 422 Carolina Cir, Durham, NC 27707

GRANT JR, Blount (SeFla) 8500 Bluebonnet Blvd Apt 31, Baton Rouge, LA 70810

GRANT, Hugh (Oly) PO Box 632, Eastsound, WA 98245

GRANT, Jared (WNC) 1910 10th Street Blvd NW, Hickory, NC 28601

GRANT, Joan (WNC) 290 Old Haw Creek Rd, Asheville, NC 28805

GRANT, Priscilla Percy R (O) 2230 Euclid Ave, Cleveland, OH 44115

GRANT, Rebecca Ann (Me) 16 Alton Road, Apt 219, Augusta, ME 04330

GRANT, Sandra Marceau (SC)

GRANTZ, Brian Glenn (NI) 117 N Lafayette Blvd, South Bend, IN 46601

GRATZ, Louis Paul (Vt) 208 Silver St, Bennington, VT 05201

GRAUER, David Ernst (Chi) 808 S Seminary Ave, Park Ridge, IL 60068

GRAUNKE, Kristine (WTex) PO Box 68, Hebbronville, TX 78361

GRAVATT, Jacqueline Segar (SVa) 301 49th St, Virginia Beach, VA 23451

GRAVES JR, Bob (CGC) 1302 E Avery St, Pensacola, FL 32503

GRAVES, Carol Carson (NMich) 4341 Se Satinleaf Pl, Stuart, FL 34997

GRAVES IV, Charles Cornelius (Tex)

GRAVES JR, Farrell (EC) 5 Mill Pond Rd, Stony Brook, NY 11790

GRAVES, Jon C (NJ) 210 S Mchenry Ave, Crystal Lake, IL 60014

GRAVES, Lisa (NJ) 164 Neptune Dr, Manahawkin, NJ 08050

GRAVES, Rena B (Pa) 5421 Germantown Ave, Philadelphia, PA 19144

GRAVES, Richard (Ia) 1247 7th Ave N, Fort Dodge, IA 50501

GRAY, Bruce William (Ind) 4538 Sylvan Rd, Indianapolis, IN 46228

GRAY, Calvin (Colo) 1625 Larimer St Apt 2501, Denver, CO 80202

GRAY, Cathy J (Ind) 11120 El Arco Dr, Whittier, CA 90604

GRAY, Chris (SwFla) 8005 25th Street East, Parrish, FL 34219

GRAY, Cindra Dee (Ore) PO Box 358, Newberg, OR 97132

GRAY, Donna Claire (Ct)

GRAY, Douglas Alan (USC) 927 Naples Ave, Cayce, SC 29033

✠ **GRAY III**, Duncan (Miss) 110 Philip Rd, Oxford, MS 38655

✠ **GRAY**, Frank (NI) 3820 Nall Ct, South Bend, IN 46614

GRAY, Giuliana C (Miss) 4600 Saint Charles Ave, New Orleans, LA 70115

GRAY, Katherine Tupper (SVa) 84 Post St, Newport News, VA 23601

GRAY, Melvin K (Fla) 715 Sleepyvale Ln, Houston, TX 77018

GRAY, Michael Fred (Va) 712 Amanda Ct, Culpeper, VA 22701

GRAY, Patrick Terrell (Mass) 151 Asbury St, South Hamilton, MA 01982

GRAY, Peter Whittlesey (Miss) Trinity Church, 1329 Jackson Ave, New Orleans, LA 70130

GRAY, Priscilla Grace-Gloria (Minn) 611 19th St N, Sartell, MN 56377

GRAY, Robert Edward (Tex)

GRAY, Svea Blomquist (Mich) 306 N Division St, Ann Arbor, MI 48104

GRAY, Victoria Stephanie (Cal)

GRAYBILL, Richard Martin (NMich) First And Canda St, Ishpeming, MI 49849

GRAYBILL, Virginia K (NMich) 301 N 1st St, Ishpeming, MI 49849
GRAYDEN, Margaret Miller (The Episcopal NCal)
GRAY-FOW, Michael John Gregory (Mil) 120 S Ridge St, Whitewater, WI 53190
✠ **GRAY-REEVES**, Mary (ECR) 154 Central Ave, Salinas, CA 93901
GRAYSON, Timothy Holiday (Md) 536 Kinsale Rd, Timonium, MD 21093
GREATHOUSE, William Matthew (WTenn) 103 S Poplar St, Paris, TN 38242
GREATWOOD, Richard Neil (CFla) 1167 Adair Park Place, Orlando, FL 32804
GREELEY, Horace (Cal)
GREELEY III, Paul William (USC) 206 Kings Mountain St, York, SC 29745
GREEN, Andrew (SanD) 39326 Moronga Canyon Dr, Palm Desert, CA 92260
GREEN, Andrew T (WTex) Church of the Holy Spirit, 11093 Bandera Rd, San Antonio, TX 78250
GREEN III, Anthony Roy (Spok) 1705 5th St, Wenatchee, WA 98801
GREEN, Daniel (The Episcopal NCal) 40 5th St, Petaluma, CA 94952
GREEN, David Keith (CGC)
GREEN, David Robert (Be) 302 Coventry Pointe Ln, Pottstown, PA 19465
GREEN, Dru (Chi) 971 First St, Batavia, IL 60510
GREEN, Frazier L (Ga) 1041 Fountain Lake Dr, Brunswick, GA 31525
GREEN, Gary (Mil) 6502 51st Ave, Kenosha, WI 53142
GREEN, Gretchen Hall (O) 35 Cohasset Dr, Hudson, OH 44236
GREEN JR, Joseph Nathaniel (SVa) 3826 Wedgefield Ave, Norfolk, VA 23502
GREEN, Kenneth William (Spok) 539 3rd Ave, Havre, MT 59501
GREEN, Larry A (Chi) 1424 N Dearborn St, Chicago, IL 60610
GREEN, Linda (Chi) 971 First St, Batavia, IL 60510
GREEN, Lisa (SVa) 1333 Jamestown Rd, Williamsburg, VA 23185
GREEN, Mary Emily (Tex) 4633 Tanner View Dr, Clinton, WA 98236
GREEN, Patricia Anne (MWich) 28 Easton Ave, Portsmouth, RI 02871
GREEN, Patricia Lynn (RG) 1678 Tierra Del Rio NW, Albuquerque, NM 87107
GREEN, Randy (WNC) 343 Dogwood Knl, Boone, NC 28607
GREEN, Richard (Oly) 2442 Park Hill Dr, Longview, WA 98632
GREEN, Ronnie Dillon (Ala)
GREEN JR, Roy Donald (EO) 275 N Main St, Providence, RI 02903
GREEN, Susan Louise (SanD) 125 W El Alameda, Palm Springs, CA 92262

GREEN, Tamara Melanie (Cal) 7211 Garden Glen Ct Apt 318, Huntington Beach, CA 92648
GREENAWAY, Douglas Andrew Gordon (WA) 1116 Lamont St NW, Washington, DC 20010
GREENE, Adam S (Fla) 4620 Algonquin Ave, Jacksonville, FL 32210
GREENE, Catie (Colo) 1300 N Washington St, Denver, CO 80203
GREENE, Dorothy Anne (NY) 27 Willow Ave, Larchmont, NY 10538
GREENE, Everett Henry (RI) 1117 Capella S, Newport, RI 02840
GREENE, Hilary (Mass)
GREENE III, Joe (NY) 1451 Carriage Ridge Dr, Greensboro, GA 30642
GREENE, Jon Alan (SwVa)
GREENE, Judith (Ct) 60 Bywatyr Ln, Bridgeport, CT 06605
GREENE, Kim Harlene (WNY) St Paul's Cathedral, 128 Pearl St, Buffalo, NY 14202
GREENE, Lynne Tuthill (SwFla) 1369 Vermeer Drive, Nokomis, FL 34275
GREENE, Mary (Cal) 151 Carmel Way, Portola Valley, CA 94028
GREENE, Michael Paul Thomas (Alb) 75 Mosher Rd, Delmar, NY 12054
GREENE, Patrick (RI) 55 Main St, N Kingstown, RI 02852
GREENE, Roger Stewart (SO) 8101 Beechmont Ave, Cincinnati, OH 45255
GREENE-MCCREIGHT, Kathryn (Ct) 198 Mckinley Ave, New Haven, CT 06515
GREENEY, Dawnlynn (Minn)
GREENLAW, William A (NY) 529 W 42nd St Apt 4j, New York, NY 10036
GREENLEAF, Debra Lynn (Az)
GREENLEAF, Richard Edward (NH) 325 Pleasant St, Concord, NH 03301
GREENMAN, Elizabeth Travis Rees (SVa) 2959 Apalachee Pkwy Apt J6, Tallahassee, FL 32301
GREENSHIELDS, Kay Conner (Okla) 405 Roserock Dr, Norman, OK 73026
GREENWELL, Gail (SO) 318 E 4th St, Cincinnati, OH 45202
GREEN-WITT, Margaret Evelyn Ashmead (SwFla) 2499 Mapleleaf Ct, Spring Hill, FL 34606
GREENWOOD, April Valeria Trew (Va) 2910 Stratford Rd, Richmond, VA 23225
GREENWOOD, Don Robert (SO) 10414 NW 13th Pl, Vancouver, WA 98685
GREENWOOD JR, Eric Sutcliffe (Tenn) 404 Northridge Ct, Nashville, TN 37221
GREENWOOD, Jody (EC) 4925 Oriole Dr, Wilmington, NC 28403
GREENWOOD III, Rick (SVa) 2910 Stratford Rd, Richmond, VA 23225
GREENWOOD, Susan A (Colo) 53 Paradise Rd, Golden, CO 80401

GREENWOOD, Walter Merritt (O) 322 S Mason St, Arroyo Grande, CA 93420
GREER, Broderick L (Colo) 1720 Peabody Ave, Memphis, TN 38104
GREER, David (WLa) 208 Bruce Ave, Shreveport, LA 71105
GREER JR, George Holeman (NC) 4645 Ashley Dr, Battleboro, NC 27809
GREER, Hilary A (Pa) 47 W Afton Ave, Yardley, PA 19067
GREER JR, James Gossett (O) 13710 Shaker Blvd Apt 404, Cleveland, OH 44120
GREGG, Catherine (Nev) 2235 S 1400 E Unit 19, Saint George, UT 84790
GREGG, Jennifer E (WMass) St Stephens Episcopal Church, 67 East St, Pittsfield, MA 01201
GREGG, Robert Clark (Cal) 659 Salvatierra St, Stanford, CA 94305
✠ **GREGG**, William O (NC) 310 Majestic Heights Dr, Salisbury, NC 28144
GREGORIUS, Mary B (NY) 378 Bedford Rd, Pleasantville, NY 10570
GREGORY, Brian (Oly) 5201 NE 188th St, Lake Forest Park, WA 98155
GREGORY, Emma Jean (Nev) 4201 W Washington Ave, Las Vegas, NV 89107
GREGORY, Marie Christine (Spr) 130 W Eldorado St, Decatur, IL 62522
GREGORY, Pam (RI) 251 Danielson Pike, North Scituate, RI 02857
GREGORY, Phillip Richard (Chi) 2612 Gateshead Dr, Naperville, IL 60564
GREGORY, Rachael (Chi) 410 Grand Ave, Waukegan, IL 60085
✠ **GREIN**, Richard Frank (NY) 150 West End Avenue, Apt. 9H, New York, NY 10013
GREINER, Robert Charles (Mass) 138 Tremont St, Boston, MA 02111
GREISER, Ronald Edmond (WNC) 5601 Oak Ridge Ave, New Port Richey, FL 34652
GREMILLION, Dorothy (Tex) 2708 Butler National Dr, Pflugerville, TX 78660
GRENNEN, Thomas Kyle (Alb) Grace Church, 32 Montgomery St, Cherry Valley, NY 13320
GRENZ, Linda (RI) 275 N Main St, Providence, RI 02903
GRESSLE, Richard (NY) 130 1st Ave, Nyack, NY 10960
GREVE, James Randall (NY)
GREVE, John Haven (Ia) New Song Episcopal Church, 912 20th Ave, Coralville, IA 52241
GREVE JR, Paul Andrew (NI) 611 W Berry St, Fort Wayne, IN 46802
✠ **GREW II**, J Clark (O) One Huntington Avenue, 304, Boston, MA 02116
GREWELL, Genevieve Michael (Oly) 1551 Tenth Ave. E, Seattle, WA 98102
GRIBBLE, Robert Leslie (Tex) 301 E 8th St, Austin, TX 78701

GRIBBON, Robert T (Eas) 1510 Woodland Rd, Salisbury, MD 21801

GRIEB, Katherine (WA) 3737 Seminary Rd, Alexandria, VA 22304

GRIESBACH, Sigrid Jane (WMass) 921 Pleasant St, Worcester, MA 01602

GRIESER, Jonathan (Mil) 116 W Washington Ave, Madison, WI 53703

GRIESHEIMER, James Cade (Ia) 506 W Broadway St, Decorah, IA 52101

GRIEVES, Brian (The Episcopal Church in Haw) 25 Captains Cv, Oakland, CA 94618

GRIFFIN, Barry (At) PO Box 169, Morrow, GA 30260

GRIFFIN, Christopher E (Chi) 1356 W Jarvis Ave # 1, Chicago, IL 60626

GRIFFIN, Donald J (SeFla)

GRIFFIN, Emily (WA) St. Alban's Episcopal Church, 3001 Wisconsin Ave Nw, Washington, DC 20016

GRIFFIN, Gerrianne (LI)

GRIFFIN, Horace Leeolphus (At)

GRIFFIN, Jan (Spok) 803 Symons St, Richland, WA 99354

GRIFFIN, Jeremiah (RG) PO Box 175, Marfa, TX 79843

GRIFFIN, Jon Edward (Spr) 449 State Highway 37, West Frankfort, IL 62896

GRIFFIN, Mary-Carol Ann (Me) 862 Eagle Lake Rd, Bar Harbor, ME 04609

GRIFFIN, Patrick Corrigan (Colo) 127 W Archer Pl, Denver, CO 80223

GRIFFIN, Pauline Ruth (USC) 605 Woodland St, Spartanburg, SC 29302

GRIFFIN, P Joshua (Cal) St David Of Wales, 2800 SE Harrison St, Portland, OR 97214

GRIFFIN, Ronald Wayne (ECR) 2644 Bainbridge Ln, The Villages, FL 32162

GRIFFIN, Russell Agnew (NJ) 84 W Dehart Ave, Clayton, NJ 08312

GRIFFIN, Tim (Pa) 2730 Cranston Rd, Philadelphia, PA 19131

GRIFFIN JR, William Leonard (Ark) 40 Cliffdale Dr, Little Rock, AR 72223

GRIFFITH, Bernard Macfarren (SeFla) 15100 Sw 141st Ter, Miami, FL 33196

GRIFFITH, Bruce Derby (LI) 604 Hollywood Ave, Copiague, NY 11726

GRIFFITH, Charles (WK) 8631 Beulah Land Dr, Ozark, AR 72949

GRIFFITH, David M (Los) 821 Valley Crest St, La Canada, CA 91011

GRIFFITH, Gregory (O) 705 Main St, Coshocton, OH 43812

GRIFFITH, Nicholas (Los)

GRIFFITH JR, Robert L (LI) 4750 41st St Apt 6a, Sunnyside, NY 11104

GRIFFITH, Robert Talmadge (CFla) 2310 Holder Rd, Mims, FL 32754

GRIFFITH, Shawn Lynn (WNC) 3658 Gaston Day School Rd, Gastonia, NC 28056

GRIFFITHS, Robert Stephen (Fla) 2613 Vista Cove Rd, Saint Augustine, FL 32084

GRIFO, Lynne Ann (Ct)

GRIGGS, Linda Mackie (RI) 50 Orchard Ave, Providence, RI 02906

GRIM, Leland Howard (Minn) 2636 County Road 94, International Falls, MN 56649

GRIMELLI, Jennifer N (Md)

GRIMES, Charles Gus (Tenn) 510 W Main St, Franklin, TN 37064

GRIMES, Eve Lyn (Colo) 624 W 19th St, Pueblo, CO 81003

GRIMM, Susan (SVa) 1104 Lakepoint Dr, Clarksville, VA 23927

GRIMSHAW, Gretchen Sanders (Mass) 28 Robbins Rd, Watertown, MA 02472

GRINDON, Carri Patterson (Los) 1014 E. Altadena Dr., Altadena, CA 91001

GRINDON, Sharon Lee (Vt) 386South St, Middlebury, VT 05753

GRINER, Robert (Nwk) 115 Cedar Dr, Newton, NJ 07860

GRINNELL, Janice Louise (RI) 263 Orchard Woods Drive, Saunderstown, RI 02874

GRINNELL, Lynn Dean (SwFla) 15102 Amberly Dr, Tampa, FL 33647

GRISCOM, Donald Wayne (SwFla) 3324 Chicago Ave, Bradenton, FL 34207

GRISHAM JR, Lowell (Ark) 310 N Washington Aveue, Fayetteville, AR 72701

GRISSOM, Preston Reid (CFla)

GRISWOLD, David Alton (WA) 4201 Albemarle St NW, Washington, DC 20016

✠ **GRISWOLD III**, Frank Tracy (Chi)

GRISWOLD-KUHN, Karl E (Tex) 6 Silvester St, Kinderhook, NY 12106

GRITTER, Joshua Michael (CFla) 1875 19th Ave SW, Vero Beach, FL 32962

GRIZZLE, Anne Fletcher (SwVa) 123 W Washington St, Lexington, VA 24450

GROB, Bruce Russell (Fla) 151 Nc Highway 9 Pmb 227, Black Mountain, NC 28711

GRODT, Eileen Patricia (Oly) 722 N 145th St, Shoreline, WA 98133

GROENINGER, Mary (Minn)

GROFF, Mary Elizabeth (Ala) 6141 Sherry Dr, Guntersville, AL 35976

GROFF JR, Sanford (SeFla) 3395 Burns Rd, Palm Beach Gardens, FL 33410

GROH, Clifford Herbert (Mich)

GROHOWSKI, Elizabeth (Be)

GRONEK, Marianna L (Mich) Church of the Epiphany, 423 N Beaver St, Flagstaff, AZ 86001

GRONEMAN, Leslie Joyce (Alb)

GROSCHNER, Peter Kingston (Mich) 19759 Holiday Rd, Grosse Pointe Woods, MI 48236

GROSE, Fayette Powers (O) 310 E Lincoln Way, Lisbon, OH 44432

GROSH, Christine Marie (Neb) 7921 N Hazelwood Dr, Lincoln, NE 68510

GROSHART, Nancy Louise (U) 1051 Allen Peak Cir, Ogden, UT 84404

GROSJEAN, Lyle Wood (ECR) 3255 Amber Dr, Paso Robles, CA 93446

GROSKOPH, Elizabeth May (Roch) PO Box 541, Hancock, NY 13783

GROSKOPH, Ralph Gordon (Roch) PO Box 541, 211 Somerset Lake Rd, Hancock, NY 13783

GROSS, Brian K (Wyo) 234 40th St NE, Cedar Rapids, IA 52402

GROSS, Daniel La Rue (Be) 33 James St, Kingston, PA 18704

GROSSMAN, Stacey (Cal) 121 Martin Dr, Novato, CA 94949

GROSSO, Andrew (Dal) Trinity Episcopal Cathedral, 1100 Sumter St, Columbia, SC 29201

GROSSOEHME, Daniel Huck (O) Pulmonary Medicine Mlc2021, Cchmc, Cincinnati, OH 45229

GROSSOEHME, Henrietta H (Mich) 111 S Grant St, Bloomington, IN 47408

GROTZINGER, Terri Ann (Mont) Holy Spirit Episcopal Church, 130 S 6th St E, Missoula, MT 59801

GROUBERT, Gerri Helen (Nev) 3665 Largo Verde Way, Las Vegas, NV 89121

GROUT III, Earl Leroy (Oly) 6801 30th Ave Ne, Seattle, WA 98115

GROVER III, Charles Lowell (Roch) 4006 Brick Kiln Dr, Chittenango, NY 13037

GROVES, Barbara T (CNY) 141 Main St, Whitesboro, NY 13492

GRUBB, Eric Keith (EC)

GRUBB, Sarah Ann (Neb) 8800 Holdrege St, Lincoln, NE 68505

GRUBBS, Lucas (Ak) 4164 New Moon Cir, Santa Fe, NM 87507

GRUBE, David Quinn (Nev) 777 Sage St., Elko, NV 89801

GRUBERTH, Cole (CNY)

GRUMAN, Steve (Ala) 131 Silver Lake Cir, Madison, AL 35758

GRUMHAUS, Jennifer Wood (Mass) 23 Loew Cir, Milton, MA 02186

GRUNDY, Elizabeth A (Mass) 421 Wianno Ave, Osterville, MA 02655

GRUNDY, Sandra A (Colo) 9345 Carr St, Westminster, CO 80021

GRUNFELD, Matthew Theodore (SwFla) 4408 Gulf Dr, Holmes Beach, FL 34217

GRUSELL, Katrina L (Md) 5057 Stone Hill Dr, Ellicott City, MD 21043

GRUSENDORF, William Connor (WTex) 401 W Dry St, San Saba, TX 76877

GUAILLAS CARANGUI, Raul (DomRep) Cafetos Oe-3-76 Y Nazareth, Quito, 00593, Ecuador

GUAMAN AYALA, Francisco (EcuC) Brasilia Y Buenos Aires, Ambato, Ecuador

GUANSON, Lou Ann Haaheo (The Episcopal Church in Haw) 1515 Wilder Ave, Honolulu, HI 96822

GUBACK, Thomas Henry (WMich) 6300 N Manitou Trl, Northport, MI 49670

GUCK, Sarah St John (RG) PO Box 2795, Silver City, NM 88062

GUELZO, Allen Carl (Pa)

GUENTHER, Nancy Louise (WNY) 200 East Center St., Medina, NY 14103

GUERNSEY, Justine Marie (Alb) 563 Kenwood Ave, Delmar, NY 12054

GUERRA, Carrie Lee (WTex) Trinity Episcopal Church, 1501 N Glass St, Victoria, TX 77901

GUERRA, Irma N (At) 400 Holcomb Bridge Rd, Norcross, GA 30071

GUERRA, Norma Yanira (Los)

GUERRA-DIAZ, Juan Antonio (Ore) Po Box 1731, Hillsboro, OR 97123

✠ **GUERRERO**, Orlando Jesus (Ve) Centro Diocesano, Avenue Caroni No 100, Caracas, Venezuela

GUERRERO-STAMP, Carmen Bruni (Az) 114 W Roosevelt, Phoenix, AZ 85003

GUERRIER, Michel Marguy (Hai)

GUERRIER, Panel Marc (SwFla) 3901 Davis Blvd, Naples, FL 34104

GUEVARA-CUENCE, Leticia R (At)

GUEVARA RODRIGUEZ, Carlos Eduardo (Colom) Calle 30 No 17-08, Barrio Armenia, Teusaquillo Bogota, Colombia

GUFFEY, Andrew Ryan (Mich)

GUFFEY, Emily Williams (Mich) 4550 N Hermitage Ave, Chicago, IL 60640

GUGLIERMETTO, Gian Luigi Luigi (Los)

GUIDA, Angela G (Az) 2480 Virginia St Apt 4, Berkeley, CA 94709

GUIDERO, Kirsten (NI)

GUIDRY, Robert Turner (WNC) 869 Daylily Ln, Hayesville, NC 28904

GUILFOYLE, David Martin (SO)

GUILLAUME-SAM, Sully (LI) 1405 Bushwick Ave, Brooklyn, NY 11207

GUILLEN, Anthony Anthony (Los) 198 Via Baja, Ventura, CA 93003

GUILMETTE, Paul Arthur (Alb)

GUINN, Leslie Joan (Tex)

GUINN, Patricia J (WNY) The Hermitage, 6353 Wooglin Rd, Dewittville, NY 14728

GUINTA, Denise (SwVa) 1032 Harper Valley Rd, Luray, VA 22835

GUISER, Kim D (Pa)

GUISTOLISE, Kate (Chi) 5555 N Sheridan Rd #608, Chicago, IL 60640

✠ **GULICK JR**, Ted (Va) 425 S 2nd St, Louisville, KY 40202

GUMBS, Delores Elvida (Episcopal VI) PO Box 6454, Christiansted, St Croix, VI 00823

✠ **GUMBS**, Edward (Episcopal VI) P.O. Box 7488, St Thomas, VI 00801

GUMULAUSKAS, Michael P (Ga)

GUNDERSON, David John (Mont) 313 S Yellowstone St, Livingston, MT 59047

GUNDERSON, Gretchen Anne (Oly) 629 Taft Ave, Raymond, WA 98577

GUNN, Daniel Cube (NJ) 402 Whiton Rd, Branchburg, NJ 08853

GUNN, Kevin Paul (Los) All Saints Parish, 5619 Monte Vista St, Los Angeles, CA 90042

GUNN, Nancy Emmel (Mo)

GUNN, Sally Watkins Pope (Va)

GUNN, Scott Alan (SO) Forward Movement, 412 Sycamore St, Cincinnati, OH 45202

✠ **GUNTER**, Matthew A (FdL) 22w400 Hackberry Dr, Glen Ellyn, IL 60137

GUNTHORPES, Alexander (LI) 2666 E 22nd St, Brooklyn, NY 11235

GUSTAFSON, Diana Vivian (WA) 2300 Cathedral Ave NW, Washington, DC 20008

GUSTAFSON, Elyse Marie (Chi) 1100 Stockton St, Jacksonville, FL 32204

GUSTAFSON III, Karl Edmund (Nev) 4201 W Washington Ave, Las Vegas, NV 89107

GUSTAFSON, Mary (WMass) 1840 University Ave W Apt 201, Saint Paul, MN 55104

GUSTIN, Pete (Va) 301 W Broad St Apt 762, Falls Church, VA 22046

GUTGSELL, Jessie D (O)

GUTHRIE, Bill (Nwk) 2812 Sequoyah Drive, Haines City, FL 33844

GUTHRIE, Emily (WA) 7215 Arthur Dr, Falls Church, VA 22046

GUTHRIE, Suzanne Elizabeth (The Episcopal NCal) 4 Erin Ct, Poughkeepsie, NY 12601

✠ **GUTIERREZ**, Daniel (Pa) 601 Montano Rd NW, Albuquerque, NM 87107

GUTIERREZ, Hayr (PR) Villas De Castro, Calle 25 Ee-19, Caguas, PR 00726

GUTIERREZ, Janssen J (Tex) 6635 Alder Dr, Houston, TX 77081

GUTIERREZ, Jorge Martin (Roch) 48 Whitcomb Rd, Boxborough, MA 01719

GUTIERREZ, Jorge Pablo (SeFla) 1003 Allendale Rd, West Palm Beach, FL 33405

GUTIERREZ-DUARTE, Edgar (Mass) 32 Franklin Ave, Chelsea, MA 02150

GUTIERREZ FERRO, Jose Angel (Cu)

GUTWEIN, Dorothy (Az)

GUTWEIN, Martin (NJ) 527 N 2nd St, Camden, NJ 08102

GUY, Kenneth Gordon (FdL) N11052 Norway Ln, Tomahawk, WI 54487

GUZMAN, Pedro (NJ) 7709 Piersanti Ct, Pennsauken, NJ 08109

GUZMAN HERRERA, Diana (PR)

GUZMAN REYES, Rosaina A (PR)

GUZMAN VELEZ, Francisco Inocencio (PR) PO Box 902, Saint Just, PR 00978

GWIN, Connor Brindley (NC) 8201 Bellfield Pl, Charlotte, NC 28270

GWINN, Thomas Wallace (Alb) Box 286, North Stratford, NH 03590

GWYN III, Lewis R. (CFla) 5855 39th Ln, Vero Beach, FL 32966

GWYN, Roxane Stewart (At) 1618 Morgan Copeland Rd, Hamilton, GA 31811

GWYNN, Caron A (WA) St. Timothy's Episcopal Church, 3601 Alabama Avenue, S.E., Washington, DC 20020

GWYNNE, Geoff Carrington (Tex) 1104 Peregrine Dr, Friendswood, TX 77546

H

HAACK, Christopher Allyn (Minn) 877 Jessie St, Saint Paul, MN 55130

HAACK, Marcus John (Ia)

HAAS, Kirk (WVa) 112 S Walnut St, Morgantown, WV 26501

HAAS, Margaret Ann (Mich) 2923 Roundtree Blvd Apt A2, Ypsilanti, MI 48197

HAASE, Sylvia Anne (Oly) Po Box 208, Vaughn, WA 98394

HABECKER, Elizabeth Ann (RI) PO Box 743, Bristol, RI 02809

HABECKER, John Christian (Nwk) 47 Av Sur 723 Cfb, Apartado 01 274, San Salvador, CA 000

HABERSANG, Paul (Vt) 110 S Jefferson Rd Unit 103, South Burlington, VT 05403

HABIBY, Samir Jamil (Ga) 24 Sawyers Crossing Rd, Swanzey, NH 03446

HACKBARTH, Michael George (FdL)

HACKER, Craig A (Alb) PO Box 775, Waddington, NY 13694

HACKER, David (Spok) PO Box 356, Zillah, WA 98953

HACKETT, Ann Riley (At) Po Box 169, Morrow, GA 30260

HACKETT JR, Charles Dudleigh (At) 10298 Big Cnoe, Big Canoe, GA 30143

HACKETT, Christopher James (ETenn) 413 Cumberland Ave, Knoxville, TN 37902

HACKETT, David Robert (ETenn) 7994 Prince Dr, Ooltewah, TN 37363

HACKETT, Michael George (La)

HACKLER, Wendy Kaye Douglas (Az) 10486 N. Autumn Hill Lane, Tucson, AZ 85737

HACKNEY, Lisa E (Chi) 165 N Canal 1313, Chicago, IL 60606

HADAWAY, Elizabeth Leigh (WNY) 913 Briarwood Ct, Morgantown, WV 26505

HADAWAY JR, Michael (WNY) PO Box 205, Kingsville, MD 21087

HADDAD, Mary E (Eur) 87 Ave Raymond Poincare, Paris, 75116, France

HADDIX JR, Ted (Va) 505 Broad Leaf Circle, Raleigh, NC 27613

HADDOX, Jason M (Okla) 4739 Guerley Rd, Cincinnati, OH 45238

HADE, Lynn Augustine (Md) Grace Memorial Church, 1022 Main St, Darlington, MD 21034

HADEN JR, Robert Lee (NC) 798 Evans Rd., Hendersonville, NC 28739

HADLER JR, Jacques (WA) 1736 Columbia Rd NW Apt 201, Washington, DC 20009

HADLEY, Arthur Clayton (SO) 1500 Shasta, McAllen, TX 78504

HAENKE, Roger Alan (SanD)

HAFER, Joel Gilbert (WNC) 1024 Orleans Ave, Hendersonville, NC 28791

HAGAN, Erika P (Ct)

HAGAN JR, John (WVa) 3510 ALBON RD, MAUMEE, OH 43537

HAGANS, Michele (WA) 1645 Myrtle St NW, Washington, DC 20012

HAGBERG, Joseph Alan (CGC) 6329 Causeway Road, Panama City, FL 32408

HAGE, Raymond Joseph (WVa) 275 High Dr, Huntington, WV 25705

HAGEN, Amelia (Me) 39 Highland Ave, Millinocket, ME 04462

HAGEN, James Barlow (NY) 21-15 34th Ave apt 14C, Astoria, NY 11106

HAGEN, Maureen (Ore) 3030 Se Bybee Blvd, Portland, OR 97202

HAGENBUCH, Chris (Spok) 311 S Hall St, Grangeville, ID 83530

HAGER, Alicia (WMich)

HAGER, Marty Monroe (Va) St Thomas Episcopal Church, 8991 Brook Rd, McLean, VA 22102

HAGERMAN, Steven William (Colo) 1110 Saint Stephens Church Rd, Crownsville, MD 21032

HAGERTY, Stephen P (Md) 84 Ehrhardt Rd, Pearl River, NY 10965

HAGGENJOS, Babette Florence (The Episcopal NCal)

HAGGENJOS JR, Cliff (The Episcopal NCal) 1905 Third St, Napa, CA 94559

HAGGERTY, Mary (Mo) 7774 Wise Ave, Richmond Heights, MO 63117

HAGLER, James Robert (ETenn) 933 S. 17th St., Newark, NJ 07108

HAGNER, Nancy (Mass)

HAGUE, Bill (WA) 4001 Franklin St, Kensington, MD 20895

HAGUE, Elizabeth Ann (WA) 4507 Leland St, Chevy Chase, MD 20815

HAGUE, Jane Milliken (WA) 8 All Saints Rd, Princeton, NJ 08540

HAGUE, Leslie (SeFla) 333 Tarpon Dr, Fort Lauderdale, FL 33301

HAHN, Dorothee Elisabeth (Eur) 815 2nd Ave, New York, NY 10017

HAHN, William Douglas (Lex) 713 Edgewater Dr, Lexington, KY 40502

HAHNE, Ruth Olive (CFla) 9260-C Sw 61st Way, Boca Raton, FL 33428

HAHNEMAN, Geoffrey (Ct) 180 Battery Park Dr, Bridgeport, CT 06605

HAHNEMAN, Lisa (Ct) 154 Jackman Ave, Fairfield, CT 06825

HAIG, Karen (Oly) St Barnabas Episcopal Church, 1187 Wyatt Way NW, Bainbridge Island, WA 98110

HAIGHT, Margaret (Va) 7610 Heths Salient St Apt 200, Spotsylvania, VA 22553

HAILEY, Victor (Md) 1110 Saint Stephens Church Rd, Crownsville, MD 21032

HAIN, John Walter (NJ) 13 Madison Ave, Flemington, NJ 08822

HAINES, Harry Jeffrey (WNY) 24 Cobb Ter, Rochester, NY 14620

HAINES, Mike (Pa) 31 Kleyona Ave, Phoenixville, PA 19460

HAINES III, Ralph Edward (SVa) 42 Park Ave, Newport News, VA 23607

HAINES-MURDOCCO, Sandra Paula (RI) 109 Old Post Rd, Wakefield, RI 02879

HAIRSTON, James McArthur (Mass) Grace Church Everett, 67 Norwood St, Everett, MA 02149

HAIRSTON, Raleigh Daniel (EC) 3183 Kings Bay Cir, Decatur, GA 30034

HAKIEL, Nicholas Edward (Ida) 1014 Wildwood St, Sultan, WA 98294

HALE, Douglas J (Ore) 92725 Hyland Ln, Coos Bay, OR 97420

HALE, Jane Currie (Ct) Trinity Episcopal Church, Po Box 276, Brooklyn, CT 06234

HALE, Linda Mosier (EO) PO Box 456, Sunnyside, WA 98944

HALE, Patricia Ann (Ore) 92725 Hyland Ln, Coos Bay, OR 97420

HALE, William Charles (Mich) 1067 Hubbard St, Detroit, MI 48209

HALEY-RAY, Judith (Pa) 163 Colket Ln, Devon, PA 19333

HALFORD, Cathrine Nance (Miss) 147 Daniel Lake Blvd, Jackson, MS 39212

HALKETT, Thomas (Me) PO Box 564, Machias, ME 04654

HALL, Addison Curtis (Mass) 79 Denton Rd, Wellesley, MA 02482

HALL, Albert Benjamin (WMass) 775 Columbia Northwest, Port Charlotte, FL 33952

HALL, Caroline J A (ECR) PO Box 6359, Los Osos, CA 93412

HALL, Charles William (Tenn)

HALL, Charlotte Melissa (Nwk) 11 S Kingman Rd, South Orange, NJ 07079

HALL, Daniel Charles (NJ) 114 Willow Dr, North Cape May, NJ 08204

HALL, Daniel Emerson (Pgh) 412 Locust St, Pittsburgh, PA 15218

HALL, David A (Ala) 2753 11th Ave S, Birmingham, AL 35205

HALL, David Moreland (WMass) 20 Winchester Ave, Auburn, MA 01501

HALL, Dianne Costner (Ga) 212 N Jefferson St, Albany, GA 31701

HALL, Donna (SeFla) 941 Allendale Rd, West Palm Beach, FL 33405

HALL, Elizabeth (CFla)

HALL, Ernest Eugene (Spr) 1808 Lakeside Dr Unit A, Champaign, IL 61821

HALL, Gary (Los) Cath of St Peter & St Paul, 3101 Wisconsin Ave NW, Washington, DC 20016

HALL, John C N (Va) 2500 W Twinoaks Dr, Prescott, AZ 86305

HALL, John Liston (Ia) 20 Mcclellan Blvd, Davenport, IA 52803

HALL, Jon (Lex) 15764 Clayton Rd, Ellisville, MO 63011

HALL, Laurens Allen (Tex) 3725 Chevy Chase Dr, Houston, TX 77019

HALL, Leigh (NY) 28 Bancroft Rd, Poughkeepsie, NY 12601

HALL, Mark (Episcopal SJ) 2212 River Dr, Stockton, CA 95204

HALL, Mark R (Dal) 5100 Ross Ave, Dallas, TX 75206

HALL, Mavis Ann (Neb) 3214 Davy Jones Dr, Plattsmouth, NE 68048

HALL, Melinda (NwPa) Holy Trinity Church, 62 Pickering St, Brookville, PA 15825

HALL, Michael Gregory (CFla) Shepherd Of The Hills, 2540 W Norvell Bryant Hwy, Lecanto, FL 34461

HALL, Natalie (Pgh)

HALL, Patrick (Tex) 915 Saulnier St # B, Houston, TX 77019

HALL, Paula Claire (WLa) 361 Cypress Loop, Farmerville, LA 71241

HALL, Rosalind Katherine (SwFla) Episcopal Church of Nativity, 5900 N Lockwood Ridge Rd, Sarasota, FL 34243

HALL, Ryan Ashley (SD) St. Paul's Episcopal Church, 726 6th St, Brookings, SD 57006

HALL, Tod Latham (NH) 140 Muzzy Hill Rd, Milan, NH 03588

HALL, Virginia Badgeley (Ind) 705 S. Washington St., Bloomington, IN 47401

HALLADAY, Richard Allen (Ind) 448 Freeman Ridge Rd, Nashville, IN 47448

HALLAHAN JR, Eugene (SO)

HALLAHAN, T Mark (Los)

HALLANAN, Sunny (Eur) Chaussee de Charleroi 2, 1420 Braine-lAlleud, Belgium

HALLE, Michael Addenbrooke (Az) 241 S.Beverly Street, Chandler, AZ 85225

HALLENBECK, Edwin F (RI) 101 Larchmont Rd, Warwick, RI 02886

HALLER, Robert Bennett (NJ) Trinity Episcopal Church, Vincentown, NJ 08088

HALLER, Tobias Stanislas (NY) 305 W Lafayette Ave, Baltimore, MD 21217

HALLETT, Timothy Jerome (Spr) 3007 N Ramble Rd W, Bloomington, IN 47408

HALLEY, Marcus (Ct) 6401 Wornall Ter, Kansas City, MO 64113

HALLISEY, L Ann (The Episcopal NCal) 1711 Westshore St, Davis, CA 95616

HALLMARK, Charlotte A (WMich) PO Box 306, Middleburg, VA 20118

HALLOCK JR, Harold H (Va) 920 Flordon Dr, Charlottesville, VA 22901

HALLORAN, Sarah Katherine Smith (Ala) 917 Gordon Woods Rd, Wilmington, NC 28411

HALLY, Jane Eloise (At) 18 Lenox Pointe NE Ste A, Atlanta, GA 30324

HALSTEAD, Jan (Tex) Christ Episcopal Church, 3520 Whitestone Blvd, Cedar Park, TX 78613

HALT, David Jason (Dal) 3102 Bethany Ln, Texarkana, TX 75503

HALTON IV, John Charles (Lex)

HALVERSON-RIGATUSO, Kathryn (Ia) 111 N Vine St, Glenwood, IA 51534

HALVERSTADT JR, Albert Nast (Colo) 1244 Detroit St, Denver, CO 80206

HALVORSEN, Douglas C (NJ) 28 Oakhurst Ln, Mount Laurel, NJ 08054

HAMBLETON, Coralie Voce (NMich) St Paul's Episcopal Church, 201 E Ridge St, Marquette, MI 49855

HAMBLIN, Jeffrey L (LI) 9048 Willow Brook Dr, Sarasota, FL 34238

HAMBLIN, Sheldon (LI) 2115 Albemarle Ter, Brooklyn, NY 11226

HAMBY, Daniell Carl (Pa) 10 Lorile Cir, Eufaula, AL 36027

HAMBY, Timothy Christopher (Lex) 25 S 3rd St, Wilmington, NC 28401

HAMER, Donald (Ct) 240 Kenyon St, Hartford, CT 06105

HAMERSLEY, Andrew C (NJ) 15 Kara Ann Dr, Framingham, MA 01701

HAMES, Patty Margaret (Ct) 21 N Main St, Niantic, CT 06357

HAMILL, Allardyce Armstrong (CFla) Church of our Saviour, 200 NW 3rd St, Okeechobee, FL 34972

HAMILL, Charles Bw (Ct) Christ Tec Ch N Hills, 5910 Babcock Blvd, Pittsburgh, PA 15237

HAMILL, Jan Elizabeth (Md) 703 Peppard Dr, Bel Air, MD 21014

HAMILTON, Abigail W (Nwk) 681 Prospect Ave # 7052, West Orange, NJ 07052

HAMILTON, David (Vt) 129 Cumberland Rd, Burlington, VT 05408

HAMILTON, Gordon (USC) 101 Woodside Dr, Gaffney, SC 29340

HAMILTON SR, James (Tex) 13618 Brighton Park Dr, Houston, TX 77044

HAMILTON, James G (Md) Bmore Ch Plant, 1025 S Potomac St, Baltimore, MD 21224

HAMILTON, Jamie (NH) 20 Main St, Exeter, NH 03833

HAMILTON, John (At) 248 Arcadia St Apt B, Dahlonega, GA 30533

HAMILTON, Lisa Lucy B (SwFla) 626 Hibiscus Dr, Venice, FL 34285

HAMILTON, Olivia Rae (SO)

HAMILTON, Paul Edward Connell (LI) 8230 N Sussex Dr, Citrus Springs, FL 34434

HAMILTON, Reid Henry (At) 364 Ridgewood Dr, Hartwell, GA 30643

HAMILTON, Robert Earl (NC) 1200 N Elm St, Greensboro, NC 27401

HAMILTON, Roger John (CFla) 4018 Shorecrest Drive, Orlando, FL 32804

HAMILTON, Terrell Eugene (Episcopal SJ) 401 N Marilyn Ave, Wenatchee, WA 98801

HAMILTON, W Michael (WMass) 19 Bradford Rd, Natick, MA 01760

HAMLIN, Richard Lee (Roch) 6258 County Road 31a, Friendship, NY 14739

HAMLIN, W Richard (Mich) 1016 Poxson Ave, Lansing, MI 48910

HAMMATT JR, Edward Augustus (SeFla) 16330 Sw 80th Ave, Miami, FL 33157

HAMMON, LeRoy R (Ore) 820 Berwick Ct, Lake Oswego, OR 97034

HAMMOND, Blaine Randol (ECR) PO Box 293, Ben Lomond, CA 95005

HAMMOND, Constance Ann (Ore) 4045 S.E. Pine St., Portland, OR 97214

HAMMOND, Henry L (Md) 6705 Maxalea Rd, Baltimore, MD 21239

HAMMOND, James Allen (Va) 102 Cottage Drive, Winchester, VA 22603

HAMMOND, Jeff (WTex) 14526 Spaulding Dr, Corpus Christi, TX 78410

HAMMONDS, Joanie (Ala) 755 Plantation Dr, Selma, AL 36701

HAMNER IV, James Edward (At) 143 Sea Foam Dr, Raleigh, NC 27610

HAMP, Gary (WMich) 245 Rose Bud Ct, Traverse City, MI 49696

HAMPSON, Tom L (Episcopal SJ)

HAMPTON, Carol McDonald (Okla) 1414 N Hudson Ave, Oklahoma City, OK 73103

HAMPTON, Cynthia Marie (SO) 410 Torrence Ct, Cincinnati, OH 45202

HAMPTON, Roger Keith (Los) Po Box 260304, Corpus Christi, TX 78426

✠ **HAMPTON**, Sanford Zangwill Kaye (Oly) La Vida Real, 11588 Via Rancho San Diego, Apt D 3049, El Cajon, CA 92019

HAN, Heewoo Daniel (Va) 2 All Souls Place, London England, W1B 3DA, Great Britain (UK)

HAN, Valentine S (Va) 4060 Championship Dr, Annandale, VA 22003

HANAHAN, Gwin Hunter (At) 2744 Peachtree Rd NW, Atlanta, GA 30305

HANAVAN, Julianne (RI) 674 Westminster St, Providence, RI 02903

HANBACK, Holly (Va) 14 Cornwall St NW, Leesburg, VA 20176

HANCOCK, Art (Minn) 13705 Perry Lake Rd, Cable, WI 54821

HANCOCK, Carol Jean (Va) 7317 Dress Blue Cir, Mechanicsville, VA 23116

HANCOCK, Melinda Bowne (NI)

HANCOCK, Paul B (Ga) 1317 Gordon Ave, Thomasville, GA 31792

HAND, Gary Dean (Los) 69/659 Moo Ban Far Rangsit, Bungyeetho, Thanyaburi, Pathum Thani Thailand, 12130, Thailand

HANDI, Matt (Ct)

HANDLOSS, Pattie (Mass) 115 Bayridge Ln, Duxbury, MA 02332

HANDS, Don (Mil) 6 Becks Retreat, Savannah, GA 31411

HANDSCHY, Daniel John (CNY) 9373 Garber Rd, Saint Louis, MO 63126

HANDWERK, Larry Wayne (Chi) 9517 Springfield Ave, Evanston, IL 60203

HANEN, Patricia (O) 10 Premier Ct, Durham, NC 27713

HANEY, Jack Howard (NH) 2 Leeward Way, Fairhaven, MA 02719

HANEY, James Paul (NwT) 4904 14th Street, Lubbock, TX 79416

HANEY V, James Paul (NwT) St Pauls-on-the-Plains, 1510 Avenue X, Lubbock, TX 79401

HANISIAN, Jim (SO) 1409 W Gantry Ct, Leland, NC 28451

HANISIAN, Matthew R (Md) St Martins-in-the-Field, 375 Benfield Rd, Severna Park, MD 21146

HANK, Daniel H (USC) 4621 Kilbourne Rd, Columbia, SC 29206

HANKINS, Samuel Scott (Az) 2501 W Zia Rd Apt 8205, Santa Fe, NM 87505

HANKINSON JR, Benjamin D (Spr) W352n5317 Lake Dr, Oconomowoc, WI 53066

HANKS JR, Alexander Hamilton (WNC) Po Box 8893, Asheville, NC 28814

HANKS, Paige Alvarez (SwFla) 1704 Woodland Ave, Austin, TX 78741

HANLEY, Elise Ashley (NY) 10460 Queens Blvd Apt 3g, Forest Hills, NY 11375

HANLEY, Ian David (Los) 59131 Wilcox Ln, Yucca Valley, CA 92284

✠ **HANLEY**, Michael (Ore) Episcopal Diocese of Oregon, 11800 S Military Ln, Portland, OR 97219

HANLEY, Nicole Regina (NY) PO Box 708, 13 Walnut St, Walden, NY 12586

HANNA, Gerald Benson (Oly) 11527 9th Ave Ne, Seattle, WA 98125

HANNA, Nancy Wadsworth (NY) 100 Edward Bentley Rd., Lawrence, NY 11559

HANNA, Raymond (EC) PO Box 1043, Mount Airy, NC 27030

HANNAH, Joseph (CNY)

HANNEMAN, Jonathan Whitney (Oly)

HANNIBAL, Preston Belfield (WA) Washington National Cathedral, Mount St Alban, Washington, DC 20016

HANNON, Timothy Robert (CNY)

HANNUM, Christopher Cary Lee (At) 2148 Winding Creek Ln Sw, Marietta, GA 30064

HANSEL, Bob (SO) PO Box 217, Little Switzerland, NC 28749

HANSELL, Susan Weir (CFla) 2048 Ryan Way, Winter Haven, FL 33884
HANSELMAN, David (CNY) PO Box 88, Greene, NY 13778
HANSEN, Carl R (ECR) 429 Park Pl, King City, CA 93930
HANSEN, Elisa Marie (SwFla) 5615 Midnight Pass Rd, Sarasota, FL 34242
HANSEN, Janis Lee (Mont) 2430 SW Crestdale Dr, Portland, OR 97225
HANSEN, Jessica V (Cal) 1532 Burlingame Ave, Burlingame, CA 94010
HANSEN, Karen Sue (Okla) 310 E. Noble Ave., Guthrie, OK 73044
HANSEN, Knute Coates (Ct)
HANSEN, Marcia E (The Episcopal NCal) 190 Kaseberg Dr, Roseville, CA 95678
HANSEN, Michelle H (Ct) 125 Parklawn Dr, Waterbury, CT 06708
HANSEN, Nancy (Nwk)
HANSEN JR, Robert F (ECR) 16 Salisbury Dr Apt 7217, Asheville, NC 28803
HANSEN, Thomas Parker (NI) 3717 N Washington Rd, Fort Wayne, IN 46802
HANSKNECHT, Jeanne Marie (Mich) 10 Mill St, Cazenovia, NY 13035
HANSLEY, Mary (SVa) 301 7th St W Unit 2207, Unit 2207, Northfield, MN 55057
HANSON III, Aquilla (Fla) 406 Glenridge Rd, Perry, FL 32348
HANSON, Deborah Ann (Miss) 5400 Old Canton Rd, Jackson, MS 39211
HANSON, Jeffrey (Mass)
HANSON, Norma (Del) 405 Lady Huntingdon Ln, Asheville, NC 28803
HANSON-FOSS, Patricia Jean (Alb) PO Box 237, Au Sable Forks, NY 12912
HANSTINE, Barbara Ann (Alb) 287 Leonard St, Hancock, NY 13783
HANWAY JR, Donald Grant (Neb) 5700 Fremont St Apt 242, Lincoln, NE 68507
HANWAY, Wayne Edward (Okla)
HANYZEWSKI, The Rev'd Andrew (NJ) 404 Sunset Rd, Burlington, NJ 08016
HAPTONSTAHL, Stephen R (Minn) 807 Louisiana Ave, Cumberland, MD 21502
HARBER, Mike (Ala) 11245 Us Highway 80 W, Shorter, AL 36075
HARBER, Rachel (Va)
HARBIN, J Derek (SVa) 424 Washington St, Portsmouth, VA 23704
HARBOLD, Sally (NC) 221 Union St, Cary, NC 27511
HARBORT, Raymond Louis (Be) 1382 Newtown Langhorne Rd # E-207, Newtown, PA 18940
HARDAWAY IV, John Benjamin (USC) 404 North St, Anderson, SC 29621
HARDAWAY, Ripp Barton (WTex) 312 S Guenther Ave, New Braunfels, TX 78130

HARDAWAY, Susan (USC) 404 North St, Anderson, SC 29621
HARDEN, Elizabeth A (Roch)
HARDEN, Rosa Lee (Cal) 15 Riparian Way, Swannanoa, NC 28778
HARDENSTINE, Autumn Hecker (Pa) 126 Grist Mill Rd, Schuylkill Haven, PA 17972
HARDER, Cheryl Anne (Okla) 10 E Penton Blvd, Duluth, MN 55808
HARDIE JR, John Ford (WTex) 6709 Pharaoh Dr, Corpus Christi, TX 78412
HARDIN, Ann Marie (EO) 241 SE 2nd St, Pendleton, OR 97801
HARDIN, Crystal J (Va)
HARDIN, Glennda Cecile (Tex) PO Box 10357, Liberty, TX 77575
HARDIN, Nancy H (SO)
HARDING, Kerith (The Episcopal Church in Haw)
HARDING, Leander Samuel (Alb) Trinity School For Ministry, 311 Eleventh Street, Ambridge, PA 15003
HARDING, Rona (WA) 22968 Esperanza Drive, Lexington Park, MD 20653
HARDING, Sahra (O) 1734 Bridlewood Dr, Pittsburg, CA 94565
HARDING, Scott (At) 48 Trestle Pt, Toccoa, GA 30577
HARDING, Stephen Riker (Mass) 1047 Amsterdam Ave, New York, NY 10025
HARDING, Susannah Greer (Va) 3301 Hidden Meadow Dr, Oak Hill, VA 20171
HARDMAN, JOhn (Chi) 222 Kenilworth Ave., Kenilworth, IL 60043
HARDWICK, Bill (Oly) 19 1 2 Murray St, Norwalk, CT 06851
HARDWICK, Dana (Lex) 7620 Summerglen Dr, Raleigh, NC 27615
HARDWICK, Lada Eldredge (Colo) 4490 Hanover Ave, Boulder, CO 80305
HARDWICK, Linda Cornelius (Mo) 1001 Pheasant Hill Drive, Rolla, MO 65401
HARDY, Cameron (NY) 696 Deep Hollow Rd., Millbrook, NY 12545
HARDY, Karen (WNY) 200 Cazenovia St, Buffalo, NY 14210
HARDY, Kim (Vt) 4 St James Pl, Essex Junction, VT 05452
HARDY, Mary Elizabeth Holsberry (La) Po Box 3654, Durango, CO 81302
HARDY, Velinda Elaine (NC) P.O. Box 86, 4880 Highway 561 East, Tillery, NC 27887
HARE, Ann DuBuisson (NY) 255 Huguenot St Apt 1712, New Rochelle, NY 10801
HARE, Delmas (At) 104 Sequoyah Hills Dr, Fletcher, NC 28732
HARER, Peter (CPa) 251 S Derr Dr, Lewisburg, PA 17837
HARGETT JR, Ernest Augustus (CFla)
HARGIS, Kathleen A (Neb) PO Box 1414, Dodge City, KS 67801

HARGREAVES, Helen (Ark) 10 Camp Mitchell Rd, Morrilton, AR 72110
HARGREAVES, Mark Kingston (SanD) St James Episcopal Church, 743 Prospect St, La Jolla, CA 92037
HARGREAVES, Robert Alan (Me) Po Box 96, Nobleboro, ME 04555
HARGROVE, Thomas J (Pa) 1628 Prospect St, Ewing, NJ 08638
HARIDIS, Margaret (Nwk) 6095 Summerlake Dr, Port Orange, FL 32127
HARING, Charlotte (Az) 3942 E Monte Vista Dr, Tucson, AZ 85712
HARKER, Margaret Ann Griggs (NI) 1364 N Pinebluff Dr, Marion, IN 46952
HARKINS III, John William (At) 11086 Big Canoe, 125 Choctaw Ridge, Jasper, GA 30143
HARKNESS SR, Robert D (WLa)
HARLAN, Barry S (WVa) 3887 Carriage Ln SW, Conyers, GA 30094
HARLAN, James (SeFla) 11827 Canon Blvd Ste 101, Newport News, VA 23606
HARLAND, Mary Frances (Spok) Po Box 1510, Medical Lake, WA 99022
HARMAN, Torrence (Va) 6812 Kensington Ave, Richmond, VA 23226
HARMON, Andrew Miles (Mil) 4574 Tupello St, Baton Rouge, LA 70808
HARMON, Jessica Louise (Episcopal SJ)
HARMON, John (WA) 7005 Piney Branch Rd NW, Washington, DC 20012
HARMON, Jude Aaron (Cal) 1035 Pine St, Menlo Park, CA 94025
HARMON, Judith Lynn (Mich) 8874 Northern Ave, Plymouth, MI 48170
HARMON, Robert Dale (Spr) 1119 Oakland Ave, 1119 Oakland Ave, Mount Vernon, IL 62864
HARMON, Zachary C (NH) 1444 Liberty St SE, Salem, OR 97302
HARMUTH, Karl Michael (Dal) 9021 Church Rd, Dallas, TX 75231
HARNEY, Margaret Ferris (At) 4393 Garmon Rd Nw, Atlanta, GA 30327
HARPER, Anna Katherine (CFla) St Mary's Church, 5750 SE 115th St, Belleview, FL 34420
HARPER, Barbara Anne (ETenn) 1155 Woodlawn Rd, Lenoir City, TN 37771
HARPER, Catherine Ann (Mass) 124 Front St, Marion, MA 02738
HARPER, David Scott (CPa) 5598 Arminda St, Harrisburg, PA 17109
HARPER, Fletcher (Nwk) 241A Johnson Ave Apt M1, Hackensack, NJ 07601
HARPER, Harry Taylor (WA) 36303 Notley Manor Ln, Chaptico, MD 20621
HARPER, Helen Othelia (WNY) 210 Drummond Ave, Ridgecrest, CA 93555
HARPER, John Brammer (Ia) 1310 Bristol Dr, Iowa City, IA 52245

HARPER, John Harris (Ala) 2600 Arlington Ave S Apt 62, Birmingham, AL 35205

HARPER, Katherine Stuart (Ala) 3775 Crosshaven Dr, Birmingham, AL 35223

HARPER, William Roland (Oly) 5836 Packard Ln Ne, Bainbridge Island, WA 98110

HARPFER, Nancy Jean Fuller (EMich) St Andrews Episcopal Church, PO Box 52, Harrisville, MI 48740

HARPSTER, Chris (ETenn) St Pauls Episcopal Church, 161 E Ravine Rd, Kingsport, TN 37660

HARRELL, Linda J (Ore) 99 Brattle St, Cambridge, MA 02138

HARRELSON, Larry Eugene (Ida) 3095 W. Ravenhurst St., Meridian, ID 83646

HARRES, Elisa P (At) 13479 Spring View Dr, Alpharetta, GA 30004

HARRIES, Susan (NMich) 1111 Bingham Ave, Sault Sainte Marie, MI 49783

HARRIES, Thomas (Minn) 10520 Beard Ave S, Bloomington, MN 55431

HARRIGAN, Kate (CPa) 1105 Old Quaker Rd, Etters, PA 17319

HARRIMAN, Barbara June (Nwk)

HARRINGTON, Clayton Doyle (At)

HARRINGTON, Debra Lynn (Chi) 1250 Averill Dr, Batavia, IL 60510

HARRINGTON, James (Tex)

HARRINGTON, Lynn Beth (NY) 203 Salem Rd, Pound Ridge, NY 10576

HARRINGTON, Thomas Anthony (Okla) 2961 N 23rd St W, Muskogee, OK 74401

HARRIS, Anne (Miss) 705 Rayburn Ave, Ocean Springs, MS 39564

HARRIS, Carl Burton (Va) 2727 Fairview Ave E Apt 3b, Seattle, WA 98102

HARRIS, Cheryl Jeanne (Neb) 820 Weat 9th Street, Alliance, NE 69301

HARRIS, Christopher Ross (Mich)

HARRIS, Donald Bell (SVa) 121 Jordans Journey, Williamsburg, VA 23185

HARRIS, Edmund Immanuel (Oly) 1336 Pawtucket Ave, Rumford, RI 02916

HARRIS, Gareth Scott (At) Po Box 191708, Atlanta, GA 31119

✠ **HARRIS**, Gayle (Mass) 138 Tremont St, Boston, MA 02111

HARRIS, Helen (Alb)

HARRIS, Henry G (O) 735 Woodrich St Sw, Massillon, OH 44646

HARRIS, Herman (USC) 633 Swallow Rd, Elgin, SC 29045

HARRIS JR, James Wesley (WMo) 1700 N Westmoreland Rd, Desoto, TX 75115

HARRIS, John E (Ga) 30 Anderson Ave., Holden, MA 01520

HARRIS, John T (The Episcopal NCal) PO Box 1291, Gridley, CA 95948

HARRIS, Jonathan (SwVa) 3286 Avenham Ave Sw, Roanoke, VA 24014

HARRIS, Judy Beth (Tex)

HARRIS, Julie (WVa) 200 W King St, Martinsburg, WV 25401

HARRIS, Ladd Keith (WMich) 5527 N Sierra Ter, Beverly Hills, FL 34465

HARRIS JR, Lawrence (WA) 10450 Lottsford Rd Apt 1218, Mitchellville, MD 20721

HARRIS, Lorraine Denise (Pa) PO Box 1551, Camden, NJ 08101

HARRIS, Margaret Stilwell (Ia) 1120 45th St, Des Moines, IA 50311

HARRIS, Mark (Del) 207 E Market St, Lewes, DE 19958

HARRIS, Mark Hugh (Ore) 385 Doral Dr, Pinehurst, NC 28374

HARRIS, Mark Paul (Ark) 200 N Elm St, Searcy, AR 72143

HARRIS, Martha Caldwell (CGC) 79 6th St., Apalachicola, FL 32320

HARRIS, Martha Lester (CPa)

HARRIS, Melissa Anderson (Okla)

HARRIS, Michael William Henry (SwFla) 24311 Narwhal Lane, Port Charlotte, FL 33983

HARRIS, Patricia Lyn (WMich)

HARRIS JR, Paul Sherwood (Pa) 810 Pine St, Philadelphia, PA 19107

HARRIS, Paula (Mil) 3010 Ashford Ln, Madison, WI 53713

HARRIS, Phillip Jay (SO) 88 S Parkview Ave, Bexley, OH 43209

HARRIS, Rebecca (NwPa)

HARRIS, Robert Carradine (WTex) PO Box 314, 395 State Highway 173 N, Bandera, TX 78003

HARRIS, Steve (CPa) 1138 Boyds School Rd, Gettysburg, PA 17325

HARRIS, Suzanne Love (NJ) Box 864, Wilson, WY 83014

HARRIS, Vincent Powell (WA) 3917 Peppertree Ln, Silver Spring, MD 20906

HARRIS-BAYFIELD, Maeva Hair (Tex) 300 Westmnstr Cantrbry Dr, Apt 405, Winchester, VA 22603

✠ **HARRISON**, Dena Arnall (Tex) 3402 Windsor Rd, Austin, TX 78703

HARRISON JR, Edward (SanD) 1114 9th St, Coronado, CA 92118

HARRISON, Elizabeth Arendt (CFla) 215 S Lake Florence Dr, Winter Haven, FL 33884

HARRISON JR, G Hendree (Lex) 533 E Main St, Lexington, KY 40508

HARRISON, Harold Donald (At) 3823 Cherokee Frd, Gainesville, GA 30506

HARRISON, Jim (EMich) All Saints Episcopal Church, 100 N Drew St, Appleton, WI 54911

HARRISON, Merle Marie (Colo) 816 Harrison Ave, Canon City, CO 81212

HARRISON, Rachel (O)

HARRISON JR, Robert (WA) Churchillplein 6, The Hague, 2517 JW, Netherlands

HARRISON, Ronald Edward (Alb) 24 Summit Ave, Latham, NY 12110

HARRISON, Shari Bishop (Ala) 2185 Heritage Dr, Guntersville, AL 35976

HARRISON, Sherridan (WTex) 2503 Wood Run, San Antonio, TX 78251

HARRISS, Susan Carol (NY) 209 Garth Rd Apt 2l, Scarsdale, NY 10583

HARRITY, Alison (CFla) 5151 Lake Howell Rd, Winter Park, FL 32792

HARRON II, Frank Martin (WA) 10708 Brewer House Rd, North Bethesda, MD 20852

HARROP, Stephen (Tai) 16 W 3rd St, Essington, PA 19029

HART, Alan Reed (Alb) 120 Waters Rd, Scotia, NY 12302

HART, Benjamin James (Ky) Grace Episcopal Church, 216 E 6th St, Hopkinsville, KY 42240

HART, Curtis Webb (NY) 132 N Broadway 1NW, Tarrytown, NY 10591

✠ **HART**, Donald Purple (The Episcopal Church in Haw) P.O. Box 461, Peterborough, NH 03458

HART, Donnalee (The Episcopal NCal) St Francis in the Redwoods, 66 E Commercial St, Willits, CA 95490

HART JR, George Barrow (Ark) 3802 Hwy 82 W, Crossett, AR 71635

HART, J. Joseph (Md) 6701 N Charles St, Towson, MD 21204

HART, Lois Ann (Me) 1100 Washington St, Bath, ME 04530

HART, Lorraine M (Alb) 1154 Hedgewood Ln, Niskayuna, NY 12309

HART, Mary Carol (Alb) 120 Waters Rd, Scotia, NY 12302

HART, Patricia Peterson (U)

HART, Robert (Colo) 1471 Bennavile Ave, Birmingham, MI 48009

HART, Stephen Anthony (Alb) 8312 Daisy Cutter Xing, Georgetown, TX 78626

HART, Valerie Ann (ECR) 17100 Cambridge Way Unit 310, Tustin, CA 92782

HART, William Gardner (NY) 414 Haines Rd # 4, Mount Kisco, NY 10549

HARTE, Barry Jay (Be) 800 E Homestead Ln, Easton, PA 18042

HARTE JR, John Joseph Meakin (Az) 1000 E Ponderosa Pkwy, Flagstaff, AZ 86001

HARTE, Kathleen Audrey (LI)

HARTE, Susan Brainard (Az) 1000 E. Ponderosa Parkway, Flagstaff, AZ 86001

HART GARNER, Eleanor E (Be) 125 Mount Joy St, Mount Joy, PA 17552

HARTJEN JR, Raymond Clifton (Kan) 1015 S. 5th St., Leavenworth, KS 66048

HARTL, Palmer (Pa) 240 S 3rd St, Philadelphia, PA 19106

HARTLEY, Anne E (SwFla)

HARTLEY, Chris (Ala) 1000 W 18th St, Anniston, AL 36201

[For Corrections see p. C1] *Clergy List*

HARTLEY, Harold Aitken (Mich) 1106 Riverview St, Rogers City, MI 49779

HARTLEY, James Peyton (USC)

HARTLEY, Loyde Hobart (CPa) St James Church, 119 N Duke St, Lancaster, PA 17602

HARTLEY, Melissa M (At) 735 University Ave, Sewanee, TN 37383

HARTLEY, Robert Henry (The Episcopal NCal) 14530 N Line Post Ln, Tucson, AZ 85755

HARTLEY, Tim (Los) 609 S Hudson Ave, Pasadena, CA 91106

HARTLING, David Charles (CFla) 1606 Fort Smith Blvd, Deltona, FL 32725

HARTLING, Gardner J (Lex) 1013 Marshall Park Dr, Georgetown, KY 40324

HARTMAN, Anthony Eden (EMich) 3458 E Mckinley Rd, Midland, MI 48640

HARTMAN, Holly H (Mass) PO Box 920372, Needham, MA 02492

HARTMAN, John Franklin (Be) 30 Butler St, Kingston, PA 18704

HARTMAN, Kathleen Thomas (Vt) PO Box 383, Bethel, VT 05032

HARTMAN, Phyllis Colleen (Tex) 1803 Highland Hollow Dr, Conroe, TX 77304

HARTMAN, Salli (Va)

HARTMAN, Samuel Henry (Eas) 5 Schoolhouse Ln, North East, MD 21901

HARTMANS, Robert Gerrit (ETenn) 5008 14th Ave, Chattanooga, TN 37407

HARTNETT, John Godfrey (Nwk) 27 Bethany Woods Rd, Bethany, CT 06524

HARTNEY, Michael Elton (Roch) 210 Reading Rd, Watkins Glen, NY 14891

HARTSFIELD, Paula Kindrick (Mo)

HARTSOUGH, Bernadette Marie (NI)

HARTSUFF, Jadon (WA)

HARTT, Paul Jonathan (Alb) 8 Loudon Hts S, Loudonville, NY 12211

HARTT, Walter Fred (NJ) 408 Kingfisher Rd, Tuckerton, NJ 08087

HARTWELL, Michael (Mass) 620 Flick Cir., Thomasville, NC 27360

HARTY, George (Wyo)

HARTZELL, Susan (Va) 5911 Fairview Woods Dr, Fairfax Station, VA 22039

HARTZOG, Dorothy C (Tenn) 215 Maplemere Dr, Clarksville, TN 37040

HARVALA, Eileen Gay (Minn) Trinity Episcopal Church, 345 Main St, Portland, CT 06480

HARVEY, Errol (NY) 800 N Miami Ave Apt 302, Miami, FL 33136

HARVEY, Rick E (Ida) 2080 S Bodine St, Boise, ID 83705

HARVEY, Robert William (WNY) Tec Ch Of Our Saviour, 1700 Powder Mill Road, Silver Spring, MD 20903

HARWOOD, John Thomas (CPa) 137 3rd St, Renovo, PA 17764

HASEN, Elizabeth Sorchan (Spok) 497 Golf Course Rd, South Burlington, VT 05403

HASKELL, Robert Finch (Alb) 9 Long Creek Dr, Burnt Hills, NY 12027

HASS, Caroline Vada (WNY) Po Box 161, Alexander, NY 14005

HASSAN, Rose Cohen (Nwk) 954 Avenue C, Bayonne, NJ 07002

HASSE III, Ed (Nwk) 4 Woodland Rd, Montvale, NJ 07645

HASSELBROOK, Audrey Caroline (Nwk) 18 Shepard Pl, Nutley, NJ 07110

HASSELL, Mariann Barbara (Tenn) 1204 Jackson Dr, Pulaski, TN 38478

HASSEMER, Donald William (RG) Po Box 747, Medanales, NM 87548

HASSETT, Miranda Katherine (Mil) 6325 Shoreham Dr, Madison, WI 53711

HASSETT, Steve (Cal) 61 La Cresta Rd, Orinda, CA 94563

HASTINGS, Brian J (Chi) 857 W. Margate Terrace, #1-W, Chicago, IL 60640

HASTINGS, Mark Wayne (Mich) PO Box 287, Onsted, MI 49265

HATCH, Jessica Ann (U) 2586 S Elizabeth St Apt 6, Salt Lake City, UT 84106

HATCH, Mark (WMass) 267 Locust St Apt 2k, Apt 2K, Florence, MA 01062

HATCH, Rebekah (Ct) 2852 Kimmeridge Dr, Atlanta, GA 30344

HATCH, Victoria Theresa (Los) 1095 Dysar Rd, Banning, CA 92220

HATCHER, Spencer Elizabeth (Md)

HATFIELD, Adele Dees (Eas) 519 Long Lake Dr, Fuquay Varina, NC 27526

HATFIELD JR, Chuck (Eas) 519 Long Lake Dr, Fuquay Varina, NC 27526

HATFIELD, Joel (Dal) 7545 E Northwest Hwy Apt 354, Apt. 354, Dallas, TX 75238

HATFIELD, Russ (SwVa) 101 Logan St, Bluefield, VA 24605

HATHAWAY, Dale Caldwell (The Episcopal Church in Haw) 2648 Camille Dr, Palm Harbor, FL 34684

HATZENBUEHLER, Robin (WTenn) 1544 Carr Ave, Memphis, TN 38104

HAUCK, Barbara Horsley (Minn) 32 W College St, Duluth, MN 55812

HAUCK, Mary Rockett (The Episcopal NCal) 11489 Phoebe Ct, Penn Valley, CA 95946

HAUFF, DFMS (Minn) 2820 Voyageur Dr, Woodbury, MN 55125

HAUG, Phillip (Lex) 100 Daisey Dr, Richmond, KY 40475

HAUGAARD, Jeffrey James (CNY) 101 E Williams St, Waterloo, NY 13165

HAUGEN, Alice Bordwell Fulton (Ia) 1483 Grand Ave, Iowa City, IA 52246

HAUGHN, Terry Lee (WMich) 111 W Brighton St, Plainwell, MI 49080

HAUSER, NancyTayler (Pa) 27 Stannard Dr, Essex Junction, VT 05452

HAUSMAN, Sharon (Nwk)

HAVENS, Helen Markley Morris (Tex) 2401 Dryden Rd, Houston, TX 77030

HAVERKAMP, Heidi (Chi) 365 Rolfe Rd, Dekalb, IL 60115

HAVERLY, Tom (NJ) 5201 S Cornell Ave Apt 14b, Chicago, IL 60615

HAWES, Peter Wortham (USC) 32 Locust Ln, Tryon, NC 28782

HAWKES, Daphne (NJ) 50 Patton Ave, Princeton, NJ 08540

HAWKINS IV, Barney Barney (WNC) 3737 Seminary Rd, Alexandria, VA 22304

HAWKINS, Charles (Miss) 3003 Curran Rd, Louisville, KY 40205

HAWKINS, Deborah (Cal) 230 Grande Ave, Davis, CA 95616

HAWKINS JR, Frank Jay (Tex) 1827 Green Gate Dr, Rosenberg, TX 77471

HAWKINS, Gary Altus (WVa) 1803 New Windsor Road, New Windsor, MD 21776

HAWKINS, Jean Hufford (Az)

HAWKINS, Jodene (The Episcopal Church in Haw) 203 Kuli Puu St, Kihei, HI 96753

HAWKINS, Linda (Va) 4801 Ravensworth Rd, Annandale, VA 22003

HAWKINS, Meredith Ann Marguerite (NY)

HAWKINS, Penelope Elizabeth (Vt) Po Box 492, North Bennington, VT 05257

HAWKINS, Richard Thurber (Pa) W396 N5918 Meadow Ln, Oconomowoc, WI 53066

HAWKINS, Tom (WNY) 401 E Tyler Pkwy, Payson, AZ 85541

HAWKINS, William Mills (Ark)

HAWKS, Shanna (Spok)

HAWLEY, Carter R (Pgh) St Thomas Episcopal Church, 1465 Coburg Rd, Eugene, OR 97401

HAWLEY, Christian N (Tex) 800 S Northshore Dr, Knoxville, TN 37919

HAWLEY, Frank Martin (WTex) 4518 Winlock Dr, San Antonio, TX 78228

HAWLEY, Kristen (WA) Christ Church, 3116 O St NW, Washington, DC 20007

HAWLEY, Madeline Shelton (Tex)

HAWLEY, Oral Robers (Ak)

HAWORTH, Mark (The Episcopal Church in Haw) 60 N Beretania St Apt 801, Honolulu, HI 96817

HAWS, Molly Elizabeth (Cal) Episcopal Church Of The Good Shepherd, 1823 Ninth St, Berkeley, CA 94710

HAWTHORNE, Nanese Arnold (Eas) All Hallows Episcopal Church, 109 W Market St, Snow Hill, MD 21863

C77

HAWTHORNE, Ryan (Tex) 3818 Eastside St Apt 19205, Houston, TX 77098

HAY, Audrey Leona (NMich) 4955 12th Rd, Escanaba, MI 49829

HAY, Charles (Ga) 1014 Shore Acres Dr, Leesburg, FL 34748

HAY, Daryl (Tex) 2917 Fairfax Dr, Tyler, TX 75701

HAY, Lesley J H (Cal) 1100 California St, San Francisco, CA 94108

HAYASHI, Koji (Ida) 2282 S Southshore Way, Boise, ID 83706

✠ **HAYASHI**, Scott (U) 121 Rainier Ln, Port Ludlow, WA 98365

HAYDE, Ronald Edward (SeFla) St Mark the Evangelist, 1750 E Oakland Park Blvd, Oakland Park, FL 33334

HAYDEN, Andrea (SwFla) 1002 4th Ave, Asbury Park, NJ 07712

HAYDEN JR, Daniel Frank (Mass)

HAYDEN, John (O) 206 S Oval Dr, Chardon, OH 44024

HAYDEN JR, Louis Harold (Tex) 7193 Neshoba Cir, Germantown, TN 38138

HAYDON, Nathan John (Mo)

HAYEK, Hal T (Mil) 11211 N Shoes Way, Edgerton, WI 53534

HAYES III, Christopher Thomas (Va) 1131 Oaklawn Dr, Culpeper, VA 22701

HAYES JR, E Perren (NY) 33165 W Chesapeake St, Lewes, DE 19958

HAYES, John Michael (Md) 217 N Carey St, Baltimore, MD 21223

HAYES, Margaret Leigh (CFla)

HAYES, Pamela T. (EC) 1004 Bonner Bussells Dr, Southport, NC 28461

HAYES, Valerie Jean (Va) 543 Beulah Rd NE, Vienna, VA 22180

HAYES-MARTIN, Gianetta Marie (SO) 700 High Street, Worthington, OH 43085

HAYMAN, Robert Fleming (Oly) 1102 E Boston St, Seattle, WA 98102

HAYNES, Alice (USC) 3136 Cimarron Trl, West Columbia, SC 29170

HAYNES, Argola Electa (Los) 1979 Newport Ave, Pasadena, CA 91103

HAYNES, Brandon Shane (Ark)

HAYNES, Elizabeth Stephenson (Be) 621 Prices Dr, Cresco, PA 18326

HAYNES, John Connor (NJ) 45 W Broad St, Burlington, NJ 08016

HAYNES, Kendall Thomas (Oly) PO Box 6906, Tacoma, WA 98417

HAYNES SR, Larry Lee (NY) 34 Point St, New Hamburg, NY 12590

HAYNES, Pamela Rich (NC)

HAYNES, Peter Davis (Los) 45 Acacia Tree Ln, Irvine, CA 92612

HAYNES, Rachel Fowler (NC) PO Box 504, Davidson, NC 28036

✠ **HAYNES**, Susan (SVa) 616 Lincolnway E, Mishawaka, IN 46544

HAYNES, Thomas E (SVa) 133 Blackheath, Williamsburg, VA 23188

HAYNIE, Amy Peden (NwT) 5501 Heartland Ct, Midland, TX 79707

HAYS, Bret B (Fla) 48 Middle St, Gloucester, MA 01930

HAYS, Joseph Spurgeon (At) 666 E College St, Griffin, GA 30224

HAYS, Lloyd Philip Whistler (Pgh) Po Box 43, Ambridge, PA 15003

HAYS, Louis B (Pgh) 1525 Quarrier St, Charleston, WV 25311

HAYWARD, Stephen H (WA) Stephen H Hayward, 154 Mills Point Rd, Brooksville, ME 04617

HAYWORTH, Joseph Allison (NC) 910 Croyden St, High Point, NC 27262

HAZEL, Dorothy (Va) 609 Dutchmans Creek Trl, Irmo, SC 29063

HAZEL, Jim (Tex) 6828 Woodstock Rd, Fort Worth, TX 76116

HAZELRIGG, Dennis Russell (CFla)

HAZEN, Albie (Ore) 5944 SE Glen Eagle Way, Stuart, FL 34997

HAZEN, Susan Marcotte (Be) St John's Episcopal Church, PO Box 246, Bandon, OR 97411

HAZLETT, Brant Vincent (Spr) 600 N Mulberry St # 674, Mount Carmel, IL 62863

HEACOCK, Donald Dee (WLa) 3218 Line Ave # 101, Shreveport, LA 77104

HEAD, Janice (Colo)

HEAD, Paul Anthony (CFla) 656 Avenue L, NW, Winter Haven, FL 33881

HEALD, David Stanley (Me) 8 Pine Ln, Cumberland Foreside, ME 04110

HEALEY, Joseph Patrick (NY) 1045 Cook Rd, Grosse Pointe, MI 48236

HEALY, Catherine Elizabeth (Chi) 4350 S Oakenwald Ave Apt 201, Chicago, IL 60653

HEALY, Denise Catherine (SwFla) 1502 Paddock Dr, Plant City, FL 33566

HEALY, Linda (Miss)

HEALY, Ruth (At) 1403 Oakridge Cir, Decatur, GA 30033

HEANEY, David Lloyd (SanD) 690 Oxford St, Chula Vista, CA 91911

HEARD, Fred (Ore) 1239 Wigh St SE, Salem, OR 97302

HEARD, Thomas (CGC) 1119 N La Salle Dr, Chicago, IL 60610

HEARD, Victoria RT (Dal) 1630 N Garrett Ave, Diocese of Dallas, Dallas, TX 75206

HEARN, Roger Daniel (Va) 24 Oxford Rd, Wellesley, MA 02481

HEARNSBERGER, Keith (Ark) 1304 S Schiller St, Little Rock, AR 72202

HEATH, Claudia H (U) 326 Fairfax Dr, Little Rock, AR 72205

HEATH, Susan Blackburn (USC) 1115 Marion Street, Columbia, SC 29201

HEATHCOCK, Deborah Beth (WLa) 404 Ansley Blvd Apt B, Alexandria, LA 71303

HEATHCOCK, J Edwin (Mo) 14485 Brittania Dr, Chesterfield, MO 63017

HEATHERLY, Rose Temple (Wyo) 4700 S Poplar St, Casper, WY 82601

HEBERT, Frank (NJ) 33 Throckmorton St, Freehold, NJ 07728

HEBERT, Susanne Darnell (Tex) 710 Texas Star Dr, Richmond, TX 77469

HECK, John Hathaway (SwVa) 65 Rock Ridge Rd, Callaway, VA 24067

HECKEL, Deborah Lee (FdL) Church of the Holy Apostles, 2937 Freedom Rd, Oneida, WI 54155

HECOCK, Georgia Ingalis (Minn) St. 868, Detroit Lakes, MN 56502

HECTOR JR, Bob (WMich) 348 Waltonia Rd, Drake, CO 80515

HEDEN, Eileen (WK) 311 N 4th St, Sterling, KS 67579

HEDGES, David Benedict (Az) 602 N Wilmot Rd, Tucson, AZ 85711

HEDGES, Merry Helen (Ark) 8201 Hood Rd, Roland, AR 72135

HEDGIS, Sarah Emily (Pa) 5421 Germantown Ave, Philadelphia, PA 19144

HEDGPETH, Marty (NC) 4338 Silo Ln, Charlotte, NC 28226

HEDIN, Joanne Christine (SD) 802 E Iowa St, Rapid City, SD 57701

HEDLUND, Arnold Melvin (ECR) PO Box 2131, Salinas, CA 93902

HEDMAN, James Edward (SwFla) 9719 33rd Ave E, Palmetto, FL 34221

HEDQUIST, Ann Whitney (Kan) 3205 Sw 33rd Ct, Topeka, KS 66614

HEE, Malcolm Keleawe (Haw) The Cathedral Of St Andrew, 229 Queen Emma Sq, Honolulu, HI 96813

HEFFNER, John H (Be) 129 Fairfax Rd, Bryn Mawr, PA 19010

HEFFNER, Meredith (WA) 11815 Seven Locks Rd, Potomac, MD 20854

HEFFRON, Judy (Los) 4959 Ridgeview St, La Verne, CA 91750

HEFLIN, Rev Tim (WLa) St James Episcopal Church, 1620 Murray St, Alexandria, LA 71301

HEFLING JR, Charles (Mass) 1619 Massachusetts Ave, Cambridge, MA 02138

HEFLING, David (Roch) St Johns Episcopal Church, 183 N Main St, Canandaigua, NY 14424

HEFNER, Judith Ann (WNY) 1307 Ransom Rd, Grand Island, NY 14072

HEFTI, William Joseph (The Episcopal NCal) 24300 Green Valley Rd, Auburn, CA 95602

HEGE, Andrew Joseph (WNC)

HEGEDUS, Frank (Los) 12340 Seal Beach Blvd Ste B, Seal Beach, CA 90740

HEGG, Camille (At) 753 College St, Macon, GA 31201

HEGLUND, Janice N (Cal) 84 San Gabriel Dr, Fairfax, CA 94930

HEGNEY, Georgina (CNY) 210 Twin Hills Dr, Syracuse, NY 13207

HEGWOOD JR, Joseph Leslie (Miss)

HEHR, Randy (SwFla) 3200 N Mcmullen Booth Rd, Clearwater, FL 33761

HEICHLER, Katherine (WA) Saint Columbas Church, 4201 Albemarle St NW, Washington, DC 20016

HEIDECKER, Eric Vaughn (Nev) 14645 Rim Rock Dr, Reno, NV 89521

HEIDEL, Jerry (SwVa) PO Box 779, Hot Springs, VA 24445

HEIDEL, John W (The Episcopal NCal) 1438 Dreamy Way, Sacramento, CA 95835

HEIDMANN, Tina Jeanine (ECR) 98 Kip Dr, Salinas, CA 93906

HEIDT, James Kevin (CNY) St Johns Church, 341 Main St, Oneida, NY 13421

HEIJMEN, Rutger-Jan Spencer (SeFla) St Martins Episcopal Church, 717 Sage Rd, Houston, TX 77056

HEILIGMAN, Sara Sally (CNY) 187 Brookside Ave, Amsterdam, NY 12010

HEIMERL, Amy Marie (FdL)

HEIN, Charles Gregory (CGC) 89 Brook Haven Dr, Spruce Pine, NC 28777

HEINE, Mary Anne (La) 15249 Brandon Dr, Ponchatoula, LA 70454

HEINE JR, William AJ (SwVa) 436 Jefferson Ave, Metairie, LA 70005

HEINEMANN, Ann E (Ga) 539 N Westover Blvd Apt 103, Albany, GA 31707

HEINRICH, Judith Capstaff (Chi) 853 Oak Hill Rd, Barrington, IL 60010

HEISCHMAN, Daniel R (Ct) 270 Bronxville Rd Apt B71, Bronxville, NY 10708

HEISE, Kimberly (Minn)

HEISLER, Steven G (CFla)

HEISTAND, Virginia (RI) Saint Pauls Church, 55 Main St, North Kingstown, RI 02852

HEITMANN, Katherine A (Dal) 511 Foote St, Mckinney, TX 75069

HEKEL, Dean (Mil) 7017 Colony Dr, Madison, WI 53717

HELFERTY, Scott Hanson (Mass) 4511 Oakridge Rd, Lake Oswego, OR 97035

HELGESON, Gail Michele (Oly) 2909 7th St, Port Townsend, WA 98368

HELLER, Amy (Dal) 15746 Quorum Dr, Addison, TX 75001

HELLER, Jan C (Oly) 1663 Bungalow Way NE, Poulsbo, WA 98370

HELLER, Richard C (WVa) 266 Paw Paw Ln, Saint Marys, WV 26170

HELLMAN, Gary L (NY) 224 W 11th St Apt 2, New York, NY 10014

HELMAN, Peter Alan (Az) 3071 N Wilson Ave, Tucson, AZ 85719

HELMER, Ben Edward (Ark) 28 Prospect Ave, Eureka Springs, AR 72632

HELMER, Richard Edward (Cal) Church of Our Saviour, 10 Old Mill St, Mill Valley, CA 94941

HELMS III, David Clarke (SO) 1 Marlborough Avenue, Bromsgrove, B6O 2PG, Great Britain (UK)

HELMS, William Travis (Wyo) PO Box 1690, Jackson, WY 83001

HELMUTH, Bradley M (The Episcopal NCal) Holy Trinity Church, 202 High St, Nevada City, CA 95959

HELT, Dwight (Okla) 130 Rue de Montserrat, Norman, OK 73071

HEMINGSON, Celeste (NH) 340 Main St # 3229, Hopkinton, NH 03229

HEMMERS, Louis Emanuel (Los) 1634 Crestview Rd, Redlands, CA 92374

HEMPHILL, Margaret Ayars (Chi) 53 Loveland Rd, Norwich, VT 05055

HEMPSTEAD, James Breese (Ind) 512 Woodland Ave, Petoskey, MI 49770

HENAULT JR, Armand Joseph (Vt) 374 Spring Street, St Johnsbury, VT 05819

HENAULT, Rita (At)

HENDERSON, Catherine Ann Graves (Ga) St Francis of the Islands, 590 Walthour Rd, Savannah, GA 31410

HENDERSON, Don Keith (Colo) 40 Cougar Trl, Ridgway, CO 81432

HENDERSON, Dorsey (USC) 1115 Marion St, Columbia, SC 29201

HENDERSON, Dumont Biglar (Me) 65 Eustis Pkwy., Waterville, ME 04901

HENDERSON JR, George Raymond (Fla) 1932 Finnish Ln, Kennesaw, GA 30152

HENDERSON, Harvey George (ND) 801 2nd St N, Wahpeton, ND 58075

HENDERSON, Jane Pataky (Chi) 624 Colfax St, Evanston, IL 60201

HENDERSON, Luther Owen (WMo) 288 Cedar Glen Dr Unit 4B, Camdenton, MO 65020

HENDERSON, Mark William (Cal) 795 Buena Vista Ave W Apt 6, San Francisco, CA 94117

HENDERSON, Michael Brant (Lex) 381 Bon Haven Rd, Maysville, KY 41056

HENDERSON, Michael Jack (Fla) 1746 Hillgate Ct, Tallahassee, FL 32308

HENDERSON, Patricia Ann (Tex) St Francis Episcopal Church, 432 Forest Hill Rd, Macon, GA 31210

HENDERSON, Robert (NC) 5375 Us Highway 231, Wetumpka, AL 36092

HENDERSON III, Samuel G (Me) 134 Park St, Portland, ME 04101

HENDERSON, Sterling Archibald (Fla) 1746 Hillgate Ct, Tallahassee, FL 32308

HENDERSON, Susan (SwFla) 12630 Panasoffkee Dr, North Fort Myers, FL 33903

HENDERSON JR, Theodore Herbert (Pa) 236 Glen Pl, Elkins Park, PA 19027

HENDRICK, Elizabeth (At) 1520 Oak Rd, Snellville, GA 30078

HENDRICKS III, Frisby (SeFla) 2303 N.E. Seaview Drive, Jensen Beach, FL 34957

HENDRICKS, Mary D (Neb)

HENDRICKS, Rebecca Lanham (EO) Po Box 293, Milton Freewater, OR 97862

HENDRICKSON, Patricia Dee (Los) 265 W Sidlee St, Thousand Oaks, CA 91360

HENDRICKSON III, Robert J (Az) Saint Johns Cathedral, 1350 N Washington St Fl 3, Denver, CO 80203

HENDRICKSON, Thomas Samuel (Va) 3845 Village Views Pl, Glen Allen, VA 23059

HENDRIX, Elizabeth (USC)

HENDRIX, Julia Roane (FdL)

HENERY, Charles Robert (Mil) 20 Oakwood Dr, Delafield, WI 53018

HENLEY, Carol (Pgh) 1212 Trevanion Ave, Pittsburgh, PA 15218

HENLEY JR, Ed (SwFla) 404 Park Ridge Ave, Temple Terrace, FL 33617

HENLEY, Robert P (ETenn) 351 Hardin Ln, Sevierville, TN 37862

HENNAGIN, Bob (NwT) Church Of The Holy Comforter, 2911 Woodley Rd, Montgomery, AL 36111

HENNE, Bruce Charles (Minn) 1270 118th Ave NW, Coon Rapids, MN 55448

HENNESSEY, Nancy H (Md) 66 Highland Ave, Short Hills, NJ 07078

HENNESSY, Frank Scott (SVa) 6001 Startwood Pl, Raleigh, NC 27609

HENNESSY, Jeanne Katherine (Minn) 4875 Boatman Ln, Inver Grove Heights, MN 55076

HENNIES, Ronald Gene (SD) 3004 S West Ave, Sioux Falls, SD 57105

HENNING, Joel Peter (HB) 2607 Grant St, Berkeley, CA 94703

HENNING, Kristina Louise (FdL) 6426 S 35th St, Franklin, WI 53132

HENNINGER, Annie (SD) 105 E 12th St, Gregory, SD 57533

HENRICHSEN, Robert Anton (Neb)

HENRICK, Mother Joan (Ala) 5789 Tydan Ln, Gadsden, AL 35907

HENRICKSON, Mark (Los) 32A Wingate Street, Avondale, Auckland, 0600, New Zealand (Aotearoa)

HENRY, Barbara Dearborn (WA) 5333 N Sheridan Rd Apt.8H, Chicago, IL 60640

HENRY, Dean (NJ) 14 Winding Ln, Southwest Harbor, ME 04679

HENRY, Earl (SeFla) 4401 W Oakland Park Blvd, Fort Lauderdale, FL 33313

HENRY, Eric Lynn (CPa) 1 N Hanover St, Carlisle, PA 17013

HENRY, George Kenneth Grant (NC) 34 Red Fox Lane, Brevard, NC 28712

HENRY, John Reeves (Spr) 12844 Apache Ln, Plainview, IL 62685

HENRY II, John W (Alb) P.O. Box 175, Clifton Park, NY 12065

HENRY, Karen E J (NY) St John's Church, 365 Strawtown Rd, New City, NY 10956

HENRY, Lloyd I (LI) 4607 Avenue H, Brooklyn, NY 11234

HENRY, Richard Arlen (Episcopal SJ) 1155 Leavell Park Cir, Lincoln, CA 95648

HENRY, Richard Lynn (Nev) 228 Hillcrest Dr, Henderson, NV 89015

HENRY JR, Wayman Wright (USC) 116 Sedgewood Ct, Easley, SC 29642

HENRY-MCKEEVER, Elizabeth Anne (Ark)

HENSARLING JR, Reid (CFla) 146 Oak Sq S, Lakeland, FL 33813

HENSEL, Charles Howard (Chi) 2625 TEchny Rd Apt 620, Northbrook, IL 60062

HENSLEY, Erin Seltzer (Tex) 1110 Vasquez St, Austin, TX 78741

HENSLEY JR, Joe (Va) 905 Princess Anne St, Fredericksbrg, VA 22401

HENSLEY, Lane Goodwin (SanD) 4225 Fleur Dr Pmb 114, Des Moines, IA 50321

HENSLEY, Paul Michael (Episcopal SJ)

HENSLEY, Robert Eugene (Chi) 444 E. McClure St., Kewanee, IL 61443

HENSLEY-ECHOLS, Beth Marie (WA) Brooke Army Medical Center, 3851 Roger Brooke Dr, San Antonio, TX 78234

HENSON, David R (WNC)

HENSON, John Craig (WLa) 144 Patton Ave, Shreveport, LA 71105

HENSON, Paula (NAM) Good Shepherd Mission, PO Box 618, Fort Defiance, AZ 86504

HENSON, Tula (USC) 253 Bridleridge Rd, Lexington, SC 29073

HENTON, David Luke (RG)

HENWOOD, Karen Lee (Colo) 5604 E Nichols Pl, Centennial, CO 80112

HERALD, Erin Carol (NwPa) St Jude's Episc Church, PO Box 1714, Hermitage, PA 16148

HERASIMTSCHUK, Alexander James (NY)

HERBST, Gary (Dal) 8320 Jack Finney Blvd., Greenville, TX 75402

HERGENRATHER, Lynda May Stevenson (Va) 5904 Mount Eagle Dr Apt 318, Alexandria, VA 22303

HERKNER JR, Robert Thomas (O) 328 Windsor Ct, Huron, OH 44839

HERLOCKER, Thomas Dean (Kan) 1704 E 10th Ave, Winfield, KS 67156

HERMAN, Alice McWreath (SO) 345 Ridgedale Dr N, Worthington, OH 43085

HERMAN, Elizabeth Frances (Minn) 615 Vermillion St, Hastings, MN 55033

HERMANSON, David Harold (NJ) 56 Grace Dr, Old Bridge, NJ 08857

HERMES, Jonathan Robert (ETenn) 143 Union St, Kingsport, TN 37660

HERNANDEZ, Alejandro Felix (SeFla) 14213 SW 55th St, Miami, FL 33175

HERNANDEZ, Gustavo (Los) Po Box 893, Downey, CA 90241

HERNANDEZ, Jorge A (Nev) 2000 S Maryland Pkwy, Las Vegas, NV 89104

HERNANDEZ, Luis Alfonso (Hond)

HERNANDEZ, Miguel Angel (Nwk)

HERNANDEZ JR, Nicolas (Alb) Trinity Episcopal Church, 1336 1st Ave, Watervliet, NY 12189

HERNANDEZ-GUTIERREZ, Cesar Arnoldo (Colo) c o Joe Delacruz, 712 Jefferson St, Bentonville, AR 72712

HERNANDEZ MARTINEZ, Lis Margarita (Cu)

HERNANDEZ ROJAS, Martin Antonio (Colom) Carrera 6 No 49-85, Piso 2, Bogota, Colombia

HERNDON, James C (Ida) 1055 Riverton Rd, Blackfoot, ID 83221

HERON, James (NY) 1005 SW Park Ave Unit 603, Unit 603, Portland, OR 97205

HERON, Marsha (U) 4447 E Lake Cir S, Centennial, CO 80121

HERRERA, Lourden Del Carmen (Hond) PO Box 523900, Miami, FL 33152-3900, Honduras

HERRERA, Maria I (Pa) Po Box 40382, Philadelphia, PA 19106

HERRERA CHAGNA, Raul (EcuC) Avenue Amazonas #4430, Igl Epis Del Ecuador, Quito, Ecuador

HERRICK, Bob (NY) 15900 Riverside Dr W Apt 6k70, New York, NY 10032

HERRING, Holly (Az) All Sts Tec Ch Day Sch, 6300 N Central Ave, Phoenix, AZ 85012

HERRING, John Foster (At) 634 W Peachtree St NW, Atlanta, GA 30308

HERRING, Joseph Dahlet (At) 100 Somerby Dr Apt 2164, Alpharetta, GA 30009

HERRING, Sally L (Ala)

HERRMANN, Herbert W (Dal) 623 Ector St, Denton, TX 76201

HERRON, Daniel Peter (Az) St Mark's Church, 322 N Horne, Mesa, AZ 85203

HERRON-PIAZZA, Katharine Ann (Ct) 22 Coulter Ave, Pawling, NY 12564

HERSHBELL, Jackson Paul (SwVa) 274 Still House Dr, Lexington, VA 24450

HERTH, Daniel Edwin (Cal) 32 Mallorie Park Drive, The Garden House, Ripon North Yorkshire, HG42QF, Great Britain (UK)

HERTLEIN, Chris (Ore) 2490 NE Highway 101, Lincoln City, OR 97367

HERZOG, Carole Regina (Los) 1471 Cloister Dr, La Habra Heights, CA 90631

HERZOG, Kenneth Bernard (Fla) 3545 Olympic Dr, Green Cove Springs, FL 32043

HESCHLE, John Henry (Chi) 7100 N Ashland Blvd, Chicago, IL 60626

HESS, Elizabeth Parker (NH) PO Box 545, Berlin, NH 03570

HESS, Howard (ETenn) 8500 Cambridge Woods Ln, Knoxville, TN 37923

HESS III, Raymond Leonard (The Episcopal NCal) 9001 Crowley Way, Elk Grove, CA 95624

HESSE, Alan Roger (Mass)

HESSE, Vicki K (Colo) 1364 County Road 75, Woodland Park, CO 80863

HESSE, William Arthur (Okla) 1805 N Canary Dr, Edmond, OK 73034

HETHERINGTON, Robert Gunn (Va) 1500 Westbrook Ct Apt 2133, Richmond, VA 23227

HETLER, Gwendolyn Kay (NMich) 3135 County Road 456, Skandia, MI 49885

HETRICK JR, Budd Albert (Ida) 7470 Sundance Dr, Boise, ID 83709

HETZEL, Alan Dorn (WNC) Po Box 442, Highlands, NC 28741

HEUETT, Bradley Allen (Mich)

HEUETT, Krista D (Mich)

HEUSS, Bill (Mass) 15 Thimbleberry Ln, South Yarmouth, MA 02664

HEVERLY, Craig Brian (Ore) 925 Se Center St, Portland, OR 97202

HEWETSON, Richard Walton (Cal)

HEWIS, Clara Mae (CGC) 7979 N 9th Ave, Pensacola, FL 32514

HEWITT, Emily Clark (NY) 1848 Commonwealth Ave Apt 56, Boston, MA 02135

HEYBOER, BJ (WMich) 30 Justice St, Newaygo, MI 49337

HEYD, Matthew F (NY) 74 Trinity Pl, New York, NY 10006

HEYDT, Charles Read (SwFla) 523 S Palm Ave Apt 7, Sarasota, FL 34236

HEYDUK, Terri (U) 2606 E Creighton Way, Cottonwood Heights, UT 84121

HEYES, Andrew Robin (SwFla) 706 W 113th Ave, Tampa, FL 33612

HEYING, R Christopher (Tex) 442 N Franklin St, La Grange, TX 78945

HEYVAERT, Bruce T (NC) Saint James Church, PO Box 846, Magnolia, AR 71754

HEYWARD, Isabel Carter (Mass) PO Box 449, Cedar Mountain, NC 28718

HIATT, Anthony Ray (Tex) PO Box 22, Decatur, TX 76234

HIATT, Kathleen Mary (Nev) PO Box 146, Pioche, NV 89043

HICKENLOOPER, Morgan (CGC) Po Box 27120, Panama City, FL 32411

HICKEY, John D (Mil) 7845 N River Rd, River Hills, WI 53217

HICKEY-TIERNAN, Joseph (Oly) 255 SW Harrison St Apt 22b, Portland, OR 97201

HICKMAN, Clare L (Mich) 851 Reagan St, Canton, MI 48188

HICKS, Catherine D (Va) PO Box 399, Port Royal, VA 22535

HICKS, Janice Marie (WA)

HICKS, Mary Kohn (WMass) 88 Masonic Home Rd, #R404, Charlton, MA 01507

HICKS, Paul L (WVa) 590 W Washington St, Wytheville, VA 24382

HICKS, Richard William (La) 2507 Portola Ave Apt 20, Livermore, CA 94551

HICKS, Warren Earl (SVa) PO Box 7430, Hampton, VA 23666

HIERHOLZER, Evan (WTex) 7880 Highway 290 W Apt 6305, Austin, TX 78736

HIERS JR, John (SwFla) 1004 Woodcrest Ave, Clearwater, FL 33756

HIGGINBOTHAM, John E (RI) 99 S Pierce Rd, East Greenwich, RI 02818

HIGGINBOTHAM, Richard Cann (Chi) 3800 N Lake Shore Dr # 1j, Chicago, IL 60613

HIGGINBOTHAM, Stuart Craig (At) 422 Brenau Ave, Gainesville, GA 30501

HIGGINS, Kent (WVa) 1520 Dogwood Rd, Charleston, WV 25314

HIGGINS, Pam (Cal) 272 W I St, Benicia, CA 94510

HIGGINS, Rock (Va)

HIGGINS, Teddy John (USC)

HIGGINS, Timothy John (Me) 25 Twilight Ln, Gorham, ME 04038

HIGGINS, William Harrison (Va) 8000 Hermitage Rd, Richmond, VA 23228

HIGGINSON, Paul Howard (NH) 472 Swazey La, Bethlehem, NH 03574

HIGGINS-SHAFFER, Diane Hazel (Ore) 503 N Holladay Dr, Seaside, OR 97138

HIGGITT, Noel (ECR) 1325 San Mateo Dr, Menlo Park, CA 94025

HIGH JR, Rayford (Tex) 4709 Marbella Cir, Fort Worth, TX 76126

HIGHLAND, Terrence Irving (Pa)

HIGHSMITH, Jennifer Lynn (Ga) 102 Borrell Blvd, Saint Marys, GA 31558

HIGMAN, Thomas James (Alb)

HILDEBRAND, Nancy Steakley (WA) St Nicholas Episcopal Church, 14100 Darnestown Rd Ste B, Germantown, MD 20874

HILDEBRANDT, Lise (Mass) 1400 1st Ave, Longmont, CO 80501

HILDESLEY, Christopher Hugh (NY) 570 Park Ave Apt 6-D, New York, NY 10021

HILE, Jeanette Theresa (Nwk) 16 Day Rd, Landing, NJ 07850

HILEMAN, Mary Esther (Okla) 2809 W 28th Ave, Stillwater, OK 74074

HILFIKER, Gerald Milton (WNY) 10085 Pfarner Road, Boston, NY 14025

HILGARTNER, Elizabeth (Vt) 27 Camp St, Barre, VT 05641

HILL, Charleen Diane (RG) 2005 Beringer Rd Apt 201, Suffolk, VA 23435

HILL, David Ernest (Minn) 103 West Oxford Street, Duluth, MN 55803

HILL, Deborah (Colo) Cathedral Church of the Advent, 2017 6th Ave N, Birmingham, AL 35203

HILL, Derrick C (ETenn) 626 Mississippi Ave, Signal Mountain, TN 37377

HILL, Donald B (Roch) 321 E Market St, Jeffersonville, IN 47130

HILL, Ellen R (Los) 5066 Berean Ln, Irvine, CA 92603

HILL, Gary Hill (Tex) 9541 Highland View Dr, Dallas, TX 75238

HILL III, George Aldrich (SO) 22 Vintage Walk, Cincinnati, OH 45249

HILL, Gordon Carman (Az) 2257 E Becker Ln, Phoenix, AZ 85028

HILL IV, Harvey (WMass) 19 Ward Avenue, Northampton, MA 01060

HILL, Heather L (Eau) 1515 Wilder Ave, Honolulu, HI 96822

HILL, H Michael (CGC) 2255 Valle Escondido Dr, Pensacola, FL 32526

HILL III, James Allen (Fla) 3528 Carrington Dr, Tallahassee, FL 32303

HILL, Jesse Jaron (Okla)

HILL, John Spencer (Colo) St Margarets Episcopal Church, 5310 Stahl Rd, San Antonio, TX 78247

HILL, Joshua Ashton (Me) 950 Episcopal School Way, Knoxville, TN 37932

HILL, Jude (The Episcopal NCal) 573 Dolores St, San Francisco, CA 94110

HILL, Mary Ann (Okla) 5635 E 71st St, Tulsa, OK 74136

HILL, Mary Madeleine (Tex)

HILL, Rachel (Fla)

HILL, Ralph Julian (SD) 9021 E Amherst Dr Apt C, Denver, CO 80231

HILL, Renee Leslie (NY) 575 Grand St Apt 1801, New York, NY 10002

HILL, Robert Samuel (Ky)

HILL, Susan Diane (Ga) 3101 Waters Ave, Savannah, GA 31404

HILL, Susan Elizabeth (NY) 225 W 99th St, New York, NY 10025

HILL, Vernon Willard (Episcopal SJ) PO Box 153, Bakersfield, CA 93302

HILL, Wesley Allen (Pgh)

HILLEBRAND, The Very Rev Dr Walter V (LI) 23 Cedar Shore Dr, Massapequa, NY 11758

HILLEGAS, Eric (CPa) St John The Baptist Episcopal Church, 140 N Beaver St, York, PA 17401

HILLENBRAND, Pam (Chi) 412 North Church St, Rockford, IL 61103

HILLER, Michael T (Cal) 278 Hester Ave, San Francisco, CA 94134

HILLGER, Cindy Lou (Minn) 2801 Westwood Rd, Minnetonka Beach, MN 55361

HILLIARD-YNTEMA, Katharine Arnold (At) 737 Woodland Ave Se, Atlanta, GA 30316

HILLIN JR, Harvey Henderson (WK)

HILLMAN, George Evans (FdL) P O Box 215, Sturgeon Bay, WI 54235

HILLS, Frances Ann (WMass) 2 Amy Ct, Pittsfield, MA 01201

HILLS, John Bigelow (WMich) 1450 S Ferry St Apt 104, Grand Haven, MI 49417

HILLS, Julian Victor (Mil) 3046 N Cambridge Ave, Milwaukee, WI 53211

HILLS, Nancy Hays (Mil)

HILLS, Wesley Bert (Chi) 266 Tull Ct, Bellingham, WA 98226

HILLS JR, William Leroy (SC) 820 Pinckney St, Mc Clellanville, SC 29458

HILSABECK, Polly H (NC) 184 Grey Elm Trl, Durham, NC 27713

HILTON, Duncan Lindsley (NH) 16 Bradley Ave, Brattleboro, VT 05301

HILTON, Olivia Parsons Lillich (WA)

HIMES, John Martin (Tex) 802 Shadowood Dr, Marshall, TX 75672

HINCAPIE LOAIZA, David Hernan (Colom)

HINCHLIFFE, George (Fla) 11418 Lowndesboro Drive, Jacksonville, FL 32223

HINDE, Daniel (O)

HINDLE, Darren E (RG)

HINDS, Eric (Cal) 1 S El Camino Real, San Mateo, CA 94401

HINDS, Gilberto Antonio (LI) 8 L, 9707 Horace Harding Expy Apt 8l, Corona, NY 11368

HINES, Caroline V (NH) 3 Furbush St, Rochester, NH 03867

HINES JR, Chester (Mo) 1210 Locust St, St. Louis, MO 63103

HINES, Donna Lee (SVa)

HINES, John C (Tex) 4603 Pro Ct, College Station, TX 77845

HINES, John Moore (Ky) 5722 Coach Gate Wynde, Louisville, KY 40207

HINES, John S (WNC) 219 Chunns Cove Rd, Asheville, NC 28805

HINKLE, Daniel Wayne (Be) 234 High St, Atglen, PA 19310

HINKLE, Robin Hansen (Ala)

HINO, Moki (The Episcopal Church in Haw) Good Shepherd Episcopal Church, 2140 Main St, Wailuku, HI 96793

HINRICHS, Bill (Alb) 1201 Vineyard St, Cohoes, NY 12047

HINSE, Mary N (Cal) 2230 Huron Dr., Concord, CA 94519

HINSON, Bryan T (At) 136 Red Fox Run, Macon, GA 31210

HINSON, Jerome Andrew (WMo) 5 Averil Ct, Fredericksburg, VA 22406

HINTON, Brad (Del) 2320 Grubb Rd, Wilmington, DE 19810

HINTON, Gregory (CPa) 147 Ridgebury Dr, Xenia, OH 45385

HINTON, Michael (Episcopal VI) Box 199, Cruz Bay, Saint John, VI 00831

HINTON, Wes (SO) 5907 Castlewood Xing, Milford, OH 45150

HINTZ, Mary Louise (Cal) 623 28th St, Richmond, CA 94804

HINXMAN, Frederic William (Lex) 5639 Highway #1, Granville Ferry, NS B0S 1K0, Canada

HIPP JR, Thomas Allison (USC) 910 Hudson Rd, Greenville, SC 29615

HIPPLE, Judy Kay (Chi) 4511 Newcastle Rd, Rockford, IL 61108

HIRDES, Carrie D (Tex)

✠ **HIRSCHFELD**, A Robert (NH) 103 Hedgerose Ln, Hopkinton, NH 03229

HIRSCHMAN, Portia Royall Conn (Md) 11860 Weller Hill Dr, Monrovia, MD 21770

HIRST, Dale Eugene (SVa) 4127 Columbus Ave, Norfolk, VA 23504

HIRST, Robert Lynn (Kan) Po Box 1859, Wichita, KS 67201

HITCH, Catherine Elizabeth (Colo) 1320 Arapahoe Street, Golden, CO 80401

HITCH, Kenneth R (Alb) 405 N Saginaw Rd, Midland, MI 48640

HITCHCOCK JR, Horace Gaylord (The Episcopal Church in Haw) 1420 E Palomar St Apt 303, Chula Vista, CA 91913

HITCHCOCK, Jessica (WA) 5225 Pooks Hill Rd, 1208 S, Bethesda, MD 20814

HITE, Jean (SwFla) 6804 Satinleaf Rd S Apt 103, Naples, FL 34109

HITE SPECK, Nancy J (NJ) 201 Meadow Ave, Point Pleasant Beach, NJ 08742

HIXON, Beth (Pa) 1201 Lower State Rd, North Wales, PA 19454

HIZA, Douglas William (Minn) 10 Meynal Crescent, South Hackney, London, E97AS, Great Britain (UK)

HIZER, Cynthia A (NAM) 550 Jenkins Rd, Covington, GA 30014

HLASS, Lisa (Ark) 2606 Beach Head Ct, Richmond, CA 94804

HLAVACEK, Frances (Be) 110 W Catherine St, Milford, PA 18337

HO, Edward HC (Mass) 24 Greenleaf St, Malden, MA 02148

HO, Jeng-Long (Tai) #200 Ziqiang 1st Rd, Samin Dist, Kaohsiung, Taiwan

HO, Jui-En (Tai)

HOAG, David Stewart (NY) 503 North Causeway 102, New Smyrna Beach, FL 32169

HOARE, Geoffrey Michael St John (WA)

HOBART, James (Nev) 1816 Derbyshire Dr, Las Vegas, NV 89117

HOBART, Terri (Colo) 3621 N Cook St, Denver, CO 80205

HOBBS, Bryan (SeFla) 751 SW 98th Ter, Pembroke Pines, FL 33025

HOBBS, Mercy (SD) 405 N Madison Ave, Pierre, SD 57501

HOBBS, William (WMass) 45 Park Ave., Athol, MA 01331

HOBBS, William Ebert (O) 18 Donlea Dr, Toronto, ON M4G 2M2, Canada

HOBBS MIRACKY, Tammany (Mass)

HOBBY, Kim A (ETenn) Christ Church Episcopal, PO Box 347, South Pittsburg, TN 37380

HOBDEN, Brian Charles (RG) 3160 Executive Hills Rd, Las Cruces, NM 88011

HOBGOOD, Bob (EC) 1870 Holly St SW, Ocean Isle Beach, NC 28469

HOBGOOD JR, Walter P (Ga) 1036 Cherry Creek Dr, Valdosta, GA 31605

HOBSON, Carol Gordon (Dal)

HOBSON JR, George Hull (Eur) 119 Blvd. Du Montparnasse, Paris, 75006, France

HOBSON III, Jenks (Va) Po Box 247, Washington, VA 22747

HOBSON, Patricia Shackelford (SO) 2955 Thrushfield Terrace, Cincinnati, OH 45238

HOCH, Helen Elizabeth (Kan) 314 N 3rd St, Burlington, KS 66839

HOCH, Sarah (Minn)

HOCHE-MONG, Raymond (Cal) Box 937, Montara, CA 94037

HOCKENSMITH, David Albert (Pa) PO Box 90, Morgan, VT 05853

HOCKER, Will (Cal) 6135 Laird Ave, Oakland, CA 94605

HOCKING, Charles Edward (NC) 632 Hughes Rd, Hampstead, NC 28443

HOCKRIDGE, Ann Elizabeth (Pa) Po Box 716, Lyndonville, VT 05851

HODAPP, Timothy Leo (Ct) 3372 Main St, Rocky Hill, CT 06067

HODGE, Nancy P (Mil)

HODGE, Reginald Roy (Episcopal VI)

HODGE, Sonia H (Mass) 111 High St, Taunton, MA 02780

HODGE SR, Vincent (Va) Po Box 767, West Point, VA 23181

HODGES, Corinne (RG) Holy Family Episcopal Church, 10a Bisbee Ct, Santa Fe, NM 87508

HODGES SR, David Burton (Mo) 1 Wickersham Ln, Saint Louis, MO 63124

HODGES, Michael (Mass) 29 Central St, Andover, MA 01810

✠ **HODGES-COPPLE**, Anne (NC) 1104 Watts St, Durham, NC 27701

HODGKINS, Margaret S. R. (Ct) Trinity Episcopal Church, PO Box 400, Southport, CT 06890

HODGSON, Carla (Minn)

HODGSON, Gregory Scott (SVa) 11940 Fairlington Lane, Midlothian, VA 23113

HODSDON, Douglas Graham (Fla) 1439 N Market St, Jacksonville, FL 32206

HODSDON, Joseph Graham (EC)

HOEBERMANN, Christine Marie (Oly) 123 L St NE, Auburn, WA 98002

HOECKER, Maria (Me) 32 Emery Ln, Boothbay Harbor, ME 04538

HOECKER, Marsha (Mass) 188 Center Rd, Shirley, MA 01464

HOEDEL, Barbara Anne (Ak) PO Box 1661, Kodiak, AK 99615

HOEKSTRA, Robert Bruce (ND) 411 2nd Ave NE, Jamestown, ND 58401

HOELTZEL, George Anthony (NY) 721 Warburton Ave, Yonkers, NY 10701

HOELZEL III, William N (Chi) 3257 Anika Dr, Fort Collins, CO 80525

HOEY, Anne Knight (Tex) 5608-A Jim Hogg Ave., Austin, TX 78756

HOEY, Lori Jean (CFla) 901 Clearmont St, Sebastian, FL 32958

HOFER, Christopher David (LI) 1653 19th St, Cuyahoga Falls, OH 44223

HOFER, Larry John (CPa) 32801 Ocean Reach Dr, Lewes, DE 19958

HOFF, Timothy Joseph (Ala) 2601 Lakewood Cir, Tuscaloosa, AL 35405

HOFFACKER, Charles Edward Niblett (WA) 9a Parkway 202, Greenbelt, MD 20770

HOFFER, Jack Lee (CPa) 830 Washington Avenue, Tyrone, PA 16686

HOFFER, Wilma Marie (EO) 64849 Casa Ct, Bend, OR 97701

HOFFMAN, Arnold (Spr) 1226 Olive St Unit 505, Saint Louis, MO 63103

HOFFMAN, Charles Lance (Ct) 8 Sharon Ln, Old Saybrook, CT 06475

HOFFMAN JR, Edgar Henry Hap (Ark) 7 Rubra Ct, Little Rock, AR 72223

HOFFMAN, Ellendale Mccollam (Ct) 8 Sharon Ln, Old Saybrook, CT 06475

HOFFMAN JR, Henry J (Az)

HOFFMAN, Jeffrey Paul (CNY)

HOFFMAN, Lisa A (NJ) St Barnabas By The Bay Church, 13 W Bates Ave, Villas, NJ 08251

HOFFMAN, Mary E (Ia) 2704 E Garfield St, Davenport, IA 52803

HOFFMAN, Michael Patrick (CGC) Christ Episcopal Church, 18 W Wright St, Pensacola, FL 32501

HOFFMAN, Roy E (SVa) 3100 Shore Dr Apt 916, Virginia Beach, VA 23451

HOFFMANN, Beth (Ore) 2409 Crescent Rd, Navarre, FL 32566

HOFFMANN, Holly Christine (Me) 885 Shore Rd, Cape Elizabeth, ME 04107

HOFF NOLAN, Daryce (Chi) 7600 Wolf Rd, Burr Ridge, IL 60527

HOFMANN, Therese Marie (Mass) 108 Stratford St, West Roxbury, MA 02132

HOGAN, Claudia S M (Eau)

HOGAN, Lucy Lind (WA) 4500 Massachusetts Ave Nw, Washington, DC 20016

HOGG, Douglas (EC) 347 S Creek Dr, Osprey, FL 34229

HOGG, John Edwin (Va)

HOGG JR, Peter (SVa) 7858 Sunset Dr, Hayes, VA 23072

HOGIN, Christopher W (ETenn) Church Of The Ascension, 800 S Northshore Dr, Knoxville, TN 37919

HOGUE, Kelsey (Colo) 5256 Mt Arapaho Cir, Frederick, CO 80504

HOGUE, Marlene Christine Harshfield (Eau) PO Box 637, Hayward, WI 54843

HOGUE JR, Richard R (SanD) 3163 Cedar St, San Diego, CA 92102

HOHENFELDT, Robert John (Mil) 1310 Rawson Ave, South Milwaukee, WI 53172

HOIDRA, Carol (Ct) 245 E 72nd St Apt 2d, New York, NY 10021

Clergy List

HOKE, Stuart Hubbard (Ark) 127 N Tryon St Unit 513, Charlotte, NC 28202

HOLBEN, Lawrence Robert (The Episcopal NCal) 701 Lassen Ln, Mount Shasta, CA 96067

HOLBERT, John Russell (La) 1645 Carol Sue Ave, Terrytown, LA 70056

HOLBROOK JR, Paul Evans (Lex) 308 Madison Pl, Lexington, KY 40508

HOLCOMB, Justin (CFla) 533 Legacy Park Dr, Casselberry, FL 32707

HOLCOMB, Steve A-Retired (WNC) 1500 Maltby Rd, Marble, NC 28905

HOLCOMBE, Matthew P (Colo) 1412 Providence Rd, Charlotte, NC 28207

HOLCOMBE, Scott Thorne (CFla) 4146 Millstone Dr, Melbourne, FL 32940

HOLDBROOKE, Charles Henry (LI) Calvary St Cyprians Church, Brooklyn, NY 11221

HOLDEN, Elizabeth G (Tex) 4709 Laurel St, Bellaire, TX 77401

HOLDER, Anthony Brian (SeFla) 2801 N University Dr, Pembroke Pines, FL 33024

HOLDER, Arthur Glenn (Cal) 510 Baylor Ct, Benicia, CA 94510

HOLDER, Charles Richard (Md) PO Box A, Rohrersville, MD 21779

HOLDER, Jennifer Sutton (NwT) 1318 Amarilla St, Abilene, TX 79602

HOLDER, Lauren R (At) 435 Peachtree St NE, Atlanta, GA 30308

HOLDER, Michael Rawle (SVa) 926 Thomasson Lane, South Hill, VA 23970

HOLDER, Timothy (ETenn) 142 Lovers Ln, Elizabethton, TN 37643

HOLDER-JOFFRION, Kerry (The Episcopal Church in Haw) P. O. Box 1037, Kekaha, HI 96752

HOLDING, Megan (Mass) 77 Monadnock Rd, Wellesley, MA 02481

HOLDING, Suzann (Chi) 2728 6th Ave, San Diego, CA 92103

HOLDORPH, Jedediah D (EO) 1829 NE Berg Way, Bend, OR 97701

HOLE, Jeremy (Fla) 4141 Nw 18th Dr, Gainesville, FL 32605

✠ **HOLGUIN-KHOURY**, Julio (DomRep) Agape Flights Dms 13602, 100 Airport Ave E, Venice, FL 34285

HOLICKY, Kathryn Elizabeth (Me)

HOLLAND, Albert L (Del) 1101 Saint Paul St Apt 412, Baltimore, MD 21202

HOLLAND JR, Bud (Pa) 121 Penns Grant Dr, Morrisville, PA 19067

HOLLAND, Carol L (Va) P.O. Box 1626, Kilmarnock, VA 22482

HOLLAND, Clayton Theodore (Dal) 517 W Hull St, Denison, TX 75020

HOLLAND, Donald Keith (Ga)

HOLLAND, Eleanor Lois (Md) 3204 Bayonne Ave, Baltimore, MD 21214

HOLLAND, J Mark (ETenn)

HOLLAND, Janet M (Cal) 1042 Dead Indian Memorial Road, Ashland, OR 97520

HOLLAND, John Stewart (HB)

HOLLAND III, Jule Carr (NC) 7404 Halifax Rd, Youngsville, NC 27596

HOLLAND, Katharine Grace (Ore) 13265 Nw Northrup St, Portland, OR 97229

HOLLAND, Nancy R (SanD)

HOLLAND-SHUEY, Marilyn Basye (Ala) 3740 Meridian St N, Huntsville, AL 35811

HOLLAR, Sarah (NC) 19107 Southport Dr, Cornelius, NC 28031

HOLLEMAN, Virginia Falconer (Dal) 5518 Merrimac Ave, Dallas, TX 75206

HOLLENBECK, Jon (Dal) 2215 Tracey Ann Ln, Killeen, TX 76543

HOLLENBECK, Scott Warren (Colo) 820 2nd St, Meeker, CO 81641

✠ **HOLLERITH IV**, Herman (SVa) 600 Talbot Road, Norfolk, VA 23505

HOLLERITH, Melissa Kaye Zuber (Va) 5503 Toddsbury Rd, Richmond, VA 23226

HOLLERITH, Randolph M (WA) 1205 W Franklin St, Richmond, VA 23220

HOLLIDAY, Charles Thomas (Va) 3001 Stonewall Ave, Richmond, VA 23225

HOLLIDAY, Fran (Chi) 5057 W Devon Ave, Chicago, IL 60646

HOLLIGER, John Charles (O) 70 Welshire Court, Delaware, OH 43015

HOLLINGER, Ranee Marie (U)

✠ **HOLLINGSWORTH JR**, Mark (O) 2230 Euclid Ave, Cleveland, OH 44115

HOLLINGSWORTH-GRAVES, Judy Lynn (SD) 1508 S Rock Creek Dr # 168, Sioux Falls, SD 57103

HOLLIS, Joanna (NJ) 5 Paterson St, New Brunswick, NJ 08901

HOLLIS, Randolph Newton (Ark)

HOLLIS, Robin Buckholtz (Az) St James The Ap Tec Ch, 975 E Warner Rd, Tempe, AZ 85284

HOLLIS, Tony (Md) 712 Murdock Rd, Baltimore, MD 21212

HOLLOWAY, Alexandra (WTex)

HOLLOWAY, Eric Andre Cole (WTex)

HOLLOWELL II, James Rhoads (Colo) 11675 Flatiron Dr, Lafayette, CO 80026

HOLLY, William David (Okla)

HOLLYWOOD, Trula Louise (CNY) 701 S Main St, Athens, PA 18810

HOLM, Margie (SVa) 400 N High St, Franklin, VA 23851

HOLMAN, Emily Clark (NJ) 96 Fairacres Dr, Toms River, NJ 08753

HOLMAN, John Earl (Tex) 2400 Spring Raindrive, #1018, Spring, TX 77379

HOLMAN, J(oseph) Lawrence (Be) RR 1 Box 125A, Towanda, PA 18848

HOLMAN, Kathryn Daneke (At) 1883 Clinton Dr, Marietta, GA 30062

HOLMBERG, Sandi (Minn) 14266 E Fox Lake Rd, Detroit Lakes, MN 56501

HOLMES, Francine Reynolds (NY) 944 Thistlegate Rd, Oak Park, CA 91377

HOLMES, Jane Victoria Frances (NC) 2540 Bricker Drive, Charlotte, NC 28273

HOLMES, Jim (WA) 10450 Lottsford Rd Apt 5005, Mitchellville, MD 20721

HOLMES, Joyce Ann Woolever (SwFla) St Wilfred Episcopal Church, 3773 Wilkinson Rd, Sarasota, FL 34233

HOLMES, Kristine Marie (Mass) 91 Main St, Bridgewater, MA 02324

HOLMES, Marsha Evans (Fla) 400 San Juan Dr, Ponte Vedra Beach, FL 32082

HOLMES, Martha (Ala) 1109 26th St S Apt 4, Birmingham, AL 35205

HOLMES, Phillip Wilson (WNY) 418 Virginia St, Buffalo, NY 14201

HOLMES, Rebecca Elizabeth (NC) 237 N Canterbury Rd, Charlotte, NC 28211

HOLMES, Rilla (USC) 205 Meadowlark Ln, Fountain Inn, SC 29644

HOLMES, Stanley W (WVa) PO Box 79, Hansford, WV 25103

HOLMGREN, Stephen Carl (La) 13650 Oakley Ln, Saint Francisville, LA 70775

HOLMQUIST, David Wendell (Neb) St Augustine of Canterbury, 285 S 208th St, Elkhorn, NE 68022

HOLROYD, David D (Me) 3 Elizabeth Rd, South Berwick, ME 03908

HOLSTON III, George (Fla) 804 Doubles Ct, Harker Heights, TX 76548

HOLSTROM, Sue (Chi) 1218 Avery Ranch Rd, Silver City, NM 88061

HOLT, Ann Case (NJ) 60 Main St, Clinton, NJ 08809

HOLT, Charles L (Tex) 3946 Saint Johns Ave Apt 306, Jacksonville, FL 32205

HOLT, Jane L Bonnie (Minn) 224 2nd St N, Cannon Falls, MN 55009

HOLT, Joseph (Cal) 2237 Fulton #103, San Francisco, CA 94117

HOLT, Stephen (Md)

HOLT III, William Therrel (Az) 854 E Florida Saddle Dr, Green Valley, AZ 85614

HOLTHUS, Jess (Va) 106 W Church St, Frederick, MD 21701

HOLTKAMP, Patrick John (LI) 7712 35th Ave Apt A64, Jackson Heights, NY 11372

HOLTMAN, Kimberly (Nwk) Private, Austin, TX 78704

HOLTON, Edie H (Md) 120 E J St, Benicia, CA 94510

HOLTON, Stephen C (Ct) Christ Episcopal Church, 84 Broadway, New Haven, CT 06511

HOLTON, Steve (NY) 91 Greenwood Ln, White Plains, NY 10607

HOLTZEN, Thomas Lee (Mil) 2777 Mission Rd, Nashotah, WI 53058

HOLZ JR, John Clifford (Ak)

HOLZHALB, Leon (La) 100 Christwood Blvd, Covington, LA 70433

HOMEYER, Charlie (WMich) 3539 Quiggle Ave Se, Ada, MI 49301

HOMEYER, Peter Carey (SO) Christ Episcopal Church, 20 West First Street, Dayton, OH 45402

HONAKER, Martha (Ind) 111 Ivy Lane, Sparta, NC 28675

HONDERICH, Thomas E (Ind) 3941 N Delaware St, Indianapolis, IN 46205

HONEA, Janice Bailey (Dal) 6909 Studebaker Dr, Mckinney, TX 75071

HONEYCHURCH, John Robert (Los) 1000 Concha St, Altadena, CA 91001

HONNOLD, Sandra Elizabeth (The Episcopal NCal) PO Box 7063, PMB 295, Ocean View, HI 96737

HONODEL, Jill (Cal) 285 Kaanapali Dr, Napa, CA 94558

HONSE, Robert Wayne (Kan)

HOOD, Nancy E (Dal) 6883 Lagoon Dr, Grand Prairie, TX 75054

HOOD, Stephen D (Colo) 2030 Country Meadows Ct, Grand Junction, CO 81507

HOOD, Suzanne (EC)

HOOD, William Rienks (La) 1808 Prospect St, Houston, TX 77004

HOOGERHYDE, Scott Matthew (Spr) 7 E Main St, Mendham, NJ 07945

HOOK, Andrew S (Spr) Cath Ch Of St Paul The Ap, 815 South Second Street, Springfield, IL 62704

HOOK, Edward Lindsten (Colo) PO Box 1388, Green Valley, AZ 85622

HOOKE, Ruthanna Brinton (WMass) 3737 Seminary Rd, Alexandria, VA 22304

HOOKER, Al (Va) 6645 Northumberland Hwy, Heathsville, VA 22473

HOOKER, Hannah (Ark) Christ Episcopal Church, 509 Scott St, Little Rock, AR 72201

HOOKER, John L (WMass) 22c Castle Hill Rd, Agawam, MA 01001

HOOKS, Rhonda Lynn Lynn (La)

HOOP, Kimberly Ann (WMich) 4155 S Norway St Se, Grand Rapids, MI 49546

HOOPER, Elizabeth E (Los) 1014 E Altadena Dr, Altadena, CA 91001

HOOPER, Jack (Mich) 42 Cottage Circle, West Lebanon, NH 03784

HOOPER, Larry (SeFla) 401 Duval St, Key West, FL 33040

HOOPER, Phillip Russell (NI)

HOOPER III, Robert Channing (Ct) 10 Cumberland Rd, West Hartford, CT 06119

HOOPER, Ruth Isabelle (Az) 1710 W. Dalehaven Cir, Tucson, AZ 85704

HOOPES, David Bryan (LI) Church of St Edward the Martyr, 14 E 109th St, New York, NY 10029

HOOS, AnnaMarie (Cal) Church of the Epiphany, 1839 Arroyo Ave, San Carlos, CA 94070

HOOVER, Greg T (Ark) 735 W Kingsley St, Springfield, MO 65807

HOOVER, Joshua Aaron (Mich) 355 W Maple Rd, Birmingham, MI 48009

HOOVER, Judy Verne Hanlon (Minn) 2020 Orkla Dr, Golden Valley, MN 55427

HOOVER, Melvin Aubrey (SO) 1870 Commonwealth Ave., Auburndale, MA 02466

HOOVER, Richard A (CFla) 209 S Iowa Ave, Lakeland, FL 33801

HOOVER, Todd (SeFla) 605 Lakeside Cir, Pompano Beach, FL 33060

HOOVER-DEMPSEY, Randy (Tenn) 1829 Hudson Rd, Madison, TN 37115

HOPEWELL, Gloria (Chi) 210 S High St, Galena, IL 61036

HOPKINS, Christine Carroll (Spr) 102 E Mchenry St, Urbana, IL 61801

HOPKINS, Daniel W (Colo) 7127 S Quemoy St, Aurora, CO 80016

HOPKINS, John Leonard (Alb) 34 Velina Dr, Burnt Hills, NY 12027

HOPKINS, Lydia Elliott (La)

HOPKINS, Michael Warren (Roch) 67 E Main St, Hornell, NY 14843

HOPKINS, Portia (The Episcopal NCal)

HOPKINS, Terry Robert (Minn) P.O. Box 402, Monticello, MN 55362

HOPKINS, Vivian Louise (Oly) 32820 20th Ave S #61, Federal Way, WA 98003

HOPKINS-GREENE, Nancy (SO) 6255 Stirrup Rd, Cincinnati, OH 45244

HOPLAMAZIAN, Julie M (NY) St Luke St Matthew, 520 Clinton Ave, Brooklyn, NY 11238

HOPNER, Kathryn Ann (The Episcopal NCal) St Pauls Episcopal Church, PO Box 737, Sparks, NV 89432

HOPPE, Robert Donald (FdL) 806 4th St, Algoma, WI 54201

HOPWOOD, Alfred Joseph (Minn) 1417 Blue Flag Ct, Northfield, MN 55057

HORD, Christine D (CGC)

HOREN, Anna Lynn (Colo) 10159 Jill Ave, Highlands Ranch, CO 80130

HORKEY, Patricia Lynn (SanD) PO Box 506, Idyllwild, CA 92549

HORLE, Garrison Locke (Colo) 720 Downing St, Denver, CO 80218

HORN, Huston (Los) 1428 Peartree Ct, Encinitas, CA 92024

HORN, John C (Ia) Trinity Episcopal Cathedral, 121 W 12th St, Davenport, IA 52803

HORN, Mike (ND) 1652 Peacock Blvd, Oceanside, CA 92056

HORN, Raisin (Ia) Christ Episcopal Church, 2100 N 2nd St, Clinton, IA 52732

HORNADAY, Evelyn (WMo) Stpeter All Sts Tec Ch, 100 E Red Bridge Rd, Kansas City, MO 64114

HORNBECK, Jen (Cal) 1001 Norton St, San Mateo, CA 94401

HORNE, Lance Cameron (Fla) 3275 Tallavana Trl, Havana, FL 32333

HORNE, Martha (Va) 3809 Fort Worth Ave, Alexandria, VA 22304

HORNER, John (O) 813 W Main St, Elizabeth City, NC 27909

HORNER, William McKinley (Miss) 14981 W Verde Ln, Goodyear, AZ 85338

HORNING, David (Mich) 104 Mount Homestake Dr., Leadville, CO 80461

HORNSBY, Jim (Mass) 260 Lake Ave, Fall River, MA 02721

HORST, Diane Elizabeth (NMich) 12769 W Lakeshore Dr, Brimley, MI 49715

HORTON, Carol J (NJ) 3 Plumstead Ct, Annandale, NJ 08801

HORTON, Fred Lane (NC) 2622 Weymoth Rd, Winston Salem, NC 27103

HORTON JR, James Taylor (Tex) 7413 Hillstone Dr, Benbrook, TX 76126

HORTON, Jim (EC) 1060 Dixie Trl, Williamston, NC 27892

HORTON, Sarah (Vt) 17 Mack Ave, West Lebanon, NH 03784

HORTON-HOWE, Carole Lee (Los) 7056 Washington Ave, Whittier, CA 90602

HORTON-SMITH, Sandra (Kan) St Paul's Episcopal Church, 601 Poyntz Ave, Manhattan, KS 66502

HORTUM, John (Va) 1407 N Gaillard St, Alexandria, VA 22304

HORVATH, Leslie Ferguson (USC) 639 Ponden Dr, Greer, SC 29650

HORVATH, Michael J (RI)

HORVATH, Victor John (Vt) 6 South St, Bellows Falls, VT 05101

HOSEA, Beverly Ann (Spok) 1822 E 34th Ave, Spokane, WA 99203

HOSEA, Jan (RG) 7171 Tennyson St NE, Albuquerque, NM 87122

HOSKINS, Charles L (Ga) 4629 Sylvan Dr, Savannah, GA 31405

HOSKINS, Jo Ann Smith (Fla) 4241 Duval Dr, Jacksonville Beach, FL 32250

HOSLER, Carol Smith (Az) 815 S 216th St Apt 117, Des Moines, WA 98198

HOSLER, Joshua Luke (Oly) 2117 Walnut St, Bellingham, WA 98225

HOSPADOR, Dorothea Cecelia (NJ) 247 Carr Ave, Keansburg, NJ 07734

HOSTER JR, David (Tex) 30003 Edgewood Drive, Georgetown, TX 78628

HOSTER, Elizabeth M (O) Trinity Episcopal Church, 316 Adams Street, Toledo, OH 43604

HOSTETTER, Jane (USC) 2303 NE Seaview Dr, Jensen Beach, FL 34957

HOTCHKISS, Margaret Peterson (Wyo) PO Box 250, Saratoga, WY 82331

HOTCHKISS, Thomas S (Dal) 11122 Midway Rd, Dallas, TX 75229

HOTRA, Nancy (WMich) 9733 Sterling Rd, Richland, MI 49083

HOTZE, Janice A (Ak) Po Box 91, Haines, AK 99827

HOUCK III, Ira Chauncey (USC) 120 Norse Dr, Columbia, SC 29229

HOUCK, John Bunn (Chi) 5236 S Cornell Ave, Chicago, IL 60615

HOUCK, Kay M (WMich)

HOUGH III, Charles (Dal) 2900 Alemeda St, Fort Worth, TX 76108

HOUGH, George Willard (NwPa) 904 Holliday Hills Dr, Hollidaysburg, PA 16648

HOUGHTON, Frederick Lord (EMich) 4138 N Francis Shores Ave, Sanford, MI 48657

HOUGHTON, John William (NI) 609 Houghton St., Culver, IN 46511

HOUGHTON, William Clokey (NwT) 27 Painted Canyon Place, The Woodlands, TX 77381

HOUGLAND, Erin Elizabeth (Ind)

HOUGLAND JR, Whayne (WMich) Tec Dio Of Wern Mi, 535 S Burdick St, Kalamazoo, MI 49007

HOUK, David Jay (Dal) 848 Harter Rd, Dallas, TX 75218

HOULE, Michael Anthony (EMich) 4525 Birch Run Rd, Birch Run, MI 48415

HOULIK, Michael Andrew (Colo) 2712 Geneva Pl, Longmont, CO 80503

HOULTBERG, Loren Andrew (Kan)

HOUPT, Cameron Wheeler (Colo) 10222 W Ida Ave Unit 238, Littleton, CO 80127

HOUSE, Karen Ellen (CFla) 1120 Sunshine Ave, Leesburg, FL 34748

HOUSER III, Richard Truett (Tex) 13131 Fry Rd, Cypress, TX 77433

HOUSER, Teresa (Neb)

HOUSNER-RITTER, Jenny Lee (Mich)

HOUSTON, Barbara Pearce (EC) 206 North Fairlane Drive, Box 939, Grifton, NC 28530

HOUZE, Jared Foster (NwT)

HOVENCAMP, Otis (WNY) 85 Wide Beach Rd, Irving, NY 14081

HOVEY, Diane Lane (Ct)

HOWANSTINE JR, John Edwin (Md) 3090 Broomes Island Rd, Port Republic, MD 20676

HOWARD, Alex (Colo) 7168 Burnt Mill Rd, Beulah, CO 81023

HOWARD, Anne (Los) 950 Dena Way, Santa Barbara, CA 93111

HOWARD, Charles Lattimore (Pa)

HOWARD, Coleen Gayle (Ore) PO Box 1319, Gresham, OR 97030

HOWARD III, George Williams (Spr) 811 Highland Vw, Mount Vernon, IL 62864

HOWARD, Harry Lee (ETenn) 2668 Larenwood Dr, Maryville, TN 37804

HOWARD II, Joseph B (Tenn) 2458 Centerpoint Rd, Hendersonville, TN 37075

HOWARD, Karin D (SwVa) 4461 S Main St Apt 111, Acworth, GA 30101

HOWARD, Ken Wayne (WA) 9 Liberty Heights Court, Germantown, MD 20874

HOWARD, Leonard Rice (The Episcopal Church in Haw) 98-1128 Malualua St, Aiea, HI 96701

HOWARD, Lois Waser (Lex) 713 Dicksonia Ct, Lexington, KY 40517

HOWARD, Noah B (NC) 206 Maryland Ave, Roanoke, NC 27886

HOWARD, Sally Anne (Los) 132 N Euclid Ave, Pasadena, CA 91101

✠ **HOWARD**, Samuel Johnson (Fla) 325 N Market St, Jacksonville, FL 32202

HOWARD, Sylvia Lord (Spr) 1811 Highland Vw, Mount Vernon, IL 62864

HOWARD, Ted (Colo) 1419 Pine St, Boulder, CO 80302

HOWCOTT, Jeffernell Ophelia Green (Mich) 19320 Santa Rosa Dr, Detroit, MI 48221

✠ **HOWE**, Barry (WMo) PO Box 413227, Kansas City, MO 64141

HOWE, Garth (Chi) 3232 N Halsted St Unit H302, Chicago, IL 60657

HOWE, Heath (Chi) 333 Warwick Rd, Kenilworth, IL 60043

HOWE, Jeffrey Newman (Lex) 201 Price Rd Apt 216, Lexington, KY 40511

HOWE JR, Ralph (La) 8965 Bayside Ave, Baton Rouge, LA 70806

HOWE, Ray (Be) 833 Gillinder Pl, Cary, NC 27519

HOWE, Wendy (ECR) 203 Lighthouse Ave, Pacific Grove, CA 93950

HOWELL, Edward Allen (The Episcopal NCal) 1953 Terry Rd, Santa Rosa, CA 95403

HOWELL, Laura (Be) 44 E Market St, Bethlehem, PA 18018

HOWELL, Margery E (SVa) 3316 Hyde Cir, Norfolk, VA 23513

HOWELL, Melissa Lynn Oliver (Mass) Grace Episcopal Church, 133 School St, New Bedford, MA 02740

HOWELL, Miguelina (Ct) Christ Church Cathedral, 45 Church St, Hartford, CT 06103

HOWELL, Robert M (SO) 69081 Mount Herman Rd, Cambridge, OH 43725

HOWELL, Sydney C (Va) 495 Melrose Dr, Monticello, FL 32344

HOWELL, Terry Robert (At) 2135 Zelda Dr Ne, Atlanta, GA 30345

HOWELL-BURKE, Undine Jean (Neb) 7425 Stevens Ridge Rd, Lincoln, NE 68516

HOWELLS, Donald Arthur (Be) 1936 Chestnut Hill Road, Mohnton, PA 19540

HOWLETT, Louise (NH) 131 E Harrisville Rd, Dublin, NH 03444

HOWSER, Carol Louise Jordan (Ore) 192 Harrison St, Ashland, OR 97520

HOWZE, Lynn Corpening (CFla) 215 West Park, Lakeland, FL 33803

HOXIE, George (Dal)

HOY, Lois (Cal) 36 dos Posos, Orinda, CA 94563

HOY, Mary Ann (Me) 6 Old Mast Landing Rd, Freeport, ME 04032

HOYT, Calvin Van Kirk (CPa) 1418 Walnut St, Camp Hill, PA 17011

HOYT, Tim (WNC) 479 Whispering Woods Dr, Saluda, NC 28773

HROSTOWSKI, Susan (Miss) 1861 Tryon Dr Unit 3, Fayetteville, NC 28303

HSIEH, Nathaniel (Eur) 44 Rue Docteur Robert, Chatillon Sur Seine, 21400, France

HU, Kuo-Hua (Tai) Chieh Shou Road 5, Kangshan, 82018, Taiwan

HUACANI, Amy J (NC) PO Box 2263, Durham, NC 27702

HUAL, Jeffrey C (Md) 3600 Solomons Island Rd, Edgewater, MD 21037

HUANG, Peter P (Los) 840 Echo Park Ave, Los Angeles, CA 90026

HUBBARD, Carol Murphy (WNC) 211 Montford Ave, Asheville, NC 28801

HUBBARD JR, Charles Clark (Ala) 227 McDuffie Drive, Richmond Hill, GA 31324

HUBBARD, Colenzo (WTenn) 604 Saint Paul Ave, Memphis, TN 38126

HUBBARD, Cynthia (Mass) 45 White Trellis, Plymouth, MA 02360

HUBBARD, Francis Appleton (NJ) 5 North Rd, Berkeley Heights, NJ 07922

HUBBARD, James (SwVa) 384 Waughs Ferry Rd, Amherst, VA 24521

HUBBARD JR, Joseph L (ND)

HUBBARD, Lani Marie (Oly) 225 Mar Vista Way, Port Angeles, WA 98362

HUBBARD, Martha (Mass) The Episcopal Diocese of Massachusetts, 138 Tremont St, Boston, MA 02111

HUBBARD, Mavourneen Ann (NY) 17 South Ave, 855 Wolcott Ave, Beacon, NY 12508

HUBBARD, Philip R (LI) 161 Ponquogue Ave, Hampton Bays, NY 11946

HUBBELL, Gilbert Leonard (O) 1094 Clifton Ave # 2, Akron, OH 44310

HUBBELL, Sally Hanes (The Episcopal NCal) 209 Matheson St, Healdsburg, CA 95448

HUBBY III, Turner Erath (Tex) 329 Meadowbrook Dr, San Antonio, TX 78232

HUBER, Amy Whitcombe (Eau) 234 Avon St, La Crosse, WI 54603

HUBER, Donald Marvin (Neb) 10807 Scott Peddler Rd, Cattaraugus, NY 14719

HUBER, Ellen (SD) 171 Old Tannery Rd # 6468, Monroe, CT 06468

HUBER, E Wendy (Colo) 76 Spring Ridge Ct, Glenwood Springs, CO 81601

HUBER, Glenna (WA) 1820 Greenberry Rd, Baltimore, MD 21209

HUBER, Joshua David (Mo) 413 Thilly Ave, Columbia, MO 65203

HUBER, Kurt J (SD) PO Box 552, Eagle Butte, SD 57625

HUBER, Steve (Los) 506 N. Camden Drive, Beverly Hills, CA 90210

HUBERT, Deven Ann (Roch) 66 Little Briggins Cir, Fairport, NY 14450

HUCK, Beverly (Nwk) 155 Rainbow Dr # 5549, Livingston, TX 77399

HUCKABAY JR, Harry Hunter (ETenn) 1706 Glenroy Ave., Chattanooga, TN 37405

HUDAK, Bob (EC) St Paul's Church, 401 E. 4th St, Greenville, NC 27858

HUDAK, Catherine Ann (RG)

HUDDLESTON, Kevin Douglas (Okla) 1010 S West St, Stillwater, OK 74074

HUDDLESTON, Nathan (WA)

HUDLOW, A Kelley (Ala) 521 20th St N, Birmingham, AL 35203

HUDSON, Aaron (NY) 40 Old Mill Rd, Staten Island, NY 10306

HUDSON, Andrew (SeFla) 7538 Granville Dr, Tamarac, FL 33321

HUDSON, Andrew George (SeFla) 2250 SW 31st Ave, Fort Lauderdale, FL 33312

HUDSON, Betty (SVa) 120 John Bratton, Williamsburg, VA 23185

HUDSON, Brandon James (Ark)

HUDSON, Daniel Mark (La) 1329 Jackson Ave, New Orleans, LA 70130

HUDSON, Henry Lee (Ala) 1424 4th St, New Orleans, LA 70130

HUDSON, Joseph Dale (SwFla)

HUDSON, Kimberly Karen (WA) 11403 Trillum St, Bowie, MD 20721

HUDSON, Linda Ann (Wyo) 860 S 3rd St, Lander, WY 82520

HUDSON, Mary Bowen (CFla) 4345 Indian River Dr, Cocoa, FL 32927

HUDSON, Mary Jo (EMich)

HUDSON, Michael (WMo) Po Box 152, Cullowhee, NC 28723

HUDSON, Thomas James (Md)

HUDSON-LOUIS, Holly (ECR) 65 Highway 1, Carmel, CA 93923

HUDSPETH, Denise (CFla) 208 Nw Avenue H, Belle Glade, FL 33430

HUERTA, Efrain (Tex) 12607 Banchester Ct, Houston, TX 77070

HUERTA GARCIA, Huerta (Tex) Chamela 33 A, Tlaquepaque, JAL 45589, Mexico

HUESCHEN, Micheal Gordon (WMich)

HUESTIS, Warren (SO)

HUFF, Carolyn Tuttle (Pa) 1121 N Trooper Rd, Norristown, PA 19403

HUFF II, Charles Richard (Oly)

HUFF, Christopher Mercer (SC) 1612 Dryden Ln, Charleston, SC 29407

HUFF, Clark Kern (Tex) 2252 Garden Court, San Marcos, TX 78666

HUFF, Holly A (U)

HUFF, Susan Ellen (At) 1031 Eagles Ridge Ct, Lawrenceville, GA 30043

HUFFMAN, Charles Howard (Tex) 8124 Greenslope Dr, Austin, TX 78759

HUFFORD, Robert Arthur (SO) 52 Bishopsgate Dr Apt 703, Cincinnati, OH 45246

HUFFSTETLER, Joel W (ETenn) 3920 Clairmont Dr Ne, Cleveland, TN 37312

HUFT, Jerry Ray (CGC) Po Box 595, Wewahitchka, FL 32465

HUGGARD, Linda (Episcopal SJ) 4300 Keith Way, Bakersfield, CA 93309

✠ **HUGHES**, Carlye J (Nwk) Diocese Of Newark, Episcopal House, 31 Mulberry S, Newark, NJ 07102

HUGHES, Frank W (WLa) 299 Milton Rd, Spearsville, LA 71277

✠ **HUGHES**, Gethin Benwil (SanD) 461 Quail Run Rd, Buellton, CA 93427

HUGHES, James Anthony (Va) 9320 West St, Manassas, VA 20110

HUGHES, J Daniel (Chi)

HUGHES, Jennifer Scheper (Mass) 1147 Walnut St, Berkeley, CA 94707

HUGHES, John Richard (Mil) 8231 W Highlander Dr, Mequon, WI 53097

HUGHES, Laura K (WMo) St George Episcopal Church, 423 N Business Route 5, Camdenton, MO 65020

HUGHES, Linda (Ia) 103 Melissa St, Elizabethtown, KY 42701

HUGHES, Mary London (ECR) 902 California Ave, San Jose, CA 95125

HUGHES III, Robert Davis (SO) 335 Tennessee Ave, Sewanee, TN 37383

HUGHES, Rosalind Claire (O)

HUGHES, Thomas Downs (WNC) 16 Salisbury Dr Apt 7206, Asheville, NC 28803

HUGHES JR, Thomas Roddy (Eas) 852 Spring Valley Dr, Fredericksburg, VA 22405

HUGHES-EMPKE, Sheryl (Ia) PO Box 486, Perry, IA 50220

HUGHES-HABEL, Deborah Jean (Ore) 4615 S 3200 W, West Valley City, UT 84119

HUGHS, Leslie Curtis (LI) 114 Mountain View Ln, Stamford, VT 05352

HUINER, Peter Bruce (Del) 500 Woodlawn Rd, Wilmington, DE 19803

HULEN, Jennifer L (Chi) 9 S Bompart Ave, Saint Louis, MO 63119

HULET, Jefferson R (NJ) 14 Saint Remy Ct, Newport Coast, CA 92657

HULIN, Kathy Elizabeth (CFla) 209 S Iowa Ave, Lakeland, FL 33801

HULL, Carol (SO) 14590 Wilmot Way, Lake Oswego, OR 97035

HULL, George Andrew (Chi) 509 Brier St, Kenilworth, IL 60043

HULL, Nicholas Andrew (SwVa) PO Box 1146, Columbus, GA 31902

HULL, S (Los) 13025 Bloomfield St., Studio City, CA 91604

HULL IV, William Franklin (Fla) 630 S Sapodilla Ave Apt 214, West Palm Beach, FL 33401

HULLAR, Leonard Earl (Ct) 115 W Main St, Plainville, CT 06062

HULLINGER, Jon M (Kan) 3750 E Douglas Ave, Wichita, KS 67208

HULL-RYDE, Norman Arthur (WNC) 2535 Sheffield Dr, Gastonia, NC 28054

HULME, Steven Edward (Ct) 26 Colony Rd, East Lyme, CT 06333

HULS II, Frederick Eugene (Az) 2812 N 69th Pl, Scottsdale, AZ 85257

HULTMAN, Eugene Bradlee (Mass) 255 N Central Ave, Quincy, MA 02170

HUMBER, Michael Reagan (Colo) 4506 Fillmore St, Denver, CO 80216

HUMKE, Richard (Ky) 320 Joe Conway Ct Apt 2107, Masonic Home, KY 40041

HUMM, Charity A (Md)

HUMM, Richard Matthew (Md) St Pauls Church, 25 Church St, Prince Frederick, MD 20678

HUMMEL, Thomas Charles (Va) 1200 N Quaker Ln, Alexandria, VA 22302

HUMMELL, Mark (NY) 160 Cabrini Blvd Apt 36, New York, NY 10033

HUMPHREY, Christine Ann (Mich) 544 W Iroquois Rd, Pontiac, MI 48341

HUMPHREY, Georgia Lehman (Ia) 15064 Sheridan Ave, Clive, IA 50325

HUMPHREY JR, Howard MacKenzie (O) 6295 Chagrin River Rd, Chagrin Falls, OH 44022

HUMPHREY, Marian Teresa (WA) 9801 Livingston Rd, Fort Washington, MD 20744

HUMPHREY, Mary Beth (WA) 302 Ridgecrest Dr, Chapel Hill, NC 27514

HUMPHREY, Nathan J A (RI) Mem Ch Of St John, 61 Poplar St, Newport, RI 02840

HUMPHREY, Tyler Jason (Mil)

HUMPHREYS, Eugene L (NC) 425 E 17th St, Charlotte, NC 28206

HUMPHREYS, Walter Lee (ETenn) 7113 Hampshire Dr, Knoxville, TN 37909

HUMPHRIES, Charles Emerson (SeFla)

HUMPHRIES JR, John Curtis (CNY) 405 Euclid Avenue, Elmira, NY 14905

HUNDLEY, Brooks (WA)

HUNGATE, Carla Valinda (At) 4318 Windmill Trce, Douglasville, GA 30135

HUNGERFORD, Eric Paul (Pa) 18 E Chestnut Hill Ave, Philadelphia, PA 19118

HUNGERFORD, Roger (CGC) 2805 32nd Avenue Dr, Moline, IL 61265

HUNKINS, Orin James (Okla) 3724 Bonaire Pl, Edmond, OK 73013

HUNLEY, Deborah (SwVa) 2042 Lee Hi Rd SW, Roanoke, VA 24018

HUNN, Meg Buerkel (NC) 412 N East Street, Raleigh, NC 27604

HUNN, Michael (RG) 412 N East St, Raleigh, NC 27604

HUNNICUTT, Samuel Austin (WTex)

HUNSINGER, Jimmie Ruth Coffey (Fla) 350 Sw Stallion Gln, Lake City, FL 32024

HUNT, Anthony (Minn)

HUNT, Ashley Stephen (EC) 1 Palmerston Road, Melton Mowbray, Great Britain (UK)

HUNT, Edward (SVa) 20475 Sunningdale Park, Grosse Pointe Woods, MI 48236

HUNT III, Ernest Edward (Eur) 3310 Fairmount St Apt 9b, Dallas, TX 75201

HUNT, Hazel Bailey (Be) Po Box 86, Towanda, PA 18848

HUNT, J Patrick (NJ) 57 Putters Pl, Savannah, GA 31419

HUNT, John C (O) 44267 Route 511 East, Oberlin, OH 44074

HUNT, John Marsden (LI)

HUNT, Karla Westfall (Va) 5724 White Oak Road, Sandston, VA 23150

HUNT, Katherine Ann (Ak) 2006 W 31st Ave, Anchorage, AK 99517

HUNT, Lisa (Tex) 419 Woodland St, Nashville, TN 37206

HUNT, Mary (ETenn) 100 Steven Ln., Harriman, TN 37748

HUNT, Meredith (WMich) 1 Gates Cir Apt 504, Buffalo, NY 14209

HUNT, Paul Stuart (Pa) 212 S High St, West Chester, PA 19382

HUNT, Teresa Gioia (Pgh) 1335 Berryman Avenue, Bethel Park, PA 15102

HUNT, Terry Lynn (Nev) 79 Northwood Commons Pl, Chico, CA 95973

HUNT, Victoria Wells (Mass) Po Box 1205, East Harwich, MA 02645

HUNT, William Gilbert (Miss) 510 Godsey Rd., Apt. 183, Bristol, TN 37620

HUNTER, Christina M (Alb) 2331 15th St, Troy, NY 12180

HUNTER, Colenthia (SO) 8387 Vicksburg Dr, Cincinnati, OH 45249

HUNTER, Elizabeth Lane (Miss) 327 N First St, Rolling Fork, MS 39159

HUNTER, Elizabeth Sue (U) 231 E 100 S, Salt Lake City, UT 84111

HUNTER JR, Herschel Miller (Va) PO Box 37, Ivy, VA 22945

HUNTER II, James Nathaniel (Ak) 322 Cross Way, North Pole, AK 99705

HUNTER, James Wallace (RG) St Marys Church, 1500 Chelwood Park Blvd NE, Albuquerque, NM 87112

HUNTER, Karen (Ida) 204 Courthouse Dr, Salmon, ID 83467

HUNTER, Kenneth (Alb) 29 Walnut St., Oneonta, NY 13820

HUNTER, Lars J (Vt) PO Box 662, West Dover, VT 05356

HUNTER, Lawrence Scott (Cal) 542 Siskiyou Blvd, Ashland, OR 97520

HUNTER, Marcia (Lex) 104 Dellwood Dr, Berea, KY 40403

HUNTER, Mary Veronica (Alb) 305 Main St, Oneonta, NY 13820

HUNTER, Paul A (Alb) Christ Episcopal Church, 69 Fair St, Cooperstown, NY 13326

HUNTER, S Scott (Mich) The Cathedral Church Of St Paul, 4800 Woodward Ave, Detroit, MI 48201

HUNTER, Teri (Alb) Trinity Episc Church, 18 Trinity Pl, Plattsburgh, NY 12901

HUNTER, Walcott Wallace (SwFla) Po Box 646, Kinderhook, NY 12106

HUNTER-SPENCER, Dorothy Elaine (CFla)

HUNTINGTON, Carol L (Me) 121 Bowery St, Bath, ME 04530

HUNTINGTON, Francis Cleaveland (NY) 11 Rassapeague, Saint James, NY 11780

HUNTINGTON, Frederic Dubois (Va) 3720 Dunston Ave, Richmond, VA 23225

HUNTLEY, Stuart Michael (LI) 9 Carlton Ave, Port Washington, NY 11050

HUPF, Jeffrey Lee (Minn) 2459 Winthrop Ct, Mendota Heights, MN 55120

HUR, Won-Jae (Cal) 206 Arborway Apt 3, Boston, MA 02130

HURD JR, Austin Avery (Pgh) 102 Fountain Cv, 160 Marwood Rd Apt 3314, Cabot, PA 16023

HURLBERT, Sarah Frances (Mich) 9208 Legacy Oaks Pl, Asheville, NC 28803

HURLBURT, Martha Cornue (EO) 801 Jefferson St, Klamath Falls, OR 97601

HURLBUT, Terence James (WMass) 7 Woodbridge St, South Hadley, MA 01075

HURLEY, Hal Owen (SeFla) 418 N Sapodilla Ave, West Palm Beach, FL 33401

HURLEY, Janet (Los) St John Episcoapl Ch, PO Box 183, Needles, CA 92363

HURLEY, Regina Maria (RG)

HURLEY, Thomas James (Neb) 113 N 18th St, Omaha, NE 68102

HURST, Hassell J (Ga) PO Box 50555, Nashville, TN 37205

HURST, Michael Logan (Dal)

HURST, Michael W (SwFla) 301 S Gulfstream Ave Unit 204, Sarasota, FL 34236

HURST, Rodney Shane (RG) 508 W Fox St, Carlsbad, NM 88220

HURST, William George (NH) 108 Wecuwa Dr, Fort Myers, FL 33912

HURST, William Jeffrey (WMo)

HURT, Lynda Ann (WMo)

HURTADO, Homero (EcuC) Guallabamba 214, Cuenca, Ecuador

HURTT, Annie Lawrie (Pa) 659 W Johnson St, Philadelphia, PA 19144

HURWITZ, Ellen Sara (Md) 12147 Pleasant Walk Rd, Myersville, MD 21773

HUSBY, Mary Eloise Brown (SD) 1504 S Park Ave, Sioux Falls, SD 57105

HUSHION, Timothy V (NC) 328 6th St, Pittsburgh, PA 15215

HUSSEY, David Payne (SD) 405 N Madison Ave, Pierre, SD 57501

HUSSEY-SMITH, Teddra R (EC) 5071 Voorhees Rd, Denmark, SC 29042

HUSSON, Brenda G (NY) 865 Madison Ave, New York, NY 10021

HUSTAD, Siri Hauge (Minn) 519 Oak Grove St, Minneapolis, MN 55403

HUSTON, Jeffrey Clayton (Okla)

HUSTON, Julie Winn (At) 2950 Mount Wilkinson Pkwy SE Unit 817, Atlanta, GA 30339

HUSTON, Mary Ann (Tex) 3816 Bellaire Blvd, Houston, TX 77025

HUSTON, Nancy Williams (Neb) 923 S 33rd St, Omaha, NE 68105

HUTCHENS, Marquita L (WVa) St. John's Episcopal Churh, 1105 Quarrier Street, Charleston, WV 25301

HUTCHERSON, Anne V (WMo) 624 W 61st Ter, Kansas City, MO 64113

HUTCHERSON, Brian (SwVa) 74 Peterson Pl, Fishersville, VA 22939

HUTCHERSON, Robert (WMo) 624 West 64th Terrace, Kansas City, MO 64113

HUTCHINS, Margaret Smith (EC) 7909 Blue Heron Dr W Apt 2, Wilmington, NC 28411

HUTCHINS, Susan Ellen (RG) St Lukes Episcopal Church, PO Box 1258, Deming, NM 88031

HUTCHINSON, Anthony Alonzo (Ore) Trinity Episcopal Church, 44 N 2nd St, Ashland, OR 97520

HUTCHINSON, Barbara (CPa) 9 Carlton Ave, Port Washington, NY 11050

HUTCHINSON JR, John Fuller (Del) 350 Noxontown Rd, Middletown, DE 19709

HUTCHINSON, Ninon N (CNY) 7029 Texas Rd, Croghan, NY 13327

HUTCHION, Hal (ETenn) 2703 Upper Stone Mountain Rd, Unicoi, TN 37692

HUTCHISON, Jonathan (Ind) Hc 81 Box 6009, Questa, NM 87556

HUTCHISON, Sheldon Butt (ECR) 921 Eton Way, Sunnyvale, CA 94087

HUTCHSON, Lee Allen (Va) 18256 Oxshire Ct, Montpelier, VA 23192

HUTJENS, Dale Henry (FdL) 123 Nob Hill Ln, De Pere, WI 54115

HUTSON, Blake Robert (CGC) 1624 Oakmont Cir, Niceville, FL 32578

HUTSON, Linda Darlene (Az) 12111 N La Cholla Blvd, Oro Valley, AZ 85755

HUTTAR BAILEY, Julia Ruth (Mich)

HUTTO, Kelsey (Ind) 422 N 13th Ave, Beech Grove, IN 46107

HUTTON, Linda Vaught (Va)

HUTTON III, Skip (SVa) 3429 Boyce Court, Norfolk, VA 23509

HUXLEY, Dave (NwT) Saint Luke's Church, 146 S Church St, Whitewater, WI 53190

HUYCK, Jonathan Taylor (RI) 175 Mathewson St, Providence, RI 02903

HUYNH, Tinh Trang (Va) 64 Horseshoe Ln N, Columbus, NJ 08022

HYATT, David (Pa) 404 Donna Ln, Phoenixville, PA 19460

HYCHE, Jerald (Tex) 1803 Highland Hollow Dr, Conroe, TX 77304

HYDE, Ian Geoffrey (Dal) 205 W Brin St, Terrell, TX 75160

HYDE, John Ernest Authur (SwFla) 4650 Cove Cir Apt 407, Madeira Beach, FL 33708

HYDE, Lillian (Tex) Po Box 580117, Houston, TX 77258

HYDE, Pamela Willson (Az) 4290 N Fanning Dr, Flagstaff, AZ 86004

HYDE III, Robert Willis (Tex) 208 Seawall Blvd, Galveston, TX 77550

HYLDEN, Emily R (Dal) 1302 W Kiest Blvd, Dallas, TX 75224

HYLDEN, Jordan (Dal) 6345 Wydown Blvd, Saint Louis, MO 63105

HYLTON, George Hartwell (RI)

HYMES, Adrienne Renita (SwFla) 8005 25th St E, Parrish, FL 34219

HYNDMAN, David Lee (NI) 8981 E 5th Ave Apt 101, Gary, IN 46403

I

IALONGO, Donna Marie (Chi) 2s697 Parkview Dr, Glen Ellyn, IL 60137

IBE, Morgan Kelechi (Okla) 1843 Chelsea Dr, Edmond, OK 73013

IDEMA III, Henry (WMich) 13562 Redbird Ln, Grand Haven, MI 49417

IDICULA, Mathew (Chi) St Columba Of Iona, 1800 Irving Park Rd, Hanover Park, IL 60133

IFILL, Angela Sylvia S (O) 64 Bayley Ave, Yonkers, NY 10705

IGO, Nancy Elle (RG) PO Box 1414, Cloudcroft, NM 88317

IHIASOTA, Isaac (WNY) 8283 Effie Drive, Niagara Falls, NY 14304

✠ **IHLOFF**, Robert Wilkes (Md) 1200 Steuart St Unit 1020, Baltimore, MD 21230

IKENYE, Ndungu John Brown (Chi) 1930 Darrow Ave, Evanston, IL 60201

ILLINGWORTH, David Paul (Me) 28 Wayne St, Portland, ME 04102

ILLUECA, Marta Del Carmen (Del)

IMBODEN, Stanley Franklin (CPa) 315 Dead End Rd, Lititz, PA 17543

IMMEL, Otto Wigaart (NJ) Po Box 2379, Tybee Island, GA 31328

IMPEY, Paul (Az)

IMPICCICHE, Frank S (Ind) 522 3rd Ave NE, Carmel, IN 46032

INAPANTA, Martha E (EcuC)

INAPANTA PAEZ, Lourdes Esther (EcuC)

INCORVATI, Rick (SO)

INESON JR, John Henry (Me) 53 High St, Damariscotta, ME 04543

INFANTE PINZON, John Edwin (WMich) 524 Washington Ave, Grand Haven, MI 49417

INGALLS JR, Brad (Md) PO Box 25, Churchville, MD 21028

INGALLS, Clayton Dean (Tenn) 5501 Franklin Pike, Nashville, TN 37220

INGALLS, Jason T (Tex) 1100 N. 15th St., Waco, TX 76707

INGALLS, Meg (WA) 2046 Cullum Park, San Antonio, TX 78253

INGEMAN, Peter Lyle (Ga) 3128 Huntington Ridge Circle, Valdosta, GA 31602

INGERSOLL, Russ (WNC) 52 Sturbridge Lane, Greensboro, NC 27408

INGRAHAM, Doris Williams (SeFla) 15955 Nw 27th Ave, Opa Locka, FL 33054

INIESTA-AVILA, Bernardo (Nev) 4201 W Washington Ave, Las Vegas, NV 89107

INMAN, John Wesley (WMich) 135 Old York Rd, New Hope, PA 18938

INMAN, Virginia Bain (NC) 607 N Greene St, Greensboro, NC 27401

INSCOE, Laura D (Va) 2319 E Broad St, Richmond, VA 23223

INSERRA, John Michael (WTex) 1417 E Austin Ave, Harlingen, TX 78550

IRELAND, Joel T (LI) 532 E 1st St, Tucson, AZ 85705

IRIZARRY, Gladys Esther (PR)

IRIZARRY, J E (PR)

IRONSIDE, Susan R (Nwk) 6 Delbarton Dr, Madison, NJ 07940

IRSCH, Leona M (WNY) 108 S Thomas Ave, Kingston, PA 18704

IRVIN, Cynthia Diane (Colo) 546 N Elm St # 1496, Cortez, CO 81321

IRVINE, Peter Bennington (Mil) 1140 Blaine Ave, Janesville, WI 53545

IRVING, Anthony Tuttle (Oly) 5445 Donnelly Dr Se, Olympia, WA 98501

IRVING, Jocelyn (WA) 9713 Summit Cir Apt 1b, Upper Marlboro, MD 20774

IRWIN, Margaret Bertha (Mil) 6205 Mineral Point Rd Apt 722, Apt 722, Madison, WI 53705

IRWIN, Sara (Pgh)

IRWIN, Zachary Tracy (NwPa) 4216 E South Shore Dr, Erie, PA 16511

ISAAC III, Frank Reid (O) 2181 Ambleside Dr Apt 412, Cleveland, OH 44106

✠ **ISAAC**, Telesforo A (SwFla) JP 8600, PO Box 025284, Miami, FL 33102

ISAACS, James (WA) St James Church, 11815 Seven Locks Rd, Potomac, MD 20854

ISADORE, Daniel Joseph (Pgh) 5801 Hampton St, Pittsburgh, PA 15206

ISHLER, Dina Carter (CPa)

ISHMAN, Martha S (NwPa) 245 Valley Trails Ln, Franklin, PA 16323

ISLEY, Carolyn W (ETenn) 118 Oak Grove Rd, Greeneville, TN 37745

ISRAEL, Carver (LI) 322 Clearbrook Ave, Lansdowne, PA 19050

ISRAEL JR, Fielder (Md) 4720 Winterberry Ct, Williamsburg, VA 23188

ISWARIAH, James Chandran (Va) 465 Walnut Ln, King William, VA 23086

✠ **ITTY**, Johncy (Ore) 10 Avalon Rd, Garden City, NY 11530

IVATTS, Justin Anthony (Va)

IVELL, Elizabeth (Nwk) 80 Maple Ave Apt B, Morristown, NJ 07960

IVERSEN, Rachel Shannon (CGC)

IVES, Joel (Mass) 23 Monmouth St., Brookline, MA 02446

IVES, Nathan Warren (Mass) 19R Norwood Avenue, Rockport, MA 01966

IVEY, Betsy (Pa) 1401 S 22nd St, Philadelphia, PA 19146

IVEY, Valerie Ann (Ore) 15240 Nw Courting Hill Dr, Banks, OR 97106

IWICK, Richard Edward (Mich) 25755 Kilreigh Ct, Farmington Hills, MI 48336

IX, Victoria Shippee (WMass) 37 Chestnut St, Springfield, MA 01103

IZQUIERDO-VELAZQUEZ, Jesus B (EcuC)

IZUTSU, Margaret W (Mich) 18 Fairview Ave, Arlington, MA 02474

IZZI SR, Robert Peter (RI)

IZZO, Joanne (NJ) 8411 13th Ave # 2nd Floor, Brooklyn, NY 11228

J

JABLONSKI, Carol (WA) 64 Pinnacle Pt, Asheville, NC 28805

JACKSON, Andy (Ark) PO Box 36, Roland, AR 72135

JACKSON, Brad (Va) PO Box 305, Madison, VA 22727

JACKSON, Bruce A (Az) 7719 W Bluefield Ave, Glendale, AZ 85308

JACKSON, Carl Thomas (Va) 2940 Corries Way, Conneaut, OH 44030

JACKSON III, Chandler Cheshire (WMo) PO Box 704, 1932 E Highway 14, Ozark, MO 65721

JACKSON, Darlene A (SVa)

JACKSON, David (SwFla) All Souls Episcopal Church, 14640 N Cleveland Ave, North Fort Myers, FL 33903

JACKSON, David G (Chi) 203 S Kensington Ave, La Grange, IL 60525

JACKSON, David Hilton (The Episcopal Church in Haw) 245 Cavalier Dr, Greenville, SC 29607

JACKSON, Deborah Mitchell (Fla) 4849 Hampshire Pl, Hixson, TN 37343

JACKSON JR, Gary (CFla) 7 Whispering Pines Trl, Ormond Beach, FL 32174

JACKSON, Gary Jon (Ga) St Mark's Episcopal Church, 900 Gloucester St, Brunswick, GA 31520

JACKSON, Hugo T (At) 4246 Glenforest Way NE, Roswell, GA 30075

C88

Clergy List

JACKSON, Ira Leverne (Ga) Grace Episcopal Church, PO Box 617, Sandersville, GA 31082

JACKSON, Jeffery R (At) 69 Mobley Rd, PO Box 752, Hamilton, GA 31811

JACKSON, Jimmy (Kan) St Matts Tec Ch, 2001 Windsor Dr, Newton, KS 67114

JACKSON, Judy Ann (Chi)

JACKSON, Kimberly (At) 3737 Seminary Rd, Alexandria, VA 22304

JACKSON, Margaret Ruth Brosz (Ia)

JACKSON, Micah (Chi) 1407 E 60th St, Chicago, IL 60637

JACKSON, Patricia Gladys (Ct) 120 Sigourney St, Hartford, CT 06105

JACKSON, Paula Marie (SO) 1009 Egan Hills Dr, Cincinnati, OH 45229

JACKSON, Peter (Nwk) 130 Bessida St, Bloomfield, NJ 07003

JACKSON, Peter Jonathan Edward (WA) 1 The Green, London, N14 7EG, Great Britain (UK)

JACKSON, Phillip A (NY) 50 Pine St, New York, NY 10005

JACKSON, Reginald Fitzroy (LI) 1695 E 55th St, Brooklyn, NY 11234

JACKSON, Rosemary H (WNC) 145 Old Mt Olivet Rd, Zirconia, NC 28790

JACKSON, Terry Allan (NY) 600 W 246th St Apt 1515, Bronx, NY 10471

JACKSON, Thomas C (Cal) 111 Whalley Avenue, 111 Whalley Ave, New Haven, CT 06511

JACKSON-ESSIEM, Erika (Mo) 801 Figueroa St, Folsom, CA 95630

JACKSON-MCKINNEY, Statha Frances (SwFla) 484 E Shade Dr, Venice, FL 34293

JACOB, James Neithelloor (RI)

JACOB, Jerry Elias (Ala) 305 Arnold St NE, Cullman, AL 35055

JACOB, Michelet (Hai)

JACOB, Renard (Hai)

JACOBS, Allston Alexander (Md) 2019 Division St, Baltimore, MD 21217

JACOBS, Connie Hartquist (Episcopal SJ) 2635 2nd Ave Apt 730, San Diego, CA 92103

JACOBS, Gregory Alexander (NC) 420 Jerome Rd, Durham, NC 27713

JACOBS, John (NC) 21 Riviera Dr, Pinehurst, NC 28374

JACOBS, Marlene (Oly) 1917 Logan Ave S, Minneapolis, MN 55403

JACOBS III, Philip Chauncey (Mass) 12 Antassawamock Rd, Mattapoisett, MA 02739

JACOBS, Robert Alexander (NY) 20 Trestle Way, Dayton, NJ 08810

JACOBSEN, Hailey Robison (Mass)

JACOBSON, Harold Knute (Mo) 123 S Ninth Street, Columbia, MO 65201

JACOBSON, Jeanne (CPa) 616 Spruce St, Hollidaysburg, PA 16648

JACOBSON, Marc R (Pgh) Quezon City, 4604 Crewe Hall Ln, Waxhaw, NC 28173

JACOBSON, Matthew Daniel (NY) 145 W 46th St, New York, NY 10036

JACOBSON, Mr Jacobson (Pa) 9 Esty Way, Groveland, MA 01834

JACOBSON, Paul Alan (Ind) 859 E Broadway, Stratford, CT 06615

JACOBSON, Stephen K (Pa) 155 Bayside Dr, Eastham, MA 02642

✠ **JACOBUS**, Russell Edward (FdL) 17786 Valley View Rd, Townsend, WI 54175

JACOBY, Lisa Anne (Episcopal SJ) St George Episcopal Church, 23802 Avenida De La Carlota, Laguna Hills, CA 92653

JAEGER, Nick (Ky) 2502 Jefferson St., Paducah, KY 42001

JAENKE, Karen Ann (NJ) 24 Woodland Rd, Fairfax, CA 94930

JAKOBSEN, Wilma (ECR) St Jude the Apostle Church, 20920 McClellan Rd, Cupertino, CA 95014

JALLOUF, Georges (Chi) 218 Somonauk St, Sycamore, IL 60178

JAMBOR, Christopher Noel (Tex) 1805 Malibar Rd, Fort Worth, TX 76116

JAMES, Adam Anthony (WMo)

JAMES, Alan (Chi) 165 N Canal St Apt 1313, Chicago, IL 60606

JAMES, Charles (CGC) Po Box 29, Bon Secour, AL 36511

JAMES, Darryl Farrar (LI) 3312 S Indiana Ave, Chicago, IL 60616

JAMES, Edmund Ludwig (Okla) 104 W Hanover St, Hoyt, OK 74472

JAMES, Jan (Az) 423 N. Beaver St., Flagstaff, AZ 86001

JAMES, Jay Carleton (NC) 950 E Broadway Apt 2, APT 2, South Boston, MA 02127

JAMES, John Hugh Alexander (Ct) South Cottage, Llanerchydol, Welshpool Powys, SA21 9PG, Great Britain (UK)

JAMES, Marcus Gilbert (Roch)

JAMES, Molly F (Ct) 779 Prospect Ave Apt B4, West Hartford, CT 06105

JAMES, Nancy (Ak) 713 E St Ne, Washington, DC 20002

JAMES JR, Ralph Matthew (WVa) PO Box 145, Union, WV 24983

JAMES, Reynelda Cordelia (Nev)

JAMES, Robin L (WMo) 12212 Wyandotte Ct., Kansas City, MO 64145

JAMES, Sally Patricia (NMich) 402 W Fleshiem St, Iron Mountain, MI 49801

JAMESON, Elizabeth Butler (Chi) 654 Little Prospect Rd, Estes Park, CO 80517

JAMESON, Jonathan Isaac (CFla)

JAMESON, Parker (Tex) 7909 Lynchburg Dr, Austin, TX 78738

JAMIESON, Sandra Swift Cornett (SwFla) 301 Jasmine Way, Clearwater, FL 33756

JAMIESON JR, William Stukey (WNC) 15 Macon Ave, Asheville, NC 28801

JAMIESON-DRAKE, Victoria (NC)

JAMISON, Dale Martin (NMich) 901 Dakota Ave, Gladstone, MI 49837

JAMISON, Dorothy Lockwood (Cal) 501 Portola Rd Apt 12J, Portola Valley, CA 94028

JAMISON, Walter Kay (Fla)

JANDA, Mary Sheridan (U)

JANELLE, Nicole Simonne (Los) St Stephens Anglican Church, 1121 14th Ave SW, Calgary, AB T2R 0P3, Canada

JANE REDDICK, Mary (Tex) 2525 Seagler Rd, Houston, TX 77042

JANESS, Nancy Kingswood (Nev)

JANG, Teduan Vincent (Cal) 5072 Diamond Heights Blvd, San Francisco, CA 94131

JARA, Francisco Gonzalo (EcuC)

JARRELL, Robin Campbell (Pgh) 229 Alana Ln, Lewisburg, PA 17837

JARRETT III, John J (SeFla) 1052 Nw 65th St, Miami, FL 33150

JARRETT, Shancia Ralna (Ct)

JARRETT-SCHELL, Peter (WA) 1700 Powder Mill Rd, Silver Spring, MD 20903

JARRETT-SCHELL, Rondesia (WA) 9815 Berrywood Ct, Springdale, MD 20774

JARVIS, Victoria McGaughey (At)

JASMER, Gerald Bruce (Mont) 36 30th St W, Billings, MT 59102

JAVIER, Nazareno C (Pa)

JAWORSKI, Karen Loomis (Tex)

JAY, Lynn (Los) 26084 Viento Ct, Valencia, CA 91355

JAYAWARDENE, Thomas Devashri (Los) 1141 Westmont Rd, Santa Barbara, CA 93108

JAYNES, Ronald Paul (Pa) 210 N President Ave Apt B3, B3, Lancaster, PA 17603

JAYNES, Ruth (Neb) 1322 S 52nd St, Omaha, NE 68106

JEAN, Jean Junior (Hai)

JEAN, MacDonald (Hai) Box 1309, Port-Au-Prince, Haiti

JEAN, Markendy (Hai)

JEANES III, Paul (NJ) 33 Mercer St, Princeton, NJ 08540

JEAN GILLES, Belange (Hai)

JEAN-JACQUES, Harry (Hai) Boite Postale 1309, Port-Au-Prince, Haiti

JEAN-PHILIPPE, Jean-Alphonse (Hai) PO Box 407139, C/O Lynx Air, Fort Lauderdale, FL 33340

JEFFERS, Mary Elisabeth (USC) 711 S McDuffie St, Anderson, SC 29624

JEFFERSON, Alyce Lee (La) 1329 Jackson Ave, New Orleans, LA 70130

JEFFERSON, Paula Kaye (Tex)

JEFFERSON, Rita (WLa)

✠ **JEFFERTS SCHORI**, Katharine Jefferts (Nev) 8631 Eagle Chase Trl, Reno, NV 89523

JEFFERY, Anne-Marie (WA) St Peters Episcopal Church, 183 Rector St, Perth Amboy, NJ 08861

JEFFERY, Vincent James (Nev) 1500 Mount Rose St, Reno, NV 89509

JEFFREY, Kathryn G (CFla) 29 Nord Circle Rd, North Oaks, MN 55127

JEFFREY, Peter Leigh (Mass) 8 Kirk St, Lowell, MA 01852

JEKABSONS, Wendie Susan Scudds (ETenn) 334 Sourwood Hills Rd, Bristol, TN 37620

✠ **JELINEK**, James Louis (Minn) 957 25th St NW, Washington, DC 20037

JELLICO, Jerry J (SC)

JELLISON, Mary (Wyo) 3129 Pinewood Ave, Bellingham, WA 98225

JEMMOTT, Brian Anthony Lester (NJ) 2005 S Columbia Pl, Decatur, GA 30032

JENCKS, Jeff (CGC) 7979 N 9th Ave, Pensacola, FL 32514

JENKINS, Al W (CFla) 103 W Christina Blvd, Lakeland, FL 33813

JENKINS JR, Harry Oliver (La) 1534 7th St, Slidell, LA 70458

JENKINS, James Morgan (CPa) St. Paul's Episcopal Church, 101 E Main St, Bloomsburg, PA 17815

JENKINS, John Stone (La) 708 Forest Point Dr, Brandon, MS 39047

JENKINS, John William Andrew (Va)

JENKINS, Judith Ann (RG) 601 Montano Rd Nw, Albuquerque, NM 87107

JENKINS, Kathryn E (Va) 3507 Pond Chase Dr, Midlothian, VA 23113

JENKINS, Marilyn Hamilton (WA)

JENKINS, Mark A (NH) 20260 Williamsville Rd, Gregory, MI 48137

JENKINS, Martha L (SVa) 120 Reykin Dr, Richmond, VA 23236

JENKINS, Michael Lemon (WNC) 5165 Hayes Waters Rd, Morganton, NC 28655

JENKINS, Stephanie (Okla) 835 SW Polk St, Topeka, KS 66612

JENKINS, William David (Kan) 314 N Adams St, Junction City, KS 66441

JENKS, Peter Q (Me) 200 Main St, Thomaston, ME 04861

JENNEKER, Bruce (WA) 75 Peterborough St. Apt. 617, Boston, MA 02215

JENNER, Helen McLeroy (NC) 1079 Ridge Dr, Clayton, NC 27520

JENNEY, Joe Allen (EMich)

JENNINGS, Albert (O) 8667 Shepard Rd # 204, Macedonia, OH 44056

JENNINGS, Gay Clark (O) 168 Hiram College Dr, Sagamore Hills, OH 44067

JENNINGS, James Courtney (HB) 5701 Snead Rd, Richmond, VA 23224

JENNINGS, Kelly Kathleen (Tex)

JENNINGS, Margaret Herring (USC) 301 W Liberty St, Winnsboro, SC 29180

JENNINGS, Mary Kay (RG) Yankton Mission Cluster, 126 N Park NE, Wagner, SD 57380

JENNINGS, Nathan Grady (Tex) PO Box 2247, Austin, TX 78768

JENNINGS, Robert Tallmadge (Ky) 2002 High Ridge Rd, Louisville, KY 40207

JENNINGS III, William Worth (NC) 702 Hillandale Ln, Garner, NC 27529

JENSEN, Anne (Cal) 865 Walavista Ave., Oakland, CA 94610

JENSEN, Barbara Ann (NJ) 238 Main St, South River, NJ 08882

JENSEN, Jan D (Tex) 11 Sherwood St, Dayton, TX 77535

JENSEN, Jonathon W (Pgh) 315 Shady Ave, Pittsburgh, PA 15206

JENSEN, Julia Kooser (Ore) 2020 SW Knollcrest Dr., Portland, OR 97225

JENSEN, Patricia Ann (CFla) 9301 Hunters Park Way, Tampa, FL 33647

JENSON, Constance (WA) 17413 Audrey Road, Cobb Island, MD 20625

JERGENS, Andrew MacAoidh (SO) 3030 Erie Ave, Apt 512, Cincinnati, OH 45208

JERGER, Robert C (Tex)

JERNAGAN III, Luke (Mo) 22 Dromara Rd, Saint Louis, MO 63124

JEROME, Joseph (LI) 3956 44th St, Sunnyside, NY 11104

JERSEY, Jean Staffeld (Vt) 32 Liberty St, Montpelier, VT 05602

JESION, Lawrence Michael (Ga) Christ Episcopal Church, 1904 Greene St, Augusta, GA 30904

JESKE, Mark William (WMo) 4401 Wornall Rd, Kansas City, MO 64111

JESSETT, Frederick Edwin (Oly) 5309 S Myrtle Ln, Spokane, WA 99223

JESSUP, Dorothy Margaret Paul (Pa) 278 Friendship Dr, Paoli, PA 19301

JESSUP, Elaine Anderson (SeFla) 464 NE 16th St, Miami, FL 33132

JESTER, Pamela Jean (Cal) 911 Dowling Blvd, San Leandro, CA 94577

JETT, Charles D (SC) 3501 Merrill Pl Apt 234, Mt Pleasant, SC 29466

JETT, Mary J (NY) Church of St Mary the Virgin, 145 W 46th St, New York, NY 10036

JEULAND, Eric Vincent (Ct) 25 Church St, Shelton, CT 06484

JEULAND, Jane Catherine Eppley (Ct) 300 Main St, Wethersfield, CT 06109

JEVNE, Lucretia (The Episcopal NCal) 120 Loraine Ct, Vacaville, CA 95688

JEW, Cynthia Lynne (Los) Trinity Episcopal Church, 600 Saratoga, Fillmore, CA 93016

JEWELL, Kenneth Arthur (Nev) 732 Aesop Dr, Spring Creek, NV 89815

JEWETT, Ethan A (Pa) 2013 Appletree St, Philadelphia, PA 19103

JEWISS, Tony (Los) 1290 Kent Street, Brooklyn, NY 11222

JEWSON, Dayna (Mo) 7511 Rannells Ave, Saint Louis, MO 63143

JILLARD, Christina Liggitt (Oly) 647 Polo Rd Apt 613, Columbia, SC 29223

JIM, Rosella A (NAM) Po Box 5854, Farmington, NM 87499

JIMENEZ, Darla Sue (NwT)

JIMENEZ, Juan (Los) 311 W South St, Anaheim, CA 92805

JIMENEZ, Maria Jesus (Oly) 2020 E. Terrace St., Seattle, WA 98122

JIMENEZ-IRIZARRY, Edwin (Ct) Urb El Vedado, Calle 12 de Octubre 428-A, San Juan, PR 00918

JINETE, Alvaro E (Chi) 3241 Calwagner St, Franklin Park, IL 60131

JIZMAGIAN, Mary Gibson (Cal) 2570 Chestnut St, San Francisco, CA 94123

JODKO, Juliusz Siegmond (Ct) St Michaels Parish, 210 Church St, Naugatuck, CT 06770

JOE-KINALE, Rose Mary (Nev)

JOFFRION JR, Felix Hughes (Ala) 1180 11th Ave S, Birmingham, AL 35205

JOHANNSEN, Carole (NY) 8 Pine Rd, Bedford Hills, NY 10507

JOHANNSON, Johanna-Karen (NY) PO Box 1412, Bucksport, ME 04416

JOHANSON, Norman Lee (Neb) 116 S Sunset Pl, Monrovia, CA 91016

JOHANSSEN, John (SO) 9429 Lighthouse Cut, Thornville, OH 43076

JOHN, Abidhananthar (Roch) PO Box 466, Savona, NY 14879

JOHN, James Howard (Kan) 7603 E Morris St, Wichita, KS 67207

JOHN, Rene (NJ) 1525 Betty Ln, Ewing, NJ 08628

JOHNS, Martha (Los) 30382 Via Con Dios, Rancho Santa Margarita, CA 92688

JOHNS, Michael Richard (WMo)

JOHNS III, Norm (Oly) 5787 Lenea Dr Nw, Bremerton, WA 98312

JOHNSON JR, Al (Chi) 212 Biltmore Dr, N Barrington, IL 60010

JOHNSON, Alston Boyd (WLa) 550 Dunmoreland Dr, Shreveport, LA 71106

JOHNSON, Andrew (Roch) 1957 Five Mile Line Rd., Penfield, NY 14526

JOHNSON, Andy (Okla) 2408 NW 55th St, Oklahoma City, OK 73112

JOHNSON, Ann L (Ct) 1105 Quarrier St, Charleston, WV 25301

JOHNSON, Ann Ruth (Az) 701 N Apollo Way, Flagstaff, AZ 86001

JOHNSON, Anthony Troy (NY)

JOHNSON, Anthony (Miss) 1052 Deer Dr, Bay Saint Louis, MS 39520

✠ **JOHNSON**, Bob (WNC) 21 Lincolnshire Loop, Asheville, NC 28803

JOHNSON, Brett Randall (Mass) 66 Lowell Rd, North Reading, MA 01864

JOHNSON, Brian David (SanD) 1836 N Mira Loma Way, Palm Springs, CA 92262

JOHNSON, Candine E (Va)

JOHNSON, Carolynn Elayne (Mich)

JOHNSON, Charlotte Marie (Chi)

JOHNSON, Christopher Allen (Mich) 45 Woodland Ave, Glen Ridge, NJ 07028

JOHNSON, Daniel Edward (Va)

JOHNSON, Darrell Joseph (Pgh)

JOHNSON, David (Miss) 116 Cedar Pointe, Fairhope, AL 36532

JOHNSON, David A (CFla) 1700 Ashwood Blvd, Charlottesville, VA 22911

JOHNSON, David George (NMich) 1021 E E St, Iron Mountain, MI 49801

JOHNSON, Dennis Lee (Wyo) Po Box 3485, Jackson, WY 83001

✠ **JOHNSON**, Deon K (Mo) 200 W Saint Paul St, Brighton, MI 48116

JOHNSON, Diana (U) 1854 E Kensington Ave, Salt Lake City, UT 84108

✠ **JOHNSON**, Don (WTenn) 692 Poplar Ave, Memphis, TN 38105

JOHNSON, Donald Keith (Dal) 2026 Cherrywood Ln, Denton, TX 76209

JOHNSON, Doris (Ga) 3 Westridge Rd, Savannah, GA 31411

JOHNSON, Douglas Peter (WMo) 9905 N Hawthorne Ave, Kansas City, MO 64157

JOHNSON, Edwin (Mass) 14 Cushing Ave, Dorchester, MA 02125

JOHNSON, Eric N (Oly) Christ Episcopal Anacortes, 1216 7th St, Anacortes, WA 98221

JOHNSON, Erin Minta (WNC) PO Box 32, Cashiers, NC 28717

JOHNSON, Frank T (SanD) 651 Eucalyptus Ave, Vista, CA 92084

JOHNSON JR, Fred Hoyer (NY) 118 Lake Emerald Drive - #409, Oakland Park, FL 33309

JOHNSON, GREGORY (The Episcopal Church in Haw) PO Box 893788, Mililani, HI 96789

JOHNSON JR, Harold Vance (WA) 12194 Cathedral Dr, Lake Ridge, VA 22192

JOHNSON, Herbert Alan (WNC) 245 Laurel Falls Rd, Franklin, NC 28734

JOHNSON, Horace S (Ct) 3404 Castlebar Cir, Ormond Beach, FL 32174

JOHNSON, Ida (Cal) 535 Joaquin Ave #D, San Leandro, CA 94577

JOHNSON, James Baxter (Colo) 1715 Holly Way, Fort Collins, CO 80526

JOHNSON, Jane Margaret (FdL) 1316 Ellis St, Stevens Point, WI 54481

JOHNSON, Jay Brooks (NC) 2690 Fairlawn Dr, Winston Salem, NC 27106

JOHNSON, Jay Emerson (WMich) 212 Grand St, Saugatuck, MI 49453

JOHNSON, Joan Cottrell (Mass) 4833 Europa Dr, Naples, FL 34105

JOHNSON, Johan (NY) 521 W 126th St, New York, NY 10027

JOHNSON, John Brent (Tex) St Johns Episcopal Church, 1305 Roosevelt Dr, Silsbee, TX 77656

JOHNSON, Juanita Hanger (Neb) 10761 Izard St, Omaha, NE 68114

JOHNSON, Julie Anna (Tenn) St Mary Magdalene Church, PO Box 150, Fayetteville, TN 37334

JOHNSON, June (Ga) 519 Parker Ave, Decatur, GA 30032

JOHNSON, June B (Oly) 114 20th Ave SE, Olympia, WA 98501

JOHNSON, Karen Brown (WA) 18404 Tea Rose Pl, Gaithersburg, MD 20879

JOHNSON, Katherine Bradley (NC) 2504 Englewood Ave, Durham, NC 27705

JOHNSON, Kellaura Beth Jones (Tex) 4629 Creekbend Dr, Houston, TX 77035

JOHNSON, Kenneth William (Mass) 11699 Bennington Woods Rd, Reston, VA 20194

JOHNSON, Kent William (LI) 6626 52nd Rd, #1, Maspeth, NY 11378

JOHNSON, Kevin Allen (Tex) St Albans Episcopal Church, 316 W Main St, Arlington, TX 76010

JOHNSON, Kristine (ECR) 146 Twelfth Street, Pacific Grove, CA 93950

JOHNSON, Lee (Episcopal SJ) 310 Audubon Dr, Lodi, CA 95240

JOHNSON, Linda Catherine (Ind) Iu Episcopal Campus Ministry, PO Box 127, Bloomington, IN 47402

JOHNSON, Linda Marie (Oly) Po Box 354, Westport, WA 98595

JOHNSON, Lori Elaine (EMich) 315 1/2 N Maple St, Flushing, MI 48433

JOHNSON, Lydia Knizley (CGC)

JOHNSON, Lynn H (NJ) 3 Azalea Dr, Lumberton, NJ 08048

JOHNSON, Maeve Maud Vincent (Az) 114 W Roosevelt St., Phoenix, AZ 85003

JOHNSON, Malinda Margaret Eichner (Ct) 9 Arrow Head Rd, Westport, CT 06880

JOHNSON, Marcus Peter (CFla) 320 Franklin St, Geneva, IL 60134

JOHNSON, Marietta (Mont) Po Box 78, Red Lodge, MT 59068

JOHNSON, Marta D V (Md) PO Box 103, 4603 Rocks Rd, Street, MD 21154

JOHNSON, Mary Peterson (ND) 356 20th Ave NW, Turtle Lake, ND 58575

JOHNSON, Mary Richardson (NMich) 1021 E E St, Iron Mountain, MI 49801

JOHNSON, Matthew (NC) Am Roethenfeld 8, Ingolstadt, 85051, Germany

JOHNSON, Michael R (SD) PO Box 434, Deadwood, SD 57732

JOHNSON, Michaela (Kay) (RI) 1214 Noyes Dr, Silver Spring, MD 20910

JOHNSON, Natalie S (Oly)

JOHNSON, Neil Edward (WNY) 18 Harrogate Square, Williamsville, NY 14221

JOHNSON, Nora (Pa)

JOHNSON, Patricia A (Ia) 2222 McDonald St, Sioux City, IA 51104

JOHNSON, Paul (Tex) 17706 Linkview Dr, Dripping Springs, TX 78620

JOHNSON, Qiana (Chi)

JOHNSON, Randy Wayne (Minn) 2175 1st St, White Bear Lake, MN 55110

JOHNSON, Richard E (Mont) 902 Logan St, Helena, MT 59601

JOHNSON, Robert Gaines (SVa) 1411 25th St, Galveston, TX 77550

JOHNSON, Robert Wallace (CFla)

JOHNSON, Ronald A (O) 7514 Peachmont Ave NW, North Canton, OH 44720

JOHNSON, Ronald Norman (SeFla) 320 Dudley Creek Rd, Hardy, VA 24101

JOHNSON, Ronda (Mich)

JOHNSON, Russell L (SwFla) 13555 Heron Cir, Clearwater, FL 33762

JOHNSON, Russell Michael (The Episcopal Church in Haw) 296 Nikolau Pl, Hilo, HI 96720

JOHNSON JR, Russell Woodrow (WMo) 5220 Eden Ave Apt 532, Edina, MN 55436

JOHNSON, Sandra Parnell (SwFla) 14640 N Cleveland Ave, N Ft Myers, FL 33903

JOHNSON, Sanford Ralph (WMass) 50 Shaker Farm Rd N, Marlborough, NH 03455

JOHNSON, Simeon O (NY) 165 Saint Marks Pl Apt 10H, Staten Island, NY 10301

JOHNSON, Stephanie Mcdyre (Ct) 51 Summit Rd, Riverside, CT 06878

JOHNSON, Susan (At) 571 Holt Rd NE, Marietta, GA 30068

JOHNSON, Susan Elaine (Eur) Schiesstaettberg 44, Eichstatt, AL 498421-4125, Germany

JOHNSON, Sydney (Wyo)

JOHNSON, Thalia Felice (Mich) 8261 Cypress Way, Dexter, MI 48130

JOHNSON, Theodore William (WA) PO Box 386, Basye, VA 22810

JOHNSON, Tim (Pa) 201 Crestline Dr, Kennett Square, PA 19348

JOHNSON, Vicki Lynn (Spok) 1322 Kimball Ave, Richland, WA 99354

JOHNSON, Walter S (Los) 1264 N Kings Rd Apt 17, West Hollywood, CA 90069

JOHNSON, Ward Kendall (ND) 1003 Crescent Ln, Bismarck, ND 58501

JOHNSON, William Alexander (NY) 27 Fox Meadow Rd, Scarsdale, NY 10583

JOHNSON, william g (Az) PO Box 30742, Tucson, AZ 85751

JOHNSON RUSSELL, Tracy Johnson (Ct) 89 Lenox St Unit N, New Haven, CT 06513

JOHNSON-SMITH, Janis Lynn (Oly) 7002 Southwick Ct SW, Tumwater, WA 98512

JOHNSON-TAYLOR, Allan (WA) 4211 Enterprise Rd, Bowie, MD 20720

JOHNSON-TOTH, Louise M (Roch) 243 Genesee Park Blvd, Rochester, NY 14619

JOHNSTON, Cathy Lynn (ETenn) 2152 Hawthorne St, Kingsport, TN 37664

JOHNSTON, Clifford A (CPa) 3147 Grahamton Rd, Morrisdale, PA 16858

JOHNSTON, Copeland David (EC)

JOHNSTON, David Knight (Mass) 78 Bishop Dr, Framingham, MA 01702

JOHNSTON, David L (WVa)

JOHNSTON, Duncan (Ala) 414 E Broad St, Westfield, NJ 07090

JOHNSTON, Edward (NY) 1215 5th Ave Apt 12d, New York, NY 10029

JOHNSTON, Gregory B (Mass) 147 Concord Rd, Lincoln, MA 01773

JOHNSTON, Hewitt (NJ) 41087 Calla Lily St, Indian Land, SC 29707

JOHNSTON, Laurel (ECR) 2767 Delpha Court, Thousand Oaks, CA 91362

JOHNSTON, Madelynn (RG) PO Box 8716, Santa Fe, NM 87504

JOHNSTON, Mark Wylie (Ala) 105 Delong Rd, Nauvoo, AL 35578

JOHNSTON, Martha Suzanne (Tenn) 1216 Sneed Rd W, Franklin, TN 37069

JOHNSTON, Nature (Colo)

JOHNSTON, Philip Gilchrist (Va) 4773 Thornbury Dr, Fairfax, VA 22030

JOHNSTON III, Robert Hugh (Dal) 5311 Ridgedale Dr, Dallas, TX 75206

JOHNSTON JR, Robert Hugh (WTex) 102 E. Live Oak St., Cuero, TX 77954

JOHNSTON, Robert Owen (SVa) 207 Marshall St, Petersburg, VA 23803

JOHNSTON, Sally (USC) 392 Stonemarker Rd, Mooresville, NC 28117

✠ **JOHNSTON**, Shannon Sherwood (Va) 110 W Franklin St, Richmond, VA 23220

JOHNSTON, Suzanne Elaine (Roch) 1245 Culver Rd., Rochester, NY 14609

JOHNSTON, William Merrill (FdL) 1010 Congress St, Neenah, WI 54956

JOHNSTON, Zula J (Oly) 8527 46th Ct Ne, Olympia, WA 98516

JOHNSTONE, Elise (Oly)

JOHNSTONE, Mary (RI) 39 Washington St, Newport, RI 02840

JOINER, James (Ore) St David Of Wales Epis Ch, 2800 SE Harrison St, Portland, OR 97214

JOLLY, Anne B (Chi) 3201 Windsor Rd, Austin, TX 78703

JOLLY, Marshall A (WNC) Grace Episcopal Church, 303 S King St, Morganton, NC 28655

JONES, Abram Paschal (Miss) 3921 Oakridge Dr, Jackson, MS 39216

JONES, Alan (Cal) 1100 California St, San Francisco, CA 94108

JONES, Andrew Lovell (Ct) 13 Locust St, Norwalk, CT 06855

JONES, Andy (Mil) 2920 Pelham Rd, Madison, WI 53713

JONES, Angela Louise (Neb) 1555 14Th St, Mitchell, NE 69357

JONES, Anthony Edward (LI) St Augustines Episcopal Church, 4301 Avenue D, Brooklyn, NY 11203

JONES III, Arthur (Be)

JONES II, Ben (WMass) 569 Main St, Fitchburg, MA 01420

JONES, Bernie (Mass) PO Box 1785, Salem, VA 24153

JONES, Beverly Jean (CNY) 7460 Se Concord Pl, Hobe Sound, FL 33455

✠ **JONES**, Bob Gordon (Wyo) 900 Cottonwood Dr, Fort Collins, CO 80524

JONES, Bonnie Quantrell (Lex) 1801 Glenhill Dr, Lexington, KY 40502

JONES, Bryan (Los) 5306 Arbor Road, Long Beach, CA 90808

JONES, Carolyn G (WMass) 4 Carousel Ln, Lunenburg, MA 01462

✠ **JONES III**, Charles I (Mont) PO Box 86, Gulf Shores, AL 36547

JONES, Charles James (CNY) 16 Vistaview Ln Apt 108, Endwell, NY 13760

JONES, Christine Ann (Vt)

JONES, Christopher David (Mass) 152 Sontag Dr, Franklin, TN 37064

JONES, Chuck (RG) 200 Mulberry St NE, Apt 2023, Albuquerque, NM 87106

JONES, Claiborne (At) 5668 Stillwater Court, Stone Mountain, GA 30087-1645, Virgin Islands (U.S.)

JONES, Connie (SVa) 6214 Monroe Pl, Norfolk, VA 23508

JONES, Corey Matthew (Ala)

JONES, Curtis Carl (Ark) 20900 Chenal Pkwy, Little Rock, AR 72223

JONES, Curtis M (ETenn)

JONES, Daniel Gwilym (Be) 315 Calvin St, Dunmore, PA 18512

✠ **JONES**, David Colin (Va) 6043 Burnside Landing Dr, Burke, VA 22015

JONES, David G (ECR) 1061 Garcia Rd, Santa Barbara, CA 93103

JONES, David James (ECR) Le Bourg, 47120 Loubes-Bernac, Duras, 47120 FR, France

JONES, David Lyall (NJ) 908 Ravine Rd, Califon, NJ 07830

JONES, Derek Leslie (Cal) 786 Tunbridge Rd, Danville, CA 94526

JONES, Donald Avery (Ind) 2652 E Windermere Woods Dr, Bloomington, IN 47401

JONES, Dorothy Kovacs (Cal) Po Box 768, Tiburon, CA 94920

JONES, Duncan Haywood (NC) 102 E Calhoun St, Jackson, NC 27845

JONES JR, Eddie Ellsworth (Fla) 160 Bear Pen Rd, Ponte Vedra Beach, FL 32082

JONES, Edward Wilson (Va) Diocese Of Virginia, 110 W Franklin St, Richmond, VA 23220

JONES, Elizabeth Goodyear (Miss) 201 Plantation Club Dr Apt 1116, Melbourne, FL 32940

JONES, Erin Courtney (NwT) 2435 Bakerview Park Dr, Ferndale, WA 98248

JONES, Eustan Ulric (LI) 721 E 96th St Apt 2, Brooklyn, NY 11236

JONES, Gary (Va) 412 Maple Ave, Richmond, VA 23226

JONES, Gary Harned (Tex) 3806 Kiamesha Dr, Missouri City, TX 77459

JONES, Gerald Dean (Nev)

JONES, Greg (NC) 1520 Canterbury Rd, Raleigh, NC 27608

JONES, Helen Hammon (Ky) 30 River Hill Rd, Louisville, KY 40207

JONES, Herbert H (Va)

JONES JR, Hugh Burnett (ETenn) PO Box 1408, Ridgeland, MS 39158

JONES, Jack Monte (WTex) 1615 S Monroe St, San Angelo, TX 76901

JONES, Jacqueline Sydney (Alb) 8 Byard St, Johnstown, NY 12095

JONES, James (NJ) Oceanview Towers 30, 510 Ocean Ave, Long Branch, NJ 07740

JONES, James Place (SeFla) 9013 SW 62nd Ter, Miami, FL 33173

JONES, James Walter (Mont)

JONES, Jane Denton (Los) 457 W 39th St, San Pedro, CA 90731

JONES, Janice (Tex) 1314 E University Ave, Georgetown, TX 78626

JONES, Jared Lane (CFla)

JONES, Jerry Steven (WK) 1113 Pinehurst St, Hays, KS 67601

JONES, Joann Bradley (Pa) 230 Pennswood Rd, Bryn Mawr, PA 19010

JONES, John Tyler (WA) 11040 Baltimore Ave, Beltsville, MD 20705

JONES, Judith A (Ore) 4929 SW Seneca Pl, Waldport, OR 97394

JONES, Kathleen Andrea Andie (Okla) 1901 Skyline Place, Bartlesville, OK 74006

JONES, Kenneth Leon (Mass) 62 Hopetown Road, Mt.Pleasant, SC 29464

JONES, Kent Trevor (Chi) 3706 W Saint Paul Ave, McHenry, IL 60050

JONES, Leland Bryant (SanD) 1118 W Country Club Ln, Escondido, CA 92026

JONES, Lynne (SeFla) 206 Pendleton Ave, Palm Beach, FL 33480

JONES, Margaret W (WTenn) 4757 Walnut Grove Rd, Memphis, TN 38117

JONES, Mark Andrew (SeFla) 1111 E Sample Rd, Pompano Beach, FL 33064

JONES, Mark Stephen (Ga) 212 N Jefferson St, Albany, GA 31701

JONES, Mary Alice (Mont)

JONES, Mary-Frances (Minn) 911 - 8th Avenue Northwest, Austin, MN 55912

JONES, Michael Stephen (CNY) 785 Forest Ridge Dr, Youngstown, OH 44512

JONES, Nelson Bradley (Alb) 970 State St, Schenectady, NY 12307
JONES, Patricia Loraine (Alb) 1295 Myron St, Schenectady, NY 12309
JONES, Patricia Wayne (WNC) 260 21st Ave Nw, Hickory, NC 28601
JONES, Rebecca (Colo) 8235 W 44th Ave, Wheat Ridge, CO 80033
JONES, Rich (SwVa) 2455 N Stevens St, Alexandria, VA 22311
JONES, Richmond A (At) 432 Forest Hill Rd, Macon, GA 31210
JONES, Robert Michael (WNC) PO Box 729, Highlands, NC 28741
JONES, Ross (Okla) 385 Racquet Club Rd, Asheville, NC 28803
JONES, Ruth Elise (NwT) 3010 - 60th, Lubbock, TX 79413
JONES, Sandra Lee Spoar (U) PO Box 981208, Park City, UT 84098
JONES, Scott Daniel (CFla) 10716 E Medina Ave, Mesa, AZ 85209
JONES, Sondra Kay (RG)
JONES, Stephanie Annie R (Ark)
JONES, Stephen Bradley (ETenn)
JONES, Stephen Chad (Tenn) 1216 Sneed Rd W, Franklin, TN 37069
JONES JR, Stewart H (Colo) 2421 S Krameria St, Denver, CO 80222
JONES, Tammy Lynn (Ida) PO Box 324, Rupert, ID 83350
JONES, Theodore Grant (Md) 2604 Halcyon Avenue, Baltimore, MD 21214
JONES, Thomas A (Neb)
JONES, Thomas Glyndwr (At) 4425 Colchester Ct, Columbus, GA 31907
JONES, Timothy Dale (WNC) 290 Old Haw Creek Rd, Asheville, NC 28805
JONES, Timothy Kent (SVa) 111 Waddell Ct, South Boston, VA 24592
JONES, Tyler (NY) 161 Mansion St, Poughkeepsie, NY 12601
JONES, Vern Edward (Cal) 3814 Jefferson Ave, Emerald Hills, CA 94062
JONES, Walton (Miss) 308 South Commerce St., Natchez, MS 39120
JONES, William Henry (O) 2651 Cheltenham Rd, Toledo, OH 43606
JONES, William Ogden (SVa) 8137 Brown Rd, Bon Air, VA 23235
JONES MAGEE, Heidi Tanya (Mont)
JOO, Paul (Chi) 1300 Hallberg Ln, Park Ridge, IL 60068
JOOS, Heidi L (Minn) 3105 W 40th St, Minneapolis, MN 55410
JOPLIN, Susan Colley (Okla) 2513 Sw 123rd St, Oklahoma City, OK 73170
JOPLING, Mal (Fla)
JORDAN, Elizabeth Joy (Mass)
JORDAN, Johannas (Minn)
JORDAN SR, John E (Nev) 7560 Splashing Rock Dr., Las Vegas, NV 89131
JORDAN, Jon R. (Dal)
JORDAN, Ryan Christopher (Dal)

JORIS, Stan (Okla) 2141 Sw 25th St, Oklahoma City, OK 73108
JOSE, Nancy (WA) 8213 Bald Eagle Ln, Wilmington, NC 28411
JOSEPH, Annette Beth (Mo) 206 Bradley Dr, Sikeston, MO 63801
JOSEPH, Arthur E (NY) 450 Convent Ave, New York, NY 10031
JOSEPH, Hyvenson (NJ)
JOSEPH, Jean (Hai) PO Box 1390, Port-Au-Prince, Haiti
JOSEPH, Pierre (Ve) Calle Tiuna y Callejon, Sta Elena, Venezuela, Venezuela
JOSEPH, Rogenor (Hai)
JOSEPH, Similé (Hai)
JOSEPH, Winston (SeFla)
JOSEPH, Yves-Eugene (Ct)
☩ **JOSLIN**, David Bruce (CNY) 10 Meadow Ridge Rd, Westerly, RI 02891
JOSLIN, Roger (LI) 13225 Sound Ave, Mattituck, NY 11952
JOSLYN-SIEMIATKOSKI, Daniel Edmond (Tex) 80 Pleasant St Unit 2, Arlington, MA 02476
JOY, Charles (SVa) 1009 W Princess Anne Rd, Norfolk, VA 23507
JOY, Patricia Cutler (Ct)
JOYCE, KD (Az)
JOYNER, Thomas (Ala) 136 E Magnolia Ave, Auburn, AL 36830
JOYNER JR, William Henry (NC) 5327 Ashlar Ave, Crozet, VA 22932
JOYNER-GIFFIN, Sally (Md) 13736 Catoctin Furnace Rd, Thurmont, MD 21788
JUAREZ, Jose Martin (ECR) 113 Morcroft Ln, Durham, NC 27705
JUAREZ VILLAMAR, Betty (Litoral Diocese Of Ecuador) Coop Esperanza Mz.1 Sl.7, Canton Catarama, Ecuador
JUBINSKI, Chris (LI) Christ Episcopal Church, PO Box 8, Chaptico, MD 20621
JUCHTER, Mark Russell (NwPa) 5804 Callaway Circlee, Callaway, FL 32404
JUDD, Steven William (Minn) 460 Willow Creek Dr, Owatonna, MN 55060
JUDSON, Marguerite Ann (Cal)
JULIAN, Mercedes I (RI) Ascension Church, 390 Pontiac Ave, Cranston, RI 02910-3322, Panama
JULNES-DEHNER, Noel (SO) 3491 Forestoak Ct, Cincinnati, OH 45208
JUMP, Douglas Brian (CFla)
JUNCO SOTOLONGO, Gilberto (Cu)
JUNG, Annie K (La)
JUNK, Dixie Roberts (Kan) 2701 W 51st Ter, Westwood, KS 66205
JUNKIN, Hays Maclean (NH) 35 Mont Vernon St, Milford, NH 03055
JUPIN, J MICHAEL (SO) 4147 Marla Dr NE, Albuquerque, NM 87109
JURADO, Ruben Dario (Nwk) 326 Westervelt Pl, Lodi, NJ 07644

JURKOVICH-HUGHES, Jocelynn Lena (SanD) 216 A Street, Davis, CA 95616
JUSTICE, Brian (Va)
JUSTICE, Simon (Ore) 445 NW Elizabeth Dr, Corvallis, OR 97330
JUSTIN, Daniel (Los) 14311 Dickens St Apt 111, Sherman Oaks, CA 91423

K

KADEL, Andrew (NY) 5700 Arlington Ave, Bronx, NY 10471
KAEHR, Michael G (SanD) 9503 La Jolla Farms Rd, La Jolla, CA 92037
KAESTNER, James Andrew (Mil) N52w37111 Washington St, Oconomowoc, WI 53066
KAETON, Elizabeth (Nwk) 35647 Joann Dr, Millsboro, DE 19966
KAHL, Eric (SwFla) 1142 Coral Way, Coral Gables, FL 33134
KAHL JR, Robert Mathew (NJ) 107 E Tampa Ave, Villas, NJ 08251
KAHLE, George Frank (SVa) 16711 Holly Trail Dr, Houston, TX 77058
KAHLER, Jerome Evans (Los) 9061 Santa Margarita Rd, Ventura, CA 93004
KAHN, Paul Stewart (NY) 552 West End Avenue, New York, NY 10024
KAIGHN, Reuel Stewart (Be) 145 The Hideout, Lake Ariel, PA 18436
KAISCH, Kenneth Burton (Los) 2112 Camino Del Sol, Fullerton, CA 92833
KALAS, Steven Curtis (Nev) 3607 Blue Dawn Dr, North Las Vegas, NV 89032
KALEMKERIAN, Louise Knar (Ct) 5030 Main St, Trumbull, CT 06611
KALISZEWSKI, Jeanne Elizabeth (Ore) 1535 NE 17th Ave, Portland, OR 97232
KALLENBERG, Richard (NI) 55805 Oak Manor Pl, Elkhart, IN 46514
KALLIO, Craig (ETenn) 119 Newell Ln, Oak Ridge, TN 37830
KALOM, Judith Christine Lilly (At)
KALUNIAN, Peter John (Spok) 5506 W 19th Ave, Kennewick, WA 99338
KAMANO, Charles Lansana (Ct) 28 Church St, West Haven, CT 06516
KAMIHACHI, James Dennis (Eas)
KAMINSKAS, Karen A (Pa)
KAMINSKI, Neil (CGC) 188 Elcano Dr, Hot Springs Village, AR 71909
KAMINSKI, Radhajyoti T-D (WMich)
KAMM, Wayne Kenneth (Ia) 1451 Salem Rd., Salem, IA 52649
KAMRAN, Celal Jesher (Va)
KANE, Maria A (WA) 4535 Piney Church Rd, Waldorf, MD 20602
KANE, Paul (SeFla) St James In The Hills Tec, 3329 Wilson St, Hollywood, FL 33021
KANE, Ross Ross (Va) 3737 Seminary Rd, Alexandria, VA 22304
KANELLAKIS, Theodore (NY) 10 Rawson Ave, Camden, ME 04843

KANESTROM, Glenn (FdL) 6443 Estelle Ave, Riverbank, CA 95367

KANG, Peter (Los) 700 Tiffany Dr, Santa Maria, CA 93454

KANGAS, John Gilbert (NMich) 302 E Arch St, Ironwood, MI 49938

KANO, Mia B (Mass)

KANOUR, Marion Elizabeth (SwVa) 817 Greenway Cir, Waynesboro, VA 22980

KANYI, Peter (ETenn) 630 Mississippi Ave, Signal Mtn, TN 37377

KANZLER JR, Jay Lee (Mo) 20 Southmoor Dr, Clayton, MO 63105

KAOMA, Kapya John (Mass) Christ Church, PO Box 366202, Hyde Park, MA 02136

KAPP, John Deane (Az) 2800 W Ina Rd, Tucson, AZ 85741

KAPPEL, Roger D (EC) 13518 Pegasus Rd, Cypress, TX 77429

KAPURCH, Linda Marie (Md) 343 Elizabeth Dr, Kennett Square, PA 19348

KARANJA, Daniel Njoroge (SVa) PO Box 604, Schertz, TX 78154

KARAS, Erik (WMass) 194 Main St, Sheffield, MA 01257

KARASHIN, Kimberly Macy (Pgh)

KARCHER, David Pirritte (SeFla) 5374 Sw 80th St, Miami, FL 33143

KARCHER, Steven Michael (Colo)

KARELIUS, Bradford Lyle (Los) 29602 Via Cebolla, Laguna Niguel, CA 92677

KARKER, Arthur Lee (Me) Po Box 277, West Rockport, ME 04865

KARL JR, John (Roch) 995 Park Ave, Rochester, NY 14610

KARL, Sharon Leith (Roch) 995 Park Ave, Rochester, NY 14610

KARN, Jack Mann (Tex)

KARPF, Jessie Olive (Ct) 345 Main St, Portland, CT 06480

KARPF, Ted (WA) 16 Casita Dr # G8, Hc 77, Ojo Caliente, NM 87549

KASEY, Philip Howerton (NJ) 4326 Teall Beach Rd, Geneva, NY 14456

KASEY, Polly Mcwilliams (NJ) 4326 Teall Beach Rd, Geneva, NY 14456

KASIO, Joseph Lelit (Nev)

KASSABIAN, Robin Lynn (Los) 25 E Laurel Ave, Sierra Madre, CA 91024

KASSEBAUM, John Albert (NY) 53 S Clinton Ave, Hastings On Hudson, NY 10706

KASWARRA, George (NY) 23 N Willow St, Montclair, NJ 07042

KATER JR, John (Cal) 141 Fulton Ave Apt 311, Apt 311, Poughkeepsie, NY 12603

KATHMANN, Charmaine M (La) St. John's Episcopal Church, 2109 17th Street, Kenner, LA 70062

KATON, Joanne Catherine (SeFla) 1800 Southwest 92nd Place, Miami, FL 33165

KATONA, Kenneth J (Del)

KATULIC, Samuel (CFla)

KATZ, Nathaniel Peter (Eur) 514 W Adams Blvd, Los Angeles, CA 90007

KAUFFMAN, Bette Jo (WLa) 79 Quail Ridge Dr, Monroe, LA 71203

KAUFMAN, Linda Margaret (WA) 701 S Wayne St, Arlington, VA 22204

KAUTZ, Richard Arden (Ind) 913 Brentwood Ct, New Albany, IN 47150

KAVROS, Peregrine Murphy (NC) 1311 Lawrence Rd, Hillsborough, NC 27278

KAY, Frances Creveling (WLa) 2914 W Prien Lake Rd, Lake Charles, LA 70605

KAY, Lauren (Me)

KAYIGWA, Beatrice Mbatudde (WMass) 209 Union St, Clinton, MA 01510

KAYNOR, Robert K (NC) 3605 Rugby Rd, Durham, NC 27707

KAZANJIAN, Rosanna (Mass) Po Box 1215, Sonoita, AZ 85637

KAZANJIAN JR, Victor (Mass) 1872 Cerros Colorados, Santa Fe, NM 87501

KE, Jason Chau-sheng (Tai) 37 Jen-Chih St., Nanton City, Taiwan

KEARLEY, David Arthur (Ala) 154 Morgans Steep Rd, Sewanee, TN 37375

KEARNS, Jada Dart (CFla) 1601 Alafaya Trl, Oviedo, FL 32765

KEATOR, Marnie Knowles (The Episcopal Church in Haw) PO Box 2037, 1 Carley Lane, South Londonderry, VT 05155

KEBBA, Elaine Marguerite Bailey (NC) 6003 Quail Ridge Dr, Greensboro, NC 27455

KEBLESH JR, Joe (O) 4617 Crestview Dr, Sylvania, OH 43560

KECK, Carolyn (Tenn) 505 N 5th St, Maquoketa, IA 52060

KEEBLE, Mac (WTex) 4201 Adina Way, Corpus Christi, TX 78413

KEECH, April Irene (NY)

KEEDY, Susan Shipman (SeFla) 1200 Heron Ave, Miami Springs, FL 33166

KEEFER, John S (Pa) 124 High St, Sharon Hill, PA 19079

KEEGAN, Meaghan Joan (Alb)

KEEHN, Randy P (ND)

KEEL, Ron (WMo) 4801 W 133rd Street, Leawood, KS 66209

KEELER, Donald Franklin (Ia) 121 W Marina Rd, Storm Lake, IA 50588

KEELER, Elizabeth Franklin (Va) PO Box 299, Washington, VA 22747

KEELER, John Dowling (At) 225 Brookhaven Cir, Elberton, GA 30635

KEEN JR, Charles (Dal) 206 Mansfield Blvd, Sunnyvale, TX 75182

KEEN, George Comforted (CFla) 1225 W Granada Blvd, Ormond Beach, FL 32174

KEEN, Lois (Ct) 20 Hudson St, Norwalk, CT 06851

KEENAN, John P (Vt) 73 Oak St, Newport, VT 05855

KEENAN, Mary Louise (Tex)

KEENE, Christopher Paul (Del) Immanuel Church, 100 Harmony St, New Castle, DE 19720

KEENE, Claire Claire (ETenn) 4000 Shaw Ferry Rd, Lenoir City, TN 37772

KEENE, Katheryn C (Ct) 92 Bryn Mawr Ave, Auburn, MA 01501

KEENE-JOHNSON, Benita D (Md) 2629 Huntingdon Ave, Baltimore, MD 21211

KEENER, E Michaella (Pa) P.O. Box 594, 36 Bayview Avenue, Stonington, ME 04681

KEENER JR, Ross Fulton (SVa) 117 Cove Rd, Newport News, VA 23608

KEENEY, Albert J (Roch) 2901 Capen Dr, Bloomington, IL 61704

KEENEY, Randall James (NC) PO Box 1547, Clemmons, NC 27012

KEE-REES, James Louis (WTex) 1501 N Glass St, Victoria, TX 77901

KEESE, Peter Gaines (ETenn) 905 Chateaugay Rd, Knoxville, TN 37923

KEESHIN, Joyce Jenkins (SO) St James Episcopal Church, 3207 Montana Ave, Cincinnati, OH 45211

KEGGI, J John (Me) 62 Crest Rd, Wellesley, MA 02482

KEILL, David (Va) 8212 Pilgrim Ter, Richmond, VA 23227

KEIM, Robert (ECR) 301 Trinity Ave, Arroyo Grande, CA 93420

KEITH, Briggett (Nwk) 3004 Overton Rd, Henrico, VA 23228

KEITH, Caitlyn Jordan (USC)

KEITH, George Arthur (SanD) 4424 44th St Apt 305, San Diego, CA 92115

KEITH JR, John Matthew (Ala) 15001 Searstone Dr Apt 111, Cary, NC 27513

KEITH, Judith Ann (Ga) PO Box 33, 216 Remington Avenue, Thomasville, GA 31799

KEITH III, Stuart Brooks (Colo) PO Box 1591, Edwards, CO 81632

KEITH, Thomas Aaron (NwT)

KEITH, William J (SC) PO Box 145, Lookout Mountain, TN 37350

KEITH-LUCAS, Diane Dorothea (Mass) 1 Hilltop Ave, Lexington, MA 02421

KEIZER, Garret John (Vt) 770 King George Farm Rd, Sutton, VT 05867

KELAHER, Edward Thomas (NC) 3 Chevy Chase Cir, Chevy Chase, MD 20815

KELDERMAN, Kate E (Ct) 24 Elizabeth St, Kent, CT 06757

KELLAM, Patricia Marie (SVa) PO Box 468, Amelia Court House, VA 23002

KELLAWAY, Jim (Ct) 123 Babbitt Hill Road, Pomfret Center, CT 06259

KELLER, Anthony (Los) 808 Foothill Blvd, La Canada, CA 91011

KELLER III, Christoph (Ark) 5224 Country Club Blvd, Little Rock, AR 72207

KELLER JR, David (WNC) 524 Lanigan Way SE, Saint Joseph, MN 56374

KELLER, John (O) 20508 Hilliard Blvd, Rocky River, OH 44116

KELLER, Susan (Md) Trinity St Philips Cath, 24 Rector St, Newark, NJ 07102

KELLERMANN, Alan Seth (The Episcopal NCal) 245 S Church St, Grass Valley, CA 95945

KELLEY, Barbara A (Pa) 159 Windsor Ave, Southampton, PA 18966

KELLEY, Carlton F (Chi) 57607 M-51 South, Dowagiac, MI 49047

KELLEY, James Vincent (Nev)

KELLEY III, Mark Hazen (WMich)

KELLEY, Patrick (Mil) 212 S Michigan St, Prairie Du Chien, WI 53821

KELLEY, Theresa M (Mont) 3350 Keokuk St, Butte, MT 59701

KELLIHER, James William (RI)

KELLINGTON, Brian T (Spr) 17085 SE 93rd Yondel Cir, The Villages, FL 32162

KELLINGTON, Laurie R (Spr) 17085 SE 93rd Yondel Cir, The Villages, FL 32162

KELLNER, Andrew L (Pa)

KELLO, Rebecca Ruth (Ky) 1215 State St, Bowling Green, KY 42101

KELLOGG, Alicia Sue (Me) 27 Forest Ave, Winthrop, ME 04364

KELLOGG III, Edward Samuel (SanD) 3407 Larga Cir, San Diego, CA 92110

KELLOGG, John A (WA) 618 G St SE, Washington, DC 20003

KELLUM, Rose Edna (Miss)

KELLY, Arthur James (Pa) 1171 Sandy Ridge Rd, Doylestown, PA 18901

KELLY, Christopher Douglas (SeFla) 110 Selfridge Rd, Gansevoort, NY 12831

KELLY III, Colin Purdie (RG) 4 Inca Ln, Los Alamos, NM 87547

KELLY III, Francis J (CFla) 1250 Paige Pl, The Villages, FL 32159

KELLY, Jane Young (SwFla) The Ch Of The Good Shpd, 401 W Henry St, Punta Gorda, FL 33950

KELLY, Karen Joy (WMich)

KELLY, Katherine T (Spok) 731 8th St, Lewiston, ID 83501

KELLY, Kathleen M (SanD) 308 E Acacia Ave, Hemet, CA 92543

KELLY, Linda (NwT) 218 Oak Hill Dr, Kerrville, TX 78028

KELLY, Margaret I (Ida) 1800 N Cole Rd Apt E204, Boise, ID 83704

KELLY, Roger K (Ga) 3101 Waters Ave, Savannah, GA 31404

KELLY, Sarah Elizabeth (O) 9160 Putnam Rd, Pandora, OH 45877

KELLY, Shannon (Mass) 37 Grandwood Dr, Forestdale, MA 02644

KELLY, Stacy (Va) 1527 Dahlia Ct, Mclean, VA 22101

KELLY, Steven Joseph Patrick (Mich) 791 Westchester Rd, Grosse Pointe Park, MI 48230

KELLY, Tracey (Va) 419 Turnpike Rd, Mills River, NC 28759

KELLY, Verneda Joan (Neb) 1014 N 6th St, Seward, NE 68434

KELM, Mark William (Minn) 109 Lawn Terrace, Golden Valley, MN 55416

KELMEREIT, Alan (SwFla) 4554 Springview Cir, Labelle, FL 33935

KELSEY, Anne (Mo) PO Box 4740, Saint Louis, MO 63108

KELSEY, Julie Vietor (Ct) 38 Brocketts Point Rd, Branford, CT 06405

KELSEY II, Preston Telford (Ct) 80 Lyme Rd, Apt 213, Hanover, NH 03755

KELSEY, Stephen (Az) 138 N White Willow Pl, Tucson, AZ 85710

KELSON, Laura Jayne (CGC) 1 Saint Francis Dr, Gulf Breeze, FL 32561

KELTON, Barbara Smoot (Dal) PO Box 13, Farmersville, TX 75442

KEM, Robert Andrew (Ia) 1611 NW Northwood Dr, Ankeny, IA 50023

KEMEZA, Maureen (Mass) 17 Munroe Pl., Concord, MA 01742

KEMMERER, Stanley Courtright (Ct) Po Box 2025, Burlington, CT 06013

KEMMLER, Richard Sigmund (NY) 1420 Pine Bay Dr, Sarasota, FL 34231

KEMP, Drusilla Rawlings (Ky) Church Of The Advent, 901 Baxter Ave, Louisville, KY 40204

KEMP, Matthew (Spr) 189 N 92nd St, Milwaukee, WI 53226

KEMP, Rowena Jessica (Ct) 55 New Park Ave, Hartford, CT 06106

KEMPF, Barb (Ind) St Christophers Tec Ch, 1402 W Main St, Carmel, IN 46032

KEMPF, Victoria N (Colo) 2220 Katahdin Dr, Fort Collins, CO 80525

KEMPSELL JR, Howard Frederic (Va) PO Box 2360, Centreville, VA 20122

KEMPSON-THOMPSON, Deborah (Nev) 1776 Us Highway 50, Glenbrook, NV 89413

KENDAGOR, Rita Jo Carson (WMo)

KENDALL, John Thomas (CGC)

KENDALL, Michael Jonah (Ida) 403 E Main St, Durham, NC 27701

KENDALL, Michael Samuel (NY) 9 1/2 Church St, Bristol, RI 02809

KENDALL-SPERRY, David (SO) St Peters Episcopal Church, 45 W Winter St, Delaware, OH 43015

KENDRICK, David (WMo) St Johnh's Church, 515 E Division St, Springfield, MO 65803

✠ **KENDRICK**, Russell (CGC) 3557 Hampshire Dr, Birmingham, AL 35223

KENDRICK, William Barton (The Episcopal NCal) 19 Five Iron Ct, Chico, CA 95928

KENNA, Jennifer Anne (CNY) 235 John St, Clayton, NY 13624

KENNARD, Susan (Tex) 3000 Avenue L, Bay City, TX 77414

KENNEDY, Arthur Thomas (Ida) 261 Los Lagos, Twin Falls, ID 83301

KENNEDY, David Kittle (The Episcopal Church in Haw) 1 Keahole Pl Apt 3409, Honolulu, HI 96825

KENNEDY, Dennis (Colo)

KENNEDY, Ellen Kathleen (Ct) 243 Harbor St, Branford, CT 06405

KENNEDY, Gary Grant (Kan) 1900 E Front St, Galena, KS 66739

KENNEDY III, John Ira (Ala)

KENNEDY JR, John Ira (Ala)

KENNEDY III, John Martin (Ct)

KENNEDY, Joseph M (EMich)

KENNEDY, Karen (Oly)

KENNEDY, Nan N (Tex) 304 Krupp Ave, Liberty Hill, TX 78642

KENNEDY, Palmer Bourne (SC)

KENNEDY, Thomas B (Mass) 46 Glen Road, Brookline, MA 02445

KENNEDY, Tim (WA)

KENNELLY, Margery (Tenn) 379 Hammond St, Chestnut Hill, MA 02467

KENNINGTON, Spergeon Albert (CGC) 212 Margaret Dr, Fairhope, AL 36532

KENNY, Susie Fowler (Los) 1020 N Brand Blvd, Glendale, CA 91202

KENT, David Williamson (Kan) 1900 Spyglass Court, Lawrence, KS 66047

KENT, Stuart Matthews (Dal) PO Box 429, North Stonington, CT 06359

KENWORTHY, Stuart A (WA) 2801 Mexico Avenue NW, Apt 711, Washington, DC 20007

KENYI, Alex Lodu (ND) 3725 30th St, San Diego, CA 92104

KEPLINGER, Steve (Az) 2331 E Adams St, Tucson, AZ 85719

KEPPELER, Lisa (Pa) 124 S Main St, Coopersburg, PA 18036

KEPPY, Susan (WNY) 429 Cherry Ln, Lewiston, NY 14092

KERBEL, Carol Ann (NJ) 232 Camino De La Sierra, Santa Fe, NM 87501

KERBEL, Walter J (NY) 1418 E 57th St, Chicago, IL 60637

KERN, David Paul (Nwk) PO Box 1703, North Eastham, MA 02651

KERN, Karl Lee (Be) 182 Gable Dr/, Myerstown, PA 17067

KERN, Roy Allen (CPa) 613 Eschol Ridge Rd, Elliottsburg, PA 17024

KERNER, Sandi (SVa) 2755 Buckstone Dr, Powhatan, VA 23139

KERR, Catherine D (Pa) 123 N Main St, New Hope, PA 18938

KERR, Donald G (Episcopal VI)

KERR, Kyra Anne (RG) P.O. Box 188, Tesuque, NM 87574

KERR, Lauri (CPa) 1435 Scott St, Williamsport, PA 17701

KERR, Linda (Pa) 1603 Yardley Commons, Yardley, PA 19067

KERR, Robert Anthony (Mich) 21731 Southfield Rd, Southfield, MI 48075

KERR, Verdery (NC) 3148 Champaign St, Charlotte, NC 28210

KERRICK, Mike (The Episcopal NCal) 2612 Colin Rd, Placerville, CA 95667

KERSCHEN, Charles Thomas (WK) 520 East Ave S, Lyons, KS 67554

KERTLAND, Gail Ellen (LI) 36 Cathedral Ave, Garden City, NY 11530

KESHGEGIAN, Flora A (Pa) 601 Montgomery Ave Apt 308, Bryn Mawr, PA 19010

KESLER, Walter Wilson (Tex) 3937 Anewby Way, Fort Worth, TX 76133

KESSEL-HANNA, Kay Lynn (Oly) 11527 9th Ave NE, Seattle, WA 98125

KESSELUS, Kenneth William (Tex) 1301 Church St, Bastrop, TX 78602

KESSLER, Edward Scharps (Pa) 44 Hinde Street, Sheffield, S4 8HJ, Great Britain (UK)

KESSLER, Judith Maier (CNY) 17 Elizabeth St, Binghamton, NY 13901

KESSLER, Rachel Cheryl (O) Harcourt Parish, PO Box 377, Gambier, OH 43022

KESTER, Martha (Ia) 1916 Merklin Way, Des Moines, IA 50310

KETNER, Thomas Howard (Wyo) 411 E Center St, Douglas, WY 82633

KETNER, Virginia Lynn (Wyo) 930 Leal St, Douglas, WY 82633

KETTLEWELL, Paula Swaebe (Va) 5903 Willow Oaks Dr Apt E, Apt E, Richmond, VA 23225

KEUCHER, Gerald Werner (LI) 1 Pendleton Pl, Staten Island, NY 10301

KEVERN, John (WVa) C/O Trinity Epis Church, PO Box P, Moundsville, WV 26041

KEW, William Richard (Tenn) 2272 Lewisburg Pike, Franklin, TN 37064

KEY, Nancy Anne (Episcopal SJ) PO Box 7446, Visalia, CA 93290

KEY, Sandy (NC) 1308 Langdon Pl, Pittsboro, NC 27312

KEYDEL JR, John F (Md) 970 Running Brook Way, Annapolis, MD 21401

KEYES, Charles Don (NY) 5801 Hampton St, Pittsburgh, PA 15206

KEYES, John Irvin (SD) 513 Douglas Ave, Yankton, SD 57078

KEYS, Joel Thompson (Tenn) 409 Indigo, Saint Simons Island, GA 31522

KEYSE, Andrew Carl (WMo) 6914 NW Pleasant View Ct, Kansas City, MO 64152

KEYSER, Patrick Lee (WA)

KEYWORTH, Gill (Tex) 1215 Ripple Creek Dr, Houston, TX 77057

KEZAR, Dennis Dean (SwFla) 4030 Manatee Ave W, Bradenton, FL 34205

KHALIL, Adeeb Mikhail (WVa) 127 Brookwood Ln, Beckley, WV 25801

KHAMIN, Alexei (Nwk) All Saints Episcopal Church, 230 E 60th St, New York, NY 10022

KIBLER SR, Bryant C (Lex) 607 HWY 1746, 607 Highway 1746, Irvine, KY 40336

KIBLINGER, Charles Edward (Va) 651 Rivendell Blvd, Osprey, FL 34229

KIDD, Dave (At) 10952 NW 32nd Ave, Gainesville, FL 32606

KIDD, Reggie M (CFla)

KIDD, Saundra Kay (Fla) 4129 Oxford Ave, Jacksonville, FL 32210

KIDD, Scott (At) 44 Tesnatee Landing Dr, Cleveland, GA 30528

KIDD, Stephen (Miss) 11322 E Taylor Rd, Gulfport, MS 39503

KIDDER, Ann (O) PO Box 519, Gates Mills, OH 44040

KIDDER, Frederick Elwyn (PR)

KIEFER, Lee (EO) 428 King St, Wenatchee, WA 98801

KIENZLE, Edward Charles (Mass) 109 Dobbins St, Waltham, MA 02451

KIESCHNICK, Frannie (Cal) 134 La Goma St, Mill Valley, CA 94941

KIESSLING, Donna Jean (Del) 22 N Union St, Smyrna, DE 19977

KIKER, Norman Wesley (Okla) 5705 Earl Dr, Shawnee, OK 74804

KILBOURN, Lauren Michelle (NC) 221Union St, Cary, NC 27511

KILBOURN, Thomas Lewis (Ct) 51 Paddy Hollow Rd, Bethlehem, CT 06751

KILBOURN-HUEY, Mary Esther (Lex) 310 Edgemont Rd, Maysville, KY 41056

KILGORE, John W (Mo) 320 Union Blvd, Saint Louis, MO 63108

KILIAN, Joan M (NC) 9003 Oakfield Dr, Statesboro, GA 30461

KILLEEN, David (Fla) St Johns Episcopal Church, 211 N Monroe St, Tallahassee, FL 32301

KILLELEA, Lauren Banks (Mass)

KILLIAN, David Allen (Mass) 882 Watertown St, West Newton, MA 02465

KILLIAN, Kathleen Erin (Me)

KILPATRICK, Brenda (Chi)

KILPATRICK, George Michael (SanD)

KIM, Andrew (Los) 13091 Galway St, Garden Grove, CA 92844

KIM, Grace Woongja (RG)

KIM, John (Pa) 3204 Ashy Way, Drexel Hill, PA 19026

KIM, John D (Los) St James Episcopal Church, 3903 Wilshire Blvd, Los Angeles, CA 90010

KIM, Jonathan Jang-Ho (WNY) Kumi Box 1039, Kumi Kyungbuk, 730-600, Korea (South)

KIM, Kyrie (NY)

KIM, Richard (Mich) 19983 E Doyle Pl, Grosse Pointe, MI 48236

KIM, Sean (WMo)

KIM, Stephen Yongchul (Los) 45267 Sancroft Ave, Lancaster, CA 93535

KIM, Yein (NY) 117 Main St, East Setauket, NY 11733

KIM, Yong Gul Ninian (LI) 2235 36th St, Astoria, NY 11105

KIMBALL, Anne (Ct) 14890 David Dr, Fort Myers, FL 33908

KIMBALL JR, George Allen (Mil) 320 E Pleasant St Unit 301, Oconomowoc, WI 53066

KIMBALL, Jennifer Warfel (Va) 125 Beverly Rd, Ashland, VA 23005

KIMBALL, Melodie Irene (Ore) 257 E Milton St, Lebanon, OR 97355

KIMBLE, Shell Teyssier (WA) 5316 Taylor Rd, Riverdale, MD 20737

KIMBROUGH, Timothy Edward (Tenn) 435 Patina Cir, Nashville, TN 37209

KIMES, Nicki Sagendorf (Ct) 134 East Ave, New Canaan, CT 06840

KIMMEL, Joseph Lee (Mass) 24 Peabody Ter Apt 1301, Cambridge, MA 02138

KIMMELMAN, Sandra Sue (Miss)

KIMMICK, Donald William (Nwk) 9625 Miranda Dr, Raleigh, NC 27617

KIMSEY, Hillary (Oly) 1318 N Callow Ave, Bremerton, WA 98312

KIMURA, Gregory W (Los) 50 Bedford Cv, San Rafael, CA 94901

KIN, Nancy E (O) 1249 3rd St, Rensselaer, NY 12144

KINARD III, George Oscar (SeFla)

KINCAID III, Samuel Thomas (Dal) 708 Harrison St, La Porte, IN 46350

KINDEL JR, William H (Colo) 1534 44th Avenue Ct, Greeley, CO 80634

KINDERGAN, Walter Bradford (CGC)

KING, Alisha Monique (Eas)

KING, Allan Brewster (Mass) 222 Sayre Drive, Princeton, NJ 08540

KING, Benjamin John (Mass) Sch of Theology U of the S, 335 Tennessee Ave, Sewanee, TN 37383

KING, Brandon D (NJ)

KING JR, Charles Baldwin (Alb) 5 Jodiro Ln Apt 100, Colonie, NY 12205

KING, Darlene Dawn (EMich) 3201 Gratiot Ave, Port Huron, MI 48060

KING JR, Earle (WNY) 2595 Baseline Rd, Grand Island, NY 14072

KING, Ed (WMass) 4571 Lakeshore Rd, Lexington, MI 48450

KING, Francis Marion Covington (WNC) 140 Saint Marys Church Rd, Morganton, NC 28655

KING, Frank Walter (WNC) 4425 Huntington Dr, Gastonia, NC 28056

KING, Giovan Venable (The Episcopal Church in Haw) The Parish of St. Christopher, 93 N. Kainalu Drive, Kailua, HI 96734

KING, Janet Gay Felland (Ida) 678 E 400 N, Rupert, ID 83350

KING, Karen (Chi) 125 E 26th St, Chicago, IL 60616

KING, Karen Gail (Mont) PO Box 158, Troy, MT 59935

KING, Karen L (Ind) 3401 Lindel Ln, Indianapolis, IN 46268

KING, Kathryn Louise (NJ) 28 Ralph St, Bergenfield, NJ 07621

KING JR, Kenneth Vernon (EO) 702 Grant St, Summit, MS 39666

KING, L A (The Episcopal NCal) 572 Bokman Place, Sonoma, CA 95476

KING, Leyla (ETenn) 1607 W 43rd St, Chattanooga, TN 37409

KING, Margaret Creed (Fla) 704 Vauxhall Dr, Nashville, TN 37221

KING, Mary Howard (Miss) PO Box 1225, Corinth, MS 38835

KING, Steven (WMo) 113 N 18th St, Omaha, NE 68102

KING, Tom Earl (NC) 2725 SE 39th St, Moore, OK 73160

KING, William Michael (Ala) 905 Castlemaine Drive, Birmingham, AL 35226

KINGDON, Art (Vt) 334 Oak Grove Rd, Vassalboro, ME 04989

KINGMAN, Donna Watkins (WMass) 3 Newington Ln, Worcester, MA 01609

KINGSLEY, Josh (Ore) 11229 NE Prescott St, Portland, OR 97220

KINGSLEY, Myra Jessica (Az) 100 W Roosevelt St, Phoenix, AZ 85003

KINGSLEY, Timothy Miles (Minn) 519 Oak Grove St, Minneapolis, MN 55403

KINGSLIGHT, Kathleen Anne (Oly) St Pauls Episcopal Church, 700 Callahan Dr, Bremerton, WA 98310

KINGSTON, Louise (NJ) 85 Westcott Rd, Princeton, NJ 08540

KINMAN, Mike (Los) 540 Woodland, Pasadena, CA 91106

KINMAN, Thomas David (Az) PO Box 40126, Tucson, AZ 85717

KINNER, Heidi Ellen (Mont) St. Peters Episcopal Cathedral, 511 N. Park Avenue, Helena, MT 59601

KINNEY, Elise (Mass) 193 Clifton St, Malden, MA 02148

KINNEY, Genie (Cal) 1746 29th Ave, San Francisco, CA 94122

KINNEY, Kate (Oly) 610-906-9690, Eastsound, WA 98245

KINNEY, Patricia May (CNY) 14 Church St, Moravia, NY 13118

KINNEY, Robert Paul (SwFla)

KINNEY, Robert Sturgis (Okla) 5231 Wedgefield Rd, Granbury, TX 76049

KINNEY, Stephen W (Tex) 2306 Cypress Pt W, Austin, TX 78746

KINNUNEN, Victor J (NwPa)

KINSER, Dixon (NC) St Paul's Episcopal Church, 520 Summit St, Winston Salem, NC 27101

KINSEY, Douglas Andrew (Pgh)

KINSEY, Elizabeth A (WMich)

KINSEY, Kevin Lee (Me) 650 Main St Ste A, Caribou, ME 04736

KINSEY, Theron Harvey (Cal) 917 Avis Dr, El Cerrito, CA 94530

KINSEY, Thomas Burton (SO) 5004 Upton Ave S, Minneapolis, MN 55410

KINSOLVING, John Armistead (RG) 107 Washington Ave, Santa Fe, NM 87501

KINYON, Brice Wayne (USC) 1900 Woodvalley Drive, Columbia, SC 29212

KIRBY, Elisa Mabley (EC) 320 Pollock St, New Bern, NC 28560

KIRBY, Erin C (WNC) PO Box 1539, Marion, NC 28752

KIRBY, Gary Lee (Okla)

KIRBY, Harry Scott (Eau) 1712 Lehman St., Eau Claire, WI 54701

KIRBY, Jacquelyn Walsh (RI) PO Box 317, Jamestown, RI 02835

KIRBY, Kelly Ellen (Ky) 330 N Hubbards Ln, Louisville, KY 40207

KIRBY, Richard Allen (Neb)

KIRBY, Robert Douglas (WA)

KIRBY, Whitney B (Tex) 100 W. Roosevelt, Phoenix, AZ 85003

KIRCHER, Kathleen L (SwFla) 1741 Winding Oaks Way, Naples, FL 34109

KIRCHMIER, Anne Ruth (SVa) 45 Main St, Newport News, VA 23601

KIRK, Deborah (WA) 14300 Saint Thomas Church Rd, Upper Marlboro, MD 20772

KIRK, Jeffrey Malcolm (NJ) 102 Pearlcroft Rd, Cherry Hill, NJ 08034

KIRK, Patricia Lanier (USC) 501 S La Posada Cir Apt 118, Green Valley, AZ 85614

KIRKALDY, David (Tex) 612 Duroux Rd, La Marque, TX 77568

KIRKHAM II, Hall (Mass) 112 Randolph Avenue, Milton, MA 02186

KIRKING, Kerry Clifton (Spok) 912 3rd Ave W Apt 402, Seattle, WA 98119

KIRKLAND, Patricia Ann (Ia)

KIRKLEY, John Lawrence (Cal) 4616 California St, San Francisco, CA 94118

KIRK-NORRIS, Barbara (WTenn) PO Box 2949, Big Spring, TX 79721

KIRKPATRICK, Daisy (CNY) 741 West Second St, Elmira, NY 14905

KIRKPATRICK, Frank Gloyd (Ct) 154 Clearfield, Wethersfield, CT 06109

KIRKPATRICK, Martha (Del) St Barnabas Church, 2800 Duncan Rd, Wilmington, DE 19808

KIRKPATRICK, Nathan Elliott (NC) 8410 Merin Rd, Chapel Hill, NC 27516

KIRKPATRICK, Rebecca Blair (Oly) 111 NE 80th St, Seattle, WA 98115

KIRKPATRICK JR, Robert Jr Frederick (Lex) 9801 Germantown Pike Apt 115, Lafayette Hill, PA 19444

KISNER, Mary (CPa) 218 S. 18th Street, Lebanon, PA 17042

KISS, Margaret Mary (Mil) 3775 S 27th St Apt 210, Milwaukee, WI 53221

KISSAM, Todd William (Eas) 105 Church Lane, Church Hill, MD 21623

KISSINGER, Debra Jean (Minn) 5000 Estate Coakley Bay, Apt. J-3, Christiansted, VI 00820

KITAGAWA, John Elliott (Az) 1700 E Chula Vista Rd, Tucson, AZ 85718

KITAYAMA, Scott D (WTex)

KITCH, Anne E (Nwk) 500 Hillcrest Blvd, Phillipsburg, NJ 08865

KITCH, Sarah Underhill (Los) 280 Royal Ave, Simi Valley, CA 93065

KITT, Michael (SwFla) 523 Courtland Ave, Park Ridge, IL 60068

KITTELSON, Alan Leslie (Vt) 6 Park St, Vergennes, VT 05491

KITTREDGE, Cynthia Briggs (Tex) Seminary of the Southwest, 501 E 32nd St, Austin, TX 78705

KIVEL, Virginia McDermott (Dal)

KLAM, Warren Peter (Va) 4200 Harbor Blvd., Oxnard, CA 93035

KLAMER, Mark (Spr)

KLEE, Gillian Marie (WTenn) 1516 Willow St, Blytheville, AR 72315

KLEFFMAN, Todd Aaron (Ind) 5757 Rosslyn Ave, Indianapolis, IN 46220

KLEIN, Craig Alan (Kan) 67 SW Pepper Tree Ln, Topeka, KS 66611

KLEIN, Elizabeth Gordon (Ore)

KLEIN, Everett H (WMich) 7521 Anthony St, Whitehall, MI 49461

KLEIN, John Conrad (Mich) 231 E Grand Blvd, Detroit, MI 48207

KLEIN, Susan Webster (Los) 9606 Oakmore Rd, Los Angeles, CA 90035

KLEIN-LARSEN, Martha Susan (Ct) 117 Oenoke Rdg, New Canaan, CT 06840

KLEMMT, Pierce (Va) 1208 N Pitt St, Alexandria, VA 22314

KLENZMANN, Joseph G (Va)

KLEVEN, Terence J (Ia) 1334 N Prairie St, Pella, IA 50219

KLICKMAN, John Michael (Dal) 4017 Hedgerow Dr, Plano, TX 75024

KLIMAS, Marcella Louise (CPa) 4355 Georgetown Sq Apt 141, Atlanta, GA 30338

KLINE, Andy (Colo) 5 Brookside Dr, Greenwood Village, CO 80121

KLINE, Catherine (Episcopal SJ)

KLINE, Daniel John (SanD)

KLINE, Nancy Wade (CFla) St. Barnabas Episcopal Church, 319 W. Wisconsin Ave, Deland, FL 32720

KLINEFELTER, Aaron (SO)

KLINE-MORTIMER, Sandra L (Md) Po Box 3298, Shepherdstown, WV 25443

KLINGELHOFER, Stephan Ernest (Eas) 545 Fey Rd # 21620-, Chestertown, MD 21620

KLINGENBERG, Ralph Gerard (SeFla)

KLINGENSMITH, Roxanne Elizabeth Pearson (Mont) 1715 S Black Ave, Bozeman, MT 59715

KLINGSTEDT, Luke A (CFla)

KLITZKE, Dale (USC) 1816 Crestwood Ln, Menomonie, WI 54751

KLITZKE, Paul Kenneth (Dal) 8787 Greenville Avenue, Dallas, TX 75243

KLOPFENSTEIN, Timothy David (CGC) 106 Galaxy Ave, Bonaire, GA 31005

KLOTS, Stephen Barrett (Ct) 40 Bulls Bridge Rd, South Kent, CT 06785

KLOZA, Wanda Margaret (CPa) 101 Pine St, Harrisburg, PA 17101

✠ **KLUSMEYER**, William (WVa) 1 Roller Rd, Charleston, WV 25314

KLUTTERMAN, David Lee (FdL) 330 Mcclellan St, Wausau, WI 54403
KNAPICK, Veronica Helene (Ak) 6816 E. Riverwood Cir, Palmer, AK 99645
KNAPP, Carl Jude (Pa) 584 Fairway Ter, Philadelphia, PA 19128
KNAPP, Clayton L (WMass) 3003 Dick Wilson Dr, Sarasota, FL 34240
KNAPP, Cynthia Clark (At) 43 Twin Oak Ln, Wilton, CT 06897
KNAPP, Donald Hubert (Be) 162 Springhouse Rd, Allentown, PA 18104
KNAPP, Gretchen Bower (Mont) Po Box 794, Hilger, MT 59451
KNAPP, Ron (Eas) 11240 Gail Dr, Princess Anne, MD 21853
KNAUFF, Elizabeth Ann (Ct) 155 Wyllys St, Hartford, CT 06106
KNAUP JR, Daniel Joseph (O) 4954 Valencia Dr, Toledo, OH 43623
KNEE, Jacob S (Mont) St Stephen's Episcopal Ch, 1241 Crawford Dr, Billings, MT 59102
KNEIPP, Lee Benson (WTenn) Po Box 3874, Pineville, LA 71361
KNIGHT, Arthur James (NJ) 3 Blueberry Rd, Shamong, NJ 08088
KNIGHT, David Hathaway (Va) 6005 S Crestwood Ave, Richmond, VA 23226
KNIGHT IV, F Michael (Pa) 1517 N Hunting Horn Turn, Glen Mills, PA 19342
KNIGHT, Hollinshead T (Cal) 485 Bridgeway Apt 1, Sausalito, CA 94965
KNIGHT, J David (CGC) Saint Simon's On The Sound, 28 Miracle Strip Pkwy SW, Fort Walton Beach, FL 32548
KNIGHT, Joseph Sturdevant (CGC) 436 Lapsley Street, Selma, AL 36701
KNIGHT, Mother Kimberly (La) 200 Chapel Crk Apt 116, Mandeville, LA 70471
KNIGHT, Samuel Theodore (Mich) 28725 Sunset Boulevard West, Lathrup Village, MI 48076
KNIGHT, Skully (La) 3200 Woodland Ridge Blvd, Baton Rouge, LA 70816
KNIGHT, Theolinda Lenore Johnson (Cal) 806 Jones St, Berkeley, CA 94710
KNIGHT, W Allan (Md) 58 Hanson Rd, Chester, NH 03036
KNIPP, Vicki Waynne (Tex)
KNISELY, Harry (Ct) 365 Hickory Rd, Carlisle, PA 17015
✠ **KNISELY JR**, W Nicholas (RI) Tec Dio Of Ri, 275 N Main St, Providence, RI 02903
KNOCKEL, Wayne J (WNY) Saint Peter's Episcopal Church, 205 Longmeadow Rd, Eggertsville, NY 14226
KNOLL LENON, Katherine G (Ga)
KNOTT, Joseph Lee (Ala) 5528 - 11th Court South, Birmingham, AL 35222
KNOTTS, Harold Wayne (Mich) 26431 W Chicago, Redford, MI 48239

KNOUSE, Amanda (CPa) 9668 Maidstone Rd, Delaplane, VA 20144
KNOWLES, Bobbie (SeFla) 2704 Rossedale Street, Houston, TX 77004
KNOWLES, Melody D (Va) 3737 Seminary Rd, Alexandria, VA 22304
KNOWLES, Walter (Oly) 1010 Hoyt Ave Apt 4, Everett, WA 98201
KNOWLTON, Beth (WTex) 315 E Pecan St, San Antonio, TX 78205
KNOX, David Paul (CFla) 216 Sheridan Ave, Longwood, FL 32750
KNOX, David Ray (Spr)
KNOX, Dena (Wyo)
KNOX, Jeffrey Donald (CNY) 1755 State Route 48, Fulton, NY 13069
KNOX, John Michael (WK) 16019 W 80th St, Lenexa, KS 66219
KNOX, Regina G (Me) 143 State St, Portland, ME 04101
✠ **KNUDSEN**, Chilton Richardson (Me) Diocese of Maryland, 4 E University Pkwy, Baltimore, MD 21218
KNUDSON, Kay Francis (Neb) 1304 Wade St, Lexington, NE 68850
KNUTH, Charles H (Mont)
KNUTSEN, Jamie (The Episcopal NCal) 1354 Yulupa Ave Apt H, Santa Rosa, CA 95405
KNUTSON, Randy Alan (The Episcopal NCal) 201 E Fir St, PO Box 124, Fort Bragg, CA 95437
KNUTSON, William Ralph (Los)
KOCH, Adrienne Marie (O) 32263 Plumbrook Ct, Avon Lake, OH 44012
KOCH, Eunice Jane (Minn) PO Box 513, Ely, MN 55731
KOCH, Janie (Okla) 325 E Washington Ave, PO Box 534, Mcalester, OK 74501
KOCH, William Christian (RG) P.O. Box 1614, Blue Hill, ME 04614
KOCHENBURGER, Philip (Tex) 2740 Dove Meadow Ct, Cameron Park, CA 95682
KOCHTITZKY, Rodney Morse (Tenn) The Pastoral Ctr For Healing, 1024 Noelton Ave, Nashville, TN 37204
KODERA, T James (Mass) 212 Old Lancaster Rd, Sudbury, MA 01776
KOEHLER, Anne E (Nwk) PO Box 611, East Orleans, MA 02643
KOEHLER, Michael Alban Collins (WTex) 6000 Fm 3237 Unit A, Wimberley, TX 78676
KOEHLER III, Norman Elias (Pgh) 408 Forest Highlands Dr, Pittsburgh, PA 15238
KOEHLER, Robert Brien (Spr) 19206 Boca Del Mar, San Antonio, TX 78258
KOELLIKER, Karulynn Travis (Va)
KOELLN, Theodore Frank (CFla) 505 Ne 1st Ave, Mulberry, FL 33860
KOENIG, Diane L (Chi) 86 Pomeroy Ave # 2, Crystal Lake, IL 60014
KOENIG, John (NJ) 17546 Drayton Hall Way, San Diego, CA 92128
KOENIGER, Margaret Smithers (Nwk) 574 Ridgewood Rd, Maplewood, NJ 07040

KOEPKE III, John Frederick (SO) 179 Strathmoor Xing, Dayton, OH 45429
KOERNER, Travers (WA) 314 Lincoln Ave, Rockville, MD 20850
KOFFRON-EISEN, Elizabeth Mary (Ia) 945 Applewood Ct #1, Coralville, IA 52241
KOGGANI, Mtipe D (Mo)
KOH, Aidan Y (Los) 4344 Lemp Ave, Studio City, CA 91604
KOHL, Stacey (Ct)
KOHLMEIER, Susan (Roch) 1017 Silvercrest Dr, Webster, NY 14580
KOHN, Jeff (ECR) 980 W Franklin St, Monterey, CA 93940
KOHN-PERRY, Ellen Marie (Nwk)
KOLANOWSKI, Ron (Ct) St. James Episcopal Church, 95 Route 2A, Preston, CT 06365
KOLB, Jerry Warren (WMo) 8256 Outlook Ln, Prairie Village, KS 66208
KOLBET, Paul Robert (Mass) 8 Ivy Cir, Wellesley, MA 02482
KOLLIN, Harriet (Pa) 1034 Broadview Dr, Jim Thorpe, PA 18229
KOLLIN JR, James T (NJ) 120 Sussex St Apt 1b, Hackensack, NJ 07601
KONDRATH, William Michael (Mass) 25 Richards Ave, Sharon, MA 02067
✠ **KONIECZNY**, Ed (Okla) Episcopal Diocese Of Oklahoma, 924 N Robinson Ave, Oklahoma City, OK 73102
KONYHA, Dorothy Margaret (NwPa) 134 W 7th St, Erie, PA 16501
KOONCE, Kelly Montgomery (Tex) 6625 Whitemarsh Valley Walk, Austin, TX 78746
KOONCE, Nancy (Ida)
KOONS, Zachary Gunnar (Tex) 1420 E Palm Valley Blvd, Round Rock, TX 78664
KOOPERKAMP, Sarah Jennifer (LI) 612 Greenwood Ave, Brooklyn, NY 11218
KOOPERKAMP, William Earl (Vt) Church Of The Good Shepherd, 39 Washington St, Barre, VT 05641
KOOR, Margaret Platt (SwFla) 4017 Heaton Ter, North Port, FL 34286
KOPERA, Dorothy Jean (NMich) 214 E Avenue A, Newberry, MI 49868
KOPP, Vincent Joseph (NC) 4523 Six Forks Rd, Raleigh, NC 27609
KOPPEL, Mary E (Miss) PO Box 5176, Austin, TX 78763
KOPPELBERGER, Sarah G (NC)
KOPREN, Kristin C (RG) 151 S Resler Dr Apt 2, El Paso, TX 79912
KORIENEK, Martha (ECR) Diocese of El Camino Real, PO Box 689, Salinas, CA 93902
KORN, Elizabeth Louise (NMich) N2809 River Dr, Wallace, MI 49893
KORTE, Mary Jane (Mo) Christ Church, 1000 N Main St, Rolla, MO 65401
KOSHNICK, Loxley Jean (Minn) PO Box 868, Detroit Lakes, MN 56502
KOSHY, Jayan (Minn)

KOSKELA, David Michael (Colo) 5433 South Buckskin Pass, Colorado Springs, CO 80917

KOSKELA, Robert N (Mil) 1260 Deming Way Apt 310, Madison, WI 53717

KOSKI, John Arthur (FdL)

KOSSLER, Robert Joseph (Cal) 484 Florence Ave, Oakland, CA 94618

KOSTIC, Elizabeth M (Pa) 2523 E Madison St, Philadelphia, PA 19134

KOTUBY, Janice (NY) 860 Wolcott Ave, Beacon, NY 12508

KOTVAL, Amanda (Va) 3090 Glen Valley Dr, Crozet, VA 22932

KOULOURIS, Beulah (Mass) 12 Sunrise Ave, Plymouth, MA 02360

KOUNTZ, Peter James (Pa)

KOVACH, Gary David (WNC) 19 Old Youngs Cove Rd, Candler, NC 28715

KOVALOVICH, Kurt Kriztofer (Be) 200 S 2nd St, Pottsville, PA 17901

KOVITCH, Joseph Gerard (SO) PO Box 176, Westerville, OH 43086

KOVOOR, George (Lex) 400 Humphrey St, New Haven, CT 06511

KOWALEWSKI, Mark Robert (Los) 252 Vineyard Rd, Huntington, NY 11743

KOWALEWSKI, Paul James (Los) 54280 Avenida Montezuma, La Quinta, CA 92253

KOWALSKI, Jim (NY) Cath Of St John The Dvn, 1047 Amsterdam Ave, New York, NY 10025

KOWALSKI, Mark Joseph (Neb) Diocese of Nebraska, 109 N 18th St, Omaha, NE 68102

KOWALSKI, Ronald Chester (SwFla) 7349 Ulmerton Rd, Lot# 1398 Balboa St., Largo, FL 33771

KOWALSKI, Vesta (Me) 2635 2nd Ave Apt 828, San Diego, CA 92103

KOZAK, Jan (EO) PO Box 214, Madras, OR 97741

KOZAK, Paul Shoaf (Mass)

KOZIELEC, Mark A (Mo) Saint Marks Church, 4714 Clifton Ave, Saint Louis, MO 63109

KOZIKOWSKI, Mary Carol (NMich) 922 10th Ave, Menominee, MI 49858

KOZLOWSKI, Joseph Felix (WNY) 4532 Van Dusen Rd, Lockport, NY 14094

KOZLOWSKI, Matthew William (WA) 623 SE Ocean Blvd, Stuart, FL 34994

KOZLOWSKI, Robin E (WNY)

KOZUSZEK, Jeffrey Frank (Spr) 512 W Main St, Salem, IL 62881

KRADEL, Adam (Pa) 311 S Orange St, Media, PA 19063

KRAEMER, C Jeff (Dal) 760 Burchart Dr, ., Prosper, TX 75078

KRAFT, Carol Joyce (Chi) 124 West Prairie Street, Wheaton, IL 60187

KRAFT JR, Kenneth M (SC)

KRAFT, Roberta A (FdL)

KRAKOWSKY, Posey (NY) 12 W 11th St, New York, NY 10011

KRAMER, Aron M (Minn) 3011 E Superior St, Duluth, MN 55812

KRAMER, Beaman K (SwVa) 1904 Old Stage Rd, Alexandria, VA 22308

KRAMER, Caroline Anne (WNC)

KRAMER, Chuck (NY) 4536 Albany Post Rd, Hyde Park, NY 12538

KRAMER, Esther (Mil) 1023 Milwaukee St, Delafield, WI 53018

KRAMER, Linda Jean (SD) 23120 S Rochford Rd, Hill City, SD 57745

KRANICHFELD, Bram (Vt)

KRANTZ, Jeffrey Hoyt (LI) 43 Cedar Shore Dr, Massapequa, NY 11758

KRANTZ, Kristin (Md) 1307 N Main St, Mount Airy, MD 21771

KRANTZ, Saralouise Camlin (LI) 555advent Street, Westbury, NY 11590

KRAPF, Richard D (Roch) 15 Granger Street, Canandaigua, NY 14424

KRASINSKI, Joseph Alexander (Ct) 2 Cannondale Dr, Danbury, CT 06810

KRAULAND, Lesley Werner (WA) 1317 G St NW, Washington, DC 20005

KRAUS, Susan (Me) PO Box 1002, 77 Bristol Rd, Damariscotta, ME 04543

KRAUSE, David (Dal) 12109 Mossygate Trl, Manor, TX 78653

KRAUSE, Janice (Tex) 12109 Mossygate Trl, Manor, TX 78653

KRAUSS, Harry Edward (NY) 2 W 90th St Apt 5b, New York, NY 10024

KREAMER, Martha (CGC) PO Box 57, Lillian, AL 36549

KREITLER, Peter Gwillim (Los) 16492 El Hito Ct, Pacific Palisades, CA 90272

KREJCI, Richard Scott (Va) 346 Laurel Farms Ln, Urbanna, VA 23175

KRELL, Thomas William (Mich) 16200 W 12 Mile Rd, Southfield, MI 48076

KRELLER, Daniel Ward (Nwk) 2933 N Sheridan Rd Apt 509, Chicago, IL 60657

KREMER, Gregory J (Roch)

KRENGEL, William Erich (Ct) 191 Margarite Rd, Middletown, CT 06457

KREUTZER, Michael Alan (SO) 7 Lonsdale Ave, Dayton, OH 45419

KRIEGER, Frederick Gordon (SO) 707-5450 Kaye Street, Halifax, NS B3K 0G7, Canada

KRIEGER, Walter Lowell (Be) 25 Spruce St, Topton, PA 19562

KRISS, Gary W (Alb) PO Box 26, Cambridge, NY 12816

KROH, Timothy E (NwPa)

KROLL, Brenda M (Ark) 1402 Pagosa Trl, Carrollton, TX 75007

KROM, Judith Sue (NJ) 410 S Atlantic Ave, Beach Haven, NJ 08008

KROMHOUT, Linda Adams (CFla) 2104 Golden Arm Rd, Deltona, FL 32738

KRONENBERG, Elizabeth Grace (Los)

KROOHS, Ken (NC) 700 Sunset Dr, High Point, NC 27262

KROOHS, Mary (NC) 1700 Queen St, Winston Salem, NC 27103

KROPP, Catherine Amy (Ak)

✠ **KROTZ**, James (Neb) 3484 520th Rd, Rushville, NE 69360

KRUDYS, Emily Judin (Va) PO Box 11, Montpelier, VA 23192

KRUEGER, Albert Peter (Ore) 1926 W Burnside St Unit 909, Portland, OR 97209

KRUGER, Andrew David (NJ) 205 North Ave E, Cranford, NJ 07016

KRUGER, Ann (CFla) 167 Clear Lake Cir, Sanford, FL 32773

KRUGER, Diane Renee (Kan) 7404 E Killarney Pl, Wichita, KS 67206

KRUGER, Matthew Carl (Mass) 81 Elm St, Concord, MA 01742

KRUGER, Susan Marie (Minn) 1711 Stanford Ave, Saint Paul, MN 55105

KRULAK JR, Victor Harold (SanD) 3118 Canon St Apt 4, San Diego, CA 92106

KRULAK, William Morris (Md) 113 W Hughes St, Baltimore, MD 21230

KRUMBHAAR, Andrew Ramsay (CFla) 144 Carretera Chapala-Ajijic, Pmb 108, San Antonio Tlaycapan, JAL 45900, Mexico

KRUMLAUF, Dennis Skyler (CFla)

KRUMME, Judith Sterner (Mass) 349 Simon Willard Rd, Concord, MA 01742

KRUTZ, Charles (La) 14205 Woodland Ridge Ave, Baton Rouge, LA 70816

KRYDER-REID, Thomas Marshall (Ind) 5354 Olympia Dr, Indianapolis, IN 46228

KRYZAK, Andrew Astwood (Ct) 628 Main St, Stamford, CT 06901

KUBBE, AnnaLeigh (EMich) Diocese of Eastern Michigan, 924 N Niagara St, Saginaw, MI 48602

KUBICEK, Chief (Md) 8400 Greenspring Ave, Stevenson, MD 21153

KUBLER, Barry P (SwFla) 1223 Wild Daisy Dr, Plant City, FL 33563

KUEHN, Craig (The Episcopal NCal) 2821 Bronzecrest St, Placerville, CA 95667

KUEHN, Jerome Frederick (FdL) 806 4th St, Algoma, WI 54201

KUENNETH, John (Tenn) 538 Hickory Trail Dr, Nashville, TN 37209

KUGLER, Michael (Ia)

KUHLMANN, Martha Chandler (Cal) 107 Franciscan Dr, Danville, CA 94526

KUHN, Darlene (WMich)

KUHN, Michael (La) Trinity Episcopal School, 1315 Jackson Ave, New Orleans, LA 70130

KUHN, Philip James (Mass) 25 Wood lane, Maynard, MA 01754

KUHN, Thomas Randall (EC) 328 Kelly Ave, Oak Hill, WV 25901

KUHNS, Patricia Drost (Eas) 7 Chadwick Terrace, Easton, MD 21601

KUHR, Carolyn S (Mont) 2409 West Irene Street, Boise, ID 83702
KUHR, Elisabeth Schader (Spok) 2490 Thompson Rd, Cowiche, WA 98923
KUJAWA-HOLBROOK, Sheryl Anne (Los) 1644 Carmel Cir E, Upland, CA 91784
KUKOWSKI, Richard George (WA) 10450 Lottsford Rd Apt 154, Mitchellville, MD 20721
KULAK, Joshua B (Tex) 103 W 30th St Apt 401, Apt 401, Austin, TX 78705
KULP, John Eugene (SwFla) 17 W Vernon Ave Unit 301, Phoenix, AZ 85003
KUNDINGER, Hazel Doris (CFla) 2404 Fairway Dr, Melbourne, FL 32901
KUNHARDT III, Philip B (NY) Po Box 33, Waccabuc, NY 10597
KUNKLE JR, George Owen (RG) 1914 Tijeras Rd, Santa Fe, NM 87505
KUNZ JR, Carl (Del) PO Box 5856, Wilmington, DE 19808
KUNZ, Phyllis Ann (Minn) 67982 260th Ave, Kasson, MN 55944
KUNZ, Rich (NY) 99 Ridgetop Cir Unit 202, Brevard, NC 28712
KUOL, Agook Kon (Tex) 1225 Texas St, Houston, TX 77002
KUOL, Daniel Kuch (Ky) 8701 Shepherdsville Rd, Louisville, KY 40219
KURATKO, Lauren (NY) 3110 Ashford Dunwoody Rd NE, Atlanta, GA 30319
KURATKO, Ryan (NY) PO Box 788, Mechanicsville, VA 23111
KURIA, Janet Kabui (Md) 6515 Loch Raven Blvd, Loch Hill, MD 21239
KURKOWSKI, Nicole P (NJ)
KURTH, Michael Benjamin Evington (Del) 2 Rectory St, Rye, NY 10580
KURTZ, James Edward (CFla) 1352 Seburn Rd, Apopka, FL 32703
KURTZ, Kelli Grace (Los) 4451 Ramona Dr, Riverside, CA 92506
KURTZ, Margaret Eileen (Ida) 3185 E Rivernest Dr, Boise, ID 83706
KUSCHEL, Catherine Mary (Eau) 3774 Goodwin Ave N, Oakdale, MN 55128
KUSKY, Donna Lee Stewart (EMich) 13685 Block Rd, Birch Run, MI 48415
KWAN, Franco (Cal) 425 Swallowtail Ct, Brisbane, CA 94005
KWIATKOWSKI, Jan (Mil) 9333 W Goodrich Ave, Milwaukee, WI 53224
KYLE, Anne Meredith (WMo) Calvary Episcopal Church, 713 S Ohio Ave, Sedalia, MO 65301
KYLE, Michael Raymond (Mo) 3932 Oxford Rd, Jefferson City, MO 65109

L

LABARRE, Barbara L Root (Okla) 10901 S Yale Ave, Tulsa, OK 74137
LABATT, Walter Bruce (Mo) 520 Coventry Cir, Dexter, MI 48130

LABELLE, Philip N (Mass) 27 Main St, Southborough, MA 01772
LABORDA HARRIS, Christy (The Episcopal NCal) St. Stephen's Episcopal Church, PO Box 98, Sebastopol, CA 95472
LABORDE, Jean Jonas (Hai)
LABUD, Richard John (CFla) 28097 Se Highway 42, Umatilla, FL 32784
LACEY, Maryanne (SanD) 3208 Old Heather Rd, San Diego, CA 92111
LACOMBE III, Edgar Arthur (Alb) 607 Curtis St, Ogdensburg, NY 13669
LACROSSE, Diana Parsons (Dal) 2700 Warren Cir, Irving, TX 75062
LACY, Mimi (SVa) 1245 Hartford Dr, Virginia Beach, VA 23464
LACY II, Thomas Alonzo (Fla) St Annes Episcopal Church, PO Box 889, Tifton, GA 31793
✠ **LADEHOFF SR**, Robert Louis (Ore) 1330 SW 3rd Ave Apt P8, Portland, OR 97201
LAFFLER, Brian H (Nwk) 72 Lodi St, Hackensack, NJ 07601
LAFLER, Mark Alan (CFla) 33929 Venice Ln, Sorrento, FL 32776
LAFON, Kirk David (At) 950 Episcopal School Way, Knoxville, TN 37932
LAFOREST, Charlotte (WMass) St Andrews Episcopal Church, 335 Longmeadow St, Longmeadow, MA 01106
LAFRANCE, Shawn Vincent (NH)
LAGANA, Gaye Lynn (Nev) PO Box 18917, Spokane, WA 99228
LAGER, Michael A (Ark) 2708 Canterbury Cir, Fort Smith, AR 72903
LAGMAN, Jo Ann J (Chi)
LAGO, Ana Mercedes (PR)
LAGUERRE, Jackson (Hai)
LAHAR, Teresa Rosanne (WK)
LAHEY, Stephen Edmund (Neb) 1935 Sewell St, Lincoln, NE 68502
✠ **LAI**, David (Tai) 7- Lane 105, Hangchow S - Road Sec 1, Taipei, 10060, Taiwan
LAI, Paul C (LI) 1321 College Point Blvd, College Point, NY 11356
LAINE, Jeanty (SeFla) 404 Sw 3rd St, Delray Beach, FL 33444
LAINSON, Vinnie (Va) 9325 West Street, Manassas, VA 20110
LAIRD, Daniel Dale (NC) 1737 Hillandale Rd, Durham, NC 27705
LAIRD, I Bruce (Colo) 606 Newnan St, Carrollton, GA 30117
LAIRD, Lucinda Rawlings (Eur) 330 N Hubbards Ln, Louisville, KY 40207
LAIRD, Robert C (Oly) 316 E 88th St, New York, NY 10128
LAITE JR, Robert Emerson (Me) 200 Main St, Thomaston, ME 04861
LAKE, Mark William (RG) 2602 S 2nd St, Tucumcari, NM 88401
LALONDE, Kathryn Nan (Pgh) 100 Great Pl Ne, Albuquerque, NM 87113

LALONDE, Walter Joseph (Ala) 139 N Jefferson Ave, Canonsburg, PA 15317
LALOR, Donald Jene (Minn)
LAM, Connie M Ng (Los) 133 E Graves Ave, Monterey Park, CA 91755
LAM, Peter (LI) 33 Howard Pl, Waldwick, NJ 07463
LAM, Vivian P (LI) 500 S Country Rd, Bay Shore, NY 11706
LA MACCHIA, James R (Mass) 32 Mountain Ash Dr, Kingston, MA 02364
LAMAZARES, Gabe (NC) 2412 Cascadilla St, Durham, NC 27704
LAMB, Jan M (NC) 3064 Colony Rd Apt D, Durham, NC 27705
✠ **LAMB**, Jerry Alban (The Episcopal NCal) 1065 Villita Loop, Las Cruces, NM 88007
LAMB, Ridenour Newcomb (Ga) 2425 Cherry Laurel Ln., Albany, GA 31705
LAMB, Thomas Jennings (Chi) 503 Macon Dr, Rockford, IL 61109
LAMB, Trevor Vanderveer (CFla) 316 Ocean Dunes Rd, Daytona Beach, FL 32118
LAMB, Watson (La) 10701 Saint Francis Dr, Philadelphia, MS 39350
LAMBELET, Nicole (NI)
LAMBERS, August Jacob (Ak)
LAMBERT, Bob (SD) 1568 Addison Ave, Rapid City, SD 57702
LAMBERT, Dave (Ala) TEC Ch Of The Epiphany, 1338 Montevallo Rd, Leeds, AL 35094
LAMBERT, Gary (Mil) 205 Nichols Rd, Monona, WI 53716
LAMBERT, George A (Me) 259 Essex St Apt 3, Bangor, ME 04401
LAMBERT, John Peck (Oly) 26621 128th Ave Se, Kent, WA 98030
LAMBERT, Leandra Lisa (LI) 254 Hicks St, Brooklyn, NY 11201
✠ **LAMBERT JR**, Rt Rev Paul E (Dal) 123 Wild Heron Rd, Savannah, GA 31419
LAMBERT, Vicki (Minn)
✠ **LAMBERT III**, William Jay (Eau) 603 Gibson Street, Leesburg, FL 34748
LAMBIS, Luz Maria (Colom)
LAMBORN, Amy (Tenn) The General Theo Sem, 440 West 21st Street, New York, NY 10011
LAMBORN, Rob (Tenn) Otey Memorial Parish, PO Box 267, Sewanee, TN 37375
LAMKIN, Melissa (Ct) 139 W 91st St, New York, NY 10024
LAMMING, Sarah Rebecca (WA) 2 Horseshoe Way, Market Rasen, LN8 3FN, Great Britain (UK)
LAMONTAGNE, Allen Allen (Eas) 167b Beach Rd, Banner Elk, NC 28604
LAMPE, Christine Kay (WK) 710 N Main St, Garden City, KS 67846
LAMPERT, Richard B (SwFla) 826 Hampton Wood Ct, Sarasota, FL 34232

Clergy List

LAMPHERE, Mary Kathryn (Spok) 15319 E 8th Ave, Spokane Valley, WA 99037

LANCASTER, James Mansell (Miss) 2721 Brumbaugh Rd, Ocean Springs, MS 39564

LANCE, Philip J (Los) 839 N June St, Los Angeles, CA 90038

LANDER, Barbara Temple (ND) 319 S 5th St, Grand Forks, ND 58201

LANDER III, James Rollin (Los) 1101 E Terrace St 202, Seattle, WA 98122

LANDER, Stephen King (Minn) 5029 Girard Ave S, Minneapolis, MN 55419

LANDERS, Davidson Texada (Ala) 5220 Midway Cir, Tuscaloosa, AL 35406

LANDERS JR, Edward Leslie (Tenn) 6536 Jocelyn Hollow Rd, Nashville, TN 37205

LANDERS, Gail Joan (Md) 12400 Manor Road, PO Box 4001, Glen Arm, MD 21057

LANDERS, Greg Leroy (NY) 2150 Baileys Corner Rd, Wall Township, NJ 07719

LANDERS, Kay Marie (Los) 1136 Scenic View St, Upland, CA 91784

LANDERS, Sylvia C (Neb) 206 Westridge Drive, Norfolk, NE 68701

LANDEWEER, Marc Yeong Hoon (Minn)

LANDRETH, Robert Dean (Mass) 7 Mechanic Sq, Marblehead, MA 01945

LANDRITH, Richard Stanley (EO) 123 S G St, Lakeview, OR 97630

LANDRY, Brad (Ala) St Pauls Episcopal Church, 1018 E Grayson St, San Antonio, TX 78208

LANDRY, Robert W (Me)

LANE III, Calvin (SO) St Georges Episcopal Church, 5520 Far Hills Ave, Dayton, OH 45429

LANE, Charles Lewis (Ia)

LANE III, Edward Jacob (Ky)

LANE, John Charles (Oly) 311 Ridge Dr, Port Townsend, WA 98368

LANE, Johnny (Ga) Route #4, Leslie Road, Box 1455, Americus, GA 31709

LANE, Joseph Andrew (Cal) 527 E Woodbury Rd, Altadena, CA 91001

LANE, Keith Cecil (NY) 487 Hudson St, New York, NY 10014

LANE, Nancy Upson (CNY)

LANE, Peter (Chi) 1346 E Madison Park, Chicago, IL 60615

LANE, Peter Austin (SwFla) 1601 Curlew Rd, Palm Harbor, FL 34683

LANE, Stephen E (WNY) 15 Fernhill Ave, Buffalo, NY 14215

LANE, Stephen Taylor (Me) 1400 East Ave Apt 313, #313, Rochester, NY 4610

LANE, William Benjamin (Del) 117 Millers Run, Glen Mills, PA 19342

LANG, Anne Adele (FdL)

LANG, Deborah L. (Chi) 8206 PENNY LN, Richmond, IL 60071

LANG, Ellen Davis (SD) 3504 E. Woodsedge St., Sioux Falls, SD 57108

LANG, Mark William (NwT) 727 W Browning Ave, Pampa, TX 79065

LANG, Martha Ellen (Ia) 2101 Nettle Ave, Muscatine, IA 52761

LANG, Nicholas Gerard (Ct) 14 France St, Norwalk, CT 06851

LANG, Thomas Andrew (Ore) 2812 Ne Kaster Dr, Hillsboro, OR 97124

LANGDON, Clarence (Chi) 1249 Hedgerow Dr, Grayslake, IL 60030

LANGDON, David (Miss) PO Box 40, Parchman, MS 38738

LANGENFELD, Robert Joseph (Minn) 615 Vermillion St, Hastings, MN 55033

LANGE-SOTO, Anna Beatriz (Cal) 1503 E Campbell Ave, Campbell, CA 95008

LANGEVIN, Ann Elizabeth (Nev) St Thomas Episcopal Church, 5383 E Owens Ave, Las Vegas, NV 89110

LANGFELDT, John Addington (EO) 1000 Vey Way Apt 361, The Dalles, OR 97058

LANGFORD, Thomas William (Spr) 873 S Park Ave, Springfield, IL 62704

LANGILLE, David (Minn) Messiah Episcopal Church, 1631 Ford Pkwy, Saint Paul, MN 55116

LANGLE, Susan (NH) Unit 6, 26 Myrtle St, Claremont, NH 03743

LANGLEY III, Raleigh (CFla) 6710 Wolf Pen Branch Rd, Harrods Creek, KY 40027

LANGLOIS, Donald Harold (Spr) 916 W Loughlin Dr, Chandler, AZ 85225

LANGSTON, Michael Griffith (NC) 3916 N Potsdam Ave Pmb 4544, Sioux Falls, SD 57104

LANIER, Justin (Vt) 200 Pleasant St, Bennington, VT 05201

LANIER, Stanley Lin (At) PO Box 637, Waycross, GA 31502

LANIGAN, Sean Robert (Pa) 36 Ardmore Ave, Ardmore, PA 19003

LANNING JR, James Clair (Chi) 1315 W. Roosevelt Rd., Wheaton, IL 60187

LANPHERE, Lynette (Ala) 8132 Becker Ln, Leeds, AL 35094

LAPENTA-H, Sarah (ECR) 4775 Cambridge St, Boulder, CO 80301

LAPRE, Alfred Charles (Ct) 616 Shamrock Dr, Fredericksburg, VA 22407

LAQUINTANO, David (NJ) 2998 Bay Ave, Ocean City, NJ 08226

LARA, Juana (Dal) St Barnabas Episcopal Church, 1200 N Shiloh Rd, Garland, TX 75042

LARA, Lino (Dal) 5923 Royal Ln, Dallas, TX 75230

LARA, Pedro De Jesus (Mil) 115 N 5th St, Delavan, WI 53115

LARCOMBE, David John (Vt) 37 Premo Rd, Roxbury, VT 05669

LAREMORE, Darrell Lee (SeFla) 6003 Back Bay Ln, Austin, TX 78739

LARGE, Alexander R (Tex) 717 Sage Rd, Houston, TX 77056

LARGENT, Lacy (Tex) PO Box 151, Navasota, TX 77868

LARIBEE JR, Richard (CNY) 230 Owensville Rd, West River, MD 20778

LARIMORE, Collin Kenneth (WMo)

LARIVE, Armand Edward (Spok) 4812 Fremont Ave, Bellingham, WA 98229

LARKIN, Greg (Los) 1251 Las Posas Rd, Camarillo, CA 93010

LARKIN, Lauren Renee Ellis (Colo)

LAROCCA, Lucy D(riscoll) (Ct) 1109 Main St, Branford, CT 06405

LAROCHE WILSON, Jill Monica (Pa) 246 Fox Rd, Media, PA 19063

LAROM JR, Richard U (NY) PO Box 577, Ivoryton, CT 06442

LARRIMORE, Chip Barker (Cal) 61 Santa Rosa Ave, Sausalito, CA 94965

LARSEN, Amy Louise (Episcopal SJ)

LARSEN, Gilbert Steward (Ct) 9160 Sw 193rd Cir, Dunnellon, FL 34432

LARSEN JR, Jim (Pa) PO Box 341490, Dayton, OH 45434

LARSEN, Matthew David (Dal) 3966 McKinney Ave, Dallas, TX 75204

LARSEN, Peter Michael (LI) 515 Eastlake Dr, Muscle Shoals, AL 35661

LARSON, Derek Michael (SeFla)

LARSON, Donna J (WMass) 958 North 32nd Street, Allentown, PA 18104

LARSON, Frances Jean (Minn) 1010 1st Ave N, Wheaton, MN 56296

LARSON, John Milton (Los) 2665 Tallant Rd Apt W307, Santa Barbara, CA 93105

LARSON JR, Lawrence John (Cal) 1835 NW Lantana Dr, Corvallis, OR 97330

LARSON, Robert Anton (Colo) P.O. Box 563, Ouray, CO 81427

LARSON, Rowan Julian (Mass) 76 Normandy Ave, Cambridge, MA 02138

LARSON, Steven Shaw (Ga) PO Box 74, Swainsboro, GA 30401

LARSON, Wayne Harold (Md) 1751 Firestone Plaza, Palm Springs, CA 92264

LARSON-MILLER, Lizette (Cal) 926 Santa Fe Ave, Albany, CA 94706

LA RUE, Howard Arlen (Va) PO Box 72, Searsport, ME 04974

LA RUE, Michael Dreyer (Tex)

LASCH, Ian (Ga) 8605 Spoon Dr, Saint Louis, MO 63132

LASCH, Loren V (Ga) Diocese Of Missouri, 1210 Locust St # 3, Saint Louis, MO 63103

LASH, Rebecca Henry (NwPa) 870 Diamond Park, Meadville, PA 16335

LASITER JR, Douglas Norman (La) 302 Greenwood St, Morgan City, LA 70380

LASKOWSKI, Kevin R (Va)

LASLEY, Jerry Drew (EMich)

LASSALLE, David Fredric (SVa) 1336 Bolling Ave, Norfolk, VA 23508

LASSEN, Coryl J (Cal) 2601 Hilltop Dr., 1311, Richmond, CA 94806

LASSITER, Jesse Ray (NJ)

LASSITER, Richard Bruce (Nev) 1311 Ramona Ln, Boulder City, NV 89005

LATHAM, Betty Craft (ETenn) 628 Magnolia Vale Dr, Chattanooga, TN 37419

LATHAM, Jennifer Briggs (The Episcopal Church in Haw)

LATHROP, Brian Albert (NY) 63 Downing St Apt 4-A, New York, NY 10014

LATHROP, John (Me) 101 Paseo Encantado Ne, Santa Fe, NM 87506

LATIMER, Susan (SanD) 28813 Snead Dr, Sun City, CA 92586

LATOUR, Charles H (La)

LATTA, Dennis James (Ind) 2742 S Hickory Corner Rd, Vincennes, IN 47591

✠ **LATTIME**, Mark A (Ak) 1205 Denali Way, Fairbanks, AK 99701

LAU, Ronald Taylor Christensen (LI) 326 Clinton St, Brooklyn, NY 11231

LAU, Wai Lun (Los)

LAUCHER, Bill (Tex) 2811 Laporte Ave, Fort Collins, CO 80521

LAUDISIO, Patricia Devin (Colo) 3328 Sentinel Dr, Boulder, CO 80301

LAUER, Daniel Donald (WTex) 2006 Pinetree Ln, San Antonio, TX 78232

LAUGHERY, Martha Christine (Wyo)

LAUGHLIN III, Ledlie (WA) 4201 Albemarle St NW, Washington, DC 20016

LAUGHLIN, Ophelia (NJ) Waterman Avenue, Rumson, NJ 07760

LAUGHMAN JR, Richard (The Episcopal NCal) StJames of Jerusalem TEC Ch, 556 N G W Blvd, Yuba City, CA 95993

LAUK, Candice Ruth (NMich) 1003 Wickman Dr, Iron Mountain, MI 49801

LAURA, Ronald Samuel (Vt) 158 Concord Rd Apt K9, Billerica, MA 01821

LAURINEC, Jennene Ellen (Tex) 308 Cottage Rd., Carthage, TX 75633

LAURITZEN, Ruth (Wyo)

LAUTENSCHLAGER, Paul John (Colo) 11 W Madison St, Colorado Springs, CO 80907

LAUZON, Marcia (Mont)

LAVALLEE, Armand Aime (Ct) 5523 Birchhill Rd, Mint Hill, NC 28227

LAVALLEE, Donald Alphonse (RI) 1665 Broad St, Cranston, RI 02905

LAVANN, Jason Gary (Mil) 216 E Chandler Blvd, Burlington, WI 53105

LAVELLE, Jon Frederick (CNY) 51 Colonial Cir, Buffalo, NY 14222

LAVENGOOD, Henrietta Louise (NJ) 211 Falls Ct, Medford, NJ 08055

LAVENGOOD, Martin (NJ) 211 Falls Ct, Medford, NJ 08055

LAVER, Michael Scott (Roch) 121 Crawford St, Rochester, NY 14620

LAVERY, Patricia Anne (NwPa) PO Box 287, Grove City, PA 16127

LAVETTY, Denise Jean (NY) 224 Waverly Pl, New York, NY 10014

LAVINE, Patricia Iva (Alb) 323 Lakeshore Dr, Norwood, NY 13668

LAVOE, John F (CNY) 210 Yoxall Ln, Oriskany, NY 13424

LAW, Eric H F (Los) PO Box 1189, Rancho Mirage, CA 92270

LAWBAUGH, William (CPa) 813 Franklin Ave, Aliquippa, PA 15001

LAWLER, Gary Elwyn Andrew (Chi) 6033 N Sheridan Rd Apt 27j, Chicago, IL 60660

LAWLER, Karen (The Episcopal NCal)

LAWLER, Kathy (The Episcopal NCal)

LAWLER, Rick (WNC) PO Box 2680, Blowing Rock, NC 28605

LAWLER, Steven W (Mo) 600 Lee Ave, Saint Louis, MO 63119

LAWLOR, Jay R (WMich) Diocese of Western Michigan, 535 S Burdick St Ste 1, Kalamazoo, MI 49007

LAWRENCE JR, Albert Sumner (Tex) 14 Sedgewick Pl, The Woodlands, TX 77382

LAWRENCE, Amy (Cal) 2711 Harkness St, Sacramento, CA 95818

LAWRENCE, Bruce Bennett (NC) C/O Department Of Religion, Duke University, Durham, NC 27706

LAWRENCE, Catherine Abbott (NY) 1415 Pelhamdale Ave, Christ Church, Pelham, NY 10803

LAWRENCE, Dean (WVa) 221 E Washington St, Charles Town, WV 25414

LAWRENCE, Eric John (Nev) 2306 Paradise Dr Apt 222, Reno, NV 89512

LAWRENCE, Gerard Martin (Mass) 22874 NE 127th Way, Redmond, WA 98053

LAWRENCE JR, Harry Martin (ETenn) 1800 Lula Lake Rd, Lookout Mountain, GA 30750

LAWRENCE, John Elson (WA) 4336 Wordsworth Way, Venice, FL 34293

LAWRENCE, Matthew Richard (Ore) 1515 NW 28th Ave Apt 15, Portland, OR 97210

LAWRENCE, Phil (Okla) 32251 S 616 Rd, Grove, OK 74344

LAWRENCE JR, Raymond Johnson (SwVa) 913 Ash Tree Ln., Niskayuna, NY 12309

LAWRENCE, Wade William (Pgh) 6911 Prospect Ave, Pittsburgh, PA 15202

LAWS III, Robert J (NJ) 30513 Washington St, Princess Anne, MD 21853

LAWS, Tom (Nwk) 11 Harvard St, Montclair, NJ 07042

LAWSON, Daniel Matthew Custance (Mich) 1631 Stoney Brook Dr, Rochester Hills, MI 48309

LAWSON, Frederick Quinney (U) 4294 S Adonis Dr, Salt Lake City, UT 84124

LAWSON, Neil-St Barnabas J (Episcopal SJ) P.O. Box 7606, Stockton, CA 95267

LAWSON, Paul (Los) 567 Mayflower Rd, Claremont, CA 91711

LAWSON, Peter Raymond (Cal) 805 N Webster St, Petaluma, CA 94952

LAWSON, Richard (Colo) 1350 N Washington St, Denver, CO 80203

LAWSON, Rolfe Adrian (Vt)

LAWSON, Shirley May (NY)

LAWSON-BECK, David Roswell (NJ) 143 W Milton Ave, Apt 4, Rahway, NJ 07065

✠ **LAWTON**, Fraser Wynn (Dal)

LAWYER, Evelyn Virden (Minn) 4539 Keithson Dr, Arden Hills, MN 55112

LAYCOCK, John Emerson (Mich) PO Box 137, 7112 Kauffman Blvd, Presque Isle, MI 49777

LAYCOCK JR, Ralph Bradley (SwVa) 2725 Wilshire Ave SW, Roanoke, VA 24015

LAYDEN, Daniel Keith (NI) 11009 Brandy Oak Run, Fort Wayne, IN 46845

LAYNE, Robert Patterson (Kan) The Cedars, 807 N Maxwell St, Mc Pherson, KS 67460

LAYTON, Mindy Jane (NY) 61 Gramercy Park N Fl 2, New York, NY 10010

LAZARD, Amirold (Hai)

LAZO, Andrew (CFla) 1257 S Park Ave, Winter Garden, FL 34787

LAZZURI, Jennifer Lynn (Ha)

LEA, Gail Ann (U) PO Box 96, Moab, UT 84532

LEA, William Howard (Ga) 1 Fair Hope Ln, Savannah, GA 31411

LEACH, Alex (The Episcopal NCal) 3006 Goshawk St, Davis, CA 95616

LEACH, JoAnn Zwart (Ore) 3721 N Kingswood Way, Flagstaff, AZ 86004

LEACH, Marilyn May (Minn)

LEACH, Shannon (Nev) 8400 Paseo Vista Dr, Las Vegas, NV 89128

LEACOCK, Rob (Ark) 8605 Verona Trl, Austin, TX 78749

LEAMAN, Kris (Ia) 120 1st St NE, Mason City, IA 50401

LEANILLO, Ricardo Ivan (SwFla) 5033 9th St, Zephyrhills, FL 33542

LEANNAH, Scott Robert (Mil) 3734 S 86th St, Milwaukee, WI 53228

LEARY, Charles Randolph (SO) 133 Croskey Boulevard, Medway, OH 45341

LEARY, Kevin David (Ct) 15 Rimmon Rd, Woodbridge, CT 06525

LEAS, Bercry Eleanor (Mich) 7051 Wakan Ln., Corryton, TN 37721

LEAVITT, Christie Plehn (Nev) 1739 Carita Ave, Henderson, NV 89014

LE BARRON, Bruce Erie (WK) 3218 White Tail Way, Salina, KS 67401

LEBEAU, Philip Henry (ECR) 23 Millar Ave, San Jose, CA 95127

LEBENS ENGLUND, Paul (Minn) 519 Oak Grove St, Minneapolis, MN 55403

LE BLANC, Fran Andre Telles (Md) 204 Monument Rd, Orleans, MA 02653

LEBLANC, Tracy Jean (Ore) 15416 Ne 90th St, Vancouver, WA 98682

LEBRIJA, Lorenzo (SanD) 3737 Seminary Rd, Alexandria, VA 22304

LEBROCQ JR, Eric Francis (Tex) St. John's Episcopal Church, PO Box 1477, Sealy, TX 77474

LEBRON, Robert Emmanuel (Mil) 409 E. Court St., Janesville, WI 53545

LEBUS, Jesse Williams (LI) 1670 Route 25a, Cold Spring Harbor, NY 11724

LECLAIR, Arthur Anthony (Colo) 8221 E Fremont Cir, Englewood, CO 80112

LECLAIR, Paul Joseph (Mich) 1434 E 13 Mile Rd, Madison Heights, MI 48071

LECLAIRE, Patrick Harry (Nev) 620 W B St, Fallon, NV 89406

LECLERC, Charles Edward (NH) 1873 Dover Rd, Epsom, NH 03234

LECORBEILLER, Suzanne Hayden (Ida)

LECOUTEUR II, Eugene Hamilton (Va) PO Box 622, Middleburg, VA 20118

LEDERHOUSE, Susan (Mass) 237 N Main St Apt 409, South Yarmouth, MA 02664

LEDERMAN, Maureen Elizabeth (Ct) 124 Midland Dr, Meriden, CT 06450

LEDFORD, Marcia (Mich) 959 Sherman St, Ypsilanti, MI 48197

LEDGERWOOD, Mary Jayne (CGC) 1900 Dauphin St, Mobile, AL 36606

LEDIARD SR, Daniel E (EO) PO Box 681, Virginia City, NV 89440

LEDIARD, Jo Anne (Spok) 1609 W 10th Ave, Kennewick, WA 99336

LEDYARD, Flo (Md) 1021 Bosley Rd, Cockeysville, MD 21030

LEE, Alan C (NY)

LEE, Alison (Az) 423 N Beaver St, Flagstaff, AZ 86001

LEE III, Arthur R (SwFla) 3217 SW 126th Ter, Archer, FL 32618

LEE, Betsy A. (Minn) 4901 Triton Dr, Golden Valley, MN 55422

LEE, Caleb J (EC) 215 Ann St, Beaufort, NC 28516

LEE, Chen-Cheng (Tai) No. 311 Sec.2, Chieding Rd, Chieding District, Kaohsiung City, 85241, Taiwan

LEE, Christine Kim (NY) St Peters Chelsea, 346 W 20th St, New York, NY 10011

LEE, David Edward (Va) 2343 Highland Ave, Charlottesville, VA 22903

LEE, Deborah Annette (NY) 54 E 83rd St Apt 3c, New York, NY 10028

LEE, Donald Dearman (WTex) Po Box 545, Bandera, TX 78003

LEE JR, Edward Lewis (WMich) The Quadrangle Apt 3315, 3300 Darby Rd, Haverford, PA 19041

LEE, Enoch (Tai) North 1-6, Ming-Shin Street, Hualien, Taiwan

LEE, Grace (Va)

LEE, Hosea Mun-Yong (Nwk) 1600 Parker Ave Apt 3-D, Fort Lee, NJ 07024

LEE, Hyacinth Evadne (NY) 50 Guion Pl, 5H, New Rochelle, NY 10801

LEE, Hyangnam (Los) 408 S Broadway, Redondo Beach, CA 90277

LEE, James Kyung-Jin (Los) Tec Ch Of The Messiah, 614 N Bush St, Santa Ana, CA 92701

LEE JR, James Oliver (Dal) 1729 S Beckley Ave, Dallas, TX 75224

✠ **LEE**, Jeff (Chi) 65 E Huron St, Chicago, IL 60611

LEE JR, John E (NMich) Rr 1 Box 586, Newberry, MI 49868

LEE, Judith (WMass) 36 Marion Rd E # 8540, Princeton, NJ 08540

LEE, Jui-Chiang (U) 163 Tung-Ming Rd., Keelung, Taiwan

LEE, Julia Hamilton (Ala)

LEE, Kristin Hope (Wyo) 2822 Olive Dr, Cheyenne, WY 82001

LEE, Linda (Ore)

LEE, Marc DuPlan (Kan) 4515 W Moncrieff Pl, Denver, CO 80212

LEE, Margaret Will (Chi) 3412 54th St, Moline, IL 61265

LEE, Mark Chong (RG) 23126 Airedale Lane, San Antonio, TX 78260

LEE, Maurice Charles (Spr) 3231 Alton Rd, Atlanta, GA 30341

LEE, Nathaniel Jung-Chul (NY) 209 Madison Ave, New York, NY 10016

LEE, Rhonda Mawhood (NC)

LEE, Richard Stanley (SanD) 4026 Ampudia St, San Diego, CA 92110

LEE, Robert Bruce (Vt) 51 Park St., Canaan, VT 05903

LEE III, Robert Vernon (Fla) 1131 N Laura St, Jacksonville, FL 32206

LEE, Samuel Sroun-Houi (Oly) 34608 8th Ave SW, Federal Way, WA 98023

LEE, Sang (Dal) 2783 Valwood Pkwy, Farmers Branch, TX 75234

LEE, Scott Charles (Ct) PO Box 3264 - 120 Short Road, Sewanee, TN 37375

LEE, Scott R (RI) St James the Apostle Epis Ch, 1803 Highland Hollow Dr, Conroe, TX 77304

LEE, Shirley Lynne (Ak) 1205 Denali Way, Fairbanks, AK 99701

LEE, Stedwart Warren Rubinstein (Episcopal VI) 261 Mount Pleasant, Frederiksted, VI 00840

LEE, Steven (NY) 1047 Amsterdam Ave, New York, NY 10025

LEE, Susan Hagood (Mass) 336 Maple St, New Bedford, MA 02740

LEE, Tammy (EC) 304 E Franklin St, Chapel Hill, NC 27514

LEE, Terence A (NY) 204 W 134th St, New York, NY 10030

LEE III, Thomas Carleton (LI) 3000 Galloway Ridge Apt D104, Pittsboro, NC 27312

LEE, Thomas Moon (Los) 510 Mable Mason Cv, La Vergne, TN 37086

LEE, Wanhong Barnabas (Md) St Johns Episcopal Church, 9120 Frederick Rd, Ellicott City, MD 21042

LEE, Wen-Hui (Tai) 5F No 7 Kee-King 2nd Road, Kee Lung City, 20446, Taiwan

LEE III, William Forrest (Md) PO Box 2188, Mountain Lake Park, MD 21550

LEECH, John (Oly)

LEED, Rolf (WMo) 2901 NE 72nd St # 188, Gladstone, MO 64119

LEEMHUIS, Guy Anthony (Los) 260 N Locust St, Inglewood, CA 90301

LEE PAE, Ju Young (LI)

LEES, Everett (Okla) 2613 W Broadway St, Broken Arrow, OK 74012

LEESON, Gary William (Los) 4457 Mont Eagle Pl, Los Angeles, CA 90041

LEFEVRE, Ann Raynor (Be) 1190 Bianca Dr Ne, Palm Bay, FL 32905

LEGER, Don Curtis (WLa) 919 Anthony Ave, Opelousas, LA 70570

LEGER, Jean Bob (Hai)

LEGG, Carolyn Ingrid Christensen (Ct)

LEGNANI, Bob (NJ) 22 Ashley Dr, Delran, NJ 08075

LEHMAN, Kitty (Cal) 705 W Main St, Kerrville, TX 78028

LEHMAN, Susan (SwVa) 550 E 4th St Unit U, Cincinnati, OH 45202

LEHRER, Christian Anton (WA) 13301 Baden Westwood Rd, Brandywine, MD 20613

LEIBHART, Linda (Roch) 9406 Chipping Dr, Richmond, VA 23237

LEIBOVITCH, Warren Neil (Az)

LEIDER, Jennifer (O) St. Paul's Episcopal Church, 798 S. Coy Rd., Oregon, OH 43616

LEIDHEISER-STODDARD, Margaret Clare (NC) Saint Marys School, 900 Hillsborough St, Raleigh, NC 27603

LEIGH, Joel Joseph (NJ) 238 Twilight Ave, Keansburg, NJ 07734

LEIGH-KOSER, Charlene M (CPa) 115 Nahant St, Lynn, MA 01902

LEIGHT, Susan Elaine (Eas)

LEIGH-TAYLOR, Christine (The Episcopal NCal) 4231 Oak Meadow Rd, Placerville, CA 95667

LEIGHTON, Tim (Spr) 1920 E Oakland Avenue, Bloomington, IL 61705

LEIKER, Diana Louise (WNY)

LEIN, Clay (Neb) 1102 Highland St, Houston, TX 77009

LEIN, John Elliott (Ark)

LEINBACH, Jeanne A (O) 2747 Fairmount Blvd, Cleveland Heights, OH 44106

LEININGER, Austin L (Colo) 6219 E 122nd Dr, Brighton, CO 80602

LEIP, Harry Louis (Mo) 600 N Euclid Ave, Saint Louis, MO 63108

LEISERSON, Joanna (SO) 2218 Oakland Ave, Covington, KY 41014
LEMA, Julio M (At) 1379 Craighill Ct, Norcross, GA 30093
LEMAIRE JR, Michael E (Cal) 2220 Cedar St, Berkeley, CA 94709
LEMAY, Anne Rae (NJ) 576 West Ave, Sewaren, NJ 07077
LEMBURG, David Wesley (Ga) 110 Dove Ln, Savannah, GA 31406
LEMBURG, Melanie Dickson (Ga) 1909 15th St, Gulfport, MS 39501
LEMERY, Gary Conrad (RI) 45 Bay View Drive North, Jamestown, RI 02835
LEMLER, James (Ind) Christ Church, 254 E Putnam Ave, Greenwich, CT 06830
LEMLEY, Daniel James (SwFla) 701 Orange Ave, Clearwater, FL 33756
LEMLEY, Kent Christopher (At) 764 Springlake Ln Nw, Atlanta, GA 30318
LEMMING, Craig P (Minn) St John TEC Ch, 60 Kent St, Saint Paul, MN 55102
LEMON, Karen Dillenbeck (WK) 20081 Sw 20th Ave, Pratt, KS 67124
LEMONS, Catherine (Minn) 12621 Old Columbia Pike, Silver Spring, MD 20904
LENARTOWICZ, Pam (EMich) 525 Weiss Rd, Gaylord, MI 49735
LENNE, Laurent Pierre (Eur)
LENNON, Evelyn Cromartie (Minn) 65a Lovell Rd, Fryeburg, ME 04037
LENNOX, Daniel Duncan (NY) 707 Washington St, Hoboken, NJ 07030
LENNSTROM, Brian (Oly) 1216 7th St, Anacortes, WA 98221
LENOIR, Robert Scott (Miss) 7416 Riverview St, Gautier, MS 39553
LENOW, Joseph Earl (Md)
LENT, Morris J (SC) 1855 Houghton Dr, Charleston, SC 29412
LENTEN, John William (NMich) 11 Longyear Dr, Negaunee, MI 49866
LENTZ, Benjamin Lee (Be) 9758 N Rome Rd, Athens, PA 18810
LENTZ III, Julian Carr (ECR) 1001 Sleepy Hollow Ln, Plainfield, NJ 07060
LENTZ, Preston (The Episcopal Church in Haw) 999 Wilder Ave Apt 1204, Honolulu, HI 96822
LENZO, Alex (RG) 1525 33rd Cir SE, Rio Rancho, NM 87124
LEO, Agnes Patricia (The Episcopal Church in Haw) 665 Paopua Loop, Kailua, HI 96734
LEO, Denise Florence (Pa) 400 S Jackson St, Media, PA 19063
LEO, Jason (SeFla) 3780 Clifton Ave, Cincinnati, OH 45220
LEON, Luis (WA) 4912 41st St NW, Washington, DC 20016
LEON, Sadoni (Hai) Eglesi Episcopal DHaiti, Boite Postale 1309, Port-au-Prince, Haiti
LEONARD, Alan (NJ) 320 Linda Anne Ave, Cape May, NJ 08204

LEONARD, Jaime (Mont) PO Box 267, Ennis, MT 59729
LEONARD, Sean T (Mass) St Dunstans Tec Ch, 18 Springdale Ave, Dover, MA 02030
LEONARD, Thomas Edgar (Az) 11 Avenida de la Herran Rd, Tubac, AZ 85646
LEONARD-PASLEY, Tricia (Ct) 680 Racebrook Rd, Orange, CT 06477
LEONETTI, Stephen (The Episcopal NCal) PO Box 6194, Vacaville, CA 95696
✠ **LEON-LOZANO**, Cristobal (Litoral Diocese Of Ecuador) Casilla 13-05-179, Manta, Ecuador
LEOPOLD, Bobby (Vt) 1616 Read Ave, Chattanooga, TN 37408
LEPLEY, Rebecca (EMich) 539 N William St, Marine City, MI 48039
LERENA, Angela Joy (Colo)
LERMOND, Sally Ann (WA)
LEROUX, Donald Francis (ND) 319 S 5th St, Grand Forks, ND 58201
LEROUX JR, Grant Meade (Ga) 5 Mooregate Square, Atlanta, GA 30327
LE ROY, Melinda Louise Perkins (WNC) 4 Flycatcher Way Unit 302, Arden, NC 28704
LERUD, Nathanael D (Ore) Trinity Episcopal Cathedral, 147 Nw 19th Ave, Portland, OR 97209
LESESNE JR, Gray (Ind) 125 Monument Cir, Indianapolis, IN 46204
LESH, Ryan Edwin (NY) 7423 S Broadway, Red Hook, NY 12571
LESIEUR, Betsy Ann (RI) 200 Heroux Blvd # 2001, Cumberland, RI 02864
LESIEUR, David Dexter (WTex)
LESLIE, Jo Marie (Md) 130 W Seminary Ave, Lutherville, MD 21093
LESLIE, Joanne (Los) 1351 Grant St, Santa Monica, CA 90405
LESLIE III, Richard B (ECR) 520 Lobos Ave, Pacific Grove, CA 93950
LESSMANN, Mary T (Dal) 8011 Douglas Avenue, Dallas, TX 75225
LESTER, Elmore William (LI) 1440 Tanglewood Pkwy, Fort Myers, FL 33919
LE SUEUR, Susan Dianne Lassey (NH) 18 Gaita Dr, Derry, NH 03038
LESWING, James B (Chi) 1003 Claremont Dr, Downers Grove, IL 60516
LETHIN, Judith Lynn Wegman (Ak) 3509 Wentworth St, Anchorage, AK 99508
LETHIN, Kris Walter (Ak) 175 Main St, Seldovia, AK 99663
LEVANWAY, William Douglas (ETenn)
LEVENSALER, Kurt H (The Episcopal NCal) St Timothys Church, 1550 Diablo Rd, Danville, CA 94526
LEVENSON JR, Russell J (Tex) St Martins Episcopal Church, 717 Sage Rd, Houston, TX 77056
LEVENSTRONG, Peter Townsend (Cal)

LEVESCONTE, Suzanne (SO) Trinity Episcopal Church, 115 N 6th St, Hamilton, OH 45011
LEVINE, Paul H (ECR) 720 S 3rd St Apt 5, San Jose, CA 95112
LEVY, Sandra Maria (Va) 9107 Donora Dr, Richmond, VA 23229
LEVY, William Turner (NY) 22121 Lanark St, Canoga Park, CA 91304
LEWALLEN, Jerrie (Ala) 174 Carpenter Cir, Sewanee, TN 37375
LEWALLEN, Theresa Cammarano (Va) St Albans Episcopal Church, 6800 Columbia Pike, Annandale, VA 22003
LEWELLEN, Donald S (Chi) 523 W Glen Ave, Peoria, IL 61614
LEWELLIS, Bill (Be) 3235 Clear Stream Dr, Whitehall, PA 18052
LEWIS III, Albert Davidson (ETenn) 340 Chamberlain Cove Rd, Kingston, TN 37763
LEWIS, Alice LaReign (EMich) 437n County Road 441, Manistique, MI 49854
LEWIS, Amy (Alb)
LEWIS, Barbara (Tex) 1401 Calumet St Unit 312, Houston, TX 77004
LEWIS, Barbara Ann (Nev) 1511 Cardinal Peak Ln Unit 101, Las Vegas, NV 89144
LEWIS, Barbara J (Pa) 88 Glen Mawr Dr, Ewing, NJ 08618
LEWIS, Catherine Blanc (Roch) 7086 Salmon Creek Rd, Williamson, NY 14589
LEWIS, Cynthia Jean (Nev)
LEWIS, Earl James (Del) 1313 Lee St E Apt 112, Charleston, WV 25301
LEWIS, Edwin L (Ct) 1864 Post Rd, Darien, CT 06820
LEWIS, Ernest Loran (The Episcopal NCal) 640 Hawthorne Ln, Davis, CA 95616
LEWIS JR, Irwin Morgan (SVa) 356 Westover Ave, Norfolk, VA 23507
LEWIS, Jason (Ky) 204 Monroe Ave, Belton, MO 64012
LEWIS, Jeffrey Clement (Me) St George's School, PO Box 1910, Newport, RI 02840
LEWIS, John (WTex) St Benedicts Workshop, 315 E Pecan St, San Antonio, TX 78205
LEWIS, John Walter (Me) 33 Knowlton St, Camden, ME 04843
LEWIS, Karen Burke (NJ) PO Box 605, Gladstone, NJ 07934
LEWIS, Karen Cichowski (Mich) 218 W Ottawa St, Lansing, MI 48933
LEWIS, Kate (Los) 265 W Sidlee St, Thousand Oaks, CA 91360
LEWIS, Katherine (Minn) 13000 Saint Davids Rd, Minnetonka, MN 55305
LEWIS, Kenneth Rutherford (Ala) 708 Fairfax Dr, Fairfield, AL 35064
LEWIS, Kristina Jean (Colo)
LEWIS, Laurie Ann (Kan) 3705 Edgemont St, Wichita, KS 67208
LEWIS, Lawrence Bernard (WMo) 415 Market Street, Osceola, MO 64776

Clergy List

LEWIS JR, Lloyd Alexander (LI) 5501 Seminary Rd Apt 812, Falls Church, VA 22041
LEWIS, Mabel (NY) 40 Barton St, Newburgh, NY 12550
LEWIS, Mark (Nwk) PO Box 93, Rensselaerville, NY 12147
LEWIS, Matthew W (Tenn) 900 Broadway, Nashville, TN 37203
LEWIS, Melanie Krosnes (Va)
LEWIS III, Philip Gregory (Oly)
LEWIS, Richard H (CNY) 52 Lawrence Dr Apt 211, Lowell, MA 01854
LEWIS, Richard Irvin (Spr)
LEWIS, Robert Michael (SanD) 2231 S Elks Ln Unit 64, Yuma, AZ 85364
LEWIS, Sarah Elizabeth (Md) 1055 Via Nandina Pl, Henderson, NV 89011
LEWIS, Sarah V (CNY) 52 Lawrence Drive Apt 211, Lowell, MA 01854
LEWIS, Sharon (SwFla) 3773 Wilkinson Rd, Sarasota, FL 34233
LEWIS, Stephen Charles (Okla)
LEWIS, Thom (SVa) 2702 W Market St, Greensboro, NC 27403
LEWIS, Timothy J (LI) PO Box 264, Wainscott, NY 11975
LEWIS, Walter England (Nwk) 60 Dryden Rd, Montclair, NJ 07043
LEWIS, William Benjamin (WA) 14110 Royal Forest Ln, Silver Spring, MD 20904
LEWIS, William George (CFla) 442 Sanderling Dr, Indialantic, FL 32903
LEWIS-HEADDEN, Margaret (Oly) P.O. Box 1997, 1036 Golf Course Rd., Friday Harbor, WA 98250
LEWIS-THEERMAN, Kristina D (NY) 91 Church St, Seymour, CT 02630
LEY, James Lawrence (Pa) 101 Lydia Ln, West Chester, PA 19382
LEYS, Donovan I (LI) 20931 111th Avenue, Queens Village, NY 11429
L'HOMMEDIEU, J Gary (CFla) 1433 Fairview St, Orlando, FL 32804
LIANG, Fan-Wei (Tai)
LIBBEY, Elizabeth Weaver (USC) 1140 Fork Creek Rd, Saluda, NC 28773
LIBBEY, Robert Edward (USC) 16 Salisbury Dr Apt 7410, Asheville, NC 28803
LIBBY, Glenn (Los) 835 W 34th Street 203, Los Angeles, CA 90089
LIBERATORE, James Vincent (Tex) 2706 Pebble Creek Dr, Pearland, TX 77581
LICARI, Luigi (Cal) 904-9 Deer Park Crescent, Toronto, ON M4V 2C4, Canada
LIEB, James Marcus (ECR) PO Box 293, Ben Lomond, CA 95005
LIEBER, William Louis (SanD) 8975 Lawrence Welk Dr Spc 77, Escondido, CA 92026
LIEBERT-HALL, Linda Ann (CFla) Shepherd of the Hills, 2540 W Norvell Bryant Hwy, Lecanto, FL 34461

LIEBLER, John (CFla) 2254 6th Ave SE, Vero Beach, FL 32962
LIEF, Richard C (SanD) 3212 Eichenlaub St, San Diego, CA 92117
LIEM, Jennifer E (Chi) 10 N Lake St Apt 315, Grayslake, IL 60030
LIENESCH, Elizabeth F (Minn)
LIERLE, Deane (Okla) 5037 E Via Montoya Dr, Phoenix, AZ 85054
LIESKE, Mark Stephen (Los) 4635 Border Village Rd # F1 Pmb 300, San Ysidro, CA 92173
LIETZ, Dennis Eugene (Chi) 935 Knollwood Rd, Deerfield, IL 60015
LIGGETT JR, Jim (NwT) 3518 Hyde Park Ave., Midland, TX 79707
✠ **LIGHT**, Arthur Heath (SwVa) 2524 Wycliffe Ave Sw, Roanoke, VA 24014
LIGHTCAP, Torey Lynn (Kan) 835 SW Polk St, Topeka, KS 66612
LIGHTSEY, Pamela Sue Willis (Ga) 2700 Pebblewood Dr, Valdosta, GA 31602
LIGHTSEY, Richard Brian (NI) 602 W Superior St, Kokomo, IN 46901
LIGON, Michael Moran (EC) 517 Brandywine Cir, Greenville, NC 27858
LIKOS, Mark Steven (Ala)
LIKOWSKI, James Boyd (Ore) 2818 Lilac St, Longview, WA 98632
LIKWARTZ, Judy Saima (Ore) Po Box 51447, Casper, WY 82605
LILE JR, James Elbert (WMo)
LILES, Allison Sandlin (Tex) 6615 Saddleback Ct, Crozet, VA 22932
LILES, Eric (Va) 6605 Bevington Rd, Dallas, TX 75248
LILES, Kathleen Kathleen (NY) 120 W 69th St, New York, NY 10023
LILLARD SR, Eddie Lee (NJ) 1819 Columbus Ave, Neptune, NJ 07753
LILLEY, Lin S (RG) 8300 Wyoming Blvd NE Apt 2112, Albuquerque, NM 87113
✠ **LILLIBRIDGE**, Gary Richard (WTex) PO Box 6885, San Antonio, TX 78209
LILLIE, Paul Andrew (The Episcopal Church in Haw) 3311 Campbell Avenue, Honolulu, HI 96815
LILLIS, Rosemary (Roch) 2 Woodchuck Ln, Brick, NJ 08724
LILLVIS, David (Mich) 1 Gates Cir Apt 504, Buffalo, NY 14209
LILLY, Beth Cobb (WNC) 1700 Verrazzano Pl, Wilmington, NC 28405
LIM, You-Leng Leroy (Los) 12172 9th St, Garden Grove, CA 92840
LIMATO, Richard Paul (NY) 225 W 99th St, New York, NY 10025
LIMATU, Hector (Los) Chapantongo, Col Chapantongo Centro, Chapantongo, HID 42900, Mexico
LIMBACH, Mary Evelyn (Eau) 2034 Upper Ridge Road, Port Washington, WI 53074
LIMBURG, Megan (Va) St Christophers School, 711 Saint Christophers Rd, Richmond, VA 23226
LIMEHOUSE III, Frank F (Ala) 3538 Lenox Rd, Birmingham, AL 35213

LIMO, John Edward (Los) 15757 Saint Timothy Rd, Apple Valley, CA 92307
LIMOZAINE, Bruce John (Ark) 30 Gettysburg N, Cabot, AR 72023
LIMPERT JR, Robert Hicks (Alb) 731 Old Piseco Rd, Piseco, NY 12139
LIN, Justin Chun-Min (Tai) 3/F, 262 Chung-Hsiao I Road, Hsin Hsing Dis, Kaohsiung, 800, Taiwan
LIN, Philip Li-Feng (Tai) 23 Wu-Chuan West Road Sec. 1, Taichung, TAIWAN, Taiwan
LIN, Samuel Ying-Chiu (Tai) #280 Fuhsing S Rd, Sec 2, C/O Diocese Of Taiwan, Taipei, Taiwan
LIN, Shu-Hwa (Tai) 1 F 29 Alley 6, Lane 168 Chung-her Rd, Keelung, 20347, Taiwan
LINARES-RIVERA, Ivette (PR)
LINBOOM, Bradley A (Chi) 412 55th St, Clarendon Hills, IL 60514
LINCOLN, Matt (WNY) Trinity Church, 371 Delaware Ave, Buffalo, NY 14202
LINCOLN, Richard (Los) 15114 Archwood St, Van Nuys, CA 91405
LINCOLN, Thomas Clarke (Nwk) 1156 Carolina Cir Sw, Vero Beach, FL 32962
LIND, Douglass Theodore (Ct) 17080 Harbour Point Dr, Apt 1017, Fort Myers, FL 33908
LIND, Tracey (O) 2970 Scarborough Rd, Cleveland Heights, OH 44118
LINDAHL, Rosa Vera (Ala)
LINDBERG, Robert Morris (CPa) 16 Winch Hill Rd, Swanzey, NH 03446
LINDELL, John Allen (Mont) 6629 Merryport Ln, Naples, FL 34104
LINDELL, Thomas Jay (Az) 4460 N Camino Del Rey, Tucson, AZ 85718
LINDEMAN, Eileen Cornish (RI) 830 Mohican Way, Redwood City, CA 94062
LINDEMAN, Matthew James (Ct) 4 Glen St, Milford, CT 06460
LINDEMAN, Mitchell James (RI) Church of the Ascension, 370 Main St, Wakefield, RI 02879
LINDENBERG, Juliana T (NC) 231 N Church St, Rocky Mount, NC 27804
LINDER, Callie Maebelle (Mich) 2034 S 69th East Pl, Tulsa, OK 74112
LINDER, Mark (Ky) 2500 Crossings Blvd Unit 518, Bowling Green, KY 42104
LINDER, Philip Conrad (SC) 25 Otranto Lane, Columbia, SC 29209
LINDH-PAYNE, Kristofer Hans (Md) 2216 Pot Spring Rd., Timonium, MD 21093
LINDLEY, James B (Ore) 97955 Hallway Rd, PO Box 3190, Harbor, OR 97415
LINDLEY, Susie (Okla) 1202 W Elder Ave, Duncan, OK 73533
LINDQUIST, Mary Dail (Vt) 16 Bradley Ave, Brattleboro, VT 05301
LINDSAY JR, Spencer Hedden (La) 273 Monarch Dr Apt L-26, Houma, LA 70364

LINDSAY, Steven William (Pa)

LINDSEY, Richard Carroll (SC) 3001 Meeting St, Hilton Head Island, SC 29926

LINDSLEY, James Elliott (NY) Maplegarth, Box 881, Millbrook, NY 12545

LINDSTROM JR, Donald Fredrick (CGC) 269 Rainbow Falls Rd, Franklin, NC 28734

LINDSTROM, Justin Alan (WTex) 7731 Broadway Unit A1, San Antonio, TX 78209

LINDSTROM, Marjorie Dawson (Nwk) 91 Francisco Ave, Rutherford, NJ 07070

LINDWRIGHT, Pippa (Mil) 342 W 3rd St, Oconomowoc, WI 53066

LINEBAUGH, Jonathan Andrew (CFla) 5910 NE 22nd Ter, Fort Lauderdale, FL 33308

LING, Steven (Ct) Trinity Episcopal Church, 345 Main St, Portland, CT 06480

LINGLE, Mark Duane (Ct) 503 Old Long Ridge Rd, Stamford, CT 06903

LINLEY, Eliza (ECR) 210 Lake Court, Aptos, CA 95003

LINNENBERG, Daniel M (Roch) 5829 Jaqui Ln, Franklin, OH 45005

LINSCOTT, Stephanie (Tex) 3838 N Braeswood Blvd Apt 251, Apt 251, Houston, TX 77025

LINTON, Adam (Mass) 204 Monument Rd, Orleans, MA 02653

LINVILLE, Harriet Burton (ECR) 10372 S W Windwood Way, Portland, OR 97225

LINZEL, Claire Benedict (SwFla) 411 Nottinghill Gate St, 805, 1207, Arlington, TX 76014

LIOTTA, Thomas Mark (NY) 629 County Route 12, New Hampton, NY 10958

LIPP, Beth Ann (ND) P.O. Box 1241, Bismarck, ND 58502

LIPPART SR, Thomas Edward (NMich) 5207 Eleuthra Cir, Vero Beach, FL 32967

LIPPE, Amanda J (ETenn) PO Box 29, Norris, TN 37828

LIPSCOMB III, CHarles Lloyd (SwVa) 501 V E S Rd Apt B513, Lynchburg, VA 24503

LIPSCOMB III, John (CFla) 317 S Mary St, Eustis, FL 32726

LIPSCOMB, Leonard Scott (WA) 301 A St SE, Washington, DC 20003

LIPSCOMB, Steve (Kan) 3324 NW Bent Tree Ln, Topeka, KS 66618

LIRIANO MARTINEZ, Jorge Antonely (NJ) 3050 River Rd, Camden, NJ 08105

LIRO, Judith (Tex) 4301 N I H 35, Austin, TX 78722

LITMAN, Eric Robert (Mass) 1 Linden St, Quincy, MA 02170

LITSEY, Kim Jeanne (Az) 3635 Brave Dr, Lake Havasu City, AZ 86406

✠ **LITTLE II**, Edward Stuart (NI) 1526 Pine Top Trce, Mishawaka, IN 46545

LITTLE, Geoffrey Alan (Ct) 358 Lenox St, New Haven, CT 06513

LITTLE, Tracie L (EMich) 543 Michigan Ave, Marysville, MI 48040

LITTLEFIELD, Jeff (Ore) 11265 SW Cabot St, Beaverton, OR 97005

LITTLEJOHN, Luchy (Tex) 6307 Hickory Holw, Windcrest, TX 78239

LITTLEPAGE, Dorothella Michel (Ct) 120 Sigourney St, Hartford, CT 06105

LITTMAN, Val J (Eur) C Punta Colon - Edificio Trump - JWMarriott, Val Littman Apartment 3901, Ciudad de Panama, Panama

LITTRELL, James H (Pa) 213 E Cliveden St, Philadelphia, PA 19119

LITWINSKI, Anthony (Eur) Calle de Cervantes 35 4-4a, Valencia, 46007, Spain

LITZENBERGER, Caroline Jae (Ore) 1605 NE Clackamas St Apt 300c, Portland, OR 97232

LIU, Ting-Hua (Tai) I-105-7 Hang Chou South Road, Silo, Taiwan

LIVELY, James W (SwVa) 111 Pleasant St, Sturgis, MI 49091

LIVELY, Paula Kay (WMo) 601 E Benton St, Monett, MO 65708

LIVERMORE, Charles Whittier (ETenn) 7604 Windwood Dr, Powell, TN 37849

LIVINGOOD, Abigail Zoeann (Ia)

LIVINGSTON, Bill (Miss) 37 Sheffield Pl, Brevard, NC 28712

LIVINGSTON, Diane Howard (WNC) 37 Sheffield Place, Brevard, NC 28712

LIVINGSTON, James John (Los) 31641 La Novia Ave, San Juan Capistrano, CA 92675

LIVINGSTON, James Leo (NMich) 3135 County Road 456, Skandia, MI 49885

LIZ LOPEZ, Tony (PR) 231 Garfield Ave, Trenton, NJ 08629

LJUNGGREN, M Lorraine (NC) 5400 Crestview Rd, Raleigh, NC 27609

LJUNGGREN, Timothy Merle (Mont) 62 Greenway Dr, Goshen, IN 46526

LLERENA FIALLOS, Angel Polivio (EcuC) Apartado 89, Guaranda, Provincia De Bolivar, Ecuador

LLOYD, Bonnie Jean (Tenn) 1420 Wilson Pike, Brentwood, TN 37027

LLOYD, Dennis (Pa) 233 S Bay Dr, Dover, DE 19901

LLOYD, Elizabeth Anne (Chi) 322 Farragut St, Park Forest, IL 60466

LLOYD, Emily (WA) 487 Hudson St, New York, NY 10014

LLOYD, Kevin (NC) 67 Mount Hope Ave, Jamestown, RI 02835

LLOYD, Margaret Ewing (Mass) 115 Standish Ave, Plymouth, MA 02360

LLUMIGUANO AREVALO, Nancy (EcuC) Sarmiento, Quito, Ecuador

LO, Kwan (Los) 133 E Graves Ave, Monterey Park, CA 91755

LO, Pei-Han Peggy (Tex)

LOBB, Mark Andrew (Md)

LOBBAN, Andy (Cal) Grace Cathedral, 1100 California St, San Francisco, CA 94108

LOBDELL, Gary Thomas (Oly) 2610 E Section St Unit 92, Mount Vernon, WA 98274

LOBS, Donna Burkard (CFla) 128 Legacy Dr, Advance, NC 27006

LOBS III, George Richard (CFla) 128 Legacy Dr, Advance, NC 27006

LOCH, C Louanne (Fla) Holy Trinity Episcopal Church, 100 NE 1st St, Gainesville, FL 32601

LOCH, Jerry Lynn (Chi) 446 Somonauk St, Sycamore, IL 60178

LOCHER, Elizabeth A (Pgh) 106 Greyfriar Dr, Pittsburgh, PA 15215

LOCHNER, Charlie (NJ) 2106 5th Ave, Spring Lake, NJ 07762

LOCK, John Mason (NJ) Trinity Episcopal Church, 65 W Front St, Red Bank, NJ 07701

LOCKE, Carol Ann (Los) 61 Painter St Apt 1, Pasadena, CA 91103

LOCKE, Kathleen Newell (Nwk) 15 Norwood Ave, Summit, NJ 07901

LOCKE, William Russell (RI) 63 Pidge Ave, Pawtucket, RI 02860

LOCKETT, Donna A (CGC) 102 Shadow Ln, Troy, AL 36079

LOCKETT, HAROLD J (At) 586 Lynn Valley Rd SW, Atlanta, GA 30311

LOCKETT, Tina (CGC) Trinity Episcopal Cathedral, 1100 Sumter St, Columbia, SC 29201

LOCKEY JR, Myron Willis (Miss)

LOCKHART, Donna Lee (Mich)

LOCKLEY, Linda Sue (SwFla) 6006 Braden Run, Bradenton, FL 34202

LOCKWOOD II, Frank Robert (Alb) 14 Spencer Blvd, Coxsackie, NY 12051

LOCKWOOD, Marcia (ECR) PO Box 345, Carmel Valley, CA 93924

LODER, Debra Jayne (Az)

LODU, Hellen Juan (ND)

LODWICK, James Nicholas (NY) 132 S Scott St Apt 2, South Bend, IN 46601

LOESCHER, Candyce Jean (Ky) St Marks Episcopal Church, 2822 Frankfort Ave, Louisville, KY 40206

LOEWE, Richard (Los) 1907 W West Wind, Santa Ana, CA 92704

LOFGREN, Claire (NY) St. Joseph of Arimathea, 2172 Saw Mill River Road, White Plains, NY 10607

LOGAN, Christie Larson (Oly) 720 E Road Of Tralee, Shelton, WA 98584

LOGAN, Jeffery Allen (Tex)

LOGAN, Linda Marie (CNY) 405 N Madison Ave, Pierre, SD 57501

LOGAN JR, Willis (SwVa) 100 W Jefferson St, Charlottesville, VA 22902

LOGAN, Yvonne Luree (NY) 1185 Park Ave Apt 12j, New York, NY 10128

LOGILDES COROA, Gerardo (Cu)

LOGSDON, Tami Davis (NwT) 4207 Emil Ave, Amarillo, TX 79106

✠ **LOGUE**, Frank S (Ga) 1309 E 38th St, Savannah, GA 31404

LOHSE, Dana May (Wyo) Po Box 291, Kaycee, WY 82639

LOKEN, Gail (Ak) 6211 Geronimo Cir, Anchorage, AK 99504

LOKEY, Michael Paul (Eas) 29618 Polks Rd, Princess Anne, MD 21853

LOLCAMA, Thirza A (Oly) 10630 Gravelly Lake Dr SW, Lakewood, WA 98499

LOLK, Otto Lothar Manfred (Pa) 3135 Clark Ave, Trevose, PA 19053

LOMAS, Bruce (Mass) 3 Gould St, Melrose, MA 02176

LOMBARDO, Janet Marie Vogt (NH) 17 Rockey Brook Rd, Meredith, NH 03253

LONDON, Daniel DeForest (The Episcopal NCal) 2451 Ridge Rd, Berkeley, CA 94709

LONDON, Gary Loo (Los) 122 S California Ave, Monrovia, CA 91016

LONE, Jose Francisco (Hond)

LONERGAN, Kit (Mass) 119 Washington Street, c/o St James Episcopal Church, Groveland, MA 01834

LONERGAN, Wallace Gunn (Ida) 812 E Linden St, Caldwell, ID 83605

LONG, Amy Laurel (WK)

LONG, Benjamin Isaac (Tex) 1941 Webberville Rd, Austin, TX 78721

LONG, Beth (At) 165 Meredith Ridge Rd, Athens, GA 30605

LONG, Betty Ann (Ct) 2 Viking Ln, Sandwich, MA 02563

LONG, Cynthia A (The Episcopal NCal) 7041 Verdure Way, Elk Grove, CA 95758

LONG, Eric (SwVa) PO Box 257, Roanoke, VA 24002

LONG, Gail Ann (SVa) 2441 Tuxedo Pl, Albany, GA 31707

LONG, Jean M (WMo)

LONG II, John Michael (Neb) 1615 Brent Blvd, Lincoln, NE 68506

LONG, Michael Richardson (Chi) 1003 Olympic Dr, Pflugerville, TX 78660

LONG, Shirley Dube (WNC) Po Box 72, Deep Gap, NC 28618

LONG, Thomas Mcmillen (Colo) 4155 E Jewell Ave Ste 1117, Denver, CO 80222

LONGACRE, Seth T (SanD) 70 Garfield St, Apt 16, Ashland, OR 97520

LONGE, Neal Patrick (Alb) 58 Reber St, Colonie, NY 12205

✠ **LONGEST**, Charles Lindsay (Md) 7200 Third Ave Apt C035, Sykesville, MD 21784

LONGHI, Anthony Peter (Chi) 1850 Landre Ct, Burlington, WI 53105

LONGSTAFF, Thomas Richmond Willis (Me) 39 Pleasant St, Waterville, ME 04901

LONSWAY, Rose Anne (O) Grace Episcopal Church, 36200 Ridge Road, Willoughby, OH 44094

LONTO, Michael J (WNY) 99 Wildwood Ave, Salamanca, NY 14779

LOOMIS, Julia Dorsey (SVa) 1 Crawford Pkwy Apt 201, Portsmouth, VA 23704

LOOP, Dick (Ore) 36489 Florence Ct., Astoria, OR 97103

LOOR CEDENO, Mary (Litoral Diocese Of Ecuador) 22 Ava & 3er Callejon P, Bahia De Caraquez, Ecuador

LOPEZ, Abel E (Los) 2396 Mohawk St Unit 7, Pasadena, CA 91107

LOPEZ, Angel Jesus (CFla)

LOPEZ, Antonio (Nev) 832 N Eastern Ave, Las Vegas, NV 89101

LOPEZ, Bienvenido (DomRep) Ch TEC Divina Providencia, Calle Mc d Rosario #39, San Antonio de Guerra, Republica Dominicana, Dominican Republic

LOPEZ, Eddie (SeFla) 1200 Heron Ave, Miami Springs, FL 33166

LOPEZ, Luis Fernando (Colom)

LOPEZ, Mary Alice (SwFla) 504 Columbia Dr, Tampa, FL 33606

LOPEZ, Nicolas Antonio (PR)

LOPEZ, Oscar Obdulio (Hond) 12 Calle B 10-11 Ave SE, Casa No 1023, San Pedro Sula, Honduras

LOPEZ, Pedro (Tex) Saint Peter's Church, 705 Williams St, Pasadena, TX 77506

LOPEZ JR, Ramiro Eduardo (WTex) 1247 Vista Del Juez, San Antonio, TX 78216

LOPEZ, Ricardo Ramirez (NwT) 907 Adams Ave, Odessa, TX 79761

LOPEZ, Sarah (Ia)

LOPEZ, Sunny (Chi) 3115 W Jerome St, Chicago, IL 60645

LOPEZ, Uriel (Tex) 40 Center St, Elgin, IL 60120

LOPEZ BOLANOS, Eddy E (RI)

LOPEZ-CHAVERRA, Hector (SwFla) Episc Ch St. Francis, P.O. Box 9332, Tampa, FL 33674

LOPEZ ZAMUDIO, Rocio Patricia (Okla) PO Box 10722, Midwest City, OK 73140

LOPOSER, Ellen Fogg (Spok) St Andrew's Episcopal Church, 2404 N Howard St, Spokane, WA 99205

LOR, Cher John (Minn) Holy Apostles Episcopal Church, 2200 Minnehaha Ave E, Saint Paul, MN 55119

LOR, Nor Annie (Minn)

LORD, James Raymond (Ky) 3001 Myrshine Dr, Pensacola, FL 32506

LORD, Mary George (NwPa) 2425 Glendale Ave, Erie, PA 16510

LORD, Richard (Va) 543 Beulah Rd NE, Vienna, VA 22180

LORD, Robert Charles (CFla) 1312 Bridgeport Dr, Winter Park, FL 32789

LORENSON, Ruth Lorraine (LI) 9 Warton Pl, Garden City, NY 11530

LORENZ, Connie (LI) 49 Hudson Watch Dr, Ossining, NY 10562

LORENZE, James Dennis (Eau) 2304 Country Club Ln, Eau Claire, WI 54701

LORENZETTI, Dominick J (Episcopal SJ)

LORING III, Richard Tuttle (Mass) 114 Badger Ter, Bedford, MA 01730

LORING, William Delano (Ct) 16613 Ashwood Dr, Tampa, FL 33624

LOSCH, Richard Rorex (Ala) Po Box 1560, Livingston, AL 35470

LOSE, Cynthia Agnes (RG)

LOTESTA, Brenda (Chi)

LOUA, Cece Alfred-S (NY) 1021 Norwich Dr, Troy, MI 48084

LOUD JR, Johnson D (Minn) 740 Shane Park Cir Apt 2, Prescott, WI 54021

LOUDEN, Molly O'Neill (Ct) 37 Gin Still Ln, West Hartford, CT 06107

LOUDENSLAGER, Samuel Charles (Ark) 20000 Hwy 300-Spur, Bigelow, AR 72016

LOUGHRAN JR, Eugene James (SwFla) 633 Coquina Court, Fort Myers, FL 33908

LOUGHREN, James Patrick (The Episcopal Church in Haw) 4879 Lake Shore Dr, Bolton Landing, NY 12814

LOUIS CHARLES, Samuel (Hai)

LOUIS DEAN SKIPPER, James Louis Dean (Ala) 1426 Gilmer Ave, Montgomery, AL 36104

LOUTREL, William Frederic (Ct) 7 Rattlesnake Mtn Rd, Stockbridge, MA 01262

LOUTTIT SR, James William (CFla) 331 Lake Ave, Maitland, FL 32751

LOVE, Melva Charlottee (Tex)

LOVEJOY, Margaret Helen (WLa)

LOVELACE, David (CPa) 3754 Cayuga Ln, York, PA 17402

LOVELACE, Logan Chas (WNC)

LOVELADY, Eldwin M (Oly) 3700 14th Ave SE Unit 3, Olympia, WA 98501

LOVETT, G David (ETenn) 7900 High Heath, Knoxville, TN 37919

LOVING, John Harnish (NwT) 8009 Ladera Verde, Austin, TX 78739

LOW, James (Ct) 57 Willow Grove Rd, Brunswick, ME 04011

LOW, Salin Miller (Ct) 12 Meadowview Ct, Canton, CT 06019

LOWE, Dianne Louise (Spok) St James Episcopal Church, 1410 NE Stadium Way, Pullman, WA 99163

LOWE, Edward Charles (Ga) 1881 East Pkwy, Deland, FL 32724

LOWE, Edward William (NJ)

LOWE JR, Eugene Yerby (NY) 624 Colfax St, Evanston, IL 60201

LOWE, Harold Chapin (Dal) 2212 Saint Andrews, Mckinney, TX 75072

LOWE, John Leon (Ind) 200 Glennes Ln Apt 205, Dunedin, FL 34698

LOWE, Robert Steven (Chi) 2009 Regency Ct, Geneva, IL 60134

LOWE JR, Thomas (RG) Episcopal Church of St. John, P.O. Box 449, Alamogordo, NM 88310
LOWE, Walter James (At) 1647 N Rock Springs Rd NE, Atlanta, GA 30324
LOWERY, Don (NC) 210 S Chestnut St, Henderson, NC 27536
LOWERY, Hermon Lee (Ga) 2705 Michael Rd, Albany, GA 31721
LOWERY, Thomas Ethan (Va)
LOWREY, Edward Sager (NwPa) Box 54, 107 Harvey Rd, Foxburg, PA 16036
LOWREY III, Pierce Lang (At) 3830 Randall Farm Rd SE, Atlanta, GA 30339
LOWRY, David B (LI) Po Box 51777, New Orleans, LA 70151
LOWRY, Robert Lynn (Tex) Trinity in the Woodland Texas, 3901 S Panther Creek Dr, The Woodlands, TX 77381
LOWRY III, William M (CGC) PO Box 224, Tunica, MS 38676
LOW-SKINNER, Debra (Cal) 137 Redding Rd Apt C, Campbell, CA 95008
LOY, Reed J (NH) 885 Shore Rd, Cape Elizabeth, ME 04107
✠ **LOYA**, Craig William (Minn) 113 N 18th St, Omaha, NE 68102
LOYD, Janet Ellen (Oly) 56738 Sturgeon Rd, Darrington, WA 98241
LOYD, Michael Corman (Kan) 8021 W 21st St N, Wichita, KS 67205
LOYOLA, Leo (The Episcopal Church in Haw) Diocese o f Hawaii, 229 Queen Emma Sq, Honolulu, HI 96813
LOZAMA, Abiade (Hai)
LOZANO, Kathleen Barbara (Los) St Matthias Episcopal Church, 7056 Washington Ave, Whittier, CA 90602
LUAL, Anderia Arok (Az) Diocese of Arizona, 114 W Roosevelt St, Phoenix, AZ 85003
LUBELFELD, Nicholas (Va) 7418 Spring Village Dr, APT 311, Springfield, VA 22150
LUBIN, Gary Robert (SO)
LUCAS, Jeremy (Ore) 1060 Chandler Rd, Lake Oswego, OR 97034
✠ **LUCAS**, Kimberly Danielle (Colo) 1830 Connecticut Ave NW, Washington, DC 20009
LUCAS, Mary Louise (Mass) 136 Bay Street 501, Hamilton, ON L8P 3H8, Canada
LUCAS, Paul Nahoa (The Episcopal Church in Haw) 47-074 Lihikai Dr, Kaneohe, HI 96744
LUCAS, T Stewart (Md) 540 Vinington Ct, Atlanta, GA 30350
LUCAS-GREEN, Jason Bryan (Minn) 2947 Blanding Ct, Hayward, CA 94541
LUCEY, David James (Va) 94 Interpromontory Road, Great Falls, VA 22066
LUCHS, Lewis Richard (Chi) 6417 81st St, Cabin John, MD 20818
LUCK, Diana Nelson (Dal) 6912 Merrilee Ln, Dallas, TX 75214

LUCK, G Thomas (WTex) 403 Summit Cir, Fredericksburg, TX 78624
LUCKENBACH, David Andrew (Tex) 1709 S College Ave, Tyler, TX 75701
LUCKETT JR, David Stafford (Miss) 4241 Otterlake Cv, Niceville, FL 32578
LUCKEY, Marion Isabelle Aiken (NMich) 1531 Vardon Rd, Munising, MI 49862
LUCKRITZ, Denzil John (Chi) 558 Kingsway Dr, Aurora, IL 60506
LUDBROOK, Helen Christine (Mo) 1422 Lawnwood Dr, Des Peres, MO 63131
LUDWIG, Nancy Greig (Me)
LUECKENHOFF, James Joseph (WLa) 1518 Griffith St, Lake Charles, LA 70601
LUECKERT, Diana Rowe (The Episcopal NCal) 4800 Olive Oak Way, Carmichael, CA 95608
LUEDDE, Christopher S (Roch) 31 Kitty Hawk Dr, Pittsford, NY 14534
LUETHE, Robin Lewis (Oly) 789 Highway 603, Chehalir, WA 98532
LUFKIN, alison (Ore) 16702 Westpoint Dr, Nehalem, OR 97131
LUFKIN II, George S (Ore) PO Box 243, Leadville, CO 80461
LUGER, Virginia M (ND) 821 N 4th St Apt 3, Bismarck, ND 58501
LUGO, Beverley Lee (Ida) 411 10th Ave S, Nampa, ID 83651
LUGO MARRERO, Haydee (Cu)
LUHRING, Peggy Williams (SVa) 4449 N Witchduck Rd, Virginia Beach, VA 23455
LUI, David Suikwei (Cal) 1011 Harrison St # 202, Oakland, CA 94607
LUJAN, Mary (EO) PO Box 25, Hood River, OR 97031
LUKANICH, Emily A (NY) Christ Episcopal Church, PO Box 1000, Vail, CO 81658
LUKAS, Arlene (WNC) 416 N Haywood St, Waynesville, NC 28786
LUKAS, Randolph Edgar (Alb) PO Box 827, New Lebanon, NY 12125
LUKASON, Lauren Sayre (Mass)
LUKENS JR, Alexander M (Colo) 536 Seneca Cir, Walsenburg, CO 81089
LUKENS, Ann Pierson (Oly) 2015 Killarney Way, Bellevue, WA 98004
LUKENS, Matthew M (Mich) 183 Alala Rd, Kailua, HI 96734
LUKENS, Susan Ackley (Va)
LULLO, Milania (WNY) 200 Cazenovia St, Buffalo, NY 14210
LUMBARD, Carolyn Mary Dunsmore (Roch) 326 Frederick Douglass St, Rochester, NY 14608
LUNA JR, Eulalio Gallardo (WTex) 234 W Mariposa Dr, San Antonio, TX 78212
LUNA, Julie (Minn) 60 Kent St, Saint Paul, MN 55102
LUND, Joseph Walter (WA) 70381 Placerville Rd, Rancho Mirage, CA 92270

LUND, Judith Ann (Ark) 8280 Spanker Ridge Dr, Bentonville, AR 72712
LUND, Virginia U Sapienza (Mil) 1101 Greenough Dr W Apt E 6, Missoula, MT 59802
LUNDEN, Michael Carl (NY) 118 S Church St, Goshen, NY 10924
LUNDGREN, Linda Lou (The Episcopal Church in Haw) 8 3rd St, Proctor, MN 55810
LUNDGREN, Richard John (Chi) 165 Le Grande Blvd, Aurora, IL 60506
LUNDIN, George Edward (Miss) 705 Southern Ave, Hattiesburg, MS 39401
LUNDQUIST, Rob (WNC) 63 Forest Lake Dr, Asheville, NC 28803
LUNNUM, Lindsay (LI) Zion Episcopal Church, 243-01 Northern Blvd, Douglaston, NY 11363
LUNTSFORD, Sharon Lorene (ND) Po Box 18, Alexander, ND 58831
LUONI, Rick (CFla) 2499 N Westmoreland Dr, Orlando, FL 32804
LUPFER JR, William (Colo) 120 Broadway Fl 38, New York, NY 10271
LUPTON JR, Jim (Ark) 241 Riverview St., Belhaven, NC 27810
LUTAS, Donald M (Mich) 563 E Boston Blvd, The Connolly House, Detroit, MI 48202
LUTES, Kathy (Mil) 1112 Harmony Cir NW, Janesville, WI 53545
LUTHER, Carol Luther (Cal) St Paul's Episcopal School, 46 Montecito Ave., Oakland, CA 94610
LUTHER, Diane Marie (Chi)
LUTTER, Linda F (Chi) 5725 Stearns School Rd, Gurnee, IL 60031
LUTTRELL, John Sidney (LI) 1289 Old York Road, Robbinsville, NJ 08691
LUTZ, Alison W (NY) 39 Chestnut St, South Hamilton, MA 01982
LUTZ, Bill (CNY) 82 Scott Ave, Elmira, NY 14905
LUTZ, Joseph Anthony (WVa)
LUTZ, Richard Herbert (LI) Cashelmara 40, 23200 Lake Rd, Bay Village, OH 44140
LUTZ, Ruth Jeanne (RG) 1330 Renoir Ct., Las Cruces, NM 88007
LUZARDO JR, Joseph Peter (NJ)
LWEBUGA-MUKASA, Katherine N (WNY) 168 Schimwood Ct, Getzville, NY 14068
LYGA, Robert Michael (Minn) N36457 State Road 93/121, Independence, WI 54747
LYLE, Jerry (Tex) St. Joseph's Episcopal Church, PO Box 797, Salado, TX 76571
LYLE, Patsy Rushworth (La) 19344 Links Ct, Baton Rouge, LA 70810
LYLE, Randall R (Ia) 875 Dry Run Creek Ct, Hiawatha, IA 52233
LYLE, William Edward (SO) 1547 Stratford Dr, Kent, OH 44240
LYMAN, Janyce Rebecca (Cal) 115 Sheridan Way, Woodside, CA 94062

LYNCH JR, Bobby (WNC) Po Box 561, Rutherfordton, NC 28139

LYNCH, David Ross (WMo) 1433 NW R D Mize Rd, Blue Springs, MO 64015

LYNCH, Gwynn (SanD) 13319 Fallen Leaf Rd, Poway, CA 92064

LYNCH, John J (RI) 12 Clinton St, Central Falls, RI 02863

LYNCH, Suzanne Mchugh Stryker (WMo) 1342 S Ventura Ave, Springfield, MO 65804

LYNCH, William David (NC) 8849 Ray Rd, Raleigh, NC 27613

LYNN, Connor Kay (Los) 1902 Park Ave Apt 316, Los Angeles, CA 90026

LYNN, Jackie (Chi)

LYNTON, Devadas Peter (At)

LYON, Don (CFla) 1628 Bent Oaks Blvd, Deland, FL 32724

LYON IV, James Fraser (USC) 28 Lake Ct, Columbia, SC 29206

LYON, Lauren Jean (Ia) Trinity Church, 320 E College St, Iowa City, IA 52240

LYON, Susan Loy (Ark) 1000 N Mississippi St, Little Rock, AR 72207

LYONS JR, James Hershel (Nev) All Saints Episcopal Church, 4201 W Washington Ave, Las Vegas, NV 89107

LYONS, Judith F (Los)

LYONS, Leroy A (NJ) 1208 Prospect Ave, Plainfield, NJ 07060

LYONS, Patricia M (WA) 1511 Frazier St, Alexandria, VA 22304

LYTHGOE, Amy U (Colo) 1533 Kearney St, Denver, CO 80220

LYTLE, Ashley Alexandra Gabriella (At) 515 E Ponce de Leon Ave, Decatur, GA 30030

LYTLE, William Adam (Alb) 912 NY-146, Clifton Park, NY 12065

M

MAAS, Benjamin Wells (Va) 1374 S Brook St, Louisville, KY 40208

MAAS, Jan A (NY) 4403 Kirke Ct, Alexandria, VA 22304

MABERRY, Lois Rayner (WLa)

MACARTHUR III, Robert Stuart (Mo) 334 Maple Ridge Rd, Center Sandwich, NH 03227

MACATEE, Louise Mae (Los) Church of the Epiphany, 5450 Churchwood Dr, Oak Park, CA 91377

MACAULEY JR, Robert Conover (Vt) 175 Hills Point Road, Charlotte, VT 05445

MACBETH, Andy (WTenn) 1640 Harbert Ave, Memphis, TN 38104

MACCOLL, Craig (Colo) 9305 Wolfe St, Highlands Ranch, CO 80129

MACCONNELL, James Stuart (Wyo) 103 15th St #1, Dallas Center, IA 0063

MACDONALD, Daniel (Mass) 147 Concord Rd, Lincoln, MA 01773

MACDONALD, David Roberts (LI) 53 Glen Ave, Sea Cliff, NY 11579

MACDONALD, Heyward Hunter (Md) 2551 Summit Ridge Trl, Charlottesville, VA 22911

MACDONALD, Jean A (Vt) 7 N College St, Montpelier, VT 05602

MACDONALD, John Alexander (Spok)

MACDONALD, Linda Jean (Mich) 1780 Nemoke Trl, Haslett, MI 48840

✠ **MACDONALD**, Mark Lawrence (Ak) 93 First Ave., Toronto, ON M4M1W9, Canada

MACDONALD, Susan Savage (Va) 723 S Braddock St, Winchester, VA 22601

MACDONALD, Terrence Cameron (O) 207 Weed St, New Canaan, CT 06840

MACDONALD, Walter Young (Mich) 2796 Page Ave, Ann Arbor, MI 48104

MACDOUGALL, Matthew Bradstock (NwPa) 343 E Main St, Youngsville, PA 16371

MACDOWELL, Barry Scott (Ind) 138 S 18th St, Richmond, IN 47374

MACDUFFIE, Bruce Lincoln (CNY) 836 5th Ave. West, Dickinson, ND 58601

MACEK, Kathryn Ellen (EO) 1273 Yuma St Unit 201, Colorado Springs, CO 80909

MAC EWEN, Suzanne Marie (Wyo) Po Box 137, Evanston, WY 82931

MACFARLANE, Robert John (Chi) 3724 Farr Ave, Fairfax, VA 22030

MACFIE JR, Tom (Tenn) 117 Carruthers Rd, Sewanee, TN 37375

MACGILL, Martha (Md)

MACGILL III, William D (WVa) 5909 Cedar Landing Rd, Wilmington, NC 28409

MACGREGOR, Laird S (WK) 322 S Ash St, Mcpherson, KS 67460

MACGREGOR, Ro (SO) 1045 S Court St Apt 5, Circleville, OH 43113

MACHOWSKI, Matthew (Va)

MACIAS, Ryan (Los)

MACIAS PEREZ, Franklin Oswaldo (Litoral Diocese Of Ecuador) CALLE AMARILIS FUENTES N, 603 Y CALLE D, GUAYAQUIL, 09-01-5250, Ecuador

MACINNIS, Elyn G (NY) 64 Memorial Rd, Providence, RI 02906

MACINTIRE, Morgan Montelepre (La) 2050 Bert Kouns Industrial Loop, Shreveport, LA 71118

MACK, Arthur Robert (Mich) 13 Dover Ln., Hendersonville, NC 28739

MACK, Ross Julian (NI) PO Box 462, Valparaiso, IN 46384

MACKAY III, Donald (Oly) 6354 Evergreen Dr., West Linn, OR 96078

MACKAY VINSON, Jean Annette (SVa) 4032 Rampart Ave, Virginia Beach, VA 23455

MACKE, Beth (Ind) 4713 Housebridge Rd, Corydon, KY 42406

MACKENZIE, ALexander James (The Episcopal NCal) 2714 S 10th St, Lebanon, OR 97355

MACKENZIE, Andrea Shortal (ECR) 13601 Saratoga Ave, Saratoga, CA 95070

MACKENZIE, Carol (NH) 12 Moore St, Chelmsford, MA 01824

MACKENZIE, John Anderson Ross (WNY) 11819 Eastkent Sq, Richmond, VA 23238

MACKENZIE, Katharine Helen (Los) 948 W Sierra Nevada Way, Orange, CA 92865

MACKENZIE, Lester V (Los) 428 Park Ave, Laguna Beach, CA 92651

MACKENZIE, Mary (Oly) 16060 Ne 28th St, Bellevue, WA 98008

MACKENZIE, Vanessa Mildred (Los) 1739 Buckingham Rd, Los Angeles, CA 90019

MACKEY, Guy (RG) 312 N Orchard Ave, Farmington, NM 87401

MACKEY, Jeffrey A (Fla) 2589 Lail Rd, Morganton, NC 28655

MACKEY, Judith P (Los) 801 Haslam Dr, Santa Maria, CA 93454

MACKEY, Kyle Christopher (At) 372 Hiden Blvd, Newport News, VA 23606

MACKEY, Peter David (Mich) 614 Company St, Adrian, MI 49221

MACKILLOP SR, Alan (SanD) 73 Windward Ln, Manchester, NH 03104

MACKINTOSH, Leigh Partridge (NY) 9625 Wendhurst Dr, Glen Allen, VA 23060

MACKNIGHT, Jeff (WA) 5450 Massachusetts Ave, Bethesda, MD 20816

MACKOV, Elwyn Joseph (WVa) 118 Five Point Ave, Martinsburg, WV 25404

MACLEOD, Jay (NH) Episcopal Church Of St Andrew, PO Box 294, New London, NH 03257

MACLEOD III, Norman M (RI) 25 Mumford Ave, Newport, RI 02840

MACLIN, Charles Waite (Me) PO Box 1259, Portland, ME 04104

MACNALLY, Janet Lee (Minn)

MACORT, John Gilbert (Ct) 5227 Rancho Ave, Sarasota, FL 34234

MACPHAIL, Alexander Douglas (SwVa) 1101 Franklin Rd SW, Roanoke, VA 24016

MACPHAIL, Karin L (SwVa) 335 Eagle Street, Woodstock, VA 22664

MACQUEEN, Karen (Los) 23730 Gold Nugget Ave, Diamond Bar, CA 91767

MACSWAIN, Robert Carroll (EC) U Of The S Sch Of Theology, 335 Tennessee Ave, Sewanee, TN 37383

✠ **MACVEAN-BROWN**, Shannon (Vt) 8850 Woodward Ave, Detroit, MI 48202

MACWHINNIE II, Anthony Eugene (CGC) 7810 Navarre Pkwy, Navarre, FL 32566

MADDISON, Ben (NJ)

MADDOX III, William Edward (NC) 5718 Catskill Court, Durham, NC 27713

MADDUX, Carole Frauman (At) 9695 Hillside Dr, Roswell, GA 30076

MADDUX, Donald Jess (Oly) 706 West Birch Street, Shelton, WA 98584

MADDY, Marta Tuff (Minn)

MADER, Carol Ann (Mich) 6092 Beechwood Dr, Haslett, MI 48840

MADISON, David (Tex) 1420 4th Ave Ste 29, Canyon, TX 79015

MADISSON LOPEZ, Vaike (Hond) Km 119 Crr al Norte, Jugo de Cane, Siguatepeque, 21105, Honduras

MADRID, Hector (Hond) Apartado Postal 30, Siguatepeque, Comayagua, Honduras

MADSEN, David Lloyd (SanD) Saint Albans Episcopal Church, 490 Farragut Cir, El Cajon, CA 92020

MAESTRETTI, Carolyn Fern (Nev)

MAFLA SILVA, Daniel Antonio (Colom) Apartado Aereo 52964, Iglesia Episcopal En Colombia, Bogota, 52964, Ecuador

MAGALA, Joy (Los) 8341 de Soto Ave, Canoga Park, CA 91304

MAGDALENE, Deborah (NY) 12 Saterlee Pl, Wappingers Falls, NY 12590

MAGEE JR, Lynwood Cresse (SC) 98 Wentworth St, Charleston, SC 29401

MAGEVNEY, Laura Mann (Fla)

MAGGIANO, Grey (Md) Memorial Episcopal Church, 1407 Bolton St, Baltimore, MD 21217

MAGIE, William Walter (Ia) 301 S 2nd St, Polk City, IA 50226

MAGILL, Peter George (CFla) 8310 Crosswicks Dr, Orlando, FL 32819

MAGLIULA, Robert James (NY) Holy Cross Monastery, PO Box 99, West Park, NY 12493

✠ **MAGNESS**, James Beattie (SVa) 2309 Point Chesapeake Quay, Unit 4021, Virginia Beach, VA 23451

MAGNUS, Elsie Linda (ND) PO Box 704, Walhalla, ND 58282

MAGNUS, Robert Frederick (Be) 105 Baird Rd, Mars Hill, NC 28754

MAGNUSON, Paulette Williams (Tex)

MAGOOLA, Robert (Neb)

MAGUIRE III, Bernard Leonard (Pa) 224 Flourtown Rd, Plymouth Meeting, PA 19462

MAGUIRE, Rebecca Maria (Va)

MAHAFFEY, Glenn G (CNY) 201 S Wilbur Ave, Sayre, PA 18840

MAHAFFY II, Richard James (SwFla)

MAHAN, Charles Earl (Mo) 444 Brightfield Trl, Manchester, MO 63021

MAHER JR, John (Va) 14331 Forest Row Trl, Midlothian, VA 23112

MAHER III, John Francis (Mil) 2045 Atwood Ave Apt 304, Madison, WI 53704

MAHLER, Linda Lorraine (WA)

MAHON, Paul Kelly (EO)

MAHONEY, James Michael (Ida) 1912 Delmar St, Boise, ID 83713

MAHOOD, Sharon M (Ia) 3705 Washington Ave, Des Moines, IA 50310

MAHR, Wineva P (Ia)

MAHURIN, Shanda (SwFla) 1021 Greenturf Rd, Spring Hill, FL 34608

MAIER, Andrea R (Oly) 10841 Whipple St Apt 105, North Hollywood, CA 91602

MAIER, Beth Ann (Vt) 1924 Blake St A, Berkeley, CA 94704

MAIL, Mary Jean (Mil) 509 East University, Bloomington, IN 47401

MAILS, Ryan Fredrick (Me) 407 Hillmont Ave, Longview, TX 75601

MAINWARING, Monica Burns (At) 562 Greenwood Ave NE, Atlanta, GA 30308

MAINWARING, Simon (At) Christchurch School, 49 Seahorse Ln, Christchurch, VA 23031

MAIOCCO III, Joseph F (SwFla) 500 Park Shore Dr, Naples, FL 34103

MAJOR, John Charles (Be) 325 Parke Sreet, West Pittston, PA 18643

MAJOR, Joseph Kenneth (SeFla) 1835 Nw 54th St, Miami, FL 33142

MAJOR, Kathryn S (CNY) 97 Underhill Rd, Ossining, NY 10562

MAJOR, Maureen Maeve (O) 2055 Akron Peninsula Rd, Akron, OH 44313

MAJOR, Philip S (CNY) St Pauls Syracuse, 310 Montgomery St Ste 1, Syracuse, NY 13202

MAKINS, Claire T (Chi)

MAKOWSKI, Chester Joseph (Tex) 1410 Jack Johnson Blvd., Galveston, TX 77550

MALANUK, Patsy (USC) 6045 Lakeshore Dr, Columbia, SC 29206

MALARKEY, Shawn O (Pgh) 33 Alice St, Pittsburgh, PA 15205

MALAVE TORRES, Hector (PR)

MALCOLM, Frieda (Ias) 1006 Beaglin Park Dr Apt 201, Salisbury, MD 21804

MALCOLM, Karen Gottwald (Alb)

MALCOLM, Kenneth A (Tex) 910 E 3rd Ave, Durango, CO 81301

MALCOLM, Patricia Ann (Del) PO Box 1374, Dover, DE 19903

MALDONADO-MERCADO, Roberto (SanD) 56 Fourth Ave Apt 108, Chula Vista, CA 91910

MALEK, David J (Mo)

MALERI, Karen D (Ct) 145 Canal St Unit 514, Shelton, CT 06484

MALIA, Linda Merle (WNY) 209 Columbus Ave, Buffalo, NY 14220

MALIA, Phyllis Terri (CFla)

MALIAMAN, Irene Egmalis (The Episcopal Church in Haw) ECIM, 911 N Marine Corps Dr, Tamuning, GU 96913

MALIN, Katherine Murphy (NY) 2 Rectory St, Rye, NY 10580

MALIONEK, Judith (Alb) 21 Hackett Blvd, Albany, NY 12208

MALIONEK, Thomas V (Alb) St Paul Church, Po Box 637, Kinderhook, NY 12106

MALLARY JR, Raymond Dewitt (NY) 80 Lyme Rd #161, Hanover, NH 03755

MALLETTE STEPHENS, Hershey A (WA)

MALLIN, Caroll Sue Driftmeyer (SeFla) 1150 Stanford Dr, Coral Gables, FL 33146

MALLON, Beth Kohlmeyer (Ore) 11511 SW Bull Mountain Rd, Tigard, OR 97224

MALLONEE, Anne Floyd (NY) 19 E 34th St, New York, NY 10016

MALLORY, Richard Deaver (Az) 455 Hope St Apt 3d, Stamford, CT 06906

MALLORY, Steven Michael (Okla) 1808 Cedar Ln, Ponca City, OK 74604

MALLOW, Sherod Earl (Ala) 2131 Sw 23rd Ave, Fort Lauderdale, FL 33312

MALLOY, Nancy (Colo) St Laurences Tec Mission, 26812 Barkley Rd, Conifer, CO 80433

MALLOY, Patrick L (NY) The General Theo Sem, 440 W 21st St, New York, NY 18102

MALM, Bob (Va) 3601 Russell Rd, Alexandria, VA 22305

MALONE, Bonnie (Oly) 24219 Witte Rd SE, Maple Valley, WA 98038

MALONE JR, Elmer Taylor (NC) 308 Wilcox St, Warrenton, NC 27589

MALONE, Michael James (Dal) 430 Greenwood Drive, Petersburg, VA 23805

MALONE, Tim (WA) 2609 N Glebe Rd, Arlington, VA 22207

MALONE, Trawin E (Tex) 4115 Paint Rock Dr, Austin, TX 78731

MALONEY, Linda Mitchell (Vt) PO Box 294, Enosburg Falls, VT 05450

MALONEY, Sean Patrick Henry (Mass) 622 Airline Rd, Corpus Christi, TX 78412

MALPHURS, Elisabeth Jane (Miss)

MALSEED, Caroline Frey (Ak) 4032 Deborah Dr, Juneau, AK 99801

MALTBIE, Colin Snow (Minn) 1000 Shumway Ave, Faribault, MN 55021

MALTESE NEHRBASS, Michelleslie Monnett (NJ)

MAMOUR, Samson James (SwVa)

MANASEK, Robert Wesley (Neb) St Francis Episcopal Church, PO Box 1201, Scottsbluff, NE 69361

MANASTERSKI, Myron` Julian (CFla) 5108 Landing Ln, Ocala, FL 34476

MANCHESTER, Sean (RI) 19 Trinity Pkwy, Providence, RI 02908

MANCIA COTO, Nimia Margarita (Hond)

MANCIL, Eric Nathan (CGC)

MANDEVILLE, Kathleen C (NY) PO Box 450, Tivoli, NY 12583

MANDILE, Luigi (La)

MANGELS III, John (The Episcopal NCal) 6725 Hillglen Way, Fair Oaks, CA 95628

MANHARDT, Catherine (WA)

MANIACI, Maria Kathleen (NMich) 824 Dakota Ave, PO Box 411, Gladstone, MI 49837

MANION, James Edward (Del) 20 Olive Ave, Rehoboth Beach, DE 19971

MANIYATT, John Kuriakose (Md) 4 E University Pkwy, Baltimore, MD 21218

MANLEY, David Brent (Mil)

MANLEY JR, Derrill Byrne (NwT) 1615 S Carpenter Ln, Cottonwood, AZ 86326

MANLEY, Wendy T (Cal) 1090 Brookfield Rd., Berlin, VT 05602

MANN, Alice (Mass) 51 Leroy Ave, Haverhill, MA 01835

MANN, Carl Douglas (Ia) 19372 140th St, Danville, IA 52623

MANN, Charles Henry (SwFla) 5900 N Lockwood Ridge Road, Sarasota, FL 34243

MANN, Frederick Earl (SwFla) 7835 Moonstone Dr, Sarasota, FL 34233

MANN III, Harold Vance (WNC) 15 Creekside View Dr, Asheville, NC 28804

MANN, Henry Rezin (SanD) 7981 Hemingway Ave, San Diego, CA 92120

MANN, karen (WMo) 16514 E 53rd Street Ct S, Independence, MO 64055

MANN, Louise (Mass) 8399 Breeding Rd, Edmonton, KY 42129

MANN, Lucretia Winslow (ECR) 5271 Scotts Valley Dr, Scotts Valley, CA 95066

MANN, Mary Anne (Ct) 36 Convent Drive 1a31, Bethesda, MD 20892

MANNEN, Daniel Joseph (SVa) 414 Pine St, Titusville, FL 32796

MANNEY, Thomas Michael (EMich) 2128 Miles Rd, Lapeer, MI 48446

MANNING, Gary Briton (Mil) 1717 Church St, Wauwatosa, WI 53213

MANNING, Gene Bentley (Tenn) 900 Broadway, Nashville, TN 37203

MANNING, Jean Louise (FdL) 1344 M-64, Ontonagon, MI 49953

MANNING, Jeanette Belle (SO) 164 Community Dr, Dayton, OH 45404

MANNING, Slaven L (USC) PO Box 220, Prosperity, SC 29127

MANNING, William B (WNC)

MANNING-LEW, Sharon Janine (NY) 522 Washington St, Peekskill, NY 10566

MANNISTO, Virginia Lee (NMich) N4354 Black Creek Rd, Chatham, MI 49816

MANNSCHRECK, Mary Lou Cowherd (SwVa) St Luke's Episcopal Church, 801 S Osage Ave, Bartlesville, OK 74003

MANOFF, Maribeth Scholten (ETenn)

MANOLA, John Edwin (NJ)

MANOOGIAN, Phyllis (Cal) 2300 Bancroft Way, Berkeley, CA 94704

MANSELLA, Thomas G (Va) 3705 S George Mason Dr Apt 2105s, Falls Church, VA 22041

MANSFIELD, Charles Kirk (Vt) 157 Parker Hill Rd, Bellows Falls, VT 05101

MANSFIELD, Gregory James Edward (SeFla) St Bernard Tec Ch, 16711 W Dixie Hwy, North Miami Beach, FL 33160

MANSFIELD, Meribah Ann (SO) 2282 Fernleaf Lane, Columbus, OH 43235

MANSFIELD JR, Richard Huntington (Ct) 41 Gatewood, Avon, CT 06001

MANSFIELD, Robert Grant (Nwk) 550 Ridgewood Rd, Maplewood, NJ 07040

MANSFIELD, Vic (WNC) PO Box 531, Skyland, NC 28776

MANSIR, Kerry Rhoads (Me) 2 Dresden Ave, Gardiner, ME 04345

MANSON, Anne Leslie Yount (Va) The Prestwould, 612 West Franklin St. #12C, Richmond, VA 23220

MANSON, Malcolm (Cal) 35 Keyes Avenue, San Francisco, CA 94129

MANTILLA-BENITEZ, Haydee (EcuC) Avenue Libertad Parada 8, Esmeralda, Ecuador

MANUEL, Anandsekar Joseph (LI) 3907 61st St, Woodside, NY 11377

MANZANARES, Zoila Manzanares-Rodriguez (Ind) 6613 El Paso Dr, Indianapolis, IN 46214

MARANVILLE, Irvin Walter (Vt) 6809 23rd Ave W, Bradenton, FL 34209

MARCANTONIO, John (Be) 39 Johnson Rd, West Orange, NJ 07052

MARCETTI, Alvin Julian (RI) 81 Warren Ave, East Providence, RI 02914

MARCH, Amanda (Mass) 1135 Walnut St, Newton, MA 02461

MARCH, Bette Ann (Mont) 34 Thomas The Apostle Rd, Cody, WY 82414

MARCH, Theresa Dianne (Episcopal SJ)

MARCHAND, R Richard (NY) 1802 17th Ave Apt 113, Seattle, WA 98122

MARCHL III, William Henry (NC) 719 S 1st St, Smithfield, NC 27577

MARCIALES ARENAS, Alberto Camilo (Colom) Carrera 6 No 49-85, Piso 2, Bogota, Colombia

MARCOUX, Kent (WA) St George's Parish, 160 U St NW, Washington, DC 20001

MARCUCCI, Jean D (NJ)

MARCURE, Johanna M (RI) 209 E Main St, Waterville, NY 13480

MAREE, Donna (Pa) 2112 Delancey Pl, Philadelphia, PA 19103

MAREK, Joseph J (Tenn) 204-A Courthouse Dr., Salmon, ID 83467

MARGERUM, Michael C (Nev) 11205 Carlsbad Rd, Reno, NV 89506

MARGRAVE, Tom (CNY) 29 William St, Cortland, NY 13045

MARICONDA, Thomas Nicholas (Ct) 36 Main St, Newtown, CT 06470

MARIE, Christine (Ore)

MARIN, Carlos Heli (CFla) 438 Magpie Ct, Kissimmee, FL 34759

MARIN, Mario R (Cal)

MARIN, Nora (Cal)

MARINCO, Judith Ann (EMich) 1434 E 13 Mile Rd, Madison Heights, MI 48071

MARINCO, Vincent Michael (EMich) 1434 E 13 Mile Rd, Madison Heights, MI 48071

MARINO, Matthew A (Fla) 114 W Roosevelt St, Phoenix, AZ 85003

MARION, Mark Vincent (SD)

MARIS, Margo (Ore) 13201 Se Blackberry Cir, Portland, OR 97236

MARKEVITCH, Diane (Mil) 17 Dumont Cir, Madison, WI 53711

MARKHAM, Eva Melba Roberts (Ky) 1604 Whippoorwill Rd., Louisville, KY 40213

MARKHAM, Ian (Va) 3737 Seminary Rd, Alexandria, VA 22304

MARKIE, Patrick Gregory (Minn) 770 Parkview Ave, Saint Paul, MN 55117

MARKLE, Ann (WNY) 1076 Sparta Hwy, Crossville, TN 38572

MARKS, Chas (WMo) 2732 Benton Blvd, Kansas City, MO 64128

MARKS, Patrica (Ga) 814 W Alden Ave, Valdosta, GA 31602

MARKS, Sharla J (Tex) 2431 St Gregory St, Arlington, TX 76013

MARLER, Malcolm Lewis (Ala)

MARLIN, John Henry (Okla) 1818 Coventry Ln, Oklahoma City, OK 73120

MARMON, Mark Mccarter (Tex) 10416 Highway 6, Hitchcock, TX 77563

MARONDE, James A (Los)

MARONEY III, Gordon Earle (Ark) PO Box 202, Smackover, AR 71762

MARQUES, Barbara (Va) 7411 Moss Side Ave, Richmond, VA 23227

MARQUEZ, Juan I (DomRep) Calle Santiago 114, Gazcue, Santo Domingo, Dominican Republic

MARR JR, Andrew (Chi) 56500 Abbey Rd, Three Rivers, MI 49093

✠ **MARRAY**, Santosh K (Eas) The Diocese of Easton, 314 North St, Easton, MD 21601

MARRERO-AYALA, Angel (Mass)

MARRERO CAMACHO, Luis Fernando (PR)

MARRONE, Michael J (Mass) 410 Washington St, Duxbury, MA 02332

MARRS JR, James David (SD)

MARSDEN, Richard Conlon (SwFla) 222 S Palm Ave, Sarasota, FL 34236

MARSH, Abigail (Colo) 6931 E Girard Ave, Denver, CO 80224

MARSH, Caryl (U) 4316 S Adonis Dr, Salt Lake City, UT 84124

MARSH, Elizabeth (Me) 368 Kings Hwy W, 358 Farwood Rd, Haddonfield, NJ 08033

MARSH, Gayle (Minn) 1644 Cohansey St, Saint Paul, MN 55117

MARSH, Graham (Okla)

MARSH, Keith A (Pa) Church of the Messiah, PO Box 127, Gwynedd, PA 19436

MARSH, Mike (WTex) 343 N Getty St, Uvalde, TX 78801

MARSH JR, Robert Francis (Fla) 2462 C H Arnold Rd, Saint Augustine, FL 32092

MARSH IV, Wallace (Ga) St. James' Episc Church, 161 Church St. N.E., Marietta, GA 30060

MARSHALL, David Allen (Oly) 722 N 145th St, Shoreline, WA 98133

MARSHALL, David J (SwFla) Grace Episcopal Church, 1020 Rose Ranch Rd, San Marcos, CA 92069

MARSHALL, Elizabeth (Mass)

MARSHALL, John Anthony (WNY) 7145 Fieldcrest Dr, Lockport, NY 14094

MARSHALL, John Harris (NwT)

MARSHALL, McAlister Crutchfield (Va) 2316 E Grace St # 8011, Richmond, VA 23223

MARSHALL, Mercedes Concepcion (SwFla) 5326 Charles St, New Port Richey, FL 34652

☩ **MARSHALL**, Paul Victor (Be) 2234 Overlook Ln, Fogelsville, PA 18051

MARSHALL III, Wally (Chi) 710 Crab Tree Ln, Bartlett, IL 60103

MARSTON, Robert Dandridge (SVa) 128 Prince St Unit 47, Tappahannock, VA 22560

MARTA, Dale Charles (Mo) 112 N Ray Ave, Maryville, MO 64468

MARTENS, Ann F (Va) 6113 Madison Crest Ct, Falls Church, VA 22041

MARTIEN, Augusta Grace (SVa) 2310 Oakengate Ln, Midlothian, VA 23113

MARTIN, Alexander David (O) 415 Pellett Dr, Bay Village, OH 44140

MARTIN, Alison Jane (WNY) 285 Crestmount Ave, Apr 151, Tonawanda, NY 14150

MARTIN, Andrea Brooke (Mich) 163 Oak Street, Hillsdale, MI 49242

MARTIN, Chad (Va) 20645 Smollet Ter, Ashburn, VA 20147

MARTIN, Christopher (Cal) 1123 Court St, San Rafael, CA 94901

MARTIN, Christopher S (Fla) 2205 Fleet Landing Blvd, Atlantic Beach, FL 32233

MARTIN, David Aaron (RG) 431 Richmond Pl NE, Albuquerque, NM 87106

MARTIN, Derrick Antonio (SeFla) 17 Fernhill Ave, Buffalo, NY 14215

MARTIN, Donald Graham (WK) 1715 W 5th St, Colby, KS 67701

MARTIN JR, Ed (NJ) 1281 Venezia Ave, Vineland, NJ 08361

MARTIN, George H (Minn) 10720 Wentworth Ave S, Bloomington, MN 55420

MARTIN, Gregory Alexander (Cal) 162 Hickory St, San Francisco, CA 94102

MARTIN, Hallock (SeFla) 5042 El Claro N, West Palm Beach, FL 33415

MARTIN, Helena L (Ct)

MARTIN, Irene Elizabeth (Oly) PO Box 83, Skamokawa, WA 98647

MARTIN, James Mitchell (WVa) 177 Edison Dr, Huntington, WV 25705

MARTIN JR, John Charles (Md) 610 Brookfield Ave, Cumberland, MD 21502

MARTIN, Kathleen A (NY) 900 W End Ave, New York, NY 10025

MARTIN, Kenneth Earl (Fla) 125 Holly Vw, Holly Lake Ranch, TX 75765

MARTIN, Kevin E (Dal) 202 Kickapoo Creek Ln, Georgetown, TX 78633

MARTIN, Lydia Adriana Peter (Md) 10800 Greenpoint Rd, Lavale, MD 21502

MARTIN, Mary J (NY) 900 W End Ave Apt 10-C, New York, NY 10025

MARTIN, Mary Nadine (Az) 7750 E Oakwood Cir, Tucson, AZ 85750

MARTIN, Maureen Louise (Mich)

MARTIN, Nancee (Fla) 1023 N Fletcher Ave, Fernandina Beach, FL 32034

MARTIN, Nancy K (WVa) 222 5th Ave, Hinton, WV 25951

MARTIN, Patricia L (NMich)

MARTIN, Paul Dexter (WLa) 275 Southfield Rd, Shreveport, LA 71105

MARTIN, Peter Thomas (SanD)

MARTIN, Rene Elizabeth (Md) Sugarloaf Pkwy, Frederick, MD 21704

MARTIN, Rex L (Wyo) PO Box 64, Hartville, WY 82215

MARTIN JR, Robert James (SwFla) 9727 Bay Colony Dr, Riverview, FL 33578

MARTIN, Robin (Pa) 8114 Heacock Ln, Wyncote, PA 19095

MARTIN, William (Okla) PO Box 1153, Pryor, OK 74362

MARTIN, William L (Be) 5114 Hilltop Cir, East Stroudsburg, PA 18301

MARTIN, Wm Thomas (At) 3207 Pristine Vw, Williamsburg, VA 23188

MARTINDALE, James Lawrence (NMich) 14 Stonegate Hts, Marquette, MI 49855

MARTINDALE, Kyle T (NY) 9302 Blondo St, Omaha, NE 68134

MARTINDALE, Richard James (Ky) 5 S Green St, Henderson, KY 42420

MARTINER, John (Del) 65 Continental Dr, Harwich, MA 02645

MARTINEZ, Bernardo (NwT) 907 Adams Ave, Odessa, TX 79761

MARTINEZ, Isaac Provencio (Mass) 962 Highland Ave, Medford, MA 02155

MARTINEZ, Jacqueline Michelle (Ore)

MARTINEZ, Joel (WMass)

MARTINEZ, Jose (Ct) 155 Wyllys St, Hartford, CT 06106

MARTINEZ, Kim Renee (RG) Po Box 1434, Santa Cruz, NM 87567

MARTINEZ, Luke (Episcopal SJ)

MARTINEZ, Mario Ancizar (NY) 802 Broadway, New York, NY 10003

MARTINEZ AMENGUAL, Margarita (Hond)

MARTINEZ AMENGUAL, Roberto Aaron (Hond)

MARTINEZ GAMA OLIVARES, Jose I (Dal)

MARTINEZ-JANTZ, Jeanie (Va) 2408 Fairhill Dr, Suitland, MD 20746

MARTINEZ-MORALES, Roberto (Los) 1011 S Verdugo Rd, Glendale, CA 91205

MARTINEZ RAPALO, Arturo (Hond) IMS SAP Dept 215, PO BOX 523900, Miami, FL 33152-3900, Honduras

MARTINEZ TOLEDO, Eduardo (PR)

MARTINEZ TORO, Jorge De Jesus (Colom) Carrera 80 #53a-78, Medellin, Antioquia, Colombia

MARTINHAUK, Jeff (SanD) 2728 6th Ave, San Diego, CA 92103

MARTINICHIO, John Robert (CNY) 89 Fairview Ave, Binghamton, NY 13904

MARTINO, Rose Marie (LI) 612 Forest Ave, Massapequa, NY 11758

MARTIN-RHODES, Lilla Rebecca (LI) 27002 Arrowbrook Way, Wesley Chapel, FL 33544

☩ **MARTINS**, Daniel Hayden (Spr) 821 S 2nd St, Springfield, IL 62704

MARTZ, Jeannie (Los) 3107 Pepperwood Ct, Fullerton, CA 92835

MARTZ, Steve (Chi) 947 Oxford Rd, Glen Ellyn, IL 60137

MARVIC, Paula A (NMich) 501 Ogden Ave, Escanaba, MI 49829

MARX, Jeffery Wayne (WTenn) 484 Riding Brook Way, Collierville, TN 38017

MARX, Lily Esther (WMich) 1200 Seminole Rd, Norton Shores, MI 49441

MASADA, Jennifer Ann (The Episcopal Church in Haw) 912 20th Ave, Coralville, IA 52241

MASILLEM, Benedict Baguyos (Ak) 6510 E 10th Ave Apt B, Anchorage, AK 99504

MASON, Alan Newell (Ct) 211 Senexet Rd, Woodstock, CT 06281

MASON, Brooks Kevin (SanD)

MASON, Bruce (Ct) PO Box 443, Litchfield, CT 06759

MASON JR, Charles Thurston (Ind) 224 N Alden Rd, Muncie, IN 47304

MASON, Christopher P (SwVa) 128 Laurel Mountain Estates Dr, Todd, NC 28684

MASON, David Raymond (O) 2277 N Saint James Pkwy, Cleveland Heights, OH 44106

MASON, Eric (Oly) Church of the Redeemer, 6211 NE 182nd St, Kenmore, WA 98028

MASON, Jack Malleroyal (Eas) 114 S Harrison St, Easton, MD 21601

MASON, Joan M (NJ) 417 Washington St, Toms River, NJ 08753

MASON, Joel (NY) 39 Morton Pl, Chappaqua, NY 10514

MASON, John Skain (HB) Rr 2 Box 542b, Inwood, WV 25428

MASON, Lisa P (NY) 1300 Wiltshire Ave, San Antonio, TX 78209

MASON, Marilyn (Los) PO Box 743, Bristol, RI 02809

MASON, Philip Caldwell (Colo) 280 Peregrine Dr, San Marcos, TX 78666

MASON, Samuel Alison (NC) 2181 Jameson Ave Unit 1207, Alexandria, VA 22314

MASON, Victoria Anne (Tex) 6500 Halsey Court, Austin, TX 78739

MASSENBURG, Barbara Jean (Ak) 7962 N Tongass Hwy, Ketchikan, AK 99901

MASSENBURG, Raymond Douglas (Chi) 1514 15th St NW, Washington, DC 20005

MASSEY, Hoyt B (SwFla) PO Box 2161, Franklin, NC 28744

MASSEY, Nigel (NY) 111 E 60th St Ph, New York, NY 10022

MASSIE IV, Robert Kinloch (Mass) 140 Sycamore St, Somerville, MA 02145

MASTER II, George (Pa) 7 Azalea Ln, Media, PA 19063

MASTERMAN, Brenda Patricia (RG) 119 N Golfview Road, Box 9, Lake Worth, FL 33460

MASTERMAN, Frederick James (SeFla) 15170 N Rugged Lark Dr, Tucson, AZ 85739

MASTERSON, Elizabeth Rust (Del) 1 Southerly Ct., Apt. 606, Towson, MD 21286

MASTERSON, Laura Jean (At)

MASZTAL, Gregory Thomas (Episcopal SJ)

MATA, Edwin Geovanny (SwFla)

MATAMOROS, Delia Patricia (Hond) Iglesia Episcopal San Isidro, Colonia Florencia Norte, Primeraentrada Boulevard Suyapa, Tegucigalpa MDC, 11101, Honduras

MATARAZZO, Laura Rice (Nwk) 10 Doe Hollow Lane, Belvidere, NJ 07823

MATHAUER, Margaret Ann (Vt) 7 Holy Cross Rd, Colchester, VT 05446

MATHENY, Clint Michael (CFla) 130 N Magnolia Ave, Orlando, FL 32801

MATHER, Ashley L (Kan)

MATHER, Nicholas S (Oly) 1428 22nd Ave, Longview, WA 98632

MATHER-HEMPLER, Portia (ECR) 950 30th St, Port Townsend, WA 98368

MATHES, Hester (WTenn) 4645 Walnut Grove Rd, Memphis, TN 38117

✠ **MATHES**, Jim (SanD) 5302 E Palisades Rd, San Diego, CA 92116

MATHESON, M Jennings (Ct) 74 South St # 809, Litchfield, CT 06759

MATHEUS, Robert Day (SO) 36 Old Sycamore Ln, Granville, OH 43023

MATHEW, Cherian (ND)

MATHEWS, Keith (SO) 662 N 600 E, Firth, ID 83236

MATHEWS, Koshy (Pa) 2256 Mountain View Dr, Concord, CA 94520

MATHEWS, Miriam Atwell (Md) 3433 Manor Ln, Ellicott City, MD 21042

MATHEWS, Ranjit Koshy (Ct) 120 Old Tannery Ln, Rocky Hill, CT 06067

MATHEWS JR, Tom (Nwk) 5 Surrey Ln, Madison, NJ 07940

MATHEWS, Weston (Va) 7434 Tillman Dr, Falls Church, VA 22043

MATHEWSON, Colin J (SanD) St Paul's Episcopal Cathedral, 2728 6th Ave, San Diego, CA 92103

MATHEWSON, Kathryn Carroll (ETenn) 412 silverberry, Pittsboro, NC 27312

MATHEWSON, Laurel (SanD) St Paul's Cathedral, 2728 6th Ave, San Diego, CA 92103

MATHIAS, Barbara Helen (Minn) 110 S Oak St, Lake City, MN 55041

MATHIESON, James West (SVa) 183 Grove Park Cir, Danville, VA 24541

MATHIS, Judy (CFla) 86 Dianne Dr., Ormond Beach, FL 32176

MATHIS, Thelma Monique (At) 306 Peyton Rd SW, Atlanta, GA 30311

MATHISON, Mary Alice (CGC) 28788 N Main St, Daphne, AL 36526

MATIJASIC, Ernie (SwFla) 401 W Shoreline Dr Unit 253, Sandusky, OH 44870

MATIS, Glenn Marshall (Pa) 45 Latham Ct, Doylestown, PA 18901

MATISSE, Jackie (SO) 232 E Main St, Lebanon, OH 45036

MATKIN, Jeromy Michael (Okla) 701 Wicklow St Apt 502, Stillwater, OK 74074

MATLAK, David John (Mil) 1101 Forest Ave, Richmond, VA 23229

MATNEY, Rex H (Kan) The Church of the Covenant, PO Box 366, Junction City, KS 66441

MATO, Sarah (Mass) Church of the Holy Spirit, 204 Monument Rd, Orleans, MA 02653

MATOS FLORESTAL, Divina Providencia (DomRep)

MATOTT, Michele Louise (Mass) 80 Fisher Rd Unit 90, Cumberland, RI 02864

MATSON, David (Me) 26 Heron Ln, Harpswell, ME 04079

MATTER, Janice Louise (Me) 5 Boynton Ln, Billerica, MA 01821

MATTERS, Rick (Spok) 430 W 24th Ave, Spokane, WA 99203

MATTHEW, John Clifford (Ida) 5301 E Warm Springs Ave E102, Boise, ID 83716

MATTHEWS JR, Allen Russel (WTex) PO Box 348, Luling, TX 78648

MATTHEWS, Anne (Miss) PO Box 804, Brookhaven, MS 39602

MATTHEWS, Bonnie Anne (Ct) Trinity Episc Church, 120 Sigourney St, Hartford, CT 06105

✠ **MATTHEWS**, Clay (Va) PO Box 12686, New Bern, NC 28561

MATTHEWS, Daniel Paul (NY) 1047 Amsterdam Ave, New York, NY 10025

MATTHEWS JR, Daniel Paul (At) 435 Peachtree St, Atlanta, GA 30308

MATTHEWS, Don (CNY) 375 W Clinton St, Elmira, NY 14901

MATTHEWS III, James Houston (WNC) 2232 Water Oak Ln, Gastonia, NC 28056

MATTHEWS, Joyce (Mich) 37906 Glengrove Dr, Farmington Hills, MI 48331

MATTHEWS, Judith (Wyo)

MATTHEWS, Kevin Brian (NC) 625 Candlewood Dr, Greensboro, NC 27403

MATTHEWS, Mary Theresa (RI) 2721 Woodson Dr, 2721 Woodson Dr, Mckinney, TX 75072

MATTHEWS, Patricia Gail (Ark)

MATTHEWS, Richard L (Minn) 8895 Bradford Pl, Eden Prairie, MN 55347

MATTHEWS, William Thompson (Tex)

MATTIA, Joan Plubell (Va) 16 Grande Rue, Gilley, 52500, France

MATTIA JR, Louis Joseph (Va) 622 Worchester St, Herndon, VA 20170

MATTILA, Daniel E (Ct) 104 Walnut Tree Hill Rd, Sandy Hook, CT 06482

MATTLIN, Margaret Baker (Minn) 2085 Buford Ave, Saint Paul, MN 55108

MATTSON, Bradley L (CPa)

MATTSON, Jennifer (CPa) 33 Wilson Dr, Lancaster, PA 17603

MATTSON, Sherry (Ind) 11974 State Highway M26, Eagle Harbor, MI 49950

MAUAI, Brandon Lee (ND) 500 S Main Ave, Sioux Falls, SD 57104

MAUGHAN III, Webster (O) 1226 Waverly Rd, Sandusky, OH 44870

MAULDEN, Kristina Ann (RG) 318 Silver Ave SW, Albuquerque, NM 87102

MAUMUS, Priscilla Guderian (La) Episcopal Diocese of Louisiana, 1623 Seventh St., New Orleans, LA 70115

MAUNEY, James Patrick (RI) PO Box 1236, Sagamore Beach, MA 02562

MAURER, Karen Diane (Los) 211 Calle Potranca, San Clemente, CA 92672

MAURER, Sally Beth (NJ) St Johns Episcopal Church, 76 Market St, Salem, NJ 08079

MAURY, James L (Ga) PO Box 61297, Savannah, GA 31420

MAXFIELD, Christian D (Mil) 14640 N Cleveland Ave, North Fort Myers, FL 33903

MAXSON, John Hollis (The Episcopal Church in Haw) 447 Kawaihae St, Honolulu, HI 96825

MAXWELL, Anne M (Miss) 259 W Hickory St, Ponchatoula, LA 70454

MAXWELL, Barbara Jean (O) 120 Charles Ct, Elyria, OH 44035

MAXWELL, Daniel L (EMich)

MAXWELL, Elizabeth Gail (NY) 225 W 99th St, New York, NY 10025

MAXWELL JR, George (At) 2744 Peachtree Rd Nw, Atlanta, GA 30305

MAXWELL, James (Mich) 281 W Drayton St, Ferndale, MI 48220

MAXWELL, Kate (Minn)

MAXWELL, Kevin Burns (Cal) 2 Meadow Park Circle, Belmont, CA 94002

MAXWELL, Max (Ct) Grace Episcopal Church, 4 Madison Ave, Madison, CT 06443

MAXWELL, Sally Dawn (Minn) St Davids Episcopal Church, 304 E 7th St, Austin, TX 78701

MAY, Amanda Gwyn (Cal) 613 Parkhaven Ct, Pleasant Hill, CA 94523

MAY, David Hickman (Va) 9608 January Dr, Richmond, VA 23238

MAY JR, Frederick Barnett (NJ) 916 Lagoon Ln., Mantoloking, NJ 08738

MAY JR, Jim (Fla) 16178 Williams Pl, King George, VA 22485

MAY IV, Lynde Eliot (Mil) 982 Hunters Trl, Sun Prairie, WI 53590

MAY, Philip Walter (WTex) 700 S Upper Broadway St, Corpus Christi, TX 78401

MAY, Richard Ernest (Va) Po Box 155, Campton, NH 03223

MAY, Richard Leslie (SVa) 349 Archers Mead, Williamsburg, VA 23185

MAY, Thomas Richard (NJ) 65 W Front St, Red Bank, NJ 07701

MAYBERRY, Richard (Ct) 16 Southport Woods Dr, Southport, CT 06890

MAYCOCK, Roma (Va) 5210 Patriots Colony Dr, Williamsburg, VA 23188

MAYEN, John Mabior (SD) 1415 S Bahnson Ave, Sioux Falls, SD 57105

MAYER, Annette Cleary (Chi)

MAYER, Charles D (NY)

MAYER, Linda Margaret (Spok) PO Box 1226, Chelan, WA 98816

MAYER JR, Nicholas Max (WTex) Po Box 1265, Castroville, TX 78009

MAYER, Peter Woodrich (Md) 1601 Pleasant Plains Rd, Annapolis, MD 21409

MAYER, Sandra (CGC) 5158 Border Dr N, Mobile, AL 36608

✠ **MAYER**, Scott (NwT) 1802 Broadway, Lubbock, TX 79401

MAYERS, Tom (Mich) 3837 W. 7 Mile Rd., Detroit, MI 48221

MAYES, Amy Kathryn (Wyo) 519 E Park Ave, Riverton, WY 82501

MAYFIELD, Donna Jeanne (O) 515 N Chillicothe Rd, Aurora, OH 44202

MAYFIELD JR, Ellis (ETenn) 1449 Stage Coach Rd, Sewanee, TN 37375

MAYHALL, Monna (Tenn) 1509 Jaybee Ct, Franklin, TN 37064

MAYHEW, Nancy (EMich) 105 S Erie St # 5, Bay City, MI 48706

MAYHOOD, Gary William (LI) 509 W Plane St, Hackettstown, NJ 07840

MAYNARD, Beth H (Spr) 12 Lothrop St Apt 4, Beverly, MA 01915

MAYNARD, Dennis Roy (SanD) 49 Via Del Rossi, Rancho Mirage, CA 92270

MAYNARD, Jane (Oly) 1829 Cascadia Cir, Medford, OR 97504

MAYNUS, Cody (Minn)

MAYO, HArold Jonathan (Be) 3900 Mechanicsville Rd, Whitehall, PA 18052

MAYO, Valerie Joan (Ky)

MAYOM, Abraham Mabior (SD)

MAYOR, Mike (Oly) 2541 S Meridian Apt U304, Puyallup, WA 98373

MAYORGA-GONZALEZ, Mary Mayorga (Ct) 3 Oakwood Ave, Lawrence, MA 01841

MAYPOLE, Sara (Va) 6988 Woodchuck Hill Rd, Fayetteville, NY 13066

MAYRER, Jane Goodhue (Md) 2010 Sulgrave Ave, Baltimore, MD 21209

MAYS, Foster (NC) 140 Windmill Trl, High Point, NC 27265

MAYS-STOCK, Barbara L (RI) 50 Charles St, Cranston, RI 02920

✠ **MAZE**, Larry (Ark) 102 Midland St, Little Rock, AR 72205

MAZINGO, Stephen L (NC) Saint Peters Church, 801 Atlantic Ave, Fernandina Beach, FL 32034

MAZUJIAN, Harry (NJ) 44 Broad St, Flemington, NJ 08822

MAZUR, Meghan J (Tex)

MAZZA, Joseph (Colo) 1737 Mayview Rd, Jacksonville, FL 32210

MAZZA, Joseph Edward (FdL) 4569 Glidden Dr, Sturgeon Bay, WI 54235

MAZZACANO, Leslie G (NJ) 379 Huntington Dr, Delran, NJ 08075

MAZZARELLA, Virginia (Roch) 327 Mendon Center Rd, Pittsford, NY 14534

MCADAM, Gavin Edward (Dal)

MCADAMS, James Lee (Ala) 3775 Crosshaven Dr, Birmingham, AL 35223

MCADAMS, Kathy (Mass) PO Box 287, Franklin, MA 02038

MCAFEE JR, Ernest (Dal) 1106 Richland Oaks Drive, Richardson, TX 75081

MCALHANY, Julie Ann (Me) St John's Episcopal Church, 234 French St, Bangor, ME 04401

MCALISTER, Donald Beaton (Chi)

MCALISTER, Joel (Tex)

MCALISTER, L Jett (Ct) 92 Locust Ave, Danbury, CT 06810

MCALLEN, Robert (WTex) 1112 S Westgate Dr, Weslaco, TX 78596

MCALPINE, Thomas Hale (FdL) 4526 Crescent Rd, Fitchburg, WI 53711

MCAULAY, Roderick Neil (The Episcopal NCal) 7803 Stefenoni Ct, Sebastopol, CA 95472

MCBAY, Susannah E (Tex) 717 Sage Rd, Houston, TX 77056

MCBEATH, Susan Audrey (Ind) 13088 Tarkington Commons, Carmel, IN 46033

MCBEE, David (O)

MCBRIDE, Bill (WLa) 9105 Colonial Gdns, Shreveport, LA 71106

MCBRIDE, Ronald Winton (Cal) 34043 Calle Mora, Cathedral City, CA 92234

MCBRYDE, Greer (CFla) 1155 C.R. 753 South, Webster, FL 33597

MCCABE, Chad P (WMass)

MCCABE, Paul Charles (At) 1785 Benningfield Dr Sw, Marietta, GA 30064

MCCAFFREY, Susan Maureen (CFla) 4110 S Ridgewood Ave, Port Orange, FL 32127

MCCAIN, Heather (Mo) 2425 Calder Court, Columbia, MO 65201

MCCAIN, Michael T (Ark)

MCCALEB, Doug (SeFla) 464 NE 16th Street, Miami, FL 33132

MCCALL, Chad (Tex)

MCCALL JR, John Keith William (Me) 300 Page St, San Francisco, CA 94102

MCCALL, Ramelle Lorenzo (SC) 1815 Shoremeade Rd Ste 309, Mt Pleasant, SC 29464

MCCALL, Terry A (Mass) 5117 N Chatham Dr, Bloomington, IN 47404

MCCALLISTER, Katlin E (The Episcopal Church in Haw) 1407 Kapiolani St, Hilo, HI 96720

MCCANDLESS, Clelie Fleming (Miss) 8245 Getwell Rd, Southaven, MS 38672

MCCANDLESS, Richard Lawrence (O) 1106 Bell Ridge Rd., Akron, OH 44303

MCCANDLESS, Richard William (Kan) 3028 Washington Ave, Parsons, KS 67357

MCCANLESS, Debra (WTenn)

MCCANN, Christopher Richard (O) 16267 Oakhill Rd, Cleveland Heights, OH 44112

MCCANN, John Harrison (WMo) 1010 W Meyer Blvd, Kansas City, MO 64113

MCCANN, Michael Louis (HB)

MCCANN, Michael Wayne (At) 975 Longstreet Cir, Gainesville, GA 30501

MCCANN, Robert Emmett (Cal) 4023 Canyon Rd, Lafayette, CA 94549

MCCANN, Sandy (At)

MCCANN, Susan Griffen (WMo) 1010 W Meyer Blvd, Kansas City, MO 64113

MCCARD, John (Va) 3110 Ashford Dunwoody Rd NE, Atlanta, GA 30319

MCCARLEY, Daniel Lambert (Dal)

MCCARLEY, Melanie (Mass) Zion Church, 221 E. Washington St., Charles Town, WV 25414

MCCARROLL, Connie Jo (SO) 4381 S.Rangeline Rd., West Milton, OH 45383

MCCARRON, Charles F (LI) 11 Violet Ave, Mineola, NY 11501

MCCARTHY, Bartlett A (Dal) 7335 Inwood Rd, Dallas, TX 75209

MCCARTHY, Bill (Ore) 5060 SW Philomath Blvd Pmb 165, PMB 165, Corvallis, OR 97333

MCCARTHY, Ian (Fla) St Marys Episcopal Church, 623 SE Ocean Blvd, Stuart, FL 34994

MCCARTHY, Jean Elizabeth Rinner (Ia) 2906 39th St, Des Moines, IA 50310

MCCARTHY, Laura Jean (Eas)

MCCARTHY, Marty (NC) 4205 Quail Hunt Ln, Charlotte, NC 28226

MCCARTHY, Mary Katharine (NY) 135 Grant Ave, White Plains, NY 10604

MCCARTHY, Melissa (Los) 6860 Poppyview Dr, Oak Park, CA 91377

MCCARTHY, Nancy Horton (SeFla) 24 Highbridge Xing, Apt 1002, Asheville, NC 28803

MCCARTHY JR, Stephen J (Mass) Corpus Christi College, Merton Street, Oxford, OX1 4JF, Great Britain (UK)

MCCARTY, Marje (EC) 100 E Sherwood Dr, Havelock, NC 28532

MCCARTY, Mary Sharon (WA) 1831 Parkers Creek Road, Port Republic, MD 20676

MCCARTY, Patricia (WTenn) 1720 Peabody Ave, Memphis, TN 38104

MCCARTY, Steven Lynn (Md) St Andrews Tec Ch, 22 Cmbrlnd St PO Box 189, Clear Spring, MD 21722

MCCASLIN, Allan (WNC) 5198 Nc Highway 194 S, Banner Elk, NC 28604

MCCASLIN, H Kenneth (Pa) 694 Kennedy Ln, Wayne, PA 19087

MCCAUGHAN, Patricia Susanne (Los) 1554 N Shelley Ave, Upland, CA 91786

MCCAULEY, Margaret Hudley (Los) 4215 W 61st St, Los Angeles, CA 90043

MCCAULEY, Shana (Ore) 1550 Diablo Rd, Danville, CA 94526

MCCAULLEY, Barbara Marie (Ia) 620 Briarstone Dr Apt 28, Mason City, IA 50401

MCCAUSLAND, John (NH) 111 Peaked Hill Rd, Hopkinton, NH 03229

MCCAW, Mary Ann (Oly) 6 Lincoln Rd, Wellesley, MA 02481

MCCLAIN, Charles (Tenn)

MCCLAIN, Daniel W (SVa) 1505 Shroyer Rd Apt 2, Oakwood, OH 45419

MCCLAIN, Marion Roy Sam (Tex) 3650 Chicora Ct Apt 330, Fort Worth, TX 76116

MCCLAIN, Mikel (EO) 7875 SW Alden St, Portland, OR 97223

MCCLAIN, Rebecca Lee (Oly) Saint Pauls Cathedral, 2728 6th Ave, San Diego, CA 92103

MCCLATCHY, Johnny Edward (Nev)

MCCLEERY III, Bill (SO) 7265 Edgewood Ln, Athens, OH 45701

MCCLELLAN, Robert Farrell (NMich) Po Box 841, Saint Helena, CA 94574

MCCLELLAN, Thomas Lee (Pa) Po Box 642, Lafayette Hill, PA 19444

MCCLELLAND, Carol Jean (EO) 12019 SE 15th St, Vancouver, WA 98683

MCCLENDON, Brenda (Miss)

MCCLOGHRIE, Kathleen Lesley (NY) 4259 Forest Hills Dr, Fortuna, CA 95540

MCCLOUD, Christine L (Md) 4020 Silvage Rd, Nottingham, MD 21236

MCCLOUGH, Jeffrey David (Chi) 3801 Central Ave, Western Springs, IL 60558

MCCLOY, Randolph McKellar (WTenn) 42 S Goodlett St, Memphis, TN 38117

MCCLURE JR, Bill (EMich) 232 N E St, Cheboygan, MI 49721

MCCLURE, Robert Coke (Neb) Saint Matthews Church, 312 W 16th St, Alliance, NE 69301

MCCOART JR, Charles Carroll (Va) Emmanuel Episcopal Church, 1608 Russell Rd, Alexandria, VA 22301

MCCOLL, Scott Joseph (Eur)

MCCOMAS, Scot Alexander (Az) 21596 N 59th Ln, Glendale, AZ 85308

MCCOMBS, Lauren (Cal) 1040 Border Rd, Los Altos, CA 94024

MCCONCHIE, Leann P. (WNY) 119 Royal Pkwy E, Williamsville, NY 14221

MCCONE, Susan (Ct) 80 Green Hill Rd, Washington, CT 06793

MCCONKEY, David Benton (Alb) 6 Albion Place, Northampton, NN1 1UD, Great Britain (UK)

✠ MCCONNELL, Dorsey (Pgh) Tec Dio Of Pittsburgh, 4099 William Penn Hwy, Monroeville, PA 15146

MCCONNELL JR, James Bert (SwFla) 2916 Palm Dr, Punta Gorda, FL 33950

MCCONNELL, Linda (ECR) 61 Corral de Tierra Rd, Salinas, CA 93908

MCCONNELL, Ted (Va) 7319 Habeas Ct, Mechanicsville, VA 23111

MCCONNELL, Theodore A (Alb) 106 East Farm Woods Ln, Fort Ann, NY 12827

MCCOOK, Carla Benae (SwFla) 1929 Par Pl, Sarasota, FL 34240

MCCORMICK, Brendan (Ct) 5 Sea Ln, Old Saybrook, CT 06475

MCCORMICK, Matthew W (SC) Calvary Episcopal Church, 106 Line St, Charleston, SC 29403

MCCORMICK, Phyllis Ann (SwFla) 2850 Countrybrook Dr Apt 13, Apt. 13, Palm Harbor, FL 34684

MCCORMICK, Reid (CFla) 210 Church St, Greenville, AL 36037

MCCORMICK, Thomas Ray (Del) PO Box 1478, Bethany Beach, DE 19930

MCCOWN, Rusty (Tenn) 510 W Main St, Franklin, TN 37064

MCCOY, Adam (NY) Mount Calvary Monastery, 505 E Los Olivos St, Santa Barbara, CA 93105

MCCOY, David Ormsby (SO) 24 Old Coach Rd, Athens, OH 45701

MCCOY, Elaine K (O) 3785 W 33rd St, Cleveland, OH 44109

MCCOY, Robert Martin (Md) 521 Sixth St., Annapolis, MD 21403

MCCOY, William Keith (NJ) 14 Second Street, Edison, NJ 08837

MCCRACKEN, Jennifer Anne (Mass) 112 Randolph Ave, Milton, MA 02186

MCCRACKEN-BENNETT, Rick (SO) 9019 Johnstown Alexandria Rd, Johnstown, OH 43031

MCCRAY-GOLDSMITH, Julia (ECR) 147 Nw 19th Ave, Portland, OR 97209

MCCREARY, Ernest Cannon (USC) 8530 Geer Hwy, Cleveland, SC 29635

MCCREATH, Amy (Mass) 23 Gilbert St, Waltham, MA 02453

MCCRICKARD, Bonnie Mixon (Pa) Church of the Nativity, 208 Eustis Ave SE, Huntsville, AL 35801

MCCRUM, Lewis Lamb (NJ) 415 Washington St, Toms River, NJ 08753

MCCUE, Allan Homer (Mass) 12 Regwill Ave, Wenham, MA 01984

MCCUE, Mary Madeline (WA)

MCCUE, Michael Edlow (WMass) 123 Eileen Dr, Rochester, NY 14616

MCCULLOCH, Kent (Oly) 10630 Gravelly Lake Dr Sw, Lakewood, WA 98499

MCCULLOUGH, Brian Duncan (SanD) 332 N Massachusetts St, Winfield, KS 67156

MCCULLOUGH, Mary (Pa) 708 S Bethlehem Pike, Ambler, PA 19002

MCCUNE, Henry Ralph (Dal) 11560 Drummond Dr, Dallas, TX 75228

MCCURDY III, Alexander (Pa) 613 Maplewood Avenue, Wayne, PA 19087

MCCURDY, Lani (Cal) 3973 17th St, San Francisco, CA 94114

MCCURRY MILLIKEN, Cathleen Ann (Mil) 1734 Fairhaven Dr., Cedarburg, WI 53012

MCCURTAIN, Glad (SwFla) 261 1st Ave SW, Largo, FL 33770

MCCUSKER III, Thomas Bernard (Va) Orchid Garden Homes, 229 103 Thepprasit Rd Moo 12, Pattaya, 20150, Thailand

MCDADE, Shelley D (Del) 12 W 11th St, New York, NY 10011

MCDANIEL, Eleanor B (SwVa) 205 Race Course St, Ashland, VA 23005
MCDANIEL, Elna Irene (Eau) 408 W Nott St, Tomah, WI 54660
MCDANIEL, Judith Maxwell (Oly) 3971 Point White Dr NE, Bainbridge Island, WA 98110
MC DARBY, Mark Daniel (Alb) 8 Summit St, Philmont, NY 12565
MCDERMOT, Joanna (NwPa) 19556 E Cole Rd, Meadville, PA 16335
MCDERMOTT, James Patrick (LI) 1709 Rue Saint Patrick Apt 504, Montreal, QC H3K 3G9, Canada
MCDERMOTT, John Roy (Md) 4493 Barberry Ct, Concord, CA 94521
MCDERMOTT, Matthew (Cal) 580 Colorado Ave, Palo Alto, CA 94306
MCDERMOTT, Megan K (CPa)
MCDERMOTT, Nelda Grace (Ark) 1204 Hunter St, Conway, AR 72032
MCDONALD, David Forrest (NY) PO Box 783, Cornwall, NY 12518
MCDONALD, Dawn (CFla) 1457 Barn Owl Loop, Sanford, FL 32773
MCDONALD, Durstan R (Tex) 811 E 46th St, Austin, TX 78751
MCDONALD, James (Alb) 1937 The Plz, Schenectady, NY 12309
MCDONALD, James Roy (NY) PO Box 161897, Austin, TX 78716
MCDONALD, James Wallace (Episcopal SJ) 627 Goshen Ave, Clovis, CA 93611
MCDONALD, Janet Strain (Va) Po Box 233, Free Union, VA 22940
MCDONALD, Jim (Ark) 106 S 5th St, Batesville, AR 72501
MCDONALD, Karen Loretta (WMich) 89513 Shorelane Dr, Lawton, MI 49065
MCDONALD, Kendrah (WTex) 1215 W 22 1 2 St, Austin, TX 78705
MCDONALD, Lauren (SVa) Spiritworks Foundation, 5800 Mooretown Rd, Williamsburg, VA 23188
MCDONALD, Marc E (Kan) 828 Commercial St, Emporia, KS 66801
MCDONALD, Mark (Tex) Ascension Episcopal Church, 2525 Seagler Rd, Houston, TX 77042
MCDONALD, Norval (Md) 7824 St Andrews Ln, Stanley, NC 28164
MCDONALD, Reverend Timothy Mark (The Episcopal NCal)
MCDONALD, Vickie Lynn (SwFla)
MCDONALD, William Kenneth (Mich) 421 East Ellen Street, Fenton, MI 48430
MCDONNELL, Brian K (Md) 8 Loveton Farms Ct, Sparks, MD 21152
MCDONNELL, George Anne (Minn) PO Box 3811, Lacey, WA 98509
MCDOUGLE, Jane (Cal) 537 Chenery St, San Francisco, CA 94131
MCDOWELL, Glenda Irene (WNC) Cathedral of All Souls, 9 Swan St, Asheville, NC 28803

MCDOWELL JR, John S (CPa) 176 E Pomfret St, Carlisle, PA 17013
MCDOWELL, Joseph Lee (CFla) 116 Jamaica Dr, Cocoa Beach, FL 32931
MCDOWELL, Maria Gwyn (Ore) 5301 NE 73rd Ave, Portland, OR 97218
MCDOWELL, The Rev Mthr Mia Chelynn (USC)
MCDOWELL, Todd S (Mo) Grace Episcopal Church, 514 E Argonne Dr, Kirkwood, MO 63122
MCDOWELL-FLEMING, Dave (CGC) 1606 Ursulines Ave, New Orleans, LA 70116
MCDUFFIE, John Stouffer (WA) 5320 Westpath Way, Bethesda, MD 20816
MCELRATH, James Devoe (WNC) 22 Edgewater Ln, Canton, NC 28716
MCELROY, Catherine DeLellis (NY) 191 Larch Ave, Teaneck, NJ 07666
MCELROY, Elizabeth (Ia)
MCELROY, Gary Austin (O) 8437 Eaton Dr, Chagrin Falls, OH 44023
MCELROY, Jamie (CGC) 3921 Oakridge Dr, Jackson, MS 39216
MCELWAIN, David Marc (Wyo) 104 Ta Bi Dr, Worland, WY 82401
MCELWEE, Michael R (Eau) W5668 County Road F, La Crosse, WI 54601
MCEVOY, Susan E (Wyo)
MCEWEN JR, Billy Wayne (ND)
MCEWEN, Michael Thomas (Okla) PO Box 338, 514 Big Rock Rd, Medicine Park, OK 73557
MCFADDEN, Cheryl Culley (Ct) 203 Vandemere St, Oriental, NC 28571
MCGARRY, Susan Ellen (Vt) Saint Stephens Church, 3 Main St, Middlebury, VT 05753
MCGARRY-LAWRENCE, Marla (Ore) 2136 NE Cesar E Chavez Blvd., Portland, OR 97212
MCGAVERN III, Cecil George (Tex) 15015 Memorial Dr, Houston, TX 77079
MCGAVRAN, Frederick Jaeger (SO) 3528 Traskwood Cir, Cincinnati, OH 45208
MCGEE JR, Hubert (Ind) 1609 Rivershore Rd, Elizabeth City, NC 27909
MCGEE, Robert Maurice (CFla)
MCGEE, William Earl (ETenn) 3404-A Taft Hwy, Signal Mountain, TN 37377
MCGEHEE, Andrew Austin (Miss) 1790 Lavista Rd NE, Atlanta, GA 30329
MCGEHEE, Pitman Pittman (Tex) 1307 Westover Rd, Austin, TX 78703
MCGEHEE, Steve Yarnall (Va) 6000 Grove Ave, Richmond, VA 23226
MCGEHEE, Margaret Evalyn (Kan)
MCGILL JR, Dennis Madison (Ga)
MCGILL, Jim (Tex) 1514 Lake Bank Ct, El Lago, TX 77586
MCGILL JR, William James (CPa) Po Box 682, Cornwall, PA 17016

MCGIMPSEY, Ralph Gregory (Mich) 8207 Nice Way, Sarasota, FL 34238
MCGINN, John Edward (Mass) 29 Oak Ridge Rd, East Sandwich, MA 02537
MCGINNIS, Brandon Scott (Ore)
MCGINTY, John P (LI) 17 Exeter Dr, Auburn, MA 01501
MCGINTY, William Joseph (Be) 110 Ave M., Matamoras, PA 18336
MCGIRR, Joyce Bearden (Nwk)
MCGLANNAN, Dorian (Mich) 1241 Long Dr, Freeland, WA 98249
MCGLASHON JR, Hugh (CFla) PO Box 3303, Haines City, FL 33845
MCGOWAN, Carole (RG) 2805 Don Pablo Rd NW, Albuquerque, NM 87104
MCGOWAN, Diane Darby (Minn) 5029 2nd Ave S, Minneapolis, MN 55419
MCGOWAN, Neal Scott (Tex) 5402 Indigo St, Houston, TX 77096
MCGOWAN, Sandra Maria (Alb)
MCGOWEN, Willetta Hulett (Ga) 900 Gloucester St, Brunswick, GA 31520
MCGRADY, Jacqueline Ann (Mass) PO Box 2847, Nantucket, MA 02584
MCGRANE, Kevin John (Mo) 3664 Arsenal St, Saint Louis, MO 63116
MCGRATH, Nancy Hunnewell (EO) 18160 Cottonwood Rd Pmb 719, Sunriver, OR 97707
MCGRATH, Victoria (Nwk) 113 Center Ave, Chatham, NJ 07928
MCGRAW, Jean (SC) 2341 Wofford Rd, Charleston, SC 29414
MCGRAW, Stanley Earle (At) 1878 Oleander Ct, Charleston, SC 29414
MCGRAW, Tara L (SwFla)
MCGREGOR, Claudia Kathleen (Ark)
MCGREGOR, Patsy (SeFla) PO Box 399, Ambridge, PA 15003
MCGRIFF, Amanda Perkins (WTenn)
MCGUGAN, Terry (Colo) 2950 S University Blvd, Denver, CO 80210
MCGUINNESS, David (NC) 4330 Pin Oak Dr, Durham, NC 27707
MCGUIRE, Malcolm (Pa) 1300 Lombard St Apt 711, Philadelphia, PA 19147
MCGUIRE, Mark Alan (WMo) 908 SW Hackney Ct, Lees Summit, MO 64081
MCGURK, Brian (Mass) 625 Main St, Chatham, MA 02633
MCHALE, Stephen (Cal) 1700 Santa Clara Ave, Alameda, CA 94501
MCHALE O'CONNOR, Colleen (WNY) 1 E Main St, Le Roy, NY 14482
MCHENRY, Richard Earl (Tex) 1010 Willowcreek Rd, Cleburne, TX 76033
MCHUGH III, John Michael (NJ) 324 Rio Grande Blvd Nw, Albuquerque, NM 87104
MCILHINEY, David B (NH) 701 E High St Apt 211, Charlottesville, VA 22902

MCILMOYL, Mac (The Episcopal NCal) 1314 Spring St, Saint Helena, CA 94574

MCILVAIN, Jean Christine (Pgh) 5622 Alan St, Aliquippa, PA 15001

MCILVEEN, Richard William (Me) 26 Concord St, Portland, ME 04103

MCINDOO, Lisa (WTenn) Diocese Of West Tennessee, 692 Poplar Ave, Memphis, TN 38105

MCINNIS, Victor Erwin (Miss) Po Box 63, Lexington, MS 39095

MCINTIRE, Rhonda (RG) 17 Camino Redondo, Placitas, NM 87043

MCINTOSH, David Kevin (Ct) PO Box 309, 1 N Main St, Kent, CT 06757

MCINTOSH, Eric (Pgh) St James Episcopal Church, 11524 Frankstown Rd, Pittsburgh, PA 15235

MCINTOSH, Justin Michael (Va) 575 Gillums Ridge Rd, Charlottesville, VA 22903

MCINTOSH, Kendra Lea (Nwk) 26 W 84th St, New York, NY 10024

MCINTOSH, Wayne S (SD) Trinity Episcopal Church, 500 14th Ave NW, Watertown, SD 57201

MCINTYRE, Calvin Carney (NY) 4401 Matilda Ave, Bronx, NY 10470

MCINTYRE, Gregory Edward (NC) 258 W Franklin Blvd, Gastonia, NC 28052

MCINTYRE, John George (Md) 326 Pintail Dr, Havre De Grace, MD 21078

MCINTYRE, Moni (Pgh) 4601 5th Ave #825, Pittsburgh, PA 15213

MCJILTON, Sheila N (WA) St Philips Church, 522 Main St, Laurel, MD 20707

MCKAY IV, Bob (NwPa) 1267 Treasure Lk, Du Bois, PA 15801

MCKAY, Judy Aileen (Ida) 5301 E Warm Springs Ave, # E102, Boise, ID 83716

MCKAY, Paige Higley (NwT) 1101 Slide Rd, Lubbock, TX 79416

MCKAY, William Martin (RG)

MCKEAN, Samantha Kate (Ga) 615 E 49th St, Savannah, GA 31405

MCKEE, Christianne (Spok) 1909 W. Clearview Dr., Ellensburg, WA 98926

MCKEE, Elizabeth Shepherd (NC) 408 Woodlawn Ave, Greensboro, NC 27401

MCKEE, Helen Louise (SVa) 405 Avondale Dr., Danville, VA 24541

MCKEE, Lewis Kavanaugh (WTenn) 57 Wychewood Dr, Memphis, TN 38117

MCKEE, Martha Marcella (NJ) 246 Tanzanite Cir, Buda, TX 78610

MCKEE, Michael Dale (Los) 815 Emerald Bay, Laguna Beach, CA 92651

MCKEE, Stephen (Okla) 501 S Cincinnati Ave, Tulsa, OK 74103

MCKEE, Susan Rose (CGC) PO Box 9, Bon Secour, AL 36511

MCKEE, Todd Anderson (Vt) 105 Hickory Rdg, White River Junction, VT 05001

MCKEEFRY, Hailey Lynne (Cal) 28 Cobblestone Ln, Belmont, CA 94002

MCKEEVER, Anne Dryden (The Episcopal NCal) 2620 Capitol Ave., Sacramento, CA 95816

✠ **MCKELVEY**, Jack Marston (Roch) 8 Grove St, Rochester, NY 14605

MCKENNA, Cynthia Ann (Va) 6102 New Pembrook Ln, Fredericksburg, VA 22407

MCKENNA, Keith (NY) 429 Lakeshore Drive, Putnam Valley, NY 10579

MCKENNEY, Mary Lou (ECR)

MCKENNEY, Walter (Ct) 38 Clover Dr, West Hartford, CT 06110

MCKENZIE, Bryan Keith (Tex) 2117 Ruea St, Grand Prairie, TX 75050

MCKENZIE, Jennifer Gaines (Va) 33 Elmers Green, Skelmersdale, WN8 6RZ, Great Britain (UK)

MCKENZIE JR, William Bruce (Ore) 1873 Sw High St, Portland, OR 97201

MCKENZIE-HAYWARD, Renee (Pa) 34 East Hodges Ave, Philadelphia, PA 19121

MCKEON, Julia (Cal) 1590 Cabrillo Hwy S, Half Moon Bay, CA 94019

MCKEON JR, Richard (NY) Church of the Messiah, PO Box 248, Rhinebeck, NY 12572

MCKEY-DUNAR, Kathryn (Ct)

MCKIM, Laurie J. (WTex) Church of the Advent, 104 W Elizabeth St, Brownsville, TX 78520

MCKINLEY, Ellen Bacon (Ct) 47 Valley Rd # B1, Cos Cob, CT 06807

MCKINLEY, Mele Senitila Tuineau (Ore) 1817 E Alsea Hwy, Waldport, OR 97394

MCKINNEY, Catherine R (Va) Varina Episcopal Church, 2385 Mill Rd, Henrico, VA 23231

MCKINNEY, Chantal (NC) 242 Flintshire Rd, Winston Salem, NC 27104

MCKINNEY, Douglas Walton (Los) 401 S Detroit St Apt 311, Los Angeles, CA 90036

MCKINNEY, Helen Katherine (Mass)

MCKINNON, Michael John (Mass) 9 Svenson Ave, Worcester, MA 01607

MCKINNON, Stanley A (Ark) PO Box 767, Siloam Springs, AR 72761

MCKONE-SWEET, Mark C (SVa) 2121 Ferguson Loop, Chesapeake, VA 23322

MCLACHLAN, Suhail Shepard (Mass) 10 Searle Street, Cambridge, CB4 3DB, Great Britain (UK)

MCLAIN, Madge (WLa) PO Box 1101, Abbeville, LA 70511

MCLAIN III, Paul King (WTenn) 102 N 2nd St, Memphis, TN 38103

MCLAREN, Christopher Todd (RG) 6730 Green Valley Pl NW, Los Ranchos, NM 87107

MCLARTY JR, Andrew (Miss)

MCLAUGHLIN, Debra K (SeFla) Stbenedicts Tec Ch, 7801 NW 5th St, Plantation, FL 33324

MCLAUGHLIN, Eleanor (NH) 38 Nekal Ln, Randolph, NH 03593

MCLAUGHLIN, John Norris (Mass) 406 Paradise Rd Apt 1b, Swampscott, MA 01907

MCLAUGHLIN, Marlys Jean (Az) 10926 W Topaz Dr, Sun City, AZ 85351

MCLAURIN, Malcolm (Oly) 2127 N 186th St, Shoreline, WA 98133

MCLEAN JR, James Rayford (Ark) PO Box 524, Leland, MI 49654

MCLEAN, Jean Medding (Mont)

MCLEAN, Katherine Sharp (La) 600 W. Church St., Hammond, LA 70401

MCLEAN, Richard (WTex) 3821 Sandia Dr, Plano, TX 75023

MCLEAVEY, Lauren (LI) 9 Carlton Ave, Port Washington, NY 11050

MCLELLAN, Brenda Jean (Mont) 350 Janet St Apt 2b Apt 2b, Helena, MT 59601

MCLEMORE, Ann Rossington (Miss) 13604 Caldwell Dr Apt 62, Austin, TX 78750

MCLEMORE, William Pearman (Chi) 711 1st Ave, Sterling, IL 61081

MCLEOD, Harrison Marvin (USC) Christ Church, 10 N Church St, Greenville, SC 29601

MCLEOD III, Henry Marvin (Vt) 301 Georgetown Cir, Charleston, WV 25314

MCLEOD, Robert Boutell (CFla) 6661 N Placita Alta Reposa, Tucson, AZ 85750

MCLEON IV, Richard (WTex) PO Box 698, Henderson, TX 75653

✠ **MCLOUGHLIN**, Jose Antonio (WNC) 924 N Robinson Ave, Oklahoma City, OK 73102

MCLUEN, Roy (CGC) 25450 144th Pl SE, Kent, WA 98042

MCMAHAN, Larry Wayne (CGC) 3902 E Jamie Ln, Bloomington, IN 47401

MCMAHON, Kathryn Evans (WA) 818 University Blvd W, Silver Spring, MD 20901

MCMANUS, Bridget (CNY) 531 Cumberland Ave, Syracuse, NY 13210

MCMANUS, Elizabeth C (Tex)

MCMANUS, Mary Christie (Cal) 215 10th Ave, San Francisco, CA 94118

MCMANUS, Michael (Colo) P. O. Box 33022, Palm Beach Gardens, FL 33420

MCMICHAEL JR, Ralph Nelson (Spr) 1210 Locust St, Saint Louis, MO 63103

MCMILLAN, Bruce Dodson (Miss) PO Box 596, Holly Springs, MS 38635

MCMILLAN, Daniel (SanD)

MCMILLAN, John (Alb) 4531 Ethel St, Okemos, MI 48864

MCMILLAN, Marilyn Ayres (Mass) 205 Old Main St, South Yarmouth, MA 02664

MCMILLEN II, Chuck (WTenn) St James Episcopal Church, PO Box 838, Union City, TN 38281

MCMILLIN, Andrea McMillin (Oly) 1600 Knox Ave, Bellingham, WA 98225

MCMULLEN, Andrew L (The Episcopal Church in Haw) St Matthias Tec Ch, 18320 Furrow Rd, Monument, CO 80132

MCMURREN, Margaret (Ore) 1525 Glen Creek Rd Nw, Salem, OR 97304

MCMURTRY, Herbert Charles (Ak) 1915 Lindsay Loop, Mount Vernon, WA 98274

MCNAB, Charles Bruce (Colo) 2 Park Plaza Rd, Bozeman, MT 59715

MCNAB, Joan T (Colo) 536 W North St, Aspen, CO 81611

MCNABB, Christopher Ward (LI) 33 Mercer St, Princeton, NJ 08540

MCNAIR, David (WNC) C Of Holy Spirit, PO Box 956, Mars Hill, NC 28754

MCNAIR, Kent Stevens (The Episcopal NCal) 2200 Country Club Dr, Cameron Park, CA 95682

MCNALLY, Jennifer Steckel (Minn) 2035 Charlton Rd, Sunfish Lake, MN 55118

MCNAMARA, Beth Cooper (Md) 8015 Rider Ave, Towson, MD 21204

MCNAMARA, Dawn (Va)

MCNAMARA, Joseph Francis (CPa) Po Box 474, Mansfield, PA 16933

MCNAMARA, Kim (Oly) PO Box 156, Allyn, WA 98524

MCNAMARA, Patrick (NH) Holy Trinity, 768 Main St, Greenport, NY 11944

MCNAUGHTON, Bonnie Eleanor (Los) 2571 Via Campesina Unit G, Palos Verdes Estates, CA 90274

MCNAUGHTON, Margaret (WA) 720 Upland Pl, Alexandria, VA 22314

MCNEELEY, David Fielden (Hai) 566 Standish Rd, Teaneck, NJ 07666

MCNEELY, Virginia Diane (The Episcopal NCal) Trinity Cathedral, 2620 Capitol Ave, Sacramento, CA 95816

MCNEILL, Nayan (ECR) 20 University Ave, Los Gatos, CA 95030

MCNELLIS, Kathleene Kernan (RG) 6200 Coors NW, Albuquerque, NM 87120

MCNIEL, Donna (Mich) 800 Abbot Rd, East Lansing, MI 48823

MCNIFF, Susie M (NY)

MCNISH, Jill (Pa) 199 W Baltimore Ave, Clifton Heights, PA 19018

✠ **MCNUTT JR**, Charlie Fuller (CPa) 5225 Wilson Ln Apt 2137, Mechanicsburg, PA 17055

MCNUTT, Robin Lee (Neb) 3020 Belvedere Blvd, Omaha, NE 68111

MCPARTLIN, Julie (Alb) 5101 Highway A1a Apt 203, Vero Beach, FL 32963

MCPEAK, Christopher (Oly)

MCPEAK, Helen (Oly) 4016 Ridge Way, Mount Vernon, WA 98273

MCPEEK, Steve (Eur)

MCPHAIL, Donald Stewart (SC) 22 Saint Augustine Dr, Charleston, SC 29407

MCPHERSON, Bruce (Md) 214 Wardour Drive, Annapolis, MD 21401

MCPHERSON, Clair W (NY) 1234 Midland Ave Apt 5e, Bronxville, NY 10708

MCPHERSON, Phebe (Md) 214 Wardour Dr, Annapolis, MD 21401

MCPHERSON, Thomas Dale (WMich) 224 Chauncey Ct, Marshall, MI 49068

MCQUADE, Lynne (NY) 900 Palmer Rd Apt 7l, Bronxville, NY 10708

MCQUEEN, Dale (Oly) 3230 Chanute Dr., Lake Havasu city, AZ 86404

MCQUEEN, Henry (WA) St Johns Church, 3427 Olney Laytonsville Rd, Olney, MD 20832

MCQUEEN, Paul (CFla) 1332 Bramley Ln, Deland, FL 32720

MCQUERY, Andy (O)

MCQUIN, Randall Lee (Kan) 3141 Fairview Park Dr Ste 250, Falls Church, VA 22042

MCRAE, Marcia O (Ga) 511 E Broughton St, Bainbridge, GA 39817

MCREE, Tim (WNC) 274 Sunset Hts, Canton, NC 28716

MCSWAIN, William D (SC) 7313 Highway 162, Hollywood, SC 29449

MCTERNAN, Vaughan Durkee (Colo) 2609 Rigel Drive, Colorado Springs, CO 80906

MCVEY, Arthur William (Kan) 9218 Cherokee Pl, Leawood, KS 66206

MCVEY, Brian (Tenn) 4403 High Ct, Davenport, IA 52804

MCWHORTER, Betty (NY) 1304 NW Meadows Drive, McMinnville, OR 97128

MCWHORTER, Shirley R (Mich) St Thomas Episcopal Church, 2441 Nichols Drive, Trenton, MI 48183

MCWHORTER, Stephen (Ala) 570 Lovely Ln, Sylacauga, AL 35151

MEACHEN, Jerome Webster (Ct) 20 W Canal St Apt 423, Winooski, VT 05404

MEAD, Alan Champ (CPa) 3159 Silver Sands Circle #103, Virginia Beach, VA 23451

MEAD, Andrew Craig (NY) 321 Wandsworth Street, Narragansett, RI 02882

MEAD, Carol Lynn (Miss) 105 Montgomery Rd, Starkville, MS 39759

MEAD, Matthew Hoxsie (NY) 1415 Pelhamdale Avenue, Pelham, NY 10803

MEADE, Elizabeth Gordon (Mil) 805 Devils Ln, Walworth, WI 53184

MEADE, Gary J (WTenn) St Marys Episcopal Church, 108 N King Ave, Dyersburg, TN 38024

MEADE, Jean (La) 1314 Jackson Ave, New Orleans, LA 70130

MEADERS III, Calvin Judson (Miss) 305 S Commerce St, Natchez, MS 39120

MEADERS JR, Jud (Miss) 200 E Academy St., Canton, MS 39046

MEADOWS JR, Richard Dean (Md) St James Episcopal Church, 1607 Grace Church Rd, Silver Spring, MD 20910

MEAIRS, Babs Marie (SanD) 11650 Calle Paracho, San Diego, CA 92128

MEANS, Carl T (Wyo) 300 Mt. Arter Loop, Lander, WY 82520

MEANS, Jackie (Ind) 834 Mount Dora Ln, Indianapolis, IN 46229

MEANS-KOSS, Brian Jeremy (Va)

MEARS, Catherine (Ia)

MEARS JR, Preston Kennard (NH) 15101 Candy Hill Rd, Upper Marlboro, MD 20772

MEASE, Carole Ann (CPa) 359 Schoolhouse Rd, Middletown, PA 17057

MEAUX, Amy Dafler (Ark) 320 W Main St, Danville, KY 40422

MEBANE JR, Will (Mass) St Barnabass Memorial, 103 Main St, Falmouth, MA 02540

MECK III, Daniel Stoddart (Md) 5620 Greenspring Avenue, Baltimore, MD 21209

MECK, Nancy (SVa) 13530 Heathbrook Rd, Midlothian, VA 23112

MECKLING, Jude (Pa) 730 S Highland Ave, Merion Station, PA 19066

MEDELA, Jean (Hai) Eglesi Episcopal DHaiti, Boite Postale 1309, Port-au-Prince, Haiti

MEDINA, Ernesto (Neb) 16611 Castelar St, Omaha, NE 68130

MEDINA, Felix R (PR) Po Box 2156, Bridgeport, CT 06608

MEDINA MEJIA, Jorge Reynaldo (Hond)

MEDINA-SALABARRIA, Ricardo Santiago (NC)

MEDLEY, James (Mass) 496 S Almond St, Fall River, MA 02724

MEECH, Michelle (NY) 4800 Woodward Ave, Detroit, MI 48201

MEEKS, Edward Gettys (USC) 405 S Chapel St, Baltimore, MD 21231

MEENGS, John Richard (WMich) 622 Lawndale Ct, Holland, MI 49423

MEGEATH, Sally Holme (Colo) 343 Canyon St, Lander, WY 82520

MEGGINSON JR, Marshall Elliot (HB) 5689 Utrecht Rd, Baltimore, MD 21206

MEGINNISS, David (Ala) 801 Pin Brook Ln, Tuscaloosa, AL 35406

MEIER, Kermit Irwin (Ore) 1209 Fleet Landing Blvd, Atlantic Beach, FL 32233

MEIROW, Lisa Marie (Fla)

MEISS, Marion (Be) 46 S. Laurel St., Hazleton, PA 18201

MEISTER, Deborah (Ct) 3001 Wisconsin Ave NW, Washington, DC 20016

MEISTER, Stephen George (Roch) 400 S Main St, Newark, NY 14513

MEISTER BOOK, Nancy D (Az)
MEJIA, Jairo (ECR) 12149 Saddle Rd, Carmel Valley, CA 93924
MEJIA, Jose Arnaldo (Hond) Calle Principal, La Estrada, HN, Honduras
MEJIA, Maria Esmeralda (Hond)
MEJIA, Nelson Yovany (Hond) Roatan Islas De La Bahia, Apartado 193, Roatan Coxen Hole, Honduras
MEJIA BALLESTEROS, Francisco Javier (Colom) C 1 N 48-95 Barrio Leon XIII, Villavicencio Meta, Colombia
MEJIA ESPINOSA, Jose Vicente (EcuC) Avenue La Castellana 40-06, Zona 8, Guatemala City, 01008, Guatemala
MEJIA-MONTESDEOCA, Marco (EcuC) P.O. Box 588, Ibarra, Ecuador
MELANCON, Sylvia A (WTex)
MELBERGER, MaryJo (Pa) 734 Twining Way, Collegeville, PA 19426
MELCHER, John (Mich) 2441 Nichols St, Trenton, MI 48183
MELCHIONNA, Elizabeth Marie Marie (NC) 104 Nuttal Pl, Chapel Hill, NC 27514
MELENDEZ, Mario (SVa)
MELENDEZ, Michael Paul (Mass) 138 Tremont St, Boston, MA 02111
MELIN, Marilyn Joyce (Chi) 206 South Maple Street, Libertyville, IL 60048
MELIS, Alberto Manuel (Tex) 305 N 30th St, Waco, TX 76710
MELLO, Jeffrey William (Ct) 112 Church St, Wethersfield, CT 06109
MELLO, Mary Ann (RI) 114 George St, Providence, RI 02906
MELLO-MAKI, Christine Helene (NMich) 470 North Us 141, Crystal Falls, MI 49920
MELLON, Bob (Pa) 10551 Machrihanish Cir, San Antonio, FL 33576
MELLOTT, Emily Alice (NJ) 207 W Main St, Moorestown, NJ 08057
MELNYK, James (NC) 5400 Crestview Rd, Raleigh, NC 27609
MELTON, Betty Anne (Miss)
MELTON, Brent (NC) 210 Ellington St, Fayetteville, NC 28305
MELTON, Heather L (NAM) 288 Harrison Ave, Harrison, NY 10528
MELTON, Jk (Colo) Fordham University, 441 E Fordham Rd, Bronx, NY 10458
MELTON, Jonathan Randall (Dal) 1360 Regent St # 157, Madison, WI 53715
MELTON, Mark Randall (Dal) 101 Meadowood Rd, Enchanted Oaks, TX 75156
MEMBA, Joseluis (Pa) PO Box 502, Red Bank, NJ 07701
MENAUL, Marjorie (CPa) 6288 Peach Tree Rd, Columbus, OH 43213
MENDEZ, Noe (Dal) The H Nativity Tec Ch, 2200 18th St, Plano, TX 75074

MENDEZ, Richard (U) RR 2 Box 64, Pocatello, ID 83202
MENDEZ, Troy Douglas (Az) Trinity Cathedral, 100 W Roosevelt St, Phoenix, AZ 85003
MENDEZ COLON, Ana Rosa (PR) Urbanizacion Venus Gardens, 1770 Calle Peliux, San Juan, PR 00926
MENDOZA, Christine Love (Va) 9350 Braddock Rd, Burke, VA 22015
MENDOZA, Lidia (SanD)
MENDOZA, Loretta (Mil) 2708 Red Fawn Ct, Racine, WI 53406
MENDOZA, Nelson (NY)
MENDOZA CEDENO, Victor Eduardo (Litoral Diocese Of Ecuador)
MENDOZA MARMOLEJOS, Milquella Rosanna (DomRep)
MENDOZA PEREZ, Julio Cesar (Ve) Dio de Venezuela, CD Av Caroni No 100, Caracas, Venezuela
MENDOZA QUIROZ, Hugo Eligio (Litoral Diocese Of Ecuador) Calle #19, #208, Calderon, Ecuador
MENEELEY, Beverly Ann (Be)
MENELAS, Frederic (Hai)
MENGER, James Andrew (Ga) 3521 Nassau Dr, Augusta, GA 30909
MENJIVAR, Natividad (Okla) St Mark's Episcopal Church, 6744 S Kings Hwy, Alexandria, VA 22306
MENJIVAR, Nicholas (NC) Po Box 218, Durham, NC 27702
MENNELL, John (Nwk) 75 S Fullerton Ave, Montclair, NJ 07042
MENTZER, Scott Allen (WK) 916 E 7th St, Goodland, KS 67735
MENZI, Donald Wilder (Mich) 5 E 10th St, New York, NY 10003
MERCER JR, Charles Spencer (Md) The Tec Ch Of Smv, 3121 Walbrook Ave, Baltimore, MD 21216
MERCER, Emmanuel A (Md) Saint Paul's Church, 22 E Chestnut Hill Ave, Philadelphia, PA 19118
MERCER, Jarred A (Mass)
MERCER, Karen (Md)
MERCER JR, Roy Calvin (CFla) 4932 Willowbrook Cir, Winter Haven, FL 33884
MERCER, Thomas Robert (NY) Po Box A, Granite Springs, NY 10527
MERCER LADD, Morgan (LI)
MERCHANT, John Edward (At) 474 Sunset Dr, Asheville, NC 28804
MERCHANT, Patricia (At) 120 Warren St NE, Atlanta, GA 30317
MERCHANT II, Wilmot (SC) 801 11th Ave N, North Myrtle Beach, SC 29582
MERCIER, Darcey (Vt)
MERCURE, Joan Carol (Minn) 4557 Colfax Ave S, Minneapolis, MN 55419
MEREDITH, Carol Ann (Colo) 316 Oakland St, Aurora, CO 80010
MEROLA SR, Carl Robert (CFla) 705 Victory Lane, Hendersonville, NC 28739
MEROLA JR, Carl Robert (Va) 402 Valencia Cir, Oviedo, FL 32765

MERONEY, Anne Elrod (At) 4919-B Rivoli Dr, Macon, GA 31210
MERRELL, Robin Nicholas (Cal) 3886 Balcom Rd, San Jose, CA 95148
MERRICK, Barbara Robinson (Ky) 8110 Saint Andrews Church Rd, Louisville, KY 40258
MERRILL JR, Robert C (Tex) 1321 Upland Dr # 5192, Houston, TX 77043
MERRILL, Russell Walter (EMich) 262 Raleigh Pl, Lennon, MI 48449
MERRILL, Wendy Wheadon (NC)
MERRIMAN, Michael Walter (Minn) 2012 Stain Glass Dr, Plano, TX 75075
MERRIN, Susie (Colo)
MERRITT, Claudia W (Va) 3401 Hawthorne Ave, Richmond, VA 23222
MERRITT, Frederick Deen (Neb)
MERRITT, Robert E (CFla) 864 Summerfield Dr, Lakeland, FL 33803
MERROW, Andrew T P (Va) 2609 N Glebe Rd, Arlington, VA 22207
MERTZ, Annie Pierpoint (The Episcopal NCal) St Pauls Episcopal School, 116 Montecito Ave, Oakland, CA 94610
MERTZ, Mary Ann (Pa) 116 Lancaster Pike, Oxford, PA 19363
MERZ, John (LI) 129 Kent St, Brooklyn, NY 11222
MESENBRING, David Gary (Oly) 1245 10th Ave E, Seattle, WA 98102
MESSENGER, William Glen (Mass) 29 Saint John St, Jamaica Plain, MA 02130
MESSENGER-HARRIS, Beverly Ann (CNY) 124 W Hamilton Ave, Sherrill, NY 13461
MESSER, Chuck (NJ) PO Box 452, Glen Riddle, PA 19037
MESSER, Kenneth Blaine (Ia)
MESSER-CROTEAU, Julia (SVa) 2357 Inlynnview Rd, Virginia Beach, VA 23454
MESSERSMITH, Daphne (CPa) PO Box 125, Cornwall, PA 17016
MESSERSMITH, Merton (CPa) 909 Alison Ave, Mechanicsburg, PA 17055
MESSICK, Joshua E (Md) 20 3rd St, Pocomoke City, MD 21851
MESSIER, Daniel Joseph (Az) 600 S La Canada Dr, Green Valley, AZ 85614
MESSINA JR, Michael Frank (CFla) 94 Pecan Run, Ocala, FL 34472
MESTETH, Rhoda Yvonne (SD) Po Box 9, Pine Ridge, SD 57770
MESTRE JR, Jos Wilfredo (Ct) 2340 North Ave Apt. 7D, Bridgeport, CT 06614
METCALF, Michael Patrick (Dal) 3205 Landershire Ln, Plano, TX 75023
METCALFE, Steven (WNY) 10640 Clarence Center Rd, Clarence, NY 14031
METELLUS, Donald (Hai)
METHVEN, Susanne (Okla) 3328 S Marion Ave, Tulsa, OK 74135
METIVIER, Catherine A (Okla)

METOYER, Eric (Cal) Tec Dio Of Ca, 1055 Taylor St, San Francisco, CA 94108

METRO, Michael (Be)

METTLER, Garrett M (NY) 160 Southern Blvd, Danbury, CT 06810

METZGER, Curtis (NH) PO Box 1541, Concord, NH 03302

METZGER, Jim (Mo) 3402 Sawgrass Ln, Cincinnati, OH 45209

METZLER, Carolyn (RG) 1611 Sunset Gardens Rd SW, Albuquerque, NM 87105

METZLER, Martie (Mo) 5305 Kenrick View Drive, Saint Louis, MO 63119

METZLER, Paul Arthur (CNY) 5305 Kenrick View Dr, Saint Louis, MO 63119

MEULENDYK, John (Mich) St Philips Episcopal Church, 100 Romeo Rd, Rochester, MI 48307

MEUSCHKE, Marty O (Ga) 145 River Ridge Loop, Hortense, GA 31543

MEYER, Alan King (Az) 5909 SW Karla Ct, Portland, OR 97239

MEYER, Erika (NY) 240 E 31st St, New York, NY 10016

MEYER, John (Mich) 1353 Labrosse St, Detroit, MI 48226

MEYER, John Anthony (LI) 423 Falcon Ridge Dr, Sheridan, WY 82801

MEYER, Kerri (Minn)

MEYER, Mark David (Colo) 1365 Fairview Ave, Canon City, CO 81212

MEYER, Nancy Ruth (NH) St Peter's Episcopal Church, 621 W Belmont Ave, Chicago, IL 60657

MEYER, Robert (FdL) PO Box 184, Tremont, IL 61568

MEYER, Wendel William (Mass) 7502 Heyburn Ct, Louisville, KY 40222

MEYERS, David Craig (WMich) Church Of The Holy Spirit, 1200 Post Dr NE, Belmont, MI 49306

MEYERS, Frederick W Rick (Colo) 420 Cantril St, Castle Rock, CO 80104

MEYERS, Ruth (Cal) Cdsp, 2451 Ridge Rd, Berkeley, CA 94709

MEYERS, Timothy M (At)

MEZACAPA, Nicklas A (Minn) 111 3rd Ave SW, Rochester, MN 55902

MICHAEL, Mark A (WA) 10033 River Rd, Potomac, MD 20854

MICHAELS, Glen Francis (Alb) PO Box 2123, Plattsburgh, NY 12901

MICHAELS, Laurie Jane (Chi) 647 Dundee Ave, Barrington, IL 60010

MICHAELSON, Peter Ruhl (RI) 2 Gaspee Point Dr, Warwick, RI 02888

MICHAUD, Bruce Alan (EMich) 2090 Wyndham Ln, Alpena, MI 49707

MICHAUD, David Norman (Eas) St Peters Church, 115 Saint Peters St, Salisbury, MD 21801

MICHAUD, Eleanor Jean (Eau)

MICHAUD, Jean (Hai) Eglesi Episcopal DHaiti, Boite Postale 1309, Port-au-Prince, Haiti

✠ **MICHEL**, Rodney (LI) 600 E Cathedral Rd Apt G304, Philadelphia, PA 19128

MICHELFELDER, Susan Rebecca (SO) 1824 Ridgecliff Rd, Columbus, OH 43221

MICHELL, Neal O (Dal) 5100 Ross Ave, Dallas, TX 75206

MICHELS, Sandra B (Tex) 1231 Roaring Springs Rd, Ft Worth, TX 76114

MICHIE, Mike (WTex) 8701 Tiercels Dr, Mckinney, TX 75070

MICKELSON, Margaret Belle (Ak) PO Box 849, Cordova, AK 99574

MICKLOW, Patricia L (NMich)

MIDDLETON, Mark Leslie (Chi) 509 Hessel Blvd, Champaign, IL 61820

MIDDLETON, Tracie Gail (Tex) 1280 East Dr, Beaumont, TX 77706

MIDENCE VALDES, Francisco (Hond) Comercio, Tela, Honduras

MIDURA, Louis (Alb) 351 Maggies Run, Sunderland, VT 05250

MIDWOOD JR, John Earle (Pa) 300 N Lawrence St, Philadelphia, PA 19106

MIEDKE, Warren Giles (Tex) 13131 Fry Rd, Cypress, TX 77433

MIESCHER III, Walter Henry (Kan) 2630 N Ridgewood Ct, Wichita, KS 67220

MIHALYI, David (CNY) 472 Washington St, Geneva, NY 14456

MIKAYA, Henry C (WMich) Box 1315, Gabrone, Botswana

MIKEL, Joseph F (Oly) 15945 Cascade Ln Se, Monroe, WA 98272

MILAM, Dave (Mass) 108 Lakeside Ave, Lakeville, MA 02347

MILAM, Thomas Richerson (SwVa) 715 Forest Hills Dr, Wilmington, NC 28403

MILANO, Mary Lucille (Chi) 8765 W Higgins Rd, Chicago, IL 60631

MILES, Allan Wayne (Ore)

MILES, Frank William (Colo) 1175 Vine St Apt 207, Denver, CO 80206

MILES, Glenworth Dalmane (LI) 2714 Lurting Ave, Bronx, NY 10469

MILES, James B (HB)

MILES, John P (SVa) 268 Mill Stream Way, Williamsburg, VA 23185

MILES, Kristin K (NY) 21 S End Ave Ph 2h, New York, NY 10280

MILES, Richard Alan Knox (NC) 36525 Navigator St, Kenai, AK 99611

MILES, Tom (Kan) 1308 Overlook Dr, Manhattan, KS 66503

MILESKI, Annette Marie (Mich)

MILFORD, Sara M (Ark) PO Box 3090, Bentonville, AR 72712

MILHAN, Pamela Hope Arnold (SwFla)

MILHOAN, Charles Everett (Az) 4102 W Union Hills Dr, Glendale, AZ 85308

MILHOLEN, Linda Scott (WMo) PO Box 109, Houston, MO 65483

MILHOLLAND, Nancy Elizabeth (Mass) 58 Stanford Heights Ave, San Francisco, CA 94127

MILHON-MARTIN, Jana (Los) 569 Carleton Pl, Claremont, CA 91711

MILIAN, Mario Emilio (SwFla) 3617 S Omar Ave, Tampa, FL 33629

MILIEN, Marivel (SeFla) 6744 N Miami Ave, Miami, FL 33150

MILIEN, Smith (SeFla) 6744 North Miami Ave, Miami, FL 33150

MILKOVICH, Edward Frank (Los) 28211 Pacific Coast Hwy, Malibu, CA 90265

MILLER, Alan Clayborne (Fla) 1637 NW 19th Cir, Gainesville, FL 32605

MILLER, Alfred Franklin (Colo) 2701 S York St, Denver, CO 80210

MILLER, Anthony Glenn (Los) 350 S Madison Ave Apt 207, Pasadena, CA 91101

MILLER, Arthur Burton (ECR) 2050 California St Apt 20, Mountain View, CA 94040

MILLER, Barbara Ruth (ECR) 207 Lippizan Ln, Paso Robles, CA 93446

MILLER, Barry William (Ct) 99 Timberwood Rd, West Hartford, CT 06117

MILLER, Bill (Tex) PO Box 1745, Lihue, HI 96766

MILLER, Charlene Ida (Tex) 14300 66th St N Lot 900, Clearwater, FL 33764

MILLER, Christopher (At) 291 Leland Ter NE, Atlanta, GA 30317

MILLER, Christopher H (Va) 1000 Saint Stephens Rd, Alexandria, VA 22304

MILLER, Clark Stewart (NI) 319 7th St, Logansport, IN 46947

MILLER, David Dallas (Dal) 1700 N Westmoreland Rd, Desoto, TX 75115

MILLER, David Walton (Los) 1037 16th St Apt 1, Santa Monica, CA 90403

MILLER, Derek Harris (Md)

MILLER, Donald Stewart (Cal) 45602 State Hwy 14, Stevenson, WA 98648

MILLER, Duane Alexander (WTex)

MILLER JR, Ed (Va) 7807 Foxhound Rd, Mclean, VA 22102

MILLER JR, Edwin (Okla) 3300 N Vermont Ave, Oklahoma City, OK 73112

MILLER, Elizabeth (Me) 286 Lincoln St, South Portland, ME 04106

MILLER, Elizabeth Ann (Tex)

MILLER, Elizabeth M (Be) 44 E Market St, Bethlehem, PA 18018

MILLER, Eric Lee (SO) 321 Worthington Ave, Cincinnati, OH 45215

MILLER JR, Ernest Charles (NY) 611 Broadway Rm 520, New York, NY 10012

MILLER, Fred (CPa) 547 Brighton Pl, Mechanicsburg, PA 17055

MILLER, Frederic (LI) 41 Reid Ave, Port Washington, NY 11050

MILLER, Isaac J (Pa) 18th & Diamond, Philadelphia, PA 19121

MILLER, Janice Mary Howard (NI) 2117 E Jefferson Blvd, South Bend, IN 46617

MILLER, Jason Michael (WNY) 64 Green Forest Ct, East Amherst, NY 14051

MILLER, Jean Louise (EC) 9191 Daly Rd., Cincinnati, OH 45231

MILLER, Jerry (WMo) 4258 E Whitehall Dr, Springfield, MO 65809

MILLER, Jo Anne (Ore) P.O. Box 413, Bandon, OR 97411

MILLER, Joel (ECR) 160 Robideaux Rd, Aptos, CA 95003

MILLER, John Edward (Alb) PO Box 12, Ancram, NY 12502

MILLER, John Edward (Va) 4209 Monument Ave, Richmond, VA 23230

MILLER, John Leonard (NY) 23 Cedar Ln, Princeton, NJ 08540

MILLER, John Sloan (La) 12679 N Highmeadow Ct, Baton Rouge, LA 70816

MILLER, Joseph Potter (Los)

MILLER, Judith Joelynn Walker (Oly) PO Box 1782, Westport, WA 98595

MILLER JR, Kenny (Mil) 3906 W Mequon Rd, Mequon, WI 53092

MILLER, Kurt David (Ga) 3665 Bermuda Cir, Augusta, GA 30909

MILLER, Laura Jean (Alb) 41 Gardiner Pl, Walton, NY 13856

MILLER, Lee (SwFla) 4279 70th St Cir E, Palmetto, FL 34221

MILLER, Mark Joseph (Oly) 913 2nd St, Snohomish, WA 98290

MILLER, Megan P (NY)

MILLER, Michaelene (Ark) 220 Brown St, Little Rock, AR 72205

MILLER, Nancy Fay (RI) 82 Rockmeadow Rd, Westwood, MA 02090

MILLER, pastor (Ct) 2227 NW 79th Ave, Doral, FL 33198

MILLER, Patricia L (WMo) 1840 Hickory Station Cir, Snellville, GA 30078

MILLER, Patrick Jameson (Tex) 3514 Corondo Ct., Houston, TX 77005

MILLER, Paula (Mich) 1325 Champaign Rd, Lincoln Park, MI 48146

MILLER, R Cameron (Roch) 40 Solar Dr, Geneva, NY 14456

MILLER, Rene (Tenn) PO Box 1903, Monterey, CA 93942

MILLER, Robert Mcgregor (Pa) 2039 Serendipity Way, Schwenksville, PA 19473

MILLER, Robert William (Minn) 11030 Batello Dr, Venice, FL 34292

MILLER, Roger Edward (CFla) 11620 Claymont Cir, Windermere, FL 34786

MILLER, Sandra Siegel (Chi)

MILLER, Sarah L (Minn)

MILLER, Sarah Taylor (Va) 826 S Lee St, Alexandria, VA 22314

MILLER, Stephen Arthur (WNC) 290 Hillside Oaks Dr, Jefferson, NC 28640

MILLER, Stephen Howard (Okla) 701 N 7th St, Perry, OK 73077

✠ **MILLER**, Steve (Mil) 804 E Juneau Ave, Milwaukee, WI 53202

MILLER, Susan Heilmann (ECR) 25020 Pine Hills Dr, Carmel, CA 93923

MILLER, Suzanne Margaret (U)

MILLER, Terry (Va) 25928 Kilreigh Dr, Farmington Hills, MI 48336

MILLER, Thomas Paul (NY) 165 Christopher St Apt 5W, New York, NY 10014

MILLER, Todd (Mass) 12 Ridge Ave, Newton, MA 02459

MILLER, Vicki Lynn (Miss)

MILLER, Victoria C (Ct) 350 Sound Beach Ave, Old Greenwich, CT 06870

MILLER, William Charles (Pgh) 18297 W 155th Ter, Olathe, KS 66062

MILLER, William Robert (CPa) 182 Dew Drop Rd Apt G, York, PA 17402

MILLER IV, Woodford Decatur (CFla) 2508 Creekside Dr., Fort Piece, FL 34981

MILLER-MARCIN, Christine Ann (Del)

MILLER-MUTIA, Sylvia J (RG) 3310 Mackland Ave NE, Albuquerque, NM 87106

MILLETTE, Carol Leslie (RI) 19 Midway Dr, Warwick, RI 02886

MILLICAN JR, Ford Jefferson (La) 3919 Morris Pl, Jefferson, LA 70121

MILLIEN, Jean (Hai) Ecole Le Bon Samaritan, 26 Rue Jonathas, Carrefour, 06134, Haiti

MILLIEN, Wilner (PR)

MILLIGAN, Donald Arthur (Mass) 222 Bowdoin St, Winthrop, MA 02152

MILLIGAN, Kathleen Sue (Ia) 3714 PA Ave, I-86, Dubuque, IA 52002

MILLIGAN, Michael (U) 430 W 400 N Apt 311, Apt 311, Bountiful, UT 84010

MILLIKEN, Jean Louise (Va) 3732 N Oakland St, Arlington, VA 22207

✠ **MILLIKEN**, Mike (WK) 1 N Main Sreet - Suite 418, Hutchinson, KS 67501

MILLIKIN, Gregory L (Chi) 114 N Pine St, New Lenox, IL 60451

MILLNER JR, Bo (Va) 2817 Floyd Ave, Richmond, VA 23221

MILLOTT, Donna Evans (SwFla) 1236 Santa Barbara Blvd, Cape Coral, FL 33991

MILLS, Alice Marie (USC) St Timothys Episcopal Church, 900 Calhoun St, Columbia, SC 29201

MILLS JR, Arthur Donald (SO) 2696 Cedarbrook Way, Beavercreek, OH 45431

MILLS, Byron Keith (Az) 596 W. Ord Mountain Rd, Globe, AZ 85501

MILLS, Carol Ann (Tex) 205 Hillcrest Dr, Alvin, TX 77511

MILLS, Christen H (Mass)

MILLS III, Edward James (ETenn) 2104 Lamont St, Kingsport, TN 37664

MILLS, Eric Christopher (EC) 194 St Brendan Ct, Southport, NC 28461

MILLS, Fred Thomas (Ky) 685 West Dr, Madisonville, KY 42431

MILLS III, Joseph Edmund (LI) 1118 9th St Apt 9, Santa Monica, CA 90403

MILLS JR, Joseph Milton (Tex) 205 Hillcrest Dr, Alvin, TX 77511

MILLS, Joy Anna Marie (Pa) 2103 Quail Ridge Dr, Paoli, PA 19301

MILLS III, Ladson Frazier (SC) 3114 Mayfair Ln, Johns Island, SC 29455

MILLS, Michael S (Dal) 11122 Midway Rd, Dallas, TX 75229

MILLS, Nancy Thompson (Ga) PO Box 3136, Thomasville, GA 31799

MILLS, Stephen (ECR) 713 Helen Dr, Hollister, CA 95023

MILLS, Susan Patricia (SO) 9222 Garrison Dr Apt 203c, Indianapolis, IN 46240

MILLS, Wallace Wilson (Ak)

MILLSAP, William Richard (Nev) PO Box 2246, Reno, NV 89505

MILLS-CURRAN, Lori (Mass) 7 Kimball Rd, Westborough, MA 01581

MILLS-CURRAN, Mary (Mass)

MILLS-POWELL, Mark Oliver Mclay (Eur)

MILNER, LIz (Cal)

MILNER JR, Raymond Joseph (SanD) 200 E 22nd St Apt 32, Roswell, NM 88201

MILTENBERGER, Gordon (Dal) 10 Oak Village Rd, Greenville, TX 75402

MINARIK JR, Harry J (ETenn) 69 Hickory Trail, Norris, TN 37828

MINDRUM, Alice Anderson (Ct) 60 Range Rd, Southport, CT 06890

MINEAU, Charles Douglas (NMich)

MINER, Bob (Ct) 15 Morningside Ter, Wallingford, CT 06492

MINER, Darren R (Cal) 1750 29th Ave, San Francisco, CA 94122

MINER, David R. (Fla) 3212 Wind Lake Ln, Tallahassee, FL 32312

MINER II, James Stevens (SO) 2929 Summer Wind Ln Apt Lr3203, Highlands Ranch, CO 80129

MINER-PEARSON, Anne (Minn) 15601 Island Road, Burnsville, MN 55306

MINGLEDORFF, Paschal Schirm (Ga) 9541 Whitfield Ave, Savannah, GA 31406

MINICH, Henry Nichols Faulconer (SeFla) 250 Pantops Mountain Rd Apt 5406, Charlottesville, VA 22911

MINIFIE, Charles Jackson (NY) 23 Sherman Dr, Hilton Head Island, SC 29928

MINNICH-LOCKEY, Laura (Va) 79 Laurel St, Harrisonburg, VA 22801

MINNICK, Maggie (Ct) 381 Main St # 187, Middletown, CT 06457

MINOR, Cheryl Vasil (Mass) 65 Common Street, Belmont, MA 02478

MINOR, Paul Lawrence (Mass) 65 Common St., Belmont, MA 02478

MINSHEW, Jim (SeFla) PO Box 1596, Port Salerno, FL 34992

MINSHEW, Nancy Elizabeth (CFla) 3735 Us Highway 17 92 N, Davenport, FL 33837

MINTER, Larry Clifton (Ky) 5409 Hickory Hill Rd, 5409 Hickory Hill Rd, Louisville, KY 40214

MINTON, Anne Mansfield (Mass) 35 Riverwalk Way Unit 303, Lowell, MA 01854

MINTON, Sarah L (Fla)

MINTZ, Elsa (Pa) 3716 Abercrombie Ct, Mount Pleasant, SC 29466

MINX, Patricia Ann (Kan) 105 S Indian Wells Dr, Olathe, KS 66061

MIRATE, Galen Alderman (Ga) 245 Oakland Pkwy Apt 1107, Leesburg, GA 31763

MIRON, Jane Elizabeth (CPa)

MIRON, Mary Louise (NMich)

MIS, Claire (LI) 7 Redbridge Ct, East Setauket, NY 11733

MISKELLEY, Audrey (Cal)

MISNER, Mary Jane Brain (Mil) N1639 Six Corners Rd, Walworth, WI 53184

MISSEL, Ryan (Mo)

MISSNER, Heath McDonell (Chi) 470 Maple St, Winnetka, IL 60093

MITCHEL III, Glen Henry Hank (Los) 1072 Casitas Pass Road #317, Carpinteria, CA 93014

MITCHELL, Barbara Louise (Alb) 172 Ottawa St, Lake George, NY 12845

MITCHELL JR, Charles Albert (Los) 111 S 6th St, Burbank, CA 91501

MITCHELL, Dawn-Victoria (CNY) 3206 Pleasant St, Hannibal, MO 63401

MITCHELL III, James L (WMich) 4631 S Spruce Ave, White Cloud, MI 49349

MITCHELL, Jeffrey Jay (WK) PO Box 250, Liberal, KS 67905

MITCHELL, Joe T (NC) 505 Mountain Rd, Asheboro, NC 27205

MITCHELL, John Patrick (NJ) 8 Chadwell Pl, Morristown, NJ 07960

MITCHELL, Karin Rasmussen (NJ) 125 Orchard Ave, Hightstown, NJ 08520

MITCHELL, Katherine N (EC) 515 Pamlico River Dr, Washington, NC 27889

MITCHELL, Lisa Sauber (NJ) 380 Sycamore Ave, Shrewsbury, NJ 07702

MITCHELL, Marilyn Dean (NC) 90 Worcester Rd Unit 12, Washington Depot, CT 06794

MITCHELL, Patricia Rhonda (LI) 732 Scarsdale Rd, Tuckahoe, NY 10707

MITCHELL, Phyllis Susan (Ak)

MITCHELL, Preston Wade (SwVa)

MITCHELL JR, Richard Cope (Colo) 3107 Nevermind Ln, Colorado Springs, CO 80917

MITCHELL, Sadie S (Pa) 600 E Cathedral Rd, Apt H320, Philadelphia, PA 19128

MITCHELL, Thomas James (WNY) 7145 Fieldcrest Drive, Lockport, NY 14094

MITCHELL, Tim (Ky) 901 Baxter Ave, Louisville, KY 40204

MITCHELL, Winnie (Colo) 3821 Elk Ln, Pueblo, CO 81005

MITCHENER, Gary Asher (O) 13800 Shaker Blvd Apt 206, Cleveland, OH 44120

MITCHENER, Julia B (At) PO Box 6124, Charlotte, NC 28207

MITCHICAN, Jonathan A (Pa) 1000 Burmont RD, Drexel Hill, PA 19026

MITHEN III, Thomas Scott (Ga) 516 E Broughton St, Bainbridge, GA 39817

MITMAN, John Louis (Ct) 31 Steep Hollow Ln, West Hartford, CT 06107

MIX, Lucas John (Az) Lucas Mix, Redmond, WA 98053

MIZIRL, Sandi (Tex) 3015 Fleeton Rd, Reedville, VA 22539

MKHIZE, Danana Elliot (La) 1222 N Dorgenois St, New Orleans, LA 70119

MOBERLY, Paul Benjamin (Va)

MOCZYDLOWSKI, Ann (WA) 10120 Brock Dr, Silver Spring, MD 20903

MODESITT, Lori Jane (Wyo) 1357 Loomis St, Wheatland, WY 82201

MODISETT, Cara Ellen (SwVa)

MOEHL, Thomas Joseph (Ore) 12360 Summit Loop SE, Turner, OR 97392

MOELLER, Linda Lee Breitung (NJ)

MOERMOND, Curt (Ia)

MOESER, Annelies Gisela (Tex)

MOHN, Michael Collver (Va) 1527 Senseny Rd, Winchester, VA 22602

MOIR, Tory Kuepper (Colo) 2201 Dexter St, Denver, CO 80207

MOISE, Burnet (SeFla)

MOISE, Joe (LI) 1227 Pacific St, Brooklyn, NY 11216

MOJALLALI, Darius (Alb) 5 Snowden Ave, Delmar, NY 12054

MOLEGODA, Shariya (Ct) 232 Durham Rd, Madison, CT 06443

MOLINA-MOORE, Amanda E (WA) PO Box 3510, Wilmington, DE 19807

MOLINE, Mark Edwin (Az) 2000 Shepherds Lane, Prescott, AZ 86301

MOLITOR, Jerome Peter (FdL)

MOLITORS, Elizabeth A (Los) 393 N Main St, Glen Ellyn, IL 60137

MOLLARD, Elizabeth McCarter (CPa) 235 N Spruce St, Elizabethtown, PA 17022

MOLLER, Nels D (Ida) 902 E Lakeview Ln, Spokane, WA 99208

MOLLISON, Carol Suzanne (Okla) 721 N Thomas St, Altus, OK 73521

MOLNAR, Annette June (RG) St Elizabeths Episcopal Church, 1 Morse Rd, Sudbury, MA 01776

MOLNAR, Joshua (WTex)

MOLONY, Roberta Diane (Chi) 2009 Boehme St, Lockport, IL 60441

MOMBERG, Tom (WTenn) 3235 Overland Pl, Memphis, TN 38111

MONAHAN, Anne (WA) 404 S Lee St, Alexandria, VA 22314

MONASTIERE, Sally (Los) 900 E Harrison Ave Apt B9, Pomona, CA 91767

MONCRIEFF, Stephanie Christen Patterson (Ia) 4535 Kimball Ave, Waterloo, IA 50701

MONCURE, Peggy (Va)

MONETTE, Ruth Alta (Los) 104-5990 E Blvd, Vancouver, BC V6T 1Z3, Canada

MONGE-MANCIA, Israel (Hond)

MONGE-SANTIAGO, Juan Angel (NJ) 213 Madison Ave, Lakewood, NJ 08701

MONGILLO, Gary Anthony (Ct)

MONK, Edward R (Dal) Saint Johns Church, 101 N 14th St, Corsicana, TX 75110

MONNAT, Thomas Leonard (Pa) 213 Earlington Road, Havertown, PA 19083

✠ **MONNOT**, Elizabeth Lockwood (Ia) 3310 Southern Hills Dr, Des Moines, IA 50321

MONNOT, Michael (Ia) 1225 41st Ave, Sacramento, CA 95822

MONREAL, Anthony A (Episcopal SJ) 9323 South Westlawn, Fresno, CA 93706

MONREAL, Linda Carey (Episcopal SJ)

MONROE, George Wesley (Chi) 2866 Vacherie Ln, Dallas, TX 75227

MONROE, Sarah Beth (Oly) 2422 Leach Ct SE, Olympia, WA 98501

MONROE, Virginia Hill (Ala) 430 Newman Ave. Se, Huntsville, AL 35801

MONROE LOES, Brenda Frances (At) 304 E 6th St, West Point, GA 31833

MONSON, Scott Bradley (Minn) 1015 Sibley Memorial Hwy Apt 303, Saint Paul, MN 55118

MONSOUR, John (SwFla) 2114 W Destiny Point Cir, St George, UT 84790

MONTAGNO, Karen (SO) 536 Main St # 2, Medford, MA 02155

MONTAGUE, Cynthia Russell (ECR) 17574 Winding Creek Rd, Salinas, CA 93908

MONTELLA, Christopher (Los)

✠ **MONTERROSO GONZALEZ**, Hector (Tex) 2417 North Blvd, Houston, TX 77098

MONTES, Alejandro (Tex) 10426 Towne Oak Ln, Sugar Land, TX 77478

MONTES, Alex G (Tex) 2227 Woodland Springs St, Houston, TX 77077

MONTES, Eli (Kan) St Francis Community Services, 4155 E Harry St, Wichita, KS 67218

MONTES, Luz D (Tex)

MONTGOMERY, Brandt Leonard (Md) Saint James School, 17641 College Road, Hagerstown, MD 21740

Clergy List

MONTGOMERY, Bruce (NJ) 1310 Tullo Rd, Martinsville, NJ 08836
MONTGOMERY, Cathy (SwVa) 2231 Timberlake Dr, Lynchburg, VA 24502
MONTGOMERY, Ellen Maddigan (WNY) 41 Saint Georges Sq, Buffalo, NY 14222
MONTGOMERY JR, Errol Linn (Miss) 4 Patrick Pl, Bella Vista, AR 72715
MONTGOMERY, Fletcher (Fla) 100 NE 1st St, Gainesville, FL 32601
MONTGOMERY, Ian (Alb) 26 Gaskill Rd, Chester, VT 05143
MONTGOMERY, Ian Bruce (Ct) 304 E 65th St Apt 21a, New York, NY 10065
MONTGOMERY, Jennifer Born (Va) 4000 Lorcom Ln, Arlington, VA 22207
MONTGOMERY, John Alford (Lex)
MONTGOMERY, Lee Allen (U) 70 N 200 W, Cedar City, UT 84720
MONTGOMERY, Terri Lynn (Mich)
MONTGOMERY, Tyler Lindell (SVa) PO Box 3520, Williamsburg, VA 23187
MONTIEL, Robert Michael (WTenn) 103 S Poplar St, Paris, TN 38242
MONTILEAUX, Charles Thomas (SD) Po Box 246, Kyle, SD 57752
MONTJOY IV, Gid (Md) 609 Collins Creek Dr., Murrells Inlet, SC 29576
MONTOOTH, Cynthia Hooton (SwFla) 15 Knob Hill Circle, Decatur, GA 30030
MONTOYA CARPIO, S Leonardo (EcuC) Apartado #17-01-3108, Quito, Ecuador
MOODY, John Wallace (NY) 42 W 9th St Apt 18, New York, NY 10011
✠ **MOODY**, Robert Manning (Okla) 4001 Fillmore Avenue, Apt 550, Alexandria, VA 22311
MOON, Abigail White (Fla) 91 Manthorne Rd, Boston, MA 02132
MOON, Anthony Bernard (Okla) 2401 N Westminster Road, Arcadia, OK 73007
MOON, Catherine Joy (Cal) The Curate's House, 7 Walton Village, Liverpool, AL L4 6TJ, Great Britain (UK)
MOON JR, Don Pardee (Chi) 438 N Sheridan Rd # A500, Waukegan, IL 60085
MOON, James Fred (WMo) 43 Old Mill Ln, South Greenfield, MO 65752
MOON, Richard Warren (Neb) PO Box 1012, West Plains, MO 65775
MOON, Robert Michael (Los) 1294 Westlyn Pl, Pasadena, CA 91104
MOONEY, Michelle Puzin (Mil) 2633 N Hackett Ave Apt A, Milwaukee, WI 53211
MOORE, Albert Lee (NC) 8705 Gleneagles Dr, Raleigh, NC 27613
MOORE, Allison (NY) 161 Main St, New Paltz, NY 12561
MOORE, Andrew York (Va) 2727 S Quincy St Apt 624, Arlington, VA 22206

MOORE, Andy (NJ) 25 Meckes St, Springfield, NJ 07081
MOORE, Anne Elizabeth Olive (Ore) 630 B St, Silverton, OR 97381
MOORE, Bob (Cal) 4230 Langland St, Cincinnati, OH 45223
MOORE, Bob (Tex) 3285 Park Falls Ct, League City, TX 77573
MOORE JR, Charles (SVa) 12800 Nightingale Drive, Chester, VA 23836
MOORE, Charlotte Elizabeth (Eas)
MOORE, Cheryl P (U) 2378 East 1700 South Street, Salt Lake City, UT 84108
MOORE, Chris (Pa) 51 Springhouse Ln, Media, PA 19063
MOORE III, Clint (Chi) 750 Pearson Street Apt 902, Des Plaines, IL 60016
MOORE, Courtland Manning (Tex) 2341 Monticello Cir, Plano, TX 75075
MOORE, Cynthia (Dal)
MOORE, Daniel T (Pa) 448 North St, Doylestown, PA 18901
MOORE, David (Oly) 116 Rossel Ln, PO Box 702, Eastsound, WA 98245
MOORE, Delrece Lorraine (Colo) 3665 Overton St, Colorado Springs, CO 80910
MOORE, Denise Maureen (Alb)
MOORE, Dominic C (Az) 533 E Main St, Lexington, KY 40508
MOORE, Donald (Eas) 3946 Rock Branch Rd, North Garden, VA 22959
MOORE, Frederick Ashbrook (Ore) 1675 Chester Ave, Arcata, CA 95521
MOORE, James Raymond (The Episcopal Church in Haw) 911 N Marine Corps Dr, Tamuning, GU 96913
MOORE, Jan Marie (Miss) PO Box 1483, Hattiesburg, MS 39403
MOORE, Judith (O) 7125 North Hills Blvd NE, Albuquerque, NM 87109
MOORE, Julia Gibert (Miss) 208 S Leflore Ave, Cleveland, MS 38732
MOORE, Katherine Joanne (Wyo) PO Box 246, Sundance, WY 82729
MOORE, Kathleen A (NwPa)
MOORE, Kathleen M (Los)
MOORE, Landon Mccord (LI)
MOORE, Linda June (Vt) 1919 Old Coach Rd, Lyndonville, VT 05851
MOORE, Lynda Foster (WNC) 138 Murdock Ave, Asheville, NC 28801
MOORE, Margaret Jo (The Episcopal NCal) 516 Clayton Ave, El Cerrito, CA 94530
MOORE, Marie Loudette (O)
MOORE, Mark Ross (Ct) 85 Viscount Dr Unit 12c, Milford, CT 06460
MOORE, Mark Thomas (Mil) 142 Lakefield Ct, Racine, WI 53402
MOORE, Mary Diane (Oly) 7796 S Harrison Cir, Centennial, CO 80122
MOORE, Mary Navarre (ETenn) 715 E Brow Rd, Lookout Mountain, TN 37350
MOORE, Matthew (LI) 139 Saint Johns Pl, Brooklyn, NY 11217

MOORE, Melvin Leon (Va) 219 Cornwallis Ave, Locust Grove, VA 22508
MOORE, Michael D (Fla)
MOORE, Nancy Lee (Me) 403 Harrison Rd, Norway, ME 04268
MOORE, Orral Margarite (Neb) 714 N 129th Plz, Omaha, NE 68154
MOORE, Pamela Andrea (The Episcopal NCal) Po Box 4791, Santa Rosa, CA 95402
MOORE, Patricia Elaine (The Episcopal NCal) 342 Wilson St, Petaluma, CA 94952
MOORE, Paul R (Oly) St Pauls Resurreccin Churches, 415 S 18th St, Mount Vernon, WA 98274
MOORE JR, Ralph M (Me) 191 W Meadow Rd, Rockland, ME 04841
MOORE, Richard Wayne (La) 4500 Lake Borgne Ave, Metairie, LA 70006
MOORE, Robert Allen (Minn) 19 Lea Road, Whittle-le-Woods, Chorley, Lancs, PR6-7PF, Great Britain (UK)
MOORE JR, Robert Raymond (SwVa) 110 Clinton Avenue, Big Stone Gap, VA 24219
MOORE, Robin Adair (Oly) PO Box 584, Grapeview, WA 98546
MOORE, Rodney Allen (Colo) 1306 Charles Dr, Knoxville, TN 37918
MOORE, Scott Alan (Eur)
MOORE, Stephen D (Pa)
MOORE, Stephen Edward (Oly) 716 Third Street, Unit 202, Mukilteo, WA 98275
MOORE, Steven Paul (CNY) St Marys Episcopal Church, 1917 Third St, Napa, CA 94559
MOORE, Theodore Edward (NJ) 17 Cray Ter., Fanwood, NJ 07023
MOORE, Trenton Scott (Va)
MOORE, Vassilia Shelton (SwFla) 16500 Gulf Blvd Apt 755, North Redington Beach, FL 33708
MOORE JR, Walter Taylor (Miss) 103 Waterstone Dr, Oxford, MS 38655
MOOREHEAD, Kate Bingham (Fla) 240 N Belmont Ave, Wichita, KS 67208
MOOREHEAD, Susan Jo (CFla)
MOORE-LEVESQUE, Christa (RI) 87 Narragansett Ave, PO Box 317, Jamestown, RI 02835
MOORER, Dawson Delayne (O) 281 E 244th St Apt D5, Euclid, OH 44123
MOORHEAD, Bill (Ia) 107 Washington Park Rd, Iowa City, IA 52245
MOOTE, Kimberly Ann (NMich) E9494 Maple St, Munising, MI 49862
MOQUETE, Clemencia Rafaela (NY) 821 Central Trinity Avenue, Bronx, NY 10456
MORALES, Evelyn Ruth (NC) 2009 Hickswood Rd, High Point, NC 27265
MORALES JR, Frank R (NY) 3115 S High St, Arlington, VA 22202
MORALES, Loyda (Ct) 347 Chiquita Ct, Kissimmee, FL 34758

MORALES, Roberto (Va)

MORALES COLON, Francisco Javier (PR)

MORALES COLON, Nancy (PR)

MORALES GAVIRIA, Jose Ricardo (Colom) Barrio Las Delicias, El Bagne, Antioquia, Colombia

✠ MORALES MALDONADO, Rafael L (PR) Ch Tec Puetorriquene, PO Box 902, Saint Just, PR 00978

MORALES PEREZ, Francisco Alberto (PR)

MORALES-VEGA, Emilia (PR) D10 Calle Pomarrosa, Guaynabo, PR 00969

MORAN, John Jay (Mont) 2415 Hauser Blvd, Helena, MT 59601

✠ MORANTE-ESPANA, Terencio Alfredo (Litoral Diocese Of Ecuador) Ulloa 213 Y Carrion, Box 17-0-353-A, Quito, Ecuador

MORA VILLEGA, Carlos Donato (Litoral Diocese Of Ecuador) Amarilis F 603 C D Ave T, Guayaquil, Ecuador

MORCK, Christopher Robert (Mass) 257 Grape St, New Bedford, MA 02740

MOREAU, Joseph Raoul (LI) 15524 90th Ave, Jamaica, NY 11432

MOREAU, Walter Jerome (NJ) 211 Willow Valley Sq # D-319, Lancaster, PA 17602

MOREHEAD, Carol (Mass) Grace Church, 160 High St, Medford, MA 02155

MOREHOUS, Amy Hodges (ETenn) 800 S Northshore Dr, Knoxville, TN 37919

MOREHOUSE JR, Merritt Dutton (FdL) 1920 Green Tree Road, Washington Island, WI 54246

MOREHOUSE, Rebecca (Cal) 21 Sonora Way, Corte Madera, CA 94925

MOREHOUSE, Tim (The Episcopal Church in Haw) 1837 Kalakaua Ave, Apt 3408, Honolulu, HI 96815

MORELL, Ellen Jones (Az) 8110 Saint Andrews Church Rd, Louisville, KY 40258

MORELLI, Thomas Carlo Anthony (SanD) 1114 9th St, Coronado, CA 92118

MORELL MONTALVO, Louise Esthella (PR)

MORENO, Victor Fernando (Ga)

MORENO CASAS, Alberto Moreno (Okla) San Miguel Arcangel, 907 Adams Ave, Odessa, TX 79761

MORENO CASTRO, Susana (DomRep)

MORESCHI, Alexander Thomas (Ga)

MORETZ, Matthew John (NY) 202 W 58th St # 11n, New York, NY 10019

MORETZSOHN, Jeffrey Paul (Pa)

MOREY, Erin K (Pgh)

MORFORD, Norman L (Ind) PO Box 55085, Indianapolis, IN 46205

MORFORD, Samuel Allen (Neb) 9302 Blondo St, Omaha, NE 68134

MORGAN, Daniel (Ct) 489 Mansfield Ave, Darien, CT 06820

MORGAN, Dennis Lee (Eas) 6242 Oxbridge Dr, Salisbury, MD 21801

MORGAN, Diane Elizabeth (Mich) 15102 Fox, Redford, MI 48239

MORGAN, Dwight (SeFla) 2201 S.W. 25th Street, Coconut Grove, FL 33133

MORGAN, E F Michael (Pa) 33 Baltusrol Way, Springfield, NJ 07081

MORGAN III, Harold Edgar (USC) 204 Derby Ln, Clinton, SC 29325

MORGAN, J Gregory (NY) St Simon The Cyrenian Church, 135 Remington Place, New Rochelle, NY 10801

MORGAN, James Charles (Tex) 235 Royal Oaks St, Huntsville, TX 77320

MORGAN JR, James Hanly (WVa) 520 11th St, Huntington, WV 25701

MORGAN, Keely (Minn) 60 Kent St, Saint Paul, MN 55102

MORGAN, Mamie Elizabeth (USC) 204 Derby Lane, Clinton, SC 29325

MORGAN, Marilyn Kay (Ark) 1475 Stone Crest Dr, Conway, AR 72034

MORGAN, Michael T (Mont) W 3817 Fort Wright Dr 1-204, Spokane, WA 99204

MORGAN, Michele H (WA) 301 A St NE, Washington, DC 20002

MORGAN, Pamela (Ark) 1410 E Walnut St, Rogers, AR 72756

MORGAN, Philip (Eau) 240 Aspen Dr, Somerset, WI 54025

MORGAN, Ralph Baier (Tex)

MORGAN V, Richard (RI) 19 Castle Way, Westerly, RI 02891

MORGAN, Richard (Pa) Church of the Good Samaritan, 212 W Lancaster Ave, Paoli, PA 19301

MORGAN, Ruth Margaret (RG) 8017 Krim Dr. NE, Albuquerque, NM 87109

MORGAN, Walter (ETenn) 3475 Edgewood Cir Nw, Cleveland, TN 37312

MORGAN-HIGGINS, Stanley Ethelbert (Nwk) 3828 Leprechaun Ct, Decatur, GA 30034

MORICAL, Robin E (CFla) 1631 Ford Pkwy, Saint Paul, MN 55116

MORIN, Geoffrey S (Colo) 841 Shenton Road, West Chester, PA 19380

MORIYAMA, Jerome Tomokazu (WA) Rossbrin Cove, Schull, Co Cork, Ireland

MORLAN, Lynette K (Episcopal SJ) 2803 Stratford Dr, San Ramon, CA 94583

MORLEY, Anthony J (Minn) 825 Summit Ave Apt 806, Minneapolis, MN 55403

MORLEY, Richard Matthew (NJ) 140 S Finley Ave, Basking Ridge, NJ 07920

MORLEY, William Harris (NC) 3454 Rugby Rd, Durham, NC 27707

MORNARD, Jean Elisabeth (SD) 635 Montana Ave SW, Huron, SD 57350

MORONEY, Kevin John (NY) 440 W 21st St, New York, NY 10011

MORONTA, Buddelov Adolfo (NY)

MORPETH, Robert Park (Ala) 521 20th St N, Birmingham, AL 35203

MORRIGAN, Cedar Abrielynne (Minn) 309 13th St Sw, Little Falls, MN 56345

MORRIS, Bonnie (WNY) 20 Milton Street, Williamsville, NY 14221

MORRIS, Charles (Be) 24 Forsythia Dr, Harwich, MA 02645

MORRIS, Danielle Dubois (CFla) 444 Covey Cv, Winter Park, FL 32789

MORRIS, David John (Pa) 449 Newgate Ct Apt B2, Andalusia, PA 19020

MORRIS, David Wayne (NY) 15 Pine St, Lake Peekskill, NY 10537

MORRIS, Gregg A (Chi) 1125 Franklin St, Downers Grove, IL 60515

MORRIS, Janie Kirt (Tex) 439 NW 44th Street, Oklahoma City, OK 73118

MORRIS, John (Vt) 37 Thompson Rd, East Corinth, VT 05040

MORRIS III, John Glen (Va) 1021 Aquia Dr, Stafford, VA 22554

MORRIS, John Karl (The Episcopal NCal) 3663 Solano Ave Apt 204, Napa, CA 94558

MORRIS, John William (CPa) St Johns Episcopal Church, 321 W Chestnut St, Lancaster, PA 17603

MORRIS, Jonathan Edward (USC) 717 Dupre Dr, Spartanburg, SC 29307

MORRIS, Julie H (Los) P.O. Box 1028, Camarillo, CA 93011

MORRIS, Karen Lynn (WTex)

MORRIS, Kevin L (LI) 176 Palisade Ave, Jersey City, NJ 07306

MORRIS, Matthew David (Ore)

MORRIS, Robert Corin Veal (Nwk) 422 Clark, South Orange, NJ 07079

MORRIS III, Robert Lee (Va)

MORRIS, Roberta Louise (Los) 1733 N New Hampshire Ave, Los Angeles, CA 90027

MORRIS, Robert Bob (Fla) 4450 Tropea Way Unit 1445, Jacksonville, FL 32246

MORRIS, Sarah (NC) 1962 Tyler Rd, Christiansburg, VA 24073

MORRIS, Stephen B (SwFla) 140 4th St N, St Petersburg, FL 33701

MORRIS, Stephen Michael (NY) 510 W 149th St, New York, NY 10031

MORRIS, Thomas Rand (Tex) 4410 Westheimer Rd Apt 3320, Houston, TX 77027

MORRIS JR, William Russell (Ind)

MORRIS-KLIMENT, Nicholas M (Mass) 44 Seminole Rd, Acton, MA 01720

MORRISON, Alistair James (Alb) 132 Duanesburg Churches Rd, Duanesburg, NY 12056

MORRISON, Enid Ann (Ind) 8320 E. 10th St., Indianapolis, IN 46219

MORRISON, Glenn David (Mich) 171 W Pike St, Pontiac, MI 48341

MORRISON JR, Henry T Nick (Az) Po Box 610, Ketchum, ID 83340

Clergy List

MORRISON, James R (La) 1329 Jackson Ave, New Orleans, LA 70130

MORRISON, Jillian B (Ct)

MORRISON, John Ainslie (SO) Calvary Episcopal Church, 3766 Clifton Ave, Cincinnati, OH 45220

MORRISON III, John E (LI) 510 Manatuck Blvd, Brightwaters, NY 11718

MORRISON, Karl Frederick (NJ) 75 Linwood Circle, Princeton, NJ 08540

MORRISON, Larry Clair (NJ) PO Box 100, Front Royal, VA 22630

MORRISON, Leroy Oran (NwT) 6535 Amber Dr, Odessa, TX 79762

MORRISON, Mary K (ECR) 1217vanderbilt Way, Sacramento, CA 95825

MORRISON, Mikel Anne (Oly) 760 Kristen Ct, Santa Barbara, CA 93111

MORRISON, Pauline (Ore) St John's Episcopal Church, 110 NE Alder St, Toledo, OR 97391

MORRISON, Richard (Az) 720 West Elliot Road, Gilbert, AZ 85233

MORRISON, Robert (Ore) Po Box 789, Lincoln City, OR 97367

MORRISON JR, Robert Dabney (EC) 119 Briarwood St, Lynchburg, VA 24503

MORRISON, Sam (FdL) 101 S Wythe St, Pentwater, MI 49449

MORRISON-CLEARY, Douglas Vaughn (Minn)

MORRIS-RADER, Patricia (Ore) 8045 Sw 56th Ave, Portland, OR 97219

MORRISS, Jerry Davis (Dal) 132 Baywood Blvd, Mabank, TX 75156

MORRISSETTE, Paul E (WMass) 14 Enaya Cir, Worcester, MA 01606

MORRISSEY, Terri Jo (Chi)

MORROW, Andrea (Mich) 2803 1st St, Wyandotte, MI 48192

MORROW, Dan (Eur) 101 Pine St, Harrisburg, PA 17101

MORROW, Gabriel Charles Daniel (Alb) PO Box 41, Burnt Hills, NY 12027

MORROW JR, Harold Frederick (CPa) 2453 Harrisburg Pike, Lancaster, PA 17601

MORROW, Jerry Dean (Mass) 89 Msgr Patrick J Lydon Way, Dorchester, MA 02124

MORROW, John Thomas (NJ) PO Box 424, Pine Beach, NJ 08741

MORROW, Mildred K (WNC) 9 Swan St, Asheville, NC 28803

MORROW, Penelope (Eas) St Pauls Tec Ch, PO Box 1207, Ocean City, MD 21843

MORROW, Quintin Gregory (Tex) 17 Lamar St, Fort Worth, TX 76102

MORSCH, Joel (Spr) 3011 Champions Dr, Maryville, TN 37801

MORSE, Alice Janette (Mich) 3899 Ryans Rdg, Monroe, MI 48161

MORSE, Davidson Rogan (Tex) 2916 Caprock Ct, Grapevine, TX 76051

MORSE, Elizabeth (Ore) 661 NW Kersey Dr, Dallas, OR 97338

MORT, Kevin Duane (SwFla)

MORTON III, James Hamilton Bates (Va)

MORTON, John (WNC) PO Box 185, Flat Rock, NC 28731

MORTON SR, Kell (Pa) 316 High St, Pottstown, PA 19464

MORTON, Paula (WNC) 901 Big Raven Ln, Saluda, NC 28773

MORTON, Ronald Dean (ETenn) 5401 Tiffany Ln, Knoxville, TN 37912

MORTON III, Woolridge Brown (Va) 212 Wirt St NW, Leesburg, VA 20176

MOSELEY, Christine Carr (Vt) PO Box 125, Newport, VT 05855

MOSER, Albert E (Alb) 133 Saratoga Rd Apt. 109-8, Glenville, NY 12302

MOSER, Frederick Perkins (Vt) 5167 Shelburne Rd, Shelburne, VT 05482

MOSER, Patricia Mariann (Chi) 621 W Belmont Ave, Chicago, IL 60657

MOSER, Paul Henry (Md) 15 Brooks Rd, Bel Air, MD 21014

MOSES, George David (WVa) 20 Alexander Dr, Morgantown, WV 26508

MOSES, Michael David (Minn) 11078 Nichols Spring Dr, Chatfield, MN 55923

MOSES, Robert Emilio (CFla) 145 E Edgewood Dr, Lakeland, FL 33803

MOSES, Sarah Marie (Miss)

MOSHER, Steve (Eas) PO Box S, Saint Michaels, MD 21663

MOSIER, James David (EO) 1237 Sw 12th St, Ontario, OR 97914

MOSKAL, Jason Edward (LI) 3350 82nd St, Jackson Heights, NY 11372

MOSLEY, Carl Ernest (Eas) 111 76th St Unit 205, Ocean City, MD 21842

MOSLEY, Lathrop H (USC) 202 E Augusta Pl, Greenville, SC 29605

MOSQUEA, Jose Luis (DomRep)

MOSS JR, Alfred Alfonso (Chi) 1500 N Lancaster St, Arlington, VA 22205

MOSS III, David M (At) 3880 N Stratford Rd NE, Atlanta, GA 30342

MOSS, Denise S (At)

MOSS, Eliot (WMass) 7 Kestrel Ln, Amherst, MA 01002

MOSS III, Frank (WMass) 17910 NW Chestnut Lane, Portland, OR 97231

MOSS, Susan Maetzold (Minn) 175 Woodlawn Ave, Saint Paul, MN 55105

MOSSBARGER, David (NwT) 1402 Wilshire Dr, Odessa, TX 79761

MOSSMAN, Christie A (Los)

MOSSO, Karen Ann (Minn) 721 Roma Ave, Jeffersonville, IN 47130

MOTE, Donna Susan (SeFla) 1296 Fork Creek Trl, Decatur, GA 30033

MOTE, Larry H. (RG) 1016 E 1st St, Portales, NM 88130

MOTES, Brantley Eugene (Ala) Po Box 5556, Decatur, AL 35601

MOTHERSELL, Lawrence Lavere (Roch) Po Box 1, Geneseo, NY 14454

MOTIS, John Ray (CFla) Church Of The Good Shepherd, 221 S 4th St, Lake Wales, FL 33853

MOTT, Pam (Me) 23 Mae Ln, Topsham, ME 04086

MOTTL, Christine Elizabeth (Pa) 27074 Saint Peters Church Rd, Crisfield, MD 21817

MOTTL, Paul Edward (Neb) 3211 Grays Gable Rd, Laramie, WY 82072

MOUA, Bao (Minn) Holy Apostles Episcopal Church, 2200 Minnehaha Ave E, Saint Paul, MN 55119

MOUER, Patty (WNC) 500 Christ School Rd, Arden, NC 28704

MOUGHTY, Kelly Patricia (Va) 115 E Fairfax Street, Falls Church, VA 22046

MOUILLE, David Ronald (Kan) 4786 Black Swan Dr, Shawnee, KS 66216

MOULDER, John (Chi)

MOULINIER, Deirdre Ward (Az)

MOULTON, Elizabeth Jean (Be) 109 Cruser St, Montrose, PA 18801

MOULTON, Eric Morgan (EC) 1219 Forest Hills Dr, Wilmington, NC 28403

MOULTON II, John (Fla) 1631 Blue Heron Ln, Jacksonville Beach, FL 32250

MOULTON, Roger Conant (Mass) 291 Washington St, Arlington, MA 02474

MOUNCEY, Perry (CNY) 127 Brookview Ln, Liverpool, NY 13088

MOUNT, Jeremy Philip (RG)

MOUNTFORD, Helen Harvene (Los) 1566 Edison St, Santa Ynez, CA 93460

MOUNTFORD SR, Robert Tatton (CFla) 160 Heron Bay Cir, Lake Mary, FL 32746

MOURADIAN, Victoria Kirk (Los) 1047 Senda Verde Unit A, Santa Barbara, CA 93105

MOUSIN, Tom (Me) 29 Lakeview Rd, Winchester, MA 01890

MOWERS, Culver Lunn (CNY) Po Box 130, Brooktondale, NY 14817

MOWERS, David M (Mil) 111 Sixth St, Baraboo, WI 53913

MOYER, Dale Luther (SeFla) 4851a Nursery Rd, Dover, PA 17315

MOYER JR, J Douglas (Be) 205 North Seventh Street, Stroudsburg, PA 18360

MOYER, Laureen H (Cal) 412 Centre Ct, Alameda, CA 94502

MOYER, Michael David (Eas) 1 Church St, Berlin, MD 21811

MOYER, Michelle M (Be) 321 Wyandotte St, Bethlehem, PA 18015

MOYERS, William Riley (SwFla) 2008 Isla De Palma Cir, Naples, FL 34119

MOYLE, Sandra K (Fla) St Catherines Episcopal Church, 3123 Palmetto Street, Florence, SC 29501

MOYSER, George H (SC) 58 Raven Glass Ln, Bluffton, SC 29909

MOZELIAK JR, Leon (CNY) St Pauls Ch All Sts Ch, 204 Genesee St, Chittenango, NY 13037

MOZINGO, Brandon Thomas (At) 325 Oliver Ave, Pittsburgh, PA 15222

MRAZ, Barbara E (Minn) 4201 Sheridan Ave S, Minneapolis, MN 55410

MROCZKA, Mary Ann (Roch) PO Box 462, Geneseo, NY 14454

MUCUUTHI NG'ETHE, Christine (LI) 215 Forward Support Battalion, Battalion & 74th St, Fort Hood, TX 76544

MUDD, Gwynneth (SVa) 797 Casual Ct, Virginia Beach, VA 23454

MUDGE, Hiram Thomas (Kan) PO Box 99, West Park, NY 12493

MUDGE, Julia Hamilton (Alb) 204 Worthington Ter, Wynantskill, NY 12198

MUDGE, Melanie (NC) 2820 Rue Sans Famille, Raleigh, NC 27607

MUDGE JR, Shaw (Ct) 25 Rushforde Dr, Manchester, CT 06040

MUELLER, Denise Ray (SO) 412 Sycamore St., Cincinnati, OH 45202

MUELLER, Heather (The Episcopal Church in Haw) PO Box 628, Kapa'au, HI 96755

MUELLER, Kay (CFla)

MUELLER, Mary Margaret (WTex) 1045 Shook Ave Apt 105, San Antonio, TX 78212

MUGAN JR, Robert Charles (WNC) 894 Indian Hill Rd, Hendersonville, NC 28791

MUHLHEIM, Nancy Colleen Collins (Ore) 98 Fairway Loop, Eugene, OR 97401

MUINDE, Sandra Laverne (FdL) 311 Division St, Oshkosh, WI 54901

MUIR, George Daniels (Ga) St Pauls Church, 605 Reynolds St, Augusta, GA 30901

MUIR, Richard Dale (Chi) 181 Wildwood Rd, Lake Forest, IL 60045

MUKHWANA-NAFUMA, Joel Eric (NY)

MULDER, Timothy John (Nwk) 1075 Pottersville Rd, Gladstone, NJ 07934

MULDOON, Maggie R (Minn) 18350 67 Avenue, Cloverdale, BC V3S 1E5, Canada

MULFORD, Marie Lynne (WVa) 2585 State Route 7 N, Gallipolis, OH 45631

MULKIN, Suzanne Devine (CFla) 875 Brock Rd, Bartow, FL 33830

MULL, Judson Gary (At) 499 Trabert Ave Nw, Atlanta, GA 30309

MULLALY JR, Charles (Va) 888 Summit View Ln, Charlottesville, VA 22903

MULLARKEY, Meghan Mullarkey K (Oly) 4223 N 26th St, Tacoma, WA 98407

MULLEN, Melanie B (WA) St Paul's Episcopal Church, 815 E Grace St, Richmond, VA 23219

MULLEN, Sean E (Pa) St Mark's Church, 1625 Locust St, Philadelphia, PA 19103

MULLER, Albert J (O)

MULLER, Denise (Az)

MULLER, Donald (NJ) 30 Orchard Ave, Nanticoke, PA 18634

MULLER, John (Colo) 513 E 19th St, Delta, CO 81416

MULLER, Michael A (Nwk) St Peter's Episc Church, 215 Boulevard, Mountain Lakes, NJ 07046

MULLER, Thomas G (Eur) Via de Renai 19, Pelago FI, 50060, Italy

MULLER JR, William C (SVa) 20708 Baskerville Mill Rd, Mc Kenney, VA 23872

MULLIGAN IV, Edward B (At) Holy Innocents' Episc Ch, 805 Mount Vernon Hwy NW, Atlanta, GA 30327

MULLIN, Mark Hill (Okla) 2091 Brownstone Ln, Charlottesville, VA 22901

MULLINS, Andrew (NY) 230 E 50th St Apt 4c, New York, NY 10022

MULLINS, Earl (Mass) 6922 Hollenberry Rd, Sykesville, MD 21784

MULLINS, Edward L (Mich) 730 E Knot Ct, Corolla, NC 27927

MULLINS, Judith Pierpont (Oly) 80 E Roanoke St Apt 16, Seattle, WA 98102

MULLINS, Perry Emerson (Dal)

MULLIS, Brad (NC) 405 Baymount Dr., Statesville, NC 28625

MULVEY, Dorian (Az) 31129 Bowery Ct, Menifee, CA 92584

MULVEY JR, Thomas Patrick (Mass)

MUMFORD, Nigel William David (SVa)

MUMITA, Joseph Thairu (Mass) Grace Episcopal Church, 67 Norwood St, Everett, MA 02149

MUMMA-WAKABAYASHI, Diane Carole (NJ)

MUN, Paul Shinkyu (Tenn) Church Of The Holy Spirit, 5325 Nolensville Pike, Nashville, TN 37211

MUNCEY, Marilee Elliott (Episcopal SJ) 915 E Main St, Turlock, CA 95380

MUNCIE, Margaret Ann (NY) 1 Chipping Ct, Greenville, SC 29607

MUNCIE, Steve D. (LI) 65 Joralemon Street, Brooklyn, NY 11201

MUNDIA, Wilberforce Omusala (NC) 204 W Salisbury St, Pittsboro, NC 27312

MUNDY, Robert (RG)

MUNGOMA, Stephen Masette (Los) 1401 W 123rd St, Los Angeles, CA 90047

MUNOZ, Antonio (Dal) 5100 Ross Ave, Dallas, TX 75206

MUNOZ JR, Frank (SanD) Grace Episcopal Church, San Marcos, CA 92069

MUNOZ, Joel (Ind)

MUNOZ, Maria E (Cal) Nuestra Senora de las Americas, 2610 N Francisco Ave, Chicago, IL 60647

MUNOZ PENA, Munoz (PR) 2703 Paseo de la Reina, Ponce, PR 00716

MUNOZ QUINTANA, Dimas D (PR) Po Box 8106, Humacao, PR 00792

MUNRO, Edward Henry (Md) 12310 Firtree Ln, Bowie, MD 20715

MUNRO, Michael (Kan) 1430 W Myrtle Ave, Phoenix, AZ 85021

MUNROE, Jim (WMass) 235 State St Apt 413, Springfield, MA 01103

MUNROE, Sally G (Colo) 1127 Westmoreland Rd, Colorado Springs, CO 80907

MUNSELL, Richard Francis (Colo)

MUNSON, Peter (Colo) 9972 W 86th Ave, Arvada, CO 80005

MUNZ, Catherine (Pgh) 106 Spyglass Dr, Pittsburgh, PA 15229

MURANGI, Samuel Bacwa (Pa) 8201 Frankford Ave, Philadelphia, PA 19136

MURASAKI-WEKALL, Ellen S (Los) 330 East Cordova St Unit 366, Pasadena, CA 91101

MURBARGER, Jason Andrew (CFla) Trinity Episcopal Church, 2365 Pine Ave, Vero Beach, FL 32960

MURCHIE, Alan Cameron (Ct) 21 Brightwood Ln, West Hartford, CT 06110

MURDOCH, Judith Carolyn (Fla) 4227 Columbia Rd, Martinez, GA 30907

MURDOCH, Julie (NC) 75 Old Cheat Rd., Morgantown, WV 26508

MURDOCH, Richard Dorsey (SVa) 214 Archers Mead, Williamsburg, VA 23185

MURDOCK, Audrey (Ct) 831 Stafford Ave, Bristol, CT 06010

MURDOCK, Linda Lee (EC) PO Box 626, Havelock, NC 28532

MURIUKI, James Kamau (Spr) 493 S Jackson St, Montgomery, AL 36104

MURPH, Jeff (Pgh) 530 10th St, Oakmont, PA 15139

MURPHEY, William Frederick (CPa) 2306 Edgewood Rd, Harrisburg, PA 17104

MURPHY, Diane Gensheimer (Va) 9374 Mount Vernon Cir, Alexandria, VA 22309

MURPHY, Edward John (NJ) 10 Rupells Rd, Clinton, NJ 08809

MURPHY JR, Edward John (CNY) 7639 Reed Ter, Lowville, NY 13367

MURPHY, Gwyneth MacKenzie (NY) 31 Birchwood Dr, Rhinebeck, NY 12572

MURPHY JR, Hartshorn (Los) 1630 Greenfield Ave. Apt 105, Los Angeles, Los Angeles, CA 90025

MURPHY, James T (SwFla) 1605 Banchory Cir, Walhalla, SC 29691

MURPHY, Jo-Ann R (Va) 3605 S Douglas Rd, Miami, FL 33133

MURPHY, Kyle (CPa)

MURPHY, Linda Estelle (Va) 15 Hamilton St, Colonial Beach, VA 22443

MURPHY, Madeline (Me)

MURPHY, Michael John (Tenn) 219 Jennings Cir, Tullahoma, TN 37388

MURPHY, Michael Robert (SVa) 421 Barr Dr., Clarksville, TN 37043

MURPHY JR, P L (Dal)

MURPHY, Patricia Ann (Kan) 7515 W 102nd St, Overland Park, KS 66212
MURPHY, Robert A (WMo) 4225 Sw Clipper Ln, Lees Summit, MO 64082
MURPHY JR, Russell Edward (Wyo) 11506 Wornall Rd, Kansas City, MO 64114
MURPHY, Sue (Me) 37 Chancery Ln, Sanford, ME 04073
MURPHY, Susan (Ind)
MURPHY, T Abigail (LI) 15 Stewart Ave, Stewart Manor, NY 11530
MURPHY, Terri Marie (WA) 15575 Germantown Rd, Germantown, MD 20874
MURPHY, Thomas Lynch (WNC) 9 Swan St, Asheville, NC 28803
MURPHY, Thomas M (Md) 38 Duncan Ave, Jersey City, NJ 07304
MURPHY, Timothy Hunter (Ala) 801 The Trce W, Jasper, AL 35504
MURPHY, Warren C (Wyo) 50 Diamond View Rd, Cody, WY 82414
MURPHY, William Mckee (WMich) N 2794 Summerville Park Road, Lodi, WI 53555
MURPHY-GILL, Meghan (Chi)
MURRAY, Ann Elena Williams (Okla) 325 E 1st St, Edmond, OK 73034
MURRAY, Austin B (The Episcopal Church in Haw) 2853 Panepoo St, Kihei, HI 96753
MURRAY IV, Bill S (At) 8011 Douglas Ave, Dallas, TX 75225
MURRAY, Diane Marie (FdL) W5766 Winooski Rd, Plymouth, WI 53073
MURRAY, Elizabeth Ann (CFla) 144 Sea Park Blvd, Satellite Beach, FL 32937
MURRAY JR, George Ralph (Eas) 4453 Eastwicke Dr, Salisbury, MD 21804
MURRAY III, John William (CGC) 1326 Live Oak Ln, Jacksonville, FL 32207
MURRAY, Kathleen (Va)
MURRAY, Kathleen Fontaine (SO) 6795 E Calle La Paz Unit 9101, Unit 9101, Tucson, AZ 85715
MURRAY, Laura Jane (Oly) 7701 Skansie Ave, Gig Harbor, WA 98335
MURRAY, Lois Thompson (SeFla) 1521 Alton Rd # 219, Miami Beach, FL 33139
MURRAY, Mac (WMass) 2107 23rd Ave W, Seattle, WA 98199
MURRAY, Mary Janet (Ark)
MURRAY, Milton Hood (Fla) 3750 Peachtree Rd NE # 422, Atlanta, GA 30319
MURRAY, Noland Patrick (Ark) 14300 Chenal Pkwy Apt 1316, Little Rock, AR 72211
MURRAY, Robert Scott (Episcopal SJ) 1104 Kitanosho-Cho, Ohmihachiman, Shiga, 523-0806, Japan
MURRAY III, Roderic Lafayette (Ala) 634 Timber Ln, Nashville, TN 37215
MURRAY III, Thomas Holt (WTex) 1120 Lake Dr, Kerrville, TX 78028

MURRAY, Thomas P (Fla) 4129 Oxford Ave, Jacksonville, FL 32210
MURRAY, Timothy (Chi)
MURRAY, Trilby Ometa (Chi) 3801 S Wabash Ave, Chicago, IL 60653
MURRAY, Vincent Devitt (Oly) 306 Lopez Ave, Port Angeles, WA 98362
MURRAY-SMITH, Jihan Brittany (Chi) 1424 N Dearborn St, Chicago, IL 60610
MURRELL, William Lewis (NY) 2400 Johnson Ave Apt 10c, Bronx, NY 10463
MURSULI, Modesto (SeFla) 399a Himrod St, Brooklyn, NY 11237
MUSCO, John Robert (LI) 1099 Ocean Ave, Brooklyn, NY 11230
MUSGRAVE, David Charles (Chi) 11112 Bayberry Hills Dr, Raleigh, NC 27617
MUSOKE-LUBEGA, Benjamin Kiwomutemero (NY) 27 Compton Dr, East Windsor, NJ 08520
MUSSER, David N (Colo)
MUSSER, Jonathan David (WA) 3737 Seminary Rd # 107, Alexandria, VA 22304
MUSSER, Lisa Flores (Colo) 3800 W 20th St, Greeley, CO 80634
MUSTARD, George Thomas (SwVa) 6437 Monarch Ct, Hoschton, GA 30548
MUSTERED, Jeremiah John (Pa)
MUSTERMAN, Amanda E (At) 206 W Columbia St, Somerset, KY 42501
MUTCHLER, Marlene Kay-Scholten (Ore) 147 Nw 19th Ave, Portland, OR 97209
MUTH, Donald Charles (La) 4920 Cleveland Pl, Metairie, LA 70003
MUTOLO, Frances (Colo) 85 Long Bow Cir, Monument, CO 80132
MUWINA, Derrick (Mass)
MWANGI, Isaac (Okla)
MYCOFF JR, Walt (SO) 892 W Webster Rd, Summersville, WV 26651
MYERS, Amy Slaughter (Md) Epiphany Episcopal Church, 2216 Pot Spring Rd, Timonium, MD 21093
MYERS, Annwn (Miss) 335 Tennessee Ave, Sewanee, TN 37383
MYERS, Bethany Leigh (Mass) 800 N Saint Asaph St # 202, Alexandria, VA 22314
MYERS, Brooke (Mo) 4141 Flora Pl, Saint Louis, MO 63110
MYERS, Charles Thomas (CFla)
MYERS, David John (Ark) 12599 Timberline Dr, Garfield, AR 72732
MYERS, Elizabeth Williams (Be) 798 Willow Grove St # 3a, Hackettstown, NJ 07840
MYERS, Fredrick Eugene (SanD) 65565 Acoma Ave Spc 3, Spc3, Desert Hot Springs, CA 92240
MYERS, Jason Phillip (Tex)
MYERS, Jeannette (The Episcopal NCal) 38 Payran Street, Petaluma, CA 94952

MYERS, John Geenwood (Tex) 833 Clarence St, Lake Charles, LA 70601
MYERS, Jonathan (Spok) St Stephen Episcopal Church, 4805 NE 45th St, Seattle, WA 98105
MYERS, Max Arthur (Ct) 247 New Milford Tpke, New Preston Marble Dale, CT 06777
MYERS, Nicholas A (Mass) 29 Lakeview Rd, Winchester, MA 01890
MYERS, Rebecca Sue (CPa) 53 S 4th St, Newport, PA 17074
MYERS II, Robert (Ind) 8014 River Bay Drive West, Indianapolis, IN 46240
MYERS JR, Robert Keith (Chi) 452 Woodward Ct, Lake Forest, IL 60045
MYERS, Roy (WLa) 1906 Evangeline Dr, Bastrop, LA 71220
MYERS, Thomas (NJ) 2502 Central Ave, North Wildwood, NJ 08260
MYHR, Laura Parmer (WNC) 100 Summit Street, Marion, NC 28752
MYNATT, Belva Charlene (WMo) 3523 S Kings Hwy, Independence, MO 64055
MYRICK, Bill (Mil) PO Box 528, 503 E Walworth Ave, Delavan, WI 53115
MYSEN, Andrea Leigh (Chi) 3015 Indianwood Rd, Wilmette, IL 60091
MYSINGER, Kellie Ann (Ky) 1215 State St, Bowling Green, KY 42101

N

NABE, Clyde Milton (Mo) 4742 Burlington Ave N, Saint Petersburg, FL 33713
NABORS JR, Mark Steven (Ark)
NACHTRIEB, John David (Chi) 131 N Brainard Ave, La Grange, IL 60525
NAECKEL, Lynn Miles (Minn) Po Box 43, Ranier, MN 56668
NAEF, Linda (Miss) 655 Eagle Ave, Jackson, MS 39206
NAEGELE III, John Aloysius (CPa) 982 Spa Rd. Apt. 201, Annapolis, MD 21403
NAGARAJAH, Bertram (ECR)
NAGATA, Ada (Los) Church of Our Saviour, 535 West Roses Road, San Gabriel, CA 91775
NAGEL, Ginger (CNY) 100 Wilson Pl, Syracuse, NY 13214
NAGLE, George Oberholser (CNY) 65 Glenwood Dr, Saranac Lake, NY 12983
NAGLEY, Stephanie Jane (WA) 6030 Grosvenor Ln, Bethesda, MD 20814
NAGY, Robert Arthur (NJ) 865 Hunters Dr, Deptford, NJ 08096
NAGY, Stephen R (Ct)
NAILOR, Willis Michael (CPa) 221 N Front St, Harrisburg, PA 17101
NAIRN, Frederick William (Minn) 5895 Stoneybrook Dr, Minnetonka, MN 55345
NAKAMURA RENGERS, Katherine Toshiko (Ala) 521 20th St N, Birmingham, AL 35203

NAKO, Jim (Chi) 9300 S Pleasant Ave, Chicago, IL 60643

NALVEN, Claudia (WTex) 327 S 4th St, Geneva, IL 60134

NANCARROW, Arthur Paul (Mich) 148 W Eagle Lake Dr, Maple Grove, MN 55369

NANCARROW, Margaret Grace (Minn) 422 N 13th Ave E, Duluth, MN 55805

NANCARROW, Paul Steven (SwVa) 25 Church St, Staunton, VA 24401

NANCEKIVELL, Diane (NJ) 1008 Hemenway Rd, Bridport, VT 05734

NANNY, Susan Kathryn (Mo) 2831 Eads Ave, Saint Louis, MO 63104

NANTHICATTU, Jacob Philip (NY) 182 Ridge Rd, Valley Cottage, NY 10989

NANTON-MARIE, Allan Anselm (Fla) PO Box 1-5442, Fort Lauderdale, FL 33318

NAPIER, Graeme Stewart Patrick Columbanus (NY)

NAPOLIELLO, Susan Foster (The Episcopal NCal) 2412 Foothill Blvd No. 31, Calistoga, CA 94515

NARAIN, Errol (Chi) 125 E 26th St, Chicago, IL 60616

NARVAEZ ADORNO, Jose A (PR)

NASH, Cynthia Gordon (WNC) 15 Hemlock Ave, Spruce Pine, NC 28777

NASH, Penny Annette (Va) 5404 Kingsbury Rd, Richmond, VA 23226

NATHAN, Johnson L (Okla)

NATHANIEL, Mary (Ak) PO Box 56, Chalkyitsik, AK 99788

NATIONS, Christopher Cameron (Tex) 1420 E Palm Valley Blvd, Round Rock, TX 78664

NATTA, Laura E (Cal)

NATTERMANN, Peggy (WMich) 06685 M-66n, Charlevoix Estates Lot 124, Charlevoix, MI 49720

NATZKE, Vicki (FdL) 7221 Country Village Dr, Wisconsin Rapids, WI 54494

NAUGHTON, Ezra A (Episcopal VI) 398 N St Sw, Washington, DC 20024

NAUGHTON, Mary Anne (SeFla) 3300A S Seacrest Blvd, Boynton Beach, FL 33435

NAUGHTON, Sharon Yvonne (EMich) St Paul's Episcopal Church, 711 S Saginaw St, Flint, MI 48502

NAUMANN, John Frederick (Mont) 1241 Crawford Dr., Billings, MT 59102

NAUMANN, Richard Donald (Wyo) 3487 S 27th Ave Unit 3, Bozeman, MT 59718

NAUSKA, Gayle (Ak) 1703 Richardson Dr, Anchorage, AK 99504

NAWROCKI, Cynthia Lynn (WMich) 3006 Bird Ave Ne, Grand Rapids, MI 49525

NAYLOR, Susan B (Mo) 2905 Wingate Ct, Saint Louis, MO 63119

NCACA, Mawethu (NC)

NDAI, Domenic M (Pa) 801 Macdade Blvd, Collingdale, PA 19023

NDISHABANDI, William K (NJ) 147 Daniel Lake Blvd, Jackson, MS 39212

NDUNGU, Samuel Kirabi (Pa) 6361 Lancaster Ave, Philadelphia, PA 19151

NEAD III, Prescott Eckerman (USC) 714 Michaels Crk, Evans, GA 30809

NEAKOK, Willard Payne (Ak)

NEAL, Deonna Denice (Ala) St. John's Episcopal Church, 113 Madison Avenue, Montgomery, AL 36104

NEAL, Kristi Hasskamp (WNC) 100 Spring Ln, Black Mountain, NC 28711

NEAL, Linda (ECR) 41-884 Laumilo St, Waimanalo, HI 96795

NEAL, Scott (Vt) PO Box 410, Arlington, VT 05250

NEAL, William Everett (FdL)

NEALE, Alan James Robert (Pa) 316 S 16th St, Philadelphia, PA 19102

NEARY, Marlyn Mason (NH) 1935 Us Route 3, Colebrook, NH 03576

NEAT, William J (Lex) 739 Isaac Shelby Cir W, Frankfort, KY 40601

NEBEL, Sue (Chi) 2023 Lake Ave, Wilmette, IL 60091

NECKERMANN, Ernest Charles (Los) 1107 Foothills Dr, Newberg, OR 97132

NEDELKA, Jerome Joseph (LI) PO Box 2016, Miller Place, NY 11764

NEED, Merrie Anne Dunham (Colo) 7726 S Trenton Ct, Englewood, CO 80112

NEEL, Doug (Colo) 225 S Pagosa Blvd, Pagosa Springs, CO 81147

NEEL-RICHARD, Joanne Louise (Ct) 39 Mckinley Ave, New Haven, CT 06515

NEELY, Christopher Fones (SO) 3580 Shaw Ave 409, Cincinnati, OH 45208

NEFF, Shanna (WTex) St Pauls Episcopal Church, PO Box 1148, San Antonio, TX 78294

NEFSTEAD, Eric (Cal) 275 Burnett Ave Apt 8, San Francisco, CA 94131

NEGLIA, Dwight (Nwk) 116 Oakmont Dr, Mays Landing, NJ 08330

NEGRON CARABALLO SR, Luis (PR)

NEIDLINGER, Theodore (NI) 125 S Mccann St, Kokomo, IN 46901

NEIGHBORS, Dolores (Chi) 5555 S Everett Ave Apt C-4, Chicago, IL 60637

NEIL, Earl Albert (WA) 4545 Connecticut Ave Nw, Apt 929, Washington, DC 20008

NEIL, Judy Kay (Ala) Grace Episcopal Church, 5712 1st Ave N, Birmingham, AL 35212

NEIL, Kevin (Cal)

NEILSON, Kurt (Ore) 2736 SE 63rd Ave, Portland, OR 97206

NEILSON, Lisa (Tex) 902 George Bush Dr, College Station, TX 77840

NEILY, Robert Edward (Mich) 704 15th St Apt 360, Durham, NC 27705

NEISLAR, Ranie H (Ga)

NEITZEL, Anna C (Dal) 6525 Inwood Road, Dallas, TX 75209

NELSON, Angela (NC)

NELSON III, Benjamin Howard (WTex) 3039 Ranch Rd 12, San Marcos, TX 78666

NELSON, Beth Anne (Tex)

NELSON SR, Bob (SanD) 330 11th St, Del Mar, CA 92014

NELSON, Charles Herbert (LI) 19451 Murdock Ave, Saint Albans, NY 11412

NELSON, David (Tex) 2727 Bens Branch Dr Apt 1001, Kingwood, TX 77339

NELSON, Elizabeth (SwFla) 705 Jefferson Ave, Lehigh Acres, FL 33936

NELSON, Elizabeth Anne (Ida)

NELSON, Genevieve Elizabeth (SVa) 7400 Hampton Blvd, Norfolk, VA 23505

NELSON, Geri Lee (Ga) 129 Viewcrest Dr, Hendersonville, NC 28739

NELSON, J Douglas (SD) 21 rue du Sourdonnet, Les Mathes, SD 17570, France

NELSON, James Craig (WTex) 2500 N 10th St, Mcallen, TX 78501

NELSON, Jeffrey Scott (Colo) 1313 Steele St Apt 101, Unit 101, Denver, CO 80206

NELSON, Jennifer Claire (Cal)

NELSON, Joseph Reed Peter (NJ) 715 Magie Ave, Elizabeth, NJ 07208

NELSON, Joshua D (SO)

NELSON, Julie (ECR) 532 Tyrella Ave Apt 30, Mountain View, CA 94043

NELSON JR, Levine S (Pa) Po Box 1105, Norristown, PA 19404

NELSON, Richard A (Ga) 7607 Lynes Ct, Savannah, GA 31406

NELSON JR, Richard Louis (NwT) 3737 Seminary Rd Pmb Vh103, Alexandria, VA 22304

NELSON, Rita (Del) 30895 Crepe Myrtle Dr Unit 66, Millsboro, DE 19966

NELSON JR, Robert Mitchell (Nev) 3609 Casa Grande Ave, Las Vegas, NV 89102

NELSON, Robert William (Ak) 93 Laukahi St, Kihei, HI 96753

NELSON, Roger (Mass) 557 Salem St, Malden, MA 02148

NELSON, Sarah Lee (Del) Saint James Episcopal Church, 2 S Augustine St, Newport, DE 19804

NELSON-AMAKER, Melana (WA) 8001 Annapolis Rd, New Carrollton, MD 20784

NELSON-LOW, Jane (Spok) 719 W. Montgomery Ave, Spokane, WA 99205

NEMBHARD, Ralston Bruce (CFla) 8413 Clematis Ln, Orlando, FL 32819

NEMES, John Dale (Oly) 16920 Se 40th Pl, Bellevue, WA 98008

NERN JR, William B (Cal)

NERUD, Barbara Jeanne (Neb)

NESBIT, Pamela (Pa) 16 Belmont Sq, Doylestown, PA 18901

NESBIT JR, William Reed (Mo) 2006 Trenton Ct, Jefferson City, MO 65109

NESBITT, John Russell (EO) 3846 NE Glisan St, Portland, OR 97232

NESBITT, Katharine Lynne (EO)

NESBITT, Paula Diane (Cal) 577 Forest St., Oakland, CA 94618

NESHEIM, Donald Oakley (Minn) CO Deborah Alexander, 3032 Walden Dr, Chaska, MN 55318

NESIN, Leslie Frances (Me) Po Box 358, Howland, ME 04448

NESMITH, Elizabeth Clare (LI) 305 Carlls Path, Deer Park, NY 11729

NESS, Jerry (Neb) 5605 N Ave, Kearney, NE 68847

NESS, Louisett Marie (Chi) 466 W Jackson St, Woodstock, IL 60098

NESS, Zanne Bartlett (ND) 1971 Mesquite Loop, Bismarck, ND 58503

NESTA, Paul (Dal)

NESTLEHUTT, Abigail Crozier (Pa) PO Box 517, Saint Michaels, MD 21663

NESTLEHUTT, Mark Stevens (Pa) 1426 Pennsylvania Ave, Berwyn, PA 19312

NESTLER, Mary June (U)

NESTOR, Elizabeth M (RI) 57 South Rd, Wakefield, RI 02879

NESTROCK, Frederick (Mich) 4633 Fairway Ct, Waterford, MI 48328

NETTLES, Duane Joseph (Va) The Church Of The Annunciation, 4505 S Claiborne Ave, New Orleans, LA 70125

NETTLETON, Edwin Bewick (Colo) Po Box 22, Lake City, CO 81235

NETTLETON, Jerome Paul (Eas) 525 E 6th St, Cookeville, TN 38501

NETZLER, Sherryl Kaye (Nev) 1631 Esmeralda Pl, Minden, NV 89423

NEUBAUER, Nicholas Lawrence (Nev)

NEUBAUER, Zachary D (The Episcopal NCal)

NEUBERGER, Jeffrey Lynn (Spok) 1453 SW Xavier Drive, Oak Harbor, WA 98277

NEUBURGER, James Edward (USC) 301 W Liberty St, Winnsboro, SC 29180

NEUFELD, Ellen Christine (Alb) 6349 Milgen Rd Apt 12, Columbus, GA 31907

NEUFELD, Michael John (Alb) 52 Sacandaga Rd, Scotia, NY 12302

NEUHARDT, Kerry (Az) 975 E Warner Rd, Tempe, AZ 85284

NEVELS JR, Harry V (O) 2532 Potomac Hunt Ln Apt 1B, Richmond, VA 23233

NEVILLE, Robert E (ECR) 5170 Madison Ave, Trumbull, CT 06611

NEVILLE, Robyn M (SeFla) 1299 Quaker Hill Dr, Alexandria, VA 22314

NEVIN-FIELD, Claire Margaret (Eas) 436 Pear Tree Point Rd, Chestertown, MD 21620

NEVINS, Nancy Ruth (WMo) 416 SE Grand, Lee's Summit, MO 64063

NEWAGO, Michael Jeffrey (SD) 812 W 8th St., Yankton, SD 57078

NEWBERRY, Hancella Warren (SO) 840 Middlebury Dr N, Worthington, OH 43085

NEWBERT, Russell Anderson (WNY) 185 Norwood Ave, Buffalo, NY 14222

NEWBERY, Charles Gomph (LI) 1322 Shattuck Ave Apt 306, Berkeley, CA 94709

NEWBOLD SR, Simeon Eugene (SeFla) PO Box 540668, Opa Locka, FL 33054

NEWCOMB, Blair Deborah (Md) PO Box 301, Center Sandwich, NH 03227

NEWCOMB, Deborah Johnson (Va) 25260 County Route 54, Dexter, NY 13634

NEWCOMB, Thomason League (NY) 35 Parkview Ave Apt 4l, Bronxville, NY 10708

NEWCOMBE, David Gordon (NY) 113 Gilbert Road, Cambridge, CB43N, Great Britain (UK)

NEWELL, Kevin Michael (Va)

NEWELL, Tige John E (SVa) 1562 Heathrow Ln, Keswick, VA 22947

NEWELL-LARGE, Amy (Colo)

NEWHART, David George (CFla) 120 Larchmont Ter, Sebastian, FL 32958

NEWLAND, Benjamin (Colo) Saint Johns Episcopal Church, 1419 Pine St, Boulder, CO 80302

NEWLIN, Melissa Dollie (ECR) 1965 Luzern St, Seaside, CA 93955

NEWLUN, Connor J (Md) Aquia Episcopal Church, PO Box 275, Stafford, VA 22555

NEWMAN, Georgia Ann (At)

NEWMAN II, James Arthur (Los) 1445 Westerly Ter, Los Angeles, CA 90026

NEWMAN, Jenny M (Miss)

NEWMAN, Michael Werth (Pa) 1806 Half Mile Post S, Garnet Valley, PA 19060

NEWMAN, Robin Lee Ritter (NY)

NEWMAN, Ryan D (Episcopal SJ) 31152 Oakmont Pl, Laguna Niguel, CA 92677

NEWMAN, Thomas Frank (SD) 20120 SE 39th St, Harrah, OK 73045

NEWTON, Alissabeth Anne (Oly) Diocese Of Olympia, 1551 10th Ave E, Seattle, WA 98102

NEWTON IV, John (Tex) 209 W 27th St, Austin, TX 78705

NEWTON, John David (Minn) 1631 Ford Pkwy, Saint Paul, MN 55116

NEYLAND, Thomas Allen (Colo) 474 S Camino Holgado, Green Valley, AZ 85614

NEYLON, Jean Carla (Md)

NG, Joshua (Cal) 15930 Annellen St, Hacienda Heights, CA 91745

NGUYEN, Herman Hong Xuan (Los) 10795 Garza Ave, Anaheim, CA 92804

NI, Huiliang (Los) St Edmunds Episcopal Church, 1175 S San Gabriel Blvd, San Marino, CA 91108

NICHOLS, Alice (Ky) 216 E 6th St, Hopkinsville, KY 42240

NICHOLS, Catherine (Vt) PO Box 554, East Middlebury, VT 05740

NICHOLS JR, Charlie (NH) 43 Pine St, Exeter, NH 03833

NICHOLS, David Wilson (Tenn) 1431 Tannin Dr, Durham, NC 27713

NICHOLS, Jacob Robert (Dal) 12660 Jupiter Rd Apt 1116, Dallas, TX 75238

✠ **NICHOLS**, Kevin Donnelly (Be) 21 Hampshire Hills Dr, Bow, NH 03304

NICHOLS, Liane Christoffersen (Ia) 2013 Minnetonka Dr, Cedar Falls, IA 50613

NICHOLS III, Robert George (Tex) 15 Hannon Ave, Mobile, AL 36604

NICHOLS, Sarah (Los) 837 S Orange Grove Blvd, Pasadena, CA 91105

NICHOLSON, Anne L (Md) 1830 Connecticut Ave NW, Washington, DC 20009

NICHOLSON, Kedron (WNC) 245 Kingsley Ave, Orange Park, FL 32073

NICKEL, Rebecca (Ind) S2601 E Thompson Rd, Indianapolis, IN 46227

NICKELSON, Marian L (Ak) 1133 Walnut Ave, Kenai, AK 99611

NICKERSON, Audra M (WMich) 141 Broad St N, Battle Creek, MI 49017

NICKERSON, Bruce Edward (Mass) 77 South Rd, Bedford, MA 01730

NICKLES, Amanda L (Fla) PO Box 10472, Tallahassee, FL 32302

NICKLES, Brenda Joyce (Alb) 12 Woodbridge Ave., Chatham, NY 12037

NICKLES, Megan Woods (Wyo) 349 N Douglas St, Powell, WY 82435

NICOLL, Tom (NY) 16 Claret Dr, Greenville, SC 29609

NICOLOSI, Gary (Az) Law Office of Gary Nicolosi, 12356 W Gilia Way, Peoria, AZ 85383

NIELSEN III, Peter W (O) 5811 Vrooman Rd, Painesville, OH 44077

NIEMAN, John S (USC) PO Box 234, Newcastle, ME 04553

NIEMEYER, David (Va) 501 W Nine Mile Rd, Highland Springs, VA 23075

NIETERT, Jack (SC) 2830 W Royal Oaks Dr, Beaufort, SC 29902

NILES, Sally (Az)

NIPPS, Leslie (Cal) 592 Jean St Apt 202, Oakland, CA 94610

NISBETT, Joshua (LI) 11738 Cross Island Pkwy, Cambria Heights, NY 11411

NISSEN, Peter Boy (WK) 312 S Kansas Ave, Norton, KS 67654

NITZ, Theodore Allen (Spok) 2300 NW Ridgeline Drive, Pullman, WA 99163

NIX JR, William Dale (NwT) 11355 Nix Ranch Road, Canadian, TX 79014

NIXON, Barbara Elizabeth (Ct) 399 Windward Way, Sacramento, CA 95831

NIXON, James Thomas (At) 5622 N Wayne Ave Apt 1, Unit #1, Chicago, IL 60660

NIXON, Thomas E (CGC) 1580Deese Road, Ozark, AL 36360

NJOKU, Benjamin (Mass)

NNAJI, Benjamin Udochukwu (NY) 1905 Morris Ave, Bronx, NY 10453

NOALL, Nancy Jo (WA) 312 Hillmoor Dr, Silver Spring, MD 20901

NOBLE, Anthony Norman (SanD) 625 Pennsylvania Ave, San Diego, CA 92103

NOBLE, Bill (NJ) 1941 Wayside Rd, Eatontown, NJ 07724

NOBLE, Mitzi McAlexander (WA) 508 Tranquility Rd., Moneta, VA 24121

NOCHER, Janet Gregoire (Tex) 4408 Foxfire Way, Fort Worth, TX 76133

NOEL, Virginia Lee (Mo) 15826 Clayton Rd Apt 131, Ellisville, MO 63011

NOGLE, Rosaleen (WNY)

NOLAND, Elisabeth Hooper (RG) 2 Pino Pl, Santa Fe, NM 87508

NOLEN, Kenneth (CFla) 414 Pine St, Titusville, FL 32796

NONKEN, Scott Eugene (SwFla)

NOON, Anna Catherine Christian (NJ) Rua da Carreira do Conde 18, 2A, Santiago de Compostela, 15701, Spain

NOONAN, Deborah (Az) 2331 E Adams St, Tucson, AZ 85719

NORBY, Laura L (Mil) 508 Rupert Rd, Waunakee, WI 53597

NORCROSS, Stephen (Ore) 8949 SW Fairview Pl, Portland, OR 97223

NORD, Christina Virginia (Pa) 108 N 5th St, Allentown, PA 18102

NORDQUIST, Conrad (Los) 4063 Ruis Ct, Jurupa Valley, CA 92509

NORDSTROM JR, Eugene Alexander (HB)

NORDWICK, Brian P (ECR) 670 Clearview Dr, Hollister, CA 95023

NORFLEET, Laurence (Del)

NORGARD, David (Los) PO Box 691458, West Hollywood, CA 90069

NORMAN, Curt (EMich) St Johns Episcopal Church, 123 N Michigan Ave, Saginaw, MI 48602

NORMAN, Joseph Gary (Alb) PO Box 800, Morris, NY 13808

NORMAN, Lynn (ETenn) Trinity Episcopal Church, 1900 Dauphin St, Mobile, AL 36606

NORMAN JR, Richard Hudson (SwFla) 12213 Clubhouse Dr, Lakewood Ranch, FL 34202

NORMAND, Ann (Tex) 1225 Texas St, Houston, TX 77002

NORRIS, David (Ct) 5 Briar Brae Rd, Stamford, CT 06903

NORRIS, M Brent (CGC) 337 Charlotte St, Asheville, NC 28801

NORRIS, Mark Joseph Patrick (Neb) 155 Strozier Rd # B, West Monroe, LA 71291

NORRIS III, Paul Haile (At) 951 Williams St, Madison, GA 30650

NORRIS, Stephen Allen (Ga) 2493 Chandler Dr, Valdosta, GA 31602

NORRIS, Susy (NJ) 6355 Pine Dr, Chincoteague, VA 23336

NORRO, Hugo (Los) 4200 Summers Ln Unit 15, Klamath Falls, OR 97603

NORTH JR, Bill (Tex) 570 Marietta Ave, Swarthmore, PA 19081

NORTH, Bob (Chi) 7 Huron Trce, Galena, IL 61036

NORTH, Joseph James (Alb) 144 Prospect Ave, Gloversville, NY 12078

NORTHCRAFT, Linda (Mich) 19120 Eldridge Ct, Southfield, MI 48076

NORTHRUP, Michael C (Nev) 507 Churchill St, Fallon, NV 89406

NORTHUP, Frederick Bowen (At) 1118 Chicory Ln, Asheville, NC 28803

NORTHUP, Lesley Armstrong (NY) 1298 NE 95th St, Miami, FL 33138

NORTHWAY, Daniel Page (Kan) 3531 SW Ashworth Ct, Topeka, KS 66614

NORTON JR, James Frederick (Ia) 1621 E River Ter, Minneapolis, MN 55414

NORTON, Jerry R (Ak)

NORTON, Marlee R (Va) 2416 N Florida St, Arlington, VA 22207

NORTON, Mary (NwPa) 218 Center St, Ridgway, PA 15853

NORTON, Mary Julyan (Ak) St Georges In The Arctic Ch, Po Box 269, Kotzebue, AK 99752

NORVELL, John David (Okla) 530 Northcrest Dr, Ada, OK 74820

NOVAK, Barbara Ellen Hosea (Spok) 1107 E 41st Ave, Spokane, WA 99203

NOVAK, Margaret Anne (Oly) 15502 30th Ave Ne, Shoreline, WA 98155

NOVAK, Nick (Tex) 5215 Honey Crk, Baytown, TX 77523

NOVAK-SCOFIELD, Eleanor Patricia (SwVa) 124 E Main St, Abingdon, VA 24210

NOVES, W David Peter (WNY) 840 Bataan Ave, Dunkirk, NY 14048

NOWLIN, Ben G (Mo) 61 Dames Ct, Ferguson, MO 63135

NOYES, Daphne B (Mass) Church Of The Advent, 30 Brimmer St, Boston, MA 02108

NSENGIYUMVA, Samuel (CFla) 1223 Huron Trail, Sheboygan Falls, WI 53085

NSUBUGA, Thomas (WLa) 538 Main St, Grambling, LA 71245

NTAGENGWA, Jean Baptiste (Mass) 464 Newport Ave, Attleboro, MA 02703

NUAMAH, Reggie (LI) 3607 Glenwood Rd, Brooklyn, NY 11210

NULL, John A (WK) 636 E Iron Ave, Salina, KS 67401

NUNEZ, Tim (CFla) 221 4th St S, Lake Wales, FL 33853

NUNLEY, Jan (NY) 1414 Elm St, Peekskill, NY 10566

NUNNALLY, Peter E (Va)

NURDING, Brian Frank (The Episcopal Church in Haw) 1144 Kumukumu St Apt E, Honolulu, HI 96825

NUSSER-TELFER, Hiltrude Maria (O) 9868 Ford Rd, Perrysburg, OH 43551

NUTTER, James Wallace (Tex) 6221 Main St, Houston, TX 77030

NWACHUKU, Chukwuemeka Polycarp (Chi) St Andrew's -, 1928 Darrow Ave, Evanston, IL 60201

NWANKWO, Chizoba Uzoamaka (NJ)

NYATSAMBO, Tobias (NH) PO Box 737, Ashland, NH 03217

NYBACK, Rachel (Los) 1818 Monterey Blvd, Hermosa Beach, CA 90254

NYBERG, Kristina Yvette (Los) 700 S. Myrtle Avenue, Apt 514, Monrovia, CA 91016

NYE, Linda Wade (NC) Grace Mem Tec Ch, 871 Merrimon Ave, Asheville, NC 28804

NYEIN, Zack (At) 325 Park Ave, New York, NY 10022

NYGAARD, Richard Lowell (NwPa)

NYGAARD, Steven Bickham (NMich) 6144 Westridge 21.25 Dr, Gladstone, MI 49837

NYRE-THOMAS, Beryl Jean (Los) 1117 Bennett Ave, Long Beach, CA 90804

NYSTROM, Brian Eric (Wyo) PO Box 1690, Jackson, WY 83001

O

OAK, Carol Pinkham (Md) St. John's Episcopal Church, 9120 Frederick Road, Ellicott City, MD 21042

OAKES, Leonard (Cal) 777 Southgate Ave, Daly City, CA 94015

OAKES, Sara Elizabeth Herr (Cal) 622 Terra California Dr Apt 7, Walnut Creek, CA 94595

OAKES, Susan L (Ala)

OAKLAND, Mary Jane (Ia) 1612 Truman Dr, Ames, IA 50010

OASIN, Elizabeth Jayne (NJ) 344 B Delancey Pl, Mount Laurel, NJ 08054

OATS, Louis (NC) 1325 Hickory Lane, Dandridge, TN 37725

OBENCHAIN, John Colin (Pa) 98 Ayers Dr, Rising Sun, MD 21911

OBERHEIDE, Rick (Ala) 155 N Twining St, Montgomery, AL 36112

OBIER, Cynthia Andrews (La) 4255 Hyacinth Ave, Baton Rouge, LA 70808

OBREGON, Ernesto M (Ala) 5424 Wisteria Trce, Trussville, AL 35173

O'BRIEN, Donald Richard (SwFla)

O'BRIEN, Eileen Elizabeth (Tex)

O'BRIEN, Julie (Az) 9502 W Hutton Dr, Sun City, AZ 85351

O' BRIEN, Richard L (Nev) Epiphany Episcopal Church, 10450 Gilespie St, Las Vegas, NV 89183

O'BROCHTA, Joseph William (Lex)

O'CALLAGHAN, Beth (WA) 11800 Old Georgetown Rd Unit 1432, North Bethesda, MD 20852

O'CARROLL, Bryan (SwFla) 2627 Green Valley St, Valrico, FL 33596

OCCHIUTO, Joseph John (LI)
O'CONNELL, Kelly (Mass) 138 Tremont St, Boston, MA 02111
O'CONNELL, Patricia Marie (WMass) 2205 Boston Road, Apt K97, Wilbraham, MA 01095
O'CONNOR, Andrew T (Kan) 2406 N Spring Meadow Cir, Wichita, KS 67205
O'CONNOR, Christopher Duane (WNY) 30 Favor St, Attica, NY 14011
O'CONNOR, Maureen Nicole (Chi)
O'CONNOR JR, Terrence (NJ) 2998 Bay Ave, Ocean City, NJ 08226
ODDERSTOL, Sarah Dodds (WA) St. Mary's Episcopal Church, 306 S Prospect Avenue, Park Ridge, IL 60068
ODEKIRK, Dennis Russell (Los) 830 Columbine Ct, San Luis Obispo, CA 93401
O'DELL, Thomas Peyton (WMich) 123 W Washington St, Lexington, VA 24450
ODEN, Jason Daniel (SO)
ODGERS, Marie Christine Hanson (Neb) 8800 Holdrege St, Lincoln, NE 68505
ODIERNA, Robert Odie (NH) 46 Turtle Rock Rd, Windham, NH 03087
ODOM, Robert (Tex) 5923 Royal Ln, Dallas, TX 75230
O'DONNELL, John J (NH) 315 Mason Rd, Milford, NH 03055
O'DONNELL, Michael Alan (Alb) 4940 Shirley Pl, Colorado Springs, CO 80920
OESTERLIN, Peter William (RG) 3232 Renaissance Dr SE, Rio Rancho, NM 87124
OFFINGER, Julia Macy (NY)
O'FLINN, Nancy C (Ala)
O'FLYNN, Donnel (Mont) Christ Church, 215 3rd Ave E, Kalispell, MT 59901
OFOEGBU, Daniel Okwuchukwu (Dal) Church Of The Ascension, 8787 Greenville Ave., Dallas, TX 75243
OGBURN JR, John Nelson (NC) 330 W Presnell St Apt 44, Asheboro, NC 27203
OGBURN, William L (LI) 487 Hudson St, New York, NY 10014
OGDEN, Virginia Louise (Alb) 51 Brockley Dr, Delmar, NY 12054
OGIER JR, Dwight (At) 125 Betty Street, Clarkesville, GA 30523
OGLE, Albert Joy (NY) 3634 Seventh Ave Unit 6B, San Diego, CA 92103
OGLE SR, Louis Knox (La) 43 Hyacinth Dr, Covington, LA 70433
OGLESBY, Charles Lucky (NC) 325 Glen Echo Ln Apt J, Cary, NC 27518
OGLESBY, Keith (Fla)
OGLESBY, Patricia A (Pa) 1734 Huntington Tpke, Trumbull, CT 06611
OGUIKE, Martin Ugochukwu (NJ) 17 Woodbridge Ave, Sewaren, NJ 07077
OGUS, Mary H (EC) 175 9th Ave, New York, NY 10011
OGUS, Rebecca (NC)

OGWAL-ABWANG, Benoni Y (NY) 135 Remington Pl, New Rochelle, NY 10801
OH, David Yongsam (Nwk) 1224 McClaren Drive, Carmichael, CA 95608
OH, KyungJa (Chi) Bexley Seabury Sem Fed, 1407 E 60th St, Chicago, IL 60637
O'HAGIN, Zarina Eileen Suarez (Vt) 215 Corner Rd, Hardwick, VT 05843
O'HARA, Christina Swenson (SD) 2707 W 33rd St, Sioux Falls, SD 57105
O'HARA, Ellen (NY) 141 Fulton Ave Apt 609, Poughkeepsie, NY 12603
O'HARA-TUMILTY, Anne (Los) 26029 Laguna Court, Valencia, CA 91355
✠ **OHL**, C Wallis (NwT) 3205 Skye Ridge Dr, Norman, OK 73069
OHLEMEIER, Mark William (Spr) 105 E D St, Belleville, IL 62220
OHLIDAL, Susan Marie (Vt)
OHLSON, Elizabeth Anderson (NJ) 5752 West Ave, Ocean City, NJ 08226
OHLSTEIN, Allen Michael (Kan) 310 W 17th St, Leavenworth, KS 66048
OHMER, John (Va) 2502 E Grace St, Richmond, VA 23223
OKTOLLIK, Carrie Ann (Ak) PO Box 446, Point Hope, AK 99766
OKUNSANYA, Adegboyega Gordon (At) 711 Saint Saginaw Street, Flint, MI 48502
OKUSI, George Otiende (Los) 312 S Oleander Ave, Compton, CA 90220
OLANDESE, Jan Susan (Nev) 2830 Phoenix St, Las Vegas, NV 89121
OLBRYCH, Jennie Clarkson (SC) 26 Saint Augustine Dr, Charleston, SC 29407
OLDFATHER, Susan Kay (Md) PO Box 187, Kingsville, MD 21087
OLDHAM ROBINETT, Lynn Margaret (Cal) 211 Forbes Ave, San Rafael, CA 94901
OLDS, Kevin (Ct) 4670 Congress St, Fairfield, CT 06824
OLDSTONE-MOORE, Jennifer (Ind) St Anne Episcopal Church, 6461 Tylersville Rd, West Chester, OH 45069
O'LEARY, Jane (Md) 6011 Chesworth Rd., Baltimore, MD 21228
O'LEARY, Timothy Robert (Chi)
OLEXICK, Nancy Morris (NMich)
OLIVER, Aaron J (Nev)
OLIVER, Kyle M (Chi) 16160 W Arlington Dr, Libertyville, IL 60048
OLIVER, Nancy Diesel (CFla) 2951 Mulberry Dr, Titusville, FL 32780
OLIVERO, Cesar Olivero (SwFla) 17241 Edgewater Dr, Port Charlotte, FL 33948
OLIVEROS, Sandra Milena (Colom)
OLIVO, David Andrew (Nwk) 207 Fairmount Rd, Ridgewood, NJ 07450
OLLER, Jan (Ind) St Johns Episcopal Church, PO Box 445, Crawfordsville, IN 47933

OLMEDO-JAQUENOD, Nina (Cal) 1321 Webster St, Alameda, CA 94501
OLMSTED, Nancy Kay Young (RI) Po Box 245, Lincoln, RI 02865
OLOIMOOJA, Edith Ipiso (Los) 3303 W Vernon Ave, Los Angeles, CA 90008
OLOIMOOJA, Joseph Mtende (Los) 1501 N Palos Vevoler Dr. #128, Harbor City, CA 90710
OLSEN, Christiana (WNC) 11 Flycatcher Way Unit 301, Arden, NC 28704
OLSEN, Daniel Kevin (Pa) Box 681, Oaks, PA 19456
OLSEN, Donna Jeanne Hoover (Ind) 2601 East Thompson Road, Indianapolis, IN 46227
OLSEN, L Michael (RG) 318 Vegas De Taos Loop, 208 Camino de Santiago, Taos, NM 87571
OLSEN JR, Lloyd Lein (CFla) 992-B E Michigan St, Orlando, FL 32806
OLSEN, Meredith Dk (Md) 4127 Chadds Xing, Marietta, GA 30062
OLSEN, Robert M (The Episcopal NCal) 8070 Glen Creek Way, Citrus Heights, CA 95610
OLSON, Anna (Los) 4274 Melrose Ave, Los Angeles, CA 90029
OLSON, Barbara Jane (ND)
OLSON, Britt Elaine (Oly) 262 Swenson Ct, Auburn, CA 95603
OLSON, Cori (SeFla) 208 S Lakeside Dr Apt 203, Lake Worth Beach, FL 33460
OLSON, Ellen Elizabeth (Neb) 609 Avenue C, Plattsmouth, NE 68048
OLSON, John Seth (Ala) 202 Gordon Dr SE, Decatur, AL 35601
OLSON, Theodore Evor (Del)
OLSON, Thomas Mack (The Episcopal NCal) 300 West St, Vacaville, CA 95688
OLSSON, John (Mass)
OLSSON, Paul V (Vt) 78 Seminary Street Ext, Middlebury, VT 05753
OLULORO, Emmanuel Bola (Az) 848 E Dobbins Rd, Phoenix, AZ 85042
OLVER, Matthew S C (Dal) 2777 Mission Rd, Nashotah, WI 53058
O'MALLEY, Donald Richard (WNC) 208 Stanley Dr, Winchester, VA 22602
OMERNICK, Marilyn (Los) 2766 Mountain View Dr, La Verne, CA 91750
OMONIYI, Ayodeji Oloyede (Tex)
ONATE-ALVARADO, Gonzalo Antonio (EcuC) Apartado Postal 5250, Guayaquil, Ecuador
O'NEIL, Janet Anne (Mo) 808 N Mason Rd, Saint Louis, MO 63141
O'NEILL, Bruce Douglas (Cal) 2833 Claremont Blvd, Berkeley, CA 94705
O'NEILL, Joanne Carbone (Nwk) 97 Highwood Ave, Tenafly, NJ 07670
✠ **O'NEILL**, Robert John (Colo) 7937 E 24th Ave, Denver, CO 80238

O'NEILL, Vince (The Episcopal Church in Haw) 98-939 Moanalua Rd, Aiea, HI 96701

ONG, Dian Marie (Ia) 803 W Tyler Ave, Fairfield, IA 52556

ONG, Merry Chan (Cal) 1011 Harrison St, Oakland, CA 94607

ONUIGBO, Ebele Patience Okonkwo (WA)

ONYENDI, Matthias E (Tex)

OPARE-ADDO, Frederick Akwetey (LI) 13304 109th Ave, South Ozone Park, NY 11420

OPAT, Kris (Pgh) 1066 Washington Rd, Pittsburgh, PA 15228

OPEL, William A (NH) 395 Locust Road, Eastham, MA 02642

O'PRAY, Denis Michael (Minn) 2412 Seabury Ave, Minneapolis, MN 55406

OPRENDEK, Matt (NY) 33 Jefferson ave, Garden City, NY 11530

ORCHARD, Carolyn Gertrude (NMich) 311 S 4th St, Crystal Falls, MI 49920

O'REAR, Joseph Allen (Be)

O'REAR, Lisa Ellen (O) 1412 Ardoon St, Cleveland Heights, OH 44121

O'REILLY, Eileen (SO) 6873 Fieldstone Pl, Mason, OH 45040

O'REILLY, Patricia (Los) 402 S. Oakland Ave Apt 6, Pasadena, CA 91101

OREM, Becky Jane Tilton (NwT) St Pauls Tec Ch, 1510 Avenue X, Lubbock, TX 79401

ORENS, Elizabeth Mills Pickering (Md) St James Church, 19200 York Rd, Parkton, MD 21120

ORESKOVICH JR, Steve John (Mont) 1405 Sunflower Dr, Missoula, MT 59802

ORIHUELA, Roberto Opolinar (Va) 7000 Arlington Blvd, Falls Church, VA 22042

O'RILEY, Lori Cameron (SO) 46 Erie Ave, Glendale, OH 45246

ORLANDO, Helen Marie (NJ) 10 Iris Ct, Marlton, NJ 08053

ORLANDO, Patricia Roberts (CFla)

ORME-ROGERS, Charles Arthur (Mil) 7634 Mid Town Rd - #212, Madison, WI 53719

ORMOS, Patrick Patrick (WTex) 12933 Latchwood Ln, Austin, TX 78753

ORNDORFF, Vivian (Tex) 3901 S Panther Creek Dr, The Woodlands, TX 77381

O'ROURKE, Brian (Los) 5011 Acampo Ave, Glendale, CA 91214

O'ROURKE, David Carter (Colo) 2840 Signal Creek Place, Thornton, CO 80241

OROZCO, Benjamin Manuel (SanD) 3568 Elmwood Ct, Riverside, CA 92506

ORR, Daniel (O) 62 Orchard St, Oberlin, OH 44074

ORR, Kristin Elizabeth (Mont) 8 Palomino Dr, Livingston, MT 59047

ORRALA MONCADA, Francisco (Litoral Diocese Of Ecuador)

ORRIN, Dyana Vail (Ak) 1501 N Adams St, Fredericksburg, TX 78624

ORSBURN, Kenneth Ray (Okla)

ORSO, Thomas Ray (NY) 100 Dehaven Dr Apt 405, Yonkers, NY 10703

ORT, Larry Victor (SD) St Pauls Episcopal Church, 726 6th St, Brookings, SD 57006

ORTEGA, Guido Andres (EcuC) Ave Amz 4430 Y VLG, Casilla, 17116165, Ecuador

ORTEGA CABALLERO, Hector Amilcar (Hond) Catedral TEC El Buen Pastor, 21 Calle 23 Ave C Col Trejo, San Pedro Sula, Honduras

ORTEZ, Leonel (SeFla)

ORTT, William (Eas) 111 S Harrison St, Easton, MD 21601

ORTUNG, Thomas Edward (Oly) 105 State St, Kirkland, WA 98033

ORVILLE, Lynn D (WNC) PO Box 491, Little Compton, RI 02837

ORWIG, Dana Lynn Maynard (Okla) 2710 Nw 17th St, Oklahoma City, OK 73107

OSBERGER, Charles Edward (Eas) 14084 Old Wye Mills Rd, Wye Mills, MD 21679

OSBORN, Bradley Scott (Chi)

OSBORN, Mary Anne (Ct) 560 Lake Dr, Guilford, CT 06437

OSBORN, Sherrell A (Vt) 78 Lyman Park Rd Apt 3, Hinesburg, VT 05461

OSBORNE, Bill (Spok) 5720 S Perry St, Spokane, WA 99223

OSBORNE, Caroline Joy (Tenn) 95 Fairway Dr, Nashville, TN 37214

OSBORNE, Jamie (Ala) 113 Madison Ave, Montgomery, AL 36104

OSBORNE, Janne Alr (Tex) PO Box 150535, Austin, TX 78715

OSBORNE, Laura Jean (Colo)

OSBORNE, Ralph Everett (FdL) 2420 Marathon Ave, Neenah, WI 54956

OSBORNE, Richard L (Kan) 102 Southfork Cir, Pottsboro, TX 75076

OSBORNE, Robert Allen (Tenn) 95 Fairway Dr, Nashville, TN 37214

OSBORNE-MOTT, Susan Elizabeth (NJ) 503 Asbury Ave, Asbury Park, NJ 07712

OSGOOD, John A (NY) 201 Old Mountain Rd N, Nyack, NY 10960

OSGOOD, Lynn Ann Kalsched (Tex)

OSGOOD, Thomas Marston (Cal) 6471 Coopers Hawk Rd, Klamath Falls, OR 97601

O'SHEA, Eileen Elizabeth (Ida) 524 Ruth Ln, Nampa, ID 83686

O'SHEA, Nancy Corinne Tucker (WTenn) 6294 Venus Ave, Bartlett, TN 38134

OSMUN, Andrew (Ct) 120 Roydon Rd, New Haven, CT 06511

OSNAYA-JIMENEZ, Uriel (Tex) 9600 Huntington Place Dr, Houston, TX 77099

OSORIO-CAMACHO, Nabor (Ve)

OST, Gary (Cal) 499 Ellsworth St Apt A, San Francisco, CA 94110

OSTENSO MOORE, Anna Victoria (Minn) 519 Oak Grove St, Minneapolis, MN 55403

OSTLUND, Holly Lisa (SeFla) 15730 88th Pl N, Loxahatchee, FL 33470

OSTRANDER, Paul Copeland (Okla) 2321 Northwest 48th Street, Oklahoma City, OK 73112

OSTUNI, Elizabeth Ellen (Nwk) 10 Hampton Downes, Newton, NJ 07860

O'SULLIVAN, Ann Kathlyn (Me)

OSWALD, Todd D (USC) 2200 Wilson Rd, Newberry, SC 29108

OTA, David Yasuhide (Cal) 963 Vasco da Gama Ln, Foster City, CA 94404

OTERO-RUIZ, Edgar (At)

OTIS, Violetta Lansdale (Me) 17 Foreside Rd, Falmouth, ME 04105

OTT, Bob (ECR) 1490 Mark Thomas Dr., Monterey, CA 93940

OTT, Janet Sanderson (Miss) 1200 Meadowbrook Rd Apt 44, Jackson, MS 39206

OTT, Luther (Miss) 1200 Meadowbrook Road, #44, Jackson, MS 39206

OTT, Paula Lee (Lex) 2410 Lexington Rd, Winchester, KY 40391

OTTERBURN, Margaret (Nwk) 219 Ivy Rd, Egg Harbor Township, NJ 08234

✠ **OTTLEY**, Jim (LI) 3 E Fairway Ct, Bay Shore, NY 11706

OTTO, Ronald Lee (EMich) St Andrews Church, PO Box 52, Harrisville, MI 48740

OTTO, Susan Wanty (EMich) St Andrews Church, PO Box 52, Harrisville, MI 48740

OTTSEN, David (Tex) 360 Timberlake Dr W, Holland, MI 49424

OU, Chun-Shih Shih (Tai) 200 Chu Chang 1st Road, Kaohsiung, Taiwan

OUELLETTE, Sue E (Roch) 1957 Five Mile Line Rd, Penfield, NY 14526

OUGHTON, Marjorie Knapp (Pa) Church St Paul's, 301 E 9th St, Chester, PA 19013

OUSLEY, David Kenneth (Alb) Saint Eustace Episcopal Church, 2450 Main St, Lake Placid, NY 12946

OUSLEY, John Douglas (NY) 402 E 90th St Apt 5f, New York, NY 10128

OUSLEY, Patrick Lance (Tex) 1551 10th Ave E, Seattle, WA 98102

✠ **OUSLEY**, Steven Todd (EMich) 1821 Avalon Ave, Saginaw, MI 48638

OUTMAN-CONANT, Robert Earl (Mass) 482 Beech St, Rockland, MA 02370

OUTWIN, Edson (WNY) 316 Park Ave, Medina, NY 14103

OVENSTONE, Jenni (Va) 810 Mockingbird Ln Apt 301, Towson, MD 21286

OVERALL, Martha (NY) 345 E 86th St Apt 16d, New York, NY 10028

C132

OVERBO, Terry (ND)

OWEN, Charles Bryan (La) St Lukes Episcopal Church, 8833 Goodwood Blvd, Baton Rouge, LA 70806

OWEN, David Allen (Ct) 92 E Hill Rd, Canton, CT 06019

OWEN, Donald Edward (Ala) 1921 Chandaway Ct, Pelham, AL 35124

OWEN, Harrison Hollingsworth (WA)

OWEN, Jennifer Marie (NY)

OWEN II, Keith Keith (O) 18001 Detroit Ave, Lakewood, OH 44107

OWEN, Ron (Fla) 4483 Twinview Ln, Orlando, FL 32814

OWEN, Sam (NY) 661 E 219th St, Bronx, NY 10467

OWEN, Shelby Ochs (SwVa) 4609 Leonard Pkwy, Richmond, VA 23226

OWEN, Stephen Lee (Miss) PO Box 3400, Meridian, MS 39303

OWEN, William Bonner (NY) PO Box 99, West Park, NY 12493

OWENS IV, Bernard J (O) 4407 Westbourne Rd, Greensboro, NC 27410

OWENS, Brent (Fla) Episcopal Church of the Good Shepherd, 1100 Stockton St, Jacksonville, FL 32204

OWENS JR, Donald P (La) 712 Saddleridge Drive, Wimberley, TX 78676

OWENS, John Alfred (Fla) 4180 Julington Creek Rd, Jacksonville, FL 32223

OWENS, Jonathan Michael (Cal) 1707 Gouldin Rd, Oakland, CA 94611

OWENS, Michael (At) P.O. Box 86, 637 University Ave, Sewanee, TN 37375

OWENS, Miriam Elizabeth (Roch) 515 Oakridge Dr, Rochester, NY 14617

OWENS, U'Neice Yvette (Ga) 4033 Foxborough Blvd, Valdosta, GA 31602

OWENS, Wendy S (Wyo) P. O. Box 3259, GILLETTE, WY 82717

OWENSBY, Jacob W (WLa) 335 Main St, Pineville, LA 71360

OWREN, David (The Episcopal NCal) 99 Pampas Ln, Fortuna, CA 95540

OWSLEY, Rebecca D (EMich) Christ Episcopal Church, 202 W Westover St, East Tawas, MI 48730

OWUOR, Shadrack (EMich)

OWUSU-AFRIYIE, Kwabena (Pa) 811 Longacre Blvd, Yeadon, PA 19050

OXFORD, Scott (WNC) 520 New Haw Creek Rd, Asheville, NC 28805

OXLEY, Sara (CFla) 14638 Black Quill Dr, Winter Garden, FL 34787

P

PACE, Bradley (Ind) St Johns Episcopal Church, 600 Ferry St, Lafayette, IN 47901

PACE, David Frederick (ECR) 514 Central Ave, Menlo Park, CA 94025

PACE, David Taylor (Ore) 1729 Northeast Tillamook St, Portland, OR 97212

PACE, James Conlin (NY) 145 W 46th St Apt 5, New York, NY 10036

PACE, Joseph Leslie (Ct) 1 Gold St Apt 16e, Hartford, CT 06103

PACE, Robert F (Tex) 6200 Adirondack Trl, Amarillo, TX 79106

PACE, Stephanie Anne Heflin (O) 3677 Hughstowne Dr, Akron, OH 44333

PACE, Stephen (Va)

PACHECO, Jose (SanD) 209 Clay St, Weed, CA 96094

PACHECO OSARIO, Jesus Isaias (Colom)

✠ **PACKARD**, George Elden (NY) 26 Oakwood Ave, Rye, NY 10580

PACKARD, Jeff (CPa) 208 W Foster Ave, State College, PA 16801

PACKARD, Laurence Kent (Va) 9350 Braddock Rd, Burke, VA 22015

PACKARD, Linda Axelson (Chi) 1 Prairie Ridge Dr Apt 220, apt.220, Galena, IL 61036

PACKARD, Nancy Meader (Be) 359 Whitehall Rd, Hooksett, NH 03106

PACKARD, William Laurence (Va) 43600 Russell Branch Pkwy, Ashburn, VA 20147

PACKER, Barbara J (Nwk) Po Box 240, Mendham, NJ 07945

PACKER III, George Leonard (Los) 5700 Rudnick Ave, Woodland Hills, CA 91367

PADASDAO, Imelda Sumaoang (The Episcopal Church in Haw) 1326 Konia St, Honolulu, HI 96817

PADDOCK, Andrea Lee (Los) 31551 Catalina St., Laguna Beach, CA 92651

PADDOCK, John Sheldon (SO) 1837 Ruskin Rd, Dayton, OH 45406

PADGETT, John (WTex) 12431 Modena Bay, San Antonio, TX 78253

PADGETT, Judy Malinda Pitts (At) 980 W Mill Bnd Nw, Kennesaw, GA 30152

PADILLA, Manuel Jack (NMich) 711 Michigan Ave, Crystal Falls, MI 49920

PADILLA, Margaret E (NMich) 711 Michigan Ave, Crystal Falls, MI 49920

PADILLA-MORALES, Luis Fernando (PR)

PADZIESKI, Virginia Sue (Minn) 7 Terrace Point, P. O. Box 788, Grand Marais, MN 55604

PAE, Joseph S (LI) 191 Kensington Rd, Garden City, NY 11530

PAE, Keun-Joo (Nwk) 76 E Main St, Newark, OH 43055

PAETZOLD, Ryan Richard (NJ) 17 Barclay Rd, Hainesport, NJ 08036

PAGANO, Joseph Samuel (Md)

PAGE, Anna Skae (Mass)

PAGE, Donald Richard (Ct) 11 Nassau Rd., Somers Point, NJ 08244

PAGE JR, Hugh Rowland (NI) 1526 Cedar Springs Ct, Mishawaka, IN 46545

PAGE, Michelle Rene (EC) 18115 State Road 23 Ste 112, South Bend, IN 46637

PAGE, Samira (Dal) 6941 Kingdom Estates Dr, Dallas, TX 75236

PAGE JR, William Russell (Mass) 217 Holland St Pt 2A, Somerville, MA 02144

PAGER, Deng Alaak (Dal) 8787 Greenville Ave, Dallas, TX 75243

PAGET, Joshua N (Los)

PAGLINAUAN, Cristina (Md) 5603 N Charles St, Baltimore, MD 21210

PAGUIO, Ruth Alegre (ECR) 212 Swain Way, Palo Alto, CA 94304

PAHL JR, James Larkin (NC) 302 College St, Oxford, NC 27565

PAINE, Michael Jackson (WVa) 13 Byron St, Boston, MA 02108

PAINTER JR, Borden Winslow (Ct) 110 Ledgewood Rd, West Hartford, CT 06107

PAINTER, R Scott (Tex) 1805 W Alabama St, Houston, TX 77098

PAIVA III, Fernando (NJ) 2131 Woodbridge Ave, Edison, NJ 08817

PALACIO BEDOYA, Luis Hernan (Colom) Carrera 6 No 49-85, Piso 2, Bogota, Colombia

PALARINE, John (Fla) 12236 Mandarin Rd, Jacksonville, FL 32223

PALASI, Dario (LI) 13424 96th St, Ozone Park, NY 11417

PALLARD SR, John J (CFla) PO Box 142, Peckham Lane RR#2, Coventry, RI 03/01/2816

PALLARES ARELLANO, Jorge Enrique (Episcopal SJ) 10154 Mountain Ave, Tujunga, CA 91042

PALMA, Jose (WMo) 420 W 14th St, Kansas City, MO 64105

PALMER, Alison (WA) 70 Lookout Rd, Wellfleet, MA 02667

PALMER JR, Archie (Nwk) 459 Passaic Ave Apt 315, Cottage 315, West Caldwell, NJ 07006

PALMER, Beth (Miss) 1415 Baum St, Vicksburg, MS 39180

PALMER, Brian (ECR) 2700 Eton Rd, Cambria, CA 93428

PALMER, John Avery (ECR) 981 South Clover Ave, San Jose, CA 95128

PALMER, John M (NY) 33 E 10th St Apt 2-G, New York, NY 10003

PALMER, Laura E (Pa)

PALMER, Richard Rainer (Colo) 400 Summit Blvd Unity 1503, Broomfield, CO 80021

PALMER, Richard William (Wyo) 4753 Estero Blvd Apt 1601, Fort Myers Beach, FL 33931

PALMER, Sara (Va) 108 W Farriss Ave, High Point, NC 27262

PALMGREN, Charles Leroy (At) 4482 Hunters Ter, Stone Mountain, GA 30083

PALMISANO, Michael (Pa)

PALUMBO, Candace Ann (Alb)

PANG, Lisa A (The Episcopal Church in Haw) 911 N Marine Corps Dr, Tamuning, GU 96913

PANG, Pui-Kong Thomas (Mass) 138 Tremont St, Boston, MA 02111

PANKEY, Steve (Ky) 923 Cherry Dr, Bowling Green, KY 42101
PANNELL, Terry (Mass) 202 Wildwing Park Ln, Catskill, NY 12414
PANTLE, Thomas Alvin (Dal) 617 Star St # 81, Bonham, TX 75418
PANTON, Rosalyn Way (Ga) 2200 Birnam Pl, Augusta, GA 30904
PANZARELLA, Michael T (NJ)
PAPANEK, Nicolette (Kan) 545 Greenup St #3, Covington, KY 41011
PAPAZOGLAKIS, Elizabeth (Alb) 912a Route 146, Clifton Park, NY 12065
PAPAZOGLAKIS, Thomas W (Alb) 912a Route 146, Clifton Park, NY 12065
PAPE, Cynthia Dale (Mass) 1 Linden St, Quincy, MA 02170
PAPILE, Jim (Va) 8801 Nadie Ln, Wilmington, NC 28411
PAPINI, Heber Mauricio (Okla) 5230 Peach Creek Dr, Houston, TX 77017
PAPPAS III, Jim (At) 735 University Ave, Sewanee, TN 37383
PARACHINI, David Charles (Ct) 42 Blue Jay Dr, Northford, CT 06472
PARADINE, Philip James (Va) 118 Monte Vista Ave., Charlottesville, VA 22903
PARADISE, Gene Hooper (Ga) 10 Iron Bound Pl NW, Atlanta, GA 30318
PARAISON, Edwin Mardochee (DomRep) Calle Tony Mota Ricart #16, Box 132, Barahona, Dominican Republic
PARAISON, Maud (Hai) PO Box 5826, Fort Lauderdale, FL 33310
PARDO ARCINIEGAS, Angel Maria (Colom) c/o Diocese of Colombia, Cra 6 No. 49-85 Piso 2, Bogota, BDC, Colombia
PARDOE III, Edward Devon (Ct) St Barnabas Episcopal Church, 954 Lake Ave, Greenwich, CT 06831
PARDY, William Goehl (SwFla)
PAREDES MUNGUIA, Delma Ibel (Hond) La Visitacion De La BVM, 23 Ave C, San Pedro Sula, Honduras
PARHAM, Alfred Philip (RG) 6148 Los Robles Dr, El Paso, TX 79912
PARHAM, Michael (WLa) 605 Terra Ave, Alexandria, LA 71303
PARINI, Barbara Dennison (Mass) 2957 Barbara St., Ashland, OR 97520
PARISH, Nurya (WMich) 1025 3 Mile Rd NE, Grand Rapids, MI 49505
PARK, Ciritta Boyer (WA) 1927 Shore Dr, Bellbrook, OH 45305
PARK, Cynthia (At) 74 Cottage Settings, Black Mountain, NC 28711
PARK, John Hayes (Hond) 520 Park Rd, Ambridge, PA 15003
PARK, Patricia Ann (The Episcopal NCal) 124 Orange St, Auburn, CA 95603
PARK, Stephen Radcliffe (NH) 4060 Barrows Point Rd, Nisswa, MN 56468
PARK, Theodore Allen (Minn) 19 S 1st St Apt B2208, Minneapolis, MN 55401

PARKER, Betsee (Va) 110 W Franklin St, Richmond, VA 23220
PARKER, Carol Ann (EO) 9333 Nw Winters Ln, Prineville, OR 97754
PARKER, David Clinton (Ind) 224 Davis Ave, Elkins, WV 26241
PARKER, Dennis James Sagun (Ore) 4320 S Corbett Ave Apt 317, Portland, OR 97239
PARKER, Donald Harry (Mass) 28 Cambridge Cir., Smithfield, RI 02917
PARKER, Elizabeth (Tex) 200 Oyster Creek Dr, Lake Jackson, TX 77566
PARKER, Emily (NC)
PARKER, Gary Joseph (LI) 9 Barrow St Apt 3b, New York, NY 10014
PARKER, James Frank (HB) 2409 Cheshire Woods Rd, Toledo, OH 43617
PARKER, Jesse Leon Anthony (Md) 105 W 6th St, New Castle, DE 19720
PARKER JR, Jim (Ga) 402 E 46th St, Savannah, GA 31405
PARKER, Lisa (SwFla) 2346 Gull Ln, Sarasota, FL 34237
PARKER, Mark (The Episcopal NCal)
PARKER, Matthew Ross (Dal)
PARKER, Phillip Don (Miss) PO Box 366, Sumner, MS 38957
PARKER, Robert Coleman (Tex) 832 W Jones St, Livingston, TX 77351
PARKER, Ronald Mark (Tex) 200 N Bailey Ave, Fort Worth, TX 76107
PARKER, Ronald Wilmar (Pa) 254 Williams Rd, Bryn Mawr, PA 19010
PARKER, Stephanie Eve (WNC) 2543 US Hwy 21 S, Sparta, NC 28675
PARKER JR, Stephen Dwight (Ct) 4607 Chandlers Forde, Sarasota, FL 34235
PARKER, Susan D (Az)
PARKER, William Curtis (Ky) 200 Armitage Ct, Lincoln University, PA 19352
PARKIN, Jason Lloyd (Chi) 575 Drexel Ave, Glencoe, IL 60022
PARKINSON, Caroline Smith (Va) 7321 Swift Rd, Greenbrier, TN 37073
PARKS, James Joseph (Fla)
PARKS, Ken Thomas (Ark) 1001 Kingsland Rd, Bella Vista, AR 72714
PARKS, Larry Joseph (EMich) St John the Baptist, PO Box 217, Otter Lake, MI 48464
PARKS, Sarah J (EMich) St John the Baptist, PO Box 217, Otter Lake, MI 48464
PARKS, Theodore Edward Michael (Mil) PO Box 590, Milwaukee, WI 53201
PARLIER, Susan Taylor (USC) 1238 Evergreen Ave, West Columbia, SC 29169
PARMAN IV, Fritz Quinn (ETenn) St Peters Episcopal Church and School, 848 Ashland Ter, Chattanooga, TN 37415
PARMETER JR, George (SD) Po Box 1361, Huron, SD 57350

PARNELL, Pilar F (Va) 648 Middle Gate, Irvington, VA 22480
PARNELL, Scott Daniel (Va) 648 Middle Gate, Irvington, VA 22480
PARNELL, William Clay (Mass) 138 Tremont St, Boston, MA 02111
PARR, Heather Katheryn (Ore) 835 E 43rd Ave, Eugene, OR 97405
PARRIS, Cheryl (Ga) PO Box 690408, Bronx, NY 10469
PARRIS, Kenneth W (Cal)
PARRISH, David Leroy (Neb) 647 Sussex Dr, Janesville, WI 53546
PARRISH JR, Joseph (NJ) 5914 Nottingham Rd, Knoxville, TN 37918
PARRISH, Judy (SwVa) 989 Pigeon Hill Rd, Roseland, VA 22967
PARRISH, Larry (Neb) PO Box 117, Falls City, NE 68355
PARROTT, Sally F (USC) 100 Deerfield Dr, Greer, SC 29650
PARRY, Tyler (Be)
PARRY-MOORE, Joyce (Oly) St James Episcopal Church, 24447 94th Ave S, Kent, WA 98030
PARSELL, Harry Irvan (SwFla) 738 Pinellas Point Dr S, St Petersburg, FL 33705
✠ **PARSLEY JR**, Henry (Ala) Episcopal Diocese Of Easton, 314 North St, Easton, MD 21601
PARSLEY, Jamie (ND) 117 20th Ave N, Fargo, ND 58102
PARSONS, Ann Roberts (Ak) Po Box 1445, Sitka, AK 99835
PARSONS, Berry Ed (LI) 20 Apache Ln, Sedona, AZ 86351
PARSONS, Susan Diane (Cal)
PARSONS, Timothy Hamilton (CNY) 12 Oak Ave, Norway, ME 04268
PARSONS-CANCELLIERE, Rebecca Anne (Be) Tec Par Of St Mark, 21 Race St, Jim Thorpe, PA 18229
PARTANEN, Robert Carl (Cal) 62 Valais Ct, Fremont, CA 94539
PARTEE CARLSEN, Mariclair Elizabeth (Pa) 6167 Sweet Birch Ct, Acworth, GA 30101
PARTHUM III, Chuck (Mass) 1415 Victoria Cir N, Elm Grove, WI 53122
PARTLOW, John Michael Owen (WVa) 809 Chestnut Ct, Winnetka, IL 60093
PARTLOW, Ruth (SVa) 1600 Westbrook Ave Apt 510, Apartment 510, Richmond, VA 23227
PARTRIDGE, Cameron (Cal) 747 Humboldt Rd, Brisbane, CA 94005
PARTRIDGE JR, Henry Roy (Me) 3 Old Colony Ln, Scarborough, ME 04074
PASALO, Annalise C (The Episcopal Church in Haw)
PASALO JR, Ernesto Castro (The Episcopal Church in Haw)
PASAY, Marcella Claire (CFla) 11251 SW Highway 484, Dunnellon, FL 34432

PASCHALL JR, Fred William (NC) 4341 Bridgewood Ln, Charlotte, NC 28226

PASHTURRO, James Joseph (Mich) 6321 Fernridge Ln, Ann Arbor, MI 48103

PASTERNAK POST, Alyssa R (CPa)

PATHIK, Happy (Cal)

PATIENCE, Rodger L (FdL) 130 Cherry Ct, Appleton, WI 54915

PATNAUDE, Robert J (O) 7146 Hesperides Dr, Warrenton, VA 20186

PATRONIK JR, Joseph Andrew (SanD) PO Box 1283, Marina, CA 93933

PATTEN, Kenneth Lloyd (Hond)

PATTERSON JR, Baldo Alfred Kaleo (The Episcopal Church in Haw) 229 Queen Emma Sq, Honolulu, HI 96813

PATTERSON, Barbara Anne Bowling (At) 437 S Candler St, Decatur, GA 30030

PATTERSON, Beverly A (WTex) 3701 Cimarron Blvd Apt 2604, Corpus Christi, TX 78414

PATTERSON, Brice Joel (SO)

PATTERSON JR, Dennis Delamater (At) St Lukes Episc Ch, 435 Peachtree St NE, Atlanta, GA 30308

PATTERSON, Helene C (Alb)

PATTERSON, Jane (WTex) Seminary of the Southwest, PO Box 2247, Austin, TX 78768

PATTERSON, Keith F (Roch) 71 Delray Rd, Rochester, NY 14610

PATTERSON, Margaret Pittman (Del) 555 Pierce Street, No. 804, Albany, CA 94706

PATTERSON, Michael Steven (Nev) PO Box 1041, Fernley, NV 89408

PATTERSON, Robert Place (Md) 3 Cobb Ln, Topsham, ME 04086

PATTERSON, Sharon (NJ)

PATTERSON, Tim (NC) 607 N Greene St, Greensboro, NC 27401

PATTERSON JR, William Brown (NC) 195 N Carolina Ave, Sewanee, TN 37375

PATTERSON-URBANIAK, Penelope Ellen (CFla) 676 Nettles Ridge Rd, Banner Elk, NC 28604

PATTISON, Ruth Lindberg (At) 1501 Dinglewood Dr, Columbus, GA 31906

PATTON, Kathleen (Oly) 2442 Park Hill Dr, Longview, WA 98632

PATTON, Thomas Dunstan (Spr)

PATTON-GRAHAM, Heather Lynn (The Episcopal Church in Haw) 2611 Ala Wai Blvd Apt 1206, Honolulu, HI 96815

PAUL, Jeffrey (Nev) 305 N Minnesota St, Carson City, NV 89703

PAUL, Linda Joy (Okla) 501 S Cincinnati Ave, Tulsa, OK 74103

PAUL, Marcea E (Tex) 10600 Caribbean Blvd, Cutler Bay, FL 33189

PAUL, Michael (Tex) 6419 15th St S, Fargo, ND 58104

PAUL, Richard (Colo)

PAUL, Rocks-Anne (SwFla) 1200 4th St W, Palmetto, FL 34221

PAUL, Wectnick (Ct) Box 1309, Port-Au-Prince, Haiti

PAULEY, Perry Michael (Az)

PAULIKAS, Steve (LI) 286-88 7th Ave, Brooklyn, NY 11215

PAULSON, Diane Theresa (Ida) 1785 Arlington Dr, Pocatello, ID 83204

PAULSON, Donald Leonard (Ida) 1785 Arlington Dr, Pocatello, ID 83204

PAULUS, Ruth (SO) 1401 Vanderlyn Ct, Fairborn, OH 45324

PAVLAC, Brian Alexander (Be) 513 Abbyshire Dr, Berea, OH 44017

PAXTON, Richard Edwin (Colo) 820 Broadway St, Paducah, KY 42001

PAYDEN-TRAVERS, Christine (NC) 108 E Devonshire St, Winston Salem, NC 27127

✠ **PAYNE**, Claude Edward (Tex) 2702 Charter House Dr, Abilene, TX 79606

PAYNE, Edward Thomas (SO) 8363 Cannon Knoll Ct, West Chester, OH 45069

PAYNE, Harold Womack (Ark) 3412 W 7th St, Little Rock, AR 72205

PAYNE, John Douglas (Tex) 4902 George St, Wichita Falls, TX 76302

PAYNE, No Saluation-- Pam (Be)

PAYNE, Susan Strauss (Ark) 1723 Center St, Little Rock, AR 72206

PAYNE-CARTER, Gloria (WNY) 15 Fernhill Ave, Buffalo, NY 14215

PAYNE-HARDIN, Mary Elizabeth (CNY) 1608 Baker Ct, Panama City, FL 32401

PAYNE WHITE, Robin Adair (Okla)

PAYNE-WIENS, Reginald A (NC) 1941 Webberville Rd, Austin, TX 78721

PAYSON, Charles Beck (Chi) 230 Benjamin St, Fernandina Beach, FL 32034

PAYSON, Deborah (Pa) 531 Maison Place, Bryn Mawr, PA 19010

PAYSON, Evelyn (Mil) N1133 Vinne Ha Ha Rd, Fort Atkinson, WI 53538

PEABODY, Morrill (RG) Po Box 247, Lemitar, NM 87823

PEABODY, S Walton (Pa) 234 Yahoola Shoals Dr, Dahlonega, GA 30533

PEACOCK, Andrea Coffee (SC)

PEACOCK, Caroline (NY) St Luke Tec Ch, 487 Hudson St, New York, NY 10014

PEACOCK, Joan Louise (Va) 7515 Snowpea Ct Unit M, Alexandria, VA 22306

PEACOCK, Margaret Ann (NMich) Po Box 66, Saint Ignace, MI 49781

PEAK, Ronald Robert (Kan) 609 Gould St, Eustis, FL 32726

PEALER, Judson Paul (Me) 2614 Main St, Rangeley, ME 04970

PEARCE, Clyde Willard (Ala) 1301 Paradise Cove Ln, Wilsonville, AL 35186

PEARCE JR, Robert Charles (Kan) 1720 Westbank Way, Manhattan, KS 66503

PEARCE, Sherilyn (Lex) Christ Church Cathedral, 318 E 4th St, Cincinnati, OH 45202

PEARCE, William Philip Daniel (ECR) 1037 Olympic Ln, Seaside, CA 93955

PEARSALL, Arlene Epp (SD) 115 N Dakota Ave Apt 117, Sioux Falls, SD 57104

PEARSALL, Martin A (Colo) 4939 Harvest Rd, Colorado Springs, CO 80917

PEARSON, Albert Claybourn (Tex) 261 Fell St, San Francisco, CA 94102

PEARSON II, Alonzo Lawrence (FdL) 421 Lowell Pl, Neenah, WI 54956

PEARSON, Anna (NY) 235 W 102nd St Apt 15n, New York, NY 10025

PEARSON, Bryan Austin (Mass)

PEARSON, Cedric Eugene (O) 14778 Dexter Falls Rd, Perrysburg, OH 43551

PEARSON, Daniel (Minn) 1970 Nature View Lane, W. St. Paul, MN 55118

PEARSON, David Ernest (NI)

PEARSON, Francis J (Be) 10 Chapel Rd, New Hope, PA 18938

PEARSON, Jan (Colo)

PEARSON, Jim (SD) Christ Episcopal Church, 513 Douglas Ave, Yankton, SD 57078

PEARSON, John Norris (Oly) 2831 Marietta St, Steilacoom, WA 98388

PEARSON, Joseph Herbert (At) 1280 Berkeley Rd, Avondale Estates, GA 30002

PEARSON, Katie Curran (Colo) 1350 N Washington St, Denver, CO 80203

PEARSON, Kevin David (Oly) 16617 Marine View Dr SW, Burien, WA 98166

PEARSON, Michael A (Pa) 2 Blount Circle, Barrington, RI 02806

PEARSON, Patricia Waychus (Cal) 1219 Dutch Mill Drive, Danville, CA 94526

PEARSON, Wendy L (WMich)

PEARSON, William Arthur (Alb) 27 Trottingham Road, Saratoga Springs, NY 12866

PEASE JR, Edwin C (Mass) 2 Kennedy Ln, Walpole, MA 02081

PECARO, Bernie (SeFla) 140 Se 28th Ave, Pompano Beach, FL 33062

PECH, Meredith Ayer (Ore) 371 Idaho St, Ashland, OR 97520

PECK, David W (CPa) 119 N Duke St, Lancaster, PA 17602

PECK SR, Donald Morrow (Ore) 304 Spyglass Dr, Eugene, OR 97401

PECK JR, Edward Jefferson (CPa) 7041 Fairway Oaks, Fayetteville, PA 17222

PECK, Felicity Lenton Clark (ETenn) 3333 Love Cir, Nashville, TN 37212

PECK, Frederick (Ore) 18205 SE 42nd St, Vancouver, WA 98683

PECK, Maryjane (Mich) Christ Episcopal Church, 120 N Military St, Dearborn, MI 48124

PECKHAM, Ashley Hall (RI) 31 W Main Rd, Portsmouth, RI 02871

PECKHAM CLARK, Margaret A (Nwk) 1579 Northern Boulevard, Roslyn, NY 11576

PECOY III, James (SC)

PEDERSEN, Kyle (Ct)

PEDRAZA ARIAS, Bladimir Ivan (Colom) Kra 15 # 71-15, Barrio 7 de Agosto, Cartagena Bolivar, 472, Colombia

PEDRICK, Jennifer (RI) 1336 Pawtucket Ave, Rumford, RI 02916

PEEK, Charles Arthur (Neb) 2010 Fifth Avenue, Kearney, NE 68845

PEEL, Richard Charles (Mont) 1726 Cannon St Apt 4, Helena, MT 59601

PEELER, Amy Lauren (Chi) 320 Franklin St, Geneva, IL 60134

PEEL-SHAKESPEARE, Margaret (Colo) 13151 W 28th Ave, Golden, CO 80401

PEEPLES, David H (Ala) 2354 Wildwood Dr, Montgomery, AL 36111

PEERMAN III, C(Harles) Gordon (Tenn) 4416 Harding Pl, Nashville, TN 37205

PEET, Donald Howard (Ct) PO Box 681, Sandisfield, MA 01255

PEETE, Brandon Ben (SwFla) 5503 Effingham Dr, Houston, TX 77035

PEETE, Nan (WA) 3001 Veazey Ter NW Apt 1208, Washington, DC 20008

PEETS, Patricia Ann Dunne (Mo) 429 Martindale Dr, Albany, GA 31721

PEGLAR VANLOO, Marion Andrea (Mich)

PELKEY, Richard Elwood (Tex) 7860 SW 86th Way, Gainesville, FL 32608

PELKEY, Wayne Lloyd (Ia) 13218 State Road #17, West Plains, MO 65775

PELLA, Diane Maria (Az) Po Box 753, Hartsdale, NY 10530

PELLATON, Tom (NY) 2186 5th Ave Apt 7d, New York, NY 10037

PELLEGRINI, Lucy Carr Bergen (Vt) 48 East St, Bristol, VT 05443

PELLETIER, Ann Dietrich (RI) 57 Grandeville Ct, Apt#3323, Wakefield, RI 02879

PELNAR, William Donald (Mil) 2544 Tilden Ave, Delavan, WI 53115

PEMBERTON, Barbara Louise (CFla) 668 Whispering Pines Ct, Inverness, FL 34453

PENA-REGALADO JR, Jose (Hond) Col Victoria, Bloque J-3, Choloma Cortes, Honduras

PENA TAVAREZ, Vicente A (DomRep) Ch TEC Todos Los Stos, Calle Dr. Ferry Esq, La Romna, Dominical Republic, Dominican Republic

PENCE, George Edgar (Spr) 5125 Americo Ln, Elkton, FL 32033

PENDERGAST, Margaret Mcshane (Be) PO Box 1094, Reading, PA 19603

PENDERGRAFT, Randall Scott (Mont) Po Box 367, Red Lodge, MT 59068

PENDLETON, Mark (NH) Christ Church, 43 Pine St, Exeter, NH 03833

PENDLETON, William Beasley (NC) 1205-B Brookstown Ave. NW, Winston Salem, NC 27101

PENFIELD, Joyce A (RI) 25 Pomona Ave, Providence, RI 02908

PENICK, Fern Marjorie (Eau) 538 N 4th St, River Falls, WI 54022

PENLAND, Michael R (SeFla) 236 Fennel Dun Cir, Biltmore Lake, NC 28715

PENNEKAMP, Nancy (Cal)

PENNER, Loree (Md) 623 Monkton Rd, Monkton, MD 21111

PENNINGTON, Jasper Green (Mich) 204 Elm St, Ypsilanti, MI 48197

PENNINGTON, John Joseph (Lex) 24 Thompson Ave, Ft Mitchell, KY 41017

PENNINGTON, Richard Gregory (WVa)

PENNOYER II, Robert Morgan (NY)

PENNYBACKER, Kathleen Joanne (CFla) 320 S Canaday Dr, Inverness, FL 34450

PENROD, Scott (WTex) 14819 Turkey Trl, San Antonio, TX 78232

PEOPLES, David Brandon (CFla) 2627 Brookside Bluff Loop, Lakeland, FL 33813

PEPE, Carol Ann (NJ)

PEPIN, Ken (Roch) 53 Lee Road 974, Phenix City, AL 36870

PEPPLER, Connie Jo (Ind) 4131 W Woodyard Rd, Bloomington, IN 47404

PERALTA, Ercilia (DomRep)

PERCIVAL, Joanna Vera (ECR) Flat 5 Waterside, Mill Lane, Uplyme, Lyme Regis, Dorset, DT7 3TZ, Great Britain (UK)

PERCIVAL, Jonathan (NJ) 4051 Westbourne Cir, Sarasota, FL 34238

PERCIVAL, Michael John (Colo) 381 Baltusrol Dr, Aptos, CA 95003

PERDUE, David (NwT) 1101 Slide Rd, Lubbock, TX 79416

PERDUE, Lane (Be) Trinity Cathderal, 100 W Roosevelt St, Phoenix, AZ 85003

PERDUE, Melody Mae (SVa)

PERDUE, Thomas Hayes (EC) 3981 Fairfax Sq, Fairfax, VA 22031

PEREIRA ALVAREZ, Rafael Alexis (Nev) 4201 W Washington Ave, Las Vegas, NV 89107

PERES LEITE, Dessordi (WA)

PEREZ, Gregory Gerard (Mass) 74 S Common St, Lynn, MA 01902

PEREZ, Jon (ECR)

PEREZ-BULLARD, Altagracia (NY) 1047 Amsterdam Ave, New York, NY 10025

PEREZ MACIAS, Jesus Eduardo (Colom) Ap Aer 2704, Barranquilla, Atlantico, Colombia

PEREZ MOREIRA, Hector Amado (EcuC) Cd Sauces 5 Mz 225 V2, Guayaquil, Ecuador

PEREZ-QUINONES, Juan Pablo (PR)

PEREZ RISCO, Rody (Cu)

PEREZ RUBI, Evelio (Cu)

PEREZ-VEGA, Rodrigo (Nwk) 214 Washington St, Hackettstown, NJ 07840

PERICA, Raymond William (CFla) 145 E Edgewood Dr, Lakeland, FL 33803

PERIDANS, Dominique F (WA) 1217 Massachusetts Ave NW, Washington, DC 20005

PERINE, Everett Craig (Ct) 60 Church St, Hebron, CT 06248

PERKINS, Aaron C (Me) 26 Moulton Ln, York, ME 03909

PERKINS, Cecil Patrick (FdL) 215 Houston St, Ripon, WI 54971

PERKINS, David W (Ga) None, 389 Ambrose Rucker Rd, Monroe, VA 24574

PERKINS, Ezgi S (FdL) 420 W 14th St, Kansas City, MO 64105

PERKINS, Jesse (Chi) St Michaels Episcopal Church, 647 Dundee Ave, Barrington, IL 60010

PERKINS, Lynn Jones (Az) PO Box 4330, Gallup, NM 87305

PERKINS, Patrick R (WMass) 679 Farmington Ave, West Hartford, CT 06119

PERKINS, Roger S (Az) 1409 Linda Drive, Gallup, NM 87301

PERKINSON, Ed (O) 3 Fox Hollow, Plymouth, MA 02360

PERKO, F Michael (RG) 2 Paa Ko Ct, Sandia Park, NM 87047

PERO, David Edward (Ore) 1609 Elm St, Forest Grove, OR 97116

PERRA, James Francis (WMich) 1401 Towson St, Baltimore, MD 21230

PERREAULT, Matthew Denis (CFla)

PERRIN, Charlie (LI) 27521 Pine Straw Rd, Leesburg, FL 34748

PERRIN, Henry Keats (SO) 10129 Springbeauty Ln, Cincinnati, OH 45231

PERRIN, Mary (WMich) 2512 Highpointe Dr, Kalamazoo, MI 49008

PERRIN, Ronald Van Orden (NY) 3409 Hollywood Ave, Austin, TX 78722

PERRIN, Susan Elizabeth (USC)

PERRINO, Robert Anthony (SeFla) 1103 Duncan Cir Apt 103, Palm Beach Gardens, FL 33418

PERRIS, John David (NY) 581 Valley Rd, Upper Montclair, NJ 07043

PERRIZO, Faith Crook (WVa) 541 Deer Ridge Ln S, Maplewood, MN 55119

PERROTT, Ann Marie (Ct)

PERRY, Ally (Ala) 3125 Debra Ln, Westlake, LA 70669

✠ **PERRY**, Bonnie Anne (Mich) 4550 N Hermitage Ave # 103, Chicago, IL 60640

PERRY, Cecilia Carolyn (RI) PO Box 872, Bristol, RI 02809

PERRY, David Warner (Ore) 12701 SE River Rd Apt 408np, Portland, OR 97202

PERRY, John Wallis (Vt) 431 Union St, Hudson, NY 12534

PERRY, Kenneth M (Roch) PO Box 147, Geneva, NY 14456

PERRY, Margaret Rose (Az) St Francis in-the-Valley, 600 S La Canada Dr, Green Valley, AZ 85614

PERRY, Nandra Loraine (Tex)

PERRY, Raymond Glenn (NMich) 251 Monongahela Rd, Crystal Falls, MI 49920

PERRY, Robert Kendon (Ida) 411 Capitol Ave, Salmon, ID 83467

PERSCHALL JR, Don (Dal) 909 W Gandy St, Denison, TX 75020

✠ **PERSELL**, Bill (Chi) 28 Haskell Dr, Bratenahl, OH 44108

PERSHOUSE, Gayle (Mass)

PERSON, Kathryn Jeanne (NY) 1803 Glenwood Rd, Brooklyn, NY 11230

PESSAH, Elizabeth Jayne (Fla) 1225 W Granada Blvd, Ormond Beach, FL 32174

PESSAH, Stephen Michael (Fla) 1225 W Granada Blvd, Ormond Beach, FL 32174

PETERMAN, Lynn (EC) 115 John L Hurst Dr, Swansboro, NC 28584

PETERS JR, August William (WA) 1000 Hilton Ave, Catonsville, MD 21228

PETERS, David W (Tex) PO Box 178, Mount Vernon, IL 62864

PETERS, Diana (Colo) 161 W Whidbey Ave Apt 32, Cottage #32, Oak Harbor, WA 98277

PETERS, Greg (Oly) 4424 SW 102nd St, Seattle, WA 98146

PETERS, Helen Sarah (Ak) 1340 23rd Ave, Fairbanks, AK 99701

PETERS, John (Minn) 14434 Fairway Dr, Eden Prairie, MN 55344

PETERS, Peter William (Roch) 239 Yarmouth Rd, Rochester, NY 14610

PETERS, Thomas Word (Ct) 480 Budding Ridge Rd, Cheshire, CT 06410

PETERS, Yejide (NY) 1414 Greycourt Ave, Richmond, VA 23227

PETERSEN, Barbara Jean (WNC) 2047 Paint Fork Rd, Mars Hill, NC 28754

PETERSEN, Brian (SanD)

PETERSEN, Carolyn Sherman (CFla) 4708 Waterwitch Point Dr, Orlando, FL 32806

PETERSEN, Duane Eric (WLa) 1030 Johnston Street, Lafayette, LA 70501

PETERSEN, William Herbert (Roch) 49 Winding Brook Dr, Fairport, NY 14450

PETERSEN-SNYDER, Christine (LI) 290 Conklin St, Farmingdale, NY 11735

PETERS-MATHEWS, Joseph (Oly) 1122 Broadway E Unit 301, UNIT 301, Seattle, WA 98102

PETERSMEYER, Julie Andrews (WA)

PETERSON, Alison (U)

PETERSON, Amy Lepine (NI)

PETERSON, Barbara (Mass) 17 Sandy Neck Rd, East Sandwich, MA 02537

PETERSON, Bryan Anthony (Neb) 9302 Blondo St, Omaha, NE 68134

PETERSON, Carol Elizabeth (Tex) 1908 Central Ave, Cheyenne, WY 82001

PETERSON, Diane Mildred (Ct) 5160 Madison Avenue, 4670 Congress Street, Trumbull, CT 06611

PETERSON JR, Frank Lon (NY) 969 Park Ave Apt 8C, New York, NY 10028

PETERSON, Iris E (Be) 56 Franklin St Unit 16, Danbury, CT 06810

PETERSON JR, John Henry (FdL) 129 5th St, Neenah, WI 54956

PETERSON, John Louis (WA) 1001 Red Oak Dr, Hendersonville, NC 28791

PETERSON JR, John Raymond (SwFla) 5020 Bayshore Blvd Apt 301, Tampa, FL 33611

PETERSON-WLOSINSKI, Cindy (Minn) 1121 W Morgan St, Duluth, MN 55811

PETERSON ZUBIZARRETA, Dorenda C (SeFla)

PETIT, Charles David (USC) 5220 Clemson Ave, Columbia, SC 29206

PETITE, Robert (Chi) 4717 S. Greenwood Ave. Unit 1, Chicago, IL 60615

PETITFRERE, Mondesir (Hai)

PETIT-HOMME, Jean Pierre (Hai)

PETRASH, David (Dal) 1300 Overlook Dr, Kaufman, TX 75142

PETROCCIONE, Jim (Nwk) 28 Ross Rd, Stanhope, NJ 07874

PETROCHUK, Michael Aaron (O) St Andrew's Episcopal Church, 583 W Hopocan Ave, Barberton, OH 44203

PETRONE, Ayden James (NJ)

PETROTTA, Anthony Joseph (Ore) PO Box 445, Wilsonville, OR 97070

PETTEE, Abigail Bower (Me) 33 Chestnut St, Camden, ME 04843

PETTENGILL SR, David E (Az) 1558 E Gary St, Mesa, AZ 85203

PETTENGILL-RASURE, Rachael Marie (Mass) 453 Adams St, Milton, MA 02186

PETTIGREW, Thomas John (Alb) 3764 Main St, Warrensburg, NY 12885

PETTIT, Robert Trent (Dal)

PETTITT, Robert Riley (ND) 1201 49th Avenue, Rt 6, Fargo, ND 58103

PETTY, Carol Ross (Tex) Episcopal Diocese of Texas, PO Box 2247, Austin, TX 78768

PETTY, Isaac Ross (WMo)

PETTY JR, Jess Joseph (O) 35 B Pond St, Marblehead, MA 01945

PETTY, Rachel Lei (NwT)

PETTY JR, Tyrus Cecil (Kan) 5841 Sw 26th St, Topeka, KS 66614

PETZAK, Rodney Ross (Nev) 1965 Golden Gate Dr, Reno, NV 89511

PEVEHOUSE, James Melvin (Tex) 680 Calder St, Beaumont, TX 77701

PEYTON III, Allen Taylor (Alb) 2401 Ben Hill Rd, Atlanta, GA 30344

PEYTON IV, Francis Bradley (WA) 1919 York Rd Fl 2, Timonium, MD 21093

PEYTON JR, Lee (At) 2230 E Deerfield Dr, Media, PA 19063

PEYTON, Linda (Me) 42 Flying Point Rd, Freeport, ME 04032

PEYTON, William Parish (Va) St. Paul's Memorial Church, 1701 University Ave, Charlottesville, VA 22903

PFAB, Penny (Fla) 724 Lake Stone Cir, Ponte Vedra Beach, FL 32082

PFAFF, Brad Hampton (NY) 126 W 83rd St Apt 3p, New York, NY 10024

PFAFF, David Anthony (SO) 965 Forest Ave, Glendale, OH 45246

PFEIFFER, Dorothea Koop (WNC) 2 Sweet Gum Ct, Hilton Head, SC 29928

PFISTER, Kathleen Rock (Tex) PO Box 5176, Austin, TX 78763

PHALEN, John Richard (Los) 5772 Garden Grove Blvd Spc 487, Westminster, CA 92683

PHAM, J Peter (Chi) 1499 Massachusetts Ave. N.W., Apt. 1001, Washington, DC 20005

PHANORD, Jean Berthold (Hai)

PHARES, Nicholas Isaak (Ala) 3200 N 12th Ave, Pensacola, FL 32503

PHELAN JR, John (Minn)

PHELAN, Shane (Nwk) 43 Massachusetts Ave, Haworth, NJ 07641

PHELPS, Gerald Edward (WTex)

PHELPS, Joan (Ct) A 2124, 400 Seabury Dr, Bloomfield, CT 06002

PHELPS, John Edward (Me) 4 Glendale Rd, Kennebunk, ME 04043

PHELPS JR, Kenneth Oliver (Md) PO Box 40, Sunderland, MD 20689

PHELPS, Mary M (Minn) 6085 Lincoln Dr Apt 212, 212, Edina, MN 55436

PHELPS, Nicholas Barclay (Pa) 1906 Trenton Ave, Bristol, PA 19007

PHELPS, Sarah E (NC) 306 Bayoak Dr, Cary, NC 27513

PHELPS, Shannon David (SanD) Po Box 234, Del Mar, CA 92014

PHENNA, Timothy Peter (Colo) 1320 Arapahoe St, Golden, CO 80401

PHILBROOK, Maryann (Be) PO Box 5385, Bethlehem, PA 18015

PHILIP, Kristi (Spok) 22 W 37th Ave, Spokane, WA 99203

PHILIPS, Modayil Philips (Pa) 1831 Bainbridge St, Philadelphia, PA 19146

PHILIPS, Ronald K (Wyo) PO Box 950, Thermopolis, WY 82443

PHILLIPS III, Arthur William (WLa) Diocese Of Western Louisiana, PO Box 20131, Alexandria, VA 22320

PHILLIPS, Benjamin T S (SO)

PHILLIPS, Beth (Cal) 815 Portola Rd, Portola Valley, CA 94028

PHILLIPS, Christopher (Chi)

PHILLIPS, Craig (Va) 4818 Old Dominion Dr, Arlington, VA 22207

PHILLIPS, Debbie (Mass) 35 Settlers Way, Salem, MA 01970

PHILLIPS, Douglas Cecil (Ind) 40 Trapelo St, Brighton, MA 02135

PHILLIPS, Jennifer Mary (Mass) PO Box 1168, 100 Indian Hill Rd, Barnstable, MA 02630

PHILLIPS, Jerry Ray (La) PO Box 199, Rosedale, LA 70772

PHILLIPS, John Bradford (Cal) 891 Skeel Drive, Camarillo, CA 93010

PHILLIPS II, John Walter (CGC) 590 Parker Dr, Pensacola, FL 32504

PHILLIPS, Julia Coleman (CGC) 127 Hamilton Ave, Panama City, FL 32401

PHILLIPS, Kevin (The Episcopal NCal) 2094 Grant Rd, Mountain View, CA 94040

PHILLIPS, Linda (Nwk) 50 State Route 24, Chester, NJ 07930

PHILLIPS, Marie (O) 50 Sunnycliff Dr, Euclid, OH 44123

PHILLIPS, Michael (NY) 316 E 88th St, New York, NY 10128

PHILLIPS, Paul (Spok) 1416 S Grand Blvd Apt 3, Spokane, WA 99203

PHILLIPS JR, Raymond Leland (USC) 701 Unity St, Fort Mill, SC 29715

PHILLIPS, Richard Oliver (NY) 10 Badger St, Littleton, NH 03561

PHILLIPS, Robert Taylor (WA) 1525 Newton St NW, Washington, DC 20010

PHILLIPS, Roger V (Minn) 1801 Santa Maria Pl, Orlando, FL 32806

PHILLIPS JR, Roy Allen (Neb)

PHILLIPS, Sara Dulaney (CGC) 4875 Highway 188, Coden, AL 36523

PHILLIPS, Stuart John Tristram (Tenn) 654 Long Hollow Pike, Goodlettsville, TN 37072

PHILLIPS, Susan Elizabeth (Del) 18 Olive Ave, Rehoboth Beach, DE 19971

PHILLIPS, Thomas Larison (Spr) 1015 Frank Dr, Champaign, IL 61821

PHILLIPS, Thomas M (CFla)

PHILLIPS, Trey B (At)

PHILLIPS, Wendell Roncevalle (NC) 4211 Sharon View Rd, Charlotte, NC 28226

PHILLIPS-GAINES, Lynn (Miss) 105 N Montgomery St, Starkville, MS 39759

PHILPUTT JR, Frederick Chapman (Dal) 5811 Penrose Ave, Dallas, TX 75206

PHINNEY, James Mark (Oly) 4246 South Discovery Road, Port Townsend, WA 98368

PHIPPS, Marion Elizabeth (Chi) 5403 W Greenbrier Dr, Mchenry, IL 60050

PHIPPS JR, Robert Stirling (Va) PO Box 33430, San Antonio, TX 78265

PIATKO, Joann (NwPa) 26 Chautauqua Pl, Bradford, PA 16701

PICKARD, Brian Andrew (RG)

PICKARD, Joe (Nwk) 91 Ann Rustin Dr, Ormond Beach, FL 32176

PICKEN, Robert Andrew (Roch) 191 Kensington Rd, Garden City, NY 11530

PICKENS, Bradley Jefferson (NMich)

PICKENS, Gregory Doran (Dal) 8011 Douglas Ave, Dallas, TX 75225

PICKERAL, Gretchen Marta (Minn) 3454 26th Ave S, Minneapolis, MN 55406

PICKERING, LouAnn (Ore) 7610 Sw 49th Ave, Portland, OR 97219

PICKERING, William Todd (Va) 208 N 28th St, Richmond, VA 23223

PICKERRELL, Nina (Cal) 1100 California St, San Francisco, CA 94108

PICKERSGILL, Erin (Mo)

PICKUP JR, Ed (NC) PO Box 146, Franklin, VA 23851

PICOT, Katherine Frances (Tex) The Harnhill Centre of Christian Healing, Harnhill, Cirencester, GL75PX, Great Britain (UK)

PICOU, Michael David (SeFla) St Stephen's Episc Ch, 2750 McFarlane Rd, Coconut Grove, FL 33133

PIERCE, Adam Miller (Ind) 16 N 16th St, Wilmington, NC 28401

PIERCE, C (Chi) Grace Episcopal Church, 120 E 1st St, Hinsdale, IL 60521

PIERCE, Dorothy Kohinke (CNY) PO Box 458, Chenango Bridge, NY 13745

PIERCE, Graham Towle (Me) 35 Pine Ledge Dr, Scarborough, ME 04074

PIERCE, Jacob Evan (NC)

PIERCE, Johanna M (Va) 62 Pickering St, Brookville, PA 15825

PIERCE, Kenneth Allen (Lex)

PIERCE, Nathaniel (Eas) 3864 Rumsey Dr, Trappe, MD 21673

PIERCE, Patricia Daniels (NJ) 203 Wildwood Ave, Pitman, NJ 08071

PIERCE, Patrick Arthur (CPa) 306 N Main St, Mercersburg, PA 17236

PIERCE, Raymond (Wyo)

PIERCE, Roderick John (Tex) 1428 N Cromwell Ct, Springfield, MO 65802

PIERCE, Terry Lee (Tex) PO Box 268, Taylor, TX 76574

PIERJOK, Joseph Anton (WMo)

PIERRE, Kesma (Hai)

PIERRE, Marie Yolaine (Hai)

PIERRE, Robin (NJ)

PIERRE, Yonel (Hai)

PIERRE LOUIS, Guimond (Hai)

PIERSON, Anne Susan (The Episcopal NCal)

PIERSON, Peter (Alb) PO Box 183, 156 Josh Hall Pond Road, Grafton, NY 12082

PIERSON, Robert Michael (NY) 220 NE Village Squire Ave Unit 8, Gresham, OR 97030

PIERSON, Stew (Vt) 232 High Rock Rd, Hinesburg, VT 05461

PIETSCH, Louise Parsons (NY) 80 Lyme Rd Apt 347, Hanover, NH 03755

PIETTE, Joseph Leroy (Minn) 204 8th St, Cloquet, MN 55720

PIFKE, Lauran Kretchmar (Ak) 3400 Stevenson Blvd Apt Q37, Fremont, CA 94538

PIGGINS, Deborah Hanwell (NJ)

PIGOTT, Susan Marie (NwT)

PIKE, Clifford Arthur Hunt (Pa) 105 Elm St, Lawrenceburg, KY 40342

PIKE, David (WMich) 1519 Elmwood Rd, Lansing, MI 48917

PIKE, Diane (WMich) 925 S 84th St, Omaha, NE 68114

PIKE, Richard S (NY) St Matthews Episcopal Church, PO Box 293, Bedford, NY 10506

PIKE, Stephen Phillip (Ky) RCT 1 HQ Co, UIC 40145, FPO, AP 96426

PIKE, Thomas Frederick (NY) 26 Gramercy Park S Apt 9h, New York, NY 10003

PILARSKI, Terri C (Mich) 120 N Military St, Dearborn, MI 48124

PILAT, Ann Ferres (USC) St Mary's Episcopal Church, 170 St Andrews Rd, Columbia, SC 29210

PILAT, Jennifer (LI)

PILLOT, Anne (O) 4292 Elmwood Rd, South Euclid, OH 44121

PILLSBURY, Jeannette Noyes (Ia) PO Box 4, Decorah, IA 52101

PILLSBURY, Samuel Hale (L₀s) 919 Albany St, Los Angeles, CA 90015

PINCELLI, Brigitte Julianna (NJ) 90 Leonardine Ave, South River, NJ 08882

PINDER, Churchill (CPa) Ststephens Tec Cath, 221 N Front St, Harrisburg, PA 17101

PINELL MENDIETA, Jose Daniel (NC)

PINEO, Linda (At) 3404 Doral Ln, Woodstock, GA 30189

PINHO, Joseph T (Mass) 1 Summit Dr Apt 48, Reading, MA 01867

PINKERTON, Patricia Edith Long (ECR) The Vicarad,St Annes Way, St.Briavels., Gloucestershire, GL15 6UE, Great Britain (UK)

PINKERTON, Susan B (Ct) 4225 Upper Park Dr, Fairfax, VA 22030

PINKSTON JR, Frederick William (NC) 7225 Saint Clair Dr, Charlotte, NC 28270

PINNOCK, Betty Lou (Ore) 459 Herbert St, Ashland, OR 97520

PINTI, Daniel John (WNY) 13021 W. Main St., Alden, NY 14004

PINTO DE ARIZA, Myriam (Colom) CRA 6 49-85, Bogota DC, Colombia
PINZINO, Gwendolyn (SeFla) 3300a S Seacrest Blvd, Boynton Beach, FL 33435
PINZON, Alvaro (Tex)
PINZON, Samuel Eduardo (WA) 15570 SW 143rd Ter, Miami, FL 33196
PINZON CASTRO, Luis Alberto (Colom) Carrera 6 No 49-85, Piso 2, Bogota, Colombia
PINZON DUQUE, Alvaro Felipe (Colom)
PIOTROWSKI, Mary Triplett (Az) 2035 N Southern Hills Dr, Flagstaff, AZ 86004
PIOVANE, Michael (Be) Po Box 368, Trexlertown, PA 18087
PIPER, Charles Edmund (NMich) 1676 Lander Ln, Lafayette, CO 80026
PIPER, Dominique N (Los)
PIPER, Geoffrey Tindall (Mass) 600 Point Rd, Marion, MA 02738
PIPER, Katherine Mae (Colo) 390 Garnet Ave, Granby, CO 80446
PIPER, Linda Lee (NMich) 1676 Lander Ln, Lafayette, CO 80026
PIPER, Mary Elizabeth Meacham (Ore) 4757 Highway 66, Ashland, OR 97520
PIPKIN, Michael (Minn) 1730 Clifton Pl Ste 201, Minneapolis, MN 55403
PIPPIN, Jacqueline Lynne (SanD)
PIPPIN, Tina (At) 25 Second Avenue, Atlanta, GA 30317
PIRAINO, Liz (Los)
PIRET, Michael John (LI) Christ Church, 61 E Main St, Oyster Bay, NY 11771
PITCHER, Trenton Langland (Chi) 145 E Columbia Ave, Elmhurst, IL 60126
PITMAN JR, Ralph William (O) 14431 Gleaming Rose Dr, Cypress, TX 77429
PITT-HART, Barry Thomas (SD) 1409 S 5th Ave, Sioux Falls, SD 57105
PITTMAN, David (NC) 218 Pine Cove Drive, Inman, SC 29349
PITTMAN, Warren (NC) 2903 County Clare Rd, Greensboro, NC 27407
PITTS, John Robert (Tex) 3652 Chevy Chase Dr, Houston, TX 77019
PITTS, Kristen Tossell (WA) St Andrew's Episcopal Church, 4512 College Ave, College Park, MD 20740
PITZER, Elaine Virginia (Spok) St Stephen's Episcopal Church, 5720 S Perry St, Spokane, WA 99223
PITZER, John M (La)
PIVER, Jane (Va) 53 Ridgemont Road, Ruckersville, VA 22968
PIXCAR-POL, Tomas (PR) PO Box 3184, Guayama, PR 00785
PIZZONIA, Wanda (Mass) Post Road & Ring'S End Road, Darien, CT 06820
PIZZUTO, Vincent Anthony (Cal) 171 Forrest Ave, Fairfax, CA 94930

PLACE, Donald Gordon (WMass) 52 County Road, Pownal, VT 05261
PLACKETT-FERGUSON, Jane (Tex)
PLANK, David Bellinger (LI) 26 Hampton Towne Est, Hampton, NH 03842
PLANTIN, Jean Ernso (Hai)
PLANTIN, Jean Wilfrid (Hai)
PLANTZ, Chris (Neb) 605 S Chestnut St, Kimball, NE 69145
PLATSON, Julie L (Ak) PO Box 1130, Sitka, AK 99835
PLATT, Gretchen Mary (SwFla) 1562 Dormie Dr, Gladwin, MI 48624
PLATT, Warren Christopher (NY) 255 W 23rd St Apt 3-DE, New York, NY 10011
PLATT-HENDREN, Barbara (NC) 554 Shuford Circle Dr, Newton, NC 28658
PLAZAS, Carlos Alberto (Chi) 1333 W Argyle St, Chicago, IL 60640
PLEKON, Michael P (SanD) 590 Pointing Rock Dr, PO Box 831, Borrego Springs, CA 92004
PLESTED, Robert William Harvey (LI) 5402 Timber Trace St, San Antonio, TX 78250
PLIMPTON, Barbara Wilson (WNC) PO Box 968, Marion, NC 28752
PLOVANICH, Ede Marie (CGC)
PLUCKER, Susan (The Episcopal NCal) 1200 Fulton Ave Apt 227, Sacramento, CA 95825
PLUMMER, Catherine B (NAM) Episcopal Church in Navajoland, PO Box 720, Farmington, NM 87499
PLUMMER, Cathlena Arnette (NAM) PO Box 720, Farmington, NM 87499
PLUMMER, Dale W (Okla) 505 N Pennsylvania Ave, Roswell, NM 88201
PLUMMER, Lilly Arnese (NwT)
PLUMMER, Lynn Whitman (NC) 8600 Mount Holly Hntrsvlle Rd, Huntersville, NC 28078
PLUMMER, Mark Alton (NC) 102 Teachs Ct, Surf City, NC 28445
PLUNKET-BREWTON, Callie Dawn (Ala) 410 N Pine St, Florence, AL 35630
POGGEMEYER JR, Lewis Eugene (U) 2849 Polk Ave, Ogden, UT 84403
POGOLOFF, Stephen Mark (NC) 218 Forestwood Dr, Durham, NC 27707
POGUE, Blair Alison (Minn) 2136 Carter Ave, Saint Paul, MN 55108
POGUE, Ronald D (Tex) 5616 Shady Hill Ln, Arlington, TX 76016
POIRIER, Esther (Oly) 4426 133rd Ave SE, Bellevue, WA 98006
POISSON, Ellen Francis (USC) Order of St Helena, 414 Savannah Barony Dr, North Augusta, SC 29841
POIST, David (Va) 341 Woodlands Rd, Charlottesville, VA 22901
POLANCO DE LA CRUZ, Leonel (Ga)
POLING, Jason Alder (Md) 2 Seiler Ct, Reisterstown, MD 21136

POLK, Perry Willis (The Episcopal NCal) Grace Episcopal Church, 1405 Kentucky St, Fairfield, CA 94533
POLLACH, Gideon Liam (LI) 125 Court St # 11sh, Brooklyn, NY 11201
POLLARD III, Robert (NY) 119 Executive Center Dr Apt 102, West Palm Beach, FL 33401
POLLEY, Seth (Az) 5 Gardner St, Bisbee, AZ 85603
POLLINA, Roy (SwVa) 311 E Church St, Martinsville, VA 24112
POLLITT, Michael James (Chi) 1376 Telegraph Rd., West Caln, MI 19320
POLLOCK, Douglas Stephen (Oly) 7701 Skansie Ave, Gig Harbor, WA 98335
POLLOCK, John (EC) 1912 Shepard St, Morehead City, NC 28557
POLLOCK, Margaret (Va) 21517 Laytonsville Rd, Laytonsville, MD 20882
POLLOCK, Ron (NJ) 154 W High St, Somerville, NJ 08876
POLVINO, Andrea Regina (WNY) 515 Columbus Ave., Waco, TX 76701
POLYARD, Karen Marie (Minn) PO Box 27, Wabasha, MN 55981
POMMERSHEIM, Hannah G (Tex)
POMMIER, Suellen Jane (Ore)
POMPA, Tony (Be) 19 E Cochran St, Middletown, DE 19709
PONADER, Martha Downs (Ind) 1337 Eagle Run Dr, Sanibel, FL 33957
PONCE MARTINEZ, Jacqueline (PR) 659 Deauville Ct, Kissimmee, FL 34758
POND, Finn Richard (Spok) 7315 N Wall St, Spokane, WA 99208
POND JR, Walter Edward (WNY) 171 N Maple St, Warsaw, NY 14569
PONDER, James Brian (Miss) 118 N Congress St, Jackson, MS 39201
PONDER, Savannah C (WA)
PONSOLDT, Megan (Los) Grace Episcopal Church, 301 S Main St, Kilmarnock, VA 22482
PONS SANTANA, Halbert (Cu)
POOL, Jayne Collins (Ala) 106 Stratford Road, Birmingham, AL 35209
POOLE, Charles Lane (The Episcopal NCal) 6342 Paso Dr, Redding, CA 96001
POOLE, John Huston (CFla) 603 Spring Island Way, Orlando, FL 32828
POOLEY, Nina Ranadive (WMass) 152 Princes Point Rd, Yarmouth, ME 04096
POOSER, William Craig (Chi) 2423 Blue Quail, San Antonio, TX 78232
POPE, Charles Maurice (Ia) 505 Edgehill Dr, Saint Albans, WV 25177
POPE III, Daniel Stuart (Roch) 406 Canandaigua St, Palmyra, NY 14522
POPE, Nadine Karen (Colo) PO Box 1010, Cumming, GA 30028
POPE, Robert Gardner (Colo) 108 Sawmill Cir, Bayfield, CO 81122

POPE, Steven Myron (Tex) 905 Whispering Wind Dr, Georgetown, TX 78633

POPE, Stina (Cal) 934 W 14th St, Port Angeles, WA 98363

POPHAM, James J (CGC) Saint David's Episcopal Church, 401 S Broadway, Englewood, FL 34223

POPHAM, Jo P (CGC)

POPLE, David (Ct) 95 Greenwood Ave, 22 Golden Hill St, Bethel, CT 06801

POPPE, Bernard (WMass) 14 Whitman Rd, Worcester, MA 01609

POPPE, Kenneth Welch (Vt) 2 Cherry St, Burlington, VT 05401

POPPLEWELL, Elizabeth D (Ia) 1808 NW 121st Cir, Clive, IA 50325

POPPOFF, Robin Marie (ECR) 7269 Santa Teresa Blvd, San Jose, CA 95139

PORCHER, Philip (SC) 1494 Stratton Pl, Mount Pleasant, SC 29466

PORRAS, Samuel Edison (At) 498 Prince Ave, Athens, GA 30601

PORTARO JR, Sam Anthony (Chi) 1250 N Dearborn St Apt 19c, Chicago, IL 60610

PORTER, Elizabeth Streeter (Ark) 10 Thunderbird Dr, Holiday Island, AR 72631

PORTER III, Fulton (Chi) 2720 2nd Private Rd, Flossmoor, IL 60422

PORTER, George Vernon (Ga) 1201 Fairfield St, Cochran, GA 31014

PORTER, James Robert (Az) 2200 Lester Dr NE Apt 460, Albuquerque, NM 87112

PORTER, Joe Thomas (WTenn) 43 Carriage Ln, Sewanee, TN 37375

PORTER, John Harvey (Cal) 551 Ivy St, San Francisco, CA 94102

PORTER, John Joseph (At) 215 Abington Dr NE, Atlanta, GA 30328

PORTER, Lloyd Brian (Tex) 1701 W TC Jester Blvd, Houston, TX 77008

PORTER, Nicholas (Ct) Trinity Church, 651 Pequot Ave, P.O. Box 400, Southport, CT 06890

PORTER, Pam (WMass) PO Box 19, Heath, MA 01346

PORTER, Roger Cliff (CGC) 6500 Middleburg Ct, Mobile, AL 36608

PORTER, Shirley (At)

PORTER-ACEE III, John Marshall (EC) 413 Kempton Dr, Greenville, NC 27834

PORTEUS, James Michael (Az) Triskele, Rinsey, Ashton, Helston, TR13 9TS, Great Britain (UK)

PORTILLA GOMEZ, Israel Alexander (Ak) 2210 E Tudor Rd Apt 1, Anchorage, AK 99507

PORTO LOPEZ, Estiven David (DomRep)

POST, Suzanne Marie (SwFla) 14511 Daffodil Dr Apt 1402, Fort Myers, FL 33919

POSTON, Ronald Glen (Az) 2174 E Loma Vista Dr, Tempe, AZ 85282

POTEAT, Sally Tarler (EC) 4181 Cambridge Cove Cir SE # 2, Southport, NC 28461

POTEET, David Bertrand (Tex) Po Box 6828, Katy, TX 77491

POTEET, Fred (SVa) 2317 Mariners Mark Way Apt 303, Virginia Beach, VA 23451

POTTER, Christopher (NH)

POTTER, David (WA)

POTTER, Frances Dickinson (NH) 1010 Waltham St Apt 352, Lexington, MA 02421

POTTER, Jack C (U) 231 E 100 S, Salt Lake City, UT 84111

POTTER, Linda (Chi) 1240 NE 64th Ln, Hillsboro, OR 97124

POTTER, Lorene Heath (WNY) 537 S Park Ave, Buffalo, NY 14204

POTTER, Meredith (Chi) 317 Satinwood Ct S, Buffalo Grove, IL 60089

POTTER, Paul Christopher (Los) 37 Sepulveda, Rancho Santa Margarita, CA 92688

POTTER, Sara (The Episcopal NCal) 1776 Old Arcata Rd, Bayside, CA 95524

POTTER JR, Spencer (SeFla) 7700 SW 181st Ter, Palmetto Bay, FL 33157

POTTERTON, Carol Thayer (SO) 5825 Woodmont Ave, Cincinnati, OH 45213

POTTS, David G (SD) 1728 Mountain View Rd, Rapid City, SD 57702

POTTS, Kathleen (Miss) 1421 Goodyear Blvd., Picayune, MS 39466

POTTS, Matthew L (Mass)

POULIN, Sue (NH) Saint John the Baptist, 118 High St, Sanbornville, NH 03872

POUNDERS, Marci J (Dal) St James Episcopal Church, 9845 Mccree Rd, Dallas, TX 75238

POVEY, John Michael (Mass) 3901 Glen Oaks Dr E, Sarasota, FL 34232

POWELL, Anne Margrete (The Episcopal NCal) 20248 Chaparral Cir, Penn Valley, CA 95946

POWELL, Anthony F (Fla) 657 SE 2nd Ave, Melrose, FL 32666

POWELL, Art (NJ) 16 Copperfield Dr, Hamilton, NJ 08610

POWELL, Betty (WA) 2361 Elliott Island Rd, Vienna, MD 21869

POWELL, Blanche Lee (Del) 304 Taylor Ave, Hurlock, MD 21643

POWELL, Brent Cameron (WTenn) 346 Hawthorne St, Memphis, TN 38112

POWELL, Catherine Ravenel (EC) 505 S Front St, Wilmington, NC 28401

POWELL, Christopher (Chi) Christ Church, 470 Maple St, Winnetka, IL 60093

POWELL, David Brickman (Ala) PO Box 467, Selma, AL 36702

POWELL, Elizabeth Jennings (Ala) P.O. Box 467, Selma, AL 36702

POWELL, Everett (Cal) 417 44th Ave, San Francisco, CA 94121

POWELL, Greg (Eas) 29497 Hemlock Ln, Easton, MD 21601

POWELL, Gwendolen Mair (Minn)

POWELL, John Charles (NJ) 307 Red Lion Road, Southampton, NJ 08088

POWELL, Kenneth James (Ore) All Saints Parish, 1355 Waller St, San Francisco, CA 94117

POWELL, Kevin Thomas (Ia)

POWELL, Lewis (The Episcopal NCal) 20248 Chaparral Cir, Penn Valley, CA 95946

POWELL, Mark M (EC) St Ews On-The-Sound Tec Ch, 101 Airlie Rd, Wilmington, NC 28403

POWELL, Murray Richard (Tex) 951 Curtin St, Houston, TX 77018

✠ **POWELL**, Neff (SwVa) 295 W 22nd Ave, Eugene, OR 97405

POWELL JR, Peter Ross (Ct) 6 Gorham Ave, Westport, CT 06880

POWELL, R Bingham (Ore) St Marys Episcopal Church, 1300 Pearl St, Eugene, OR 97401

POWELL, Rita Teschner (Mass) Trinity Church Episcopal, 206 Clarendon St, Boston, MA 02116

POWELL IV, Robert Jefferson (ETenn) 1101 N Broadway St, Knoxville, TN 37917

POWELL, Sydney Roswell (NY) 3405 Grace Ave, Bronx, NY 10469

POWELL, William Vincent (Okla) 124 Randolph Ct, Stillwater, OK 74075

POWELL IV, Woodson Lea (NC) 560 Water Tower Rd, Moncure, NC 27559

POWER, William Joseph Ambrose (Dal) 8011 Douglas Ave, Dallas, TX 75225

POWERS JR, Clarence (LI) 3520 Oaks Way Apt 809, Pompano Beach, FL 33069

POWERS, David Allan (CGC) 959 Charleston St, Mobile, AL 36604

POWERS, Elizabeth Ann (SD) 5398 SE Malden Dr, Portland, OR 97206

POWERS, Fairbairn (Los) 531 Harrison Ave, Claremont, CA 91711

POWERS, Lee (NJ) 119 Saint Georges Dr, Galloway, NJ 08205

POWERS, Nancy Chambers (Dal) 1232 Old Glory Dr, Aubrey, TX 76227

POWERS, Pat (SwFla) Caixa Postal 11510, Porto Alegre, 91720-15, Brazil

POWERS, Sharon Kay (Mass) 49 Puritan Rd, Buzzards Bay, MA 02532

POWERS, Steve (FdL) 311 Division St, Oshkosh, WI 54901

POZO, Francisco (NJ) 61 Kristopher Dr, Trenton, NJ 08620

POZZUTO, Keith (Tex) 5210 Friars Loop, Temple, TX 76502

PRADA, Alvaro Javier (Colom)

PRADAT, Paul Gillespie (Ala) 12200 Bailey Cove Rd SE, Huntsville, AL 35803

PRAKTISH, Carl Robert (Va) 2572 Lemon Rd Apt 903, Honolulu, HI 96815

PRALL, Brian R (Chi)

PRATER, Joy (Ark)

PRATER, Willard Gibbs (O) 2490 Moore Ln, Hatfield, PA 19440

PRATHER, Joel A (Mil) 1636 Valley Rd, Oconomowoc, WI 53066

PRATHER, Lynn (Ga) 3504 Professional Cir Ste A, Martinez, GA 30907

PRATI, Jason M (SO) PO Box 421, New Albany, OH 43054

PRATOR, Lloyd Eugene (NY) 15620 Riverside Dr W Apt 13i, New York, NY 10032

PRATT, Dorothy (ETenn) 5409 Jacksboro Pike, Knoxville, TN 37918

PRATT JR, Earle (LI) 3240 N Caves Valley Path, Lecanto, FL 34461

PRATT, Grace Atherton (Va) 8009 Fort Hunt Rd, Alexandria, VA 22308

PRATT, Jennifer Julian (Oly) 2109 N Lafayette Ave, Bremerton, WA 98312

PRATT, Mary Florentine Corley (Vt) 865 Otter Creek Hwy, New Haven, VT 05472

PRAY, Frederick Russell (NJ) 221 Ivy Rd, Edgewater Park, NJ 08010

PREAS, Barbara Jean (Nev) 10328 SUMMER RIVER AV., Las Vegas, NV 89144

PRECHTEL, Daniel L (Chi) 3424 Belmont Ave, El Cerrito, CA 94530

PREECE, Mark (Vt) 220 E 6th Ave, Conshohocken, PA 19428

PREHM, Katherine T. (Spok) 3401 W Lincoln Ave, Yakima, WA 98902

PREHN III, Walter Lawrence (WTex) 5308 Carrington Ct, Midland, TX 79707

PRENDERGAST, James David (Los) 1325 Monterey Rd, South Pasadena, CA 91030

PRENTICE, David Ralph (Mass) All Saints Episcopal Church, 46 Cherry St, Danvers, MA 01923

PRESCOTT, Clarke W (Los) 8830 Mesa Oak Dr, Riverside, CA 92508

PRESCOTT, Vicki (Roch) 2500 East Avenue, Apartment 5H, Rochester, NY 14610

PRESLER, Henry Airheart (NC) Po Box 293, Monroe, NC 28111

PRESLER, Jane Crosby (Vt) 2534 Hill West Rd., Montgomery, VT 05471

PRESLER, Titus Leonard (Vt) PO Box 501, Montgomery, VT 05471

PRESSENTIN, Elsa (EMich) 7562 Alex Ct, Freeland, MI 48623

PRESTEGARD, Joann Maxine (Oly) 55 Irving St, Cathlamet, WA 98612

PRESTON, Elizabeth Cone (Ia) PO Box 85, Spirit Lake, IA 51360

PRESTON II, James Montgomery (Tex) 1310 Malmaison Ridge Dr, Spring, TX 77379

PRESTON, Leigh (ETenn) 335 Tennessee Ave, Sewanee, TN 37383

PRESTON, Shannon (Tex)

PRESTON, Troy Lynn (Roch) Christ Episcopal Church, 33 E 1st St, Corning, NY 14830

PRETTI, Victoria (Del) 893 Main St, West Newbury, MA 01985

PREVATT JR, James Thomas (NC) 5104 Ainsworth Dr, Greensboro, NC 27410

PREVIL, Myldred (LI) 1227 Pacific St, Brooklyn, NY 11216

PREVIL, Philome (LI) 1227 Pacific St, Brooklyn, NY 11216

PREVOST, Ned (Chi) 6 Brookshire Rd, Worcester, MA 01609

PREYSNER, Elizabeth (NH)

PRICE, Barbara Deane (Ak) Po Box 56419, North Pole, AK 99705

PRICE, Barbara Jean (WNY) 77 Huntington Ave, Buffalo, NY 14214

PRICE, Basil Hayes (WK)

PRICE, Darwin Ladavis (LI) PO Box 280, Brewster, MA 02631

PRICE, David William (Tex) 302 S Hardie St, Alvin, TX 77511

PRICE, George (SeFla) 2300 Spanish River Rd, Boca Raton, FL 33432

PRICE, George N (Me) 290 Baxter Blvd Apt B3, Portland, ME 04101

PRICE, Gloria Maccormack (EC) 130 Quail Dr, Dudley, NC 28333

PRICE, Harold Thomas (Ky) 409 Wendover Ave, Louisville, KY 40207

PRICE, John Randolph (Md) 772 Ticonderoga Ave, Severna Park, MD 21146

PRICE, Joyce Elizabeth (WNC) 75 Echo Lake Dr, Fairview, NC 28730

PRICE, Kathie (WA) 199 Rolfe Rd, Williamsburg, VA 23185

✠ **PRICE**, Kenneth Lester (SO) 4754 Shire Ridge Rd. W, Hilliard, OH 43026

PRICE, Marston (Ct) 33 Old Field Hill Rd # Unit48, Southbury, CT 06488

PRICE, Paul Alexander (Los) 1630 NW Camellia Loop, Oak Harbor, WA 98277

PRICE, Phyllis Anne (Mass) 12191 Clipper Dr, Lake Ridge, VA 22192

PRICE, Robert Paul (Dal) 1023 Compass Cove Cir, Spring, TX 77379

PRICE, Sarah Kye (Va) St Marks Episcopal Church, 520 N Arthur Ashe Blvd, Richmond, VA 23220

PRICE, Stephen Marsh (NY) 133 Grove St, Peterborough, NH 03458

PRICE, Susan Medlicott (Spok) 2029 Sheridan Pl, Richland, WA 99352

PRICE-HADZOR, Robert Baylor (La)

PRICHARD, Albert Hughes (WVa) 75 Old Cheat Rd, Morgantown, WV 26508

PRICHARD, Robert W (Va) Virginia Theological Seminary, 3737 Seminary Rd, Alexandria, VA 22304

PRICHARD, Thomas Morgan (Pgh) 10508 James Wren Way, Fairfax, VA 22030

PRICKETT, Gerald Stanley (WNC) 360 Asheville School Rd., Asheville, NC 28806

PRIDEMORE JR, Charles Preston (NY) PO Box 149, Ossining, NY 10562

PRIEST JR, WIlliam Hunt (Ga) 4400 86th Ave SE, Mercer Island, WA 98040

PRINCE, Elaine (Md) 10913 Knotty Pine Dr, Hagerstown, MD 21740

PRINGLE, Amy (Los) 5332 Mount Helena Ave, Los Angeles, CA 90041

PRINGLE, Charles Derek (SVa) 419 Elizabeth Lake Dr, Hampton, VA 23669

PRINGLE-MEJIA, Isaac Emilio (DomRep)

PRINZ, Susan Moore (USC) 6408 Bridgewood Rd, Columbia, SC 29206

✠ **PRIOR**, Brian N (Minn) 1101 W Broadway Ave Ste 2, Minneapolis, MN 55411

PRIOR, Eleanor (Me) 47 Outlook Rd, North Billerica, MA 01862

PRIOR, Greg (RI) 7 Trillium Ln, Hilton Head Island, SC 29926

PRIOR, Randall Leavitt (Va) 9515 Holly Prospect Ct, Burke, VA 22015

PRITCHER, Joan Jean (At) 1098 Saint Augustine Pl Ne, Atlanta, GA 30306

PRITCHETT JR, Harry Houghton (NY) 1290 Peachtree Battle Ave Nw, Atlanta, GA 30327

PRITCHETT JR, James H (WNC) 209 Nut Hatch Loop, Arden, NC 28704

PRIVETTE, William Herbert (EC) 1119 Hendricks Ave., Jacksonville, FL 28540

PRIVITERA, Linda Fisher (Mass) 21 Marathon St, Arlington, MA 02474

PROBERT, Walter Leslie (Mil) 125 Cedar Ridge Dr, West Bend, WI 53095

PROBST, David (At) 169 Lakeport Rd, Macon, GA 31210

PROCTOR, Frederick Gregory (Miss) 5527 Ridgewood Rd, Jackson, MS 39211

PROCTOR, Judith Harris (Va) St Paul's Episcopal Church, 228 S Pitt St, Alexandria, VA 22314

PROCTOR, Richard Gillespie (CGC) 4129 Oxford Ave., Jacksonville, FL 32210

PROFFITT, Darrel D (Tex) 1225 W Grand Pkwy S, Katy, TX 77494

PROFFITT III, John (Ark) 1608 Mcentire Cir, Chatsworth, GA 30705

PROUD, James (Pa) 111 W Walnut Ln, Philadelphia, PA 19144

✠ **PROVENZANO**, Larry C (LI) TEC Dio of LI, 36 Cathedral Ave, Garden City, NY 11530

PROVINE, Marion Kay (Minn) 3424 Willow Ave, White Bear Lake, MN 55110

PRUITT, Albert (CGC) 729 Brown Pl, Decatur, GA 30030

PRUITT, Alonzo C (Chi) 222 N Marion St, Unit 1 M, Oak Park, IL 60302

PRUITT JR, George Russell (Md) 1246 Summit Ave Sw, Roanoke, VA 24015

PRUITT, Mark (O) false, 23 Westwick Way, Copley, OH 44321

PRUITT, R Allen (NC) 7511 Bedfordshire Dr, Charlotte, NC 28226

PRYNE, Carla Valentine (Oly) 1745 NE 103rd St, Seattle, WA 98125

PUCA JR, Anthony J (Nwk) 9 Harrington Ave, Westwood, NJ 07675

PUCHALLA, Daniel Andrew (Chi) 3739 N Pine Grove Ave Apt 2n, Chicago, IL 60613

PUCIK, Jonathan (NC)

PUCKETT, David Forrest King (Tex) 12535 Perthshire Rd, Houston, TX 77024

PUCKETT, Douglas Arnold (Va) 111 Aiken Rd # 323, Graniteville, SC 29829

PUCKLE, Donne Erving (Az) 125 E Kayetan Dr, Sierra Vista, AZ 85635

PUGH, Charles Dean (Md) 128 S Hilltop Rd, Catonsville, MD 21228

PUGH III, Willard Jerome (HB) 1700 E 56th St Apt 3806, Chicago, IL 60637

PUGLIESE, Bill (Ia) 108 Eden Way Ct, Cranberry Twp, PA 16066

PUGLIESE, Richard A (Spr) 744 Parker Road, West Glover, VT 05875

PULIMOOTIL, Cherian Pilo (Va) 7124 Dijohn Court Dr, Alexandria, VA 22315

PUMPHREY, Charles Michael (Ia) 6217 Thornwood Drive, ALEXANDRIA, VA 22310

PUMPHREY SR, David William (O) 4001 Glacier Hills Dr Unit 334, Ann Arbor, MI 48105

PUMPHREY, John Blair (Del) 146 Fairhill Dr, Wilmington, DE 19808

PUMPHREY, Patricia Tilton (Nev) Trinity Episcopal Church, PO Box 2246, Reno, NV 89505

PUMPHREY, Thomas Claude (At) 64 Powderhorn Dr, Phoenixville, PA 19460

PUNNETT, Ian Case (Minn) 901 Portland Ave, Saint Paul, MN 55104

PUNZO, Thomas Edward (WMo) 10910 N Hull Ave, Kansas City, MO 64154

PUOPOLO JR, Angelo (SO) 3550 Shaw Ave, Cincinnati, OH 45208

PURCELL, Christine (Los) 1031 Bienveneda Ave, Pacific Palisades, CA 90272

PURCELL, Mary Frances Fleming (Lex) 835 Pinkney Dr, Lexington, KY 40504

PURCELL-CHAPMAN, Diana Barnes (Roch) Po Box 492, Wellsville, NY 14895

PURCHAL, John Jeffrey (LI) 45 Willow St. Apt. 420, Springfield, MA 01103

PURDOM III, Allen Bradford (O) 4089 Colony Rd, South Euclid, OH 44121

PURDUM, Ellen Echols (At) 3098 Saint Annes Ln Nw, Atlanta, GA 30327

PURDY, James Hughes (Mo) 448 Conway Meadows Dr, Chesterfield, MO 63017

PURDY, Thomas Clayton (Ga) Christ Church, 6329 Frederica Rd, Saint Simons Island, GA 31522

PURNELL, Erl Gould (Ct) 12 Pine Glen Rd, Simsbury, CT 06070

PURNELL, Susan Ann (Los) 19682 Verona Ln, Yorba Linda, CA 92886

PURRINGTON, Sandra Jean (NMich) 201 E Ridge St, Marquette, MI 49855

PURSER, Phil Philip (USC) 635 Timberlake Dr, Chapin, SC 29036

PURSLEY, George William (SO) 332 Mount Zion Rd NW, Lancaster, OH 43130

PURVIS, Robert David (Ind) 31 Hampshire Ct, Noblesville, IN 46062

PURYEAR, Jim (SwFla) 2606 E Randolph Ave, Alexandria, VA 22301

PURYEAR, Sarah Elizabeth (Tenn)

PUSKARZ, Cathy Jayne (Ct)

PUSNUR, Barnabas Eliah (Chi)

PUTMAN, Richard Byron (Ala) 3927 Clairmont Ave S Apt 2, Birmingham, AL 35222

PUTNAM, Kevin Todd (Cal) 849 Spruance Ln, Foster City, CA 94404

PUTNAM, Sarah Thompson (SC) PO Box 888, Marion, SC 29571

PUTNAM, Thomas Clyde (Ia) 397 Huron Ave, Cambridge, MA 02138

PYATT, Petrina Margarette (NJ) 100 E Maple Ave, Penns Grove, NJ 08069

PYLES, Chris (Md) 707 Park Ave, Baltimore, MD 21201

PYRON JR, Wilson Nathaniel (Mo) 1422 Shadycreek Ct, Saint Louis, MO 63146

Q

QUAINTON, Rodney F (Chi) 1725 Northfield Square, Northfield, IL 60093

QUATORZE, Jean Lenord (NY)

QUEEN, Jeffrey Denver (Lex) 3 Chalfonte Place, Fort Thomas, KY 41075

QUEEN, Laura Virginia (Los) Church Pension Group, 19 E 34th St, New York, NY 10016

QUEEN JR, William L (Va) 514 N 25th St, Richmond, VA 23223

QUEHL-ENGEL, Catherine Mary (Ia) 103 Oak Ridge Dr Se, Mount Vernon, IA 52314

QUESENBERRY-NELSON, Jane E (Minn) 4903 Maple Grove Rd, Hermantown, MN 55811

QUEVEDO-BOSCH, Juan A (LI) First Floor, 1317 34th Ave, Astoria, NY 11106

✠ **QUEZADA MOTA**, Moises (DomRep) Calle Costa Rica No 21, Ens Ozama Santo Domingo, Dominican Republic

QUICK, Alexander Loren (WMich)

QUICK, Judy Goins (Ala) 224 Bentley Cir, Shelby, AL 35143

QUIGGLE, George Willard (Ala) 384 Windflower Dr, Dadeville, AL 36853

QUIGLEY, James E (WA) St Albans Church, 3001 Wisconsin Ave NW, Washington, DC 20016

QUIJADA-DISCAVAGE, Thomas Damian (Los) 2563 Sale Pl, Walnut Park, CA 90255

QUILA GARCIA, Pedro Perfecto (EcuC) Box 235, Tena, Ecuador

QUILL, Margaret (Chi) Gn Angels Of Elk River Inc, 400 Evans Ave NW, Elk River, MN 55330

QUIN, Alison (NY) 3021 State Route 213 E, Stone Ridge, NY 12484

QUINES JR, Brent Bagni (Los) Holy Trinity and St Benedict, 416 N Garfield Ave, Alhambra, CA 91801

QUINLAN, Leila N (Fla)

QUINN, Carolee Elizabeth Sproull (USC) 1402 Wenwood Ct, Greenville, SC 29607

QUINN, Catherine Alyce Rafferty (Nwk) 66 Pomander Walk, Ridgewood, NJ 07450

QUINN, Derek James (WMich) 222 Boardman Ave Apt B, Apt B, Traverse City, MI 49684

QUINN, Michele (Colo) 3153 S Forest St, Denver, CO 80222

QUINN, Peter Darrell (Ct) 120 Ford Ln, Torrington, CT 06790

QUINN, Scott (Pgh) 537 Hamilton Rd, Pittsburgh, PA 15205

QUINNELL, Carolyn T (CFla) 517 Dominican Ter, Sebastian, FL 32958

QUINNELL, Robert Douglass (CFla) PO Box 2373, Belleview, FL 34421

QUINNEY, Sarah Howell (The Episcopal NCal) 2351 Pleasant Grove Blvd, Roseville, CA 95747

✠ **QUINONEZ-MERA**, Juan Carlos (EcuC)

QUINTON, Dean Lepidio (Nev) 8500 Doniphan Dr, Unit 17, Anthony, TX 79821

R

RAASCH, Timothy (Minn) 743 5th St Apt 108, West Sacramento, CA 95605

✠ **RABB**, John (Md) 4 E University Pkwy, Baltimore, MD 21218

RABONE, Christian Robert (NwT)

RABY, Edith Gilliam (CFla) 111 S Church St, Smithfield, VA 23430

RACHAL, Paula C (NC) 2803 Watauga Dr, Greensboro, NC 27408

RACHAL, Robert T (NC) 2803 Watauga Dr, Greensboro, NC 27408

RACINE, Jean-Joel (Hai) Box 1309, Port-Au-Prince, Haiti

RACIOPPI, Jerry (Nwk) 36 Gould St, Verona, NJ 07044

RACKLEY, Kenneth Ira (Nev)

RACKLEY, M Kathryn (O) 1730 Wright Ave, Rocky River, OH 44116

RACUSIN, Michele (Cal) 5267 San Jacinto Ave, Clovis, CA 93619

RADANT, William Fred (Mil) PO Box 442, Manitowish Waters, WI 54545

RADCLIFF III, Cecil Darrell (CFla) 3010 Big Sky Blvd, Kissimmee, FL 34744

RADCLIFF, Irene Evelyn (SO)

RADCLIFF, Jason (Alb)

RADCLIFFE, Ernest Stanley (Oly) 3732 Colonial Ln SE, Port Orchard, WA 98366

RADCLIFFE JR, William Eugene (Md) 2846 Angus Circle, Molino, FL 32577

RADER, Kyle Gordon (NJ)

RADIX, Shelton Nkhrumah (NJ)

RADLEY, Charles Perrin (Me) 3701 R St NW, Washington, DC 20007

RADNER, Ephraim Louis (Colo) 410 W 18th St, Pueblo, CO 81003

RADTKE, Warren (Mass) 301 Brooksby Village Dr Unit 513, Peabody, MA 01960

RADZIK, David Robert (O)

RAFFALOVICH, Francis Dawson (Dal) 306 Cobalt Cv, Georgetown, TX 78633

RAFFERTY, Joseph Patrick (Be) 220 Montgomery Ave, West Pittston, PA 18643

RAFFERTY, Robert Douglas (NMich) 421 Cherry St, Iron River, MI 49935

RAFTER, John Wesley (Me) 59 Simonton Rd, Camden, ME 04843

RAGAN, Raggs (Ore) 640 Southshore Blvd, Lake Oswego, OR 97034

RAGLAND, Rebecca B (Mo) 1210 Locust St, Saint Louis, MO 63103

RAGSDALE, Eliza Robinson (SeFla) 213 Princess St, Alexandria, VA 22314

RAGSDALE, James Lewis (Colo) 3143 S Nucla St, Aurora, CO 80013

RAGSDALE, Katherine H (Nwk) 99 Brattle St, Cambridge, MA 02138

RAGSDALE III, Lee Morris (ETenn)

RAHHAL, Michele Duff (Okla) 721 Franklin Dr, Ardmore, OK 73401

RAHM, Kent David (Va) 1240 S 2nd St Unit 626, Minneapolis, MN 55415

RAHN, Gaynell M (Va) 905 Princess Anne St, Fredericksburg, VA 22401

RAICHE, Brian Michael (Mass) 26 White St, Haverhill, MA 01830

RAILEY, Robert Macfarlane (NMich) 3029 N Lakeshore Blvd, Marquette, MI 49855

RAINEY, Gregory (Ore)

RAINING, Hillary (Pa) 226 Righters Mill Rd, Gladwyne, PA 19035

RAINS JR, Harry James (WNC) 8 Nicole Lane, Weaverville, NC 28787

RAISH, John Woodham (WLa) 6315 Cindy Ln, Houston, TX 77008

RAJ, Seelam Sujanna (Mo)

RAJ, Vincent S (ECR) 3600 High Meadow Dr Apt 31, Carmel, CA 93923

RAJAGOPAL, Doris Elizabeth (Pa) 763 Valley Forge Rd, Wayne, PA 19087

RALLISON, Brian Gary (Pa) 261 S 900 E, Slc, UT 84102

RALPH, Michael Jay (SO) 127 W Mound St, Circleville, OH 43113

RALSTON, Betty Marie (Colo) Po Box 773627, Steamboat Springs, CO 80477

RALSTON, D Darwin (O) 711 College Ave, Lima, OH 45805

RAMAN, Neil Kumar (Pgh) 7916 Graff Ave, Pittsburgh, PA 15218

RAMBO JR, Charles B (CFla) Po Box 46, Rutherfordton, NC 28139

RAMBO, Thomas (SwVa) 323 Catherine St, Walla Walla, WA 99362

RAMBOW, George (Miss) 319 University Dr, Starkville, MS 39759

RAMERMAN, Diane Gruner (Oly) 1216 7th St, Anacortes, WA 98221

RAMEY, Bernard (Va) St Albans Episcopal Church, 6800 Columbia Pike, Annandale, VA 22003

RAMIREZ, Lucia (PR)

RAMIREZ, Mark Lloyd (Chi) St Barnabas Episc Church, 22W415 Butterfield Rd, Glen Ellyn, IL 60137

RAMIREZ-MILLER, Gerardo Carlos (NY) 351 W 24th St Apt 6-C, New York, NY 10011

RAMIREZ-NIEVES, Aida Iris (Episcopal VI) PO Box 1796, Kingshill, VI 00851

RAMIREZ-SEGARRA, Cesar E (PR) PO Box 1967, Yauco, PR 00698

RAMOS, Leon (PR)

RAMOS, Mary Serena (Minn) 700 S 2nd Street, Unit 41, Minneapolis, MN 55401

RAMOS, Pablo (U) 1904 W Dale Ridge Ave, Salt Lake City, UT 84116

RAMOS-GARCIA, Ramon (PR)

✠ **RAMOS-ORENCH**, Wilfrido (PR) 77 Linnmoore St, Hartford, CT 06114

RAMSEY, Ron (SVa) 8 Meacham Rd, Cambridge, MA 02140

RAMSEY, Walter Albert (Cal) 162 Hickory St, San Francisco, CA 94102

RAMSEY-MUSOLF, Michael Jeffrey (Los) Department Of Physics, U Mass Amherst, 710 N Pleasant St 416, Amherst, MA 01003

RAMSHAW, Lance Arthur (Del) 106 Alden Rd, Concord, MA 01742

RAMSHAW, Lynn Cecelia Homeyer (Chi) 12 Jolynn Dr, Ormond Beach, FL 32174

RAMSTAD, Philip Robert (Minn) 901 Como Boulevard East, #304, Osceda, WI 54020

RANDALL, Anne E (Dal) 924 N Robinson Ave, Oklahoma City, OK 73102

RANDALL, Ben (Tenn) 105 Edgewood Ave, McMinnville, TN 37110

RANDALL, Catharine Louise (Ct) 91 Minortown Rd, Woodbury, CT 06798

RANDALL, Elizabeth Penney (Colo) 735 S Vine St, Denver, CO 80209

RANDALL, Jeanne Rice (Ala)

RANDALL, Richard Alan (CPa) 222 N 6th St, Chambersburg, PA 17201

RANDALL JR, Robert James (SVa) 716 Abbey Dr, Virginia Beach, VA 23455

RANDALL, Sarah Archais (Mass) PO Box C, Duxbury, MA 02331

RANDLE, Cameron D (SVa) 6125 Carlos Ave, Los Angeles, CA 90028

RANDOLPH, Barry Trent (Mich) 231 E Grand Blvd, Detroit, MI 48207

RANDOLPH JR, Henry G (NI) 117 N Lafayette Blvd, South Bend, IN 46601

RANEY III, Raymond Raymond (RG) 04 Tano Road, Santa Fe, NM 87506

RANK, Andrew Peter Robert (SanD) PO Box 34548, San Diego, CA 92163

RANKIN, Annette Reiser (Ore) 10 Old Mill St, Mill Valley, CA 94910

RANKIN, Deborah (WVa) 2220 2nd St, Cuyahoga Falls, OH 44221

RANKIN, Edward Harris (Oly) 5610 N Washington St Apt 4211, Stillwater, OK 74075

RANKIN, Jerry Dean (Kan) 406 Hillside St, Abilene, KS 67410

RANKIN-WILLIAMS, Christopher N (Cal) Po Box 217, Ross, CA 94957

RANNA, Claire Dietrich (Cal)

RANNENBERG, Pamela Lamb (RI) 442 Wickford Point Rd, North Kingstown, RI 02852

RANOULL, Mary Elizabeth (Fla)

RANSOM, James Clifford (Md) 89 Hilltop Pl, New London, NH 03257

RANSOM, Lisa (Vt) 2016 Us RR 2, Waterbury, VT 05676

RAO, Chitra Dasu Sudarshan (Los) 10833 Le Conte Ave, Los Angeles, CA 90095

RAPALO, Milton Omar (Hond)

RAPALO DE RUIZ, Jaqueline Siomara (Hond) 23 Ave 21 Calle SO Col Trejo, San Pedro Sula Cortes, Honduras

RAPP, Phillip James (WK) 6529 Clifton Rd, Clifton, VA 20124

RARDIN, Thomas Michael (Tex) 4132 N Summercrest Loop, Round Rock, TX 78681

RASCHKE, Gerald Wesley (Spr) 2921 Haverford Rd, Springfield, IL 62704

RASCHKE, Vernon Joseph (SD) 625 W Main, Lead, SD 57754

RASICCI, Michael Dominic (Chi) 222 S Batavia Ave, Batavia, IL 60510

RASMUS, John (Eau) 5318 Regent St, Madison, WI 53705

RASMUS, Paul (SeFla) 3740 Holly Dr, Palm Beach Gardens, FL 33410

RASMUSSEN, Cynthia M (Roch) 215 Parkview Dr, Rochester, NY 14625

RASMUSSEN, Jeanne Louise (Az) 520 N Pokegama Ave, Grand Rapids, MN 55744

RASMUSSEN, Rik Lorin (The Episcopal NCal) St Paul's Episcopal Church, PO Box 160914, Sacramento, CA 95816

RASNER, Richard Lewis (SO) 143 State St, Portland, ME 04101

RASNICK, Thomas (ETenn) 6804 Glenbrook Cir, Knoxville, TN 37919

RATCLIFF, Elizabeth Rogers (WLa)

RATH, Erin (Neb) PO Box 988, Scottsbluff, NE 69363

RATHBONE, Cristina (Mass) 138 Tremont St, Boston, MA 02111

RATLIFF, Ruth Evelyn (Ia) St Luke's Episcopal Church, 2410 Melrose Dr, Cedar Falls, IA 50613

RATTERREE, Gretchen S (Roch)

RAU, Michael S (SwFla) St Marks Episcopal Church, 513 Nassau St S, Venice, FL 34285

RAULERSON, Aaron D (Ala) 5529 Cedar Mill Dr, Guntersville, AL 35976

RAUSCHER JR, William V. (NJ) 663 N Evergreen Ave, Woodbury, NJ 08096

RAVEN, Margaret Hilary (NJ) 324 Edgewood Dr, Toms River, NJ 08755

RAVNDAL III, Eric (CFla) 1302 Country Club Oaks Cir, Orlando, FL 32804

RAWLINS, Allister (LI) 744 Havemeyer Ave, Bronx, NY 10473

RAWLINSON, John Edward (Cal) 891 Dowling Blvd, San Leandro, CA 94577

RAWSON, William Leighton (Nwk) 10960 Big Canoe, Jasper, GA 30143

RAY, Douglass E (Colo) 5601 Collins Ave Apt 706, Miami Beach, FL 33140

RAY, Harvey H (Cal) 1354 Primavera Dr E, Palm Springs, CA 92264

RAY, John (At)

RAY, John Sewak (At) 4808 Glenwhite Dr, Duluth, GA 30096

RAY, Michael Fleming (Ct) 88 Palmer St, Norwich, CT 06360

RAY, Pratik Kumar (RG)

✠ **RAY**, Rayford J (NMich) 9922 U.65 Ln, Rapid River, MI 49878

RAY, Suzanne Patricia (NMich) 9922 U 65 Lane, Rapid River, MI 49878

RAY, Todd Abert (WK)

RAY, Wanda (O) 101 Cluster Oaks Ct, Foley, AL 36535

RAY, Wayne Allen (Miss) 116 Siowan Ave, Ocean Springs, MS 39564

RAYBOURN JR, Fred Loren (Neb) 1204 Sunshine Blvd, Bellevue, NE 68123

RAYBURG-ELLIOTT, Jason (Chi) 12219 S 86th Ave, Palos Park, IL 60464

RAYLS, John William (WTex) PO Box 6885, San Antonio, TX 78209

RAYMOND, Patrick (Chi) 647 Dundee Ave, Barrington, IL 60010

RAYMOND, Seth (Mil) 2657 N 115th St, Wauwatosa, WI 53226

RAYMOND, Sue Ann (Ia) Lot 17A, 1771 Golf Course Blvd., Independence, IA 50644

RAYSA, Mary G (SO)

RAZEE, George Wells (Ct) 234 Essex Mdws, Essex, CT 06426

RAZIM, Genevieve (Tex)

RAZZINO, Robin (Va) 1701 N Quaker Ln, Alexandria, VA 22302

REA, Robert Allen (NC) 1226 21st Ave, San Francisco, CA 94122

READ, Allison (Ct) 300 Summit St, Hartford, CT 06106

READ, David Glenn (WTex) PO Box 1765, Boerne, TX 78006

READ, Nancy Ann (Nwk) 12 Northfield Ter, Clifton, NJ 07013

READ II, Philip Daugherty (SwFla) 11698 Pointe Cir, Fort Myers, FL 33908

REANS, Douglas J (NJ) 512 Sycamore Ter, Cinnaminson, NJ 08077

REARDON, John Paul (RI) 474 Fruit Hill Ave, North Providence, RI 02911

REARDON, Michael Joseph (Ct)

REASONER, Rand (Los) 5700 Rudnick Ave, Woodland Hills, CA 91367

REAT, Lee Anne (SO) 2318 Collins Dr, Worthington, OH 43085

REBHOLTZ, Brian L (The Episcopal NCal) 11310 Bosal Cir, Auburn, CA 95603

REBOUCHE, Madeleine (WLa)

RECHTER, Elizabeth (Los) 2744 Peachtree Rd NW, Atlanta, GA 30305

RECTENWALD, Marion Bridget (SD) 371 New College Dr, Sewanee, TN 37375

✠ **REDDALL**, Jennifer (Az) 114 W Roosevelt St, Phoenix, AZ 85003

REDDELL, Ronald Kirk (Oly) 910 Harris Ave Unit 408, Bellingham, WA 98225

REDDIE, Grover Tyrone (Alb) 11192 State Route 9W, Coxsackie, NY 12051

REDDIG, Mike (Cal) 1400 Geary Blvd Apt 3a, San Francisco, CA 94109

REDDIMALLA, Samuel (NY) 4673 Flatlick Branch Dr, Chantilly, VA 20151

REDDING, Pam (Cal) 2925 Bonifacio St, Concord, CA 94519

REDFIELD, William (CNY) 225 Pelham Rd, Syracuse, NY 13214

REDMON, Caroline (Los) 1050 E Ramon Rd Unit 125, Palm Springs, CA 92264

RED OWL, Cordelia (SD) Po Box 354, Porcupine, SD 57772

REDPATH, Valerie Jean (NJ) 329 Estate Point Rd, Toms River, NJ 08753

REECE, Herbert Anderson (O) 9522 Lincolnwood Dr, Evanston, IL 60203

REECE, Jennifer M (Me) 41 Mount Desert St, Bar Harbor, ME 04609

REECE, Mark Spencer (SeFla) Iglesia Catedral del Redentor, Calle Beneficencia 18, Madrid, 28004, Spain

REED, Anne L (SO) 1617 E Mcmillan St Apt 301, Cincinnati, OH 45206

REED, Bobette P (O) Deer Hill Rr#1, East Hampton, CT 06424

REED, Craig Andrew (Dal) 9714 Lanward Dr, Dallas, TX 75238

✠ **REED**, David (Ky) 5226 Moccasin Trl, Louisville, KY 40207

✠ **REED**, David (WTex) PO Box 6885, San Antonio, TX 78209

REED, Davies (Ind) 1525 Mulberry St, Zionsville, IN 46077

REED, Elizabeth H (Be) 108 N 5th St, Allentown, PA 18102

REED, Jeffrey Bruce (Az) PO Box 42618, Tucson, AZ 85733

REED, Jim (EC) 1718 East Macon Rd, Atlantic Beach, NC 28512

REED, Juan Y (Chi) 1617 E 50th Place, Apt 4D, Chicago, IL 60615

REED, Loreen Hayward Rogers (At) 355 Porter St, Madison, GA 30650

✠ **REED JR**, Poulson (Okla) 6300 N Central Ave, Phoenix, AZ 85012

REED, Richard Wayne (RG) Hc 31 Box 17-B, Las Vegas, NM 87701

REED, Robin Allison (CFla)

REED, Ronald Lind (Kan) 4810 W 67th St, Prairie Village, KS 66208

REED, Stephen K (Ak) 1722 Linden St, Longmont, CO 80501

REED, Thomas Louis (Pa) 16 Nestlenook Dr, Middleboro, MA 02346

REEDER, Tom (Fla) 400 San Juan Dr, Ponte Vedra, FL 32082

REEMAN, Karen Baehr (NJ) 69 Broad St, Eatontown, NJ 07724

REES, Elizabeth (Va) 1501 River Farm Dr, Alexandria, VA 22308

REES, Emily Frances (At) Po Box 223, Braselton, GA 30517

REESE, Carol Sue (Chi) 1525 W Birchwood Ave, Chicago, IL 60626

REESE, Donnis Jean (EMich) 200 E Page St, Rose City, MI 48654

REESE, Jeannette Ellis (Ga) 45 Spooks Branch Ext, Asheville, NC 28804

REESE, John (SwFla) 509 E Twiggs St, Tampa, FL 33602

REESE, John Victor (Ark) 406 W Central Ave, Bentonville, AR 72712

REESE, Judith Foster (WTenn) 800 Rountree Ave, Kinston, NC 28501

REESE, Mary (EC) 404 E. New Hope Rd., Goldsboro, NC 27534

REESE, Robert Emory (Ga) 45 Spooks Branch Ext, Asheville, NC 28804

REESE, Thomas Francis (LI) 141 Ascan Ave, Forest Hills, NY 11375

REESON, Geoffrey Douglas (EcuC) Casilla 17-16-95, Quito, Ecuador

REESON, Marta Lidia (EcuC) Casilla 17-16-95, Quito, Ecuador

REEVE, Keith John (NC) 3613 Clifton Ct, Raleigh, NC 27604

REEVE, Susan Margaret (The Episcopal NCal) 146 Saint Gertrude Ave, Rio Vista, CA 94571

REEVES, Bernice Brysch (WTex)

REEVES, Daniel (NC) 22 Lansgate Ct, Durham, NC 27713

REEVES, Diane Delafield (Fla) 13588 NE 247th Lane, Box 18, Orange Springs, FL 32182

REEVES, Jack William (LI) 23 Old Mamaroneck Rd Apt 5r, White Plains, NY 10605

REEVES, Jess Leonidas (Tenn) 24 Longmeadow, Pine Bluff, AR 71603

REEVES, Thomas Daniel (Spr)

Clergy List

REEVES-KAUTZ, Robin K (Tex) 610 Duck Ct, Clute, TX 77531

REGAN, Natalie M (Va)

REGAN, Thomas Francis (SD) 708 Sawyer St, Lead, SD 57754

REGEN, Catharine Louise Emmert (Tenn) 306 Broadview Dr, Dickson, TN 37055

REGISFORD, Sylvanus Hermus Alonzo (SeFla) 7580 Derby Ln, Shakopee, MN 55379

REGIST, Antonio Alberto (WTex) 1310 Pecan Valley Dr, Antonio, TX 78210

REHAGEN, Gerry (EMich) 2093 Michaywe Dr, Gaylord, MI 49735

REHBERG, Gloria Irene (RG) 7104 Montano Rd Nw, Albuquerque, NM 87120

REHBERG, Gretchen (Spok) 245 E 13th Ave, 731 E 8th Ave, Spokane, WA 99202

REHO, James Hughes (SwFla) Lamb Of God Episcopal Church, 19691 Cypress View Dr, Fort Myers, FL 33967

REICH, Jeffrey Walker (Miss) 834 N 5th Ave, Laurel, MS 39440

REICHARD, Bernice Dorothy (Be) P.O. Box 368, Trexlertown, PA 18087

REICHEL, Sonya Joan (The Episcopal NCal)

REICHERT, Elaine Starr Gilmer (Cal) 1605 Vendola Dr, San Rafael, CA 94903

REICHMAN, Amy L (Ct) PO Box 698, Sharon, CT 06069

REICHMANN, Jeffrey H (At) 26 Oakwood Ct, Jacksonville Beach, FL 32250

REID, Allison (La)

REID, Brian S (NwPa) 99 Manor Dr, Dubois, PA 15801

REID, Catharine Brannan (Oly) 1123 19th Ave East, Seattle, WA 98112

REID, Courtney (Chi)

REID, Dennis Joseph (Ida)

REID, Franklin Lionel (NY) 1064 E 219th St, Bronx, NY 10469

REID, Gordon (Pa) 1027 Arch St, Apt 406, Philadelphia, PA 19107

REID, Jennie Lou (SeFla) 3840 Alhambra Ct, Coral Gables, FL 33134

REID, M Sue (Oly) 315 Burns Ln, Williamsburg, VA 23185

REID, Michael (ECR) 146 12th St, Pacific Grove, CA 93950

REID, Paul (Pa) 7809 Old York Rd, Elkins Park, PA 19027

REID, Richard William (Vt) PO Box 70070, North Dartmouth, MA 02747

REID-LEVY, Schelly (Md) 3002 Holly St, Edgewater, MD 21037

REIDT, Donna (Vt) 124 Willis Rd, West Charleston, VT 05872

REILEY, Jennifer B S (Mass) 48 Prospect St, North Andover, MA 01845

REIMER, Leslie (Pgh) 5426 Wilkins Ave, Pittsburgh, PA 15217

REIMER, Susan (RG) 184 Boutwell Ct, Loveland, CO 80537

REINERS JR, Alwin (Va) 1600 Westbrook Ave, Richmond, VA 23227

REINERS, Diane (NY)

REINHARD, Kathryn Louise (NY) Christ Church, 84 Broadway, New Haven, CT 06511

REINHARDT, Connie (WA) 27 Broad St, Newburyport, MA 01950

REINHEIMER, John Jay (NH) 227 W 6th St, Port Clinton, OH 43452

REINHEIMER, Philip (The Episcopal NCal) 13948 Gold Country Drive, Penn Valley, CA 95945

REINHOLZ, Andrew C (NJ) 203 Wildwood Ave, Pitman, NJ 08071

REINHOLZ, Kimberly (Va) Christ Church, 205 N 7th St, Stroudsburg, PA 18360

REINKE, Michael Barton (NH)

REINKEN, Dirk Christian (NJ) 5208 Biltmore Dr, Freehold, NJ 07728

REISCHMAN, Charles J (Spr) 4767 Redbud Cr, Decatur, IL 62526

REISHUS, John William (WMich) 5161 E 50 N, Kokomo, IN 46901

REISNER, Terry Ralph (Dal)

REISS, James E (LI)

REJOUIS, Mary Kate (Colo) 2700 University Heights Ave, Boulder, CO 80302

RELLER, Wilfred Herman (Colo) 71 Aspen Ln, Golden, CO 80403

RELYEA, Michael Johl (NY) 127b east terminal blvd, Atlantic Beach, NC 28512

REMBOLDT, Cherry Ann (SanD) 47535 State Highway 74, Palm Deset, CA 92260

REMENTER, Nancy Sandra (CPa) 239 E Market St, Marietta, PA 17547

REMER, Douglas E (SwFla) 5231 S Jules Verne Ct, Tampa, FL 33611

REMINGTON, Melissa (WVa) 821 Edgewood Dr, Charleston, WV 25302

REMPPEL, Paulette Evelyn (NY) 52 Brookside Pl, New Rochelle, NY 10801

REMY, Joseph Michel Jean (Hai) 5935 Del Lago Cir, Sunrise, FL 33313

RENCHER, Ollie (WTenn) 1720 Peabody Ave, Memphis, TN 38104

RENDON, Carlos H (Colom)

RENDON OSPINA, Gonzalo Antonio (Colom) Cra 80 No 53a-78, Medelin Antioquia, 99999, Colombia

RENEGAR, Douglas Mcbane (Ga) 224 Lakefield Rd, Waterloo, SC 29384

RENFREW, William Finch (Mich) 2101 Wellesley Dr, Lansing, MI 48911

RENG, Zecharia (ND)

RENGERS, Josiah (Ala) 109 Woodcrest Circle, Eutaw, AL 35462

RENN, Wade (Nwk) 558 Highland Ave, Montclair, NJ 07043

RENNA, Pamela Stacey (EMich) 123 N Michigan Ave, Saginaw, MI 48602

RENNER, Melissa Elaine (NI) 2527 Riverview Pl., Elkhart, IN 46516

REPLOGLE, Jennifer (Chi) 33 Mercer St, Princeton, NJ 08540

REPP, Jeanette (Los) 1648 W 9th St, San Pedro, CA 90732

RESSLER, Richard Alan (SD) St Pauls Episcopal Church, 309 S Jackson St, Jackson, MI 49201

RESTREPO CARDONA, Juan Carlos (Colom) Calle 51 # 6-49, Bogota, 111166, Colombia

RETAMAL, M Regina (Mass) 59 Lawrence St, Framingham, MA 01702

RETZLAFF, Georg (USC) 1612 Goldfinch Ln, West Columbia, SC 29169

REUMAN, Gene (CFla) 2915 W Henley Ln, Dunnellon, FL 34433

REUSS, Patricia Ann Osborne (WNC) 133 Liberty Ct, Oak Ridge, TN 37830

REVEL, Anna Carter (Ky) 5146 Sunnybrook Dr, Paducah, KY 42001

REX III, Charles Walton (WNC) 2739 Prairie Ave, Evanston, IL 60201

REX JR, William Moyer (Pa) 407 N Broad St, Lansdale, PA 19446

REXFORD, William Nelson (Mich) 7213 Meadow Wood Way, Clarksville, MD 21029

REYES, J Sierra (Chi) St Lukes Episcopal Church, 1270 Poplar St, Denver, CO 80220

REYES, Jesus (Oly) 30955 SW Fir Ave, Wilsonville, OR 97070

REYES, Juan P (WA) 3001 Wisconsin Ave NW, Washington, DC 20016

REYES, Omar (SwFla)

REYES, Oscar Alejandro (RG)

REYES GUILLEN, Karla Patricia (Hond) Catedral TEC Sta Maria De LA, Colonia Florencia N Primera, Tegucigalpa MDC, 11101, Honduras

REYES PEREZ, Jose R (WMass) 4 W End Ave, Westborough, MA 01581

REYNES, Stephen Alan (Vt) 64 State St, Montpelier, VT 05602

REYNOLDS, Bettye (The Episcopal NCal) 4706 Oakbough Way, Carmichael, CA 95608

REYNOLDS, Bo Daniel (NY) 487 Hudson St, New York, NY 10014

REYNOLDS, Dawn Marie (Ore)

REYNOLDS, Eleanor Francis (Nwk) PO Box 240, Mendham, NJ 07945

REYNOLDS, Fred (Roch) 589 Sagamore Ave Unit 84, Portsmouth, NH 03801

REYNOLDS, Gail Ann (Kan) 9119 Dearborn St, Overland Park, KS 66207

REYNOLDS, James Ronald (Tex) 3717 Cook Ct, Fort Worth, TX 76244

REYNOLDS, Joe D (Tex) 145 15th St NE Apt 1006, Atlanta, GA 30309

REYNOLDS, Katharine Sylvia (Minn) Loring Green East, 1201 Yale Pl Apt 610, Minneapolis, MN 55403

REYNOLDS, Kay (ETenn) 4017 Sherry Dr, Knoxville, TN 37918

REYNOLDS, Roger James (Ore) 18271 SW Ewen Dr, Aloha, OR 97003

REYNOLDS, Sarah Anne (Los) 1519 Otis St NE, Washington, DC 20017

REYNOLDS JR, Wallace Averal (CFla) 5626 Avenwood Cir NW, Cleveland, TN 37312

REZAC, Laura Anne (SC)

REZACH, Karen Beverly (Nwk) 74 Edgewood Pl, Maywood, NJ 07607

REZIN, Mary Ellen (Eau) 27042 State Highway 21, Tomah, WI 54660

RHEA, Pamela Towery (Miss) 318 College St, Columbus, MS 39701

RHEA, Robert E (Tenn) 1401 Lee Victory Pkwy, Smyrna, TN 37167

RHOADES, Mary Ann (Chi) PO Box 494, Dixon, IL 61021

RHOADES, Stephen James (USC) Saint James Episcopal Church, 301 Piney Mountain Rd, Greenville, SC 29609

RHOADS, Bob (Oly) 181 W Maple St, Sequim, WA 98382

RHOADS, Tommy L (WTenn) PO Box 442, Humboldt, TN 38343

RHODENHISER, Imogen Leigh (NC) 410 Church Rd, Bloomfield Hills, MI 48304

RHODENHISER, James Cousins (Az) Stclare Tec Ch, 2309 Packard St, Ann Arbor, MI 48104

RHODES, Charlotte Dimmick (CFla) 414 Pine St, Titusville, FL 32796

RHODES, David Hughes (Ct) 44 Twin Oak Trl, Beacon Falls, CT 06403

RHODES, Debra G (NI)

RHODES, Judith Louise (Ct) 661 Old Post Rd, Fairfield, CT 06824

RHODES, Margaret Diana Clark (WMo) 1815 NE Independence Ave, Lees Summit, MO 64086

RHODES, Matthew W (SwVa) 1659 Perrowville Rd, Forest, VA 24551

RHODES, Robert Richard (NI) 9 Harrington Ave, Westwood, NJ 07675

RHODES, Robert Wayne (Oly) 300 W 8th St Unit 314, Vancouver, WA 98660

RHOTON, Lissie (SVa) 3608 Burns Ct, Virginia Beach, VA 23462

RHYNE, Patty (NC) Christ Church, 1412 Providence Rd, Charlotte, NC 28207

RICE, Arianne V (Md) 8129 Dotty Rd, Rosedale, MD 21237

✠ **RICE**, David Wayne C (Episcopal SJ) Diocese Of San Joaquin, 1528 Oakdale Rd, Modesto, CA 95355

RICE, Debra Harsh (WNC) PO Box 2319, Franklin, NC 28744

RICE, Doreen Ann (Kan)

RICE, Edward G (NH) 37 Harbor Way Unit 13, Wolfeboro, NH 03894

RICE, Glenda Ann (Ak) PO Box 1130, Sitka, AK 99835

RICE JR, John (Va) 240 Old Main St, South Yarmouth, MA 02664

RICE, John David Sayre (WNC) 51 N View Cir, Hayesville, NC 28904

RICE, Lawrence Allen (NMich) 5526 S Baker Side Rd, Sault Sainte Marie, MI 49783

RICE, Rodney Vincent (NY) 914 Adana Rd, Pikesville, MD 21208

RICE, Sandra Kay (Md) Retired, Frederick, MD 21701

RICE, Steven C (NC) 2575 Parkway Dr, Winston Salem, NC 27103

RICE, Whitney (Mo) 1210 Locust St, Saint Louis, MO 63103

RICE, Winston Edward (La) 512 E Boston St, Covington, LA 70433

RICH, Bill (Mass) 333 Ricciuti Dr Apt 1526, Quincy, MA 02169

RICH III, Edward Robins (SwFla) 11315 Linbanks Pl, Tampa, FL 33617

RICH, Nancy Willis (O) 5650 Grace Woods Dr Unit 203, Willoughby, OH 44094

RICH, Noel David (Minn) 808 Eldo Ln SW, Alexandria, MN 56308

RICH, Sara (Fla)

RICH, Sue (EMich) Trinity Episcopal Church, 815 N Grant Street, Bay City, MI 48708

RICH, Tim (RI) St Lukes Episc Ch, 99 S Pierce Rd, East Greenwich, RI 02818

RICHARD, Mary B (WLa) PO Box 1627, Shreveport, LA 71165

RICHARDS, Anne Marie (Md) Emmanuel Episcopal Church, 811 Cathedral St, Baltimore, MD 21201

RICHARDS, Bramwell Trevor (Mil)

RICHARDS, Bruce (Del)

✠ **RICHARDS**, Daniel Paul (USC) 23 Catesby Cir, Columbia, SC 29206

RICHARDS, Dennison Sherman (LI) 107-66 Merrick Blvd, Jamaica, NY 11433

RICHARDS, Edward Thomas (CGC) PO Box 7359, Panama City Beach, FL 32413

RICHARDS, Emily Barr (Pa) 654 N Easton Rd, Glenside, PA 19038

RICHARDS, Erin Kathleen (ND) 301 Main St S, Minot, ND 58701

RICHARDS, Fitzroy Ivan (Oly) 75 Gladstone Gardens SW, Calgary, AB T3E 7E4, Canada

RICHARDS, Jeffery Martin (O) 2510 Olentangy Dr, Akron, OH 44333

RICHARDS, Michael Gregory (Los) PO Box 220383, Newhall, CA 91322

RICHARDS, Rosalie (NY) 536 Old Glen Ave, Berlin, NH 03570

RICHARDS, Susan M (Pa) 1074 BROADMOOR RD, BRYN MAWR, PA 19010

RICHARDS, Tyler Clayton (FdL) 220 N Superior St, De Pere, WI 54115

RICHARDSON, Carolyn Garrett (SanD) 3515 Lomas Serenas Dr., Escondido, CA 92029

RICHARDSON, Christopher C (SO) 2151 Dorset Rd, Columbus, OH 43221

RICHARDSON, David Anthony (Az) 227 S Montgomery Ave, Vail, AZ 85641

RICHARDSON, Ellen (EC) 311 10th St W, Tifton, GA 31794

RICHARDSON JR, Grady Wade (Ala) 605 Country Club Dr, Gadsden, AL 35901

RICHARDSON, Janet (Ind) 310 Del Mar Dr, Lady Lake, FL 32159

RICHARDSON, Jeffrey Roy (SC)

RICHARDSON, Jim (The Episcopal NCal) 1700 University Ave, Charlottesville, VA 22903

RICHARDSON JR, John Dowland (CGC) 19 Gaywood Cir, Birmingham, AL 35213

RICHARDSON, John Marshall (WMo) 23405 S Waverly Rd, Spring Hill, KS 66083

RICHARDSON, Jon M (Nwk) 90 Kiel Ave, Kinnelon, NJ 07405

RICHARDSON, Marcia Ann Kelley (Me) 6 Jewett Cove Rd, Westport Is, ME 04578

RICHARDSON, Mark Stanton (Fla)

RICHARDSON, Mary M (Cal) 5833 College Ave, San Diego, CA 92120

RICHARDSON, Matthew Paul (Ark)

RICHARDSON, Michael Wm (Colo) 16181 Parkside Dr, Parker, CO 80134

RICHARDSON, Shelie (Vt)

RICHARDSON, Susan (Pa) 20 N American St, Philadelphia, PA 19106

RICHARDSON, W Mark (Cal) Cdsp, 2451 Ridge Rd, Berkeley, CA 94709

RICHAUD III, Mickey (Tenn) PO Box 808, Townsend, TN 37882

RICHEY, Donald Delose (Ct) 99 Willowbrook Rd, Cromwell, CT 06416

RICHMOND III, Allen Pierce (Ak) 2602 Glacier St, Anchorage, AK 99508

RICHMOND, John David (Spr) 11 Independence Sq, Bloomington, IL 61704

RICHMOND, Seth Gunther (Colo) 460 Prospector Ln, Estes Park, CO 80517

RICHMOND, Susan (Mass) 197 8th St Apt 801, Charlestown, MA 02129

RICHNOW, Douglas Wayne (Tex) 4014 Meadow Lake Ln, Houston, TX 77027

RICHTER, Amy Elizabeth (Md) 6150 Aster View Ln, Frederick, MD 21703

RICHTER, Anne (Colo) St Thomas Episcopal Church, 9616 Westport Rd, Louisville, KY 40241

RICHTER, Kerlin (Ore) 7030 SE Boise St., Portland, OR 97206

RICHTER JR, William Thompson (Tex) 2929 Woodland Hills Dr, Kingwood, TX 77339

RICK II, John William (Ct) 625 S St Andrews Pl, Los Angeles, CA 90005

RICKARDS JR, Joseph Asher (Ind) Spring Mills, 109 Jamestown Dr, Falling Waters, WV 25419

✠ **RICKEL**, Gregory Harold (Oly) 3209 42nd Ave SW, Seattle, WA 98116

RICKENBAKER, James Robert (Va) PO Box 255, Stafford, VA 22555

RICKENBAKER, Rachel Amelia (Va) PO Box 127, Upperville, VA 20185

RICKENBAKER, Thomas (EC) Box 548, Edenton, NC 27932

Clergy List

RICKER, Linda Seay (SVa)
RICKER, Mark (Colo) St Andrews Episcopal Church, PO Box 427, Ashland, WI 54806
RICKERT, David (Az)
RICKETTS, Linda (Mass) 12607 Cascade Hls, San Antonio, TX 78253
RICKETTS, Marcia Carole Couey (NwT) 133 Olivias Ct, Tuscola, TX 79562
RICKETTS, Nancy Lee (Tex) 1500 N Capital of Texas Hwy, Austin, TX 78746
RICKEY, David Bruce (Cal) 1602 W Pierson St Apt 232, Phoenix, AZ 85015
RICO, Bayani Depra (The Episcopal NCal) 2420 Tuolumne St, Vallejo, CA 94589
RIDDICK, Daniel Howison (SwVa) 240 Blackwater Ridge Ln, Glade Hill, VA 24092
RIDDLE, Jennifer (Ala) 530 Hurst Rd, Odenville, AL 35120
RIDEOUT, Robert Blanchard (SO) 7121 Muirfield Dr., Dublin, OH 43017
RIDER, David (NY) 424 W End Ave Apt 9c, New York, NY 10024
RIDER, Joe (CFla) 400 18th St, Vero Beach, FL 32960
RIDER, Paul G (Minn) 401 S 1st St Unit 610, Minneapolis, MN 55401
RIDER, Wm Blake (Tex) Diocese of Texas, 1225 Texas St, Houston, TX 77002
RIDGE, Charles Searls (Oly) 2658 48th Ave SW, Seattle, WA 98116
RIDGWAY, Michael Wyndham (ECR) 365 Stowell Ave, Sunnyvale, CA 94085
RIEKER, Scott (Md)
RIERDAN, Pastor Jill (WMass) 128 Main St, Easthampton, MA 01027
RIETH, Sarah Melissa (WNY) 500 E Rhode Island Ave, Southern Pines, NC 28387
RIETMANN, Paul David (Oly) 3615 N Gove St, Tacoma, WA 98407
RIGGALL, Daniel John (Me) Po Box 165, Kennebunk, ME 04043
RIGGALL, George Gordon (CGC) 524 Artesian Springs Dr, Fairhope, AL 36532
RIGGIN, Jean Monroe Porter (NC)
RIGGIN, John Harris (CGC) 4051 Old Shell Rd, Mobile, AL 36608
RIGGINS, Patricia Readon (WTex) 1310 Pecan Valley Dr, San Antonio, TX 78210
RIGGLE JR, John Field (SwFla) 9267 Sun Isle Dr Ne, Saint Petersburg, FL 33702
RIGHTMYER, Tom (WNC) 16 Salisbury Dr Apt 7304, Asheville, NC 28803
RIIS, Susan (SO) 144884 Harbor Dr E, Thornville, OH 43076
RIKER JR, William Chandler (Nwk) 249 Hartshorne Rd, Locust, NJ 07760
RILEY, Clay (SD) 1333 Jamestown Rd, Williamsburg, VA 23185

RILEY, Diane Napolitano (Nwk)
RILEY, Elizabeth R (Oly)
RILEY, George Daniel (NY) 39 Minnesota Ave, Long Beach, NY 11561
RILEY, Gregg Les (WLa) 3203 Claiborne Cir, Monroe, LA 71201
RILEY JR, James Foster (Minn) 132 Maj Hornbrook Road, Christchurch, Canterbury, New Zealand (Aotearoa)
RILEY, Linda (Ak)
RILEY, Mark D (SVa) 3928 Pacific Ave, Virginia Beach, VA 23451
RILEY, Reese Milton (Los) 1414 East Grovemont, Santa Ana, CA 92705
RIMASSA, Paul Stephen (NJ) 215 Briner Ln, Hamilton Square, NJ 08690
RIMER, Kathleen Pakos (Mass) 330 Brookline Ave., Boston, MA 02115
RIMKUS, William Allen (Chi) 14755 Eagle Ridge Dr, Homer Glen, IL 60491
RINCON, Virginia M (Me) 121 Margaret St Apt C, South Portland, ME 04106
RINEHART, James (Be) 108 Arbor Drive, Myerstown, PA 17067
RINES, Charles Tedford (The Episcopal NCal) 3641 Mari Dr, Lake Elsinore, CA 92530
RING, Anthony Richard (Eau) W10601 Pine Rd, Thorp, WI 54771
RING, Bonnie (Cal) 2011 Carlos Street, Moss Beach, CA 94038
RINGLAND, Robin Lynn (Oly) 415 S 18th St, Mount Vernon, WA 98274
RINGLE, Lorena May (Pgh) Christ Episcopal Church, 5910 Babcock Blvd, Pittsburgh, PA 15237
RIOS, Austin (Eur) Dio Of Wern N Ca, 900-B Centrepark Dr, Asheville, NC 28805
RIOS, Lajunta Michelle (Tex) Trinity Episcopal Church, 5010 N Main St, Baytown, TX 77521
RISARD, Frederick William (Episcopal SJ) 5001 3rd Ave, Marina, CA 93933
RISK III, Jay (Chi) 901 N Delphia Ave, Park Ridge, IL 60068
RITCHIE, Anne Gavin (Va) 1002 Janneys Ln, Alexandria, VA 22302
RITCHIE, Harold (Fla) 12013 SW 1st St, Micanopy, FL 32667
RITCHIE, Patricia Ritter (Tex) 4090 Delaware St, Beaumont, TX 77706
RITCHIE, Robert Joseph (Pa) 7712 Brous Ave, Philadelphia, PA 19152
RITCHIE, Sandra Lawrence (Pgh) 1808 Kent Rd, Pittsburgh, PA 15241
RITCHINGS, Frances Anne (Pa) 36 E Abington Ave, Philadelphia, PA 19118
RITONIA, Ann M (Md) 9120 Frederick Rd, Ellicott City, MD 21042
RITSON, Veronica Merita (Az) 6556 N Villa Manana Dr, Phoenix, AZ 85014
RITTER, Christine (Pa) 1771 Sharpless Rd, Meadowbrook, PA 19046

RITTER, Cynthia Anne (Okla) 1604 S Fir Ave, Broken Arrow, OK 74012
RITTER, Kenneth Phillip (Miss) 20 Belvoir Ave, Chattanooga, TN 37411
RITTER, Nathan Philip (Alb) 69 Fair St, Cooperstown, NY 13326
RIVAS, Vidal (WA) Tec Ch Hse, Mount Saint Alban, Washington, DC 20016
RIVERA, Aristotle C (Cal) PO Box 101, Brentwood, CA 94513
☩ **RIVERA**, Bavi Edna (Oly) PO Box 1548, The Dalles, OR 97058
RIVERA, Felix Arnaldo (Ct)
RIVERA, Johnny Abel (PR)
RIVERA, Jorge Juan (PR)
RIVERA-GEORGESCU, Ana Maria (CNY) St James Episcopal Church, 14216 Nys Route 9n, Au Sable Forks, NY 12912
RIVERA PEREZ, Francisco Javier (PR) PO Box 902, Saint Just, PR 00978
RIVERA-RIVERA, Luis Antonio (NY) 550 W 155th St, New York, NY 10032
RIVERA RIVERA, Luis Guillermo (PR)
RIVERA-RODRIGUEZ, Angel (PR)
RIVEROS MAYORGA, Jose Aristodemus (Colom) c/o Diocese of Colombia, Cra 6 No. 49-85 Piso 2, Bogota, BDC, Colombia
RIVERS, Barbara White Batzer (Pa) 378 Paoli Woods, Paoli, PA 19301
RIVERS, David Buchanan (Pa) 148 Heacock Ln, Wyncote, PA 19095
RIVERS III, Joseph Tracy (Pa) 2902 Monterey Ct, Springfield, PA 19064
RIVET, E (Colo) 7102 E Briarwood Dr, Centennial, CO 80112
RIVETTI, Mary Beth (Spok) 1436 Pine Cone Rd Apt 3, Moscow, ID 83843
RIVOLTA, Agostino Cetrangolo (NJ) 69 Broad St, Eatontown, NJ 07724
ROACH, Michelle Mona (CFla)
ROADMAN, Betsy Johns (NY) 91 Mystic Dr, Ossining, NY 10562
☩ **ROAF**, Phoebe Alison (WTenn) 692 Poplar Ave, Memphis, TN 38105
ROANE, Wilson (FdL) E2382 Pebble Run Rd, Waupaca, WI 54981
ROARK III, Hal (NY) 39 Granite Springs Rd, Granite Springs, NY 10527
ROBAYO HIDALGO, Daniel Dario (Tex) 11801 Carrizo Springs Path, Manor, TX 78653
ROBB, George Kerry (SeFla) 521 Rhine Rd, Palm Beach Gardens, FL 33410
ROBB, Polly Holcomb (Ala)
ROBB, Stephen Sargeant (Roch) 1130 Webster Rd, Webster, NY 14580
ROBBINS, Buckley (ETenn) 781 Shearer Cove Rd, Chattanooga, TN 37405
ROBBINS, Charlotte Ann (ND) 3600 25th St. S., Fargo, ND 58104
ROBBINS, Herbert John (RG) 104 East Circle Drive, Ruidoso Downs, NM 88346

ROBBINS, Janice M (ETenn) 3425 Alta Vista Dr, Chattanooga, TN 37411

ROBBINS, Lance (Roch) 1130 Webster Rd, Webster, NY 14580

ROBBINS, Mary Elizabeth (Tex) 562 Elkins lk, Huntsville, TX 77340

ROBBINS, Mary Elizabeth (Tex)

ROBBINS-COLE, Adrian (Mass) Saint Andrew's Church, 79 Denton Rd, Wellesley, MA 02482

ROBBINS-COLE, Sarah Jane (Mass) 49 Concord St, Peterborough, NH 03458

ROBBINS-PENNIMAN, Sylvia Beckman (SwFla) Church of the Good Shepherd, 639 Edgewater Dr, Dunedin, FL 34698

ROBERSON, Jason Daniel (SeFla)

ROBERSON, Keith James (Dal) 5733 Kay Dr, Fort Worth, TX 76119

ROBERSON, Mary Moore Mills (USC) 3123 Oakview Rd, Columbia, SC 29204

ROBERT, Mary Christopher (CGC) 551 W Barksdale Dr, Mobile, AL 36606

ROBERTS, Alice (NH) 2 Moore Rd, Newport, NH 03773

ROBERTS, Caleb S (Okla) 208 W University Ave, Champaign, IL 61820

ROBERTS, Charles Jonathan (SwFla) Calvary Episcopal Church, 1615 First St, Indian Rocks Beach, FL 33785

ROBERTS, Colby (Spok) 5706 Englewood Ave, Yakima, WA 98908

ROBERTS, George C (Ct) Saint James Episcopal Church, 3 Mountain Rd, Farmington, CT 06032

ROBERTS, Harold (Miss) 7417 Falcon Cir, Ocean Springs, MS 39564

ROBERTS, Harvey William (Ky) 330 N Hubbards Ln, Louisville, KY 40207

ROBERTS III, Henry Pauling (EC) 260 Houser Road, Blacksburg, SC 29702

ROBERTS, James Beauregard (Miss) 2441 S Shore Dr, Biloxi, MS 39532

ROBERTS, James Christopher (Mont) 208 Jefferson St, PO Box 113, Sheridan, MT 59749

ROBERTS, Jason (WTex) 8514 Heraldry St, Helotes, TX 78023

ROBERTS JR, John Bannister Gibson (CFla) 860 Ohlinger Rd, Babson Park, FL 33827

ROBERTS, John Charles (WNC) 500 Christ School Rd, Arden, NC 28704

ROBERTS, Jose (RI) 236 Central Ave, Pawtucket, RI 02860

ROBERTS, Judith S (Ind) 342 Red Ash Cir, Englewood, FL 34223

ROBERTS, Kim Elaine (Neb) 2312 J St, Omaha, NE 68107

ROBERTS, Leonard (Nwk)

ROBERTS, Les Allen (Md) 507 Towson Ave, Lutherville Timonium, MD 21093

ROBERTS III, Malcolm (EC) 520 Taberna Way, New Bern, NC 28562

ROBERTS, Matthew James (NwT)

ROBERTS, Mollie (EC) 3702 Mays Bend Rd, Pell City, AL 35128

ROBERTS, Patricia Joyce (Ia) 3226 S Clinton St, Sioux City, IA 51106

ROBERTS, Patricia Kant (CFla) 35 Willow Dr, Orlando, FL 32807

ROBERTS, Paul Benjamin (At) 33 Cross Crk E, Dahlonega, GA 30533

ROBERTS, Peter (CFla) 5500 N Tropical Trl, Merritt Island, FL 32953

ROBERTS, Rebecca N (CNY)

ROBERTS, Steven Michael (La) 1613 7th St, New Orleans, LA 70115

ROBERTS, Susan Jean (WMo) 261 S 900 E, Salt Lake City, UT 84102

ROBERTS, Suzanne (Me) 143 State St, Portland, ME 04101

ROBERTS, William Bradley (Va) 8633 Devara Ct, Richmond, VA 23235

ROBERTS, William D (Chi) 720 Ambria Dr, Mundelein, IL 60060

ROBERTS, William Tudor (Mich) 43050 12 Oaks Crescent Dr Apt 3066 Unit 3066, Unit 3066, Novi, MI 48377

ROBERTSHAW III, Arthur Bentham (Ct) 88 Notch Hill Rd Apt 240, North Branford, CT 06471

ROBERTSHAW, Michelle (SwFla) St Andrews Episcopal Church, PO Box 272, Boca Grande, FL 33921

ROBERTSON, Amanda Kucik (USC) 2701 Park Rd, Charlotte, NC 28209

ROBERTSON IV, Ben G (Miss) The Chapel Of The Cross, 674 Mannsdale Rd, Madison, MS 39110

ROBERTSON, Bruce Edward (NMich) 452 Silver Creek Rd, Marquette, MI 49855

ROBERTSON, Charles Kevin (Az) 815 2nd Ave, New York, NY 10017

ROBERTSON, Claude Richard (Ark) 1605 E Republican Rd, Jacksonville, AR 72076

ROBERTSON, James Bruce (CPa) 4824 Bell Street, Kansas City, MO 64112

ROBERTSON, John (Minn) 38378 Reservation Highway 101, PO Box 369, Morton, MN 56270

ROBERTSON, John Brown (EC) St Timothy's Epis Church, 107 Louis St, Greenville, NC 27858

ROBERTSON, Josephine (Oly) St John's Kirkland, 105 State St S, Kirkland, WA 98033

ROBERTSON, Karen (Suzi) Sue (Oly) 1757 244th Ave NE, Sammamish, WA 98074

ROBERTSON, Kristin C (Los)

ROBERTSON, Marilyn Sue (Okla) 127 NW 7th St, Oklahoma City, OK 73102

ROBERTSON, Patricia Rome (Oly) 313 Bromley Pl NW, Bainbridge Island, WA 98110

ROBESON, Terry Ann (Wyo) 665 Cedar St, Lander, WY 82520

ROBINSON, Allen (LI) 2729 Moores Valley Dr, Baltimore, MD 21209

✠ **ROBINSON**, Bishop Gene Gene (NH) Diocese Of New Hampshire, 63 Green St., Washington, DC 20005

ROBINSON, Carla Lynn (Oly) 15220 Main St, Bellevue, WA 98007

ROBINSON, Charles (SVa) 9470 Astilbe Ln, Toano, VA 23168

ROBINSON, Charles Edward (U) PO Box 981208, Park City, UT 84098

ROBINSON, Chris (Miss) 113 S 9th St, Oxford, MS 38655

ROBINSON, Constance Diane (Eas) 5820 Haven Ct, Rock Hall, MD 21661

ROBINSON, Cristopher Allan (WTex) 21126 Marin Hls, San Antonio, TX 78259

ROBINSON, David (Me) PO Box 7554, Ocean Park, ME 04063

ROBINSON JR, David Gordon (NH) 91 Osprey Dr, Portsmouth, NH 03801

ROBINSON, David Gordon (Eas) 5820 Haven Ct, Rock Hall, MD 21661

ROBINSON, David Scott (Pa) 603 Misty Hollow Dr, Maple Glen, PA 19002

ROBINSON, Dorothy Linkous (Tex) 7700 Pleasant Meadow Cir, Austin, TX 78731

ROBINSON, Fred (SwFla) 222 South Palm Avenue, Sarasota, FL 34236

ROBINSON, Janet Rohrbach (Ga) 3565 Bemiss Rd, Valdosta, GA 31605

ROBINSON, Joseph O (Mass) 120 High St, Wareham, MA 02571

ROBINSON, Katherine Sternberg (Wyo) 2350 S Poplar St, Casper, WY 82601

ROBINSON, Linda Gail H Hornbuckle (Ala) 6324 Woodlake Dr., Buford, GA 30518

ROBINSON, Mark K J (Ct) 5 Mccurdy, Old Lyme, CT 06371

ROBINSON, Michael Eric (Mass) 171 Goddard Ave, Brookline, MA 02445

ROBINSON, Michael Kevin (Ark) 305 Pointer Trl W, Van Buren, AR 72956

ROBINSON, Paula (Mo) 123 S 9th St, Columbia, MO 65201

ROBINSON, Sonja Douglas (EC) 1009 Midland Dr, Wilmington, NC 28412

ROBINSON JR, Virgil Austin Anderson (Chi) 1527 Chapel Ct, Northbrook, IL 60062

ROBINSON-COMO, Glenice (Tex) 1117 Texas St, Houston, TX 77002

ROBISON, Bruce (Pgh) 5801 Hampton St, Pittsburgh, PA 15206

ROBISON, Jeannie (Ala) Church of the Nativity, 208 Eustis Ave SE, Huntsville, AL 35801

ROBISON, Sandra L(ee) (Spok) 1407 Thayer Dr, Richland, WA 99354

ROBLES, Daniel (DomRep)

ROBLES, Lawrence A (ECR) C O Rev La Robles, 1441 Constitution Blvd, Salinas, CA 93906

ROBSON, David (CPa) 2985 Raintree Rd, York, PA 17404

ROCCOBERTON, Marjorie Ruth Smith (Ct) 82 Shoddy Mill Rd, Bolton, CT 06043

ROCK, Ian Eleazar (Episcopal VI)

ROCK, Jean Baptiste Kenol (Ct) 3061 Bainbridge Ave, Bronx, NY 10467

ROCK, J Konrad (WK) 706 E 74th Ave, Hutchinson, KS 67502

ROCK, John Sloane (Minn) PO BOX 1178, Bemidji, MN 56619

ROCK, Thomas A (Vt)

ROCKHILL, Cara M (Mass)

ROCKMAN, Jane Linda (NJ) 559 Park Ave, Scotch Plains, NJ 07076

ROCKWELL, Cristine Van Kirk (WMass) 51 Perkins St, Springfield, MA 01118

ROCKWELL, Hays H (Mo) Po Box 728, West Kingston, RI 02892

ROCKWELL, Melody Neustrom (Ia) 220 40th St NE, Cedar Rapids, IA 52402

ROCKWELL, Raymond Eugene (Alb)

ROCKWELL III, Reuben L (Del) 604 Marilyn Ct, Townsend, DE 19734

ROCKWELL, Sarah (NH) 10 Pond Rd, Derry, NH 03038

ROCKWOOD, David Alan (Ak) Po Box 23003, Ketchikan, AK 99901

RODDY, Bonnie Joia (Ore) 266 E 4th Ave Apt 601, Salt Lake City, UT 84103

RODDY, Jack Edward (Ore) 266 E 4th Ave Apt 601, Salt Lake City, UT 84103

RODENBECK, Benjamin Daniel (Az) Trinity Episcopal Church, PO Box 590, Kingman, AZ 86402

RODGERS, Beverly (Okla)

RODGERS, Carol Ellen (NJ)

RODGERS, James Devin (SO) 1935 Bryant Ave S Apt 7, Minneapolis, MN 55403

RODGERS, Paul Benjamin (Mass) 359 Elm St, Dartmouth, MA 02748

RODGERS, Peter R (Ct) 400 Humphrey St, New Haven, CT 06511

RODGERS, Stephen M (NY) 14160 SW Teal Blvd. 32 B, Beaverton, OR 97008

RODIN, Carol Jane Strandoo (Oly) Christ Episcopal Church, 1216 7th St, Anacortes, WA 98221

RODMAN, Edward Willis (Mass) 8 Yorks Rd, Framingham, MA 01701

RODMAN, Janet Laura (EC) 218 Fairway Drive, Washington, DC 27889

RODMAN III, Samuel (NC) 112 Randolph Ave, Milton, MA 02186

RODRICK, David Andrew (USC)

RODRIGUEZ, Al (Tex) 2503 Ware Rd, Austin, TX 78741

RODRIGUEZ, Christopher Michael (CFla) 2365 Pine Ave, Vero Beach, FL 32960

RODRIGUEZ, Edwin (Az)

RODRIGUEZ, Gladys (CFla) 1601 Alafaya Trl, Oviedo, FL 32765

RODRIGUEZ, Hector Raul (Md) 6960 Sunfleck Row, Columbia, MD 21045

RODRIGUEZ, Isaas (At) 3004 Mccully Dr NE, Atlanta, GA 30345

RODRIGUEZ, Jose Santiago (Va)

RODRIGUEZ, Julius Sophia (Va)

RODRIGUEZ, Julius M (Episcopal SJ) 5286 Kalanianaole Hwy, Honolulu, HI 96821

RODRIGUEZ, Omar (Az)

RODRIGUEZ JR, Pedro Luis (NY)

RODRIGUEZ, Ramiro (Los) 7540 Passons Blvd, Pico Rivera, CA 90660

RODRIGUEZ ESPINEL, Neptali (Minn) 1524 Summit Ave, Saint Paul, MN 55105

RODRIGUEZ GERMAN, Domingo Antonio (DomRep)

RODRIGUEZ-HOBBS, Joshua (Md) Tec Ch Of The Good Shpd, 1401 Carrollton Ave, Ruxton, MD 21204

RODRIGUEZ-LAUREANI, Yuriria (Ind)

RODRIGUEZ-PADRON, Francisco (LI) 418 50th St, Brooklyn, NY 11220

RODRIGUEZ RODRIGUEZ, Santiago (Cu)

RODRIGUEZ SANCHEZ, Mario Hiram (PR) PO Box 9262, San Juan, PR 00908

RODRIGUEZ-SANJURJO, Jose (CFla) Church of the Incarnation, 1601 Alafaya Trl, Oviedo, FL 32765

RODRIGUEZ-SANTOS, Carlos (Hond)

RODRIGUEZ SANTOS, Noel Josue (Cu)

RODRIGUEZ-SANTOS, Toribio (NJ) 38 W End Pl, Elizabeth, NJ 07202

RODRIGUEZ TOUCET, Maritza (PR)

RODRIGUEZ-YEJO, Ruben (Del) 1005 Pleasant St, Wilmington, DE 19805

ROECK, Gretchen Elizabeth (Minn) 5330 Oliver Ave S, Minneapolis, MN 55419

ROEHL, Cynthia Ann (SwFla) 639 Edgewater Dr, Dunedin, FL 34698

ROEHNER, Rodney (CFla) 919 Tennis Ave, Maple Glen, PA 19002

ROESCHLAUB, Robert Friedrich (Ind) 20 Pannatt Hill, Millom, Cumbria, LA18 5DB, Great Britain (UK)

ROESKE, Michael Jerome (NI) 35 Bowdoin St, Boston, MA 02114

ROESSLER, Richard (Alb)

ROFF, Lucinda Lee (Ala) 812 5th Ave, Tuscaloosa, AL 35401

ROFINOT, Laurie Ann (Mass) 88 Lexington Ave # 2, Somerville, MA 02144

ROGERS, Annis Humphries (Pgh) 335 Locust St, Johnstown, PA 15901

ROGERS, Diana (Ct) 20 Shepherd Ln, Orange, CT 06477

ROGERS III, George M (Alb) 325 East 80th Street, 1D, New York, NY 10021

ROGERS, Henry Stanley Fraser (Oly) 4770 116th Ave Se, Bellevue, WA 98006

ROGERS JR, Jack (WTenn) 225 Birch Tree Loop, Oxford, MS 38655

ROGERS, James Arthur (Tex) 4302 Wynnwood Dr, Wichita Falls, TX 76308

ROGERS, John Sanborn (RI) 106 Osprey Dr, Saint Marys, GA 31558

ROGERS, Joy Edith Stevenson (Chi) 65 E Huron St, Chicago, IL 60611

ROGERS, Larry Samuel (Okla) 1310 N Sioux Ave, Claremore, OK 74017

ROGERS, Linda Franks (SVa) All Saints Episcopal Church, 1969 Woodside Ln, Virginia Beach, VA 23454

ROGERS, Martha C (Ia)

ROGERS, Matthew Arnold (Md) 3100 Monkton Rd, Monkton, MD 21111

ROGERS, Norma Jean (Az) PO Box 4567, Tubac, AZ 85646

ROGERS, Page (Ct) 99 Lee Farm Dr, Niantic, CT 06357

ROGERS, Rhonda (Tex)

ROGERS, Sandra K (SwFla)

ROGERS, Sean Michael (EO)

ROGERS III, Thomas Sherman (Chi) 1653 West Congress Parkway, Chicago, IL 60612

ROGERS, Tim (Mass) 2920 NE 8th Ter Apt 101, Wilton Manors, FL 33334

ROGERS, Victor (Ct) 111 Whalley Ave, New Haven, CT 06511

ROGERS, William Burns (Tenn) 510 W Main St, Franklin, TN 37064

ROGGE, Joel Jay (WA) 23 State St Apt 2, Marblehead, MA 01945

ROGINA, Julius M (Nev) 1080 Del Webb Pkwy West, Reno, NV 89523

ROGNAS, Alice Anita (Mont) 713 8th St, Lewiston, ID 83501

ROHDE, John W (CNY)

ROHDE, Kay M (NAM) 1326 East A St., Casper, WY 82601

ROHLEDER, Catherine Christine (Kan)

ROHMAN, Suzannah (Me) St. Paul's Episcopal Church, 145 Main St., Southington, CT 06489

ROHRBACH, Marissa S (Ct) St Andrews Episcopal Church, 20 Catlin St, Meriden, CT 06450

ROHRER, Jane Carolyn (Oly) Tec Ch Of The H Cross, 11526 162nd Ave NE, Redmond, WA 98052

ROHRS, Andrea (SVa) 3 Bisley Ct, Henrico, VA 23238

ROHRS, John D (Va) 3 Bisley Ct, Henrico, VA 23238

ROJAS-ARROYO, Padre Sergio (PR)

ROJAS POVEDA, Jesus A (EC) 737 Delma Grimes Rd, Coats, NC 27521

ROLAND, Carla (NY) Ch of St Matthew St Timothy, 26 W 84th St, New York, NY 10024

ROLDAN, Roman D (Tex) 11621 Ferdinand St, Saint Francisville, LA 70775

ROLES, Elizabeth J (WNC) 175 9th Ave # 123, New York, NY 10011

ROLFE-BOUTWELL, Suzan Jane (Mass) 7588 N Meredith Blvd, Tucson, AZ 85741

ROLLE, Denrick Ephriam (SeFla)

ROLLE, Yolanda Antoinette (Mass) 54 Williams Ave Unit A, Unit A, Boston, MA 02136

ROLLINS, Andrew Sloan (La) 640 Carriage Way, Baton Rouge, LA 70808

ROLLINS, John August (Nwk) 11 Fine Road, High Bridge, NJ 08829

ROLLINS, Wayne (SO) 2919 N Knightsbridge Cir, Ann Arbor, MI 48105

ROLLO, Katherine (Nwk)

ROMACK, Gay Harpster (Az) 609 N Old Litchfield Rd, Litchfield Park, AZ 85340

ROMANELLI, Leah L (O)

ROMANIK, David F (NwT) 230 Pennswood Rd, Bryn Mawr, PA 19010

ROMANS, Nicholas J (Chi) 514 S Mountain Road, Mesa, AZ 85208

ROMER, William Miller (NH) 128 Audubon Dr, Acton, MA 01720

ROMERIL, Gwendolyn Jane (Be) 26 W Market St, Bethlehem, PA 18018

ROMERO, Arnoldo L (WTex)

✠ **ROMERO**, Sylvestre Donato (NJ) 808 W State St, Trenton, NJ 08618-5326, Guatemala

ROMERO-GUEVARA, Antonio N (EcuC) Dias De La Madrid 943, Quito, Ecuador

ROMERO MARTE, Francisco Alfredo (DomRep)

ROMO-GARCIA, Gerardo (LI) 147 Shade Tree Ln, Riverhead, NY 11901

RONALDI, Lynn P (Va) Episcopal Church Of The Advent, PO Box 366, Sumner, MS 38957

RONDEAU, Daniel James (SanD) 44910 Calle Placido, La Quinta, CA 92253

RONKOWITZ, George (SeFla) 8310 SW 60th Ave, South Miami, FL 33143

RONN, Denise (Ga) 4 Mulberry Way, Cartersville, GA 30120

RONNINGEN, Greta (ECR)

RONTANI, Aidan A (The Episcopal NCal)

RONTANI JR, William (The Episcopal NCal) 104 Main St., Wheatland, CA 95692

ROOD JR, Peter (Los) 702 W Alegria Ave, Sierra Madre, CA 91024

ROOS, Michelle Kate (Ind) 720 Dr Martin Luther King Jr St, Indianapolis, IN 46202

ROOS, Rich (Ind) 2033 Paradise Oaks Ct, Atlantic Beach, FL 32233

ROOSEVELT, Nancy (O) 17100 Van Aken Blvd, Shaker Heights, OH 44120

ROOSEVELT, Nick (Ga) 1007 Persimmon Ave, Sunnyvale, CA 94087

ROOT, Diane (Vt) 2 Jones Ave, West Lebanon, NH 03784

ROPER, Jeffrey Howard (Kan) 3750 E Douglas Ave, Wichita, KS 67208

ROPER, John Dee (Kan) 14802 E Willowbend Cir, Wichita, KS 67230

ROPER, Terence Chaus (Pa) 1815 John F Kennedy Blvd, Philadelphia, PA 19103

ROQUE, Christopher Collin (WTex) 2019 Douglas Dr, San Angelo, TX 76904

RORABACK, Leslie Enid (EC)

RORKE, Stephen Ernest (Roch) 6727 Royal Thomas Way, Alexandria, VA 22315

ROS, Salvador Patrick (NJ)

ROSA, Thomas Phillip (Chi) 121 W Macomb St, Belvidere, IL 61008

ROSADA, Miguel Andres (Fla)

ROSA-MALDONADO, Jorge R (PR) 248 Smith Rd SW, Rome, GA 30165

ROSANAS, Louis (Hai) Box 1309, Port-Au-Prince, Haiti

ROSARIO-CRUZ, Eliacin (Oly) 111 NE 80th St, Seattle, WA 98115

ROSARIO DE LA CRUZ, P. Guelmy (Nwk) 3901 Park Ave, Union City, NJ 07087

ROSE, Ann W (Ore) 7 Saint Johns Rd Apt 30, Cambridge, MA 02138

ROSE, Christopher Lee (Ct) 30 Woodland St Unit 10np, Hartford, CT 06105

ROSE, David D (SwVa) 210 4th St., Radford, VA 24141

ROSE, David Jonathan (Ga) 2421 Menokin Dr Apt 103, Alexandria, VA 22302

ROSE, Heather (Az)

ROSE, Joseph (Ct)

ROSE, Josie Rodriguez (NwT) 5539 7th Ave N, Saint Petersburg, FL 33710

ROSE, Joy Ann (Nwk) 4376 Caliquen Dr, Brooksville, FL 34604

ROSE, Leland Gerald (WNY) 602 Crescent Ave, East Aurora, NY 14052

ROSE, L(oran) A(nson) Paul (WA) 6101 Edsall Rd Apt 508, Alexandria, VA 22304

ROSE, Margaret (NY) 531 E 72nd St Apt 3c, New York, NY 10021

ROSE, Patricia M (SO)

ROSE, Philip John (Minn) 7708 Upton Ave S, Minneapolis, MN 55423

ROSE-CROSSLEY, Ramona (Vt) 327 University Ave, Sewanee, TN 37375

ROSE-CROSSLEY, Remington (Vt)

ROSEN, Carolyn (Me) 119 N 33rd St, Billings, MT 59101

ROSEN, Elisabeth Payne (Cal) P O Box 1306, Ross, CA 94957

ROSENBERG, Elma Joy Van Fossen (SwFla) 125 56th Ave S Apt 314, Saint Petersburg, FL 33705

ROSENBLUM, Nancy Jo (Alb) 22 Buckingham Dr, Albany, NY 12208

ROSENDAHL, Mary (CFla) 1043 Genesee Avenue, Sebastian, FL 32958

ROSENDALE, Mary (WMass)

ROSENGREN, Linda W (Fla) 5054 Ripple Rush Dr N, Jacksonville, FL 32257

ROSERO-NORDALM, Ema (Mass) St Stephen's Episcopal Church, 419 Shawmut Ave, Boston, MA 02118

ROSHEUVEL, Terrence Winst (NJ) 25 Sunset Ave E, Red Bank, NJ 07701

✠ **ROSKAM**, Catherine Scimeca (NY) 15502 Friar St, Van Nuys, CA 91411

ROSOLEN, Emil J (SeFla) 100 NE Mizner Blvd # 1503, Boca Raton, FL 33432

ROSOLOWSKI, Robert (Eau)

ROSS, Anne M (NY) 88 Ridge Rd, Valley Cottage, NY 10989

ROSS, David Jeffrey (Cal) Po Box 774, Pinole, CA 94564

ROSS, Donna Baldwin (ECR) 3291 Pickwick Ln, Cambria, CA 93428

ROSS, Ellen Marie (Neb) 106 Robin Rd, Council Bluffs, IA 51503

ROSS, George Mark (Minn) Po Box 1231, Cass Lake, MN 56633

ROSS, Jeffrey Austin (Del) 224 Second St, Lewes, DE 19958

ROSS, John (ETenn) 413 Cumberland Ave, Knoxville, TN 37902

ROSS, Johnnie (Roch) 250 Danbury Cir S, Rochester, NY 14618

ROSS, Jonathan (Vt)

ROSS, Nancy J (Oly) 2225 Mattison Ln Apt B, Apt B, Santa Cruz, CA 95062

ROSS, Patricia Lynn (Cal) 215 10th Ave, San Francisco, CA 94118

ROSS, Robert (Md) 91 Miry Brook Rd, Danbury, CT 06810

ROSS, Rowena Jane (RG)

ROSS, Sue (Dal) 2679 Orchid Dr, Richardson, TX 75082

ROSSER SR, James Bernard (At) 2703 Sanibel Ln Se, Smyrna, GA 30082

ROSS-HUNT, Lindsay S (Oly)

ROSSI, Anna Elaine (Cal)

ROSSI, Kim Elizabeth (WNY) St Stephen's Episcopal Church, PO Box 446, Olean, NY 14760

ROSSI, Matthew Jordan (Dal)

ROTCHFORD, Lisa Marie (Los) 24352 Via Santa Clara, Mission Viejo, CA 92692

ROTH, Marilyn Lee (EO) 1805 Minnesota St, The Dalles, OR 97058

ROTH, Ralph C (Be) Phoebe Berks Village, 1 Reading Dr Apt 107, Wernersville, PA 19565

ROTHAUGE, Arlin John (Ore) 197 Lighthouse Ln, Friday Harbor, WA 98250

ROTTGERS, Steve (WMo) 3521 NW Winding Woods Dr, Lees Summit, MO 64064

ROUFFY, Edward Albert (Colo) 950 SW 21st Ave Apt 402, Portland, OR 97205

ROUMAS, Peisha Geneva (WMo) 91 E 100th Ter, Kansas City, MO 64131

ROUNDS, James Arlen (Wyo) PO Box 1194, Laramie, WY 82073
ROUNDTREE, Ella Louise (Ga) 101 Herons Bill Dr, Bluffton, SC 29909
ROUNTREE, Philip (Cal) 60 Martinez Ct, Novato, CA 94945
ROUSE, Charles Ernest (The Episcopal NCal)
ROUSER, John Richard (ETenn) 7555 Ooltewah Georgetown Rd, Ooltewah, TN 37363
ROUSSEAU, Sean Kenneth (Va) St Pauls Episcopal Church, 6750 Fayette St, Haymarket, VA 20169
ROUSSELL, Chris (SwVa) Emmanuel Episcopal Church, 717 Quincy St, Rapid City, SD 57701
ROWAN, Mary Elizabeth (Minn)
ROWE, Deryl Tobias (Ark)
ROWE, Gary (Del) 2013 Dogwood Ln, Wilmington, DE 19810
ROWE, Grayce O'Neill (Az) 1423 E Blue Wash Rd, New River, AZ 85087
ROWE, Jacquelyn (NJ) PO Box 326, Pine Beach, NJ 08741
ROWE, Mary Stone (Mont)
ROWE, Matthew (NwT) Emmanuel Episcopal Church, 3 S Randolph St, San Angelo, TX 76903
ROWE, Michael (SwFla) 9213 Estero River Cir, Estero, FL 33928
ROWE, Randi Hicks (WNY) 9 Cedar St, Lockport, NY 14094
ROWE, Richard (WNC) 64 Oak Gate Dr, Hendersonville, NC 28739
ROWE, Richard Charles (NwPa) 706 Wilhelm Rd, Hermitage, PA 16148
ROWE, Sandra Jeanne (CFla) PO Box 2206, Breckenridge, CO 80424
ROWE, Sean (NwPa) 4024 State St, Erie, PA 16508
ROWE-GUIN, Kathy (Va) 5911 Fairview Woods Dr, Fairfax Station, VA 22039
ROWELL, Emily Elizabeth (Ala) 5801 Candler Ave, Tuscaloosa, AL 35406
ROWELL, Melanie Gibson (At)
ROWELL, Rebecca E (Ga) 6329 Frederica Rd, St Simons Island, GA 31522
ROWINS, Charles Howard (Los) 1 Warrenton Rd, Baltimore, MD 21210
ROWLAND, Thomas Dayle (RG) St Paul's Episcopal Church, PO Box 949, Truth Or Consequences, NM 87901
ROWLES, Stephen Paul (Va) 9116 Shewsbury Dr, New Kent, VA 23124
ROWLEY, Angela (Ct) Yale New Haven Hospital, 20 York Street, New Haven, CT 06510
ROWTHORN, Jeffery William (Ct) 17 Woodland Dr, Salem, CT 06420
ROY, Derik Justin Hurd (Alb) 10 W High St, Ballston Spa, NY 12020
ROY, Jeffrey A (NJ) 7 Lincoln Ave, Rumson, NJ 07760
ROY, Robert Royden (Minn) 1289 Galtier St, Saint Paul, MN 55117
ROY, Thomas D (Minn)

ROYAL, Dorothy Kaye (Neb) St Mary's Episcopal Church, 116 S 9th St, Nebraska City, NE 68410
ROYALS, Debbie (Az) 401 E Lawton St, Tucson, AZ 85704
ROYALTY, Beth (Minn) 1422 13th Ave NE, Rochester, MN 55906
ROYCE, Geoffrey Swenson (Pgh)
ROZENDAAL, Jay Calvin (Oly) 1134 Finnegan Way # 302, Bellingham, WA 98225
ROZENE, Wendy Anne (Me) 17 Fox Run Rd, Cumberland, ME 04021
ROZO, Oscar Andres (WNC) 321 N Cedar St, Lincolnton, NC 28092
ROZZELLE, Stephen (Nwk) 400 Ramapo Avenue, Pompton Lakes, NJ 07442
RUBEL, Christopher Scott (Los) 250 N Live Oak Ave, Glendora, CA 91741
RUBENDALL III, Charles Wesley (NJ)
RUBIANO-ALVARADO, Raul (CFla) 2851 Afton Cir, Orlando, FL 32825
RUBIN, Richard Louis (Los) 163 W. 11th St., Claremont, CA 91711
RUBINSON, Rhonda Joy (NY) 400 W 119th St Apt 11l, New York, NY 10027
RUBRIGHT, Elizabeth Alice Shemet (SwFla)
RUCKER, Eric Joseph (Ia)
RUCKER, James Cliff (Tex) 203 Ivy Terrace St, Lufkin, TX 75901
RUDACILLE, Stephen L (SwFla) 2702 Saint Cloud Oaks Dr, Valrico, FL 33594
RUDE, David B (Nwk) 109 Wisperwood Dr, Dingmans Ferry, PA 18328
RUDER, John Williams (Oly) 602 6th St, Castlegar, BC V1N2G1, Canada
RUDER, Rhonda (Minn)
RUDOLPH, Patrick Charles (FdL) 1036 Pine Beach Rd, Marinette, WI 54143
RUEDY, Shirley Eloise (SwVa) 302 N New St, Staunton, VA 24401
RUEHLEN, Petroula Kephala (Tex) 3541 Adrienne Ln, Lake Charles, LA 70605
RUETTEN, Mary K (SwVa) St John's Episcopal Church, PO Box 257, Roanoke, VA 24002
RUFFIN, Hunter (Az) 8011 Douglas Ave, Dallas, TX 75225
RUFFINO, Russell Gabriel (Eur) Corso Cavour 110, CP 81, Orvieto, 05018, Italy
RUGG, Stephen Peter (NH)
RUGGABER, Michael Paul (Nev)
RUGGER, Mildred Susan (NwT) St Andrew's Episcopal Church, 1601 S Georgia St, Amarillo, TX 79102
RUGGLES, Roxanne (Lex) Church of the Nativity, PO Box 3, Maysville, KY 41056
RUGH, Nathan (Los) 1227 4th St, Santa Monica, CA 90401
RUHLE, Kay West (CFla)

RUIZ, Ana L (EcuC)
✠ **RUIZ RESTREPO**, Luis Fernando (DomRep) Carrera 80 #53 A 78, Medellin, Colombia
RUIZ-RIQUER, Cynthia S (Tex) 5910 Black Oak Ln, River Oaks, TX 76114
RUK, Michael (Pa) 10 Chapel Rd, New Hope, PA 18938
RULE II, John Henry (Okla) 1122 E 20th St, Tulsa, OK 74120
RUMPLE, John G (Chi) 550 University Blvd # 1410, Indianapolis, IN 46202
RUNDLETT, Brad (Va) St Timothys Episcopal Church, 432 Van Buren St, Herndon, VA 20170
RUNGE, Phillip Diedrich (RG) 338 Lakeview Dr, Baxley, GA 31513
RUNGE, Thomas Leonard (Lex) 7 Court Pl, Newport, KY 41071
RUNKLE, John Ander (Tenn) PO Box 815, Sewanee, TN 37375
RUNNELS, Stan (WMo) 11 E 40th St, Kansas City, MO 64111
RUNNER, Paul W (NJ) 370 Main St, Wakefield, RI 02879
RUNNING JR, Joseph Martin (EC) 3207 Notting Hill Rd, Fayetteville, NC 28311
RUPP, Lawrence Dean (SO) 13 Balsam Acres, New London, NH 03257
RUPP, Tuesday Jane (Ct) 249 Main St S, Woodbury, CT 06798
RUPPE, David (SO) 25005 SR 26, New Matamoras, OH 45767
RUPPE-MELNYK, Glyn Lorraine (Pa) 689 Sugartown Road, Malvern, PA 19355
RUSCHMEYER, Henry Cassell (NY) 2929 SE Ocean Blvd Apt M9, Stuart, FL 34996
RUSH, Joyce Anne (Minn) 407 Nw 7th St, Brainerd, MN 56401
RUSHTON, Joseph Michael (Eas) 12305 Wight St, Ocean City, MD 21842
RUSK, Michael Frederick (Eur) 3 rue de Monthoux, Geneva, 01201, Switzerland
RUSLING, Julia G (La) 432 Lockwood Ter, Decatur, GA 30030
RUSS JR, Frank D (SC) 1159 Wyndham Rd, Charleston, SC 29412
RUSSELL, Ann Veronica (Episcopal VI) Box 3066, Sea Cow's Bay, Tortola, British Virgin Island VG 1110, British Virgin Islands
RUSSELL, Carlton Thrasher (Mass) 27 Abnaki Way, Stockton Springs, ME 04981
RUSSELL, Charles A (Ind)
RUSSELL, John Alan (WNY) 768 Potomac Ave, Buffalo, NY 14209
RUSSELL, Kathleen Sams (Tex) 1823 Montana Sky Drive, Austin, TX 78727
RUSSELL, Kenneth Paul (Ore) 5311 Sw Wichita St, Tualatin, OR 97062
RUSSELL, Margaret Ellen Street (Me) 9 Perkins Rd, Boothbay Harbor, ME 04538

RUSSELL, Michael (Tex) 3112 James St, San Diego, CA 92106
RUSSELL, Patricia Griffith (NwT) 1802 Broadway, Lubbock, TX 79401
RUSSELL, Scott (NJ) 2365 McAleer Rd, Sewickley, PA 15143
RUSSELL, Sherrill Ann (WMo) 7110 N State Route 9, Kansas City, MO 64152
RUSSELL, Steven Scott (Eau)
RUSSELL, Susan (Los) 680 Mountain View St, Altadena, CA 91001
RUSSELL, Susan Hayden (Mass) 72 Cavendish Cir, Salem, MA 01970
RUTENBAR, C Harles Mark (WTenn) 7774 Grand Point Rd, Presque Isle, MI 49777
RUTENBAR, LaRae (WMich) 8238 Greengate Cv, Cordova, TN 38018
RUTHERFORD, Allen (Ind) 420 Locust St, Mount Vernon, IN 47620
RUTHERFORD, Ellen C (NJ) 1115 New Pear St, Vineland, NJ 08360
RUTHERFORD, Thomas Houston (CFla) 1260 Log Landing Dr, Ocoee, FL 34761
RUTHERFORD, Timothy (CFla)
RUTHVEN, Carol (Lex) 926 Mason Headley Rd, Lexington, KY 40504
RUTHVEN, Scott (RG) 805 Lenox Ave., Las Cruces, NM 88005
RUTHY, Rosemary (Eau)
RUTLEDGE, Andrew Brooks (Md)
RUTLEDGE, Fleming (NY) 38 Hillandale Rd, Rye Brook, NY 10573
RUTLEDGE, Lynn V (Me) 13 Garnet Head Rd, Pembroke, ME 04666
RUTLEDGE, Shawn Joseph (Az)
RUTTAN, Karl D (Ky) 324 E Main St Unit 213, Unit 213, Louisville, KY 40202
RUTTER, Deborah Wood (Va) PO Box 1306, Front Royal, VA 22630
RUVALCABA, Carlos Enrique (Los)
RUYAK, Mark A (Cal) 5 Weatherly Drive Apt 109, Mill Valley, CA 94941
RUYLE, Everett Eugene (At) 1195 Terramont Dr, Roswell, GA 30076
RWAMASIRABO, Nfikije Mugisha (NJ)
RYAN, Adele Marie (Mass) 50 Harden Hill Rd, Box C, Duxbury, MA 02331
RYAN, Bartholomew Grey (Chi) 2713 6 3/16 Ave, New Auburn, WI 54757
RYAN, Dennis L (Miss) 3507 Pine St, Pascagoula, MS 39567
RYAN III, Frances Isabel Sells (Az) 3150 N Winding Brook Rd, Flagstaff, AZ 86001
RYAN, Katherine (WNC) 1091 Copper Canyon Dr, Prosper, TX 75078
✠ **RYAN**, Kathryn McCrossen (Tex) 3402 Windsor Rd, Austin, TX 78703
RYAN, Matthew Wayne (NwPa) 67 Thomas-Ryan Road, Emporium, PA 15834
RYAN, Meg (Mo) 602 Broadmoor Dr Apt B, Chesterfield, MO 63017

RYAN, Michael James (WMich) St Johns Episcopal Church, 127 State St S, Kirkland, WA 98033
RYAN, Michelle Ann (Colo)
RYAN, William Wilson (WTenn) 9233 Speerberry Ln, #14101, Cordova, TN 38016
RYDER, Anne Elizabeth (WMass) PO Box 1294, Sheffield, MA 01257
RYDER, Barbara (SVa) 12 Spring St, Decatur, GA 30030
RYMER, Lionel Simon (Episcopal VI) Po Box 7335, St Thomas, VI 00801

S

SAAGER, Rebecca A (Lex) 311 Washington St, Frankfort, KY 40601
SAARE, Keith Robert (RG)
SABAS, Christine Janet (Eas)
SABETTI III, Henry Martin (Eas) 12822 Shrewsbury Church Rd, Kennedyville, MD 21645
SABOGAL GUTIERREZ, Diego Fernando (Colom)
SABOM, William Stephen (At) 1143 Sanden Ferry Dr, Decatur, GA 30033
SABUNE, Petero Aggrey Nkurunziza (NY) 293 Highland Ave, Newark, NJ 07104
SACCAROLA FAVARO, Flavio (EcuC) Apdo 08-01-404, Esmeraldas, Ecuador
SACHS, The Reverend Patti (Md) 1601 Pleasant Plains Rd, Annapolis, MD 21409
SACHS, William Lewis (Va) 509 Saint Christophers Road, Richmond, VA 23226
SADBERRY, Marcia L (Tex)
SADIQ, Nadeem (Alb)
SAFFORD, Timothy Browning (Eur) 24 School St, Dartmouth, MA 02748
SAHDEV, Michael Clifford (SeFla) 1829 Malcolm Ave Apt 5, Los Angeles, CA 90025
SAID, James T (Ga) 6742 Fox Club Ln, Brownsburg, IN 46112
SAIK, Robert (Az) 70 Kettle Point Ave Unit E, East Providence, RI 02914
SAILER, David Walter (WNC) 3 Oak Leaf Ln, Arden, NC 28704
SAINTILVER, Margarette (Hai)
SAINT JEAN, Santochena (Hai)
SAINT JUSTE, Vanel (DomRep)
SAINT LOUIS, Martial (Hai)
SAINT-PIERRE, Nathanael L B (NY) Haiti Con Of The Good Sam, 661 E 219th St, Bronx, NY 10467
SAINT ROMAIN, Brad (Tex) 3333 Castle Ave, Waco, TX 76710
SAINT-VIL, Renaud (Hai)
SAJNA, Barbara Jean Reiser (FdL) 2100 Ridges Rd, Baileys Harbor, WI 54202
SAKIN, Charles Robert (NJ) 1812 Rue De La Port Drive, Wall, NJ 07719
SAKRISON, David L (U) 280 E 300 S, Moab, UT 84532

SALAMONE, Robert Emmitt (At) 2490 Orchard Walk, Bogart, GA 30622
SALAMONY, Columba (Roch) 130 Water St Apt 308, Apt 308, Penn Yan, NY 14527
SALAZAR TAPIAS, Julio A (Colom)
SALCEDO, Federico B (PR) Cotto Station, PO Box 9699, Arecibo, PR 00613
SALIK, Lamuel Gill (Dal) 138 Liveoak St, Hereford, TX 79045
SALINARO, Katherine Ella Mae (Cal) 121 Sheffield, Hercules, CA 94547
SALISBURY, Katherine Ann (LI) 157 Montague St, Brooklyn, NY 11201
SALLES, Stacy (Mich) 67640 Van Dyke Rd # 10, Washington, MI 48095
SALMON JR, Abraham Dickerson (Md) 7351 Willow Rd Apt 2, Frederick, MD 21702
SALMON, Alan Kent (NJ) 4 Tara Ln, Delran, NJ 08075
SALMON JR, John Frederick (Nwk) 551 Medford Leas, Medford, NJ 08055
SALMON, Nina (SwVa) 1308 Crenshaw Ct, Lynchburg, VA 24503
SALMON, Walter Burley Stattmann (Va)
SALT, Alfred Lewis (Nwk) 4822 Martinique Way, Naples, FL 34119
SALTZGABER, Jan Mcminn (Ga) 225 W Point Dr, Saint Simons Island, GA 31522
SALVATIERRA SERIAN, Juan E (EcuC) Juan Salvatierra Serian, Apdo 17-11-6165, Quito, Ecuador
SAM, Albert Abuid Samuel (WNY) 7469 Dysinger Rd, Lockport, NY 14094
SAM, Helen (WNY) PO Box 14, Dunkirk, NY 14048
SAM, Rachelle (WA)
SAMILIO, Jamie (Va) 2455 Gallows Rd, Dunn Loring, VA 22027
SAMMIS, Robert Lyle (Los)
SAMMONS, Gregory P (O) 4684 Brittany Rd, Toledo, OH 43615
SAMPEY, Amanda (NH) PO Box 44, Mirror Lake, NH 03853
SAMPSON, Leon (NAM) PO Box 28, Bluff, UT 84512
SAMPSON, Paula Kathryn (Ak) 4317 Birch Avenue, Terrace, BC V8G 1X2, Canada
SAMRA, Gordon L (NI) 14823 Waterbrook Rd, Fort Wayne, IN 46814
SAMS, David Lee (Minn) 203 Aspenwood Drive, Redwood Falls, MN 56283
SAMS, Jonathan (Mich) 6402 Fredmoor Dr, Troy, MI 48098
SAMSON, Clive E P (Mo)
SAMUEL, Amjad John (Ct) 1361 W Market St, Akron, OH 44313
SAMUEL, Jason Wade (U) 650 S 100 E Apt K105, Logan, UT 84321
SAMUEL, Joshua (LI)
SAMUEL, Pauline Ann (At)

SAMUEL, Samuel (DomRep) Aptd 764, Santo Domingo, Dominican Republic

SAMUELS, Marguerite Anne (Eas)

SAMUELS, Robert Marshall (WNY) 201 Saint Francis Dr, Green Bay, WI 54301

SAMUELSON, Frank W (Tex) 3901 S Panther Creek Dr, The Woodlands, TX 77381

SAMUELSON, Louise B (Tex) 2450 River Oaks Blvd, Houston, TX 77019

SANBORN, Calvin (Me) Po Box 823, York Harbor, ME 03911

SANCHEZ, Jose D (Tex) 525 NE 15th St, Miami, FL 33132

SANCHEZ, Patricia Anne (U) 1579 S State St, Clearfield, UT 84015

SANCHEZ NAVARRO, Connie (Hond)

SANCHEZ NAVARRO, Jose Israel (Hond)

SANCHEZ NUNEZ, Carlos A (PR) PO Box 327, Manati, PR 00674

SANCHEZ ORTIGAS, Tulia Yoset (Cu)

SANCHEZ PUJOL, Sandino (DomRep) Santiago #114, Santo Domingo, Dominican Republic

SANCHEZ-SANCHEZ, Benjamin (Tex)

SANCHEZ-SHABAZZ, Jacqueline Marie (NY) 236 E 31st St, New York, NY 10016

SAND, David Allan (NMich) PO Box 805, Iron Mountain, MI 49801

SANDERS, Edwin Benjamin (Ky) 3812 Burning Bush Rd, Louisville, KY 40241

SANDERS, Harvel Ray (Mo) 110 Walnut Park Dr, Sedalia, MO 65301

SANDERS, Jaime Mw (Ore) 2190 Crest Dr, Lake Oswego, OR 97034

SANDERS, Lynn Coggins (NY) 5 Maitland Dr, Greenville, SC 29617

SANDERS, Marilyn Mae (CNY) 33092 Bay Ter, Lewes, DE 19958

SANDERS, Megan (NY) 226 E 60th St, Apt 3, New York, NY 10022

SANDERS, Patrick W (Miss)

SANDERS, Richard Devon (At)

SANDERS, Richard Evan (Ga) 605 Reynolds St, Augusta, GA 30901

SANDERS, The Rev Dr Joanne (Cal) 732 Laurel Ave, Menlo Park, CA 94025

SANDERS, Wayne Francis Michael (SanD) 3563 Merrimac Ave, San Diego, CA 92117

SANDERSON, Dow (SC) 218 Ashley Ave, Charleston, SC 29403

SANDERSON, Holladay Worth (Ida) All Saints Episcopal Church, 704 S Latah St, Boise, ID 83705

SANDERSON, Meredith Kadet (NY) 501 Cypress St, Liverpool, NY 13088

SANDFORT, Candace C (Nwk)

SANDLIN, Allan (At) 1881 Edinburgh Ter NE, Atlanta, GA 30307

SANDOE, Deirdre Etheridge (WA) 400 Rouen Dr Apt H, Deland, FL 32720

SANDOVAL, Carlos Juan (SeFla) 1000 NW North River Dr Apt 110, Miami, FL 33136

SANDOVAL, Juan (At) 161 Church St NE, Marietta, GA 30060

SANDS, Melissa Marie (SwFla)

SANDS, Robin Osborne (NC)

SANDS, Stacey Erin (SO)

SANDWELL-WEISS, Rosa Leah (Az) 8502 N Deer Valley Dr, Tucson, AZ 85742

SANFILIPPO, Matthew Paul (LI)

SANFORD, Carol Webb (WMo)

SANFORD, Gary Lee (NwT) 1801 Edmund Blvd, San Angelo, TX 76901

SANG, Clive Oscar (NJ) 26 E. Sunset Avenue, Red Bank, NJ 07701

SANGREY, William Frederick (SO)

SANON, Jean-Louis Felix (NY) 2757 Jacob Ln, Douglasville, GA 30135

SANTANA, Carlos Enrique (DomRep) (Md) Apartado 128, San Pedro De Macoris, Dominican Republic

SANTANA MERA, Goldi Amparo (Litoral Diocese Of Ecuador) Calle Ch Y La 29 Ava S N, Ambato, Ecuador

SANTANA-RUIZ, Benjamin (PR) 222 S Palm Ave, Sarasota, FL 34236

SANTIAGO, Vicente C (Pgh) 132 Sherwood Drive, Greensburg, PA 15601

SANTIAGO MERCADO, Carlos Geraldo (PR)

SANTIAGO-PADILLA, Gilberto (PR) Carr 187 KM 5.8, Mediana Alta, Loiza, PR 00772

SANTIBANEZ, Susana (Az)

SANTIVIAGO-ESPINAL, Maria Isabel (NY) 2453 78th St # 2, East Elmhurst, NY 11370

SANTMAN, Linda (Oly)

SANTOS, Elenito Bravo (NC) 221 Union St, Cary, NC 27511

SANTOS ABREGO, Concepcion (Hond) Espiritu Santo, Barrio Las Brisas, Santa Rita, Honduras

SANTOS-MONTES, Margarita (PR)

SANTOSUOSSO, John Edward (SwFla) 4860 Highlands Place Drive, Lakeland, FL 33813

SANTUCCI, Mark Albert (Ct) 166 Lambtown Rd, Ledyard, CT 06339

SANZO, Maria B (NJ) 318 Huxley Dr, Brick, NJ 08723

SAPP, Rose Marie (CFla)

SARAI-CLARK, Wilhelmina Olivia (Spok) 503 E D St, Moscow, ID 83843

SARDINAS IGLESIAS, Loida (Colom)

SARGENT, Arthur Lloyd (Dal) 213 Sierra Ridge Dr, San Marcos, TX 78666

SARRAZIN, Victor (NY) 12 Depot St, Middletown, NY 10940

SARTIN, George Randall (Fla) 3480 Lakeshore Dr, Tallahassee, FL 32312

SARTIN, Nancy Avera (Ga) 1521 N Patterson St, Valdosta, GA 31602

SASSER JR, Howell Crawford (Del) Saint Pauls Church, PO Box 764, Bloomsburg, PA 17815

SATERSTROM, Roger Thomas (Tenn) Christ Church Cathedral, 900 Broadway, Nashville, TN 37203

SATHER, Jerry (SwFla) 6 Deer Spg, Irvine, CA 92604

SATO, Judith Ann (Colo) 13741 Windrush dr, Colorado Springs, CO 80921

SATORIUS, Joanna (Los) PO Box 512164, Los Angeles, CA 90051

SATTERLY, Hazel (NMich)

SATTERLY, Norris Jay (NMich) 132 Henford Ave, Kingsford, MI 49802

SATULA, John A (Mass) 6schoolhouse Hill Road, Newtown, CT 06470

SAUCEDO SICA, Susan (Nwk) 407 N Broad St, Lansdale, PA 19446

✠ **SAULS**, Stacy F (Lex) 929 Star Shoot Pkwy, Lexington, KY 40509

SAUNDERS, Cora Germaine (At) 607 River Run Dr, Sandy Springs, GA 30350

SAUNDERS, John (Ga) General Theological Seminary, 175 9th Ave, New York, NY 10011

SAUNDERS III, Kenneth H (ETenn) 2094 Suncrest Village Ln, Gray, TN 37615

SAUNDERS, Lisa (NC) 3029 Mountainbrook Rd, Charlotte, NC 28210

SAUNDERSON, Ann Marie (Oly) 3918 N 24th St, Tacoma, WA 98406

SAUNKEAH, Bobby Reed (Okla) 110 E 17th St, Ada, OK 74820

SAVAGE-KING, Ruthann (NC) 148 Helena Ln, Archer Lodge, NC 27527

SAVASTANO, Peter (Nwk)

SAVIDGE, Karen (WMo) 207 N 7th St, Saint Joseph, MO 64501

SAVILLE III, John (Los) PO Box 152, Corona, CA 92878

SAVINO, Bella Jean (Ak) Po Box 70786, Fairbanks, AK 99707

SAWICKY, Blake (Cal) St Marks Berkeley, 2300 Bancroft Way, Berkeley, CA 94704

SAWTELLE, Gary Donald (Roch) 2171 Scottsville Rd, Scottsville, NY 14546

SAWYER, Alice Sherman (Mich) 205 Holly Ln, Dothan, AL 36301

SAWYER, Anne M (NY) 737 N 6th Ave, Tucson, AZ 85705

SAWYER, Frank D (USC) 210 S Indian River Dr, Fort Pierce, FL 34950

SAWYER, Gary Alan (Az)

SAWYER, Robert Claremont (NC) PO Box 28024, Raleigh, NC 27611

SAWYER, Stanley Whitfield (SVa) 2200 Cape Arbor Dr, Virginia Beach, VA 23451

SAWYER, Susan (Kan) 1640 Sunflower Rd, Clay Center, KS 67432

SAWYER, Vivian Ruth (CFla)

SAWYER HARMON, Cecily Judith (Del) 262 S College Ave, Newark, DE 19711

SAXE, Joshua Andrew (WVa) 218 Church St, Lewisburg, WV 24901

SAXE, Sarah (RI) 176 Wunnegin Cir, East Greenwich, RI 02818

SAXON, Mary-Margaret (Colo) 5527 Harrison Street, Kansas City, MO 64110

SAXON, Miriam (NC) 2214 Buck Quarter Farm Rd, Hillsborough, NC 27278

SAXTON II, Carl (Ala) 97 Mountain Meadow Rd, Gadsden, AL 35901

SAYLOR, Kristin Lee (Chi)

SAYLORS, Joann L (Tex) 1225 Texas St, Houston, TX 77002

SCALES, Linda (Ga) 4344 Miller Dr, Evans, GA 30809

SCALES JR, Louie Grady (Ga) 4344 Miller Drive, Evans, GA 30809

SCALIA, Deborah White (La) 10136 Walden Dr, River Ridge, LA 70123

SCALIA, Derek Michael (NH)

SCALISE, Margaret Mary (Ala) 8816 Old Greensboro Rd, 19103, Tuscaloosa, AL 35405

✠ **SCANLAN**, Audrey (CPa) 124 Brindle Rd, Mechanicsburg, PA 17055

SCANLAN, Paul Joseph (SO)

SCANLON, Geoffrey Edward Leyshon (Spr) 2910 E Stone Creek Blvd, Urbana, IL 61802

SCANNELL, Ann Frances (WMass)

SCANNELL, John Scott (Ore) 1350 NE 17th Ave Unit 1c, Portland, OR 97232

SCARBOROUGH, Anjel Lorraine (CPa) 300 Chervil Ct, Harrisburg, PA 17112

SCARBOROUGH, Stuart Kirby (CPa)

SCARCIA, Steven Angelo (Alb) 5989 State Route 5, PO Box 169, Herkimer, NY 13350

✠ **SCARFE**, Alan (Ia) 225 37th St, Des Moines, IA 50312

SCARFF, Stephen D (Alb) 129 Ledge Hill Rd, Guilford, CT 06437

SCARLETT, Jamal (RG)

SCARLETT, William George (Md)

SCARPACE, Ramona (Minn) 2035 Charlton Rd, Sunfish Lake, MN 55118

SCHAAL, Richard (CNY) 1504 76th Rd, Berkshire, NY 13736

SCHADT, Stuart Everett (Va) 6070 Greenway Ct, Manassas, VA 20111

SCHAEFER, Christine Marie (Ark)

SCHAEFER III, John (Neb) 7236 County Road 34, Fort Calhoun, NE 68023

SCHAEFER, Joslyn (WNC) 349 N Haywood St, Waynesville, NC 28786

SCHAEFER, Lee (Ind) 444 South Harbour Drive, Noblesville, IN 46062

SCHAEFER, Lynette Golderman (The Episcopal Church in Haw) PO Box 1233, Kaunakakai, HI 96748

SCHAEFER, Norma Jane (Chi) 417 N Beck Rd, Lindenhurst, IL 60046

SCHAEFFER, John R (Eas) 317 S Main St, North East, MD 21901

SCHAEFFER, Phillip Negley (NMich) 1803 N Schaeffer Rd, N4244 Gladhaven Road, Moran, MI 49760

SCHAEFFER, Susan Edwards (NY) 17 Perkins Ave, Northampton, MA 01060

SCHAFFENBURG, Karl Christian (Miss) 800 W 15th St, Laurel, MS 39440

SCHAFFNER, Philip Perry (Minn) 2401 33rd Ave. S, Minneapolis, MN 55406

SCHAFROTH, Stephen Louis (EO) 1107 Lewis St, The Dalles, OR 97058

SCHAIBLE II, Donald J (Be) Christ and Trinity Parishes, 58 River St, Carbondale, PA 18407

SCHAITBERGER, Stephen Harold (Minn) 1402 S 8th St, Brainerd, MN 56401

SCHALLER, Joseph G (Pa) 303 W. Lancaster Avenue, Suite 2C, Wayne, PA 19087

SCHALLER JR, Warren August (Va) 7 Lost Ridge Lane, Galena, IL 61036

SCHAPER, Richard (Cal) 646 Ridgewood Avenue, Mill Valley, CA 94941

✠ **SCHARF**, Douglas Frederick (SwFla) 296 River Dr, Tequesta, FL 33469

SCHARF JR, Frederick E (SwFla) 11644 Spindrift Loop, Hudson, FL 34667

SCHARK, Frederick J (WMich) St Mark Episcopal Church, 27 E Chicago St, Coldwater, MI 49036

SCHEDA, Claudia (WNY) 39 Lennox Ave, Amherst, NY 14226

SCHEEL, William Preston (Ark) 26 Cypress Point, Wimberley, TX 78676

SCHEELER, Joseph L (Oly) All Saints Episc Church, 2206 Nw 99th St, Vancouver, WA 98665

SCHEELER, Richard Edward Gerhart (Mil) 1540 S 166th St, New Berlin, WI 53151

SCHEEPERS, Noble (Mass) 62 Cedar St, Dedham, MA 02026

SCHEFF, Tanya (Fla) 338 N 10th St, Quincy, FL 32351

SCHEIBLE, Anne Clare Elsworth (Minn) 225 5th St Se, Chatfield, MN 55923

SCHEIBLE, Gordon Kenneth (WTex) 2151 Bella Vista, Canyon Lake, TX 78133·

SCHEID, Daniel S (EMich) 922 Blanchard Ave, Flint, MI 48503

SCHEIDE, Diana Southwick (NY) PO Box 296, Callicoon, NY 12723

SCHEIDER, Dave (Tex) 2750 Hester Way, Salado, TX 76571

SCHELB, Holly Greenmam (NC) 1323 Irving St, Winston Salem, NC 27103

SCHELL, Anita Louise (Ct) 82 Shore Rd, Old Lyme, CT 06371

SCHELL, Donald J (Cal) 555 De Haro St Ste 330, San Francisco, CA 94107

SCHELL, Richardson Whitfield (Ct) Kent School, Kent, CT 06757

SCHELLENBERG, Roger Thomas (Va) 5775 Barclay Drive Suite G, Kingstowne, VA 22315

SCHELLHAMMER, Judith Lynn (Mich) PO Box 287, Onsted, MI 49265

SCHELLHASE, Peter C (Alb)

SCHELLING, Robert Louis (Colo) 393 Private Road 5730, Jefferson, TX 75657

SCHELLINGERHOUDT, Liz (At) 450 Clairmont Ave, Atlanta, GA 30030

SCHEMBS, Lois Jean (Nwk) 321 Lamberts Mill Rd, Westfield, NJ 07090

SCHENCK, Tim (Mass) 172 Main St, Hingham, MA 02043

SCHENEMAN, Mark (CPa) 226 Acre Dr, Carlisle, PA 17013

SCHENKEL JR, Robert Downes (Be) 6539 Betsy Ross Cir, Bethlehem, PA 18017

SCHENONE, Janine L (SanD) 4321 Eastgate Mall, San Diego, CA 92121

SCHERCK, Steven H (Alb) PO Box 397, Guilderland, NY 12084

SCHERER, Anna (SVa) 1830 Kirby Rd, McLean, VA 22101

SCHERER-HOOCK, Joyce Lynn (Mass) PO Box 308, Topsfield, MA 01983

SCHERFF, Holly D (Ia)

SCHERM, Mary Cecelia (WMass) 75 Silver Crest Ln, Greenfield, MA 01301

SCHEYER, Joyce Mack (NJ)

SCHIAVONE, Denise Marie (Md)

SCHIEFELBEIN, Leslie Colleen (Va)

SCHIEFEN, Patricia Ann (WK)

SCHIEFFELIN JR, John Jay (WMass)

SCHIEFFLER, Danny (Ark) 19 Woodberry Rd., Little Rock, AR 77212

SCHIERING, Janet Christine (EO) PO Box 1323, Hood River, OR 97031

SCHIESLER, Robert Alan (WMich) 30 Kerry Ct, Mechanicsburg, PA 17050

SCHIESZ, Catherine Murdock (Ala) PO Box M, Florence, AL 35631

SCHIFFMAYER, Jeffrey Paul (Tex) 8739 Serenade Ln, Houston, TX 77040

SCHILLING III, Walter Bailey (CFla) 2948 Wyndham Way, Melbourne, FL 32940

SCHILLREFF, Kathy (SwFla) 278 Sawgrass Ct, Naples, FL 34110

SCHINDLER, Gary (WNY) 591 E Main St, Springville, NY 14141

SCHINK, Susan Alma (Nwk)

SCHIRMACHER, Michael G (Md) 69471 i vallarta 130 local 3, Col E Zapata, Pto Vallarta, JAL 48380, Mexico

SCHISLER, Richard Thomas (SO) 2210 Cleveland Ave, Portsmouth, OH 45662

SCHISLER, Sallie Chellis (SO) 2210 Cleveland Ave, Portsmouth, OH 45662

SCHISSER, Janet (Mo) 1203 Castle Bay Pl, Columbia, MO 65203
SCHIVELY, John Alrik (The Episcopal NCal) 1441 Marseille Ln, Roseville, CA 95747
SCHJONBERG, Mary Frances Frances (Nwk) 407 Seaview Cir, Neptune, NJ 07753
SCHLABACH, Karen E (Kan) 10003 W 70th Ter, Merriam, KS 66203
SCHLACHTER, Melvin Harlan (Ia) 7 Glenview Knl NE, Iowa City, IA 52240
SCHLAFER, David John (Mil) 5213 Roosevelt Street, Bethesda, MD 20814
SCHLISMANN, Robert (Neb) 1309 R St, Lincoln, NE 68508
SCHLOSSBERG, Jacob Z (CFla)
SCHLOSSBERG, Stephen Kk (Va) 1574 Spring Avenue Ext, Wynantskill, NY 12198
SCHLOTTERBECK, Marilou Jean (WMich) 12530 Cinder Rd, Beulah, MI 49617
SCHMALING, Pamela Jane (Oly) 7913 W Golf Course Dr, Blaine, WA 98230
SCHMIDT, Ann W (Ark) 726 Davemar Dr, Saint Louis, MO 63123
SCHMIDT, Carolyn Jean Decker (Minn) PO Box 278, 1633 Croftville Rd, Grand Marais, MN 55604
SCHMIDT JR, Frederick William (Tenn) Gar-Evn Theo Sem, 2121 Sheridan Rd, Evanston, IL 60201
SCHMIDT, John David (NY)
SCHMIDT, Kenneth John (Mass)
SCHMIDT, Kenneth L (Cal) 1350 Waller St, San Francisco, CA 94117
SCHMIDT, Kevin Lynn (Kan) 15309 W 153rd St, Olathe, KS 66062
SCHMIDT, Linda Marie (FdL) N2592 State Highway 17, Merrill, WI 54452
SCHMIDT, Norma (Ct) 661 Old Post Rd, Fairfield, CT 06824
SCHMIDT, Richard (CGC) 101 Fairwood Blvd, Fairhope, AL 36532
SCHMIDTETTER, Todd T (CFla)
SCHMITT, Barbara Joyce (SO) 115 N 6th St, Hamilton, OH 45011
SCHMITT, Geoffrey (WLa) 3910 Parkway Dr, 1605 Gray Lake Dr, Princeton, LA 71067
SCHMITT, Jacqueline (CNY) 1085 Warburton Ave Apt 818, Yonkers, NY 10701
SCHMITZ, Barbara G (CNY)
SCHMITZ, Lance Aaron (Okla)
SCHMOETZER, Jane Ellen (Spok) 1940 Thayer Dr, Richland, WA 99354
SCHNAARE, Anne Elizabeth (WMich) 538 Cosmopolitan, Marshall, MI 49068
SCHNABEL, Charles Edward (LI) 143 Lakeside Trail, Ridge, NY 11961
SCHNABL, Emily (Neb) 4036 Neptune Dr, Oklahoma City, OK 73116
SCHNACK, Peggy Ellan (NH)

SCHNATTERLY, Michael Dean (USC) 4 Cottage Knoll Cir, Greenville, SC 29609
SCHNAUFER, Eric (USC) 6 Del Norte Blvd, Greenville, SC 29615
SCHNEIDER, Gregg Alan (Mil) 703 Milwaukee Road, Beloit, WI 53511
SCHNEIDER, Harold (EMich)
SCHNEIDER, Judith Irene (Colo) 2187 Canyon Ct W, Grand Junction, CO 81507
SCHNEIDER, Marian Helen (Roch) 13 E Water St, Friendship, NY 14739
SCHNEIDER, Marilyn (Colo) 7900 E Dartmouth Ave Apt 58, Denver, CO 80231
SCHNEIDER, Marni Jacqueline (Los) 2972 Cadence Way, Virginia Beach, VA 23456
SCHNEIDER, Matthew C (Ala) 166 Canterbury Rd, Springfield, MA 01118
SCHNEIDER, Mp (Vt) 164 Milton Rd, Warwick, RI 02888
SCHNEIDER, Shane Bernard (WK)
SCHNEIDER, Stephen (Ore) 2427 Ne 17th Ave, Portland, OR 97212
SCHNEIDER, Thomas Carl (ETenn) 1038 Sparta Hwy, Crossville, TN 38572
SCHNEIDER, William J (Mass) 276 Riverside Dr Apt 4e, New York, NY 10025
SCHOECK, Lauren Lenoski (CPa) 6300 N Central Ave, Phoenix, AZ 85012
SCHOECK, Robert H (CPa) 119 N Duke St, Lancaster, PA 17602
SCHOENBRUN, Zoila Collier (Cal) 327 San Rafael Ave, Belvedere, CA 94920
✠ **SCHOFIELD JR**, Cal (SeFla) 7900 E Dartmouth Ave Apt 77, Denver, CO 80231
SCHOFIELD, Kathlyn Elizabeth (CNY) St Paul's Episcopal Church, 204 Genesee St, Chittenango, NY 13037
SCHOFIELD, Peter (Alb) 39 Imperial Dr., Niskayuna, NY 12309
SCHOFIELD-BROADBENT, Carrie (CNY) 941 Euclid Ave., Syracuse, NY 13210
SCHOLER, Linda Carlson (NJ) P O Box 1206, Chincoteague Island, VA 23336
SCHOMBURG, Karen (Spok) Episcopal Diocese Of Spokane, 245 E 13th Ave, Spokane, WA 99202
SCHOOLER, William Thomas (Cal) 352 Bay Rd, Atherton, CA 94027
SCHOOMAKER, Ronald William (CFla)
SCHOONMAKER, Dan (O) 231 Rosebury Ct, Mayfield Heights, OH 44124
SCHOONMAKER, Lisa Katherine (CPa) 21 S Main St, Lewistown, PA 17044
SCHOTTO, Kathleen (Md)
SCHRAMM, George T (WVa) Po Box 308, Shepherdstown, WV 25443

SCHRAMM, John Eldon (NI) PO Box 695, Plymouth, IN 46563
SCHRANZ, Donald Jerome (Roch)
SCHRAPLAU, Frederick William (NY) 182 Nixon Avenue, Staten Island, NY 10304
SCHREIBER, Mary (WMass) 6 Wall St, Shelburne Falls, MA 01370
SCHREIBER, Michael Nelson (Cal) 162 Hickory St, San Francisco, CA 94102
SCHREINER, Shawn M (Chi) 5 North 047 Route 83, Bensenville, IL 60106
SCHRIDER, James Edward (Los) 620 D Street, SE, Washington, DC 20003
SCHRIMSHER, Alyce Marie (Dal) 6132 Yellow Rock Trl, Dallas, TX 75248
SCHRODER, Edward Amos (Fla) 15 Hickory Lane, Amelia Island, FL 32034
SCHROEDER, Catherine Ann (Ia)
SCHROEDER, Cecelia (Los) 314 Ayrlee Ave NW, Leesburg, VA 20176
SCHROEDER, H.B.W. (Eas)
SCHUBERT, Jill Marie (Minn) 520 N Pokegama Ave, Grand Rapids, MN 55744
SCHUBERT, Kevin Lane Johnson (WTex) 3307 Garden Villa Ln, Austin, TX 78704
SCHUBERT, Rebecca Malcolm (WMo) 3700 West 83 Terrace, Prairie Village, KS 66206
SCHUEDDIG JR, Louis Charles (At) 345 9th St NE, Atlanta, GA 30309
SCHUETZ, Mary (EMich) 3536 West River Road, Sanford, MI 48657
SCHUILING, Alice Catherine (NMich) 1100 Sunview Dr Apt 201, Saint Johns, MI 48879
SCHULE, Andrew (WNY)
SCHULENBERG, George W (ND) 135 Skogmo Blvd, Fergus Falls, MN 56537
SCHULENBERG, Michael A (Minn) 715 N High St, Lake City, MN 55041
SCHULER, Rock Hal (Md) St Andrew Tec, PO Box 175, Mayo, MD 21106
SCHULLER, Chris (Nev) 555 E Silverado Ranch Blvd Unit 1153, Las Vegas, NV 89183
SCHULTZ, Alison (Ore) PO Box 2492, Cashiers, NC 28717
SCHULTZ, Gregory Allen (FdL) West 7145 County Road U, Plymouth, WI 53073
SCHULTZ, Mark Daniel (NY) PO Box 65840, Tucson, AZ 85728
SCHUNEMAN, Steven Lawrence (SanD) 200 N El Camino Real Spc 179, Oceanside, CA 92058
SCHUNIOR, Rebecca Justice (NC) 85 S Union Blvd Apt 448, #340, Lakewood, CO 80228
SCHUNK, Steve (NY) PO Box 913, Highland, NY 12528
SCHUSTER III, Franklin Phillip (RG) PO Box 586, Arroyo Seco, NM 87514

SCHUSTER WELTNER, Alicia Dawn (At) 2744 Peachtree Rd NW, Atlanta, GA 30305
SCHUTZ, Christine Elizabeth (O) 843 Tarra Oaks Dr, Findlay, OH 45840
SCHUTZ, Regan M (SanD) PO Box 3331, Sewanee, TN 37375
SCHUYLER, William Kearns (Me) 19 Ridgeway Ave, Sanford, ME 04073
SCHWAB, Susan (Mass) 280 Village St Apt G1, Medway, MA 02053
SCHWAHN, Vincent (Los) 117 Avenida S Jeronimo, San Angel, Mexico City, CMX 01000, Mexico
SCHWARTZ, William (Mil) 4146 Cosmo St, San Diego, CA 92111
SCHWARTZ CROUCH, Emily (Ky) 7304 Westport Rd, Louisville, KY 40222
SCHWARZ, Robert Carl (SD) 500 S Main Ave, Sioux Falls, SD 57104
SCHWARZ, Robert Louis (LI) 324 Fairington Dr, Summerville, SC 29485
SCHWARZER, Margaret (Mass) 321 Tappan St Apt 5, Brookline, MA 02445
SCHWEINSBURG JR, Richard Lyle (RI) 46 Fairway Dr, Coventry, RI 02816
SCHWENK, Christopher Lee (Pa) 23 E Airy St, Norristown, PA 19401
SCHWENKE, Carol (SwFla) 3000 S Schiller St, Tampa, FL 33629
SCHWENZFEIER, Paul Macleod (Mass) 32 Arlington Rd., Wareham, MA 02571
SCHWERT, Douglas Peters (WTex) 433 Trojan St, Port Aransas, TX 78373
SCHWOYER, Robin Lynn Vanhorn (Pa) 232 American Dr, Richboro, PA 18954
SCIAINO, Elizabeth Rauen (NJ) 88 Claremont Rd, Bernardsville, NJ 07924
SCIME, Michael S (Ind)
SCIPIO, Clarence Tyrone (Episcopal VI) PO Box 1148, St Thomas, VI 00804
SCISSONS, Anne (EO) 719 38th Ave SE, Albany, OR 97322
SCOFIELD, Lawrence F (NwPa) 24 W Frederick St, Corry, PA 16407
SCOLARE, Michael Charles (WTex)
SCOOPMIRE, Leslie Barnes (Mo) 11538 Patty Ann Dr, Saint Louis, MO 63146
SCOTT JR, Ben (Minn) 8429 55th St Sw, Byron, MN 55920
SCOTT, Catherine F (Neb) 1903 Pleasantview Ln, Bellevue, NE 68005
SCOTT, Cathy Ann (Ind) Holy Family Episcopal Church, 11445 Fishers Point Blvd, Fishers, IN 46038
SCOTT, David Thomas (NwT) Po Box 88, Perryton, TX 79070
SCOTT, Dick (Oly) 4885 Nw Chad Ct, Silverdale, WA 98383
SCOTT, Donna Jeanne (Tenn) 404 Siena Drive, Nashville, TN 37205
SCOTT, Edward C (NC) 1740 Park Grove Pl NW, Concord, NC 28027

SCOTT, George Michael (Ga) PO Box 294, Cochran, GA 31014
SCOTT, Horton James (NY) 489 Saint Pauls Pl, Bronx, NY 10456
SCOTT JR, James Edward (Tex) 8407 Glenscott St., Houston, TX 77061
SCOTT, Jean Pearson (NwT) 1101 Slide Rd., Lubbock, TX 79416
SCOTT, John Charles (Ala) St Stephens Episcopal Church, PO Box 839, Eutaw, AL 35462
SCOTT III, John Llewellyn (Alb) 86 Lake Hill Rd, Burnt Hills, NY 12027
SCOTT, Keith (RI) 103 Union Ave, Delmar, NY 12054
SCOTT, Marshall (WMo) 209 Upper Meadows Rd, Sparta, TN 38583
SCOTT, Matthew Rhoades (NwPa) 209 West St, Warren, PA 16365
SCOTT, Michael B (NMich)
SCOTT, Miriam Gabriel (NwT)
SCOTT, Peggy King (La) 607 E Main St, New Roads, LA 70760
SCOTT, Rebecca Jean (Oly)
SCOTT, Robert (The Episcopal NCal) 556 Port Cir, Cloverdale, CA 95425
SCOTT II, Robert Alfred (Okla)
SCOTT, Robert W (Neb) 13054 Thomas Drive, Bellevue, NE 68005
SCOTT, Roger Timothy (Az)
SCOTT, Sheila M (Mil) 11958 W Mill Rd, Unit 5, Milwaukee, WI 53225
SCOTT, Shelby (Okla) 9119 S 89th E Ave, Broken Arrow, OK 74133
SCOTT, Thomas (WMich) 2327 Park Place 2, Evanston, IL 60201
SCOTT JR, William Tayloe (Cal) 95 Winfield St, San Francisco, CA 94110
SCOTT-HAMBLEN, Shane (Cal) 34 Andrew Dr Apt 134, Tiburon, CA 94920
SCOTT-JONES, Jennifer M (CNY) 18300 Upper Bay Rd, Houston, TX 77058
SCOTTO, Vincent Francis (SwFla) 1324 Red Oak Ln, Port Charlotte, FL 33948
SCRANTON, Susan (Los) 1420 E Foothill Blvd, Glendora, CA 91741
SCRIBNER, Jean (Neb) 1725 Old Haywood Rd, Asheville, NC 28806
SCRIVEN, Elizabeth A (Ind) 5070 Bosuns Way Apt B1, Ypsilanti, MI 48197
SCRIVENER, William Eugene (SO) 7193 Foxview Dr, Cincinnati, OH 45230
SCRUGGS JR, Charles Perry (ETenn) 187 Hunziker Rd, Tracy City, TN 37387
SCRUTCHINS, Arthur Paul (Okla) PO Box 3141, Shawnee, OK 74802
✠ **SCRUTON**, Gordon (WMass) 40 Carriage Hill Dr, Wethersfield, CT 06109
SEABURY, Scott Hamor (WMass) 10 Rawlins Brook Rd, Suffield, CT 06078
SEADALE, Vincent Gerald (Mass)
✠ **SEAGE**, Brian (Miss) 4110 Robin Dr, Jackson, MS 39206

SEAGE, Kyle Dice (Miss) 7 Sierra Ct, Tiburon, CA 94920
SEAGLE, Teresa Ryan (Fla) 301 Brooks Cir E, Jacksonville, FL 32211
SEAL, Chris Houston (The Episcopal NCal) 201 Nevada St, Nevada City, CA 95959
SEALES, Hea Suk (Ala)
SEALS, William Frederick (CFla) 23 Surrey Run, Hendersonville, NC 28791
SEAMAN, Kelly S (NH) 52 Gould Rd, New London, NH 03257
SEAMAN, Martha Lee (Az) 7419 E Palm Ln, Scottsdale, AZ 85257
SEAMANS, Timothy Joseph Sommer (Cal) A, 249 27th Ave, San Francisco, CA 94121
SEARLE, S Elizabeth (Nwk) 200 W 79th St Apt 14p, New York, NY 10024
SEARS, Barbara Anne (Md) 1000 Weller Cir Apt 221, Westminster, MD 21158
SEATON, Anne Christine (Minn) 168 W Arizona St, Holbrook, AZ 86025
SEATON, Robert Deane (WK) 137 Aspen Rd, Salina, KS 67401
SEATVET, John (WK) St Cornelius Episcopal Church, 200 W Spruce St, Dodge City, KS 67801
SEAVER, Maurice Blanchard (WNC) 3500 Carmel Rd, Charlotte, NC 28226
SEAVEY, SuZanne Elane (ETenn) 135 Fountainhead Ct, Lenoir City, TN 37772
SEBOLD, Mary (WA)
SEBRO, Jacqueline Marie (ECR) 815 Sycamore Canyon Rd, Paso Robles, CA 93446
SECAUR, Stephen (Mil) 435 Som Center Rd, Mayfield Village, OH 44143
SECKINGER, Ralph Raymond (CFla)
SEDDON, Anne Christine (Ct) 4 Maybury Rd, Suffield, CT 06078
SEDDON, Matthew T (Ind) Trinity Episcopal Church, 111 South Grant Street, Bloomington, IN 47408
SEDGWICK, Roger (O) 647 Reid Ave, Lorain, OH 44052
SEDLACEK, Carol Westerberg (Ore) 2103 Desiree Pl, Lebanon, OR 97355
SEDLACEK, Wes (Ore) 2103 Desiree Pl, Lebanon, OR 97355
SEDWICK, Katherine (Oly) 5128 40th Ave S, Minneapolis, MN 55417
SEEBER, Laurian (Vt) 47 Shadow Lang Berlin, Barre, VT 05641
SEEFELDT, Scott Allen (Mil)
SEEGER, Elisabeth Ann (Oly) 4467 S 172nd St, Seatac, WA 98188
SEEGER, Sue Fisher (Mass) 28 Seagrave Rd, Cambridge, MA 02140
SEEKINS, Sheila (Me)
SEELEY, Janet Lynne (Wyo)
SEELEY JR, Walt (Wyo) 2024 Rolling Hills Road, Kemmerer, WY 83101
SEELY, Shirley Ann (EMich) 3201 Gratiot Ave, Port Huron, MI 48060
SEELY, Steven (WA)

Clergy List

SEELYE FOREST, Elizabeth Jane (Mich) 14191 Ivanhoe Dr Apt 3, Sterling Heights, MI 48312
SEFCHICK, Frank Stephen (Be) 1498 Quakake Rd, Weatherly, PA 18255
SEFTON, Kate (The Episcopal NCal)
SEGAL, Joy Joy (Pa) 916 S Swanson St, Philadelphia, PA 19147
SEGER, David L (NI) 13259 Hisega Dr, Rapid City, SD 57702
SEGER, Nikki Elizabeth Louise (SwFla)
SEGERBRECHT, Stephen Louis (Kan) 1715 Prestwick Dr, Lawrence, KS 66047
SEGUIN, Jean-Pierre Martin (NY)
SEIBERT, Joanna Johnson (Ark) 27 River Ridge Rd, Little Rock, AR 72227
SEIBERT, Stephen Christopher (Fla)
SEIDMAN, Kim (NwT) H Comforter Tec Ch, PO Box 412, Broomfield, CO 80038
SEIFERT, Cynthia (Tenn) 5041 English Village Dr, Nashville, TN 37211
SEIFERT, Robert Joseph (ECR) 161 Palo Verde Ter, Santa Cruz, CA 95060
SEIFERT, Sarah Lavonne (WMass) 14301 S Blackbob Rd, Olathe, KS 66062
SEILER, Jeffrey (Va) 4003 St Erics Turn, Williamsburg, VA 23185
SEILER, MIchael (Los) PO Box 1105, 28843 Manitoba Dr, Lake Arrowhead, CA 92352
SEILS, Donald Davis (Colo) 5749 N Stetson Ct, Parker, CO 80134
SEIPEL, James Russell (Los) 25769 Player Dr, Valencia, CA 91355
SEITER, Claudia (U) 540 W 2350 S, Brigham City, UT 84302
SEITZ, Christopher R (CFla) Wycliffe College, University Of Toronto, Toronto, ON M5S 1H7, Canada
SEITZ, Mark Ellis (WVa) 115 Cornerstone Dr., Springfield, GA 31329
SEITZ, Phil (EMich) 3003 Mill Station Road, Hale, MI 48739
SEITZ JR, Tom (CFla) 221 4th St S, Lake Wales, FL 33853
SELDEN, Elizabeth Ann (Minn) 6212 Crest Ln, Edina, MN 55436
SELES, Deb (SanD) 75325 Pino Dr, Palm Desert, CA 92211
SELF, Debbie (SwFla)
SELFE-VERRONE, Ann Christine (NY) Chapel of St. Francis, 3621 Brunswick Ave., Los Angeles, CA 90039
SELLERS, Randal Hugh (CGC)
SELLERS, ROBERT CLAYTON (Tex) 145 N Halifax Ave Apt 202, APT 202, Daytona Beach, FL 32118
SELLERY, David F (NC) 213 Council Gap Ct, Cary, NC 27513
SELL-LEE, William Merle (WA) 965 Winslow Way E Unit 103, Bainbridge Island, WA 98110

SELLS, Jeffery Edward (Oly) Po Box 3090, Salt Lake City, UT 84110
SELLS, Michael (NAM)
SELLS, Patti (Los)
SELNICK, Thomas Conrad (O) 5040 Wright Terrace, Skokie, IL 60077
SELVAGE, Dan (CPa) 102 Faust Cir, Bellefonte, PA 16823
SELVEY, Mark F (Neb) 3427 N 161st Ave, Omaha, NE 68116
SELZER, David Owen (WNY) 4 Phylis St, Ottawa, ON K2J 1V2, Canada
SEME, Gregory (Tex)
SEME, Yves (Hai)
SEMES, Robert Louis (Ore) 1354 Primavera Dr E, Palm Springs, CA 92264
SEMON-SCOTT, Deborah Anne (Mich) 3 N Broad St, Hillsdale, MI 49242
SEMPARI, Izabella (Cal) 1012 1 2 Allston Way, Berkeley, CA 94710
SENECHAL, Roger Edward (WMass) 7601 Harper Road, Joelton, TN 37080
SENEY SR, Robert William (WMo) 14165 Denver West Cricle #3407, Lakewood, CO 80401
SENTIGAR, Betsy Welliver (Be)
SENUTA, Lisa (Kan) 550 Sunset Ridge Rd, Northfield, IL 60093
SENYONI, Christian (WTenn) Grace Episcopal Church, 405 2nd Ave NE, Jamestown, ND 58401
SERAS, Barbara (Md) 67 River Bend Park, Lancaster, PA 17602
SERFES, Patricia May (Me) 2524 Casa Dr, New Port Richey, FL 34655
SERIO, Robert Andrew (Ala) Church of the Nativity, 208 Eustis Ave Se, Huntsville, AL 35801
SERRANO, Francisco De Jesus (WA)
SERRANO, Marco Gabriel (Kan)
SERRANO POVEDA, Nelson Evelio (Episcopal SJ)
SERVAIS, Jean Neal (Okla) PO Box 165, Coalgate, OK 74538
SERVELLON, Maria Filomena (NY) 30 Pine Grove Ave, Kingston, NY 12401
SERVETAS, Linda Anne (Alb) 16 Dean St, Deposit, NY 13754
SERVETAS, Nickolas (Alb) 1071 New Jersey Ave, Hellertown, PA 18055
SESSIONS, Judy Karen (WTex) 2910 Treasure Hills Blvd Apt B, Harlingen, TX 78550
SESSIONS, Marcia A (RI) 45 Fales Rd, Bristol, RI 02809
SESSUM, Bob Lee (Lex) 12000 Diamond Creek Rd Apt 102, Raleigh, NC 27614
SETMEYER, Robert Charles (Chi) 711 S River Rd Apt 508, Des Plaines, IL 60016
SETTLES, Russell Lee (NC) 9118 Kings Canyon Dr, Charlotte, NC 28210

SETZER, Stephen F (Del) 635 E 14th St Apt 02e, Unit 02-E, New York, NY 10009
SEUFERT, Carmen Rae (Roch) 103 Williams St, Newark, NY 14513
SEUTTER, Jennifer M (Ak)
SEVAYEGA, Reginald Delano (HB) 4701 Belfiore Rd, Warrensville Heights, OH 44128
SEVER, Cynthia A (Spr) 3390 Lyell Rd, Rochester, NY 14606
SEVICK, Gerald (Tex) 3901 S. Panther Creek, The Woodlands, TX 77381
SEVILLE, Joe (CPa) 1405 Wedgewood Way, Mechanicsburg, PA 17050
SEVILLE, John C (Chi) 802 Foxdale Ave, Winnetka, IL 60093
SEWARD, Barbara J (Be) Church of St Benedict, 909 Lily Cache Ln, Bolingbrook, IL 60440
SEWELL, John Wayne (WTenn) 53 Shepherd Ln, Memphis, TN 38117
SEXTON, Jessica Elaine (Md) 1401 Carrollton Ave, Baltimore, MD 21204
SEXTON, Patricia (USC) 1001 12th St, Cayce, SC 29033
SEXTON, Tim (The Episcopal Church in Haw) PO Box 181, Des Moines, NM 88418
SEYMOUR, John Jack David (Chi) 1631 N Tripp Ave, Chicago, IL 60639
SEYMOUR, Marlyne Joyce (Mil) 862 No. Sandy Lane, Elkhorn, WI 53121
SGRO, Anthony Huston (WNC)
SHACKELFORD, Lynn Clark (Okla) 404 Washington Avenue, Sand Springs, OK 74063
SHACKLEFORD, Richard Neal (LI) Timber Ridge, 711 John Green Rd, Jonesborough, TN 37659
SHADLE, Jennifer L (Colo)
SHADOW, Burton Alexander (Tex) 3540 Manderly Place, Fort Worth, TX 76109
SHAEFER, Susan A (Mich) 1605 E Stadium Blvd, Ann Arbor, MI 48104
SHAFER, Gail Ann (Mich)
SHAFER, Lee Franklin (Ky) 821 S 4th St, Louisville, KY 40203
SHAFER, Linda Jean (Mich) 151 N Main St, Brooklyn, MI 49230
SHAFER, Mike (NY) 21 Decker Road, Stanfordville, NY 12581
SHAFER, Samuel H (RG) 630 66th St, Oakland, CA 94609
SHAFFER, Brian Keith (Mich) Cathedral Church of St. Paul, Detroit, MI 48201
SHAFFER, Charles Omer (Md) 7200 Third Ave, Cottage 119, Eldersburg, MD 21784
SHAFFER, Dee (NC) 1008 Saint Patrick St, Tarboro, NC 27886
SHAFFER, James M (SC) 102 Blue Heron Pond Rd, Kiawah Island, SC 29455
SHAFFER, John Alfred (CNY) PO Box 1219, Shepherdstown, WV 25443

SHAFFER, Tracy (Me)

SHAH, Anil Virendra (Los)

SHAHINIAN, Katharine Anne (Md) St Annes Episcopal Church, Church Circle, Annapolis, MD 21401

SHAIN-HENDRICKS, Christy (Colo) PO Box 10000, Silverthorne, CO 80498

SHAKESPEARE, Lyndon (Colo) Church of the Holy Comforter, 1700 W 10th Ave, Broomfield, CO 80020

SHALLCROSS, Lexa (Be) 150 Elm St, Emmaus, PA 18049

SHAMBAUGH, Benjamin Albert (Me) 143 State St, Portland, ME 04101

SHAMEL, Andrew (Cal) 55 Monument Cir Ste 600, Indianapolis, IN 46204

SHAN, Becky (ECR) 578 Ironwood Ter Apt 5, Sunnyvale, CA 94086

SHANAHAN, Thomazine Weinstein (CPa) 4426 Reservoir Rd Nw, Washington, DC 20007

✠ **SHAND**, James J (Eas) 208 Somerset Ct, Queenstown, MD 21658

SHAND III, William Munro (WA) PO Box 326, Saluda, NC 28773

SHANDS, Harriet Goodrich (WNC) 21 Chestnut Ridge Road, Pisgah Forest, NC 28768

SHANE, Janette (Chi) 102 Marquette St, Park Forest, IL 60466

SHANK, Jason Nathaniel (NwPa)

SHANK, Nancy (CPa) 111 Pine St, Danville, PA 17821

SHANKLES, Jeffrey Scott (Va) 6800a Columbia Pike, Annandale, VA 22003

SHANKS, Margaret R (Lex) 367 Stratford Dr, Lexington, KY 40503

SHANKS, Stephen Ray (Ala) 5302 Dorchester Rd, Richmond, VA 23225

SHANLEY-ROBERTS, EILEEN (Chi) 1245 Saint Johns Ave, Highland Park, IL 60035

SHANNON JR, Carl (Tex) 102 Pecan Grv Apt 121, Houston, TX 77077

SHANNON, Carolyn Louise (Nev) 2366 Aqua Vista Ave, Henderson, NV 89014

SHANNON, James (Pa) 112 Lansdowne Ct, Lansdowne, PA 19050

SHANNON, James Michael (ND) 319 S 5th St, Grand Forks, ND 58201

SHANNON II, Robert Lloyd (Roch) 17 Uncle Bens Way, Orleans, MA 02653

SHAPTON, Eleanor (Spok) 240 Maringo Rd, Ephrata, WA 98823

SHARP, Carolyn Jackson (Ct) Yale Divinity School, 409 Prospect St., New Haven, CT 06511

SHARP, James L (ETenn) 135 Scenic Shores Dr, Dandridge, TN 37725

SHARP, Jeffrey Robert (Oly) 205 East 96th St, Tacoma, WA 98445

SHARP, Lynne (Roch) St Pauls, 1924 Trinity Ave, Walnut Creek, CA 94596

SHARP, Virginia Gale (ETenn) PO Box 1780, Dandridge, TN 37725

SHARP, Wesley Eric (Ala) 700 Rinehart Rd, Lake Mary, FL 32746

SHARPE, Sheila Gast (Del) 65 East Stephen Drive, Newark, DE 19713

SHARPE, Virginia Edna (CFla) 210 Fallen Timber Trl, Deland, FL 32724

SHARPTON, Larry (Ala) 8501 Olde Gate, Montgomery, AL 36116

SHARROW, Charles (WTex) 960 Toledo Dr, Brownsville, TX 78526

SHATAGIN, Theodore Ivan (Vt) Po Box 1807, Ardmore, OK 73402

SHATTUCK JR, Gardiner Humphrey (RI) 190 North St, Warwick, RI 02886

SHAUBACH, Sheila Kathryn (Episcopal SJ) Po Box 164, Raymond, CA 93653

SHAVER, Ellen (Me) 139 High Head Rd, Harpswell, ME 04079

SHAVER, Stephen (The Episcopal NCal) 550 Mendocino Ave, Santa Rosa, CA 95401

SHAW, Adrianna S (Kan) St Philip's Episcopal Church, 302 E. General Stewart Way, Hinesville, GA 31314

SHAW, Jane Alison (Cal) 110 California St, San Francisco, CA 94111

SHAW, Martini (Pa) 6361 Lancaster Ave, Philadelphia, PA 19151

SHAW, Philip Algie (Az) Trinity Episcopal Church, P.O. Box 590, Kingman, AZ 86402

SHAW, Samuel Gates (Ala) 4112 Abingdon Ln, Birmingham, AL 35243

SHAW, Warren Ervin (Pa) 1029 Bristlecone Ln, Charlottesville, VA 22911

SHEARER, Donald Robert (Nwk) 156 Mountain Dr, Greentown, PA 18426

SHEARIN, Phillip Haywood (WMass)

SHEATS, George Sabin (Me)

SHEAY, Virginia M (NJ) 12 Glenwood Ln, Stockton, NJ 08559

SHECTER, Teri Ann (Colo) 2461 F 1/4 Road #231, Grand Junction, CO 81505

SHEEHAN JR, David (Del) 3401 Greenbriar Ln, West Grove, PA 19390

SHEEHAN, John (Va) 512 Duff Rd NE, Leesburg, VA 20176

SHEEN RODRIGUEZ, Juan Enrique (DomRep)

SHEETZ, David Allan (Cal) 901 E Van Buren St Apt 1001, Phoenix, AZ 85006

SHEFFIELD, John Joseph (Tex) PO Box 12615, San Antonio, TX 78212

SHEFFIELD, Sharon (Los) 10354 Downey Ave, Downey, CA 90241

SHEHANE, Mary (Oly) 9416 1st Ave Ne Apt 408, Seattle, WA 98115

SHELBY, F Stuart (CFla) All Saints Church, 338 E Lyman Ave, Winter Park, FL 32789

SHELBY, Jason (Miss) 106 Sharkey Ave, Clarksdale, MS 38614

SHELDON, Carren (Ore) 1500 State Street, Santa Barbara, CA 93101

SHELDON, Jaclyn Struff (Ct) 85 Holmes Rd, East Lyme, CT 06333

SHELDON, Karen Sears (Vt) 86 S Main St, Hanover, NH 03755

SHELDON, Patricia Lu (Neb) 3818 N 211th St, Elkhorn, NE 68022

SHELDON, Peggy Ann (SeFla) 2000 Sw Racquet Club Dr, Palm City, FL 34990

SHELDON, Raymond S (Oly) 1075 Alexander Pl Ne, Bainbridge Island, WA 98110

SHELDON, Terry Lynn (CNY) 21 White St, Clark Mills, NY 13321

SHELL, Lawrence S (NMich) 201 E. Ridge St., Marquette, MI 49855

SHELLITO, John (Va) St Georges Church, 915 N Oakland St, Arlington, VA 22203

SHELLY, Marshall (NJ) 505 Main St, Spotswood, NJ 08884

SHELTON, Benson Eldridge (Va) 8061 Saint Pauls Church Rd, Hanover, VA 23069

SHELTON, Edna S (Mich) 18270 Northlawn St, Detroit, MI 48221

SHELTON, Linda Ross (Tex) 3507 Plumb St, Houston, TX 77005

SHEMATEK, Jon Paul (Md) 9120 Frederick Rd, Ellicott City, MD 21042

SHEMAYEV, Roman Aeired (Mil) 3528 Valley Ridge Rd, Middleton, WI 53562

SHEPARD, Diane Elise Rucker (Pgh) 1155 Brintell St, Pittsburgh, PA 15201

SHEPARD, Kenneth (Neb)

SHEPARD, Margaret Smith (CGC) 1608 Baker Ct, Panama City, FL 32401

SHEPHERD, Angela Fontessa (At) St Bartholomews Episcopal Church, 1790 Lavista Rd NE, Atlanta, GA 30329

SHEPHERD, Burton Hale (WTex) 185 Towerview Dr Unit 1101, Saint Augustine, FL 32092

SHEPHERD, Karlyn Ann (RG) 22 Bowersville Rd, Algodones, NM 87001

SHEPHERD, Nancy DeLane (At) 1150 Pimbury Ct, Indianapolis, IN 46260

SHEPHERD, Nancy Hamilton (Mass) 172 Harvard Rd, Stow, MA 01775

SHEPHERD, Stephen (Va) 6019 Hibbling Ave, Springfield, VA 22150

SHEPHERD, Thomas Charles (Mass) 6600 Ne 22nd Way Apt 2323, Fort Lauderdale, FL 33308

SHEPHERD, Thomas E (WMo) 1107 Saratoga Drive, Euless, TX 76040

SHEPHERD JR, William Henry (At) 1150 Pimbury Ct, Indianapolis, IN 46260

SHEPHERD, William John (Pa) 110 W Johnson St, Philadelphia, PA 19144

SHEPIC, Charlotte (Colo) 14031 W Exposition Dr, Lakewood, CO 80228

SHEPLER, Dawn (Tex)

SHEPLEY, Joseph (Ct) 65 Grey Rock Rd, Southbury, CT 06488

SHEPLEY, Tara B (Ct) 65 GreyRock Rd, Southbury, CT 06488

SHEPPARD, Dale Eugene (WVa) 1051 Walker Road, Follansbee, WV 26037

Clergy List

SHEPPARD, Patricia (Fla) 919 San Fernando St, Fernandina Beach, FL 32034

SHEPPARD, Ricardo Wayne (WA)

SHERARD, Susan (NC) 402 West Smith Street, 4J, Greensboro, NC 27401

SHERER, Valori (Mo) PO Box 1872, Shelby, NC 28151

SHERFICK, Kenneth L (WMich) 1517 Emoriland Blvd, Knoxville, TN 37917

SHERIDAN, Dennis Arnol (Los) 242 E Alvarado St, Pomona, CA 91767

SHERIDAN, Samuel R (Va)

SHERIDAN-CAMPBELL, Laura M (Ore) 124 Alida St, Ashland, OR 97520

SHERMAN, Andrew James (SeFla) 245 NE 2nd St, Boca Raton, FL 33432

SHERMAN, Beth (RI) St Francis Episcopal Church, San Francisco, CA 94127

SHERMAN, Clark Michael (Mont) 5 W Olive St, Bozeman, MT 59715

SHERMAN, Guy Charles (Oly) 12527 Roosevelt Way NE Apt 405, Seattle, WA 98125

SHERMAN JR, Lev (Me) 130 Cedar St, Bangor, ME 04401

SHERMAN, Merrell Scot (Cal)

SHERMAN, Russell E (WTex) 202 Primera Dr, San Antonio, TX 78212

SHERMAN, Walter (Ind) 701 NW 24th Street, Wilton Manors, FL 33311

SHERRADEN, Shawn Travis (Kan)

SHERRER, Wayne (Nwk) 150 Elm St, Emmaus, PA 18049

SHERRILL III, Alex (At)

SHERRILL, Christopher Ralph (NJ) PO Box 45, Southport, ME 04576

SHERRILL II, Edmund Knox (NH) Church Farm School, 1001 E Lincoln Hwy, Exton, PA 19341

SHERRILL JR, George (LI) 15117 14th Rd, Whitestone, NY 11357

SHERRILL, Joan Lee (NC)

SHERRILL, Karen Flynt (LI) Grace Episcopal Church, 1415 Clintonville St, Whitestone, NY 11357

SHERROUSE, Wanda Gail (CFla) 121 W 18th St, Sanford, FL 32771

SHERWOOD, Robert Leon (Mass) 165 Main St, Buzzards Bay, MA 02532

SHERWOOD, Zalmon Omar (Mich) 315 W. Oak St., Arcadia, FL 34266

SHEW, Debbie (Colo) 910 E 3rd Ave, Durango, CO 81301

SHEWMAKER, David Paul (The Episcopal NCal) St Paul's Episcopal Ch, 220 E. Macken, Crescent City, CA 95531

SHIELD, Catherine Ann (Kan) 13420 E Harry St, Wichita, KS 67230

SHIELDS, John (NC) 520 Summit St, Winston Salem, NC 27101

SHIELDS, Kelly Ann (Ia)

SHIELDS, Mary Mac (EC)

SHIELDS, Richard Edward (The Episcopal Church in Haw) 1441

Victoria St Apt 403, Honolulu, HI 96822

SHIELDS, Wes (CFla) 2508 Amity Ave, Gastonia, NC 28054

SHIER, Marshall (Los) 1348 E Wilshire Ave, Fullerton, CA 92831

SHIER, Pamela C (WVa) 164 Mason Ridge Rd, Mount Morris, PA 15349

SHIFLET JR, Bill (Md) 4520 Cornflower Ct, Ellicott City, MD 21043

SHIGAKI, Jerry Moritsune (Oly) 6963 Ca Ave SW U 102, Seattle, WA 98136

SHIGAKI, Pauline Yuri (Oly)

SHILEY, Earl Edward (Pa) 224 Cambridge Chase, Exton, PA 19341

SHIMONKEVITZ, Amy Ruth (Md)

✠ **SHIN**, Allen K (NY) Episcopal Diocese of New York, 1047 Amsterdam Ave, New York, NY 10025

SHINE, Anna Colleen (WNC) PO Box 645, Valle Crucis, NC 28691

SHIPMAN, Bruce MacDonald (Ct) 241 Monument St Apt 6, Groton, CT 06340

SHIPMAN, Josh (Miss)

SHIPP, Mary Jane Mccoy (Mont) 120 Antelope Dr, Dillon, MT 59725

SHIPPEE, Richard C (RI) 29 11th St, Providence, RI 02906

SHIPPEN II, Joseph (USC) PO Box 1213, Griffin, GA 30224

SHIPPEN, Sallie Elliot (Cal) 756 14th Way SW, Edmonds, WA 98020

SHIRE, James Robert (The Episcopal Church in Haw)

SHIRLEY, Diana Frangoulis (SO) 664 Glacier Pass, Westerville, OH 43081

SHIRLEY, Fredric C (SO) 664 Glacier Pass, Westerville, OH 43081

SHIRLEY, John Robert (LI) 7 Warner Ln, Lake Ronkonkoma, NY 11779

SHIRLEY, Sarah A (WA) PO Box 690, Waynesburg, PA 15370

SHIRLEY, Sylvia (Okla) St John's Episcopal Church, 5201 N Brookline Ave, Oklahoma City, OK 73112

SHIROTA, Andrew Kunihito (Ky) 4700 Lowe Rd, Louisville, KY 40220

SHISLER, Sara (The Episcopal Church in Haw) 480 Olinda Rd, Makawao, HI 96768

SHIVES, Beverly Mason (SeFla) 159 Biscayne Ave, Tampa, FL 33606

SHIVES, Robert Edward (WVa) 154 East St, Kearneysville, WV 25430

SHOBE, Melody W (RI) 2407 Cranston St., Cranston, RI 02920

SHOBE, Robert Casey (Dal) 7956 Roundrock Rd, Dallas, TX 75248

SHOCKLEY, Stephanie Elizabeth (NJ) 316 E 88th St, New York, NY 10128

SHODA, David Brian (WVa) 108 S Washington St, Berkeley Springs, WV 25411

SHOEMAKER, Adam (SC) The Tec Ch Of The H Comforter, 320 East Davis Street, Burlington, NC 27215

SHOEMAKER, Eric Wayne (CFla) 8795 Lowell Road, Pomfret, MD 20675

SHOEMAKER, Patricia Ross Pittman (NC) 22 Mayflower Ln, Lexington, NC 27295

SHOEMAKER, Stephanie (RI) 96 Washington St, Newport, RI 02840

SHOFSTALL, Sarah (O) 25400 Fort Meigs Rd Apt 104, Perrysburg, OH 43551

SHOLANDER, Mark Earl (CFla) 721 Governor Morrison St Unit 426, Charlotte, NC 28211

SHOLTY JR, Henry Edward (Dal) 5942 Abrams Rd # 209, Dallas, TX 75231

SHORES-FOSTER, Robyn (SD)

SHORT, James Healy (Colo) 797 Tower Hill Rd., Appomattox, VA 24522

SHORT, James Ritchie (Episcopal SJ) Casanova & ocean, Carmel, CA 93921

SHORT, Molly (Tenn) 290 Quintard Rd, Sewanee, TN 37375

SHORTELL, Bruce Mallard (At) PO Box 1293, Flowery Branch, GA 30542

SHORTES, Stephen Edward (The Episcopal NCal) 2883 Coloma St, Placerville, CA 95667

SHORTESS, Stephen A (WTex)

SHORTRIDGE, Delores J (Nev) 973 S. Fulton St., Denver, CO 80247

SHORTT, Mary J (EMich) P.O. Box 151, West Branch, MI 48661

SHOUCAIR, James Douglas (Pgh) 130 Westchester Dr, Pittsburgh, PA 15215

SHOULAK, Jim (Minn) 20475 County Road 10, Corcoran, MN 55340

SHOWERS, David (Md) Middleham St Peter Ep Par, PO Box 277, Lusby, MD 20657

SHOWS, William Derek (NC) 1077 Fearrington Post, Pittsboro, NC 27312

SHOWS CAFFEY, Elizabeth Kristen (At) 634 W Peachtree St NW, Atlanta, GA 30308

SHRIVER, Domingo Frances (WMich) 301 N James St, Ludington, MI 49431

SHUART, Steve (NwPa) PO Box 368, South Harwich, MA 02661

SHUFORD, Carlton Lamont (Ga) 131 Avondale Dr, Augusta, GA 30907

SHUFORD, Sheila Cathcart (Nwk) 12 Sorman Ter, Randolph, NJ 07869

SHUKAIR, Halim Adel (Mich) 120 N Military St, Dearborn, MI 48124

SHULDA, David Leroy (Ore) 2139 Berwin Ln, Eugene, OR 97404

SHUMAKER, Jack (Episcopal SJ) 1317 Gold Hunter Rd, San Andreas, CA 95249

SHUMARD, Jim (Wyo) 701 S Wolcott St, Casper, WY 82601

SHUMATE, Jonathan Kale Gavin (Ore)

SIBERINE, Katherine H (NH) 1704 Ne 43rd Ave, Portland, OR 97213

SIBLEY, David C (Spok) 59 Chapelwood Ave, Walla Walla, WA 99362

SICHANGI, Nicholas Nyongesa (Eas)

SICILIANO, Elizabeth Diana (Md)

SICKELS, Peter L (Ia) 4814 Amesbury Ct, Davenport, IA 52807

SICKLER, Brenda Pamela (WMo) 5 E 337th Rd, Humansville, MO 65674

SIDEBOTHAM, John Nelson (EC) 16 Fayetteville St W, Wrightsville Beach, NC 28480

SIDERIUS, Donna-Mae (SVa) 3 Mizzen Cir, Hampton, VA 23664

SIDES, Serena Wille (WA) 620 G St SE, Washington, DC 20003

SIEGEL II, Carl De Haven (WMo) 1405 Boyce Ave, Baltimore, MD 21204

SIEGFRIEDT, Karen (The Episcopal NCal) 170 Verdon St, Morro Bay, CA 93442

SIEGMUND, Mary Kay (Kan) 3 Ne 83rd Ter, Kansas City, MO 64118

SIENER, George Richard (NH) 6 Whippoorwill Ln, Exeter, NH 03833

SIERACKI, Emily (Ida) 518 N 8th St, Boise, ID 83702

SIERRA, Alfredo Nuno (Cu)

SIERRA, Federico (Los) 425 N Stoneman Ave Apt A, Alhambra, CA 91801

SIERRA, Frank (WMo) 2718 Alabama Ct, Joplin, MO 64804

SIERRA, Jesus (NC) Ch TEC PR, PO Box 902, Saint Just, PR 00978

SIERRA ECHEVERRY, Gabriel Alcides (Colom) Par La Anunciacion, El Bagre, Apartado Aereo 52964, Bogota, Colombia

SIFFORD, Thomas Andrew (Ark) 74 Sierra Dr, Hot Springs Village, AR 71909

SIFONTES, Marisa Anne (NC)

SIGAFOOS, Richard Vaughn (Colo) 131 31 Rd, Grand Junction, CO 81503

SIGAMONEY, Christopher (LI)

SIGLER, James (The Episcopal NCal) PO Box 467, Wimberley, TX 78676

SIGLER JR, Richard Eugene (NC) 930 Walker Ave, Greensboro, NC 27403

SIGLOH, Jane Engleby (SwVa) 4068 Garth Rd, Crozet, VA 22932

SIGNORE, Richard S (WMass) 19 Briggs Ave, Bourne, MA 02532

SIGNORELLI, Barry M (NY) 278 Monmouth St Apt 4-L, Jersey City, NJ 07302

SILBAUGH, Morgan Collins (Cal) 914 Mountain Meadows Cir, Ashland, OR 97520

SILBEREIS, Richard M (Ct) 155 Wyllys St, Hartford, CT 06106

SILCOX JR, James Heyward (Va) Wicomico Parish Church, PO Box 70, Wicomico Church, VA 22579

SILIDES JR, George Constantine (NC) 830 W Bonita Ave, Claremont, CA 91711

SILIDES, Hunter (NC) 411 Gold St, Juneau, AK 99801

SILK-WRIGHT, Margaret E (CFla) 1813 Palo Alto Ave, Lady Lake, FL 32159

SILLA, Suzeanne Marie (ETenn) Diocese of Northern Indiana, 117 N Lafayette Blvd, South Bend, IN 46601

SILTON, Margaret Kanze (NC) 2 Magnolia Ct, Greensboro, NC 27401

SILVA-GONZALEZ, Alvaro (PR)

SILVA PAREZ, Jose Espar (Colom)

SILVER, Deborah Lee (At) 3005 St James Pl, Grovetown, GA 30813

SILVER, Gay (Fla) 14557 Basilham Ln, Jacksonville, FL 32258

SILVERSTRIM, Elaine Margaret (CPa) 110 Dry Run Rd., Coudersport, PA 16915

SIMEONE, Richard (Mass) 100 Sarah Ln Apt 14, Simsbury, CT 06070

SIMMONS, Charles Winston (NY) St Andrews Church, 781 Castle Hill Ave, Bronx, NY 10473

SIMMONS, David (Mil) 808 S East Ave, Waukesha, WI 63186

SIMMONS, Harriet (Miss) 4911 Country Club Dr, Meridian, MS 39305

SIMMONS, Harriette (At) Saint Pauls Church, 605 Reynolds St, Augusta, GA 30901

SIMMONS, Lydia (SD)

SIMMONS, Mary Rose (NMich) 5976 Whitney 19.8 Blvd, Gladstone, MI 49837

SIMMONS, Michele (ETenn)

SIMMONS IV, Tom (Va) 1807 Hungary Rd, Richmond, VA 23228

SIMMONS, Warren Reginald (At) 106 Ardsley Run, Canton, GA 30115

SIMON JR, Ken (SanD) 6556 Park Ridge Blvd, San Diego, CA 92120

SIMONIAN, Marlene Jenny (RI) 1346 Creek Nine Dr, North Port, FL 34290

SIMONS, Daniel J (NY) 311 Newtown Tpke, Wilton, CT 06897

SIMONS, Jim (Pgh) 736 18th Ct, Vero Beach, FL 32962

SIMONSEN, Douglas C (Oly) PO Box 1974, Anacortes, WA 98221

SIMOPOULOS, Nicole M (SanD) 563 Kamoku St, Honolulu, HI 96826

SIMPLE, Margaret (Ak)

SIMPSON, Ashley Danielle (EC) 609 Broad St, Beaufort, NC 28516

SIMPSON, Christopher Ben (Spr) 402 Pekin St., Lincoln, IL 62656

SIMPSON, Cindy (EC) Christ Episcopal School, 107 S Washington St, Rockville, MD 20850

SIMPSON, Dawn Marie (Colo) Po Box 291, Monte Vista, CO 81144

SIMPSON, Elizabeth Bass (Mo) St Matthews Episcopal Church, 1100 Grove St, Mexico, MO 65265

SIMPSON, Geoffrey Stewart (Pa) Church Of The Good Samaritan, 212 W Lancaster Ave, Paoli, PA 19301

SIMPSON IV, John C. (SwVa)

SIMPSON, Matthew David (Me) PO Box 387, Buckingham, PA 18912

SIMPSON, Richard Edmund (LI) 405 Ragan Rd, Oriental, NC 28571

SIMPSON, Richard Michael (WMass) 88 Highland St, Holden, MA 01520

SIMPSON, Richard Roy (RI) 7009 SE 117th Pl, Portland, OR 97266

SIMPSON, Sallie O'Keef (NC) 1315 Oakwood Ave, Raleigh, NC 27610

SIMPSON, Ward Howard (SD) 500 S Main Ave, Sioux Falls, SD 57104

SIMRILL, Spenser (At) 4945 Dupont Ave S, Minneapolis, MN 55419

SIMS, Ashton Lane-Ross (ETenn)

SIMS, Carol Carruthers (SVa) 3929 Ocean Cut Lane, Virginia Beach, VA 23451

SIMS, Elizabeth Erringer (Cal) 1700 Santa Clara Ave, Alameda, CA 94501

SIMS, Gordon C (CFla)

SIMS, Gregory Brian (Chi) 4233 Ahlstrand Dr, Rockford, IL 61101

SIMS, Gregory Knox (Cal) Po Box 1, Boonville, CA 95415

SIMS, Rebekah Elizabeth (Ind) Chapel of the Good Shepherd, 610 Meridian St, West Lafayette, IN 47906

SIMS, Richard Osborn (Nev) 24 Elysium Dr, Ely, NV 89301

SIMS, William David (Ark) 3686 Savanna Way, Palm Springs, CA 92262

SIMSON, John (Mass) 4773 Abargo St, Woodland Hills, CA 91364

SINCLAIR, Barbara Louise (Chi) St James Episcopal Church, 425 E MacArthur Ave, Lewistown, IL 61542

SINCLAIR, Elisabeth Anne (WMo) 7110 N State Route 9, Kansas City, MO 64152

SINCLAIR, Gregory Lynn (NwT) 801 Ross Ave, Abilene, TX 79605

SINCLAIR, Nancy (Los) 502 Hawk Ln, Fountain Valley, CA 92708

SINCLAIR, Scott Gambrill (Cal) 663 Coventry Rd, Kensington, CA 94707

SINCLAIR, Thomas Roy (WA) 1001 4th St SW Apt 710, 710, Washington, DC 20024

SINCLAIR JR, William Carter (SVa) 5181 Singleton Way, Virginia Beach, VA 23462

SINGER, Allen Michael (EC) 2429 Tara Forest Drive, Leland, NC 28451

SINGER, Ann Kilpen (Va)

SINGER, Blake A (Va)

SINGER, Susanna Jane (Cal) 1233 Howard St Apt 714, San Francisco, CA 94103

✠ **SINGH**, Prince Grenville (Roch) 4 Cathedral Oaks, Fairport, NY 14450

SINGH, Simon Peter (Chi) 261 W Army Trail Rd, Bloomingdale, IL 60108

SINGLETON, Jill (Nwk) 38 Duncan Ave, Jersey City, NJ 07304

SINGLETON, Richard Oliver (Mich) 1520 W River Rd, Scottsville, VA 24590

SINISI, Gabriel A (Az) 18995 W Cholla St, Surprise, AZ 85388

SINK, Thomas Leslie (NJ) Po Box 3010, Pt Pleasant, NJ 08742

SINNING, Thomas John (Minn) 1517 Rosewood Cir, Alexandria, MN 56308

SINNOTT, Lynn (Roch) 4577 Townsley Rd, Cedarville, OH 45314

SINTIM, Tim (NC) 1925 Waters Dr, Raleigh, NC 27610

SIPE, Robert Billie (Ore) 59048 Whitetail Ave, Saint Helens, OR 97051

SIPES, David Sheldon (O) 446 Shepard Rd, Mansfield, OH 44907

SIPOS, Elizabeth Anne Margaret (Md) 11901 Belair Rd, Kingsville, MD 21087

SIPPLE, Peter Warren (Pa) 45 Bay View Avenue, Cornwall on Hudson, NY 12520

SIPTROTH, Stephen Michael (Cal)

SIRCY, Micheal John (SwFla)

SIRENO, Robert (Ct)

SIRIANI, Laura Eustis (Los) 1221 Wass St, Tustin, CA 92780

SIRMON JR, Thomas Forbes (CGC) 860 N Section St, Fairhope, AL 36532

SIROTA, Victoria (NY) 7 Sirota Dr, Searsmont, ME 04973

SISK, Heather (NY)

✠ **SISK**, Mark (NY) PO Box 53, Jefferson, NY 12093

SISK, Robert Buchanan (Mont) Rr 1 Box 241, Wilsall, MT 59086

SISSON, Duane (Cal) 2973 California St, Oakland, CA 94602

SISSON, Penny Ray (Miss) 414 Turnberry Cir, Oxford, MS 38655

SITES, Melissa Jo (WA) 13 Hillside Rd Unit T, Greenbelt, MD 20770

SITTS, C Joseph (CFla) 271 New Waterford Pl, Longwood, FL 32779

SIVE, Marian (Alb) 17 Pond Ln, Troy, NY 12182

SIVLEY, John Stephen (CPa) 869E Rhue Haus Ln, Hummelstown, PA 17036

SIWEK, Peter (Chi) 733 Hayes Ave, Oak Park, IL 60302

SIZE, Patricia Barrett (Mil) 2215 Commonwealth Ave, Madison, WI 53726

SKAGGS, Richard Lee (WVa) 1410 Chapline St, Wheeling, WV 26003

SKALA, Kira (Va) 241 Signal Ridge Ln, Winchester, VA 22603

SKALESKI, Elizabeth Harris (Ct)

SKAU, Laurie Jean (Minn) 6727 France Ave N, Brooklyn Center, MN 55429

SKAUG, Jon (Az)

SKEATES, Winifred June (NH) 32 Pickering Farm Rd, Hancock, NH 03449

SKEITH, Minerva Camarena (Tex)

SKEITH, Paul (Tex) 1502 Eva St, Austin, TX 78704

SKELLEN, Bonnie Jean (NwPa) 425 E Main St, Ridgway, PA 15853

SKELLY, Herbert Cope (Mass) 40 Woodland Way, Eastham, MA 02642

SKEWES-COX, Peter Dunne (Nev)

SKIDMORE, Joanne Louise (FdL) 2389 Penny Ln, Sister Bay, WI 54234

SKIFFINGTON, Steven Wayne (Episcopal SJ) Trinity Cathedral, 2620 Capitol Ave, Sacramento, CA 95816

SKILLICORN, Gerald Amos (WMo) 2207 Conrad Way, Somerset, NJ 08873

SKILLINGS, Thomas (Mo) 1104 Mills Ave, Burlingame, CA 94010

SKINNER, Beatrice (SD)

SKINNER, Jean Mary (CNY) 40 Faxton St, Utica, NY 13501

SKINNER, Susan (Mo) 400 Mark Dr, Saint Louis, MO 63122

✠ **SKIRVING**, Robert Stuart (EC) TEC Dio Of E Ca, PO Box 1336, Kinston, NC 28503

SKOGLUND, Lars (Mil) 4635 Erie St, Racine, WI 53402

SKOGLUND, Melesa Hope Mcewan (Mil) St Andrews Episcopal Church, 1833 Regent St, Madison, WI 53726

SKORBURG, R. Chase (Dal)

SKORNIK, Andria (Ore) St Andrews Episcopal Church, 1125 Franklin St, Downers Grove, IL 60515

SKUTCH, Patrick J (Chi) 306 S Prospect Ave, Park Ridge, IL 60068

SLABACH, Brock Allen (WMo) 16808 S State Route D, Belton, MO 64012

SLACK, Sean (Pa) St Pauls Church, 89 Pinewood Dr, Levittown, PA 19054

SLADE, Debra Katherine Ann (Ct) 503 Old Long Ridge Rd, Stamford, CT 06903

SLADE, Kara N (NJ) Saint Davids Episcopal Church, PO Box 334, Laurinburg, NC 28353

SLAKEY, Anne Elisa Margaret (The Episcopal NCal) 110 N. 10th St., Payette, ID 83661

SLANE, Christopher D (SO)

SLANE, Melanie West Jianakoplos (SO) 3524 Glen Edge Ln, Cincinnati, OH 45213

SLANGER, George Comfort (ND) 8435 207th St. W., Lakeville, MN 55044

SLATER, Amy A (Fla) 44 Dewees Ave, Atlantic Beach, FL 32233

SLATER, Chadwick M (WVa) 200 Duhring St, Bluefield, WV 24701

SLATER, Joan (NMich) PO Box100, Mackinac Island, MI 49757

SLATER, Jo Ann Kennedy (Mich) 5416 Parkgrove Rd, Ann Arbor, MI 48103

SLATER, Michael (Nev) 7900 Pueblo Dr, Stagecoach, NV 89429

SLATER, Sarah Elizabeth (WA)

SLATER, Scott (Md) 4 E University Pkwy, Baltimore, MD 21218

SLAUGHTER, Susan (Tex) 1612 Boardwalk Ct, Arlington, TX 76011

SLAVIN, Nancy (Cal)

SLAWNWHITE, Virginia Ann (NH) Po Box 433, Portsmouth, NH 03802

SLAWSON III, H Thomas (Miss) 2456 Sunkist Country Club Rd, Biloxi, MS 39532

SLAYMAKER, Lorraine P (Ark) 1112 Alcoa Rd, Benton, AR 72015

SLEMP, Dennett Clinton (SVa) 11001 Ashburn Rd, North Chesterfield, VA 23235

SLENSKI, Mary (Ind) 5256 Central Ave, Indianapolis, IN 46220

SLIGH, John Lewis (SeFla) 2422 W Stroud Ave, Tampa, FL 33629

SLOAN, Ellen Margaret (SwFla) St Michael All Angels, 2304 Periwinkle Way, Sanibel, FL 33957

✠ **SLOAN SR**, John Mckee (Ala) 521 20th St N, Birmingham, AL 35203

SLOAN, Richard D (NY) 90 Gilbert Road, Ho-Ho-kus, NJ 07423

SLOAN, Stan Jude (RG) 2313 N Kedzie Blvd # 2, Chicago, IL 60647

SLOAN, Susan (Ala) 821 Baylor Drive, Huntsville, AL 35802

SLOCUM, Robert Boak (Lex) PO Box 2505, Danville, KY 40423

SLONE, Remington (At) 105 Benmore Bay, Johns Creek, GA 30022

SLOVAK, Anita M (Az) Christ The King Tec Ch, 2800 W Ina Rd, Tucson, AZ 85741

SLUSHER, Bonnie G (SD) 5314 Somerset Dr, Rowlett, TX 75089

SLUSHER, Montie Bearl (Ak) 1133 Park Dr., Fairbanks, AK 99709

SLUSS, Mark Duane (Spok) 2365 Copperbrook Ct, Richland, WA 99354

SMALL, Timothy K (CPa) 370 Spring Hill Ln, Columbia, PA 17512

SMALLEY, H Bud (Ida) 5170 Leonard Rd, Pocatello, ID 83204

SMALLEY, Nancy T (Dal) 416 Victorian Dr, Waxahachie, TX 75165

SMALLEY, Richard Craig (Ala) 2017 6th Avenue North, Birmingham, AL 35203

SMALLEY, Stephen Mark (Pgh) 210 Strawberry Cir, Cranberry Township, PA 16066

✠ **SMALLEY**, William Edward (Ind) 13809 E 186th St, Noblesville, IN 46060

SMALLWOOD, Kevin A (WMass)

SMART, Dennis (At) 442 Euclid Ter Ne, Atlanta, GA 30307

SMART JR, James Hudson (NwT) 1826 Elmwood Dr, Abilene, TX 79605

SMART, John A (Pa) 5100 N Northridge Cir, Tucson, AZ 85718

SMART, LuLa Grace Grace (Pa) 147 7th Ave, Folsom, PA 19033

SMARTT, Cleda (Mich)

SMEDLEY IV, Wes (Chi) 900 N Wood St Apt 1s, Chicago, IL 60622

SMELSER, Todd Dudley (At) 1358 E Rock Springs Rd NE, Atlanta, GA 30306

SMILEY-LYKINS, Brenda (SVa) 2817 Mohawk Dr, North Chesterfield, VA 23235

SMIRAGLIA, Richard Paul (Pa) 340 Fitzwater Street, Philadelphia, PA 19147

SMITH, Aaron William (Fla) 4775 Godwin Ave, Jacksonville, FL 32210

SMITH, Adeline (CFla)

SMITH, Aidan (Pgh)

SMITH, Alan Bruce (SO) 627 Yaronia Dr N, Columbus, OH 43214

SMITH, Aloha (Los) 5848 Tower Rd, Riverside, CA 92506

SMITH, Andrea (Ct) 16 Clam Shell Alley, P.O. Box 412, Vinalhaven, ME 04863

SMITH, Ann (Chi)

SMITH, Anne (Chi)

SMITH, Anne Largent (The Episcopal NCal) 7718 Turtle Cove Way, Elk Grove, CA 95758

SMITH, Ann-Lining (Cal) 750 47th Ave Spc 34, Capitola, CA 95010

SMITH, Arthur Wells (CNY) 341 Main St, Oneida, NY 13421

SMITH, Barbara Joan (U) Tec Carmel Of St Teresa, 123 Little New York Rd, Rising Sun, MD 21911

SMITH, Bert Orville (At) 841 Kings Grant Dr NW, Atlanta, GA 30318

SMITH, Betty Lorraine (NMich) 8114 Trout Lake Rd, Naubinway, MI 49762

SMITH JR, Bob (Me) 35 Prospect St, Caribou, ME 04736

SMITH, Bob (Eas) 35 Spruance Ct, Elkton, MD 21921

SMITH, Bobby (Chi) 724 Highland Ave, Salina, KS 67401

SMITH, Bonnie (EC) 501 S Harding Dr Apt 1002, Goldsboro, NC 27534

SMITH, Bradford Ray (NC) 116 S Church St, PO Box 293, Monroe, NC 28111

SMITH, Brian E (Fla) 2402 San Pedro Ave, Tallahassee, FL 32304

SMITH, Bruce (Cal) 14 Ardmore Ct, Pleasant Hill, CA 94523

SMITH, Carol Diane (Minn) 1211 Jackson Ave, Detroit Lakes, MN 56501

SMITH, Carol Kay Huston (Mil) 4522 Aztec Trl, Fitchburg, WI 53711

SMITH, Carter Aestin (WNC) 2499 N Westmoreland Dr, Orlando, FL 32804

SMITH, Cathleen Anne (WNY) 410 N Main St, Jamestown, NY 14701

SMITH, Cecilia Mary Babcock (Tex) PO Box 2247, Austin, TX 78768

SMITH, Channing (Tex) 13601 Saratoga Avenue, Saratoga, CA 95070

SMITH, Charles J (USC) St Michael and All Angels, 6408 Bridgewood Rd, Columbia, SC 29206

SMITH, Charles Rodney (Tex) 156 Fairacres Ln, Sewanee, TN 37375

SMITH, Charles Stuart (Alb) 45 Pierrepont Ave., Potsdam, NY 13676

SMITH, Chris (Alb) 12 Main St., Hagaman, NY 12086

SMITH, Claudia L (Me) 810 Morgan Bay Rd, Blue Hill, ME 04614

SMITH, Coleen Haas (SO)

SMITH III, Colton Mumford (SC) 1 Bishop Gadsden Way Apt 346, Charleston, SC 29412

SMITH, Craig Faulkner (Vt) 5 Lake Forest Dr, Burlington, VT 05401

SMITH, Craig Loren (Az)

☩ **SMITH**, Dabney (SwFla) The Dio Of SW Florida, 8005 25th St E, Parrish, FL 34219

SMITH, Dale Leroy (Los) 10451 Jordan Pkwy, Hopewell, VA 23860

SMITH, David Grant (Cal) 655 Colby Cir Apt 17, Claremont, CA 91711

SMITH, David Gregory (Mont) 5 W Olive St, Bozeman, MT 59715

SMITH, David Hayes (Va) 800 Chatham Hall Cir., Chatham, VA 24531

SMITH, David Lester (WNY) 5448 Broadway St, Lancaster, NY 14086

SMITH, Don Leland (Oly) 8989 S Pine Dr, Beulah, CO 81023

SMITH, Donald Hedges (Roch) 2492 Keystone Lake Drive, Cape Coral, FL 33909

SMITH III, Donald M (WLa) 860 N Section St, Fairhope, AL 36532

SMITH, Doris Graf (At) 282 Hemlock Ct, Clarkesville, GA 30523

SMITH, Douglas Cameron (CPa) 779 Long Ln, Gettysburg, PA 17325

☩ **SMITH**, Drew (Ct) 106 Vista Way, Bloomfield, CT 06002

SMITH, Duane Andre (Lex) 110 Chestnut Ct, Berea, KY 40403

SMITH, Edward D (CFla) 1210 Locust St, Saint Louis, MO 63103

SMITH, Edwin Earl St Clair (Pa) 154 Locksley Rd, Glen Mills, PA 19342

SMITH JR, Frank Warner (Neb) 2303 Elk, Beatrice, NE 68310

SMITH, Gail S (Mass) 35 Skyline Dr, Chatham, MA 02633

SMITH, Geoffrey T (NH) 400 E 58th St Apt 3c, New York, NY 10022

SMITH III, George (Chi) 792 Forest Ave, Glen Ellyn, IL 60137

SMITH, Georgianna (Minn)

SMITH, Glenn Colyer (Chi) 754 Main St, Islip, NY 11751

SMITH, Gregory (EC)

SMITH, Gregory Louis (SC) 314 Grove St, Charleston, SC 29403

SMITH JR, Harmon Lee (NC) 3510 Randolph Rd, Durham, NC 27705

SMITH, H Gregory (Pa) 5421 Germantown Ave, Philadelphia, PA 19144

SMITH, Hilary Borbon (Va) 4924 Bethlehem Rd., Richmond, VA 23230

SMITH, H Mark (Mass) 10 Linda Ln Apt 2-8, Dorchester, MA 02125

SMITH, Hubert (CNY) 2891 Oran Delphi Rd, Manlius, NY 13104

SMITH, Jacob Andrew (NY) 61 Gramercy Park N Apt 7, New York, NY 10010

SMITH, Jacqueline Kay (Oly) 6208 83rd St Sw, Lakewood, WA 98499

SMITH, James Clare (Be) 302 Pine St, Ashland, PA 17921

SMITH, James Dinard (SVa) 3235 Sherwood Ridge Dr, Powhatan, VA 23139

SMITH JR, James Owen (EC) 113 S Woodlawn Ave, Greenville, NC 27858

SMITH, Jane Gravlee (WNC) 40 Wildwood Ave., Asheville, NC 28804

SMITH, Jay (NY) 145 W 46th St # 4, New York, NY 10036

SMITH, Jean (Ia) St Timothys Epscopal Ch, 1020 24th St, West Des Moines, IA 50266

SMITH, Jean Ann (Ind) 6033 Gladden Dr, Indianapolis, IN 46220

SMITH, Jean Reinhart (NJ) 58 Jenny Ln, Brattleboro, VT 05301

SMITH, Jeffry Bradford (Episcopal SJ) 10 St Theresa'S Avenue, W Roxbury, MA 02132, Great Britain (UK)

SMITH, Jennifer Dorothy (Dal) 3609 Steven Dr, Plano, TX 75023

SMITH, Jerry W (Fla) 4800 Belmont Park Ter, Nashville, TN 37215

SMITH IV, Jess Wayne (Wyo) 33 Windy Ridge Rd, Laramie, WY 82070

SMITH, Jesse George (Tex) 2825 Winterhaven Dr, Hurst, TX 76054

SMITH, Jessica (Los) St Anne's Episcopal Church, 2350 Main St, Washougal, WA 98671

SMITH, Jethroe Larrie (At) 46 S Main St, Wadley, GA 30477

SMITH, Joan (Ky) 1077 Merrick Dr, Lexington, KY 40502

SMITH, John (Md) 6108 River Crescent Dr, Annapolis, MD 21401

SMITH, John Perry (Fla) 256 E Church St, Jacksonville, FL 32202

SMITH, John Peterson (WLa) 1904 Jasmine Dr, Opelousas, LA 70570

SMITH JR, John Robert (Az) 602 N Wilmot Rd, Tucson, AZ 85711

SMITH, Jonathan R (Ct)

SMITH, Joseph Kershaw (Pa) 101 Shelton Dr, Spartanburg, SC 29307

SMITH, Juanita Dawn (Wyo) 15 S Tschirgi St, Sheridan, WY 82801

SMITH, Julie (Ore) 335 SE 8th Ave, Hillsboro, OR 97123

SMITH, Julie Lynn (Pgh)

SMITH, Karen (Colo) 19580 Pilgrims Pl, Parker, CO 80138

SMITH, Kate E (Dal)

SMITH, Kathryn Barr (Ala) St Stephen's Episcopal Church, 3775 Crosshaven Dr, Vestavia, AL 35223

SMITH, Kent Clarke (Ct) 112 Sconset Ln, Guilford, CT 06437

SMITH, Kerry Jon (Md) 6097 Franklin Gibson Rd, Tracys Landing, MD 20779

SMITH, Kevin Corbin (Oly) 507 Mcgraw St, Seattle, WA 98109

SMITH, Kirby (SanD) 2083 Sunset Cliffs Blvd, San Diego, CA 92107

☩ **SMITH**, Kirk Stevan (Az) 114 W Roosevelt St, Phoenix, AZ 85003

SMITH, Kristy K (Ia) 4339 W Sawmill Ct, Castle Rock, CO 80109

SMITH, Larry Phillip (Dal) 3208 Bloomfield Ct, Plano, TX 75093

SMITH, Leslie Carl (NJ) 153 Seamans Rd, New London, NH 03257

SMITH, Letitia Lee (NC) 2725 Wilshire Ave. S.W., Roanoke, VA 24015

SMITH, Linda Becker (Nev) St Paul's Episcopal Church, PO Box 737, Sparks, NV 89432

SMITH, Lisa White (Minn) 4900 Nathan Lane, Plymouth, MN 55442

SMITH, Lizabeth (Nwk) 653 Courtney Hollow Lane, Madison, VA 22727

SMITH, Lora Alison (Alb) 531 County Route 59, Potsdam, NY 13676

SMITH III, Louis Murdock (NC) 4320 Innisfree Ct, Indian Trail, NC 28079

SMITH, Marc D (Mo) 4520 Lucas and Hunt Rd, Saint Louis, MO 63121

SMITH, Margaret Mary Stapleton (Ct)

SMITH, Mark (NJ) 1904 Walnut St, Philadelphia, PA 19103

SMITH, Martin L (WA) 429 N St SW Apt S306, Washington, DC 20024

SMITH, Mary Jo (Vt) 973 Route 106, Reading, VT 05062

SMITH, Melissa (Tenn) 84 Broadway, New Haven, CT 06511

SMITH JR, Merle Edwin (Ia) 715 W 7th St S, Newton, IA 50208

✠ **SMITH**, Michael (ND) PO Box 8, Naytahwaush, MN 56566

SMITH, Michael Allen (Az) 7101 N Perugia Way, Tucson, AZ 85741

SMITH, Michael John (SO)

SMITH, Michael W (SC) 218 Ashley Ave., Charleston, SC 29403

SMITH, Miles Miles (Va) Grace Church, 5607 Gordonsville Rd, PO Box 43, Keswick, VA 22947

SMITH, Miriam Ruth (Ia)

SMITH, Mitchell T (USC) 1329 Jackson Ave, New Orleans, LA 70130

SMITH, Molly Dale (NJ) 805 Timber Ln., Nashville, TN 37215

SMITH, Nancy Metze (SwFla) 13011 Sandy Key Bend, Apt 1, North Fort Myers, FL 33903

SMITH, Nancy Spencer (Mass) 29 W Cedar St, Boston, MA 02108

SMITH, Nora (NY) 136 Hover Ave, Germantown, NY 12526

SMITH, Paul (Ak) 9631 Noaya Cir, Eagle River, AK 99577

SMITH, Paul Weeghman (Ky) 3724 Hillsdale Rd, Louisville, KY 40222

SMITH, Rebecca Jean (Neb)

SMITH, Rebecca Marie (Miss)

SMITH, Richard Byron (NC) 6 Natchez Ct, Greensboro, NC 27455

SMITH, Richard Leslie (Cal) 226 Clinton Park, San Francisco, CA 94103

SMITH JR, Richard Winton (Pa) 305 E 83rd St Apt 4g, New York, NY 10028

SMITH, Robert E (Mich) 22326 Cherry Hill St, Dearborn, MI 48124

SMITH, Robert Kennedy (CFla) 3224 Carleton Circle East, Lakeland, FL 33803

SMITH, Roberts (Los)

SMITH, Robin (Pa) 107 Allison Rd, Oreland, PA 19075

SMITH, Robin Penman (Dal) 2712 E Aspen CT, Plano, TX 75075

SMITH, Roger W (SC) 15 Newpoint Rd, Beaufort, SC 29907

SMITH, Ron (Tex) 1403 Preston Ave, Austin, TX 78703

SMITH, Rose Ann (NwT) 3500 Barclay Dr, Amarillo, TX 79109

SMITH, Samantha Ruth Elizabeth (Tex)

SMITH, Samuel J (WMass) PO BOX 1524, PO Box 1524, Stockbridge, MA 01262

SMITH, Sarah E (Okla)

SMITH, Sarah W (Va)

SMITH, Smith (SO) 333 S Drexel Ave, Bexley, OH 43209

SMITH, Stanley James (O) 249 E 7th St, New York, NY 10009

SMITH, Stephen (SO) 7121 Muirfield Dr, Dublin, OH 43017

SMITH, Stephen (Tex) 3310 Nathanael Rd., Greensboro, NC 27408

SMITH, Stephen H (Tex) 10 North Lavender, Ranchos de Taos, NM 87557

SMITH, Stephen John Stanyon (WNY) 100 Beard Ave, Buffalo, NY 14214

SMITH, Stephen Richard (Los)

SMITH, Steven Ronald (Eur) Church of the Ascension, Seybothstrasse 4, 81545 Munich, Germany

SMITH, Stuart (Nwk) 2112 North St, Orange, VA 22960

SMITH, Susan (Ark) 1809 Canal Pointe, Little Rock, AR 72202

SMITH, Susannah Rankin (NY) 219 Old Franklin Grove Dr, Chapel Hill, NC 27514

SMITH, Suzanne Gail (Tex) 909 Manor Dr, Angleton, TX 77515

SMITH, Taylor Magavern (SC) 120 Brailsford St, Daniel Island, SC 29492

SMITH, Ted (Tex) PO Box 10357, Liberty, TX 77575

SMITH, Thee (At) 3530 Fairlane Dr NW, Atlanta, GA 30331

SMITH, Thomas A (Dal)

SMITH, Thomas Eugene (EMich) 1523 N Oak Rd, Davison, MI 48423

SMITH, Thomas Gibson (Chi) 118 Tanglewood Dr, Elk Grove Village, IL 60007

SMITH JR, Thomas Parshall (NY) 225 W 99th St, New York, NY 10025

SMITH, Timothy Clarke (Cal) 2325 Union St, San Francisco, CA 94123

SMITH, Travis H (Tex) H Comforter Tec Ch, PO Box 786, Angleton, TX 77516

SMITH, Travis K (Md) St Michaels Episcopal Church, 1520 Canterbury Rd, Raleigh, NC 27608

SMITH, Twila (WNY) Cathedral Commons, 128 Pearl Street Apt 6, Buffalo, NY 14202

SMITH, Vicki (Kan) 10104 Sorrills Creek Ln, Raleigh, NC 27614

SMITH, Vickie Mitchel (Ark) 601 Brookside Dr Apt 12, Little Rock, AR 72205

SMITH III, Walter Frederick (RG) 10328, Albuquerque, NM 87114

✠ **SMITH**, Wayne (Mo) 823 Carillon Ct, Saint Louis, MO 63141

SMITH, Wendy M (ECR) 4061 Sutherland Dr, Palo Alto, CA 94303

SMITH, Wesley Wesley (At) 210 Willie Six Road, Sewanee, TN 37375

SMITH, Whitney B (Ind) 1323 N Dequincy St, Indianapolis, IN 46201

SMITH, WillaMarie Eileen (CFla) 381 N Lincoln St, Daytona Beach, FL 32114

SMITH, Willard Boardman (Okla)

SMITH, William Charles (NwT) St Matthew's Episcopal Church, 727 W Browning Ave, Pampa, TX 79065

SMITH, William Herbert (WMich) 2073 SE North Blackwell Dr, Port St Lucie, FL 34952

SMITH, William Louis (Md) 24 Lake Dr, Bel Air, MD 21014

SMITH III, William Paul (Fla) PO Box 1005, Hilliard, FL 32046

SMITH, Willie (Nwk)

SMITH, Winston Teal (Pa)

SMITH-ALLEN, Serita Verner (EO) Po Box 186, Union, OR 97883

SMITH BOOTH, Rebecca "Beccy" (Tex) 114 Otter Trail SW, Huntsville, AL 35824

SMITH-CRIDDLE, Linda C (O) 19 Pent Road, Madison, CT 06443

SMITHDEAL JR, Foss Tyra (NC) 8050 Ravenwood Ln, Stanley, NC 28164

SMITHERMAN, Suzanne Nichols (ETenn) 1108 Meadow Ln, Kingsport, TN 37663

SMITH-FIRESTONE, Tammy (The Episcopal NCal)

SMITHGRAYBEAL, Felicia Marie (Colo) 252 Hillspire Dr, Windsor, CO 80550

SMITH-JONES, Kathleen Aidan (Md)

SMITH-KURTZ, Mary Bonnagean (WMich) 7280 Deepwater Point Rd, Williamsburg, MI 49690

SMITH-MCGEHEE, Lionel Eby (NY) 225 W 99th St, New York, NY 10025

SMITH-MORAN, Barbara Putney (Mass) 93 Anson Road, Concord, MA 01742

SMOKE, Joan C (Ind) 1813 Linwood Dr, Bedford, IN 47421

SMOLKO, Regis Joseph (Pgh) 2365 Mcaleer Rd, Sewickley, PA 15143

SMUCKER III, John Reed (Mich) 108 N Quaker Ln, Alexandria, VA 22304

SMULLEN, Thelma (Md) 15708 Bradford Dr, Laurel, MD 20707

✠ **SMYLIE**, John (Wyo) 123 S Durbin St, Casper, WY 82601

SMYTH, Margaret Emma Ferrell (NJ) 53 Mulberry St, Medford, NJ 08055

SMYTH, Toneh Alana (Pa)

SMYTH, William E (NC) 76 Louisiana Ave, Asheville, NC 28806

SMYTHE JR, Colville (Az) 692 E. Fruit Stand Way, Queen Creek, AZ 85140

SMYTHE, Sally Lee (ND) 301 Main St S, Minot, ND 58701

SNAPP, JAmes Russell (Ark) 102 Antonine Heights, City Walk, London, SE1 3DB, Great Britain (UK)

SNARE, Pamela Porter (Tenn) 1024 Chicamauga Ave, Nashville, TN 37206

SNEARY, Jerry (WTex) 164 Fox Rdg, Canyon Lake, TX 78133

SNELLING, Kathryn Sue (Ak) PO Box 1130, Sitka, AK 99835

SNEVE, Paul (SD) 2501 S Glendale Ave, Sioux Falls, SD 57105

SNIBBE, Jane (The Episcopal NCal)

SNICKENBERGER, Patricia Wolcott (Chi) 179 School St, Libertyville, IL 60048

SNIDER II, Mike (Fla) St Patrick's Episcopal Church, 1532 Stratford Ct, Saint Johns, FL 32259

SNIDER, Stephen B (Pa) 10527 W Albany St, Boise, ID 83704

SNIECIENSKI, Ed (Los) 908 N AVENUE 65, LOS ANGELES, CA 90042

SNIFFEN, Ernest Timothy (Me) P0 Box 368, Readfield, ME 04355

SNIFFEN, Michael Thomas (LI) 85 5th St, Garden City, NY 11530

SNIVELY, Candace Foley (NC)

SNODGRASS, A Bowie (Nwk) 60 Knollwood Rd, Short Hills, NJ 07078

SNODGRASS, Cynthia Jean (SO) 5146 SW 9th Lane, Gainesville, FL 32607

SNODGRASS, Galen D (WMo) 3317 N 103rd Ct, Kansas City, KS 66109

SNODGRASS, Thomas James (Md) 705 Gladstone Ave, Baltimore, MD 21210

✠ **SNOOK**, Susan Brown (SanD) 510 Tarento Dr, San Diego, CA 92106

SNOW, George Richard (WLa) 151 Washakie Dr, Evanston, WY 82930

SNOW, Peter David (Oly) 927 36th Ave, Seattle, WA 98122

SNOW, Robert Gerald (Neb) PO Box 407052, Fort Lauderdale, FL 33340

SNYDER, Bindy (WTenn) 539 Cherry Rd, Memphis, TN 38117

SNYDER, Daniel (WMich)

SNYDER, David L (NJ) St. Andrew's Episcopal Church, 121 High Street, Mt. Holly, NJ 08060

SNYDER, Erick (Be) 290 Conklin St, Farmingdale, NY 11735

SNYDER, George Lewis (SO)

SNYDER, Judith (Be) 4621 Ashley Ln, Bethlehem, PA 18017

SNYDER, Katharine (Colo)

SNYDER, Larry Alan (Chi) 240 S 4th St, Warsaw, IL 62379

SNYDER, Paul Leech (Okla) PO Box 10722, Midwest City, OK 73140

SNYDER, Philip (CNY) 248 Buckfield Dr, Lititz, PA 17543

SNYDER, Philip L (Dal) 2220 Susan Cir, Plano, TX 75074

SNYDER, Sharon Boublitz (Eas) 12842 Fox Ridge Ct, Bishopville, MD 21813

SNYDER, Susanna Jane (Mass) 99 Brattle St, Cambridge, MA 02138

SNYDER, Tina Bel (Nev)

SNYDER, William Delpharo (O) 4920 Woodview Rd, Ravenna, OH 44266

SOARD II, John Robert (Tex) 207 Bob O Link Ln, Wharton, TX 77488

SOJWAL, Imlijungla (LI) 27 Church St, Stonington, CT 06378

SOL, Brenda (SanD) 8011 Douglas Ave, Dallas, TX 75225

SOLA, Geri Ely (Eau) 6579 W Center Dr, Hurley, WI 54534

✠ **SOLAK**, Ketlen A (Pgh) 913 Wilson Rd, Wilmington, DE 19803

SOLAQUA, Virginia Lisbeth (Cal) 14 Lagunitas Rd, Ross, CA 94957

SOLBAK, Mary Martha (CPa) 1001 E Oregon Rd, Lititz, PA 17543

SOLDWEDEL, Erik (Nwk) 31 Mulberry St, Newark, NJ 07102

SOLLER, Robin (NH) 23 Old Bristol Rd, New Hampton, NH 03256

SOLOMON, Dana Lee (Colo) St Stephen's Episcopal Church, 1303 S Bross Ln, Longmont, CO 80501

SOLOMON, Rhett Berard (At)

SOLON JR, Robert Francis (O) PO Box 248, 619 Catawba Ave, Put In Bay, OH 43456

SOLON, Terry Tim (Wyo) 3251 Acacia Dr, Cheyenne, WY 82001

SOLTER, Katrina Howard (NH) St Patricks Episcopal Church, 4700 Whitehaven Pkwy NW, Washington, DC 20007

SOLTYS, Jacqueline Rebecca (SVa) 65 E Huron St, Chicago, IL 60611

SOMERS, Daniel E (NJ)

SOMERS, David Wayne (CFla) 5873 N Dean Rd, Orlando, FL 32817

SOMERS, Faye Veronica (SeFla) 2707 NW 37th St, Boca Raton, FL 33434

SOMERVILLE II, Ben (Az) 542 Raymond Dr, Sierra Vista, AZ 85635

SOMERVILLE, David James (Ga) 128 King Cotton Rd, Brunswick, GA 31525

SOMES, Norman (ECR) 85 Anna Laura Rd, 85 Anna Laura Rd, Jacksonville, OR 97530

SOMMER, Robert Lane (ECR) All Saints Church/Cristo Rey, 437 Rogers Ave, Watsonville, CA 95076

SOMMER, Sue (Chi) 415 Kelly Cir, Duluth, MN 55811

SOMODEVILLA, Rene (Dal) 4018 S Lakewood Dr, Memphis, TN 38128

SONDEREGGER, Kathrine Ann (Va) 669 Weybridge St # 5753, Middlebury, VT 05753

SONLEY, Joseph (Hai)

SONNEN, Jon Anton (Tex) 4403 Seneca St, Pasadena, TX 77504

SONNESYN, Roger Earl (Minn) 12908 Hideaway Trl, Minnetonka, MN 55305

SOPER, Robert Arthur (WTex) 300 Hollywood Dr, Edinburg, TX 78539

SORENSEN, John Thomas (Pa) 1400 Lakecrest Court, Mt Pleasant, SC 29466

SORENSEN, Lael (Me) St Peter's Episcopal Church, 11 White St, Rockland, ME 04841

SORENSEN, Richard Todd (Nev) 1580 G St, Sparks, NV 89431

SORENSEN, Todd W (Colo) 9901 Brodie Ln Ste 160, Austin, TX 78748

SORENSON, James Ronald (EMich) 226 W Nicolet Blvd, Marquette, MI 49855

SOREY, Gene Christine (Fla) 4304 Redtail Hawk Dr, Jacksonville, FL 32257

SOREY, Katie O (Miss)

SORVILLO SR, James (SwFla) 1124 Austin Ct, Dunedin, FL 34698

SOSA, Gary Rafael (NAM) Po Box 216, Bluff, UT 84512

SO-SCHOOS, Alistair (Md) Church Pension Group, 19 E 34th St, New York, NY 10016

SOSNOWSKI, John William (NJ) 3751 Friendly Orange Ct NE, Leland, NC 28451

SOTELO, Fabio A (At) St Bedes Episcopal Church, 2601 Henderson Mill Rd NE, Atlanta, GA 30345

SOTO, Luis Fernando (DomRep)

SOTOMAYOR, Ricardo S (Tex)

SOUCEK, Paul (Nwk)

SOUDER, Diane J (Az) Po Box 1077, Winter Park, FL 32790

SOUFFRANT, Anthony (Hai)

SOUGHERS, Tara (Mass) 23 Horseshoe Dr., Plainville, MA 02762

SOUKUP, Patricia Marie (RG) 3700 Parsifal St NE, Albuquerque, NM 87111

SOULE, Patrick Ross (Tenn) 151 Kingsley Ave, Orange Park, FL 32073

SOULIS, Cameron J (Pgh) Calvary Episcopal Church, 315 Shady Ave, Pittsburgh, PA 15206

SOUTH, Lynn Crisco (The Episcopal Church in Haw) 100 Kulanihakoi St, Kihei, HI 96753

SOUTHALL, Jennifer Lea (Miss) 606 Starling Crest, Oxford, MS 38655

SOUTHERLAND, Thomas Rudolph (SO) 10555 Montgomery Rd., Apt 32, Cincinnati, OH 45242

SOUTHERN, Susannah (Eas)

SOUTHWICK, Susan Bowman (Ala)

SOUZA, Raymond Manuel (EC) 846 Wide Waters, Bath, NC 27808

SOWAH, Constance Kate (Minn) 4180 Lexington Ave S, Eagan, MN 55123
SOWALE, Moses O (Mass)
SOWARDS, William Michael (Pa) St James Episcopal Church, 3768 Germantown Pike, Collegeville, PA 19426
SOWERS, Susan R (CGC) 3200 N 12th Ave, Pensacola, FL 32503
SOWINSKI, Charles Paul (Az) 6300 N Central Ave, Phoenix, AZ 85012
SOYARS, Jonathan E (Chi) 115 W 7th St, Charlotte, NC 28202
SPACCARELLI, Cara Elizabeth (Ind) 620 G St SE, Washington, DC 20003
SPAETH, Colleen Grayce (NJ) 247 Merion Ave, Haddonfield, NJ 08033
SPAFFORD, Donald Wick (Dal) 5903 Bonnard Dr, Dallas, TX 75230
SPAGNA, Amy L (Vt)
SPAINHOUR, John Robert (Vt) 4616 Mcclelland Dr Unit 203, Unit 203, Wilmington, NC 28405
SPALDING, Kirsten Snow (Cal) 333 Ellen Dr, San Rafael, CA 94903
SPALDING, Rita Capitan (Ga)
SPANGENBERG, Carol (WMich) 1612 Stoney Point Dr, Lansing, MI 48917
SPANGLER, DeLiza (WNY) 128 Pearl St, Buffalo, NY 14202
SPANGLER, Haywood B (Va) 1205 Swan Lake Dr Apt 303, Charlottesville, VA 22902
SPANN, Ron (Mich) 2971 Iroquois St, Detroit, MI 48214
SPANNAUS, Timothy Wise (Mich) 27786 Rainbow Cir, Lathrup Village, MI 48076
SPARKS, Douglas E (NI) 853 Forest Ave, South Bend, IN 46616
SPARKS, Rebecca Jo (Tex) PO Box 1015, Salado, TX 76571
SPARROW, Kevin H (Vt) 23 Pleasant St, Montpelier, VT 05602
SPARROW SAVAGE, Brittany (WMo)
SPAULDING, Mark (Cal) 19179 Center St, Castro Valley, CA 94546
SPEAR, Kimberley K (CFla)
SPEARE-HARDY II, Benjamin (SO) 5301 Free Pike, Trotwood, OH 45426
SPEAR-JONES, Michael W (SVa) 12 Milnor Ter, Crossville, TN 38558
SPECK-EWER, Nathan Stewart (SwFla)
SPEEKS, Mark William (NY) 267 Humphrey St # 3, New Haven, CT 06511
SPEER, James D (Ct) 63 Clyde Ave, Waterbury, CT 06708
SPEER, Richard (WTex) 800 S Indiana Ave, 800 S Indiana Ave, Weslaco, TX 78596
SPEER, Robert Hazlett (Md) 5732 Cross Country Blvd, Baltimore, MD 21209
SPEER, William Roth (NJ) 2000 Miller Ave Apt 12, Millville, NJ 08332
SPEIR, Edmund L (Ida)

SPELLERS, Stephanie (LI) 82 Commonwealth Ave Apt 2, Boston, MA 02116
SPELLMAN, Lynne (Ark) 1219 W Lakeridge Dr, Fayetteville, AR 72703
SPELLMEYER, Shane Allan (Chi)
SPELMAN, Harold James (HB)
SPELMAN, Katherine (Chi) 3430 Highland Ave, Berwyn, IL 60402
SPENCER, Adam P (Chi)
SPENCER, Allison D (LI) 12706 Se Pinehurst Ct, Hobe Sound, FL 33455
SPENCER, Bonnie (Colo) 3006 S Holly Pl, Denver, CO 80222
SPENCER, Carol (Miss) 3000 Saint Charles Ave, 201, New Orleans, LA 70115
SPENCER, Cindy (ECR) 15163 N Cutler Dr, Tucson, AZ 85739
SPENCER, Dorothy Jane (NMich) PO Box 302, Manistique, MI 49854
SPENCER, James Scott (CFla) 4220 Saxon Dr, New Smyrna Beach, FL 32169
SPENCER, Leon P (NC) 4705 Andorra Ct, Greensboro, NC 27410
SPENCER, Michael (NH) 325 Pleasant St, Concord, NH 03301
SPENCER, Michael Paul (SO) 412 Sycamore St, Cincinnati, OH 45202
SPENCER, Patricia Ann (CGC) 851 Village Lake Dr S, Deland, FL 32724
SPENCER, Robert (Miss) 1623 Acadia Court, Jackson, MS 39211
SPENCER, Robert Paul (NMich) PO Box 302, Manistique, MI 49854
SPENCER, Ronald Dwight (WMo) 521 2nd St NE Apt B, Washington, DC 20002
SPEROPULOS IV, Peter James (Mo)
SPERRY, Rebecca Lynne (Chi) 2056 Vermont St, Blue Island, IL 60406
SPICER JR, Clyde Allen (Md) 724 Morningside Dr, Towson, MD 21204
SPICER, John M (WMo) St Andrews Episcopal Church, 6401 Wornall Ter, Kansas City, MO 64113
SPICER, Stephen L (Ky) 304 E Stockbridge St, Eagle Lake, TX 77434
✠ SPIEGEL, Phyllis (U) 252 E Kelsey Ave, Salt Lake City, UT 84111
SPIERS, Linda Mitchell (Ct) 3 Whirling Dun, Canton, CT 06019
SPIGNER, Charles Bailey (Va) 10355 Spencer Trail Pl, Ashland, VA 23005
SPINA, Frank Anthony (Oly) 414 W Newell St, Seattle, WA 98119
SPINELLA, Linda Jean (NH) 270 Stark Hwy N, Dunbarton, NH 03046
SPINILLO GRZYWA, Jonathan Michael Francis (Minn) 111 3rd Ave SW, Rochester, MN 55902
SPOON, Bryan William (WMo)
SPOOR, Cameron S (Tex)
SPORS, Daniel Paul (Cal)
SPRAGUE, James W (Los) PO Box 303, Santa Barbara, CA 93102
SPREIER, Raymond (EO) PO Box 6073, Bend, OR 97708

SPRICK, Lynne Ann (Minn) 110 S Oak St, Lake City, MN 55041
SPRIGGS, Sunhwan (Nwk)
SPRINGER, Alice E (Dal) 1410 S Goliad St Apt 2007, Rockwall, TX 75087
SPRINGER, David R (Alb) 12 Shannon Ct, West Sand Lake, NY 12196
SPRINGER, Nancy (WTex) 4000 W Loop 250 N, Midland, TX 79707
SPRINGER, Susan W (Colo) St Johns Episcopal Church, 1419 Pine St, Boulder, CO 80302
SPROAT, Jim (WTex) 2109 Sawdust Rd Apt 27102, Spring, TX 77380
SPROTT-GOLDSON, Marion C (NC) 731 Raleigh Rd, Chapel Hill, NC 27514
SPROUL, James Renfro (EC) 881 Lakeside Dr, Lenoir City, TN 37772
SPROUSE, Herbert Warren (CPa) The Mem Ch Of The Pofp, 20 W High St, Gettysburg, PA 17325
SPRUHAN, Judy (SD) 720 Diamond Rd, Salem, VA 24153
SPRUILL, Robert Leigh (Tex) 5825 Robert E Lee Dr, Nashville, TN 37215
SPULNIK, Frederick Joseph (RI) 4873 Collwood Blvd unit B, San Diego, CA 92115
SPURGIN, Joyce M (Okla) 516 McLish St, Ardmore, OK 73401
SPURLOCK, Paul Allan (Colo) 10000 E Yale Ave Apt 4, 10000 E Yale Ave Apt43, Denver, CO 80231
SQUIER, Timothy J (Ct) 500 E Depot St, Antioch, IL 60002
SQUIRE, James Richard (Pa) Episcopal Academy, 1785 Bishop White Dr, Newtown Square, PA 19073
SQUIRE JR, Willard Searle (CFla) 748 Hammond Pl, The Villages, FL 32162
SRAMEK JR, Tom (Ore) PO Box 2631, Hillsboro, OR 97123
SROKA, Joe (NC) 5778 Siler Cty Snow Cp Rd, Siler City, NC 27344
SSERWADDA, Emmanuel (NY) 69 Georgia Ave, Bronxville, NY 10708
STACE, April (NMich)
STACEY, Caroline (NY) 487 Hudson St, New York, NY 10014
STACK JR, AJ (NY) 40 Leedsville Rd, Amenia, NY 12501
STACY, Charles Herrick (Los) 1509 Eucalyptus Dr, Solvang, CA 93463
STADEL, Jerold Russell (SwFla) 725 Parsons Mooring Ct, Seffner, FL 33584
STAFFORD, Gil (Az)
STAFFORD, Robert Holmes (NY) 401 S El Cielo Rd Unit 71, Palm Springs, CA 92262
STAFFORD, William Sutherland (Fla) 4316 Hampshire Pl, San Jose, CA 95136
STAFFORD-WHITTAKER, William Paul (WA) 3248 Robert Clifton Weaver Way NE, Washington, DC 20018

STAGGS, Katresia Anne (Ark) 501 S Phoenix Ave, Russellville, AR 72801

STAHL, Daryl (RI) 91 Pratt St, providence, RI 02906

STAHLECKER, Linzi Ann (Oly) 8788 22nd Ave NW, Seattle, WA 98117

STAHURA, Denise H (Minn)

STAIR, Adrian (Mass) 51 Longmeadow Dr, Amherst, MA 01002

STALEY, Mary (Va) PO Box 482, Put In Bay, OH 43456

STALLER, Margaretmary B (Cal) 4821 Wolf Way, Concord, CA 94521

STALLINGS, Buddy Monroe (NY) 244 Eastbrooke St, Jackson, MS 39216

STAMBAUGH, Doran Bartlett (SanD) PO Box 127, Carlsbad, CA 92018

STAMBAUGH, James Ryan (Pa) 1020 Remington Rd, Wynnewood, PA 19096

STAMM, George (Eau) 13497 45th Ave, Chippewa Falls, WI 54729

ST AMOUR III, Frank Shalvey (Eas) 7591 Sandy Bottom Rd, Chestertown, MD 21620

STANFORD, Bill (Tex) 3550 SW Loop 820, Fort Worth, TX 76133

STANFORD, Daryl Clayton (Kan)

STANFORD, David Dewitt (Chi) 2705 Armfield Rd, Hillsborough, NC 27278

STANFORD, Donna Lynn (WMo) 100 E Red Bridge Rd, Kansas City, MO 64114

STANFORD, Iain M (Cal)

STANFORD, Virginia Francene (Md) 370 River Rd, Cambridge, VT 05444

STANG, Christine Simmons (Minn)

STANGER, Mark E (Cal) 9790 SW 163rd Ave, Beaverton, OR 97007

STANLEY, Anne G (Me) 45 Washington St, Eastport, ME 04631

STANLEY, Arthur Patrick (Ia) 9 Westbourne Court, Cooden Drive, Bexhill On Sea TN39 3AA, Great Britain (UK)

STANLEY, E Bevan (Ct) 25 South St, PO Box 248, Litchfield, CT 06759

STANLEY, Gordon John (Chi) 340 W Diversey Pkwy, Chicago, IL 60657

STANLEY, James Martin (Chi) 320 Franklin St, Geneva, IL 60134

STANLEY JR, John Hiram (Tex) 4105 Hartwood Dr, Fort Worth, TX 76109

STANLEY, Lauren Regina (SD) PO Box 256, Mission, SD 57555

STANLEY, Marjorie Jean (Spok) 255 W Shore Ln, Sandpoint, ID 83864

STANLEY, Mark (Md) Old St Pauls Church, 309 Cathedral St, Baltimore, MD 21201

STANLEY, Mary Luck (Md) Old St Pauls Church, 309 Cathedral St, Baltimore, MD 21201

STANLEY, Stephen Ranson (SwVa) 1826 Mount Vernon Rd SW, Roanoke, VA 24015

STANLEY, William S (Va)

STANSBURY, Noah (Tex) 5521 Springdale Rd Apt 2212, Austin, TX 78723

STANSFIELD, Patricia J (Los) PO Box 152, Corona, CA 92878

STANTON, Chelsea (Minn)

STANTON, James Malcom (Ind) 321 Market St, Jeffersonville, IN 47130

✠ **STANTON**, James Monte (Dal) 1630 N Garrett Ave, Dallas, TX 75206

STANTON, John Frank (SeFla) 7900 Harbor Island Dr Apt 1501, North Bay Village, FL 33141

STANTON, John Robert (At) 4906 Sulky Dr Apt 204, Richmond, VA 23228

STANTON, Sarah Morningstar (EO) 4701 7th Ave SW Unit 303, Olympia, WA 98502

STANTON, Susan A (Los)

STANTON, William B (Colo) 220 57th Ave, Greeley, CO 80634

STAPLES, Ann McDonald (Pgh) Po Box 1, Marion Center, PA 15759

STAPLETON JR, Jack (Colo) 2683 Pinehurst Dr, Evergreen, CO 80439

STARBUCK, Elizabeth (Ct) 88 N Main St, PO Box 983, Kent, CT 06757

STARK, Gregory (O) 162 S Main St Apt 1/2, Oberlin, OH 44074

STARKES, Lionel Alfonso (Nev) Po Box 50763, Henderson, NV 89016

STARKWEATHER, Betty (ND) 679 Lehigh Dr., Merced, CA 95348

STARR, Charles Michael (Pgh) 4048 Circle Dr, Bakerstown, PA 15007

STARR, Chris (Ak) C of the Atonement, 4945 High Point Road, Sandy Springs, GA 30342

STARR III, David H (Los) 424 Montecito Ave, Monterey, CA 93940

STARR, Mark Lowell (CGC) 41 Olympic Blvd, Port Townsend, WA 98368

STARR, Nancy Barnard (Mil) 76 Grange Road, Mount Eden, Auckland, 1024, New Zealand (Aotearoa)

STARR, Therese Ann (Okla) PO Box 759, Eufaula, OK 74432

STASSER, Nina (U) 2225 S Jasmine St Unit 310, Denver, CO 80222

STATER, Catherine J (CFla) 319 W Wisconsin Ave, Deland, FL 32720

STATEZNI, Gregory George (Episcopal SJ) 7000 College Ave Apt 21, Bakersfield, CA 93306

STAYNER, David (Ct) 28 Myra Rd, Hamden, CT 06517

STAYNER, Sandra (Ct) 39 Pleasant Drive, Cheshire, CT 06410

STAYTON, Darrell Lynn (Ark) PO, Box 726, Stuttgart, AR 72160

ST CLAIR, Melinda Lee (Mont) Saint Lukes Church, 119 N 33rd St, Billings, MT 59101

ST CLAIRE II, Kyle (Pa) 1650 Franklin Dr, Furlong, PA 18925

STEADMAN, Darren F (Va)

STEADMAN, Larry Kenneth (WK) 705 W 31st Ave, Hutchinson, KS 67502

STEADMAN, Marguerite Alexandra (Me) 3116 O St Nw, Washington, DC 20007

STEAGALL, Patricia V (Ore) 735 20th St NE, Salem, OR 97301

STEARNS, Fellow Clair (ECR) Po Box 2789, Saratoga, CA 95070

STEBBING, Alyssa C (Tex) 1122 Ryon St Apt B, Houston, TX 77009

✠ **STEBBINS**, Marty (Mont)

STEBINGER, Peter A R (Minn) 615 Bethmour Rd, Bethany, CT 06524

STECH, Ernest William (Mich) 20500 W Old US Highway 12, Chelsea, MI 48118

STECKER IV, Rick (NH) PO Box 293, New London, NH 03257

STECKLINE, Donna L (SwVa) P.O. Box 345, Gilbertsville, NY 13776

STEDMAN, David Algernon (WNY) Po Box 7488, St Thomas, VI 00801

STEED, Ronald Scott (Ct) 95 Route 2a, Preston, CT 06365

STEEDMAN SANBORN, Marda (Oly) Diocese of Olympia, 1551 10th Ave E, Seattle, WA 98102

STEELE, Chris C (Oly) 9061 Seward Park Ave S Apt 6-183, Seattle, WA 98118

STEELE, Christopher Andrew (Dal) 11122 Midway Rd, Dallas, TX 75229

STEELE, David Regan (NY) 777 E 222nd St, Bronx, NY 10467

STEELE, Gary Ross (Ak) 2708 W 65th Ave, Anchorage, AK 99502

STEELE, James Logan (Chi) 317 Goold Park Dr, Morris, IL 60450

STEELE, Kelly Ann (Ga)

STEELE, Robert Emanuel (The Episcopal Church in Haw) 250 Kawaihae St Apt 1b, Honolulu, HI 96825

STEELE, Sean (Tex) St Isidore Episcopal, 24803 Oakhurst Dr, Spring, TX 77386

STEEN, S James (WMich) 3482 Palmer Dr, Saugatuck, MI 49453

STEEVER JR, Raymond George Edward (Los) Route 1, Box 109, Pullman, WA 99163

STEEVES, Joan Altpeter (Colo) 6337 Deframe Way, Arvada, CO 80004

STEEVES, Timothy (Pa) 409 E Lancaster Ave, Downingtown, PA 19335

STEFANIK, Alfred Thomas (Vt) 49 Raintree Circle, Palm Coast, FL 32164

STEFANOVSKY, Derek (Ct)

STEFFENHAGEN, Leverne Richard (WNY) 9705 Niagara Falls Blvd Apt 19, Niagara Falls, NY 14304

STEFFENHAGEN, Louis Keith (Pa)

STEFFENSEN, Leslie Nunez (Va) Armed Forces and Fed Ministries, 310 Wisconsin Ave NW, Washington, DC 20016

STEFKO, Nadia M (Chi) 3857 N Kostner Ave, Chicago, IL 60641

STEGELMANN, Dawn (Ct) 651 Pequot Ave, Southport, CT 06890
STEIDL, Gerald Scobie (CFla) 127 E Cottesmore Cir, Longwood, FL 32779
STEIG, George Terrance (Oly) 5241 12th Ave Ne, Seattle, WA 98105
STEILBERG, Isabel Fourqurean (SVa) 221 34th St, Newport News, VA 23607
STEIN, Edward Lee (Tex) 717 Sage Rd, Houston, TX 77056
STEINBACH, Frederick Leo (Ia) PO Box 838, Chariton, IA 50049
STEINBRENNER, Peter Dean (Nev)
STEINER, Scott A (Mich)
STEINER IV, Skip (Md) 7474 Washington Blvd, Elkridge, MD 21075
STEINHAUER, Roger Kent (Roch) 25 Chadbourne Rd, Rochester, NY 14618
STEINHAUSER, Elizabeth (Mass) 419 Shawmut Ave., Boston, MA 02118
STELLE, Eric Arthur (Oly) 7701 Skansie Ave, Gig Harbor, WA 98335
STEN, Pamela V (WMich) 605 W 4th St Apt 2, Buchanan, MI 49107
STENNER, David Anthony (Md) 203 E Chatsworth Ave, Reisterstown, MD 21136
STENNETTE, Lloyd Roland (SeFla) PO Box 11383, Miami, FL 33101
STENNING, Gordon J (RI) 36 Brant Rd, Portsmouth, RI 02871
STEPHEN, Christopher (Dal)
STEPHENS, Jefferson (U) 2141 Horizon View Dr, St George, UT 84790
STEPHENS, Josh (WNC) Bruton Parish Episcopal Church, PO Box 3520, Williamsburg, VA 23187
STEPHENS, Paul Jeffery (Miss) 717 Forest Ave, Long Beach, MS 39560
STEPHENS, Steve Daniel (RG) 400 Huning Ranch Loop W, Los Lunas, NM 87031
STEPHENS, Thomas Lee (Okla) 1560 Pecan Pl, Bartlesville, OK 74003
STEPHENS, Wyatt E (Mil) 1538 N 58th St, Milwaukee, WI 53208
STEPHENSON, Amanda C (NC)
STEPHENSON, Elizabeth Ann (WTex)
STEPHENSON, John William (Kan) Rr 1 Box 190, Riverton, KS 66770
STEPHENSON, Michael (Okla) 3621 24th Ave SE Apt 3, Norman, OK 73071
STEPHENSON, Randolph (WA) 4 Jeb Stuart Ct, Rockville, MD 20854
STEPHENSON-DIAZ, Lark (SanD) 1023 Iris Ct, Carlsbad, CA 92011
STEPP, Jonathan (WNC) 84 Church St, Franklin, NC 28734
STER, David (CPa) 1363 Princeton Rd, Mechanicsburg, PA 17050
STERCHI, Margaret (NJ) 501 Huntington Pl, Harrison, AR 72601
STERKEN, Janet Leigh (Eau) 322 N. Water St., Sparta, WI 54656

STERLING III, Edward Arthur (Oly) 3762 Palisades Pl W, University Place, WA 98466
STERLING, Leslie (Mass) St Bartholomews Church, 239 Harvard St, Cambridge, MA 02139
STERN, Linda Sue (Okla) 516 Mclish St, Ardmore, OK 73401
STERNE, Colleen Kathryn (Los) Trinity Episcopal Church, 1500 State St, Santa Barbara, CA 93101
STERNE, Martha (At) 805 Mount Vernon Hwy, Atlanta, GA 30327
STERRY, Steven Chapin (Los) Anglican Ch Of The Epiphany, 5151 Cordova Rd, La Mirada, CA 90638
STEVENS JR, Arthur Grant (WMass) 904B West Victoria St, Santa Barbara, CA 93101
STEVENS, George (Mass) St. John's Church, P.O. Box 5610, Beverly, MA 01915
STEVENS, Judy (WMass) 904b W Victoria St, Santa Barbara, CA 93101
STEVENS, Karl Peter Bush (SO) St Stephens Tec Ch, 30 W Woodruff Ave, Columbus, OH 43210
STEVENS, Merrill Richard (EO) St Pauls Episcopal Church, 1805 Minnesota St, The Dalles, OR 97058
STEVENS, Nancy (Roch) 60 Ridgeway Ests, Rochester, NY 14626
STEVENS, Patricia D (At) 2039 Linden Rd, winter Park, FL 32792
STEVENS JR, Rob (NH) 1113 Macon Ave, Pittsburgh, PA 15218
STEVENS, Robert Ellsworth (CFla) 2346 Colfax Ter, Evanston, IL 60201
STEVENS, Scott J (Ct) PO Box 151, Hampton, CT 06247
STEVENS III, Walter Alexander (The Episcopal Church in Haw) P.O. Box 207, Kapaau, HI 96755
STEVENS, William Clair (RG)
STEVENS-HUMMON, Rebecca M (Tenn) 2902 Overlook Dr, Nashville, TN 37212
STEVENSON, Ann (NH) 7502 Heyburn Ct, Louisville, KY 40222
STEVENSON, Anne B (Tenn) 216 Chestnut Hill Dr, Nashville, TN 37215
STEVENSON, Carolyn Eve (NH) 231 Main St, Salem, NH 03079
STEVENSON, Frank Beaumont (SO) School Lane, Stanton Saint John, Oxford, OX33 1ET, Great Britain (UK)
STEVENSON, Frederic George (CPa) 890 Mccosh St, Hanover, PA 17331
STEVENSON, Janis Jordan (Mich) 430 Nicolet St, Walled Lake, MI 48390
STEVENSON, Jeffrey Neal (LI) 6401 Wornall Ter, Kansas City, MO 64113
✠ **STEVENSON**, Mark Mark (Va) 8737 River Rd, Henrico, VA 23229
STEVENSON, RIchard Hugh (The Episcopal NCal) 411 Cortland Ter, Brentwood, CA 94513
STEVENSON, Thomas Edward (Ore) PO Box 29, Alsea, OR 97324

STEVENS-TAYLOR, Sally Hodges (Az) PO Box 65840, Tucson, AZ 85728
STEWART, Audrey (Mass) Parish of the Epiphany, 70 Church St, Winchester, NJ 01890
STEWART, Barbara (Los) 1014 Presidio Dr, Costa Mesa, CA 92626
STEWART, Bonnie (Ore) St Michael All Angels Ch, 1704 NE 43rd Ave, Portland, OR 97213
STEWART, Carol Wendt (Roch) 3074 O'Donnell Rd, Wellsville, NY 14895
STEWART, Caroline (Md) 4024 Stewart Rd, Stevenson, MD 21153
STEWART, Charles N (CNY) 18 E Elizabeth St, Skaneateles, NY 13152
STEWART, Daniel R (Oly) 322 Aoloa St Apt 1101, Kailua, HI 96734
STEWART, James Allen (Wyo) St Mark's Episcopal Church, 1908 Central Ave, Cheyenne, WY 82001
STEWART, James Macgregor (NC)
STEWART, Jane Louise (Ia) 912 20th Ave., Coralville, IA 52241
STEWART, John Bruce (Va) 4327 Ravensworth Rd Apt 210, Annandale, VA 22003
STEWART JR, John Plummer (Ala) St Matthias Episc Church, 2310 Skyland Blvd E, Tuscaloosa, AL 35405
STEWART, Kevin Paul (Mil) 4722 N 104th St, Wauwatosa, WI 53225
STEWART, Leslie (Tex) PO Box 292365, Lewisville, TX 75029
STEWART, Matt (Mass) 11 W. Grove St., Middleboro, MA 02346
STEWART, Natalie Ann (ECR) PO Box 515, Aromas, CA 95004
STEWART, Natasha (Mass) 407 Rochester St, Fall River, MA 02720
STEWART, Pamela Fay (Colo) 126 W 2nd Ave, Denver, CO 80223
STEWART, Sarah C (Cal)
STEWART-SICKING, Joseph (Md) 8890 McGaw Rd, Columbia, MD 21045
STEWART-SICKING, Megan Elizabeth (Md) 1509 Glencoe Rd, Glencoe, MD 21152
STEWMAN, Kerry Jo (O) Po Box 366274, Bonita Springs, FL 34136
ST GEORGE, David (Nwk) 8 Binney Rd, Old Lyme, CT 06371
ST. GERMAIN, Beverly Anne Lavallee (Vt) Three Cathedral Square 3a, Burlington, VT 05401
ST GERMAIN JR, Paul (SO) 410 Cumberland Ave, Portland, ME 04101
ST GERMAIN-ILER III, Robert (Ala) 347 S Central Ave, Alexander City, AL 35010
STICHWEH, Michael Terry (CFla) 410 N Meridian St Apt 604, Indianapolis, IN 46204
STICKLEY, David (CNY) 29 Lincoln Ave Apt 2, Binghamton, NY 13905
STICKNEY, Jane Burr (Ct) 14 Lone Pine Trl, Higganum, CT 06441
STICKNEY, Jim (Cal) 1324 Devonshire Ct, El Cerrito, CA 94530

STICKNEY, Joyce (Los) 28211 Pacific Coast Hwy, Malibu, CA 90265
STIEFEL, Robert (NH) 10715 County Road Id, Blue Mounds, WI 53517
STIEGLER, Mark A (Roch) 3835 Oneill Rd, Lima, NY 14485
STIER, Diane L (WMich)
STIFLER, Linnea (WMich) 2010 Nichols Rd, Kalamazoo, MI 49004
STILES, Katherine Mitchell (Me) 2 Longfellow Rd, Cambridge, MA 02138
STILES-RANDAK, Susan (RI) Peace Dale Estates, 1223 Saugatucket Rd Apt A102, Peace Dale, RI 02879
STILL, Kimberly L (Fla) 919 San Fernando St, Fernandina Beach, FL 32034
STIMPSON, Peter K (NJ) 220 W Kilbride, Williamsburg, VA 23188
STINE, Stephen Blaine (Tex) 1220 Quirby Lane, Tyler, TX 75701
STINNETT, Roger Allen (WMo) 804 Wendy Ln, Carthage, MO 64836
STINSON, Marian (Oly) 84 Ledgewood Dr, Glastonbury, CT 06033
STINSON, Richard Lyon (Pgh) 191 Ashby Ln, Front Royal, VA 22630
STIPE, Nickie Maxine (Ak) 280 Northern Ave Apt 10-A, Avondale Estates, GA 30002
STISCIA, Ronald (CPa) 5092 Riverfront Dr, Bradenton, FL 34208
STITT, David (WLa) 713 Circle C, Hastings, NE 68901
STIVERS, Dana (Me) PO Box 577, Ivoryton, CT 06442
ST JOHN, Andrew Reginald (NY) 1 E 29th St, New York, NY 10016
ST LOUIS, Allison (CPa) 180 Shannon Ln, Hellam, PA 17406
ST LOUIS, Jean (Hai)
ST LOUIS, Leslie (WA) 13106 Annapolis Rd, Bowie, MD 20720
ST LOUIS, Samuel (Hai)
STOCK, David (Neb) 4036 Neptune Dr, Oklahoma City, OK 73116
STOCKBRIDGE, Nancy Starr (WA)
STOCKDALE, William Barrington (NJ)
STOCKSDALE, Robert (Ct) 183 Pin Oak Dr, Southington, CT 06489
STOCKTON, Jim (Tex) 16306 Ascent Cv, Pflugerville, TX 78660
STOCKTON, Marietta Grace (WK) 406 W. Kingman Ave., Lakin, KS 67860
STOCKWELL-TANGEMAN, Carolyn Lee (WMo) 5618 Wyandotte St, Kansas City, MO 64113
STODDARD, Gary David (Colo)
STODDART, David Michael (Va) Church Of Our Saviour, 1165 Rio Road East, Charlottesville, VA 22901
STODGHILL, Dawnell S (WLa) St Thomas Episcopal Church, 3706 Bon Aire Dr, Monroe, LA 71203
STODGHILL, Marion (Ky) Norton Hospital, Chaplain, 200 E. Chesnut Street, Louisville, KY 40202

STODGHILL III, Thomas Whitfield (WLa) 3435 Westminister Ave, Monroe, LA 71201
STOESSEL, Andrew (Mass) 51 Barbour Farm Rd, PO Box 304, Stonington, ME 04681
STOFEL, Alvin Dale (NwT)
STOFFAN, Eileen Bowman (WMich)
STOFFREGEN, Diana Lynn Jacobson (Spok) 5609 S Custer Street, Spokane, WA 99223
STOFFREGEN, Megan Amy (Spok) 5609 S Custer Rd, Spokane, WA 99223
✠ **STOKES**, Chip (NJ) TEC Dio Of NJ, 808 W State St, Trenton, NJ 08618
STOKES, Grant A (SVa) Trinity Episcopal Church, 500 Court St, Portsmouth, VA 23704
STOKES, Keisha (Roch)
STOKES III, William Alexander (Fla)
STOMSKI, William (Nev) 3300b S Seacrest Blvd, Boynton Beach, FL 33435
STONE, Carey Don (Ark) 112 Traveler Ln, Maumelle, AR 72113
STONE, Dean Putnam (Kan) 9201 W 82nd St, Overland Park, KS 66204
STONE, Mary Ruth (NJ) 40 - B Center St, Highlands, NJ 07732
STONE, Matt (Tex) 603 Spring St, Smithville, TX 78957
STONE, Michael Lee (SVa) 12120 Diamond Hill Dr, Midlothian, VA 23113
STONE, Mike (Tex) 18300 Upper Bay Rd, Houston, TX 77058
STONE, Thomas Michael (Chi) 3601 N North St, Peoria, IL 61604
STONER, D Scott (Mil) 2017 E Olive St, Milwaukee, WI 53211
STONER, Suzanne (Ark)
STONESIFER, John DeWitt (WA) 3603 Gleneagles Dr Apt 3c, Silver Spring, MD 20906
STOPFEL, Barry Lee (Nwk) 404 Union St, Milton, DE 19968
STOPPEL, Gerald Corwin (WMich) PO Box 65, Saugatuck, MI 49453
STOREY, Wayne Alton (CNY) 311 S Massey St, Watertown, NY 13601
STORM, Astrid J (NY) 19 Kent St, Beacon, NY 12508
STORMENT, JOhn Douglas (WTex) 1635 Thrush Court Cir, San Antonio, TX 78248
STORMER, Eugene Allen (Spr) 825 Lorraine Ave, Springfield, IL 62704
STORRS, Sherry (NC)
STORY, Mark (Okla) 1701 Mission Rd, Edmond, OK 73034
STOUDEMIRE, Stewart Mcbryde (WNC) 950 - 36th Ave Circle NE, Hickory, NC 28601
STOUT, Arla Jeanne (Mich) 204 Sunnyside Ave, Cameron, WI 54822
STOUT, David Alan (The Episcopal Church in Haw) St James Church, PO Box 278, Kamuela, HI 96743
STOUTE, Barclay Lenardo (LI) 28 Fallon Ct, Elmont, NY 11003

STOUT-KOPP, Ronnie T (Nwk) 50 Brams Hill Dr, Mahwah, NJ 07430
STOWE, Barbara E (Mass) 33 Washington St, Topsfield, MA 01983
STOWE, Howard Timothy Wheeler (NY) 79 Ne 93rd St, Miami Shores, FL 33138
STOWE, Mallene Wells (CFla)
STOWELL, Philip Werner (NJ) 929 E Laddoos Ave, Queen Creek, AZ 85140
ST PIERRE, Joanne Madelyn (EMich) PO Box 217, Otter Lake, MI 48464
STRADER-SASSER, Jim William (CPa) 103 Old Oak Rd, Newark, DE 19711
STRAHAN, Linda C (RI) 103 Kay St, Newport, RI 02840
STRALEY, Benjamin Pearce (RI)
STRAND, Jon (Va) 543 Beulah Rd NE, Vienna, VA 22180
STRANDE, Dana (Minn) 7305 Afton Rd, Woodbury, MN 55125
STRANDLUND, Daniel P (WTex) 113 Madison Ave, Montgomery, AL 36104
STRANDLUND, Lucy B (NC)
STRANE, Steven Roberts (SanD) 4489 Caminito Cuarzo, San Diego, CA 92117
STRANGE, Phillip Ross (Los) 10223 Gerald Ave, North Hills, CA 91343
STRASBURGER, Frank C (NJ) 27 Tidal Run Ln, Brunswick, ME 04011
STRASSER, Gabor (Va) 18525 Bear Creek Ter, Leesburg, VA 20176
STRATFORD, Jane (Cal) 4683 Roosevelt Dr, Brentwood, CA 94513
STRATTON, Jonathan Robert (Mo) 523 Smiley Ave, Fountain Hill, PA 18015
STRAUB, Gregory (Eas) 1920 S Ocean Dr Apt 1004, Fort Lauderdale, FL 33316
STRAUSS, Arlen Richard (CNY) 109 Glenside Rd, Ithaca, NY 14850
STRAVERS, Cynthia A (NY) 2 E 90th St, New York, NY 10128
STRAVERS, Richard L (WMich) 3363 Dunns Rdg, Kalamazoo, MI 49006
STRAWBRIDGE, Jennifer R (Va) Mansfield College, Mansfield Road, Oxford, OX1 3TF, Great Britain (UK)
STREEPY, Shawn (Kan) 10700 W 53rd St, Shawnee, KS 66203
STREET, Terry (WTenn) 210 Walnut Trace Dr, Cordova, TN 38018
STREETER, Christopher Michael (CPa) 900 Kent Dr, Mechanicsburg, PA 17050
STREEVER, Hilary Brandt (Va) St Jamess Episcopal Church, 1205 W Franklin St, Richmond, VA 23220
STREIFF, Suzanne (Oly) 305 Burma Rd, Castle Rock, WA 98611
STREIT JR, Jep (Mass) 325 Slip Rd, Greenfield, NH 03047
STRENTH, Robert Sean (CFla) 357 Forest Park Cir, Longwood, FL 32779

STREUFERT, Nancy Stimac (The Episcopal NCal) 625 15th St, Eureka, CA 95501
STRIBLING, Anna Jones (Va) 4540 Carrington Rd, Markham, VA 22643
STRIBLING, Emily B (WA) 4621 Laverock Pl NW, Washington, DC 20007
STRIBLING JR, Jess Hawkins (Va) 1 Colley Ave Apt 600, Norfolk, VA 23510
STRICKLAND, Thomas James (Ga)
✠ **STRICKLAND**, Vernon Edward (WK) 665 N Desmet Ave, Buffalo, WY 82834
STRICKLAND JR, William Earl (Alb) 4 Avery Pl, Clifton Park, NY 12065
STRICKLIN, Paul (USC) 6408 Bridgewood Rd., Columbia, SC 29206
STRIDIRON, Andrea Renee (Roch) 2000 Highland Ave, Rochester, NY 14618
STRING, Jansen Edward (Md) 2900 Dunleer Rd, Baltimore, MD 21222
STRINGER, Pam (EC) 111 N King St, Bath, NC 27808
STRINGER, Stacy Bussy (Tex) 1225 Texas St, Houston, TX 77002
STRINGFELLOW III, Howard (Be) 333 Wyandotte St, Bethlehem, PA 18015
STRIPP, Sarah Lynn (Miss)
STRIZAK, Jenna (At) Holy Trinity Parish, 515 E Ponce de Leon Ave, Decatur, GA 30030
STROBEL, Mark Alan (ND) 3600 25th St S, Fargo, ND 58104
STROBEL, Pam Owen (NY) 123 Henry St, Greenwich, CT 06830
STROH, Nancy Marshall (Pa) 3440 Norwood Pl, Holland, PA 18966
STROHM, Ralph (WVa) 2248 Adams Ave, Huntington, WV 25704
STROHMAIER, Gretchen (Mont) Holy Spirit Episcopal Church, 130 S 6th St E, Missoula, MT 59801
STROM, Aune Juanita (Mo) PO Box 972, Rolla, MO 65402
STROMBERG, Matthew Roy (Alb)
STRONG, Anne Lorraine (Az) PO Box 65840, Tucson, AZ 85728
STRONG, Daniel (WMass) 17 Exeter Dr, Auburn, MA 01501
STRONG III, Maurice Leroy (Chi) 26 E Stonegate Dr, Prospect Heights, IL 60070
STRONG, Nancy (WMass) 17 Exeter Dr, Auburn, MA 01501
STROO, Eric Edward (Oly) 111 NE 80th St, Seattle, WA 98115
STROTHEIDE, Cassandra (Colo) 48 Ruth Rd, Broomfield, CO 80020
STROUD, Daniel (Pa) PO Box 247, Ft Washington, PA 19034
STROUD, Ethan (EC)
STROUD, Lara (Pa) PO Box 247, Fort Washington, PA 19034
STROUD, Nancy Webb (WMass) 64 Westwood Dr, Westfield, MA 01085

STROUP, Susan Louise (Oly)
STROUT, Shawn Owen (WA) 3737 Seminary Rd, Alexandria, VA 22304
STRUBEL, Gary F (Alb) 457 3rd St, Troy, NY 12180
STRUBLE, Kenneth (At) 573 Currahee Pt, Toccoa, GA 30577
STUART, Judith Lynne (Mass)
STUART, Lawrence Earl (Mich) 3901 Cheyenne Rd, Richmond, VA 23235
STUART, Marianne D(esmarais) (Ala) 249 Arch St, Philadelphia, PA 19106
STUART, Mark (Los) 2260 N Cahuenga Blvd Apt 507, Los Angeles, CA 90068
STUART V, Mose Wadsworth (Ala)
STUART, Toni (The Episcopal NCal) 4881 8th St, Carpinteria, CA 93013
STUBE, Peter (Pa) 125 Timothy Cir, Wayne, PA 19087
STUBER, Richard Leonard (Wyo) 1320 Landon Ave, Yakima, WA 98902
STUCKEY, Ross W (WMo) 1654 E Cardinal St, Springfield, MO 65804
STUDENNY, Ronald Roman (Dal) 977 W Highway 243, Canton, TX 75103
STUDLEY, Richard E (Minn) 9817 W. Pinecrest Dr, Sun City, AZ 85351
STUDWELL, Cathleen M (Nwk)
STUERKE, Pamela S (Mo) 5315 Pershing Ave Apt 1, Saint Louis, MO 63112
STUHLMAN, Byron (CNY) 22 River Rd Rm 24, Box 24, Newcastle, ME 04553
STUHLMANN, Robert (Vt) 2000 Main St, Stratford, CT 06615
STUMP, Celeste (Los) 330 E 16th St, Upland, CA 91784
STURE, Keehna (EO)
STURGEON, Mary Sue (Neb) 5176 S 149th Ct, Omaha, NE 68137
STURGEON, Stephen C (Cal) 85 E 100 N, Logan, UT 84321
STURGES, Harriette Horsey (WA) 3001 Wisconsin Ave Nw, Washington, DC 20016
STURGES, Kathleen McAuliffe (Va) 113 Melbourne Park Cir Apt A, Charlottesville, VA 22901
STURGESS, Amber (ECR) PO Box 5538, Carmel By The Sea, CA 93921
STURGIS, Janet Elizabeth (Neb) PO Box 2567, Mountain View, AR 72560
STURNI, Gary Kristan (WTenn) 6922 Great Oaks Rd, Germantown, TN 38138
STURTEVANT, Henry Hobson (NY) 484 W 43rd St Apt 33h, New York, NY 10036
STUTLER, Jamie (At) 1029 Wellesley Crest Dr, Woodstock, GA 30189
STUTSO, Michael (Mich)
SUAREZ, Eva Noemi (NY) 865 Madison Ave, New York, NY 10021
SUAREZ ELLES, Jose Armando (Colom) Cr 3 Sur # 11-A-02, Malambo, ATLANTICO, Colombia
SUBRAMANI, Vasu (NJ)

SUELLAU, Nancy Shebs (Fla) St Catherines Episcopal Church, 4758 Shelby Ave, Jacksonville, FL 32210
SUGENO, David Senkichi (Tex)
SUHAR, John Charles (SwFla) 771 34th Ave N, Saint Petersburg, FL 33704
SUHR, Esther Jean (Mont) 2584 Mt Hwy 284, Townsend, MT 59644
SUIT, Marvin Wilson (Lex) 440 Fountain Avenue, Flemingsburg, KY 41041
SUITTER, Andrew M (Mass) 1210 Locust St, Saint Louis, MO 63103
SULERUD, Mary (Md) 1222 Berry St, Baltimore, MD 21211
SULLIVAN, Ann Mary (The Episcopal NCal) 5850 Crestmoor Dr, Paradise, CA 95969
SULLIVAN, Bernadette Marie (LI) Po Box 243, Hampton Bays, NY 11946
SULLIVAN, Bradley Joseph (Tex) 3003 Memorial Ct Apt 2405, Houston, TX 77007
SULLIVAN, Brian Christopher (At) 2602 Peterboro Row, Marietta, GA 30062
SULLIVAN, David Andrew (Alb) P.O. Box 146, Elizabethtown, NY 12932
SULLIVAN, John Paul (Minn) 811 5th St NW, Austin MN, MN 55912
SULLIVAN, Judith A (Pa) Philadelphia Episc Cath, 3717 Chestnut St Ste 200, Philadelphia, PA 19104
SULLIVAN, Karen Sue Racer (Ind) 1770 N Layman Ave, Indianapolis, IN 46218
SULLIVAN, Kristin Louise (Tex)
SULLIVAN, Margaret L (La) 726 Maple St, Denham Springs, LA 70726
SULLIVAN, Mark Campbell (Del) 463 Nicole Ct, Smyrna, DE 19977
SULLIVAN, Mary Patricia (NMich) 201 E Ridge St, Marquette, MI 49855
SULLIVAN, Maryalice (Mass) 91 Bella Vista Cir, Chepachet, RI 02814
SULLIVAN, Mary Bea (Ala)
SULLIVAN JR, Matthew Robert (SeFla) 8144 Bridgewater Ct Apt C, West Palm Beach, FL 33406
SULLIVAN, Michael Radford (At) 805 Mount Vernon Hwy, Atlanta, GA 30327
SULLIVAN, Paul David (Mass) 138 Tremont St., Boston, MA 02111
SULLIVAN, Peggy (NY) P.O. Box 708, Walden, NY 12586
SULLIVAN JR, Robert Edmund (NJ) 3450 Wild Oak Bay Blvd Apt 138, Bradenton, FL 34210
SULLIVAN, Rosemari Gaughan (Va) 402 Virginia Avenue, Alexandria, VA 22302
SULLIVAN-CLIFTON, Sonia (Ga) 5873 N Dean Rd, Orlando, FL 32817
SUMMERFIELD, Leroy James (WNC) 5365 Pine Ridge Dr, Connellys Springs, NC 28612
SUMMEROUR, Toby (WNC) 233 Deep Ford Fls, Lake Toxaway, NC 28747

SUMMERS, Joseph Holmes (Mich) 1435 South Blvd, Ann Arbor, MI 48104

SUMMERSON, Stephen Lyn (Me) PO Box 8, Presque Isle, ME 04769

SUMNER JR, Edwin Roberts (NJ) 8 Heath Vlg, Hackettstown, NJ 07840

✠ **SUMNER JR**, George Robinson (Dal) 20 Queens Park Crescent West, Toronto, ON M5S 2W2, Canada

SUMNERS III, Charles Abram (WTex) 3704 Bunyan Cir, Lago Vista, TX 78645

SUNDARA, John Deepak (Tex) 2345 Sage Rd Apt 429, Apt 429, Houston, TX 77056

SUNDARA, Naomi (Dal)

SUNDERLAND, Douglas Clark (Wyo) 18 Manning Rd, Cody, WY 82414

SUNDERLAND, Edward (NY) 405 W 23rd St Apt 5b, New York, NY 10011

SUNDERLAND, Melanie (O) 1103 Castleton Rd, Cleveland Heights, OH 44121

SUNDIN, Chad Ludwig (Az) 1735 S College Ave, Tempe, AZ 85281

SUNDIN, Jana Patrice (Az)

SUPIN, Charles Robert (Nev) 554 East Landing Ridge Circle, Jefferson, NC 28640

SURGEON, Ornoldo A (SeFla) 20011 Nw 39th Ct, Miami Gardens, FL 33055

SURINER, Noreen (WMass) PO Box 464, Middlefield, MA 01243

SUTCLIFFE, David (Alb) 75 Willett St. Apt. 41, Albany, NY 12210

SUTHERLAND, Alan (Okla) 848 N Rainbow Blvd # 5108, Las Vegas, NV 89107

SUTHERLAND, Linda Ann (Tex) 830 County Road 109, Hamilton, TX 76531

SUTHERLAND, Mark (RI) St Martin of Tours, 50 Orchard Ave, Providence, RI 02906

SUTHERLAND, Melody (Eas) 219 Somerset Rd, Stevensville, MD 21666

SUTHERS, Derwent (At) 1178 Circulo Canario, Rio Rico, AZ 85648

SUTOR JR, Jack Thomas (Va) PO Box 120, Hanover, VA 23069

SUTTERFIELD, Ragan K (Ark)

SUTTERISCH, Anna (O)

SUTTERISCH, Noah M (O)

SUTTON, Audrey J (Dal)

SUTTON, Christine Marie (Be) PO Box 198, Lehman, PA 18627

✠ **SUTTON**, Eugene Taylor (Md) 4 E University Pkwy, Baltimore, MD 21218

SUTTON, John (Cal) 1045 Neilson St, Albany, CA 94706

SUTTON, Norma Sarah (Chi)

SUTTON, Sharon Laverne (NJ) St Stephens Episcopal Church, 324 Bridgeboro St, Riverside, NJ 08075

SVIHEL, David Mark (SwFla)

SVOBODA-BARBER, Helen (NC) St Lukes Tec Ch, 1737 Hillandale Rd, Durham, NC 27705

SWAIN, Barry Edward Bailey (NY) Church of the Resurrection, 119 East 74th Street, New York, NY 10021

SWAIN, Kathryn F (Kan)

SWAIN, Storm Kirsten (NY) United Lutheran Seminary, 7301 Germantown Ave, Philadelphia, PA 19119

SWAN, Clinton E (Ak) Po Box 50037, Kivalina, AK 99750

SWAN, Craig (RI) 72 Central St, Narragansett, RI 02882

SWAN, Richard A (Spr) PO Box 1513, Decatur, IL 62525

SWANLUND, Callie E (Pa) 6703 Wissahickon Ave, Philadelphia, PA 19119

SWANN, Albert Henry (ETenn) 2304 E Lamar Alexander Pkwy Apt 314, Maryville, TN 37804

SWANN, Catherine Williams (Va) 387 Harbor Drive, Reedville, VA 22539

SWANN, Stuart Alan (Los) 1560 S Fredrica Ave, Clearwater, FL 33756

SWANSON, Geraldine Ann (NY) 155 Bay St Apt 6H, Staten Island, NY 10301

SWANSON, Karen (The Episcopal Church in Haw) St Andrews Tec Ch, 1600 Santa Lucia Ave, San Bruno, CA 94066

SWANSON, Kenneth Banford (At) 1015 Old Roswell Rd, Roswell, GA 30076

SWANSON, Richard Alden (Cal) 3101 Peninsula Rd Apt 301, Oxnard, CA 93035

SWANSON, Rick (Vt) PO Box 1175, Stowe, VT 05672

SWARR, J Peter (Me) 1 Porter Rd, East Longmeadow, MA 01028

SWARTHOUT, James Edward (Chi) 10275 N. River Rd, Barrington Hills, IL 60102

SWARTSFAGER, Ames Kent (LI) 1022 Marine Dr NE Unit 2, Olympia, WA 98501

SWARTZELL, Steven Phillip (Los)

SWAYZE, Mother Marie (Pa) 540 Lowell St, Wakefield, MA 01880

SWEENEY, Craig Chandler (Be) 2411 SW 35th Ter, Topeka, KS 66611

SWEENEY, David Cameron (Ore) 503 N Holladay Dr, Seaside, OR 97138

SWEENEY, Joseph Francis (NJ) 25 Quail Hollow Drive, Westampton, NJ 08060

SWEENEY, Meghan T (Mass) All Saints Episcopal Church, 121 N Main St, Attleboro, MA 02703

SWEENEY, Michael (Va) 7419 Tanglewood Rd, Richmond, VA 23225

SWEENEY, Sylvia A (Los) Bloy Hse At Claremont, 1325 N College Ave, Claremont, CA 91711

SWEET, Fran Maciver (Cal) Po Box 1384, Alameda, CA 94501

SWEET, Portia Ann (Tex) 1656 Blalock Rd, Houston, TX 77080

SWEIGERT, Cynthia (Minn) 5700 Forbes Ave, Pittsburgh, PA 15217

SWENSON, Richard Clive (Minn)

SWENSON, Warren Thomas (WMo)

SWESEY, Jean Elizabeth (Minn) 1008 Transit Ave, Roseville, MN 55113

SWETMAN, Margarita O (Nwk) 2528 Palmer Ave, New Orleans, LA 70118

SWIEDLER, Anne Elizabeth (At) 216 Riverview Trl, Roswell, GA 30075

SWIFT, Daniel Willard (Los) 24874 Olive Tree Ln, Los Altos, CA 94024

SWIFT, John Kohler (WMo) 6 Hunter Dr, Guilford, CT 06437

SWIFT, Steve Albert (Md) 8403 Nunley Dr Apt E, Parkville, MD 21234

SWINDELL, Kay Howard (EC) 1514 Clifton Rd, Jacksonville, NC 28540

SWINDLE, Frank (NwT) 649 Hwy 577, Pioneer, LA 71266

SWINEHART, Bruce Howard (Colo) 1404 Orchard Ave, Boulder, CO 80304

SWINEHART JR, Charles (Mich) 1615 Ridgewood Dr, East Lansing, MI 48823

✠ **SWING**, William Edwin (Cal) 105 Pepper Ave, Burlingame, CA 94010

SWINNEA, Stephanie Lavenia (Neb) 8 El Charman Lake Pl, Gibbon, NE 68840

SWINSKI, Grace (RI)

SWITZ, Robert (Cal) 5825 Spanish River Rd, Fort Pierce, FL 34951

SWITZER, John B (Miss) 4412 Gautier Vancleave Rd, Gautier, MS 39553

SWITZER, Michael Paul (CFla)

SWONGER, Timothy Lee (Nev) 1560 Jamielinn Ln Unit 103, Las Vegas, NV 89110

SWOPE, Bob (Ak)

SWORD, Carl Richard (NY) 200 E 33rd St, Apt 14-J, New York, NY 10016

SY, Jonathan J (Los) 21202 Spurney Ln, Huntington Beach, CA 92646

SYDNOR JR, Charles Raymond (Va) 175 Rogue Point Ln, Heathsville, VA 22473

SYEDULLAH, Masud Ibn (NY) 12 Beadart Pl, Hyde Park, NY 12538

SYER, Nathan George (Nev)

SYLER, Gregory Charles (WA) St George Church, PO Box 30, Valley Lee, MD 20692

SYLVESTER, Heather (Me)

SYLVESTER, Kay (Los)

SYMINGTON, Ann Pritzlaff (Los) 4450 E Camelback Rd, Phoenix, AZ 85018

SYMINGTON, Sid (ECR) 545 Shasta Ave, Morro Bay, CA 93442

SYMONS, Frederic (The Episcopal NCal) 5301 Whitney Ave, Carmichael, CA 95608

SYNAN, Thomas (WMass) Church of The Heavenly Rest, 2 E 90th St, New York, NY 10128

SZARKE, Christopher J (U) 7486 S Union Park Ave, Midvale, UT 84047

SZCZERBA JR, Thomas John (NJ) 121 Francis Ave, Wayne, PA 19087

Clergy List

SZOBOTA, Nick (Va) 230 Owensville Rd, West River, MD 20778

SZOKE, Robyn J (CPa) 6 Kitszell Dr, Carlisle, PA 17015

SZOST, Lois Anne Whitcomb (NY) 57 Goodwin Rd, Stanfordville, NY 12581

SZYMANOWSKI, Michael Peter (SC) 100 Lewisfield Ct, Summerville, SC 29485

SZYMANSKI, Michael Stephen (WNY) 21 Modern Ave, Lackawanna, NY 14218

T

TABB, Stewart (SVa) 405 Talbot Hall Rd, Norfolk, VA 23505

TABER II, Ken (SwFla) 200 College Ave NE, Grand Rapids, MI 49503

TABER-HAMILTON, Nigel john (Oly) 7317 Cedar House Ct, Clinton, WA 98236

TABER-HAMILTON, Rachel Kathryn (Oly) 7317 Cedar House Ct, Clinton, WA 98236

TABONE, Marcel M (NJ)

TABOR, Henry Caleb Coleman (NC) 2208 Hope St, Raleigh, NC 27607

TACKKETT, Antoinette Vance (Kan) 613 Elm St, Coffeyville, KS 67337

TADKEN, Neil (Los) 122 S California Ave, Monrovia, CA 91016

TAFLINGER, Mary (Ind) 5553 Leumas Rd, Cincinnati, OH 45239

TAFOYA, Stacey T (Colo) 315 Leyden St, Denver, CO 80220

TAFT JR, Paul Eberhart (Tex) 5504 Andover Dr, Tyler, TX 75707

TAGGART, Mary Heller (Vt) PO Box 249, Stowe, VT 05672

TAKACS, Erika (NC) 6055 Glenacre Dr, Kernersville, NC 27284

TAKES WAR BONNETT, Ray Lee (SD) 840 Spruce St Lot 38, Rapid City, SD 57701

TALBERT, John Keith (CGC)

TALBERT, Thomas Keith (CGC) 701 N Pine St, Foley, AL 36535

TALBIRD JR, John D (ETenn) 5450 Whitley Park Ter Apt 210, Bethesda, MD 20814

TALBOT, Jared C (Me)

TALCOTT, Barbara Geer (NH) St Marks School, 25 Marlboro Rd, Southborough, MA 01772

TALIAFERRO, Bob (Mo) St Pauls Episcopal Church, 1010 N Main St, Sikeston, MO 63801

TALK IV, John Gordon (NC) 946 Sheldon Rd, Southern Pines, NC 28387

TALLANT, Greg (At) 3285 Kensington Road, Avondale Estates, GA 30002

TALLEVAST, William Dalton (CPa) 1501 N Campbell Ave, Dept of Pastoral Care, Tucson, AZ 85724

TALLEY, Jennie (NY) St Johns Episcopal Church, 11 Wilmot Rd, New Rochelle, NY 10804

TALLMAN JR, Samuel Vose (WNC) St Mary of the Hills Church, PO Box 14, Blowing Rock, NC 28605

✠ **TALTON**, Chester Lovelle (Los) 1528 Oakdale Rd, Modesto, CA 95355

TAMAYO LOPEZ, Carlos Alberto (Cu)

TAMKE, Stephen (LI) 54 George St, Manhasset, NY 11030

TAMM, Daniel A (Los)

TAMMEARU, Deborah Gibson (NY) 633 W Sierra Madre Blvd Apt 12, Sierra Madre, CA 91024

TAN, Courtney Ann Urquhart (Los)

TAN, Wee Chung (Minn)

TANABE, Irene (Oly) 4533 52nd Ave S, Seattle, WA 98118

TAN CRETI, Michael J (Neb) 2051 N 94th St, Omaha, NE 68134

TANG, Chris (Md) 3118 Cape Hill Ct, Hampstead, MD 21074

TANG, Pamela W (NY)

TANKERSLEY, Rebecca (Dal) 14115 Hillcrest Rd, Dallas, TX 75254

TANNER, Michael Abbott (At)

TANTIMONACO, Dan Frank (Az) 2008 W Olive Way, Chandler, AZ 85248

TAPLEY, William Clark (WTex) 1604 W Kansas Ave, Midland, TX 79701

TAPPE, Ibba (Fla) 2935 Tidewater St, Fernandina Beach, FL 32034

TARBOX, Janet (USC) 318 Palmer Dr, Lexington, SC 29072

TARDIFF, Dick (The Episcopal Church in Haw) PO Box 545, Kealakekua, HI 96750

TARPLEY, Kent W (SwVa) 375 E Pine St, Wytheville, VA 24382

TARRANT, Paul John (RI) 39 Jeffrey Street, Edinburgh, EH1 1DH, Great Britain (UK)

TARTT JR, Jo Cowin (WA) 2727 34th Pl Nw, Washington, DC 20007

TARVER, Brian M (WTex) 311 E Corpus Christi St, Beeville, TX 78102

TASY, Beverly Ann Moore (Oly) St Christophers Tec Ch, 207 E Permian Dr, Hobbs, NM 88240

TATE, Mary Katherine (Del) 18 Olive Ave, Rehoboth Beach, DE 19971

TATE, Robert Lee (Pa) 7209 Lincoln Dr, Philadelphia, PA 19119

TATE, Russell Eric (Eau) 510 S Farwell St Ste 2, Eau Claire, WI 54701

TATE, Ruth Newman (At) 201 Ellen Ct, Warner Robins, GA 31088

TATEM, Catherine Leigh (USC) The Church of the Redeemer, 120 Mauldin Rd, Greenville, SC 29605

TATEM, Sandra Lou (Alb) 39 Greyledge Dr, Loudonville, NY 12211

TATEM, William Arthur (Alb) 39 Graystone Rd, Loudonville, NY 12211

TATLIAN, Edward Anthony (CFla) 6400 N Socrum Loop Rd, Lakeland, FL 33809

TATLOCK, Alan Ralph (Alb) 2938 Birchton Rd, Ballston Spa, NY 12020

TATRO, Marie A (LI) St Gabriels Episcopal Church, 331 Hawthorne St, Brooklyn, NY 11225

TATTERSALL, Elizabeth Russell (Nev) 1048 Wisteria Dr., Minden, NV 89423

TAUBE, Kimberly Lynn (WMo) 524 4th St, Boonville, MO 65233

TAUPIER, Linda (WMass)

TAVOLARO, Dante A (RI) 1 Smith Ave, PO Box 505, Greenville, RI 02828

TAYEBWA, Onesmus OT (Los) 5700 Rudnick Ave, Woodland Hills, CA 91367

TAYLOR, A(lice) Susan (NJ) 13 Forsythia Ct, Marlton, NJ 08053

TAYLOR, Andrea Maija (Mass) St Davids Church, 205 Old Main St, South Yarmouth, MA 02664

TAYLOR, Barbara (At) PO Box 1030, Clarkesville, GA 30523

TAYLOR, Bob (Ct) 4 Harbor View Drive, Essex, CT 06426

TAYLOR, Brenda M (CFla) 221 Wading Bird Cir SW, Palm Bay, FL 32908

TAYLOR, Brian (Chi) 1401 Los Arboles Ave NW, Albuquerque, NM 87107

TAYLOR, Bruce W (Episcopal VI) The Valley, Box 65, Virgin Gorda, VG1150, British Virgin Islands

TAYLOR, Carlene Holder (Ga)

TAYLOR, Charles Henry (WNC) 84 Keasler Rd, Asheville, NC 28805

TAYLOR, Courtney Stacy (Miss)

TAYLOR, Cynthia nan (Ga) 973 Hunting Horn Way W, Evans, GA 30809

TAYLOR, David Edwin (SwVa) PO Box 527, Rocky Mount, VA 24151

TAYLOR, David Kenneth (Nwk) 124 Franklin Ct, Flemington, NJ 08822

TAYLOR, Dean (At) 1600 Southmont Dr, Dalton, GA 30720

TAYLOR, Dennis (Oly) 4218 Montgomery Pl, Mount Vernon, WA 98274

TAYLOR, Edgar Garland (La) 1716 Soniat St, New Orleans, LA 70115

TAYLOR, George Williamson (NY) 311 Huguenot St, New Rochelle, NY 10801

TAYLOR, Gregory Blackwell (Va) 250 Pantops Mountain Rd, 5407, Charlottesville, VA 22911

TAYLOR, James Delane (CFla) 10 Fox Cliff Way, Ormond Beach, FL 32174

TAYLOR JR, James Edward (CFla) 1150 E Montague Ave, North Charleston, SC 29405

TAYLOR, James Maurice (Pa) 160 Marvin Rd, Elkins Park, PA 19027

TAYLOR, Jo (SVa) 3100 Shore Dr Apt 625, Virginia Beach, VA 23451

✠ **TAYLOR**, John Harvey (Los) 19968 Paseo Luis, Yorba Linda, CA 92886

TAYLOR, LeBaron (SwVa) PO Box 709, Covington, VA 24426

TAYLOR, Linda Sue (Tex) 2305 Ashland Ave, Fort Worth, TX 76107

TAYLOR, Lloyd (LI) 13304 109th Ave, South Ozone Park, NY 11420

TAYLOR, Marjorie Beth (Mich) St. John's Episcopal Church, 26998 Woodward Ave, Royal Oak, MI 48067

TAYLOR, Mary Ann Demetsenaere (Me) 83 Indian Hill Ln, Frankfort, ME 04438

TAYLOR, Patricia Lois (Oly) 75 E Lynn St Apt 104, Seattle, WA 98102

TAYLOR, Paul N (WMass) 34 Boylston Cir, Shrewsbury, MA 01545

TAYLOR, Phyllis (Pa) 401 Central Ave, Cheltenham, PA 19012

✠ **TAYLOR**, Porter (WNC) 44 Ravenwood Dr, Fletcher, NC 28732

TAYLOR, Porter Case (CFla)

TAYLOR, Ralph Douglas (Az) St Philips in the Hills, PO Box 65840, Tucson, AZ 85728

TAYLOR JR, Raymond George (NC) 461 Pemaquid Harbor Rd, Pemaquid, ME 04558

TAYLOR, Richard Louis (WLa) 108 Jason Ln, Natchitoches, LA 71457

TAYLOR, Robert (NC) 813 Darby St, Raleigh, NC 27610

TAYLOR, Robert C (USC) 511 Roper Mtn Rd, Greenville, SC 29615

TAYLOR, Robert Stuart (SeFla) 3325 E Community Dr, Jupiter, FL 33458

TAYLOR, Robert Vincent (Oly) 32508 W Kelly Rd, Benton City, WA 99320

TAYLOR, Robin (WA) 8005 Deepwater View Dr, Port Tobacco, MD 20677

TAYLOR, Ronald Brent (WNC) 7545 Sarah Dr, Denver, NC 28037

TAYLOR, Scott C (Los) 146 12th St, Pacific Grove, CA 93950

TAYLOR, Stanley Richard (HB) 157 Patrick Crescent, Essex, ON N8M 1X2, Canada

TAYLOR, Stefanie Elizabeth (At) 3110 Ashford Dunwoody Rd NE, Atlanta, GA 30319

TAYLOR, Susan (Me)

TAYLOR, Sylvester Oneal (LI) 485 Linwood St, Brooklyn, NY 11208

TAYLOR, Terrence Alexander (SeFla) 20822 San Simeon Way Apt 109, Miami, FL 33179

TAYLOR JR, Timus Gayle (Tenn) 4715 Harding Pike, Nashville, TN 37205

TAYLOR JR, Willard Seymour (EC) 245 Mcdonald Church Rd, Rockingham, NC 28379

TAYLOR JR, William Brown (SVa) 4025 Reese Dr S, Portsmouth, VA 23703

TAYLOR, Williamson (NY) 29 Drake St, Mount Vernon, NY 10550

TAYLOR LYMAN, Susan May (SD) 325 N Plum St, Vermillion, SD 57069

TAYLOR-MONTOYA, Amanda (RG)

TCHAMALA, Theodore K (Md) 6515 Loch Raven Blvd, Baltimore, MD 21239

TEAGUE, Charles Steven (NC) 337 Marley Was, Fuquay Varina, NC 27526

TEASLEY, Rrobintteasleygmailcomobin (SVa) 11406 Glenmont Rd, North Chesterfield, VA 23236

TEDERSTROM, John Patton (Ky) 1007 Hess Ln, Louisville, KY 40217

TEDESCO, Robert Lincoln (Va) 407 Russell Ave Apt 605, Gaithersburg, MD 20877

TEDESCO, William Nicholas (Ct) 20 Erickson Way, South Yarmouth, MA 02664

TEED, Lee B (SanD) 4860 Circle Dr, San Diego, CA 92116

TEES, Matthew B (LI)

TEETS, James C (SwFla) 37637 Magnolia Ave, Dade City, FL 33523

TEETZ, Margaret Lou-Sarah (Alb) Christ Church, 970 State St, Schenectady, NY 12307

TELFER, Barbara Jean (O)

TEMBECKJIAN, Renee Melanie (CNY) 4782 Hyde Rd, Manlius, NY 13104

TEMME, Louis (Pa)

TEMPLE, Charles Sloan (NY) 1 E 29th St, New York, NY 10016

TEMPLE, Gordon Clarence (ETenn) 6808 Levi Rd, Hixson, TN 37343

TEMPLE JR, Gray (At) 10685 Bell Rd, Duluth, GA 30097

TEMPLE, Palmer Collier (At) 1883 Wycliff Rd Nw, Atlanta, GA 30309

TEMPLEMAN, Mark Alan (Mass) 60 Monument Avenue, Swampscott, MA 01907

TEMPLETON, Gary Lynn (Okla) 903 N Primrose St, Duncan, OK 73533

TEMPLETON, John (At) 274 Hershey Lane, Clayton, GA 30525

TEMPLETON, Patricia Dale (At) 4393 Garmon Rd NW, Atlanta, GA 30327

TEMS, Robin (Colo)

TENCH, Jack Marvin (Oly) 1919 NE Ridgewood Ct, Poulsbo, WA 98370

TENDICK, James Ross (U) 1780 Plateau Cir, Moab, UT 84532

✠ **TENNIS**, Cabell (Oly) 725 9th Ave Apt 904, Apt. 904, Seattle, WA 98104

TENNISON, George Nelson (La) 401 Magnolia Ln, Mandeville, LA 70471

TENNY, Claire Mary (Chi) Po Box 426, Vails Gate, NY 12584

TEPAVCHEVICH, Kathie Elaine (Chi) 6588 Shabbona Rd, Indian Head Park, IL 60525

TEPE, Donald James (EMich) 3226 Meadowview Ln, Saginaw, MI 48601

TEPPER, Peter Wesley (CFla)

TERHUNE, Jason Scott (Tenn)

TERHUNE, Rebecca Claudia (Mil)

TERHUNE JR, Robert Dawbarn (Tex) 2605A Spring Ln, Austin, TX 78703

TERRY, Andrew (Tex) 8830 Blue Horizon Ct, Cypress, TX 77433

TERRY, Eleanor Applewhite (Mass) 193 Salem St, Boston, MA 02113

TERRY, Susan (Kan) 3209 W 25th St, Lawrence, KS 66047

TERRY, Teresa F (Dal)

TERRY, William Hutchinson (La) 626 Congress St., New Orleans, LA 70117

TERVINE, Denise (Hai)

TERWILLIGER, David R (Ak) 11451 Spyglass Hill Cir, Anchorage, AK 99515

TESCHNER, David (SVa) 10960 Bland Ridge Dr, South Prince George, VA 23805

TESKA, William Jay (Minn) 940 Franklin Ter, Apt 409, Minneapolis, MN 55406

TESS, Mike (Mil) 124 Dewey St, Sun Prairie, WI 53590

TESTA, Dennis Arthur (Md) 302 Homewood Rd, Linthicum, MD 21090

TESTER, Elizabeth B (WNC)

TESTER, Helen Whitener (Miss) 743 Milwaukee Rd, Beloit, WI 53511

TESTIN, Joan Marie (RI) Emmanuel Episcopal Church, 120 Nate Whipple Hwy, Cumberland, RI 02864

TETRAULT, David Joseph (SVa) 22501 Cypress Point Rd, Williamsburg, VA 23185

TETRAULT, Joanne Russell (Md) 6400 Belair Rd, Baltimore, MD 21206

TETZLAFF, Chana (Ind) St Christophers Episcopal Church, 1402 W Main Street, Carmel, IN 46032

TETZLAFF, Tyler J (Ind)

THABET, David George (WVa) 1305 15th St, Huntington, WV 25701

THACKER, Bob (SwVa) 207 Lookout Point Dr, Osprey, FL 34229

THADDEUS JR, Aloysius Peter (WTex) 115 Northwood Dr, Cuero, TX 77954

THADEN, Timothy Robert (Colo) 14397 59 1 2 Rd, Collbran, CO 81624

THAETE JR, William Elwood (Oly) 10239 Old Frontier Rd NW, Silverdale, WA 98383

THAMES, David Blake (Tex) 4419 Taney Ave No 202, Alexandria, VA 22304

THAO, Choua May (Minn) 2200 Minnehaha Ave E, Saint Paul, MN 55119

THAO, Thomas Zaxao (Minn)

THARAKAN, Angeline H (Ark) 2535 E Bennett St, Springfield, MO 65804

✠ **THARAKAN**, Jos (Ida) 9537 W Homewood Dr, Boise, ID 83709

THATCHER, Anne C (Nwk) 8000 Saint Martins Ln, Philadelphia, PA 19118

THAYER, Andrew Richard (La) 1329 Jackson Ave, Church of the Ascension, Montgomery, AL 36104

THAYER, Evan (Ala) 201 S Main Ave, Demopolis, AL 36732

THAYER II, Fred (SanD) 12103 Caminito Corriente, San Diego, CA 92128

THAYER, Judith Ann (Mil) 912 20th Ave, Coralville, IA 52241

THAYER, Steven Allen (NJ) Po Box 440, Jamison, PA 18929

THEUS SR, James Graves (WLa) 6291 Old Baton Rouge Hwy, Alexandria, LA 71302

THEW, Richard H (EO) Po Box 125, Cove, OR 97824

THEW FORRESTER, Kevin L (Ore) 7476 SW Applegate Dr, Beaverton, OR 97007

THEW FORRESTER, Rise Fay (Ore) 7476 SW Applegate Dr, Beaverton, OR 97007

THIBODAUX, Louise Ruprecht (Ala)

THIBODEAUX, James L (Oly) 7904 Manzanita Dr NW, Olympia, WA 98502

THIELE, William C (Nwk) 215 Lafayette Ave., Passaic, NJ 07055

THIM, Paul Russell (At) 697 Densley Dr, Decatur, GA 30033

THOBER, Ellie Thober (Neb) 4718 18th St, Columbus, NE 68601

THOENI, Thomas Andrew (SwFla) 302 Carey St, Plant City, FL 33563

THOM, Ashley Jane Squier (Chi) 3626 N. Francisco Ave., Chicago, IL 60618

THOM, Brian (Ida) 1858 W Judith Ln, Boise, ID 83705

THOM, Ken (Eas) 3849 Sirman Dr, Snow Hill, MD 21863

THOMAS, Adam P (Ct) 15 Pearl St, Mystic, CT 06355

THOMAS, Allisyn (SanD) St Pauls Cathedral, 2728 Sixth Avenue, San Diego, CA 92103

THOMAS JR, Arthur Robert (Ak) PO Box 1872, Seward, AK 99664

THOMAS JR, Benjamin A (SeFla)

THOMAS, Benjamin Randall (WK) 402 S 8th St, Salina, KS 67401

THOMAS, Bethany (Colo) 1221 Illinois St. Apt 2A, Golden, CO 80401

THOMAS, Christopher Blake (Dal) 1200 Main St Apt 906, Dallas, TX 75202

THOMAS, David L (Okla)

THOMAS, Douglas Earl (WTex) 2722 Old Ranch Rd, San Antonio, TX 78217

THOMAS, Douglas Paul (NwT) 602 Meander St, Abilene, TX 79602

THOMAS, Elaine Ellis (Nwk) All Saints Episcopal Parish, 701 Washington St, Hoboken, NJ 07030

THOMAS, Jaime Alfredo (Dal) PO Box 15, Fort Ord, CA 93941

THOMAS, James McCormack (Mass) P.O. Box 1073, East Sandwich, MA 02537

THOMAS JR, James Morris (The Episcopal NCal) 18402 Yale Ct, Sonoma, CA 95476

THOMAS, John (Va) 17 Laurel Ct, Nellysford, VA 22958

THOMAS, John Alfred (Va) 3800 Powell Ln Apt 813, Falls Church, VA 22041

THOMAS, John Paul (Dal) 739 Middale Rd, Duncanville, TX 75116

THOMAS, Jonathan R (Chi) 1864 Post Rd, Darien, CT 06820

THOMAS, Joshua (Oly) 370 Lexington Ave Rm 1201, New York, NY 10017

THOMAS, Kathryn Pauline (Va) 214 Church St, Madison, VA 22727

THOMAS, Kathy (NI) 10010 Aurora Pl, Fort Wayne, IN 46804

THOMAS, Keila Carpenter (Lex) 145 E 5th St, Morehead, KY 40351

THOMAS, Kenneth Dana (Ct) 5 Bassett St Apt B10, West Haven, CT 06516

THOMAS, Larry Todd (WA)

THOMAS, Laughton (Fla) 516 Howard Ave, Tallahassee, FL 32310

THOMAS, Lauren (Colo) 8155 Sterling Ranch Ave, Littleton, CO 80125

THOMAS, Leonard Everett (EC) 916 Lord Granville Dr., Morehead City, NC 28557

THOMAS, Margaret Ann (Me) 297 Wardwell Point Rd, Penobscot, ME 04476

THOMAS, Margaret Warren (Minn) 9426 Congdon Blvd, Duluth, MN 55804

THOMAS, Marilu James (Va)

THOMAS, Megan Evans (NJ) 16 All Saints Rd, Princeton, NJ 08540

THOMAS, Michael Jon (WNY) 703 W Ferry St Apt C9, Buffalo, NY 14222

THOMAS, Michael Joseph (Tex)

THOMAS, Micki-Ann (SwFla) 7250 Quarry St, Englewood, FL 34224

THOMAS, Natalie (Mass)

THOMAS, Patricia Menne (EC) 136 Saint Andrews Cir, New Bern, NC 28562

THOMAS, Peter Glyn (Tex) 831 Walker Stone Dr Apt 104, Cary, NC 27513

THOMAS, Rachel Woodall (Ct) 155 Essex St, Deep River, CT 06417

THOMAS, Rhonda Ann (EC)

THOMAS, Robert William (NC) 413 Dogwood Creek Pl, Fuquay Varina, NC 27526

THOMAS, Roy Abraham (Dal)

THOMAS, Sarah D. (Los)

THOMAS, Sherry (Ct) 386 N Anna Dr, Louisa, VA 23093

THOMAS, Teresa Ann Collingwood (Ak) PO Box 76, Fort Yukon, AK 99740

THOMAS, Timothy Bosworth (SeFla) 3434 N Ocean Shore Blvd, Flagler Beach, FL 32136

THOMAS, Valerie Bricker (Fla) 244 Ashley Lake Dr, Melrose, FL 32666

THOMAS, Victor J (Tex) 3129 Southmore Blvd, Houston, TX 77004

THOMAS, Wayland Eugene (Md) 55 Brooklyn Hts Rd, Thomaston, ME 04861

THOMAS, William Carl (EC) 4832 Bluebell Trce, New Bern, NC 28562

THOMAS, William Steven (SeFla) 14445 Horseshoe Trce, Wellington, FL 33414

THOMASON, Clayton Leslie (Chi) 42 Ashland Ave, River Forest, IL 60305

THOMASON, Steven (Oly) 1245 10th Ave E, Seattle, WA 98102

THOMPSON, Barkley Stuart (Ark) 8600 Evergreen Dr, Little Rock, AR 72227

THOMPSON, Carla Eva (Va) 322 N Alfred St, Alexandria, VA 22314

THOMPSON, Catherine M (Dal) Tec Ch Of The Annunciation, 602 N Old Orchard Lane, Lewisville, TX 75077

THOMPSON, Chris Christopher (WVa) Church of the Holy Communion, 218 Ashley Ave, Charleston, SC 29403

THOMPSON, Danielle L (Ala) 1910 12th Ave S, Birmingham, AL 35205

THOMPSON, David Frank Ora (USC) 510 Sikes Ave, North Augusta, SC 29841

THOMPSON, David J (Dal) 30 Brimmer St, Boston, MA 02108

THOMPSON, David Joel (Colo) 360 Scrub Oak Cir, Monument, CO 80132

THOMPSON, Donald Frederick (Ct) 11 Lenox Ave, Norwalk, CT 06854

THOMPSON, Edward (Pa) 301 N Chester Rd, Swarthmore, PA 19081

THOMPSON, Edward Hnebe (Tex) 3608 Mocha Trl, Austin, TX 78728

THOMPSON, Elena M (WA) PO Box 1167, Baxley, GA 31515

THOMPSON JR, Fred Edward (SC) 2138 Allandale Plantation Rd, Wadmalaw Island, SC 29487

THOMPSON, Fred Leonard (NC) 538 Furth Ln, Southern Pines, NC 28387

THOMPSON, Helen Plemmons (At) 91 Wylde Wood Dr, McDonough, GA 30253

THOMPSON III, Henry Lawrence (Pgh) 2310 Meadow Vue Dr, Moon Township, PA 15108

THOMPSON, James E (Episcopal SJ) 3930 SE 162nd Ave Spc 22, Portland, OR 97236

THOMPSON, Jerry A (Neb) Stmarks - Campus, Lincoln, NE 68508

THOMPSON, Jessica R (SanD)

THOMPSON, John Eric (Roch) 26 N Clinton St, Dansville, NY 14437

THOMPSON, John Kell (Oly) 65600 E Desert Side Dr, Tucson, AZ 85739

THOMPSON, John Paul (Alb) PO Box 180, Copake Falls, NY 12517

THOMPSON JR, Joseph Downing (Mo)

THOMPSON, Karen Elizabeth (EMich) 18890 Fireside Hwy, Presque Isle, MI 49777

THOMPSON, Kenneth David (Ky) 1768 Plum Ridge Rd, Taylorsville, KY 40071

THOMPSON, Kenya (At)

THOMPSON, Lori Lee L (ETenn) 590 Walthour Rd, Savannah, GA 31410

THOMPSON, Marisa Tabizon (Neb) 9320 Blondo St, Omaha, NE 68134

THOMPSON, Mark (Vt) 700 Douglas Ave Apt 907, Minneapolis, MN 55403

THOMPSON, M Dion (Md) 1208 John St, Baltimore, MD 21217

THOMPSON, Michael Bruce (EC) Dashwood House, Sidgwick Avenue, Cambridge, CB3 9DA, Great Britain (UK)

THOMPSON, Michael King (NC) 103 Sheffield Rd, Williamsburg, VA 23188

✠ THOMPSON JR, Morris (La) 1623 7th St, New Orleans, LA 70115

THOMPSON III, Morris King (Miss) 3831 35th Ave, Meridian, MS 39305

THOMPSON, Owen C (SO) Grace Church, 130 1st Ave, Nyack, NY 10960

THOMPSON, Paul Mason (Vt) 4323 Main Street Rt 6a, Cummaquid, MA 02637

THOMPSON, Peggy Reid (ECR) 451 Vivienne Dr, Watsonville, CA 95076

THOMPSON, Peter D (Ct) 325 Park Ave, New York, NY 10022

THOMPSON, Richelle L (Ala) Church Of The Resurrection, 113 Brown Ave, Rainbow City, AL 35906

THOMPSON, Robert Wildan (Ky) 1206 Maple Ln, Anchorage, KY 40223

THOMPSON, Roderick James Marcellus (Cal) 4048 17th St, San Francisco, CA 94114

THOMPSON, Scott A (Tex) Holy Cross Episc Church, 5653 W. River Park Dr., Sugar Land, TX 77479

THOMPSON SR, Stephen Lafoia (ETenn) 134 Iris Pl, Newport, TN 37821

THOMPSON, Sue (Cal) St Edmund's Episcopal Church, PO Box 688, Pacifica, CA 94044

THOMPSON, Tommy Alan (Pa) Washington Memorial Chapel, Valley Forge, PA 19481

THOMPSON, Wanda Jean (Me) 1375 Forest Ave. Apt. H14, Portland, ME 04103

THOMPSON, Zachary R (NY) 805 Mount Vernon Hwy, Atlanta, GA 30327

THOMPSON DE MEJIA, Kara Ann (Hond) Spring Garden, Islas De La Bahia, Roatan, Honduras

THOMPSON-QUARTEY, C John (At) 131 Fawn Pl, Marietta, GA 30062

THOMPSON-UBERUAGA, William (Ida) 518 N 8th St, Boise, ID 83702

THOMS, Benjamin (WLa)

THOMSEN, William Robert (WNC) 299 Locust Grove Rd, Weaverville, NC 28787

THOMSON, Jacqueline (Va) 9405 Shouse Dr, Vienna, VA 22182

THOMSON, James (Okla) 501 S Cincinnati Ave, Tulsa, OK 74103

THOMSON, Malcolm Davis (WMich)

THOMSON, Ronald Reed (RG) 733 Lakeway Dr, El Paso, TX 79932

THON, Susan Cecelia (WA) 34 Wellesley Circle, Glen Echo, MD 20812

THOR, Margaret Carlson (Minn) 60 Kent St, Saint Paul, MN 55102

THOR, Peter Chianeng (Minn) 2200 Minnehaha Ave E, Saint Paul, MN 55119

THORME, Trisha Ann (NJ) 1040 Yardville Allentown Rd, Trenton, NJ 08620

THORNBERG, Anne (Los) 3321 Rustburg Dr, Fayetteville, NC 28303

THORNBERG, Jeff (Los) 617 W Roses Rd, San Gabriel, CA 91775

THORNE, Joyce Terrill (RI) 670 Weeden Street, Pawtucket, RI 02860

THORNE, Sara M (WA) 3525 Woodley Road, NW, Washington, DC 20016

THORNE, Walter Joseph (Los)

THORNELL, Kwasi (SeFla) 1525 Casino Cir, Silver Spring, MD 20906

THORNLEY, Edward Charles (WA) 4700 Whitehaven Parkway NW, Washington, DC 20007

THORNTON, Corey Todd (The Episcopal Church in Haw) PSC 473 Box 10, FPO, AP 96349-0001, Japan

THORNTON, Daniel Ingram (Ala) 1402 Prier Dr, Marion, AL 36756

✠ THORNTON, John Stuart (Ida) 323 W Jefferson St Apt 204, Boise, ID 83702

THORNTON, Norman Edward (Del) Box 2805, Northfield, MA 01360

THORNTON, Theresa Joan (SO) 10345 Montgomery Rd, Cincinnati, OH 45242

THORP, Steven Tanner (Spr) 1717 Park Haven Dr, Champaign, IL 61820

THORPE, John A (Okla) 2117 North 4th Ave East, Newton, IA 50208

THORPE, Mary Brennan (Va) 110 W Franklin St, Richmond, VA 23220

THORSEN, Heidi (Ct)

THORSTAD, Anita Fortino (SeFla) 951 De Soto Rd Apt 330, Boca Raton, FL 33432

THRALL, Barbara (WMass) 19 Hadley St Apt D12, South Hadley, MA 01075

THREADGILL, Nancy (Pgh) 335 Locust St, Johnstown, PA 15901

THROOP, John R (FdL) PO Box 29, Adams, NY 13605

THULLBERY, Marion (NC) Durham Va Medical Center, 508 Fulton St, Durham, NC 27705

THURBER, Lorraine Theresa (Alb)

THURSTON, Bud (Ore) 39 Greenridge Ct, Lake Oswego, OR 97035

THWEATT III, Richmond Fitzgerald (WLa) 7109 Woodridge Ave, Oklahoma City, OK 73132

THWING, Robert C (Ak) PO Box 91943, Anchorage, AK 99509

TIAPULA, Imo Siufanua (The Episcopal Church in Haw) Po Box 2030, Pago Pago, AS 96799

TIBBETTS, Cathy (Va) The Falls Chruch Episcopal, 225 E Broad St, Falls Church, VA 22046

TIBBETTS, Ronald Creighton (Mass) 9 Cooney Ave, Plainville, MA 02762

TICHENOR, Liz (Cal) All Souls Episcopal Parish, 2220 Cedar St, Berkeley, CA 94709

TICKNOR, Patricia Horan (WMo) 12270 N New Dawn Ave, Oro Valley, AZ 85755

TICKNOR, William Howard Correa (Md) 5757 Solomons Island Rd, Lothian, MD 20711

TIDWELL, Janet Ruth (At) 582 Walnut St, Macon, GA 31201

TIDY, John Hylton (SeFla) 96114 Piney Island Dr, Fernandina Beach, FL 32034

TIEDERMAN, Nancy (Oly) 920 Cherry Ave NE, Bainbridge IS, WA 98110

TIEGS, Karen (Ore) All Saints' Episcopal Church, 3847 Terracina Dr., Riverside, CA 92506

TIELENS, Mees (Cal)

TIELKING, Claudia Gould (WA) 6533 Mulroy Street, Mc Lean, VA 22101

TIERNEY, Bridget (La) 114 N Pine St, New Lenox, IL 60451

TIERNEY, Dennis Stanley (Oly) 6973 Island Center Rd NE, Bainbridge Island, WA 98110

TIERNEY III, Peter George (RI) 28 Hamlet Ave, Woonsocket, RI 02895

TIERNEY, Philip Joseph (RI) 10 Murray Ave, North Kingstown, RI 02852

TIERNEY, Veronica M (RI) FourTwelve LLC, 28 Hamlet Ave, Woonsocket, RI 02895

TIFF II, Richard Olin (At)

TIFFANY, Susan Jean (O) 53720 Ironwood Rd, South Bend, IN 46635

TIFFENSON, Stephen (Cal)

TIGHE, Maureen (Ore) 1001 B-Ne 90th Ave, Portland, OR 97220

TILDEN, Roger (Md) 8089 Harmony Rd, Denton, MD 21629

TILING, Robert Henry (Chi) 1691 Campos Dr., The Villages, FL 32162

TILLER, Darrell Lamont (Pa)

TILLER, Monte Jackson (SeFla) 6409 Lantana Pines Dr, Lantana, FL 33462

TILLITT, Jay Lanning (LI) 1021 N University St, Redlands, CA 92374

TILLMAN, Ann Marie (WNY) 24 Maple Rd, East Aurora, NY 14052

TILLMAN, Christine Wylie (WMich) 3828 Cook Ct. S.W., Wyoming, MI 49519

TILLMAN, Jane Guion (WMass)

TILLOTSON, Ellen (Ct) 38 Fair St, Guilford, CT 06437

TILSON, Alan Russell (Kan) 1649 Alabama Ave S, Saint Louis Park, MN 55416

Clergy List

TILSON, Brent Edward (Spok) St Martins Episcopal Church, 416 E Nelson Rd, Moses Lake, WA 98837
TILSON JR, Hugh Arval (NC) 3819 Jones Ferry Rd, Chapel Hill, NC 27516
TIMMERMAN, Melissa (SC) 484 Lymington Rd, Severna Park, MD 21146
TINDALL, Byron Cheney (SC) 102 Fir Court Unit 1260, Waleska, GA 30183
TINGLEY, Harry William (Chi) 6007 N Sheridan Rd Apt 30k, Apt 30K, Chicago, IL 60660
TINNON, Becky (The Episcopal Church in Haw) 2121 San Diego Ave, San Diego, CA 92110
TINNON, Michael Scott (The Episcopal Church in Haw) 98-939 Moanalua Rd, Aiea, HI 96701
TINSLEY JR, Fred Haley (WLa) 3535 Santa Fe St Unit 41, Corpus Christi, TX 78411
TINSLEY, Pamela Byam (Oly)
TIPPETT, Michael R (Minn) 2202 Lexington Ave S, Saint Paul, MN 55120
TIPTON, Tommy (USC) 1029 Old Plantation Dr, Pawleys Island, SC 29585
TIRADO, Hernan (Colom)
TIRADO, Vincent (SeFla) 18601 Sw 210th St, Miami, FL 33187
TIRRELL, Charles David (Tex) 9701 Meyer Forest Dr Apt 12112, Houston, TX 77096
TIRRELL, John Alden (Cal) Box 456, Athens, 125, Greece
TISDALE JR, William Alfred (NC) 27 Church St, Stonington, CT 06378
TISDELLE, Celeste (Fla) St Marys Episcopal Church, 400 Saint Johns Ave, Green Cove Springs, FL 32043
TITCOMB, Cecily Johnson (SeFla) 141 S. County rd, Palm Beach, FL 33480
TITTLE, Darlene Anne Duryea (Nwk) 11 Overhill Dr, Budd Lake, NJ 07828
TITUS, Bessie Charlotte (Ak)
TITUS, John Clark (At) 5428 Park Cir, Stone Mountain, GA 30083
TITUS, Luke (Ak) Saint Barnabas Mission, Minto, AK 99758
TITUS, Nancy Espenshade (NC) 1739 Berwickshire Cir, Raleigh, NC 27615
TJELTVEIT, Maria Washington Eddy (Be) 124 S Madison St, Allentown, PA 18102
TJOFLAT, Marie Elizabeth (Fla) 1255 Peachtree St, Jacksonville, FL 32207
TLUCEK, Laddie (Okla) 1509 Nw 198th St, Edmond, OK 73012
TOALSTER, Rebecca D (CFla) 1015 S Floral Ave, Bartow, FL 33830
TOBER, John Milton (RG) 102 Saint James, Las Cruces, NM 88005
TOBERMAN, Harold Frederick (Ark) 329 Colony Green Dr, Bloomingdale, IL 60108
TOBIN, Barbara Kinzer (Pa) 313 Pine St, Philadelphia, PA 19106

TOBIN, Florence Lane (Roch) PO Box 304, Corning, NY 14830
TOBIN JR, Robert Wallace (Mass) 355 Blackstone Blvd Apt 307, Providence, RI 02906
TOBIN, Roger Martin (SeFla) 5690 N Kendall Dr, Miami, FL 33156
TOBOLA, Cynthia Pruet (Tex) PO Box 895, Palacios, TX 77465
TODARO, Alicia Butler (Alb) St Paul's Church, 58 3rd St, Troy, NY 12180
TODD, Charles E (Ga) St Paul Episcopal Church, 1802 Abercorn St, Savannah, GA 31401
TODD, Christopher Howard (SeFla) 30243 Coconut Hwy, Big Pine Key, FL 33043
TODD, Edward Pearson (Eur) 18 Hall Pond Lane, Copake, NY 11516-1400, Afghanistan
TODD, Kevin (WNC)
TODD, Michael P (Alb) 1620 Boathouse Cir, GR 208, Sarasota, FL 34231
TODD, Richard Alfred (Minn) 38378 Glacier Dr, North Branch, MN 55056
TOEBBEN, Warren B (Mil)
TOFANI, Ann Lael (Spr) 427 W 4th St, Mount Carmel, IL 62863
TOFFEY, Judith E (Ct) 314 Sperry Rd, Bethany, CT 06524
TOLA, Elaine M (NC)
TOLAND, Paula (Nwk) 119 Main St, Millburn, NJ 07041
TOLES, John F (Okla) 518 W Randolph Ave, Enid, OK 73701
TOLIVER, Jeffrey Thomas (RG) 1601 S Saint Francis Dr, Santa Fe, NM 87505
TOLL, Dick (Ore) PO Box 220112, 1707 SE Courtney Rd, Milwaukie, OR 97269
TOLLEFSON, Jane Jill Carol (Minn) 2700 Canby Ct, Northfield, MN 55057
TOLLETT, Mitchell Joseph (Tex) 121 Rowland Pl, Tyler, TX 75701
TOLLISON, Ann Black (Va) PO Box 100, Gum Spring, VA 23065
TOLLISON JR, Henry Ernest (USC) 105 Freeport Dr, Greenville, SC 29615
TOLLIVER, Lisa (Ky) 7504 Westport Rd, Louisville, KY 40222
TOLLIVER, Richard (Chi) 4729 S. Drexel Blvd, Chicago, IL 60615
TOLZMANN, Lee Ann (Ct) Tec Ch In Connecticut, 219 Pratt St, Meriden, CT 06450
TOMAINE, Jane (Nwk) 349 Short Dr, Mountainside, NJ 07092
TOMBAUGH, Richard Franklin (Ct) 58 Terry Rd, Hartford, CT 06105
TOMCZAK, Beth Lynn (WMich) 321 N Main St, Three Rivers, MI 49093
TOMEI, Gail Robbins (Pa) St Marys Bonita Springs, 9803 Bonita Springs Road, Bonita Springs, FL 34133
TOMLIN, Kyle R (Va) 6769 Ridge Ave # A, Philadelphia, PA 19128
TOMLINSON, Diane B (Chi)

TOMLINSON, Liz (Va) 3439 Payne St, Falls Church, VA 22041
TOMLINSON, Ruth (Neb) 5704 N 159th St, Omaha, NE 68116
TOMMASEO, Ellis (LI)
TOMOSO, John Hau'oli (The Episcopal Church in Haw) 51 Kuula St, Kahului, HI 96732
TOMPKINS JR, Douglas (Pa) 310 S Chester Rd, Swarthmore, PA 19081
TOMPKINS, Joyce L (Pa) 310 S Chester Rd, Swarthmore, PA 19081
TOMTER, Patrick Austin (Oly) PO Box 10785, Portland, OR 97296
TONEY, Martha Ann (CFla)
TONGE, Samuel Davis (Ga) 1023 Woods Road, Waycross, GA 31501
TONGUE, Mary Jane (Md) 203 Star Pointe Ct Unit 3d, Abingdon, MD 21009
TONSMEIRE SR, Louis (At) 224 Trammell St, Calhoun, GA 30701
TONTONOZ, David Costa (Eas) 5211 Dove Point Ln, Salisbury, MD 21801
TOOF, Jan Jarred (CNY) 2006 Manchester Rd, Wheaton, IL 60187
TOOKEY, Carol (NAM) PO Box 436, Aztec, NM 87410
TOOMEY, David C (NY) 45 Orchard St, Boston, MA 02130
TOONE, Susan (U) 1579 S State St, Clearfield, UT 84015
TORNQUIST, Frances C (Cal) 2748 Wemberly Dr, Belmont, CA 94002
TORO, Arthur N (Los) 135 Loden Pl, Jackson, MS 39209
TORO, Suzanne Frances Rosemary (NY) 70 Clinton St, Cornwall, NY 12518
TORRES, Julio Orlando (NY) 232 E 11th St # 3, New York, NY 10003
TORRES, Michele Angier (Mass) 103 Harvard Ave, Medford, MA 02155
TORRES, Tony (PR)
TORRES BAYAS, Javier (Cal) Guerrero 589, Tuxtepec, OAX 68313, Mexico
TORRES FUENTES, Pascual Pedro (Hond) Apdo 16, Puerto Cortes, Honduras
TORRES MARTINEZ, Wilfrido Oswaldo (EcuC) Convencion Y Solanda 056, Guaranda, Ecuador
TORREY, Bruce (Ct) 187 Dewitt Rd, Accord, NY 12404
TORREY, Dorothy Ellen (The Episcopal NCal) 901 Lincoln Rd Apt 40, Yuba City, CA 95991
TORREY, Leah Fredrickson (NH)
TORTORA, Rosario F (SC)
TORVEND, Samuel Edward (Oly) 15 Roy St, Seattle, WA 98109
TOTHILL, Marlene Grey (NwT) 19 Winchester Ct, Midland, TX 79705
TOTTEN, Julia Kay (Spok) PO Box 15, Florence, OR 97439
TOTTEN, William (Spok) PO Box 15, Florence, OR 97439
TOTTEY JR, Alfred George (CNY) 7385 Norton Ave, Clinton, NY 13323

TOTTY, Jonathan Paul (Tex)

TOUCHSTONE, G Russell (Los) 1069 S Gramercy Pl, Los Angeles, CA 90019

TOURANGEAU, Edward J (Ind) 260 Elm Ct, Troy, VA 22974

TOURNOUX, Gregory Allen (Spr) 2056 Cherry Rd, Springfield, IL 62704

TOVEN, Kenneth H (Minn) 1505 13th St N, Princeton, MN 55371

TOWELL, Gail Richards (CFla)

TOWERS, Crystal Daphne (ND)

TOWERS, Paul (Be) St Paul's Church, 276 Church St, Montrose, PA 18801

TOWERS, Richard A (ECR) 980 W Franklin St, Monterey, CA 93940

TOWLER, Lewis Wilson (Mich) 1711 Pontiac Trl, Ann Arbor, MI 48105

TOWNE, Jane Clapp (ND) 1111 N 1st St Apt 10, Bismarck, ND 58501

TOWNER, Philip Haines (NY) 552 W End Ave, New York, NY 10024

TOWNER, Robert Arthur (Mo) 38 N Fountain St, Cape Girardeau, MO 63701

TOWNLEY, Katherine Sue (NI)

TOWNSEND, Bowman (Tex) 2205 Matterhorn Ln, Austin, TX 78704

TOWNSEND, Craig D (NY) 445 Degraw St, Brooklyn, NY 11217

✠ **TOWNSEND**, Martin (Eas) HC 86 Box 48 C-1, Springfield, WV 26763

TOWNSEND III, Thomas Pinckney (Ga) 544 Bartow St, Saint Simons Island, GA 31522

TOWSON, Louis Albert (CFla) 348 Sherwood Ave, Satellite Beach, FL 32937

TOY, Fran (Cal) 4151 Laguna Ave, Oakland, CA 94602

TRACHE, Robert G (SeFla) 1750 E Oakland Park Blvd, Fort Lauderdale, FL 33334

TRACHMAN, Michael David (Okla) 2213 Galaxy Dr, Altus, OK 73521

TRACY, Dick Blaylock (Kan) 3020 Oxford Cir, Lawrence, KS 66049

TRACY, Edward J (SVa) 11827 Canon Blvd Ste 101, Newport News, VA 23606

TRACY, Paul John (NI) 1025 Park Pl Apt 159, Mishawaka, IN 46545

TRACY, Rita Vanessa (Kan) 3020 Oxford Cir, Lawrence, KS 66049

TRAFFORD, Edward John (RI) 45 Rotary Dr, West Warwick, RI 02893

TRAFTON, Clark Wright (Cal) 875 S Nueva Vista Dr, Palm Springs, CA 92264

TRAGER, Jane (O) 222 Eastern Heights Blvd, Elyria, OH 44035

TRAINOR, Christine (Cal)

TRAINOR, Helen C (WA) Legal Aid & Justice Center, 1000 Preston Ave. Ste A, Charlottesville, VA 22903

TRAINOR, Jim (FdL) E942 Whispering Pines Rd, Waupaca, WI 54981

TRAINOR, Mary Patricia (Los) 10925 Valley Home Ave, Whittier, CA 90603

TRAINOR, Mary Stoddard (FdL) E942 Whispering Pines Rd, Waupaca, WI 54981

TRAKEL, Debra Lynn (Mil) 4535 N 92nd St Apt R107, Wauwatosa, WI 53225

TRAMBLEY, Adam Thomas (NwPa) 343 Forker Blvd, Sharon, PA 16146

TRAMEL, Stephanie M (Ia) 2300 Bancroft Way, Berkeley, CA 94704

TRAMMELL, Robert William (Okla) St Augustine Qf Canterbury, 14700 N May Ave, Oklahoma City, OK 73134

TRAN, Catherine (Colo) 6556 High Dr, Morrison, CO 80465

TRAPANI, Kathleen (Cal) 30 Greenridge Pl, Danville, CA 94506

TRAPP, Grace J (SwVa) PO Box 328, Harpswell, ME 04079

TRAPP, James E (NY) PO Box 40697, Portland, OR 97240

✠ **TRAQUAIR**, Megan Mcclure (The Episcopal NCal) 10222 S 44th Ln, Laveen, AZ 85339

TRASK III, Bob (EMich) 13 Circle Ave, Wheaton, IL 60187

TRAVIS, Doug (Tex) 9701 Shadows Ct, Granbury, TX 76049

TRAVIS, Kathleen Ann (Ia) 3120 E 24th St, Des Moines, IA 50317

TRAVIS, Michelle Halsall (Mont) 1821 Westlake Dr Apt 124, Austin, TX 78746

TRAVIS, R Carroll (CFla) 2103 N Indian River Dr, Cocoa, FL 32922

TRAVIS, Robert P (NC) 326 Kenyon Ave, Wakefield, RI 02879

TRAVIS, Sherry (Miss) 1365 Sweetwater Dr, Brentwood, TN 37027

TRAVIS, Veronika E (Pa)

TRAYLOR, Thomas Wallace (Cal) 1801 Jackson St Apt 4, San Francisco, CA 94109

TRAYNHAM, Warner Raymond (Los) 6125 Alviso Ave, Los Angeles, CA 90043

TREADWELL III, Chuck (Tex) 11704 Via Grande Dr, Austin, TX 78739

TREANOR, Susan Mary (Be) PO Box 325, Jeffersonville, NY 12748

TREES, Thomas H (CFla) 1616 Sterns Dr, Leesburg, FL 34748

TREGO, Randall (Tex) 3106 Heritage Creek Oaks, Houston, TX 77008

TREI, Rosemary (Dal) 5923 Royal Ln, Dallas, TX 75230

TREJO-BARAHONA, Oscar (Hond)

TRELEASE, Murray Lincoln (Oly) 343 Eagles Roost Ln, Lopez Island, WA 98261

TRELOAR, Zeb (Ky) 806 Main St, Murray, KY 42071

TREMMEL, Marcia Ann (SwFla) 11588 57th Street Cir. E., Parrish, FL 34219

TRENARY, Jen L (CPa) 245 N 4th St, Columbia, PA 17512

TREPPA, Joyce Lynn (Mich) 1150 Tarpon Center Dr. #503, Venice, FL 34285

TREVATHAN, W Illiam Andre (Ky) 1 Franklin Town Blvd Apt 1515, Philadelphia, PA 19103

TREVER, Stephen Cecil (NY) 2300 Bancroft Way, Berkeley, CA 94704

TREWHELLA, Charles Keith (Ore) 19691 Nw Meadow Lake Rd, Yamhill, OR 97148

TREZEVANT, Margaret Anne (Cal) 1755 Clay St, San Francisco, CA 94109

TRIGG, Joseph (WA) Po Box 760, La Plata, MD 20646

TRIGLETH, John Paul (Mil) S3919A Highway 12, Baraboo, WI 53913

TRILLOS, Alejandra (ECR) 111 San Miguel Ave, Salinas, CA 93901

TRIMBLE, James Edward (Lex) 511 College St, Winchester, KY 40391

TRIMBLE, Sally (Va) 3401 Chantarene Dr, Pensacola, FL 32507

TRIMBLE JR, William Bradley (EC) 4619 Bentley Dr, Wilmington, NC 28409

TRIPLETT, Laurie Ann (RG)

TRIPP, Roy (SC) PO Box 761, Port Royal, SC 29935

TRIPP, Thomas Norman (WNY) 354 Burroughs Dr, Amherst, NY 14226-909

TRISTRAM, Geoffrey (Mass) 980 Memorial Dr, Cambridge, MA 02138

TRIVELY, Tim (SwFla) 4 Gatehouse Ct, Asheville, NC 28803

TROGDON, Denise (SC) 1700 Wainwright Dr, Reston, VA 20190

TROIANO, Susan (Alb) 107 State St, Albany, NY 12207

TRONCALE, John E (NJ) 301 Meadows Dr, Forest, VA 24551

TROTTER, Scott (Ark) 1103 Oakdale Dr, West Memphis, AR 72301

TROUTMAN-MILLER, Jana Lee (Mil) 1840 N Prospect Ave, Milwaukee, WI 53202

TROW, Chester John (SwFla)

TROWBRIDGE, Dustin (Ct) St James Episcopal Church, 25 West St, Danbury, CT 06810

TRUAX, Heidi (Ct) 31 Hilltop Rd, Sharon, CT 06069

TRUBY, Laura (Ore) 14221 Livesay Rd, Oregon City, OR 97045

TRUE, Jerry Erwin (WMass) 936 Grayson Drive Apt. 326, Springfield, MA 01119

TRUE SR, Timothy Emmett (Az) 225 Cumberland St W, Cowan, TN 37318

TRUIETT SR, Melvin Edward (Md) 2322 Ivy Ave, Baltimore, MD 21214

TRUITT, Ann Harris (SVa) 5428 Club Head Rd, Virginia Beach, VA 23455

TRULL, Scott (NJ) 327 s juniper st, Philadelphia, PA 19107

TRUMBLE JR, John (O) 51 Walnut St, Tiffin, OH 44883

TRUMBLE, Jordan Elizabeth (WVa)

TRUSCOTT, Nancy Jean Baldwin (Alb) 10 Orchard Street, Delhi, NY 13753

TRUTNER, Thomas Kirk (Cal) 22 Cedar Lane, Orinda, CA 94563

TRYGAR SR, Earl P (Be) RR 2, Box 2229, Moscow, PA 18444

TRYTTEN, Patricia Shoemaker (Oly) 310 N K St, Tacoma, WA 98403

TSAI, Ching-Yi (Tai)

TSOU, Tsai-Hsin (Tai) 1 F #5 Ln 348 Lishan St, Neihu Dist, Taipei, 11450, Taiwan

TUBBS, Adrian Quentin (Az) 168 W Arizona St, Holbrook, AZ 86025

TUBBS, James Collin (Tenn) 5256 Village Tree, Nashville, TN 37211

TUBBS, Suzanne (Tex) 604 Tryon Ct, Tyler, TX 75703

TUCHOLS, Franklin Joseph (Ct) 661 Old Post Rd, Fairfield, CT 06824

TUCK, Michael G (WMass) 114 George St, Providence, RI 02906

TUCKER, Alice Elizabeth (Tex) 2900 Bunny Run, Austin, TX 78746

TUCKER, Brian J (Los)

TUCKER, Elizabeth (CFla) 1020 Keyes Ave, Winter Park, FL 32789

TUCKER, Gene Richard (CPa) 212 Penn St, Huntingdon, PA 16652

TUCKER, James M (NJ) 130 Prince St, Bordentown, NJ 08505

TUCKER, Jennifer L (U)

TUCKER, Jim (Tex) 107 Oakstone Dr, Chapel Hill, NC 27514

TUCKER, Julia (SVa) C O Eleanor Baird, 1273 Helmsdale Dr, Forest, VA 24551

TUCKER, Kenneth Merrill (USC) 1502 Greenville Street, Abbeville, SC 29620

TUCKER, Martha D (Ct)

TUCKER, Tamra E (Mass)

TUCKER-GRAY, Lisa (O) 4225 Walden Dr, Ann Arbor, MI 48105

TUCKER-PARSONS, Lou (ETenn) 8321 Georgetown Bay Dr, Ooltewah, TN 37363

TUDELA, Mary Elizabeth (Chi) 4364 Hardy Street, Lihue, HI 96766

TUDOR, Richard Beresford (Mo) 3106 Aberdeen Dr, Florissant, MO 63033

TUDOR, William Ellis (Ind) 3021 94th Ave E, Edgewood, WA 98371

TUDOR-FOLEY, Hugh (NC) 3168 Dona Sofia Dr, Studio City, CA 91604

TUELL IV, Henry Offord (NY) 1333 Bay St, Staten Island, NY 10305

TUFF, Roy (SwFla) 401 W Henry St, Punta Gorda, FL 33950

TULIS, Edward (CNY)

TULL, Sandra Ann (Fla) 1021 Oxford Dr, Saint Augustine, FL 32084

TULLER, Stuart (Va) 2132 Owls Cove Ln, Reston, VA 20191

TULLY, Coleen Marie (Minn) 101 N 5th St, Marshall, MN 56258

TULLY, William M (NY) 801 S Grand Ave Apt 1310, Los Angeles, CA 90017

TUMMINIO HANSEN, Danielle (Tex) 12 Quincy Ave, Quincy, MA 02169

TUNKLE, Paul (Md) 200 Common Rd, Dresden, ME 04342

TUNNELL, Janet A (SwFla) St Thomas Episcopal Church, 1200 Snell Isle Blvd NE, St Petersburg, FL 33704

TUNNEY, Liz (LI)

TURBERG, Judith Evelyn (Az) 100 S Laura Ln, Casa Grande, AZ 85194

TURBEVILLE, Keith (Dal) P.O. Box 292, Buda, TX 78610

TURCZYN, Jeffrey Robert (NY) 40 Running Hill Road, Scarborough, ME 04074

TURK, Davette Lois (Fla) 8256 Wallingford Hills Ln, Jacksonville, FL 32256

TURMO, Joel (WMich) 9798 E Bc Ave, Richland, MI 49083

TURNAGE, Benjamin Whitfield (Ala) 1124 Lakeview Crescent, Birmingham, AL 35205

TURNBULL, Malcolm Edward (Va) 13342 Beachcrest Dr, Chesterfield, VA 23832

TURNER, Alice Camp (WNY) 90 South Dr, Lackawanna, NY 14218

TURNER, Alicia Beth (WNC) PO Box 2723, Weaverville, NC 28787

TURNER, Amy (CFla) 1100 Sam Perry Blvd, Fredericksburg, VA 22401

TURNER, Anne (Va) 5814 19th St N, Arlington, VA 22205

TURNER, Arlie Raymond (RG) 397 Old Offen PO Rd, Traphill, NC 28685

TURNER, Barry (ECR) 891 Vista Del Brisa, San Luis Obispo, CA 93405

TURNER, Bonnie L (NMich) 510 E Park Dr, Peshtigo, WI 54157

TURNER, Brian William (CFla) 1250 Deggen Ct NW, Palm Bay, FL 32907

TURNER, Carl Francis (NY) 1 W 53rd St, New York, NY 10019

TURNER, Clay Howard (USC) 2285 Armstrong Creek Rd, Marion, NC 28752

TURNER, Cody Anthony (Dal)

TURNER, Diana Serene (The Episcopal NCal) 605 Tahoe Island Dr., South Lake Tahoe, CA 96150

TURNER, Donald L (CNY) 243 West Vw, Carlisle, PA 17013

TURNER, Elizabeth Zarelli (Tex) 9520 Anchusa Trl, Austin, TX 78736

TURNER SR, Eric Wood (CFla) 4581 Bellaluna Dr., West Melbourne, FL 32904

TURNER, John Edward (The Episcopal Church in Haw) 19446 N. 110th Lane, Sun City, AZ 85373

TURNER, Linnea (Va) 5701 Hunton Wood Dr, Broad Run, VA 20137

TURNER, Maurice Edgar (Cal) 4222 Churchill Dr, Pleasanton, CA 94588

TURNER, Mollie Douglas (SVa) PO Box 925, 77 Chestnut St Unit 201, Tryon, NC 28782

TURNER III, Philip Williams (Tex) 9520 Anchusa Trl, Austin, TX 78736

TURNER, Pippa (NY) 2 E 90th St, New York, NY 10128

TURNER, Robert (NJ) 525 Pleasant Ave, Piscataway, NJ 08854

TURNER, Saundra Lee (Ga) 2104 Amberley Pass, Evans, GA 30809

TURNER, Scott Scott (Colo) St Pauls Episcopal Church, PO Box 770722, Steamboat Springs, CO 80477

TURNER, Sharon Richey (Dal) 6728 Mayer Road, La Grange, TX 78945

TURNER, Shawna Kaye (Okla) 501 N Broadway Ave, Shawnee, OK 74801

TURNER, Stephen Deree (EC)

TURNER III, Thomas (WTex) 200 N. Wright Streed, Alice, TX 78332

TURNER, Timothy Jay (WTex) 120 Herweck Dr, San Antonio, TX 78213

TURNER-JONES, Nancy Marie (SO) 318 E. 4th St., Cincinnati, OH 45202

TURNEY, Nancy J (O) 1632 Hilltown Pike, Hilltown, PA 18927

TURNHAM, Rena Marie (Minn) 519 Oak Grove St, Minneapolis, MN 55403

TURRELL, James Fielding (Be) Sch of Theology, U Of The South, Sewanee, TN 37383

TURRIE, Anne Elizabeth (RG) PO Box 2427, Mesilla Park, NM 88047

TURTLE, Jonathan (CFla)

TURTON, Neil Christopher (NJ) 509 Lake Ave, Bay Head, NJ 08742

TUSKEN, Mark (Chi) 327 S 4th St, Geneva, IL 60134

TUTASIG TENORIO, Digna Mercedes (Eur)

TUTON, Dan (RG) 8409 La Ventura Ct NW, Albuquerque, NM 87120

TUTTLE, Eric J (NJ)

TUTTLE, Johnny (ETenn) 1125 Wateree St, Kingsport, TN 37660

TUTTLE, Margaret Constance (Nwk) 19 Oberlin St, Maplewood, NJ 07040

TUTU, Mpho A (WA) 3001 Park Center Dr Apt 1119, Alexandria, VA 22302

TUTU, Nontombi N (Tenn)

TUYISHIME, Emmanuel (SO)

TWAIT, Aaron Thomas (Minn)

TWEEDALE, David Lee (Colo) 423 E Thunderbird Dr, Fort Collins, CO 80525

TWEEDIE, William Duane (Tex) 301 E 8th St, Austin, TX 78701

TWEEDY, Jeanette Elizabeth (NY) PO Box 172, Peacham, VT 05862

TWELVES, Paul Douglass (RI) 355 Blackstone Blvd Apt 108, Providence, RI 02906

TWENTYMAN JR, Donald Graham (Ia) 120 24th St, Spirit Lake, IA 51360

TWIGGS, Frances R (Spok) 428 King St, Wenatchee, WA 98801

TWINAMAANI, Benjamin (SwFla) 9533 Pebble Glen Ave, Tampa, FL 33647

TWISS, Ian (Mich) Trinity Episcopal Church, 11575 Belleville Rd, Belleville, MI 48111

TWO BEARS, Neil V (ND) Po Box 685, Fort Yates, ND 58538

TWO BULLS, Robert (Minn) 3317 33rd Ave S, Minneapolis, MN 55406

TWO BULLS, Twilla Ramona (SD)

TWOMEY, Patrick Timothy (FdL) 415 E Spring St, Appleton, WI 54911

TWYMAN, Thomas Wellwirth (CNY) 122 Metropolitan Ave, Ashland, MA 01721

TYLER, Adelyn (Ark)

TYLER, Lera (WTex) 116 US Highway 87, Comfort, TX 78013

TYLER, Pamela (Los) 37529 Meridian Ave, Dade City, FL 33525

TYLER, Rachel Emily (NJ)

TYLER SMITH, Virginia Stewart (Roch) 11 Episcopal Ave, Honeoye Falls, NY 14472

TYNDALL, Constance Flanigan (WMo) 4239 E Valley Rd, Springfield, MO 65809

TYNDALL, Jeremy (Ore) The Rectory, 55 Cove Road, Farnborough Hants, GU140EX, Great Britain (UK)

TYO JR, Charles Hart (Roch) 16 Elmwood Ave, Friendship, NY 14739

TYREE, James Scott (Okla) 235 W Duffy St, Norman, OK 73069

TYREE-CUEVAS, Susan Mccorkle (Oly) 1804 Pointe Woodworth Dr NE, Tacoma, WA 98422

TYRIVER, Marcia Rivenburg (Mich) 255 Ba Wood Ln, Janesville, WI 53545

TYSON, Lynda (Ct) 23 Evarts Ln, Madison, CT 06443

TYSON, Stephen Alfred (Ore) 370 Market Ave., Coos Bay, OR 97420

TZENG, Wen-Bin (Tai) No. 7 Lane 105, Section 1, Hang Chow South Road, Taipei, Taiwan

U

UBIERA, Ramon (NJ) 207 Summer Ave Apt 1, Newark, NJ 07104

UDELL, George Morris Edson (Tex) 1436 Daventry Dr, DeSoto, TX 75115

UEDA, Lisa Marie (FdL)

UFFELMAN, Stephen Paul (EO) 915 Ne Crest Dr, Prineville, OR 97754

UFFMAN, Craig David (Roch) 2000 Highland Ave, Rochester, NY 14618

UHLIK, Charles R (Ky) 2641 E Southern Hills Blvd, Springfield, MO 65804

UITTI, Aaron (At) 124 Commercial Ave, East Palatka, FL 32131

ULISSE, Maccene (Hai)

ULLMAN, Richard L (O) 241 S 6th St Apt 2408, Philadelphia, PA 19106

ULLMANN, Clair Filbert (Eur)

ULRICH, Stephanie Lyn (Neb) 9302 Blondo St, Omaha, NE 68134

UMEOFIA, Christian Chinedu (NC) Po Box 1333, Goldsboro, NC 27533

UMPHLETT, David Alton (NC) 108 W. Farriss Ave., High Point, NC 27262

UNANGST, Joanna Dehaan (WMich)

UNANGST, Kurt Aaron (WMich)

UNDEM, John (Minn)

UNDERHILL, William Dudley (WA) 25 Nottingham Dr, Kingston, MA 02364

UNDERWOOD, Bonnie Gordy (At) 411 Stathams Way, Warner Robins, GA 31088

UNDERWOOD, Deborah Ann (Okla) 501 S. Cincinnati Ave., Tulsa, OK 74103

UPHAM, Judith Elizabeth (Tex) 9805 Livingston Rd, Fort Washington, MD 20744

UPTON, David Hugh (USC) 206 W Prentiss Ave, Greenville, SC 29605

UPTON, Thomas Lee (Neb) 14017 Washington St, Omaha, NE 68137

URANG, Gunnar (Vt) PO Box 306, Norwich, VT 05055

URBANEK, Virginia (Me) PO Box 455, Houlton, ME 04730

URINOSKI, Ann Kathryne (NJ) 18b Ryers Ln, Matawan, NJ 07747

URMSON-TAYLOR, Ralph (Okla) 47a Via Porta Perlici PG, Assisi, OK 06081, Italy

URQUIDI, Ashley Elizabeth (SVa) 1969 Woodside Ln, Virginia Beach, VA 23454

USHER JR, Guy Randolph (Eau) 303 S Hollybrook Dr, Chillicothe, IL 61523

V

VACA TAPIA, Harold Alexander (EcuC) C Calderon Ar Y Ch, Tulcan Carchi, Ecuador

VACCARO, Anthony Joseph (Chi) Church of Our Saviour, 530 W Fullerton Pkwy, Chicago, IL 60614

VADERS, Nancy Johnson (NC) St Anne's Episc Ch, 2690 Fairlawn Dr, Winston Salem, NC 27106

VAFIS, John Symon (The Episcopal NCal) PO Box 1044, Colusa, CA 95932

VAGUENER, Martha (SwFla) 3105 Short Leaf St, Zephyrhills, FL 33543

VAIL, Jean (Chi) 305 Sutherland Ct, Durham, NC 27712

VALADEZ-JAIME, Agustin (Ore) 2025 W Indian School Rd Apt 907, Phoenix, AZ 85015

VALANDRA, Linda Beth (SD) 410 University Ave, Hot Springs, SD 57747

VALANTASIS, Richard L (Mo) 17 Wildflower Way, Santa Fe, NM 87506

VALCOURT, Theodore Philippe-Francois (CGC) 401 Live Oak Ave, Pensacola, FL 32507

VALDEMA, Pierre-Henry Fritz (Hai) 117 Mountain Ash Ln Unit C, Myrtle Beach, SC 29579

VALDERRAMA SANABRIA, Juan Pablo (Colom) c/o Diocese of Colombia, Cra 6 No. 49-85 Piso 2, Bogota, BDC, Colombia

VALDES, Fernando Joaquin (Los) 514 W Adams Blvd, Los Angeles, CA 90007

VALDEZ LEIVA, Pedro Antonio (Gua) 826 Howard St, Carthage, MO 64836

VALDIVIA MELO, Yannel (Cu)

VALENTINE III, A Wilson (Ak) 924 C St, Juneau, AK 99801

VALENTINE, Darcy Adrian (Minn) 615 Vermillion St, Hastings, MN 55033

VALENTINE JR, John Carney (WVa) 206 E 2nd St, Weston, WV 26452

VALENTINE, Peggy Lee (NwT) St Mark's Episcopal Church, 3150 Vogel St, Abilene, TX 79603

VALENTINE, Ron (Chi) St James The Less Tec Ch, 550 Sunset Ridge Rd, Northfield, IL 60093

VALENTINE DAVIS, Melinda R (Mil)

VALIATH, Abraham J (Be) 365 Lafayette Ave., Palmerton, PA 18071

VALLE, Jose Francisco (WA) 1700 Powder Mill Rd, Silver Spring, MD 20903

VALLE-PLAZA, Juan Nelson (EcuC) Casilla 0901-5250, Guayaquil, Ecuador

VALLIERE, Pierre R (Hai)

VALOVICH, Stephen Anthony (SeFla) 3395 Burns Rd, Palm Beach Gardens, FL 33410

VAN, Maron Ines (Ore) 4435 Fox Hollow Rd, Eugene, OR 97405

VAN ANTWERPEN, Alanna Mary (NH) 214 Main St, Nashua, NH 03060

VANAUKER, Margaret Elizabeth (Md) 225 Bowie Trl, Lusby, MD 20657

VANBAARS, Sven (Va) PO Box 146, Gloucester, VA 23061

VAN BLACK, Barbara Ann (Tex)

VAN BRUNT, Thomas Harvey (SO) 534 Chapel Rd, Amelia, OH 45102

VANBUREN, Andrew (Be) 1 Welsh Dr, Douglassville, PA 19518

VAN BUREN, Barrett (Los) 15524 Pintura Dr, Hacienda Heights, CA 91745

VANCAMP, John Raymond (Tex)

VANCE, Craig Douglas (The Episcopal Church in Haw) 2140 Main St, Wailuku, HI 96793

VANCE, Marcus Patrick (SVa) 2651 California St, Columbus, IN 47201

VANCE, Timothy (SwVa) PO Box 344, Sewanee, TN 37375

VANCE, William Walter (CFla) 26 Willow Dr, Orlando, FL 32807

VANCOOTEN-WEBSTER, Jennifer Elizabeth (LI) 286-88 7th Ave, Brooklyn, NY 11215

VAN CULIN JR, Samuel (WA) 3900 Watson Pl NW # 5d-B, Washington, DC 20016

VAN CULIN, Thomas Andrew K (Mich) 61 Grosse Pointe Blvd, Grosse Pointe Farms, MI 48236

VANDAGRIFF, Mary Cordelia (Ala) 220 S Wood Rd, Homewood, AL 35209

VANDERAU JR, Robert Julian (RI) 2305 Edgewater Drive, Apt 1718, Orlando, FL 32804

VANDERBRUG, Abby (NH) 1025 3 Mile Rd NE, Grand Rapids, MI 49505

VANDERCOOK, Ross Allan (Mich) 9900 N Meridian Rd, Pleasant Lake, MI 49272

VANDERCOOK, Susan Elizabeth (Mich) 9900 N Meridian Rd, Pleasant Lake, MI 49272

VANDER LEE, Jerome Neal (SD) 500 S Main Ave, Sioux Falls, SD 57104

VANDERMEER, Leigh A (Chi) 410 Christian Loop, Havana, FL 32333

VANDERVEEN, Peter Todd (Pa) 230 Pennswood Rd, Bryn Mawr, PA 19010

VAN DERVOORT, Ann (Tenn) 1106 Chickering Park Dr, Nashville, TN 37215

VAN DE STEEG, Franklin Exford (Minn) PO Box 155, Hastings, MN 55033

VAN DEUSEN, Robert Reed (CPa) 205 King St, Northumberland, PA 17857

VAN DEUSEN, Robert Wayne (Mil) 9360 W Terra Ct, Milwaukee, WI 53224

VANDEVENTER, Heather A (Spok) 118 N Washington St, Alexandria, VA 22314

VAN DINE JR, John Henry (Nwk) St John's Church of Boonton, 226 Cornelia St, Boonton, NJ 07005

VANDIVORT JR, Paul M (Mo) 12366 Federal Dr, Des Peres, MO 63131

VAN DOOREN, John David (NY) 5749 N Kenmore Ave, Chicago, IL 60660

VANDOREN JR, Robert Lawson (WTenn) 5097 Greenway Cv, Memphis, TN 38117

VAN DUFFELEN, Marilyn (Ia) PO Box 895, Sioux City, IA 51102

VAN DYKE, Bude (Ala) PO Box 824, Sewanee, TN 37375

VAN DYKE, Elizabeth (Oly)

VAN EENWYK, John Richter (Roch) P. O. Box 1961, Olympia, WA 98507

VAN ES, Kenneth (Eau) 2603 Yorktown Ct, Eau Claire, WI 54703

VANG, Marshall Jacob (Alb) 88 Circular St Apt1, Saratoga Springs, NY 12866

VANG, Toua (Minn) 2200 Minnehaha Ave E, Saint Paul, MN 55119

VAN GORDEN SR, Schuyler Humphrey (Eau) 120 10th Ave, Eau Claire, WI 54703

VAN GULDEN, Sarah Ann (Mass) 74 S Common St, Lynn, MA 01902

VAN HORN, Johnny R (Miss)

VAN HORN, Nicholas M (NC)

VAN HORNE, Beverly (Mo) 11907 Bardmont Dr, Saint Louis, MO 63126

VAN HORNE, Peter (Mo) 11907 Bardmont Dr, Saint Louis, MO 63126

VANHOUTEN, Patricia Delores (Minn)

VAN HUSS, Teri Hewett (Episcopal SJ) PO Box 7446, Visalia, CA 93290

VANI, Benedict S (CFla) 2341 Port Malabar Blvd NE, Palm Bay, FL 32905

VAN KIRK, Andrew D (Dal) 6400 Mckinney Ranch Pkwy, Mckinney, TX 75070

VAN KIRK, Natalie Beam (Tenn) 22W415 Butterfield Rd, Glen Ellyn, IL 60137

VAN KLAVEREN, Dina Els (Md) 1216 Seminole Dr, Arnold, MD 21012

VAN KOEVERING, Helen E (Lex) 3216 Sebastian Ln, 1891 Parkers Mill Rd, Lexington, KY 40504

✠ **VAN KOEVERING**, Mark Allan (Lex) 3216 Sebastian Ln, Lexington, KY 40513

VAN KUIKEN, Ali (NJ) 100 Sullivan Way, Trenton, NJ 08628

VAN LIEW, Christina (LI)

VANN, Deborah Louise (CFla) 380 Royal Palm Dr, Melbourne, FL 32935

VANN, Tim E (Ia) 6651 Park Crest Dr, Papillion, NE 68133

VAN NIEL, Noah (NC) 4321 Hermitage Rd, Virginia Beach, VA 23455

VANO, Mary Foster (Ark) 20900 Chenal Pkwy, Little Rock, AR 72223

VAN OSS, Bill (SwFla) 690 Durion Ct, Sanibel, FL 33957

VAN OSS SR, Earl T (U) 737 East Center, Orem, UT 84057

VANOVER, Debra A (The Episcopal Church in Haw) 25 Hiatt St, Lebanon, OR 97355

VAN PARYS, Cynthia Leigh (NI) 1464 Glenlake Dr, South Bend, IN 46614

VAN PLETZEN, Blane Frederik (WNY) 2097 Abbey Road, APT 304, Onalaska, WI 54650

VAN SANT, Mark Richard (NJ) 27 Tocci Ave, Monmouth Beach, NJ 07750

VAN SANT, Paul (NJ) 38 Anne Dr, Tabernacle, NJ 08088

VAN SANTEN, Frans Nicolaas (CFla)

VAN SICKLE, Kathleen (Cal) 555 Pierce St Apt 340e, Albany, CA 94706

VAN SICLEN, John (Me) PO Box 523, Damariscotta, ME 04543

VAN SLYKE, Charlotte Sturgis (Ala)

VANUCCI, Anthony Joseph (Pa) 9700 Entrada Pl NW, Albuquerque, NM 87114

VANVLIET-PULLIN, Dana Mae (SVa) St Peter's Episc Church, 224 S Military Hwy, Norfolk, VA 23502

VAN WASSENHOVE, Mark (Ind) 8755 Washington Blvd West Dr, Indianapolis, IN 46240

VAN WELY, Richard Francis (Ct) 223 Weaver St Apt 20D, Greenwich, CT 06831

VAN WORMER JR, Dale William (SwFla)

VAN ZANDT, James K Polk (Tenn) 1307 Clifftops Ave, Monteagle, TN 37356

VAN ZANDT, Jane Whitbeck (NH) 58 Hanson Rd, Chester, NH 03036

VAN ZANTEN JR, Peter Eric (Oly) 1111 Archwood Dr Sw Unit 442, Olympia, WA 98502

VARAS, Dwayne Anthony (Ga) 3901 Davis Blvd, Naples, FL 34104

VARDEMANN, Brady Jodoka (Mont) 556 S Rodney St, Helena, MT 59601

VARELA SOLORZANO, Marco Antonio (Hond) Colonia La Sabana, Samparo Sula, Honduras

VARELA ZUNIGA, Nery Yolanda (Hond) Colonia Los Robles, Atlantida, Ceiba, 31105, Honduras

VARGAS POLANCO, Luis Arnaldo (PR)

VARGHESE, Roy (Tex)

VARGHESE, Winnie Sara (At) 134 W 18th St Fl 2, New York, NY 10011

VARNELL, Bradley (Tex)

VARNER, Joshua H (Ga) Diocese Of Georgia, 611 E Bay St, Savannah, GA 31401

VARNUM, Ben (Neb) 285 S 208th St, Elkhorn, NE 68022

VASQUEZ, Adela (WA)

VASQUEZ, Jaime Armando (Hond) IMS SAP Dept 215, PO Box 523900, Miami, FL 33152-3900, Honduras

VASQUEZ, Martha Sylvia Ovalle (Cal) 301 E Cevallos Apt 223, San Antonio, TX 78204

VASQUEZ, Martir (Az) Saint Andrews Church, 6300 W Camelback Rd, Glendale, AZ 85301

VASQUEZ, Otto Rene (Los)

VASQUEZ AVILA, Rudy Alberto (Hond) Iglesia la Resureccion, Barrio San Jose, El Paraiso, 15023, Honduras

VASQUEZ SANCHEZ, Vicente (Hond)

VASQUEZ-VERA, G Elisa (EcuC) U 213 Y C Ap 17-02-5304, Quito, Ecuador

VATH, Jennifer Marie (Mass) 25 Central St, Andover, MA 01810

VAUGHAN, Jesse L (The Episcopal NCal) 5801 River Oak Way, Carmichael, CA 95608

VAUGHAN, John (CFla) 3295 Timucua Cir, Orlando, FL 32837

VAUGHN, Barry (Nev) Saint Albans Church, 429 Cloudland Dr, Birmingham, AL 35226

VAUGHN, Denise C (Ga) 1512 Meadows Ln, Vidalia, GA 30474

VAUGHN, Robert Joseph (SwFla) 327 W Hickory St, Arcadia, FL 34266

VAUGHN, S Chadwick (At) St Bedes Episcopal Church, 2601 Henderson Mill Rd NE, Atlanta, GA 30345

VAUGHT, Samuel Thomas (Ind) 1620 Central Ave Apt 201, Indianapolis, IN 46202

VAZQUEZ-GELI, Jose R (PR)

VAZQUEZ-SCHMITT, Peter John (RG)

VEACH, Deborah Joan (Ind) 215 N. 7th St., Terre Haute, IN 47807

VEAL, David (NwT) 3026 54th St Apt 410, Lubbock, TX 79413

VEALE, David Scott (Vt) 8 Bishop St, Saint Albans, VT 05478

VEALE, Donald Meier (Ore) 5346 Don Miguel Dr, Carlsbad, CA 92010

VEALE JR, Erwin Olin (Ga) 3120 Exeter Rd, Augusta, GA 30909

VEAL EBY, Rosemary Anne (Ala)

VEGA ESTRELLA, Ramiro Eduardo (EcuC) Box 1801-288, Ambato, Ecuador

VEINOT, William Paul (Ct) 327 Orchard St, Rocky Hill, CT 06067

VEIT JR, Rick (Wyo) 7711 Hawthorne Dr, Cheyenne, WY 82009

VEITINGER, Kevin E (NY) 96 Scarborough Rd, Briarcliff Manor, NY 10510

VELA, Debra Kay (Dal)

VELARDE, Inez Jean (NAM) St Lukes-In-The-Desert, PO Box 720, Farmington, NM 87499

VELASQUEZ BORJAS, Gladis (Hond) Aldea Santa Cruz, Tegucigalpa, Tegucigalpa M.D.C., FM 15023, Honduras

VELASQUEZ MARTINEZ, Victor Manuel (Hond)

VELAZQUEZ-MORALES, Juan Alberto (PR)

VELEZ CASTRO, Edwin Orlando (PR)

VELEZ GARCIA, Bryan Alexis (PR)

VELEZ-RIVERA, Daniel (Va) 11625 Vantage Hill Rd Unit 11c, Reston, VA 20190

VELEZ-VELAZQUEZ, Carlos (PR)

VELLA, Joan C (WNC) 600 Bilyeu Street, Apt 258, Raleigh, NC 27606

VELLA JR, Joseph Agius (SwFla) 125 Lamara Way NE, Saint Petersburg, FL 33704

VELLOM, Lee Sherwin (Az) 1741 N Camino Rebecca, Nogales, AZ 85621

VELLOM, Timothy John (WTex) 8210 Robin Rest Dr, San Antonio, TX 78209

VELTHUIZEN, Tina (NI) 608 Cushing St, South Bend, IN 46616

VENABLE, Charles Wallace (Ala)

VENEZIA, Deborah L (CFla) 7725 Indian Ridge Trail South, Kissimmee, FL 34747

VENKATESH, Catherine (Mass) 281 Renfrew St, Arlington, MA 02476

VENTRIS, Margaret Pyre (Los) 72348 Larrea Ave, Twentynine Palms, CA 92277

VERBECK III, Guido Fridolin (WLa) 4741 Crescent Dr, Shreveport, LA 71106

VERDON, John Thomas (Md)

VERGARA, Winfred Bagao (LI) 4011 68th St Apt 2, Woodside, NY 11377

VERGARA GRUESO, Edison (Colom) Carrera 6 No 49-85, Piso 2, Bogota, Colombia

VERHAEGHE, Ronald Edward (WMo) 4401 Wornall Rd, Kansas City, MO 64111

VERNON, Valerie Veronica (SeFla) Po Box 22462, West Palm Beach, FL 33416

VERRET, Joan Claire (CFla) 220 E Palm Dr, Lakeland, FL 33803

VERSHURE, Claude Edward (SD) 25413 He Sapa Trl, Custer, SD 57730

VERVYNCK, Jennifer R (Oly) 290 Oak Shore Dr, Port Townsend, WA 98368

VESGA-ARDILA, Ramon (Ve)

VETINEL, Jean Marc (Hai)

VETOVITZ, Pamela Kay (Okla)

VETTEL-BECKER, Richard A (Cal) 706 Tabriz Dr, Billings, MT 59105

VIA, John Albert (At) 8340 Main St., Port Republic, VA 24471

VICE, Julie D (Nev) 916 Silver St, Elko, NV 89801

VICENS, Leigh Christiana (SD)

VICKERS, David (WMich) 8119 M 68, Indian River, MI 49749

VICKERY JR, Robby (Tex) 3512 Peregrine Falcon Dr, Austin, TX 78746

VIDAL, Gene Vance (Az) Po Box 13647, Phoenix, AZ 85002

VIE, Todd (SwVa) 3536 Willow Lawn Dr, Lynchburg, VA 24503

VIECHWEG, Edrice Veronica (Ct) 503 Old Long Ridge Rd, Stamford, CT 06903

VIEL, Brian John (WK) 800 W. 32nd Ave., Hutchinson, KS 67502

VIERECK, Alexis (Mass)

VIGGIANO, Alyse Elizabeth (Va)

VIGGIANO, Robert Peter (Tex) 5156 Cornetto Blfs, Round Rock, TX 78665

VIGIL, Vaughn (Md)

VIL, Jean (Hai) PO Box 407139, C O Lynx Air, Fort Lauderdale, FL 33340-7139, Haiti

VILAR MENDEZ, Jose Francisco (Ga)

VILAR-SANTIAGO, Jose E (PR) 3735 Lancewood Pl, Delray Beach, FL 33445

VILAR-SANTIAGO, Miguel E (Md) PO Box 264, Brooklanville, MD 21022

VILAS, Franklin Edward (Nwk) 18 Greylawn Dr, Lakewood, NJ 08701

VILLACIS MACIAS, Carlos Emilio (Litoral Diocese Of Ecuador)

VILLAGOMEZA, Christian (SwFla)

VILLALOBOS, Fabian (Dal) 534 W 10th St, Dallas, TX 75208

VILLARREAL, Arthur Wells (At) 405 Vista Cir., Macon, GA 31204

VILLEMUER-DRENTH, Lauren Anne (NC) 321 S Cleveland Rd, Lexington, KY 40515

VILORD, Charles Louis (SwFla)

VINCENT, Elizabeth (The Episcopal NCal) 100 Sanborn Ct, Folsom, CA 95630

VINCENT, Janet (NY) 19 Coxing Rd, PO Box 190, Cottekill, NY 12419

VINCENT-ALEXANDER, Samantha (SVa) 178 W Leicester Ave, Norfolk, VA 23503

VINE, Walter James (Mil) 2655 N Grant Blvd, Milwaukee, WI 53210

VINGE, Patricia Gay (WMich) 2010 Nichols Rd, Kalamazoo, MI 49004

VINSON, Richard Lee (Pa) 4712 Beach Bay Ct, Virginia Beach, VA 23455

VIOLA JR, Carmen Joseph (NJ) 51 N Main St, Mullica Hill, NJ 08062

VIOLA, Harry Alexander (WNC) Po Box 1046, Hendersonville, NC 28793

VIOLA, William Michael (LI) 52 Maryland Blvd, Hampton Bays, NY 11946

VISCONTI, Richard Dennis (LI) 15938 Cobble Mill Dr, Wimauma, FL 33598

VISGER, James Robert (Neb) 610 Sycamore Dr, Lincoln, NE 68510

VISMINAS, Christine Elizabeth (Mass) 70 Dennison Ave, Framingham, MA 01702

VITET, Kino (LI) 1417 Union St, Brooklyn, NY 11213

VIVIAN, Tim (Episcopal SJ) 10105 Mountaingate Ln, Bakersfield, CA 93311

VIZCAINO, Roberto (EcuC) Jose Herboso 271, Cdla, La Flo, Quito, Ecuador

VOCELKA, Craig Robert (Oly) 3769 NE Bahia Vista Dr, Bremerton, WA 98310

VOELKER, Sharon L (EMich) St Stephen's, 5500 N Adams Rd, Troy, MI 48098

VOETS, Keith (LI) St Alban The Martyr, 11642 Farmers Blvd, Saint Albans, NY 11412

VOGEL, Caroline (ETenn) 425 N Cedar Bluff Rd, Knoxville, TN 37923

VOGELE, Nancy (NH) 97 Victory Cir, White River Junction, VT 05001

VOGEL-POLIZZI, Virginia Margaret (WMass)

VOIEN, Cindy (Los) 1645 W 9th St # 2, San Pedro, CA 90732

VOLKMANN, Jan Elizabeth (NY) 60 Pine Hill Park, Valatie, NY 12184

VOLLAND, Mary Catherine (RG) 126 Woodsmoke Ln, Rochester, NY 14612

VOLLKOMMER, Marsha Merritt (Chi) Grace Episcopal Church, 309 Hill St, Galena, IL 61036

VOLLMAN, Michael (Ky) 400 Fairway TRL, Springfield, TN 37172

VOLPE, Gina (Chi) 9300 S Pleasant Ave, Rectory, Chicago, IL 60643

VOLQUEZ-PEREZ, Huascar (PR) Mision Episcopal Cristo Rey, 24 Calle Palmeras, Salinas, PR 00751

VON GRABOW, Richard Henri (The Episcopal NCal) 580 Cooper Dr, Benicia, CA 94510

VONGSANIT, Sam Chanpheng (Episcopal SJ) 709 N Jackson Ave, Fresno, CA 93702

VON HAAREN, Barbara Elizabeth (Minn) 1862 W 6th St, Red Wing, MN 55066

VON HAAREN, Erika Shivers (Az) 6715 N Mockingbird Ln, Scottsdale, AZ 85253

VONO, Michael (RG) TEC Dio of the Rio Gr&e, 4304 Carlisle Blvd NE, Albuquerque, Italy
VON RAUTENKRANZ, Sue (WA) The Tec Dio Of Wa, Mount St Alban, Washington, DC 20016
VON ROESCHLAUB, Kurt (LI) 4 Cornwall Ln, Port Washington, NY 11050
VONROSENBERG, Charles (ETenn) 23 St. Giles Place, Asheville, NC 28803
VON WRANGEL, Carola (Tenn) Church of the Advent, 5501 Franklin Pike, Nashville, TN 37220
VOORHEES, Cynthia Evans (Los) 1308 Santiago Dr, Newport Beach, CA 92660
VOORHEES JR, Ted (O) 115 Washington St, St Augustine, FL 32084
VORKINK II, Peter (NH) 20 Main St, Exeter, NH 03833
VOSBURGH, Linda Ann (Colo) PO Box 1023, Broomfield, CO 80038
VOTAW, Al (SC) 657 Wampler Dr, Charleston, SC 29412
VOYLE, Rob (Ore) 24965 NW Pederson Rd, Hillsboro, OR 97124
VOYSEY, Stephen Otte (Mass) 1 Colpitts Road, Weston, MA 02493
VROON, Daron Jon (At) 939 James Burgess Rd, Suwanee, GA 30024
VRYHOF, David B (Mass) 980 Memorial Dr, Cambridge, MA 02138
VUKICH, Dawn (Los) 26391 Bodega Ln, Mission Viejo, CA 92691
VUKMANIC, Paula (Los) 1513 S Dodson Ave, San Pedro, CA 90732
VUKOVIC, Robert (Eur)
VUONO, Reverend Deacon Dorothy (Del) 19337 Fleatown Rd, Lincoln, DE 19960

W

WACASTER, David C (WA) 4706 31st St S, Arlington, VA 22206
WACHNER, Emily J (NY) 400 Aster St, Nyack, NY 10960
WACHTER, Jessica B (Mo)
WACHTER, Steven Edward (RG)
WACOME, Karen Ann Halvorsen (Ia) 415 3rd St NW, Orange City, IA 51041
WADDELL, Clayton Burbank (SeFla) 141 S County Rd, Palm Beach, FL 33480
WADDELL, Jonathan H (Ala) 5014 Lakeshore Dr, Pell City, AL 35128
WADDELL, Thomas Robert (Va) 5911 Edsall Rd Ph 5, Alexandria, VA 22304
WADDINGHAM, Gary Brian (Mont) 119 N 33rd St, Billings, MT 59101
WADDLE, Helen Ann (Okla) PO Box 2402, Oklahoma City, OK 73157
WADE, Carol (Lex) Christ Church Cathedral, 166 Market St, Lexington, KY 40507

WADE, Francis Howard (WA) 4800 Fillmore Ave Apt 1452, Apt 1452, Alexandria, VA 22311
WADE III, Herschel Vonedward (Md)
WADE, J Merrill (Tex) 15709 Circuit Ln, Austin, TX 78728
WADE, Karin Elizabeth (Mass) PO Box 372, Rockport, MA 01966
WADE, Libby (WMass) 1110 Fairview St, Lee, MA 01238
WADE, Mary Macsherry (Miss) 2681 Lake Cir, Jackson, MS 39211
WADE, Stephen Hamel (Va) 132 N Jay St, Middleburg, VA 20117
WADE, Suzanne (Mass) 75 Cold Spring Rd, Westford, MA 01886
WADE, William St Clair (Tenn) 1 Casey Road, East Kingston, NH 03827
WAFER-CROSS, Melissa Lee (NwT) 3502 47th St, Lubbock, TX 79413
WAFF, Kay Childers (SwVa) 314 N Bridge St, Bedford, VA 24523
WAFF, William Dubard Razz (Mil) 78 Hillcrest Dr, Weaverville, NC 28787
WAFLER, Donald Samuel (Minn) 628 1st St Se, Faribault, MN 55021
WAGAMAN, Stanley Warner (Az) Episc Ch Of St Francis, 600 S La Canada Dr, Green Valley, AZ 85614
WAGAR, Catherine (Los) St Mark's Episcopal Church, 14646 Sherman Way, Van Nuys, CA 91405
WAGEMAN, Carole A (Vt) 173 Hollow Road, North Ferrisburgh, VT 05473
WAGENSEIL JR, Robert Arthur (SwFla) 1700 Patlin Cir S, Largo, FL 33770
WAGENSELLER, Joseph Paul (Ct) 6 Clifford Ln, Westport, CT 06880
✠ **WAGGONER JR**, James E (Spok) 8028 N Pamela St, Spokane, WA 99208
WAGGONER, Janet Cuff (Tex) 4713 Darla Dr, Fort Worth, TX 76132
WAGGONER, Leigh (Colo) 110 W. North St., Cortez, CO 81321
WAGNER, Barbara Jean (WMich) 2430 Greenbriar, Harbor Springs, MI 49740
WAGNER, Beth Anne (Eur) 4815 Neptune Rd, Venice, FL 34293
WAGNER, Daniel Andrew (USC)
WAGNER, David W (At) 465 Clifton Rd NE, Atlanta, GA 30307
WAGNER, Jennifer Lynne (Los)
WAGNER, John C (Be) 1185 Santamont Rd, Potsdam, NY 13676
WAGNER, Mary M (Ia)
WAGNER, Sharon Lavonne (Cal) 1921 Hemlock Dr, Oakley, CA 94561
WAGNER, Wm Beau (Me) St Matthew's Episcopal Church, PO Box 879, Lisbon, ME 04250
WAGNER-PIZZA, Ken E (CPa) 1540 Hidden Valley Dr, Montoursville, PA 17754
WAGNER SHERER, Kara (Chi) 3857 N. Kostner Ave, Chicago, IL 60641

WAGNON, William S (WA) 9225 Crestview Dr, Indianapolis, IN 46240
WAHL, Eugene Richard (Colo) 4400 Wellington Rd, Boulder, CO 80301
WAHL, Hughes Edward (Md) 5010 Marina Cove Dr Apt 203, Naples, FL 34112
WAHLGREN, Matthew David (O) 206 N Park Ave, Fremont, OH 43420
WAID, Anna (Del) 301 Woodlawn Rd, Wilmington, DE 19803
WAINWRIGHT, Philip (Pgh) 326 Maple Ter, Pittsburgh, PA 15211
WAINWRIGHT-MAKS, Laurence Christopher (Roch) 105 N Montgomery St, Starkville, MS 39759
WAIT, Curtis (Colo) 228 S Jefferson Ave, Louisville, CO 80027
WAIT, Roger Lee (Neb) 3711 A St, Lincoln, NE 68510
WAITE, Paula Jean (Del) 307 Federal St, Milton, DE 19968
WAJDA, Kathryn (Md) 1505 Sherbrook Rd, Lutherville Timonium, MD 21093
WAJNERT, Theresa Altmix (Nwk) PO Box 37, Calistoga, CA 94515
WAKABAYASHI, Allen Mitsuo (NJ) PO Box 605, Gladstone, NJ 07934
WAKEEN, Teresa M (Mich) 4800 Woodward Ave, Detroit, MI 48201
WAKELEE PIERCE, Julia (The Episcopal NCal) 1501 Washington Ave, Albany, CA 94706
WAKELY, Nancy Kay (Okla) PO Box 2088, Norman, OK 73070
WAKEMAN, Nancy Ann (CPa)
WAKITSCH, Randal John (Chi) 503 W Jackson St, Woodstock, IL 60098
WALBERG, Elsa Phyllis (Mass) PO Box 245, Danville, VT 05828
WALCOTT, Robert (O) 5300 Zebulon Rd Unit 35, Macon, GA 31210
WALDEN, Jan (Mass) 22 Henry Dr, Moosup, CT 06354
WALDHAUSER, Mason M (CFla)
WALDIE, Nanette Marie (Oly) 4228 Factoria Blvd SE, Bellevue, WA 98006
WALDING, Jennifer Maureen (Minn) 4180 Lexington Ave S, Eagan, MN 55123
WALDO JR, Mark E (Ala) 311 Lindsey Rd, Coosada, AL 36020
✠ **WALDO**, William Andrew (USC) 2244 Sargent Ave, Saint Paul, MN 55105
WALDON, Mark W (Nwk) 2 Marble Ct Apt 1, Apt 1, Clifton, NJ 07013
WALDON JR, Raymond J (Tex) 601 Columbus Ave, Waco, TX 76701
WALDRON, Teresa Jane (Cal) PO Box 35, Inverness, CA 94937
WALDROP, Charlotte (USC) 137 Summerwood Way, Aiken, SC 29803
WALK, Everett (SwFla) 8700 State Road 72, Sarasota, FL 34241
WALKER, Ansley Elizabeth (CGC)
WALKER, Aurilla Kay (Neb)
WALKER, David Bruce (Spok) 127 E 12th Ave, Spokane, WA 99202

WALKER, Elizabeth (Oly)
WALKER, Elizabeth Ann (WVa) 3343 Davis Stuart Road, Fairlea, WV 24902
WALKER, Frederick Walker (LI) 17802 Hillside Ave Apt 314, Jamaica, NY 11432
WALKER JR, Harold William (SeFla) St Thomas Episcopal Parish, 5690 N Kendall Dr, Coral Gables, FL 33156
WALKER, James Arvie (NwT)
WALKER, James Lee (Los) 4114 S Norton Ave, Los Angeles, CA 90008
WALKER, Janice Ficke (WNC) 2709 Pleasant Run Dr, Richmond, VA 23233
WALKER, Jeffrey (Ct) 4124 Berkman Dr, Austin, TX 78723
WALKER, Karen (Wyo)
WALKER, Kathalin (U) PO Box 125, Page, AZ 86040
WALKER, Kathleen D (NC) 5518 Sharpe Dr, Raleigh, NC 27612
WALKER, Lynell Elizabeth (The Episcopal NCal) 2380 Wyda Way, Sacramento, CA 95825
WALKER, Michelle (NI) 708 Harrison St, Laporte, IN 46350
WALKER, Paul Edward (Ia) 510 Columbia St, Burlington, IA 52601
WALKER, Paul Nelson (Va) 100 W Jefferson St, Charlottesville, VA 22902
WALKER, Peggy (WNC) 37 Newbridge Pkwy Unit 302, Asheville, NC 28804
WALKER, Randolf D (Oly)
WALKER, Roger D (Ky) PO Box 8101, Louisville, KY 40257
WALKER, Samuel Clevenger (WA) Zach Fowler Road, PO Box 8, Chaptico, MD 20621
WALKER, Scott D (CFla)
WALKER, Seldon Matthew (SVa) 131 Tuckahoe Trce, Yorktown, VA 23693
WALKER, Skip (EC) 1337 Hamlet St, Fayetteville, NC 28306
WALKER, Stacy (Chi) 1340 Brook St Apt L, Apt L, Saint Charles, IL 60174
WALKER, Stephen Bruce (WNC) 168 Cherry Birch Ln, Saluda, NC 28773
WALKER, Susan (WA) 1317 G St NW, Washington, DC 20005
WALKER, Terrence Alaric (SVa) PO Box 753, Lawrenceville, VA 23868
WALKER, William Ray (CPa) St. Paul's Episcopal Church, P.O. Box 170, Philipsburg, PA 16866
WALKER, William Royce (Wyo) 157 Pleasant Valley Rd, Hartville, WY 82215
WALKER MILLER, Joy (Tex)
WALKLEY, Richard Nelson (Ga) 918 E Ridge Village Dr, Cutler Bay, FL 33157
WALL, Anne Fuller (ECR) 535 Torrey Pine Pl, Arroyo Grande, CA 93420
WALL, Daniel S (NC)
WALL,·Henry Pickett (USC) 5220 Clemson Ave, Columbia, SC 29206
WALL JR, John Furman (Spr) 507 Hanover St, Fredericksburg, VA 22401

WALL, John N (NC) English Dept Of Box 8105, Nc State University, Raleigh, NC 27695
WALL, Richard David (WA) 2430 K Street NW, Washington, DC 20037
WALL, Sean (Ida) 2201 SW Vermont St, Portland, OR 97219
WALLACE, Allan Ray (Ind)
WALLACE, Arland Lee (Kan) 8021 W 21st St N, Wichita, KS 67205
WALLACE, Charles F (Alb)
WALLACE, Gene Richard (Los) 1650 E Old Badillo St # C-207, Covina, CA 91724
WALLACE, Jeff (SC) 211 River Landing Dr Unit 458, Daniel Island, SC 29492
WALLACE JR, Jim (ETenn) 83 Charissa Run, Rochester, NY 14623
WALLACE, John Bruce (EMich) 5845 Berry Lane, Indian River, MI 49749
WALLACE, John Robert (Pa) 736 11th Ave, Prospect Park, PA 19076
WALLACE, Kathryn McLaughlin (The Episcopal NCal) 4308 Wood St, Dunsmuir, CA 96025
WALLACE, Lance S (SwFla) 5250 Championship Cup Ln, Spring Hill, FL 34609
WALLACE, Martha Ellen (WA) 530 SW Cove Pt, Depoe Bay, OR 97341
WALLACE, Peter Marsden (At) 2920 Landrum Education Dr, Oakwood, GA 30566
WALLACE, Robert Edgar (Ky) 2140 Bonnycastle Ave Apt 9b, Louisville, KY 40205
WALLACE, Sean M (LI) 119 E 74th St, New York, NY 10021
WALLACE, Tanya R (WMass) 7 Woodbridge St, South Hadley, MA 01075
WALLACE, Thomas Allen (Tex) 213 Lisa Ln, Bellville, TX 77418
WALLACE, William Lewis (Los) 1448 15th St Ste 203, Santa Monica, CA 90404
WALLACE-WILLIAMS, Fr Joseph Anthony (Pa) 265 Union Blvd Apt 616, Saint Louis, MO 63108
WALLENS, Michael Gary (RG) 510 N 2nd St, Alpine, TX 79830
WALLER, Allen Ranson (NC) 4523 Six Forks Rd, Raleigh, NC 27609
WALLER, Clifford Scott (WTex) Po Box 12349, San Antonio, TX 78212
WALLER, Stephen Jay (Dal) 8108 Crowberry Ln, Irving, TX 75063
WALLEY, Kent R (NJ) PO Box 605, 182 Main St, Gladstone, NJ 07934
WALLEY, Seth (Miss) 113 S 9th St, Oxford, MS 38655
WALLING, Ann Boult (Tenn) 6501 Pennywell Dr, Nashville, TN 37205
WALLING, Carolyn M (U)
WALLING, Charles Edward (Miss) 4394 E Falcon Dr, Fayetteville, AR 72701
WALLINGFORD, Kit (Tex) 6221 Main St, Houston, TX 77030

WALLIS, Benjamin E (Pa) Church of the Epiphany, 115 Jefferson Ave, Danville, VA 24541
WALLIS, James Howard (Nev) 2528 Silverton Dr, Las Vegas, NV 89134
WALLNER, Frank (Pa) 404 Levering Mill Rd., Bala Cynwyd, PA 19004
WALLNER, Ludwig John (Alb) 11631 Scenic Hills Blvd., Hudson, FL 34667
WALLS, Alfonso S (Los) 9324 Capobella, Aliso Viejo, CA 92656
WALMER, Corey Ann (Me) St Luke's Episcopal Church, PO Box 249, Farmington, ME 04938
WALMER, Tim (Me) 368 Knowlton Corner Rd, Farmington, ME 04938
WALMISLEY, Andrew John (The Episcopal Church in Haw) Po Box 625, Point Reyes Station, CA 94956
WALMSLEY, John W (CFla) 367 Jaybee Ave, Davenport, FL 33897
WALN, William W (WK)
WALPOLE, Lisa Calhoun (SC) 464 Golf Dr, Georgetown, SC 29440
WALSH, Eileen (SVa) 519 W 20th St Apt 303, Norfolk, VA 23517
WALSH, Lora (Ark) 224 N East Ave, Fayetteville, AR 72701
WALSH, Paul David (Ida) 1565 E 10th N, Mountain Home, ID 83647
WALSH, Peter F (Ct) 111 Oenoke Rdg, New Canaan, CT 06840
WALSH-MINOR, Gina (SwFla) 1a Hamilton Ave, Cranford, NJ 07016
WALTER, Andrew (WA) Grace Episcopal Church, 1607 Grace Church Rd, Silver Spring, MD 20910
WALTER, Aran Evan (FdL) St Thomas Episcopal Church, 226 Washington St, Menasha, WI 54952
WALTER, Cynthia (WVa) PO Box 4063, Table Rock Lane, Wheeling, WV 26003
WALTER, Francis Xavier (Ala) 100 Rattlesnake Spring Ln, Sewanee, TN 37375
WALTER II, George Avery (Ore) 77287 S Ash Rd, Stanfield, OR 97875
WALTER, Kathy Marie (SwFla) 2222 Americus Blvd N Apt 12, Clearwater, FL 33763
WALTER, Verne L (FdL) 16899 Crestview Dr Unit A, Sonora, CA 95370
WALTERS, Delores Marie (ND) PO Box 214, Fort Yates, ND 58538
WALTERS, Fred Ashmore (USC) 1001 12th St, Cayce, SC 29033
WALTERS, Gloria Louise (Okla) St Mark Episcopal Church, 800 S 3rd St, Hugo, OK 74743
WALTERS, Jennifer L (NH) 49 Concord St, Peterborough, NH 03458
WALTERS, Joshua D (Va) 1025 Douglass Dr, Mclean, VA 22101
WALTERS, Karen Graf (SVa) 150 Bella Vista Ter, Unit D, North Venice, FL 34275
WALTERS, Larry (Mich) 11179 Delight Creek Rd, Fishers, IN 46038

WALTERS, Robert Carroll (WMass) 17 Briarwood Cir, Worcester, MA 01606

WALTERS, Roxanne S (Cal) 1217 Skycrest Dr Apt 3, Walnut Creek, CA 94595

WALTERS, Scott (WTenn)

WALTERS, William Harry (USC) 1109 W Woodmont Dr, Lancaster, SC 29720

WALTERS MALONE, Sandra A (Episcopal VI)

WALTERS-PACE, Jill A (Tex) 9700 Saints Cir, Fort Worth, TX 76108

WALTHALL, Chuck (Eas) 4015 W Palm Aire Dr Apt 708, Pompano Beach, FL 33069

WALTHER, Aileen Dianne Pallister (CFla) 753 Creekwater Ter Apt 101, Lake Mary, FL 32746

WALTMAN, Lynne M (Tex) 5820 Lyle St, Westworth Village, TX 76114

WALTON, Billy R (Miss) 608 W Jefferson St, Tupelo, MS 38804

WALTON, Carol Leighann (Nev) 2214 Kimra Ln, Cedar Park, TX 78613

WALTON JR, Harry E (Mass) 3250 NE 28th St Apt 611, Fort Lauderdale, FL 33308

WALTON, James (Pa) 9601 Frankford Ave, Philadelphia, PA 19114

WALTON, Joy Edemy (Del) 2550 Kensington Gdns Unit 103, Ellicott City, MD 21043

WALTON, Lori Ann (Cal) 7688 Shady Hollow Dr, Newark, CA 94560

WALTON, Lynne A (CNY)

WALTON, Macon Brantley (SVa) 202 Ridgeland Dr, Smithfield, VA 23430

WALTON, Mary Fish (Md) 1810 Park Ave, Richmond, VA 23220

WALTON, Rebecca (Miss)

WALTON, Regina Laba (Mass) Parish Of The Good Shepherd, 1671 Beacon St, Waban, MA 02468

WALTON, Robert Harris (WMich) 2186 Tamarack Dr, Okemos, MI 48864

WALTON, Sandra Lee (Colo) 10751 W 69th Ave, Arvada, CO 80004

WALTZ, Bill (Colo) 207 Rainbow Acres Lane, PO Box 21, Gunnison, CO 81230

WALWORTH, Diana Lynn (Mich) PO Box 287, Onsted, MI 49265

WALWORTH, James Curtis (LI) 443 River Rd Ste 210, Highland Park, NJ 08904

WALWORTH, Roy Chancellor (Wyo) 216 Southridge Rd, Evanston, WY 82930

WAMSLEY, Shawn Earl (Pa) Diocese Of Pennsylvania, 3717 Chestnut St Ste 300, Philadelphia, PA 19104

WAN, Sze-Kar (Mass) 87 Herrick Rd, Newton Center, MA 02459

WANAMAKER, Katherine Elizabeth (Minn) 615 Vermillion St, Hastings, MN 55033

WAND, Thomas C (Pa) 301 Norristown Rd Apt E 101, Ambler, PA 19002

WANDALL, Frederick Summerson (Va) Green Spring Village, 7416 Spring Village Dr Apt 116, Springfield, VA 22150

WANDREY, Bryce Philip (SC) 701 Reading Ave Apt 208, Reading, PA 19611

WANG, Kit M David Nathan (Me) PO Box 158, East Waterboro, ME 04030

WANTLAND, David Cuenod (Ga) 6221 Main St, Houston, TX 77030

WAPLE, Gary (WVa) RR 2 Box 243, Lewisburg, WV 24901

WARD, Barbara Pyle (Ida) 450 W Highway 30, Burley, ID 83318

WARD, Elizabeth Howe (Chi) 79 Meadow Hill Rd, Barrington, IL 60010

WARD, Geoffrey F (Mil) 8314 N Regent Rd, Fox Point, WI 53217

WARD, Horace (SeFla) 18501 Nw 7th Ave, Miami, FL 33169

WARD, James (Cal) 202 El Prado Ave., San Rafael, CA 94903

WARD, Jeremiah (Tex) 43 N High Oaks Cir, Spring, TX 77380

WARD, Karen Marie (Oly) 4272 Fremont Ave N, Seattle, WA 98103

WARD, Mary Christine Mollie (Spr) 1104 N Roosevelt Ave, Bloomington, IL 61701

WARD, Meredith (NY) 60 W 13th St Apt 7d, New York, NY 10011

WARD, Meredyth (WMass) 44 Elm St Unit 104, Worcester, MA 01609

WARD, Patrick Carroll (Mass) 249 S Orleans Rd, Orleans, MA 02653

WARD JR, Patrick John (NY) 75a Prospect Ave, Ossining, NY 10562

WARD, Richard Philip (Spok) 2885 Elinor St, Eugene, OR 97403

WARD, Suzanne Lynn (Episcopal SJ) 1934 S Santa Fe St, Visalia, CA 93292

WARD JR, Tom (Tenn) Po Box 3270, Sewanee, TN 37375

WARD, Valerie K (Los) PO Box 1868, Santa Maria, CA 93456

WARDE, Erin J (Okla) 110 E 17th St, Ada, OK 74820

WARDER, Oran (Va) 228 S Pitt St, Alexandria, VA 22314

WARE, Anita Faye (WNC) 1201 S New Hope Rd, Gastonia, NC 28054

WARE, David (Md) 5603 N Charles St, Baltimore, MD 21210

WARE DUNN, Philene M (Va)

WAREHAM, George Ludwig (NwPa) 3111 Pearl Dr, New Castle, PA 16105

WAREING, Robert (Tex) 3122 Red Maple Dr, Friendswood, TX 77546

WARFEL, John (NY) 17 Crescent Pl, Middletown, NY 10940

WARING, James Donald (NY) 802 Broadway, New York, NY 10003

WARLEY, Dianne Goodwin (Ct) 73 Ayers Point Rd, Old Saybrook, CT 06475

WARNE, Nathaniel Adam (NI)

WARNE II, William Thomas (Be) 197 Urie Ave, Lake Winola, PA 18625

WARNE III, William Thomas (Oly) 2915 SE 173rd Ct, Vancouver, WA 98683

WARNECKE JR, Frederick John (NC) 3017 Lake Forest Dr, Greensboro, NC 27408

WARNER, Anthony Francis (Md) 2434 Cape Horn Rd, Hampstead, MD 21074

WARNER, Brian Douglas (WLa)

WARNER, Christopher Scott (At) 1275 Wappetaw Pl, Mount Pleasant, SC 29464

WARNER, Deborah (Mass) Church of the Messiah, 13 Church St, Woods Hole, MA 02543

WARNER, Donald Emil (Neb) 422 W 2nd St # 1026, Grand Island, NE 68801

WARNER, Donald Nelson (Colo) 6961 S Cherokee St, Littleton, CO 80120

WARNER, Janet Avery (EO) 444 NW Apollo Rd, Prineville, OR 97754

WARNER, John Seawright (Ga) 2211 Dartmouth Rd, Augusta, GA 30904

WARNER, Katherine Wakefield (SwFla) PO Box 272, Boca Grande, FL 33921

WARNER, Kevin (SwFla) 622 Tanana Fall Dr, Ruskin, FL 33570

WARNER JR, Richard Wright (EC) 835 Calabash Rd NW, Calabash, NC 28467

WARNER, Suzanne McCarroll (Ky) 1265 Bassett Ave, Louisville, KY 40204

✠ **WARNER**, Vincent Waydell (Oly) PO Box 12126, Seattle, WA 98102

WARNKE, James William (Nwk) 680 Albin St, Teaneck, NJ 07666

WARNOCK, James H (NI) 5513 Bridgeport Way W Unit A, University Place, WA 98467

WARREN III, Allan Bevier (Mass) 30 Brimmer St, Boston, MA 02108

WARREN, Annika Laurin (Ct) 31 Woodland St, Hartford, CT 06105

WARREN, Daniel (Me) 730 Mere Point Rd, Brunswick, ME 04011

WARREN, George Henry (WMass) 12 Walnut Hill Rd, Pascoag, RI 02859

WARREN, Gregory G (Ark) 925 Mitchell St, Conway, AR 72034

WARREN, Harold Robert (Colo) 6625 Holyoke Ct, Fort Collins, CO 80525

WARREN, Heather Anne (Va) 170 Reas Ford Rd, Earlysville, VA 22936

WARREN, J Lewis (Neb) 1524 Cuming St Apt 222, Omaha, NE 68102

WARREN, John Wells (Mont) 1347 Shelton Mill Rd, Auburn, AL 36830

WARREN, Joseph Palmer (Ala) 2017 6th Ave N, Birmingham, AL 35203

WARREN, Laurie Elizabeth (The Episcopal NCal)

WARREN, Matthew Douglas (The Episcopal NCal) Christ The King Tec Ch, 545 Lawrence St, Quincy, CA 95971

WARREN, Penelope Sandra Muehl (Minn) 3124 Utah Ave N, Crystal, MN 55427

WARREN JR, Ralph (SeFla) 223 East Tall Oaks Circle, Palm Beach Gardens, FL 33410

WARREN, Randall R (WMich) 247 W Lovell St, Kalamazoo, MI 49007

WARREN, Robert James (Eur) Christ Church, 8 rue d Bon Pasteur, Clermont-Ferrand, 63000, France

WARREN, Tom (EC) 800 Rountree Ave, Kinston, NC 28501

WARREN, Victoria Daniel (Nev) 1776 Us Highway 50, Glenbrook, NV 89413

WARREN-BROWN, Judith Anne (CFla)

WARTHAN, Frank Avery (Chi) 298 S Harrison Ave, Kankakee, IL 60901

WARWICK, Charles C (Be) PO Box 406, New Milford, PA 18834

WARWICK, Eilene Robinson (Miss) 25 Twelve Oaks Dr, Madison, MS 39110

WARWICK-SABINO, Debra Ann (The Episcopal NCal) 1405 Kentucky St, Fairfield, CA 94533

WAS, Brent (Me) 120 Main St, Amesbury, MA 01913

WASDYKE, Wesley (NH) 744 Cedar Club Cir, Chapel Hill, NC 27517

WASHAM JR, Charles W (Lex) 2734 Chancellor Drive, Suite 202, Crestview Hills, KY 41017

WASHBURN, Elizabeth Lane (WMass)

WASHINGTON, Derek (Eau) 931 Leroy Ct, River Falls, WI 54022

WASHINGTON, Lynne (At) 8076 Crown Colony Pkwy, Mechanicsville, VA 23116

WASHINGTON III, Vant (Minn)

WASINGER, Doug (WTex) 4502 Corona Dr Apt 8c, Corpus Christi, TX 78411

WASTLER, Mark William (Md) 1415 Foxwood Ct, Annapolis, MD 21409

WASZCZAK, Brigid (Az) St Matthew's Episcopal Church, 9071 E Old Spanish Trail, Tucson, AZ 85710

WATAN, Jay Sapaen (Cal) 3010 Alemany Blvd, San Francisco, CA 94112

WATERS, Elliott (Pa) 325 Cameron Station Blvd, Alexandria, VA 22304

WATERS, Margaret (Tex) 4902 Ridge Oak Dr, Austin, TX 78731

WATERS, Sonia E (NJ) 369 Sand Shore Rd, Budd Lake, NJ 07828

WATERSONG, Auburn Lynn (Vt) Christ Episcopal Church, 64 State St, Montpelier, VT 05602

WATKINS, Gilbert Harold (WVa) 2721 Riverside Dr, Saint Albans, WV 25177

WATKINS, Jane Hill (CGC) 10100 Hillview Dr Apt 2311, Pensacola, FL 32514

WATKINS, Laurel Josephine (Ore) 210 E 9th St, Bartlesville, OK 74003

WATKINS, LeeAnne (Minn) 1895 Laurel Ave, Saint Paul, MN 55104

WATKINS, Linda (CPa) 407 Greenwood St, Mont Alto, PA 17237

WATKINS, LindaMay (SO) 20 W 1st St, Dayton, OH 45402

WATKINS, Lucien Alexander (SwFla) 1545 54th Ave S, Saint Petersburg, FL 33705

WATKINS, Michael Mack (Ore) 210 E 9th St, Bartlesville, OK 74003

WATROUS, Janet Couper (NC) 415 S Boylan Ave, Raleigh, NC 27603

WATSON, Amanda Jane Price (NwT) 701 Amarillo St, Abilene, TX 79602

WATSON, George Stennis (WTenn) 1319 Cheyenne Dr, Richardson, TX 75080

WATSON, Jack Lee (Fla) 23 Cameo Drive, Flat Rock, NC 28731

WATSON, James Darrell (Tex) 1101 Tiffany Ln, Longview, TX 75604

WATSON, Janice McKee (The Episcopal Church in Haw) Episcopal Church in Micronesia, 911 N Marine Corps Dr, Tamuning, GU 96913

WATSON JR, Joel Joel (LI) 3216 Kensington Ave, Richmond, VA 23221

WATSON, Karen (Neb) 925 S. 84th St., Omaha, NE 68114

WATSON, Margaret (SD) 503 Main St., Eagle Butte, SD 57625

WATSON, Martha (Nev) St Peter's, 3695 Rogers Ave, Ellicott City, MD 21043

WATSON, Michael Townes (NY) 85 E Main Street, Mount Kisco, NY 10549

WATSON, Richard Avery (SVa) 9 Westwood Drive, East Haddam, CT 06469

WATSON, Shayna Jamillah (CPa) 119 N Duke St, Lancaster, PA 17602

WATSON, Suzanne E (SanD) 5 Rainey Ln, Westport, CT 06880

WATSON, Wendy (The Episcopal NCal) 81 Iris Dr, Calistoga, CA 94515

WATSON III, William John (SC) 25 Waterfowl Rd, Bluffton, SC 29910

WATSON EPTING, Susanne K (Ia) 86 Broadmoor Ln, Iowa City, IA 52245

WATT, Jacqueline Tyndale (At) 605 Dunwoody Chace Ne, Atlanta, GA 30328

WATT, Tanya Chere (RI)

WATT, Tim (RI) 1 Queen Anne Sq, Newport, RI 02840

WATTON, Sharon L (Mich) 3772 S Livernois Rd, Rochester Hills, MI 48307

WATTS, Charles Melvin (O) 4113 West State Street, Route 73, Wilmington, OH 45177

WATTS, Janice Diane (Az) St. Andrew's Episcopal Church, 6300 W. Camelback Rd., Glendale, AZ 85301

WATTS, Marilyn Ruth (The Episcopal Church in Haw) 1525 Wilder Ave Apt 304, Honolulu, HI 96822

WATTS, Sarah Elizabeth (Ala)

WATTS, Sharon Lee Jones (Md) 4 E University Pkwy, Baltimore, MD 21218

WATTS JR, William Joseph (WMass) 19 Pleasant St, Chicopee, MA 01013

WAUTERS JR, Will (Los) 1722 Timber Oak, San Antonio, TX 78232

WAVE, John Erford (CGC) 3615 Phillips Ln, Panama City, FL 32404

WAWERU, David G (LI) 2142 Modoc Dr, Harker Heights, TX 76548

WAY, Edson (NwT) 2807 42nd St., Lubbock, TX 79413

WAY, Harry L (Az) 4102 W Union Hills Dr, Glendale, AZ 85308

WAY, Michael (NJ) 503 Asbury Ave, Asbury Park, NJ 07712

WAYLAND, David Frazee (Va) 1342 Allister Green, Charlottesville, VA 22901

WAYMAN, Eugene (EC)

WAYMAN, Teresa Lachmann (WVa) 3085 Sycamore Run Road, Glenville, WV 26351

✠ WAYNICK, Cate (Ind) 5537 Woodacre Ct., Indianapolis, IN 46234

WEATHERFORD, David William (SanD) 10835 Gabacho Dr, San Diego, CA 92124

WEATHERHOLT, Anne (Md) 712 David Ave, Westminster, MD 21157

WEATHERHOLT JR, Floyd Allan (Md) 2 E High St, Hancock, MD 21750

WEATHERLY, Joe (Tenn) 885 Spring Valley Rd, Cookeville, TN 38501

WEATHERLY, John (Va) 8441 Porter Ln, Alexandria, VA 22308

WEATHERLY, Robert H (EC) 1414 Chambers St, Vicksburg, MS 39180

WEATHERWAX, Elizabeth May (Pgh) 402 Royal Ct, Pittsburgh, PA 15234

WEAVER III, David (Chi) 3835 Johnson Ave, Western Springs, IL 60558

WEAVER, Eric James (LI) 8 Oceanside Ct, Northport, NY 11768

WEAVER, Evelyn Jean (SD) 2018 13th Ave, Belle Fourche, SD 57717

WEAVER, Ivan Michael (SD)

WEAVER, Joshua L (ETenn)

WEAVER, Lorne Edward (Los) 1725 Partridge Ave., Upland, CA 91784

WEAVER, Robert Crew (O) 2553 Derbyshire Rd, Cleveland Heights, OH 44106

WEAVER, Sally (Mo) 2575 Sunrise Dr, Eureka, MO 63025

WEAVER, Shahar Caren (Chi) 3801 S Wabash Ave, Chicago, IL 60653

WEBB II, Alexander Henderson (WTenn) 4645 Walnut Grove Rd, Memphis, TN 38117

WEBB, Anne (NH) 43 Thorndike Pond Rd, Jaffrey, NH 03452

WEBB, Benjamin Sewell (Ia)

WEBB, Estelle C (Ct) 1651 Dickson Ave Apt 124, Scranton, PA 18509

WEBB, Fain Murphey (Nwk) P.O. Box 336, Columbia, NJ 07832

WEBB, Frieda Van Baalen (WNY) 3360 McKinley Parkway, Buffalo, NY 14219

WEBB JR, James Wilson (Miss) 309 E Parkway Dr, Indianola, MS 38751

WEBB III, Joseph (Va) 4074 Thorngate Dr, Williamsburg, VA 23188

WEBB III, Joseph Baxtar (Eau) 6101 Bannocks Dr., San Antonio, TX 78239

WEBB, Katherine (Eas) 210 David Dr, Chestertown, MD 21620

WEBB, Nathan John (Dal)

WEBB, Pamela Connor (SVa) 8221 Old Mill Ln, Williamsburg, VA 23188

WEBB, Richard Cassius Lee (NH) 43 Thorndike Pond Rd., Jaffrey, NH 03452

WEBB, Robert Joseph (Ind) 721 W Main St, Madison, IN 47250

WEBB, Ross Allan (USC) 2534 Shiland Dr, Rock Hill, SC 29732

WEBB, William Charles (WNY) 29 Grove St, Angola, NY 14006

WEBBER, Ann (Mich) 152 Good Hill Rd, Weston, CT 06883

WEBBER, Bruce Milton (NJ) 19105 35th Avenue, Apt. J, Flushing, NY 11358

WEBBER, Christopher L (Ct) 1601 19th Ave, San Francisco, CA 94122

WEBBER, Michael Basquin (NY) PO Box 121, Paradox, NY 12858

WEBER, Claudia Jo (ECR) 1217 Vanderbilt Way, Sacramento, CA 95825

WEBER, Dean A (Nwk) 81 Highwood Ave, Tenafly, NJ 07670

WEBER, Lynne Bleich (Nwk) 81 Highwood Ave, Tenafly, NJ 07670

WEBER-JOHNSON, Jered Paul (Minn) 3001 Wisconsin Ave NW, Washington, DC 20016

WEBSTER, Alan Kim (WVa) 36 Norwood Rd, Charleston, WV 25314

WEBSTER, Alice Elizabeth (EC) 12903 Saint Georges Ln NW, Mount Savage, MD 21545

WEBSTER, Daniel Joseph (Md) 2215 New York Ave SW Apt B, Albuquerque, NM 87104

WEBSTER, Kiah S (USC) 11540 Ferguson Rd, Dallas, TX 75228

WEBSTER, Pamela Ball (Minn) 435 Sunset Rd, Ely, MN 55731

WEBSTER II, Phillip (USC) St Mary's Church, 170 Saint Andrews Rd, Columbia, SC 29210

WEBSTER, Randy Lee (Ia) 510 Columbia St, Burlington, IA 52601

WEBSTER, Richmond Rudolphus (Ala) 202 Gordon Dr Se, Decatur, AL 35601

WEBSTER, Valerie Minton (Mont) 311 S 3rd Ave, Bozeman, MT 59715

WEBSTER II, W Raymond (Chi) 51 Pine Grove, Amherst, MA 01002

WEDDERBURN, Derrick Hexford (NJ) Broadway & Royden, Cadmen, NJ 08104

WEDGWOOD-GREENHOW, Stephen John Francis (NwT) 21618 Liberty St Unit 419 Apt 419, Lexington Park, MD 20653

WEEDON, Sarah Lipscomb (CPa) 150 E Lincoln St, Shamokin, PA 17872

WEEKS, Ann Gammon (ETenn)

WEEKS, Jo Ann (Los) 23446 Swan St, Moreno Valley, CA 92557

WEEKS, Lawrence Biddle (Me) 628 N Treat Ave, Tucson, AZ 85716

WEEKS, WIlliam Bradley (ETenn) Grace Episcopal Church, 20 Belvoir Ave, Chattanooga, TN 37411

WEEKS WULF, Marta Joan (SeFla) 7350 SW 162nd Street, Palmetto Bay, FL 33157

WEGENER, Barbara Jean (WMo)

WEGER, Rohani Ann (SeFla) 1225 Texas St, Houston, TX 77002

WEGLARZ, Eileen (NY) 98 Stewart Ave, Eastchester, NY 10709

WEGMAN, Jay D (NY) Cathedral Station, Box 1111, New York, NY 10025

WEHMILLER, Paula Jean Lawrence (Pa) 612 Ogden Ave., Swarthmore, PA 19081

WEHNER, Paul (Tex) 7327 Timberlake Dr, Sugar Land, TX 77479

WEI, Fei-jan Elizabeth (Tai) 114 Fuh Rd 6FL, Yunghe City, Taipei 23449, Taiwan

WEIDMAN, Hal J (ND) 712 N 7th St, Bismarck, ND 58501

WEIDNER, David (Fla) 128 Bilbao Dr, Saint Augustine, FL 32086

WEIERBACH, Cornelia Miller (Va) 5613 23rd St N, Arlington, VA 22205

WEIHER, Joie Muir Clee (Va) 7057 Blackwell Rd, Warrenton, VA 20187

WEIKERT, Robert Curtis (Mich) 4212 Wylie Rd, Dexter, MI 48130

WEILER, Matthew Gordon Beck (CFla) 3538 Lenox Rd, Birmingham, AL 35213

WEINBERG, Richard Mosson (WA) St Margarets Episcopal Church, 1830 Connecticut Ave NW, Washington, DC 20009

WEINER, Margaret Yoder (Ia) 3801 Grand Ave Unit 106, Des Moines, IA 50312

WEINER, Mary Lou (Ida) 4933 W View Dr, Meridian, ID 83642

WEINER TOMPKINS, Rebecca (NY) 145 W 46th St, New York, NY 10036

WEINREICH, Gabriel (Mich) 2116 Silver Maples Drive, Chelsea, MI 48118

WEIR, Daniel Sargent (WNY) 337 NH 16A, Intervale, NH 03845

WEIR, Silas Michael (Colo) 4009 Histead Way, Evergreen, CO 80439

WEIS, Christopher A (Tex)

WEISER, Samuel Ivan (RG) 848 Camino De Levante, Santa Fe, NM 87501

WEISS, Chuck (Del) PO Box, Dover, DE 19903

WEISS, Edward Allen (CFla) 200 Nw 3rd St, Okeechobee, FL 34972

WEISS, James Michael Egan (Mass) Dept of Theology, Stokes Hall, Boston College, Chestnut Hill, MA 02467

WEISS, Louise Lindecamp (RG) 3900 Trinity Dr, Los Alamos, NM 87544

WEISS, Molly M (Minn)

WEISSMAN, Stephen (Mo) 434 Gorman Bridge Rd, Asheville, NC 28806

WEITZEL, Mark Augustin (Los) 1020 N Brand Blvd, Glendale, CA 91202

WELCH, Barbara Leigh (Pa) 110 Llanfair Rd, Ardmore, PA 19003

WELCH, Elizabeth Jean (Cal) Sojourn Chaplain, SFO General Hospital, 1001 Potrero Ave Rm 2F4, San Francisco, CA 94110

WELCH, George Truman (Mass) 1692 Beacon St, Waban, MA 02468

WELCH, Geraldine T (NJ)

WELCH, Jimmy Dean (Okla) 4250 W Houston St, Broken Arrow, OK 74012

WELCH, Lauren Marie (Md) 7 Overpark Ct, Baltimore, MD 21234

WELDON JR, Jay (Mass) 4800 Old Dawson Rd, Albany, GA 31721

WELDON, Jonathan Naylor (Oly) 415 S Garden St, Bellingham, WA 98225

WELDY JR, Robert Lee (Cal) PO Box 430, Inverness, CA 94937

WELIN, Amy Doyle (CPa) 1917 Roxbury Ct, Mechanicsburg, PA 17055

WELIN, Gregory William (CPa) 58 Brookfield Rd, Seymour, CT 06483

WELLBORN, Gay S (RG)

WELLER, Edith (Oly) 8216 14th Ave Ne, Seattle, WA 98115

WELLER, Gordon (Mich) 218 Ottawa St., Lansing, MI 48933

WELLER, Gretchen (Lex) 435 SOM Center Road, Mayfield Village, OH 44143

WELLER JR, Tom (CGC) 2300 W Beach Dr, Panama City, FL 32401

WELLES JR, George H (Mass) 810 Monterrosa Dr, Myrtle Beach, SC 29572

WELLES, Hope Virginia (Mo) 4455 Atlantic Blvd, Jacksonville, FL 32207

WELLFORD, Eleanor (Va) 514 S Gaskins Rd, Richmond, VA 23238

WELLNER, Robert Harry (Ct) 4750 Welby Drive, P.O. Box 142, Schnecksville, PA 18078

WELLS, Ben Reid (At) St Francis Episcopal Church, 432 Forest Hill Rd, Macon, GA 31210

WELLS, Bob (Tex) 9302 Sunlake Dr, Pearland, TX 77584

WELLS, Charlotte E (EO) 241 Se 2nd St, Pendleton, OR 97801

WELLS, David L (Spr) Cath Of Stpaul The Ap, 815 S Second Street, Springfield, IL 62704

WELLS, Della Wager (RI)

WELLS, Dorothy Sanders (WTenn) St. George's Episcopal Church, 2425 S.

Germantown Road, Germantown, TN 38138

WELLS, Jane Ely (Minn) 105 S Cedar St, Oberlin, OH 44074

WELLS, Jason (NH) 18 Kimball St, Pembroke, NH 03275

WELLS SR, John T (Tex) 14043 Horseshoe Cir, Woodway, TX 76712

WELLS, Lloyd Francis (At) 335 Forest Heights Dr, Athens, GA 30606

WELLS, Mary Beth (SeFla) 231 Spring Hill Dr, Gordonsville, VA 22942

WELLS JR, Roy Draydon (Ala) 3608 Montclair Rd, Birmingham, AL 35213

WELLS, William E (Los) 18631 Chapel Ln, Huntington Beach, CA 92646

WELLS JR, William Smith (Va) 6914 West Grace Street, Richmond, VA 23226

WELLS MILLER, Tracy J (ECR) Ep Ch of St Jn the Baptist, 125 Canterbury Dr, Aptos, CA 95003

WELSAND, Randy Arthur (Minn) 1928 38th St S, St Cloud, MN 56301

WELSCH, Matthew A (NY)

WELTY III, Terrence Anthony (Tex) 106 E Crawford St, Palestine, TX 75801

WELTY, Winston W (Pa) Santa Clara 613, Riberas del Pilar, Chapala, JAL 45906, Mexico

WENDEL JR, David Deaderick (Ala) 210 Oak Ct, New Braunfels, TX 78132

WENDEL, Richard (Chi) 536 W Fullerton Pkwy, Chicago, IL 60614

WENDELL, Chris (Mass) St. Paul's Church, 100 Pine Hill Road, Bedford, MA 01730

WENDELL, Martin Paul (Alb) 405 Master St, Valley Falls, NY 12185

WENDER, Sarai Tucker (ETenn) The Tec Ch In E Tennessee, 814 Episcopal School Way, Knoxville, TN 37932

WENDFELDT, Steve (SanD) 2728 Sixth Avenue, San Diego, CA 92103

WENGROVIUS, John H (Colo) 108 Crawford Cir, Golden, CO 80401

WENGROVIUS, Steve (Colo) 3712 W 99th Ave, Westminster, CO 80031

WENNER, Peter (Mass) 210 Nahanton St Apt 107, Newton Center, MA 02459

WENNER GARDNER, Rachel E (Pa) The Church Of The Holy Trinity, 1904 Walnut St, Philadelphia, PA 19103

WENRICK, Heather (Oly) 3407 40th Ave W, Seattle, WA 98199

WENTZIEN, Marilyn Lawrence (Ia) 522 Walnut St, Mamaroneck, NY 10543

WERDAL, Evelyn Paige (NY) 522 Walnut St, Mamaroneck, NY 10543

WERNER, Frederick John Emil (Mich) 13070 Independence Ave, Utica, MI 48315

WERNER, George (Pgh) 106 Sewickley Heights Dr, Sewickley, PA 15143

WERNER, Mark (USC) 2 N Hill Ct, Columbia, SC 29223

WERNICK, Mike (WMich) 1800 Bloomfield Dr Se, Kentwood, MI 49508

WERNTZ, Pamela Louise (Mass) 120 Marshall St, Watertown, MA 02472

WERT, Susan Mitchell (Md)

WESCH, Kate (Ct) 7 Maywood Dr, Old Lyme, CT 06371

WESEN, Vicki (Oly) 1500A E College Way # 447, Mount Vernon, WA 98273

WESLEY, Carol A (Mo) 5519 Alaska Ave, Saint Louis, MO 63111

WESLEY JR, John (Fla) 338 N 10th St, Quincy, FL 32351

WESSELL, David E (FdL) 2805 Elgin St, Durham, NC 27704

WEST, Anne Elizabeth (Va) PO Box 432, Madison, VA 22727

WEST, Barbara Field (Ct) 7 Hillcrest Rd, Manchester, CT 06040

WEST, Clark Russell (CNY) G3 Anabel Taylor Hall, Ithaca, NY 14853

WEST, Geoffrey George (NJ) 525 Willowbrook Dr, Jeffersonville, PA 19403

WEST, Hilary (EC) 411 W Bridge Ln, Nags Head, NC 27959

WEST, Hillary T (Va) 4212 Kingcrest Pkwy, Richmond, VA 23221

WEST, Jan Hickman (Cal) 171 Prospect Ave, San Anselmo, CA 94960

WEST, Jennifer Kezirian (RI)

WEST JR, John (Ga) 720 Talison Ave Apt 202, Daniel Island, SC 29492

WEST, John Thomas (NMich) 301 N 1st St, Ishpeming, MI 49849

WEST, Philip (RG) 2243 Henry Rd Sw, Albuquerque, NM 87105

WEST, Randolph Harrison (Ct) 1402 Stratman Cir Unit A, Chattanooga, TN 37421

WEST, Scott (SwVa) PO Box 164, 120 Church St NE, Blacksburg, VA 24063

WEST, Tim (SO) 600 Dorothy Moore Avenue, Unit 10, Urbana, OH 43078

WESTBROOK, Carl (Tex)

WESTBURY JR, Rick (Fla) 15 N Wilderness Trl, Ponte Vedra Beach, FL 32082

WEST-DOOHAN, Sue (Be) HC 75 Box 32, Strange Creek, WV 25063

WESTERBERG, George Arthur (Mass) PO Box 530, Fryeburg, ME 04037

WESTFALL, Doris Ann (Mo) 28 Whinhill Ct, Saint Peters, MO 63304

WESTHORP, Peter H (RI) 2574 Creve Coeur Mill Rd, Maryland Heights, MO 63043

WESTON, Jane Mitchell (At) PO Box 102, Conyers, GA 30012

WESTON, Stephen Richard (Colo) 1125 Windsor Ave, Pulaski, VA 24301

WESTPFAHL, Carol E (ETenn) 210 Redwolf Way, Lenoir City, TN 37772

WESTPHAL, Stacey Elizabeth (CFla) 522 Summerset Ct, Indian Harbour Beach, FL 32937

WETHERED, Stephanie (Nwk) 224 Cornelia St, Boonton, NJ 07005

WERNICK, Robert (Ark) 525 Hilton St, El Dorado, AR 71730

WETHERINGTON, Timothy R (CFla) Church Of The Messiah, 241 N Main St, Winter Garden, FL 34787

WETHERN, James Douglas (Ga) PO Box 20327, Saint Simons Island, GA 31522

WETMORE, Ian (LI) St Michael's Episcopal Church, 111 Ofallon Troy Rd, O Fallon, IL 62269

WETTSTEIN, David (Ida) 6925 Copper Dr, Boise, ID 83704

WETZEL, Luke A (Chi) St Paul's Parish, 60 Akenside Rd, Riverside, IL 60546

WETZEL, Mary (At) PO Box 4548, Atlanta, GA 30302

WETZEL, Todd Harold (Dal) Po Box 429, Cedar Hill, TX 75106

WEYLS, Richard Coleman (Oly) 6312 185th Pl SW, Lynnwood, WA 98037

WEYMOUTH, Richard Channing (NH) RR3 Box 18, Plymouth, NH 03264

WEZA, Barbra Lee (Oly)

WHALEN, Dena Stokes (WNC) P.O. Box 490, Clarkesville, GA 30523

WHALEN, Donald (Eas) 2929 SE Ocean Blvd O-5, Stuart, FL 34996

WHALEY, Mary Susan (Okla)

WHALEY, Stephen Foster (Tex) 605 Dulles Ave, Stafford, TX 77477

WHALLON, Diane (Fla) 1640 NE 40th Ave Apt 106, Ocala, FL 34470

✠ **WHALON**, Pierre W (Eur) 23 Avenue George V, Paris, 75008, France

WHARFF GALVIS, Arian Hernando (NJ)

WHARTON, Roger (ECR) 1404 Arnold Ave, San Jose, CA 95110

WHATLEY, Virginia (Nwk)

WHEATLEY, Gail J (Oly) 470 Cedar Park Dr, Port Angeles, WA 98362

WHEATLEY, Paul David (Dal) Church Of The Incarnation, 3966 McKinney Ave, Dallas, TX 75204

WHEATLEY-JONES, Elizabeth (Miss) PO Box 345, Grenada, MS 38902

WHEELER, Charles R (WNY) 161 E Main St, Westfield, NY 14787

WHEELER, Diana Roberta (Cal) 573 Dolores st., San Francisco, CA 94110

WHEELER, Elisa Desportes (Va) 638 Burton Point Rd, Mathews, VA 23068

WHEELER, Evelyn (Ind)

WHEELER, Frances Marie (Kan) 14301 S Blackbob Rd, Olathe, KS 66062

WHEELER, Jim (Ct) PO Box 10, Woodbury, CT 06798

WHEELER, John Bevan (Md) 2795 Topmast Ct, Annapolis, MD 21401

WHEELER, Kathryn Brown (CGC) 2002 W Lakeridge Dr, Albany, GA 31707

WHEELER JR, Louis (WA) 2001 14th St SE, Washington, DC 20020

WHEELER, Rhonda Estes (SVa) Emmanuel Episcopal Church, 179 E Mercury Blvd, Hampton, VA 23669
WHEELOCK, Janet (SVa) St Marys Ch, 1010 12th St, Ramona, CA 92065
WHEELOCK, Leslie Gail (RI) 8 Neptune St, Jamestown, RI 02835
WHELAN, Janet Kay (WMo) 13500 Rinehart Ln, Parkville, MO 64152
WHELCHEL, Judith Hester (WNC) 67 Windsor Rd, Asheville, NC 28804
WHENNEN, John (Chi) 2640 Park Dr, Flossmoor, IL 60422
WHETSTONE, Raymond David (Ala) Grace Episcopal Church, PO Box 1791, Anniston, AL 36202
WHIDDON, Ennis Howard (USC) 301 Piney Mountain Rd, Greenville, SC 29609
WHISTLER, Tamsen (Mo) 1020 N Duchesne Dr, Saint Charles, MO 63301
WHITAKER, Ann Latham (Miss) 806 Prairie View Road, Oxford, MS 38655
WHITAKER, Bradford G (ETenn) 305 W 7th St, Chattanooga, TN 37402
WHITAKER III, Howard Wilson (Nwk) PO Box 596, Scottsboro, AL 35768
WHITAKER, Monica (Az) 100 Arroyo Pinon Dr, Sedona, AZ 86336
WHITBECK, Marjorie Bailey Ogden (Mass) 29 Princess Rd, West Newton, MA 02465
WHITCOMB SLEMMER, Amy Whitcomb (Mass) 32 S St, Hull, MA 02045
WHITE, Andrew D'Angio (Me) Saint Davids Episcopal Church, 138 York St, Kennebunk, ME 04043
WHITE JR, Bain (Colo) St Mark's Episcopal Church, PO Box 534, Craig, CO 81626
WHITE, Barbara (Ky)
WHITE, Bruce Alan (Az) 7267 E Onda Cir, Tucson, AZ 85715
WHITE, Chellie (Nwk) 707 Washington St, Hoboken, NJ 07030
WHITE, Deborah (Cal) 130 Muir Station Rd., Martinez, CA 94553
WHITE, Dorothy A (Minn) 2420 Penn Ave S # 2, Minneapolis, MN 55405
WHITE, Harold Naylor (Va) PO Box 326, Wicomico Church, VA 22579
WHITE, Helen Slingluff (Ga) 15 Willow Rd, Savannah, GA 31419
WHITE, James Lee (Del) 39 Gainsborough Dr, Lewes, DE 19958
WHITE, Jon (CNY) St Luke's Episcopal Church, 5402 W Genesee St, Camillus, NY 13031
WHITE, K Alon (NY) 79 Cedar Hill Ave Apt 1, Nyack, NY 10960
WHITE, Karin Kay (ECR) 390 N Winchester Blvd Apt 9B, Santa Clara, CA 95050
WHITE, Kathryn (Chi) 3052 Jeffrey Dr, Joliet, IL 60435
WHITE, Kathryn (WMass) 129 Roseland Park Road, Woodstock, CT 06281

WHITE, Kenneth Orgill (WLa) 2320 Wooster Ln Apt 6, Sanibel, FL 33957
WHITE, Konrad Shepard (Los) 524 E Duffy St, Savannah, GA 31401
WHITE, Krstin (Ind) 1100 W 42nd St, Indianapolis, IN 46208
WHITE, Laura Dale (Me) 522 NW 8th St, Pendleton, OR 97801
WHITE, Lynn Scott (Chi) 1100 Pembridge Dr Apt 330, Apt 330, Lake Forest, IL 60045
WHITE, Mary (Vt) 10 N Main Ave, Albany, NY 12203
WHITE, Michael S (Ga) 308a Bradley Point Rd, Savannah, GA 31410
WHITE, M Joanna (Md) 2125 Beach Village Court, Annapolis, MD 21403
WHITE, Nancy Anne (Md) 3267 Stepney St, Edgewater, MD 21037
WHITE, Nicholson Barney (O) 1109 Hollyheath Ln, Charlotte, NC 28209
WHITE JR, Paul Donald (La) 3553 Windgarden Cv, Memphis, TN 38125
WHITE, Paul T (WLa)
WHITE, R Scott (WNC) Trinity Church, 60 Church St, Asheville, NC 28801
WHITE, Rita Ellen (Va) 138 Pier Pl, Kinsale, VA 22488
WHITE, Robert J (LI)
WHITE, Roger Bradley (Ct) PO Box 309, Kent, CT 06757
WHITE, Rowena Ruth (WLa) 8212 Argosy Ct, Baton Rouge, LA 70809
WHITE, Sara D (Me) 143 State St, Portland, ME 04101
WHITE, Stephen James (Me) 140 Bluff Rd, Yarmouth, ME 04096
WHITE, Steve (NJ) 5 Thrushwood Ln, Great Barrington, MA 01230
WHITE, Steve (CNY) 1101 N Broadway St, Knoxville, TN 37917
✠ **WHITE**, Terry Allen (Ky) 425 S Second St Suite 200, Louisville, KY 40202
WHITE, Thomas Rees (Ct) 9 Joshuas Way, Kennebunk, ME 04043
WHITEHAIR, Eric Ian (Md)
WHITE-HASSLER, Jane (Ct) 130 Vincent Dr, Newington, CT 06111
WHITEHEAD, Danny (Ala) 1159 Henson Dr, Florence, AL 35630
WHITEHEAD, Philip Hoyle (USC) 6026 Crabtree Rd, Columbia, SC 29206
WHITE HORSE-CARDA, Pat (SD) 500 S Main Ave, Sioux Falls, SD 57104
WHITEHURST, Joseph Stewart (USC) 173 Kendallwood Ct, Aiken, SC 29803
WHITELAW, Eleanor Drake (CGC) 343 N Randolph Ave, Eufaula, AL 36027
WHITELEY, Raewynne Jean (LI) 15 Highland Ave, Saint James, NY 11780
WHITEMAN, Christopher William (Mass) 5 Chauncy Ln, Cambridge, MA 02138

WHITESEL, Ann Brier (CPa) 12 Strawberry Dr, Carlisle, PA 17013
WHITESIDE, Henry B (EC) 7 Masonic Ave, Shelburne Falls, MA 01370
WHITE-SPUNNER, Kenneth Paul (CGC) 180 Louise St, Monroeville, AL 36460
WHITFIELD, Ann (Nev) 10810 NE Sherwood Dr., Vancouver, WA 98686
WHITFIELD, Deirdre (Pa) 126 Westminster Dr, Wallingford, PA 19086
WHITFIELD, Jacqueline Rutledge (NC)
WHITFIELD, Stephen Ray (Tex) 2301 Lauren Loop, Leander, TX 78641
WHITFORD, Michele E (FdL) 1220 N 7th St, Sheboygan, WI 53081
WHITING, Raymond Arthur (Ga)
WHITING, William Richard (WMich) 2165 Chesapeake Dr NE, Grand Rapids, MI 49505
WHITLEY, Ryan R (SwFla) 1 W Ardmore Ave, Ardmore, PA 19003
WHITLOCK III, Robin (SwFla) 949 41st Ave N, Saint Petersburg, FL 33703
WHITMAN III, Frank Lewis (Minn) 4900 Nathan Ln N, Plymouth, MN 55442
WHITMAN, Marian Chandler (WTenn) 2425 S Germantown Rd, Germantown, TN 38138
WHITMER, Marlin Lee (Ia) 2602 250th St, De Witt, IA 52742
WHITMER, Ronald Delane (La) 5400 Courtyard Dr., Gonzales, LA 70737
WHITMIRE JR, Norman (LI) 8545 96th St, Woodhaven, NY 11421
WHITMORE, Bruce Gregory (Tex) 1401 Avenue O #F, Huntsville, TX 77340
WHITMORE, Chuck (WNY) 3802 James St Unit 30, Bellingham, WA 98226
WHITMORE, Elizabeth Needham (Mass) 1391 Hyannis Barnstable Rd, Barnstable, MA 02630
✠ **WHITMORE**, Keith (Eau) 90 N National Ave, Fond Du Lac, WI 54935
WHITMORE, Paula Michele (Spok) 602 NW 10th St, Pendleton, OR 97801
WHITNAH JR, John C (Pa) Gethsemane Cathedral, 3600 25th St S, Fargo, ND 58104
WHITNAH, Michael David (Tenn) 116 N Academy St, Murfreesboro, TN 37130
WHITNEY, Ann (Ak) PO Box 870995, Wasilla, AK 99687
WHITNEY, Marilla Jane (Minn) 1421 Lucia Ave, Fairmont, MN 56031
WHITNEY, Wayne V (Az) TEC Ch of the Nativity, 22405 N Miller Rd, Scottsdale, AZ 85255
WHITNEY WISE, Stephen (Ore) 4033 SE Woodstock Blvd., Portland, OR 97202
WHITSITT, Helen Bonita (WMo) PO Box 57, Fayette, MO 65248

WHITTAKER, Brendan Joseph (NH) 1788 Vt Route 102, Guildhall, VT 05905

WHITTAKER JR, Richard Russell (U) 1784 Aaron Dr, Tooele, UT 84074

WHITTAKER-NAVEZ, Christine Ruth (Mass) 223 Pond St, Hopkinton, MA 01748

WHITTED, Warren Rohde (Neb) 8141 Farnam Dr Apt 328, Omaha, NE 68114

WHITTEN, James Austin (CFla) St Mary of the Angels, 6316 Matchett Rd, Orlando, FL 32809

WHITTEN, Wesley Roy (The Episcopal NCal) 11197 Via Vis, Nevada City, CA 95959

WHITTINGTON, Nancy Susan (WNC) 140 Chestnut Cir, Blowing Rock, NC 28605

WHITTINGTON, Richard Culbertson (Tex)

WHITTLE, Natalie Wang (Ga) 102 S Jackson Rd, Statesboro, GA 30461

WHITWORTH, Jana L (Oly)

WHITWORTH, Julia E (Ind) Trinity Episcopal Church, 3243 N Meridian St, Indianapolis, IN 46208

WHRITENOUR, Jack Raymond (Alb) 588 Albany St, Little Falls, NY 13365

WHYTE, Horace Maxwell (NY) 170 W End Ave Apt 30-H, New York, NY 10023

WIBLE, Christina Karen Kirchner (NJ) 10 N Slope, Clinton, NJ 08809

WIBLE, Terry (Be) 57 Piper Dr, New Oxford, PA 17350

WICHAEL, Karen (Kan) 5648 W 92nd Pl, Overland Park, KS 66207

WICHELNS, Anne (CNY) Church Of The Resurrecton, 120 West Fifth Street, Oswego, NY 13126

WICHELNS, Jerome Bailey (CNY) 10751 Limburg Forks Rd, Carthage, NY 13619

WICHMAN, James Henry (O) 2314 Oak Glen Ct, Akron, OH 44333

WICK, Calhoun W (Del) 4031 Kennett Pike Apt 72, Wilmington, DE 19807

WICKERSHAM, Kristin Price Robinson (Va)

WICKHAM, Jonathan (WTex) 15670 Robin Ridge, San Antonio, TX 78248

WICKHAM III, William (Del) 9410 Creek Summit Cir, Richmond, VA 23235

WICKIZER, Bob (Okla) 218 N 6th St, Muskogee, OK 74401

WIDING, Jon (Ct) 47 Fox Holw, Avon, CT 06001

WIDLAKE, Dina Elaine (Va) 6715 Georgetown Pike, Mclean, VA 22101

WIECKING III, Frederick August (Ind) 4 Sunnyside Rd, Silver Spring, MD 20910

WIECZOREK, Catherine Lane (NJ)

WIED, Gethin James (Los)

WIEHE, Philip (NC) 3616 Laurel Park Hwy, Hendersonville, NC 28739

WIELAND, William David (Ind) Same As Above, Greencastle, IN 46135

WIENK, Dennis Leslie (Roch) 1760 Blossom Rd, Rochester, NY 14610

WIENS, Dolores Flaming (NI) 304 N 390 E, Ivins, UT 84738

WIENS HEINSOHN, Lisa Marie (Minn) 2136 Carter Ave, Saint Paul, MN 55108

WIESNER, August Donald (NJ) 2104 Bristol Lake Court, Blc 2104, Charlotte, NC 28215

WIESNER, Kurt Christopher (U) 261 S 900 E, Salt Lake City, UT 84102

WIETSTOCK, Anne Kimberley (NI) 117 N Lafayette Blvd, South Bend, IN 46601

WIGGERS, John Mark (ETenn) 1101 N Broadway St, Knoxville, TN 37917

WIGGIN, Jane-Allison E (La)

WIGGINS JR, Eschol Vernon (Ga) 1009 Hillcrest Dr, Cochran, GA 31014

WIGGINS, Reese H (La) 17764 Jefferson Ridge Dr, Baton Rouge, LA 70817

WIGG-MAXWELL, Elizabeth Parker (Nwk) 38 Lynn St, Harrington Park, NJ 07640

WIGHT, Andrea (Chi) 7398 Bell Vista Ter, Rockford, IL 61107

WIGHT, Bill (USC) 5 Blackhawk Ct, Blythewood, SC 29016

WIGHT, Susan (USC) 5 Blackhawk Ct, Blythewood, SC 29016

WIGLE, John Whitcombe (O) 814 Westport Dr, Youngstown, OH 44511

WIGMORE, William Joseph (Tex) 1701 Rock Creek Dr, Round Rock, TX 78681

WIGNER JR, J Douglas (Va) 1802 Dover Pointe Ct, Henrico, VA 23238

WIGNER, Sarah Leann (NwT)

WIKE, Antoinette Ray (NC) 221 Union St, Cary, NC 27511

WIKSELL, Ryan David (WMo)

WILBERT, Brian Kurt (O) 42 S Cedar St, Oberlin, OH 44074

WILBURN, James Mark (Tex) 24 Mcfaddan Ln, Temple, TX 76502

WILBURN, Merry I (Tex) 16830 Blairstone, Houston, TX 77084

WILCHES GARCIA, Guillermo A (PR)

WILCOX II, David S (WMo) 335 Tennessee Ave, Sewanee, TN 37383

WILCOX, Diana L (Nwk) Christ Church, 74 Park Ave, Glen Ridge, NJ 07028

WILCOX JR, Jack Franklyn (Okla) 101 Great Oaks Dr, Norman, OK 73071

WILCOX, Melissa Quincy (Mil) 250 Mooreland Ave, Carlisle, PA 17013

WILCOXSON, Frederick Dean (CFla) 154 Terry Lane, Benton, TN 37307

WILCOXSON, JoAnn Vanessa (CFla) 154 Terry Lane, Benton, TN 37307

WILD, Geoffrey Mileham (NwPa) PO Box 287, Grove City, PA 16127

WILD, Janet (ECR) 13601 Saratoga Ave, Saratoga, CA 95070

WILD III, Philip Charles (La) 120 S New Hampshire St, Covington, LA 70433

WILDE, Gregory Dean (Spr) 6164 Colfax Ln S, Minneapolis, MN 55419

WILDER, Ginny (NC) Trinity Episcopal Church, 1108 N Adams St, Wilmington, DE 19801

WILDER, Hannah (SanD) 3688 Cactusview Dr, San Diego, CA 92105

WILDER, Marilyn (Spok) 617 10th St, Oroville, WA 98844

WILDGOOSE, Angelo Stanley (NJ) 400 E Front St Apt 222, Plainfield, NJ 07060

WILDMAN, Rachel Preston (Mass) 100 Pine Hill Rd, Bedford, MA 01730

WILE, Mary Lee (Me) 46 Willow Grove Rd, Brunswick, ME 04011

WILEMON, Zane Howard (Cal) 81 N 2nd St, San Jose, CA 95113

WILEY, George Bell (Kan) 2313 Willow Crk, Lawrence, KS 66049

WILEY, Henrietta Lovejoy (Md) Trinity Episcopal Church, 120 Allegheny Ave, Towson, MD 21204

WILEY, Judi (SO) 234 N. High St., Hillsboro, OH 45133

WILHELM, Joseph Franklin (Los) 404 W Santa Ana St, Ojai, CA 93023

WILHELM, Quinn Jay (Colo) 2950 S University Blvd, Denver, CO 80210

WILKERSON, Bonnie Carver (Ia) St Lukes Episcopal Church, 605 Avenue E, Fort Madison, IA 52627

WILKERSON, Charles Edward (Md) St Luke's Episcopal Church, 1101 Bay Ridge Ave, Annapolis, MD 21403

WILKERSON, Christopher T (FdL)

WILKES, Hugh E (Alb) 2717 2nd Ave, Watervliet, NY 12189

WILKES III, Joseph Warren (Mass) 186 Upham St, Melrose, MA 02176

WILKES, Nancy Schreiber (Tex)

WILKINS, Christopher Ian (WA) St Philips Episcopal Church, 13801 Baden Westwood Rd, Brandywine, MD 20613

WILKINS, Tamara Lee (Ala)

WILKINSON, Donald Charles (Mo) 17210 Fawn Cloud Ln, San Antonio, TX 78248

WILKINSON, Ernest Benjamin (NwT) 727 W Browning Ave, Pampa, TX 79065

WILKINSON, James Royse (Ky) 1804 Leawood Ct, Louisville, KY 40222

WILKINSON, Joyce (WTex)

WILKINSON, Kirsteen (Ind) 2824 S Pennsylvania St, Indianapolis, IN 46225

WILKINSON, Marcia Campbell (Ala) 6634 31st Pl NW, Washington, DC 20015

WILKINSON, Mark (Tex) 5373 Franz Rd, Katy, TX 77493

WILKINSON, Mary Suzanne (NwT) 727 W Browning Ave, Pampa, TX 79065

WILKINSON, Randy (WA) Church Of The Ascension, 205 S Summit Ave, Gaithersburg, MD 20877

WILKINSON, Shivaun Renee (WA) 3820 Aspen Hill Rd, Silver Spring, MD 20906

WILKINSON, Wendy (Tex) Good Sam TEC Ch, 848 Baker Rd, Virginia Beach, VA 23462

WILLARD V, John Dayton (SD) 11400 Rodophil Rd, Amelia Court House, VA 23002

WILLARD, Neil Alan (Tex) Palmer Memorial Church, 6221 Main St, Houston, TX 77030

WILLARD JR, Wilson Howard (SO) 1305 Cutter St, Cincinnati, OH 45203

WILLARD-WILLIFORD, Joy (CFla) 5625 Holy Trinity Dr, Melbourne, FL 32940

WILLCOX, Halley L (At) Wellness Ctr, 901 Preston Ave, Charlottesville, VA 22903

WILLE, Elizabeth Suzanne (Chi) 1559 Central Ave, Indianapolis, IN 46202

WILLEMS, James Rutherford (Los) 561 48th Street, Oakland, CA 94609

WILLERER, Rhonda (Fla) 475 Cloisterbane Dr, Saint Johns, FL 32259

WILLIAMS JR, A Lenwood (Miss) 9378 Harroway Rd, Summerville, SC 29485

WILLIAMS, Alfredo (Dal) 1516 N Leland Ave, Indianapolis, IN 46219

WILLIAMS, Alina Somodevilla (La) 4101 Sigma Rd, Dallas, TX 75244

WILLIAMS, Alton Paul (CPa) 5 Greenway Dr, Mechanicsburg, PA 17055

WILLIAMS, Anne Elizabeth (Ia) PO Box 33, Anamosa, IA 52205

WILLIAMS JR, Arthur (O) 25530 Edgecliff Dr, Euclid, OH 44132

WILLIAMS, Arthur Wordsworth Lonfellow (NY) 3412 103rd St, Corona, NY 11368

WILLIAMS, Barbara Farrar (SVa) P O Box 62184, Virginia Beach, VA 23466

WILLIAMS, Brandon E (Cal) 601 N Tejon St, Colorado Springs, CO 80903

WILLIAMS JR, Bud (Los) 1438 Coronado Ter, Los Angeles, CA 90026

WILLIAMS, Bunny Simon (Ga)

WILLIAMS, Carolynne Juanita Grant (At) 2088 Cloverdale Dr Se, Atlanta, GA 30316

WILLIAMS, Cecil David (Nwk) 515 Parker St, Newark, NJ 07104

WILLIAMS, Colin Harrington (CNY) 2850 SW Scenic Drive, Portland, OR 97225

WILLIAMS, Court (Chi) 3025 Walters Ave, Northbrook, IL 60062

WILLIAMS, David R (NC) 1406 Victoria Ct, Elon, NC 27244

WILLIAMS, Donald B (Kan) 2510 Grand Blvd Apt 1103, Kansas City, MO 64108

WILLIAMS, Douglas M (Colo) 28 Cunningham Pond Rd, Peterborough, NH 03458

WILLIAMS, Edward Earl (NY)

WILLIAMS, Elizabeth Ann (Los) 512 E Williams St, Barstow, CA 92311

WILLIAMS, Eric (Mich) 1948 Hunters Ridge Dr, Bloomfield Hills, MI 48304

WILLIAMS, Florence Darcy (Eas) Emmanuel Episcopal Church, PO Box 875, Chestertown, MD 21620

WILLIAMS, Francis Edward (RG) 1020 Sable Circle, Las Cruces, NM 88001

WILLIAMS, Glenn Thomas (ND) 3613 River Dr S, Fargo, ND 58104

WILLIAMS, Henrietta R (Ind) 115 Ne 66th St, Oak Island, NC 28465

WILLIAMS JR, Hollis (Oly) 725 9th Ave Apt 2007, Seattle, WA 98104

WILLIAMS, Howard (LI) 1102 E 73rd St Apt C, Brooklyn, NY 11234

WILLIAMS III, Hugh Elton (CFla) Po Box 91777, Lakeland, FL 33804

WILLIAMS, Ian (WNC)

WILLIAMS, Jacqueline Miller (SO) 6461 Tylersville Rd, West Chester, OH 45069

WILLIAMS II, James Edward (Los) 580 Hilgard Ave, Los Angeles, CA 90024

WILLIAMS, Jerome Tywan (RG)

WILLIAMS JR, Jerre Stockton (WTex) 372 Englewood Dr, Kerrville, TX 78028

WILLIAMS, Jeryln Ann (SD) 431 Sweden St, Caribou, ME 04736

WILLIAMS, Jill (Nwk)

WILLIAMS, Jill Barton (USC) 337 Nichols Branch Ln, Irmo, SC 29063

WILLIAMS, Joe Curtis (Okla) 3127 E 4th St, Tulsa, OK 74104

WILLIAMS II, John F (NY) 860 Wolcott Ave, Beacon, NY 12508

WILLIAMS, Jon Ryan (WMo)

WILLIAMS, Joseph David (NwT) 1105 1/2 Madison St, Borger, TX 79007

WILLIAMS, Josie Marie (Miss) 5930 Warriors Trl, Vicksburg, MS 39180

WILLIAMS, Julie (Az) 100 Arroyo Pinon Dr, Sedona, AZ 86336

WILLIAMS, Kay Ann (Ala)

WILLIAMS, Larry C (At) PO Box 1117, Hot Springs, AR 71902

WILLIAMS, Lloyd Clyde (Ind) 702 Dr Martin Luther King Jr St, Indianapolis, IN 46202

WILLIAMS, Lois Vander Wende (Cal) 455 Fair Oaks St., San Francisco, CA 94110

WILLIAMS, Lorna H (Pa) 50 Greenhill Ave, Dover, DE 19901

WILLIAMS, Margaret (Chi) 707 1st Ave, Sterling, IL 61081

WILLIAMS, Marge (Tex) 18319 Otter Creek Trl, Humble, TX 77346

WILLIAMS, Mary Grace (NY) 9 Chestnut St, Rhinebeck, NY 12572

WILLIAMS, Melody Sue (SO) 60 S Dorset Rd, Troy, OH 45373

WILLIAMS, Michael David (Colo)

WILLIAMS, Michael Robert (Ak) MNC-I Chaplain, Camp Victory, APO, AE 09342

WILLIAMS, Mildred (Alb) 2304 Deer Trl, Lampasas, TX 76550

WILLIAMS JR, Milton (NC) 1133 N La Salle Dr, Chicago, IL 60610

WILLIAMS, Mollie (Ind) 11335 Winding Wood Ct, Indianapolis, IN 46235

WILLIAMS, Pamela Mary (Neb) 1014 N 6th St, Seward, NE 68434

WILLIAMS, Patricia S. (Mo) 336 N Lorimier St, Cape Girardeau, MO 63701

WILLIAMS, Patrick J (NY) 1660 Madison Ave Apt 5a, New York, NY 10029

WILLIAMS, Paul Brazell (SO) 270 Blue Jacket Cir, Pickerington, OH 43147

WILLIAMS, Persis (Alb) Po Box 1662, Blue Hlll, ME 04614

WILLIAMS, Peter A (CNY) PO Box 170, 13 Court Street, Cortland, NY 13045

WILLIAMS, R Jane (Be) 1670 Lindberg St, Bethlehem, PA 18020

WILLIAMS, Rick (NC) PO Box 1852, Salisbury, NC 28145

WILLIAMS, Robert (Ore) 10450 SW 153rd Ave, Beaverton, OR 97007

WILLIAMS, Robert Harry (Oly) 1805 38th Ave, Seattle, WA 98122

WILLIAMS, Robert Lewis (Oly) 3300 Carpenter Rd SE, Electra 109, Lacey, WA 98503

WILLIAMS, R(obert) Samuel (NwPa) 22633 Phillips Dr, Pleasantville, PA 16341

WILLIAMS, Sandra Kaye (SD) 509 Jackson St, Belle Fourche, SD 57717

WILLIAMS, Sandy (Mass) 173 Georgetown Rd, Boxford, MA 01921

WILLIAMS, Scott Eugene (Miss) 1909 15th St, Gulfport, MS 39501

WILLIAMS, Sharon E (O) 2171 E 49th St, Cleveland, OH 44103

WILLIAMS, Sharon Vaughan (Tex)

WILLIAMS, Shawn McNown (LI) 22 Highland RD, Glen Cove, NY 11542

WILLIAMS, Shearon Sykes (Va) 2500 Cameron Mills Rd, Alexandria, VA 22302

WILLIAMS, Stephen Junior Cherrington (RG) PO Box 387, Stephentown, NY 12168

WILLIAMS, Stephen Lee (Los) 14252 Suffolk St, Westminster, CA 92683

WILLIAMS, Susan Anslow (Mich) 1948 Hunters Ridge Dr, Bloomfield Hills, MI 48304

WILLIAMS, Thomas (SwFla) 9404 Oak Meadow Ct, Tampa, FL 33647

WILLIAMS, Thomas Donald (CFla) 3015 Indian River Drive, Palm Bay, FL 32905

WILLIAMS, Wendy (SeFla) 400 Seabrook Rd, Tequesta, FL 33469

WILLIAMS, Wesley Danford (Ve) Dio de Venezuela, CD Av Caron No 100, Caracas, Venezuela

WILLIAMS JR, Wesley Samuel (Episcopal VI) 6501 Red Hook Plz Ste 201, St Thomas, VI 00802

WILLIAMS-BELT, Christine V (CNY)

WILLIAMS-DUNCAN, Stacy (Va) 372 El Camino Real, Atherton, CA 94027

WILLIAMS FANNING, Rhonda Artrea (Tex)

WILLIAMSON, Anne (NH) 101 Chapel St, Portsmouth, NH 03801

WILLIAMSON, Barbara (Mass) 210 Nahanton St Apt 107 Unit 107, Newton Center, MA 02459

WILLIAMSON, Emmanuel (Pa) 1101 2nd Street Pike, Southampton, PA 18966

WILLIAMSON JR, James Gray (SwFla) 8005 25th St E, Parrish, FL 34219

WILLIAMSON, Jeremiah D (Colo) Grace St Stephens Tec Ch, 601 N Tejon St, Colorado Springs, CO 80903

WILLIAMSON, Randolph Lewis (Pa) 343 Michigan Ave, Swarthmore, PA 19081

WILLIAMSON, Rebecca Ann (Az) 1735 S College Ave, Tempe, AZ 85281

WILLIARD, Julie S (At)

WILLIS, Anisa Cottrell (Lex) St Pauls Episcopal Church, 7 Court Pl, Newport, KY 41071

WILLIS, Barbara Creighton (Va) 1905 Wildflower Ter, Richmond, VA 23238

WILLIS JR, Dick (SwVa) 501 Woods Ave SW, Roanoke, VA 24016

WILLIS JR, Frederick Webber (SVa) 5119 Blake Point Rd, Chincoteague Island, VA 23336

WILLIS, Laurie Joy (Chi) 1050 Borregas Ave SPC 103, Sunnyvale, CA 94089

WILLIS, Nancy Appleby (RI) 86 Dendron Rd, Wakefield, RI 02879

WILLIS JR, Robert Eugene (Okla)

WILLIS, Ron W. (Cal) 631 Ofarrell St Apt 714, San Francisco, CA 94109

WILLIS, Ryan Lee (Kan)

WILLISTON, Ashton K (Ga) 6329 Frederica Rd, Saint Simons Island, GA 31522

WILLMANN JR, Robert Everett (SO) 155 N 6th St, Zanesville, OH 43701

WILLMS, Ann (Va) P.O. Box 426, Ivy, VA 22945

WILLOUGHBY III, William (Ga) The Ibert, 224 E 34th St, Savannah, GA 31401

WILLOW, Mary Margaret Gregory (SwFla) 127 Gesner St, Linden, NJ 07036

WILLS JR, Edwin Francis (Ark) 515 Booker St, Little Rock, AR 72205

WILLS, Robert Murlin (Mich) 1506 Eagle Crest Dr, Prescott, AZ 86301

WILMER, Amelie (Va) 6309 Ridgeway Rd, Richmond, VA 23226

WILMINGTON, Richard Newton (Cal) 2 Columbia Dr, Rancho Mirage, CA 92270

WILMOT, Susan Elizabeth (Az) 975 E Warner Rd, Tempe, AZ 85284

WILMOTH, Danny Stewart (Va) 3440 S Jefferson St, Falls Church, VA 22041

WILS, Duane Michael (NMich) 6971 Days River 24.5 Rd, Gladstone, MI 49837

WILSON, Adwoa (Mass)

WILSON, Anne (SO) 7730 Tecumseh Trl, Cincinnati, OH 45243

WILSON, Barbara Anne (Chi) 9713 Oakview Dr, Portage, MI 49024

WILSON, Barrie Andrew (CFla)

WILSON JR, Charles (SO) 77 Sherman Ave, Columbus, OH 43205

WILSON, Charleston D (SwFla) 222 S Palm Ave, Sarasota, FL 34236

WILSON, Clinton M (Ky) 4715 Harding Pike, Nashville, TN 37205

WILSON, Conrad Bruce (WTex) 10 Tanglewood St, San Marcos, TX 78666

WILSON, Dana Jane Gant (Tex) 124 Oakmont Dr, Weatherford, TX 76088

WILSON, Dianne Louise (WMass)

WILSON, Donald Rexford (Ore) 7065 S.W. Molalla Bend Rd., Wilsonville, OR 97070

WILSON, Donald Robert (Mass) 76 Old Pine Hill Rd N, Berwick, ME 03901

WILSON, Edward Adrian (ECR) 90 Cashew Blossom Drive, San Jose, CA 95123

WILSON, Eugenia Theresa (NY) 5030 Henry Hudson Pkwy E, Bronx, NY 10471

WILSON JR, Frank E (Minn) 16376 7th Street Lane S, Lakeland, MN 55043

WILSON, Frank F(enn) (At) 803 Wilkins Dr, Monroe, GA 30655

WILSON, George Steil (Oly) 3607 214th St SW, Brier, WA 98036

WILSON, Gregory Maclean (NJ) 208 Jackdaw Aly, Media, PA 19063

WILSON, Harold David (CFla) 1629 Championship Blvd, Franklin, TN 37064

WILSON, James Barrett (Ky) 7619 Beech Spring Ct, Louisville, KY 40241

WILSON, James G (Ct) 54 Harbour View Place, Stratford, CT 06615

WILSON II, James Nyebe (NJ) 114 W Bayview Ave, Pleasantville, NJ 08232

WILSON, Janey (USC) 144 Caldwell St, Rock Hill, SC 29730

WILSON, Jennifer Mccormick (SeFla)

WILSON, Kate (ECR) 611 Dellingham Dr Apt A, Indianapolis, IN 46260

WILSON, Kellie C (USC) 10 N Church St, Greenville, SC 29601

WILSON, Kenneth Wayne (CNY) 7863 Russell Ln, Manlius, NY 13104

WILSON, Linda (RG) 109 Chaparral Loop, Socorro, NM 87801

WILSON, Linda Tardy (Pgh) Na, Pittsburgh, PA 15213

WILSON, Mary Elizabeth (Tex) 717 Sage Road, Houston, TX 77056

WILSON, Mauricio Jose (Cal) 114 Montecito Ave, Oakland, CA 94610

WILSON, Mike (SwFla) 5108 Plainfield St, Midland, MI 48642

WILSON III, Morris Karl (Tenn) 3002 Westmoreland Dr, Nashville, TN 37212

WILSON, Nathan Patrick (Ga)

WILSON, Norbert Lance Weston (Ala) 136 E Magnolia Ave, Auburn, AL 36830

WILSON, Phillip (Nwk) 36 South St, Morristown, NJ 07960

WILSON, Ray E (Tex) PO Box 1943, Lenox, MA 01240

WILSON, Raymond G (LI) 165 Pine St, Freeport, NY 11520

WILSON, Richard (Az)

WILSON, Richard Lawrence (SwFla)

WILSON, Robert Arthur (Vt) PO Box 244, Newport, VT 05855

WILSON, Roy Dennis (Miss) 1954 Spillway Rd, Brandon, MS 39047

WILSON, Sandra Antoinette (Nwk) 116 Turrell Ave, South Orange, NJ 07079

WILSON, Stefanie G (Los) Campbell Hall School, 4533 Laurel Canyon Blvd, North Hollywood, CA 91607

WILSON, Stephen (Colo) 1000 E 16th Ave Ste 210, Denver, CO 80218

WILSON, Thomas (SanD) 339 Brightwood Ave, Chula Vista, CA 91910

WILSON, Tom (EC) 101 Bear Track Ln, Kitty Hawk, NC 27949

WILSON, Tom (SC) 1853 Grovehurst Dr, Charleston, SC 29414

WILSON, William Henry (Ala) 800 Lake Colony Cir, Birmingham, AL 35242

WILSON-BARNARD, Letha (Minn) 2753 41st Ave S, Minneapolis, MN 55406

WILT, David (SeFla) 415 Duval St, Key West, FL 33040

WILTFONG, Michele (WNC)

WILTON, Glenn Warner Paul (Oly) 10 Lichfield Avenue, CANTERBURY, CT1 3YA, Great Britain (UK)

WILTSEE JR, Lamont (ECR) 138 White Oaks Ln, Carmel Valley, CA 93924

✠ **WIMBERLY**, Don Adger (Tex) 3515 Plumb St, Houston, TX 77005

WIMBUSH, Claire S (SVa) 1333 Jamestown Rd, Williamsburg, VA 23185

WIMMER, Lisa Jan (CFla) PO Box 2373, Belleview, FL 34421

WINBORN JR, James Henderson (SVa) 8880 Colonnades Ct W Apt 412, Bonita Springs, FL 34135

WINCHELL, Ron (Mil) 128 Eagle Ct, Locust Grove, VA 22508

WINDEL, Marian Kathleen (Va) 5783 Orkney Grade, Mount Jackson, VA 22842

WINDOM, Barbara Sewell (At) 432 Forest Hill Rd, Macon, GA 31210

WINDSOR, Janice Priebe (Colo) 33741 State Highway 257, Windsor, CO 80550

WINDSOR, Robert Grover (Mass) 34 Exeter St, West Newton, MA 02465

WINDSOR, Walter Van Zandt (Miss) PO Box 2164, Woodville, MS 39669

WINELAND, Richard Kevin (NI) 5484 Village Way, Nashville, TN 37211

WINGER, Nordon W (Az) 1721 Chelsea Way, Roseville, CA 95661

WINGERT, Anita LaVonne (Me) 550 N Ravine St, Sault Sainte Marie, MI 49783

WINGFIELD, Vest Garrett (Tex) PO Box 540742, Houston, TX 77254

WINGO, Pat (ETenn) 345 Homestead Dr, Cropwell, AL 35054

WINGO, Sara-Scott Nelson (Ala) 800 S Northshore Dr, Knoxville, TN 37919

WINKLER, Anne Louise (Ind) 7300 Lantern Rd, Indianapolis, IN 46256

WINKLER JR, Richard Edward (The Episcopal Church in Haw) 202 Pin Oak Dr, Harker Heights, TX 76548

WINKLER, Thomas Earl (Minn) 39259 K-C Dr, Winona, MN 55987

WINKLER JR, William Edward (NY)

WINN, John Barrington (Oly) Po Box 1961, Silverdale, WA 98383

WINN, Mary Margaret (Va)

WINNER, Lauren Frances (NC) 1737 Hillandale Rd, Durham, NC 27705

WINSETT, Steve (Chi) 2514 Bradley Ave, Louisville, KY 40217

WINSLETT JR, Hoyt (Ala) 1224 - 37th Avenue East, Tuscaloosa, AL 35404

WINSLOW, Gail George (NwPa) Church of the Ascension, 26 Chautauqua Pl, Bradford, PA 16701

WINSLOW JR, K Dennis (NY) PO Box 93, Rensselaerville, NY 12147

WINSOR, Michael Michael (NY) 7602 Woodthrush Drive, Dallas, TX 75230

WINSTON, William (Tex) 3313 Minot Ave, Fort Worth, TX 76133

WINTER, Brian William (Colo) 12408 Prospect Ave. NE, Albuquerque, NM 87112

WINTER, Cheryl (WVa) PO Box 424, Hurricane, WV 25526

WINTER, James L (Miss) 684 White Oak Ln, Starkville, MS 39759

WINTER, Laren Royce (RG) Po Box 2963, Ruidoso, NM 88355

WINTER CHASER, Vivian Janice (Az) 725 S. Beck Ave, Tempe, AZ 85281

WINTERROWD, William Jerry (Colo)

WINTERS, Richard (Ind) 5502 Washington Blvd, Indianapolis, IN 46220

WINTERS, William Michael (Ala) PO Box 116, Guntersville, AL 35976

WINTON, Keith (Neb) 9302 Blondo St, Omaha, NE 68134

WINTON, Paul Steve (NC) Saint John's Episcopal Church, 1623 Carmel Rd, Charlotte, NC 28226

WINWARD, Mark Scott (SwFla) 4354 Redwood Rd, Fort Meade, MD 20755

WIRENIUS, John Francis (NY)

WIRES, John William (At) 4900 English Dr, Annandale, VA 22003

WIRT, Linda (Los) 4 Sobrante, Aliso Viejo, CA 92656

WIRTH, Bradley S (Mont) All Saints' Church, PO Box 1923, Whitefish, MT 59937

WISCHMEYER, Kara (Tex) 226 Chuck Wagon Rd, Lubbock, TX 79404

WISE, C Matthew William (WTex) 315 E Pecan St, San Antonio, TX 78205

WISE JR, Eugene Field (Tenn) Po Box 261, Murfreesboro, TN 37133

WISE, John K (NwPa)

WISE, Leah Caitlin (Va)

WISELEY, Jerry Lee (SC) 1746 Summit Rd, Hot Springs, SD 57747

WISEMAN, Grant Buchanan (SeFla) 1830 NW 36th St, Oakland Park, FL 33309

WISEMAN, Heather Buchanan (SO) 2489 Walnutview Ct, Cincinnati, OH 45230

WISEMAN, Philip M (SO) 2489 Walnutview Ct, Cincinnati, OH 45230

WISKUS, Richard Joseph (Mo) 1151 W Columbia St, Farmington, MO 63640

WISMER, Robert (Tex) 11310 Meadow Lake Dr, Houston, TX 77077

WISNER, Stephen Forster (NJ) 304 Woodmere Ave, Neptune, NJ 07753

WISNEWSKI JR, Robert Carew (Ala) 113 Madison Ave, Montgomery, AL 36104

WISNIEWSKI, Richard Joseph (NJ) The Church Of St Mark And All Saints, 429 South Pitney Road, Galloway, NJ 08205

WISSLER, Kenneth John (Pa) 201 W Evergreen Ave Apt 904, Philadelphia, PA 19118

WISZ, Katherine (NC)

WITCHGER, Anne Marie (NY) 1085 5th Ave, New York, NY 10128

WITH, Jan Louise (Neb) St Marys Episcopal Church, 212 Clark St, Bassett, NE 68714

WITHROCK JR, John William (CGC) 401 W College St, Troy, AL 36081

WITKE, E(Dward) Charles (Mich) 3000 Glazier Way, Ann Arbor, MI 48105

WITT, Anne Lane (Va) PO Box 1059, Kilmarnock, VA 22482

WITT, Bonnie Rae (WNY) Po Box 66, Gasport, NY 14067

WITT JR, Richard Cyril (NY) 16 Lawrence Rd, Accord, NY 12404

WITT JR, Robert Edward (Alb) 26400 George Zeiger Dr Apt 109, Beachwood, OH 44122

WITTIG, Nancy Constantine Hatch (Pa) 21801 Elizabeth Ave, Fairview Park, OH 44126

WITTMAYER, Kevin Edward (Tex) 906 Padon St, Longview, TX 75601

WIZOREK, Julie C (Md) 249 Double Oak Rd N, Prince Frederick, MD 20678

WLOSINSKI, Stephen Stanley (Minn) 1121 W Morgan St, Duluth, MN 55811

WODEHOUSE, Priscilla Davis (WNC)

WOEHLER, Charles (WTex) 1416 North Loop 1604 East, San Antonio, TX 78232

WOESSNER, David H (WMass)

WOGGON, Karla Marie (WNC) 1048 15th Ave NW, Hickory, NC 28601

WOHLERS, Lee Ferry (Vt) 7297 Vt Route 14, Hardwick, VT 05843

WOHLEVER, Russell J (CFla) All Saints Church, 338 E Lyman Ave, Winter Park, FL 32789

WOJCIEHOWSKI, Arthur Anthony (Minn) 1500 Prospect Ave, Cloquet, MN 55720

WOLCOTT, Sarah Elizabeth (Neb) 512 N Oak St, Gordon, NE 69343

WOLF, David B (WA) 1516 Hamilton St NW, Washington, DC 20011

✠ **WOLF**, Gerry (RI) 275 N Main St, Providence, RI 02903

WOLF, Max (Mass) 20 Olive Ave, Rehoboth Beach, DE 19971

WOLFE, Alexander (ND) Po Box 8340, Fargo, ND 58109

WOLFE, Ari (Cal)

✠ **WOLFE**, Dean (NY) 835 SW Polk St, Topeka, KS 66612

WOLFE, Dorothy Annabell (Neb) 603 3rd Ave, Bayard, NE 69334

WOLFE, Vernon Eugene (Oly) 53565 W Ferndale Rd, Milton Freewater, OR 97862

WOLFENBARGER, Mary Suzanne (WLa) 55 Magnolia Dr, Belleville, IL 62221

WOLFF, Edda Stephanie (Eur)

WOLFF, William George (Kan) 4524 77th St, Urbandale, IA 50322

WOLFORD, Rachael Rossiter (Oly) PO Box 522, Cathlamet, WA 98612

WOLLARD, Robert Foster (Mich) 4505 Westlawn Pkwy, Waterford, MI 48328

WOLSONCROFT III, Arthur Mathew (NY) 414 E 52nd St, New York, NY 10022

WOLTER, Jack M (WNY) 668 Shadow Mountain Dr, Prescott, AZ 86301

WOLTERSTORFF, Claire Kingma (WMich) 58 Sunnybrook Ave Se, Grand Rapids, MI 49506

WOLTZ, Charles Morris (Okla) 924 N Robinson Ave, Oklahoma City, OK 73102

WOLYNIAK, Joseph Geoffrey (Colo) 1151 Walton Rd, Blue Bell, PA 19422

WOMACK, Debbie Jaye (NwT)

WOMACK, Lawrence (LI) 8725 Sedgeburn Dr, Charlotte, NC 28278

WOMELSDORF, Charles Stowers (CGC) 327 Honeysuckle Hill, Tallassee, AL 36078

WON, Hogil Hilary (Nwk) 403 79th St, North Bergen, NJ 07047

WONDRA, Ellen K (Chi) 1354 Oak View Cir Apt 126, Rohnert Park, CA 94928

WONG, Diane (Mass) 5b Park Ter, Arlington, MA 02474

WONG, George C (The Episcopal Church in Haw) 8992 Kula Hwy, Kula, HI 96790

WONG, Gloria Violet Lee (Mass) Po Box 825, Oak Bluffs, MA 02557

WONG, Peter Reginald (La) 1733 Cloverdale Ave, Baton Rouge, LA 70808

WONG, Philip (Oly) 62 Pine St, Rockville Centre, NY 11570

WONG, Sally (ECR)

WOO, Raymond A (The Episcopal Church in Haw) 45 N Judd St, Honolulu, HI 96817

WOOD, Ann Patricia (WMass) 13 Kelleher Dr, South Deerfield, MA 01373

WOOD, Camille Carpenter (La) 3552 Morning Glory Ave, Baton Rouge, LA 70808

WOOD, Christian Michael (SwFla) 4111 W Barcelona St, Tampa, FL 33629

WOOD, Colette (NC) 16 Highland Ave, Cohasset, MA 02025

WOOD, Grace Marie (EC) 198 Dogwood Trl, Elizabeth City, NC 27909

WOOD, Gretchen A (SO) 24 High Ridge Loop Apt 605, Pawleys Island, SC 29585

WOOD, Henry Palmer (CFla) 720 S Lakeshore Blvd, Lake Wales, FL 33853

WOOD, Howard Fitler (Pa) 526 Washington Ave, Hulmeville, PA 19047

WOOD, Hunter (Va) 250 Pantops Mountain Rd, 5126, Charlottesville, VA 22911

WOOD, Jan (O) Grace Episcopal Church, 315 Wayne St, Sandusky, OH 44870

WOOD, Joseph A (Md) 4202 E Fowler Ave Stop Fao226, Tampa, FL 33620

WOOD, Kathrine Ringold (Ore) 437 Franklin St, Denver, CO 80218

WOOD, Linda (Cal) 3080 Birdsall Ave, Oakland, CA 94619

WOOD, Mark Raymond (Ct) 89 Eddy St, Providence, RI 02903

WOOD, Michael J (WMich)

WOOD, Nancy Currey (SVa) 1524 Southwick Rd, Virginia Beach, VA 23451

WOOD, Nikky (Cal)

WOOD, Priscilla Peacock (Mass) 302 Linden Ponds Way Unit 512, Hingham, MA 02043

✠ **WOOD JR**, R aymond Stewart (Mich) Kendal 157, 80 Lyme Rd, Hanover, NH 03755

WOOD, Robert (WNC) PO Box 222, Cashiers, NC 28717

WOOD, Robert Earl (WMo) 1009 W 57th St, Kansas City, MO 64113

WOOD, Rodgers Taylor (WVa) 1223 Stanford Ct, Coraopolis, PA 15108

WOOD, Roger Lee (EMich) 106 S Kennefic St, Yale, MI 48097

WOOD, Sammy L (Tenn) 30 Brimmer St, Boston, MA 02108

WOOD, Sarah Anne (Va) 86 Fourth Ave., New York, NY 10003

WOOD, Stuart Clary (Va) 7120 Ore Bank Rd, Port Republic, VA 24471

WOOD III, William Hoge (Pa) 251 Montgomery Ave Unit 9, Haverford, PA 19041

WOOD, William James (Kan) 30 Spofford Lane, Trevett, ME 04571

WOOD JR, William R (WVa) 107 Elma Dr, Williamstown, WV 26187

WOODALL, Carolyn Louise (Episcopal SJ) Episcopal Church of St. Anne, 1020 W Lincoln Rd, Stockton, CA 95207

WOODALL JR, Percy J (At) 3663 SE Cambridge Drive, Stuart, FL 34997

WOODARD, Sarah Wilson (NC) 400 Moline St., Durham, NC 27707

WOODBERRY, Robin Rae (O) 427 Gypsy Ln., Youngstown, OH 44504

WOODBURY, Robert Lane (Mil) 5558 N Berkeley Blvd, Whitefish Bay, WI 53217

WOODCOCK, Bruce W (SeFla) 108 Castle Heights Ave, Nyack, NY 10960

WOODEN, Lorentho (SO) 550 E 4th St, Cincinnati, OH 45202

WOODFIN, Joseph Robert (Fla) 801 Atlantic Ave, Fernandina Beach, FL 32034

WOODHAM, Lorna Althea (Nwk)

WOODHOUSE, Michelle M (Los) 4125 Creciente Dr, Santa Barbara, CA 93110

WOOD-HULL, L D (Chi) PO Box 173, Western Springs, IL 60558

WOODLEY, Claire (LI) 2 Glendale Rd, Ossining, NY 10562

WOODLIEF, Vern Andrews (Az) 1069 N Paseo Iris, Green Valley, AZ 85614

WOODLIFF III, George (Miss) 712 S Montgomery St, Starkville, MS 39759

WOODLIFF, Kirk Alan (Nev) 2125 Stone View Dr, Sparks, NV 89436

✠ **WOODLIFF-STANLEY**, Ruth M (SC) 1945 Ivanhoe St, Denver, CO 80220

WOODLING, Edith (At) 25 Battle Ridge Pl, Atlanta, GA 30342

WOODROOFE III, Robert (Ct) 42 Christian Street, New Preston, CT 06777

WOODRUFF, Jennifer Lynn (Lex) 302 Jackson St, Berea, KY 40403

WOODRUFF, Karen (Va) Po Box 367, Lively, VA 22507

WOODRUM, Donald Lee (Fla) Po Box 1238, Live Oak, FL 32064

WOODS, Blake (Okla) 5635 E 71st St, Tulsa, OK 74136

WOODS, Cynthia (The Episcopal NCal)

WOODS, Harold Dean (Vt) 233 South Street, South Hero, VT 05486

WOODS JR, J (Mass) 62 Las Casas St, Malden, MA 02148

WOODS, Joshua Wayne (WTex) 1300 Wiltshire Ave, San Antonio, TX 78209

WOODS, Michael Timothy (WTex) 178 Brooks Ranch Dr, Kyle, TX 78640

WOODS, Robert Douglas (Episcopal SJ) PO Box 1837, Kernville, CA 93238

WOODS, Stephen I (NY) Above, Above, NM 87507

WOODSON, Elizabeth D (Tex)

WOODSUM, Mark (Me) 2808 Lakemont Dr, Fallbrook, CA 92028

WOODWARD JR, Brinton Webb (NH) RR3 Box 18, Plymouth, NH 03264

WOODWARD, Deborah Marshall (Mass) 1080 Hillside St, Milton, MA 02186

WOODWARD III, George Frederick (Los) 1294 Westlyn Pl, Pasadena, CA 91104

WOODWARD, Matthew Thomas (The Episcopal NCal) 1328 27th St, Sacramento, CA 95816

WOODWARD, Thomas Bullene (RG) 13 Calle Loma, Santa Fe, NM 87507

WOODWORTH, Laura T(Ufts) (NMich) 2500 South Hill Road, Gladstone, MI 49837

WOODWORTH, Nanette L (EC) 114 Breezewood Dr Apt G, Greenville, NC 27858

WOODWORTH-HILL, Nancy (WVa) 17 Lynwood Ave, Wheeling, WV 26003

WOODY, Robert (WTex) 13638 Liberty Oak St, San Antonio, TX 78232

WOOFENDEN, Anna (WMass)

WOOLERY-PRICE, Edward Raymond (Tex) All Saints' Episcopal Church, 209 W 27th St, Austin, TX 78705

WOOLIVER, Tammy (Okla) 264 Woodbriar, Noble, OK 73068

WOOLLEN, Nancy Sewell (Ind)

WOOLLETT JR, Donald M (WLa)

WOOLLEY JR, Stan (WMass) 868 Butler Dr, Livingston, SC 29107

WOOLLEY, Steven Eugene (Spok) 1803 Crestline Dr, Walla Walla, WA 99362

WOOLSEY, Deborah J (SO) St Paul's Episcopal Church, 33 W Dixon Ave, Dayton, OH 45419

WOOMER JR, Harold Gerard (Nev)

WOOTEN, David (Episcopal SJ)

WOOTTEN, Jo Ann H (Ark) 346 Rock Spring Rd, Wake Forest, NC 27587

WOOTTEN III, Mid L (Ark) 379 Springmoor Dr, Raleigh, NC 27615

WORTH, Elsa H (NH) St James Church, 44 West St, Keene, NH 03431

WORTHINGTON, Cynthia Muirhead (RG) 6043 Royal Crk, San Antonio, TX 78239

WORTHINGTON JR, Daniel Owen (Va) P O Box 83, Gloucester, VA 23061

WORTHINGTON, Douglas (Ct)

WORTHINGTON, William Ray (Ga) 207 Hermitage Way, Saint Simons Island, GA 31522

WORTHLEY, Christopher Thomas (WA) 2114 De La Vina St Unit 1, Santa Barbara, CA 93105

WOS, Edward John (ND)

WRAMPELMEIER, Christopher Kent (NwT) 2602 Parker St, Amarillo, TX 79109

WRATHALL, Susan L (RI) 70 Moore St, Warwick, RI 02889

WRATTEN, Ken (ECR) 8640 Solera Dr, San Jose, CA 95135

WREDE, Anne McRae (NJ) 544 King St, Woodbury, NJ 08096

WREDE, Richard (NJ) 500 Fourth St, Riverton, NJ 08077

WREN, Dane Clark (CFla) 302 Bent Way Ln, 700 Rinehart Rd, Lake Mary, FL 32746

WREN, Katherine A (Ark)

WRIDER, Anne Johnson (SO) 5455 N Sheridan Rd Apt 3912, Chicago, IL 60640

WRIGHT, Allan McLean (WMass) Po Box 3504, Annapolis, MD 21403

WRIGHT, Andrew Ray (Nwk) 3401 Bellaire Dr S, Fort Worth, TX 76109

WRIGHT, Angus Dale (NMich) PO Box 302, Manistique, MI 49854

WRIGHT, Anne Coghill (Md) 20370 Marguritte Sq, Sterling, VA 20165

WRIGHT, Benjamin R (RG) 363 Park St, Beaver, PA 15009

WRIGHT, Bill (NwT) 3549 Clearview Dr, San Angelo, TX 76904

WRIGHT, Brian Theodore (Oly) 10875 176th Cir NE Apt 1815, Redmond, WA 98052

◄ **WRIGHT**, Carl W (Md) Apo Ae 0962, PSC2 Box 9808, Ramstein, Germany

WRIGHT, Catherine Louise (Tex) 1012 Banyon St, Austin, TX 78757

WRIGHT, Diana Lee (Ia)

WRIGHT, Elizabeth Louise (RI) 10 Eustis Ave, Newport, RI 02840

WRIGHT, Elton Stanley (Colo) 342 Old Cahaba Trl, Helena, AL 35080

WRIGHT, Eugene Nat (WA) 205 S Summit Ave, Gaithersburg, MD 20877

WRIGHT, Gwynne (Chi) 43 Rawcliffe Croft, York, YO305US, Great Britain (UK)

WRIGHT, Hollis (Colo) 6402w Hillcrest Dr, Manistique, MI 49854

WRIGHT, James D (Fla) 3231 Nw 47th Pl, Gainesville, FL 32605

WRIGHT, James O. Pete (Los) 1505 Monticello Ct., Redlands, CA 92373

WRIGHT, Janice Bracken (At) 7 Creek Side Way SW, Rome, GA 30165

WRIGHT, Jean Ann Frances (At) 5228 Stone Village Cir Nw, Kennesaw, GA 30152

WRIGHT, Jo (Okla) 2184 Rosewood Ln N, Roseville, MN 55113

WRIGHT, John Hamil Spedden (Del) 54 Ridge Ave, Edgewater, MD 21037

WRIGHT, Jonathan Michael (SC) 1295 Abercorn Trce, Mount Pleasant, SC 29466

WRIGHT, Korey J (Tex)

WRIGHT, Lonell (La) 7696 Stevenson Way, San Diego, CA 92120

WRIGHT, Mark R (Dal) 2019 Highland Forest Dr, Highland Village, TX 75077

WRIGHT III, Martin Luther (Pgh) 1249 Main Street, PO Box 175, Shanksville, PA 15560

WRIGHT, Matthew L (NY) St Gregorys Episcopal Church, PO Box 66, Woodstock, NY 12498

WRIGHT, Michael Alfred (Oly) 1428 22nd Ave, Longview, WA 98632

WRIGHT, Milton King (Minn) 707 Saint Olaf Ave, Northfield, MN 55057

WRIGHT, Rick Lynn (At)

✠ **WRIGHT**, Robert Christopher (At) 306 Peyton Rd SW, Atlanta, GA 30311

WRIGHT, Ross (SVa) 4203 Springhill Ave, Richmond, VA 23225

WRIGHT, Ryan A (SwFla) St Marys, 9801 Bonita Beach Rd SE, Bonita Springs, FL 34135

WRIGHT, Scot R (Oly) 650 Bellevue Way NE Unit 2401, Bellevue, WA 98004

WRIGHT, Stanalee (Spok)

WRIGHT, Stuart Wayne (Md) 4 E University Pkwy, Baltimore, MD 21218

✠ **WRIGHT**, Wayne (Del) 1841 North St, Philadelphia, PA 19130

WRIGHT, William J (Alb) 14 Monument St, Deposit, NY 13754

WRIGHT, Winston (SeFla) 1466 39th St, West Palm Beach, FL 33407

WRIGHT-NAVA, C Susanne (Los)

WRIGHT-PRUSKI, Dorota (Va) St Andrew Church, 4000 Lorcom Ln, Arlington, VA 22207

WU, Chia-Kuei (Tai)

WU, Hsing-Hsiang (Tai) 499 Sec 4 Danjin Rd, Tamsui Dist, New Taipei City, 25135, Taiwan

WU, Ming-Lung (Tai) No 1-6 Mingxin St, Hualien City, 97050, Taiwan

WU, Peter (The Episcopal Church in Haw) 229 Queen Emma Sq, Honolulu, HI 96813

WURM, Laurie J (Nwk)

WYATT, Andrea Castner (Ct) 133 School St, New Bedford, MA 02740

WYATT, Benjamin Keith (Ind)

WYATT II, Robert Odell (Chi) 110 S Marion St Unit 307, Oak Park, IL 60302

WYCKOFF, Mike (Tex) 2857 Grimes Ranch Rd, Austin, TX 78732

WYER, George William (Va) Po Box 638, Ivy, VA 22945

WYLAND, Richard Rees (Roch) 41 Great Oak Ln, Redding, CT 06896

WYLD, Kevin Andrew (CFla) 3440 N Goldenrod Rd Apt 1016, Winter Park, FL 32792

WYLIE, Craig Robert (SwVa) 170 Crestview Dr, Abingdon, VA 24210

WYLY JR, David F (EC)

WYMAN, Deborah Little (Mass) 986 Memorial Dr, Cambridge, MA 02138

WYMER, Seth Thomas (SO) 5101 Johnstown Rd, New Albany, OH 43054

WYNDER JR, Charles Allen (WA)

WYNDHAM, Beth (WTex) St Thomas Episcopal Church, 1416 N Loop 1604 E, San Antonio, TX 78232

WYNEN, Nancy (Oly) 1399 Sw 17th St, Boca Raton, FL 33486

WYNN, James E (Pa) 520 S 61st St, Philadelphia, PA 19143

WYNN, Ronald Lloyd (Ore) 355 Stadium Dr S, Monmouth, OR 97361

WYPER, Susan (Ct) Saint Lukes Parish, 1864 Post Rd, Darien, CT 06820

WYSOCK, Christine Phillips (Spok) 535 Shelokum Dr, Silverton, OR 97381

WYSONG, Terry (Ct) PO Box 606, Marion, CT 06444

X

XIE, Paul Songling (LI) 13532 38th Ave, Flushing, NY 11354

Y

YABROFF, Martin Irving (Oly) 172 View Cir, Felton, CA 95018

YAGEL, William Westwood (SwVa)

YAGERMAN, Steve (NY) 234 E 60th St, New York, NY 10022

YAGER-WIGGAN, Bonnie-Marie C (Pgh)

YAK, Atem (Mass)

YAKUBU-MADUS, Fatima Emitsela (Ind) 1100 W 42nd St, Indianapolis, IN 46208

YALE, Richard Barrington (The Episcopal NCal) 4 Quista Dr, Chico, CA 95926

YAMAMOTO, Keith Akio (Los) 330 E 16th St, Upland, CA 91784

YANCEY, David Warren (Tenn) 1390 Jones Creek Rd, Dickson, TN 37055

YANCEY, Nancy (At) 5480 Clinchfield Trl, Norcross, GA 30092

YANCEY, Preston G (Tex)

YANCY, Stephanie Pauline (NC) 5606 Carey Pl, Durham, NC 27712

YANDELL, George Shaw (At) Church of the Holy Family, 202 Griffith Rd, Jasper, GA 30143

YANNI, Timothy J (Az) 3133 E Beryl Ave, Phoenix, AZ 85028

YARBOROUGH, Buzz (WTex) 121 Peppertree Crossing Ave, Brunswick, GA 31525

YARBOROUGH, Clare Mcjimsey (Az) 5671 E Copper St, Tucson, AZ 85712

YARBROUGH, C Denise (Roch) St. Mark's Episcopal Church, 179 Main St., Penn Yan, NY 14527

YARBROUGH, Douglas (Ida) 346 E Alexis Loop, Nampa, ID 83686

YARBROUGH, Oliver Larry (Ala) 24 Oak Dr, Middlebury, VT 05753

YARBROUGH, Rebecca Ricketts (NC) PO Box 970, Davidson, NC 28036

YARSIAH, James (NJ) 1324 Marvin Ave, Charleston, SC 29407

YATES, Adam (Ct) 205-1880 57th Ave W, Vancouver, BC V6P 1T7, Canada

YATES, Christopher Garrett (Pgh) 1066 Washington Rd, Mt Lebanon, PA 15228

YATES, Robert Gordon (SwFla) 37505 Moore Dr, Dade City, FL 33525

YATES, William J (CFla) 3400 Wingmann Rd., Avon Park, FL 33825

YAW, Chris (Mich) St David's Episcopal Church, 16200 W 12 Mile Rd, Southfield, MI 48076

YAW, David Dixon (Ak) 3195 Jackson Heights St, Ketchikan, AK 99901

YAWN, Justin (Fla) 613 Treehouse Cir, St Augustine, FL 32095

YAZELL, William James (WLa)

YEAGER, Alice Elizabeth (ND) 301 Main St S, Minot, ND 58701

YEAGER, Linda (WMo) 11701 Wedd St Apt 9, Overland Park, KS 66210

YEAGER, Robert Timothy (Chi) 924 Lake Street, Oak Park, IL 60301

YEARWOOD, Kirtley (Oly) Holy Cross Health, 1500 Forest Glen Rd, Silver Spring, MD 20910

YEATES, Judith Ann (Neb) 6615 N 162nd St, Omaha, NE 68116

YEPES LOPEZ, Alvaro Nelson (DomRep) Iglesia Episcopal Dominicana, Calle Santiago No 114, Santo Domingo, 764, Dominican Republic

YERKES, Kenneth Bickford (Mo) 1 Macarthur Blvd Apt S503, Haddon Township, NJ 08108

YESKO, Francis Michael (Pgh) Tec Dio Of Pittsburgh, 4099 William Penn Hwy 502, Monroeville, PA 15146

YETTER, Joan (Mont) 932 Avenue F, Billings, MT 59102

YODER, Christopher (Okla)

YODER, John Henry (Nev) 1006 33rd St Apt 15w, Vero Beach, FL 32960

YOE, Sara (Md)

YONKERS, Michael Allan (Chi) 920 S Aldine Ave, Park Ridge, IL 60068

YOO, Sung W (Tex)

YOON, Paul Hwan (Los) Box 22, Taejon, 300, Korea (South)

YOON, Young (Nwk) 818 Park Ave, River Edge, NJ 07661

YORK, Susan Spence (WMich) 2490 Basswood St, Jenison, MI 49428

YORK-SIMMONS, Noelle M (Va) 118 N Washington St, Alexandria, VA 22314

YOSHIDA, Thomas Kunio (The Episcopal Church in Haw) 1410 Makiki St, Honolulu, HI 96814

YOST, Martin C (Alb) 50 William St, Catskill, NY 12414

YOTTER, Katherine Ann (CFla) 6400 N Socrum Loop Rd, Lakeland, FL 33809

YOULL MARSHALL, Lynda Mary (Va)

YOUMANS, Timothy Sean (Okla) Casady School, 9500 N Pennsylvania Ave, Oklahoma City, OK 73120

YOUNG, Adam A (Fla) 2017 6th Ave N, Birmingham, AL 35203

YOUNG, Bernard Orson Dwight (LI) 18917 Turin Dr, Saint Albans, NY 11412

YOUNG, Bruce Alan (Mass) 46 Laurel St., Gloucester, MA 01930

YOUNG, Francene (Tex) 605 W 9th St, Houston, TX 77007

YOUNG, Frank Whitman (Ala) 109 Hannah Ln, Oak Grove, AL 35150

YOUNG, G Todd (Md) 101 S Prospect St, Hagerstown, MD 21740

YOUNG, Gary (EO) 665 Parsons Rd, Hood River, OR 97031

✠ **YOUNG III**, George (ETenn) 814 Episcopal School Way, Knoxville, TN 37932

YOUNG, James (Minn) 2105 Ontario Ln, Northfield, MN 55057

YOUNG, James Joseph (Los) 12868 Hacienda Dr., Studio City, CA 91604

YOUNG, James Oliver (Okla) 2207 Ridgeway St, Ardmore, OK 73401

YOUNG, James Robert (The Episcopal NCal) Po Box 2334, Avila Beach, CA 93424

YOUNG, Jim (SwVa) 5260 Triad Ct SE, Salem, OR 97306

YOUNG, Kammy Mary (CGC) 302 N Reus St, Pensacola, FL 32501

YOUNG, Kathryn McMillan (Tenn) 704 Park Blvd, Austin, TX 78751

YOUNG, Linda M (Spok) 1410 NE Stadium Way, Pullman, WA 99163

YOUNG, Malcolm Clemens (Cal) 2674 Saint Giles Ln, Mountain View, CA 94040

YOUNG, Mary Catherine (NC) Canterbury Downtown, 12 W 11th St, New York, NY 10011

YOUNG, Ronald Bruce (Roch) Christ Episcopal Church, 26 S Main St, Pittsford, NY 14534

YOUNG, S Matthew (Lex) 7 Court Pl, Newport, KY 41071

YOUNG, Shari Maruska (Cal) PO Box 872, Tiburon, CA 94920

YOUNG, Sherry Lawry (EMich) 5584 Lapeer Rd Apt 1D, Kimball, MI 48074

YOUNG, Tammy M (NJ)

YOUNGBLOOD, Susan Russell (Chi) 825 N Taylor Ave, Oak Park, IL 60302

YOUNGER, Maryann D (NC)

YOUNGSON, Charles Mitchell (Ala) 509 Tamworth Ln, Birmingham, AL 35209

YOUNKIN, Randy John (Pgh) 431 Alameda Ave, Youngstown, OH 44504

YOUNKIN, Ronald Willingham (Pgh)

YOUNT, Amy Clark (WA) 6006 Benalder Dr, Bethesda, MD 20816

YOUSE JR, Don C (Pgh) 955 W North Ave, Pittsburgh, PA 15233

YSKAMP, Janis (CPa) 813 Valley Rd, Mansfield, PA 16933

YUDASZ, Mitchell Victor (Mich)

YULE, Marilynn Fritz (Spok) PO Box 6318, Kennewick, WA 99336

YUNG, Bernard (The Episcopal Church in Haw) 10504 Center St, Fairfax, VA 22030

YUNKER, Judy Lee (Lex) 562 University Dr, Prestonburg, KY 41653

Z

✠ **ZABALA**, Artemio M (Los) 5048 Brunswick Dr, Fontana, CA 92336

ZABANEH SR, Raja Benny (Fla)

ZABRISKIE, Marek P (Ct) 212 Washington Ln, Fort Washington, PA 19034

ZACHARIA, The Rev Dr Manoj Mathew (Md) 199 Duke Of Gloucester St, Annapolis, MD 21401

ZACHRITZ, John Louis (RG) 13 County Road 126, Espanola, NM 87532

ZACKER, John G W (NY) 64 Weir Ln, Locust Valley, NY 11560

ZADIG SR, Alfred Thomas Kurt (WMass) 12 Briarwood Cir, Worcester, MA 01606

ZAHARIA, Paul Michael (ND) 301 Main St S, Minot, ND 58701

ZAHER, Holly Ann Rankin (Ind)

ZAHL, John A (NY) 382 Cantitoe St, Bedford Hills, NY 10507

ZAHL, Paul Francis Matthew (WA) 506 N Dillard St, Winter Garden, FL 34787

ZAHN, Marianne (Los) St Wilfred Of York, 18631 Chapel Ln, Huntington Beach, CA 92646

ZAINA, Lisa Marie (WA) 3601 Connecticut Ave NW Apt 414, Washington, DC 20008

ZAISS, John Deforest (Nev) 7832 Magnolia Glen Ave, Las Vegas, NV 89128

ZAKRZEWSKI, Joy Lael (FdL) 2336 Canterbury Ln, Sister Bay, WI 54234

ZALESAK, Richard Joseph (Tenn) 1601 Campbell Ln, Galveston, TX 77551

ZALNERAITIS JR, Herbert Benedict (Mass) 93 Main St Apt 3, Brattleboro, VT 05301

ZAMBONI, Jack (NJ) 400 New Market Rd, Dunellen, NJ 08812

ZAMBRANO RECALDE, Hugo Edmundo (Colom)

ZANETTI, Diane P (Be) 4484 Heron Dr, Reading, PA 19606

ZAPATA-GARCIA, Carlos Alberto (EcuC) Calle Hernando Sarmiento, N 39-54 Y Portete, Setor El Batan Quito, Ecuador

ZAPPA, Cathy C (At) Episc Ch Of The Holy Spirit, 724 Pilgrim Mill Rd, Cumming, GA 30040

ZARTMAN, Rebecca Ann (Tex)

ZAUCHA, Scott Lybrand (Chi) 503 W Jackson St, Woodstock, IL 60098

ZAVACKY, Ryan A (WMo)

ZEIGLER, Luther (Mass) Tec Chaplaincy At Harvard, 2 Garden St, Cambridge, MA 02138

ZEILFELDER, Eugene Walter (NJ) 10913 Trestles Rd, Frisco, TX 75035

ZELLER, Maggie (ETenn) 1108 Meadow Ln, Kingsport, TN 37663

ZELLERMAYER, Charles Clayton (Mil) 400 Garland Ct, Waukesha, WI 53188

ZELLEY III, Edmund W (NJ) 18 Oak Ave, Metuchen, NJ 08840

ZELLEY JR, Walt (NJ) PO Box 2, Copake Falls, NY 12517

ZELLNER, John Clement (USC) 230 Depot St, Tryon, NC 28782

ZEMAN, Andy (Ct) 135 Ball Farm Rd, Oakville, CT 06779

ZEPEDA PADILLA, Jorge Alberto (Hond)

ZEPHIER, Richard (SD) 1410 N Kline St, Aberdeen, SD 57401

ZEREN, Corby (Md)

ZERRA, Luke D (Pgh)

ZETTINGER, Bill (SanD) 1920 Hamilton Ln, Escondido, CA 92029

ZEVALLOS, Guillermina Sara (Ga)

ZHANG, Lu (LI)

ZIEGENHINE, Kathleen Roach (NwPa) 458 E 23rd St, Erie, PA 16503

ZIELINSKI, Frances Gertrude (Chi) 710 S Paulina St # 904, Chicago, IL 60612

ZIEMANN, Judith Jon (The Episcopal NCal) 5905 W. 30th Ave., Wheat Ridge, CO 80214

ZIFCAK, Patricia (Mass) 2100 County St Apt 31, South Attleboro, MA 02703

ZILE, Eric Neil (CGC) 2640 Cameron Way, Frederick, MD 21701

ZIMBRICK-ROGERS, Emily (Pa)

ZIMMERMAN, Aaron M G (Tex) 305 N 30th St, Waco, TX 76710

ZIMMERMAN, Curtis Roy (Oly) 2014 N Saginaw Rd, 406, Midland, MI 48640

ZIMMERMAN, Douglas Lee (SwFla) 205 S. Occident St, Tampa, FL 33609

ZIMMERMAN, Gretchen Densmore (NJ) 106 Green St, Church Hill, MD 21623

ZIMMERMAN, Janet Whaley (WMass) PO Box 114, Great Barrington, MA 01230

ZIMMERMAN, John Paul (Alb) 6459 Vosburgh Rd, Altamont, NY 12009

ZIMMERMAN, Stephen Francis (Colo) Grace St Stephens Ch, 601 North Tejon St, Colorado Springs, CO 80903

ZIMMERMANN, Matt (Kan) 214 Laura Ln, Bastrop, TX 78602

ZIMMERSCHIED, Jill Whitney (Wyo) 202 12th St, Wheatland, WY 82201

ZINK, Jesse (WMass)

ZIOBRO, Albert Fredrick (WA) 3909 Albemarle St Nw, Washington, DC 20016

ZITO, Robert John Amadeus (NY) 95 Reade St, New York, NY 10013

ZITTLE, Twyla Jeanne (Colo) 2902 Airport Rd Apt 123, Colorado Springs, CO 80910

ZIVANOV, ELIZABETH Ann (Nev) 2505 Old Town Dr, North Las Vegas, NV 89031

ZLATIC, Martin (SeFla) 6321 Lansdowne Cir, Boynton Beach, FL 33472

ZOBEL, Jeanette Lynn (Mil)

ZOGG, Jennifer G (RI) 1336 Pawtucket Ave, Rumford, RI 02916

ZOLLER, Joan Duncan (WMo) Po Box 967, Blue Springs, MO 64013

ZOLLICKOFFER, Joseph Paul (Md)

ZOOK, Aaron (Eau) 709 Miles Street, CHIPPEWA FALLS, WI 54729

ZOOK-JONES, Jill (SVa) 6148 Rutledge Hill Rd, Columbia, SC 29209

ZORAWICK, Joseph Marion (NY) 40 W 67th St, New York, NY 10023

ZORRILLA-BALSEIRO, Rafael (PR) PO Box 270196, San Juan, PR 00928

ZOTALIS, James (Minn) 601 N 4th St, Bismarck, ND 58501

ZOUTENDAM, Philip (WMich)

ZÉPHIRIN, Odette (Hai)

ZSCHEILE, Dwight J (Minn) 18 Crescent Lane, North Oaks, MN 55127

ZUBIETA, Augustin Teodoro (Pgh) 5660 Lonesome Dove Ct, Clifton, VA 20124

ZUBLER, Eric John (CGC) St Pauls Episcopal Chapel, PO Box 2, Magnolia Springs, AL 36555

ZUG, Albert Edward Roussel (Pa) 2 E Spring Oak Cir, Media, PA 19063

ZULL, Aaron Beatty (Mich) 250 E Harbortown Dr, Detroit, MI 48207

ZUMPF, Michael (NC) 600 Morgan Rd, Eden, NC 27288

ZUST, Vicki Diane (SO) 3324 Kioka Ave, Columbus, OH 43221

ZWICK, Patricia Diane (Lex) 1337 Winchester Ave, Ashland, KY 41101

ZWIFKA, David Alan (Be) St Luke's Church, 22 S 6th St, Lebanon, PA 17042

ALPHABETICAL INDEX

Alphabetical Index

Alphabetical Index

Alphabetical Index

Index of Advertisers

We thank you for your support.

CLASSIFIED BUYER'S GUIDE

CLASSIFIED BUYER'S GUIDE

CLASSIFIED BUYER'S GUIDE

CLASSIFIED BUYER'S GUIDE